# ROTHMANS FOOTBALL YEARBOOK 1982–83

EDITOR: JACK ROLLIN

QUEEN ANNE PRESS
MACDONALD & CO (PUBLISHERS) LTD
LONDON

Front Cover: British involvement in the 1982 World Cup finals in Spain is reflected in photographs of Scotland's Kenny Dalglish (Colorsport), Northern Ireland's Pat Jennings (Colorsport) and England's Kevin Keegan (Sporting Pictures [UK] Ltd). FIFA World Cup photo (Sporting Pictures [UK] Ltd).

ISBN 0356 07887 6 (hardcover)
0356 07888 4 (limp)

Published by Queen Anne Press,
Macdonald & Co (Publishers) Ltd,
Maxwell House, Worship Street, London EC2A 2EN

Filmset, printed and bound in Great Britain by
Hazell Watson & Viney Ltd, Aylesbury, Bucks

# CONTENTS

4

## EUROPEAN FOOTBALL

## RECORDS SECTION

## OTHER LEAGUE, YOUTH AND SCHOOLS FOOTBALL

## INFORMATION SECTION

## MISCELLANEOUS

# FOREWORD FROM ROTHMANS OF PALL MALL

Everyone associated with the game of football is stimulated by the World Cup. Whether standards are high or the matches exciting, the glamour and importance of the competition never fail to capture the imagination of all football followers.

England re-emerged as a world force and returned unbeaten. Scotland were unlucky to be drawn in the strongest original group. Yet the performances of Northern Ireland really underlined all that is good in British football. As underdogs Billy Bingham's men played with the spirit and determination which won admirers throughout the world. But what was quite obvious to all who saw them was the sheer enjoyment they derived from their matches. Surely this is how football was meant to be played. Together with the sometimes naïve, but very entertaining, open football played by such emerging football nations as Algeria and Cameroon, and the sheer magic of the Brazilians on the attack, the Irish reminded us all of the romance and beauty of the game.

This is the 13th edition of *Rothmans Football Yearbook* and certainly it isn't reporting an unlucky year for British football. Hopefully, the good omens of the World Cup will see our international side build on the confidence gained in Spain, where the behaviour of our fans was better than expected and the sportsmanship was overall at a high standard.

Tradition plays an important rôle in the game of football, so perhaps it isn't surprising to see Aston Villa's name on the European Cup, considering they have won the FA Cup and the Championship on seven occasions each, plus three triumphs in the Football League Cup. Similarly, for a World Cup held in Europe, previous form would have pointed to Italy and West Germany reaching the final, and, of course, they did. Hopefully, again, the tradition and quality of *Rothmans Football Yearbook* have also produced a reputation for the publication which will stand for many years to come.

Although attendances have dropped, Association Football is still Britain's most popular sport, and with senior administrators dedicated to promote the spirit of the game and to develop missing flair at League level, we look forward to a year of very real progress in Britain. Last year we hoped for an increase in attacking football, and the introduction of three points for a win certainly produced a more positive attitude throughout the game. So let us hope that in the coming season we will see the improvement of the national teams supplemented by a continuation of European Cup dominance and, above all, a spirit of enjoyment and sportsmanship which has been universally appreciated when seen in the recent World Cup.

EDITORIAL PANEL

Jack Rollin, Ted Croker, Geoff Peters, Trevor Morris OBE.

# INTRODUCTION

The thirteenth edition of *Rothmans Football Yearbook* includes the results of all World Cup final tournament matches played, including the full list of teams and goalscorers. FIFA were unable to supply a complete list of all qualifying competition line-ups because they intend to include them in their own publication at a later date, but we have been able to feature all European and South American details as well as examples of other teams who reached the finals.

In addition, there is full coverage of domestic football with line-ups, goalscorers and attendances of matches played in the Football League and Scottish League, as well as the League Cup, FA Cup, Scottish League Cup and Scottish Cup. Transfers affecting players being signed by Football League clubs are given, together with any transfer fee noted at the time. As there is no official figure for such moves, the fees quoted are estimated, and with the addition of levies, including VAT, they are merely a guide to the value of the players in question.

This year's edition also marks the return of the former style of Diary which appeared in earlier issues of *Rothmans Football Yearbook*.

The Editor would like to thank Norman Barrett, Lionel Francis and Alan Elliott respectively for their assistance in the compilation of the Diary, Non-League Football and the Scottish season; also the invaluable assistance rendered in the completion of the book by Christine Forrest and Graeme Wright.

The Editor would also like to pay tribute to the various organisations who have helped to make this edition complete, especially Mrs Sandra Whiteside of the Football League, Mike McNamara of the Football Association, and the secretaries of all the Football League and Scottish League clubs for their kind cooperation. The ready availability of Football League secretary Graham Kelly and his staff to answer queries was as usual most appreciated. Thanks are also due to Jim Farry, the Scottish League secretary, and his staff.

## ACKNOWLEDGEMENTS

The Editor would like to express his appreciation of the following individuals and organisations for their cooperation: Glynis Firth, Mike Foster, Chris J. Whalley, Debbie Singleton (all from the Football League); Adrian Titcombe (The Football Association); The Scottish Football Association, The Welsh Football Association, Tom Cairns of The Scottish League, the secretaries of all Football League and Scottish League clubs, Alan Dick, Malcolm Brodie, A. Rice (The English Schools FA), W. P. Goss (AFA), Maurice Golesworthy, Ken Goldman, Peter Dunk, Karen Spink, Christine Phillips, Elaine Morgan and Glenda Rollin.

# EDITORIAL

The professional game may be on the gallows with a noose of insolvency around its neck, but it has cried wolf so often to threats of financial ruin that its critics remain unimpressed. It was ironic, then, that it should be Wolves who came closest to extinction at the end of the 1981–82 season.

However, the affairs at Molineux brought a disturbing development with them. In putting the club in the hands of an Official Receiver, it would seem to have initiated a kind of Russian roulette. It is hoped that by sifting through the diary of events of last season, and their revelations of fiscal failure with Bristol City, Hull City and Oxford United among the more serious candidates for bankruptcy, other clubs will not imagine that a saviour can always be found somewhere.

If and when the financial aspect is put right, an equally important move must be made to redefine the word success. It must be taken completely out of the context of the game being 'all about winning' and the obsession with matches being simply won, drawn and slaughtered. Winners provide losers, and there will always be more losers than winners. The short-sighted and narrow attitude towards success in what is a professional entertainment has already led to a type of football which has no obviously universal appeal to the uncommitted as a spectacle, based as it is on the concept that victory, whatever the manner of it, is the only answer.

The Football League's new system of three points for a win did produce an improvement in goalscoring, but by a margin too small to make any definite conclusions. Indeed, the First Division provided fewer goals than in 1980–81. But it did nothing in the continuing recession to attract more spectators to the stands and terraces. In fact, there was another chilling drop in support for the game, with overall attendances falling to a new low post-war level of just over 20 million. Manchester United had the highest attendance average at 44,570. Tottenham Hotspur came next with 35,099, followed by Liverpool on 35,060 and Manchester City with 34,063. But half of the rest of the teams in Division One recorded less than 20,000 on average, Notts County being the poorest supported with 11,627. Oddly enough, because of Sheffield United's incredible 14,891 average in the Fourth Division, this division actually showed an increase of attendances on the previous term. And there were only two clubs with less than 2000 on average: Rochdale on 1837 and Tranmere Rovers with 1735.

It is a sobering thought, when taking note of an article previously produced by the author, to read: 'Down and down go the soccer gates in Britain. The game is fast running into a cul-de-sac of decreasing receipts and increasing costs . . . attendances will improve only when the standard of play goes up.' That was written in November 1964.

To put attendances in some kind of perspective, here are some illuminating figures:

| Season | Attendances | Average |
|--------|-------------|---------|
| 1906–07 | 10,929,000 | 14,380 |
| 1937–38 | 28,132,933 | 15,225 |
| 1958–59 | 33,610,985 | 16,573 |
| 1963–64 | 28,535,022 | 14,075 |
| 1981–82 | 20,006,961 | 9865 |

Though the table deliberately omits the artificial boom days of the 1940s when more than a million people watched League football each weekend, in 1981–82 attendance was less than half that figure.

Every professional sport needs live spectators to support it. Sponsorship will lessen the burden of costs, but unless the intention is to drive a wedge between winning and losing teams, thereby consigning unsuccessful clubs to be watched by mere handfuls of people, the product has to be improved.

The World Cup in Spain provided just two teams whose approach had to be admired – Brazil and France. They alone played with a carefree fluency which caught the imagination of everyone sitting in his TV armchair. Alas, they were not destined to reach the final. Instead it was Italy who won. The home of *catenaccio* proved supreme, thanks to the Italians' expertise of converting virtually every goal chance.

This, of course, remains the dilemma: attractive football which will not necessarily produce results or safety first? What is certain is that the game will have greater overall appeal the first way rather than the second. But if professional football is to thrive, let alone survive, it will have to change its attitude.                    JACK ROLLIN

# ROTHMANS
# 100 YEARS OF FOOTBALL
# 1870 to 1969

**Rothmans**

**The complete Rothmans Football statistical record:**
**Rothmans One Hundred Years of Football.**
**Only 2,000 individually-numbered sets are available for sale.**
**Four superb royal blue and gold especially-bound volumes**
**with leather spines, measuring 205mm. × 245mm. each**
**containing 500 pages.**

|  |  |
|---|---|
| Volume One: | 1870-1914 |
| Volume Two: | 1918-1939 |
| Volume Three: | 1940-1959 |
| Volume Four: | 1960-1969 |

These volumes will record:
- the development of the game, season by season
- statistical records
- all League clubs' statistics, highlighting results,
- appearances and goals scored

Plus comprehensive details featuring:
- F A Cup
- International Football
- Scottish Football
- Non-League competitions

Plus all senior competitions since Football was first organised.

The first Rothmans Football Yearbook was published in 1970 so Rothmans One Hundred Years of Football will complete the statistical list and factual record of every senior match ever played, presented in Rothmans own inimitable style.

The four volumes will cost £250 and to ensure you get a set of these special editions a deposit of £30 should be sent to:

**G.E. Peters**
**Rothmans One Hundred Years of Football**
**74 Worship Street**
**London EC2A 3EN**

Cheques should be made payable to "ROTHMANS ONE HUNDRED YEARS OF FOOTBALL".

On receipt of the £30 deposit a personal number will be issued and will eventually appear in gold blocking on all four volumes registered in your name.

The books can only be bought in sets and may only be obtained from the above address.

Final and complete payment of £220 will be required no later than 1st September 1983.

# ROTHMANS FOOTBALL AWARDS 1982

The following six special awards have been made by Rothmans to mark a worthwhile contribution to the game in season 1981–82.

**KEITH BURKINSHAW.** Tottenham Hotspur made a brave attempt to win a number of honours in various domestic and European spheres. In the end, as much hit by outside forces – the arduous nature of our domestic game and consequential injuries – as hampered by their own shortcomings, they had to be content with taking the FA Cup for a seventh time. None the less, manager Keith Burkinshaw pursued throughout the season his policy of playing attractive, entertaining football which drew the uncommitted as well as the dedicated to Spurs' matches. The entire country must applaud this approach.

**BILLY McNEILL.** In the comparatively short time that the Premier Division has operated in Scotland, Celtic have already made an impression on the competition, and under the direction of Billy McNeill, who graced the centre-half position in his playing days at Parkhead, Celtic added another championship to their substantial array of trophies. Although they had to struggle through a poor patch towards the end of the season, they had by then established a lead which proved unassailable. Their achievement was all the more praiseworthy because of an uncharacteristic slump in the League Cup.

**CORINTHIAN-CASUALS.** In the present era of high-powered professionalism, the stance of the Corinthian-Casuals club as upholders of the real spirit of the game remains an example to all. It was appropriate that, entering their Centenary Year, they enjoyed their best season for many a day with a fine FA Cup run reminiscent of their golden era and a high final placing in their division of the Berger Isthmian League. These play-for-fun boys often even refuse their legitimate expenses; a unique situation in senior non-League circles.

**ASTON VILLA.** Ensuring that the European Cup of the Champion Clubs returned to England for the sixth season in succession was a meritorious performance for Aston Villa in what for them was a difficult campaign in several ways. A change of manager during the season brought assistant Tony Barton to the fore at a time when the European Cup battles were at their highest. He assumed control in a quiet but effective fashion, and the whole club's response was worthy of those traditions long established at Villa Park.

**KEITH EDWARDS.** Proving that it is not always a mistake to return to a former club, Keith Edwards revelled in Sheffield United's storming season in Division Four after going back to Bramall Lane from Hull City. His 35 League goals for United put him level with Craig Madden of Bury, but Edwards had managed a last goal for Hull which gave him the edge over his rival and made him the Football League's top marksman for 1981–82 with 36 goals. It also hoisted him to a personal career total in excess of a century, and his contribution to the Sheffield club's 94 goals was well received.

**GRAEME SOUNESS.** Captaining Liverpool to their 13th League title was Graeme Souness, who grew in stature more during 1981–82 than in any other season of a career which he began as a youth player on the books of Tottenham Hotspur. It was at Middlesbrough that he first emerged with credit, and his midfield talents eventually came to the notice of the Anfield club. For Scotland, he has also succeeded in stamping an authoritative air of generalship, and he was seen to marked purpose for his country during the World Cup finals in Spain.

# MILESTONES DIARY 1981–82

**August**

2 Aberdeen win the £15,000 top prize in their own four-club tournament, beating Southampton 5-1, while West Ham United earn third place with a single-goal win over Manchester United.

3 Liverpool and England goalkeeper Ray Clemence is transfer-listed . . . Tottenham Hotspur goalkeeper Barry Daines is granted a free transfer by the League after a dispute with the club, when it was alleged they had failed to enclose his new contract in a registered envelope. Daines insisted he had not received it . . . Spurs' Don McAllister, with a similar claim, is also granted a 'free' . . . Stoke City's England Under-21 international Adrian Heath, who wants a transfer, is told by manager Richie Barker: 'If you want another job it will be outside football.'

5 Leeds United are having problems raising the £1 million to pay for Peter Barnes, the West Bromwich Albion and England winger . . . Norwich City's similarly rated centre-forward Justin Fashanu, back after seven weeks playing for Adelaide City, says: 'I'm definitely moving on. I would like a big challenge and a big First Division club – with Norwich's permission. There is a lot more to this than just money.' . . . Rumanian Footballer of the Year, Marcel Raducanu, defects to West Germany.

6 Manchester United manager Ron Atkinson is optimistic that Arsenal's centre-forward Frank Stapleton will sign for them. He is also interested in signing Bryan Robson from his former club, West Bromwich Albion.

7 Paul Gilchrist (Hereford United), who won an FA Cup medal with Southampton in 1976, has to retire on medical advice, as does Preston North End's forward Ricky Thomson.

8 Tottenham manager Keith Burkinshaw refuses to be panicked into buying Ray Clemence at £350,000 despite drawing 3-3 with Glentoran in a friendly. 'They are asking an awful lot of money for a 33-year-old,' he says.

10 Wolverhampton Wanderers expect to sign Rene Van de Kerkhof, the Dutch World Cup player, from PSV Eindhoven . . . Millwall are interested in buying back their former midfield player, Dave Mehmet, after five months with Tampa Bay Rowdies. His wife Linda has been unable to settle in America.

11 Arsenal are in a race to sign Tony Woodcock from the West German club Cologne before Friday's deadline for eligibility in the coming season's European competitions.

12 Nottingham Forest learn from League tribunal that they must pay £425,000 for Mark Proctor. The figure is £325,000 below Middlesbrough's valuation but exceeds Forest's offer by £175,000.

13 Tottenham striker Garth Crooks will miss the start of the season after breaking down in training. He will have a cartilage operation . . . David O'Leary agrees to stay with Arsenal and Lee Chapman signs a new contract for Stoke.

14 Liverpool, in a flurry of transfer activity, move for Brighton and Hove Albion's Eire international defender Mark Lawrenson while preparing to shed Jimmy Case to Brighton, Colin Irwin to Swansea City and goalkeeper Clemence to Spurs. 'I've got one or two questions to ask Keith Burkinshaw,' says Clemence.

15 Woodcock is now sought by Leeds . . . The League's new competition, the Group Cup, begins quietly. Only three of the 16 ties top crowds of 3000 . . . In Auckland, New Zealand set up a record score in the World Cup, beating Fiji 13-0. Captain Steve Sumner scores six goals . . . Sheffield United complete a back-room clear-out with the departure of assistant manager Danny Bergara. He follows Harry Haslam, Martin Peters, chief scout Arthur Turner, physiotherapist Geoff Goodall and coach Geoff Vowden . . . Jimmy Greenhoff, back from a stint in Canada with Toronto, expects to link up with Port Vale.

17 Aston Villa whack East Germany's World Cup team 4-2 at Villa Park . . . Middlesbrough line up two Dutchmen: Heini Otto, an Under-23 international from Twente Enschede, and Peter Holyheuk, a 6-foot defender and amateur from The Hague . . . Stoke City will be sponsored by the Japanese photographic company Ricoh . . . Ted MacDougall, 34, now a Romsey publican, will make a comeback with Salisbury . . . Coventry City sack their third-team goalkeeper, 20-year-old Steve Murcott, for disciplinary reasons. Two years ago he made his senior début after the regular choice was injured in the pre-match warm-up . . . After crowd trouble at Halifax the club decide not to play neighbours Huddersfield Town in friendlies and improve security arrangements. 'We will make it like Alcatraz,' says chairman Sam Rorke.

18    Charlton Athletic open their new Jimmy Seed stand at The Valley. Ex-players present include Don Welsh, Leslie Fell, George Green, Alec Stock, Peter and Ted Croker, Frank Rist, Harold Hobbis, Seamus D'Arcy, Benny Fenton, Bill Dodgin senior, Charlie Hall and Fred Lucas ... Some clubs in North America want revolutionary new rules, including the enlargement of the goal by a foot in every direction ... Bass are to sponsor the Northern Premier League for £25,000 covering a three-year period.

19    Arsenal hope to persuade Frank Stapleton, their Eire centre-forward, to stay at Highbury and turn down Manchester United's offer while awaiting the outcome of an independent tribunal chaired by Professor Sir John Wood. Stapleton, who has been training with United, is valued by Arsenal at £2 million while United have cut their offer from £750,000 to £650,000 ... Rene Van de Kerkhof is to stay with PSV Eindhoven, but Birmingham City sign Dutch 'B' international winger Bud Brocken from Willem II Tilburg for £110,000.

20    The Welsh FA decide to allow their four League clubs to appoint one paid director each. Cardiff City expect to provide Ron Jones, their general manager and Britain's former Olympic athlete, with the first such position ... The League appeals Committee fix the Stapleton fee at £1.1 million including levies and VAT ... Norwich, having transferred Fashanu to Nottingham Forest, hope to sign Imre Varadi from Everton as a replacement ... Bobby Gould, former Chelsea assistant manager, signs a one-year playing contract for Wimbledon. He was soon to go to Aldershot as assistant manager.

21    Arsenal manager Terry Neill, commenting on the Stapleton fee following his return from Italy and a 2-2 draw with Juventus (Liam Brady's team), says: 'These fees are ridiculous.' Paul Vaessen, scorer of the goal which beat Juventus in the 1979–80 European Cup-Winners' Cup, has recovered from a fractured leg ... The Welsh FA announce a profit of £37,813 ... Since switching to Wembley, the FA Charity Shield has raised £723,310 ... Clydebank's Bill Munro resigns after six years in charge.

22    The Charity Shield attracts a record 92,500 crowd, receipts £431,000 ... At the launching of the 12th edition of *Rothmans Football Yearbook*, Fulham manager Malcolm Macdonald calls for Football League clubs to 'stand on their own feet'.

24    Two more transfer deals of £1 million plus are rumoured with Manchester City interested in Forest's Trevor Francis and Manchester United continuing their liking for Albion midfield player Bryan Robson ... Sunderland make John Hawley, Steve Whitworth and Sam Allardyce available for transfer ... Liverpool play their seventh pre-season friendly and beat Crusaders 5-0 at Seaview, Belfast in a match before 10,000 to inaugurate the Irish club's new £250,000 stand ... Manchester United physiotherapist Jim Headridge dies after collapsing at the club's training ground.

25    Wolves are thwarted in the transfer market again when 18-year-old Ally McCoist prefers to join Sunderland. Middlesbrough and Glasgow Rangers were other disappointed clubs seeking the signature of the St Johnstone player ... Arsenal and Ipswich Town both announce sponsorship deals with Japanese electronic companies. The Gunners will receive £500,000 from JVC over three years, Ipswich £400,000 from Pioneer.

26    Norwich announce a loss of £327,000 ... England's 18-strong squad for the World Youth Cup in Australia includes Paul Allen, the FA Cup's youngest finalist ... Ally MacLeod, ex-Scotland boss, is sacked by Motherwell. Bill Samuel, the club's chairman, says: 'It is an extremely unpleasant and difficult task to dismiss Mr MacLeod, as we all like him as a person at Motherwell.' ... The League announce incentives, to clubs, to reward goalscoring on a monthly basis and for each division's highest scorers at the end of the season ... Coventry chairman Jimmy Hill hits out at the game's big spenders. 'The lust for success by some managers and chairmen at a few clubs will put players into a pressure cooker out of which can only come disaster', he says. City announce incentives for players, who can earn up to £400 a man.

27    Jimmy Bloomfield leaves his position as Orient manager 'by mutual consent' ... Brighton decline to pay the £125,000 decreed by the tribunal for Plymouth Argyle centre-half George Foster ... England's squad to play Norway in the World Cup is announced in almost unique circumstances: the season proper begins tomorrow! ... Spurs striker Steve Archibald has damaged foot ligaments.

28    Middlesbrough directors are to report Brian Clough to the FA alleging that he brought the game into disrepute. 'He should stick to his full-time job and keep out of the affairs of other clubs', says Charles Amer, Middlesbrough chairman. 'I think Clough is furious over missing out when Craig Johnston left us for Liverpool.' Boro had also reported Forest concerning an alleged illegal approach to Mark Proctor, who later joined the Nottingham club ... Wales' World Cup players have been offered an £80,000 incentive to qualify for the finals, £20,000 from Adidas and £60,000 as a share

from FIFA's pool . . . Celtic, on the eve of their new League season, have failed to reach the League Cup quarter-finals for the first time since 1963. 'Football is about disappointments as much as glory and we have pushed this to the back of our minds', said manager Billy McNeill. 'I'm convinced we're on the right lines and we'll make a strong bid to retain the title.'

29  The League season opens with modest attendances, the highest being 36,187 at Maine Road, Manchester . . . Quickest goal by Steve Neville (Sheffield United) in 35 seconds at home to Hereford United . . . Young marksman: 17-year-old Keith Curle, Bristol Rovers apprentice, against Chester . . . Sunderland manager Alan Durban is the first critic of the new system of three points for a win. Speaking after the 3-3 draw with Ipswich he says: 'It is outrageous that the clubs should lose two points each for drawing after giving a superb exhibition like that.'

30  Diego Maradona, 20, will return to Argentinos Juniors next year because Boca Juniors have failed to pay the first instalment on his transfer, having been caught by a revaluing of the peso against the dollar.

31  Scottish manager Jock Stein picks experience for his squad to play Sweden in the World Cup and has three over-age performers in the Under-21 side . . . Bank Holiday crowd of 51,496 sees a goalless draw at Old Trafford between Manchester United and Nottingham Forest . . . Eire recall Liam Brady to their side for the crucial World Cup qualifier with the Netherlands.

## September

1  Wales include four Swansea City players in their 16-strong squad to play Czechoslovakia in the World Cup . . . The Football League is to inquire into allegations of illegal payments by Halifax Town at the request of the club's board . . . Spanish footballers call for an indefinite strike unless clubs pay £1·5 million owed to players and agree to other demands.

2  Graham Turner, Shrewsbury Town's manager, denies he has a players' revolt on his hands. 'The majority of them are happy to serve out their contracts', he says . . . Manchester City expect to end 10 days of negotiations by signing Trevor Francis from Nottingham Forest . . . League Cup tie at Chester abandoned after 78 minutes when a goal post is broken.

3  Manchester City hope to unload utility player Tony Henry and striker Dave Bennett, while paying £350,000 for their manager's son Kevin Bond from Seattle Sounders, and Age Hareide, the Norwegian international defender from Molde, for £10,000 when a work permit is issued . . . At the launch of the *Football League Review*, Jack Dunnett, president of the Football League, predicts a new era of harmony with the Football Association after a meeting with Bert Millichip, chairman of the FA . . . Finnish international Aki Lahtinen joins Notts County.

6  England have injury problems, with Dave Watson, Steve Coppell and Trevor Brooking likely absentees against Norway . . . Scotland's Graeme Souness is also sidelined.

5  Gates slump again; only 457,303 for the weekend's programme of 46 matches in just the second week of the new campaign.

7  Leeds United seek a central defender on loan, Paul Hart having undergone an operation for appendicitis, Neil Firm suffering an Achilles tendon injury, and Keith Parkinson out with back trouble . . . Australian soccer clubs in the Philips League voted to switch from winter to summer in an attempt to attract larger crowds . . . Tony Knapp, Norwegian-based English coach of Viking Stavanger, predicts an England win over Norway. 'The trouble with the Norwegians is that they respect England too much', he says. 'They need to be much more positive.'

8  Charlie George signs for the Hong Kong club Bulova for £50,000 . . . Scarborough announce a profit of £40,000 . . . Cardiff City are to send Chelsea a letter of protest concerning some of their supporters who misbehaved at Ninian Park on Saturday . . . England's Under-21 side use 16 players in the match with Norway but can only draw 0-0 . . . George Best stars in a benefit game for Middlesbrough. The crowd chant 'sign him on'.

9  Norway's seniors go one better, beating England 2-1 in an Oslo World Cup upset. 'We let Norway play for five minutes and they scored two goals', says Greenwood . . . Scotland beat Sweden 2-0, but Eire are held 2-2 by the Netherlands and Wales lose 2-0 in Prague against Czechoslovakia . . . England lose 1-0 to Denmark in a women's soccer match in Tokyo.

10  Jimmy Guthrie, Portsmouth's captain in the 1939 Cup Final and later chairman of the PFA, dies at 68.

11 Stoke refute Wolves' allegations of breach of contract over Richie Barker, who left Molineux to join Stoke as manager in July.

14 Manchester United offer £2 million to West Bromwich Albion for Bryan Robson and Remi Moses . . . Wigan Athletic defender Neil Davids breaks his right leg for the second time in a year while playing for the reserves . . . Newport County announce a testimonial match for manager Len Ashurst.

15 Frank Worthington re-signs for Birmingham City after playing the summer in North America with Tampa Bay Rowdies . . .

16 European night of mixed fortunes: Aberdeen hold Ipswich at Portman Road, Dundee United slam Monaco 5-2 in Monte Carlo, Spurs beat Ajax 3-1 in Amsterdam, but Rangers crash by three goals in Prague against Dukla . . . Laurie Cunningham, Real Madrid winger, undergoes surgery for the third time – this operation concerns his left knee ligaments; the others were on his crushed big toe . . . California Surf pack up because of financial problems.

17 Moses goes to Old Trafford after all, the club he supported from the terraces as a youth . . . Henry joins Bolton after first being turned down by them for medical reasons and having had a move to Norwich squashed.

18 Fit again, Trevor Brooking plays in West Ham's reserves while England youth captain Paul Allen retains his place for tomorrow's match at West Bromwich . . . Don Masson rejoins Notts County from Minnesota Kicks and David Moss returns to the Luton team sheet after a summer with Tampa Bay Rowdies . . . Another bound for home shores from the USA is Willie Donachie, the former Manchester City defender recently with Portland Timbers and heading now for Norwich.

19 Forest manager Brian Clough sends winger John Robertson home before the match with Stoke after a disagreement following a transfer request the previous weekend.

21 The FA will discuss the question of paid directors on 19 November . . . Best might sign on a match-to-match basis for Oldham.

22 Ron Jones, 46, becomes football's first paid director at Cardiff.

23 Czechoslovakia's 1-1 draw in Iceland gives Wales some World Cup hope, but England prospects are poor after Rumania and Hungary play a goalless draw in Bucharest . . . Rotherham United are almost £1 million in debt. The annual report reveals the 1980–81 season's deficit is £438,000 . . . Keith Edwards, Hull City's centre-forward transfer-listed at £150,000, is offered improved terms after the club turned down a player-exchange with his former club Sheffield United.

24 Edwards rejoins United . . . Arsenal make a pre-tax loss of £488,341 . . . Best may rejoin Manchester United . . . The FA rule that Dean Neal is a Queen's Park Rangers player after all, despite his signing for Millwall after a summer with Tulsa Rough-necks . . . League Secretary Graham Kelly fears saturation TV coverage of the World Cup finals in Spain could hit League gates in 1982–83. 'We felt the backlash after the European Championships last year', he says . . . Trevor Francis, with damaged knee ligaments, might be out for five weeks.

25 The League Management Committee propose the scrapping of the Fourth Division and creation of three regional sections of Division Three, each comprising 18 clubs.

26 Gates creep up slightly but at 492,326 are still reflecting the recession in the game.

27 Bob Lord, Burnley's chairman, decides to dispose of his controlling interest in the club. He and his family have 2800 shares . . . Chicago Sting win the North American League, beating New York Cosmos with a shootout goal before 36,971 spectators in Toronto . . . Fans throw missiles and light bonfires in Hong Kong when Charlie George fails for a second time to make his début because of a back injury.

28 Cardiff City, seeking a new manager, have unsuccessfully tried for Birmingham City's Archie Gemmill, Vancouver Whitecaps' Terry Yorath and Arsenal's John Hollins. Now Crewe's Arfon Griffiths expresses interest.

29 Bill Shankly dies in Broadgreen Hospital, Liverpool, aged 67. Before his retirement in July 1974 he spent 15 years as Liverpool's manager, during which time he made them one of the most outstandingly successful teams in the world . . . Bob Lord sells his shares to a consortium including two directors – for £50,000.

30 Celtic bow out to Juventus in the European Cup . . . Rangers follow them in the European Cup-Winners' Cup, but Aberdeen account for Ipswich and, despite losing their home leg, Dundee United hold enough aces from their Monte Carlo trip to despatch Monaco . . . Hereford United ban all their players from attending the ground, owing to an influenza virus . . . Brentford's new chairman, Martin Lange, intends to improve the club's finances. They are alleged to be losing £3000 per week . . . AFC Bournemouth expect to elevate Alec Stock to the board . . . Brighton

will have to leave their 8-foot fencing where it stands for the moment . . . David Hay is appointed manager of Motherwell.

## October

1 Bryan Robson's transfer to Manchester United sets a new record £1·5 million, in the wake of a long drawn-out deal during which West Bromwich manager Ronnie Allen said 'He leaves over my dead body' and chairman Bert Millichip added 'Robson is the one player who is not for sale at any price'. . . . Oxford United announce a loss of £77,104.

2 Despite the failure of many clubs to release youth internationals for the World Youth Cup in Australia, England coach John Cartwright is optimistic: 'I've got a good team and I am sure we'll surprise a few people.'

3 George Best is included in Northern Ireland's squad for the World Cup qualifying match against Scotland. At 35, the San José Earthquakes forward appears to be on the point of another breakthrough . . . England youths beat Cameroon 2-0 down under . . . Colchester United, losing £2000 a week, may have to drop out at the end of the season. Chairman Maurice Cadman says: 'We are suffering enormous losses.' . . . Bright scoring spot: 139 goals in the weekend programme is the best of the season to date.

5 Police permit the removal of some of the Brighton barriers . . . England draw 1-1 with Argentina amid fights between rival supporters in Sydney . . . Blackburn Rovers to complain to the Football League about the artificial pitch at Queen's Park Rangers. 'We felt the surface was not suited to good football', says manager David Brown.

6 Dean Neal, subject of a High Court case to decide his own club, has officially joined Millwall from Queen's Park Rangers . . . A compensation tribunal decrees that Kilmarnock must pay Dumbarton £47,500 for Alastair McLeod and Arbroath £12,500 to Brechin City for Stewart Glover.

7 Best is unimpressive playing for San José Earthquakes in a 1-1 draw with Linfield.

8 Having watched Best twice in a week, Billy Bingham says: 'I did not consider him fit enough for this standard of football.' . . . England achieve 1-1 draw with Australia in the World Youth Cup . . . Watford announce a £500,000 loss but chairman Elton John gives them a loan of £1·2 million, thus avoiding gift tax of £325,000 . . . Tom Morris (Leeds) resigns as a League referee to become the League's deputy secretary designate on 4 January.

11 Weekend matches leave Scotland without Joe Jordan and David Provan, both unfit for World Cup duty . . . Switzerland's 2-1 win in Rumania gives England a lifeline . . . The youth side beats Egypt 4-2 after trailing by two goals in the first five minutes.

12 Steve Coppell will stay with Manchester United and not join Coventry . . . Wembley are inundated with applications for tickets to see England's World Cup decider with Hungary . . . Paul Went resigns after 20 days as Orient manager . . . Brentford beat Best's San José Earthquakes 8-2 . . . Birmingham City full-back Mark Dennis, sent off on Saturday along with Southampton's Alan Ball, has been fined a week's wages and loses his win bonus as a result of action by manager Jim Smith.

13 The London FA, in their centenary match, are beaten 4-3 at Highbury by an England XI . . . Ken Knighton is appointed Orient manager . . . Ten clubs are fined by the FA for accumulating too many disciplinary points . . . John Jackson, a 42-year-old barrister, becomes chairman of Burnley.

14 The floodlights fail temporarily at Swansea, and Welsh hopes fade with them after a 2-2 draw with Iceland . . . Eire show spirit in beating France 3-2 and Scotland's goalless draw in Northern Ireland makes them the first home country to reach the World Cup finals . . . Third and Fourth Division clubs turn down the regional reorganisation suggested by the Management Committee . . . England lose 2-1 to Qatar in the World Youth Cup. One of Qatar's officials says: 'We used to have British coaches but they were no good' . . . Sunderland cut prices of admission . . . Dave Mehmet, former Millwall midfield player, is to have a trial with Ipswich.

15 Derby County launch a £350,000 survival scheme . . . Wembley is sold out for Hungary . . . George Burley (Ipswich), out for eight months with a serious knee injury, reports fit after a reserve run-out on Wednesday.

16 Swansea discover promotion cost them a loss of £269,000.

17 Allan Ball, the Queen of the South goalkeeper, plays his 800th match for the club . . . Kevin Beattie, after five operations on his right knee, complains of further pains.

18 England lose 1-0 to Rumania in the World Youth Cup match for third place.

19 The facelift for Hampden Park starts. It will cost £2·2 million . . . West Bromwich Albion hope to sign Martin Jol from Twente Enschede for £250,000.

20 Scotland appoint Ross Mathie, coach of Clyde, as assistant director of coaching . . .
Bristol Rovers dismiss Terry Cooper as manager.
21 Liverpool hold AZ 67 2-2 in Holland, Glentoran's physiotherapist, Bobby McGregor,
dies in Sofia attending an injured player, Southampton crash 4-2 at home to Malcolm
Allison's Sporting Lisbon, and Aberdeen tan Arges Pitesti 3-0. But Aston Villa's
Tony Morley scores twice in their sparkling away win over Dynamo Berlin . . . Leeds
axe backroom stalwarts Maurice Lindley, Bob English and Tony Collins . . . Darlington give Billy Elliott a new five-year contract as manager.
22 Cup Final share-out gives Tottenham and Manchester City each £306,600. Gate
money for their two games yielded £1,049,967 . . . Bobby Gould, previously assistant
manager at Aldershot, becomes Bristol Rovers' manager.
24 Leicester City manager Jock Wallace is unhappy about the Rangers surface at Loftus
Road, following his team's 2-0 defeat there.
28 England's match with Hungary in November to be shown live on TV.
29 Ex-Liverpool and Swansea forward Ian Callaghan signs for Crewe Alexandra . . .
Willie Young, Arsenal's Scottish-born defender, is ordered by manager Terry Neill to
stay away from the club's training ground . . . Bristol City are reported to be losing
£3000 a week and had a deficit of £466,000 on the 1980–81 season. Their total debt is
£700,000, including £120,000 owed in income tax and VAT . . . However, Ipswich
made a profit of £116,451.
31 Hungary clinch a place in England's group for the World Cup finals, beating Norway
4-1 . . . League gates exceed half a million with 521,622 – the best since the first day
of the season.

**November**
1 Scottish League Cup final crowd will be limited to 57,000 because of work on the
renovation of Hampden's east terracing.
2 Colchester announce a profit of £8742, thanks only to surplus in transfer fees and
increase in lottery income . . . Tranmere Rovers' overdraft of £250,000 has been eased
by the sale of the sports centre and social club for an undisclosed fee . . . Port Vale
make a loss of £12,496 . . . Derby County announce a new public issue of 60,000
shares at £10 each.
3 UEFA celebrations for Dundee United who overcome a two-goal deficit to whack
Borussia Moenchengladbach 5-0, but dismay for Arsenal who lose out on away goals
to lowly Belgian club Winterslag . . . Wigan Athletic set an all-ticket limit of 20,000
for their League Cup tie with Chelsea next week.
4 Away goals are decisive for Villa, who lose 1-0 at home to Dynamo Berlin, and only
a late goal by Liverpool enables them to avoid extra time against AZ 67 Alkmaar . . .
Spurs edge through 1-0 against Dundalk . . . Millwall plan to try more Sunday home
fixtures in the New Year.
6 Birmingham City, losing £5000 a week, reveal liabilities of £1·2 million. They had an
operating deficit of £260,000 . . . Stoke prepare to give Steve Ford, a former National
League basketball player, his début.
9 Graham Williams, former West Bromwich Albion and Welsh international full-back,
quits his health club business in Weymouth to become Cardiff's chief coach.
10 England manager Ron Greenwood selects blend of youth and experience for the vital
game with Hungary. The relatively inexperienced Alvin Martin and Alan Devonshire,
plus untried Paul Goddard and Tony Morley, are in the 22, along with established
players like Ray Clemence, Dave Watson, Ray Wilkins, Trevor Brooking and Kevin
Keegan . . . Dario Gradi is sacked as Crystal Palace manager after poor results. Steve
Kember becomes the caretaker . . . Terry Cooper, at 37, is to play for Doncaster
Rovers . . . Irish League football will be sponsored by Smirnoff for three years at
£15,000 a season . . . Port Vale defender Lee Harwood has to retire after 15 months
of knee trouble . . . Dennis Tueart signs a two-year contract with Manchester City at
the age of 31.
11 Switzerland draw 0-0 with Rumania. England now need just one point against Hungary . . . Wigan's League Cup gate is just over 12,000 but they beat Chelsea 4-2 . . .
Ray Hankin joins Arsenal from Vancouver Whitecaps for £400,000.
12 Manchester United report a loss of £277,582 after tax, but their recent transfer deal-
ings are not included in the year ending 31 May . . . Swansea chairman Malcolm Struel
becomes the second paid director with a Welsh club . . . Brian Clough, Forest manager, threatens to close the City Ground's Trent End terracing if bad behaviour
persists.
13 Portsmouth announce a profit of £9608, aided by average gates in 1980–81 of

13,500 . . . Former England goalkeeper Gordon Banks settles his unfair dismissal claim against Telford United.

14 All but two of The Football League's First Division games are postponed to prevent World Cup casualties.

15 Colin Jackson, Rangers' long-serving centre-half, earns around £60,000 from a 25,000 Ibrox gate for his benefit game against Everton, which was drawn 1-1 but won 3-1 by the Scots on penalties. Howard Kendall, with a 14-minute appearance as substitute in the first half, makes a playing comeback as boss of the Goodison Park club.

16 England may be without Trevor Brooking (knee injury) against Hungary. The gates at Wembley will be opened at 6 p.m.

17 England Under-21s beat the Hungarians by two clear goals and the seniors pick Martin for centre-half . . . Steve Smith, who last played for Huddersfield four years ago and now coaches the juniors, may be recalled for the FA Cup tie with Workington, because of injuries and suspensions.

18 England win 1-0. Greenwood says: 'There was no great euphoria afterwards in the dressing-room, just satisfaction and gratitude that we were able to benefit from the second chance we were given by Switzerland's results.' . . . Scotland lose 2-1 in Portugal but have already made the finals. Not so Wales, who were beaten 3-0 in Tbilisi by USSR. Joy, however, for Northern Ireland, whose single goal against Israel is enough to put them in the finals.

19 Fulham manager Malcolm Macdonald becomes the first paid director of a Football League club in England . . . A new road scheme jeopardises Luton's Kenilworth Road ground. The club, who recently announced an operating loss of more than £200,000, claim a new stadium would cost £1 million . . . Belfast's Windsor Park is hopeful of a £1 million government injection.

20 David Bradford, 27, the last player sold by Washington Diplomats before their bankruptcy, awaits his Coventry début after a £60,000 move and three reserve outings . . . Forest sign West German 'B' international midfield player Jurgen Rober for £250,000 from Chicago Sting . . . Brentford announce a loss of £67,764.

21 England's success in the World Cup fails to inspire League attendances. The day's best gate is in Scotland at Parkhead with 48,600 watching Celtic and Rangers.

22 The Scottish PFA want a percentage of transfer fees donated to their pension fund.

23 Queen's Park Rangers threaten to quit the FA Cup if their synthetic pitch can be used in the competition only for a year's trial . . . Stoke decide against signing the 27-year-old Iranian midfield player, Hedy Shoar, after a trial period . . . Two cracked pylons force Bradford City to postpone their forthcoming League Cup tie, which will now be played on 2 December.

24 Newcastle United announce a loss of £877,381 and are now nearly £1 million in debt . . . Queen's Park Rangers receive assurances from the FA about their Omniturf and withdraw their threat to quit the FA Cup . . . Reg Rowlands resigns as Chester chairman after 25 years on the board.

25 Einar Aas, the Norwegian international defender from Forest, breaks an ankle playing against Sunderland . . . Celtic win the *Daily Express* National Five-a-Side tournament at Wembley, beating Southampton 1-0 in the Arena with a goal from Charlie Nicholas . . . St Johnstone winger John Pelosi is banned for six months. At Dunfermline he was sent off in an incident in which Jim Brown broke his leg . . . Hamburg lose 3-2 at Aberdeen in the UEFA Cup.

26 Bert Millichip, chairman of the FA, calls for government action against soccer hooliganism. Speaking at the CCPR's annual conference at Bournemouth he says: 'The FA has insufficient muscle to act further on its own.' . . . Jeremy Charles (Swansea) has a cartilage operation.

27 Bristol Rovers say they are to share a ground with rivals City. Both would play at Ashton Gate, with Rovers leaving the Eastville ground they have occupied since 1897. The club is in dispute over the terms of a lease renewal with Bristol Stadium Ltd who purchased the freehold from Rovers in 1940 for £12,500 . . . Leicester City announce a loss of £319,000.

28 Rangers win the Scottish League Cup, beating Dundee United 2-1.

29 Czechoslovakia draw 1-1 with the USSR in Bratislava and so Wales lose interest in the World Cup . . . Mick Mills may leave Ipswich: 'Bobby Robson, the manager, has said that there is no place for me in a fully fit squad', he says.

30 Bill Taylor, coach to the England team since 1974, dies aged 42. He had a brain operation in 1980, after contracting a virus infection which affected the nervous system . . . Sunderland axe secretary Ron Linney.

## December

1  Trevor Francis is sidelined again – this time for an operation on a thigh injury . . . Best may sign for Middlesbrough . . . Dismissals reach 68 – 8 more than for the corresponding period last season. They comprise 48 in the League, 17 in the League Cup and 3 in the FA Cup . . . Dundee United draw 0-0 in Belgium against Winterslag.

2  Preston North End announce a loss of £344,000 . . . Coventry submit a new shirt design to the Football League to try to retain TV coverage. The 'T' on their shirts is alleged to be an advertisement for the club's sponsor, Talbot . . . Norwich City announce a loss of £327,000. 'I'm afraid there will be hundreds of players on the dole at the end of the season', says chairman Sir Arthur South. The club sack seven members of the backroom staff.

3  The FA announce an advertising promotion for the World Cup with a new mascot for Spain called Bulldog Bobby. It is hoped that this and other commercial enterprises will raise at least £750,000 . . . Preston sack Tommy Docherty after 17 matches. Alan Kelly becomes caretaker . . . Ron Atkinson tells the Manchester United AGM that there will be concentration on home-grown talent . . . Best's former club, Hibernian, claim San José Earthquakes owe them £10,000.

5  France beat Cyprus and end the miniscule hopes of Eire reaching Spain . . . League gates hit their lowest of the term: 445,946.

7  Northern Ireland announce their World Cup mascot, a jovial fan with an Irish scarf called 'Yer Man' . . . Derby want to ban Chelsea fans from their ground after incidents nine days earlier.

8  The reserve game on the all-weather pitch at Queen's Park Rangers is called off; groundstaff are late arriving because of the snow . . . Bob Lord dies aged 73. He had been Burnley chairman for 26 years, until his earlier resignation, and a senior vice-president of the League.

9  Aberdeen lose 3-1 in Hamburg but Dundee celebrate manager Jim McLean's new contract by hitting five past Winterslag . . . Mills rejects a move from Ipswich to Sunderland . . . Gillingham pay £10,000 for Maidstone's Frank Ovard . . . Oxford beat Cambridge 2-0 in Wembley's Varsity Match . . . Gordon Lee is appointed manager of Preston . . . Hearts sack Tony Ford, and Alex MacDonald, the team captain, takes over as player-coach.

10  France will stage the finals of the 1984 European Championship . . . Martin Flook, 37-year-old self-made millionaire, becomes chairman of Bristol Rovers.

11  The Pools Panel prepare for a rare December outing because of snow and ice . . . Liverpool head for Tokyo and the World Club Championship with Brazil's Flamengo . . . Best promises to sign for Middlesbrough on Tuesday . . . Northampton Town have put their 11-acre training ground up for sale.

12  Neil Macfarlane, Minister for Sport, welcomes the FA's inquiry into the behaviour of Chelsea supporters at Derby on 28 November. 'These hooligans are undoubtedly putting at risk the future of this great club', he says . . . Only five League games, including Rangers' at Loftus Road, four FA Cup ties and four Scottish games survive the weather.

13  Flamengo beat Liverpool 3-0 at the National Stadium in Tokyo before 62,000.

14  Best decides against joining Middlesbrough. 'I'm shattered', says manager Bobby Murdoch. 'He wanted a First Division platform for the World Cup finals in Spain, but that has all gone now that he has gone back to America.' Another blow to the club – they must play their third-round tie in the FA Cup on Rangers' much-criticised pitch, despite a protest . . . Stoke expect to sign Robert Prytz, Malmo's Swedish international midfield player for £80,000 after a two-week trial.

15  The League appoint a sponsorship, promotional and PR Agency, CSS Promotions Ltd, to inject income-earning opportunities for all 92 clubs.

16  An FA disciplinary commission decides that all Chelsea's away games from New Year's Day to the end of the season must be all-ticket. Chelsea must also pay £1000 to each of the home clubs involved to offset losses and expenses . . . Billy Bingham is given a three-year contract on a part-time basis at £10,000 a year from February as Northern Ireland manager.

18  Bristol City directors Stephen Kew and Peter West resign after two local businessmen, Deryn Coller and Ken Sage, promise to raise more than £½ million for the club provided Kew and West resign.

19  Weather again decimates the programme; only seven English and four Scottish games survive. Undersoil heating helps several of them . . . Kevin Beattie, 28, decides to retire because of crippling arthritis in his right knee, and an Achilles injury puts Denis

Tueart out for the season . . . Dismissals reach 71 – 50 in the League, 16 in the League Cup and 5 in the FA Cup.

21 Neil Macfarlane indicates he would like the FA to change the Bulldog to a Lion . . . Bradford City, hoping to beat the snow by flying to Jersey for a friendly with Forest, had to call it off because of a waterlogged pitch . . . Gillingham sell Danny Westwood to Barnet for a four-figure fee . . . New Zealand manager John Adshead wants Norwich to postpone signing 18-year-old reserve striker Wynton Rufer to allow him to play in the World Cup qualifying decider with China.

22 Amid the weather adversities, Liverpool play a friendly at Ibrox Park to inaugurate Rangers' new Govan Stand to mark the final phase of the ground's £10 million development. They win 2-0 . . . Queen's Park Rangers offer their pitch to the England team.

23 Jim Prentice is appointed financial director and administrator of Tottenham Hotspur.

26 Only eight League games survive the Boxing Day weather.

28 Only 12 of the scheduled 43 games are completed and the backlog increases.

29 Eastville stages its last Bristol derby in which 12,355 watch Rovers beat City 1-0 . . . Paul McGee, on loan to Burnley for two months, is wanted back by Preston, though the Turf Moor club say they had a verbal agreement with North End's former boss Tommy Docherty to transfer him for £25,000.

30 Bert Millichip says: 'Watch out for England in the World Cup. We are not going to Spain as poor relations. We have the players and there is no reason why we should not do well.'. . . Doncaster forward Ian Nimmo breaks his leg in two places during training . . . Manchester United attract a best gate of the season at Portsmouth – 14,000 for their 3-0 friendly win.

## January

1 Burnley report a net loss on the year of £342,000 . . . Swansea manager John Toshack receives the MBE . . . Preston get McGee back.

2 Alan Ball senior, father of the Southampton player, is killed in a car crash in Cyprus.

3 Bob Houghton resigns as Bristol City manager. 'There is nothing more I can do', he says. His assistant, Roy Hodgson, takes over.

4 Alex Sabella, the Leeds United midfield player, is transferred to Estudiantes in his native Argentina for £100,000 . . . Thurlestone Reserves from South Devon earn their first League point in two years, drawing 3-3 with Centrax . . . Watford draw West Ham in the fourth round of the FA Cup, having just made record receipts of £53,203 from their victory over Manchester United on Saturday . . . Bristol City are undergoing a financial investigation to pull them out of trouble and possible bankruptcy . . . Walsall put four players on the transfer list.

5 Portsmouth axe assistant manager Stan Harland . . . Martin Edwards becomes chief executive at Manchester United . . . Arsenal's assistant manager, Don Howe, is set to become number two to Ron Greenwood.

7 Robert Maxwell, the millionaire publisher and new chairman of Oxford United, tells his players: 'You must be in the Second Division by 1984.' United, losing £2000 a week, have been saved by a £120,000 cash injection from Maxwell . . . West Ham United pay New York Cosmos £400,000 for the Belgian international, François Van der Elst . . . Brighton move in for 21-year-old Barnet defender Graham Pearce, for £10,000 . . . Spurs unveil details of their £4½ million West Stand which seats 6500 and has 72 executive boxes . . . Wolves chairman Harry Marshall gives manager John Barnwell an ultimatum: 'Accept the terms of a new contract or resign.'

8 European Championship draw finds England in with Hungary again . . . In the Under-21 championship quarter-finals they are paired with Poland and hope the political situation there will be easier by the spring . . . The Pools Panel prepare to sit for the fifth week running, and fixture congestion begins to threaten the World Cup plans. However, it's still a far cry from the winter of 1962–63 when, on 10 successive Saturdays between 29 December and 2 March, 337 of a scheduled 443 games were postponed. On 5 January there were only three third-round ties played in the FA Cup . . . John Barnwell resigns as Wolves' manager.

9 Eight League, one FA Cup, one Scottish Premier Division game and two Scottish friendlies survive the arctic conditions. Rangers' undersoil heating pays off again with 42,000 for the Celtic game. Scotland's only other heated pitch, at Hibs, stages one of the friendlies.

10 Paul Halford, Derby County's 19-year-old reserve striker, accepts an offer to join Napier City Rovers of New Zealand . . . The Kiwis beat China 2-1 in a Singapore play-off to clinch the last World Cup spot, with Wynton Rufer scoring the second

goal . . . Belgium are to complain to FIFA about England's likely seeding in the World Cup draw.

11 Difficult to keep the All-Whites out of the news – Colin Walker, 23, a former dustman who emigrated to New Zealand after breaking his leg as a Barnsley amateur, is starring again for the club he returned to in 1979 . . . George Kerr, who was 39 on Saturday, is sacked as manager at Grimsby . . . Martin Spencer, chief executive and director of Chelsea, warns clubs about the financial crisis facing the majority of them. 'Something drastic is called for and perhaps the current fixture hold-up will lift a few heads out of the sand', he says . . . Halifax Town need £100,000 immediately to survive . . . Luton have lost £38,000 in gate money alone because of postponements . . . FA Secretary Ted Croker makes it clear that the Cup Final stays on 22 May . . . Forty applications are received for the managerial vacancy at Bristol City, who are losing £4000 a week.

12 Leeds' Welsh international Brian Flynn decides to remain with the club after turning down a £300,000 move to Stoke . . . Fulham's boss Malcolm Macdonald advocates summer soccer.

14 The PFA and representatives of the Football League meet to discuss the former's attempt at a ceiling on transfer fees and introduction of the multiplication system which operates in Europe . . . Brighton list six players . . . Chesterfield, who lost £140,000 in the year, are £345,000 in debt . . . Chipman Ltd of Horsham, of whom Denis Thatcher is chairman, have become the UK Licensees of a Swiss invention, cellsystem, which aims to beat the menace of waterlogged pitches. The cost will be £130,000 . . . Shuffle across Sheffield for Jeff King, who joins United from Wednesday on a free transfer.

16 The World Cup draw in Madrid puts England with Czechoslovakia, France and Kuwait; Scotland with Brazil, New Zealand and the USSR, and Northern Ireland with Spain, Honduras and Yugoslavia.

18 England agree to cancel their friendly with France on 24 March . . . Ray Westwood, former Bolton Wanderers and England forward, dies at 69 . . . Bristol City are banned by the League from buying players after falling behind on payments to Newcastle for Mick Harford . . . Ricki Herbert, New Zealand's 20-year-old World Cup defender, is to have a trial with Southampton.

19 Arsenal are fined £1500 by UEFA after crowd trouble against Winterslag in October, though the club were able to prove that none of the members of the club's official travel group was guilty . . . Derby shareholders approve the new £600,000 shares sale . . . Southend increase ticket prices by 30 per cent.

20 Jack Barker, former Derby County and England centre-half, dies at 75 . . . Aberdeen manager Alex Ferguson turns down Wolves job.

21 Findus are to invest £250,000 in Grimsby Town over four years. The club's new £400,000 stand will be called The Findus Family Stand . . . Northern's Ireland's PFA becomes affiliated to the GMWU . . . Plans for a merger of Halifax's soccer and rugby clubs founder again.

22 The Football League postpone the inaugural Associate Members Floodlit Cup because of the fixture chaos.

23 John Hewitt scores the fastest goal in Scottish Cup history for Aberdeen at Motherwell in 9·6 seconds, beating the 10-second goal of Davie McLelland 53 years ago . . . Rangers defender Gregor Stevens is sent off against Kilmarnock after a tackle on Killie substitute Albert Morrison, who had been on the field only a minute. Morrison had his leg broken in two places. Stevens, a £150,000 signing from Leicester in 1979, has been sent off five times and booked on 19 occasions since joining Rangers. He also had a five-game suspension recently.

24 Non-League clubs agree to a new structure as Berger Isthmian League clubs vote 14–9 in favour of a pyramid system with the Alliance Premier at the top and Isthmian, Southern and Northern Premier clubs linking as feeder competitions. The change involves 152 clubs in all.

25 Derby County axe Colin Addison as manager . . . Forest place John Robertson on the transfer list at £600,000 . . . Darlington will fold unless they receive £50,000 within six weeks. They are £100,000 in debt and losing £1000 a week . . . Bristol City players call in the PFA to thrash out the club's plan to give eight leading players immediate free transfers to cut the £350,000 annual wage bill.

26 Bristol City chairman Archie Gooch states that 'the club will have to close down within two weeks if agreement with the players is not reached' . . . Celtic's £200,000 offer for 24-year-old Airdrie striker Sandy Clark is turned down. The Parkhead club have Charlie Nicholas (broken leg) and Davie Provan (knee) injured.

27 Swansea manager John Toshack is fined £200 by the Welsh FA for foul and abusive language to the referee of his club's Southern Junior Floodlit Cup game with Southampton on 8 December ... Brian Clough dismisses talk of a return to manage Derby ... Rachid Harkouk (Notts County) declines World Cup place with Algeria, the country of his father's birth ... An action group threatens a boycott of Wolves' match with Sunderland on Saturday ... Stoke decide not to sign Falkirk striker Willie Herd, 21, who has been on trial and is rated at £100,000. They suspend their captain Ray Evans for two weeks as a result of internal disciplinary measures.

28 Despite their overdraft, Manchester United plan to install undersoil heating ... League Cup final referee will be Peter Willis, 43, a Road Safety Officer who works for County Durham Police. He is a former Newcastle United amateur ... Terry Butcher (Ipswich Town) undergoes an exploratory operation on his nose to deal with persistent bleeding following an injury at Luton last Saturday ... Norwich claim Manchester City owe them £400,000 of the £1 million fee for Kevin Reeves in March 1980.

29 Richie Barker, Stoke manager, claims 'There is no crisis at this club'. Two transferred players have criticised the club and two others have been fined, one of them Lee Chapman for his press comments ... Chelsea may be forced to sell Stamford Bridge ... A new company, BCFC (1982), is formed to rescue Bristol City ...

30 The first full League programme for eight weeks fails to bring back the crowds; only 468,612 watch the 46 matches ... A special gate at Hearts, offering free admission for the unemployed, is used by only 1100 in a crowd of 11,054 ... Scottish club chairmen, at a meeting in Dunblane, favour a winter break and a bonus system for goals.

## February

1 FA Chairman Bert Millichip blames Football League boards for the financial crisis facing several of them. 'They do not want to know', he says. 'I say to all chairmen that unless they do match income with expenditure, a lot more clubs are going to be in trouble.' ... Bristol City make an improved severance pay offer of £80,000 to the eight players ... Bristol Stadium Ltd plan to develop Eastville as a sport and entertainment centre.

2 Charlie George has his contract cancelled by Bulova after seven games for them. 'His style of play did not suit Hong Kong', says coach Ron Wylie ... Cork United £40,000 in debt and with gates under 2000 face worrying times ... Oxford chairman Robert Maxwell refuses to accept the resignation of manager Ian Greaves, who has apparently agreed to take the Wolves job. The manager claims he has no written contract.

3 The Bristol City 'eight' agree to cancel their contracts. They are Geoff Merrick, Trevor Tainton, Chris Garland, Julian Marshall, Gerry Sweeney, Jimmy Mann, Peter Aitken and David Rogers. The total, £250,000 ... Dundee hope to raise £500,000 by switching from a private to a public company ... Darlington now need £50,000 in five weeks to live ... Cork obtain a six weeks' reprieve. They owe Manchester City £8000 following a recent match ... Bobby Robson, commenting on his hospitalised centre-half Terry Butcher, says: 'He is on his ninth pint of blood and may have to have another operation.' ... Peter Swales, Manchester City chairman, calls for across-the-board restraint on players' wages. 'We now have a rat-race with top players demanding and getting £1000 per week.'

4 Port Vale offer the brothers Chamberlain, Neville and Mark, at £300,000 ... Bristol City receive unpaid hotel and restaurant bills of £5000, alleged to emanate from the period under former manager Bob Houghton ... Ipswich problems: John Wark has a virus infection and Russell Osman a gashed knee. They may recall Allan Hunter, 35, who has played no senior football for 15 months ... Bristol City prepare to play Jon Economou, 20, Wayne Bray and Steve Thompson, both 18, against Fulham.

5 Northampton Town part company with manager Bill Dodgin for the second time ... Aston Villa manager Ron Saunders' future is placed in doubt by a boardroom decision to restrict the terms of his contract over the next three years ... John McGinley, signed from Gateshead for £3000, may make his Sunderland début.

6 Some 3000 Chelsea fans beat the away ban and travel to Watford ... Gates hit their lowest point of the term: 435,661.

8 Newport County sack Len Ashurst and appoint Colin Addison, who had left Newport once before in June 1978.

9 Ron Saunders resigns as Villa boss ... England XI beat Manchester City at Maine Road in a benefit for the late Bill Taylor with 11,106 present. Alvin Martin breaks his collarbone ... The Department of Employment refuse Wynton Rufer a work permit.

10 Nottingham Forest list two £1 million strikers, Justin Fashanu and Ian Wallace, together with skipper John McGovern. The announcement is made by assistant man-

ager Peter Taylor while Brian Clough is away on holiday . . . David Webb resigns as Bournemouth manager.

11    Scunthorpe United, £130,000 in debt and losing £1500 a week, sack their general manager and secretary and replace their chairman . . . Harry Gregg joins Swansea as goalkeepers' coach . . . Hereford United have withdrawn from the Football Combination, saving £2000 but losing £450 as the result of a fine for their action . . . Bristol City reduce seat prices by 50p but ask season-ticket holders to pay 30p for each match they attend . . . Webb decides to stay at Bournemouth.

12    The FA lift the away ban on Chelsea fans three days before a test ruling in the High Court . . . Middlesbrough chairman Charles Amer, concerned over physical attacks and the threat of them against himself and his family, resigns after nine years . . . Leeds winger Peter Barnes loses his appeal against a £750 fine imposed by manager Allan Clarke for comments in a newspaper article . . . Stoke's Lee Chapman has his fine reduced on a similar charge from £300 to £100 by a League Management Committee hearing.

13    Nine Argentine players from River Plate are banned following a pay dispute. This could hit Argentina's World Cup hopes . . . League managers pledge early release for British World Cup players.

15    Uncapped Steve Foster (Brighton) is in England's squad against Northern Ireland because of the centre-half crisis . . . Alex MacDonald, 33, is appointed Hearts manager . . . The Irish League draw 3-3 with OFK Belgrade at Windsor Park . . . Birmingham City axe manager Jim Smith . . . Stoke coach Wally Gould leaves by mutual consent . . . Leeds give a trial to Anders Giske, Brann Bergen's Norwegian international midfield player . . . Manchester City defender Nicky Reid faces disciplinary action after failing to turn out in a friendly with Poole Town.

16    Stoke appoint Bill Asprey, a former player, as assistant manager . . . Hereford chairman Peter Hill says: 'The board are working on a survival package.' . . . Richard Vernon Stokes, a former Portsmouth chairman and FA member, dies at 80 . . . Exeter City's first team, which lost 5-1 to Millwall on Sunday, return to lose a Midweek League match 1-0 to Millwall Reserves.

17    Port Vale are to spend £10,000 on better floodlighting, helped by a grant of £8000 from the Football Grounds Improvement Trust . . . Bristol City obtain two months' delay in the battle against liquidation.

18    Morton managing director Hal Stewart warns: 'Scottish football is on a disaster course.' The League Management Committee call for a Premier Division of 16 clubs and either a First Division of 22 or a First of 10 and a Second Division of 12 . . . Chester announce a loss of £137,000; they are losing more than £3000 a week . . . Ron Saunders is poised to become Birmingham City manager . . . Ken Knighton sacks captain Tommy Taylor because of 'his behaviour on and off the field last week'.

19    Jasper Carrott resigns as a director of Birmingham because he was not consulted by colleagues over the dismissal of Jim Smith.

21    The 92 Football League chairmen, at a crisis meeting in Solihull, want to amend some of the football Laws to improve the product and the image of the game . . . Reading manager Maurice Evans denies that long-serving goalkeeper Steve Death has walked out of the club.

22    League chairmen endorse a £5 million advertising campaign to win back support to the game. Six-a-side football, popular in the United States, will also be tried . . . Malcolm Page (Oxford United) retires because of a knee injury at 35 . . . Bristol City prepare a £25,000 debenture scheme, available for 10 companies, as part of their £1 million share issue due next month.

23    Goal by Bryan Robson in less than 60 seconds puts England on the way to beating Northern Ireland 4-0 at Wembley. Cyrille Regis makes his début as a 66th-minute substitute for the injured Trevor Francis. Foster is the other débutant . . . Southampton discuss a possible deal to sign Dutch international winger Tscheu La Ling, 26, after he impressed in a trial against IFK Gothenburg, scoring twice in a 4-4 draw . . . Tommy Taylor is reinstated at Orient after an amicable meeting.

24    Scotland, despite impressing, lose 3-0 in Spain, after two late goals . . . Swansea exchange David Giles for Ian Walsh of Crystal Palace.

25    Hull City, with debts of £350,000, call in the receiver but hope to complete the season. Chairman Christopher Needler recently gave the club an interest-free loan of £325,000, with a bank guarantee of a further £225,000, but was told by his financial advisors that it would be unwise for him to continue his support on such a scale . . . Bristol Rovers plan cuts in expenditure and new methods of increasing revenue . . . Derby owe £10,000 in tax bills . . . According to a *Daily Telegraph* survey, Barrow

made a small profit in 1981, Dagenham £25,000 and Boston United a remarkable £163,000, although Altrincham lost £10,000 . . . Bobby Charlton opens a soccer school in Manchester.

26 Phil Hoadley, Norwich City centre-half, is to be loaned to Eastern AA in Hong Kong for a month.

27 The Manchester derby at Old Trafford produces a gate of 57,872 with 5000 more locked out; the result, 1-1.

28 Southampton manager Lawrie McMenemy considers La Ling to be 'a luxury player because I couldn't play him in all games' . . . Laurie Cunningham makes a comeback for Real Madrid after 17 months of injuries.

## March

1 Halifax Town's playing staff go up for sale. Chairman Sam Rorke says: 'If the financial position does not improve by the end of the month I will close the club down.' They are losing £3000 a week and have debts of £254,000. One player was alleged to be earning £350 a week while others were receiving less than £120 . . . Oxford appoint Jim Smith as manager on a two-year contract . . . The League complete a £2 million sponsorship deal with the National Dairy Board, as a result of which the League Cup will be called the Milk Cup for the next four years . . . Gordon Taylor, secretary of the PFA, warns club chairmen: 'We shall have to force clubs into liquidation if they copy what Bristol City are doing.' The club have signed two new players and are moving for a third, despite axing eight on contract . . . Derby County offer John Newman, their caretaker manager, the job proper . . . Norwich sell Willie Donachie back to Portland Timber for the £200,000 fee they paid for him in September. The club's striker, John Fashanu, is suspended for two matches after being sent off in an East Anglian League game. City are also thinking of erecting a missile barrier behind one goal at Carrow Road.

2 Frank Worthington joins Leeds and Byron Stevenson goes to Birmingham in an exchange deal . . . Newman takes the Derby post . . . Charlie George signs for Bournemouth . . . Barnsley boss Norman Hunter fines defender Neil Cooper a week's wages and puts him on the list while planning to make a comeback himself . . . Southampton striker Steve Moran, 21, will miss the rest of the season with the persistent back injury which sidelined him in January . . . Halifax launch survival plan.

3 Cardiff sack manager Richie Morgan, along with his chief coach Graham Williams, and appoint Len Ashurst as manager. Earlier in the week Ashurst had a testimonial match at Newport . . . York axe Kevin Randall, who took over from Barry Lyons in December on a caretaker basis . . . All Hull players will receive free transfers . . . Villa earn a 0-0 draw in Simferopol against Dynamo Kiev, Liverpool take a slender single-goal lead over CSKA Sofia, while both Tottenham and Dundee United establish 2-0 wins over Eintracht Frankfurt and Radnicki Nis respectively.

4 Hull dismiss manager Mike Smith, assistant Cyril Lea and commercial manager Gordon Dimbleby. Youth development officer Bobby Brown agrees to halve his £15,000 salary and take charge of the team . . . West Bromwich plan to sign Twente's Dutchman Romeo Zondervan, 23, in a £250,000 transfer . . . Chelsea will break their receipts record for the second time in three weeks. The expected 45,000 for the FA Cup game with Spurs will pay £150,000, compared with £130,000 for Liverpool's visit . . . Manchester City's Kevin Bond may leave the club.

5 Blackpool, with debts of over £500,000, may be taken over by a local businessman . . . Glasgow Rangers' long-serving Sandy Jardine will have a benefit match on 16 May after 17 years.

6 Spurs, Leicester, Queen's Park Rangers and West Bromwich are the successful sixth-round teams in the FA Cup; Forfar win the minnows battle in the Scottish Cup, Gordon Leitch celebrating his 22nd birthday by scoring his first goal of the season for them . . . Spurs Argentine star Ossie Ardiles tries to obtain an extension of his 1 April deadline to join the World Cup holders' training camp.

8 Harry Haslam, who helped sign Ardiles and Ricky Villa for Spurs, is Argentina bound again seeking talent . . . Ipswich launch scheme to borrow additional money to provide 4600 more seats . . . Gregor Stevens (Rangers) is suspended for six months . . . England will play a benefit game in Bilbao, their World Cup headquarters . . . Leeds are £1.5 million in debt, having lost £433,000 in the year ending 31 July primarily owing to compensation payments to former manager Jimmy Adamson and other backroom staff . . . Doncaster Rovers plan to increase their share capital . . . Cork United, with debts of £40,000, face closure.

9  Hereford's survival may depend on the city council. The club seek a long-term lease on their Edgar Street home to enable them to pay off a tax debt of £80,000.

10 Alun Evans, secretary of the UAU, is to succeed Trevor Morris as FA of Wales secretary. Morris is retiring through ill health ... Bristol City to sell Swedish goalkeeper Jan Moller to Toronto Blizzard for £85,000 ... Crystal Palace pull out of the £250,000 deal to buy back David Swindlehurst from Derby ... A 14,525 gate braves rain to pay £30,000 for Kevin Beattie's testimonial at Ipswich, a 2-2 draw with Moscow Dynamo ... Three players sent off in the first half at Lincoln bring the total of dismissals to 100 ... Sunderland chairman Tom Cowie blames the board for the club's plight. 'The directors, like many others elsewhere, have to accept responsibility.'

11 The FA decide to take no action after the Boxing Day incident at Liverpool in which Manchester City goalkeeper Joe Corrigan was struck by an object from the crowd ... Tommy Craig moves from Swansea to Carlisle on a free.

12 Bristol City are ordered to return Ray Gooding (Coventry), Les Carter (Crystal Palace) and Aidan McCaffery (Bristol Rovers) to their former clubs ... Laurie Cunningham is included in England's squad for Bilbao ... Cork United will have to play their next 'home' game away.

13 Liverpool beat Spurs 3-1 after extra time in the League Cup final, which produces record receipts of £720,000 ... Charlie George is introduced to the Derby crowd before the game with Palace, having agreed to return to his former club.

14 Tom Forsyth, 33, Rangers' defender, accepts medical advice and retires with a serious knee complaint ... Dunfermline captain Jim Brown is to sue John Pelosi, the St Johnstone winger, in the first civil action taken in Scotland over an on-the-field incident. Brown, 31, who suffered a broken leg, is unlikely to play again.

15 Ron Greenwood denies England's World Cup headquarters are sub-standard ... England's one referee in the World Cup will be Clive White. Malcolm Moffat (Northern Ireland) and Bob Valentine (Scotland) are the other UK nominees. White will also referee the FA Cup final ... A consortium of 10 businessmen have made Hull an increased offer of £814,000.

16 Graham Kelly, Secretary of the Football League, says: 'There is no reason why the membership of the League should be maintained at 92 clubs.' ... Crystal Palace, about to announce a profit of £98,000 on 1980–81, place Steve Wicks and Jim Cannon on the transfer list ... Hull will keep most of the players they made available for transfer ... Hereford secretary Peter Grange agrees to leave at the end of the season as part of staff cuts ... Brighton agree to a transfer request from Mickey Thomas once a replacement has been signed.

17 Aston Villa beat Kiev 2-0, and a late goal from Glenn Hoddle enables Spurs to go through. Liverpool lose to CSKA after extra time with Mark Lawrenson sent off, and Dundee United crash by three clear goals in Yugoslavia ... England Under-21 win in Poland 2-1 ... Queen's Park Rangers plan a roof over their ground.

18 The FA begin their search for a successor to Ron Greenwood ... Birmingham's hopes of signing Les Mutrie and Tony Norman from Hull dashed when the Hull board asked for a joint fee of £170,000 ... Hereford council refuses to amend the United's ground lease ... Laurie Cunningham, one of three Real players sent off in a UEFA Cup tie with Kaiserslautern, may be banned from playing for England in Bilbao ... Liverpool manager Bob Paisley, back from their controversial defeat in Sofia, says: 'The officials were the worst I have seen in Europe since the trouble we had with Inter-Milan in 1965.'

19 Arsenal await a work permit for Vladimir Petrovic, the Yugoslav World Cup star they hope to sign from Red Star Belgrade ... Steve Kember stays as caretaker manager of Crystal Palace.

20 Argentina deny an Arsenal bid for Diego Maradona.

21 Morton are the subject of a take-over inquiry from Dallas Tornado ... Keith Burkinshaw, Spurs' manager, calls for a First Division of 18 clubs. 'The League chairmen won't help – they won't reduce the League because they cling to the idea that we should play as many matches as possible.'

22 Bristol City are saved. The Football League waive the £250,000 guarantee that next season's fixtures will be fulfilled, but City's £95,000 share-out from the League Cup pool with be withheld for a year ... West Bromwich may try to buy Cunningham back from Real Madrid.

23 England draw 1-1 with Athletic Bilbao in José Rojo's benefit game ... Scotland beat the Netherlands 2-1 at Hampden Park before 71,843 ... Directors' wives at Hereford volunteer for the office cleaning at Edgar Street ... 13 Scottish clubs plan a campaign to advertise their lotteries.

24 Scotland Under-21 are through to the semi-finals of the UEFA Championship . . . Wales draw 1-1 with Spain in Valencia but Ireland crash by four goals in France . . . Oxford sell Keith Cassells and Mark Wright to Southampton while Trevor Hebberd makes the reverse journey. Hebberd is rated at £80,000 in the £230,000 transaction . . . Keith MacRae, back from Portland Timbers, will join Leeds . . . Martin Jol (WBA) has a cartilage operation . . . Walsall obtain John Teasdale, 19, free from Wolves.

25 Transfer-deadline activity includes Mick Harford moving to Birmingham City for £100,000 from Bristol City with the fee going to Newcastle, who were owed £100,000 by City . . . Godfrey Ingham joins San José Earthquakes from Luton for £60,000 . . . Martin Peters, 38, declines to play again with Cardiff . . . Scottish clubs will keep the present League set-up . . . Hereford will carry on – for the moment . . . Norwich free nine players.

26 Dundee United are fined £2000 for failing to turn up for the final of the Scottish Second XI Cup at Ayr earlier in the month.

27 England Boys are the top scorers of the day, beating the Netherlands 7-0 at Wembley.

29 Darlington announce their target of £50,000 has been reached . . . Steve Kember is offered a three-year contract at Crystal Palace . . . Ipswich striker Paul Mariner resumes training after an Achilles tendon operation six weeks previously . . . Hereford council gives United a lifeline by varying the club's lease on their corporation-owned ground.

30 Airdrie manager Bobby Watson resigns. A director of a steel stock-holding company, he was the only part-time manager in the Scottish Premier Division . . . Courageous Hull defender Steve Hoolickin, 30, retires because of a heart condition he has had since 1975 . . . Middlesbrough free eight players, Chelsea five . . . Sheffield United play Bradford City in Division Four in front of 24,593.

31 Don Masson, 35, Notts County's captain, is to retire . . . Gary Mills (Nottingham Forest) moves to Seattle Sounders . . . Billy McCulley, East Stirling's longest-serving player, is transferred to Ayr United for less than £10,000. McCulley, 29, was signed in 1973 and at 5ft 4in is said to be the smallest player in Scottish football . . . Alan Oakes is sacked as Chester's player-manager at 39, the same age as Portsmouth's departing boss Frank Burrows. Bobby Campbell, assistant manager of Aldershot earlier in the season, takes over from Burrows . . . Rangers, at home, are watched by just 3000 against Airdrie.

**April**

1 Tony Barton is appointed as Aston Villa's manager after standing in since February. He has a three-year contract. Roy McLaren, the club coach, is promoted to assistant manager . . . David Fairclough, 25, joins Toronto Blizzard from Liverpool for £150,000.

2 Aldershot announce a loss of £92,000 for the year ending June 1981, almost double the previous deficit . . . Rochdale, expected to lose £30,000 this season, say they will close unless the next five home matches double their attendances.

3 Queen's Park Rangers and Spurs reach the FA Cup final . . . In Scotland both semi-finals are drawn, including Second Division Forfar with Rangers . . . For Ossie Ardiles, due to return to Buenos Aires for World Cup training, Spurs' victory over Leicester could be his last appearance in England because of the Falkland Islands crisis.

4 Manchester United's Northern Ireland international Tom Connell is to move to Glentoran, where he can play part-time.

5 Stockport County consider changing their colours because they match the Argentine national strip.

6 Rangers edge Forfar out, 2-1, in the Scottish Cup semi-final replay . . . Spurs hope Ricky Villa, their other Argentine, will be able to overcome political pressures.

7 A Tony Morley goal gives Aston Villa a slender lead over Anderlecht, but Tottenham have to settle for a 1-1 draw in a bruising game with Barcelona . . . Arsenal are informed that a work permit has been granted by the Department of Employment for Vladimir Petrovic, their £750,000-rated midfield player known at home as 'The Pidgeon' . . . Aberdeen secure their Scottish Cup final spot . . . Former Clydebank manager Bill Munro is appointed at Airdrie . . . England Under-21 hold Poland 2-2.

9 Colchester United manager Bobby Roberts refuses to resign . . . Scarborough boss Jim McAnearney resigns after three home defeats . . . Hull's three sacked managerial and commercial administrators settle for compensation.

11 Fulham might install a Cellsystem pitch which could cost £400,000.

14 Tottenham are fined £2500 and Barcelona £7000 by UEFA after considering reports from the official observer and referee Egbert Mulder of The Netherlands . . . Tottenham become the first club to attract a million spectators in the season. The milestone was reached when the 18,226th spectator passed through the turnstiles in their 28th game.

15 Norwich are cleared of blame for an incident the previous Saturday when a lighter thrown from the crowd hit the referee . . . Ten new clubs are elected to the Southern League . . . Joe Royle (Norwich) is forced to retire with a knee injury.

17 Linfield clinch their 34th Irish League title . . . Alvin Martin injures his shoulder for the second time in the year.

19 Terry Butcher, after only two senior outings since recovering from his badly damaged nose, is in England's squad of 22 for the match with Wales . . . England Under-21 beat Scotland 1-0.

20 Bryan Robson (Carlisle) scores the 250th League goal of his distinguished career.

21 Spurs lose 1-0 in Barcelona but Villa reach the final of the European Cup by holding Anderlecht to a goalless draw in Belgium. However, fighting fans threaten action by UEFA . . . Don Masson decides to join Bulova in Hong Kong . . . Bristol City's share issue produces only £75,000 in four weeks . . . Chester have the lowest gate of the season, 1034, their lowest in history.

23 Anderlecht ask UEFA to have Aston Villa expelled from the European Cup . . . Mike England, the Wales manager, accuses Tottenham of favouritism in withdrawing Paul Price, the Welsh skipper, from the international with England . . . Trevor Francis loses an appeal against the £2000 he was fined for being sent off against Everton last month . . . Manchester United name Norman Whiteside, 16, youth international from Northern Ireland, as substitute against Brighton . . . Manager Jimmy McGuigan leaves Stockport County by mutual consent. Eric Webster, who doubles as assistant manager and groundsman, takes over . . . Grimsby give Alec King, commercial manager, a five-year contract. Fund raising is up to £500,000 annually.

24 Attendances at 442,922 are the second worst of the season . . . Linfield clinch a League and Cup double.

25 Michel Platini, 26, French international midfield player and captain, has apparently had offers from Manchester United, Everton and Arsenal, while Manchester City and Tottenham are also reported to be interested. His contract with St Etienne expires in June . . . Dundalk take the League of Ireland Championship.

26 The Scottish League decides to retain the two-points system for a win . . . A back injury keeps Kevin Keegan out of the match with Wales . . . Watford beat Manchester United 3-2 before 7280 at Old Trafford in the first leg of the Youth Cup final . . . Blackpool manager Allan Brown and his assistant Bobby Smith will be leaving at the end of the season. This brings the number of League club managerial changes in three years to 47: 10 in Division One, 14 in Two, 10 in Three, and 13 in Four.

27 Trevor Francis scores the goal that beats Wales . . . Glasgow Rangers line up Robert Prytz, who almost joined Stoke earlier this season. He will cost £100,000 . . . Halifax Town will carry on next season, according to chairman Sam Rorke . . . Manchester United sign a two-year sponsorship deal with Sharp Electronics for £500,000 . . . Southampton manager Lawrie McMenemy says: 'I am sure if the injury to Keegan had been serious then someone in the England camp would have contacted me. I'm hoping the stories about the injury are being exaggerated.' . . . Reading manager Maurice Evans relegates his entire senior side to the reserves.

28 Northern Ireland draw 1-1 with Scotland, the weakened Irish giving first caps to Bobby Campbell (Bradford City), Jim Cleary (Glentoran) and Felix Healy (Coleraine) . . . England Under-21 are held 1-1 by Scotland but reach the UEFA final . . . Bristol City are saved. Though only £90,000 of the £300,000 had been raised, the caretaker board contacts several businessmen and raises the balance.

29 The 70-year-old Central League plans to expand, inviting 10 more League clubs . . . Ken Bates, who purchased Chelsea Football Club on 2 April, becomes chairman.

30 Aston Villa are fined £14,500 but may play in the European Cup final against Bayern Munich. Anderlecht are fined £4375 . . . Bristol City sack manager Roy Hodgson.

## May

1 The Arsenal v West Ham match is held up for nearly 12 minutes because of fighting on the terraces. Terry Neill, the Arsenal manager, says: 'It makes you wonder what sort of parents produce mindless morons like this.' His opposite number, John Lyall, offers: 'There seems to be nothing we can do about it.' After the match a man is fatally stabbed outside the ground, the second North London fatality of the season,

following the death of a young man at the foot of an escalator at Seven Sisters underground station last November after Tottenham's match with Manchester United.

2   Arsenal are reported to be interested in re-signing Liam Brady from Juventus.

3   Bobby Roberts is sacked as Colchester's manager.

4   Southampton and Coventry draw 5-5, the first score draw of 10 goals in the First Division since Chelsea v West Ham in December 1966 . . . The FA launch an inquiry into the crowd disturbances at Highbury . . . According to a directors guide to the solvency of football clubs, published by the accountants to the FA, three of the points emerging are: 1. Gate receipts do not always pay the wages; 2. Increased gate receipts have failed to keep pace with increased expenses; 3. Clubs are finding it hard to maintain and repair grounds as well as carry out improvements to them . . .Mickey Thomas (Brighton) is fined two weeks' wages after failing to report for training . . . Tony Parkes, the Blackburn midfield player, retires after a year-long fight to recover from a broken leg. He will continue on the coaching staff . . . The FA of Ireland are pessimistic about their game in Buenos Aires against Argentina. The likelihood is that English clubs will not release their players.

5   Allan Hunter (Ipswich Town) becomes player-manager of Colchester . . . West Bromwich part with their coach Gerry Summers at the end of his six months' contract . . . IFK Gothenburg establish a 1-0 lead over Hamburg in the UEFA Cup final first leg . . . Wyndham Evans, 30, in his first Division One match for Swansea, is carried off in the 24th minute with a badly twisted knee . . . Mixenden '76, beaten 1-0 in the Halifax and District FA Dunkley Cup final by Golden Fleece on Halifax Town's ground, had to turn out a 10-man team because the rules prevented them from including two players who had not taken part in earlier rounds.

6   Peter Taylor, the Nottingham Forest assistant manager, is to retire. 'I have been in football for 36 years and it is having its effect on me now', he says. His partnership with Brian Clough had embraced Hartlepool United, Derby County, Brighton and then Forest. Taylor also led Brighton alone for a spell . . . UEFA reject Anderlecht's appeal and confirm Aston Villa's European Cup final place, but reduce the Belgian club's fine to £1458 . . . The funeral of Denis Hill-Wood, the Arsenal chairman who died earlier in the week, is to be held on Tuesday . . . Watford 4 Manchester United 4 in the Youth Cup final second leg means that the trophy goes to Watford.

7   Peter Shilton may leave Forest if he so desires, although there has been no disagreement between player and club . . . Rangers will have Robert Prytz next season, provided that they pay £100,000 for him and that he obtains a work permit and avoids serious injury until July . . . Bruce Rioch, Torquay's player-coach, declines the chance to manage the club . . . Manchester City expect to transfer Nick Reid to Seattle Sounders for £400,000 and sign him back in September at a lower fee.

9   The FAs of England, Scotland and Northern Ireland will each be fined £4400 if they boycott the World Cup because of the Falklands crisis . . . New Zealand beat the touring League of Ireland 1-0 in the first of five such matches . . . Rangers defeat Southampton by a single goal in Sandy Jardine's testimonial. Some 10,000 pay £30,000.

10  England's World Cup 40 includes nine uncapped players . . . Ipswich sign David Barnes, the Coventry defender, after a six-weeks trial. They once rejected him as a schoolboy striker . . . Aston Villa are to control tickets for the European Cup final through their official travellers club . . . Preston release four players on free transfers.

11  Hereford are banned from buying new players until they pay Portsmouth the £15,000 owed from the sale of two players in December 1980 . . . Norman Whiteside signs as a professional for Manchester United.

12  Barcelona beat Standard Liège 2-1 in a bruising European Cup-Winners' Cup final on their own Nou Camp ground . . . Wrexham chairman Fred Tomlinson offers his resignation if someone is prepared to take over his personal guarantees towards the club's bank debts, believed to be approaching £500,000 . . . Eire call off their match in Argentina, but it is too late to prevent some English clubs agreeing to release players for the tour, which also takes in Brazil, Chile and Trinidad . . . Steve Hunt, Coventry's midfield player, may return to New York Cosmos for the summer months . . . Kettering Town have launched an appeal for £50,000 to enable them to pay off debts.

13  Speculation increases that the three British teams will withdraw from the World Cup finals. Meanwhile Spanish stadium workers are threatening to strike during the finals over pay and conditions . . . Bristol City are retaining only 10 players, Halifax just eight. Halifax are scrapping their reserve team . . . Bristol Rovers have decided not to share Ashton Gate with City next season. They have signed a five-year agreement to

stay at Eastville for £1000 a week rent. The club will also receive £28,000 in compensation from their landlords, agreed in the High Court.

14  Scotland's World Cup 40 is full of experienced players . . . Denis Smith, 34, prepares to make one of his last appearances for Stoke before joining York as player-manager . . . Brentford manager Fred Callaghan receives a further two-year contract . . . Wrexham axe manager Mel Sutton and his assistant Mickey Evans.

15  Liverpool win their 13th League Championship. Manager Bob Paisley says: 'I'm proudest of this one because there was so much to do.' In January the club were ninth with 27 points from 18 matches. Despite this success, gates at Anfield are down 25 per cent over the past two seasons and the staff has been cut from 31 to 23 . . . Celtic win their 33rd title in Scotland . . . Enfield beat Altrincham 1-0 in the FA Trophy final . . . Tony Woodcock may join Arsenal . . . Dismissals reach 150.

17  Keith Burkinshaw admits he might have to leave Ricky Villa out of Spurs' Cup final team because of the Falklands crisis . . . Wrexham, who dismissed manager Mel Sutton earlier in the week, free three experienced players; Peterborough axe five and scrap their reserve and youth teams; Oxford release five, and Chesterfield put the entire staff on offer.

18  Leeds United fans riot at West Bromwich as defeat endangers their First Division status . . . Brian Little, who has had to retire with a knee injury, plays in his own testimonial match, scoring twice in a 3-2 win for Villa over an England team. A crowd of 9229 provide £25,000 . . . West Ham prepare to sign Sandy Clark, the Airdrie centre-forward, for £200,000.

19  Gothenburg shake Hamburg, beating them 3-0 on their own ground in the second leg of the UEFA Cup final . . . Swansea clinch a European spot by beating Cardiff 2-1 in the second leg of the Welsh Cup final.

20  Terry Cooper becomes the third Bristol City manager of the season . . . Northampton promote Clive Walker to manager for the second time. He took over for a spell in 1979.

21  England beat Fulham 3-0 in a testimonial game for Les Strong; it produces receipts of £17,000 . . . Bobby Campbell is confirmed as Portsmouth's manager.

22  Spurs and Rangers draw the FA Cup final 1-1 after extra time. Gate receipts of £918,000 are a British record. Villa left himself out of Spurs' team . . . In Scotland, Aberdeen also need extra time to beat Rangers 4-1.

24  Scotland beat Wales 1-0 . . . John Bond and assistant John Benson decide to stay at Manchester City, despite a tempting offer from Portugal's Benfica . . . Alex Cropley, the Portsmouth midfield player, retires at 31 with a persistent knee injury.

25  England have a 2-0 win over The Netherlands at Wembley . . . Peterborough United manager Peter Morris, 38, is to leave the club . . . Glenn Roeder misses the Cup final replay as skipper of Queen's Park Rangers because of suspension incurred in a League game . . . John McDowell (Norwich) joins Bristol Rovers as player-coach . . . Hampden Park is to have undersoil heating with a gas-operated system. The decaying North Stand will be demolished in the £440,000 improvement.

26  Aston Villa win the European Cup with a goal from Peter Withe, though the hero is substitute goalkeeper Nigel Spink, 23, in only his second senior game. He came on for Jimmy Rimmer after eight minutes . . . David Hay, having steered Motherwell to promotion, resigns to become manager of a sports complex in Florida . . . Leicester line up Alan Smith, 19, a striker from Alvechurch, for £15,000.

27  A Glenn Hoddle penalty goal gives Spurs their seventh FA Cup win in seven finals against an injury-weakened but gallant Rangers side . . . Wales beat Northern Ireland 3-0 at Wrexham before 2315 spectators, the lowest British International Championship crowd since before the First World War. The attendance was hit by the television showing of the FA Cup final replay . . . Liverpool are to be sponsored for the next three years by Crown Paints in a £500,000 deal . . . Bryan Robson resigns as Carlisle player-coach after Bob Stokoe's recommendation that he should become team manager was rejected by the board . . . Norwich to increase admission prices by an average 10 per cent; Leicester, who made no increase last season, will raise their seating charges by an average 14 per cent . . . George Best might play for Marconi Leopards in the Philips Soccer League in Australia. For six matches he wants £3000 a game, accommodation and fares.

28  Keith Burkinshaw is likely to sign a new three-year contract for Spurs . . . Bob Paisley is voted Manager of the Year . . . Diego Maradona, 21, joins Barcelona for a world-record fee of £4,235,000.

29  England win the 100th match against Scotland by a Paul Mariner goal . . . Asa Hartford may sign for Chelsea after the World Cup at £200,000. Ken Bates, the Chelsea

chairman, recently signed David Speedie from Darlington for £70,000 ... Malcolm Allison takes Sporting Lisbon to a League and Cup double in Portugal ... Scotland win the UEFA Youth Tournament, beating Czechoslovakia 3-1 in Helsinki ... Ray Stewart and Tommy Burns are omitted from Scotland's World Cup 22.

31   Norman Whiteside, 17, with two Football League appearances, one as a substitute, is in Northern Ireland's World Cup squad.

## June

1   Nottingham Forest become a limited company after 117 years of being run by a committee with 209 club members ... Alan Mullery resigns as Charlton Athletic manager, hours after Mike Gliksten stepped down as chairman after 20 years. Mark Hulyer, 28, a South London businessman, takes over from Gliksten .. Bolton Wanderers are trying to contact Pelé in the hope he will take over as player-manager from George Mulhall, who was dismissed earlier ... Blackpool have appointed Sam Ellis, the Watford coach, as manager.

2   England draw 1-1 with Iceland in Reykjavik with a virtual 'B' team, while Wales surprise France by beating them 1-0 in Paris ... West Bromwich may be making managerial changes, with Ronnie Allen moving to an administrative role ... Charlton Athletic appoint Ken Craggs as team manager, with Leighton Phillips becoming player-coach ... A £2,200,000 appeal fund for the redevelopment of Hampden Park is boosted by the promise of £250,000 from the Scottish Sports Council. The fund already stands at £750,000.

3   The England senior squad beats Finland 4-1 in Helsinki as part of their final preparations for the World Cup, but Cyrille Regis, injured the day before against Iceland, will miss the trip ... Manchester United sign Peter Bodak, the Coventry City winger on a free transfer ... Telford United are nominated as the non-League candidate for a Football League place as Alliance Premier League champions Runcorn and runners-up Enfield have unsuitable grounds for League status ... Halifax chairman Sam Rorke resigns, but he will become club president and leave his money with the club ... Chesterfield are to sue Wolves for a £30,000 instalment on the transfer fee of Alan Birch, who has since moved on to Barnsley.

4   Ron Greenwood axes wingers from his final 22. There is no room for either Tony Morley or Peter Barnes. The squad will be the oldest of the 24 teams competing in Spain, with an average age of 28 ... Brian Clough signs a three-year contract with Forest ... Leicester give free transfers to seven players ... Ardiles says he will not honour the last year of his Spurs contract ... Portsmouth snap up ex-England winger Dave Thomas from Middlesbrough and Ernie Howe from Queen's Park Rangers ... Scottish FA secretary Ernie Walker pleads to World Cup fans: 'Be proud of your team, be Scottish – but, above all, behave!'

5   With a week to go before the World Cup, Spain's leading newspaper, *El Pais*, describes Mundial '82 as 'the great national disaster'. Grounds are still being completed, ticket sales are disappointing, and the organisers hope merely to break even ... Wolves finally cancel the contract of Peter Knowles, 36, who walked out on the club in 1969 to become a Jehovah's Witness.

6   Ipswich agree to waive the last year of Bobby Robson's contract in the likelihood that he will take over as England manager after the World Cup ... Wolves are to sell their sports and social club at Molineux because of their near-£2 million debts ... Billy Bingham bans his players from sunbathing in Brighton ... Scotland plan two games against local teams in Portugal.

7   Tottenham may release Ardiles on loan to a European club.

8   Greenwood is confident. 'We are all delighted with the way things are going and are quietly confident about our chances. If we can get that little bit of luck in Spain, who knows what will happen?' ... Leeds axe assistant manager Martin Wilkinson ... Promoted Burnley announce season-ticket sales have passed £61,000, some £10,000 more than for all last term ... Grimsby and their former manager George Kerr reach settlement over compensation ... Colin Appleton is appointed Hull manager by new chairman Don Robinson, who once sacked him as manager of Scarborough ... Ray Houghton joins Fulham on a free transfer from West Ham.

9   Scotland beat Portuguese Third Division side Torralta 9-1 ... Bert Millichip wants England fans who misbehave in Spain to be sent home ... Arsenal, having signed Tony Woodcock and Vladimir Petrovic, are still hoping to recapture Liam Brady, though he may move from Juventus to Sampdoria for £780,000 ... Northampton sign Dave Syrett on a free transfer from Peterborough ... Hermann Neuberger, vice-president of FIFA, says that Colombia may not be able to stage the 1986 World Cup

if the 24-team format is retained . . . Harry Marshall remains chairman of Wolves after a secret ballot of shareholders gives him 4211 votes against 4107. Vice-chairman Wilf Sproson is not so lucky and is voted out after 24 years . . . Wrexham appoint Bobby Roberts as manager.

10 England receive a warm welcome from locals in Bilbao . . . Scotland beat Torralta 7-0 . . . Bristol City re-sign Tom Ritchie from Sunderland for nothing, 18 months after selling him for £180,000 . . . Neil Martin resigns as manager of Walsall . . . Drew Busby, 34, the Morton and former Airdrie and Hearts player, who also had a spell with Toronto Blizzard, is appointed player-manager of Queen of the South . . . Eric McManus, Stoke goalkeeper, falls through a glass door at his home, severing a nerve and tendon in an arm . . . Chris Nicholl damages his ankle in a fall at the Irish headquarters in Spain . . . Tom Finney loses £112 when his hotel room is burgled there . . . FIFA President João Havelange calls off dress rehearsal of the World Cup ceremony to prevent further damage to the pitch.

11 At the League's AGM the four clubs seeking re-election are voted back without trouble: Crewe 50 votes, Northampton 53, Rochdale 48, Scunthorpe 48, leaving Telford with the unlucky 13 . . . Scottish doubts remain over Kenny Dalglish, who has been struggling to find form in practice . . . Kevin Keegan celebrates his OBE in the Honours List. His room-mate, Trevor Brooking, received a similar honour last year. They share something else: both are injured and doubtful for England's opening match.

12 Jimmy Frizzell, the Oldham Athletic manager, is sacked. He has been at the club as player and manager for 23 years.

13 For the first time in 20 years the opening match in the World Cup finals produces a goal. Belgium, quoted at 7-1 against winning 1-0 by the bookmakers, do just that against the holders Argentina.

14 Dino Zoff, Italy's 40-year-old goalkeeper, keeps a clean sheet on his 100th appearance . . . Manchester United expect to sign Arnold Muhren from Ipswich on the expiry of his contract on 31 July.

15 Hungary's 10 goals against El Salvador are the highest in the World Cup final tournament . . . Deaths announced of Bob Hesford, former Huddersfield Town goalkeeper, at 66 and of Albert Henshall, president of Stoke, at 69.

16 England start smartly with a 27-seconds goal from Bryan Robson against France and go on to win 3-1 . . . Algeria shake West Germany with a 2-1 win . . . Hungary ask FIFA to withdraw cautions against two players for drinking water at the side of the pitch . . . Havelange confirms that 24 teams will take part in 1986 . . . Harry Marshall resigns as Wolves chairman. 'The activities of the past few weeks and in particular a writ, which has recently been issued, have made it impossible for the present board to continue to run the club.' . . . Arsenal are cleared by an FA commission over crowd trouble on 1 May . . . Coventry transfer Rudi Kaiser, their Dutch Under-21 cap, to Nice for £50,000. City will play Portsmouth in August to raise money for relatives of people killed on HMS Coventry in the Falklands conflict.

17 Northern Ireland hold Yugoslavia to a goalless draw, 17-year-old Norman Whiteside leading their attack.

18 Scotland the brave lead Brazil but are finally beaten 4-1 . . . Doug Ellis, former Aston Villa chairman and Birmingham director, becomes Wolves chairman. He discloses that debts could be as high as £2.5 million. 'The club was saved from extinction with just 24 hours to spare', he says . . . John Newman decides he cannot afford to offer a new contract to Charlie George.

20 England win again, thanks to defensive errors by the Czechs.

21 Chaos in Valladolid as France beat Kuwait 4-1. Play is held up for seven minutes after Kuwait protest about a goal, which the Russian referee eventually disallows to the annoyance of France! . . . Northern Ireland held by Honduras . . . Leeds chairman Manny Cussins will meet his manager amid speculation that Allan Clarke might be replaced.

22 Scotland fail to reach the second stage on goal difference after drawing 2-2 with USSR . . . Kuwait are fined £6000 by FIFA . . . Ipswich say that Bobby Robson could combine his roles as club manager and leader of the England team . . . Chester appoint Cliff Sear, their caretaker manager, as manager . . . Malcolm Finlayson, former Wolves goalkeeper, becomes the club's vice-chairman . . . Terry Curran might join Sheffield United from rivals Wednesday . . . Lincoln are £200,000 in debt . . . Trevor Phillips joins Stockport from Chester after being loaned to them towards the end of the season. He is County's second capture, the other being Paul Bowles from Port Vale.

23 Paul Mariner, credited with the own goal from Czechoslovakia's Jozef Barmos, has

the chance of equalling the 94-year-old British record for scoring in consecutive internationals . . . Italy reach the second stage without winning a match.

24 Keegan is in a clinic having treatment on his back injury . . . Alan Mullery is appointed manager of Crystal Palace. He appoints Ken Shellito as assistant manager and Ian Salter as reserve and youth team coach.

25 Northern Ireland, with 10 men, beat Spain . . . England do the same with 11 against Kuwait . . . West Germany and Austria stroll it together.

26 FIFA reject Algeria's protest that the West Germany v Austria game was fixed.

28 Bobby Robson confirms that he has been offered the England job. 'I think I have to take it', he says.

29 England and West Germany draw 0-0. 'The game was very difficult but we feel we now have a stepping-stone for the semi-finals', says Greenwood . . . Italy manage to win at last, beating Argentina 2-1 in an impressive if unruly encounter . . . Martin Wilkinson is appointed Peterborough manager.

30 Derby promote Alan Ashman, the chief scout, to assistant manager while Ritchie Norman becomes coach . . . England manager Ron Greenwood says: 'All members of the squad are fit and available for selection.'

## July

1 England officials are shocked when Joseph Blatter, the FIFA secretary, says: 'If two or even three teams finish level in the second-round group after goal difference and goals scored have been taken into consideration, then the position the teams filled in the first round will decide the semi-finalists. If this fails to separate them, lots will be drawn.' . . . Northern Ireland draw 2-2 with Austria . . . Alan Buckley is re-appointed player-manager of Walsall . . . Dean Emerson becomes a Stockport professional after his début in the past season as a non-contract player.

2 West Germany's 2-1 win over Spain means England have to win 2-0 against the Spanish or 3-2 or more . . . Diego Maradona (Argentina) is sent off against Brazil . . . Wolves call in the receiver. Last season their loss was £725,000 . . . Tommy Docherty receives £15,000 as compensation from Preston.

3 FIFA reject England's appeal not to make final placings in the first phase the only possible tie-breaker in the second round.

4 Northern Ireland's gallant bid ends in a 4-1 defeat by France . . . Poland also reach the semi-finals, at the expense of USSR . . . Eddie Gray is appointed player-manager of Leeds in succession to Allan Clarke.

5 England are unable to beat Spain. Despite a desperate double-substitution of Keegan and Brooking for Woodcock and Rix with 27 minutes left, the game remains goalless . . . Paolo Rossi's hat-trick stuns the Brazilians . . . Steve Biggins joins Oxford United from Shrewsbury . . . Middlesbrough centre-forward Billy Ashcroft may join Dutch club Twente Enschede . . . Ardiles will play for Paris St Germain in 1982–83.

6 Bobby Robson's successor at Ipswich will be Bobby Ferguson, the club's coach. 'Although we do not wish to anticipate the FA announcement, we have to make contingency plans.' . . . Chelsea sign Bryan Robson, 36, from Carlisle . . . Rossi is to be given the equivalent of a British knighthood, the civic title of Commendatore . . . Crystal Palace sign Ian Edwards, the Wrexham centre-forward.

7 FIFA reject the Football League's experimental rules . . . Robson is appointed England manager on a five-year contract . . . Manchester United winger Steve Coppell may need a cartilage operation . . . York sign ex-Derby goalkeeper Roger Jones and Stoke full-back Chris Evans, a former youth international once with Arsenal.

8 A Rossi double sinks Poland, but the drama is in the other semi-final, with West Germany beating France 5-4 on penalty kicks after the match, which went into extra-time, finished 3-3 . . . Ferguson, 44, is confirmed as Robson's successor . . . Jurgen Rober moves from Forest to West German club Bayer Leverkusen for £150,000 . . . Wimbledon sign Wayne Entwistle (Crewe), Gary Peters (Fulham) plus Tony Tagg and Chris Dibble (both Millwall).

9 Arnaldo Coelho, 39, a Brazilian businessman, will become the first non-European to referee a World Cup final.

10 Poland take third place, edging France out 3-2.

11 Italy beat West Germany 3-1 in the World Cup final . . . a rebel tour of South Africa is planned.

12 FA Secretary Ted Croker warns that any English players involved in the South African tour could throw their careers into jeopardy . . . Jimmy Lumsden is appointed assistant to Eddie Gray at Leeds . . . Sandy Jardine becomes assistant manager to

Alex MacDonald at Hearts . . . Terry Gray moves to Bradford City from Southend United . . . Jock Wallace resigns as Leicester manager and takes over Motherwell.

13 Cardiff sign Jeff Hemmerman from Portsmouth and will have Martin Thomas, the Bristol Rovers goalkeeper, on loan . . . Crystal Palace swap Neil Smillie for Brighton's Gary Williams . . . Halifax manager Mick Bullock signs Jimmy Hallybone from Orient . . . Leicester want to keep Wallace. 'We are not accepting the resignation', says Terry Shipman, City's chairman . . . John Wark enters hospital for a minor knee operation . . . Steve Moran (Southampton) is in light training again.

14 Joe Royle is appointed manager of Oldham Athletic . . . Real Betis are interested in signing Peter Barnes from Leeds . . . Wolves are hoping to form a new company to enable them to carry on.

15 Spurs refuse permission for Ardiles to tour South Africa because it might affect his transfer to Paris St Germain. Jimmy Hill's involvement as one of the tour's organisers is criticised by Ted Croker. 'Mr Hill is acting irresponsibly. It is not South Africa's interest he has at heart', he says . . . Gerry Armstrong (Watford), the Northern Ireland striker, wins the Golden Boot award as the British player of the World Cup series . . . Allen Wade, 56, is sacked as the FA's director of coaching. Robson will become national coach and will have overall responsibility for the game in England . . . Bolton sign Ray Deakin (Port Vale) and Vernon Allatt (Halifax), and their centre-half Paul Jones accepts less money after first being released by the club.

16 Sir Matt Busby, resigns as a vice-president of the Football League for 'personal reasons' . . . Kevin Beattie may return to League soccer.

17 South African 'rebels' 0 Western Province 0.

18 The rebels win the second game of their tour, beating Durban Amazulu 1-0 . . . Jack Hayward, millionaire, whose father was born in Wolverhampton, says that he does not wish to see the club die.

19 Brentford sign Graham Wilkins from Chelsea . . . Frank Van Hattum, the New Zealand World Cup goalkeeper, signs a two-year contract for Feyenoord (Netherlands) . . . Ricky Sbragia joins Rochdale from Blackpool.

20 Southend line up another Greaves, 16-year-old Andy, younger son of Jimmy and brother of Danny . . . Tottenham hope Ricky Villa will return once visa restrictions are lifted . . . David Webb is unhappy at Bournemouth . . . Doncaster re-sign goalkeeper Dennis Peacock from Bolton and release David Harle to Exeter . . . Drybrough's, who sponsor the Northern League, are to double their contribution to the competition, which is being enlarged.

21 John Toshack, Swansea's manager, is fined £150 by the Welsh FA after remarks made to the referee at Vetch Field on 15 May . . . Richard Hartley, 35, a Nottingham businessman, has made a successful offer for Mansfield Town . . . Colchester sign Kevin Beattie . . . Rebels 1 Transvaal XI 1.

22 Wolves are granted a weeks' stay of execution by the Football League and the Official Receiver . . . Webb agrees to sign a new contract at Bournemouth.

23 The Football League instruct referees to send players off if they commit 'professional fouls' . . . Derek Dougan is behind the latest group to try a salvage operation at Wolves . . . David Jeffrey, 19, joins Linfield from Manchester United.

24 Figures issued by BBC and ITV reveal that only 13 million saw the World Cup final between Italy and West Germany, a drop of nearly half compared with the 23 million who watched the 1978 final. England's last 1982 game with Spain was seen by 13,667,000 on ITV.

25 Gary Mabbutt, the Bristol Rovers and England Under-21 international, may move to Tottenham Hotspur . . . Wolves expect to sell Willie Carr to Millwall for £10,000.

26 Graham Kelly, the League Secretary, says: 'We will have to find a formula so that clubs can satisfy us that they can meet their commitments regarding transfers, salaries and stadia.' . . . The Milk Cup (ex-League Cup) draw is made and the National Dairy Council announce the launching of a £2 million sponsorship over four years . . . Brian Little is appointed Aston Villa's youth coach . . . Craig Paterson moves from Hibs to Rangers for £200,000 . . . Wolves have a deadline for survival: Friday.

27 Alastair Jones, the Receiver responsible for Wolves, gives a glimmer of hope. There are four different consortia bidding . . . West Bromwich appoint Ron Wylie as manager. He was coaching in Hong Kong for a year . . . England may play Scotland at Wembley in midweek at the end of the season and have yet to finalise details of a summer tour to South America . . . George Best may play in a match as part of the centenary celebrations of Arbroath Vics, a Scottish Junior club.

28 A fifth consortium joins in the Wolves fight . . . Trevor Francis is being sought by

Sampdoria, the Italian club who recently signed Liam Brady. Manchester City may replace him with David Cross from West Ham.

29   Ken Wheldon, the Walsall chairman, backed by millionaire Jack Hayward, is thought to have the advantage over the Derek Dougan group in the consortium struggle for Wolves . . . The first tour of the USSR by a British schools team begins with the departure of Warwickshire Schools Under-16s to play in Moscow, Sukhumi, Sochi, Leningrad and Tbilisi . . . Stoke are furious with the Department of Employment, who have granted Robert Prytz a work permit for Rangers after refusing them one for the same player.

30   Wolves are saved – with three minutes to go before the deadline. The favourite falls at the post, giving a win to Dougan's group . . . Trevor Francis joins Sampdoria from Manchester City . . . Clive White, the World Cup referee, resigns from the League list. He was fined £1500 two weeks earlier after admitting deception offences in court . . . Don Howe is staying with Arsenal . . . Reading are £107,000 in debt.

31   The prodigal son obtains absolution for sinners: Rossi's six World Cup goals prompt the Italian FA to remit two years of suspension imposed on 11 players involved in the bribery scandals.

# SPORT AND THE LAW

Soccer's playing laws are the key to its existence, differentiating it from rugby and all other forms of football. Yet as the game becomes progressively torn by commercial, violent and social pressures, national laws are required to fill gaps which were never envisaged when the game's own laws were first created by the Corinthian-orientated law-makers in Queen Victoria's Britain. Previous seasons have reflected these trends through charities, commerce, companies, tax and violence – notably the latter. The 1981–82 season saw this confirmed at four levels separate from the playing game itself: Parliament, courts of law, boardroom and soccer's council chambers.

Parliament's last legislation for the whole of British sport was the Safety of Sports Grounds Act in 1975, following the Ibrox disaster in 1971. In early 1981 Mr Jack Dunnett, MP – solicitor, President of the Football League and Notts County Chairman – was associated with an attempt to face at parliamentary level the problem of football violence. The Football Crowds (Control) Bill, which made little progress, was intended 'To make further provision for the control of spectators at association football matches; and for connected purposes'. His fellow solicitor and Chairman of the FA, Mr Bert Millichip, at the Annual General Meeting of the Central Council for Physical Recreation in November 1981, called for Government intervention; in mid-May the Minister for Sport, Mr Neil Macfarlane, consulted with the four British Associations on what has become a running sore within the game, both overseas and at home.

Another approach to Parliament came via an all-party Committee for seeking tax and VAT relief, especially where grounds are improved for community use. Government assistance came to Arsenal when the Department of Employment was persuaded to reject FL and PFA advice and to grant a permit for Vladimir Petrovic from Yugoslavia.

In the courts of law activity concerned both civil and criminal judgements. In the High Court Billy Bremner was awarded £100,000 for libel damages following an allegation that he had 'fixed' a match. Mr John Malam, physiotherapist, was awarded £3600 by a Birmingham industrial tribunal for unfair dismissal by Wolverhampton Wanderers, and a Lincolnshire/Humberside fireman lost an appeal to a Hull industrial tribunal for unfair dismissal when he was sacked after admitting a charge of threatening behaviour likely to cause a breach of the peace at a football match. Still in the pipeline at the time of writing is the first-ever claim for damages by one professional player against another for a broken leg sustained in a Scottish League match. Meanwhile, a Fourth Division club coach was fined £200 by Hereford magistrates for using insulting words and behaviour to local officials, and streams of hooligans appear in courts almost daily.

Companies Acts receivers for ailing club finances became as newsworthy as the usual managerial merry-go-round. Bristol City was liquidated and replaced by another company; and Chelsea were involved in a complex company and property deal which in detail concerned the City of London's square mile rather than the Stamford Bridge playing surface.

The Football League Chairmen's seminar resulted in the formation of a sub-committee, including Sir Matt Busby and Jimmy Hill, to examine among other issues the laws of the game in relation to the so-called cynical or professional foul. This particular part of their brief is concerned with the *penal* laws of the game rather than its *playing* laws, for on the basis that this offence is a criminal or civil assault when committed deliberately or intentionally, the problem arises as to how the game's playing laws should deal with it. The League sendings-off having reached an all-time high of 150 in 1981–82, the sub-committee's role is not an idle one.

Overriding all else, however, is the problem of crowd violence and mindless hooliganism. Events throughout the season were almost a deliberate and insolent affront to the game's protests and attempts to protect itself. At the CCPR Conference in Bournemouth in November, the FA Chairman condemned the hooligan 'scum', and the following Saturday £2500 worth of damage was done by Chelsea supporters at Derby County's Baseball Ground. This resulted in FA restraints on Chelsea's followers – innocent as well as guilty – for within the game it is impossible to differentiate between the good, the bad and the ugly. Nearly six months later, UEFA fined Aston Villa £14,000 for violence committed by followers unconnected with the club; within 24 hours, rioting on Highbury's hitherto trouble-free terraces, at the beginning of the League match with West Ham United, ended outside the ground with a fatal stabbing, treated by the police as murder.

Sadly this was not the only recorded death in 1981–82. In September, after a Spurs–Manchester United game, a youth died from asphyxia following an underground escalator fracas in north London, and two courts recorded manslaughter verdicts from other fatalities: Nottingham Crown Court imposed a four-year jail sentence for a killing at Middlesbrough in September 1980, as did London's Old Bailey at the Central Criminal Court for a killing in February 1981 at Tottenham. There is, however, no suggestion that any local club was connected with the offences and it is tragic that a game of beauty should be desecrated by the minority.

A lighter side was seen through the contrasting treatment accorded to Twickenham and Newcastle streakers. The lady who paraded topless across the rugby pitch was not prosecuted on the basis that the public interest would not be served by focusing further attention on her, whereas a sailor who followed suit at St James' Park, Newcastle, was fined £100.

This discretion to prosecute and sentence is arguably at the root of the problem, for there is always the possibility of an offender escaping scot-free or with a moderate penalty. With this in mind, I set out in an Appendix to *Sport and the Law*, published by the *Sunday Telegraph* in 1978, a draft Safety of Sports Persons Act equating soccer hooligans with drunken drivers, and recommending compulsory disqualification. The practical operation would be effected by supervision or attendance orders requiring the offender's presence away from grounds at such times as games are played.

FIFA awarded a 'fair play' trophy for good conduct by teams competing in the World Cup in Spain and the Berger Isthmian League has been operating a similar scheme in the South of England's premier non-Football League competition for some years. Perhaps some imaginative sponsor could introduce a parallel scheme for 'fair play' crowds. Then the law could take a rest and soccer return to its role as a game of fun and joy.

EDWARD GRAYSON

# ROTHMANS FOOTBALL YEARBOOK

## PAST EDITIONS

The following editions of
ROTHMANS FOOTBALL YEARBOOK
are still available:

| | | |
|---|---|---|
| 1973/74 | Limp | £1.30 |
| 1978/79 | Cased | £4.95 |
| 1979/80 | Limp | £3.75 |
| 1979/80 | Cased | £5.50 |
| 1980/81 | Limp | £4.95 |
| 1981/82 | Limp | £5.95 |
| 1981/82 | Cased | £7.95 |

# AWARDS 1981–82

## FOOTBALLER OF THE YEAR

The Football Writers' Association award for the Footballer of the Year went to Steve Perryman, the captain of Tottenham Hotspur and a long-serving player for the White Hart Lane club, who won a further justified honour by being selected for the first time to play for his country at full international level against Iceland.

**Award Winners**
1947–48 Stanley Matthews (Blackpool), 1948–49 Johnny Carey (Manchester U), 1949–50 Joe Mercer (Arsenal), 1950–51 Harry Johnston (Blackpool), 1951–52 Billy Wright (Wolverhampton W), 1952–53 Nat Lofthouse (Bolton W), 1953–54 Tom Finney (Preston NE), 1954–55 Don Revie (Manchester C), 1955–56 Bert Trautmann (Manchester C), 1956–57 Tom Finney (Preston NE), 1957–58 Danny Blanchflower (Tottenham H), 1958–59 Syd Owen (Luton T), 1959–60 Bill Slater (Wolverhampton W), 1960–61 Danny Blanchflower (Tottenham H), 1961–62 Jimmy Adamson (Burnley), 1962–63 Stanley Matthews (Stoke C), 1963–64 Bobby Moore (West Ham U), 1964–65 Bobby Collins (Leeds U), 1965–66 Bobby Charlton (Manchester U), 1966–67 Jackie Charlton (Leeds U), 1967–68 George Best (Manchester U), 1968–69 Dave Mackay (Derby Co) shared with Tony Book (Manchester C), 1969–70 Billy Bremner (Leeds U), 1970–71 Frank McLintock (Arsenal), 1971–72 Gordon Banks (Stoke C), 1972–73 Pat Jennings (Tottenham H), 1973–74 Ian Callaghan (Liverpool), 1974–75 Alan Mullery (Fulham), 1975–76 Kevin Keegan (Liverpool), 1976–77 Emlyn Hughes (Liverpool), 1977–78 Kenny Burns (Nottingham F), 1978–79 Kenny Dalglish (Liverpool), 1979–80 Terry McDermott (Liverpool), 1980–81 Frans Thijssen (Ipswich T), 1981–82 Steve Perryman (Tottenham H).

## THE PFA AWARDS 1982

**Player of the Year** – Kevin Keegan (Southampton)
*Previous Winners* – Andy Gray (Aston V); Pat Jennings (Tottenham H); Colin Todd (Derby Co); Norman Hunter (Leeds U); Peter Shilton (Nottingham F); Liam Brady (Arsenal); Terry McDermott (Liverpool); John Wark (Ipswich T).
**Young Player of the Year** – Steve Moran (Southampton).
*Previous Winners* – Andy Gray (Aston V); Peter Barnes (Manchester C); Mervyn Day (West Ham U); Kevin Beattie (Ipswich T); Tony Woodcock (Nottingham F); Cyrille Regis (WBA); Glenn Hoddle (Tottenham H); Gary Shaw (Aston V).
**PFA Merit Award** – Joe Mercer OBE
*Previous Winners* – Jack Taylor; George Eastham; Denis Law; Bobby Charlton; Bill Shankly; Tom Finney; Sir Matt Busby; John Trollope.

*The following four teams were selected by the Professional Footballers' Association to represent the divisions of the Football League.*

**Division 1:** Peter Shilton (Nottingham F); Kenny Swain (Aston Villa), David O'Leary (Arsenal), Alan Hansen (Liverpool), Kenny Sansom (Arsenal), Graeme Souness (Liverpool), Glenn Hoddle (Tottenham H), Bryan Robson (Manchester U), Trevor Francis (Manchester C), Kevin Keegan (Southampton), Cyrille Regis (WBA).

**Division 2:** Mark Wallington (Leicester C); Kirk Stephens (Luton T), Mike McCarthy (Barnsley), Glenn Roeder (QPR), Steve Buckley (Derby Co), Ricky Hill (Luton T), Ian Banks (Barnsley), Brian Horton (Luton T), David Moss (Luton T), Simon Stainrod (QPR), Paul Walsh (Charlton Ath).

**Division 3:** Gerry Peyton (Fulham); Malcolm Brown (Huddersfield T), Tony Gale (Fulham), Martin Dobson (Burnley), Dave Rushbury (Carlisle U), Phil Bonnyman (Chesterfield), Danny Wilson (Chesterfield), Dick Tydeman (Gillingham), Gordon Davies (Fulham), Keith Cassells (Oxford U), Tony Kellow (Exeter C).

**Division 4:** Keith Waugh (Sheffield U); Cec Podd (Bradford C), Paul Hilton (Bury), Colin Methven (Wigan Ath), Steve Sherlock (Stockport Co), Billy Kellock (Peterborough U), Roger Osborne (Colchester U), Mick Gynn (Peterborough U), Bobby Campbell (Bradford C), Mark Chamberlain (Port Vale), Craig Madden (Bury).

## BELL'S FOOTBALL MANAGER OF THE YEAR 1981–82

**Bob Paisley** was elected Manager of the Year in the Bell's Scotch Whisky Award for a record fifth time. Under his guidance Liverpool, who were written off by many in December, achieved the double of League and League Cup in 1981–82. Other winners were David Pleat of Luton Town (Division Two), Burnley's Brian Miller (Division Three) and Ian Porterfield of Sheffield United (Division Four). Special awards went to Tony Barton of Aston Villa, who brought the European Cup back to England for the sixth successive season, and to Graham Taylor, who took Watford from Division Four to Division One in five seasons.

SEPTEMBER
*Manager of the Month:* **John Lyall** (West Ham U); *Division Two:* **Jack Charlton** (Sheffield W); *Division Three:* **Billy Bremner** (Doncaster R); *Division Four:* **Frank O'Farrell** (Torquay U).

OCTOBER
*Manager of the Month:* **Keith Burkinshaw** (Tottenham H); *Division Two:* **Graham Taylor** (Watford); *Division Three:* **Keith Peacock** (Gillingham); *Division Four:* **Ian Porterfield** (Sheffield U).

NOVEMBER
*Manager of the Month:* **David Pleat** (Luton T); *Division One:* **Terry Neill** (Arsenal); *Division Three:* **Bob Stokoe** (Carlisle U); *Division Four:* **Bobby Roberts** (Colchester U).

DECEMBER
*Manager of the Month:* **Ronnie Allen** (WBA); *Division Two:* **John Neal** (Chelsea); *Division Three:* **Malcolm Macdonald** (Fulham); *Division Four:* **Bobby Roberts** (Colchester U).

JANUARY
*Manager of the Month:* **Bob Paisley** (Liverpool); *Division Two:* **Ken Knighton** (Orient); *Division Three:* **Gordon Lee** (Preston NE); *Division Four:* **Larry Lloyd** (Wigan Ath).

FEBRUARY
*Manager of the Month:* **Emlyn Hughes** (Rotherham U); *Division One:* **Keith Burkinshaw** (Tottenham H); *Division Three:* **Brian Miller** (Burnley); *Division Four:* **Peter Morris** (Peterborough U).

MARCH
*Manager of the Month:* **Bob Paisley** (Liverpool); *Division Two:* **Jock Wallace** (Leicester C); *Division Three:* **Colin Murphy** (Lincoln C); *Division Four:* **Roy McFarland** (Bradford C).

APRIL
*Manager of the Month:* **Tony Barton** (Aston Villa); *Division Two:* **Terry Venables** (QPR); *Division Three:* **Jimmy Smith** (Oxford U); *Division Four:* **David Webb** (AFC Bournemouth).


## BELL'S BEST ACHIEVEMENT BY A BRITISH MANAGER IN THE WORLD CUP

Billy Bingham of Northern Ireland was unanimously selected for the Bell's Scotch Whisky special award for the best achievement by a British manager in the World Cup. Bob Paisley of Liverpool said: 'Northern Ireland's performances exceeded all our expectations and gave their fans and television viewers more real enjoyment than either of the other British teams. But they all did us proud.'

# DIVISION 1 LEAGUE POSITION PROGRESS CHART

**1981 – 1982**

| Team | Sep 12 | Sep 19 | Sep 26 | Oct 3 | Oct 10 | Oct 17 | Oct 24 | Oct 31 | Nov 7 | Nov 14 | Nov 21 | Nov 28 | Dec 5 | Dec 12 | Dec 19 | Dec 26 | Jan 2 | Jan 9 | Jan 16 | Jan 23 | Jan 30 | Feb 6 | Feb 13 | Feb 20 | Feb 27 | Mar 6 | Mar 13 | Mar 20 | Mar 27 | Apr 3 | Apr 10 | Apr 17 | Apr 24 | May 1 | May 8 | May 15 | Final Position |
|---|---|---|---|---|---|---|---|---|---|---|---|---|---|---|---|---|---|---|---|---|---|---|---|---|---|---|---|---|---|---|---|---|---|---|---|---|---|
| Arsenal | 16 | 17 | 13 | 16 | 18 | 16 | 17 | 14 | 11 | 11 | 10 | 8 | 6 | 9 | 9 | 9 | 10 | 11 | 11 | 10 | 9 | 7 | 4 | 4 | 5 | 5 | 4 | 6 | 6 | 6 | 6 | 7 | 7 | 7 | 6 | 5 | 5 |
| Aston Villa | 14 | 14 | 16 | 17 | 16 | 13 | 10 | 12 | 14 | 15 | 14 | 13 | 16 | 17 | 17 | 17 | 14 | 14 | 15 | 16 | 17 | 15 | 15 | 15 | 13 | 14 | 13 | 14 | 13 | 11 | 12 | 11 | 12 | 11 | 11 | 11 | 11 |
| Birmingham C | 18 | 8 | 14 | 15 | 11 | 11 | 14 | 15 | 13 | 14 | 15 | 20 | 20 | 19 | 19 | 19 | 19 | 19 | 20 | 20 | 19 | 19 | 17 | 17 | 17 | 18 | 17 | 18 | 17 | 19 | 20 | 17 | 17 | 16 | 18 | 16 | 16 |
| Brighton & HA | 10 | 12 | 10 | 8 | 7 | 9 | 8 | 7 | 9 | 9 | 11 | 11 | 11 | 8 | 8 | 8 | 10 | 9 | 10 | 8 | 7 | 8 | 9 | 9 | 8 | 9 | 8 | 9 | 10 | 10 | 12 | 13 | 13 | 13 | 12 | 13 | 13 |
| Coventry C | 8 | 9 | 8 | 9 | 12 | 14 | 11 | 13 | 15 | 16 | 17 | 14 | 12 | 12 | 13 | 14 | 15 | 15 | 16 | 17 | 15 | 17 | 18 | 18 | 18 | 18 | 19 | 17 | 18 | 18 | 16 | 15 | 15 | 15 | 14 | 14 | 14 |
| Everton | 10 | 19 | 7 | 11 | 14 | 8 | 7 | 8 | 12 | 12 | 13 | 15 | 14 | 13 | 13 | 11 | 8 | 10 | 5 | 8 | 10 | 5 | 7 | 5 | 6 | 7 | 11 | 11 | 12 | 13 | 15 | 13 | 9 | 8 | 8 | 8 | 8 |
| Ipswich T | 3 | 2 | 1 | 1 | 1 | 3 | 2 | 2 | 2 | 2 | 2 | 3 | 3 | 3 | 3 | 5 | 5 | 1 | 1 | 1 | 1 | 6 | 7 | 5 | 6 | 4 | 7 | 5 | 5 | 2 | 2 | 2 | 2 | 2 | 2 | 2 | 2 |
| Leeds U | 20 | 20 | 22 | 22 | 22 | 20 | 18 | 18 | 16 | 17 | 20 | 19 | 18 | 16 | 16 | 16 | 16 | 17 | 14 | 15 | 16 | 18 | 18 | 19 | 19 | 19 | 18 | 19 | 19 | 18 | 19 | 21 | 21 | 19 | 20 | 18 | 20 |
| Liverpool | 16 | 17 | 12 | 13 | 8 | 10 | 12 | 9 | 7 | 7 | 9 | 10 | 10 | 11 | 12 | 12 | 12 | 9 | 7 | 8 | 9 | 7 | 6 | 5 | 6 | 5 | 4 | 3 | 4 | 1 | 1 | 1 | 1 | 1 | 1 | 1 | 1 |
| Manchester C | 4 | 7 | 6 | 8 | 10 | 13 | 15 | 16 | 10 | 8 | 9 | 9 | 9 | 7 | 7 | 4 | 2 | 2 | 2 | 4 | 8 | 6 | 3 | 7 | 8 | 8 | 8 | 8 | 9 | 9 | 9 | 10 | 10 | 10 | 9 | 10 | 10 |
| Manchester U | 22 | 16 | 11 | 4 | 5 | 6 | 1 | 11 | 1 | 1 | 1 | 1 | 1 | 2 | 2 | 2 | 4 | 3 | 3 | 3 | 3 | 2 | 2 | 3 | 3 | 3 | 5 | 4 | 5 | 4 | 3 | 3 | 3 | 3 | 3 | 3 | 3 |
| Middlesbrough | 19 | 21 | 18 | 20 | 19 | 19 | 20 | 20 | 21 | 21 | 21 | 21 | 21 | 22 | 22 | 22 | 22 | 22 | 22 | 22 | 22 | 22 | 22 | 22 | 22 | 22 | 22 | 22 | 22 | 21 | 22 | 22 | 22 | 22 | 22 | 22 | 22 |
| Nottingham F | 12 | 6 | 4 | 6 | 6 | 4 | 5 | 5 | 5 | 5 | 5 | 7 | 7 | 8 | 6 | 6 | 7 | 6 | 6 | 7 | 11 | 11 | 10 | 10 | 9 | 10 | 10 | 12 | 10 | 11 | 12 | 13 | 11 | 12 | 13 | 11 | 12 |
| Notts Co | 6 | 10 | 17 | 14 | 10 | 12 | 13 | 9 | 19 | 19 | 18 | 18 | 18 | 20 | 20 | 20 | 20 | 18 | 14 | 13 | 14 | 16 | 12 | 12 | 13 | 13 | 14 | 14 | 13 | 13 | 14 | 14 | 15 | 15 | 15 | 15 | 15 |
| Southampton | 5 | 3 | 9 | 7 | 9 | 10 | 8 | 8 | 8 | 6 | 8 | 6 | 3 | 5 | 3 | 2 | 2 | 4 | 4 | 2 | 4 | 2 | 1 | 1 | 1 | 1 | 1 | 2 | 1 | 3 | 4 | 5 | 6 | 6 | 7 | 7 | 7 |
| Stoke C | 7 | 11 | 15 | 15 | 17 | 15 | 17 | 15 | 19 | 18 | 13 | 12 | 12 | 15 | 15 | 15 | 15 | 16 | 17 | 18 | 18 | 18 | 13 | 13 | 15 | 15 | 16 | 16 | 17 | 16 | 17 | 21 | 18 | 20 | 16 | 20 | 18 |
| Sunderland | 13 | 13 | 20 | 19 | 20 | 17 | 15 | 16 | 18 | 13 | 12 | 12 | 22 | 22 | 22 | 21 | 21 | 16 | 17 | 18 | 18 | 13 | 21 | 21 | 21 | 21 | 21 | 21 | 22 | 22 | 18 | 16 | 17 | 17 | 17 | 17 | 19 |
| Swansea C | 2 | 4 | 3 | 3 | 2 | 1 | 3 | 4 | 3 | 4 | 4 | 2 | 4 | 4 | 1 | 1 | 1 | 5 | 5 | 6 | 5 | 5 | 5 | 5 | 2 | 2 | 1 | 2 | 3 | 3 | 3 | 4 | 5 | 4 | 5 | 6 | 6 |
| Tottenham H | 9 | 5 | 5 | 5 | 5 | 3 | 2 | 4 | 4 | 3 | 4 | 4 | 5 | 5 | 6 | 5 | 6 | 6 | 9 | 9 | 11 | 9 | 8 | 7 | 7 | 7 | 7 | 7 | 7 | 7 | 6 | 6 | 5 | 5 | 4 | 4 | 4 |
| WBA | 14 | 14 | 21 | 18 | 19 | 19 | 19 | 17 | 17 | 18 | 16 | 16 | 14 | 14 | 14 | 13 | 13 | 13 | 13 | 13 | 14 | 14 | 16 | 16 | 16 | 16 | 15 | 16 | 15 | 15 | 17 | 20 | 18 | 18 | 19 | 19 | 17 |
| West Ham U | 1 | 1 | 2 | 2 | 4 | 5 | 6 | 6 | 6 | 6 | 5 | 5 | 7 | 10 | 10 | 10 | 10 | 12 | 12 | 12 | 12 | 12 | 14 | 12 | 14 | 12 | 11 | 11 | 9 | 8 | 8 | 8 | 8 | 9 | 10 | 9 | 9 |
| Wolverhampton W | 21 | 22 | 19 | 21 | 21 | 21 | 21 | 21 | 20 | 19 | 19 | 19 | 16 | 18 | 18 | 18 | 18 | 19 | 19 | 19 | 20 | 20 | 20 | 20 | 20 | 20 | 20 | 20 | 20 | 20 | 20 | 16 | 19 | 21 | 21 | 21 | 21 |

# DIVISION 2 LEAGUE POSITION PROGRESS CHART

*1981* — *1982*

| Team | Sep 12 | Sep 19 | Sep 26 | Oct 3 | Oct 10 | Oct 17 | Oct 24 | Oct 31 | Nov 7 | Nov 14 | Nov 21 | Nov 28 | Dec 5 | Dec 12 | Dec 19 | Dec 26 | Jan 2 | Jan 9 | Jan 16 | Jan 23 | Jan 30 | Feb 6 | Feb 13 | Feb 20 | Feb 27 | Mar 6 | Mar 13 | Mar 20 | Mar 27 | Apr 3 | Apr 10 | Apr 17 | Apr 24 | May 1 | May 8 | May 15 | Final Position |
|---|---|---|---|---|---|---|---|---|---|---|---|---|---|---|---|---|---|---|---|---|---|---|---|---|---|---|---|---|---|---|---|---|---|---|---|---|---|
| Barnsley | 4 | 8 | 8 | 13 | 16 | 14 | 9 | 6 | 5 | 4 | 3 | 6 | 4 | 5 | 5 | 6 | 7 | 7 | 8 | 7 | 7 | 7 | 6 | 7 | 10 | 10 | 10 | 10 | 8 | 7 | 7 | 10 | 8 | 6 | 7 | 6 | 6 |
| Blackburn R | 11 | 7 | 6 | 12 | 9 | 8 | 8 | 9 | 8 | 8 | 10 | 7 | 8 | 8 | 7 | 6 | 6 | 6 | 4 | 4 | 4 | 4 | 5 | 4 | 5 | 5 | 3 | 5 | 5 | 6 | 9 | 10 | 9 | 9 | 10 | 10 | 10 |
| Bolton W | 22 | 22 | 22 | 21 | 21 | 21 | 21 | 21 | 22 | 21 | 20 | 22 | 22 | 18 | 19 | 19 | 20 | 20 | 20 | 20 | 19 | 19 | 19 | 17 | 17 | 16 | 17 | 17 | 18 | 18 | 18 | 17 | 18 | 20 | 19 | 19 | 19 |
| Cambridge U | 15 | 13 | 19 | 18 | 16 | 14 | 8 | 7 | 7 | 7 | 9 | 15 | 18 | 18 | 11 | 11 | 19 | 18 | 13 | 14 | 16 | 13 | 13 | 14 | 14 | 14 | 14 | 14 | 14 | 15 | 19 | 16 | 16 | 16 | 14 | 14 | 14 |
| Cardiff C | 20 | 20 | 17 | 20 | 20 | 19 | 14 | 12 | 9 | 12 | 16 | 18 | 18 | 18 | 11 | 11 | 13 | 13 | 14 | 17 | 20 | 20 | 20 | 20 | 17 | 21 | 21 | 21 | 14 | 16 | 14 | 19 | 19 | 20 | 20 | 20 | 20 |
| Charlton Ath | 18 | 16 | 18 | 17 | 20 | 15 | 14 | 16 | 16 | 13 | 16 | 16 | 18 | 15 | 15 | 15 | 15 | 10 | 13 | 14 | 17 | 20 | 20 | 8 | 8 | 5 | 7 | 8 | 10 | 11 | 16 | 16 | 19 | 19 | 13 | 13 | 13 |
| Chelsea | 9 | 14 | 9 | 5 | 5 | 7 | 11 | 10 | 10 | 12 | 6 | 10 | 8 | 7 | 7 | 7 | 5 | 5 | 5 | 8 | 5 | 8 | 9 | 9 | 9 | 8 | 9 | 7 | 8 | 6 | 9 | 6 | 6 | 5 | 6 | 5 | 5 |
| Crystal Palace | 10 | 15 | 15 | 14 | 11 | 7 | 12 | 14 | 15 | 17 | 15 | 18 | 11 | 13 | 13 | 13 | 15 | 16 | 16 | 15 | 15 | 18 | 18 | 19 | 19 | 18 | 18 | 16 | 15 | 19 | 18 | 15 | 17 | 16 | 15 | 15 | 15 |
| Derby Co | 12 | 9 | 12 | 17 | 18 | 17 | 16 | 15 | 17 | 14 | 17 | 19 | 13 | 16 | 16 | 16 | 17 | 17 | 13 | 13 | 12 | 14 | 15 | 15 | 15 | 15 | 15 | 15 | 16 | 14 | 14 | 14 | 14 | 17 | 16 | 16 | 16 |
| Grimsby T | 2 | 3 | 10 | 6 | 12 | 15 | 17 | 17 | 19 | 19 | 20 | 21 | 22 | 22 | 22 | 22 | 22 | 22 | 22 | 22 | 21 | 21 | 21 | 22 | 22 | 22 | 22 | 22 | 22 | 21 | 21 | 21 | 21 | 15 | 17 | 17 | 17 |
| Leicester C | 6 | 11 | 7 | 11 | 8 | 6 | 11 | 10 | 9 | 9 | 14 | 9 | 9 | 9 | 9 | 9 | 12 | 12 | 12 | 14 | 14 | 12 | 14 | 13 | 13 | 11 | 12 | 12 | 11 | 7 | 8 | 10 | 5 | 4 | 8 | 8 | 8 |
| Luton T | 3 | 2 | 2 | 1 | 1 | 1 | 1 | 1 | 1 | 1 | 1 | 1 | 1 | 1 | 1 | 1 | 1 | 1 | 1 | 1 | 1 | 1 | 1 | 1 | 1 | 2 | 1 | 2 | 2 | 1 | 1 | 1 | 1 | 1 | 1 | 1 | 1 |
| Newcastle U | 19 | 16 | 10 | 6 | 11 | 10 | 14 | 12 | 12 | 8 | 10 | 10 | 10 | 10 | 10 | 10 | 11 | 11 | 11 | 11 | 10 | 10 | 8 | 11 | 9 | 8 | 8 | 6 | 6 | 5 | 7 | 9 | 10 | 9 | 9 | 9 | 9 |
| Norwich C | 7 | 5 | 3 | 7 | 13 | 9 | 13 | 11 | 11 | 7 | 12 | 12 | 12 | 12 | 12 | 12 | 10 | 10 | 10 | 11 | 11 | 11 | 12 | 12 | 12 | 12 | 8 | 8 | 12 | 6 | 5 | 8 | 5 | 4 | 2 | 3 | 3 |
| Oldham Ath | 16 | 12 | 5 | 4 | 4 | 3 | 6 | 5 | 5 | 5 | 4 | 4 | 3 | 2 | 3 | 2 | 2 | 2 | 2 | 2 | 2 | 2 | 3 | 3 | 3 | 3 | 6 | 7 | 8 | 10 | 11 | 12 | 12 | 12 | 12 | 11 | 11 |
| Orient | 17 | 18 | 21 | 22 | 22 | 22 | 22 | 19 | 20 | 22 | 22 | 20 | 21 | 19 | 21 | 20 | 20 | 14 | 15 | 13 | 16 | 16 | 16 | 16 | 16 | 7 | 7 | 8 | 10 | 11 | 12 | 12 | 12 | 12 | 22 | 22 | 22 |
| QPR | 8 | 6 | 14 | 9 | 7 | 10 | 4 | 5 | 3 | 3 | 5 | 4 | 4 | 4 | 5 | 4 | 4 | 4 | 4 | 5 | 6 | 5 | 7 | 6 | 7 | 9 | 9 | 7 | 7 | 9 | 8 | 6 | 6 | 5 | 6 | 5 | 5 |
| Rotherham U | 13 | 17 | 11 | 15 | 18 | 18 | 16 | 18 | 18 | 16 | 15 | 18 | 17 | 17 | 17 | 17 | 18 | 18 | 19 | 20 | 15 | 11 | 8 | 4 | 3 | 5 | 5 | 9 | 9 | 8 | 6 | 4 | 7 | 7 | 4 | 7 | 7 |
| Sheffield W | 1 | 1 | 1 | 2 | 3 | 4 | 3 | 3 | 4 | 6 | 6 | 5 | 6 | 6 | 6 | 8 | 8 | 7 | 6 | 8 | 20 | 15 | 8 | 4 | 5 | 4 | 5 | 4 | 5 | 4 | 4 | 4 | 4 | 7 | 4 | 4 | 4 |
| Shrewsbury T | 14 | 10 | 13 | 8 | 10 | 13 | 15 | 16 | 18 | 15 | 13 | 13 | 14 | 14 | 14 | 14 | 15 | 15 | 16 | 17 | 18 | 17 | 17 | 18 | 18 | 18 | 17 | 18 | 16 | 15 | 17 | 20 | 20 | 21 | 18 | 18 | 18 |
| Watford | 5 | 4 | 4 | 3 | 2 | 2 | 2 | 2 | 2 | 2 | 2 | 3 | 2 | 3 | 3 | 3 | 3 | 3 | 3 | 3 | 3 | 2 | 2 | 2 | 2 | 2 | 2 | 2 | 1 | 2 | 2 | 2 | 2 | 2 | 2 | 2 | 2 |
| Wrexham | 21 | 21 | 20 | 19 | 19 | 20 | 20 | 20 | 21 | 20 | 21 | 21 | 20 | 20 | 21 | 21 | 19 | 19 | 20 | 21 | 21 | 21 | 21 | 21 | 21 | 20 | 19 | 19 | 20 | 20 | 20 | 15 | 17 | 18 | 21 | 21 | 21 |

## DIVISION 3 LEAGUE POSITION PROGRESS CHART

| | Sept | | | Oct | | | | | Nov | | | | Dec | | | | Jan | | | | | Feb | | | | Mar | | | | Apr | | | | May | | | Final Position |
|---|---|---|---|---|---|---|---|---|---|---|---|---|---|---|---|---|---|---|---|---|---|---|---|---|---|---|---|---|---|---|---|---|---|---|---|---|---|
| | 12 | 19 | 26 | 3 | 10 | 17 | 24 | 31 | 7 | 14 | 21 | 28 | 5 | 12 | 19 | 26 | 2 | 9 | 16 | 23 | 30 | 6 | 13 | 20 | 27 | 6 | 13 | 20 | 27 | 3 | 10 | 17 | 24 | 1 | 8 | 15 | |
| | | | | | | | 1981 | | | | | | | | | | | | | | | | | | | | | | 1982 | | | | | | | | | |
| Brentford | 7 | 9 | 19 | 19 | 20 | 18 | 17 | 16 | 15 | 13 | 13 | 10 | 7 | 7 | 7 | 6 | 6 | 6 | 8 | 11 | 12 | 15 | 14 | 12 | 14 | 12 | 14 | 12 | 10 | 11 | 9 | 7 | 7 | 7 | 7 | 7 | 8 |
| Bristol C | 19 | 13 | 13 | 20 | 19 | 20 | 16 | 15 | 14 | 17 | 17 | 19 | 20 | 20 | 20 | 21 | 21 | 20 | 20 | 21 | 18 | 21 | 22 | 18 | 21 | 22 | 22 | 22 | 22 | 23 | 23 | 23 | 23 | 23 | 23 | 23 | 23 |
| Bristol R | 13 | 6 | 7 | 6 | 8 | 6 | 11 | 11 | 13 | 8 | 9 | 9 | 11 | 12 | 12 | 12 | 12 | 8 | 10 | 6 | 7 | 9 | 6 | 9 | 8 | 9 | 7 | 8 | 9 | 11 | 13 | 12 | 12 | 15 | 16 | 14 | 15 |
| Burnley | 16 | 17 | 22 | 22 | 21 | 21 | 21 | 21 | 20 | 20 | 20 | 20 | 18 | 18 | 18 | 18 | 19 | 19 | 18 | 18 | 15 | 8 | 5 | 5 | 4 | 6 | 6 | 6 | 7 | 5 | 5 | 5 | 5 | 5 | 6 | 4 | 1 |
| Carlisle U | 11 | 14 | 12 | 7 | 9 | 6 | 7 | 10 | 10 | 6 | 6 | 3 | 3 | 3 | 3 | 2 | 2 | 2 | 2 | 5 | 3 | 3 | 1 | 1 | 1 | 2 | 5 | 4 | 2 | 1 | 1 | 1 | 1 | 1 | 1 | 1 | 2 |
| Chester | 8 | 10 | 16 | 16 | 18 | 19 | 20 | 22 | 22 | 23 | 23 | 22 | 23 | 23 | 22 | 22 | 22 | 22 | 22 | 21 | 21 | 23 | 23 | 23 | 23 | 24 | 24 | 24 | 24 | 24 | 24 | 24 | 24 | 24 | 24 | 24 | 24 |
| Chesterfield | 10 | 4 | 2 | 1 | 1 | 3 | 2 | 1 | 2 | 1 | 2 | 2 | 2 | 1 | 1 | 2 | 1 | 2 | 2 | 1 | 2 | 1 | 3 | 3 | 3 | 1 | 3 | 1 | 5 | 6 | 7 | 6 | 8 | 8 | 10 | 11 | 11 |
| Doncaster R | 9 | 5 | 3 | 2 | 3 | 2 | 5 | 5 | 5 | 5 | 5 | 10 | 10 | 10 | 10 | 10 | 12 | 16 | 10 | 11 | 14 | 18 | 19 | 17 | 19 | 19 | 17 | 15 | 16 | 16 | 20 | 20 | 19 | 19 | 18 | 19 | 19 |
| Exeter C | 14 | 18 | 18 | 16 | 14 | 13 | 14 | 13 | 12 | 12 | 12 | 13 | 13 | 13 | 13 | 13 | 16 | 12 | 12 | 14 | 16 | 13 | 17 | 18 | 21 | 17 | 15 | 16 | 16 | 15 | 17 | 16 | 16 | 18 | 17 | 17 | 18 |
| Fulham | 12 | 18 | 8 | 9 | 15 | 9 | 5 | 7 | 7 | 7 | 7 | 1 | 5 | 5 | 4 | 4 | 4 | 4 | 5 | 2 | 5 | 2 | 2 | 2 | 2 | 3 | 4 | 2 | 3 | 3 | 3 | 2 | 3 | 2 | 4 | 3 | 3 |
| Gillingham | 15 | 16 | 14 | 13 | 7 | 5 | 5 | 3 | 2 | 4 | 1 | 4 | 6 | 8 | 6 | 6 | 5 | 4 | 5 | 2 | 1 | 2 | 2 | 3 | 1 | 4 | 11 | 10 | 8 | 6 | 10 | 10 | 11 | 9 | 8 | 6 | 6 |
| Huddersfield T | 21 | 21 | 15 | 15 | 12 | 16 | 15 | 17 | 14 | 16 | 14 | 11 | 16 | 9 | 12 | 10 | 8 | 9 | 8 | 9 | 13 | 15 | 13 | 15 | 15 | 11 | 16 | 17 | 18 | 14 | 12 | 12 | 13 | 14 | 16 | 16 | 17 |
| Lincoln C | 6 | 8 | 9 | 14 | 10 | 15 | 18 | 18 | 19 | 16 | 16 | 16 | 10 | 10 | 11 | 13 | 17 | 16 | 18 | 10 | 18 | 10 | 11 | 13 | 13 | 7 | 4 | 3 | 1 | 2 | 2 | 2 | 3 | 3 | 3 | 3 | 4 |
| Millwall | 3 | 7 | 4 | 8 | 11 | 4 | 8 | 12 | 9 | 3 | 3 | 5 | 8 | 8 | 8 | 9 | 11 | 11 | 13 | 13 | 11 | 14 | 10 | 11 | 12 | 14 | 12 | 14 | 12 | 15 | 15 | 9 | 8 | 9 | 8 | 9 | 9 |
| Newport Co | 1 | 2 | 6 | 12 | 6 | 12 | 14 | 11 | 16 | 18 | 18 | 18 | 18 | 18 | 16 | 16 | 16 | 13 | 13 | 15 | 17 | 19 | 14 | 19 | 16 | 21 | 21 | 21 | 21 | 20 | 19 | 20 | 19 | 20 | 21 | 18 | 16 |
| Oxford U | 5 | 11 | 20 | 11 | 14 | 11 | 11 | 8 | 8 | 6 | 10 | 10 | 6 | 9 | 9 | 9 | 9 | 14 | 14 | 17 | 17 | 7 | 9 | 9 | 5 | 4 | 7 | 9 | 9 | 7 | 4 | 4 | 4 | 4 | 2 | 5 | 5 |
| Plymouth Arg | 24 | 23 | 23 | 24 | 23 | 24 | 23 | 24 | 24 | 23 | 21 | 21 | 21 | 21 | 14 | 14 | 15 | 15 | 15 | 15 | 10 | 14 | 12 | 13 | 14 | 13 | 13 | 8 | 11 | 13 | 9 | 7 | 9 | 9 | 11 | 10 | 10 |
| Portsmouth | 20 | 22 | 11 | 10 | 17 | 17 | 19 | 19 | 18 | 19 | 19 | 19 | 20 | 18 | 18 | 16 | 17 | 19 | 18 | 18 | 19 | 20 | 18 | 16 | 17 | 15 | 15 | 11 | 16 | 17 | 14 | 14 | 14 | 13 | 15 | 15 | 13 |
| Preston NE | 18 | 20 | 21 | 21 | 22 | 22 | 22 | 20 | 22 | 22 | 22 | 22 | 23 | 23 | 23 | 23 | 23 | 23 | 23 | 23 | 20 | 21 | 20 | 19 | 20 | 20 | 20 | 20 | 19 | 18 | 18 | 18 | 11 | 18 | 12 | 12 | 14 |
| Reading | 4 | 3 | 1 | 3 | 4 | 7 | 9 | 4 | 9 | 11 | 11 | 13 | 11 | 11 | 11 | 11 | 12 | 7 | 7 | 5 | 7 | 5 | 7 | 6 | 10 | 6 | 5 | 2 | 2 | 4 | 8 | 11 | 11 | 12 | 13 | 13 | 12 |
| Southend U | 17 | 12 | 17 | 13 | 9 | 10 | 12 | 8 | 8 | 8 | 7 | 7 | 4 | 4 | 4 | 7 | 6 | 5 | 5 | 3 | 3 | 4 | 4 | 10 | 12 | 9 | 10 | 10 | 18 | 20 | 6 | 8 | 6 | 8 | 6 | 5 | 7 |
| Swindon T | 2 | 1 | 5 | 5 | 2 | 5 | 1 | 6 | 12 | 15 | 15 | 6 | 19 | 19 | 21 | 21 | 20 | 20 | 21 | 20 | 22 | 19 | 21 | 18 | 18 | 18 | 18 | 18 | 18 | 21 | 21 | 21 | 21 | 21 | 20 | 19 | 22 |
| Walsall | 22 | 15 | 10 | 4 | 5 | 4 | 5 | 5 | 4 | 4 | 2 | 4 | 6 | 8 | 7 | 8 | 9 | 3 | 3 | 4 | 4 | 6 | 8 | 7 | 2 | 2 | 9 | 11 | 13 | 15 | 16 | 17 | 17 | 17 | 17 | 19 | 20 |
| Wimbledon | 23 | 24 | 24 | 24 | 24 | 23 | 24 | 24 | 23 | 24 | 24 | 24 | 24 | 24 | 24 | 24 | 24 | 24 | 24 | 24 | 24 | 24 | 24 | 24 | 24 | 24 | 23 | 23 | 23 | 22 | 22 | 22 | 22 | 22 | 22 | 22 | 21 |

# DIVISION 4 LEAGUE POSITION PROGRESS CHART

*1981* — *1982*

| Team | Sept | | | Oct | | | | | Nov | | | | Dec | | | | Jan | | | | | Feb | | | | Mar | | | | Apr | | | | May | | | Final Position |
|---|---|---|---|---|---|---|---|---|---|---|---|---|---|---|---|---|---|---|---|---|---|---|---|---|---|---|---|---|---|---|---|---|---|---|---|---|---|
| | 12 | 19 | 26 | 3 | 10 | 17 | 24 | 31 | 7 | 14 | 21 | 28 | 5 | 12 | 19 | 26 | 2 | 9 | 16 | 23 | 30 | 6 | 13 | 20 | 27 | 6 | 13 | 20 | 27 | 3 | 10 | 17 | 24 | 1 | 8 | 15 | |
| Aldershot | 11 | 8 | 14 | 17 | 16 | 13 | 10 | 10 | 12 | 14 | 14 | 13 | 13 | 13 | 13 | 13 | 13 | 13 | 13 | 14 | 12 | 11 | 12 | 12 | 11 | 11 | 12 | 14 | 13 | 14 | 14 | 14 | 15 | 14 | 16 | 15 | 16 |
| Blackpool | 3 | 4 | 5 | 4 | 2 | 2 | 4 | 7 | 8 | 9 | 9 | 10 | 10 | 10 | 10 | 10 | 10 | 10 | 9 | 9 | 9 | 12 | 12 | 9 | 9 | 9 | 9 | 9 | 10 | 10 | 12 | 13 | 13 | 11 | 13 | 13 | 12 |
| AFC Bournemouth | 1 | 1 | 1 | 1 | 1 | 4 | 6 | 5 | 5 | 5 | 6 | 6 | 6 | 6 | 6 | 6 | 4 | 3 | 4 | 4 | 5 | 3 | 3 | 2 | 3 | 4 | 5 | 5 | 5 | 5 | 5 | 3 | 3 | 4 | 4 | 4 | 4 |
| Bradford C | 10 | 5 | 3 | 2 | 3 | 1 | 1 | 5 | 3 | 3 | 3 | 3 | 3 | 3 | 3 | 3 | 3 | 4 | 3 | 4 | 5 | 5 | 4 | 5 | 4 | 5 | 4 | 6 | 5 | 5 | 5 | 3 | 3 | 3 | 3 | 2 | 2 |
| Bury | 7 | 7 | 4 | 5 | 4 | 3 | 5 | 2 | 3 | 2 | 2 | 4 | 4 | 4 | 4 | 1 | 5 | 5 | 6 | 6 | 6 | 6 | 7 | 7 | 7 | 7 | 6 | 6 | 7 | 7 | 8 | 9 | 9 | 7 | 10 | 9 | 9 |
| Colchester U | 6 | 2 | 7 | 8 | 10 | 6 | 3 | 6 | 4 | 4 | 4 | 4 | 1 | 1 | 1 | 2 | 2 | 2 | 2 | 3 | 3 | 3 | 6 | 6 | 7 | 6 | 7 | 7 | 5 | 6 | 6 | 6 | 6 | 6 | 6 | 6 | 6 |
| Crewe Alex | 24 | 24 | 24 | 24 | 24 | 24 | 24 | 24 | 23 | 22 | 22 | 23 | 23 | 23 | 24 | 24 | 24 | 24 | 24 | 23 | 23 | 23 | 23 | 23 | 24 | 24 | 24 | 24 | 24 | 24 | 24 | 24 | 24 | 24 | 24 | 24 | 24 |
| Darlington | 20 | 18 | 22 | 21 | 21 | 19 | 18 | 16 | 15 | 15 | 17 | 15 | 15 | 15 | 15 | 15 | 15 | 15 | 15 | 16 | 17 | 18 | 20 | 18 | 17 | 16 | 16 | 16 | 16 | 17 | 12 | 10 | 11 | 13 | 11 | 12 | 13 |
| Halifax T | 19 | 18 | 21 | 20 | 20 | 22 | 19 | 18 | 19 | 19 | 11 | 21 | 21 | 21 | 21 | 21 | 21 | 21 | 20 | 18 | 18 | 18 | 20 | 20 | 17 | 18 | 17 | 21 | 20 | 22 | 23 | 23 | 21 | 19 | 20 | 19 | 19 |
| Hartlepool U | 14 | 13 | 11 | 11 | 9 | 11 | 11 | 11 | 11 | 11 | 12 | 12 | 12 | 12 | 12 | 12 | 12 | 12 | 15 | 11 | 15 | 11 | 11 | 13 | 13 | 13 | 13 | 12 | 15 | 16 | 17 | 16 | 16 | 17 | 15 | 14 | 14 |
| Hereford U | 9 | 15 | 15 | 13 | 13 | 15 | 16 | 14 | 15 | 13 | 13 | 14 | 16 | 16 | 16 | 16 | 16 | 16 | 18 | 19 | 18 | 19 | 19 | 16 | 15 | 15 | 15 | 14 | 11 | 11 | 10 | 10 | 10 | 10 | 9 | 10 | 10 |
| Hull C | 12 | 9 | 17 | 18 | 17 | 18 | 20 | 20 | 20 | 20 | 16 | 14 | 14 | 14 | 14 | 14 | 14 | 14 | 14 | 14 | 14 | 15 | 16 | 15 | 14 | 14 | 16 | 10 | 10 | 9 | 9 | 9 | 9 | 9 | 7 | 8 | 8 |
| Mansfield T | 22 | 21 | 13 | 13 | 12 | 16 | 19 | 21 | 21 | 21 | 20 | 16 | 20 | 20 | 20 | 20 | 20 | 20 | 20 | 17 | 16 | 16 | 15 | 14 | 16 | 18 | 17 | 17 | 17 | 16 | 17 | 16 | 17 | 16 | 17 | 20 | 20 |
| Northampton T | 17 | 22 | 23 | 23 | 23 | 23 | 23 | 23 | 24 | 23 | 23 | 24 | 24 | 24 | 24 | 24 | 24 | 24 | 24 | 24 | 24 | 24 | 24 | 24 | 23 | 23 | 23 | 21 | 19 | 19 | 20 | 20 | 22 | 22 | 22 | 22 | 22 |
| Peterborough U | 4 | 6 | 6 | 10 | 7 | 7 | 7 | 4 | 6 | 6 | 3 | 5 | 5 | 5 | 6 | 6 | 6 | 6 | 8 | 7 | 7 | 7 | 7 | 5 | 2 | 3 | 3 | 2 | 2 | 4 | 2 | 4 | 5 | 5 | 5 | 5 | 5 |
| Port Vale | 13 | 12 | 10 | 7 | 9 | 10 | 12 | 12 | 10 | 10 | 10 | 8 | 8 | 8 | 8 | 5 | 8 | 8 | 8 | 8 | 8 | 8 | 8 | 8 | 8 | 8 | 8 | 8 | 8 | 8 | 7 | 7 | 8 | 8 | 8 | 7 | 7 |
| Rochdale | 16 | 20 | 20 | 22 | 22 | 17 | 18 | 20 | 18 | 18 | 18 | 18 | 18 | 18 | 18 | 18 | 18 | 19 | 19 | 21 | 20 | 21 | 21 | 22 | 22 | 20 | 19 | 21 | 23 | 23 | 21 | 22 | 23 | 20 | 21 | 21 | 21 |
| Scunthorpe U | 18 | 16 | 16 | 19 | 20 | 21 | 22 | 22 | 24 | 24 | 22 | 22 | 22 | 22 | 22 | 22 | 22 | 22 | 19 | 22 | 22 | 21 | 19 | 19 | 20 | 19 | 22 | 23 | 23 | 21 | 22 | 23 | 23 | 23 | 23 | 23 | 23 |
| Sheffield U | 5 | 10 | 8 | 5 | 5 | 2 | 1 | 2 | 2 | 4 | 2 | 2 | 2 | 2 | 2 | 2 | 3 | 1 | 1 | 2 | 1 | 3 | 4 | 2 | 4 | 4 | 3 | 3 | 3 | 4 | 4 | 2 | 1 | 1 | 1 | 1 | 1 |
| Stockport C | 14 | 11 | 9 | 12 | 14 | 13 | 13 | 13 | 12 | 12 | 11 | 11 | 11 | 11 | 11 | 11 | 11 | 11 | 11 | 13 | 15 | 14 | 14 | 17 | 18 | 18 | 18 | 18 | 18 | 18 | 18 | 18 | 18 | 18 | 19 | 18 | 18 |
| Torquay U | 2 | 3 | 2 | 3 | 6 | 9 | 9 | 8 | 8 | 9 | 8 | 9 | 9 | 9 | 9 | 9 | 9 | 10 | 10 | 10 | 10 | 10 | 10 | 10 | 10 | 12 | 12 | 15 | 12 | 15 | 15 | 15 | 14 | 14 | 16 | 16 | 15 |
| Tranmere R | 23 | 23 | 19 | 16 | 18 | 14 | 13 | 15 | 16 | 16 | 16 | 19 | 18 | 18 | 12 | 12 | 13 | 13 | 11 | 12 | 13 | 13 | 13 | 13 | 13 | 14 | 13 | 14 | 13 | 13 | 12 | 12 | 12 | 12 | 11 | 11 | 11 |
| Wigan Ath | 21 | 17 | 12 | 11 | 8 | 8 | 8 | 8 | 7 | 7 | 7 | 7 | 7 | 7 | 7 | 7 | 7 | 5 | 5 | 6 | 3 | 1 | 1 | 2 | 1 | 2 | 2 | 2 | 4 | 1 | 1 | 2 | 1 | 2 | 2 | 3 | 3 |
| York C | 8 | 14 | 18 | 15 | 15 | 17 | 17 | 17 | 17 | 17 | 17 | 17 | 17 | 17 | 17 | 17 | 17 | 18 | 17 | 18 | 19 | 21 | 22 | 22 | 22 | 21 | 20 | 19 | 22 | 19 | 19 | 21 | 19 | 18 | 17 | 17 | 17 |

# THE FOOTBALL LEAGUE

**Featuring full details of each of the 92 clubs in the Football League.**

**Officials, statistics, ground information, full 1981–82 League record and career details of the players.**

### THE FOOTBALL LEAGUE OFFICIALS

**President**
J. J. Dunnett MA (Cantab), LLB, MP
(*Notts County*)

**Vice-Presidents**
R. Wragg F Inst BM, FIOR (*Sheffield United*)
J. F. Wiseman (*Birmingham City*)

**Management Committee**
Dr C. S. Grossmark MB, BS, MRCS, LRCP (*Gillingham*)
G. H. C. Needler MA, FCA (*Hull City*)
J. W. Smith CBE, JP
R. Daniel (*Plymouth Argyle*)
Sir Arthur South JP (*Norwich City*)
B. B. Winston (*Orient*)

**Life Members**
F. A. Would (*Grimsby Town*)
E. M. Gliksten (*Charlton Athletic*)
L. T. Shipman CBE (*Leicester City*)
Lord Westwood JP, FCIS

**Secretary**
R. H. G. Kelly FCIS

**Deputy Secretary**
G. E. Readle MBE

**Deputy Secretary Designate**
T. L. Morris

**Assistant Secretary**
N. J. Thomas FCA

## INTRODUCTION TO CLUB SECTION

For the first time in the history of *Rothmans Football Yearbook*, a major alteration in the listing of career totals for Football League players was incorporated in the 1981–82 edition. On the fourth page of each club's section, the accumulative figures of League appearances include both full appearances and those made as a substitute.

However, in order that these figures can be broken down each season, they will continue to be split on the third page of the club's section as in previous years. For example, the 29+1s will still be shown on page three, but will go forward to page four as 30 – to be added to any previous total for that particular player.

It should be stressed that these substitute appearances are confined only to those players who actually appeared in the match in question and not to nominated substitutes who did not get on to the field of play during the game.

The actual players' appearances have been checked and re-checked while this change has been effected. Wherever discovered, alterations from previous years, including changes in goalscorers, have been included.

Over the years there have been a number of queries raised concerning the attendance figures which appear on these club pages. Those which feature on page two of each club are taken either from press sources at the time of the match or from estimated figures. But the final attendance figures for the season, which also incorporate the club's average crowd at home, are those officially supplied by the Football League.

On page four of the club section, the asterisk * which appears with the name of a player means that he was given a free transfer by that club at the end of the 1981–82 season. The list of players on the club's page four is based on the retained list. Any subsequent transfers appear under the section provided elsewhere in the yearbook, and the record of such players will appear under their former club. The asterisk against a number on page three of the club section denotes the player substituted. In the Scottish League, the additional dagger refers to the second substituted player.

Because of the pressure of space, it is not possible to include a list of apprentices, non-contract players and associated schoolboys retained by clubs, but those under these categories who made appearances in the Football League during 1981–82 are included.

Another innovation this year has been the award of three points for a win in Football League matches instead of two. Many clubs have therefore passed their previous record totals and, in order to keep a sense of proportion, the former record has been retained and where appropriate any higher figure for 1981–82 has also been included.

# ALDERSHOT Division 4

*Chairman:* R. J. Driver.

*Vice-Chairman:* F. G. Wiltshire FSVA.

*Directors:* R. H. Lamarre, A. English, L. Kennett, Major A. Dobson MBE.

*Team Manager:* Len Walker.

*Secretary/Commercial Manager:* M. A. Cosway.

*Year Formed:* 1926. *Turned Professional:* 1927.

*Limited Company:* 1927

**Football League Record:**
1932 Elected to Division 3(S); 1958–73 Division 4; 1973–76 Division 3; 1976– Division 4.

**Honours:** *Football League:* best season: 8th, Division 3, 1973–74. *FA Cup* best season: 5th rd, 1932–33, 5th rd replay, 1978–79. *Football League Cup:* never past 2nd rd.

*Record Victory:* 8-1 v Gateshead, Division 4, 13 Sept, 1958.

*Record Defeat:* 0-9 v Bristol C, Division 3(S), 28 Dec, 1946.

*Most League Points:* 57, Division 4, 1978–79.

*Most League Goals:* 83, Division 4, 1963–64.

*Highest League Scorer in Season:* John Dungworth, 26, Division 4, 1978–79.

*Most League Goals in Total Aggregate:* Jack Howarth, 171, 1965–71; 1972–77.

*Most Capped Player:* Peter Scott, 1 (10), Northern Ireland.

*Most League Appearances:* Len Walker, 450, 1964–76.

*Record Transfer Fee Received:* £100,000 from Shrewsbury T for John Dungworth, Nov 1979.

*Record Transfer Fee Paid:* £54,000 to Portsmouth for Colin Garwood, Feb 1980.

*Previous Managers since the War:* Bill McCracken, Gordon Clark, Harry Evans, Dave Smith, Tommy McAnearney, Jimmy Melia, Cliff Huxford, Tommy McAnearney.

*Address of Supporters Club:* 213 High St, Aldershot.

---

**Recreation Ground, High St, Aldershot GU11 1TW.** Telephone Aldershot 20211. *Record attendance:* 19,138 v Carlisle U, FA Cup 4th rd replay, 28 January, 1970. *Record receipts:* £11,850 v Shrewsbury T, FA Cup 5th rd, 20 February, 1979. *Ground capacity:* 16,000 (14,000 under cover).

*How to get there:* Aldershot railway station is on the main line from London's Waterloo; the ground is five minutes walk from the station. Many buses run from the town centre on match days.

*Match tickets:* Can be booked in advance by telephoning ground. Available 2 weeks prior to match.

*Car parking:* Car parks within ¾ mile of the ground.

*Entertainments/catering facilities:* Vice-Presidents' club, Sportsman's club.

*Club shop:* Run by Supporters' Club; sells all types of souvenirs.

*Handbooks/programmes:* Programmes only available on sale.

*Extra information:* Harry Brooks scored five goals for Aldershot in each of two successive FA Cup ties in the 1945–46 season.

*Club Colours:* Red and blue striped shirts, blue edge on collar and cuffs, blue shorts, red stockings with two blue hoops.

*Change Colours:* White shirts, red edge on collar and cuffs, white shorts with blue stripe, white stockings with two blue hoops.

*Club Captain:*

*Trainer:* John Anderson.

*Player-Coach:* Ian Gillard.

*Club Nickname:* Shots.

## ALDERSHOT 1981–82 LEAGUE RECORD

| Match No. | Date | Venue | Opponents | Result | H/T Score | Goalscorers | Attendance |
|---|---|---|---|---|---|---|---|
| 1 | Aug 29 | H | Darlington | D 0-0 | 0-0 | | 1918 |
| 2 | Sept 4 | A | Stockport Co | L 2-4 | 2-3 | Sanford 2 | 2239 |
| 3 | 12 | H | Halifax T | W 3-1 | 1-1 | Sanford, Wanklyn, Lucas | 1733 |
| 4 | 18 | A | Crewe Alex | W 3-2 | 2-1 | Garwood 2 (1 pen), Sanford | 1956 |
| 5 | 22 | A | Colchester U | D 1-1 | 0-1 | Crosby | 2719 |
| 6 | 26 | H | Mansfield T | L 2-3 | 2-1 | Brodie, Sanford | 2486 |
| 7 | 29 | H | York C | L 0-1 | 0-1 | | 2056 |
| 8 | Oct 4 | A | Rochdale | D 0-0 | 0-0 | | 1821 |
| 9 | 11 | A | Bradford C | L 1-4 | 1-0 | Lucas | 6254 |
| 10 | 17 | H | Blackpool | W 3-2 | 1-1 | French 2, Edwards | 2600 |
| 11 | 20 | H | AFC Bournemouth | W 2-0 | 1-0 | Garwood, Crosby | 3704 |
| 12 | 24 | A | Hull C | W 2-1 | 1-1 | Lucas, Sanford | 2999 |
| 13 | 31 | H | Hartlepool U | L 1-2 | 0-1 | Sanford | 2658 |
| 14 | Nov 4 | A | Peterborough U | L 1-7 | 1-2 | Sanford | 3781 |
| 15 | 7 | H | Bury | L 1-2 | 0-0 | Lucas | 2164 |
| 16 | 14 | A | Port Vale | L 0-1 | 0-1 | | 2811 |
| 17 | 28 | H | Tranmere R | W 2-1 | 2-0 | Scott, Lucas | 1878 |
| 18 | Dec 5 | A | Sheffield U | L 0-2 | 0-0 | | 11,541 |
| 19 | Jan 3 | H | Torquay U | D 1-1 | 1-0 | Garwood | 2260 |
| 20 | 23 | A | Darlington | W 1-0 | 0-0 | McDonald | 1504 |
| 21 | 31 | H | Crewe Alex | W 3-0 | 0-0 | Lucas, Briley, Robinson | 2053 |
| 22 | Feb 3 | A | Hereford U | W 1-0 | 0-0 | Sanford | 2253 |
| 23 | 6 | A | Halifax T | D 2-2 | 1-2 | French, Bennett | 1754 |
| 24 | 9 | H | Colchester U | D 1-1 | 1-1 | Jopling | 2324 |
| 25 | 14 | H | Rochdale | D 2-2 | 0-1 | French 2 | 2079 |
| 26 | 17 | A | Wigan Ath | L 0-1 | 0-0 | | 5120 |
| 27 | 20 | A | Mansfield T | L 0-1 | 0-1 | | 2001 |
| 28 | 23 | H | Northampton T | W 2-1 | 1-0 | French, Garwood | 1171 |
| 29 | 28 | H | Bradford C | L 0-2 | 0-2 | | 2721 |
| 30 | Mar 6 | A | Blackpool | W 2-0 | 2-0 | Garwood, French | 2655 |
| 31 | 9 | A | AFC Bournemouth | D 2-2 | 1-2 | Garwood, Jopling | 5333 |
| 32 | 12 | H | Hull C | L 0-3 | 0-0 | | 2059 |
| 33 | 16 | H | Peterborough U | L 0-1 | 0-1 | | 1453 |
| 34 | 20 | A | Hartlepool U | D 2-2 | 0-0 | Brodie, Robinson | 1702 |
| 35 | 23 | A | Scunthorpe U | D 1-1 | 1-0 | Sanford | 1658 |
| 36 | 27 | H | Bury | D 1-1 | 0-0 | Wanklyn | 3068 |
| 37 | Apr 3 | H | Port Vale | L 1-2 | 0-2 | McDonald | 1594 |
| 38 | 6 | H | Stockport Co | D 1-1 | 0-0 | Lucas | 1304 |
| 39 | 10 | A | Northampton T | D 0-0 | 0-0 | | 2365 |
| 40 | 12 | A | Hereford U | D 2-2 | 1-1 | Sanford, McDonald | 1748 |
| 41 | 17 | H | Sheffield U | D 1-1 | 1-1 | Jopling | 4100 |
| 42 | 24 | A | Tranmere R | L 0-1 | 0-1 | | 1242 |
| 43 | May 1 | H | Scunthorpe U | W 4-0 | 4-0 | French 2, Brodie, Lucas | 1304 |
| 44 | 4 | A | York C | L 0-4 | 0-1 | | 1571 |
| 45 | 8 | A | Torquay U | L 1-2 | 1-1 | Lucas | 1447 |
| 46 | 15 | H | Wigan Ath | W 2-0 | 0-0 | Briley, French (pen) | 2493 |

**Final League Position: 16**

### Goalscorers

*League* (57): Sanford 11, French 10 (1 pen), Lucas 9, Garwood 7 (1 pen), Brodie 3, Jopling 3, McDonald 3, Briley 2, Crosby 2, Robinson 2, Wanklyn 2, Bennett 1, Edwards 1, Scott 1.
*League Cup* (5): Garwood 2, Crosby 1, Lucas 1, Robinson 1.
*FA Cup* (6): Garwood 2, Brodie 1, French 1, McDonald 1, Robinson 1.

| | | | |
|---|---|---|---|
| **League Cup** | First Round | Wimbledon (h) | 0-0 |
| | | (a) | 3-1 |
| | Second Round | Wigan Ath (h) | 2-2 |
| | | (a) | 0-1 |
| **FA Cup** | First Round | Leytonstone (h) | 2-0 |
| | Second Round | Oxford U (h) | 2-2 |
| | | (a) | 2-4 |

| Johnson | Edwards | Wooler | Briley | Bennett | Jopling | McGregor | Brodie | Lucas | Garwood | Crosby | Robinson | Scott | Sanford | Wanklyn | French | McDonald | Horn | Hampshire | Fielder | Match No. |
|---|---|---|---|---|---|---|---|---|---|---|---|---|---|---|---|---|---|---|---|---|
| 1 | 2 | 3 | 4 | 5 | 6 | 7 | 8* | 12 | 9 | 10 | 11 | | | | | | | | | 1 |
| 1 | 2 | 3 | 4 | 5 | 6 | | | | 9 | 10 | 11 | 7 | 8 | | | | | | | 2 |
| 1 | | 3 | | 5 | 6 | | 7 | | 9 | 10 | 11 | 2 | 8 | 4 | | | | | | 3 |
| 1 | 2 | 3 | 4 | 5 | 6 | | 11 | | 9 | | 8 | | 10 | 7 | | | | | | 4 |
| 1 | 2 | 3 | 4 | 5 | 6 | | 11 | | 9 | | 8 | | 10 | 7 | | | | | | 5 |
| 1 | 2 | 3 | 4 | 5 | 6 | | 11 | | 9 | | 8 | | 10 | 7 | | | | | | 6 |
| 1 | 2 | 3 | 4 | 5 | 6 | | 11 | 12 | 9 | | 8 | | 10 | 7* | | | | | | 7 |
| 1 | 2 | 3 | 4 | 5 | 6* | | 11 | | 9 | | 8 | | 10 | 7 | 12 | | | | | 8 |
| 1 | 2 | 3 | 4 | 5 | | | 7 | 9 | 8 | | 11 | 6 | 10 | | | | | | | 9 |
| 1 | 2 | | 6 | 4 | 5 | | 7 | 9 | 8 | | 11 | 3 | | | | 10 | | | | 10 |
| 1 | 2 | | 6 | 4 | 5 | | 7 | 9 | 8 | | 11 | 3 | | | | 10 | | | | 11 |
| 1 | 2 | | 6 | 4 | 5 | | 7 | 9 | 8 | | 11 | 3 | | | | 10 | | | | 12 |
| 1 | 2 | | 4 | 5 | 6 | 11* | 7 | 9 | 8 | | | 3 | 10 | | 12 | | | | | 13 |
| 1 | | 6 | | 5 | | | 7 | 9 | 3 | | 11 | 2 | 10 | 4 | | 8 | | | | 14 |
| 1 | 2 | | 6 | 5 | | | 7 | 9 | | | 11 | 3 | 8 | 4 | | 10 | | | | 15 |
| 1 | 2 | | 6 | 4 | 5 | | 7* | 9 | | | 11 | 3 | 10 | | 12 | 8 | | | | 16 |
| 1 | 2 | | 6 | 4 | 5 | | 10 | 7 | 9 | | 11 | 3 | | | | 8 | | | | 17 |
| 1 | 2 | | 6 | 5 | 4 | | 10 | 7* | 9 | | 11 | 3 | | | 12 | 8 | | | | 18 |
| 1 | | 4 | 5 | 6 | | 11 | 8* | 9 | 7 | | | 3 | 12 | | 10 | 2 | | | | 19 |
| 1 | 2 | | 4 | 5 | 6 | | 10* | 9 | | | 11 | 3 | 12 | 7 | | 8 | | | | 20 |
| 1 | 2 | | 4 | 5 | 6 | | | 7 | | | 11 | 3 | 9 | | 10 | 8 | | | | 21 |
| | 2 | | 4 | 5 | 6 | | | 7 | | | 11 | 3 | 9 | | 10 | 8 | 1 | | | 22 |
| 1 | 2 | 3 | | 5 | 6 | | 12 | 7 | | | 11 | 9* | 4 | | 10 | 8 | | | | 23 |
| 1 | 2 | | 4 | 5 | 6 | | | 7 | 9 | | 11 | 3 | | | 10 | 8 | | | | 24 |
| 1 | 2 | | 4 | 5 | 6 | | 12 | 7* | 9 | | 11 | 3 | | | 10 | 8 | | | | 25 |
| 1 | 2 | | 4 | 5 | 6 | | 11 | 7 | 9 | | | 3 | | | 10 | 8 | | | | 26 |
| 1 | 2 | | 4 | 5 | 6 | | | 7 | 9 | | 11 | 3 | 12 | | 10* | 8 | | | | 27 |
| 1 | 2 | | 4 | 5 | 6 | | | 7 | 9 | | 11 | 3* | 12 | | 10 | 8 | | | | 28 |
| 1 | 2 | 3 | | 5 | | | 12 | 7 | 9 | | 11* | 6 | 4 | | 10 | 8 | | | | 29 |
| 1 | 2 | 3 | 11 | 5 | 6 | | 10 | 7 | 9 | | 8 | 4 | | | | | | | | 30 |
| 1 | 2 | 3 | 4 | 5 | 6 | | 11 | 7 | 9 | | | | | | 10 | 8 | | | | 31 |
| 1 | 2 | 3* | 4 | 5 | 6 | | 11 | 7 | 9 | | | | 12 | | 10 | 8 | | | | 32 |
| 1 | 2 | 3 | 4* | 5 | 6 | 7 | 11 | 12 | 9 | | | | | | 10 | 8 | | | | 33 |
| 1 | 2 | 3 | | 5 | 6 | 7 | 11 | 12 | 9 | | | | 4* | | 10 | 8 | | | | 34 |
| 1 | 2 | | 6 | 5 | | | 7 | 11 | | | | 3 | 9 | 4 | 10 | 8 | | | | 35 |
| 1 | 2* | 3 | 6 | 5 | | | 7 | 11 | 4 | | 9 | | 12 | | 10 | 8 | | | | 36 |
| 1 | | 3 | 4 | 5 | 6 | 7 | 11 | | | | | 2 | 9 | | 10 | 8 | | | | 37 |
| 1 | | 2 | 5 | 6 | | | 10 | 7 | 9 | | 11 | 3 | 4 | | | 8 | | | | 38 |
| 1 | | 3 | 4 | 5 | 6 | | 11 | 7 | | | | 2 | 9 | 8 | 10 | | | | | 39 |
| 1 | 2 | | 4 | 5 | 6 | | 10* | 7 | | | 11 | 3 | 9 | | 12 | 8 | | | | 40 |
| 1 | 2 | | 4 | 5 | 6 | | | 7 | | | 11 | 3 | 8 | | 9 | 10 | | | | 41 |
| | 2 | | 5 | 6 | | | 11 | 7* | 12 | | | 3 | 8 | 4 | 9 | 10 | 1 | | | 42 |
| 1 | 2 | | 4 | 5 | 6 | | 9 | 7 | | | 11 | 3 | 8 | | | 10 | | | | 43 |
| 1 | 2 | | 4 | 5 | 6 | | 10 | 7 | | | 11* | 3 | 12 | | 9 | 8 | | | | 44 |
| 1 | 2 | | 6 | 4 | 5 | | 9 | 7 | | | | 3 | | | | 10 | | 8 | 11 | 45 |
| 1 | 2 | | 4 | 5 | 6 | | 11 | 7 | | | | 3 | 8 | | 9 | 10 | | | | 46 |
| 44 | 42 | 27 | 37 | 46 | 34 | 7 | 26 | 33 | 30 | 14 | 28 | 33 | 27 | 15 | 28 | 31 | 2 | 1 | 1 | |
| | | | | | | | + | + | | | | + | + | + | + | + | | | | |
| | | | | | | | 3s | 2s | | | | 2s | 1s | 6s | 3s | 3s | | | | |

## ALDERSHOT

| | Ht | Wt | Birthplace | Clubs | League App. | League Gls |
|---|---|---|---|---|---|---|
| **Goalkeepers** | | | | | | |
| Glen Johnson | 6 2 | 13 6 | Barrow | Arsenal | — | — |
| | | | | Doncaster R | 95 | — |
| | | | | Walsall (on loan) | 3 | — |
| | | | | Aldershot | 378 | — |
| Graham Horn* | 6 2 | 14 1 | Westminster | Arsenal | — | — |
| | | | | Portsmouth (on loan) | 22 | — |
| | | | | Luton T | 58 | — |
| | | | | Brentford (on loan) | 3 | — |
| | | | | Charlton Ath | — | — |
| | | | | Kettering T | (not known) | |
| | | | | Southend U | 9 | — |
| | | | | Aldershot | 9 | — |
| **Defenders** | | | | | | |
| Joe Jopling | 6 0 | 12 13 | South Shields | Aldershot | 35 | 2 |
| | | | | Leicester C | 3 | — |
| | | | | Torquay U (on loan) | 6 | — |
| | | | | Aldershot | 269 | 11 |
| Alan Wooler | 6 0 | 11 0 | Poole | Reading | 38 | — |
| (Contract cancelled April 1982) | | | | West Ham U | 4 | — |
| | | | | Aldershot | 231 | 3 |
| Peter Scott | 5 10 | 11 4 | Liverpool | Everton | 44 | 1 |
| (N Ireland) | | | | Southport (on loan) | 4 | — |
| | | | | York C | 100 | 4 |
| | | | | Aldershot | 88 | 2 |
| Nigel Edwards* | 5 11 | 11 10 | Wrexham | Chester | 290 | 15 |
| | | | | Rotherham U (on loan) | — | — |
| | | | | Aldershot | 137 | 6 |
| Paul Bennett* | 6 0 | 12 6 | Southampton | Southampton | 116 | 1 |
| | | | | Reading | 105 | 3 |
| | | | | Aldershot | 113 | 2 |
| **Midfield** | | | | | | |
| Les Briley | 5 6 | 9 11 | London | Chelsea | — | — |
| | | | | Hereford U | 61 | 2 |
| | | | | Wimbledon | 61 | 2 |
| | | | | Aldershot | 93 | 2 |
| Stuart Robinson | 5 7 | 10 5 | Middlesbrough | Newcastle U | 12 | 2 |
| | | | | Aldershot | 63 | 8 |
| Wayne Wanklyn* | 5 7 | 10 7 | Hull | Reading | 54 | 3 |
| | | | | Aldershot | 18 | 2 |
| Ian McDonald | 5 7 | 10 5 | Barrow | Barrow | 35 | 2 |
| | | | | Workington | 42 | 4 |
| | | | | Liverpool | — | — |
| | | | | Colchester U (on loan) | 5 | 2 |
| | | | | Mansfield T | 56 | 4 |
| | | | | York C | 175 | 29 |
| | | | | Aldershot | 31 | 3 |
| Colin Fielder | 5 8 | 10 7 | Winchester | Aldershot | 1 | — |
| **Forwards** | | | | | | |
| Colin Garwood* | 5 9 | 10 13 | Heacham | Peterborough U | 66 | 31 |
| | | | | Oldham Ath | 92 | 36 |
| | | | | Huddersfield T | 28 | 8 |
| | | | | Colchester U | 87 | 25 |
| | | | | Portsmouth | 71 | 34 |
| | | | | Aldershot | 81 | 25 |
| Murray Brodie | 6 0 | 12 13 | Glasgow | Leicester C | 3 | 2 |
| | | | | Aldershot | 427 | 81 |
| Alex McGregor* | 5 10 | 10 8 | Glasgow | Ayr U | 29 | 1 |
| | | | | Hibernian | — | — |
| | | | | Shrewsbury T | 49 | 7 |
| | | | | Aldershot | 177 | 17 |
| Brian Lucas | 5 7 | 10 12 | Farnborough | Aldershot | 79 | 12 |
| Mickey French* | 6 0 | 12 4 | Eastbourne | QPR | — | — |
| | | | | Brentford | 65 | 16 |
| | | | | Swindon T | 10 | 1 |
| | | | | Doncaster R | 36 | 5 |
| | | | | Aldershot | 74 | 16 |
| Paul Hampshire* | 5 6 | 10.7 | Guildford | Aldershot | 5 | 2 |
| Mark Sanford | 6 0 | 11 8 | London | Aldershot | 63 | 21 |
| Bobby Gould | 5 10 | 11 5 | Coventry | Coventry C | 81 | 40 |
| (Contract cancelled) | | | | Arsenal | 65 | 16 |
| | | | | Wolverhampton W | 40 | 18 |
| | | | | WBA | 52 | 18 |
| | | | | Bristol C | 35 | 15 |
| | | | | West Ham U | 51 | 15 |
| | | | | Wolverhampton W | 34 | 13 |
| | | | | Bristol R | 36 | 12 |
| | | | | Hereford U | 45 | 13 |
| | | | | Chelsea | — | — |
| | | | | Wimbledon | — | — |
| | | | | Aldershot | — | — |

# ARSENAL                                    Division 1

*Chairman:* P. D. Hill-Wood.

*Directors:* Sir Robert Bellinger CBE,DSC, S. C. McIntyre MBE, FCIS, The Rev N. F. Bone TD, A. Wood, R. G. Gibbs, C. E. B. L. Carr, R. C. L. Carr.

*Manager:* Terry Neill.   *Secretary:* K. J. Friar.

*Assistant Manager/Chief Scout:* Wilf Dixon.

*Chief Coach:* Don Howe.

*Year Formed:* 1886.   *Turned Professional:* 1891.   *Limited Company:* 1893.

*Former Names:* 1886–91, Royal Arsenal; 1891–1914, Woolwich Arsenal.

*Former Grounds:* 1886–87, Plumstead Common; 1887–88, Sportsman Ground; 1888–90, Manor Ground; 1890–93, Invicta Ground; 1893–1913, Manor Ground; 1913– Highbury.

**Football League Record:**
1893 Elected to Division 2; 1904–13 Division 1; 1913–19 Division 2; 1919– Division 1.

**Honours:** *Football League:* Division 1 – Champions 1930–31, 1932–33, 1933-34, 1934–35, 1937–38, 1947–48, 1952–53, 1970–71; Runners-up 1925–26, 1931–32, 1972–73; Division 2 – Runners-up 1903–04. *FA Cup:* Winners 1929–30, 1935–36, 1949–50, 1970–71, 1978–79; Runners-up 1926–27, 1931–32, 1951–52, 1971–72, 1977–78, 1979–80. *Double Performed:* 1970–71. *League Cup:* Runners-up 1967–68, 1968–69. **European Competitions:** *Fairs Cup:* 1963–64, 1969–70 (winners), 1970–71; *European Cup:* 1971–72; *UEFA Cup:* 1978–79, 1981–82; *European Cup-Winners' Cup:* 1979–80 (runners-up).

*Record Victory:* 12–0 v Loughborough T, Division 2, 12 Mar, 1900.

*Record Defeat:* 0-8 v Loughborough T, Division 2, 12 Dec, 1896.

*Most League Points:* 66, Division 1, 1930–31. *Three points win:* 71, Division 1, 1981–2.

*Most League Goals:* 127, Division 1, 1930–31.

*Highest League Scorer in Season:* Ted Drake, 42, 1934–35.

*Most League Goals in Total Aggregate:* Cliff Bastin, 150, 1930–47.

*Most Capped Player:* Pat Rice, 49, Northern Ireland.

*Most League Appearances:* George Armstrong, 500, 1960–77.

*Record Transfer Fee Received:* £1,250,000 from Crystal Palace for Clive Allen, August 1980.

*Record Transfer Fee Paid:* £1,250,000 to QPR for Clive Allen, June 1980.

*Previous Managers since the War:* George Allison, Tom Whittaker, Jack Crayston, George Swindin, Billy Wright, Bertie Mee.

*Address of the Club Shop or Boutique:* Gunners Shop, Arsenal Stadium, Highbury, N5.

---

**Arsenal Stadium, Highbury, London N5.** Telephone 01-226 0304. *Ground capacity:* 60,000. *Record attendance:* 73,295 v Sunderland, Div 1, 9 March, 1935. *Record receipts:* £116,498 v Juventus, Cup-Winners' Cup semi-final, 9 April, 1980. *Telegraphs:* 'Gunneretic London N5.' *Pitch measurements:* 110yd×71yd.

*How to get there:* Arsenal Underground Station (Piccadilly Line) is within one minute of the ground. Finsbury Park (Piccadilly and Victoria) and Drayton Park are also within walking distance. Buses 4a, 19, 106, 141a, 236.

*Match tickets:* Postal application one calendar month prior to the match. Prices and availability of tickets can be checked with the club on their Ansafone Service 01-359 0131.

*Car parking:* Parking is allowed in the adjacent streets under the control of the Police.

*Entertainments/catering facilities:* West Stand restaurant is open Mon–Fri for the general public and on match days for ticket holders in the West Stand Upper tier. East Stand restaurant is open on match days only for ticket holders in the East Stand Upper tier. Reservations for both restaurants can be made by telephoning 01-226 4968. There are also extensive refreshment bars around the ground.

*Club shop:* Shop in Avenell Road, Highbury, is open Mon–Fri 9.30 am–5 pm. On Saturday first team matches it is open from 1.00 pm–5.30 pm. Other shops in the ground are open on match days.

*Handbooks/programmes:* Programmes can be obtained from the club shop. Programmes available on subscription. subscription.

*Club Colours:* Red shirts with white sleeves, white shorts, red and white stockings.

*Change Colours:* Yellow shirts with blue shorts, yellow stockings.

*Club Captain:* David O'Leary.

*Club Nickname:* Gunners.

# ARSENAL 1981-82 LEAGUE RECORD

| Match No. | Date | Venue | Opponents | Result | H/T Score | Goalscorers | Attendance |
|---|---|---|---|---|---|---|---|
| 1 | Aug 29 | H | Stoke C | L 0-1 | 0-1 | | 28,212 |
| 2 | Sept 2 | A | WBA | W 2-0 | 2-0 | Talbot, Sunderland | 17,104 |
| 3 | 5 | A | Liverpool | L 0-2 | 0-1 | | 35,269 |
| 4 | 12 | H | Sunderland | D 1-1 | 0-0 | Sunderland | 26,471 |
| 5 | 19 | A | Leeds U | D 0-0 | 0-0 | | 21,410 |
| 6 | 22 | H | Birmingham C | W 1-0 | 1-0 | Talbot | 19,504 |
| 7 | 26 | H | Manchester U | D 0-0 | 0-0 | | 39,797 |
| 8 | Oct 3 | A | Notts Co | L 1-2 | 1-0 | Hawley | 10,848 |
| 9 | 10 | A | Swansea C | L 0-2 | 0-1 | | 20,600 |
| 10 | 17 | H | Manchester C | W 1-0 | 0-0 | Meade | 25,470 |
| 11 | 24 | A | Ipswich T | L 1-2 | 0-1 | Sunderland | 24,362 |
| 12 | 31 | H | Coventry C | W 1-0 | 0-0 | Thomas (og) | 23,102 |
| 13 | Nov 7 | A | Aston Villa | W 2-0 | 2-0 | Rix, Talbot | 27,316 |
| 14 | 21 | A | Nottingham F | W 2-1 | 0-1 | Sunderland, Talbot | 20,912 |
| 15 | 28 | H | Everton | W 1-0 | 0-0 | McDermott | 25,860 |
| 16 | Dec 5 | A | West Ham U | W 2-1 | 2-0 | Whyte, Hollins (pen) | 33,833 |
| 17 | Jan 20 | A | Stoke C | W 1-0 | 1-0 | Sunderland | 9625 |
| 18 | 23 | A | Southampton | L 1-3 | 1-1 | O'Leary | 22,263 |
| 19 | 26 | H | Brighton & HA | D 0-0 | 0-0 | | 17,922 |
| 20 | 30 | H | Leeds U | W 1-0 | 1-0 | Vaessen | 22,408 |
| 21 | Feb 2 | H | Wolverhampton W | W 2-1 | 0-0 | Rix, Vaessen | 15,163 |
| 22 | 6 | A | Sunderland | D 0-0 | 0-0 | | 16,345 |
| 23 | 13 | H | Notts Co | W 1-0 | 0-0 | Meade | 18,229 |
| 24 | 16 | H | Middlesbrough | W 1-0 | 0-0 | Rix | 13,738 |
| 25 | 20 | A | Manchester U | D 0-0 | 0-0 | | 43,833 |
| 26 | 27 | A | Swansea C | L 0-2 | 0-1 | | 29,724 |
| 27 | Mar 6 | A | Manchester C | D 0-0 | 0-0 | | 30,288 |
| 28 | 13 | H | Ipswich T | W 1-0 | 1-0 | Robson | 25,977 |
| 29 | 16 | H | WBA | D 2-2 | 0-1 | Meade, Sunderland | 15,799 |
| 30 | 20 | A | Coventry C | L 0-1 | 0-0 | | 11,965 |
| 31 | 27 | H | Aston Villa | W 4-3 | 2-2 | Sunderland, Rix 2, Meade | 24,756 |
| 32 | 29 | A | Tottenham H | D 2-2 | 2-0 | Sunderland 2 | 40,940 |
| 33 | Apr 3 | A | Wolverhampton W | D 1-1 | 0-0 | Davis | 11,532 |
| 34 | 10 | A | Brighton & HA | L 1-2 | 0-0 | Talbot | 21,019 |
| 35 | 12 | H | Tottenham H | L 1-3 | 0-1 | Hawley | 48,897 |
| 36 | 17 | H | Nottingham F | W 2-0 | 1-0 | Talbot, Rix | 21,986 |
| 37 | 24 | A | Everton | L 1-2 | 1-1 | Rix | 19,136 |
| 38 | May 1 | H | West Ham U | W 2-0 | 2-0 | Rix, Sunderland | 34,977 |
| 39 | 4 | A | Birmingham C | W 1-0 | 0-0 | Whyte | 13,133 |
| 40 | 8 | A | Middlesbrough | W 3-1 | 1-1 | Talbot, Davis, Rix | 9565 |
| 41 | 11 | H | Liverpool | D 1-1 | 0-1 | Sunderland | 30,932 |
| 42 | 15 | H | Southampton | W 4-1 | 3-0 | Davis 2, Robson, Hawley | 28,534 |

**Final League Position: 5**

### Goalscorers

*League* (48): Sunderland 11, Rix 9, Talbot 7, Davis 4, Meade 4, Hawley 3, Robson 2, Vaessen 2, Whyte 2, Hollins 1 (pen), McDermott 1, O'Leary 1, own goal 1.
*League Cup* (3): Nicholas 1, Sunderland 1, Young 1.
*FA Cup* (0).

| League Cup | Second Round | Sheffield U (a) | 0-1 |
|---|---|---|---|
| | | (h) | 2-0 |
| | Third Round | Norwich C (h) | 1-0 |
| | Fourth Round | Liverpool (h) | 0-0 |
| | | (a) | 0-3 |
| FA Cup | Third Round | Tottenham H (a) | 0-1 |

| Jennings | Devine | Sansom | Talbot | O'Leary | Young | Davis | Sunderland | McDermott | Nicholas | Rix | Vaessen | Hollins | Hawley | Whyte | Meade | Robson | Wood | Gorman | Match No. |
|---|---|---|---|---|---|---|---|---|---|---|---|---|---|---|---|---|---|---|---|
| 1 | 2* | 3 | 4 | 5 | 6 | 7 | 8 | 9 | 10 | 11 | 12 | | | | | | | | 1 |
| 1 | 2 | 3 | 4 | 5 | 6 | 7 | 8 | 9 | 10 | 11 | | | | | | | | | 2 |
| 1 | 2 | 3 | 4 | 5 | 6 | 12 | 8 | 9 | 10* | 11 | | 7 | | | | | | | 3 |
| 1 | | 3 | 4 | 5 | 6 | 7 | 8 | 9 | 10 | 11 | | 2 | | | | | | | 4 |
| 1 | 12 | 3 | 4 | 5 | 6 | 7* | 8 | 9 | 10 | 11 | | 2 | | | | | | | 5 |
| 1 | 2 | 3 | 4 | 5 | 6 | 7 | 8 | 9 | | 11 | | 10 | | | | | | | 6 |
| 1 | 2 | 3 | 4 | 5 | 6 | 11 | 8 | | 10 | | | 7 | 9 | | | | | | 7 |
| 1 | | 3 | 4 | 5 | 6 | 7 | 8 | 12 | 10 | 11 | | 2 | 9* | | | | | | 8 |
| 1 | 2 | 3 | 4 | 5 | 6 | 7 | 8 | | 10 | | | 11 | 9 | | | | | | 9 |
| 1 | | 3 | 4 | 5 | | | 8 | 7 | 10 | 11 | | 2 | 9 | 6 | | | | | 10 |
| 1 | | 3 | 4 | 5 | 6 | 7 | 8 | | 10 | 11 | | 2 | 9 | | | | | | 11 |
| 1 | | 3 | 4 | 5 | | | 8 | 7 | 10 | 11 | 8 | 2 | 9 | 6 | | | | | 12 |
| 1 | 2 | 3 | 4 | 5 | | 9 | | | 10 | 11 | 8 | 7 | | 6 | | | | | 13 |
| 1 | 2 | 3 | 4 | 5 | | 9 | 8 | | 10 | 11 | | 7 | | 6 | | | | | 14 |
| 1 | 2* | 3 | 4 | 5 | | 9 | 8 | 12 | 10 | 11 | | 7 | | 6 | | | | | 15 |
| 1 | | 3 | 4 | 5 | | 9 | 8 | | 10 | 11 | | 7 | | 6 | | 2 | | | 16 |
| | | 3 | 4 | 5 | | 9 | 8 | | 10 | 11 | | 7 | | 6 | | 2 | 1 | | 17 |
| | | 3 | 4 | 5* | | 9 | 8 | 12 | 10 | 11 | | 7 | | 6 | | 2 | 1 | | 18 |
| | | 3 | 4 | | | 9* | 8 | 7 | 10 | 11 | | 5 | | 6 | 12 | 2 | 1 | | 19 |
| | | 3 | 4 | 5 | | 9 | 8 | | 10 | 11 | 7 | 2 | | 6 | | | 1 | | 20 |
| | | 3 | 4 | 5 | | 9 | 8* | | 10 | 11 | 7 | 2 | 12 | 6 | | | 1 | | 21 |
| | | 3 | 4 | 5 | | 9 | 8 | | 10 | 11 | 7 | 2 | | 6 | | | 1 | | 22 |
| | | 3 | 4 | 5 | | 9 | 8 | | 10* | 11 | 7 | 2 | | 6 | 12 | | 1 | | 23 |
| | | 3 | 4 | 5 | | 9 | 8 | | 10* | 11 | 7 | 2 | | 6 | 12 | | 1 | | 24 |
| | | 3 | 4 | 5 | | 9 | 8 | | 10 | 11 | 7* | 2 | | 6 | 12 | | 1 | | 25 |
| | | 3 | 4 | 5 | | 9 | 8 | | 10 | 11 | 7* | 2 | | 6 | 12 | | 1 | | 26 |
| | | 3 | 4 | 5 | | 9 | 8 | | | 11 | | 2 | | 6 | 10 | | 1 | 7 | 27 |
| | | 3 | 4 | 5 | | 9 | 8 | | | 11 | | 2 | | 6 | 10 | | 1 | 7 | 28 |
| | | 3 | 4 | 5 | | 9 | 8 | | | 11 | | 2 | | 6 | 12 | 10 | 1 | 7* | 29 |
| | 5 | 3 | 4 | | | 9 | 8 | | | 11 | | 2 | | 6 | 12 | 10 | 1 | 7* | 30 |
| | | 3 | 4 | 5 | | 9 | 8 | | | 11 | | 2 | | 6 | 7 | 10 | 1 | | 31 |
| | | 3 | 4 | 5 | | 9* | 8 | | 12 | 11 | | 2 | | 6 | 7 | 10 | 1 | | 32 |
| | | 3 | 4 | 5 | | 9 | 8 | | | 11 | | 2 | 12 | 6 | 7* | 10 | 1 | | 33 |
| | | 3 | 4 | 5 | | 9 | 8 | | | 11 | | 2 | | 6 | 7 | 10 | 1 | | 34 |
| | | 3 | 4 | 5 | | | 12 | | 9 | 11 | | 2 | 8 | 6 | 7 | 10* | 1 | | 35 |
| | | 3 | 4 | 5 | | 9 | | | | 11 | | 2 | 8 | 6 | 7 | 10 | 1 | | 36 |
| | | 3 | 4 | 5 | | 9 | 8 | | 12 | 11 | | 2* | | 7 | 6 | 10 | 1 | | 37 |
| | | 3 | 4 | 5 | | 9 | 8 | | | 11 | | 2 | | 7 | 6 | 10 | 1 | | 38 |
| | | 3 | 4 | 5 | | 9 | 8 | | | 11 | | 2 | | 7 | 6 | 10 | 1 | | 39 |
| | | 3 | 4 | 5 | | 7* | 8 | | 12 | 11 | | 2 | 9 | 6 | | 10 | 1 | | 40 |
| | | 3 | 4 | 5 | | | 8 | | 7 | 11 | | 2 | 9* | 6 | 12 | 10 | 1 | | 41 |
| | | 3 | 4 | 5 | | 7 | 8 | | | 11 | | 2 | 9 | 6 | | 10 | 1 | | 42 |
| 16 | 10 | 42 | 42 | 40 | 10 | 37 | 38 | 9 | 28 | 39 | 9 | 40 | 12 | 32 | 8 | 20 | 26 | 4 | |

+ 1s (Devine)   + 1s (Young)   + 4s (Sunderland)   + 3s (McDermott)   + 1s (Rix)   + 2s (Hawley)   + 8s (Meade)

# ARSENAL

| | Ht | Wt | Birthplace | Clubs | League App. | League Gls |
|---|---|---|---|---|---|---|
| **Goalkeepers** | | | | | | |
| Pat Jennings | 6 0 | 12 6 | Newry, | Watford | 48 | — |
| (N Ireland) | | | Co. Down | Tottenham H | 472 | — |
| | | | | Arsenal | 165 | — |
| Rhys Wilmot | 6 1 | 12 0 | Wales | Arsenal | — | — |
| George Wood | 6 3 | 14 0 | Douglas | East Stirling | 22 | 1 |
| (Scotland) | | | | Blackpool | 117 | — |
| | | | | Everton | 103 | — |
| | | | | Arsenal | 37 | — |
| **Defenders** | | | | | | |
| David O'Leary | 5 11 | 11 3 | London | Arsenal | 236 | 8 |
| (Eire) | | | | | | |
| John Devine | 5 10½ | 12 1 | Dublin | Arsenal | 80 | — |
| (Eire) | | | | | | |
| Chris Whyte | 6 1 | 11 10 | London | Arsenal | 32 | 2 |
| Kenny Sansom | 5 6 | 11 8 | Camberwell | Crystal Palace | 172 | 3 |
| (England) | | | | Arsenal | 84 | 3 |
| Danny O'Shea | | | London | Arsenal | — | — |
| John Kay | | | Sunderland | Arsenal | — | — |
| James Watt* | | | Scotland | Arsenal | — | — |
| **Midfield** | | | | | | |
| Graham Rix | 5 9 | 11 0 | Doncaster | Arsenal | 197 | 24 |
| (England) | | | | | | |
| Brian Talbot | 5 10 | 12 0 | Ipswich | Ipswich T | 177 | 25 |
| (England) | | | | Arsenal | 144 | 15 |
| John Hollins | 5 8 | 11 7 | Guildford | Chelsea | 436 | 47 |
| (England) | | | | QPR | 151 | 5 |
| | | | | Arsenal | 104 | 7 |
| Peter Nicholas | 5 8½ | 11 8 | Newport, | Crystal Palace | 127 | 7 |
| (Wales) | | | Gwent | Arsenal | 39 | 1 |
| Stewart Robson | | | Billericay | Arsenal | 20 | 2 |
| Paul Gorman | | | Dublin | Arsenal | 4 | — |
| David Cork | | | Doncaster | Arsenal | — | — |
| **Forwards** | | | | | | |
| Alan Sunderland | 5 9 | 11 6¼ | Mexborough | Wolverhampton W | 158 | 29 |
| (England) | | | | Arsenal | 169 | 45 |
| Brian McDermott | 5 8 | 9 12 | London | Arsenal | 39 | 6 |
| Paul Vaessen | | | Bermondsey | Arsenal | 32 | 6 |
| Brian Sparrow | 5 7 | 10 2 | London | Arsenal | — | — |
| Paul Davis | 5 8 | 9 7 | London | Arsenal | 50 | 5 |
| John Hawley | 6 0 | 13 12 | Withernsea | Hull C | 114 | 22 |
| | | | | Leeds U | 33 | 16 |
| | | | | Sunderland | 25 | 11 |
| | | | | Arsenal | 14 | 3 |
| David Harrison | | | Leeds | Arsenal | — | — |
| (Contract cancelled April 1982) | | | | | | |
| Ray Hankin | 6 2 | 14 0 | Wallsend | Burnley | 112 | 37 |
| (Contract cancelled Jan 1982) | | | | Leeds U | 83 | 32 |
| | | | | Vancouver W | (not known) | |
| | | | | Arsenal | — | — |
| Raphael Meade | | | London | Arsenal | 16 | 4 |
| Colin Hill | | | Uxbridge | Arsenal | — | — |

# ASTON VILLA                                    Division 1

*Chairman:* R. F. Bendall.

*Vice Chairman:* D. J. Bendall.

*Directors:* J. H. Kartz, A. T. Gill.

*Manager:* Tony Barton.   *Secretary:* Steven Stride.

*Commercial Manager:* Sue Walker.   *Year Formed:* 1874.

*Turned Professional:* 1885.   *Limited Company:* 1896.

*Previous Grounds:* 1874–76, Aston Park; 1876–97, Perry Barr; 1897–Villa Park.

**Football League Record:**
1888 Original Member of the League; 1936–38 Division 2; 1938–59 Division 1; 1959–60 Division 2; 1960–67 Division 1; 1967–70 Division 2; 1970–72 Division 3; 1972–75 Division 2; 1975– Division 1.

*Honours: Football League:* Division 1 – Champions 1893–94, 1895–96, 1896–97, 1898–99, 1899–1900, 1909–10, 1980–81; Runners-up 1888–89, 1902–03, 1907–08, 1910–11, 1912–13, 1913–14, 1930–31, 1932–33; Division 2 – Champions 1937–38, 1959–60; Runners-up 1974–75; Division 3 – Champions 1971–72. *FA Cup:* Winners 1887, 1895, 1897, 1905, 1913, 1920, 1957 (7 wins stands as the record); Runners-up 1892, 1924. *Double Performed:* 1896–97. *Football League Cup:* Winners 1961, 1975, 1977; Runners-up 1963, 1971. **European Competitions:** *European Cup:* 1981–82 (winners); *UEFA Cup:* 1975–76, 1977–78.

*Record Victory:* 13-0 v Wednesbury Old Athletic, FA Cup 1st rd, 1886.

*Record Defeat:* 1-8 v Blackburn R, FA Cup 3rd rd, 1888–89.

*Most League Points:* 70, Division 3, 1971–72.

*Most League Goals:* 128, Division 1, 1930–31.

*Highest League Scorer in Season:* 49, 'Pongo' Waring, Division 1, 1930–31.

*Most League Goals in Total Aggregate:* 213, Harry Hampton, 1904–20, and Billy Walker, 1919–34.

*Most Capped Player:* Peter McParland, 33 (34), Northern Ireland.

*Most League Appearances:* 560, Charlie Aitken, 1961–76.

*Record Transfer Fee Received:* £1,469,000 (£1,175,000 basic fee) from Wolverhampton W for Andy Gray, Sept 1979.

*Record Transfer Fee Paid:* £500,000 to Newcastle U for Peter Withe, May 1980.

*Previous Managers since the War:* Alex Massie, George Martin, Eric Houghton, Joe Mercer, Dick Taylor, Tommy Cummings, Tommy Docherty, Vic Crowe, Ron Saunders.

*Address of the Club Shop or Boutique:* c/o Villa Park.

---

**Villa Park, Trinity Rd, Birmingham B6 6HE.** Telephone 021-327 6604. 24-hour answering service 021-328 1722. *Telegraphic Address:* 'Villa, Birmingham 6'. *Ground capacity:* 48,000. *Record attendance:* 76,588 v Derby Co, FA Cup 6th rd, 2 March, 1946. *Record receipts:* £167,753, FA Cup semi-final, Everton v West Ham U, 12 April, 1980. *Club record:* £90,000 UEFA Cup quarter-final v Barcelona, 1 Mar, 1978. *Pitch measurements:* 115yd×75yd.

*How to get there:* Bus 5 from Corporation Street to Witton Square. Special buses from Priory Ringway and Hall of Memory (city centre). Birmingham New Street railway station is near the centre. The ground is ½ mile from link to the motorway.

*Match tickets:* Applications for any games can be made by post or in person, any time during the season.

*Car parking:* Asda Car Park in Aston Hall Road. Side-street parking also available.

*Entertainments/catering facilities:* Many refreshment points around the ground.

*Club shop:* Adjacent to the ground; sells all types of souvenirs.

*Handbooks/programmes:* Programmes available on seasonal subscription.

*Club Colours:* Claret shirts with light blue trim, white shorts, blue stockings.   *Change Colours:* White shirts with claret and light blue collar and cuffs, blue shorts, white stockings.

*Club Nickname:* The Villans.

## ASTON VILLA 1981–82 LEAGUE RECORD

| Match No. | Date | Venue | Opponents | Result | | H/T Score | Goalscorers | Attendance |
|---|---|---|---|---|---|---|---|---|
| 1 | Aug 29 | H | Notts Co | L | 0-1 | 0-1 | | 30,097 |
| 2 | Sept 2 | A | Sunderland | L | 1-2 | 1-1 | Donovan | 29,372 |
| 3 | 5 | A | Tottenham H | W | 3-1 | 3-0 | Donovan 2, Mortimer | 31,265 |
| 4 | 12 | H | Manchester U | D | 1-1 | 1-1 | Cowans | 37,661 |
| 5 | 19 | A | Liverpool | D | 0-0 | 0-0 | | 37,474 |
| 6 | 23 | H | Stoke C | D | 2-2 | 1-0 | Withe 2 | 25,637 |
| 7 | 26 | H | Birmingham C | D | 0-0 | 0-0 | | 40,763 |
| 8 | Oct 3 | A | Leeds U | D | 1-1 | 1-0 | Shaw | 21,065 |
| 9 | 10 | A | Coventry C | D | 1-1 | 1-1 | Shaw | 16,306 |
| 10 | 17 | H | West Ham U | W | 3-2 | 3-1 | Morley, Geddis, Mortimer | 32,064 |
| 11 | 24 | A | Wolverhampton W | W | 3-0 | 2-0 | Shaw 2, Palmer (og) | 19,942 |
| 12 | 31 | H | Ipswich T | L | 0-1 | 0-1 | | 32,652 |
| 13 | Nov 7 | H | Arsenal | L | 0-2 | 0-2 | | 27,316 |
| 14 | 21 | A | Middlesbrough | D | 3-3 | 1-1 | Withe, Cowans, Shaw | 12,522 |
| 15 | 28 | H | Nottingham F | W | 3-1 | 2-0 | Bremner 2, Withe | 26,847 |
| 16 | Dec 5 | A | Manchester C | L | 0-1 | 0-0 | | 32,487 |
| 17 | 15 | A | Swansea C | L | 1-2 | 1-2 | Thompson (og) | 15,191 |
| 18 | 19 | A | Everton | L | 0-2 | 0-1 | | 16,538 |
| 19 | 28 | A | Brighton & HA | W | 1-0 | 0-0 | Morley | 24,287 |
| 20 | Jan 16 | A | Notts Co | L | 0-1 | 0-0 | | 9597 |
| 21 | 30 | H | Liverpool | L | 0-3 | 0-2 | | 35,947 |
| 22 | Feb 2 | H | Sunderland | W | 1-0 | 0-0 | Geddis | 19,916 |
| 23 | 6 | A | Manchester U | L | 1-4 | 1-1 | Geddis | 43,184 |
| 24 | 10 | H | Southampton | D | 1-1 | 0-1 | Withe | 24,287 |
| 25 | 17 | H | Tottenham H | D | 1-1 | 0-1 | Withe | 23,877 |
| 26 | 20 | A | Birmingham C | W | 1-0 | 0-0 | Withe | 32,779 |
| 27 | 27 | H | Coventry C | W | 2-1 | 2-1 | Cowans (pen), Shaw | 24,474 |
| 28 | Mar 6 | A | West Ham U | D | 2-2 | 1-1 | Cowans, Withe | 26,894 |
| 29 | 13 | H | Wolverhampton W | W | 3-1 | 2-1 | Donovan, Morley, Shaw | 26,790 |
| 30 | 20 | A | Ipswich T | L | 1-3 | 0-2 | McNaught | 20,407 |
| 31 | 27 | A | Arsenal | L | 3-4 | 2-2 | Shaw, Morley, Heard | 24,756 |
| 32 | 30 | H | WBA | W | 2-1 | 0-0 | Shaw, Withe | 28,440 |
| 33 | Apr 10 | A | Southampton | W | 3-0 | 0-0 | Nicholl (og), McNaught, Morley | 22,801 |
| 34 | 12 | H | Brighton & HA | W | 3-0 | 0-0 | Geddis 2, Evans | 22,731 |
| 35 | 17 | H | Middlesbrough | W | 1-0 | 1-0 | Evans | 21,098 |
| 36 | 24 | A | Nottingham F | D | 1-1 | 0-1 | Cowans (pen) | 18,213 |
| 37 | 28 | H | Leeds U | L | 1-4 | 1-1 | Geddis | 20,566 |
| 38 | May 1 | H | Manchester C | D | 0-0 | 0-0 | | 22,150 |
| 39 | 5 | A | Stoke C | L | 0-1 | 0-1 | | 10,363 |
| 40 | 8 | A | WBA | W | 1-0 | 0-0 | Heard | 19,615 |
| 41 | 15 | H | Everton | L | 1-2 | 1-1 | Cowans | 20,446 |
| 42 | 21 | H | Swansea C | W | 3-0 | 2-0 | Morley, Bremner, Withe | 18,294 |

**Final League Position: 11**

### Goalscorers

*League* (55): Withe 10, Shaw 9, Cowans 6 (2 pens), Geddis 6, Morley 6, Donovan 4, Bremner 3, Evans 2, Heard 2, McNaught 2, Mortimer 2, own goals 3.
*League Cup* (9): Cowans 4 (3 pens), Withe 2, Blair 1, Bremner 1, Morley 1.
*FA Cup* (7): Geddis 3, Shaw 2, Cowans 1 (pen), own goal 1.

| | | | |
|---|---|---|---|
| **League Cup** | Second Round | Wolverhampton W (h) | 3-2 |
| | | (a) | 2-1 |
| | Third Round | Leicester C (a) | 0-0 |
| | | (h) | 2-0 |
| | Fourth Round | Wigan Ath (a) | 2-1 |
| | Fifth Round | WBA (h) | 0-1 |
| **FA Cup** | Third Round | Notts Co (a) | 6-0 |
| | Fourth Round | Bristol C (a) | 1-0 |
| | Fifth Round | Tottenham H (a) | 0-1 |

| Rimmer | Swain | Gibson | Evans | McNaught | Mortimer | Bremner | Geddis | Withe | Cowans | Morley | Blair | Ormsby | Donovan | Shaw | Williams | Deacy | Linton | Blake | Bullivant | Shelton | Jones | Heard | Walters | Match No. |
|---|---|---|---|---|---|---|---|---|---|---|---|---|---|---|---|---|---|---|---|---|---|---|---|---|
| 1 | 2 | 3 | 4 | 5* | 6 | 7 | 8 | 9 | 10 | 11 | 12 | | | | | | | | | | | | | 1 |
| 1 | 2 | 3 | 4 | | 6 | 7 | | 9 | 10 | 11 | | 5 | | 8 | | | | | | | | | | 2 |
| 1 | 2 | 3 | 4 | | 6 | 7 | | 9 | 10 | 11 | | 5 | | 8 | | | | | | | | | | 3 |
| 1 | 2 | 3 | 4 | | 6 | 7 | | 9 | 10 | 11 | | 5 | | 8 | | | | | | | | | | 4 |
| 1 | 2 | 3 | 4 | 5 | 6 | 7 | | 9 | 10 | 11 | | | | 8 | | | | | | | | | | 5 |
| 1 | 2 | 3 | 4 | 5* | 6 | 7 | | 9 | 10 | 11 | 12 | | | 8 | | | | | | | | | | 6 |
| 1 | 2 | 3 | 4 | | 6 | 7 | | 9 | 10 | 11 | 8 | 5 | | | | | | | | | | | | 7 |
| 1 | 2 | 3 | 4 | | 6 | 7 | | 9 | 10 | 12 | 11 | 5 | | 8* | | | | | | | | | | 8 |
| 1 | 2 | 3 | 4 | | 6 | 7 | | 9 | 10 | 11 | | 5 | | 8 | | | | | | | | | | 9 |
| 1 | | 3 | 4 | | 6 | 7 | | 9* | 10 | 11 | 12 | 5 | | 8 | 2 | | | | | | | | | 10 |
| 1 | | 3 | 4 | | 6 | 7 | | 9 | 10 | 11 | | 5 | | 8 | 2 | | | | | | | | | 11 |
| 1 | 2 | 3 | 4 | | 6 | 7 | | 9 | 10 | 11 | | 5 | | 8 | | | | | | | | | | 12 |
| 1 | 2 | 3 | 4 | | 6 | 7 | | 9 | 10 | 11 | 12 | | | 8* | 5 | | | | | | | | | 13 |
| 1 | 2 | 3 | 4 | | | 7 | | 9 | 10 | 11 | | | | 8 | 5 | 6 | | | | | | | | 14 |
| 1 | 2 | 3 | 4 | | | 7 | | 9 | 10 | 11 | | | | 8 | 5 | 6 | | | | | | | | 15 |
| 1 | 2 | 3 | 4 | | | 7 | | 9 | 10 | 11 | | | | 8 | 5 | 6 | | | | | | | | 16 |
| 1 | 2 | 3 | 4 | | | 7 | | 9 | 10 | 11 | | | | 8 | 5 | 6* | | | 12 | | | | | 17 |
| 1 | 2 | 3 | 4 | | | 7 | | 9 | 10 | 11 | | | | 8 | 5 | 6 | | | | | | | | 18 |
| 1 | 2 | 3 | 4 | | 6 | 7 | | 9 | 10 | 11 | | | | 8 | 5 | | | | | | | | | 19 |
| 1 | 2 | 3 | 4 | | 6* | 7 | | 9 | 10 | 11 | | | | 8 | 5 | | | | 12 | | | | | 20 |
| 1 | 2 | 3 | 4 | | 6 | 7 | 8 | 9 | 10 | 11 | 12 | | | | 5* | | | | | | | | | 21 |
| 1 | 2 | 3* | | | 6 | 7 | 8 | 9 | 10 | | | 4 | 5 | | | | | | 12 | 11 | | | | 22 |
| 1 | 2 | 3 | 4 | | 6 | 7 | 8 | 9 | 10 | | | 5 | | | | | | | 11 | | | | | 23 |
| 1 | 2 | | 4 | 5 | 6 | 7 | 8 | 9 | 10 | 11 | | | | | 3 | | | | | | | | | 24 |
| 1 | 2 | | 4 | 5 | 6 | 7 | | 9 | 10 | 11 | | | | 8 | 3 | | | | | | | | | 25 |
| 1 | 2* | | 4 | 5 | 6 | 7 | | 9 | 10 | 11 | | | | 8 | 3 | | | | 12 | | | | | 26 |
| 1 | | | 4* | 5 | 6 | 7 | | 9 | 10 | 11 | 12 | | | 8 | 3 | | | | | | 2 | | | 27 |
| 1 | 2 | | | 5 | 6 | 4 | | 9 | 10 | 11 | 7 | | | 8 | 3 | | | | | | | | | 28 |
| 1 | 2 | | 4 | 5 | 6 | 7 | | | 10 | 11 | 9 | | | 8 | 3 | | | | | | | | | 29 |
| 1 | 2 | | 4 | 5 | | | | | 10 | 11 | 7* | | 9 | 8 | 3 | | | | 6 | | | 12 | | 30 |
| 1 | 2 | | 4 | 5 | | | | 9 | 10 | 11 | 8 | | | 7 | 3 | | | | 6 | | | | | 31 |
| 1 | 2 | | 4 | 5 | 6 | | | 9 | 10 | 11 | 8 | | | | 3 | | | | | | | 7 | | 32 |
| 1 | 2 | | 4 | 5 | 6 | 7 | | 9 | 10 | 11 | 8 | | | | 3 | | | | | | | | | 33 |
| 1 | 2 | | 4 | 5 | 6 | 7 | 8 | 9 | 10 | 11 | | | | | 3* | | | | 12 | | | | | 34 |
| 1 | 2 | | 4 | 5 | | | 8 | 9 | 10 | 11 | 7 | | | | 3 | | | | 6 | | | | | 35 |
| 1 | 2 | | 4 | 5 | 6* | 7 | | 9 | 10 | 11 | 12 | | | 8 | 3 | | | | | | | | | 36 |
| 1 | 2 | | | 5 | | 7 | 8 | 9 | 10 | 11* | 6 | | | 4 | 3 | | | | | | | 12 | | 37 |
| 1 | 2 | | | 5 | | 7 | | 9 | 10 | 11 | 4 | | | 8 | 3 | | | | 6 | | | | | 38 |
| 1 | 2 | | 4 | 5 | 6 | 7 | | 9 | 10 | 11* | 12 | | | 8 | 3 | | | | | | | | | 39 |
| 1 | 2 | | 4 | 5 | 6 | 7 | | 9 | 10 | | | | | 8 | 3 | | | | | | | 11 | | 40 |
| 1 | 2 | | 4 | 5 | 6 | 7 | | 9 | 10 | 12 | | | | 8* | 3 | | | | | | | 11 | | 41 |
| 1 | 2 | | 4 | 5 | 6 | 7 | 8 | 9 | 10 | 11 | | | | | 3 | | | | | | | | | 42 |
| 42 | 39 | 23 | 38 | 22 | 32 | 38 | 14 | 35 | 42 | 36 | 9 | 12 | 8 | 26 | 28 | 4 | — | 1 | 4 | 1 | 2 | 6 | — | |

Substitute appearances: +1s 9s (Mortimer / Bremner); +1s 3s (Williams / Deacy); +2s 1s (Jones / Heard).

## ASTON VILLA

| | Ht | Wt | Birthplace | Clubs | League App. | League Gls |
|---|---|---|---|---|---|---|
| **Goalkeepers** | | | | | | |
| Nigel Spink | 6 1 | 13 10 | Chelmsford | Aston V | 1 | — |
| Jimmy Rimmer | 5 11 | 11 12 | Southport | Manchester U | 34 | — |
| (England) | | | | Swansea C (on loan) | 17 | — |
| | | | | Arsenal | 124 | — |
| | | | | Aston V | 209 | — |
| Mark Kendall | 6 0 | 12 10 | Nuneaton | Aston V | — | — |
| Kevin Poole | 5 8 | 11 1 | Bromsgrove | Aston V | — | — |
| **Defenders** | | | | | | |
| Colin Gibson | 5 8 | 10 10 | Bridport | Aston V | 87 | 2 |
| Ken McNaught | 5 11 | 11 1 | Kirkcaldy | Everton | 66 | 3 |
| | | | | Aston V | 166 | 6 |
| Allan Evans | 6 0 | 11 12 | Dunfermline | Dunfermline Ath | 98 | 14 |
| (Scotland) | | | | Aston V | 158 | 24 |
| Gary Williams | 5 9 | 11 7 | Wolverhampton | Aston V | 75 | — |
| | | | | Walsall (on loan) | 9 | — |
| Noel Blake | 6 0 | 13 5 | Jamaica | Aston V | 4 | — |
| | | | | Shrewsbury T (on loan) | 6 | — |
| Mark Jones | 5 6 | 10 1 | Warley | Aston V | 2 | — |
| Kenny Swain | 5 11 | 11 7 | Liverpool | Chelsea | 119 | 26 |
| | | | | WBA (on loan) | — | — |
| | | | | Aston V | 146 | 2 |
| Kevin Rogers | 5 9 | 11 3 | Mertlye | Aston V | — | — |
| Raymond Walker | 5 9 | 11 0 | N. Shields | Aston V | — | — |
| Paul Birch | | | Birmingham | Aston V | — | — |
| Dean Glover | 5 9 | 11 2 | Birmingham | Aston V | — | — |
| **Midfield** | | | | | | |
| Dennis Mortimer | 5 10 | 12 0 | Liverpool | Coventry C | 193 | 10 |
| | | | | Aston V | 235 | 22 |
| Gordon Cowans | 5 8 | 9 2 | County Durham | Aston V | 214 | 31 |
| Brendan Ormsby | 5 10½ | 11 3 | Birmingham | Aston V | 37 | — |
| Gary Stirland* | 5 8½ | 10 2 | Middlesbrough | Aston V | — | — |
| Eamonn Deacy | 5 8½ | 10 10 | Galway | Aston V | 16 | — |
| (Eire) | | | | | | |
| Des Bremner | 5 10 | 11 11 | Aberchider | Hibernian | 199 | 18 |
| (Scotland) | | | | Aston V | 116 | 8 |
| Terry Bullivant | 5 7½ | 10 11 | London | Fulham | 101 | 2 |
| | | | | Aston V | 13 | — |
| Pat Heard | 5 10 | 11 0½ | Hull | Everton | 11 | — |
| | | | | Aston V | 17 | 2 |
| Robert Hopkins | 5 7 | 10 5 | Birmingham | Aston V | 2 | 1 |
| Andy Blair | 5 9 | 10 9 | Kirkcaldy | Coventry C | 93 | 6 |
| | | | | Aston V | 18 | — |
| Mark Hutchinson | 5 8½ | 10 7 | Stoke | Aston V | — | — |
| Martin MacKenzie | 5 6 | 10 1 | Pwhelli | Aston V | — | — |
| **Forwards** | | | | | | |
| Brian Little | 5 8 | 11 2 | Durham | Aston V | 247 | 60 |
| (England)   (Retired, injury) | | | | | | |
| Ivor Linton* | 5 10 | 10 13 | West Bromwich | Aston V | 27 | — |
| Gary Shaw | 5 10 | 11 9 | Birmingham | Aston V | 97 | 36 |
| Terry Donovan | 5 11 | 10 12 | Liverpool | Grimsby T | 64 | 23 |
| (Eire)   (Contract cancelled April 1982) | | | | Aston V | 17 | 6 |
| David Geddis | 5 10½ | 12 2 | Carlisle | Ipswich T | 43 | 5 |
| | | | | Luton T (on loan) | 13 | 4 |
| | | | | Aston V | 43 | 12 |
| Tony Morley | 5 8½ | 11 8½ | Ormskirk | Preston NE | 84 | 15 |
| (England) | | | | Burnley | 91 | 5 |
| | | | | Aston V | 97 | 19 |
| Peter Withe | 6 2 | 12 0 | Liverpool | Southport | 3 | — |
| (England) | | | | Barrow | 1 | — |
| | | | | Arcadia Shepherds | (not known) | |
| | | | | Wolverhampton W | 17 | 3 |
| | | | | Birmingham C | 35 | 9 |
| | | | | Nottingham F | 75 | 28 |
| | | | | Newcastle U | 76 | 25 |
| | | | | Aston V | 71 | 30 |
| Mark Walters | 5 9 | 10 12 | Birmingham | Aston V | 1 | — |
| (Apprentice) | | | | | | |

# BARNSLEY
## Division 2

*Chairman:* G. Buckle LLB.

*Directors:* A. Raynor JP, R. F. Potter, G. Pallister, N. W. B. Moody JP, C. Williams, J. Steele.

*Secretary:* Michael Spinks.

*Team Manager:* Norman Hunter.

*Year Formed:* 1887. *Turned Professional:* 1888.

*Limited Company:* 1899.

*Previous Name:* Barnsley St Peter's.

**Football League Record:**
1898 Elected to Division 2; 1932–34 Division 3(N); 1934–38 Division 2; 1938–39 Division 3(N); 1946–53 Division 2; 1953–55 Division 3(N); 1955–59 Division 2; 1959–65 Division 3; 1965–68 Division 4; 1968–72 Division 3; 1972–79 Division 4; 1979–81 Division 3; 1981– Division 2.

**Honours:** *Football League:* best season: 3rd, Division 2, 1914–15, 1921–22; Division 3(N) – Champions 1933–34, 1938–39, 1954–55; Runners-up 1953–54; Division 3 – Runners-up 1980–81; Division 4 – Runners-up 1967–68; Promoted 1978–79. *FA Cup:* Winners 1912; Runners-up 1910. *Football League Cup* best season: 5th rd, 1981–82.

*Record Victory:* 9-0 v Loughborough T, Division 2, 28 Jan, 1899 and v Accrington Stanley, Division 3(N), 3 Feb, 1934.

*Record Defeat:* 0-9 v Notts Co, Division 2, 19 Nov, 1927.

*Most League Points:* 67, Division 3(N), 1938–39. *Three points win:* 67, Division 2, 1981–82.

*Most League Goals:* 118, Division 3(N), 1933–34.

*Highest League Scorer in Season:* Cecil McCormack, 33, Division 2, 1950–51.

*Most League Goals in Total Aggregate:* Ernest Hine, 123, 1921–26, 1934–38.

*Most Capped Player:* Eddie McMorran, 9 (15), Ireland.

*Most League Appearances:* Barry Murphy, 514, 1962-78.

*Record Transfer Fee Received:* £60,000 from West Ham U for Anton Otulakowski, Oct 1976.

*Record Transfer Fee Paid:* £95,000 to Crystal Palace for Ian Evans, March 1980.

*Previous Managers since the War:* Angus Seed, Tim Ward, Johnny Steele, John McSeveney, Jim Iley, Allan Clarke.

---

**Oakwell Ground, Grove St, Barnsley.** Telephone Barnsley (0226) 295353. *Ground capacity:* 35,554 (15,000 under cover). *Record attendance:* 40,255 v Stoke C, 15 Feb, 1936, FA Cup 5th rd. *Record receipts:* £16,146 v Rotherham U, 16 Dec, 1978, FA Cup 2nd rd. *Pitch measurements:* 111yd×75yd.

*How to get there:* Fairly frequent train service from Sheffield and Leeds to Exchange Station Barnsley. No special buses, just the normal services, and no buses from town centre because the ground is so close.

*Match tickets:* Stand seats bookable two weeks in advance.

*Car parking:* Two official club parks adjacent to the ground holding 1200 cars; parking fee 25p. There is a free public park in Queens Road, two minutes from the ground. The M1 runs approximately two miles from the ground.

*Entertainments/catering facilities:* Football club social club is adjacent to the ground. Seven tea bars sited around the ground sell refreshments; three of them sell alcoholic drinks.

*Club shop:* Inside the ground; sells all types of souvenirs.

*Handbooks/programmes:* Programmes available on subscription.

*Extra information:* For post-match entertainment, there is Rebeccas night club in Queens Road.

*Club Colours:* Red shirts, white shorts, red stockings.

*Change Colours:* White shirts, black shorts, white stockings.

*Club Captain:* Phil Chambers.

*Club Nickname:* The Tykes.

## BARNSLEY 1981–82 LEAGUE RECORD

| Match No. | Date | Venue | Opponents | Result | H/T Score | Goalscorers | Attendance |
|---|---|---|---|---|---|---|---|
| 1 | Aug 29 | H | Shrewsbury T | W 4-0 | 2-0 | Aylott 2, Parker, Banks (pen) | 13,344 |
| 2 | Sept 5 | A | Norwich C | D 1-1 | 1-1 | Parker | 13,677 |
| 3 | 8 | A | Leicester C | L 0-1 | 0-0 | | 15,447 |
| 4 | 12 | H | Bolton W | W 3-0 | 2-0 | Aylott 2, McCarthy | 13,844 |
| 5 | 19 | A | Cambridge U | L 1-2 | 1-1 | Banks | 5586 |
| 6 | 22 | H | Sheffield W | W 1-0 | 1-0 | Banks | 28,870 |
| 7 | 26 | H | Cardiff C | L 0-1 | 0-0 | | 12,114 |
| 8 | Oct 3 | A | Watford | L 1-3 | 1-2 | Aylott | 10,803 |
| 9 | 10 | A | Blackburn R | L 1-2 | 1-1 | Banks (pen) | 10,522 |
| 10 | 17 | H | Newcastle U | W 1-0 | 1-0 | Aylott | 18,477 |
| 11 | 24 | A | Chelsea | W 2-1 | 1-1 | Banks, Glavin | 15,268 |
| 12 | 31 | H | Orient | W 1-0 | 0-0 | Aylott | 13,435 |
| 13 | Nov 7 | H | Oldham Ath | W 3-1 | 1-0 | Banks 2 (1 pen), Parker | 14,918 |
| 14 | Nov 14 | A | Rotherham U | W 4-2 | 1-2 | Banks 3 (1 pen), Glavin | 18,324 |
| 15 | 21 | H | Wrexham | D 2-2 | 2-1 | Parker 2 | 14,544 |
| 16 | 24 | A | Sheffield W | D 2-2 | 1-0 | Parker, Glavin | 30,621 |
| 17 | 28 | A | Charlton Ath | L 1-2 | 0-2 | Aylott | 5553 |
| 18 | Dec 5 | H | Crystal Palace | W 2-0 | 0-0 | Glavin 2 | 14,877 |
| 19 | 12 | A | QPR | L 0-1 | 0-0 | | 10,972 |
| 20 | Jan 23 | A | Orient | W 3-1 | 2-0 | Walker, Banks, Aylott | 3620 |
| 21 | 30 | H | Cambridge U | D 0-0 | 0-0 | | 13,114 |
| 22 | Feb 2 | A | Shrewsbury T | W 2-0 | 0-0 | Walker, Banks | 4382 |
| 23 | 6 | A | Bolton W | L 1-2 | 0-1 | Cooper | 11,680 |
| 24 | 9 | H | Watford | D 0-0 | 0-0 | | 17,070 |
| 25 | 20 | A | Cardiff C | D 0-0 | 0-0 | | 4503 |
| 26 | 24 | H | Norwich C | L 0-1 | 0-1 | | 15,360 |
| 27 | 27 | H | Blackburn R | L 0-1 | 0-0 | | 13,150 |
| 28 | Mar 6 | A | Newcastle U | L 0-1 | 0-1 | | 18,636 |
| 29 | 12 | H | Chelsea | W 2-1 | 0-1 | Banks, Glavin | 12,706 |
| 30 | 16 | H | Luton T | W 4-3 | 1-1 | Walker 2, Banks, Evans | 14,004 |
| 31 | 23 | H | Grimsby T | W 3-2 | 2-0 | Aylott, Walker, Banks | 15,383 |
| 32 | 27 | A | Oldham Ath | D 1-1 | 1-1 | Glavin | 8939 |
| 33 | Apr 2 | H | Rotherham U | W 3-0 | 2-0 | Birch 2, Walker | 23,059 |
| 34 | 9 | A | Grimsby T | L 2-3 | 2-0 | Walker 2 | 12,338 |
| 35 | 10 | H | Derby Co | D 0-0 | 0-0 | | 13,457 |
| 36 | 17 | A | Wrexham | D 0-0 | 0-0 | | 4860 |
| 37 | 24 | H | Charlton Ath | W 1-0 | 0-0 | Walker | 9287 |
| 38 | 28 | H | Derby Co | W 1-0 | 1-0 | Walker | 11,296 |
| 39 | May 1 | A | Crystal Palace | W 2-1 | 0-1 | Walker, Birch | 7500 |
| 40 | 4 | H | Leicester C | L 0-2 | 0-1 | | 15,418 |
| 41 | 8 | H | QPR | W 3-0 | 0-0 | Birch 2, Aylott | 10,579 |
| 42 | 15 | A | Luton T | D 1-1 | 0-0 | Birch (pen) | 14,463 |

**Final League Position: 6**

**Goalscorers**

*League* (59): Banks 15 (4 pens), Aylott 11, Walker 11, Glavin 7, Birch 6 (1 pen), Parker 6, Cooper 1, Evans 1, McCarthy 1.

*League Cup* (19): Glavin 6, Aylott 4, Parker 2, Barrowclough 1, Cooper 1, Evans 1, Joyce 1, McCarthy 1, Riley 1, Walker 1.

*FA Cup* (0).

| | | | |
|---|---|---|---|
| **League Cup** | First Round | Peterborough U (a) | 3-2 |
| | | (h) | 6-0 |
| | Second Round | Swansea C (h) | 2-0 |
| | | (a) | 2-3 |
| | Third Round | Brighton & HA (h) | 4-1 |
| | Fourth Round | Manchester C (h) | 1-0 |
| | Fifth Round | Liverpool (a) | 0-0 |
| | | (h) | 1-3 |
| **FA Cup** | Third Round | Blackpool (h) | 0-2 |

| Horn | Joyce | Chambers | Glavin | Banks | McCarthy | Evans | Parker | Aylott | McHale | Barrowclough | Riley | Campbell | Cooper | Walker | Law | Wilkes | Birch | Mann | Longden | Match No. |
|---|---|---|---|---|---|---|---|---|---|---|---|---|---|---|---|---|---|---|---|---|
| 1 | 2 | 3 | 4 | 5 | 6 | 7 | 8 | 9 | 10 | 11 | | | | | | | | | | 1 |
| 1 | 2 | 3 | 4 | 5 | 6 | 7 | 8 | 9 | 10 | 11 | | | | | | | | | | 2 |
| 1 | 2 | 3 | 4 | 5 | 6 | 7 | 8 | 9* | 10 | 11 | 12 | | | | | | | | | 3 |
| 1 | 2 | 3 | 4 | 5 | 6 | 7 | 8 | 9 | 10 | 11 | | | | | | | | | | 4 |
| 1 | 2 | 3 | 4 | 5 | 6 | 7 | 8 | 9 | 10 | 11* | 12 | | | | | | | | | 5 |
| 1 | 2 | 3 | 4 | 5 | 6 | 7 | 8 | 9 | 10 | 11 | | | | | | | | | | 6 |
| 1 | 2 | 3 | 4 | 5 | 6 | 7 | 8* | 9 | 10 | 11 | 12 | | | | | | | | | 7 |
| 1 | 2 | 3 | 4 | 5 | 6 | 7 | 8 | 9* | 10 | 11 | 12 | | | | | | | | | 8 |
| 1 | 2 | 3 | 4 | 5 | 6 | 7 | 8 | | 10 | 12 | 9* | 11 | | | | | | | | 9 |
| 1 | 2 | 3 | 4 | 5 | 6 | 7 | 8 | 9 | 10 | | | 11 | | | | | | | | 10 |
| 1 | 2 | 3 | 4 | 5 | 6 | 7 | 8 | 9 | 10 | | | 11 | | | | | | | | 11 |
| 1 | 2 | 3 | | 5 | 6 | 7 | 8 | 9 | 10 | | | 11 | 4 | | | | | | | 12 |
| 1 | 2 | 3 | | 5 | 6 | 7 | 8 | 9 | 10 | | | 11 | 4 | | | | | | | 13 |
| 1 | 2 | 3 | 4 | 5 | 6 | 7 | 8 | 9 | 10 | 11 | | | | | | | | | | 14 |
| 1 | 2 | 3 | 4 | 5 | 6 | 7 | 8 | 9 | 10 | 11 | | | | | | | | | | 15 |
| 1 | 2 | 3 | 4 | 5 | 6 | 7 | 8 | 9 | 10 | 11 | | | | | | | | | | 16 |
| 1 | 2 | 3 | 4 | 5 | 6 | 7 | | 9 | 10 | 11 | | 8 | | | | | | | | 17 |
| 1 | 2 | 3 | 4 | 5 | 6 | 7 | | 9 | 10 | 11 | 8 | | | | | | | | | 18 |
| 1 | 2 | 3 | 4 | 5 | 6 | 7 | | 9 | 10 | 11 | 8 | | | | | | | | | 19 |
| 1 | 2 | 3 | | 5 | 6 | 7 | | 9 | 10 | 11 | | | 4 | 8 | | | | | | 20 |
| 1 | | 3 | 4 | 5 | 6 | 7 | | 9 | 10 | 11 | | | 2 | 8 | | | | | | 21 |
| 1 | | 3 | | 5 | 6 | 7 | | 9 | 10 | | | | 4 | 8 | 2 | | 11 | | | 22 |
| 1 | | 3 | | 5 | 6 | 7 | | 9 | 10 | | 12 | | 4 | 8 | 2 | | 11* | | | 23 |
| 1 | | 3 | | 5 | 6 | 7 | | 9 | 10 | 11* | 12 | | 4 | 8 | 2 | | | | | 24 |
| 1 | | 3 | | 5 | 6 | 7 | 8 | 9 | 10 | 11 | | | 4 | | 2 | | | | | 25 |
| 1 | | 3 | 12 | 5 | 6 | 7 | 8* | 9 | 10 | | | | 4 | | 2 | | 11 | | | 26 |
| 1 | | 3 | 4 | 12 | 6 | 7 | | 9 | 10 | | | 8 | 5* | | 2 | | 11 | | | 27 |
| 1 | | 3 | 4 | 5 | 6 | 7 | | 9 | 10 | | | 11* | | | 2 | | 8 | 12 | | 28 |
| 1 | | 3 | 4 | 5 | 6 | 7 | | 9 | 10 | | | | | 8 | 2 | | 11 | | | 29 |
| 1 | | 3 | 4 | 5 | 6 | 7 | | 9 | | | | | | 8 | 2 | | 11 | 10 | | 30 |
| 1 | | 3 | 4 | 5 | 6 | 7 | | 9 | | | | | | 8 | | | 11 | 10 | 2 | 31 |
| 1 | | 3 | 4 | 5 | 6 | 7* | | 9 | | | | | | 8 | | | 11 | 10 | 2 | 32 |
| 1 | | 3 | | 5 | 6 | | | 9 | 10 | | | | | 8 | 2 | 7 | 11 | 4 | | 33 |
| 1 | | 3 | 4 | 5 | 6 | | | 9 | 10 | | | | | 8 | 2 | 7 | 11 | | | 34 |
| 1 | | 3 | 4 | 5 | 6 | 7 | | 9 | 10 | | | 12 | | 8 | 2 | | 11* | | | 35 |
| 1 | | 3 | | 5 | 6 | 7 | | 9 | 10 | | | | | 8 | 2 | | 11 | 4 | | 36 |
| 1 | | 3 | | 5 | 6 | 7 | | 9 | 10 | | | | | 8 | 2 | | 11 | 4 | | 37 |
| 1 | | 3 | | 5 | 6 | 7 | | 9 | 10 | | | | | 8 | 2 | | 11 | 4 | | 38 |
| 1 | | 3 | | 5 | 6 | 7 | | 9 | 10 | | | | | 8 | 2 | | 11 | 4 | | 39 |
| 1 | | 3 | | 5 | 6 | 7 | | 9 | 10 | | | 12 | | 8 | 2 | | 11 | 4* | | 40 |
| 1 | | 3 | | 5 | 6 | 7 | | 9 | 10 | | | 4 | | 8 | 2 | | 11 | | | 41 |
| 1 | | 3 | | 5 | 6 | 7 | | 9 | 10 | | | 4 | | 8 | 2 | | 11 | | | 42 |
| 42 | 20 | 42 | 26 | 41 | 42 | 40 | 18 | 41 | 39 | 17 | 7 | 7 | 10 | 19 | 19 | 2 | 17 | 9 | 4 | |

```
        +  +                    +  +  +                    +
        1s 1s                   1s 1s 8s                   1s
```

# BARNSLEY

| | Ht | Wt | Birthplace | Clubs | League App. | League Gls |
|---|---|---|---|---|---|---|
| **Goalkeepers** | | | | | | |
| Gary Pierce | 6 1 | 12 9 | Bury | Huddersfield T | 23 | — |
| | | | | Wolverhampton W | 98 | — |
| | | | | Barnsley | 59 | — |
| Martin New | 5 11 | 13 5 | Swindon | Arsenal | — | — |
| | | | | Mansfield T | 21 | — |
| | | | | Barnsley | 24 | — |
| Bobby Horn | 6 1 | 14 1 | Westminster | Crystal Palace | — | — |
| | | | | Barnsley | 42 | — |
| **Defenders** | | | | | | |
| Phil Chambers | 5 7½ | 11 1 | Barnsley | Barnsley | 359 | 7 |
| Mick McCarthy | 6 1½ | 13 3 | Barnsley | Barnsley | 221 | 6 |
| Norman Hunter | 5 11½ | 12 6 | Eighton Banks | Leeds U | 541 | 18 |
| (England) | | | | Bristol C | 108 | 4 |
| (Non-contract) | | | | Barnsley | 30 | — |
| Joe Joyce | 5 9 | 10 5 | Consett | Barnsley | 61 | — |
| Ian Evans | 6 2½ | 12 6 | Egham | QPR | 39 | 2 |
| (Wales) | | | | Crystal Palace | 137 | 14 |
| | | | | Barnsley | 100 | 3 |
| Nicky Law | 6 0 | 13 5 | Greenwich | Arsenal | — | — |
| | | | | Barnsley | 19 | — |
| Paul Longden | 5 7 | 10 3 | Wakefield | Barnsley | 4 | — |
| David Glover | 5 9 | 10 3 | Barnsley | Barnsley | — | — |
| Philip Dunstone | 5 11 | 11 3 | Barnsley | Barnsley | — | — |
| **Midfield** | | | | | | |
| Ray McHale | 5 8 | 12 6 | Sheffield | Chesterfield | 124 | 27 |
| | | | | Halifax T | 86 | 21 |
| | | | | Swindon T | 173 | 33 |
| | | | | Brighton & HA | 11 | — |
| | | | | Barnsley | 53 | 1 |
| Ian Banks | 5 10½ | 12 2 | Mexborough | Barnsley | 127 | 32 |
| Ronnie Glavin | 5 10 | 12 6 | Glasgow | Partick T | 126 | 34 |
| (Scotland) | | | | Celtic | 102 | 36 |
| | | | | Barnsley | 106 | 45 |
| Bobby Downes* | 5 7½ | 11 4 | Bloxwich | WBA | — | — |
| | | | | Peterborough | 26 | 3 |
| | | | | Rochdale | 174 | 10 |
| | | | | Watford | 199 | 19 |
| | | | | Barnsley | 43 | 1 |
| Winston Campbell | 5 8 | 11 6 | Sheffield | Barnsley | 9 | — |
| Gary Walters* | 5 7 | 10 0 | Doncaster | Barnsley | — | — |
| Ian Hughes* | 5 9 | 11 1 | Sunderland | Sunderland | 1 | — |
| | | | | Barnsley | — | — |
| Philip Watkin | 5 7 | 10 0 | Doncaster | Barnsley | — | — |
| David Wilkes | 5 8 | 10 2 | Barnsley | Barnsley | 2 | — |
| Dean Whitehouse | 5 5 | 9 1 | Mexborough | Barnsley | — | — |
| Alan Birch | 5 6 | 10 5 | West Bromwich | Walsall | 171 | 23 |
| | | | | Chesterfield | 90 | 35 |
| | | | | Wolverhampton W | 15 | — |
| | | | | Barnsley | 17 | 6 |
| Jimmy Mann | 5 10 | 11 6 | Goole | Leeds U | 2 | — |
| | | | | Bristol C | 231 | 31 |
| | | | | Barnsley | 10 | — |
| **Forwards** | | | | | | |
| Glyn Riley* | 5 10 | 11 11 | Barnsley | Doncaster R (on loan) | 8 | 2 |
| | | | | Barnsley | 130 | 16 |
| Stewart Barrowclough | 5 9 | 10 5 | Barnsley | Barnsley | 9 | — |
| | | | | Newcastle U | 219 | 20 |
| | | | | Birmingham C | 29 | 2 |
| | | | | Bristol R | 61 | 14 |
| | | | | Barnsley | 31 | — |
| Derrick Parker | 5 9½ | 11 8 | Wallsend | Burnley | 6 | 2 |
| | | | | Southend U | 129 | 43 |
| | | | | Barnsley | 75 | 20 |
| Trevor Aylott | 6 1½ | 14 0 | London | Chelsea | 29 | 2 |
| | | | | QPR (on loan) | — | — |
| | | | | Barnsley | 96 | 27 |
| Colin Walker | 5 8 | 11 8 | Rotherham | Barnsley | 21 | 11 |
| John Bukovina | 5 6½ | 10 8 | Barnsley | Barnsley | — | — |

# BIRMINGHAM CITY     Division 1

*President:*
*Chairman:* C. K. Coombs.
*Vice Chairman:* J. F. Wiseman.
*Directors:* N. B. A. Bosworth LLB, D. M. Coombs, R. Burman.
*Manager:* Ron Saunders. *Limited Company:* 1888.
*Secretary:* Alan Instone. *Coach:* Norman Bodell.
*Year Formed:* 1875. *Turned Professional:* 1885.
*Previous Grounds:* Waste ground near Arthur St, 1875; Muntz St, Small Heath, 1877; St Andrew's, 1906.
*Previous Names:* 1875–88, Small Heath Alliance; 1888, dropped 'Alliance'; became Birmingham 1905; became Birmingham City 1945.

**Football League Record:**
Division One: 1894–96; 1901–02; 1903–08; 1921–39; 1948–50; 1955–65; 1972–79; 1980–
Division Two: 1892–94; 1896–1901; 1902–03; 1908–21; 1946–48; 1950–55; 1965–72; 1979–80.

**Honours:** *Football League:* Division 1 best season: 6th, 1955–56; Division 2 – Champions 1892–93, 1920–21, 1947–48, 1954–55; Runners-up 1893–94, 1900–01, 1902–03, 1971–72. *FA Cup:* Runners-up 1931, 1956. *Football League Cup:* Winners 1963. **European Competitions:** *European Fairs Cup:* 1955–58, 1958–60 (runners-up), 1960–61 (runners-up), 1960–62.

*Record Victory:* 12-0 v Walsall Town Swifts, Division 2, 17 Dec, 1892 and v Doncaster R, Division 2, 11 April, 1903.
*Record Defeat:* 1-9 v Sheffield W, Division 1, 13 Dec, 1930.
*Most League Points:* 59, Division 2, 1947–48.
*Most League Goals:* 103, Division 2, 1893–94 (only 28 games).
*Highest League Scorer in Season:* Joe Bradford, 29, Division 1, 1927–28.
*Most League Goals in Total Aggregate:* Joe Bradford, 249, 1920–35.
*Most Capped Player:* Malcolm Page, 28, Wales.
*Most League Appearances:* Gil Merrick, 486, 1946–60.
*Record Transfer Fee Received:* £975,000 from Nottingham F for Trevor Francis, Feb 1979.
*Record Transfer Fee Paid:* £350,000 to Derby Co for David Langan, June 1980.
*Previous Managers since the War:* Ted Goodier, Harry Storer, Bob Brocklebank, Arthur Turner, Pat Beasley, Gil Merrick, Joe Mallett, Stan Cullis, Fred Goodwin, Willie Bell, Sir Alf Ramsey, Jim Smith.
*Address of Supporters Club:* St Andrew's Club, St Andrew's, Birmingham 9.
*Address of the Club Shop or Boutique:* City Souvenirs, 26 Cattell Road, Birmingham 9.

---

**St Andrews, Birmingham B9 4NH.** Telephone 021-772 0101/2689, (Information Service) 021-773 7161. *Ground capacity:* 44,500 (9,009 seats). *Record Attendance:* 66,844 v Everton, FA Cup 5th rd, 11 Feb, 1939. *Record Receipts:* £48,505 v Aston Villa, Division 1, 11 Oct, 1980. *Pitch measurements:* 115yd×75yd.

*How to get there:* Buses 97 from Carr's Lane, City Centre, 98, 99 from Bus Station, 58, 60 from High Street; Specials from Albert Street and Hall of Memory, Broad Street. Nearest railway station, Birmingham New Street. By road; via M1, M45, and A45 to Small Heath area of Birmingham and via Cattell Road (sixth turning on the right past Small Heath Park) to the ground; via M6 (exit 6, Gravelly Hill) and A38M (Aston Expressway), leave Expressway at first exit, left into Dartmouth Street, and then via Lawley Street and Watery Lane onto the Coventry Road. Turn left and then take left fork into Cattell Road.
*Match tickets:* Bookable three weeks in advance.
*Car parking:* Public car park in Coventry Road and Cattell Road.
*Entertainments/catering facilities:* Catering points inside the ground.
*Club shop:* Sells all types of souvenirs.
*Handbooks/programmes:* Programmes on sale on match days in and outside the ground; subscription rates available on request.
*Extra information:* In their away League programme in 1947–48, Birmingham let in only 11 goals; this is the best away performance in Division 2 since World War II.
*Club Colours:* Royal blue shirts, three white vertical stripes on sleeves, white shorts blue trim, white stockings with blue hoops on turnover.
*Change Colours:* Yellow shirts, three blue vertical stripes on sleeves, yellow shorts blue trim, yellow stockings with blue hoops on turnover.
*Club Captain:*     *Chief Scout:*     *Club Nickname:* Blues.

## BIRMINGHAM CITY 1981–82 LEAGUE RECORD

| Match No. | Date | Venue | Opponents | Result | H/T Score | Goalscorers | Atten-dance |
|---|---|---|---|---|---|---|---|
| 1 | Aug 29 | A | Everton | L 1-3 | 1-1 | Van Mierlo | 33,045 |
| 2 | Sept 1 | H | Ipswich T | D 1-1 | 1-0 | Evans | 17,328 |
| 3 | 5 | H | Nottingham F | W 4-3 | 2-2 | Broadhurst, Evans, Whatmore 2 | 19,035 |
| 4 | 12 | A | Middlesbrough | L 1-2 | 0-2 | Whatmore | 13,189 |
| 5 | 19 | H | Manchester C | W 3-0 | 1-0 | Evans 3 | 20,109 |
| 6 | 22 | A | Arsenal | L 0-1 | 0-1 | | 19,504 |
| 7 | 26 | A | Aston Villa | D 0-0 | 0-0 | | 40,763 |
| 8 | Oct 3 | H | West Ham U | D 2-2 | 1-1 | Langan, Dillon | 22,290 |
| 9 | 10 | H | Southampton | W 4-0 | 0-0 | Worthington 2, Whatmore 2 | 16,938 |
| 10 | 17 | A | Manchester U | D 1-1 | 1-0 | Worthington (pen) | 48,514 |
| 11 | 24 | A | Stoke C | L 0-1 | 0-0 | | 15,399 |
| 12 | 31 | H | WBA | D 3-3 | 1-2 | Gemmill, Evans, Worthington (pen) | 21,301 |
| 13 | Nov 7 | A | Brighton & HA | D 1-1 | 1-0 | Evans | 18,292 |
| 14 | 21 | H | Wolverhampton W | L 0-3 | 0-1 | | 18,223 |
| 15 | 28 | A | Swansea C | L 0-1 | 0-0 | | 15,097 |
| 16 | Dec 5 | H | Notts Co | W 2-1 | 1-1 | Evans 2 (1 pen) | 11,914 |
| 17 | Jan 5 | A | Ipswich T | L 2-3 | 0-2 | Van Mierlo, Broadhurst | 19,188 |
| 18 | 9 | A | Nottingham F | L 1-2 | 0-0 | Worthington | 15,906 |
| 19 | 26 | H | Coventry C | D 3-3 | 1-2 | Broadhurst, Evans 2 | 13,023 |
| 20 | 30 | A | Manchester C | L 2-4 | 2-4 | Worthington 2 | 28,438 |
| 21 | Feb 6 | H | Middlesbrough | D 0-0 | 0-0 | | 10,715 |
| 22 | 13 | A | West Ham U | D 2-2 | 1-0 | Whatmore, Van Mierlo | 22,512 |
| 23 | 16 | H | Sunderland | W 2-0 | 1-0 | Van Mierlo, Worthington | 10,776 |
| 24 | 20 | H | Aston Villa | L 0-1 | 0-0 | | 32,779 |
| 25 | 27 | A | Southampton | L 1-3 | 1-1 | Worthington (pen) | 20,620 |
| 26 | Mar 6 | H | Manchester U | L 0-1 | 0-1 | | 19,637 |
| 27 | 13 | H | Stoke C | W 2-1 | 1-0 | Curbishley, Hawker | 12,018 |
| 28 | 20 | A | WBA | D 1-1 | 0-0 | Evans | 21,160 |
| 29 | 23 | H | Tottenham H | D 0-0 | 0-0 | | 17,708 |
| 30 | 27 | H | Brighton & HA | W 1-0 | 0-0 | Harford | 13,234 |
| 31 | 30 | A | Liverpool | L 1-3 | 0-1 | Harford | 24,224 |
| 32 | Apr 6 | H | Everton | L 0-2 | 0-1 | | 12,273 |
| 33 | 10 | H | Leeds U | L 0-1 | 0-0 | | 14,497 |
| 34 | 12 | A | Sunderland | L 0-2 | 0-2 | | 14,821 |
| 35 | 17 | A | Wolverhampton W | D 1-1 | 0-0 | Harford | 18,964 |
| 36 | 24 | H | Swansea C | W 2-1 | 1-0 | Broadhurst, Harford | 14,973 |
| 37 | 28 | A | Tottenham H | D 1-1 | 1-0 | Harford | 25,470 |
| 38 | May 1 | A | Notts Co | W 4-1 | 1-1 | Phillips, Evans 2, Harford | 10,710 |
| 39 | 4 | H | Arsenal | L 0-1 | 0-0 | | 13,133 |
| 40 | 8 | H | Liverpool | L 0-1 | 0-0 | | 26,381 |
| 41 | 12 | A | Leeds U | D 3-3 | 2-2 | Harford 2, Evans | 18,583 |
| 42 | 15 | A | Coventry C | W 1-0 | 0-0 | Harford | 15,905 |

**Final League Position: 16**

### Goalscorers

*League* (53): Evans 15 (1 pen), Harford 9, Worthington 9 (3 pens), Whatmore 6, Broadhurst 4, Van Mierlo 4, Curbishley 1, Dillon 1, Gemmill 1, Hawker 1, Langan 1, Phillips 1.
*League Cup* (3): Evans 1, Whatmore 1, Worthington 1.
*FA Cup* (2): Curbishley 1, Worthington 1 (pen).

| **League Cup** | Second Round | Nottingham F (h) | 2-3 |
|---|---|---|---|
| | | (a) | 1-2 |
| **FA Cup** | Third Round | Ipswich T (h) | 2-3 |

| Weelands | Langan | Dennis | Broadhurst | Hawker | Todd | Brocken | Dillon | Evans | Gemmill | Van Mierlo | Handysides | Whatmore | Worthington | Van Den Hauwe | Curbishley | Coton | Scott | Jones | Phillips | Stevenson | Linney | MacDowall | Harford | Match No. |
|---|---|---|---|---|---|---|---|---|---|---|---|---|---|---|---|---|---|---|---|---|---|---|---|---|
| 1 | 2 | 3 | 4 | 5 | 6 | 7* | 8 | 9 | 10 | 11 | 12 | | | | | | | | | | | | | 1 |
| 1 | 2 | 3 | | 5 | 6 | 7 | 4 | 9 | 10 | 11 | | 8 | | | | | | | | | | | | 2 |
| 1 | 2 | 3 | | 5 | 6 | 7* | 4 | 9 | 10 | 11 | 12 | 8 | | | | | | | | | | | | 3 |
| 1 | 2 | 3 | | 5 | 6 | 7* | 4 | 9 | 10 | 11 | 12 | 8 | | | | | | | | | | | | 4 |
| 1 | 2 | 3 | | 5 | 6 | 7 | 4 | 9 | | 11* | 10 | 8 | 12 | | | | | | | | | | | 5 |
| 1 | 2 | 3 | | 5 | 6 | | 4 | 9* | 10 | 11 | 7 | 8 | 12 | | | | | | | | | | | 6 |
| 1 | 2 | 3 | | 5 | 6 | 7* | 4 | 10 | | 11 | 12 | 8 | 9 | | | | | | | | | | | 7 |
| 1 | 2 | 3 | | 5 | 6 | 7 | 4 | 10 | | 11* | 12 | 8 | 9 | | | | | | | | | | | 8 |
| 1 | 2 | 3 | | 5 | 6 | 7 | 4 | 10 | | 11 | | 8 | 9 | | | | | | | | | | | 9 |
| 1 | | 3* | | 5 | 6 | 7 | 4 | 10 | | 11 | 12 | 8 | 9 | 2 | | | | | | | | | | 10 |
| 1 | | 5 | 3 | | 6 | 7 | 4 | 8 | 10 | 11 | | | 9 | 2 | | | | | | | | | | 11 |
| 1 | | 5 | 3 | | 6 | 7 | | 8 | 10 | 11* | 12 | | 9 | 2 | 4 | | | | | | | | | 12 |
| | | | 5 | | 6 | 7 | | 8 | 10 | 11 | | 3 | 9 | 2 | 4 | 1 | | | | | | | | 13 |
| | 2 | 3 | | | 6 | 7* | | 8 | 10 | 11 | 12 | | 9 | 5 | 4 | 1 | | | | | | | | 14 |
| | 2 | 3 | | | 6 | 7 | | | 10 | 11* | 12 | 8 | 9 | 5 | 4 | 1 | | | | | | | | 15 |
| | 2 | 3 | | | 6 | 7 | | 9 | 10 | 11 | | 8 | | 5 | 4 | 1 | | | | | | | | 16 |
| | 2 | 3 | 5 | | 6 | 7 | | | 10 | 11 | | 8 | 9 | | 4 | 1 | | | | | | | | 17 |
| | 2 | 3 | 5 | | 6 | 7 | | | 10 | 11 | | 8 | 9 | | 4 | 1 | | | | | | | | 18 |
| | 2 | | 5 | | 6 | 7 | | 8 | 10 | 11 | | | 9 | 3 | 4 | 1 | | | | | | | | 19 |
| 1 | 2 | 3 | 10 | | 6 | | 4 | 8 | | 11 | | | 9 | 5 | 7 | | | | | | | | | 20 |
| 1 | 2 | 3 | | | 6 | | 4 | 8 | 10 | 11 | | | 9 | | 7 | | 5 | | | | | | | 21 |
| | 2 | 3* | | | 6 | 7 | | | | 11 | | 8 | 9 | 12 | 4 | 1 | 5 | 10 | | | | | | 22 |
| | 2 | | | | 6 | 7 | | | | 11 | | 8 | 9 | 3 | 4 | 1 | 5 | 10 | | | | | | 23 |
| | 2 | | | | 6 | 7 | | | | 11 | | 8 | 9 | 3 | 4 | 1 | 5 | 10 | | | | | | 24 |
| | 2 | | | | 6 | | | | 10 | 11 | 7* | 8 | 9 | 3 | 4 | 1 | 5 | 12 | | | | | | 25 |
| 1 | 2 | 3 | | | | 7* | 12 | 9 | | 11 | | 8 | | | 10 | 6 | 5 | | | 4 | | | | 26 |
| 1 | 2 | 3 | 4 | | | 7 | | 9 | | 11 | | 8* | | | 10 | 6 | 5 | | | 12 | | | | 27 |
| 1 | 2 | 10 | 12 | | | 7 | 8* | 9 | | 11 | | | | 3 | 6 | | 5 | | | 4 | | | | 28 |
| 1 | 2 | 10 | 3 | | | 7 | | 9 | | 11 | | | | 4 | 6 | | 5 | | | | | 8 | | 29 |
| 1 | 2 | 10 | 3 | | | 7 | 8 | | | 11 | | | | | 6 | | 5 | | | 4 | | | 9 | 30 |
| 1 | 2 | 10 | 3 | | | 7 | 8* | | | 11 | | 12 | | 4 | 6 | | 5 | | | | | | 9 | 31 |
| 1 | 2 | | 3 | | | | 8 | 10 | | | | 7* | 11 | 4 | 6 | | 5 | | | 12 | | | 9 | 32 |
| 1 | 2 | | 3 | | | | 8 | 10 | | | | 12 | 11 | 4 | 6 | | 5 | 7 | | | | | 9* | 33 |
| 1 | | 10 | 3 | 11* | | 7 | 8 | | | | | | | 4 | 6 | | 5 | | | 12 | | 2 | 9 | 34 |
| | 2 | 10 | 3 | | | 7 | 8 | | | | | 11 | | 5 | 6* | 1 | 12 | | | 4 | | | 9 | 35 |
| | 2 | 10 | 3 | | | 7 | 8 | | | 11 | | | 12 | 5 | 6 | 1 | | | | 4* | | | 9 | 36 |
| | 2 | | 3 | | | 7 | 8 | | | 11 | | | 12 | 4 | 6 | 1 | 10* | | | 5 | | | 9 | 37 |
| | 2 | | 3 | | | 7 | 8 | | | 11 | | | | 5 | 6 | 1 | 10 | | | 4 | | | 9 | 38 |
| | 2 | 10 | 3* | | | 7 | 8 | | | 11 | | | | 5 | 6 | 1 | 12 | | | 4 | | | 9 | 39 |
| | 2 | 10 | 3 | | | 7 | 8 | | | 11 | | | | 5 | 6 | 1 | | | | 4 | | | 9 | 40 |
| | 2 | 10 | 3 | | | 7 | 8 | | | 11 | | | | 5 | 6 | 1 | | | | 4 | | | 9 | 41 |
| | 2 | | 3 | | | 7 | 8 | | | 11* | | | 12 | 5 | 6 | 1 | 10 | | | 4 | | | 9 | 42 |
| 23 | 36 | 17 | 35 | 19 | 19 | 17 | 35 | 29 | 19 | 40 | 8 | 22 | 18 | 30 | 29 | 15 | 14 | 4 | 7 | 12 | — | 2 | 12 | |

Substitute markers: + 1s (Hawker), + 1s (Brocken), + 12s (Van Mierlo), + 2s (Whatmore), + 2s (Worthington), + 1s (Van Den Hauwe), + 1s (Coton), + 4s (Phillips), + 1s (Stevenson)

## BIRMINGHAM CITY

| | Ht | Wt | Birthplace | Clubs | League App. | League Gls |
|---|---|---|---|---|---|---|
| **Goalkeepers** | | | | | | |
| Tony Coton | 6 1 | 11 8 | Tamworth | Birmingham C | 18 | — |
| | | | | Hereford U (on loan) | — | — |
| Jeff Wealands | 6 0½ | 12 0 | Darlington | Wolverhampton W | — | — |
| | | | | Northampton T (on loan) | — | — |
| | | | | Darlington | 28 | — |
| | | | | Hull C | 240 | — |
| | | | | Birmingham C | 102 | — |
| David Coles | 6 0 | 11 0 | Wandsworth | Birmingham C | — | — |
| **Defenders** | | | | | | |
| Mark Dennis | 5 9 | 10 8 | Streatham | Birmingham C | 107 | — |
| Pat Van Den Hauwe | 5 10 | 10 6 | Dendermonde, Belgium | Birmingham C | 44 | — |
| Kevan Broadhurst | 5 9½ | 11 2 | Dewsbury | Birmingham C | 102 | 8 |
| | | | | Walsall (on loan) | 3 | — |
| Colin Todd (England) | 5 9 | 11 5 | Chester-le-Street | Sunderland | 173 | 3 |
| | | | | Derby Co | 293 | 6 |
| | | | | Everton | 32 | 1 |
| | | | | Birmingham C | 93 | — |
| Geoff Scott | 5 10¼ | 12 4¾ | Birmingham | Stoke C | 78 | 3 |
| | | | | Leicester C | 39 | — |
| | | | | Birmingham C | 15 | — |
| David Langan (Eire) | 5 10 | 11 2 | Dublin | Derby Co | 143 | 1 |
| | | | | Birmingham C | 78 | 1 |
| Phil Hawker | 6 1 | 11 6 | Solihull | Birmingham C | 31 | 1 |
| Tony McGarr | 5 9 | 10 5 | Bermondsey | Birmingham C | — | — |
| Nigel Winterburn | 5 8 | 10 5 | Nuneaton | Birmingham C | — | — |
| Martin Howles (Contract cancelled April 1982) | | | | | | |
| **Midfield** | | | | | | |
| Les Phillips | 5 8 | 10 6 | Lambeth | Birmingham C | 11 | 1 |
| Kevin Dillon | 5 11 | 10 13 | Sunderland | Birmingham C | 159 | 12 |
| Byron Stevenson (Wales) | 6 1 | 11 0 | Llanelli | Leeds U | 95 | 4 |
| | | | | Birmingham C | 12 | — |
| Archie Gemmill (Scotland) | 5 5 | 11 2 | Paisley | St Mirren | 67 | 9 |
| (Contract cancelled March 1982) | | | | Preston NE | 99 | 13 |
| | | | | Derby Co | 261 | 18 |
| | | | | Nottingham F | 58 | 4 |
| | | | | Birmingham C | 97 | 12 |
| Alan Curbishley | 5 9 | 11 6 | Forest Gate | West Ham U | 85 | 4 |
| | | | | Birmingham C | 100 | 10 |
| Carl Francis | 5 11 | 10 9 | West Ham | Birmingham C | — | — |
| Alex Gibson | | | Nottingham | Birmingham C | — | — |
| Duncan MacDowall | 6 1 | 12 0 | Paddington | Birmingham C | 2 | — |
| David Linney* | | | Birmingham | Birmingham C | 1 | — |
| Derek McKay | 5 10 | 10 8 | Glasgow | Birmingham C | — | — |
| Brian Stewart | 5 10 | 10 8 | Glasgow | Birmingham C | — | — |
| Ian Handysides | 5 6 | 10 6 | Jarrow | Birmingham C | 28 | — |
| **Forwards** | | | | | | |
| Neil Whatmore | 5 9½ | 11 8 | Ellesmere Port | Bolton W | 277 | 102 |
| | | | | Birmingham C | 24 | 6 |
| Paul Ivey | 5 11 | 10 8 | Westminster | Birmingham C | 7 | — |
| (Contract cancelled March 1982) | | | | | | |
| Tony Evans | 5 8 | 11 7 | Liverpool | Blackpool | 6 | — |
| | | | | Cardiff C | 124 | 47 |
| | | | | Birmingham C | 59 | 26 |
| Terry Goode* | 5 8 | 11 3 | Islington | Birmingham C | 2 | — |
| Mike Sturridge | 5 11 | 11 0 | Birmingham | Birmingham C | — | — |
| Bud Brocken | 5 9 | 11 0 | Tilburg | Tilburg | (not known) | |
| | | | | Birmingham C | 17 | — |
| Toine Van Mierlo (Netherlands) | 6 0 | 11 6 | Sorendonk | Tilburg | (not known) | |
| | | | | Birmingham C | 40 | 4 |
| Mick Harford | 6 1 | 12 4 | Sunderland | Lincoln C | 115 | 41 |
| | | | | Newcastle U | 19 | 4 |
| | | | | Bristol C | 30 | 11 |
| | | | | Birmingham C | 12 | 9 |

Free transfers: Tony Knight*, Geoff Craig*, Gary Fillery*, John Whitehouse*, Tony Hinchey*.

# BLACKBURN ROVERS Division 2

*President:* W. H. Bancroft.

*Chairman:* W. Fox.

*Vice-Chairman:* R. D. Coar BSC.

*Directors:* T. W. Ibbotson LLB, A. Sharples, Dr M. Jeffries TD, K. C. Lee.

*Secretary:* John W. Howarth AAAI.

*Manager:* Bobby Saxton.  *Year Formed:* 1875.

*Limited Company:* 1897.  *Turned Professional:* 1880.

*Previous Grounds:* 1875, Brookhouse Ground; 1876, Alexandra Meadows; 1881, Leamington Road; 1890, Ewood Park.

*Previous Name:* Blackburn Grammar School OB.

**Football League Record:**
1888 Original Member of the League; 1936–39 Division 2; 1946–47 Division 1; 1947–57 Division 2; 1957–66 Division 1; 1966–71 Division 2; 1971–75 Division 3; 1975–79 Division 2; 1979–80 Division 3; 1980– Division 2.

**Honours:** *Football League:* Division 1 – Champions 1911–12, 1913–14; Division 2 – Champions 1938–39; Runners-up 1957–58; Division 3 – Champions 1974–75; Runners-up 1979–80. *FA Cup:* Winners 1884, 1885, 1886, 1890, 1891, 1928; Runners-up 1882, 1960. *Football League Cup:* Semi-final 1961–62.

*Record Victory:* 11-0 v Rossendale U, FA Cup, 1884–85.

*Record Defeat:* 0-8 v Arsenal, Division 1, 25 Feb, 1933.

*Most League Points:* 60, Division 3, 1974–75.

*Most League Goals:* 114, Division 2, 1954–55.

*Highest League Scorer in Season:* Ted Harper, 43, Division 1, 1925–26.

*Most League Goals in Total Aggregate:* Tommy Briggs, 140, 1952–58.

*Most Capped Player:* Bob Crompton, 41, England.

*Most League Appearances:* Ronnie Clayton, 580, 1950–69 (and 57 FA Cup games).

*Record Transfer Fee Received:* £357,000 from Leeds U for Kevin Hird, Feb 1979.

*Record Transfer Fee Paid:* £100,000 to Chelsea for Duncan McKenzie, March 1979.

*Previous Managers since the War:* Eddie Hapgood, Will Scott, Jack Bruton, Jackie Bestall, John Carey, Dally Duncan, Jack Marshall, Eddie Quigley, John Carey, Ken Furphy, Gordon Lee, Jim Smith, Jim Iley, Howard Kendall.

---

**Ewood Park, Blackburn BB2 4JF.** Telephone Blackburn 55432/55433. *Telegraphic Address:* 'Rovers, Blackburn'. *Ground capacity:* 25,000. *Record attendance:* 61,783 v Bolton W, FA Cup 6th rd, 2 Mar, 1929. *Record receipts:* £40,686 v Aston Villa, FA Cup 5th rd, 16 Feb, 1980. *Pitch measurements:* 116yd 2ft×72yd 2ft.

*How to get there:* Blackburn is the nearest railway station and Corporation buses run from there to the ground.

*Club shop:* Open every day selling all types of souvenirs.

*Handbooks/programmes:* No handbook. Programmes available on subscription from the club shop.

*Extra information:* In 1881–82, Blackburn Rovers were unbeaten for 35 successive matches.

*Club Colours:* Blue and white halved shirts, white shorts, blue stockings with red and white tops.

*Change Colours:*

*Reserve Team Manager:* Jim Furnell

*Club Nickname:* Blue and Whites.

# BLACKBURN ROVERS 1981–82 LEAGUE RECORD

| Match No. | Date | Venue | Opponents | Result | H/T Score | Goalscorers | Atten- dance |
|---|---|---|---|---|---|---|---|
| 1 | Aug 29 | H | Sheffield W | L 0-1 | 0-1 | | 14,980 |
| 2 | Sept 1 | A | Shrewsbury T | W 2-1 | 0-1 | Lowey, Brotherston | 4220 |
| 3 | 5 | A | Charlton Ath | L 0-2 | 0-1 | | 6141 |
| 4 | 12 | H | Orient | W 2-0 | 1-0 | Keeley, Crawford | 7043 |
| 5 | 19 | A | Cardiff C | W 3-1 | 2-1 | Stonehouse 2, Pontin (og) | 4253 |
| 6 | 23 | H | Cambridge U | W 1-0 | 0-0 | Crawford | 7518 |
| 7 | 26 | H | Leicester C | L 0-2 | 0-1 | | 8925 |
| 8 | Oct 3 | A | QPR | L 0-2 | 0-1 | | 9541 |
| 9 | 10 | H | Barnsley | W 2-1 | 1-1 | Garner 2 | 10,522 |
| 10 | 17 | A | Derby Co | D 1-1 | 1-0 | Keeley | 10,572 |
| 11 | 24 | A | Grimsby T | D 1-1 | 1-0 | Garner | 7450 |
| 12 | 31 | H | Wrexham | D 0-0 | 0-0 | | 8159 |
| 13 | Nov 7 | A | Crystal Palace | W 2-1 | 2-0 | Garner 2 | 9452 |
| 14 | 14 | H | Luton T | L 0-1 | 0-0 | | 9862 |
| 15 | 21 | A | Watford | L 2-3 | 0-2 | Burke, Stonehouse (pen) | 11,822 |
| 16 | 25 | H | Shrewsbury T | D 0-0 | 0-0 | | 6892 |
| 17 | 28 | H | Norwich C | W 3-0 | 1-0 | Garner 2, Miller | 8153 |
| 18 | Dec 5 | A | Newcastle U | D 0-0 | 0-0 | | 18,721 |
| 19 | 19 | A | Chelsea | D 1-1 | 0-0 | Miller | 11,768 |
| 20 | 26 | A | Oldham Ath | W 3-0 | 3-0 | Garner, Stonehouse, Bell | 15,400 |
| 21 | 28 | H | Bolton W | D 2-2 | 2-1 | Arnott, Stonehouse (pen) | 16,577 |
| 22 | Jan 13 | H | Charlton Ath | L 0-2 | 0-1 | | 5825 |
| 23 | 16 | A | Sheffield W | D 2-2 | 0-2 | Stonehouse, Keeley | 13,120 |
| 24 | 23 | H | Rotherham U | W 2-0 | 1-0 | Stonehouse, Arnott | 7706 |
| 25 | 30 | H | Cardiff C | W 1-0 | 0-0 | Garner | 7001 |
| 26 | Feb 6 | A | Orient | D 0-0 | 0-0 | | 3990 |
| 27 | 16 | H | QPR | W 2-1 | 0-0 | Stonehouse, Brotherston | 6884 |
| 28 | 20 | A | Leicester C | L 0-1 | 0-1 | | 10,890 |
| 29 | 27 | A | Barnsley | W 1-0 | 0-0 | Garner | 13,150 |
| 30 | Mar 6 | H | Derby Co | W 4-1 | 2-0 | Miller, Stonehouse (pen), Bell, Garner | 8364 |
| 31 | 13 | A | Grimsby T | W 2-0 | 1-0 | Stonehouse (pen), Garner | 8676 |
| 32 | 20 | A | Wrexham | L 0-1 | 0-1 | | 5780 |
| 33 | 27 | H | Crystal Palace | W 1-0 | 0-0 | Bell | 8362 |
| 34 | Apr 3 | A | Luton T | L 0-2 | 0-1 | | 10,721 |
| 35 | 9 | H | Oldham Ath | D 0-0 | 0-0 | | 11,044 |
| 36 | 12 | H | Bolton W | L 0-2 | 0-1 | | 11,912 |
| 37 | 17 | H | Watford | L 1-2 | 1-0 | Stonehouse (pen) | 7284 |
| 38 | 24 | A | Norwich C | L 0-2 | 0-2 | | 16,309 |
| 39 | May 1 | H | Newcastle U | W 4-1 | 2-0 | Bell, Branagan, Rathbone, Garner | 5207 |
| 40 | 4 | A | Cambridge U | L 0-1 | 0-1 | | 3203 |
| 41 | 8 | A | Rotherham U | L 1-4 | 1-0 | Fazackerley | 8333 |
| 42 | 15 | H | Chelsea | D 1-1 | 0-0 | Garner | 6133 |

**Final League Position: 10**

### Goalscorers

*League* (47): Garner 14, Stonehouse 11 (5 pens), Bell 4, Keeley 3, Miller 3, Arnott 2, Brotherston 2, Crawford 2, Branagan 1, Burke 1, Fazackerley 1, Lowey 1, Rathbone 1, own goal 1.
*League Cup* (3): Garner 2, Lowey 1.
*FA Cup* (2): Garner 2.

| | | | | |
|---|---|---|---|---|
| **League Cup** | Second Round | Sheffield W (h) | | 1-1 |
| | | (a) | | 2-1 |
| **FA Cup** | Third Round | WBA (a) | | 2-3 |

| Gennoe | Hamilton | Rathbone | Speight | Keeley | Fazackerley | Miller | Burke | Lowey | Crawford | Brotherston | Stonehouse | Branagan | Williamson | Garner | Comstive | Arnott | Bell | Butcher | Murphy | Salmon | Match No. |
|---|---|---|---|---|---|---|---|---|---|---|---|---|---|---|---|---|---|---|---|---|---|
| 1 | 2 | 3 | 4 | 5 | 6 | 7 | 8 | 9* | 10 | 11 | 12 | | | | | | | | | | 1 |
| 1 | 6 | 3 | 4 | 5 | | 7 | 8 | 9 | 10 | 11 | | 2 | | | | | | | | | 2 |
| 1 | 2 | 3 | | 5* | | 7 | 8 | 9 | 10 | 11 | 6 | 4 | | 12 | | | | | | | 3 |
| 1 | 4 | 3 | | 5 | 6 | 7 | 8 | | 10 | 11 | 9 | 2 | | | | | | | | | 4 |
| 1 | 4 | 3 | | 5 | 6 | 7 | 8 | | 10 | 11 | 9 | 2 | | | | | | | | | 5 |
| 1 | | 3 | | 5 | 6 | 7 | 8 | | 10 | 11 | 9 | 2 | | 4 | | | | | | | 6 |
| 1 | 4 | 3 | | 5 | 6 | 7 | 8 | | 10* | 11 | 9 | 2 | | 12 | | | | | | | 7 |
| 1 | 4 | 3 | | 5 | 6 | 7 | 8 | 12 | 10 | 11* | 9 | 2 | | | | | | | | | 8 |
| 1 | | 3 | 4 | 5 | 6 | 7 | 8 | 9 | | 11 | | 2 | | 10 | | | | | | | 9 |
| 1 | | 3 | 4 | 5 | 6 | 7 | 8 | 9 | | 11 | | 2 | | 10 | | | | | | | 10 |
| 1 | 4* | 3 | | 5 | 6 | 7 | 8 | 9 | | 11 | 12 | 2 | | 10 | | | | | | | 11 |
| 1 | 4 | 3 | | 5 | 6 | 7 | 8 | 9 | | 11 | | 2 | | 10 | | | | | | | 12 |
| 1 | | 3 | | 5 | 6 | 7 | 8 | 9 | | 11 | 4 | 2 | | 10 | | | | | | | 13 |
| 1 | | 3 | | 5* | 6 | 7 | 8 | 9 | | 11 | 4 | 2 | | 10 | 12 | | | | | | 14 |
| 1 | | 3 | | 5 | 6 | 7 | 8 | 9 | | 11 | 4 | 2 | | 10 | | | | | | | 15 |
| 1 | | 3 | | 5 | 6 | 7 | | | | 11 | | 2 | | 10 | 8 | 4 | 9 | | | | 16 |
| 1 | | 3 | | 5 | 6 | 7 | | | | 11 | 8 | 2 | | 10 | | 4 | 9 | | | | 17 |
| 1 | | 3 | | 5 | 6 | 7 | | | | 11 | 8 | 2 | | 10 | | 4 | 9 | | | | 18 |
| 1 | 3 | | | 5 | 6 | 7 | | | | 11 | 8 | 2 | | 10 | | 4 | 9 | | | | 19 |
| 1 | | 3 | | 5 | 6 | 7 | | | | 11 | 8 | 2 | | 10 | | 4 | 9 | | | | 20 |
| 1 | | 3 | | 5 | 6 | 7 | | | | 11 | 8 | 2 | | 10 | | 4 | 9 | | | | 21 |
| 1 | | 3 | | 5 | 6 | 7* | 12 | | | 11 | 8 | 2 | | 10 | | 4 | 9 | | | | 22 |
| 1 | | 3 | | 5 | 6 | 7 | 12 | | | 11 | 8 | 2 | | 10* | | 4 | 9 | | | | 23 |
| 1 | | 3 | | 5 | 6 | 7 | | | | 11 | 8 | 2 | | 10 | | 4 | 9 | | | | 24 |
| 1 | | 3 | | 5 | 6 | 7 | | | | 11 | 8 | 2 | | 10 | | 4 | 9 | | | | 25 |
| 1 | | 3 | | 5 | 6 | 7 | | | | 11 | 8 | 2 | | 10 | | 4 | 9 | | | | 26 |
| 1 | 2 | 3 | | 5 | | 7 | | | | 11 | 8 | 6 | | 10 | | 4 | 9 | | | | 27 |
| 1 | | 3 | | 5 | 6 | 7 | | | | 11 | 8 | 2 | | 10 | | 4 | 9 | | | | 28 |
| 1 | | 3 | | 5 | 6 | 7 | | | | 11 | 8 | 2 | | 10 | | 4 | 9 | | | | 29 |
| 1 | | 3 | | 5 | 6 | 7 | | | | 11 | 8 | 2 | | 10 | | 4 | 9 | | | | 30 |
| 1 | 2 | 3 | | 5 | 6 | 7 | | | | 11 | 8 | | | 10 | | 4 | 9 | | | | 31 |
| 1 | | 3 | | 5 | 6 | 7 | | | | 11 | 8 | 2 | | 10 | | 4 | 9 | | | | 32 |
| 1 | | 3 | 4 | 5 | 6 | 7 | | | | 11 | 8 | 2 | | 10 | | | 9 | | | | 33 |
| 1 | 12 | 3 | 4 | 5 | 6 | 7 | | | | 11 | 8 | 2 | | 10* | | | 9 | | | | 34 |
| 1 | | 3 | 4 | 5 | 6 | 7 | | | | 11 | 8 | 2 | | 10 | | | 9 | | | | 35 |
| | | 3 | 4 | 5 | 6 | 7 | 12 | | | 11 | 8 | 2 | | 10 | | | | 9* | 1 | | 36 |
| | 11 | 3 | 4 | 5 | 6 | 7 | | 9 | | | 8 | 2 | | 10 | | | 1 | | | | 37 |
| | 11 | 3 | 4 | 5 | 6 | 7 | | 9* | | | 8 | 2 | | 10 | | | 1 | 12 | | | 38 |
| | 2 | 3 | 4 | | 6 | 7 | | | | 11* | 8 | 5 | | 10 | | | 1 | 9 | | 12 | 39 |
| | | 3 | 4 | 5 | 6 | 7 | | | | 11 | 8 | 2 | | 10 | | | 1 | 9 | | | 40 |
| | | 3 | 4 | 5 | 6 | 7* | 12 | | | 11 | 8 | 2 | | 10 | | | 1 | 9 | | | 41 |
| | 4 | 3 | | 5 | 6 | 7 | 8 | | | 11 | | 2 | | 10 | | | 1 | 9 | | | 42 |
| 35 | 16 | 41 | 13 | 41 | 39 | 42 | 16 | 12 | 8 | 38 | 35 | 40 | — | 35 | 1 | 17 | 25 | 6 | 1 | 1 | |
| +1s | | | | | | | +3s | +2s | | | +1s | +1s | +1s | | | | | | +2s | | |

## BLACKBURN ROVERS

| | Ht | Wt | Birthplace | Clubs | League App. | League Gls |
|---|---|---|---|---|---|---|
| **Goalkeepers** | | | | | | |
| John Butcher* | 6 2 | 12 3 | Newcastle | Blackburn R | 104 | — |
| Chris Pearce* | 6 0 | 11 4 | Newport | Wolverhampton W | — | — |
| | | | | Rochdale (on loan) | 5 | — |
| | | | | Barnsley (on loan) | — | — |
| | | | | Blackburn R | — | — |
| Terry Gennoe | 6 2½ | 13 5 | Shrewsbury | Bury | 3 | — |
| | | | | Blackburn R (on loan) | — | — |
| | | | | Leeds U (on loan) | — | — |
| | | | | Halifax T | 78 | — |
| | | | | Everton (on loan) | — | — |
| | | | | Crystal Palace (on loan) | 3 | — |
| | | | | Southampton | 36 | — |
| | | | | Blackburn R | 35 | — |
| Michael Salmon | | | Leyland | Blackburn R | 1 | — |
| **Defenders** | | | | | | |
| Derek Fazackerley | 5 11 | 11 6 | Preston | Blackburn R | 436 | 14 |
| Glenn Keeley | 5 10 | 12 0 | Barking | Ipswich T | 4 | — |
| | | | | Newcastle U | 44 | 2 |
| | | | | Blackburn R | 214 | 8 |
| Mike Rathbone | 5 10 | 11 13 | Birmingham | Birmingham C | 20 | — |
| | | | | Blackburn R | 111 | 2 |
| Jim Branagan | 5 10 | 11 5 | Barton | Oldham Ath | 27 | — |
| | | | | Huddersfield T | 38 | — |
| | | | | Blackburn R | 113 | 2 |
| David Hamilton | 5 7½ | 9 12 | South Shields | Sunderland | — | — |
| | | | | Blackburn R | 20 | — |
| Julian Marshall | 6 3 | 12 0 | Swansea | Hereford U | 92 | 4 |
| | | | | Bristol C | 29 | — |
| | | | | Blackburn R | — | — |
| Phil Williamson* | | | Macclesfield | Blackburn R | 1 | — |
| **Midfield** | | | | | | |
| Kim Walters* | | | Pilsley | Heanor T | (not known) | |
| | | | | Blackburn R | — | — |
| Tony Parkes | 5 7½ | 11 2 | Sheffield | Blackburn R | 350 | 38 |
| (Retired, injury) | | | | | | |
| Noel Brotherston | 5 8½ | 10 8 | Belfast | Tottenham H | 1 | — |
| (N Ireland) | | | | Blackburn R | 187 | 25 |
| Mick Speight | 5 10½ | 12 7 | Upton | Sheffield U | 199 | 14 |
| | | | | Blackburn R | 51 | 4 |
| Paul Comstive | | | Southport | Blackburn R | 5 | — |
| David Mail | | | Bristol | Aston V | — | — |
| | | | | Blackburn R | — | — |
| Donal Murphy | 5 11 | 11 0 | Dublin | Coventry C | 43 | 10 |
| | | | | Millwall (on loan) | 3 | — |
| | | | | Torquay U | 85 | 20 |
| | | | | Plymouth Arg | 48 | 9 |
| | | | | Torquay U (on loan) | 3 | — |
| | | | | Blackburn R | 3 | — |
| **Forwards** | | | | | | |
| Norman Bell | 6 0¼ | 13 2 | Sunderland | Wolverhampton W | 80 | 17 |
| | | | | Blackburn R | 25 | 4 |
| Simon Garner | 5 8 | 11 3 | Boston | Blackburn R | 122 | 35 |
| Kevin Stonehouse | 5 11 | 11 10 | Bishop Auckland | Shildon | (not known) | |
| | | | | Blackburn R | 70 | 23 |
| Viv Busby* | 6 0 | 11 12 | Slough | Luton T | 77 | 16 |
| | | | | Newcastle U (on loan) | 4 | 2 |
| | | | | Fulham | 118 | 29 |
| | | | | Norwich C | 22 | 11 |
| | | | | Sheffield U (on loan) | 3 | 1 |
| | | | | Stoke C | 50 | 9 |
| | | | | Tulsa R | (not known) | |
| | | | | Blackburn R | 8 | 1 |
| John Lowey | 5 11 | 12 7 | Manchester | Manchester U | — | — |
| | | | | California S | (not known) | |
| | | | | Blackburn R | — | — |
| | | | | Port Vale | — | — |
| | | | | Sheffield W | 42 | 4 |
| | | | | Blackburn R | 33 | 3 |
| Marshall Burke | 5 7 | 9 1 | Glasgow | Burnley | 24 | 5 |
| | | | | Leeds U | — | — |
| | | | | Blackburn R | 39 | 7 |
| Ian Miller | 5 9 | 11 7 | Perth | Bury | 15 | — |
| | | | | Nottingham F | — | — |
| | | | | Doncaster R | 124 | 14 |
| | | | | Swindon T | 127 | 9 |
| | | | | Blackburn R | 42 | 3 |

# BLACKPOOL Division 4

*Chairman:* K. Chadwick LLB.
*Directors:* G. Bloor, F. J. Hessey, B. A. Pemberton,
T. White.
*Manager:* Sam Ellis.
*Secretary:* D. Johnson.
*Year Formed:* 1887.   *Limited Company:* 1896.
*Turned Professional:* 1887.
*Previous Grounds:* 1887, Raikes Hall Gardens; 1897, Athletic
Grounds; 1899, Raikes Hall Gardens; 1899, Bloomfield Road.
*Previous Name:* 'South Shore' combined with Blackpool in 1899,
twelve years after the latter had been formed on the breaking up of
the old 'Blackpool St John's club.

**Football League Record:**
1896 Elected to Division 2; 1899 Failed Re-election; 1900 Re-elected; 1900–30 Division 2; 1930–33
Division 1; 1933–37 Division 2; 1937–67 Division 1; 1967–70 Division 2; 1970–71 Division 1; 1971–78
Division 2; 1978–81 Division 3; 1981– Division 4.

**Honours:** *Football League:* Division 1 – Runners-up 1955–56; Division 2 – Champions 1929–30; Runners-up 1936–37, 1969–70. *FA Cup:* Winners 1953; Runners-up 1948, 1951. *Football League Cup:* Semi-final 1962. *Anglo-Italian Cup:* Winners 1971; Runners-up 1972.

*Record Victory:* 10-0 v Lanerossi Vicenza, Anglo-Italian tournament, 10 June, 1972.
*Record Defeat:* 1-10 v Small Heath, Division 2, 2 March, 1901 and 1-10 v Huddersfield, Division 1, 13
Dec, 1930.
*Most League Points:* 58, Division 2, 1929–30 and 1967–68. *Three points win:* 58, Division 4, 1981–82.
*Most League Goals:* 98, Division 2, 1929–30.
*Highest League Scorer in Season:* Jimmy Hampson, 45, Division 2, 1929–30.
*Most League Goals in Total Aggregate:* Jimmy Hampson, 247, 1927–38.
*Most Capped Player:* Jimmy Armfield, 43, England.
*Most League Appearances:* Jimmy Armfield, 568, 1952–71.
*Record Transfer Fee Received:* £325,000 from Everton for Mickey Walsh, August 1978.
*Record Transfer Fee Paid:* £110,000 to Peterborough U for Bob Doyle, July 1979.
*Previous Managers since the War:* Joe Smith, Ron Suart, Stan Mortensen, Les Shannon, Jimmy
Meadows, Bob Stokoe, Harry Potts, Allan Brown, Jimmy Meadows, Bob Stokoe, Stan Ternent, Alan
Ball Jnr, Allan Brown.
*Address of Supporters Club:* Blackpool FC Supporters' Club, Bloomfield Road, Blackpool, Lancs.
(*Shop:* Same address as ground.)

---

**Bloomfield Rd Ground, Blackpool FY1 6JJ.** Telephone Blackpool 404331. *Telegraphic address:* 'Football Blackpool'. *Ground capacity:* 18,000. *Record attendance:* 39,118 v Manchester U, Division 1, 19
April, 1952. *Record receipts:* £28,986.52 v Everton, League Cup 2nd rd, 2nd leg, 3 Sept, 1980. *Pitch
measurements:* 111yd×73yd.
*How to get there:* Coliseum bus station, Lytham Road, 10 minutes' walk. Railway: South station (a few minutes' walk from ground) and North station.
*Match tickets:* Bookable four weeks in advance of the match.
*Car parking:* Car park for 1,000 cars. Street parking available.
*Entertainments/catering facilities:* Refreshment and licensed bars. Entertainment after the game at the Supporters' Club by prior arrangement.
*Club shop:* In Bloomfield Road sells all types of souvenirs.
*Handbooks/programmes:* Programmes available from the development shop.
*Extra information:* When England lost 6-3 to Hungary in November 1953, there were four Blackpool players – Stanley Matthews, Stan Mortensen, Harry Johnston, and Ernie Taylor – in the team.
*Club Colours:* Tangerine shirts with white stripe on sleeves, collars and cuffs, white shorts, tangerine with white trim stockings.
*Change Colours:* White shirts, tangerine shorts and tangerine stockings.
*Club Captain:* Terry Pashley.   *First Team Coach:*
*Club Nickname:* The Seasiders.

## BLACKPOOL 1981–82 LEAGUE RECORD

| Match No. | Date | Venue | Opponents | Result | H/T Score | Goalscorers | Attendance |
|---|---|---|---|---|---|---|---|
| 1 | Aug 29 | H | Stockport Co | W 2-0 | 1-0 | Blair, Morris | 4556 |
| 2 | Sept 5 | A | Scunthorpe U | D 1-1 | 0-0 | Noble | 2200 |
| 3 | 12 | H | Crewe Alex | W 5-0 | 3-0 | Bamber, Goddard 2, Morris, Hockaday | 4506 |
| 4 | 19 | A | Darlington | D 2-2 | 1-0 | Bamber, Morris | 2485 |
| 5 | 22 | A | Rochdale | D 0-0 | 0-0 | | 2763 |
| 6 | 26 | H | Hull C | W 3-1 | 1-0 | Bamber 2, Morris | 4838 |
| 7 | 30 | H | Halifax T | W 7-1 | 2-0 | Hockaday, Bamber 3, Simmonite, Noble, Harrison | 5084 |
| 8 | Oct 3 | A | Mansfield T | D 2-2 | 1-1 | Hockaday, McEwan (pen) | 3466 |
| 9 | 10 | H | Torquay U | W 2-1 | 1-0 | Noble, Morris | 6716 |
| 10 | 13 | A | Northampton T | W 1-0 | 1-0 | Morris | 2376 |
| 11 | 17 | A | Aldershot | L 2-3 | 1-1 | Pashley, Bamber | 2600 |
| 12 | 20 | A | York C | W 4-0 | 2-0 | Hockaday, Morris, Blair, Noble | 2657 |
| 13 | 31 | A | Sheffield U | L 1-3 | 0-0 | McEwan | 15,566 |
| 14 | Nov 4 | H | Bury | D 1-1 | 0-1 | Blair | 7805 |
| 15 | 7 | A | Peterborough U | L 1-3 | 0-2 | McEwan (pen) | 5442 |
| 16 | 11 | H | Port Vale | L 2-3 | 2-2 | Noble, Morris | 4785 |
| 17 | 14 | H | AFC Bournemouth | L 0-3 | 0-1 | | 4665 |
| 18 | Dec 4 | A | Colchester U | L 1-2 | 1-1 | Bamber | 3875 |
| 19 | Jan 9 | H | Scunthorpe U | W 2-0 | 0-0 | Morris 2 | 4136 |
| 20 | 13 | H | Tranmere R | L 1-2 | 1-0 | Bamber | 3329 |
| 21 | 30 | H | Darlington | W 1-0 | 1-0 | Entwistle | 3825 |
| 22 | Feb 1 | A | Stockport Co | W 3-2 | 2-1 | Entwistle, Bamber, Hockaday | 5008 |
| 23 | 5 | A | Crewe Alex | D 1-1 | 1-0 | Lewis (og) | 2513 |
| 24 | 10 | A | Rochdale | D 1-1 | 1-1 | Entwistle | 3294 |
| 25 | 13 | H | Mansfield T | L 2-3 | 1-3 | McEwan (pen), Hockaday | 3017 |
| 26 | 17 | H | Northampton T | W 1-0 | 1-0 | Noble | 2231 |
| 27 | 20 | A | Halifax T | D 0-0 | 0-0 | | 2245 |
| 28 | 27 | A | Torquay U | D 1-1 | 1-1 | Harrison | 2177 |
| 29 | Mar 3 | H | Bradford C | W 1-0 | 1-0 | Stewart | 4004 |
| 30 | 6 | H | Aldershot | L 0-2 | 0-2 | | 2655 |
| 31 | 10 | H | York C | W 3-1 | 2-0 | Brockbank, McEwan (pen), Bamber | 2164 |
| 32 | 13 | A | Port Vale | L 0-2 | 0-2 | | 3439 |
| 33 | 20 | H | Sheffield U | L 0-1 | 0-0 | | 7542 |
| 34 | 27 | H | Peterborough U | D 2-2 | 0-1 | Bamber 2 | 2855 |
| 35 | 30 | A | Wigan Ath | L 1-2 | 0-2 | Morgan | 7329 |
| 36 | Apr 3 | A | AFC Bournemouth | L 0-1 | 0-0 | | 5146 |
| 37 | 9 | H | Wigan Ath | L 1-2 | 0-0 | Hockaday | 9439 |
| 38 | 10 | A | Tranmere R | L 1-3 | 0-2 | Morgan | 1828 |
| 39 | 17 | H | Colchester U | D 0-0 | 0-0 | | 2298 |
| 40 | 21 | A | Hereford U | L 1-2 | 0-2 | Musial (og) | 2617 |
| 41 | 24 | A | Bradford C | L 0-1 | 0-0 | | 4898 |
| 42 | 28 | A | Hartlepool U | D 2-2 | 2-0 | Noble, Bamber | 1387 |
| 43 | May 1 | H | Hereford U | W 1-0 | 0-0 | Noble | 1881 |
| 44 | 4 | A | Hull C | L 0-1 | 0-1 | | 3206 |
| 45 | 15 | H | Hartlepool U | D 2-2 | 0-1 | Stewart 2 | 1824 |
| 46 | 18 | A | Bury | W 1-0 | 1-0 | Noble | 2041 |

**Final League Position: 12**

### Goalscorers

*League* (66): Bamber 15, Morris 10, Noble 9, Hockaday 7, McEwan 5 (4 pens), Blair 3, Entwistle 3, Stewart 3, Goddard 2, Harrison 2, Morgan 2, Brockbank 1, Pashley 1, Simmonite 1, own goals 2.
*League Cup* (1): Bamber 1.
*FA Cup* (7): Harrison 2, Morris 2, Bamber 1, Entwistle 1, Wann 1.

| | | | |
|---|---|---|---|
| **League Cup** | First Round | Bradford C (a) | 1-3 |
| | | (h) | 0-0 |
| **FA Cup** | First Round | Horden Colliery Welfare (a) | 1-0 |
| | Second Round | Kettering T (a) | 3-0 |
| | Third Round | Barnsley (a) | 2-0 |
| | Fourth Round | QPR (h) | 0-0 |
| | | (a) | 1-5 |

| Hesford | Simmonite | Pashley | Blair | Greenall | McEwan | Morris | Noble | Bamber | Hockaday | Harrison | Morgan | Wann | Hart | Pollard | Goddard | Entwistle | Sbragia | Gardner | Rush | Fletcher | Deary | McAvoy | Stewart | Brockbank | Bardsley | Butler | Match No. |
|---|---|---|---|---|---|---|---|---|---|---|---|---|---|---|---|---|---|---|---|---|---|---|---|---|---|---|---|
| 1 | 2 | 3 | 4 | 5 | 6 | 7 | 8 | 9 | 10* | 11 | 12 | | | | | | | | | | | | | | | | 1 |
| 1 | 2 | 3 | | 5 | | 7 | 8 | 9 | 10* | 11 | | 4 | 6 | 12 | | | | | | | | | | | | | 2 |
| 1 | 2 | 3 | 4 | 5 | | 7 | 8* | 9 | 12 | 11 | | | 6 | | | 10 | | | | | | | | | | | 3 |
| 1 | 2 | 3 | 4 | | 6 | 7 | 8* | 9 | 12 | 11 | | | | 5 | | 10 | | | | | | | | | | | 4 |
| 1 | 2 | 3 | 4 | 5 | | 7 | 8 | 9 | | 11 | | | 6 | | | 10 | | | | | | | | | | | 5 |
| 1 | 2 | 3 | 4 | | 6 | 7 | 8* | 9 | 12 | 11 | | | | 5 | | 10 | | | | | | | | | | | 6 |
| 1 | 2 | 3 | 4* | | 6 | 7 | 8 | 9 | 10 | 11 | | 12 | 5 | | | | | | | | | | | | | | 7 |
| 1 | 2 | 3 | 4 | | 6 | 7 | 8 | | 10* | 11 | | 12 | 5 | | 9 | | | | | | | | | | | | 8 |
| 1 | 2 | 3 | 4 | | 6 | 7 | 8 | 9 | 10 | 11 | | | 5 | | | | | | | | | | | | | | 9 |
| 1 | 2 | 3 | 4 | | 6 | 7 | 8 | 9 | 10 | 11 | | | | | | | 5 | | | | | | | | | | 10 |
| 1 | | 3 | 4 | | 6 | 7 | 8 | 9 | 10 | 11 | 12 | | 5 | | | | | 2* | | | | | | | | | 11 |
| 1 | | 3 | 4 | | 6 | 7 | 8 | 9 | 10* | 11 | 12 | | 5 | | | | | 2 | | | | | | | | | 12 |
| | | 3 | 4 | | 6 | 7 | 8 | | 10 | 11 | 12 | | 5 | | 9* | | | 2 | 1 | | | | | | | | 13 |
| | | 3 | 4 | | 6 | 7 | 8 | | 10 | 11* | | | 5 | | 9 | | | 2 | 1 | 12 | | | | | | | 14 |
| | | 3 | 4* | | 6 | 7 | 8 | 9 | 10 | | | 11 | 5 | | | | 12 | 2 | 1 | | | | | | | | 15 |
| | 2 | 3 | 4 | | 6 | 7 | 8 | 9 | 10* | | | 11 | 5 | | | | | | 1 | | 12 | | | | | | 16 |
| | 2 | 3 | 4 | | | 7 | 8 | 9 | | 11* | | | 5 | | 6 | | | | 1 | | 12 | 10 | | | | | 17 |
| 1 | 2 | 3 | 4 | | | 7 | 8 | 9 | 10 | 11 | | | 6 | 5 | | | | | | | | | | | | | 18 |
| 1 | 2 | 3 | 4 | | 6* | 7 | 8 | 9 | 10 | 11 | | | 5 | | | | | | | 12 | | | | | | | 19 |
| 1 | 2 | 3 | 4 | | | 7 | 8 | 9 | 10 | 11 | | 5* | 12 | | | | | | | 6 | | | | | | | 20 |
| 1 | | 3 | 4 | 5 | | 7 | 8 | 9 | 10 | | | | 6 | | | 11 | | 2 | | | | | | | | | 21 |
| 1 | | 3 | 4 | 5 | | 7 | 8 | 9 | 10 | 12 | | | 6 | | | 11* | | 2 | | | | | | | | | 22 |
| 1 | | 3 | 4 | 5 | 12 | | 8 | 9 | 10* | 11 | | | 6 | | | 7 | | 2 | | | | | | | | | 23 |
| 1 | | 3 | 4 | 5 | | | 8 | 9* | | 11 | 7 | 6 | | | 10 | | | 2 | | | | | 12 | | | | 24 |
| 1 | | 3 | 4 | | 6 | | 8 | 9 | 12 | 11* | 7 | 5 | | | 10 | | | 2 | | | | | | | | | 25 |
| 1 | | 10 | 4 | | 6 | | 8 | 9 | | | | | 5 | | | 11 | | | | | 2 | 7 | | 3 | | | 26 |
| 1 | | 10 | 4 | | 6 | | 8 | 9 | | | | | 5* | | | 11 | | | | | 2 | 7 | 12 | 3 | | | 27 |
| 1 | | 10 | 4 | 12 | 6 | | 8 | 9 | | | | | 5 | | | | | | | | 2 | 7 | 11* | 3 | | | 28 |
| 1 | 7 | | 4 | | 6 | | 8 | 9 | 10 | | | | 5 | | | | | | | | 2 | | 11 | 3 | | | 29 |
| | 7 | | 4 | | 6 | | 8 | 9 | 10 | | | | 5 | | | | | | 1 | | 2 | 12 | 11* | 3 | | | 30 |
| 1 | | 10 | | | 6 | | 8 | 9 | 4 | | | | 5 | 7 | | | | | | | 2 | | 11 | 3 | | | 31 |
| 1 | | 10 | | | 6 | | 8 | 9 | 4 | | | | 5 | | | 12 | | | | | 2 | 7 | 11* | 3 | | | 32 |
| 1 | 2 | 10 | | | 6 | | 8 | 9 | 7 | | | | 5* | 12 | | | | | | | 11 | 4 | | 3 | | | 33 |
| 1 | 2 | 11 | | | 6 | | | 9 | 10 | 7 | | | 5 | | | | | | | | 4 | 8 | | 3 | | | 34 |
| 1 | 2 | 11 | | 6 | | | 9 | 10 | 12 | 7 | | | 5 | | | | | | | | 4 | 8* | | 3 | | | 35 |
| 1 | 2 | 11* | 6 | | 4 | | 9 | 10 | 12 | 7 | | | 5 | | | | | | | | | 8 | | 3 | | | 36 |
| 1 | 2 | 11 | | | 6 | | 9 | 10 | 12 | 7 | | | 5 | | | | | | | | 4 | 8* | | 3 | | | 37 |
| 1 | 2 | 11 | 12 | 5* | | 9 | 10 | 8 | | 7 | | | 4 | | | | | | | | 6 | | | 3 | | | 38 |
| 1 | 2 | 11 | | 5 | | | 6 | | | 8 | 7 | | | | | | | | | | 4 | 10 | 9 | 3 | | | 39 |
| 1 | 2 | 11 | | 5 | | 6 | 9 | 8 | 4* | 7 | | | | | | | | | | | 12 | 10 | | 3 | | | 40 |
| 1 | 2 | 11 | 8* | 5 | 6 | | 9 | 10 | | 7 | | | | | | | | | | | 4 | 12 | | 3 | | | 41 |
| | 2 | 11 | 12 | 5 | | 10 | 9 | 8 | | 7* | | 6 | | | | | | | 1 | | 4 | | | 3 | | | 42 |
| 1 | 2 | 11 | 4 | 5 | | 10 | 9 | 7 | | | | | 6 | | | | | | | | 8 | | | 3 | | | 43 |
| 1 | 2 | 11* | 4 | 5 | | 10 | 9 | 7 | | | | | 6 | | | | | | | | 8 | 12 | | 3 | | | 44 |
| 1 | 2 | 3 | 4* | 5 | | 10 | 9 | 7 | | 11 | | | 6 | | | | | | | | 8 | 12 | | | | | 45 |
| 1 | 2 | 3 | | 5 | | 10 | 6 | 4 | | | | | | | | | | | | | 4 | 8 | 9 | 7 | 11 | | 46 |
| 39 | 29 | 46 | 35 | 16 | 24 | 22 | 44 | 38 | 37 | 31 | 11 | 13 | 27 | — | 4 | 11 | 2 | 12 | 7 | — | 22 | 6 | 9 | 19 | 1 | 1 | |
| | | | | +1s | +2s | +1s | | | | | +4s | +4s | +1s | +6s | +1s | +1s | | +1s | +1s | | +1s | +5s | +5s | | | | |

# BLACKPOOL

| | Ht | Wt | Birthplace | Clubs | League App. | League Gls |
|---|---|---|---|---|---|---|
| **Goalkeepers** | | | | | | |
| Iain Hesford | 6 1½ | 14 2½ | Noola, Kenya | Blackpool | 158 | — |
| Jon Rush | 6 0 | 12 9 | Wellington, NZ | Blackpool | 11 | — |
| (Contract cancelled March 1982) | | | | | | |
| Glan Letheran | 6 2 | 13 10 | Llanelli | Leeds U | 1 | — |
| (Contract cancelled) | | | | Scunthorpe U (on loan) | 27 | — |
| | | | | Chelsea (on loan) | — | — |
| | | | | Notts Co (on loan) | — | — |
| | | | | Chesterfield | 63 | — |
| | | | | Swansea C | 21 | — |
| | | | | Blackpool | — | — |
| | | | | | | |
| **Defenders** | | | | | | |
| Ricky Sbragia | 6 0 | 11 0 | Lennoxtown | Birmingham C | 15 | 1 |
| (Contract cancelled March 1982) | | | | Morton (on loan) | 4 | — |
| | | | | Walsall | 77 | 4 |
| | | | | Blackpool | 26 | 1 |
| Paul Gardner | 5 9 | 12 6 | Southport | Blackpool | 152 | 1 |
| (Contract cancelled March 1982) | | | | | | |
| Terry Pashley | 5 8 | 12 0 | Chesterfield | Burnley | 18 | — |
| | | | | Blackpool | 155 | 4 |
| Gordon Simmonite | 5 10 | 11 4 | Sheffield | Sheffield W | 1 | — |
| | | | | Boston U | (not known) | |
| | | | | Blackpool | 47 | 1 |
| Colin Greenall | | | Billinge | Blackpool | 30 | — |
| Nigel Hart | 6 0 | 12 13 | Golborne | Wigan Ath | 1 | — |
| | | | | Leicester C | — | — |
| | | | | Blackpool | 28 | — |
| David Bardsley | 5 10 | 10 0 | Manchester | Blackpool | 1 | — |
| (Apprentice) | | | | | | |
| Roger Kenyon | 6 0 | 11 8 | Blackpool | Everton | 267 | 6 |
| (Contract cancelled) | | | | Vancouver W | (not known) | |
| | | | | Blackpool | — | — |
| John Butler | 5 9 | 10 10 | Salford | Blackpool | 1 | — |
| (Apprentice) | | | | | | |
| | | | | | | |
| **Midfield** | | | | | | |
| Peter Noble | 5 9 | 10 7½ | Newcastle | Newcastle U | 25 | 7 |
| (Contract cancelled March 1982) | | | | Swindon T | 216 | 62 |
| | | | | Burnley | 243 | 63 |
| | | | | Blackpool | 71 | 12 |
| Wayne Harrison* | 5 6 | 10 2 | Whitehaven | Workington | 4 | — |
| | | | | Blackpool | 86 | 6 |
| Andy Brockbank | 5 10 | 10 9½ | Havering | Blackpool | 28 | 1 |
| John Deary | 5 8 | 11 2 | Ormskirk | Blackpool | 37 | — |
| Willie Morgan* | 5 8½ | 10 8 | Glasgow | Burnley | 183 | 19 |
| (Scotland) | | | | Manchester U | 238 | 24 |
| | | | | Burnley | 13 | — |
| | | | | Bolton W | 134 | 7 |
| | | | | Blackpool | 42 | 4 |
| Stan McEwan | 5 11 | 12 8 | Cambusrethan | Blackpool | 214 | 24 |
| (Contract cancelled April 1982) | | | | | | |
| Ronnie Blair | 5 9 | 11 0 | Coleraine | Oldham Ath | 76 | 1 |
| | | | | Preston NE (on loan) | — | — |
| | | | | Rochdale | 71 | 3 |
| | | | | Oldham Ath | 295 | 22 |
| | | | | Blackpool | 36 | 3 |
| Dennis Wann | 5 8 | 10 11 | Blackpool | Blackpool | 17 | — |
| (Contract cancelled March 1982) | | | | York C | 66 | 7 |
| | | | | Southend U (on loan) | — | — |
| | | | | Chesterfield (on loan) | 3 | — |
| | | | | Hartlepool U (on loan) | 2 | — |
| | | | | Darlington | 121 | 13 |
| | | | | Rochdale | 67 | 7 |
| | | | | Blackpool | 19 | — |
| Jeff Bourne | 5 9 | 11 7 | Linton | Derby Co | 49 | 9 |
| (Contract cancelled) | | | | Crystal Palace | 32 | 10 |
| | | | | Sheffield U | 26 | 11 |
| | | | | Atlanta C | (not known) | |
| | | | | Blackpool | — | — |
| | | | | | | |
| **Forwards** | | | | | | |
| David Hockaday | 5 10 | 10 9½ | Billingham | Blackpool | 107 | 16 |
| Dave Bamber | 6 3 | 13 10 | St Helens | Blackpool | 60 | 19 |
| Paul Fletcher | 5 9½ | 12 10 | Bolton | Bolton W | 36 | 5 |
| (Contract cancelled) | | | | Burnley | 293 | 71 |
| | | | | Blackpool | 20 | 8 |
| Andy Welsh | 5 5 | 8 10 | Fleetwood | Blackpool | 1 | — |
| (Contract cancelled March 1982) | | | | | | |
| Alan McAvoy | 5 6 | 9 12 | Wigton | Blackpool | 6 | — |
| Gerry Hendrick | 5 11 | 10 6 | Dublin | St Patrick's Ath | (not known) | |
| (Contract cancelled March 1982) | | | | Blackpool | — | — |
| Paul Stewart | 5 11 | 11 10 | Manchester | Blackpool | 14 | 3 |

# BOLTON WANDERERS　Division 2

*President:* J. Battersby.

*Chairman:* T. Edge.

*Vice-Chairman:* N. Riley.

*Directors:* G. Ball, G. Hargreaves, S. Jones, G. Seymour, G. Warburton.

*Player Manager:* John McGovern.

*Secretary:* Des McBain.　*Year Formed:* 1874.

*Turned Professional:* 1880.　*Limited Company:* 1895.

*Previous Grounds:* Park Recreation Ground and Cockle's Field before moving to Pike's Lane Ground 1881; Burnden Park 1895.

*Previous Name:* 1874–77, Christ Church FC; 1877 became Bolton Wanderers.

**Football League Record:**
1888 Founder Member of the League; 1899–1900 Division 2; 1900–03 Division 1; 1903–05 Division 2; 1905–08 Division 1; 1908–09 Division 2; 1909–10 Division 1; 1910–11 Division 2; 1911–33 Division 1; 1933–35 Division 2; 1935–64 Division 1; 1964–71 Division 2; 1971–73 Division 3; 1973–78 Division 2; 1978–80 Division 1; 1980– Division 2.

**Honours:** *Football League:* Division 1 best season: 3rd 1891–92, 1920–21, 1924–25. Division 2 – Champions 1908–09, 1977–78; Runners-up 1899–1900, 1904–05, 1910–11, 1934–35. Division 3 – Champions 1972–73. *FA Cup:* Winners 1923, 1926, 1929, 1958; Runners-up 1894, 1904, 1953. *Football League Cup:* Semi-final 1976–77.

*Record Victory:* 13-0 v Sheffield U, FA Cup, 2nd rd, 1 Feb, 1890.

*Record Defeat:* 0-7 v Manchester C, Division 1, 21 Mar, 1936.

*Most League Points:* 61, Division 3, 1972–73.

*Most League Goals:* 96, Division 2, 1934–35.

*Highest League Scorer in Season:* Joe Smith, 38, Division 1, 1920–21.

*Most League Goals in Total Aggregate:* Nat Lofthouse, 255, 1946–61.

*Most Capped Player:* Nat Lofthouse, 33, England.

*Most League Appearances:* Eddie Hopkinson, 519, 1956–70.

*Record Transfer Fee Received:* £340,000 from Birmingham C for Neil Whatmore, Aug 1981.

*Record Transfer Fee Paid:* £350,000 to WBA for Len Cantello, May 1979.

*Previous Managers since the War:* Walter Rowley, Bill Ridding, Nat Lofthouse, Jimmy McIlroy, Jimmy Meadows, Nat Lofthouse, Jimmy Armfield, Ian Greaves, Stan Anderson, George Mulhall.

*Address of Supporters Club:* Supporters Club, Burnden Park, Manchester Road, Bolton.

*Address of the Club Shop or Boutique:* 'The Happy Shop', Burnden Park, Bolton.

**Burnden Park, Bolton BL3 2QR.** Telephone Bolton 389200. Information Service: Bolton 21101. *Ground capacity:* 43,000. *Record attendance:* 69,912 v Manchester C, FA Cup 5th rd, 18 Feb, 1933. *Record receipts:* £53,931 v Everton, League Cup, semi-final 2nd leg, 15 Feb, 1977. *Pitch measurements:* 113yd×76yd.
*How to get there:* Local buses 8, 524, 523, 542, 543. The nearest station is Trinity St in the town centre.
*Match tickets:* Bookable in advance.
*Car parking:* Private car parking only on Burnden forecourt. Large park only 200 yards from the ground. Limited street parking in the vicinity. Multi-storey parks in the town centre.
*Entertainments/catering facilities:* Prerecorded programmes of news, interviews, and record requests. Burnden Sporting Club not now available to the general public. Refreshment bars in each section of the ground and in the Sporting Club.
*Club shop:* On main car park. Open Mon-Sat. Send SAE for mail order list.
*Handbooks/programmes:* Programmes available on subscription from club shop.
*Extra information:* History of club written by Dr Percy Young.
*Club Colours:* White shirts, navy blue shorts, white stockings.
*Change Colours:* All green.
*Club Captain:* Mike Doyle.　*Club Coach:* Walter Joyce.
*Reserve Team Coach:* Charlie Wright.　*Physiotherapist/Trainer:* Peter Nightingale.
*Club Nickname:* Trotters.

# BOLTON WANDERERS 1981–82 LEAGUE RECORD

| Match No. | Date | Venue | Opponents | Result | | H/T Score | Goalscorers | Attendance |
|---|---|---|---|---|---|---|---|---|
| 1 | Aug 29 | A | Chelsea | L | 0-2 | 0-2 | | 16,606 |
| 2 | Sept 5 | H | Luton T | L | 1-2 | 0-0 | Gowling | 6911 |
| 3 | 12 | A | Barnsley | L | 0-3 | 0-2 | | 13,844 |
| 4 | 19 | H | Oldham Ath | L | 0-2 | 0-2 | | 7222 |
| 5 | 23 | A | Derby Co | W | 2-0 | 2-0 | McElhinney, Thompson | 12,066 |
| 6 | 26 | A | Rotherham U | L | 0-2 | 0-2 | | 6998 |
| 7 | 29 | H | Newcastle U | W | 1-0 | 1-0 | Thompson | 6429 |
| 8 | Oct 3 | H | Grimsby T | L | 1-2 | 0-1 | Thomas | 7217 |
| 9 | 10 | H | Leicester C | L | 0-3 | 0-1 | | 7361 |
| 10 | 17 | A | Cardiff C | L | 1-2 | 0-0 | Cantello | 3879 |
| 11 | 24 | H | Cambridge U | L | 3-4 | 2-2 | Henry 2, Kidd | 5751 |
| 12 | 31 | A | Norwich C | D | 0-0 | 0-0 | | 12,991 |
| 13 | Nov 7 | H | Watford | W | 2-0 | 1-0 | Henry, Thompson | 7066 |
| 14 | 14 | A | Shrewsbury T | L | 0-2 | 0-1 | | 4062 |
| 15 | 21 | H | Orient | W | 1-0 | 0-0 | Carter | 5737 |
| 16 | 24 | A | Luton T | L | 0-2 | 0-0 | | 8889 |
| 17 | 28 | A | Crystal Palace | L | 0-1 | 0-0 | | 8839 |
| 18 | Dec 5 | H | QPR | W | 1-0 | 0-0 | Hoggan | 6076 |
| 19 | 19 | H | Charlton Ath | W | 2-0 | 1-0 | Henry, Chandler | 5085 |
| 20 | 28 | H | Blackburn R | D | 2-2 | 1-2 | Thompson, Henry | 16,577 |
| 21 | Jan 16 | A | Chelsea | D | 2-2 | 0-1 | Foster, Henry | 7278 |
| 22 | 30 | A | Oldham Ath | D | 1-1 | 0-1 | Thompson | 9271 |
| 23 | Feb 3 | A | Newcastle U | L | 0-2 | 0-1 | | 14,761 |
| 24 | 6 | H | Barnsley | W | 2-1 | 1-0 | Henry, Thompson | 11,680 |
| 25 | 16 | A | Sheffield W | W | 1-0 | 0-0 | Foster | 16,555 |
| 26 | 20 | H | Rotherham U | L | 0-1 | 0-1 | | 9466 |
| 27 | 27 | A | Leicester C | L | 0-1 | 0-0 | | 10,678 |
| 28 | Mar 2 | A | Grimsby T | D | 1-1 | 1-0 | Henry | 6525 |
| 29 | 6 | H | Cardiff C | W | 1-0 | 0-0 | Jones (pen) | 6269 |
| 30 | 9 | A | Wrexham | L | 1-2 | 1-2 | Thompson | 3202 |
| 31 | 13 | A | Cambridge U | L | 1-2 | 1-1 | Henry | 3430 |
| 32 | 20 | H | Norwich C | L | 0-1 | 0-0 | | 6199 |
| 33 | 27 | A | Watford | L | 0-3 | 0-1 | | 12,937 |
| 34 | Apr 3 | H | Shrewsbury T | D | 1-1 | 1-0 | Thompson | 5833 |
| 35 | 10 | H | Wrexham | W | 2-0 | 0-0 | Henry (pen), Reid | 6221 |
| 36 | 12 | A | Blackburn R | W | 2-0 | 1-0 | Thompson 2 | 11,912 |
| 37 | 17 | A | Orient | L | 0-3 | 0-2 | | 2851 |
| 38 | 24 | H | Crystal Palace | D | 0-0 | 0-0 | | 6280 |
| 39 | 28 | A | Charlton Ath | L | 0-1 | 0-1 | | 3379 |
| 40 | May 1 | A | QPR | L | 1-7 | 0-4 | Henry (pen) | 10,002 |
| 41 | 4 | H | Derby Co | W | 3-2 | 1-2 | Thompson 2, Henry | 5226 |
| 42 | 8 | H | Sheffield W | W | 3-1 | 1-1 | Chandler, Gowling, Henry | 13,656 |

**Final League Position: 19**

### Goalscorers

*League* (39): Henry 13 (2 pens), Thompson 12, Chandler 2, Foster 2, Gowling 2, Cantello 1, Carter 1, Hoggan 1, Jones 1 (pen), Kidd 1, McElhinney 1, Reid 1, Thomas 1.
*League Cup* (4): Berry 1, Kidd 1, Thomas 1, Thompson 1.
*FA Cup* (3): Foster 1, Gowling 1, Thompson 1.

| **League Cup** | First Round | Oldham Ath (h) | 2-1 |
|---|---|---|---|
| | | (a) | 2-4 |
| **FA Cup** | Third Round | Derby Co (h) | 3-1 |
| | Fourth Round | Crystal Palace (a) | 0-1 |

| McDonagh | Nicholson | Brennan | McElhinney | Jones | Gowling | Thomas | Thompson | Hoggan | Cantello | Reid | Bennett | Kidd | Nikolic | Henry | Carter | Hebberd | Peacock | Chandler | Whitworth | Foster | Bailey | Langley | Doyle | Berry | Match No. |
|---|---|---|---|---|---|---|---|---|---|---|---|---|---|---|---|---|---|---|---|---|---|---|---|---|---|
| 1 | 2 | 3 | 4 | 5 | 6 | 7 | 8 | 9 | 10 | 11 |  |  |  |  |  |  |  |  |  |  |  |  |  |  | 1 |
| 1 | 2 |  | 4 | 5 | 6 | 7 |  | 9 | 10 | 11 | 3 | 8 |  |  |  |  |  |  |  |  |  |  |  |  | 2 |
| 1 | 2 |  | 4 | 5 | 6 |  | 12 | 9 | 10* | 11 | 3 | 8 | 7 |  |  |  |  |  |  |  |  |  |  |  | 3 |
| 1 | 12 |  | 4 | 5 | 6 |  | 7 | 9 | 10* |  | 3 | 8 |  | 2 | 11 |  |  |  |  |  |  |  |  |  | 4 |
| 1 | 2 |  |  | 5 | 6 | 7 |  | 9 | 10 |  | 3 | 8 |  | 4 |  | 11 |  |  |  |  |  |  |  |  | 5 |
|  |  |  | 2 | 5 | 6 |  | 7 | 9 | 10 |  | 3 | 8 |  | 4 |  | 11 | 1 |  |  |  |  |  |  |  | 6 |
|  |  |  | 2 | 5 | 6 |  | 7 | 9 | 10 |  | 3 | 8 |  | 4 |  | 11 | 1 |  |  |  |  |  |  |  | 7 |
|  |  |  | 2 | 5 | 6 |  | 7 | 9* | 10 | 12 | 3 | 8 |  | 4 |  | 11 | 1 |  |  |  |  |  |  |  | 8 |
| 1 |  |  | 2 | 5* | 6 |  | 12 | 9 | 10 |  | 3 | 8 |  | 4 | 11 | 7 |  |  |  |  |  |  |  |  | 9 |
| 1 |  |  | 2 | 5 | 6 |  |  | 9 | 10 |  | 3 | 8 |  | 4 | 11 | 7 |  |  |  |  |  |  |  |  | 10 |
| 1 |  | 3* |  | 5 | 6 |  |  | 9 | 10 | 11 |  | 8 |  | 4 |  |  |  | 7 | 2 | 12 |  |  |  |  | 11 |
| 1 |  |  |  | 5 | 6 |  |  | 9 | 10 | 11 | 3 | 8 |  | 4 |  |  |  | 7 | 2 |  |  |  |  |  | 12 |
| 1 |  |  |  | 5 | 6 |  |  | 9 | 10 | 11 | 3 | 8 |  | 4 |  |  |  | 7 | 2 |  |  |  |  |  | 13 |
| 1 |  |  |  | 5 | 6 |  |  | 9 | 10 | 11 | 3 | 8* |  | 4 | 12 |  |  | 7 | 2 |  |  |  |  |  | 14 |
| 1 |  |  |  | 5 | 6 |  | 8* | 9 | 10 | 11 | 3 |  |  | 4 |  |  |  | 7 | 2 | 12 |  |  |  |  | 15 |
| 1 |  |  |  | 5 | 6 |  | 8* | 9 | 10 | 11 | 3 |  |  | 4 |  |  |  | 7 | 2 | 12 |  |  |  |  | 16 |
| 1 |  |  |  | 5 | 6 |  | 12 | 9 | 10 | 11 |  |  |  | 4 |  |  |  | 7* | 2 | 8 |  | 3 |  |  | 17 |
| 1 |  |  |  | 5 | 6 |  |  | 9 | 10 | 11 |  |  |  | 4 |  |  |  | 7 | 2 | 8 |  | 3 |  |  | 18 |
| 1 |  |  |  | 5 | 6 |  |  | 9 | 10 | 11 |  |  |  | 4 |  |  |  | 7 | 2 | 8 |  | 3 |  |  | 19 |
| 1 |  |  | 4 | 5 | 6 |  |  | 9 | 10* | 11 | 3 | 8 |  |  |  |  |  | 7 | 2 |  | 12 |  |  |  | 20 |
| 1 |  |  |  | 5 | 6 |  |  | 9 |  | 11 | 3 |  |  | 4 |  |  |  | 7 | 2 | 8 | 10 |  |  |  | 21 |
| 1 |  |  |  | 5 | 6 |  | 12 | 9 | 10 | 11 | 3 |  |  | 4 |  |  |  | 7* | 2 | 8 |  |  | 6 |  | 22 |
| 1 |  |  |  | 5 | 6 | 7 |  | 9 | 10 | 11* | 3 |  |  | 4 | 12 |  |  |  | 2 | 8 |  |  | 6 |  | 23 |
| 1 |  |  |  | 5 | 6 |  |  | 9 | 10 | 11 | 3 |  |  | 4 |  |  |  | 7 | 2 | 8 |  |  | 6 |  | 24 |
| 1 |  |  |  | 5 | 6 |  | 12 | 9 | 10* | 11 | 3 |  |  | 4 |  |  |  | 7 | 2 | 8 |  |  | 6 |  | 25 |
| 1 |  |  |  | 5 | 6 |  |  | 9 | 10 | 11 | 3 |  |  | 4 |  |  |  | 7 | 2 | 8 |  |  |  |  | 26 |
| 1 |  |  |  | 5 | 6 |  |  | 9 | 10 | 11 | 3 |  |  | 4 |  |  |  | 7 | 2 | 8 |  |  |  |  | 27 |
| 1 |  | 3 |  | 5 |  |  |  | 9 | 10 | 11 | 3 |  |  | 4 |  |  |  | 7 | 2 | 8 |  |  | 6 |  | 28 |
| 1 |  |  |  | 5 |  |  |  | 9 | 10 | 11 | 3 |  |  | 4 |  |  |  | 7 | 2 | 8 |  |  | 6 |  | 29 |
| 1 | 12 |  |  | 5 |  |  |  | 9 | 10* | 11 | 3 |  |  | 4 |  |  |  | 7 | 2 | 8 |  |  | 6 |  | 30 |
| 1 | 3 |  |  | 5 |  |  |  | 9 | 10 | 11 |  |  |  | 4 |  |  |  | 7 | 2 | 8 |  | 12 | 6* |  | 31 |
| 1 |  |  |  | 5 | 6 |  |  | 9 | 10 |  | 3 |  |  | 4 |  |  |  | 7 | 2 | 8 | 11 |  |  |  | 32 |
| 1 |  |  |  | 5 | 6 |  |  | 9 | 10 |  | 3 |  |  | 4 |  |  |  | 7 | 2 | 8 | 11* | 12 |  |  | 33 |
| 1 |  |  |  | 5 | 6 |  | 8 | 9 | 10 | 11 | 3 |  |  | 4* |  |  |  | 7 | 2 |  | 12 |  |  |  | 34 |
| 1 |  |  |  | 5 | 6 |  | 8 | 9 | 10 | 11* | 3 |  |  | 4 | 12 |  |  | 7 | 2 | 9 |  |  |  |  | 35 |
| 1 |  |  |  | 5 | 6 |  | 8 |  | 10 | 11 | 3 |  |  | 4 |  |  |  | 7 | 2 | 9 |  |  |  |  | 36 |
| 1 |  |  |  | 5 | 6 |  | 8 |  | 10 | 11 | 3 |  |  | 4 | 12 |  |  | 7 |  | 9* |  |  |  | 2 | 37 |
| 1 |  |  | 12 | 5 | 6 |  | 8 |  | 10 | 11* | 3 |  |  | 4 |  |  |  | 7 | 2 | 9 |  |  |  |  | 38 |
| 1 | 2* |  |  | 5 | 6 |  | 8 |  | 10 | 11 | 3 |  |  | 4 |  |  |  | 7 | 12 | 9 |  |  |  |  | 39 |
| 1 |  |  |  | 5 | 6 |  | 8 |  | 10 | 11 | 3 |  |  | 4 |  |  |  | 7 | 2 | 9 |  |  |  |  | 40 |
| 1 |  |  |  | 5 |  |  | 8 | 9 | 10 | 11 | 3 |  |  | 4 |  |  |  | 7 | 2 |  |  |  | 6 |  | 41 |
| 1 |  |  |  | 5 |  |  | 8 | 9 | 10 | 11 | 3 |  |  | 4 |  |  |  | 7 | 2 |  |  |  | 6 |  | 42 |
| 39 | 6 | 4 | 18 | 41 | 40 | 3 | 34 | 25 | 34 | 12 | 35 | 10 | 1 | 39 | 11 | 6 | 3 | 32 | 29 | 20 | 5 | 3 | 10 | 2 |  |
|  | +2s |  | +1s | +2s | +2s | +4s |  |  |  |  |  |  |  | +2s |  |  |  | +1s | +3s |  |  | +3s | +1s |  |  |

## BOLTON WANDERERS

| | Ht | Wt | Birthplace | Clubs | League App. | League Gls |
|---|---|---|---|---|---|---|
| **Goalkeepers** | | | | | | |
| Dennis Peacock* | 6 2 | 14 1 | Lincoln | Nottingham F | 22 | — |
| | | | | Walsall (on loan) | 10 | — |
| | | | | Doncaster R | 199 | — |
| | | | | Bolton W | 16 | — |
| Jim McDonagh | 6 0 | 13 9 | Rotherham | Rotherham U | 121 | — |
| (Eire) | | | | Manchester U (on loan) | — | — |
| | | | | Bolton W | 161 | — |
| | | | | Everton | 40 | — |
| | | | | Bolton W | 39 | — |
| Simon Farnworth | 5 11 | 10 11 | Chorley | Bolton W | — | — |
| **Defenders** | | | | | | |
| Paul Jones* | 6 1½ | 12 9 | Ellesmere Port | Bolton W | 411 | 36 |
| Peter Nicholson* | 6 0 | 12 0 | Cleator Moor | Blackpool | 6 | — |
| | | | | Bolton W | 318 | 12 |
| Mike Bennett | 5 7 | 10 0 | Bolton | Bolton W | 49 | 1 |
| Gerry McElhinney | 6 2 | 13 0 | Londonderry | Distillery | (not known) | |
| | | | | Bolton W | 36 | 1 |
| Ian Brennan | 5 10½ | 11 11 | Easington | Burnley | 175 | 11 |
| (Contract cancelled April 1982) | | | | Bolton W | 17 | — |
| Neil Berry | 5 11 | 10 4 | Edinburgh | Bolton W | 3 | — |
| Steve Whitworth | 6 0 | 12 0 | Coalville | Leicester C | 353 | — |
| (England) | | | | Sunderland | 83 | — |
| | | | | Bolton W | 29 | — |
| Mike Doyle | 6 0 | 12 2 | Manchester | Manchester C | 448 | 32 |
| (England) | | | | Stoke C | 115 | 5 |
| | | | | Bolton W | 10 | — |
| **Midfield** | | | | | | |
| Peter Reid | 5 7 | 11 5 | Huyton | Bolton W | 210 | 22 |
| Len Cantello* | 5 10 | 11 13 | Newton Heath | WBA | 301 | 13 |
| | | | | Bolton W | 90 | 3 |
| Dusan Nikolic | 5 8 | 11 10 | Belgrade | Red Star | (not known) | |
| (Yugoslavia) (Contract cancelled Dec 1981) | | | | Bolton W | 22 | 2 |
| Barry Taylor* | 5 7½ | 10 2 | Bolton | Bolton W | — | — |
| Brian Atherton | 5 6 | 9 0 | Bolton | Bolton W | — | — |
| (Contract cancelled Feb 1982) | | | | | | |
| David Kay* | | | Prestwich | Bolton W | — | — |
| Tony Henry | 5 11 | 12 0 | Newcastle | Manchester C | 79 | 6 |
| | | | | Bolton W | 39 | 13 |
| David Hoggan | 5 9 | 10 0 | Falkirk | Bolton W | 65 | 5 |
| **Forwards** | | | | | | |
| Chris Thompson | 5 10 | 11 6 | Walsall | Bolton W | 57 | 14 |
| Alan Gowling* | 6 1 | 12 0 | Stockport | Manchester U | 71 | 18 |
| | | | | Huddersfield T | 128 | 58 |
| | | | | Newcastle U | 92 | 30 |
| | | | | Bolton W | 149 | 28 |
| Geoff Langley* | 5 8 | 10 8 | Gateshead | Bolton W | 6 | — |
| Brian Kidd | 6 0 | 13 0 | Manchester | Manchester U | 203 | 53 |
| (England) | | | | Arsenal | 77 | 30 |
| (Contract cancelled Jan 1982) | | | | Manchester C | 98 | 44 |
| | | | | Everton | 40 | 11 |
| | | | | Bolton W | 43 | 14 |
| Mike Carter* | 5 9 | 10 7 | Warrington | Bolton W | 49 | 8 |
| | | | | Mansfield T (on loan) | 18 | 4 |
| | | | | Swindon T (on loan) | 5 | — |
| John Thomas* | 5 8 | 11 3 | Birmingham | Everton | — | — |
| | | | | Halifax T (on loan) | 5 | — |
| | | | | Tranmere R (on loan) | 11 | 2 |
| | | | | Bolton W | 22 | 6 |
| Wayne Foster | 5 8½ | 11 0 | Leigh | Bolton W | 23 | 2 |
| Jeff Chandler | 5 6½ | 10 0 | Hammersmith | Blackpool | 37 | 7 |
| (Eire) | | | | Leeds U | 30 | 1 |
| | | | | Bolton W | 33 | 2 |

# AFC BOURNEMOUTH

# Division 3

*Chairman:* H. G. Walker LLB.

*Directors:* E. G. Keep, P. W. Hayward, W. J. L. Mackeen, D. R. Lever, G. P. Pound, S. A. Latter, A. W. R. Stock, J. Davidson.

*Secretary:* Mrs C. B. Dowsett.

*Manager:* David Webb.

*Commercial Manager:* D. Dowsett.

*Year Formed:* 1899.

*Turned Professional:* 1912.   *Limited Company:* 1914.

*Previous Names:* Boscombe St Johns, 1890–99; Boscombe FC, 1899–1923; Bournemouth & Boscombe Ath FC, 1923–71.

*Previous Grounds:* 1899–1910, Castlemain Road, Pokesdown; 1910, Dean Court.

**Football League Record:**
Elected to Division 3(S), 1923. Remained a Third Division Club for record number of years until 1970; 1970–71 Division 4; 1971–75, Division 3; 1975–82 Division 4; 1982– Division 3.

**Honours:** *Football League:* Division 3 best season: 3rd, 1961–62, 1971–72; Division 3(S) – Runners-up 1947–48. Promotion from Division 4 1970–71 (2nd), 1981–82 (4th). *FA Cup* best season: 6th rd, 1956–57. *Football League Cup* best season: 4th rd, 1962, 1964.

*Record Victory:* 11-0 v Margate, FA Cup 1st rd, 20 Nov, 1971.

*Record Defeat:* 1-8 v Bradford C, Division 3, 24 Jan, 1970.

*Most League Points:* 62, Division 3, 1971–72. *Three points win:* 88, Division 4, 1981–82.

*Most League Goals:* 88, Division 3(S), 1956–57.

*Highest League Scorer in Season:* Ted MacDougall, 42, 1970–71.

*Most League Goals in Total Aggregate:* Ron Eyre, 202, 1924–33.

*Most Capped Player:* Tommy Godwin, 4 (13), Eire.

*Most League Appearances:* Ray Bumstead, 412, 1958–70.

*Record Transfer Fee Received:* £195,000 from Manchester U for Ted MacDougall, Sept 1972.

*Record Transfer Fee Paid:* £70,000 to Cardiff C for Brian Clark, Oct 1972.

*Previous Managers since the War:* Harry Kinghorn, Harry Lowe, Jack Bruton, Freddie Cox, Don Welsh, Bill McGarry, Reg Flewin, Freddie Cox, John Bond, Trevor Hartley, John Benson, Alec Stock.

*Address of Club Shop:* The Cherry Bees Shop, Dean Court, Bournemouth, BH7 7AF.

---

**Dean Court Ground, Bournemouth.** Telephone Bournemouth 35381. *Telegraphic address:* 'Football Bournemouth'. *Ground capacity:* 19,175. *Record attendance:* 28,799 v Manchester U, FA Cup 6th rd, 2 March, 1957. *Record Receipts:* £15,466 v Portsmouth, Division 4, 2 Oct, 1979. *Pitch measurements:* 112yd×75yd.

*How to get there:* Nearest station Bournemouth on the main line from London (Waterloo). Corporation bus 25.

*Car parking:* Adequate parking for 1500 cars.

*Entertainments/catering facilities:* Refreshment points around the ground.

*Club shop:* Sells all types of souvenirs.

*Handbooks/programmes:* No handbook. Programmes available on subscription.

*Extra information:* The club did not compete in the FA Cup in 1923–24, their first League season, because their election came too late for them to be exempt from the preliminary rounds.

*Club Colours:* All red with single white stripe under arm and down side.

*Change Colours:* All white with single red stripe under arm and down side.

*Club Captain:* John Impey.

*Trainer:* John Kirk.   *Coach:* Harry Redknapp.

*Club Nickname:* Cherries.

## AFC BOURNEMOUTH 1981–82 LEAGUE RECORD

| Match No. | Date | Venue | Opponents | Result | H/T Score | Goalscorers | Attendance |
|---|---|---|---|---|---|---|---|
| 1 | Aug 29 | H | Crewe Alex | W 2-0 | 1-0 | Morgan, Dawtry | 3244 |
| 2 | Sept 5 | A | Mansfield T | W 1-0 | 0-0 | Edmunds | 2950 |
| 3 | 12 | H | Darlington | W 2-0 | 0-0 | Smith, Morgan | 3900 |
| 4 | 19 | A | Halifax T | D 1-1 | 0-1 | Funnell | 1588 |
| 5 | 22 | A | York C | W 1-0 | 1-0 | Dawtry | 2252 |
| 6 | 26 | H | Rochdale | W 1-0 | 1-0 | Dawtry | 5146 |
| 7 | 29 | H | Wigan Ath | D 0-0 | 0-0 | | 4952 |
| 8 | Oct 3 | A | Stockport Co | W 2-1 | 2-0 | Funnell 2 | 2718 |
| 9 | 10 | H | Northampton T | D 1-1 | 1-0 | Morgan | 5241 |
| 10 | 17 | A | Peterborough U | L 0-1 | 0-1 | | 4673 |
| 11 | 20 | A | Aldershot | L 0-2 | 0-1 | | 3704 |
| 12 | 24 | H | Bury | W 3-2 | 2-0 | Graham 2, Funnell | 4894 |
| 13 | 31 | A | Tranmere R | W 1-0 | 1-0 | Heffernan | 1730 |
| 14 | Nov 3 | H | Scunthorpe U | W 2-0 | 0-0 | Spackman, Graham | 5032 |
| 15 | 7 | H | Port Vale | D 1-1 | 1-0 | Spackman | 5798 |
| 16 | 14 | A | Blackpool | W 3-0 | 1-0 | Funnell, Crawford, Brignull | 4665 |
| 17 | 28 | H | Sheffield U | D 0-0 | 0-0 | | 9855 |
| 18 | Dec 5 | A | Hartlepool U | D 1-1 | 0-0 | Heffernan | 1760 |
| 19 | 26 | H | Colchester U | D 1-1 | 1-0 | Goddard | 8829 |
| 20 | 28 | A | Torquay U | W 2-1 | 1-0 | Heffernan, Brignull | 2831 |
| 21 | Jan 23 | A | Crewe Alex | D 0-0 | 0-0 | | 1597 |
| 22 | 30 | H | Halifax T | D 1-1 | 0-1 | Funnell | 4690 |
| 23 | Feb 2 | H | Bradford C | L 0-2 | 0-1 | | 5084 |
| 24 | 6 | A | Darlington | W 1-0 | 1-0 | Crawford | 2443 |
| 25 | 9 | H | York C | W 5-1 | 2-1 | Crawford 2, Williams (pen), Funnell, Edmunds | 4373 |
| 26 | 13 | H | Stockport Co | W 1-0 | 0-0 | Crawford | 5628 |
| 27 | 20 | A | Rochdale | W 1-0 | 0-0 | Heffernan | 1295 |
| 28 | 23 | H | Mansfield T | W 1-0 | 1-0 | Funnell | 5725 |
| 29 | 27 | A | Northampton T | L 0-1 | 0-1 | | 2125 |
| 30 | Mar 6 | H | Peterborough U | D 1-1 | 0-0 | Funnell | 7351 |
| 31 | 9 | H | Aldershot | D 2-2 | 2-1 | Dawtry 2 | 5333 |
| 32 | 13 | A | Bury | D 2-2 | 1-1 | Spackman, Carter | 4087 |
| 33 | 16 | A | Scunthorpe U | W 2-0 | 0-0 | Morgan, Funnell | 1441 |
| 34 | 20 | H | Tranmere R | D 1-1 | 0-0 | Crawford | 5302 |
| 35 | 27 | A | Port Vale | D 1-1 | 0-1 | Morgan | 3004 |
| 36 | 31 | A | Hereford U | W 2-1 | 1-0 | Morgan, Funnell | 3145 |
| 37 | Apr 3 | H | Blackpool | W 1-0 | 0-0 | Funnell | 5146 |
| 38 | 10 | A | Colchester U | W 2-1 | 2-0 | Funnell, Crawford | 2662 |
| 39 | 13 | H | Torquay U | W 4-0 | 1-0 | Morgan, Heffernan 2 (1 pen), Impey | 6398 |
| 40 | 17 | H | Hartlepool U | W 5-1 | 3-0 | Funnell 2, Crawford 2, Impey | 6567 |
| 41 | 24 | A | Sheffield U | D 0-0 | 0-0 | | 18,593 |
| 42 | May 1 | H | Hull C | W 1-0 | 0-0 | Heffernan | 8055 |
| 43 | 4 | A | Wigan Ath | D 0-0 | 0-0 | | 9021 |
| 44 | 8 | A | Bradford C | D 2-2 | 1-1 | Crawford, Goddard | 9768 |
| 45 | 11 | A | Hull C | D 0-0 | 0-0 | | 3387 |
| 46 | 15 | H | Hereford U | D 1-1 | 0-0 | Funnell | 9925 |

**Final League Position: 4**

### Goalscorers

*League* (62): Funnell 16, Crawford 10, Heffernan 7 (1 pen), Morgan 7, Dawtry 5, Graham 3, Spackman 3, Brignull 2, Edmunds 2, Goddard 2, Impey 2, Carter 1, Smith 1, Williams 1 (pen).
*League Cup* (0).
*FA Cup* (4): Funnell 2, Crawford 1, Williams 1.

| League Cup | First Round | Fulham (h) | 0-1 |
|---|---|---|---|
| | | (a) | 0-2 |
| FA Cup | First Round | Reading (h) | 1-0 |
| | Second Round | Dorchester T (a) | 1-1 |
| | | (h) | 2-1 |
| | Third Round | Oxford U (h) | 0-2 |

| Allen | Heffernan | Sulley | Smith | Compton | Impey | Edmunds | Dawtry | Mooney | Morgan | Williams | Brignull | Kelly | Funnell | Speckman | Leigh | Graham | Crawford | Dawkins | Goddard | O'Donnell | George | Carter | Match No. |
|---|---|---|---|---|---|---|---|---|---|---|---|---|---|---|---|---|---|---|---|---|---|---|---|
| 1 | 2 | 3 | 4 | 5 | 6 | 7 | 8 | 9 | 10 | 11 | | | | | | | | | | | | | 1 |
| 1 | 2 | 3 | 4 | 5 | 6 | 7 | 8 | 9 | 10 | 11 | | | | | | | | | | | | | 2 |
| 1 | 2 | 3 | 4 | | 6 | 7 | 8 | 9 | 10 | 11 | 5 | | | | | | | | | | | | 3 |
| 1 | 2 | 3 | 4 | 5 | 6 | | 8 | 9 | 10 | 11 | | 7* | 12 | | | | | | | | | | 4 |
| 1 | 2 | 3 | 4 | 5 | 6 | 7* | 8 | | 10 | 11 | | 9 | 12 | | | | | | | | | | 5 |
| 1 | 2 | 3 | 4 | 5 | 6 | | 8 | | 10 | 11 | | 7 | 9 | | | | | | | | | | 6 |
| 1 | 2 | 3 | 4 | 5 | 6 | | 8 | | 10 | | | 7 | 9 | 11 | | | | | | | | | 7 |
| 1 | 2 | 3 | 4 | 5 | 6 | 11 | 8 | | 10 | | | 7 | 9 | | | | | | | | | | 8 |
| 1 | 2 | 3 | 4 | 5 | 6 | 12 | 8 | | 10 | 11* | | 7 | 9 | | | | | | | | | | 9 |
| | 2 | 3 | 4 | 5 | 6 | | 8 | 11 | 10* | | 12 | 7 | 9 | | 1 | | | | | | | | 10 |
| | 2 | 3 | 4 | 5 | 6 | | 8 | 11 | 10 | | | 7 | 9 | | 1 | | | | | | | | 11 |
| | 2 | 3 | 4 | 5 | 6 | | | | | 11 | | 7 | 9 | 10 | 1 | | 8 | | | | | | 12 |
| | 2 | 3 | 4 | | 6 | | | | | 11 | 5 | 7 | 9 | 10 | 1 | | 8 | | | | | | 13 |
| | 2 | 3 | 4 | | 6 | | | | | 11 | 5 | 7 | 9 | 10 | 1 | | 8 | | | | | | 14 |
| | 2 | 3 | 4 | | 6 | | | | | 11 | 5 | 7 | 9 | 10 | 1 | | 8 | | | | | | 15 |
| | 2 | 3 | 4 | | 6 | | | | | 11 | 5 | 7 | 9 | 10 | 1 | | 8 | | | | | | 16 |
| | 2 | 3 | 4 | | 6 | 12 | | | | 11 | 5 | 7 | 9 | 10* | 1 | | 8 | | | | | | 17 |
| | 2 | 3 | 7 | | 4 | | 6 | | 8 | 5 | | | 11 | 9 | 1 | 10 | | | | | | | 18 |
| | 2 | 3 | 4 | | 6 | 7* | | | | 11 | 5 | | 9 | | 1 | | 8 | | 12 | | | 10 | 19 |
| | 2 | 3 | | | 6 | | | | | 11 | 5 | | 9 | 7 | 1 | | 8 | | 4 | | | 10 | 20 |
| | 2 | 3 | 4 | | 6 | 10 | | | | 11 | 5 | | 9 | 7 | 1 | | 8* | | 12 | | | | 21 |
| | 2 | 3 | | | 6 | 4 | | | | 11 | 5 | | 9 | 7 | 1 | | 8* | 12 | 10 | | | | 22 |
| | 2 | 3 | | | 6 | 10 | 12 | | | 11 | 5 | | 9 | 7* | 1 | | | 4 | 8 | | | | 23 |
| | 2 | 3 | 5 | | 6 | 7 | 10 | | | 11 | | | 9 | 4 | 1 | | 8 | | | | | | 24 |
| | 2 | 3 | 5 | | 6 | 7 | 10 | | | 11 | | | 9 | 4* | 1 | | 8 | | 12 | | | | 25 |
| | 2 | 3 | 5 | | 6 | 7 | 10 | | | 11 | | | 9 | 4 | 1 | | 8 | | | | | | 26 |
| | 2 | 3 | 5 | | 6 | 7 | 10 | | | | | | 9 | 4 | 1 | | 8 | | | 11 | | | 27 |
| | 2 | 3 | 5 | | 6 | 7 | 10 | | | 11 | | | 9 | 4 | 1 | | 8 | | | | | | 28 |
| | 2 | 3 | 10 | 5 | 6 | 7* | | | | 11 | | | 9 | 4 | 1 | | 8 | | 12 | | | | 29 |
| | 2 | 3 | 10 | | 6 | | | | | 11 | 5 | | 9 | 4 | 1 | | 8* | 7 | 12 | | | | 30 |
| | 2 | 3 | | | 6 | | | | 10 | 11 | 5 | | 9 | 4 | 1 | | 8 | 7 | | | | | 31 |
| | 2 | 3 | 5 | | 7 | | 10 | | 11 | | 6 | | 9 | 4 | 1 | | | | | | | 8 | 32 |
| | 2 | 3 | 5 | | 11 | | 10 | 8 | | | 6 | | 9 | 4 | 1 | | | | | | | 7 | 33 |
| | 2 | 3 | 8 | | 6 | | 11 | 10 | | | 5 | | 9* | 4 | 1 | | | | 12 | | | 7 | 34 |
| | 2 | 3 | | | 6 | | 11* | 10 | 8 | | 5 | 12 | | 4 | 1 | | 9 | | | | | 7 | 35 |
| | 2 | 3 | | | 6 | | 10 | 8 | | | 5 | | 11 | 4 | 1 | | 9 | | | | | 7 | 36 |
| | 2 | 3 | | | 6 | | 10 | 8 | | | 5 | | 11 | 4 | 1 | | 9* | | 12 | | | 7 | 37 |
| | 2 | 3 | | | 6 | | 10 | 8 | | | 5 | | 11 | 4 | 1 | | 9 | | 12 | | | 7* | 38 |
| | 2 | 3 | | | 6 | | 10 | 8 | | | 5 | | 11 | 4 | 1 | | 9 | | | | | 7 | 39 |
| | 2 | 3 | | | 6 | | 10 | 8* | | | 5 | | 11 | 4 | 1 | | 9 | | 12 | | | 7 | 40 |
| | 2 | 3 | | | 6 | | 10 | | | | 5 | | 11 | 4 | 1 | | 9 | | 8 | | | 7 | 41 |
| | 2 | 3 | | | 6 | | 10 | 8 | | | 5 | | 11 | 4 | 1 | | 9 | | | | | 7 | 42 |
| | 2 | 3 | | | 6 | | 10 | 8 | | | 5 | | 11 | 4 | 1 | | 9 | | 12 | | | 7* | 43 |
| | 2 | 3 | | | 6 | | | 8 | | | 5 | | 11 | 4 | 1 | | 9 | | 10 | | | 7 | 44 |
| 1 | | 3 | 6 | | | | 4 | | | | | | 5 | 12 | | 8 | 9 | 2 | 10* | 11 | | 7 | 45 |
| | 2 | 3 | | | 6 | | 10 | 8 | | | 5 | | 11 | 4 | 1 | | 9 | | | | | 7 | 46 |
| 10 | 45 | 46 | 22 | 20 | 43 | 13 | 27 | 6 | 25 | 36 | 29 | 13 | 40 | 34 | 36 | 5 | 27 | 3 | 6 | 3 | 2 | 15 | |
| | | | | | | + | + | | | + | | + | + | | | | + | + | + | + | + | | |
| | | | | | | 1s | 2s | | | 1s | | 3s | 1s | | | | 1s | 2s | 3s | 4s | 1s | | |

## AFC BOURNEMOUTH

| | Ht | Wt | Birthplace | Clubs | League App. | League Gls |
|---|---|---|---|---|---|---|
| **Goalkeepers** | | | | | | |
| Ken Allen | 6 4 | 13 8 | Thornaby on Tees | Bournemouth | 134 | — |
| Ian Leigh | 5 11 | 12 3 | Ilfracombe | Bournemouth | 36 | — |
| **Defenders** | | | | | | |
| John Impey | 5 11 | 11 12 | Exeter | Cardiff C | 21 | — |
| | | | | Bournemouth | 257 | 7 |
| David Webb | 5 10½ | 12 11 | London | Orient | 62 | 3 |
| (Non-contract) | | | | Southampton | 75 | 2 |
| | | | | Chelsea | 230 | 21 |
| | | | | QPR | 116 | 7 |
| | | | | Leicester C | 33 | — |
| | | | | Derby Co | 26 | 1 |
| | | | | Bournemouth | 10 | — |
| Paul Compton | 6 1½ | 13 1 | Stroud | Trowbridge T | (not known) | |
| | | | | Bournemouth | 51 | — |
| Phil Brignull | 6 0 | 11 2 | Stratford | West Ham U | 1 | — |
| | | | | Bournemouth | 29 | 2 |
| Derek Dawkins | 5 10 | 11 3 | Edmonton | Leicester C | 3 | — |
| | | | | Mansfield T | 73 | — |
| | | | | Bournemouth | 5 | — |
| Chris Sulley | 5 8 | 10 0 | Camberwell | Chelsea | — | — |
| | | | | Bournemouth | 54 | — |
| **Midfield** | | | | | | |
| Tom Heffernan | 6 2 | 12 7 | Dublin | Tottenham H | — | — |
| | | | | Bournemouth | 111 | 11 |
| Billy Elliott | 5 10 | 11 6 | Poole | Plymouth Arg | — | — |
| (Contract cancelled June 1981) | | | | Bournemouth | 11 | 1 |
| Gary Pugh | 6 1 | 12 10 | Ramsgate | Dover | (not known) | |
| (Contract cancelled April 1982) | | | | Bournemouth | 3 | 1 |
| Keith Williams | 5 9 | 11 7 | Burtwood | Aston V | — | — |
| | | | | Northampton T | 131 | 6 |
| | | | | Bournemouth | 37 | 1 |
| Brian O'Donnell | 5 8½ | 10 12 | Port Glasgow | Bournemouth | — | — |
| | | | | Bristol R | — | — |
| | | | | Blacktown C | (not known) | |
| | | | | Bournemouth | 7 | — |
| Howard Goddard | 5 9 | 12 0 | Over Wallop | Bournemouth | 64 | 18 |
| | | | | Swindon T | 13 | — |
| | | | | Newport Co | 105 | 42 |
| | | | | Blackpool (on loan) | 4 | 2 |
| | | | | Bournemouth | 9 | 2 |
| Milton Graham | 5 10½ | 12 4 | Tottenham | Bournemouth | 5 | 3 |
| Paul Edmunds | 5 8 | 10 10 | Leicester | Leicester C | 8 | 2 |
| (Contract cancelled April 1982) | | | | Bournemouth | 14 | 2 |
| Tony Funnell | 5 6½ | 10 10 | Eastbourne | Southampton | 17 | 8 |
| | | | | Gillingham | 33 | 10 |
| | | | | Brentford | 32 | 8 |
| | | | | Bournemouth | 43 | 16 |
| **Forwards** | | | | | | |
| Andy Crawford | 5 7 | 10 4 | Filey | Derby Co | 21 | 4 |
| | | | | Blackburn R | 56 | 21 |
| | | | | Bournemouth | 28 | 10 |
| Steve Carter | 5 8 | 10 10 | Gt Yarmouth | Manchester C | 6 | 2 |
| (Non-contract) | | | | Notts Co | 188 | 21 |
| | | | | Derby Co | 33 | — |
| | | | | Notts Co | — | — |
| | | | | Bournemouth | 16 | 1 |
| Nigel Spackman | 6 1 | 12 4 | Romsey | Bournemouth | 79 | 6 |
| Danny Bailey | | | Leyton | Bournemouth | 2 | — |
| (Apprentice) | | | | | | |
| Neil Prosser | 5 7 | 10 10 | Edmonton | Harlow T | (not known) | |
| (Contract cancelled Nov 1981) | | | | Bournemouth | 2 | — |
| Dean Mooney | 6 2 | 12 12 | Paddington | Orient | 22 | 3 |
| | | | | Walthamstow A | (not known) | |
| | | | | Haugar | (not known) | |
| | | | | Gais (Sweden) | (not known) | |
| | | | | Bournemouth | 27 | 10 |
| Trevor Morgan | 6 1 | 13 1 | Forest Gate | Leytonstone | (not known) | |
| | | | | Bournemouth | 53 | 13 |
| | | | | Mansfield T | 12 | 6 |
| | | | | Bournemouth | 14 | 4 |
| Kevin Dawtry | 5 6 | 9 10 | Hythe | Southampton | 1 | — |
| | | | | Crystal Palace | — | — |
| | | | | Bournemouth | 38 | 6 |
| Brian Mundee | | | London | Bournemouth | — | — |

# BRADFORD CITY Division 3

*Chairman:* R. Martin.
*Vice-Chairman:* J. H. Garside.
*Directors:* E. Sutcliffe, R. Stead.
*Manager:* Roy McFarland.
*Secretary:* T. F. Newman.
*Year Formed:* 1903.
*Turned Professional:* 1903.
*Limited Company:* 1908.

**Football League Record:**
1903 Elected to Division 2; 1908–22 Division 1; 1922–27 Division 2; 1927–29 Division 3(N); 1929–37 Division 2; 1937–61 Division 3; 1961–69 Division 4; 1969–72 Division 3; 1972–77 Division 4; 1977–78 Division 3; 1978–82 Division 4; 1982– Division 3.

**Honours:** *Football League:* Division 1 best season: 5th, 1910–11; Division 2 – Champions 1907–08; Division 3(N) – Champions 1928–29. *FA Cup:* Winners 1911 (first holders of the present trophy). *Football League Cup* best season: 5th rd, 1965.

*Record Victory:* 11-1 v Rotherham U, Division 3(N), 25 Aug, 1928.

*Record Defeat:* 1-9 v Colchester U, Division 4, 30 Dec, 1961.

*Most League Points:* 63, Division 3(N), 1928–29. *Three points win:* 91, Division 4, 1981–82.

*Most League Goals:* 128, Division 3(N), 1928–29.

*Highest League Scorer in Season:* David Layne, 34, Division 4, 1961–62.

*Most League Goals in Total Aggregate:* Frank O'Rourke, 88, 1906–13.

*Most Capped Player:* Harry Hampton, 9, Ireland.

*Most League Appearances:* Ian Cooper, 443, 1965–77.

*Record Transfer Fee Received:* £50,000 from Walsall for Stephen Baines, July 1980.

*Record Transfer Fee Paid:* £31,000 to Burnley for Billy Ingham, Aug 1980.

*Previous Managers since the War:* Jack Barker, John Milburn, David Steele, Ivor Powell, Peter Jackson, Bob Brocklebank, Bill Harris, Willie Watson, Grenville Hair, Jimmy Wheeler, Bryan Edwards, Bobby Kennedy, John Napier, George Mulhall.

---

**Valley Parade Ground, Bradford BD8 7DY.** Telephone Bradford 306062. *Ground capacity:* 16,000. *Record attendance:* 39,146 v Burnley, FA Cup 4th rd, 11 March, 1911. *Record receipts:* £27,000 v Southampton, FA Cup 6th rd, 6 March, 1976. *Pitch measurements:* 110yd×76yd.

*How to get there:* Ground situated approximately ¾ mile from city centre along Manningham Lane. Corporation buses 23–26 from Cheapside plus specials. West Yorkshire buses from Chester St bus station. The nearest railway station is Bradford Exchange. By road, the ground is approximately ¼ mile from Ring Road towards Bradford.

*Car parking:* Street parking in most side-streets. No parking in Valley Parade or South Parade.

*Entertainments/catering facilities:* Hot drinks, pies, crisps, etc. available at snack bars in the ground.

*Club shop:* Adjacent to ground entrance; sells all types of souvenirs.

*Handbooks/programmes:* Programmes will be sent on receipt of remittance and SAE c/o City Shop, Valley Parade.

*Extra information:* A Bradford firm designed the present FA Cup, the third actual trophy, in 1910. The first club to win it was Bradford City in 1911.

*Club Colours:* White shirts with amber and claret trimmings, claret shorts, claret stockings.

*Change Colours:* Amber shirts with amber shorts, amber stockings.

*Club Captain:* Joe Cooke.

*Coach:* Mick Jones. *First Team Trainer:* Brian Edwards.

*Club Nickname:* The Bantams.

## BRADFORD CITY 1981–82 LEAGUE RECORD

| Match No. | Date | Venue | Opponents | Result | H/T Score | Goalscorers | Atten-dance |
|---|---|---|---|---|---|---|---|
| 1 | Aug 29 | H | Wigan Ath | D 3-3 | 2-3 | Campbell 2, Black | 4229 |
| 2 | Sept 5 | A | Hull C | L 1-2 | 0-1 | Campbell | 3916 |
| 3 | 12 | H | York C | W 6-2 | 3-1 | Campbell 3 (1 pen), Jackson 2, Black | 3601 |
| 4 | 19 | A | Hereford U | W 2-1 | 2-0 | Gallagher, Campbell | 2802 |
| 5 | 22 | A | Darlington | W 5-1 | 2-0 | Gallagher 2, McNiven 2, Ingham | 2303 |
| 6 | 26 | H | Colchester U | W 2-1 | 1-0 | Gallagher, Staniforth | 4772 |
| 7 | 30 | H | Rochdale | W 2-0 | 2-0 | Gallagher, McNiven | 5388 |
| 8 | Oct 3 | A | Scunthorpe U | W 3-1 | 1-1 | Gallagher, Partridge (og), McNiven | 3229 |
| 9 | 11 | H | Aldershot | W 4-1 | 0-1 | Black (pen), McFarland, Campbell, McNiven | 6254 |
| 10 | 17 | A | Northampton T | W 2-0 | 0-0 | Campbell 2 | 2053 |
| 11 | 19 | A | Stockport Co | W 3-2 | 2-2 | Staniforth, Campbell, McNiven | 3684 |
| 12 | 24 | H | Sheffield U | L 0-2 | 0-2 | | 13,711 |
| 13 | 31 | A | Torquay U | L 0-2 | 0-2 | | 3144 |
| 14 | Nov 4 | H | Port Vale | W 1-0 | 1-0 | Black (pen) | 4043 |
| 15 | 8 | H | Hartlepool U | W 1-0 | 1-0 | Jackson | 5753 |
| 16 | 14 | A | Tranmere R | D 1-1 | 1-0 | Gallagher | 3218 |
| 17 | Dec 5 | H | Peterborough U | W 2-0 | 2-0 | Jackson, McNiven | 4875 |
| 18 | Jan 3 | H | Darlington | W 3-0 | 2-0 | Jackson, Gallagher, Staniforth | 4473 |
| 19 | 9 | H | Hull C | D 1-1 | 0-1 | Staniforth | 5183 |
| 20 | 20 | H | Mansfield T | L 3-4 | 1-1 | Gallagher 2 (2 pens), Wood | 3729 |
| 21 | 23 | A | Wigan Ath | L 1-4 | 1-2 | Campbell | 7107 |
| 22 | 30 | H | Hereford U | D 0-0 | 0-0 | | 3734 |
| 23 | Feb 2 | A | AFC Bournemouth | W 2-0 | 1-0 | McNiven, Gallagher | 5084 |
| 24 | 6 | A | York C | W 3-0 | 2-0 | Jackson, Campbell, Black (pen) | 3093 |
| 25 | 14 | H | Scunthorpe U | D 0-0 | 0-0 | | 5103 |
| 26 | 19 | A | Colchester U | W 2-1 | 1-0 | Jackson, McNiven | 3975 |
| 27 | 24 | H | Bury | D 1-1 | 0-1 | Staniforth | 5468 |
| 28 | 28 | A | Aldershot | W 2-0 | 2-0 | McNiven 2 | 2721 |
| 29 | Mar 3 | A | Blackpool | L 0-1 | 0-1 | | 4004 |
| 30 | 7 | H | Northampton T | W 2-1 | 1-0 | McNiven, Campbell | 4836 |
| 31 | 10 | H | Stockport Co | W 5-1 | 0-1 | Campbell 2, Staniforth, Chapman, McNiven | 3941 |
| 32 | 15 | A | Port Vale | D 1-1 | 0-0 | Campbell | 4325 |
| 33 | 21 | H | Torquay U | W 3-0 | 2-0 | Lester, Gallagher (pen), Jones (og) | 4774 |
| 34 | 23 | A | Halifax T | D 0-0 | 0-0 | | 5926 |
| 35 | 27 | A | Hartlepool U | W 2-0 | 2-0 | Gallagher (pen), Bird (og) | 2512 |
| 36 | 30 | A | Sheffield U | D 1-1 | 0-1 | Gallagher (pen) | 24,593 |
| 37 | Apr 3 | H | Tranmere R | D 1-1 | 0-1 | Campbell | 4489 |
| 38 | 10 | H | Halifax T | W 5-2 | 2-0 | Gallagher 2 (1 pen), Cooke, Campbell, McNiven | 5179 |
| 39 | 12 | A | Bury | D 1-1 | 0-0 | Campbell | 5231 |
| 40 | 17 | A | Peterborough U | L 0-2 | 0-1 | | 6756 |
| 41 | 24 | H | Blackpool | W 1-0 | 0-0 | Campbell | 4898 |
| 42 | 26 | H | Crewe Alex | W 1-0 | 0-0 | Campbell | 2009 |
| 43 | May 1 | A | Rochdale | D 1-1 | 1-1 | Staniforth | 3080 |
| 44 | 5 | H | Crewe Alex | W 4-1 | 2-0 | McNiven 4 | 5393 |
| 45 | 8 | H | AFC Bournemouth | D 2-2 | 1-1 | Campbell 2 | 9768 |
| 46 | 15 | A | Mansfield T | W 2-0 | 1-0 | McNiven, Jackson | 3107 |

**Final League Position: 2**

### Goalscorers

*League* (88): Campbell 24 (1 pen), McNiven 19, Gallagher 16 (6 pens), Jackson 8, Staniforth 7, Black 5 (3 pens), Chapman 1, Cooke 1, Ingham 1, Lester 1, McFarland 1, Wood 1, own goals 3.
*League Cup* (11): Campbell 3, Black 2 (1 pen), Gallagher 2 (1 pen), Ingham 1, Watson 1, own goals 2.
*FA Cup* (0).

| | | | |
|---|---|---|---|
| **League Cup** | First Round | Blackpool (h) | 3-1 |
| | | (a) | 0-0 |
| | Second Round | Mansfield T (h) | 3-4 |
| | | (a) | 2-0 |
| | Third Round | Ipswich T (a) | 1-1 |
| | | (h) | 2-3 |
| **FA Cup** | First Round | Scunthorpe U (a) | 0-1 |

| Smith | Podd | Watson | Ingham | Jackson | McFarland | Gallagher | Black | Campbell | McNiven | Chapman | Thompson | Staniforth | Wood | Ramsbottom | Ellis | Cooke | Lester | Match No. |
|---|---|---|---|---|---|---|---|---|---|---|---|---|---|---|---|---|---|---|
| 1 | 2 | 3 | 4 | 5 | 6 | 7 | 8 | 9 | 10 | 11 | | | | | | | | 1 |
| 1 | 2 | 3 | 4 | 5 | 6 | 7 | 8 | 9 | 10 | 11 | | | | | | | | 2 |
| 1 | 2 | 3 | 4 | 5 | | 7* | 8 | 9 | 10 | 11 | 6 | 12 | | | | | | 3 |
| 1 | 2 | 3 | 4 | 5 | 6 | 7 | 8 | 9 | 10 | 11 | | | | | | | | 4 |
| 1 | 2 | 3 | 4 | 5 | 6 | 7 | 8 | 9 | 10 | 11 | | | | | | | | 5 |
| 1 | 2 | 3 | 4 | 5 | 6 | 7 | | 9 | 10 | 11 | | 8 | | | | | | 6 |
| 1 | 2 | 3 | 4 | 5 | 6 | 7 | 8 | 9 | 10 | 11 | | | | | | | | 7 |
| 1 | 2 | 3 | 4 | 5 | | 7 | 8 | 9 | 10 | 11 | 6 | | | | | | | 8 |
| 1 | 2 | 3 | 4 | 5 | 6 | | 8 | 9 | 10 | 11 | | 7 | | | | | | 9 |
| 1 | 2 | 3 | 4 | 5 | 6 | | 8 | 9 | 10 | 11 | | 7 | | | | | | 10 |
| 1 | 2 | 3 | 4 | 5 | 6* | | 8 | 9 | 10 | 11 | | 7 | 12 | | | | | 11 |
| 1 | 2 | 3 | 4 | 5 | 6* | | 8 | 9 | 10 | 11 | | 7 | 12 | | | | | 12 |
| | 2 | 3 | 4 | 5 | | 7 | 8 | 9 | 10 | 11* | | 6 | | 1 | 12 | | | 13 |
| | 2 | 3 | 4 | 5 | | 7 | 8 | 9 | 10 | 11 | | 6 | | 1 | | | | 14 |
| | 2 | 3 | 4 | 5 | | 7 | 8 | 9 | 10 | 11 | | 6 | | 1 | | | | 15 |
| | 2 | | 4 | 5 | 6 | 7 | 8 | 9 | 10 | 11 | | 3 | | 1 | | | | 16 |
| | 2 | 3 | 4 | 5 | | 7 | | 9 | 10* | 12 | | 8 | 6 | 1 | 11 | | | 17 |
| | 2 | 3 | 4 | 5 | | 7 | | 9 | 10 | | | 8 | 6 | 1 | 11 | | | 18 |
| | 2 | 3 | 4 | 5 | | 7 | | 9 | 10 | | | 8 | 6 | 1 | 11 | | | 19 |
| | 2 | 3 | 4 | 5 | | 7 | | 9 | 10 | 12 | | 8 | 6 | 1 | 11* | | | 20 |
| | 2 | 12 | 4 | | 6 | 7 | | 9 | 10 | | | 8 | 3 | 1 | 11* | 5 | | 21 |
| | 2 | | 4 | | 6 | 7 | | 9 | 10 | | | 8 | 3 | 1 | 11 | 5 | | 22 |
| | 2 | 3 | 4 | | 6 | 7 | | 9 | 10 | | | 8 | | 1 | 11 | 5 | | 23 |
| | 2 | | | 5 | 6 | 7 | 4 | 9 | 10 | | | 8 | 3 | 1 | 11 | | | 24 |
| | 2 | | 4 | 5 | 6 | 7 | | 9 | 10 | | | 8 | 3 | 1 | 11 | | | 25 |
| | 2 | 3 | 4 | 5 | 6 | 7 | | 9 | 10 | | | 8 | | 1 | 11 | | | 26 |
| | 2 | 3 | 4 | | 6 | 7* | | 9 | 10 | | | 8 | | 1 | 11 | 5 | 12 | 27 |
| | 2 | 3 | 4 | | 6 | 7 | | 9 | 10 | | | 8 | | 1 | 11* | 5 | 12 | 28 |
| | 2 | 3 | 4 | | | 7 | | 9 | 10 | | | 8 | 6 | 1 | 11 | 5* | 12 | 29 |
| | 2 | 3 | 4 | | 6 | | 12 | 9 | 10 | | | 8 | | 1 | 11* | 5 | 7 | 30 |
| | 2 | 3 | 4* | | 6 | | 12 | 9 | 10 | 11 | | 8 | | 1 | | 5 | 7 | 31 |
| | 2 | 3 | 4 | | 6 | 7 | | 9 | 10 | 11 | | | | 1 | | 5 | 8 | 32 |
| | 2 | 3 | 4 | 5 | 6 | | 8 | | 10 | 11 | | 9 | | 1 | 7 | | | 33 |
| | 2 | 3 | 4 | | 6 | | 8 | 9 | 10 | 11 | | | | 1 | | 5 | 7 | 34 |
| | 2 | 3 | 4 | | 6 | | 8 | 9* | 10 | 11 | | 12 | | 1 | | 5 | 7 | 35 |
| | 2 | 3 | 4 | 12 | 6 | 7 | | 9 | 10 | 11 | | 8 | | 1 | | 5* | | 36 |
| | 2 | 3 | 4* | | 6 | 7 | | 9 | 10 | 11 | | 12 | | 1 | | 5 | 8 | 37 |
| | 2 | 3 | | | 6 | 7 | | 9 | 10 | 11 | | 8 | | 1 | | 5 | 4 | 38 |
| | 2 | 3 | | | 6 | 7 | | 9 | 10 | 11 | | 8 | | 1 | | 5 | 4 | 39 |
| | 2 | | | | 6 | 7 | 12 | 9 | 10 | 11 | | 8* | | 1 | 3 | 5 | 4 | 40 |
| | 2 | 3 | | | 6 | 7 | | 9 | 10 | 11 | | 8 | | 1 | | 5 | 4 | 41 |
| | 2 | 3 | 12 | | 6* | 7 | | 9 | 10 | 11 | | 8 | | 1 | | 5 | 4 | 42 |
| | 2 | 3 | | | 6 | 7 | | 9 | 10 | 11 | | 8 | | 1 | | 5 | 4 | 43 |
| | 2 | 3 | | | 6 | 7 | | 9 | 10 | 11 | | 8 | | 1 | | 5 | 4 | 44 |
| | 2 | 3* | | | 6 | 7 | | 9 | 10 | 11 | | 8 | | 1 | 12 | 5 | 4 | 45 |
| | 2 | 3 | | | 6 | 7 | | 9 | 10 | 4 | | 8 | | 1 | 11 | 5 | | 46 |
| 12 | 46 | 40 | 36 | 30 | 30 | 40 | 16 | 45 | 46 | 32 | 2 | 31 | 13 | 34 | 16 | 22 | 15 | |

```
      +       +       + +         +       + +       +       +
      1s      2s      2s 1s       2s      3s 2s     2s      3s
```

## BRADFORD CITY

| | Ht | Wt | Birthplace | Clubs | League App. | League Gls |
|---|---|---|---|---|---|---|
| **Goalkeepers** | | | | | | |
| Steve Smith* | 6 0 | 12 5 | Lydney | Birmingham C | 2 | — |
| | | | | Bradford C | 105 | — |
| Neil Ramsbottom | 6 1 | 13 0 | Blackburn | Bury | 174 | — |
| | | | | Blackpool | 13 | — |
| | | | | Crewe Alex (on loan) | 3 | — |
| | | | | Coventry C | 51 | — |
| | | | | Sheffield W | 18 | — |
| | | | | Plymouth Arg | 39 | — |
| | | | | Blackburn R | 10 | — |
| | | | | Sheffield U | 2 | — |
| | | | | Bradford C | 54 | — |
| **Defenders** | | | | | | |
| Cec Podd | 5 9 | 10 0 | St Kitts, W Indies | Bradford C | 435 | 1 |
| Mick Wood | 5 11 | 10 13 | Bury | Blackburn R | 147 | 2 |
| | | | | Bradford C | 146 | 9 |
| Peter Jackson | 6 1 | | Bradford | Bradford C | 98 | 10 |
| Alan Hebditch* | | | Wigan | Bradford C | 2 | — |
| Roy McFarland (England) | 5 11½ | 11 4 | Liverpool | Tranmere R | 35 | — |
| | | | | Derby Co | 434 | 44 |
| | | | | Bradford C | 30 | 1 |
| Gary Watson | 5 8 | 10 6 | Bradford | Bradford C | 250 | 28 |
| **Midfield** | | | | | | |
| Barry Gallagher | | | Bradford | Bradford C | 57 | 19 |
| Les Chapman* | 5 7 | 10 4 | Oldham | Oldham Ath | 76 | 9 |
| | | | | Huddersfield T | 133 | 8 |
| | | | | Oldham Ath | 187 | 11 |
| | | | | Stockport Co | 32 | 1 |
| | | | | Bradford C | 93 | 3 |
| Billy Ingham* | 5 5½ | 9 10 | Stakeford | Burnley | 212 | 22 |
| | | | | Bradford C | 78 | 4 |
| John Black | 5 8 | 10 10½ | Glasgow | Wolverhampton W | 6 | — |
| | | | | Bradford C | 40 | 10 |
| Mike Lester | 5 9½ | 11 8 | Manchester | Oldham Ath | 27 | 1 |
| | | | | Manchester C | 2 | — |
| | | | | Stockport Co (on loan) | 9 | 1 |
| | | | | Washington D | (not known) | |
| | | | | Grimsby T | 48 | 10 |
| | | | | Barnsley | 64 | 11 |
| | | | | Exeter C | 19 | 6 |
| | | | | Bradford C | 18 | 1 |
| **Forwards** | | | | | | |
| David McNiven | 5 6 | 11 4 | Stonehouse | Leeds U | 22 | 6 |
| | | | | Bradford C | 188 | 60 |
| David Staniforth* | 6 0 | 12 1 | Chesterfield | Sheffield U | 26 | 3 |
| | | | | Bristol R | 153 | 31 |
| | | | | Bradford C | 115 | 25 |
| Bobby Campbell (N Ireland) | 5 11 | 12 7 | Belfast | Aston V | 10 | 1 |
| | | | | Halifax T (on loan) | 15 | — |
| | | | | Huddersfield T | 31 | 9 |
| | | | | Sheffield U | 37 | 11 |
| | | | | Vancouver W | (not known) | |
| | | | | Huddersfield T | 7 | 3 |
| | | | | Halifax T | 22 | 3 |
| | | | | Bradford C | 108 | 51 |
| John Hanson* | 5 11 | 11 9 | Bradford | Bradford C | 1 | — |
| Mark Ellis | 5 7 | 10 5 | Bradford | Bradford C | 22 | 1 |
| Joe Cooke | 5 11 | 12 7 | Dominica | Bradford C | 204 | 62 |
| | | | | Peterborough U | 18 | 5 |
| | | | | Oxford U | 72 | 13 |
| | | | | Exeter C | 17 | 3 |
| | | | | Bradford C | 22 | 1 |

# BRENTFORD Division 3

*Chairman:* M. M. Lange.

*Directors:* R. J. J. Blindell LLB, E. J. Radley-Smith MS, FRCS, LRCP, D. Tana.

*Manager:* Fred Callaghan.

*Chief Development Executive:* Miss C. Mathews.

*Press Officer/Programme Editor:* Eric White (01-574 3047).

*Year Formed:* 1889.

*Turned Professional:* 1899. *Limited Company:* 1901.

*Previous Grounds:* Clifden Road 1889–91; Benns Fields, Little Ealing 1891–95; Shotters Field 1895–98; Cross Road, S. Ealing 1898–1900; Boston Park 1900–04; Griffin Park 1904.

**Football League Record:**
1920 Original Member of Division 3; 1921–33 Division 3(S); 1933–35 Division 2; 1935–47 Division 1; 1947–54 Division 2; 1954–62 Division 3(S); 1962–63 Division 4; 1963–66 Division 3; 1966–72 Division 4; 1972–73 Division 3; 1973–78 Division 4; 1978– Division 3.

**Honours:** *Football League:* Division 1 best season: 5th, 1935–36; Division 2 – Champions 1934–35; Division 3(S) – Champions 1932–33; Runners-up 1929–30, 1957–58; Division 4 – Champions 1962–63. *FA Cup* best season: 6th rd, 1938, 1946, 1949. *Football League Cup* best season: 3rd rd, 1961, 1969.

*Record Victory:* 9–0 v Wrexham, Division 3, 15 Oct, 1963.

*Record Defeat:* 0–7 v Swansea T, Division 3(S), 8 Nov, 1924; 0–7 v Walsall, Division 3(S), 19 Jan, 1957.

*Most League Points:* 62, Division 3(S), 1932–33; 62, Division 4, 1962–63. *Three points win:* 68, Division 3, 1981–82.

*Most League Goals:* 98, Division 4, 1962–63.

*Highest League Scorer in Season:* Jack Holliday, 38, Division 3(S), 1932–33.

*Most League Goals in Total Aggregate:* Jim Towers, 153, 1954–61.

*Most Capped Player:* Idris Hopkins, 12, Wales.

*Most League Appearances:* Ken Coote, 514, 1949–64.

*Record Transfer Fee Received:* £60,000 from Sheffield W for Andy McCulloch, June 1979.

*Record Transfer Fee Paid:* £65,000 to Bury for Alan Whitehead, July 1981.

*Previous Managers since the War:* Harry Curtis, Jackie Gibbons, Jimmy Bain, Tom Lawton, Bill Dodgin (Snr), Malcolm McDonald, Tommy Cavanagh, Billy Gray, Jimmy Sirrel, Frank Blunstone, Mike Everitt, John Docherty, Bill Dodgin (Jnr).

*Address of Supporters Club:* Same as Football Club.

*Address of the Club Shop or Boutique:* c/o the Club.

---

**Griffin Park, Braemar Rd, Brentford, Middlesex TW8 0NT.** Telephone 01-560 2021. *Ground capacity:* 37,000 (30,500 under cover). *Record attendance:* 39,626 v Preston NE, FA Cup 6th rd, 5 March, 1938. *Record receipts:* £16,799 v Fulham, Division 3, 13 Sept, 1980. *Pitch measurements:* 114yd×75yd.

*How to get there:* South Ealing (Underground, Piccadilly line). Southern Region trains from Waterloo to Brentford Central. Buses 91, 65, 117, E1, E2, 267. The ground is within a mile of the M4 and A4 roads.

*Match tickets:* Admission mainly by cash through the turnstiles on the day but tickets for Block B only are available at £2.60 each a fortnight prior to each match. Postal applications should include SAE.

*Car parking:* Confined to streets around the ground.

*Entertainments/catering facilities:* Catering kiosks in the ground. A members' social club, the 'Centre Circle' in Braemar Road.

*Club shop:* Applications for price lists, etc., should be sent to the Commercial Manager, Brentford FC, Braemar Road, Brentford, Middlesex, TW8 0NT, accompanied by SAE.

*Handbooks/programmes:* Programmes not available on subscription.

*Extra information:* One of only six clubs to win all their home games in a season; Brentford accomplished this feat in 1929–30.

*Club Colours:* Red and white striped shirts, black shorts, black stockings with red and white hoop tops.

*Change Colours:* All blue.

*Physiotherapist:* A. E. Lyons. *Player-Coach:* Ron Harris.

*Club Nickname:* Bees.

## BRENTFORD 1981–82 LEAGUE RECORD

| Match No. | Date | Venue | Opponents | Result | H/T Score | Goalscorers | Attendance |
|---|---|---|---|---|---|---|---|
| 1 | Aug 29 | A | Fulham | W 2-1 | 2-1 | Tucker (pen), Brown (og) | 7632 |
| 2 | Sept 5 | H | Walsall | D 0-0 | 0-0 | | 5315 |
| 3 | 12 | A | Portsmouth | D 2-2 | 0-0 | Crown, Booker | 10,364 |
| 4 | 19 | H | Plymouth Arg | D 0-0 | 0-0 | | 4890 |
| 5 | 21 | H | Gillingham | L 0-1 | 0-0 | | 5420 |
| 6 | 26 | A | Doncaster R | L 0-1 | 0-0 | | 5494 |
| 7 | 29 | A | Newport Co | W 1-0 | 0-0 | Tucker | 4026 |
| 8 | Oct 3 | H | Carlisle U | L 1-2 | 0-0 | Johnson G. | 4590 |
| 9 | 10 | A | Exeter C | L 1-3 | 1-0 | Crown | 3689 |
| 10 | 17 | H | Lincoln C | W 3-1 | 3-0 | Booker, Whitehead, Tucker | 4180 |
| 11 | 19 | H | Southend U | L 0-1 | 0-0 | | 5400 |
| 12 | 24 | A | Chesterfield | W 2-0 | 0-0 | Bowen, Roberts | 5525 |
| 13 | 31 | H | Burnley | D 0-0 | 0-0 | | 6930 |
| 14 | Nov 3 | A | Swindon T | W 3-0 | 2-0 | Johnson G., Bowen, Kamara | 6369 |
| 15 | 7 | H | Bristol C | L 0-1 | 0-0 | | 6760 |
| 16 | 14 | A | Oxford U | W 2-1 | 1-0 | Johnson G. 2 | 5461 |
| 17 | 28 | H | Chester | W 1-0 | 1-0 | McNichol | 5200 |
| 18 | Dec 5 | A | Preston NE | W 3-1 | 1-1 | Bowen 2, Johnson G. | 4162 |
| 19 | 28 | A | Millwall | W 1-0 | 0-0 | Roberts | 7474 |
| 20 | Jan 2 | H | Huddersfield T | L 0-1 | 0-0 | | 5440 |
| 21 | 19 | A | Walsall | L 0-3 | 0-2 | | 3853 |
| 22 | 23 | H | Fulham | L 0-1 | 0-0 | | 10,830 |
| 23 | 27 | A | Reading | L 1-4 | 1-2 | Sweetzer | 3481 |
| 24 | 30 | A | Plymouth Arg | L 0-1 | 0-1 | | 5008 |
| 25 | Feb 6 | H | Portsmouth | D 2-2 | 1-1 | Tucker (pen), Bowles | 5950 |
| 26 | 9 | A | Gillingham | D 1-1 | 1-1 | Bowles | 3931 |
| 27 | 13 | A | Carlisle U | L 0-1 | 0-0 | | 4942 |
| 28 | 20 | H | Newport Co | W 2-0 | 0-0 | Roberts, Kamara | 4297 |
| 29 | 27 | H | Exeter C | W 2-0 | 0-0 | Whitehead, Bowen | 4931 |
| 30 | Mar 6 | A | Lincoln C | L 0-1 | 0-0 | | 2827 |
| 31 | 8 | A | Southend U | D 1-1 | 1-1 | Kemp | 3765 |
| 32 | 13 | H | Chesterfield | W 2-0 | 1-0 | Roberts, Kamara | 5360 |
| 33 | 20 | A | Burnley | D 0-0 | 0-0 | | 7871 |
| 34 | 22 | H | Bristol R | W 1-0 | 1-0 | Bowles (pen) | 5843 |
| 35 | 27 | A | Bristol C | W 1-0 | 0-0 | Bowen | 5997 |
| 36 | Apr 3 | H | Oxford U | L 1-2 | 1-2 | Booker | 5786 |
| 37 | 9 | H | Millwall | W 4-1 | 0-0 | Johnson G., Booker, McNichol, Roberts | 7460 |
| 38 | 12 | A | Wimbledon | W 2-1 | 0-1 | Hurlock, Roberts | 4513 |
| 39 | 17 | H | Préston NE | D 0-0 | 0-0 | | 5627 |
| 40 | 19 | H | Swindon T | W 4-2 | 2-0 | Hurlock, Bowen, Bowles, McNichol | 5374 |
| 41 | 24 | A | Chester | W 2-1 | 1-0 | Kamara, Johnson G. | 1304 |
| 42 | 26 | H | Wimbledon | L 2-3 | 2-0 | Bowles, Johnson G. | 6612 |
| 43 | May 1 | H | Doncaster R | D 2-2 | 1-0 | Bowen, Whitehead | 4124 |
| 44 | 3 | A | Bristol R | W 2-1 | 2-1 | Roberts, Kamara | 4314 |
| 45 | 8 | A | Huddersfield T | D 1-1 | 1-0 | Bowles (pen) | 4542 |
| 46 | 15 | H | Reading | L 1-2 | 1-2 | Roberts | 4502 |

**Final League Position: 8**

**Goalscorers**

*League* (56): Bowen 8, Johnson G. 8, Roberts 8, Bowles 6 (2 pens), Kamara 5, Booker 4, Tucker 4 (2 pens), McNichol 3, Whitehead 3, Crown 2, Hurlock 2, Kemp 1, Sweetzer 1, own goal 1.
*League Cup* (0).
*FA Cup* (3): Bowen 2, Roberts 1.

| | | | | | |
|---|---|---|---|---|---|
| **League Cup** | First Round | | Oxford U (a) | | 0-1 |
| | | | (h) | | 0-2 |
| **FA Cup** | First Round | | Exeter C (h) | | 2-0 |
| | Second Round | | Colchester U (h) | | 1-1 |
| | | | (a) | | 0-1 |

| McKellar | Tucker | Hill | Salman | Whitehead | Hurlock | Shrubb | Roberts | Booker | Harris | Crown | Walker | Johnson R. | Bowen | Johnson G. | McNichol | Kamara | Bowles | Priddy | Kruse | Sweetzer | Tonge | Rowe | Kemp. | Spencer | Match No. |
|---|---|---|---|---|---|---|---|---|---|---|---|---|---|---|---|---|---|---|---|---|---|---|---|---|---|
| 1 | 2 | 3 | 4 | 5 | 6 | 7 | 8 | 9 | 10* | 11 | 12 | | | | | | | | | | | | | | 1 |
| 1 | 2 | 3 | 4 | 5 | 6 | 7 | 8 | 9 | 10 | 11 | | | | | | | | | | | | | | | 2 |
| 1 | 2 | 3 | 4 | 5 | 6 | | 8 | 9 | 10 | 11 | 7 | | | | | | | | | | | | | | 3 |
| 1 | 2 | 3 | 4 | 5 | 6 | 7 | 8 | 9 | 10 | | 11 | | | | | | | | | | | | | | 4 |
| 1 | | | 4 | 5 | 6 | 2 | 11 | 9 | 10 | | 7 | 3 | 8 | | | | | | | | | | | | 5 |
| 1 | 2 | 3 | 4 | 5 | 6 | | | 10 | 11 | 7 | | | 8 | 9 | | | | | | | | | | | 6 |
| 1 | 2 | 3 | 4 | 5 | 6 | | | 12 | 10 | 11 | 7* | | 8 | 9 | | | | | | | | | | | 7 |
| 1 | 2 | 3 | 4 | 5 | 6 | | | 12 | 7 | 10 | 11 | | 8* | 9 | | | | | | | | | | | 8 |
| 1 | 2 | 3 | 4 | 5 | 6 | | | 10 | 7 | 11 | | | 8 | 9 | | | | | | | | | | | 9 |
| 1 | 2 | 3 | 4 | 5 | 6 | | | 11 | 7 | | | | 8 | 9 | 10 | | | | | | | | | | 10 |
| 1 | 2 | 3 | 4 | 5 | 6 | | | 11 | 7* | 12 | | | 8 | 9 | 10 | | | | | | | | | | 11 |
| 1 | | 3 | 2 | 5 | 6 | | | 11 | 7 | 10 | | | 8 | 9 | 4 | | | | | | | | | | 12 |
| 1 | | 3 | 2 | 5 | 6 | | | 11 | | | | | 8 | 9 | 4 | 7 | 10 | | | | | | | | 13 |
| 1 | | 3 | 2* | 5 | 6 | | | 11 | 12 | | | | 8 | 9 | 4 | 7 | 10 | | | | | | | | 14 |
| 1 | | 3 | 2 | 5 | 6 | | | 11 | 12 | | | | 8 | 9* | 4 | 7 | 10 | | | | | | | | 15 |
| 1 | | 3 | | 5 | 6 | | | 11 | 10 | 2 | | | 8 | 9 | 4 | 7 | | | | | | | | | 16 |
| | | 3 | | | | | | 11 | 10 | 2 | | | 8 | 9 | 4 | 7 | | 1 | | | | | | | 17 |
| 1 | | 3 | 2 | 5 | 6 | | | 11 | | | | | 8 | 9 | 4 | 7 | 10 | | | | | | | | 18 |
| 1 | | 3 | 2 | 5 | 6 | | | 11 | | | | | 8 | 9 | 4 | 7 | 10 | | | | | | | | 19 |
| 1 | | 3 | 2 | 5 | 6 | | | 11 | 12 | | | | 8 | 9* | 4 | 7 | 10 | | | | | | | | 20 |
| 1 | | 3 | 2* | 5 | | | | 11 | | 6 | 12 | | 8 | 9 | 4 | 7 | 10 | | | | | | | | 21 |
| 1 | | 3 | | 5* | | | | 11 | 12 | 2 | 6 | | 8 | 9 | 4 | 7 | 10 | | | | | | | | 22 |
| 1 | | 3 | | | 6 | | 8 | | 2 | | | 11* | | | 4 | 7 | 10 | | | 5 | 9 | 12 | | | 23 |
| 1 | | 3 | 2 | 5 | 6 | | | 11* | 8 | | | | 12 | | 4 | 7 | 10 | | | 9 | | | | | 24 |
| 1 | | 3 | 2 | 5 | 6 | | | 11* | 12 | | | | 8 | | 4 | 7 | 10 | | | 9 | | | | | 25 |
| 1 | | 3 | 11 | 2 | 5 | 6 | | | | | | | 8 | | 4 | 7 | 10 | | | 9 | | | | | 26 |
| 1 | | 3 | 2 | 5 | 6 | | | 11 | | | | | 9 | | 4 | 7 | 10 | | | 8 | | | | | 27 |
| 1 | | 3 | 4 | 5 | | | | 11 | | 6 | | | 9 | | | 7 | 10 | | | 8 | | 2 | | | 28 |
| 1 | | 3 | 4 | 5 | | | | 11 | | 6 | 7 | | 9 | 12 | | | 10 | | | 8* | | 2 | | | 29 |
| 1 | | 3 | 12 | 4 | 5 | 6 | | 11 | 7* | | | | 9 | | 10 | | | | | | | 2 | 8 | | 30 |
| 1 | | 3 | 11 | 4 | 5 | 6 | | 12 | | | | | 7 | | 10 | | | | | 9 | | 2* | 8 | | 31 |
| 1 | | 3 | 4 | 5 | 6 | | | 11 | 12 | | | | 9 | | | 7 | 10 | | | | | 2 | 8* | | 32 |
| 1 | | 3 | 4 | 5 | 6 | | | 11 | 10 | | | | 9 | 8 | | 7 | | | | | | 2 | | | 33 |
| 1 | | 3 | 4 | 5 | 6 | | | 11 | 12 | | | | 9 | 8 | | 7 | 10 | | | | | 2* | | | 34 |
| 1 | | 3 | 4 | 5 | 6 | | | 11 | | | | | 9 | 8 | 2 | 7 | 10 | | | | | | | | 35 |
| 1 | | 3 | 4 | 5 | | | | 11* | | 6 | | | 9 | 8 | 2 | 7 | 10 | | | 12 | | | | | 36 |
| 1 | | 3 | 4 | 5 | | | | 11 | | 6 | | | 9 | 8 | 2 | 7 | 10 | | | | | | | | 37 |
| 1 | | 3 | 4 | 5* | 6 | | | 11 | 7 | 12 | | | 9 | 8 | 2 | | 10 | | | | | | | | 38 |
| 1 | | 3 | 4 | | 6 | | | 11 | | 5 | | | 9 | 8 | 2 | 7 | 10 | | | | | | | | 39 |
| 1 | | 3 | 4 | | 6 | | | 11 | | 5 | | | 9 | 8 | 2 | 7 | 10 | | | | | | | | 40 |
| 1 | | 3 | 4 | 12 | 6 | | | 11* | | 5 | | | 9 | 8 | 2 | 7 | 10 | | | | | | | | 41 |
| 1 | | 3 | 4 | 5 | 6 | | | 11 | 12 | | | | 9* | 8 | 2 | 7 | 10 | | | | | | | | 42 |
| 1 | 2 | 3 | 4* | 5 | 6 | | | 11 | 12 | | | | 9 | 8 | | 7 | 10 | | | | | | | | 43 |
| 1 | | | | 5 | 6 | | | 11 | 4 | 7 | | | 9 | 8 | 10 | | | | | | | 2 | | 3 | 44 |
| 1 | | | | 5 | 6 | | | 11 | 4 | 8 | | | 9 | | | 7 | 10 | | | | | 2 | | 3 | 45 |
| 1 | | | 4 | 5 | 6 | | | 11 | | | | | 9 | 8 | | 7 | 10 | | | | | 2 | | 3 | 46 |
| 45 | 38 | 17 | 40 | 42 | 40 | 4 | 39 | 27 | 19 | 7 | 7 | 1 | 37 | 29 | 26 | 31 | 31 | 1 | 1 | 8 | — | 10 | 3 | 3 | |
| | + | | | | + | | | + | + | + | + | | + | + | | | | | | | | + | + | | |
| | 1s | | | | 1s | | | 1s | 1s | 1s | 2s | | 1s | 1s | | | | | | | | 1s | 1s | | |

88

# BRENTFORD

| | Ht | Wt | Birthplace | Clubs | League App. | League Gls |
|---|---|---|---|---|---|---|
| **Goalkeepers** | | | | | | |
| David McKellar | 6 0 | 11 8 | Irvine | Ipswich T | — | — |
| | | | | Colchester U (on loan) | — | — |
| | | | | Peterborough U (on loan) | — | — |
| | | | | Derby Co | 41 | — |
| | | | | Brentford | 84 | — |
| Paul Priddy | 6 0 | 11 8 | Isleworth | Brentford | 121 | — |
| | | | | Wimbledon | 1 | — |
| | | | | Brentford | 1 | — |
| **Defenders** | | | | | | |
| Danis Salman | 5 10 | 11 8 | Famagusta | Brentford | 220 | 5 |
| Barry Tucker | 5 6 | 10 12 | Swansea | Northampton T | 214 | 3 |
| | | | | Brentford | 164 | 5 |
| Pat Kruse | 5 11 | 12 10 | Biggleswade | Leicester C | 2 | — |
| (Contract cancelled April 1982) | | | | Mansfield T (on loan) | 6 | 1 |
| | | | | Torquay U | 79 | 4 |
| | | | | Northampton T (on loan) | 18 | — |
| | | | | Brentford | 186 | 12 |
| Jim McNichol | 6 0 | 12 10 | Glasgow | Ipswich T | — | — |
| | | | | Luton T | 15 | — |
| | | | | Brentford | 103 | 15 |
| Robbie Johnson | 5 8 | 10 13 | London | Arsenal | — | — |
| (Contract cancelled April 1982) | | | | Brentford | 2 | — |
| Mark Hill | 6 0 | 12 0 | Perivale | QPR | — | — |
| (Contract cancelled April 1982) | | | | Brentford | 56 | 3 |
| Alan Whitehead | 6 3 | 12 0 | Bury | Bury | 99 | 13 |
| | | | | Brentford | 43 | 3 |
| Terry Rowe | 5 7 | 9 7 | Fulham | Brentford | 10 | — |
| (Apprentice) | | | | | | |
| Kevin Teer | | | | Brentford | 1 | — |
| (Contract cancelled April 1982) | | | | | | |
| Tony Spencer | | | | Brentford | 3 | — |
| (Apprentice) | | | | | | |
| **Midfield** | | | | | | |
| Paul Walker | 5 6 | 10 10 | London | Brentford | 55 | 4 |
| Paul Shrubb* | 5 7¾ | 10 4 | Guildford | Fulham | 1 | — |
| | | | | Hellenic (S Africa) | (not known) | |
| | | | | Brentford | 182 | 8 |
| Ron Harris | 5 8 | 11 7 | Hackney | Chelsea | 655 | 13 |
| (Non-contract) | | | | Brentford | 49 | — |
| Terry Hurlock | 5 9 | 13 2 | Hackney | Leytonstone | (not known) | |
| | | | | Brentford | 82 | 6 |
| Stan Bowles | 5 10 | 11 4 | Manchester | Manchester C | 17 | 2 |
| (England) | | | | Bury | 5 | — |
| | | | | Crewe Alex | 51 | 18 |
| | | | | Carlisle U | 33 | 12 |
| | | | | QPR | 255 | 70 |
| | | | | Nottingham F | 19 | 2 |
| | | | | Orient | 46 | 7 |
| | | | | Brentford | 31 | 6 |
| Chris Kamara | 6 1 | 12 0 | Middlesbrough | Portsmouth | 63 | 7 |
| | | | | Swindon T | 147 | 21 |
| | | | | Portsmouth | 11 | — |
| | | | | Brentford | 31 | 5 |
| Bob Booker | 6 2½ | 12 4 | Watford | Brentford | 79 | 17 |
| **Forwards** | | | | | | |
| Gary Roberts | 6 0 | 11 6 | Rhyl | Wembley | (not known) | |
| | | | | Brentford | 59 | 11 |
| Gary Johnson | 5 11¾ | 11 8 | Camberwell | Chelsea | 19 | 9 |
| | | | | Brentford | 52 | 13 |
| Keith Bowen | 6 1 | 11 2 | Northampton | Northampton T | 65 | 24 |
| | | | | Brentford | 38 | 8 |
| Gordon Sweetzer | 6 0 | 11 8 | Toronto | Brentford | 72 | 40 |
| (Contract cancelled April 1982) | | | | Cambridge U | 9 | 3 |
| | | | | USA | (not known) | |
| | | | | Brentford | 9 | 1 |
| Kevin Tonge | | | | Brentford | 1 | — |
| (Apprentice) | | | | | | |

# BRIGHTON & HOVE ALBION Division 1

*Chairman:* M. K. Bamber.

*Vice-Chairman:* K. Wickenden.

*Directors:* N. J. Hyams, D. Sizen, T. Appleby.

*Manager:* Mike Bailey.

*Secretary:* Kenneth Calver. *Year Formed:* 1900.

*Turned Professional:* 1900. *Limited Company:* 1901.

*Previous Name:* Brighton & Hove Rangers.

*Previous Grounds:* 1900, Withdean; 1901, County Ground; 1902, Goldstone Ground.

**Football League Record:**
1920 Original Member of Division 3; 1921–58 Division 3(S); 1958–62 Division 2; 1962–63 Division 3; 1963–65 Division 4; 1965–72 Division 3; 1972–73 Division 2; 1973–77 Division 3; 1977–79 Division 2; 1979– Division 1.

**Honours:** *Football League:* Division 1 best season: 16th, 1979–80; Division 3(S) – Champions 1957–58; Runners-up 1953–54, 1955–56; Division 3 – Runners-up 1971–72, 1976–77; Division 4 – Champions 1964–65. *FA Cup* best season: 5th rd, 1929–30, 1932–33, 1945–46, 1959–60; old 3rd rd 1913–14, 1923–24. *Football League Cup* best season: 5th rd, 1978–79.

*Record Victory:* 10-1 v Wisbech, FA Cup 1st rd, 13 Nov, 1965.

*Record Defeat:* 0-9 v Middlesbrough, Division 2, 23 Aug, 1958.

*Most League Points:* 65, Division 3(S), 1955–56, and Division 3, 1971–72.

*Most League Goals:* 112, Division 3(S), 1955–56.

*Highest League Scorer in Season:* Peter Ward, 32, Division 3, 1976–77.

*Most League Goals in Total Aggregate:* Tommy Cook, 113, 1922–29.

*Most Capped Player:* Mark Lawrenson, 13 (16), Eire.

*Most League Appearances:* 'Tug' Wilson, 509, 1922–36.

*Record Transfer Fee Received:* £900,000 from Liverpool for Mark Lawrenson, Aug 1981.

*Record Transfer Fee Paid:* £400,000 to Glasgow Rangers for Gordon Smith, June 1980.

*Previous Managers since the War:* Tommy Cook, Don Welsh, Billy Lane, George Curtis, Archie Macaulay, Freddie Goodwin, Pat Saward, Brian Clough, Peter Taylor, Alan Mullery MBE.

*Address of Supporters Club:* Albion Shop, Goldstone Ground, Hove.

---

**Goldstone Ground, Old Shoreham Rd, Hove, Sussex BN3 7DE.** Telephone Brighton 739535. *Ground capacity:* 32,500. *Record attendance:* 36,747 v Fulham, Division 2, 27 December, 1958. *Pitch measurements:* 112yd×75yd.

*How to get there:* Buses 5, B5, 9, 26, 40, 55, 19 from Old Steyne and 11 via Brighton station and Old Shoreham Rd. Hove station is five minutes walk from the ground.

*Match tickets:* Postal bookings for tickets four weeks in advance if available.

*Car parking:* Car parking facilities are available a few minutes away at the Greyhound Stadium, Neville Road, and in Hove Station Goods Yard, Sackville Road. There is limited parking adjacent to the stadium.

*Entertainments/catering facilities:* Bars and tea stands around the ground.

*Club shop:* At the ground; sells all types of souvenirs.

*Handbooks/programmes:* Programmes available by post from the club shop.

*Extra information:* In 1933–34 Oliver Brown was Brighton's leading scorer with 12 goals; yet he played in only 8 matches! Missed promotion to Division 1, 1977–78 on goal difference.

*Club Colours:* All blue.

*Change Colours:* All yellow.

*Physiotherapist:* M. Yaxley.

*First Team Coach:* John Collins.

*Club Nickname:* The Seagulls.

## BRIGHTON & HOVE ALBION 1981–82 LEAGUE RECORD

| Match No. | Date | Venue | Opponents | Result | | H/T Score | Goalscorers | Attendance |
|---|---|---|---|---|---|---|---|---|
| 1 | Aug 29 | A | West Ham U | D | 1-1 | 0-0 | McNab (pen) | 30,468 |
| 2 | Sept 1 | H | Swansea C | L | 1-2 | 1-2 | Ritchie | 19,885 |
| 3 | 5 | H | Middlesbrough | W | 2-0 | 1-0 | Case, Otto (og) | 13,386 |
| 4 | 12 | A | Everton | D | 1-1 | 0-0 | Robinson | 27,352 |
| 5 | 19 | H | Coventry C | D | 2-2 | 1-1 | Robinson, McNab (pen) | 15,262 |
| 6 | 22 | A | Wolverhampton W | W | 1-0 | 1-0 | Ritchie | 12,586 |
| 7 | 26 | A | Nottingham F | L | 1-2 | 1-0 | Smith | 19,220 |
| 8 | Oct 3 | H | Manchester C | W | 4-1 | 0-0 | Robinson, Ritchie 2, Williams | 18,300 |
| 9 | 10 | A | WBA | D | 0-0 | 0-0 | | 13,704 |
| 10 | 17 | H | Liverpool | D | 3-3 | 0-2 | Foster, Case, Ritchie | 26,321 |
| 11 | 24 | A | Tottenham H | W | 1-0 | 0-0 | Robinson | 37,294 |
| 12 | 31 | H | Stoke C | D | 0-0 | 0-0 | | 17,862 |
| 13 | Nov 7 | H | Birmingham C | D | 1-1 | 0-1 | Robinson | 18,292 |
| 14 | 21 | H | Notts Co | D | 2-2 | 0-2 | Case, Gatting | 13,854 |
| 15 | 24 | A | Swansea C | D | 0-0 | 0-0 | | 14,459 |
| 16 | 28 | A | Manchester U | L | 0-2 | 0-1 | | 41,911 |
| 17 | Dec 5 | H | Sunderland | W | 2-1 | 1-1 | Smith, Ritchie | 14,251 |
| 18 | 8 | A | Southampton | W | 2-0 | 0-0 | Ritchie, Gatting | 22,128 |
| 19 | 28 | H | Aston Villa | L | 0-1 | 0-0 | | 24,287 |
| 20 | Jan 16 | H | West Ham U | W | 1-0 | 0-0 | Ritchie | 22,620 |
| 21 | 26 | A | Arsenal | D | 0-0 | 0-0 | | 17,922 |
| 22 | 30 | A | Coventry C | W | 1-0 | 1-0 | Ritchie | 11,023 |
| 23 | Feb 6 | H | Everton | W | 3-1 | 1-0 | Grealish, Ryan, Foster | 16,148 |
| 24 | 13 | A | Manchester C | L | 0-4 | 0-2 | | 30,038 |
| 25 | 20 | H | Nottingham F | L | 0-1 | 0-1 | | 17,175 |
| 26 | 27 | H | WBA | D | 2-2 | 1-0 | Ritchie, Robinson | 14,553 |
| 27 | Mar 2 | H | Leeds U | W | 1-0 | 1-0 | Stille | 12,857 |
| 28 | 6 | A | Liverpool | W | 1-0 | 1-0 | Ritchie | 28,574 |
| 29 | 9 | H | Tottenham H | L | 1-3 | 0-1 | Gatting | 27,090 |
| 30 | 20 | A | Stoke C | D | 0-0 | 0-0 | | 9120 |
| 31 | 27 | A | Birmingham C | L | 0-1 | 0-0 | | 13,234 |
| 32 | 30 | A | Ipswich T | L | 1-3 | 0-1 | Robinson | 19,361 |
| 33 | Apr 3 | H | Southampton | D | 1-1 | 1-0 | McNab (pen) | 20,977 |
| 34 | 10 | H | Arsenal | W | 2-1 | 0-0 | Ritchie, Robinson | 21,019 |
| 35 | 12 | A | Aston Villa | L | 0-3 | 0-0 | | 22,731 |
| 36 | 17 | A | Notts Co | L | 1-4 | 0-2 | Robinson | 7920 |
| 37 | 20 | A | Middlesbrough | L | 1-2 | 1-1 | Ritchie | 9788 |
| 38 | 24 | H | Manchester U | L | 0-1 | 0-0 | | 20,755 |
| 39 | May 1 | A | Sunderland | L | 0-3 | 0-1 | | 16,224 |
| 40 | 4 | H | Wolverhampton W | W | 2-0 | 2-0 | Robinson, Nelson | 10,429 |
| 41 | 8 | H | Ipswich T | L | 0-1 | 0-1 | | 17,786 |
| 42 | 15 | A | Leeds U | L | 1-2 | 1-0 | Robinson | 19,831 |

**Final League Position: 13**

### Goalscorers

*League* (43): Ritchie 13, Robinson 11, Case 3, Gatting 3, McNab 3 (3 pens), Foster 2, Smith 2, Grealish 1, Nelson 1, Ryan 1, Stille 1, Williams 1, own goal 1.
*League Cup* (3): Gatting 1, Grealish 1, Ritchie 1.
*FA Cup* (3): Case 1, McNab 1 (pen), Thomas 1.

| | | | | |
|---|---|---|---|---|
| **League Cup** | Second Round | Huddersfield T (a) | 0-1 | |
| | | (h) | 2-0 | |
| | Third Round | Barnsley (a) | 1-4 | |
| **FA Cup** | Third Round | Barnet (a) | 0-0 | |
| | | (h) | 3-1 | |
| | Fourth Round | Oxford U (h) | 0-3 | |

| Moseley | Shanks | Williams | Grealish | Foster | Stevens | Case | Ritchie | Robinson | McNab | Ryan | Smith | Gatting | Digweed | Thomas | Nelson | Stille | Ring | Match No. |
|---|---|---|---|---|---|---|---|---|---|---|---|---|---|---|---|---|---|---|
| 1 | 2 | 3 | 4 | 5 | 6 | 7 | 8* | 9 | 10 | 11 | 12 | | | | | | | 1 |
| 1 | 2 | 3 | 4* | 5 | 6 | 7 | 8 | 9 | 10 | 11 | 12 | | | | | | | 2 |
| 1 | 2 | 3 | 4 | 5 | 6 | 7 | 8* | 9 | 10 | 11 | 12 | | | | | | | 3 |
| 1 | 2 | 3 | 4 | 5 | | 7 | 8 | 9 | 10 | | 11 | 6 | | | | | | 4 |
| 1 | 2 | 3 | 4 | 5 | 12 | 7 | 8* | 9 | 10 | | 11 | 6 | | | | | | 5 |
| 1 | 2 | 3 | 4 | 5 | 12 | 7 | 10* | 9 | 8 | | 11 | 6 | | | | | | 6 |
| 1 | 2 | 3 | 4 | 5 | | 7 | 8 | 9 | 10 | | 11 | 6 | | | | | | 7 |
| 1 | 2 | 3 | 4* | 5 | 12 | 7 | 8 | 9 | 10 | | 11 | 6 | | | | | | 8 |
| 1 | 2 | 3 | 4* | 5 | 12 | 7 | 8 | 9 | 10 | | 11 | 6 | | | | | | 9 |
| | 2 | 3 | 4 | 5 | | 7 | 8 | 9 | 10 | | 11 | 6 | 1 | | | | | 10 |
| 1 | 2 | 3 | 4 | 5 | | 7 | 8 | 9 | 10 | | 11 | 6 | | | | | | 11 |
| 1 | 2 | 3 | 4* | 5 | 12 | 7 | 8 | 9 | 10 | | 11 | 6 | | | | | | 12 |
| 1 | 2 | 3 | 4 | 5 | | 7 | 8* | 9 | 10 | | 11 | 6 | | 12 | | | | 13 |
| 1 | 2 | | | 5 | 6* | 7 | | 9 | 10 | 12 | 8 | 4 | | 11 | 3 | | | 14 |
| 1 | 2 | | 4 | 5 | | 7 | | 9 | 10 | | 8 | 6 | | 11 | 3 | | | 15 |
| 1 | 2 | | 4 | 5 | | 7 | | 9 | 10 | | 8 | 6 | | 11 | 3 | | | 16 |
| 1 | 2 | | 4 | 5 | | 12 | 9* | 10 | 7 | 8 | | 6 | | 11 | 3 | | | 17 |
| 1 | 2 | | 4 | 5 | | | 9 | 10 | 7 | 8 | | 6 | | 11 | 3 | | | 18 |
| 1 | 2 | | 4 | 5 | 12 | 7 | 8 | 10 | 9 | | | 6 | | 11* | 3 | | | 19 |
| 1 | 2 | | 4 | 5 | | 8 | 10 | 7 | 9 | | | 6 | | 11 | 3 | | | 20 |
| 1 | 2 | | 4 | 5 | 12 | 9 | 10 | 7* | 8 | | | 6 | | 11 | 3 | | | 21 |
| 1 | 2 | | 4 | | 5 | 8 | 10 | 7 | 9 | | | 6 | | 11 | 3 | | | 22 |
| 1 | | | 4 | 5 | 2 | 7 | 8 | 10 | 9 | 11 | | 6 | | | 3 | | | 23 |
| 1 | | | 4 | 5 | 2 | 7 | 8 | 10 | 9 | 11 | | 6 | | | 3 | | | 24 |
| 1 | | | 4* | 5 | 2 | 7 | 8 | 12 | 10 | 9 | | 6 | | 11 | 3 | | | 25 |
| 1 | | | 4 | 5 | 2 | 7 | 8 | 9* | 10 | 12 | | 6 | | 11 | 3 | | | 26 |
| 1 | | | 4 | 5 | 2 | 7 | 8 | 9 | | | | 6 | | 11 | 3 | 10 | | 27 |
| | 12 | | 4 | 5 | 2 | 7 | 8 | 9 | | 11 | | 6 | 1 | | 3 | 10* | | 28 |
| | | | 4 | 5 | 2 | 7 | 8 | 9 | 12 | 11 | | 6 | 1 | | 3 | 10* | | 29 |
| | 2 | | 4 | 5 | | 7 | 8 | 9 | 10 | 12 | 11* | 6 | 1 | | 3 | | | 30 |
| | 3 | | 4 | 5 | 2 | 8 | 9 | 10 | 7* | 11 | | 6 | 1 | 12 | | | | 31 |
| | 2 | | 4* | 5 | | 7 | 8 | 9 | 10 | | | 6 | 1 | 11 | 3 | 12 | | 32 |
| | 2 | | 4 | 5 | | 7 | 8 | 9 | 10 | | | 6 | 1 | 11 | 3 | | | 33 |
| | 2 | | | 5 | | 7 | 4 | 8 | 9 | 10 | | 6 | 1 | 11 | 3 | | | 34 |
| | 2 | | 4 | 5 | | 7 | 8 | 9 | 10* | | | 6 | 1 | 11 | 3 | 12 | | 35 |
| | 2 | | | 5 | 4 | 7 | 8 | 9 | 10 | 11 | | 6 | 1 | | 3 | | | 36 |
| | 2 | | | 5 | 4 | 7 | 8 | 9 | 10 | 11 | | 6 | 1 | | 3 | | | 37 |
| | 2 | | | 5 | 4 | 7 | 8 | 9 | 10 | 11 | | 6 | 1 | | 3 | | | 38 |
| 1 | 2 | 12 | | 5 | 4 | 7 | 8* | 9 | 10 | 11 | | 6 | | | 3 | | | 39 |
| 1 | 2 | 12 | | 5 | 4 | 7* | 8 | 9 | 10 | | | 6 | | | 3 | 11 | | 40 |
| 1 | 2 | 12 | | 5 | 4 | 7 | 8 | 9 | 10* | | | 6 | | 11 | 3 | | | 41 |
| 1 | 2 | 3 | 4 | 5 | 6 | 7 | 8* | 9 | 12 | 10 | 11 | | | | | | | 42 |
| 30 | 35 | 14 | 34 | 40 | 25 | 33 | 38 | 34 | 38 | 17 | 24 | 39 | 12 | 18 | 27 | 3 | 1 | |
| +1s | | | +3s | +7s | | +1s | +1s | +2s | +3s | +3s | | | | +2s | +2s | | | |

## BRIGHTON & HOVE ALBION

| | Ht | Wt | Birthplace | Clubs | League App. | League Gls |
|---|---|---|---|---|---|---|
| **Goalkeepers** | | | | | | |
| Graham Mosley | 6 0 | 11 8 | Manchester | Blackburn R | — | — |
| | | | | Derby Co | 32 | — |
| | | | | Aston V (on loan) | 3 | — |
| | | | | Walsall (on loan) | 3 | — |
| | | | | Brighton | 110 | — |
| Perry Digweed | 6 0½ | 11 4 | London | Fulham | 15 | — |
| | | | | Brighton | 27 | — |
| **Defenders** | | | | | | |
| Gary Williams | 5 10 | 11 0 | Liverpool | Preston NE | 112 | 2 |
| | | | | Brighton | 158 | 7 |
| Tony Vessey | 5 9 | 11 10 | Derby | Brighton | 1 | — |
| (Contract cancelled March 1982) | | | | | | |
| Gary Stevens | 5 11 | 11 10 | Ipswich | Ipswich T | — | 2 |
| | | | | Brighton | 92 | 2 |
| Steve Foster | 6 0 | 12 8 | Portsmouth | Portsmouth | 109 | 6 |
| (England) | | | | Brighton | 120 | 4 |
| Jacob Cohen* | 5 8 | 11 10 | Israel | Maccabi Tel Aviv | (not known) | |
| (Israel) | | | | Brighton | 6 | — |
| Chris Ramsey | 5 9 | 10 12 | Birmingham | Bristol C | — | — |
| | | | | Brighton | 3 | — |
| Tommy Mason* | 5 8 | 10 6 | London | Fulham | 6 | — |
| | | | | Brighton | — | — |
| Sammy Nelson | 5 10 | 11 0 | Belfast | Arsenal | 255 | 10 |
| (N Ireland) | | | | Brighton | 27 | 1 |
| Don Shanks | 5 11 | 10 8 | London | Luton T | 90 | 2 |
| | | | | QPR | 180 | 10 |
| | | | | Brighton | 36 | — |
| Steve Gatting | 5 11 | 11 11 | Middlesex | Arsenal | 58 | 5 |
| | | | | Brighton | 39 | 3 |
| Graham Pearce | 5 9 | 11 0 | London | Barnet | (not known) | |
| | | | | Brighton | — | — |
| **Midfield** | | | | | | |
| Paul Clark | 5 10 | 12 5 | S Benfleet | Southend U | 33 | 1 |
| | | | | Brighton | 79 | 9 |
| | | | | Reading (on loan) | 2 | — |
| Giles Stille | 5 9 | 11 9 | London | Brighton | 16 | 4 |
| Neil McNab | 5 7 | 10 10 | Greenock | Morton | 14 | — |
| | | | | Tottenham H | 72 | 3 |
| | | | | Bolton W | 35 | 4 |
| | | | | Brighton | 89 | 4 |
| Moshe Gariani | 5 5 | 9 0 | Israel | Maccabi Nathanya | (not known) | |
| (Israel) (Contract cancelled Sept 1981) | | | | Brighton | 1 | — |
| Tony Grealish | 5 7 | 11 7 | Paddington | Orient | 171 | 10 |
| (Eire) | | | | Luton T | 78 | 2 |
| | | | | Brighton | 37 | 1 |
| Jimmy Case | 5 9 | 12 7 | Liverpool | Liverpool | 186 | 23 |
| | | | | Brighton | 33 | 3 |
| **Forwards** | | | | | | |
| Mike Ring | 5 10 | 10 6 | Brighton | Brighton | 1 | — |
| | | | | Morton (on loan) | — | — |
| Gerry Ryan | 5 10 | 10 12 | Dublin | Bohemians | — | — |
| (Eire) | | | | Derby Co | 30 | 4 |
| | | | | Brighton | 100 | 15 |
| Andy Ritchie | 5 9½ | 11 11 | Manchester | Manchester U | 33 | 13 |
| | | | | Brighton | 65 | 18 |
| Mick Robinson | 6 0 | 13 4 | Leicester | Preston NE | 48 | 15 |
| (Eire) | | | | Manchester C | 30 | 8 |
| | | | | Brighton | 77 | 30 |
| Gordon Smith | 5 11 | 12 0 | Kilwinning | Kilmarnock | 163 | 36 |
| | | | | Rangers | 98 | 35 |
| | | | | Brighton | 65 | 12 |
| Tommy Kristiansen (Contract cancelled March 1982) | | | | Brighton | — | — |
| Mickey Thomas | 5 6 | 10 6 | Mochdre | Wrexham | 230 | 33 |
| (Wales) | | | | Manchester U | 90 | 11 |
| | | | | Everton | 10 | — |
| | | | | Brighton | 20 | — |

Also retained: Mark Fleet*, Matt Wiltshire*, Daniel Deans*.

# BRISTOL CITY
Division 4

*Chairman:* D. Williams.

*Vice-Chairman:* L. J. Kew.

*Directors:* D. N. Coller, K. J. Sage, O. W. Newland, W. I. Williams, B. Boyd, B. Marshall.

*Manager:* Terry Cooper.

*Secretary:* J. Lillington.

*Year Formed:* 1894.

*Turned Professional:* 1897.

*Limited Company:* 1897. BCFC (1982) PLC.

*Previous Grounds:* 1894, St John's Lane; 1904, Ashton Gate.

*Previous Name:* 1894–97, Bristol South End.

**Football League Record:**

1901 Elected to Division 2; 1906–11 Division 1; 1911–22 Division 2; 1922–23 Division 3(S); 1923–24 Division 2; 1924–27 Division 3(S); 1927–32 Division 2; 1932–55 Division 3(S); 1955–60 Division 2; 1960–65 Division 3; 1965–76 Division 2; 1976–80 Division 1; 1980–81 Division 2; 1981–82 Division 3; 1982–Division 4.

**Honours:** *Football League:* Division 1 – Runners-up 1906–07; Division 2 – Champions 1905–06; Runners-up 1975–76; Division 3(S) – Champions 1922–23, 1926–27, 1954–55; Runners-up 1937–38; Division 3 – Runners-up 1964–65. *FA Cup:* Runners-up 1909. *Football League Cup:* Semi-final 1970–71. *Welsh Cup:* Winners 1934. *Anglo-Scottish Cup:* Winners 1977–78.

*Record Victory:* 11-0 v Chichester, FA Cup, 1st rd, 5 Nov, 1960.

*Record Defeat:* 0-9 v Coventry C, Division 3(S), 28 Apr, 1934.

*Most League Points:* 70, Division 3(S), 1954–55.

*Most League Goals:* 104, Division 3(S), 1926–27.

*Highest League Scorer in Season:* Don Clark, 36, Division 3(S), 1946–47.

*Most League Goals in Total Aggregate:* John Atyeo, 315, 1951–66.

*Most Capped Player:* Billy Wedlock, 26, England.

*Most League Appearances:* John Atyeo, 597, 1951–1966 (+48 cup ties).

*Record Transfer Fee Received:* £325,000 from Coventry C for Gary Collier, July 1979.

*Record Transfer Fee Paid:* £235,000 to St Mirren for Tony Fitzpatrick, July 1979.

*Previous Managers since the War:* Bob Hewison, Bob Wright, Pat Beasley, Peter Doherty, Fred Ford, Alan Dicks, Bob Houghton, Roy Hodgson.

*Address of Supporters Club:* Supporters Club, Bristol City FC, Ashton Gate, Bristol BS3 2EJ.

*Address of the Club Shop or Boutique:* City Shop, Ashton Gate, Bristol BS3 2EJ.

---

**Ashton Gate, Bristol BS3 2EJ.** Telephone Bristol 632812 (5 lines). *Telegraphic address:* 'City Bristol'. *Ground capacity:* 30,868. *Record attendance:* 43,335 v Preston NE, FA Cup 5th rd, 16 Feb, 1935. *Record receipts:* £45,000 v Aston Villa, FA Cup 4th rd, 23 Jan, 1982. *Pitch measurements:* 115yd×75yd.

*How to get there:* Buses 79, 59. Parsons St station is available within walking distance for special trains. Also certain scheduled trains stop there.

*Match tickets:* Tickets can be booked any length of time before the match; Postal application must include remittance and SAE. Personal applications not accepted until 4 weeks before the match.

*Car parking:* Season-ticket holders can obtain season car park parking tickets. Coach parking at Cannons Marsh. There is limited street parking around the ground.

*Entertainments/catering facilities:* Social club in the main stands. Tea bars in the ground. Alcoholic beverages only obtainable by members of a bona-fide Supporters' Club. There is a wide variety of pre-match entertainment, and some matches are sponsored, so throw-away gifts to the crowd, and programme prizes, are a regular feature.

*Club shop:* One of the biggest in the country, sells all types of souvenirs, clothing and many other items.

*Handbooks/programmes:* Programmes not available on subscription but postal applications are accepted.

*Extra information:* Indoor bowling area in the main stand. Large room available for functions caters for 200 people.

*Club Colours:* Red shirts, white shorts, red and white stockings.

*Change Colours:* White shirts, black shorts, black stockings.

*Club Captain:*

*Club Nickname:* Robins.

# BRISTOL CITY 1981–82 LEAGUE RECORD

| Match No. | Date | Venue | Opponents | Result | H/T Score | Goalscorers | Attendance |
|---|---|---|---|---|---|---|---|
| 1 | Aug 29 | A | Carlisle U | D 2-2 | 0-2 | Harford, Mann | 3930 |
| 2 | Sept 5 | H | Doncaster R | D 2-2 | 2-0 | Mabbutt, Harford | 6586 |
| 3 | 12 | A | Fulham | L 1-2 | 1-0 | Mann | 4169 |
| 4 | 19 | H | Newport Co | W 2-1 | 0-1 | Mann 2 | 7552 |
| 5 | 22 | H | Plymouth Arg | W 3-2 | 1-2 | Harford, Nicholls, Mann | 7471 |
| 6 | 26 | A | Portsmouth | L 0-2 | 0-1 | | 10,203 |
| 7 | 29 | A | Gillingham | D 1-1 | 0-0 | Harford | 3887 |
| 8 | Oct 3 | H | Walsall | L 0-1 | 0-1 | | 6033 |
| 9 | 10 | H | Preston NE | D 0-0 | 0-0 | | 5389 |
| 10 | 17 | A | Oxford U | L 0-1 | 0-1 | | 3906 |
| 11 | 20 | H | Reading | W 2-0 | 0-0 | Devine, Tainton | 5006 |
| 12 | 24 | A | Lincoln C | W 2-1 | 2-0 | Harford 2 | 3683 |
| 13 | 31 | H | Chesterfield | D 0-0 | 0-0 | | 8442 |
| 14 | Nov 3 | A | Millwall | L 0-2 | 0-1 | | 5002 |
| 15 | 7 | A | Brentford | W 1-0 | 0-0 | Harford | 6760 |
| 16 | 14 | H | Southend U | L 0-2 | 0-0 | | 6381 |
| 17 | 28 | H | Burnley | L 2-3 | 1-1 | Mann (pen), Garland | 4862 |
| 18 | Dec 5 | A | Swindon T | D 0-0 | 0-0 | | 6949 |
| 19 | 29 | A | Bristol R | L 0-1 | 0-1 | | 12,355 |
| 20 | Jan 2 | H | Wimbledon | L 1-3 | 1-1 | Stevens | 4660 |
| 21 | 16 | H | Huddersfield T | D 0-0 | 0-0 | | 4921 |
| 22 | 30 | A | Newport Co | D 1-1 | 1-1 | Harford | 5927 |
| 23 | Feb 6 | H | Fulham | D 0-0 | 0-0 | | 9228 |
| 24 | 9 | A | Plymouth Arg | L 1-2 | 0-1 | Chandler | 5260 |
| 25 | 13 | A | Walsall | W 1-0 | 1-0 | Newman | 4020 |
| 26 | 20 | H | Portsmouth | L 0-1 | 0-0 | | 9397 |
| 27 | 23 | H | Exeter C | W 3-2 | 2-1 | Harford 2, Chandler | 6612 |
| 28 | 27 | A | Preston NE | W 3-1 | 1-1 | McCaffery, Bray, Harford | 6411 |
| 29 | Mar 6 | H | Oxford U | L 0-2 | 0-0 | | 8155 |
| 30 | 10 | A | Reading | L 1-3 | 0-0 | Dixon (og) | 3107 |
| 31 | 13 | H | Lincoln C | L 0-1 | 0-1 | | 6341 |
| 32 | 20 | A | Chesterfield | L 0-1 | 0-0 | | 4230 |
| 33 | 27 | H | Brentford | L 0-1 | 0-0 | | 5997 |
| 34 | Apr 3 | A | Southend U | L 0-3 | 0-0 | | 3133 |
| 35 | 6 | H | Carlisle U | D 1-1 | 0-1 | Chandler | 4329 |
| 36 | 10 | A | Exeter C | L 0-4 | 0-2 | | 4580 |
| 37 | 12 | H | Bristol R | L 1-2 | 0-1 | Bray | 10,791 |
| 38 | 17 | H | Swindon T | L 0-3 | 0-1 | | 6524 |
| 39 | 21 | A | Chester | D 0-0 | 0-0 | | 1034 |
| 40 | 24 | A | Burnley | L 0-2 | 0-0 | | 7039 |
| 41 | May 1 | H | Gillingham | W 2-1 | 1-0 | Williams, Economou | 3931 |
| 42 | 4 | A | Huddersfield T | L 0-5 | 0-3 | | 3468 |
| 43 | 8 | A | Wimbledon | D 0-0 | 0-0 | | 2114 |
| 44 | 12 | H | Millwall | W 4-1 | 2-1 | Newman 2 (1 pen), Chandler 2 | 2696 |
| 45 | 15 | H | Chester | W 1-0 | 1-0 | Chandler | 3934 |
| 46 | 18 | A | Doncaster R | D 2-2 | 0-2 | Thompson, Chandler | 4252 |

**Final League Position: 23**

## Goalscorers

*League* (40): Harford 11, Chandler 7, Mann 6 (1 pen), Newman 3 (1 pen), Bray 2, Devine 1, Economou 1, Garland 1, McCaffery 1, Mabbutt 1, Nicholls 1, Stevens 1, Tainton 1, Thompson 1, Williams 1, own goal 1.
*League Cup* (4): Mann 2 (1 pen), Harford 1, Rodgers 1.
*FA Cup* (6): Harford 2, Mann 2, Chandler 1, Tainton 1.

| | | | | |
|---|---|---|---|---|
| **League Cup** | First Round | Walsall (h) | | 2-0 |
| | | (a) | | 0-1 |
| | Second Round | Carlisle U (a) | | 0-0 |
| | | (h) | | 2-1 |
| | Third Round | QPR (a) | | 0-3 |
| **FA Cup** | First Round | Torquay U (h) | | 0-0 |
| | | (a) | | 2-1 |
| | Second Round | Northampton T (h) | | 3-0 |
| | Third Round | Peterborough U (a) | | 1-0 |
| | Fourth Round | Aston Villa (h) | | 0-1 |

| Moller | Stevens | Merrick | Mann | Rodgers | Marshall | Tainton | Musker | Mabbutt | Harford | Devine | Hay | Sweeney | Aitken | Nicholls | Whitehead | Williams | Boyle | Chandler | Garland | Newman | Smith | Bray | Economou | McCaffery | Carter | Gooding | Shaw | Down | Thompson | Match No. |
|---|---|---|---|---|---|---|---|---|---|---|---|---|---|---|---|---|---|---|---|---|---|---|---|---|---|---|---|---|---|---|
| 1 | 2 | 3 | 4 | 5 | 6 | 7 | 8 | 9 | 10 | 11 | | | | | | | | | | | | | | | | | | | | 1 |
| 1 | 2 | 3 | 4 | 5 | 6 | 7 | 8 | 9 | 10 | 11 | | | | | | | | | | | | | | | | | | | | 2 |
| 1 | 2 | 6 | 4 | 5 | | 7 | 8 | 10 | 9 | 11 | 3 | | | | | | | | | | | | | | | | | | | 3 |
| 1 | 2 | | 8 | 5 | 6 | 7 | 9 | 10 | 11 | | 3 | 4 | | | | | | | | | | | | | | | | | | 4 |
| 1 | 2 | | 8 | 5* | | 7 | 12 | 9 | 10 | 11 | 3 | 4 | 6 | | | | | | | | | | | | | | | | | 5 |
| 1 | 2 | | 8 | 5 | | 7 | 9 | 10 | 11 | | 3 | 4 | 6 | | | | | | | | | | | | | | | | | 6 |
| 1 | 2 | | 8 | 5 | | 7 | 11 | 9 | 10 | | 3 | 4 | 6 | | | | | | | | | | | | | | | | | 7 |
| 1 | 2 | | 8 | 5 | | 7 | 11 | 9 | 10 | | 3 | 4 | | 6 | | | | | | | | | | | | | | | | 8 |
| 1 | 2 | | 8 | 5 | | 7 | 9 | 10 | | | 3 | 4 | 6 | 11 | | | | | | | | | | | | | | | | 9 |
| 1 | 2 | | 8 | 5 | | 9 | 10 | 7 | | | 3 | 6 | 4 | 11 | | | | | | | | | | | | | | | | 10 |
| 1 | 2 | | 8 | 5 | | 7 | 9 | 10 | | | 3 | 6 | 4 | 11 | | | | | | | | | | | | | | | | 11 |
| 1 | 2 | | 8 | 5 | | 3 | 9 | 10 | 7 | | 6 | 4 | 11 | | | | | | | | | | | | | | | | | 12 |
| 1 | 2 | | 8 | 5 | | 7 | 9 | 10 | | | 4 | 11 | 3 | 6 | | | | | | | | | | | | | | | | 13 |
| 1 | 2 | | 8 | 5 | | 7 | 9 | 10 | | | 4 | | | 3 | 6 | 11 | | | | | | | | | | | | | | 14 |
| 1 | 2 | | 8 | 5 | | 7 | 9 | 10 | | | 4 | | | 3 | 6 | 11 | | | | | | | | | | | | | | 15 |
| 1 | 2 | | 8* | 5 | | 7 | 11 | 9 | 10 | 12 | 4 | | | 3 | 6 | | | | | | | | | | | | | | | 16 |
| 1 | 2 | | 8 | 5 | | 11 | 9 | 7 | | | 4 | | | 3 | 6 | 10 | | | | | | | | | | | | | | 17 |
| 1 | 2 | | 8 | | | 11 | 10 | 7 | | | 4 | 6 | | 3 | 5 | 9 | | | | | | | | | | | | | | 18 |
| 1 | 2 | | 8 | 5 | | 7 | 10 | 11 | | | 4 | | | 3 | 6 | 9 | | | | | | | | | | | | | | 19 |
| 1 | 2 | | 8 | | | 7 | 10 | 11* | 12 | | 4 | 6 | | 3 | 5 | 9 | | | | | | | | | | | | | | 20 |
| 1 | 2 | | 8 | | | 7 | 11 | 10 | | | 4 | 6 | | 3 | 5 | 9* | 12 | | | | | | | | | | | | | 21 |
| 1 | 2 | | 8 | | | 7 | 11 | 10 | | | 12 | 6 | 4 | 3 | 5* | 9 | | | | | | | | | | | | | | 22 |
| 1 | 2 | | | | | 7 | 10 | | | | 3 | | | 6 | | 5 | 9 | 4*12 | | | | 8 | 11 | | | | | | | 23 |
| 1 | 2 | | | | | 7 | 10 | | | | 3 | | | 6 | | 5 | 9 | 4 | | | | 8 | 11 | | | | | | | 24 |
| 1 | 2 | | | | | 7 | 10 | | | | 3 | | | 6 | | 5 | 9 | 4 12 | | | | 8 | 11* | | | | | | | 25 |
| 1 | 2 | | | | | 7 | 10 | 11 | | | 6 | | | 3 | | 9 | 4 | | | | | 5 | 8 | | | | | | | 26 |
| 1 | 2 | | | | | 7 | 10 | 11 | | | 5 | | | 3 | | 9 | 4* | | | 12 | 6 | 8 | | | | | | | | 27 |
| 1 | 2 | | | | | 7* | 10 | 11 | | | 6 | | | 3 | | 9 | 12 | 4 | | | 5 | 8 | | | | | | | | 28 |
| 1 | 2 | | | | | | 10 | 11 | | | 6 | | | 3 | | 9 | | 4 | | 5 | 8 | 7 | | | | | | | | 29 |
| 1 | 2 | | | | | 7 | | 11 | | | 6 | | | 3 | | 9 | 12 | 4 | | 5 | 8 | 10* | | | | | | | | 30 |
| 1 | 2 | | | | | 3 | | | | | 6 | | | 9 | | 4 | 7 | 11 | | 5 | 8 | 10 | | | | | | | | 31 |
| | 2 | | | | | 7 | 10 | | | | 3 | | | 6 | | 5 | | 4 | | 8 | 11 | | 9 | 1 | | | | | | 32 |
| | 2 | | | | | 7 | | | | | 3 | | | 5 | | 6 12 | 9 | 4* | | 8 | 11 | | 10 | 1 | | | | | | 33 |
| | 2 | | | | | 4 | | | | | 11 | | | 6 | | 3 | 5 | 9 | 12 | 8 | 7* | | 10 | 1 | | | | | | 34 |
| | 2 | | | | | 4 | | | | | 11 | | | 6 | | 3 | 5 | 8 | | 9 | 7 | | 10 | 1 | | | | | | 35 |
| | 2 | | | | | 4 | | | | | 11 | | | 6 | | 3 | 5 | 8 | | 9 | 7 12 | | 10* | 1 | | | | | | 36 |
| | 2 | | | | | 4 | | | | | 12 11 | | | 6 | | 3 | 5 | 8 | | 9* | 7 10 | | | 1 | | | | | | 37 |
| | 2 | | | | | 4 | | | | | 7* 3 | | | 6 | | 5 | 9 | 12 | | 8 | 11 | | 10 | 1 | | | | | | 38 |
| | 2 | | | | | 4 | | | | | 12 3 | | | 6 | | 7 | 5 | 9 | | 8*11 | | | 10 | 1 | | | | | | 39 |
| | 2 | | | | | 4 | | | | | 8 3 | | | 6 | | 7 | 5 | 9 | 12 | | 11 | | 10* | 1 | | | | | | 40 |
| 10 | | | | | | 4 | | | | | 8 3 | | | 6 | | 2 | 5 | 9 | | | 7 | | 11 | 1 | | | | | | 41 |
| 10 | | | | | | 4 | | | | | 8 3 | | | 6 | | 2 | 5 | 9 | 12 | | 7 | | 11* | 1 | | | | | | 42 |
| | 2 | | | | | 4 | | | | | 8 3 | | | 5 | | 6 | 9 | 10 | | 7 11 | | | | 1 | | | | | | 43 |
| | 3 | 5 | | 4 | | 7 | | | | | | 2 | 6 | 9 | | 10 12 | 8*11 | | | | | | | 1 | | | | | | 44 |
| 8 | | | | 4 | | 3 | | | | | 6 | | 2* | 5 | 9 | | 10 12 | 7 11 | | | | | | 1 | | | | | | 45 |
| | 2 | | | | | 4 | | | | | 6 | | | 5 | | 9 | 10 | 11 | | 8* | 7 | | | 1 | | | 3 | 12 | | 46 |
| 31 | 46 | 3 | 22 | 18 | 3 | 19 | 32 | 11 | 30 | 19 | 33 | 8 | 19 | 27 | 6 | 33 | 22 | 30 | 1 | 15 | 1 | 19 | 17 | 6 | 16 | 3 | 15 | 1 | — | |
| | | | | | | | + | | | + | + | + | | | | + | | + | + | + | | + | | | | | + | | | |
| | | | | | | | 1s | | | 2s | 1s | 2s | | | | 1s | | 1s | 6s | 4s | | 2s | | | | | 1s | | | |

## BRISTOL CITY

| | Ht | Wt | Birthplace | Clubs | League App. | League Gls |
|---|---|---|---|---|---|---|
| **Goalkeepers** | | | | | | |
| John Shaw* | 6 1 | 13 7 | Stirling | Leeds U | — | — |
| | | | | Bristol C | 162 | — |
| David Mogg | 5 9½ | 10 5 | Bristol | Bristol C | — | — |
| Jan Moller | 6 1 | 13 0 | Malmo | Malmo | (not known) | |
| (Sweden) (Contract cancelled April 1982) | | | | Bristol C | 48 | — |
| **Defenders** | | | | | | |
| Geoff Merrick | 5 9 | 11 0 | Bristol | Bristol C | 367 | 10 |
| (Contract cancelled Feb 1982) | | | | | | |
| Paul Stevens | 5 7 | 9 9½ | Bristol | Bristol C | 61 | 1 |
| Allan Hay* | 5 11 | 11 3 | Scotland | Bolton W | — | 1 |
| | | | | Bristol C | 74 | 1 |
| | | | | St Mirren (on loan) | — | — |
| Alan Nicholls | 6 2 | 12 0 | Plymouth | Bristol C | 31 | 2 |
| Gary Williams | 5 8 | 10 1½ | Bristol | Bristol C | 34 | 1 |
| Terry Boyle | 5 10 | 12 4 | Ammerford | Tottenham H | — | — |
| (Wales) | | | | Crystal Palace | 26 | 1 |
| | | | | Wimbledon (on loan) | 5 | 1 |
| | | | | Bristol C | 23 | — |
| Billy Down* | | | | Bristol C | 1 | — |
| Ray Perlee | | | | Bristol C | — | — |
| **Midfield** | | | | | | |
| Ricky Chandler | 5 10 | 11 1 | Bristol | Bristol C | 38 | 7 |
| Joe Economou* | 5 6 | 10 6 | London | Bristol C | 19 | 1 |
| Tony Fitzpatrick | 5 7 | 10 7 | Glasgow | St Mirren | '160 | 9 |
| (Transferred to St Mirren June 1981) | | | | Bristol C | 75 | 1 |
| Wayne Bray | | | | Bristol C | 19 | 2 |
| Steve Thompson | | | | Bristol C | 1 | 1 |
| Mark Smith* | | | | Bristol C | 5 | — |
| Bobby Newman | | | | Bristol C | 21 | 3 |
| **Forwards** | | | | | | |
| Chris Garland | 5 9½ | 11 12 | Bristol | Bristol C | 142 | 32 |
| (Contract cancelled Feb 1982) | | | | Chelsea | 92 | 22 |
| | | | | Leicester C | 55 | 15 |
| | | | | Bristol C | 55 | 10 |
| Russell Musker | 5 7 | 10 0 | Plymouth | Bristol C | 37 | — |
| Gary Smith* | 5 9 | 11 2 | Warminster | Bristol C | 14 | — |
| Peter Devine* | | | | Bristol C | 21 | 1 |
| Steven Wherry | | | | Bristol C | — | — |
| Les Carter | 5 9 | 11 2 | Farnborough | Crystal Palace | 2 | — |
| | | | | Bristol C | 16 | — |

# BRISTOL ROVERS

# Division 3

*President:* Duke of Beaufort. *Vice-Presidents:* E. W. H. Godfrey, H. E. L. Brown.

*Chairman:* Martin R. Flook.

*Directors:* C. A. L. Stevens, G. A. Holmes, A. Palmer, G. H. Hole, N. Roydon, B. W. Bradshaw.

*Manager:* Bobby Gould.

*Hon. Company Secretary:* A. E. Hill FCA.

*Chief Executive:* G. J. Bennett.

*Year Formed:* 1883. *Turned Professional:* 1897.

*Limited Company:* 1896.

*Previous Names:* 1883, Black Arabs; 1884, Eastville Rovers; 1897, Bristol Eastville Rovers; 1898, Bristol Rovers.

*Previous Grounds:* Purdown, Ashley Hill and Ridgeway Ground.

**Football League Record:**
1920 Original Member of Division 3; 1921–53 Division 3(S); 1953–62 Division 2; 1962–74 Division 3; 1974–81 Division 2; 1981– Division 3.

**Honours:** *Football League:* Division 2 best season: 6th, 1955–56, 1958–59; Division 3(S) – Champions 1952–53; Division 3 – Runners-up 1973–74. *FA Cup* best season: 6th rd, 1950–51, 1957–58. *Football League Cup* best season: 5th rd, 1970–71, 1971–72.

*Record Victory:* 7-0 v Swansea T, Division 2, 2 Oct, 1954, v Brighton, Division 3(S), 29 Nov, 1952 and v Shrewsbury T, Division 3, 21 Mar, 1964.

*Record Defeat:* 0-12 v Luton T, Division 3(S), 13 Apr, 1936.

*Most League Points:* 64, Division 3(S), 1952–53.

*Most League Goals:* 92, Division 3(S), 1952–53.

*Highest League Scorer in Season:* Geoff Bradford, 33, Division 3(S), 1952–53.

*Most League Goals in Total Aggregate:* Geoff Bradford, 245, 1949–64.

*Most Capped Player:* Matt O'Mahoney, 6, Eire, and 1, Ireland.

*Most League Appearances:* Stuart Taylor, 545, 1966–80.

*Record Transfer Fee Received:* £200,000 from Luton T for Steve White, Dec 1979.

*Record Transfer Fee Paid:* £100,000 to Birmingham C for Stewart Barrowclough, July 1979.

*Previous Managers since the War:* Brough Fletcher, Bert Tann, Fred Ford, Bill Dodgin (Snr), Don Megson, Bobby Campbell, Harold Jarman, Terry Cooper.

*Address of Supporters Club:* 468 Stapleton Road, Bristol.

*Address of the Club Shop or Boutique:* The Rovers Shop, 468 Stapleton Road, Bristol 5.

---

**Bristol Stadium, Eastville, Bristol BS5 6NN.** Telephone Bristol 511050. *Ground capacity:* 12,500 (7,500 covered). *Record attendance:* 38,472 v Preston NE, FA Cup 4th rd, 30 Jan, 1960. *Record receipts:* £23,275 v Southampton, FA Cup 4th rd, 28 Jan, 1978. *Pitch measurements:* 110yd×70yd.

NB All correspondence should be sent to Hambrook Training Ground, Filton Road, Hambrook, Bristol BS16 1JG. Telephone Bristol 566756.

*How to get there:* Buses 51 from Temple Meads Station to Stapleton Rd, five minutes from ground. By car, leave M4 or M5 at M32 junction; M32 runs direct to the ground.

*Match tickets:* Stand tickets available two weeks prior to the match.

*Car parking:* Large car parks at Stapleton Rd and Muller Rd entrances.

*Entertainments/catering facilities:* Bar open to the public in stand. Tea bar on the terraces.

*Club shop:* In Stapleton Rd; sells all types of souvenirs.

*Handbooks/programmes:* Handbooks and programmes available from club shop; programmes can be ordered on subscription.

*Extra information:* Bristol Rovers went 27 games without defeat in 1952–53, a Division 3 (South) record, and 27 games in Division 3 from the start of the season 1973–74 (a Division 3 record).

*Club Colours:* Blue and white quartered shirts, blue shorts, white stockings with two blue rings on top.

*Change Colours:* Green and black.

*Club Nickname:* The Pirates.

## BRISTOL ROVERS 1981–82 LEAGUE RECORD

| Match No. | Date | Venue | Opponents | Result | H/T Score | Goalscorers | Attendance |
|---|---|---|---|---|---|---|---|
| 1 | Aug 29 | H | Chester | D 2-2 | 0-2 | Curle, Williams D. | 5554 |
| 2 | Sept 5 | A | Chesterfield | L 0-2 | 0-1 | | 3501 |
| 3 | 12 | H | Burnley | W 2-1 | 1-0 | Stephens 2 | 5083 |
| 4 | 19 | A | Reading | W 3-0 | 1-0 | Randall, Stephens 2 | 4947 |
| 5 | 23 | A | Exeter C | W 3-1 | 2-1 | Williams D., McCaffery, Randall | 5510 |
| 6 | 26 | H | Lincoln C | L 0-2 | 0-1 | | 6112 |
| 7 | 29 | H | Wimbledon | D 2-2 | 0-0 | Mabbutt 2 | 5364 |
| 8 | Oct 3 | A | Preston NE | W 1-0 | 1-0 | Stephens | 4964 |
| 9 | 9 | A | Southend U | L 0-1 | 0-0 | | 4530 |
| 10 | 17 | H | Swindon T | L 1-4 | 0-2 | Stephens | 8779 |
| 11 | 21 | A | Oxford U | D 1-1 | 0-1 | Randall | 4422 |
| 12 | 24 | H | Huddersfield T | W 3-2 | 1-0 | Randall, Stephens, McCaffery | 5064 |
| 13 | 31 | A | Doncaster R | L 2-4 | 0-2 | Mabbutt, Stephens | 6694 |
| 14 | Nov 3 | H | Newport Co | W 2-0 | 1-0 | Randall, Williams D. | 6464 |
| 15 | 7 | H | Gillingham | W 2-0 | 0-0 | Randall, Curle | 5518 |
| 16 | 14 | A | Millwall | D 0-0 | 0-0 | | 5970 |
| 17 | 28 | A | Walsall | L 1-2 | 1-1 | Barrett | 4311 |
| 18 | Dec 5 | H | Fulham | L 1-2 | 0-1 | Williams B. | 4489 |
| 19 | 19 | H | Carlisle U | L 0-1 | 0-1 | | 3759 |
| 20 | 26 | A | Portsmouth | D 0-0 | 0-0 | | 11,395 |
| 21 | 29 | H | Bristol C | W 1-0 | 1-0 | McCaffery | 12,355 |
| 22 | Jan 2 | A | Plymouth Arg | L 0-4 | 0-0 | | 7058 |
| 23 | 19 | A | Chesterfield | W 1-0 | 0-0 | Randall | 4853 |
| 24 | 23 | A | Chester | D 1-1 | 0-1 | Randall | 2040 |
| 25 | 30 | H | Reading | D 1-1 | 0-1 | Mabbutt | 5355 |
| 26 | Feb 6 | A | Burnley | L 0-4 | 0-2 | | 5724 |
| 27 | 9 | H | Exeter C | W 3-2 | 2-0 | Parkin, Randall 2 | 4987 |
| 28 | 13 | H | Preston NE | W 2-0 | 0-0 | Williams D., Stephens | 5003 |
| 29 | 20 | A | Wimbledon | L 0-1 | 0-0 | | 2408 |
| 30 | 27 | H | Southend U | W 2-1 | 0-0 | Barrett, Williams D. | 4910 |
| 31 | Mar 6 | A | Swindon T | L 2-5 | 1-1 | Parkin, Stephens | 6689 |
| 32 | 13 | A | Huddersfield T | W 2-0 | 1-0 | Williams B., Valentine (og) | 6156 |
| 33 | 16 | A | Newport Co | D 1-1 | 1-1 | Williams B. (pen) | 5312 |
| 34 | 20 | H | Doncaster R | W 3-0 | 3-0 | Mabbutt, Randall, Williams D. | 4597 |
| 35 | 22 | A | Brentford | L 0-1 | 0-1 | | 5843 |
| 36 | 27 | A | Gillingham | L 0-2 | 0-1 | | 5100 |
| 37 | Apr 3 | H | Millwall | L 0-1 | 0-1 | | 4279 |
| 38 | 10 | H | Portsmouth | D 1-1 | 1-1 | Williams D. | 4833 |
| 39 | 12 | A | Bristol C | W 2-1 | 1-0 | Williams D., Randall | 10,791 |
| 40 | 17 | A | Fulham | L 2-4 | 0-2 | Williams D. (pen), Slatter | 6849 |
| 41 | 24 | H | Walsall | W 2-1 | 0-1 | Stephens, Bailey | 3677 |
| 42 | May 1 | A | Lincoln C | L 0-1 | 0-1 | | 4024 |
| 43 | 3 | H | Brentford | L 1-2 | 1-2 | Williams D. | 4314 |
| 44 | 8 | H | Plymouth Arg | L 2-3 | 2-1 | Williams B. (pen), Williams D. | 4025 |
| 45 | 11 | H | Oxford U | W 1-0 | 1-0 | Penny | 4754 |
| 46 | 15 | A | Carlisle U | W 2-1 | 2-1 | Hughes 2 | 6653 |

**Final League Position: 15**

### Goalscorers

*League* (58): Randall 12, Stephens 11, Williams D. 11 (1 pen), Mabbutt 5, Williams B. 4 (2 pens), McCaffery 3, Barrett 2, Curle 2, Hughes 2, Parkin 2, Bailey 1, Penny 1, Slatter 1, own goal 1.
*League Cup* (4): Mabbutt 1, Parkin 1, Stephens 1, Williams D. 1.
*FA Cup* (1): Williams D. 1 (pen).

| | | | |
|---|---|---|---|
| **League Cup** | First Round | Crewe Alex (a) | 1-1 |
| | | (h) | 1-0 |
| | Second Round | Northampton T (h) | 1-2 |
| | | (a) | 1-3 |
| **FA Cup** | First Round | Fulham (h) | 1-2 |

| Kite | Gillies | Slatter | McCaffery | Parkin | Williams B. | Curle | Williams D. | Mabbutt | Randall | Barrett | Cooper | Stephens | Hughes | Williams G. | Jones | Thomas | Pendrey | Penny | Westaway | Bailey | Kelly | Holloway | Smith | Match No. |
|---|---|---|---|---|---|---|---|---|---|---|---|---|---|---|---|---|---|---|---|---|---|---|---|---|
| 1 | 2 | 3 | 4 | 5 | 6 | 7 | 8 | 9 | 10* | 11 | 12 | | | | | | | | | | | | | 1 |
| 1 | 2 | 3 | 4 | 5 | 6 | 7 | 8 | 9 | 10* | | 11 | 12 | | | | | | | | | | | | 2 |
| 1 | 2 | 3 | 4* | 5 | | 12 | 8 | 9 | | 7 | 11 | 10 | 6 | | | | | | | | | | | 3 |
| 1 | 2 | 3 | 4 | 5 | | 12 | 8 | 9 | 6 | 7 | 11* | 10 | | | | | | | | | | | | 4 |
| 1 | 2 | 3 | 4 | 5 | | 12 | 8 | 9 | 6 | 7 | 11 | 10* | | | | | | | | | | | | 5 |
| 1 | 2 | 3 | 4* | 5 | | 12 | 8 | 9 | 6 | 7 | 11 | 10 | | | | | | | | | | | | 6 |
| 1 | 2 | 3 | 4 | 5 | | | 8 | 9 | 10 | 7 | | | 6 | 11 | | | | | | | | | | 7 |
| 1 | 2 | 3 | 4 | 5 | | | 8 | 9 | 10* | 7 | 12 | | 6 | 11 | | | | | | | | | | 8 |
| 1 | | 3 | 4 | 5 | | | 8 | 9 | 10 | 7 | | | 6 | 11 | 2 | | | | | | | | | 9 |
| 1 | | 3* | 4 | 5 | 8 | | 7 | 9 | | 11 | 12 | 10 | | 6 | 2 | | | | | | | | | 10 |
| 1 | 2 | | 4 | 5 | 11 | | 8 | 9 | 12 | 6 | | 10* | 7 | 3 | | | | | | | | | | 11 |
| 1 | 3 | | 4 | 5 | 6 | | 8 | 10 | 11 | 12 | | 9 | | 7* | 2 | | | | | | | | | 12 |
| 1 | 3 | 7* | 4 | | 6 | 12 | 8 | 10 | 11 | | | 9 | 5 | | 2 | | | | | | | | | 13 |
| | 7 | | 4 | | 3 | 8 | 9 | 6 | 11 | | | 10 | 5 | | 2 | 1 | | | | | | | | 14 |
| | 7 | | 4 | | 11 | 3 | 8 | 6 | 10 | | | 9 | 5 | | 2 | 1 | | | | | | | | 15 |
| | 7 | | 4 | | 11 | 3 | 8 | 6 | 10 | | | 9 | 5 | | 2 | 1 | | | | | | | | 16 |
| | 8 | | 4 | | 11 | 12 | 3 | 6 | 10* | 7 | | 9 | 5 | | 2 | 1 | | | | | | | | 17 |
| | 8 | | 4 | 12 | 3 | | 11* | 6 | 10 | 7 | | 9 | 5 | | 2 | 1 | | | | | | | | 18 |
| | 8 | | | 3 | 12 | 11 | 6 | | 7* | | 4 | 10 | | | 2 | 1 | 5 | 9 | | | | | | 19 |
| | 7 | 3 | 8 | 5 | 11 | | 9 | 4 | | 6 | | 12 | | | 2 | 1 | | 10* | | | | | | 20 |
| | 8 | 10 | 4 | 5 | 3 | | 11 | 6 | | 7* | | 12 | | | 2 | 1 | | 9 | | | | | | 21 |
| | 3 | 7 | 4* | 5 | 11 | | 8 | 6 | | 12 | | 9 | | | 2 | 1 | | 10 | | | | | | 22 |
| 12 | 7 | | 4 | 5 | 11 | 3 | 8 | 6 | 10* | | | 9 | | | 2 | 1 | | | | | | | | 23 |
| 12 | 3 | | 4 | 5 | 11 | 7* | 8 | 6 | 10 | | | 9 | | | 2 | 1 | | | | | | | | 24 |
| 9 | 3 | | 4 | 5 | 11 | | 8 | 6 | 10 | | | 7 | | | 2 | 1 | | | | | | | | 25 |
| 9 | | | 4* | 5 | 11 | | 7 | 6 | 10 | | 12 | | 8 | | 2 | 1 | | | 3 | | | | | 26 |
| 1 | | | | | 5 | 11 | 8 | 6 | 10 | 7 | | 9* | 3 | | 2 | | | | | 4 | 12 | | | 27 |
| 1 | | | | | 5 | 11 | 8 | 6 | 10 | 7 | | 9 | 3 | | 2 | | | | | 4 | | | | 28 |
| 1 | | | | 3 | 7 | 12 | 6 | 4 | 10 | 9* | | | 2 | | | | | | 5 | 11 | 8 | | | 29 |
| 1 | 4 | | | 5 | 11 | | 8 | 3 | 10 | 7 | | | 6 | | | | | | 2 | 9 | | | | 30 |
| 1 | 4 | | | 5 | 11 | | 8 | 3 | 10 | 7 | | 9 | 6 | | | | | | | 2 | | | | 31 |
| 1 | 11 | | | 5 | 10 | 3 | 7 | 9 | 6 | | | 8 | | | 2 | | | | | 4 | | | | 32 |
| 1 | 3 | | | 5 | 11 | | 8 | | 10 | 7 | | 9 | 6 | | 2 | | | | | 4 | | | | 33 |
| 1 | 3 | | | 5 | | 12 | 8 | 11 | 10 | 7 | | 9 | 6 | | 2* | | | | | 4 | | | | 34 |
| 1 | 7 | | | 5 | | 12 | 8 | 6 | 10* | 11 | | 9 | 3 | | 2 | | | | | 4 | | | | 35 |
| 1 | 3 | | | 5 | 10 | | 8 | | 11 | 7 | | 9 | 6 | | 2 | | | | | 4* | 12 | | | 36 |
| 1 | 3 | | | 5 | 11 | | 8 | 10 | 12 | 7 | | 9 | 6 | 4 | 2* | | | | | 4 | | | | 37 |
| 1 | 2 | | | 5 | 11 | | 8 | 10 | 3 | 7* | | 9 | 6 | | | | | 12 | | 4 | | | | 38 |
| 1 | 3 | 12 | | 5 | 11 | | 8 | 4 | 10 | 7 | | 9* | | | 2 | | | | | 6 | | | | 39 |
| 1 | 3 | | | 5 | 11* | | 8 | | 10 | 4 | 7 | | 6 | | 2 | | | | | 12 | 9 | | | 40 |
| | 3 | | | 5 | 11* | | 8 | 10 | 4 | 7 | | 9 | 6 | 2 | 1 | | | | | 4 | | 12 | | 41 |
| | 3 | | | 5 | 11 | | 8 | 6 | 10 | | | 9 | 4 | 2 | 1 | | | | | 7 | | | | 42 |
| | 3 | | | 5 | 11 | | 8 | 6 | 10 | 12 | | 9 | 4 | 2 | 1 | | | | | 7* | | | | 43 |
| | 3 | 4 | | 5 | 11 | 10 | 8 | 6 | 12 | 7* | | 9 | | 2 | 1 | | | | | | | | | 44 |
| | 3 | | | 5 | 11 | 7 | 8 | 6 | | | | 9 | 4 | 2 | 1 | | 10 | | | | | | | 45 |
| | 2 | | | 5 | 11 | 7 | 8 | 6 | | | | 9 | 10 | 4 | 3 | 1 | | | | | | | | 46 |
| 27 | 26 | 28 | 28 | 39 | 37 | 10 | 46 | 45 | 34 | 29 | 5 | 35 | 22 | 16 | 34 | 19 | 1 | 5 | 1 | 15 | 3 | 1 | — | |
| | +2s | | | +1s | +1s | | +10s | | +3s | +3s | +3s | +4s | | | | | | +1s | | +1s | +2s | +1s | | |

## BRISTOL ROVERS

| | Ht | Wt | Birthplace | Clubs | League App. | League Gls |
|---|---|---|---|---|---|---|
| **Goalkeepers** | | | | | | |
| Martin Thomas | 6 1 | 13 0 | Senghenydd | Bristol R | 162 | — |
| Phillip Kite | 6 1½ | 13 12 | Bristol | Bristol R | 31 | — |
| **Defenders** | | | | | | |
| Vaughan Jones* | 5 8½ | 11 11 | Tonyrefail | Bristol R | 101 | 3 |
| Mark Hughes | 6 0 | 11 4 | Port Talbot | Bristol R | 61 | 3 |
| Don Gillies | 5 10 | 11 5 | Glencoe | Morton | 47 | 23 |
| (Contract cancelled June 1982) | | | | Bristol C | 200 | 26 |
| | | | | Bristol R | 59 | — |
| Aidan McCaffery | 5 11 | 11 2 | Newcastle | Newcastle U | 59 | 4 |
| | | | | Derby Co | 37 | 4 |
| | | | | Bristol R | 63 | 8 |
| | | | | Bristol C | 6 | 1 |
| | | | | Bristol R | 4 | — |
| Kevin Westaway* | 5 9 | 11 5 | Bristol | Bristol R | 2 | — |
| Gary Pendrey* | 5 10 | 12 0 | Birmingham | Birmingham C | 304 | 4 |
| | | | | WBA | 18 | — |
| | | | | Torquay U | 12 | — |
| | | | | Bristol R | 1 | — |
| Tim Parkin | 6 1 | 12 10 | Penrith | Blackburn R | 13 | — |
| | | | | Malmo | (not known) | |
| | | | | Bristol R | 40 | 2 |
| Neil Slatter | 5 11 | 10 10 | Cardiff | Bristol R | 32 | 1 |
| David Smith | 6 0 | 12 12 | Frome | Bristol R | 1 | — |
| (Apprentice) | | | | | | |
| **Midfield** | | | | | | |
| David Williams | 5 9 | 11 12 | Cardiff | Bristol R | 266 | 48 |
| Geraint Williams | 5 7 | 10 8 | Treorchy | Bristol R | 44 | 1 |
| Gary Mabbutt | 5 10 | 10 6 | Bristol | Bristol R | 131 | 10 |
| Alan Routledge | 5 9 | 11 5 | Wallsend | Bristol R | 1 | — |
| (Contract cancelled March 1982) | | | | | | |
| Ian Holloway | 5 8½ | 11 9 | Kingswood | Bristol R | 2 | — |
| Brian Williams | 5 8 | 12 2 | Manchester | Bury | 159 | 19 |
| | | | | QPR | 19 | — |
| | | | | Swindon T | 99 | 8 |
| | | | | Bristol R | 37 | 4 |
| Steve Bailey | | | Bristol | Bristol R | 16 | 1 |
| **Forwards** | | | | | | |
| Shaun Penny* | 5 8 | 10 13 | Bristol | Bristol C | — | — |
| | | | | Bristol R | 60 | 13 |
| Mike Barrett | 5 10 | 10 6 | Bristol | Bristol R | 58 | 5 |
| Paul Randall | 5 11 | 12 6 | Liverpool | Bristol R | 52 | 33 |
| | | | | Stoke C | 46 | 7 |
| | | | | Bristol R | 52 | 15 |
| Steve Williams* | 5 10 | 10 10 | Barry | Bristol R | 8 | 1 |
| Archie Stephens | 5 11 | 12 7 | Liverpool | Melksham T | (not known) | |
| | | | | Bristol R | 39 | 11 |
| Errington Kelly* | 5 8 | 11 7 | St Vincent | Ledbury T | (not known) | |
| | | | | Bristol R | 5 | — |
| Keith Curle | 6 0 | 11 9 | Bristol | Bristol R | 20 | 2 |

# BURNLEY

## Division 2

*Chairman:* J. E. Jackson.

*Vice-Chairman:* Dr R. D. Iven MRCS (Eng), LRCP (Lond), MRCGP

*Directors:* J. Eglin, D. Gill, A. R. Hutchinson.

*Team Manager:* Brian Miller.

*Secretary:* Albert Maddox. *Deputy Secretary:* Robert Bradshaw.

*Commercial Manager:* Bill Read.

*Year Formed:* 1882. *Turned Professional:* 1883.

*Limited Company:* 1897.

*Previous Name:* 1881–82, Burnley Rovers.

*Previous Grounds:* 1881, Calder Vale; 1882 Turf Moor.

**Football League Record:**
1888 Original Member of the Football League; 1897–98 Division 2; 1898–1900 Division 1; 1900–13 Division 2; 1913–30 Division 1; 1930–47 Division 2; 1947–71 Division 1; 1971–73 Division 2; 1973–76 Division 1; 1976–80 Division 2; 1980–82 Division 3; 1982– Division 2.

**Honours:** *Football League:* Division 1 – Champions 1920–21, 1959–60; Runners-up 1919–20, 1961–62; Division 2 – Champions 1897–98, 1972–73; Runners-up 1912–13, 1946–47; Division 3 – Champions 1981–82. Record 30 consecutive Division 1 games without defeat 1920–21. *FA Cup:* Winners 1913–14; Runners-up 1946–47, 1961–62. *Football League Cup:* semi-final 1960–61, 1968–69. *Anglo-Scottish Cup:* Winners 1978–79. **European Competitions:** *European Cup:* 1960–61; *European Fairs Cup:* 1966–67.

*Record Victory:* 9-0 v Darwen, Division 1, 9 Jan, 1892; v C Palace, FA Cup 2nd rd replay 1908–09; v New Brighton, FA Cup 4th rd, 26 Jan, 1957.

*Record Defeat:* 0-10 v Aston Villa, Division 1, 29 Aug, 1925 and v Sheffield U, Division 1, 19 Jan, 1929.

*Most League Points:* 62, Division 2, 1972–73. *Three points win:* 80, Division 3, 1981–82.

*Most League Goals:* 102, Division 1, 1960–61.

*Highest League Scorer in Season:* George Beel, 35, Division 1, 1927–28.

*Most League Goals in Total Aggregate:* George Beel, 178, 1923–32.

*Most Capped Player:* Jimmy McIlroy, 52 (55) Northern Ireland.

*Most League Appearances:* Jerry Dawson, 530, 1906–29.

*Record Transfer Fee Received:* £300,000 from Everton for Martin Dobson, Aug 1974; and from Derby Co for Leighton James, Nov 1975.

*Record Transfer Fee Paid:* £165,000 to QPR for Leighton James, Sept 1978.

*Previous Managers since the War:* Cliff Britton, Frank Hill, Alan Brown, Billy Dougall, Harry Potts, Jimmy Adamson, Joe Brown, Harry Potts.

*Address of the Club Shop or Boutique:* The Claret and Blue Shop, Brunshaw Road, Burnley, Lancs.

---

**Turf Moor, Burnley BB10 4BX.** *Telephone: Office:* Burnley (0282) 27777/38021; *Ticket Office and Shop:* Burnley 27777 and 38021. *Ground capacity:* 23,000. *Record attendance:* 54,775 v Huddersfield T, FA Cup 3rd rd, 23 Feb, 1924. *Pitch measurements:* 115yd×73yd.
*How to get there:* Central bus station and the Central railway station are both within 5 minutes' walk of the ground, which is near the town centre.
*Match tickets:* None. Pay at turnstiles £3.50 and £2.90.
*Car parking:* Parks in Church St and Fulledge Recreation Ground are both chargeable. Each holds about 500 cars, and both are about 5 minutes' walk from stadium.
*Entertainments/catering facilities:* 'Centre Spot' Social Club underneath Bob Lord Stand. Seating for 300. Members and bona-fide guests only on match days. Snack, licensed bars are sited around the ground and under the stands.
*Club shop:* Attached to the Development Office in Brunshaw Rd, Burnley. Telephone: Burnley 27777 and 38021.
*Handbooks/programmes:* Centenary Handbook on sale £1.50. There is a subscription list for League programmes on a seasonal basis; enquiries c/o Club shop.
*Club Colours:* Claret shirts with light blue sleeves, white shorts, white stockings.
*Change Colours:* All yellow.
*Club Captain:* Martin Dobson.
*First Team Trainer:* Frank Casper.
*Physiotherapist:* Jimmy Holland MCSP
*Club Nickname:* Clarets.

102

## BURNLEY 1981–82 LEAGUE RECORD

| Match No. | Date | Venue | Opponents | Result | | H/T Score | Goalscorers | Attendance |
|---|---|---|---|---|---|---|---|---|
| 1 | Aug 29 | A | Gillingham | L | 1-3 | 0-1 | Taylor | 4663 |
| 2 | Sept 5 | H | Plymouth Arg | W | 1-0 | 0-0 | Dobson (pen) | 4022 |
| 3 | 12 | A | Bristol R | L | 1-2 | 0-1 | Kite (og) | 5083 |
| 4 | 19 | H | Huddersfield T | D | 0-0 | 0-0 | | 6485 |
| 5 | 22 | H | Doncaster R | L | 0-1 | 0-0 | | 3789 |
| 6 | 26 | A | Millwall | L | 3-4 | 3-2 | Laws, Potts, Overson | 4877 |
| 7 | 29 | A | Carlisle U | L | 0-1 | 0-0 | | 3983 |
| 8 | Oct 3 | H | Swindon T | L | 0-2 | 0-2 | | 3359 |
| 9 | 10 | A | Portsmouth | W | 2-1 | 1-0 | Young, Wharton | 9891 |
| 10 | 17 | H | Exeter C | D | 3-3 | 1-2 | Taylor, Overson, Laws (pen) | 3975 |
| 11 | 20 | A | Preston NE | D | 1-1 | 0-0 | Wharton | 7527 |
| 12 | 24 | H | Fulham | D | 2-2 | 2-0 | Hamilton, Taylor | 4224 |
| 13 | 31 | A | Brentford | D | 0-0 | 0-0 | | 6930 |
| 14 | Nov 3 | H | Chester | W | 1-0 | 0-0 | Cassidy | 3455 |
| 15 | 7 | H | Wimbledon | D | 2-2 | 1-0 | Hamilton, Overson | 4231 |
| 16 | 14 | A | Reading | D | 1-1 | 0-1 | Steven | 4089 |
| 17 | 28 | A | Bristol C | W | 3-2 | 1-1 | Young, McGee 2 (1 pen) | 4862 |
| 18 | Dec 5 | H | Oxford U | W | 2-1 | 0-0 | Cassidy, Hamilton | 4346 |
| 19 | Jan 9 | A | Plymouth Arg | D | 1-1 | 0-0 | Young | 5065 |
| 20 | 16 | H | Newport Co | W | 2-1 | 0-1 | Taylor, Overson | 4716 |
| 21 | 30 | A | Huddersfield T | W | 2-1 | 0-0 | Taylor 2 | 10,269 |
| 22 | Feb 2 | H | Gillingham | W | 1-0 | 0-0 | Wharton | 5845 |
| 23 | 6 | H | Bristol R | W | 4-0 | 2-0 | Hamilton, Mabbutt (og), Scott, Taylor | 5724 |
| 24 | 9 | A | Doncaster R | W | 1-0 | 0-0 | Wharton | 5638 |
| 25 | 13 | A | Swindon T | W | 2-1 | 2-1 | Taylor, Cassidy | 4838 |
| 26 | 20 | H | Millwall | D | 1-1 | 1-0 | Hamilton | 7094 |
| 27 | 27 | H | Portsmouth | W | 3-0 | 1-0 | Taylor, Phelan, Scott | 7024 |
| 28 | Mar 2 | A | Walsall | D | 1-1 | 0-0 | Hamilton | 4196 |
| 29 | 6 | A | Exeter C | L | 1-2 | 0-0 | Allen | 3136 |
| 30 | 13 | A | Fulham | D | 1-1 | 1-1 | Young | 7214 |
| 31 | 17 | A | Chester | W | 1-0 | 1-0 | Laws (pen) | 3261 |
| 32 | 20 | H | Brentford | D | 0-0 | 0-0 | | 7871 |
| 33 | 27 | H | Wimbledon | D | 0-0 | 0-0 | | 2641 |
| 34 | 31 | A | Lincoln C | D | 1-1 | 0-0 | Steven | 6148 |
| 35 | Apr 3 | H | Reading | W | 3-0 | 2-0 | Hamilton 2, Young | 6622 |
| 36 | 10 | H | Lincoln C | W | 1-0 | 0-0 | Hamilton | 10,915 |
| 37 | 12 | A | Chesterfield | W | 2-1 | 2-1 | Laws, Dobson | 7200 |
| 38 | 17 | A | Oxford U | D | 0-0 | 0-0 | * | 10,171 |
| 39 | 20 | H | Southend U | L | 3-5 | 2-2 | McGee, Steven, Otulakowski (og) | 8126 |
| 40 | 24 | H | Bristol C | W | 2-0 | 0-0 | Laws, Dobson | 7039 |
| 41 | May 1 | A | Newport Co | D | 0-0 | 0-0 | | 4094 |
| 42 | 4 | H | Carlisle U | W | 1-0 | 0-0 | McGee | 9899 |
| 43 | 8 | H | Walsall | W | 2-1 | 1-0 | McGee, Young | 8543 |
| 44 | 11 | H | Preston NE | W | 2-0 | 0-0 | Hamilton 2 | 13,871 |
| 45 | 14 | A | Southend U | W | 4-1 | 2-1 | McGee 2, Wharton, Laws | 4829 |
| 46 | 18 | H | Chesterfield | D | 1-1 | 0-1 | Young | 18,655 |

**Final League Position: 1**

### Goalscorers
*League* (66): Hamilton 11, Taylor 9, McGee 7 (1 pen), Young 7, Laws 6 (2 pens), Wharton 5, Overson 4, Cassidy 3, Dobson 3 (1 pen), Steven 3, Scott 2, Allen 1, Phelan 1, Potts 1, own goals 3.
*League Cup* (5): Holt 2, Cassidy 1, Hamilton 1, Potts 1.
*FA Cup* (11): Hamilton 4, Taylor 3, McGee 2, Steven 2.

| League Cup | First Round | Tranmere R (a) | 2-4 |
|---|---|---|---|
| | | (h) | 3-3 |
| FA Cup | First Round | Runcorn (h) | 0-0 |
| | | (a) | 2-1 |
| | Second Round | Bury (a) | 1-1 |
| | | (h) | 2-1 |
| | Third Round | Altrincham (h) | 6-1 |
| | Fourth Round | Shrewsbury T (a) | 0-1 |

| Stevenson | Laws | Holt | Scott | Phelan | Dobson | Cavener | Taylor | Hamilton | Cassidy | Potts | Young | Overson | Robertson | Steven | Dixon | Wharton | Anderson | McGee | Allen | Flynn | Match No. |
|---|---|---|---|---|---|---|---|---|---|---|---|---|---|---|---|---|---|---|---|---|---|
| 1 | 2 | 3 | 4* | 5 | 6 | 7 | 8 | 9 | 10 | 11 | 12 |  |  |  |  |  |  |  |  |  | 1 |
| 1 | 2 | 3 |  |  | 6 | 7 | 8 | 9 | 10 | 11 | 4 | 5 |  |  |  |  |  |  |  |  | 2 |
| 1 | 2 | 3 | 4 |  | 6 | 7* | 8 | 9 |  | 11 |  | 5 | 12 | 10 |  |  |  |  |  |  | 3 |
| 1 | 2 | 3 | 4 |  | 6 | 7 |  | 9 | 10 |  |  | 5 | 11 | 8 |  |  |  |  |  |  | 4 |
| 1 | 2 | 3 | 10 |  | 6 |  | 12 | 9 | 8* | 7 |  | 5 | 11 | 4 |  |  |  |  |  |  | 5 |
| 1 | 2 | 3 | 4 |  | 6 |  | 10 | 9* |  | 7 |  | 5 | 11 | 8 | 12 |  |  |  |  |  | 6 |
| 1 | 2 |  | 4 | 9 | 6 |  | 10 |  |  | 7 |  | 5 | 11 | 8 |  | 3 |  |  |  |  | 7 |
| 1 | 2 |  | 4 | 10 | 6 |  |  | 9 |  | 7 | 12 | 5 | 11* | 8 |  | 3 |  |  |  |  | 8 |
| 1 | 2 |  | 4* | 7 | 6 |  | 10 | 9 | 12 | 11 |  | 5 |  | 8 |  | 3 |  |  |  |  | 9 |
| 1 | 2 |  | 4 | 7 | 6 |  | 10 | 9 |  | 11 |  | 5 |  | 8 |  | 3 |  |  |  |  | 10 |
| 1 | 2 |  | 9 | 3 | 4 |  | 11 | 10 |  | 7 |  | 5 |  | 6 |  | 8 |  |  |  |  | 11 |
| 1 | 2 |  | 4 | 7 | 6 |  | 10 | 9 |  | 11 |  | 5 |  | 8 |  | 3 |  |  |  |  | 12 |
| 1 | 2 |  | 4* | 7 | 6 |  | 10 | 9 |  | 11 |  | 5 |  | 8 |  | 3 | 12 |  |  |  | 13 |
| 1 | 2 |  |  | 7 | 6 |  | 10 | 9 | 4 | 12 | 11* | 5 |  | 8 |  | 3 |  |  |  |  | 14 |
| 1 | 2 |  |  |  | 6 |  |  | 9 | 4 | 7 | 11 | 5 |  | 8 |  | 3 |  | 10 |  |  | 15 |
| 1 | 2 |  |  |  | 6 |  |  | 9 | 4 | 7 | 11 | 5 |  | 8 |  | 3 |  | 10 |  |  | 16 |
| 1 | 2 |  |  |  | 6 | 7 |  | 9 | 4 | 12 | 11 | 5 |  | 8* |  | 3 |  | 10 |  |  | 17 |
| 1 | 2 |  |  |  | 6 | 7 |  | 9 | 4 |  | 11 | 5 |  | 8 |  | 3 |  | 10 |  |  | 18 |
| 1 | 2 |  |  |  | 6 |  | 10 | 9 | 8 |  | 11 | 5 |  | 7 | 4 | 3 |  |  |  |  | 19 |
| 1 | 2 |  |  |  | 6 |  | 10 | 9 | 7 |  | 11 | 5 |  | 8 | 4 | 3 |  |  |  |  | 20 |
| 1 | 2 | 6 | 12 |  |  | 7 | 10 | 9 | 4 |  | 11 | 5 |  | 8* |  | 3 |  |  |  |  | 21 |
| 1 | 2 | 6 | 8 |  |  | 7 | 10 | 9 | 4 |  | 11 | 5 |  |  |  | 3 |  |  |  |  | 22 |
| 1 | 2 | 6 | 8 |  |  | 7 | 10 | 9 | 4 |  | 11 | 5 |  |  |  | 3 |  |  |  |  | 23 |
| 1 | 2 | 6 | 8 | 12 |  | 7 | 10 | 9 | 4 |  | 11 | 5* |  |  |  | 3 |  |  |  |  | 24 |
| 1 | 2 | 6 | 8 | 5* | 7 | 12 | 10 | 9 | 4 | 11 |  |  |  |  |  | 3 |  |  |  |  | 25 |
| 1 | 2 | 6 | 8 | 5 | 7 |  | 10 | 9 | 4 |  | 11 |  |  |  |  | 3 |  |  |  |  | 26 |
| 1 | 2 | 6 | 8 | 5 | 7 |  | 10* | 9 | 4 | 12 | 11 |  |  |  |  | 3 |  |  |  |  | 27 |
| 1 | 2 | 6 | 8 | 5 | 7 |  |  | 9 | 4 | 10 | 11 |  |  |  |  | 3* |  |  |  | 12 | 28 |
| 1 | 2 | 6 | 8* | 5 | 7 |  |  | 9 | 4 | 10 | 11 |  |  |  |  | 3 |  |  |  | 12 | 29 |
| 1 | 2 | 3 | 4 |  | 6 | 7 |  | 9 |  |  | 11 | 5 |  | 8 |  |  |  | 10 |  |  | 30 |
| 1 | 2 | 3 | 4 |  | 6 | 7 |  | 9 |  | 12 | 11 | 5 |  | 8 |  |  |  | 10* |  |  | 31 |
| 1 | 2 | 3 | 4 |  | 6 | 7 |  | 9 |  |  | 11 | 5 |  | 8 |  |  |  | 10 |  |  | 32 |
| 1 | 2 |  | 4 | 6* |  | 7 |  | 9 |  | 12 | 11 | 5 |  | 8 |  | 3 |  | 10 |  |  | 33 |
| 1 | 2 |  |  |  |  | 7 |  | 9 | 4 |  | 11 | 5 |  | 8 | 6 | 3 |  | 10 |  |  | 34 |
| 1 | 2 | 6 |  |  |  | 7 | 4 | 9 |  |  | 11 | 5* |  | 8 |  | 3 | 12 | 10 |  |  | 35 |
| 1 | 2 | 6 | 4 |  |  | 7 | 12 | 9 |  |  | 11 |  |  | 8 | 5 | 3* |  | 10 |  |  | 36 |
| 1 | 2 | 6 |  |  |  | 7 | 4 | 9 |  |  | 11 |  |  | 8 | 5 | 3 |  | 10 |  |  | 37 |
| 1 | 2 | 6 | 4 |  |  | 7 |  | 9 |  |  | 11 |  |  | 8 | 5 | 3 |  | 10 |  |  | 38 |
| 1 | 2 | 6 | 4 |  |  | 7 | 12 | 9 |  |  | 11 |  |  | 8 | 5 | 3* |  | 10 |  |  | 39 |
| 1 | 2 | 6 |  |  |  | 7 |  | 9 | 4 |  | 11 | 5 |  | 8 |  | 3 |  | 10 |  |  | 40 |
| 1 |  | 6 | 2 |  |  | 7 |  | 9 | 4 |  | 11 | 5 |  | 8 |  | 3 |  | 10 |  |  | 41 |
| 1 | 2 | 6 |  |  |  | 7 |  | 9 | 4 |  | 11 | 5 |  | 8 |  | 3 |  | 10 |  |  | 42 |
| 1 |  | 6 | 2* |  |  | 7 |  | 9 | 4 | 12 | 11 | 5 |  | 8 |  | 3 |  | 10 |  |  | 43 |
| 1 | 2 | 6 |  |  |  | 7 |  | 9 | 4 |  | 11 | 5 |  | 8 |  | 3 |  | 10 |  |  | 44 |
| 1 | 2 | 6 |  |  |  | 7 |  | 9 | 4 |  | 11 | 5 |  | 8 |  | 3 |  | 10 |  |  | 45 |
| 1 | 2 | 6 |  |  |  | 7 |  | 9 | 4 |  | 11 |  |  | 8 | 5 | 3 |  | 10 |  |  | 46 |
| 46 | 44 | 30 | 29 | 22 | 44 | 6 | 21 | 44 | 27 | 14 | 37 | 36 | 5 | 36 | 8 | 34 | 2 | 19 | — | 2 |  |
|  |  | +1s | +1s |  | +3s | +1s |  |  |  | +7s | +2s | +1s |  | +1s |  |  |  | +2s | +2s |  |  |

## BURNLEY

| | Ht | Wt | Birthplace | Clubs | League App. | League Gls |
|---|---|---|---|---|---|---|
| **Goalkeepers** | | | | | | |
| Alan Stevenson | 6 1 | 12 3 | Staveley | Chesterfield | 104 | — |
| | | | | Burnley | 406 | — |
| Billy O'Rourke | 6 0 | 12 7 | Nottingham | Burnley | 4 | — |
| | | | | Newport Co (on loan) | — | — |
| Dave Reynolds | 6 0 | 13 0 | Belfast | Burnley | — | — |
| (Contract cancelled April 1982) | | | | | | |
| **Defenders** | | | | | | |
| Derek Scott | 5 8 | 11 12 | Gateshead | Burnley | 181 | 17 |
| Ian Wood | 5 9 | 12 0 | Radcliffe | Oldham Ath | 525 | 22 |
| (Contract cancelled Nov 1981) | | | | Burnley | 17 | — |
| Brian Laws | 5 8 | 11 0 | Wallsend | Burnley | 87 | 8 |
| Vince Overson | 6 0 | 13 0 | Kettering | Burnley | 97 | 5 |
| David Holt | 5 10 | 11 0 | Padiham | Bury | 178 | 9 |
| | | | | Oldham Ath | 142 | 1 |
| | | | | Burnley | 65 | 1 |
| Garnett Cromie* | | | Belfast | Crusaders | (not known) | |
| | | | | Burnley | — | — |
| David Miller | 5 10½ | 10 3 | Burnley | Burnley | — | — |
| **Midfield** | | | | | | |
| Paul Dixon | 5 11 | 10 10 | Londonderry | Burnley | 24 | 1 |
| Martin Dobson | 5 9 | 11 7 | Blackburn | Bolton W | — | — |
| (England) | | | | Burnley | 224 | 43 |
| | | | | Everton | 190 | 29 |
| | | | | Burnley | 119 | 15 |
| Tom Cassidy | 5 11 | 12 5 | Belfast | Glentoran | (not known) | |
| (N Ireland) | | | | Newcastle U | 180 | 22 |
| | | | | Burnley | 54 | 4 |
| Eric Potts* | 5 6 | 10 5 | Liverpool | Sheffield W | 159 | 21 |
| | | | | Brighton | 33 | 5 |
| | | | | Preston NE | 57 | 5 |
| | | | | Burnley | 56 | 5 |
| Mike Phelan | 5 10½ | 11 11½ | Nelson | Burnley | 39 | 3 |
| Kevin Young | 5 9 | 10 9 | Burnley | Burnley | 94 | 10 |
| **Forwards** | | | | | | |
| Philip Cavener | 5 8 | 10 7 | South Shields | Burnley | 63 | 4 |
| Billy Hamilton | 6 1 | 12 0 | Belfast | Linfield | (not known) | |
| (N Ireland) | | | | QPR | 12 | 2 |
| | | | | Burnley | 115 | 27 |
| Colin Anderson* | 5 7 | 10 0 | Newcastle | Burnley | 6 | — |
| Andrew Wharton | 5 5½ | 10 6 | Burnley | Burnley | 40 | 5 |
| Steve Taylor | 5 10 | 10 9 | Oldham | Bolton W | 40 | 16 |
| | | | | Port Vale (on loan) | 4 | 2 |
| | | | | Oldham Ath | 47 | 25 |
| | | | | Luton T | 20 | 1 |
| | | | | Mansfield T | 37 | 7 |
| | | | | Burnley | 60 | 25 |
| William Wright | 6 0 | 10 11 | Corbridge | Burnley | — | — |
| Trevor Steven | 5 10 | 11 7 | Berwick | Burnley | 37 | 3 |
| Martin Lowe* | | | | Burnley | — | — |
| Mark Allen | 5 11 | 11 13 | Newcastle | Burnley | 2 | 1 |
| Paul McGee | 5 10 | 13 4 | Dublin | Sligo R | (not known) | |
| (Eire) | | | | Toronto M | (not known) | |
| | | | | QPR | 39 | 7 |
| | | | | Preston NE | 66 | 13 |
| | | | | Burnley | 19 | 7 |

# BURY Division 4

*Chairman:* R. A. Clarke BSC TECH, FIOB.
*Vice-Chairman:* Canon J. R. Smith MA.
*Directors:* G. A. Black, A. Metcalfe, Mrs A. Allen.
*Team Manager:* Jim Iley.
*Secretary:* John Heap.
*Year Formed:* 1885. *Turned Professional:* 1885.
*Limited Company:* 1897.

**Football League Record:**
1894 Elected to Division 2; 1895–1912 Division 1; 1912–24
Division 2; 1924–29 Division 1; 1929–57 Division 2; 1957–61
Division 3; 1961–67 Division 2; 1967–68 Division 3; 1968–69
Division 2; 1969–71 Division 3; 1971–74 Division 4; 1974–80
Division 3; 1980– Division 4.

**Honours:** *Football League:* Division 1 best season: 4th, 1925–26; Division 2 – Champions 1894–95; Runners-up 1923–24; Division 3 – Champions 1960–61; Runners-up 1967–68. *FA Cup:* Winners 1900, 1903. *Football League Cup:* Semi-final 1963.

*Record Victory:* 12-1 v Stockton, FA Cup 1st rd replay, 1896–97.

*Record Defeat:* 0-10 v Blackburn R, FA Cup, 1887–88.

*Most League Points:* 68, Division 3, 1960–61. *Three points win:* 68, Division 4, 1981–82.

*Most League Goals:* 108, Division 3, 1960–61.

*Highest League Scorer in Season:* Craig Madden, 35, Division 4, 1981–82.

*Most League Goals in Total Aggregate:* Norman Bullock, 124, 1920–35.

*Most Capped Player:* Bill Gorman, 11 (14), Eire, and (4), Ireland.

*Most League Appearances:* 506, Norman Bullock, 1920–35.

*Record Transfer Fee Received:* £85,000 from Swindon T for Andy Rowland, Sept 1978.

*Record Transfer Fee Paid:* £30,000 to Stoke C for David Gregory and £30,000 to Port Vale for Ken Beamish, Sept 1978.

*Previous Managers since the War:* Norman Bullock, John McNeil, Dave Russell, Bob Stokoe, Bert Head, Les Shannon, Jack Marshall, Les Hart, Colin McDonald, Tommy McAnearney, Allan Brown, Bobby Smith, Bob Stokoe, Dave Hatton, Dave Connor.

*Address of the Club Shop or Boutique:* Bury FC Souvenir Shop, Gigg Lane. Telephone 061-764 7475.

---

**Gigg Lane, Bury BL9 9HR.** Telephone 061-764 4881/2. *Ground capacity:* 35,000. *Record attendance:* 35,000 v Bolton, FA Cup 3rd rd, 9 Jan, 1960. *Record receipts:* £22,200 v Nottingham F, League Cup quarter-final, 17 Jan, 1978. *Pitch measurements:* 112yd×72yd.

*How to get there:* Buses 35, 472, 481, 488, 524 from Kay Gardens to within walking distance. The nearest railway station is Bury. Buses run from the station to the ground.

*Match tickets:* 500 seats in the Reserved Chair section of the main stand may be booked two weeks before the match.

*Car parking:* Season-ticket holders only may use the car park on match days. But there is ample parking space in the side-streets around the ground.

*Entertainments/catering facilities:* Social club open during normal licensing hours.

*Club shop:* At the ground; sells all types of souvenirs.

*Handbooks/programmes:* Programmes available from club shop.

*Extra information:* The social club has large dance hall, lounge, and cocktail bars. These facilities may be hired for private functions; tel: 061-764 6771.

*Club Colours:* White shirts, royal blue shorts, white stockings.

*Change Colours:* Yellow shirts, yellow shorts, yellow stockings.

*Club Captain:* Joe Jakub.

*First Team Trainer:*

*Club Nickname:* The Shakers.

## BURY 1981–82 LEAGUE RECORD

| Match No. | Date | Venue | Opponents | Result | | H/T Score | Goalscorers | Atten- dance |
|---|---|---|---|---|---|---|---|---|
| 1 | Aug 29 | H | Rochdale | W | 3-0 | 3-0 | Madden, Hilton P., Johnson | 3925 |
| 2 | Sept 5 | A | Hereford U | L | 0-3 | 0-1 | | 2508 |
| 3 | 12 | H | Stockport Co | W | 2-0 | 0-0 | Madden 2 | 3077 |
| 4 | 19 | A | Mansfield T | D | 1-1 | 1-1 | Gore | 2501 |
| 5 | 23 | A | Crewe Alex | W | 2-1 | 0-1 | Madden, Butler | 2033 |
| 6 | 26 | H | Darlington | W | 2-0 | 0-0 | Johnson 2 | 2562 |
| 7 | 29 | H | Scunthorpe U | W | 4-0 | 1-0 | Madden 2, Gore, Jakub | 2684 |
| 8 | Oct 3 | A | Halifax T | L | 1-2 | 0-1 | Madden | 2420 |
| 9 | 10 | A | Tranmere R | W | 3-1 | 1-0 | Madden 2, Johnson | 1985 |
| 10 | 17 | H | Port Vale | W | 3-2 | 2-2 | Johnson 2 (1 pen), Butler | 3565 |
| 11 | 20 | H | Wigan Ath | W | 5-3 | 1-1 | Madden 2, Butler, Hilton P., McMahon (og) | 6249 |
| 12 | 24 | A | AFC Bournemouth | L | 2-3 | 0-2 | Madden, Howard | 4894 |
| 13 | 31 | H | Northampton T | W | 7-1 | 4-0 | Johnson 2, Howard, Madden 3, Hilton P. | 3459 |
| 14 | Nov 4 | A | Blackpool | D | 1-1 | 1-0 | Butler | 7805 |
| 15 | 7 | A | Aldershot | W | 2-1 | 0-0 | Madden, Cruickshank | 2164 |
| 16 | 14 | H | Peterborough U | W | 3-1 | 2-1 | Kellock (og), Johnson, Madden | 6426 |
| 17 | 28 | H | Hull C | L | 0-2 | 0-0 | | 4508 |
| 18 | Dec 5 | A | Torquay U | D | 1-1 | 0-1 | Johnson | 2386 |
| 19 | Jan 16 | A | Colchester U | D | 1-1 | 1-1 | Hilton P. | 3504 |
| 20 | 19 | H | Hartlepool U | D | 1-1 | 0-0 | Johnson | 2997 |
| 21 | 23 | A | Rochdale | D | 1-1 | 1-0 | Johnson | 3581 |
| 22 | 30 | H | Mansfield T | W | 3-2 | 1-2 | Johnson, Butler, Cruickshank | 2954 |
| 23 | Feb 2 | A | York C | D | 0-0 | 0-0 | | 1713 |
| 24 | 6 | A | Stockport Co | L | 1-2 | 0-0 | Butler | 3155 |
| 25 | 9 | H | Crewe Alex | W | 2-1 | 1-0 | Madden, Butler | 2900 |
| 26 | 13 | H | Halifax T | D | 1-1 | 1-0 | Madden | 3590 |
| 27 | 20 | A | Darlington | W | 3-2 | 0-1 | Madden 2, Bradley | 2039 |
| 28 | 24 | A | Bradford C | D | 1-1 | 1-0 | Madden | 5468 |
| 29 | 27 | H | Tranmere R | W | 4-0 | 3-0 | Madden 3, Gore | 3295 |
| 30 | Mar 6 | A | Port Vale | D | 0-0 | 0-0 | | 3729 |
| 31 | 9 | A | Wigan Ath | L | 2-3 | 1-0 | Hilton M., Madden | 7508 |
| 32 | 13 | H | AFC Bournemouth | D | 2-2 | 1-1 | Hilton M., Madden | 4087 |
| 33 | 20 | A | Northampton T | L | 0-1 | 0-1 | | 2109 |
| 34 | 27 | H | Aldershot | D | 1-1 | 0-0 | Hilton M. | 3068 |
| 35 | Apr 3 | A | Peterborough U | L | 0-1 | 0-1 | | 4931 |
| 36 | 6 | H | Hereford U | D | 1-1 | 1-1 | Madden | 2398 |
| 37 | 10 | H | Sheffield U | D | 1-1 | 0-0 | Madden | 14,705 |
| 38 | 12 | H | Bradford C | D | 1-1 | 0-0 | Gore | 5231 |
| 39 | 17 | H | Torquay U | L | 0-1 | 0-1 | | 2346 |
| 40 | 24 | A | Hull C | L | 2-3 | 2-2 | Roberts D. (og), Madden | 3602 |
| 41 | 27 | H | Sheffield U | D | 1-1 | 1-0 | Madden (pen) | 6650 |
| 42 | May 1 | H | Colchester U | W | 4-3 | 3-1 | Butler, Madden 2 (1 pen), Hilton P. | 1720 |
| 43 | 4 | A | Scunthorpe U | D | 2-2 | 1-1 | Hilton P., Madden | 1106 |
| 44 | 8 | A | Hartlepool U | L | 0-1 | 0-1 | | 1370 |
| 45 | 15 | H | York C | W | 3-1 | 1-0 | Hilton P., Jakub, Madden | 2002 |
| 46 | 18 | H | Blackpool | L | 0-1 | 0-1 | | 2041 |

**Final League Position: 9**

### Goalscorers

*League* (80): Madden 35 (1 pen), Johnson 13 (1 pen), Butler 8, Hilton P. 7, Gore 4, Hilton M. 3, Cruickshank 2, Howard 2, Jakub 2, Bradley 1, own goals 3.
*League Cup* (4): Madden 3, Johnson 1 (pen).
*FA Cup* (6): Madden 4, Johnson 2.

| | | | | |
|---|---|---|---|---|
| League Cup | First Round | Carlisle U (h) | | 3-3 |
| | | | (a) | 1-2 |
| FA Cup | First Round | Tranmere R (a) | | 1-1 |
| | | | (h) | 3-1 |
| | Second Round | Burnley (h) | | 1-1 |
| | | | (a) | 1-2 |

| Platt | Bradley | Kennedy | Gore | Hilton P. | Howard | Madden | Butler | Johnson | Jakub | Hilton M. | Mullen | Cruickshank | Constantine | Brown | Baines | Bramhall | Smith | Hughes | Cutler | Match No. |
|---|---|---|---|---|---|---|---|---|---|---|---|---|---|---|---|---|---|---|---|---|
| 1 | 2 | 3 | 4 | 5 | 6 | 7 | 8* | 9 | 10 | 11 | 12 | | | | | | | | | 1 |
| 1 | 2 | 3 | 4 | 5 | 6 | 7 | 8* | 9 | 10 | 11 | | 12 | | | | | | | | 2 |
| 1 | 2* | 3 | 4 | 5 | 6 | 7 | 8 | 9 | 10 | 11 | 12 | | | | | | | | | 3 |
| 1 | | 3 | 4 | 5 | 2 | 7 | 8 | 9 | 10 | 11* | 12 | 6 | | | | | | | | 4 |
| 1 | | 3 | 4 | 5 | 6 | 7 | 8 | 9 | 10 | | 12 | 11* | 2 | | | | | | | 5 |
| 1 | | 3 | 4 | 5 | 6 | 7* | 8 | 9 | 10 | | 12 | 11 | 2 | | | | | | | 6 |
| 1 | | 3 | 4 | 5 | 6 | 9 | 8 | | 10 | | 7 | 11 | 2 | | | | | | | 7 |
| 1 | | 3 | 4 | 5 | 6 | 9 | 8 | | 10 | 12 | 7* | 11 | 2 | | | | | | | 8 |
| | | 3 | 4 | 5 | 6 | 7 | 8 | 9 | 10 | 11 | | 12 | 2* | 1 | | | | | | 9 |
| 1 | | 3 | 4 | 5 | 6 | 7 | 8 | 9 | 10 | 11 | | | 2 | | | | | | | 10 |
| 1 | | 3 | 4 | 5 | 6 | 7 | 8 | 9 | 10 | 11 | | | 2 | | | | | | | 11 |
| 1 | | 3 | 4 | 5 | 6 | 7 | 8 | 9 | 10 | 11 | | | 2 | | | | | | | 12 |
| | | 3 | 4 | 5 | 2 | 7 | 8* | 9 | 10 | 11 | 12 | 6 | | 1 | | | | | | 13 |
| | | 3 | 4 | 5 | 2 | 7 | 8 | 9 | 10 | 11 | | 6 | | 1 | | | | | | 14 |
| | | 3 | 4 | 5 | 2 | 7 | 8 | 9 | 10 | 11 | | 6 | | 1 | | | | | | 15 |
| | | 3 | | 5 | 2 | 7 | 8 | 9 | 10 | 11 | 4 | 6 | | 1 | | | | | | 16 |
| | | 3 | 4 | 5 | 2 | 7 | 8* | 9 | 10 | 11 | 12 | 6 | | 1 | | | | | | 17 |
| | | 3 | 4 | 5 | 2 | 7 | | 9 | 10 | 11* | 8 | 6 | 12 | 1 | | | | | | 18 |
| | | 3 | 4 | 5 | | 7 | 8 | 9 | 10 | | | 11 | 2 | 1 | 6 | | | | | 19 |
| | | 3 | 4 | | 6 | 7 | 8* | 9 | 10 | | 12 | 11 | 2 | 1 | 5 | | | | | 20 |
| | | 3 | 4 | | 6 | 7 | 8 | 9 | 10 | | | 11 | 2 | 1 | 5 | | | | | 21 |
| | | 3 | 4 | 5 | 2 | 7 | 8 | 9 | 10 | 11* | 12 | 6 | | 1 | | | | | | 22 |
| | | 3 | 4 | 5 | 2 | 7 | 8* | 9 | 10 | | 12 | 11 | | 1 | 6 | | | | | 23 |
| 12 | | 3 | 4 | 5 | 2 | 7 | 8 | 9* | 10 | | | 6 | | 1 | 11 | | | | | 24 |
| | | 3 | 4 | 5 | 2 | 9 | 8 | | 10 | | 7 | 11 | | 1 | 6 | | | | | 25 |
| 12 | | 3 | 4 | 5 | 2 | 9 | 8 | | 10 | | 7 | 11* | | 1 | 6 | | | | | 26 |
| | 2 | 3 | 4 | 5 | 6 | 9 | 8 | 12 | 10 | | 7* | 11 | | 1 | | | | | | 27 |
| | 2* | 3 | 4 | 5 | 6 | 9 | 8 | | 10 | | 7 | 11 | 12 | 1 | | | | | | 28 |
| | | 3 | 4 | 5 | 6* | 9 | 8 | | 10 | | 7 | 12 | 11 | 2 | 1 | | | | | 29 |
| | | 3 | 4 | 5 | 6 | 7 | 8 | 9 | 10 | 11 | | | 2 | 1 | | | | | | 30 |
| 12 | | 3 | 4 | 5 | 6 | 7 | | 9 | 10* | 11 | 8 | | 2 | 1 | | | | | | 31 |
| | | 3 | 4 | 5 | 6 | 7 | | 9 | 10 | 11 | 12 | 8 | 2* | 1 | | | | | | 32 |
| | 2 | 3 | 4 | 5 | 6 | 7* | 8 | 9 | 12 | 10 | | 11 | | 1 | | | | | | 33 |
| | 2 | 3 | 4 | | 6 | 9 | 8 | | | | | 11 | 10 | 1 | | 5 | 7 | | | 34 |
| | 2 | 3 | 12 | | 6 | 9 | 8 | | 10 | | 7* | 11 | | 1 | | 5 | 4 | | | 35 |
| | | 3 | 4* | 5 | 2 | 7 | 8 | 9 | 10 | | 12 | | | 1 | | 6 | 11 | | | 36 |
| | | 3 | 4 | 5 | 2 | 7 | 8* | 9 | 10 | | 12 | | | 1 | | 6 | 11 | | | 37 |
| | | 3 | 4 | 5 | 2 | 7 | 8 | 9 | 10 | | 12 | | | 1 | | 6* | 11 | | | 38 |
| 1 | 2 | 3 | 4 | 5 | 6 | 7 | 8 | 9 | 10 | | 12 | | | | | | 11* | | | 39 |
| 1 | | 3 | 2 | 5 | 12 | 9 | 8 | | 10 | | 7 | 11 | | | | 6 | 4* | | | 40 |
| 1 | | 3 | 2 | | 6 | 7 | 8 | 9* | 10 | | 12 | | 4 | 11 | | 5 | | | | 41 |
| 1 | 2 | 3 | 4 | 9 | 6 | 7 | 8 | | 10 | | | | | 11 | | 5 | | | | 42 |
| 1 | 2 | 3 | 4 | 11 | 7 | 9 | 8 | | 10 | | 12 | | | 5 | | 6* | | | | 43 |
| 1 | 2 | 3 | 4 | 5 | 6 | 9 | 8 | | 10 | | 7 | 11 | | | | | | | | 44 |
| 1 | 2 | 3 | 4 | 5 | 6 | 9 | 8 | | 10 | | 7 | 11* | | | | | | | 12 | 45 |
| 1 | 2* | 3 | 4 | 5 | 6 | 9 | 8 | | 10 | | 7 | 11 | | | | | | | 12 | 46 |
| 19 | 15 | 45 | 44 | 41 | 44 | 46 | 43 | 31 | 44 | 27 | 9 | 33 | 15 | 27 | 7 | 9 | 6 | 1 | — | |
| +3s | | +1s | | +1s | | | | | | | +2s | +3s | +13s | +5s | +2s | | | | +2s | |

## BURY

| | Ht | Wt | Birthplace | Clubs | League App. | League Gls |
|---|---|---|---|---|---|---|
| **Goalkeepers** | | | | | | |
| David Brown | 6 1 | 12 8 | Hartlepool | Middlesbrough | 10 | — |
| | | | | Oxford U | 21 | — |
| | | | | Plymouth Arg (on loan) | 5 | — |
| | | | | Bury | 27 | — |
| John Platt | 5 10 | 11 7 | Ashton | Oldham Ath | 109 | — |
| | | | | Bury | 19 | — |
| **Defenders** | | | | | | |
| John Hughes* | 5 7 | 10 6 | Manchester | Bury | 1 | — |
| Mike Spencer | 5 6 | 10 0 | Manchester | Bury | — | — |
| (Contract cancelled Sept 1981) | | | | | | |
| Brian Edwards* . | 5 11 | 11 0 | Manchester | Bury | — | — |
| Keith Kennedy* | 5 7 | 10 8 | Sunderland | Newcastle U | 1 | — |
| | | | | Bury | 405 | 4 |
| Dave Constantine* | 5 8 | 10 3 | Dukinfield | Hyde U | — | — |
| | | | | Bury | 70 | 2 |
| Pat Howard* | 5 11 | 12 0 | Dodworth | Barnsley | 178 | 6 |
| | | | | Newcastle U | 184 | 7 |
| | | | | Arsenal | 16 | — |
| | | | | Birmingham C | 40 | — |
| | | | | Bury | 118 | 5 |
| Noel Bradley* | 5 11½ | 11 4 | Manchester | Manchester C | — | — |
| | | | | Bury (on loan) | 27 | 1 |
| Steve Kenworthy | 6 1 | 12 8 | Wrexham | Wrexham | 20 | — |
| | | | | Bury | | |
| John Bramhall | 6 2 | 13 6 | Warrington | Tranmere R | 170 | 7 |
| | | | | Bury | 9 | — |
| **Midfield** | | | | | | |
| Craig Madden | 5 8 | 10 2 | Manchester | Bury | 128 | 56 |
| Joe Jakub | 5 6 | 9 6 | Falkirk | Burnley | 42 | — |
| | | | | Bury | 79 | 3 |
| Tommy Gore | 5 7 | 11 8 | Liverpool | Liverpool | — | — |
| | | | | Tranmere R | — | — |
| | | | | Wigan Ath | 102 | 14 |
| | | | | Bury | 75 | 7 |
| Brian Smith | 5 7 | 11 8 | Bolton | Bolton W | 49 | 3 |
| (Contract cancelled April 1982) | | | | Bradford C (on loan) | 8 | — |
| | | | | Blackpool | 19 | 1 |
| | | | | Bournemouth | 40 | 2 |
| | | | | Bury | 6 | — |
| Mark Hilton* | 5 9 | 10 3 | Middleton | Oldham Ath | 50 | 2 |
| | | | | Bury | 30 | 3 |
| **Forwards** | | | | | | |
| Paul Hilton | 6 1 | 11 6 | Oldham | Bury | 110 | 26 |
| Steve Johnson | 6 0 | 12 9 | Liverpool | Bury | 120 | 42 |
| Steve Mullen* | 5 7 | 10 2 | Glasgow | Darwen | — | — |
| | | | | Bury | 93 | 5 |
| Paul Cruickshank | 5 11 | 11 1 | Oldham | Blackpool | — | — |
| | | | | Bury | 67 | 4 |
| Mick Butler* | 5 9 | 10 0 | Barnsley | Barnsley | 120 | 57 |
| | | | | Huddersfield T | 79 | 21 |
| | | | | Bournemouth | 69 | 19 |
| | | | | Bury | 82 | 15 |
| Chris Cutler | 5 11 | 11 0 | Manchester | Bury | 2 | — |
| Free Transfer: Jim Woodyer* | | | | | | |

# CAMBRIDGE UNITED Division 2

CAMBRIDGE UNITED F.C.

*Chairman:* D. A. Ruston.

*Vice-Chairman:* A. R. Douglas.

*Directors:* C. R. Brett, J. E. Cooke, S. W. Cutter, A. E. Harris, B. Peacock.

*Manager:* John Docherty. *Secretary:* L. S. Holloway.

*Year Formed:* 1919. *Turned Professional:* 1946.

*Limited Company:* 1948.

*Previous Name:* Abbey United until 1949.

**Football League Record:**
1970 Elected to Division 4; 1973–74 Division 3; 1974–77 Division 4; 1977-78 Division 3; 1978– Division 2.

**Honours:** *Football League:* Division 2 best season: 8th, 1979–80. Division 3 – Runners-up 1977–78; Division 4 – Champions 1976–77. *FA Cup* best season: 4th rd, 1979–80. *Football League Cup:* 4th rd, 1980–81.

*Record Victory:* 6-0 v Darlington, 18 Sept, 1971.

*Record Defeat:* 0-6 v Aldershot, Division 3, 13 April, 1974, and v Darlington, Division 4, 28 Sept, 1974.

*Most League Points:* 65, Division 4, 1976–77.

*Most League Goals:* 87, Division 4, 1976–77.

*Highest League Scorer in Season:* Alan Biley, 21, 1977–78.

*Most League Goals in Total Aggregate:* Alan Biley, 74, 1975–80.

*Most Capped Player:* Tom Finney, 7 (14), Northern Ireland.

*Most League Appearances:* Steve Fallon, 297, 1975–82.

*Record Transfer Fee Received:* £350,000 from Derby Co for Alan Biley, Jan 1980.

*Record Transfer Fee Paid:* £140,000 to Northampton T for George Reilly, Nov 1979.

*Previous Managers since the War:* Bill Whittaker, Gerald Williams, Bert Johnson, Roy Kirk, Alan Moore, Bill Leivers, Ron Atkinson.

*Address of Supporters Club:* 530 Newmarket Rd, Cambridge.

---

**Abbey Stadium, Newmarket Rd, Cambridge.** Telephone Teversham (02205) 2170/3555. *Ground capacity:* 12,500. *Record attendance:* 14,000 v Chelsea, Friendly, 1 May, 1970. *Record receipts:* £18,811 v Aston Villa, FA Cup 4th rd, 26 Jan, 1980. *Pitch measurements:* 115yd×75yd.

*How to get there:* Nearest railway station: Cambridge. Buses 180 and 181 run from the station to the town centre; then buses 182 and 183 to the ground, which is situated on the east side of the city.

*Match tickets:* Reserved seats bookable 14 days in advance. Postal applications must be accompanied by remittance and SAE.

*Car parking:* Limited parking at main entrance; off-street parking allowed, and at Coldhams Common.

*Entertainments/catering facilities:* Entertainments each evening organised by Supporters' Club. Three canteens open in the ground on match days.

*Club shop:* Two shops, one at the main entrance, the other inside the ground.

*Handbooks/programmes:* Handbooks not available.

*Extra information:* Cambridge are the third youngest professional club in the Football League; they turned professional in 1946.

*Club Colours:* Shirts amber with black trim, shorts amber with black trim, stockings amber with black trim.

*Change Colours:* White.

*Club Captain:*

---

## CAMBRIDGE UNITED 1981–82 LEAGUE RECORD

| Match No. | Date | Venue | Opponents | Result | | H/T Score | Goalscorers | Attendance |
|---|---|---|---|---|---|---|---|---|
| 1 | Aug 29 | A | Crystal Palace | L | 1-2 | 0-2 | Spriggs (pen) | 11,201 |
| 2 | Sept 1 | H | Derby Co | L | 1-2 | 1-1 | Spriggs (pen) | 5071 |
| 3 | 5 | H | Rotherham U | W | 3-0 | 2-0 | Finney 2, Streete | 4385 |
| 4 | 12 | A | Newcastle U | L | 0-1 | 0-0 | | 14,699 |
| 5 | 19 | H | Barnsley | W | 2-1 | 1-1 | Mayo 2 | 5586 |
| 6 | 23 | A | Blackburn R | L | 0-1 | 0-0 | | 7518 |
| 7 | 26 | A | Oldham Ath | L | 0-2 | 0-0 | | 4549 |
| 8 | Oct 3 | H | Chelsea | W | 1-0 | 0-0 | Reilly | 8806 |
| 9 | 10 | A | Grimsby T | W | 2-1 | 1-0 | Mayo, Streete | 7450 |
| 10 | 17 | H | Watford | L | 1-2 | 0-1 | Mayo | 7239 |
| 11 | 24 | A | Bolton W | W | 4-3 | 2-2 | Spriggs (pen), Turner, Gibbins, Mayo | 5751 |
| 12 | 31 | H | Cardiff C | W | 2-1 | 1-0 | Spriggs, Gibbins | 4041 |
| 13 | Nov 7 | H | Shrewsbury T | W | 2-0 | 1-0 | Mayo 2 | 3851 |
| 14 | 14 | A | Norwich C | L | 1-2 | 0-1 | Fallon | 13,467 |
| 15 | 21 | H | Sheffield W | L | 1-2 | 1-0 | Spriggs (pen) | 6461 |
| 16 | 25 | A | Derby Co | L | 1-2 | 0-1 | Taylor | 8470 |
| 17 | 28 | A | Leicester C | L | 1-4 | 0-1 | Christie | 9524 |
| 18 | Dec 5 | H | Wrexham | L | 2-3 | 2-0 | Taylor, Reilly | 3172 |
| 19 | Jan 23 | A | Charlton Ath | D | 0-0 | 0-0 | | 4766 |
| 20 | 26 | H | Crystal Palace | D | 0-0 | 0-0 | | 3505 |
| 21 | 30 | A | Barnsley | D | 0-0 | 0-0 | | 13,114 |
| 22 | Feb 6 | H | Newcastle U | W | 1-0 | 1-0 | Spriggs | 5092 |
| 23 | 9 | H | QPR | W | 1-0 | 0-0 | O'Neill | 4822 |
| 24 | 13 | A | Rotherham U | L | 0-1 | 0-1 | | 7312 |
| 25 | 20 | H | Oldham Ath | D | 0-0 | 0-0 | | 3408 |
| 26 | 27 | H | Grimsby T | D | 2-2 | 0-0 | Mayo, Smith | 3542 |
| 27 | Mar 2 | A | Luton T | L | 0-1 | 0-0 | | 10,597 |
| 28 | 6 | A | Watford | D | 0-0 | 0-0 | | 11,804 |
| 29 | 13 | H | Bolton W | W | 2-1 | 1-1 | Gibbins, O'Neill | 3430 |
| 30 | 20 | A | Cardiff C | L | 4-5 | 2-5 | Reilly, Gibbins, Fallon, Streete | 3242 |
| 31 | 27 | A | Shrewsbury T | L | 0-1 | 0-1 | | 3159 |
| 32 | Apr 3 | H | Norwich C | L | 1-2 | 0-0 | Fallon | 7035 |
| 33 | 7 | A | Chelsea | L | 1-4 | 0-3 | Smith (pen) | 6196 |
| 34 | 10 | H | Luton T | D | 1-1 | 0-0 | Reilly | 8815 |
| 35 | 12 | A | Orient | D | 0-0 | 0-0 | | 3162 |
| 36 | 17 | A | Sheffield W | L | 1-2 | 0-1 | Streete | 18,314 |
| 37 | 20 | H | Orient | W | 2-0 | 2-0 | Goldsmith 2 | 3660 |
| 38 | 24 | H | Leicester C | L | 1-2 | 0-1 | Fallon | 7212 |
| 39 | May 1 | A | Wrexham | D | 0-0 | 0-0 | | 3351 |
| 40 | 4 | H | Blackburn R | W | 1-0 | 1-0 | Reilly | 3203 |
| 41 | 8 | H | Charlton Ath | W | 4-0 | 1-0 | Spriggs, Reilly 2, Streete | 4281 |
| 42 | 15 | A | QPR | L | 1-2 | 1-1 | Fallon | 10,467 |

**Final League Position: 14**

**Goalscorers**

*League* (48): Mayo 8, Reilly 7, Spriggs 7 (4 pens), Fallon 5, Streete 5, Gibbins 4, Finney 2, Goldsmith 2, O'Neill 2, Smith 2 (1 pen), Taylor 2, Christie 1, Turner 1.
*League Cup* (4): Gibbins 3, Reilly 1.
*FA Cup* (1): Taylor 1.

| League Cup | Second Round | Colchester U (a) | 1-3 |
|---|---|---|---|
| | | (h) | 3-2 |
| FA Cup | Third Round | Doncaster R (a) | 1-2 |

| Webster | Donaldson | Murray | Reilly | Fallon | O'Neill | Gibbins | Spriggs | Lyons | Streete | Finney | Polycarpou | Goldsmith | Mayo | Christie | Lockhart | Turner | Taylor | Smith | Key | Cartwright | Nicholls | Match No. |
|---|---|---|---|---|---|---|---|---|---|---|---|---|---|---|---|---|---|---|---|---|---|---|
| 1 | 2 | 3 | 4 | 5 | 6 | 7 | 8 | 9* | 10 | 11 | 12 |  |  |  |  |  |  |  |  |  |  | 1 |
| 1 | 2 | 3 | 4 | 5 | 6 |  | 8 |  | 12 | 10 |  | 11 | 7 | 9* |  |  |  |  |  |  |  | 2 |
| 1 | 2 | 3 | 4 | 5 | 6 | 10 | 8 |  | 7 | 11 |  | 9 |  |  |  |  |  |  |  |  |  | 3 |
| 1 | 2 | 3 | 4 | 5 | 6 | 10 | 8 |  | 7 | 11 |  |  | 9 |  |  |  |  |  |  |  |  | 4 |
| 1 | 2 | 3 | 4 | 5 | 6 | 10 | 8 |  | 7 | 11 |  |  | 9 |  |  |  |  |  |  |  |  | 5 |
| 1 | 2 | 3 | 4 | 5 | 6 | 10 | 8 |  | 7 | 11 |  |  | 9 |  |  |  |  |  |  |  |  | 6 |
| 1 | 2 | 3 | 4 | 5 | 6 | 10 | 8 |  | 7 | 11 |  |  | 9 |  |  |  |  |  |  |  |  | 7 |
| 1 |  | 3 | 4 | 5 | 6 | 10 | 8 |  | 7 | 11 |  | 9 | 2 |  |  |  |  |  |  |  |  | 8 |
| 1 | 2 | 3 | 4 | 5 |  | 10 | 8 |  | 9 | 6 |  | 11 | 7 |  |  |  |  |  |  |  |  | 9 |
| 1 | 2 | 3 | 4 | 5 | 6 | 10 | 8 |  | 9* | 12 |  | 11 | 7 |  |  |  |  |  |  |  |  | 10 |
| 1 | 2 | 3 | 4 | 5 |  | 10 | 8 |  |  |  |  | 11 | 7 | 9 | 6 |  |  |  |  |  |  | 11 |
| 1 | 2 | 3 |  | 5 | 6 | 10 | 8 |  | 11 |  |  | 9 | 7* | 12 | 4 |  |  |  |  |  |  | 12 |
| 1 | 2 | 3 | 11 | 5 | 6 | 10 | 8 |  | 12 | 7 |  | 9 |  |  | 4* |  |  |  |  |  |  | 13 |
| 1 |  | 3 | 10 | 5 | 6 | 11 | 8 |  | 2 | 7 |  | 9 |  |  |  | 4 |  |  |  |  |  | 14 |
| 1 |  | 3 | 10 | 5 | 6 | 11 | 8 |  | 12 | 7* |  | 9 | 4 |  |  | 2 |  |  |  |  |  | 15 |
| 1 | 6 | 3 | 10 | 5 |  | 11 | 8 |  |  | 7 |  | 9* | 4 |  |  | 12 | 2 |  |  |  |  | 16 |
|  | 2 | 3 | 10 | 5 | 12 | 11 | 8 |  | 9* |  |  |  | 4 |  |  | 7 | 6 | 1 |  |  |  | 17 |
|  | 2 | 3 | 10 | 5 | 6 | 11 | 8 |  | 9 |  |  | 4* |  |  |  | 7 | 12 | 1 |  |  |  | 18 |
|  | 2 | 3 | 4 | 5 | 10 | 11 | 8 |  | 7 |  |  |  |  |  |  | 9 | 6 | 1 |  |  |  | 19 |
|  | 2 | 3 | 10 | 5 | 6 | 11 | 8 |  | 9* | 12 |  |  |  |  |  | 7 | 4 | 1 |  |  |  | 20 |
|  | 2 | 3 | 10 | 5 | 7 | 9 | 8* |  | 6 | 12 |  |  |  |  |  | 11 | 4 | 1 |  |  |  | 21 |
|  | 2 | 3 | 10 | 5 | 7 | 9 | 8 |  | 6 |  |  |  |  |  |  | 11 | 4 | 1 |  |  |  | 22 |
|  | 2 | 3 | 10 | 5 | 7 | 9 | 8 |  | 6 |  |  |  |  |  |  | 11 | 4 | 1 |  |  |  | 23 |
|  | 2 | 3 | 10 | 5 | 7 | 9 | 8 |  | 6 | 12 |  |  |  |  |  | 11* | 4 | 1 |  |  |  | 24 |
|  | 2 | 3 | 10 | 5 | 7* | 9 | 8 |  | 6 |  |  | 11 |  |  |  |  | 4 | 1 | 12 |  |  | 25 |
|  | 2 | 3 | 10 | 5 |  | 9 | 8 |  | 7* |  |  | 11 |  | 12 |  |  | 4 | 1 | 6 |  |  | 26 |
|  | 2 | 3 | 10 | 5 | 7* | 9 | 8 |  |  |  |  | 11 |  | 6 |  |  | 4 | 1 | 12 |  |  | 27 |
|  |  | 3 | 10 | 5 | 2 | 9 | 8 |  |  |  |  | 11 |  |  |  |  | 4 | 1 | 7 | 6 |  | 28 |
|  | 2 | 3 | 10 | 5 | 12 | 9 | 8 |  |  |  |  | 11* |  |  |  |  | 4 | 1 | 7 | 6 |  | 29 |
|  | 2 | 3 | 10 | 5 |  | 8 | 9 |  | 11 |  |  |  |  |  |  |  | 4 | 1 | 7 | 6 |  | 30 |
|  | 2 | 3 | 10 | 5 |  | 8 | 9 |  | 11 | 12 |  |  |  |  |  |  | 4 | 1 | 7 | 6* |  | 31 |
|  | 2 | 3 |  | 5 | 6 | 9 | 8* |  | 10 |  |  | 11 |  | 12 |  |  | 4 | 1 | 7 |  |  | 32 |
|  | 2 | 3 | 10* | 5 | 8 | 9 |  |  | 11 |  |  | 12 |  |  |  |  | 4 | 1 | 7 | 6 |  | 33 |
| 1 | 2 | 3 | 8 | 5 |  | 9 |  |  | 6 | 10 |  |  |  | 11 |  |  | 4 | 7 |  |  |  | 34 |
| 1 | 2 | 3 | 8 | 5 |  | 9 |  |  | 6 | 10 |  |  |  | 11 |  |  | 4 | 7 |  |  |  | 35 |
| 1 |  | 3 | 5 | 12 | 9 |  |  |  | 6 | 10 |  | 8 |  | 11 |  |  | 2 | 4 | 7* |  |  | 36 |
| 1 | 7 | 3 | 5 | 9 |  |  |  |  | 6 | 10 |  | 8 |  | 11 |  |  | 2 | 4 |  |  |  | 37 |
| 1 | 7 | 3 | 5 | 9 |  |  |  |  | 6 | 10 |  | 8 |  | 11* |  |  | 2 | 4 |  |  | 12 | 38 |
| 1 | 7 | 3 | 9 | 5 |  |  |  |  | 6 | 10 |  |  |  | 11 |  |  | 2 | 4 |  |  | 8 | 39 |
| 1 | 7 | 3 | 9 | 5 |  |  | 8 |  | 6 | 10 |  |  |  |  |  |  | 2 | 4 |  |  | 11 | 40 |
| 1 | 7 | 3 | 9 | 5 |  |  | 8 |  | 6 | 10 |  |  |  |  |  |  | 2 | 4 |  |  | 11 | 41 |
|  | 7 | 3 | 9 | 5 | 12 |  | 8* |  | 6 | 10 |  |  |  |  |  |  | 2 | 4 | 1 |  | 11 | 42 |
| 24 | 37 | 42 | 37 | 42 | 29 | 35 | 33 | 1 | 29 | 26 | 1 | 6 | 20 | 15 | 1 | 11 | 9 | 27 | 18 | 14 | 5 |  |

Substitutes: + 4s (Reilly) | + + + + + + 1s 2s 1s 4s 1s 1s | + + + + 1s 2s 1s 1s | + 3s

## CAMBRIDGE UNITED

| | Ht | Wt | Birthplace | Clubs | League App. | League Gls |
|---|---|---|---|---|---|---|
| **Goalkeepers** | | | | | | |
| Malcolm Webster | 5 10½ | 12 6 | Rossington | Arsenal | 3 | — |
| | | | | Fulham | 95 | — |
| | | | | Southend | 96 | — |
| | | | | Cambridge U | 200 | — |
| Richard Key | 6 0 | 12 4 | Coventry | Coventry C | — | — |
| | | | | Exeter C | 109 | — |
| | | | | Cambridge U | 49 | — |
| **Defenders** | | | | | | |
| Steve Fallon | 6 1 | 12 7 | Whittlesey | Cambridge U | 297 | 23 |
| Jamie Murray | 5 9 | 10 12 | Scotland | Cambridge U | 163 | 3 |
| Lindsay Smith | 5 11 | 12 0 | London | Colchester U | 212 | 16 |
| | | | | Cambridge U | 169 | 7 |
| | | | | Charlton Ath (on loan) | 1 | — |
| | | | | Millwall (on loan) | 5 | — |
| | | | | Lincoln C (on loan) | 5 | — |
| Dave Donaldson | 5 10 | 13 0 | London | Arsenal | — | — |
| | | | | Millwall | 216 | 1 |
| | | | | Cambridge U | 88 | — |
| Chris Turner | 6 1 | 14 0 | St Neots | Peterborough U | 312 | 37 |
| | | | | Luton T | 30 | 5 |
| | | | | Cambridge U | 19 | — |
| | | | | New England TM | (not known) | |
| | | | | Swindon T | 3 | — |
| | | | | Cambridge U | 22 | 1 |
| **Midfield** | | | | | | |
| Floyd Streete | 6 1 | 13 11 | West Indies | Cambridge U | 111 | 15 |
| Stephen Spriggs | 5 3 | 10 2 | Doncaster | Huddersfield T | 4 | — |
| | | | | Cambridge U | 278 | 43 |
| Doug Evans | 5 10 | 11 10 | Swansea | Norwich C | 18 | 1 |
| (Contract cancelled Jan 1982) | | | | Cambridge U | 12 | 2 |
| Roger Gibbins* | 5 11 | 11 11 | Enfield | Tottenham H | — | — |
| | | | | Oxford U | 19 | 2 |
| | | | | Norwich C | 48 | 12 |
| | | | | New England | (not known) | |
| | | | | Cambridge U | 100 | 12 |
| Graham Cox | 5 8 | 9 11 | Hitchin | Cambridge U | — | — |
| (Contract cancelled April 1982) | | | | | | |
| Les Cartwright | 5 9 | 10 13 | Aberdare | Coventry C | 68 | 3 |
| (Wales) | | | | Wrexham | 115 | 6 |
| | | | | Cambridge U | 17 | — |
| Andy Beattie | 6 2 | 11 6 | Lincoln | Cambridge U | — | — |
| Ray Nicholls | 5 6 | 10 6 | Peterborough | Cambridge U | 5 | — |
| (Apprentice) | | | | | | |
| Tom O'Neill | 5 7 | 10 11 | Glasgow | Cambridge U | 94 | 8 |
| **Forwards** | | | | | | |
| Tom Finney | 5 10 | 11 8 | Belfast | Luton T | 14 | 5 |
| (N Ireland) | | | | Sunderland | 15 | 1 |
| | | | | Cambridge U | 215 | 55 |
| Derrick Christie | 5 8 | 11 0 | Bletchley | Northampton T | 138 | 18 |
| | | | | Cambridge U | 98 | 14 |
| Martin Goldsmith | 6 0 | 10 11 | Wales | Cambridge U | 10 | 3 |
| George Reilly | 6 3 | 13 5 | Bellshill | Northampton T | 127 | 46 |
| | | | | Cambridge U | 99 | 26 |
| Graham Watson | 5 10 | 11 6 | Doncaster | Doncaster R | 48 | 11 |
| | | | | Rotherham U | 13 | — |
| | | | | Doncaster R | 109 | 23 |
| | | | | Cambridge U | 209 | 24 |
| | | | | Lincoln C | 43 | 2 |
| | | | | Cambridge U | 1 | — |
| Alan Taylor | 5 9 | 10 6 | Lancaster | Rochdale | 55 | 7 |
| (Contract cancelled March 1982) | | | | West Ham U | 98 | 25 |
| | | | | Norwich C | 24 | 5 |
| | | | | Vancouver W | (not known) | |
| | | | | Cambridge U | 18 | 4 |
| Steve Pyle | 5 7 | 10 3 | Newcastle | Cambridge U | 1 | — |
| Keith Lockhart | 6 0 | 11 0 | Newcastle | Cambridge U | 2 | — |
| (Apprentice) | | | | | | |
| Joe Mayo | 6 2½ | 13 6 | Tipton | Walsall | 7 | 1 |
| | | | | WBA | 73 | 16 |
| | | | | Orient | 155 | 35 |
| | | | | Cambridge U | 21 | 8 |

# CARDIFF CITY

# Division 3

*Chairman:* R. Grogan c ENG, MIEE, MI GAS E, AMBIM.

*Vice-Chairman:* J. A. Clemo, DIP PE.

*Directors:* C. Griffiths, J. P. Leonard.

*Executive Director:* J. D. Evans, MA (Cantab).

*Team Manager:* Len Ashurst.

*Asst. Manager:*

*Managing Director:* Ron Jones.

*Secretary:*

*Year Formed:* 1899.  *Turned Professional:* 1910.

*Limited Company:* 1910.

*Previous Grounds:* Riverside, Sophia Gardens, Old Park and Fir Gardens. Moved to Ninian Park, 1910.

*Previous Name:* 1899–1910, Riverside.

**Football League Record:**
1920 Elected to Division 2; 1921–29 Division 1; 1929–31 Division 2; 1931–47 Division 3(S); 1947–52 Division 2; 1952–57 Division 1; 1957–60 Division 2; 1960–62 Division 1; 1962–75 Division 2; 1975–76 Division 3; 1976–82 Division 2; 1982– Division 3.

**Honours:** *Football League:* Division 1 – Runners-up 1923–24; Division 2 – Runners-up 1920–21, 1951–52, 1959–60; Division 3(S) – Champions 1946–47; Division 3 – Runners-up 1975–76. *FA Cup:* Winners 1926–27 (only occasion the Cup has been won by a club outside England); Runners-up 1925. *Football League Cup:* semi-final 1965–66. *Welsh Cup:* Winners 20 times. *Charity Shield:* 1927. **European Competitions:** *European Cup-Winners' Cup:* 1964–65, 1965–66, 1967–68, 1968–69, 1969–70, 1970–71, 1971–72, 1973–74, 1974–75, 1976–77, 1977–78.

*Record Victory:* 9-2 v Thames, Division 3(S), 6 Feb, 1932.

*Record Defeat:* 2-11 v Sheffield U, Division 1, 1 Jan, 1926.

*Most League Points:* 66, Division 3(S), 1946–47.

*Most League Goals:* 93, Division 3(S), 1946–47.

*Highest League Scorer in Season:* Stan Richards, 31, Division 3(S), 1946–47.

*Most League Goals in Total Aggregate:* Len Davies, 127, 1921–29.

*Most Capped Player:* Alf Sherwood, 39 (41), Wales.

*Most League Appearances:* Tom Farquharson, 445, 1922–35.

*Record Transfer Fee Received:* £110,000 for John Toshack from Liverpool, Nov 1970.

*Record Transfer Fee Paid:* £130,000 to Blackpool for Billy Ronson, July 1979.

*Previous Managers since the War:* Bill McCandless, Cyril Spiers, Trevor Morris, Bill Jones, George Swindin, Jimmy Scoular, Frank O'Farrell, Jimmy Andrews, Richie Morgan.

*Address of Supporters Club:* Bluebirds Club, Bluebirds Office, Ninian Park, Cardiff CF1 8SX.

*Address of the Club Shop or Boutique:* Bluebirds Shop, Ninian Park, Cardiff CF1 8SX.

---

**Ninian Park, Cardiff CF1 8SX.** Telephone Cardiff 398636/7/8. *Telegraphic address:* 'Soccer Cardiff'. *Ground capacity:* 43,000. *Record attendance:* 61,566, Wales v England, 14 Oct, 1961. *Club record:* 57,800 v Arsenal, Division 1, 22 April, 1953. *Record receipts:* £31,728 v Everton, FA Cup 5th rd, 26 Feb, 1977. *Pitch measurements:* 114yd×78yd.
*How to get there:* Corporation bus 2 runs past the ground; special buses run to Ninian Park from the bus station, returning after the match. Nearest railway station: Cardiff Central.
*Match tickets:* Bookable.
*Entertainments/catering facilities:* Refreshment points around the ground.
*Club shop:* Open on match days; souvenirs available during the week from the Pools Office.
*Handbooks/programmes:* No handbook. Back numbers of programmes available from Programme Dept, Ninian Park.
*Extra information:* In 1928–29 Cardiff conceded the fewest number of goals in the First Division – but were relegated.
*Club Colours:* Blue shirts, blue shorts and white stockings.
*Change Colours:* All yellow.
*Club Nickname:* Bluebirds.

# CARDIFF CITY 1981–82 LEAGUE RECORD

| Match No. | Date | Venue | Opponents | Result | | H/T Score | Goalscorers | Attendance |
|---|---|---|---|---|---|---|---|---|
| 1 | Aug 29 | A | Oldham Ath | D | 2-2 | 1-2 | Stevens, Dwyer | 4383 |
| 2 | Sept 5 | H | Chelsea | L | 1-2 | 1-1 | Kitchen | 8898 |
| 3 | 12 | A | Rotherham U | L | 0-1 | 0-0 | | 7197 |
| 4 | 19 | H | Blackburn R | L | 1-3 | 1-2 | Ronson | 4253 |
| 5 | 22 | A | Luton T | W | 3-2 | 2-1 | Kitchen (pen), Sayer, Stevens | 9015 |
| 6 | 26 | A | Barnsley | W | 1-0 | 0-0 | Stevens | 12,114 |
| 7 | Oct 3 | H | Newcastle U | L | 0-4 | 0-2 | | 5764 |
| 8 | 10 | A | Sheffield W | L | 1-2 | 1-0 | Bennett D. | 15,621 |
| 9 | 17 | H | Bolton W | W | 2-1 | 0-0 | Stevens, Bennett D. | 3879 |
| 10 | 24 | H | Shrewsbury T | D | 1-1 | 0-0 | Stevens | 4357 |
| 11 | 31 | A | Cambridge U | L | 1-2 | 0-1 | Micallef | 4041 |
| 12 | Nov 4 | H | Wrexham | W | 3-2 | 1-1 | Micallef, Stevens, Lewis | 4625 |
| 13 | 7 | H | Norwich C | W | 1-0 | 0-0 | Bennett D. | 5704 |
| 14 | 14 | A | Watford | D | 0-0 | 0-0 | | 13,907 |
| 15 | 21 | H | Leicester C | W | 3-1 | 0-0 | Micallef, Bennett D., Stevens | 6687 |
| 16 | 24 | A | Wrexham | L | 1-3 | 0-0 | Dwyer | 3635 |
| 17 | 28 | A | QPR | L | 0-2 | 0-0 | | 10,225 |
| 18 | Dec 4 | H | Derby Co | W | 1-0 | 1-0 | Micallef | 5515 |
| 19 | 28 | H | Charlton Ath | L | 0-1 | 0-1 | | 7887 |
| 20 | Jan 20 | H | Oldham Ath | L | 0-1 | 0-0 | | 4097 |
| 21 | 30 | A | Blackburn R | L | 0-1 | 0-0 | | 7001 |
| 22 | Feb 6 | H | Rotherham U | L | 1-2 | 1-1 | Kitchen | 3800 |
| 23 | 13 | A | Newcastle U | L | 1-2 | 0-2 | Stevens | 15,049 |
| 24 | 17 | A | Chelsea | L | 0-1 | 0-0 | | 9710 |
| 25 | 20 | H | Barnsley | D | 0-0 | 0-0 | | 4503 |
| 26 | 27 | H | Sheffield W | L | 0-2 | 0-2 | | 5674 |
| 27 | Mar 6 | A | Bolton W | L | 0-1 | 0-0 | | 6269 |
| 28 | 9 | A | Crystal Palace | L | 0-1 | 0-0 | | 6526 |
| 29 | 13 | A | Shrewsbury T | D | 1-1 | 0-1 | Bennett G. | 4089 |
| 30 | 20 | H | Cambridge U | W | 5-4 | 5-2 | Stevens 3, Kitchen 2 | 3242 |
| 31 | 27 | A | Norwich C | L | 1-2 | 0-0 | Gilbert | 12,720 |
| 32 | 30 | H | Grimsby T | W | 2-1 | 2-1 | Stevens, Moore D. (og) | 3924 |
| 33 | Apr 3 | H | Watford | W | 2-0 | 0-0 | Bennett D., Micallef | 6734 |
| 34 | 10 | H | Orient | W | 2-1 | 1-1 | Bennett D., Kitchen | 5689 |
| 35 | 13 | A | Charlton Ath | D | 2-2 | 0-2 | Stevens, Mullen | 4186 |
| 36 | 17 | A | Leicester C | L | 1-3 | 1-1 | Kitchen | 13,650 |
| 37 | 24 | H | QPR | L | 1-2 | 1-2 | Micallef | 5979 |
| 38 | 28 | A | Orient | D | 1-1 | 0-0 | Maddy | 2527 |
| 39 | May 1 | A | Derby Co | D | 0-0 | 0-0 | | 10,111 |
| 40 | 8 | H | Crystal Palace | L | 0-1 | 0-0 | | 5762 |
| 41 | 15 | A | Grimsby T | W | 1-0 | 0-0 | Micallef | 8148 |
| 42 | 17 | H | Luton T | L | 2-3 | 0-1 | Kitchen, Micallef | 10,277 |

**Final League Position: 20**

**Goalscorers**

*League* (45): Stevens 13, Kitchen 8 (1 pen), Micallef 8, Bennett D. 6, Dwyer 2, Bennett G. 1, Gilbert 1, Lewis 1, Maddy 1, Mullen 1, Ronson 1, Sayer 1, own goal 1.
*League Cup* (3): Stevens 2, Sugrue 1.
*FA Cup* (1): Maddy 1.

| League Cup | First Round | Exeter C (h) | 2-1 |
|---|---|---|---|
| | | (a) | 1-3 |
| FA Cup | Third Round | Manchester C (a) | 1-3 |

| Healey | Jones | Sullivan | Grapes | Pontin | Dwyer | Lewis | Kitchen | Stevens | Ronson | Buchanan | Micallef | Sayer | Maddy | Bennett D. | Sugrue | Gilbert | Giles | Thomas | Hughes | Grotier | Bennett G. | Francombe | Sanders | Mullen | Henderson | Polycarpou | Dibble | Match No. |
|---|---|---|---|---|---|---|---|---|---|---|---|---|---|---|---|---|---|---|---|---|---|---|---|---|---|---|---|---|
| 1 | 2 | 3 | 4 | 5 | 6 | 7 | 8 | 9 | 10 | 11 | | | | | | | | | | | | | | | | | | 1 |
| 1 | 2 | 3 | 4* | 5 | 6 | 7 | 8 | 9 | 10 | 11 | 12 | | | | | | | | | | | | | | | | | 2 |
| 1 | 2 | 3 | 4 | 5 | 6 | 7 | 8 | 9 | 10 | 11 | | | | | | | | | | | | | | | | | | 3 |
| 1 | 2* | 3 | | 5 | 6 | 7 | 8 | 9 | 10 | | 12 | | 4 | 11 | | | | | | | | | | | | | | 4 |
| 1 | 2 | 3 | | 5 | 6 | 7 | 8 | 9 | 10 | | 11 | | 4 | | | | | | | | | | | | | | | 5 |
| 1 | 2 | 3 | | 5 | 6 | | 11 | 9 | 10 | | | | 4 | 7 | 8 | | | | | | | | | | | | | 6 |
| 1 | 2 | 3 | | 5 | 6 | | 11 | 9 | 10 | | 12 | | 4* | 7 | 8 | | | | | | | | | | | | | 7 |
| 1 | 2 | | | 5 | 6 | | 11 | 9 | | | | 8 | | 7 | | 3* | 12 | 4 | 10 | | | | | | | | | 8 |
| | 2* | | | 5 | 6 | | 11 | 9 | | | | 8 | 4 | 7 | | 3 | 12 | | 10 | 1 | | | | | | | | 9 |
| | | 2 | | 5 | 6 | | 11 | 9 | | | | 8 | 4* | 7 | | 3 | 12 | | 10 | 1 | | | | | | | | 10 |
| | | 2 | | 5 | 6 | | 11 | 9 | | | | 8 | 4 | 7 | | 3 | | | 10 | 1 | | | | | | | | 11 |
| | 2 | | | | 6 | | 11 | 9 | | | 8 | | 4 | 7 | | 3 | | | 10 | 1 | 5 | | | | | | | 12 |
| | 2 | | | | | | 11 | 9 | | | 8 | | 4 | 7 | | 3 | | 5 | 10 | 1 | 6 | | | | | | | 13 |
| | 2 | | | 5 | | | 11 | 9 | | | 8 | | 4 | 7 | | 3 | | | 10 | 1 | 6 | | | | | | | 14 |
| | 2 | | | 5 | | | 11 | 9 | | | 8 | | 4* | 7 | 12 | 3 | | | 10 | 1 | 6 | | | | | | | 15 |
| | 2 | | | 5 | | 12 | 11 | 9 | | | 8 | | 4* | 7 | | 3 | | | 10 | 1 | 6 | | | | | | | 16 |
| | 2 | | | 5 | | 4 | 11 | 9 | | | 8 | | | 7* | 12 | 3 | | | 10 | 1 | 6 | | | | | | | 17 |
| 1 | 2 | | | 5 | | | 11 | 9 | | | 8 | | 4 | 7 | | 3 | | | 10 | | 6 | | | | | | | 18 |
| 1 | 2 | | | 5 | 3 | | 11 | 9 | | | 8 | | 4* | 7 | 12 | | | | 10 | | 6 | | | | | | | 19 |
| 1 | 2 | | | 5 | | | 10 | 9 | | | 8 | | 4 | 7 | | 3 | | | 11 | | 6 | | | | | | | 20 |
| 1 | 2 | | | 5 | | | 10 | 9 | | | 8 | | 4 | 7 | | 3 | | | 11 | | 6 | | | | | | | 21 |
| 1 | | | | 5 | 10 | | 11 | 9* | | | 8 | | 4 | 7 | | 3 | | | 12 | | 6 | | 2 | | | | | 22 |
| 1 | 2 | | | 5 | 10 | | 11 | 9 | | | 8 | | 4 | 7 | | 3 | | | | | 6* | 12 | | | | | | 23 |
| 1 | 2 | | | 5 | 10 | | 11 | 9 | | | 8 | | 4 | 7 | | 3 | | | | | 6 | | | | | | | 24 |
| 1 | 2 | | 4 | 5 | | | 10 | 9 | | | 12 | | | 7 | 8* | 3 | | | 11 | | 6 | | | | | | | 25 |
| 1 | 2 | 12 | 4* | 5 | | | 10 | 9 | | | 8 | | | 7 | | 3 | | | 11 | | 6 | | | | | | | 26 |
| 1 | 2 | 8 | | 5 | 10* | | | 9 | | | 12 | | | 7 | | 3 | | | | | 6 | 4 | 11 | | | | | 27 |
| 1 | 2 | | 4 | 5 | | | 10 | 9* | | | 8 | | | 7 | | 3 | | | 11 | | 6 | 12 | | | | | | 28 |
| 1 | 2 | | 4 | 5 | | | 10 | 9 | 12 | | 8* | | | 7 | | 3 | | | 11 | | 6 | | | | | | | 29 |
| 1 | 2 | | 4 | 5 | | 7* | 11 | 9 | | | 12 | | | 8 | | 3 | | | 10 | | | | | | 6 | | | 30 |
| 1 | 2 | | 4 | | | 7 | 11 | 9 | | | 12 | | | 5* | | 3 | | | 10 | | | | | | 6 | 8 | | 31 |
| 1 | 2 | | 4 | | | 7 | 11 | 9 | | | 5 | | | 10 | | 3 | | | | | | | | | 6 | 8 | | 32 |
| 1 | 2 | | 4 | | | 7 | 11 | 9 | | | 5 | | | 10 | | 3 | | | | | | | | | 6 | 8 | | 33 |
| 1 | 2 | | 4 | | | 7 | 11 | 9* | | | 12 | | | 8 | | 5 | | | 10 | | 3 | | | | 6 | | | 34 |
| 1 | 2 | | 4 | | | 7 | 11 | 9 | | | 5 | | | 10* | | 12 | | | | | | | | | 6 | 8 | 3 | 35 |
| 1 | 2 | | 4 | | | 7 | 11 | 9 | | | 5 | | | 12 | | 10* | | | | | | | | | 6 | 8 | 3 | 36 |
| 1 | 2 | | 4 | | | 7 | 9 | | | | 5* | | | 11 | | 10 | | | 12 | | | | | | 6 | 8 | 3 | 37 |
| 1 | 2 | | 4 | | | 7 | 9 | | | | 11 | | | 10 | | 5 | | | | | | | | | 6 | 8 | 3 | 38 |
| 1 | 2 | | 4 | | | 7 | 9 | | | | 11 | | | 10 | | 5 | | | | | | | | | 6 | 8 | 3 | 39 |
| | 2 | | 4 | | | 9* | 11 | | | | 5 | | | 12 | | 10 | | | 8 | | | | | | 6 | 3 | 1 | 40 |
| 1 | 2 | | 4 | | | 7 | | | | | 10 | | | 5 | | 11 | | | 8 | | 9 | | | | 6 | 3 | | 41 |
| 1 | 2 | | 4 | | 7* | | | | | | 12 | | | 10 | | 5 | | | 11 | | 8 | 9 | | | 6 | 3 | | 42 |
| 32 | 36 | 7 | 24 | 40 | 21 | 19 | 25 | 38 | 7 | 3 | 29 | 4 | 23 | 35 | 2 | 28 | 3 | 2 | 22 | 9 | 19 | 2 | 1 | 12 | 11 | 7 | 1 | |
| | + | | + | | + | | | + | | | | | + | + | + | | + | + | + | | | | | + | + | | | |
| | 1s | | 1s | | 2s | | | 4s | | | | | 4s | 1s | 3s | | 3s | 2s | 2s | | | | | 1s | 1s | | | |

## CARDIFF CITY

| | Ht | Wt | Birthplace | Clubs | League App. | League Gls |
|---|---|---|---|---|---|---|
| **Goalkeepers** | | | | | | |
| Ron Healey | 5 11 | 13 0 | Manchester | Manchester C | 30 | — |
| (Eire) | | | | Coventry C (on loan) | 3 | — |
| | | | | Preston NE (on loan) | 6 | — |
| | | | | Cardiff C | 216 | — |
| Andy Dibble | | | | Cardiff C | 1 | — |
| (Apprentice) | | | | | | |
| **Defenders** | | | | | | |
| Phil Dwyer* | 6 0 | 13 0 | Cardiff | Cardiff C | 357 | 33 |
| (Wales) | | | | | | |
| Keith Pontin | 6 1½ | 12 7 | Pontyclun | Cardiff C | 189 | 5 |
| (Wales) | | | | | | |
| Linden Jones | 5 6 | 10 8 | New Tredegar | Cardiff C | 96 | 2 |
| Tim Gilbert* | 5 9 | 11 12 | South Shields | Sunderland | 36 | 3 |
| | | | | Cardiff C | 33 | 1 |
| Gary Bennett | 6 1 | 12 1 | Manchester | Manchester C | — | — |
| | | | | Cardiff C | 19 | 1 |
| Peter Francombe | | | | Cardiff C | 3 | — |
| (Contract cancelled April 1982) | | | | | | |
| **Midfield** | | | | | | |
| Steve Grapes* | 5 7 | 10 11 | Norwich | Norwich C | 41 | 3 |
| | | | | Bournemouth (on loan) | 7 | 1 |
| | | | | Cardiff C | 147 | 6 |
| John Lewis | 5 9 | 11 3 | Tredegar | Cardiff C | 95 | 4 |
| Wayne Hughes* | 6 0 | 12 5 | Port Talbot | WBA | 6 | 2 |
| | | | | Tulsa R | (not known) | |
| | | | | Cardiff C | 46 | 1 |
| Paul Maddy | | | Cwycarn | Cardiff C | 35 | 3 |
| Dean Holtham | | | | Cardiff C | — | — |
| (Contract cancelled April 1982) | | | | | | |
| Alan Sanders | | | | Cardiff C | 2 | — |
| Andy Polycarpou | 5 9 | 11 3 | London | Southend U | 63 | 10 |
| | | | | Cambridge U | 5 | — |
| | | | | Cardiff C | 7 | — |
| Mick Henderson* | 5 10 | 11 4½ | Gosforth | Sunderland | 84 | 2 |
| | | | | Watford | 51 | — |
| | | | | Cardiff C | 11 | — |
| **Forwards** | | | | | | |
| Paul Davies* | 5 11 | 12 9 | Kidderminster | Cardiff C | 2 | — |
| Gary Stevens | 6 1 | 12 0 | Birmingham | Cardiff C | 150 | 44 |
| Constantinous | 5 5 | 11 4 | Cardiff | Cardiff C | 61 | 10 |
| Micallef | | | | | | |
| Peter Kitchen* | 5 8 | 11 1 | Mexborough | Doncaster R | 228 | 89 |
| | | | | Ipswich T (on loan) | — | — |
| | | | | Orient | 65 | 28 |
| | | | | Fulham | 24 | 6 |
| | | | | Cardiff C | 67 | 21 |
| Paul Sugrue* | 5 7 | 9 10 | Coventry | Nuneaton B | (not known) | |
| | | | | Manchester C | 6 | — |
| | | | | Cardiff C | 5 | — |
| Dave Bennett | 6 0 | 11 2 | Manchester | Manchester C | 52 | 9 |
| | | | | Cardiff C | 36 | 6 |
| Stan Maynard | | | | Cardiff C | — | — |
| (Contract cancelled April 1982) | | | | | | |

# CARLISLE UNITED

## Division 2

*President:* H. Sherrard.

*Vice-Presidents:* J. Johnstone JP, T. L. Sibson.

*Chairman:* J. A. Bendall.

*Directors:* J. C. Monkhouse, H. A. Jenkins, J. R. Sheffield, R. S. Liddell, I. Ward, Dr T. Gardner MB, CHB.

*General Manager:* Colin Hutchinson.

*Team Manager:* Bob Stokoe.

*Match Secretary:* Margita Lynch.

*Asst Manager:*

*Year Formed:* 1904. *Limited Company:* 1921.

*Previous Grounds:* 1903–5, Milholme Bank; 1906–9, Devonshire Park; 1910– Brunton Park.

**Football League Record:**
1928 Elected to Division 3(N); 1958–62 Division 4; 1962–63 Division 3; 1963–64 Division 4; 1964–65 Division 3; 1965–74 Division 2; 1974–75 Division 1; 1975–77 Division 2; 1977–82 Division 3; 1982– Division 2.

**Honours:** *Football League:* Division 1 best season: 22nd, 1974–75; Promoted from Division 2 (3rd) 1973–74; Division 3 – Champions 1964–65; Division 4 – Runners-up 1963–64. *FA Cup:* 6th rd, 1974–75. *Football League Cup:* Semi-final 1969–70.

*Record Victory:* 8-0 v Hartlepools U, Division 3(N), 1 Sept, 1928 and v Scunthorpe U, Division 3(N), 25 Dec, 1952.

*Record Defeat:* 1-11 v Hull C, Division 3(N), 14 Jan, 1939.

*Most League Points:* 62, Division 3(N), 1950–51. *Three points win:* 80, Division 3, 1981–82.

*Most League Goals:* 113, Division 4, 1963–64.

*Highest League Scorer in Season:* Jimmy McConnell, 42, Division 3(N), 1928–29.

*Most League Goals in Total Aggregate:* Jimmy McConnell, 126, 1928–32.

*Most Capped Player:* Eric Welsh, 4, Ireland.

*Most League Appearances:* Alan Ross, 466, 1963–79.

*Record Transfer Fee Received:* £150,000 from Hull C for Mick Tait, Sept 1979 and £150,000 from Chesterfield for Phil Bonnyman, March 1980.

*Record Transfer Fee Paid:* £120,000 to York C for Gordon Staniforth, Oct 1979.

*Previous Managers since the War:* W. Clark, Ivor Broadis, Bill Shankly, Fred Emery, Andy Beattie, Ivor Powell, Alan Ashman, Tim Ward, Bob Stokoe, Ian MacFarlane, Alan Ashman, Dick Young, Bobby Moncur, Martin Harvey.

---

**Brunton Park, Carlisle CA1 1LL.** Telephone Carlisle (0228) 26237. *Record attendance:* 27,500 v Birmingham C, FA Cup 3rd rd, 5 Jan, 1957, and v Middlesbrough, FA Cup 5th rd, 7 Feb, 1970. *Record receipts:* £20,506 v Manchester U, FA Cup 3rd rd, 7 Jan, 1978. *Ground capacity:* 25,000. *Pitch measurements:* 117yd×78yd.

*How to get there:* City centre one mile away. Ribble buses from the Town Hall. Nearest railway station, Carlisle. By road – exit 43 from the M6, ground ¾ mile away; this avoids the town centre.

*Match tickets:* Bookable 1–2 weeks in advance by post or personal application.

*Car parking:* Car park holding 1500 vehicles adjacent to the ground. Limited street parking available.

*Entertainments/catering facilities:* Supporters Club with extensive bar facilities. Refreshment points around the ground.

*Club shop:* Brunton House open on match days and week days.

*Handbooks/programmes:* No handbook. Programmes available on subscription.

*Extra information:* In 1949, Carlisle's player-manager Ivor Broadis transferred himself to Sunderland for £18,000.

*Club Colours:* Blue shirts with red and white trim, blue shorts, white stockings with red and white trim.

*Change Colours:* Yellow shirts, blue shorts, yellow stockings.

*Club Trainer:*

*Club Nickname:* Cumbrians.

## CARLISLE UNITED 1981–82 LEAGUE RECORD

| Match No. | Date | Venue | Opponents | Result | H/T Score | Goalscorers | Attendance |
|---|---|---|---|---|---|---|---|
| 1 | Aug 29 | H | Bristol C | D 2-2 | 2-0 | Lee, Robson | 3930 |
| 2 | Sept 5 | A | Exeter C | L 1-2 | 0-0 | Robson | 3533 |
| 3 | 12 | H | Southend U | W 3-2 | 1-2 | Robson, Moody (og), Crabbe (pen) | 3596 |
| 4 | 19 | A | Lincoln C | D 0-0 | 0-0 | | 3623 |
| 5 | 22 | H | Chesterfield | L 0-1 | 0-1 | | 4710 |
| 6 | 26 | H | Oxford U | W 2-1 | 0-0 | Lee, Beardsley | 3085 |
| 7 | 29 | H | Burnley | W 1-0 | 0-0 | Staniforth | 3983 |
| 8 | Oct 3 | A | Brentford | W 2-1 | 0-0 | Lee, Staniforth | 4590 |
| 9 | 10 | A | Swindon T | L 1-2 | 1-0 | Beardsley | 5265 |
| 10 | 17 | H | Plymouth Arg | W 3-1 | 1-0 | Staniforth 3 (1 pen) | 3630 |
| 11 | 20 | A | Huddersfield T | L 1-2 | 1-2 | Robson | 7185 |
| 12 | 24 | H | Walsall | W 2-1 | 1-0 | Crabbe, Beardsley | 3956 |
| 13 | 31 | A | Newport Co | L 0-2 | 0-2 | | 3972 |
| 14 | Nov 3 | H | Doncaster R | W 2-0 | 1-0 | Coughlin, Staniforth | 3725 |
| 15 | 7 | H | Fulham | L 1-2 | 0-2 | Robson | 4385 |
| 16 | 14 | A | Portsmouth | W 2-1 | 1-0 | Robson, Lee | 8858 |
| 17 | 28 | H | Gillingham | W 2-0 | 2-0 | Bannon, Crabbe | 4196 |
| 18 | Dec 5 | A | Millwall | W 2-1 | 1-1 | Bannon 2 | 4740 |
| 19 | 19 | A | Bristol R | W 1-0 | 1-0 | Lee | 3759 |
| 20 | Jan 30 | H | Lincoln C | W 1-0 | 1-0 | Bannon | 3893 |
| 21 | Feb 2 | H | Preston NE | W 1-0 | 1-0 | Houghton | 5044 |
| 22 | 6 | A | Southend U | D 1-1 | 0-1 | Lee | 4911 |
| 23 | 9 | H | Chesterfield | W 3-0 | 0-0 | Robson, Crabbe, Lee | 5575 |
| 24 | 13 | H | Brentford | W 1-0 | 0-0 | Bannon | 4942 |
| 25 | 20 | A | Oxford U | L 1-2 | 1-2 | Lee | 4797 |
| 26 | 27 | H | Swindon T | D 1-1 | 1-1 | Beardsley | 4633 |
| 27 | Mar 6 | A | Plymouth Arg | L 0-1 | 0-0 | | 3272 |
| 28 | 9 | H | Huddersfield T | D 2-2 | 1-1 | Staniforth 2 | 3643 |
| 29 | 13 | A | Walsall | D 1-1 | 0-0 | Robson | 3507 |
| 30 | 16 | A | Doncaster R | D 1-1 | 1-0 | Bannon | 3431 |
| 31 | 20 | H | Newport Co | D 2-2 | 2-0 | Bannon, Coughlin | 4042 |
| 32 | 23 | H | Reading | W 2-1 | 2-0 | Coughlin, Robson | 4557 |
| 33 | 27 | A | Fulham | L 1-4 | 0-3 | Robson | 7477 |
| 34 | Apr 3 | H | Portsmouth | W 2-0 | 2-0 | Staniforth, Ashurst | 3919 |
| 35 | 6 | A | Bristol C | D 1-1 | 1-0 | Lee | 4329 |
| 36 | 10 | A | Preston NE | W 1-0 | 1-0 | Robson | 7802 |
| 37 | 13 | H | Chester | W 3-0 | 1-0 | Craig, Bannon, Lee | 5340 |
| 38 | 17 | H | Millwall | W 2-1 | 0-0 | Craig, Bannon | 4917 |
| 39 | 20 | H | Exeter C | W 3-2 | 2-1 | Robson 3 | 5220 |
| 40 | 24 | A | Gillingham | D 0-0 | 0-0 | | 5809 |
| 41 | May 1 | H | Wimbledon | W 2-1 | 0-1 | Staniforth (pen), Leslie (og) | 4466 |
| 42 | 4 | A | Burnley | L 0-1 | 0-0 | | 9899 |
| 43 | 8 | A | Reading | D 2-2 | 1-1 | Craig, Coughlin | 2715 |
| 44 | 11 | A | Wimbledon | L 1-3 | 0-1 | Coughlin | 2022 |
| 45 | 15 | H | Bristol R | L 1-2 | 1-2 | Staniforth (pen) | 6653 |
| 46 | 19 | A | Chester | W 1-0 | 1-0 | Robson | 2535 |

**Final League Position: 2**

### Goalscorers

*League* (65): Robson 15, Staniforth 11 (3 pens), Lee 10, Bannon 9, Coughlin 5, Beardsley 4, Crabbe 4 (1 pen), Craig 3, Ashurst 1, Houghton 1, own goals 2.
*League Cup* (6): Lee 2, Coady 1, Haigh 1, Staniforth 1, own goal 1.
*FA Cup* (8): Robson 3, Bannon 2, Beardsley 1, Lee 1, Staniforth 1.

| | | | |
|---|---|---|---|
| **League Cup** | First Round | Bury (a) | 3-3 |
| | | (h) | 2-1 |
| | Second Round | Bristol C (h) | 0-0 |
| | | (a) | 1-2 |
| **FA Cup** | First Round | Darlington (a) | 2-2 |
| | | (h) | 3-1 |
| | Second Round | Bishop Auckland (h) | 1-0 (at Workington) |
| | Third Round | Huddersfield T (h) | 2-3 |

| Swinburne | Ashurst | Rushbury | Coady | Houghton | Parker | Coughlin | Campbell | Lee | Robson | Crabbe | Bannon | Hamilton | Haigh | Larkin | Beardsley | Staniforth | Collins | Craig | Ritchie | Match No. |
|---|---|---|---|---|---|---|---|---|---|---|---|---|---|---|---|---|---|---|---|---|
| 1 | 2 | 3* | 4 | 5 | 6 | 7 | 8 | 9 | 10 | 11 | 12 | | | | | | | | | 1 |
| 1 | 2 | 3 | 4* | 5 | 6 | | 8 | 9 | 10 | 11 | | 12 | 7 | | | | | | | 2 |
| 1 | 5 | 3 | 4 | | | 7 | | 9 | 10* | 11 | | | 2 | 6 | 8 | 12 | | | | 3 |
| 1 | 5 | 3 | | | 2 | 7 | | 9 | 10 | | | | 4 | 6 | 8 | 11 | | | | 4 |
| 1 | 5 | 3 | 12 | | 2 | 7 | | 9 | 10* | | | | 4 | 6 | 8 | 11 | | | | 5 |
| 1 | 5 | 3 | | | 2 | 7 | | 9 | 10 | | | | 4 | 6 | 8 | 11 | | | | 6 |
| 1 | 5 | 3 | | | 2 | 7 | | 9 | 10 | | | | 4 | 6 | 8 | 11 | | | | 7 |
| 1 | 5 | 3 | | | 2 | 7 | | 9 | 10 | | | | 4 | 6 | 8 | 11 | | | | 8 |
| 1 | 5 | 3 | | | 2 | 7 | | 9 | 10 | | | | 4 | 6 | 8 | 11 | | | | 9 |
| 1 | 5 | 3 | | | 2 | 7 | | 9 | 10 | | | | 4 | 6 | 8 | 11 | | | | 10 |
| 1 | 5 | 3 | | | 2 | | 12 | 9 | 8 | 7 | | | 4* | 6 | 10 | 11 | | | | 11 |
| 1 | 5 | 3 | | | 2 | | | 9 | 8 | 7 | | | 4 | 6 | 10 | 11 | | | | 12 |
| 1 | 4 | 3 | | | 2 | | 12 | 6 | 9 | 8 | 7 | | 5* | | 10 | 11 | | | | 13 |
| 1 | 5 | 3 | 12 | | 2 | 4 | | 9 | 8 | 7 | | | | 6 | 10 | 11* | | | | 14 |
| 1 | 5 | 3 | 10* | | 2 | 4 | | 9 | 8 | 7 | | 12 | 6 | | 10 | 11 | | | | 15 |
| 1 | 5 | 3* | | | 2 | 4 | | 9 | 8 | 7 | 12 | | | 6 | 10 | 11 | | | | 16 |
| 1 | 5 | 3 | | | 2 | | 12 | 9 | 8 | 7 | 11 | | 4 | 6 | 10* | | | | | 17 |
| 1 | 5 | 3 | | | 2 | | | 9 | 8 | 7 | 10 | | 4 | 6 | | 11 | | | | 18 |
| 1 | 5 | | | | | | | 9 | 8 | 7 | 10 | | 3 | 6 | 4 | 11 | | | | 19 |
| 1 | 5 | 3 | | | 4 | 2 | | 8 | 10 | 9 | | | 7 | 6* | 12 | 11 | | | | 20 |
| 1 | 5 | 3 | | | 4 | 7 | | 8 | 6 | 9 | | | 2 | | 10 | 11 | | | | 21 |
| 1 | 5 | 3 | | | 4 | 7 | | 8 | 6 | 9 | 10 | | 2 | | 12 | 11* | | | | 22 |
| 1 | 5 | 3 | | | 4 | 2 | 7 | 10 | 8* | 6 | 9 | 12 | | | | 11 | | | | 23 |
| 1 | 5 | 3 | | | 4 | 2 | 7* | 10 | 8 | 6 | 9 | 12 | | | | 11 | | | | 24 |
| 1 | 5 | 3 | | | 4 | 2 | 7 | 10 | 6 | 9 | | | 8 | | 12 | 11* | | | | 25 |
| 1 | 5 | 3 | | | 4 | 2 | 12 | 7* | 10 | 8 | 6 | | | | 11 | 9 | | | | 26 |
| 1 | 5 | 3 | | | 4 | 2 | 7 | 10 | 8 | 6* | 9 | | | | 12 | 11 | | | | 27 |
| 1 | 5 | 3 | | | 4 | 2 | 7 | 10 | 8 | | 9 | | | 6 | | 11 | | | | 28 |
| 1 | 6 | 4 | 5 | 3 | 8 | | | 10 | 9 | | 12 | | | | | 11 | 7* | 2 | | 29 |
| 1 | 5 | 3 | | | 4 | 2 | | 8 | 10 | 9 | 7 | | | | | 11 | 6 | | | 30 |
| 1 | 5 | 3 | | | 4 | 2 | | 8 | 10 | 9* | 7 | | | | | 11 | 12 | 6 | | 31 |
| 1 | 5 | 3 | | | 4 | 2 | | 8 | 10 | 9 | | | | | | 11 | | 6 | 7 | 32 |
| 1 | 5 | 3 | | | 4 | 2 | | 8 | 10 | 9 | | | | | | 11 | | 6 | 7 | 33 |
| 1 | 5 | 3 | | | 2 | | | 10 | 9 | | | | 8 | 4 | | 11 | | 6 | 7 | 34 |
| 1 | 5 | 3 | | | 2 | | | 10 | 9 | | | | 8 | 4 | | 11 | | 6 | 7 | 35 |
| 1 | 5 | 3 | | | 2 | 8 | | 10 | 9 | | | | 11 | 4 | | | | 6 | 7 | 36 |
| 1 | 5 | 3 | | | 2 | 8 | | 10 | 9 | | | | 11 | 4 | | | | 6 | 7 | 37 |
| 1 | 5 | 3 | | | 2 | 8* | | 10 | 9 | | | | 11 | 4 | 12 | | | 6 | 7 | 38 |
| 1 | 5 | 3 | | | 2 | 8 | | 9 | 10 | | | | 4 | | | 11 | | 6 | 7 | 39 |
| 1 | 5 | 3 | | | 2 | 8 | | 9 | 10 | | | | 4 | | | 11 | | 6 | 7 | 40 |
| 1 | 5 | 3 | | | 2 | 8 | | 10 | 9 | | | | 4 | | | 11 | | 6 | 7 | 41 |
| 1 | 5 | 3 | | | 2 | 8 | | 10 | 9 | | | | 11 | 4 | 12 | | | 6 | 7* | 42 |
| 1 | 5 | 3 | | | 2 | 8 | | 10 | 9 | | | | 11 | 4 | | | | 6 | 7 | 43 |
| 1 | 5 | 3 | | | 4 | 2 | 8 | 10* | 9 | | | | 11 | | 12 | | | 6 | 7 | 44 |
| 1 | 5 | 3 | | | 2 | 8 | 12 | 9 | 10 | | | | 4 | | | 11 | | 6 | 7* | 45 |
| 1 | 5 | 3 | 8 | | 2 | 7 | | 9 | 10* | | | | 4 | | | 11 | | 6 | 12 | 46 |
| 46 | 46 | 45 | 4 | 18 | 43 | 33 | 6 | 40 | 39 | 26 | 23 | — | 21 | 30 | 19 | 33 | 2 | 18 | 14 | |
| | | | + | | + | + | + | | | | | + | + | + | + | + | + | + | + | |
| | | | 2s | | 4s | 2s | 1s | | | | | 2s | 1s | 2s | 1s | 3s | 4s | 1s | 1s | |

## CARLISLE UNITED

| | Ht | Wt | Birthplace | Clubs | League App. | League Gls |
|---|---|---|---|---|---|---|
| **Goalkeepers** | | | | | | |
| Trevor Swinburne | 6 0 | 12 12 | East Rainton | Sunderland | 10 | — |
| | | | | Sheffield U (on loan) | — | — |
| | | | | Carlisle U | 206 | — |
| Tony Harrison* | 6 1 | 13 0 | Gateshead | Southport | 48 | — |
| | | | | Carlisle U | 8 | — |
| **Defenders** | | | | | | |
| Bob Parker | 5 9 | 10 12 | Coventry | Coventry C | 81 | — |
| | | | | Carlisle U | 307 | 5 |
| Ian MacDonald | 6 1 | 12 4 | Rinteln, | St Johnstone | 108 | 2 |
| (Transferred to Dundee July 1981) | | | West Germany | Carlisle U | 187 | 7 |
| Andy Collins | 5 10 | 10 9 | Carlisle | Carlisle U | 54 | 1 |
| (Contract cancelled April 1982) | | | | | | |
| Gary Watson | 6 2 | 11 7 | Easington | Oxford U | 24 | — |
| (Contract cancelled April 1982) | | | | Carlisle U | 18 | — |
| Mike Coady | 5 11 | 11 0 | Dipton | Sunderland | 6 | — |
| (Contract cancelled April 1982) | | | | Carlisle U | 51 | 1 |
| Paul Haigh | 5 10 | 11 6 | Scarborough | Hull C | 180 | 8 |
| | | | | Carlisle U | 51 | — |
| Tony Larkin | 6 0 | 11 12 | Wrexham | Wrexham | — | — |
| | | | | Shrewsbury T | 55 | — |
| | | | | Carlisle U | 31 | — |
| Jack Ashurst | 6 0 | 12 4 | Renton | Sunderland | 140 | 4 |
| | | | | Blackpool | 53 | 3 |
| | | | | Carlisle U | 46 | 1 |
| Dave Rushbury | 5 10 | 11 4 | Wolverhampton | WBA | 28 | — |
| | | | | Sheffield W | 112 | 7 |
| | | | | Swansea C | 52 | — |
| | | | | Carlisle U | 45 | — |
| **Midfield** | | | | | | |
| Jimmy Hamilton | 5 11½ | 11 4 | Uddingston | Sunderland | 17 | 2 |
| (Contract cancelled April 1982) | | | | Plymouth Arg | 8 | — |
| | | | | Bristol R | 20 | 1 |
| | | | | Carlisle U | 154 | 12 |
| | | | | Morton (on loan) | — | — |
| Keith Houghton | 6 2 | 12 4 | Newcastle | Carlisle U | 58 | 2 |
| Stuart Metcalfe | 5 7 | 9 0 | Blackburn | Blackburn R | 386 | 21 |
| (Contract cancelled May 1981) | | | | Carlisle U | 25 | 3 |
| Russell Coughlin | 5 8 | 11 6 | Swansea | Manchester C | — | — |
| | | | | Blackburn R | 24 | — |
| | | | | Carlisle U | 62 | 8 |
| Alan Campbell* | 5 8 | 11 7 | Arbroath | Charlton Ath | 198 | 28 |
| | | | | Birmingham C | 175 | 12 |
| | | | | Cardiff C | 167 | 2 |
| | | | | Carlisle U | 31 | — |
| John Crabbe | 5 8 | 11 0 | Weymouth | Southampton | 12 | — |
| | | | | Gillingham | 181 | 12 |
| | | | | Carlisle U | 26 | 4 |
| Tommy Craig* | 5 8 | 11 9 | Aberdeen | Aberdeen | 45 | 8 |
| (Scotland) | | | | Sheffield W | 214 | 38 |
| | | | | Newcastle U | 124 | 23 |
| | | | | Aston V | 27 | 2 |
| | | | | Swansea C | 52 | 9 |
| | | | | Carlisle U | 18 | 3 |
| **Forwards** | | | | | | |
| Paul Bannon* | 6 2 | 11 2 | Dublin | Carlisle U | 101 | 33 |
| George McVitie | 5 9¾ | 11 1 | Carlisle | Carlisle U | 128 | 21 |
| (Contract cancelled May 1981) | | | | WBA | 42 | 5 |
| | | | | Oldham Ath | 113 | 19 |
| | | | | Carlisle U | 198 | 20 |
| Hugh McGrogan | 5 9 | 11 0 | Dumbarton | Oxford U | 126 | 13 |
| (Contract cancelled April 1982) | | | | Carlisle U | 2 | — |
| Peter Beardsley | 5 8 | 11 4 | Newcastle | Carlisle U | 104 | 22 |
| (Contract cancelled March 1982) | | | | | | |
| Gordon Staniforth | 5 6 | 9 12 | Hull | Hull C | 12 | 2 |
| | | | | York C | 128 | 33 |
| | | | | Carlisle U | 100 | 31 |
| Bryan Robson | 5 7 | 11 8 | Sunderland | Newcastle U | 206 | 81 |
| | | | | West Ham U | 120 | 47 |
| | | | | Sunderland | 90 | 34 |
| | | | | West Ham U | 107 | 47 |
| | | | | Sunderland | 52 | 23 |
| | | | | Carlisle U | 48 | 21 |
| Bob Lee | 6 2 | 13 10 | Melton Mowbray | Leicester C | 63 | 17 |
| | | | | Doncaster R (on loan) | 14 | 4 |
| | | | | Sunderland | 109 | 32 |
| | | | | Bristol R | 23 | 2 |
| | | | | Carlisle U | 41 | 10 |

# CHARLTON ATHLETIC      Division 2

*Chairman:* M. Hulyer.
*Managing Director:* R. D. Collins.
*Directors:* E. M. Glicksten, W. J. Jenner, M. Stanley, P. Crystal.
*Secretary:* W. J. Jenner.
*Manager:* Ken Craggs.
*General Manager:* Benny Fenton.
*Commercial Manager:* Andy Nelson.

*Year Formed:* 1905. *Turned Professional:* 1920.
*Limited Company:* 1919.
*Previous Grounds:* 1906, Siemen's Meadow; 1907, Woolwich Common; 1909, Pound Park; 1913, Horn Lane; 1920, The Valley; 1922, Catford; 1922, The Valley.

**Football League Record:**
1921 Elected to Division 3(S); 1929–33 Division 2; 1933–35 Division 3(S); 1935–36 Division 2; 1936–57 Division 1; 1957–72 Division 2; 1972–75 Division 3; 1975–80 Division 2; 1980–81 Division 3; 1981– Division 2.

**Honours:** *Football League:* Division 1 – Runners-up 1936–37; Division 2 – Runners-up 1935–36; Division 3(S) – Champions 1928–29, 1934–35; Promoted from Division 3 (3rd) 1974–75, 1980–81. *FA Cup:* Winners 1947; Runners-up 1946. *Football League Cup* best season: 4th rd, 1962–63, 1964–65, 1978–79.

*Record Victory:* 8-1 v Middlesbrough, Division 1, 12 Sept, 1953.
*Record Defeat:* 1-11 v Aston Villa, Division 2, 14 Nov, 1959.
*Most League Points:* 61, Division 3(S), 1934–35.
*Most League Goals:* 107, Division 2, 1957–58.
*Highest League Scorer in Season:* Ralph Allen, 32, Division 3(S), 1934–35.
*Most League Goals in Total Aggregate:* Stuart Leary, 153, 1953–62.
*Most Capped Player:* John Hewie, 19, Scotland.
*Most League Appearances:* Sam Bartram, 583, 1934–56.
*Record Transfer Fee Received:* £650,000 from Crystal Palace for Mike Flanagan, Aug 1979.
*Record Transfer Fee Paid:* £135,000 to Tampa Bay for Nicky Johns, Aug 1979.
*Previous Managers since the War:* Jimmy Seed, Jimmy Trotter, Frank Hill, Bob Stokoe, Eddie Firmani, Theo Foley, Andy Nelson, Mike Bailey.
*Address of Supporters Club:* Same address as Club.
*Address of the Club Shop or Boutique:* 'The Valley Shop', The Valley, Floyd Road, London SE7 8AW. 01-858 6006.

---

**The Valley, Floyd Rd, Charlton, London SE7 8AW.** Telephone 01-858 3711/2. *Ground capacity:* 20,000. *Record attendance:* 75,031 v Aston Villa, FA Cup 5th rd, 12 Feb, 1938. *Record receipts:* £31,120 v West Ham U, League Cup 3rd rd, 23 Sept, 1980. *Pitch measurements:* 114yd×78yd.
*How to get there:* Buses 53, 54, 75, 177, 180. Nearest railway station, Charlton, is on the line from London from Charing Cross and Waterloo East. The ground is 3 minutes walk from the station.
*Car parking:* In ground for season-ticket holders only. Off-street parking available.
*Entertainments/catering facilities:* The Valley Club, Harvey Gardens (01-858 1495), and Beer and Snack Bars in the ground.
*Club shop:* The Valley Shop in ground is open on match days.
*Handbooks/programmes:* Both available in shops, and programmes on subscription.
*Extra information:* Charlton are the only club to go from the third to the first division in successive seasons (1934–36) and then finish runners-up.
*Club Colours:* Red shirts, white shorts, red stockings.
*Change Colours:* Yellow and blue.
*Club Captain:*
*Club Coach:*
*First Team Trainer/Physiotherapist:* Charlie Hall.
*Club Nickname:* Haddicks, Robins, or Valiants.

---

## CHARLTON ATHLETIC 1981–82 LEAGUE RECORD

| Match No. | Date | Venue | Opponents | Result | H/T Score | Goalscorers | Attendance |
|---|---|---|---|---|---|---|---|
| 1 | Aug 29 | A | Luton T | L 0-3 | 0-2 | | 8776 |
| 2 | Sept 5 | H | Blackburn R | W 2-0 | 1-0 | McAllister, Walsh | 6141 |
| 3 | 12 | A | Crystal Palace | L 0-2 | 0-1 | | 14,227 |
| 4 | 19 | H | Grimsby T | W 2-0 | 1-0 | Walsh 2 | 6075 |
| 5 | 23 | A | Chelsea | D 2-2 | 1-1 | Walsh 2 | 15,329 |
| 6 | 26 | A | Wrexham | L 0-1 | 0-0 | | 3076 |
| 7 | Oct 3 | H | Derby Co | W 2-1 | 1-0 | Hales 2 | 6686 |
| 8 | 10 | A | Shrewsbury T | D 1-1 | 0-1 | Hales | 4336 |
| 9 | 17 | H | Sheffield W | W 3-0 | 2-0 | Walsh 2, Robinson | 8258 |
| 10 | 20 | H | Oldham Ath | W 3-1 | 1-1 | Robinson, Lansdowne, Futcher (og) | 6575 |
| 11 | 25 | A | Orient | D 1-1 | 0-1 | Elliott | 8265 |
| 12 | 31 | H | QPR | L 1-2 | 0-2 | Hales | 11,333 |
| 13 | Nov 7 | H | Leicester C | L 1-4 | 1-1 | Walsh | 8212 |
| 14 | 14 | A | Newcastle U | L 1-4 | 1-1 | Madden (pen) | 15,200 |
| 15 | 21 | A | Rotherham U | L 1-2 | 0-0 | Hales | 7177 |
| 16 | 24 | H | Chelsea | L 3-4 | 2-3 | Robinson, Hales, Ambrose | 11,082 |
| 17 | 28 | H | Barnsley | W 2-1 | 2-0 | Smith, Madden | 5553 |
| 18 | Dec 5 | A | Watford | D 2-2 | 0-2 | Hales, Rice (og) | 12,113 |
| 19 | 19 | A | Bolton W | L 0-2 | 0-1 | | 5085 |
| 20 | 28 | A | Cardiff C | W 1-0 | 1-0 | Hales | 7887 |
| 21 | 30 | H | Norwich C | D 0-0 | 0-0 | | 6277 |
| 22 | Jan 13 | A | Blackburn R | W 2-0 | 1-0 | Hales, Gritt | 5825 |
| 23 | 19 | H | Luton T | D 0-0 | 0-0 | | 7013 |
| 24 | 23 | H | Cambridge U | D 0-0 | 0-0 | | 4766 |
| 25 | 30 | A | Grimsby T | D 3-3 | 1-2 | Hales, McAllister, Walsh | 7088 |
| 26 | Feb 6 | H | Crystal Palace | W 2-1 | 1-0 | Walsh, McAllister | 9072 |
| 27 | 13 | A | Derby Co | D 1-1 | 1-1 | McAllister | 10,846 |
| 28 | 20 | H | Wrexham | W 1-0 | 0-0 | Gritt | 4561 |
| 29 | 27 | H | Shrewsbury T | W 1-0 | 0-0 | Robinson | 4575 |
| 30 | Mar 6 | A | Sheffield W | D 1-1 | 1-1 | Robinson | 12,853 |
| 31 | 12 | H | Orient | W 5-2 | 1-1 | Phillips L., Walsh, Lansdowne 2, Gritt | 5871 |
| 32 | 20 | A | QPR | L 0-4 | 0-1 | | 13,118 |
| 33 | 27 | A | Leicester C | L 1-3 | 1-0 | Hales | 13,681 |
| 34 | Apr 3 | H | Newcastle U | L 0-1 | 0-1 | | 6357 |
| 35 | 10 | A | Norwich C | L 0-5 | 0-2 | | 14,908 |
| 36 | 13 | H | Cardiff C | D 2-2 | 2-0 | Smith, Lansdowne | 4186 |
| 37 | 17 | H | Rotherham U | L 1-2 | 0-0 | Walsh | 5011 |
| 38 | 24 | A | Barnsley | L 0-1 | 0-0 | | 9287 |
| 39 | 28 | H | Bolton W | W 1-0 | 1-0 | Walsh | 3379 |
| 40 | May 1 | H | Watford | D 1-1 | 1-0 | Mehmet | 9747 |
| 41 | 4 | A | Oldham Ath | L 0-1 | 0-1 | | 2904 |
| 42 | 8 | A | Cambridge U | L 0-4 | 0-1 | | 4281 |

**Final League Position: 13**

### Goalscorers

*League* (50): Walsh 13, Hales 11, Robinson 5, Lansdowne 4, McAllister 4, Gritt 3, Madden 2 (1 pen), Smith 2, Ambrose 1, Elliott 1, Mehmet 1, Phillips L. 1, own goals 2.
*League Cup* (5): Hales 2 (1 pen), Elliott 1, Lansdowne 1, Robinson 1.
*FA Cup* (0).

| | | | | |
|---|---|---|---|---|
| **League Cup** | First Round | Reading (a) | | 2-2 |
| | | (h) | | 3-1 |
| | Second Round | Norwich C (a) | | 0-1 |
| | | (h) | | 0-1 |
| **FA Cup** | Third Round | Orient (a) | | 0-1 |

| Phillips J. | Naylor | Harrison | Gritt | McAllister | Phillips L. | Walker | Walsh | Hales | Lansdowne | Ferns | Johns | Smith | Robinson | Elliott | Dickenson | Madden | Berry | Ambrose | Mehmet | Browne | Match No. |
|---|---|---|---|---|---|---|---|---|---|---|---|---|---|---|---|---|---|---|---|---|---|
| 1 | 2 | 3 | 4 | 5 | 6 | 7 | 8 | 9 | 10 | 11 | | | | | | | | | | | 1 |
| | 2 | 3 | | 5 | 6 | 7 | 8 | 9 | 10 | 11 | 1 | 4*12 | | | | | | | | | 2 |
| | 2 | 3 | | 5 | 6 | 7 | | 9 | 10 | 11 | 1 | 8 | 4 | | | | | | | | 3 |
| | 2 | | 4 | 5 | 6 | | 8 | 9 | 10 | 3 | 1 | | 11 | 7 | | | | | | | 4 |
| | 2 | | 4 | 5 | 6 | | 8 | 9 | 10 | 3 | 1 | | 11 | 7 | | | | | | | 5 |
| | 2 | | 4 | 5 | 6 | | 8 | 9 | 10 | 3 | 1 | | 11 | 7 | | | | | | | 6 |
| | 2 | | 4 | 5 | 6 | | 8 | 9 | 10 | 3 | 1 | | 11 | 7 | | | | | | | 7 |
| | 2 | | 4 | 5 | 6 | | 8 | 9 | 10 | 3* | 1 | | 7 | 12 | 11 | | | | | | 8 |
| | 2 | | 4 | 5 | 6 | | 8 | 9 | 10* | | 1 | | 11 | 7 | 3 | 12 | | | | | 9 |
| | 2 | | 4 | 5 | 6 | | 8 | 9 | 10 | | 1 | | 11 | 7 | 3 | | | | | | 10 |
| | 2 | | 4 | 5 | 6 | | 8 | 9 | 10 | | 1 | | 11 | 7 | 3 | | | | | | 11 |
| | 2 | | 4 | 5 | 6 | | 8 | 9 | | | 1 | | 11 | 7 | 3 | 10 | | | | | 12 |
| | 2 | | 4 | 5 | 6 | | 8 | 9 | 12 | | 1 | | 11 | 7 | 3* | 10 | | | | | 13 |
| | 2 | | 4 | 5 | 6 | | 8 | 9 | | 3 | 1 | 12 | 11 | 7 | 10* | | | | | | 14 |
| | 2 | | 4 | 5 | 6 | | | 9 | | 3 | 1 | | 11 | 7 | | 8 | 10 | | | | 15 |
| | 2 | | 6* | 7 | 8 | | 9 | | | 3 | 1 | 12 | 11 | 4 | | 5 | 10 | | | | 16 |
| | 2 | | | | 6 | | 9* | | | 3 | 1 | 4 | 11 | 7 | | 12 | 5 | 8 | 10 | | 17 |
| | 2 | | | | 6 | | 8 | 9 | | 3 | 1 | 4 | 11 | 7 | | | 5* | 10 | 12 | | 18 |
| | 2 | | | 5 | 6 | | 8 | 9 | | 3 | 1 | 4* | 11 | 7 | | | | 10 | 12 | | 19 |
| | 2 | | 4 | 5 | 6 | | 8 | 9 | 7 | 3 | 1 | | 11 | | | | 10 | | | | 20 |
| | 2* | | 4 | 5 | 6 | | 8 | 9 | 7 | 3 | 1 | | 11 | 12 | | | 10 | | | | 21 |
| | 2 | | 4 | 5 | 6 | | 8 | 9 | | 3 | 1 | | 11 | | | | 10 | 7 | | | 22 |
| | 2 | | 4 | | 6 | | 8 | 9 | | 3 | 1 | | 11 | 5 | | | 10 | 7 | | | 23 |
| | 2 | | 4 | 5 | 6 | | 8 | 9 | | 3* | 1 | | 11 | 12 | | | 10 | 7 | | | 24 |
| | 2 | | 4 | 5 | 6 | | 8 | 9 | | | 1 | | 11 | 3 | | | 10 | 7 | | | 25 |
| | 2 | | 4* | 5 | 6 | | 8 | 9 | | | 1 | 12 | 11 | 3 | | | 10 | 7 | | | 26 |
| | 2 | | 12 | 5* | 6 | | 8 | 9 | | | 1 | | 11 | 3 | | | 10 | 7 | 4 | | 27 |
| | 2 | | 7 | 5 | 6* | | 8 | 9 | | | 1 | | 11 | 3 | | | 10 | 4 | 12 | | 28 |
| | 2 | | | 5 | 6 | | 8 | 9 | | | 1 | | 11 | 3 | | | 10 | 7 | 4 | | 29 |
| | 2 | | | 5 | 6 | | 8 | 9 | 12 | | 1 | | 11 | 3 | | | 10 | 7* | 4 | | 30 |
| | 2 | | | 5 | 6 | | 8 | 9 | 7 | | 1 | | 11 | 3 | | | 10 | | 4 | | 31 |
| | 2 | | | 5 | 6 | | 8 | 9* | 7 | | 1 | 12 | 11 | 3 | | | 10 | | 4 | | 32 |
| 1 | 2 | | | 5 | 6 | | 8 | 9 | 12 | | | | 11 | 3 | | | 10 | 7* | 4 | | 33 |
| | 2 | | | 5 | 6 | | 8 | 9 | 12 | | 1 | | 11* | 3 | | | 10 | 7 | 4 | | 34 |
| | 2 | | | 5 | 6 | | 8 | 9 | 12 | | 1 | | 11 | 3 | | | 10 | 7* | 4 | | 35 |
| | 2 | | | | 6 | | 8 | 9 | 10 | 11 | 1 | | 5 | 3 | | | | 7 | 4 | | 36 |
| | 2 | | | | 6 | | 8 | 9* | 10 | 7 | 1 | 5 | 11 | 3 | | | 12 | | 4 | | 37 |
| | 2 | | | 5 | 6 | | 8 | | 10 | 7 | 1 | | 11 | 3 | | | | 9 | 4 | | 38 |
| | 2 | | | 5 | 6 | | 8 | | 10 | 7 | 1 | | 11 | 3 | | | 12 | 9 | 4* | | 39 |
| | 2 | | | 5 | 6 | | 8 | | 10 | 7 | 1 | | 11 | 3 | | | | 9 | 4 | | 40 |
| | 2 | | | 5 | 6 | | 8 | | 10 | 7 | 1 | | 11* | 3 | | | 9 | 12 | 4 | | 41 |
| | 2 | | | 5 | 6 | | 8 | | 10 | 7* | 1 | 12 | | 3 | | | 9 | 11 | 4 | | 42 |
| 2 | 42 | 3 | 33 | 26 | 42 | 3 | 38 | 35 | 24 | 26 | 40 | 6 | 37 | 36 | 5 | 6 | 24 | 18 | 16 | — | |
| | | | +1s | | | | | | +3s | +2s | | +4s | +2s | +2s | +2s | +1s | +1s | +4s | +1s | | |

## CHARLTON ATHLETIC

| | Ht | Wt | Birthplace | Clubs | League App. | League Gls |
|---|---|---|---|---|---|---|
| **Goalkeepers** | | | | | | |
| Nicky Johns | 6 3½ | 11 8 | Bristol | Millwall | 50 | — |
| | | | | Tampa Bay R | (not known) | |
| | | | | Charlton Ath (on loan) | 10 | — |
| | | | | Sheffield U (on loan) | 1 | — |
| | | | | Charlton Ath | 111 | — |
| John Phillips | 6 0 | 10 8 | Shrewsbury | Shrewsbury T | 51 | — |
| (Wales) | | | | Aston V | 15 | — |
| | | | | Chelsea | 125 | — |
| | | | | Swansea C (on loan) | — | — |
| | | | | Crewe Alex (on loan) | 6 | — |
| | | | | Brighton | 1 | — |
| | | | | Charlton Ath | 2 | — |
| **Defenders** | | | | | | |
| Leslie Berry | 6 2 | 12 5 | Plumstead | Charlton Ath | 244 | 10 |
| Tony Hazell | 5 10 | 12 12½ | High Wycombe | QPR | 369 | 4 |
| (Contract cancelled April 1982) | | | | Millwall | 153 | 6 |
| | | | | Crystal Palace | 5 | — |
| | | | | Charlton Ath | 37 | — |
| Kevin Dickenson | 5 5 | 10 3½ | London | Tottenham H | — | — |
| | | | | Charlton Ath | 8 | — |
| Terry Naylor | 5 10 | 11 10 | Islington | Tottenham H | 243 | — |
| | | | | Charlton Ath | 67 | — |
| Paul Elliott | 6 1½ | 11 11½ | London | Charlton Ath | 38 | 1 |
| Frank Clark* | 6 0 | 11 7½ | Bromley | Charlton Ath | — | — |
| Steve Harrison | 5 7 | 11 1½ | Blackpool | Blackpool | 148 | — |
| (Contract cancelled April 1982) | | | | Vancouver W | (not known) | |
| | | | | Watford | 83 | — |
| | | | | Charlton Ath | 3 | — |
| Phil Ferns | 5 11 | 11 4 | Liverpool | Bournemouth | 95 | 6 |
| | | | | Charlton Ath | 28 | — |
| Leighton Phillips | 5 10 | 10 11 | Briton Ferry | Cardiff C | 180 | 11 |
| (Wales) | | | | Aston V | 140 | 4 |
| | | | | Swansea C | 97 | — |
| | | | | Charlton Ath | 42 | 1 |
| **Midfield** | | | | | | |
| Steven Gritt | 5 10 | 10 10 | Bournemouth | Bournemouth | 6 | 3 |
| | | | | Charlton Ath | 178 | 16 |
| Phil Walker | 5 9½ | 12 1 | London | Millwall | 146 | 17 |
| | | | | Charlton Ath | 78 | 12 |
| Kevin Smith | 5 8 | 10 7 | St Paul's Cray, Kent | Charlton Ath | 46 | 6 |
| Viggo Jacobsen* | 5 6 | 9 11½ | Denmark | Kastrup | (not known) | |
| | | | | Charlton Ath | 9 | — |
| Billy Lansdowne | 6 0 | 11 6 | Epping | West Ham U | 9 | 1 |
| | | | | Charlton Ath | 27 | 4 |
| Don McAllister | 5 10 | 11 2 | Radcliffe | Bolton W | 156 | 2 |
| | | | | Tottenham H | 172 | 9 |
| | | | | Charlton Ath | 26 | 4 |
| David Mehmet | 5 9 | 11 9 | London | Millwall | 114 | 15 |
| | | | | Charlton Ath | 16 | 1 |
| **Forwards** | | | | | | |
| Martin Robinson | 5 8½ | 11 5½ | Ilford | Tottenham H | 6 | 2 |
| | | | | Charlton Ath | 163 | 44 |
| Leroy Ambrose | 5 9 | 10 11 | St Vincent, W Indies | Charlton Ath | 33 | 1 |
| Derek Hales | 5 9½ | 11 8½ | Lower Halstow | Luton T | 7 | 1 |
| | | | | Charlton Ath | 129 | 73 |
| | | | | Derby Co | 23 | 4 |
| | | | | West Ham U | 24 | 10 |
| | | | | Charlton Ath | 118 | 44 |
| Johnny Ostergaard | 5 10½ | 13 2½ | Denmark | Ikast | (not known) | |
| (Contract cancelled June 1981) | | | | Charlton Ath | 12 | 1 |
| Paul Walsh | 5 7 | 10 1 | London | Charlton Ath | 87 | 24 |
| Stephen Browne | | | | Charlton Ath | 1 | — |
| (Apprentice) | | | | | | |

Also retained: Paul Curtis, Paul Kay.
Free transfers: James Clare*, Henry Laville*.

# CHELSEA

# Division 2

*President:* The Right Hon Earl Cadogan MC, DL.

*Chairman:* K. W. Bates.

*Directors:* Viscount Chelsea, D. Mears BSC, N. J. Spencer FCA, G. Webb.

*Chief Executive:* Martin Spencer FCA.

*Manager:* John Neal.  *Asst Manager:* Ian McNeill.

*Secretary:* Sheila Marson.

*Marketing Executive:* Mike Barker.

*Year Formed:* 1905.  *Turned Professional:* 1905.

*Limited Company:* 1905.

**Football League Record:**
1905 Elected to Division 2; 1907–10 Division 1; 1910–12 Division 2; 1912–24 Division 1; 1924–30 Division 2; 1930–62 Division 1; 1962–63 Division 2; 1963–75 Division 1; 1975–77 Division 2; 1977–79 Division 1; 1979– Division 2.

**Honours:** *Football League:* Division 1 – Champions 1954–55; Division 2 – Runners-up 1906–07, 1911–12, 1929–30, 1962–63, 1976–77. *FA Cup*; Winners 1970; Runners-up 1914–15, 1966–67. *Football League Cup:* Winners 1964–65, Runners-up 1971–72. **European Competitions:** *European Fairs Cup:* 1958–60, 1965–66, 1968–69; *European Cup-Winners' Cup:* 1970-71 (winners), 1971–72.

*Record Victory:* 13-0 v Jeunesse Hautcharage, European Cup-Winners' Cup 1st rd, 29 Sept, 1971.

*Record Defeat:* 1-8 v Wolverhampton W, Division 1, 26 Sept, 1953.

*Most League Points:* 57, Division 2, 1906–07. *Three points win:* 57, Division 2, 1981–82.

*Most League Goals:* 98, Division 1, 1960–61.

*Highest League Scorer in Season:* Jimmy Greaves, 41, 1960–61.

*Most League Goals in Total Aggregate:* Bobby Tambling, 164, 1958–70.

*Most Capped Player:* Ray Wilkins, 24 (52) England.

*Most League Appearances:* Ron Harris, 655, 1962–80.

*Record Transfer Fee Received:* £825,000 from Manchester U for Ray Wilkins, Aug 1979.

*Record Transfer Fee Paid:* £225,000 to Celtic for David Hay, July 1974.

*Previous Managers since the War:* Billy Birrell, Ted Drake, Tommy Docherty, Dave Sexton, Ron Suart, Eddie McCreadie, Ken Shellito, Danny Blanchflower, Geoff Hurst.

*Address of Supporters Club:* Same as Football Club.

*Address of the Club Shop or Boutique:* Stamford Bridge, SW6.

---

**Stamford Bridge, London SW6.** Telephone 01-385 5545/6, (Information Service) 01-381 0111. *Telegraphic address:* 'Chelstam, London SW6.' *Ground capacity:* 45,000 (21,500 covered). *Record attendance:* 82,905 v Arsenal, Division 1, 12 Oct, 1935. *Record receipts:* £158,227 v Tottenham H, FA Cup 6th rd, 6 March, 1982. *Pitch measurements:* 114yd×71yd.

*How to get there:* Nearest station is Fulham Broadway on the Underground (District Line). London Transport regular buses to Fulham Broadway, Kings Road, Fulham Road, or Stamford Bridge.

*Match tickets:* Advance tickets available by postal or personal application. No telephone bookings.

*Car parking:* Street parking only.

*Entertainments/catering facilities:* Licensed bars at all points of the ground.

*Club shop:* Run by the Football Club; sells all types of souvenirs.

*Handbooks/programmes:* Programmes available on subscription.

*Club Colours:* All royal blue with white stripe on shorts. White stockings.

*Change Colours:* Yellow, blue, yellow.

*First Team Trainer:* Norman Medhurst.

*Physiotherapist:* Eddie Franklin, MCSP.

*Club Nickname:* Blues.

## CHELSEA 1981–82 LEAGUE RECORD

| Match No. | Date | Venue | Opponents | Result | H/T Score | Goalscorers | Atten-dance |
|---|---|---|---|---|---|---|---|
| 1 | Aug 29 | H | Bolton W | W 2-0 | 2-0 | Lee, Droy | 16,606 |
| 2 | Sept 5 | A | Cardiff C | W 2-1 | 1-1 | Mayes 2 | 8898 |
| 3 | 12 | H | Watford | L 1-3 | 1-1 | Walker | 20,036 |
| 4 | 19 | A | Shrewsbury T | L 0-1 | 0-0 | | 5616 |
| 5 | 23 | H | Charlton Ath | D 2-2 | 1-1 | Driver 2 | 15,329 |
| 6 | 26 | H | Norwich C | W 2-1 | 1-1 | Bumstead (pen), Driver | 14,509 |
| 7 | 28 | A | Orient | W 2-0 | 1-0 | Fillery, Mayes | 9698 |
| 8 | Oct 3 | A | Cambridge U | L 0-1 | 0-0 | | 8806 |
| 9 | 10 | H | Wrexham | W 2-0 | 0-0 | Fillery, Lee | 14,170 |
| 10 | 16 | A | Leicester C | D 1-1 | 1-1 | Fillery | 18,358 |
| 11 | 24 | H | Barnsley | L 1-2 | 1-1 | Mayes | 15,268 |
| 12 | 31 | A | Rotherham U | L 0-6 | 0-3 | | 10,145 |
| 13 | Nov 7 | H | Newcastle U | W 2-1 | 2-0 | Lee, Fillery | 16,059 |
| 14 | 14 | A | Oldham Ath | L 0-1 | 0-1 | | 9773 |
| 15 | 21 | H | Grimsby T | D 1-1 | 1-1 | Lee | 11,931 |
| 16 | 24 | A | Charlton Ath | W 4-3 | 3-2 | Walker 2, Bumstead 2 | 11,082 |
| 17 | 28 | A | Derby Co | D 1-1 | 1-0 | Walker | 13,963 |
| 18 | Dec 5 | H | Sheffield W | W 2-1 | 1-0 | Hales, Lee | 17,033 |
| 19 | 19 | H | Blackburn R | D 1-1 | 0-0 | Lee | 11,768 |
| 20 | 26 | A | QPR | W 2-0 | 0-0 | Walker, Mayes | 22,022 |
| 21 | Jan 16 | A | Bolton W | D 2-2 | 1-0 | Mayes, Bumstead | 7278 |
| 22 | 30 | H | Shrewsbury T | W 3-1 | 1-0 | Walker 3 | 11,446 |
| 23 | Feb 6 | A | Watford | L 0-1 | 0-0 | | 17,101 |
| 24 | 17 | H | Cardiff C | W 1-0 | 0-0 | Walker | 9710 |
| 25 | 20 | A | Norwich C | L 1-2 | 1-2 | Walker | 16,018 |
| 26 | 27 | A | Wrexham | L 0-1 | 0-0 | | 3935 |
| 27 | Mar 9 | H | Leicester C | W 4-1 | 1-0 | Hales, Locke, Mayes 2 | 10,586 |
| 28 | 12 | A | Barnsley | L 1-2 | 1-0 | Lee | 12,706 |
| 29 | 17 | H | Crystal Palace | L 1-2 | 0-2 | Mayes | 13,894 |
| 30 | 20 | H | Rotherham U | L 1-4 | 1-3 | Rhoades-Brown | 11,900 |
| 31 | 27 | A | Newcastle U | L 0-1 | 0-1 | | 26,887 |
| 32 | Apr 3 | H | Oldham Ath | D 2-2 | 1-0 | Mayes 2 | 8938 |
| 33 | 7 | H | Cambridge U | W 4-1 | 3-0 | Hutchings, Lee 2, Fillery | 6196 |
| 34 | 10 | H | QPR | W 2-1 | 0-1 | Droy, Lee | 18,365 |
| 35 | 12 | A | Crystal Palace | W 1-0 | 1-0 | Walker | 17,189 |
| 36 | 17 | A | Grimsby T | D 3-3 | 2-1 | Walker 3 | 9164 |
| 37 | 20 | A | Luton T | D 2-2 | 1-1 | Walker, Fillery | 16,185 |
| 38 | 24 | H | Derby Co | L 0-2 | 0-0 | | 11,005 |
| 39 | May 1 | A | Sheffield W | D 0-0 | 0-0 | | 19,259 |
| 40 | 5 | H | Orient | D 2-2 | 2-0 | Lee, Mayes | 6009 |
| 41 | 8 | H | Luton T | L 1-2 | 1-1 | Walker | 15,044 |
| 42 | 15 | A | Blackburn R | D 1-1 | 0-0 | Pates | 6133 |

**Final League Position: 12**

### Goalscorers

*League* (60): Walker 16, Mayes 12, Lee 11, Fillery 6, Bumstead 4 (1 pen), Driver 3, Droy 2, Hales 2, Hutchings 1, Locke 1, Pates 1, Rhoades-Brown 1.
*League Cup* (5): Fillery 3, Bumstead 1, Walker 1.
*FA Cup* (9): Mayes 4, Bumstead 1, Droy 1, Fillery 1, Lee 1, Rhoades-Brown 1.

| | | | |
|---|---|---|---|
| League Cup | Second Round | Southampton (a) | 1-1 |
| | | (h) | 2-1 |
| | Third Round | Wigan Ath (a) | 2-4 |
| FA Cup | Third Round | Hull C (h) | 0-0 |
| | | (a) | 2-0 |
| | Fourth Round | Wrexham (h) | 0-0 |
| | | (a) | 1-1 |
| | | (a) | 2-1 |
| | Fifth Round | Liverpool (h) | 2-0 |
| | Sixth Round | Tottenham H (h) | 2-3 |

| Borota | Locke | Rofe | Viljoen | Droy | Pates | Walker | Bumstead | Lee | Mayes | Fillery | Driver | Chivers | Iles | Rhoades-Brown | Hutchings | Britton | Wilkins | Francis | Hales | Nutton | Canoville | Match No. |
|---|---|---|---|---|---|---|---|---|---|---|---|---|---|---|---|---|---|---|---|---|---|---|
| 1 | 2 | 3 | 4 | 5 | 6 | 7 | 8* | 9 | 10 | 11 | 12 | | | | | | | | | | | 1 |
| 1 | 2 | 3 | 4 | 5* | 6 | 7 | 8 | 9 | 10 | 11 | 12 | | | | | | | | | | | 2 |
| 1 | 2 | 3 | 4 | | 5* | 7 | 8 | 9 | 10 | 11 | 12 | 6 | | | | | | | | | | 3 |
| 1 | 2 | 3 | 4 | | 5 | 7 | 8 | 9 | 10* | 11 | 12 | 6 | | | | | | | | | | 4 |
| | 2 | 3* | 4 | 5 | | | 8 | 9 | 10 | 11 | 7 | 6 | 1 | 12 | | | | | | | | 5 |
| 1 | 2 | | | 5 | | | 8 | 9 | 10 | 11 | 7 | 6 | | 4 | 3 | | | | | | | 6 |
| 1 | 2 | | | 5 | | | 8 | 9 | 10 | 11 | 7 | 6 | | 4 | 3 | | | | | | | 7 |
| 1 | 2 | | | 5 | 12 | | 8 | 9 | 10 | 11 | 7* | 6 | | 4 | 3 | | | | | | | 8 |
| 1 | 2 | | 4 | 5 | | | | 9 | 10 | 11 | | 6 | | 7 | 3 | 8 | | | | | | 9 |
| 1 | 2 | | 4 | 12 | 5 | | | 9 | 10* | 11 | | 6 | | 7 | 3 | 8 | | | | | | 10 |
| 1 | 2 | | 12 | 5 | | 4 | | 9 | 10 | 11 | | 6 | | 7 | 3 | 8* | | | | | | 11 |
| 1 | | | 4 | 5 | 6 | 10 | 8 | 9 | 12 | 11 | | 2 | | 7* | 3 | | | | | | | 12 |
| 1 | | | 4 | 11 | 7 | 10 | | 9 | | | | 3 | | 6 | 5 | 8 | 2 | | | | | 13 |
| | | | 12 | 5 | 10 | 8 | | 9 | | 11 | | 6 | | 7 | 3 | 4* | 2 | 1 | | | | 14 |
| | | | 5 | 6 | 10 | 8 | | 9 | 12 | 11 | | | | 7 | 3 | 4* | 2 | 1 | | | | 15 |
| | | | 5 | 6 | 10 | 8 | | 9 | 7 | 11 | | | | | 3 | | 2 | 1 | 4 | | | 16 |
| | | | 5 | 6 | 10 | 8 | | 9 | 7 | 11 | | | | | 3 | | 2 | 1 | 4 | | | 17 |
| | | | 5 | 6 | 10 | 8 | | 9 | 7 | 11 | | | | 12 | 3 | | 2* | 1 | 4 | | | 18 |
| | | | 5 | 6 | 10 | 8 | | 9 | 7 | 11 | | | | | 3 | | 2 | 1 | 4 | | | 19 |
| | | | 5 | 6 | 10 | 8 | | 9 | 7 | 11 | | | | | 3 | | 2 | 1 | 4 | | | 20 |
| | | | 5 | 6 | 10 | 8 | | 9 | 7 | 11 | | | | | 3 | | 2 | 1 | 4 | | | 21 |
| | 2 | | 5 | 6 | 10 | 8 | | | 7 | 11* | | | | 9 | 3 | 4 | | 1 | 12 | | | 22 |
| | 2 | | 5 | 6 | 10 | 8* | | 9 | 7 | 12 | | | | 11 | 3 | | | 1 | 4 | | | 23 |
| | 2 | | 5 | 6 | 10 | | | 9 | | 11 | | | | 7 | 3 | 1 | 8 | | 4 | | | 24 |
| | 2 | | 5* | 6 | 10 | | | 9 | 12 | 11 | | | | 7 | 3 | 1 | 8 | | 4 | | | 25 |
| | 2 | | | 6 | 10 | | | 9 | 12 | 11 | | 5 | | 7 | 3 | 8* | | 1 | 4 | | | 26 |
| | 2 | | | 6 | 10 | | | 9 | | 11 | | 5 | | 7 | 3 | 1 | 8 | | 4 | | | 27 |
| | 2 | | | 6 | 12 | | | 9 | 10 | 11 | | 5 | | 7 | 3 | 1 | 8* | | 4 | | | 28 |
| | 2 | | | 6* | 12 | | | 9 | 10 | 11 | | 5 | | 7 | 3 | 8 | | 1 | 4 | | | 29 |
| | 2 | | | 6 | 12 | | | 9 | 10 | 11 | | 5 | | 7 | 3 | 8* | | 1 | 4 | | | 30 |
| | 2 | 8 | | 6 | 12 | | | 9 | 10 | 11 | | 5 | | 7* | 3 | | | 1 | 4 | | | 31 |
| | 2 | | | 6 | 8 | | | 9 | 10 | 11 | | 5 | | 7 | 3 | | | 1 | 4 | | | 32 |
| | | | | 5 | 6 | 9* | | 2 | 10 | 11 | | 8 | | 7 | 3 | 12 | | 1 | 4 | | | 33 |
| 3 | | | | 5 | 6 | 9 | | 2 | 10 | | | 8 | | 7* | 11 | 12 | | 1 | 4 | | | 34 |
| | 2 | | | 6 | 8* | | | 9 | 10 | 11 | | 5 | | 7 | 3 | | | 1 | 4 | 12 | | 35 |
| | 2 | | | | 6 | 9 | | 5 | 10 | 11 | | 8 | | 7 | 3 | | | 1 | 4 | | | 36 |
| | 2 | | | | 6 | 9 | | 5 | 10 | 11 | | 8 | | 7 | 3 | | | 1 | 4 | | | 37 |
| | 2 | | | | 6 | 9 | | 5 | 10 | 11 | | 8* | | 12 | 3 | 7 | | 1 | 4 | | | 38 |
| | 2 | 12 | | 5 | 6 | 9 | | 11 | 10 | | | 8 | | 7 | 3 | | | 1 | 4* | | | 39 |
| | 2 | 3* | 5 | 6 | 7 | | | 9 | 10 | 11 | | 12 | | 4 | 8 | | | 1 | | | | 40 |
| | 2 | | 5 | 6 | 9 | 4 | | | 10 | 11 | | 8 | | 7* | 3 | | | 1 | | 12 | | 41 |
| | 2 | | 5 | 4 | 8* | | | 9 | 10 | 11 | | 6 | | | 3 | | | 1 | | 12 | 7 | 42 |
| 12 | 31 | 6 | 9 | 20 | 42 | 31 | 21 | 40 | 35 | 39 | 4 | 28 | 1 | 24 | 35 | 17 | 10 | 29 | 10 | 17 | 1 | |
| | +1s | | +3s | | +5s | | | +4s | +1s | +4s | +1s | | | +3s | | +1s | +1s | | +2s | +2s | | |

## CHELSEA

| | Ht | Wt | Birthplace | Clubs | League App. | League Gls |
|---|---|---|---|---|---|---|
| **Goalkeepers** | | | | | | |
| Petar Borota* | 6 0 | 12 7 | Yugoslavia | Belgrade SC | — | — |
| (Yugoslavia) | | | | Partizan | — | — |
| | | | | Chelsea | 107 | — |
| Bob Iles | 6 1 | 12 7 | Leicester | Weymouth | — | — |
| | | | | Chelsea | 9 | — |
| Steve Francis | 5 11 | 11 5 | Billericay | Chelsea | 29 | — |
| **Defenders** | | | | | | |
| Gary Locke | 5 11 | 11 5 | Park Royal | Chelsea | 266 | 3 |
| Micky Droy | 6 4½ | 15 5 | Highbury | Chelsea | 239 | 10 |
| Graham Wilkins | 5 6½ | 10 2 | Hayes | Chelsea | 137 | 1 |
| Michael Nutton | 5 11 | 10 12 | St John's Wood | Chelsea | 71 | — |
| Gary Chivers | 5 11 | 11 5 | Stockwell | Chelsea | 103 | 4 |
| Kevin Hales | 5 7 | 10 4 | Dartford | Chelsea | 17 | 2 |
| Colin Pates | 5 11 | 11 0 | Carshalton | Chelsea | 73 | 1 |
| Dennis Rofe* | 5 7 | 10 11 | Fulham | Orient | 171 | 6 |
| | | | | Leicester C | 290 | 5 |
| | | | | Chelsea | 59 | — |
| Paul Williams | 6 0 | 11 7 | Lambeth | Chelsea | — | — |
| **Midfield** | | | | | | |
| John Bumstead | 5 7 | 10 0 | Rotherhithe | Chelsea | 98 | 9 |
| Mike Fillery | 5 10 | 11 12 | Mitcham | Chelsea | 124 | 23 |
| Ian Britton | 5 5 | 9 7 | Dundee | Chelsea | 263 | 33 |
| Colin Viljoen | 5 8 | 10 10 | Johannesburg | Ipswich T | 305 | 46 |
| (England) | | | | QPR (on loan) | — | — |
| | | | | Manchester C | 27 | — |
| | | | | Chelsea | 20 | — |
| Chris Hutchings | 5 10 | 11 0 | Winchester | Harrow B | (not known) | |
| | | | | Chelsea | 47 | 2 |
| Timmy Elmes | 5 10 | 12 0 | Thornton Heath | Chelsea | 4 | — |
| Jasper Dale | 5 6 | 10 0 | Croydon | Chelsea | — | — |
| **Forwards** | | | | | | |
| Clive Walker | 5 8½ | 11 4 | Oxford | Chelsea | 163 | 51 |
| Colin Lee | 6 1 | 11 9 | Plymouth | Bristol C | — | — |
| | | | | Hereford U (on loan) | 9 | — |
| | | | | Torquay U | 35 | 14 |
| | | | | Tottenham H | 62 | 18 |
| | | | | Chelsea | 80 | 27 |
| Peter Rhoades- | 5 9 | 10 6 | Hampton | Chelsea | 65 | 2 |
| Brown | | | | | | |
| Phil Driver | 5 10 | 10 12 | Huddersfield | Luton T | — | — |
| | | | | Wimbledon | 16 | 3 |
| | | | | Chelsea | 31 | 4 |
| Alan Mayes | 5 7 | 10 10 | London | QPR | — | — |
| | | | | Watford | 133 | 31 |
| | | | | Northampton T (on loan) | 10 | 4 |
| | | | | Swindon T | 89 | 38 |
| | | | | Chelsea | 52 | 16 |
| Paul Canoville | 5 10 | 11 0 | Hillingdon | Hillingdon B | (not known) | |
| | | | | Chelsea | 3 | — |
| Paul Ward | 5 11 | 12 5 | Sedgefield | Chelsea | — | — |

# CHESTER Division 4

*President:* Duke of Westminster.   *Chairman:* R. Rowlands.
*Vice-Chairman:* C. Thompson.
*Directors:* L. Lloyd, E. J. Owen, R. S. Tresidder, D. Darlington.
*Team Manager:* Cliff Sear.   *Secretary:* S. Gandy.
*Year Formed:* 1884.   *Turned Professional:* 1902.
*Limited Company:* 1909.
*Previous Grounds:* Faulkner Street; Old Showground; 1904, Whipcord Lane; 1906, Sealand Road.

**Football League Record:**
1931 Elected Division 3(N); 1958–75 Division 4; 1975–82 Division 3; 1982– Division 4.

**Honours:** *Football League:* Division 3 best season: 5th, 1977–78; Division 3(N) – Runners-up 1935–36. FA Cup best season: 5th rd, 1976–77, 1979–80. *Football League Cup:* Semi-final 1974–75. *Welsh Cup:* Winners 1908, 1933, 1947. *Debenhams Cup:* Winners 1977.
*Record Victory:* 12-0 v York C, Division 3(N), 1 Feb, 1936.
*Record Defeat:* 2-11 v Oldham Ath, Division 3(N), 19 Jan, 1952.
*Most League Points:* 56, Division 3(N), 1946–47; Division 4, 1964–65.
*Most League Goals:* 119, Division 4, 1964–65.
*Highest League Scorer in Season:* Dick Yates, 36, Division 3(N), 1946–47.
*Most League Goals in Total Aggregate:* Gary Talbot, 83, 1963–67, 1968–70.
*Most Capped Player:* Bill Lewis, 9 (30), Wales.
*Most League Appearances:* Ray Gill, 408, 1951–62.
*Record Transfer Fee Received:* £300,000 from Liverpool for Ian Rush, May 1980.
*Record Transfer Fee Paid:* £45,000 to Carlisle U for Steve Ludlam, May 1980.
*Previous Managers since the War:* Frank Brown, Louis Page, John Harris, Stan Pearson, Bill Lambton, Peter Hauser, Ken Roberts, Alan Oakes.
*Address of the Club Shop or Boutique:* 18 Grosvenor St, Chester.

---

**The Stadium, Sealand Rd, Chester CH1 4LW.** Telephone Chester 371376. *Ground capacity:* 20,000. *Record attendance:* 20,500 v Chelsea, FA Cup 3rd rd replay, 16 Jan, 1952. *Record receipts:* £15,854 v Aston Villa, FL Cup semi-final first leg, 15 Jan, 1975. *Pitch measurements:* 114yd×76yd.
*How to get there:* Nearest railway station, Chester. Corporation bus to Town Hall Square, where special buses run from the Odeon Cinema to the ground.
*Match tickets:* No advance booking.
*Car parking:* Extensive parking at ground.
*Entertainments/catering facilities:* Catering facilities on ground.
*Club shop:* In town centre; stocks all types of souvenirs.
*Handbooks/programmes:* Programmes not available on subscription.
*Extra information:* Additional programme shop inside the ground.
*Club Colours:* Royal blue shirts with white stripes, royal blue shorts with red and white trim, white stockings with red and blue ringed top.
*Change Colours:* All yellow.
*First Team Trainer:* Jim Walker.
*Club Nickname:* The Seals.

## CHESTER 1981−82 LEAGUE RECORD

| Match No. | Date | Venue | Opponents | Result | H/T Score | Goalscorers | Atten- dance |
|---|---|---|---|---|---|---|---|
| 1 | Aug 29 | A | Bristol R | D 2-2 | 2-0 | Zelem, Oakes | 5554 |
| 2 | Sept 5 | H | Swindon T | D 0-0 | 0-0 | | 1798 |
| 3 | 12 | A | Gillingham | W 1-0 | 0-0 | Simpson | 3990 |
| 4 | 19 | H | Millwall | D 0-0 | 0-0 | | 2052 |
| 5 | 23 | H | Walsall | D 0-0 | 0-0 | | 1978 |
| 6 | 26 | A | Fulham | L 0-2 | 0-2 | | 3629 |
| 7 | 29 | A | Huddersfield T | W 2-1 | 1-1 | Simpson 2 | 7747 |
| 8 | Oct 10 | H | Oxford U | D 2-2 | 1-1 | Phillips, Sutcliffe | 2008 |
| 9 | 17 | A | Wimbledon | L 0-1 | 0-1 | | 1659 |
| 10 | 21 | H | Chesterfield | L 0-2 | 0-0 | | 2329 |
| 11 | 24 | A | Plymouth Arg | L 1-5 | 1-2 | Jones | 2646 |
| 12 | 31 | H | Reading | L 2-3 | 2-2 | Phillips, Needham | 1765 |
| 13 | Nov 3 | A | Burnley | L 0-1 | 0-0 | | 3455 |
| 14 | 7 | A | Preston NE | W 1-0 | 1-0 | Storton | 5181 |
| 15 | 14 | H | Exeter C | L 0-2 | 0-0 | | 2125 |
| 16 | 28 | A | Brentford | L 0-1 | 0-1 | | 5200 |
| 17 | Dec 2 | H | Doncaster R | D 1-1 | 0-0 | Cooke | 1555 |
| 18 | 5 | H | Southend U | D 1-1 | 0-0 | Cooke | 1388 |
| 19 | 26 | A | Newport Co | W 1-0 | 1-0 | Ludlam | 4908 |
| 20 | Jan 19 | H | Portsmouth | W 3-2 | 1-1 | Sutcliffe, Jones, Simpson | 1444 |
| 21 | 23 | H | Bristol R | D 1-1 | 1-0 | Simpson | 2040 |
| 22 | 30 | A | Millwall | L 1-2 | 1-1 | Cooke | 3250 |
| 23 | Feb 3 | A | Lincoln C | L 0-3 | 0-0 | | 2120 |
| 24 | 6 | H | Gillingham | D 0-0 | 0-0 | | 1543 |
| 25 | 9 | A | Walsall | L 1-2 | 1-2 | Henderson | 3668 |
| 26 | 13 | A | Doncaster R | L 3-4 | 1-2 | Henderson, Simpson 2 | 4098 |
| 27 | 20 | H | Huddersfield T | W 3-1 | 1-0 | Henderson, Cooke, Simpson | 3120 |
| 28 | 27 | A | Oxford U | L 1-3 | 0-1 | Cooke | 5049 |
| 29 | Mar 9 | A | Chesterfield | W 5-3 | 1-2 | Simpson 2, Raynor, Henderson 2 | 4291 |
| 30 | 13 | H | Plymouth Arg | L 0-3 | 0-1 | | 1988 |
| 31 | 17 | H | Burnley | L 0-1 | 0-1 | | 3261 |
| 32 | 20 | A | Reading | L 1-4 | 0-3 | Simpson | 3093 |
| 33 | 27 | H | Preston NE | L 0-1 | 0-0 | | 2842 |
| 34 | 31 | H | Wimbledon | D 1-1 | 0-0 | Simpson | 1359 |
| 35 | Apr 3 | A | Exeter C | L 0-3 | 0-1 | | 2498 |
| 36 | 10 | H | Newport Co | L 0-2 | 0-0 | | 1451 |
| 37 | 13 | A | Carlisle U | L 0-3 | 0-1 | | 5340 |
| 38 | 17 | A | Southend U | L 0-2 | 0-1 | | 3427 |
| 39 | 21 | H | Bristol C | D 0-0 | 0-0 | | 1034 |
| 40 | 24 | H | Brentford | L 1-2 | 0-1 | Storton | 1304 |
| 41 | 27 | A | Swindon T | L 0-3 | 0-1 | | 3848 |
| 42 | May 1 | A | Portsmouth | L 0-2 | 0-0 | | 6196 |
| 43 | 5 | H | Fulham | L 0-2 | 0-1 | | 1174 |
| 44 | 8 | H | Lincoln C | L 1-2 | 0-0 | Jones | 1176 |
| 45 | 15 | A | Bristol C | L 0-1 | 0-1 | | 3934 |
| 46 | 19 | H | Carlisle U | L 0-1 | 0-1 | | 2535 |

**Final League Position: 24**

### Goalscorers

*League* (36): Simpson 12, Cooke 5, Henderson 5, Jones 3, Phillips 2, Storton 2, Sutcliffe 2, Ludlam 1, Needham 1, Oakes 1, Raynor 1, Zelem 1.
*League Cup* (1): Jones 1.
*FA Cup* (0).

| | | | | |
|---|---|---|---|---|
| **League Cup** | First Round | Plymouth Arg (h) | | 1-1 |
| | | | (a) | 0-1 |
| **FA Cup** | First Round | Penrith (a) | | 0-1 |

| Millington | Needham | Raynor | Storton | Zelem | Oakes | Jones | Simpson | Ludlam | Phillips | Sutcliffe | Cottam | Howat | Cooke | Allen | Burns | Blackwell | Hornsby | Henderson | Harrington | Dean | Williams | Match No. |
|---|---|---|---|---|---|---|---|---|---|---|---|---|---|---|---|---|---|---|---|---|---|---|
| 1 | 2 | 3 | 4 | 5 | 6 | 7 | 8 | 9 | 10 | 11* | 12 |  |  |  |  |  |  |  |  |  |  | 1 |
| 1 | 2 | 3 | 4 | 5 | 6 | 7 | 8 | 9 | 10* | 11 |  | 12 |  |  |  |  |  |  |  |  |  | 2 |
| 1 | 2 | 3 | 4 |  | 6 | 7 | 8 | 9 |  | 11 | 5 | 10 |  |  |  |  |  |  |  |  |  | 3 |
| 1 | 2 | 3 | 4 | 5 | 6 | 7 | 8 | 9 |  | 11 |  |  | 10* | 12 |  |  |  |  |  |  |  | 4 |
| 1 | 2 | 3 | 4 | 5 | 6 | 7 | 8 | 9 |  | 11* |  |  | 10 | 12 |  |  |  |  |  |  |  | 5 |
| 1 | 2 | 3 | 4 | 5 | 6 | 7 | 8 | 9 |  | 11 | 12 |  | 10* |  |  |  |  |  |  |  |  | 6 |
| 1 | 2 | 3 | 4 | 5 | 6 | 7 | 8 | 9 | 10 | 11 |  |  |  |  |  |  |  |  |  |  |  | 7 |
| 1 | 2 | 3 | 4 | 5 | 6 | 7 | 8 | 9 | 10 | 11 |  |  |  |  |  |  |  |  |  |  |  | 8 |
| 1 | 2 | 3 | 4 |  | 6 | 7* | 8 | 9 | 10 | 11 | 5 |  |  |  | 12 |  |  |  |  |  |  | 9 |
| 1 | 2 | 3 | 4 |  | 6 | 7 | 8 | 9 | 10 | 11* | 5 |  |  |  | 12 |  |  |  |  |  |  | 10 |
| 1 | 2 | 3 | 4 |  | 6 | 7 | 8* | 9 | 10 |  | 5 | 12 |  |  | 11 |  |  |  |  |  |  | 11 |
| 1 | 6 | 3 | 4 | 5 |  | 7 |  | 9* | 10 | 11 | 2 | 8 | 12 |  |  |  |  |  |  |  |  | 12 |
| 1 | 2* | 3 | 4 |  | 6 |  |  | 9 | 10 | 7 | 5 | 8 |  | 11 | 12 |  |  |  |  |  |  | 13 |
| 1 |  | 4 |  |  | 2 | 6 |  | 9 | 10 | 11 | 5 |  |  | 7 | 3 | 8 |  |  |  |  |  | 14 |
| 1 |  | 4 |  |  | 2 | 6 | 12 | 9 | 10 | 11 | 5 |  |  | 7* | 3 | 8 |  |  |  |  |  | 15 |
| 1 | 2 | 4 |  |  |  |  | 8 | 9 | 10 | 11 | 5 |  |  |  | 3 | 6 | 7 |  |  |  |  | 16 |
| 1 | 2* | 4 |  |  |  |  | 8 | 9 | 10 | 11 | 5 |  |  | 12 | 3 | 6 | 7 |  |  |  |  | 17 |
| 1 | 2 | 4 |  |  |  |  | 8 | 9 | 10 | 7 | 5 |  |  | 11 | 3 | 6 |  |  |  |  |  | 18 |
| 1 | 2 | 4 |  |  |  | 6 | 8 | 9 |  |  | 5 |  |  | 11 | 3 | 7 |  | 10 |  |  |  | 19 |
| 1 | 2 | 4 |  |  |  | 6 | 8 | 9 |  | 7 | 5 |  |  |  | 3 | 10 |  | 11 |  |  |  | 20 |
| 1 | 2 | 4 |  |  |  | 6 | 8 | 9* |  | 7 | 5 |  |  | 12 | 3 | 10 |  | 11 |  |  |  | 21 |
| 1 | 2 | 4 |  |  |  | 6 | 8* |  | 10 |  | 5 |  |  | 11 | 12 | 3 | 7 | 9 |  |  |  | 22 |
| 1 | 2 | 4 | 10 |  |  | 6 | 8* |  |  |  | 5 |  |  | 11 | 12 | 3 | 7 | 9 |  |  |  | 23 |
| 1 | 2 | 4 | 5 |  |  | 6 | 8 |  |  | 12 | 7 |  |  | 11* | 3 | 10 |  | 9 |  |  |  | 24 |
| 1 | 2 | 3 | 4 | 5 |  |  | 8 | 9 |  | 12 | 7 |  |  | 6* |  | 10 |  | 11 |  |  |  | 25 |
| 1 | 2 | 3 | 4 | 5 |  |  | 8 | 9 |  | 12 | 7* |  |  | 6 |  | 10 |  | 11 |  |  |  | 26 |
|  | 2 | 4 | 5 | 6 |  |  | 8 | 9 |  |  |  |  |  | 7 | 3 | 10 |  | 11 | 1 |  |  | 27 |
|  | 2 | 4 | 5 | 6 |  |  | 8 | 9 |  |  |  |  |  | 7 | 3 | 10 |  | 11 | 1 |  |  | 28 |
|  | 10 | 3 | 4 | 5 | 6 |  | 8 | 9 |  |  |  |  |  | 2 |  | 7 |  | 11 | 1 |  |  | 29 |
|  | 10 | 3 | 4 | 5 | 6 |  | 8 | 9 |  |  |  | 12 |  | 2 |  | 7* |  | 11 | 1 |  |  | 30 |
|  | 8 | 3 | 4 | 5 | 6 |  |  | 9 |  |  |  |  |  | 7 | 2 | 10 |  | 11 | 1 |  |  | 31 |
|  | 2 | 3 | 4 |  | 6 |  |  | 9 |  | 7 | 5 |  |  | 12 | 10 | 8* |  | 11 | 1 |  |  | 32 |
|  | 2 | 4 | 5 | 6 |  |  | 8 | 9 | 10 |  | 7 |  |  | 12 | 3 |  |  | 11* | 1 |  |  | 33 |
| 1 | 2 |  |  | 5 |  |  | 8 | 9 | 10 |  | 7 |  |  | 4 | 3 | 6 |  | 11 | 1 |  |  | 34 |
|  | 6 | 2 | 4 | 5 |  |  | 9 | 8 | 10 |  | 7 |  |  |  | 3 |  |  | 11 | 1 |  |  | 35 |
|  | 6 | 2 | 4 | 5 |  |  | 9 | 8 | 10 |  | 7 |  |  |  | 3 |  |  | 11 | 1 |  |  | 36 |
|  | 6 | 2 | 4 | 5 |  |  | 8 | 9 | 10 | 12 | 7 |  |  |  | 3* |  |  | 11 | 1 |  |  | 37 |
| 1 | 2 | 3 | 5 |  |  |  | 8 | 9* | 10 | 12 | 4 |  |  | 7 |  | 6 |  | 11 |  |  |  | 38 |
| 1 |  | 4 | 5 |  |  |  | 8 |  | 10 | 7 | 2 |  |  | 9 | 3 | 6 |  | 11 |  |  |  | 39 |
| 1 |  | 4 | 5 |  | 12 |  | 10 |  | 8 |  | 2 |  |  | 9 | 3 | 6 |  | 11* | 7 |  |  | 40 |
| 1 | 2 | 4 |  |  | 8 | 12 | 10 |  | 7* | 5 |  |  |  | 9 | 3 | 6 |  | 11 |  |  |  | 41 |
| 1 | 3 | 2 | 4 | 5 |  |  | 8 | 9 | 10 |  | 6 |  |  | 7 | 12 |  |  | 11* |  |  |  | 42 |
| 1 | 3 | 2 | 4 |  |  |  | 8 | 9 |  |  | 5 |  |  | 7 | 11 | 6 |  | 10 |  |  |  | 43 |
| 1 | 3 | 4 |  |  |  | 12 | 10 |  |  | 7* | 5 |  |  | 9 | 6 |  |  | 11 |  | 2 | 8 | 44 |
| 1 | 3 | 4 |  |  |  | 10 | 9 | 6 |  |  | 5 |  |  | 7 | 12 |  |  | 11 |  | 2 | 8* | 45 |
| 1 | 3 |  | 5 |  |  | 10 | 12 | 6 |  | 7* | 4 |  |  | 9 | 8 |  |  | 11 |  | 2 |  | 46 |
| 36 | 27 | 40 | 42 | 31 | 25 | 33 | 33 | 33 | 17 | 32 | 30 | 3 | 11 | 15 | 29 | 21 | 4 | 28 | 10 | 4 | 2 |  |

+1s (Raynor), +4s (Storton), +4s (Oakes), +1s (Jones), +3s (Ludlam), +2s (Phillips), +2s (Sutcliffe), +7s (Burns), +3s (Blackwell), +2s (Henderson)

## CHESTER

| | Ht | Wt | Birthplace | Clubs | League App. | League Gls |
|---|---|---|---|---|---|---|
| **Goalkeepers** | | | | | | |
| Gren Millington | 5 10 | 11 6 | Queensferry | Chester | 1 | — |
| | | | | Brighton | — | — |
| | | | | Chester | 278 | — |
| Phil Harrington | 5 10 | 11 2 | Bangor | Chester | 10 | — |
| **Defenders** | | | | | | |
| Trevor Storton | 6 1 | 12 2 | Keighley | Tranmere R | 118 | 9 |
| | | | | Liverpool | 5 | — |
| | | | | Chester | 341 | 15 |
| Jim Walker* | 5 10 | 10 10 | Northwich | Derby Co | 42 | 3 |
| | | | | Hartlepool U (on loan) | 10 | — |
| | | | | Brighton | 28 | 4 |
| | | | | Peterborough U | 31 | 1 |
| | | | | Chester | 172 | 4 |
| Paul Raynor* | 5 11 | 11 0 | Chester | Chester | 197 | 9 |
| Paul Needham | 5 10 | 11 4 | Chester | Chester | 36 | 1 |
| John Cottam | 5 10 | 13 3 | Nottingham | Nottingham F | 95 | 4 |
| | | | | Mansfield T (on loan) | 2 | 1 |
| | | | | Lincoln C (on loan) | 1 | — |
| | | | | Chesterfield | 120 | 7 |
| | | | | Chester | 120 | 1 |
| David Burns* | 5 8 | 10 6 | Ellesmere Pt | Chester | 78 | 1 |
| Peter Zelem | 6 0 | 11 6 | Manchester | Chester | 37 | 1 |
| Gregory Moffat | 5 11 | 10 9 | Liverpool | Chester | — | — |
| Mark Dean (Apprentice) | | | | Chester | 4 | — |
| **Midfield** | | | | | | |
| Alan Oakes* | 6 0 | 12 10 | Winsford | Manchester C | 565 | 26 |
| | | | | Chester | 211 | 15 |
| Steve Ludlam | 5 7 | 10 10 | Chesterfield | Sheffield U | 27 | 1 |
| | | | | Carlisle U | 96 | 11 |
| | | | | Chester | 73 | 8 |
| Mike Keen* | | | | Chester | — | — |
| Paul Blackwell | 5 10 | 11 5 | Mancot | Chester | 23 | — |
| Mike Williams (Apprentice) | | | | Chester | 2 | — |
| **Forwards** | | | | | | |
| Bryn Jones* | 5 8 | 10 0 | St Asaph | Chester | 162 | 17 |
| Peter Sutcliffe* | 5 6 | 9 0 | Manchester | Manchester U | — | — |
| | | | | Stockport Co | 27 | 2 |
| | | | | Port Vale | 50 | 6 |
| | | | | Chester | 109 | 7 |
| Trevor Phillips | 5 6 | 11 2 | Barnsley | Rotherham U | 322 | 81 |
| | | | | Hull C | 22 | 3 |
| | | | | Stockport Co (on loan) | 13 | 4 |
| | | | | Chester | 64 | 11 |
| Terry Cooke | 5 10 | 10 8 | Wrexham | Chester | 27 | 10 |
| Gary Simpson | 6 0 | 13 7 | Chesterfield | Chesterfield | 43 | 8 |
| | | | | Chester | 37 | 12 |
| John Allen | 6 0 | 12 1 | Mancot | Chester | 22 | — |
| Peter Henderson* | 6 0 | 12 4 | Berwick-on-Tweed | Witton A | (not known) | |
| | | | | Chester | 64 | 10 |
| | | | | Gillingham | 7 | 3 |
| | | | | Crewe Alex (on loan) | 7 | — |
| | | | | Chester | 28 | 5 |

# CHESTERFIELD Division 3

*President:* His Grace the Duke of Devonshire MC, DL, JP.

*Chairman:* E. I. Gaunt.

*Vice-Chairman:* A. Bates.

*Directors:* F. Tuckley, E. Brocklehurst, P. C. J. T. Kirkman OBE, J. Leedham.

*Team Manager:* Frank Barlow.

*Secretary:* R. F. Pepper.

*Year Formed:* 1866. *Turned Professional:* 1891.

*Limited Company:* 1871.

*Previous Name:* Chesterfield Town, 1904.

**Football League Record:**
1899 Elected to Division 2; 1909 failed re-election; 1921–31 Division 3(N); 1931–33 Division 2; 1933–36 Division 3(N); 1936–51 Division 2; 1951–58 Division 3(N); 1958–61 Division 3; 1961–70 Division 4; 1970– Division 3.

**Honours:** *Football League:* Division 2 best season: 4th, 1946–47; Division 3(N) – Champions 1930–31, 1935–36; Runners-up 1933–34; Division 4 – Champions 1969–70. *FA Cup* best season: 5th rd, 1932–33, 1937–38, 1949–50. *Football League Cup* best season: 4th rd, 1964–65. *Anglo-Scottish Cup:* Winners 1980–81.

*Record Victory:* 10-0 v Glossop North End, Division 2, 17 Jan, 1903.

*Record Defeat:* 1-9 v Port Vale, Division 2, 24 Sept, 1932.

*Most League Points:* 64, Division 4, 1969–70. *Three points win:* 64, Division 3, 1981–82.

*Most League Goals:* 102, Division 3(N), 1930–31.

*Highest League Scorer in Season:* Jimmy Cookson, 44, Division 3(N), 1925–26.

*Most League Goals in Total Aggregate:* Ernie Moss, 127, 1969–76; 1979–81.

*Most Capped Player:* Walter McMillen, 4(7), Ireland.

*Most League Appearances:* Dave Blakey, 613, 1948–67.

*Record Transfer Fee Received:* £200,000 from Wolverhampton W for Alan Birch, Aug 81.

*Record Transfer Fee Paid:* £150,000 to Carlisle U for Phil Bonnyman, March 1980.

*Previous Managers since the War:* Bob Brocklebank, Bob Marshall, Ted Davison, Duggie Livingstone, Tony McShane, Jimmy McGuigan, Joe Shaw, Arthur Cox.

*Address of Supporters Club:* 132 Saltergate, Chesterfield. Contact secretary P. Tooley (0246) 853162 or chairman H. Borrell (0246) 75862.

*Address of the Club Shop or Boutique:* 132 Saltergate, Chesterfield.

---

**Recreation Ground, Chesterfield S40 4SX.** Telephone Chesterfield 32318. *Ground capacity:* 19,750 (12,000 covered). *Record attendance:* 30,968 v Newcastle U, Division 2, 7 April, 1939. *Record receipts:* £24,640 v Barnsley, Division 3, 26 Dec, 1980. *Pitch measurements:* 114yd×72yd.

*How to get there:* Chesterfield railway station is one mile from the ground, via Corporation St, Holywell St, to Saltergate.

*Match tickets:* Seats in the Centre and Wing Stands may be booked in advance.

*Car parking:* Street parking permitted around the ground. Also car parks in Saltergate within ½ mile of the ground.

*Entertainments/catering facilities:* A social club (members only) is sited on the ground at the Saltergate entrance. Refreshment bars around the ground.

*Club shop:* A wide range of souvenirs available as well as programmes and handbooks.

*Extra information:* In 1980–81 Chesterfield played 65 competitive games (46 League, 6 FA Cup, 4 League Cup, 9 Anglo-Scottish Cup) – a record for a Division 3 club. Arnold Birch, Chesterfield's goalkeeper, scored five goals in 1923–24, all from penalties.

*Club Colours:* Royal blue shirts, white shorts, white stockings with three blue rings.

*Change Colours:* Red shirts, black shorts, red stockings.

*Club Player/Coach:* Bill Green.

*First and Second Team Coach:* Bill Dearden.

*Physiotherapist:* John Short.

*Club Nickname:* Blues or Spireites.

## CHESTERFIELD 1981−82 LEAGUE RECORD

| Match No. | Date | Venue | Opponents | Result | H/T Score | Goalscorers | Atten-dance |
|---|---|---|---|---|---|---|---|
| 1 | Aug 29 | A | Newport Co | L 0-1 | 0-1 | | 5079 |
| 2 | Sept 5 | H | Bristol R | W 2-0 | 1-0 | Kowalski, Bonnyman | 3501 |
| 3 | 12 | A | Walsall | D 1-1 | 0-1 | Green | 3280 |
| 4 | 19 | H | Fulham | W 3-0 | 0-0 | Bonnyman, Windridge 2 | 4019 |
| 5 | 22 | H | Carlisle U | W 1-0 | 1-0 | Henderson | 4710 |
| 6 | 26 | A | Plymouth Arg | W 2-0 | 0-0 | Nisbet (og), Henderson | 3451 |
| 7 | 29 | A | Swindon T | W 2-1 | 1-1 | Crawford, Ridley | 5365 |
| 8 | Oct 3 | H | Portsmouth | D 2-2 | 0-1 | Windridge, Ridley | 6150 |
| 9 | 10 | A | Reading | W 2-0 | 1-0 | Windridge, Crawford | 4690 |
| 10 | 17 | H | Southend U | L 1-2 | 0-1 | Bonnyman (pen) | 6146 |
| 11 | 21 | A | Chester | W 2-0 | 0-0 | Bonnyman, Henderson | 2329 |
| 12 | 24 | H | Brentford | L 0-2 | 0-0 | | 5525 |
| 13 | 31 | A | Bristol C | D 0-0 | 0-0 | | 8442 |
| 14 | Nov 3 | H | Huddersfield T | W 1-0 | 0-0 | Bonnyman (pen) | 6847 |
| 15 | 7 | H | Oxford U | D 2-2 | 0-0 | Henderson, Windridge | 5295 |
| 16 | 14 | A | Lincoln C | L 1-2 | 1-1 | Ridley | 5878 |
| 17 | 28 | H | Wimbledon | W 2-0 | 2-0 | Henderson, Walker | 4604 |
| 18 | Dec 5 | A | Exeter C | W 3-0 | 1-0 | Bonnyman, Green, Wilson | 3947 |
| 19 | Jan 5 | H | Preston NE | D 0-0 | 0-0 | | 3964 |
| 20 | 19 | A | Bristol R | L 0-1 | 0-0 | | 4853 |
| 21 | 23 | H | Newport Co | W 1-0 | 0-0 | Walker | 4234 |
| 22 | 30 | A | Fulham | L 0-1 | 0-1 | | 9213 |
| 23 | Feb 2 | A | Doncaster R | W 3-1 | 2-0 | Bonnyman, Henderson, Parkinson (og) | 6157 |
| 24 | 6 | H | Walsall | W 1-0 | 0-0 | Bonnyman | 5989 |
| 25 | 9 | A | Carlisle U | L 0-3 | 0-0 | | 5575 |
| 26 | 13 | A | Portsmouth | L 1-5 | 1-2 | Bonnyman | 8046 |
| 27 | 20 | H | Plymouth Arg | D 2-2 | 1-1 | Ridley, Crawford | 4381 |
| 28 | 27 | H | Reading | W 2-1 | 1-0 | Henderson, Crawford | 4462 |
| 29 | Mar 5 | A | Southend U | W 2-0 | 1-0 | Henderson 2 | 5819 |
| 30 | 9 | H | Chester | L 3-5 | 2-1 | Henderson, Wilson, Bonnyman (pen) | 4291 |
| 31 | 13 | A | Brentford | L 0-2 | 0-1 | | 5360 |
| 32 | 20 | H | Bristol C | W 1-0 | 0-0 | Wilson | 4230 |
| 33 | 23 | A | Huddersfield T | D 1-1 | 0-1 | Windridge | 6721 |
| 34 | 27 | A | Oxford U | D 1-1 | 0-0 | Bonnyman (pen) | 6215 |
| 35 | Apr 3 | H | Lincoln C | L 0-2 | 0-1 | | 7443 |
| 36 | 6 | A | Gillingham | L 2-3 | 2-0 | Henderson 2 | 5111 |
| 37 | 10 | A | Doncaster R | D 0-0 | 0-0 | | 5221 |
| 38 | 12 | H | Burnley | L 1-2 | 1-2 | Bonnyman (pen) | 7200 |
| 39 | 17 | H | Exeter C | W 2-1 | 1-1 | Crawford, Henderson | 2867 |
| 40 | 24 | A | Wimbledon | L 1-3 | 0-1 | Walker | 2138 |
| 41 | 27 | H | Millwall | L 0-1 | 0-1 | | 2377 |
| 42 | May 1 | H | Swindon T | W 2-1 | 2-0 | Walker, Bonnyman | 2028 |
| 43 | 4 | A | Millwall | L 2-3 | 1-1 | Hunter, Kowalski | 2265 |
| 44 | 8 | A | Preston NE | L 0-2 | 0-2 | | 5445 |
| 45 | 15 | H | Gillingham | L 1-3 | 0-2 | Bonnyman | 2259 |
| 46 | 18 | A | Burnley | D 1-1 | 1-0 | Carroll | 18,655 |

**Final League Position: 11**

**Goalscorers**

*League* (57): Bonnyman 14 (5 pens), Henderson 13, Windridge 6, Crawford 5, Ridley 4, Walker 4, Wilson 3, Green 2, Kowalski 2, Carroll 1, Hunter 1, own goals 2.
*League Cup* (1): Green 1.
*FA Cup* (4): Bonnyman 2, Henderson 1, Walker 1.

| **League Cup** | First Round | Doncaster R (a) | 0-0 |
|---|---|---|---|
| | | (h) | 1-1 (lost on away goals rule) |
| **FA Cup** | First Round | Preston NE (h) | 4-1 |
| | Second Round | Huddersfield T (h) | 0-1 |

| Turner | Bellamy | O'Neill | Wilson | Green | Ridley | Tartt | Crawford | Bonnyman | Kowalski | Walker | Windridge | Pollard | Henderson | Athersych | Hunter | Carroll | Stirk | Salmons | Henson | Gregory | Partridge | Robinson | Match No. |
|---|---|---|---|---|---|---|---|---|---|---|---|---|---|---|---|---|---|---|---|---|---|---|---|
| 1 | 2 | 3 | 4 | 5 | 6 | 7 | 8 | 9 | 10 | 11 |  |  |  |  |  |  |  |  |  |  |  |  | 1 |
| 1 | 2 | 3 | 4 | 5 | 6 | 7* | 8 | 9 | 10 | 11 | 12 |  |  |  |  |  |  |  |  |  |  |  | 2 |
| 1 | 2 |  | 4 | 5 | 6 |  | 11 | 9 | 10 |  | 7 | 3 | 8 |  |  |  |  |  |  |  |  |  | 3 |
| 1 | 2 | 3 | 4 | 5 | 6 |  | 11 | 9 | 10 |  | 7* | 12 | 8 |  |  |  |  |  |  |  |  |  | 4 |
| 1 | 2 | 3 | 4* | 5 | 6 |  | 11 | 9 | 10 |  | 7 |  | 8 | 12 |  |  |  |  |  |  |  |  | 5 |
| 1 | 2 | 3 |  | 5 | 6 | 4 | 11 | 9 | 10 |  | 7 |  | 8 |  |  |  |  |  |  |  |  |  | 6 |
| 1 | 2 | 3 |  | 5 | 6 | 4 | 11 | 9 | 10 | 12 | 7* |  | 8 |  |  |  |  |  |  |  |  |  | 7 |
| 1 | 2 | 3 | 4 | 5 | 6 |  | 11 | 9 | 10 | 12 | 7 |  | 8* |  |  |  |  |  |  |  |  |  | 8 |
| 1 | 2 | 3 | 4 |  | 6 |  | 11 | 9 | 10 |  | 7 |  | 8 | 5 |  |  |  |  |  |  |  |  | 9 |
| 1 | 2* | 3 | 4 |  | 6 |  | 11 | 9 | 10 | 12 | 7 |  | 8 | 5 |  |  |  |  |  |  |  |  | 10 |
| 1 | 2 | 3 | 4 | 5 | 6 |  | 11 | 9 | 10 |  | 7 |  | 8 |  |  |  |  |  |  |  |  |  | 11 |
| 1 | 2* | 3 | 4 | 5 | 6 |  | 11 | 9 | 10 |  | 7 |  | 8 |  | 12 |  |  |  |  |  |  |  | 12 |
| 1 |  | 3 | 4 | 5 | 6 |  | 11 | 9 | 10 | 12 | 7* |  | 8 |  |  |  | 2 |  |  |  |  |  | 13 |
| 1 |  | 3 | 4 | 5* | 6 |  | 11 | 9 | 10 | 12 | 7 |  | 8 |  |  |  | 2 |  |  |  |  |  | 14 |
| 1 |  | 3 | 4 |  | 6 |  | 11 | 9 | 10 | 12 | 7 |  | 8 |  | 5* |  | 2 |  |  |  |  |  | 15 |
| 1 |  | 3 | 4 | 5 | 6 |  | 11 | 9 | 10 |  | 7 |  | 8 |  |  |  | 2 |  |  |  |  |  | 16 |
| 1 |  | 3 | 4 | 5 |  |  |  | 9 | 10 | 11 | 7 | 6 | 8 |  |  |  | 2 |  |  |  |  |  | 17 |
| 1 |  | 3 | 4 | 5 |  |  |  | 9 | 10 | 11 | 7 | 6 | 8 |  |  |  | 2 |  |  |  |  |  | 18 |
| 1 |  | 3 | 4 | 5 |  |  |  | 9 | 10 | 11 | 7* | 6 | 8 |  |  |  | 2 | 12 |  |  |  |  | 19 |
| 1 |  | 3 |  | 5 | 4 |  | 7 | 9 | 10 | 11 | 12 | 6* | 8 |  |  |  | 2 |  |  |  |  |  | 20 |
| 1 |  | 3 | 4 | 5 | 6 |  | 7 | 9 | 10* | 11 | 12 |  | 8 |  |  |  | 2 |  |  |  |  |  | 21 |
| 1 |  | 3 | 4 | 5 | 6 |  | 12 | 9 | 10 | 11 | 7 | 2* | 8 |  |  |  |  |  |  |  |  |  | 22 |
| 1 |  | 3 | 4 | 5 | 6 |  | 11 | 9 | 10 |  | 7 | 2 | 8 |  |  |  |  |  |  |  |  |  | 23 |
| 1 |  | 3* | 4 | 5 | 6 |  | 11 | 9 | 10 | 12 | 7 | 2 | 8 |  |  |  |  |  |  |  |  |  | 24 |
| 1 |  | 3 | 4* | 5 | 6 |  | 11 | 9 | 10 | 12 | 7 | 2 | 8 |  |  |  |  |  |  |  |  |  | 25 |
| 1 |  | 3 | 4 | 5 | 6 |  | 11 | 9 | 10 |  | 7 |  | 8* |  | 12 |  | 2 |  |  |  |  |  | 26 |
| 1 |  | 3 | 4 | 5 | 6 |  | 11 | 9 | 10 | 12 |  |  | 8 |  | 7* |  | 2 |  |  |  |  |  | 27 |
| 1 |  | 3 | 4 | 5 | 6 |  | 11 | 9 | 10 | 12 |  |  | 8* |  |  |  | 2 |  | 7 |  |  |  | 28 |
| 1 |  | 3 | 4 | 5 | 6 |  | 11 | 8 | 10 | 12 | 9 |  |  |  |  |  | 2 |  | 7* |  |  |  | 29 |
| 1 |  | 3 | 4 | 5 | 6 |  | 11 | 9 | 10* | 12 |  |  | 8 |  |  |  | 2 |  | 7 |  |  |  | 30 |
| 1 |  | 3 | 4 | 5 | 10 |  | 11 | 9 |  | 12 |  | 6 | 8 |  |  |  | 2 |  | 7* |  |  |  | 31 |
| 1 |  | 3 | 4 | 5* | 10 |  | 11 | 9 |  |  | 7 | 6 | 8 |  | 12 |  | 2 |  |  |  |  |  | 32 |
| 1 |  | 3 | 4 |  | 10 |  | 11 | 9 |  |  | 7 | 6 | 8 | 5* | 12 |  | 2 |  |  |  |  |  | 33 |
|  | 5 |  | 4 |  | 6 |  | 11 | 9 |  |  | 7* | 3 | 8 |  | 10 |  | 2 |  |  | 1 | 12 |  | 34 |
| 1 | 12 | 3 | 4 |  | 6 |  | 11 | 9 |  |  |  | 5 | 8 |  | 10 |  | 2 |  |  |  | 7* |  | 35 |
| 1 | 12 | 3 | 4 |  | 6 |  | 11 | 9 |  |  |  | 5 | 8 |  | 10 |  | 2 |  |  |  | 7* |  | 36 |
| 1 | 2 | 3 | 4 | 5 | 12 |  | 11 | 9 |  |  | 7 | 6 | 8 |  | 10* |  |  |  |  |  |  |  | 37 |
| 1 | 2* | 3 | 4 | 5 | 12 |  | 11 | 9 |  |  |  | 6 | 8 |  | 10 |  |  |  |  |  | 7 |  | 38 |
| 1 | 2 | 3 | 4 | 5 |  |  | 11* | 9 | 10 |  |  | 6 | 8 |  | 12 |  |  |  |  |  | 7* |  | 39 |
| 1 | 2 | 3 | 4 | 5 |  |  | 11 | 9 | 10 | 12 |  | 6 | 8 |  |  |  |  |  |  |  | 7* |  | 40 |
| 1 | 2 | 3 | 4 | 5 |  |  | 11 | 9 | 10 |  | 7 | 6 | 8 |  |  |  |  |  |  |  |  |  | 41 |
| 1 | 2 | 3 | 4 | 5 |  |  | 11 | 9 | 10 |  | 7 | 6 | 8 |  |  |  |  |  |  |  |  |  | 42 |
| 1 | 2 |  | 4 |  | 6 |  | 11 | 9 | 10 |  | 7 |  | 8 | 5 |  |  |  |  |  |  | 3 |  | 43 |
| 1 | 2 |  | 4* |  | 6 |  | 11 | 9 | 10 |  | 7 | 12 | 8 | 5 |  |  |  |  |  |  | 3 |  | 44 |
| 1 | 6 | 2 | 4 |  |  |  |  | 9 | 10 | 11 | 7* | 12 | 8 | 5 |  |  |  |  |  |  | 3 |  | 45 |
| 1 | 2 | 3 | 4 | 5 |  |  |  | 9 |  |  | 7 | 6 | 8 |  | 10 | 11 |  |  |  |  |  |  | 46 |
| 45 | 23 | 42 | 43 | 35 | 36 | 4 | 40 | 46 | 37 | 15 | 25 | 17 | 44 | 6 | 12 | 2 | 20 | 3 | 4 | 1 | 3 | 3 |  |
|  | +2s |  |  | +2s | +1s |  |  |  |  |  | +10s | +9s |  |  | +4s |  | +1s | +1s | +2s |  | +1s |  |  |

## CHESTERFIELD

| | Ht | Wt | Birthplace | Clubs | League App. | League Gls |
|---|---|---|---|---|---|---|
| **Goalkeepers** | | | | | | |
| Paul Gregory | 5 10 | 11 7 | Sheffield | Chesterfield | 3 | — |
| John Turner | 5 11 | 12 8 | Peterlee | Derby Co | — | — |
| | | | | Doncaster R (on loan) | 4 | — |
| | | | | Brighton (on loan) | — | — |
| | | | | Peterborough U (on loan) | — | — |
| | | | | Huddersfield T (on loan) | 1 | — |
| | | | | Reading | 31 | — |
| | | | | Torquay U | 76 | — |
| | | | | Chesterfield | 100 | — |
| | | | | Everton (on loan) | — | — |
| **Defenders** | | | | | | |
| Sean O'Neill | 5 9 | 12 2 | Belfast | Leeds U | — | — |
| | | | | Chesterfield | 304 | 3 |
| Les Hunter | 6 2 | 11 10 | Middlesbrough | Chesterfield | 165 | 8 |
| Bill Green | 6 3 | 12 8 | Newcastle | Hartlepool U | 131 | 9 |
| | | | | Carlisle U | 119 | 4 |
| | | | | West Ham U | 35 | 1 |
| | | | | Peterborough U | 30 | — |
| | | | | Chesterfield | 116 | 4 |
| John Stirk | 5 6 | 11 1 | Consett | Ipswich T | 6 | — |
| | | | | Watford | 46 | — |
| | | | | Chesterfield | 43 | — |
| Gary Bellamy | 6 1¾ | 11 5 | Worksop | Chesterfield | 28 | — |
| John Partridge | 5 11 | 11 8 | Chesterfield | Chesterfield | 4 | — |
| Gary Pollard | 6 1 | 11 10 | Staveley | Chesterfield | 55 | — |
| John Ridley* | 6 1½ | 12 6 | Consett | Port Vale | 156 | 3 |
| | | | | Leicester C | 24 | — |
| | | | | Chesterfield | 124 | 8 |
| **Midfield** | | | | | | |
| Geoff Salmons* | 5 10¾ | 10 11½ | Mexborough | Sheffield U | 180 | 8 |
| | | | | Stoke C | 118 | 14 |
| | | | | Sheffield U (on loan) | 5 | — |
| | | | | Leicester C | 26 | 4 |
| | | | | Chesterfield | 120 | 15 |
| Phil Bonnyman | 6 0 | 12 0 | Glasgow | Rangers | — | — |
| | | | | Hamilton A | 71 | 7 |
| | | | | Carlisle U | 152 | 26 |
| | | | | Chesterfield | 99 | 25 |
| Danny Wilson | 5 7 | 10 3 | Wigan | Wigan Ath | (not known) | |
| | | | | Bury | 90 | 8 |
| | | | | Chesterfield | 76 | 6 |
| Tony Henson | 5 10 | 11 7 | Dronfield | Sheffield W | — | — |
| | | | | Chesterfield | 6 | — |
| Richard Denby* | | | | Chesterfield | — | — |
| Andy Kowalski | 5 10 | 11 0 | Mansfield | Chesterfield | 323 | 29 |
| **Forwards** | | | | | | |
| Phil Walker | 6 0 | 12 1 | Kirkby | Chesterfield | 153 | 33 |
| Alan Crawford* | 5 7½ | 9 10 | Rotherham | Rotherham U | 237 | 49 |
| | | | | Mansfield T (on loan) | 2 | — |
| | | | | Chesterfield | 94 | 20 |
| Dave Windridge | 5 9 | 11 0 | Atherstone | Sheffield U | — | — |
| | | | | Chesterfield | 36 | 6 |
| Russ Athersych | 5 9 | 11 4 | Sheffield | Chesterfield | 10 | — |
| Micky Carroll | 5 7 | 11 0 | | Whickham | (not known) | |
| | | | | Chesterfield | 3 | 1 |
| Martin Henderson | 6 0 | 12 9 | Kirkcaldy | Rangers | 33 | 10 |
| | | | | Hibernian (on loan) | 6 | — |
| | | | | Philadelphia F | (not known) | |
| | | | | Leicester C | 91 | 12 |
| | | | | Chesterfield | 44 | 13 |
| Steven Robinson (Apprentice) | 5 10 | 10 10 | Sheffield | Chesterfield | 3 | — |

# COLCHESTER UNITED Division 4

*Patron:* A. Buck QC, MP.
*President:* R. G. R. Chapman FRICS.
*Chairman:* M. J. Cadman.  *Vice-Chairman:* H. R. Piper.
*Directors:* N. F. Fitch, R. F. West, J. W. Rippingale.
*Player-Manager:* Allan Hunter.  *Secretary:* Martin R. Bennet.
*Year Formed:* 1937.  *Turned Professional:* 1937.
*Limited Company:* 1937.

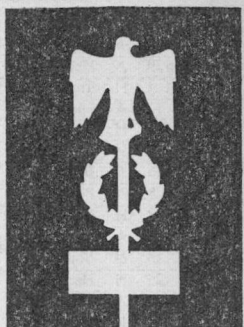

**Football League Record:**
1950 Elected to Division 3(S); 1958–61 Division 3; 1961–62 Division 4; 1962–65 Division 3; 1965–66 Division 4; 1966–68 Division 3; 1968–74 Division 4; 1974–76 Division 3; 1976–77 Division 4; 1977–81 Division 3; 1981– Division 4.

**Honours:** *Football League:* Division 3(S) best season: 3rd, 1956–57; Division 4 – Runners-up 1961–62. *FA Cup* best season: 1970–71, 6th rd (record for a Fourth Division club shared with Oxford United and Bradford City). *Football League Cup* best season: 5th rd, 1974–75.

*Record Victory:* 9-1 v Bradford C, Division 4, 30 Dec, 1961.
*Record Defeat:* 0-7 v Leyton Orient, Division 3(S), 5 Jan, 1952; 0-7 v Reading, Division 3(S), 18 Sept, 1957.
*Most League Points:* 60, Division 4, 1973–74. *Three points win:* 72, Division 4, 1981–82.
*Most League Goals:* 104, Division 4, 1961–62.
*Highest League Scorer in Season:* Bobby Hunt, 37, Division 4, 1961–62.
*Most League Goals in Total Aggregate:* Martyn King, 131, 1959–65.
*Most Capped Player:* None.
*Most League Appearances:* Micky Cook, 536, 1969–82.
*Record Transfer Fee Received:* £90,000 from Gillingham for Trevor Lee, Jan 1981.
*Record Transfer Fee Paid:* £25,000 to Ipswich T for Roger Osborne, Feb 1981.
*Previous Managers since the War:* Ted Fenton, Jimmy Allen, Jack Butler, Benny Fenton, Neil Franklin, Dick Graham, Jim Smith, Bobby Roberts.

---

**Layer Rd Ground, Colchester.** Telephone (0206) 74042. *Telegraphic address:* 'United Colchester'. *Ground capacity:* 16,150. *Record attendance:* 19,072 v Reading, FA Cup 1st rd, 27 Nov, 1948. *Record receipts:* £20,265 v Manchester U, FA Cup 5th rd, 20 Feb, 1979. *Pitch measurements:* 110yd×71yd.
*How to get there:* Buses from Osborne Street in Colchester, which is about 2 miles from the railway station.
*Match tickets:* Stand seats can be booked two weeks in advance (Ticket Office tel: Colchester 72202 or 74042.) All bookings will be accepted and held, *provided* the tickets are *paid for* and *collected* at least 48 hours before kick-off. During the 48 hours prior to the game, tickets will be available *only* to cash customers at the ground. This method should not affect people who live outside the immediate area of Layer Road, for postal applications with the appropriate remittance will still be accepted up to 72 hours before kick-off provided that such applications are accompanied by a stamped (first class) addressed envelope.
*Car parking:* Parking facilities in Butt Road and Layer Road, approximately 150 yards past the ground on the south side of Colchester. Free parking in Army Barracks (150 yards).
*Entertainments/catering facilities:* Refreshment points on the ground.
*Club shop:* Sells all types of souvenirs; mailing list on request.
*Handbooks/programmes:* Back numbers of CUFC programmes can be ordered from the club shop.
*Extra information:* In 1947–48, Colchester, then a non-League side, reached the 5th round of the FA Cup.
*Club Colours:* Blue and white vertical stripes, blue shorts, white stockings.
*Change Colours:* Red shirts, black shorts, black stockings.
*Club Trainer/Coach:*
*Club Nickname:* The U's.

## COLCHESTER UNITED 1981–82 LEAGUE RECORD

| Match No. | Date | Venue | Opponents | Result | H/T Score | Goalscorers | Attendance |
|---|---|---|---|---|---|---|---|
| 1 | Aug 29 | A | Hartlepool U | W 3-1 | 2-0 | Bremner 2, Packer (pen) | 2007 |
| 2 | Sept 4 | H | Tranmere R | W 4-0 | 2-0 | Allinson 2 (1 pen), Cook, Bremner | 2474 |
| 3 | 12 | A | Sheffield U | L 0-1 | 0-1 | | 11,293 |
| 4 | 18 | H | Torquay U | W 3-0 | 1-0 | Adcock 2, Cook | 2820 |
| 5 | 22 | H | Aldershot | D 1-1 | 1-0 | Coleman | 2719 |
| 6 | 26 | A | Bradford C | L 1-2 | 0-1 | Leslie | 4772 |
| 7 | 28 | A | Port Vale | L 1-2 | 0-0 | McDonough | 3351 |
| 8 | Oct 2 | H | Northampton T | W 5-1 | 2-0 | Coleman, Allinson (pen), Bremner 2, McDonough | 2760 |
| 9 | 11 | A | Rochdale | W 2-1 | 0-0 | Allinson, McDonough | 1366 |
| 10 | 16 | H | York C | W 4-0 | 2-0 | McDonough, Bremner, Leslie, Allinson | 3139 |
| 11 | 20 | H | Hereford U | W 4-0 | 2-0 | Allinson, Bremner, Osborne 2 | 3064 |
| 12 | 24 | A | Halifax T | W 2-0 | 1-0 | Allinson (pen), McDonough | 1374 |
| 13 | 30 | H | Wigan Ath | L 1-2 | 0-2 | Coleman | 3882 |
| 14 | Nov 2 | A | Mansfield T | W 3-1 | 1-0 | Allinson 3 (1 pen) | 2294 |
| 15 | 7 | A | Hull C | W 3-2 | 1-1 | Bremner, McDonough 2 | 3040 |
| 16 | 13 | H | Scunthorpe U | W 2-1 | 1-1 | Allinson, Cook | 3838 |
| 17 | 28 | A | Darlington | W 2-1 | 1-1 | Bremner, Osborne | 1456 |
| 18 | Dec 4 | H | Blackpool | W 2-1 | 1-1 | Allinson, Noble (og) | 3875 |
| 19 | 26 | A | AFC Bournemouth | D 1-1 | 0-1 | McDonough | 8829 |
| 20 | Jan 16 | H | Bury | D 1-1 | 1-1 | Adcock | 3504 |
| 21 | 23 | A | Hartlepool U | D 3-3 | 1-3 | McDonough, Fagan (og), Allinson (pen) | 2862 |
| 22 | 30 | A | Torquay U | L 0-1 | 0-0 | | 2037 |
| 23 | Feb 6 | H | Sheffield U | W 5-2 | 4-1 | Lyons, McDonough, Allinson 2, Bremner | 5194 |
| 24 | 9 | A | Aldershot | D 1-1 | 1-1 | Lyons | 2324 |
| 25 | 14 | A | Northampton T | W 2-1 | 1-0 | Allinson, Bremner | 3102 |
| 26 | 19 | H | Bradford C | L 1-2 | 0-1 | Cook | 3975 |
| 27 | 26 | H | Rochdale | W 3-2 | 2-1 | Adcock 2, Bremner | 2760 |
| 28 | Mar 2 | A | Tranmere R | L 1-2 | 0-2 | Bremner | 1252 |
| 29 | 5 | A | York C | L 0-3 | 0-1 | | 1854 |
| 30 | 10 | A | Hereford U | D 2-2 | 0-1 | Allinson (pen), Osborne | 2060 |
| 31 | 12 | H | Halifax T | D 1-1 | 1-1 | Bremner | 2464 |
| 32 | 16 | H | Mansfield T | L 0-1 | 0-0 | | 2000 |
| 33 | 20 | A | Wigan Ath | L 2-3 | 0-2 | Bremner, Osborne | 6747 |
| 34 | 22 | A | Stockport Co | D 0-0 | 0-0 | | 1740 |
| 35 | 26 | H | Hull C | W 2-0 | 0-0 | Bremner, Coleman | 2193 |
| 36 | 30 | H | Crewe Alex | D 1-1 | 1-1 | Allinson | 1904 |
| 37 | Apr 2 | A | Scunthorpe U | L 1-2 | 0-1 | Bremner | 1762 |
| 38 | 10 | H | AFC Bournemouth | L 1-2 | 0-2 | Allinson | 2662 |
| 39 | 13 | A | Peterborough U | D 2-2 | 0-0 | Allinson, McDonough | 5402 |
| 40 | 17 | A | Blackpool | D 0-0 | 0-0 | | 2298 |
| 41 | 24 | H | Darlington | W 1-0 | 0-0 | Bremner | 1764 |
| 42 | 27 | H | Peterborough U | D 1-1 | 1-0 | Bremner | 2212 |
| 43 | May 1 | A | Bury | L 3-4 | 1-3 | Lyons, Bremner, McDonough | 1720 |
| 44 | 3 | H | Port Vale | W 1-0 | 1-0 | McDonough | 1470 |
| 45 | 7 | H | Stockport Co | L 0-1 | 0-0 | | 2132 |
| 46 | 15 | A | Crewe Alex | W 3-1 | 3-1 | Bremner, Allinson, McDonough | 1226 |

**Final League Position: 6**

### Goalscorers

*League* (82): Allinson 21 (6 pens), Bremner 21, McDonough 14, Adcock 5, Osborne 5, Coleman 4, Cook 4, Lyons 3, Leslie 2, Packer 1 (pen), own goals 2.
*League Cup* (8): Bremner 3, Allinson 2 (1 pen), McDonough 2, Cook 1.
*FA Cup* (8): Allinson 3 (2 pens), Adcock 1, Cook 1, Leslie 1, Wignall 1, own goal 1.

| | | | |
|---|---|---|---|
| **League Cup** | First Round | Gillingham (h) | 2-0 |
| | | (a) | 1-1 |
| | Second Round | Cambridge U (h) | 3-1 |
| | | (a) | 2-3 |
| | Third Round | Tranmere R (a) | 0-1 |
| **FA Cup** | First Round | Newport Co (h) | 2-0 |
| | Second Round | Brentford (a) | 1-1 |
| | | (h) | 1-0 |
| | Third Round | Newcastle U (a) | 1-1 |
| | | (h) | 3-4 |

| Walker | Cook | Packer | Leslie | Wignall | Wright | Osborne | Bremner | Longhorn | McDonough | Allinson | Adcock | Coleman | Foley | Rowles | Cotton | Lyons | Groves | Ward | Hunter | Match No. |
|---|---|---|---|---|---|---|---|---|---|---|---|---|---|---|---|---|---|---|---|---|
| 1 | 2 | 3 | 4 | 5 | 6 | 7* | 8 | 9 | 10 | 11 | 12 | | | | | | | | | 1 |
| 1 | 2 | | 4 | 5 | 6 | | 8 | 9* | 10 | 11 | 7 | 3 | 12 | | | | | | | 2 |
| 1 | 2 | | 4 | 5 | 6 | 7 | 8 | | 10 | 11 | 12 | 3 | 9* | | | | | | | 3 |
| 1 | 2 | | 4 | 5 | 6 | 7 | 8 | | 10 | 11 | 9 | 3 | | | | | | | | 4 |
| 1 | 2 | | 4 | 5 | 6 | 9 | 8 | | 10 | 11 | 7 | 3 | | | | | | | | 5 |
| 1 | 2 | | 4 | 5 | 6 | 9 | 8 | | 10 | 11 | 7 | 3 | | | | | | | | 6 |
| 1 | 2 | | 4 | 5 | 6 | 9 | 8 | | 10 | 11 | 7 | 3 | | | | | | | | 7 |
| 1 | 2 | | 4* | 5 | 6 | 9 | 8 | 12 | 10 | 11 | 7 | 3 | | | | | | | | 8 |
| 1 | 2 | | 4 | 5 | 6 | 9 | 8 | | 10 | 11 | 7 | 3 | | | | | | | | 9 |
| 1 | 2 | | 4 | 5 | 6 | 9 | 8 | 12 | 10 | 11 | 7* | 3 | | | | | | | | 10 |
| 1 | 2 | | 4 | 5 | 6 | 9 | 8 | | 10 | 11 | 7 | 3 | | | | | | | | 11 |
| 1 | 2 | | 4 | 5 | 6 | 9 | 8 | 12 | 10 | 11 | 7* | 3 | | | | | | | | 12 |
| 1 | 2 | | 4 | 5 | | 9 | 8 | 6* | 10 | 11 | 7 | 3 | 12 | | | | | | | 13 |
| 1 | 2 | | 4 | 5 | | 9 | 8 | | 10 | 11 | 12 | 3 | 6 | 7* | | | | | | 14 |
| 1 | 2 | | 4 | 5 | 6 | 9 | 8 | | 10 | 11 | 7 | 3 | | | | | | | | 15 |
| 1 | 2 | | 4* | 5 | 6 | 9 | 8 | 12 | 10 | 11 | 7 | 3 | | | | | | | | 16 |
| 1 | 2 | | 4 | 5 | 6 | 9 | 8 | | | 11 | 7 | 3 | 10 | | | | | | | 17 |
| 1 | 2 | | 4 | 5 | 6 | 9 | 8 | | 10 | 11 | 7* | 3 | 12 | | | | | | | 18 |
| 1 | 2 | | 4 | 5 | 6 | 9 | 8 | | 10 | 11 | 12 | 3* | 7 | | | | | | | 19 |
| 1 | 2 | | 4 | 5 | 6 | 9 | 8 | 12 | 10 | 11 | 7 | 3* | | | | | | | | 20 |
| 1 | 2* | 6 | | 5 | | 9 | 8 | 12 | 10 | 11 | 7 | 3 | 4 | | | | | | | 21 |
| 1 | 2 | 4* | | 5 | 6 | 9 | 8 | | 10 | 11 | 12 | 3 | | 7 | | | | | | 22 |
| 1 | 2 | | | 5 | 6 | 9 | 8 | 3* | 10 | 11 | 7 | 12 | | | | 4 | | | | 23 |
| 1 | 2 | 12 | | 5 | 6 | 9* | 8 | 3 | 10 | 11 | 7 | | | | | 4 | | | | 24 |
| 1 | 2 | 7* | | 5 | 6 | 9 | 8 | 3 | 10 | 11 | 12 | | | | | 4 | | | | 25 |
| 1 | 2 | | | 5 | 6 | 9 | 8 | 3 | 10 | 11 | 7 | | | | | 4 | | | | 26 |
| 1 | 2 | | | | 6 | 9 | 8 | 3 | 10 | 11* | 7 | 5 | | | | 4 | 12 | | | 27 |
| 1 | 2 | | | | 6 | 9 | 8 | 5 | 10 | 11 | 7* | 3 | | | | 4 | 12 | | | 28 |
| 1 | 2 | 4* | | | 6 | 9 | 8 | 3 | 10 | 11 | | 5 | | | 7 | | 12 | | | 29 |
| 1 | 2 | | | 5 | 6 | 9 | 8* | | 10 | 11 | 12 | 3 | | | | 4 | | 7 | | 30 |
| 1 | 2 | | | 5 | 6 | 9 | 8 | | 10 | 11 | 12 | 3 | | | | 4 | | 7* | | 31 |
| 1 | 2 | | 4 | 5 | 6 | 9 | 8 | | 10 | 11 | 7 | 3 | | | | | | | | 32 |
| 1 | 2 | 10* | 4 | 5 | 6 | 9 | 8 | 12 | | 11 | | 3 | | | 7 | | | | | 33 |
| 1 | 2 | | 4 | 5 | 6 | 9 | 8 | | 10 | 11 | | 3 | | | 7 | | | | | 34 |
| 1 | 2 | | 4 | 5 | 6 | 9 | 8 | | | 11 | 12 | 3 | 10 | | 7* | | | | | 35 |
| 1 | 2 | | 4 | 5 | 6 | 9 | 8 | | 10 | 11 | | 3 | | | 7 | | | | | 36 |
| 1 | 2 | | 4 | 5 | 6 | 9 | 8 | | 10 | 11 | 7 | 3 | | | | | | | | 37 |
| 1 | 2 | 6 | 4 | 5 | | 9 | 8 | 3* | 10 | 11 | 7 | | | | | | 12 | 10 | | 38 |
| 1 | 2 | 6 | 12 | 5 | | 10 | 8 | 9 | | 11 | | 3 | | | 7* | 4 | | | | 39 |
| 1 | 2 | 6 | 12 | 5 | | 9* | 8 | | 10 | 11 | | 3 | | | 7 | 4 | | | | 40 |
| 1 | 2 | 6 | 4 | 5 | | | 8 | | 10 | 11* | 12 | | | | 7 | 9 | 3 | | | 41 |
| 1 | 2 | 6 | 4 | 5 | 3 | | 8 | | 10 | 11 | | | | | 7* | 9 | 12 | | | 42 |
| 1 | 2 | 6 | 4 | 5 | 3 | | 8 | | 10 | 11 | 12 | | | | 7* | 9 | | | | 43 |
| 1 | 2 | 6 | | 5 | 4 | | 8 | | 10 | 11 | | | | | 7 | 9 | 3 | | | 44 |
| 1 | 2 | 6 | | 5* | 4 | | 8 | | 10 | 11 | 12 | | | | 7 | 9 | 3 | | | 45 |
| 1 | 2 | 6 | | 5 | | | 8 | 4 | 10 | 11* | | | | | 7 | 9 | 12 | 3 | | 46 |
| 46 | 46 | 14 | 31 | 43 | 38 | 39 | 46 | 14 | 40 | 41 | 31 | 34 | 1 | 4 | 9 | 16 | 9 | 3 | 1 | |
| | | +3s | | | | | +7s | | +1s | +9s | +3s | +1s | +2s | +2s | +2s | +2s | | | | |

## COLCHESTER UNITED

| | Ht | Wt | Birthplace | Clubs | League App. | League Gls |
|---|---|---|---|---|---|---|
| **Goalkeepers** | | | | | | |
| Mike Walker | 6 1 | 13 2 | Colwyn Bay | Reading | — | — |
| | | | | Shrewsbury T | 6 | — |
| | | | | York C | 60 | — |
| | | | | Watford | 137 | — |
| | | | | Charlton Ath (on loan) | 1 | — |
| | | | | Colchester U | 409 | — |
| Jeff Wood | 6 1 | 10 9 | London | Charlton Ath | 147 | — |
| (Contract cancelled April 1982) | | | | Colchester U | — | — |
| **Defenders** | | | | | | |
| Micky Cook | 5 7 | 10 11 | Enfield | Colchester U | 536 | 18 |
| Mick Packer | 5 10 | 11 0 | London | Watford | 67 | 2 |
| | | | | Crewe Alex (on loan) | 12 | — |
| | | | | Colchester U | 332 | 20 |
| Steve Wignall | 5 11 | 11 11 | Liverpool | Doncaster R | 130 | 1 |
| | | | | Nottingham F (on loan) | — | — |
| | | | | Colchester U | 201 | 10 |
| Steve Wright | 6 0 | 10 11 | Clacton | Colchester U | 117 | 2 |
| Phil Coleman | 5 11 | 11 9 | Woolwich | Millwall | 36 | 1 |
| | | | | Colchester U | 41 | 4 |
| Allan Hunter | 6 0 | 12 8 | Sion Mills | Coleraine | (not known) | |
| (N Ireland) | | | | Oldham Ath | 83 | 1 |
| | | | | Blackburn R | 84 | 1 |
| | | | | Ipswich T | 280 | 8 |
| | | | | Colchester U | 1 | — |
| Wayne Ward | | | | Colchester U | 5 | — |
| **Midfield** | | | | | | |
| Steve Leslie | 5 10 | 11 0 | Brentwood | Colchester U | 378 | 38 |
| Russell Cotton* | 5 10 | 11 8 | Wellington | Colchester U | 37 | 1 |
| Dennis Longhorn | 5 11 | 11 0 | Southampton | Bournemouth | 30 | 1 |
| | | | | Mansfield T | 96 | 5 |
| | | | | Sunderland | 40 | 3 |
| | | | | Sheffield U | 36 | 1 |
| | | | | Aldershot | 53 | 3 |
| | | | | Colchester U | 43 | — |
| Roger Osborne | 5 9 | 10 11 | Otley | Ipswich T | 124 | 9 |
| | | | | Colchester U | 51 | 5 |
| Tony Adcock | 5 10 | 10 8 | Bethnal Green | Colchester U | 41 | 5 |
| Perry Groves | | | | Colchester U | 9 | — |
| (Apprentice) | | | | | | |
| **Forwards** | | | | | | |
| Steve Foley | 6 0 | 11 4 | Clacton | Colchester U | 283 | 54 |
| Ian Allinson | 5 10 | 11 0 | Hitchin | Colchester U | 262 | 47 |
| Eddie Rowles | 5 9 | 11 2 | Gosport | Bournemouth | 66 | 12 |
| | | | | York C | 67 | 14 |
| | | | | Torquay U | 59 | 13 |
| | | | | Darlington | 103 | 21 |
| | | | | Colchester U | 91 | 17 |
| Kevin Bremner | 5 9½ | 12 3 | Banff | Keith | (not known) | |
| | | | | Colchester U | 80 | 29 |
| Roy McDonough | 6 1 | 11 11 | Solihull | Birmingham C | 2 | 1 |
| | | | | Walsall | 82 | 15 |
| | | | | Chelsea | — | — |
| | | | | Colchester U | 52 | 16 |
| John Lyons | 5 10 | 11 6 | Buckley | Wrexham | 86 | 23 |
| | | | | Millwall | 55 | 20 |
| | | | | Cambridge U | 21 | 6 |
| | | | | Colchester U | 18 | 3 |

# COVENTRY CITY

## Division 1

*Life President:* Derrick H. Robins.

*President:* J. R. Mead JP.

*Chairman:* J. W. T. Hill.

*Directors:* M. F. French FCA, J. W. Jamieson, P. D. H. Robins, T. Sergeant FRCS.

*Executive Manager:* Gordon Milne.

*Team Manager:* Dave Sexton.

*General Secretary:* J. D. Dent.

*Commercial Manager:* George Curtis.

*Year Formed:* 1883. *Turned Professional:* 1908.

*Limited Company:* 1907. *Former Names:* 1883–98 Singers FC; 1898 Coventry City FC.

**Football League Record:**
1919 Elected to Division 2; 1925–26 Division 3(N); 1926–36 Division 3(S); 1936–52 Division 2; 1952–58 Division 3(S); 1958–59 Division 4; 1959–64 Division 3; 1964–67 Division 2; 1967– Division 1.

**Honours:** *Football League:* Division 1 best season: 6th, 1969–70; Division 2 – Champions 1966–67; Division 3 – Champions 1963–64; Division 3(S) – Champions 1935–36; Runners–up 1933–34. Division 4 – Runners-up 1958–59. *FA Cup* best season: 6th rd, 1962–63, 1966–67, 1972–73, 1981–82; old 4th rd, 1909–10. *Football League Cup* best season: Semi-final 1980–81. **European Competition:** *European Fairs Cup:* 1970–71.

*Record Victory:* 9-0 v Bristol C, Division 3(S), 28 Apr, 1934.

*Record Defeat:* 2-10 v Norwich C, Division 3(S), 15 Mar, 1930.

*Most League Points:* 60, Division 4, 1958–59; and Division 3, 1963–64.

*Most League Goals:* 108, Division 3(S), 1931–32.

*Highest League Scorer in Season:* Clarrie Bourton, 49, Division 3(S), 1931–32.

*Most League Goals in Total Aggregate:* 171, Clarrie Bourton, 1931–37.

*Most Capped Player:* Dave Clements, 21 (48), Northern Ireland.

*Most League Appearances:* George Curtis, 486, 1956–70.

*Record Transfer Fee Received:* £365,000 from Portland Timbers for Gary Collier, March 1980.

*Record Transfer Fee Paid:* £325,000 to Bristol C for Gary Collier, July 1979.

*Previous Managers since the War:* Dick Bayliss, Billy Frith, Harry Storer, Jack Fairbrother, Jesse Carver, Harry Warren, Billy Frith, Jimmy Hill, Noel Cantwell, Bob Dennison, Gordon Milne.

*Address of Supporters Club:* Freehold St, Coventry. Telephone: 26268.

*Address of Club Shop:* 'Sky Blue Shop', Highfield Road, Coventry.

---

**Highfield Road Stadium, King Richard Street, Coventry CV2 4FW.** Telephone Coventry 57171. *Telex:* 312132, answer back code COV AFC. *Telegraphic address:* 'City Football Coventry'. *Ground capacity:* 20,000 all-seater stadium. *Record attendance:* 51,455 v Wolverhampton W, Division 2, 29 April, 1967. *Record receipts:* £68,029·70 v West Ham U, League Cup semi-final 1st leg, 27 Jan, 1981. *Pitch measurements:* 110yd×75yd.

*How to get there:* Buses from Coventry railway station to town centre (Pool Meadow bus station). Then buses 16, 17 (Hospital), 32 (Potters Green), 33 (Bell Green) to ground. Also taxi service from station.

*Match tickets:* Stand seat tickets can be booked 21 days in advance of any home League fixture. Postal applications accepted if sent with correct remittance to the Ticket Office Manager, Coventry City FC, Highfield Rd Stadium, Coventry.

*Car parking:* Street parking permitted all around the ground. Special coach/car park situated at Gosford Green (200 yards from stadium) on Walsgrave Road (A46).

*Entertainments/catering facilities:* Pre-match entertainment at all League and Cup games by Radio Sky Blue; live entertainment from groups and bands at special matches. The Sky Blue Buttery is open for hot and cold snacks before matches for main stand patrons. There are 16 licensed refreshment rooms and lounges, and 11 unlicensed refreshment rooms and lounges around the ground; all are open before the game, at half-time, and after the match. The Grandstand restaurant, recommended by Egon Ronay, is open for lunch Mon. to Fri. and is available in the evening for private dinner parties. On match days it is used as the Vice-Presidents' Club. An executive suite, with accommodation for 60 and full buffet facilities, can also be hired on match days, during the afternoon. Grandstand Restaurant, Highfield Road, Coventry.

*Club shop:* Sited in the main stand; sells all types of souvenirs. There is a similar shop at the Thackhall St side of the stadium, attached to the Sky Blue Pools Office.

*Handbooks/programmes:* Programmes available through a postal service.

*Extra information:* Coventry City Supporters' Club under the Sky Blue stand, Thackhall St, welcomes visiting supporters on production of the membership card of their own club. They can attend the evening entertainment if they give 48-hours' notice by post to the secretary, Frank Fountaine, Coventry City SC, Thackhall St, Coventry.

*Club Colours:* Sky blue shirts and shorts with navy and white trim, sky blue stockings.

*Change Colours:* Red shirts and shorts with navy and white trim, red stockings.

*Club Nickname:* Sky Blues.

# COVENTRY CITY 1981–82 LEAGUE RECORD

| Match No. | Date | Venue | Opponents | Result | H/T Score | Goalscorers | Attendance |
|---|---|---|---|---|---|---|---|
| 1 | Aug 29 | H | Manchester U | W 2-1 | 1-1 | Whitton, Bodak | 20,050 |
| 2 | Sept 2 | A | Stoke C | L 0-4 | 0-2 | | 13,914 |
| 3 | 5 | A | Notts Co | L 1-2 | 0-1 | Daly | 10,889 |
| 4 | 12 | H | Leeds U | W 4-0 | 2-0 | Kaiser, Thompson 2, Whitton | 13,065 |
| 5 | 19 | A | Brighton & HA | D 2-2 | 1-1 | Kaiser, Hunt | 15,262 |
| 6 | 22 | H | Liverpool | L 1-2 | 1-2 | Daly | 16,731 |
| 7 | 26 | H | Southampton | W 4-2 | 1-1 | Hunt 2, Thompson 2 | 12,610 |
| 8 | Oct 3 | A | Sunderland | D 0-0 | 0-0 | | 19,269 |
| 9 | 10 | H | Aston Villa | D 1-1 | 1-1 | Hateley | 16,306 |
| 10 | 17 | A | Nottingham F | L 1-2 | 1-0 | Hunt | 20,101 |
| 11 | 24 | H | Swansea C | W 3-1 | 2-0 | Hateley 2, Kaiser | 14,050 |
| 12 | 31 | A | Arsenal | L 0-1 | 0-0 | | 23,102 |
| 13 | Nov 7 | A | Wolverhampton W | L 0-1 | 0-0 | | 13,193 |
| 14 | 21 | A | West Ham U | L 2-5 | 1-2 | Hunt 2 | 26,065 |
| 15 | 24 | H | Stoke C | W 3-0 | 2-0 | Daly, Thompson, Bradford | 10,250 |
| 16 | 28 | H | Middlesbrough | D 1-1 | 1-0 | Hateley | 11,309 |
| 17 | Dec 5 | A | Tottenham H | W 2-1 | 1-1 | Hunt, Gillespie | 28,073 |
| 18 | 12 | H | Manchester C | L 0-1 | 0-1 | | 12,393 |
| 19 | 26 | H | WBA | L 0-2 | 0-1 | | 15,033 |
| 20 | 28 | A | Everton | L 2-3 | 2-3 | Thomas, Bodak | 23,895 |
| 21 | Jan 16 | H | Ipswich T | L 2-4 | 1-1 | Hunt, Daly | 11,719 |
| 22 | 26 | A | Birmingham C | D 3-3 | 2-1 | Hunt, Hateley, Thompson | 13,023 |
| 23 | 30 | H | Brighton & HA | L 0-1 | 0-1 | | 11,023 |
| 24 | Feb 6 | A | Leeds U | D 0-0 | 0-0 | | 16,385 |
| 25 | 16 | H | Notts Co | L 1-5 | 1-2 | Hateley | 10,203 |
| 26 | 20 | A | Liverpool | L 0-4 | 0-3 | | 28,286 |
| 27 | 27 | A | Aston Villa | L 1-2 | 1-2 | Thompson | 24,474 |
| 28 | Mar 9 | H | Nottingham F | L 0-1 | 0-1 | | 9720 |
| 29 | 13 | A | Swansea C | D 0-0 | 0-0 | | 16,425 |
| 30 | 17 | A | Manchester U | W 1-0 | 1-0 | Whitton | 34,499 |
| 31 | 20 | H | Arsenal | W 1-0 | 0-0 | Hateley | 11,965 |
| 32 | 27 | H | Wolverhampton W | D 0-0 | 0-0 | | 11,514 |
| 33 | Apr 3 | A | Ipswich T | L 0-1 | 0-1 | | 20,411 |
| 34 | 10 | A | WBA | W 2-1 | 1-1 | Thompson, Whitton | 12,718 |
| 35 | 13 | H | Everton | W 1-0 | 1-0 | Singleton | 11,858 |
| 36 | 17 | H | West Ham U | W 1-0 | 1-0 | Hateley | 13,398 |
| 37 | 24 | A | Middlesbrough | D 0-0 | 0-0 | | 10,968 |
| 38 | 27 | H | Sunderland | W 6-1 | 2-1 | Gillespie, Thompson 2, Francis, Hateley 2 | 11,227 |
| 39 | May 1 | H | Tottenham H | D 0-0 | 0-0 | | 15,431 |
| 40 | 4 | A | Southampton | D 5-5 | 2-1 | Whitton 2, Hateley 3 | 18,522 |
| 41 | 8 | A | Manchester C | W 3-1 | 2-0 | Whitton 3 | 27,580 |
| 42 | 15 | H | Birmingham C | L 0-1 | 0-0 | | 15,905 |

**Final League Position: 14**

### Goalscorers

*League* (56): Hateley 13, Thompson 10, Hunt 9, Whitton 9, Daly 4, Kaiser 3, Bodak 2, Gillespie 2, Bradford 1, Francis 1, Singleton 1, Thomas 1.
*League Cup* (1): Hateley 1.
*FA Cup* (10): Hateley 4, Hunt 3, Thompson 2, Bodak 1.

| League Cup | Second Round | Everton (a) | 1-1 |
|---|---|---|---|
| | | (h) | 0-1 |
| FA Cup | Third Round | Sheffield W (h) | 3-1 |
| | Fourth Round | Manchester C (a) | 3-1 |
| | Fifth Round | Oxford U (h) | 4-0 |
| | Sixth Round | WBA (a) | 0-2 |

| Blyth | Thomas | Roberts | Jacobs | Dyson | Gillespie | Bodak | Daly | Thompson | Whitton | Hunt | Kaiser | Hateley | Gooding | Bradford | Hendrie | English | Barnes | Francis | Hormantschuk | Hagan | Sealey | Butterworth | Singleton | Match No. |
|---|---|---|---|---|---|---|---|---|---|---|---|---|---|---|---|---|---|---|---|---|---|---|---|---|
| 1 | 2 | 3 | 4 | 5 | 6 | 7 | 8 | 9 | 10 | 11 | | | | | | | | | | | | | | 1 |
| 1 | 2 | 3 | 4 | 5 | 6 | 7* | 8 | 9 | 10 | 11 | 12 | | | | | | | | | | | | | 2 |
| 1 | 2 | 3 | 4 | 5 | 6 | | 8 | 9 | 10 | 11 | 7 | | | | | | | | | | | | | 3 |
| 1 | 2 | 3 | 4 | 5 | 6 | | 8 | 9 | 10 | 11 | 7 | | | | | | | | | | | | | 4 |
| 1 | 2 | 3 | 4 | 5 | 6 | | 8 | 9 | 10 | 11 | 7 | | | | | | | | | | | | | 5 |
| 1 | 2 | 3 | 4 | 5 | 6 | | 8 | 9 | 10* | 11 | 7 | 12 | | | | | | | | | | | | 6 |
| 1 | 2 | 3 | 4 | 5 | 6 | | 8 | 9 | 10* | 11 | 7 | 12 | | | | | | | | | | | | 7 |
| 1 | 2 | 3 | 4 | 5 | 6 | | 8* | 9 | 10 | 11 | 7 | 12 | | | | | | | | | | | | 8 |
| 1 | 2 | 3 | 4 | 5 | 6 | | | 9 | 8 | 11 | 7 | 10 | | | | | | | | | | | | 9 |
| 1 | 2 | 3 | 4 | 5 | 6 | | | 9 | 8 | 10 | 7 | 11 | | | | | | | | | | | | 10 |
| 1 | 2 | 3 | 4 | 5 | 6 | | | 9 | 8 | 11 | 7 | 10 | | | | | | | | | | | | 11 |
| 1 | 2 | 3 | 4 | 5 | 6 | | | 9 | | 11 | 7 | 8 | 10 | | | | | | | | | | | 12 |
| 1 | 2 | 3 | 4 | 5 | 6 | | 8 | 9 | 10 | 11 | 7 | | | | | | | | | | | | | 13 |
| 1 | 2 | 3 | 4 | 5 | 6 | | 8 | 9 | | 11 | | 10 | | | 7 | | | | | | | | | 14 |
| 1 | 2 | 3 | 4 | 5 | 6 | | 8 | 9 | | 11 | | 10 | | | 7 | | | | | | | | | 15 |
| 1 | 2 | 3 | 4 | 5 | 6 | | 8 | 9 | | 11 | 12 | 10 | 7* | | | | | | | | | | | 16 |
| 1 | 2 | 3 | 4 | 5 | 6 | | 8* | 9 | | 11 | 12 | 10 | | | 7 | | | | | | | | | 17 |
| 1 | 2 | 3 | 4 | 5 | 6 | | 8 | 9 | | 11 | 12 | 10 | | | 7 | | | | | | | | | 18 |
| 1 | 2 | 3 | 4 | 5 | 6 | | 8 | 9 | 12 | 11 | | 10* | | | 7 | | | | | | | | | 19 |
| 1 | 2 | 3 | 4 | 5 | 6 | 7 | 8 | 9 | | 11 | 12 | | | | 10* | | | | | | | | | 20 |
| 1 | 2 | | | 5 | 6 | 7 | 8 | | | 11 | | 9 | | 10 | | 3 | 4* | 12 | | | | | | 21 |
| 1 | 2 | 12 | | 5 | 6 | 7 | 8* | | 10 | 11 | | 9 | | | | 3 | | 4 | | | | | | 22 |
| 1 | 2 | 12 | | 5 | 6 | 7 | 8* | | 10 | 11 | | 9 | | | | 3 | | 4 | | | | | | 23 |
| 1 | 2 | | 4 | | 6 | 7 | | | 10 | 11 | | 9 | | 8 | | 3 | | 5 | | | | | | 24 |
| 1 | 2 | | | 5 | 6 | 7 | | | 10 | 11 | | 9 | | 8 | | 3 | | 4 | | | | | | 25 |
| 1 | 2 | 3 | 8 | 5 | | | | | 10 | 11 | | 9 | | | 7 | | | 4 | | 6 | | | | 26 |
| 1 | 8 | 2 | | 5 | | 7 | | | 10 | 11 | | 9 | | | | 3 | | 4 | | 6 | | | | 27 |
| | 2 | 3 | 4 | 5 | 6 | | | | 12 | 11* | | 9 | | 7 | | 10 | | 8 | | | 1 | | | 28 |
| | 2 | 3 | 4 | 5 | 6 | | | | | 11 | | 9 | | 7* | | 10 | | 8 | | | 1 | 12 | | 29 |
| | 2 | 3 | 4 | 5 | 6 | | | | | | | 9 | | 7 | | 10 | | 8 | | | 1 | 11 | | 30 |
| | 2 | 3 | 4 | 5 | 6 | | | | | | | 9 | | 7 | | 10 | | 8 | | | 1 | 11 | | 30 |
| | 2 | 3 | 4 | 5 | 6 | | | | | | | 9 | | 7 | | 10 | | 8 | | | 1 | 11 | | 32 |
| | 2* | 3 | 4 | 5 | 6 | | | | 12 | | | 9 | | 7 | | 10 | | 8 | | | 1 | 11 | | 33 |
| | | 3 | 4 | 5 | 6 | | | | 10 | 7 | | 11 | | | 9 | | | 8 | | | 1 | 2 | | 34 |
| | | 3 | 4 | 5 | 6 | | | | 10 | 7 | | 11 | | | 9 | 12 | | | | | 1 | 2 | 8* | 35 |
| | 2 | 3 | 8 | 5 | 6 | | | | 10 | 7* | | 11 | | | 9 | 12 | | | | | 1 | 4 | | 36 |
| | 2 | 3 | | 5 | 6 | | | | 10 | 7 | | 11 | | | 9 | | | 8 | | | 1 | 4 | | 37 |
| | 2 | 3 | | 5 | 6 | | | | 10 | 7 | | 11 | | | 9 | | | 8 | | | 1 | 4 | | 38 |
| | 2 | 12 | 3 | 5 | 6 | | | | 10 | 7 | | 11* | | | 9 | | | 8 | | | 1 | 4 | | 39 |
| | 2 | 3 | | 5 | 6 | | | | 10 | 7 | | 11 | | | 9 | | | 8 | | | 1 | 4 | | 40 |
| | 3 | 2 | | 5 | 6 | | | | 10 | 7 | | 11 | | | 9* | 12 | | | | | 1 | 4 | 8 | 41 |
| | 2 | 3 | | 6 | 5 | | | | 10 | 7 | | 9 | | | 8 | 12 | | | | | 1 | 4* | 11 | 42 |
| 27 | 39 | 33 | 37 | 40 | 40 | 9 | 19 | 35 | 26 | 36 | 11 | 31 | 1 | 6 | 6 | 8 | 6 | 18 | — | 3 | 15 | 13 | 3 | |

|  | + | + |  |  |  |  |  |  | + | + |  | + | + |  |  |  |  |  | + |  | + |  |  |  |
|  | 1s | 2s |  |  |  |  |  |  | 1s | 2s |  | 5s | 3s |  |  |  |  |  | 5s |  | 1s |  |  |  |

## COVENTRY CITY

| | Ht | Wt | Birthplace | Clubs | League App. | League Gls |
|---|---|---|---|---|---|---|
| **Goalkeepers** | | | | | | |
| Jim Blyth | 6 1¼ | 13 3 | Perth | Preston NE | 1 | — |
| (Scotland) | | | | Coventry C | 151 | — |
| | | | | Hereford U (on loan) | 7 | — |
| Les Sealey | 6 1 | 11 6½ | Bethnal Green | Coventry C | 119 | — |
| Steve Murcott | 6 0 | 12 0 | Birmingham | Coventry C | 1 | — |
| (Contract cancelled July 1981) | | | | | | |
| Derek Richardson* | 6 2½ | 15 0 | London | Chelsea | — | — |
| | | | | QPR | 31 | — |
| | | | | Sheffield U | 42 | — |
| | | | | Coventry C | — | — |
| **Defenders** | | | | | | |
| Brian Roberts | 5 8¼ | 11 3½ | Manchester | Coventry C | 147 | — |
| | | | | Hereford U (on loan) | 5 | — |
| Paul Dyson | 6 2 | 13 7 | Birmingham | Coventry C | 101 | 4 |
| Steve Jacobs | 5 8 | 11 0 | London | Coventry C | 51 | — |
| David Jones | 5 10 | 12 7 | Liverpool | Everton | 86 | 1 |
| (Contract cancelled April 1982) | | | | Coventry C | 11 | — |
| Gary Gillespie | 6 2 | 12 1 | Scotland | Falkirk | 22 | — |
| | | | | Coventry C | 130 | 4 |
| Peter Hormantschuk | 5 10 | 10 8 | Coventry | Coventry C | 5 | — |
| Danny Thomas | 5 7 | 11 0 | Worksop | Coventry C | 67 | 2 |
| Ian Butterworth | 6 1 | 12 6 | Crewe | Coventry C | 14 | — |
| Jim Hagan* | 5 11 | 11 8½ | Monkstown | Larne | (not known) | |
| | | | | Torquay U (on loan) | 7 | — |
| | | | | Coventry C | 13 | — |
| | | | | Detroit E | (not known) | |
| | | | | Seiko, Hong Kong | (not known) | |
| | | | | Coventry C | 3 | — |
| **Midfield** | | | | | | |
| Ray Gooding* | 5 8 | 11 4½ | Hartlepool | Coventry C | 49 | 5 |
| | | | | Bristol C (on loan) | 3 | — |
| Andy Blair | 5 8½ | 10 10 | Bedworth | Coventry C | 93 | 6 |
| Steve Whitton | 6 0 | 12 7 | London | Coventry C | 36 | 9 |
| Gerry Daly | 5 10 | 10 6 | Dublin | Bohemians | (not known) | |
| (Eire) | | | | Manchester U | 111 | 23 |
| | | | | Derby Co | 112 | 31 |
| | | | | Coventry C | 54 | 12 |
| Gary Howlett* | 5 8 | 10 4 | Dublin | Home Farm | (not known) | |
| | | | | Coventry C | — | — |
| Martin Singleton | 5 9 | 10 0 | Banbury | Coventry C | 3 | 1 |
| David Bradford | 5 5 | 9 8 | Manchester | Blackburn R | 60 | 3 |
| (Contract cancelled April 1982) | | | | Sheffield U | 54 | 3 |
| | | | | WBA | — | — |
| | | | | Peterborough U (on loan) | 4 | — |
| | | | | Michigan | (not known) | |
| | | | | Detroit E | (not known) | |
| | | | | Washington D | (not known) | |
| | | | | Coventry C | 6 | 1 |
| Gerry Francis | 5 9 | 12 4 | London | QPR | 293 | 53 |
| (England) | | | | Crystal Palace | 59 | 7 |
| | | | | QPR | 17 | 4 |
| | | | | Coventry C | 18 | 1 |
| **Forwards** | | | | | | |
| Gary Barnett* | 5 5 | 9 4 | Stratford | Coventry C | — | — |
| Garry Thompson | 6 0 | 12 9 | Birmingham | Coventry C | 114 | 34 |
| Steve Hunt | 5 7 | 10 11 | Birmingham | Aston V | 7 | 1 |
| (Contract cancelled April 1982) | | | | New York C | (not known) | |
| | | | | Coventry C | 135 | 21 |
| Mark Hateley | 6 1 | 11 7 | Liverpool | Coventry C | 58 | 16 |
| Tom English | 5 9 | 11 6 | Cirencester | Coventry C | 66 | 17 |
| Roger van Gool | 5 9 | 11 10 | Belgium | FC Bruges | (not known) | |
| (Belgium) | | | | Cologne | (not known) | |
| (Contract cancelled Aug 1981) | | | | Coventry C | 17 | — |
| Peter Bodak* | 5 8 | 9 10 | Birmingham | Coventry C | 32 | 5 |
| John Hendrie | 5 8½ | 10 11 | Lennoxtown | Coventry C | 6 | — |
| Rudi Kaiser | 5 6 | 10 10 | Amsterdam | Antwerp | (not known) | |
| | | | | Coventry C | 16 | 3 |

Free transfers: Andy Willock*, Russell Gordon*, Gregory Abbott*.

# CREWE ALEXANDRA     Division 4

*President:* D. Godfrey.

*Chairman:* N. Rowlinson.

*Vice-Chairman:* N. Hassall.

*Directors:* J. McHugh, K. Potts, E. Tagg, D. Rowlinson, R. Clayton, J. McMillan, J. Bowler.

*Manager:* Arfon Griffiths.

*Secretary:* Mrs Gill Palin.

*Year Formed:* 1877.    *Turned Professional:* 1893.

*Limited Company:* 1892.

**Football League Record:**
1892 Original Member of Division 2; 1896 Failed re-election; 1921 Re-entered Division 3(N); 1958–63 Division 4; 1963–64 Division 3; 1964–68 Division 4; 1968–69 Division 3; 1969– Division 4.

**Honours:** *Football League:* Division 2 best season: 10th, 1892–93. *FA Cup* best season: semi-final 1888. *Football League Cup* best season: 3rd rd, 1974–75, 1975–76, 1978–79.

*Record Victory:* 8-0 v Rotherham U, Division 3(N), 1 Oct, 1932.

*Record Defeat:* 2-13 v Tottenham H, FA Cup 4th rd replay, 3 Feb, 1960.

*Most League Points:* 59, Division 4, 1962–63.

*Most League Goals:* 95, Division 3(N), 1931–32.

*Highest League Scorer in Season:* Terry Harkin, 34, Division 4, 1964–65.

*Most League Goals in Total Aggregate:* Bert Swindells, 126, 1928–37.

*Most Capped Player:* Bill Lewis, 12 (30), Wales.

*Most League Appearances:* Tommy Lowry, 436, 1966–78.

*Record Transfer Fee Received:* £40,000 from Port Vale for Paul Bowles, Sept 1979.

*Record Transfer Fee Paid:* £10,000 to Derby Co for Colin Chesters, Sept 1979, and to Sheffield U for Mike Guy, Sept 1979.

*Previous Managers since the War:* George Lillycrop, Frank Hill, Arthur Turner, Harry Catterick, Ralph Ward, Maurice Lindley, Harry Ware, Jimmy McGuigan, Ernie Tagg, Dennis Viollet, Jimmy Melia, Ernie Tagg, Harry Gregg, Warwick Rimmer, Tony Waddington.

*Address of Supporters Club:* Registered Office, Crewe Alexandra Supporters' Association, 131 Edleston Road, Crewe, Cheshire.

*Address of the Club Shop or Boutique:* Gresty Road, Crewe.

---

**Football Ground, Gresty Rd, Crewe.** Telephone Crewe 213014. *Telegraphic address:* 'Alex Football Crewe'. *Ground capacity:* 17,000. *Record attendance:* 20,000 v Tottenham H, FA Cup 4th rd, 30 Jan, 1960. *Record receipts:* £5,388 v Wigan Ath, League Cup 1st rd, 13 Aug, 1980. *Pitch measurements:* 112yd×74yd.

*How to get there:* Local bus services from outlying districts. The ground is situated just five minutes' walk from Crewe railway station.

*Match tickets:* Advance booking for important cup ties only.

*Car parking:* Parking at the ground for 200 cars.

*Entertainments/catering facilities:* The Alexandra Club adjoining the ground is owned by the club. Refreshment points inside the ground.

*Club shop:* Situated at the ground; sells all types of souvenirs.

*Handbooks/programmes:* Handbooks on sale at matches.

*Extra information:* In 1956–57 the club set an unenviable League record of playing 30 consecutive games without a win.

*Club Colours:* Red shirts, white shorts, red stockings.

*Change Colours:* Sky blue shirts and stockings, black shorts.

*Club Nickname:* The Railwaymen.

## CREWE ALEXANDRA 1981–82 LEAGUE RECORD

| Match No. | Date | Venue | Opponents | Result | | H/T Score | Goalscorers | Attendance |
|---|---|---|---|---|---|---|---|---|
| 1 | Aug 29 | A | AFC Bournemouth | L | 0-2 | 0-1 | | 3244 |
| 2 | Sept 6 | H | Torquay U | L | 0-1 | 0-1 | | 2054 |
| 3 | 12 | A | Blackpool | L | 0-5 | 0-3 | | 4506 |
| 4 | 18 | H | Aldershot | L | 2-3 | 1-2 | Haslegrave, Chesters (pen) | 1956 |
| 5 | 23 | H | Bury | L | 1-2 | 1-0 | Palios | 2033 |
| 6 | 26 | A | Peterborough U | L | 0-3 | 0-2 | | 3775 |
| 7 | 29 | A | Sheffield U | L | 0-4 | 0-2 | | 11,512 |
| 8 | Oct 2 | H | Port Vale | L | 0-2 | 0-1 | | 4604 |
| 9 | 10 | H | Scunthorpe U | W | 3-0 | 2-0 | Chesters, Ricketts, Palios | 1586 |
| 10 | 16 | A | Stockport Co | L | 0-2 | 0-0 | | 2669 |
| 11 | 21 | H | Rochdale | L | 1-2 | 0-1 | Palios | 1827 |
| 12 | 24 | A | Mansfield T | W | 1-0 | 0-0 | Scott | 2513 |
| 13 | 31 | H | Halifax T | L | 0-1 | 0-0 | | 2291 |
| 14 | Nov 4 | A | Hartlepool U | W | 2-1 | 2-1 | Linacre P. (og), Palios | 2338 |
| 15 | 8 | A | Northampton T | L | 0-3 | 0-0 | | 2794 |
| 16 | 14 | H | Darlington | W | 1-0 | 1-0 | Scott | 1858 |
| 17 | 28 | H | York C | D | 1-1 | 0-1 | Palios | 1881 |
| 18 | Dec 5 | A | Hull C | L | 0-1 | 0-0 | | 3184 |
| 19 | Jan 19 | A | Tranmere R | L | 0-3 | 0-1 | | 1609 |
| 20 | 23 | H | AFC Bournemouth | D | 0-0 | 0-0 | | 1597 |
| 21 | 26 | H | Wigan Ath | L | 0-1 | 0-1 | | 3874 |
| 22 | 31 | A | Aldershot | L | 0-3 | 0-0 | | 2053 |
| 23 | Feb 5 | H | Blackpool | D | 1-1 | 0-1 | Gwyther | 2513 |
| 24 | 9 | A | Bury | L | 1-2 | 0-1 | Lewis | 2900 |
| 25 | 13 | A | Port Vale | D | 0-0 | 0-0 | | 6542 |
| 26 | 19 | H | Peterborough U | L | 0-1 | 0-1 | | 1628 |
| 27 | 24 | A | Torquay U | D | 1-1 | 1-0 | Lewis | 1601 |
| 28 | 28 | A | Scunthorpe U | W | 1-0 | 0-0 | Howat | 2591 |
| 29 | Mar 6 | H | Stockport Co | L | 0-2 | 0-0 | | 1827 |
| 30 | 9 | A | Rochdale | L | 0-1 | 0-1 | | 1060 |
| 31 | 13 | H | Mansfield T | L | 0-2 | 0-0 | | 1476 |
| 32 | 16 | H | Hartlepool U | L | 1-2 | 1-1 | Ricketts | 1116 |
| 33 | 20 | A | Halifax T | L | 1-2 | 0-1 | Palios | 2128 |
| 34 | 23 | H | Hereford U | W | 1-0 | 0-0 | Palios | 1326 |
| 35 | 27 | H | Northampton T | D | 2-2 | 0-2 | Palios, Williams | 1801 |
| 36 | 30 | A | Colchester U | D | 1-1 | 1-1 | Palios | 1904 |
| 37 | Apr 4 | A | Darlington | L | 0-1 | 0-0 | | 2206 |
| 38 | 10 | A | Wigan Ath | L | 0-3 | 0-1 | | 6142 |
| 39 | 12 | H | Tranmere R | D | 1-1 | 0-0 | Griffiths (pen) | 2015 |
| 40 | 17 | H | Hull C | D | 1-1 | 1-1 | Palios | 1595 |
| 41 | 23 | A | York C | L | 0-6 | 0-3 | | 1753 |
| 42 | 26 | H | Bradford C | L | 0-1 | 0-0 | | 2009 |
| 43 | May 1 | H | Sheffield U | L | 2-3 | 1-1 | Williams, Palios | 6186 |
| 44 | 5 | A | Bradford C | L | 1-4 | 0-2 | Williams | 5393 |
| 45 | 8 | A | Hereford U | L | 1-4 | 1-3 | Palios | 3058 |
| 46 | 15 | H | Colchester U | L | 1-3 | 1-3 | Scott | 1226 |

**Final League Position: 24**

### Goalscorers

*League* (29): Palios 12, Scott 3, Williams 3, Chesters 2 (1 pen), Lewis 2, Ricketts 2, Griffiths 1 (pen), Gwyther 1, Haslegrave 1, Howat 1, own goal 1.
*League Cup* (1): Ricketts 1.
*FA Cup* (2): Haslegrave 1, Scott 1.

| **League Cup** | First Round | Bristol R (h) | 1-1 |
|---|---|---|---|
| | | (a) | 0-1 |
| **FA Cup** | First Round | Willenhall T (a) | 1-0 |
| | Second Round | Scunthorpe U (h) | 1-3 |

| Mulhearn | Salathiel | Lewis | Heath | Scott | Haslegrave | Keighley | Ricketts | Chesters | Palios | Williams | Griffiths | Hanlon | Bowers | Henderson | Callaghan | Gwyther | Waller | Howat | Entwistle | Longley | Cook | Match No. |
|---|---|---|---|---|---|---|---|---|---|---|---|---|---|---|---|---|---|---|---|---|---|---|
| 1 | 2 | 3 | 4 | 5 | 6 | 7* | 8 | 9 | 10 | 11 | 12 | | | | | | | | | | | 1 |
| 1 | 2 | 3 | 4 | 5 | 6 | 9 | 8 | | 10 | 11* | | 7 | 12 | | | | | | | | | 2 |
| 1 | 2 | 3 | 4 | 5 | 6* | 9 | 8 | | 10 | | 12 | 7 | 11 | | | | | | | | | 3 |
| 1 | 2 | 3 | | 5 | 6 | 7 | 8 | 12 | 10 | | 4 | | 11* | 9 | | | | | | | | 4 |
| 1 | 2 | 3 | | 5 | 6 | 7 | 12 | 9* | 10 | | 4 | | 8 | 11 | | | | | | | | 5 |
| 1 | 2 | 3 | | 5 | 6 | 7 | | 9 | 10 | | 4 | 11 | | 8 | | | | | | | | 6 |
| 1 | 2 | 3 | 11 | 5 | 6 | 7 | | 12 | 10 | | 4* | 8 | | 9 | | | | | | | | 7 |
| 1 | 2 | 3 | | 5 | 6 | 7 | 12 | 9 | 10 | | 4 | 11 | | 8* | | | | | | | | 8 |
| 1 | | 3 | | 5 | 6 | | 8* | 9 | 10 | 7 | 4 | 11 | 2 | 12 | | | | | | | | 9 |
| 1 | | 3 | | 5 | 6 | 12 | | 9* | 10 | 7 | 4 | 11 | 2 | 8 | | | | | | | | 10 |
| 1 | 12 | 2 | | 5 | | 6 | 8* | 9 | 10 | 7 | 4 | 11 | 3 | | | | | | | | | 11 |
| 1 | 6 | 2 | 12 | 5 | | | 8 | 9 | 10 | 11* | 4 | 7 | 3 | | | | | | | | | 12 |
| 1 | 4 | 2 | | 5 | 6 | | | 9 | 10 | 11 | | 7 | 3 | | 8 | | | | | | | 13 |
| 1 | 4 | 2 | | 5 | 6 | | | 9 | 10 | 7 | 8 | | 3 | | 11 | | | | | | | 14 |
| 1 | 4 | 2 | | 5 | | 7 | | 9 | 10 | 11 | 6 | | 3 | | 8 | | | | | | | 15 |
| 1 | 4 | 2 | | 5 | | 7 | | 9 | 10 | 11 | 6 | | 3 | | 8 | | | | | | | 16 |
| 1 | 4 | 2 | | 5 | | 7 | 9* | 12 | 10 | 11 | 6 | | 3 | | 8 | | | | | | | 17 |
| 1 | 4 | 2 | | 5 | | 7* | 9 | 12 | 10 | 11 | 6 | | 3 | | 8 | | | | | | | 18 |
| 1 | 4 | 2* | | 5 | | 7 | | 9 | 10 | 11 | 6 | 12 | 3 | | 8 | | | | | | | 19 |
| 1 | 4* | 2 | | 5 | | 7 | | 12 | | 11 | 6 | | 3 | | 8 | 9 | | 10 | | | | 20 |
| 1 | 4 | 2 | | 5 | | 7 | 10* | 12 | | 11 | 6 | | 3 | | 8 | 9 | | | | | | 21 |
| 1 | 4 | 2 | 12 | 5 | | 7 | | 10 | | 11 | 6 | | 3 | | 8* | 9 | | | | | | 22 |
| 1 | 4 | 2 | 6 | 5 | | 7 | 12 | | 10 | 8 | 11* | | 3 | | | 9 | | | | | | 23 |
| 1 | 4 | 2 | 6 | 5 | | 7 | 10* | 12 | | 8 | 11 | | 3 | | | 9 | | | | | | 24 |
| 1 | 4 | 2 | 12 | 5 | 6 | | 9* | | | 8 | 11 | | 3 | | 7 | 10 | | | | | | 25 |
| 1 | 4 | 2 | | 5 | | 7 | | 9 | 10 | 11 | | | 3 | | 6 | 8 | | | | | | 26 |
| 1 | 4 | 2 | 12 | 5 | | 7 | | 9 | | 6 | 11 | | 3 | 8* | | | | 10 | | | | 27 |
| 1 | 4 | 2 | | 5 | | 7 | | 9 | | 6 | 11 | | 3 | 8 | | | | 10 | | | | 28 |
| 1 | 4 | 2 | 8 | 5 | | 7* | 12 | 9 | | 6 | 11 | | 3 | | | | | 10 | | | | 29 |
| 1 | 4 | 2 | 7 | 5 | | | 12 | 9 | | 6 | 11 | | 3 | 8* | | | | 10 | | | | 30 |
| 1 | 4 | 2 | 8 | 5 | | 7 | | 9 | | 6 | 11 | | 3 | | | | | 10 | | | | 31 |
| 1 | 4 | 2 | 7 | 5 | | 8 | | 9 | | 6 | 11 | | 3 | | | | | 10 | | | | 32 |
| 1 | 4 | 2 | 12 | 5 | | 7 | | 9 | | 6 | 11 | | 3 | 8* | | | | 10 | | | | 33 |
| 1 | 4 | 2 | | 5 | | 7 | 8 | 9 | | 6 | 11 | | 3 | | | | | 10 | | | | 34 |
| 1 | 4 | 2 | 12 | 5 | | 7 | 8* | | | 6 | 11 | | 3 | | | | | 10 | 9 | | | 35 |
| 1 | 4 | 2 | | 5 | | 7 | 8 | 10 | | 6 | 11 | | 3 | | | | | | 9 | | | 36 |
| | 4 | 2 | | 5 | | 7 | 8 | 10 | 1 | 6 | 11 | | 3 | | | | | | 9 | | | 37 |
| | 4 | 2 | | 5 | | 8 | 7 | 10 | | 6* | 11 | | 3 | | | | | 12 | 9 | 1 | | 38 |
| | 4 | 2 | | 5 | | 7 | 8 | 6 | | | 11 | | 3 | | | | | 10 | 9 | 1 | | 39 |
| 1 | 4 | 2 | 3 | 5 | | 7 | 8* | 12 | | 6 | 11 | | | | | | | 10 | 9 | | | 40 |
| 1 | 4 | 3 | 2 | 5 | | | 8 | 12 | | 6 | 11* | | | | | | | 10 | 9 | 7 | | 41 |
| 1 | 4 | 2 | 3 | 5 | | 7 | 8* | 12 | | 6 | 11 | | | | | | | 10 | 9 | | | 42 |
| 1 | 4 | 2 | 3 | 5 | | 7 | 8 | | | 6 | 11 | | | | | | | 10 | 9 | | | 43 |
| 1 | 4 | 3 | 2 | 5 | | 8 | 7 | 12 | | 6 | 11 | | | | | | | 10 | 9* | | | 44 |
| 1 | 4 | 3 | 2 | 5 | | 7 | 8 | 9 | | 6 | | | | | | | | 10 | | | 11 | 45 |
| | 4 | 2 | 3 | 5 | | 7 | 8* | 9 | | 6 | 11 | | | | | | | | 10 | 1 | 12 | 46 |
| 42 | 43 | 46 | 17 | 46 | 40 | 25 | 14 | 28 | 42 | 39 | 32 | 14 | 17 | 6 | 15 | 7 | 1 | 16 | 11 | 3 | 2 | |
| | + | | | | + | | + | + | + | + | + | + | + | + | | | | + | | | + | |
| | 1s | | | | 6s | | 4s | 3s | 8s | 2s | 2s | 1s | 1s | 1s | | | | 1s | | | 1s | |

## CREWE ALEXANDRA

| | Ht | Wt | Birthplace | Clubs | League App. | League Gls |
|---|---|---|---|---|---|---|
| **Goalkeepers** | | | | | | |
| Ken Mulhearn* | 6 0 | 13 11 | Liverpool | Everton | — | — |
| | | | | Stockport Co | 100 | — |
| | | | | Manchester C | 50 | — |
| | | | | Shrewsbury T | 370 | — |
| | | | | Crewe Alex | 88 | — |
| Nick Longley | | | | Crewe Alex | 3 | — |
| (Non-contract) | | | | | | |
| **Defenders** | | | | | | |
| Kevin Lewis* | 5 9 | 11 13 | Hull | Manchester U | — | — |
| | | | | Stoke C | 15 | — |
| | | | | Crewe Alex | 122 | 2 |
| Bob Scott | 6 2½ | 13 4 | Liverpool | Wrexham | 19 | — |
| | | | | Reading (on loan) | 5 | — |
| | | | | Hartlepool U | 37 | — |
| | | | | Rochdale | 71 | 3 |
| | | | | Crewe Alex | 134 | 7 |
| Danny Bowers* | 5 8¾ | 10 2 | Stoke | Stoke C | 39 | 2 |
| | | | | Shrewsbury T (on loan) | 6 | — |
| | | | | Crewe Alex | 108 | 2 |
| Colin Prophett | 5 11 | 12 2 | Crewe | Sheffield W | 117 | 7 |
| (Contract cancelled) | | | | Norwich C | 35 | — |
| | | | | Swindon T | 160 | 10 |
| | | | | Chesterfield | 37 | 1 |
| | | | | Crewe Alex | 79 | 1 |
| Duncan Heath* | 5 9 | 10 13 | Stoke | Aston Villa | — | — |
| | | | | Crewe Alex | 23 | — |
| Neil Salathiel | | | Wrexham | Sheffield W | — | — |
| | | | | Wrexham | 4 | — |
| | | | | Crewe Alex | 44 | — |
| **Midfield** | | | | | | |
| Steve Hanlon | 5 10 | 10 6 | Chester | Crewe Alex | 18 | — |
| (Contract cancelled April 1982) | | | | | | |
| Neil Griffiths* | 5 11 | 11 10 | Stoke | Chester | 90 | 4 |
| | | | | Port Vale | 218 | 13 |
| | | | | Crewe Alex | 34 | 1 |
| Sean Haslegrave | 5 8 | 10 7 | Stoke | Stoke C | 113 | 5 |
| | | | | Nottingham F | 7 | 1 |
| | | | | Preston NE | 113 | 2 |
| | | | | Crewe Alex | 40 | 1 |
| Phil Williams* | | | Swansea | Arsenal | — | — |
| | | | | Blackpool | — | — |
| | | | | USA | (not known) | |
| | | | | Crewe Alex | 39 | 3 |
| Tony Cook | | | | Crewe Alex | 3 | — |
| (Non-contract) | | | | | | |
| Ian Callaghan | 5 7 | 11 11 | Liverpool | Liverpool | 640 | 49 |
| (England) (Retired) | | | | Swansea C | 76 | 1 |
| | | | | Cork Hibs | (not known) | |
| | | | | Crewe Alex | 15 | — |
| **Forwards** | | | | | | |
| Mark Palios | 5 8 | 10 13 | Birkenhead | Tranmere R | 190 | 25 |
| | | | | Crewe Alex | 104 | 23 |
| Colin Chesters* | 5 11 | 11 0 | Crewe | Derby Co | 9 | 1 |
| | | | | Crewe Alex | 61 | 6 |
| Paul Keighley* | 5 7½ | 10 5 | Ribchester | Bolton W | — | — |
| | | | | Crewe Alex | 29 | — |
| Ian Howat* | 5 8 | 10 12 | Wrexham | Chester | 57 | 10 |
| | | | | Crewe Alex | 17 | 1 |
| Alan Ricketts | | | | Wrexham | — | — |
| (Contract cancelled April 1982) | | | | Crewe Alex | 17 | 2 |
| Wayne Entwistle | 5 11 | 11 8 | Bury | Bury | 31 | 7 |
| | | | | Sunderland | 45 | 12 |
| | | | | Leeds U | 11 | 2 |
| | | | | Blackpool | 32 | 6 |
| | | | | Crewe Alex | 11 | — |
| David Waller | | | | Crewe Alex | 1 | — |
| (Non-contract) | | | | | | |

# CRYSTAL PALACE    Division 2

*Chairman:* R. G. Noades.

*Deputy Chairman:* B. Bishop.

*Directors:* B. Coleman, A. S. C. De'Souza, R. O. Faulkner, R. J. Easterby, C. D. Richards, B. Bishop, J. C. C. M. Rose, E. G. Libby, R. M. Marsden.

*Team Manager:* Alan Mullery MBE.

*Secretary:* Alan Leather.

*Year Formed:* 1905.    *Limited Company:* 1905.

*Turned Professional:* 1905.

*Previous Grounds:* 1905, Crystal Palace; 1915, Herne Hill; 1919, The Nest; 1924, Selhurst Park.

**Football League Record:**
1920 Original Members of Division 3; 1921–25 Division 2; 1925–58 Division 3(S); 1958–61 Division 4; 1961–64 Division 3; 1964–69 Division 2; 1969–73 Division 1; 1973–74 Division 2; 1974–77 Division 3; 1977–79 Division 2; 1979–81 Division 1; 1981– Division 2.

**Honours:** *Football League:* Division 1 best season: 13th, 1979–80; Division 2 – Champions 1978–79; Runners-up 1968–69; Division 3 – Runners-up 1963–64; Division 3(S) – Champions 1920–21; Runners-up 1928–29, 1930–31, 1938–39; Division 4 – Runners-up 1960–61. *FA Cup* best season: semifinal 1975–76. *Football League Cup* best season: 5th rd, 1968–69, 1970–71.

*Record Victory:* 9–0 v Barrow, Division 4, 10 Oct 1959.

*Record Defeat:* 4–11 v Manchester C, FA Cup 5th rd, 20 Feb, 1926.

*Most League Points:* 64, Division 4, 1960–61.

*Most League Goals:* 110, Division 4, 1960–61.

*Highest League Scorer in Season:* Peter Simpson, 46, Division 3(S), 1930–31.

*Most League Goals in Total Aggregate:* Peter Simpson, 154, 1930–36.

*Most Capped Player:* Ian Evans, 13, Wales.

*Most League Appearances:* Terry Long, 432, 1956–69.

*Record Transfer Fee Received:* £800,000 (nett) from Arsenal for Kenny Sansom, Aug 1980.

*Record Transfer Fee Paid:* £800,000 (nett) to Arsenal for Clive Allen, Aug 1980.

*Previous Managers since the War:* George Irwin, Jack Butler, Ronnie Rooke, Fred Dawes, Charlie Slade, Laurie Scott, Cyril Spiers, George Smith, Arthur Rowe, Dick Graham, Bert Head, Malcolm Allison, Terry Venables, Ernie Walley, Malcolm Allison, Dario Gradi, Steve Kember.

*Address of Supporters Club:* Selhurst Park, SE25 6PU.

*Address of Club Shop:* Palace Shop, Selhurst Park SE25 6PU.

---

**Selhurst Park, London, SE25 6PU.** Telephone 01-653 4462. *Ground capacity:* 38,500 (18,000 covered). *Record attendance:* 51,482 v Burnley, Division 2, 11 May, 1979. *Record receipts:* £74,868 v Tottenham H, Division 1, 6 Oct, 1979. *Pitch measurements:* 112yd×74yd.
*How to get there:* Ground served by three stations – Selhurst (5 minutes walk), Norwood Junction (7 minutes) and Thornton Heath (10 minutes). Buses 68, 75, 154, 157, 12 (to Norwood Junction).
*Match tickets:* Seats bookable in advance, postal applications accepted one month in advance and personal application two weeks in advance. Postal applications must be accompanied by SAE and the correct remittance. Cheques must be made payable to Crystal Palace FC and name and address must be written on the back. Separate application must be made for each match.
*Car parking:* By prior arrangement only through the Secretary.
*Entertainments/catering facilities:* Extensive match-day catering facilities within the ground, including Strikers, a fully licensed high-class restaurant – for reservations ring 01-653 1876. Comprehensive range of non-match-day function rooms for all occasions – for details ring Tony Francis on 01-653 4462.
*Club shop:* Sells all types of souvenirs.
*Handbooks/programmes:* Programmes available on subscription.
*Extra information:* Vic Rouse, the Crystal Palace goalkeeper, was the first Fourth Division player to be capped when he played for Wales v Ireland in 1959.
*Club Colours:* White shirts with 4-inch diagonal band red over blue, white shorts, white stockings.
*Change Colours:* Light blue shirts with 4-inch diagonal red band from left shoulder; light blue shorts; light blue stockings.
*Club Nickname:* The Eagles.

## CRYSTAL PALACE 1981–82 LEAGUE RECORD

| Match No. | Date | Venue | Opponents | Result | H/T Score | Goalscorers | Attendance |
|---|---|---|---|---|---|---|---|
| 1 | Aug 29 | H | Cambridge U | W 2-1 | 2-0 | Hinshelwood 2 (2 pens) | 11,201 |
| 2 | Sept 2 | A | Norwich C | L 0-1 | 0-1 | | 14,434 |
| 3 | 5 | A | Sheffield W | L 0-1 | 0-0 | | 18,476 |
| 4 | 12 | H | Charlton Ath | W 2-0 | 1-0 | Walsh 2 | 14,227 |
| 5 | 19 | A | QPR | L 0-1 | 0-1 | | 17,039 |
| 6 | 22 | H | Orient | W 1-0 | 1-0 | Hilaire | 11,061 |
| 7 | 26 | H | Shrewsbury T | L 0-1 | 0-0 | | 9037 |
| 8 | Oct 3 | A | Leicester C | D 1-1 | 0-0 | Hilaire | 12,558 |
| 9 | 10 | H | Rotherham U | W 3-1 | 0-1 | Smillie, Brooks, Langley | 8021 |
| 10 | 17 | A | Wrexham | W 1-0 | 0-0 | Lovell | 4795 |
| 11 | 24 | H | Derby Co | L 0-1 | 0-1 | | 11,127 |
| 12 | 31 | A | Luton T | L 0-1 | 0-1 | | 11,712 |
| 13 | Nov 7 | H | Blackburn R | L 1-2 | 0-2 | Cannon (pen) | 9452 |
| 14 | 21 | A | Oldham Ath | D 0-0 | 0-0 | | 5581 |
| 15 | 24 | H | Norwich C | W 2-1 | 0-0 | Mabbutt 2 | 9010 |
| 16 | 28 | H | Bolton W | W 1-0 | 0-0 | Jones (og) | 8839 |
| 17 | Dec 5 | A | Barnsley | L 0-2 | 0-0 | | 14,877 |
| 18 | Jan 19 | H | Sheffield W | L 1-2 | 1-1 | Wicks | 8289 |
| 19 | 26 | A | Cambridge U | D 0-0 | 0-0 | | 3505 |
| 20 | 30 | H | QPR | D 0-0 | 0-0 | | 15,267 |
| 21 | Feb 6 | A | Charlton Ath | L 1-2 | 0-1 | Brooks | 9072 |
| 22 | 21 | A | Orient | D 0-0 | 0-0 | | 5132 |
| 23 | 27 | A | Rotherham U | L 0-2 | 0-1 | | 10,007 |
| 24 | Mar 9 | H | Cardiff C | W 1-0 | 0-0 | Langley | 6526 |
| 25 | 13 | A | Derby Co | L 1-4 | 1-2 | McAlle (og) | 10,248 |
| 26 | 17 | A | Chelsea | W 2-1 | 2-0 | Mabbutt, Murphy | 13,894 |
| 27 | 20 | H | Luton T | D 3-3 | 2-3 | Smillie 2, Mabbutt | 12,001 |
| 28 | 23 | H | Leicester C | L 0-2 | 0-2 | | 9506 |
| 29 | 27 | A | Blackburn R | L 0-1 | 0-0 | | 8362 |
| 30 | 31 | A | Newcastle U | D 0-0 | 0-0 | | 21,610 |
| 31 | Apr 3 | H | Grimsby T | L 0-3 | 0-1 | | 7541 |
| 32 | 9 | A | Watford | D 1-1 | 1-0 | Giles | 18,224 |
| 33 | 12 | H | Chelsea | L 0-1 | 0-1 | | 17,189 |
| 34 | 17 | H | Oldham Ath | W 4-0 | 1-0 | Hilaire 2, Mabbutt 2 | 6720 |
| 35 | 20 | A | Grimsby T | W 1-0 | 1-0 | Hilaire | 7646 |
| 36 | 24 | A | Bolton W | D 0-0 | 0-0 | | 6280 |
| 37 | 27 | H | Watford | L 0-3 | 0-1 | | 12,355 |
| 38 | May 1 | H | Barnsley | L 1-2 | 1-0 | Mabbutt | 7500 |
| 39 | 4 | A | Shrewsbury T | L 0-1 | 0-0 | | 3159 |
| 40 | 8 | A | Cardiff C | W 1-0 | 0-0 | Mabbutt | 5762 |
| 41 | 11 | H | Wrexham | W 2-1 | 2-0 | Wilkins 2 | 7272 |
| 42 | 15 | H | Newcastle U | L 1-2 | 0-0 | Murphy (pen) | 8453 |

**Final League Position: 15**

**Goalscorers**

*League* (34): Mabbutt 8, Hilaire 5, Smillie 3, Brooks 2, Hinshelwood 2 (2 pens), Langley 2, Murphy 2 (1 pen), Walsh 2, Wilkins 2, Cannon 1 (pen), Giles 1, Lovell 1, Wicks 1, own goals 2.
*League Cup* (4):Cannon 2 (1 pen), Langley 1, Murphy 1.
*FA Cup* (5): Hilaire 2, Cannon 1 (pen), Price 1, Smillie 1.

| League Cup | Second Round | Doncaster R (a) | 0-1 |
|---|---|---|---|
| | | (h) | 2-0 |
| | Third Round | Sunderland (a) | 1-0 |
| | Fourth Round | WBA (h) | 1-3 |
| FA Cup | Third Round | Enfield (a) | 3-2 |
| | Fourth Round | Bolton W (h) | 1-0 |
| | Fifth Round | Orient (h) | 0-0 |
| | | (a) | 1-0 |
| | Sixth Round | QPR (a) | 0-1 |

| Barron | Hinshelwood | Dare | Price | Cannon | Gilbert | Smillie | Murphy | Walsh | Langley | Hilaire | Hughes | Bason | Brooks | Lovell | Wicks | Leahy | Galliers | Mabbutt | Boulter | Giles | Fry | Wilkins | Baxter | Nebbeling | Match No. |
|---|---|---|---|---|---|---|---|---|---|---|---|---|---|---|---|---|---|---|---|---|---|---|---|---|---|
| 1 | 2 | 3 | 4 | 5 | 6* | 7 | 8 | 9 | 10 | 11 | 12 | | | | | | | | | | | | | | 1 |
| 1 | 2 | 3 | 4 | 5 | 6 | 7 | | 9 | 10 | | | 8 | 11* | 12 | | | | | | | | | | | 2 |
| 1 | 2 | 3 | 4 | 5 | 6 | 7 | | 9 | 10 | 12 | 11 | | | 8* | | | | | | | | | | | 3 |
| 1 | 2 | | 4 | 3 | 6 | 8 | | 9 | 10 | 11 | | 7 | | | 5 | | | | | | | | | | 4 |
| 1 | 2 | | 6 | 3 | 5 | 8 | | 9 | 10 | 11* | 12 | 7 | | | 4 | | | | | | | | | | 5 |
| 1 | | | 4 | 3 | 6 | 8 | | 9 | 10 | 11 | | 7 | 2 | 5 | | | | | | | | | | | 6 |
| 1 | | | 4 | 3 | 6 | 8 | | 9 | 10 | 11* | | 7 | 2 | 5 | 12 | | | | | | | | | | 7 |
| 1 | 3 | 4 | 5 | 6 | | 8 | | | 10 | 11 | | 9 | 2 | 7* | 12 | | | | | | | | | | 8 |
| 1 | | | | 5 | 6 | 8 | 4 | 12 | 10 | | | 9 | 2 | 7 | 3 | 11* | | | | | | | | | 9 |
| 1 | | | | 5 | 6 | 8 | 4 | 9* | 10 | 11 | | 12 | 2 | 7 | 3 | | | | | | | | | | 10 |
| 1 | | | | 5 | 6 | 8 | 4 | 10 | | 11 | | 9* | 2 | 7 | 3 | | | 12 | | | | | | | 11 |
| 1 | 12 | | | 5 | 6 | 8 | 4 | | 10 | | | 2 | 11* | 3 | | | 7 | 9 | | | | | | | 12 |
| 1 | 11 | | | 5 | 6 | 8 | 4* | | 10 | 12 | | 2 | | 3 | | | 7 | 9 | | | | | | | 13 |
| 1 | 7 | | | 5 | | 8 | 4 | 10* | | 11 | | | 2 | 6 | | | 12 | 9 | 3 | | | | | | 14 |
| 1 | 7* | | | 5 | | 8 | 4 | 9 | | 11 | | | 2 | 6 | | | 12 | 10 | 3 | | | | | | 15 |
| 1 | | | | 5 | | 8 | 4 | 9 | | 11 | | 7 | | 6 | | | 2 | 10 | 3 | | | | | | 16 |
| 1 | | | | 5 | | 8 | 4 | 9 | | 11 | | 7 | | 6 | | | 2 | 10 | 3 | | | | | | 17 |
| 1 | 2 | | 6 | | | 8 | 4 | 9 | | 11 | | | 12 | 7* | 5 | | | 10 | 3 | | | | | | 18 |
| 1 | 2 | | 6 | | | 8 | 4 | 9* | | 11 | | | 7 | | 5 | | 12 | 10 | 3 | | | | | | 19 |
| 1 | 2 | | 6 | | | 8 | 4 | 9 | | 11 | | | 7 | | 5 | | | 10 | 3 | | | | | | 20 |
| 1 | 2 | | 6 | | | 8 | 4 | 9 | | 11 | | 12 | | | 5 | | | 10* | 3 | 7 | | | | | 21 |
| 1 | 2 | | 12 | 6 | | 8 | | 9 | | 11 | | | 7 | | 5 | | | 10 | 3 | 4* | | | | | 22 |
| 1 | 2* | | 4 | | 6 | 8 | | 9 | | 11 | | | 7 | | 5 | | | 10 | 3 | 12 | | | | | 23 |
| | | | 9 | | 6 | 8* | 4 | 12 | | 11 | | | 2 | | 5 | 1 | | 10 | 3 | 7 | | | | | 24 |
| 1 | 2 | | | 5 | 6 | 8 | 4 | | | 11 | | 9 | | 3 | | | | 10 | | 7 | | | | | 25 |
| 1 | 2 | | 9 | | 6 | 8 | 4 | | | 11 | | | | | 5 | | | 10 | 3 | 7 | | | | | 26 |
| 1 | 2 | | 11 | | 6 | 8 | 4 | 9* | | 12 | | | | | 5 | | | 10 | 3 | 7 | | | | | 27 |
| 1 | 2 | | 11 | | 6 | 8 | 4 | 9 | | 7 | | 12 | | | 5 | | | 10 | 3* | | | | | | 28 |
| 1 | 2 | | 4 | 11 | | | | 9 | 8 | | | 12 | 5 | 6* | | | | 10 | 3 | 7 | | | | | 29 |
| 1 | 3 | | 4 | 5 | 6 | 8 | | 9 | | 2 | | 11 | | | | | | 10 | | 7 | | | | | 30 |
| 1 | 3 | | | 5 | 6 | 8 | | 9 | 12 | 2* | | 11 | 4 | | | | | 10 | | 7 | | | | | 31 |
| 1 | 3 | | 4 | 5 | 6 | 8 | | | | 11 | | 9 | 2 | | | | | 10 | | 7 | | | | | 32 |
| 1 | 3 | | 4 | 5 | 6 | 8 | | | | 11 | | 9 | 2 | | | | | 10 | | 7 | | | | | 33 |
| 1 | 3 | | | 5 | 6 | 8 | | | | 11 | | 9 | 2 | | 4 | | | 10 | | 7 | | | | | 34 |
| 1 | 3 | | | 5 | 6 | 8 | | | | 11 | | 9 | 2 | | 4 | | | 10 | | 7 | | | | | 35 |
| 1 | 3 | | | 5 | 6 | 8 | | | | 11 | | 9 | 2 | | 4 | | | 10 | | 7 | | | | | 36 |
| 1 | 3 | | | 5 | 6 | 8 | 12 | | | 11 | | 9 | 2 | | 4* | | | 10 | | 7 | | | | | 37 |
| 1 | 3 | | | 5 | 6 | 8 | 4 | | | 11 | | 9 | | | | | | 10 | 2 | 7* | 12 | | | | 38 |
| 1 | 3 | | 4 | 5 | 6 | 8 | | 9 | | 11* | | | 2 | | | | | 10 | | 7 | 12 | | | | 39 |
| 1 | 2 | | 9* | 5 | 6 | 8 | 4 | | | 11 | | | 3 | | | | | 10 | | 7 | 12 | | | | 40 |
| 1 | | | | 5 | 6* | 8 | 4 | | | 11 | | 2 | | 3 | 12 | | | 10 | | 7 | 9 | | | | 41 |
| | | | | 5 | | 8 | 4 | | | 11 | | 2 | | | | | | 10 | | 7 | 1 | 9 | 3 | 6 | 42 |
| **40** | **27** | **4** | **17** | **42** | **31** | **41** | **24** | **12** | **25** | **33** | **3** | **17** | **22** | **28** | **14** | **1** | **8** | **31** | **16** | **20** | **2** | **2** | **1** | **1** | |
| | | | +2s | | | +1s | +1s | +1s | +3s | +4s | +1s | +3s | +2s | | +1s | +5s | | | +1s | +3s | | | | | |

## CRYSTAL PALACE

| | Ht | Wt | Birthplace | Clubs | League App. | League Gls |
|---|---|---|---|---|---|---|
| **Goalkeepers** | | | | | | |
| David Fry | 6 1 | 12 7 | Bournemouth | Crystal Palace | 15 | — |
| Paul Barron | 6 2 | 13 5 | London | Plymouth Arg | 44 | — |
| | | | | Arsenal | 8 | — |
| | | | | Crystal Palace | 73 | — |
| **Defenders** | | | | | | |
| Jim Cannon | 6 0 | 13 0 | Glasgow | Crystal Palace | 336 | 19 |
| Kevin Dare | 5 9 | 11 13 | Finchley | Crystal Palace | 6 | — |
| (Contract cancelled Feb 1982) | | | | | | |
| Billy Gilbert | 5 11 | 12 0 | Lewisham | Crystal Palace | 169 | 2 |
| Paul Hinshelwood | 6 0 | 12 6 | Bristol | Crystal Palace | 241 | 16 |
| Neil Banfield | 5 11 | 12 0 | London | Crystal Palace | 3 | — |
| (Contract cancelled Feb 1982) | | | | | | |
| David Boulter | 5 8 | 11 3 | London | Crystal Palace | 16 | — |
| Steve Lovell | 5 9 | 11 3 | Swansea | Crystal Palace | 55 | 3 |
| (Wales) | | | | Stockport Co (on loan) | 12 | — |
| Gavin Nebbeling | 6 0 | 12 4 | Johannesburg | Crystal Palace | 1 | — |
| Paul Baxter | 5 7 | 10 8 | Hackney | Crystal Palace | 1 | — |
| Brian Bason | 5 9 | 11 0 | Epsom | Chelsea | 19 | 1 |
| | | | | Plymouth Arg | 130 | 10 |
| | | | | Crystal Palace | 27 | — |
| | | | | Portsmouth (on loan) | 9 | — |
| Keith Oakley | 5 10 | 12 0 | Durham | Crystal Palace | — | — |
| **Midfield** | | | | | | |
| Jerry Murphy | 5 9 | 11 10 | Stepney | Crystal Palace | 131 | 12 |
| (Éire) | | | | | | |
| Tony Paul | 5 9 | 11 0 | Islington | Crystal Palace | 1 | — |
| (Contract cancelled Feb 1982) | | | | | | |
| Shaun Brooks | 5 7 | 11 0 | London | Crystal Palace | 43 | 2 |
| David Price | 5 11 | 12 0 | Caterham | Arsenal | 126 | 16 |
| | | | | Peterborough U (on loan) | 6 | 1 |
| | | | | Crystal Palace | 27 | 2 |
| Steve Leahy | 5 7 | 10 9 | Battersea | Crystal Palace | 4 | — |
| (Contract cancelled March 1982) | | | | | | |
| Steve Galliers | 5 6 | 9 7 | Chorley | Wimbledon | 155 | 10 |
| | | | | Crystal Palace | 13 | — |
| Graeme Smith | 5 8 | 10 7 | Hartlepool | Crystal Palace | — | — |
| **Forwards** | | | | | | |
| Neil Smillie | 5 6 | 10 7 | Barnsley | Crystal Palace | 83 | 7 |
| | | | | Brentford (on loan) | 3 | — |
| Vince Hilaire | 5 6 | 10 0 | Forest Hill | Crystal Palace | 173 | 22 |
| Mike Elwiss | 6 0 | 12 6 | Doncaster | Doncaster R | 97 | 30 |
| (Retired, injury) | | | | Preston NE | 192 | 60 |
| | | | | Crystal Palace | 20 | 7 |
| | | | | Preston NE (on loan) | 10 | 3 |
| Tommy Langley | 5 11 | 11 7 | Elephant and Castle | Chelsea | 142 | 40 |
| | | | | QPR | 25 | 8 |
| | | | | Crystal Palace | 35 | 5 |
| Mark Annon | 5 8 | 10 12 | London | Crystal Palace | — | — |
| (Non-contract) | | | | | | |
| Peter Nott | | | London | Fulham | — | — |
| (Contract cancelled Feb 1982) | | | | Crystal Palace | — | — |
| Gary Allen | 5 10 | 11 4 | London | Crystal Palace | — | — |
| Paul Wilkins | 6 2 | 12 0 | Hackney | Crystal Palace | 5 | 2 |
| Trevor Ames | 6 0 | 11 1 | Poole | Aston V | — | — |
| (Contract cancelled Feb 1982) | | | | Hereford U | 8 | — |
| | | | | Crystal Palace | — | — |
| Kevin Mabbutt | 5 7 | 10 2 | Bristol | Bristol C | 129 | 29 |
| | | | | Crystal Palace | 31 | 8 |
| David Giles | 5 7 | 10 4½ | Cardiff | Cardiff C | 59 | 3 |
| (Wales) | | | | Wrexham | 38 | 2 |
| | | | | Swansea C | 54 | 13 |
| | | | | Orient (on loan) | 3 | 2 |
| | | | | Crystal Palace | 21 | 1 |

# DARLINGTON Division 4

*Chairman:* J. L. T. Moore.
*Directors:* D. Mason, A. Brown, J. B. Hadley, A. Moore, K. Warne, C. Parias.
*Manager:* Billy Elliott.
*Secretary:* David Thorne.
*Year Formed:* 1883. *Turned Professional:* 1908.
*Limited Company:* 1891.

**Football League Record:**
1921 Original Member Division 3(N); 1925–27 Division 2; 1927–58 Division 3(N); 1958–66 Division 4; 1966–67 Division 3; 1967– Division 4.

**Honours:** *Football League:* Division 2 best season: 15th, 1925–26; Division 3(N) – Champions 1924–25; Runners-up 1921–22; Division 4 – Runners-up 1965–66. *FA Cup* best season: 3rd rd, 1910–11, 5th rd, 1957–58. *Football League Cup* best season: 5th rd, 1967–68.

*Record Victory:* 9-2 v Lincoln C, Division 3(N), 7 Jan, 1928.
*Record Defeat:* 0-10 v Doncaster R, Division 4, 25 Jan, 1964.
*Most League Points:* 59, Division 4, 1965–66.
*Most League Goals:* 108, Division 3(N), 1929–30.
*Highest League Scorer in Season:* David Brown, 39, Division 3(N), 1924–25.
*Most League Goals in Total Aggregate:* David Brown, 74, 1923–26.
*Most Capped Player:* None.
*Most League Appearances:* Ron Greener, 442, 1955–68.
*Record Transfer Fee Received:* £65,011 from Chelsea for David Speedie, May 1982.
*Record Transfer Fee Paid:* £17,000 to Notts Co for Eric Probert, Oct 1978.
*Previous Managers since the War:* Bill Forrest, George Irwin, Bob Gurney, Dick Duckworth, Eddie Carr, Lol Morgan, Jimmy Greenhalgh, Ray Yeoman, Len Richley, Frank Brennan, Allan Jones, Ralph Brand, Dick Conner, Billy Horner, Peter Madden, Len Walker.
*Address of Supporters Club:* Same as Football Club.
*Statistician:* Frank Tweddle.

---

**Feethams Ground, Darlington.** Telephone Darlington (0325) 65097/67712. *Ground capacity:* 20,000. *Record attendance:* 21,023 v Bolton W, League Cup 3rd rd, 14 Nov, 1960. *Record receipts:* £15,059 v Sheffield U, Division 4, 15 May, 1982. *Pitch measurements:* 110yd×74yd.
*How to get there:* Darlington railway station, five minutes walk.
*Match tickets:* Postal and telephone bookings accepted in advance of the match.
*Car parking:* Ample parking in surrounding side-streets.
*Entertainments/catering facilities:* Three nearby cafés. Three snack bars in the ground.
*Club shop:* Shop inside the ground sells all types of souvenirs.
*Handbooks/programmes:* No handbook. Programmes available on subscription.
*Extra information:* The club will make every effort to cater for the disabled, the blind, or any person who has some difficulty seeking entrance because of illness.
*Club Colours:* White shirts with black collar and cuffs, black shorts, black stockings with white hoop round top.
*Change Colours:* All royal blue or all red.
*First Team Trainer/Coach:* George Herd.
*Club Nickname:* The Quakers.

## DARLINGTON 1981–82 LEAGUE RECORD

| Match No. | Date | Venue | Opponents | Result | H/T Score | Goalscorers | Attendance |
|---|---|---|---|---|---|---|---|
| 1 | Aug 29 | A | Aldershot | D 0-0 | 0-0 | | 1918 |
| 2 | Sept 5 | H | Port Vale | D 1-1 | 1-0 | Speedie | 1872 |
| 3 | 12 | A | AFC Bournemouth | L 0-2 | 0-0 | | 3900 |
| 4 | 19 | H | Blackpool | D 2-2 | 0-1 | Speedie, Hamilton | 2485 |
| 5 | 22 | H | Bradford C | L 1-5 | 0-2 | Hamilton | 2303 |
| 6 | 26 | A | Bury | L 0-2 | 0-0 | | 2562 |
| 7 | 29 | A | Tranmere R | D 1-1 | 0-0 | Speedie | 1345 |
| 8 | Oct 3 | H | Peterborough U | D 0-0 | 0-0 | | 1628 |
| 9 | 9 | A | York C | D 2-2 | 1-2 | Walsh, McLean | 2407 |
| 10 | 17 | H | Mansfield T | W 1-0 | 0-0 | Hamilton | 1576 |
| 11 | 20 | H | Halifax T | D 1-1 | 0-0 | Hamilton | 1642 |
| 12 | 24 | A | Hereford U | D 1-1 | 0-1 | Wicks | 2217 |
| 13 | 31 | H | Rochdale | W 2-0 | 2-0 | Wicks, Hamilton | 1454 |
| 14 | Nov 4 | A | Wigan Ath | L 1-2 | 1-0 | Walsh | 4512 |
| 15 | 7 | H | Stockport Co | W 2-0 | 1-0 | Mitchell, Speedie | 1556 |
| 16 | 14 | A | Crewe Alex | L 0-1 | 0-1 | | 1858 |
| 17 | 28 | H | Colchester U | L 1-2 | 1-1 | Speedie | 1456 |
| 18 | Dec 5 | A | Northampton T | W 1-0 | 0-0 | Walsh | 1669 |
| 19 | Jan 3 | A | Bradford C | L 0-3 | 0-2 | | 4473 |
| 20 | 20 | A | Port Vale | D 2-2 | 1-0 | Speedie, Walsh | 3529 |
| 21 | 23 | H | Aldershot | L 0-1 | 0-0 | | 1504 |
| 22 | 26 | A | Sheffield U | D 0-0 | 0-0 | | 11,517 |
| 23 | 30 | A | Blackpool | L 0-1 | 0-1 | | 3336 |
| 24 | Feb 3 | H | Hartlepool U | W 2-1 | 1-1 | McLean, Stalker | 4548 |
| 25 | 6 | H | AFC Bournemouth | L 0-1 | 0-1 | | 2443 |
| 26 | 13 | A | Peterborough U | L 1-3 | 1-1 | Stalker | 3202 |
| 27 | 17 | H | Scunthorpe U | W 4-1 | 1-1 | Speedie, McLean (pen), Skipper, Walsh (pen) | 1663 |
| 28 | 20 | H | Bury | L 2-3 | 1-0 | Hamilton 2 | 2039 |
| 29 | 28 | H | York C | W 3-1 | 1-1 | Speedie 3 | 3212 |
| 30 | Mar 6 | A | Mansfield T | W 3-2 | 1-1 | Speedie, McLean, Walsh | 1538 |
| 31 | 9 | A | Halifax T | D 3-3 | 2-0 | Stalker 2, Speedie | 1508 |
| 32 | 14 | H | Hereford U | L 0-1 | 0-1 | | 2557 |
| 33 | 16 | H | Wigan Ath | W 3-1 | 1-0 | Walsh (pen), Hamilton, McFadden | 2147 |
| 34 | 20 | A | Rochdale | L 2-3 | 1-1 | Speedie 2 | 1252 |
| 35 | 23 | H | Hull C | W 2-1 | 2-0 | Speedie, Walsh | 2651 |
| 36 | 26 | A | Stockport Co | L 0-1 | 0-0 | | 1831 |
| 37 | Apr 4 | H | Crewe Alex | W 1-0 | 0-0 | McFadden | 2206 |
| 38 | 10 | A | Hull C | W 3-1 | 2-0 | Booth (og), Stalker, McFadden | 4589 |
| 39 | 12 | H | Hartlepool U | W 5-2 | 1-2 | McLean, Walsh 4 (1 pen) | 4575 |
| 40 | 17 | H | Northampton T | W 3-0 | 1-0 | Smith, Wicks, Speedie | 1729 |
| 41 | 24 | A | Colchester U | L 0-1 | 0-0 | | 1764 |
| 42 | 30 | H | Tranmere R | L 1-2 | 0-0 | McLean (pen) | 1612 |
| 43 | May 5 | A | Torquay U | W 2-1 | 2-0 | Walsh, Skipper | 1278 |
| 44 | 8 | A | Scunthorpe U | D 1-1 | 1-0 | Speedie | 1274 |
| 45 | 15 | H | Sheffield U | L 0-2 | 0-2 | | 11,130 |
| 46 | 18 | H | Torquay U | D 1-1 | 0-0 | McLean (pen) | 1283 |

**Final League Position: 13**

### Goalscorers

*League* (61): Speedie 17, Walsh 13 (3 pens), Hamilton 8, McLean 7 (3 pens), Stalker 5, McFadden 3, Wicks 3, Skipper 2, Mitchell 1, Smith 1, own goal 1.
*League Cup* (2): Charlton 1, Walsh 1.
*FA Cup* (3): Speedie 1, Smith 1, Walsh 1.

| **League Cup** | First Round | Rotherham U (h) | 1-3 |
|---|---|---|---|
| | | (a) | 1-2 |
| **FA Cup** | First Round | Carlisle U (h) | 2-2 |
| | | (a) | 1-3 |

| Cuff | Kamara | McLean | Smith | Mitchell | Skipper | Speedie | Hawker | McFadden | Hamilton | Walsh | Ball | Stalker | Charlton | Wilson | Wicks | Liddle | Honour | Match No. |
|---|---|---|---|---|---|---|---|---|---|---|---|---|---|---|---|---|---|---|
| 1 | 2 | 3 | 4 | 5 | 6 | 7 | 8 | 9 | 10 | 11 |  |  |  |  |  |  |  | 1 |
| 1 | 2 | 3 | 4 |  | 5 | 8 | 7 |  | 10 | 11 | 6 | 9 |  |  |  |  |  | 2 |
| 1 | 2 | 3 | 4 | 6 | 5 | 8 | 7 |  | 10 | 11 |  | 9 |  |  |  |  |  | 3 |
| 1 | 2 | 3 | 4 | 6 | 5 | 8 | 7*12 |  | 10 | 11 |  |  | 9 |  |  |  |  | 4 |
| 1 | 2 | 3 | 4 | 6 | 5 | 8 | 7 | 9* | 10 | 11 |  | 12 |  |  |  |  |  | 5 |
| 1 | 2 |  | 4 |  | 5 | 8 | 7 |  | 10 | 11 | 6 | 9* |  | 3 | 12 |  |  | 6 |
| 1 |  | 3 | 4 |  | 5 | 8 | 7 |  | 10 | 11* | 6 | 9 |  | 2 | 12 |  |  | 7 |
| 1 |  | 3 | 4 |  | 5 | 8 | 7 | 11 | 10 |  | 6 | 9 |  | 2 |  |  |  | 8 |
| 1 | 6 | 3 | 4 | 12 | 5 | 8 | 7 |  | 10 | 11 |  | 9 |  | 2* |  |  |  | 9 |
| 1 | 6 | 3 | 4 | 9 | 5 | 8 | 7 |  | 10 | 11 |  |  |  | 2 |  |  |  | 10 |
| 1 | 6 | 3 | 4 | 9* | 5 | 8 | 7 |  | 10 | 11 |  | 12 |  | 2 |  |  |  | 11 |
| 1 | 2 | 8 | 4 | 7 | 5 | 6 |  |  | 10 | 11 |  | 9* |  | 3 | 12 |  |  | 12 |
| 1 | 2 | 8 | 4 | 7 | 5 | 6 |  |  | 10 | 11 |  |  |  | 3 | 9 |  |  | 13 |
| 1 | 2 | 8 | 4 | 7 | 5 | 6 |  |  | 10 | 11* |  | 12 |  | 3 | 9 |  |  | 14 |
| 1 | 2 | 8 | 4 | 7 | 5 | 6 |  |  | 10 | 11 |  |  |  | 3 | 9 |  |  | 15 |
| 1 | 2 | 8 | 4 | 7 | 5 | 6 |  |  | 10 | 11 |  |  |  | 3 | 9 |  |  | 16 |
| 1 | 2 | 8 | 4 | 3 | 5 | 6 | 7 |  | 10* | 11 |  | 12 |  | 9 |  |  |  | 17 |
| 1 | 2 | 8 | 4 |  | 5 | 6 |  |  | 10 | 11 |  | 7 |  | 3 | 9 |  |  | 18 |
| 1 | 2 | 8 | 4 |  | 5 | 6 | 12 |  | 10 | 11 |  | 7* |  | 3 | 9 |  |  | 19 |
| 1 | 2 | 8 | 4 |  | 5 | 6 | 7 |  | 10 | 11 |  | 9 |  | 3 |  |  |  | 20 |
| 1 | 2 | 8 | 4 |  | 5 | 6 | 9 |  | 10 | 11 |  | 7* |  | 3 | 12 |  |  | 21 |
| 1 | 2 | 8 | 4 |  | 5 | 6 | 9 |  | 10 | 11 |  | 7 |  | 3 |  |  |  | 22 |
| 1 | 2 | 8 | 4 |  | 5 | 6 | 9 |  | 10 | 11 |  | 7 |  | 3 |  |  |  | 23 |
| 1 | 2 | 8 | 4 |  | 5 | 6 | 9 |  | 10 | 11 |  | 7 |  | 3 |  |  |  | 24 |
| 1 | 2 | 8 | 4 |  | 5 | 6 | 9 |  | 10 | 11 |  | 7 |  | 3*12 |  |  |  | 25 |
| 1 | 2* | 8 | 4 |  | 5 | 6 | 9 | 12 | 10 | 11 |  | 7 |  | 3 |  |  |  | 26 |
| 1 | 2 | 8 | 4 |  | 5 | 6 | 9 |  | 10 | 11 |  | 7 |  | 3 |  |  |  | 27 |
| 1 | 2 | 8 | 4 |  |  | 6 | 9 |  | 10 | 11 |  | 7 |  | 3 | 5 |  |  | 28 |
| 1 | 2 | 8 | 4 |  | 5 | 6 | 9 |  | 10 | 11 |  | 7 |  | 3 |  |  |  | 29 |
| 1 | 2 | 8 | 4 |  | 5 | 6 | 9 |  | 10 | 11 |  | 7 |  | 3 |  |  |  | 30 |
| 1 | 2 | 8 | 4 |  | 5 | 6 | 9 |  | 10 | 11 |  | 7 |  | 3 |  |  |  | 31 |
| 1 | 2 | 8 | 4 |  | 5 | 6 | 9 | 12 | 10 | 11 |  | 7* |  | 3 |  |  |  | 32 |
| 1 | 2 | 8 | 4 |  | 5 | 6 | 9 | 7 | 10 | 11 |  |  |  | 3 |  |  |  | 33 |
| 1 | 2 | 8 | 4 |  | 5 | 6 | 9 | 7*10 |  | 11 |  | 12 |  | 3 |  |  |  | 34 |
| 1 | 2 | 8 | 4 |  | 5 | 6 | 9 | 7 | 10 | 11 |  |  |  | 3 |  |  |  | 35 |
| 1 | 2 | 8 | 4 |  | 5 | 6 | 9 | 7 | 10 | 11 |  |  |  |  | 3 |  |  | 36 |
| 1 | 2 | 8 |  |  | 5 |  | 9 | 7 | 10* | 11 |  | 6 |  | 4 | 3 | 12 |  | 37 |
| 1 | 2 | 8 | 4 |  | 5 |  | 9 | 10 |  | 11 |  | 7 |  |  | 6 | 3 |  | 38 |
| 1 | 2 | 8 | 4 |  | 5 | 6 | 9 | 7 |  | 11 |  |  |  |  | 10 | 3 |  | 39 |
| 1 | 2 | 8 | 4 |  | 5 | 6 | 9 | 7* |  | 11 |  | 12 |  |  | 10 | 3 |  | 40 |
| 1 | 2 | 8 | 4 |  | 5 | 6* | 9 | 7 |  | 11 |  | 12 |  |  | 10 | 3 |  | 41 |
| 1 | 2 | 8 | 4 |  | 5 | 6 | 9* | 7 |  | 11 |  | 12 |  |  | 10 | 3 |  | 42 |
| 1 | 2 | 8 | 4 |  | 5 | 6 | 9 | 7 |  | 11 |  |  |  |  | 10 | 3 |  | 43 |
| 1 | 2 | 8 | 4 |  | 5 | 6 | 7 | 9 |  | 11 |  |  |  |  | 10 | 3 |  | 44 |
| 1 | 2 | 8 | 4 |  | 5 | 6 | 9 | 7* |  | 11 |  | 12 |  |  | 10 | 3 |  | 45 |
| 1 | 2 | 8 | 4 |  | 5 | 6 | 7 |  |  | 11 |  | 9 |  |  | 10 | 3 |  | 46 |
| 46 | 43 | 46 | 45 | 12 | 45 | 44 | 37 | 17 | 38 | 45 | 4 | 25 | 1 | 29 | 17 | 12 | — |  |

Substitute appearances: Smith +1s; Skipper +1s; Speedie +3s; Stalker +9s; Wicks +5s; Liddle +1s.

## DARLINGTON

| | Ht | Wt | Birthplace | Clubs | League App. | League Gls |
|---|---|---|---|---|---|---|
| **Goalkeepers** | | | | | | |
| Kevin Barry | 5 10 | 11 7 | Newcastle | Nottingham F | — | — |
| (Contract cancelled Aug 1981) | | | | Darlington | 18 | — |
| Pat Cuff | 6 0 | 12 6 | Middlesbrough | Middlesbrough | 31 | — |
| | | | | Grimsby T (on loan) | 2 | — |
| | | | | Millwall | 42 | — |
| | | | | Darlington | 76 | — |
| Fred Barber | 5 10 | 11 7 | Ferryhill | Darlington | — | — |
| **Defenders** | | | | | | |
| Kevan Smith | 6 3 | 11 9 | Eaglescliffe | Darlington | 119 | 4 |
| Donald Ball* | 5 11 | 11 3 | Barnard Castle | Darlington | 60 | 2 |
| Peter Skipper | 5 11 | 12 6½ | Hull | Hull C | 23 | 2 |
| | | | | Scunthorpe U (on loan) | 1 | — |
| | | | | Darlington | 91 | 4 |
| Alan Kamara | 5 9 | 10 12 | Sheffield | York C | 10 | — |
| | | | | Darlington | 88 | — |
| Kevin Glendinning* | | | Corbridge | Darlington | 4 | — |
| Harry Wilson | 5 9½ | 10 12 | Hetton-le-Hole | Burnley | 10 | — |
| | | | | Brighton | 130 | 4 |
| | | | | Preston NE | 42 | — |
| | | | | Darlington | 55 | — |
| David McLean | 5 8 | 11 0 | Newcastle | Newcastle U | 9 | — |
| | | | | Carlisle U | 15 | — |
| | | | | Darlington | 123 | 15 |
| Gavin Liddle | 5 10 | 12 7 | Houghton-le-Spring | Darlington | 12 | — |
| (Non-contract) | | | | | | |
| **Midfield** | | | | | | |
| David Hawker* | 5 7 | 9 12 | Hull | Hull C | 35 | 2 |
| | | | | Darlington | 77 | 2 |
| Harry Charlton | 5 7¾ | 10 8 | Newcastle | Middlesbrough | 10 | — |
| (Retired, injury) | | | | Hartlepool U (on loan) | 3 | — |
| | | | | Chesterfield | 21 | — |
| | | | | Buxton | (not known) | |
| | | | | Darlington | 72 | 4 |
| David Speedie | 5 7 | 10 4 | Glenrothes | Barnsley | 23 | — |
| | | | | Darlington | 88 | 21 |
| Scott Duncan | | | Darlington | Scarborough | (not known) | |
| (Contract cancelled April 1982) | | | | Darlington | — | — |
| Barry Stell | 5 8½ | 10 10 | Felling | Sheffield W | — | — |
| (Contract cancelled April 1982) | | | | Darlington | 9 | — |
| Roger Wicks | 6 0 | 11 0 | Warrington | Darlington | 32 | 4 |
| Ken Mitchell | 5 11 | 11 12 | Sunderland | Newcastle U | 66 | 2 |
| (Contract cancelled April 1982) | | | | Darlington | 13 | 1 |
| Brian Honour | 5 7 | 12 5 | Horden | Darlington | 1 | — |
| (Non-contract) | | | | | | |
| **Forwards** | | | | | | |
| Alan Walsh | 6 0 | 11 0 | Hartlepool | Middlesbrough | 3 | — |
| | | | | Darlington | 167 | 59 |
| John Stalker | 5 11 | 11 7 | Musselburgh | Leicester C | — | — |
| | | | | Darlington | 109 | 34 |
| Ian Hamilton* | 5 7½ | 10 7 | South Shields | Darlington | 103 | 19 |
| Tony McFadden | 5 10 | 12 0 | Hexham | Racing Jet | (not known) | |
| | | | | Reyrothes | (not known) | |
| | | | | Darlington | 20 | 3 |

# DERBY COUNTY

## Division 2

*Chairman:* W. Stevenson.

*Vice-Chairman:* J. N. Kirkland.

*Directors:* F. W. Fern, M. McGarry, B. G. Holmes, R. J. Moore, R. J. Mulholland, E. Strachan.

*Manager:* John Newman.

*Secretary:* Michael Durnford.

*Year Formed:* 1884. *Turned Professional:* 1884.

*Limited Company:* 1896.

*Former Grounds:* 1884–95, Racecourse Ground; 1895, Baseball Ground.

**Football League Record:**
1888 Founder Member of the Football League; 1907–12 Division 2; 1912–14 Division 1; 1914–15 Division 2; 1915–21 Division 1; 1921–26 Division 2; 1926–53 Division 1; 1953–55 Division 2; 1955–57 Division 3(N); 1957–69 Division 2; 1969–80 Division 1; 1980– Division 2.

**Honours:** *Football League:* Division 1 – Champions 1971–72, 1974–75; Runners-up 1895–96, 1929–30, 1935–36; Division 2 – Champions 1911-12, 1914–15, 1968–69; Runners-up 1925–26; Division 3(N) – Champions 1956–57; Runners-up 1955–56. *FA Cup:* Winners 1945–46; Runners-up 1897–98, 1898–99, 1902–03. *Football League Cup:* Semi-final 1967–68. *Texaco Cup:* 1971–72. *Charity Shield:* 1975. **European Competitions:** *European Cup:* 1972–73, 1975–76; *UEFA Cup:* 1974–75, 1976–77.

*Record Victory:* 12-0 v Finn Harps, UEFA Cup 3rd rd, 1st leg, 15 Sept, 1976.

*Record Defeat:* 2-11 v Everton, FA Cup 1st rd, 1889–90.

*Most League Points:* 63, Division 2, 1968–69 and 63, Division 3(N), 1955–56, 1956–57.

*Most League Goals:* 111, Division 3(N), 1956–57.

*Highest League Scorer in Season:* Jack Bowers, 37, Division 1, 1930–31 and Ray Straw, 37, Division 3(N), 1956–57.

*Most League Goals in Total Aggregate:* Steve Bloomer, 291, 1892–1906 and 1910–14.

*Most Capped Player:* Roy McFarland, 28, England.

*Most League Appearances:* Kevin Hector, 486, 1966–78; 1980–82.

*Record Transfer Fee Received:* £400,000 from Southampton for Charlie George, Dec 1978.

*Record Transfer Fee Paid:* £410,000 to Crystal Palace for Dave Swindlehurst, April 1980.

*Previous Managers since the War:* Stuart McMillan, Jack Barker, Harry Storer, Tim Ward, Brian Clough, Dave Mackay, Colin Murphy, Tommy Docherty, Colin Addison.

*Address of Supporters Club:* Baseball Ground, Derby.

*Address of the Club Shop or Boutique:* The Ramtique, 57 Osmaston Road, Derby.

---

**Baseball Ground, Shaftesbury Crescent, Derby DE3 8NB.** Telephone Derby 40105. *Telegraphic address:* 'Football Derby'. *Ground capacity:* 33,000 (16,000 seats.) *Record attendance:* 41,826 v Tottenham H, Division 1, 20 Sept, 1969. *Record receipts:* £65,000 v Juventus, European Cup semi-final, 25 April, 1973. *Pitch measurements:* 110yd×71yd.

*How to get there:* Buses from town centre 159, 188 and 189. Nearest railway station Derby Midland.

*Match tickets:* Available 14 days prior to game (£2.70, £3.30, £3.80). Children £1.50.

*Car parking:* Eight car parks within half a mile of the ground run by the club in connection with the local corporation. Street parking half a mile from the ground.

*Entertainments/catering facilities:* Sportsmen's Club (members only). Licensed and refreshment bars in all parts of the ground. Executive Box complex.

*Club shop:* The Ramtique, 57 Osmaston Road.

*Programmes: The Ram Newspaper,* the official club programme, is available on match days priced 35p and on subscription care of the Programme Editor, Derby County Football Club, or from local newsagents.

*Club Colours:* White shirts, blue shorts, white stockings.

*Change Colours:* Orange, blue, orange.

*Club Captain:* Steve Powell.

*Club Nickname:* The Rams.

## DERBY COUNTY 1981–82 LEAGUE RECORD

| Match No. | Date | Venue | Opponents | Result | H/T Score | Goalscorers | Attendance |
|---|---|---|---|---|---|---|---|
| 1 | Aug 29 | H | Orient | L 1-2 | 0-1 | Hector | 12,423 |
| 2 | Sept 1 | A | Cambridge U | W 2-1 | 1-1 | Emery, Swindlehurst | 5071 |
| 3 | 5 | A | Shrewsbury T | L 1-4 | 0-1 | Swindlehurst | 4373 |
| 4 | 12 | H | Leicester C | W 3-1 | 3-0 | Hector, Buckley, Ramage | 16,046 |
| 5 | 19 | A | Sheffield W | D 1-1 | 1-0 | Powell S. | 23,764 |
| 6 | 23 | H | Bolton W | L 0-2 | 0-2 | | 12,066 |
| 7 | 26 | H | QPR | W 3-1 | 1-0 | Hector 2, Ramage | 11,246 |
| 8 | Oct 3 | A | Charlton Ath | L 1-2 | 0-1 | Emson | 6686 |
| 9 | 10 | A | Newcastle U | L 0-3 | 0-2 | | 17,243 |
| 10 | 17 | H | Blackburn R | D 1-1 | 0-1 | Powell B. | 10,572 |
| 11 | 24 | A | Crystal Palace | W 1-0 | 1-0 | Swindlehurst | 11,127 |
| 12 | 31 | H | Grimsby T | D 1-1 | 1-0 | Clayton | 11,706 |
| 13 | Nov 7 | A | Luton T | L 2-3 | 0-1 | Osgood, Clayton | 10,784 |
| 14 | 14 | H | Wrexham | W 2-1 | 1-0 | Buckley, Edwards (og) | 10,956 |
| 15 | 21 | A | Norwich C | L 1-4 | 0-2 | Osgood | 13,457 |
| 16 | 25 | H | Cambridge U | W 2-1 | 1-0 | Swindlehurst, Clayton | 8470 |
| 17 | 28 | H | Chelsea | D 1-1 | 0-1 | Osgood | 13,963 |
| 18 | Dec 4 | A | Cardiff C | L 0-1 | 0-1 | | 5515 |
| 19 | Jan 16 | A | Orient | L 2-3 | 2-2 | Hill, Fisher (og) | 4595 |
| 20 | 23 | H | Oldham Ath | W 1-0 | 0-0 | Swindlehurst | 10,171 |
| 21 | 26 | A | Watford | L 1-6 | 0-3 | Emson | 12,643 |
| 22 | 30 | H | Sheffield W | W 3-1 | 0-1 | Sheridan, Wilson 2 | 11,215 |
| 23 | Feb 2 | A | Rotherham U | L 1-2 | 1-0 | Hill | 7487 |
| 24 | 6 | A | Leicester C | L 1-2 | 0-0 | Emson | 14,132 |
| 25 | 13 | H | Charlton Ath | D 1-1 | 1-1 | Sheridan | 10,846 |
| 26 | 20 | A | QPR | L 0-3 | 0-2 | | 8890 |
| 27 | 27 | H | Newcastle U | D 2-2 | 1-0 | Emson, Wilson | 12,257 |
| 28 | Mar 6 | A | Blackburn R | L 1-4 | 0-2 | Swindlehurst | 8364 |
| 29 | 10 | A | Shrewsbury T | D 1-1 | 1-0 | Wilson | 7518 |
| 30 | 13 | H | Crystal Palace | W 4-1 | 2-1 | Buckley, Skivington, Wilson 2 | 10,248 |
| 31 | 20 | A | Grimsby T | L 0-1 | 0-1 | | 7573 |
| 32 | 27 | H | Luton T | D 0-0 | 0-0 | | 15,836 |
| 33 | Apr 3 | A | Wrexham | D 1-1 | 1-0 | Emson | 4073 |
| 34 | 10 | A | Barnsley | D 0-0 | 0-0 | | 13,457 |
| 35 | 12 | H | Rotherham U | W 3-1 | 1-0 | Skivington, Wilson, Buckley | 14,080 |
| 36 | 17 | H | Norwich C | L 0-2 | 0-1 | | 12,508 |
| 37 | 24 | A | Chelsea | W 2-0 | 0-0 | Powell B., George | 11,005 |
| 38 | 28 | H | Barnsley | L 0-1 | 0-1 | | 11,296 |
| 39 | May 1 | H | Cardiff C | D 0-0 | 0-0 | | 10,111 |
| 40 | 4 | A | Bolton W | L 2-3 | 2-1 | Attley, George | 5226 |
| 41 | 8 | A | Oldham Ath | D 1-1 | 1-0 | Wilson | 4296 |
| 42 | 15 | H | Watford | W 3-2 | 1-0 | Buckley, Wilson, Hector | 14,946 |

**Final League Position: 16**

**Goalscorers**

*League* (53): Wilson 9, Swindlehurst 6, Buckley 5, Emson 5, Hector 5, Clayton 3, Osgood 3, George 2, Hill 2, Powell B. 2, Ramage 2, Sheridan 2, Skivington 2, Attley 1, Emery 1, Powell S. 1, own goals 2.
*League Cup* (2): Hector 1, own goal 1.
*FA Cup* (1): Powell B. 1.

| League Cup | Second Round | West Ham U (h) | 2-3 |
|---|---|---|---|
| | | (a) | 0-2 |
| FA Cup | Third Round | Bolton W (a) | 1-3 |

| Jones | Coop | Richards | Powell S. | Ramage | Hector | Spooner | Reid | Wilson | Swindlehurst | Emson | Emery | Buckley | Powell B. | Cherry | Osgood | Gamble | Sheridan | Clayton | Skivington | Gibson | Money | Dalziel | Hill | Banovic | Attley | Lovatt | McAlle | George | Barton | Match No. |
|---|---|---|---|---|---|---|---|---|---|---|---|---|---|---|---|---|---|---|---|---|---|---|---|---|---|---|---|---|---|---|
| 1 | 2 | 3 | 4 | 5 | 6 | 7 | 8 | 9* | 10 | 11 | 12 | | | | | | | | | | | | | | | | | | | 1 |
| 1 | 2 | 3 | 4 | 5 | 9 | 6 | 8 | | 10 | | | 7 | 11 | | | | | | | | | | | | | | | | | 2 |
| 1 | 2 | 3 | 4 | 5 | 9 | 6* | 8 | | 10 | 12 | | 7 | 11 | | | | | | | | | | | | | | | | | 3 |
| 1 | 2 | | 4 | 5 | 9 | | 8 | | 10 | 11 | | 7 | 3 | 6 | | | | | | | | | | | | | | | | 4 |
| 1 | 2 | | 4 | 5 | 9* | | 8 | 12 | 10 | 11 | | 7 | 3 | 6 | | | | | | | | | | | | | | | | 5 |
| | 2 | | 4 | 5 | 9 | | 8 | 12 | 10 | 11* | | 7 | 3 | 6 | 1 | | | | | | | | | | | | | | | 6 |
| | 2 | | 4 | 5 | 9 | | 8 | | 10 | 11 | | | | 6 | 1 | 3 | 7* | 12 | | | | | | | | | | | | 7 |
| | 2 | | 4 | 5 | | 7 | 8 | 9 | 10* | 11 | | | 3 | 6 | 1 | | 12 | | | | | | | | | | | | | 8 |
| | 2 | | 4 | 5* | 9 | | | | 10 | 11 | | | 3 | 8 | 1 | | 6 | 12 | 7 | | | | | | | | | | | 9 |
| 1 | 2 | | 4 | | | | 8 | | 10 | 11 | | 7 | 3 | 6 | | | 5 | 9 | | | | | | | | | | | | 10 |
| 1 | 2 | | 4 | | | | 8 | | 10 | 11 | | 7 | 3 | 6 | | | 5 | 9 | | | | | | | | | | | | 11 |
| 1 | 2 | | 4 | | | 7 | 8 | | 10 | 11* | | | 3 | 6 | | | 5 | 9 | 12 | | | | | | | | | | | 12 |
| 1 | 2 | | 4 | | | 7 | 8* | | 10 | 11 | | | 3 | 6 | | 12 | 5 | 9 | | | | | | | | | | | | 13 |
| 1 | 2 | | 4 | | | | 8 | | 10 | 11 | | 7 | 3 | 6 | | 12 | 5 | 9* | | | | | | | | | | | | 14 |
| 1 | 2 | | 4* | | | | 8 | | 10 | 11 | | 7 | 3 | 6 | | 12 | 5 | 9 | | | | | | | | | | | | 15 |
| 1 | 12 | 3 | | | | | 8 | | 10 | 11 | | 7* | 4 | 6 | 2 | | 5 | 9 | | | | | | | | | | | | 16 |
| 1 | 7 | 3* | | | | | 8 | | 10 | 11 | | | 4 | 6 | 2 | | 5 | 9 | 12 | | | | | | | | | | | 17 |
| 1 | 7 | 3 | | | | | 8* | 9 | 10 | 11 | | | 4 | 6 | 2 | | 5 | 12 | | | | | | | | | | | | 18 |
| 1 | 3 | | | | | 7 | | | 10 | 11 | 2 | 4 | 8 | | | | | | | | 5 | 6 | 9 | | | | | | | 19 |
| 1 | | | | | | 7 | | | 10 | 11 | 2 | 3 | 8 | | | | 5 | | | | 6 | 4 | 9 | | | | | | | 20 |
| 1 | 11* | | | | | 7 | | | 10 | 12 | 2 | 3 | 8 | | | | 5 | | | | 6 | 4 | 9 | | | | | | | 21 |
| | | | | | | 7 | | | 10 | 11 | 2 | 3 | 8 | | | | 5 | | 12 | | 6 | 4* | 9 | 1 | | | | | | 22 |
| | 12 | | | | | 7 | | | 10 | 11 | 2* | 3 | 8 | | | | 5 | | 4 | | 6 | | 9 | 1 | | | | | | 23 |
| | | 4* | | | | 7 | 8 | | 10 | 11 | | 3 | | | | | 5 | 9 | 6 | | | | | 1 | 2 | 12 | | | | 24 |
| | | | | | | 7 | | | 10 | 11 | | 3 | 8 | | | | 5 | 9 | 4 | | | | | 1 | 2 | | 6 | | | 25 |
| | | | | | | 7 | | | 10 | 11 | | 3 | 8 | | | | 5 | 9 | 4 | | | | | 1 | 2 | | 6 | | | 26 |
| | | | | | | · | | | 10 | 11 | | 3 | 8 | | | | 5 | 9 | 4 | | | | | 1 | 7 | | 2 | 6 | | 27 |
| | | 4 | | | | | | | 10 | 11 | | 3 | 8 | | | | 9 | 5 | | | | | | 1 | 7 | | 2 | 6 | | 28 |
| | | | | | | 7 | | 9 | 10 | 11 | | 3 | 8 | | | | 5 | 4 | | | | | | 1 | 2* | 12 | 6 | | | 29 |
| | | | | | | 7 | | 9 | 10 | 11 | | 3 | 8 | | | | 5 | 4 | | | | | | 1 | 2 | | 6 | | | 30 |
| | | | | | | | 12 | 9 | 10 | 11 | | 3 | 8 | | | | 5 | 4 | | | | | | 1 | 2* | | 6 | 7 | | 31 |
| | | | | | | | | 9 | 10 | 11 | | 3 | | | | | 5 | 4 | | | | | | 1 | 8 | | 6 | 7 | 2 | 32 |
| | | | | | | | | 9 | 10 | 11 | | 3 | | | | | 5 | 4 | | | | | | 1 | 8 | | 6 | 7 | 2 | 33 |
| | | | | | | | 12 | 9* | 10 | 11 | | 3 | | | | | 5 | 4 | | | | | | 1 | 8 | | 6 | 7 | 2 | 34 |
| | | | | | | | | 9 | 10 | 11 | | 3 | | | | | 5 | 4 | | | | | | 1 | 8 | | 6 | 7 | 2 | 35 |
| | | | | | | | 12 | 9* | 10 | 11 | | 3 | | | | | 5 | 4 | | | | | | 1 | 8 | | 6 | 7 | 2 | 36 |
| | | | | | | | | | 10 | 11 | | 3 | 7 | | | | 5 | 4 | | | | | | 1 | 8 | | 6 | 9 | 2 | 37 |
| | | | | | | | 12 | | 10 | 11 | | 3 | 7 | | | | 5 | 4* | | | | | | 1 | 8 | | 6 | 9 | 2 | 38 |
| | | | | | | | | | 10 | 11 | | 3 | 7 | | | | 5 | 4 | | | | | | 1 | 8 | | 6 | 9 | 2 | 39 |
| | | | | | | | 12 | | 10 | 11 | | 3 | 7 | | | | 5 | 4 | | | | | | 1 | 8 | | 6 | 9 | 2* | 40 |
| | | | | | | | 12 | 9 | 10 | 11 | | 3 | 8 | | | | 5 | 4 | | | | | | 1 | 2 | | 6 | 7* | | 41 |
| | | | | | | 7 | 8 | | 10 | 11 | | 3 | | | | | 5 | 9 | | | | | | 1 | 4 | | 6 | | 2 | 42 |
| 17 | 17 | 8 | 16 | 9 | 27 | 4 | 12 | 20 | 36 | 39 | 15 | 40 | 32 | 4 | 4 | 1 | 31 | 13 | 21 | — | 5 | 4 | 6 | 21 | 19 | 2 | 18 | 11 | 10 | |
| + | + | | | | + | | | + | | + | + | | | | + | + | + | + | + | | | | | | + | | | | | |
| 1s | 1s | | | | 4s | | | 4s | | 2s | 1s | | | | 3s | 1s | 1s | 3s | 1s | | | | | | 2s | | | | | |

## DERBY COUNTY

| | Ht | Wt | Birthplace | Clubs | League App. | League Gls |
|---|---|---|---|---|---|---|
| **Goalkeepers** | | | | | | |
| Steve Cherry | 5 11 | 11 0 | Nottingham | Derby Co | 8 | — |
| | | | | Port Vale (on loan) | 4 | — |
| Roger Jones* | 5 10 | 12 12 | Upton-on-Severn | Bournemouth | 160 | — |
| | | | | Blackburn R | 242 | — |
| | | | | Newcastle U | 5 | — |
| | | | | Stoke C | 101 | — |
| | | | | Derby Co | 59 | — |
| | | | | Birmingham C (on loan) | 4 | — |
| Yakka Banovic | 5 10 | 11 8 | Yugoslavia | Heidelberg U | (not known) | |
| (Yugoslavia) | | | | Derby Co | 21 | — |
| **Defenders** | | | | | | |
| Steve Buckley | 5 11 | 12 4 | Brinsley | Luton T | 123 | 9 |
| | | | | Derby Co | 174 | 11 |
| Frank Sheridan* | 6 0 | 11 0 | London | Derby Co | 43 | 5 |
| John Lovatt | 5 7 | 10 0 | Newcastle | Derby Co | 4 | — |
| Wayne Richards* | 5 8 | 11 0 | Scunthorpe | Derby Co | 19 | — |
| Alan Ramage | 6 2 | 13 8 | Guisborough | Middlesbrough | 71 | 2 |
| (Contract cancelled March 1982) | | | | Derby Co | 33 | 2 |
| Ian Dalziel | 5 8 | 11 10 | Sunderland | Derby Co | 4 | — |
| Steve Powell | 5 9 | 12 0 | Derby | Derby Co | 267 | 18 |
| Mick Coop | 5 11 | 11 5½ | Leamington | Coventry C | 424 | 18 |
| (Contract cancelled Feb 1982) | | | | York C (on loan) | 4 | — |
| | | | | Derby Co | 18 | — |
| Brian Attley | 5 9 | 9 12 | Cardiff | Cardiff C | 79 | 1 |
| | | | | Swansea C | 89 | 6 |
| | | | | Derby Co | 19 | 1 |
| John McAlle | 6 0 | 11 3 | Liverpool | Wolverhampton W | 407 | — |
| | | | | Sheffield U | 18 | — |
| | | | | Derby Co | 18 | — |
| John Barton | 5 10 | 11 0 | Birmingham | Everton | 20 | — |
| | | | | Derby Co | 10 | — |
| **Midfield** | | | | | | |
| Steve Emery | 5 10 | 11 10 | Hereford | Hereford U | 204 | 10 |
| | | | | Derby Co | 75 | 4 |
| Barry Powell* | 5 7½ | 10 2 | Kenilworth | Wolverhampton W | 64 | 7 |
| | | | | Coventry C | 164 | 28 |
| | | | | Derby Co | 84 | 7 |
| Glen Skivington | 5 10 | 11 3 | Barrow | Barrow | (not known) | |
| | | | | Derby Co | 34 | 2 |
| David King | 5 9 | 10 7 | Colchester | Derby Co | — | — |
| (Contract cancelled April 1982) | | | | | | |
| Tony Reid | 5 9 | 10 10 | Nottingham | Derby Co | 27 | 1 |
| Kevin Hector* | 5 8 | 11 6 | Leeds | Bradford PA | 176 | 113 |
| (England) | | | | Derby Co | 430 | 147 |
| | | | | Vancouver W | (not known) | |
| | | | | Burton A | (not known) | |
| | | | | Derby Co | 56 | 8 |
| Francis Gamble | 5 9 | 11 0 | Liverpool | Burscough | (not known) | |
| | | | | Derby Co | 2 | — |
| Paul Halford | | | | Derby Co | — | — |
| (Contract cancelled Jan 1982) | | | | | | |
| **Forwards** | | | | | | |
| John Clayton | 5 11 | 11 7 | Elgin | Derby Co | 24 | 4 |
| Paul Emson | 5 11 | 11 3 | Lincoln | Brigg T | (not known) | |
| | | | | Derby Co | 111 | 13 |
| David Swindlehurst | 6 2 | 13 3 | Edgware | Crystal Palace | 237 | 73 |
| | | | | Derby Co | 82 | 21 |
| Kevin Wilson* | 5 7 | 10 7 | Banbury | Derby Co | 55 | 16 |
| Aidan Gibson* | | | Clayton | Derby Co | 2 | — |
| Colin Murphy (Contract cancelled Feb 1982) | | | | | | |
| Andy Hill | 6 1 | 12 0 | Ilkeston | Kimberley | (not known) | |
| | | | | Derby Co | 6 | 2 |
| Charlie George* | 5 11 | 12 7 | London | Arsenal | 133 | 31 |
| (England) | | | | Derby Co | 106 | 34 |
| | | | | Nottingham F (on loan) | 2 | — |
| | | | | Southampton | 44 | 11 |
| | | | | Hong Kong | (not known) | |
| | | | | Bournemouth | 2 | — |
| | | | | Derby Co | 11 | 2 |

# DONCASTER ROVERS

*President:* J. C. Morris.

*Chairman:* I. M. Jones.

*Directors:* H. Bates, A. Phillips, K. Jackson, B. E. Boldry, J. J. Burke, G. Smith.

*Vice-Presidents:* B. Bailey, R. Jones.

*Manager:* Billy Bremner.

*Secretary:* Roger Reade.

*Year Formed:* 1879. *Turned Professional:* 1885.

*Limited Company:* 1905 and 1920.

*Previous Grounds:* 1880–1916, Intake Ground; 1920–22, Benetthorpe Ground; 1922, Low Pasture, Belle Vue.

**Doncaster Rovers Football Club Ltd.**
(Founded 1879)

**Football League Record:**
1901 Elected to Division 2; 1903 Failed re-election; 1904 Re-elected; 1905 Failed re-election; 1923 Re-elected to Division 3(N); 1935–37 Division 2; 1937–47 Division 3(N); 1947–48 Division 2; 1948–50 Division 3(N); 1950–58 Division 2; 1958–59 Division 3; 1959–66 Division 4; 1966–67 Division 3; 1967–69 Division 4; 1969–71 Division 3; 1971–81 Division 4; 1981– Division 3.

**Honours:** *Football League:* Division 2 best season: 7th, 1901–02; Division 3(N) – Champions 1934–35, 1946–47, 1949–50; Runners-up 1937–38, 1938–39; Division 4 – Champions 1965–66, 1968–69; Promoted 1980–81 (3rd). *FA Cup* best season: 5th rd, 1951–52, 1953–54, 1954–55, 1955–56. *Football League Cup* best season: 5th rd, 1975–76.

*Record Victory:* 10-0 v Darlington, Division 4, 25 Jan, 1964.

*Record Defeat:* 0-12 v Small Heath, Division 2, 11 Apr, 1903.

*Most League Points:* 72, Division 3(N), 1946–47.

*Most League Goals:* 123, Division 3(N), 1946–47.

*Highest League Scorer in Season:* Clarrie Jordan, 42, Division 3(N), 1946–47.

*Most League Goals in Total Aggregate:* Tom Keetley, 180, 1923–29.

*Most Capped Player:* Len Graham, 14, Ireland.

*Most League Appearances:* Fred Emery, 406, 1925–36.

*Record Transfer Fee Received:* £70,000 from Preston NE for Mike Elwiss, Feb 1974 and £70,000 from Bolton W for Dennis Peacock, March 1980.

*Record Transfer Fee Paid:* £30,000 to Barnsley for Alan Little, Dec 1979.

*Previous Managers since the War:* Bill Marsden, Jackie Bestall, Peter Doherty, Jack Hodgson, Syd Bycroft, Jack Crayston, Jack Bestall, Norman Curtis, Danny Malloy, Oscar Hold, Bill Leivers, Keith Kettleborough, George Raynor, Lawrie McMenemy, Maurice Setters, Stan Anderson.

*Address of Supporters Club:* Secretary, K. J. Avis, 64 Harrowden Road, Doncaster.

*Address of the Club Shop or Boutique:* On ground.

---

**Belle Vue Ground, Doncaster.** Telephone Doncaster 535281. *Telegraphic address:* 'Rovers Doncaster'. *Ground capacity:* 21,150. *Record attendance:* 37,149 v Hull C, Division 3(N), 2 Oct, 1948. *Record receipts:* £15,220.66 v Huddersfield T, Division 3, 6 Nov, 1981. *Pitch measurements:* 110yd×77yd.

*How to get there:* Buses from town centre (Duke St) – Race Course, Hyde Park, and Cantley Estate services. Doncaster railway station is near the town centre.

*Match tickets:* No advance booking except for Cup ties.

*Car parking:* Very large car and coach park adjoining the ground. Entrance direct from Great North Road.

*Entertainments/catering facilities:* Refreshment bars in Main Stand and around the ground, including licensed bars. Social club adjoining ground.

*Club shop:* In Main Stand, stocks all types of souvenirs.

*Handbooks/programmes:* Annual handbook on sale at 20p post free or at shop or Supporters Club office. Programmes on sale at shop but not on subscription.

*Extra information:* Development Association office on ground. Supporters Club office on ground – minimum subscription 15p (Children and OAPs 10p). Handbook free to members. Phone 539679.

*Club Colours:* White shirts with red trim on sleeves, white shorts with red stripes on side, red with white turnover stockings.

*Change Colours:* Green shirts with white sleeves, green shorts, green stockings, all with white trim.

*Assistant Manager:* Dave Bentley. *Physiotherapist:* Gerry Delahunt. *Club Nickname:* Rovers.

## DONCASTER ROVERS 1981–82 LEAGUE RECORD

| Match No. | Date | Venue | Opponents | Result | H/T Score | Goalscorers | Attendance |
|---|---|---|---|---|---|---|---|
| 1 | Aug 29 | H | Reading | L 0-1 | 0-0 | | 4192 |
| 2 | Sept 5 | A | Bristol C | D 2-2 | 0-2 | Dawson, Mell | 6586 |
| 3 | 11 | H | Exeter C | W 3-0 | 2-0 | Warboys, Harle, Dowd | 4369 |
| 4 | 19 | A | Wimbledon | W 1-0 | 0-0 | Warboys | 2364 |
| 5 | 22 | A | Burnley | W 1-0 | 0-0 | Dawson | 3789 |
| 6 | 26 | H | Brentford | W 1-0 | 0-0 | Warboys | 5494 |
| 7 | 29 | H | Preston NE | W 1-0 | 0-0 | Pugh | 7513 |
| 8 | Oct 10 | A | Newport Co | L 0-1 | 0-0 | | 4379 |
| 9 | 17 | H | Millwall | W 1-0 | 0-0 | Russell | 6466 |
| 10 | 20 | H | Lincoln C | W 4-1 | 1-0 | Mell, Dawson 2, Pugh | 8201 |
| 11 | 24 | A | Swindon T | D 2-2 | 0-1 | Lister, Russell | 6750 |
| 12 | 31 | H | Bristol R | W 4-2 | 2-0 | Lister, Douglas, Pugh, Snodin G. | 6694 |
| 13 | Nov 3 | A | Carlisle U | L 0-2 | 0-1 | | 3725 |
| 14 | 6 | H | Huddersfield T | L 1-2 | 1-1 | Warboys (pen) | 11,319 |
| 15 | 14 | A | Gillingham | L 0-3 | 0-2 | | 8189 |
| 16 | 28 | A | Plymouth Arg | L 2-4 | 2-2 | Nimmo, Snodin I. | 4341 |
| 17 | Dec 2 | A | Chester | D 1-1 | 0-0 | Snodin G. | 1555 |
| 18 | 5 | H | Portsmouth | D 0-0 | 0-0 | | 5912 |
| 19 | Jan 16 | A | Southend U | D 1-1 | 0-0 | Pugh | 4741 |
| 20 | 29 | H | Wimbledon | L 1-3 | 1-2 | Dawson | 5849 |
| 21 | Feb 2 | A | Chesterfield | L 1-3 | 0-2 | Snodin G. | 6157 |
| 22 | 6 | A | Exeter C | L 1-2 | 0-1 | Lister (pen) | 3193 |
| 23 | 9 | H | Burnley | L 0-1 | 0-0 | | 5638 |
| 24 | 13 | H | Chester | W 4-3 | 2-1 | Snodin G., Little, Lister, Pugh | 4098 |
| 25 | 17 | A | Reading | D 3-3 | 1-3 | Little, Dawson, Pugh | 2361 |
| 26 | 20 | A | Preston NE | L 1-3 | 1-1 | Dawson | 5830 |
| 27 | 27 | H | Newport Co | L 0-2 | 0-1 | | 4190 |
| 28 | Mar 6 | A | Millwall | W 2-0 | 1-0 | Mell, Douglas | 4055 |
| 29 | 10 | A | Lincoln C | L 0-5 | 0-2 | | 5187 |
| 30 | 12 | H | Swindon T | D 0-0 | 0-0 | | 3532 |
| 31 | 16 | A | Carlisle U | D 1-1 | 0-1 | Lister | 3431 |
| 32 | 20 | A | Bristol R | L 0-3 | 0-3 | | 4597 |
| 33 | 23 | H | Oxford U | D 1-1 | 0-1 | Lister | 3800 |
| 34 | 27 | A | Huddersfield T | W 2-1 | 0-1 | Cawthorne, Harle | 6871 |
| 35 | Apr 3 | H | Gillingham | D 1-1 | 0-0 | Wigginton | 3902 |
| 36 | 6 | A | Fulham | L 1-3 | 1-1 | Snodin I. | 5081 |
| 37 | 10 | H | Chesterfield | D 0-0 | 0-0 | | 5221 |
| 38 | 12 | A | Oxford U | L 1-3 | 0-1 | Russell | 8278 |
| 39 | 17 | A | Portsmouth | D 0-0 | 0-0 | | 8657 |
| 40 | 20 | H | Walsall | W 1-0 | 0-0 | Liddell | 3903 |
| 41 | 24 | H | Plymouth Arg | D 2-2 | 2-0 | Dawson, Douglas | 3894 |
| 42 | May 1 | A | Brentford | D 2-2 | 0-1 | Snodin G., Lister (pen) | 4124 |
| 43 | 4 | H | Southend U | D 1-1 | 1-0 | Mell | 3734 |
| 44 | 8 | H | Fulham | W 2-1 | 1-1 | Mell 2 | 4729 |
| 45 | 15 | A | Walsall | D 0-0 | 0-0 | | 3799 |
| 46 | 18 | H | Bristol C | D 2-2 | 2-0 | Snodin G. 2 | 4252 |

**Final League Position: 19**

### Goalscorers

*League* (55): Dawson 8, Lister 7 (2 pens), Snodin G. 7, Mell 6, Pugh 6, Warboys 4 (1 pen), Douglas 3, Russell 3, Harle 2, Little 2, Snodin I. 2, Cawthorne 1, Dowd 1, Liddell 1, Nimmo 1, Wigginton 1.
*League Cup* (2): Douglas 1, Mell 1.
*FA Cup* (7): Warboys 3, Dawson 1, Douglas 1, Little 1, own goal 1.

| **League Cup** | First Round | Chesterfield (h) | 0-0 |
|---|---|---|---|
| | | (a) | 1-1 (won on away goals rule) |
| | Second Round | Crystal Palace (h) | 1-0 |
| | | (a) | 0-2 |
| **FA Cup** | First Round | Mansfield T (a) | 1-0 |
| | Second Round | Penrith (h) | 3-0 |
| | Third Round | Cambridge U (h) | 2-1 |
| | Fourth Round | Norwich C (a) | 1-2 |

| Boyd | Russell | Dawson | Snodin I. | Lister | Dowd | Pugh | Nimmo | Warboys | Snodin G. | Lally | Harle | Douglas | Mell | Humphries G. | Humphries S. | Little | Swan | Cooper | Parkinson | Bremner | Cawthorne | Wigginton | Liddell | Bennett | Allanson | Match No. |
|---|---|---|---|---|---|---|---|---|---|---|---|---|---|---|---|---|---|---|---|---|---|---|---|---|---|---|
| 1 | 2 | 3 | 4 | 5 | 6 | 7 | 8 | 9 | 10* | 11 | 12 |  |  |  |  |  |  |  |  |  |  |  |  |  |  | 1 |
| 1 | 2 | 3 | 4 | 10* | 6 | 7 |  | 9 |  | 5 | 8 | 12 | 11 |  |  |  |  |  |  |  |  |  |  |  |  | 2 |
| 1 | 2 | 3 | 4 | 10 | 6 | 7 |  | 9 |  | 5 | 8 | 11 |  |  |  |  |  |  |  |  |  |  |  |  |  | 3 |
| 1 | 2 | 3 | 4 | 10 | 6 | 7 | 12 | 9 |  | 5* | 8 | 11 |  |  |  |  |  |  |  |  |  |  |  |  |  | 4 |
| 1 | 3 | 11 | 4* | 2 | 6 | 9 | 12 | 5 |  | 7 | 8 | 10 |  |  |  |  |  |  |  |  |  |  |  |  |  | 5 |
| 1 | 2 | 3 | 4* | 10 | 6 | 7 | 12 | 9 |  | 5 | 8 | 11 |  |  |  |  |  |  |  |  |  |  |  |  |  | 6 |
| 1 | 2 | 3 |  | 4 | 6 | 7 | 12 | 9* | 10 | 5 | 8 | 11 |  |  |  |  |  |  |  |  |  |  |  |  |  | 7 |
| 1 | 2 | 3 |  | 4 | 6 | 7 |  | 9 | 10* | 5 | 8 | 11 | 12 |  |  |  |  |  |  |  |  |  |  |  |  | 8 |
| 1 | 2 | 3 |  | 4 | 6 | 7 |  | 9 | 10 | 5 | 8 | 11* | 12 |  |  |  |  |  |  |  |  |  |  |  |  | 9 |
| 1 | 2 | 3 |  | 4 | 6 | 7 |  | 9 | 10 |  | 8 | 11 | 5 |  |  |  |  |  |  |  |  |  |  |  |  | 10 |
| 1 | 2 | 3 |  | 4 | 6 | 7 |  | 9 | 10 | 5 | 8 | 11 |  |  |  |  |  |  |  |  |  |  |  |  |  | 11 |
|  |  | 3 | 2 | 4 | 6 | 7 |  | 9* | 10 | 5 | 8 | 11 | 12 | 1 |  |  |  |  |  |  |  |  |  |  |  | 12 |
| 1 | 3* | 2 | 4 | 6 | 7 |  |  |  | 10 | 5 | 8 | 11 | 12 |  |  | 9 |  |  |  |  |  |  |  |  |  | 13 |
| 1 |  | 2 | 4 | 6 | 7 |  | 9 | 10 |  | 5 |  | 11 |  |  |  | 8 | 3 |  |  |  |  |  |  |  |  | 14 |
| 1 | 12 |  | 4 | 2 | 6 | 7 |  |  | 10 | 5 | 8* | 9 |  | 11 |  |  |  | 3 |  |  |  |  |  |  |  | 15 |
| 1 | 2 |  | 4 | 5 | 6 | 7 | 8 |  | 10 |  | 9 |  |  | 11 |  |  |  | 3 |  |  |  |  |  |  |  | 16 |
| 1 | 2 |  | 4 | 5 | 6 | 7 | 8 |  | 10 |  | 11* | 9 | 12 |  |  |  |  | 3 |  |  |  |  |  |  |  | 17 |
| 1 | 2 | 12 | 4 | 11 | 6 | 7 | 8* | 9 | 10 | 5 |  |  |  |  |  |  |  | 3 |  |  |  |  |  |  |  | 18 |
|  |  | 8 |  | 4 | 6 | 7 |  |  | 10 | 2 |  | 9 |  | 1 | 11 |  |  | 3 | 5 |  |  |  |  |  |  | 19 |
| 12 |  | 8 |  | 4 | 11 | 6 | 7* |  | 10 | 2 |  | 9 |  | 1 |  |  |  | 3 | 5 |  |  |  |  |  |  | 20 |
|  | 2 | 8* |  | 4 | 6 | 7 |  |  | 10 | 11 |  | 9 |  | 1 | 12 |  |  | 3 | 5 |  |  |  |  |  |  | 21 |
| 1 | 2 | 8 |  | 4 | 11 | 6* | 7 |  | 10 | 5 | 12 | 9 |  |  |  |  |  | 3 |  |  |  |  |  |  |  | 22 |
| 1 | 9 |  |  | 4 | 6 |  | 7 |  | 10 | 2 | 8 | 12 | 11 |  |  |  |  | 3 | 5* |  |  |  |  |  |  | 23 |
| 1 | 2 | 8* |  | 4 | 6 |  | 12 |  | 10 | 7 |  | 9 |  |  | 11 |  |  | 3 | 5 |  |  |  |  |  |  | 24 |
| 1 | 2 | 8 |  | 4 | 6 |  | 7 |  | 10 | 5 |  | 9 |  |  | 11 |  |  | 3 |  |  |  |  |  |  |  | 25 |
| 1 | 2 | 8 |  | 4 |  | 6 | 7 | 10 | 5 | 12 | 9 |  |  |  | 11* |  |  | 3 |  |  |  |  |  |  |  | 26 |
| 1 | 2 | 8 |  | 4 | 11 | 6 | 7 |  | 10* | 9 |  | 5 |  |  |  |  |  | 3 | 12 |  |  |  |  |  |  | 27 |
| 1 | 2 |  |  | 4 | 5 | 6 | 7 | 10 |  |  | 8 | 9 | 11 |  |  |  |  | 3 |  |  |  |  |  |  |  | 28 |
| 1 | 2 | 12 |  | 4 | 5 | 6 | 7* | 10 |  |  | 8 | 9 | 11 |  |  |  |  | 3 |  |  |  |  |  |  |  | 29 |
| 1 | 2 | 3 |  | 4 | 5 | 6* | 7 | 10 | 11 |  | 9 | 12 |  |  |  |  |  | 8 |  |  |  |  |  |  |  | 30 |
| 1 |  |  |  | 4 | 5 |  | 7 | 10 | 2 | 8 | 9 | 11 | 6 |  |  |  |  | 3 |  |  |  |  |  |  |  | 31 |
| 1 | 2 |  |  | 4 | 6 |  | 7 | 10 | 5 | 8 | 9 | 11* | 12 |  |  |  |  | 3 |  |  |  |  |  |  |  | 32 |
| 1 | 2 | 3 |  | 4 | 5 |  | 7* | 10 |  | 12 | 9 | 11 | 6 |  |  | 8 |  |  |  |  |  |  |  |  |  | 33 |
| 1 |  | 3* | 4 | 11 |  | 7 |  | 10 |  | 12 | 9 |  | 2 |  |  |  |  |  |  |  | 5 | 6 | 8 |  |  | 34 |
| 1 |  |  | 4 | 11 |  | 7* |  | 10 | 12 | 3 | 9 |  | 2 |  |  |  |  |  |  |  | 5 | 6 | 8 |  |  | 35 |
| 1 | 2 |  | 4 |  |  |  |  | 10 | 7 |  | 9 |  |  | 11 |  |  |  | 3 |  |  | 5 | 6 | 8 |  |  | 36 |
| 1 | 2 |  | 4 | 11 |  | 12 |  | 10 | 3* |  | 9 |  |  | 7 |  |  |  |  |  |  | 5 | 6 | 8 |  |  | 37 |
|  | 2 |  | 4 | 3 |  | 7 |  | 10 | 12 |  | 9 | 1 | 11 |  |  |  |  |  |  |  | 5* | 6 | 8 |  |  | 38 |
|  | 2 |  | 4 |  |  | 12 |  | 10 | 7 |  | 9 | 3 | 1 | 11 |  |  |  |  |  |  | 5 | 6 | 8* |  |  | 39 |
|  | 2 |  | 4* | 12 |  | 7 |  | 10 | 11 |  | 9 | 3 | 1 |  |  |  |  |  |  |  | 5 | 6 | 8 |  |  | 40 |
|  | 2 | 11 | 4 |  |  | 7 |  | 10 |  |  | 9 | 3 | 1 |  |  |  |  |  |  |  | 5 | 6 | 8* | 12 |  | 41 |
|  |  | 3 | 4 |  |  | 7 |  | 10 |  | 9* | 12 | 2 | 1 | 11 |  |  |  |  |  |  | 5 | 6 | 8 |  |  | 42 |
|  |  | 4 |  |  |  | 7 |  | 10 |  |  | 9 | 2 | 1 | 11 |  | 3 |  |  |  |  | 5 | 6 | 8 |  |  | 43 |
|  | 2 | 4* |  |  |  | 7 |  | 10 |  | 12 | 9 | 3 | 1 | 11 |  |  |  |  |  |  | 5 | 6 | 8 |  |  | 44 |
|  | 2 |  | 4 |  |  | 7 |  | 10 |  |  | 9 | 3 | 1 | 11 |  |  |  |  |  |  | 5 | 6 | 8 |  |  | 45 |
|  | 3 |  | 4 |  |  | 7 |  | 10 |  | 12 | 9 | 5 | 1 | 11 |  |  |  |  |  |  |  | 6 | 8 |  | 2* | 46 |
| 33 | 35 | 28 | 33 | 40 | 27 | 42 | 4 | 14 | 40 | 30 | 21 | 38 | 12 | 12 | 13 | 19 | 1 | 20 | 5 | — | 12 | 13 | 13 | — | 1 | |
| + | + |  | + | + | + |  | + | + | + | + | + |  |  |  |  | + |  |  |  |  | + |  | + |  |  | |
| 2s | 2s |  | 1s | 3s | 4s |  | 2s | 5s | 4s | 6s | 2s |  |  |  |  | 1s |  |  |  |  | 1s |  | 1s |  |  | |

## DONCASTER ROVERS

| | Ht | Wt | Birthplace | Clubs | League App. | League Gls |
|---|---|---|---|---|---|---|
| **Goalkeepers** | | | | | | |
| Willie Boyd | 5 10 | 11 4 | Bellshill | Hull C | — | — |
| | | | | Doncaster R | 89 | — |
| Steve Humphries | 5 11 | 12 10 | Hull | Leicester C | — | — |
| | | | | Doncaster R | 13 | — |
| **Defenders** | | | | | | |
| Hugh Dowd* | 6 1 | 13 0 | Lurgan | Glenavon | (not known) | |
| (N Ireland) | | | | Sheffield W | 113 | — |
| | | | | Doncaster R | 88 | 3 |
| Billy Russell | 5 10 | 11 4 | Glasgow | Everton | — | — |
| | | | | Celtic | — | — |
| | | | | Doncaster R | 125 | 4 |
| Stewart Mell | 5 10 | 11 0 | Doncaster | Doncaster R | 44 | 11 |
| Carl Swan | 6 2 | 11 10 | Sheffield | Burton A | (not known) | |
| | | | | Doncaster R | 14 | 1 |
| Terry Cooper | 5 7½ | 10 9 | Castleford | Leeds U | 249 | 7 |
| (England) | | | | Middlesbrough | 105 | 1 |
| | | | | Bristol C | 11 | — |
| | | | | Bristol R | 59 | — |
| | | | | Doncaster R | 20 | — |
| Graham Cawthorne | 6 3 | 11 12 | Doncaster | Grimsby T | 1 | — |
| | | | | Doncaster R | 12 | 1 |
| Gary Allanson | | | | Doncaster R | 1 | — |
| (Apprentice) | | | | | | |
| Keith Parkinson | 6 1 | 12 6 | Preston | Leeds U | 31 | — |
| (Contract cancelled) | | | | Hull C (on loan) | 1 | — |
| | | | | Doncaster R | 5 | — |
| **Midfield** | | | | | | |
| Steve Lister | 6 1 | 11 10 | Doncaster | Doncaster R | 129 | 22 |
| Pat Lally* | 5 10 | 10 9 | Paddington | Millwall | 1 | — |
| | | | | York C | 72 | 5 |
| | | | | Swansea C | 160 | 10 |
| | | | | Aldershot (on loan) | 3 | — |
| | | | | Doncaster R | 122 | — |
| Dave Harle | 5 8 | 9 10 | Doncaster | Doncaster R | 61 | 3 |
| Ian Snodin | 5 7 | 8 11½ | Rotherham | Doncaster R | 74 | 5 |
| Glynn Snodin | 5 6 | 9 5 | Rotherham | Doncaster R | 185 | 16 |
| Daral Pugh | 5 8 | 10 7 | Sunderland | Doncaster R | 148 | 15 |
| Alan Little | 5 11½ | 12 12 | Newcastle | Aston V | 3 | — |
| | | | | Southend U | 103 | 12 |
| | | | | Barnsley | 91 | 14 |
| | | | | Doncaster R | 79 | 11 |
| **Forwards** | | | | | | |
| Ian Nimmo | 5 11 | 11 12 | Boston | Sheffield W | 45 | 10 |
| | | | | Peterborough U (on loan) | 4 | 1 |
| | | | | Doncaster R | 86 | 29 |
| Alan Warboys | 6 0½ | 14 0 | Goldthorpe | Doncaster R | 39 | 11 |
| | | | | Sheffield W | 71 | 13 |
| | | | | Cardiff C | 60 | 27 |
| | | | | Sheffield U | 7 | — |
| | | | | Bristol R | 144 | 53 |
| | | | | Fulham | 19 | 2 |
| | | | | Hull C | 49 | 9 |
| | | | | Doncaster R | 89 | 21 |
| Billy Bremner | 5 5½ | 10 7 | Stirling | Leeds U | 586 | 92 |
| (Scotland) | | | | Hull C | 61 | 6 |
| (Non-contract) | | | | Doncaster R | 5 | — |
| Richard Dawson* | 5 9 | 11 12 | Chesterfield | Rotherham U | 24 | 3 |
| | | | | Doncaster R | 43 | 14 |
| Des Bennett | | | Doncaster | Doncaster R | 2 | — |
| (Apprentice) | | | | | | |
| Russell Wilcox | | | Hemsworth | Doncaster R | 1 | — |
| (Non-contract) | | | | | | |
| Glenn Humphries | | | Hull | Doncaster R | 15 | — |
| (Apprentice) | | | | | | |
| Garry Liddell | 5 9 | 11 4 | Stirling | Leeds U | 3 | — |
| | | | | Grimsby T | 105 | 24 |
| | | | | Hearts | 24 | 6 |
| | | | | Doncaster R | 13 | 1 |
| Colin Douglas | 6 1 | 11 0 | Hurlford | Celtic | — | — |
| | | | | Doncaster R | 42 | 3 |

# EVERTON

## Division 1

*Chairman:* P. D. Carter.

*Vice-Chairman:* T. H. W. Scott.

*Directors:* A. W. Waterworth, G. A. Watts, K. M. Tamlin, J. Search, D. A. B. Newton.

*Manager:* Howard Kendall.

*Secretary:* Jim Greenwood.

*Year Formed:* 1878.  *Limited Company:* 1892.

*Turned Professional:* 1885.

*Former Grounds:* 1878, Stanley Park; 1882, Priory Road; 1884, Anfield Road; 1892, Goodison Park.

**Football League Record:**
1888 Founder Member of the Football League; 1930–31 Division 2; 1931–51 Division 1; 1951–54 Division 2; 1954– Division 1.

**Honours:** *Football League:* Division 1 – Champions 1890–91, 1914–15, 1927–28, 1931–32, 1938–39, 1962–63, 1969–70; Runners-up 1889–90, 1894–95, 1901–02, 1904–05, 1908–09, 1911–12; Division 2 – Champions 1930–31; Runners-up 1953–54. *FA Cup:* Winners 1906, 1933, 1966; Runners-up 1893, 1897, 1907, 1968. *Football League Cup:* Runners-up 1976–77. **European Competitions:** *European Cup:* 1963–64, 1970–71; *European Cup-Winners' Cup:* 1966–67. *European Fairs Cup:* 1962–63, 1964–65, 1965–66. *UEFA Cup:* 1975–76, 1978–79, 1979–80.

*Record Victory:* 11-2 v Derby Co, FA Cup 1st rd, 1889–90.

*Record Defeat:* 4-10 v Tottenham H, Division 1, 11 Oct, 1958.

*Most League Points:* 66, Division 1, 1969–70.

*Most League Goals:* 121, Division 2, 1930–31.

*Highest League Scorer in Season:* Dixie Dean, 60, 1927–28.

*Most League Goals in Total Aggregate:* Dixie Dean, 349, 1925–37.

*Most Capped Player:* Alan Ball, 39 (72), England.

*Most League Appearances:* Ted Sagar, 465, 1929–53.

*Record Transfer Fee Received:* £325,000 from Wolverhampton W for Dave Thomas, Oct 1979.

*Record Transfer Fee Paid:* £650,000 to Aston Villa for John Gidman, Oct 1979.

*Previous Managers since the War:* Theo Kelly, Cliff Britton, Ian Buchan, John Carey, Harry Catterick, Billy Bingham, Gordon Lee.

*Address of Supporters Club:* 38 City Road, Liverpool 4.

---

**Goodison Park, Liverpool L4 4EL.** Telephone 051-521 2020. *Match ticket information:* 051-523 6642 (24 hr. service). *Ground capacity:* 53,091 (25,000 seats). *Record attendance:* 78,299 v Liverpool, Division 1, 18 Sept, 1948. *Record receipts:* £174,945, Liverpool v Manchester U, FA Cup semi-final replay, 4 April, 1979. *Pitch measurements:* 112yd×78yd.

*How to get there:* Corporation buses 19 and 44 from Pierhead, 68 from Old Swan, 3, 22, 25, 500 from South End of the City and 30, 92, 92a, 92b, 93 from City centre. Nearest railway station, Liverpool Lime Street.

*Match tickets:* Reserved stand seats are available for all home fixtures (except the match v Liverpool) at any time during the season, either by post or by personal application to the Box Office at the Goodison Rd side of the ground. The Box Office is open each weekday from 9 am to 5 pm. Postal applications should be addressed to the Box Office manager and contain the correct remittance and SAE.

*Car parking:* Extensive parking facilities on site at the corner of Priory Rd and Utting Ave.

*Entertainments/catering facilities:* Royal Blue Restaurant open to the public for lunch on Mondays to Fridays but restricted to members on match days.

*Club shop:* All souvenirs available from The Toffee Shop in Goodison Rd; send SAE for mail order list.

*Handbooks/programmes:* Match-day magazine available on seasonal subscription.

*Club Colours:* Royal blue shirts with white trim, white shorts, blue trim, white stockings.

*Change Colours:* Amber shirts, blue trim, amber shorts, blue trim, amber stockings – also all blue.

*Club Coach:* Mike Heaton.

*Team Captain:* Billy Wright.

*Club Nickname:* Toffeemen or Blues.

## EVERTON 1981–82 LEAGUE RECORD

| Match No. | Date | Venue | Opponents | Result | | H/T Score | Goalscorers | Attendance |
|---|---|---|---|---|---|---|---|---|
| 1 | Aug 29 | H | Birmingham C | W | 3-1 | 1-1 | Ainscow, Eastoe, Biley | 33,045 |
| 2 | Sept 2 | A | Leeds U | D | 1-1 | 1-1 | Biley | 26,502 |
| 3 | 5 | A | Southampton | L | 0-1 | 0-0 | | 21,624 |
| 4 | 12 | H | Brighton & HA | D | 1-1 | 0-0 | Wright | 27,352 |
| 5 | 19 | A | Tottenham H | L | 0-3 | 0-0 | | 31,219 |
| 6 | 22 | H | Notts Co | W | 3-1 | 2-0 | Eastoe, Ross, O'Keefe | 22,175 |
| 7 | 26 | H | WBA | W | 1-0 | 0-0 | Lyons | 23,871 |
| 8 | Oct 3 | A | Stoke C | L | 1-3 | 0-1 | McBride | 16,007 |
| 9 | 10 | A | West Ham U | D | 1-1 | 1-1 | McMahon | 31,608 |
| 10 | 17 | H | Ipswich T | W | 2-1 | 2-1 | Ferguson, Stevens | 25,146 |
| 11 | 24 | A | Middlesbrough | W | 2-0 | 1-0 | Ferguson 2 | 13,423 |
| 12 | 31 | H | Manchester C | L | 0-1 | 0-0 | | 31,305 |
| 13 | Nov 7 | A | Liverpool | L | 1-3 | 0-0 | Ferguson | 48,861 |
| 14 | 21 | H | Sunderland | L | 1-2 | 0-0 | Eastoe | 19,759 |
| 15 | 24 | A | Notts Co | D | 2-2 | 1-0 | Biley, Sharp | 7771 |
| 16 | 28 | A | Arsenal | L | 0-1 | 0-0 | | 25,860 |
| 17 | Dec 5 | H | Swansea C | W | 3-1 | 0-0 | Sharp, O'Keefe 2 | 23,860 |
| 18 | 19 | H | Aston Villa | W | 2-0 | 1-0 | Lyons, Eastoe | 16,538 |
| 19 | 28 | H | Coventry C | W | 3-2 | 3-2 | Higgins 2, Sharp | 23,895 |
| 20 | Jan 6 | A | Manchester U | D | 1-1 | 1-0 | Sharp | 40,451 |
| 21 | 19 | A | Southampton | D | 1-1 | 1-0 | Richardson | 22,355 |
| 22 | 23 | A | Wolverhampton W | W | 3-0 | 2-0 | Richardson, Irvine 2 | 11,784 |
| 23 | 30 | H | Tottenham H | D | 1-1 | 1-0 | Sharp | 30,717 |
| 24 | Feb 6 | A | Brighton & HA | L | 1-3 | 0-1 | Heath | 16,148 |
| 25 | 13 | H | Stoke C | D | 0-0 | 0-0 | | 20,656 |
| 26 | 20 | A | WBA | D | 0-0 | 0-0 | | 14,819 |
| 27 | 27 | H | West Ham U | D | 0-0 | 0-0 | | 28,618 |
| 28 | Mar 6 | A | Ipswich T | L | 0-3 | 0-1 | | 19,360 |
| 29 | 13 | H | Middlesbrough | W | 2-0 | 1-0 | Higgins, Sharp | 15,807 |
| 30 | 20 | A | Manchester C | D | 1-1 | 1-1 | Heath | 33,002 |
| 31 | 27 | H | Liverpool | L | 1-3 | 1-1 | Sharp | 51,847 |
| 32 | Apr 3 | A | Nottingham F | W | 1-0 | 0-0 | McMahon | 17,323 |
| 33 | 6 | A | Birmingham C | W | 2-0 | 1-0 | Heath, Ainscow | 12,273 |
| 34 | 10 | A | Manchester U | D | 3-3 | 1-1 | Sharp, Lyons, Heath | 29,317 |
| 35 | 13 | A | Coventry C | L | 0-1 | 0-1 | | 11,858 |
| 36 | 17 | A | Sunderland | L | 1-3 | 1-1 | Irvine | 18,359 |
| 37 | 20 | H | Nottingham F | W | 2-1 | 0-0 | Sharp 2 | 15,460 |
| 38 | 24 | H | Arsenal | W | 2-1 | 1-1 | Wright, Heath | 19,136 |
| 39 | May 1 | A | Swansea C | W | 3-1 | 1-0 | Heath, Sharp 2 (1 pen) | 16,243 |
| 40 | 4 | H | Leeds U | W | 1-0 | 0-0 | Sharp | 17,137 |
| 41 | 8 | H | Wolverhampton W | D | 1-1 | 1-1 | Eastoe | 20,124 |
| 42 | 15 | A | Aston Villa | W | 2-1 | 1-1 | Sharp 2 | 20,446 |

**Final League Position: 8**

**Goalscorers**

*League* (56): Sharp 15 (1 pen), Heath 6, Eastoe 5, Ferguson 4, Biley 3, Higgins 3, Irvine 3, Lyons 3, O'Keefe 3, Ainscow 2, McMahon 2, Richardson 2, Wright 2, McBride 1, Ross 1, Stevens 1.
*League Cup* (5): Ferguson 2, McMahon 2, O'Keefe 1.
*FA Cup* (1): Eastoe 1.

| League Cup | Second Round | Coventry C (h) | 1-1 |
|---|---|---|---|
| | | (a) | 1-0 |
| | Third Round | Oxford U (h) | 1-0 |
| | Fourth Round | Ipswich T (h) | 2-3 |
| FA Cup | Third Round | West Ham U (a) | 1-2 |

| Arnold | Wright | Bailey | Walsh | Lyons | Thomas | Ainscow | Eastoe | Biley | Hartford | Ross | Ratcliffe | McMahon | Ferguson | O'Keefe | McBride | Sharp | Stevens | Higgins | Lodge | Richardson | Kendall | Southall | Irvine | Heath | Borrows | Rimmer | Match No. |
|---|---|---|---|---|---|---|---|---|---|---|---|---|---|---|---|---|---|---|---|---|---|---|---|---|---|---|---|
| 1 | 2 | 3 | 4 | 5 | 6 | 7 | 8 | 9 | 10 | 11 |  |  |  |  |  |  |  |  |  |  |  |  |  |  |  |  | 1 |
| 1 | 2 |  | 4 | 5 | 6 | 11 |  | 8 | 9 | 10 |  | 3 | 7 |  |  |  |  |  |  |  |  |  |  |  |  |  | 2 |
| 1 | 2 |  | 4 | 5 | 6 | 11 |  | 8 | 9 | 10 |  | 3 | 7* | 12 |  |  |  |  |  |  |  |  |  |  |  |  | 3 |
| 1 | 2 |  | 4 | 5 | 6 | 11 |  | 8 | 9 | 10 |  | 3 | 7 |  |  |  |  |  |  |  |  |  |  |  |  |  | 4 |
| 1 | 2 |  | 4 | 5 | 6 | 11 | 8 | 9 | 10 |  |  | 3 | 7* |  | 12 |  |  |  |  |  |  |  |  |  |  |  | 5 |
| 1 | 2 |  | 4 | 5 | 6 | 11 | 8 | 9* | 10 | 7 |  | 3 |  |  | 12 |  |  |  |  |  |  |  |  |  |  |  | 6 |
| 1 | 2 |  | 4 | 5 | 6 |  |  | 9 | 10 | 7 |  | 3 | 8* | 11 | 12 |  |  |  |  |  |  |  |  |  |  |  | 7 |
| 1 | 2 | 3* | 4 | 5 | 6 |  |  | 9 | 10 | 7 |  | 8 | 11 | 12 |  |  |  |  |  |  |  |  |  |  |  |  | 8 |
| 1 |  | 3 |  | 5 | 6 |  | 8* |  | 10 | 7 |  | 9 |  | 12 | 11 |  | 2 | 4 |  |  |  |  |  |  |  |  | 9 |
|  |  | 3 | 4 | 5 | 6* |  |  | 12 | 10 | 7 |  | 9 | 8 | 11 |  |  | 2 |  |  |  |  | 1 |  |  |  |  | 10 |
| 1 |  | 3 |  | 5 |  |  |  | 10* | 12 | 7 |  | 9 | 8 | 11 |  |  | 2 | 4 | 6 |  |  |  |  |  |  |  | 11 |
| 1 |  | 3 |  | 5 |  |  |  | 10* |  | 7 |  | 9 | 8 | 11 | 12 |  | 2 | 4 | 6 |  |  |  |  |  |  |  | 12 |
| 1 |  | 3 |  | 5 |  |  |  | 10* | 12 | 7 |  | 9 | 8 | 11 |  |  | 2 | 4 | 6 |  |  |  |  |  |  |  | 13 |
| 1 |  | 3 | 4 | 5 |  |  | 10 | 8* | 9 | 7 |  |  |  | 11 |  |  | 2 |  | 6 | 12 |  |  |  |  |  |  | 14 |
| 1 |  |  | 4 | 5 |  |  |  | 11* | 10 |  | 3 | 7 |  |  |  | 9 | 2 |  | 6 | 12 |  |  |  | 8 |  |  | 15 |
| 1 |  |  | 4 | 5 |  |  |  |  | 10 | 8 | 3 | 7 |  | 11 |  | 9 | 2 |  | 6 |  |  |  |  |  |  |  | 16 |
| 1 |  |  | 4 | 5 |  |  |  |  | 10 | 8 | 3 | 7 |  | 11 |  | 9 | 2 |  |  | 6 |  |  |  |  |  |  | 17 |
|  |  |  |  | 5 |  |  |  |  | 10 | 8 | 3 |  |  |  |  | 9 | 2 | 4 | 11 | 6 |  | 1 | 7 |  |  |  | 18 |
|  |  |  |  | 5 |  |  |  |  | 10 | 8 | 3 | 7 |  |  |  | 9 | 2 | 4 |  | 6 |  | 1 | 11 |  |  |  | 19 |
|  |  |  |  | 5 |  |  |  |  | 10 |  | 3 | 7 |  |  |  | 9 | 2 | 4 | 11 | 8 |  | 1 | 6 |  |  |  | 20 |
|  |  |  |  | 5 |  |  |  |  | 10 |  | 3 |  |  |  |  | 9 | 2 | 4 | 11 | 6 |  | 1 | 7 | 8 |  |  | 21 |
|  |  |  |  | 5 |  |  |  |  | 10 |  | 3 |  |  |  |  | 9 | 2 | 4 | 11 | 6 |  | 1 | 7 | 8 |  |  | 22 |
|  |  |  |  | 5 |  |  |  |  | 10 |  | 3 |  |  |  |  | 9 | 2 | 4 | 11 | 6 |  | 1 | 7 | 8 |  |  | 23 |
|  |  |  |  | 5* |  |  |  |  | 10 | 12 | 3 |  |  |  |  | 9 | 2 | 4 | 11 | 6 |  | 1 | 7 | 8 |  |  | 24 |
|  | 5 |  |  |  |  |  |  |  |  | 11 | 3 | 10 |  |  |  | 9 |  | 4 |  | 6 |  | 1 | 8 | 7 | 2 |  | 25 |
|  | 5 | 3 |  |  |  |  |  |  |  | 10 | 11 |  |  |  |  | 9 |  | 4 |  | 6 |  | 1 | 7 | 8 | 2 |  | 26 |
|  | 5 | 3 |  |  |  |  |  |  |  | 10 | 11 |  |  |  |  | 9 |  | 4 |  | 6 |  | 1 | 7 | 8 | 2 |  | 27 |
|  | 5 | 3 |  |  |  |  |  |  |  | 10* | 11 | 12 |  |  |  | 9 |  | 4 |  | 6 |  | 1 | 7 | 8 | 2 |  | 28 |
|  | 5 | 3 |  |  |  | 12 |  |  |  | 11 | 10* |  |  |  |  | 9 |  | 4 |  | 6 |  | 1 | 7 | 8 | 2 |  | 29 |
|  | 5 |  |  |  |  |  |  |  |  | 11 | 3 | 10 |  |  |  | 9 |  | 4 |  | 6 |  | 1 | 7 | 8 | 2 |  | 30 |
|  | 5 |  |  |  |  |  |  |  |  | 11 | 3 | 10 |  |  |  | 9 |  | 4 |  | 6 |  | 1 | 7 | 8 | 2 |  | 31 |
|  | 5 |  |  |  |  | 12 |  |  | 10 | 11 | 3 | 6 |  |  |  | 9* |  | 4 |  |  |  | 1 | 7 | 8 | 2 |  | 32 |
|  | 5* |  |  |  |  |  |  |  | 10 | 12 | 11 | 3 | 6 |  |  | 9 |  | 4 |  |  |  | 1 | 7 | 8 | 2 |  | 33 |
|  |  |  |  | 5 |  |  |  |  | 10 | 11 | 3 | 6 |  |  |  | 9 |  | 4 |  | 12 |  | 1* | 7 | 8 | 2 |  | 34 |
|  |  |  |  | 5 |  |  |  |  | 10 | 11 | 3 | 6 |  |  |  | 9 |  | 4 |  |  |  | 1 | 7 | 8 | 2 |  | 35 |
|  | 5 |  |  |  |  | 12 |  | 10 |  |  | 3 | 6 |  |  |  | 9 |  | 4 | 11 |  |  | 1 | 7* | 8 | 2 |  | 36 |
|  | 5 |  |  |  |  |  |  |  |  | 11 | 3 | 6 |  |  |  | 9 |  | 4 |  | 10 |  | 1 | 7 | 8 | 2 |  | 37 |
|  | 5 | 3 |  |  |  |  |  |  |  | 11 |  | 6 |  |  |  | 9 | 2 | 4 |  | 10 |  | 1 | 7 | 8 |  |  | 38 |
|  | 5 | 3 |  |  |  |  |  |  |  | 11 |  | 6 |  |  |  | 9 | 2 | 4 |  | 12 |  | 1 | 7 | 8 |  | 10* | 39 |
|  | 5 | 3 |  |  |  | 12 |  |  |  | 11 |  | 6 |  |  |  | 9 | 2 | 4 |  |  |  | 1 | 7 | 8 |  | 10* | 40 |
|  | 5 | 3 |  |  |  | 10 |  |  |  | 11 |  | 6 |  |  |  | 9 |  | 4 |  |  |  | 1 | 7 | 8 | 2 |  | 41 |
|  | 5 | 3 |  |  |  | 10 |  |  |  | 11 |  | 6 |  |  |  | 9 |  | 4 |  |  |  | 1 | 7 | 8 | 2 |  | 42 |
| 16 | 24 | 12 | 18 | 26 | 10 | 15 | 17 | 16 | 7 | 27 | 25 | 31 | 7 | 8 | 7 | 27 | 19 | 29 | 12 | 15 | 4 | 26 | 25 | 22 | 15 | 2 |  |
|  |  |  | +1s |  | +2s | +2s | +3s |  | +1s |  |  | +1s | +1s | +3s | +1s | +2s |  |  |  |  |  | +1s | +3s |  |  |  |  |

## EVERTON

| | Ht | Wt | Birthplace | Clubs | League App. | League Gls |
|---|---|---|---|---|---|---|
| **Goalkeepers** | | | | | | |
| Martin Hodge | 6 0 | 13 2 | Southport | Plymouth Arg | 43 | — |
| | | | | Everton | 25 | — |
| | | | | Preston NE (on loan) | 28 | — |
| Simon Steele | 6 0 | 11 0 | Southport | Everton | — | — |
| Neville Southall | 6 1 | 12 0 | Llandudno | Winsford U | (not known) | |
| (Wales) | | | | Bury | 39 | — |
| | | | | Everton | 26 | — |
| Jim Arnold | 6 1 | 11 5 | Stafford | Stafford R | (not known) | |
| | | | | Blackburn R | 58 | — |
| | | | | Everton | 16 | — |
| | | | | | | |
| **Defenders** | | | | | | |
| Billy Wright | 5 11 | 12 7 | Liverpool | Everton | 149 | 7 |
| Mike Lyons | 6 0 | 12 2 | Liverpool | Everton | 390 | 48 |
| Mark Higgins | 6 1 | 13 4 | Buxton | Everton | 99 | 5 |
| Kevin Ratcliffe | 5 11 | 12 8 | Mancot | Everton | 48 | — |
| (Wales) | | | | | | |
| Brian Borrows | 5 10 | 10 12 | Liverpool | Everton | 15 | — |
| John Bailey | 5 8 | 11 3 | Liverpool | Blackburn R | 120 | 1 |
| | | | | Everton | 85 | 2 |
| Mike Walsh | 6 0 | 12 1 | Manchester | Bolton W | 177 | 4 |
| (Eire) | | | | Everton | 18 | — |
| Mark Kearney | 5 10 | 11 0 | Ormskirk | Marine | (not known) | |
| | | | | Everton | — | — |
| Gary Stevens | 5 11 | 10 12 | Barrow | Everton | 19 | 1 |
| | | | | | | |
| **Midfield** | | | | | | |
| Steve McMahon | 5 7 | 10 9 | Liverpool | Everton | 66 | 7 |
| Trevor Ross | 5 9½ | 11 10 | Ashton-under- | Arsenal | 58 | 5 |
| | | | Lyne | Everton | 124 | 16 |
| Kevin Richardson | 5 7 | 10 2 | Newcastle | Everton | 18 | 2 |
| Paul Lodge | 5 8½ | 10 11 | Liverpool | Everton | 24 | — |
| Alan Ainscow | 5 6½ | 9 4 | Bolton | Blackpool | 192 | 28 |
| | | | | Birmingham C | 108 | 16 |
| | | | | Everton | 17 | 2 |
| Keith Tierney | 5 6 | 10 4 | Manchester | Everton | — | — |
| Adrian Heath | 5 6 | 10 1 | Stoke | Stoke C | 95 | 16 |
| | | | | Everton | 22 | 6 |
| Howard Kendall | 5 7 | 10 13 | Ryton-on-Tyne | Preston NE | 104 | 13 |
| (Contract cancelled) | | | | Everton | 230 | 21 |
| | | | | Birmingham C | 115 | 16 |
| | | | | Stoke C | 82 | 9 |
| | | | | Blackburn R | 79 | 6 |
| | | | | Everton | 4 | — |
| | | | | | | |
| **Forwards** | | | | | | |
| Joe McBride | 5 8 | 10 8 | Glasgow | Everton | 57 | 9 |
| Peter Eastoe | 5 9 | 11 1 | Tamworth | Wolverhampton W | 6 | — |
| | | | | Swindon T | 91 | 43 |
| | | | | QPR | 72 | 15 |
| | | | | Everton | 95 | 26 |
| Dean Kelly | 5 7 | 10 2 | Liverpool | Everton | — | — |
| (Contract cancelled April 1982) | | | | | | |
| Graeme Sharp | 6 1 | 11 8 | Glasgow | Dumbarton | 40 | 16 |
| | | | | Everton | 35 | 15 |
| Gerry Mullan | | | Limavady | Ballymena U | (not known) | |
| (Transferred to Glentoran Nov 1981) | | | | Everton | — | — |
| Alan Irvine | 5 8 | 11 4 | Glasgow | Queen's Park | — | — |
| | | | | Everton | 25 | 3 |
| Alan Biley | 5 8 | 10 9 | Leighton | Luton T | — | — |
| | | | Buzzard | Cambridge U | 165 | 74 |
| | | | | Derby Co | 47 | 19 |
| | | | | Everton | 19 | 3 |
| | | | | Stoke C (on loan) | 8 | 1 |
| Mick Ferguson | 6 1 | 12 8 | Newcastle | Coventry C | 127 | 51 |
| | | | | Everton | 8 | 4 |
| Mark Leonard | 5 11 | 11 10 | St Helens | Witton A | (not known) | |
| | | | | Everton | — | — |
| Stuart Rimmer | 5 7 | 9 2 | Southport | Everton | 2 | — |
| (Apprentice) | | | | | | |

# EXETER CITY

## Division 3

*President:* F. E. J. Dart.

*Chairman:* L. G. Vallance.

*Vice-Chairman:* C. Hill.

*Directors:* F. E. J. Dart, I. Webb ICMA, S. J. West FIB, R. M. L. Williams.

*Manager:* Brian Godfrey.

*Secretary:* P. R. Wakeham.

*Commercial Manager:* E. R. Ellis.

*Year Formed:* 1904.  *Turned Professional:* 1908.

*Limited Company:* 1908.

**Football League Record:**
1920 Elected Division 3; 1921–1958 Division 3(S); 1958–64 Division 4; 1964–66 Division 3; 1966–77 Division 4; 1977– Division 3.

**Honours:** *Football League:* Division 3 best season: 8th, 1979–80; Division 3(S) – Runners-up 1932–33; Division 4 – Runners-up 1976–77. *FA Cup* best season: 6th rd replay, 1931. *Football League Cup:* never beyond 4th rd. *Division 3(S) Cup:* Winners 1934.

*Record Victory:* 8-1 v Coventry C, Division 3(S), 4 Dec, 1926 and v Aldershot, Division 3(S), 4 May, 1935.

*Record Defeat:* 0-9 v Notts Co, Division 3(S), 16 Oct, 1948 and v Northampton T, Division 3(S), 12 Apr, 1958.

*Most League Points:* 62, Division 4, 1976–77.

*Most League Goals:* 88, Division 3(S), 1932–33.

*Highest League Scorer in Season:* Fred Whitlow, 34, Division 3(S), 1932–33.

*Most League Goals in Total Aggregate:* Alan Banks, 105, 1963–66, 1967–73.

*Most Capped Player:* Dermot Curtis, 1 (17), Eire.

*Most League Appearances:* Arnold Mitchell, 495, 1952–66.

*Record Transfer Fee Received:* £105,000 from Blackpool for Tony Kellow, Nov 1978.

*Record Transfer Fee Paid:* £65,000 to Blackpool for Tony Kellow, March 1980.

*Previous Managers since the War:* George Roughton, Norman Kirkman, Norman Dodgin, Bill Thompson, Frank Broome, Glen Wilson, Cyril Spiers, Jack Edwards, Ellis Stuttard, Jock Basford, Frank Broome, John Newman, Bobby Saxton.

*Address of Supporters Club:* The 'Near Post', 2 Blackboy Road, Exeter.

*Address of the Club Shop or Boutique:* The 'Near Post', 2 Blackboy Road, Exeter.

---

**St James Park, Exeter EX4 6PX.** Telephone Exeter 54073. *Ground capacity:* 17,500. *Record attendance:* 20,984 v Sunderland, FA Cup 6th rd replay, 4 March, 1931. *Record receipts:* £32,007 v Newcastle U, FA Cup 5th rd replay, 18 Feb, 1981. *Pitch measurements:* 114yd×73yd.

*How to get there:* City buses A, D, J, K, S from city centre to The Fountain (one-minute walk to the ground). Routes G and J pass both railway stations – Exeter St David's and Exeter Central.

*Match tickets:* Tickets may be booked in advance usually two weeks before home matches.

*Car parking:* No car park at the ground. Limited street parking permitted.

*Entertainments/catering facilities:* Members social club. Subscription £1.25; joint membership £2.50. The club is situated at the ground.

*Club shop:* Sells all types of souvenir.

*Handbooks/programmes:* Programmes can be ordered on subscription.

*Extra information:* Membership of the Supporters Association at 25p per year.

*Club Colours:* Red and white vertical stripes, black shorts, black stockings with red and white turnover.

*Change Colours:* Green shirts, green shorts, green stockings.

*Coaches:* Alan Beer, Malcolm Musgrove.

*Club Nickname:* The Grecians.

## EXETER CITY 1981–82 LEAGUE RECORD

| Match No. | Date | Venue | Opponents | Result | H/T Score | Goalscorers | Attendance |
|---|---|---|---|---|---|---|---|
| 1 | Aug 29 | A | Huddersfield T | D 1-1 | 1-0 | Pratt | 8647 |
| 2 | Sept 5 | H | Carlisle U | W 2-1 | 0-0 | Hatch, Kellow | 3533 |
| 3 | 11 | A | Doncaster R | L 0-3 | 0-2 | | 4369 |
| 4 | 19 | H | Swindon T | L 1-2 | 0-1 | Kellow (pen) | 4372 |
| 5 | 23 | H | Bristol R | L 1-3 | 1-2 | Kellow | 5510 |
| 6 | 26 | A | Gillingham | W 3-2 | 1-1 | Lester, Roberts L., Rogers P. | 4158 |
| 7 | 29 | A | Portsmouth | L 0-2 | 0-2 | | 10,989 |
| 8 | Oct 3 | H | Millwall | W 5-4 | 3-1 | Kellow, Lester 3, Rogers P. | 7169 |
| 9 | 10 | H | Brentford | W 3-1 | 0-1 | Kellow, Cooke, Prince | 3689 |
| 10 | 17 | A | Burnley | D 3-3 | 2-1 | Kellow, Lester, Cooke | 3975 |
| 11 | 20 | A | Fulham | L 1-4 | 1-2 | Cooke | 4500 |
| 12 | 24 | H | Preston NE | W 4-3 | 2-1 | Rogers P., Kellow 2 (1 pen), Roberts L. | 3642 |
| 13 | 31 | A | Wimbledon | D 1-1 | 0-1 | Lester | 2152 |
| 14 | Nov 4 | H | Oxford U | L 1-2 | 1-0 | Roberts L. | 3349 |
| 15 | 7 | H | Reading | W 4-3 | 1-2 | Kellow 2 (1 pen), Rogers P., Pullar | 3765 |
| 16 | 14 | A | Chester | W 2-0 | 0-0 | Sparrow, Pratt | 2125 |
| 17 | 28 | A | Newport Co | D 1-1 | 0-1 | Hatch | 4149 |
| 18 | Dec 5 | H | Chesterfield | L 0-3 | 0-1 | | 3947 |
| 19 | 28 | H | Plymouth Arg | D 1-1 | 0-0 | Kellow | 9144 |
| 20 | Jan 1 | A | Southend U | L 1-2 | 0-2 | Fisher | 5985 |
| 21 | 16 | H | Walsall | W 2-0 | 0-0 | Kellow 2 | 3118 |
| 22 | 31 | A | Swindon T | L 2-3 | 1-1 | Rogers M., Pullar | 5656 |
| 23 | Feb 6 | H | Doncaster R | W 2-1 | 0-0 | Rogers M., Delve | 3193 |
| 24 | 9 | A | Bristol R | L 2-3 | 0-2 | Rogers M., Kellow (pen) | 4987 |
| 25 | 14 | A | Millwall | L 1-5 | 0-2 | Rogers P. | 3628 |
| 26 | 20 | H | Gillingham | D 1-1 | 1-1 | Kellow (pen) | 2888 |
| 27 | 23 | H | Bristol C | L 2-3 | 1-2 | Roberts L., Rogers P. | 6612 |
| 28 | 27 | A | Brentford | L 0-2 | 0-0 | | 4931 |
| 29 | Mar 6 | H | Burnley | W 2-1 | 0-0 | Rogers P. 2 | 3136 |
| 30 | 10 | H | Fulham | W 1-0 | 0-0 | Rogers P. | 3367 |
| 31 | 13 | A | Preston NE | L 0-1 | 0-1 | | 4770 |
| 32 | 17 | A | Oxford U | D 0-0 | 0-0 | | 5098 |
| 33 | 20 | H | Wimbledon | W 2-1 | 2-1 | Pratt, Kellow | 3002 |
| 34 | 24 | H | Lincoln C | L 1-2 | 0-0 | Rogers M. | 3081 |
| 35 | 27 | A | Reading | L 0-4 | 0-2 | | 3365 |
| 36 | Apr 3 | H | Chester | W 3-0 | 1-0 | Raynor (og), Kellow (pen), Giles | 2498 |
| 37 | 9 | A | Plymouth Arg | L 1-2 | 0-1 | Kellow (pen) | 9458 |
| 38 | 10 | H | Bristol C | W 4-0 | 2-0 | Kellow 2 (1 pen), Pratt, Rogers P. | 4580 |
| 39 | 17 | A | Chesterfield | L 1-2 | 1-1 | Pratt | 2867 |
| 40 | 20 | A | Carlisle U | L 2-3 | 1-2 | Pratt, Delve | 5220 |
| 41 | 24 | H | Newport Co | W 1-0 | 1-0 | Delve | 3168 |
| 42 | May 1 | A | Walsall | L 1-2 | 0-1 | Pratt | 2487 |
| 43 | 5 | H | Portsmouth | D 3-3 | 2-1 | Kellow, Pratt 2 | 2596 |
| 44 | 8 | H | Southend U | D 1-1 | 0-1 | Marker | 3174 |
| 45 | 12 | H | Huddersfield T | W 1-0 | 0-0 | Hatch | 2888 |
| 46 | 15 | A | Lincoln C | L 0-2 | 0-0 | | 5447 |

**Final League Position: 18**

### Goalscorers

*League* (71): Kellow 21 (8 pens), Rogers P. 10, Pratt 9, Lester 6, Roberts L. 4, Rogers M. 4, Cooke 3, Delve 3, Hatch 3, Pullar 2, Fisher 1, Giles 1, Marker 1, Prince 1, Sparrow 1, own goal 1.
*League Cup* (4): Cooke 2, Fisher 1, Kellow 1 (pen).
*FA Cup* (0).

| League Cup | First Round | Cardiff C (a) | 1-2 |
|---|---|---|---|
| | | (h) | 3-1 |
| | Second Round | Liverpool (a) | 0-5 |
| | | (h) | 0-6 |
| FA Cup | First Round | Brentford (a) | 0-2 |

| Main | Rogers M. | Hatch | Davey | Cooke | Roberts L. | Rogers P. | Pratt | Kellow | Lester | Pullar | Bond | Roberts P. | Prince | Mitchell | Sparrow | Fisher | Delve | Marker | Shaw | Foster | Howarth | Kirkup | Giles | Robertson | Match No. |
|---|---|---|---|---|---|---|---|---|---|---|---|---|---|---|---|---|---|---|---|---|---|---|---|---|---|
| 1 | 2 | 3 | 4 | 5 | 6 | 7 | 8 | 9 | 10 | 11 | | | | | | | | | | | | | | | 1 |
| | 2 | 11 | 4 | 5 | 3 | 7* | 8 | 9 | 10 | | 1 | 6 | 12 | | | | | | | | | | | | 2 |
| | 2 | 11* | 4 | 5 | 3 | 7 | 8 | 9 | 10 | | 1 | 6 | 12 | | | | | | | | | | | | 3 |
| | | 11 | 4 | 5 | 3 | | 8 | 9 | 10 | | 1 | 6 | 12 | | 2* | 7 | | | | | | | | | 4 |
| | 11* | 2 | | 5 | 6 | | 8 | 9 | 4 | | 1 | | | | 3 | 7 | 10 | | | | | | | | 5 |
| | | 2 | | 5* | 6 | 7 | | 9 | 4 | 11 | 1 | 12 | 8 | | 3 | | 10 | | | | | | | | 6 |
| | | 2 | | 5 | 6 | 7 | | 9 | 4 | 11 | 1 | | 8 | | 3 | | 10 | | | | | | | | 7 |
| | | 2 | | 5 | 6 | | 8 | 9 | 4 | 11 | 1 | | 7 | | 3 | | 10 | | | | | | | | 8 |
| 12 | 2 | | | 5 | 6 | | 8 | 9 | 4 | 11* | 1 | | 7 | | 3 | | 10 | | | | | | | | 9 |
| | 2 | | 4 | | 7 | 6 | 8 | 9 | | 11 | 1 | | | | 3 | | 10 | | | 5 | | | | | 10 |
| | 2 | | 4* | | 7 | 6 | 8 | 9 | | 11 | 1 | 12 | | | 3 | | 10 | | | 5 | | | | | 11 |
| | 2 | | 4 | | 6 | | 8 | 9 | 11 | 7 | 1 | | | | 3 | | 10 | | | 5 | | | | | 12 |
| | 2 | | | | 6 | 7* | 8 | 9 | 4 | 11 | 1 | | | 12 | 3 | | 10 | | | 5 | | | | | 13 |
| 1 | 2* | | 4 | | 6 | 7 | 12 | 9 | | 11 | | | 8 | | 3 | | 10 | | | 5 | | | | | 14 |
| 1 | 2 | | | | 6 | 7 | 8 | 9 | 4 | 11 | | | | | 3 | | 10 | | | 5 | | | | | 15 |
| 1 | 2 | | | | 6 | 7* | 8 | 9 | 4 | 11 | | | | 12 | 3 | | 10 | | | 5 | | | | | 16 |
| 1 | 2 | 11 | | | 6* | 7 | 8 | 9 | 4 | | | | | 12 | 3 | | 10 | | | 5 | | | | | 17 |
| 1 | 2 | 11 | | 5 | | | 8 | 9 | 4 | | | 6* | 7 | 12 | 3 | | 10 | | | | | | | | 18 |
| 1 | | 3 | | | 6 | 7 | 8 | 9 | | 11 | | 4 | 2 | | | | 10 | | | 5 | | | | | 19 |
| 1 | | 3 | | | 6 | 7* | | 9 | | 11 | | 4 | 2 | 12 | | 8 | 10 | | | 5 | | | | | 20 |
| 1 | | | 4 | | 6 | 7 | 8 | 9 | | 11 | | 2 | 3 | | | | 10 | | | 5 | | | | | 21 |
| 1 | | | 4 | | 6 | 7* | 8 | 9 | | 11 | | 2 | 3 | 12 | | | 10 | | | 5 | | | | | 22 |
| | | | 4 | | 6 | 7 | 8 | 9 | | 11 | 1 | 2 | 3 | | | | 10 | | | 5 | | | | | 23 |
| | | 11 | 4 | | 6 | 7 | 8 | 9 | | | 1 | 2 | 3 | | | | 10 | | | 5 | | | | | 24 |
| | | 11* | 4 | | 6 | 7 | 8 | 9 | | | 1 | 2 | 3 | 12 | | | 10 | | | 5 | | | | | 25 |
| | | 11* | 4 | | 6 | 7 | 8 | 9 | | | 1 | 2 | 3 | 12 | | | 10 | | | 5 | | | | | 26 |
| | | | 4 | | 6 | 7 | 8 | 9 | | 11 | 1 | 2* | 3 | | | | 10 | | | 5 | | | | | 27 |
| | 2 | | | | | 7 | 8 | 9 | 12 | | 1 | 6 | | | 3 | | 10 | 4 | | 5 | 11* | | | | 28 |
| | | | | | | 7 | 8 | 9* | | 11 | 1 | 6 | | | 3 | | 10 | 4 | | 5 | | 12 | 2 | | 29 |
| | | 11 | | | | 7 | 8 | 9 | | | 1 | 6 | | | 3 | | 10 | 4 | | 5 | | | 2 | | 30 |
| | | 11 | | | | 7 | 8 | 9 | 12 | | 1 | 6 | | | 3 | | 10 | 4* | | 5 | | | 2 | | 31 |
| | | | | | | 7 | 8 | 9 | | 11 | 1 | 6 | | | 3 | | 10 | 4 | | 5 | | | 2 | | 32 |
| 1 | | | 4 | | | 7 | 8 | 9* | 10 | | | 6 | | | 3 | | 11 | 12 | | 5 | | | 2 | | 33 |
| | | | 4 | | | 7 | 8 | 9 | | 11 | 1 | 6 | | | 3 | | 10 | | | 5 | | | 2 | | 34 |
| | | | | | | | 8 | 9 | 12 | 11 | 1 | 6 | 4* | | 3 | | | | | 5 | | 2 | 7 | 10 | 35 |
| | 2 | 12 | | | | 7 | 8 | 9 | | 11* | 1 | 6 | | | 3 | | | | | 5 | | 4 | 10 | | 36 |
| | 2 | 12 | | | | 7* | 8 | 9 | | | 1 | 6 | 3 | | | | 10 | | | 5 | | 4 | 11 | | 37 |
| | 2 | 11 | | | | 7 | 8 | 9 | | | 1 | 6 | | | 3 | | 10 | | | 5 | | 4 | | | 38 |
| | 2 | 11 | | | | 7 | 8 | 9 | | | 1 | 6 | | | 3 | | 10 | | | 5 | | 4 | | | 39 |
| 1 | 2 | 11 | | | | 7 | 8 | 9 | | | | 6 | 3* | | | | 10 | | | 5 | | 4 | 12 | | 40 |
| 1 | 2 | 3 | | | | 7 | 8 | 9 | | | | 6 | | | | | 10 | | | 5 | | 4 | 11 | | 41 |
| 1 | 2 | | 4 | | | 7 | 8 | 9 | | | | 6 | | | 3 | | 10 | 12 | | 5 | | | 11* | | 42 |
| 1 | | 11 | | | | 7 | 12 | 9 | 8* | | | 6 | | | 3 | | 10 | 4 | | 5 | | 2 | | | 43 |
| | 2 | 11 | | | | | 8 | 9 | | | 1 | 6 | | | 3 | | 10 | 4 | | 5 | 7 | | | | 44 |
| | 2 | 11 | | | | 7 | 8 | 9 | | | 1 | 6 | | | 3 | | 10 | 4 | | 5 | | | | | 45 |
| | 2 | 11 | | | | 7 | 12 | 9 | 8* | | 1 | 6 | | | 3 | | 10 | | | 5 | | 4 | | | 46 |
| 15 | 35 | 20 | 15 | 17 | 23 | 42 | 23 | 46 | 18 | 27 | 31 | 26 | 6 | 13 | 38 | 6 | 40 | 11 | 3 | 28 | 1 | 8 | 9 | 5 | |

| | + | + | | + | | + | | | + | + | | + | + | | | + | + | | | + | + | | + | | |
| | 1s | 2s | | 2s | | 7s | | | 1s | 3s | | 1s | 4s | | | 2s | 3s | | | 1s | | | 1s | | |

## EXETER CITY

| | Ht | Wt | Birthplace | Clubs | League App. | League Gls |
|---|---|---|---|---|---|---|
| **Goalkeepers** | | | | | | |
| Ian Main* | 6 0 | 13 2 | Swindon | Gloucester C | (not known) | |
| | | | | Exeter C | 78 | — |
| Len Bond | 6 0 | 12 7 | Ilminster | Bristol C | 30 | — |
| | | | | Exeter C (on loan) | 30 | — |
| | | | | Cardiff C (on loan) | — | — |
| | | | | Torquay U (on loan) | 3 | — |
| | | | | Scunthorpe U (on loan) | 8 | — |
| | | | | Colchester U (on loan) | 3 | — |
| | | | | Brentford | 122 | — |
| | | | | St Louis SS | (not known) | |
| | | | | Exeter C | 48 | — |
| **Defenders** | | | | | | |
| Peter Hatch* | 5 11 | 11 6 | Henley on Thames | Oxford U | 19 | 2 |
| | | | | Exeter C | 346 | 18 |
| Phil Roberts* (Wales) | 5 11 | 12 12 | Cardiff | Bristol R | 176 | 6 |
| | | | | Portsmouth | 153 | 1 |
| | | | | Hereford U | 3 | — |
| | | | | Exeter C | 105 | — |
| Martyn Rogers | 5 9 | 11 6 | Bristol | Bristol C | — | — |
| | | | | Bath C | (not known) | |
| | | | | Exeter C | 84 | 4 |
| Tony Mitchell* | 5 7 | 11 0 | London | Exeter C | 60 | — |
| Lee Roberts | 6 0 | 12 2 | Wolverhampton | Shrewsbury T | 15 | 1 |
| | | | | Exeter C | 142 | 12 |
| John Sparrow | 5 10 | 12 0 | Bethnal Green | Chelsea | 69 | 2 |
| | | | | Millwall (on loan) | 7 | — |
| | | | | Exeter C | 53 | 2 |
| Graeme Kirkup (Apprentice) | | | | Exeter C | 8 | — |
| Steve Davey (Contract cancelled Feb 1982) | 5 9 | 11 0 | Plymouth | Plymouth Arg | 226 | 48 |
| | | | | Hereford U | 107 | 32 |
| | | | | Portsmouth | 92 | 8 |
| | | | | Exeter C | 15 | — |
| Nick Marker (Apprentice) | | | | Exeter C | 14 | 1 |
| **Midfield** | | | | | | |
| John Delve | 5 7 | 11 0 | Isleworth | QPR | 15 | — |
| | | | | Plymouth Arg | 132 | 6 |
| | | | | Exeter C | 171 | 15 |
| David Pullar | 6 0 | 11 0 | Co. Durham | Portsmouth | 93 | 4 |
| | | | | Exeter C | 98 | 17 |
| Frankie Prince (Contract cancelled Jan 1982) | 5 9 | 11 5 | Penarth | Bristol R | 361 | 23 |
| | | | | Exeter C | 31 | 2 |
| Stuart Robertson* | 5 4 | 10 0 | Glasgow | Burnley | 32 | — |
| | | | | WBA (on loan) | — | — |
| | | | | Exeter C | 6 | — |
| Paul Giles | 5 10 | 9 12 | Cardiff | Cardiff C | 17 | 1 |
| | | | | Exeter C | 9 | 1 |
| **Forwards** | | | | | | |
| Peter Rogers | 5 9 | 10 12 | Bristol | Bristol C | — | — |
| | | | | Minehead | (not known) | |
| | | | | Bath C | (not known) | |
| | | | | Exeter C | 137 | 24 |
| Ian Pearson (Contract cancelled Sept 1982) | 5 11 | 11 3 | Leeds | Plymouth Arg | 12 | — |
| | | | | Millwall | 44 | 9 |
| | | | | Exeter C | 69 | 10 |
| Tony Kellow | 5 11 | 12 7 | Budock Water | Falmouth | (not known) | |
| | | | | Exeter C | 107 | 40 |
| | | | | Blackpool | 57 | 23 |
| | | | | Exeter C | 102 | 51 |
| Ray Pratt | 5 10 | 12 0 | Merthyr | Merthyr T | (not known) | |
| | | | | Exeter C | 54 | 15 |
| Phil Fisher* | 5 9 | 10 10 | Ammanford | Exeter C | 11 | 1 |
| Frank Howarth (Apprentice) | | | | Exeter C | 2 | — |

# FULHAM

## Division 2

*Life-Presidents:* Tommy Trinder CBE., Ted Drake.

*Chairman:* E. Clay.

*Directors:* G. Clay, B. Dalton, E. Drake, M. Macdonald.

*Manager:* Malcolm Macdonald.

*Club Secretary:* Mrs Y. Haines.   *Year Formed:* 1879.

*Turned Professional:* 1898.   *Limited Company:* 1903.

*Previous Name:* 1879–98, Fulham St Andrew's.

*Previous Grounds:* Lillie Road, Fulham Cross; Barn Elms, Barnes; Ranelagh House; Stansfield's Field, Fulham Road; Half-Moon Cricket Ground, Putney; 1896, Craven Cottage.

**Football League Record:**
1907 Elected to Division 2; 1928–32 Division 3(S); 1932–49 Division 2; 1949–52 Division 1; 1952–59 Division 2; 1959–68 Division 1; 1968–69 Division 2; 1969–71 Division 3; 1971–80 Division 2; 1980–82 Division 3; 1982– Division 2.

**Honours:** *Football League:* Division 1 best season: 10th, 1959–60; Division 2 – Champions 1948–49; Runners-up 1958–59; Division 3(S) – Champions 1931–32; Division 3 – Runners-up 1970–71. *FA Cup:* Runners-up 1974–75. *Football League Cup* best season: 5th rd, 1967–68, 1970–71.

*Record Victory:* 10-1 v Ipswich T, Division 1, 26 Dec, 1963.

*Record Defeat:* 0-9 v Wolverhampton W, Division 1, 16 Sept, 1959.

*Most League Points:* 60, Division 2 1958–59, and Division 3, 1970–71. *Three points win:* 78, Division 3, 1981–82.

*Most League Goals:* 111, Division 3(S), 1931–32.

*Highest League Scorer in Season:* Frank Newton, 41, Division 3(S), 1931–32.

*Most League Goals in Total Aggregate:* Bedford Jezzard, 154, 1948–56.

*Most Capped Player:* Johnny Haynes, 56, England.

*Most League Appearances:* Johnny Haynes, 594, 1952–70.

*Record Transfer Fee Received:* £333,333 from Liverpool for Richard Money, May 1980.

*Record Transfer Fee Paid:* £150,000 to Orient for Peter Kitchen, Feb 1979 and £150,000 to Brighton & HA for Teddy Maybank, Dec 1979.

*Previous Managers since the War:* Jack Peart, Frank Osborne, Doug Livingstone, Bill Dodgin (Snr), Bedford Jezzard, Vic Buckingham, Bobby Robson, Johnny Haynes, Bill Dodgin (Jnr), Alec Stock, Bobby Campbell.

*Address of Supporters Club:* Fulham Travel Club, Craven Cottage, Stevenage Road, SW6.

---

**Craven Cottage, Stevenage Rd, Fulham, London SW6.** Telephone 01-736 6561/2/3. Pools Office: 01-736 4634. *Telegraphic address:* 'Fulhamish, London SW6'. *Ground capacity:* 20,000. *Record attendance:* 49,335 v Millwall, Division 2, 8 Oct, 1938. *Record receipts:* £44,763 v Manchester U, FA Cup 4th rd, 27 Jan, 1979. *Pitch measurements:* 110yd×75yd.

*How to get there:* Underground stations, Putney Bridge (District Line) and Hammersmith (District, Metropolitan, Piccadilly). Then by bus – 30, 74, 85, 93, 220.

*Match tickets:* The Box Office is now computerised, and seats are bookable at any time during the season 9.30–4.30.

*Car parking:* Parking in streets around the ground.

*Entertainments/catering facilities:* Social amenities available. Snack bars and licensed bars around the ground. The Riverside Suite is available for conferences, weddings, parties, etc.

*Club shop:* Sells all types of souvenir. Open only on match days.

*Handbooks/programmes:* Programmes available.

*Extra information:* Fulham Travel Club runs trips to away matches.

*Club Colours:* White shirts with black collar, black shorts, white stockings with three black hoops on turnover.

*Change Colours:* Red shirts, red shorts, black stockings with three red hoops on turnover.

*Club Captain:* Les Strong.

*First Team Trainer:* Derek Wright.

*Club Nickname:* Cottagers.

## FULHAM 1981–82 LEAGUE RECORD

| Match No. | Date | Venue | Opponents | Result | H/T Score | Goalscorers | Attendance |
|---|---|---|---|---|---|---|---|
| 1 | Aug 29 | H | Brentford | L 1-2 | 1-2 | Davies | 7632 |
| 2 | Sept 5 | A | Lincoln C | D 1-1 | 0-0 | Beck | 3934 |
| 3 | 12 | H | Bristol C | W 2-1 | 0-1 | Davies, Brown | 4169 |
| 4 | 19 | A | Chesterfield | L 0-3 | 0-0 | | 4019 |
| 5 | 22 | A | Wimbledon | W 3-1 | 1-0 | Coney 2, Davies | 5554 |
| 6 | 26 | H | Chester | W 2-0 | 2-0 | O'Driscoll, Lewington (pen) | 3629 |
| 7 | 29 | H | Southend U | W 2-1 | 0-1 | Davies, Wilson | 4556 |
| 8 | Oct 3 | A | Oxford U | L 0-2 | 0-1 | | 4244 |
| 9 | 10 | A | Huddersfield T | L 0-1 | 0-1 | | 8258 |
| 10 | 17 | H | Newport Co | W 3-1 | 1-1 | Davies 2, Lewington (pen) | 3918 |
| 11 | 20 | H | Exeter C | W 4-1 | 2-1 | Davies 2, O'Driscoll, Brown | 4500 |
| 12 | 24 | A | Burnley | D 2-2 | 0-2 | Davies 2 | 4224 |
| 13 | 31 | H | Portsmouth | D 1-1 | 0-0 | Wilson | 7542 |
| 14 | Nov 3 | A | Plymouth Arg | L 1-3 | 0-1 | Davies | 4915 |
| 15 | 7 | A | Carlisle U | W 2-1 | 2-0 | Davies, Coney | 4385 |
| 16 | 14 | H | Walsall | D 1-1 | 1-1 | Brown | 6168 |
| 17 | 28 | H | Millwall | D 0-0 | 0-0 | | 8343 |
| 18 | Dec 5 | A | Bristol R | W 2-1 | 1-0 | Coney, Davies | 4489 |
| 19 | 30 | A | Swindon T | W 4-1 | 2-0 | Davies 2, Lock, O'Driscoll | 5641 |
| 20 | Jan 20 | A | Reading | W 3-0 | 2-0 | Gale, Coney, Lewington (pen) | 3762 |
| 21 | 23 | A | Brentford | W 1-0 | 0-0 | O'Sullivan | 10,830 |
| 22 | 30 | H | Chesterfield | W 1-0 | 1-0 | Davies | 9213 |
| 23 | Feb 6 | A | Bristol C | D 0-0 | 0-0 | | 9228 |
| 24 | 9 | H | Wimbledon | W 4-1 | 1-0 | Coney 2, Downes (og), Wilson | 7802 |
| 25 | 19 | A | Southend U | D 0-0 | 0-0 | | 7715 |
| 26 | 23 | A | Oxford U | D 0-0 | 0-0 | | 5959 |
| 27 | 27 | H | Huddersfield T | D 2-2 | 0-1 | Coney, Lock (pen) | 5963 |
| 28 | Mar 7 | A | Newport Co | W 3-1 | 0-0 | Brown, Wilson, Coney | 5178 |
| 29 | 10 | A | Exeter C | L 0-1 | 0-0 | | 3367 |
| 30 | 13 | H | Burnley | D 1-1 | 1-1 | Davies | 7214 |
| 31 | 16 | H | Plymouth Arg | L 1-3 | 1-2 | Tempest | 5105 |
| 32 | 20 | A | Portsmouth | D 1-1 | 0-1 | Lock (pen) | 10,712 |
| 33 | 27 | H | Carlisle U | W 4-1 | 3-0 | Brown 2, Davies, O'Driscoll | 7477 |
| 34 | Apr 3 | A | Walsall | D 1-1 | 0-0 | O'Driscoll | 3120 |
| 35 | 6 | H | Doncaster R | W 3-1 | 1-1 | Coney, Davies, Brown | 5081 |
| 36 | 10 | A | Gillingham | L 0-2 | 0-1 | | 9895 |
| 37 | 13 | H | Swindon T | W 2-0 | 2-0 | Brown 2 | 6665 |
| 38 | 17 | H | Bristol R | W 4-2 | 2-0 | Davies, Lock (pen), Brown, O'Driscoll | 6849 |
| 39 | 20 | A | Preston NE | W 3-1 | 1-1 | Davies 2, Lock (pen) | 6009 |
| 40 | 25 | A | Millwall | L 3-4 | 0-2 | Brown, O'Driscoll, Stevens (og) | 6484 |
| 41 | May 1 | H | Reading | D 2-2 | 0-1 | Wilson, Lewington | 6773 |
| 42 | 5 | A | Chester | W 2-0 | 1-0 | Coney, Tempest | 1174 |
| 43 | 8 | A | Doncaster R | L 1-2 | 1-1 | Coney | 4729 |
| 44 | 11 | H | Gillingham | D 0-0 | 0-0 | | 7176 |
| 45 | 15 | H | Preston NE | W 3-0 | 2-0 | Davies 2, Coney | 7985 |
| 46 | 18 | H | Lincoln C | D 1-1 | 0-0 | Brown | 20,398 |

**Final League Position: 3**

### Goalscorers

*League* (77): Davies 24, Coney 13, Brown 12, O'Driscoll 7, Lock 5 (4 pens), Wilson 5, Lewington 4 (3 pens), Tempest 2, Beck 1, Gale 1, O'Sullivan 1, own goals 2.
*League Cup* (11): Coney 4, Wilson 3, Beck 1, Davies 1, Hopkins 1, Lewington 1.
*FA Cup* (2): Coney 2.

| League Cup | First Round | Bournemouth (a) | 1-0 |
|---|---|---|---|
| | | (h) | 2-0 |
| | Second Round | Newcastle U (a) | 2-1 |
| | | (h) | 2-0 |
| | Third Round | Oldham Ath (a) | 1-1 |
| | | (h) | 3-0 |
| | Fourth Round | Tottenham H (a) | 0-1 |
| FA Cup | First Round | Bristol R (a) | 2-1 |
| | Second Round | Hereford U (a) | 0-1 |

| Peyton | Hopkins | Strong | Brown | Banton | Beck | Davies | Day | Coney | O'Sullivan | Lewington | Wilson | Gale | O'Driscoll | Scott | Tempest | Peters | Lock | Parker | Reeves | Stannard | Match No. |
|---|---|---|---|---|---|---|---|---|---|---|---|---|---|---|---|---|---|---|---|---|---|
| 1 | 2 | 3 | 4 | 5 | 6 | 7 | 8* | 9 | 10 | 11 | 12 | | | | | | | | | | 1 |
| 1 | 2 | 3 | 5 | | 4 | 7 | | 9 | 10 | 11 | 8 | 6 | | | | | | | | | 2 |
| 1 | 2 | 3 | 5 | | 4 | 7 | | 9 | 10 | 11 | 8 | 6 | | | | | | | | | 3 |
| 1 | 2 | 3 | 5 | | 4 | 7 | | 9 | 10 | 11 | 8 | 6 | | | | | | | | | 4 |
| 1 | 2 | 3 | 5 | | | 7 | | 9 | 10 | 11 | 8 | 6 | 4 | | | | | | | | 5 |
| 1 | 2 | 3 | 5 | | | 7 | | 9 | 10 | 11 | 8 | 6 | 4 | | | | | | | | 6 |
| 1 | 2 | 3 | 5 | | | 7 | | 9 | 10 | 11 | 8 | 6 | 4 | | | | | | | | 7 |
| 1 | 2 | 3 | 5 | | | 7 | 12 | 9 | 10 | 11 | 8 | 6 | 4* | | | | | | | | 8 |
| 1 | 2 | 3 | 5 | | | 7 | 12 | 9 | 10 | | 8 | 6 | 4* | 11 | | | | | | | 9 |
| 1 | 2 | 3 | 5 | | | 7 | | 9 | 10 | 11 | 8 | 6 | 4 | | | | | | | | 10 |
| 1 | 2 | 3 | 5 | | | 7 | | 9 | 10 | 11 | 8 | 6 | 4 | | | | | | | | 11 |
| 1 | 2 | 3 | 5 | | | 7 | | | 10 | 11 | 8 | 6 | 4 | 9 | | | | | | | 12 |
| 1 | 2 | 3 | 5 | | | 7 | | 9 | 10 | 11 | 8 | 6 | 4 | | | | | | | | 13 |
| 1 | 2 | 3 | 5 | | | 7 | | 9 | 10 | 11 | 8 | 6 | 4* | | 12 | | | | | | 14 |
| 1 | 2 | 3 | 5 | | | 7 | | 9 | 10 | 11 | 8 | 6 | 4 | | | | | | | | 15 |
| 1 | 2 | 3 | 5* | | | 7 | 12 | 9 | 10 | 11 | 8 | 6 | 4 | | | | | | | | 16 |
| 1 | 2 | 3 | 5 | | | 7 | | 9 | 10 | 11 | 8 | 6 | 4 | | | | | | | | 17 |
| 1 | 2 | 3 | 5 | | | 7 | | 9 | 10 | 11 | 8 | 6 | 4 | | | | | | | | 18 |
| 1 | 2 | 3 | 5 | | | 7 | | 9* | 10 | 11 | 8 | 6 | 4 | | 12 | | | | | | 19 |
| 1 | | 3 | 5 | | | 7* | | 9 | 10 | 11 | | 6 | 4 | | | | 2 | 12 | 8 | | 20 |
| 1 | | 3 | 5 | | | | | 9 | 10 | 11 | | 6 | 4 | | 7 | | 2 | | 8 | | 21 |
| 1 | | 3 | 5 | | | 7* | | 9 | 10 | 11 | 8 | 6 | 4 | 12 | | | 2 | | | | 22 |
| 1 | | 3 | 5 | | | | | 9 | 10 | 11 | 8 | 6 | 4 | 7 | | | 2 | | | | 23 |
| 1 | | 3 | 5 | | | 7 | | 9 | 10 | 11 | 8 | 6 | 4 | | | | 2 | | | | 24 |
| 1 | 12 | 3 | 5 | | | 7 | | 9 | 10 | 11* | 8 | 6 | 4 | | | | 2 | | | | 25 |
| 1 | | 3 | 5 | | | 7 | | 9 | 10 | | 8 | 6 | 4 | | | | 2 | 12 | 11* | | 26 |
| 1 | | 3 | 5 | | | 7 | | 9 | 10 | | 8 | 6 | 4 | | | | 2 | | 11 | | 27 |
| 1 | | 3 | 5 | | | 7 | | 9 | 10 | | 8 | 6 | 4 | | | | 2 | | 11 | | 28 |
| 1 | | 3 | 5 | | | 7 | | 9 | 10 | | 8 | 6 | 4 | | | | 2 | | 11 | | 29 |
| 1 | 12 | 3 | 5 | | | 7 | | 9 | 10 | | 8 | 6 | 4 | | | | 2 | | 11* | | 30 |
| 1 | 6 | 3 | 5 | 12 | | 7 | | | 10 | | 8 | | 4* | 9 | | | 2 | 11 | | | 31 |
| 1 | 2 | 3 | 5 | | | 7 | | | 10 | | 8 | 6 | 4 | 9* | | | 11 | 12 | | | 32 |
| 1 | 2 | 3 | 5 | | | 7 | | | 10 | | 8 | 6 | 4 | 9 | | | 11 | | | | 33 |
| 1 | 2 | 3 | 5 | | | 7 | | 9 | | | 8 | 6 | 4 | | | | 11 | 10 | | | 34 |
| 1 | 2 | 3 | 5 | | | 7 | | 9 | 10 | | 8 | 6 | 4 | | | | 11 | | | | 35 |
| 1 | 2 | 3 | 5 | | | 7 | | 9 | 10 | | 8 | 6 | 4 | | | | 11 | | | | 36 |
| 1 | 2 | 3 | 5 | | | 7 | | 9 | 10 | | 8 | 6 | 4 | | | | 11 | | | | 37 |
| 1 | 2 | 3 | 5 | | | 7 | | 9 | 10 | | 8 | 6 | 4 | | | | 11 | | | | 38 |
| | 2 | 3 | 5 | | | 7 | | 9 | 10 | | 8 | 6 | 4 | | | | 11 | | | 1 | 39 |
| | 2 | 3 | 5* | | | 7 | | 9 | 10 | | 8 | 6 | 4 | 12 | | | 11 | | | 1 | 40 |
| 1 | 2 | | 5 | | | 7* | | 9 | 10 | 11 | 8 | 6 | 4 | 12 | | | 3 | | | | 41 |
| 1 | 12 | 2 | 5 | | | | | 9 | 10 | 11 | 8 | 6* | 4 | 7 | | | 3 | | | | 42 |
| 1 | 2 | | 5 | | | | | 9 | 10 | 11 | 8 | 6 | 4 | 7 | | | 3 | | | | 43 |
| 1 | 12 | 2 | 5 | | | | | 9 | 10 | 11 | 8 | 6 | 4 | 7 | | | | 3* | | | 44 |
| 1 | 2 | 3* | 5 | | | 7 | | 9 | 10 | 11 | 8 | 6 | 4 | 12 | | | | | | | 45 |
| 1 | 2 | 3* | 5 | | | 7 | | 9 | 10 | 11 | 8 | 6 | 4 | 12 | | | | | | | 46 |
| 44 | 31 | 46 | 46 | 1 | 4 | 41 | 1 | 42 | 45 | 31 | 42 | 44 | 42 | 1 | 9 | — | 25 | 2 | 7 | 2 | |
| +4s | | | | | +1s | | +3s | | +1s | | | | | +5s | +1s | +1s | +3s | | | | |

## FULHAM

| | Ht | Wt | Birthplace | Clubs | League App. | League Gls |
|---|---|---|---|---|---|---|
| **Goalkeepers** | | | | | | |
| Gerry Peyton (Eire) | 6 2 | 13 11 | Birmingham | Aston V | — | — |
| | | | | Burnley | 30 | — |
| | | | | Fulham | 208 | — |
| Jim Stannard | 6 0 | 13 1 | London | Fulham | 19 | — |
| **Defenders** | | | | | | |
| Les Strong | 5 9 | 10 7 | London | Crystal Palace | — | — |
| | | | | Fulham | 369 | 5 |
| Steve Hatter | 6 2 | 13 0 | London | Fulham | 26 | 1 |
| Tony Gale | 6 1½ | 12 4 | London | Fulham | 200 | 16 |
| Kevin Lock | 6 0 | 11 6 | London | West Ham U | 132 | 2 |
| | | | | Fulham | 132 | 18 |
| Geoff Banton* | 5 11 | 11 7 | Ashton-under-Lyne | Bolton W | — | — |
| | | | | Plymouth Arg | 7 | — |
| | | | | Fulham | 38 | 3 |
| Gary Peters | 5 11 | 11 12 | Surrey | Reading | 156 | 7 |
| | | | | Fulham | 64 | 2 |
| Roger Brown | 6 1 | 11 10 | Tamworth | Bournemouth | 63 | 3 |
| | | | | Norwich C | 16 | — |
| | | | | Fulham | 86 | 14 |
| Paul Parker | 5 7 | 10 8 | London | Fulham | 6 | — |
| Jeff Hopkins | 6 0 | 11 9 | Swansea | Fulham | 36 | — |
| Steve Tapley | 5 11 | 11 0 | London | Fulham | — | — |
| **Midfield** | | | | | | |
| John Beck | 5 10½ | 11 9 | Edmonton | QPR | 40 | 1 |
| | | | | Coventry C | 69 | 6 |
| | | | | Fulham | 114 | 13 |
| Robert Wilson | 5 10 | 11 2 | London | Fulham | 80 | 8 |
| Clive Day | 6 0 | 11 0 | Essex | Fulham | 10 | — |
| Ray Lewington | 5 6 | 10 5 | London | Chelsea | 85 | 4 |
| | | | | Wimbledon | 23 | — |
| | | | | Fulham | 61 | 5 |
| Sean O'Driscoll (Eire) | 5 8 | 10 6 | Birmingham | Alvechurch | (not known) | |
| | | | | Fulham | 94 | 11 |
| Tony Finnigan* | | | Wimbledon | Crystal Palace | — | — |
| | | | | Fulham | — | — |
| John Reeves | 5 7 | 9 10 | London | Fulham | 7 | — |
| Peter O'Sullivan (Wales) | 5 6 | 10 0 | Colwyn Bay | Manchester U | — | — |
| | | | | Brighton | 435 | 38 |
| | | | | Fulham | 45 | 1 |
| Peter Scott | 5 8 | 10 7 | London | Fulham | 1 | — |
| **Forwards** | | | | | | |
| Brian Greenaway | 5 9 | 10 1 | London | Fulham | 85 | 8 |
| Tony Mahoney | 6 0 | 11 12 | Barking | Fulham | 59 | 10 |
| | | | | Northampton T (on loan) | 6 | — |
| Gordon Davies (Wales) | 5 7 | 10 6 | S Wales | Fulham | 162 | 67 |
| Dale Tempest | 5 11 | 12 0 | Leeds | Fulham | 15 | 2 |
| Dean Coney | 6 0 | 12 6 | Dagenham | Fulham | 49 | 16 |

Hilton Phillips (Contract cancelled Feb 1982)
Free transfers: Charles Johnson*, Mark Aspinall*

# GILLINGHAM Division 3

*Chairman:* Dr C. S. Grossmark.

*Vice-Chairman:* C. A. L. Cox.

*Directors:* J. W. Leech, B. B. Moore.

*Manager:* Keith Peacock. *Club Secretary:* R. J. Dennison.

*Assistant Manager:* Paul Taylor.

*Year Formed:* 1893. *Turned Professional:* 1894.

*Limited Company:* 1893.

*Previous Name:* New Brompton, 1893–1913.

Founded 1893

**Football League Record:**
1920 Original Member of Division 3; 1921 Division 3(S); 1938 Failed re-election; 1950 Re-elected to Division 3(S); 1958–64 Division 4; 1964–71 Division 3; 1971–74 Division 4; 1974– Division 3.

**Honours:** *Football League:* Division 3 best season: 4th, 1978–79; Division 4 – Champions 1963–64; Runners-up 1973–74. *FA Cup* best season: 5th rd, 1969–70. *Football League Cup* best season: 4th rd, 1964.

*Record Victory:* 10-1 v Gorleston, FA Cup 1st rd, 16 Nov, 1957.

*Record Defeat:* 2-9 v Nottingham F, Division 3(S), 18 Nov, 1950.

*Most League Points:* 62, Division 4, 1973–74. *Three points win:* 71, Division 3, 1981–82.

*Most League Goals:* 90, Division 4, 1973–74.

*Highest League Scorer in Season:* Ernie Morgan, 31, Division 3(S), 1954–55; Brian Yeo, 31, Division 4, 1973–74.

*Most League Goals in Total Aggregate:* Brian Yeo, 135, 1963–75.

*Most Capped Player:* Damien Richardson, 2 (3), Eire.

*Most League Appearances:* John Simpson, 571, 1957–72.

*Record Transfer Fee Received:* £60,000 from Charlton Ath for Dick Tydeman, Dec 1976.

*Record Transfer Fee Paid:* £90,000 to Colchester U for Trevor Lee, Jan 1981.

*Previous Managers since the War:* Archie Clark, Harry Barratt, Freddie Cox, Basil Hayward, Andy Nelson, Len Ashurst, Gerry Summers.

*Address of Supporters Club:* Gillingham FC Supporters' Association, Gordon Road, Gillingham.

---

**Priestfield Stadium, Gillingham.** Telephone Medway 51854. *Telegraphic address:* 'Football Gillingham, Kent'. *Ground capacity:* 22,000. *Record attendance:* 23,002 v QPR, FA Cup 3rd rd, 10 Jan, 1948. *Record receipts:* £33,285 v WBA, FA Cup 4th rd, 23 Jan, 1982. *Pitch measurements:* 114yd×75yd.

*How to get there:* Gillingham railway station (six or seven minutes' walk). Bus services are 10 minutes from ground.

*Match tickets:* Can be reserved by postal application enclosing correct remittance and SAE.

*Car parking:* Park for 500 cars adjoining the ground, entrance in Toronto Rd.

*Entertainments/catering facilities:* A club house, and several bars around the ground.

*Club shop:* Sells all types of souvenir.

*Handbooks/programmes:* Programmes available on subscription. Handbooks also available.

*Extra information:* Enquiries about supporters association to Gillingham FC Supporters Association, Gordon Rd, Gillingham.

*Club Colours:* Blue shirts, white shorts, white stockings, white and blue trim.

*Change Colours:* All red.

*Club Captain:* Dick Tydeman.

*Club Nickname:* The Gills.

## GILLINGHAM 1981–82 LEAGUE RECORD

| Match No. | Date | Venue | Opponents | Result | H/T Score | Goalscorers | Attendance |
|---|---|---|---|---|---|---|---|
| 1 | Aug 29 | H | Burnley | W 3-1 | 1-0 | Price, Laws (og), Lee | 4663 |
| 2 | Sept 5 | A | Reading | L 2-3 | 0-0 | Lee, Price | 3496 |
| 3 | 12 | H | Chester | L 0-1 | 0-0 | | 3990 |
| 4 | 19 | A | Preston NE | D 1-1 | 0-0 | Westwood | 4563 |
| 5 | 21 | A | Brentford | W 1-0 | 0-0 | Tydeman | 5420 |
| 6 | 26 | H | Exeter C | L 2-3 | 1-1 | Bowman, Price | 4158 |
| 7 | 29 | H | Bristol C | D 1-1 | 0-0 | Price | 3887 |
| 8 | Oct 3 | A | Wimbledon | W 2-0 | 1-0 | Bowman 2 (1 pen) | 2510 |
| 9 | 10 | A | Plymouth Arg | W 2-1 | 1-0 | Lee, Bowman | 3094 |
| 10 | 17 | H | Huddersfield T | W 3-2 | 3-1 | Price, Bruce, White | 4432 |
| 11 | 20 | H | Portsmouth | W 4-2 | 1-2 | Bowman (pen), White 2, Price | 5546 |
| 12 | 24 | A | Millwall | W 2-1 | 1-0 | White 2 | 5763 |
| 13 | 31 | H | Swindon T | W 1-0 | 0-0 | White | 8410 |
| 14 | Nov 2 | A | Southend U | L 0-3 | 0-1 | | 6009 |
| 15 | 7 | A | Bristol R | L 0-2 | 0-0 | | 5518 |
| 16 | 14 | H | Doncaster R | W 3-0 | 2-0 | Lee, White 2 | 8189 |
| 17 | 28 | A | Carlisle U | L 0-2 | 0-2 | | 4196 |
| 18 | Dec 5 | H | Walsall | L 1-4 | 0-1 | White (pen) | 5845 |
| 19 | 28 | H | Newport Co | D 1-1 | 1-0 | Kemp | 6055 |
| 20 | Jan 16 | A | Lincoln C | L 0-2 | 0-0 | | 2756 |
| 21 | 30 | H | Preston NE | L 0-2 | 0-1 | | 5379 |
| 22 | Feb 2 | A | Burnley | L 0-1 | 0-0 | | 5845 |
| 23 | 6 | A | Chester | D 0-0 | 0-0 | | 1543 |
| 24 | 9 | H | Brentford | D 1-1 | 1-1 | White | 3931 |
| 25 | 13 | H | Wimbledon | W 6-1 | 3-1 | White (pen), Price 2, Bruce, Duncan, Cascarino | 4214 |
| 26 | 20 | A | Exeter C | D 1-1 | 1-1 | Duncan | 2888 |
| 27 | 27 | H | Plymouth Arg | W 3-2 | 1-2 | Bruce, Cascarino, Kemp | 4835 |
| 28 | Mar 6 | A | Huddersfield T | L 0-2 | 0-0 | | 5338 |
| 29 | 9 | A | Portsmouth | L 0-1 | 0-1 | | 6711 |
| 30 | 12 | H | Millwall | D 1-1 | 1-0 | Cascarino | 5508 |
| 31 | 16 | H | Southend U | W 2-0 | 1-0 | Bruce, Price | 3782 |
| 32 | 20 | A | Swindon T | W 1-0 | 1-0 | Adams | 4908 |
| 33 | 27 | H | Bristol R | W 2-0 | 1-0 | White (pen), Price | 5100 |
| 34 | 31 | A | Oxford U | D 1-1 | 1-1 | Adams | 5223 |
| 35 | Apr 3 | A | Doncaster R | D 1-1 | 0-0 | Sitton | 3902 |
| 36 | 6 | H | Chesterfield | W 3-2 | 0-2 | Sitton, Lee 2 | 5111 |
| 37 | 10 | H | Fulham | W 2-0 | 1-0 | Bruce, Powell | 9895 |
| 38 | 12 | A | Newport Co | L 2-4 | 1-3 | Price 2 | 4353 |
| 39 | 17 | A | Walsall | L 0-1 | 0-0 | | 2684 |
| 40 | 24 | H | Carlisle U | D 0-0 | 0-0 | | 5809 |
| 41 | May 1 | A | Bristol C | L 1-2 | 0-1 | Lee | 3931 |
| 42 | 4 | H | Lincoln C | W 1-0 | 0-0 | Cascarino | 3245 |
| 43 | 8 | H | Oxford U | W 2-1 | 0-1 | Bruce, Weatherly | 4690 |
| 44 | 11 | A | Fulham | D 0-0 | 0-0 | | 7176 |
| 45 | 15 | A | Chesterfield | W 3-1 | 2-0 | Cascarino, Grewcock, Pollard (og) | 2259 |
| 46 | 18 | H | Reading | W 2-1 | 0-1 | Sharpe, Lee | 3920 |

**Final League Position: 6**

### Goalscorers

*League* (64): Price 12, White 12 (3 pens), Lee 8, Bruce 6, Bowman 5 (2 pens), Cascarino 5, Adams 2, Duncan 2, Kemp 2, Sitton 2, Grewcock 1, Powell 1, Sharpe 1, Tydeman 1, Weatherly 1, Westwood 1, own goals 2.
*League Cup* (1): Price 1.
*FA Cup* (7): White 2 (1 pen), Bowman 1, Bruce 1, Kemp 1, Powell 1, Price 1.

| | | | |
|---|---|---|---|
| **League Cup** | First Round | Colchester U (a) | 0-2 |
| | | (h) | 1-1 |
| **FA Cup** | First Round | Plymouth Arg (a) | 0-0 |
| | | (h) | 1-0 |
| | Second Round | Barking (h) | 1-1 |
| | | (a) | 3-1 |
| | Third Round | Oldham Ath (h) | 2-1 |
| | Fourth Round | WBA (h) | 0-1 |

| Sutton | Sharpe | Ford | Bruce | Weatherly | Bowman | Powell | Duncan | Tydeman | Lee | Price | White | Young | Adams | Hillyard | Sitton | Westwood | Ovard | Bottiglieri | Kemp | Donn | Cascarino | Miller | Shaw | Grewcock | Sage | Match No. |
|---|---|---|---|---|---|---|---|---|---|---|---|---|---|---|---|---|---|---|---|---|---|---|---|---|---|---|
| 1 | 2 | 3 | 4 | 5 | 6 | 7 | 8 | 9 | 10 | 11* | 12 | | | | | | | | | | | | | | | 1 |
| 1 | | 3 | 4 | 5 | 6 | 7* | 8 | 9 | 10 | 11 | | 2 | 12 | | | | | | | | | | | | | 2 |
| | 2 | 3 | 4 | 5 | 6 | 7 | 8* | 9 | 10 | 11 | 12 | | | 1 | | | | | | | | | | | | 3 |
| | | 3 | 4 | 5 | 6 | 7 | 8 | 9 | | 11 | | | | 1 | 2 | 10 | | | | | | | | | | 4 |
| | | 3 | 4 | 5 | 6 | 7 | 8 | 9 | | 11 | | | 12 | 1 | 2 | 10* | | | | | | | | | | 5 |
| | | 3 | 4 | 5 | 6 | 7* | 8 | 9 | 12 | 11 | | | | 1 | 2 | 10 | | | | | | | | | | 6 |
| 12 | | 3 | 4 | 5 | 6 | | 8 | 9* | 10 | 11 | | 7 | | 1 | 2 | | | | | | | | | | | 7 |
| | | 3 | 4 | 5 | 6 | | 8 | 9 | 10 | 11 | | 7 | | 1 | 2 | | | | | | | | | | | 8 |
| | | 3 | 4 | 5 | 6 | | 8 | | 10 | 11 | 9 | 7 | | 1 | 2 | | | | | | | | | | | 9 |
| 12 | | 3 | 4 | 5 | 6 | 7* | 8 | | 10 | 11 | 9 | | | 1 | 2 | | | | | | | | | | | 10 |
| | 2 | 3 | 4 | 5 | 6 | 7 | 8 | | 10 | 11 | 9 | | | 1 | | | | | | | | | | | | 11 |
| | 2 | 3 | 4 | 5 | 6 | 7 | 8 | | 10 | 11 | 9 | | | 1 | | | | | | | | | | | | 12 |
| | 2 | 3 | 4 | 5 | 6 | 7 | 8 | | 10 | 11 | 9 | | | 1 | | | | | | | | | | | | 13 |
| | 2 | 3 | 4 | 5 | 6 | 7* | 8 | | 10 | 11 | 9 | | | 1 | | | 12 | | | | | | | | | 14 |
| | 2 | 3 | 4 | 5 | 6 | 7 | 8 | 12 | 10* | 11 | 9 | | | 1 | | | | | | | | | | | | 15 |
| | 2 | 3 | 4 | 5 | 6 | 7 | 8 | | 10 | 11 | 9 | | | 1 | | | | | | | | | | | | 16 |
| | 2 | 3 | 4 | 5 | 6 | 7 | 12 | 8 | | 11 | 9 | | | 1 | | | | 10* | | | | | | | | 17 |
| | 2 | 3* | 4 | 5 | 6 | 7 | | 8 | 10 | 11 | 9 | | | 1 | | | 12 | | | | | | | | | 18 |
| | 2 | 3 | 4 | 5 | | 7 | 8 | 6 | | 11 | 9 | | | 1 | | | 10 | | | | | | | | | 19 |
| | 2 | | 4 | | | | 6 | 8 | | 11 | 9 | 12 | 3 | 1 | 5 | | 7* | | | | 10 | | | | | 20 |
| | 2 | | 4 | | | 7 | 6 | 8* | | 11 | 9 | | 3 | 1 | 5 | | | | | | 10 | 12 | | | | 21 |
| | 2 | | 4 | | 6 | 7* | 8 | | | | 9 | | 3 | 1 | 5 | | | | 12 | | 10 | 11 | | | | 22 |
| | 2 | | 4 | | | | 6 | 8 | | | 9 | | 3 | 1 | 5 | | | | | | 10 | 11 | 7 | | | 23 |
| | 2 | | 4 | | | | 6 | 8 | | 11 | 9 | | 3 | 1 | 5 | | | | | | 10 | 12 | 7* | | | 24 |
| | 2 | | 4 | | | 7 | 6 | 8 | | 11 | 9* | | 3 | 1 | 5 | | | | | | 10 | 12 | | | | 25 |
| | 2 | | 4 | | | 7 | 6 | 8 | | 11 | | | 3 | 1 | | | | | | | 10 | 12 | 9* | 5 | | 26 |
| | 2 | | 4 | | | 7 | 6 | 8 | | 11 | | | 3 | 1 | | | | | | | 10 | 12 | 9* | 5 | | 27 |
| | 2 | | 4 | | | 7 | | 8 | | 11 | 9 | | 3 | 1 | 12 | | 6* | | | | 10 | | 5 | | | 28 |
| | 2 | | 4 | | | | | 8 | | 11 | 9 | | 3 | 1 | 6 | | 7 | 12 | | | 10* | | 5 | | | 29 |
| | 2 | | 4 | | | | | 8 | | 11 | 9 | | 3 | 1 | 6 | | 7 | | | | 10 | | 5 | | | 30 |
| | 2 | | 4 | 12 | | | | 8 | | 11 | 9 | | 3 | 1 | 6 | | 7* | | | | 10 | | 5 | | | 31 |
| | 2 | | 4 | 5 | | | | 8 | | 11 | 9 | | 3 | 1 | 7 | | | | | | 10 | | 6 | | | 32 |
| | 2 | | 4 | 5 | | | | 8 | | 11 | 9 | | 3 | 1 | 7 | | | | | | 10 | | 6 | | | 33 |
| | 2 | | 4 | 5 | | | | 8 | | 11 | 9 | | 3 | 1 | 7 | | | | | | 10 | | 6* | 12 | | 34 |
| | 2 | | 4 | 5 | | 7* | | 8 | | 11 | 9 | | 3 | 1 | 6 | | | | | | 12 | | 10 | | | 35 |
| | 2 | | 4 | 5 | | 7 | | 8* | 12 | 11 | | | 3 | 1 | 6 | | | | | | 10 | | 9 | | | 36 |
| | 2 | | 4 | 5 | | 7 | | 8 | | 11 | | | 3 | 1 | 6 | | | | | | 10 | | 9 | | | 37 |
| | 2 | | 4 | 5 | | 7 | | 8* | | 11 | 12 | | 3 | 1 | 6 | | | | | | 10 | | 9 | | | 38 |
| | 2 | | | 5 | | 7 | | 8 | 12 | 11 | | | 3 | 1 | 6 | | | | | | 10* | | 4 | 9 | | 39 |
| | 2 | | 4 | 5 | | 7 | | 8 | 10* | 11 | 12 | | 3 | 1 | | | | | | | | | 6 | 9 | | 40 |
| | | | 4 | 5 | | 7 | | 8 | | 11 | 2 | | 3 | 1 | | | | | | | 10 | | 6* | 9 | 12 | 41 |
| | 2 | | 4 | 5 | | 7 | | 8 | | 11 | | | 3 | 1 | 6 | | | | | | 10 | | 9 | | | 42 |
| | 2 | | 4 | 9 | | 7 | | 8* | 12 | | | | 3 | 1 | 6 | | | | | | 10 | | 5 | 11 | | 43 |
| | 2 | | 4 | 9 | | 7 | | 8 | | | | | 3 | 1 | 6 | | | | | | 10 | | 5 | 11 | | 44 |
| | 2 | | 4 | | | 7 | | 9 | 8 | | | | 3 | 1 | 6 | | | | | | 10 | | 5 | 11 | | 45 |
| | 2 | | 4 | | | 7* | | 8 | 9 | | | | 3 | 1 | 6 | | | | | | 10 | 12 | 5 | 11 | | 46 |
| 2 | 37 | 20 | 45 | 32 | 18 | 34 | 24 | 32 | 24 | 39 | 27 | 1 | 29 | 44 | 29 | 3 | 4 | 2 | 9 | — | 19 | 4 | 16 | 12 | — | |

+ 2s | + 1s | + 1s | + 1s | + 3s | + 5s | + 1s | + 2s | + 1s | + 2s 2s | + 1s 5s | + 1s | + 1s 1s

## GILLINGHAM

| | Ht | Wt | Birthplace | Clubs | League App. | League Gls |
|---|---|---|---|---|---|---|
| **Goalkeepers** | | | | | | |
| Ron Hillyard | 5 11 | 11 4 | Rotherham | York C | 61 | — |
| | | | | Hartlepool (on loan) | 23 | — |
| | | | | Bury (on loan) | — | — |
| | | | | Brighton (on loan) | — | — |
| | | | | Gillingham | 332 | — |
| Gary Sutton | 5 10½ | 11 0 | Folkestone | Gillingham | 11 | — |
| **Defenders** | | | | | | |
| Charles Young* | 6 1 | 11 12 | Nicosia | Aston V | 10 | — |
| | | | | Gillingham | 28 | 1 |
| John Sharpe | 5 11 | 11 5 | Portsmouth | Southampton | 21 | — |
| | | | | Gillingham | 138 | 2 |
| Andy Ford* | 5 11 | 12 0 | Minehead | Bournemouth | | |
| | | | | Southend U | 138 | 3 |
| | | | | Swindon T | 98 | — |
| | | | | Gillingham | 62 | 3 |
| Mark Weatherly | 6 0 | 11 12 | Ramsgate | Gillingham | 231 | 15 |
| John Sitton | 5 11 | 12 4 | Hackney | Chelsea | 13 | — |
| | | | | Millwall | 45 | 1 |
| | | | | Gillingham | 30 | 2 |
| Peter Shaw | 6 2½ | 13 11 | Northolt | Charlton Ath | 105 | 5 |
| | | | | Exeter C (on loan) | 3 | — |
| | | | | Gillingham | 16 | — |
| Mick Adams | 5 6 | 10 4 | Sheffield | Gillingham | 48 | 2 |
| Melvyn Sage | 5 8 | 10 4 | Gillingham | Gillingham | 1 | — |
| **Midfield** | | | | | | |
| John Overton | 5 11 | 10 10 | Rotherham | Aston V | 3 | — |
| | | | | Halifax T (on loan) | 14 | 2 |
| | | | | Gillingham | 178 | 10 |
| Steve Bruce | 6 0 | 11 2 | Durham | Gillingham | 126 | 15 |
| Nigel Donn | 5 10 | 10 8 | Maidstone | Gillingham | 3 | — |
| (Contract cancelled April 1982) | | | | | | |
| Colin Duncan | 5 10½ | 11 0 | Plymouth | Oxford U | 189 | 6 |
| | | | | Gillingham | 76 | 3 |
| Trevor Lee | 5 11 | 11 7 | London | Millwall | 108 | 22 |
| | | | | Colchester U | 96 | 35 |
| | | | | Gillingham | 45 | 14 |
| Richie Bowman | 5 6 | 10 7 | Lewisham | Charlton Ath | 96 | 7 |
| | | | | Reading | 194 | 30 |
| | | | | Gillingham | 18 | 5 |
| Dick Tydeman | 6 2 | 12 6 | Gillingham | Gillingham | 295 | 12 |
| | | | | Charlton Ath | 158 | 7 |
| | | | | Gillingham | 33 | 1 |
| Tony Bottiglieri | 5 9½ | 10 4 | Gillingham | Gillingham | 9 | — |
| **Forwards** | | | | | | |
| Danny Westwood | 5 10½ | 11 5 | Dagenham | QPR | 1 | 1 |
| (Contract cancelled April 1982) | | | | Gillingham | 211 | 74 |
| Ken Price | 5 10½ | 11 3 | Dudley | Southend U | 1 | — |
| | | | | Gillingham | 235 | 78 |
| Pat Walker | 5 9½ | 11 2 | Dublin | Gillingham | 51 | 3 |
| (Contract cancelled April 1982) | | | | | | |
| Dean White | 5 10 | 11 4 | Hastings | Chelsea | — | — |
| | | | | Gillingham | 102 | 23 |
| David Young | 5 10½ | 11 0 | Rochester | Gillingham | — | — |
| (Contract cancelled Jan 1982) | | | | | | |
| Colin Powell | 5 10 | 11 13½ | Hendon | Stevenage | (not known) | |
| | | | | Barnet | (not known) | |
| | | | | New England TM | (not known) | |
| | | | | Charlton Ath | 321 | 30 |
| | | | | Gillingham | 34 | 1 |
| Mark Miller | 5 8 | 10 10 | Newcastle | Whitley Bay | (not known) | |
| | | | | Gillingham | 5 | — |
| Frank Ovard | 5 9 | 10 10 | Folkestone | Maidstone U | (not known) | |
| (Contract cancelled April 1982) | | | | Gillingham | 6 | — |
| Tony Cascarino | 6 2 | 11 10 | Swanley | Crockenhill | (not known) | |
| | | | | Gillingham | 24 | 5 |

# GRIMSBY TOWN                     Division 2

*Chairman:* R. K. Middleton.

*Vice-Chairman:* T. J. Lindley.

*Directors:* T. Wilkinson, T. W. Bygott, D. B. Ramsden, W. R. Ramsden, P. Sheffield, D. P. Everitt FCA.

*Manager:* David Booth.   *Secretary:* D. J. Dowse.

*Year Formed:* 1878.   *Turned Professional:* 1890.

*Limited Company:* 1890.   *Previous Name:* Grimsby Pelham.

*Previous Grounds:* Clee Park; Abbey Park.

**Football League Record:**
1892 Original Member Division 2; 1901–03 Division 1; 1903 Division 2; 1910 Failed Re-election; 1911 Re-elected Division 2; 1920–21 Division 3; 1921–26 Division 3(N); 1926–29 Division 2; 1929–32 Division 1; 1932–34 Division 2; 1934–48 Division 1; 1948–51 Division 2; 1951–56 Division 3(N); 1956–59 Division 2; 1959–62 Division 3; 1962–64 Division 2; 1964–68 Division 3; 1968–72 Division 4; 1972–77 Division 3; 1977–79 Division 4; 1979–80 Division 3; 1980– Division 2.

**Honours:** *Football League:* Division 1 best season: 5th, 1934–35; Division 2 – Champions 1900–01, 1933–34; Runners-up 1928–29; Division 3(N) – Champions 1925–26, 1955–56; Runners-up 1951–52; Division 3 – Champions 1979–80; Runners-up 1961–62; Division 4 – Champions 1971–72; Runners-up 1978–79. *FA Cup:* Semi-finals, 1936, 1939. *Football League Cup* best season: 5th rd, 1979–80. *League Group Cup:* 1981–82.

*Record Victory:* 9-2 v Darwen, Division 2, 15 Apr, 1899.

*Record Defeat:* 1-9 v Arsenal, Division 1, 28 Jan, 1931.

*Most League Points:* 68, Division 3(N), 1955–56.

*Most League Goals:* 103, Division 2, 1933–34.

*Highest League Scorer in Season:* Pat Glover, 42, Division 2, 1933–34.

*Most League Goals in Total Aggregate:* Pat Glover, 182, 1930–39.

*Most Capped Player:* Pat Glover, 7, Wales.

*Most League Appearances:* Keith Jobling, 448, 1953–69.

*Record Transfer Fee Received:* £125,000 from Aston Villa for Terry Donovan, July 1979.

*Record Transfer Fee Paid:* £80,000 to Vancouver Whitecaps for Trevor Whymark, Dec 1980.

*Previous Managers since the War:* Charlie Spencer, Bill Shankly, Billy Walsh, Allenby Chilton, Tim Ward, Tom Johnston, Jimmy McGuigan, Don McEvoy, Bill Harvey, Bobby Kennedy, Lawrie McMenemy, Ron Ashman, Tommy Casey, John Newman, George Kerr.

*Address of Supporters Club:* Souvenir Shop, Blundell Park, Cleethorpes DN35 7PY.

---

**Blundell Park, Cleethorpes, South Humberside DN35 7PY.** Telephone Cleethorpes (0472) 691420. *Telegraphic address:* 'Football Grimsby'. *Ground capacity:* 22,000. *Record attendance:* 31,657 v Wolverhampton W, FA Cup 5th rd, 20 Feb, 1937. *Record receipts:* £29,228, v Wolverhampton W, FL Cup 5th rd, 4 Dec, 1979. *Pitch measurements:* 111yd×74yd.
*How to get there:* Buses 3A, 3F, 9 run to the ground; also football specials from the town centre. Nearest railway stations are Cleethorpes and Grimsby Town.
*Match tickets:* Seating can be booked two weeks in advance.
*Car parking:* Parking permitted in all side streets around the ground.
*Entertainments/catering facilities:* A licensed bar and several snack bars.
*Club shop:* There are 5 club shops, around the ground, selling all types of souvenir.
*Handbooks/programmes:* Programmes on sale at matches, and souvenir shops.
*Extra information:* Grimsby have played in all six divisions of the Football League – First, Second, Third, Third South, Third North and Fourth.
*Club Colours:* Black and white striped shirts, black shorts, white stockings.
*Change Colours:* Red shirts, red shorts and red stockings.
*Club Captain:* Joe Waters.
*Coach:*
*Club Nickname:* The Mariners.

## GRIMSBY TOWN 1981–82 LEAGUE RECORD

| Match No. | Date | Venue | Opponents | Result | H/T Score | Goalscorers | Attendance |
|---|---|---|---|---|---|---|---|
| 1 | Aug 29 | H | Leicester C | D 2-2 | 1-1 | Kilmore, Drinkell | 11,032 |
| 2 | Sept 1 | A | Watford | W 2-0 | 0-0 | Ford 2 | 11,257 |
| 3 | 5 | A | Orient | W 2-1 | 2-1 | Ford, Kilmore | 3764 |
| 4 | 12 | H | QPR | W 2-1 | 2-0 | Cumming 2 | 9490 |
| 5 | 19 | A | Charlton Ath | L 0-2 | 0-1 | | 6075 |
| 6 | 22 | H | Norwich C | L 1-2 | 0-2 | Whymark | 10,185 |
| 7 | 26 | H | Sheffield W | L 0-1 | 0-0 | | 13,110 |
| 8 | Oct 3 | A | Bolton W | W 2-1 | 1-0 | Drinkell, Mitchell | 7217 |
| 9 | 10 | H | Cambridge U | L 1-2 | 0-1 | Ford | 7450 |
| 10 | 17 | A | Luton T | L 0-6 | 0-3 | | 9090 |
| 11 | 24 | H | Blackburn R | D 1-1 | 0-1 | Wigginton | 7450 |
| 12 | 31 | A | Derby Co | D 1-1 | 0-1 | Moore K. | 11,706 |
| 13 | Nov 7 | A | Wrexham | L 0-2 | 0-0 | | 3351 |
| 14 | 21 | A | Chelsea | D 1-1 | 1-1 | Ford | 11,931 |
| 15 | 28 | H | Newcastle U | D 1-1 | 1-1 | Mitchell | 9257 |
| 16 | Dec 5 | A | Oldham Ath | L 1-3 | 1-1 | Ford | 5907 |
| 17 | Jan 9 | H | Orient | L 1-2 | 0-1 | Waters | 6877 |
| 18 | 30 | A | Charlton Ath | D 3-3 | 2-1 | Moore K., Drinkell 2 | 7088 |
| 19 | Feb 6 | A | QPR | L 0-1 | 0-1 | | 8753 |
| 20 | 9 | H | Rotherham U | L 1-2 | 1-0 | Waters (pen) | 8629 |
| 21 | 20 | A | Sheffield W | D 1-1 | 1-1 | Waters (pen) | 14,654 |
| 22 | 27 | A | Cambridge U | D 2-2 | 0-0 | Brolly, Drinkell | 3542 |
| 23 | Mar 2 | H | Bolton W | D 1-1 | 0-1 | Waters | 6525 |
| 24 | 6 | H | Luton T | D 0-0 | 0-0 | | 7733 |
| 25 | 13 | A | Blackburn R | L 0-2 | 0-1 | | 8676 |
| 26 | 16 | H | Watford | L 0-2 | 0-0 | | 6146 |
| 27 | 20 | H | Derby Co | W 1-0 | 1-0 | Kilmore | 7573 |
| 28 | 23 | A | Barnsley | L 2-3 | 0-2 | Drinkell, Whymark | 15,383 |
| 29 | 27 | H | Wrexham | D 1-1 | 0-0 | Kilmore | 6216 |
| 30 | 30 | A | Cardiff C | L 1-2 | 1-2 | Whymark (pen) | 3924 |
| 31 | Apr 3 | A | Crystal Palace | W 3-0 | 1-0 | Kilmore, Moore K., Whymark | 7541 |
| 32 | 9 | H | Barnsley | W 3-2 | 0-2 | Whymark, Moore K., Waters | 12,338 |
| 33 | 10 | A | Rotherham U | D 2-2 | 1-1 | Whymark, Ford | 10,011 |
| 34 | 17 | H | Chelsea | D 3-3 | 1-2 | Moore D., Cooper, Kilmore | 9164 |
| 35 | 20 | H | Crystal Palace | L 0-1 | 0-1 | | 7646 |
| 36 | 24 | A | Newcastle U | W 1-0 | 0-0 | Brolly | 14,101 |
| 37 | 27 | H | Shrewsbury T | W 5-1 | 1-1 | Whymark, Waters (pen), Crosby, Brolly, Moore D. | 7051 |
| 38 | May 1 | H | Oldham Ath | W 2-1 | 1-0 | Whymark, Waters (pen) | 7656 |
| 39 | 5 | A | Norwich C | L 1-2 | 0-0 | Whymark | 18,360 |
| 40 | 8 | A | Shrewsbury T | L 0-2 | 0-1 | | 4036 |
| 41 | 12 | A | Leicester C | W 2-1 | 2-0 | Whymark 2 | 13,914 |
| 42 | 15 | H | Cardiff C | L 0-1 | 0-0 | | 8148 |

**Final League Position: 17**

**Goalscorers**

*League* (53): Whymark 11 (1 pen), Ford 7, Waters 7 (4 pens), Drinkell 6, Kilmore 6, Moore K. 4, Brolly 3, Cumming 2, Mitchell 2, Moore D. 2, Cooper 1, Crosby 1, Wigginton 1.
*League Cup* (2): Moore K. 1, Whymark 1.
*FA Cup* (9): Drinkell 3, Cumming 2, Brolly 1, Kilmore 1, Moore K. 1, Whymark 1.

| | | | |
|---|---|---|---|
| **League Cup** | Second Round | Watford (h) | 1-0 |
| | | (a) | 1-3 |
| **FA Cup** | Third Round | Millwall (a) | 6-1 |
| | Fourth Round | Newcastle U (a) | 2-1 |
| | Fifth Round | QPR (a) | 1-3 |

| Batch | Stone | Crombie | Waters | Wigginton | Moore K. | Brolly | Whymark | Drinkell | Mitchell | Kilmore | Ford | Cumming | Moore D. | Czuczman | Steeples | Ward | Beacock | O'Dell | Crosby | Cooper | Match No. |
|---|---|---|---|---|---|---|---|---|---|---|---|---|---|---|---|---|---|---|---|---|---|
| 1 | 2 | 3 | 4 | 5 | 6 | 7* | 8 | 9 | 10 | 11 | 12 | | | | | | | | | | 1 |
| 1 | 2 | 3 | 4 | 5 | 6 | 7 | 8* | 9 | 10 | 11 | 12 | | | | | | | | | | 2 |
| 1 | 2 | 3 | 4 | 5 | 6 | 7 | | 9 | 10 | 11* | 8 | 12 | | | | | | | | | 3 |
| 1 | 2 | 3 | 4 | 5 | 6 | 7 | | 9 | 10* | 12 | 8 | 11 | | | | | | | | | 4 |
| 1 | 2 | 3* | 4 | 5 | 6 | | 8 | 9 | 10 | 12 | 7 | 11 | | | | | | | | | 5 |
| 1 | 2 | 3* | 4 | 5 | 6 | 7 | 8 | 9 | 10 | 12 | | 11 | | | | | | | | | 6 |
| 1 | | 3 | 4 | 5 | 6 | 7 | 8 | 9 | 10 | 12 | | 11* | 2 | | | | | | | | 7 |
| 1 | | 3 | 4 | 5 | 6 | 7 | 8 | 9 | 10 | | 12 | 11* | 2 | | | | | | | | 8 |
| 1 | | 3 | 4 | | 6 | 7 | 8 | 9* | 10 | | 12 | 11 | 2 | 5 | | | | | | | 9 |
| 1 | | 3 | 4 | | 6 | 7 | 8 | 9 | 10 | 12 | 11* | | 2 | 5 | | | | | | | 10 |
| 1 | 2* | 3 | 4 | 5 | 6 | | 9 | | 10 | 12 | 8 | 11 | | | 7 | | | | | | 11 |
| 1 | | 3 | 4* | 5 | 6 | 12 | 9 | | 10 | | 7 | 11 | 2 | | | 8 | | | | | 12 |
| 1 | | 3 | | 5 | 6 | 4 | 9 | | 10 | 8 | 7 | 11* | 2 | | | | 12 | | | | 13 |
| 1 | | | 5 | 3 | 7 | 9 | 12 | 10 | | 11 | | 2 | 6 | | | | 8 | 4* | | | 14 |
| 1 | | 3 | | 5 | 6 | 7 | | 9 | 10 | | 8 | 11 | 2 | | | | 12 | 4* | | | 15 |
| 1 | | 3 | | 5 | 6 | 7 | | 9 | 12 | 10 | 8 | 11 | 2 | | | | | 4* | | | 16 |
| 1 | | 3 | 4 | 5 | 6 | 7* | 8 | | 10 | 12 | 9 | 11 | 2 | | | | | | | | 17 |
| 1 | 4 | 3 | | | 5 | 12 | | 9 | 10 | 8 | 7 | | 2 | | | | 11* | | 6 | | 18 |
| 1 | 4 | 12 | 5 | | 6 | 11 | | 9 | 10 | 8 | 7* | | 2 | | | | | | 3 | | 19 |
| 1 | 7 | | 4 | 5 | 6 | 11* | | 9 | 10 | 8 | 12 | | 2 | | | | | | 3 | | 20 |
| 1 | 7 | 3 | 4 | 5 | 6 | 11 | | 9 | 10 | | 8 | | 2 | | | | | | | | 21 |
| 1 | 7 | 3 | 4 | 5 | 6 | 11 | | 9 | 10 | | 8 | | 2 | | | | | | | | 22 |
| 1 | | 3 | 4 | 5 | 6 | 11 | | 9 | 10 | | 8 | | 2* | 12 | | 7 | | | | | 23 |
| 1 | | 3 | 4 | | 6 | 7 | | 9 | 10 | | 8 | 11 | 2 | | | | | | | 5 | 24 |
| 1 | | 3 | 4 | | 6 | 7 | 12 | 9 | | | 8* | 11 | 2 | | | | 10 | | | 5 | 25 |
| 1 | | 3 | 4 | | 6 | 7 | 12 | 9 | | | 8 | 11* | 2 | | | | 10 | | | 5 | 26 |
| 1 | | 3 | 4 | | 6 | 7 | 12 | 9 | | | 8* | 11 | 2 | | | | 10 | | | 5 | 27 |
| 1 | | 3 | 4 | | 6 | 7 | 12 | 9 | | | 8 | 11* | 2 | | | | 10 | | | 5 | 28 |
| 1 | | 3 | 4 | | 6 | 7 | 12 | 9 | | | 8 | 11 | 2 | | | | 10* | | | 5 | 29 |
| 1 | 4 | 3 | | | 6 | 7 | | 9 | 10 | 8 | 12 | 11 | 2 | | | | | | | 5* | 30 |
| 1 | 5 | 3* | 4 | | 6 | 7 | | 9 | 10 | | 8 | 11 | 2 | | | | | | 12 | | 31 |
| 1 | 5 | | 4 | | 6 | 7* | | 9 | 10 | 8 | 12 | 11 | 2 | | | | | | 3 | | 32 |
| 1 | | 6 | 4 | | 11 | | 9* | | 10 | 8 | 7 | | 2 | | | | 12 | | 3 | 5 | 33 |
| 1 | | 6 | 4 | | 11 | | 9 | 12 | 10 | 8 | 7 | | 2* | | | | | | 3 | 5 | 34 |
| 1 | | 6 | 4 | | 11 | | 9 | 12 | 10* | 8 | 7 | | 2 | | | | | | 3 | 5 | 35 |
| 1 | 7 | 6 | 4 | | 11 | | 9 | | | 8* | 12 | | 2 | | | | 10 | | 3 | 5 | 36 |
| 1 | 7 | 6 | 4 | | 10* | 11 | 9 | | | 8 | 12 | | 2 | | | | | | 3 | 5 | 37 |
| 1 | 7 | 6 | 4 | | 10 | 11* | 9 | | | 8 | 12 | | 2 | | | | | | 3 | 5 | 38 |
| 1 | 2 | 6 | 4 | | 10* | 11 | 9 | | | 8 | 7 | | 2 | | | | 12 | | 3 | 5 | 39 |
| 1 | 10 | 6 | 4 | | 12 | 9 | 8 | | | | 7 | 11* | 2 | | | | | | 3 | 5 | 40 |
| 1 | 7 | 6 | 4 | | | 9 | | | | 8 | | 11 | 2 | | | | 10 | | 3 | 5 | 41 |
| 1 | | 6 | 4 | 5 | | | 9 | 12 | | 8 | 7 | 11 | 2 | | | | 10* | | 3 | | 42 |
| 42 | 21 | 38 | 35 | 20 | 36 | 35 | 28 | 23 | 30 | 23 | 25 | 23 | 34 | 3 | 1 | 2 | 10 | 3 | 14 | 16 | |

+1s (Stone); +3s (Moore K.), +5s (Brolly), +5s (Whymark); +7s (Mitchell), +10s (Kilmore), +1s (Ford); +1s (Ward), +1s (Beacock), +3s (O'Dell); +1s (Crosby)

# GRIMSBY TOWN

| | Ht | Wt | Birthplace | Clubs | League App. | League Gls |
|---|---|---|---|---|---|---|
| **Goalkeepers** | | | | | | |
| Nigel Batch | 5 10 | 12 5 | Huddersfield | Grimsby T | 194 | — |
| Len Robinson* | 5 10 | 12 0 | Bridlington | Brigg T | (not known) | |
| | | | | Grimsby T | — | — |
| Peter Grotier | 5 11 | 12 10 | West Ham | West Ham U | 50 | — |
| | | | | Cardiff C (on loan) | 2 | — |
| | | | | Lincoln C | 233 | — |
| | | | | Cardiff C | 38 | — |
| | | | | Grimsby T | — | — |
| **Defenders** | | | | | | |
| Kevin Moore | 5 11 | 11 7 | Grimsby | Grimsby T | 234 | 15 |
| David Moore | 5 10 | 12 13 | Grimsby | Grimsby T | 98 | 2 |
| Clive Wigginton* | 6 0 | 12 1 | Sheffield | Grimsby T | 171 | 6 |
| | | | | Scunthorpe U | 88 | 7 |
| | | | | Lincoln C | 60 | 6 |
| | | | | Grimsby T | 122 | 2 |
| | | | | Doncaster R (on loan) | 13 | 1 |
| Dean Crombie | 5 11 | 11 7 | Lincoln | Lincoln C | 33 | — |
| | | | | Grimsby T | 156 | 1 |
| John Stone | 6 0 | 12 5 | Saltburn, Yorks | Middlesbrough | 2 | — |
| | | | | York C | 86 | 5 |
| | | | | Darlington | 120 | 14 |
| | | | | Grimsby T | 82 | 2 |
| Phil Crosby | | | Leeds | Grimsby T | 29 | 1 |
| Jimmy Fell* | 5 10 | 12 0 | Newcastle | Grimsby T | — | — |
| Neil Cooper | 5 10½ | 11 1 | Aberdeen | Aberdeen | 12 | 1 |
| | | | | Barnsley | 60 | 6 |
| | | | | Grimsby T | 16 | 1 |
| **Midfield** | | | | | | |
| Bob Cumming | 5 8 | 11 4 | Airdrie | Grimsby T | 235 | 41 |
| Joe Waters | 5 5 | 10 5 | Limerick | Leicester C | 13 | 1 |
| (Eire) | | | | Grimsby T | 280 | 50 |
| Bob Mitchell* | 5 10 | 11 0 | S Shields | Sunderland | 3 | — |
| | | | | Blackburn R | 29 | 6 |
| | | | | Grimsby T | 142 | 6 |
| Andy O'Dell | 5 8 | 10 8 | Hull | Grimsby T | 3 | — |
| **Forwards** | | | | | | |
| Tony Ford | 5 9 | 12 2 | Grimsby | Grimsby T | 199 | 33 |
| Mike Brolly | 5 9 | 10 4 | Kilmarnock | Chelsea | 8 | 1 |
| | | | | Bristol C | 30 | 2 |
| | | | | Grimsby T | 254 | 27 |
| Kevin Drinkell | 5 10 | 11 10 | Grimsby | Grimsby T | 160 | 43 |
| Kevin Kilmore | 5 9 | 11 10 | Scunthorpe | Scunthorpe U | 102 | 28 |
| | | | | Grimsby T | 84 | 23 |
| Garry Beacock | 5 10 | 11 10 | Scunthorpe | Grimsby T | 15 | — |
| John Steeples | 5 10 | 11 13 | Doncaster | Grimsby T | 7 | — |
| Trevor Whymark | 6 0 | 11 0 | Norfolk | Ipswich T | 260 | 74 |
| (England) | | | | Vancouver W | (not known) | |
| | | | | Sparta Rotterdam | (not known) | |
| | | | | Derby Co | 2 | — |
| | | | | Grimsby T | 54 | 14 |

# HALIFAX TOWN Division 4

*Chairman:* J. Turner. *Vice-Chairman:* J. S. Crowther.

*Directors:* D. Sharp, M INST BM, P. Dawson, T. Dawson, J. Robinson, A. E. D. Pateman.

*Manager:* Mickey Bullock.

*Secretary:* Mrs Carol Bell.

*Commercial Manager:* Tony Thwaites.

*Year Formed:* 1911. *Turned Professional:* 1911.

*Limited Company:* 1911.

*Previous Grounds:* Sandhall and Exley.

**Football League Record:**
1921 Original Member; Division 3(N); 1958–63 Division 3; 1963–69 Division 4; 1969–76 Division 3; 1976– Division 4.

**Honours:** *Football League:* Division 3 best season: 3rd, 1970–71; Division 3(N) – Runners-up 1934–35; Division 4 – Runners-up 1968–69. *FA Cup* best season: 5th rd, 1932–33, 1952–53. *Football League Cup* best season: 4th rd, 1964.

*Record Victory:* 7-0 v Bishop Auckland, FA Cup 2nd rd replay, 10 Jan, 1967.

*Record Defeat:* 0-13 v Stockport Co, Division 3(N), 6 Jan, 1934.

*Most League Points:* 57, Division 4, 1968–69.

*Most League Goals:* 83, Division 3(N), 1957–58.

*Highest League Scorer in Season:* Albert Valentine, 34, Division 3(N), 1934–35.

*Most League Goals in Total Aggregate:* Ernest Dixon, 129, 1922–30.

*Most Capped Player:* None.

*Most League Appearances:* John Pickering, 367, 1965–74.

*Record Transfer Fee Received:* £55,000 from Huddersfield T for Mick Kennedy, Aug 1980.

*Record Transfer Fee Paid:* £25,000 to Huddersfield T for Kevin Johnson, Aug 1978.

*Previous Managers since the War:* Jack Breedon, W. Wootton, Jimmy Thomson, Gerald Henry, Bobby Browne, Willie Watson, Billy Burnicle, Harry Hooper, Willie Watson, Vic Metcalfe, Alan Ball (Snr), George Kirby, Ray Henderson, George Mulhall, John Quinn, Alan Ball (Snr), Jimmy Lawson, George Kirby.

*Address of Supporters Club:* Same as Football Club.

*Address of the Club Shop or Boutique:* Club Shop, 11 Horton Street, Halifax, Yorks.

---

**Shay Ground, Halifax HX1 2YS.** Telephone Halifax 53423. *Ground capacity:* 16,500. *Record attendance:* 36,885 v Tottenham H, FA Cup 5th rd, 14 Feb, 1953. *Record receipts:* £14,000 v Manchester C, FA Cup 3rd rd, 4 Jan, 1980. *Pitch measurements:* 110yd×70yd.

*How to get there:* Near the town centre within a few minutes walking distance of the bus station and railway station.

*Match tickets:* Advance booking on application to the secretary.

*Car parking:* Car park is available; entrance in Shaw Hill.

*Entertainments/catering facilities:* High-class restaurant and social club adjacent to club office.

*Club shop:* Shop on ground and also in town centre. Programmes, souvenirs, etc (wide range always available) from the Promotions Office, 11 Horton Street, Halifax. P & p must always accompany requests.

*Handbooks/programmes:* Handbooks and programmes available from Supporters Club, c/o Halifax Town AFC.

*Extra information:* In 1929, Halifax played a goalkeeper, Bob Suter, who was 47 years old.

*Club Colours:* Royal blue shirts with white trim, collar and cuffs, white shorts, blue trim, blue stockings with white tops.

*Change Colours:* Yellow shirts, blue trim, blue shorts, yellow stockings with blue tops.

*Team Captain:* Billy Ayre.

*Club Nickname:* The Shaymen.

## HALIFAX TOWN 1981–82 LEAGUE RECORD

| Match No. | Date | Venue | Opponents | Result | H/T Score | Goalscorers | Attendance |
|---|---|---|---|---|---|---|---|
| 1 | Aug 29 | A | Port Vale | D 0-0 | 0-0 | | 3382 |
| 2 | Sept 5 | H | Peterborough U | D 1-1 | 0-0 | Davison | 1809 |
| 3 | 12 | A | Aldershot | L 1-3 | 1-1 | Graham | 1733 |
| 4 | 19 | H | AFC Bournemouth | D 1-1 | 1-0 | Davison | 1588 |
| 5 | 22 | H | Tranmere R | L 0-2 | 0-2 | | 1943 |
| 6 | 26 | A | Hartlepool U | L 2-3 | 2-1 | Davison, McIlwraith | 1800 |
| 7 | 30 | A | Blackpool | L 1-7 | 0-2 | Davison | 5084 |
| 8 | Oct 3 | H | Bury | W 2-1 | 1-0 | Allatt, Graham | 2420 |
| 9 | 10 | A | Hereford U | D 2-2 | 1-1 | Davison, Graham | 2359 |
| 10 | 17 | H | Rochdale | D 0-0 | 0-0 | | 2140 |
| 11 | 20 | A | Darlington | D 1-1 | 0-0 | Graham | 1642 |
| 12 | 24 | H | Colchester U | L 0-2 | 0-1 | | 1374 |
| 13 | 31 | A | Crewe Alex | W 1-0 | 0-0 | Allatt | 2291 |
| 14 | Nov 3 | H | Torquay U | L 1-2 | 0-0 | Graham | 1523 |
| 15 | 7 | H | Mansfield T | W 2-1 | 2-0 | Evans, Allatt | 1447 |
| 16 | 13 | A | Stockport Co | L 1-2 | 1-1 | Allatt | 2493 |
| 17 | 28 | H | Scunthorpe U | L 1-2 | 1-1 | Graham | 1396 |
| 18 | Dec 5 | A | Wigan Ath | L 0-2 | 0-0 | | 4022 |
| 19 | Jan 2 | A | Sheffield U | D 2-2 | 0-1 | Ward 2 | 11,623 |
| 20 | 13 | A | Rochdale | W 1-0 | 1-0 | Davison | 1122 |
| 21 | 22 | H | Port Vale | D 1-1 | 0-1 | Ward | 2965 |
| 22 | 26 | A | Peterborough U | D 0-0 | 0-0 | | 3016 |
| 23 | 30 | A | AFC Bournemouth | D 1-1 | 1-0 | Ward | 4690 |
| 24 | Feb 6 | H | Aldershot | D 2-2 | 2-1 | Ayre, Davison | 1754 |
| 25 | 9 | A | Tranmere R | D 1-1 | 0-0 | Ayre | 1454 |
| 26 | 13 | A | Bury | D 1-1 | 0-1 | Ward | 3590 |
| 27 | 20 | H | Blackpool | D 0-0 | 0-0 | | 2245 |
| 28 | 27 | H | Hereford U | L 1-2 | 1-1 | Davison | 2098 |
| 29 | Mar 2 | A | Hull C | L 0-2 | 0-0 | | 6952 |
| 30 | 9 | H | Darlington | D 3-3 | 0-2 | Davison 2, Ayre | 1508 |
| 31 | 12 | A | Colchester U | D 1-1 | 1-1 | Ayre | 2464 |
| 32 | 20 | H | Crewe Alex | W 2-1 | 1-0 | Spooner, Ward | 2128 |
| 33 | 23 | H | Bradford C | D 0-0 | 0-0 | | 5926 |
| 34 | 27 | A | Mansfield T | L 2-3 | 1-1 | Davison 2 | 2197 |
| 35 | Apr 2 | H | Stockport Co | W 4-1 | 2-0 | Firth, Davison 2, Spooner | 2135 |
| 36 | 10 | A | Bradford C | L 2-5 | 0-2 | Davison, Graham | 5179 |
| 37 | 12 | H | Sheffield U | L 1-5 | 1-1 | Hendrie | 8077 |
| 38 | 17 | H | Wigan Ath | D 0-0 | 0-0 | | 3660 |
| 39 | 20 | A | Northampton T | W 1-0 | 0-0 | Graham | 1935 |
| 40 | 24 | A | Scunthorpe U | D 0-0 | 0-0 | | 1643 |
| 41 | 27 | A | Torquay U | D 2-2 | 1-2 | Davison 2 | 1331 |
| 42 | May 1 | H | Hartlepool U | W 2-0 | 1-0 | Evans, Ward | 1305 |
| 43 | 4 | H | Northampton T | W 2-1 | 0-1 | Davison 2 | 1730 |
| 44 | 7 | A | York C | L 0-4 | 0-1 | | 2423 |
| 45 | 11 | H | York C | D 0-0 | 0-0 | | 1903 |
| 46 | 14 | H | Hull C | D 2-2 | 1-1 | Davison, Hendrie | 2293 |

**Final League Position: 19**

### Goalscorers

*League* (51): Davison 20, Graham 8, Ward 7, Allatt 4, Ayre 4, Evans 2, Hendrie 2, Spooner 2, Firth 1, McIlwraith 1.
*League Cup* (1): Davison 1.
*FA Cup* (0).

| **League Cup** | First Round | Preston NE (h) | 1-2 |
|---|---|---|---|
| | | (a) | 0-0 |
| **FA Cup** | First Round | Peterborough U (h) | 0-3 |

| Kilner | Ward | Carr | Evans | Ayre | Hendrie | Graham | Davison | Allatt | Chamberlain | McIlwraith | Firth | Whiteley | O'Neil | Bullock | Smelt | Walker | Spooner | Kendall | Keys | Goodman | Match No. |
|---|---|---|---|---|---|---|---|---|---|---|---|---|---|---|---|---|---|---|---|---|---|
| 1 | 2 | 3 | 4 | 5 | 6 | 7 | 8 | 9 | 10 | 11 |  |  |  |  |  |  |  |  |  |  | 1 |
| 1 | 2 | 3 | 4 | 5 | 6 | 9 | 8 |  | 10 | 11 | 7 |  |  |  |  |  |  |  |  |  | 2 |
| 1 | 2 | 3 | 4 | 5 | 6 | 9 | 8* | 12 | 10 | 11 | 7 |  |  |  |  |  |  |  |  |  | 3 |
| 1 | 2 | 3 | 4 | 5 | 6 | 11 | 8 | 9* | 10 | 12 | 7 |  |  |  |  |  |  |  |  |  | 4 |
| 1 | 2 | 3 | 4 | 5 | 6 | 11 | 8 | 9* | 10 | 12 | 7 |  |  |  |  |  |  |  |  |  | 5 |
| 1 | 2 | 3 | 4 | 5 |  | 7 | 8 | 9 | 10 | 11* | 12 | 6 |  |  |  |  |  |  |  |  | 6 |
| 1 | 2 | 3 | 4 | 5 | 6 | 9 | 8 |  | 10 |  | 7* | 12 | 11 |  |  |  |  |  |  |  | 7 |
|  | 7 | 3 | 4 | 5 | 6 | 11 | 8 | 9 | 10 |  | 2 |  |  |  | 1 |  |  |  |  |  | 8 |
|  | 7 | 3 | 4 | 5 | 6 | 11 | 8 | 9 | 10 |  | 2 |  |  |  | 1 |  |  |  |  |  | 9 |
|  | 7 | 3 | 4 | 5 | 6 |  | 8 | 9 | 10 |  | 2 | 11 |  |  | 1 |  |  |  |  |  | 10 |
|  | 7 | 3 | 4* | 5 | 6 | 11 | 8 | 9 | 10 | 12 | 2 |  |  |  | 1 |  |  |  |  |  | 11 |
|  | 7 | 3 | 4 | 5 | 6 | 11 | 8 | 9 | 10 |  | 2 |  |  |  | 1 |  |  |  |  |  | 12 |
|  | 7* | 3 | 4 | 5 | 6 | 11 | 8 | 9 | 10 | 12 | 2 |  |  |  | 1 |  |  |  |  |  | 13 |
|  | 7 | 3 | 4 | 5 | 6 | 11* | 8 | 9 | 10 | 12 | 2 |  |  |  | 1 |  |  |  |  |  | 14 |
|  | 7 | 3 | 4 | 5 | 6 | 11 | 8 | 9 | 10 | 12 | 2* |  |  |  | 1 |  |  |  |  |  | 15 |
|  | 2 | 3 | 4 | 5 | 6 | 11 | 8 | 9 | 10* |  | 7 |  |  |  | 1 |  | 12 |  |  |  | 16 |
|  | 7 | 3 | 4 | 5 | 6 | 9 | 8 |  | 10 | 11 | 2 |  |  |  | 1 |  |  |  |  |  | 17 |
|  | 7 | 3 | 4 | 5 | 6 | 9* | 8 |  |  |  | 2 | 11 | 12 |  | 1 |  | 10 |  |  |  | 18 |
|  | 7 |  | 4 | 5 | 6 | 9 | 8 |  |  |  | 2 | 12 | 3 | 11* | 1 |  | 10 |  |  |  | 19 |
|  | 7 |  | 4 | 5 | 6 | 11 | 8* | 9 |  |  | 2 | 12 | 3 |  | 1 |  | 10 |  |  |  | 20 |
|  | 7 |  | 4 | 5 | 6 | 11 | 8 | 9* |  |  | 2 | 12 | 3 |  | 1 |  | 10 |  |  |  | 21 |
|  | 7* |  | 4 | 5 | 6 | 11 | 8 | 9 |  |  | 2 | 12 | 3 |  | 1 |  | 10 |  |  |  | 22 |
|  | 7 |  | 4 | 5 | 6 | 11 | 8 | 9* |  |  | 2 | 12 | 3 |  | 1 |  | 10 |  |  |  | 23 |
|  | 2 | 11* | 4 | 5 | 6 |  | 8 |  | 12 |  | 7 |  |  | 9 | 1 |  | 10 | 3 |  |  | 24 |
|  | 7 |  | 4 | 5 | 6 |  | 8 | 9* |  |  | 2 | 11 | 12 |  | 1 |  | 10 | 3 |  |  | 25 |
|  | 7 |  | 4 | 5 | 6 |  | 8 |  |  |  | 2 | 11 |  | 9 | 1 |  | 10 | 3 |  |  | 26 |
|  | 7 | 12 | 4 | 5 | 6 |  | 8 |  |  |  |  | 11 | 3 | 9 | 1 |  | 10 | 2* |  |  | 27 |
|  | 7 | 12 | 4 | 5 | 6 |  | 8 | 9 |  |  |  | 11 | 3 |  | 1 |  | 10 | 2* |  |  | 28 |
|  | 7 | 12 | 4 | 5 | 6 |  | 8 | 9 |  |  |  | 11 | 3 |  | 1 |  | 10 | 2* |  |  | 29 |
|  | 7 | 3 | 4 | 5 | 6 |  | 8 | 9 |  |  | 2 | 11 |  |  | 1 |  | 10 |  |  |  | 30 |
|  | 7 | 3 | 4 | 5 | 6 |  | 8 | 9 |  |  | 2 | 11 |  |  | 1 |  | 10 |  |  |  | 31 |
|  | 7 | 3 | 4 | 5 | 6 | 12 | 8 |  |  |  | 2 | 11* |  |  | 1 |  | 10 | 9 |  |  | 32 |
| 1 | 7 | 3 | 4 | 5 | 6 | 9 | 8 |  |  |  | 2 | 11 |  |  |  |  | 10 |  |  |  | 33 |
| 1 | 7 |  | 4 | 5 | 6 | 9 | 8 |  |  |  | 2 | 11 | 3* |  |  |  | 10 | 12 |  |  | 34 |
| 1 | 7 | 3 | 4 | 5 | 6 | 9 | 8 |  |  |  | 2 | 11 |  |  |  |  | 10 |  |  |  | 35 |
| 1 | 7* | 3 | 4 | 5 | 6 | 9 | 8 | 12 |  |  | 2 | 11 |  |  |  |  | 10 |  |  |  | 36 |
| 1 |  | 3 | 4 | 5 | 6 | 9 | 8 |  |  |  |  | 7 | 12 | 11 |  |  | 10 |  |  | 2* | 37 |
|  | 11* | 3 | 4 | 5 | 6 | 9 | 8 |  |  |  |  | 7 |  |  | 1 |  | 10 | 12 |  | 2 | 38 |
|  | 11 | 3 | 4 | 5* | 6 | 9 | 8 |  |  |  |  | 7 |  |  | 1 |  | 10 | 12 |  | 2 | 39 |
|  | 11* | 3 | 4 | 5 | 6 | 9 | 8 |  |  |  |  | 7 |  |  | 1 |  | 10 | 12 |  | 2 | 40 |
|  | 11 | 3 | 4 | 5 | 6 | 9 | 8 |  |  |  |  | 7 |  |  | 1 |  | 10 |  |  | 2 | 41 |
|  | 11 | 3 | 4 | 5 | 6 | 9 | 8 |  |  |  |  | 7 |  |  | 1 |  | 10 |  |  | 2 | 42 |
|  |  | 3 | 4 | 5 | 6 | 9 | 8 |  |  |  |  | 7 |  |  | 1 |  | 10 | 11 |  | 2 | 43 |
|  | 11 | 3 | 4* | 5 | 6 | 9 | 8 |  |  |  |  | 7 |  |  | 1 |  | 10 | 12 |  | 2 | 44 |
|  | 2 | 11 | 4 |  | 6 | 9 | 8 |  |  |  |  | 7 |  |  | 1 |  | 10 | 3 | 5 |  | 45 |
|  | 11 | 3 | 4 |  | 6 | 9 | 8 |  |  |  |  | 7 | 12 |  | 1 |  | 10 | 2* | 5 |  | 46 |
| 12 | 44 | 35 | 46 | 44 | 45 | 36 | 46 | 22 | 35 | 4 | 29 | 10 | 8 | 7 | 34 | — | 29 | 9 | 1 | 10 |  |

+ 3s    + 1s  + 2s   + + + + +   + 1s   + + 4s 1s
         3s        1s   2s   3s 8s 5s 1s 1s   1s

## HALIFAX TOWN

| | Ht | Wt | Birthplace | Clubs | League App. | League Gls |
|---|---|---|---|---|---|---|
| **Goalkeepers** | | | | | | |
| John Kilner* | 6 0 | 11 7 | Bolton | Preston NE | — | — |
| | | | | Halifax T | 114 | — |
| Lee Smelt | 6 1 | 13 2 | Edmonton | Colchester U | — | — |
| | | | | Gravesend | (not known) | |
| | | | | Nottingham F | 1 | — |
| | | | | Peterborough U (on loan) | 5 | — |
| | | | | Halifax T | 34 | — |
| **Defenders** | | | | | | |
| Billy Ayre | 5 11 | 12 10 | Crookhills | Scarborough | (not known) | |
| | | | | Hartlepool U | 141 | 27 |
| | | | | Halifax T | 63 | 5 |
| Malcolm Goodman | 6 2 | 12 12 | Bromsgrove | Halifax T | 61 | 1 |
| Dave Evans | 5 11 | 12 6 | West Bromwich | Aston V | 2 | — |
| | | | | Halifax T | 130 | 6 |
| Clive Nattress (Contract cancelled July 1981) | 6 0 | 12 4½ | Durham | Blackpool | — | — |
| | | | | Darlington | 302 | 15 |
| | | | | Halifax T | 37 | 5 |
| Ken Burton (Contract cancelled July 1981) | 5 7½ | 11 8 | Sheffield | Sheffield W | 56 | 2 |
| | | | | Peterborough U (on loan) | 4 | — |
| | | | | Chesterfield | 237 | 6 |
| | | | | Halifax T | 27 | 1 |
| Everton Carr* | 5 7 | 11 6 | Antigua | Leicester C | 12 | — |
| | | | | Halifax T | 38 | — |
| Paul Kendall (Apprentice) | 6 0 | 12 6 | Halifax | Halifax T | 13 | — |
| **Midfield** | | | | | | |
| Franny Firth* | 5 10 | 11 0 | Dewsbury | Huddersfield T | 27 | 4 |
| | | | | Halifax T | 168 | 19 |
| Paul Hendrie | 5 6 | 10 3 | Glasgow | Birmingham C | 23 | 1 |
| | | | | Bristol R | 30 | 1 |
| | | | | Halifax T | 113 | 8 |
| Steve Ward | 6 0 | 12 12 | Derby | Brighton | — | |
| | | | | Northampton T | 15 | 2 |
| | | | | Halifax T | 79 | 8 |
| Tom O'Neil* | 5 6½ | 10 4 | St Helens | Manchester U | 53 | — |
| | | | | Blackpool (on loan) | 7 | — |
| | | | | Southport | 197 | 16 |
| | | | | Tranmere R | 74 | 10 |
| | | | | Halifax T | 40 | 2 |
| Glyn Chamberlain* | 5 9 | 11 4 | Chesterfield | Burnley | — | |
| | | | | Chesterfield | 18 | — |
| | | | | Halifax T | 35 | — |
| Steven Walker* | | | | Halifax T | 1 | — |
| Steve Spooner | 5 11 | 12 10 | London | Derby Co | 8 | — |
| | | | | Halifax T | 29 | 2 |
| **Forwards** | | | | | | |
| Andy Whiteley* | 5 10 | 11 0 | Halifax | Halifax T | 36 | 1 |
| Vernon Allatt* | 5 11 | 11 8 | Hednesford | Halifax T | 70 | 7 |
| Simon Bullock* | 5 11 | 11 9 | Stoke | Stoke C | — | |
| | | | | Halifax T | 17 | 1 |
| Tommy Graham* | 5 9 | 10 10 | Glasgow | Aston V | | |
| | | | | Barnsley | 38 | 13 |
| | | | | Halifax T | 71 | 17 |
| Jimmy McIlwraith* | 5 8 | 10 4 | Troon | Motherwell | 28 | 6 |
| | | | | Bury | 89 | 21 |
| | | | | Portsmouth | 19 | — |
| | | | | Bury | 29 | 3 |
| | | | | Halifax T | 36 | 6 |
| Bobby Davison | 5 10 | 11 5 | South Shields | Seaham CW | (not known) | |
| | | | | Huddersfield T | 2 | — |
| | | | | Halifax T | 46 | 20 |

# HARTLEPOOL UNITED Division 4

*President:* S. Spaldin.

*Chairman:* J. V. Barker.

*Vice-Chairman:* B. H. Crosby.

*Directors:* B. Maxwell, J. S. Fullard, T. Shepherd, D. Jukes, S. I. Levinson.

*Manager:* Billy Horner.  *Secretary:* W. P. Hillan.

*Year Formed:* 1908.  *Turned Professional:* 1908.

*Limited Company:* 1908.

*Previous Names:* Hartlepools United until 1968; Hartlepool until 1977.

**Football League Record:**
1921 Original Member of Division 3(N); 1958–68 Division 4; 1968–69 Division 3; 1969– Division 4.

**Honours:** *Football League:* Division 3 best season: 22nd, 1968–69; Division 3(N) – Runners-up 1956–57. *FA Cup* best season: 4th rd, 1954–55, 1977–78. *Football League Cup* best season: 4th rd, 1974–75.

*Record Victory:* 10-1 v Barrow, Division 4, 4 Apr, 1959.

*Record Defeat:* 1-10 v Wrexham, Division 4, 3 Mar, 1962.

*Most League Points:* 60, Division 4, 1967–68.

*Most League Goals:* 90, Division 3(N), 1956–57.

*Highest League Scorer in Season:* William Robinson, 28, Division 3(N), 1927–28.

*Most League Goals in Total Aggregate:* Ken Johnson, 98, 1949–64.

*Most Capped Player:* Ambrose Fogarty, 1 (11), Eire.

*Most League Appearances:* Wattie Moore, 448, 1948–64.

*Record Transfer Fee Received:* £60,000 from Brighton for Malcolm Poskett, Feb 1978.

*Record Transfer Fee Paid:* £10,000 to Sunderland for Ambrose Fogarty, Nov 1963.

*Previous Managers since the War:* Fred Westgarth, Ray Middleton, Bill Robinson, Allenby Chilton, Bob Gurney, Alvan Williams, Geoff Twentyman, Brian Clough, Angus McLean, John Simpson, Len Ashurst, Ken Hale.

*Club Shop:* On ground.

---

**The Victoria Ground, 18 Scarborough Street, Hartlepool** Telephone Hartlepool 72584; (Office) 73492. *Ground capacity:* 18,000. *Record attendance:* 17,426 v Manchester U, FA Cup 3rd rd, 5 Jan, 1957. *Record receipts:* £17,000 v Leeds U, FA Cup 3rd rd, 18 Jan, 1979. *Pitch measurements:* 113yd×77yd.

*How to get there:* Hartlepool railway station is only a few hundred yards from the ground. Local bus services run scheduled services to Hartlepool.

*Match tickets:* No pre-booking of tickets.

*Car parking:* Ample side-street parking.

*Entertainments/catering facilities:* Two refreshment kiosks inside the ground.

*Club shop:* Open on match days; stocks all types of souvenirs.

*Handbooks/programmes:* No handbooks. Programmes available on subscription.

*Extra information:* Just three years after finishing second in Division 3(N) in 1956–57, the club conceded a Fourth Division record 109 goals.

*Club Colours:* Blue and white shirts, white shorts, blue stockings.

*Change Colours:* All red with white stripe on shirt and emblem, red shorts and stockings.

*Club Nickname:* The Pool.

---

## HARTLEPOOL UNITED 1981–82 LEAGUE RECORD

| Match No. | Date | Venue | Opponents | Result | H/T Score | Goalscorers | Attendance |
|---|---|---|---|---|---|---|---|
| 1 | Aug 29 | H | Colchester U | L 1-3 | 0-2 | Harding | 2007 |
| 2 | Sept 5 | A | Rochdale | L 1-2 | 1-1 | Houchen | 1481 |
| 3 | 12 | H | Wigan Ath | W 2-1 | 0-0 | Linacre J., Hampton | 1715 |
| 4 | 18 | A | York C | W 2-1 | 1-0 | Houchen, Newton | 2244 |
| 5 | 22 | A | Scunthorpe U | L 1-2 | 1-1 | Newton | 1998 |
| 6 | 26 | H | Halifax T | W 3-2 | 1-2 | Hampton 2, Houchen | 1800 |
| 7 | 30 | H | Hull C | W 3-2 | 2-2 | Houchen (pen), Hampton, Newton | 2654 |
| 8 | Oct 3 | A | Hereford U | D 1-1 | 0-0 | Houchen | 2247 |
| 9 | 10 | H | Peterborough U | L 0-1 | 0-0 | | 2450 |
| 10 | 17 | A | Sheffield U | D 1-1 | 0-0 | Bird | 12,752 |
| 11 | 20 | A | Tranmere R | L 0-1 | 0-1 | | 1431 |
| 12 | 24 | H | Torquay U | D 0-0 | 0-0 | | 2099 |
| 13 | 31 | H | Aldershot | W 2-1 | 1-0 | Newton, Linacre J. | 2658 |
| 14 | Nov 4 | H | Crewe Alex | L 1-2 | 1-2 | Houchen | 2338 |
| 15 | 8 | A | Bradford C | L 0-1 | 0-1 | | 5753 |
| 16 | 14 | H | Northampton T | W 3-1 | 1-0 | Newton 2, Hogan | 1637 |
| 17 | 28 | A | Port Vale | L 2-5 | 0-1 | Howard, Hogan | 2477 |
| 18 | Dec 5 | H | AFC Bournemouth | D 1-1 | 0-0 | Newton | 1760 |
| 19 | Jan 16 | A | Mansfield T | L 2-3 | 1-0 | Brown, Houchen | 2011 |
| 20 | 19 | A | Bury | D 1-1 | 0-0 | Houchen (pen) | 2997 |
| 21 | 23 | A | Colchester U | D 3-3 | 3-1 | Houchen 2, Bird | 2862 |
| 22 | 25 | A | Stockport Co | W 2-0 | 1-0 | Bird, Brown | 1924 |
| 23 | 30 | H | York C | W 3-2 | 0-0 | Houchen, Fagan, Newton | 2291 |
| 24 | Feb 3 | H | Darlington | L 1-2 | 1-1 | Bird | 4548 |
| 25 | 6 | A | Wigan Ath | D 1-1 | 0-1 | Newton | 6315 |
| 26 | 10 | H | Scunthorpe U | D 3-3 | 1-2 | Houchen (pen), Johnson 2 | 2001 |
| 27 | 13 | H | Hereford U | W 2-1 | 0-1 | Howard 2 | 1811 |
| 28 | 20 | A | Hull C | L 2-5 | 0-2 | Houchen 2 | 2825 |
| 29 | 27 | A | Peterborough U | D 4-4 | 4-3 | Houchen 3 (1 pen), Staff | 4610 |
| 30 | Mar 6 | H | Sheffield U | L 2-3 | 1-2 | Linacre P., Staff | 4145 |
| 31 | 10 | H | Tranmere R | D 0-0 | 0-0 | | 1633 |
| 32 | 13 | A | Torquay U | D 1-1 | 1-0 | Staff | 1619 |
| 33 | 16 | A | Crewe Alex | W 2-1 | 1-1 | Houchen, Hogan | 1116 |
| 34 | 20 | H | Aldershot | D 2-2 | 0-0 | Newton, Bainbridge | 1702 |
| 35 | 27 | H | Bradford C | L 0-2 | 0-2 | | 2512 |
| 36 | 31 | H | Rochdale | D 1-1 | 1-0 | Brown | 1259 |
| 37 | Apr 3 | A | Northampton T | L 1-2 | 1-1 | Bird | 1890 |
| 38 | 10 | H | Stockport Co | D 2-2 | 1-2 | Stimpson, Brown | 1506 |
| 39 | 12 | A | Darlington | L 2-5 | 2-1 | Harding, Clarke | 4575 |
| 40 | 17 | A | AFC Bournemouth | L 1-5 | 0-3 | Hogan | 6567 |
| 41 | 24 | H | Port Vale | W 3-1 | 1-1 | Linacre P., Newton (pen), Staff | 1429 |
| 42 | 28 | H | Blackpool | D 2-2 | 0-2 | Newton 2 | 1387 |
| 43 | May 1 | A | Halifax T | L 0-2 | 0-1 | | 1305 |
| 44 | 5 | H | Mansfield T | W 3-0 | 0-0 | Newton, Staff, Linacre J. | 1202 |
| 45 | 8 | H | Bury | W 1-0 | 1-0 | Linacre P. | 1370 |
| 46 | 15 | A | Blackpool | D 2-2 | 1-0 | Linacre P., Newton | 1824 |

**Final League Position: 14**

**Goalscorers**

*League* (73): Houchen 18 (4 pens), Newton 15 (1 pen), Bird 5, Staff 5, Brown 4, Hampton 4, Hogan 4, Linacre P. 4, Howard 3, Linacre J. 3, Harding 2, Johnson 2, Bainbridge 1, Clarke 1, Fagan 1, Stimpson 1.
*League Cup* (2): Houchen 1, Newton 1.
*FA Cup* (3): Newton 2, Linacre P. 1.

| | | | | |
|---|---|---|---|---|
| **League Cup** | First Round | Northampton T (a) | 0-2 | |
| | | (h) | 2-1 | |
| **FA Cup** | First Round | Wigan Ath (a) | 2-2 | |
| | | (h) | 1-0 | |
| | Second Round | Hull C (a) | 0-2 | |

| Burleigh | Brown | Stimpson | Hogan | Bird | Linighan A. | Kerr | Sweeney | Staff | Houchen | Harding | Hampton | Fagan | Johnson | Linacre J. | Newton | Linacre P. | Howard | Bainbridge | Lowe | Dobson | Watson | Clarke | Lawrence | Linighan D. | Match No. |
|---|---|---|---|---|---|---|---|---|---|---|---|---|---|---|---|---|---|---|---|---|---|---|---|---|---|
| 1 | 2 | 3 | 4 | 5 | 6 | 7* | 8 | 9 | 10 | 11 | 12 | | | | | | | | | | | | | | 1 |
| 1 | 2 | 3 | 4 | | 6 | 7 | 8 | 9* | 10 | 11 | | 5 | 12 | | | | | | | | | | | | 2 |
| 1 | 7 | 3 | 4 | 5 | | | 2 | | 10 | | 9 | 6 | 11 | | 8 | | | | | | | | | | 3 |
| 1 | 6 | 3 | 4 | 5 | | | 2 | | 10 | | 9 | | 11 | 7 | 8 | | | | | | | | | | 4 |
| 1 | 6 | 3 | 4 | 5 | | | 2 | | 10 | | 9 | | 11 | 7 | 8 | | | | | | | | | | 5 |
| 1 | 12 | 3 | 4* | 5 | 6 | | 2 | | 10 | | 9 | | 11 | 7 | 8 | | | | | | | | | | 6 |
| 1 | 12 | 3 | 4* | 5 | 6 | | 2 | | 10 | | 9 | | 11 | 7 | 8 | | | | | | | | | | 7 |
| 1 | 3 | | 4 | 5 | 6 | | 2 | | 10 | | 9 | | 11 | 7 | 8 | | | | | | | | | | 8 |
| 1 | 3 | | 4 | 5 | 6 | | 2 | 12 | 10 | | 9 | | 11* | 7 | 8 | | | | | | | | | | 9 |
| 1 | | 3 | 4* | 5 | 6 | | 2 | | 10 | 12 | 9 | | 11 | 7 | 8 | | | | | | | | | | 10 |
| 1 | | 3 | 4 | 5 | 6 | | 2 | | 10 | 12 | 9 | | 11* | 7 | 8 | | | | | | | | | | 11 |
| 1 | 2 | 3 | 12 | 5 | | | | | 10 | 4 | 9 | | | 7 | 8 | 11* | | | | | | | | | 12 |
| 1 | 2 | 3 | | 5 | 6 | | | | 10 | 4 | 9 | | | 7 | 8 | 11 | | | | | | | | | 13 |
| 1 | 2 | 3 | 12 | 5 | 6** | | | | 10 | 4 | 9 | | | 7 | 8 | 11 | | | | | | | | | 14 |
| 1 | 2 | 3 | 12 | 5 | 6 | | | 9 | 10 | 4* | | | | 7 | 8 | 11 | | | | | | | | | 15 |
| 1 | 2 | 3 | 4 | 5 | 6 | | | | 10 | | | | 11 | 7 | 8 | 9 | | | | | | | | | 16 |
| 1 | 2 | 3 | 7 | 4 | 5 | | | 12 | 10 | | | | 8 | | 9 | 11* | 6 | | | | | | | | 17 |
| 1 | 2 | | 4 | 5 | 6 | | | 9 | 10 | | | | 11 | 7 | 8 | 3 | | | | | | | | | 18 |
| 1 | 4 | 3 | | 5 | | | 2* | 9 | 10 | | | 6 | 11 | 7 | 8 | 12 | | | | | | | | | 19 |
| 1 | 4 | | | 5 | | | 2 | 11 | 10 | | | 6 | 8* | 7 | 9 | 3 | 12 | | | | | | | | 20 |
| 1 | 4 | | 8 | 5 | | | 2 | 11 | 10 | | | 6 | | 7 | 9 | 3 | | | | | | | | | 21 |
| 1 | 4 | | 8 | 5 | | | 2 | 11 | 10 | | | 6 | | 7 | 9 | 3 | | | | | | | | | 22 |
| 1 | 4 | | 8 | 5 | | | 2 | 11 | 10 | | | 6 | | 7 | 9 | 3 | | | | | | | | | 23 |
| 1 | 4 | | 8 | 5 | | | 2 | 11 | 10 | | | 6 | 12 | 7 | 9* | 3 | | | | | | | | | 24 |
| 1 | 4 | | 8 | 5 | | | 2 | 11 | 10* | | | 6 | 12 | 7 | 9 | 3 | | | | | | | | | 25 |
| 1 | 4 | | 8 | | 6 | | 2* | | 10 | | | 5 | 11 | 7 | 9 | 3 | | | | | 12 | | | | 26 |
| 1 | 2 | | 4 | 5 | | | 8 | | 10 | | | | 11 | 7 | | 3 | 9 | 6 | | | | | | | 27 |
| 1 | 2 | | 4 | 5* | | | | | 10 | | 12 | | 11 | 7 | | 3 | 9 | 6 | 8 | | | | | | 28 |
| 1 | 2 | 3 | 4 | 5 | | | 8 | | 10 | | | 6 | | 7 | 9 | 11 | | | | | | | | | 29 |
| 1 | 2 | 3 | | 5 | | | 8 | | 10 | | | | 4 | 7 | 9 | 11 | 6 | | | | | | | | 30 |
| 1 | 6 | 3 | | 5 | | | 2 | 8 | 10 | | | | 4 | 7 | 9 | 11 | | | | | | | | | 31 |
| 1 | 6 | 3 | 4 | 5 | | | 8 | | 10 | 7* | | | 11 | 2 | 9 | 12 | | | | | | | | | 32 |
| 1 | 6 | 12 | 4 | | | | 8 | | 10 | 7 | | | 11* | 2 | 9 | 3 | 5 | | | | | | | | 33 |
| 1 | 6 | | 4 | 5 | | | 8 | | 10 | | | | 11 | 2 | 9 | 3 | 7 | | | | | | | | 34 |
| | 6 | | 4 | 5 | | | 8 | | | | | | 11 | 2 | 3 | 9* | 7 | 12 | 1 | | | | 10 | | 35 |
| | 9 | | 4 | 5 | | | 8 | | | | | | 11 | 2 | 3 | | 6 | 12 | 10* | 1 | | 7 | | | 36 |
| | 9 | | 7 | 6 | | | 8 | 12 | | | | | 11 | 2 | 3 | | 4 | 10* | 1 | | 5 | | | | 37 |
| | 9 | 3* | 4 | 5 | | | 8 | 12 | 10 | | | | 11 | 2 | | | 6 | | 1 | | | 7 | | | 38 |
| 1 | 9 | 3 | 4 | 5 | | | 2 | 12 | 8* | | | | 11 | 7 | | | | | | | 10 | 6 | | | 39 |
| 1 | 9 | 3 | 4 | 5 | | | 2 | 11 | | | | | | 7 | 10 | 12 | | | | | 8* | 6 | | | 40 |
| | 6 | 3 | 4 | 5 | | | 2 | 8 | | | | | 11* | 7 | 9 | 10 | | | | | | 1 | 12 | | 41 |
| | 6 | 3 | | 5 | | | 2 | | | | | | 11 | 7 | 9 | 10 | | | | 4* | | 1 | 8 | 12 | 42 |
| | 6 | 3 | | 5 | | | 2 | | | | | | 11 | 7 | 9 | 10 | | | | | 8* | 1 | 12 | 4 | 43 |
| | 6 | 3 | 4 | 5 | | | 2 | 8 | | | | | | 7 | 9 | 10 | | | | | | 1 | 12 | 11* | 44 |
| | 6 | 3 | 4 | 5 | | | 2 | | | | | | | 7 | 9 | 10 | | | | | 12 | 1 | 8 | 11* | 45 |
| | 6 | 3 | 4 | 5 | | | 2* | 11 | | | | | | 7 | 9 | 10 | | | | | | 1 | 8 | 12 | 46 |
| 36 | 42 | 29 | 36 | 42 | 17 | 2 | 32 | 24 | 32 | 10 | 15 | 11 | 29 | 42 | 34 | 31 | 4 | 9 | 3 | 2 | 10 | 5 | 3 | 6 | |
| +<br>2s | +<br>1s | +<br>3s | | | +<br>1s | | +<br>3s | | +<br>3s | +<br>2s | | +<br>3s | | | +<br>1s | +<br>2s | +<br>1s | +<br>1s | +<br>3s | | +<br>2s | +<br>3s | | | |

## HARTLEPOOL UNITED

| | Ht | Wt | Birthplace | Clubs | League App. | League Gls |
|---|---|---|---|---|---|---|
| **Goalkeepers** | | | | | | |
| Graham Richardson | 5 10 | 11 4 | Sedgefield | Hartlepool U | 89 | — |
| John Watson | 6 1 | 13 1 | Huddersfield | Huddersfield T | — | — |
| | | | | Hartlepool U | 30 | — |
| Martin Burleigh | 5 11 | 12 10 | Newcastle | Newcastle U | 11 | — |
| | | | | Darlington | 30 | — |
| | | | | Carlisle U | 26 | — |
| | | | | Darlington | 71 | — |
| | | | | Hartlepool U | 84 | — |
| Trevor Ramshaw | 5 11 | 12 2 | Durham | Hartlepool U | — | — |
| **Defenders** | | | | | | |
| Michael Fagan | 5 11 | 12 0 | Newcastle | Carlisle U | — | — |
| | | | | Hartlepool U | 36 | 1 |
| Alan Sweeney | 5 7 | 11 10 | Glasgow | Huddersfield T | 66 | 1 |
| | | | | Hartlepool U | 97 | 2 |
| John Bird | 6 1 | 13 0 | Doncaster | Doncaster R | 50 | 3 |
| | | | | Preston NE | 166 | 9 |
| | | | | Newcastle U | 87 | 5 |
| | | | | Hartlepool U | 87 | 9 |
| Andy Linighan | 6 6 | 12 6 | Hartlepool | Smiths BC | (not known) | |
| | | | | Hartlepool U | 23 | — |
| Barry Stimpson | 5 10 | 11 10 | Billingham | Hartlepool U | 34 | 1 |
| Phil Brown | 5 11 | 11 6 | Hartlepool | Hartlepool U | 100 | 5 |
| Neil Black | 5 11 | 11 0 | Blaydon | Hartlepool U | — | — |
| (Contract cancelled April 1982) | | | | | | |
| Terry Bainbridge | | | | Hartlepool U | 10 | 1 |
| (Non-contract) | | | | | | |
| **Midfield** | | | | | | |
| Roy Hogan | 5 8 | 10 6 | Hartlepool | Hartlepool U | 116 | 12 |
| Derek Loadwick | 5 7 | 12 0 | Middlesbrough | Leeds U | — | — |
| | | | | Stockport Co | 84 | — |
| | | | | Hartlepool U | 51 | 1 |
| Ken Lowe | 5 10 | 11 4 | Hartlepool | Hartlepool U | 4 | — |
| Bobby Kerr* | 5 4½ | 9 3 | Alexandria | Sunderland | 368 | 57 |
| | | | | Blackpool | 22 | 2 |
| | | | | Hartlepool U | 49 | 2 |
| Paul Dobson | 5 11 | 11 2 | | Hartlepool U | 5 | — |
| Philip Linacre | 6 0 | 11 0 | Middlesbrough | Coventry C | — | — |
| | | | | Hartlepool U | 33 | 4 |
| Harry Clarke | 5 10 | 11 7 | Sunderland | Middlesbrough | — | — |
| | | | | Hartlepool U | 7 | 1 |
| Mark Lawrence | 6 0 | 11 2 | Middlesbrough | Hartlepool U | 132 | 18 |
| John Linacre | 5 9 | 11 10 | Middlesbrough | Hartlepool U | 196 | 12 |
| David Linighan | 6 2 | 11 12 | Hartlepool | Hartlepool U | 6 | — |
| **Forwards** | | | | | | |
| Bob Newton | 5 11 | 12 6 | Chesterfield | Huddersfield T | 42 | 7 |
| | | | | York C (on loan) | — | — |
| | | | | Hartlepool U | 147 | 48 |
| Alan Harding | 5 9 | 11 4 | Sunderland | Darlington | 129 | 38 |
| | | | | Lincoln C | 209 | 38 |
| | | | | Hartlepool U | 83 | 8 |
| Derek Hampton* | 5 10 | 11 4 | Middlesbrough | Whitby | (not known) | |
| | | | | Hartlepool U | 74 | 17 |
| Paul Staff | 5 9 | 10 12 | Hartlepool | Hartlepool U | 36 | 5 |
| Kevin Johnson | 5 9 | 10 12 | Doncaster | Sheffield W | 1 | — |
| | | | | Southend U | 17 | 1 |
| | | | | Gillingham (on loan) | 1 | — |
| | | | | Workington | 15 | 1 |
| | | | | Hartlepool U | 61 | 9 |
| | | | | Huddersfield T | 81 | 23 |
| | | | | Halifax T | 57 | 10 |
| | | | | Hartlepool U | 46 | 2 |
| David Howard | 6 0 | 11 7 | Hartlepool | Newcastle U | — | — |
| | | | | Hartlepool U | 9 | 4 |
| Gerry McNamee | 5 11 | 11 4 | Consett | Hartlepool U | 3 | 1 |

Mike Spelman (Contract cancelled April 1982)

# HEREFORD UNITED Division 4

*Chairman:* P. S. Hill FRICS.

*Vice-Chairman:* M. B. Roberts.

*Directors:* D. Vaughan, A. J. Phillips, G. Rivers, J. E. Jackson, G. C. E. Hales.

*Manager:* Frank Lord. *Secretary:* P. J. Grange.

*Year Formed:* 1924. *Turned Professional:* 1924.

*Limited Company:* 1939.

*Ground:* Edgar Street Athletic Ground.

**Football League Record:**
1972 Elected to Division 4; 1973–76 Division 3; 1976–77 Division 2; 1977–78 Division 3; 1978– Division 4.

**Honours:** *Football League:* Division 3 – Champions 1975–76; Division 4 – Runners-up 1972–73. *FA Cup* best season: 4th rd, 1971–72, 1976–77, 1981–82. *Football League Cup* best season: 3rd rd, 1974–75.

*Record Victory:* 11-0 v Thynnes (FA Cup), Sept 1947.

*Record Defeat:* 0-5 v Wrexham, 22 Dec, 1973; 1-6 v Tranmere R, 29 Nov, 1975; 1-6 v Wolverhampton W, 2 Oct, 1976.

*Most League Points:* 63, Division 3, 1975–76. *Three points win:* 67, Division 4, 1981–82.

*Most League Goals:* 86, Division 3, 1975–76.

*Highest League Scorer in Season:* Dixie McNeil, 35, 1975–76.

*Most League Goals in Total Aggregate:* Dixie McNeil, 85, 1974–77.

*Most Capped Player:* Brian Evans, 1 (7) Wales.

*Most League Appearances:* Tommy Hughes, 240, 1973–82.

*Record Transfer Fee Received:* £100,000 from Derby Co for Steve Emery, Sept 1979.

*Record Transfer Fee Paid:* £25,000 to Aston Villa for David Cunningham, Aug 1979.

*Previous Managers since the War:* George Tranter, Alex Massie, Joe Wade, Ray Daniel, Bob Dennison, John Charles, Colin Addison, John Sillett, Tony Ford, Mike Bailey.

*Address of Supporters Club:* Edgar Street, Hereford.

*Address of the Club Shop or Boutique:* Edgar Street, Hereford.

---

**Edgar Street, Hereford.** Telephone Hereford (0432) 276666. *Ground capacity:* 17,500. *Record attendance:* 18,114 v Sheffield W, FA Cup 3rd rd, 4 Jan, 1958. *Record receipts:* £12,666 v Bristol C, FA Cup 4th rd, 26 Jan, 1974. *Pitch measurements:* 111yd×80yd.

*How to get there:* Ground very close to town centre, within five minutes walking distance from Hereford railway station and the bus station.

*Match tickets:* Tickets can be booked in advance.

*Car parking:* Parking is available around the ground for approximately 1,000 vehicles.

*Entertainments/catering facilities:* Canteens on the ground. A social club next to ground.

*Club shop:* All types of souvenirs sold.

*Handbooks/programmes:* Programmes available on application to the club shop.

*Extra information:* As a non-League Club, Hereford reached the first round proper of the FA Cup for 21 consecutive seasons.

*Club Colours:* White shirts with red and black trim, black shorts, white with red and black top stockings.

*Change Colours:* Red shirts, white and black trim, white shorts, red stockings, white and black trim.

*Club Trainer:* Peter Isaac. *Club Nickname:* United.

## HEREFORD UNITED 1981–82 LEAGUE RECORD

| Match No. | Date | Venue | Opponents | Result | H/T Score | Goalscorers | Attendance |
|---|---|---|---|---|---|---|---|
| 1 | Aug 29 | A | Sheffield U | D 2-2 | 0-2 | Phillips, Laidlaw | 11,906 |
| 2 | Sept 5 | H | Bury | W 3-0 | 1-0 | White 2, Phillips | 2508 |
| 3 | 12 | A | Tranmere R | D 0-0 | 0-0 | | 1413 |
| 4 | 19 | H | Bradford C | L 1-2 | 0-2 | Bray | 2802 |
| 5 | 23 | H | Torquay U | L 0-3 | 0-3 | | 2408 |
| 6 | 26 | A | Northampton T | W 3-2 | 1-1 | Bray, McGrellis, Dobson | 1552 |
| 7 | Oct 3 | H | Hartlepool U | D 1-1 | 0-0 | Overson | 2247 |
| 8 | 10 | H | Halifax T | D 2-2 | 1-1 | Dungworth, Binney | 2359 |
| 9 | 17 | A | Scunthorpe U | D 2-2 | 0-1 | White (pen), Binney | 1499 |
| 10 | 20 | A | Colchester U | L 0-4 | 0-2 | | 3064 |
| 11 | 24 | H | Darlington | D 1-1 | 1-0 | Phillips | 2217 |
| 12 | 28 | A | Peterborough U | L 1-3 | 1-1 | Price | 3040 |
| 13 | 31 | A | York C | W 4-3 | 2-1 | Laidlaw, Dungworth 2, Phillips | 1600 |
| 14 | Nov 4 | H | Stockport Co | D 0-0 | 0-0 | | 2350 |
| 15 | 7 | A | Wigan Ath | D 1-1 | 1-0 | White | 4715 |
| 16 | 14 | H | Hull C | D 2-2 | 2-0 | Phillips, White | 2652 |
| 17 | 28 | A | Mansfield T | L 1-2 | 1-1 | White | 1898 |
| 18 | Dec 5 | H | Rochdale | D 0-0 | 0-0 | | 2312 |
| 19 | Jan 30 | A | Bradford C | D 0-0 | 0-0 | | 3734 |
| 20 | Feb 3 | H | Aldershot | L 0-1 | 0-0 | | 2253 |
| 21 | 6 | H | Tranmere R | D 1-1 | 0-1 | Phillips | 2071 |
| 22 | 10 | A | Torquay U | W 2-1 | 0-1 | Harvey, Dobson | 1914 |
| 23 | 13 | A | Hartlepool U | L 1-2 | 1-0 | Laidlaw | 1811 |
| 24 | 17 | H | Sheffield U | D 1-1 | 1-1 | Dobson | 3058 |
| 25 | 20 | H | Northampton T | W 2-1 | 1-0 | Showers, Laidlaw | 2229 |
| 26 | 27 | A | Halifax T | W 2-1 | 1-1 | Showers, Harvey | 2098 |
| 27 | Mar 6 | H | Scunthorpe U | W 2-1 | 1-1 | Showers, Price | 2159 |
| 28 | 10 | H | Colchester U | D 2-2 | 1-0 | Phillips 2 | 2060 |
| 29 | 14 | A | Darlington | W 1-0 | 1-0 | Laidlaw | 2557 |
| 30 | 15 | A | Stockport Co | D 1-1 | 1-0 | Harvey | 1357 |
| 31 | 20 | H | York C | W 2-1 | 0-1 | Price, White | 2703 |
| 32 | 23 | A | Crewe Alex | L 0-1 | 0-0 | | 1326 |
| 33 | 27 | H | Wigan Ath | W 3-0 | 1-0 | Phillips, Price 2 | 4191 |
| 34 | 31 | H | AFC Bournemouth | L 1-2 | 0-1 | Showers | 3145 |
| 35 | Apr 3 | A | Hull C | L 1-2 | 0-2 | Price | 3713 |
| 36 | 6 | A | Bury | D 1-1 | 1-1 | Laidlaw | 2398 |
| 37 | 10 | H | Port Vale | W 1-0 | 0-0 | Price | 2973 |
| 38 | 12 | A | Aldershot | D 2-2 | 1-1 | Price, Phillips | 1748 |
| 39 | 17 | A | Rochdale | W 1-0 | 0-0 | Bartley | 1342 |
| 40 | 21 | H | Blackpool | W 2-1 | 2-0 | Price, Bartley | 2617 |
| 41 | 24 | H | Mansfield T | W 3-1 | 1-0 | Harvey, Showers, Phillips | 2852 |
| 42 | 26 | A | Port Vale | D 1-1 | 0-0 | Laidlaw | 2160 |
| 43 | May 1 | A | Blackpool | L 0-1 | 0-0 | | 1881 |
| 44 | 5 | H | Peterborough U | W 2-1 | 1-0 | Spiring, Showers | 2357 |
| 45 | 8 | H | Crewe Alex | W 4-1 | 3-1 | Harvey (pen), Phillips, Price, White | 3058 |
| 46 | 15 | A | AFC Bournemouth | D 1-1 | 0-0 | Showers | 9925 |

**Final League Position: 10**

### Goalscorers

*League* (64): Phillips 12, Price 10, White 8 (1 pen), Laidlaw 7, Showers 7, Harvey 5 (1 pen), Dobson 3, Dungworth 3, Bartley 2, Binney 2, Bray 2, McGrellis 1, Overson 1, Spiring 1.
*League Cup* (1): Phillips 1.
*FA Cup* (9): Harvey 2, Laidlaw 2, Phillips 2, Showers 2, Overson 1.

| | | | | |
|---|---|---|---|---|
| **League Cup** | First Round | Port Vale (h) | | 1-1 |
| | | (a) | | 0-2 |
| **FA Cup** | First Round | Southend U (h) | | 3-1 |
| | Second Round | Fulham (h) | | 1-0 |
| | Third Round | Scunthorpe U (a) | | 1-1 |
| | | (h) | | 4-1 |
| | Fourth Round | Leicester C (h) | | 0-1 |

| Hughes | Price | Pejic | Hicks | Cornes | Spring | Harvey | Laidlaw | Phillips | Bartley | White | Overson | Bray | Showers | Ames | Dobson | McGrellis | Binney | Dungworth | Lane | Brand | Sullivan | Musial | Match No. |
|---|---|---|---|---|---|---|---|---|---|---|---|---|---|---|---|---|---|---|---|---|---|---|---|
| 1 | 2 | 3* | 4 | 5 | 6 | 7 | 8 | 9 | 10 | 11 | 12 |  |  |  |  |  |  |  |  |  |  |  | 1 |
| 1 | 2 |  | 4 |  | 6 | 7 | 8 | 9 |  | 11 | 5 | 3 | 10 |  |  |  |  |  |  |  |  |  | 2 |
| 1 | 2 |  | 4 | 5 | 6 | 7 | 8 | 9 |  | 11 |  | 3 | 10 |  |  |  |  |  |  |  |  |  | 3 |
| 1 | 2 |  | 4 | 5 | 6 | 7 | 8 | 9 |  | 11 |  | 3 | 10* | 12 |  |  |  |  |  |  |  |  | 4 |
| 1 | 2 |  | 4 | 5 | 6 | 7 | 8 | 9 |  | 11 |  | 3 | 10* | 12 |  |  |  |  |  |  |  |  | 5 |
| 1 | 2 |  | 4 |  | 6* | 7 | 8 | 9 |  | 11 |  | 3 | 10 |  | 5 | 12 |  |  |  |  |  |  | 6 |
| 1 | 2 |  | 4 |  | 6 | 7 | 8 | 9 |  | 11 | 12 | 3 |  |  | 5 | 10* |  |  |  |  |  |  | 7 |
| 1 | 2 |  | 4 | 5 |  | 7 | 8 | 9* |  | 11 |  | 3 |  |  | 6 | 12 |  | 10 |  |  |  |  | 8 |
| 1 | 2 |  |  | 5 | 6 | 7 | 8 | 9* |  | 11 |  | 3 |  |  | 4 | 12 |  | 10 |  |  |  |  | 9 |
| 1 | 2 |  | 4 | 5 |  | 7 | 8 | 9 |  | 11 |  | 3 |  |  | 6 |  |  | 10 |  |  |  |  | 10 |
| 1 | 2 |  | 4 |  | 6 | 7* | 8 | 9 |  | 11 |  | 3 |  |  | 5 | 12 |  | 10 |  |  |  |  | 11 |
| 1 | 2 |  | 4 |  | 6 | 7 | 8 | 9 |  | 11 |  | 3 |  |  | 5 |  |  | 10 |  |  |  |  | 12 |
| 1 | 2* |  | 4 |  | 6 | 7 | 8 | 9 |  | 11 |  | 3 |  |  | 5 | 10 |  | 12 |  |  |  |  | 13 |
| 1 | 2 |  | 4 |  | 6 | 7 | 8 | 9* |  | 11 |  | 3 |  |  | 5 | 10 |  | 12 |  |  |  |  | 14 |
|  | 2 |  | 4 |  | 6 | 7 | 8 | 9 |  | 11 |  | 3 |  |  | 5 |  |  |  | 10 | 1 |  |  | 15 |
|  | 2 |  | 4 |  | 6 | 7 | 8 | 9 |  | 11 |  | 3 |  |  | 5 |  |  |  | 10 | 1 |  |  | 16 |
|  | 2 |  | 4 |  | 6 | 7 | 8 | 9 |  | 11 |  | 3 | 10 |  | 5 |  |  |  |  | 1 |  |  | 17 |
|  | 2 |  | 4 |  | 6 | 7 | 8 | 9 |  | 11 |  |  | 10 |  | 5 |  |  |  |  | 1 | 3 |  | 18 |
|  | 2 |  | 4 |  | 9 | 7 | 8 |  |  | 11 |  |  | 10 |  | 5 |  |  |  |  | 1 | 3 | 6 | 19 |
|  | 2 |  | 4 |  | 9* | 7 | 8 |  |  | 11 |  |  | 10 |  | 5 |  |  | 12 |  | 1 | 3 | 6 | 20 |
|  | 2 |  | 4 |  |  | 7 | 8 | 9 |  | 11 | 5 |  | 10 |  |  |  |  |  |  | 1 | 3 | 6 | 21 |
|  | 2 |  | 4 |  |  | 7 | 8 | 9 |  | 11 |  |  | 10 |  | 5 |  |  |  |  | 1 | 3 | 6 | 22 |
|  | 2 |  | 4* |  |  | 7 | 8 | 9 |  | 11 |  |  | 10 |  | 5 |  |  | 12 |  | 1 | 3 | 6 | 23 |
|  | 2 |  |  |  |  |  | 8 | 9 |  | 11 | 4 |  | 10 |  | 5 |  |  | 7 |  | 1 | 3 | 6 | 24 |
|  | 2 |  |  |  |  |  | 8 | 9 |  | 11 | 4 |  | 10 |  | 5 |  |  | 7 |  | 1 | 3 | 6 | 25 |
|  | 2 | 3 | 4 |  |  | 7 | 8 | 9 |  | 11 |  |  | 10 |  | 5 |  |  |  |  | 1 |  | 6 | 26 |
|  | 2 | 3 | 4 |  |  | 7 | 8 | 9 |  | 11 |  |  | 10 |  | 5 |  |  |  |  | 1 |  | 6 | 27 |
|  | 2 | 3 | 4 |  |  | 7 | 8 | 9 |  | 11 |  |  | 10 |  | 5 |  |  |  |  | 1 |  | 6 | 28 |
|  | 2 | 3 | 4 |  | 12 | 7 | 8 | 9* |  | 11 |  |  | 10 |  | 5 |  |  |  |  | 1 |  | 6 | 29 |
|  | 2 | 3 | 4 |  | 12 | 7 | 8 | 9* |  | 11 |  |  | 10 |  | 5 |  |  |  |  | 1 |  | 6 | 30 |
|  | 2 | 3 | 4 |  | 6 | 7 | 8 | 9 | 5 | 11 |  |  | 10 |  |  |  |  |  |  | 1 |  |  | 31 |
|  | 2 | 3 | 4 |  | 6 |  | 8 | 9 | 5 | 11 |  |  | 10 |  | 7 |  |  |  |  | 1 |  |  | 32 |
|  | 2 | 3 | 4 | 5 | 6 | 7 | 8 | 9 |  | 11 |  |  | 10 |  |  |  |  |  |  | 1 |  |  | 33 |
|  | 2 | 3 | 4 |  | 6 | 7 | 8 | 9 | 5 | 11 |  |  | 10 |  |  |  |  |  |  | 1 |  |  | 34 |
|  | 2 | 3 | 4 |  | 6 | 7 | 8 | 9 | 5 | 11 |  |  | 10 |  |  |  |  |  |  | 1 |  |  | 35 |
|  | 2 | 3 | 4 | 5 |  | 7 | 8 |  |  | 11 |  |  | 10 |  | 9 |  |  |  |  | 1 |  | 6 | 36 |
|  | 2 | 3 | 4 |  |  | 7 | 8 | 9 | 5 | 11 |  |  | 10 |  |  |  |  |  |  | 1 |  | 6 | 37 |
|  | 2 | 3 | 4* |  | 6 | 7 | 8 | 9 | 5 | 11 |  |  | 10 |  |  |  |  | 12 |  | 1 |  | 4* | 38 |
|  | 2 | 3 | 4 |  | 6 | 7 | 8 | 9 | 5 | 11 |  |  | 10 |  |  |  |  |  |  | 1 |  | 5 | 39 |
|  | 2 | 3 | 4 |  |  | 7 | 8 | 9 | 5 | 11 |  |  | 10 |  |  |  |  |  |  | 1 |  | 6 | 40 |
|  | 2 | 3 | 4 |  |  | 7 | 8* | 9 | 5 | 11 |  |  | 10 |  |  |  |  | 12 |  | 1 |  | 6 | 41 |
|  | 2 | 3 | 4 |  |  | 7 | 8 | 9 | 5 | 11 |  |  | 10 |  |  |  |  |  |  | 1 |  | 6 | 42 |
|  | 2 | 3 | 4 |  |  | 7 | 8 | 9 | 5 | 11 | 12 |  | 10 |  |  |  |  |  |  | 1 |  | 6* | 43 |
|  | 2 | 3 | 4 |  |  | 7 | 8 | 9 | 5 | 11 |  |  | 10 |  |  |  |  |  |  | 1 |  | 6 | 44 |
|  | 2 | 3 | 4 |  |  | 7 | 8 | 9 | 5 | 11 |  |  | 10 |  |  |  |  |  |  | 1 |  | 6 | 45 |
|  | 2 | 3 | 4 |  |  | 7 | 8 | 9 | 5 | 11 |  |  | 10 |  |  |  |  | 12 |  | 1 |  | 6* | 46 |
| 14 | 41 | 27 | 42 | 7 | 26 | 42 | 42 | 43 | 17 | 46 | 5 | 16 | 35 | — | 24 | 6 | — | 7 | 2 | 32 | 8 | 24 |  |
|  |  |  |  |  | +3s |  |  |  |  |  |  |  | +3s | +2s | +3s | +4s |  |  | +3s |  |  |  |  |

## HEREFORD UNITED

| | Ht | Wt | Birthplace | Clubs | League App. | League Gls |
|---|---|---|---|---|---|---|
| **Goalkeepers** | | | | | | |
| Tommy Hughes* | 6 1 | 12 4 | Dalmuir | Chelsea | 11 | — |
| | | | | Aston V | 16 | — |
| | | | | Brighton (on loan) | 3 | — |
| | | | | Hereford U | 240 | — |
| Drew Brand | 6 1 | 11 1 | Edinburgh | Everton | 2 | — |
| | | | | Crewe Alex (on loan) | 15 | — |
| | | | | Hereford U | 54 | — |
| | | | | Sheffield U (on loan) | — | — |
| **Defenders** | | | | | | |
| Stuart Cornes* | 6 0 | 11 1 | Usk | Hereford U | 93 | 3 |
| Chris Price | 5 7 | 10 2 | Hereford | Hereford U | 169 | 12 |
| Danny Bartley* | 5 8½ | 11 4½ | Paulton | Bristol C | 100 | 7 |
| | | | | Swansea C | 199 | 8 |
| | | | | Hereford U | 73 | 6 |
| Richard Overson* | 5 11 | 12 2 | Kettering | Burnley | 6 | — |
| | | | | Hereford U | 11 | 1 |
| Ian Dobson | 5 10 | 11 1 | Hull | Hull C | 92 | 7 |
| (Contract cancelled March 1982) | | | | Hereford U | 41 | 5 |
| Mel Pejic | 5 7½ | 10 6 | Stoke | Stoke C | 1 | — |
| | | | | Hereford U | 40 | — |
| Adam Musial* | 5 8 | 10 10 | Poland | Arka Gydnia | (not known) | |
| (Poland) | | | | Hereford U | 40 | — |
| Keith Hicks | 6 0 | 13 2 | Oldham | Oldham Ath | 242 | 11 |
| | | | | Hereford U | 81 | 1 |
| **Midfield** | | | | | | |
| Winston White | 5 10½ | 10 12 | Leicester | Leicester C | 12 | 1 |
| | | | | Hereford U | 138 | 18 |
| Paul Gilchrist | 5 11 | 11 6 | Dartford | Charlton Ath | 7 | — |
| (Retired, injury) | | | | Fulham (on loan) | — | — |
| | | | | Doncaster R | 22 | 8 |
| | | | | Southampton | 107 | 17 |
| | | | | Portsmouth | 39 | 3 |
| | | | | Swindon T | 17 | 6 |
| | | | | Hereford U | 11 | 1 |
| Jimmy Harvey | 5 9½ | 11 4 | Lurgan | Glenavon | (not known) | |
| | | | | Arsenal | 3 | — |
| | | | | Hereford U | 83 | 6 |
| Gary Lowe | 5 11 | 11 10 | Manchester | Crystal Palace | — | — |
| (Contract cancelled Nov 1981) | | | | Manchester C | — | — |
| | | | | Hereford U | 9 | — |
| Sean Lane | | | Bristol | Hereford U | 18 | — |
| (Contract cancelled March 1982) | | | | | | |
| **Forwards** | | | | | | |
| Peter Spiring* | 5 8 | 11 0 | Glastonbury | Bristol C | 61 | 16 |
| | | | | Liverpool | — | — |
| | | | | Luton T | 15 | 2 |
| | | | | Hereford U | 209 | 19 |
| Stuart Phillips | 6 0½ | 11 7 | Halifax | Hereford U | 71 | 15 |
| Frank McGrellis* | 5 10 | 11 6 | Falkirk | Coventry C | — | — |
| | | | | Huddersfield T (on loan) | 5 | — |
| | | | | Hereford U | 85 | 24 |
| Fred Binney | 5 10 | 11 7 | Plymouth | Torquay U | 12 | 1 |
| (Non-contract) | | | | Exeter C (on loan) | 17 | 11 |
| | | | | Torquay U | 22 | 9 |
| | | | | Exeter C | 160 | 79 |
| | | | | Brighton | 70 | 35 |
| | | | | Plymouth Arg | 71 | 39 |
| | | | | Hereford U | 27 | 6 |
| Ian Bray | | | Neath | Hereford U | 16 | 2 |
| (Contract cancelled March 1982) | | | | | | |
| Joe Laidlaw | 5 8½ | 11 12 | Wallsend | Middlesbrough | 111 | 20 |
| | | | | Carlisle U | 151 | 44 |
| | | | | Doncaster R | 128 | 27 |
| | | | | Portsmouth | 60 | 19 |
| | | | | Hereford U | 62 | 8 |
| Derek Showers | 5 11 | 11 4 | Merthyr Tydfil | Cardiff C | 83 | 10 |
| (Wales) | | | | Bournemouth | 60 | 19 |
| | | | | Portsmouth | 39 | 8 |
| | | | | Hereford U | 57 | 11 |

# HUDDERSFIELD TOWN  Division 3

*Chairman:* K. S. Longbottom.
*Directors:* J. Christie, K. C. Padley, C. Senior, M. Ryan, E. A. Lodge, C. Hodgkinson.
*Manager:* Mick Buxton.
*Secretary:* G. S. Binns.
*Year Formed:* 1908.
*Turned Professional:* 1908.  *Limited Company:* 1908.

**Football League Record:**
1910 Elected to Division 2; 1920–52 Division 1; 1952–53 Division 2; 1953–56 Division 1; 1956–70 Division 2; 1970–72 Division 1; 1972–73' Division 2; 1973–75 Division 3; 1975–80 Division 4; 1980– Division 3.

**Honours:** *Football League:* Division 1 – Champions 1923–24, 1924–25, 1925–26; Runners-up 1926-27, 1927–28, 1933–34; Division 2 – Champions 1969–70; Runners-up 1919–20, 1952–53; Division 4 – Champions 1979–80. *FA Cup:* Winners 1922; Runners-up 1920, 1928, 1930, 1938. *Football League Cup:* Semi-final, 1967–68.

© 1973

*Record Victory:* 10-1 v Blackpool, Division 1, 13 Dec, 1930.

*Record Defeat:* 0-8 v Middlesbrough, Division 1, 30 Sept, 1950.

*Most League Points:* 66, Division 4, 1979–80.

*Most League Goals:* 101, Division 4, 1979–80.

*Highest League Scorer in Season:* Sam Taylor, 35, Division 2, 1919–20; George Brown, 35, Division 1, 1925–26.

*Most League Goals in Total Aggregate:* George Brown, 142, 1921–29.

*Most Capped Player:* Jimmy Nicholson, 31 (41), Northern Ireland.

*Most League Appearances:* Billy Smith, 520, 1914–34.

*Record Transfer Fee Received:* £100,000 from Leeds U for Trevor Cherry, June 1972.

*Record Transfer Fee Paid:* £110,000 to Mansfield T for Terry Austin, Dec 1980.

*Previous Managers since the War:* David Steele, George Stephenson, Andy Beattie, Bill Shankly, Eddie Boot, Tom Johnston, Ian Greaves, Bobby Collins, Tom Johnston.

*Address of Supporters Club:* Supporters Club Offices, 286 Leeds Road, Huddersfield, Yorkshire.

*Address of the Club Shop or Boutique:* The Terriers Souvenir Shop, 286 Leeds Road, Huddersfield.

---

**Leeds Rd., Huddersfield HD1 6PE.** Telephone Huddersfield 20335/6. *Ground capacity:* 48,000. *Record attendance:* 67,037 v Arsenal, FA Cup 6th rd, 27 Feb, 1932. *Record receipts:* £36,997 v Barnsley, Division 3, 7 Feb, 1981. *Pitch measurements:* 115yd×75yd.

*How to get there:* The ground is one mile from the town centre via Corporation buses 40, 41, 42. On match days special buses run from the centre. By road, the ground can be reached along Leeds Road either from the town centre or from Leeds.

*Match tickets:* Admission to all parts is by payment at the turnstiles except for special matches (Tel: Huddersfield 36100).

*Car parking:* Ample parking accommodation on all four sides of the ground; in the region of 6000 cars can be parked within 200 yards of the turnstiles.

*Entertainments/catering facilities:* Licensed Presidents Club – members only. 11 unlicensed snack bars around the ground.

*Club shop:* Close to the ground; sells all types of souvenirs (Tel: Huddersfield 31028). Open match days.

*Handbooks/programmes:* Programmes available on subscription from the club shop.

*Extra information:* In 1952–53 the club fielded an unchanged defensive line-up throughout the season.

*Club Colours:* Blue and white striped shirts, white shorts, white stockings.

*Change Colours:* All yellow.

*Club Captain:* David Sutton.

*Coach:* Jim Robson.

*Physiotherapist/Coach:* John Haselden.

*Club Nickname:* The Terriers.

## HUDDERSFIELD TOWN 1981−82 LEAGUE RECORD

| Match No. | Date | Venue | Opponents | Result | H/T Score | Goalscorers | Attendance |
|---|---|---|---|---|---|---|---|
| 1 | Aug 29 | H | Exeter C | D 1-1 | 0-1 | Kindon (pen) | 8647 |
| 2 | Sept 5 | A | Oxford U | L 0-1 | 0-0 | | 3976 |
| 3 | 12 | H | Wimbledon | D 1-1 | 0-0 | Fletcher | 7326 |
| 4 | 19 | A | Burnley | D 0-0 | 0-0 | | 6485 |
| 5 | 22 | A | Preston NE | D 1-1 | 1-1 | Kennedy | 6483 |
| 6 | 26 | H | Southend U | W 3-2 | 2-1 | Kindon (pen), Robins, Kennedy (pen) | 7254 |
| 7 | 29 | H | Chester | L 1-2 | 1-1 | Robins | 7747 |
| 8 | Oct 3 | A | Reading | W 2-1 | 2-0 | Kindon (pen), Hicks (og) | 4971 |
| 9 | 10 | H | Fulham | W 1-0 | 1-0 | Robins | 8258 |
| 10 | 17 | A | Gillingham | L 2-3 | 1-3 | Weatherly (og), Hanvey | 4432 |
| 11 | 20 | H | Carlisle U | W 2-1 | 2-1 | Burke, Cowling | 7185 |
| 12 | 24 | A | Bristol R | L 2-3 | 0-1 | Lillis, Kennedy (pen) | 5064 |
| 13 | 31 | H | Millwall | L 1-2 | 0-0 | Robins | 8546 |
| 14 | Nov 3 | A | Chesterfield | L 0-1 | 0-0 | | 6847 |
| 15 | 6 | A | Doncaster R | W 2-1 | 1-1 | Kennedy, Laverick | 11,319 |
| 16 | 14 | H | Swindon T | W 3-0 | 1-0 | Laverick 2, Hanvey | 7802 |
| 17 | 28 | A | Portsmouth | L 1-2 | 1-1 | Aizlewood (og) | 8155 |
| 18 | Dec 5 | H | Plymouth Arg | D 0-0 | 0-0 | | 6949 |
| 19 | Jan 2 | A | Brentford | W 1-0 | 0-0 | Fletcher | 5440 |
| 20 | 9 | H | Oxford U | W 2-0 | 0-0 | Cowling, Brown | 7070 |
| 21 | 16 | A | Bristol C | D 0-0 | 0-0 | | 4921 |
| 22 | 30 | H | Burnley | L 1-2 | 0-0 | Cowling | 10,269 |
| 23 | Feb 6 | A | Wimbledon | L 0-2 | 0-1 | | 2499 |
| 24 | 9 | H | Preston NE | L 2-3 | 2-1 | Fletcher 2 | 6674 |
| 25 | 13 | H | Reading | W 6-1 | 2-0 | Fletcher 2, Lillis, Hicks (og), Cowling, Stanton | 6022 |
| 26 | 16 | A | Walsall | D 1-1 | 0-0 | Austin | 3362 |
| 27 | 20 | A | Chester | L 1-3 | 0-1 | Purdie | 3120 |
| 28 | 27 | A | Fulham | D 2-2 | 1-0 | Austin, Stanton | 5963 |
| 29 | Mar 2 | H | Lincoln C | L 0-2 | 0-1 | | 5874 |
| 30 | 6 | A | Gillingham | W 2-0 | 0-0 | Robins, Fletcher | 5338 |
| 31 | 9 | A | Carlisle U | D 2-2 | 1-1 | Robins, Lillis | 3643 |
| 32 | 13 | H | Bristol R | L 0-2 | 0-1 | | 6156 |
| 33 | 23 | H | Chesterfield | D 1-1 | 1-0 | Lillis | 6721 |
| 34 | 27 | H | Doncaster R | L 1-2 | 1-0 | Hanvey | 6871 |
| 35 | 30 | H | Newport Co | W 2-0 | 1-0 | Kennedy (pen), Hotte | 4205 |
| 36 | Apr 3 | A | Swindon T | W 5-1 | 1-1 | Hanvey, Hotte 2, Cowling, Kennedy | 3872 |
| 37 | 6 | A | Millwall | W 3-1 | 2-0 | Lillis, Cowling, Wilson | 3507 |
| 38 | 10 | H | Walsall | W 2-1 | 0-0 | Cowling, Hotte | 6572 |
| 39 | 12 | A | Lincoln C | L 0-2 | 0-1 | | 8203 |
| 40 | 17 | A | Plymouth Arg | D 1-1 | 0-1 | Kennedy (pen) | 5434 |
| 41 | 24 | H | Portsmouth | L 0-1 | 0-0 | | 5658 |
| 42 | May 1 | A | Southend U | L 0-4 | 0-1 | | 4470 |
| 43 | 4 | H | Bristol C | W 5-0 | 3-0 | Boyle (og), Cowling, Robins, Stanton, Wilson | 3468 |
| 44 | 8 | H | Brentford | D 1-1 | 0-1 | Valentine | 4542 |
| 45 | 12 | A | Exeter C | L 0-1 | 0-0 | | 2888 |
| 46 | 15 | A | Newport Co | L 0-1 | 0-0 | | 4169 |

**Final League Position: 17**

### Goalscorers

*League* (64): Cowling 8, Fletcher 7, Kennedy 7 (4 pens), Robins 7, Lillis 5, Hanvey 4, Hotte 4, Kindon 3 (3 pens), Laverick 3, Stanton 3, Austin 2, Wilson 2, Brown 1, Burke 1, Purdie 1, Valentine 1, own goals 5.
*League Cup* (8): Fletcher 4, Austin 1, Kindon 1, Robins 1, Wilson 1.
*FA Cup* (11): Fletcher 3, Brown 2, Laverick 2, Austin 1, Cowling 1, Lillis 1, Robins 1.

| | | | | |
|---|---|---|---|---|
| **League Cup** | First Round | Rochdale (h) | 3-1 | |
| | | (a) | 4-2 | |
| | Second Round | Brighton & HA (h) | 1-0 | |
| | | (a) | 0-2 | |
| **FA Cup** | First Round | Workington (a) | 1-1 | |
| | | (h) | 5-0 | |
| | Second Round | Chesterfield (a) | 1-0 | |
| | Third Round | Carlisle U (a) | 3-2 | |
| | Fourth Round | Orient (h) | 1-1 | |
| | | (a) | 0-2 | |

| Rankin | Brown | Burke | Stanton | Sutton | Hanvey | Lillis | Kennedy | Fletcher | Kindon | Cowling | Wilson | Austin | Robins | Purdie | Taylor | Laverick | Bell | Hotte | Valentine | Cox | Match No. |
|---|---|---|---|---|---|---|---|---|---|---|---|---|---|---|---|---|---|---|---|---|---|
| 1 | 2 | 3 | 4 | 5 | 6 | 7 | 8 | 9 | 10 | 11 |  |  |  |  |  |  |  |  |  |  | 1 |
| 1 | 2 | 3 |  | 5 | 6 | 7 | 8 |  | 10 | 11* |  | 4 | 9 | 12 |  |  |  |  |  |  | 2 |
| 1 | 2 | 3 | 4* | 5 |  | 7 | 8 | 9 | 10 | 11 |  | 12 | 6 |  |  |  |  |  |  |  | 3 |
| 1 | 2 | 3 |  | 5 | 6 | 7 | 8 | 9 | 10 | 11 |  | 4 |  |  |  |  |  |  |  |  | 4 |
| 1 | 2 | 3 |  | 5 | 6 | 7 | 8 | 9*10 |  | 11 |  | 4 | 12 |  |  |  |  |  |  |  | 5 |
| 1 | 2 | 3 |  | 5 | 6 | 7 | 8 | 9 |  |  | 11 | 4 | 10 |  |  |  |  |  |  |  | 6 |
| 1 | 2 | 3 |  | 5 | 6 | 7 | 8 | 9 |  |  | 11* | 4 | 12 | 10 |  |  |  |  |  |  | 7 |
| 1 | 2 | 3 |  | 5 | 6 | 7 | 8 | 9 |  |  | 11 | 4 | 10 |  |  |  |  |  |  |  | 8 |
| 1 | 2 | 3 |  | 5 | 6 | 7 | 8 | 9 |  |  | 11 | 4 | 10 |  |  |  |  |  |  |  | 9 |
| 1 | 2 | 3 |  | 5 | 6 | 7 | 8 | 9 |  |  | 11 | 4 | 10 |  |  |  |  |  |  |  | 10 |
| 1 | 2 | 3 |  | 5 | 6 | 7 | 8*11 |  |  | 12 |  | 4 | 9 | 10 |  |  |  |  |  |  | 11 |
| 1 | 2 | 3 |  |  | 6 | 7 | 8 | 11 |  |  |  | 4 | 9 | 10 | 5 |  |  |  |  |  | 12 |
| 1 | 2 | 3 |  | 5 | 6 | 7 | 8 | 11 |  |  |  | 4 | 9 | 10 |  |  |  |  |  |  | 13 |
|  | 2 | 3 |  | 5 | 6 |  | 8 |  |  |  | 11 | 4 | 9 | 10 | 1 | 7 |  |  |  |  | 14 |
|  | 2 | 3 |  | 5 | 6 |  | 8 |  |  |  | 11 | 4 | 9 | 10 | 1 | 7 |  |  |  |  | 15 |
|  | 2 | 3 |  | 5 | 6 |  |  |  |  |  | 11 | 9 | 10 | 8 | 1 | 7 | 4 |  |  |  | 16 |
|  | 2 |  |  | 5 | 6 | 8 | 12 |  |  |  | 11 | 9*10 | 3 |  | 1 | 7 | 4 |  |  |  | 17 |
|  | 2 | 3 | 7 | 5 |  | 4 | 8 | 12 |  | 11 | 6 | 9*10 |  |  | 1 |  |  |  |  |  | 18 |
|  | 2 | 7* | 5 | 6 | 4 | 8 | 9 | 11 | 12 |  | 3 | 1 |  |  |  |  |  | 10 |  |  | 19 |
|  | 2 | 3 | 4 | 5 | 6 | 7 | 8 | 9 | 11 |  |  | 1 |  |  |  |  |  | 10 |  |  | 20 |
|  | 2 | 3 | 4 | 5 | 6 | 7 | 8 | 9 | 11 |  |  | 1 |  |  |  |  |  | 10 |  |  | 21 |
|  | 2 | 3 | 4 | 5 | 6 | 7 | 8 | 9* | 11 | 12 | 10 |  | 1 |  |  |  |  |  |  |  | 22 |
|  | 2 | 3 | 4 | 5 | 6 | 7 | 8 | 11 | 12 | 10 |  | 1 |  |  |  |  |  | 9* |  |  | 23 |
| 1 | 2 | 3 | 4 | 5 | 6 | 7 | 8 | 9* | 11 | 10 | 12 |  |  |  |  |  |  |  |  |  | 24 |
| 1 | 2 |  | 4 | 5 | 6 | 7 | 8 | 9 | 11 | 10 | 3 |  |  |  |  |  |  |  |  |  | 25 |
| 1 | 2 |  | 4 | 5 | 6 | 7 | 8 | 9 | 11 | 10 | 3 |  |  |  |  |  |  |  |  |  | 26 |
|  | 2 |  | 4* | 5 | 6 | 7 | 8 | 9 | 11 | 10 | 12 | 3 | 1 |  |  |  |  |  |  |  | 27 |
|  | 2 | 5 | 4 |  | 6 | 7 |  | 9 | 11 | 8 | 10 | 3 | 1 |  |  |  |  |  |  |  | 28 |
|  | 2 | 3 | 4 |  | 6 | 7 |  | 9 | 11 | 8 | 10*12 | 5 | 1 |  |  |  |  |  |  |  | 29 |
| 1 | 2 | 3 | 4 |  | 6 |  | 8 | 9 | 11 | 7 | 10 |  |  |  |  |  |  |  | 5 |  | 30 |
| 1 | 2 | 3 | 4 |  | 6 | 7 |  | 9 | 11 | 8 | 10*12 |  |  |  |  |  |  |  | 5 |  | 31 |
| 1 | 2 | 3 | 4 |  | 6 | 7 |  | 9 | 11 | 8* | 10 | 12 |  |  |  |  |  |  | 5 |  | 32 |
|  | 2 | 3 | 4 | 5 | 6 | 7 | 8 | 9 | 11 | 10 |  |  |  |  |  |  |  |  |  | 1 | 33 |
|  | 2 | 3 | 4 | 5 | 6 | 7 | 8 | 12 | 11* |  | 10 |  |  |  |  |  | 9 |  |  | 1 | 34 |
|  | 2 | 3 | 4 | 5 | 6 | 7 | 8 |  | 11 |  | 10 |  |  |  |  |  | 9 |  |  | 1 | 35 |
|  | 2 | 3 | 4 |  | 6 | 7 | 8 |  | 11 | 10 |  |  |  |  |  |  | 9 |  | 5 | 1 | 36 |
|  | 2 | 3 | 4 |  | 6 | 7 | 8 |  | 11 | 10 |  |  |  |  |  |  | 9 |  | 5 | 1 | 37 |
|  | 2 | 3 | 4 |  | 6 | 7 |  | 8 | 11 | 10 |  |  |  |  |  |  | 9 |  | 5 | 1 | 38 |
|  | 2 | 3 | 4 |  | 6 | 7 | 8 | 12 | 11 | 10* |  |  |  |  |  |  | 9 |  | 5 | 1 | 39 |
|  | 2 | 3 | 4 |  | 6 | 7 | 8 |  | 11 | 10 | 12 |  |  |  |  |  | 9* |  | 5 | 1 | 40 |
|  | 2 | 3 | 4 |  | 6 | 7 | 8 |  | 12 | 10 | 11 |  |  |  |  |  | 9* |  | 5 | 1 | 41 |
|  | 2 | 3 | 4 |  | 6 | 7 | 8 |  | 11 | 10 | 12 |  |  |  |  |  | 9* |  | 5 | 1 | 42 |
|  | 2 | 3 | 4 |  | 6 | 7 | 8 |  | 11 | 10 | 9 |  |  |  |  |  |  |  | 5 | 1 | 43 |
|  | 2 | 3 | 4 |  | 6 | 7 | 8 |  | 11 | 10 | 9 |  |  |  |  |  |  |  | 5 | 1 | 44 |
|  | 2 | 3 | 4 |  | 6* | 7 | 8 |  | 11 | 10 | 9 |  |  |  |  |  | 12 |  | 5 | 1 | 45 |
|  | 2 | 3 | 4 |  |  | 7 | 8 |  | 11 | 10 | 9 | 6 |  |  |  |  |  |  | 5 | 1 | 46 |
| 19 | 46 | 41 | 31 | 29 | 43 | 42 | 39 | 22 | 10 | 36 | 31 | 20 | 26 | 11 | 13 | 4 | 2 | 13 | 14 | 14 |  |

Substitute indicators: Stanton +4s, Cowling +2s, Wilson +3s, Austin +1s, Robins +6s, Purdie +4s; Hotte +1s.

## HUDDERSFIELD TOWN

| | Ht | Wt | Birthplace | Clubs | League App. | League Gls |
|---|---|---|---|---|---|---|
| **Goalkeepers** | | | | | | |
| Richard Taylor* | 6 0½ | 12 9 | Huddersfield | Huddersfield T | 105 | — |
| | | | | Wolverhampton W (on loan) | — | — |
| | | | | Sunderland (on loan) | — | — |
| | | | | York C (on loan) | 2 | — |
| Alan Starling | 6 1 | 13 4 | Barking | Luton T | 7 | — |
| | | | | Torquay U (on loan) | 1 | — |
| | | | | Northampton T | 238 | 1 |
| | | | | Huddersfield T | 112 | — |
| Andy Rankin* | 6 0 | 12 0 | Bootle | Everton | 85 | — |
| | | | | Watford | 299 | — |
| | | | | Huddersfield T | 71 | — |
| Robert Picton* | 6 2 | 13 0 | Barnsley | Huddersfield T | — | — |
| **Defenders** | | | | | | |
| Malcolm Brown | 6 2 | 13 0 | Salford | Bury | 11 | — |
| | | | | Huddersfield T | 210 | 7 |
| Dave Sutton | 6 1 | 12 2 | Tarleton | Plymouth Arg | 61 | — |
| | | | | Reading (on loan) | 9 | — |
| | | | | Huddersfield T | 167 | 8 |
| Keith Hanvey | 6 0 | 12 7 | Manchester | Manchester C | — | — |
| | | | | Swansea C | 11 | — |
| | | | | Rochdale | 121 | 10 |
| | | | | Grimsby T | 54 | 2 |
| | | | | Huddersfield T | 153 | 9 |
| Fred Robinson* | 5 10 | 11 4 | Rotherham | Doncaster R | 119 | 3 |
| | | | | Huddersfield T | 72 | 2 |
| David Burke | 5 10 | 10 7 | Liverpool | Bolton W | 69 | 1 |
| | | | | Huddersfield T | 41 | 1 |
| Tony Hall (Contract cancelled) | | | Jarrow | Ipswich T | — | — |
| | | | | Huddersfield T | — | — |
| Peter Valentine | 5 10 | 12 0 | Huddersfield | Huddersfield T | 14 | 1 |
| **Midfield** | | | | | | |
| Mark Lillis | 6 0 | 12 2 | Manchester | Huddersfield T | 88 | 12 |
| David Cowling | 5 7 | 10 6 | Doncaster | Mansfield T | — | — |
| | | | | Huddersfield T | 147 | 23 |
| Brian Stanton | 5 7 | 10 7 | Liverpool | Bury | 83 | 14 |
| | | | | Huddersfield T | 116 | 24 |
| Micky Kennedy | 5 10 | 10 6 | Salford | Halifax T | 76 | 4 |
| | | | | Huddersfield T | 81 | 9 |
| Edward Burrows (Contract cancelled) | | | Halifax | Leeds U | — | — |
| | | | | Huddersfield T | — | — |
| Philip Wilson | 5 6 | 10 4 | Hemsworth | Bolton W | 39 | 4 |
| | | | | Huddersfield T | 34 | 2 |
| Tim Hotte (Non-contract) | | | Bradford | Arsenal | — | — |
| | | | | Huddersfield T | 14 | 4 |
| **Forwards** | | | | | | |
| Ian Robins* | 5 9 | 11 4 | Bury | Oldham Ath | 220 | 40 |
| | | | | Bury | 49 | 5 |
| | | | | Huddersfield T | 156 | 59 |
| Peter Fletcher* | 6 1 | 12 0 | Manchester | Manchester U | 7 | — |
| | | | | Hull C | 36 | 5 |
| | | | | Stockport Co | 51 | 13 |
| | | | | Huddersfield T | 99 | 37 |
| Bernard Purdie* | 5 9 | 11 0 | Wrexham | Wrexham | 10 | 3 |
| | | | | Chester | 63 | 14 |
| | | | | Crewe Alex | 213 | 44 |
| | | | | Huddersfield T | 46 | 1 |
| Steve Kindon* | 6 0 | 12 12 | Warrington | Burnley | 109 | 28 |
| | | | | Wolverhampton W | 138 | 28 |
| | | | | Burnley | 76 | 18 |
| | | | | Huddersfield T | 73 | 35 |
| Terry Austin | 6 1 | 12 6 | Isleworth | Crystal Palace | — | — |
| | | | | Ipswich T | 19 | 1 |
| | | | | Plymouth Arg | 58 | 18 |
| | | | | Walsall | 47 | 19 |
| | | | | Mansfield T | 84 | 31 |
| | | | | Huddersfield T | 39 | 10 |
| Ian Thompson* | | | | Huddersfield T | — | — |

# HULL CITY

## Division 4

*Chairman:* D. Robinson.

*Vice-Chairman:*

*Directors:*

*Team Manager:* Colin Appleton.

*Assistant Manager/Coach:*

*Secretary:* Paul King.

*General Manager (Development):*

*Youth Development Officer:* Bobby Brown.

*Year Formed:* 1904. *Turned Professional:* 1905.

*Limited Company:* 1905.

*Previous Grounds:* 1904, Boulevard Ground (Hull RFC); 1905, Anlaby Road (Hull CC); 1946, Boothferry Park.

**Football League Record:**
1905 Elected to Division 2; 1930–33 Division 3(N); 1933–36 Division 2; 1936–49 Division 3(N); 1949–56 Division 2; 1956–58 Division 3(N); 1958–59 Division 3; 1959–60 Division 2; 1960–66 Division 3; 1966–78 Division 2; 1978–81 Division 3; 1981– Division 4.

**Honours:** *Football League:* Division 2 best season: 3rd, 1909–10; Division 3(N) – Champions 1932–33, 1948–49; Division 3 – Champions 1965–66; Runners-up 1958–59. *FA Cup* best season: Semi-final, 1930. *Football League Cup* best season: 4th rd, 1973–74, 1975–76, 1977–78.

*Record Victory:* 11-1 v Carlisle U, Division 3(N), 14 Jan, 1939.

*Record Defeat:* 0-8 v Wolverhampton W, Division 2, 4 Nov, 1911.

*Most League Points:* 69, Division 3, 1965–66. *Three points win:* 69, Division 4, 1981–82.

*Most League Goals:* 109, Division 3, 1965–66.

*Highest League Scorer in Season:* Bill McNaughton, 39, Division 3(N), 1932–33.

*Most League Goals in Total Aggregate:* Chris Chilton, 195, 1960–71.

*Most Capped Player:* Terry Neill, 15 (59), Northern Ireland.

*Most League Appearances:* Andy Davidson, 511, 1952–67.

*Record Transfer Fee Received:* £200,000 from Manchester U for Stuart Pearson, May 1974.

*Record Transfer Fee Paid:* £150,000 to Carlisle U for Mick Tait, Sept 1979.

*Previous Managers since the War:* Ernest Blackburn, Major Frank Buckley, Raich Carter, Bob Jackson, Bob Brocklebank, Cliff Britton, Terry Neill, John Kaye, Bobby Collins, Ken Houghton, Mike Smith.

*Club Shop:* Club Shop, Boothferry Park, Hull. On match days, in main car park. Also in South Stand. Weekdays; articles may be purchased from the Development Association, 101 Boothferry Road, Hull. (0482) 51119.

**Boothferry Park, Hull HU4 6EU.** Telephone (0482) 52195. *Telegraphic address:* 'Tigers Hull'. *Ground capacity:* 42,000. *Record attendance:* 55,019 v Manchester U, FA Cup 6th rd, 26 Feb, 1949. *Record receipts:* £22,229 v Stoke City, FA Cup 6th rd, 6 March, 1971. *Pitch measurements:* 112yd×75yd.

*How to get there:* Buses 63c, 67 (Hull Corporation), 6, 155 (East Yorkshire) from coach station, Ferensway, Hull. Nearest railway stations, Hull and Boothferry Park Halt. Special trains on match days from Hull Paragon to Boothferry Park Halt; admittance to ground through turnstiles on station. Ground situated on A63 to the west of the city.

*Car parking:* At Kempton Road, five minutes walk from ground (opposite Three Tuns Hotel).

*Entertainments/catering facilities:* Catering facilities at points around the ground.

*Handbooks/programmes:* Programmes available on subscription.

*Extra information:* The club's 31 wins in 1965–66 was a Third Division record.

*Club Colours:* Amber shirts with red pin stripe, black collar and cuffs, black shorts with amber and red stripe down side, amber stockings.

*Change Colours:* All white.

*Club Nickname:* The Tigers.

## HULL CITY 1981–82 LEAGUE RECORD

| Match No. | Date | Venue | Opponents | Result | | H/T Score | Goalscorers | Attendance |
|---|---|---|---|---|---|---|---|---|
| 1 | Aug 29 | A | Torquay U | L | 1-2 | 0-0 | Mutrie | 2651 |
| 2 | Sept 5 | H | Bradford C | W | 2-1 | 1-0 | Mutrie, Ferguson | 3916 |
| 3 | 12 | A | Northampton T | D | 1-1 | 0-1 | Mutrie | 1938 |
| 4 | 19 | H | Sheffield U | W | 2-1 | 1-1 | Booth, Edwards | 7219 |
| 5 | 22 | H | Peterborough U | D | 1-1 | 1-0 | Ferguson | 3713 |
| 6 | 26 | A | Blackpool | L | 1-3 | 0-1 | Mutrie | 4838 |
| 7 | 30 | A | Hartlepool U | L | 2-3 | 2-2 | Whitehurst, Mutrie (pen) | 2654 |
| 8 | Oct 3 | H | Tranmere R | L | 1-2 | 0-2 | Whitehurst | 3087 |
| 9 | 10 | A | Mansfield T | D | 3-3 | 1-2 | Deacy, Mutrie (pen), Marwood | 3464 |
| 10 | 17 | H | Wigan Ath | L | 0-2 | 0-1 | | 3600 |
| 11 | 20 | A | Scunthorpe U | D | 4-4 | 2-1 | Roberts G., Richards, Marwood 2 | 3575 |
| 12 | 24 | H | Aldershot | L | 1-2 | 1-1 | Mutrie | 2999 |
| 13 | 31 | A | Port Vale | L | 1-2 | 0-2 | Mutrie | 2591 |
| 14 | Nov 3 | H | York C | W | 2-0 | 1-0 | Marwood, Roberts G. | 3340 |
| 15 | 7 | H | Colchester U | L | 2-3 | 1-1 | Mutrie, Roberts G. | 3040 |
| 16 | 14 | A | Hereford U | D | 2-2 | 0-2 | Whitehurst 2 | 2652 |
| 17 | 28 | A | Bury | W | 2-0 | 0-0 | McClaren, Roberts G. | 4508 |
| 18 | Dec 5 | H | Crewe Alex | W | 1-0 | 0-0 | Mutrie | 3184 |
| 19 | Jan 9 | A | Bradford C | D | 1-1 | 1-0 | Roberts G. | 5183 |
| 20 | 23 | H | Torquay U | W | 1-0 | 0-0 | Flounders | 3003 |
| 21 | 30 | A | Sheffield U | D | 0-0 | 0-0 | | 12,612 |
| 22 | Feb 6 | H | Northampton T | L | 0-1 | 0-1 | | 3341 |
| 23 | 10 | A | Peterborough U | L | 0-3 | 0-1 | | 3161 |
| 24 | 13 | A | Tranmere R | D | 2-2 | 1-0 | Mutrie 2 | 1737 |
| 25 | 20 | H | Hartlepool U | W | 5-2 | 2-0 | Mutrie 4, Lowe (og) | 2825 |
| 26 | 27 | H | Mansfield T | W | 2-0 | 1-0 | Flounders, Mutrie | 4958 |
| 27 | Mar 2 | H | Halifax T | W | 2-0 | 0-0 | Davis, Mutrie | 6952 |
| 28 | 6 | A | Wigan Ath | L | 1-2 | 1-1 | Mutrie | 6008 |
| 29 | 9 | H | Scunthorpe U | W | 2-0 | 2-0 | Mutrie, McClaren | 6121 |
| 30 | 12 | A | Aldershot | W | 3-0 | 0-0 | Mutrie 2, Marwood | 2059 |
| 31 | 16 | A | York C | W | 3-1 | 1-0 | Mutrie, Whitehurst, Marwood | 4771 |
| 32 | 20 | H | Port Vale | W | 3-1 | 0-0 | Booth, Mutrie, Deacy | 5506 |
| 33 | 23 | A | Darlington | L | 1-2 | 0-2 | Flounders | 2651 |
| 34 | 26 | A | Colchester U | L | 0-2 | 0-0 | | 2193 |
| 35 | Apr 3 | H | Hereford U | W | 2-1 | 2-0 | Flounders 2 | 3713 |
| 36 | 6 | A | Rochdale | W | 1-0 | 0-0 | Mutrie | 1738 |
| 37 | 10 | H | Darlington | L | 1-3 | 0-2 | McClaren | 4589 |
| 38 | 12 | A | Stockport Co | W | 2-1 | 0-0 | McClaren, Mutrie | 2450 |
| 39 | 17 | A | Crewe Alex | D | 1-1 | 1-1 | Marwood | 1595 |
| 40 | 20 | H | Stockport Co | D | 0-0 | 0-0 | | 3526 |
| 41 | 24 | H | Bury | W | 3-2 | 2-2 | Roberts G., Mutrie (pen), Whitehurst | 3602 |
| 42 | May 1 | A | AFC Bournemouth | L | 0-1 | 0-0 | | 8055 |
| 43 | 4 | A | Blackpool | W | 1-0 | 1-0 | Marwood | 3206 |
| 44 | 8 | H | Rochdale | W | 2-1 | 1-1 | Marwood 2 | 3012 |
| 45 | 11 | H | AFC Bournemouth | D | 0-0 | 0-0 | | 3387 |
| 46 | 14 | A | Halifax T | D | 2-2 | 1-1 | Marwood 2 | 2293 |

**Final League Position: 8**

### Goalscorers

*League* (70): Mutrie 27 (3 pens), Marwood 12, Roberts G. 6, Whitehurst 6, Flounders 5, McClaren 4, Booth 2, Deacy 2, Ferguson 2, Davis 1, Edwards 1, Richards 1, own goal 1.
*League Cup* (1): Ferguson 1.
*FA Cup* (7): McClaren 2, Whitehurst 2, Marwood 1, Mutrie 1, Swann 1.

| | | | | |
|---|---|---|---|---|
| **League Cup** | First Round | Lincoln C (a) | 0-3 | |
| | | (h) | 1-1 | |
| **FA Cup** | First Round | Rochdale (a) | 2-2 | |
| | | (h) | 2-2 | |
| | | (a) | 1-0 | (at Leeds) |
| | Second Round | Hartlepool U (h) | 2-0 | |
| | Third Round | Chelsea (a) | 0-0 | |
| | | (h) | 0-2 | |

| Norman | McNeil | Booth | Richards | Eccleston | Horswill | Roberts G. | Edwards | Whitehurst | Mutrie | Ferguson | Deacy | Hoolickin | Marwood | McClaren | Roberts D. | Swann | Davies | Kynman | Parkinson | Norrie | Flounders | Thompson | Davis | Match No. |
|---|---|---|---|---|---|---|---|---|---|---|---|---|---|---|---|---|---|---|---|---|---|---|---|---|
| 1 | 2 | 3 | 4 | 5 | 6 | 7 | 8 | 9 | 10* | 11 | 12 |  |  |  |  |  |  |  |  |  |  |  |  | 1 |
| 1 |  | 3 | 4 | 5 | 6 |  | 8 | 12 | 10* | 11 | 9 | 2 | 7 |  |  |  |  |  |  |  |  |  |  | 2 |
| 1 |  | 3 | 4 | 5 |  |  | 8 |  | 10 | 11 | 9 | 2 | 7 | 6 |  |  |  |  |  |  |  |  |  | 3 |
| 1 |  | 3 | 4 | 5 | 6 |  | 8 | 9 | 10 | 11 |  | 2 | 12 | 7* |  |  |  |  |  |  |  |  |  | 4 |
| 1 |  | 3 | 4 | 5 | 6 |  | 8 | 9 | 10 | 11 |  | 2 | 7 |  |  |  |  |  |  |  |  |  |  | 5 |
| 1 |  | 3 | 4 | 5 | 6 |  | 8* |  | 10 | 11 | 9 | 12 | 2 | 7 |  |  |  |  |  |  |  |  |  | 6 |
| 1 |  | 3 | 5 |  | 6 |  |  | 9 | 10 | 11 |  | 2 | 7 | 8 | 4 |  |  |  |  |  |  |  |  | 7 |
| 1 |  | 3 | 5 |  | 6 |  |  | 9 | 10 | 11* |  | 2 | 8 | 12 | 7 | 4 |  |  |  |  |  |  |  | 8 |
| 1 |  | 3 | 4* |  | 6 |  |  | 9 | 10 |  | 8 | 2 | 11 | 7 | 5 | 12 |  |  |  |  |  |  |  | 9 |
| 1 |  | 3 | 4 |  | 6 |  | 8 | 9 | 10 | 11* |  | 2 | 7 | 12 | 5 |  |  |  |  |  |  |  |  | 10 |
|  | 2 | 4 | 5 | 3 | 6 |  |  | 9 | 10 |  |  |  | 7 | 8 |  | 1 | 11 |  |  |  |  |  |  | 11 |
|  | 2 | 4 | 5 | 3 | 6 |  |  | 9* | 10 |  | 12 |  | 7 | 8 |  | 1 | 11 |  |  |  |  |  |  | 12 |
|  | 2* | 4 | 5 | 3 | 6 |  |  | 9 | 10 |  | 12 |  | 7 | 8 |  | 1 | 11 |  |  |  |  |  |  | 13 |
|  | 2 | 11 | 4 | 5 | 3 | 6 |  | 9 | 10 |  |  |  | 7 | 8 |  | 1 |  |  |  |  |  |  |  | 14 |
|  | 2 | 11 | 4 | 5 | 3* | 6 |  | 9 | 10 |  | 12 |  | 7 | 8 |  | 1 |  |  |  |  |  |  |  | 15 |
| 1 | 2 | 3 |  |  | 6 |  |  | 9 | 10 |  |  | 5 | 7 | 8 | 4 | 11 |  |  |  |  |  |  |  | 16 |
| 1 | 2 | 3 |  |  | 6 |  |  | 9 | 10 |  |  | 5 | 7* | 8 | 4 | 11 |  | 12 |  |  |  |  |  | 17 |
| 1 | 2 | 3 |  |  | 6 |  |  | 9 | 10 |  |  | 5 | 7 | 8 | 4 | 11 |  |  |  |  |  |  |  | 18 |
| 1 | 2 | 3 |  |  | 6 |  |  |  | 10 |  |  | 5 | 7 | 8 | 4 | 11 |  |  |  |  | 9 |  |  | 19 |
|  | 2 | 3 |  |  | 6 |  |  |  | 10 |  | 8 | 5 | 7 |  | 4 | 11 | 1 |  |  |  | 9 |  |  | 20 |
|  | 2 | 3 |  |  | 6 |  |  | 9 | 10 |  | 8 | 5 | 7* |  | 4 | 11 | 1 |  |  |  | 12 |  |  | 21 |
|  | 2* | 3 |  |  | 6 |  |  | 9 |  |  | 8 | 5 | 7 | 12 | 4 | 11 | 1 |  |  |  | 10 |  |  | 22 |
| 1 | 2 | 3* | 12 |  | 6 |  |  | 9 | 10 |  |  | 5 | 7 | 8 | 4 | 11 |  |  |  |  |  |  |  | 23 |
| 1 | 2* |  |  | 5 | 6 |  |  | 9 | 10 | 11 |  |  | 7 | 8 | 4 | 12 |  |  |  |  | 3 |  |  | 24 |
| 1 |  |  |  | 5 | 6 |  |  | 9 | 10 | 11 |  |  | 7 | 8 | 4 | 2 |  |  |  |  | 3 |  |  | 25 |
| 1 |  |  |  | 5 | 6* |  |  | 12 | 10 | 11 |  |  | 7 | 8 | 4 | 2 |  |  |  |  | 3 | 9 |  | 26 |
| 1 |  |  | 12 |  | 2 | 11 |  |  |  |  |  | 5 | 7 | 8 | 4* | 3 |  |  |  |  | 10 | 6 | 9 | 27 |
| 1 | 4 |  |  |  |  | 5 |  | 9 | 10 | 11 |  |  | 7 | 8 | 2 |  |  |  |  |  | 3 | 6 |  | 28 |
| 1 |  | 3 |  |  |  | 5* |  | 9 | 10 | 11 |  |  | 7 | 8 | 4 | 2 |  |  |  |  | 12 | 6 |  | 29 |
| 1 |  | 3 |  |  |  |  |  | 9 | 10 | 11 |  |  | 7 | 8 | 4 | 2 |  |  |  |  |  | 5 | 6 | 30 |
| 1 |  | 3 |  |  |  |  |  | 9 | 10 | 11 |  |  | 7 | 8 | 4 | 2 |  |  |  |  |  | 5 | 6 | 31 |
| 1 |  | 3 | 12 |  |  |  |  | 9 | 10 | 11 |  |  | 7 | 8 | 4 | 2* |  |  |  |  |  | 5 | 6 | 32 |
| 1 |  | 3 | 2 |  |  |  |  | 9 |  | 11 |  |  | 7 | 8 | 4 |  |  |  |  |  | 10 | 5 | 6 | 33 |
| 1 |  | 3 | 2* |  |  |  |  | 9 |  | 11 | 12 |  | 7 | 8 | 4 |  |  |  |  |  | 10 | 5 | 6 | 34 |
| 1 | 2 | 3 | 11 |  |  |  |  |  | 10 |  |  |  | 7 | 8 | 4 |  |  |  |  |  | 9 | 5 | 6 | 35 |
| 1 | 2 | 3 | 11 |  |  |  |  |  | 10 |  | 12 |  | 7 | 8* | 4 |  |  |  |  |  | 9 | 5 | 6 | 36 |
| 1 | 2 | 3 | 11 |  |  |  |  | 12 | 10 |  |  |  | 7 | 8 | 4 |  |  |  |  |  | 9 | 5 | 6* | 37 |
| 1 | 2 | 3 | 11 |  |  |  |  |  | 10 |  |  |  | 7 | 8 | 4 |  |  |  |  |  | 9 | 5 | 6 | 38 |
| 1 | 2 | 11 |  |  |  |  |  | 9 | 10 |  |  | 3 | 7 | 8 | 4 |  |  |  |  |  |  | 5 | 6 | 39 |
| 1 | 3* | 2 |  |  |  | 5 |  |  | 10 | 11 |  | 7 | 9 | 8 | 4 |  |  |  |  |  |  | 6 | 12 | 40 |
| 1 |  | 3 | 11 |  |  |  |  | 9 | 10 |  |  | 6 | 7 | 8 | 4 |  |  |  |  |  |  | 5 | 2 | 41 |
| 1 |  | 3 | 11 |  |  |  |  |  | 10 |  |  | 6 | 7 |  | 4 |  | 8 |  |  |  | 9 | 5 | 2 | 42 |
| 1 |  | 3 | 11 |  |  |  |  |  | 10 |  |  | 6 | 7 |  | 4 |  | 8 |  |  |  | 9 | 5 | 2 | 43 |
| 1 | 2 |  | 4 |  |  | 7 |  |  | 10 | 11 |  |  | 9 | 5 | 3 | 6 |  |  |  |  |  | 12 | 8* | 44 |
|  |  | 3 | 11 |  |  | 5 |  | 9 | 10 |  |  |  | 7 |  | 4 | 2* | 1 | 8 |  |  |  | 6 | 12 | 45 |
|  |  | 3 | 11 |  |  | 5 |  | 9 | 10 |  |  |  | 7 |  | 4 | 1 |  | 8 |  |  |  | 6 | 2 | 46 |
| 36 | 21 | 37 | 28 | 13 | 17 | 29 | 5 | 34 | 43 | 12 | 25 | 9 | 40 | 35 | 34 | 18 | 10 | 8 | — | 1 | 12 | 21 | 18 |  |
|  |  |  | + | + | + |  |  |  | + |  |  |  | + | + | + | + | + |  |  | + | + | + | + |  |
|  |  |  | 1s | 1s | 1s |  |  |  | 2s |  |  |  | 3s | 5s | 2s | 2s | 2s |  |  | 1s | 1s | 2s | 2s |  |

## HULL CITY

| | Ht | Wt | Birthplace | Clubs | League App. | League Gls |
|---|---|---|---|---|---|---|
| **Goalkeepers** | | | | | | |
| Tony Norman* | 6 1½ | 12 8 | Mancot | Burnley | — | — |
| | | | | Hull C | 95 | — |
| John Davies | 6 3 | 13 2 | Llandyssul | Cardiff C | 7 | — |
| | | | | Hull C | 14 | — |
| **Defenders** | | | | | | |
| John Roberts | 6 0 | 12 2 | Swansea | Swansea C | 37 | 16 |
| (Wales)   (Retired, injury) | | | | Northampton T | 62 | 11 |
| | | | | Arsenal | 59 | 4 |
| | | | | Birmingham C | 66 | 1 |
| | | | | Wrexham | 145 | 5 |
| | | | | Hull C | 26 | 1 |
| Dale Roberts | 5 10½ | 11 5 | Newcastle | Ipswich T | 18 | — |
| | | | | Hull C | 70 | 2 |
| Steve Richards | 6 0 | 12 0 | Hull | Hull C | 55 | 2 |
| Bobby McNeil* | 5 8½ | 10 9 | Bellshill | Hull C | 35 | — |
| Steve Hoolickin | 5 11 | 11 2 | Manchester | Oldham Ath | 8 | — |
| (Contract cancelled March 1982) | | | | Bury | 140 | 5 |
| | | | | Carlisle U | 143 | 2 |
| | | | | Hull C | 31 | — |
| Stuart Eccleston* | 5 11 | 11 5 | Stoke | Stoke C | — | — |
| | | | | Hull C | 23 | — |
| Dennis Booth | 5 7½ | 10 5 | Stenley Common | Charlton Ath | 77 | 5 |
| | | | | Blackpool | 12 | — |
| | | | | Southend U | 78 | 1 |
| | | | | Lincoln C | 162 | 9 |
| | | | | Watford | 100 | 2 |
| | | | | Hull C | 74 | 2 |
| Gary Swann* | 5 8¾ | 10 10 | Hull | Hull C | 40 | 2 |
| **Midfield** | | | | | | |
| Steve McClaren | 5 7½ | 9 4 | York | Hull C | 58 | 5 |
| Brian Marwood | 5 7 | 9 13 | Easington | Hull C | 79 | 16 |
| Mike Horswill | 5 10½ | 11 0 | Annfield Plain | Sunderland | 69 | 3 |
| (Contract cancelled April 1982) | | | | Manchester C | 14 | — |
| | | | | Plymouth Arg | 102 | 3 |
| | | | | Hull C | 84 | 6 |
| Garreth Roberts | 5 4 | 10 2 | Hull | Hull C | 112 | 14 |
| Dave Kynman | 5 10 | 9 12 | Hull | Hull C | 11 | — |
| (Non-contract) | | | | | | |
| Brian Ferguson* | 5 10 | 10 6 | Irvine | Mansfield T | — | — |
| | | | | Newcastle U | 5 | 1 |
| | | | | Hull C | 28 | 2 |
| Ian Davis | | | | Hull C | 20 | 1 |
| (Apprentice) | | | | | | |
| Neil Thompson | | | Beverley | Nottingham F | — | — |
| (Non-contract) | | | | Hull C | 23 | — |
| **Forwards** | | | | | | |
| Craig Norrie | 5 10½ | 10 11½ | Hull | Hull C | 31 | 4 |
| (Contract cancelled February 1982) | | | | | | |
| Nick Deacy | 6 0½ | 12 7 | Cardiff | Merthyr T | (not known) | |
| (Wales) | | | | Hereford U | 17 | 2 |
| (Contract cancelled April 1982) | | | | Workington (on loan) | 5 | 2 |
| | | | | PSV Eindhoven | (not known) | |
| | | | | Beringen | (not known) | |
| | | | | Vitesse | (not known) | |
| | | | | Hull C | 87 | 7 |
| Billy Whitehurst* | 6 0 | 13 0 | Rotherham | Mexborough | (not known) | |
| | | | | Hull C | 62 | 7 |
| Les Mutrie | 6 1 | 11 6 | Newcastle | Gateshead | (not known) | · |
| | | | | Carlisle U | 5 | — |
| | | | | Blyth S | (not known) | |
| | | | | Hull C | 63 | 32 |
| Andy Flounders* | | | Hull | Hull C | 18 | 5 |

# IPSWICH TOWN Division 1

*President:* Lady Blanche Cobbold.

*Chairman:* P. M. Cobbold.

*Directors:* W. Kerr, H. R. Smith, J. M. Sangster, K. H. Brightwell, J. C. Cobbold.

*Manager:* Bobby Ferguson.

*Secretary:* D. C. Rose.

*PRO:* Mel Henderson.

*Year Formed:* 1887. *Turned Professional:* 1936.

*Limited Company:* 1936.

**Football League Record:**
1938 Elected to Division 3(S); 1954–55 Division 2; 1955–57 Division 3(S); 1957–61 Division 2; 1961–64 Division 1; 1964–68 Division 2; 1968– Division 1.

**Honours:** *Football League:* Division 1 – Champions 1961–62; Runners-up 1980–81, 1981–82; Division 2 – Champions 1960–61, 1967–68; Division 3(S) – Champions 1953–54, 1956–57. *FA Cup:* Winners 1977–78. *Football League Cup* best season: Semi-final 1981–82. *Texaco Cup:* 1972–73. **European Competitions:** *European Cup:* 1962–63; *European Cup-Winners' Cup:* 1978–79; *UEFA Cup:* 1973–74, 1974–75, 1975–76, 1977–78, 1979–80, 1980–81 (winners), 1981–82.

*Record Victory:* 10-0 v Floriana, Malta, European Cup 1st rd, 25 Sept, 1962.

*Record Defeat:* 1-10 v Fulham, Division 1, 26 Dec, 1963.

*Most League Points:* 64, Division 3(S), 1953–54, 1955–56. *Three points win:* 83, Division 1, 1981–82.

*Most League Goals:* 106, Division 3(S), 1955–56.

*Highest League Scorer in Season:* Ted Phillips, 41, Division 3(S), 1956–57.

*Most League Goals in Total Aggregate:* Ray Crawford, 203, 1958–63, 1966–69.

*Most Capped Player:* Allan Hunter, 47 (53), Northern Ireland.

*Most League Appearances:* Mick Mills, 580, 1966–82.

*Record Transfer Fee Received:* £450,000 from Arsenal for Brian Talbot, Jan 1979.

*Record Transfer Fee Paid:* £250,000 to Millwall for Kevin O'Callaghan, Jan 1980.

*Previous Managers since the War:* A. Scott Duncan, Alf Ramsey, Jackie Milburn, Bill McGarry, Bobby Robson.

*Address of Supporters Club:* Same as Football Club.

*Address of the Club Shop or Boutique:* Same as Football Club.

---

**Portman Road, Ipswich, Suffolk IP1 2DA.** Telephone Ipswich 219211 (4 lines). *Ground capacity:* 37,000. *Record attendance:* 38,010 v Leeds U, FA Cup 6th rd, 8 March, 1975. *Record receipts:* £105,950 v AZ 67 Alkmaar, UEFA Cup final 1st leg, 6 May, 1981. *Pitch measurements:* 112yd×72yd.

*How to get there:* The ground is central and only two minutes walk from Ipswich railway station; the town centre is five minutes away. Local buses run past the ground.

*Match tickets:* On sale 12 days prior to match, price £4.00 and £4.50. Postal bookings accepted.

*Car parking:* Large parks in Portman Road, Portman's Walk, and off Princess Street at Greyfriars Park.

*Entertainments/catering facilities:* 'Centre Spot' bar and restaurant in Portman Road. Bars around the ground. Executive boxes available.

*Club shop:* Four on the ground stock all types of souvenirs.

*Handbooks/programmes:* Programmes available on subscription and an Annual is published.

*Extra information:* When Ipswich won the First Division title in 1962, five of the side – Bailey, Carberry, Phillips, Elsworthy, and Leadbetter – had been regulars in the Third Division side of the middle fifties.

*Club Colours:* Blue shirts with three white stripes down each arm, white shorts with three blue stripes, blue stockings with three white stripes.

*Change Colours:* White shirts with three black stripes down each arm, black shorts with three white stripes, white stockings with three black stripes.

*Club Captain:* Mick Mills.

*First Team Trainer:*

*Club Nickname:* Town or Blues.

# IPSWICH TOWN 1981–82 LEAGUE RECORD

| Match No. | Date | | Venue | Opponents | Result | | H/T Score | Goalscorers | Attendance |
|---|---|---|---|---|---|---|---|---|---|
| 1 | Aug 29 | H | | Sunderland | D | 3-3 | 0-1 | Wark, Gates 2 | 24,060 |
| 2 | Sept 1 | A | | Birmingham C | D | 1-1 | 0-1 | Brazil | 17,328 |
| 3 | | 5 | A | Manchester U | W | 2-1 | 2-1 | Brazil, Wark | 45,645 |
| 4 | | 12 | H | Liverpool | W | 2-0 | 1-0 | Neal (og) Wark (pen) | 26,703 |
| 5 | | 19 | A | Notts Co | W | 4-1 | 1-0 | Brazil 2, Wark, Muhren | 12,559 |
| 6 | | 22 | H | WBA | W | 1-0 | 0-0 | Deehan (og) | 20,524 |
| 7 | | 26 | H | Leeds U | W | 2-1 | 0-1 | Butcher, Gates | 22,319 |
| 8 | Oct 3 | A | | Southampton | L | 3-4 | 3-1 | Wark 2 (1 pen), Mariner | 22,552 |
| 9 | | 10 | H | Wolverhampton W | W | 1-0 | 1-0 | O'Callaghan | 20,498 |
| 10 | | 17 | A | Everton | L | 1-2 | 1-2 | Gates | 25,146 |
| 11 | | 24 | H | Arsenal | W | 2-1 | 1-0 | Mariner, Mills | 24,362 |
| 12 | | 31 | A | Aston Villa | W | 1-0 | 1-0 | Osman | 32,652 |
| 13 | Nov 7 | H | | Swansea C | L | 2-3 | 0-1 | Mariner, Muhren | 24,190 |
| 14 | | 21 | A | Stoke C | L | 0-2 | 0-0 | | 13,802 |
| 15 | | 28 | H | Manchester C | W | 2-0 | 0-0 | Wark (pen), D'Avray | 20,476 |
| 16 | Dec 5 | A | | Middlesbrough | W | 1-0 | 1-0 | D'Avray | 13,577 |
| 17 | Jan 5 | H | | Birmingham C | W | 3-2 | 2-0 | Mariner 2, Brazil | 19,188 |
| 18 | | 16 | A | Coventry C | W | 4-2 | 1-1 | Wark, Muhren, Mariner, Brazil | 11,719 |
| 19 | | 30 | H | Notts Co | L | 1-3 | 0-1 | Thijssen | 21,570 |
| 20 | Feb 6 | A | | Liverpool | L | 0-4 | 0-3 | | 41,316 |
| 21 | | 16 | H | Southampton | W | 5-2 | 3-1 | Brazil 5 | 20,264 |
| 22 | | 20 | A | Leeds U | W | 2-0 | 0-0 | Brazil, Mills | 20,287 |
| 23 | | 27 | A | Wolverhampton W | L | 1-2 | 1-2 | Gates | 12,439 |
| 24 | Mar 2 | A | | West Ham U | L | 0-2 | 0-1 | | 24,846 |
| 25 | | 6 | H | Everton | W | 3-0 | 1-0 | Wark, Brazil, Gates | 19,360 |
| 26 | | 13 | A | Arsenal | L | 0-1 | 0-1 | | 25,977 |
| 27 | | 17 | A | Nottingham F | D | 1-1 | 0-0 | Wark (pen) | 16,686 |
| 28 | | 20 | H | Aston Villa | W | 3-1 | 2-0 | Wark, McCall, Gates | 20,407 |
| 29 | | 27 | A | Swansea C | W | 2-1 | 1-1 | Brazil, Gates | 20,750 |
| 30 | | 30 | H | Brighton & HA | W | 3-1 | 1-0 | Brazil 2, Wark | 19,361 |
| 31 | Apr 3 | H | | Coventry C | W | 1-0 | 1-0 | Wark | 20,411 |
| 32 | | 7 | A | Sunderland | D | 1-1 | 0-0 | Steggles | 11,845 |
| 33 | | 10 | A | Tottenham H | L | 0-1 | 0-0 | | 45,215 |
| 34 | | 13 | H | West Ham U | W | 3-2 | 2-1 | Brazil, Wark (pen), Osman | 28,767 |
| 35 | | 17 | H | Stoke C | W | 2-0 | 1-0 | Mariner, Wark | 20,309 |
| 36 | | 20 | H | Manchester U | W | 2-1 | 1-1 | Wark 2 | 25,763 |
| 37 | | 24 | A | Manchester C | D | 1-1 | 1-0 | Brazil | 30,329 |
| 38 | May 1 | H | | Middlesbrough | W | 3-1 | 2-1 | Wark, Muhren, Brazil | 17,980 |
| 39 | | 5 | A | WBA | W | 2-1 | 1-0 | Gates, Brazil | 12,564 |
| 40 | | 8 | A | Brighton & HA | W | 1-0 | 1-0 | Mariner | 17,786 |
| 41 | | 15 | H | Nottingham F | L | 1-3 | 0-0 | Brazil | 19,937 |
| 42 | | 17 | H | Tottenham H | W | 2-1 | 1-0 | Mills, Brazil | 20,764 |

**Final League Position: 2**

## Goalscorers

*League* (75): Brazil 22, Wark 18 (5 pens), Gates 9, Mariner 8, Muhren 4, Mills 3, D'Avray 2, Osman 2, Butcher 1, McCall 1, O'Callaghan 1, Steggles 1, Thijssen 1, own goals 2.

*League Cup* (15): Gates 4, Brazil 3, Wark 3, Mariner 1, Muhren 1, O'Callaghan 1, Steggles 1, Turner 1.

*FA Cup* (7): Brazil 3, Gates 2, D'Avray 1, Wark 1.

| | | | | |
|---|---|---|---|---|
| **League Cup** | Second Round | Leeds U (a) | 1-0 | |
| | | (h) | 3-0 | |
| | Third Round | Bradford C (h) | 1-1 | |
| | | (a) | 3-2 | |
| | Fourth Round | Everton (a) | 3-2 | |
| | Fifth Round | Watford (h) | 2-1 | |
| | Semi-final | Liverpool (h) | 0-2 | |
| | | (a) | 2-2 | |
| **FA Cup** | Third Round | Birmingham C (a) | 3-2 | |
| | Fourth Round | Luton T (a) | 3-0 | |
| | Fifth Round | Shrewsbury T (a) | 1-2 | |

| Cooper | Mills | McCall | Thijssen | Osman | Butcher | Wark | Muhren | Mariner | Brazil | Gates | Turner | Parkin | O'Callaghan | Steggles | Burley | D'Avray | Sivell | Gernon | Jackson | Match No. |
|---|---|---|---|---|---|---|---|---|---|---|---|---|---|---|---|---|---|---|---|---|
| 1 | 2 | 3 | 4 | 5 | 6 | 7 | 8 | 9 | 10 | 11 | | | | | | | | | | 1 |
| 1 | 2 | 3 | 4 | 5 | 6 | 7 | 8 | 9 | 10 | 11 | | | | | | | | | | 2 |
| 1 | 2 | 3 | 4 | 5 | 6 | 7 | 8 | 9 | 10 | 11 | | | | | | | | | | 3 |
| 1 | 2 | 3 | 4 | 5 | 6 | 7 | 8 | 9 | 10 | 11 | | | | | | | | | | 4 |
| 1 | 2 | 3 | 4* | 5 | 6 | 7 | 8 | 9 | 10 | 11 | 12 | | | | | | | | | 5 |
| 1 | 2 | 3 | | | 6 | 7 | 8 | 9 | 10 | 11 | | 4* | 12 | | 5 | | | | | 6 |
| 1 | 2 | 3 | | | 6 | 7 | 8 | 9 | | 11 | | 4 | 10 | | 5 | | | | | 7 |
| 1 | 4 | 3 | | 6 | 5 | 7 | 8 | 9 | | 11 | | 10* | 12 | | 2 | | | | | 8 |
| 1 | 2 | 3 | 4 | 5 | 6 | 7 | 8 | 9 | | 11 | | | 10 | | | | | | | 9 |
| 1 | 2 | 3 | 4 | 5 | 6 | 7 | 8 | 9 | | 11 | | | 10 | | | | | | | 10 |
| 1 | 10 | 3 | 4 | 5 | 6 | 7 | 8 | 9 | | 11 | | | 2 | | | | | | | 11 |
| 1 | 2 | 3 | 4 | 5 | 6 | 7 | 8 | 9 | 10 | 11 | | | | | | | | | | 12 |
| 1 | 2 | 3 | 4 | 5 | 6 | 7 | 8 | 9 | 10 | 11 | | | | | | | | | | 13 |
| 1 | 4 | 3 | | 5 | 6 | 7 | 8 | 9 | 10 | 11 | | | | | 2 | | | | | 14 |
| 1 | 4 | 3 | | 5 | 6 | 7 | 8 | | 10 | 11* | | 12 | 9 | | 2 | | | | | 15 |
| 1 | 4 | 3 | | 5 | 6 | 7 | 8 | | 10 | 11 | | | | | 2 | 9 | | | | 16 |
| 1 | 4* | 3 | | 5 | 6 | 7 | 8 | 9 | 10 | 11 | | | 12 | | 2 | | | | | 17 |
| 1 | 4 | 3 | | 5 | 6 | 7 | 8 | 9 | 10 | 11 | | | | | 2 | | | | | 18 |
| 1 | 4 | 3 | 9 | 5 | | 7 | 8 | | 10 | 11 | | | 12 | 6* | 2 | | | | | 19 |
| 1 | 4 | 3 | | 5 | | 7 | 8 | 9 | | 11 | | 10* | 12 | 6 | 2 | | | | | 20 |
| 1 | 4 | 3 | | 5 | | 7 | 8 | | 10 | 11 | | | | 6 | 2 | 9 | | | | 21 |
| 1 | 4 | 3 | | 5 | | 7 | 8 | | 10 | 11 | | | | 6 | 2 | 9 | | | | 22 |
| 1 | 4* | 3 | | 5 | | 7 | 8 | | 10 | 11 | | | 12 | 6 | 2 | 9 | | | | 23 |
| 1 | 4 | 3 | | 5 | | 7 | 8 | | 10 | 11 | | | 12 | 6* | 2 | 9 | | | | 24 |
| | 4 | 3 | | 5 | | 7 | 8 | | 10 | 11 | | | | 6 | 2 | 9 | 1 | | | 25 |
| | 4 | 3 | | 5 | | 7 | 8 | | 10 | 11 | | | | 6 | 2 | 9 | 1 | | | 26 |
| | 4* | 9 | | 5 | | 7 | 8 | | 10 | 11 | | | 12 | 6 | 2 | | 1 | 3 | | 27 |
| | 4 | 3 | | 5 | | 7 | 8 | | 10 | 11 | | | 9 | 6 | 2 | | 1 | | | 28 |
| | 4 | 3 | | 5 | | 7 | 8 | | 10 | 11 | | | | 6 | 2 | 9 | 1 | | | 29 |
| | 4 | 3 | | 5 | | 7 | 8 | | 10 | 11 | | | | 6 | 2 | 9 | 1 | | | 30 |
| 1 | 4 | 3 | | 5 | | 7 | 8 | | 10 | 11 | | | | | 2 | 9 | | 6 | | 31 |
| 1 | 4* | 3 | | 5 | | 7 | 8 | | 10 | 11 | | | 12 | 6 | 2 | 9 | | | | 32 |
| 1 | 4 | 3 | | 5 | | 7* | 8 | | 10 | 11 | | | 12 | 6 | 2 | 9 | | | | 33 |
| 1 | 4 | 3 | | 5 | 6 | 7 | 8 | 9 | 10 | 11 | | | | | 2 | | | | | 34 |
| 1 | 4 | 3 | | 5 | 6 | 7 | 8 | 9 | 10 | 11 | | | | | 2 | | | | | 35 |
| | 4 | 3 | | 5 | 6 | 7 | 8 | 9 | 10 | 11 | | | | | 2 | | 1 | | | 36 |
| 1 | 4* | 3 | | 5 | 6 | 7 | 8 | 9 | 10 | 11 | | | 12 | | 2 | | | | | 37 |
| 1 | 4 | 3 | | 5 | 6 | 7 | 8 | 9* | 10 | 11 | | | 12 | | 2 | | | | | 38 |
| 1 | 4 | 9 | | 5 | 6 | 7 | 8 | | 10 | 11* | | | 12 | | 2 | | | 3 | | 39 |
| | 4 | 11 | | 5 | 6 | 7 | 8 | 9 | 10 | | | | | | 2 | | 1 | 3 | | 40 |
| | 4* | 3 | | 5 | 6 | 7 | 8 | 9 | 10 | 11 | | | 12 | | 2 | | 1 | | | 41 |
| | 4 | 3 | | 5 | 6 | 7 | 8 | 9 | 10 | 11 | | | | | 2 | | 1 | | | 42 |
| 32 | 42 | 42 | 12 | 39 | 27 | 42 | 42 | 25 | 35 | 38 | 1 | 5 | 7 | 18 | 29 | 12 | 9 | 4 | 1 | |
| | | | | | | | | | | | +2s | +1s | +12s | | +1s | | | | | |

# IPSWICH TOWN

| | Ht | Wt | Birthplace | Clubs | League App. | League Gls |
|---|---|---|---|---|---|---|
| **Goalkeepers** | | | | | | |
| Paul Cooper | 5 11 | 12 7 | Brierley Hill | Birmingham C | 17 | — |
| | | | | Ipswich T | 268 | — |
| Laurie Sivell | 5 8 | 11 0 | Lowestoft | Ipswich T | 128 | — |
| | | | | Lincoln C (on loan) | 2 | — |
| Gary Westwood | 6 0 | 13 0 | Barrow | Ipswich T | — | — |
| | | | | Charlton Ath (on loan) | — | — |
| John Jackson | 6 0 | 13 13 | Hammersmith | Crystal Palace | 346 | — |
| | | | | Orient | 226 | — |
| | | | | Millwall | 79 | — |
| | | | | Ipswich T | 1 | — |
| **Defenders** | | | | | | |
| George Burley | 5 9½ | 11 0 | Cumnock | Ipswich T | 292 | 4 |
| (Scotland) | | | | | | |
| Terry Butcher | 6 4 | 14 0 | Singapore | Ipswich T | 127 | 9 |
| (England) | | | | | | |
| Mick Mills | 5 7½ | 11 10 | Godalming | Ipswich T | 580 | 22 |
| (England) | | | | | | |
| Kevin Beattie | 5 10½ | 12 4 | Carlisle | Ipswich T | 228 | 24 |
| (England)   (Contract cancelled Feb 1982) | | | | | | |
| Russell Osman | 6 0 | 11 10 | Repton | Ipswich T | 190 | 7 |
| (England) | | | | | | |
| Don Souter* | 5 11 | 11 8 | Hammersmith | Ipswich T | — | — |
| Kevin Steggles | 6 0 | 11 1 | Ditchingham | Ipswich T | 24 | 1 |
| Ron Burns | 5 8 | 10 7 | Londonderry | Coleraine | — | — |
| | | | | Ballymena U (on loan) | — | — |
| | | | | Ipswich T | — | — |
| Irvin Gernon | 6 2 | 11 13½ | Birmingham | Ipswich T | 4 | — |
| Ian Templeton | 5 9½ | 10 7 | Sunderland | Ipswich T | — | — |
| Frank Yallop | 5 10½ | 10 3 | Watford | Ipswich T | — | — |
| David Barnes | 5 10 | 10 8 | Westminster | Coventry C | 9 | — |
| | | | | Ipswich T | — | — |
| **Midfield** | | | | | | |
| John Wark | 5 10½ | 11 12 | Glasgow | Ipswich T | 222 | 69 |
| (Scotland) | | | | | | |
| Tommy Parkin | 5 7 | 10 4 | Gateshead | Ipswich T | 15 | — |
| | | | | Grimsby T (on loan) | 6 | — |
| | | | | Peterborough U (on loan) | 3 | — |
| Bryan Klug | 5 8 | 10 10 | Coventry | Ipswich T | — | — |
| | | | | Wimbledon (on loan) | 11 | — |
| Steve McCall | 5 11 | 11 3 | Carlisle | Ipswich T | 83 | 2 |
| Arnold Muhren | 5 11 | 11 1 | Volendam | Ajax | (not known) | |
| (Netherlands) | | | | Twente | (not known) | |
| | | | | Ipswich T | 161 | 21 |
| Frans Thijssen | 5 11 | 11 2 | Heumen | NEC | (not known) | |
| (Netherlands) | | | | Twente | (not known) | |
| | | | | Ipswich T | 96 | 7 |
| Jim King | 5 7 | 11 0 | Dumfries | Ipswich T | — | — |
| Mark Lomas | 5 9 | 11 7 | Manchester | Ipswich T | — | — |
| (Contract cancelled Jan 1982) | | | | | | |
| Tony Kinsella | 5 8 | 10 4 | Grays | Millwall | 61 | 1 |
| | | | | Tampa Bay R | (not known) | |
| | | | | Ipswich T | — | — |
| Trevor Putney | 5 9½ | 10 3 | Harold Hill | Brentwood & W | (not known) | |
| | | | | Ipswich T | — | — |
| **Forwards** | | | | | | |
| Eric Gates | 5 6 | 10 4 | Ferryhill | Ipswich T | 194 | 44 |
| (England) | | | | | | |
| Robin Turner | 5 9 | 10 8 | Carlisle | Ipswich T | 33 | — |
| Paul Mariner | 6 0 | 12 2 | Bolton | Plymouth Arg | 135 | 56 |
| (England) | | | | Ipswich T | 200 | 72 |
| Alan Brazil | 6 0 | 12 4 | Glasgow | Ipswich T | 126 | 60 |
| (Scotland) | | | | | | |
| Mich D'Avray | 6 1 | 12 0 | Johannesburg | Ipswich T | 20 | 3 |
| Kevin O'Callaghan | 5 8½ | 10 9 | London | Millwall | 20 | 3 |
| (Eire) | | | | Ipswich T | 47 | 1 |
| Russell Irving | 5 8 | 11 2½ | Wallsend | Ipswich T | — | — |
| John Linford | 6 2 | 11 12 | Norwich | Ipswich T | — | — |

Free transfers: George Ainsley*, Alec Chamberlain*, Gary McManus*, Dale Brooks*.

# LEEDS UNITED

# Division 2

*President:* The Right Hon The Earl of Harewood LLD.

*Chairman:* M. Cussins.

*Vice-Chairman:* L. Silver.

*Directors:* R. Barker MCIT, MBIM, B. Woodward, J. W. G. Marjason, S. G. Simon, W. J. Fotherby, M. Holmes.

*Player Manager:* Eddie Gray.

*Asst Manager:* Jimmy Lumsden.

*General Manager/Secretary:* Keith Archer.

*Year Formed:* 1919, as Leeds United after disbandment (by FA order) of Leeds City in 1904.

*Turned Professional:* 1920.  *Limited Company:* 1920.

**Football League Record:**
1920 Elected to Division 2; 1924–27 Division 1; 1927–28 Division 2; 1928–31 Division 1; 1931–32 Division 2; 1932–47 Division 1; 1947–56 Division 2; 1956–60 Division 1; 1960–64 Division 2; 1964–82 Division 1; 1982– Division 2.

**Honours:** *Football League:* Division 1 – Champions 1968–69, 1973–74; Runners-up 1964–65, 1965–66, 1969–70, 1970–71, 1971–72; Division 2 – Champions 1923–24, 1963–64; Runners-up 1927–28, 1931–32, 1955–56. *FA Cup:* Winners 1972; Runners-up 1965, 1970, 1973. *Football League Cup:* Winners 1967–68. **European Competitions:** *European Cup:* 1969–70, 1974–75 (runners-up). *European Cup-Winners' Cup:* 1972–73 (runners-up). *European Fairs Cup:* 1965–66, 1966–67 (runners-up), 1967–68 (winners), 1968–69, 1970–71 (winners). *UEFA Cup:* 1971–72, 1973–74, 1979–80.

*Record Victory:* 10-0 v Lyn Oslo, European Cup 1st rd 1st leg, 17 Sept, 1969.

*Record Defeat:* 1-8 v Stoke C, Division 1, 27 Aug, 1934.

*Most League Points:* 67, Division 1, 1968–69.

*Most League Goals:* 98, Division 2, 1927–28.

*Highest League Scorer in Season:* John Charles, 42, Division 2, 1953–54.

*Most League Goals in Total Aggregate:* John Charles, 154, 1948–57 and 1962.

*Most Capped Player:* Billy Bremner, 54, Scotland.

*Most League Appearances:* Jack Charlton, 629, 1953–73.

*Record Transfer Fee Received:* £500,000 from Nottingham F for Frank Gray, July 1979.

*Record Transfer Fee Paid:* £930,000 to WBA for Peter Barnes, Aug 1981.

*Previous Managers since the War:* Billy Hampson, Willis Edwards, Major Frank Buckley, Raich Carter, Bill Lambton, Jack Taylor, Don Revie OBE, Brian Clough, Jimmy Armfield, Jock Stein, Jimmy Adamson, Allan Clarke.

*Address of Supporters Club:* Leeds United Supporters Club, Fullerton Park, Elland Road, Leeds 11.

*Address of the Club Shop or Boutique:* Leeds United Club Shop, Elland Road, Leeds 11.

---

**Elland Road, Leeds LS11 0ES.** Telephone Leeds 716037 (3 lines). *Telegraphic Address:* 'Football Leeds'. *Ground capacity:* 43,900. *Record attendance:* 57,892 v Sunderland, FA Cup 5th rd replay, 15 March, 1967. *Record receipts:* £146,483, FA Cup semi-final replay, Everton v West Ham U, 16 April, 1980. *Pitch measurements:* 117yd×76yd.
*How to get there:* Nearest railway station, Leeds. The city centre is within walking distance from the station and then by Corporation buses to the ground.
*Match tickets:* Computer installed for sale of match-by-match tickets.
*Car parking:* Within one minute of the ground there is a large park owned by the Leeds Greyhound Association; this holds about 1000 cars.
*Entertainments/catering facilities:* Supporters' social club adjacent to the ground. Snack bars around the ground.
*Club shop:* This operates at the ground next to the Pools Office and stocks all types of souvenirs.
*Handbooks/programmes:* Programmes are available from the club shop, and on subscription.
*Extra information:* The club have a Robotphone Answering System – the Leeds United Information Service: Leeds 702621. New Football League record established in 1973–74 with a 29-game run of matches without defeat from beginning of the season. Leeds United have an official fan club aimed at young supporters aged 6–16.
*Club Colours:* All white with blue and yellow stripe.
*Change Colours:* All yellow with blue and white trim.
*Club Captain:* Kenny Burns.
*Deputy Manager:*

## LEEDS UNITED 1981–82 LEAGUE RECORD

| Match No. | Date | Venue | Opponents | Result | H/T Score | Goalscorers | Attendance |
|---|---|---|---|---|---|---|---|
| 1 | Aug 29 | A | Swansea C | L 1-5 | 1-1 | Parlane | 23,489 |
| 2 | Sept 2 | H | Everton | D 1-1 | 1-1 | Graham | 26,502 |
| 3 | 5 | H | Wolverhampton W | W 3-0 | 1-0 | Graham 3 | 20,216 |
| 4 | 12 | A | Coventry C | L 0-4 | 0-2 | | 13,065 |
| 5 | 19 | H | Arsenal | D 0-0 | 0-0 | | 21,410 |
| 6 | 23 | A | Manchester C | L 0-4 | 0-2 | | 35,077 |
| 7 | 26 | A | Ipswich T | L 1-2 | 1-0 | Barnes | 22,319 |
| 8 | 30 | A | Manchester U | L 0-1 | 0-0 | | 47,019 |
| 9 | Oct 3 | H | Aston Villa | D 1-1 | 0-1 | Balcombe | 21,065 |
| 10 | 10 | A | Liverpool | L 0-3 | 0-2 | | 35,840 |
| 11 | 17 | H | WBA | W 3-1 | 0-0 | Graham, Cherry, Connor | 19,164 |
| 12 | 24 | H | Sunderland | W 1-0 | 0-0 | Gray E. | 25,220 |
| 13 | 31 | A | Nottingham F | L 1-2 | 1-1 | Butterworth | 25,272 |
| 14 | Nov 7 | H | Notts Co | W 1-0 | 1-0 | Butterworth | 19,552 |
| 15 | 21 | A | Southampton | L 0-4 | 0-3 | | 21,127 |
| 16 | 28 | H | West Ham U | D 3-3 | 1-0 | Graham, Hird (pen), Cherry | 25,637 |
| 17 | Dec 5 | A | Stoke C | W 2-1 | 2-0 | Graham, Hamson | 13,901 |
| 18 | 12 | H | Tottenham H | D 0-0 | 0-0 | | 28,780 |
| 19 | Jan 16 | H | Swansea C | W 2-0 | 1-0 | Stevenson, Butterworth | 18,709 |
| 20 | 30 | A | Arsenal | L 0-1 | 0-1 | | 22,408 |
| 21 | Feb 6 | H | Coventry C | D 0-0 | 0-0 | | 16,385 |
| 22 | 20 | H | Ipswich T | L 0-2 | 0-0 | | 20,287 |
| 23 | 27 | H | Liverpool | L 0-2 | 0-1 | | 33,689 |
| 24 | Mar 2 | A | Brighton & HA | L 0-1 | 0-1 | | 12,857 |
| 25 | 10 | H | Manchester C | L 0-1 | 0-0 | | 20,797 |
| 26 | 13 | A | Sunderland | W 1-0 | 0-0 | Worthington | 20,285 |
| 27 | 16 | A | Wolverhampton W | L 0-1 | 0-1 | | 11,729 |
| 28 | 20 | H | Nottingham F | D 1-1 | 1-1 | Worthington (pen) | 18,036 |
| 29 | 27 | A | Notts Co | L 1-2 | 1-0 | Worthington | 13,316 |
| 30 | Apr 3 | H | Manchester U | D 0-0 | 0-0 | | 31,118 |
| 31 | 6 | A | Middlesbrough | D 0-0 | 0-0 | | 15,494 |
| 32 | 10 | A | Birmingham C | W 1-0 | 0-0 | Hart | 14,497 |
| 33 | 13 | H | Middlesbrough | D 1-1 | 0-1 | Parlane | 20,458 |
| 34 | 17 | H | Southampton | L 1-3 | 1-3 | Worthington | 21,353 |
| 35 | 24 | A | West Ham U | L 3-4 | 1-0 | Connor, Graham, Flynn | 24,748 |
| 36 | 28 | A | Aston Villa | W 4-1 | 1-1 | Graham, Worthington 2, Connor | 20,566 |
| 37 | May 1 | H | Stoke C | D 0-0 | 0-0 | | 17,775 |
| 38 | 4 | A | Everton | L 0-1 | 0-0 | | 17,137 |
| 39 | 8 | A | Tottenham H | L 1-2 | 0-1 | Worthington | 35,020 |
| 40 | 12 | H | Birmingham C | D 3-3 | 2-2 | Worthington 2 (1 pen), Connor | 18,583 |
| 41 | 15 | H | Brighton & HA | W 2-1 | 0-1 | Hamson, Hird | 19,831 |
| 42 | 18 | A | WBA | L 0-2 | 0-0 | | 23,118 |

**Final League Position: 20**

### Goalscorers

*League* (39): Graham 9, Worthington 9 (2 pens), Connor 4, Butterworth 3, Cherry 2, Hamson 2, Hird 2 (1 pen), Parlane 2, Balcombe 1, Barnes 1, Flynn 1, Gray E. 1, Hart 1, Stevenson 1.
*League Cup* (0).
*FA Cup* (3): Gray E. 1, Hamson 1, Hird 1.

| League Cup | Second Round | Ipswich T (h) | 0-1 |
|---|---|---|---|
| | | (a) | 0-3 |
| FA Cup | Third Round | Wolverhampton W (a) | 3-1 |
| | Fourth Round | Tottenham H (a) | 0-1 |

| Lukic | Hird | Gray F. | Flynn | Hart | Cherry | Harris | Graham | Parlane | Gray E. | Barnes | Greenhoff | Stevenson | Firm | Connor | Hamson | Arins | Thomas | Balcombe | Burns | Butterworth | Aspin | Worthington | Match No. |
|---|---|---|---|---|---|---|---|---|---|---|---|---|---|---|---|---|---|---|---|---|---|---|---|
| 1 | 2 | 3 | 4 | 5 | 6 | 7 | 8 | 9 | 10 | 11 | | | | | | | | | | | | | 1 |
| 1 | | | 4 | 5 | 6 | 7 | 8 | 9 | 3 | 11 | 2 | 10 | | | | | | | | | | | 2 |
| 1 | 12 | | 4 | | 6 | 7 | 8 | 9 | 3 | 11 | 2* | 10 | 5 | | | | | | | | | | 3 |
| 1 | 12 | | 4 | | 6 | 7* | 8 | | 3 | 11 | 2 | 10 | 5 | 9 | | | | | | | | | 4 |
| 1 | | 5 | 4 | | 6 | 7 | 8 | | 3 | 11 | 2 | 10 | | 9 | | | | | | | | | 5 |
| 1 | 8 | 5 | 4 | | 6 | 7 | | | 3* | 11 | 2 | 10 | | 9 | 12 | | | | | | | | 6 |
| 1 | 10 | 3 | 4 | | 6 | 7 | 8 | | | 11 | 2* | 5 | | 12 | 9 | | | | | | | | 7 |
| 1 | 2 | 3 | 4* | | 6 | 7 | 8 | | | 11 | | 5 | 12 | 10 | 9 | | | | | | | | 8 |
| 1 | 4 | 3 | | 5 | 6 | 7 | 8 | | | 11 | 2 | 10 | | 9 | | | | | | | | | 8 |
| 1 | 2 | 3 | | 5 | 6 | 7 | 8 | 10 | 11 | 12 | | 4* | | 9 | | | | | | | | | 10 |
| 1 | 4 | 3 | | 5 | 2 | 7* | 8 | | | 11 | 12 | | | | 10 | | | | 6 | 9 | | | 11 |
| 1 | 4 | 3 | | 5 | 2 | | 8 | | 7 | 11 | | 9 | | 10 | | | | | 6 | | | | 12 |
| 1 | 4 | 3 | | 5 | 2 | | 8 | | 7 | | 11 | | | 10 | | | | | 6 | 9 | | | 13 |
| 1 | 2 | 3 | | 5 | 6 | | 8 | | 7 | 11 | 4 | | | 10 | | | | | | 9 | | | 14 |
| 1 | | 3 | 4 | 5 | 2 | | 8 | | 11 | 7 | | | | 10 | | | | | 6 | 9 | | | 15 |
| 1 | 11 | | 3 | 5 | 2 | 7 | 8 | | 4 | | | | | 10 | | | | | 6 | 9 | | | 16 |
| 1 | 11 | | 3 | 5 | 2 | 7 | 8 | | 4 | | | | | 10 | | | | | 6 | 9 | | | 17 |
| 1 | 11 | | 3 | 5 | 2 | 7 | 8 | | 4 | 12 | | | | 10 | | | | | 6 | 9* | | | 18 |
| 1 | 11 | | 3 | 5 | 2 | | 8* | 7 | 12 | 4 | | | | 10 | | | | | 6 | 9 | | | 19 |
| 1 | 11* | 3 | | 5 | 2 | 12 | 8 | 7 | | 4 | | | | 10 | | | | | 6 | 9 | | | 20 |
| 1 | 11 | 3 | 4 | 5 | 2 | | 8 | 9 | 7 | | | | 6 | 10 | | | | | | | | | 21 |
| 1 | 2 | 3 | | 5 | | | 8 | 9 | 10 | 11 | 4 | | | | | | | | 7 | 6 | | | 22 |
| 1 | 7 | 3 | | 5 | 2 | | 8 | | 10* | 11 | 4 | 12 | | | | | | | 6 | 9 | | | 23 |
| 1 | 11 | 3 | 12 | 5* | 2 | 7 | 8 | | 4 | | | | | 10 | | | | | 6 | 9 | | | 24 |
| 1 | 4 | | 5 | 11 | 3 | 2 | | | 10 | | | | | | | | 8 | | 6 | 7 | | 9 | 25 |
| 1 | 4 | 11 | | 5 | | 7 | 3 | 2 | 10 | | | | | | | | 8 | | 6 | | | 9 | 26 |
| 1 | 4 | 11 | | 5 | 12 | 7 | 3 | 2* | 10 | | | | | | | | 8 | | 6 | | | 9 | 27 |
| 1 | 2 | 4 | | 5 | | 8 | 7* | 3 | 11 | | | | | 10 | | | 12 | | 6 | | | 9 | 28 |
| 1 | 2 | 10 | | 5 | 6 | 4 | 3 | 11 | 7 | | | | | | | | 8 | | | | | 9 | 29 |
| 1 | 2 | 4 | | 5 | 6 | 8 | 3 | 11 | 10 | | | | | | | | 7 | | | | | 9 | 30 |
| 1 | 4 | 3 | | 5 | 2 | 8 | 11 | | 10 | | | | | | | | 7 | | 6 | | | 9 | 31 |
| 1 | 2 | 3 | | 5 | 8 | 7 | 11 | | 10 | | | | | | | | 4 | | 6 | | | 9 | 32 |
| 1 | 2* | 3 | | 5 | 8 | 7 | 11 | | 10 | | | | | | | | 4 | | 6 | 12 | | 9 | 33 |
| 1 | 2 | 3* | | 5 | 12 | 8 | 7 | 11 | 10 | | | 4 | | | | | | | 6 | | | 9 | 34 |
| 1 | 2 | 3 | 4 | 5 | 6 | | 8 | 7 | 11 | | | 12 | | | | | | | | 10* | | 9 | 35 |
| 1 | 2 | 3 | 4 | 5 | 6 | | 8 | 7 | 11 | | | | | 10 | | | | | | | | 9 | 36 |
| 1 | 2* | 3 | 4 | 5 | 6 | | 8 | 7 | 11 | | | 10 | | | | | | | 12 | | | 9 | 37 |
| 1 | | 3 | 4 | 5 | 2 | | 8 | 7 | 11 | | | 10 | | | | | | | 6 | | | 9 | 38 |
| 1 | 12 | 3 | 4 | 5 | 2 | | 8 | 7 | 11 | | | 10 | | | | | | | 6* | | | 9 | 39 |
| 1 | 2 | 3 | 4* | 5 | 6 | | 8 | 7 | 11 | | | 10 | | | 12 | | | | | | | 9 | 40 |
| 1 | 2 | | | 5 | 6 | 8 | 7 | 11 | 10 | | | 3 | | | 4 | | | | | | | 9 | 41 |
| 1 | 2 | 12 | | 5 | 6 | 8 | 7 | 11 | 10 | | | 9* | | | 4 | | 3 | | | | | | 42 |
| 42 | 35 | 36 | 16 | 32 | 38 | 16 | 38 | 12 | 29 | 30 | 10 | 18 | 3 | 23 | 17 | — | 13 | 1 | 22 | 13 | 1 | 17 | |
| +3s | +1s | +1s | | +3s | | | | | | | | +2s | +1s | +4s | +1s | +1s | +2s | | +1s | +1s | | | |

## LEEDS UNITED

| | Ht | Wt | Birthplace | Clubs | League App. | League Gls |
|---|---|---|---|---|---|---|
| **Goalkeepers** | | | | | | |
| John Lukic | 6 4 | 13 7 | Chesterfield | Leeds U | 117 | — |
| David Seaman | 6 2 | 13 0 | Rotherham | Leeds U | — | — |
| Keith MacRae | 6 0 | 11 9 | Glasgow | Motherwell | 111 | — |
| | | | | Manchester C | 56 | — |
| | | | | Portland T | (not known) | — |
| | | | | Leeds U | — | — |
| **Defenders** | | | | | | |
| Paul Hart | 6 2 | 12 8 | Manchester | Stockport Co | 88 | 5 |
| | | | | Blackpool | 143 | 17 |
| | | | | Leeds U | 152 | 13 |
| Kevin Hird | 5 7 | 10 6 | Colne | Blackburn R | 132 | 20 |
| | | | | Leeds U | 124 | 14 |
| Neil Firm | 6 3 | 13 7 | Bradford | Leeds U | 12 | — |
| | | | | Oldham Ath (on loan) | 9 | — |
| Brian Greenhoff* (England) | 5 10 | 12 2 | Barnsley | Manchester U | 221 | 13 |
| | | | | Leeds U | 72 | 1 |
| Trevor Cherry (England) | 5 9 | 11 6 | Huddersfield | Huddersfield T | 186 | 10 |
| | | | | Leeds U | 383 | 24 |
| Frank Gray (Scotland) | 5 10 | 11 10 | Glasgow | Leeds U | 193 | 17 |
| | | | | Nottingham F | 81 | 5 |
| | | | | Leeds U | 37 | — |
| Kenny Burns (Scotland) | 5 10 | 11 0 | Glasgow | Birmingham C | 170 | 45 |
| | | | | Nottingham F | 137 | 13 |
| | | | | Leeds U | 23 | — |
| Mark Hinchcliffe | 5 11 | 11 6½ | Leeds | Leeds U | — | — |
| Colin Thacker | 5 11 | 10 5 | Mansfield | Leeds U | — | — |
| Neil Aspin (Apprentice) | 6 1 | 12 3 | Gateshead | Leeds U | 1 | — |
| Martin Dickinson | 5 10 | 11 0 | Leeds | Leeds U | 7 | — |
| **Midfield** | | | | | | |
| Brian Flynn (Wales) | 5 4 | 12 3 | Port Talbot | Burnley | 120 | 8 |
| | | | | Leeds U | 152 | 11 |
| Eddie Gray (Scotland) | 5 11 | 12 6 | Glasgow | Burnley (on loan) | 2 | — |
| | | | | Leeds U | 427 | 52 |
| Gary Hamson | 5 8 | 10 12 | Nottingham | Sheffield U | 108 | 8 |
| | | | | Leeds U | 48 | 3 |
| John Sheridan | 5 9 | 10 8 | Stretford | Leeds U | — | — |
| Gerald Hill | | | Leeds | Leeds U | — | — |
| Gwyn Thomas | 5 8 | 11 0 | Swansea | Leeds U | 33 | 2 |
| **Forwards** | | | | | | |
| Carl Harris (Wales) | 5 9 | 11 0 | Neath | Leeds U | 154 | 26 |
| Arthur Graham (Scotland) | 5 8 | 11 10 | Glasgow | Aberdeen | 220 | 34 |
| | | | | Leeds U | 184 | 32 |
| Alex Sabella (Contract cancelled Jan 1982) | 5 8 | 10 13 | Buenos Aires | River Plate | (not known) | — |
| | | | | Sheffield U | 76 | 8 |
| | | | | Leeds U | 23 | 2 |
| Derek Parlane (Scotland) | 6 0 | 11 10 | Helensburgh | Queen's Park | — | — |
| | | | | Rangers | 218 | 80 |
| | | | | Leeds U | 49 | 10 |
| Terry Connor | 5 7 | 10 0 | Leeds | Leeds U | 77 | 14 |
| Steve Balcombe* | 6 1 | 11 0 | Bangor | Leeds U | 1 | 1 |
| David Matthews* | 5 11 | 11 4 | Shipley | Leeds U | — | — |
| Alan Clarke* | 5 9 | 10 0 | Dublin | Leeds U | — | — |
| Frank Worthington (England) | 5 10 | 11 10 | Halifax | Huddersfield T | 171 | 42 |
| | | | | Leicester C | 210 | 72 |
| | | | | Bolton W | 84 | 35 |
| | | | | Birmingham C | 75 | 30 |
| | | | | Leeds U | 17 | 9 |
| Peter Barnes (England) | 5 10 | 11 0 | Manchester | Manchester C | 115 | 15 |
| | | | | WBA | 77 | 23 |
| | | | | Leeds U | 30 | 1 |
| Robert Peel | | | Garforth | Leeds U | — | — |
| Aiden Butterworth | 5 8 | 11 0 | Leeds | Leeds U | 15 | 3 |

Free transfers: Mark Gavin*, Michael Imlach*, Steve Maddock*, Richard Nuttall*.

# LEICESTER CITY Division 2

*Chairman:* T. W. Shipman.
*Vice-Chairman:* T. E. Bloor.
*Directors:* W. G. Page, D. E. Sharp, W. K. Shooter FCA, T. Smeaton.
*Manager:* Gordon Milne. *Gen Secretary:* A. K. Bennett.
*PRO:* Graham Clark.
*Year Formed:* 1884.
*Previous Grounds:* 1884, Victoria Park; 1887, Belgrave Road; 1888, Victoria Park; 1891, Filbert Street.
*Previous Name:* 1884–1919, Leicester Fosse.

**Football League Record:**
1894 Elected to Division 2; 1908–09 Division 1; 1909–25 Division 2; 1925–35 Division 1; 1935–37 Division 2; 1937–39 Division 1; 1946–54 Division 2; 1954–55 Division 1; 1955–57 Division 2; 1957–69 Division 1; 1969–71 Division 2; 1971–78 Division 1; 1978–80 Division 2; 1980–81 Division 1; 1981– Division 2.

**Honours:** *Football League:* Division 1 – Runners-up 1928–29; Division 2 – Champions 1924–25, 1936–37, 1953–54, 1956–57, 1970–71, 1979–80; Runners-up 1907–08. *FA Cup:* Runners-up 1949, 1961, 1963, 1969. *Football League Cup:* Winners 1964; Runners-up 1965. **European Competitions:** *European Cup-Winners' Cup:* 1961–62.

*Record Victory:* 10-0 v Portsmouth, Division 1, 20 Oct, 1928.

*Record Defeat:* 0-12 (as Leicester Fosse) v Nottingham F, Division 1, 21 Apr, 1909.

*Most League Points:* 61, Division 2, 1956–57. *Three points win:* 66, Division 2, 1981–82.

*Most League Goals:* 109, Division 2, 1956–57.

*Highest League Scorer in Season:* Arthur Rowley, 44, Division 2, 1956–57.

*Most League Goals in Total Aggregate:* Arthur Chandler, 262, 1923–35.

*Most Capped Player:* Gordon Banks, 37 (73), England.

*Most League Appearances:* Adam Black, 530, 1920–35.

*Record Transfer Fee Received:* £325,000 from Stoke C for Peter Shilton, Nov 1974.

*Record Transfer Fee Paid:* £250,000 to FC Bruges, Belgium, for Roger Davies, Dec 1977; to Oldham Ath for Alan Young, July 1979; to Partick T for Jim Melrose, July 1980.

*Previous Managers since the War:* Johnny Duncan, Norman Bullock, David Halliday, Matt Gillies, Frank O'Farrell, Jimmy Bloomfield, Frank McLintock, Jock Wallace.

*Address of Supporters Club:* 69 Burnmoor Street, Leicester LE2 7JL

---

**City Stadium, Filbert St, Leicester, LE2 7FL.** Telephone Leicester 555000 (Match information Leicester 551155). *Ground capacity:* 32,000. *Record attendance:* 47,298 v Tottenham H, FA Cup 5th rd, 18 Feb, 1928. *Record receipts:* £70,633 v Shrewsbury T, FA Cup 6th rd, 6 March, 1982. *Pitch measurements:* 112yd×75yd.
*How to get there:* Corporation buses from Humberstone Gate and Waterloo St (opposite railway station) in city centre. Nearest station Leicester. Midland Red run bus services to the town centre from outlying districts.
*Match tickets:* Seats can be booked from 2 months prior to the date of match & SAE.
*Car parking:* Parking adjacent to the ground is for season-ticket holders only. There is nearby street parking and also a public car park about five minutes walk from the ground.
*Entertainments/catering facilities:* A private season-ticket members bar in the main stand, and catering bars in all sections of the ground.
*Club shop:* Situated under the main stand; sells all types of souvenirs.
*Handbooks/programmes:* Both handbooks and programmes are available from the club shop.
*Extra information:* A League inquiry after Leicester's record defeat discovered that the players had been celebrating a team-mate's wedding!
*Club Colours:* Blue shirts with white collar and cuffs, white shorts with LCFC initials on thigh, white stockings with blue tops.
*Club Captain:* Mark Wallington.
*Physiotherapist:* John McVey.
*Club Nickname:* Filberts or Foxes.

---

## LEICESTER CITY 1981–82 LEAGUE RECORD

| Match No. | Date | Venue | Opponents | Result | H/T Score | Goalscorers | Attendance |
|---|---|---|---|---|---|---|---|
| 1 | Aug 29 | A | Grimsby T | D 2-2 | 1-1 | Lineker, Melrose | 11,032 |
| 2 | Sept 5 | H | Wrexham | W 1-0 | 0-0 | Hamill | 12,905 |
| 3 | 8 | H | Barnsley | W 1-0 | 0-0 | Hamill | 15,447 |
| 4 | 12 | A | Derby Co | L 1-3 | 0-3 | Melrose | 16,046 |
| 5 | 19 | H | Luton T | L 1-2 | 1-0 | Lynex (pen) | 14,159 |
| 6 | 22 | A | Rotherham U | D 1-1 | 0-0 | May | 7781 |
| 7 | 26 | A | Blackburn R | W 2-0 | 1-0 | May, Melrose | 8925 |
| 8 | Oct 3 | H | Crystal Palace | D 1-1 | 0-0 | Lineker | 12,558 |
| 9 | 10 | A | Bolton W | W 3-0 | 1-0 | Melrose 2, Young | 7361 |
| 10 | 16 | H | Chelsea | D 1-1 | 1-1 | Melrose | 18,358 |
| 11 | 24 | A | QPR | L 0-2 | 0-1 | | 12,419 |
| 12 | 31 | H | Sheffield W | D 0-0 | 0-0 | | 19,125 |
| 13 | Nov 7 | A | Charlton Ath | W 4-1 | 1-1 | Melrose, Lynex (pen), Lineker 2 | 8212 |
| 14 | 14 | H | Orient | L 0-1 | 0-0 | | 11,733 |
| 15 | 21 | A | Cardiff C | L 1-3 | 0-0 | Welsh | 6687 |
| 16 | 28 | H | Cambridge U | W 4-1 | 1-0 | Lynex, Hebberd, Peake, Lineker | 9524 |
| 17 | Dec 5 | A | Norwich C | D 0-0 | 0-0 | | 13,367 |
| 18 | 12 | H | Watford | D 1-1 | 1-1 | Lineker | 10,340 |
| 19 | 28 | A | Oldham Ath | D 1-1 | 1-0 | Lynex | 9174 |
| 20 | Jan 30 | A | Luton T | L 1-2 | 0-1 | Lineker | 11,810 |
| 21 | Feb 6 | H | Derby Co | W 2-1 | 0-0 | Lynex (pen), Lineker | 14,132 |
| 22 | 20 | H | Blackburn R | W 1-0 | 1-0 | Peake | 10,890 |
| 23 | 27 | H | Bolton W | W 1-0 | 0-0 | Lynex (pen) | 10,678 |
| 24 | Mar 2 | H | Newcastle U | W 3-0 | 2-0 | Young, Lineker 2 | 12,497 |
| 25 | 9 | A | Chelsea | L 1-4 | 0-1 | Lynex | 10,586 |
| 26 | 13 | H | QPR | W 3-2 | 1-1 | Lynex (pen), Young, Melrose | 17,821 |
| 27 | 17 | H | Rotherham U | W 1-0 | 0-0 | Melrose | 21,123 |
| 28 | 20 | A | Sheffield W | L 0-2 | 0-0 | | 18,962 |
| 29 | 23 | A | Crystal Palace | W 2-0 | 2-0 | Lynex, Lineker | 9506 |
| 30 | 27 | H | Charlton Ath | W 3-1 | 0-1 | Young 2, MacDonald | 13,681 |
| 31 | 30 | A | Shrewsbury T | D 1-1 | 1-1 | Lineker | 5340 |
| 32 | Apr 10 | A | Newcastle U | D 0-0 | 0-0 | | 25,545 |
| 33 | 13 | H | Oldham Ath | W 2-1 | 1-1 | Melrose, Lineker | 14,298 |
| 34 | 17 | H | Cardiff C | W 3-1 | 1-1 | Lineker 2, Lynex | 13,650 |
| 35 | 20 | A | Wrexham | D 0-0 | 0-0 | | 4913 |
| 36 | 24 | A | Cambridge U | W 2-1 | 1-0 | Lineker, Welsh | 7212 |
| 37 | May 1 | H | Norwich C | L 1-4 | 0-1 | May | 19,630 |
| 38 | 4 | A | Barnsley | W 2-0 | 1-0 | Welsh, Lineker | 15,418 |
| 39 | 8 | A | Watford | L 1-3 | 0-3 | Melrose | 20,859 |
| 40 | 12 | H | Grimsby T | L 1-2 | 0-2 | Welsh (pen) | 13,914 |
| 41 | 15 | H | Shrewsbury T | D 0-0 | 0-0 | | 11,368 |
| 42 | 18 | A | Orient | L 0-3 | 0-2 | | 2107 |

**Final League Position: 8**

**Goalscorers**

*League* (56): Lineker 17, Melrose 11, Lynex 10 (5 pens), Young 5, Welsh 4 (1 pen), May 3, Hamill 2, Peake 2, Hebberd 1, MacDonald 1.
*League Cup* (4): Lynex 1, Melrose 1, Robson 1, own goal 1.
*FA Cup* (11): Young 3, Lineker 2, May 2, Melrose 2, O'Neill 1, own goal 1.

| **League Cup** | Second Round | Preston NE (a) | 0-1 |
|---|---|---|---|
| | | (h) | 4-0 |
| | Third Round | Aston Villa (h) | 0-0 |
| | | (a) | 0-2 |
| **FA Cup** | Third Round | Southampton (h) | 3-1 |
| | Fourth Round | Hereford U (a) | 1-0 |
| | Fifth Round | Watford (h) | 2-0 |
| | Sixth Round | Shrewsbury T (h) | 5-2 |
| | Semi-final | Tottenham H | 0-2 (at Villa Park) |

| Wallington | Williams | Gibson | Peake | May | O'Neill | Lynex | Melrose | Lineker | Wilson | MacDonald | Smith | Hamill | Young | Robson | Ramsay | Leet | Scott | Welsh | Hebberd | Kelly | Friar | Walker | Buchanan | Match No. |
|---|---|---|---|---|---|---|---|---|---|---|---|---|---|---|---|---|---|---|---|---|---|---|---|---|
| 1 | 2 | 3 | 4* | 5 | 6 | 7 | 8 | 9 | 10 | 11 | 12 | | | | | | | | | | | | | 1 |
| 1 | 2 | 3 | 4 | 5 | 6 | 7 | 8* | 9 | 10 | 12 | | 11 | | | | | | | | | | | | 2 |
| 1 | 2 | 3 | 4 | 5 | 6 | 7 | 8 | 9 | 10 | | | 11 | | | | | | | | | | | | 3 |
| 1 | 2 | 3 | 4 | 5 | 6 | 7 | 8 | 12 | 10 | | | | 9* | 11 | | | | | | | | | | 4 |
| 1 | 2 | 3 | 4 | 5 | 6 | 7 | 8 | 9 | 10 | | | | | 11 | | | | | | | | | | 5 |
| 1 | 2 | 3 | 4 | 5 | 6 | 7 | 8 | | 10 | | | | 9 | 11 | | | | | | | | | | 6 |
| 1 | 2 | 3 | | 5 | 6 | 7 | 8 | | 10 | 11 | | | 9 | | 4 | | | | | | | | | 7 |
| 1 | 2 | 3 | | 5 | 6 | 7 | 8 | 12 | 10* | 11 | | | 9 | | 4 | | | | | | | | | 8 |
| 1 | 2 | | | | 6 | 12 | 8 | 7 | 9 | | | | 11 | 10 | 4* | 3 | 5 | | | | | | | 9 |
| 1 | 2 | | | | 6 | | 8 | 7 | 10 | | | | 9 | 11 | 4 | 3 | 5 | | | | | | | 10 |
| 1 | 2 | | | | 6 | 12 | 8 | 7 | 10 | | | | 9* | 11 | 4 | 3 | 5 | | | | | | | 11 |
| 1 | 2 | | | | 6 | 7 | 8 | 9 | 10 | 4 | | | 11 | | | 3 | 5 | | | | | | | 12 |
| 1 | 2 | | | | 6 | 7 | 8 | 9 | 10 | 4 | | | 11* | | | 3 | 5 | 12 | | | | | | 13 |
| 1 | 2 | | | | 6 | 7 | 8* | 9 | 10 | 4 | | | 11 | | | 3 | 5 | 12 | | | | | | 14 |
| 1 | 2 | 4 | | | 6 | 7 | | 9 | 10 | 11 | | | 8 | | | 3 | 5 | | | | | | | 15 |
| 1 | 2 | 4 | | 5 | 6 | 7 | | 9 | 10 | 11* | | | 12 | | | 3 | | | 8 | | | | | 16 |
| 1 | 2 | 4 | | 5 | 6 | 7 | | 9 | 10 | | | | | | | 3 | | | 8 | 11 | | | | 17 |
| 1 | 2 | 4 | | 5 | 6 | 7 | | 9 | 10 | | | | | | | 3 | | | 8 | 11 | | | | 18 |
| 1 | 2 | | | 5 | 6 | 7 | 8 | | 10 | | | | 9 | | 4 | 3 | | | | 11 | | | | 19 |
| 1 | 2 | 4 | | 5 | 6 | 7 | 12 | 8 | 10 | | | | 9 | | | | | | | 11* | 3 | | | 20 |
| 1 | 2 | 4 | | 5 | 6 | 7 | 12 | 8 | 10 | | | | 9 | | | | | | | 11* | 3 | | | 21 |
| 1 | 2 | 4 | | 5 | 6 | 7* | 12 | 8 | 10 | | | | 9 | | | | | | | 11 | 3 | | | 22 |
| 1 | 2 | 4 | | 5 | 6 | 7 | 12 | 8 | 10 | | | | 9* | | | | | | | 11 | 3 | | | 23 |
| 1 | 2 | 4 | | 5 | 6 | 7 | 12 | 8 | 10 | | | | 9 | | | | | | | 11* | 3 | | | 24 |
| | 2 | 4 | | 5 | 6 | 7 | 12 | 8 | 10* | | | | 9 | | | | | | | 11 | 3 | 1 | | 25 |
| | 2 | 4 | | 5 | 6 | 7 | 12 | 8 | 10 | | | | 9* | | | | | | | 11 | 3 | 1 | | 26 |
| | 2 | 4 | | 5 | 6 | 7* | 9 | 8 | 10 | 11 | | | 12 | | | | | | | | 3 | 1 | | 27 |
| | 2 | 4 | | 5 | 6 | 7* | 12 | 8 | 10 | 11 | | | 9 | | | | | | | | 3 | 1 | | 28 |
| | 2 | 4 | | 5 | | 7* | 12 | 8 | 10 | 11 | | | 9 | | | | | | | 6 | 3 | 1 | | 29 |
| | 2 | 4 | | 5 | 6* | 7 | 12 | 8 | 10 | 11 | | | 9 | | | | | | | | 3 | 1 | | 30 |
| 1 | 2 | 4 | | 5 | 6 | 7 | 12 | 8 | 10 | | | | 9* | | | | | | | 11 | 3 | | | 31 |
| 1 | | 4 | | 5 | 6 | 7 | 9* | 8 | 10 | 11 | | | 12 | | | 3 | | | | | 2 | | | 32 |
| 1 | | 4 | | 5 | 6 | 7 | 9* | 8 | 10 | 11 | | | 12 | | | 3 | | | | | 2 | | | 33 |
| 1 | | | | 5 | 6 | 7 | | 8 | 10* | 11 | | | 9 | | 4 | 3 | | | | 12 | 2 | | | 34 |
| 1 | | | | 5 | 6 | | 9 | 8 | 10* | 4 | | | 7 | | | 3 | | 12 | | 11 | 2 | | | 35 |
| 1 | | 4 | | 5 | 6 | 7 | 9 | 8 | 10 | | | | | | | 3 | | | | 11 | 2 | | | 36 |
| 1 | | 4 | | 5 | 6 | 7 | 9 | 8 | 10 | | | | | | | 3 | | | | 11 | 2 | | | 37 |
| 1 | | 4 | | 5 | 6 | 7 | 9 | 8 | 10 | 11 | | | | | | 3 | | | | 12 | 2* | | | 38 |
| 1 | | 4 | | 5 | 6 | 7 | 8* | | 10 | 11 | | | 9 | | 2 | | | | | 12 | 3 | | | 39 |
| 1 | | 4 | | 5 | 6 | 7 | | 8 | 10* | 11 | | | 9 | | | 3 | | 12 | | | 2 | | | 40 |
| 1 | | 4 | | 5 | 6 | 7* | | 8 | 10 | 11 | | | 9 | | | 3 | | 12 | | | 2 | | | 41 |
| 1 | | 4 | | | 6 | 7 | | 8 | 10* | 11 | | | 9 | | | 3 | | | | 5 | 2 | | 12 | 42 |
| 36 | 31 | 8 | 31 | 34 | 41 | 37 | 24 | 37 | 35 | 24 | 2 | 2 | 24 | 8 | 10 | 17 | 7 | 7 | 4 | 14 | 23 | 6 | — | |
| | | | + | + | + | | + | + | | | | | | | | | | | | + | | + | | |
| | | | 4s | 11s | 2s | | 1s | 2s | | | | | | | | | | | | 9s | | 1s | | |

## LEICESTER CITY

| | Ht | Wt | Birthplace | Clubs | League App. | League Gls |
|---|---|---|---|---|---|---|
| **Goalkeepers** | | | | | | |
| Mark Wallington | 6 1 | 14 2½ | Sleaford | Walsall | 11 | — |
| | | | | Leicester C | 324 | — |
| Nicky Walker | 6 2½ | 12 10¼ | Aberdeen | Elgin | (not known) | — |
| | | | | Leicester C | 6 | — |
| **Defenders** | | | | | | |
| Tommy Williams | 5 10¼ | 10 12 | West Lothian | Leicester C | 180 | 10 |
| Larry May | 6 0¼ | 12 6 | Sutton Coldfield | Leicester C | 152 | 11 |
| John O'Neill (N Ireland) | 5 11¾ | 13 3 | Derry | Leicester C | 129 | 2 |
| Billy Gibson | 5 9¾ | 11 5¾ | Lanark | Leicester C | 28 | — |
| Peter Welsh | 6 0¾ | 13 2¼ | Coatbridge | Leicester C | 41 | 4 |
| Norman Leet | 6 2½ | 13 12 | Leicester | Leicester C | 18 | — |
| Paul Friar | 5 8 | 10 11 | Glasgow | Leicester C | 38 | — |
| Ian Sherwood | 5 8 | 10 12 | Smethwick | Leicester C | — | — |
| Derek Thomson | 5 9 | 10 6 | Aberdeen | Leicester C | — | — |
| **Midfield** | | | | | | |
| Andy Peake | 5 9½ | 11 2½ | Market Harborough | Leicester C | 98 | 8 |
| Colin Bell (Contract cancelled April 1982) | 5 9¼ | 10 10½ | Braunstone | Leicester C | — | — |
| Bobby Smith | 5 7 | 11 7¾ | Dalkeith | Hibernian | 152 | 19 |
| | | | | Peterborough U (on loan) | 5 | — |
| | | | | Leicester C | 75 | 19 |
| Ian Wilson | 5 7¼ | 10 10½ | Aberdeen | Leicester C | 99 | 3 |
| Paul Ramsey | 5 10 | 12 0 | Derry | Leicester C | 13 | — |
| Eddie Kelly | 5 8 | 12 3 | Glasgow | Arsenal | 175 | 13 |
| | | | | QPR | 28 | 1 |
| | | | | Leicester C | 85 | 4 |
| | | | | Notts Co | 27 | 1 |
| | | | | Bournemouth | 13 | — |
| | | | | Leicester C | 14 | — |
| Brandon Knowles (Contract cancelled Jan 1982) | | | | Leicester C | — | — |
| Kevin MacDonald | 6 0¼ | 11 11¼ | Inverness | Inverness Caley | (not known) | |
| | | | | Leicester C | 45 | 3 |
| Keith Robson | 6 0 | 11 4 | Hetton-le-Hole | Newcastle U | 14 | 3 |
| | | | | West Ham U | 68 | 13 |
| | | | | Cardiff C | 21 | 5 |
| | | | | Norwich C | 65 | 13 |
| | | | | Leicester C | 8 | — |
| **Forwards** | | | | | | |
| Gary Lineker | 5 9¾ | 11 10½ | Leicester | Leicester C | 74 | 23 |
| Neil Grewcock | 5 5½ | 11 3 | Leicester | Leicester C | 8 | 1 |
| | | | | Gillingham (on loan) | 13 | 1 |
| Dave Buchanan | 5 7¼ | 11 0 | Newcastle | Leicester C | 29 | 6 |
| Gavin Drummond (Contract cancelled March 1982) | 5 10¾ | 10 13½ | Derry | Leicester C | — | — |
| Richard Pell | 5 8 | 11 0 | Leicester | Leicester C | — | — |
| Alan Young | 6 0 | 12 7 | Kirkcaldy | Oldham Ath | 122 | 30 |
| | | | | Leicester C | 104 | 26 |
| Jim Melrose | 5 9 | 10 1 | Glasgow | Partick T | 122 | 31 |
| | | | | Leicester C | 67 | 20 |
| Stewart Hamill | 5 9 | 10 8 | Glasgow | Pollock | (not known) | |
| | | | | Scunthorpe U (on loan) | 4 | — |
| | | | | Leicester C | 10 | 2 |
| Steve Lynex | 5 9 | 11 5 | West Bromwich | WBA | — | — |
| | | | | Shamrock R | (not known) | |
| | | | | Birmingham C | 46 | 10 |
| | | | | Leicester C | 53 | 15 |
| Richard Hill | 5 11½ | 11 10 | Hinckley | Leicester C | — | — |
| Barry Cliff | 5 7 | 10 6 | Motherwell | Leicester C | — | — |

Free transfers: Paul Culpin*, Steve Saxby*.

# LINCOLN CITY

## Division 3

*Chairman:* G. T. Blades.

*Vice-Chairman:* H. W. Dove.

*Directors:* G. T. Blades, A. C. Davey, H. C. Sills, M. J. Green.

*Manager:* Colin Murphy.

*Secretary:* Philip M. Hough.

*Year Formed:* 1883. *Turned Professional:* 1892.

*Limited Company:* 1892.

*Previous Grounds:* 1883, John O'Gaunt's; 1894, Sincil Bank.

**Football League Record:**
1892 Original Member of Division 2. Remained in Division 2 until 1920 when they failed re-election but also missed seasons 1908–09 and 1911–12, when not re-elected. 1921–32 Division 3(N); 1932–34 Division 2; 1934–48 Division 3(N); 1948–49 Division 2; 1949–52 Division 3(N); 1952–61 Division 2; 1961–62 Division 3; 1962–76 Division 4; 1976–79 Division 3; 1979–81 Division 4; 1981– Division 3.

**Honours:** *Football League: Division 2* best season: 5th, 1901–02; Division 3(N) – Champions 1931–32, 1947–48, 1951–52; Runners-up 1927–28, 1930–31, 1936–37; Division 4 – Champions 1975–76; Runners-up 1980–81. *FA Cup* best season: 1st rd of Second Series (5th rd equivalent), 1886–87, 2nd rd (5th rd equivalent), 1889–90, 1901–02. *Football League Cup* best season: 4th rd, 1967–68.

*Record Victory:* 11-1 v Crewe Alex, Division 3(N), 29 Sept, 1951.

*Record Defeat:* 3-11 v Manchester C, Division 2, 23 Mar, 1895.

*Most League Points:* 74, Division 4, 1975–76 (former League record). *Three points win:* 77, Division 3, 1981–82.

*Most League Goals:* 121, Division 3(N), 1951–52.

*Highest League Scorer in Season:* Allan Hall, 42, Division 3(N), 1931–32.

*Most League Goals in Total Aggregate:* Andy Graver, 144, 1950–55 and 1958–61.

*Most Capped Player:* David Pugh, 3 (7), Wales; Con Moulson, 3 (6) Eire; George Moulson, 3, Eire.

*Most League Appearances:* Tony Emery, 402, 1946–59.

*Record Transfer Fee Received:* £180,000 from Newcastle U for Mick Harford, Dec 1980.

*Record Transfer Fee Paid:* £45,000 to Southampton for George Shipley, Jan 1980.

*Previous Managers since the War:* Bill Anderson, Bob Chapman, Ron Gray, Bert Loxley, David Herd, Graham Taylor, George Kerr, Willie Bell.

*Address of the Club Shop or Boutique:* Red Imps Shop on ground.

---

**Sincil Bank, Lincoln.** Telephone Lincoln 22224 and Commercial Dept 42333. *Ground capacity:* 16,225. *Record attendance:* 23,196 v Derby Co, League Cup 4th rd, 15 Nov, 1967. *Record receipts:* £12,512.49 v Watford, League Cup 3rd rd replay, 25 Nov, 1981. *Pitch Measurements:* 110yd×75yd.

*How to get there:* There is a regular bus service from Lincoln Central Station to the ground, although there are no special buses. Nearest stations are Lincoln Central and Lincoln St Marks.

*Match tickets: Car parking:* Limited to 150 cars at the ground.

*Entertainments/catering facilities:* Social club at the ground with light catering before and after the match.

*Club shop:* Sited on the ground; sells all types of souvenirs.

*Handbooks/programmes:* Programmes available at each game or by subscription.

*Extra information:* Frank Keetley scored six times in 21 minutes for Lincoln against Halifax Town, 16 January 1932. Most points, most wins, fewest defeats and fewest goals against in a season in Division 4.

*Club Colours:* Red with white vertical striped shirts, black shorts, red and white stockings.

*Change Colours:* Green shirts, black shorts.

*Assistant Manager:* John Pickering.

*Reserve Team Manager:* Lennie Lawrence.

*Physiotherapist:* Bert Loxley.

*Club Nickname:* The Red Imps.

## LINCOLN CITY 1981–82 LEAGUE RECORD

| Match No. | Date | Venue | Opponents | Result | | H/T Score | Goalscorers | Attendance |
|---|---|---|---|---|---|---|---|---|
| 1 | Aug 29 | A | Portsmouth | D | 1-1 | 0-0 | Cammack | 10,698 |
| 2 | Sept 5 | H | Fulham | D | 1-1 | 0-0 | Shipley (pen) | 3934 |
| 3 | 12 | A | Plymouth Arg | W | 2-0 | 1-0 | Gilbert, Cockerill | 3323 |
| 4 | 19 | H | Carlisle U | D | 0-0 | 0-0 | | 3623 |
| 5 | 23 | H | Millwall | L | 0-1 | 0-1 | | 3923 |
| 6 | 26 | A | Bristol R | W | 2-0 | 1-0 | Cunningham, Cammack | 6112 |
| 7 | 29 | A | Walsall | L | 1-2 | 1-0 | Cunningham | 3653 |
| 8 | Oct 3 | H | Newport Co | D | 2-2 | 0-1 | Cammack, Hobson | 3351 |
| 9 | 10 | H | Wimbledon | W | 5-1 | 2-1 | Cockerill 2, Cunningham, Cammack, Hobson | 3168 |
| 10 | 17 | A | Brentford | L | 1-3 | 0-3 | Cunningham | 4180 |
| 11 | 20 | A | Doncaster R | L | 1-4 | 0-1 | Bell | 8201 |
| 12 | 24 | H | Bristol C | L | 1-2 | 0-2 | Bell | 3683 |
| 13 | 31 | A | Oxford U | D | 1-1 | 0-0 | Bell | 3985 |
| 14 | Nov 4 | H | Preston NE | L | 1-2 | 1-2 | Shipley | 3587 |
| 15 | 7 | A | Southend U | W | 2-0 | 0-0 | Cockerill, Shipley | 5016 |
| 16 | 14 | H | Chesterfield | W | 2-1 | 1-1 | Cunningham, Shipley (pen) | 5878 |
| 17 | 28 | H | Swindon T | W | 2-0 | 0-0 | Lewis (og), Cunningham | 3132 |
| 18 | Dec 5 | A | Reading | L | 2-3 | 1-1 | Cammack, Shipley (pen) | 2973 |
| 19 | Jan 16 | H | Gillingham | W | 2-0 | 0-0 | Thompson S., Bell | 2756 |
| 20 | 23 | H | Portsmouth | D | 1-1 | 0-0 | Bell | 3297 |
| 21 | 30 | A | Carlisle U | L | 0-1 | 0-1 | | 3893 |
| 22 | Feb 3 | H | Chester | W | 3-0 | 0-0 | Peake, Cammack, Shipley (pen) | 2120 |
| 23 | 6 | H | Plymouth Arg | W | 2-0 | 1-0 | Thompson S., Cockerill | 2970 |
| 24 | 9 | A | Millwall | D | 1-1 | 0-1 | Shipley | 3198 |
| 25 | 13 | A | Newport Co | D | 0-0 | 0-0 | | 3735 |
| 26 | 20 | H | Walsall | D | 1-1 | 0-0 | Shipley (pen) | 3243 |
| 27 | 27 | A | Wimbledon | D | 1-1 | 0-1 | Cockerill | 2094 |
| 28 | Mar 2 | A | Huddersfield T | W | 2-0 | 1-0 | Cunningham, Peake | 5874 |
| 29 | 6 | H | Brentford | W | 1-0 | 0-0 | Hobson | 2827 |
| 30 | 10 | H | Doncaster R | W | 5-0 | 2-0 | Hobson 3, Turner P., Hibberd | 5187 |
| 31 | 13 | A | Bristol C | W | 1-0 | 1-0 | Cunningham | 6341 |
| 32 | 16 | A | Preston NE | D | 1-1 | 1-0 | Cunningham | 4879 |
| 33 | 20 | H | Oxford U | W | 2-1 | 1-0 | Peake, Cockerill | 4474 |
| 34 | 24 | A | Exeter C | W | 2-1 | 0-0 | Hibberd 2 (2 pens) | 3081 |
| 35 | 27 | H | Southend U | D | 1-1 | 0-0 | Stead (og) | 5455 |
| 36 | 31 | H | Burnley | D | 1-1 | 0-0 | Cockerill | 6148 |
| 37 | Apr 3 | A | Chesterfield | W | 2-0 | 1-0 | Cunningham, Hobson | 7443 |
| 37 | 10 | A | Burnley | L | 0-1 | 0-0 | | 10,915 |
| 39 | 12 | H | Huddersfield T | W | 2-0 | 1-0 | Cunningham, Neale | 8203 |
| 40 | 17 | H | Reading | W | 2-1 | 0-0 | Shipley, Peake | 4888 |
| 41 | 24 | A | Swindon T | L | 0-1 | 0-0 | | 3981 |
| 42 | May 1 | H | Bristol R | W | 1-0 | 1-0 | Cockerill | 4024 |
| 43 | 4 | A | Gillingham | L | 0-1 | 0-0 | | 3245 |
| 44 | 8 | A | Chester | W | 2-1 | 0-0 | Cockerill, Shipley (pen) | 1176 |
| 45 | 15 | H | Exeter C | W | 2-0 | 0-0 | Shipley (pen), Cockerill | 5447 |
| 46 | 18 | A | Fulham | D | 1-1 | 0-0 | Carr | 20,398 |

**Final League Position: 4**

### Goalscorers

*League* (66): Cockerill 11, Cunningham 11, Shipley 11 (7 pens), Hobson 7, Cammack 6, Bell 5, Peake 4, Hibberd 3 (2 pens), Thompson S. 2, Carr 1, Gilbert 1, Neale 1, Turner P. 1, own goals 2.
*League Cup* (12): Cunningham 4, Shipley 3, Carr 1, Cockerill 1, Hobson 1, Peake 1, Turner W. 1.
*FA Cup* (2): Cammack 1, Thompson S. 1.

| League Cup | First Round | Hull C (h) | 3-0 |
|---|---|---|---|
| | | (a) | 1-1 |
| | Second Round | Notts Co (h) | 1-1 |
| | | (a) | 3-2 |
| | Third Round | Watford (a) | 2-2 |
| | | (h) | 2-3 |
| FA Cup | First Round | Port Vale (h) | 2-2 |
| | | (a) | 0-0 |
| | | (a) | 0-2 |

| Felgate | Thompson T. | McVay | Gilbert | Peake | Carr | Shipley | Cammack | Hobson | Cunningham | Cockerill | Creane | Turner P. | Neale | Smith | Bell | Naylor | Beavon | Turner W. | Thompson S. | Hibberd | Rodgers | Ward | Match No. |
|---|---|---|---|---|---|---|---|---|---|---|---|---|---|---|---|---|---|---|---|---|---|---|---|
| 1 | 2 | 3 | 4 | 5 | 6 | 7 | 8 | 9 | 10 | 11 | | | | | | | | | | | | | 1 |
| 1 | 2 | 3 | 4 | | 6 | 7 | 11 | 9 | 10 | 8 | 5* | 12 | | | | | | | | | | | 2 |
| 1 | 2 | 3 | 4* | | 6 | 7 | 11 | 9 | 10 | 8 | 5 | 12 | | | | | | | | | | | 3 |
| 1 | 2 | 3 | 4 | | 6 | 7 | 11 | 9 | 10 | 8 | | | | 5 | | | | | | | | | 4 |
| 1 | 2 | 3 | 4 | | 6 | 7 | 11 | 9 | 10 | | | | 8 | 5 | | | | | | | | | 5 |
| 1 | 2 | 3 | 4 | | 6 | 7 | 11 | 9 | 10 | | | | 8 | 5 | | | | | | | | | 6 |
| 1 | 2 | 3* | 4 | | 6 | 7 | 11 | 9 | 10 | 12 | | | 8 | 5 | | | | | | | | | 7 |
| 1 | 2 | 3 | | | 6 | 8 | 7 | 9 | 10 | 4 | | 11* | 5 | 12 | | | | | | | | | 8 |
| 1 | 2 | 3 | | 5 | 6 | 8 | 7 | 9 | 10 | 4 | | 11* | | 12 | | | | | | | | | 9 |
| 1 | 2 | 3 | | 5 | 6 | 8 | 7 | 9 | 10 | 4 | | 11 | | | | | | | | | | | 10 |
| 1 | 2 | 3 | | 5 | 6 | 8 | 7 | 9 | 10 | 4 | | 11* | | 12 | | | | | | | | | 11 |
| | 2 | 3 | 12 | 5 | 6 | 8 | 7* | 9 | 10 | 4 | | | 11 | 1 | | | | | | | | | 12 |
| 1 | | 2 | 11 | 5 | 6 | 8 | | 7 | 10 | 4 | | 3 | 9 | | | | | | | | | | 13 |
| 1 | | | 11 | 5 | 6 | 8 | 7 | 12 | 10 | 4 | | 2 | 9 | | | 3* | | | | | | | 14 |
| 1 | | | 11 | 5 | 4 | 7 | | | 10 | 8 | | 2 | 9 | | 1 | | | 3 | 6 | | | | 15 |
| 1 | | | 11 | 5 | 8 | 7 | | | 10 | 4 | | 2 | 9 | | 1 | | | 3 | 6 | | | | 16 |
| 1 | | | 11 | 5 | 8 | 7 | | 9 | 10 | 4 | | 2 | | | | | | 3 | 6 | | | | 17 |
| 1 | | | | 5 | 8 | 7 | | 9 | 10 | 4 | | 2 | 11 | | | | | 3 | 6 | | | | 18 |
| 1 | | | | 5 | 2 | 7 | | 9 | | 4 | | | 3 | | | 10 | 11 | 8 | 6 | | | | 19 |
| 1 | 12 | | | 5 | 2 | | | 9 | | 4 | | | 3 | | | 10 | 11* | 8 | 6 | 7 | | | 20 |
| 1 | 12 | | | | 2 | 7 | | 9 | 10 | 4 | 5 | | 3 | | | | 11* | 8 | 6 | | | | 21 |
| 1 | | | 11 | 5* | 2 | 7 | | 9 | 10 | 4 | | | 3 | | | | | 8 | 6 | 12 | | | 22 |
| 1 | | | 11 | 5 | 2 | 7 | | 9 | 10 | 4 | | | 3 | | | | | 8 | 6 | | | | 23 |
| 1 | | | 11* | 5 | 2 | 7 | | 9 | 10 | 4 | | | 3 | | | | | 8 | 6 | 12 | | | 24 |
| 1 | | | | 5 | 2 | 7 | | 9 | 10 | 4 | | | 3 | | | | | 8 | 6 | 11 | | | 25 |
| 1 | 12 | | | 5 | 2* | 7 | | 9 | 10 | 4 | | | 3 | | | | | 8 | 6 | 11 | | | 26 |
| 1 | 12 | | | 5 | 2 | 7 | | 9 | 10 | 4 | | | 3 | | | | | 8 | 6 | 11* | | | 27 |
| 1 | | | | 5 | 2 | 7 | | 9 | 10 | 4 | | | 3 | | | | | 8 | 6 | 11 | | | 28 |
| 1 | | | | 5 | 2 | 7 | | 9 | 10 | 4 | | | 3 | | | | | 8 | 6 | 11 | | | 29 |
| 1 | | | | 5 | 2 | 7 | | 9 | 10 | 4 | | | 3 | | | | | 8 | 6 | 11 | | | 30 |
| 1 | | | | 5 | 2 | 7 | | 9 | 10 | 4 | | | 3 | | | | | **8** | 6 | 11 | | | 31 |
| 1 | | | | 5 | 2 | 7 | | 9 | 10 | 4 | | 8 | 3 | | | | | | 6 | 11 | | | 32 |
| 1 | | | | 5 | 2 | 7 | | 9 | 10 | 4 | | 8 | 3 | | | | | | 6 | 11 | | | 33 |
| 1 | | | | 5 | 2 | | | 9 | 10 | 4 | | 8 | 3 | | | | 7 | | 6 | 11 | | | 34 |
| 1 | 12 | | | 5 | 2 | | | 9 | 10 | 4 | | 8 | 3 | | | | 7* | | | 11 | 6 | | 35 |
| 1 | 12 | | | 5 | 2 | 7 | | 9 | 10 | 4 | | 8 | 3 | | | | | | | 11 | 6* | | 36 |
| 1 | | | | 5 | 2 | 7 | | 9 | 10 | 4 | | 8 | 3 | | | | | | 6 | 11 | | | 37 |
| 1 | 12 | | | 5 | 2* | 7 | | 9 | 10 | 4 | | 8 | 3 | | | | | | 6 | 11 | | | 38 |
| 1 | | | | 5 | 2 | 7 | | 9 | 10 | 4 | | 8 | 3 | | | | | | 6 | 11 | | | 39 |
| 1 | 12 | | | 5 | 2 | 7 | | 9 | 10 | 4 | | 8 | 3 | | | | | | 6 | 11* | | | 40 |
| 1 | 12 | | | 5 | 2 | 7 | | | 10 | 4 | | 8 | 3 | | | | | | 6 | 11* | | 9 | 41 |
| 1 | | | | | 2 | 7 | | | 10 | 4 | | 8 | 3 | | | | 9 | | 6 | 11 | 5 | | 42 |
| 1 | 12 | | | 5 | 2 | 7 | | | 10 | 4 | | 8 | 3 | | | | 9 | | 6 | 11* | | | 43 |
| 1 | 12 | | | 5 | 2 | 7 | | | 10 | 4 | | 8 | 3 | | | | 9 | | 6* | 11 | | | 44 |
| 1 | 12 | | | 5 | 2* | 7 | | | 10 | 4 | | 8 | 3 | | | | 9 | | 6 | 11 | | | 45 |
| 1 | 12 | | | 5 | 2 | 7 | | 9 | 10 | 4 | | 8 | 3 | | | | | | 6 | 11* | | | 46 |
| 43 | 12 | 13 | 15 | 37 | 46 | 43 | 18 | 31 | 46 | 43 | 2 | 27 | 31 | 5 | 11 | 3 | 7 | 16 | 30 | 23 | 3 | 1 | |
| | | | +14s | | | | | +1s | +1s | | | +1s | +1s | | +3s | | | | +2s | | | | |

## LINCOLN CITY

| | Ht | Wt | Birthplace | Clubs | League App. | League Gls |
|---|---|---|---|---|---|---|
| **Goalkeepers** | | | | | | |
| Colin Boulton | 5 10 | 13 1 | Cheltenham | Derby Co | 273 | — |
| (Contract cancelled Feb 1982) | | | | Southampton (on loan) | 5 | — |
| | | | | Los Angeles A | (not known) | |
| | | | | Lincoln C | 4 | — |
| David Felgate | 6 1 | 13 13 | Blaenau | Bolton W | — | — |
| | | | Ffestiniog | Rochdale (on loan) | 47 | — |
| | | | | Bradford C (on loan) | — | — |
| | | | | Crewe Alex (on loan) | 14 | — |
| | | | | Lincoln C | 85 | — |
| Stuart Naylor | 6 2 | 11 13 | Leeds | Lincoln C | 3 | — |
| **Defenders** | | | | | | |
| Phil Neale | 5 10 | 11 5 | Scunthorpe | Lincoln C | 231 | 19 |
| Steve Ward | 6 0 | 10 13 | Sheffield | Lincoln C | 2 | — |
| (Contract cancelled Aug 1981) | | | | | | |
| David Carr | 5 11 | 11 0 | Aylesham | Luton T | 43 | — |
| | | | | Lincoln C | 137 | 4 |
| Trevor Peake | 6 0 | 12 9 | Nuneaton | Nuneaton B | (not known) | |
| | | | | Lincoln C | 125 | 6 |
| Steve Thompson | 6 0 | 14 7½ | Sheffield | Boston U | (not known) | |
| | | | | Lincoln C | 61 | 4 |
| Trevor Thompson* | 5 9 | 11 13¾ | Newcastle | WBA | 20 | — |
| | | | | Newport Co | 35 | 2 |
| | | | | Lincoln C | 80 | 1 |
| Nolan Keeley* | 5 11 | 11 2 | East Barsham | Scunthorpe U | 259 | 37 |
| | | | | Lincoln C | 52 | 3 |
| Gerard Creane | 6 0 | 13 12 | Lincoln | Lincoln C | 6 | — |
| David McVay | 6 1 | 12 11 | Workington | Notts Co | 113 | 2 |
| (Contract cancelled Nov 1981) | | | | Torquay U (on loan) | 8 | — |
| | | | | Peterborough U | 49 | 1 |
| | | | | Lincoln C | 13 | — |
| David Rodgers | 6 1¼ | 13 2 | Bristol | Bristol C | 192 | 15 |
| | | | | Torquay U | 5 | 1 |
| | | | | Lincoln C | 3 | — |
| David Beavon | 5 9 | 10 9 | Nottingham | Notts Co | 5 | — |
| | | | | Lincoln C | 7 | — |
| **Midfield** | | | | | | |
| David Hughes* | 5 9 | 12 5 | Birmingham | Aston V | 4 | 1 |
| | | | | Lincoln C | 62 | 1 |
| | | | | Scunthorpe U | 21 | — |
| | | | | Lincoln C | — | — |
| George Shipley | 5 7 | 10 2¾ | Newcastle | Southampton | 3 | — |
| | | | | Reading (on loan) | 12 | 1 |
| | | | | Blackpool (on loan) | — | — |
| | | | | Lincoln C | 112 | 21 |
| Phil Turner | 5 8 | 10 7 | Sheffield | Lincoln C | 80 | 6 |
| Stuart Hibberd | 6 0 | 11 13½ | Sheffield | Lincoln C | 28 | 3 |
| Glenn Cockerill | 6 0 | 11 13 | Grimsby | Lincoln C | 71 | 10 |
| | | | | Swindon T | 26 | 1 |
| | | | | Lincoln C | 44 | 11 |
| **Forwards** | | | | | | |
| Gordon Hobson | 5 8 | 10 5 | Sheffield | Lincoln C | 157 | 46 |
| Tony Cunningham | 6 1 | 13 2½ | Kingston, | Lincoln C | 118 | 29 |
| | | | Jamaica | | | |
| Derek Bell | 5 8 | 10 4½ | Wyberton | Derby Co | — | — |
| | | | | Halifax T | 112 | 21 |
| | | | | Sheffield W (on loan) | 5 | 1 |
| | | | | Barnsley | 46 | 20 |
| | | | | Lincoln C | 48 | 10 |
| Craig Ramsey* | 5 7 | 11 13½ | Dunfermline | Lincoln C | 5 | 2 |
| David Gilbert* | | | | Lincoln C | 30 | 1 |
| John Ward* | 5 8 | 10 7 | Lincoln | Lincoln C | 240 | 91 |
| | | | | Workington (on loan) | 11 | 3 |
| | | | | Watford | 27 | 6 |
| | | | | Grimsby T | 3 | — |
| | | | | Lincoln C | 1 | — |

# LIVERPOOL Division 1

*Chairman:* J. W. Smith JP

*Directors:* C. J. Hill, Coun. S. J. Moss JP, S. C. Reakes JP, H. Cartwright, J. T. Cross, W. D. Corkish.

*Team Manager:* Bob Paisley. *Asst. Manager:* Joe Fagan.

*General Secretary:* P. B. Robinson.

*Year Formed:* 1892. *Turned Professional:* 1892.

*Limited Company:* 1892.

**Football League Record:**
1893 Elected to Division 2; 1894–95 Division 1; 1895–96 Division 2; 1896–1904 Division 1; 1904–05 Division 2; 1905–54 Division 1; 1954–62 Division 2; 1962– Division 1.

**Honours:** *Football League:* Division 1 – Champions 1900–01, 1905–06, 1921–22, 1922–23, 1946–47, 1963–64, 1965–66, 1972–73, 1975–76, 1976–77, 1978–79, 1979–80, 1981–82 (Liverpool have a record number of 13 League Championship wins); Runners-up 1898–99, 1909–10, 1968–69, 1973–74, 1974–75, 1977–78; Division 2 – Champions 1893–94, 1895–96, 1904–05, 1961–62; *FA Cup:* Winners 1965, 1974; Runners-up 1914, 1950, 1971, 1977; *Football League Cup:* Winners 1981, 1982; Runners-up 1977–78. **European Competitions:** *European Cup:* 1964–65, 1966–67, 1973–74, 1976–77 (winners), 1977–78 (winners), 1978–79, 1979–80, 1980–81 (winners), 1981–82; *European Cup-Winners' Cup:* 1965–66 (runners-up), 1971–72, 1974–75; *European Fairs Cup:* 1967–68, 1968–69, 1969–70, 1970–71; *UEFA Cup:* 1972–73 (winners), 1975–76 (winners); *Super Cup:* 1977 (winners), 1978. *World Club Championship:* 1981 (runners-up).

*Record Victory:* 11–0 v Strömsgodset, European Cup-Winners' Cup, 17 Sept, 1974.

*Record Defeat:* 1–9 v Birmingham C, Division 2, 11 Dec, 1954.

*Most League Points:* 68, Division 1, 1978–79 (former First Division record). *Three points win:* 87, Division 1, 1981–82.

*Most League Goals:* 106, Division 2, 1895–96.

*Highest League Scorer in Season:* Roger Hunt, 41, Division 2, 1961–62.

*Most League Goals in Total Aggregate:* Roger Hunt, 245, 1959–69.

*Most Capped Player:* Emlyn Hughes, 59 (62) England.

*Most League Appearances:* Ian Callaghan, 640, 1960–78.

*Record Transfer Fee Received:* £500,000 from Hamburg SV for Kevin Keegan, June 1977.

*Record Transfer Fee Paid:* £900,000 to Brighton & HA for Mark Lawrenson, Aug 1981.

*Previous Managers since the War:* George Kay, Don Welsh, Phil Taylor, Bill Shankly.

*Address of Supporters Club:* 212 Lower Breck Road.

*Address of the Club Shop or Boutique:* Same as ground.

---

**Anfield Road, Liverpool 4.** Telephone 051-263 2361. *Telegraphic address:* 'Goalkeeper Liverpool'. *Ground capacity:* 45,000. *Record attendance:* 61,905 v Wolverhampton W, FA Cup 4th rd, 2 Feb, 1952. *Record receipts:* £154,000 Wales v Scotland, World Cup qualifying tie, 12 Oct, 1977. *Pitch measurements:* 110yd×75yd.

*How to get there:* Buses 17d from Pier Head and 26, 27 from Castle Street. Nearest stations, Bankhall and Kirkdale.

*Match tickets:* Postal applications 19 days before the match.

*Car parking:* Limited street parking around the ground. Large privately owned car park in Priory Road within five minutes walk of the ground.

*Entertainments/catering facilities:* Licensed refreshment bars in all parts of the ground.

*Club shop:* Main shop run by the Development Association open Monday–Saturday. Small kiosks in the ground open on match days only.

*Handbooks/programmes:* No handbook. Programmes available on subscription from the secretary.

*Extra information:* Liverpool's defensive record of only 16 goals conceded in 1978–79 is the best in First Division history.

*Club Colours:* All red with white facings.

*Change Colours:* Yellow shirts, red pin stripes, yellow shorts, yellow stockings.

*Captain:* Phil Thompson. *First Team Trainer:* Ron Moran.

*Club Nickname:* Reds or Pool.

# LIVERPOOL 1981–82 LEAGUE RECORD

| Match No. | Date | Venue | Opponents | Result | | H/T Score | Goalscorers | Attendance |
|---|---|---|---|---|---|---|---|---|
| 1 | Aug 29 | A | Wolverhampton W | L | 0-1 | 0-0 | | 28,001 |
| 2 | Sept 1 | H | Middlesbrough | D | 1-1 | 0-1 | Neal (pen) | 31,963 |
| 3 | 5 | H | Arsenal | W | 2-0 | 1-0 | McDermott, Johnson | 35,269 |
| 4 | 12 | A | Ipswich T | L | 0-2 | 0-1 | | 26,703 |
| 5 | 19 | H | Aston Villa | D | 0-0 | 0-0 | | 37,474 |
| 6 | 22 | A | Coventry C | W | 2-1 | 2-1 | Kennedy A., McDermott (pen) | 16,731 |
| 7 | 26 | A | West Ham U | D | 1-1 | 0-1 | Johnson | 30,802 |
| 8 | Oct 3 | H | Swansea C | D | 2-2 | 0-1 | McDermott 2 (2 pens) | 48,645 |
| 9 | 10 | H | Leeds U | W | 3-0 | 2-0 | Rush 2, Cherry (og) | 35,840 |
| 10 | 17 | A | Brighton & HA | D | 3-3 | 2-0 | Dalglish, Kennedy R., McDermott | 26,321 |
| 11 | 24 | H | Manchester U | L | 1-2 | 0-1 | McDermott (pen) | 41,438 |
| 12 | 31 | A | Sunderland | W | 2-0 | 0-0 | Souness, McDermott | 27,854 |
| 13 | Nov 7 | H | Everton | W | 3-1 | 0-0 | Dalglish 2, Rush | 48,861 |
| 14 | 21 | A | WBA | D | 1-1 | 0-0 | Dalglish | 20,871 |
| 15 | 28 | H | Southampton | L | 0-1 | 0-0 | | 37,189 |
| 16 | Dec 5 | A | Nottingham F | W | 2-0 | 0-0 | Lawrenson, Kennedy R. | 24,521 |
| 17 | 26 | H | Manchester C | L | 1-3 | 0-1 | Whelan | 37,929 |
| 18 | Jan 5 | H | West Ham U | W | 3-0 | 2-0 | McDermott, Whelan, Dalglish | 28,427 |
| 19 | 16 | H | Wolverhampton W | W | 2-1 | 0-1 | Whelan, Dalglish | 26,438 |
| 20 | 26 | A | Notts Co | W | 4-0 | 1-0 | Whelan, Rush 3 | 14,407 |
| 21 | 30 | A | Aston Villa | W | 3-0 | 2-0 | Rush, McDermott 2 | 35,947 |
| 22 | Feb 6 | H | Ipswich T | W | 4-0 | 3-0 | McDermott, Rush, Dalglish, Whelan | 41,316 |
| 23 | 16 | A | Swansea C | L | 0-2 | 0-0 | | 22,604 |
| 24 | 20 | H | Coventry C | W | 4-0 | 3-0 | Souness, Lee, Rush, McDermott (pen) | 28,286 |
| 25 | 27 | A | Leeds U | W | 2-0 | 1-0 | Souness, Rush | 33,689 |
| 26 | Mar 6 | H | Brighton & HA | L | 0-1 | 0-1 | | 28,574 |
| 27 | 9 | A | Stoke C | W | 5-1 | 2-0 | McDermott, Dalglish, Souness, Lee, Whelan | 16,758 |
| 28 | 20 | H | Sunderland | W | 1-0 | 1-0 | Rush | 30,344 |
| 29 | 27 | A | Everton | W | 3-1 | 1-1 | Whelan, Souness, Johnston | 51,847 |
| 30 | 30 | H | Birmingham C | W | 3-1 | 1-0 | Rush 2, McDermott | 24,224 |
| 31 | Apr 2 | H | Notts Co | W | 1-0 | 0-0 | Dalglish | 30,126 |
| 32 | 7 | A | Manchester U | W | 1-0 | 0-0 | Johnston | 50,969 |
| 33 | 10 | A | Manchester C | W | 5-0 | 2-0 | Lee, Neal (pen), Johnston, Kennedy A., Rush | 40,112 |
| 34 | 13 | H | Stoke C | W | 2-0 | 2-0 | Kennedy A., Johnston | 30,419 |
| 35 | 17 | H | WBA | W | 1-0 | 0-0 | Dalglish | 34,286 |
| 36 | 24 | A | Southampton | W | 3-2 | 1-1 | Rush, Whelan 2 | 24,704 |
| 37 | May 1 | H | Nottingham F | W | 2-0 | 0-0 | Johnston 2 | 34,321 |
| 38 | 3 | A | Tottenham H | D | 2-2 | 0-2 | Dalglish 2 | 38,091 |
| 39 | 8 | A | Birmingham C | W | 1-0 | 0-0 | Rush | 26,381 |
| 40 | 11 | A | Arsenal | D | 1-1 | 1-0 | Rush | 30,932 |
| 41 | 15 | H | Tottenham H | W | 3-1 | 0-1 | Lawrenson, Dalglish, Whelan | 48,122 |
| 42 | 18 | A | Middlesbrough | D | 0-0 | 0-0 | | 17,431 |

**Final League Position: 1**

## Goalscorers

*League* (80): Rush 17, McDermott 14 (4 pens), Dalglish 13, Whelan 10, Johnston 6, Souness 5, Kennedy A. 3, Lee 3, Johnson 2, Kennedy R. 2, Lawrenson 2, Neal 2 (2 pens), own goal 1.
*League Cup* (28): Rush 8, Dalglish 5, Johnson 3, McDermott 3 (1 pen), Whelan 3, Sheedy 2, Johnston 1, Neal 1, Souness 1, own goal 1.
*FA Cup* (7): Rush 3, Dalglish 2, Hansen 1, Lawrenson 1.

| **League Cup** | Second Round | Exeter C (h) | 5-0 |
|---|---|---|---|
| | | (a) | 6-0 |
| | Third Round | Middlesbrough (h) | 4-1 |
| | Fourth Round | Arsenal (a) | 0-0 |
| | | (h) | 3-0 |
| | Fifth Round | Barnsley (h) | 0-0 |
| | | (a) | 3-1 |
| | Semi-final | Ipswich T (a) | 2-0 |
| | | (h) | 2-2 |
| | Final | Tottenham H | 3-1 (at Wembley) |
| **FA Cup** | Third Round | Swansea C (a) | 4-0 |
| | Fourth Round | Sunderland (a) | 3-0 |
| | Fifth Round | Chelsea (a) | 0-2 |

| Grobbelaar | Neal | Lawrenson | Thompson | Kennedy R. | Hansen | Dalglish | Lee | Johnson | McDermott | Souness | Johnston | Kennedy A. | Whelan | Sheedy | Rush | Match No. |
|---|---|---|---|---|---|---|---|---|---|---|---|---|---|---|---|---|
| 1 | 2 | 3 | 4 | 5* | 6 | 7 | 8 | 9 | 10 | 11 | 12 |  |  |  |  | 1 |
| 1 | 2 | 3 | 4 | 5 | 6 | 7 | 8 | 9 | 10 | 11 |  |  |  |  |  | 2 |
| 1 | 2 | 3 | 4 | 5 | 6 | 7 | 8 | 9 | 10 | 11* | 12 |  |  |  |  | 3 |
| 1 | 2 |  | 4 | 5 | 6 | 7 | 8 | 9 | 10* | 11 | 12 | 3 |  |  |  | 4 |
| 1 | 2 |  | 4 | 5 | 6 | 7 | 8 | 9 | 10 | 11 |  | 3 |  |  |  | 5 |
| 1 | 2 | 12 | 4 | 5 | 6 | 7 | 8 | 9* | 10 | 11 |  | 3 |  |  |  | 6 |
| 1 | 2 |  | 4 | 5 | 6 | 7 | 8 | 9 | 10 | 11 |  | 3 |  |  |  | 7 |
| 1 | 2 | 5 | 4 |  |  | 7 | 8 | 9* | 10 | 11 |  | 3 | 6 |  | 12 | 8 |
| 1 | 2 | 5 | 4 | 6 |  | 7 | 8 |  | 10 | 11 |  | 3 |  |  | 9 | 9 |
| 1 | 2 | 12 | 4 | 5 | 6 | 7 | 8 |  | 10 | 11 |  | 3 |  |  | 9* | 10 |
| 1 | 2 | 3 | 4 | 5 | 6 | 7 | 8 | 9* | 10 | 11 |  |  | 12 |  |  | 11 |
| 1 | 2 | 3 | 4 | 5 | 6 | 7 |  |  | 10 | 11 |  | 8 |  |  | 9 | 12 |
| 1 | 2 | 3 | 4 | 5* | 6 | 7 |  | 12 | 10 | 11 |  | 8 |  |  | 9 | 13 |
| 1 | 2 | 3 | 4 | 5* | 6 | 7 |  | 9 | 10 | 11 | 12 | 8 |  |  |  | 14 |
| 1 | 2 | 3 | 4 | 5 | 6 | 7 |  | 12 | 10* | 11 |  | 8 |  |  | 9 | 15 |
| 1 | 2 | 3 | 4 | 5 | 6 | 7 |  |  | 10 | 11 |  | 8 |  |  | 9 | 16 |
| 1 | 2 | 3 | 4 |  | 6 | 7 | 8 |  |  | 11 | 10* | 12 | 5 |  | 9 | 17 |
| 1 | 2 | 3 | 4 |  | 6 | 7 |  |  | 10 | 11 |  | 8 | 5 |  | 9 | 18 |
| 1 | 2 | 3 | 4 |  | 6 | 7 |  | 12 | 10 | 11 |  | 8* | 5 |  | 9 | 19 |
| 1 | 2 | 3 |  |  | 6 | 7 | 8 |  | 10 | 11 |  | 4 | 5 |  | 9 | 20 |
| 1 | 2 | 3 |  |  | 6 | 7 | 8 |  | 10 | 11 |  | 4 | 5 |  | 9 | 21 |
| 1 | 2 | 3 |  |  | 6 | 7 | 8 |  | 10 | 11 |  | 4 | 5 |  | 9 | 22 |
| 1 | 2 | 3 |  |  | 6 | 7 | 8 |  | 10 | 11 |  | 4 | 5 |  | 9 | 23 |
| 1 | 2 | 3 |  |  | 6 | 7 | 8 |  | 10 | 11 |  | 4 | 5 |  | 9 | 24 |
| 1 | 2 | 3 |  |  | 6 | 7 | 8 | 12 | 10 | 11 |  | 4 | 5 |  | 9* | 25 |
| 1 | 2 | 3 |  |  | 6 | 7 | 8* |  | 10 | 11 |  | 4 | 5 | 12 | 9 | 26 |
| 1 | 2 | 3 |  |  | 6 | 7 | 8 |  | 10 | 11 |  | 4 | 5 |  | 9 | 27 |
| 1 | 2 | 3 | 6 |  |  | 7 | 8 | 12 |  | 11 | 10* | 4 | 5 |  | 9 | 28 |
| 1 | 2 | 3 | 6 |  |  | 7 | 8 |  |  | 11 | 10 | 4 | 5 |  | 9 | 29 |
| 1 | 2 | 3 | 6 |  |  | 7 | 8 |  | 10 | 11 |  | 4 | 5 |  | 9 | 30 |
| 1 | 2 | 3 | 6 |  |  | 7 | 8 |  | 10 | 11 |  | 4 | 5 |  | 9 | 31 |
| 1 | 2 | 3 | 6 |  |  | 7 | 8 | 12 |  | 11* | 10 | 4 | 5 |  | 9 | 32 |
| 1 | 2 | 3 | 6 |  | 11 | 7 | 8 |  | 10 |  |  | 4 | 5 |  | 9 | 33 |
| 1 | 2 | 3 | 6 |  | 11 | 7 | 8 |  | 10 |  |  | 4 | 5 |  | 9 | 34 |
| 1 | 2 | 3 | 6 |  | 11 | 7 | 8 |  | 10 |  |  | 4 | 5 |  | 9 | 35 |
| 1 | 2 | 3 | 6 |  | 11 | 7 | 8 |  | 10 |  |  | 4 | 5 |  | 9 | 36 |
| 1 | 2 | 3 | 6 |  | 11 | 7 | 8 |  | 10 |  |  | 4 | 5 |  | 9 | 37 |
| 1 | 2 | 3 | 6 |  | 11 | 7 | 8 | 12 | 10* |  |  | 4 | 5 |  | 9 | 38 |
| 1 | 2 | 3 | 6 |  | 10 | 7 | 8 |  |  | 11 | 12 | 4 | 5* |  | 9 | 39 |
| 1 | 2 | 3 | 6 |  | 10 | 7 | 8* |  |  | 11 | 12 | 4 | 5 |  | 9 | 40 |
| 1 | 2 | 3 | 6 |  | 10 | 7 | 8 |  |  | 11 |  | 4 | 5 |  | 9 | 41 |
| 1 | 2 | 3 | 6 |  | 10 | 7 | 8 |  |  | 11 |  | 5 | 4 |  | 9 | 42 |
| 42 | 42 | 37 | 34 | 15 | 35 | 42 | 35 | 10 | 28 | 34 | 13 | 32 | 31 | — | 32 |  |
|  | + |  |  |  |  |  | + | + | + | + | + | + | + |  |  |  |
|  | 2s |  |  |  |  |  | 5s | 1s | 1s | 5s | 2s | 1s | 2s |  |  |  |

# LIVERPOOL

| | Ht | Wt | Birthplace | Clubs | League App. | League Gls |
|---|---|---|---|---|---|---|
| **Goalkeepers** | | | | | | |
| Steve Ogrizovic | 6 3 | 14 7 | Mansfield | Chesterfield | 16 | — |
| | | | | Liverpool | 4 | — |
| Bruce Grobbelaar | 6 1 | 13 0 | Durban, SA | Crewe Alex | 24 | 1 |
| (Zimbabwe) | | | | Vancouver W | (not known) | |
| | | | | Liverpool | 42 | — |
| | | | | | | |
| **Defenders** | | | | | | |
| Phil Neal | 5 11 | 12 2 | Irchester | Northampton T | 186 | 29 |
| (England) | | | | Liverpool | 317 | 27 |
| Phil Thompson | 6 0 | 11 8 | Liverpool | Liverpool | 316 | 7 |
| (England) | | | | | | |
| Alan Hansen | 6 1 | 13 0 | Alloa | Partick T | 86 | 6 |
| (Scotland) | | | | Liverpool | 161 | 6 |
| Alan Harper | 5 8 | 9 7 | Liverpool | Liverpool | — | — |
| Alan Kennedy | 5 9 | 10 7 | Sunderland | Newcastle U | 158 | 9 |
| | | | | Liverpool | 127 | 9 |
| Michael Halsall | 5 10 | 11 4 | Liverpool | Liverpool | — | — |
| Avi Cohen | 5 11½ | 11 11 | Tel Aviv | Maccabi | (not known) | |
| (Israel) (Contract cancelled Nov 1981) | | | | Liverpool | 18 | 1 |
| Tim Bredbury | | | Hong Kong | Liverpool | — | — |
| (Contract cancelled April 1982) | | | | | | |
| Mark Lawrenson | 6 0 | 11 7 | Preston | Preston NE | 73 | 2 |
| (Eire) | | | | Brighton | 152 | 5 |
| | | | | Liverpool | 39 | 2 |
| Steve Nicol | 5 10 | 12 0 | Irvine | Ayr U | 70 | 7 |
| | | | | Liverpool | — | — |
| | | | | | | |
| **Midfield** | | | | | | |
| Terry McDermott | 5 9 | 12 13 | Kirkby | Bury | 90 | 8 |
| (England) | | | | Newcastle U | 56 | 6 |
| | | | | Liverpool | 230 | 54 |
| Howard Gayle | 5 10½ | 10 9 | Liverpool | Liverpool | 4 | 1 |
| | | | | Fulham (on loan) | 14 | — |
| Bob Savage | 5 7 | 11 1 | Liverpool | Liverpool | — | — |
| Graeme Souness | 5 11 | 12 13 | Edinburgh | Tottenham H | — | — |
| (Scotland) | | | | Middlesbrough | 176 | 22 |
| | | | | Liverpool | 169 | 22 |
| Kevin Sheedy | 5 7 | 9 2 | Hereford | Hereford U | 51 | 4 |
| | | | | Liverpool | 3 | — |
| Ron Whelan | 5 9 | 10 13 | Dublin | Home Farm | (not known) | |
| (Eire) | | | | Liverpool | 33 | 11 |
| Craig Johnston | 5 9 | 11 2 | Johannesburg | Lake McQuarrie | (not known) | |
| | | | | Sydney C | (not known) | |
| | | | | Middlesbrough | 64 | 16 |
| | | | | Liverpool | 18 | 6 |
| | | | | | | |
| **Forwards** | | | | | | |
| David Fairclough | 5 9 | 11 0 | Liverpool | Liverpool | 90 | 31 |
| (Contract cancelled April 1982) | | | | | | |
| Sammy Lee | 5 7 | 10 1 | Liverpool | Liverpool | 83 | 8 |
| David Johnson | 5 10 | 12 4 | Liverpool | Everton | 50 | 11 |
| (England) | | | | Ipswich T | 137 | 35 |
| | | | | Liverpool | 149 | 55 |
| Kenny Dalglish | 5 8 | 11 13 | Glasgow | Celtic | 204 | 112 |
| (Scotland) | | | | Liverpool | 202 | 78 |
| Colin Russell | 5 7 | 10 7 | Liverpool | Liverpool | 1 | — |
| Ian Rush | 6 0½ | 12 6 | Flint | Chester | 34 | 14 |
| (Wales) | | | | Liverpool | 39 | 17 |
| Steven Foley | 5 7 | 10 12 | Liverpool | Liverpool | — | — |

# LUTON TOWN Division 1

*President:* T. Hodgson.

*Chairman:* D. Mortimer.

*Directors:* R. J. Smith, E. S. Pearson LLM, BSC, R. L. Banks, D. J. Evans.

*General Secretary:* G. H. Mackrell FCCA.

*Club Secretary:* J. S. Wilkinson.

*Executive Director:* J. R. Smith.

*Team Manager:* David Pleat.

*Year Formed:* 1885. *Turned Professional:* 1890.

*Limited Company:* 1897.

*Previous Grounds:* 1885, Excelsior, Dallow Lane; 1897, Dunstable Road; 1905, Kenilworth Road.

**Football League Record:**

1897 Elected to Division 2; 1900 failed re-election; 1920 Division 3; 1921 Division 3(S); 1937–55 Division 2; 1955–60 Division 1; 1960–63 Division 2; 1963–65 Division 3; 1965–68 Division 4; 1968–70 Division 3; 1970–74 Division 2; 1974–75 Division 1; 1975–82 Division 2; 1982– Division 1.

**Honours:** *Football League:* Division 1 best season: 8th, 1957–58; Division 2 – Champions 1981–82, Runners-up 1954–55, 1973–74; Division 3 – Runners-up 1969–70; Division 4 – Champions 1967–68. Division 3(S) – Champions 1936–37, Runners-up 1935–36. *FA Cup:* Runners-up 1959. *Football League Cup* best season: 5th rd, 1978–79.

*Record Victory:* 12-0 v Bristol R, Division 3(S), 13 Apr, 1936.

*Record Defeat:* 0-9 v Small Heath, Division 2, 12 Nov, 1898.

*Most League Points:* 66, Division 4, 1967–68 (equalled former Division 4 record). *Three points win:* 88, Division 2, 1981–82.

*Most League Goals:* 103, Division 3(S), 1936–37.

*Highest League Scorer in Season:* Joe Payne, 55, Division 3(S), 1936–37.

*Most League Goals in Total Aggregate:* Gordon Turner, 243, 1949–64.

*Most Capped Player:* George Cummins, 19, Eire.

*Most League Appearances:* Bob Morton, 494, 1948–64.

*Record Transfer Fee Received:* £350,000 from Manchester C for Paul Futcher, June 1978.

*Record Transfer Fee Paid:* £200,000 to Mansfield T for Mike Saxby, July 1979 and £200,000 to Bristol R for Steve White, Dec 1980.

*Previous Managers since the War:* George Martin, Dally Duncan, Syd Owen, Sam Bartram, Bill Harvey, Allan Brown, Alec Stock, Harry Haslam.

*Address of Supporters Club:* Bobbers Club, Beech Hill Path, Luton.

---

**70–72 Kenilworth Rd, Luton.** Telephone Luton (0582) 411622. 24-hour answering service: 0582-33010. *Ticket office:* 0582-30748. *Telegraphic address:* 'Football Luton'. *Ground capacity:* 22,601 (17,000 covered). *Record attendance:* 30,069 v Blackpool, FA Cup 6th rd replay, 4 March, 1959. *Record receipts:* £42,870 v Ipswich T, FA Cup 4th rd, 23 Jan, 1982. *Pitch measurements:* 112yd×72yd.

*How to get there:* Nearest railway station, Luton (six minutes walk). There is also a frequent bus service to and from the town centre to the ground, but the ground is central.

*Match tickets:* Seats can be booked two weeks before the game.

*Car parking:* Ample parking facilities adjacent to the ground entrance in Maple Road.

*Entertainments/catering facilities:* Licensed bars and refreshment bars on ground.

*Club shop:* Sells all types of souvenirs.

*Programmes:* Programmes can be obtained from club shop.

*Extra information:* Joe Payne scored 10 goals against Bristol Rovers in April 1936, a record individual score in a Football League match.

*Club Colours:* White shirts with orange sleeves and shoulders with 3 white and 2 navy ½" stripes across shoulders and sleeves, white shorts with 2 orange and 3 navy vertical stripes down side, orange stockings with white and navy trim.

*Change Colours:* Orange shirts with navy sleeves and shoulders with white and navy stripes across shoulders and sleeves, navy shorts with white and orange trim, orange stockings with white and navy trim.

*Club Captain:* Brian Horton.

*First Team Trainer:* John Sheridan.

*Club Nickname:* Hatters.

## LUTON TOWN 1981–82 LEAGUE RECORD

| Match No. | Date | Venue | Opponents | Result | | H/T Score | Goalscorers | Attendance |
|---|---|---|---|---|---|---|---|---|
| 1 | Aug 29 | H | Charlton Ath | W | 3-0 | 2-0 | Donaghy, McAllister (og), White | 8776 |
| 2 | Sept 1 | A | QPR | W | 2-1 | 0-1 | Aizlewood, Hill | 18,703 |
| 3 | 5 | A | Bolton W | W | 2-1 | 0-0 | Stein, Aizlewood | 6911 |
| 4 | 12 | H | Sheffield W | L | 0-3 | 0-0 | | 12,131 |
| 5 | 19 | A | Leicester C | W | 2-1 | 0-1 | White 2 | 14,159 |
| 6 | 22 | H | Cardiff C | L | 2-3 | 1-2 | Saxby, Antic | 9015 |
| 7 | 26 | H | Watford | W | 4-1 | 3-0 | Moss 2 (2 pens), Stein 2 | 12,839 |
| 8 | Oct 3 | A | Orient | W | 3-0 | 2-0 | Aizlewood, Hill, White | 5084 |
| 9 | 10 | A | Oldham Ath | D | 1-1 | 0-1 | White | 8403 |
| 10 | 17 | H | Grimsby T | W | 6-0 | 3-0 | Fuccillo, Moss (pen), White 4 | 9090 |
| 11 | 24 | A | Wrexham | W | 2-0 | 0-0 | Donaghy, White | 4069 |
| 12 | 31 | H | Crystal Palace | W | 1-0 | 1-0 | Moss (pen) | 11,712 |
| 13 | Nov 7 | H | Derby Co | W | 3-2 | 1-0 | Moss, Goodyear, Donaghy | 10,784 |
| 14 | 14 | A | Blackburn R | W | 1-0 | 0-0 | Moss (pen) | 9862 |
| 15 | 21 | A | Newcastle U | L | 2-3 | 0-2 | Moss (pen), Donaghy | 21,037 |
| 16 | 24 | H | Bolton W | W | 2-0 | 0-0 | Stein, Moss | 8889 |
| 17 | 28 | H | Rotherham U | W | 3-1 | 0-0 | White, Donaghy, Stein | 11,061 |
| 18 | Dec 5 | A | Shrewsbury T | D | 2-2 | 1-2 | White, Donaghy | 5259 |
| 19 | 28 | A | Norwich C | W | 3-1 | 3-1 | Antic, White, Stein | 19,348 |
| 20 | Jan 19 | A | Charlton Ath | D | 0-0 | 0-0 | | 7013 |
| 21 | 30 | H | Leicester C | W | 2-1 | 1-0 | White, Donaghy | 11,810 |
| 22 | Feb 6 | A | Sheffield W | D | 3-3 | 1-1 | White, Moss (pen), Stein | 18,012 |
| 23 | 20 | A | Watford | D | 1-1 | 1-1 | Stein | 22,580 |
| 24 | 27 | H | Oldham Ath | W | 2-0 | 1-0 | Moss 2 (1 pen) | 11,506 |
| 25 | Mar 2 | H | Cambridge U | W | 1-0 | 0-0 | Horton | 10,597 |
| 26 | 6 | A | Grimsby T | D | 0-0 | 0-0 | | 7733 |
| 27 | 12 | H | Wrexham | D | 0-0 | 0-0 | | 10,880 |
| 28 | 16 | A | Barnsley | L | 3-4 | 1-1 | Stein 2, Law (og) | 14,004 |
| 29 | 20 | A | Crystal Palace | D | 3-3 | 3-2 | Antic, Moss (pen), Stein | 12,001 |
| 30 | 27 | A | Derby Co | D | 0-0 | 0-0 | | 15,836 |
| 31 | 30 | H | Orient | W | 2-0 | 0-0 | Moss (pen), Hill | 9716 |
| 32 | Apr 3 | H | Blackburn R | W | 2-0 | 1-0 | Stein, White | 10,721 |
| 33 | 10 | A | Cambridge U | D | 1-1 | 0-0 | Turner | 8815 |
| 34 | 12 | H | Norwich C | W | 2-0 | 0-0 | Stein, Jennings | 15,061 |
| 35 | 17 | H | Newcastle U | W | 3-2 | 0-1 | Stein 3 (2 pens) | 13,041 |
| 36 | 20 | H | Chelsea | D | 2-2 | 1-1 | Antic, Donaghy | 16,185 |
| 37 | 24 | A | Rotherham U | D | 2-2 | 1-1 | Fuccillo, Money | 11,290 |
| 38 | 30 | H | Shrewsbury T | W | 4-1 | 1-0 | Stein, Hill, White, Moss | 14,563 |
| 39 | May 8 | A | Chelsea | W | 2-1 | 1-1 | Antic, Stein | 15,044 |
| 40 | 11 | H | QPR | W | 3-2 | 1-0 | Hill, White, Moss (pen) | 16,657 |
| 41 | 15 | H | Barnsley | D | 1-1 | 0-0 | Stein | 14,463 |
| 42 | 17 | A | Cardiff C | W | 3-2 | 1-0 | Stein 2, Donaghy | 10,277 |

**Final League Position: 1**

### Goalscorers

*League* (86): Stein 21 (2 pens), White 18, Moss 15 (11 pens), Donaghy 9, Antic 5, Hill 5, Aizlewood 3, Fuccillo 2, Horton 1 Goodyear 1, Jennings 1, Money 1, Saxby 1, Turner 1, own goals 2.
*League Cup* (1): White 1.
*FA Cup* (2): Horton 1, Moss 1 (pen).

| League Cup | Second Round | Wrexham (h) | 0-2 |
|---|---|---|---|
| | | (a) | 1-0 |
| FA Cup | Third Round | Swindon T (h) | 2-1 |
| | Fourth Round | Ipswich T (h) | 0-3 |

| Findlay | Stephens | Aizlewood | Horton | Saxby | Donaghy | Hill | Stein | White | Antic | Ingram | Small | Turner | Moss | Fuccillo | Bunn | Goodyear | Aleksic | Judge | Money | Jennings | Match No. |
|---|---|---|---|---|---|---|---|---|---|---|---|---|---|---|---|---|---|---|---|---|---|
| 1 | 2 | 3 | 4 | 5 | 6 | 7 | 8 | 9 | 10 | 11 |  |  |  |  |  |  |  |  |  |  | 1 |
| 1 | 2 | 3 | 4 | 5 | 6 | 7 | 8 | 9 | 10 | 11 |  |  |  |  |  |  |  |  |  |  | 2 |
| 1 | 2 | 3 | 4 | 5 | 6 | 7 | 8 | 9 | 10 | 11* | 12 |  |  |  |  |  |  |  |  |  | 3 |
| 1 | 2 | 3 | 4 | 5 | 6 | 7 | 8 | 9 | 10 |  | 12 | 11* |  |  |  |  |  |  |  |  | 4 |
| 1 | 2 | 3 | 4 | 5 | 6 | 7 | 8 | 9 | 10 |  |  |  | 11 |  |  |  |  |  |  |  | 5 |
| 1 | 2 | 3* | 4 | 5 | 6 | 7 | 8 | 9 | 10 |  | . |  | 11 | 12 |  |  |  |  |  |  | 6 |
| 1 | 2 | 3 | 4 | 5 | 6 | 7 | 8 | 9 |  |  |  |  | 11 | 10 |  |  |  |  |  |  | 7 |
| 1 | 2 | 3 | 4 | 5 | 6 | 7 | 8 | 9 | 12 |  |  |  | 11* | 10 |  |  |  |  |  |  | 8 |
| 1 | 2 | 3 | 4 | 5* | 6 | 7 | 8 | 9 | 12 |  |  |  | 11 | 10 |  |  |  |  |  |  | 9 |
| 1 | 2 | 3* | 4 | 5 | 6 | 7 | 9 | 8 |  |  |  |  | 11 | 10 | 12 |  |  |  |  |  | 10 |
| 1 | 2 |  | 4 | 5 | 6 | 7 | 9 | 8 |  |  |  |  | 11 | 10 |  | 3 |  |  |  |  | 11 |
| 1 | 2 |  | 4 | 5* | 6 | 7 | 8 | 9 | 12 |  |  |  | 11 | 10 |  | 3 |  |  |  |  | 12 |
| 1 | 2 | 5 | 4 |  | 6 | 7 | 8 | 9 |  |  |  |  | 11 | 10 |  | 3 |  |  |  |  | 13 |
|  | 2 | 3 | 4 |  | 6 | 7 | 8 | 9 |  |  |  |  | 11 | 10 |  | 5 | 1 |  |  |  | 14 |
|  | 2 | 3 | 4 |  | 6 | 7 | 8 | 9 | 12 |  |  |  | 11 | 10 |  | 5* | 1 |  |  |  | 15 |
|  | 2 | 3 | 4 |  | 6 | 7 | 8 | 9 | 12 |  |  |  | 11 | 10 |  | 5 | 1* |  |  |  | 16 |
|  | 2 | 3 | 4 |  | 6 | 7 | 8 | 9 |  |  |  |  | 11 | 10 |  | 5 | 1 |  |  |  | 17 |
|  | 2 | 3 | 4 |  | 6 | 7* | 8 | 9 | 12 |  |  |  | 11 | 10 |  | 5 |  | 1 |  |  | 18 |
| 1 | 2 | 3 | 4 |  | 6 |  | 9 | 10 | 7 |  |  |  | 11 | 8 |  | 5 |  |  |  |  | 19 |
| 1 | 2 | 3 |  |  | 6 | 7 | 8 | 9 | 4 |  |  |  | 11 | 10 |  | 5 |  |  |  |  | 20 |
|  | 2 | 3 | 4 |  | 6 | 7 | 8 | 9 | 12 |  |  |  | 11 | 10* |  | 5 |  | 1 |  |  | 21 |
|  | 2 | 3 | 4 |  | 6 | 7 | 8 | 9 | 12 |  |  |  | 11* | 10 |  | 5 |  | 1 |  |  | 22 |
| 1 | 2 | 3 | 4 |  | 6 | 7 | 8 | 9 |  |  |  |  | 11 | 10 |  | 5 |  |  |  |  | 23 |
| 1 | 2 | 3 | 4 |  | 6 | 7 | 8 | 9 |  |  |  |  | 11 | 10 |  | 5 |  |  |  |  | 24 |
| 1 | 2 | 3 | 4 |  | 6 | 7 | 8 | 9 | 12 |  |  |  | 11 | 10* |  | 5 |  |  |  |  | 25 |
| 1 | 2 | 3 | 4 |  | 6 | 7 | 8 | 9 | 10 |  |  |  | 11 |  |  | 5 |  |  |  |  | 26 |
| 1 | 2 | 3* | 4 |  | 6 | 7 | 8 | 9 | 10 |  |  |  | 11 |  | 12 | 5 |  |  |  |  | 27 |
| 1 | 2 | 3 | 4 |  | 6 | 7 | 8 | 9 | 12 |  |  |  | 11 | 10* |  | 5 |  |  |  |  | 28 |
| 1 | 2 |  | 4 |  | 6 | 7 | 8 | 9 | 10 |  |  | 3 | 11 |  |  | 5 |  |  |  |  | 29 |
| 1 | 2 |  | 4 |  | 6 | 7 | 8 | 9 |  |  |  | 10 | 11 |  |  | 5 |  |  | 3 |  | 30 |
| 1 | 2 |  | 4 |  | 6 | 7 | 8 | 9 |  |  |  | 10 | 11 |  |  | 5 |  |  | 3 |  | 31 |
| 1 | 2 |  | 4 |  | 6 | 7* | 8 | 9 |  |  |  | 10 | 11 |  |  | 5 |  |  | 3 | 12 | 32 |
| 1 | 2 |  | 4 |  | 6 |  | 8 | 9 | 7 |  |  | 10* | 11 | 12 |  | 5 |  |  | 3 |  | 33 |
| 1 | 2 |  | 4 |  | 6 | 7 | 8 | 9 |  |  |  |  | 11* | 10 |  | 5 |  |  | 3 | 12 | 34 |
| 1 | 2 |  | 4 |  | 6 |  | 8 | 9 | 7 |  |  |  | 11 | 10 |  | 5 |  |  | 3 |  | 35 |
| 1 | 2 |  | 4 |  | 6 | 7 | 8 | 9 |  |  |  |  | 11 | 10 |  | 5 |  |  | 3 |  | 36 |
|  | 2 |  | 4 |  | 6 | 7* | 8 | 9 | 12 |  |  |  | 11 | 10 |  | 5 |  | 1 | 3 |  | 37 |
| 1 | 2 |  | 4 |  | 6 | 7 | 8 | 9 | 12 |  |  |  | 11 | 10* |  | 5 |  |  | 3 |  | 38 |
| 1 | 2 |  | 4 |  | 6 |  | 8 | 9 | 7 |  |  |  | 11 | 10 |  | 5 |  |  | 3 |  | 39 |
| 1 | 2 |  | 4 |  | 6 | 7 | 8 | 9 | 10 |  |  |  | 11 |  |  | 5 |  |  | 3 |  | 40 |
| 1 | 2 |  | 4 |  | 6 | 7 | 8 | 9 | 12 |  |  |  | 11 | 10* |  | 5 |  |  | 3 |  | 41 |
| 1 | 2 |  | 4 |  | 6 | 7 | 8 | 9 | 10 |  |  | 12 | 11* |  |  | 5 |  |  | 3 |  | 42 |
| 34 | 42 | 26 | 41 | 12 | 42 | 38 | 42 | 42 | 17 | 3 | — | 7 | 36 | 27 | — | 32 | 4 | 4 | 13 | — |  |
|  |  |  |  |  |  |  |  |  |  | +13s | +3s |  | +2s | +2s |  |  |  |  | +2s |  |  |

## LUTON TOWN

| | Ht | Wt | Birthplace | Clubs | League App. | League Gls |
|---|---|---|---|---|---|---|
| **Goalkeepers** | | | | | | |
| Alan Judge | 5 11 | 11 5½ | Kingsbury | Luton T | 7 | — |
| Jake Findlay | 6 1 | 14 1 | Blairgowrie | Aston V | 14 | — |
| | | | | Luton T | 138 | — |
| Andrew Beasley | 6 1¼ | 12 2 | Wolverhampton | Luton T | — | — |
| **Defenders** | | | | | | |
| Wayne Turner | 5 9 | 11 5 | Luton | Luton T | 11 | 1 |
| | | | | Lincoln C (on loan) | 16 | — |
| Mal Donaghy | 5 10 | 12 7 | Belfast | Larne | — | — |
| (N Ireland) | | | | Luton T | 166 | 10 |
| Kirk Stephens | 5 9 | 11 8 | Coventry | Luton T | 147 | 2 |
| Mark Aizlewood | 6 0 | 11 4 | Newport | Newport Co | 38 | 1 |
| | | | | Luton T | 98 | 3 |
| Mike Saxby | 6 0 | 13 10 | Mansfield | Mansfield T | 79 | 5 |
| | | | | Luton T | 82 | 6 |
| Richard Money | 5 11½ | 11 5 | Lowestoft | Scunthorpe U | 173 | 4 |
| | | | | Fulham | 106 | 3 |
| | | | | Liverpool | 14 | — |
| | | | | Luton T | 13 | 1 |
| | | | | Derby Co (on loan) | 5 | — |
| **Midfield** | | | | | | |
| Pasqualle Fuccillo | 5 11 | 11 4 | Bedford | Luton T | 151 | 24 |
| Ricky Hill | 5 9 | 11 10 | London | Luton T | 211 | 31 |
| Clive Goodyear | 5 11 | 11 4 | Lincoln | Luton T | 38 | 2 |
| Robert Johnson | 5 6 | 9 12 | Bedford | Luton T | — | — |
| Neil Madden* | 5 6 | 9 4 | Luton | Luton T | 1 | — |
| Raddy Antic | | | Yugoslavia | Zaragoza | (not known) | |
| (Yugoslavia) | | | | Luton T | 54 | 6 |
| Paul Keys | | | Ipswich | Luton T | — | — |
| (Contract cancelled April 1982) | | | | Halifax T (on loan) | 2 | — |
| Brian Horton | 5 10 | 11 4 | Hednesford | Port Vale | 236 | 33 |
| | | | | Brighton | 218 | 33 |
| | | | | Luton T | 41 | 1 |
| **Forwards** | | | | | | |
| Godfrey Ingram | 5 7 | 10 3 | Luton | Luton T | 27 | 6 |
| (Contract cancelled April 1982) | | | | Northampton T (on loan) | 10 | 4 |
| Brian Stein | 5 10 | 11 8 | South Africa | Luton T | 184 | 60 |
| David Moss | 5 9 | 11 7 | Witney | Swindon T | 230 | 60 |
| | | | | Luton T | 147 | 68 |
| Seamus Heath | 5 9 | 10 5 | Belfast | Luton T | 3 | — |
| Michael Small | 6 0 | 12 4 | Birmingham | Luton T | — | — |
| Steve White | 5 11 | 11 10 | Chipping | Bristol R | 50 | 20 |
| | | | Sodbury | Luton T | 72 | 25 |
| Frankie Bunn | 5 11 | 10 6 | Birmingham | Luton T | 5 | 1 |
| Ray Brammer* | | | | Luton T | — | — |
| Billy Jennings* | 5 9 | 10 2 | Hackney | Watford | 92 | 33 |
| | | | | West Ham U | 99 | 33 |
| | | | | Orient | 67 | 21 |
| | | | | Luton T | 2 | 1 |

# MANCHESTER CITY

## Division 1

*Chairman:* P. J. Swales.

*Executive President:* S. H. Cussons.

*Directors:* S. S. Rose MB, FRCS, A. E. Alexander MSIA, R. Harris, J. B. Muir, I. L. G. Niven, M. T. Horwich, W. C. Adams.

*Secretary:* J. B. Halford.

*Team Manager:* John Bond.

*Assistant Team Manager:* John Benson.

*Year Formed:* 1887 as Ardwick FC; 1895 as Manchester City.

*Limited Company:* 1894.

*Turned Professional:* 1887 as Ardwick FC.

*Previous Names:* 1887–94, Ardwick FC (Formed through the amalgamation of West Gorton and Gorton Athletic, the latter having been formed in 1880).

*Previous Grounds:* 1880–81, Clowes Street; 1881–82, Kirkmanshulme Cricket Ground; 1882–84, Queens Road; 1884–87, Pink Bank Lane; 1887–1923, Hyde Road (1894–1923, as City); 1923, Maine Road.

**Football League Record:**
1892 Ardwick elected founder member of Division 2; 1894 Newly-formed Manchester C elected to Division 2; Division 1 1899–1902, 1903–09, 1910–26, 1928–38, 1947–50, 1951–63, 1966– ; Division 2 1902–03, 1909–10, 1926–28, 1938–47, 1950–51, 1963–66.

**Honours:** *Football League:* Division 1 – Champions 1936–37, 1967–68; Runners-up 1903–04, 1920–21, 1976–77; Division 2 – Champions 1898–99, 1902–03, 1909–10, 1927–28, 1946–47, 1965–66; Runners-up 1895–96, 1950–51. *FA Cup:* Winners 1904, 1934, 1956, 1969; Runners-up 1926, 1933, 1955, 1981. *Football League Cup:* Winners 1970, 1976; Runners-up 1973–74. **European Competitions:** *European Cup:* 1968–69. *European Cup-Winners' Cup:* 1969–70 (winners), 1970–71. *UEFA Cup:* 1972–73, 1976–77, 1977–78, 1978–79.

*Record Victory:* 11-3 v Lincoln C, Division 2, 23 Mar, 1895.

*Record Defeat:* 1-9 v Everton, Division 1, 3 Sept, 1906.

*Most League Points:* 62, Division 2, 1946–47.

*Most League Goals:* 108, Division 2, 1926–27.

*Highest League Scorer in Season:* Tommy Johnson, 38, Division 1, 1928–29.

*Most League Goals in Total Aggregate:* Tommy Johnson, 158, 1919–30.

*Most Capped Player:* Colin Bell, 48, England.

*Most League Appearances:* Alan Oakes, 565, 1959–76.

*Record Transfer Fee Received:* £748,000 from WBA for Peter Barnes, July 1979.

*Record Transfer Fee Paid:* £1,437,500 to Wolverhampton W for Steve Daley, Sept 1979. (£1,150,000 basic fee).

*Previous Managers since the War:* Wilf Wild, Sam Cowan, Jock Thomson, Les McDowall, George Poyser, Joe Mercer, Malcolm Allison, John Hart, Ron Saunders, Tony Book, Malcolm Allison.

*Address of Supporters Club:* OK Souvenir Sports Ltd, Maine Road, Moss Side, Manchester M14 7WN.

---

**Maine Road, Moss Side, Manchester M14 7WN.** Telephone 061-226 1191/2. *Telegraphic address:* 'Football, Manchester 14'. *Ground capacity:* 52,500. *Record attendance:* 84,569 v Stoke C, FA Cup 6th rd, 3 March, 1934 (British record for any game outside London or Glasgow). *Record receipts:* £165,000 Liverpool v Manchester U, FA Cup semi-final, 31 March, 1979. *Pitch measurements:* 119yd×79yd.

*How to get there:* Corporation specials from Aytoun Street, Piccadilly, in centre of city. Nearest railway station, Manchester Piccadilly.

*Match tickets:* Advance booking 14 days prior to the match.

*Car parking:* Kippax Street car park holds approximately 400 cars. Also street parking.

*Entertainments/catering facilities:* Social club can be used by visiting supporters (contact Mr Roy Clarke). Licensed refreshment points around the ground.

*Club shop:* Open all week at the ground.

*Handbooks/programmes:* Handbook available. Programmes can be obtained on a mailing list.

*Extra information:* Manchester City scored more goals in 1937–38 than any other First Division side – but were relegated!

*Club Colours:* Sky blue shirts with white collar and cuffs, white stripe down sleeve, sky blue shorts with white trimmings, sky blue stockings with white rings on top.

*Change Colours:* White shirts with red/black stripe diagonally across chest, black shorts, black stockings.

*Club Captain:* Joe Corrigan. *Team Captain:* Paul Power.

*Club Nickname:* Citizens.

## MANCHESTER CITY 1981–82 LEAGUE RECORD

| Match No. | Date | Venue | Opponents | Result | | H/T Score | Goalscorers | Attendance |
|---|---|---|---|---|---|---|---|---|
| 1 | Aug 29 | H | WBA | W | 2-1 | 2-0 | Hutchison, Tueart | 36,187 |
| 2 | Sept 1 | A | Notts Co | D | 1-1 | 0-1 | McDonald | 14,546 |
| 3 | 5 | A | Stoke C | W | 3-1 | 1-0 | Francis 2, Boyer | 25,256 |
| 4 | 12 | H | Southampton | D | 1-1 | 1-1 | Reeves | 42,003 |
| 5 | 19 | A | Birmingham C | L | 0-3 | 0-1 | | 20,109 |
| 6 | 23 | H | Leeds U | W | 4-0 | 2-0 | Tueart 2, Reeves 2 | 35,077 |
| 7 | 26 | H | Tottenham H | L | 0-1 | 0-0 | | 39,085 |
| 8 | Oct 3 | A | Brighton & HA | L | 1-4 | 0-0 | Reeves | 18,300 |
| 9 | 10 | H | Manchester U | D | 0-0 | 0-0 | | 52,037 |
| 10 | 17 | A | Arsenal | L | 0-1 | 0-0 | | 25,470 |
| 11 | 24 | H | Nottingham F | D | 0-0 | 0-0 | | 34,881 |
| 12 | 31 | A | Everton | W | 1-0 | 0-0 | Tueart | 31,305 |
| 13 | Nov 7 | H | Middlesbrough | W | 3-2 | 2-1 | Francis, Reeves, Tueart (pen) | 32,025 |
| 14 | 21 | H | Swansea C | W | 4-0 | 1-0 | Tueart 2 (1 pen), Reeves 2 | 34,744 |
| 15 | 28 | A | Ipswich T | L | 0-2 | 0-0 | | 20,476 |
| 16 | Dec 5 | H | Aston Villa | W | 1-0 | 0-0 | Tueart | 32,487 |
| 17 | 12 | A | Coventry C | W | 1-0 | 1-0 | Tueart | 12,393 |
| 18 | 19 | H | Sunderland | L | 2-3 | 0-1 | Francis 2 | 29,462 |
| 19 | 26 | A | Liverpool | W | 3-1 | 1-0 | Hartford, Bond (pen), Reeves | 37,929 |
| 20 | 28 | H | Wolverhampton W | W | 2-1 | 0-0 | Hartford, Francis | 40,298 |
| 21 | Jan 9 | H | Stoke C | D | 1-1 | 0-1 | Francis | 31,941 |
| 22 | 30 | H | Birmingham C | W | 4-2 | 4-2 | Francis 2, Reeves 2 | 28,438 |
| 23 | Feb 2 | A | West Ham U | D | 1-1 | 0-0 | Bond (pen) | 26,552 |
| 24 | 6 | A | Southampton | L | 1-2 | 0-0 | McDonald | 22,645 |
| 25 | 13 | H | Brighton & HA | W | 4-0 | 2-0 | Francis, Reeves, McDonald, Stevens (og) | 30,038 |
| 26 | 20 | H | Tottenham H | L | 0-2 | 0-0 | | 46,181 |
| 27 | 27 | A | Manchester U | D | 1-1 | 1-1 | Reeves | 57,827 |
| 28 | Mar 6 | H | Arsenal | D | 0-0 | 0-0 | | 30,288 |
| 29 | 10 | A | Leeds U | W | 1-0 | 0-0 | Reeves | 20,797 |
| 30 | 13 | A | Nottingham F | D | 1-1 | 1-0 | Caton | 20,927 |
| 31 | 20 | H | Everton | D | 1-1 | 1-1 | Bond | 33,002 |
| 32 | 27 | A | Middlesbrough | D | 0-0 | 0-0 | | 11,709 |
| 33 | Apr 3 | H | West Ham U | L | 0-1 | 0-0 | | 30,875 |
| 34 | 10 | A | Liverpool | L | 0-5 | 0-2 | | 40,112 |
| 35 | 12 | A | Wolverhampton W | L | 1-4 | 0-4 | McDonald | 14,891 |
| 36 | 17 | A | Swansea C | L | 0-2 | 0-2 | | 19,212 |
| 37 | 21 | A | WBA | W | 1-0 | 1-0 | Francis | 11,073 |
| 38 | 24 | H | Ipswich T | D | 1-1 | 0-1 | Hartford | 30,329 |
| 39 | May 1 | A | Aston Villa | D | 0-0 | 0-0 | | 22,150 |
| 40 | 5 | H | Notts Co | W | 1-0 | 0-0 | Power | 24,443 |
| 41 | 8 | H | Coventry C | L | 1-3 | 0-2 | Francis | 27,580 |
| 42 | 15 | A | Sunderland | L | 0-1 | 0-1 | | 26,167 |

**Final League Position: 10**

### Goalscorers

*League* (49): Reeves 13, Francis 12, Tueart 9 (2 pens), McDonald 4, Bond 3 (2 pens), Hartford 3, Boyer 1, Caton 1, Hutchison 1, Power 1, own goal 1.
*League Cup* (5): Tueart 2, Hartford 1, McDonald 1, own goal 1.
*FA Cup* (4): Francis 2, Bond 1 (pen), McDonald 1.

| | | | |
|---|---|---|---|
| **League Cup** | Second Round | Stoke C (h) | 2-0 |
| | | (a) | 0-2 (won 9-8 on pens) |
| | Third Round | Northampton T (h) | 3-1 |
| | Fourth Round | Barnsley (a) | 0-1 |
| **FA Cup** | Third Round | Cardiff C (h) | 3-1 |
| | Fourth Round | Coventry C (h) | 1-3 |

| Corrigan | Ranson | McDonald | Reid | Power | Caton | O'Neill | Boyer | Tueart | Hutchison | Reeves | Henry | Williams | Gow | Francis | Bond | Booth | Hartford | Hareide | Kinsey | Wilson | Ryan | Jackson | May | Elliott | Match No. |
|---|---|---|---|---|---|---|---|---|---|---|---|---|---|---|---|---|---|---|---|---|---|---|---|---|---|
| 1 | 2 | 3 | 4 | 5 | 6* | 7 | 8 | 9 | 10 | 11 | 12 | | | | | | | | | | | | | | 1 |
| | 2 | 3 | 4 | 5 | 6 | 7 | 9 | | 10 | 11* | 12 | 1 | 8 | | | | | | | | | | | | 2 |
| 1 | 2 | 3 | 4 | 5* | 6 | 7 | 12 | | 10 | 11 | | | 8 | 9 | | | | | | | | | | | 3 |
| 1 | 2 | 3 | 4 | | 6 | 7 | 5 | | 10 | 11 | | | 8 | 9 | | | | | | | | | | | 4 |
| 1 | | | 4 | | 3 | 7 | 12 | 6 | 10 | 11* | | | 8 | 9 | 2 | 5 | | | | | | | | | 5 |
| 1 | 2 | 3 | 4 | 5 | 6 | 12 | | 7 | 10 | 11 | | | 8 | 9* | | | | | | | | | | | 6 |
| 1 | 2 | 3 | 4 | | 6 | 5 | 9* | 7 | 10 | 11 | | | 8 | 12 | | | | | | | | | | | 7 |
| 1 | 2 | 3 | 4 | | 6 | 8 | 9 | 7 | 10 | 11 | | | | 5 | | | | | | | | | | | 8 |
| 1 | 2 | | 4 | 9 | 5 | 7 | | 10 | 6 | 11 | | | | 3 | | 8 | | | | | | | | | 9 |
| 1 | 2 | | 4 | 5 | 6 | 8 | | 7 | 9 | 11 | | | | 3 | | 10 | | | | | | | | | 10 |
| 1 | 2 | | 4 | 5 | 6 | 8* | | 7 | 9 | 11 | | | | 3 | | 10 | 12 | | | | | | | | 11 |
| 1 | 2 | 3 | 4* | 10 | 6 | | 9 | 7 | 12 | 11 | | | | 5 | | 8 | | | | | | | | | 12 |
| 1 | 2 | 3 | 4 | 8* | 6 | | 7 | | 12 | 11 | | | | 9 | 5 | 10 | | | | | | | | | 13 |
| 1 | 2 | 3 | 4 | | 6* | | 7 | 11 | 8 | | | | | 9 | 5 | 10 | 12 | | | | | | | | 14 |
| 1 | 2 | 3 | 4 | | 6 | | 7 | 11 | 8 | | | | | 9 | 5 | 10 | | | | | | | | | 15 |
| 1 | 2 | 3 | 4 | | 6 | | 7 | 11 | 8 | | | | | 9 | 5 | 10 | | | | | | | | | 16 |
| 1 | 2 | 3 | 4 | | 6 | | 7 | 11 | 8 | | | | | 9 | 5 | 10 | | | | | | | | | 17 |
| 1 | 2 | 3 | 4 | | 6 | | 7* | 11 | 8 | | | | | 9 | 5 | 10 | 12 | | | | | | | | 18 |
| 1 | 2 | 3 | 4 | | 6 | | | 11 | 8 | | | | | 9 | 5 | 10 | | 7 | | | | | | | 19 |
| 1 | 2 | | 4 | | 6 | | | 11 | 8 | | | | | 9 | 5 | 10 | | 7 | 3 | | | | | | 20 |
| 1 | | 3 | 4 | | 6 | 7 | | 11 | 8 | | | | | 9 | 5 | 10 | | | 2 | | | | | | 21 |
| 1 | 2 | 3 | | 11 | 6 | | | 8 | | | | | | 9 | 5 | 10 | | 7 | 4 | | | | | | 22 |
| 1 | 2 | 3 | | 11 | 6 | | | 8 | | | | | | 9 | 5 | 10 | 12 | 7 | 4* | | | | | | 23 |
| 1 | 2 | 3 | | 11 | 6 | | | 10* | 8 | | | | | 9 | 5 | | 12 | 7 | 4 | | | | | | 24 |
| 1 | 2 | 3 | 4 | 11 | 6 | | | 8 | | | | | | 9 | 5* | 10 | 12 | 7 | | | | | | | 25 |
| 1 | 2 | 3 | 4 | 11 | 6 | | | 8 | | | | | | 9 | 5* | 10 | | 7 | 12 | | | | | | 26 |
| 1 | 2 | 3 | 4 | 11 | 6 | | | 8 | | | | | | | 5 | 10 | | 7 | 9 | | | | | | 27 |
| 1 | 2 | 3 | 4 | 11 | 6 | | | 8 | | | | | | 9* | 5 | 10 | | 7 | 12 | | | | | | 28 |
| 1 | 2 | 3 | 4 | 11 | 6 | | | 8 | | | | | | | 5 | 9 | | 7 | 10 | | | | | | 29 |
| 1 | 2 | 3 | 4 | 11* | 6 | | | 8 | | | | | | | 5 | 10 | 9 | 12 | | 7 | | | | | 30 |
| 1 | 2 | 3 | 4 | | 6 | | | 8 | | | | | | 9 | 5 | 10 | 11 | | | 7 | | | | | 31 |
| 1 | 2 | | 4 | | 6 | | | 8 | | | | | | 9 | | 11 | 7 | 3 | | | 5* | 12 | 10 | | 32 |
| 1 | 2 | 3 | 4 | 5 | 6 | | | 8 | | | | | | | | 10 | 9 | 7 | 11 | | | | | | 33 |
| 1 | 2 | 3 | 4 | | 6 | | | 8 | | | | | | | 5 | 10 | 9 | 11 | | 7 | | | | | 34 |
| 1 | 2 | 3 | | | | | | 8 | | | | | | 9 | 5 | 10 | 4 | 11 | | 7 | | 6* | 12 | | 35 |
| | 2 | 3 | 4 | | 6 | | | 8 | 1 | | | | | 9 | 5 | 10 | 12 | 11 | | | 7* | | | | 36 |
| 1 | 2 | 3 | 4 | 6 | | | | 8 | | | | | | 9 | 5 | 10 | 12 | 11* | | 7 | | | | | 37 |
| 1 | 2* | 3 | | 4 | 6 | | | 8 | | | | | | 9 | 5 | 10 | 11 | 7 | | | | 12 | | | 38 |
| 1 | | 3 | 4 | 11 | 6 | | 9 | 8 | | | | | | | 5 | 10 | 12 | 7 | | | | 2* | | | 39 |
| 1 | | 3 | 4 | 11 | 6 | | 9 | 8 | | | | | | | 5 | 10 | 7 | | | | | 2 | | | 40 |
| | | 3 | 4 | 11 | 6 | | | 7 | 8 | | | 1 | | 9 | 5 | 10 | | | | | | 2 | | | 41 |
| 1 | | 3 | 5 | | 6 | | 9 | 8 | | | | | | 4 | | 10 | 7* | 12 | 2 | 11 | | | | | 42 |
| 39 | 36 | 36 | 36 | 25 | 39 | 12 | 10 | 15 | 20 | 42 | — | 3 | 6 | 26 | 32 | 1 | 30 | 9 | 13 | 3 | 19 | 6 | 3 | 1 | |
| | | | | +1s | +2s | | +2s | | +2s | | | | | +1s | | | +7s | +3s | +1s | | +2s | +3s | | | |

## MANCHESTER CITY

| | Ht | Wt | Birthplace | Clubs | League App. | League Gls |
|---|---|---|---|---|---|---|
| **Goalkeepers** | | | | | | |
| Joe Corrigan (England) | 6 5 | 14 12 | Manchester | Manchester C | 451 | — |
| Alex Williams | 6 2 | 12 12 | Moss Side | Manchester C | 5 | — |
| **Defenders** | | | | | | |
| John Ryan | 5 11 | 11 8 | Lewisham | Fulham | 45 | 1 |
| | | | | Luton T | 266 | 10 |
| | | | | Norwich C | 116 | 26 |
| | | | | Seattle S | (not known) | |
| | | | | Sheffield U | 56 | 2 |
| | | | | Manchester C | 19 | — |
| Ray Ranson | 5 9 | 11 13 | St Helens | Manchester C | 117 | 1 |
| Nicky Reid | 5 9 | 12 1 | Davyhulme | Manchester C | 104 | — |
| (Contract cancelled April 1982) | | | | | | |
| Tommy Caton | 6 2 | 13 0 | Kirkby | Manchester C | 111 | 1 |
| Bobby McDonald | 5 10 | 12 5 | Aberdeen | Aston V | 39 | 3 |
| | | | | Coventry C | 161 | 14 |
| | | | | Manchester C | 64 | 8 |
| Geoff Lomax | 5 8 | 11 5 | Droysiden | Manchester C | — | — |
| Kevin Bond | 6 0 | 12 4 | West Ham | Norwich C | 142 | 12 |
| | | | | Seattle S | (not known) | |
| | | | | Manchester C | 33 | 3 |
| Age Hareide (Norway) | 6 1 | 12 4 | Hareid | Molde FK | (not known) | |
| | | | | Manchester C | 16 | — |
| **Midfield** | | | | | | |
| Paul Power | 5 10 | 11 7 | Openshaw | Manchester C | 217 | 21 |
| Tommy Hutchison (Scotland) | 5 11½ | 11 2 | Cardenden | Alloa | 68 | 4 |
| | | | | Blackpool | 165 | 10 |
| | | | | Coventry C | 314 | 24 |
| | | | | Manchester C | 46 | 4 |
| | | | | Bulova, Hong Kong (on loan) | (not known) | |
| Asa Hartford (Scotland) | 5 7 | 11 4 | Clydebank | WBA | 213 | 18 |
| | | | | Manchester C | 185 | 22 |
| | | | | Nottingham F | 3 | — |
| | | | | Everton | 81 | 6 |
| | | | | Manchester C | 30 | 3 |
| Andy May | 5 8 | 10 10 | Bury | Manchester C | 7 | — |
| Gary Jackson | 5 6 | 10 3 | Swinton | Manchester C | 8 | — |
| Andy Elliott* | 5 6 | 10 4 | Hadfield | Manchester C | 1 | — |
| **Forwards** | | | | | | |
| Dennis Tueart (England) | 5 8 | 11 4 | Newcastle | Sunderland | 178 | 46 |
| | | | | Manchester C | 140 | 59 |
| | | | | New York Cosmos | (not known) | |
| | | | | Manchester C | 48 | 22 |
| Kevin Reeves (England) | 5 9 | 12 1 | Burley | Bournemouth | 63 | 20 |
| | | | | Norwich C | 119 | 37 |
| | | | | Manchester C | 90 | 27 |
| Steve Kinsey | 5 7 | 9 9 | Gorton | Manchester C | 17 | — |
| Dave Wiffill | 6 1 | 10 12 | Bristol | Bath C | (not known) | |
| | | | | Manchester C | — | — |
| | | | | Bulova, Hong Kong (on loan) | (not known) | |
| Clive Wilson | 5 5 | 9 4 | Greenheys | Manchester C | 4 | — |
| Phil Boyer (England) | 5 8 | 11 7 | Nottingham | Derby Co | — | — |
| | | | | York C | 109 | 27 |
| | | | | Bournemouth | 141 | 46 |
| | | | | Norwich C | 116 | 34 |
| | | | | Southampton | 138 | 49 |
| | | | | Manchester C | 19 | 2 |
| Keith Parkinson* | 5 7 | 10 12 | Wigan | Manchester C | — | — |
| Steve Evans* | 5 6 | 9 6 | Hamilton | Glasgow R | — | — |
| | | | | Manchester C | — | — |
| Trevor Francis (England) | 5 10 | 11 7 | Plymouth | Birmingham C | 280 | 118 |
| | | | | Nottingham F | 70 | 28 |
| | | | | Manchester C | 26 | 12 |

# MANCHESTER UNITED     Division 1

*President:* Sir Matt Busby CBE, KCSG.

*Chairman:* C. M. Edwards.   *Vice-Chairman:* J. A. Gibson.

*Directors:* W. A. Young, D. D. Haroun JP, Sir Matt Busby CBE, KCSG, J. G. Gulliver, R. L. Edwards.

*Manager:* Ron Atkinson.   *Secretary:* R. L. Olive.

*Year Formed:* 1878 as Newton Heath; 1902, Manchester United.

*Turned Professional:* 1885.   *Limited Company:* 1907.

*Previous Name:* Newton Heath, 1880–1902.

*Previous Grounds:* 1880–93, North Road, Monsall Road; 1893, Bank Street; 1910, Old Trafford (Played at Maine Rd 1941-49).

**Football League Record:**
1892 Newton Heath elected to Division 1; 1894–1906 Division 2; 1906–22 Division 1; 1922–25 Division 2; 1925–31 Division 1; 1931–36 Division 2; 1936–37 Division 1; 1937–38 Division 2; 1938–74 Division 1; 1974–75 Division 2; 1975– Division 1.

**Honours:** *Football League:* Division 1 – Champions 1907–08, 1910–11, 1951–52, 1955–56, 1956–57, 1964–65, 1966–67; Runners-up 1946–47, 1947–48, 1948–49, 1950–51, 1958–59, 1963–64, 1967–68, 1979–80; Division 2 – Champions 1935–36, 1974–75; Runners-up 1896–97, 1905–06, 1924–25, 1937–38. *FA Cup:* Winners 1909, 1948, 1963, 1977; Runners-up 1957, 1958, 1976, 1979. *Football League Cup:* Semi-final 1969–70, 1970–71, 1974–75, 1978–79. **European Competitions:** *European Cup:* 1956–57 (s-f), 1957–58 (s-f), 1965–66 (s-f)1967–68 (winners), 1968–69 (s-f). *European Cup-Winners' Cup:* 1963–64, 1977–78. *European Fairs Cup:* 1964–65. *UEFA Cup:* 1976–77, 1980–81.

*Record Victory:* 10-0 v Anderlecht, European Cup preliminary rd, 26 Sept, 1956.

*Record Defeat:* 0-7 v Blackburn R, Division 1, 10 April, 1926 and v Aston Villa, Division 1, 27 Dec, 1930 and v Wolverhampton W, Division 2, 26 Dec, 1931.

*Most League Points:* 64, Division 1, 1956–57. *Three points win:* 78, Division 1, 1981–82.

*Most League Goals:* 103, Division 1, 1956–57 and 1958–59.

*Highest League Scorer in Season:* Dennis Viollet, 32, 1959–60.

*Most League Goals in Total Aggregate:* Bobby Charlton, 198, 1956–73.

*Most Capped Player:* Bobby Charlton, 106, England.

*Most League Appearances:* Bobby Charlton, 606, 1956–73.

*Record Transfer Fee Received:* £500,000 from Brighton & HA for Andy Ritchie, Oct 1980.

*Record Transfer Fee Paid:* £1,500,000 to WBA for Bryan Robson, Oct 1981.

*Previous Managers since the War:* Matt Busby, Wilf McGuinness, Sir Matt Busby, Frank O'Farrell, Tommy Docherty, Dave Sexton.

*Address of Supporters Club:* Football Ground, Old Trafford (sae for details). Tel: 061-872 6000.

*Address of the Club Shop or Boutique:* Red Devils Souvenir Shop, Old Trafford. Tel: 061-872 3398.

---

**Old Trafford, Manchester M16 0RA.** Telephone 061-872 1661/2. *Telegraphic address:* 'Stadium Manchester'. *Ground capacity:* 58,504. *Record attendance:* 76,962 Wolverhampton W v Grimsby T, FA Cup semi-final, 25 March, 1939. *Club record:* 70,504 v Aston Villa, Division 1, 27 Dec, 1920. *Record receipts:* £124,441, League Cup Final replay, Liverpool v Nottingham F, 22 March, 1978; £102,457 v Tottenham H, League Cup 2nd rd second leg, 28 Oct, 1981. *Pitch measurements:* 116yd×76yd.

*How to get there:* Special buses from Aytoun Street, Cannon Street, and various points in Manchester and Salford. Frequent train service from Manchester Oxford Road station direct to the Football Ground station, returning after the match. Schedule services from Oxford Road and Knott Mill, Manchester, or from Altrincham, Timperley, and intermediate stations, run to Warwick Road station, only a few minutes walk from the ground.

*Match tickets:* Seats can be booked from one calendar month before the match. Any not sold by Monday before a Saturday match can be reserved by personal application. For up-to-date ticket information, tel: 061-872 7771 (24 hour service). Tickets for over-subscribed matches are allocated by ballot.

*Car parking:* Large car parks within easy reach of the ground at Lancashire County Cricket Ground, Talbot Rd and Great Stone Rd (1,200). White City Stadium, Chester Rd (900). Alternatively, cars can be parked in Manchester, Altrincham, or at outside intermediate stations and the rest of the journey made by the above train services.

*Entertainments/catering facilities:* Licensed bars around the ground. Restaurant in conference complex (not match days).

*Club shop:* The souvenir shop alongside the ticket office is open throughout the week. Price lists sent on receipt of SAE.

*Programmes:* Available on subscription and application with remittance can be sent to the ground for individual matches. The supporters' club publishes an annual handbook and newsletters.

*Extra information:* The Manchester United Development Association has monthly draws for special prizes and a weekly draw. New agents are always welcome; tel: 061-872 4676/5208 for full details. There is a travel club for away matches. The club also run their own lottery.

*Club Colours:* Red shirts with red, white and black trim, white shorts, black stockings with red tops and three white bands.

*Club Nickname:* Red Devils.

## MANCHESTER UNITED 1981–82 LEAGUE RECORD

| Match No. | Date | Venue | Opponents | Result | | H/T Score | Goalscorers | Attendance |
|---|---|---|---|---|---|---|---|---|
| 1 | Aug 29 | A | Coventry C | L | 1-2 | 1-1 | Macari | 20,050 |
| 2 | 31 | H | Nottingham F | D | 0-0 | 0-0 | | 51,496 |
| 3 | Sept 5 | H | Ipswich T | L | 1-2 | 1-2 | Stapleton | 45,645 |
| 4 | 12 | A | Aston Villa | D | 1-1 | 1-1 | Stapleton | 37,661 |
| 5 | 19 | H | Swansea C | W | 1-0 | 1-0 | Birtles | 47,309 |
| 6 | 22 | A | Middlesbrough | W | 2-0 | 1-0 | Stapleton, Birtles | 19,772 |
| 7 | 26 | A | Arsenal | D | 0-0 | 0-0 | | 39,797 |
| 8 | 30 | H | Leeds U | W | 1-0 | 0-0 | Stapleton | 47,019 |
| 9 | Oct 3 | H | Wolverhampton W | W | 5-0 | 2-0 | Stapleton, McIlroy 3, Birtles | 46,837 |
| 10 | 10 | A | Manchester C | D | 0-0 | 0-0 | | 52,037 |
| 11 | 17 | H | Birmingham C | D | 1-1 | 0-1 | Coppell | 48,514 |
| 12 | 21 | H | Middlesbrough | W | 1-0 | 0-0 | Moses | 38,342 |
| 13 | 24 | A | Liverpool | W | 2-1 | 1-0 | Moran, Albiston | 41,438 |
| 14 | 31 | H | Notts Co | W | 2-1 | 1-1 | Birtles, Moses | 45,928 |
| 15 | Nov 7 | A | Sunderland | W | 5-1 | 1-1 | Moran, Robson, Stapleton 2, Birtles | 27,070 |
| 16 | 21 | A | Tottenham H | L | 1-3 | 1-2 | Birtles | 35,534 |
| 17 | 28 | H | Brighton & HA | W | 2-0 | 1-0 | Birtles, Stapleton | 41,911 |
| 18 | Dec 5 | A | Southampton | L | 2-3 | 1-2 | Stapleton, Robson | 24,404 |
| 19 | Jan 6 | H | Everton | D | 1-1 | 0-1 | Stapleton | 40,451 |
| 20 | 23 | A | Stoke C | W | 3-0 | 1-0 | Coppell, Stapleton (pen), Birtles | 19,682 |
| 21 | 27 | A | West Ham U | W | 1-0 | 0-0 | Macari | 41,291 |
| 22 | 30 | A | Swansea C | L | 0-2 | 0-0 | | 23,900 |
| 23 | Feb 6 | H | Aston Villa | W | 4-1 | 1-1 | Moran 2, Robson, Coppell | 43,184 |
| 24 | 13 | A | Wolverhampton W | W | 1-0 | 1-0 | Birtles | 22,481 |
| 25 | 20 | H | Arsenal | D | 0-0 | 0-0 | | 43,833 |
| 26 | 27 | H | Manchester C | D | 1-1 | 1-1 | Moran | 57,827 |
| 27 | Mar 6 | A | Birmingham C | W | 1-0 | 1-0 | Birtles | 19,637 |
| 28 | 17 | H | Coventry C | L | 0-1 | 0-1 | | 34,499 |
| 29 | 20 | A | Notts Co | W | 3-1 | 1-0 | Coppell 2, Stapleton | 17,056 |
| 30 | 27 | H | Sunderland | D | 0-0 | 0-0 | | 40,776 |
| 31 | Apr 3 | A | Leeds U | D | 0-0 | 0-0 | | 31,118 |
| 32 | 7 | H | Liverpool | L | 0-1 | 0-0 | | 50,969 |
| 33 | 10 | A | Everton | D | 3-3 | 1-1 | Coppell 2, Grimes | 29,317 |
| 34 | 12 | H | WBA | W | 1-0 | 0-0 | Moran | 38,717 |
| 35 | 17 | H | Tottenham H | W | 2-0 | 0-0 | Coppell (pen), McGarvey | 50,724 |
| 36 | 20 | A | Ipswich T | L | 1-2 | 1-1 | Gidman | 25,763 |
| 37 | 24 | A | Brighton & HA | W | 1-0 | 0-0 | Wilkins | 20,755 |
| 38 | May 1 | H | Southampton | W | 1-0 | 0-0 | McGarvey | 40,038 |
| 39 | 5 | A | Nottingham F | W | 1-0 | 1-0 | Stapleton | 18,449 |
| 40 | 8 | A | West Ham U | D | 1-1 | 0-0 | Moran | 26,337 |
| 41 | 12 | A | WBA | W | 3-0 | 2-0 | Robson, Birtles, Coppell | 19,772 |
| 42 | 15 | H | Stoke C | W | 2-0 | 2-0 | Robson, Whiteside | 43,072 |

**Final League Position: 3**

**Goalscorers**

*League* (59): Stapleton 13 (1 pen), Birtles 11, Coppell 9 (1 pen), Moran 7, Robson 5, McIlroy 3, McGarvey 2, Macari 2, Moses 2, Albiston 1, Gidman 1, Grimes 1, Whiteside 1, Wilkins 1.
*League Cup* (0).
*FA Cup* (0).

| | | | | |
|---|---|---|---|---|
| **League Cup** | Second Round | Tottenham H (a) | | 0-1 |
| | | (h) | | 0-1 |
| **FA Cup** | Third Round | Watford (a) | | 0-1 |

| Bailey | Gidman | Albiston | Wilkins | McQueen | Buchan | Coppell | Birtles | Stapleton | Macari | McIlroy | Duxbury | Moses | Moran | Robson | Roche | Nicholl | McGarvey | Grimes | Whiteside | Davies | Match No. |
|---|---|---|---|---|---|---|---|---|---|---|---|---|---|---|---|---|---|---|---|---|---|
| 1 | 2 | 3 | 4 | 5 | 6 | 7 | 8 | 9 | 10 | 11 |  |  |  |  |  |  |  |  |  |  | 1 |
| 1 | 2 | 3 | 4 | 5 | 6 | 7 | 8 | 9 | 10 | 11 |  |  |  |  |  |  |  |  |  |  | 2 |
| 1 | 2 | 3 | 4 | 5 | 6 | 7 | 8 | 9 | 10 | 11* | 12 |  |  |  |  |  |  |  |  |  | 3 |
| 1 | 2 | 3 | 4 | 5 | 6 | 7 | 8 | 9 | 10 | 11 |  |  |  |  |  |  |  |  |  |  | 4 |
| 1 | 2 | 3 | 4 | 5 | 6 | 7 | 8 | 9 | 10 | 11* |  |  | 12 |  |  |  |  |  |  |  | 5 |
| 1 | 2 | 3 | 4 | 5 | 6* | 7 | 8 | 9 | 10 | 11 |  |  | 12 |  |  |  |  |  |  |  | 6 |
| 1 | 2 | 3 | 4 | 5 | 6 | 7 | 8 | 9 | 10 | 11 |  |  |  |  |  |  |  |  |  |  | 7 |
| 1 | 2 | 3 | 4 | 5* | 6 | 7 | 8 | 9 | 10 | 11 |  |  | 12 |  |  |  |  |  |  |  | 8 |
| 1 | 2 | 3 | 4 |  | 6 | 7 | 8 | 9 | 10 | 11 |  |  | 5 |  |  |  |  |  |  |  | 9 |
| 1 | 2 | 3 | 4 |  | 6 | 12 | 8* | 9 | 10 | 11 |  |  | 5 | 7 |  |  |  |  |  |  | 10 |
| 1 | 2 | 3 | 4 |  | 6 | 11 | 8 | 9 |  |  |  | 10 | 5 | 7 |  |  |  |  |  |  | 11 |
| 1 | 2 | 3 | 4 |  | 6 | 11 | 8 | 9 |  | 5 |  | 10 |  | 7 |  |  |  |  |  |  | 12 |
| 1 | 2 | 3 | 4 |  | 6 | 11 | 8 | 9 |  |  |  | 10 | 5 | 7 |  |  |  |  |  |  | 13 |
| 1 | 2 | 3 | 4 |  | 6 | 11 | 8 | 9 | 12 |  |  | 10 | 5 | 7* |  |  |  |  |  |  | 14 |
| 1 | 2* | 3 | 4 |  | 6 | 11 | 8 | 9 | 12 |  |  | 10 | 5 | 7 |  |  |  |  |  |  | 15 |
|  |  | 3 | 4 |  | 6* |  | 8 | 9 |  | 11 | 2 | 10 | 5 | 7 | 1 |  |  | 12 |  |  | 16 |
|  | 2 | 3 | 4 | 6 |  |  | 8 | 9 |  | 11 |  | 10 | 5 | 7 | 1 |  |  |  |  |  | 17 |
|  | 2 | 3 | 4 | 6 |  |  | 8 | 9 |  | 11 |  | 10 | 5 | 7 | 1 |  |  |  |  |  | 18 |
| 1 | 2 | 3 | 4 |  | 6 | 11 |  | 9 |  |  |  | 10 | 5 | 7 |  |  | 8 |  |  |  | 19 |
| 1 |  | 3 | 4 | 5 |  | 11 | 8 | 9 |  |  | 2 | 10 | 6 | 7 |  |  |  |  |  |  | 20 |
| 1 |  | 3 | 4 |  | 6 | 11 | 8 | 9 |  |  | 2 | 10 | 5 | 7 |  |  |  |  |  |  | 21 |
| 1 | 12 | 3 | 4 |  | 6* | 11 | 8 | 9 |  |  | 2 | 10 | 5 | 7 |  |  |  |  |  |  | 22 |
| 1 | 2 | 3 | 4 |  | 6 | 11 | 8* | 9 |  |  |  | 10 | 5 | 7 |  |  | 12 |  |  |  | 23 |
| 1 | 2 | 3 | 4 |  | 6 | 11 | 8 | 9 |  |  |  | 10 | 5 | 7 |  |  |  |  |  |  | 24 |
| 1 | 2 | 3 | 4 |  | 6 | 11 | 8 | 9 |  |  |  | 10 | 5 | 7 |  |  |  |  |  |  | 25 |
| 1 | 2 | 3 | 4 |  | 6 | 11 | 8 | 9 |  |  |  | 10 | 5 | 7 |  |  |  |  |  |  | 26 |
| 1 | 2 | 3 | 4 |  | 6 | 11 | 8 | 9 |  |  |  | 10 | 5* | 7 |  |  | 12 |  |  |  | 27 |
| 1 | 2 | 3 | 4 |  | 6 | 11 | 8 | 9 | 12 |  |  | 10 | 5 | 7* |  |  |  |  |  |  | 28 |
| 1 | 2 | 3 | 4 |  | 6 | 11 | 8 | 9 |  |  |  | 10 | 5* | 7 |  |  | 12 |  |  |  | 29 |
| 1 | 2 | 3 | 4 | 5 | 6 | 11 | 8* | 9 |  |  |  | 10 |  |  |  |  | 12 |  |  |  | 30 |
| 1 |  | 3 | 4 |  | 6 | 11 |  | 9 |  |  | 2 | 10 | 5 | 7 |  |  | 8 |  |  |  | 31 |
| 1 |  | 3 | 4 |  | 6* | 11 |  | 9 |  |  | 2 | 10 | 5 | 7 |  |  | 8 | 12 |  |  | 32 |
| 1 | 2 | 3 | 4 |  | 6 | 11 |  | 9 |  |  |  | 10* | 5 | 7 |  |  | 8 | 12 |  |  | 33 |
| 1 | 2 | 3 | 4 |  | 6 | 11 |  | 9 |  |  |  |  | 5 | 7 |  |  | 8 | 10 |  |  | 34 |
| 1 | 2 | 3 | 4 |  | 6 | 11 |  | 9 |  |  |  |  | 5 | 7 |  |  | 8 | 10 |  |  | 35 |
| 1 | 2 | 3 | 4* |  | 6 | 12 |  | 9 |  |  |  | 11 | 5 | 7 |  |  | 8 | 10 |  |  | 36 |
| 1 | 2 | 3 | 4 |  | 6 | 11* |  | 9 |  |  |  |  | 5 | 7 |  |  | 8 | 10 | 12 |  | 37 |
| 1 | 2 | 3 | 4 |  | 6 |  |  | 9 |  |  |  |  | 5 | 7 |  |  | 8 | 10 | 11 |  | 38 |
| 1 | 2 | 3 | 4 |  | 6 | 11 |  | 9 |  |  |  |  | 5 | 7 |  |  | 8 | 10 |  |  | 39 |
| 1 | 2 | 3 | 4 |  | 6 | 11 | 8* | 9 |  |  |  | 10 | 5 | 7 |  |  |  | 12 |  |  | 40 |
| 1 | 2 | 3 | 4 |  | 6 | 11 | 8 | 9 |  |  |  |  | 5 | 7 |  |  |  | 10 |  |  | 41 |
| 1 | 2 | 3 | 4 |  | 6 | 11 | 8* |  |  |  |  | 10 | 5 | 7 |  |  |  | 12 |  | 9 | 42 |
| 39 | 36 | 42 | 42 | 21 | 27 | 35 | 32 | 41 | 10 | 12 | 19 | 20 | 30 | 32 | 3 | — | 10 | 9 | 1 | 1 |  |

Substitute appearances:

| Bailey | | | | | Coppell | Birtles | | Macari | McIlroy | | | Moran | Robson | | | McGarvey | Grimes | Whiteside | Davies |
|---|---|---|---|---|---|---|---|---|---|---|---|---|---|---|---|---|---|---|---|
| + | | | | | + | + | | + | + | | | + | + | | | + | + | + | + |
| 1s | | | | | 1s | 1s | | 5s | 1s | | | 1s | 6s | | | 1s | 6s | 2s | 1s |

## MANCHESTER UNITED

| | Ht | Wt | Birthplace | Clubs | League App. | League Gls |
|---|---|---|---|---|---|---|
| **Goalkeepers** | | | | | | |
| Paddy Roche* (Eire) | 6 1 | 11 9 | Dublin | Shelbourne | (not known) | |
| | | | | Manchester U | 46 | — |
| Gary Bailey | 6 1½ | 12 10 | Ipswich | Manchester U | 149 | — |
| Stephen Pears | 5 11½ | 11 10 | Brandon | Manchester U | — | — |
| **Defenders** | | | | | | |
| Martin Buchan (Scotland) | 5 10 | 12 2 | Aberdeen | Aberdeen | 131 | 10 |
| | | | | Manchester U | 373 | 4 |
| Arthur Albiston (Scotland) | 5 7½ | 10 13 | Edinburgh | Manchester U | 192 | 2 |
| James Nicholl (N Ireland) (Contract cancelled April 1982) | 5 9½ | 11 12 | Canada | Manchester U | 197 | 3 |
| | | | | Sunderland (on loan) | 3 | — |
| Gordon McQueen (Scotland) | 6 3 | 13 7 | Kilbirnie | St Mirren | 57 | 5 |
| | | | | Leeds U | 140 | 15 |
| | | | | Manchester U | 115 | 18 |
| Martin Lane* | 5 9 | 11 4 | Altrincham | Manchester U | — | — |
| David Jeffrey* | 5 11 | 11 11 | Newtonards | Manchester U | — | — |
| Nikola Jovanovic (Yugoslavia) | 6 3 | 14 0 | Cetinje | Red Star | (not known) | |
| | | | | Buducnost (on loan) | (not known) | |
| | | | | Manchester U | 21 | 4 |
| Gareth Orritt* | 5 7½ | 10 8 | Middlesbrough | Manchester U | — | — |
| Tom Connell (N Ireland) (Contract cancelled April 1982) | 5 9½ | 10 12 | Newry | Coleraine | — | — |
| | | | | Manchester U | 2 | — |
| Kevin Moran (Eire) | 5 10½ | 12 8½ | Dublin | Manchester U | 72 | 8 |
| Tony Whelan | 6 0 | 12 0 | Dublin | Bohemians | (not known) | |
| | | | | Manchester U | 1 | — |
| John Gidman (England) | 5 11 | 12 2 | Liverpool | Liverpool | — | — |
| | | | | Aston V | 197 | 9 |
| | | | | Everton | 64 | 2 |
| | | | | Manchester U | 37 | 1 |
| Paul McGrath | | | Ealing | St Patrick's Ath | (not known) | |
| | | | | Manchester U | — | — |
| **Midfield** | | | | | | |
| Sean Williams* | 5 4 | 9 9 | Trebanog | Manchester U | — | — |
| Mike Duxbury | 5 9 | 10 11½ | Accrington | Manchester U | 57 | 2 |
| Alan Davies | 5 8 | 10 4 | Manchester | Manchester U | 1 | — |
| Ray Wilkins (England) | 5 8 | 11 0 | Hillingdon | Chelsea | 179 | 30 |
| | | | | Manchester U | 92 | 3 |
| Lou Macari (Scotland) | 5 5½ | 10 13 | Edinburgh | Celtic | 56 | 27 |
| | | | | Manchester U | 315 | 76 |
| Danny Keough | 5 7½ | 9 9 | Bacup | Manchester U | — | — |
| Alan Stevenson* | 5 6½ | 9 10 | Rotherham | Manchester U | — | — |
| David Wynn | 5 6½ | 10 1 | Ormskirk | Manchester U | — | — |
| Kel McDermott* | 5 6½ | 9 6 | Belfast | Manchester U | — | — |
| Tom Sloan (N Ireland) | 5 5½ | 9 11 | Ballymena | Ballymena U | — | — |
| | | | | Manchester U | 11 | — |
| Remi Moses | 5 6 | 10 7 | Manchester | WBA | 63 | 5 |
| | | | | Manchester U | 21 | 2 |
| Bryan Robson (England) | 5 10½ | 11 9 | Chester-le-Street | WBA | 197 | 39 |
| | | | | Manchester U | 32 | 5 |
| Mark Dempsey | 5 7 | 8 9 | Manchester | Manchester U | — | — |
| Ashley Grimes (Eire) | 5 11½ | 11 7 | Dublin | Manchester U | 74 | 8 |
| **Forwards** | | | | | | |
| Steve Coppell (England) | 5 7 | 11 11 | Liverpool | Tranmere R | 38 | 10 |
| | | | | Manchester U | 293 | 49 |
| Joe Jordan (Scotland) | 6 1 | 12 0 | Carluke | Morton | 10 | 1 |
| | | | | Leeds U | 169 | 35 |
| (Transferred to AC Milan June 1981) | | | | Manchester U | 109 | 37 |
| Gary Worrall | 5 9 | 11 5 | Salford | Manchester U | — | — |
| Chris Lynam* | 5 6 | 9 6 | Manchester | Manchester U | — | — |
| Andy Reynolds | 5 4½ | 9 13 | Neath | Manchester U | — | — |
| Scott McGarvey | 6 0 | 11 5 | Glasgow | Manchester U | 18 | 2 |
| Garry Birtles (England) | 5 11 | 11 8 | Nottingham | Nottingham F | 87 | 32 |
| | | | | Manchester U | 58 | 11 |
| Mark Hughes | 5 9 | 11 12 | Wrexham | Manchester U | — | — |
| Frank Stapleton (Eire) | 5 11 | 13 0 | Dublin | Arsenal | 225 | 75 |
| | | | | Manchester U | 41 | 13 |
| Norman Whiteside (N Ireland) (Apprentice) | 6 0 | 12 3 | Belfast | Manchester U | 2 | 1 |

# MANSFIELD TOWN Division 4

*President:* A. F. Patrick.

*Chairman:* J. B. Almond JP.   *Vice-Chairman:* J. W. Pratt.

*Directors:* J. A. Brown, Dr S. S. Scott MB, CHB, MRCGP, J. N. Lea.

*Player-Manager:* Stuart Boam.   *Secretary:* J. D. Eaton.

*Year Formed:* 1905.

*Turned Professional:* 1905.   *Limited Company:* 1905.

**Football League Record:**
1931 Elected to Division 3(S); 1932–37 Division 3(N); 1937–47
Division 3(S); 1947–58 Division 3(N); 1958–60 Division 3;
1960–63 Division 4; 1963–72 Division 3; 1972–75 Division 4;
1975–77 Division 3; 1977–78 Division 2; 1978–80 Division 3;
1980– Division 4.

**Honours:** *Football League:* Division 3 – Champions 1976–77; Division 4 – Champions 1974–75; Division 3(N) – Runners-up 1950–51. *FA Cup* best season: 6th rd, 1968–69. *Football League Cup* best season: 5th rd, 1975–76.

*Record Victory:* 9-2 v Rotherham U, Division 3(N), 27 Dec, 1932 and v Hounslow T, FA Cup 1st rd replay, 5 Nov 1962.

*Record Defeat:* 1-8 v Walsall, Division 3(N), 19 Jan, 1933.

*Most League Points:* 68, Division 4, 1974–75.

*Most League Goals:* 108, Division 4, 1962–63.

*Highest League Scorer in Season:* Ted Harston, 55, Division 3(N), 1936–37.

*Most League Goals in Total Aggregate:* Harry Johnson, 104, 1931–36.

*Most Capped Player:* John McClelland, 6 (15), Northern Ireland.

*Most League Appearances:* Sandy Pate, 413, 1967–78.

*Record Transfer Fee Received:* £200,000 from Luton T for Mike Saxby, July 1979.

*Record Transfer Fee Paid:* £75,000 to Luton T for Steve Taylor, July 1979.

*Previous Managers since the War:* Roy Goodall, Freddie Steele, Stan Mercer, Charlie Mitten, Sam Weaver, Raich Carter, Tommy Cummings, Tommy Eggleston, Jock Basford, Danny Williams, David Smith, Peter Morris, Billy Bingham, Mick Jones.

*Address of Supporters Club:* Club Shop, c/o the ground.

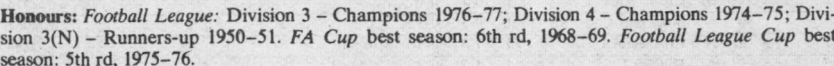

**Field Mill Ground, Quarry Lane, Mansfield.** Telephone Mansfield 23567. *Telegraphic address:* 'Football Mansfield'. *Ground capacity:* 23,500. *Record attendance:* 24,467 v Nottingham F, FA Cup 3rd rd, 10 Jan, 1953. *Record receipts:* £19,227 v Sheffield W, Division 3, 15 Mar, 1980. *Pitch measurements:* 115yd×72yd.

*How to get there:* Buses from town centre to within 300 yards of the ground. Nearest railway station, Alfreton and Mansfield Parkway.

*Match tickets:* Advance booking 5 days prior to match.

*Car parking:* Room for 500 cars at the ground and another 3,000 within 500 yards.

*Entertainments/catering facilities:* No club room. Licensed tea bars in the ground.

*Club shop:* Adjacent to the ground; sells all types of souvenirs.

*Handbooks/programmes:* Both on sale at the club shop.

*Extra information:* Mansfield became famous giant-killers as a non-League side in 1929. They went to Molineux in the FA Cup 3rd round and beat Wolves 1-0.

*Club Colours:* Amber shirts with blue trim, blue shorts, amber stockings.

*Change Colours:* White shirts with blue and amber trimmings, white shorts, white stockings.

*Club Trainer/Coach:* Geoff Allen.

*Club Nickname:* The Stags.

## MANSFIELD TOWN 1981–82 LEAGUE RECORD

| Match No. | Date | Venue | Opponents | Result | H/T Score | Goalscorers | Attendance |
|---|---|---|---|---|---|---|---|
| 1 | Aug 29 | A | Peterborough U | L 0-1 | 0-0 | | 4310 |
| 2 | Sept 5 | H | AFC Bournemouth | L 0-1 | 0-0 | | 2950 |
| 3 | 12 | A | Port Vale | D 0-0 | 0-0 | | 3043 |
| 4 | 19 | H | Bury | D 1-1 | 1-1 | Lumby | 2501 |
| 5 | 21 | H | Northampton T | W 4-1 | 2-0 | Nicholson, Lumby, Burrows, Mann | 2612 |
| 6 | 26 | A | Aldershot | W 3-2 | 1-2 | Burrows, Boam, Lumby | 2486 |
| 7 | 30 | A | Torquay U | L 0-2 | 0-1 | | 3100 |
| 8 | Oct 3 | H | Blackpool | D 2-2 | 1-1 | Bird, Caldwell | 3466 |
| 9 | 10 | H | Hull C | D 3-3 | 2-1 | Lumby 2, Caldwell | 3464 |
| 10 | 17 | A | Darlington | L 0-1 | 0-0 | | 1576 |
| 11 | 20 | A | Sheffield U | L 1-4 | 1-3 | Caldwell | 12,727 |
| 12 | 24 | H | Crewe Alex | L 0-1 | 0-0 | | 2513 |
| 13 | 30 | A | Stockport Co | L 0-3 | 0-1 | | 2081 |
| 14 | Nov 2 | H | Colchester U | L 1-3 | 0-1 | Morgan | 2294 |
| 15 | 7 | A | Halifax T | L 1-2 | 0-2 | Caldwell | 1447 |
| 16 | 14 | H | Rochdale | W 4-3 | 1-1 | Parkinson (pen), Bell 2, Morgan | 2300 |
| 17 | 28 | H | Hereford U | W 2-1 | 1-1 | Wood, Lumby | 1898 |
| 18 | Dec 5 | A | Tranmere R | D 2-2 | 0-1 | Morgan 2 | 1317 |
| 19 | Jan 2 | H | Wigan Ath | L 1-2 | 1-1 | Wood | 2173 |
| 20 | 16 | H | Hartlepool U | W 3-2 | 0-1 | Caldwell, Parkinson, Morgan | 2011 |
| 21 | 20 | A | Bradford C | W 4-3 | 1-1 | Lumby 2, Parkinson, Morgan | 3729 |
| 22 | 23 | H | Peterborough U | L 1-2 | 0-2 | Parkinson (pen) | 3242 |
| 23 | 30 | A | Bury | L 2-3 | 2-1 | Bell, Lumby | 2954 |
| 24 | Feb 2 | A | Scunthorpe U | L 0-1 | 0-0 | | 2099 |
| 25 | 6 | H | Port Vale | L 1-3 | 1-0 | Bell | 2690 |
| 26 | 9 | A | Northampton T | D 1-1 | 0-1 | Lumby | 1945 |
| 27 | 13 | A | Blackpool | W 3-2 | 3-1 | Parkinson, Cannell, Lumby | 3017 |
| 28 | 20 | H | Aldershot | W 1-0 | 1-0 | Parkinson | 2001 |
| 29 | 23 | A | AFC Bournemouth | L 0-1 | 0-1 | | 5725 |
| 30 | 27 | A | Hull C | L 0-2 | 0-1 | | 4958 |
| 31 | Mar 6 | H | Darlington | L 2-3 | 1-1 | Lumby, Nicholson | 1538 |
| 32 | 8 | H | Sheffield U | D 1-1 | 1-0 | Wood | 8951 |
| 33 | 13 | A | Crewe Alex | W 2-0 | 0-0 | Bell, Cannell | 1476 |
| 34 | 16 | A | Colchester U | W 1-0 | 0-0 | Lumby | 2000 |
| 35 | 20 | H | Stockport Co | D 2-2 | 0-1 | Lumby, Parkinson (pen) | 2159 |
| 36 | 27 | H | Halifax T | W 3-2 | 1-1 | Caldwell 2, Cannell | 2197 |
| 37 | Apr 3 | A | Rochdale | D 1-1 | 1-1 | Parkinson | 1276 |
| 38 | 5 | H | York C | L 0-2 | 0-1 | | 2388 |
| 39 | 10 | A | York C | L 1-2 | 1-1 | Wood | 2155 |
| 40 | 13 | H | Scunthorpe U | D 1-1 | 1-1 | Caldwell | 2202 |
| 41 | 17 | H | Tranmere R | W 3-0 | 1-0 | Nicholson, Bird, Parkinson (pen) | 1995 |
| 42 | 24 | A | Hereford U | L 1-3 | 0-1 | Cannell | 2852 |
| 43 | May 1 | H | Torquay U | W 3-1 | 1-0 | Caldwell, Nicholson 2 | 1392 |
| 44 | 5 | A | Hartlepool U | L 0-3 | 0-0 | | 1202 |
| 45 | 8 | A | Wigan Ath | L 1-3 | 1-2 | Burrows | 8517 |
| 46 | 15 | H | Bradford C | L 0-2 | 0-1 | | 3107 |

**Final League Position: 20**

### Goalscorers

*League* (63): Lumby 14, Caldwell 9, Parkinson 9 (4 pens), Morgan 6, Bell 5, Nicholson 5, Cannell 4, Wood 4, Burrows 3, Bird 2, Boam 1, Mann 1.
*League Cup* (6): Lumby 3, Bird 1, Wood 1, own goal 1.
*FA Cup* (0).

| League Cup | First Round | Scunthorpe U (a) | 0-0 |
|---|---|---|---|
| | | (h) | 2-0 |
| | Second Round | Bradford C (a) | 4-3 |
| | | (h) | 0-2 |
| FA Cup | First Round | Doncaster R (h) | 0-1 |

| Arnold | McJannet | Wood | Bell | Boam | Bird | Thomson | Parkinson | Lumby | Woodhead | Nicholson | Mann | Caldwell | Burrows | Foster | Morgan | Cannell | Brown | Calderwood | Match No. |
|---|---|---|---|---|---|---|---|---|---|---|---|---|---|---|---|---|---|---|---|
| 1 | 2 | 3 | 4 | 5 | 6 | 7 | 8 | 9 | 10 | 11* | 12 | | | | | | | | 1 |
| 1 | 2 | 3 | 4 | 5 | 6 | 7 | 8* | 9 | 10 | 11 | 12 | | | | | | | | 2 |
| 1 | 3 | 2 | 4 | 5 | 6 | 7 | | 9 | | 11 | | 8 | 10 | | | | | | 3 |
| 1 | 2 | 3 | 4 | 5 | 6 | 7 | | 9 | | 11 | | 8 | 10 | | | | | | 4 |
| 1 | 2 | 3 | 4 | | 6 | 7 | | 9 | | 11 | | 8 | 10 | 5 | | | | | 5 |
| 1 | 2 | 3 | 4 | 12 | 6 | 7* | | 9 | | 11 | | 8 | 10 | 5 | | | | | 6 |
| 1 | 2 | 3 | 4 | 12 | 6 | 7* | | 9 | | 11 | | 8 | 10 | 5 | | | | | 7 |
| 1 | 2 | | 4 | 12 | 6 | 7* | | 9 | | 11 | | 8 | 10 | 5 | 3 | | | | 8 |
| 1 | 2 | | 4 | | 6 | 7 | 12 | 9* | | 11 | | 8 | 10 | 5 | 3 | | | | 9 |
| 1 | 2 | | 4 | | 6 | 7 | 12 | | 9* | 11 | | 8 | 10 | 5 | 3 | | | | 10 |
| 1 | 2 | | 4 | | 6 | 7 | | 9 | | 11 | | 8 | 10 | 5 | 3 | | | | 11 |
| 1 | 2 | | 4 | 12 | 6 | 7* | | 9 | | 11 | | 8 | 10 | 5 | 3 | | | | 12 |
| 1 | 2 | 3 | 4 | | 6 | 7 | | 9 | | 11 | | 8 | 10 | 5 | | | | | 13 |
| 1 | 2 | 3* | 4 | | 6 | 7 | 12 | | | 11 | | 9 | 10 | 5 | 8 | | | | 14 |
| 1 | 2 | 3 | 4 | | 6 | 7* | 11 | | | 12 | | 9 | 10 | 5 | 8 | | | | 15 |
| 1 | 2 | 6 | 4 | | | 7 | 11 | 9 | | | | | 10 | 5 | 3 | 8 | | | 16 |
| 1 | 2 | 6 | 4 | | | 7 | 11 | 9 | | | | | 10 | 5 | 3 | 8 | | | 17 |
| 1 | 2 | 6 | 4 | | | 7 | 11 | 9 | | | | | 10 | 5 | 3 | 8 | | | 18 |
| 1 | 2 | 6 | 4 | | | 7 | 11 | 9 | | | | | 10 | 5 | 3 | 8 | | | 19 |
| 1 | 2 | 6 | 4 | | | 7 | 11 | 9 | | | | | 10 | 5 | 3 | 8 | | | 20 |
| 1 | 2 | 6 | 4 | 12 | | 7 | 11 | 9 | | | | | 10* | 5 | 3 | 8 | | | 21 |
| 1 | 2 | 6 | 4* | 12 | | 7 | 11 | 9 | | | | | 10 | 5 | 3 | 8 | | | 22 |
| 1 | 2 | 6 | 4 | 12 | | 7 | 11 | 9 | | | | | 10 | 5 | 3 | 8* | | | 23 |
| | 2 | 6 | 4 | 12 | | 7 | 11 | 9 | | | | | 10 | 5 | 3 | 8* | | 1 | 24 |
| 1 | 2 | 6 | 4 | | | 7 | 11 | 9 | | | | | 10 | 5 | 3 | 8 | | | 25 |
| 1 | 2 | 6 | 4 | | | 7 | 11 | 9 | | | | | 10 | 5 | 3 | 8 | | | 26 |
| 1 | 2 | 6 | 4 | | | 7 | 11 | 9 | | | | | 10 | 5 | 3 | 8 | | | 27 |
| 1 | 2 | 6 | 4 | | | 7 | 11 | 9 | | | | | 10 | 5 | 3 | 8 | | | 28 |
| 1 | 2 | 6 | 4 | | | 7* | 11 | 9 | | | 12 | | 10 | 5 | 3 | 8 | | | 29 |
| 1 | 2 | 6 | 4 | | | 7 | 11 | 9* | | | 12 | | 10 | 5 | 3 | 8 | | | 30 |
| 1 | 2 | 6 | 4 | | | 7 | 11 | 9 | | | | | 10 | 5 | 3 | 8 | | | 31 |
| 1 | 2 | 6 | 4 | 12 | | 7 | 11 | 9* | | | | | 10 | 5 | 3 | 8 | | | 32 |
| 1 | 2 | 3 | 4 | | | 7 | 11 | 9 | | | | | 10 | 5 | | 8 | 6 | | 33 |
| 1 | 2 | 6 | 4 | | | 7 | 11 | 9 | | | | | 10 | 5 | 3 | 8 | | | 34 |
| 1 | 2 | 6 | 4 | 12 | | 7 | 11* | 9 | | | | | 10 | 5 | 3 | 8 | | | 35 |
| 1 | | 6 | 4 | | 2 | 7 | | 9 | | 11 | | | 10 | 5 | 3 | 8 | | | 36 |
| 1 | | 6 | 4 | | 2 | 7 | | 9 | | 11 | | 8 | 10 | 5 | 3 | | | | 37 |
| 1 | | 6 | 4 | | 2 | 7 | | 9 | | 11 | 12 | | 10 | 5 | 3 | 8* | | | 38 |
| 1 | | 6 | 4 | | 2 | 7 | | 9 | | 11 | | | 10 | 5 | 3 | 8 | | | 39 |
| 1 | | 6 | 4 | | 2 | 7 | | 9 | | 11 | | | 10 | 5 | 3 | 8 | | | 40 |
| 1 | | 6 | 4 | | 2 | 7 | | 9 | | 11 | | | 10 | 5 | 3 | 8 | | | 41 |
| 1 | | 6 | 4 | 12 | 2 | 7 | | 9* | | 11 | | | 10 | 5 | 3 | 8 | | | 42 |
| 1 | 12 | 6 | 4 | | 2 | 7* | | 9 | | 11 | | | 10 | 5 | 3 | 8 | | | 43 |
| 1 | 2 | 6 | 4 | | | 7 | | 9 | | 11 | | 8 | 10 | 5 | 3 | | | | 44 |
| 1 | 2 | 6 | 4 | | | 7 | | 9 | | 11 | | | 10 | 5 | 3 | 8 | | | 45 |
| 1 | 2 | 6 | 4 | | | 7 | | 9 | | 11 | | | 10 | 5 | 3 | 8 | | | 46 |
| 45 | 37 | 36 | 45 | 4 | 25 | 25 | 31 | 38 | 11 | 37 | 35 | 31 | 41 | 28 | 12 | 23 | 1 | 1 | |
| + | | | | | + | + | + | + | + | + | + | + | | | | | | | |
| 1s | | | | | 4s | 1s | 4s | 1s | 1s | 1s | 2s | 2s | | | | | | | |

## MANSFIELD TOWN

| | Ht | Wt | Birthplace | Clubs | League App. | League Gls |
|---|---|---|---|---|---|---|
| **Goalkeepers** | | | | | | |
| Rod Arnold | 5 10 | 11 4 | Wolverhampton | Wolverhampton W | — | — |
| | | | | Mansfield T | 386 | — |
| Colin King | 6 0 | 11 8 | Edinburgh | Blackpool | — | — |
| (Contract cancelled Oct 1981) | | | | Clydebank | 6 | — |
| | | | | Notts Co | — | — |
| | | | | Rotherham U (on loan) | — | — |
| | | | | Mansfield T | — | — |
| Graham Brown | 5 11 | 12 8 | Matlock | Millwall | — | — |
| (Non-contract) | | | | Brighton | — | — |
| | | | | Crawley T | (not known) | |
| | | | | Watford | — | — |
| | | | | Mansfield T | 142 | — |
| | | | | Doncaster R | 53 | — |
| | | | | Swansea C | 4 | — |
| | | | | Southport | — | — |
| | | | | Portland | (not known) | |
| | | | | York C | 69 | — |
| | | | | Rotherham U | 31 | — |
| | | | | Mansfield T | 1 | — |
| **Defenders** | | | | | | |
| Kevin Bird | 5 9 | 10 12 | Doncaster | Doncaster R | — | — |
| | | | | Mansfield T | 348 | 53 |
| Barry Foster* | 5 9 | 10 4 | Worksop | Mansfield T | 287 | — |
| Ian Wood* | 5 10 | 10 7 | Kirkby in Ashfield | Mansfield T | 149 | 9 |
| John McClelland | 6 1 | 11 4 | Belfast | Portadown | — | — |
| (N Ireland) | | | | Cardiff C | 4 | 1 |
| (Transferred to Rangers May 1981) | | | | Bangor | — | — |
| | | | | Mansfield T | 125 | 8 |
| Leslie McJannet* | | 10 4 | Cumnock | Mansfield T | 74 | — |
| Adrian Burrows* | 5 11 | 11 12 | Sutton | Mansfield T | 78 | 6 |
| Iain Jamieson | 5 10 | 10 9 | Ayr | Mansfield T | — | — |
| (Contract cancelled March 1982) | | | | | | |
| Stuart Boam | 6 1 | 13 5 | Kirkby | Mansfield T | 175 | 2 |
| | | | | Middlesbrough | 320 | 14 |
| | | | | Newcastle U | 69 | 1 |
| | | | | Mansfield T | 8 | 1 |
| **Midfield** | | | | | | |
| Arthur Mann* | 5 9 | 10 8 | Burntisland | Hearts | 32 | — |
| | | | | Manchester C | 35 | — |
| | | | | Blackpool (on loan) | 3 | — |
| | | | | Notts Co | 253 | 21 |
| | | | | Shrewsbury T | 8 | 1 |
| | | | | Mansfield T | 116 | 3 |
| Noel Parkinson | 5 8 | 10 7 | Hull | Ipswich T | — | — |
| | | | | Bristol R (on loan) | 5 | 1 |
| | | | | Brentford (on loan) | 10 | — |
| | | | | Mansfield T | 70 | 13 |
| Charlie Bell | 5 9 | 10 10 | Middlesbrough | Middlesbrough | 10 | 1 |
| | | | | Mansfield T | 45 | 5 |
| Gary Nicholson | 5 7½ | 9 11 | Newcastle | Newcastle U | 12 | — |
| | | | | Mansfield T | 38 | 5 |
| Alex Livingstone* | | | | Mansfield T | — | — |
| Colin Calderwood | | | Glasgow | Mansfield T | 1 | — |
| **Forwards** | | | | | | |
| Brian Thomson* | 5 8 | 10 2 | Morecambe | West Ham U | — | — |
| | | | | Mansfield T | 63 | 1 |
| Dave Caldwell | 5 10 | 11 6 | Aberdeen | Mansfield T | 64 | 17 |
| Simon Woodhead | 5 10 | 11 0 | Wakefield | Mansfield T | 13 | — |
| Jim Lumby* | 5 11 | 11 4 | Grimsby | Grimsby T | 31 | 12 |
| | | | | Boston U | (not known) | |
| | | | | Gainsborough T | (not known) | |
| | | | | Brigg T | (not known) | |
| | | | | Scunthorpe U | 55 | 28 |
| | | | | Carlisle U | 27 | 7 |
| | | | | Tranmere R | 46 | 21 |
| | | | | Mansfield T | 51 | 18 |
| Paul Cannell | 5 10 | 11 0 | Newcastle | Newcastle U | 48 | 13 |
| | | | | Washington D | (not known) | |
| | | | | Mansfield T | 23 | 4 |

# MIDDLESBROUGH

Division 2

*Chairman:* G. T. Kitching.

*Vice-Chairman:* M. McCullagh.

*Directors:* E. Varley, J. D. Hatfield, K. C. Amer, C. Amer, K. Varley, G. R. Kitching.

*Manager:* Bobby Murdoch.

*Executive Officer (Football):* Harold Shepherdson MBE.

*General Secretary:* T. H. C. Green FAAI.

*Year Formed:* 1876.

*Turned Professional:* 1889; became amateur 1892, and professional again, 1899.

*Limited Company:* 1892.

*Previous Grounds:* 1877, Old Archery Ground, Linthorpe Rd; 1903, Ayresome Park.

**Football League Record:**
1899 Elected to Division 2; 1902–24 Division 1; 1924–27 Division 2; 1927–28 Division 1; 1928–29 Division 2; 1929–54 Division 1; 1954–66 Division 2; 1966–67 Division 3; 1967–74 Division 2; 1974–82 Division 1; 1982– Division 2.

**Honours:** *Football League:* Division 1 best season: 3rd, 1913–14. Division 2 ᵣ Champions 1926–27, 1928–29, 1973–74; Runners-up 1901–02. Division 3 – Runners-up 1966–67. *FA Cup* best season: 6th rd, 1935–36, 1946–47, 1969–70, 1974–75, 1976–77, 1977–78; old last eight 1900–01, 1903–04. *Football League Cup:* Semi-final 1975–76. *Amateur Cup:* Winners 1895, 1898. *Anglo-Scottish Cup:* Winners 1975–76.

*Record Victory:* 9-0 v Brighton & HA, Division 2, 23 Aug, 1958.

*Record Defeat:* 0-9 v Blackburn R, Division 2, 6 Nov, 1954.

*Most League Points:* 65, Division 2, 1973–74.

*Most League Goals:* 122, Division 2, 1926–27.

*Highest League Scorer in Season:* George Camsell, 59, Division 2, 1926–27 (record for Division 2).

*Most League Goals in Total Aggregate:* George Camsell, 326, 1925–39.

*Most Capped Player:* Wilf Mannion, 26, England.

*Most League Appearances:* Tim Williamson, 563, 1902–23.

*Record Transfer Fee Received:* £575,000 from Liverpool for Craig Johnston, April 1981.

*Record Transfer Fee Paid:* £475,000 to Newcastle U for Irving Nattrass, Aug 1979.

*Previous Managers since the War:* David Jack, Walter Rowley, Bob Dennison, Raich Carter, Stan Anderson, Jack Charlton OBE, John Neal.

*Address of the Club Shop or Boutique:* Warwick Street, Middlesbrough.

---

**Ayresome Park, Middlesbrough, Teesside.** Telephone Middlesbrough 819659/815996. Special Answering Service available on 0642-825383. *Telegraphic address:* 'Football, Middlesbrough'. *Ground capacity:* 42,000. *Record attendance:* 53,596 v Newcastle U, Division 1, 27 Dec, 1949. *Record receipts:* £57,710 v Barnsley, FA Cup 5th rd, 14 Feb, 1981. *Pitch measurements:* 115yd×75yd.

*How to get there:* Regular buses from the Exchange in Middlesbrough to the ground. Buses also from bus station next to Middlesbrough railway station.

*Match tickets:* By postal or personal application two weeks prior to the match.

*Car parking:* Off-street parking near the ground.

*Entertainments/catering facilities:* Social club (members only); refreshment bars around the ground.

*Handbooks/programmes:* Programmes available on subscription.

*Extra information:* When Middlesbrough bought Alf Common from Sunderland in 1905, they paid the first £1,000 transfer fee.

*Club Colours:* Red shirts with three narrow stripes down sleeve in white, red shorts with same markings and red stockings.

*Change Colours:* All white.

*Club Captain:* Tony McAndrew. *Club Physiotherapist:* Lew Clayton.

*Club Coaches:* Micky Burns and Cyril Knowles.

*Club Nickname:* The Boro.

## MIDDLESBROUGH 1981–82 LEAGUE RECORD

| Match No. | Date | Venue | Opponents | Result | | H/T Score | Goalscorers | Attendance |
|---|---|---|---|---|---|---|---|---|
| 1 | Aug 29 | H | Tottenham H | L | 1-3 | 1-2 | Otto | 20,464 |
| 2 | Sept 1 | A | Liverpool | D | 1-1 | 1-0 | Shearer | 31,963 |
| 3 | 5 | A | Brighton & HA | L | 0-2 | 0-1 | | 13,386 |
| 4 | 12 | H | Birmingham C | W | 2-1 | 2-0 | Otto, Hodgson | 13,189 |
| 5 | 19 | A | Southampton | L | 0-2 | 0-2 | | 20,105 |
| 6 | 22 | H | Manchester U | L | 0-2 | 0-1 | | 19,772 |
| 7 | 26 | H | Stoke C | W | 3-2 | 1-1 | Cochrane, Woof, Shearer | 11,604 |
| 8 | Oct 3 | A | WBA | L | 0-2 | 0-0 | | 12,840 |
| 9 | 10 | H | Nottingham F | D | 1-1 | 0-0 | Gunn (og) | 15,043 |
| 10 | 17 | A | Wolverhampton W | D | 0-0 | 0-0 | | 12,061 |
| 11 | 21 | A | Manchester U | L | 0-1 | 0-0 | | 38,342 |
| 12 | 24 | H | Everton | L | 0-2 | 0-1 | | 13,423 |
| 13 | 31 | A | West Ham U | L | 2-3 | 0-2 | Woof, Thomson (pen) | 27,604 |
| 14 | Nov 7 | A | Manchester C | L | 2-3 | 1-2 | Angus, Thomson | 32,025 |
| 15 | 14 | H | Sunderland | D | 0-0 | 0-0 | | 21,019 |
| 16 | 21 | H | Aston Villa | D | 3-3 | 1-1 | McAndrew (pen), Ashcroft 2 | 12,522 |
| 17 | 28 | A | Coventry C | D | 1-1 | 0-1 | Woof | 11,309 |
| 18 | Dec 5 | H | Ipswich T | L | 0-1 | 0-1 | | 13,577 |
| 19 | Jan 27 | A | Tottenham H | L | 0-1 | 0-1 | | 22,819 |
| 20 | 30 | H | Southampton | L | 0-1 | 0-1 | | 12,693 |
| 21 | Feb 6 | A | Birmingham C | D | 0-0 | 0-0 | | 10,715 |
| 22 | 13 | H | Swansea C | D | 1-1 | 0-1 | McAndrew (pen) | 11,209 |
| 23 | 16 | A | Arsenal | L | 0-1 | 0-0 | | 13,738 |
| 24 | 20 | A | Stoke C | L | 0-2 | 0-1 | | 10,473 |
| 25 | 27 | A | Nottingham F | D | 1-1 | 1-0 | Hodgson | 16,464 |
| 26 | Mar 6 | H | Wolverhampton W | D | 0-0 | 0-0 | | 10,155 |
| 27 | 9 | H | WBA | W | 1-0 | 1-0 | Hodgson | 9884 |
| 28 | 13 | A | Everton | L | 0-2 | 0-1 | | 15,807 |
| 29 | 20 | H | West Ham U | L | 2-3 | 0-2 | McAndrew (pen), Ashcroft | 12,134 |
| 30 | 27 | H | Manchester C | D | 0-0 | 0-0 | | 11,709 |
| 31 | Apr 3 | A | Sunderland | W | 2-0 | 1-0 | Ashcroft, Baxter | 19,006 |
| 32 | 6 | H | Leeds U | D | 0-0 | 0-0 | | 15,494 |
| 33 | 10 | H | Notts Co | W | 3-0 | 1-0 | Wood, Bolton, Bailey | 10,402 |
| 34 | 13 | A | Leeds U | D | 1-1 | 1-0 | Shearer | 20,458 |
| 35 | 17 | A | Aston Villa | L | 0-1 | 0-1 | | 21,098 |
| 36 | 20 | H | Brighton & HA | W | 2-1 | 1-1 | Otto, McAndrew (pen) | 9788 |
| 37 | 24 | H | Coventry C | D | 0-0 | 0-0 | | 10,968 |
| 38 | May 1 | A | Ipswich T | L | 1-3 | 1-2 | Thomas | 17,980 |
| 39 | 8 | H | Arsenal | L | 1-3 | 1-1 | Baxter | 9565 |
| 40 | 11 | A | Notts Co | W | 1-0 | 0-0 | MacDonald | 6713 |
| 41 | 15 | A | Swansea C | W | 2-1 | 0-0 | Otto, Stanley (og) | 12,961 |
| 42 | 18 | H | Liverpool | D | 0-0 | 0-0 | | 17,431 |

**Final League Position: 22**

### Goalscorers

*League* (34): Ashcroft 4, McAndrew 4 (4 pens), Otto 4, Hodgson 3, Shearer 3, Woof 3, Baxter 2, Thomson 2 (1 pen), Angus 1, Bailey 1, Bolton 1, Cochrane 1, MacDonald 1, Thomas 1, Wood 1, own goals 2.
*League Cup* (3): Ashcroft 1, Shearer 1, Thomson 1.
*FA Cup* (3): Thomson 2, Otto 1.

| | | | |
|---|---|---|---|
| **League Cup** | Second Round | Plymouth Arg (h) | 2-1 |
| | | (a) | 0-0 |
| | Third Round | Liverpool (a) | 1-4 |
| **FA Cup** | Third Round | QPR (a) | 1-1 |
| | | (h) | 2-3 |

| Platt | Craggs | Bolton | Hedley | Baxter | Nattrass | Woof | Otto | MacDonald | Shearer | McAndrew | Hodgson | McCreesh | Cochrane | Angus | Ross | Bailey | Wood | Ashcroft | Askew | Thomson | Bell | Thomas | Currie | Match No. |
|---|---|---|---|---|---|---|---|---|---|---|---|---|---|---|---|---|---|---|---|---|---|---|---|---|
| 1 | 2 | 3 | 4 | 5 | 6 | 7 | 8 | 9 | 10* | 11 | 12 | | | | | | | | | | | | | 1 |
| 1 | | 3 | 4 | 5 | | 7 | 8 | | 10 | 6 | 9* | 2 | 12 | 11 | | | | | | | | | | 2 |
| 1 | | 3 | 4 | 5 | | 7* | 8 | | 10 | 6 | 9 | 2 | 12 | 11 | | | | | | | | | | 3 |
| 1 | 2 | 3 | | 5 | | | 8 | 12 | 10* | 6 | 9 | | 7 | | 4 | 11 | | | | | | | | 4 |
| 1 | 2 | 3 | | 5 | | 9 | 8 | | | | 6 | | 7 | | 4 | 11* | 10 | 12 | | | | | | 5 |
| 1 | 2 | 3 | | 5 | | 7 | 8 | | 10 | 6 | 9 | | | | 4 | | | | | 11 | | | | 6 |
| 1 | 2 | 3 | | 5 | | 10 | 8 | | 9 | 6 | | | 7 | | 4* | | | | | 11 | 12 | | | 7 |
| 1 | 2 | 3 | | 5 | | 9* | 8 | | 10 | 6 | | | 7 | | | | 12 | 11 | 4 | | | | | 8 |
| 1 | 2 | 3 | | 5 | | 12 | 8 | | 10 | 6 | | | 7 | | 4 | | | 9 | | 11* | | | | 9 |
| 1 | 2 | 3 | | 5 | | 12 | 8 | | 10 | 6 | | | 7 | | 4 | | | 9* | 11 | | | | | 10 |
| 1 | 2 | 3 | | 5 | | 9 | 8 | | 10 | 6 | | | 7 | | 4 | | | | | 11 | | | | 11 |
| 1 | 2 | 3 | | 5 | | 9 | 8 | | 10* | 6 | 12 | | 7 | | 4 | | | | | 11 | | | | 12 |
| 1 | | 3 | | 5 | 2 | 9 | 8 | | 12 | 6* | 10 | | 7 | | 4 | | | | | 11 | | | | 13 |
| 1 | 2 | | | 5 | 3 | 9 | 8 | | 10 | 6 | | | 7 | | 4 | | | | | 11 | | | | 14 |
| 1 | | 3 | | 5 | 2 | 9 | 8* | | 10 | 6 | 12 | | 7 | | 4 | | | | | 11 | | | | 15 |
| 1 | | 3 | | 5 | 2 | 9* | 8 | | 11 | 6 | 10 | | 7 | | 4 | | | 12 | | | | | | 16 |
| 1 | | 3 | | 5 | 2 | 9* | 8 | | 11 | 6 | 10 | | 7 | | 4 | | | 12 | | | | | | 17 |
| 1 | | 3 | | 5 | 2 | 9* | 8 | | | 6 | 10 | | 7 | | 4 | | | 12 | | 11 | | | | 18 |
| 1 | 2 | | | 5 | | | 8 | 12 | 10* | 6 | 9 | | 7 | | 4 | 3 | | | | 11 | | | | 19 |
| 1 | 2 | | | 5 | | | 8 | | | 6 | 9 | | 7 | | 4 | 3 | | | | 11 | | 10 | | 20 |
| 1 | 2 | | | 5 | 6 | | 8 | | 11 | 9 | | | 7 | | 4 | 3 | | | | | | 10 | | 21 |
| 1 | 2 | | | 5 | 6 | | 8 | | 11 | 9 | | | 7 | | 4 | 3 | | | | | | 10 | | 22 |
| 1 | 2 | | | 5 | 6 | | 8 | | 11* | 9 | | | 7 | | 4 | 3 | | | | 10 | | 12 | | 23 |
| 1 | 2 | | | 5 | 6 | 12 | 8 | | 11 | | | | 7 | | 4 | 3 | 10 | | | 9* | | | | 24 |
| 1 | | | | 5 | 2 | 10 | 8 | | | 6 | 9 | | 7 | | 4 | 3 | | | | 11 | | | | 25 |
| 1 | | | | 5 | 2 | 10* | 8 | | | 6 | 9 | 12 | 7 | | 4 | 3 | | | | 11 | | | | 26 |
| 1 | | | | 5 | 2 | 12 | 8 | | | 6 | 9 | | 7* | | 4 | 3 | 10 | | | 11 | | | | 27 |
| 1 | 8 | | | 5 | 2 | | | | | 6 | 9 | | 7 | | 4 | 3 | 10 | | | 11 | | | | 28 |
| 1 | 2 | | | 5 | 8 | | | | | 6 | 9 | | 7 | | 4 | 3 | 10 | | | 11 | | | | 29 |
| 1 | | | | 5 | 2 | 12 | 8 | | | 9 | | | 6 | | 4 | 3 | 7 | 10 | | 11* | | | | 30 |
| 1 | 7 | | | 5 | 2 | 12 | 8 | | | 9 | | | | | 4 | 3 | 6 | 10* | | 11 | | | | 31 |
| 1 | 7 | | | 5 | 2 | | 8 | | 4 | 9 | | | | | | 3 | | 6 | 10 | 11 | | | | 32 |
| 1 | 7 | | | 5 | 2 | | 8 | 12 | 4 | 9* | | | | | | 3 | | 6 | 10 | 11 | | | | 33 |
| 1 | 7 | | | 5 | 2 | | 8 | | 10 | 9 | | | 4 | | | 3 | | 6 | | 11 | | | | 34 |
| 1 | 7* | | | 5 | 2 | | 8 | 12 | 10 | 9 | | | 4 | | | 3 | | 6 | | 11 | | | | 35 |
| 1 | | | | 5 | 2 | | 8 | 12 | 4 | 9 | | | 7 | | | 3 | | 6 | 10 | 11* | | | | 36 |
| 1 | 2 | | | 5 | 6 | | 8 | 12 | 10 | 7 | 9 | | | | 4 | 3 | | | | | | 11* | | 37 |
| 1 | 2 | | | 5 | 6 | | 8 | | 10* | 7 | 9 | | | | 4 | 3 | | 12 | | 11 | | | | 38 |
| 1 | 2 | 4* | | 5 | | | 8 | 12 | 7 | 9 | | | | | | 3 | | 6 | 10 | 11 | | | | 39 |
| 1 | | 3 | | 5 | | | 8 | 10 | 4 | 9 | | | | 2 | | | | 6 | | 7 | | 11 | | 40 |
| 1 | 2 | 6 | | 5 | | | 8 | 10 | | 9 | | | | | | 3 | | 4 | | 7 | | 11* | 12 | 41 |
| 1 | 2 | 6 | | 5 | | | 8 | 10 | 4 | 9 | | | | | | 3 | | 12 | | 7* | | 11 | | 42 |
| 42 | 23 | 27 | 3 | 40 | 27 | 17 | 40 | 4 | 20 | 39 | 31 | 2 | 22 | 14 | 22 | 26 | 11 | 14 | 6 | 18 | 1 | 13 | — | |
| | | | | | | +6s | +4s | +4s | +3s | | | | +3s | | | +7s | +2s | | | +1s | | | | |

## MIDDLESBROUGH

| | Ht | Wt | Birthplace | Clubs | League App. | League Gls |
|---|---|---|---|---|---|---|
| **Goalkeepers** | | | | | | |
| Jim Platt | 6 1 | 12 10 | Ballymoney | Middlesbrough | 378 | — |
| (N Ireland) | | | | Hartlepool U (on loan) | 13 | — |
| | | | | Cardiff C (on loan) | 4 | — |
| Kelham O'Hanlon | 6 0 | 12 0 | Saltburn | Middlesbrough | — | — |
| Neil Connell* | 5 9½ | 11 4 | Aberdeen | Middlesbrough | — | — |
| **Defenders** | | | | | | |
| John Craggs* | 5 8½ | 12 4 | Flinthill | Newcastle U | 52 | 1 |
| | | | | Middlesbrough | 409 | 12 |
| Ian Bailey | 5 9 | 11 12 | Middlesbrough | Middlesbrough | 145 | 1 |
| | | | | Carlisle U (on loan) | 7 | 1 |
| | | | | Doncaster R (on loan) | 9 | — |
| | | | | Bolton W (on loan) | 5 | — |
| Mike Angus | 5 10 | 12 3 | Middlesbrough | Middlesbrough | 37 | 1 |
| Jeff Peters | 5 6 | 10 2 | Wideopen | Middlesbrough | 6 | — |
| (Contract cancelled March 1982) | | | | | | |
| Irving Nattrass | 5 11 | 12 0 | Fishburn | Newcastle U | 238 | 16 |
| | | | | Middlesbrough | 71 | 1 |
| Keith Nobbs* | 5 10 | 11 10 | Bishop Auckland | Middlesbrough | 1 | — |
| Billy Ashcroft* | 6 1 | 14 4 | Liverpool | Wrexham | 219 | 72 |
| | | | | Middlesbrough | 159 | 21 |
| Tony McAndrew | 5 10 | 12 4 | Lanark | Middlesbrough | 247 | 13 |
| Joe Bolton | 5 11 | 12 2 | Birtley | Sunderland | 273 | 11 |
| | | | | Middlesbrough | 27 | 1 |
| Paul Robinson* | 5 11 | 11 4 | Trimdon | Middlesbrough | — | — |
| Mick Baxter | 6 1 | 12 0 | Birmingham | Preston NE | 210 | 17 |
| | | | | Middlesbrough | 40 | 2 |
| Darren Wood | 5 10 | 11 8 | Scarborough | Middlesbrough | 11 | 1 |
| Tony Mowbray | 6 1 | 12 2 | Saltburn | Middlesbrough | — | — |
| **Midfield** | | | | | | |
| Billy Askew* | 5 6½ | 10 2 | Lumley | Middlesbrough | 12 | — |
| | | | | Blackburn R (on loan) | — | — |
| Graeme Hedley | 5 10 | 10 4 | Easington | Middlesbrough | 50 | 6 |
| (Contract cancelled March 1982) | | | | Sheffield W (on loan) | 6 | 1 |
| | | | | Darlington (on loan) | 14 | 1 |
| | | | | York C (on loan) | 5 | 1 |
| Terry Cochrane | 5 7½ | 10 9 | Killyleagh | Coleraine | — | — |
| (N Ireland) | | | | Burnley | 67 | 13 |
| | | | | Middlesbrough | 97 | 6 |
| Andy McCreesh | 5 10½ | 11 0 | Billingham | Middlesbrough | 2 | — |
| (Contract cancelled March 1982) | | | | | | |
| Colin Ross | 5 7 | 11 0 | Dailly | Middlesbrough | 27 | — |
| Mark Robinson | 5 10 | 11 8 | Middlesbrough | Middlesbrough | — | — |
| (Contract cancelled March 1982) | | | | | | |
| David McClurg | 5 9 | 10 8 | Killyleagh | Distillery | — | — |
| | | | | Middlesbrough | — | — |
| Heine Otto | 6 0 | 12 0 | Amsterdam | Twente | (not known) | |
| | | | | Middlesbrough | 40 | 4 |
| Bobby Thomson | 5 10 | 11 6 | Glasgow | St Johnstone | 118 | 17 |
| | | | | Morton | 90 | 25 |
| | | | | Middlesbrough | 20 | 2 |
| **Forwards** | | | | | | |
| Steve Bell | 5 7 | 10 4 | Middlesbrough | Middlesbrough | 1 | — |
| (Apprentice) | | | | | | |
| Billy Woof* | 5 10 | 11 9 | Gateshead | Middlesbrough | 46 | 5 |
| | | | | Brighton (on loan) | — | — |
| | | | | Peterborough U (on loan) | 3 | — |
| David Shearer | 5 10 | 12 0 | Inverness | Middlesbrough | 68 | 14 |
| | | | | Wigan Ath (on loan) | 11 | 9 |
| David Hodgson | 5 10 | 11 12 | Gateshead | Middlesbrough | 125 | 16 |
| Bozo Jankovic | 6 0 | 13 4 | Sarajevo | Zeljeznicar | 495 | † |
| (Yugoslavia) | | | | Middlesbrough | 50 | 16 |
| Garry MacDonald | 6 0 | 12 1 | Middlesbrough | Middlesbrough | 15 | 1 |
| Colin Blackburn | 5 9 | 10 9 | Richmond | Middlesbrough | 1 | — |
| (Contract cancelled March 1982) | | | | | | |
| David Currie | 6 0 | 11 13 | Stockton | Middlesbrough | 1 | — |
| Philip McMahon* | | | | Middlesbrough | — | — |
| Dave Thomas | 5 8 | 10 8 | Kirkby-in-Ashfield | Burnley | 157 | 19 |
| (England) | | | | QPR | 182 | 29 |
| | | | | Everton | 71 | 4 |
| | | | | Wolverhampton W | 10 | — |
| | | | | Vancouver W | (not known) | |
| | | | | Middlesbrough | 13 | 1 |

† Jankovic's goals for Zeljeznicar not known.

# MILLWALL

## Division 3

*Chairman:* Allan A. Thorne.

*Directors:* H. T. J. Burnige FRICS, R. I. Burr, L. C. Eppel, P. J. Martinelli, W. J. Nelan.

*General Secretary:* G. I. S. Hortop.

*Player-Manager:* Peter Anderson.

*Assistant Manager:* Terry Long.

*Year Formed:* 1885.   *Turned Professional:* 1893.

*Limited Company:* 1894.

*Previous Grounds:* 1885, Glengall Road, Millwall; 1886, Back of 'Lord Nelson'; 1890, East Ferry Road; 1901, North Greenwich; 1910, The Den.

*Previous Names:* 1885, Millwall Rovers; 1889, Millwall Athletic.

**Football League Record:**
1920 Original Members of Division 3; 1921 Division 3(S); 1928–34 Division 2; 1934–38 Division 3(S); 1938–48 Division 2; 1948–58 Division 3(S); 1958–62 Division 4; 1962–64 Division 3; 1964–65 Division 4; 1965–66 Division 3; 1966–75 Division 2; 1975–76 Division 3; 1976–79 Division 2; 1979– Division 3.

**Honours:** *Football League:* Division 2 best season: 3rd, 1971–72; Division 3(S) – Champions 1927–28, 1937–38; Division 3 – Runners-up 1965–66; Division 4 – Champions 1961–62; Runners-up 1964–65. *FA Cup:* semi-final 1900, 1903, 1937 (first Division 3 side to reach semi-final). *Football League Cup* best season: 5th rd, 1973–74, 1976–77.

*Record Victory:* 9-1 v Torquay U, Division 3(S), 29 Aug, 1927; v Coventry C, Division 3(S), 19 Nov, 1927.

*Record Defeat:* 1-9 v Aston Villa, FA Cup 4th rd, 28 Jan, 1946.

*Most League Points:* 65, Division 3(S), 1927–28; Division 3, 1965–66. *Three points win:* 67, Division 3, 1981–82.

*Most League Goals:* 127, Division 3(S), 1927–28.

*Highest League Scorer in Season:* Richard Parker, 37, Division 3(S), 1926–27.

*Most League Goals in Total Aggregate:* Derek Possee, 79, 1967–73.

*Most Capped Player:* Eamonn Dunphy, 22 (23), Eire.

*Most League Appearances:* Barry Kitchener, 523, 1967–82.

*Record Transfer Fee Received:* £250,000 from Ipswich T for Kevin O'Callaghan, Jan 1980.

*Record Transfer Fee Paid:* £100,000 to Fulham for John Mitchell, July 1978; £100,000 to Crystal P for Nick Chatterton, Nov 1978; £100,000 to Fulham for Chris Guthrie, March 1980.

*Previous Managers since the War:* Jack Cock, Charlie Hewitt, Ron Gray, Jimmy Seed, Reg Smith, Ron Gray, Billy Gray, Benny Fenton, Gordon Jago, George Petchey.

*Address of Supporters Club:* 470 New Cross Road, Deptford, London, SE8.

*Address of the Club Shop or Boutique:* Same.

---

**The Den, Cold Blow Lane, London, SE14 5RH.** Telephone 01-639 3143/4,/1474. *Ground capacity:* 32,000. *Record attendance:* 48,672 v Derby Co, FA Cup 5th rd, 20 Feb, 1937. *Record receipts:* £21,756 v Ipswich T, FA Cup 6th rd, 11 Mar, 1978. *Pitch measurements:* 112yd×74yd.

*How to get there:* Buses from Central London and West End: 36, 36A, 36B, 53, 141, 171, 177, 182. From City: 21. Nearest Underground stations; New Cross or New Cross Gate (Metropolitan Line). Also New Cross Gate British Rail station.

*Match tickets:* Bookable 10–14 days in advance from club office.

*Car parking:* Car park near the ground. Also ample street parking.

*Entertainments/catering facilities:* Several licensed refreshment points around the ground.

*Club shop:* Three shops at the ground open on match days.

*Programmes:* Programmes available on subscription.

*Extra information:* Millwall went unbeaten for 59 successive League matches at The Den between 24 Aug 1964 and 14 Jan 1967.

*Club Colours:* Blue shirts, white trim, white shorts, blue stockings.

*Change Colours:* Red shirts, white trim, red shorts, red stockings.

*Club Captain:* Nicky Chatterton.

*Club Nickname:* Lions.

## MILLWALL 1981–82 LEAGUE RECORD

| Match No. | Date | Venue | Opponents | Result | H/T Score | Goalscorers | Attendance |
|---|---|---|---|---|---|---|---|
| 1 | Aug 29 | H | Preston NE | W 2-1 | 0-0 | Horrix, Chatterton (pen) | 4549 |
| 2 | Sept 5 | A | Wimbledon | W 3-1 | 1-0 | Anderson, Dibble 2 | 5102 |
| 3 | 13 | H | Reading | L 0-1 | 0-1 | | 7178 |
| 4 | 19 | A | Chester | D 0-0 | 0-0 | | 2052 |
| 5 | 23 | A | Lincoln C | W 1-0 | 1-0 | Chatterton | 3923 |
| 6 | 26 | H | Burnley | W 4-3 | 2-3 | Chatterton, West, Bartley, Anderson | 4877 |
| 7 | 29 | H | Oxford U | L 1-2 | 0-0 | Chatterton | 5885 |
| 8 | Oct 3 | A | Exeter C | L 4-5 | 1-3 | Horrix, Anderson, Tagg, Chatterton (pen) | 7169 |
| 9 | 11 | H | Walsall | W 2-0 | 1-0 | McKenna, Massey | 6289 |
| 10 | 17 | A | Doncaster R | L 0-1 | 0-0 | | 6466 |
| 11 | 20 | A | Newport Co | D 1-1 | 0-1 | Horrix | 4609 |
| 12 | 24 | H | Gillingham | L 1-2 | 0-1 | Chatterton | 5763 |
| 13 | 31 | A | Huddersfield T | W 2-1 | 0-0 | Warman, Chatterton | 8546 |
| 14 | Nov 3 | H | Bristol C | W 2-0 | 1-0 | Boyle (og), West | 5002 |
| 15 | 7 | A | Swindon T | W 2-1 | 1-1 | Chatterton, Hayes | 5710 |
| 16 | 14 | H | Bristol R | D 0-0 | 0-0 | | 5970 |
| 17 | 28 | H | Fulham | D 0-0 | 0-0 | | 8343 |
| 18 | Dec 5 | H | Carlisle U | L 1-2 | 1-1 | Chatterton (pen) | 4740 |
| 19 | 28 | H | Brentford | L 0-1 | 0-0 | | 7474 |
| 20 | Jan 23 | A | Preston NE | L 0-1 | 0-1 | | 5085 |
| 21 | 30 | H | Chester | W 2-1 | 1-1 | Horrix, Paddon | 3250 |
| 22 | Feb 1 | A | Southend U | D 2-2 | 1-1 | Neal 2 | 5676 |
| 23 | 6 | A | Reading | L 0-4 | 0-2 | | 4120 |
| 24 | 9 | H | Lincoln C | D 1-1 | 1-0 | Peake (og) | 3198 |
| 25 | 14 | H | Exeter C | W 5-1 | 2-0 | Horrix 2, Tagg 3 | 3628 |
| 26 | 20 | A | Burnley | D 1-1 | 0-1 | Shinton | 7094 |
| 27 | 24 | H | Wimbledon | W 2-1 | 0-0 | Horrix, Chatterton (pen) | 4072 |
| 28 | 27 | A | Walsall | D 1-1 | 0-0 | Tagg | 3731 |
| 29 | Mar 6 | A | Doncaster R | L 0-2 | 0-1 | | 4055 |
| 30 | 9 | H | Newport Co | W 1-0 | 1-0 | Neal | 3084 |
| 31 | 12 | A | Gillingham | D 1-1 | 0-1 | Neal | 5508 |
| 32 | 28 | H | Swindon T | D 0-0 | 0-0 | | 4381 |
| 33 | Apr 3 | A | Bristol R | W 1-0 | 1-0 | Hayes | 4279 |
| 34 | 6 | A | Huddersfield T | L 1-3 | 0-2 | Horrix | 3507 |
| 35 | 9 | A | Brentford | L 1-4 | 0-0 | West | 7460 |
| 36 | 12 | H | Southend U | D 1-1 | 1-0 | Horrix | 3025 |
| 37 | 17 | A | Carlisle U | L 1-2 | 0-0 | Parker (og) | 4917 |
| 38 | 20 | H | Plymouth Arg | W 2-1 | 2-1 | Horrix, Allardyce | 2562 |
| 39 | 25 | H | Fulham | W 4-3 | 2-0 | Horrix 3, Martin | 6484 |
| 40 | 27 | A | Chesterfield | W 1-0 | 1-0 | Shinton | 2377 |
| 41 | May 1 | A | Oxford U | D 0-0 | 0-0 | | 7230 |
| 42 | 4 | H | Chesterfield | W 3-2 | 1-1 | Horrix, Chatterton (pen), West | 2265 |
| 43 | 8 | H | Portsmouth | W 1-0 | 1-0 | Shinton | 4969 |
| 44 | 12 | A | Bristol C | L 1-4 | 1-2 | Dibble | 2696 |
| 45 | 15 | A | Plymouth Arg | L 1-2 | 0-2 | Horrix | 3193 |
| 46 | 21 | A | Portsmouth | D 2-2 | 0-1 | Massey, Chatterton (pen) | 4902 |

**Final League Position: 9**

### Goalscorers

*League* (62): Horrix 15, Chatterton 12 (6 pens), Tagg 5, Neal 4, West 4, Anderson 3, Dibble 3, Shinton 3, Hayes 2, Massey 2, Allardyce 1, Bartley 1, McKenna 1, Martin 1, Paddon 1, Warman 1, own goals 3.
*League Cup* (7): Horrix 3, Dibble 2, Chatterton 1, West 1.
*FA Cup* (7): Chatterton 3 (1 pen), Allardyce 2, Hayes 1, Neal 1.

| League Cup | First Round | Orient (a) | 1-1 |
|---|---|---|---|
| | | (h) | 3-2 |
| | Second Round | Oxford U (h) | 3-3 |
| | | (a) | 0-1 |
| FA Cup | First Round | Portsmouth (a) | 1-1 |
| | | (h) | 3-2 |
| | Second Round | Dagenham (a) | 2-1 |
| | Third Round | Grimsby T (h) | 1-6 |

| Gleasure | Roberts | Warman | Chatterton | Tagg | Martin | Dibble | Anderson | Horrix | Bartley | West | Massey | Hayes | Allardyce | Slough | McKenna | Neal | Paddon | Stevens | Shinton | Sansome | Madden | Kitchener | Robinson | Match No. |
|---|---|---|---|---|---|---|---|---|---|---|---|---|---|---|---|---|---|---|---|---|---|---|---|---|
| 1 | 2 | 3 | 4 | 5 | 6 | 7 | 8* | 9 | 10 | 11 | 12 | | | | | | | | | | | | | 1 |
| 1 | 2 | 3 | 4 | 5 | 6 | 7 | 8 | 9 | | 11 | 12 | 10* | | | | | | | | | | | | 2 |
| 1 | 2 | 3 | 4 | 5 | 6 | 7 | 8 | 9 | 10 | 11 | | | | | | | | | | | | | | 3 |
| 1 | 2 | 3 | 4 | | 6 | 7 | 8 | 9 | 10 | 11 | | | 5 | | | | | | | | | | | 4 |
| 1 | 2 | 3 | 4 | | 6 | 7 | 8 | 9 | 10 | 11 | | | 5 | | | | | | | | | | | 5 |
| 1 | 2 | 3 | 4 | | 6 | 7 | 8 | 9 | 10 | 11 | | | 5 | | | | | | | | | | | 6 |
| 1 | 2 | 3 | 4 | 5 | 6 | 7 | 8 | 9 | 10 | 11 | | | | | | | | | | | | | | 7 |
| 1 | 2 | 3 | 4 | | 6 | 7 | 8 | 9 | 10 | 11* | 12 | | 5 | | | | | | | | | | | 8 |
| 1 | 2 | 3 | 4 | | | 7 | 8 | 10 | | 11 | | | 5 | 6 | 9 | | | | | | | | | 9 |
| 1 | 2 | 3 | 4 | | 12 | 7* | 8 | 10 | | 11 | | | 5 | 6 | 9 | | | | | | | | | 10 |
| 1 | 2 | 3 | 4 | | 12 | | 8 | 10 | 9 | 11 | | 7 | 5* | 6 | | | | | | | | | | 11 |
| 1 | 2 | 3 | 4 | 5 | | | 8 | 10 | 9 | 11 | | 7 | | 6 | | | | | | | | | | 12 |
| 1 | | 3 | 4 | 2 | 12 | | | 10 | 9* | 11 | 8 | 7 | 5 | 6 | | | | | | | | | | 13 |
| 1 | | 3 | 4 | 2 | | | | 10 | | 11 | 8 | 7 | 5 | 6 | 9 | | | | | | | | | 14 |
| 1 | | 3 | 4 | 2 | | | | 10 | | 11 | 8 | 7 | 5 | 6 | 9 | | | | | | | | | 15 |
| 1 | | 3 | 4 | 2 | | | | 10* | | 11 | 8 | 7 | 5 | 6 | 9 | 12 | | | | | | | | 16 |
| 1 | | 3 | 4 | 2 | 12 | | | 10 | | 11 | 8 | 7 | 5 | 6 | 9* | | | | | | | | | 17 |
| 1 | 6 | 3 | 4 | 2 | | | | 10 | 9 | 11 | 8 | 7* | 5 | | | 12 | | | | | | | | 18 |
| 1 | 2 | 3 | 4 | | 12 | | | 10* | 9 | 11 | | | 5 | 6 | | 7 | 8 | | | | | | | 19 |
| 1 | | 3 | | 4 | 2 | 7 | | 9 | | 11 | 12 | | 5 | 6 | | 10 | 8* | | | | | | | 20 |
| 1 | | 3 | | 4 | 2 | 7 | 9 | | | 11 | | | 5 | 6 | | 10 | 8 | | | | | | | 21 |
| 1 | | 3 | | 4 | 2 | 7 | 9 | | | 11 | | | 5 | 6 | | 10 | 8 | | | | | | | 22 |
| 1 | | 3 | | 4 | 2 | 7 | 9 | | | 11 | 12 | | 5* | 6 | | 10 | 8 | | | | | | | 23 |
| 1 | 2 | 3 | 4 | 5 | 6 | 7 | | 9 | | 11 | 8 | | | | | 10 | | | | | | | | 24 |
| 1 | 5 | 3 | | 6 | | | 9 | | | 11 | 8 | 4 | | | | 10 | | 2 | 7 | | | | | 25 |
| 1 | 6 | 3 | 12 | 5 | 2 | | | 10 | | 11 | 8 | 4* | | | 9 | | | | 7 | | | | | 26 |
| 1 | 2 | 3 | 4 | 6 | | | 9 | | | 11 | 8 | | 5 | | | 10 | | | 7 | | | | | 27 |
| 1 | 2 | 3 | 4 | 6 | | | 9 | | | 11 | 8 | 12 | 5 | | | 10 | | | 7* | | | | | 28 |
| 1 | 2 | 3 | 4 | 6 | | 12 | 9 | | | 11 | 8 | 7 | 5 | | | 10* | | | | | | | | 29 |
| 1 | 6 | 3 | 4 | | 2 | | 9 | | | 11 | 8 | 7 | 5 | | | 10 | | | | | | | | 30 |
| 1 | 6 | 3 | 4 | | 2 | 12 | 9 | | | 11 | 8 | 7* | 5 | | | 10 | | | | | | | | 31 |
| | 6 | | 4 | | 2 | | 9* | | | 11 | 8 | 12 | 5 | | | 10 | | | 7 | | 1 | 3 | | 32 |
| | 6 | | 4 | | 2 | | | 12 | | 11 | 8 | 9 | 5 | | | 10 | | | 7* | | 1 | 3 | | 33 |
| | 6 | | 4 | | 2 | | | 12 | | 11 | 8 | 9* | 5 | | | 10 | | | 7 | | 1 | 3 | | 34 |
| | 6 | | 4 | | 2 | 7 | 12 | 10 | | 11 | 8* | | 5 | | | | | | 9 | | 1 | 3 | | 35 |
| | 6 | | 4 | | 10 | | | 9 | | 11 | 8 | | 5 | | | | | | 7 | | 1 | 3 | | 36 |
| | 6 | | 4 | | 10 | | 8 | 9 | | 11 | | | 5 | | | | | 2 | 7 | | 1 | 3 | | 37 |
| | 6* | | 4 | | 10 | | 8 | 9 | | 11 | | | 5 | | | 12 | | 2 | 7 | | 1 | 3 | | 38 |
| | 6 | | 4 | | 10 | | 8 | 9 | | 11 | | | | | | 12 | 3 | 7 | 1* | 2 | 5 | | | 39 |
| 1 | 6 | | 4 | | 10 | | 8 | 9 | | 11 | | | 5 | | | | | 2 | 7 | | 3 | | | 40 |
| 1 | 6 | | 4 | | 10 | 12 | 8 | 9 | | 11 | | | 5 | | | | | 2 | 7 | | 3* | | | 41 |
| 1 | 6 | | 4 | | 10 | | 9 | | | 11 | 8 | | 5 | | | | | 2 | 7 | | | | 3 | 42 |
| 1 | 6 | | 4 | | 2 | 9 | | | 11 | 10 | 8 | | 5 | | | | | | 7 | | | | 3 | 43 |
| 1 | 2 | | 4 | | 10 | | 9 | | | 11 | 8 | 12 | 5 | | | | | | 7 | | 6* | | 3 | 44 |
| 1 | 6 | | 4 | | 2 | 12 | 9 | | | 11 | 10 | 8* | | | 7 | | | | 5 | | | | 3 | 45 |
| 1 | 6 | | 2 | | 10 | | 9 | | | 11 | 4 | 5 | | | 8 | | | | 7 | | | | 3 | 46 |
| 38 | 41 | 27 | 44 | 11 | 36 | 19 | 17 | 42 | 12 | 45 | 25 | 19 | 36 | 14 | 6 | 18 | 5 | 7 | 18 | 8 | 10 | 3 | 5 | |
| | | + | | | + | + | + | + | | | | + | + | | | | + | | | | | | | |
| | | 1s | | | 2s | 7s | 1s | 2s | | | | 4s | 4s | | | | 4s | | | | | | | |

## MILLWALL

| | Ht | Wt | Birthplace | Clubs | League App. | League Gls |
|---|---|---|---|---|---|---|
| **Goalkeepers** | | | | | | |
| Peter Gleasure | 5 11 | 12 13 | Luton | Millwall | 51 | — |
| Paul Sansome | 5 11 | 11 10 | New Addington | Millwall | 8 | — |
| **Defenders** | | | | | | |
| Lawrie Madden | 5 11 | 12 6½ | London | Arsenal | — | — |
| | | | | Mansfield T | 10 | — |
| | | | | Charlton Ath | 113 | 7 |
| | | | | Millwall | 10 | — |
| Barry Kitchener | 6 1½ | 14 9 | Dagenham | Millwall | 523 | 24 |
| Tony Tagg* | 6 2½ | 12 11 | Epsom | QPR | 4 | — |
| | | | | Millwall | 133 | 9 |
| David Gregory | 5 7 | 10 10 | Essex | Millwall | 52 | 2 |
| (Contract cancelled Aug 1981) | | | | | | |
| Paul Roberts | 5 10 | 12 0 | London | Millwall | 115 | — |
| Paul Robinson | 5 10 | 11 1 | Hampstead | Millwall | 13 | — |
| Keith Stevens | 5 11 | 11 1 | Wimbledon | Millwall | 8 | — |
| Alan Slough* | 5 10 | 12 5 | Luton | Luton T | 275 | 28 |
| | | | | Fulham | 154 | 13 |
| | | | | Peterborough U | 105 | 10 |
| | | | | Millwall | 14 | — |
| Phil Warman | 5 6½ | 10 1 | Bromley | Charlton Ath | 316 | 19 |
| | | | | Millwall | 27 | 1 |
| Sam Allardyce | 6 1½ | 14 0 | Dudley | Bolton W | 184 | 21 |
| | | | | Sunderland | 25 | 2 |
| | | | | Millwall | 36 | 1 |
| **Midfield** | | | | | | |
| Nicky Chatterton | 5 9 | 11 0 | Norwood | Crystal Palace | 151 | 31 |
| | | | | Millwall | 155 | 34 |
| Andy Massey | 5 10 | 10 9 | London | Millwall | 50 | 2 |
| David Martin | 5 11 | 10 11 | East Ham | Millwall | 74 | 2 |
| Mark Dennehy | 5 7 | 10 1 | Stratford | Millwall | — | — |
| (Contract cancelled April 1982) | | | | | | |
| David Rose* | 5 9 | 11 2 | Redhill | Millwall | — | — |
| Peter Anderson | 5 9½ | 11 4 | Hendon | Hendon | (not known) | |
| | | | | Luton T | 181 | 34 |
| | | | | Royal Antwerp | (not known) | |
| | | | | Tampa Bay R | (not known) | |
| | | | | Sheffield U (on loan) | 30 | 12 |
| | | | | Millwall | 31 | 4 |
| Alan West | 5 9 | 10 8 | Hyde | Burnley | 44 | 3 |
| | | | | Luton T | 285 | 16 |
| | | | | Millwall | 45 | 4 |
| Alan McLeary | | | London | Millwall | — | — |
| Nick Cripps | | | | Millwall | — | — |
| (Contract cancelled Dec 1981) | | | | | | |
| **Forwards** | | | | | | |
| Chris Dibble* | 5 10 | 10 6 | Surrey | Millwall | 63 | 5 |
| Austin Hayes | 5 4½ | 9 12 | London | Southampton | 31 | 5 |
| (Eire) | | | | Millwall | 35 | 4 |
| Dean Horrix | 5 10 | 10 8 | Slough | Millwall | 57 | 19 |
| Alan McKenna | 5 10 | 11 4 | Edinburgh | Millwall | 30 | 4 |
| (Transferred to Berwick R) | | | | | | |
| John Mitchell | 5 11 | 12 4 | London | Fulham | 169 | 56 |
| | | | | Millwall | 81 | 18 |
| Chris Guthrie | 6 1 | 13 6 | Dilston | Newcastle U | 3 | — |
| (Retired, injury) | | | | Southend U | 108 | 35 |
| | | | | Sheffield U | 60 | 15 |
| | | | | Swindon T | 45 | 12 |
| | | | | Fulham | 50 | 15 |
| | | | | Millwall | 7 | 1 |
| Jimmy Sweetzer | 5 8 | 11 1 | Woking | Oxford U | 8 | 1 |
| (Contract cancelled Feb 1982) | | | | Millwall | 3 | 1 |
| John Bartley | 5 9 | 12 1 | London | Welling U | (not known) | |
| (Contract cancelled April 1982) | | | | Millwall | 40 | 8 |
| Dean Neal | 5 10½ | 12 0 | London | QPR | 23 | 8 |
| | | | | Tulsa R | (not known) | |
| | | | | Millwall | 22 | 4 |
| Bobby Shinton | 5 10 | 11 12 | West Bromwich | Walsall | 79 | 20 |
| | | | | Cambridge U | 99 | 25 |
| | | | | Wrexham | 128 | 37 |
| | | | | Manchester C | 5 | — |
| | | | | Millwall (on loan) | 5 | 3 |
| | | | | Newcastle U | 42 | 10 |
| | | | | Millwall | 18 | 3 |
| Lee Batt | | | | Millwall | — | — |
| (Contract cancelled Jan 1982) | | | | | | |

# NEWCASTLE UNITED

## Division 2

*President:* F. Braithwaite OBE.

*Chairman:* S. Seymour. *Vice-Chairman:* R. Mackenzie.

*Directors:* F. Braithwaite OBE, J. Rush AFC, W. G. McKeag, Sir G. Bowman, W. P. Catesby, E. Dunn.

*Manager:* Arthur Cox. *Asst Manager:* Tommy Cavanagh.

*Secretary:* R. Cushing.

*Assistant Secretary:* A. J. Garvie.

*Year Formed:* 1882. *Turned Professional:* 1889.

*Limited Company:* 1890.

*Previous Name:* Newcastle East End until Newcastle U in 1892.

*Previous Ground:* Chillingham Road, Heaton, until 1892.

**Football League Record:**
1893 Elected to Division 2; 1898–1934 Division 1; 1934–48 Division 2; 1948–61 Division 1; 1961–65 Division 2; 1965–78 Division 1; 1978– Division 2.

**Honours:** *Football League:* Division 1 – Champions 1904–05, 1906–07, 1908–09, 1926–27; Division 2 – Champions 1964–65; Runners-up 1897–98, 1947–48. *FA Cup:* Winners 1910, 1924, 1932, 1951, 1952, 1955; Runners-up 1905, 1906, 1908, 1911, 1974. *Football League Cup:* Runners-up 1975–76. *Texaco Cup:* Winners 1973–74, 1974–75. **European Competitions:** *European Fairs Cup:* 1968–69 (winners), 1969–70, 1970–71. *UEFA Cup:* 1977–78. *Anglo-Italian Cup:* Winners 1973.

*Record Victory:* 13-0 v Newport Co, Division 2, 5 Oct, 1946.

*Record Defeat:* 0-9 v Burton Wanderers, Division 2, 15 April, 1895.

*Most League Points:* 57, Division 2, 1964–65. *Three points win:* 62, Division 2, 1981–82.

*Most League Goals:* 98, Division 1, 1951–52.

*Highest League Scorer in Season:* Hughie Gallacher, 36, Division 1, 1926–27.

*Most League Goals in Total Aggregate:* Jackie Milburn, 178, 1946–57.

*Most Capped Player:* Alf McMichael, 40, Ireland.

*Most League Appearances:* Jim Lawrence, 432, 1904–22.

*Record Transfer Fee Received:* £500,000 from Aston Villa for Peter Withe, May 1980.

*Record Transfer Fee Paid:* £250,000 to WBA for John Trewick, Dec 1980.

*Previous Managers since the War:* George Martin, Duggie Livingstone, Charlie Mitten, Norman Smith, Joe Harvey, Gordon Lee, Richard Dinnis, Bill McGarry.

*Address of the Club Shop or Boutique:* St James' Park, Newcastle-upon-Tyne NE1 4ST.

---

**St James' Park, Newcastle-upon-Tyne NE1 4ST.** Telephone Newcastle 328361. Information service 611571. *Telegraphic address:* 'Football, Newcastle-upon-Tyne'. *Ground capacity:* 38,008. *Record attendance:* 68,386 v Chelsea, Division 1, 3 Sept, 1930. *Record receipts:* £42,415 v Ujpest Dozsa, European Fairs Cup Final, 29 May, 1969. *Pitch measurements:* 115yd×75yd.

*How to get there:* The ground is central and within walking distance of the railway station and the town centre.

*Match tickets:* Personal applications accepted 10 days before a match and postal applications accepted 14 days before a match.

*Car parking:* Car park on the north side of the ground. Street parking available.

*Entertainments/catering facilities:* Excellent facilities in the New East Stand. Refreshments available in all parts of the ground.

*Club shop:* Open daily (except Sundays). Open match days 9.30 am–3.00 pm.

*Handbooks/programmes:* Programmes if available can be ordered from the secretary price 30p.

*Extra information:* United's 13-0 win over Newport County in 1946 was a second Division record score.

*Club Colours:* Black and white striped shirts, black shorts, black stockings with two white hoops on turnover.

*Change Colours:* All yellow.

*First Team Trainer/Coach:* Tommy Cavanagh.

*Club Nickname:* Magpies.

## NEWCASTLE UNITED 1981–82 LEAGUE RECORD

| Match No. | Date | Venue | Opponents | Result | H/T Score | Goalscorers | Attendance |
|---|---|---|---|---|---|---|---|
| 1 | Aug 29 | H | Watford | L 0-1 | 0-1 | | 19,376 |
| 2 | Sept 5 | A | QPR | L 0-3 | 0-1 | | 14,176 |
| 3 | 12 | H | Cambridge U | W 1-0 | 0-0 | Trewick | 14,699 |
| 4 | 19 | A | Norwich C | L 1-2 | 1-1 | Waddle | 14,384 |
| 5 | 23 | H | Shrewsbury T | W 2-0 | 1-0 | Wharton, Shinton | 13,846 |
| 6 | 26 | H | Orient | W 1-0 | 0-0 | Trewick | 13,710 |
| 7 | 29 | A | Bolton W | L 0-1 | 0-1 | | 6429 |
| 8 | Oct 3 | A | Cardiff C | W 4-0 | 2-0 | Varadi 3, Davies (pen) | 5764 |
| 9 | 10 | H | Derby Co | W 3-0 | 2-0 | Varadi 2, Wharton | 17,243 |
| 10 | 17 | A | Barnsley | L 0-1 | 0-1 | | 18,477 |
| 11 | 24 | H | Rotherham U | D 1-1 | 0-0 | Shinton | 19,039 |
| 12 | 31 | A | Oldham Ath | L 1-3 | 1-3 | Davies | 9010 |
| 13 | Nov 7 | A | Chelsea | L 1-2 | 0-2 | Waddle | 16,059 |
| 14 | 14 | H | Charlton Ath | W 4-1 | 1-1 | Wharton, Brown, Varadi 2 | 15,200 |
| 15 | 21 | H | Luton T | W 3-2 | 2-0 | Brown 2, Varadi | 21,037 |
| 16 | 24 | A | Orient | L 0-1 | 0-0 | | 4026 |
| 17 | 28 | A | Grimsby T | D 1-1 | 1-1 | Wharton | 9257 |
| 18 | Dec 5 | H | Blackburn R | D 0-0 | 0-0 | | 18,721 |
| 19 | Jan 16 | A | Watford | W 3-2 | 1-0 | Todd 2, Varadi | 12,333 |
| 20 | 30 | H | Norwich C | W 2-1 | 0-0 | Mills, Varadi | 14,447 |
| 21 | Feb 3 | A | Bolton W | W 2-0 | 1-0 | Trewick (pen), Wharton | 14,761 |
| 22 | 6 | A | Cambridge U | L 0-1 | 0-1 | | 5092 |
| 23 | 13 | H | Cardiff C | W 2-1 | 2-0 | Trewick, Varadi | 15,049 |
| 24 | 20 | A | Shrewsbury T | D 0-0 | 0-0 | | 4636 |
| 25 | 24 | H | Sheffield W | W 1-0 | 1-0 | Varadi | 18,967 |
| 26 | 27 | A | Derby Co | D 2-2 | 0-1 | Varadi, Waddle | 12,257 |
| 27 | Mar 2 | A | Leicester C | L 0-3 | 0-2 | | 12,497 |
| 28 | 6 | H | Barnsley | W 1-0 | 1-0 | Varadi | 18,636 |
| 29 | 13 | A | Rotherham U | D 0-0 | 0-0 | | 16,905 |
| 30 | 20 | H | Oldham Ath | W 2-0 | 2-0 | Mills, Brownlie | 18,488 |
| 31 | 27 | H | Chelsea | W 1-0 | 1-0 | Waddle | 26,887 |
| 32 | 31 | H | Crystal Palace | D 0-0 | 0-0 | | 21,610 |
| 33 | Apr 3 | A | Charlton Ath | W 1-0 | 1-0 | Waddle | 6357 |
| 34 | 6 | A | Wrexham | L 2-4 | 1-1 | Varadi 2 | 4517 |
| 35 | 10 | H | Leicester C | D 0-0 | 0-0 | | 25,545 |
| 36 | 12 | A | Sheffield W | L 1-2 | 1-2 | Barton | 29,917 |
| 37 | 17 | A | Luton T | L 2-3 | 1-0 | Mills, Trewick (pen) | 13,041 |
| 38 | 24 | H | Grimsby T | L 0-1 | 0-0 | | 14,101 |
| 39 | May 1 | A | Blackburn R | L 1-4 | 0-2 | Varadi | 5207 |
| 40 | 5 | H | QPR | L 0-4 | 0-3 | | 10,670 |
| 41 | 8 | H | Wrexham | W 4-2 | 2-0 | Brownlie, Waddle, Varadi, Trewick (pen) | 9447 |
| 42 | 15 | A | Crystal Palace | W 2-1 | 0-0 | Mills (pen), Waddle | 8453 |

**Final League Position: 9**

**Goalscorers**

*League* (52): Varadi 18, Waddle 7, Trewick 6 (3 pens), Wharton 5, Mills 4 (1 pen), Brown 3, Brownlie 2, Davies 2 (1 pen), Shinton 2, Todd 2, Barton 1.
*League Cup* (1): Barton 1.
*FA Cup* (6): Varadi 2, Brownlie 1, Saunders 1, Waddle 1, own goal 1.

| **League Cup** | Second Round | Fulham (h) | 1-2 |
|---|---|---|---|
| | | (a) | 0-2 |
| **FA Cup** | Third Round | Colchester U (h) | 1-1 |
| | | (a) | 4-3 |
| | Fourth Round | Grimsby T (h) | 1-2 |

| Carr | Brownlie | Davies | Trewick | Barton | Halliday | Walker | Shoulder | Varadi | Wharton | Waddle | Martin | Haddock | Carney | Shinton | Todd | Saunders | Brown | Pugh | Mills | Cartwright | Bell | Ferris | Match No. |
|---|---|---|---|---|---|---|---|---|---|---|---|---|---|---|---|---|---|---|---|---|---|---|---|
| 1 | 2 | 3 | 4 | 5 | 6* | 7 | 8 | 9 | 10 | 11 | 12 |  |  |  |  |  |  |  |  |  |  |  | 1 |
| 1 |  | 3 | 4 | 5 | 6 | 7 | 8 | 9 | 10* | 11 | 12 | 2 |  |  |  |  |  |  |  |  |  |  | 2 |
| 1 | 2 | 3 | 4 | 5 | 6 | 7 |  | 9 | 10 | 11 | 8 |  |  |  |  |  |  |  |  |  |  |  | 3 |
| 1 | 2 | 3 | 4 | 5* | 6 | 7 |  | 9 | 10 | 11 | 8 | 12 |  |  |  |  |  |  |  |  |  |  | 4 |
| 1 | 2 | 3 | 4 | 5 | 6 |  | 12 | 9* | 10 | 11 | 8 |  | 7 |  |  |  |  |  |  |  |  |  | 5 |
| 1 | 2 | 3 | 4 | 5 | 6 |  |  | 9 | 10 | 11 | 8 |  | 7 |  |  |  |  |  |  |  |  |  | 6 |
| 1 | 2 | 3 | 4 | 5 | 6 |  |  | 9 | 10 | 11 | 8 |  | 7 |  |  |  |  |  |  |  |  |  | 7 |
| 1 | 2 | 3 | 4 | 5 | 6 |  |  | 9 | 10* | 11 | 8 | 12 | 7 |  |  |  |  |  |  |  |  |  | 8 |
| 1 | 2 | 3 | 4 | 5 | 6 |  |  | 9 | 10 | 11* | 8 |  | 7 | 12 |  |  |  |  |  |  |  |  | 9 |
| 1 | 2 | 3 | 4 | 5 | 6 |  |  | 9 | 10 | 11 | 8 |  | 7 |  |  |  |  |  |  |  |  |  | 10 |
| 1 | 2 | 3 | 4 | 5 | 6 |  | 12 | 9 | 10* | 11 | 8 |  | 7 |  |  |  |  |  |  |  |  |  | 11 |
| 1 | 2 | 3* | 4 | 5 |  |  |  | 9 | 10 | 11 | 8 | 12 | 6 | 7 |  |  |  |  |  |  |  |  | 12 |
| 1 | 2 |  | 4 |  |  |  |  | 9* | 10 | 11 | 8 | 6 | 5 |  |  | 3 |  |  | 7 | 12 |  |  | 13 |
| 1 | 2 |  | 4 |  |  |  |  | 9 | 10 | 11 | 8 | 6 | 5 |  |  | 3 |  |  | 7 |  |  |  | 14 |
| 1 | 2 |  | 4 |  |  |  | 12 | 9 | 10 | 11 | 8 | 6 | 5 |  |  | 3 |  |  | 7* |  |  |  | 15 |
| 1 | 2 |  | 4 |  |  | 7 |  | 9 | 10 | 11 | 8 | 6 | 5 |  |  | 3 |  |  |  |  |  |  | 16 |
| 1 | 2 |  | 4 |  |  |  |  | 9 | 10 | 11 | 8 | 6 | 5 |  |  | 3 |  |  | 7 |  |  |  | 17 |
| 1 | 2 |  | 4 |  |  |  | 12 | 9 | 10 | 11 | 8 | 6 | 5 |  |  | 3 |  |  | 7* |  |  |  | 18 |
| 1 | 2 |  | 4 |  |  |  |  | 9 | 10 | 11 | 8 | 6 | 5 |  | 7 | 3 |  |  |  |  |  |  | 19 |
| 1 | 2 |  | 4 |  |  |  |  | 9 | 10 | 11 | 8 | 6 | 5 |  |  | 3 |  |  | 7 |  |  |  | 20 |
| 1 |  |  | 4 | 5 |  |  |  | 9 | 10 | 11 | 8 | 6 | 2 |  |  | 3 |  |  | 7 |  |  |  | 21 |
| 1 |  |  | 4* | 5 |  |  |  | 9 | 10 | 11 | 8 | 6 | 2 | 12 |  | 3 |  |  | 7 |  |  |  | 22 |
| 1 | 2 |  | 4 | 5 |  |  |  | 9 | 10 | 11 | 8 | 6 |  |  |  | 3 |  |  | 7 |  |  |  | 23 |
| 1 | 2 |  | 4 |  |  |  |  | 9 | 10 | 11 | 8* | 6 | 5 |  |  | 3 |  |  | 7 | 12 |  |  | 24 |
| 1 | 2 |  | 4 |  |  |  |  | 9 | 10 | 11 |  | 6 | 5 |  |  | 3 |  |  | 7 | 8 |  |  | 25 |
| 1 | 2 |  | 4 |  |  |  |  | 9 | 10 | 11 |  | 6 | 5 |  |  | 3 |  |  | 7 | 8 |  |  | 26 |
| 1 | 2 |  | 4 |  |  |  |  | 9 | 10 | 11 |  | 6 | 5 |  |  | 3 |  |  | 7 | 8 |  |  | 27 |
| 1 | 2 |  | 4 |  |  |  | 12 | 9 |  | 11 | 8 | 6 | 5 |  |  | 3 |  |  | 7* | 10 |  |  | 28 |
| 1 | 2 |  | 4 |  |  |  |  | 9 |  | 11 | 8 | 6 | 5 |  |  | 3 |  |  | 7 | 10 |  |  | 29 |
| 1 | 2 |  | 4 |  |  |  | 12 | 9 |  | 11 | 8 | 6* | 5 |  |  | 3 |  |  | 7 | 10 |  |  | 30 |
| 1 | 2 |  | 4 |  |  |  |  | 9 |  | 11 | 8 | 6 | 5 |  |  | 3 |  |  | 7 | 10 |  |  | 31 |
| 1 | 2 |  | 4 |  |  |  |  | 9 |  | 11 | 8 | 6 | 5 |  |  | 3 |  |  | 7 | 10 |  |  | 32 |
| 1 | 2 |  | 4 |  |  |  |  | 9 |  | 11 | 8 | 6 | 5 |  |  | 3 |  |  | 7 | 10 |  |  | 33 |
| 1 | 2 |  | 4* |  |  |  |  | 9 | 12 | 11 | 8 | 6 | 5 |  |  | 3 |  |  | 7 | 10 |  |  | 34 |
| 1 | 2 |  | 4 | 5 |  |  | 12 | 9 |  | 11 | 8* | 6 |  |  |  | 3 |  |  | 7 | 10 |  |  | 35 |
| 1 | 2 |  | 4 | 5 |  |  |  | 9 |  | 11 | 8 | 6 |  |  |  | 3 |  |  | 7 | 10 |  |  | 36 |
| 1 | 2 |  | 4 | 5* |  |  |  | 9 | 12 | 11 | 8 | 6 |  |  |  | 3 |  |  | 7 | 10 |  |  | 37 |
| 1 | 2 |  | 4 |  |  |  |  | 9 | 12 | 11 | 8 | 6 | 5 |  |  | 3* |  |  | 7 | 10 |  |  | 38 |
| 1 | 2 | 3 |  |  |  |  |  | 9 | 10 | 11* | 8 | 6 | 5 |  |  |  |  |  | 7 | 4 | 12 |  | 39 |
| 1 | 2 |  | 4* |  |  |  |  | 9 |  | 11 | 8 | 6 | 5 |  |  | 3 |  |  | 7 | 10 | 12 |  | 40 |
| 1 | 2 |  | 4 | 5 | 6 |  |  | 9 | 12 | 11 | 8 |  |  |  |  | 3* |  |  | 7 | 10 |  |  | 41 |
| 1 |  |  | 4* | 5 | 6 |  |  | 9 | 12 | 11 | 8 | 2 |  |  |  | 3 |  |  | 7 | 10 |  |  | 42 |
| 42 | 38 | 13 | 40 | 20 | 13 | 5 | 3 | 42 | 28 | 42 | 37 | 28 | 27 | 8 | 1 | 29 | 5 | — | 23 | 16 | 2 | — |  |
|  |  |  |  |  |  |  | +7s |  | +5s | +2s | +2s | +1s | +1s | +1s |  | +1s |  |  | +1s | +2s |  |  |  |

# NEWCASTLE UNITED

| | Ht | Wt | Birthplace | Clubs | League App. | League Gls |
|---|---|---|---|---|---|---|
| **Goalkeepers** | | | | | | |
| Steve Hardwick | 5 11 | 13 0 | Mansfield | Chesterfield | 38 | — |
| | | | | Newcastle U | 85 | — |
| Kevin Carr | 6 2 | 13 6 | Ashington | Newcastle U | 98 | — |
| Simon Smith* | 5 9 | 11 5½ | Newton Aycliffe | Newcastle U | — | — |
| **Defenders** | | | | | | |
| David Barton | 6 0 | 11 7 | Bishop Auckland | Newcastle U | 102 | 5 |
| John Brownlie (Scotland) | 5 11 | 11 10 | Calder-Cruix | Hibernian | 211 | 14 |
| | | | | Newcastle U | 124 | 2 |
| Bruce Halliday | 5 11 | 11 2 | Sunderland | Newcastle U | 32 | 1 |
| Steve Carney | 5 10 | 11 5 | Wallsend | Blyth S | (not known) | |
| | | | | Newcastle U | 66 | — |
| Ian Davies* | 5 8 | 10 8 | Bristol | Norwich C | 32 | 2 |
| | | | | Newcastle U | 75 | 3 |
| Peter Haddock | 5 11 | 11 5 | Newcastle | Newcastle U | 30 | — |
| Philip Leaver* | 5 9½ | 11 3 | Derbyshire | Newcastle U | — | — |
| Peter Johnson | 5 8 | 10 4 | Harrogate | Middlesbrough | 43 | — |
| | | | | Newcastle U | 16 | — |
| Chris Withe | 5 10 | 11 3 | Speke | Newcastle U | 2 | — |
| Wesley Saunders | 6 0 | 11 11 | Sunderland | Newcastle U | 29 | — |
| Chris Hedworth | 6 1 | 10 11 | Newcastle | Newcastle U | — | — |
| **Midfield** | | | | | | |
| Kevin Pugh* | 5 7 | 10 13 | Newburn | Newcastle U | 1 | — |
| Ken Wharton | 5 8 | 8 10 | Newcastle | Newcastle U | 72 | 5 |
| Mick Martin (Eire) | 5 10 | 10 11 | Dublin | Manchester U | 40 | 2 |
| | | | | WBA | 89 | 11 |
| | | | | Newcastle U | 112 | 2 |
| Peter Cartwright | 5 7 | 10 0 | Newcastle | N Shields | (not known) | |
| | | | | Newcastle U | 61 | 3 |
| Frans Koenen (Contract cancelled Jan 1982) | 5 8 | 11 2 | Waalwijk | NEC Nijmegen | (not known) | |
| | | | | Newcastle U | 12 | 1 |
| John Trewick | 5 10 | 10 13 | Bedlington | WBA | 96 | 11 |
| | | | | Newcastle U | 61 | 7 |
| Justin Robson | 5 10½ | 11 5 | Witton Gilbert | Newcastle U | — | — |
| Geoff Smith* | | | | Newcastle U | — | — |
| Derek Bell | 5 8 | 11 4 | Newcastle | Newcastle U | 2 | — |
| William Snyder* | | | | Newcastle U | — | — |
| Paul Ferris (Apprentice) | | | | Newcastle U | 2 | — |
| **Forwards** | | | | | | |
| Chris Waddle | 6 0 | 11 5 | Gateshead | Tow Law T | (not known) | |
| | | | | Newcastle U | 55 | 8 |
| Gary Walton* | 5 11 | 11 9 | Coundon | Newcastle U | — | — |
| Nigel Walker* | 5 10 | 11 11 | Gateshead | Newcastle U | 70 | 3 |
| | | | | Plymouth Arg (on loan) | — | — |
| Alan Shoulder* | 5 5 | 10 5 | Bishop Auckland | Blyth S | — | — |
| | | | | Newcastle U | 107 | 35 |
| Ray Clarke (Retired, injury) | 6 0 | 11 7 | London | Tottenham H | 1 | — |
| | | | | Swindon T | 14 | 2 |
| | | | | Mansfield T | 91 | 52 |
| | | | | Sparta | (not known) | |
| | | | | Ajax | (not known) | |
| | | | | FC Bruges | (not known) | |
| | | | | Brighton | 30 | 8 |
| | | | | Newcastle U | 14 | 2 |
| Kevin Todd | 5 9 | 12 1 | Sunderland | Ryhope CA | (not known) | |
| | | | | Newcastle U | 2 | 2 |
| Imre Varadi | 5 8 | 11 1 | Paddington | Letchworth | (not known) | |
| | | | | Sheffield U | 10 | 4 |
| | | | | Everton | 26 | 6 |
| | | | | Newcastle U | 42 | 18 |

# NEWPORT COUNTY

## Division 3

*President:* S. Jenkins.
*Chairman:* R. Ford.
*Vice-Chairman:* G. C. Thorneycroft.
*Directors:* J. Ford, A. O. Menzies.
*Manager:* Colin Addison.
*Secretary:* Mr P. Dauncey.
*Commercial Manager:* P. Jones.
*Youth Development Officer:* G. E. A. Reynolds.
*Year Formed:* 1912.
*Turned Professional:* 1912.
*Limited Company:* 1912.

**Football League Record:**
1920 Original Member of Division 3; 1921 Division 3(S); dropped out of the Football League in 1931 but re-elected 1932; 1932–39 Division 3(S); 1946–47 Division 2; 1947–58 Division 3(S); 1958–62 Division 3; 1962–80 Division 4; 1980– Division 3.

**Honours:** *Football League:* Division 3 best season: 12th, 1980–81; Division 3(S) – Champions 1938–39. *FA Cup* best season: 5th rd, 1948–49. *Football League Cup:* never past 3rd rd. *Welsh Cup:* winners 1979–80. **European Competitions:** *European Cup-Winners' Cup:* 1980–81 (quarter-finalists).

*Record Victory:* 10-0 v Merthyr Town, Division 3(S), 10 Apr, 1930.

*Record Defeat:* 0-13 v Newcastle U, Division 2, 5 Oct, 1946.

*Most League Points:* 61, Division 4, 1979–80.

*Most League Goals:* 85, Division 4, 1964–65.

*Highest League Scorer in Season:* Tudor Martin, 34, Division 3(S), 1929–30.

*Most League Goals in Total Aggregate:* Reg Parker, 99, 1948–54.

*Most Capped Player:* Fred Cook, 2 (8), Jack Nicholls, 2 (4), Alf Sherwood, 2 (41), Billy Thomas, 2, Harold Williams, 2 (4), (all for Wales).

*Most League Appearances:* Len Weare, 526, 1955–70.

*Record Transfer Fee Received:* £50,000 from Luton T for Mark Aizlewood, March 1978.

*Record Transfer Fee Paid:* £80,000 to Swansea C for Alan Waddle, Jan 1981.

*Previous Managers since the War:* Billy McCandless, Tom Bromilow, Fred Stansfield, Bill Lucas, Bobby Evans, Bill Lucas, Trevor Morris, Les Graham, Bob Ferguson, Bill Lucas, Brian Harris, Dave Elliot, Jimmy Scoular, Colin Addison, Len Ashurst.

*Address of Supporters Club:* Same as Football Club.

---

**Somerton Park, Newport, Gwent.** Telephone 277543/277271/277472. *Ground capacity:* 18,000 (seating 1,200). *Record attendance:* 24,268 v Cardiff C, Division 3(S), 16 Oct, 1937. *Record receipts:* £28,050 v Carl Zeiss Jena, European Cup-Winners' Cup quarter-final 2nd leg, 18 Mar, 1981. *Pitch measurements:* 110yd×75yd.

*How to get there:* Nearest railway station, Newport. By bus: the Chepstow Road bus to Beechwood and walk down over Somerton Hill; the Corporation Road bus to Cromwell Road and Somerton Park. All buses from bus centre in Dock Street.

*Match tickets:* Seats can be reserved from the club secretary.

*Car parking:* Street parking under police control.

*Entertainments/catering facilities:* Licensed bar in Supporters' Club. Licensed bar in the Social Club at Cromwell Road; both membership only. Licensed bars on both sides of ground.

*Club shop:* Sells all types of souvenirs, including 1979–80 promotion book. Souvenir list available from Commercial Department.

*Handbooks/programmes:* Back issues of programmes available from programme shop. Match programmes available on subscription from Commercial Department.

*Club Colours:* Amber shirts, black shorts, amber stockings.

*Change Colours:* White shirts, black shorts, white stockings.

*First Team Trainer:* Dave Williams.

*Club Nickname:* The Ironsides.

## NEWPORT COUNTY 1981–82 LEAGUE RECORD

| Match No. | Date | Venue | Opponents | Result | H/T Score | Goalscorers | Attendance |
|---|---|---|---|---|---|---|---|
| 1 | Aug 29 | H | Chesterfield | W 1-0 | 1-0 | Johnson | 5079 |
| 2 | Sept 4 | A | Southend U | W 4-0 | 1-0 | Aldridge, Gwyther, Tynan, Elsey | 4620 |
| 3 | 12 | H | Oxford U | W 3-2 | 0-2 | Aldridge, Waddle 2 | 5293 |
| 4 | 19 | A | Bristol C | L 1-2 | 1-0 | Aldridge | 7552 |
| 5 | 23 | A | Reading | L 1-2 | 0-0 | Aldridge | 4542 |
| 6 | 26 | H | Preston NE | D 1-1 | 0-0 | Anderson (og) | 5064 |
| 7 | 29 | H | Brentford | L 0-1 | 0-0 | | 4028 |
| 8 | Oct 3 | A | Lincoln C | D 2-2 | 1-0 | Tynan 2 | 3351 |
| 9 | 10 | H | Doncaster R | W 1-0 | 0-0 | Gwyther | 4379 |
| 10 | 17 | A | Fulham | L 1-3 | 1-1 | Tynan | 3918 |
| 11 | 20 | H | Millwall | D 1-1 | 1-0 | Goddard | 4609 |
| 12 | 24 | A | Portsmouth | D 0-0 | 0-0 | | 8787 |
| 13 | 31 | H | Carlisle U | W 2-0 | 2-0 | Elsey 2 | 3972 |
| 14 | Nov 3 | A | Bristol R | L 0-2 | 0-1 | | 6464 |
| 15 | 7 | A | Walsall | L 1-3 | 0-2 | Oakes | 4169 |
| 16 | 14 | H | Plymouth Arg | L 0-1 | 0-0 | | 4427 |
| 17 | 28 | H | Exeter C | D 1-1 | 1-0 | Waddle | 4149 |
| 18 | Dec 5 | A | Wimbledon | W 3-2 | 2-0 | Tynan, Elsey, Waddle | 2056 |
| 19 | 26 | H | Chester | L 0-1 | 0-1 | | 4908 |
| 20 | 28 | A | Gillingham | D 1-1 | 0-1 | Moore | 6055 |
| 21 | Jan 2 | H | Reading | W 3-1 | 3-0 | Aldridge 2, Lowndes | 2948 |
| 22 | 16 | A | Burnley | L 1-2 | 1-0 | Moore | 4716 |
| 23 | 23 | A | Chesterfield | L 0-1 | 0-0 | | 4234 |
| 24 | 30 | H | Bristol C | D 1-1 | 1-1 | Vaughan | 5927 |
| 25 | Feb 6 | A | Oxford U | D 1-1 | 1-1 | Tynan (pen) | 5653 |
| 26 | 13 | H | Lincoln C | D 0-0 | 0-0 | | 3735 |
| 27 | 20 | A | Brentford | L 0-2 | 0-0 | | 4297 |
| 28 | 27 | A | Doncaster R | W 2-0 | 1-0 | Bishop, Aldridge | 4190 |
| 29 | Mar 7 | H | Fulham | L 1-3 | 0-0 | Lowndes | 5178 |
| 30 | 9 | A | Millwall | L 0-1 | 0-1 | | 3084 |
| 31 | 13 | H | Portsmouth | D 1-1 | 0-1 | Elsey | 4209 |
| 32 | 16 | H | Bristol R | D 1-1 | 1-1 | Tynan (pen) | 5312 |
| 33 | 20 | A | Carlisle U | D 2-2 | 0-2 | Aldridge, Tynan | 4042 |
| 34 | 27 | H | Walsall | D 2-2 | 2-2 | Serella (og), Tynan | 3484 |
| 35 | 30 | A | Huddersfield T | L 0-2 | 0-1 | | 4205 |
| 36 | Apr 2 | A | Plymouth Arg | W 2-1 | 0-0 | Elsey, Bishop | 5148 |
| 37 | 10 | A | Chester | W 2-0 | 0-0 | Aldridge 2 | 1451 |
| 38 | 12 | H | Gillingham | W 4-2 | 3-1 | Tynan (pen), Vaughan, Johnson, Gwyther | 4353 |
| 39 | 17 | H | Wimbledon | D 0-0 | 0-0 | | 3900 |
| 40 | 24 | A | Exeter C | L 0-1 | 0-1 | | 3168 |
| 41 | May 1 | H | Burnley | D 0-0 | 0-0 | | 4094 |
| 42 | 4 | A | Preston NE | L 1-2 | 0-1 | Vaughan | 4972 |
| 43 | 8 | A | Swindon T | D 1-1 | 1-1 | Aldridge | 5676 |
| 44 | 11 | H | Southend U | W 3-2 | 2-1 | Tynan 2 (1 pen), Elsey | 3716 |
| 45 | 15 | H | Huddersfield T | W 1-0 | 0-0 | Lowndes | 4169 |
| 46 | 18 | H | Swindon T | W 1-0 | 0-0 | Tynan (pen) | 5906 |

**Final League Position: 16**

**Goalscorers**

*League* (54): Tynan 13 (5 pens), Aldridge 11, Elsey 7, Waddle 4, Gwyther 3, Lowndes 3, Vaughan 3, Bishop 2, Johnson 2, Moore 2, Goddard 1, Oakes 1, own goals 2.
*League Cup* (3): Aldridge 1, Moore 1, Oakes 1.
*FA Cup* (0).

| League Cup | First Round | Torquay U (a) | 3-2 |
|---|---|---|---|
| | | (h) | 0-0 |
| | Second Round | Oldham Ath (a) | 0-1 |
| | | (h) | 0-0 |
| FA Cup | First Round | Colchester U (a) | 0-2 |

| Kendall | Elsey | Lees | Davies | Oakes | Bailey | Vaughan | Johnson | Gwyther | Aldridge | Moore | Waddle | Tynan | Relish | Walden | Lowndes | Goddard | Bishop | Thomas | Match No. |
|---|---|---|---|---|---|---|---|---|---|---|---|---|---|---|---|---|---|---|---|
| 1 | 2 | 3 | 4 | 5 | 6 | 7 | 8 | 9 | 10* | 11 | 12 | | | | | | | | 1 |
| 1 | 2 | 3 | 4 | 5 | 6 | 7 | 8 | 9 | 10* | 11 | | 12 | | | | | | | 2 |
| 1 | 2 | 3* | 4 | 5 | 6 | 7 | 8 | 9 | 10 | 11 | 12 | | | | | | | | 3 |
| 1 | 2 | 3 | 4 | 5 | 6 | 7 | 8 | 9 | 10* | 11 | | 12 | | | | | | | 4 |
| 1 | 2 | 3 | 4 | 5 | 6 | 7 | 8 | 9 | 10 | 11 | | | | | | | | | 5 |
| 1 | 2 | | 4 | 5 | | 7 | 8 | 12 | 10 | | 9 | 6 | 3 | 11* | | | | | 6 |
| 1 | 2 | | 4 | 5 | 6 | 7 | | 12 | 10 | 11 | 9 | 8 | | 3* | | | | | 7 |
| 1 | 2 | | 4* | 5 | 6 | 7 | | 9 | 10 | 11 | | 8 | | 3 | 12 | | | | 8 |
| 1 | 2 | | 4 | 5 | 6 | 7 | | 9 | | 11 | | 8 | | 3 | 10 | | | | 9 |
| 1 | 2 | 4 | | 5 | 6 | 7 | | 9 | | 11 | | 8 | | 3 | 10 | | | | 10 |
| 1 | 2 | | 4* | 5 | 6 | 7 | 3 | 9 | | | 12 | 8 | | | 10 | 11 | | | 11 |
| 1 | 11 | | 4 | 5 | 6 | 7 | 8 | | 10* | | 12 | 3 | 2 | | 9 | | | | 12 |
| 1 | 9 | | 4 | 5 | 6 | 7 | 8 | 10 | | 12 | | 3 | 2 | 11* | | | | | 13 |
| 1 | 11 | | 4 | 5 | 6* | 7 | 8 | 9 | | 12 | | 3 | 2 | | 10 | | | | 14 |
| 1 | 2 | | | 5 | 6 | 7 | 8 | | 10 | | 9 | 11 | 4* | 3 | 12 | | | | 15 |
| 1 | 11 | | 4 | 5 | 6 | 7 | | 10 | | 9 | 12 | 3 | 2* | 8 | | | | | 16 |
| 1 | 11 | | 4 | 5 | 6 | 7 | | | 9 | 10 | 3* | 2 | 8 | | 12 | | | | 17 |
| 1 | 11 | | 4 | 5 | 6 | 7 | | | 9 | 10 | 3 | 2* | 8 | | 12 | | | | 18 |
| 1 | | 2 | 4 | 5 | | 7 | 6 | 9 | 10 | 11 | | 3 | | 8 | | | | | 19 |
| 1 | | 2 | 4 | 5 | | 7 | 6 | | 10 | 11 | | 9 | 3 | 8 | | | | | 20 |
| 1 | 6 | 2 | 4 | 5* | | 7 | | | 10 | 11 | 12 | 9 | 3 | 8 | | | | | 21 |
| 1 | 6 | 2 | 5 | 4 | | 7 | | | | 11 | | 9 | 3 | 8 | 10 | | | | 22 |
| 1 | 8 | 2* | 4 | 5 | | 7 | 6 | | 12 | 11 | 10 | 9 | 3 | | | | | | 23 |
| 1 | 8 | 2 | 4 | 5 | | 7 | 6 | | 9* | 11 | 10 | 12 | 3 | | | | | | 24 |
| 1 | 8 | 2 | 4 | 5 | | 7 | 6 | | | 11 | 10 | 9 | 3 | | | | | | 25 |
| 1 | | 2 | 4 | 5 | | 7 | 6 | 12 | 11 | 10 | 9* | 3 | | 8 | | | | | 26 |
| 1 | 6 | | 4 | 5 | | 7 | | 12 | 11* | 10 | 9 | 3 | 2 | 8 | | | | | 27 |
| 1 | 8 | 2 | 4 | 5 | | 7 | 6 | 9 | 11* | 12 | | 3 | | | 10 | | | | 28 |
| 1 | 8 | 2 | 4 | 5 | | 7 | 6 | 9 | | | | 3 | | 11 | 10 | | | | 29 |
| 1 | 8 | 2 | 4 | 5 | | 7 | 6 | 12 | 9 | | | 3 | | 11 | 10* | | | | 30 |
| 1 | 8 | 2 | 4 | 5 | | 7 | | 10 | 9 | 3 | | 6* | | 11 | 12 | | | | 31 |
| 1 | 8 | 2 | 4 | 5 | | 7 | | 10 | 9 | 3* | 12 | 6 | | 11 | | | | | 32 |
| 1 | 8 | 2 | 4 | 5 | | 7 | 6 | 10* | 9 | | | 3 | | 11 | 12 | | | | 33 |
| 1 | 7 | 2* | 4 | | 3 | 6 | | 11 | 10 | 12 | | 9 | | 8 | | 5 | | | 34 |
| 1 | 8 | | 4 | 5 | | 3 | 6 | 11* | 9 | | 10 | | 2 | 7 | 12 | | | | 35 |
| 1 | 7 | | | 5 | | 3 | 6 | | 10 | 11 | | 9 | | 2 | | 8 | 4 | | 36 |
| 1 | 7 | | | 5 | | 3 | 6 | 8* | 10 | 11 | | 9 | | 2 | 12 | | 4 | | 37 |
| 1 | 7 | | 4 | 5 | | 3 | 6 | 12 | 10 | 11 | | 9 | | 2* | 8 | | | | 38 |
| 1 | 7 | | 4 | 5 | | | 6 | 12 | 10* | 11 | | 9 | 3 | 2 | 8 | | | | 39 |
| 1 | 7 | | 4 | 5 | | | 6 | 12 | 10 | 11* | | 9 | 3 | 2 | 8 | | | | 40 |
| 1 | | 4 | | 5 | | 7 | 6 | 10 | | 11 | | 9 | 3 | 2 | 8 | | | | 41 |
| 1 | | | 4 | 5 | | 7 | 6 | 10 | 12 | 11 | | 9 | 3 | 2* | 8 | | | | 42 |
| 1 | 11 | 2 | 4 | 5 | | 7 | 6 | 10 | | | | 9 | 3 | | 8 | | | | 43 |
| 1 | 11 | 2* | 4 | 5 | | 7 | 6 | 10 | | | | 9 | 3 | | 8 | 12 | | | 44 |
| 1 | 11 | | 4 | 5 | | 7 | 6 | 10 | | | | 9 | 3 | 2 | 8 | | | | 45 |
| 1 | 11 | | 4 | 5 | 12 | 7 | 6 | 10* | | | | 9 | 3 | 2 | 8 | | | | 46 |
| 46 | 40 | 25 | 41 | 45 | 17 | 44 | 34 | 20 | 32 | 28 | 11 | 32 | 28 | 23 | 28 | 4 | 5 | 3 | |
| | | | | + | | | | + | + | + | + | + | | | + | + | | | |
| | | | | 1s | | | | 6s | 4s | 1s | 7s | 6s | | | 3s | 6s | | | |

## NEWPORT COUNTY

| | Ht | Wt | Birthplace | Clubs | League App. | League Gls |
|---|---|---|---|---|---|---|
| **Goalkeepers** | | | | | | |
| Mark Kendall | 6 0 | 12 4 | Blackwood | Tottenham H | 29 | — |
| | | | | Chesterfield (on loan) | 9 | — |
| | | | | Newport Co | 74 | — |
| Ian Watson | 5 11 | 12 1 | North Shields | Sunderland | 1 | — |
| | | | | Rochdale (on loan) | 33 | — |
| | | | | Newport Co | — | — |
| **Defenders** | | | | | | |
| Grant Davies | 5 10 | 11 4 | Barrow | Preston NE | — | — |
| | | | | Newport Co | 141 | 1 |
| John Relish | 5 8 | 12 0 | Liverpool | Chester | 11 | 1 |
| | | | | Bury (on loan) | — | — |
| | | | | Newport Co | 223 | 6 |
| Richard Walden* | 6 0 | 12 0 | Hereford | Aldershot | 405 | 16 |
| | | | | Sheffield W | 100 | 1 |
| | | | | Newport Co | 151 | 2 |
| Keith Oakes | 5 10 | 12 2 | Bedworth | Peterborough U | 62 | 2 |
| | | | | Newport Co | 167 | 25 |
| Terry Lees | 5 8 | 11 0 | Stoke | Stoke C | 24 | — |
| | | | | Crewe Alex (on loan) | 6 | — |
| | | | | San José E | (not known) | |
| | | | | Port Vale | 41 | 2 |
| | | | | Roda | (not known) | |
| | | | | Sparta | (not known) | |
| | | | | Birmingham C | 12 | — |
| | | | | Newport Co | 25 | — |
| Rod Thomas | 6 2½ | 13 1 | Glyncorrwg | Swindon T | 296 | 5 |
| (Wales) | | | | Derby Co | 89 | 2 |
| | | | | Cardiff C | 96 | — |
| | | | | Newport Co | 3 | — |
| **Midfield** | | | | | | |
| Nigel Vaughan | 5 5 | 8 10 | Newport | Newport Co | 174 | 20 |
| Neil Bailey | 5 9 | 11 0 | Wigan | Burnley | — | — |
| | | | | Newport Co | 89 | 3 |
| Karl Elsey | 5 10 | 11 6 | Pembroke | QPR | 7 | — |
| | | | | Newport Co | 74 | 9 |
| Jeff Johnson | 5 8 | 11 12 | Cardiff | Manchester C | 6 | — |
| | | | | Swansea C (on loan) | 39 | 4 |
| | | | | Crystal Palace | 87 | 4 |
| | | | | Sheffield W | 180 | 6 |
| | | | | Newport Co | 34 | 2 |
| **Forwards** | | | | | | |
| John Aldridge | 5 11 | 10 4 | Liverpool | Newport Co | 101 | 32 |
| Steve Lowndes | 5 7 | 10 7 | Cwmbran | Newport Co | 165 | 27 |
| Kevin Moore | 5 9 | 11 4 | Blackpool | Blackpool | 38 | 3 |
| | | | | Swansea C | 55 | 6 |
| | | | | Bury (on loan) | 4 | — |
| | | | | Newport Co | 134 | 13 |
| Tommy Tynan | 5 10 | 13 0 | Liverpool | Liverpool | — | — |
| | | | | Swansea C (on loan) | 6 | 2 |
| | | | | Sheffield W | 91 | 31 |
| | | | | Lincoln C | 9 | 1 |
| | | | | Newport Co | 137 | 41 |
| Dave Gwyther | 5 10 | 13 4 | Birmingham | Swansea | 217 | 59 |
| | | | | Halifax T | 104 | 26 |
| | | | | Rotherham U | 162 | 45 |
| | | | | Crewe Alex (on loan) | 7 | 1 |
| | | | | Newport Co | 86 | 26 |
| Alan Waddle* | 6 3 | 12 6 | Wallsend | Halifax T | 39 | 4 |
| | | | | Liverpool | 16 | 1 |
| | | | | Leicester C | 11 | 1 |
| | | | | Swansea C | 90 | 34 |
| | | | | Newport Co | 27 | 8 |
| Ray Bishop | 5 10 | 11 0 | Hengoed | Cardiff C | 101 | 26 |
| | | | | Newport Co | 18 | 2 |
| Paul Bodin* | | | | Newport Co | — | — |

# NORTHAMPTON TOWN  Division 4

*Chairman:* N. J. Ronson.

*Vice-Chairman:* S. Wilson.

*Directors:* E. P. Northover, W. M. Griggs.

*Secretary/General Manager:* Dave Bowen.

*Manager:* Clive Walker.

*Commercial Executive:* G. Moody.

*Year Formed:* 1897.   *Turned Professional:* 1901.

*Limited Company:* 1901.

**Football League Record:**
1920 Original Member of Division 3; 1921 Division 3(S); 1958–61
Division 4; 1961–63 Division 3; 1963–65 Division 2; 1965–66
Division 1; 1966–67 Division 2; 1967–68 Division 3; 1968–76 Division 4; 1976–77 Division 3; 1977–
Division 4.

**Honours:** *Football League:* Division 1 best season: 21st, 1965–66; Division 2 – Runners-up 1964–65;
Division 3 – Champions 1962–63; Division 3(S) – Runners-up 1927–28, 1949–50; Division 4 – Promoted 1960–61 (3rd); Runners-up 1975–76. *FA Cup* best season: 5th rd, 1933–34, 1949–50, 1969–70.
*Football League Cup* best season: 5th rd, 1964–65, 1966–67.

*Record Victory:* 10-0 v Walsall, Division 3(S), 5 Nov, 1927.

*Record Defeat:* 0-10 v Bournemouth, Division 3(S), 2 Sept, 1939.

*Most League Points:* 68, Division 4, 1975–76.

*Most League Goals:* 109, Division 3, 1962–63; Division 3(S), 1952–53.

*Highest League Scorer in Season:* Cliff Holton, 36, Division 3, 1961–62.

*Most League Goals in Total Aggregate:* Jack English, 135, 1947–60.

*Most Capped Player:* E. Lloyd Davies, 12 (16), Wales.

*Most League Appearances:* Tommy Fowler, 521, 1946–61 (39 FA Cup ties).

*Record Transfer Fee Received:* £140,000 from Cambridge U for George Reilly, Nov 1979.

*Record Transfer Fee Paid:* £40,000 to Brentford for Steve Phillips, Aug 1980.

*Previous Managers since the War:* T. Smith, Bob Dennison, David Smith, Dave Bowen, Tony Marchi,
Ron Flowers, Bill Baxter, Bill Dodgin (Jnr), Pat Crerand, John Petts, Mike Keen, Clive Walker, Bill
Dodgin (Jnr).

*Address of Supporters Club:* 195, Abington Avenue, Northampton.

**County Ground, Abington Avenue, Northampton NN1 4PS.** Telephone Northampton 31553. *Ground capacity:* 17,000 (seating 1,400). *Record attendance:* 24,523 v Fulham, Division 1, 23 April, 1966. *Record receipts:* £17,438 v Manchester U. *Pitch measurements:* 120yd×75yd.

*How to get there:* Nearest railway station, Northampton. Any bus to the town centre, then from Mercer's Row, buses 1, 21, 2 and 14, though only 2 goes right to the ground.

*Match tickets:* No pre-match booking.

*Car parking:* No car park, but ample space in nearby side-streets.

*Entertainments/catering facilities:* Refreshment in hotel and tea bars on ground.

*Club shop:* 195 Abington Ave – opposite club. Run by the Supporters Club; sells all types of souvenirs.

*Handbooks/programmes:* Programmes available from the Supporters Club.

*Extra information:* Ground is shared with Northamptonshire County Cricket Club.

*Club Colours:* White shirts, claret trim, claret shorts, white stockings.

*Change Colours:* Yellow shirts, claret trim, yellow shorts, yellow stockings.

*Club Nickname:* Cobblers.

## NORTHAMPTON TOWN 1981–82 LEAGUE RECORD

| Match No. | Date | Venue | Opponents | Result | H/T Score | Goalscorers | Attendance |
|---|---|---|---|---|---|---|---|
| 1 | Aug 29 | H | Scunthorpe U | D 1-1 | 1-0 | Heeley | 2064 |
| 2 | Sept 4 | A | York C | L 1-2 | 0-1 | Phillips | 2086 |
| 3 | 12 | H | Hull C | D 1-1 | 1-0 | Denyer (pen) | 1938 |
| 4 | 19 | A | Wigan Ath | L 1-3 | 0-0 | Denyer | 3996 |
| 5 | 21 | A | Mansfield T | L 1-4 | 0-2 | Brady | 2612 |
| 6 | 26 | H | Hereford U | L 2-3 | 1-1 | Phillips 2 | 1552 |
| 7 | 29 | H | Stockport Co | D 0-0 | 0-0 | | 1865 |
| 8 | Oct 2 | A | Colchester U | L 1-5 | 0-2 | Denyer (pen) | 2760 |
| 9 | 10 | A | AFC Bournemouth | D 1-1 | 0-1 | Denyer | 5241 |
| 10 | 13 | H | Blackpool | L 0-1 | 0-1 | | 2376 |
| 11 | 17 | H | Bradford C | L 0-2 | 0-0 | | 2053 |
| 12 | 21 | A | Torquay U | D 2-2 | 0-1 | Heeley, Sandy | 2414 |
| 13 | 24 | H | Tranmere R | W 3-2 | 0-2 | Buchanan 2, Bramhall (og) | 1722 |
| 14 | 31 | A | Bury | L 1-7 | 0-4 | Phillips (pen) | 3459 |
| 15 | Nov 3 | H | Sheffield U | L 1-2 | 0-0 | Phillips | 4168 |
| 16 | 8 | H | Crewe Alex | W 3-0 | 0-0 | Phillips, Saxby, Brady | 2794 |
| 17 | 14 | A | Hartlepool U | L 1-3 | 0-1 | Phillips | 1637 |
| 18 | 28 | A | Peterborough U | L 0-1 | 0-1 | | 5293 |
| 19 | Dec 5 | H | Darlington | L 0-1 | 0-0 | | 1669 |
| 20 | Jan 23 | A | Scunthorpe U | L 1-2 | 0-2 | Perrin | 1439 |
| 21 | 30 | H | Wigan Ath | L 2-3 | 2-1 | Denyer, Perrin | 2418 |
| 22 | Feb 2 | H | Port Vale | L 3-5 | 0-4 | Alexander, Phillips, Saxby | 1644 |
| 23 | 6 | A | Hull C | W 1-0 | 1-0 | Alexander | 3341 |
| 24 | 9 | H | Mansfield T | D 1-1 | 1-0 | Alexander | 1945 |
| 25 | 14 | H | Colchester U | L 1-2 | 0-1 | Coffill | 3102 |
| 26 | 17 | A | Blackpool | L 0-1 | 0-1 | | 2231 |
| 27 | 20 | A | Hereford U | L 1-2 | 0-1 | Phillips | 2229 |
| 28 | 23 | A | Aldershot | L 1-2 | 0-1 | Phillips (pen) | 1171 |
| 29 | 27 | H | AFC Bournemouth | W 1-0 | 1-0 | Gage | 2125 |
| 30 | Mar 2 | H | Rochdale | W 2-1 | 0-0 | Massey, Gage | 1916 |
| 31 | 7 | A | Bradford C | L 1-2 | 0-1 | Perrin | 4836 |
| 32 | 9 | H | Torquay U | W 2-0 | 1-0 | Massey, Alexander | 1959 |
| 33 | 13 | A | Tranmere R | W 2-0 | 1-0 | Perrin, Saxby | 1193 |
| 34 | 16 | A | Sheffield U | L 3-7 | 0-3 | Massey 2 (1 pen), Perrin | 15,016 |
| 35 | 20 | H | Bury | W 1-0 | 1-0 | Bradley (og) | 2109 |
| 36 | 23 | H | York C | W 5-0 | 3-0 | Buchanan 2, Czuczman (og), Sandy, Aitken (og) | 2452 |
| 37 | 27 | A | Crewe Alex | D 2-2 | 2-0 | Saxby 2 | 1801 |
| 38 | Apr 3 | H | Hartlepool U | W 2-1 | 1-1 | Saxby, Coffill | 1890 |
| 39 | 10 | H | Aldershot | D 0-0 | 0-0 | | 2365 |
| 40 | 12 | A | Port Vale | L 0-1 | 0-1 | | 3012 |
| 41 | 17 | A | Darlington | L 0-3 | 0-1 | | 1729 |
| 42 | 20 | H | Halifax T | L 0-1 | 0-0 | | 1935 |
| 43 | 24 | H | Peterborough U | W 1-0 | 1-0 | Saxby | 4975 |
| 44 | 30 | A | Stockport Co | D 0-0 | 0-0 | | 1658 |
| 45 | May 4 | A | Halifax T | L 1-2 | 1-0 | Sandy | 1730 |
| 46 | 15 | A | Rochdale | L 3-5 | 3-2 | Heeley, Massey (pen), Sandy | 1056 |

**Final League Position: 22**

### Goalscorers

*League* (57): Phillips 10 (2 pens), Saxby 7, Denyer 5 (2 pens), Massey 5 (2 pens), Perrin 5, Alexander 4, Buchanan 4, Sandy 4, Heeley 3, Brady 2, Coffill 2, Gage 2, own goals 4.
*League Cup* (9): Denyer 2, Mahoney 2, Alexander 1, Heeley 1, Phillips 1, Sandy 1, Saxby 1.
*FA Cup* (6): Gage 2, Carlton 1, Mahoney 1, Phillips 1, Sandy 1.

| **League Cup** | First Round | Hartlepool U (h) | 2-0 |
|---|---|---|---|
| | | (a) | 1-2 |
| | Second Round | Bristol R (a) | 2-1 |
| | | (h) | 3-1 |
| | Third Round | Manchester C (a) | 1-3 |
| **FA Cup** | First Round | Weymouth (a) | 0-0 |
| | | (h) | 6-2 |
| | Second Round | Bristol C (a) | 0-3 |

| Poole | Brady | Saunders | Farmer | Denyer | Coffill | Carlton | Heeley | Phillips | Bowen | Alexander | Sandy | Gage | Saxby | Taylor | Buchanan | Russell | Mahoney | Perrin | Kruse | Massey | Bryant | Muir | Belfon | Match No. |
|---|---|---|---|---|---|---|---|---|---|---|---|---|---|---|---|---|---|---|---|---|---|---|---|---|
| 1 | 2 | 3* | 4 | 5 | 6 | 7 | 8 | 9 | 10 | 11 | 12 | | | | | | | | | | | | | 1 |
| 1 | 2 | | 4 | 5 | | 7 | 8 | 6* | 9 | 10 | 11 | 12 | 3 | | | | | | | | | | | 2 |
| 1 | 2 | 4* | 3 | | 6 | 7 | | 9 | 10 | 11 | 8 | 5 | 12 | | | | | | | | | | | 3 |
| 1 | 2 | 12 | 4* | 7 | 6 | 3 | | 9 | | 11 | 8 | 5 | 10 | | | | | | | | | | | 4 |
| 1 | 2 | 4 | 3 | | 6 | 7 | | 9 | 10 | 11 | 8 | 5 | | | | | | | | | | | | 5 |
| 1 | 5 | 12 | | 7 | 6 | | 3* | 10 | 9 | 11 | 8 | 5 | 2 | | | | | | | | | | | 6 |
| 1 | 4 | | | 7 | 6 | | 12 | 10 | | 11* | 8 | 5 | 3 | 2 | 9 | | | | | | | | | 7 |
| 1 | 4 | | | | 6 | 7 | 3 | | 10 | 11 | 8 | 5 | | 2 | 9 | | | | | | | | | 8 |
| 1 | 4 | | | 5 | 6 | 7 | 3 | | 10 | 11* | 8 | | 12 | 2 | 9 | | | | | | | | | 9 |
| 1 | 4 | | | 5 | 6 | 7 | 3 | 9 | 10 | 11 | 8 | | 12 | 2* | | | | | | | | | | 10 |
| 1 | 11 | 12 | | 5 | | 7 | 3 | 8* | 10 | 4 | 6 | 2 | 9 | | | | | | | | | | | 11 |
| 1 | 4 | | | | 6 | 7 | 3 | 9 | 10 | 11 | 5 | | | 2 | 8 | | | | | | | | | 12 |
| 1 | 8 | | | 5 | 6* | 7 | 3 | 12 | 10 | | 4 | | | 2 | 9 | | 11 | | | | | | | 13 |
| 1 | 8 | 12 | | | 6 | 7 | 3 | 9* | 10 | | 4 | | | 2 | 5 | | 11 | | | | | | | 14 |
| 1 | 4 | 9 | | | 6 | | 8 | | 10 | | 5 | 3 | | 2 | 7 | | 11 | | | | | | | 15 |
| 1 | 5 | 7 | | | | 9 | 8 | | 10 | 12 | 4 | 3 | | 2 | 6* | | 11 | | | | | | | 16 |
| 1 | 4 | 6 | | | | | 8 | | 10 | 9 | 5 | 3 | | 2 | 7 | | 11 | | | | | | | 17 |
| 1 | 4 | 9 | | | | 7 | | | 10 | 11 | 6 | 5 | 3 | 2 | 8 | | | | | | | | | 18 |
| 1 | 5 | 9 | | | | | 8 | | 10 | 6 | 4 | 3 | 2 | 7 | | | 11 | | | | | | | 19 |
| 1 | 4 | 6 | | | 12 | | | | 7 | 11 | 8 | 10 | 5 | 3 | 2* | | | 9 | | | | | | 20 |
| 1 | 5 | | | 7 | | 2 | | 9 | | 11 | 6 | 4 | 3 | | 8 | | | 10 | | | | | | 21 |
| 1 | 4 | 6 | | 2 | | 11 | | 10 | | 7 | 5 | 3 | | | 8 | | | 9 | | | | | | 22 |
| 1 | 4* | 3 | | 6 | 2 | 11 | | 10 | 7 | 12 | 5 | | | | 8 | | | 9 | | | | | | 23 |
| 1 | 5 | 3 | | 7 | 2 | 11 | | 9 | 6 | | 4 | | | | 8 | | | 10 | | | | | | 24 |
| 1 | | 3 | | 6 | 7 | 2 | | 9 | | 11 | 8 | 5 | 4 | | | | | 10 | | | | | | 25 |
| 1 | | 3 | | 8 | 7 | 9 | | 10 | | 11 | 6 | 4 | 2 | | | | | | 5 | | | | | 26 |
| 1 | | 3 | | 11 | 6 | 2 | 7 | 9 | | 12 | 5 | | 8 | | | | | 10* | 4 | | | | | 27 |
| 1 | 8 | 3 | | 7 | 2 | 6 | | | 11 | 10 | 4 | | 9 | | | | | | 5 | | | | | 28 |
| 1 | 2 | 3 | | 6 | | | | 10 | | 9 | 5 | 8 | 11 | | | | | | 4 | 7 | | | | 29 |
| 1 | 2 | 3 | | 8 | | 12 | 10 | 6* | | 4 | 11 | 7 | | | | | | | 5 | 9 | | | | 30 |
| 1 | 2 | 3 | | 6 | 8*11 | | 12 | | | 4 | 7 | | | | | | | 9 | 5 | 10 | | | | 31 |
| 1 | 2 | 3 | | 6 | | | | 9 | 8 | 4 | 7 | | | | | | | 10 | 5 | 11 | | | | 32 |
| 1 | 2 | 3 | | 8 | | | | 6 | | 4 | 11 | 7 | | | | | | 10 | 5 | 9 | | | | 33 |
| 1 | 2 | 3 | | 6 | | 12 | | 8* | | 4 | 7 | 9 | | | | | | 11 | 5 | 10 | | | | 34 |
| 1 | 2 | | 6 | 3 | 9* | | | 12 | | 4 | 7 | 8 | | | | | | 10 | 5 | 11 | | | | 35 |
| 1 | 2 | | 7 | 3 | | 8 | | 4 | | 6 | 9 | | | | | | | 10 | 5 | 11 | | | | 36 |
| 1 | 2 | | 6 | 3 | | 4 | 7 | | | | 8 | | | | | | | 10 | 5 | 11 | 9 | | | 37 |
| 1 | 11 | | 6 | 3 | 10* | 12 | | 4 | | 7 | 8 | | | | | | | | 5 | 9 | 2 | | | 38 |
| 1 | 9 | | 6 | 3 | | 12 | | 4 | | 7 | 8* | | | | | | 11 | | 5 | 10 | 2 | | | 39 |
| 1 | 2 | 5 | | 6 | 3 | | 8 | 4 | | 7 | | 10 | | | | | | | 11 | 9 | | | | 40 |
| 1 | 2 | | 6 | 3 | | 11 | | 4 | | 7 | 8 | | | | | | | | 5 | 10 | 9 | | | 41 |
| 1 | 2 | 5 | 6 | 3 | | 10 | | 4 | | 7 | 8* | | | | | | | | 11 | 9 | 12 | | | 42 |
| 1 | 2 | | 6 | 3 | 11 | | | 4 | | 7 | 8 | | | 9 | | | | 10 | 5 | | | | | 43 |
| 1 | | 6 | 2 | 3 | | 4 | 7 | | | 8 | | 11 | | 5 | | | 10 | 9 | | | | | | 44 |
| 1 | 12 | 7 | 2 | 6* | | 10 | | 4 | 9 | 8 | | | | | | | 5 | 11 | 3 | | | | | 45 |
| 1 | | 7 | 6 | | 10 | | 4 | | | 2 | | 9 | | | | | 5 | 11 | 3 | | 8 | | | 46 |
| 46 | 38 | 21 | 4 | 22 | 34 | 37 | 23 | 30 | 3 | 21 | 30 | 43 | 32 | 17 | 34 | — | 6 | 18 | 18 | 18 | 10 | — | 1 | |
| | +1s | +3s | | +2s | +3s | +1s | +9s | | | | | +2s | | | +1s | | | | | | +1s | | | |

## NORTHAMPTON TOWN

| | Ht | Wt | Birthplace | Clubs | League App. | League Gls |
|---|---|---|---|---|---|---|
| **Goalkeepers** | | | | | | |
| Andy Poole* | 6 0 | 12 2 | Chesterfield | Mansfield T | — | — |
| | | | | Northampton T | 141 | — |
| **Defenders** | | | | | | |
| Paul Saunders | 5 10 | 12 8 | Watford | Watford | — | — |
| | | | | Northampton T | 92 | 3 |
| Des Waldock | 5 11 | 11 6 | Northampton | Northampton T | 54 | 4 |
| (Contract cancelled Sept 1981) | | | | | | |
| Wakeley Gage | 6 4 | 13 7 | Northampton | Northampton T | 95 | 4 |
| Peter Cooke | 6 0 | 12 0 | Northampton | Northampton T | 5 | 1 |
| (Non-contract) | | | | | | |
| Andy Taylor* | 5 8 | 10 8 | Stratford-on- | Aston V | — | — |
| | | | Avon | Northampton T | 17 | — |
| Paul Brady | 5 11 | 10 8 | Birmingham | Birmingham C | — | — |
| | | | | Northampton T | 39 | 2 |
| Steve Bryant* | 5 8 | 10 6 | London | Birmingham C | 36 | 1 |
| | | | | Sheffield W (on loan) | 3 | — |
| | | | | Northampton T | 97 | 5 |
| | | | | Portsmouth | 111 | 5 |
| | | | | Northampton T | 10 | — |
| **Midfield** | | | | | | |
| Peter Denyer | 5 11 | 11 9 | Haslemere | Portsmouth | 131 | 15 |
| | | | | Northampton T | 113 | 23 |
| Gary Saxby | 5 8 | 10 3 | Mansfield | Mansfield T | 16 | 1 |
| | | | | Northampton T | 68 | 8 |
| Adam Sandy | 5 10 | 11 4 | Peterborough | Northampton T | 97 | 5 |
| Gary Leonard | 5 8 | 10 10 | Northampton | Northampton T | 2 | — |
| (Contract cancelled Sept 1981) | | | | | | |
| David Carlton* | 5 10½ | 11 10 | London | Fulham | 9 | — |
| | | | | Northampton T | 104 | 6 |
| | | | | Brentford | 140 | 7 |
| | | | | Northampton T | 76 | 1 |
| Peter Coffill | 5 8 | 10 8 | Romford | Watford | 63 | 6 |
| | | | | Torquay U | 122 | 11 |
| | | | | Northampton T | 36 | 2 |
| John Buchanan | 5 9 | 10 9 | Dingwall | Northampton T | 114 | 25 |
| | | | | Cardiff C | 231 | 54 |
| | | | | Northampton T | 34 | 4 |
| Maurice Muir | 5 9 | 11 0 | Tooting | Northampton T | 2 | — |
| (Non-contract) | | | | | | |
| Mark Heeley* | 5 6 | 9 6 | Peterborough | Peterborough U | 17 | 3 |
| | | | | Arsenal | 15 | 1 |
| | | | | Northampton T | 70 | 5 |
| **Forwards** | | | | | | |
| Kevin Farmer* | 6 0 | 12 0 | Kent | Leicester C | 1 | — |
| | | | | Northampton T | 77 | 12 |
| John Alexander | 6 0 | 11 0 | Liverpool | Millwall | 15 | 2 |
| (Contract cancelled April 1982) | | | | Reading | 25 | 9 |
| | | | | Northampton T | 22 | 4 |
| Steve Perrin | 6 1 | 12 3 | London | Crystal Palace | 48 | 11 |
| (Non-contract) | | | | Plymouth Arg | 35 | 6 |
| | | | | Portsmouth | 28 | 3 |
| | | | | Northampton T | 18 | 5 |
| Steve Massey | 5 11 | 11 5 | Denton | Stockport Co | 101 | 20 |
| | | | | Bournemouth | 97 | 19 |
| | | | | Peterborough U | 18 | 2 |
| | | | | Northampton T | 18 | 5 |
| Roger Russell | 5 8 | 10 4 | Corby | Northampton T | 1 | — |
| (Non-contract) | | | | | | |
| Frank Belfon | 5 9 | 11 3 | Wellingborough | Northampton T | 1 | — |

# NORWICH CITY
## Division 1

*President:* J. L. Hanly JP.  *Chairman:* Sir A. South JP.
*Vice-Chairman:* G. C. Watling.
*Directors:* D. S. McCall, E. A. Burrell, I. D. Coutts FCA.
*Manager:* Ken Brown.
*Commercial Manager:* N. S. MacKay.
*Secretary:* N. S. Pleasants.
*Year Formed:* 1905.  *Turned Professional:* 1905.
*Limited Company:* 1905.
*Previous Grounds:* 1905, Newmarket Road; 1908, The Nest, Rosary
Road; 1935, Carrow Road.

**NORWICH CITY FC**

**Football League Record:**
1920 Original Member of Division 3; 1921 Division 3(S); 1934–39
Division 2; 1946–60 Division 3; 1960–72 Division 2; 1972–74 Division 1; 1974–75 Division 2; 1975–81
Division 1; 1981–82 Division 2; 1982– Division 1.

**Honours:** *Football League:* Division 1 best season: 10th, 1975–76; Division 2 – Champions 1971–72;
Division 3(S) – Champions 1933–34; Division 3 – Runners-up 1959–60. *FA Cup:* semi-finals 1959.
*Football League Cup:* Winners 1962; Runners-up 1973, 1975.

*Record Victory:* 10-2 v Coventry C, Division 3(S), 15 Mar, 1930.
*Record Defeat:* 2-10 v Swindon T, Southern League, 5 Sept, 1908.
*Most League Points:* 64, Division 3(S), 1950–51. *Three points win:* 71, Division 2, 1981–82.
*Most League Goals:* 99, Division 3(S), 1952–53.
*Highest League Scorer in Season:* Ralph Hunt, 31, Division 3(S), 1955–56.
*Most League Goals in Total Aggregate:* Johnny Gavin, 122, 1945–54; 1955–58.
*Most Capped Player:* Martin O'Neill, 11 (49), Northern Ireland.
*Most League Appearances:* Ron Ashman, 590, 1947–64 (plus 72 Cup games).
*Record Transfer Fee Received:* £1,000,000 from Manchester C for Kevin Reeves, March 1980 and
£1,000,000 from Nottingham F for Justin Fashanu, Aug 1981.
*Record Transfer Fee Paid:* £300,000 to Hajduk Split for Drazen Muzinic, Sept 1980.
*Previous Managers since the War:* Cyril Spiers, Dugald Lockhead, Norman Low, Tom Parker, Archie
Macauley, Willie Reid, George Swindin, Ron Ashman, Lol Morgan, Ron Saunders, John Bond.
*Address of Supporters Club:* Club Canary, Norwich City Promotions, Carrow Road, Norwich.
*Address of the Club Shop or Boutique:* Norwich City Promotions, Carrow Road, Norwich. Telephone:
Norwich 615011.

---

**Carrow Road, Norwich NR1 1JE.** Telephone Norwich 612131. *Match information:* Norwich 612591.
*Telegraphic address:* 'Football, Norwich'. *Ground capacity:* 29,000. *Record attendance:* 43,984 v Leicester C, FA Cup 6th rd, 30 March, 1963. *Record receipts:* £56,894.35 v Ipswich T, League Cup 3rd rd
replay, 8 Oct, 1980. *Pitch measurements:* 114yd×74yd.
*How to get there:* Norwich railway station is eight minutes walk from the ground; British Rail run trains from outlying
districts on match days. Coach firms also operate special services from surrounding parts. Any scheduled bus to the
station and then walk.
*Match tickets:* Personal or postal applications to the Box Office on the ground, 14 days before the match. (Postal
applications must include sae.)
*Car parking:* Several private car parks within walking distance of the ground. Multi-storey parks in Malt House Road
and St Andrews Street. Street parking in Rouen Road, Carrow Hill, Kerrison Road, Cousins Road, and side streets off
King Street. Coaches may park at Lower Clarence Road Car Park.
*Entertainments/catering facilities:* Norwich City have their own Public House, The Nest, in the River End Complex at
Carrow road (NB: closed match days). Numerous licensed bars in the ground.
*Club shop:* Sells all types of souvenirs.
*Programmes:* Programmes available on subscription (from Carrow Road).
*Extra information:* In 1958–59 Norwich became one of only four clubs (now five) from the Third Division to reach the
FA Cup semi-final.
*Club Colours:* Yellow shirts, green pinstripe, green shorts yellow trim, yellow stockings.
*Change Colours:* White shirts, green pinstripe, white shorts, green stockings.
*Team Captain:* Mick McGuire.
*Club Nickname:* Canaries.

## NORWICH CITY 1981–82 LEAGUE RECORD

| Match No. | Date | Venue | Opponents | Result | H/T Score | Goalscorers | Attendance |
|---|---|---|---|---|---|---|---|
| 1 | Aug 29 | A | Rotherham U | L 1-4 | 1-2 | Shepherd | 8919 |
| 2 | Sept 2 | H | Crystal Palace | W 1-0 | 1-0 | Cannon (og) | 14,434 |
| 3 | 5 | H | Barnsley | D 1-1 | 1-1 | Jack | 13,677 |
| 4 | 12 | A | Wrexham | W 3-2 | 1-0 | Shepherd, Jack, Barham | 4007 |
| 5 | 19 | H | Newcastle U | W 2-1 | 1-1 | Watson, Jack | 14,384 |
| 6 | 22 | A | Grimsby T | W 2-1 | 2-0 | Jack (pen), Woods | 10,185 |
| 7 | 26 | A | Chelsea | L 1-2 | 1-1 | Jack | 14,509 |
| 8 | Oct 3 | H | Oldham Ath | L 1-2 | 1-1 | Jack (pen) | 13,710 |
| 9 | 10 | A | QPR | L 0-2 | 0-0 | | 11,806 |
| 10 | 17 | H | Shrewsbury T | W 2-1 | 1-1 | Bertschin, Mendham | 11,979 |
| 11 | 24 | A | Watford | L 0-3 | 0-2 | | 14,463 |
| 12 | 31 | H | Bolton W | D 0-0 | 0-0 | | 12,991 |
| 13 | Nov 7 | A | Cardiff C | L 0-1 | 0-0 | | 5704 |
| 14 | 14 | H | Cambridge U | W 2-1 | 1-0 | Walford, McGuire | 13,467 |
| 15 | 21 | H | Derby Co | W 4-1 | 2-0 | Barham, Bertschin, Fashanu, Mendham | 13,457 |
| 16 | 24 | A | Crystal Palace | L 1-2 | 0-0 | Mendham | 9010 |
| 17 | 28 | A | Blackburn R | L 0-3 | 0-1 | | 8153 |
| 18 | Dec 5 | H | Leicester C | D 0-0 | 0-0 | | 13,367 |
| 19 | 28 | H | Luton T | L 1-3 | 1-3 | Deehan | 19,348 |
| 20 | 30 | A | Charlton Ath | D 0-0 | 0-0 | | 6277 |
| 21 | Jan 16 | H | Rotherham U | W 2-0 | 1-0 | Deehan, Bertschin | 12,750 |
| 22 | 30 | A | Newcastle U | L 1-2 | 0-0 | Downs | 14,447 |
| 23 | Feb 3 | H | Sheffield W | L 2-3 | 1-1 | O'Neill, Barham | 15,767 |
| 24 | 6 | H | Wrexham | W 4-0 | 2-0 | Bertschin, O'Neill, Watson, Bennett | 12,300 |
| 25 | 16 | A | Oldham Ath | L 0-2 | 0-1 | | 5283 |
| 26 | 20 | H | Chelsea | W 2-1 | 2-1 | Mendham, Jack | 16,018 |
| 27 | 24 | A | Barnsley | W 1-0 | 1-0 | Bertschin | 15,360 |
| 28 | 27 | H | QPR | L 0-1 | 0-1 | | 15,928 |
| 29 | Mar 13 | H | Watford | W 4-2 | 1-2 | O'Neill, Watson, Deehan (pen), Bertschin | 15,534 |
| 30 | 16 | A | Orient | D 1-1 | 1-1 | Jack | 2933 |
| 31 | 20 | A | Bolton W | W 1-0 | 0-0 | O'Neill | 6199 |
| 32 | 27 | H | Cardiff C | W 2-1 | 0-0 | Jack, Bertschin | 12,720 |
| 33 | Apr 3 | A | Cambridge U | W 2-1 | 0-0 | Mendham, Deehan | 7035 |
| 34 | 10 | H | Charlton Ath | W 5-0 | 2-0 | O'Neill, Deehan 3, Jack | 14,908 |
| 35 | 12 | A | Luton T | L 0-2 | 0-0 | | 15,061 |
| 36 | 17 | A | Derby Co | W 2-0 | 1-0 | O'Neill, Bennett | 12,508 |
| 37 | 20 | A | Shrewsbury T | W 2-0 | 2-0 | Deehan, Mendham | 3590 |
| 38 | 24 | H | Blackburn R | W 2-0 | 2-0 | Bertschin, McGuire | 16,309 |
| 39 | May 1 | A | Leicester C | W 4-1 | 1-0 | Deehan, Barham, Bertschin, Leet (og) | 19,630 |
| 40 | 5 | H | Grimsby T | W 2-1 | 0-0 | Deehan, Bertschin | 18,360 |
| 41 | 8 | H | Orient | W 2-0 | 0-0 | Bertschin (pen), Bennett | 19,197 |
| 42 | 15 | A | Sheffield W | L 1-2 | 0-0 | Bertschin | 24,687 |

**Final League Position: 3**

**Goalscorers**

*League* (64): Bertschin 12 (1 pen), Deehan 10 (1 pen), Jack 10 (2 pens), Mendham 6, O'Neill 6, Barham 4, Bennett 3, Watson 3, McGuire 2, Shepherd 2, Downs 1, Fashanu 1, Walford 1, Clive Woods 1, own goals 2.
*League Cup* (2): Jack 2.
*FA Cup* (3): Jack 2, Watson 1.

| League Cup | Second Round | Charlton Ath (h) | 1-0 |
|---|---|---|---|
| | | (a) | 1-0 |
| | Third Round | Arsenal (a) | 0-1 |
| FA Cup | Third Round | Stoke C (a) | 1-0 |
| | Fourth Round | Doncaster R (h) | 2-1 |
| | Fifth Round | WBA (a) | 0-1 |

| Woods, Chris | Barham | Muzinic | McGuire | Walford | Watson | Mendham | Shepherd | Bertschin | Paddon | Bennett | Nightingale | Downs | Jack | Symonds | Woods, Clive | Hoadley | Hart | Donachie | Fashanu | Haylock | Royle | Deehan | O'Neill | Mountford | Match No. |
|---|---|---|---|---|---|---|---|---|---|---|---|---|---|---|---|---|---|---|---|---|---|---|---|---|---|
| 1 | 2 | 3* | 4 | 5 | 6 | 7 | 8 | 9 | 10 | 11 | 12 |  |  |  |  |  |  |  |  |  |  |  |  |  | 1 |
| 1 | 7 |  | 4 | 5 | 6 | 12 | 8 | 9 | 10* |  |  | 2 | 3 | 11 |  |  |  |  |  |  |  |  |  |  | 2 |
| 1 | 7 |  | 4 | 5 | 6 | 12 | 8 | 9 | 10* |  |  | 2 | 3 | 11 |  |  |  |  |  |  |  |  |  |  | 3 |
| 1 | 7 |  | 4 | 5 | 6 |  | 8 |  | 10 |  |  | 2 | 3 | 11* | 9 |  | 12 |  |  |  |  |  |  |  | 4 |
| 1 | 7 |  | 4 | 5 | 6 |  | 8 |  | 10 |  |  | 2* | 3 | 11 | 9 |  | 12 |  |  |  |  |  |  |  | 5 |
| 1 | 7 |  | 4 | 5 | 6 |  | 8 |  | 10 |  |  | 2 | 3 | 11 | 9 |  |  |  |  |  |  |  |  |  | 6 |
| 1 | 7 |  | 4 | 5 | 6* |  | 8 |  | 10 |  | 12 | 2 | 3 | 11 | 9 |  |  |  |  |  |  |  |  |  | 7 |
| 1 | 7 |  | 4 | 5 |  |  |  | 9 | 10* | 11 | 12 | 2 | 3 | 8 |  | 6 |  |  |  |  |  |  |  |  | 8 |
| 1 | 7 | 12 |  | 5 | 6 | 4 |  | 9 | 10 | 11* |  | 2 |  | 8 |  |  |  |  |  |  |  |  |  |  | 9 |
| 1 | 7 |  | 4 | 5 |  |  |  | 9 | 10 |  |  | 2 | 3 | 11* | 6 |  | 8 | 12 |  |  |  |  |  |  | 10 |
| 1 | 7 |  | 4 | 5 |  |  |  | 9* | 10 |  |  | 2 | 6 | 11 | 12 |  | 3 | 8 |  |  |  |  |  |  | 11 |
| 1 | 7* |  | 4 | 5 | 6 | 10 | 12 |  | 11 | 9 |  | 2 | 3 |  |  |  | 8 |  |  |  |  |  |  |  | 12 |
| 1 |  |  | 4 | 5 | 6 | 10 | 7 |  | 11 | 9 |  | 2 | 3 |  |  |  | 8 |  |  |  |  |  |  |  | 13 |
| 1 |  | 8 | 4 | 5 | 6 | 12 |  |  | 11* | 9 | 7 | 3 |  |  |  |  | 2 | 10 |  |  |  |  |  |  | 14 |
| 1 | 7* | 8 | 4 | 5 | 6 | 11 |  |  | 9 | 12 | 2 | 3 |  |  |  |  | 10 |  |  |  |  |  |  |  | 15 |
| 1 | 7 | 8 | 4 | 5 | 6 | 11* |  |  | 9 | 12 | 2 | 3 |  |  |  |  | 10 |  |  |  |  |  |  |  | 16 |
| 1 |  |  | 4 | 5 | 6 | 11 | 9 | 8 | 12 | 2 |  | 3 |  |  |  |  | 10 | 7* |  |  |  |  |  |  | 17 |
| 1 |  | 8 | 4 | 5 | 6 | 12 | 10 |  | 11 | 7 | 2 | 3 |  |  |  |  | 9* |  |  |  |  |  |  |  | 18 |
| 1 | 7 | 8* | 4 | 5 | 6 | 12 | 10 |  | 11 | 3 |  | 2 |  |  |  |  | 9 |  |  |  |  |  |  |  | 19 |
| 1 |  |  | 4 | 5 | 6 | 7 | 10 |  | 11 | 3 | 8 | 2 |  |  |  |  | 9 |  |  |  |  |  |  |  | 20 |
| 1 |  |  | 4 | 5 | 6 | 7 | 10 |  | 11 | 3 | 8 | 2 |  |  |  |  | 9 |  |  |  |  |  |  |  | 21 |
| 1 | 11 |  | 4 | 5 | 6 | 7 | 10 |  |  | 3 | 8 | 2 |  |  |  |  | 9 |  |  |  |  |  |  |  | 22 |
| 1 | 12 |  | 4 | 5 | 6 | 7* | 10 |  | 11 | 3 |  | 2 |  |  |  |  |  |  |  |  | 9 | 8 |  |  | 23 |
| 1 | 7 |  | 4 | 5 | 6 | 10 | 11 |  | 3* | 12 |  | 2 |  |  |  |  |  |  |  |  | 9 | 8 |  |  | 24 |
| 1 |  |  | 4 | 5 | 6 | 11 | 10 |  | 3 | 7 |  | 2 |  |  |  |  |  |  |  |  | 9 | 8 |  |  | 25 |
| 1 |  |  | 4 | 5 | 6 | 11 | 9*10 |  | 3 | 7 |  |  |  |  |  |  |  | 2 |  |  | 8 | 12 |  |  | 26 |
| 1 |  |  | 4 | 5 | 6 | 11 | 9 10 |  | 3 | 7 |  |  |  |  |  |  |  | 2 |  |  | 8 |  |  |  | 27 |
| 1 |  |  | 4 | 5 | 6 | 11* | 10 |  | 3 | 7 |  |  |  |  |  |  |  | 2 |  |  | 9 | 8 | 12 |  | 28 |
| 1 |  |  | 4 | 5 | 6 | 11 | 10 |  | 3 | 7 |  |  |  |  |  |  |  | 2 |  |  | 9 | 8 |  |  | 29 |
| 1 |  |  | 4 | 5 | 6 | 11 | 10 | 12 | 3 | 7 |  |  |  |  |  |  |  | 2* |  |  | 9 | 8 |  |  | 30 |
| 1 |  |  |  | 5 | 6 | 4 | 10 |  | 11 | 3 | 7 |  |  |  |  |  |  | 2 |  |  | 9 | 8 |  |  | 31 |
| 1 |  |  | 4 | 5 | 6 | 11 | 10 |  | 3 | 7 |  |  |  |  |  |  |  | 2 |  |  | 9 | 8 |  |  | 32 |
| 1 |  |  | 4 | 5 | 6 | 11 | 10 |  | 7 | 3 |  |  |  |  |  |  |  | 2 |  |  | 9 | 8 |  |  | 33 |
| 1 | 4 |  | 5 | 6 | 11 | 10 | 7* |  | 3 | 12 |  |  |  |  |  |  |  | 2 |  |  | 9 | 8 |  |  | 34 |
| 1 | 7 |  | 4 | 5 | 6 | 11 | 10 |  | 3 | 12 |  |  |  |  |  |  |  | 2* |  |  | 9 | 8 |  |  | 35 |
| 1 | 7 |  | 4 | 5 |  | 11 | 10 | 6 | 3 |  |  |  |  |  |  |  |  | 2 |  |  | 9 | 8 |  |  | 36 |
| 1 | 12 |  | 4 | 5 | 6 | 11* | 10 | 7 | 3 |  |  |  |  |  |  |  |  | 2 |  |  | 9 | 8 |  |  | 37 |
| 1 | 7 |  | 4 | 5 | 6 | 10* | 11 |  | 3 | 12 |  |  |  |  |  |  |  | 2 |  |  | 9 | 8 |  |  | 38 |
| 1 | 7 |  | 4 | 5 | 6 | 10 | 11 |  | 3 |  |  |  |  |  |  |  |  | 2 |  |  | 9 | 8 |  |  | 39 |
| 1 | 7 |  | 4 | 5 | 6 | 10 | 11 |  | 3 | 12 |  |  |  |  |  |  |  | 2 |  |  | 9* | 8 |  |  | 40 |
| 1 | 7 |  | 4 | 5 | 6 | 10 | 11 |  | 3 | 12 |  |  |  |  |  |  |  | 2 |  |  | 9* | 8 |  |  | 41 |
| 1 | 7* |  | 4 | 5 | 6 | 10 | 11 |  | 3 | 12 |  |  |  |  |  |  |  | 2 |  |  | 9 | 8 |  |  | 42 |
| 42 | 25 | 6 | 39 | 42 | 38 | 25 | 12 | 35 | 8 | 21 | 8 | 28 | 24 | 18 | 8 | 3 | — | 11 | 4 | 21 | 2 | 22 | 20 | — |  |
| | +2s | +1s | | +4s | +3s | +1s | | +1s | +1s | | +11s | | | +1s | +1s | | +1s | | | +1s | | | | +2s | |

Players continued from following page.

| | | | | | App | Gls |
|---|---|---|---|---|---|---|
| William Murphy (Contract cancelled Oct 1981) | | | Hamilton | Norwich C | — | — |
| John Fashanu | 6 1 | 11 12 | Kensington | Cambridge U | — | — |
| | | | | Norwich C | 5 | 1 |
| Keith Bertschin | 6 1 | 11 8 | Enfield | Ipswich T | 32 | 8 |
| | | | | Birmingham C | 118 | 29 |
| | | | | Norwich C | 36 | 12 |
| John Deehan | 6 0 | 11 3 | Solihull | Aston V | 110 | 42 |
| | | | | WBA | 47 | 5 |
| | | | | Norwich C | 22 | 10 |

## NORWICH CITY

| | Ht | Wt | Birthplace | Clubs | League App. | League Gls |
|---|---|---|---|---|---|---|
| **Goalkeepers** | | | | | | |
| Roger Hansbury | 5 11 | 12 0 | Barnsley | Norwich C | 78 | — |
| (Contracts cancelled Nov 1981 and Jan 1982) | | | | Bolton W (on loan) | — | — |
| | | | | Cambridge U (on loan) | 11 | — |
| | | | | Orient (on loan) | — | — |
| Clive Baker | 5 9 | 11 0 | N Walsham | Norwich C | 14 | — |
| Chris Woods | 6 2 | 12 8 | Lines | Nottingham F | — | — |
| | | | | QPR | 63 | — |
| | | | | Norwich C | 52 | — |
| **Defenders** | | | | | | |
| Phil Hoadley* | 5 11 | 12 2 | Battersea | Crystal Palace | 73 | 1 |
| | | | | Orient | 255 | 9 |
| | | | | Norwich C | 77 | 1 |
| John McDowell* | 5 10 | 12 4 | East Ham | West Ham U | 249 | 8 |
| | | | | Norwich C | 41 | 1 |
| Greg Downs | 5 9½ | 10 7 | Carlton | Norwich C | 79 | 3 |
| | | | | Torquay U (on loan) | 1 | 1 |
| Richard Symonds | 6 1 | 11 5 | Langham | Norwich C | 58 | — |
| Mark Nightingale* | 5 10 | 10 7 | Salisbury | Bournemouth | 49 | 4 |
| | | | | Crystal Palace | — | — |
| | | | | Norwich C | 35 | — |
| Drazen Muzinic | | | Yugoslavia | Hajduk Split | (not known) | |
| (Yugoslavia) | | | | Norwich C | 19 | — |
| David Watson | 5 11½ | 11 12 | Liverpool | Liverpool | — | — |
| | | | | Norwich C | 56 | 6 |
| Adrian Harris* | 6 1 | 12 11 | Gorleston | Norwich C | — | — |
| Paul Haylock | 5 8 | 11 0 | Lowestoft | Norwich C | 21 | — |
| Steve Walford | 6 1 | 11 7 | Highgate | Tottenham H | 2 | — |
| | | | | Arsenal | 77 | 3 |
| | | | | Norwich C | 52 | 1 |
| Willie Donachie | 5 9 | 11 5 | Glasgow | Manchester C | 351 | 2 |
| (Scotland) | | | | Portland T | (not known) | |
| (Contract cancelled April 1982) | | | | Norwich C | 11 | — |
| Graham Reeve* | 5 11 | 11 4 | Norwich | Norwich C | — | — |
| Phil Alexander | 6 0 | 12 8 | Reading | Norwich C | — | — |
| **Midfield** | | | | | | |
| Mick McGuire | 5 7 | 10 5 | Blackpool | Coventry C | 72 | 1 |
| | | | | Norwich C | 167 | 11 |
| Graham Paddon | 5 9 | 11 7 | Manchester | Coventry C | 5 | 1 |
| (Contract cancelled Feb 1982) | | | | Norwich C | 162 | 19 |
| | | | | West Ham U | 115 | 11 |
| | | | | Millwall (on loan) | 5 | 1 |
| | | | | Norwich C | 128 | 6 |
| Peter Mountford | 5 10 | 10 6 | Stoke | Norwich C | 2 | — |
| Mark Barham | 5 7 | 11 0 | Folkestone | Norwich C | 66 | 5 |
| Clive Woods | 5 9 | 10 10 | Norwich | Ipswich T | 268 | 23 |
| (Contract cancelled April 1982) | | | | Norwich C | 32 | 4 |
| Peter Mendham | 5 10 | 11 6 | King's Lynn | Norwich C | 70 | 8 |
| Andrew Hart* | 5 8 | 11 0 | Gt Yarmouth | Norwich C | 1 | — |
| Martin O'Neill | 5 10 | 11 3 | Kilrea | Distillery | (not known) | |
| (N Ireland) | | | | Nottingham F | 285 | 48 |
| | | | | Norwich C | 11 | 1 |
| | | | | Manchester C | 13 | — |
| | | | | Norwich C | 20 | 6 |
| Grant Reid | | | Glasgow | Norwich C | — | — |
| Eric Vasco | | | Liverpool | Liverpool | — | — |
| (Contract cancelled) | | | | Norwich C | — | — |
| **Forwards** | | | | | | |
| Neil Engall* | | | | Norwich C | — | — |
| Mark Hodder | | | | Norwich C | — | — |
| (Contract cancelled Aug 1981) | | | | | | |
| George Wilson | | | | Norwich C | — | — |
| (Contract cancelled Feb 1982) | | | | | | |
| Mark Harrowing | | | | Norwich C | — | — |
| (Contract cancelled April 1982) | | | | | | |
| David Lovett* | | | | Norwich C | — | — |
| Dave Bennett | 5 11 | 11 7 | Oldham | Manchester C | — | — |
| | | | | Norwich C | 36 | 4 |
| Steve Goble | 5 11 | 10 6 | Wells | Norwich C | 30 | 2 |
| (Contract cancelled Jan 1982) | | | | | | |
| Greig Shepherd | 6 1 | 12 0 | Edinburgh | Norwich C | 16 | 2 |
| Ross Jack | 5 10 | 11 2 | Inverness | Everton | 1 | 1 |
| | | | | Cardiff C (on loan) | — | — |
| | | | | Norwich C | 46 | 10 |
| Joe Royle | 6 1 | 13 8 | Liverpool | Everton | 231 | 102 |
| (England) | | | | Manchester C | 99 | 23 |
| | | | | Bristol C | 101 | 18 |
| | | | | Norwich C | 42 | 9 |

*Note: Players continued on previous page.*

# NOTTINGHAM FOREST — Division 1

*President:* H. W. Alcock FCA.
*Chairman:* G. E. Macpherson JP.
*Vice-Chairman:* F. Reacher.
*Directors:* B. J. Appleby QC, G. T. Thorpe, F. T. C. Pell FCA, D. C. Pavis, Dr I. L. Loch, M. R. Roworth, A. L. Burnham.
*Manager:* Brian Clough.  *Sec/Treasurer:* K. Smales.
*Year Formed:* 1865.  *Turned Professional:* 1889.
*Limited Company:* 1982.
*Previous Grounds:* 1865, Forest Racecourse; 1879, The Meadows; 1880, Trent Bridge Cricket Ground; 1882, Parkside, Lenton; 1885, Gregory, Lenton; 1890, Town Ground; 1898, City Ground.

**Football League Record:**
1892 Elected to Division 1; 1906 Division 2; 1907 Division 1; 1911–22 Division 2; 1922–25 Division 1; 1925–49 Division 2; 1949–51 Division 3(S); 1951–57 Division 2; 1957–72 Division 1; 1972–77 Division 2; 1977– Division 1.

**Honours:** *Football League:* Division 1 – Champions 1977–78; Runners-up 1966–67, 1978–79. Division 2 – Champions 1906–07, 1921–22; Runners-up 1956–57; Division 3(S) – Champions 1950–51. *FA Cup:* Winners 1898, 1959. *Anglo-Scottish Cup:* Winners 1976–77. *Football League Cup:* Winners 1977–78, 1978–79; Runners-up 1979–80. **European Competitions:** *Fairs Cup:* 1961–62, 1967–68. *European Cup:* 1978–79 (winners), 1979–80 (winners), 1980–81. *Super Cup:* 1979–80 (winners), 1980–81 (runners-up). *World Club Championship:* 1980–81 (runners-up).
*Record Victory:* 14-0 v Clapton, FA Cup, 1st rd, 1890–91.
*Record Defeat:* 1-9 v Blackburn R, Division 2, 10 Apr, 1937.
*Most League Points:* 70, Division 3(S), 1950–51.
*Most League Goals:* 110, Division 3(S), 1950–51.
*Highest League Scorer in Season:* Wally Ardron, 36, Division 3(S), 1950–51.
*Most League Goals in Total Aggregate:* Grenville Morris, 199, 1898–1913.
*Most Capped Player:* Martin O'Neill, 36 (49), Northern Ireland.
*Most League Appearances:* Bob McKinlay, 614, 1951–70.
*Record Transfer Fee Received:* £1,250,000 from Manchester U for Garry Birtles, Oct 1980.
*Record Transfer Fee Paid:* £975,000 to Birmingham C for Trevor Francis, Feb 1979.
*Previous Managers since the War:* Billy Walker, Andy Beattie, John Carey, Matt Gillies, Dave Mackay, Allan Brown.
*Address of Supporters Club:* c/o City Ground, Nottingham.
*Address of the Club Shop or Boutique:* Pools Office, City Ground, Nottingham NG2 5FJ.

---

**City Ground, Nottingham NG2 5FJ.** Telephone Nottingham 868236-7-8. Information Desk: 860232. *Telegraphic Address:* 'Forestball, Nottingham'. *Telex:* 377207 Answer back code 'Forest G'. *Ground capacity:* 35,000 (14,200 seats). *Record attendance:* 49,945 v Manchester U, Division 1, 28 Oct, 1967. *Record receipts:* £132,500 v Ajax, European Cup semi-final first leg, 9 April, 1980. *Pitch measurements:* 115yd×78yd.
*How to get there:* From Nottingham station any bus marked 'Trent Bridge'. Corporation specials from Parliament Street.
*Match tickets:* Bookable 14 days in advance of the match (personal) and 12 days (postal).
*Car parking:* Room for 300 cars in the East Stand car park and street parking off the Loughborough and Radcliffe Roads.
*Entertainments/catering facilities:* Only match-day refreshment bars. Social club situated just outside the ground. Jubilee club on ground (members only).
*Club shop:* Three shops on the ground sell all types of souvenirs.
*Handbooks/programmes:* Programmes available on subscription from Carrington Publications Ltd, Wilford Crescent East, Trent Bridge, Nottingham.
*Extra information:* Forest hold the record for the highest away win in the FA Cup proper; they beat Clapton 14-0 in 1890-91. They were also the first club to adopt shinguards (1874), the Referee's whistle (1878), three half-backs (1885), the crossbar instead of tape (1891), and oval section goal-posts (1921). Nottingham Forest are the only club to have played against clubs from all four home countries in the FA Cup. They hold the Football League record with 42 successive League matches without defeat. They are the only club to have been in three successive League Cup Finals and the first club to have achieved the League Championship and League Cup double.
*Club Colours:* Red shirts with white pinstripe, white shorts, red stockings.  *Change Colours:* All yellow.
*Club Captain:*  / *First Team Trainer:* Ron Fenton. *Second Team:* Liam O'Kane.
*Club Nickname:* Reds.

## NOTTINGHAM FOREST 1981-82 LEAGUE RECORD

| Match No. | Date | Venue | Opponents | Result | H/T Score | Goalscorers | Attendance |
|---|---|---|---|---|---|---|---|
| 1 | Aug 29 | H | Southampton | W 2-1 | 2-1 | Francis 2 | 25,234 |
| 2 | 31 | A | Manchester U | D 0-0 | 0-0 | | 51,496 |
| 3 | Sept 5 | A | Birmingham C | L 3-4 | 2-2 | Wallace 3 | 19,035 |
| 4 | 12 | H | WBA | D 0-0 | 0-0 | | 22,618 |
| 5 | 19 | A | Stoke C | W 2-1 | 0-1 | Walsh, Mills | 15,653 |
| 6 | 23 | H | Sunderland | W 2-0 | 0-0 | Wallace, Proctor | 21,133 |
| 7 | 26 | H | Brighton & HA | W 2-1 | 0-1 | Burns, Wallace | 19,220 |
| 8 | Oct 3 | A | Tottenham H | L 0-3 | 0-1 | | 34,870 |
| 9 | 10 | A | Middlesbrough | D 1-1 | 0-0 | Fashanu | 15,043 |
| 10 | 17 | H | Coventry C | W 2-1 | 0-1 | Wallace 2 | 20,101 |
| 11 | 24 | A | Manchester C | D 0-0 | 0-0 | | 34,881 |
| 12 | 31 | H | Leeds U | W 2-1 | 1-1 | Ward, Robertson (pen) | 25,272 |
| 13 | Nov 7 | A | West Ham U | D 0-0 | 0-0 | | 26,327 |
| 14 | 21 | H | Arsenal | L 1-2 | 1-0 | Fashanu | 20,912 |
| 15 | 25 | A | Sunderland | W 3-2 | 1-0 | Walsh, Fashanu, Needham | 17,419 |
| 16 | 28 | A | Aston Villa | L 1-3 | 0-2 | Walsh | 26,847 |
| 17 | Dec 5 | H | Liverpool | L 0-2 | 0-0 | | 24,521 |
| 18 | 12 | A | Swansea C | W 2-1 | 0-1 | Young, Robertson (pen) | 17,550 |
| 19 | Jan 9 | H | Birmingham C | W 2-1 | 0-0 | Ward, Wallace | 15,906 |
| 20 | 23 | H | Notts Co | L 0-2 | 0-0 | | 26,158 |
| 21 | 30 | H | Stoke C | D 0-0 | 0-0 | | 16,219 |
| 22 | Feb 6 | A | WBA | L 1-2 | 0-1 | Ward | 15,006 |
| 23 | 13 | A | Southampton | L 0-2 | 0-1 | | 21,350 |
| 24 | 16 | A | Wolverhampton W | D 0-0 | 0-0 | | 11,195 |
| 25 | 20 | A | Brighton & HA | W 1-0 | 1-0 | Ward | 17,175 |
| 26 | 27 | H | Middlesbrough | D 1-1 | 0-1 | Gray | 16,464 |
| 27 | Mar 9 | A | Coventry C | W 1-0 | 1-0 | Rober | 9720 |
| 28 | 13 | H | Manchester C | D 1-1 | 0-1 | Ward (pen) | 20,927 |
| 29 | 17 | H | Ipswich T | D 1-1 | 0-0 | Plummer | 16,686 |
| 30 | 20 | A | Leeds U | D 1-1 | 1-1 | Rober | 18,036 |
| 31 | 27 | A | West Ham U | W 1-0 | 1-0 | Wallace | 24,633 |
| 32 | Apr 3 | H | Everton | L 0-1 | 0-0 | | 17,323 |
| 33 | 10 | H | Wolverhampton W | L 0-1 | 0-0 | | 15,691 |
| 34 | 12 | A | Notts Co | W 2-1 | 1-1 | Bowyer, Plummer | 19,403 |
| 35 | 17 | A | Arsenal | L 0-2 | 0-1 | | 21,986 |
| 36 | 20 | A | Everton | L 1-2 | 0-0 | Rober | 15,460 |
| 37 | 24 | H | Aston Villa | D 1-1 | 1-0 | Needham | 18,213 |
| 38 | May 1 | A | Liverpool | L 0-2 | 0-0 | | 34,321 |
| 39 | 5 | H | Manchester U | L 0-1 | 0-1 | | 18,449 |
| 40 | 8 | H | Swansea C | L 0-2 | 0-1 | | 15,037 |
| 41 | 12 | H | Tottenham H | W 2-0 | 1-0 | Davenport, Gray | 15,189 |
| 42 | 15 | A | Ipswich T | W 3-1 | 0-0 | Davenport 3 | 19,937 |

**Final League Position: 12**

**Goalscorers**

*League* (42): Wallace 9, Ward 5 (1 pen), Davenport 4, Fashanu 3, Rober 3, Walsh 3, Francis 2, Gray 2, Needham 2, Plummer 2, Robertson 2 (2 pens), Bowyer 1, Burns 1, Mills 1, Proctor 1, Young 1.
*League Cup* (8): Wallace 3, Fashanu 1, Needham 1, Proctor 1, Rober 1, Robertson 1.
*FA Cup* (1): Proctor 1.

| | | | |
|---|---|---|---|
| **League Cup** | Second Round | Birmingham C (a) | 3-2 |
| | | (h) | 2-1 |
| | Third Round | Blackburn R (a) | 1-0 |
| | Fourth Round | Tranmere R (h) | 2-0 |
| | Fifth Round | Tottenham H (a) | 0-1 |
| **FA Cup** | Third Round | Wrexham (h) | 1-3 |

| Shilton | Anderson | Gray | McGovern | Burns | Aas | Francis | Ward | Fashanu | Proctor | Robertson | Gunn | Mills | Wallace | Walsh | Needham | Rober | Young | Bowyer | Plummer | Kendall | Sutton | Davenport | Hodge | Match No. |
|---|---|---|---|---|---|---|---|---|---|---|---|---|---|---|---|---|---|---|---|---|---|---|---|---|
| 1 | 2 | 3 | 4 | 5 | 6 | 7 | 8 | 9 | 10 | 11 | | | | | | | | | | | | | | 1 |
| 1 | 2 | 3 | 4 | 5 | 6 | 7 | 8 | 9 | 10 | 11 | | | | | | | | | | | | | | 2 |
| 1 | 2 | 3 | 4 | 5* | 6 | | | 9 | 10 | 11 | 12 | 7 | 8 | | | | | | | | | | | 3 |
| 1 | 2 | 3 | 4 | 5 | 6 | | | 9 | 7 | 11 | | | 10* | 8 | 12 | | | | | | | | | 4 |
| 1 | 2 | 3 | 4 | 5 | 6 | | | 9 | 7 | | | | 10 | 8 | 11 | | | | | | | | | 5 |
| 1 | 2 | 3 | 4 | 5 | | | | 9 | 10 | 11 | 6 | 7 | 8 | | | | | | | | | | | 6 |
| 1 | 2 | 3 | 4 | 6 | 5 | | | 9 | 10 | 11 | | 7 | 8 | | | | | | | | | | | 7 |
| 1 | 2 | 3 | 4 | 5 | | | | 9 | 10 | 11* | 6 | 7 | 8 | 12 | | | | | | | | | | 8 |
| 1 | 2 | 3 | 12 | | 5 | | | 9 | 7 | 11 | 6 | 4 | 8 | 10* | | | | | | | | | | 9 |
| 1 | 2 | 7 | 4* | | 6 | | | 9 | 10 | 11 | 3 | | 8 | 12 | 5 | | | | | | | | | 10 |
| 1 | 2 | 7 | 4 | | 6 | | | 9 | 10 | 11* | 3 | | 8 | 12 | 5 | | | | | | | | | 11 |
| 1 | 2 | 7 | 4 | | 6 | | 8 | 9 | 10 | 11 | 3 | | | | 5 | | | | | | | | | 12 |
| 1 | 2 | 7 | 4 | | 6* | | | 9 | 10 | 11 | 3 | | 8 | 12 | 5 | | | | | | | | | 13 |
| 1 | 2 | 7 | 4 | | 6 | | 8 | 9 | 10* | 11 | 3 | | | 12 | 5 | | | | | | | | | 14 |
| 1 | 2 | | 4 | | 6* | | 8 | 9 | 10 | 11 | 3 | 12 | 7 | | 5 | | | | | | | | | 15 |
| 1 | 2 | 3 | 4 | | | | 8 | 9 | 12 | 11 | 6 | 7 | 10 | | 5* | | | | | | | | | 16 |
| 1 | 5 | 3 | | | | | | 9 | 4 | 11 | 6 | 2 | 8 | 10 | 7 | | | | | | | | | 17 |
| 1 | 2 | | 4 | | | | | 9 | 10 | 11 | 3 | | 8 | | 6 | 7 | 5 | | | | | | | 18 |
| 1 | 2 | 3 | 7 | | | | | 9 | 10 | 11 | 4 | | 8 | | 6* | 5 | 12 | | | | | | | 19 |
| 1 | 10* | | 4 | | | | | 9 | 7 | 11 | 2 | | 8 | 5 | 12 | 6 | 3 | | | | | | | 20 |
| 1 | 2 | | 4 | | | | | 9 | 10 | 11 | 3 | | 8 | | | 7 | 5 | 6 | | | | | | 21 |
| 1 | 2 | 3 | 4 | | | | 12 | 9 | | 11 | 6 | | 8* | | | 7 | 5 | 10 | | | | | | 22 |
| 1 | 2 | 12 | | | | | 10 | 9 | | 11 | 3 | 7 | 4 | | | 8* | 5 | 6 | | | | | | 23 |
| 1 | 2 | | 4 | | | | | 9 | | 11 | 3 | 7 | 8 | | | 6 | 5 | 10 | | | | | | 24 |
| 1 | 2 | | 4 | | | | | 9 | | 11 | 3 | 7 | 6 | | | 5 | 10 | 8 | | | | | | 25 |
| 1 | 2 | 3 | 4 | | | | | 9 | | 11* | 6 | 7 | 12 | | | 5 | 10 | 8 | | | | | | 26 |
| 1 | 2 | 11 | 4 | | | | | 9 | 10 | | 6 | | 8 | | | 7 | 5 | 3 | | | | | | 27 |
| 1 | 2 | 11* | 4 | | | | | 9 | 12 | 8 | 6 | 10 | | | | 7 | 5 | 3 | | | | | | 28 |
| 1 | 2 | | 4 | | | | | 9 | 8 | | 6 | 10 | 11 | | | 5 | 3 | 7 | | | | | | 29 |
| 1 | 2 | | 4 | | | | | 9 | 10 | | 6 | | 8 | | | 7 | 5 | 3 | 11 | | | | | 30 |
| 1 | 2 | | 4 | | | | | 9 | 10 | 11 | 6 | | 8 | | | 7 | 5 | 3 | | | | | | 31 |
| 1 | 6 | | 4 | | | | | 9* | 10 | 11 | 2 | | 8 | | | 7 | 5 | 3 | 12 | | | | | 32 |
| 1 | 6 | | | | | | | 9 | 10* | 11 | 4 | | 8 | | | 7 | 5 | 3 | 12 | 2 | | | | 33 |
| 1 | 2 | 3 | | | | | | 9 | 10 | 11 | 4 | | | | | 7 | 5 | 6 | 8 | | | | | 34 |
| 1 | 2 | 3* | 12 | | | | | 9 | 10 | 11 | 4 | | | | | 7 | 5 | 6 | 8 | | | | | 35 |
| 1 | 2 | 12 | | | | | | 9 | 10 | 11 | 3 | 4 | | | | 7 | 5 | 6 | 8* | | | | | 36 |
| 1 | 2 | | | | | | | 9 | 8 | 11 | 3 | 10 | 4 | | | 7 | 5 | 6 | | | | | | 37 |
| | 2 | 12 | | | | | | 8 | | 11 | 3 | 10 | 4 | | | 7 | 5* | 6 | | | 1 | 9 | | 38 |
| 1 | 2 | | | | | | | 8* | | 11 | 3 | 10 | 12 | | 4 | 7 | 5 | 6 | | | | 9 | | 39 |
| 1 | 2 | | | | | | | 8* | | 11 | 3 | 10 | 12 | | 4 | 7 | 5 | 6 | | | | 9 | | 40 |
| 1 | 2 | 6 | | | | | | 9 | 7 | 11 | 4 | | 8 | | | 5 | 3 | | | | | 10 | | 41 |
| 1 | 2 | 6 | 8 | | | | | | 12 | 11 | 4 | | | | | 7 | 5 | 3 | | | | 10 | 9* | 42 |
| 41 | 39 | 32 | 26 | 7 | 14 | 2 | 14 | 31 | 35 | 36 | 36 | 13 | 28 | 7 | 17 | 21 | 25 | 23 | 7 | 1 | 1 | 5 | 1 | |
| | | + | + | | | | + | + | + | | | + | + | + | + | | + | | + | + | | | | |
| | | 1s | 4s | | | | 1s | 1s | 2s | | | 1s | 1s | 1s | 8s | | 1s | | 1s | 2s | | | | | |

# NOTTINGHAM FOREST

| | Ht | Wt | Birthplace | Clubs | League App. | League Gls |
|---|---|---|---|---|---|---|
| **Goalkeepers** | | | | | | |
| Peter Shilton (England) | 6 0 | 12 10 | Leicester | Leicester C | 286 | 1 |
| | | | | Stoke C | 110 | — |
| | | | | Nottingham F | 202 | — |
| Steve Sutton | | | Derby | Nottingham F | 2 | — |
| | | | | Mansfield T (on loan) | 8 | — |
| **Defenders** | | | | | | |
| Viv Anderson (England) | 5 11 | 10 4 | Nottingham | Nottingham F | 263 | 8 |
| Bryn Gunn | 5 9 | 10 5 | Corby | Nottingham F | 77 | — |
| David Needham* | 6 1 | 12 7 | Leicester | Notts Co | 429 | 32 |
| | | | | QPR | 18 | 3 |
| | | | | Nottingham F | 86 | 9 |
| Stuart Gray | 5 9 | 11 10 | Withernsea | Nottingham F | 47 | 3 |
| Jan Einar Aas (Norway) | | | Moss, Norway | Moss | (not known) | |
| | | | | Bayern Munich | (not known) | |
| | | | | Nottingham F | 21 | 1 |
| Willie Young | 6 3 | 12 10 | Edinburgh | Aberdeen | 132 | 10 |
| | | | | Tottenham H | 54 | 3 |
| | | | | Arsenal | 170 | 11 |
| | | | | Nottingham F | 25 | 1 |
| Chris Fairclough | | | Nottingham | Nottingham F | — | — |
| Steve Kendal | | | Birtley | Nottingham F | 1 | — |
| Nigel Thrower | | | Nottingham | Nottingham F | — | — |
| **Midfield** | | | | | | |
| John McGovern | 5 10 | 10 13 | Montrose | Hartlepool | 71 | 5 |
| | | | | Derby Co | 190 | 16 |
| | | | | Leeds U | 4 | — |
| | | | | Nottingham F | 253 | 6 |
| John Robertson (Scotland) | 5 8 | 10 9 | Uddinston | Nottingham F | 352 | 55 |
| Colin Walsh | 5 9 | 11 0 | | Nottingham F | 31 | 7 |
| Raimondo Ponte (Switzerland) (Contract cancelled July 1981) | 5 10½ | 11 4 | Naples | Grasshoppers | (not known) | |
| | | | | Nottingham F | 21 | 3 |
| Calvin Plummer | | | Nottingham | Nottingham F | 9 | 2 |
| Mark Proctor | 5 10 | 11 9 | Middlesbrough | Middlesbrough | 109 | 12 |
| | | | | Nottingham F | 37 | 1 |
| Jim McKechnie | | | Glasgow | Nottingham F | — | — |
| Jurgen Rober | | | Gernrode | Werder Bremen | (not known) | |
| | | | | Bayern Munich | (not known) | |
| | | | | Calgary | (not known) | |
| | | | | Chicago S | (not known) | |
| | | | | Nottingham F | 22 | 3 |
| **Forwards** | | | | | | |
| Gary Mills (Contract cancelled March 1982) | 5 8 | 11 1 | Northampton | Nottingham F | 58 | 8 |
| Ian Wallace (Scotland) | 5 7½ | 10 9½ | Glasgow | Dumbarton | 34 | 11 |
| | | | | Coventry C | 130 | 57 |
| | | | | Nottingham F | 66 | 20 |
| Peter Ward (England) (Contract cancelled March 1982) | 5 7 | 10 3 | Lichfield | Burton A | (not known) | |
| | | | | Brighton | 178 | 79 |
| | | | | Nottingham F | 31 | 7 |
| Steve Wigley | | | Ashton-under-Lyne | Curzon Ashton | (not known) | |
| | | | | Nottingham F | — | — |
| Steve Hodge | 5 8 | 10 8 | Nottingham | Nottingham F | 1 | — |
| Justin Fashanu | 6 1 | 12 7 | Hackney | Norwich C | 90 | 35 |
| | | | | Nottingham F | 32 | 3 |
| Colin Smith (Contract cancelled Feb 1982) | 6 0 | 12 10 | Derby | Nottingham F | — | — |
| Ian Bowyer | 5 11 | 11 2½ | Ellesmere Port | Manchester C | 50 | 13 |
| | | | | Orient | 78 | 18 |
| | | | | Nottingham F | 239 | 49 |
| | | | | Sunderland | 15 | 1 |
| | | | | Nottingham F | 24 | 1 |
| Peter Davenport | | | Birkenhead | Nottingham F | 5 | 4 |

# NOTTS COUNTY Division 1

*Chairman:* J. J. Dunnett MA, LLB (CANTAB), MP.

*Directors:* L. S. Levin JP, J. Mounteney.

*Manager:* Jimmy Sirrel.

*Commercial Manager:* Stuart J. Burgan M INST M.

*Secretary:* Lance G. Hayward.

*Year Formed:* 1862 (the oldest club in the Football League).

*Turned Professional:* 1885. *Limited Company:* 1888.

*Previous Grounds:* 1862, The Park; 1863, The Meadows; 1881, Trent Bridge; 1910, Meadow Lane.

**Football League Record:**
1888 Founder Member of the Football League; 1893–97 Division 2; 1897–1913 Division 1; 1913–14 Division 2; 1914–20 Division 1; 1920–23 Division 2; 1923–26 Division 1; 1926–30 Division 2; 1930–31 Division 3(S); 1931–35 Division 2; 1935–50 Division 3(S); 1950–58 Division 2; 1958–59 Division 3; 1959–60 Division 4; 1960–64 Division 3; 1964–71 Division 4; 1971–73 Division 3; 1973–81 Division 2; 1981– Division 1.

**Honours:** *Football League:* Division 1 best season: 3rd, 1890–91, 1900–01; Division 2 – Champions 1896–97, 1913–14, 1922–23; Runners-up 1894–95, 1980–81; Division 3(S) – Champions 1930–31, 1949–50; Runners-up 1936–37; Division 4 – Champions 1970–71; Runners-up 1959–60. *FA Cup:* Winners 1893–94; Runners-up 1890–91. *Football League Cup* best season: 5th rd, 1963–64, 1972–73, 1975–76.

*Record Victory:* 15-0 v Thornhill U, FA Cup 1st rd, 24 Oct, 1885.

*Record Defeat:* 1-9 v Blackburn R, Division 1, 16 Nov, 1889; v Aston Villa, Division 1, 29 Sept, 1888; v Portsmouth, Division 2, 9 Apr, 1927.

*Most League Points:* 69, Division 4, 1970–71.

*Most League Goals:* 107, Division 4, 1959–60.

*Highest League Scorer in Season:* Tom Keetley, 39, Division 3(S), 1930–31.

*Most League Goals in Total Aggregate:* Les Bradd, 125, 1967–78.

*Most Capped Player:* Bill Fallon, 7 (9), Eire.

*Most League Appearances:* Albert Iremonger, 564, 1904–26.

*Record Transfer Fee Received:* £150,000 from Wrexham for Mick Vinter, June 1979.

*Record Transfer Fee Paid:* £600,000 to Orient for John Chiedozie, Aug 1981.

*Previous Managers since the War:* Arthur Stollery, Eric Houghton, George Poyser, Tommy Lawton, Frank Hill, Tim Coleman, Eddie Lowe, Jack Burkitt, Andy Beattie, Billy Gray, Jimmy Sirrel, Ron Fenton.

*Address of Supporters Club:* c/o Club.

*Address of the Club Shop or Boutique:* Souvenir Sales, c/o the Ground.

---

**County Ground, Meadow Lane, Nottingham NG2 3HJ.** Telephone Nottingham 861155. *Telegraphic address:* 'Notts County FC Nottingham'. *Ground capacity:* 23,680. *Record attendance:* 47,310 v York C, FA Cup 6th rd, 12 Mar, 1955. *Record receipts:* £30,654.15 v Aston Villa, FA Cup 3rd rd, 5 Jan, 1982. *Pitch measurements:* 117yd×76yd.

*How to get there:* Nearest railway station Nottingham from there any bus marked 'Trent Bridge'.

*Match tickets:* Advance bookings can be accepted by post or by personal application 14 days before each home game. SAE must be sent with remittance in postal applications.

*Car parking:* No street parking around the ground, but ample space in the City of Nottingham Corporation car park on the Cattle Market, Meadow Lane, just 400 yards from the main entrances.

*Entertainments/catering facilities:* Social club. Tea bars and refreshment points on all sides of the ground.

*Club shop:* Open daily; situated at the ground.

*Programmes:* Back copies and subscription rates available from the club.

*Extra information:* When Notts County won the FA Cup in 1893–94, they became the first winners from the Second Division. The club has recently had a Sports Hall built on the Iremonger Road car park. This is available, for hire, to the public at certain times of the day. A sports complex including executive viewing boxes, 4 squash courts and badminton courts/indoor tennis courts and social club facilities has recently been built at the ground.

*Club Colours:* Black and white striped shirts, black shorts with white stripe down the side, white stockings with black hoops at top.

*Change Colours:* Yellow shirts with blue trim, yellow shorts, yellow stockings; (or all blue).

*Club Captain:* Pedro Richards. *First Team Trainer:* Jack Wheeler.

*Club Nickname:* Magpies.

## NOTTS COUNTY 1981–82 LEAGUE RECORD

| Match No. | Date | | Venue | Opponents | Result | | H/T Score | Goalscorers | Attendance |
|---|---|---|---|---|---|---|---|---|---|
| 1 | Aug | 29 | A | Aston Villa | W | 1-0 | 1-0 | McCulloch | 30,097 |
| 2 | Sept | 1 | H | Manchester C | D | 1-1 | 1-0 | Christie | 14,546 |
| 3 | | 5 | H | Coventry C | W | 2-1 | 1-0 | Christie, Hunt | 10,889 |
| 4 | | 12 | A | Swansea C | L | 2-3 | 0-2 | O'Brien (pen), McCulloch | 14,391 |
| 5 | | 19 | H | Ipswich T | L | 1-4 | 0-1 | Osman (og) | 12,559 |
| 6 | | 22 | A | Everton | L | 1-3 | 0-2 | McCulloch | 22,175 |
| 7 | | 26 | A | Wolverhampton W | L | 2-3 | 1-1 | Berry (og), Goodwin | 11,594 |
| 8 | Oct | 3 | H | Arsenal | W | 2-1 | 0-1 | Hunt, Kilcline | 10,848 |
| 9 | | 10 | H | Sunderland | W | 2-0 | 1-0 | Christie 2 | 10,683 |
| 10 | | 17 | A | Southampton | L | 1-3 | 0-1 | Mair | 18,900 |
| 11 | | 24 | H | West Ham U | D | 1-1 | 0-0 | Masson | 12,505 |
| 12 | | 31 | A | Manchester U | L | 1-2 | 1-1 | McCulloch | 45,928 |
| 13 | Nov | 7 | A | Leeds U | L | 0-1 | 0-1 | | 19,552 |
| 14 | | 21 | A | Brighton & HA | D | 2-2 | 2-0 | McCulloch, Mair | 13,854 |
| 15 | | 24 | H | Everton | D | 2-2 | 0-1 | Hooks, McCulloch | 7771 |
| 16 | | 28 | H | Tottenham H | D | 2-2 | 1-1 | Goodwin, Kilcline | 15,572 |
| 17 | Dec | 5 | A | Birmingham C | L | 1-2 | 1-1 | McCulloch | 11,914 |
| 18 | Jan | 16 | H | Aston Villa | W | 1-0 | 0-0 | Christie | 9597 |
| 19 | | 23 | A | Nottingham F | W | 2-0 | 0-0 | Hooks, Christie | 26,158 |
| 20 | | 26 | H | Liverpool | L | 0-4 | 0-1 | | 14,407 |
| 21 | | 30 | A | Ipswich T | W | 3-1 | 1-0 | Mair, Kilcline, Hooks | 21,570 |
| 22 | Feb | 6 | H | Swansea C | L | 0-1 | 0-1 | | 10,070 |
| 23 | | 13 | A | Arsenal | L | 0-1 | 0-0 | | 18,229 |
| 24 | | 16 | A | Coventry C | W | 5-1 | 2-1 | Goodwin, Harkouk, Mair, Christie, Chiedozie | 10,203 |
| 25 | | 20 | H | Wolverhampton W | W | 4-0 | 1-0 | McCulloch 2, Mair 2 | 10,173 |
| 26 | | 27 | A | Sunderland | D | 1-1 | 0-0 | McCulloch | 12,910 |
| 27 | Mar | 6 | H | Southampton | D | 1-1 | 0-1 | Mair | 12,474 |
| 28 | | 13 | A | West Ham U | L | 0-1 | 0-0 | | 22,145 |
| 29 | | 20 | H | Manchester U | L | 1-3 | 0-1 | Harkouk | 17,056 |
| 30 | | 24 | A | WBA | W | 4-2 | 0-1 | McCulloch 3, Mair | 12,759 |
| 31 | | 27 | H | Leeds U | W | 2-1 | 0-1 | Harkouk, Hunt | 13,316 |
| 32 | Apr | 2 | A | Liverpool | L | 0-1 | 0-0 | | 30,126 |
| 33 | | 10 | A | Middlesbrough | L | 0-3 | 0-1 | | 10,402 |
| 34 | | 12 | H | Nottingham F | L | 1-2 | 1-1 | Christie | 19,403 |
| 35 | | 17 | H | Brighton & HA | W | 4-1 | 2-0 | Christie 3, Goodwin | 7920 |
| 36 | | 24 | A | Tottenham H | L | 1-3 | 1-2 | McCulloch | 38,017 |
| 37 | | 26 | H | Stoke C | W | 3-1 | 1-1 | McCulloch, Harkouk (pen), Mair | 8656 |
| 38 | May | 1 | H | Birmingham C | L | 1-4 | 1-1 | McCulloch | 10,710 |
| 39 | | 5 | A | Manchester C | L | 0-1 | 0-0 | | 24,443 |
| 40 | | 8 | A | Stoke C | D | 2-2 | 1-2 | Christie (pen), Richards | 11,011 |
| 41 | | 11 | H | Middlesbrough | L | 0-1 | 0-0 | | 6713 |
| 42 | | 15 | H | WBA | L | 1-2 | 0-1 | Christie | 8734 |

**Final League Position: 15**

### Goalscorers

*League* (61): McCulloch 16, Christie 13 (1 pen), Mair 9, Goodwin 4, Harkouk 4 (1 pen), Hooks 3, Hunt 3, Kilcline 3, Chiedozie 1, Masson 1, O'Brien 1 (pen), Richards 1, own goals 2.
*League Cup* (3): Hooks 1, Mair 1, Masson 1.
*FA Cup* (0).

| League Cup | Second Round | Lincoln C (a) | 1-1 |
|---|---|---|---|
| | | (h) | 2-3 |
| FA Cup | Third Round | Aston Villa (h) | 0-6 |

| Avramovic | Benjamin | O'Brien | Harkouk | Kildine | Richards | Chiedozie | McCulloch | Christie | Hunt | Hooks | Goodwin | Lahtinen | Masson | Mair | Worthington | McParland | Match No. |
|---|---|---|---|---|---|---|---|---|---|---|---|---|---|---|---|---|---|
| 1 | 2 | 3 | 4* | 5 | 6 | 7 | 8 | 9 | 10 | 11 | 12 |  |  |  |  |  | 1 |
| 1 | 2 | 3 | 4 | 5 | 6 | 7 | 8 | 9 | 10 | 11* | 12 |  |  |  |  |  | 2 |
| 1 | 2 | 3 |  | 5 | 6 | 7 | 8 | 9 | 10 | 11 | 4 |  |  |  |  |  | 3 |
| 1 | 2 | 3 |  | 5 | 6 | 7 | 8 | 9 | 10 | 11 | 4* | 12 |  |  |  |  | 4 |
| 1 | 2 | 3 |  | 5 | 6 | 7* | 10 | 9 | 4 | 11 |  | 12 | 8 |  |  |  | 5 |
| 1 | 2 | 3 |  | 5 | 6 |  | 7* | 9 | 10 | 11 | 4 |  | 8 | 12 |  |  | 6 |
| 1 | 2 |  |  | 5 | 6 |  | 7 | 9 | 10 | 11 | 4 |  | 8 |  | 3 |  | 7 |
| 1 | 2 |  |  | 5 | 6 |  | 7 | 9 | 10 | 11* | 4 |  | 8 | 12 | 3 |  | 8 |
| 1 | 2 | 3 |  | 5 |  | 7 | 9 |  | 10 | 11 | 4 | 6 | 8 |  |  |  | 9 |
| 1 | 2 | 3 |  | 5 | 4 | 7 | 9 |  | 10 |  |  | 6 | 8 | 11 |  |  | 10 |
| 1 |  | 3 |  |  | 6 | 7 | 9 | 4 | 10 | 2 | 5 |  | 8 | 11 |  |  | 11 |
| 1 | 2* | 3 |  |  | 6 | 9 | 12 | 4 | 10 | 7 | 5 |  | 8 | 11 |  |  | 12 |
| 1 | 2 | 3 |  | 5 | 6 | 7 | 11 | 9* | 4 | 10 |  | 12 | 8 |  |  |  | 13 |
| 1 | 2 | 3 |  | 5 | 6 | 7 | 9 | 4 | 10 |  |  |  | 8 | 11 |  |  | 14 |
| 1 | 2 | 3 |  | 5 | 6 | 7 | 9 | 4 | 10 |  |  |  | 8 | 11 |  |  | 15 |
| 1 | 2 | 3 |  | 5 | 6 | 7 | 9 | 4 | 10 |  |  |  | 8 | 11 |  |  | 16 |
| 1 | 2 | 3 |  | 5 | 6 | 7 | 9 | 4 | 10 |  |  |  | 8 | 11 |  |  | 17 |
| 1 | 2 | 3 |  |  | 6 | 9* | 12 |  | 5 | 10 | 4 |  | 8 | 11 |  | 7 | 18 |
| 1 | 2 | 3 |  | 5 | 6 |  | 9 |  | 10 |  | 4 |  | 8 | 11 |  | 7 | 19 |
| 1 | 2 | 3 |  | 5 | 6 | 12 | 9* |  | 10 |  | 4 |  | 8 | 11 |  | 7 | 20 |
| 1 | 2 | 3 |  | 5 | 6 | 7* | 9 | 12 | 10 |  | 4 |  | 8 | 11 |  |  | 21 |
| 1 | 2 | 3 |  | 5 | 6 | 7 | 9 | 12 | 10 |  | 4* |  | 8 | 11 |  |  | 22 |
| 1 | 2 | 3 |  | 5 | 6 | 7* | 9 | 12 | 10 |  | 4 |  | 8 | 11 |  |  | 23 |
| 1 | 2 | 3 | 8* | 5 | 6 | 7 | 9 | 12 | 10 |  | 4 |  |  | 11 |  |  | 24 |
| 1 | 2 | 3 | 8* | 5 | 6 | 7 | 9 | 12 | 10 |  | 4 |  |  | 11 |  |  | 25 |
| 1 | 2 | 3 | 8 | 5 | 6 | 7 | 9 | 12 | 10* |  | 4 |  |  | 11 |  |  | 26 |
| 1 | 2 | 3 | 8 | 5 | 6 | 7 | 9 |  | 10 |  | 4 |  |  | 11 |  |  | 27 |
| 1 | 2 | 3 | 8 | 5 | 6 | 7* | 9 | 12 | 10 |  | 4 |  |  | 11 |  |  | 28 |
| 1 | 2 | 3 | 8 | 5 | 6 |  | 9 |  | 10 |  | 4 |  |  | 11 |  | 7 | 29 |
| 1 | 2 | 3 | 8* | 5 | 6 |  | 9 |  | 10 | 12 | 4 |  |  | 11 |  | 7 | 30 |
| 1 | 2 | 3 | 8 | 5 | 6 |  | 9 |  | 10* | 12 | 4 |  |  | 11 |  | 7 | 31 |
| 1 | 2 | 3 | 8 | 5 | 6 | 10 | 9 | 12 |  |  | 4 |  |  | 11 |  | 7* | 32 |
| 1 | 2 | 3 | 8* |  | 6 | 7 | 9 | 12 | 5 | 10 | 4 |  |  | 11 |  |  | 33 |
| 1 | 2 | 3 | 8 |  | 6 | 7* | 9 | 10 | 5 |  | 4 |  |  | 11 |  | 12 | 34 |
| 1 | 2 | 3 | 8* |  | 6 | 7 | 9 | 10 | 5 |  | 4 |  |  | 11 |  | 12 | 35 |
| 1 | 2 | 3 |  | 5 | 6 | 7* | 9 | 10 | 8 |  | 4 |  |  | 11 |  | 12 | 36 |
| 1 | 2 | 3 | 8* | 5 | 6 | 7 | 9 | 10 | 12 |  | 4 |  |  | 11 |  |  | 37 |
| 1 | 2 | 3 | 8 | 5 | 6 | 7 | 9 | 10 |  |  | 4 |  |  | 11 |  |  | 38 |
| 1 | 2 | 3 |  | 5 | 6 | 7 | 9 | 10 | 8 |  | 4* |  |  | 11 |  | 12 | 39 |
| 1 | 2 | 3 | 12 | 5 | 6 | 7 | 9 | 10 | 8 |  | 4* |  |  | 11 |  |  | 40 |
| 1 | 2 | 3 | 10* | 5 | 6 | 7 | 9 | 12 | 8 |  | 4 |  |  | 11 |  |  | 41 |
| 1 | 2 |  |  | 5 | 6 | 7 | 9 | 10* | 8 |  | 4 | 3 |  | 11 |  | 12 | 42 |
| 42 | 41 | 39 | 17 | 36 | 40 | 32 | 39 | 24 | 26 | 28 | 36 | 5 | 16 | 32 | 2 | 7 | |

Substitutes: Harkouk + (1s); McCulloch + (1s); Christie + (11s); Hunt + (4s); Goodwin + (2s); Lahtinen + (3s); Mair + (2s); McParland + (5s)

## NOTTS COUNTY

| | Ht | Wt | Birthplace | Clubs | League App. | League Gls |
|---|---|---|---|---|---|---|
| **Goalkeepers** | | | | | | |
| Mick Leonard | 5 11 | 11 0 | Carshalton | Halifax T | 69 | — |
| | | | | Notts Co | 13 | — |
| Raddy Avramovic | 6 0 | 12 0 | Yugoslavia | NK Rijeka | (not known) | |
| (Yugoslavia) | | | | Notts Co | 113 | — |
| **Defenders** | | | | | | |
| Pedro Richards | 5 8 | 10 8 | London | Notts Co | 268 | 3 |
| Brian Stubbs | 6 2 | 12 0 | Keyworth | Notts Co | 426 | 21 |
| (Contract cancelled Nov 1981) | | | | | | |
| Tristan Benjamin | 6 0 | 11 1 | St Kitts | Notts Co | 174 | 4 |
| Ray O'Brien | 5 9 | 11 0 | Sherborne | Manchester U | — | — |
| (Eire) | | | | Notts Co | 318 | 30 |
| Gary Wood | 5 10 | 11 3 | Corby | Notts Co | 11 | — |
| Brian Kilcline | 6 2 | 12 0 | Nottingham | Notts Co | 94 | 5 |
| Nigel Worthington | 5 10 | 12 0 | Ballymena | Ballymena U | (not known) | |
| | | | | Notts Co | 2 | — |
| **Midfield** | | | | | | |
| Gordon Mair | 5 9 | 10 6 | Coatbridge | Notts Co | 89 | 15 |
| David Hunt | 5 11 | 11 0 | Leicester | Derby Co | 5 | — |
| | | | | Notts Co | 159 | 12 |
| Don Masson | 5 8 | 10 12 | Banchory | Middlesbrough | 54 | 6 |
| (Scotland) | | | | Notts Co | 273 | 81 |
| (Contract cancelled April 1982) | | | | QPR | 116 | 18 |
| | | | | Derby Co | 23 | 1 |
| | | | | Notts Co | 129 | 11 |
| Rachid Harkouk | 6 0½ | 12 5 | Chelsea | Crystal Palace | 54 | 21 |
| | | | | QPR | 20 | 3 |
| | | | | Notts Co | 43 | 8 |
| Mark Goodwin | 5 9¾ | 10 9 | Sheffield | Leicester C | 91 | 8 |
| | | | | Notts Co | 48 | 6 |
| Aki Lahtinen | 5 11 | 11 13 | Finland | Opsoulu | (not known) | |
| (Finland) | | | | Notts Co | 8 | — |
| Chris Dykes* | | | | Notts Co | — | — |
| Ian Benjamin | 5 11 | 12 4 | Nottingham | Sheffield U | 5 | 3 |
| (Contract cancelled) | | | | WBA | 2 | — |
| | | | | Notts Co | — | — |
| **Forwards** | | | | | | |
| Paul Hooks | 5 8 | 10 11 | Wallsend | Notts Co | 156 | 27 |
| Paul Manns | 5 6 | 10 7 | Staffs | Cardiff C | — | — |
| | | | | Notts Co | 7 | 1 |
| Jim Doherty* | 5 10 | 11 0 | Lanarkshire | Cumnock | (not known) | |
| | | | | Notts Co | 8 | — |
| Iain McCulloch | 5 10 | 11 0 | Kilmarnock | Kilmarnock | 106 | 12 |
| | | | | Notts Co | 159 | 41 |
| Trevor Christie | 6 2 | 12 0 | Newcastle | Leicester C | 31 | 8 |
| | | | | Notts Co | 115 | 36 |
| Ian McParland | 5 8 | 10 8 | Edinburgh | Ormiston Primrose | (not known) | |
| | | | | Notts Co | 14 | — |
| John Chiedozie | 5 7 | 11 0 | Owerri, | Orient | 145 | 20 |
| (Nigeria) | | | Nigeria | Notts Co | 32 | 1 |

# OLDHAM ATHLETIC

## Division 2

*Chairman:* H. Wilde.

*Vice-Chairman:* R. Schofield.

*Directors:* J. Kershaw, I. H. Stott, G. T. Butterworth, D. A. Brierley, G. Knight.

*Manager:* Joe Royle.

*Secretary:* T. Finn.

*Year Formed:* 1894.  *Turned Professional:* 1899.

*Limited Company:* 1906.

*Previous Names:* 1894, Pine Villa; 1899, Oldham Athletic.

*Previous Ground:* Sheepfoot Lane; 1905, Boundary Park.

**Football League Record:**
1907 Elected to Division 2; 1910–23 Division 1; 1923–35 Division 2; 1935–53 Division 3(N); 1953–54 Division 2; 1954–58 Division 3; 1958–63; Division 4; 1963–69 Division 3; 1969–71 Division 4; 1971–74 Division 3; 1974– Division 2.

**Honours:** *Football League:* Division 1 – Runners-up 1914–15; Division 2 – Runners-up 1909–10; Division 3(N) – Champions 1952–53; Division 3 – Champions 1973–74; Division 4 – Runners-up 1962–63. *FA Cup:* semi-final 1913. *Football League Cup:* never past 3rd rd.

*Record Victory:* 11-0 v Southport, Division 4, 26 Dec, 1962.

*Record Defeat:* 4-13 v Tranmere R, Division 3(N), 26 Dec, 1935.

*Most League Points:* 62, Division 3, 1973–74.

*Most League Goals:* 95, Division 4, 1962–63.

*Highest League Scorer in Season:* Tom Davis, 33, Division 3(N), 1936–37.

*Most League Goals in Total Aggregate:* Eric Gemmell, 110, 1947–54.

*Most Capped Player:* Albert Gray, 9 (23), Wales.

*Most League Appearances:* Ian Wood, 525, 1966–80.

*Record Transfer Fee Received:* £275,000 from QPR for Simon Stainrod, Nov 1980.

*Record Transfer Fee Paid:* £200,000 to Manchester C for Kenny Clements, Sept 1979.

*Previous Managers since the War:* Bob Mellor, Frank Womack, Billy Wooton, George Hardwick, Ted Goodier, Peter McKennan, Norman Dodgin, Jack Rowley, Les McDowall, Gordon Hurst, Jimmy McIlroy, Jack Rowley, Jimmy Frizzell.

*Address of Supporters Club:* Same as club.

*Address of the Club Shop or Boutique:* 'Latique', Boundary Park, Oldham OL1 2PA.

---

**Boundary Park, Oldham.** Telephone 061-624 4972. *Ground capacity:* 26,324. *Record attendance:* 47,671 v Sheffield W, FA Cup 4th rd, 25 Jan, 1930. *Record receipts:* £23,737 v Blackburn R, Division 2, 26 Dec, 1981. *Pitch measurements:* 110yd×74yd.

*How to get there:* Oldham Werneth is the nearest railway station; ordinary bus routes and specials link the station to the ground at Boundary Park.

*Match tickets:* Tickets can be purchased in advance 12 days before the day of the match by either personal or postal application from the ticket office.

*Car parking:* Parking for 800 cars on site adjacent to ground.

*Entertainments/catering facilities:* Social club (members only); refreshment bars around the ground. Licensed bars in seated sections.

*Club shop:* A new shop has been opened and sells all the usual souvenirs.

*Handbooks/programmes:* Programmes on sale at the ground or through the post for cover price plus postage and packing.

*Extra information:* Oldham's record victory in 1962 is the record for the Fourth Division.

*Club Colours:* Blue shirts with white trim on sleeves, white shorts with blue stripe down side, white stockings.

*Change Colours:* Tangerine shirts, blue shorts, tangerine stockings.

*Physiotherapist:* G. S. Wanless.  *Commercial Manager:* A. Hardy.

*Club Nickname:* The Latics.

## OLDHAM ATHLETIC 1981–82 LEAGUE RECORD

| Match No. | Date | Venue | Opponents | Result | H/T Score | Goalscorers | Attendance |
|---|---|---|---|---|---|---|---|
| 1 | Aug 29 | H | Cardiff C | D 2-2 | 2-1 | Clements, Palmer | 4383 |
| 2 | Sept 5 | A | Watford | D 1-1 | 0-0 | Palmer | 9018 |
| 3 | 12 | H | Shrewsbury T | D 1-1 | 0-1 | Palmer | 3994 |
| 4 | 19 | A | Bolton W | W 2-0 | 2-0 | Palmer, Heaton | 7222 |
| 5 | 22 | H | QPR | W 2-0 | 1-0 | Steel 2 | 6421 |
| 6 | 26 | H | Cambridge U | W 2-0 | 0-0 | Wylde, Heaton | 4549 |
| 7 | Oct 3 | A | Norwich C | W 2-1 | 1-1 | McDonough, Heaton | 13,710 |
| 8 | 10 | H | Luton T | D 1-1 | 1-0 | Wylde | 8403 |
| 9 | 17 | A | Rotherham U | W 2-1 | 1-0 | Wylde 2 | 8034 |
| 10 | 20 | A | Charlton Ath | L 1-3 | 1-1 | Steel | 6575 |
| 11 | 24 | A | Sheffield W | L 1-2 | 0-0 | Wylde | 17,839 |
| 12 | 31 | H | Newcastle U | W 3-1 | 3-1 | Wylde, Heaton, Steel | 9010 |
| 13 | Nov 7 | A | Barnsley | L 1-3 | 0-1 | Heaton | 14,918 |
| 14 | 14 | H | Chelsea | W 1-0 | 1-0 | Heaton | 9773 |
| 15 | 21 | H | Crystal Palace | D 0-0 | 0-0 |  | 5581 |
| 16 | 24 | A | QPR | D 0-0 | 0-0 |  | 9477 |
| 17 | 28 | A | Wrexham | W 3-0 | 2-0 | Wylde 3 | 4330 |
| 18 | Dec 5 | A | Grimsby T | W 3-1 | 1-1 | Heaton, Steel, Wylde (pen) | 5907 |
| 19 | 19 | H | Orient | W 3-2 | 1-2 | Heaton 2, Steel | 5006 |
| 20 | 26 | H | Blackburn R | L 0-3 | 0-3 |  | 15,400 |
| 21 | 28 | H | Leicester C | D 1-1 | 0-1 | Wylde (pen) | 9174 |
| 22 | Jan 9 | H | Watford | D 1-1 | 0-0 | Palmer | 7409 |
| 23 | 20 | A | Cardiff C | W 1-0 | 0-0 | Palmer | 4097 |
| 24 | 23 | A | Derby Co | L 0-1 | 0-0 |  | 10,171 |
| 25 | 30 | H | Bolton W | D 1-1 | 1-0 | Doyle (og) | 9271 |
| 26 | Feb 6 | A | Shrewsbury T | L 1-2 | 1-1 | Heaton | 4970 |
| 27 | 16 | H | Norwich C | W 2-0 | 1-0 | Wylde, Keegan | 5283 |
| 28 | 20 | A | Cambridge U | D 0-0 | 0-0 |  | 3408 |
| 29 | 27 | A | Luton T | L 0-2 | 0-1 |  | 11,506 |
| 30 | Mar 6 | A | Rotherham U | L 0-3 | 0-0 |  | 8640 |
| 31 | 13 | H | Sheffield W | L 0-3 | 0-1 |  | 9027 |
| 32 | 20 | A | Newcastle U | L 0-2 | 0-2 |  | 18,488 |
| 33 | 27 | H | Barnsley | D 1-1 | 1-1 | Heaton (pen) | 8939 |
| 34 | Apr 3 | A | Chelsea | D 2-2 | 0-1 | Heaton, Wylde | 8938 |
| 35 | 9 | A | Blackburn R | D 0-0 | 0-0 |  | 11,044 |
| 36 | 13 | A | Leicester C | L 1-2 | 1-1 | Steel | 14,298 |
| 37 | 17 | A | Crystal Palace | L 0-4 | 0-1 |  | 6720 |
| 38 | 24 | H | Wrexham | W 2-1 | 0-0 | Wylde, Keegan | 3755 |
| 39 | May 1 | A | Grimsby T | L 1-2 | 0-1 | Bowden | 7656 |
| 40 | 4 | H | Charlton Ath | W 1-0 | 1-0 | Keegan | 2904 |
| 41 | 8 | H | Derby Co | D 1-1 | 0-1 | Wylde (pen) | 4296 |
| 42 | 15 | A | Orient | W 3-0 | 1-0 | Wylde (pen), Palmer, Bowden | 2090 |

**Final League Position: 11**

**Goalscorers**

*League* (50): Wylde 16 (4 pens), Heaton 12 (1 pen), Palmer 7, Steel 7, Keegan 3, Bowden 2, Clements 1, McDonough 1, own goal 1.
*League Cup* (7): Palmer 3, Atkinson 1, Heaton 1, Steel 1, Wylde 1.
*FA Cup* (1): Heaton 1 (pen).

| **League Cup** | First Round | Bolton W (a) | 1-2 |
| | | (h) | 4-2 |
| | Second Round | Newport Co (h) | 1-0 |
| | | (a) | 0-0 |
| | Third Round | Fulham (h) | 1-1 |
| | | (a) | 0-3 |
| **FA Cup** | Third Round | Gillingham (a) | 1-2 |

| McDonnell | Sinclair | Ryan | Keegan | Clements | Futcher | Wylde | Atkinson | Steel | Palmer | McDonough | Heaton | Hoolickin | Nuttall | Edwards | Bowden | Anderson | Firm | Goram | Match No. |
|---|---|---|---|---|---|---|---|---|---|---|---|---|---|---|---|---|---|---|---|
| 1 | 2* | 3 | 4 | 5 | 6 | 7 | 8 | 9 | 10 | 11 | 12 | | | | | | | | 1 |
| 1 | | 3 | 4 | 5 | 6 | 7* | 8 | 9 | 10 | 12 | 11 | 2 | | | | | | | 2 |
| 1 | | 3 | 4 | 5 | 6 | | 8 | 9 | 10 | 11 | 7* | 2 | 12 | | | | | | 3 |
| 1 | | 3 | 4 | 5 | 6 | | 8 | 9 | 10 | 11 | 7 | 2 | | | | | | | 4 |
| 1 | | 3 | 4 | 5 | 6 | | 8* | 9 | 10 | 11 | 7 | 2 | 12 | | | | | | 5 |
| 1 | 2 | 3 | 4 | | 6 | 7 | | 9 | 10 | 11 | 8 | 5 | | | | | | | 6 |
| 1 | 2 | 3 | 4 | | 6 | 7 | | 9 | 10 | 11 | 8 | 5 | | | | | | | 7 |
| 1 | 4 | 3 | | 5 | 6 | 7 | 11 | 9 | 10 | | 8 | 2 | | | | | | | 8 |
| 1 | | | 4 | 5 | 6 | 7 | 11 | 9 | 10 | | 8 | 2 | | 3 | | | | | 9 |
| 1 | | | 4 | 5 | 6 | 7* | 11 | 9 | 10 | 12 | 8 | 2 | | 3 | | | | | 10 |
| 1 | | 3 | 4 | 5 | 6 | 7 | 11 | 9 | 10 | | 8 | 2 | | | | | | | 11 |
| 1 | | | 4 | 5 | 6 | 7 | 11 | 9 | 10 | | 8 | 2 | | 3 | | | | | 12 |
| 1 | | | 4 | 5 | 6 | 7* | 11 | 9 | 10 | 12 | 8 | 2 | | 3 | | | | | 13 |
| 1 | 2 | 3 | 4 | 5 | 6 | | 11 | 9 | 10 | 7 | 8 | | | | | | | | 14 |
| 1 | 2 | 3 | 4 | 5 | 6 | 7 | 11 | 9* | 10 | | 8 | | 12 | | | | | | 15 |
| 1 | | 3 | 4 | 5 | 6 | 7 | 11 | 9 | 10 | | 8 | 2 | | | | | | | 16 |
| 1 | | 3 | 4 | 5 | 6 | 7 | 11 | 9 | 10 | | 8 | 2 | | | | | | | 17 |
| 1 | | 3 | 4 | 5 | 6 | 7 | 11 | 9 | 10 | | 8 | 2 | | | | | | | 18 |
| 1 | | 3 | 4 | 5 | | 7 | 11 | 9 | 10 | | 8 | 6 | | 2 | | | | | 19 |
| 1 | | 3 | 4 | 5 | | 7 | 11 | 9 | 12 | 10 | 8 | 6 | | 2* | | | | | 20 |
| 1 | | 3 | | 5 | 6 | 7 | 11 | 9 | 10 | 4 | 8 | 2 | | | | | | | 21 |
| 1 | | 3 | 4 | 5 | 6 | | 11 | 9 | 10 | 7 | 8 | | | 2 | | | | | 22 |
| 1 | | 3 | 4 | 5 | 6 | | 11 | 9 | 10 | 7 | 8 | | | 2 | | | | | 23 |
| 1 | | 3 | 4 | 5 | 6 | 7* | | 9 | 10 | 11 | 8 | | 12 | 2 | | | | | 24 |
| 1 | | 3 | 4* | 5 | 6 | | 11 | 9 | 12 | 10 | 8 | | 7 | 2 | | | | | 25 |
| 1 | | 3 | 4 | 5 | 6 | | 11* | 9 | 10 | 7 | 8 | | | 2 | 12 | | | | 26 |
| 1 | | 3 | 4 | 5 | 6 | 7 | 11 | 12 | 9 | 10 | 8 | 2* | | | | | | | 27 |
| 1 | | 3 | 4 | 5 | 6 | | 11 | 9 | 10 | 7 | 8 | | | 2 | | | | | 28 |
| 1 | | 3 | 4 | 5 | 6 | 7 | 11 | 9 | 10 | | 8* | | | 2 | 12 | | | | 29 |
| 1 | | 3 | 4 | | 6 | 7 | 11 | 5* | 9 | 10 | 8 | | 12 | 2 | | | | | 30 |
| 1 | | 3* | 4 | | 6 | 7 | 11 | 9 | 10 | | 8 | 2 | | 12 | | | 5 | | 31 |
| 1 | | 3 | 4 | | 6 | 7 | | 9 | 10 | | 8 | 2 | | 11 | | | 5 | | 32 |
| 1 | | 3 | 4 | | 6 | 7 | 11 | 9 | 10 | | 8 | 2 | | | | | 5 | | 33 |
| 1 | | 3 | 4 | | | 7 | 11 | 9 | 10 | | 8 | 6 | | 2 | | | 5 | | 34 |
| 1 | | 3 | 4 | | | 7 | 11 | 9 | 10 | | 8 | 6 | | 2 | | | 5 | | 35 |
| 1 | | 3 | 4 | | | 7 | 11 | 9 | 10 | 6 | 8 | | | 2 | | | 5 | | 36 |
| 1 | | 3 | 4 | | 6 | 7 | 11 | 9 | 10 | 2 | 8 | | | | | | 5 | | 37 |
| 1 | | 3 | 4 | | 6 | 12 | 11 | 9 | 8 | 10 | 7* | | | 2 | | | 5 | | 38 |
| 1 | | | 4 | | 6 | 7 | 11* | 9 | 8 | 10 | | | | 2 | 3 | 12 | 5 | | 39 |
| | 2 | 3 | 4 | | 6 | 7 | | | | 10 | 11 | 8 | 5 | 9 | | | | 1 | 40 |
| | 2 | 3 | 4 | | 6 | 7 | | | 12 | 8* | 10 | 5 | | 9 | 11 | | | 1 | 41 |
| | 2* | 3 | 4 | | 6 | 7 | | | 9 | 8 | 11 | 5 | | 12 | 10 | | | 1 | 42 |
| 39 | 9 | 37 | 40 | 27 | 37 | 34 | 33 | 35 | 35 | 33 | 38 | 28 | 1 | 20 | 3 | 1 | 9 | 3 | |
| | +1s | | | | | +2s | +2s | +3s | +1s | | +5s | +2s | +2s | +1s | | | | | |

## OLDHAM ATHLETIC

| | Ht | Wt | Birthplace | Clubs | League App. | League Gls |
|---|---|---|---|---|---|---|
| **Goalkeepers** | | | | | | |
| Peter McDonnell* | 6 0½ | 13 7 | Kendal | Bury | 1 | — |
| | | | | Liverpool | — | — |
| | | | | Oldham Ath | 137 | — |
| Andrew Goram | 5 10 | 11 6 | Bury | WBA | — | — |
| | | | | Oldham Ath | 3 | — |
| **Defenders** | | | | | | |
| Gary Hoolickin | 5 11 | 11 1 | Middleton | Oldham Ath | 65 | 1 |
| Stephen Edwards | 5 9 | 11 0 | Birkenhead | Oldham Ath | 73 | — |
| Nick Sinclair | 5 11 | 11 7 | Manchester | Oldham Ath | 32 | — |
| Kenny Clements | 6 1 | 12 6 | Manchester | Manchester C | 119 | — |
| | | | | Oldham Ath | 103 | 2 |
| Paul Futcher | 6 0 | 12 3 | Chester | Chester | 20 | — |
| | | | | Luton T | 131 | 1 |
| | | | | Manchester C | 37 | — |
| | | | | Oldham Ath | 73 | 1 |
| John Ryan | 5 10 | 11 7 | Oldham | Oldham Ath | 37 | — |
| Andrew Birchenough* | 6 0 | 11 4 | Manchester | Oldham Ath | — | — |
| Mark Cooper* | | | | Oldham Ath | — | — |
| **Midfield** | | | | | | |
| Gerard Keegan | 5 6½ | 10 9 | Manchester | Manchester C | 37 | 2 |
| | | | | Oldham Ath | 123 | 5 |
| Darren McDonough | 5 11 | 11 0 | Belgium | Oldham Ath | 51 | 4 |
| Derek Egan* | 5 8 | 10 9 | Manchester | Oldham Ath | — | — |
| Paul Atkinson | 5 10 | 11 5 | Pudsey | Oldham Ath | 101 | 8 |
| **Forwards** | | | | | | |
| Paul Heaton | 5 9 | 10 2 | Hyde | Oldham Ath | 107 | 23 |
| Jim Steel | 6 3 | 11 0 | Dumfries | Oldham Ath | 101 | 24 |
| Rodger Wylde | 6 1½ | 12 0 | Sheffield | Sheffield W | 169 | 54 |
| | | | | Burnley (on loan) | — | — |
| | | | | Oldham Ath | 74 | 32 |
| Douglas Anderson | 5 11½ | 9 5 | Hong Kong | Port Glasgow | (not known) | |
| | | | | Oldham Ath | 2 | — |
| Roger Palmer | 5 10 | 10 10 | Manchester | Manchester C | 31 | 9 |
| | | | | Oldham Ath | 58 | 13 |
| John Bowden | 6 0 | 11 7 | Stockport | Oldham Ath | 5 | 2 |
| Martin Nuttall* | 5 9 | 11 2 | Oldham | Oldham Ath | 13 | 1 |
| David Brand | | | | Oldham Ath | — | — |

# ORIENT Division 3

*Chairman:* Brian B. Winston. *Deputy Chairman:* A. J. Harding.

*Directors:* A. Pincus, D. L. Weinrabe.

*Manager:* Ken Knighton.

*Secretary:* Peter Barnes.

*Chief Marketing Executive:* Malcolm Vinacour.

*Asst Secretary:* Miss Carol Stokes.

*Assistant Manager:* Frank Clark.

*Year Formed:* 1881. *Turned Professional:* 1903.

*Limited Company:* 1906.

*Previous Names:* 1881–86, Glyn Cricket and Football Club; 1886–88, Eagle Football Club; 1888–98, Orient Football Club; 1898–1946, Clapton Orient; 1946–66, Leyton Orient.

*Previous Grounds:* Glyn Road (1884–96), Whittles Athletic Ground (1896–1900), Millfields Road (1900–30), and Lea Bridge Road (1930–37).

**Football League Record:**
1905 Elected to Division 2; 1929–56 Division 3(S); 1956–62 Division 2; 1962–63 Division 1; 1963–66 Division 2; 1966–70 Division 3; 1970–82 Division 2; 1982– Division 3.

**Honours:** *Football League:* Division 1 best season: 22nd, 1962–63; Division 2 – Runners-up 1961–62; Division 3 – Champions 1969–70; Division 3(S) – Champions 1955–56; Runners-up 1954–55. *FA Cup:* Semi-final 1977–78. *Football League Cup* best season: 5th rd, 1963.

*Record Victory:* 9-2 v Aldershot, Division 3(S), 10 Feb, 1934 and v Chester, League Cup 3rd rd, 15 Oct, 1962.

*Record Defeat:* 0-8 v Aston Villa, FA Cup 4th rd, 30 Jan, 1929.

*Most League Points:* 66, Division 3(S), 1955–56.

*Most League Goals:* 106, Division 3(S), 1955–56.

*Highest League Scorer in Season:* Tom Johnston, 35, Division 2, 1957–58.

*Most League Goals in Total Aggregate:* Tom Johnston, 121, 1956–58, 1959–61.

*Most Capped Player:* Tony Grealish, 8 (30), Eire.

*Most League Appearances:* Peter Allen, 431, 1965–78.

*Record Transfer Fee Received:* £600,000 from Notts Co for John Chiedozie, Aug 1981.

*Record Transfer Fee Paid:* £150,000 to Tottenham H for Peter Taylor, Nov 1980.

*Previous Managers since the War:* Charles Hewitt, Neil McBain, Alec Stock, Les Gore, Alec Stock, John Carey, Benny Fenton, Dave Sexton, Dick Graham, Jimmy Bloomfield, George Petchey, Jimmy Bloomfield.

*Address of Supporters Club:* Same as Ground.

*Address of the Club Shop:* Orient Shop, 369 High Road, Leyton E10.

---

**Leyton Stadium, Brisbane Road, Leyton, London E10 5NE.** Telephone 01-539 2223/4. *Telegraphic address:* 'The Orient', Leyton E10. *Ground capacity:* 26,500 (7,171 seats). *Record attendance:* 34,345 v West Ham U, FA Cup 4th rd, 25 Jan, 1964. *Record receipts:* £41,765.20 v West Ham U, FA Cup 4th rd, 26 Jan, 1980. *Pitch measurements:* 110yd×75yd.

*How to get there:* Buses 69, 58, 278, 241 pass the ground. From the centre of London, journey by underground (Central Line) to Leyton station; the ground is a few minutes' walk. Nearest BR station is Leyton Midland Road (10 minutes' walk).

*Match tickets:* Can be booked at least two weeks in advance.

*Car parking:* Street parking around the ground. A National Car Park five minutes from Brisbane Road (off Oliver Road).

*Entertainments/catering facilities:* Supporters' Section Club and snack bar points around the ground.

*Club shop:* Sells all types of souvenirs and sportswear.

*Handbooks/programmes:* Programmes can be obtained on subscription, and back numbers can be ordered from the club shop. Official centenary handbook available from club shop, £1.20 including p & p, limited edition only.

*Extra information:* The club operates a Pools Section and Travel Service. All enquiries to 369 High Road, Leyton, E10 (01-539 4483/4). Club's official historian – Neil Kaufman – can answer queries connected with the history of the club; c/o the Secretary.

*Club Colours:* All red.

*Change Colours:* All blue.

*Club Captain:*      *Reserve Team Coach:* Dario Gradi.

*Club Nickname:* The O's.

278

## ORIENT 1981–82 LEAGUE RECORD

| Match No. | Date | Venue | Opponents | Result | H/T Score | Goalscorers | Attendance |
|---|---|---|---|---|---|---|---|
| 1 | Aug 29 | A | Derby Co | W 2-1 | 1-0 | Taylor P., Jennings | 12,423 |
| 2 | Sept 5 | H | Grimsby T | L 1-2 | 1-2 | Taylor P. | 3764 |
| 3 | 12 | A | Blackburn R | L 0-2 | 0-1 | | 7043 |
| 4 | 19 | H | Wrexham | D 0-0 | 0-0 | | 2899 |
| 5 | 22 | A | Crystal Palace | L 0-1 | 0-1 | | 11,061 |
| 6 | 26 | A | Newcastle U | L 0-1 | 0-0 | | 13,710 |
| 7 | 28 | H | Chelsea | L 0-2 | 0-1 | | 9698 |
| 8 | Oct 3 | H | Luton T | L 0-3 | 0-2 | | 5084 |
| 9 | 10 | A | Watford | L 0-3 | 0-0 | | 10,052 |
| 10 | 18 | H | QPR | D 1-1 | 0-0 | Cunningham | 8192 |
| 11 | 25 | H | Charlton Ath | D 1-1 | 1-0 | Bowles (pen) | 8265 |
| 12 | 31 | A | Barnsley | L 0-1 | 0-0 | | 13,435 |
| 13 | Nov 7 | H | Sheffield W | W 3-0 | 1-0 | Margerrison, Sussex, Silkman | 5179 |
| 14 | 14 | A | Leicester C | W 1-0 | 0-0 | McNeil | 11,733 |
| 15 | 21 | A | Bolton W | L 0-1 | 0-0 | | 5737 |
| 16 | 24 | H | Newcastle U | W 1-0 | 0-0 | Margerrison | 4026 |
| 17 | 28 | H | Shrewsbury T | W 2-0 | 2-0 | Godfrey 2 | 3327 |
| 18 | Dec 5 | A | Rotherham U | L 0-1 | 0-1 | | 6346 |
| 19 | 19 | A | Oldham Ath | L 2-3 | 2-1 | Giles 2 | 5006 |
| 20 | Jan 9 | A | Grimsby T | W 2-1 | 1-0 | Godfrey, Moores | 6877 |
| 21 | 16 | H | Derby Co | W 3-2 | 2-2 | Moores 2, Godfrey | 4595 |
| 22 | 23 | H | Barnsley | L 1-3 | 0-2 | Moores | 3620 |
| 23 | 30 | A | Wrexham | W 1-0 | 0-0 | Godfrey | 4221 |
| 24 | Feb 6 | H | Blackburn R | D 0-0 | 0-0 | | 3990 |
| 25 | 21 | H | Crystal Palace | D 0-0 | 0-0 | | 5132 |
| 26 | 27 | H | Watford | L 1-3 | 1-2 | Silkman (pen) | 6595 |
| 27 | Mar 12 | A | Charlton Ath | L 2-5 | 1-1 | Jennings, Silkman | 5871 |
| 28 | 16 | H | Norwich C | D 1-1 | 1-1 | Jennings | 2933 |
| 29 | 27 | A | Sheffield W | L 0-2 | 0-0 | | 16,460 |
| 30 | 30 | A | Luton T | L 0-2 | 0-0 | | 9716 |
| 31 | Apr 6 | A | QPR | L 0-3 | 0-3 | | 10,531 |
| 32 | 10 | A | Cardiff C | L 1-2 | 1-1 | Foster | 5689 |
| 33 | 12 | H | Cambridge U | D 0-0 | 0-0 | | 3162 |
| 34 | 17 | H | Bolton W | W 3-0 | 2-0 | Godfrey, McNeil, Silkman (pen) | 2851 |
| 35 | 20 | A | Cambridge U | L 0-2 | 0-2 | | 3660 |
| 36 | 24 | A | Shrewsbury T | L 0-2 | 0-0 | | 2898 |
| 37 | 28 | H | Cardiff C | D 1-1 | 0-0 | Foster | 2527 |
| 38 | May 1 | H | Rotherham U | L 1-2 | 0-0 | Margerrison | 3009 |
| 39 | 5 | A | Chelsea | D 2-2 | 0-2 | Houchen, Lock (og) | 6009 |
| 40 | 8 | A | Norwich C | L 0-2 | 0-0 | | 19,197 |
| 41 | 15 | H | Oldham Ath | L 0-3 | 0-1 | | 2090 |
| 42 | 18 | H | Leicester C | W 3-0 | 2-0 | Godfrey, Silkman, McNeil | 2107 |

**Final League Position: 22**

**Goalscorers**

*League* (36): Godfrey 7, Silkman 5 (2 pens), Moores 4, Jennings 3, McNeil 3, Margerrison 3, Foster 2, Giles 2, Taylor P. 2, Bowles 1 (pen), Cunningham 1, Houchen 1, Sussex 1, own goal 1.
*League Cup* (3): Moores 2, Jennings 1.
*FA Cup* (4): Moores 3, Foster 1.

| | | | | |
|---|---|---|---|---|
| **League Cup** | First Round | Millwall (h) | | 1-1 |
| | | (a) | | 2-3 |
| **FA Cup** | Third Round | Charlton Ath (h) | | 1-0 |
| | Fourth Round | Huddersfield T (a) | | 1-1 |
| | | (h) | | 2-0 |
| | Fifth Round | Crystal Palace (a) | | 0-0 |
| | | (h) | | 0-1 |

| Day | Fisher | Roffey | Taylor T. | Gray | Margerrison | Godfrey | Moores | Jennings | Bowles | Taylor P. | Mayo | Hughton | Cunningham | Hallybone | Silkman | McNeil | Sussex | Giles | Foster | Osgood | Blackhall | Banjo | Houchen | Peach | Cornwell | Vincent | Match No. |
|---|---|---|---|---|---|---|---|---|---|---|---|---|---|---|---|---|---|---|---|---|---|---|---|---|---|---|---|
| 1 | 2 | 3 | 4 | 5 | 6* | 7 | 8 | 9 | 10 | 11 | 12 | | | | | | | | | | | | | | | | 1 |
| 1 | 2 | 3 | 4 | 5 | 6 | 7 | 8 | 9 | 10 | 11 | | | | | | | | | | | | | | | | | 2 |
| 1 | 2 | 3 | 4 | 5 | 6 | 7 | | 9 | 8 | 10* | 11 | 12 | | | | | | | | | | | | | | | 3 |
| 1 | 2 | 3 | 4 | | 6* | 7 | | 9 | 8 | 10 | 11 | 12 | 5 | | | | | | | | | | | | | | 4 |
| 1 | 2 | 3 | 4 | 5 | | 8 | 9 | 7 | | | | 10 | 6 | 11 | | | | | | | | | | | | | 5 |
| 1 | | 3 | 4 | 5 | 10 | 7 | 9 | 8 | | | | 2 | 6 | | 11 | | | | | | | | | | | | 6 |
| 1 | | 3 | 4 | 5 | 10 | 7* | 9 | 8 | | | 12 | 2 | 6 | | 11 | | | | | | | | | | | | 7 |
| 1 | | 3 | 4 | 5 | 10 | 7 | 9 | 8 | 11* | | | 2 | 6 | | 12 | | | | | | | | | | | | 8 |
| 1 | | 3 | 4 | 5 | 10 | 7 | 9 | | 11 | | | 2 | 6 | | 8 | | | | | | | | | | | | 9 |
| 1 | | 3 | 4 | 5 | 10* | 7 | 9 | | | | | 2 | 6 | 12 | 8 | 11 | | | | | | | | | | | 10 |
| 1 | | 3 | 4 | 5* | 10 | 7 | 9 | | | | 12 | 2 | 6 | | 8 | 11 | | | | | | | | | | | 11 |
| 1 | | 3 | 4 | 5 | 10 | 7 | 9 | | | | | 2 | 6 | | 8 | 11 | | | | | | | | | | | 12 |
| 1 | | 3 | 4 | 5 | 10 | 7 | 9 | | | | | 2 | | | 8 | 11 | 6 | | | | | | | | | | 13 |
| 1 | | 3 | 4 | 5 | 10 | 7 | 9 | | | | | 2 | | | 8 | 11 | 6 | | | | | | | | | | 14 |
| 1 | | 3 | 4 | 5 | 10 | 7 | 9 | | | | | 2 | | | 8 | 11 | 6 | | | | | | | | | | 15 |
| 1 | 6 | 3* | 4 | 5 | 10 | 7 | 9 | | | | | 2 | 12 | | 8 | 11 | | | | | | | | | | | 16 |
| 1 | 6 | | 4 | 5 | 10 | 7 | | | | | | 2 | 3 | | 8 | 11 | 9 | | | | | | | | | | 17 |
| 1 | 6 | | 4 | 5 | 10 | 7 | | | | | | 2 | 3 | | 8 | 11 | 9 | | | | | | | | | | 18 |
| 1 | 6 | | 4 | 5 | 10 | 7 | | | | | | 2 | 3 | | 8 | 11 | 9 | | | | | | | | | | 19 |
| 1 | 11 | | 4 | 5 | 8 | 7 | 9 | | | | | | 3 | | 10 | | | | 2 | 6 | | | | | | | 20 |
| 1 | 11* | | 4 | 5 | 8 | 7 | 9 | | | | | | 3 | | 10 | | | | 2 | 6 | 12 | | | | | | 21 |
| 1 | | | 4 | 5* | 8 | 7 | 9 | | | | | | 3 | 11 | 10 | | | | 2 | 6 | 12 | | | | | | 22 |
| 1 | | 3 | 4 | 5 | 8 | 7 | 9 | | | | | | | | 11 | 10* | 12 | | 2 | 6 | | | | | | | 23 |
| 1 | | 3 | 4 | 5 | 8 | 7 | 9 | | | | | | | | 11 | 12 | 10* | | 2 | 6 | | | | | | | 24 |
| 1 | 4 | | 3 | 5 | 8 | 7 | 9 | | | | | | | | 11 | 6* | 10 | 12 | 2 | | | | | | | | 25 |
| 1 | 4 | | 3 | 5 | | 7 | 9 | | | | | | | | 11 | 10 | 8 | | 2 | 6 | | | | | | | 26 |
| 1 | 4 | | 3 | 5 | 6 | 7 | 9 | 8 | | | | | | | 11 | 10 | | | 2 | | | | | | | | 27 |
| 1 | 4 | | 3 | 5 | | 7* | 9 | | 10 | 11 | | 2 | 12 | | 8 | | 6 | | | | | | | | | | 28 |
| 1 | 4 | | 3 | 5 | | 7 | 9 | | 10 | 11 | | | | | | | | | 2 | 6 | | 8 | | | | | 29 |
| 1 | 4 | | | 5 | | 7 | 9* | | | | | | 12 | | 10 | 11 | | | 2 | 6 | | 8 | | 3 | | | 30 |
| 1 | 4 | | | 5 | 8 | 7 | | | | | | | | | 10 | 12 | 11* | | 2 | 6 | | | 9 | 3 | | | 31 |
| 1 | 4 | | | 5 | 8 | 7 | | | | | | | 6 | | 10 | 11 | | | 2 | | | | 9 | 3 | | | 32 |
| 1 | 4 | | | 5 | 8 | 7 | | | | | | | 6* | 12 | 10 | 11 | | | 2 | | | | 9 | 3 | | | 33 |
| 1 | 4 | | | 5 | 8 | 7 | | | | | | | 6 | | 10 | 11 | | | 2 | | | | 9 | 3 | | | 34 |
| 1 | 4 | | | 5 | 8 | 7 | | | | | | | 6 | | 10* | 11 | | | 2 | | | | 9 | 3 | | | 35 |
| 1 | 4 | | | 5 | 8 | 7* | | | | | | | 12 | | 10 | 11 | 6 | | 2 | | | | 9 | 3 | | | 36 |
| 1 | 4 | | | 5 | 11 | 7 | | | | | | | 6 | | 10 | | 8 | | 2 | | | | 9 | 3 | | | 37 |
| 1 | 4 | | | 5 | 11 | 7 | | | | | | | 6 | | 10 | | 8 | | 2 | | | | 9 | 3 | | | 38 |
| 1 | 4 | | | 5 | 11 | 7 | | | | | | | 6 | | 10* | | 8 | 12 | 2 | | | | 9 | 3 | | | 39 |
| 1 | | | | 5 | 11 | 7 | | | | | | | 6 | | 10 | | 8 | | 2 | | | | 9 | 3 | 4 | | 40 |
| 1 | | | | 5 | 11 | 7 | | | | | | | 6 | | 10 | | 8* | | 2 | 12 | | | 9 | 3 | 4 | | 41 |
| 1 | | | | 5 | 11 | 7 | | | | | | | | | 10 | | | | 2 | 6 | | | 9 | 3 | 4 | 8 | 42 |
| 42 | 31 | 18 | 33 | 38 | 34 | 42 | 23 | 10 | 7 | 10 | — | 23 | 18 | 5 | 33 | 20 | 8 | 3 | 23 | 6 | 1 | 3 | 14 | 13 | 3 | 1 | |
| | | | | | | + | | | + | + | + | | | | + | + | + | | | | | + | | | | | |
| | | | | | | 1s | | | 3s | 1s | 4s | | | | 3s | 2s | 4s | | | | | 3s | | | | | |

## ORIENT

| | Ht | Wt | Birthplace | Clubs | League App. | League Gls |
|---|---|---|---|---|---|---|
| **Goalkeepers** | | | | | | |
| Mervyn Day | 6 2 | 14 12 | Chelmsford | West Ham U | 194 | — |
| | | | | Orient | 124 | — |
| Lloyd Scott | 6 0 | 12 3 | Stepney | Orient | — | — |
| (Contract cancelled Jan 1982) | | | | | | |
| Jeff Fielding* | 6 0 | 11 7 | Stevenage | Orient | — | — |
| **Defenders** | | | | | | |
| Bill Roffey | 5 11 | 12 13 | Stepney | Crystal Palace | 24 | — |
| | | | | Orient | 257 | 5 |
| Nigel Gray | 6 3 | 13 4 | Fulham | Orient | 203 | 1 |
| Bobby Fisher | 5 8 | 11 2 | Wembley | Orient | 312 | 4 |
| Tommy Taylor | 6 1 | 13 7 | Hornchurch | Orient | 114 | 4 |
| | | | | West Ham U | 340 | 8 |
| | | | | Orient | 116 | 5 |
| Robert Waterfall* | 5 11 | 10 7 | Ilford | Orient | — | — |
| Tommy Cunningham | 6 0 | 11 3 | London | Chelsea | — | — |
| | | | | QPR | 30 | 2 |
| | | | | Wimbledon | 99 | 12 |
| | | | | Orient | 18 | 1 |
| David Peach | 5 9 | 11 6 | Bedford | Gillingham | 187 | 30 |
| | | | | Southampton | 224 | 34 |
| | | | | Swindon T | 53 | 2 |
| | | | | Orient | 13 | — |
| Keith Osgood | 5 11 | 11 2 | Ealing | Tottenham H | 113 | 13 |
| | | | | Coventry C | 25 | 1 |
| | | | | Derby Co | 69 | 10 |
| | | | | Orient | 6 | — |
| Colin Foster | 6 4 | 13 10 | Rochford | Orient | 23 | 2 |
| **Midfield** | | | | | | |
| Tunji Banjo* | 5 8 | 11 0 | Kensington | Orient | 27 | 1 |
| (Nigeria) | | | | | | |
| Henry Hughton* | 5 8½ | 11 10 | Stratford | Orient | 111 | 2 |
| Ralph Coates | 5 7½ | 12 2 | Hetton-le-Hole | Burnley | 216 | 26 |
| (England) | | | | Tottenham H | 188 | 14 |
| (Contract cancelled Aug 1981) | | | | Orient | 76 | 12 |
| Jimmy Hallybone* | 5 6 | 10 0 | Leytonstone | Orient | 8 | — |
| Mark Kane* | 5 6 | 9 12 | Hackney | Orient | — | — |
| John Margerrison* | 5 10 | 12 2 | Bushey | Tottenham H | — | — |
| | | | | Fulham | 71 | 9 |
| | | | | Orient | 80 | 6 |
| Tony Mercer | 5 9 | 10 10 | Forest Gate | Crystal Palace | — | — |
| (Contract cancelled Jan 1982) | | | | Orient | — | — |
| Peter Moles | 5 7 | 9 5 | Basildon | Orient | — | — |
| (Contract cancelled Jan 1982) | | | | | | |
| Peter Taylor | 5 9 | 11 7 | Southend | Southend U | 75 | 12 |
| (England) | | | | Crystal Palace | 122 | 33 |
| | | | | Tottenham H | 123 | 31 |
| | | | | Orient | 37 | 10 |
| Barry Silkman | 5 8 | 10 13 | London | Hereford U | 37 | 2 |
| | | | | Crystal Palace | 48 | 7 |
| | | | | Plymouth Arg | 14 | 2 |
| | | | | Luton T (on loan) | 3 | — |
| | | | | Manchester C | 19 | 3 |
| | | | | Brentford | 14 | 1 |
| | | | | QPR | 23 | 2 |
| | | | | Orient | 35 | 5 |
| Grant Sargant | | | | Orient | — | — |
| (Contract cancelled Jan 1982) | | | | | | |
| John Cornwell | | | | Orient | 3 | — |
| (Apprentice) | | | | | | |
| Jonathan Goff | | | | Orient | — | — |
| (Contract cancelled Jan 1982) | | | | | | |
| Robert Vincent | 5 8 | 11 2 | Newcastle | Sunderland | 2 | — |
| (Non-contract) | | | | Orient | 1 | — |
| **Forwards** | | | | | | |
| Kevin Godfrey | 5 10 | 10 11 | Kennington | Orient | 73 | 10 |
| Billy Hurley | 5 9½ | 12 6 | Leytonstone | Orient | 2 | — |
| Ian Moores | 6 2 | 13 8 | Chesterton | Stoke C | 50 | 14 |
| | | | | Tottenham H | 29 | 6 |
| | | | | Orient | 117 | 26 |
| Mark Blackhall | 6 0 | 12 2 | Upney | Orient | 4 | — |
| Steve Parsons | 6 0 | 12 7 | London | Wimbledon | 94 | 19 |
| | | | | Orient | 36 | 6 |
| Mark McNeil | 5 10 | 10 5 | Bethnal Green | Orient | 24 | 3 |
| Andy Sussex | | | | Orient | 8 | 1 |
| (Apprentice) | | | | | | |
| Keith Houchen | 6 2 | 11 4 | Middlesbrough | Hartlepool U | 170 | 65 |
| | | | | Orient | 14 | 1 |

# OXFORD UNITED

# Division 3

OXFORD UNITED F.C.

*President:* The Duke of Marlborough.

*Chairman:* I. R. Maxwell MC.

*Vice-Chairmen:* Dr D. Morris BSC, D PHIL, W. H. Reeves, L. Town.

*Directors:* W. Black, G. E. Coppock, E. Gibbs, H. Kimber, P. Reeves, G. Whiting.

*Manager:* Jim Smith.

*Secretary:* Jim Hunt.

*Year Formed:* 1896. *Turned Professional:* 1949.

*Limited Company:* 1949.

*Previous Names:* Headington United; 1960, Oxford United.

**Football League Record:**
1962 Elected to Division 4; 1965–68 Division 3; 1968–76 Division 2; 1976– Division 3.

**Honours:** *Football League:* Division 2 best season: 8th, 1972–73; Division 3 – Champions 1967–68; Division 4 – Promoted 1964–65 (4th). *FA Cup* best season: 6th rd, 1963–64 (record for 4th Division club), 1981–82. *Football League Cup* best season: 5th rd, 1969–70.

*Record Victory:* 7-0 v Barrow, Division 4, 19 Dec, 1964.

*Record Defeat:* 0-5 v Cardiff C, Division 2, 8 Feb, 1969, and v Cardiff C, Division 2, 12 Sept, 1973.

*Most League Points:* 61, Division 4, 1964–65. *Three points win:* 71, Division 3, 1981–82.

*Most League Goals:* 87, Division 4, 1964–65.

*Highest League Scorer in Season:* Colin Booth, 23, Division 4, 1964–65.

*Most League Goals in Total Aggregate:* Graham Atkinson, 73, 1962–73.

*Most Capped Player:* David Roberts, 6 (17), Wales.

*Most League Appearances:* John Shuker, 480, 1962–77.

*Record Transfer Fee Received:* £100,000 from Watford for Les Taylor, Nov 1980.

*Record Transfer Fee Paid:* £75,000 to Cardiff C for Andy McCulloch, July 1974.

*Previous Managers since the War:* Arthur Turner, Ron Saunders, Gerry Summers, Mike Brown, Bill Asprey, Ian Greaves.

*Address of Supporters Club:* Supporters Club Offices, Manor Ground, Headington, Oxford.

*Address of the Club Shop or Boutique:* On ground on match days.

---

**Manor Ground, Headington, Oxford.** Telephone Oxford 61503. *Ground capacity:* 17,350. *Record attendance:* 22,730 v Preston NE, FA Cup 6th rd, 29 Feb, 1964. *Record receipts:* £14,156 v Burnley, Division 3, 17 April, 1982. *Pitch measurements:* 112yd×78yd.

*How to get there:* Bus 29/6/0 from the city centre. Nearest railway station is Oxford General. From the station take Bus 501 to Queens Lane and then take Bus 29/6/0. By road, take Oxford ring road to the east of the city, following the signs for Headington. Leave the ring road at Green Road roundabout into London Road; the ground is on the right after going straight across at the traffic lights.

*Match tickets:* Subject to availability tickets may be booked 14 days prior to the match.

*Car parking:* Parking is available in certain streets around the ground.

*Entertainments/catering facilities:* Public houses, and cafés, all just minutes from the ground. Refreshments available inside the ground.

*Club shop:* Sited on the ground, open match days only selling all types of souvenirs (mail order list sent on receipt of SAE) as well as a wide range of all club programmes for both current and previous seasons.

*Handbooks/programmes:* Handbook on sale at £1+20p postage and packing. Programmes available on subscription. Applications to the Club office.

*Extra information:* In five years from joining the Fourth Division, Oxford reached Division Two.

*Club Colours:* Yellow shirts with blue trim, blue shorts, yellow stockings.

*Change Colours:* All red.

*Club Captain:* Ray Train.

*First Team Trainer:* Ken Fish.

*Club Nickname:* The U's.

## OXFORD UNITED 1981–82 LEAGUE RECORD

| Match No. | Date | Venue | Opponents | Result | | H/T Score | Goalscorers | Attendance |
|---|---|---|---|---|---|---|---|---|
| 1 | Aug 29 | A | Plymouth Arg | W | 1-0 | 1-0 | Cassells | 4089 |
| 2 | Sept 5 | H | Huddersfield T | W | 1-0 | 0-0 | Foley | 3976 |
| 3 | 12 | A | Newport Co | L | 2-3 | 2-0 | Shotton, Cassells | 5293 |
| 4 | 19 | H | Walsall | L | 0-1 | 0-0 | | 3685 |
| 5 | 23 | H | Portsmouth | L | 0-2 | 0-1 | | 4750 |
| 6 | 26 | A | Carlisle U | L | 1-2 | 0-0 | Shotton | 3085 |
| 7 | 29 | A | Millwall | W | 2-1 | 0-0 | Jones, Cassells | 5885 |
| 8 | Oct 3 | H | Fulham | W | 2-0 | 1-0 | Foley, Thomas | 4244 |
| 9 | 10 | A | Chester | D | 2-2 | 1-1 | Jones, Cassells | 2008 |
| 10 | 17 | H | Bristol C | W | 1-0 | 1-0 | Cassells (pen) | 3906 |
| 11 | 21 | H | Bristol R | D | 1-1 | 1-0 | Cassells | 4422 |
| 12 | 24 | A | Southend U | W | 1-0 | 1-0 | Thomas | 5366 |
| 13 | 31 | H | Lincoln C | D | 1-1 | 0-0 | Thomas | 3985 |
| 14 | Nov 4 | A | Exeter C | W | 2-1 | 0-1 | Thomas 2 | 3349 |
| 15 | 7 | A | Chesterfield | D | 2-2 | 0-0 | Thomas, Briggs | 5295 |
| 16 | 14 | H | Brentford | L | 1-2 | 0-1 | Foley | 5461 |
| 17 | 28 | H | Preston NE | W | 3-0 | 2-0 | Cassells 2 (1 pen), Foley | 3798 |
| 18 | Dec 5 | A | Burnley | L | 1-2 | 0-0 | Brock | 4346 |
| 19 | Jan 9 | A | Huddersfield T | L | 0-2 | 0-0 | | 7070 |
| 20 | 30 | A | Walsall | W | 3-1 | 3-0 | Thomas, Cassells, Foley | 4573 |
| 21 | Feb 3 | H | Reading | W | 1-0 | 1-0 | Jones | 9354 |
| 22 | 6 | H | Newport Co | D | 1-1 | 1-1 | Thomas | 5653 |
| 23 | 9 | A | Portsmouth | D | 1-1 | 1-1 | Thomas | 7095 |
| 24 | 20 | H | Carlisle U | W | 2-1 | 2-1 | Thomas 2 | 4797 |
| 25 | 23 | A | Fulham | D | 0-0 | 0-0 | | 5959 |
| 26 | 27 | H | Chester | W | 3-1 | 1-0 | Jeffrey, Cassells (pen), Smithers | 5049 |
| 27 | Mar 6 | A | Bristol C | W | 2-0 | 0-0 | Shotton, Kearns | 8155 |
| 28 | 13 | H | Southend U | L | 0-2 | 0-1 | | 6252 |
| 29 | 17 | H | Exeter C | D | 0-0 | 0-0 | | 5098 |
| 30 | 20 | A | Lincoln C | L | 1-2 | 0-1 | Thomas | 4474 |
| 31 | 23 | A | Doncaster R | D | 1-1 | 1-0 | Seacole | 3800 |
| 32 | 27 | H | Chesterfield | D | 1-1 | 0-0 | Lawrence | 6215 |
| 33 | 31 | H | Gillingham | D | 1-1 | 1-1 | Kearns | 5223 |
| 34 | Apr 3 | A | Brentford | W | 2-1 | 2-1 | Hebberd, Foley | 5786 |
| 35 | 7 | H | Swindon T | W | 5-0 | 2-0 | Fogg (pen), Shotton, Thomas, Lawrence, Foley | 7354 |
| 36 | 10 | A | Reading | W | 3-0 | 1-0 | Jeffrey, Brock 2 | 6926 |
| 37 | 12 | H | Doncaster R | W | 3-1 | 1-0 | Fogg (pen), Brock, Thomas | 8278 |
| 38 | 17 | H | Burnley | D | 0-0 | 0-0 | | 10,171 |
| 39 | 20 | A | Wimbledon | W | 3-2 | 1-2 | Hebberd, Lawrence, Leslie (og) | 2903 |
| 40 | 24 | A | Preston NE | D | 2-2 | 0-1 | Kearns, Brock | 5516 |
| 41 | 28 | H | Plymouth Arg | W | 1-0 | 0-0 | Kearns | 6957 |
| 42 | May 1 | H | Millwall | D | 0-0 | 0-0 | | 7230 |
| 43 | 4 | A | Swindon T | L | 2-3 | 0-0 | Jeffrey, Fogg (pen) | 7880 |
| 44 | 8 | A | Gillingham | L | 1-2 | 1-0 | Lawrence | 4690 |
| 45 | 11 | A | Bristol R | L | 0-1 | 0-1 | | 4754 |
| 46 | 15 | H | Wimbledon | L | 0-3 | 0-0 | | 4319 |

**Final League Position: 5**

### Goalscorers

*League* (63): Thomas 14, Cassells 10 (3 pens), Foley 7, Brock 5, Kearns 4, Lawrence 4, Shotton 4, Fogg 3 (3 pens), Jeffrey 3, Jones 3, Hebberd 2, Briggs 1, Seacole 1, Smithers 1, own goal 1.
*League Cup* (7): Cassells 4 (1 pen), Foley 1, Thomas 1, own goal 1.
*FA Cup* (13): Cassells 7 (1 pen), Thomas 3, Foley 2, Smithers 1.

| | | | |
|---|---|---|---|
| **League Cup** | First Round | Brentford (h) | 1-0 |
| | | (a) | 2-0 |
| | Second Round | Millwall (a) | 3-3 |
| | | (h) | 1-0 |
| | Third Round | Everton (a) | 0-1 |
| **FA Cup** | First Round | Dover (a) | 2-0 |
| | Second Round | Aldershot (a) | 2-2 |
| | | (h) | 4-2 |
| | Third Round | Bournemouth (a) | 2-0 |
| | Fourth Round | Brighton & HA (a) | 3-0 |
| | Fifth Round | Coventry C (a) | 0-4 |

| Burton | Doyle | Fogg | Jeffrey | Briggs | Shotton | Jones | Foley | Cassells | Page | Smithers | Thomas | Lythgoe | Kearns | Kingston | Wright | Brock | Berry | Seacole | Train | Lawrence | Hebberd | Match No. |
|---|---|---|---|---|---|---|---|---|---|---|---|---|---|---|---|---|---|---|---|---|---|---|
| 1 | 2 | 3 | 4 | 5 | 6 | 7 | 8 | 9 | 10 | 11 | | | | | | | | | | | | 1 |
| 1 | 2 | 3 | 4 | 5 | 6 | 7 | 8 | 9 | 10 | 11 | | | | | | | | | | | | 2 |
| 1 | 2 | 3 | 4 | 5 | 6 | 7* | 8 | 9 | 10 | 11 | 12 | | | | | | | | | | | 3 |
| 1 | 2 | 3 | 4 | 5 | 6 | 7 | 8* | 9 | 10 | 11 | 12 | | | | | | | | | | | 4 |
| 1 | 2 | 3 | 4* | 5 | 6 | 7 | | 9 | | 11 | 10 | 12 | 8 | | | | | | | | | 5 |
| 1 | 2 | 3 | 4 | 5 | 6 | 7 | | 9 | 10 | 11 | 8* | | 12 | | | | | | | | | 6 |
| 1 | 2 | 3 | 4 | 5 | 6 | 7 | 8 | 9 | | 11 | 10 | | | | | | | | | | | 7 |
| 1 | | 3 | 4 | 5 | 6 | 7 | 8 | 9 | | 11 | 10 | | | 2 | | | | | | | | 8 |
| 1 | 2 | 3 | 4 | 5 | 6 | 7* | | 9 | | 11 | 10 | 12 | 8 | | | | | | | | | 9 |
| 1 | 2 | 3 | 4 | | 6 | 7* | 8 | 9 | | 11 | 10 | 12 | | 5 | | | | | | | | 10 |
| 1 | 2 | 3 | | 5 | 6 | 7 | 8 | 9 | 4 | 11 | 10 | | | | | | | | | | | 11 |
| 1 | 2 | 3 | | 5 | 6 | 7 | 8 | 9 | 4 | 11 | 10 | | | | | | | | | | | 12 |
| 1 | 2 | 3 | 4 | 5 | 6 | 7* | 8 | | | 11 | 10 | | 9 | | 12 | | | | | | | 13 |
| 1 | 2 | 3 | 4 | 5 | 6 | 7 | 8 | 9 | | 11 | 10 | | | | | | | | | | | 14 |
| 1 | 2 | 3 | 4 | 5 | 6 | 7 | 8 | 9 | | 11 | 10 | | | | | | | | | | | 15 |
| 1 | 2 | 3 | 4 | 5 | 6 | 7* | 8 | 9 | | 11 | 10 | | | | 12 | | | | | | | 16 |
| 1 | 2 | 3 | 4 | 5 | 6 | 12 | 8 | 9 | | 11 | 10* | | | | 7 | | | | | | | 17 |
| 1 | 2* | 3 | 4 | 5 | 6 | 10 | 8 | 9 | | 11 | 12 | | | | 7 | | | | | | | 18 |
| 1 | 2 | 3 | 4 | 5 | 6 | | 8* | 9 | | 11 | 10 | | | 12 | 7 | | | | | | | 19 |
| 1 | 2 | 3 | 4 | 5 | 6* | | 8 | 9 | | 11 | 10 | 12 | | | 7 | | | | | | | 20 |
| 1 | 2 | 3 | 4 | 5 | | 7 | 8 | 9 | | 11 | 10 | | | | | 6 | | | | | | 21 |
| 1 | 2 | 3 | 4 | 5 | | 7 | 8 | 9 | | 11 | 10 | | | | | 6 | | | | | | 22 |
| 1 | 2 | 3 | 4 | 5 | | 7 | 8 | 9 | | 11 | 10 | | | | | 6 | | | | | | 23 |
| 1 | 2 | 3 | 4 | 5 | | | 8 | 9 | | 11 | 10 | | | | | 6 | 7 | | | | | 24 |
| 1 | 2 | 3 | 4 | 5 | | | 8 | 9 | | 11 | 10 | | | | | 6 | 7 | | | | | 25 |
| 1 | 2 | 3 | 4 | 5 | | | 8 | 9 | | 11 | 10 | | | | | 6 | 7 | | | | | 26 |
| 1 | 2 | 3 | 4 | 5 | 6 | | 8 | 9* | | | 10 | 12 | | | 7 | 11 | | | | | | 27 |
| 1 | 2 | 3 | 4 | 5 | 6 | | 8 | 9* | | 11 | 10 | 12 | | | | 7 | | | | | | 28 |
| 1 | 2* | 3 | | 5 | 6 | | | | | 11 | 10 | 8 | 9 | | 12 | 7 | 4 | | | | | 29 |
| 1 | | 3 | | 5 | 6 | | | | | 11 | 10 | 8* | 9 | 12 | 2 | 7 | 4 | | | | | 30 |
| 1 | 2 | 4* | | 5 | 6 | | | | | 3 | 10 | | 9 | 12 | 7 | 8 | 11 | | | | | 31 |
| 1 | 2 | | | 5 | 6 | | | | | 3 | | | 8 | | | 10 | 11 | | 4 | 7 | 9 | 32 |
| 1 | 2 | | | 5 | 6 | | | | | 3 | 12 | | 8 | | | 10 | 11* | | 4 | 7 | 9 | 33 |
| 1 | 2 | 11 | | 5 | 6 | | 8 | | | 3 | | | | | | 10 | | | 4 | 7 | 9 | 34 |
| 1 | 2 | 11* | | 5 | 6 | | 8 | | | 3 | 12 | | | | | 10 | | | 4 | 7 | 9 | 35 |
| 1 | 2 | 11 | | 5 | 6 | | 8 | | | 3 | | | | | | 10 | | | 4 | 7 | 9 | 36 |
| 1 | 2 | 11 | | 5 | 6 | | 8* | | | 3 | 12 | | | | | 10 | | | 4 | 7 | 9 | 37 |
| 1 | 2* | 11 | | 5 | 6 | | 8 | | | 3 | 12 | | | | | 10 | | | 4 | 7 | 9 | 38 |
| 1 | 2 | | | 5 | 6 | | 8* | | | 3 | 11 | 12 | | | | 10 | | | 4 | 7 | 9 | 39 |
| 1 | 2 | | | 5 | 6 | | | | | 3 | 11 | | 8 | | | 10 | | | 4 | 7 | 9 | 40 |
| 1 | 2 | | | 5 | 6 | | 8 | | | 3 | 11 | 12 | | | | 10 | | | 4 | 7 | 9* | 41 |
| 1 | 2 | | | 5 | 6 | | 8 | | | 3* | 11 | 12 | | | | 10 | | | 4 | 7 | 9 | 42 |
| 1 | 3* | 2 | 11 | 5 | 6 | | 8 | | | | 12 | | | | | 10 | | | 4 | 7 | 9 | 43 |
| 1 | 2 | 11 | | 5 | 6 | | 8 | | | 3* | 12 | | | | | 10 | | | 4 | 7 | 9 | 44 |
| 1 | 2 | 11 | | 5 | 6 | | 8 | | | 3 | 12 | | | | | 10* | | | 4 | 7 | 9 | 45 |
| 1 | 2 | 12 | | 5 | 6 | | 8 | | | 3 | 11 | | | | | 10 | | | 4 | 7* | 9 | 46 |
| 46 | 30 | 45 | 35 | 45 | 40 | 20 | 37 | 27 | 7 | 44 | 31 | 2 | 9 | 1 | 8 | 26 | 4 | 4 | 15 | 15 | 15 | |
| | + | | | | | + | | | | + | + | + | + | + | + | | | | | | | |
| | 1s | | | | | 1s | | | | 8s | 3s | 9s | 2s | 2s | 2s | | | | | | | |

## OXFORD UNITED

| | Ht | Wt | Birthplace | Clubs | League App. | League Gls |
|---|---|---|---|---|---|---|
| **Goalkeepers** | | | | | | |
| Roy Burton | 5 10 | 12 10 | Wantage | Oxford U | 385 | — |
| Steve Foyster* | 6 3 | 14 0 | Norwich | Oxford U | — | — |
| **Defenders** | | | | | | |
| David Fogg | 5 10½ | 11 5 | Liverpool | Wrexham | 161 | — |
| | | | | Oxford U | 255 | 11 |
| Andy Kingston | 5 11 | 11 2 | Oxford | Oxford U | 50 | — |
| (Contract cancelled April 1982) | | | | | | |
| John Doyle | 5 9 | 11 6 | Oxford | Oxford U | 66 | — |
| Gary Briggs | 6 3 | 12 10 | Leeds | Middlesbrough | — | — |
| | | | | Oxford U | 192 | 5 |
| Tim Smithers | 5 11 | 10 4 | Ramsgate | Nuneaton B | (not known) | |
| | | | | Oxford U | 74 | 4 |
| Malcolm Shotton | 6 3 | 13 12 | Newcastle | Nuneaton B | (not known) | |
| | | | | Oxford U | 78 | 9 |
| **Midfield** | | | | | | |
| Billy Jeffrey* | 5 10 | 12 0 | Clydebank | Oxford U | 314 | 24 |
| Kevin Brock | 5 9 | 10 12 | Middleton Stoney | Oxford U | 73 | 12 |
| Phil Lythgoe | 5 9 | 11 0 | Norwich | Norwich C | 12 | 1 |
| (Contract cancelled April 1982) | | | | Bristol R (on loan) | 6 | — |
| | | | | Oxford U | 28 | 3 |
| Malcolm Page | 5 9 | 10 11 | Knucklas | Birmingham C | 338 | 9 |
| (Wales) (Contract cancelled Feb 1982) | | | | Oxford U | 14 | 1 |
| Ray Train | 5 5 | 10 5 | Nuneaton | Walsall | 73 | 11 |
| | | | | Carlisle U | 155 | 8 |
| | | | | Sunderland | 32 | 1 |
| | | | | Bolton W | 51 | — |
| | | | | Watford | 92 | 3 |
| | | | | Oxford U | 15 | — |
| Trevor Hebberd | 5 11½ | 11 4 | Winchester | Southampton | 97 | 7 |
| | | | | Leicester C (on loan) | 4 | 1 |
| | | | | Bolton W (on loan) | 6 | — |
| | | | | Oxford U | 15 | 2 |
| Mark Jones | 5 8 | 9 12 | Berinsfield | Oxford U | 59 | 4 |
| **Forwards** | | | | | | |
| Peter Foley | 5 11 | 11 12 | Bicester | Oxford U | 262 | 65 |
| Jason Seacole* | 5 9½ | 12 0 | Oxford | Oxford U | 120 | 22 |
| Paul Berry* | 6 0 | 12 10 | Oxford | Oxford U | 110 | 20 |
| Ray Graydon | 5 8 | 11 0 | Bristol | Bristol R | 134 | 27 |
| (Non-contract) | | | | Aston V | 193 | 67 |
| | | | | Coventry C | 20 | 5 |
| | | | | Washington D | — | — |
| | | | | Oxford U | 42 | 10 |
| Andy Thomas | 6 0 | 10 10 | Oxford | Oxford U | 48 | 15 |
| Ollie Kearns* | 6 0 | 12 0 | Banbury | Reading | 86 | 40 |
| | | | | Oxford U | 18 | 4 |
| Garry Haire | | | | Oxford U | — | — |

Garry Haire
  (Contract cancelled April 1982)
David Burn (Contract cancelled May 1981)

# PETERBOROUGH UNITED Division 4

*Chairman:* W. O'Neill Wilde.

*Vice-Chairman:* C. Duddington.

*Directors:* S. E. Nicholas, A. Hand, G. H. Woodcock, D. E. Ringham.

*Manager:* Martin Wilkinson.

*General Manager/Secretary:* A. V. Blades.

*Commercial Manager:* E. Stafford.

*Year Formed:* 1923.

*Turned Professional:* 1934.

*Limited Company:* 1934.

*Previous Name:* Peterborough and Fletton United until 1934.

**Football League Record:**
1960 Elected to Division 4; 1961–68 Division 3, when they were demoted for financial irregularities; 1968–74 Division 4; 1974–79 Division 3; 1979– Division 4.

**Honours:** *Football League:* Division 3 best season: 4th, 1977–78. Division 4 – Champions 1960–61, 1973–74. *FA Cup* best season: 6th rd, 1965. *Football League Cup:* semi-final 1966.

*Record Victory:* 8-1 v Oldham Ath, Division 4, 26 Nov, 1969.

*Record Defeat:* 1-8 v Northampton T, FA Cup 2nd rd (2nd replay), 1946–47.

*Most League Points:* 66, Division 4, 1960–61. *Three points win:* 82, Division 4, 1981–82.

*Most League Goals:* 134, Division 4, 1960–61.

*Highest League Scorer in Season:* Terry Bly, 52, Division 4, 1960–61.

*Most League Goals in Total Aggregate:* Jim Hall, 120, 1967–75.

*Most Capped Player:* Ollie Conmy, 5, Eire.

*Most League Appearances:* Tommy Robson, 482, 1968–81.

*Record Transfer Fee Received:* £110,000 from Blackpool for Bob Doyle, July 1979.

*Record Transfer Fee Paid:* £60,000 to West Ham U, for Bill Green, July 1978.

*Previous Managers since Election to Football League:* Jimmy Hagan, Jack Fairbrother, Gordon Clark, Norman Rigby, Jim Iley, Noel Cantwell, John Barnwell, Billy Hails, Peter Morris.

*Address of Supporters Club:* Same as Football Club.

---

**London Road Ground, Peterborough PE2 8AL.** Telephone Peterborough (0733) 63947. *Ground capacity:* 30,000. *Record attendance:* 30,096 v Swansea T, FA Cup 5th rd, 20 Feb, 1965. *Record receipts:* £44,157.83 v Manchester C, FA Cup 5th rd, 14 Feb, 1981. *Pitch measurements:* 112yd×76yd.

*How to get there:* Peterborough Station Bus terminal (20 minutes' walking distance).

*Match tickets:* Bookable 14 days in advance.

*Car parking:* Ample parking available at the ground.

*Entertainments/catering facilities:* Supporters' Club provides entertainments. Licensed refreshment kiosks in the ground.

*Club shop:* Sells all types of souvenirs (postal requests to General Manager).

*Handbooks/programmes:* Handbooks available and programmes can be ordered on subscription.

*Extra information:* Upon joining the Football League in 1960 Peterborough United set up a record in Division Four of scoring 134 goals in their first season.

*Club Colours:* Blue shirts, white shorts, blue stockings with white top.

*Change Colours:* All yellow with Royal blue trim.

*Team Captain:*

*Club Nickname:* The Posh.

285

## PETERBOROUGH UNITED 1981–82 LEAGUE RECORD

| Match No. | Date | Venue | Opponents | Result | H/T Score | Goalscorers | Atten-dance |
|---|---|---|---|---|---|---|---|
| 1 | Aug 29 | H | Mansfield T | W 1-0 | 0-0 | Kellock (pen) | 4310 |
| 2 | Sept 5 | A | Halifax T | D 1-1 | 0-0 | Cooke | 1809 |
| 3 | 12 | H | Rochdale | W 5-1 | 2-1 | Quow, Cooke 3, Slack | 3768 |
| 4 | 18 | A | Stockport Co | L 0-3 | 0-1 | | 2382 |
| 5 | 22 | A | Hull C | D 1-1 | 0-1 | Cooke | 3713 |
| 6 | 26 | H | Crewe Alex | W 3-0 | 2-0 | Cooke, Kellock, Hodgson | 3775 |
| 7 | Oct 3 | A | Darlington | D 0-0 | 0-0 | | 1628 |
| 8 | 10 | A | Hartlepool U | W 1-0 | 0-0 | Kellock | 2450 |
| 9 | 17 | H | AFC Bournemouth | W 1-0 | 1-0 | Cooke | 4673 |
| 10 | 19 | A | Port Vale | W 3-1 | 1-1 | Massey, Chard, Cooke | 2844 |
| 11 | 24 | H | York C | L 0-1 | 0-0 | | 4220 |
| 12 | 28 | H | Hereford U | W 3-1 | 1-1 | Collins, Kellock, Syrett | 3040 |
| 13 | 31 | A | Scunthorpe U | W 1-0 | 0-0 | Syrett | 2004 |
| 14 | Nov 4 | H | Aldershot | W 7-1 | 2-1 | Cooke, Gynn, Massey, Smith T., Syrett 3 | 3781 |
| 15 | 7 | H | Blackpool | W 3-1 | 2-0 | Hodgson, Syrett, Kellock | 5442 |
| 16 | 14 | A | Bury | L 1-3 | 1-2 | Kellock | 6426 |
| 17 | 28 | H | Northampton T | W 1-0 | 1-0 | Kellock | 5293 |
| 18 | Dec 5 | A | Bradford C | L 0-2 | 0-2 | | 4875 |
| 19 | Jan 19 | A | Wigan Ath | L 0-5 | 0-2 | | 4111 |
| 20 | 23 | A | Mansfield T | W 2-1 | 2-0 | Gynn, Syrett | 3242 |
| 21 | 26 | H | Halifax T | D 0-0 | 0-0 | | 3016 |
| 22 | 30 | H | Stockport Co | W 2-0 | 1-0 | Clarke, Cooke | 3525 |
| 23 | Feb 6 | A | Rochdale | D 1-1 | 0-1 | Cooke | 1241 |
| 24 | 10 | H | Hull C | W 3-0 | 1-0 | Cooke (pen), Clarke, Chard | 3161 |
| 25 | 13 | A | Darlington | W 3-1 | 1-1 | Cooke 2, Clarke | 3202 |
| 26 | 19 | A | Crewe Alex | W 1-0 | 1-0 | Chard | 1628 |
| 27 | 23 | A | Tranmere R | W 2-1 | 1-1 | Cooke 2 | 1185 |
| 28 | 27 | H | Hartlepool U | D 4-4 | 3-4 | Cooke 3 (1 pen), Gynn | 4610 |
| 29 | Mar 6 | A | AFC Bournemouth | D 1-1 | 0-0 | Cooke | 7351 |
| 30 | 10 | A | Port Vale | W 1-0 | 0-0 | Cooke | 4151 |
| 31 | 13 | A | York C | L 3-4 | 2-2 | Syrett, Cooke, Clarke | 2178 |
| 32 | 16 | A | Aldershot | W 1-0 | 1-0 | Gynn | 1453 |
| 33 | 20 | H | Scunthorpe U | W 2-1 | 1-0 | Gynn, Hodgson | 4785 |
| 34 | 24 | H | Torquay U | W 1-0 | 1-0 | Smith T. | 4045 |
| 35 | 27 | A | Blackpool | D 2-2 | 1-0 | Cooke, Kellock | 2855 |
| 36 | Apr 3 | H | Bury | W 1-0 | 1-0 | Phillips | 4931 |
| 37 | 10 | A | Torquay U | W 2-1 | 1-0 | Kellock, Gynn | 1989 |
| 38 | 13 | H | Colchester U | D 2-2 | 0-0 | Smith T., Kellock | 5402 |
| 39 | 17 | H | Bradford C | W 2-0 | 1-0 | Phillips, Cooke | 6756 |
| 40 | 21 | H | Sheffield U | L 0-4 | 0-3 | | 13,439 |
| 41 | 24 | A | Northampton T | L 0-1 | 0-1 | | 4975 |
| 42 | 27 | A | Colchester U | D 1-1 | 0-1 | Syrett | 2212 |
| 43 | May 1 | H | Wigan Ath | L 0-3 | 0-2 | | 6229 |
| 44 | 5 | A | Hereford U | L 1-2 | 1-1 | Kellock | 2357 |
| 45 | 8 | A | Sheffield U | L 0-4 | 0-0 | | 23,923 |
| 46 | 15 | H | Tranmere R | L 1-2 | 0-2 | Slack | 1897 |

**Final League Position: 5**

### Goalscorers

*League* (71): Cooke 24 (2 pens), Kellock 11 (1 pen), Syrett 9, Gynn 6, Clarke 4, Chard 3, Hodgson 3, Smith T. 3, Massey 2, Phillips 2, Slack 2, Collins 1, Quow 1.
*League Cup* (2): Cooke 1, Slack 1.
*FA Cup* (5): Cooke 3, Chard 1, Syrett 1.

| League Cup | First Round | Barnsley (h) | 2-3 |
|---|---|---|---|
| | | (a) | 0-6 |
| FA Cup | First Round | Halifax T (a) | 3-0 |
| | Second Round | Walsall (h) | 2-1 |
| | Third Round | Bristol C (h) | 0-1 |

| Smelt | Winters | Collins | Gynn | Slack | Rodaway | Quow | Kellock | Cooke | Hodgson | Massey | Chard | Clarke | Butler | Smith T. | Freeman | Syrett | Ciss | Phillips | Smith R. | Barnard | Rayment | Match No. |
|---|---|---|---|---|---|---|---|---|---|---|---|---|---|---|---|---|---|---|---|---|---|---|
| 1 | 2 | 3 | 4 | 5 | 6 | 7 | 8 | 9 | 10* | 11 | 12 | | | | | | | | | | | 1 |
| 1 | 2 | 3 | 4 | 5 | 6 | 7 | 8 | 9 | 10 | | 12 | 11* | | | | | | | | | | 2 |
| 1 | 2 | 3 | 4 | 5 | 6 | 7 | 8 | 9 | | | 10 | 11 | | | | | | | | | | 3 |
| 1 | 2 | 3 | 4 | 5 | 6 | 7 | 8 | 9 | | 12 | 10 | 11* | | | | | | | | | | 4 |
| 1 | | 3 | 4 | | 6 | 7 | 8 | 9 | 10 | 11 | | | 2 | 5 | | | | | | | | 5 |
| | | 3 | 4 | | 6 | 7 | 8 | 9 | 10 | 11 | | | 2 | 5 | 1 | | | | | | | 6 |
| | | 3 | 4 | | 6 | 7 | 8 | 9 | 10 | 11* | 12 | | 2 | 5 | 1 | | | | | | | 7 |
| | | 3 | 4 | | 6 | 7* | 8 | 9 | 10 | | 12 | | 2 | 5 | 1 | 11 | | | | | | 8 |
| | | 3 | 4 | | 6 | 7 | 8 | 9 | 10 | 11 | | | 2 | 5 | 1 | | | | | | | 9 |
| | 2 | | 4 | | 6 | 7* | 8 | 9 | 10 | 11 | 12 | | 3 | 5 | 1 | | | | | | | 10 |
| | | 3 | 4 | | 6 | | 8 | 9 | 10 | 11* | 7 | | 2 | 5 | 1 | | 12 | | | | | 11 |
| | | 3 | 4 | | 6 | | 8 | 9 | 10 | | | | 2 | 5 | 1 | 11 | 7 | | | | | 12 |
| | | 3 | 4 | | 6 | | 8 | 9 | 10 | | | 11 | 2 | 5 | 1 | 7 | | | | | | 13 |
| | | 3 | 4 | | 6 | | 8 | 9 | 10 | 12 | 11* | | 2 | 5 | 1 | 7 | | | | | | 14 |
| | | 3 | 4 | | 6 | | 8 | 9 | 10 | | | 11 | 2 | 5 | 1 | 7 | | | | | | 15 |
| | | 3 | 4 | | 6 | | 8 | 9 | 10 | | | 11 | 2 | 5 | 1 | 7 | | | | | | 16 |
| | | 3 | 4 | | | | 8 | 9 | 10 | 12 | 11 | | 2 | 5 | 1 | 7* | | 6 | | | | 17 |
| | | 3 | 4 | | | | 8 | 9 | 10 | 12 | 11 | | 2 | 5 | 1 | 7 | | 6* | | | | 18 |
| | | 3 | 4 | | 6 | | 8 | 9 | 10 | 12 | 11* | | 2 | 5 | 1 | 7 | | | | | | 19 |
| | | 3 | 4 | | 6 | | 8 | 9 | 10 | 11* | 12 | | 2 | 5 | 1 | 7 | | | | | | 20 |
| | | 3 | 4 | | 6 | | 8 | 9 | 10 | 11* | 7 | 12 | 2 | 5 | 1 | | | | | | | 21 |
| | | 3 | 4 | | 6 | | 8 | 9 | 10* | 11 | 12 | 7 | 2 | 5 | 1 | | | | | | | 22 |
| | | 3 | 4 | | 6 | | 8 | 9 | 10 | 11* | 12 | 7 | 2 | 5 | 1 | | | | | | | 23 |
| | | 3 | 4 | | 6 | | 8 | 9 | 10 | 11 | 7 | | 2 | 5 | 1 | | | | | | | 24 |
| | | 3 | 4 | | 6 | | 8 | 9 | 10 | 11 | 7 | | 2 | 5 | 1 | | | | | | | 25 |
| | | 3 | 4 | | 6 | | 8 | 9 | 10 | 11 | 7 | | 2 | 5 | 1 | | | | | | | 26 |
| | | 3 | 4 | | 6 | | 8 | 9 | 10 | 11 | 7 | | 2 | 5 | 1 | | | | | | | 27 |
| | | 3 | 4 | | 6 | | 8 | 9 | | 11 | 7 | | 2 | 5 | 1 | | | | 10 | | | 28 |
| | | 3 | 4 | | 6 | | 8 | 9 | | 11 | 7 | | 2 | 5 | 1 | | | | 10 | | | 29 |
| | | 3 | 4 | | 6 | | 8 | 9 | | 12 | 11 | 7 | 2 | 5 | 1 | | | | 10* | | | 30 |
| | | 3 | 4 | | 6 | | 8 | 9 | | 11 | 12 | | 2 | 5 | 1 | 7 | | | 10* | | | 31 |
| | | | 4 | | 6 | | 8 | 9 | | 11 | 12 | | 2 | 5 | 1 | 7 | | 3 | 10* | | | 32 |
| | | | 4 | | 6 | | 8 | 9 | 10 | 11 | 7 | | 2 | 5 | 1 | | | 3 | | | | 33 |
| | | | 4 | | 6 | | 8 | 9 | 10 | 11 | 7* | | 2 | 5 | 1 | 12 | | 3 | | | | 34 |
| | | | 4 | | 6 | | 8 | 9 | 10 | 11 | 7 | | 2 | 5 | 1 | | | 3 | | | | 35 |
| | | | 4 | | 6 | | 8 | 9 | 10 | 11 | 7 | | 2 | 5 | 1 | | | 3 | | | | 36 |
| | | | 4 | | 6 | | 8 | 9 | 10 | 11* | 7 | | 2 | 5 | 1 | | | 3 | | 12 | | 37 |
| | | | 4 | | 6 | | 8 | 9 | 10 | 11 | 7 | | 2 | 5 | 1 | | | 3 | | | | 38 |
| | | | 4 | | 6 | | 8 | 9 | 10 | 11 | 7 | | 2 | 5 | 1 | | | 3 | | | | 39 |
| | | | 4 | | 6 | | 8 | 9 | 10 | 11 | 7 | | 2 | 5 | 1 | | | 3* | | 12 | | 40 |
| | | | 4 | | 6 | | 8 | 9 | 10* | 11 | 12 | | 2 | 5 | 1 | 7 | | 3 | | | | 41 |
| | | | 4 | | 6 | | 8 | 9 | 10 | 11 | | | 2 | 5 | 1 | 7 | | 3 | | | | 42 |
| | | | 4 | | 6 | | 8 | 9 | 10 | 11 | 12 | | 2* | 5 | 1 | 7 | | 3 | | | | 43 |
| | 2 | 10 | 4 | 5 | 6 | | 8 | 9 | | | | 11 | | | 1 | 7* | | 3 | | | 12 | 44 |
| | 2 | 10 | 4 | 5 | | | | 9 | | | 7 | | | | 1 | 11 | | 6 | | 8 | 3 | 45 |
| | 2 | 10 | 4 | 5 | | | 8 | 9 | | | | 11* | 7 | | 1 | | 12 | 6 | | | 3 | 46 |
| 5 | 7 | 34 | 46 | 7 | 42 | 10 | 43 | 46 | 38 | 13 | 31 | 22 | 39 | 39 | 41 | 16 | 2 | 17 | 5 | 1 | 2 | |
| | | | | | | | | | + | + | + | + | | | | + | + | | + | | | |
| | | | | | | | | | 1s | 5s | 8s | 5s | | | | 1s | 2s | | 3s | | | |

288

## PETERBOROUGH UNITED

| | Ht | Wt | Birthplace | Clubs | League App. | League Gls |
|---|---|---|---|---|---|---|
| **Goalkeepers** | | | | | | |
| Neil Freeman | 6 1 | 14 7 | Northampton | Arsenal | — | — |
| | | | | Northampton T (on loan) | — | — |
| | | | | Grimsby T | 33 | — |
| | | | | Southend U | 69 | — |
| | | | | Birmingham C | 31 | — |
| | | | | Walsall (on loan) | 8 | — |
| | | | | Huddersfield T (on loan) | 18 | — |
| | | | | Peterborough U | 41 | — |
| Mel Gwinnett* | 6 1½ | 11 5½ | Worcester | Peterborough U | — | — |
| **Defenders** | | | | | | |
| John Winters | 5 8 | 11 8 | Wisbech | Peterborough U | 29 | 1 |
| Ian Phillips | 5 8 | 12 2 | Edinburgh | Mansfield T | 23 | — |
| | | | | Peterborough U | 97 | 3 |
| Trevor Slack | 6 1¾ | 12 0 | Peterborough | Peterborough U | 42 | 6 |
| Steve Collins | 5 8 | 11 4 | Stamford | Peterborough U | 48 | 1 |
| Billy Rodaway | 5 10 | 13 2½ | Liverpool | Burnley | 203 | 1 |
| | | | | Peterborough U | 42 | — |
| Geoff Butler | 5 8 | 11 0 | Middlesbrough | Middlesbrough | 55 | 1 |
| (Contract cancelled) | | | | Chelsea | 9 | — |
| | | | | Sunderland | 2 | — |
| | | | | Norwich C | 153 | 1 |
| | | | | Bournemouth | 129 | 1 |
| | | | | Peterborough U | 39 | — |
| Tony Smith | 5 10 | 11 11 | Sunderland | Newcastle U | 2 | — |
| | | | | Peterborough U | 68 | 5 |
| Patrick Rayment | 5 11 | 11 9½ | Peterborough | Peterborough U | 2 | — |
| (Apprentice) | | | | | | |
| **Midfield** | | | | | | |
| Mick Gynn | 5 5 | 10 6 | Peterborough | Peterborough U | 113 | 16 |
| Phil Chard | 5 8 | 11 3 | Corby | Peterborough U | 65 | 6 |
| Billy Kellock | 5 10 | 11 10 | Glasgow | Aston V | — | — |
| | | | | Cardiff C | 35 | 2 |
| | | | | Norwich C | 3 | — |
| | | | | Millwall | — | — |
| | | | | Chelmsford | (not known) | |
| | | | | Kettering T | (not known) | |
| | | | | Peterborough U | 134 | 43 |
| Gordon Hodgson* | 5 11 | 10 7 | Newcastle under Lyne | Newcastle U | 9 | — |
| | | | | Mansfield T | 184 | 23 |
| | | | | Oxford U | 67 | 3 |
| | | | | Peterborough U | 83 | 4 |
| **Forwards** | | | | | | |
| Tony Cliss | 5 9 | 11 0 | March | Peterborough U | 82 | 11 |
| Trevor Quow | 5 6 | 10 4½ | Peterborough | Peterborough U | 91 | 8 |
| Dave Syrett* | 5 11 | 11 13 | Salisbury | Swindon T | 122 | 30 |
| | | | | Wolverhampton W (on loan) | — | — |
| | | | | Mansfield T | 65 | 20 |
| | | | | Walsall | 11 | 3 |
| | | | | Peterborough U | 79 | 24 |
| Jackie Gallacher | 5 10½ | 12 9 | Wisbech | King's Lynn | (not known) | |
| (Contract cancelled Sept 1981) | | | | Lincoln C | 1 | — |
| | | | | Peterborough U | 13 | 1 |
| Tim Gale* | 5 7 | 11 0½ | Peterborough | Peterborough U | — | — |
| Robbie Cooke | 5 9 | 10 8 | Rotherham | Mansfield T | 15 | 1 |
| | | | | Grantham T | (not known) | |
| | | | | Peterborough U | 92 | 46 |
| Colin Clarke | 5 11 | 12 10 | Newry | Ipswich T | — | — |
| | | | | Peterborough U | 27 | 4 |
| Campbell Chapman* | 5 8 | 10 0 | Sutton-in-Ashfield | Peterborough U | — | — |

# PLYMOUTH ARGYLE Division 3

*President:* G. H. Gillin.  *Chairman:* R. Daniel.

*Vice-Chairman:* S. W. Dawe.

*Directors:* P. D. Bloom, R. Burroughs ARICS, G. E. Jasper, J. E. C. Kent.

*Team Manager:* Bobby Moncur.

*Asst Manager:* Martin Harvey.

*Secretary:* Graham Little.

*Year Formed:* 1886.  *Turned Professional:* 1903.

*Limited Company:* 1903.

*Previous Name:* 1886–1903, Argyle Athletic Club.

The Pilgrims

P·A·F·C

**Football League Record:**
1920 Original Member of Division 3; 1921–30 Division 3(S); 1930–50 Division 2; 1950–52 Division 3(S); 1952–56 Division 2; 1956–58 Division 3(S); 1958–59 Division 3; 1959–68 Division 2; 1968–75 Division 3; 1975–77 Division 2; 1977– Division 3.

**Honours:** *Football League:* Division 2 best season: 4th, 1931–32, 1952–53; Division 3(S) – Champions 1929–30, 1951–52; Runners-up 1921–22, 1922–23, 1923–24, 1924–25, 1925–26, 1926–27 (record of six consecutive years); Division 3 – Champions 1958–59; Runners-up 1974–75. *FA Cup* best season: 5th rd, 1952–53. *Football League Cup:* semi-final, 1965, 1974.

*Record Victory:* 8-1 v Millwall, Division 2, 16 Jan, 1932.

*Record Defeat:* 0-9 v Stoke C, Division 2, 17 Dec, 1960.

*Most League Points:* 68, Division 3(S), 1929–30.

*Most League Goals:* 107, Division 3(S), 1925–26 and 1951–52.

*Highest League Scorer in Season:* Jack Cock, 32, Division 3(S), 1925–26.

*Most League Goals in Total Aggregate:* Sammy Black, 180, 1924–38.

*Most Capped Player:* Moses Russell, 20 (23) Wales.

*Most League Appearances:* Sammy Black, 470, 1924–38.

*Record Transfer Fee Received:* £250,000 from Everton for Gary Megson, Feb 1980.

*Record Transfer Fee Paid:* £75,000 to Carlisle U for David Kemp, Sept 1979.

*Previous Managers since the War:* Jack Tresadern, Jimmy Rae, Jack Rowley, Neil Dougall, Ellis Stuttard, Andy Beattie, Malcolm Allison, Derek Ufton, Billy Bingham, Ellis Stuttard, Tony Waiters, Mike Kelly, Malcolm Allison, Bobby Saxton.

*Address of Supporters Club:* Same as Football Club.

*Address of the Club Shop or Boutique:* The Pilgrim Shop, Home Park, Plymouth, Devon.

---

**Home Park Plymouth, Devon PL2 3DQ.** Telephone Plymouth (0752) 52561/2/3. Lottery Shop: 51041. *Ground capacity:* 38,000 (20,000 covered). *Record attendance:* 43,596 v Aston Villa, Division 2, 10 Oct, 1936. *Record receipts:* over £10,000 (official figure not disclosed by club) v Manchester C, League Cup semi-final, 23 Jan, 1974. *Pitch measurements:* 112yd×75yd.

*How to get there:* Special City buses from the Plymouth bus station at Bretonside. Nearest railway station Plymouth.

*Match tickets:* Grand Stand and Mayflower Stand tickets are available 2–3 weeks before each first-team game.

*Car parking:* Car park adjoining the ground holds 2000 cars.

*Entertainments/catering facilities:* Eight refreshment bars around the ground.

*Club shop:* Situated on the ground; sells all types of souvenirs.

*Handbooks/programmes:* Programmes sent to all parts of the world.

*Extra information:* In 1920–21, Plymouth Argyle established a Third Division record by drawing 21 matches.

*Club Colours:* White shirts green trimmings, white shorts, white stockings.

*Change Colours:* All yellow.

*Club Nickname:* The Pilgrims.

## PLYMOUTH ARGYLE 1981–82 LEAGUE RECORD

| Match No. | Date | Venue | Opponents | Result | | H/T Score | Goalscorers | Atten-dance |
|---|---|---|---|---|---|---|---|---|
| 1 | Aug 29 | H | Oxford U | L | 0-1 | 0-1 | | 4089 |
| 2 | Sept 5 | A | Burnley | L | 0-1 | 0-0 | | 4022 |
| 3 | 12 | H | Lincoln C | L | 0-2 | 0-1 | | 3323 |
| 4 | 19 | A | Brentford | D | 0-0 | 0-0 | | 4890 |
| 5 | 22 | A | Bristol C | L | 2-3 | 2-1 | Sims, Hodges | 7471 |
| 6 | 26 | H | Chesterfield | L | 0-2 | 0-0 | | 3451 |
| 7 | 29 | H | Reading | D | 1-1 | 0-1 | Hodges | 2745 |
| 8 | Oct 3 | A | Southend U | L | 0-3 | 0-2 | | 3470 |
| 9 | 10 | H | Gillingham | L | 1-2 | 0-1 | Phillips | 3094 |
| 10 | 17 | A | Carlisle U | L | 1-3 | 0-1 | Cook | 3630 |
| 11 | 20 | A | Wimbledon | L | 1-2 | 0-0 | Randell | 2114 |
| 12 | 24 | H | Chester | W | 5-1 | 2-1 | Cook 2, Randell 2, Sims | 2646 |
| 13 | 31 | A | Walsall | W | 1-0 | 1-0 | Sims | 4549 |
| 14 | Nov 3 | H | Fulham | W | 3-1 | 1-0 | Cook 2 (1 pen), Sims | 4915 |
| 15 | 7 | H | Portsmouth | D | 0-0 | 0-0 | | 6275 |
| 16 | 14 | A | Newport Co | W | 1-0 | 0-0 | Sims | 4427 |
| 17 | 28 | H | Doncaster R | W | 4-2 | 2-2 | Sims 2, Hodges, Cook | 4341 |
| 18 | Dec 5 | A | Huddersfield T | D | 0-0 | 0-0 | | 6949 |
| 19 | 26 | H | Swindon T | W | 2-1 | 2-0 | Hodges, Cook | 8185 |
| 20 | 28 | A | Exeter C | D | 1-1 | 0-0 | Harrison (pen) | 9144 |
| 21 | Jan 2 | H | Bristol R | W | 4-0 | 0-0 | Cooper 2, Cook 2 (1 pen) | 7058 |
| 22 | 9 | H | Burnley | D | 1-1 | 0-0 | Hodges | 5065 |
| 23 | 16 | A | Preston NE | L | 0-1 | 0-1 | | 4936 |
| 24 | 23 | A | Reading | D | 2-2 | 0-2 | Cooper, Hodges | 2789 |
| 25 | 30 | H | Brentford | W | 1-0 | 1-0 | Hodges | 5008 |
| 26 | Feb 6 | A | Lincoln C | L | 0-2 | 0-1 | | 2970 |
| 27 | 9 | H | Bristol C | W | 2-1 | 1-0 | Cook, Hodges | 5260 |
| 28 | 13 | H | Southend U | D | 0-0 | 0-0 | | 5058 |
| 29 | 20 | A | Chesterfield | D | 2-2 | 1-1 | Sims, Cook | 4381 |
| 30 | 27 | A | Gillingham | L | 2-3 | 2-1 | Sims 2 | 4835 |
| 31 | Mar 6 | H | Carlisle U | W | 1-0 | 0-0 | Sims | 3272 |
| 32 | 13 | A | Chester | W | 3-0 | 1-0 | Uzzell, Hodges, Sims | 1988 |
| 33 | 16 | A | Fulham | W | 3-1 | 2-1 | Sims, Cooper, Cook | 5105 |
| 34 | 20 | H | Walsall | W | 4-1 | 3-0 | Cook 2, Nisbet, Rogers | 5134 |
| 35 | 27 | A | Portsmouth | L | 0-1 | 0-0 | | 9551 |
| 36 | Apr 2 | H | Newport Co | L | 1-2 | 0-0 | Hodges | 5148 |
| 37 | 9 | H | Exeter C | W | 2-1 | 1-0 | Nisbet, Sims | 9458 |
| 38 | 10 | A | Swindon T | W | 2-0 | 0-0 | Rogers 2 | 4056 |
| 39 | 14 | H | Wimbledon | W | 2-0 | 0-0 | Nisbet, Sims | 4748 |
| 40 | 17 | H | Huddersfield T | D | 1-1 | 1-0 | Sims | 5434 |
| 41 | 20 | A | Millwall | L | 1-2 | 1-2 | Cook | 2562 |
| 42 | 24 | A | Doncaster R | D | 2-2 | 0-2 | Sims, Cook | 3894 |
| 43 | 28 | A | Oxford U | L | 0-1 | 0-0 | | 6957 |
| 44 | May 1 | H | Preston NE | L | 0-3 | 0-1 | | 3319 |
| 45 | 8 | A | Bristol R | W | 3-2 | 1-2 | Uzzell, Sims, Rogers | 4025 |
| 46 | 15 | H | Millwall | W | 2-1 | 2-0 | Hodges, Cooper | 3193 |

**Final League Position: 10**

### Goalscorers

*League* (64): Sims 18, Cook 16 (2 pens), Hodges 11, Cooper 5, Rogers 4, Nisbet 3, Randell 3, Uzzell 2, Harrison 1 (pen), Phillips 1.
*League Cup* (3): Dennis 1 (pen), Kemp 1, own goal 1.
*FA Cup* (0).

| | | | | |
|---|---|---|---|---|
| League Cup | First Round | Chester (a) | 1-1 | |
| | | (h) | 1-0 | |
| | Second Round | Middlesbrough (a) | 1-2 | |
| | | (h) | 0-0 | |
| FA Cup | First Round | Gillingham (h) | 0-0 | |
| | | (a) | 0-1 | |

| Crudgington | Nisbet | McCartney | Harrison | Phillipson-Masters | Cooper | Hodges | Kemp | Sims | Randell | Collins | Phillips | Foster | Murphy | Dennis | Uzzell | Rowe | Rogers | Cook | James | Ham | Match No. |
|---|---|---|---|---|---|---|---|---|---|---|---|---|---|---|---|---|---|---|---|---|---|
| 1 | 2 | 3 | 4 | 5 | 6 | 7 | 8 | 9 | 10 | 11* | 12 |  |  |  |  |  |  |  |  |  | 1 |
| 1 | 2 | 3 | 4* |  | 6 | 7 | 8 | 9 | 10 | 12 | 5 | 11 |  |  |  |  |  |  |  |  | 2 |
| 1 | 2 | 3 | 4 |  | 6 | 7 | 8 | 9 | 10 |  | 5 | 11* | 12 |  |  |  |  |  |  |  | 3 |
| 1 | 2 |  | 4 |  |  | 7 | 8 | 9 | 10 |  | 5 |  | 11 | 3 | 6 |  |  |  |  |  | 4 |
| 1 | 2 |  | 4 |  | 6 | 7 | 8 | 9 | 10 |  | 5 | 12 | 11* | 3 |  |  |  |  |  |  | 5 |
| 1 | 2 |  | 4 |  | 6* | 7 | 8 | 9 | 10 |  | 5 | 12 | 11 | 3 |  |  |  |  |  |  | 6 |
| 1 | 2 |  | 4 |  |  | 7 | 8 | 9 | 10 |  | 5 | 6 |  |  | 3 |  | 11 |  |  |  | 7 |
| 1 | 2 |  | 4 |  |  | 7 | 8 | 9 | 10 |  | 5 | 6 |  |  | 3 |  | 11 |  |  |  | 8 |
| 1 | 2 | 3 |  |  | 6 | 7 | 8 | 9 | 10 |  | 5 |  |  | 4 |  |  | 11 |  |  |  | 9 |
| 1 | 2 | 3 |  | 4 | 6 | 7 |  | 9 | 10 |  | 5 |  |  |  |  |  | 11 | 8 |  |  | 10 |
| 1 | 2 | 3 |  | 4 | 6 | 7 |  | 9 | 10 |  | 5 |  |  |  |  |  | 11 | 8 |  |  | 11 |
| 1 | 2 | 3 | 5 | 4 | 6 | 7 |  | 9 | 10 |  |  |  |  |  |  |  | 11 | 8 |  |  | 12 |
| 1 | 2 |  | 4 | 5 | 6 | 7 |  | 9 | 10 |  |  |  |  |  | 3 |  | 11 | 8 |  |  | 13 |
| 1 | 2 |  | 4 | 5 | 6 | 7 |  | 9 | 10 |  |  |  |  |  | 3 |  | 11 | 8 |  |  | 14 |
| 1 | 2 |  | 4 | 5 | 6 | 7 |  | 9 | 10 |  |  |  |  |  | 3 |  | 11 | 8 |  |  | 15 |
| 1 | 2 | 3 | 4 | 5 | 6 | 7 |  | 9 | 10 |  |  |  |  |  |  |  | 11 | 8 |  |  | 16 |
| 1 | 2 | 3 | 4 | 5 | 6 | 7 |  | 9 | 10 |  |  |  |  |  |  |  | 11 | 8 |  |  | 17 |
| 1 | 2 |  | 4 | 5 | 6 | 7 |  | 9 |  | 10 |  |  |  |  | 3 |  | 11 | 8 |  |  | 18 |
| 1 | 2 |  | 4 | 5 | 6 | 7 |  | 9 |  | 10 |  |  |  |  | 3 |  | 11 | 8 |  |  | 19 |
| 1 | 2 |  | 4 | 5 | 6 | 7 |  | 9 | 10 | 8* |  |  | 12 |  | 3 |  | 11 |  |  |  | 20 |
| 1 | 2 |  | 4 | 5 | 6 | 7 |  | 9 | 10 |  |  |  |  |  | 3 |  | 11 | 8 |  |  | 21 |
| 1 | 2 |  | 4 | 5 | 6 | 7 |  | 9 | 10 |  |  |  |  |  | 3 |  | 11 | 8 |  |  | 22 |
| 1 | 2 |  | 4 | 5 | 6 | 7 |  | 9 | 10 |  |  |  |  |  | 3 |  | 11 | 8 |  |  | 23 |
| 1 | 2 |  | 4 | 5* | 6 | 7 |  | 9 | 10 |  |  |  |  |  | 3 | 12 | 11 | 8 |  |  | 24 |
| 1 | 2 |  | 4 |  | 6 | 7 |  | 9 | 10 |  |  |  |  |  | 3 |  | 11 | 8 | 5 |  | 25 |
| 1 | 2 |  | 4 |  | 6 | 7 |  | 9 | 10 |  |  |  |  |  | 3 |  | 11 | 8 | 5 |  | 26 |
| 1 | 2 |  | 4 |  | 6 | 7 |  | 9 | 10 |  |  |  |  |  | 3 |  | 11 | 8 | 5 |  | 27 |
| 1 | 2 |  | 4 |  | 6 | 7 |  | 9 | 10 |  |  |  |  |  | 3 |  | 11 | 8 | 5 |  | 28 |
| 1 | 2 |  | 4 |  | 6 | 7 |  | 9 | 10 |  |  |  |  |  | 3 |  | 11 | 8 | 5 |  | 29 |
| 1 | 2 |  | 4 |  | 6 | 7 |  | 9 | 10 |  |  |  |  |  | 3 |  | 11 | 8 | 5 |  | 30 |
| 1 | 2 |  | 4 | 5 | 6 | 7 |  | 9 | 10 |  |  |  |  |  | 3 |  | 11 | 8 |  |  | 31 |
| 1 | 2 |  | 4 | 5 | 6 | 7 |  | 9 | 10 |  |  |  |  |  | 3 |  | 11 | 8 |  |  | 32 |
| 1 | 2 |  | 4 | 5 | 6 | 7 |  | 9 | 10 |  |  |  |  |  | 3 |  | 11 | 8 |  |  | 33 |
| 1 | 2 |  | 4 | 5 | 6 | 7 |  | 9 | 10 |  |  |  |  |  | 3 |  | 11 | 8 |  |  | 34 |
| 1 | 2 |  | 4 | 5 | 6 | 7 |  | 9 | 10 |  |  |  |  |  | 3 |  | 11 | 8 |  |  | 35 |
| 1 | 2 |  | 4 | 5 | 6 | 7 |  | 9 | 10 |  |  |  |  |  | 3 |  | 11 | 8 |  |  | 36 |
| 1 | 2 | 10 | 4 | 5 | 6 | 7 |  | 9 |  |  |  |  |  |  | 3 |  | 11 | 8 |  |  | 37 |
| 1 | 2 | 10 | 4 | 5 | 6 | 7 |  | 9 |  |  |  |  |  |  | 3 |  | 11 | 8 |  |  | 38 |
| 1 | 2 | 10* | 4 | 5 | 6 | 7 |  | 9 |  |  |  |  |  |  | 3 | 12 | 11 | 8 |  |  | 39 |
| 1 | 2 |  | 4 | 5 | 6 | 7 |  | 9 |  |  |  |  |  |  | 3 | 10 | 11 | 8 |  |  | 40 |
| 1 | 2 | 3 | 4 | 5 | 6 | 7 |  | 9 | 10 |  |  |  |  |  |  |  | 11 | 8 |  |  | 41 |
| 1 |  | 3 | 4 | 5 | 6 | 7 |  | 9 | 10 |  |  |  |  |  | 12 |  | 11 | 8 | 2* |  | 42 |
| 1 | 2 | 3 | 4 | 5 | 6 | 7 |  | 9 | 10 |  |  |  |  |  |  |  | 11 | 8 |  |  | 43 |
| 1 | 2 | 3 | 4 | 5 | 6 | 7 |  | 9 | 10 |  |  |  |  |  |  |  | 11 | 8 |  |  | 44 |
| 1 | 2 |  | 4 | 5 | 6 | 7 |  | 9 | 10 |  |  |  |  |  | 3 |  | 11 | 8 |  |  | 45 |
| 1 | 5 |  | 4 |  | 6 | 7 |  | 9 | 10 |  | 2 |  |  |  | 8 |  | 3 | 11 |  |  | 46 |
| 46 | 45 | 16 | 43 | 31 | 43 | 46 | 9 | 46 | 38 | 1 | 6 | 10 | 4 | 4 | 34 | 2 | 40 | 35 | 6 | 1 |  |

+2s (Collins)    +2s (Murphy)   +2s (Dennis)   +1s (Uzzell)   +2s (Rowe)

## PLYMOUTH ARGYLE

| | Ht | Wt | Birthplace | Clubs | League App. | League Gls |
|---|---|---|---|---|---|---|
| **Goalkeepers** | | | | | | |
| Geoff Crudgington | 6 0 | 12 12 | Wolverhampton | Aston V | 4 | — |
| | | | | Bradford C (on loan) | 1 | — |
| | | | | Preston NE | — | |
| | | | | Crewe Alex | 250 | — |
| | | | | Swansea C | 52 | — |
| | | | | Plymouth Arg | 129 | — |
| Neil Hards | 6 0 | 12 7 | Portsmouth | Plymouth Arg | 4 | — |
| **Defenders** | | | | | | |
| John Uzzell | 5 10 | 11 3 | Plymouth | Plymouth Arg | 117 | 3 |
| Tyrone James | 6 2 | 11 0 | Paddington | Fulham | 20 | — |
| | | | | Plymouth Arg | 81 | — |
| George Foster | 5 10 | 11 2 | Plymouth | Plymouth Arg | 212 | 6 |
| | | | | Torquay U (on loan) | 6 | 3 |
| | | | | Exeter C (on loan) | 28 | — |
| Forbes Phillipson- Masters | 6 1 | 12 10 | Bournemouth | Southampton | 9 | — |
| | | | | Exeter C (on loan) | 6 | — |
| | | | | Bournemouth (on loan) | 7 | 2 |
| | | | | Luton T (on loan) | 10 | — |
| | | | | Plymouth Arg | 113 | — |
| Vaughan Powell (Contract cancelled April 1982) | 5 6 | 9 4 | Slough | Plymouth Arg | — | — |
| Chris Jefferis* | 5 10 | 10 9 | Plymouth | Plymouth Arg | — | — |
| Michael McCartney | 5 7 | 10 12 | Edinburgh | WBA | — | — |
| | | | | Carlisle U | 156 | 17 |
| | | | | Southampton | 22 | 1 |
| | | | | Plymouth Arg | 16 | — |
| Chris Harrison | 5 8 | 10 6 | Launceston | Plymouth Arg | 206 | 5 |
| Michael Ham | 6 1 | 12 0 | Plymouth | Plymouth Arg | 1 | — |
| **Midfield** | | | | | | |
| Kevin Hodges | 5 7 | 10 0 | Bridport | Plymouth Arg | 143 | 21 |
| Leigh Cooper | 5 8 | 10 9 | Reading | Plymouth Arg | 85 | 8 |
| Jeremy Collins* | 5 8 | 10 0 | Plymouth | Plymouth Arg | 4 | — |
| Colin Randell | 5 9 | 10 8 | Skewen | Coventry C | — | — |
| | | | | Plymouth Arg | 139 | 9 |
| | | | | Exeter C | 78 | 4 |
| | | | | Plymouth Arg | 110 | 8 |
| Denis Murphy (Contract cancelled Sept 1981) | 5 9 | 10 6 | Dublin | Plymouth Arg | — | — |
| Gordon Nisbet | 5 10 | 12 2 | Wallsend | WBA | 136 | — |
| | | | | Hull C | 193 | 1 |
| | | | | Plymouth Arg | 64 | 3 |
| David Phillips | 5 9 | 10 10 | Welberg, Germany | Plymouth Arg | 8 | 1 |
| Mark Rowe | 5 6 | 10 0 | Wadebridge | Plymouth Arg | 4 | — |
| Nigel Jarvis* | | | | Plymouth Arg | — | — |
| **Forwards** | | | | | | |
| Brian Johnson (Contract cancelled Jan 1982) | 5 10 | 11 6 | London | Plymouth Arg | 197 | 40 |
| | | | | Torquay U (on loan) | 7 | 2 |
| Mark Graves* | 5 9 | 10 11 | Middlesex | Plymouth Arg | 33 | 3 |
| Dave Kemp | 5 9 | 11 0 | Harrow | Crystal Palace | 35 | 10 |
| | | | | Portsmouth | 64 | 30 |
| | | | | Carlisle U | 61 | 22 |
| | | | | Gillingham (on loan) | 9 | 2 |
| | | | | Brentford (on loan) | 3 | 1 |
| | | | | Plymouth Arg | 84 | 39 |
| John Sims | 6 0 | 12 10 | Belper | Derby Co | 3 | — |
| | | | | Luton T (on loan) | 3 | 1 |
| | | | | Oxford U (on loan) | 7 | 1 |
| | | | | Colchester U (on loan) | 2 | — |
| | | | | Notts Co | 61 | 13 |
| | | | | Exeter C | 34 | 11 |
| | | | | Plymouth Arg | 120 | 33 |
| John Peachey (Contract cancelled Jan 1982) | 6 0 | 12 1 | Cambridge | York C | 8 | 3 |
| | | | | Barnsley | 127 | 31 |
| | | | | Darlington | 26 | 7 |
| | | | | Plymouth Arg | 3 | — |
| Kelvin Howe (Contract cancelled Feb 1982) | 5 10 | 10 6 | Calstock | Plymouth Arg | — | — |
| Andy Rogers | 5 8 | 10 0 | Chatteris | Peterborough U | 29 | 1 |
| | | | | Southampton | 5 | — |
| | | | | Plymouth Arg | 40 | 4 |
| Jeff Cook | 5 9 | 11 3 | Hartlepool | Stoke C | 30 | 5 |
| | | | | Bradford C (on loan) | 8 | 1 |
| | | | | Plymouth Arg (on loan) | 7 | 5 |
| | | | | Plymouth Arg | 35 | 16 |
| Tony Dennis | 5 6 | 10 2 | Taplow | Plymouth Arg | 6 | — |

# PORTSMOUTH

## Division 3

*Vice-President*: Sir A. L. Blake MC, LLB, KCVO.

*Chairman:* B. J. Deacon.

*Vice-Chairman:* J. R. Parkhouse.

*Directors:* D. K. Deacon, S. W. Sloan, G. G. Gauntlett.

*Manager:* Bobby Campbell.

*Company Secretary:* W. J. B. Davis.

*Chief Executive:* J. W. Dickinson MBE.

*Year Formed:* 1898.

*Turned Professional:* 1898.   *Limited Company:* 1898.

**Football League Record:**
1920 Original Member of Division 3; 1921 Division 3(S);
1924–27 Division 2; 1927–59 Division 1; 1959–61 Division 2;
1961–62 Division 3; 1962–76 Division 2; 1976–78 Division 3; 1978–80 Division 4; 1980– Division 3.

**Honours:** *Football League:* Division 1 – Champions 1948–49, 1949–50; Division 2 – Runners-up 1926–27; Division 3(S) – Champions 1923–24; Division 3 – Champions 1961–62. *FA Cup:* Winners 1939; Runners-up 1929, 1934. *Football League Cup* best season: 5th rd, 1961.

*Record Victory:* 9-1 v Notts Co, Division 2, 9 Apr, 1927.

*Record Defeat:* 0-10 v Leicester C, Division 1, 20 Oct, 1928.

*Most League Points:* 65, Division 3, 1961–62.

*Most League Goals:* 91, Division 4, 1979–80.

*Highest League Scorer in Season:* Billy Haines, 40, Division 2, 1926–27.

*Most League Goals in Total Aggregate:* Peter Harris, 194, 1946–60.

*Most Capped Player:* Jimmy Dickinson, 48, England.

*Most League Appearances:* 764, Jimmy Dickinson, 1946–65.

*Record Transfer Fee Received:* £130,000 from Brighton for Steve Foster, June 1979.

*Record Transfer Fee Paid:* £155,000 to Fulham for Paul Went, Dec 1973.

*Previous Managers since the War:* Jack Tinn, Bob Jackson, Eddie Lever, Freddie Cox, George Smith, John Mortimore, Ron Tindall, Ian St John, Jimmy Dickinson MBE, Frank Burrows.

*Address of Supporters Club:* Frogmore Road, Portsmouth.

*Address of the Club Shop or Boutique:* The Club Shop, Portsmouth, 42 Frogmore Road, Portsmouth.

---

**Fratton Park, Frogmore Rd, Portsmouth PO4 8RA.** Telephone Portsmouth 731204/5. *Telegraphic address:* 'Pompey Portsm'th'. *Ground capacity:* 40,000 (14,200 covered). *Record attendance:* 51,385 v Derby Co, FA Cup 6th rd, 26 Feb, 1949. *Record receipts:* £39,521 v Middlesbrough, FA Cup 3rd rd, 9 Jan, 1980. *Pitch measurements:* 116yd×73yd.

*How to get there:* Fratton station on main line from London Waterloo is just four minutes walk from the ground. Buses 17 and 18 from Portsmouth Harbour station and Gosport Ferry Terminal to the ground. Buses also from Portsmouth station.

*Match tickets:* South Stand centre section (the best seats) bookable 10 days in advance.

*Car parking:* Only side-street parking.

*Entertainments/catering facilities:* The Pompey public house and reception rooms adjoin the ground and are owned by the club. There are also several bars around the ground.

*Club shop:* 42 Frogmore Road.

*Handbooks/programmes:* No handbook. The match-day magazine available on subscription.

*Extra information:* Portsmouth were the first club to come out of the Third Division to win the League Championship.

*Club Colours:* Blue shirts with white collars and cuffs, white shorts, red socks.

*Change Colours:* Red shirts with white collar and cuffs, red shorts, white stockings.

*Club Captain:* Bill Rafferty.

*Club Nickname:* Pompey.

## PORTSMOUTH 1981–82 LEAGUE RECORD

| Match No. | Date | Venue | Opponents | Result | H/T Score | Goalscorers | Attendance |
|---|---|---|---|---|---|---|---|
| 1 | Aug 29 | H | Lincoln C | D 1-1 | 0-0 | Rafferty | 10,698 |
| 2 | Sept 5 | A | Preston NE | L 0-1 | 0-1 | | 6112 |
| 3 | 12 | H | Brentford | D 2-2 | 0-0 | Rafferty, Hemmerman | 10,364 |
| 4 | 19 | A | Southend U | L 0-2 | 0-1 | | 4355 |
| 5 | 23 | A | Oxford U | W 2-0 | 1-0 | Doyle (pen), Rafferty | 4750 |
| 6 | 26 | H | Bristol C | W 2-0 | 1-0 | Tait, Berry | 10,203 |
| 7 | 29 | H | Exeter C | W 2-0 | 2-0 | Rafferty, Hemmerman | 10,989 |
| 8 | Oct 3 | A | Chesterfield | D 2-2 | 1-0 | Hemmerman, Tait | 6150 |
| 9 | 10 | H | Burnley | L 1-2 | 0-1 | Doyle (pen) | 9891 |
| 10 | 17 | A | Walsall | L 1-3 | 0-1 | Berry | 4408 |
| 11 | 20 | A. | Gillingham | L 2-4 | 2-1 | Tait, Rafferty | 5546 |
| 12 | 24 | H | Newport Co | D 0-0 | 0-0 | | 8787 |
| 13 | 31 | A | Fulham | D 1-1 | 0-0 | Hemmerman | 7542 |
| 14 | Nov 3 | H | Wimbledon | W 1-0 | 0-0 | Cropley | 9063 |
| 15 | 7 | A | Plymouth Arg | D 0-0 | 0-0 | | 6275 |
| 16 | 14 | H | Carlisle U | L 1-2 | 0-1 | Hemmerman | 8858 |
| 17 | 28 | H | Huddersfield T | W 2-1 | 1-1 | Cropley, Tait | 8155 |
| 18 | Dec 5 | A | Doncaster R | D 0-0 | 0-0 | | 5912 |
| 19 | 26 | H | Bristol R | D 0-0 | 0-0 | | 11,395 |
| 20 | Jan 6 | A | Reading | L 1-2 | 1-2 | Tait | 4018 |
| 21 | 19 | A | Chester | L 2-3 | 1-1 | Doyle, Hemmerman | 1444 |
| 22 | 23 | A | Lincoln C | D 1-1 | 0-0 | Tait | 3297 |
| 23 | 30 | H | Southend U | D 0-0 | 0-0 | | 7731 |
| 24 | Feb 6 | A | Brentford | D 2-2 | 1-1 | Rollings, Tait | 5950 |
| 25 | 9 | H | Oxford U | D 1-1 | 1-1 | Aizlewood | 7095 |
| 26 | 13 | H | Chesterfield | W 5-1 | 2-1 | Aizlewood, Crown, Rafferty 3 | 8046 |
| 27 | 20 | A | Bristol C | W 1-0 | 0-0 | Rafferty | 9397 |
| 28 | 23 | A | Swindon T | L 0-2 | 0-1 | | 4860 |
| 29 | 27 | A | Burnley | L 0-3 | 0-1 | | 7024 |
| 30 | Mar 6 | H | Walsall | W 1-0 | 1-0 | Aizlewood | 7133 |
| 31 | 9 | H | Gillingham | W 1-0 | 1-0 | Rafferty | 6711 |
| 32 | 13 | A | Newport Co | D 1-1 | 1-0 | Crown | 4209 |
| 33 | 20 | H | Fulham | D 1-1 | 1-0 | Rafferty | 10,712 |
| 34 | 27 | H | Plymouth Arg | W 1-0 | 0-0 | Rafferty | 9551 |
| 35 | Apr 3 | A | Carlisle U | L 0-2 | 0-2 | | 3919 |
| 36 | 6 | A | Preston NE | D 1-1 | 1-0 | Rafferty | 6712 |
| 37 | 10 | A | Bristol R | D 1-1 | 1-1 | Rafferty | 4833 |
| 38 | 12 | H | Reading | W 3-0 | 2-0 | Senior 2, Doyle (pen) | 8427 |
| 39 | 17 | H | Doncaster R | D 0-0 | 0-0 | | 8657 |
| 40 | 24 | A | Huddersfield T | W 1-0 | 0-0 | Rafferty | 5658 |
| 41 | May 1 | H | Chester | W 2-0 | 0-0 | Rafferty, Doyle (pen) | 6196 |
| 42 | 5 | A | Exeter C | D 3-3 | 1-2 | Rafferty, Tait 2 | 2596 |
| 43 | 8 | A | Millwall | L 0-1 | 0-1 | | 4969 |
| 44 | 15 | H | Swindon T | W 3-0 | 2-0 | Hemmerman 3 | 6372 |
| 45 | 18 | A | Wimbledon | L 2-3 | 1-1 | Hemmerman, Doyle (pen) | 2642 |
| 46 | 21 | H | Millwall | D 2-2 | 1-0 | Doyle 2 (2 pens) | 4902 |

**Final League Position: 13**

### Goalscorers

*League* (56): Rafferty 17, Hemmerman 10, Tait 9, Doyle 8 (7 pens), Aizlewood 3, Berry 2, Cropley 2, Crown 2, Senior 2, Rollings 1.
*League Cup* (6): Doyle 2, Rafferty 2, Berry 1, Kamara 1.
*FA Cup* (3): Hemmerman 2, Tait 1.

| | | | | |
|---|---|---|---|---|
| **League Cup** | First Round | Southend U (a) | | 0-0 |
| | | (h) | | 4-1 |
| | Second Round | QPR (a) | | 0-5 |
| | | (h) | | 2-2 |
| **FA Cup** | First Round | Millwall (h) | | 1-1 |
| | | (a) | | 2-3 |

| Knight | McLaughlin | Viney | Kamara | Aizlewood | Rollings | Gregory | Doyle | Rafferty | Berry | Rogers | Hemmerman | Tait | Ellis | Barnard | Cropley | Leworthy | Crown | Garner | Bryant | Bason | Bartlett | Sullivan | Wimbleton | Senior | Gosney | Match No. |
|---|---|---|---|---|---|---|---|---|---|---|---|---|---|---|---|---|---|---|---|---|---|---|---|---|---|---|
| 1 | 2 | 3 | 4 | 5 | 6 | 7 | 8* | 9 | 10 | 11 | 12 | | | | | | | | | | | | | | | 1 |
| 1 | 2 | 3 | 4 | 5 | 6* | 7 | 8 | 9 | 10 | 11 | | 12 | | | | | | | | | | | | | | 2 |
| 1 | 2 | 3 | 4 | 5 | | | 8 | 9 | 10* | 12 | | 7 | 11 | 6 | | | | | | | | | | | | 3 |
| 1 | 2 | 3 | 4 | 5 | | | 8 | 9 | 10 | | | 7 | 11 | 6* | 12 | | | | | | | | | | | 4 |
| 1 | 2 | 3 | 4 | 5 | | | 8 | 9 | 10 | | | 7 | 11 | 6 | | | | | | | | | | | | 5 |
| 1 | 2 | 3 | 4 | 5 | | | 8 | 9 | 10 | | | 7 | 11 | 6 | | | | | | | | | | | | 6 |
| 1 | 2 | 3 | 4 | 5 | | | 8* | 9 | 10 | 12 | | 7 | 11 | 6 | | | | | | | | | | | | 7 |
| 1 | 2 | 3 | 4* | 5 | | | 8 | 9 | 10 | 12 | | 7 | 11 | 6 | | | | | | | | | | | | 8 |
| 1 | 2 | 3 | 4 | 5 | | | 8* | 9 | 11 | | | 7 | 10 | 6 | 12 | | | | | | | | | | | 9 |
| 1 | | 3 | 4 | 5 | 6 | | 8 | 9 | 12 | | | 7 | 10 | 2 | 11* | | | | | | | | | | | 10 |
| 1 | | 3 | 4 | 5 | 6 | | 8 | 9 | 11* | | | 12 | 10 | 2 | 7 | | | | | | | | | | | 11 |
| 1 | | 3 | | 5 | 6 | 11 | 8 | 9* | | | | 7 | 10 | 2 | 4 | 12 | | | | | | | | | | 12 |
| 1 | | 3 | | 5 | 6 | | 8 | 9 | | | | 7 | 11 | 2 | 10 | 4 | | | | | | | | | | 13 |
| 1 | | 3 | 6 | 12 | | | 4 | 9* | 8 | | | 7 | | 2 | 10 | 11 | 5 | | | | | | | | | 14 |
| 1 | | 3 | | 5 | 6 | | 8 | 4 | 9 | | | 7 | 10 | 2 | 11 | | | | | | | | | | | 15 |
| 1 | | 3 | | 5 | 6 | 10 | 4 | | 8 | 11 | | 7 | | 2 | 9 | | | | | | | | | | | 16 |
| 1 | 2 | | | 5 | 6 | | 4 | | | | | 7 | 8 | 9 | 10 | | 11 | | 3 | | | | | | | 17 |
| 1 | 2 | | | 5 | 6 | | | | 12 | | | 7 | 9 | 8 | 10 | | 11* | | 3 | | | | | | | 18 |
| 1 | 2 | 3 | | 5* | 6 | | 4 | | 12 | | | 7 | 9 | 8 | 10 | | 11 | | | | | | | | | 19 |
| 1 | 2 | | | | 6 | | 4 | | 12 | | | 7* | 9 | 8 | | | 11 | 5 | 3 | 10 | | | | | | 20 |
| 1 | 2 | | | 5 | 6 | | 4 | | | | | 7 | 9 | 8 | | | 11 | | 3 | 10 | | | | | | 21 |
| 1 | 2 | | | 5 | 6 | | 4 | | 12 | | | 7 | 9 | 8 | | | 11* | | 3 | 10 | | | | | | 22 |
| 1 | | | | 5 | 6 | | 4 | | 12 | | | 7 | 9 | 2 | 8 | | 11* | | 3 | 10 | | | | | | 23 |
| 1 | 2 | | | 5 | 6 | | 4 | | 8 | | | 7 | 9 | | | | 11 | | 3 | 10 | | | | | | 24 |
| 1 | 2 | | | 5 | 6 | | 4* | | 8 | | | 7 | 9 | | 12 | | 11 | | 3 | 10 | | | | | | 25 |
| 1 | 2 | | | 5 | 12 | | 4 | | 8 | | | | 9 | | 7* | | 11 | 6 | 3 | 10 | | | | | | 26 |
| 1 | 2 | | | 5* | | | | 9 | 8 | | | 7 | | | 4 | | 11 | 6 | 3 | 10 | 12 | | | | | 27 |
| 1 | 2 | | | | | | 9 | | 8 | 12 | | 5 | | | 7 | | 11 | 6 | 3 | 10* | | | | | | 28 |
| 1 | 2 | | | | | | 9 | 7 | 8 | 11* | | | 10 | 5 | 4 | | 12 | 6 | | | | 3 | | | | 29 |
| 1 | 2 | | | 5 | | | 9 | 7 | 8 | | | | 10 | 6 | 4 | | 11 | | | | | 3 | | | | 30 |
| 1 | | | | 5* | | | 9 | 7 | 8 | 12 | | | 10 | 2 | 4 | | 11 | 6 | | | | 3 | | | | 31 |
| 1 | 2 | | | 5 | | | 9 | | 8 | 7 | | | 10 | 6 | 4 | | 11 | | | | | 3 | | | | 32 |
| 1 | 2 | | | 5 | | | | | 8 | 7* | | | 10 | 6 | 4 | | 11 | | | | | 3 | 12 | 9 | | 33 |
| 1 | 2 | | | 5 | | | 4 | | 8 | 7 | | | 10 | 6 | | | 11* | | | | | 3 | 12 | 9 | | 34 |
| 1 | 2 | | | 5* | | | 4 | | 8 | 7 | | | 10 | 6 | | | 11 | | | | | 3 | 12 | 9 | | 35 |
| 1 | 2 | | | | | | 4 | | 8 | 7 | | | | 6 | | | 11 | 5 | | 10 | | 3 | | 9 | | 36 |
| 1 | 2 | | | | | | 4 | 9 | 8 | 7 | | | 10 | 6 | | 5 | | | | | | 3 | | 11 | | 37 |
| 1 | 2 | | | | | | 4 | | 8 | 10 | 11 | | | 6 | | 7* | 5 | | | | | 3 | 12 | 9 | | 38 |
| 1 | 2 | | | 5 | | | 4 | | 8 | 10 | 11 | | | 6 | | | 12 | | | | | 3 | 7* | 9 | | 39 |
| 1 | 2 | 6 | | 5 | | | 4 | | 8 | 10 | 11 | 12 | | | | | | | | | | 3 | 7* | 9 | | 40 |
| 1 | 2 | 6 | | 5 | | | 4 | | 8 | 10 | 11 | 7 | 9 | | | | | | | | | 3 | | | | 41 |
| 1* | 2 | 6 | | 5 | | | 4 | | 8 | 10 | 11 | 7 | 9 | 12 | | | | | | | | 3 | | | | 42 |
| | 2 | 6 | | 5 | | | 4 | | | 10 | 11 | 7 | 9 | 8 | | | | | | | | 3 | | | 1 | 43 |
| 1 | 2 | 6 | | 5 | | | 4 | | | 10 | 11 | 7 | | 8 | | | | | | | | 3 | | 9 | | 44 |
| 1 | | 6 | | | | | 4 | 9 | | 10 | 11 | 7 | | 5 | 2 | | 8 | | | | | 3 | | | | 45 |
| 1 | | 6 | | | | | 4 | | | 10 | 11 | 7 | | 5 | 2 | | 8 | | | | | 3 | | 9 | | 46 |
| 45 | 36 | 24 | 11 | 36 | 19 | 12 | 43 | 35 | 26 | 14 | 29 | 34 | 31 | 16 | 8 | — | 25 | 10 | 11 | 9 | — | 18 | 4 | 9 | 1 | |

+2s  +4s  +1s  +4s  +5s  +1s  +1s  +1s  +2s  +1s  +2s     +1s  +4s

Players continued from following page.

| | | | | | | | |
|---|---|---|---|---|---|---|---|
| Mick Tait | 5 11 | 12 5 | Wallsend | Oxford U | 64 | 23 | |
| | | | | Carlisle U | 106 | 20 | |
| | | | | Hull C | 33 | 3 | |
| | | | | Portsmouth | 73 | 17 | |
| Billy Rafferty | 6 0 | 12 6 | Pt Glasgow | Coventry C | 27 | 3 | |
| | | | | Blackpool | 36 | 9 | |
| | | | | Plymouth Arg | 90 | 35 | |
| | | | | Carlisle U | 72 | 27 | |
| | | | | Wolverhampton W | 44 | 6 | |
| | | | | Newcastle U | 39 | 6 | |
| | | | | Portsmouth | 61 | 23 | |

## PORTSMOUTH

| | Ht | Wt | Birthplace | Clubs | League App. | League Gls |
|---|---|---|---|---|---|---|
| **Goalkeepers** | | | | | | |
| Peter Mellor | 6 2 | 14 0 | Presbury | Manchester C | — | — |
| (Contract cancelled Jan 1982) | | | | Burnley | 69 | — |
| | | | | Chesterfield (on loan) | 4 | — |
| | | | | Fulham | 189 | — |
| | | | | Hereford U | 32 | — |
| | | | | Portsmouth | 129 | — |
| Alan Knight | 6 1 | 13 1½ | Balham | Portsmouth | 55 | — |
| Andrew Gosney | 6 4 | 13 5 | Southampton | Portsmouth | 1 | — |
| **Defenders** | | | | | | |
| John McLaughlin | 5 8 | 10 10 | Edmonton | Colchester U | 66 | 2 |
| | | | | Swindon T | 202 | 8 |
| | | | | Portsmouth | 107 | 1 |
| Alan Garner | 6 0 | 12 4 | Lambeth | Millwall | 2 | — |
| (Non-contract) | | | | Luton T | 88 | 3 |
| | | | | Watford | 200 | 15 |
| | | | | Portsmouth | 36 | 2 |
| Peter Ellis | 5 11 | 11 6 | Portsmouth | Portsmouth | 209 | — |
| Keith Viney* | 5 11 | 11 12 | Portsmouth | Portsmouth | 166 | 3 |
| Archie Styles | 5 9 | 11 0 | Liverpool | Everton | 23 | — |
| (Contract cancelled Feb 1982) | | | | Birmingham C | 74 | 3 |
| | | | | Peterborough U | 32 | 1 |
| | | | | Portsmouth | 28 | — |
| Steve Aizlewood | 5 11 | 13 11 | Newport | Newport Co | 197 | 18 |
| | | | | Swindon T | 112 | 10 |
| | | | | Portsmouth | 111 | 6 |
| Kevin Bartlett | 5 9 | 10 5 | Portsmouth | Portsmouth | 3 | — |
| (Contract cancelled April 1982) | | | | | | |
| Andy Rollings | 6 2 | 12 12 | Portishead | Norwich C | 4 | — |
| | | | | Brighton | 168 | 10 |
| | | | | Swindon T | 12 | 1 |
| | | | | Portsmouth | 19 | 1 |
| Colin Sullivan | 5 7 | 11 3 | Saltash | Plymouth Arg | 230 | 7 |
| | | | | Norwich C | 157 | 3 |
| | | | | Cardiff C | 63 | 1 |
| | | | | Hereford U | 8 | — |
| | | | | Portsmouth | 18 | — |
| Gary Juryeff | 5 11 | 11 9 | Gosport | Portsmouth | — | — |
| (Contract cancelled April 1982) | | | | | | |
| Graham Marriner | 5 10 | 11 11 | Haslemere | Portsmouth | — | — |
| (Contract cancelled April 1982) | | | | | | |
| **Midfield** | | | | | | |
| Leigh Barnard* | 5 7½ | 9 10 | Worsley | Portsmouth | 79 | 8 |
| | | | | Peterborough U (on loan) | 4 | — |
| Ken Todd | 5 7 | 9 9 | Co Durham | Wolverhampton W | 5 | 1 |
| (Contract cancelled March 1982) | | | | Port Vale | 44 | 9 |
| | | | | Portsmouth | 3 | 1 |
| David Gregory | 5 9 | 11 6 | Peterborough | Peterborough U | 142 | 32 |
| (Non-contract) | | | | Stoke C | 23 | 3 |
| | | | | Blackburn R (on loan) | 5 | 3 |
| | | | | Bury | 52 | 13 |
| | | | | Portsmouth | 74 | 18 |
| Neil Ayrton | | | Lewisham | Maidstone U | (not known) | |
| (Contract cancelled Sept 1981) | | | | Portsmouth | 2 | — |
| Bobby Doyle | 6 0 | 11 12 | Dumbarton | Barnsley | 149 | 16 |
| | | | | Peterborough U | 130 | 10 |
| | | | | Blackpool | 49 | 2 |
| | | | | Portsmouth | 68 | 12 |
| Alex Cropley | 5 8 | 10 0 | Aldershot | Hibernian | 114 | 24 |
| | | | | Arsenal | 30 | 5 |
| | | | | Aston V | 67 | 7 |
| | | | | Newcastle U (on loan) | 3 | — |
| | | | | Portsmouth | 10 | 2 |
| Paul Wimbleton | 5 8 | 10 6 | Portsmouth | Portsmouth | 8 | — |
| Steve Berry | 5 7 | 10 6 | Gosport | Portsmouth | 27 | 2 |
| David Leworthy | 5 8½ | 11 11 | Portsmouth | Portsmouth | 1 | — |
| (Contract cancelled April 1982) | | | | | | |
| David Crown | 5 10 | 11 4 | Enfield | Walthamstow A | (not known) | |
| | | | | Brentford | 46 | 8 |
| | | | | Portsmouth | 27 | 2 |
| **Forwards** | | | | | | |
| Trevor Senior | 6 1½ | 12 8 | Dorchester | Dorchester | (not known) | |
| | | | | Portsmouth | 9 | 2 |
| Jeff Hemmerman* | 5 11 | 11 0 | Hull | Hull C | 59 | 10 |
| | | | | Scunthorpe U (on loan) | 5 | 1 |
| | | | | Port Vale | 15 | 5 |
| | | | | Portsmouth | 123 | 39 |
| Alan Rogers | 5 10 | 10 7 | Plymouth | Plymouth Arg | 117 | 5 |
| | | | | Portsmouth | 105 | 12 |

*Note: Players continued on previous page.*

# PORT VALE Division 4

*Chairman:* D. Ratcliffe JP.

*Vice-Chairman:* J. D. Lloyd.

*Directors:* D. S. Jones, A. McPherson, D. P. McGrath, J. Lloyd, J. Burgess (President).

*Manager:* John McGrath.  *Secretary:* Andrew Waterhouse.

*Chief Coach:* John Rudge.

*Year Formed:* 1876.  *Turned Professional:* 1885.

*Limited Company:* 1911.

*Previous Name:* Burslem Port Vale; became Port Vale, 1913.

*Previous Grounds:* 1876, Limekin Lane, Longport; 1881, Westport; 1884, Moorland Road, Burslem; 1886, Athletic Ground, Cobridge; 1913, Recreation Ground, Hanley; 1950, Vale Park.

**Football League Record:**
Original Member Division 2, 1892–96; Failed re-election in 1896; Re-elected 1898; Resigned 1907; Returned in Oct, 1919, when they took over the fixtures of Leeds City; 1929–30 Division 3(N); 1930–36 Division 2; 1936–38 Division 3(N); 1938–52 Division 3(S); 1952–54 Division 3(N); 1954–57 Division 2; 1957–58 Division 3(S); 1958–59 Division 4; 1959–65 Division 3; 1965–70 Division 4; 1970–78 Division 3; 1978– Division 4.

**Honours:** *Football League:* Division 2 best season: 5th, 1930–31; Division 3(N) – Champions 1929–30, 1953–54; Runners-up 1952–53; Division 4 – Champions 1958–59; Promoted 1969–70 (4th). *FA Cup:* semi-final 1954, when in Division 3. *Football League Cup:* never past 2nd rd.

*Record Victory:* 9-1 v Chesterfield, Division 2, 24 Sept, 1932.

*Record Defeat:* 0-10 v Sheffield U, Division 2, 10 Dec, 1892 and v Notts Co, Division 2, 26 Feb, 1895.

*Most League Points:* 69, Division 3(N), 1953–54. *Three points win:* 70, Division 4, 1981–82.

*Most League Goals:* 110, Division 4, 1958–59.

*Highest League Scorer in Season:* Wilf Kirkham, 38, Division 2, 1926–27.

*Most League Goals in Total Aggregate:* Wilf Kirkham, 154, 1923–29, 1931–33.

*Most Capped Player:* Sammy Morgan, 7 (18) Northern Ireland.

*Most League Appearances:* Roy Sproson, 761, 1950–72.

*Record Transfer Fee Received:* £55,000 from Leicester C for John Ridley, Sept 1978.

*Record Transfer Fee Paid:* £40,000 to Bury for Peter Farrell, Nov 1978; £40,000 to Wolverhampton W for Ken Todd, Aug 1978.

*Previous Managers since the War:* Billy Frith, Gordon Hodgson, Ivor Powell, Freddie Steele, Norman Low, Freddie Steele, Jackie Mudie, Sir Stanley Matthews, Gordon Lee, Roy Sproson, Colin Harper, Bob Smith, Dennis Butler, Alan Bloor.

*Address of Supporters Club:* Hamil Rd, Burslem, Stoke-on-Trent ST6 1AW.

---

**Vale Park, Burslem, Stoke-on-Trent.** Telephone Stoke-on-Trent 814134. *Ground capacity:* 35,000. *Record attendance:* 50,000 v Aston Villa, FA Cup 5th rd, 20 Feb, 1960. *Record receipts:* £11,991 v Burnley, FA Cup 4th rd, 29 Jan, 1977. *Pitch measurements:* 116yd×76yd.

*How to get there:* Nearest railway station, Stoke-on-Trent; there are frequent bus services from the town centre to Burslem.

*Match tickets:* Not bookable in advance.

*Car parking:* Parking is available behind the Railway Stand on Hamil Road, and on the Lorne Street side of the ground.

*Entertainments/catering facilities:* Light refreshments served on the ground. Social club on the Hamil Road side of the ground provides entertainment on certain evenings; membership by subscription.

*Club shop:* Sells all types of souvenirs.

*Handbooks/programmes:* Programmes are available on application to the club office or to the club shop.

*Extra information:* Port Vale are one of only five clubs to reach the FA Cup semi-final while in the Third Division; they did so in the 1953–54 season. Open Market every Friday.

*Club Colours:* White shirts with black trim, black shorts, white stockings.

*Change Colours:* Yellow shirts, green shorts, yellow stockings.

*Trainer:* Lol Hamlett.

*Club Nickname:* Valiants.

## PORT VALE 1981–82 LEAGUE RECORD

| Match No. | Date | Venue | Opponents | Result | H/T Score | Goalscorers | Attendance |
|---|---|---|---|---|---|---|---|
| 1 | Aug 29 | H | Halifax T | D 0-0 | 0-0 | | 3382 |
| 2 | Sept 5 | A | Darlington | D 1-1 | 0-1 | Deakin (pen) | 1872 |
| 3 | 12 | H | Mansfield T | D 0-0 | 0-0 | | 3043 |
| 4 | 19 | A | Rochdale | W 2-1 | 0-0 | Keenan, Deakin (pen) | 2750 |
| 5 | 23 | A | Wigan Ath | L 0-2 | 0-1 | | 4525 |
| 6 | 26 | H | Stockport Co | W 1-0 | 1-0 | Moss | 2757 |
| 7 | 28 | H | Colchester U | W 2-1 | 0-0 | Sproson, Moss | 3351 |
| 8 | Oct 2 | A | Crewe Alex | W 2-0 | 1-0 | Chamberlain N., Chamberlain M. | 4604 |
| 9 | 10 | H | Sheffield U | L 0-2 | 0-1 | | 7289 |
| 10 | 17 | A | Bury | L 2-3 | 2-2 | Bowles, Greenhoff | 3565 |
| 11 | 19 | H | Peterborough U | L 1-3 | 1-1 | Deakin (pen) | 2844 |
| 12 | 31 | H | Hull C | W 2-1 | 2-0 | Shankland, Chamberlain M. | 2591 |
| 13 | Nov 4 | A | Bradford C | L 0-1 | 0-1 | | 4043 |
| 14 | 7 | A | AFC Bournemouth | D 1-1 | 0-1 | Moss | 5798 |
| 15 | 11 | A | Blackpool | W 3-2 | 2-2 | Tartt 2, Chamberlain N. | 4785 |
| 16 | 14 | H | Aldershot | W 1-0 | 1-0 | Greenhoff | 2811 |
| 17 | 28 | H | Hartlepool U | W 5-2 | 1-0 | Moss 2, Chamberlain M., Chamberlain N., Armstrong | 2477 |
| 18 | Dec 5 | A | Scunthorpe U | D 0-0 | 0-0 | | 1902 |
| 19 | 19 | A | Torquay U | W 1-0 | 1-0 | Chamberlain M. | 1880 |
| 20 | Jan 20 | H | Darlington | D 2-2 | 0-1 | Hunter, Moss | 3529 |
| 21 | 22 | A | Halifax T | D 1-1 | 1-0 | Chamberlain M. | 2965 |
| 22 | 25 | H | Tranmere R | D 0-0 | 0-0 | | 4355 |
| 23 | 30 | H | Rochdale | D 1-1 | 1-1 | Tartt | 3835 |
| 24 | Feb 2 | A | Northampton T | W 5-3 | 4-0 | Hunter 2, Sproson, Chamberlain M., Greenhoff | 1644 |
| 25 | 6 | A | Mansfield T | W 3-1 | 0-1 | Chamberlain M., Moss, Sealy | 2690 |
| 26 | 8 | H | Wigan Ath | D 1-1 | 0-1 | Sealy | 8775 |
| 27 | 13 | H | Crewe Alex | D 0-0 | 0-0 | | 6542 |
| 28 | 19 | A | Stockport Co | W 2-1 | 0-1 | Sealy (pen), Moss | 3001 |
| 29 | 22 | A | York C | L 0-2 | 0-1 | | 1938 |
| 30 | 27 | A | Sheffield U | L 1-2 | 1-0 | Sealy (pen) | 13,813 |
| 31 | Mar 6 | H | Bury | D 0-0 | 0-0 | | 3729 |
| 32 | 10 | A | Peterborough U | L 0-1 | 0-0 | | 4151 |
| 33 | 13 | H | Blackpool | W 2-0 | 2-0 | Chamberlain N., Moss | 3439 |
| 34 | 15 | H | Bradford C | D 1-1 | 0-0 | Tartt | 4325 |
| 35 | 20 | A | Hull C | L 1-3 | 0-0 | Deakin | 5506 |
| 36 | 27 | H | AFC Bournemouth | D 1-1 | 1-0 | Deakin (pen) | 3004 |
| 37 | Apr 3 | A | Aldershot | W 2-1 | 2-0 | Sproson, Deakin | 1594 |
| 38 | 10 | A | Hereford U | L 0-1 | 0-0 | | 2973 |
| 39 | 12 | H | Northampton T | W 1-0 | 1-0 | Sproson | 3012 |
| 40 | 17 | H | Scunthorpe U | W 2-1 | 0-1 | Moss 2 | 2507 |
| 41 | 24 | A | Hartlepool U | L 1-3 | 1-1 | Chamberlain M. | 1429 |
| 42 | 26 | H | Hereford U | D 1-1 | 0-0 | Sproson | 2160 |
| 43 | May 1 | H | York C | D 0-0 | 0-0 | | 1924 |
| 44 | 3 | A | Colchester U | L 0-1 | 0-1 | | 1470 |
| 45 | 8 | A | Tranmere R | W 2-1 | 2-0 | Moss 2 | 1521 |
| 46 | 15 | H | Torquay U | W 2-0 | 1-0 | Bowles, Sproson | 2007 |

**Final League Position: 7**

### Goalscorers

*League* (56): Moss 13, Chamberlain M. 8, Deakin 6 (4 pens), Sproson 6, Chamberlain N. 4, Sealy 4 (2 pens), Tartt 4, Greenhoff 3, Hunter 3, Bowles 2, Armstrong 1, Keenan 1, Shankland 1.
*League Cup* (4): Moss 2, Chamberlain N. 1, Deakin 1.
*FA Cup* (8): Chamberlain N. 4, Moss 2, Armstrong 1, Chamberlain M. 1.

| League Cup | First Round | Hereford U (a) | 1-1 |
|---|---|---|---|
| | | (h) | 2-0 |
| | Second Round | Tranmere R (a) | 0-2 |
| | | (h) | 1-2 |
| FA Cup | First Round | Lincoln C (a) | 2-2 |
| | | (h) | 0-0 |
| | | (h) | 2-0 |
| | Second Round | Stockport Co (h) | 4-1 |
| | Third Round | Shrewsbury T (a) | 0-1 |

| Harrison | Keenan | Deakin | Hunter | Bowles | Sproson | Greenhoff | Moss | Chamberlain N. | Bromage | Chamberlain M. | Higgins | Armstrong | Brissett | Tartt | Bennett | Shankland | Farrell | Sealy | Bright | Match No. |
|---|---|---|---|---|---|---|---|---|---|---|---|---|---|---|---|---|---|---|---|---|
| 1 | 2 | 3 | 4 | 5 | 6 | 7 | 8 | 9 | 10 | 11 | | | | | | | | | | 1 |
| 1 | 2 | 3 | 4 | 5 | 6 | | 8 | | 10 | 11 | 7 | 9 | | | | | | | | 2 |
| 1 | 2 | 3 | 4 | 6 | 5 | | 8 . | | 10 | 11 | 7 | 9 | | | | | | | | 3 |
| 1 | 2 | 3 | 4 | 6 | 5 | | 8 | 7* | 10 | 11 | | 9 | 12 | | | | | | | 4 |
| 1 | 2 | 3 | 4 | 6 | 5 | | 8 | 12 | 10* | 11 | 7 | 9 | | | | | | | | 5 |
| 1 | 2 | 3 | 4 | 6 | 5 | 12 | 8 | 10* | | 11 | | 9 | 7 | | | | | | | 6 |
| 1 | 2 | 3 | 4 | 6 | 5 | 9 | 8 | 10 | 12 | 11 | | | 7* | | | | | | | 7 |
| 1 | 2 | 3 | 4 | 6 | 5 | 7 | 8 | 10* | 9 | 11 | | 12 | | | | | | | | 8 |
| 1 | 2 | 12 | 4 | 6 | 5* | 9 | 10 | | 8 | 11 | | 7 | | 3 | | | | | | 9 |
| 1 | 2 | 12 | 4 | 6 | | 7 | 8* | | 10 | 11 | | 9 | 5 | 3 | | | | | | 10 |
| 1 | 2 | 5 | 4 | 6 | | 7* | | | 10 | 11 | | 9 | 8 | 3 | 12 | | | | | 11 |
| 1 | 2 | | 4 | 6 | 5 | 7* | | 9 | 10 | 11 | 12 | | | 3 | | 8 | | | | 12 |
| 1 | 11 | | 4 | 6 | 5 | | 8 | 10 | 3 | 7 | | 9 | | 2 | | | | | | 13 |
| 1 | 2 | | 4 | 6 | 5 | 12 | 8 | 10 | 9 | 7 | | 11* | | 3 | | | | | | 14 |
| 1 | 2 | | 4 | 6 | 5 | | 8 | 10 | 9 | 7 | | 11 | | 3 | | | | | | 15 |
| 1 | | | 4 | 6 | 5 | 2* | 8 | 10 | 9 | 7 | | 11 | | 3 | | 12 | | | | 16 |
| 1 | | | 4 | 6 | 5 | 2 | 8 | 10 | 9 | 7 | | 11 | | 3 | | | | | | 17 |
| 1 | | | 4 | 6 | 5 | 9 | 8 | 7 | 3 | 11 | | 10 | | 2 | | | | | | 18 |
| 1 | | | 4 | 6 | 5 | 9 | 8 | 7 | 3 | 11 | | 10 | | 2 | | | | | | 19 |
| 1 | | | 4 | 6 | 5 | 9 | 8 | 7 | 3 | 11 | | 10 | | 2 | | | | | | 20 |
| 1 | | | 4 | 6 | 5 | 9* | 8 | 7 | 3 | 11 | | 10 | | 2 | | 12 | | | | 21 |
| 1 | 9* | 4 | 6 | 5 | | 8 | 7 | 3 | 11 | | | 10 | | 2 | | 12 | | | | 22 |
| 1 | | | 4 | 6 | 5 | 9 | 8 | 7 | 3 | 11 | | 10 | | 2 | | | | | | 23 |
| 1 | | | 4 | 6 | 5 | 9 | 8 | 7 | 3 | 11 | | 10 | | 2 | | | | | | 24 |
| 1 | | 4 | | 5 | 9 | 8 | 7* | 3 | 11 | | | 12 | 6 | 2 | | 10 | | | | 25 |
| 1 | | 4 | | 5 | 9 | 8 | | 3 | 11 | | | 10* | 6 | 2 | | 12 | 7 | | | 26 |
| 1 | | 4 | 9 | 5 | | 8 | | 3 | 11 | | | | 6* | 2 | 12 | 10 | 7 | | | 27 |
| 1 | 7* | 4 | 6 | 5 | 9 | 8 | | 3 | 11 | | | | | 2 | | 12 | 10 | | | 28 |
| 1 | | 4 | 6 | 5 | 9 | 8 | | 3 | 11 | | | | | 2 | | 10 | 7 | | | 29 |
| 1 | 7* | 4 | 6 | 5 | 9 | 8 | | 3 | 11 | | | 12 | 2 | | 10 | | | | | 30 |
| 1 | | 4 | 6 | 5 | 9* | 8 | 7 | 3 | 11 | | | 10 | | 2 | | 12 | | | | 31 |
| 1 | 4* | | 6 | 5 | | 8 | 7 | 3 | 11 | | | 10 | 12 | 2 | | 9 | | | | 32 |
| 1 | | | 6 | 5 | 9 | 8 | 7* | 3 | 11 | | | 10 | 4 | 2 | | 12 | | | | 33 |
| 1 | | | 6 | 5 | 9 | 8 | 7 | 3 | 11 | | | 10 | 4 | 2 | | | | | | 34 |
| 1 | 12 | 5 | | 6 | | 9 | 8 | 3 | 11 | | | 10 | 4* | 2 | | 7 | | | | 35 |
| 1 | | 5 | | 6 | | 9 | 8 | 3 | 11 | | | 10 | | 4 | 2 | 7 | | | | 36 |
| 1 | | 10 | 12 | 6 | 5 | 9 | 8 | 3 | 11 | | | | | 4 | 2 | 7* | | | | 37 |
| 1 | | 10 | 12 | 6 | 5 | 9 | 8 | 3 | 11 | | | | | 4 | 2 | 7* | | | | 38 |
| 1 | 7 | 10 | 4 | 6 | 5 | 9 | 8 | 3 | 11 | | | | | 2 | | | | | | 39 |
| 1 | 7 | 10 | 4 | 6 | 5 | 9* | 8 | 12 | 3 | 11 | | | | 2 | | | | | | 40 |
| 1 | 10* | 9 | 4 | 6 | 5 | | 8 | 7 | 3 | 11 | | 12 | | 2 | | | | | | 41 |
| 1 | 9 | | 4 | 6 | 5 | | 8 | 7 | 3 | 11 | | 10 | | 2 | | | | | | 42 |
| 1 | 9 | | 4 | 6 | 5 | | 8 | 7* | 3 | 11 | | 10 | | 2 | | | | 12 | | 43 |
| 1 | 9 | | 4 | 6 | 5 | | 8 | 7 | 3 | 11 | | 10 | | 2 | | | | | | 44 |
| 1 | | | 4 | 6 | 5 | 9 | 8 | 7 | 3 | 11 | | 10 | | 2 | | | | | | 45 |
| 1 | | | 4 | 6 | 5 | 9 | 8 | | 3 | 11 | | 10 | | 2 | | | | | 7 | 46 |
| 46 | 20 | 21 | 39 | 44 | 42 | 31 | 44 | 28 | 44 | 46 | 3 | 32 | 10 | 38 | 3 | 6 | 2 | 6 | 1 | |
| + | + | + | | | + | | + | + | + | | | + | + | + | | + | + | + | + | |
| 1s | 2s | 2s | | | 2s | | 2s | 1s | | | | 1s | 2s | 4s | | 1s | 6s | 2s | 1s | |

# PORT VALE

| | Ht | Wt | Birthplace | Clubs | League App. | League Gls |
|---|---|---|---|---|---|---|
| **Goalkeepers** | | | | | | |
| Mark Harrison | 6 0½ | 12 7 | Derby | Nottingham F | — | — |
| | | | | Southampton | — | — |
| | | | | Port Vale | 70 | — |
| | | | | Stoke C (on loan) | — | — |
| | | | | | | |
| **Defenders** | | | | | | |
| Gerry Keenan* | 5 9 | 11 0 | Liverpool | Bury | 71 | 3 |
| | | | | Port Vale | 106 | 7 |
| Phil Sproson | 6 0 | 12 0 | Trent Vale | Port Vale | 150 | 10 |
| Paul Bowles* | 6 1 | 12 11 | Manchester | Manchester U | — | — |
| | | | | Crewe Alex | 178 | 20 |
| | | | | Port Vale | 98 | 8 |
| | | | | Southampton (on loan) | — | — |
| Trevor Brissett* | 5 10½ | 11 7 | Stoke | Stoke C | — | — |
| | | | | Port Vale | 55 | — |
| Andy Higgins* | 6 3 | 12 4 | Bolsover | Chesterfield | 1 | — |
| | | | | Port Vale | 14 | — |
| Colin Tartt | 5 11 | 11 7 | Liverpool | Port Vale | 175 | 7 |
| | | | | Chesterfield | 186 | 7 |
| | | | | Port Vale | 38 | 4 |
| Gary Loughran* | 5 10 | 9 5 | Middlesbrough | Aston Villa | — | — |
| | | | | Port Vale | — | — |
| | | | | | | |
| **Midfield** | | | | | | |
| Paul Bennett* | 5 9 | 9 9 | Liverpool | Port Vale | 30 | 1 |
| Peter Farrell* | 5 7 | 10 9 | Liverpool | Bury | 54 | 9 |
| | | | | Doncaster R (on loan) | — | — |
| | | | | Shrewsbury T (on loan) | — | — |
| | | | | Port Vale | 89 | 10 |
| Felix Healy | 5 11 | 12 0 | Londonderry | Finn Harps | (not known) | — |
| (N Ireland) | | | | Port Vale | 41 | 2 |
| (Now with Coleraine but registration retained) | | | | | | |
| Russell Bromage | 5 11 | 11 5 | Blurton | Port Vale | 145 | 7 |
| Terry Armstrong | 5 10 | 12 2 | Barnsley | Huddersfield T | 40 | 2 |
| | | | | Port Vale | 51 | 3 |
| Ray Deakin* | 5 8 | 11 1 | Liverpool | Everton | — | — |
| | | | | Port Vale | 23 | 6 |
| Jimmy Greenhoff | 5 9 | 12 0 | Barnsley | Leeds U | 96 | 19 |
| | | | | Birmingham C | 31 | 14 |
| | | | | Stoke C | 274 | 76 |
| | | | | Manchester U | 97 | 26 |
| | | | | Crewe Alex | 11 | 4 |
| | | | | Port Vale | 33 | 3 |
| Geoff Hunter | 5 9 | 10 5 | Hull | Manchester U | — | — |
| | | | | Crewe Alex | 87 | 8 |
| | | | | Port Vale | 41 | 3 |
| | | | | | | |
| **Forwards** | | | | | | |
| Neville Chamberlain | 5 7½ | 11 5 | Stoke | Port Vale | 136 | 32 |
| Mark Chamberlain | 5 8½ | 9 8 | Stoke | Port Vale | 96 | 18 |
| John Miller* | 5 10 | 12 10 | Ipswich | Ipswich T | 50 | 2 |
| | | | | Norwich C | 23 | 3 |
| | | | | Mansfield T | 113 | 14 |
| | | | | Port Vale | 26 | 4 |
| Ernie Moss | 6 1½ | 13 2 | Chesterfield | Chesterfield | 271 | 94 |
| | | | | Peterborough U | 35 | 9 |
| | | | | Mansfield T | 57 | 21 |
| | | | | Chesterfield | 107 | 33 |
| | | | | Port Vale | 44 | 13 |
| Andy Shankland | 5 8 | 9 0 | Stoke | Port Vale | 12 | 1 |
| Mark Bright | 6 0 | 11 0 | Stoke | Port Vale | 2 | — |
| (Non-contract) | | | | | | |

# PRESTON NORTH END Division 3

*President:* Tom Finney OBE, JP.

*Chairman:* Alan R. W. Jones JP, FRICS.

*Vice-Chairman:* T. J. Hemmings.

*Managing Director:* B. J. Campbell.

*Directors:* T. W. S. Croft FCIOB, K. W. Leeming, T. H. Gore, E. Griffith BVSC, MRCVS, M. H. McCann LLB, A. C. Pilkington AICS, F INST FF.

*Team Manager:* Gordon Lee.

*Secretary:* D. J. Allan. *Asst Manager:* Geoff Nulty.

*Year Formed:* 1881. *Turned Professional:* 1885.

*Limited Company:* 1893.

**Football League Record:**
1888 Original Member of League; 1901–04 Division 2; 1904–12 Division 1; 1912–13 Division 2; 1913–14 Division 1; 1914–15 Division 2; 1919–25 Division 1; 1925–34 Division 2; 1934–49 Division 1; 1949–51 Division 2; 1951–61 Division 1; 1961–70 Division 2; 1970–71 Division 3; 1971–74 Division 2; 1974–78 Division 3; 1978–81 Division 2; 1981– Division 3.

**Honours:** *Football League:* Division 1 – Champions 1888–89 (first champions), 1889–90; Runners-up 1890–91, 1891–92, 1892–93, 1905–06, 1952–53, 1957–58; Division 2 – Champions 1903–04, 1912–13, 1950–51; Runners-up 1914–15, 1933–34; Division 3 – Champions 1970–71. *FA Cup:* Winners 1889, 1938; Runners-up 1888, 1922, 1937, 1954, 1964. *Double Performed:* 1888–89. *Football League Cup* best season: 4th rd, 1963, 1966, 1972, 1981.

*Record Victory:* 26-0 v Hyde, FA Cup 1st Series, 1st rd, 15 Oct, 1887.

*Record Defeat:* 0-7 v Blackpool, Division 1, 1 May, 1948.

*Most League Points:* 61, Division 3, 1970–71. *Three points win:* 61, Division 3, 1981–82.

*Most League Goals:* 100, Division 2, 1927–28 and Division 1, 1957–58.

*Highest League Scorer in Season:* Ted Harper, 37, Division 2, 1932–33.

*Most League Goals in Total Aggregate:* Tom Finney, 187, 1946–60.

*Most Capped Player:* Tom Finney, 76, England.

*Most League Appearances:* Alan Kelly, 447, 1961–75.

*Record Transfer Fee Received:* £765,000 from Manchester C for Mick Robinson, June 1979.

*Record Transfer Fee Paid:* £95,000 to Nottingham F for Steve Elliott, March 1979.

*Previous Managers since the War:* W. Scott, Scot Symon, Frank Hill, Cliff Britton, Jimmy Milne, Bobby Seith, Alan Ball Snr, Bobby Charlton CBE, Harry Catterick, Nobby Stiles, Tommy Docherty.

*Address of Supporters Club:* c/o Preston North End FC, Deepdale, Preston.

*Address of the Club Shop:* The Lilywhite Shop, Preston North End FC, Deepdale, Preston.

---

**Deepdale, Preston PR1 6RU.** Telephone Preston 795919. *Ansaphone:* Preston 709170. *Ground capacity:* 25,000. *Record attendance:* 42,684 v Arsenal, Division 1, 23 Apr, 1938. *Record receipts:* £28,303.40 v Blackburn R, Division 2, 21 April, 1981. *Pitch measurements:* 112yd×78yd.

*How to get there:* Special buses to Deepdale from outlying areas and town centre bus station. Nearest railway station: Preston.

*Match tickets:* Postal applications, including remittance and SAE, may be made 14 days before the match.

*Car parking:* Club car park on the Deepdale Road (West Stand) side of the ground, holds 500 vehicles. Only limited off-street parking.

*Entertainments/catering facilities:* The ground is well-equipped for normal match-day refreshments.

*Club shop:* Open on match days only. All postal enquiries to: The Commercial Manager, Preston North End Commercial Department, Lowthorpe Road, Deepdale, Preston PR1 6RU (Tel: Preston 795465/795156).

*Handbooks/programmes:* No handbook. Programmes available on subscription from the Commercial Manager.

*Extra information:* The first club to do the League and FA Cup double, accomplishing this feat in 1888–89.

*Club Colours:* White shirts, with navy blue collars and cuffs, navy blue shorts with white trim, white stockings with navy blue rings.

*Change Colours:* Yellow shirts, royal blue shorts, yellow stockings.

*Team Captain:* Don O'Riordan.

*First Team Trainer/Physiotherapist:* Dennis Loze.

*Club Nickname:* The Lilywhites or North End.

## PRESTON NORTH END 1981–82 LEAGUE RECORD

| Match No. | Date | Venue | Opponents | Result | H/T Score | Goalscorers | Atten-dance |
|---|---|---|---|---|---|---|---|
| 1 | Aug 29 | A | Millwall | L 1-2 | 0-0 | Walsh | 4549 |
| 2 | Sept 5 | H | Portsmouth | W 1-0 | 1-0 | Bruce | 6112 |
| 3 | 12 | A | Swindon T | L 0-4 | 0-2 | | 5695 |
| 4 | 19 | H | Gillingham | D 1-1 | 0-0 | Bruce (pen) | 4563 |
| 5 | 22 | H | Huddersfield T | D 1-1 | 1-1 | Naughton | 6483 |
| 6 | 26 | A | Newport Co | D 1-1 | 0-0 | Doyle | 5064 |
| 7 | 29 | A | Doncaster R | L 0-1 | 0-0 | | 7513 |
| 8 | Oct 3 | H | Bristol R | L 0-1 | 0-1 | | 4964 |
| 9 | 10 | A | Bristol C | D 0-0 | 0-0 | | 5389 |
| 10 | 17 | H | Reading | D 0-0 | 0-0 | | 5671 |
| 11 | 20 | H | Burnley | D 1-1 | 0-0 | O'Riordan | 7527 |
| 12 | 24 | A | Exeter C | L 3-4 | 1-2 | Bruce 2 (1 pen), Doyle | 3642 |
| 13 | 31 | H | Southend U | W 1-0 | 0-0 | Pountney (og) | 4285 |
| 14 | Nov 4 | A | Lincoln C | W 2-1 | 2-1 | Buckley, Elliott | 3587 |
| 15 | 7 | H | Chester | L 0-1 | 0-1 | | 5181 |
| 16 | 14 | A | Wimbledon | L 2-3 | 2-1 | Dunn, Bruce | 2428 |
| 17 | 28 | A | Oxford U | L 0-3 | 0-2 | | 3798 |
| 18 | Dec 5 | H | Brentford | L 1-3 | 1-1 | Bruce | 4162 |
| 19 | Jan 5 | A | Chesterfield | D 0-0 | 0-0 | | 3964 |
| 20 | 16 | H | Plymouth Arg | W 1-0 | 1-0 | Bruce | 4936 |
| 21 | 23 | H | Millwall | W 1-0 | 1-0 | Elliott (pen) | 5085 |
| 22 | 30 | A | Gillingham | W 2-0 | 1-0 | Naughton, Bruce | 5379 |
| 23 | Feb 2 | A | Carlisle U | L 0-1 | 0-1 | | 5044 |
| 24 | 6 | H | Swindon T | D 0-0 | 0-0 | | 5606 |
| 25 | 9 | A | Huddersfield T | W 3-2 | 1-2 | Bruce 2, Elliott | 6674 |
| 26 | 13 | A | Bristol R | L 0-2 | 0-0 | | 5003 |
| 27 | 20 | H | Doncaster R | W 3-1 | 1-1 | McGee, Bruce, Elliott (pen) | 5830 |
| 28 | 27 | H | Bristol C | L 1-3 | 1-1 | Kelly | 6411 |
| 29 | Mar 6 | A | Reading | L 1-2 | 0-1 | Elliott | 2655 |
| 30 | 13 | H | Exeter C | W 1-0 | 0-0 | Elliott | 4770 |
| 31 | 16 | H | Lincoln C | D 1-1 | 0-1 | O'Riordan | 4879 |
| 32 | 19 | A | Southend U | D 2-2 | 0-2 | Elliott, Bruce | 3549 |
| 33 | 27 | A | Chester | W 1-0 | 0-0 | Elliott | 2842 |
| 34 | Apr 3 | H | Wimbledon | W 3-2 | 1-0 | Bruce 2, O'Riordan | 4964 |
| 35 | 6 | A | Portsmouth | D 1-1 | 0-1 | O'Riordan | 6712 |
| 36 | 10 | H | Carlisle U | L 0-1 | 0-1 | | 7802 |
| 37 | 13 | A | Walsall | W 3-0 | 2-0 | Elliott, Bruce 2 | 3507 |
| 38 | 17 | A | Brentford | D 0-0 | 0-0 | | 5627 |
| 39 | 20 | H | Fulham | L 1-3 | 1-1 | Buckley (pen) | 6009 |
| 40 | 24 | H | Oxford U | D 2-2 | 1-0 | Kelly, Doyle | 5516 |
| 41 | 27 | H | Walsall | W 1-0 | 1-0 | Kelly | 4930 |
| 42 | May 1 | A | Plymouth Arg | W 3-0 | 1-0 | Kelly, Bell, Elliott | 3319 |
| 43 | 4 | H | Newport Co | W 2-1 | 1-0 | Bruce, Kelly | 4972 |
| 44 | 8 | H | Chesterfield | W 2-0 | 2-0 | Naughton, Bruce | 5445 |
| 45 | 11 | A | Burnley | L 0-2 | 0-0 | | 13,871 |
| 46 | 15 | A | Fulham | L 0-3 | 0-2 | | 7985 |

**Final League Position: 14**

**Goalscorers**

League (50): Bruce 18 (2 pens), Elliott 10 (2 pens), Kelly 5, O'Riordan 4, Doyle 3, Naughton 3, Buckley 2 (1 pen), Bell 1, Dunn 1, McGee 1, Walsh 1, own goal 1.
League Cup (3): Bruce 1, Clark 1, Naughton 1.
FA Cup (1): Doyle 1.

| League Cup | First Round | Halifax T (a) | 2-1 |
|---|---|---|---|
| | | (h) | 0-0 |
| | Second Round | Leicester C (h) | 1-0 |
| | | (a) | 0-4 |
| FA Cup | First Round | Chesterfield (a) | 1-4 |

| Litchfield | Taylor | Coleman | Clark | O'Riordan | Blackley | Walsh | Houston | Bruce | Doyle | Naugton | Elliott | Westwell | McGee | McAteer | Anderson | Bell | Farrelly | Booth | Kelly | Buckley | Dunn | Mullen | Sayer | Hodge | Match No. |
|---|---|---|---|---|---|---|---|---|---|---|---|---|---|---|---|---|---|---|---|---|---|---|---|---|---|
| 1 | 2 | 3 | 4 | 5 | 6 | 7 | 8 | 9 | 10 | 11* | 12 | | | | | | | | | | | | | | 1 |
| 1 | | 2 | 4 | 5 | 6 | 12 | 7* | 10 | 8 | 11 | | | 3 | 9 | | | | | | | | | | | 2 |
| 1 | 2 | | 4 | 5 | 6 | 12 | 7 | 10 | 8* | 11 | | | 3 | 9 | | | | | | | | | | | 3 |
| 1 | | 2 | 4 | 5 | | 12 | 7 | 9 | | 11 | 10* | | | | 3 | 6 | 8 | | | | | | | | 4 |
| 1 | | 2 | 4 | 5 | | | 7 | 8 | 9 | 11* | | | | 3 | 6 | 10 | 12 | | | | | | | 5 |
| 1 | | 2 | 4 | 5 | | 11 | 7 | 9 | 8 | | | | | 3 | 6 | 10 | | | | | | | | 6 |
| 1 | 2 | 6 | 5 | | | 7* | 12 | 9 | 8 | | | | | 11 | 3 | 4 | 10 | | | | | | | | 7 |
| 1 | | 2 | 4 | 5 | | 12 | 7 | 9 | 8* | | | | | 11 | 3 | 6 | 10 | | | | | | | | 8 |
| 1 | 2 | | 4 | 6 | | | | 9 | | | | | | | 3 | 10* | 12 | 5 | 7 | 8 | 11 | | | | 9 |
| 1 | 2 | | 4 | 6 | | | | 9 | | | | | | | 3 | 10* | 12 | 5 | 7 | 8 | 11 | | | | 10 |
| 1 | 12 | 2 | 4 | 6 | | | | 9 | 10 | | | | | | 3 | | | 5 | 7 | 8 | 11* | | | | 11 |
| 1 | 8 | | 4 | 6 | | | | 9 | 10 | | 2 | | | | 3 | 12 | | 5* | | 7 | 11 | | | | 12 |
| 1 | 2 | | 4 | 6 | | | | 9 | 10 | | | | | | 3 | 5 | 12 | | 7* | 8 | 11 | | | | 13 |
| 1 | 2 | | 4 | 6 | | | | 9 | 10 | 8 | | | | | 3 | 12 | | 5* | | 7 | 11 | | | | 14 |
| 1 | 2* | | 4 | 6 | | | | 9 | 10 | 8 | | | | | 3 | 5 | | | | 12 | 7 | 11 | | | 15 |
| 1 | 2* | | 4 | 6 | | | | 9 | 10 | 12 | 8 | | | | 3 | 5 | | | | | 7 | 11 | | | 16 |
| 1 | 12 | 2 | 4 | | | 7 | 8* | 9 | 10 | 11 | 9 | | | | 3 | | | 5 | | | 6 | | | | 17 |
| 1 | 2 | 8 | 4 | | | | 9 | 6 | 10 | | | | | | 3 | 7 | | 5 | | | 11 | | | | 18 |
| | 2 | | | 6 | | | 11 | 8 | 10 | 9 | | | | | 3 | 7* | 4 | 5 | 12 | | | | | 1 | 19 |
| | 2 | | | 6 | | | 11 | 8 | 10 | 9 | | | | | 3 | 7 | 4 | 5 | | | | | | 1 | 20 |
| | 2 | | | 6 | | | 11 | 8 | 10 | 9 | | | | | 3 | 7 | 4 | 5 | | | | | | 1 | 21 |
| | 2 | | | 6 | | | 11 | 8 | 10 | 9 | | | | | 3 | 7* | 4 | 5 | 12 | | | | | 1 | 22 |
| | | | | 6 | | | 12 | 11 | 8 | 10 | 9 | 2 | | | 3 | | 4* | 5 | 7 | | | | | 1 | 23 |
| | | | | 6 | | | 12 | 11 | 8 | 10 | 9 | 2* | | | 3 | | 4 | 5 | 7 | | | | | 1 | 24 |
| | 2 | | | 6 | | | 11 | 8 | 10 | 9 | | | | | 3 | | 4 | 5 | 7 | | | | | 1 | 25 |
| | | | | 6 | | | 11 | | 10* | 9 | | 8 | | | 3 | 2 | 4 | 5 | 7 | 12 | | | | 1 | 26 |
| | 2 | | | 6 | | | 11 | | 10 | 9 | | 8 | | | 3 | 5 | 4 | | 7 | | | | | 1 | 27 |
| | 2* | | | 6 | | | 11 | | 10 | 9 | | 8 | | | 3 | 12 | 4 | 5 | 7 | | | | | 1 | 28 |
| | | | | 6 | | | 11 | | 12 | 9 | | 8 | | | 3 | 2 | 4 | 5* | 7 | 10 | | | | 1 | 29 |
| | | | | 6 | | | 11 | | | 9 | | 8 | | | 3 | 2 | 4 | 5 | 7 | 10 | | | | 1 | 30 |
| | | | | 6 | | | 11 | | | 9 | | 8 | | | 3 | 2 | 4 | 5 | 7 | 10 | | | | 1 | 31 |
| | | | | 6 | | 12 | 11 | 8 | 3 | 9 | | | | | 2 | 4* | | 5 | 7 | 10 | | | | 1 | 32 |
| | | | | 6 | | | 11 | 8 | 3 | 9 | | | | | 4 | 2 | | 5 | 7 | 10 | | | | 1 | 33 |
| | | | | 6 | | | 11 | 8 | 4 | 9 | | | | | 3 | 2 | | 5 | 7 | 10 | | | | 1 | 34 |
| | | | | 6 | | 12 | 11 | 8 | 4 | 9 | | | | | 3 | 2* | | 5 | 7 | 10 | | | | 1 | 35 |
| | | | | 6 | | | 12 | 11 | 8 | 4 | 9 | | | | 3 | 2 | | 5 | 7 | 10* | | | | 1 | 36 |
| | | | | 6 | | | 11 | 8 | 4 | 9 | | | | | 3 | 2 | | 5 | 7 | 10 | | | | 1 | 37 |
| | | | | 6 | | | 11 | 8 | 4 | 9 | | | | | 3 | 2 | | 5 | 7 | 10 | | | | 1 | 38 |
| | | | | 6 | | 12 | 11 | 8 | 4 | 9 | | | | | 3 | 2 | | 5* | 7 | 10 | | | | 1 | 39 |
| | | | | 6 | | 12 | 11 | 8 | 4 | 9 | 5 | | | | 3 | 2 | | | 7 | 10* | | | | 1 | 40 |
| | | | | 6 | | 12 | 11 | 8 | 4 | 9* | 5 | | | | 3 | 2 | 10 | | 7 | | | | | 1 | 41 |
| | | | | 6 | | | 11 | 8 | 4 | 9 | 5 | | | | 3 | 2 | 10 | | 7 | | | | | 1 | 42 |
| | | | | 6 | | 4 | 11 | 8 | 3 | 9 | 5 | | | | | 2 | 10 | | 7 | | | | | 1 | 43 |
| | | | | 6 | | | 11 | 8 | 4 | 9 | 5 | | | | 3 | 2 | 10 | | 7 | | | | | 1 | 44 |
| | | | | 6 | | 12 | 11 | 8 | 4 | 9 | 5 | | | | 3 | 2 | 10* | | 7 | | | | | 1 | 45 |
| | | | | 6 | | 12 | 11 | 8 | 4 | 9 | 5 | | | | 3 | 2 | 10 | | 7* | | | | | 1 | 46 |
| 18 | 10 | 15 | 18 | 46 | 3 | 4 | 9 | 46 | 36 | 31 | 34 | 12 | 10 | 41 | 35 | 22 | 3 | 27 | 28 | 20 | 8 | 1 | 1 | 28 | |
| | + 2s | | | | | + 6s | + 9s | | | | | | | | | + 2s | + 1s | | | | | | | | |
| | | | | | | | | | | | | | | | | + 3s | | + 4s | | + 2s | + 2s | | | | |

## PRESTON NORTH END

| | Ht | Wt | Birthplace | Clubs | League App. | League Gls |
|---|---|---|---|---|---|---|
| **Goalkeepers** | | | | | | |
| Peter Litchfield | 6 1 | 12 12 | Manchester | Droylsden | — | — |
| | | | | Manchester C | — | — |
| | | | | Preston NE | 21 | — |
| **Defenders** | | | | | | |
| Daniel Cameron | 5 6½ | 11 3 | Dundee | Sheffield W | 31 | 1 |
| (Contract cancelled Aug 1981) | | | | Colchester U (on loan) | 5 | — |
| | | | | Preston NE | 122 | — |
| Brian Taylor* | 5 10 | 11 7 | Gateshead | Coventry C | — | — |
| | | | | Walsall | 216 | 25 |
| | | | | Plymouth Arg | 35 | 5 |
| | | | | Preston NE | 99 | 1 |
| | | | | Wigan Ath (on loan) | 8 | — |
| Donald O'Riordan | 5 11 | 12 0 | Dublin | Derby Co | 6 | 1 |
| | | | | Tulsa R | (not known) | |
| | | | | Doncaster R (on loan) | 2 | — |
| | | | | Preston NE | 117 | 4 |
| Simon Westwell | 5 9½ | 9 7 | Clitheroe | Preston NE | 32 | — |
| John Anderson* | 5 11 | 11 6 | Dublin | WBA | — | — |
| (Eire) | | | | Preston NE | 51 | — |
| John Blackley | 5 10 | 13 0 | Falkirk | Hibernian | 263 | 6 |
| (Scotland) | | | | Newcastle U | 46 | — |
| (Contract cancelled Oct 1981) | | | | Preston NE | 53 | — |
| Andrew McAteer | 5 10 | 11 3 | Preston | Preston NE | 82 | — |
| Jimmy Bell* | 6 1 | 12 7 | Glasgow | Preston NE | — | — |
| Neil Hanson | 5 10 | 10 11 | Blackburn | Preston NE | — | — |
| Tommy Booth | 6 2½ | 13 5 | Manchester | Manchester C | 382 | 25 |
| | | | | Preston NE | 27 | — |
| Mark Walsh | 5 10 | 10 10 | Preston | Preston NE | 10 | 1 |
| Mike Farrelly | 5 11½ | 11 11 | Manchester | Preston NE | 7 | — |
| **Midfield** | | | | | | |
| Francis Burns | 5 9 | 10 10 | Coatbridge | Manchester U | 120 | 6 |
| (Scotland) | | | | Southampton | 21 | — |
| (Contract cancelled Oct 1981) | | | | Preston NE | 273 | 9 |
| Stephen Doyle* | 5 9½ | 11 1 | Neath | Preston NE | 197 | 8 |
| Gordon Coleman | 5 9 | 10 12 | Nottingham | Preston NE | 251 | 24 |
| Alan Spavin | 5 8 | 11 4 | Lancaster | Preston NE | 426 | 26 |
| (Non-contract) | | | | | | |
| Graham Bell | 5 9 | 10 6 | Middleton | Oldham Ath | 170 | 9 |
| | | | | Preston NE | 103 | 5 |
| | | | | Huddersfield T (on loan) | 2 | — |
| Peter Sayer | 5 7 | 11 0 | Cardiff | Cardiff C | 82 | 14 |
| (Wales) | | | | Brighton | 55 | 6 |
| | | | | Preston NE | 9 | — |
| | | | | Cardiff C (on loan) | 4 | 1 |
| Jonathan Clark | 5 10 | 11 10 | Swansea | Manchester U | 1 | — |
| | | | | Derby Co | 53 | 3 |
| | | | | Preston NE | 18 | — |
| Gary Buckley | 5 5 | 10 0 | Manchester | Manchester C | 6 | — |
| | | | | Preston NE | 22 | 2 |
| John Kelly | 5 9½ | 10 6 | Bebbington | Tranmere R | 64 | 9 |
| | | | | Preston NE | 30 | 5 |
| **Forwards** | | | | | | |
| Alex Bruce | 5 8 | 11 0 | Dundee | Preston NE | 62 | 22 |
| | | | | Newcastle U | 20 | 3 |
| | | | | Preston NE | 274 | 128 |
| Ricky Thomson | 5 8 | 10 10 | Edinburgh | Preston NE | 71 | 20 |
| (Contract cancelled Oct 1981) | | | | | | |
| Graham Houston | 5 8 | 11 4 | Gibraltar | Preston NE | 36 | 1 |
| Stephen Elliott | 5 11½ | 11 10 | Haltwistle, | Nottingham F | 4 | — |
| | | | North'land | Preston NE | 119 | 35 |
| | | | | Cambridge U (on loan) | — | — |
| Willie Naughton | 6 0 | 12 8 | Catrine | Preston NE | 46 | 5 |
| Barry Dunn | 5 8½ | 10 4½ | Sunderland | Blue Star | (not known) | |
| (Contract cancelled March 1982) | | | | Sunderland | 23 | 2 |
| | | | | Preston NE | 8 | 1 |
| Chris Hunter | 5 7½ | 10 7 | Hong Kong | Preston NE | — | — |

# QUEEN'S PARK RANGERS Division 2

*President:* Sir Stanley Rous CBE
*Chairman:* J. A. Gregory. *Vice-Chairman:* J. C. Gregory.
*Executive Director:* A. Williamson.
*Directors:* C J. Armstrong FCA, A. D. Farmer MPS, B. A. V.
Henson FCA, A. Ingham, Councillor W. C. Smith JP, T. Venables.
*Team Manager:* Terry Venables.
*Secretary:* R. J. Phillips FAAI.
*Assistant Team Manager:* Alan Harris.
*Year Formed:* 1885. *Turned Professional:* 1898.
*Limited Company:* 1899.
*Previous Name:* 1885-87, St Jude's; 1887, became Queen's Park
Rangers.

*Previous Grounds:* 1885, Welford's Fields; 1888, London Scottish
Ground, Brondesbury: Home Farm: Kensal Rise Green: Gun
Club, Wormwood Scrubs: Kilburn Cricket Ground; 1899, Kensal
Rise Athletic Ground; 1901, Latimer Road, Notting Hill; 1904,
Agricultural Society, Park Royal; 1907, Park Royal Ground;
1917, Loftus Road; 1931, White City; 1933, Loftus Road; 1962, White City; 1963, Loftus Road.

**Football League Record:**
1920 Original Members of Division 3; 1921 Division 3(S); 1948-52 Division 2; 1952-58 Division 3(S);
1958-67 Division 3; 1967-68 Division 2; 1968-69 Division 1; 1969-73 Division 2; 1973-79 Division 1;
1979- Division 2.

**Honours:** *Football League:* Division 1 – Runners-up 1975-76; Division 2 – Runners-up 1967-68, 1972-73;
Division 3(S) – Champions 1947-48; Runners-up 1946-47; Division 3 – Champions 1966-67. *FA Cup:*
Runners-up 1982. *Football League Cup*: Winners 1966-67. (In 1966-67 won Division 3 and Football
League Cup.) **European Competition:** *UEFA Cup:* 1976-77.
*Record Victory:* 9-2 v Tranmere R, Division 3, 3 Dec, 1960.
*Record Defeat:* 1-8 v Mansfield T, Division 3, 15 Mar, 1965, and 1-8 v Manchester U, Division 1, 19
Mar, 1969.
*Most League Points:* 67, Division 3, 1966-67. *Three points win:* 69, Division 2, 1981-82.
*Most League Goals:* 111, Division 3, 1961-62.
*Highest League Scorer in Season:* George Goddard, 37, Division 3(S), 1929-30.
*Most League Goals in Total Aggregate:* George Goddard, 172, 1926-34.
*Most Capped Player:* Don Givens, 26 (56), Eire.
*Most League Appearances:* Tony Ingham, 519, 1950-63.
*Record Transfer Fee Received:* £1,250,000 from Arsenal for Clive Allen, June 1980.
*Record Transfer Fee Paid:* £400,000 to Leeds U for Tony Currie, Aug 1979.
*Previous Managers since the War:* Dave Mangnall, Jack Taylor, Alec Stock, Tommy Docherty, Les
Allen, Gordon Jago, Dave Sexton, Frank Sibley, Steve Burtenshaw, Tommy Docherty.
*Address of Supporters Club:* c/o Football Club.
*Address of the Club Shop or Boutique:* Supporters Club Shop, Queen's Park Rangers FC, South Africa
Road, London W12.

---

**South Africa Road, W12 7PA.** Telephone 01-743 0262/3/4/5. *Telegraphic address:* 'Queu Pear'. *Ground
capacity:* 30,000 (23,000 covered). *Record attendance:* 35,353 v Leeds U, Division 1, 28 April, 1974.
*Record receipts:* £79,660 v Tottenham H, FA Cup 3rd rd, 3 Jan, 1981. *Pitch measurements:*
112yd×72yd.
*How to get there:* Buses 12 and 207. Nos 11, 49, 72, 88, 105, 220 go near Shepherd's Bush (Metropolitan and Central
Lines) and White City (Central Line – five to ten minutes walk).
*Match tickets:* Seats bookable one month in advance of the match.
*Car parking:* No club car park, but the White City park, adjacent to the ground, is recommended. Limited parking in
side-streets.
*Entertainments/catering facilities:* Various bars around the ground.
*Club shop:* Programme shop in South Africa Road and kiosks inside the ground.
*Handbooks/programmes:* Available from programme shop.
*Extra information:* Queen's Park Rangers have had more home grounds than any other present Football League club; 12
in all, plus one game at Highbury in 1930.
*Club Colours:* Blue and white hooped shirts, white shorts, white stockings.
*Change Colours:* Red and white halved shirts, black shorts, black socks.
*Club Captain:* Glenn Roeder. *First Team Trainer:* Alan Harris.
*Club Nickname:* Rangers or R's.

## QUEEN'S PARK RANGERS 1981-82 LEAGUE RECORD

| Match No. | Date | Venue | Opponents | Result | H/T Score | Goalscorers | Attendance |
|---|---|---|---|---|---|---|---|
| 1 | Aug 29 | A | Wrexham | W 3-1 | 2-1 | King, Allen 2 | 4661 |
| 2 | Sept 1 | H | Luton T | L 1-2 | 1-0 | King | 18,703 |
| 3 | 5 | H | Newcastle U | W 3-0 | 1-0 | King, Roeder, Stainrod | 14,176 |
| 4 | 12 | A | Grimsby T | L 1-2 | 0-2 | Gregory | 9490 |
| 5 | 19 | H | Crystal Palace | W 1-0 | 1-0 | Stainrod | 17,039 |
| 6 | 22 | A | Oldham Ath | L 0-2 | 0-1 | | 6421 |
| 7 | 26 | A | Derby Co | L 1-3 | 0-1 | Gregory | 11,246 |
| 8 | Oct 3 | H | Blackburn R | W 2-0 | 1-0 | Gregory, Allen | 9541 |
| 9 | 10 | H | Norwich C | W 2-0 | 0-0 | Gregory, Stainrod | 11,806 |
| 10 | 18 | A | Orient | D 1-1 | 0-0 | Gillard | 8192 |
| 11 | 24 | H | Leicester C | W 2-0 | 1-0 | Stainrod, Gregory | 12,419 |
| 12 | 31 | A | Charlton Ath | W 2-1 | 2-0 | Stainrod, Allen | 11,333 |
| 13 | Nov 7 | H | Rotherham U | D 1-1 | 0-1 | Flanagan | 10,949 |
| 14 | 14 | A | Sheffield W | W 3-1 | 2-0 | Stainrod 3 | 17,024 |
| 15 | 21 | A | Shrewsbury T | L 1-2 | 1-1 | Flanagan | 4765 |
| 16 | 24 | H | Oldham Ath | D 0-0 | 0-0 | | 9477 |
| 17 | 28 | H | Cardiff C | W 2-0 | 0-0 | Stainrod 2 | 10,225 |
| 18 | Dec 5 | A | Bolton W | L 0-1 | 0-0 | | 6076 |
| 19 | 12 | H | Barnsley | W 1-0 | 0-0 | Flanagan | 10,972 |
| 20 | 26 | H | Chelsea | L 0-2 | 0-0 | | 22,022 |
| 21 | Jan 16 | H | Wrexham | D 1-1 | 0-1 | Stainrod | 10,066 |
| 22 | 30 | A | Crystal Palace | D 0-0 | 0-0 | | 15,267 |
| 23 | Feb 6 | H | Grimsby T | W 1-0 | 1-0 | Gregory | 8753 |
| 24 | 9 | A | Cambridge U | L 0-1 | 0-1 | | 4822 |
| 25 | 16 | A | Blackburn R | L 1-2 | 0-0 | Allen | 6884 |
| 26 | 20 | H | Derby Co | W 3-0 | 2-0 | Hazell, Fenwick, Flanagan | 8890 |
| 27 | 27 | H | Norwich C | W 1-0 | 1-0 | Roeder | 15,928 |
| 28 | Mar 9 | A | Watford | L 0-4 | 0-2 | | 16,862 |
| 29 | 13 | A | Leicester C | L 2-3 | 1-1 | Currie, Stainrod | 17,821 |
| 30 | 20 | H | Charlton Ath | W 4-0 | 1-0 | Fenwick, Allen 3 | 13,118 |
| 31 | 27 | A | Rotherham U | L 0-1 | 0-1 | | 10,472 |
| 32 | 29 | H | Sheffield W | W 2-0 | 1-0 | Flanagan, Stainrod | 11,710 |
| 33 | Apr 6 | H | Orient | W 3-0 | 3-0 | Hazell, Flanagan, Stainrod | 10,531 |
| 34 | 10 | A | Chelsea | L 1-2 | 1-0 | Gregory | 18,365 |
| 35 | 12 | H | Watford | D 0-0 | 0-0 | | 22,091 |
| 36 | 17 | H | Shrewsbury T | W 2-1 | 0-0 | Flanagan, Allen | 11,148 |
| 37 | 24 | A | Cardiff C | W 2-1 | 2-1 | Allen, Micklewhite | 5979 |
| 38 | May 1 | H | Bolton W | W 7-1 | 4-0 | Gregory, Micklewhite, Flanagan 2 Fenwick (pen), Stainrod, Allen | 10,002 |
| 39 | 5 | A | Newcastle U | W 4-0 | 3-0 | Gregory, Allen, Flanagan, Stainrod | 10,670 |
| 40 | 8 | A | Barnsley | L 0-3 | 0-0 | | 10,579 |
| 41 | 11 | A | Luton T | L 2-3 | 0-1 | Fenwick, Stainrod | 16,657 |
| 42 | 15 | H | Cambridge U | W 2-1 | 1-1 | Allen, Fenwick (pen) | 10,467 |

**Final League Position: 5**

### Goalscorers

*League* (65): Stainrod 17, Allen 13, Flanagan 10, Gregory 9, Fenwick 5 (2 pens), King 3, Hazell 2, Micklewhite 2, Roeder 2, Currie 1, Gillard 1.
*League Cup* (11): Micklewhite 3, Flanagan 2, Gregory 2, Stainrod 2, Allen 1, own goal 1.
*FA Cup* (15): Allen 7, Stainrod 5, Fenwick 1, Howe 1, Neill 1.

| | | | |
|---|---|---|---|
| **League Cup** | Second Round | Portsmouth (h) | 5-0 |
| | | (a) | 2-2 |
| | Third Round | Bristol C (h) | 3-0 |
| | Fourth Round | Watford (a) | 1-4 |
| **FA Cup** | Third Round | Middlesbrough (h) | 1-1 |
| | | (a) | 3-2 |
| | Fourth Round | Blackpool (a | 0-0 |
| | | (h) | 5-1 |
| | Fifth Round | Grimsby T (h) | 3-1 |
| | Sixth Round | Crystal Palace (h) | 1-0 |
| | Semi-final | WBA | 1-0 (at Highbury) |
| | Final | Tottenham H | 1-1 (at Wembley) |
| | Replay | | 0-1 (at Wembley) |

| Burridge | Gregory | Fenwick | Waddock | Hazell | Roeder | Flanagan | Francis | Allen | King | Stainrod | Currie | Gillard | Howe | Sealy | Micklewhite | Burke | Fereday | Stewart | O'Connor | Hucker | Neill | Wicks | Dawes | Wilkins | Match No. |
|---|---|---|---|---|---|---|---|---|---|---|---|---|---|---|---|---|---|---|---|---|---|---|---|---|---|
| 1 | 2 | 3 | 4 | 5 | 6 | 7 | 8 | 9 | 10 | 11 | | | | | | | | | | | | | | | 1 |
| 1 | 2 | 3 | 4 | 5 | 6 | 7 | 8 | 9 | 10 | 11 | | | | | | | | | | | | | | | 2 |
| 1 | 2 | 3 | | 5 | 6 | 7 | 8 | 9* | 10 | 11 | 4 | 12 | | | | | | | | | | | | | 3 |
| 1 | 2 | 3 | | | 6 | 7 | 8 | 9 | 10* | 11 | 4 | 12 | 5 | | | | | | | | | | | | 4 |
| 1 | 2 | 3 | 6 | 4 | 5 | 7 | | 9 | | | 8 | 10 | 11 | | | | | | | | | | | | 5 |
| 1 | 2 | 3 | 4 | 5 | 6 | 7 | | 9 | | | 8 | 10 | 11 | | | | | | | | | | | | 6 |
| 1 | 2 | 3 | 4 | 5 | 6 | 7* | | 9 | | | 8 | 10 | 11 | 12 | | | | | | | | | | | 7 |
| 1 | 2 | 3 | 4 | 5 | 6 | | | 9 | | | 8 | 10 | 11 | | | 7 | | | | | | | | | 8 |
| 1 | 2 | 3 | 4 | 5 | 6 | | | 9 | | | 8 | 10 | 11 | | | 7* | 12 | | | | | | | | 9 |
| 1 | 2 | 3 | 4 | 5 | 6 | 8 | | 9* | | | 10 | | 11 | | | 7 | 12 | | | | | | | | 10 |
| 1 | 2 | 3 | 4 | 5 | 6 | 7 | 8* | 9 | | | 10 | | 11 | | | 12 | | | | | | | | | 11 |
| 1 | 2 | 3 | 4 | 5 | 6 | 7 | 8 | 9 | | | 10 | | 11 | | | | | | | | | | | | 12 |
| 1 | 2 | 3 | 4 | 5 | 6 | 8 | 7* | | | | 10 | | 11 | 12 | 9 | | | | | | | | | | 13 |
| 1 | 2 | 3 | 4 | 12 | 6 | 8 | | 9* | | | 10 | | 11 | 5 | 7 | | | | | | | | | | 14 |
| 1 | 2 | 3 | | 6 | | 8 | | 9 | | | 10 | | 11 | 5 | 7 | | | | | | | | | | 15 |
| 1 | 2 | 3 | 4 | | 6 | 8 | | 9* | | | 10 | | 11 | 5 | 12 | 7 | | | | | | | | | 16 |
| 1 | 2 | 3 | 4 | | 6 | 8 | | | | | 10 | | 11 | 5 | 9 | 7 | | | | | | | | | 17 |
| 1 | 2 | 3* | 4 | | 6 | 8 | | | | | 10 | | 11 | 5 | 9 | 7 | 12 | | | | | | | | 18 |
| 1 | 2 | 3 | 4 | | 6 | 8 | | | | | | | 11 | 5 | 9* | 7 | 12 | 10 | | | | | | | 19 |
| 1 | | 3 | 4 | | 6 | 8 | | 12 | | | | | 11 | 5 | 9* | 7 | | 10 | 2 | | | | | | 20 |
| | 8 | 3 | 4 | | 6 | 12 | | 7 | | | 10 | 9 | | | 11* | 5 | | | | 1 | 2 | | | | 21 |
| | 8 | 2 | 4 | | 6 | | | 9 | | | 10 | 11 | 3 | 5 | 7 | | | | | 1 | | | | | 22 |
| 11 | | 2 | 4 | | 6 | | | 7 | | | 10 | 8 | 3 | 5 | | | 9 | | | 1 | | | | | 23 |
| 11 | | 2 | 4 | | 6 | | | 9 | | | 10 | 8* | 3 | 5 | 12 | | 7 | | | 1 | | | | | 24 |
| 11 | | 2 | | 6 | 8 | | | 9 | | | 10 | | 3 | 5 | 7 | | | | | 1 | | 4 | | | 25 |
| 11* | 2 | | 5 | 6 | 8 | | | 9 | | | 10 | | 3 | | 7 | | | | | 1 | | 4 | | 12 | 26 |
| 11 | | | 5 | 6 | 8 | | | 9 | | | 10 | 7 | 3 | 2 | | | | | | 1 | | 4 | | | 27 |
| 11 | | 4 | 5 | 6 | 8 | | | | | | 10 | 7 | 3 | 9 | | | | | | 1 | 2 | | | | 28 |
| 11* | | 4 | 5 | 6 | 8 | | | 9 | | | 10 | 7 | 3 | 2 | 12 | | | | | 1 | | | | | 29 |
| | 4 | | 5 | 6 | 8 | | | 9 | | | 10 | 7 | 3* | | 11 | 12 | | | | 1 | 2 | | | | 30 |
| | 3 | 4 | 5 | | 8 | | | 9 | 10 | | | | 7 | 12 | | | | | 1* | 2 | | 6 | 11 | | 31 |
| 11 | | | 6 | 8 | | | | 9 | | | 10 | 7 | | 4 | | | | | | 1 | 2 | 5 | 3 | | 32 |
| | 2 | 4 | 5 | 6 | 8 | | | 9 | | | 10* | 7 | 3 | 11 | | 12 | | | | 1 | | | | | 33 |
| 11 | | 4 | 5 | 6 | 8 | | | 9 | | | 10 | 7 | 3 | | | | | | | 1 | 2 | | | | 34 |
| | 4 | 5 | 7 | 8 | | | | 9 | | | 10 | | | 11 | | | | | | 1 | 2 | 6 | 3 | | 35 |
| | 2 | 4 | | 6 | 8 | | | 9 | | | 7* | | | 11 | 10 | 12 | | | | 1 | | 5 | 3 | | 36 |
| 11 | 2 | 4 | | 6 | 8 | | | 9 | | | 10 | 3 | | 7 | | | | | | 1 | | 5 | | | 37 |
| 11 | 2* | 4 | | 6 | 8 | | | 9 | | | 10 | 3 | | 7 | 12 | | | | | 1 | | 5 | | | 38 |
| 11 | 2 | 4 | | 6 | 8 | | | 9 | | | 10 | 3 | | 7* | 12 | | | | | 1 | | 5 | | | 39 |
| | 2 | 4 | 5 | 11 | 8 | | | 9 | | | 10* | 3 | | 7 | 12 | | | | | 1 | | 6 | | | 40 |
| | 11 | 4 | | 6 | 8 | | | 9 | | | 10 | | | 7 | | | | | | 1 | 2 | 5 | 3 | | 41 |
| 11 | 2 | 4* | 5 | 6 | 8 | | | 9 | | | 10 | 7 | 3 | | 12 | | | | | 1 | | | | | 42 |
| 20 | 34 | 36 | 35 | 23 | 41 | 36 | 7 | 36 | 4 | 39 | 20 | 33 | 16 | 4 | 24 | 2 | 2 | 2 | 1 | 22 | 11 | 9 | 5 | — | |
| | | | + 1s | + 1s | | + 1s | | | | | + 2s | | + 3s | + 2s | + 10s | + 2s | + 1s | | | | | | + 1s | | |

## QUEEN'S PARK RANGERS

| | Ht | Wt | Birthplace | Clubs | League App. | League Gls |
|---|---|---|---|---|---|---|
| **Goalkeepers** | | | | | | |
| Peter Hucker | 6 4½ | 13 0 | London | QPR | 23 | — |
| | | | | Cambridge U (on loan) | — | — |
| John Burridge | 5 10½ | 12 3 | Workington | Workington | 27 | — |
| | | | | Blackpool | 134 | — |
| | | | | Aston V | 65 | — |
| | | | | Southend U (on loan) | 6 | — |
| | | | | Crystal Palace | 88 | — |
| | | | | QPR | 39 | — |
| Graham Benstead | | | | QPR | — | — |
| **Defenders** | | | | | | |
| Ian Gillard | 6 2 | 13 3 | London | QPR | 408 | 9 |
| (England) | | | | | | |
| Ernie Howe | 6 2¾ | 12 12 | London | Crystal Palace | — | — |
| | | | | Fulham | 70 | 10 |
| | | | | QPR | 89 | 3 |
| Glenn Roeder | 6 2¼ | 12 8 | Woodford | Orient | 115 | 4 |
| | | | | QPR | 147 | 17 |
| Bob Hazell | 6 1½ | 14 1 | Jamaica | Wolverhampton W | 33 | 1 |
| | | | | QPR | 61 | 5 |
| Dean Wilkins | 5 8½ | 11 10 | London | QPR | 3 | — |
| Mark O'Connor | 5 6 | 9 10 | Basildon | QPR | 1 | — |
| Warren Neill | 5 10½ | 12 5 | London | QPR | 15 | — |
| Martin Duffield | | | | QPR | — | — |
| Ian Dawes | 5 8 | 10 12 | Croydon | QPR | 5 | — |
| Steve Wicks | 6 2¼ | 13 2 | Reading | Chelsea | 118 | 5 |
| | | | | Derby Co | 24 | — |
| | | | | QPR | 73 | — |
| | | | | Crystal Palace | 14 | 1 |
| | | | | QPR | 9 | — |
| **Midfield** | | | | | | |
| Gary Waddock | 5 10 | 11 12 | Kingsbury | QPR | 84 | 4 |
| (Eire) | | | | | | |
| Tony Currie | 5 11½ | 12 8 | Edgware | Watford | 18 | 9 |
| (England) | | | | Sheffield U | 313 | 55 |
| | | | | Leeds U | 102 | 11 |
| | | | | QPR | 79 | 5 |
| Terry Fenwick | 5 10 | 10 11 | Camden, | Crystal Palace | 70 | — |
| | | | Durham | QPR | 55 | 7 |
| John Gregory | 6 1 | 11 5 | Scunthorpe | Northampton T | 187 | 8 |
| | | | | Aston V | 65 | 10 |
| | | | | Brighton | 72 | 7 |
| | | | | QPR | 34 | 9 |
| Alan McDonald | | | | QPR | — | — |
| **Forwards** | | | | | | |
| Martyn Busby | 6 2 | 12 3 | Slough | QPR | 78 | 6 |
| (Retired, injury) | | | | Portsmouth (on loan) | 6 | 1 |
| | | | | Notts Co | 37 | 4 |
| | | | | Burnley (on loan) | 4 | 1 |
| | | | | QPR | 66 | 11 |
| Steve Burke | 5 10 | 10 8½ | Nottingham | Nottingham F | — | — |
| | | | | QPR | 57 | 5 |
| Gary Micklewhite | 5 8 | 9 10 | Southwark | Manchester U | — | — |
| | | | | QPR | 27 | 2 |
| Ian Stewart | 5 6½ | 11 9 | Belfast | QPR | 4 | — |
| (N Ireland) | | | | | | |
| Wayne Fereday | 5 9½ | 11 8 | Birmingham | QPR | 10 | 2 |
| Tony Sealy | 5 8¼ | 10 11 | London | Southampton | 7 | — |
| | | | | Crystal Palace | 24 | 5 |
| | | | | Port Vale (on loan) | 17 | 6 |
| | | | | QPR | 15 | 2 |
| | | | | Port Vale (on loan) | 6 | 4 |
| Clive Allen | 5 10 | 11 0 | London | QPR | 49 | 32 |
| | | | | Arsenal | — | — |
| | | | | Crystal Palace | 25 | 9 |
| | | | | QPR | 37 | 13 |
| Ian Muir | 5 6½ | 10 9 | Coventry | QPR | 2 | 2 |
| Mike Flanagan | 5 10½ | 11 10 | Ilford | Tottenham H | — | — |
| | | | | Charlton Ath | 254 | 85 |
| | | | | Crystal Palace | 56 | 8 |
| | | | | QPR | 51 | 13 |
| Simon Stainrod | 6 1½ | 11 11½ | Sheffield | Sheffield U | 67 | 14 |
| | | | | Oldham Ath | 69 | 21 |
| | | | | QPR | 54 | 21 |

# READING Division 3

*Chairman:* F. V. Waller. *Vice-Chairman:* L. Davies.

*Directors:* J. H. Brooks, K. Darvall, F. J. Briggs.

*Manager:* Maurice Evans.

*Secretary/Manager:* Roy Bentley.

*Year Formed:* 1871. *Turned Professional:* 1895.

*Limited Company:* 1895.

*Previous Grounds:* 1871, Reading Recreation; Reading Cricket Ground; 1882, Coley Park; 1889, Caversham Cricket Ground; 1896, Elm Park.

**Football League Record:**
1920 Original Member of Division 3; 1921–26 Division 3(S); 1926–31 Division 2; 1931–58 Division 3(S); 1958–71 Division 3; 1971–76 Division 4; 1976–77 Division 3; 1977–79 Division 4; 1979– Division 3.

**Honours:** *Football League:* Division 2 best season: 14th, 1926–27; Division 3(S) – Champions 1925–26; Runners-up 1931–32, 1934–35, 1948–49, 1951–52; Division 4 – Champions 1978–79. *FA Cup:* semi-final 1927. *Football League Cup* best season: 4th rd, 1965, 1966, 1978.

*Record Victory:* 10-2 v Crystal Palace, Division 3(S), 4 Sept, 1946.

*Record Defeat:* 0-18 v Preston NE, FA Cup, 1st rd, 1893–94.

*Most League Points:* 65, Division 4, 1978–79.

*Most League Goals:* 112, Division 3(S), 1951–52.

*Highest League Scorer in Season:* Ronnie Blackman, 39, Division 3(S), 1951–52.

*Most League Goals in Total Aggregate:* Ronnie Blackman, 156, 1947–54.

*Most Capped Player:* Pat McConnell, 8, Ireland.

*Most League Appearances:* Steve Death, 471, 1969–82.

*Record Transfer Fee Received:* £60,000 from Southampton for Tommy Jenkins, Dec 1969.

*Record Transfer Fee Paid:* £50,000 to Charlton Ath for Dave Shipperley, Sept 1979.

*Previous Managers since the War:* Joe Edelston, Ted Drake, Jack Smith, Harry Johnston, Roy Bentley, Jack Mansell, Charlie Hurley.

*Address of Supporters Club:* Reading Football Supporters Club, Elm Park, Norfolk Road, Reading.

---

**Elm Park, Norfolk Road, Reading.** Telephone Reading 57878/9/0. *Ground capacity:* 27,200. *Record attendance:* 33,042 v Brentford, FA Cup 5th rd, 19 Feb, 1927. *Record receipts:* £25,972 v Southampton, League Cup 4th rd, 8 Nov, 1978. *Pitch measurements:* 112yd×77yd.

*How to get there:* Corporation specials from St Mary's Butts (town centre) and from Northumberland Avenue. Usual buses within a few minutes of the ground. Nearest railway station, Reading.

*Match tickets:* Stand tickets are bookable in advance for all first-team matches 14 days before the match.

*Car parking:* Space is available for approximately 300 cars adjoining the ground entrance in Norfolk Road and Tilehurst Road.

*Entertainments/catering facilities:* Catering is available in each of the five stands and also on the terraces.

*Club shop:* Shops in Norfolk Road and on the West Terrace are open on match days selling all types of souvenirs.

*Handbooks/programmes:* The Supporters' Club produces a handbook and these are available on application to the club. Unsold programmes are available after each match at the programme shop on the West Terrace.

*Extra information:* Reading first appeared in the FA Cup 1st rd in 1877; only Notts County of the present League clubs played so long ago.

*Club Colours:* Blue shirts with white hoops, white shorts, white stockings with two blue rings.

*Change Colours:* Yellow.

*First Team Trainer:* Stewart Henderson.

*Club Nickname:* The Royals.

## READING 1981–82 LEAGUE RECORD

| Match No. | Date | Venue | Opponents | Result | H/T Score | Goalscorers | Attendance |
|---|---|---|---|---|---|---|---|
| 1 | Aug 29 | A | Doncaster R | W 1-0 | 0-0 | Earles | 4192 |
| 2 | Sept 5 | H | Gillingham | W 3-2 | 0-0 | Beavon, Heale, Hetzke (pen) | 3496 |
| 3 | 13 | A | Millwall | W 1-0 | 1-0 | Heale | 7178 |
| 4 | 19 | H | Bristol R | L 0-3 | 0-1 | | 4947 |
| 5 | 23 | H | Newport Co | W 2-1 | 0-0 | Dixon, Heale | 4542 |
| 6 | 26 | A | Swindon T | W 2-0 | 1-0 | Heale, Earles | 9316 |
| 7 | 29 | A | Plymouth Arg | D 1-1 | 1-0 | Heale | 2745 |
| 8 | Oct 3 | H | Huddersfield T | L 1-2 | 0-2 | Heale | 4971 |
| 9 | 10 | H | Chesterfield | L 0-2 | 0-1 | | 4690 |
| 10 | 17 | A | Preston NE | D 0-0 | 0-0 | | 5671 |
| 11 | 20 | A | Bristol C | L 0-2 | 0-0 | | 5006 |
| 12 | 24 | H | Wimbledon | W 2-1 | 2-0 | Webb (pen), Hicks | 3732 |
| 13 | 31 | A | Chester | W 3-2 | 2-2 | Kearney, Webb (pen), Dixon | 1765 |
| 14 | Nov 4 | H | Walsall | D 0-0 | 0-0 | | 4057 |
| 15 | 7 | A | Exeter C | L 3-4 | 2-1 | Kearney, Heale 2 | 3765 |
| 16 | 14 | H | Burnley | D 1-1 | 1-0 | Webb | 4089 |
| 17 | 27 | A | Southend U | L 0-2 | 0-0 | | 4510 |
| 18 | Dec 5 | H | Lincoln C | W 3-2 | 1-1 | Kearney, Webb (pen), Earles | 2973 |
| 19 | Jan 2 | A | Newport Co | L 1-3 | 0-3 | Sanchez | 2948 |
| 20 | 6 | H | Portsmouth | W 2-1 | 2-1 | Dixon, Webb | 4018 |
| 21 | 20 | H | Fulham | L 0-3 | 0-2 | | 3762 |
| 22 | 23 | H | Plymouth Arg | D 2-2 | 2-0 | Beavon, Dixon | 2789 |
| 23 | 27 | H | Brentford | W 4-1 | 2-1 | Webb (pen), Dixon 2, Donnellan | 3481 |
| 24 | 30 | A | Bristol R | D 1-1 | 1-0 | Donnellan | 5355 |
| 25 | Feb 3 | A | Oxford U | L 0-1 | 0-1 | | 9354 |
| 26 | 6 | H | Millwall | W 4-0 | 2-0 | Webb, Beavon, Hicks, Earles | 4120 |
| 27 | 13 | A | Huddersfield T | L 1-6 | 0-2 | Webb | 6022 |
| 28 | 17 | H | Doncaster R | D 3-3 | 3-1 | Webb, Donnellan, Earles | 2361 |
| 29 | 20 | H | Swindon T | D 1-1 | 0-0 | Allan (og) | 4130 |
| 30 | 27 | A | Chesterfield | L 1-2 | 0-1 | Webb | 4462 |
| 31 | Mar 6 | H | Preston NE | W 2-1 | 1-0 | Hetzke, Webb | 2655 |
| 32 | 10 | H | Bristol C | W 3-1 | 0-0 | Dixon 2, Beavon | 3107 |
| 33 | 13 | A | Wimbledon | D 0-0 | 0-0 | | 2551 |
| 34 | 16 | A | Walsall | W 2-1 | 0-1 | Webb, Kearney | 2789 |
| 35 | 20 | H | Chester | W 4-1 | 3-0 | Kearney, Sanchez, Dixon, Webb | 3093 |
| 36 | 23 | A | Carlisle U | L 1-2 | 0-2 | Webb (pen) | 4557 |
| 37 | 27 | H | Exeter C | W 4-0 | 2-0 | Dixon 2, Kearney, Sanchez | 3365 |
| 38 | Apr 3 | A | Burnley | L 0-3 | 0-2 | | 6622 |
| 39 | 10 | H | Oxford U | L 0-3 | 0-1 | | 6926 |
| 40 | 12 | A | Portsmouth | L 0-3 | 0-2 | | 8427 |
| 41 | 17 | A | Lincoln C | L 1-2 | 0-0 | Hicks | 4888 |
| 42 | 24 | H | Southend U | L 0-2 | 0-0 | | 2840 |
| 43 | May 1 | A | Fulham | D 2-2 | 1-0 | Earles, Beavon | 6773 |
| 44 | 8 | H | Carlisle U | D 2-2 | 1-1 | Webb (pen), Dixon | 2715 |
| 45 | 15 | A | Brentford | W 2-1 | 2-1 | Kearney, Earles | 4502 |
| 46 | 18 | A | Gillingham | L 1-2 | 1-0 | Kearney | 3920 |

**Final League Position: 12**

### Goalscorers

*League* (67): Webb 15 (6 pens), Dixon 12, Heale 8, Kearney 8, Earles 7, Beavon 5, Donnellan 3, Hicks 3, Sanchez 3, Hetzke 2 (1 pen), own goal 1.
*League Cup* (3): Earles 1, Heale 1, Hetzke 1 (pen).
*FA Cup* (0).

| | | | |
|---|---|---|---|
| **League Cup** | First Round | Charlton Ath (h) | 2-2 |
| | | (a) | 1-3 |
| **FA Cup** | First Round | Bournemouth (a) | 0-1 |

| Fearon | Williams | White | Wood | Hicks | Hetzke | Earles | Kearney | Heale | Sanchez | Webb | Lewis | Beavon | Cullen | Dixon | Clark | Joslyn | Donnellan | Barnes | Death | Moore | Court | Matthews | Henderson | Match No. |
|---|---|---|---|---|---|---|---|---|---|---|---|---|---|---|---|---|---|---|---|---|---|---|---|---|
| 1 | 2 | 3 | 4 | 5 | 6 | 7 | 8 | 9 | 10 | 11 | | | | | | | | | | | | | | 1 |
| 1 | 2 | | 5 | 6 | 7 | 8 | 9* | 10 | 11 | | 3 | 4 | | 12 | | | | | | | | | | 2 |
| 1 | 2 | | 5 | 6 | | 8 | 9 | 10 | 11 | | 3 | 4 | | 7 | | | | | | | | | | 3 |
| 1 | 2 | | 5 | 6 | 7* | 8 | 9 | 10 | 11 | | 3 | 4 | | 12 | | | | | | | | | | 4 |
| 1 | 2 | 4 | 5 | 6 | 7 | 8 | | 10 | 11 | | 3 | | | 9 | | | | | | | | | | 5 |
| 1 | 2 | 4 | 5 | 6 | 7 | 8 | | 10 | 11 | | 3 | | 12 | 9* | | | | | | | | | | 6 |
| 1 | 2 | 4 | 5 | 6 | 7 | 8 | 9 | | 10 | 11 | 3 | | | | | | | | | | | | | 7 |
| 1 | 2 | 4 | 5 | 6 | 7 | 9 | 8 | | 10 | | 3 | | | | | | 11* | 12 | | | | | | 8 |
| 1 | 2 | | 5 | 4 | 6 | 7 | 9 | 8 | 10 | | 3 | | | | | | 11 | | | | | | | 9 |
| 1 | 2 | 4 | 5 | 6 | 7 | | 9 | | 10 | 11 | 3 | | | 8 | | | | | | | | | | 10 |
| 1 | 2 | 4 | 5 | 6* | 7 | 12 | 9 | | | 11 | 3 | | 10 | 8 | | | | | | | | | | 11 |
| 1 | 2 | | 5 | 4 | 12 | 8 | 7 | 11* | 10 | | 3 | | 9 | 6 | | | | | | | | | | 12 |
| 1 | 2 | | 6 | 5 | | 8 | 9 | 10 | 11 | | 3 | 4 | | 7 | | | | | | | | | | 13 |
| 1 | 2 | | 6 | 5 | 12 | 8 | 9 | 10 | 11 | | 3 | 4 | | 7* | | | | | | | | | | 14 |
| 1 | 2 | 4 | 5 | 6 | | 8 | 9 | 10 | 11 | | 3 | 7* | | 12 | | | | | | | | | | 15 |
| 1 | 2 | 4 | 5 | 6 | | 8* | 9 | 10 | 11 | | 7 | 3 | | 12 | | | | | | | | | | 16 |
| 1 | 2 | 4 | 5 | 6 | | 8 | 10 | 7 | 12 | | 3* | 9 | | | | | 11 | | | | | | | 17 |
| 1 | 2 | | 6 | 5 | 8 | 10 | | 4 | | | 7 | 3 | | 9 | | | 11 | | | | | | | 18 |
| 1 | 2 | | 5 | | 8 | 4 | 10 | 6 | 12 | | 7* | 3 | | 9 | | | 11 | | | | | | | 19 |
| 1 | 2 | | 6 | 5 | 8 | | 4 | 10 | | | 7 | 3 | | 9 | | | 11 | | | | | | | 20 |
| 1 | 2 | | 5 | 6 | 8 | 12 | 4 | 10* | | | 7 | 3 | | 9 | | | 11 | | | | | | | 21 |
| 1 | 2* | | 5 | | 8 | 10 | 4 | 3 | | | 7 | 12 | | 9 | | | 11 | 6 | | | | | | 22 |
| 1 | 2 | | 5 | | 8 | 10 | 4 | 3 | | | 7 | | | 9 | | | 11 | 6 | | | | | | 23 |
| 1 | 2 | | 5 | 6 | 8 | 10 | 4 | 3 | | | 7 | | | 9 | | | 11* | 12 | | | | | | 24 |
| 1 | 2 | | 6 | 5 | 8 | 10 | 4 | 3 | | | 7 | | | 9 | | | 11 | | | | | | | 25 |
| | 2 | | 6 | 5 | 8 | 10 | 4 | 3 | | | 7 | | | 9 | | | 11 | 1 | | | | | | 26 |
| | 2 | | 6 | 5 | 8 | 10 | 4 | 3 | | | 7 | | | 9 | | | 11 | 1 | | | | | | 27 |
| | 2 | 7* | 5 | 6 | 8 | 10 | 4 | | | | 3 | | | 9 | | | 11 | 1 | 12 | | | | | 28 |
| | 2 | 7 | 5 | 6 | 8 | | 4 | 10 | | | 3* | | | 9 | | | 11 | 12 | | | 1 | | | 29 |
| 1 | 2 | 3 | 5 | 6 | 8 | 10 | 4 | | 11 | | 7 | 9 | | | | | | | | | | | | 30 |
| 1 | 2 | 3 | 5 | 6 | 8 | 10 | 4 | | 7 | | 9 | | | | | | 11 | | | | | | | 31 |
| 1 | 2 | 3 | 5 | 6 | 8 | 10 | 4 | 12 | 7 | | 9 | | | | | | 11* | | | | | | | 32 |
| 1 | 2 | | 5 | 6 | | 8 | 10 | 4 | 3 | | 7 | 12 | | 9 | | | 11* | | | | | | | 33 |
| 1 | 2 | 3 | 5 | 6 | | 8 | 10 | 4 | 11 | | 7 | 9 | | | | | | | | | | | | 34 |
| 1 | 2* | 3 | 6 | 5 | 8 | 10 | 4 | | 11 | | 7 | 9 | | | | | 12 | | | | | | | 35 |
| 1 | 3* | | 6 | 5 | 8 | 10 | 4 | | 11 | | 7 | 2 | | 9 | | | 12 | | | | | | | 36 |
| 1 | 2 | | 6 | 5 | 3 | 8 | 10 | 4* | 11 | | 7 | 12 | | 9 | | | | | | | | | | 37 |
| 1 | 2 | | 6 | 5 | 10 | 8 | | 4 | | | 3 | 7 | 12 | 9 | | | 11* | | | | | | | 38 |
| 1 | 2 | | 6 | 5 | 10 | 11 | 8 | 4 | | | 3 | 7 | | 9 | | | | | | | | | | 39 |
| 1 | 2 | 10 | 5 | 4 | 7 | 8 | | 11 | | | 3* | 9 | | | | | 12 | 6 | | | | | | 40 |
| 1 | 2 | 10 | 12 | 6 | 11 | 8 | 4 | | | | 3 | 9 | | | | | 7* | 5 | | | | | | 41 |
| 1 | 2 | | 6 | 5 | 3 | 11 | 10* | 4 | | | 7 | 12 | | 9 | | | | | | | 8 | | | 42 |
| 1 | 2 | | 6 | 5 | 10 | 8 | 4 | 11 | | | 7 | 9 | | | | | | | | | | | 3 | 43 |
| 1 | 2 | | 6 | 5 | 11 | 8 | 10 | 4 | | | 3 | 7 | | 9 | | | | | | | | | | 44 |
| 1 | 2 | | 6 | 5 | 10 | 8 | | 4 | | | 11 | 7 | | 9 | | | | | | | | | 3 | 45 |
| 1 | 2 | | 6 | 5 | 10 | 8 | | 4 | | | 3 | 7 | | 9 | | | 11 | | | | | | | 46 |
| 42 | 45 | 9 | 32 | 43 | 31 | 32 | 26 | 18 | 34 | 40 | 34 | 38 | 12 | 38 | 2 | — | 19 | 4 | 3 | — | 1 | 1 | 2 | |

|  |  | +1s | +1s | +1s | +1s |  |  |  |  | +1s |  | +2s | +2s | +5s | +4s |  | +1s | +3s | +2s |  | +1s |  |  | |

# READING

| | Ht | Wt | Birthplace | Clubs | League App. | League Gls |
|---|---|---|---|---|---|---|
| **Goalkeepers** | | | | | | |
| Steve Death | 5 8 | 11 7 | Elmswell | West Ham U | 1 | — |
| (Contract cancelled April 1982) | | | | Reading | 471 | — |
| Ron Fearon | 5 11 | 12 0 | Romford | QPR | — | — |
| | | | | Reading | 48 | — |
| Colin Court | | | | Reading | 1 | — |
| (Non-contract) | | | | | | |
| **Defenders** | | | | | | |
| Martin Hicks | 6 3 | 13 6 | Stratford-upon- | Charlton Ath | — | — |
| | | | Avon | Reading | 137 | 8 |
| Stewart Henderson | 5 8 | 11 8 | Bridge of Allan | Chelsea | — | — |
| | | | | Brighton | 198 | 1 |
| | | | | Reading | 161 | 6 |
| Steve Hetzke | 6 2 | 11 10 | Marlborough | Reading | 261 | 23 |
| Mark White | 5 9 | 11 0 | Sheffield | Sheffield W | — | — |
| | | | | Reading | 128 | — |
| Dave Shipperley | 6 3 | 14 0 | Hillingdon | Charlton Ath | 100 | 8 |
| (Retired, injury) | | | | Plymouth Arg (on loan) | 1 | — |
| | | | | Gillingham | 144 | 11 |
| | | | | Charlton Ath | 53 | 6 |
| | | | | Reading | 19 | — |
| Jon Cullen* | 5 7½ | 10 10 | Oxford | Reading | 20 | — |
| Steve Wood | 6 0 | 11 9 | Bracknell | Reading | 40 | — |
| Michael Barnes | | | Reading | Reading | 7 | — |
| Jerry Williams | 5 11 | 11 10 | Didcot | Reading | 106 | 7 |
| **Midfield** | | | | | | |
| Alan Lewis* | 5 8 | 10 12 | Oxford | Derby Co | 2 | — |
| | | | | Peterborough U (on loan) | 10 | 1 |
| | | | | Brighton | 3 | — |
| | | | | Sheffield W (on loan) | — | — |
| | | | | Reading | 149 | 5 |
| Roger Joslyn | 5 10 | 11 2 | Colchester | Colchester U | 98 | 4 |
| (Retired, injury) | | | | Aldershot | 186 | 17 |
| | | | | Watford | 182 | 17 |
| | | | | Reading | 68 | 1 |
| Stuart Beavon | 5 6½ | 10 4 | Oxford | Tottenham H | 4 | — |
| | | | | Notts Co (on loan) | 6 | — |
| | | | | Reading | 77 | 11 |
| Neil Webb | 5 11 | 11 6 | Reading | Reading | 72 | 22 |
| Andy Moore | | | | Reading | 1 | — |
| (Apprentice) | | | | | | |
| Mark Matthews | | | | Reading | 1 | — |
| (Non-contract) | | | | | | |
| **Forwards** | | | | | | |
| Pat Earles | 5 7 | 11 6 | Titchfield | Southampton | 12 | 1 |
| | | | | Reading | 216 | 61 |
| Mike Kearney | 6 0 | 12 0 | Glasgow | Shrewsbury T | 149 | 41 |
| | | | | Chester | 38 | 5 |
| | | | | Reading | 87 | 24 |
| | | | | Chester | 9 | — |
| | | | | Reading | 53 | 12 |
| Lawrie Sanchez | 5 11 | 11 7 | Reading | Reading | 165 | 15 |
| Gary Heale | 5 11 | 11 6¾ | Canvey | Luton T | 7 | 1 |
| | | | | Exeter C (on loan) | 4 | — |
| | | | | Reading | 76 | 20 |
| Kerry Dixon | 6 0 | 13 0 | Luton | Dunstable | (not known) | |
| | | | | Reading | 81 | 25 |
| Gary Donnellan | 5 8 | 11 12 | London | Chelsea | — | — |
| | | | | Watford | — | — |
| | | | | Reading | 22 | 3 |

# ROCHDALE Division 4

*Chairman:* D. F. Kilpatrick.

*Directors:* G. Morris FCA, C. W. Walkden, W. H. C. Dronsfield.

*Manager:* Peter Madden.

*Secretary:* T. Nichol.

*Year Formed:* 1907.

*Turned Professional:* 1907.

*Limited Company:* 1910.

**Football League Record:**
1921 Elected to Division 3(N); 1958–59 Division 3; 1959–69 Division 4; 1969–74 Division 3; 1974– Division 4.

**Honours:** *Football League:* Division 3 best season: 9th, 1969–70; Division 3(N) – Runners-up 1923–24, 1926–27. *FA Cup* best season: 4th rd, 1970–71. *Football League Cup:* Runners-up 1962 (record for 4th Division club).

*Record Victory:* 8-1 v Chesterfield, Division 3(N), 18 Dec, 1926.

*Record Defeat:* 0-8 v Wrexham, Division 3(N), 28 Dec, 1929.

*Most League Points:* 62, Division 3(N), 1923–24.

*Most League Goals:* 105, Division 3(N), 1926–27.

*Highest League Scorer in Season:* Albert Whitehurst, 44, Division 3(N), 1926–27.

*Most League Goals in Total Aggregate:* Reg Jenkins, 119, 1964–73.

*Most Capped Player:* None.

*Most League Appearances:* Graham Smith, 317, 1966–74.

*Record Transfer Fee Received:* £40,000 plus Malcolm Darling from Norwich C for David Cross, Oct 1971.

*Record Transfer Fee Paid:* £12,000 to Sunderland for Alan Weir, June 1979.

*Previous Managers since the War:* Ted Goodier, Jack Warner, Harry Catterick, Jack Marshall, Tony Collins, Bob Stokoe, Len Richley, Dick Conner, Walter Joyce, Brian Green, Mike Ferguson, Doug Collins, Bob Stokoe.

*Address of Supporters Club:* Rochdale AFC Soccer Shop, Spotland, Sandy Lane, Rochdale.

---

**Spotland, Willbutts Lane, Rochdale.** Telephone 0706-44648/9. *Ground capacity:* 28,000. *Record attendance:* 24,231 v Notts County, FA Cup 2nd rd, 10 Dec, 1949. *Record receipts:* £5330 v Sheffield U, Division 4, 16 Jan, 1982. *Pitch measurements:* 113yd×75yd.

*How to get there:* Bus station – Norden for Churchill Street; Greave for ground.

*Match tickets:* Seats can be reserved in advance.

*Car parking:* Car parking at the ground and in the adjacent side-streets.

*Entertainments/catering facilities:* A social club in the car park.

*Club shop:* Sells all types of souvenirs and programmes.

*Handbooks/programmes:* 'Forward with the Dale – A History of Rochdale AFC' £1.25 (inc P+P) from Club Shop.

*Extra information:* Social club.

*Club Colours:* Royal blue shirts with white sleeves, white collar and trim, white shorts with blue trim, blue stockings with white ring.

*Change Colours:* Red and green striped shirts, red shorts with green trim, red stockings.

*Club Nickname:* The Dale.

314

## ROCHDALE 1981–82 LEAGUE RECORD

| Match No. | Date | Venue | Opponents | Result | H/T Score | Goalscorers | Attendance |
|---|---|---|---|---|---|---|---|
| 1 | Aug 29 | A | Bury | L 0-3 | 0-3 | | 3925 |
| 2 | Sept 5 | H | Hartlepool U | W 2-1 | 1-1 | Martinez, Goodwin | 1481 |
| 3 | 12 | A | Peterborough U | L 1-5 | 1-2 | Wellings (pen) | 3768 |
| 4 | 19 | H | Port Vale | L 1-2 | 0-0 | O'Loughlin | 2750 |
| 5 | 22 | H | Blackpool | D 0-0 | 0-0 | | 2763 |
| 6 | 26 | A | AFC Bournemouth | L 0-1 | 0-1 | | 5146 |
| 7 | 30 | A | Bradford C | L 0-2 | 0-2 | | 5388 |
| 8 | Oct 4 | H | Aldershot | D 0-0 | 0-0 | | 1821 |
| 9 | 11 | H | Colchester U | L 1-2 | 0-0 | Wellings | 1366 |
| 10 | 17 | A | Halifax T | D 0-0 | 0-0 | | 2140 |
| 11 | 21 | A | Crewe Alex | W 2-1 | 1-0 | Goodwin, Wellings | 1827 |
| 12 | 24 | H | Stockport Co | W 4-1 | 3-1 | Martinez 2, Hilditch, Goodwin | 1778 |
| 13 | 31 | A | Darlington | L 0-2 | 0-2 | | 1454 |
| 14 | Nov 3 | H | Tranmere R | D 0-0 | 0-0 | | 1663 |
| 15 | 8 | H | Torquay U | W 1-0 | 0-0 | Goodwin | 1790 |
| 16 | 14 | A | Mansfield T | L 3-4 | 1-1 | Hilditch 2, Wellings (pen) | 2300 |
| 17 | 28 | H | Wigan Ath | D 1-1 | 1-1 | Hilditch | 2765 |
| 18 | Dec 5 | A | Hereford U | D 0-0 | 0-0 | | 2312 |
| 19 | Jan 13 | H | Halifax T | L 0-1 | 0-1 | | 1122 |
| 20 | 16 | H | Sheffield U | L 0-1 | 0-0 | | 3966 |
| 21 | 23 | H | Bury | D 1-1 | 0-1 | Martinez | 3581 |
| 22 | 30 | A | Port Vale | D 1-1 | 1-1 | Martinez | 3835 |
| 23 | Feb 6 | A | Peterborough U | D 1-1 | 1-0 | Hamilton | 1241 |
| 24 | 10 | A | Blackpool | D 1-1 | 1-1 | Hilditch | 3294 |
| 25 | 14 | A | Aldershot | D 2-2 | 1-0 | Cooper, Hilditch | 2079 |
| 26 | 20 | H | AFC Bournemouth | L 0-1 | 0-0 | | 1295 |
| 27 | 26 | A | Colchester U | L 2-3 | 1-2 | O'Loughlin, Hilditch | 2760 |
| 28 | Mar 2 | A | Northampton T | L 1-2 | 0-0 | O'Loughlin | 1916 |
| 29 | 9 | H | Crewe Alex | W 1-0 | 1-0 | Goodwin | 1060 |
| 30 | 12 | A | Stockport Co | W 4-0 | 2-0 | Martinez, Hilditch 2, Wellings | 2079 |
| 31 | 16 | A | Tranmere R | L 0-2 | 0-0 | | 1131 |
| 32 | 20 | H | Darlington | W 3-2 | 1-1 | O'Loughlin, Wellings (pen), Hilditch | 1252 |
| 33 | 27 | A | Torquay U | L 1-2 | 1-1 | Hilditch | 1554 |
| 34 | 31 | A | Hartlepool U | D 1-1 | 0-1 | Wellings (pen) | 1259 |
| 35 | Apr 3 | H | Mansfield T | D 1-1 | 1-1 | Hilditch | 1276 |
| 36 | 6 | H | Hull C | L 0-1 | 0-0 | | 1738 |
| 37 | 10 | A | Scunthorpe U | L 0-1 | 0-0 | | 1742 |
| 38 | 12 | H | York C | W 2-0 | 1-0 | Martinez 2, Wellings (pen) | 1421 |
| 39 | 17 | H | Hereford U | L 0-1 | 0-0 | | 1342 |
| 40 | 20 | H | Scunthorpe U | D 1-1 | 0-0 | Wellings | 1129 |
| 41 | 24 | A | Wigan Ath | D 1-1 | 1-0 | Martinez | 6153 |
| 42 | 27 | A | York C | W 2-1 | 1-0 | Hilditch 2 | 2089 |
| 43 | May 1 | H | Bradford C | D 1-1 | 1-1 | Dolan (pen) | 3080 |
| 44 | 4 | A | Sheffield U | L 1-3 | 1-2 | Wellings | 21,140 |
| 45 | 8 | A | Hull C | L 1-2 | 1-1 | Cooper | 3012 |
| 46 | 15 | H | Northampton T | W 5-3 | 2-3 | Martinez, Wellings, Warriner, O'Loughlin, Goodwin | 1056 |

**Final League Position: 21**

**Goalscorers**

*League* (50): Hilditch 14, Wellings 11 (5 pens), Martinez 9, Goodwin 6, O'Loughlin 5, Cooper 2, Dolan 1 (pen), Hamilton 1, Warriner 1.
*League Cup* (3): Cooper 1, Hilditch 1, Wellings 1.
*FA Cup* (4): Esser 2, Burke 1, Dolan 1.

| League Cup | First Round | Huddersfield T (a) | 1-3 |
|---|---|---|---|
| | | (h) | 2-4 |
| FA Cup | First Round | Hull C (h) | 2-2 |
| | | (a) | 2-2 |
| | | (a) | 0-1 (at Leeds) |

| Crawford | Weir | Snookes | Dolan | Taylor | Cooper | Hamilton | O'Laughlin | Esser | Wellings | Martinez | Hilditch | Poole | Burke | Goodwin | Warriner | Williams | Thompson | Match No. |
|---|---|---|---|---|---|---|---|---|---|---|---|---|---|---|---|---|---|---|
| 1 | 2 | 3 | 4 | 5 | 6 | 7* | 8 | 9 | 10 | 11 | 12 | | | | | | | 1 |
| | | 3 | 4* | 5 | 6 | | 8 | 9 | 10 | 11 | 7 | 1 | 2 | 12 | | | | 2 |
| | | 3 | 4 | 5 | 6 | | 8 | 9 | 10 | 11 | 7 | 1 | 2* | 12 | | | | 3 |
| | 2 | 3 | | | 6 | 11 | 4 | 8 | 10 | 7 | | 1 | 5 | 9 | | | | 4 |
| | 2 | 3 | | | 6 | | 4 | 8 | 10 | 7 | 9 | 1 | 5 | 11 | | | | 5 |
| | 2 | 3 | 12 | | 6 | | 4 | 8 | 10 | 7* | 9 | 1 | 5 | 11 | | | | 6 |
| | 2 | 3 | 7 | | 6 | | 4 | 8 | 10 | | 9 | 1 | 5 | 11 | | | | 7 |
| | | 3 | 4 | 6 | 2 | | 8 | 7 | 10 | 11 | 9* | 1 | 5 | 12 | | | | 8 |
| | | 3 | 4 | 6 | 2 | 7* | 8 | | 10 | 11 | 9 | 1 | 5 | 12 | | | | 9 |
| | | 3 | 4 | 6 | 2 | | 8 | | 10 | 11 | 9 | 1 | 5 | 7 | | | | 10 |
| | | 3 | 4 | 6 | 2 | | 8 | | 10 | 11 | 9 | 1 | 5 | 7 | | | | 11 |
| 12 | | 3 | 4 | 6 | 2 | | 8 | | 10 | 11 | 9* | 1 | 5 | 7 | | | | 12 |
| | | 3 | 4 | 6 | 2 | | 8 | | 10 | 11 | 9 | 1 | 5 | 7 | | | | 13 |
| | | 3 | 4 | 6 | 2 | | 8 | | 10 | 11 | 9 | 1 | 5 | 7 | | | | 14 |
| 12 | | 3 | 4 | 6 | 2 | | 8 | | 10 | 11 | 9 | 1 | 5* | 7 | | | | 15 |
| | | 3 | 4 | 6 | 2 | | 8 | | 10 | 11 | 9 | 1 | 5 | 7 | | | | 16 |
| | 2 | 3 | 4 | 6 | | | 8 | | 10 | 11 | 9 | 1 | 5 | 7 | | | | 17 |
| | | 3 | 4 | 6 | 2 | | 8 | 7 | 10 | | 9 | 1 | 5 | 11 | | | | 18 |
| | | 3 | 4 | 6 | 2 | 12 | 8 | | 10 | 11 | 9* | 1 | 5 | 7 | | | | 19 |
| | 2 | 3 | 4 | 6 | 5 | 7 | 8 | | 10 | 11 | 9 | 1 | | | | | | 20 |
| | 2 | 3 | 4 | 6 | 5 | | 8 | | 10 | 11 | 9 | 1 | | 7 | | | | 21 |
| | 2 | 3 | 4 | | 6 | | 8 | | 10 | 11 | 9 | 1 | 5 | 7 | | | | 22 |
| | 2 | 3 | 4 | | 6 | | 8 | | 10 | 11 | 9 | 1 | 5 | 7* | 12 | | | 23 |
| | 2 | 3 | 4 | 5 | 6 | | 8 | | 10 | 11 | 9 | 1 | | 7 | | | | 24 |
| | 2 | 3 | 4 | 5 | 6 | | 8 | | 10 | 11 | 9 | 1 | | 7 | | | | 25 |
| | 2 | 3 | 4 | 6 | 5 | | 8 | | 10 | 11 | 9 | 1 | | 7 | | | | 26 |
| | 2 | 3 | 4 | 6 | 5 | | 8 | 11 | 10 | | 9 | 1 | | 7 | | | | 27 |
| | 2 | 3 | 4 | 6 | 5 | | 8 | 11 | 10 | 12 | 9 | 1 | | 7* | | | | 28 |
| 1 | 2 | 3 | 4 | | 6 | 7* | 8 | 12 | 9 | 11 | | | 5 | 10 | | | | 29 |
| 1 | 2 | 3 | 4 | | 6 | | 8 | 12 | 10 | 11 | 9 | | 5 | 7* | | | | 30 |
| 1 | 2 | 3 | 4 | | 6 | | 8 | 7 | 10 | 11 | 9 | | 5 | | | | | 31 |
| 1 | 2 | 3 | 4 | | 6 | | 8 | 7* | 10 | 11 | 9 | | 5 | 12 | | | | 32 |
| 1 | 2 | 3 | 4 | 6 | 5 | | 8 | | 10 | 11 | 9 | | 7 | | | | | 33 |
| 1 | 2 | 3 | 4* | | 6 | | 8 | | 10 | 11 | 9 | | 5 | 7 | 12 | | | 34 |
| 1 | 2 | 3 | 4 | | 6 | | 7 | | 10 | 11 | 9 | | 5 | | 8 | | | 35 |
| 1 | 2 | 3 | 4 | | 6 | | 8 | 12 | 10 | 11 | 9 | | 5* | 7 | | | | 36 |
| 1 | 2 | 3 | 4 | 5 | 6* | 7 | 12 | | 10 | 11 | | | | 9 | 8 | | | 37 |
| 1 | 6 | 3 | 4 | 5 | | 7 | 2 | 12 | 10* | 11 | | | | 9 | 8 | | | 38 |
| 1 | 6 | 3 | 4 | 5 | | 7 | 2 | 8* | 10 | 11 | 12 | | | 9 | | | | 39 |
| 1 | 6 | 3 | 4 | 5 | | 7 | 8 | 12 | 11 | 9 | | | | 10* | 2 | | | 40 |
| 1 | 6 | 3 | 4 | 5 | | 7 | 8 | | 10 | 11 | 9 | | | | 2 | | | 41 |
| 1 | 6 | 3 | 4 | 5 | | 7 | 8 | | 10 | 11 | 9 | | | | 2 | | | 42 |
| 1 | | 3 | 4 | 5 | 6 | 7 | | | 10 | 11 | 9 | | | | 2 | 8 | | 43 |
| 1 | | 3 | 4 | 5 | 6 | | 8 | | 10 | 11 | 9 | | 7 | | 2 | | | 44 |
| 1 | | 3 | 4* | 5 | 6 | 7 | 8 | | 10 | 11 | 9 | | | | 2 | 12 | | 45 |
| 1 | 6 | 3 | | 5* | 8 | 4 | | | 10 | 11 | 9 | | | | 2 | 12 | 7 | 46 |
| 19 | 32 | 44 | 42 | 37 | 35 | 20 | 32 | 20 | 45 | 42 | 38 | 27 | 27 | 34 | 7 | 4 | 1 | |
| | +2s | | +1s | | +1s | +1s | +4s | +1s | +1s | +2s | | | | +5s | +1s | +2s | +1s | |

## ROCHDALE

| | Ht | Wt | Birthplace | Clubs | League App. | League Gls |
|---|---|---|---|---|---|---|
| **Goalkeepers** | | | | | | |
| Graeme Crawford* | 6 2 | 12 0 | Falkirk | E Stirling | 2 | — |
| | | | | Sheffield U | 2 | — |
| | | | | Mansfield T (on loan) | 2 | — |
| | | | | York C | 235 | — |
| | | | | Scunthorpe U | 104 | — |
| | | | | York C | 17 | — |
| | | | | Rochdale | 60 | — |
| Mike Poole* | 6 0 | 12 7 | Leeds | Coventry C | — | — |
| | | | | Rochdale | 192 | — |
| | | | | Portland T | (not known) | — |
| | | | | Rochdale | 27 | — |
| **Defenders** | | | | | | |
| Eric Snookes | 5 7 | 10 0 | Birmingham | Preston NE | 20 | — |
| | | | | Crewe Alex | 34 | — |
| | | | | Southport | 110 | 2 |
| | | | | Rochdale | 150 | 1 |
| Brian Taylor | 5 11 | 11 9 | Hodthorpe | Middlesbrough | 18 | 1 |
| | | | | Doncaster R | 119 | 12 |
| | | | | Rochdale | 140 | 10 |
| Alan Weir | 5 6 | 9 8 | South Shields | Sunderland | 1 | — |
| | | | | Rochdale | 98 | 3 |
| Peter Burke* | 6 0 | 11 10 | Rotherham | Barnsley | 35 | 1 |
| | | | | Halifax T | 85 | 9 |
| | | | | Rochdale | 68 | 2 |
| Bill Williams | 5 10 | 12 7 | Rochdale | Rochdale | 6 | — |
| (Non-contract) | | | | | | |
| Darren Lambert* | | | Bradford | Rochdale | — | — |
| Terry Cooper* | 5 9 | 11 7 | Cwmbran | Newport Co | 68 | 1 |
| | | | | Notts Co | 9 | — |
| | | | | Lincoln C | 270 | 12 |
| | | | | Scunthorpe U (on loan) | 4 | — |
| | | | | Bradford C | 48 | 2 |
| | | | | Rochdale | 35 | 2 |
| Steve Warriner | 5 7 | 10 0 | Liverpool | Liverpool | — | — |
| | | | | Newport Co | 36 | 2 |
| | | | | Rochdale | 8 | 1 |
| **Midfield** | | | | | | |
| Nigel O'Loughlin* | 5 8 | 10 0 | Denbigh | Shrewsbury T | 33 | 7 |
| | | | | Rochdale | 245 | 17 |
| Eugene Martinez | 5 8 | 10 10 | Chelmsford | Bradford C | 52 | 5 |
| | | | | Rochdale | 87 | 13 |
| Terry Dolan* | 6 1 | 11 3 | Bradford | Bradford C | — | — |
| | | | | Bradford PA | 48 | — |
| | | | | Huddersfield T | 162 | 14 |
| | | | | Bradford C | 195 | 43 |
| | | | | Rochdale | 43 | 1 |
| Dave Goodwin* | 5 11 | 11 7 | Alsager | Stoke C | 26 | 3 |
| | | | | Workington (on loan) | 7 | — |
| | | | | Mansfield T | 46 | 5 |
| | | | | Bury | 4 | — |
| | | | | Rochdale | 39 | 6 |
| Neville Hamilton | 5 8 | 10 0 | Leicester | Leicester C | 4 | — |
| | | | | Mansfield T | 89 | 4 |
| | | | | Rochdale | 21 | 1 |
| **Forwards** | | | | | | |
| Dave Esser* | 5 6 | 10 2 | Bowden | Everton | — | — |
| | | | | Rochdale | 180 | 24 |
| Mark Hilditch | 5 11 | 11 8 | Shaw | Rochdale | 158 | 33 |
| Barry Wellings | 5 7 | 11 0 | Liverpool | Everton | — | — |
| | | | | York C | 47 | 9 |
| | | | | Rochdale | 92 | 25 |
| Dave Thompson | 5 9 | 11 6 | Rochdale | Rochdale | 2 | — |
| (Non-contract) | | | | | | |

# ROTHERHAM UNITED　　　Division 2

*Chairman:* Anton Johnson.

*Directors:* C. R. Wright, J. Layden.

*Player-Manager:* Emlyn Hughes.　*Secretary:* J. E. Bennison.

*Year Formed:* 1884.　*Turned Professional:* 1905.

*Limited Company:* 1920.

*Previous Names:* 1884, Thornhill United; 1905, Rotherham County; 1925, amalgamated with Rotherham Town under Rotherham United.

*Previous Grounds:* Red House Ground; 1907, Millmoor.

**Football League Record:**
1893 Rotherham Town elected to Division 2; 1896 Failed re-election; 1919 Rotherham County elected to Division 2; 1923–51 Division 3(N); 1951–68 Division 2; 1968–73 Division 3; 1973–75 Division 4; 1975–81 Division 3; 1981– Division 2.

**Honours:** *Football League:* Division 2 best season: 3rd, 1954–55 (equal points with champions and runners-up); Division 3 – Champions 1980–81; Division 3(N) – Champions 1950–51; Runners-up 1946–47, 1947–48, 1948–49. *FA Cup* best season: 5th rd, 1953, 1968. *Football League Cup:* Runners-up 1961.

*Record Victory:* 8-0 v Oldham Ath, Division 3(N), 26 May, 1947.

*Record Defeat:* 1-11 v Bradford C, Division 3(N), 25 Aug, 1928.

*Most League Points:* 71, Division 3(N), 1950–51.

*Most League Goals:* 114, Division 3(N), 1946–47.

*Highest League Scorer in Season:* Wally Ardron, 38, Division 3(N), 1946–47.

*Most League Goals in Total Aggregate:* Gladstone Guest, 130, 1946–56.

*Most Capped Player:* Harold Millership, 6, Wales.

*Most League Appearances:* Danny Williams, 459, 1946–62.

*Record Transfer Fee Received:* £100,000 from Sunderland for Dave Watson, Dec 1970.

*Record Transfer Fee Paid:* £100,000 to Cardiff C for Ronnie Moore, Aug 1980.

*Previous Managers since the War:* Reg Freeman, Andy Smailes, Tom Johnston, Danny Williams, Jack Mansell, Tommy Docherty, Jimmy McAnearney, Jimmy McGuigan, Ian Porterfield.

*Address of Supporters Club:* Red and White Shop, c/o Millmoor, Rotherham.

**Millmoor Ground, Rotherham.** Telephone Rotherham 562434. *Telegraphic address:* 'Holmes Millmoor, Rotherham'. *Ground capacity:* 21,000. *Record attendance:* 25,000 v Sheffield U, Division 2, 13 Dec, 1952 and v Sheffield W, Division 2, 26 Jan, 1952. *Record receipts:* £34,217 v Sheffield W, Division 2, 4 May, 1982. *Pitch measurements:* 115yd×76yd.

*How to get there:* Corporation buses from town centre. Also regular service buses from Sheffield to town centre. Nearest railway station, Rotherham on the line from Sheffield. Station across road from ground.

*Match tickets:* Seats can be reserved one month before the match.

*Car parking:* There are parks in Kimberworth Road and Main St (the municipal car park); both are within easy reach of the ground.

*Entertainments/catering facilities:* There are refreshment kiosks on all four sides of the ground and also behind the grandstand, and the Windmill where meals may be obtained if booked in advance and drinks are served during licensing hours.

*Club shop:* Sited on the forecourt of the ground; stocks all types of souvenirs.

*Handbooks/programmes:* No handbook, but programmes may be obtained from the club or the club shop.

*Extra information:* Rotherham full-back Irvine Rhodes scored twice on his début for Rotherham against Hartlepools in March 1937.

*Club Colours:* Red shirts, white collar, white sleeves, white (or black) shorts, red stockings.

*Change Colours:* Yellow shirts with blue trim, blue shorts with yellow trim, yellow stockings.

*Club Coach:*

*Club Nickname:* The Merry Millers.

## ROTHERHAM UNITED 1981–82 LEAGUE RECORD

| Match No. | Date | Venue | Opponents | Result | | H/T Score | Goalscorers | Attendance |
|---|---|---|---|---|---|---|---|---|
| 1 | Aug 29 | H | Norwich C | W | 4-1 | 2-1 | Fern 2, Seasman, Moore | 8919 |
| 2 | Sept 5 | A | Cambridge U | L | 0-3 | 0-2 | | 4385 |
| 3 | 8 | A | Sheffield W | L | 0-2 | 0-1 | | 26,826 |
| 4 | 12 | H | Cardiff C | W | 1-0 | 0-0 | Moore | 7197 |
| 5 | 19 | A | Watford | L | 0-1 | 0-0 | | 10,644 |
| 6 | 22 | H | Leicester C | D | 1-1 | 0-0 | Moore | 7781 |
| 7 | 26 | H | Bolton W | W | 2-0 | 2-0 | Green, Henson | 6998 |
| 8 | Oct 3 | A | Shrewsbury T | L | 1-2 | 1-1 | Forrest | 4646 |
| 9 | 10 | A | Crystal Palace | L | 1-3 | 1-0 | Towner | 8021 |
| 10 | 17 | H | Oldham Ath | L | 1-2 | 0-1 | Moore | 8034 |
| 11 | 24 | A | Newcastle U | D | 1-1 | 0-0 | Gooding | 19,039 |
| 12 | 31 | H | Chelsea | W | 6-0 | 3-0 | Breckin, Fern 3, Moore 2 (1 pen) | 10,145 |
| 13 | Nov 7 | A | QPR | D | 1-1 | 1-0 | Francis (og) | 10,949 |
| 14 | 14 | H | Barnsley | L | 2-4 | 2-1 | Moore 2 | 18,324 |
| 15 | 21 | H | Charlton Ath | W | 2-1 | 0-0 | Moore (pen), Fern | 7177 |
| 16 | 28 | A | Luton T | L | 1-3 | 0-0 | Fern | 11,061 |
| 17 | Dec 5 | H | Orient | W | 1-0 | 1-0 | Towner | 6346 |
| 18 | Jan 16 | A | Norwich C | L | 0-2 | 0-1 | | 12,750 |
| 19 | 23 | A | Blackburn R | L | 0-2 | 0-1 | | 7706 |
| 20 | 30 | H | Watford | L | 1-2 | 1-0 | Fern | 8129 |
| 21 | Feb 2 | H | Derby Co | W | 2-1 | 0-1 | Richards (og), Moore | 7487 |
| 22 | 6 | A | Cardiff C | W | 2-1 | 1-1 | Gow, Fern | 3800 |
| 23 | 9 | A | Grimsby T | W | 2-1 | 0-1 | Moore, McEwan | 8629 |
| 24 | 13 | H | Cambridge U | W | 1-0 | 1-0 | Smith (og) | 7312 |
| 25 | 16 | H | Shrewsbury T | W | 3-0 | 1-0 | Fern 2, Hughes | 7497 |
| 26 | 20 | A | Bolton W | W | 1-0 | 1-0 | Seasman | 9466 |
| 27 | 23 | H | Wrexham | W | 2-0 | 0-0 | Fern, Moore | 9158 |
| 28 | 27 | H | Crystal Palace | W | 2-0 | 1-0 | Moore, Towner (pen) | 10,007 |
| 29 | Mar 6 | A | Oldham Ath | W | 3-0 | 0-0 | Seasman 2, Moore | 8640 |
| 30 | 13 | H | Newcastle U | D | 0-0 | 0-0 | | 16,905 |
| 31 | 17 | A | Leicester C | L | 0-1 | 0-0 | | 21,123 |
| 32 | 20 | A | Chelsea | W | 4-1 | 3-1 | McEwan, Moore 2, Towner | 11,900 |
| 33 | 27 | H | QPR | W | 1-0 | 1-0 | Seasman | 10,472 |
| 34 | Apr 2 | A | Barnsley | L | 0-3 | 0-2 | | 23,059 |
| 35 | 10 | H | Grimsby T | D | 2-2 | 1-1 | Seasman, Fern | 10,011 |
| 36 | 12 | A | Derby Co | L | 1-3 | 0-1 | Seasman | 14,080 |
| 37 | 17 | A | Charlton Ath | W | 2-1 | 0-0 | Moore, Seasman | 5011 |
| 38 | 24 | H | Luton T | D | 2-2 | 1-1 | Moore, Seasman | 11,290 |
| 39 | May 1 | A | Orient | W | 2-1 | 0-0 | Moore, Seasman | 3009 |
| 40 | 4 | H | Sheffield W | D | 2-2 | 1-1 | Moore, Hughes (pen) | 20,513 |
| 41 | 8 | H | Blackburn R | W | 4-1 | 0-1 | Green 2, McEwan, Moore | 8333 |
| 42 | 15 | A | Wrexham | L | 2-3 | 2-1 | Stancliffe, Moore | 3350 |

**Final League Position: 7**

**Goalscorers**

*League* (66): Moore 22 (2 pens), Fern 13, Seasman 10, Towner 4 (1 pen), Green 3, McEwan 3, Hughes 2 (1 pen), Breckin 1, Forrest 1, Gooding 1, Gow 1, Henson 1, Stancliffe 1, own goals 3.
*League Cup* (8): Fern 2, Moore 2, Breckin 1, Gooding 1, Henson 1, own goal 1.
*FA Cup* (1): Towner 1.

| **League Cup** | First Round | Darlington (a) | 3-1 |
|---|---|---|---|
| | | (h) | 2-1 |
| | Second Round | Sunderland (a) | 0-2 |
| | | (h) | 3-3 |
| **FA Cup** | Third Round | Sunderland (h) | 1-1 |
| | | (a) | 0-1 |

| Mountford | Forrest | Taylor | Green | Stancliffe | Mullen | Towner | Seasman | Moore | Fern | Henson | Gooding | Breckin | Rhodes | Hughes | Carr | Alexander | McEwan | Gow | Mimms | *Match No.* |
|---|---|---|---|---|---|---|---|---|---|---|---|---|---|---|---|---|---|---|---|---|
| 1 | 2 | 3 | 4 | 5 | 6 | 7 | 8 | 9* | 10 | 11 | 12 |  |  |  |  |  |  |  |  | 1 |
| 1 | 2 | 3 | 4* | 5 | 6 | 7 | 8 | 9 | 10 | 11 | 12 |  |  |  |  |  |  |  |  | 2 |
| 1 | 2 | 3 | 4 | 5 | 6 | 7 | 8 | 9 | 10 | 11* | 12 |  |  |  |  |  |  |  |  | 3 |
| 1 | 2 | 3 | 4 | 5 | 6 | 7 | 8 | 9 | 10 | 11* | 12 |  |  |  |  |  |  |  |  | 4 |
| 1 | 2 |  | 4 | 5 | 6 | 7 |  | 9 | 10* | 11 | 12 | 3 | 8 |  |  |  |  |  |  | 5 |
| 1 | 2 |  | 4 | 5 | 6 | 7 |  | 9 | 10 | 11 |  | 3 | 8 |  |  |  |  |  |  | 6 |
| 1 | 2 |  | 4 | 5 |  | 7 |  | 9 | 10* | 11 | 12 | 3 | 8 | 6 |  |  |  |  |  | 7 |
| 1 | 2 |  | 6 | 5 |  | 7 |  | 9 | 10* | 11 | 8 | 3 | 4 |  |  | 12 |  |  |  | 8 |
| 1 | 2 |  | 6 | 5 |  | 7 | 12 | 9 |  | 11 | 8* | 3 | 4 |  |  |  | 10 |  |  | 9 |
| 1 | 2 |  |  | 5 |  | 7 |  | 9 |  | 11* | 8 | 3 | 4 | 6 |  | 12 | 10 |  |  | 10 |
| 1 | 2 |  | 6 | 5 |  | 7 |  | 9 | 10 | 11 | 8 | 3 | 4 |  |  |  |  |  |  | 11 |
| 1 | 2 |  | 6 | 5 |  | 7 |  | 9 | 10 | 11 | 8 | 3 | 4 |  |  |  |  |  |  | 12 |
| 1 | 2 |  | 6 | 5 |  | 7 | 11 | 9 | 10 |  | 8 | 3 | 4 |  |  |  |  |  |  | 13 |
| 1 | 2 |  | 6 | 5 |  | 7 | 11 | 9 | 10* |  | 8 | 3 | 4 |  |  | 12 |  |  |  | 14 |
| 1 | 2 | 3 | 6 | 5 |  | 7 |  | 9 | 10 | 11 | 8 |  | 4 |  |  |  |  |  |  | 15 |
| 1 | 2 | 3 | 6 | 5 |  | 7 | 12 | 9 | 10* | 11 | 8 |  | 4 |  |  |  |  |  |  | 16 |
| 1 | 2 | 3 | 6 | 5 |  | 7 |  | 9 | 10 | 11 | 8 |  | 4 |  |  |  |  |  |  | 17 |
| 1 | 2 | 3 | 6 | 5 |  | 7 |  | 9 | 10* | 11 | 8 |  | 4 |  |  | 12 |  |  |  | 18 |
| 1 |  | 3 | 6 | 5 |  | 7 | 12 | 9 |  |  | 8* |  | 4 | 2 |  |  | 10 | 11 |  | 19 |
| 1 |  |  | 6 | 5 |  | 7 |  | 9 | 10 | 11 |  | 3 | 4 | 2 |  |  |  | 8 |  | 20 |
| 1 |  |  | 6 | 5 |  | 7 |  | 9 | 10 |  | 8 | 3 | 4 | 2 |  |  | 11 |  |  | 21 |
| 1 |  |  | 6 | 5 |  | 7 | 12 | 9 | 10 | 11 |  | 3 | 4 | 2* |  |  |  | 8 |  | 22 |
| 1 | 2 |  | 6 | 5 |  | 7 |  | 10 | 9 |  |  | 3 | 4 |  |  |  | 11 | 8 |  | 23 |
| 1 | 2 |  | 6 | 5 |  | 7 |  | 9 | 10 |  |  | 3 | 4 |  |  |  | 11 | 8 |  | 24 |
| 1 | 2 |  | 6 | 5 |  | 7 |  | 9 | 10 |  |  | 3 | 4 | 8 |  |  | 11 |  |  | 25 |
| 1 | 2 |  | 6 | 5 |  | 7 |  | 10 | 9 |  |  | 3 | 4 | 8 |  |  | 11 |  |  | 26 |
| 1 | 2 |  | 6 | 5 |  | 7 |  | 9 | 10 |  |  | 3 | 4 |  |  |  | 11 | 8 |  | 27 |
| 1 | 2 |  | 6 | 5 |  | 7 |  | 9 | 10 |  |  | 3 | 4 |  |  |  | 11 | 8 |  | 28 |
| 1 | 2 |  | 6 | 5 |  | 7 |  | 10 | 9 |  |  | 3 | 4 |  |  |  | 11 | 8 |  | 29 |
| 1 | 2 |  | 6 | 5 |  | 7 |  | 10 | 9 |  |  | 3 | 4 |  |  |  | 11 | 8 |  | 30 |
| 1 | 2 |  | 6 | 5 |  | 7 |  | 10 | 9 | 12 |  | 3 | 4 |  |  |  | 11* | 8 |  | 31 |
| 1 | 2 |  | 6 | 5 |  | 7 |  | 10 | 9 |  |  | 3 | 4 |  |  |  | 11 | 8 |  | 32 |
| 1 | 2 |  | 6 | 5 |  | 7 |  | 10 | 9 |  |  | 3 | 4 |  |  |  | 11 | 8 |  | 33 |
| 1 | 2* |  | 6 | 5 |  | 7 |  | 10 | 9 | 12 |  | 3 | 4 |  |  |  | 11 | 8 |  | 34 |
| 1 | 2 |  | 6 | 5 |  | 7 |  | 10 | 9 | 11* |  | 3 | 12 |  |  |  | 4 | 8 |  | 35 |
| 1 | 2 |  | 6 | 5 |  | 7 |  | 10 | 9* |  |  | 3 | 4 | 12 |  |  | 11 | 8 |  | 36 |
| 1 |  |  | 6 | 5 |  | 7 |  | 10 | 9 |  |  | 3 | 4* | 2 |  | 12 | 11 | 8 |  | 37 |
| 1 |  |  | 6 | 5 |  | 7 |  | 10 | 9 |  |  | 3 | 4* | 2 |  | 12 | 11 | 8 |  | 38 |
| 1 |  |  | 6 | 5 |  | 7 |  | 10 | 9 |  |  | 3 | 4 | 2 |  |  | 11 | 8 |  | 39 |
| 1 | 2 |  | 6 | 5 |  | 7 |  | 10 | 9 |  |  | 3 | 4 |  |  |  | 11 | 8 |  | 40 |
|  | 2 |  | 6 | 5 |  | 7 | 10 | 9 |  | 12 |  | 3 | 4* |  |  |  | 11 | 8 | 1 | 41 |
|  | 2 |  | 6 | 5 |  | 7 | 10 | 9 |  |  |  | 3 | 4 |  |  |  | 11 | 8 | 1 | 42 |
| 40 | 35 | 9 | 41 | 42 | 6 | 42 | 21 | 40 | 26 | 16 | 16 | 33 | 25 | 23 | — | 3 | 21 | 21 | 2 | |

```
                +                + + +              + + +
                4s               2s 1s 6s           1s 2s 5s
```

## ROTHERHAM UNITED

| | Ht | Wt | Birthplace | Clubs | League App. | League Gls |
|---|---|---|---|---|---|---|
| **Goalkeepers** | | | | | | |
| Ray Mountford | 6 3 | 12 7 | Mexborough | Manchester U | — | — |
| | | | | Notts Co (on loan) | — | — |
| | | | | Rotherham U | 99 | — |
| Robert Mimms | 6 4 | 12 4 | York | Halifax T | — | — |
| | | | | Rotherham U | 2 | — |
| **Defenders** | | | | | | |
| John Breckin | 5 9½ | 11 9 | Rotherham | Rotherham U | 394 | 8 |
| | | | | Darlington (on loan) | 4 | — |
| Gerald Forrest | 5 11 | 10 7 | Stockton | Rotherham U | 212 | 7 |
| John Green | 5 10 | 12 1 | Rotherham | Rotherham U | 211 | 7 |
| Paul Stancliffe | 6 0 | 11 10 | Sheffield | Rotherham U | 272 | 7 |
| Ashley Taylor | 5 10 | 10 4 | Conisborough | Rotherham U | 22 | — |
| Jimmy Mullen | 5 10½ | 11 12½ | Jarrow | Sheffield W | 230 | 10 |
| | | | | Rotherham U | 49 | 1 |
| | | | | Preston NE (on loan) | 1 | — |
| | | | | Cardiff C (on loan) | 12 | 1 |
| Emlyn Hughes | 5 10 | 12 6 | Barrow-in- | Blackpool | 28 | — |
| (England) | | | Furness | Liverpool | 474 | 35 |
| | | | | Wolverhampton W | 58 | 2 |
| | | | | Rotherham U | 24 | 2 |
| **Midfield** | | | | | | |
| Mark Rhodes | 5 9 | 10 11 | Sheffield | Rotherham U | 202 | 11 |
| Peter Carr | 5 9 | 9 12½ | Rawmarsh | Rotherham U | 36 | 3 |
| Phil Henson | 5 10 | 9 12 | Manchester | Manchester C | 17 | — |
| | | | | Swansea C (on loan) | 1 | — |
| | | | | Sheffield W | 72 | 9 |
| | | | | Stockport Co | 67 | 13 |
| | | | | Rotherham U | 68 | 7 |
| Billy McEwan | 5 10 | 11 2 | Cleland | Hibernian | 61 | 2 |
| | | | | Blackpool | 4 | — |
| | | | | Brighton | 27 | 3 |
| | | | | Chesterfield | 80 | 7 |
| | | | | Mansfield T | 32 | 3 |
| | | | | Peterborough U | 63 | 3 |
| | | | | Rotherham U | 53 | 10 |
| Tony Towner | 5 6 | 10 0 | Brighton | Brighton | 162 | 24 |
| | | | | Millwall | 68 | 13 |
| | | | | Rotherham U | 78 | 11 |
| John Seasman | 5 9 | 11 3 | Liverpool | Tranmere R | 17 | — |
| | | | | Luton T | 8 | 2 |
| | | | | Millwall | 158 | 36 |
| | | | | Rotherham U | 59 | 16 |
| Chris Waller* | | | Wath | Rotherham U | — | — |
| Gerry Gow | 5 8 | 10 8 | Glasgow | Bristol C | 375 | 47 |
| | | | | Manchester C | 26 | 5 |
| | | | | Rotherham U | 21 | 1 |
| **Forwards** | | | | | | |
| Richard Finney | 5 7 | 10 4 | Rotherham | Rotherham U | 236 | 67 |
| (Contract cancelled Feb 1982) | | | | | | |
| Ian Vaughan | 5 10 | 10 0 | Rotherham | Rotherham U | 4 | — |
| | | | | Stockport Co (on loan) | 2 | 1 |
| Rodney Fern | 5 11 | 11 0 | Burton | Leicester C | 149 | 31 |
| | | | | Luton T | 39 | 5 |
| | | | | Chesterfield | 152 | 54 |
| | | | | Rotherham U | 93 | 29 |
| Ian Porterfield | 5 11 | 12 8 | Dunfermline | Raith R | 117 | 17 |
| (Contract cancelled Aug 1981) | | | | Sunderland | 228 | 17 |
| | | | | Reading (on loan) | 5 | — |
| | | | | Sheffield W | 106 | 3 |
| | | | | Rotherham U | — | — |
| Steve Fleetwood | 5 10½ | 10 0 | Sheffield | Rotherham U | — | — |
| Mick Gooding | 5 7 | 10 7½ | Newcastle | Bishop Auckland | (not known) | |
| | | | | Rotherham U | 93 | 8 |
| Ronnie Moore | 6 0 | 12 13½ | Liverpool | Tranmere R | 249 | 72 |
| | | | | Cardiff C | 56 | 6 |
| | | | | Rotherham U | 85 | 45 |
| Ian Alexander | | | Glasgow | Rotherham U | 8 | — |

# SCUNTHORPE UNITED
# Division 4

*President:* Sir Reginald Sheffield, Bt.   *Chairman:* D. J. Wraith.

*Vice-Chairman:* J. T. Empson.

*Directors:* T. E. Belton, G. J. Alston, C. Plumtree.

*Player-Manager:* John Duncan.

*Secretary:* A. D. Rowing.

*Year Formed:* 1904.   *Turned Professional:* 1912.

*Limited Company:* 1912.

*Previous Name:* Amalgamated with Lindsey United to become Scunthorpe United, 1910.

**Football League Record:**
1950 Elected to Division 3(N); 1958–64 Division 2; 1964–68 Division 3; 1968–72 Division 4; 1972–73 Division 3; 1973– Division 4.

**Honours:** *Football League:* Division 2 best season: 4th, 1961–62; Division 3(N) – Champions 1957–58. *FA Cup* best season: 5th rd, 1957–58, 1969–70. *Football League Cup:* never past 3rd rd.

*Record Victory:* 9-0 v Boston U, FA Cup 1st rd, 21 Nov, 1953.

*Record Defeat:* 0-8 v Carlisle U, Division 3(N), 25 Dec, 1952.

*Most League Points:* 66, Division 3(N), 1957–58.

*Most League Goals:* 88, Division 3(N), 1957–58.

*Highest League Scorer in Season:* Barrie Thomas, 31, Division 2, 1961–62.

*Most League Goals in Total Aggregate:* Barrie Thomas, 92, 1959–62, 1964–66.

*Most Capped Player:* None.

*Most League Appearances:* Jack Brownsword, 600, 1950–65.

*Record Transfer Fee Received:* £60,000 from Grimsby T for Kevin Kilmore, Sept 1979.

*Record Transfer Fee Paid:* £25,000 to Notts Co for Rick Green, Aug 1979.

*Previous Managers since the War:* Leslie Jones, Bill Corkhill, Ron Suart, Tony McShane, Bill Lambton (3 days, shortest ever term of office), Frank Soo, Dick Duckworth, Freddie Goodwin, Ron Ashman, Ron Bradley, Dickie Rooks, Ron Ashman.

*Address of Supporters Club:* Scunthorpe U Official Supporters Club, c/o Old Show Ground, Scunthorpe.

---

**Old Show Ground, Scunthorpe, South Humberside.** Telephone Scunthorpe 842954/848077. *Ground capacity:* 25,000. *Record attendance:* 23, 935 v Portsmouth, FA Cup 4th rd, 30 Jan, 1954. *Record receipts:* £7895 v Newcastle U, FA Cup 4th rd replay, 30 Jan, 1974. *Pitch measurements:* 112yd×78yd.

*How to get there:* Several buses run near the ground. Nearest railway station is Scunthorpe. By road along M180, A18 from Doncaster via Berkeley Circle, Doncaster Road Hill, and Henderson Avenue; M180 and A18 from Grimsby; A15 from Lincoln via Queensway Circle, Ashby Road, Station Roundabout, Church Lane, Exeter Road, and Doncaster Road; via A1 on A638 to Retford, A620 to Gainsborough, A159 to Scunthorpe.

*Match tickets:* Tickets are bookable up to the day of the match unless advertised otherwise in the local press. No telephone bookings accepted.

*Car parking:* Club car park adjoining the ground holds 40–50 cars. Ample street parking around the ground.

*Entertainments/catering facilities:* Hot and cold refreshments served on first-team match days from various points around the ground. Sportsmans Bar due to open in 1982–83. The 1500 Club at north-west corner of ground enables members to watch matches in comfort.

*Club shop:* Sports and Leisure Shop adjoining ground sells all types of sportswear, souvenirs, lottery tickets and programmes.

*Handbooks/programmes:* Handbook, current and past programmes available at Sports and Leisure Shop at ground. Postal enquiries must enclose sae.

*Club Colours:* Sky blue shirts with claret 'V'and claret markings, sky blue shorts, sky blue stockings with claret markings.

*Change Colours:* Yellow with green 'V' and markings.

*Club Captain:* Bob Oates.   *Club Coach:* Phil McLoughlin.

*Groundsman:* Ron Barnes.

*Club Nickname:* The Iron.

## SCUNTHORPE UNITED 1981–82 LEAGUE RECORD

| Match No. | Date | Venue | Opponents | Result | H/T Score | Goalscorers | Attendance |
|---|---|---|---|---|---|---|---|
| 1 | Aug 29 | A | Northampton T | D 1-1 | 0-1 | Green | 2064 |
| 2 | Sept 5 | H | Blackpool | D 1-1 | 0-0 | Oates | 2200 |
| 3 | 12 | A | Torquay U | L 0-1 | 0-0 | | 2033 |
| 4 | 19 | H | Tranmere R | W 2-1 | 0-0 | Cowling, Moss | 1592 |
| 5 | 22 | H | Hartlepool U | W 2-1 | 1-1 | Oates, Moss | 1998 |
| 6 | 26 | A | Sheffield U | L 0-1 | 0-1 | | 11,687 |
| 7 | 29 | A | Bury | L 0-4 | 0-1 | | 2684 |
| 8 | Oct 3 | H | Bradford C | L 1-3 | 1-1 | Grimes | 3229 |
| 9 | 10 | A | Crewe Alex | L 0-3 | 0-2 | | 1586 |
| 10 | 17 | H | Hereford U | D 2-2 | 1-0 | Grimes, Moss | 1499 |
| 11 | 20 | H | Hull C | D 4-4 | 1-2 | Stewart, Green, Partridge 2 (2 pens) | 3575 |
| 12 | 24 | A | Wigan Ath | L 1-2 | 1-2 | Devries | 4553 |
| 13 | 31 | H | Peterborough U | L 0-1 | 0-0 | | 2004 |
| 14 | Nov 3 | A | AFC Bournemouth | L 0-2 | 0-0 | | 5032 |
| 15 | 7 | H | York C | L 0-3 | 0-2 | | 1622 |
| 16 | 13 | A | Colchester U | L 1-2 | 1-1 | Stewart | 3838 |
| 17 | 28 | A | Halifax T | W 2-1 | 1-1 | Cowling, Moss | 1396 |
| 18 | Dec 5 | H | Port Vale | D 0-0 | 0-0 | | 1902 |
| 19 | Jan 9 | A | Blackpool | L 0-2 | 0-0 | | 4136 |
| 20 | 23 | H | Northampton T | W 2-1 | 2-0 | Stewart, Telfer | 1439 |
| 21 | 30 | A | Tranmere R | W 1-0 | 1-0 | Green | 1520 |
| 22 | Feb 2 | H | Mansfield T | W 1-0 | 0-0 | Dall | 2099 |
| 23 | 6 | H | Torquay U | L 0-2 | 0-1 | | 1802 |
| 24 | 10 | A | Hartlepool U | D 3-3 | 2-1 | Telfer, Stewart, Moss (pen) | 2001 |
| 25 | 14 | A | Bradford C | D 0-0 | 0-0 | | 5103 |
| 26 | 17 | A | Darlington | L 1-4 | 1-1 | Stewart | 1663 |
| 27 | 20 | H | Sheffield U | W 2-1 | 1-0 | Moss, Telfer | 8105 |
| 28 | 28 | H | Crewe Alex | L 0-1 | 0-0 | | 2591 |
| 29 | Mar 6 | A | Hereford U | L 1-2 | 1-1 | Dall | 2159 |
| 30 | 9 | A | Hull C | L 0-2 | 0-2 | | 6121 |
| 31 | 12 | H | Wigan Ath | L 2-7 | 0-3 | Telfer 2 | 2511 |
| 32 | 16 | H | AFC Bournemouth | L 0-2 | 0-0 | | 1441 |
| 33 | 20 | A | Peterborough U | L 1-2 | 0-1 | Stewart | 4785 |
| 34 | 23 | H | Aldershot | D 1-1 | 0-1 | Telfer | 1658 |
| 35 | 26 | A | York C | L 1-3 | 0-1 | Arins | 2189 |
| 36 | 30 | H | Stockport Co | D 0-0 | 0-0 | | 1815 |
| 37 | Apr 2 | H | Colchester U | W 2-1 | 1-0 | Moss Telfer | 1762 |
| 38 | 10 | H | Rochdale | W 1-0 | 0-0 | Keeley (pen) | 1742 |
| 39 | 13 | A | Mansfield T | D 1-1 | 1-1 | Cowling | 2202 |
| 40 | 17 | A | Port Vale | L 1-2 | 1-0 | Cammack | 2507 |
| 41 | 20 | A | Rochdale | D 1-1 | 0-0 | Telfer | 1129 |
| 42 | 24 | H | Halifax T | D 0-0 | 0-0 | | 1643 |
| 43 | May 1 | A | Aldershot | L 0-4 | 0-4 | | 1304 |
| 44 | 4 | H | Bury | D 2-2 | 1-1 | Telfer, Cammack | 1106 |
| 45 | 8 | H | Darlington | D 1-1 | 0-1 | Cammack | 1274 |
| 46 | 14 | A | Stockport Co | D 1-1 | 1-0 | Cowling | 1945 |

**Final League Position: 23**

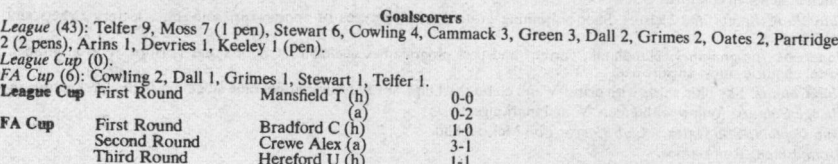

**Goalscorers**

*League* (43): Telfer 9, Moss 7 (1 pen), Stewart 6, Cowling 4, Cammack 3, Green 3, Dall 2, Grimes 2, Oates 2, Partridge 2 (2 pens), Arins 1, Devries 1, Keeley 1 (pen).
*League Cup* (0).
*FA Cup* (6): Cowling 2, Dall 1, Grimes 1, Stewart 1, Telfer 1.

| League Cup | First Round | Mansfield T (h) | 0-0 |
|---|---|---|---|
| | | (a) | 0-2 |
| FA Cup | First Round | Bradford C (h) | 1-0 |
| | Second Round | Crewe Alex (a) | 3-1 |
| | Third Round | Hereford U (h) | 1-1 |
| | | (a) | 1-4 |

| Neenan | Davy | Partridge | Keeley | Dall | Oates | Grimes | Green | O'Berg | Stewart | Pilling | Duffy | Lambert | Gowling | Hughes | Moss | Devries | Arins | Telfer | Pointon | Johnson | Duncan | Botham | Boyd | Thompson | Goodlass | Hamill | Cammack | Walker | Match No. |
|---|---|---|---|---|---|---|---|---|---|---|---|---|---|---|---|---|---|---|---|---|---|---|---|---|---|---|---|---|---|
| 1 | 2 | 3 | 4 | 5 | 6 | 7 | 9 | 10* | 11 | 12 |  |  |  | 8 |  |  |  |  |  |  |  |  |  |  |  |  |  |  | 1 |
| 1 | 2 | 12 | 4 | 5 | 6 | 7 | 9 |  | 11 | 3 | 10* |  |  | 8 |  |  |  |  |  |  |  |  |  |  |  |  |  |  | 2 |
| 1 | 2 | 8 | 4 | 5 | 6 | 7 | 9 |  | 11 |  | 10 | 3* | 12 |  |  |  |  |  |  |  |  |  |  |  |  |  |  |  | 3 |
| 1 | 2 |  | 4 | 5 | 6 | 7 | 9 |  | 11 |  |  |  | 8 | 3 | 10 |  |  |  |  |  |  |  |  |  |  |  |  |  | 4 |
| 1 | 2 |  | 4 | 5 | 6 | 7 | 9* | 12 | 11 |  |  |  | 8 | 3 | 10 |  |  |  |  |  |  |  |  |  |  |  |  |  | 5 |
| 1 | 2 |  | 4 | 5* | 6 | 7 | 9 |  | 11 |  |  | 12 | 8 | 3 | 10 |  |  |  |  |  |  |  |  |  |  |  |  |  | 6 |
| 1 | 2 | 12 | 4 | 5* | 6 | 7 | 9 |  | 11 |  |  |  | 8 | 3 | 10 |  |  |  |  |  |  |  |  |  |  |  |  |  | 7 |
| 1 | 2 | 12 | 4 | 5 | 6 | 7 | 9 |  | 11 |  |  |  | 8 | 3* | 10 |  |  |  |  |  |  |  |  |  |  |  |  |  | 8 |
| 1 | 8 | 2 | 4 | 5* | 6 | 7 | 9 |  | 11 |  |  | 12 |  |  | 10 | 3 |  |  |  |  |  |  |  |  |  |  |  |  | 9 |
| 1 |  | 2 | 4 |  | 6 | 7 | 9 | 8 | 11 |  |  | 5 |  |  | 10 | 3 |  |  |  |  |  |  |  |  |  |  |  |  | 10 |
| 1 | 12 | 2 | 4 |  | 6 | 7 | 9 | 8 | 11 |  |  | 5* |  |  | 10 | 3 |  |  |  |  |  |  |  |  |  |  |  |  | 11 |
| 1 | 2* | 8 | 4 |  | 6 | 7 | 9 |  | 11 |  |  | 5 |  |  | 10 | 3 |  |  |  |  |  |  |  |  |  |  |  |  | 12 |
| 1 |  | 8 | 4 |  | 6 | 7 | 9* |  | 11 |  |  | 12 | 2 | 5 | 10 | 3 |  |  |  |  |  |  |  |  |  |  |  |  | 13 |
| 1 |  | 8 | 4 |  | 6 | 7 | 9* |  | 11 | 10 | 12 |  | 2 | 5 |  | 3 |  |  |  |  |  |  |  |  |  |  |  |  | 14 |
| 1 | 3 | 8 | 4 |  | 6 | 7 | 9 |  | 11 |  |  |  | 2 | 5 | 10 |  |  |  |  |  |  |  |  |  |  |  |  |  | 15 |
| 1 |  | 5 | 4 |  | 6 | 7 | 9* | 8 | 11 | 3 |  | 12 | 2 | 2 | 10 |  |  |  |  |  |  |  |  |  |  |  |  |  | 16 |
| 1 | 2 |  | 4 |  | 6 | 7 |  | 8 | 11 | 3 |  |  | 9 |  | 10 |  | 5 |  |  |  |  |  |  |  |  |  |  |  | 17 |
| 1 | 2 |  | 4 |  | 6 |  |  | 8 | 11* | 3 |  | 7 | 9 |  | 10 |  | 5 | 12 |  |  |  |  |  |  |  |  |  |  | 18 |
| 1 | 2* |  | 4 | 5 | 6 |  |  |  | 11 | 3 | 8 |  | 9 | 12 | 10 |  | 7 |  |  |  |  |  |  |  |  |  |  |  | 19 |
| 1 |  |  | 4 | 5 | 6 |  |  | 8 | 11 | 3 |  |  | 9 | 2 | 10 |  | 7 |  |  |  |  |  |  |  |  |  |  |  | 20 |
| 1 | 12 |  | 4 | 5 | 6 |  |  | 9 | 11* | 3 |  | 8 | 2 |  | 10 |  | 7 |  |  |  |  |  |  |  |  |  |  |  | 21 |
| 1 |  |  | 4 | 5 | 6 |  |  | 9 | 11 | 3 |  | 8 | 2 |  | 10 |  | 7 |  |  |  |  |  |  |  |  |  |  |  | 22 |
| 1 |  |  | 4 | 5 | 6 |  |  | 9* | 11 |  |  | 7 | 12 |  | 10 |  | 2 | 8 | 3 |  |  |  |  |  |  |  |  |  | 23 |
| 1 |  |  | 4 | 5 | 6 |  |  | 9 | 11 | 3 |  | 7 | 12 |  | 10 |  | 2* | 8 |  |  |  |  |  |  |  |  |  |  | 24 |
|  | 2 |  | 4 | 5 | 6 |  |  | 9 | 11 | 3 |  | 7 |  |  | 10 |  |  | 8 |  | 1 |  |  |  |  |  |  |  |  | 25 |
|  | 2 |  | 4 |  | 6 |  |  | 9 | 11 | 3* |  | 7 | 12 |  | 10 |  | 5 | 8 |  | 1 |  |  |  |  |  |  |  |  | 26 |
| 1 | 2 |  |  | 5 | 6 |  |  | 9 | 11 | 3 |  | 7 |  |  | 10 |  | 4 | 8 |  |  |  |  |  |  |  |  |  |  | 27 |
| 1 | 2 |  | 4 | 5 | 6 |  |  | 9 | 11 | 3* |  |  |  |  | 10 |  | 7 | 8 | 12 |  |  |  |  |  |  |  |  |  | 28 |
| 1 |  |  | 4 | 5 | 6 |  |  | 9 | 11 | 3 |  |  | 2 |  | 10 |  | 7 | 8 |  |  |  |  |  |  |  |  |  |  | 29 |
| 1 | 2* |  | 4 | 5 | 6 |  |  |  | 11 | 3 |  | 12 | 9 |  | 10 |  | 7 | 8 |  |  |  |  |  |  |  |  |  |  | 30 |
| 1 | 12 |  | 4 | 5 | 6 |  |  |  |  | 3 |  | 2* |  |  | 10 |  | 7 | 8 | 11 |  |  | 9 |  |  |  |  |  |  | 31 |
| 1 | 3 |  | 4 | 5 | 6 |  |  |  | 11 |  |  | 2 |  |  | 10 |  | 7 | 8 |  |  |  | 9 |  |  |  |  |  |  | 32 |
| 1 | 2 |  | 4 | 5 | 6 |  |  |  | 12 |  |  | 3 | 11* |  | 10 |  | 7 | 8 |  |  |  | 9 |  |  |  |  |  |  | 33 |
| 1 | 2 |  |  | 5 | 6 |  |  |  | 11 |  |  | 3 |  |  | 10 |  | 7 | 8 |  |  |  | 9 | 4 |  |  |  |  |  | 34 |
| 1 |  |  | 4 | 5 | 6 |  |  |  |  |  |  |  |  |  | 10 |  | 2 | 8 |  |  |  |  | 7 | 3 | 11 |  | 9 |  | 35 |
| 1 | 3 |  |  |  | 6 |  |  |  |  |  |  |  |  |  | 10 |  | 2 | 8 |  |  |  |  | 4 | 5 | 11 | 7 | 9 |  | 36 |
| 1 | 3 |  |  |  | 6 | 7 |  |  |  |  |  |  |  |  | 10 |  | 2 | 8 |  |  |  |  | 4 | 5 | 11 |  | 9 |  | 37 |
| 1 | 3* | 5 |  |  |  |  | 2 |  | 7 |  |  |  | 12 |  | 10 |  |  | 8 |  |  |  |  | 4 | 6 | 11 |  | 9 |  | 38 |
| 1 | 3* | 5 |  |  |  |  | 2 |  | 7 |  |  |  | 9 |  | 10 |  | 4 | 8 |  |  |  |  |  | 6 | 11 |  |  | 12 | 39 |
| 1 |  | 5* |  |  |  |  | 2 |  |  |  |  | 3 |  |  | 10 |  | 4 | 8 |  |  |  |  | 12 | 6 | 11 | 7* | 9 |  | 40 |
| 1 | 3 |  | 2 |  |  |  |  |  |  |  |  | 5 |  |  | 10 |  | 4 | 8 |  |  |  |  |  | 6 | 11 | 7* | 9 |  | 41 |
| 1 | 3 |  | 2 |  |  | 7 |  |  |  |  |  | 5 |  |  | 10 |  |  | 8 |  |  |  | 12 | 4* | 6 | 11 |  | 9 |  | 42 |
| 1 | 7 | 3 | 2 |  |  |  |  |  |  |  |  | 9 |  |  | 10 |  |  | 8 |  |  |  | 12 | 4* | 6 | 11 |  |  | 5 | 43 |
| 1 | 2 |  | 6 |  |  | 7 |  |  | 12 | 8* |  |  | 5 |  | 10 |  | 9 |  | 3 |  |  |  | 4 |  |  |  | 11 |  | 44 |
| 1 |  | 3 | 2 |  |  |  |  |  | 12 | 7* |  |  | 5 |  | 10 |  | 8 |  | 11 |  |  |  | 4 | 6 |  |  | 9 |  | 45 |
| 1 | 11 |  | 2 |  |  |  |  |  | 12 |  |  |  | 5 |  | 10 |  | 7 | 8 | 3 |  |  |  | 4 | 6* |  |  | 9 |  | 46 |
| 44 | 25 | 10 | 42 | 28 | 37 | 34 | 18 | 7 | 37 | 17 | 3 | 13 | 23 | 17 | 42 | 6 | 20 | 28 | 5 | 2 | — | 4 | 10 | 11 | 9 | 4 | 9 | 1 |  |
| +3s | +3s |  |  |  | +3s | +3s | +1s | +4s | +2s | +3s | +4s |  |  |  |  |  | +1s |  | +3s |  |  |  | +1s |  |  |  | +1s |  |  |

## SCUNTHORPE UNITED

| | Ht | Wt | Birthplace | Clubs | League App. | League Gls |
|---|---|---|---|---|---|---|
| **Goalkeepers** | | | | | | |
| Joe Neenan | 6 3 | 11 13 | Manchester | York C | 56 | — |
| | | | | Scunthorpe U | 90 | — |
| Paul Johnson* | 5 11½ | 11 1 | Scunthorpe | Scunthorpe U | 2 | — |
| **Defenders** | | | | | | |
| Roger Devries | 5 8½ | 11 5 | Hull | Hull C | 318 | — |
| (Contract cancelled) | | | | Blackburn R | 13 | — |
| | | | | Scunthorpe U | 6 | 1 |
| Dean Walker | 5 9 | 11 0 | Newcastle | Burnley | — | — |
| (Non-contract) | | | | Barnsley | — | — |
| | | | | Scunthorpe U | 1 | — |
| Stuart Pilling | 5 9 | 10 2 | Sheffield | Hull C | — | — |
| (Contract cancelled March 1982) | | | | Scunthorpe U | 262 | 26 |
| Steve Davy* | 5 8½ | 10 2 | Norwich | Scunthorpe U | 134 | 1 |
| David Dall* | 6 3 | 12 7 | Scotland | Grantham T | (not known) | |
| | | | | Scunthorpe U | 77 | 2 |
| Bob Oates | 5 11½ | 11 7 | Leeds | Scunthorpe U | 295 | 17 |
| Alan Boxall* | 6 3¾ | 14 2 | Woolwich | Barton T | (not known) | |
| | | | | Scunthorpe U | 24 | 1 |
| Andy Keeley | 5 9¼ | 11 4 | Basildon | Tottenham H | 6 | — |
| | | | | Sheffield U | 28 | — |
| | | | | Scunthorpe U | 42 | 1 |
| Alan Thompson* | 5 11 | 12 0 | Liverpool | Sheffield W | 156 | 3 |
| | | | | Stockport Co | 94 | 17 |
| | | | | Portland T | (not known) | |
| | | | | Bradford C | 31 | — |
| | | | | Scunthorpe U | 11 | — |
| Tony Arins* | 6 0 | 11 8 | Chesterfield | Burnley | 29 | 2 |
| | | | | Leeds U | 1 | — |
| | | | | Scunthorpe U | 20 | 1 |
| **Midfield** | | | | | | |
| David Stewart* | 5 9 | 10 12 | Belfast | Hull C | 51 | 7 |
| (N Ireland) | | | | Chelsea | — | — |
| | | | | Scunthorpe U | 97 | 19 |
| Vince Grimes | 5 9½ | 11 10 | Scunthorpe | Hull C | 89 | 9 |
| | | | | Scunthorpe U | 143 | 12 |
| | | | | Bradford C (on loan) | 7 | 1 |
| Paul O'Berg | 5 5 | 9 4 | Hull | Bridlington T | (not known) | |
| | | | | Scunthorpe U | 71 | 12 |
| Ian Botham | 6 3 | 14 2 | Cheshire | Scunthorpe U | 6 | — |
| (Non-contract) | | | | | | |
| Vince Duffy | 5 6½ | 9 6 | Nottingham | Nottingham F | — | — |
| (Contract cancelled March 1982) | | | | Scunthorpe U | 8 | — |
| Anton Lambert | 6 0 | 11 7 | Nottingham | Long Eaton | (not known) | |
| (Contract cancelled March 1982) | | | | Scunthorpe U | 39 | 3 |
| Paul Moss | 5 7 | 10 2 | Birmingham | Wolverhampton W | — | — |
| | | | | Hull C | 54 | 7 |
| | | | | Scunthorpe U | 42 | 7 |
| Gordon Boyd* | 5 7 | 10 5 | Glasgow | Glasgow R | — | — |
| | | | | Fulham | 3 | — |
| | | | | Glasgow R | — | — |
| | | | | Barnsley | 2 | — |
| | | | | Scunthorpe U | 11 | — |
| Neil Pointon | 5 10 | 10 12 | Church Warsop | Scunthorpe U | 5 | — |
| (Apprentice) | | | | | | |
| **Forwards** | | | | | | |
| Malcolm Partridge | 6 0½ | 12 0 | Calow | Mansfield T | 69 | 20 |
| (Contract cancelled Feb 1982) | | | | Leicester C | 35 | 4 |
| | | | | Charlton Ath (on loan) | 2 | — |
| | | | | Grimsby T | 138 | 24 |
| | | | | Scunthorpe U | 97 | 21 |
| Steve Cammack | 5 10¼ | 11 9 | Sheffield | Sheffield U | 36 | 5 |
| | | | | Chesterfield | 113 | 21 |
| | | | | Scunthorpe U | 84 | 27 |
| | | | | Lincoln C | 18 | 6 |
| | | | | Scunthorpe U | 10 | 3 |
| Chris Cowling | 6 1½ | 11 0 | Scunthorpe | Scunthorpe U | 43 | 4 |
| Rick Green | 6 1½ | 13 2 | Scunthorpe | Scunthorpe U | 66 | 19 |
| (Contract cancelled April 1982) | | | | Chesterfield | 48 | 13 |
| | | | | Notts Co | 9 | — |
| | | | | Scunthorpe U | 71 | 19 |
| John Duncan | 5 11 | 11 4 | Lochee | Dundee | 124 | 62 |
| | | | | Tottenham H | 103 | 53 |
| | | | | Derby Co | 36 | 12 |
| | | | | Scunthorpe U | 3 | — |
| George Telfer | 5 10 | 11 5 | Liverpool | Everton | 99 | 20 |
| | | | | Scunthorpe U | 29 | 9 |
| Ronnie Goodlass* | 5 7 | 10 12 | Liverpool | Everton | 35 | 2 |
| | | | | Den Haag | (not known) | |
| | | | | Fulham | 22 | 2 |
| | | | | Scunthorpe U | 9 | — |

# SHEFFIELD UNITED Division 3

*Chairman:* R. J. Brealey.
*Directors:* A. H. Laver, A. H. Barrington, R. Wragg M INST BM.
*Manager:* Ian Porterfield.
*Secretary:* Richard Chester FAAI.
*Commercial Manager:* Derek Dooley.
*Year Formed:* 1889.  *Turned Professional:* 1889.
*Limited Company:* 1899.

**Football League Record:**
1892 Elected to Division 2; 1893–1934 Division 1; 1934–39 Division 2; 1946–49 Division 1; 1949–53 Division 2; 1953–56 Division 1; 1956–61 Division 2; 1961–68 Division 1; 1968–71 Division 2; 1971–76 Division 1; 1976–79 Division 2; 1979–81 Division 3; 1981–82 Division 4; 1982– Division 3.

**Honours:** *Football League:* Division 1 – Champions 1897–98; Runners-up 1896–97. 1899–1900; Division 2 – Champions 1952–53; Runners-up 1892–93, 1938–39, 1960–61, 1970–71; Division 4 – Champions 1981–82. *FA Cup:* Winners 1899, 1902, 1915, 1925; Runners-up 1901, 1936. *Football League Cup* best season: 5th rd, 1961–62, 1966–67.
*Record Victory:* 11-2 v Cardiff C, Division 1, 1 Jan, 1926.
*Record Defeat:* 0-13 v Bolton W, FA Cup, 2nd rd, 1 Feb, 1890.
*Most League Points:* 60, Division 2, 1952–53. *Three points win:* 96, Division 4, 1981–82.
*Most League Goals:* 102, Division 1, 1925–26.
*Highest League Scorer in Season:* Jimmy Dunne, 41, Division 1, 1930–31.
*Most League Goals in Total Aggregate:* Harry Johnson, 205, 1919–30.
*Most Capped Player:* Billy Gillespie, 25, Ireland.
*Most League Appearances:* Joe Shaw, 629, 1948–66.
*Record Transfer Fee Received:* £400,000 from Leeds U for Alex Sabella, May 1980.
*Record Transfer Fee Paid:* £160,000 to River Plate for Alex Sabella, July 1978.
*Previous Managers since the War:* Ted Davison, Reg, Freeman, Joe Mercer, John Harris, Arthur Rowley, John Harris, Ken Furphy, Jimmy Sirrel, Harry Haslam, Martin Peters.
*Address of Supporters Club:* Secretary, c/o SUFC, Bramall Lane, Sheffield S2 4SU.
*Address of the Club Shop or Boutique:* Lane Souvenir Shop, John Street, Sheffield S2 4SU.

---

**Bramall Lane Ground, Sheffield, S2 4SU.** Telephone Sheffield (0742) 738955/6/7. *Telegraphic address:* 'United, Sheffield'. *Ground capacity:* 49,000 (15,300 seats). *Record attendance:* 68,287 v Leeds U, FA Cup 5th rd, 15 Feb, 1936. *Record receipts:* £65,092 v Sheffield W, Division 3, 5 Apr, 1980. *Pitch measurements:* 117yd×75yd.
*How to get there:* Buses 34, 35, 38, 42, 45 from the central bus station. Sheffield railway station is within walking distance of the town centre.
*Match tickets:* Tickets bookable 14 days prior to the match.
*Car parking:* The ground is five minutes from car parks in the city centre. Ample parking in side-streets around Bramall Lane.
*Entertainments/catering facilities:* Numerous bars and buffets in the ground.
*Club shop:* Sells all types of souvenirs.
*Handbooks/programmes:* Mail order service available through the club shop.
*Extra information:* Lane Social Club offers lounge bars and bier keller.
*Club Colours:* Red and white striped shirts, black shorts, red and white stockings.
*Change Colours:*
*Club Nickname:* Blades.

## SHEFFIELD UNITED 1981–82 LEAGUE RECORD

| Match No. | Date | Venue | Opponents | Result | H/T Score | Goalscorers | Attendance |
|---|---|---|---|---|---|---|---|
| 1 | Aug 29 | H | Hereford U | D 2-2 | 2-0 | Neville, Matthews | 11,906 |
| 2 | Sept 5 | A | Wigan Ath | W 1-0 | 1-0 | Kenworthy | 8001 |
| 3 | 12 | H | Colchester U | W 1-0 | 1-0 | Hatton | 11,293 |
| 4 | 19 | A | Hull C | L 1-2 | 1-1 | Hatton | 7219 |
| 5 | 21 | A | Stockport Co | L 0-1 | 0-0 | | 5450 |
| 6 | 26 | H | Scunthorpe U | W 1-0 | 1-0 | Kenworthy | 11,687 |
| 7 | 29 | H | Crewe Alex | W 4-0 | 2-0 | Edwards 2, Hatton 2 | 11,512 |
| 8 | Oct 3 | A | York C | W 4-3 | 2-2 | Hatton, Kenworthy (pen), Trusson 2 | 5557 |
| 9 | 10 | A | Port Vale | W 2-0 | 1-0 | Edwards, Richardson | 7289 |
| 10 | 17 | H | Hartlepool U | D 1-1 | 0-0 | Edwards | 12,752 |
| 11 | 20 | H | Mansfield T | W 4-1 | 3-1 | Edwards 2, Trusson, Kenworthy (pen) | 12,727 |
| 12 | 24 | A | Bradford C | W 2-0 | 2-0 | Edwards, Neville | 13,711 |
| 13 | 31 | H | Blackpool | W 3-1 | 0-0 | Hatton 2, Trusson | 15,566 |
| 14 | Nov 3 | A | Northampton T | W 2-1 | 0-0 | Trusson 2 | 4168 |
| 15 | 7 | H | Tranmere R | W 2-0 | 1-0 | Edwards, Hatton | 13,454 |
| 16 | 14 | A | Torquay U | D 1-1 | 0-0 | Edwards | 4952 |
| 17 | 28 | A | AFC Bournemouth | D 0-0 | 0-0 | | 9855 |
| 18 | Dec 5 | H | Aldershot | W 2-0 | 0-0 | Kenworthy, Neville | 11,541 |
| 19 | Jan 2 | H | Halifax T | D 2-2 | 1-0 | Hatton, Kenworthy (pen) | 11,623 |
| 20 | 16 | A | Rochdale | W 1-0 | 0-0 | Edwards | 3966 |
| 21 | 26 | H | Darlington | D 0-0 | 0-0 | | 11,517 |
| 22 | 30 | H | Hull C | D 0-0 | 0-0 | | 12,612 |
| 23 | Feb 6 | A | Colchester U | L 2-5 | 1-4 | Kenworthy (pen), Edwards | 5194 |
| 24 | 9 | H | Stockport Co | W 4-0 | 1-0 | Matthews, King, Edwards 2 | 11,603 |
| 25 | 13 | H | York C | W 4-0 | 3-0 | Trusson, Edwards 2, Hatton | 12,901 |
| 26 | 17 | A | Hereford U | D 1-1 | 1-1 | Trusson | 3058 |
| 27 | 20 | A | Scunthorpe U | L 1-2 | 0-1 | Kenworthy (pen) | 8105 |
| 28 | 27 | H | Port Vale | W 2-1 | 0-1 | Kenworthy (pen), Edwards | 13,813 |
| 29 | Mar 6 | A | Hartlepool U | W 3-2 | 2-1 | Hatton, Edwards, Trusson | 4145 |
| 30 | 8 | A | Mansfield T | D 1-1 | 0-1 | Kenworthy | 8951 |
| 31 | 16 | H | Northampton T | W 7-3 | 3-0 | Edwards 3, Hatton 2, MacPhail, Neville | 15,016 |
| 32 | 20 | A | Blackpool | W 1-0 | 0-0 | Edwards | 7542 |
| 33 | 23 | H | Wigan Ath | W 1-0 | 0-0 | Edwards | 22,336 |
| 34 | 27 | A | Tranmere R | D 2-2 | 1-1 | Kenworthy 2 (2 pens) | 4661 |
| 35 | 30 | H | Bradford C | D 1-1 | 1-0 | Trusson | 24,593 |
| 36 | Apr 3 | H | Torquay U | W 4-1 | 4-0 | Matthews, Morris, Edwards, Trusson | 14,992 |
| 37 | 10 | H | Bury | D 1-1 | 0-0 | Edwards | 14,705 |
| 38 | 12 | A | Halifax T | W 5-1 | 1-1 | Kenworthy 2 (1 pen), Charles, Edwards 2 | 8077 |
| 39 | 17 | A | Aldershot | D 1-1 | 1-1 | Morris | 4100 |
| 40 | 21 | A | Peterborough U | W 4-0 | 3-0 | Edwards 2, King, Morris | 13,439 |
| 41 | 24 | H | AFC Bournemouth | D 0-0 | 0-0 | | 18,593 |
| 42 | 27 | A | Bury | D 1-1 | 0-1 | Edwards | 6650 |
| 43 | May 1 | A | Crewe Alex | W 3-2 | 1-1 | Edwards, King 2 | 6186 |
| 44 | 4 | H | Rochdale | W 3-1 | 2-1 | Hatton, Edwards 2 | 21,140 |
| 45 | 8 | H | Peterborough U | W 4-0 | 0-0 | Edwards 2, Kenworthy, Morris | 23,923 |
| 46 | 15 | A | Darlington | W 2-0 | 2-0 | Hatton, Edwards | 11,130 |

**Final League Position: 1**

**Goalscorers**

League (94): Edwards 35, Hatton 15, Kenworthy 15 (9 pens), Trusson 11, King 4, Morris 4, Neville 4, Matthews 3, Charles 1, MacPhail 1, Richardson 1.
League Cup (3): Hatton 2, Kenworthy 1 (pen).
FA Cup (2): Edwards 1, Hatton 1.

| League Cup | First Round | York C (h) | 1-0 |
|---|---|---|---|
| | | (a) | 1-1 |
| | Second Round | Arsenal (h) | 1-0 |
| | | (a) | 0-2 |
| FA Cup | First Round | Altrincham (h) | 2-2 |
| | | (a) | 0-3 |

| Waugh | Ryan | Kenworthy | Matthews | MacPhail | McAlle | Trussom | Tibbott | Neville | Hatton | Charles | Wiggan | Garner | Moore | Richardson | Edwards | Houston | Broddie | King | Morris | Casey | Conroy | Brazil | Match No. |
|---|---|---|---|---|---|---|---|---|---|---|---|---|---|---|---|---|---|---|---|---|---|---|---|
| 1 | 2 | 3 | 4* | 5 | 6 | 7 | 8 | 9 | 10 | 11 | 12 | | | | | | | | | | | | 1 |
| 1 | 2 | 3 | | 5 | 6 | 7 | 4 | 9 | 10 | 11 | 8 | | | | | | | | | | | | 2 |
| 1 | 2 | 3 | | 5 | 6 | 8 | 4 | 9 | 10 | 11 | 7 | | | | | | | | | | | | 3 |
| 1 | 2 | 3 | | 5 | 6 | 8 | | 9 | 10 | 4 | 7 | 11 | | | | | | | | | | | 4 |
| 1 | 9 | 3 | | 5 | 6 | 8 | | 7 | 10 | 4 | 12 | 11* | 2 | | | | | | | | | | 5 |
| 1 | 2 | 3 | | 5 | 6 | 8 | | 7 | 10 | 11 | | | | 4 | 9 | | | | | | | | 6 |
| 1 | 2 | 3 | | 5 | 6 | 8 | | 7 | 10 | 11 | | | | 4 | 9 | | | | | | | | 7 |
| 1 | 2 | 3 | | 5 | 6 | 8 | | 7 | 10 | 11 | | | | 4 | 9 | | | | | | | | 8 |
| 1 | 2 | | | 5 | 6 | 8 | | | 10 | 11 | | 7 | | 4 | 9 | 3 | | | | | | | 9 |
| 1 | 2 | 6 | | 5 | | 8 | | 12 | 10 | 11 | | 7* | | 4 | 9 | 3 | | | | | | | 10 |
| 1 | 2 | 6 | | 5 | | 8 | | 7 | 10 | 11 | | | | 4 | 9 | 3 | | | | | | | 11 |
| 1 | 2 | 6 | | 5 | | 8 | | 7 | 10 | 11 | | | | 4 | 9 | 3 | | | | | | | 12 |
| 1 | 2 | 6 | | 5 | | 8 | | 7 | 10 | 11 | | | | 4 | 9 | 3 | | | | | | | 13 |
| 1 | 2 | 6 | | 5 | | 8 | | 7 | 10 | 11 | | | | 4 | 9 | 3 | | | | | | | 14 |
| 1 | 2 | 6 | | 5 | | 8 | | 7 | 10 | 11 | | | | 4 | 9 | 3 | | | | | | | 15 |
| 1 | 2* | 6 | 12 | 5 | | 8 | | 7 | 10 | 11 | | | | 4 | 9 | 3 | | | | | | | 16 |
| 1 | 2 | 6 | | 5 | | 8 | | 7 | 10 | 11 | 4 | | | | 9 | 3 | | | | | | | 17 |
| 1 | 2 | 6 | | 5* | | 8 | | 7 | 10 | 11 | 4 | | | 12 | 9 | 3 | | | | | | | 18 |
| 1 | 2 | 6 | | | | | | 7 | 10 | 11 | 3 | | | 4 | 9 | 5 | 8 | | | | | | 19 |
| 1 | | 6 | 4 | | | | | 7 | 10 | 11 | 3 | 2 | | | 9 | 5 | | 8 | | | | | 20 |
| 1 | | 6 | 4 | | | | 8 | 7 | 10 | | 3 | 2 | | | 9 | 5 | | 11 | | | | | 21 |
| 1 | | 6 | 4 | | | | 8 | 7 | 10 | | 3 | 2 | | | 9 | 5 | | 11 | | | | | 22 |
| 1 | | 6 | 4 | | | | 8 | 7 | 10 | 12 | 3 | | 2* | 9 | 5 | | | 11 | | | | | 23 |
| 1 | | 6 | 4 | 2 | | | 8 | 12 | 10* | | 3 | | | 9 | 5 | | | 11 | 7 | | | | 24 |
| 1 | | 6 | 4 | 2 | | | 8 | 12 | 10* | | 3 | | | 9 | 5 | | | 11 | 7 | | | | 25 |
| 1 | | 6 | 4 | 2 | | | 8 | 12 | 10 | | 3 | | | 9* | 5 | | | 11 | 7 | | | | 26 |
| 1 | | 6 | 4 | 2 | | | 8 | 12 | 10 | | 3* | | | 9 | 5 | | | 11 | 7 | | | | 27 |
| 1 | | 6 | 4 | | | | 8 | | 10 | | 3 | | | 9 | 5 | | | 11 | 7 | 2 | | | 28 |
| 1 | | 6 | 4 | 11 | | | 8 | | 10 | | 3 | | | 9 | 5 | | | | 7 | 2 | | | 29 |
| | | 6 | 4 | 11 | | | 8 | | 10 | | 3 | | | 9 | 5 | | | 12 | 7 | 2* | 1 | | 30 |
| 1 | | | 4* | 6 | | | 8 | | 12 | 10 | 3 | | | 9 | 5 | | | 11 | 7 | 2 | | | 31 |
| 1 | | 6 | 4 | | | | 8 | | 10 | | 3 | | | 9 | 5 | | | 11 | 7 | 2 | | | 32 |
| 1 | | 6 | 4 | | | | 8 | | 10 | | 3 | | | 9 | 5 | | | 11 | 7 | 2 | | | 33 |
| 1 | | 6 | 4 | | | | 8 | | 10 | 12 | 3 | | | 9 | 5 | | | 11 | 7 | 2* | | | 34 |
| 1 | | 6 | 4 | | | | 8 | | 10 | | 3 | | | 9 | 5 | | | 11 | 7 | 2 | | | 35 |
| 1 | | 6 | 4 | 5 | | | 8* | | 12 | 10 | 3 | | | 9 | | | | 11 | 7 | 2 | | | 36 |
| 1 | | 6 | 4 | 5 | | | 8 | | 10 | 11 | 3 | | | 9 | | | | | 7 | 2 | | | 37 |
| 1 | | 6 | 4 | 5 | | | 8 | | 10 | 11 | 3 | | | 9 | | | | | 7 | 2 | | | 38 |
| 1 | | 6 | 4* | 5 | | | 8 | | 12 | 10 | 11 | 3 | | | 9 | | | | 7 | 2 | | | 39 |
| 1 | | 6 | | 5 | | | 8 | | 10 | 4 | 3 | | 2 | | 9 | | | 11 | 7 | | | | 40 |
| 1 | | 6 | | 5 | | | 8 | | 10 | 4 | 3 | | 2 | | 9 | | | 11 | 7 | | | | 41 |
| 1 | | 6 | | 5 | | | 8 | | 10 | 4* | 3 | | 2 | | 9 | | | 11 | 7 | | 12 | | 42 |
| 1 | | 6 | | 5 | | | 8 | | 10 | 4 | 3 | | 2 | | 9 | | | 11 | 7 | | | | 43 |
| 1 | | 6 | 4 | 5 | | | 8 | | 10 | | 3 | | 2 | | 9 | | | 11 | 7 | | | | 44 |
| 1 | | 6 | 4 | 5 | | | 8 | | 10 | | 3 | | 2 | | 9 | | | 11 | 7 | | | | 45 |
| 1 | | 6 | 4 | 5 | | | 8 | | 10 | 2 | 3 | | | | 9 | | | 11 | 7 | | | | 46 |
| 45 | 19 | 45 | 24 | 26 | 18 | 44 | 3 | 22 | 45 | 28 | 3 | 34 | 4 | 19 | 41 | 27 | 1 | 22 | 23 | 12 | 1 | — | |
| | | | | + | | | | + | | + | + | | | + | | | | + | | | + | | |
| | | | | 1s | | | | 8s | | 2s | 2s | | | 1s | | | | 1s | | | 1s | | |

## SHEFFIELD UNITED

| | Ht | Wt | Birthplace | Clubs | League App. | League Gls |
|---|---|---|---|---|---|---|
| **Goalkeepers** | | | | | | |
| Steve Conroy | 6 0¼ | 12 2½ | Chesterfield | Sheffield U | 86 | — |
| | | | | Leeds U (on loan) | — | — |
| Keith Waugh | 6 1 | 12 0 | Sunderland | Sunderland | — | — |
| | | | | Peterborough U | 195 | — |
| | | | | Sheffield U | 45 | — |
| **Defenders** | | | | | | |
| Paul Garner | 5 8¾ | 10 8 | Doncaster | Huddersfield T | 96 | 2 |
| | | | | Sheffield U | 192 | 6 |
| Phil Jones* | 6 0½ | 12 4 | Mansfield | Sheffield U | 28 | 1 |
| Les Tibbott | 5 10 | 11 7 | Oswestry | Ipswich T | 54 | — |
| | | | | Sheffield U | 78 | 2 |
| John MacPhail | 6 0½ | 12 3 | Dundee | Dundee | 68 | — |
| | | | | Sheffield U | 124 | 7 |
| John Matthews | 6 0 | 12 6 | London | Arsenal | 45 | 2 |
| | | | | Sheffield U | 103 | 14 |
| Tony Moore | 5 9 | 10 12 | Burton | Burton A | (not known) | |
| (Contract cancelled April 1982) | | | | Sheffield U | 29 | — |
| Tony Kenworthy | 5 10 | 10 7 | Leeds | Sheffield U | 223 | 30 |
| John Burke | 5 7 | 10 8 | Motherwell | Motherwell | — | — |
| | | | | Sheffield U | — | — |
| Stuart Houston | 5 11 | 12 3 | Dunoon | Chelsea | 9 | — |
| (Scotland) | | | | Brentford | 77 | 9 |
| | | | | Manchester U | 205 | 13 |
| | | | | Sheffield U | 59 | — |
| Peter Moore* | | | | Sheffield U | — | — |
| Geoff Dey | | | Sheffield | Sheffield U | — | — |
| Paul Casey* | 5 7 | 10 2 | Worksop | Sheffield U | 25 | 1 |
| Mike Trusson | 5 10 | 12 4 | Northolt | Plymouth Arg | 73 | 15 |
| | | | | Stoke C (on loan) | — | — |
| | | | | Sheffield U | 83 | 19 |
| **Midfield** | | | | | | |
| Steve Charles | 5 9 | 10 7 | Sheffield | Sheffield U | 75 | 8 |
| Gary Brazil | | | Tunbridge Wells | Crystal Palace | — | — |
| | | | | Sheffield U | 4 | — |
| Gary Marrow | 5 7 | 10 7 | Worksop | Sheffield U | — | — |
| (Contract cancelled March 1982) | | | | | | |
| Martin Peters | 5 11 | 12 4 | Plaistow | West Ham U | 302 | 80 |
| (England) | | | | Tottenham H | 189 | 46 |
| | | | | Norwich C | 207 | 44 |
| | | | | Sheeld U | 24 | 4 |
| Paul Richardson | 5 11 | 12 0 | Nottingham | Nottingham F | 221 | 18 |
| | | | | Chester | 28 | 2 |
| | | | | Stoke C | 127 | 10 |
| | | | | Sheffield U | 20 | 1 |
| Jeff King | 5 8 | 10 2 | Fauldhouse | Albion R | 42 | 7 |
| | | | | Derby Co | 15 | — |
| | | | | Notts Co (on loan) | 3 | — |
| | | | | Portsmouth (on loan) | 4 | — |
| | | | | Walsall | 51 | 4 |
| | | | | Sheffield W | 57 | 5 |
| | | | | Sheffield U | 23 | 4 |
| **Forwards** | | | | | | |
| Pedro Verde | 5 11 | 12 2 | Buenos Aires | Hercules | (not known) | |
| (Contract cancelled July 1981) | | | | Sheffield U | 10 | 3 |
| Mark Smith | 5 9 | 12 0 | Sheffield | Sheffield U | — | — |
| (Contract cancelled March 1982) | | | | | | |
| Trenton Wiggan* | | | West Indies | Sheffield U | 24 | 3 |
| Bob Hatton | 5 11 | 12 10 | Hull | Wolverhampton W | 10 | 7 |
| | | | | Bolton W | 28 | 2 |
| | | | | Northampton T | 33 | 8 |
| | | | | Carlisle U | 93 | 38 |
| | | | | Birmingham C | 175 | 58 |
| | | | | Blackpool | 75 | 32 |
| | | | | Luton T | 82 | 29 |
| | | | | Sheffield U | 89 | 33 |
| Steve Neville | 5 9½ | 11 0 | Walthamstow | Southampton | 5 | 1 |
| | | | | Exeter C | 93 | 22 |
| | | | | Sheffield U | 49 | 6 |
| Colin Morris | 5 7 | 10 5½ | Blyth | Burnley | 10 | — |
| | | | | Southend U | 133 | 25 |
| | | | | Blackpool | 87 | 26 |
| | | | | Sheffield U | 23 | 4 |
| Julian Broddle | | | | Sheffield U | 1 | — |
| (Apprentice) | | | | | | |
| Keith Edwards | 5 7 | 10 3 | Stockton | Sheffield U | 70 | 29 |
| | | | | Hull C | 132 | 57 |
| | | | | Sheffield U | 41 | 35 |

# SHEFFIELD WEDNESDAY  Division 2

*Vice-Presidents:* R. R. Gunstone, S. Ashton, C. Turner.

*Chairman:* H. E. McGee.

*Vice-Chairman:* M. Sheppard JP, FCA.

*Directors:* S. L. Speight OBE, C. Woodward, K. T. Addy, E. Barron, G. K. Hulley.

*Manager:* Jack Charlton OBE.

*Secretary:* Eric England FAAI.

*Commercial Manager:* D. Woodhead.

*Year Formed:* 1867 (fifth oldest League Club).

*Turned professional:* 1887.   *Limited Company:* 1899.

*Previous Grounds:* 1867, Highfield; 1869, Myrtle Road; 1877, Sheaf House; 1887, Olive Grove; 1899, Owlerton (since 1912 known as Hillsborough). Some games were played at Endcliffe in the 1880s. Until 1895 Bramall Lane was used for some games.

**Football League Record:**
1892 Elected to Division 1; 1899–1900 Division 2; 1900–20 Division 1; 1920–26 Division 2; 1926–37 Division 1; 1937–50 Division 2; 1950–51 Division 1; 1951–52 Division 2; 1952–55 Division 1; 1955–56 Division 2; 1956–58 Division 1; 1958–59 Division 2; 1959–70 Division 1; 1970–75 Division 2; 1975–80 Division 3; 1980– Division 2.

**Honours:** *Football League:* Division 1 – Champions 1902–03, 1903–04, 1928–29, 1929–30; Runners-up 1960–61; Division 2 – Champions 1899–1900, 1925–26, 1951–52, 1955–56, 1958–59; Runners-up 1949–50; Division 3 – Runners-up 1979–80. *FA Cup:* Winners 1896, 1907, 1935; Runners-up 1890, 1966. *Football League Cup* best season: 4th rd, 1967–68, 1976–77, 1977–78. **European Competitions:** *Fairs Cup:* 1961–62, 1963–64.

*Record Victory:* 12-0 v Halliwell, FA Cup 1st rd, 17 Jan, 1891.

*Record Defeat:* 0-10 v Aston Villa, Division 1, 5 Oct, 1912.

*Most League Points:* 62, Division 2, 1958–59. *Three points win:* 70, Division 2, 1981–82.

*Most League Goals:* 106, Division 2, 1958–59.

*Highest League Scorer in Season:* Derek Dooley, 46, Division 2, 1951–52.

*Most League Goals in Total Aggregate:* Andy Wilson, 200, 1900–20.

*Most Capped Player:* Ron Springett, 33, England.

*Most League Appearances:* Andy Wilson, 502, 1900–20.

*Record Transfer Fee Received:* £120,000 from Newcastle U for Tommy Craig, Jan 1975.

*Record Transfer Fee Paid:* £100,000 to Aberdeen for Tommy Craig, May 1969, and £100,000 to Southampton for Terry Curran, March 1979.

*Previous Managers since the War:* Secretary/Manager Eric Taylor, Harry Catterick, Vic Buckingham, Alan Brown, Jack Marshall, Danny Williams, Derek Dooley, Steve Burtenshaw, Len Ashurst.

*Address of Supporters Club:* Same as Football Club.

*Address of the Club Shop or Boutique:* Owl Shop, Hillsborough, Sheffield S6 1SW.

*Club Restaurant:* Adjoining South Stand.

---

**Hillsborough, Sheffield, S6 1SW.** Telephone Sheffield 343123. Box Office: Sheffield 343122. *Telegraphic address:* 'Wednesday, Sheffield 6'. *Ground capacity:* 50,174. *Record attendance:* 72,841 v Manchester C, FA Cup 5th rd, 17 Feb, 1934. *Record receipts:* £192,162, Tottenham H v Wolverhampton W, FA Cup semi-final, 11 April, 1981 (record for FA Cup-tie other than the Final). *Pitch measurements:* 115yd×75yd.

*How to get there:* Buses 42, 53, 81, 2 from the city centre. Sheffield railway station is close to the centre.

*Match tickets:* Seats can be booked in advance in the South and North Stands. Postal applications to the Box Office not more than 21 days before the match. Tickets are offered subject to being unsold when the application is received. Remittance and SAE must be enclosed.

*Car parking:* Street parking available. Also a park at the training ground in Middlewood Road.

*Entertainments/catering facilities:* Refreshment bars in all parts of the ground.

*Club shop:* Two shops in the ground sell all types of souvenirs.

*Handbooks/programmes:* Handbooks available from the secretary. Programmes available on subscription.

*Extra information:* When Sheffield Wednesday won the First Division title in 1929–30, they finished 10 points ahead of the runners-up.

*Club Colours:* Royal blue/white striped shirts, royal blue shorts, white stockings.

*Change Colours:* Yellow shirts with blue trim, white shorts, yellow socks with blue band.

*Club Nickname:* Owls.

## SHEFFIELD WEDNESDAY 1981–82 LEAGUE RECORD

| Match No. | Date | Venue | Opponents | Result | H/T Score | Goalscorers | Attendance |
|---|---|---|---|---|---|---|---|
| 1 | Aug 29 | A | Blackburn R | W 1-0 | 1-0 | Curran | 14,980 |
| 2 | Sept 5 | H | Crystal Palace | W 1-0 | 0-0 | Bannister | 18,476 |
| 3 | 8 | H | Rotherham U | W 2-0 | 1-0 | Williamson, McCulloch | 26,826 |
| 4 | 12 | A | Luton T | W 3-0 | 0-0 | McCulloch, Megson, Bannister | 12,131 |
| 5 | 19 | H | Derby Co | D 1-1 | 0-1 | Megson | 23,764 |
| 6 | 22 | A | Barnsley | L 0-1 | 0-1 | | 28,870 |
| 7 | 26 | A | Grimsby T | W 1-0 | 0-0 | Curran | 13,110 |
| 8 | Oct 3 | H | Wrexham | L 0-3 | 0-1 | | 18,526 |
| 9 | 10 | H | Cardiff C | W 2-1 | 0-1 | Taylor, McCulloch | 15,621 |
| 10 | 17 | A | Charlton Ath | L 0-3 | 0-2 | | 8258 |
| 11 | 24 | H | Oldham Ath | W 2-1 | 0-0 | Bannister, Peter Shirtliff | 17,839 |
| 12 | 31 | A | Leicester C | D 0-0 | 0-0 | | 19,125 |
| 13 | Nov 7 | A | Orient | L 0-3 | 0-1 | | 5179 |
| 14 | 14 | H | QPR | L 1-3 | 0-2 | Bannister | 17,024 |
| 15 | 21 | A | Cambridge U | W 2-1 | 0-1 | McCulloch (pen), Bannister | 6461 |
| 16 | 24 | H | Barnsley | D 2-2 | 0-1 | McCulloch, Taylor | 30,621 |
| 17 | 28 | H | Watford | W 3-1 | 2-0 | Pearson, Bannister, Taylor | 15,990 |
| 18 | Dec 5 | A | Chelsea | L 1-2 | 0-1 | Bannister | 17,033 |
| 19 | Jan 16 | H | Blackburn R | D 2-2 | 2-0 | McCulloch, Megson | 13,120 |
| 20 | 19 | A | Crystal Palace | W 2-1 | 1-1 | Bannister, Pickering | 8289 |
| 21 | 30 | A | Derby Co | L 1-3 | 1-0 | Bannister | 11,215 |
| 22 | Feb 3 | A | Norwich C | W 3-2 | 1-1 | Bannister 2, Peter Shirtliff | 15,767 |
| 23 | 6 | H | Luton T | D 3-3 | 1-1 | Pearson 2, Bannister | 18,012 |
| 24 | 13 | A | Wrexham | W 1-0 | 0-0 | Bannister | 4907 |
| 25 | 16 | H | Bolton W | L 0-1 | 0-0 | | 16,555 |
| 26 | 20 | H | Grimsby T | D 1-1 | 1-1 | Bannister (pen) | 14,654 |
| 27 | 24 | A | Newcastle U | L 0-1 | 0-1 | | 18,967 |
| 28 | 27 | A | Cardiff C | W 2-0 | 2-0 | Bannister (pen), Taylor | 5674 |
| 29 | Mar 2 | H | Shrewsbury T | D 0-0 | 0-0 | | 13,254 |
| 30 | 6 | H | Charlton Ath | D 1-1 | 1-1 | Taylor | 12,853 |
| 31 | 13 | A | Oldham Ath | W 3-0 | 1-0 | Pearson, Megson, Bannister | 9027 |
| 32 | 20 | H | Leicester C | W 2-0 | 0-0 | Bannister, Pearson | 18,962 |
| 33 | 27 | H | Orient | W 2-0 | 0-0 | Taylor, Megson | 16,460 |
| 34 | 29 | A | QPR | L 0-2 | 0-1 | | 11,710 |
| 35 | Apr 10 | A | Shrewsbury T | W 1-0 | 0-0 | Bannister | 8103 |
| 36 | 12 | H | Newcastle U | W 2-1 | 2-1 | Shelton, Pearson | 29,917 |
| 37 | 17 | H | Cambridge U | W 2-1 | 1-0 | Taylor, Pearson | 18,314 |
| 38 | 24 | A | Watford | L 0-4 | 0-4 | | 23,987 |
| 39 | May 1 | H | Chelsea | D 0-0 | 0-0 | | 19,259 |
| 40 | 4 | A | Rotherham U | D 2-2 | 1-1 | Bannister 2 | 20,513 |
| 41 | 8 | A | Bolton W | L 1-3 | 1-1 | Curran | 13,656 |
| 42 | 15 | H | Norwich C | W 2-1 | 0-0 | McCulloch, Bannister | 24,687 |

**Final League Position: 4**

**Goalscorers**

*League* (55): Bannister 21 (2 pens), McCulloch 7 (1 pen), Pearson 7, Taylor 7, Megson 5, Curran 3, Peter Shirtliff 2, Pickering 1, Shelton 1, Williamson 1.
*League Cup* (2): Bannister 1, Taylor 1.
*FA Cup* (1): McCulloch 1.

| | | | | |
|---|---|---|---|---|
| **League Cup** | Second Round | Blackburn R (a) | | 1-1 |
| | | (h) | | 1-2 |
| **FA Cup** | Third Round | Coventry C (a) | | 1-3 |

| Bolder | Blackhall | Williamson | Smith | Shirtliff, Peter | Taylor | Megson | Mirocevic | Bannister | McCulloch | Curran | Sterland | Mellor | Grant | Pearson | Matthewson | Pickering | King | Leman | Hornsby | Owen | Shirtliff, Paul | Shelton | Simmons | Match No. |
|---|---|---|---|---|---|---|---|---|---|---|---|---|---|---|---|---|---|---|---|---|---|---|---|---|
| 1 | 2 | 3 | 4 | 5 | 6 | 7 | 8 | 9 | 10 | 11 | | | | | | | | | | | | | | 1 |
| 1 | 2 | 3 | 4 | 5 | 6 | 7 | 8 | 9 | 10 | 11 | | | | | | | | | | | | | | 2 |
| 1 | 2 | 3 | 4 | 5 | 6 | 7 | 8 | 9 | 10 | 11 | | | | | | | | | | | | | | 3 |
| 1 | | 3 | 4 | 5 | 6 | 7 | 8 | 9 | 10 | 11 | 2 | | | | | | | | | | | | | 4 |
| 1 | | 3 | 4 | 5 | 6 | 7 | 8* | 9 | 10 | 11 | 2 | 12 | | | | | | | | | | | | 5 |
| 1 | | 3 | 4 | | 6* | 7 | 8 | 9 | 10 | 11 | 2 | 12 | | | | | | | | | | | | 6 |
| 1 | 2 | | 4 | 5 | 6 | 7 | 8 | 9 | 10 | 11 | | | 3 | | | | | | | | | | | 7 |
| 1 | 2 | | 4 | 5 | 6* | 7 | 8 | 9 | 10 | 11 | | 12 | 3 | | | | | | | | | | | 8 |
| 1 | 2 | 3 | 4 | 5 | 6 | 7 | 8* | 9 | 10 | 11 | | | | 12 | | | | | | | | | | 9 |
| 1 | 2 | 3 | 4 | 5 | 6 | 7 | 8* | 9 | 10 | 11 | | | | 12 | | | | | | | | | | 10 |
| 1 | 2 | 3 | 4 | 5 | 6 | 7 | | 9 | 10 | 11 | 8* | | | 12 | | | | | | | | | | 11 |
| 1 | | 3 | 4 | 5 | 6 | 7 | 8 | 9 | 10 | 11 | 2 | | | | | | | | | | | | | 12 |
| 1 | | 3 | 4 | 5 | 6 | 7 | 8 | 9 | | 11 | 2 | | 10 | | | | | | | | | | | 13 |
| 1 | | 3 | | | 6 | 7 | 8* | 9 | 10 | 11 | 2 | 12 | 4 | 5 | | | | | | | | | | 14 |
| 1 | | 3 | 4 | | 6 | 7 | | 9 | 10 | 11 | 2 | | | 5 | | 8 | | | | | | | | 15 |
| 1 | | 3 | 4 | | 6 | 7 | | 9 | 10* | 11 | 2 | 12 | | 5 | | 8 | | | | | | | | 16 |
| 1 | 2 | 3 | 4 | 5 | 6 | 7 | | 9 | | 11 | | 12 | | 10* | | 8 | | | | | | | | 17 |
| 1 | | 3 | 4 | 5 | 6 | 7 | | 9 | 10* | 11 | 2 | | | | | 8 | | 12 | | | | | | 18 |
| 1 | | 6 | 5 | | 7 | 8 | 9 | 10 | | | 2 | 3 | 4 | | | | | | | 11 | | | | 19 |
| 1 | | 4 | 7 | | 8 | 9 | 10 | 2 | | | 6 | 12 | 3* | 5 | | | | | | 11 | | | | 20 |
| 1 | | 6 | 5 | | 7 | 8 | 9 | 10 | | | 2 | 3 | 4 | | | | | | | 11 | | | | 21 |
| 1 | | 3 | 6 | 5 | 7 | | 9 | 2 | 10 | 11 | | | 4 | | | 12 | | | | | 8* | | | 22 |
| 1 | | 3 | 6 | 4 | 7 | | 9 | 2 | 10 | 11* | | | | 5 | | 12 | | | | | 8 | | | 23 |
| 1 | | 3 | 6 | 5 | 7 | | 9 | 2 | 10 | 11 | | | 4 | | | | | | | | 8 | | | 24 |
| 1 | | 3 | 6 | 4 | 7* | | 9 | 2 | 10 | 11 | | | | 5 | | 12 | | | | | 8 | | | 25 |
| 1 | | 3 | 4 | 2 | 6 | 7 | 9 | | 10 | 11 | | | | 5 | | | | | | | 8 | | | 26 |
| 1 | | 3 | 4 | 2 | 6 | 7* | 9 | | 10 | 11 | | | | 5 | | 12 | | | | | 8 | | | 27 |
| 1 | | 3 | 6 | 4 | 8 | 7 | | 9 | 10 | 11 | 2 | | | 5 | | | | | | | | | | 28 |
| 1 | | 3 | 8* | 4 | 6 | 7 | | 9 | 10 | 11 | 2 | | | 5 | | 12 | | | | | | | | 29 |
| 1 | | 3 | 6* | 4 | 8 | 7 | | 9 | 10 | 11 | 2 | | | 5 | | 12 | | | | | | | | 30 |
| 1 | | 3 | 6 | 4 | 8 | 7 | | 9 | 10 | 11 | 2* | | | 5 | | 12 | | | | | | | | 31 |
| 1 | 2 | 3 | 4 | | 6 | 7 | 8 | 9 | 10* | 11 | | | | 5 | | 12 | | | | | | | | 32 |
| 1 | 2 | 3 | 4 | | 6 | 7 | 8 | 9 | | 11* | | | 10 | 5 | | | | | | | | 12 | | 33 |
| 1 | 2 | 3 | 4 | | 6 | 7 | 8* | 9 | | 11 | | | 10 | 5 | | | | | | | | 12 | | 34 |
| 1 | | 3 | 4 | | 6 | 7 | | 9 | | 11 | 2 | | 10 | 5 | | | | | | | | 8 | | 35 |
| 1 | | 3 | 4 | | 6 | 7 | | 9 | | 11 | 2 | | 10 | 5 | | | | | | | | 8 | | 36 |
| 1 | | 3 | 4 | | 6 | 7 | 8 | 9 | | 11 | 2 | | 10 | 5 | | | | | | | | | | 37 |
| 1 | | 3 | 8 | 4 | 6 | | | 9 | | 11 | 2 | | 10 | 5 | | | | | | | | 7 | | 38 |
| 1 | | 3 | 4 | | 6 | 7 | | 9 | 10 | 11 | 2* | 12 | | 5 | | | | | | | | 8 | | 39 |
| 1 | 2 | 3 | 4 | 5 | 6 | 7 | | 9 | 10 | 11 | | | | | | | | | | | | 8 | | 40 |
| 1 | 2 | | 4 | 5 | 6 | 7 | | 9 | 10 | 11 | | | 3 | | | 12 | | | | | | 8* | | 41 |
| 1 | | 3 | 4 | 5 | 6 | 7 | | 9 | 10 | 11* | 2 | | | | | | | | | | | 8 | 12 | 42 |
| 42 | 18 | 32 | 41 | 31 | 35 | 40 | 20 | 42 | 28 | 35 | 27 | 9 | 4 | 13 | 1 | 24 | 2 | 2 | — | 3 | 6 | 7 | — | |
| | | | | | | | | | | | | +1s | | +5s | | +11s | | +1s | +3s | | | +2s | +1s | |

## SHEFFIELD WEDNESDAY

| | Ht | Wt | Birthplace | Clubs | League App. | League Gls |
|---|---|---|---|---|---|---|
| **Goalkeepers** | | | | | | |
| Bob Bolder | 6 1 | 14 8 | Dover | Dover | (not known) | |
| | | | | Sheffield W | 154 | — |
| Brian Cox | 6 0 | 13 3 | Sheffield | Sheffield W | 22 | — |
| | | | | Huddersfield T (on loan) | 14 | — |
| Dave Redfern | 6 1 | 13 8 | Sheffield | Sheffield W | — | — |
| **Defenders** | | | | | | |
| Dave Grant* | 6 0 | 12 8½ | Sheffield | Sheffield W | 133 | 4 |
| Mark Smith | 6 0½ | 12 2 | Sheffield | Sheffield W | 149 | 10 |
| Ray Blackhall* | 5 10 | 11 7 | Ashington | Newcastle U | 37 | — |
| | | | | Sheffield W | 115 | 1 |
| Mike Pickering | 5 11 | 12 8 | Mirfield | Barnsley | 100 | 1 |
| | | | | Southampton | 44 | — |
| | | | | Sheffield W | 106 | 1 |
| Peter Shirtliff | 5 11 | 12 2 | Chapeltown | Sheffield W | 88 | 3 |
| Charlie Williamson | 5 10 | 11 3 | Sheffield | Sheffield W | 43 | 1 |
| Gavin Oliver | 5 11 | 13 2 | Felling | Sheffield W | 2 | — |
| Trevor Matthewson | 6 1 | 12 5 | Sheffield | Sheffield W | 2 | — |
| Jim Holton | 6 1¼ | 13 7 | Lesmahagow | WBA | — | — |
| (Scotland) | | | | Shrewsbury T | 67 | 4 |
| | | | | Manchester U | 63 | 5 |
| | | | | Sunderland | 15 | — |
| | | | | Coventry C | 91 | — |
| | | | | Sheffield W | — | — |
| **Midfield** | | | | | | |
| Dennis Leman* | 5 5 | 11 4 | Newcastle | Manchester C | 17 | 1 |
| | | | | Wrexham (on loan) | 17 | 1 |
| | | | | Sheffield W | 104 | 9 |
| Kevin Taylor | 5 8 | 11 11 | Wakefield | Sheffield W | 91 | 18 |
| Brian Hornsby | 5 8 | 11 0 | Shellford | Arsenal | 26 | 5 |
| (Contract cancelled March 1982) | | | | Shrewsbury T | 75 | 16 |
| | | | | Chester (on loan) | 4 | — |
| | | | | Sheffield W | 106 | 25 |
| Mel Sterland | 5 11 | 13 2 | Sheffield | Sheffield W | 53 | 3 |
| Paul Shirtliff | 5 5 | 8 12 | Barnsley | Sheffield W | 7 | — |
| Ante Mirocevic | 5 8 | 12 6 | Titograd | Budocnost | (not known) | |
| (Yugoslavia) | | | | Sheffield W | 45 | 5 |
| Gary Megson | 5 10 | 11 6 | Manchester | Plymouth Arg | 78 | 10 |
| | | | | Everton | 22 | 2 |
| | | | | Sheffield W | 40 | 5 |
| Richard Beaumont | 5 9 | 10 6 | Sheffield | Sheffield W | — | — |
| Gary Shelton | 5 7 | 10 0 | Nottingham | Walsall | 24 | — |
| | | | | Aston V | 24 | 7 |
| | | | | Notts Co (on loan) | 8 | — |
| | | | | Sheffield W | 9 | 1 |
| **Forwards** | | | | | | |
| Gordon Owen | 5 8 | 10 9 | Barnsley | Sheffield W | 41 | 4 |
| | | | | Rotherham U (on loan) | 9 | — |
| Terry Curran | 5 10 | 12 6 | Kinsley | Doncaster R | 68 | 11 |
| | | | | Nottingham F | 48 | 12 |
| | | | | Bury (on loan) | 2 | — |
| | | | | Derby Co | 26 | 2 |
| | | | | Southampton | 26 | — |
| | | | | Sheffield W | 125 | 35 |
| Andy McCulloch | 6 2 | 13 11 | Northampton | QPR | 42 | 10 |
| | | | | Cardiff C | 58 | 24 |
| | | | | Oxford U | 41 | 9 |
| | | | | Brentford | 117 | 48 |
| | | | | Sheffield W | 97 | 37 |
| Ian Mellor* | 6 2 | 11 12 | Sale | Manchester C | 40 | 7 |
| | | | | Norwich C | 29 | 2 |
| | | | | Brighton | 122 | 31 |
| | | | | Chester | 40 | 11 |
| | | | | Sheffield W | 70 | 11 |
| John Pearson | 6 1 | 11 9½ | Sheffield | Sheffield W | 39 | 11 |
| Gary Bannister | 5 8½ | 11 3 | Warrington | Coventry C | 22 | 3 |
| | | | | Sheffield W | 42 | 21 |
| Anthony Simmons | | | | Sheffield W | 1 | — |
| (Apprentice) | | | | | | |

# SHREWSBURY TOWN     Division 2

*President:* L. Tudor-Owen.

*Chairman:* H. S. Yates.   *Vice-Chairman:* K. R. Woodhouse.

*Directors:* L. Tudor-Owen, A. C. Williams, F. C. G. Fry, P. W. Newbrook.

*Player/Manager:* Graham Turner.

*Secretary:* M. J. Starkey.

*Year Formed:* 1886.   *Turned Professional:* 1905 (approx).

*Limited Company:* 1936.

*Previous Ground:* Old Shrewsbury Racecourse.

**Football League Record:**
1950 Elected to Division 3(N); 1951–58 Division 3(S); 1958–59 Division 4; 1959–74 Division 3; 1974–75 Division 4; 1975–79 Division 3; 1979– Division 2.

**Honours:** *Football League:* Division 2 best season: 13th, 1979–80; Division 3 – Champions 1978–79; Division 4 – Runners-up 1974–75. *FA Cup* best season: 6th rd, 1978–79, 1981–82. *Football League Cup:* semi-final 1961. *Welsh Cup:* Winners 1891, 1938, 1977, 1979.

*Record Victory:* 7-0 v Swindon T, Division 3(S), 6 May, 1955.

*Record Defeat:* 1-8 v Norwich C, Division 3(S), 1952–53 and v Coventry C, Division 3, 22 Oct, 1963.

*Most League Points:* 62, Division 4, 1974–75.

*Most League Goals:* 101, Division 4, 1958–59.

*Highest League Scorer in Season:* Arthur Rowley, 38, Division 4, 1958–59.

*Most League Goals in Total Aggregate:* Arthur Rowley, 152, 1958–65 (While with Shrewsbury T, Arthur Rowley completed his League scoring record of 434 goals).

*Most Capped Player:* Jimmy McLaughlin, 5 (12) Ireland.

*Most League Appearances:* Ken Mulhearn, 370, 1971–80.

*Record Transfer Fee Received:* £262,000 from Stoke C for Paul Maguire, Sept 1980.

*Record Transfer Fee Paid:* £100,000 to Aldershot for John Dungworth, Nov 1979.

*Previous Managers since the War:* Sam Crooks, Walter Rowley, Harry Potts, John Spuhler, Arthur Rowley, Harry Gregg, Maurice Evans, Alan Durban, Richie Barker.

*Address of Supporters Club:* c/o Football Club.

---

**Gay Meadow, Shrewsbury.** Telephone Shrewsbury 60111. *Match information:* 8040. *Ground capacity:* 18,000. *Record attendance:* 18,917 v Walsall, Division 3, 26 Apr, 1961. *Record receipts:* £36,240 v Ipswich T, FA Cup 5th rd, 13 Feb, 1982. *Pitch measurements:* 116yd×76yd.

*How to get there:* Midland Red schedule bus services from main bus station in Barker Street to the ground. Special coach facilities are arranged by local companies from neighbouring districts. Shrewsbury railway station is 10 minutes walk from the ground.

*Car parking:* A park adjacent to the ground and a free public car park five minutes walk away.

*Entertainments/catering facilities:* Buffets are situated on each side of the ground.

*Club shop:* Sells all types of souvenirs.

*Handbooks/programmes:* No handbook. Programmes can be obtained through the post at 30p each plus sae to Promotions Office, Gay Meadow, Shrewsbury.

*Extra information:* In 1960–61 Shrewsbury met Swindon Town six times in League, FA Cup, and League Cup and did not lose once.

*Club Colours:* Amber shirts with blue stripes, blue shorts, amber stockings.

*Change Colours:* Red or white.

*Club Nickname:* Town.

## SHREWSBURY TOWN 1981–82 LEAGUE RECORD

| Match No. | Date | Venue | Opponents | Result | H/T Score | Goalscorers | Attendance |
|---|---|---|---|---|---|---|---|
| 1 | Aug 29 | A | Barnsley | L 0-4 | 0-2 | | 13,344 |
| 2 | Sept 1 | H | Blackburn R | L 1-2 | 1-0 | Atkins | 4220 |
| 3 | 5 | H | Derby Co | W 4-1 | 1-0 | Atkins 2, Bates, Tong | 4373 |
| 4 | 12 | A | Oldham Ath | D 1-1 | 1-0 | Bates | 3994 |
| 5 | 19 | H | Chelsea | W 1-0 | 0-0 | Biggins | 5616 |
| 6 | 23 | A | Newcastle U | L 0-2 | 0-1 | | 13,846 |
| 7 | 26 | A | Crystal Palace | W 1-0 | 0-0 | Bates | 9037 |
| 8 | Oct 3 | H | Rotherham U | W 2-1 | 1-1 | Biggins, McNally | 4646 |
| 9 | 10 | H | Charlton Ath | D 1-1 | 0-0 | Bates | 4336 |
| 10 | 17 | A | Norwich C | L 1-2 | 1-1 | Petts | 11,979 |
| 11 | 24 | A | Cardiff C | D 1-1 | 0-0 | Atkins | 4357 |
| 12 | 31 | H | Watford | L 0-2 | 0-2 | | 5672 |
| 13 | Nov 7 | A | Cambridge U | L 0-2 | 0-1 | | 3851 |
| 14 | 14 | H | Bolton W | W 2-0 | 1-0 | Bennett (og), Atkins (pen) | 4062 |
| 15 | 21 | H | QPR | W 2-1 | 1-1 | Atkins 2 (1 pen) | 4765 |
| 16 | 25 | A | Blackburn R | D 0-0 | 0-0 | | 6892 |
| 17 | 28 | A | Orient | L 0-2 | 0-2 | | 3327 |
| 18 | Dec 5 | H | Luton T | D 2-2 | 2-1 | Dungworth, Atkins | 5259 |
| 19 | Jan 30 | A | Chelsea | L 1-3 | 0-1 | Atkins | 11,446 |
| 20 | Feb 2 | H | Barnsley | L 0-2 | 0-0 | | 4382 |
| 21 | 6 | H | Oldham Ath | W 2-1 | 1-1 | Cross, Biggins | 4970 |
| 22 | 16 | A | Rotherham U | L 0-3 | 0-1 | | 7497 |
| 23 | 20 | H | Newcastle U | D 0-0 | 0-0 | | 4636 |
| 24 | 27 | A | Charlton Ath | L 0-1 | 0-0 | | 4575 |
| 25 | Mar 2 | A | Sheffield W | D 0-0 | 0-0 | | 13,254 |
| 26 | 10 | A | Derby Co | D 1-1 | 0-1 | Atkins | 7518 |
| 27 | 13 | H | Cardiff C | D 1-1 | 1-0 | Dungworth | 4089 |
| 28 | 16 | H | Wrexham | D 1-1 | 1-0 | Dungworth | 4741 |
| 29 | 20 | A | Watford | L 1-3 | 0-1 | Dungworth | 11,780 |
| 30 | 27 | H | Cambridge U | W 1-0 | 1-0 | Atkins | 3159 |
| 31 | 30 | H | Leicester C | D 1-1 | 1-1 | Atkins (pen) | 5340 |
| 32 | Apr 3 | A | Bolton W | D 1-1 | 0-1 | Atkins (pen) | 5833 |
| 33 | 10 | H | Sheffield W | L 0-1 | 0-0 | | 8103 |
| 34 | 12 | A | Wrexham | L 0-1 | 0-0 | | 6506 |
| 35 | 17 | A | QPR | L 1-2 | 0-0 | Dungworth | 11,148 |
| 36 | 20 | H | Norwich C | L 0-2 | 0-2 | | 3590 |
| 37 | 24 | H | Orient | W 2-0 | 0-0 | Atkins 2 | 2898 |
| 38 | 27 | A | Grimsby T | L 1-5 | 1-1 | Johnson | 7051 |
| 39 | 30 | A | Luton T | L 1-4 | 0-1 | Atkins | 14,563 |
| 40 | May 4 | H | Crystal Palace | W 1-0 | 0-0 | Atkins | 3159 |
| 41 | 8 | H | Grimsby T | W 2-0 | 1-0 | Cross 2 | 4036 |
| 42 | 15 | A | Leicester C | D 0-0 | 0-0 | | 11,368 |

**Final League Position: 18**

**Goalscorers**

*League* (37): Atkins 17 (4 pens), Dungworth 5, Bates 4, Biggins 3, Cross 3, Johnson 1, McNally 1, Petts 1, Tong 1, own goal 1.

*League Cup* (4): Atkins 2 (1 pen), Biggins 1, MacClaren 1.

*FA Cup* (6): Bates 3, Cross 1, Keay 1, King 1.

| League Cup | Second Round | WBA (h) | 3-3 |
|---|---|---|---|
| | | (a) | 1-2 |
| FA Cup | Third Round | Port Vale (h) | 1-0 |
| | Fourth Round | Burnley (h) | 1-0 |
| | Fifth Round | Ipswich T (h) | 2-1 |
| | Sixth Round | Leicester C (a) | 2-5 |

| Wardle | Leonard | Johnson | Petts | Griffin | Keay | Tong | McNally | Atkins | Bates | Cross | Dungworth | MacLaren | Biggins | Gibson | Edwards | King | Turner | Blake | Match No. |
|---|---|---|---|---|---|---|---|---|---|---|---|---|---|---|---|---|---|---|---|
| 1 | 2 | 3 | 4 | 5 | 6 | 7* | 8 | 9 | 10 | 11 | 12 | | | | | | | | 1 |
| 1 | 2 | 3 | 4 | 5 | 6 | 7 | 8 | 9 | 10 | | | 11 | | | | | | | 2 |
| 1 | 2 | 3 | 4 | 5 | | 7 | 8 | 9 | | 11 | | 6 | 10* | 12 | | | | | 3 |
| 1 | 2 | 3 | 4 | 5 | 12 | 7 | 8 | 9* | | 11 | | 6 | 10 | | | | | | 4 |
| 1 | 2 | 3 | 4 | 5 | | 7 | 8 | 9 | | 11 | | 6 | 10* | 12 | | | | | 5 |
| 1 | 2 | 3 | 4 | 5 | | 7 | 8 | 9 | | 11 | 12 | 6 | 10* | | | | | | 6 |
| 1 | 2 | 3 | 4 | 5 | | 7 | 8 | 9 | | 11 | | 6 | 10 | | | | | | 7 |
| 1 | 2 | 3 | 4 | 5 | | 7* | 8 | 9 | | 11 | 12 | 6 | 10 | | | | | | 8 |
| 1 | 2 | 3 | 4* | 5 | | 7 | 8 | 9 | | 11 | 12 | 6 | 10 | | | | | | 9 |
| 1 | 2 | 3 | 4 | 5 | | 7 | 8 | 9* | | 11 | 12 | 6 | 10 | | | | | | 10 |
| 1 | 2 | 3 | 4 | 5 | | 7 | 8* | 9 | 10 | 11 | | 6 | | 12 | | | | | 11 |
| 1 | 2 | | 4 | 3 | 5 | 7 | 8* | 9 | | 11 | | 6 | 10 | 12 | | | | | 12 |
| 1 | 2* | 3 | 4 | 5 | 6 | 7 | | 9 | | 11 | 8 | 12 | 10 | | | | | | 13 |
| 1 | | 3 | | 5 | 6 | 7 | | 9 | | 11 | 4 | 8 | 2 | 10 | | | | | 14 |
| 1 | | 3 | | 5 | 6 | 7 | 10 | 9 | | 11 | 4 | 8 | 2 | | | | | | 15 |
| 1 | | 3 | | 5 | 6 | 7 | 10 | 9 | | 11 | 4 | 8 | 2 | | | | | | 16 |
| 1 | | 3 | 12 | 5 | 6 | 7 | 10 | 9 | | 11 | 4 | 8* | 2 | | | | | | 17 |
| 1 | | 3 | | 5 | 6 | 7 | 10 | 9 | | 11 | 4 | 8 | 2 | | | | | | 18 |
| 1 | | 3 | 4 | 5 | 6 | 7 | 10 | 9 | | 11 | | 8 | 2 | | | | | | 19 |
| 1 | | 3 | 12 | 5 | 6 | 7 | 10 | 9 | | 11 | 4 | 8* | 2 | | | | | | 20 |
| 1 | | 3 | | 5 | 6 | 7 | 10 | 9 | | 11 | 4 | | 8 | 2 | | | | | 21 |
| 1 | | 3 | | 5 | 6 | 7* | 8 | 9 | | 11 | 4 | | 10 | 2 | | 12 | | | 22 |
| 1 | 2 | 3 | | 5 | 6 | 7 | 8 | 9 | | 11 | 4 | 12 | 10* | | | | | | 23 |
| 1 | 2 | 3 | | 5 | 6 | 7 | 8* | 9 | | 11 | 4 | 12 | | 10 | | | | | 24 |
| 1 | 2 | 3* | | 5 | 6 | 7 | | 9 | 12 | | 4 | 8 | 10 | | | | 11 | | 25 |
| 1 | 2 | 3 | | 5* | | 7 | 12 | 9 | | 11 | 4 | 10 | 6 | | | | 8 | | 26 |
| 1 | 2 | 3 | | 5 | | 7 | 8 | 9 | | 11 | 4 | 10 | 6 | | | | | | 27 |
| 1 | 2 | 3 | | 5 | | | 9 | | 11 | 4 | 10 | 6 | 7 | | | | 8 | | 28 |
| 1 | 2 | 3 | | 5 | 12 | | 9 | | 11 | 4* | 10 | 6 | 7 | | | | 8 | | 29 |
| 1 | 2 | 3 | | | | | 8 | 9 | | 11 | 4 | 10 | 6 | 7* | | 12 | 5 | | 30 |
| 1 | 2 | 3 | | | | | 8 | 9 | | | 4 | 10 | 6 | 7 | 12 | 11* | 5 | | 31 |
| 1 | 2 | 3* | 12 | | | | 8 | 9 | | | 4 | 10 | 6 | 7 | | 11 | 5 | | 32 |
| 1 | 2 | 3 | | | | | 8 | 9 | | 11 | 4 | 10 | 6 | 7* | 12 | | 5 | | 33 |
| 1 | | 3 | 7 | 2 | | | 12 | 9 | | 11 | 4* | 10 | 6 | 8 | | | 5 | | 34 |
| 1 | 2 | 3 | 9 | 5 | | 12 | 8 | | 11 | | 4 | 10 | 6 | 7* | | | | | 35 |
| 1 | | 3 | 7 | 2 | | 9 | 8 | | 11 | | 4 | 10 | 6 | | | | 5 | | 36 |
| 1 | | 3 | | 5 | 6 | 7 | 8 | 9 | 11 | | 10 | | 2 | | | | | 4 | 37 |
| 1 | | 3 | | 5 | 6 | 7 | 8 | 9 | 11 | | 10 | | 2 | | | | | 4 | 38 |
| 1 | | 3* | 12 | 5 | 6 | 7 | 8 | 9 | 11 | | 10 | | 2 | | | | | 4 | 39 |
| 1 | | 3 | | 5 | 6 | 7 | 8 | 9 | 11 | | 10 | | 2 | | | | | 4 | 40 |
| 1 | 2 | 3 | | 5 | | 7 | 8 | 9 | 11 | | 10 | | 6 | | | | | 4 | 41 |
| 1 | | 3 | | 5 | 6 | 7 | 8 | 9 | 11 | | 10 | | 2 | | | | | 4 | 42 |
| 42 | 26 | 41 | 17 | 36 | 23 | 38 | 31 | 40 | 39 | 30 | 21 | 34 | 22 | 2 | — | 2 | 12 | 6 | |

+ 4s · + 1s · + 2s · + 2s · + 1s · + 4s · + 3s · + 1s · + 4s · + 3s · + 1s

## SHREWSBURY TOWN

| | Ht | Wt | Birthplace | Clubs | League App. | League Gls |
|---|---|---|---|---|---|---|
| **Goalkeepers** | | | | | | |
| Bob Wardle | 5 11 | 11 2 | Leeds | Bristol C | — | — |
| | | | | Shrewsbury T | 131 | — |
| Steve Perks | 6 0 | 11 3½ | Shrewsbury | Shrewsbury T | — | — |
| **Defenders** | | | | | | |
| Colin Griffin | 6 0 | 11 7 | Dudley | Derby Co | — | — |
| | | | | Shrewsbury T | 263 | 6 |
| Jake King* | 5 10 | 11 0 | Glasgow | Shrewsbury T | 306 | 20 |
| Carleton Leonard* | 5 9 | 10 3 | Oswestry | Shrewsbury T | 211 | 1 |
| Jack Keay | 6 0 | 12 6 | Glasgow | Celtic | — | — |
| | | | | Shrewsbury T | 155 | 20 |
| Mark Adams | 5 11 | 10 4½ | Shrewsbury | Shrewsbury T | — | — |
| (Contract cancelled Feb 1982) | | | | | | |
| Paul Johnson | 5 9 | 11 3 | Stoke | Stoke C | 34 | — |
| | | | | Shrewsbury T | 41 | 1 |
| Wayne Williams | 5 9 | 11 3 | Telford | Shrewsbury T | — | — |
| Nigel Pearson | 6 1 | 12 6 | Nottingham | Shrewsbury T | — | — |
| **Midfield** | | | | | | |
| Steve Cross | 5 10 | 10 6 | Wolverhampton | Shrewsbury T | 113 | 7 |
| Graham Turner | 5 10 | 11 3 | Ellesmere Port | Wrexham | 77 | — |
| | | | | Chester | 218 | 5 |
| | | | | Shrewsbury T | 324 | 22 |
| David Tong* | 5 8 | 10 1 | Blackpool | Blackpool | 78 | 7 |
| | | | | Shrewsbury T | 160 | 8 |
| Ross MacLaren | | | Edinburgh | Rangers | — | — |
| | | | | Shrewsbury T | 39 | — |
| Bernard McNally | 5 7 | 9 11 | Shrewsbury | Shrewsbury T | 34 | 1 |
| **Forwards** | | | | | | |
| Ian Atkins | 5 10 | 11 0 | Birmingham | Shrewsbury T | 278 | 58 |
| Steve Biggins* | 6 0 | 11 12 | Walsall | Shrewsbury T | 146 | 41 |
| John Dungworth* | 6 0 | 10 7 | Rotherham | Huddersfield T | 23 | 1 |
| | | | | Barnsley (on loan) | 3 | 1 |
| | | | | Oldham Ath | 4 | — |
| | | | | Rochdale (on loan) | 14 | 3 |
| | | | | Aldershot | 105 | 58 |
| | | | | Hereford U (on loan) | 7 | 3 |
| | | | | Shrewsbury T | 86 | 17 |
| Dean Edwards | 5 10 | 10 6 | Wolverhampton | Shrewsbury T | 13 | 1 |
| (Contract cancelled April 1982) | | | | | | |
| Paul Petts | 5 9 | 10 11 | Hackney | Bristol R | 13 | — |
| | | | | Shrewsbury T | 45 | 1 |
| Chic Bates | 6 0 | 11 12 | West Bromwich | Stourbridge | (not known) | |
| | | | | Shrewsbury T | 160 | 45 |
| | | | | Swindon T | 63 | 15 |
| | | | | Bristol R | 29 | 4 |
| | | | | Shrewsbury T | 55 | 6 |
| Charles Gibson* | 5 10 | 11 8 | Dumbarton | Shrewsbury T | 6 | — |
| Martin Sankey | | | | Shrewsbury T | — | — |

Free transfers: Tim Cook*, John McGrath*.

# SOUTHAMPTON Division 1

*Chairman:* A. A. Woodford.

*Directors:* J. Corbett, Lt-Col Sir George Meyrick (Bart) MC, TD, B. G. W. Bowyer JP, F. G. Askham FCA, E. T. Bates.

*Manager:* Lawrie McMenemy.

*Assistant Manager:* John Mortimore.

*Secretary:* Brian Truscott.

*Year Formed:* 1885.

*Turned Professional:* 1894. *Limited Company:* 1897.

*Previous Name:* Southampton St Mary's until 1885.

*Previous Grounds:* 1885, Antelope Ground; 1897, County Cricket Ground; 1898, The Dell.

**Football League Record:**
1920 Original Members of Division 3; 1921 Division 3(S); 1922–53 Division 2; 1953–58 Division 3(S); 1958–60 Division 3; 1960–66 Division 2; 1966–74 Division 1; 1974–78 Division 2; 1978– Division 1.

**Honours:** *Football League:* Division 1 best season: 6th, 1980–81; Division 2 – Runners-up 1965–66, 1977–78; Division 3(S) – Champions 1921–22; Runners-up 1920–21; Division 3 – Champions 1959–60. *FA Cup:* Winners 1975–76; Runners-up 1900, 1902. *Football League Cup:* Runners-up 1978–79. **European Competitions:** *European Fairs Cup:* 1969–70; *UEFA Cup:* 1971-72, 1981–82; *European Cup-Winners' Cup:* 1976–77.

*Record Victory:* 11-0 v Northampton T, Southern League, 28 Dec, 1901.

*Record Defeat:* 0-8 v Tottenham H, Division 2, 28 Mar, 1936, and v Everton, Division 1, 20 Nov, 1971.

*Most League Points:* 61, Division 3(S), 1921–22, and Division 3, 1959–60. *Three points win:* 66, Division 1, 1981–82.

*Most League Goals:* 112, Div 3(S), 1957–58.

*Highest League Scorer in Season:* Derek Reeves, 39, Division 3, 1959–60.

*Most League Goals in Total Aggregate:* Mike Channon, 182, 1966–77, 1979–82.

*Most Capped Player:* Mike Channon, 45 (46), England.

*Most League Appearances:* Terry Paine, 713, 1956–74.

*Record Transfer Fee Received:* £300,000 from Manchester C for Mike Channon, July 1977.

*Record Transfer Fee Paid:* £600,000 to Middlesbrough for David Armstrong, Aug 1981.

*Previous Managers since the War:* Bill Dodgin (Snr), Sid Cann, George Roughton, Ted Bates.

*Address of Supporters Club:* Same as Football Club.

---

**The Dell, Milton Road, Southampton SO9 4XX.** Telephone Southampton 39445 and 39633. *Ground capacity:* 25,000. *Record attendance:* 31,044 v Manchester U, Division 1, 8 Oct, 1969. *Record receipts:* £63,574 v Everton, FA Cup 5th rd, 14 Feb, 1981. *Pitch measurements:* 110yd×72yd.

*How to get there:* The ground is 10 minutes' walk from Southampton Central station via Hill Lane. Buses 2 and 5 from the city centre pass the ground, which is only 10 minutes walk from the centre.

*Match tickets:* No seats available, all seats being sold to season-ticket holders. Room on the terraces for 8,800 standing, and admission is by purchasing tickets in advance (none sold on day).

*Car parking:* Only street parking in the vicinity of the ground. Municipal car parks in the city centre.

*Entertainments/catering facilities:* Licensed bars inside the ground.

*Club shop:* Situated in Milton Road, and at Hanover Buildings in City Centre.

*Handbooks/programmes:* Handbooks not published annually. Programmes available on subscription.

*Extra information:* In 1921–22, Southampton lost only four league games and conceded only 21 goals, both Division Three(South) records.

*Club Colours:* Red and white broad-striped shirts, black shorts, white stockings.

*Change Colours:* Light blue/dark blue shirts, dark blue shorts, light blue stockings.

*Club Captain:* Kevin Keegan.

*Physiotherapist:* Don Taylor MCSP, SRP.

*First Team Trainer:* Lew Chatterley   *Club Nickname:* Saints.

---

338

## SOUTHAMPTON 1981–82 LEAGUE RECORD

| Match No. | Date | Venue | Opponents | Result | H/T Score | Goalscorers | Attendance |
|---|---|---|---|---|---|---|---|
| 1 | Aug 29 | A | Nottingham F | L 1-2 | 1-2 | Keegan | 25,234 |
| 2 | Sept 1 | H | Wolverhampton W | W 4-1 | 1-0 | Channon 2, Keegan, Moran | 21,315 |
| 3 | 5 | H | Everton | W 1-0 | 0-0 | Keegan (pen) | 21,624 |
| 4 | 12 | A | Manchester C | D 1-1 | 1-1 | Keegan (pen) | 42,003 |
| 5 | 19 | H | Middlesbrough | W 2-0 | 2-0 | Baxter (og), Moran | 20,105 |
| 6 | 22 | A | West Ham U | L 2-4 | 1-2 | Armstrong, Waldron | 34,026 |
| 7 | 26 | A | Coventry C | L 2-4 | 1-1 | Keegan 2 (1 pen) | 12,610 |
| 8 | Oct 3 | H | Ipswich T | W 4-3 | 1-3 | Keegan (pen), Armstrong 2, Moran | 22,552 |
| 9 | 10 | A | Birmingham C | L 0-4 | 0-0 | | 16,938 |
| 10 | 17 | H | Notts Co | W 3-1 | 1-0 | Keegan 2, Moran | 18,900 |
| 11 | 24 | A | WBA | D 1-1 | 1-1 | Channon | 15,730 |
| 12 | 31 | H | Tottenham H | L 1-2 | 1-1 | Moran | 24,131 |
| 13 | Nov 7 | A | Stoke C | W 2-0 | 1-0 | Armstrong, Keegan | 13,864 |
| 14 | 21 | H | Leeds U | W 4-0 | 3-0 | Keegan (pen), Armstrong, Burns (og), Moran | 21,127 |
| 15 | 24 | A | Wolverhampton W | D 0-0 | 0-0 | | 15,438 |
| 16 | 28 | A | Liverpool | W 1-0 | 0-0 | Moran | 37,189 |
| 17 | Dec 5 | H | Manchester U | W 3-2 | 2-1 | Moran, Keegan, Armstrong | 24,404 |
| 18 | 8 | H | Brighton & HA | L 0-2 | 0-0 | | 22,128 |
| 19 | 28 | H | Swansea C | W 3-1 | 1-1 | Armstrong, Keegan 2 | 22,703 |
| 20 | Jan 19 | A | Everton | D 1-1 | 0-1 | Moran | 22,355 |
| 21 | 23 | H | Arsenal | W 3-1 | 1-1 | Armstrong, Puckett 2 | 22,263 |
| 22 | 30 | A | Middlesbrough | W 1-0 | 1-0 | Keegan | 12,693 |
| 23 | Feb 6 | H | Manchester C | W 2-1 | 0-0 | Baker G., Armstrong | 22,645 |
| 24 | 10 | A | Aston Villa | D 1-1 | 1-0 | Keegan | 24,287 |
| 25 | 13 | H | Nottingham F | W 2-0 | 1-0 | Keegan, Channon | 21,350 |
| 26 | 16 | A | Ipswich T | L 2-5 | 1-3 | Puckett, Keegan | 20,264 |
| 27 | 20 | H | West Ham U | W 2-1 | 2-1 | Armstrong, Channon | 24,026 |
| 28 | 27 | H | Birmingham C | W 3-1 | 1-1 | Keegan (pen), Baker G. 2 | 20,620 |
| 29 | Mar 6 | A | Notts Co | D 1-1 | 1-0 | Keegan | 12,474 |
| 30 | 10 | A | Sunderland | L 0-2 | 0-0 | | 15,747 |
| 31 | 13 | H | WBA | D 0-0 | 0-0 | | 21,376 |
| 32 | 20 | A | Tottenham H | L 2-3 | 0-2 | Baker G., Armstrong | 46,827 |
| 33 | 27 | H | Stoke C | W 4-3 | 3-0 | Waldron, Armstrong, Channon, Whitlock | 20,058 |
| 34 | Apr 3 | A | Brighton & HA | D 1-1 | 0-1 | Keegan | 20,977 |
| 35 | 10 | H | Aston Villa | L 0-3 | 0-0 | | 22,801 |
| 36 | 13 | A | Swansea C | L 0-1 | 0-1 | | 23,771 |
| 37 | 17 | A | Leeds U | W 3-1 | 3-1 | Armstrong, Keegan 2 | 21,353 |
| 38 | 24 | H | Liverpool | L 2-3 | 1-1 | Channon, Keegan (pen) | 24,704 |
| 39 | May 1 | A | Manchester U | L 0-1 | 0-0 | | 40,038 |
| 40 | 4 | H | Coventry C | D 5-5 | 1-2 | Keegan 2, Cassells 2, Ball | 18,522 |
| 41 | 8 | H | Sunderland | W 1-0 | 0-0 | Armstrong | 21,110 |
| 42 | 15 | A | Arsenal | L 1-4 | 0-3 | Armstrong | 28,534 |

**Final League Position: 7**

**Goalscorers**

*League* (72): Keegan 26 (7 pens), Armstrong 15, Moran 9, Channon 7, Baker G. 4, Puckett 3, Cassells 2, Waldron 2, Ball 1, Whitlock 1, own goals 2.
*League Cup* (2): Keegan 1, Moran 1.
*FA Cup* (1): Keegan 1.

| League Cup | Second Round | Chelsea (h) | 1-1 |
|---|---|---|---|
| | | (a) | 1-2 |
| FA Cup | Third Round | Leicester C (a) | 1-3 |

| Wells | Golac | Holmes | Williams | Waldron | Nicholl | Keegan | Channon | Moran | Baker G. | Ball | Puckett | Baker S. | Whitlock | Armstrong | Agboola | Watson | Rogers | Lawrence | Katalinic | Hebberd | Wallace | Cassells | Wright | Match No. |
|---|---|---|---|---|---|---|---|---|---|---|---|---|---|---|---|---|---|---|---|---|---|---|---|---|
| 1 | 2 | 3 | 4 | 5 | 6* | 7 | 8 | 9 | 10 | 11 | 12 |  |  |  |  |  |  |  |  |  |  |  |  | 1 |
| 1 | 2 | 3 |  | 5 |  | 7 | 8 | 9 | 4 | 11* | 12 |  | 6 | 10 |  |  |  |  |  |  |  |  |  | 2 |
| 1 | 2 | 3 |  | 5 | 6 | 7 | 8 | 9 | 4 | 11 |  |  |  | 10 |  |  |  |  |  |  |  |  |  | 3 |
| 1 | 2 | 3 |  | 5 |  | 7 | 8 | 9 | 4 | 11 |  |  |  | 10 | 6 |  |  |  |  |  |  |  |  | 4 |
| 1 | 2 | 3 |  |  | 6 | 7 | 8 | 9 | 4 | 11 |  |  |  | 10* |  | 5 | 12 |  |  |  |  |  |  | 5 |
| 1 | 2 | 3 |  |  | 6 | 7 |  |  | 8 | 11 | 9 |  |  | 10 | 4 | 5* | 12 |  |  |  |  |  |  | 6 |
| 1 | 2 | 3 |  |  | 6 | 7 | 8 | 9 | 4* | 11 | 12 |  |  | 10 |  | 5 |  |  |  |  |  |  |  | 7 |
| 1 | 2 | 3 |  |  | 6 | 7 | 8 | 9 | 4 | 11 |  |  |  | 10 |  | 5 |  |  |  |  |  |  |  | 8 |
| 1 | 2 | 3* |  |  | 6 | 7 | 8 | 9 | 4 | 11 | 12 |  |  | 10 |  | 5 |  |  |  |  |  |  |  | 9 |
| 1 | 2 | 3 | 4 |  | 6 | 7 |  | 9 |  | 11 |  |  | 5 | 10 |  |  |  | 8 |  |  |  |  |  | 10 |
|  |  | 3 | 4 | 6 | 5 | 7 | 8 |  |  | 11* | 12 | 2 |  | 10 |  |  |  | 9 | 1 |  |  |  |  | 11 |
|  |  | 3 | 4 | 6 | 5 | 7 | 8 | 9 |  | 11 |  | 2 |  | 10* |  |  |  | 12 | 1 |  |  |  |  | 12 |
|  | 2 | 3 | 4 | 6 | 5 | 7 | 8 | 9 |  | 11 |  |  |  | 10 |  |  |  |  | 1 |  |  |  |  | 13 |
|  | 2 | 3 | 4 | 6 | 5 | 7 | 8 | 9 |  | 11 |  |  |  | 10 |  |  |  |  | 1 |  |  |  |  | 14 |
|  | 2 | 3 | 4 | 6 | 5 | 7 | 8 | 9 |  | 11 |  |  |  | 10 |  |  |  |  | 1 |  |  |  |  | 15 |
|  | 2 | 3 | 4 | 6 | 5 | 7 | 8 | 9 |  | 11 |  |  |  | 10 |  |  |  |  | 1 |  |  |  |  | 16 |
|  | 2 | 3 | 4 | 6 | 5 | 7 | 8 | 9 |  | 11 |  |  |  | 10 |  |  |  |  | 1 |  |  |  |  | 17 |
|  | 2 | 3 | 4 | 6 | 5 | 7 | 8 | 9 |  | 11 |  |  |  | 10 |  |  |  |  | 1 |  |  |  |  | 18 |
|  | 2 | 3 | 4 | 6 | 5 | 7 | 8 | 9 |  | 11 |  |  |  | 10 |  |  |  |  | 1 |  |  |  |  | 19 |
|  | 2 | 3 | 4 | 6 | 5 |  | 8 | 9 | 7 | 11 |  |  |  | 10 |  |  |  |  | 1 |  |  |  |  | 20 |
|  | 2 | 3 | 4 | 6 | 5 | 7 | 8 |  |  | 11 | 9 |  |  | 10 |  |  |  |  | 1 |  |  |  |  | 21 |
|  | 2 | 3 |  | 6 | 5 | 7 | 8 |  | 4 | 11 |  |  |  | 10 |  |  |  |  | 1 | 9 |  |  |  | 22 |
|  | 2 |  |  | 6 | 5 | 7 | 8 |  | 4 | 11 |  |  |  | 10 | 3 |  |  |  | 1 | 9 |  |  |  | 23 |
|  | 2 | 3 |  | 6 | 5 | 7 | 8 |  | 4 | 11 |  |  |  | 10 |  |  |  |  | 1 | 9 |  |  |  | 24 |
|  | 2 | 3 |  | 6 | 5 | 7 | 8 |  | 4 | 11 |  |  |  | 10 |  |  |  |  | 1 | 9 |  |  |  | 25 |
|  | 2* | 3 |  | 6 | 5 | 7 | 8 |  | 4 | 11 | 9 |  |  | 10 |  |  |  | 12 | 1 |  |  |  |  | 26 |
|  | 2 | 3 |  | 6 | 5 | 7 | 8 |  | 4 | 11 | 9 |  |  | 10 |  |  |  |  | 1 |  |  |  |  | 27 |
|  | 2 | 3 |  | 6 | 5 | 7 | 8 |  | 4 | 11 | 9 |  |  | 10 |  |  |  |  | 1 |  |  |  |  | 28 |
|  | 2 | 3 |  | 6 | 5 | 7 | 8 |  | 4 | 11 | 12 |  |  | 10 |  |  |  |  | 1 |  | 9* |  |  | 29 |
|  | 2* | 3 |  | 6 | 5 | 7 | 8 |  | 4 | 11 | 12 |  |  | 10 |  |  |  |  | 1 |  | 9 |  |  | 30 |
|  | 2 | 3 |  | 6 | 5 | 7 | 8 |  | 4 | 11 | 9* |  |  | 10 |  |  |  |  | 1 |  | 12 |  |  | 31 |
|  |  | 3 | 9 | 6 | 5 | 7 | 8 |  | 4 | 11* | 12 |  |  | 10 | 2 |  |  |  | 1 |  |  |  |  | 32 |
|  | 2 | 3 | 4 | 6 |  | 7 | 8 |  |  | 11 | 9 |  | 5 | 10 |  |  |  |  | 1 |  |  |  |  | 33 |
|  | 2 | 3 | 4 | 6 | 5 | 7 | 8 |  |  | 11 | 9* |  |  | 10 |  |  |  |  | 1 |  | 12 |  |  | 34 |
|  | 2 | 3 | 4 | 6 | 5 | 7 | 8 |  |  | 11 |  |  |  | 10 |  |  |  |  | 1 |  | 9 |  |  | 35 |
|  |  | 3 | 4 | 5 |  | 7 | 8 |  |  | 11 |  | 2 | 6 | 10 |  |  |  |  | 1 |  |  | 9 |  | 36 |
|  |  | 3 |  | 5 |  | 7 | 8 |  | 4* | 11 |  | 2 | 6 | 10 |  |  |  |  | 1 |  | 12 |  | 9 | 37 |
|  | 2 | 3 |  | 5 |  | 7 | 8 |  | 4 | 11 | 12 |  |  | 10 |  |  |  |  | 1 |  | 9* | 6 |  | 38 |
|  |  |  |  | 5 |  | 7 | 8* |  | 4 | 11 |  | 2 | 9 | 10 | 3 |  |  |  | 1 |  | 12 |  | 6 | 39 |
|  | 2 | 3 | 4 | 5 |  | 7 | 8 |  |  | 11 |  |  | 6* | 10 |  |  |  |  | 1 |  | 12 |  | 9 | 40 |
|  | 2 | 3 | 4 | 5 |  | 7 | 8 |  |  | 11 |  |  | 6 | 10 |  |  |  |  | 1 |  |  | 9 |  | 41 |
|  | 2 | 3 |  | 5 |  | 7 | 8 | 9 | 4 | 11 |  |  | 6* | 10 |  |  |  |  | 1 |  | 12 |  |  | 42 |
| 10 | 36 | 40 | 21 | 34 | 34 | 41 | 40 | 18 | 26 | 41 | 8 | 5 | 9 | 41 | 5 | 5 | — | 2 | 32 | 4 | 3 | 4 | 3 |  |
|  |  |  |  |  |  |  |  |  |  |  | +9s |  |  | +2s | +2s |  |  |  |  |  | +4s | +2s |  |  |

## SOUTHAMPTON

| | Ht | Wt | Birthplace | Clubs | League App. | League Gls |
|---|---|---|---|---|---|---|
| **Goalkeepers** | | | | | | |
| Peter Wells | 6 1 | 13 4 | Nottingham | Nottingham F | 27 | — |
| | | | | Southampton | 138 | — |
| Ivan Katalinic | 6 0½ | 12 3 | Yugoslavia | Red Star Belgrade | (not known) | |
| (Yugoslavia)* | | | | Southampton | 48 | — |
| Alistair Sperring* | 6 2 | 12 10 | Portsmouth | Southampton | — | — |
| **Defenders** | | | | | | |
| Malcolm Waldron | 6 0 | 12 4 | Emsworth | Southampton | 175 | 10 |
| Chris Nicholl | 6 2 | 12 13 | Wilmslow | Burnley | — | — |
| (N Ireland) | | | | Witton A | (not known) | |
| | | | | Halifax T | 42 | 3 |
| | | | | Luton T | 98 | 6 |
| | | | | Aston V | 210 | 11 |
| | | | | Southampton | 186 | 8 |
| Mark Whitlock | 5 11 | 12 2½ | Portsmouth | Southampton | 9 | 1 |
| Ivan Golac | 5 10 | 13 1 | Yugoslavia | Partizan | — | — |
| (Yugoslavia) | | | | Southampton | 144 | 4 |
| Reuben Agboola | 5 9½ | 11 7 | London | Southampton | 11 | — |
| Steve Baker | 5 5 | 10 2 | Newcastle | Southampton | 6 | — |
| Steven Richardson* | 5 6 | 10 1 | Slough | Southampton | — | — |
| Mark Wright | 6 2¾ | 11 6 | Dorchester- | Oxford U | 10 | — |
| | | | on-Thames | Southampton | 3 | — |
| Peter Vacher* | | | | Southampton | — | — |
| Nick Holmes | 5 11 | 12 2 | Southampton | Southampton | 302 | 45 |
| Graham Baker | 5 9 | 10 8 | Southampton | Southampton | 113 | 22 |
| **Midfield** | | | | | | |
| Alan Ball | 5 6 | 10 5 | Farnworth | Blackpool | 116 | 41 |
| (England) | | | | Everton | 208 | 66 |
| | | | | Arsenal | 177 | 45 |
| | | | | Southampton | 132 | 9 |
| | | | | Blackpool | 30 | 5 |
| | | | | Southampton | 51 | 1 |
| Steve Williams | 5 10½ | 10 11 | London | Southampton | 198 | 11 |
| David Madden* | 6 0 | 11 3 | London | Southampton | — | — |
| David Armstrong | 5 8 | 11 3 | Durham | Middlesbrough | 359 | 59 |
| (England) | | | | Southampton | 41 | 15 |
| Tim Cole | | | | Southampton | — | — |
| Jeremy Stagg | | | | Southampton | — | — |
| Keith Cassells | 5 10 | 11 12 | London | Watford | 12 | — |
| | | | | Peterborough U (on loan) | 8 | — |
| | | | | Oxford U | 45 | 13 |
| | | | | Southampton | 6 | 2 |
| **Forwards** | | | | | | |
| David Wallace | 5 4½ | 9 12½ | London | Southampton | 9 | — |
| David Puckett | 5 7 | 10 2 | Southampton | Southampton | 24 | 3 |
| Mike Channon* | 6 0½ | 12 11 | Orcheston | Southampton | 392 | 155 |
| (England) | | | | Manchester C | 72 | 24 |
| | | | | Southampton | 119 | 27 |
| Joe Blochel* | 5 10½ | 11 11 | Chalfont | Southampton | — | — |
| | | | St Giles | Wimbledon (on loan) | 6 | 1 |
| Steve Moran | 5 8 | 10 11 | Croydon | Southampton | 50 | 27 |
| Kevin Keegan | 5 8 | 11 7 | Armthorpe | Scunthorpe U | 124 | 18 |
| (England) | | | | Liverpool | 230 | 68 |
| | | | | Hamburg | (not known) | |
| | | | | Southampton | 68 | 37 |
| Martin Foyle | 5 9¾ | 10 13 | Salisbury | Southampton | — | — |
| (Contract cancelled April 1982) | | | | | | |
| George Lawrence | 5 10 | 12 2 | London | Southampton | 4 | — |
| | | | | Oxford U (on loan) | 15 | 4 |
| Ian Juryeff | 5 10½ | 11 6 | Gosport | Southampton | — | — |
| Colin Dixon* | | | | Southampton | — | — |
| Paul Wiltshire | | | | Southampton | — | — |

# SOUTHEND UNITED Division 3

*President:* N. L. Mitchell. *Chairman:* M. D. Rubin ACIS.

*Directors:* J. N. Woodcock, L. H. Lesser FCA, D. A. Smith, G. C. Janes, F. Bonfield, A. R. Rubin, F. H. Walton.

*Manager:* David Smith. *Secretary:* K. Holmes FAAI, F INST CM.

*Year Formed:* 1906. *Turned Professional:* 1906.

*Limited Company:* 1919.

*Previous Grounds:* 1906, Roots Hall, Prittlewell; 1920, Kursaal; 1934, Southend Stadium; 1955, Roots Hall Football Ground.

**Football League Record:**
1920 Original Member of Division 3; 1921 Division 3(S); 1958–66 Division 3; 1966–72 Division 4; 1972–76 Division 3; 1976–78 Division 4; 1978–80 Division 3; 1980–81 Division 4; 1981– Division 3.

**Honours:** *Football League:* Division 3(S) best season: 3rd, 1931–32, 1949–50; Division 4 – Champions 1980–81; Runners-up 1971–72, 1977–78. *FA Cup* best season: old 3rd rd, 1920–21, 5th rd, 1925–26, 1951–52, 1975–76. *Football League Cup:* never past 3rd rd.

*Record Victory:* 10-1 v Golders Green, FA Cup 1st rd, 24 Nov, 1934, 10-1 v Brentwood, FA Cup 2nd rd, 7 Dec, 1968.

*Record Defeat:* 1-11 v Northampton T, Southern League, 30 Dec, 1909.

*Most League Points:* 67, Division 4, 1980–81. *Three points win:* 69, Division 3, 1981–82.

*Most League Goals:* 92, Division 3(S), 1950–51.

*Highest League Scorer in Season:* Jim Shankly, 31, 1928–29 and Sammy McCrory, 1957–58, both in Division 3(S).

*Most League Goals in Total Aggregate:* Roy Hollis, 122, 1953–60.

*Most Capped Player:* George Mackenzie, 9, Eire.

*Most League Appearances:* Sandy Anderson, 451, 1950–63.

*Record Transfer Fee Received:* £111,111 from Blackpool for Colin Morris, Dec 1979.

*Record Transfer Fee Paid:* £111,111 to Blackpool for Derek Spence, Dec 1979.

*Previous Managers since the War:* Harry Warren, Eddie Perry, Frank Broome, Ted Fenton, Alvan Williams, Ernie Shepherd, Geoff Hudson, Arthur Rowley.

*Address of Supporters Club:* 374 Victoria Ave, Southend-on-Sea, Essex.

*Address of the Club Shop or Boutique:* 374 Victoria Avenue, Southend-on-Sea.

---

**Roots Hall Football Ground, Victoria Avenue, Southend-on-Sea.** Telephone Southend 40707. *Ground capacity:* 32,000 (16,000 covered). *Record attendance:* 31,033 v Liverpool, FA Cup 3rd rd, 10 Jan, 1979. *Record receipts:* £36,599 v Liverpool, FA Cup 3rd rd, 10 Jan, 1979. *Pitch measurements:* 110yd×74yd.

*How to get there:* Regular buses from Southend Central station in the High Street; the station is on the London line from Fenchurch Street. Southend Victoria, five minutes walk from the ground, is served by trains from Liverpool Street, London.

*Match tickets:* Seats can be purchased 14 days before the match.

*Car parking:* Two car parks at the ground hold approximately 700 cars. Ample parking in side-streets.

*Entertainments/catering facilities:* Tea bars all around the ground. There is a social club for members and *bona fide* visitors.

*Club shop:* Situated in Victoria Avenue opposite the ground; sells all types of souvenirs.

*Handbooks/programmes:* Programmes are available from the club shop; programmes are available on subscription.

*Extra information:* In 1921–22 full-back Jimmy Evans topped Southend's scorers' list with 10 penalties.

*Club Colours:* White shirts with blue sleeves and blue V-neck and red and white cuffs, blue shorts, blue stockings.

*Change Colours:* Red shirts with white pinstripe, red shorts, red stockings.

*Club Captain:* Micky Stead.

*Club Trainer/Coach:* Brian Beckett.

*Club Nickname:* The Shrimpers.

## SOUTHEND UNITED 1981–82 LEAGUE RECORD

| Match No. | Date | Venue | Opponents | Result | H/T Score | Goalscorers | Atten-dance |
|---|---|---|---|---|---|---|---|
| 1 | Aug 29 | A | Walsall | W 1-0 | 1-0 | Moody | 3419 |
| 2 | Sept 4 | H | Newport Co | L 0-4 | 0-1 | | 4620 |
| 3 | 12 | A | Carlisle U | L 2-3 | 2-1 | Cusack, Gray | 3596 |
| 4 | 19 | H | Portsmouth | W 2-0 | 1-0 | Spence, Gray | 4355 |
| 5 | 21 | H | Swindon T | D 0-0 | 0-0 | | 4578 |
| 6 | 26 | A | Huddersfield T | L 2-3 | 1-2 | Gray, Pountney | 7254 |
| 7 | 29 | A | Fulham | L 1-2 | 1-0 | Otulakowski | 4556 |
| 8 | Oct 3 | H | Plymouth Arg | W 3-0 | 2-0 | Nelson, Mercer, Pennyfather | 3470 |
| 9 | 9 | H | Bristol R | W 1-0 | 0-0 | Greaves | 4530 |
| 10 | 17 | A | Chesterfield | W 2-1 | 1-0 | Greaves, Gray | 6146 |
| 11 | 19 | A | Brentford | W 1-0 | 0-0 | Yates | 5400 |
| 12 | 24 | H | Oxford U | L 0-1 | 0-1 | | 5366 |
| 13 | 31 | A | Preston NE | L 0-1 | 0-0 | | 4285 |
| 14 | Nov 2 | H | Gillingham | W 3-0 | 1-0 | Mercer 2, Cusack | 6009 |
| 15 | 7 | H | Lincoln C | L 0-2 | 0-0 | | 5016 |
| 16 | 14 | A | Bristol C | W 2-0 | 0-0 | Cusack (pen), Pennyfather | 6381 |
| 17 | 27 | H | Reading | W 2-0 | 0-0 | Mercer, Pountney | 4510 |
| 18 | Dec 5 | A | Chester | D 1-1 | 0-0 | Greaves | 1388 |
| 19 | Jan 1 | H | Exeter C | W 2-1 | 2-0 | Pountney, Cusack (pen) | 5985 |
| 20 | 16 | H | Doncaster R | D 1-1 | 0-0 | Mercer | 4741 |
| 21 | 23 | H | Walsall | W 3-2 | 3-0 | Nelson, Greaves, Pennyfather | 4684 |
| 22 | 30 | A | Portsmouth | D 0-0 | 0-0 | | 7731 |
| 23 | Feb 1 | H | Millwall | D 2-2 | 1-1 | Mercer, Hadley | 5676 |
| 24 | 6 | H | Carlisle U | D 1-1 | 1-0 | Mercer | 4911 |
| 25 | 9 | A | Swindon T | D 0-0 | 0-0 | | 4472 |
| 26 | 13 | A | Plymouth Arg | D 0-0 | 0-0 | | 5058 |
| 27 | 19 | H | Fulham | D 0-0 | 0-0 | | 7715 |
| 28 | 27 | A | Bristol R | L 1-2 | 0-0 | Moody | 4910 |
| 29 | Mar 5 | H | Chesterfield | L 0-2 | 0-1 | | 5819 |
| 30 | 8 | H | Brentford | D 1-1 | 1-1 | Phillips | 3765 |
| 31 | 13 | A | Oxford U | W 2-0 | 1-0 | Phillips 2 | 6252 |
| 32 | 16 | A | Gillingham | L 0-2 | 0-1 | | 3782 |
| 33 | 19 | H | Preston NE | D 2-2 | 2-0 | Mercer | 3549 |
| 34 | 23 | A | Wimbledon | L 0-3 | 0-2 | | 2051 |
| 35 | 27 | A | Lincoln C | D 1-1 | 0-0 | Yates | 5455 |
| 36 | Apr 3 | H | Bristol C | W 3-0 | 0-0 | Greaves 2, Phillips (pen) | 3133 |
| 37 | 9 | H | Wimbledon | W 2-0 | 2-0 | Cusack (pen), Mercer | 4779 |
| 38 | 12 | A | Millwall | D 1-1 | 0-1 | Phillips | 3025 |
| 39 | 17 | H | Chester | W 2-0 | 1-0 | Spence, Yates | 3427 |
| 40 | 20 | A | Burnley | W 5-3 | 2-2 | Spence 2, Phillips 2 (1 pen), Nelson | 8126 |
| 41 | 24 | A | Reading | W 2-0 | 0-0 | Phillips, Pountney | 2840 |
| 42 | May 1 | H | Huddersfield T | W 4-0 | 1-0 | Mercer, Spence 2, Phillips | 4470 |
| 43 | 4 | A | Doncaster R | D 1-1 | 0-1 | Nelson | 3734 |
| 44 | 8 | A | Exeter C | D 1-1 | 1-0 | Mercer | 3174 |
| 45 | 11 | A | Newport Co | L 2-3 | 1-2 | Pennyfather, Phillips | 3716 |
| 46 | 14 | H | Burnley | L 1-4 | 1-2 | Mercer | 4829 |

**Final League Position: 7**

**Goalscorers**

*League* (63): Mercer 13, Phillips 10 (2 pens), Greaves 6, Spence 6, Cusack 5 (3 pens), Gray 4, Nelson 4, Pennyfather 4, Pountney 4, Yates 3, Moody 2, Hadley 1, Otulakowski 1.
*League Cup* (1): Spence 1.
*FA Cup* (1): Gray 1.

| League Cup | First Round | Portsmouth (h) | 0-0 |
|---|---|---|---|
| | | (a) | 1-4 |
| FA Cup | First Round | Hereford U (a) | 1-3 |

This page presents a player appearance grid. Player names (column headers) read vertically; the right-hand column gives the Match No. Each cell shows the shirt number worn. Totals (appearances) appear in the bottom row, with substitute ("12th‑man") appearances noted beneath.

| Cawston | Stead | Yates | Hadley | Moody | Cusack | Gray | Pountney | Spence | Mercer | Otulakowski | Dudley | Nelson | Keeley | Walker | Pennyfather | Greaves | Phillips | Match No. |
|---|---|---|---|---|---|---|---|---|---|---|---|---|---|---|---|---|---|---|
| 1 | 2 | 3 | 4 | 5 | 6 | 7 | 8 | 9 | 10 | 11 |  |  |  |  |  |  |  | 1 |
| 1 | 2 |  | 4 | 5 | 6 |  | 8 | 9 | 10 | 11 | 3 | 7 |  |  |  |  |  | 2 |
|  | 2 | 3 |  | 5 | 6 | 7 | 8 | 9 | 10 | 11 | 4 | 1 |  |  |  |  |  | 3 |
|  | 2 | 3 |  | 5 | 6 | 7 | 4 | 9 | 10 | 8 | 11 | 1 |  |  |  |  |  | 4 |
|  | 2* | 3 | 12 | 5 | 6 | 7 | 4 | 9 | 10 | 8 | 11 | 1 |  |  |  |  |  | 5 |
| 1 | 3 | 2 |  | 5 | 6 | 7 | 4 | 9 | 10 | 8 | 12 | 11* |  |  |  |  |  | 6 |
| 1 | 3 | 2 |  | 5 | 6 | 7 | 4 | 9 | 10 | 8 | 11* | 12 |  |  |  |  |  | 7 |
| 1 | 3 | 2 |  | 5 | 6 | 7* |  | 9 | 10 | 8 |  | 11 |  |  | 4 | 12 |  | 8 |
| 1 | 3 | 2 |  | 5 | 6 | 7 |  | 9* | 10 | 8 |  | 11 |  |  | 4 | 12 |  | 9 |
| 1 | 3 | 2 |  | 5 | 6 | 7 |  |  | 10 | 8 |  | 11 |  |  | 4 | 9 |  | 10 |
| 1 | 12 | 3 | 2 | 5 | 6 | 7 |  |  | 10 | 8 |  | 11 |  |  | 4 | 9* |  | 11 |
| 1 | 8 | 3 | 2* | 5 | 6 | 7 |  | 12 | 10 |  |  | 11 |  |  | 4 | 9 |  | 12 |
| 1 | 3 | 2 |  | 5 | 6 | 7 | 12 | 9 | 10 | 8* |  | 11 |  |  | 4 |  |  | 13 |
| 1 | 3 | 2* |  | 5 | 6 | 7 | 8 | 9 | 10 |  |  | 11 |  |  | 4 | 12 |  | 14 |
|  | 2 | 3 |  | 5 | 6 | 7 | 8 | 9 | 10 | 11 |  |  | 1 |  | 4* | 12 |  | 15 |
|  | 2 | 3 |  | 5 | 6 | 7* | 8 | 9 | 10 | 11 |  |  | 1 |  | 4 | 12 |  | 16 |
|  | 2 | 3 |  | 5 | 6 |  | 8 | 9 | 10 | 11 |  |  | 1 |  | 4 | 7 |  | 17 |
|  | 2 | 3 |  | 5 | 6 |  | 8 | 9 | 10 | 11 |  |  | 1 |  | 4 | 7 |  | 18 |
|  | 2 | 3 |  | 5 | 6 | 8 | 7 | 9 | 10 | 11* |  |  | 1 |  | 4 | 12 |  | 19 |
|  | 2 | 3 |  | 5 | 6 | 7* | 8 | 9 | 10 | 11 |  |  | 1 |  | 4 | 12 |  | 20 |
|  | 2 | 3 |  | 5 | 6 |  | 8* | 12 | 10 | 11 |  | 7 | 1 |  | 4 | 9 |  | 21 |
|  | 2 | 3 | 12 | 5 | 6 |  | 8* |  | 10 | 11 |  | 7 | 1 |  | 4 | 9 |  | 22 |
|  | 2 | 3 | 12 | 5 | 6 |  |  | 8* | 10 | 11 |  | 7 | 1 |  | 4 | 9 |  | 23 |
|  | 2 | 3 | 12 | 5 | 6 | 8 |  |  | 10 | 11 |  | 7* | 1 |  | 4 | 9 |  | 24 |
|  | 2 | 3 | 12 | 5 | 6 | 8 |  |  | 10 | 11 |  | 7 | 1 |  | 4 | 9* |  | 25 |
|  | 2 | 3 | 4 | 5 | 6 | 8 |  |  | 10 | 11 |  | 9 | 7 |  | 1 |  |  | 26 |
|  | 2 | 3* | 12 | 5 | 6 | 7 |  | 9 | 10 | 11 |  | 8 | 1 |  | 4 |  |  | 27 |
|  | 2 |  | 3 | 5 | 6 | 7* |  | 9 | 10 | 11 |  | 8 | 1 |  | 4 | 12 |  | 28 |
|  | 3 | 2 |  | 5 | 6 | 12 |  | 9 | 10 | 11 |  | 7* | 1 |  | 4 |  | 8 | 29 |
|  | 3 |  | 2 | 5 | 6 | 7 |  | 9* | 10 | 11 |  | 12 | 1 |  | 4 |  | 8 | 30 |
|  | 2 | 3 | 6 | 5 |  | 7 |  |  | 10 | 11 |  | 9 | 1 |  | 4 |  | 8 | 31 |
|  | 2 | 3 |  | 5 | 6 | 7 |  |  | 10 | 11 |  | 9 | 1 |  | 4 |  | 8 | 32 |
|  | 3 | 2 |  | 5 | 6 | 7* |  | 12 | 10 | 11 |  | 9 | 1 |  | 4 |  | 8 | 33 |
|  | 3 |  |  | 5 | 6 | 7 |  | 9 | 10 | 11 |  | 2 | 1 |  | 4* | 12 | 8 | 34 |
|  | 2 | 3 | 4 | 5 | 6 | 7 |  |  | 10 | 11 |  | 9 | 1 |  |  |  | 8 | 35 |
| 1 | 2 | 3 | 6 | 5 | 4 |  |  | 12 | 10 | 11 |  | 9* |  |  | 7 |  | 8 | 36 |
| 1 | 2 | 3 |  | 5 | 6 | 4 |  | 9 | 10 | 11 |  |  |  |  | 7 |  | 8 | 37 |
| 1 | 2 | 3 |  | 5 | 6 | 4 |  | 9 | 10 | 11 |  | 12 |  |  | 7* |  | 8 | 38 |
| 1 | 2 | 3 |  | 5 | 6 | 4 |  | 9 | 10* | 11 |  | 7 |  |  |  | 12 | 8 | 39 |
| 1 | 2 | 3 |  | 5 | 6 | 4 |  | 9 |  | 11 |  | 7 |  |  | 10 |  | 8 | 40 |
| 1 | 2 | 3 |  | 5 | 6 | 4 |  | 9 |  | 11 |  | 7* |  |  | 10 | 12 | 8 | 41 |
| 1 | 2 | 3 |  | 5 | 6 | 4 |  | 9 |  | 11 |  | 7 |  |  | 10 |  | 8 | 42 |
| 1 | 2 | 3 | 6 | 5 | 4 |  |  | 9* | 10 | 11 |  | 12 |  |  | 7 |  | 8 | 43 |
|  | 2 | 3 |  | 5 | 6 | 4 |  | 9 | 10 | 11 |  |  | 1 |  | 7 |  | 8 | 44 |
|  | 2 |  |  | 5 | 6 | 4 | 7 | 9* |  | 11 |  | 3 | 1 |  | 10 | 12 | 8 | 45 |
|  | 2 |  |  | 5 | 6 | 4 | 7 | 9 |  | 11 |  | 3 | 1 |  | 10 | 12 | 8 | 46 |
| 19 | 38 | 38 | 22 | 44 | 43 | 22 | 33 | 32 | 44 | 38 | 6 | 36 | 27 | — | 33 | 13 | 18 | |

Substitute (12th‑man) appearances:  +1s  +6s   +1s +1s +4s   +1s +4s   +1s +12s

# SOUTHEND UNITED

| | Ht | Wt | Birthplace | Clubs | League App. | League Gls |
|---|---|---|---|---|---|---|
| **Goalkeepers** | | | | | | |
| Mervyn Cawston | 6 2 | 13 4 | Norwich | Norwich C | 4 | — |
| | | | | Southend (on loan) | 10 | — |
| | | | | Leicester C (on loan) | — | — |
| | | | | Newport Co (on loan) | 4 | — |
| | | | | Gillingham | 19 | — |
| | | | | Chicago S | — | — |
| | | | | Southend U | 146 | — |
| John Keeley | 6 0 | 12 3 | Plaistow | Southend U | 31 | — |
| **Defenders** | | | | | | |
| Alan Moody | 5 11 | 11 10 | Middlesbrough | Middlesbrough | 46 | — |
| | | | | Southend U | 399 | 40 |
| Tony Hadley | 6 0 | 12 2 | Rochford | Southend U | 234 | 16 |
| John Walker | 5 10 | 11 5 | Rochford | Southend U | 48 | — |
| Phil Dudley | 5 7 | 10 2 | Basildon | Southend U | 109 | 3 |
| Steve Yates | 6 0 | 12 13 | Burton upon Trent | Leicester C | 19 | — |
| | | | | Southend U | 180 | 5 |
| Dave Cusack | 6 1½ | 13 12 | Rotherham | Sheffield W | 95 | 1 |
| | | | | Southend U | 158 | 13 |
| **Midfield** | | | | | | |
| Glenn Pennyfather | 5 8 | 10 4 | Billericay | Southend U | 34 | 4 |
| Ron Pountney | 5 6 | 9 13 | Bilston | Walsall | 1 | — |
| | | | | Port Vale | — | — |
| | | | | Southend U | 234 | 19 |
| Anton Otulakowski | 5 7 | 10 10 | Dewsbury | Barnsley | 42 | 2 |
| | | | | West Ham U | 17 | — |
| | | | | Southend U | 132 | 3 |
| Micky Stead | 5 8 | 11 7 | West Ham | Tottenham H | 15 | — |
| | | | | Swansea C (on loan) | 5 | 1 |
| | | | | Southend U | 154 | 4 |
| Keith Mercer | 5 9 | 13 0 | Lewisham | Watford | 134 | 46 |
| | | | | Southend U | 96 | 27 |
| **Forwards** | | | | | | |
| Graham Franklin* | 5 9 | 11 3 | Bicester | Southend U | 6 | 1 |
| Terry Gray* | 5 8 | 10 0 | Bradford | Chelsea | — | — |
| | | | | Huddersfield T | 163 | 36 |
| | | | | Southend U | 110 | 28 |
| Garry Nelson | 5 10 | 10 10 | Braintree | Southend U | 84 | 9 |
| Derek Spence (N Ireland) | 5 10 | 11 3 | Belfast | Oldham Ath | 6 | — |
| | | | | Bury | 140 | 44 |
| | | | | Olympiakos | (not known) | |
| | | | | Blackpool | 85 | 20 |
| | | | | Southend U | 104 | 32 |
| Danny Greaves | 5 7 | 9 7 | Upminster | Southend U | 25 | 6 |
| Steve Phillips | 5 6 | 10 9 | Tottenham | Birmingham C | 20 | 1 |
| | | | | Torquay U (on loan) | 6 | — |
| | | | | Northampton T | 51 | 8 |
| | | | | Brentford | 157 | 65 |
| | | | | Northampton T | 75 | 29 |
| | | | | Southend U | 18 | 10 |

# STOCKPORT COUNTY Division 4

*President/Chairman:* A. N. Kirk.
*Directors:* P. Lukic, A. M. Barlow, J. Lewis, J. R. G. White.
*Chief Executive/Secretary:* T. R. McCreery FAAI.
*Manager:* Eric Webster.
*Assistant Secretary/Commercial Manager:* Peter Lamb.
*Year Formed:* 1883. *Turned Professional:* 1891.
*Limited Company:* 1908.
*Previous Names:* Heaton Norris Rovers 1883–88, Heaton Norris 1888–90.

*Previous Grounds:* 1883 Heaton Norris Recreation Ground, 1884 Heaton Norris Wanderers Cricket Ground, 1885 Chorlton's Farm, Chorlton's Lane, 1886 Heaton Norris Cricket Ground, 1887 Wilkes' Field, Belmont Street, 1889 Nursery Inn, Green Lane, 1902 Edgeley Park.

**Football League Record:**
1900 Elected to Division 2; 1904 failed re-election; 1905–21 Division 2; 1921–22 Division 3(N); 1922–26 Division 2; 1926–37 Division 3(N); 1937–38 Division 2; 1938–58 Division 3(N); 1958–59 Division 3; 1959–67 Division 4; 1967–70 Division 3; 1970– Division 4.

**Honours:** *Football League:* Division 2 best season: 17th, 1905–06; Division 3(N) – Champions 1921–22, 1936–37; Runners-up 1928–29, 1929–30; Division 4 – Champions 1966–67. *FA Cup* best season: 5th rd, 1935, 1950. *Football League Cup* best season: 4th rd, 1972–73.

*Record Victory:* 13-0 v Halifax T, Division 3(N), 6 Jan, 1934.

*Record Defeat:* 1-8 v Chesterfield, Division 2, 19 Apr, 1902.

*Most League Points:* 64, Division 4, 1966–67.

*Most League Goals:* 115, Division 3(N), 1933–34.

*Highest League Scorer in Season:* Alf Lythgoe, 46, Division 3(N), 1933–34.

*Most League Goals in Total Aggregate:* Jack Connor, 132, 1951–56.

*Most Capped Player:* Harry Hardy, 1, England.

*Most League Appearances:* Bob Murray, 465, 1952–63.

*Record Transfer Fee Received:* £80,000 from Manchester C for Stuart Lee, Sept 1979.

*Record Transfer Fee Paid:* £25,000 to Albion Rovers for Tony Coyle, Dec 1979.

*Previous Managers since the War:* Bob Marshall, Andy Beattie, Dick Duckworth, Willie Moir, Reg Flewin, Trevor Porteous, Bert Trautmann, Eddie Quigley, Jimmy Meadows, Walter Galbraith, Matt Woods, Brian Doyle, Jimmy Meadows, Roy Chapman, Eddie Quigley, Alan Thompson, Mike Summerbee, Jimmy McGuigan.

*Programme Editor:* Howard Jones.

---

**Edgeley Park, Hardcastle Road, Stockport, Cheshire SK3 9DD.** Telephone: 061-480 8888. *Ground capacity:* 16,500. *Record attendance:* 27,833 v Liverpool, FA Cup 5th rd, 11 Feb, 1950. *Record receipts:* £19,382 v Arsenal, League Cup 3rd rd, 22 Sept, 1980. *Pitch measurements:* 110yd×75yd.
*How to get there:* Edgeley Park is situated within a mile of Mersey Square, the town centre; the ground is a few minutes walk via Wellington Road South and Greek Street. The main line railway station lies just off Greek Street and is only a five minute walk to the Ground.
*Match tickets:* Seats can be reserved in the Main Stand by post or by telephone.
*Car parking:* Ample street parking around the ground.
*Entertainments/catering facilities:* Top class cabaret club next to the ground; four refreshment bars around the ground (not licensed).
*Supporters Club shop:* Small kiosk situated on Popular side of ground.
*Handbooks/programmes:* The *Matchday Magazine* is available outside the ground. It is also available on subscription to the Programme Editor by post.
*Extra information:* In 1934 Stockport County created a record which is still unsurpassed in a Football League game when they defeated Halifax Town 13-0, eleven goals coming in the second half.
*Club Colours:* Royal blue and white striped shirts, blue trim, white sleeves, white shorts, blue trimmings, red stockings, three white bands at top.
*Change Colours:* Yellow shirts, green shorts, green stockings with yellow bands at top.
*Club Captain:* Brian Lloyd.
*Club Nickname:* County.

## STOCKPORT COUNTY 1981–82 LEAGUE RECORD

| Match No. | Date | Venue | Opponents | Result | H/T Score | Goalscorers | Attendance |
|---|---|---|---|---|---|---|---|
| 1 | Aug 29 | A | Blackpool | L 0-2 | 0-1 | | 4556 |
| 2 | Sept 4 | H | Aldershot | W 4-2 | 3-2 | Coyle 2, Uzelac, Williams | 2239 |
| 3 | 12 | A | Bury | L 0-2 | 0-0 | | 3077 |
| 4 | 18 | H | Peterborough U | W 3-0 | 1-0 | Uzelac, Fowler, Sword | 2382 |
| 5 | 21 | H | Sheffield U | W 1-0 | 0-0 | Sword | 5450 |
| 6 | 26 | A | Port Vale | L 0-1 | 0-1 | | 2757 |
| 7 | 29 | A | Northampton T | D 0-0 | 0-0 | | 1865 |
| 8 | Oct 3 | H | AFC Bournemouth | L 1-2 | 0-2 | Power | 2718 |
| 9 | 10 | A | Wigan Ath | L 1-2 | 1-0 | Power | 4873 |
| 10 | 16 | H | Crewe Alex | W 2-0 | 0-0 | Williams, Coyle | 2669 |
| 11 | 19 | H | Bradford C | L 2-3 | 2-2 | Sword, Williams | 3684 |
| 12 | 24 | A | Rochdale | L 1-4 | 1-3 | Fowler | 1778 |
| 13 | 30 | H | Mansfield T | W 3-0 | 1-0 | Sunley, Williams, Power | 2081 |
| 14 | Nov 4 | A | Hereford U | D 0-0 | 0-0 | | 2350 |
| 15 | 7 | A | Darlington | L 0-2 | 0-1 | | 1556 |
| 16 | 13 | H | Halifax T | W 2-1 | 1-1 | Power, Sherlock | 2493 |
| 17 | 28 | H | Torquay U | W 2-1 | 2-0 | Fowler, Power | 1800 |
| 18 | Dec 5 | A | York C | D 2-2 | 2-2 | Vaughan, Park | 1762 |
| 19 | Jan 25 | H | Hartlepool U | L 0-2 | 0-1 | | 1924 |
| 20 | 30 | A | Peterborough U | L 0-2 | 0-1 | | 3525 |
| 21 | Feb 1 | H | Blackpool | L 2-3 | 1-2 | Sherlock (pen), Park | 3008 |
| 22 | 6 | H | Bury | W 2-1 | 0-0 | Park, Power | 3155 |
| 23 | 9 | A | Sheffield U | L 0-4 | 0-1 | | 11,603 |
| 24 | 13 | A | AFC Bournemouth | L 0-1 | 0-0 | | 5628 |
| 25 | 15 | H | Tranmere R | D 1-1 | 0-1 | Williams | 1934 |
| 26 | 19 | H | Port Vale | L 1-2 | 1-0 | Williams | 3001 |
| 27 | 26 | H | Wigan Ath | L 0-1 | 0-0 | | 5084 |
| 28 | Mar 6 | A | Crewe Alex | W 2-0 | 0-0 | Coyle 2 | 1827 |
| 29 | 10 | A | Bradford C | L 1-5 | 1-0 | Lloyd | 3941 |
| 30 | 12 | H | Rochdale | L 0-4 | 0-2 | | 2079 |
| 31 | 15 | H | Hereford U | D 1-1 | 0-1 | Sunley | 1357 |
| 32 | 20 | A | Mansfield T | D 2-2 | 1-0 | Williams, Emerson | 2159 |
| 33 | 22 | H | Colchester U | D 0-0 | 0-0 | | 1740 |
| 34 | 26 | H | Darlington | W 1-0 | 0-0 | Coyle | 1831 |
| 35 | 30 | A | Scunthorpe U | D 0-0 | 0-0 | | 1815 |
| 36 | Apr 2 | A | Halifax T | L 1-4 | 0-2 | Williams | 2135 |
| 37 | 6 | A | Aldershot | D 1-1 | 0-0 | Park | 1304 |
| 38 | 10 | A | Hartlepool U | D 2-2 | 2-1 | Stafford, Coyle | 1506 |
| 39 | 12 | H | Hull C | L 1-2 | 0-0 | Williams | 2450 |
| 40 | 16 | H | York C | W 4-1 | 2-0 | Phillips 2, Sherlock (pen), Park | 1938 |
| 41 | 20 | A | Hull C | D 0-0 | 0-0 | | 3526 |
| 42 | 24 | A | Torquay U | L 0-1 | 0-0 | | 1619 |
| 43 | 30 | H | Northampton T | D 0-0 | 0-0 | | 1658 |
| 44 | May 4 | A | Tranmere R | L 0-2 | 0-2 | | 1212 |
| 45 | 7 | A | Colchester U | W 1-0 | 0-0 | Phillips | 2132 |
| 46 | 14 | H | Scunthorpe U | D 1-1 | 0-1 | Phillips | 1945 |

**Final League Position: 18**

**Goalscorers**

*League* (48): Williams 9, Coyle 7, Power 6, Park 5, Phillips 4, Fowler 3, Sherlock 3 (2 pens), Sword 3, Sunley 2, Uzelac 2, Emerson 1, Lloyd 1, Stafford 1, Vaughan 1.
*League Cup* (1): Fowler 1.
*FA Cup* (4): Williams 2, Park 1, Smith 1.

| **League Cup** First Round | Wigan Ath (a) | 0-3 |
|---|---|---|
| | (h) | 1-2 |
| **FA Cup** First Round | Mossley (h) | 3-1 |
| Second Round | Port Vale (a) | 1-4 |

| Lloyd | Thorpe | Sherlock | Fowler | Sword | Uzelac | Williams | Wardrobe | Coyle | Park | Stafford | Sunley | Rutter | Power | Smith | Dwyer | Connor | Vaughan | Emerson | Seddon | Phillips | Match No. |
|---|---|---|---|---|---|---|---|---|---|---|---|---|---|---|---|---|---|---|---|---|---|
| 1 | 2 | 3 | 4 | 5 | 6 | 7 | 8* | 9 | 10 | 11 | 12 | | | | | | | | | | 1 |
| 1 | 2 | 3 | 4 | 5 | 6 | 7 | 8 | 9 | 10 | 11 | | | | | | | | | | | 2 |
| 1 | 2 | 3 | 4 | 5 | 6 | 7 | 8 | 9 | 10 | 11 | | | | | | | | | | | 3 |
| 1 | 2 | 11 | 4 | 5 | 6 | 7 | 8 | 9 | 10 | | | 3 | | | | | | | | | 4 |
| 1 | 2 | 11 | 4* | 5 | 6 | 7 | 8 | 9 | 10 | | 12 | 3 | | | | | | | | | 5 |
| 1 | 5 | 3 | 4 | 6 | | 7 | 8 | 9 | 10* | 12 | 11 | 2 | | | | | | | | | 6 |
| 1 | 5 | 3 | 4 | 6 | | 7 | | 9 | 10 | 11 | 8 | 2 | | | | | | | | | 7 |
| 1 | 5 | 3 | 4 | 6 | | 7 | 12 | 9* | 10 | 11 | | 2 | 8 | | | | | | | | 8 |
| 1 | 5 | 3 | 4 | 6 | | 7 | | 8 | 9 | 10 | 11 | 2 | | | | | | | | | 9 |
| 1 | 5 | 3 | 4 | 6 | | 7 | | 8 | 9 | 10 | 11 | 2 | | | | | | | | | 10 |
| 1 | 5 | 11 | | 6 | | 7 | | 9 | 10 | | 4 | 2 | 8 | | 3 | | | | | | 11 |
| | 5 | 11 | 4 | 6 | | 7 | | 9 | 10 | | 8 | 2 | | | 3 | 1 | | | | | 12 |
| 1 | 5 | 3 | 4 | 6 | | 7* | | 12 | 9 | 10 | 11 | 2 | 8 | | | | | | | | 13 |
| 1 | 5 | 3 | 4 | 6 | | 7 | | 9 | 10 | 11 | | 2 | 8 | | | | | | | | 14 |
| 1 | 5 | 3 | 4 | 6 | | 7 | | 9 | 10 | 11 | | 2 | 8 | | | | | | | | 15 |
| 1 | 5 | 11 | 4 | 6 | | 7 | | 9 | 10 | | | 2 | 8 | | 3 | | | | | | 16 |
| 1 | 5 | 11 | 4 | | | 7 | | 9 | 10 | 12 | | 2 | 8 | 6 | 3* | | | | | | 17 |
| 1 | 5 | 3 | 4 | | | 7 | | | 10 | | 9 | 2 | 8 | 11 | | | 6 | | | | 18 |
| 1 | 5 | 3 | 4 | | | 7 | | 9 | 10 | | | 2 | 8 | 11 | | | 6 | | | | 19 |
| 1 | 5 | 3 | 4 | | | 7 | | 9 | 10 | 11* | 12 | 2 | 8 | 6 | | | | | | | 20 |
| 1 | 5 | 3 | 4 | | | 7 | | 9 | 10 | 12 | 11* | 2 | 8 | 6 | | | | | | | 21 |
| 1 | 5 | 3 | 4 | | | 7 | | | 10 | 11 | 9 | 2 | 8 | 6 | | | | | | | 22 |
| 1 | 5 | 3 | 4 | | | 7 | | | 10 | 11 | 9 | 2 | 8 | 6 | | | | | | | 23 |
| 1 | 5 | 3 | | | | 7 | 12 | | 10 | 11 | 9* | 2 | 8 | 6 | | | | 4 | | | 24 |
| 1 | 5 | 3 | | | | 7 | 12 | | 10 | 11 | 9* | 2 | 8 | 6 | | | | 4 | | | 25 |
| 1 | 5 | 3 | 9 | | | 7 | | 11 | 10 | | | 2 | 8 | 6 | | | | 4 | | | 26 |
| 1 | 5 | 3 | 9 | | | 7 | | 11 | 10 | | 8 | 2 | | 6 | | | | 4 | | | 27 |
| 1 | 5 | 3 | 9 | | | 7 | | 11 | 10 | 12 | 8 | 2 | | 6 | | | | 4* | | | 28 |
| 1 | 5 | 3 | 9 | | | 7 | | 11* | 10 | 12 | 8 | | | 6 | | | | 4 | 2 | | 29 |
| 1 | 5 | 3 | 9 | | | 7 | | | 10 | | 8 | | 11 | 6 | | | | 4 | 2 | | 30 |
| 1 | 5 | 3 | 2 | | | 7 | | | 10 | 11 | 8 | | 9 | 6 | | | | 4 | | | 31 |
| 1 | 5 | 3 | | | | 7 | | 9 | 10 | 11 | | 2 | | 6 | | | | 4 | | 8 | 32 |
| 1 | 5 | 3 | | | | 7 | | 9 | 10 | 11 | | 2 | | 6 | | | | 4 | | 8 | 33 |
| 1 | 5 | 3 | | | | 7 | | 9 | 10 | 11 | | 2 | | 6 | | | | 4 | | 8 | 34 |
| 1 | 5 | 3 | | | | 7 | | 9 | 10 | 11 | | 2 | | 6 | | | | 4 | | 8 | 35 |
| 1 | 5 | 3 | | | | 7 | | | 10 | 11 | 9 | 2 | | 6 | | | | 4 | | 8 | 36 |
| 1 | 5 | 3 | | | | 7 | | | 10 | 11 | 9 | 2 | | 6 | | | | 4 | | 8 | 37 |
| 1 | 5 | 3 | | | | 7 | | 9 | 10 | 11 | 8 | 2 | | 6 | | | | 4 | | | 38 |
| 1 | 5 | 3 | 12 | | | 7 | | 9 | 10 | 11 | 8* | 2 | | 6 | | | | 4 | | | 39 |
| 1 | 5 | 3 | 7 | | | | | 9 | 10 | 11 | | 2 | | 6 | | | | 4 | | 8 | 40 |
| 1 | 5 | 3 | | | | 7 | | 9 | 10 | 11 | | 2 | | 6 | | | | 4 | | 8 | 41 |
| 1 | 5 | 3 | | | | 7 | | 9 | 10 | | 11 | 2 | | 6 | | | | 4 | | 8 | 42 |
| 1 | 5 | 3 | | | | 7 | | 9 | 10 | | 11 | 2 | | 6 | | | | 4 | | 8 | 43 |
| 1 | 5 | 3 | | | | 7 | | 9 | 10 | | | 2 | 11 | 6 | | | | 4 | | 8 | 44 |
| 1 | 5 | 3 | | | | 7 | | 9 | 10 | | | 2 | 11 | 6 | | | | 4 | | 8 | 45 |
| 1 | 5 | 3 | | | | 7 | | 9 | 10 | | | 2 | 11 | 6 | | | | 4 | | 8 | 46 |
| 45 | 46 | 46 | 29 | 16 | 5 | 45 | 7 | 36 | 46 | 21 | 27 | 39 | 22 | 31 | 4 | 1 | 2 | 23 | 2 | 13 | |
| | | | +1s | | | | | | | | +4s | | | +4s | +4s | | | | | | |

## STOCKPORT COUNTY

| | Ht | Wt | Birthplace | Clubs | League App. | League Gls |
|---|---|---|---|---|---|---|
| **Goalkeepers** | | | | | | |
| John Connor | 6 4 | 13 7 | Stockport | Stockport Co | 1 | — |
| (Non-contract) | | | | | | |
| Brian Lloyd | 6 1 | 13 7 | Rhyl | Stockport Co | 32 | — |
| (Wales) | | | | Southend U | 46 | — |
| | | | | Wrexham | 266 | — |
| | | | | Port Vale (on loan) | 16 | — |
| | | | | Chester | 94 | — |
| | | | | Stockport Co | 45 | 1 |
| **Defenders** | | | | | | |
| John Rutter | 5 9 | 10 10 | Warrington | Wolverhampton W | — | — |
| | | | | Bournemouth | 4 | — |
| | | | | Exeter C | 32 | 1 |
| | | | | Stockport Co | 264 | 8 |
| Andy Thorpe | 5 11 | 12 0 | Stockport | Stockport Co | 162 | 2 |
| Steve Sherlock | 5 9 | 11 8 | Birmingham | Manchester C | — | — |
| | | | | Luton T | 2 | — |
| | | | | Stockport Co | 126 | 7 |
| Steve Uzelac* | 5 11 | 12 4 | Doncaster | Doncaster R | 185 | 9 |
| | | | | Mansfield T (on loan) | 2 | — |
| | | | | Liverpool | — | — |
| | | | | Preston NE | 9 | — |
| | | | | Stockport Co | 31 | 2 |
| Alan Dwyer | 5 7 | 10 7 | Liverpool | Wrexham | 180 | 2 |
| (Contract cancelled) | | | | Stockport Co | 4 | — |
| Andy Seddon | 5 8½ | 11 0 | Worsley | Stockport Co | 2 | — |
| (Non-contract) | | | | | | |
| **Midfield** | | | | | | |
| Nigel Smith | 6 0 | 11 2 | Manchester | Blackburn R | — | — |
| | | | | Stockport Co | 34 | — |
| Terry Park | 5 11 | 11 10 | Liverpool | Wolverhampton W | — | — |
| | | | | Minnesota | (not known) | |
| | | | | Stockport Co | 144 | 14 |
| David Booth* | 6 0 | 11 7 | Handforth | Stockport Co | 28 | 4 |
| Martin Fowler* | 5 11 | 13 0 | York | Huddersfield T | 73 | 2 |
| | | | | Norwich C (on loan) | — | — |
| | | | | Hartlepool U (on loan) | 6 | — |
| | | | | Blackburn R | 38 | — |
| | | | | Stockport Co | 75 | 6 |
| Mark Leigh | | | Manchester | Manchester C | — | — |
| (Non-contract) | | | | Stockport Co | 6 | 1 |
| Dean Emerson | 5 8 | 10 8 | Salford | Stockport Co | 23 | 1 |
| (Non-contract) | | | | | | |
| **Forwards** | | | | | | |
| Oshor Williams | 5 9½ | 11 7 | Stockton | Manchester U | — | — |
| | | | | Gateshead | (not known) | |
| | | | | Southampton | 6 | — |
| | | | | Exeter C (on loan) | 3 | — |
| | | | | Stockport Co | 109 | 16 |
| Tony Coyle | 5 10 | 11 12 | Glasgow | Albion R | 46 | 5 |
| | | | | Stockport Co | 84 | 8 |
| Tommy Sword | 6 2 | 14 0 | Newcastle | Bishop Auckland | (not known) | |
| | | | | Stockport Co | 84 | 16 |
| Dave Sunley* | 5 9 | 11 6 | Lingdale | Sheffield W | 133 | 21 |
| | | | | Nottingham F (on loan) | 1 | — |
| | | | | Hull C | 69 | 11 |
| | | | | Lincoln C | 41 | 6 |
| | | | | Stockport Co | 83 | 6 |
| Mike Power | 6 0 | 12 0 | Stockport | Stockport Co | 27 | 6 |
| Andy Stafford* | 6 1½ | 11 12 | Stretford | Halifax T | 41 | 1 |
| | | | | Stockport Co | 25 | 1 |
| Micky Wardrobe | 5 11 | 12 0 | Newcastle | Burnley | 1 | — |
| | | | | Stockport Co | 11 | — |

# STOKE CITY Division 1

*Chairman:* P. Axon.

*Directors:* A. W. Clubb, F. Edwards.

*Manager:* Richie Barker.
*Assistant Manager:* Bill Asprey
*Secretary:* M. J. Potts.
*Year Formed:* 1863 (second oldest League Club).
*Turned Professional:* 1885.   *Limited Company:* 1908.
*Previous Grounds:* 1875, Sweeting's Field; 1878, Victoria Ground (previously known as the Athletic Club Ground).

**Football League Record:**
1888 Founder Members of Football League; 1890 Not re-elected; 1891 Re-elected; Relegated in 1907, and after one year in Division 2, resigned for financial reasons; Re-elected to Division 2 in 1919; 1922–23 Division 1; 1923–26 Division 2; 1926–27 Division 3(N); 1927–33 Division 2; 1933–53 Division 1; 1953–63 Division 2; 1963–77 Division 1; 1977–79 Division 2; 1979– Division 1.

**Honours:** *Football League:* Division 1 best season: 4th, 1935–36, 1946–47; Division 2 – Champions 1932–33, 1962–63; Runners-up 1921–22; Promoted 1978–79 (3rd); Division 3(N) – Champions 1926–27. *FA Cup:* Semi-finals 1899, 1971, 1972. *Football League Cup:* Winners 1971–72. **European Competitions:** *UEFA Cup:* 1972–73, 1974–75.

*Record Victory:* 10-3 v WBA, Division 1, 4 Feb, 1937.

*Record Defeat:* 0-10 v Preston NE, Division 1, 14 Sept, 1889.

*Most League Points:* 63, Division 3(N), 1926–27.

*Most League Goals:* 92, Division 3(N), 1926–27.

*Highest League Scorer in Season:* Freddie Steele, 33, Division 1, 1936–37.

*Most League Goals in Total Aggregate:* Freddie Steele, 142, 1934–49.

*Most League Appearances:* Eric Skeels, 506, 1958–76.

*Most Capped Player:* Gordon Banks 36 (73), England.

*Record Transfer Fee Received:* £600,000 from Tottenham H for Garth Crooks, July 1980.

*Record Transfer Fee Paid:* £325,000 to Leicester C for Peter Shilton, Nov 1974.

*Previous Managers since the War:* Bob McGrory, Frank Taylor, Tony Waddington, George Eastham, Alan A'Court, Alan Durban.

*Address of Social Club:* c/o Football Club.

---

**Victoria Ground, Stoke-on-Trent.** Telephone Stoke-on-Trent 413511. *Telegraphic address:* 'Football, Stoke-on-Trent'. *Ground capacity:* 35,000. *Record attendance:* 51,380 v Arsenal, Division 1, 29 Mar, 1937. *Record receipts:* £43,000 v Manchester C, Division 1, Sept 1981. *Pitch measurements:* 116yd×75yd.

*How to get there:* Stoke-on-Trent railway station, on the main line from London, is five minutes walk from the ground. No special buses from the town centre because the ground is central. By road, Stoke is well served by the M6 which passes just two miles from the city.

*Match tickets:* Bookable two weeks before the match. Ticket office tel: Stoke-on-Trent 413961.

*Car parking:* The official car park in Wheildon Road holds 2,000 cars. Street parking permitted.

*Entertainments/catering facilities:* Social club. Refreshments obtainable on the ground.

*Handbooks/programmes:* Programmes available on subscription.

*Extra information:* Neville Coleman scored seven goals for Stoke against Lincoln City in 1957, a record for a winger in English senior football.

*Club Colours:* Red and white striped shirts, white shorts and stockings.

*Change Colours:* All sky blue.

*Club Captain:* Dave Watson.

*Club Nickname:* Potters.

## STOKE CITY 1981–82 LEAGUE RECORD

| Match No. | Date | Venue | Opponents | Result | H/T Score | Goalscorers | Attendance |
|---|---|---|---|---|---|---|---|
| 1 | Aug 29 | A | Arsenal | W 1-0 | 1-0 | Chapman | 28,212 |
| 2 | Sept 2 | H | Coventry C | W 4-0 | 2-0 | Chapman 2, Heath 2 | 13,914 |
| 3 | 5 | H | Manchester C | L 1-3 | 0-1 | Chapman | 25,256 |
| 4 | 12 | A | West Ham U | L 2-3 | 1-1 | O'Callaghan, Maguire (pen) | 28,774 |
| 5 | 19 | H | Nottingham F | L 1-2 | 1-0 | Heath | 15,653 |
| 6 | 23 | A | Aston Villa | D 2-2 | 0-1 | Griffiths, Maguire (pen) | 25,637 |
| 7 | 26 | A | Middlesbrough | L 2-3 | 1-1 | Griffiths, Chapman | 11,604 |
| 8 | Oct 3 | H | Everton | W 3-1 | 1-0 | Chapman 2, Maguire | 16,007 |
| 9 | 10 | A | Tottenham H | L 0-2 | 0-0 | | 30,520 |
| 10 | 17 | H | Swansea C | L 1-2 | 1-0 | Griffiths | 14,665 |
| 11 | 24 | H | Birmingham C | W 1-0 | 0-0 | Chapman | 15,399 |
| 12 | 31 | A | Brighton & HA | D 0-0 | 0-0 | | 17,862 |
| 13 | Nov 7 | H | Southampton | L 0-2 | 0-1 | | 13,864 |
| 14 | 14 | A | WBA | W 2-1 | 2-1 | Heath, Chapman | 15,787 |
| 15 | 21 | H | Ipswich T | W 2-0 | 0-0 | Chapman, Maguire | 13,802 |
| 16 | 24 | A | Coventry C | L 0-3 | 0-2 | | 10,250 |
| 17 | 28 | A | Wolverhampton W | L 0-2 | 0-1 | | 15,314 |
| 18 | Dec 5 | H | Leeds U | L 1-2 | 0-2 | Heath | 13,901 |
| 19 | Jan 9 | A | Manchester C | D 1-1 | 1-0 | O'Callaghan | 31,941 |
| 20 | 20 | H | Arsenal | L 0-1 | 0-1 | | 9625 |
| 21 | 23 | H | Manchester U | L 0-3 | 0-1 | | 19,682 |
| 22 | 30 | A | Nottingham F | D 0-0 | 0-0 | | 16,219 |
| 23 | Feb 6 | H | West Ham U | W 2-1 | 1-0 | Chapman, Maguire | 11,987 |
| 24 | 10 | A | Sunderland | W 2-0 | 0-0 | O'Callaghan, McIlroy | 14,317 |
| 25 | 13 | A | Everton | D 0-0 | 0-0 | | 20,656 |
| 26 | 20 | H | Middlesbrough | W 2-0 | 1-0 | O'Callaghan, Chapman | 10,473 |
| 27 | 27 | H | Tottenham H | L 0-2 | 0-0 | | 20,592 |
| 28 | Mar 6 | A | Swansea C | L 0-3 | 0-1 | | 11,811 |
| 29 | 9 | H | Liverpool | L 1-5 | 0-2 | McIlroy | 16,758 |
| 30 | 13 | A | Birmingham C | L 1-2 | 0-1 | Chapman | 12,018 |
| 31 | 20 | H | Brighton & HA | D 0-0 | 0-0 | | 9120 |
| 32 | 27 | A | Southampton | L 3-4 | 0-3 | Biley, Watson, McIlroy | 20,058 |
| 33 | Apr 10 | H | Sunderland | L 0-1 | 0-1 | | 11,399 |
| 34 | 13 | A | Liverpool | L 0-2 | 0-2 | | 30,419 |
| 35 | 17 | A | Ipswich T | L 0-2 | 0-1 | | 20,309 |
| 36 | 24 | H | Wolverhampton W | W 2-1 | 1-1 | Maguire (pen), Chapman | 13,797 |
| 37 | 26 | A | Notts Co | L 1-3 | 1-1 | Chapman | 8656 |
| 38 | May 1 | A | Leeds U | D 0-0 | 0-0 | | 17,775 |
| 39 | 5 | H | Aston Villa | W 1-0 | 1-0 | Bracewell | 10,363 |
| 40 | 8 | H | Notts Co | D 2-2 | 2-1 | Watson, Maguire | 11,011 |
| 41 | 15 | A | Manchester U | L 0-2 | 0-2 | | 43,072 |
| 42 | 20 | H | WBA | W 3-0 | 2-0 | Watson, Chapman, O'Callaghan | 19,698 |

**Final League Position: 18**

**Goalscorers**

*League* (44): Chapman 16, Maguire 7 (3 pens), Heath 5, O'Callaghan 5, Griffiths 3, McIlroy 3, Watson 3, Biley 1, Bracewell 1.
*League Cup* (2): Chapman 1, Evans 1.
*FA Cup* (0).

| League Cup | Second Round | Manchester C (a) | 0-2 |
|---|---|---|---|
| | | (h) | 2-0 (lost 9-8 on pens) |
| FA Cup | Third Round | Norwich C (h) | 0-1 |

| Fox | Evans | Hampton | Dodd | O'Callaghan | Doyle | Griffiths | Heath | Chapman | Bracewell | Maguire | Ursem | Smith | Bould | Cook | Johnson | McManus | Ford | Kirk | Watson | Lumsden | McAughtrie | McIlroy | Parkin | Biley | Match No. |
|---|---|---|---|---|---|---|---|---|---|---|---|---|---|---|---|---|---|---|---|---|---|---|---|---|---|
| 1 | 2 | 3 | 4 | 5 | 6 | 7 | 8 | 9 | 10 | 11 | | | | | | | | | | | | | | | 1 |
| 1 | 2 | 3 | 4 | 5 | 6 | 7 | 8 | 9 | 10 | 11 | | | | | | | | | | | | | | | 2 |
| 1 | 2 | 3 | 4 | 5 | 6 | 7 | 8 | 9 | 10 | 11* | 12 | | | | | | | | | | | | | | 3 |
| 1 | 2 | 3 | 4 | 5 | 6 | 7 | 8 | 9 | 10 | 11 | | | | | | | | | | | | | | | 4 |
| 1 | 2 | 3 | 4* | 5 | | 7 | 8 | 9 | 10 | 11 | 12 | 6 | | | | | | | | | | | | | 5 |
| 1 | 2 | 3 | 4 | 5 | | 7 | 8 | 9 | 10 | 11 | | 6 | | | | | | | | | | | | | 6 |
| 1 | 2 | 3 | 4 | 5 | | 7 | 8* | 9 | 10 | 11 | | 6 | 12 | | | | | | | | | | | | 7 |
| 1 | 2 | 3 | 4 | 5 | | 7 | 8 | 9 | 10 | 11 | | 6 | | | | | | | | | | | | | 8 |
| 1 | 2 | 3 | 4 | 5 | | 7 | 8 | 9 | 10 | 11* | | 6 | 12 | | | | | | | | | | | | 9 |
| 1 | 2 | 3 | 4 | 5 | | 7 | 8 | 9 | 10 | 11 | | 6 | | | | | | | | | | | | | 10 |
| 1 | 2 | 3 | 4 | 5 | | 7 | 8 | 9 | 10 | 11 | | 6 | | | | | | | | | | | | | 11 |
| 1 | 2 | 3 | 4 | 5 | | 7 | 8 | 9 | 10 | | | 6 | | | 11 | | | | | | | | | | 12 |
| 1 | 2 | 3 | 4 | 5 | | 7 | 8 | 9 | 10 | 11* | | 6 | | | 12 | | | | | | | | | | 13 |
| 1 | 2 | 3 | 4 | 5 | | 7 | 8 | 9 | 10 | | | 6 | | | 11 | | | | | | | | | | 14 |
| 1 | 2 | 3 | 4 | 5 | | 7 | 8* | 9 | 10 | 12 | | 6 | | | 11 | | | | | | | | | | 15 |
| 1 | 2 | 3 | 4 | 5 | | 7 | 8* | 9 | 10 | 12 | | 6 | | | 11 | | | | | | | | | | 16 |
| | 2 | 3 | 4 | 5 | | | | 9 | 10 | 11 | | 6 | | | 7 | 1 | 8 | | | | | | | | 17 |
| | 2 | 3 | 4 | 5 | 6 | 7 | 8 | 9 | 10 | | | | | | 11 | 1 | | | | | | | | | 18 |
| 1 | 2 | | 4 | 8 | 6 | | | 9 | 10 | 11 | | | | | | | | 3 | 5 | 7 | | | | | 19 |
| 1 | 2 | | 4 | 8 | 6 | 12 | | 9 | 10 | 11 | | | | | | | | 3 | 5 | 7* | | | | | 20 |
| 1 | 2 | | 4 | 8 | 6 | 7 | | 9 | 10 | 12 | | | | | | 11* | | 3 | 5 | | | | | | 21 |
| 1 | | 3 | 4 | 8 | | 7 | | 9 | 10 | 11 | | | | | | | | 2 | 5 | | 6 | | | | 22 |
| 1 | | 3 | 4 | 8 | | 7* | | 9 | 10 | 11 | | | | | | | | 2 | 5 | 12 | 6 | | | | 23 |
| 1 | | 3 | 4 | 8 | | | | 9 | 10 | 11 | | | | | | | | 2 | 5 | | 6 | 7 | | | 24 |
| 1 | | 3 | 4 | 8 | | | | 9 | 10 | 11 | | | | | | | | 2 | 5 | | 6 | 7 | | | 25 |
| 1 | | 3 | 4 | 8 | | | | 9 | 10 | 11 | | | | | | | | 2 | 5 | | 6 | 7 | | | 26 |
| 1 | | 3 | 4* | 8 | | | | 9 | 10 | 11 | | | | | | | | 2 | 5 | 12 | 6 | 7 | | | 27 |
| 1 | | 3 | 4 | 8 | | 12 | | 9 | 10 | 11 | | | | | | | | 2* | 5 | | 6 | 7 | | | 28 |
| 1 | 2 | 3 | 4 | 8 | | 12 | | 9 | 10 | 11* | | | | | | | | | 5 | | 6 | 7 | | | 29 |
| 1 | | 3 | 4 | 8 | | 7 | | 9 | 10 | 11* | | | | | | | | 2 | 5 | 12 | 6 | | | | 30 |
| 1 | | 3 | 4 | 8 | | 12 | | 9* | 10 | 11 | | | | | | | | 2 | 5 | | 6 | 7 | | | 31 |
| 1 | | 3 | 4 | 8 | | | | 11 | 10 | | | | | | | | | | 5 | | 6 | 7 | 2 | 9 | 32 |
| 1 | | 3 | 4 | 12 | | 11 | 8 | | 10 | | | | | | | | | | 5 | | 6 | 7 | 2 | 9* | 33 |
| 1 | | 3 | 4 | 8 | | | | 9 | 10 | 11 | | | | | | | | | 5 | | 6 | 7 | 2 | | 34 |
| 1 | | 3 | 4 | 8 | | | | 9 | 10 | 11 | | | | | 2 | | | | 5 | | | 7 | | 6 | 35 |
| 1 | 2 | | | | | | | 9 | 10 | 11 | | 6 | | | 4 | | | | 5 | | | 7 | 3 | 8 | 36 |
| 1 | | 3 | 12 | | | | | 9 | 10 | 11 | | 6 | | | 4 | | | | 5 | | | 7 | 2 | 8* | 37 |
| 1 | 2 | 8 | 4 | | | | | 9 | 10 | 11 | | 6 | | | | | | | 5 | | | 7 | 3 | | 38 |
| 1 | 2 | 6 | 4 | | | | | 9 | 10 | 11 | | | | | | | | | 5 | | | 7 | 3 | 8 | 39 |
| | 2 | 6 | 4 | | | | | 9 | 10 | 11 | | | | | | 1 | | | 5 | | | 7 | 3 | 8 | 40 |
| 1 | 2 | 9 | 4* | 12 | | | | | 10 | 11 | | 6 | | | | | | | 5 | | | 7 | 3 | 8 | 41 |
| | 2 | 8 | 4 | | | | | 9 | 10 | 11* | | 6 | | | 1 | | 12 | | 5 | | | 7 | 3 | | 42 |
| 38 | 22 | 33 | 41 | 39 | 8 | 27 | 17 | 40 | 42 | 32 | 1 | 17 | 1 | — | 12 | 4 | 1 | 12 | 24 | 2 | 13 | 18 | 10 | 8 | |
| | | | | +2s | | +4s | | +1s | +3s | +2s | | +1s | | | +1s | +1s | | | +1s | | +3s | | | | |

## STOKE CITY

| | Ht | Wt | Birthplace | Clubs | League App. | League Gls |
|---|---|---|---|---|---|---|
| **Goalkeepers** | | | | | | |
| Peter Fox | 5 10½ | 12 4 | Scunthorpe | Sheffield W | 49 | — |
| | | | | West Ham U (on loan) | — | — |
| | | | | Barnsley (on loan) | 1 | — |
| | | | | Stoke C | 104 | — |
| Eric McManus | 6 1 | 12 12 | Limavady | Coventry C | 6 | — |
| | | | | Notts Co | 229 | — |
| | | | | Lincoln C (on loan) | 21 | — |
| | | | | Stoke C | 4 | — |
| **Defenders** | | | | | | |
| Denis Smith* | 6 0 | 12 2 | Stoke | Stoke C | 407 | 30 |
| | | | | York C (on loan) | 7 | 1 |
| Alan Dodd | 5 10¼ | 12 3 | Stoke | Stoke C | 354 | 3 |
| Ray Evans | 5 10 | 12 8 | Edmonton | Tottenham H | 136 | 2 |
| (Contract cancelled March 1982) | | | | Millwall | 74 | 3 |
| | | | | Fulham | 86 | 6 |
| | | | | Stoke C | 94 | 1 |
| Stephen Kirk* | 5 11½ | 10 8 | Kirkcaldy | East Fife | 25 | 2 |
| | | | | Stoke C | 12 | — |
| Dennis Thorley* | 6 0 | 11 4 | Stoke | Stoke C | 13 | — |
| | | | | Blackburn R (on loan) | 4 | — |
| David McAughtrie | 6 1 | 12 3 | Newcumnock | Stoke C | 14 | — |
| Peter Hampton | 5 7½ | 10 9 | Teeside | Leeds U | 68 | 2 |
| | | | | Stoke C | 66 | 2 |
| Dave Watson | 5 11½ | 12 0 | Nottingham | Notts Co | 23 | 1 |
| (England) | | | | Rotherham U | 121 | 20 |
| | | | | Sunderland | 177 | 27 |
| | | | | Manchester C | 146 | 4 |
| | | | | Werder Bremen | (not known) | |
| | | | | Southampton | 73 | 6 |
| | | | | Stoke C | 24 | 3 |
| Derek Parkin | 5 8½ | 11 0 | Newcastle | Huddersfield T | 61 | 1 |
| | | | | Wolverhampton W | 501 | 6 |
| | | | | Stoke C | 10 | — |
| Stephen Bould | 6 2½ | 11 13 | Stoke | Stoke C | 2 | — |
| **Midfield** | | | | | | |
| Paul A. Johnson* | 5 6½ | 11 12 | Stoke | Stoke C | 56 | — |
| Loek Ursem | 5 9 | 11 4 | Amsterdam | AZ Sportlaan | (not known) | |
| | | | | Stoke C | 38 | 7 |
| | | | | Sunderland (on loan) | 4 | — |
| John Lumsden | 5 8½ | 11 5 | Edinburgh | East Fife | 22 | 7 |
| | | | | Stoke C | 6 | — |
| Paul Bracewell | 5 8 | 10 9 | Stoke | Stoke C | 88 | 3 |
| Kevin Ronan | 5 6 | 10 7 | Thrybergh | Stoke C | — | — |
| Stephen Lennox | 5 7½ | 10 7 | Aberdeen | Stoke C | — | — |
| Sammy McIlroy | 5 9½ | 11 4 | Belfast | Manchester U | 342 | 57 |
| (N Ireland) | | | | Stoke C | 18 | 3 |
| Peter Griffiths | 5 6 | 10 8 | Barnstaple | Bideford | (not known) | |
| | | | | Stoke C | 41 | 4 |
| **Forwards** | | | | | | |
| Bren O'Callaghan | 6 2½ | 14 0 | Bradford | Doncaster R | 187 | 65 |
| (Eire) | | | | Stoke C | 170 | 39 |
| Lee Chapman | 6 1½ | 13 5 | Lincoln | Stoke C | 99 | 34 |
| | | | | Plymouth Arg (on loan) | 4 | — |
| Paul Maguire | 5 8 | 11 6 | Glasgow | Shrewsbury T | 151 | 35 |
| | | | | Stoke C | 50 | 10 |
| Stephen Ford | 6 0 | 12 7 | Shoreham | Lewes | (not known) | |
| | | | | Stoke C | 2 | — |

Free transfers: Colin Singer*, Chris Evans*.

# SUNDERLAND

## Division 1

*Chairman:* T. Cowie.

*Vice-Chairman:* K. I. Collings.

*Directors:* E. M. Evans, F. S. Cronin, J. M. Ditchburn, I. T. S. Fraser, P. J. Heyward.

*Manager:* Alan Durban.   *General Manager/Secretary:* G. Davidson.

*Assistant Manager:*

*Year Formed:* 1879.   *Turned Professional:* 1886.

*Limited Company:* 1906.

*Previous Grounds:* 1879, Blue House Field, Hendon; 1881, Ashbrooke; 1883, site of Cooper Street; 1884, Abbs Field, Fulwell; 1886, Newcastle Road; 1898, Roker Park.

*Previous Name:* 1879–81, Sunderland and District Teachers' AFC.

**Football League Record:**
1890 Elected to Division 1 (record run of 57 seasons); 1958–64 Division 2; 1964–70 Division 1; 1970–76 Division 2; 1976–77 Division 1; 1977–80 Division 2; 1980– Division 1.

*Honours: Football League:* Division 1 – Champions 1891–92, 1892–93, 1894–95, 1901–02, 1912–13, 1935–36; Runners-up 1893–94, 1897–98, 1900–01, 1922–23, 1934–35; Division 2 – Champions 1975–76; Runners-up 1963–64, 1979–80. *FA Cup:* Winners 1937, 1973; Runners-up 1913. *Football League Cup:* semi-finals: 1963. **European Competitions:** *European Cup-Winners' Cup:* 1973–74.

*Record Victory:* 11-1 v Fairfield, FA Cup 1st rd, 1894–95.

*Record Defeat:* 0-8 v West Ham U, Division 1, 19 Oct, 1968.

*Most League Points:* 61, Division 2, 1963–64.

*Most League Goals:* 109, Division 1, 1935–36.

*Highest League Scorer in Season:* Dave Halliday, 43, Division 1, 1928–29.

*Most League Goals in Total Aggregate:* Charlie Buchan, 209, 1911–25.

*Most Capped Player:* Jim Montgomery, 537, 1962–77.

*Most League Appearances:* Billy Bingham, 33 (56), Northern Ireland; Martin Harvey, 33, Northern Ireland.

*Record Transfer Fee Received:* £275,000 from Manchester C for Dennis Tueart, March 1974.

*Record Transfer Fee Paid:* £320,000 to San Lorenzo for Claudio Marangoni, Dec 1979.

*Previous Managers since the War:* Bill Murray, Alan Brown, George Hardwick, Ian McColl, Alan Brown, Bob Stokoe, Jimmy Adamson, Billy Elliott, Ken Knighton.

*Address of Supporters Club:* c/o Football Club.

---

**Roker Park Ground, Sunderland.** Telephone Sunderland 40332. *Telegraphic address:* 'Football, Sunderland'. *Ground capacity:* 47,000. *Record attendance:* 75,118 v Derby Co, FA Cup 6th rd replay, 8 Mar, 1933. *Record receipts:* £63,211 v Southampton, Division 1, 23 Aug, 1980. *Pitch measurements:* 113yd×74yd.

*How to get there:* From Sunderland railway station and Seaburn railway station take buses 123 and 124 to Redby Community Centre: the ground is five minutes walk away. Special buses from the town centre. By road via M1, A690 to Sunderland, and then route to Roker Park is signed.

*Match tickets:* Seats may be booked 10 days prior to the match.

*Car parking:* Parking for 1500 cars, 200 yards from ground.

*Entertainments/catering facilities:* Hot and cold drinks, pies, sandwiches, etc. available in the ground.

*Club shop:* Open daily; sells all types of souvenirs.

*Handbooks/programmes:* Programmes are obtainable on subscription; details from the Club Shop.

*Extra information:* Sunderland share the highest First Division away win, beating Newcastle United 9-1 in 1908; Newcastle went on to win the League that season.

*Club Colours:* Red and white striped shirts, black shorts, red stockings with white tops.

*Change Colours:* Blue shirts with red trim, red shorts with white trim, blue stockings with red tops.

*Club Coach:*

*Club Nickname:* Rokerites.

## SUNDERLAND 1981–82 LEAGUE RECORD

| Match No. | Date | | Venue | Opponents | Result | | H/T Score | Goalscorers | Attendance |
|---|---|---|---|---|---|---|---|---|---|
| 1 | Aug 29 | | A | Ipswich T | D | 3-3 | 1-0 | Ritchie, Buckley 2 | 24,060 |
| 2 | Sept 2 | | H | Aston Villa | W | 2-1 | 1-1 | Ritchie, Rowell | 29,372 |
| 3 | | 5 | H | West Ham U | L | 0-2 | 0-1 | | 28,347 |
| 4 | | 12 | A | Arsenal | D | 1-1 | 0-0 | Rowell | 26,471 |
| 5 | | 19 | H | Wolverhampton W | D | 0-0 | 0-0 | | 22,061 |
| 6 | | 23 | A | Nottingham F | L | 0-2 | 0-0 | | 21,133 |
| 7 | | 26 | A | Swansea C | L | 0-2 | 0-0 | | 17,826 |
| 8 | Oct 3 | | H | Coventry C | D | 0-0 | 0-0 | | 19,269 |
| 9 | | 10 | A | Notts Co | L | 0-2 | 0-1 | | 10,683 |
| 10 | | 17 | H | Tottenham H | L | 0-2 | 0-1 | | 25,317 |
| 11 | | 24 | A | Leeds U | L | 0-1 | 0-0 | | 25,220 |
| 12 | | 31 | H | Liverpool | L | 0-2 | 0-0 | | 27,854 |
| 13 | Nov 7 | | H | Manchester U | L | 1-5 | 1-1 | Cummins | 27,070 |
| 14 | | 14 | A | Middlesbrough | D | 0-0 | 0-0 | | 21,019 |
| 15 | | 21 | A | Everton | W | 2-1 | 0-0 | Ritchie (pen), Elliott | 19,759 |
| 16 | | 25 | H | Nottingham F | L | 2-3 | 0-1 | Hindmarch, McCoist | 17,419 |
| 17 | | 28 | H | WBA | L | 1-2 | 1-0 | Hindmarch | 15,867 |
| 18 | Dec 5 | | A | Brighton & HA | L | 1-2 | 1-1 | Ritchie | 14,251 |
| 19 | | 19 | A | Manchester C | W | 3-2 | 1-0 | Cummins, Rowell, Venison | 29,462 |
| 20 | Jan 30 | | A | Wolverhampton W | W | 1-0 | 0-0 | Cooke | 11,099 |
| 21 | Feb 2 | | A | Aston Villa | L | 0-1 | 0-0 | | 19,916 |
| 22 | | 6 | H | Arsenal | D | 0-0 | 0-0 | | 16,345 |
| 23 | | 10 | H | Stoke C | L | 0-2 | 0-0 | | 14,317 |
| 24 | | 16 | A | Birmingham C | L | 0-2 | 0-1 | | 10,776 |
| 25 | | 20 | H | Swansea C | L | 0-1 | 0-1 | | 13,163 |
| 26 | | 27 | H | Notts Co | D | 1-1 | 0-0 | Brown | 12,910 |
| 27 | Mar 10 | | H | Southampton | W | 2-0 | 0-0 | Pickering, McCoist | 15,747 |
| 28 | | 13 | H | Leeds U | L | 0-1 | 0-0 | | 20,285 |
| 29 | | 20 | A | Liverpool | L | 0-1 | 0-1 | | 30,344 |
| 30 | | 27 | A | Manchester U | D | 0-0 | 0-0 | | 40,776 |
| 31 | Apr 3 | | H | Middlesbrough | L | 0-2 | 0-1 | | 19,006 |
| 32 | | 7 | H | Ipswich T | D | 1-1 | 0-0 | West | 11,845 |
| 33 | | 10 | A | Stoke C | W | 1-0 | 1-0 | Buckley | 11,399 |
| 34 | | 12 | H | Birmingham C | W | 2-0 | 2-0 | West 2 | 14,821 |
| 35 | | 14 | A | Tottenham H | D | 2-2 | 0-2 | Rowell (pen), Pickering | 39,898 |
| 36 | | 17 | H | Everton | W | 3-1 | 1-1 | Rowell 2 (1 pen), West | 18,359 |
| 37 | | 24 | A | WBA | W | 3-2 | 2-1 | Cummins, Pickering, Rowell | 13,268 |
| 38 | | 27 | A | Coventry C | L | 1-6 | 1-2 | Cummins | 11,227 |
| 39 | May 1 | | H | Brighton & HA | W | 3-0 | 1-0 | Rowell 2 (1 pen), West | 16,224 |
| 40 | | 4 | A | West Ham U | D | 1-1 | 1-0 | West | 17,130 |
| 41 | | 8 | A | Southampton | L | 0-1 | 0-0 | | 21,110 |
| 42 | | 15 | H | Manchester C | W | 1-0 | 1-0 | Buckley | 26,167 |

**Final League Position: 19**

### Goalscorers

*League* (38): Rowell 9 (3 pens), West 6, Buckley 4, Cummins 4, Ritchie 4 (1 pen), Pickering 3, Hindmarch 2, McCoist 2, Brown 1, Cooke 1, Elliott 1, Venison 1.
*League Cup* (5): Ritchie 3, Cummins 1, Rowell 1 (pen).
*FA Cup* (2): Buckley 1, Rowell 1.

| League Cup | Second Round | Rotherham U (h) | 2-0 |
|---|---|---|---|
| | | (a) | 3-3 |
| | Third Round | Crystal Palace (h) | 0-1 |
| **FA Cup** | Third Round | Rotherham U (a) | 1-1 |
| | | (h) | 1-0 |
| | Fourth Round | Liverpool (h) | 0-3 |

| Turner | Hinnigan | Munro | Buckley | Clarke | Hindmarch | Chisholm | Ritchie | Brown | Rowell | Pickering | McCoist | Cooke | Siddall | Elliott | Arnott | Cummins | Whitworth | Venison | West | Bowyer | Nicholl | McGinley | Ursem | Match No. |
|---|---|---|---|---|---|---|---|---|---|---|---|---|---|---|---|---|---|---|---|---|---|---|---|---|
| 1 | 2 | 3 | 4 | 5 | 6 | 7 | 8 | 9* | 10 | 11 | 12 | | | | | | | | | | | | | 1 |
| 1 | 2 | 3 | 4 | 5 | 6 | 7 | 8 | | 10 | 11 | 12 | 9* | | | | | | | | | | | | 2 |
| 1 | 2 | 3 | 4 | 5 | 6 | 7 | 8 | | 10 | 11* | 12 | 9 | | | | | | | | | | | | 3 |
| | 2 | 3 | 4 | 5 | 6 | 12 | | 9 | 10 | 11 | 8* | | 1 | | 7 | | | | | | | | | 4 |
| | 2 | 3 | 4 | 5 | 6 | | | 9 | 10 | 11 | 8 | | 1 | | 7 | | | | | | | | | 5 |
| | 2 | 3 | 4 | 5 | 6 | | | 9 | 10* | 11 | 12 | | 1 | | 7 | 8 | | | | | | | | 6 |
| | 2 | | 4 | 5 | 6 | | | 9 | 10 | 11* | 12 | | 1 | 3 | 7 | 8 | | | | | | | | 7 |
| | 2 | 3 | 4 | 5 | 6 | | | 9 | 10 | | 8 | | 1 | | 7 | 11 | | | | | | | | 8 |
| | | 3 | | 5 | | | | 9 | 8* | 10 | 7 | 12 | 1 | 6 | | 11 | | 2 | 4 | | | | | 9 |
| | | | | 5 | 6 | | | 9 | | 10 | 8 | | 1 | 3 | 7 | 11 | | 2* | 4 | 12 | | | | 10 |
| | | | 4* | 5 | | 7 | | 9 | | 10 | 3 | 8 | 1 | 6 | | 11 | | 2 | 12 | | | | | 11 |
| | | 3 | 4 | 5 | | 7 | | 9* | | 10 | 8 | | 1 | 6 | | 11 | | 2 | 12 | | | | | 12 |
| | | 3 | | 5 | | | | | 8 | 10 | | | 1 | 6 | 7 | 11 | | 2 | 9 | 4 | | | | 13 |
| | | 3 | | 5 | 4 | 7 | | | | 10 | 9 | | 1 | 6 | | 11 | | 2 | 8 | | | | | 14 |
| | | 3 | 7 | 5 | 4 | 12 | | | 10* | | 8 | | 1 | 6 | | 11 | | 2 | 9 | | | | | 15 |
| | | 3 | 7* | 5 | 4 | 12 | | | 10 | | 8 | | 1 | 6 | | 11 | | 2 | 9 | | | | | 16 |
| | | 3 | 7 | 5 | 4 | | 6 | | 10* | | 8 | 12 | 1 | | | 11 | | 2 | 9 | | | | | 17 |
| | | 3* | 7 | 5 | | 12 | 6 | | 10 | | 8 | | 1 | 4 | | 11 | | 2 | 9 | | | | | 18 |
| | 2* | | 7 | 5 | 4 | | | 9 | 10 | | 3 | 8 | 1 | 6 | | 11 | | 12 | | | | | | 19 |
| | | 3 | 7 | 5 | 4 | 12 | 8 | 9 | 10 | | | | 1 | 6 | | 11* | | 2 | | | | | | 20 |
| | | 3 | | 5 | 4 | 7 | 8 | 9 | 10* | 11 | | | 1 | 6 | | | | 2 | 12 | | | | | 21 |
| | | 3 | 7 | | 4 | | | 9 | 10 | | 12 | | 1 | 6 | | 11* | | 2 | 5 | 8 | | | | 22 |
| | | 3 | 7 | 5 | | 12 | 8* | 9 | 10 | | | | 1 | 6 | 4 | | | 2 | 11 | | | | | 23 |
| | | 3* | 7 | 5 | 4 | 12 | | 9 | 10 | | | | 1 | 6 | | 11 | | 2 | 8 | | | | | 24 |
| | 2 | 3 | 7 | 5 | 4 | | | 9 | | | 8 | | 1 | 6 | | 11* | | 12 | 10 | | | | | 25 |
| | 2 | 3 | 7 | 5 | 4 | | | 9 | 10 | | | 12 | 1 | 6 | | 11 | | | | 8* | | | | 26 |
| 1 | 2 | 3 | 7 | 4 | 5 | | | | 9 | 10 | 8 | | | 6 | | 11 | | | | | | | | 27 |
| 1 | 2* | 3 | 7 | 4 | 5 | | | | 9 | 10 | 8 | | | 6 | | 11 | | | 12 | | | | | 28 |
| 1 | 2 | 3 | 7 | 4 | 5* | | | | 9 | 10 | 8 | | | 6 | | 11 | | | 12 | | | | | 29 |
| 1 | | 3 | 7 | 4 | 5 | | | | 9 | 10 | 8 | | | 6 | | 11 | | 2 | | | | | | 30 |
| 1 | | 3 | 7 | 4 | 5 | | | | 9 | 10 | 8* | | | 6 | | 11 | | 2 | | | | 12 | | 31 |
| 1 | 2 | 3 | 7 | 4 | 5 | | | | 9 | 10 | | | | 6 | | 11 | | | 8 | | | | | 32 |
| 1 | 2 | 3 | 7 | 4 | 5 | | | | 9* | 10 | | | | 6 | | 11 | | | 8 | | | 12 | | 33 |
| 1 | 2 | 3 | 7 | 4 | 5 | | | | 9* | 10 | | | | 6 | | 11 | | | 8 | | | 12 | | 34 |
| 1 | 2* | 3 | 7 | 4 | 5 | | | | 9 | 10 | | | | 6 | | 11 | | | 8 | | | 12 | | 35 |
| 1 | 2 | 3 | 7 | 4 | 5 | | | | 9 | 10 | | | | 6 | | 11 | | | 8 | | | | | 36 |
| 1 | 2 | 3 | 7 | 4 | 5 | | | | 9 | 10 | | | | 6 | | 11 | | | 8 | | | | | 37 |
| 1 | 2 | 3 | 7 | 4 | 5 | | | | 9 | 10* | 12 | | | 6 | | 11 | | | 8 | | | | | 38 |
| 1 | 2 | 3 | 7 | 4 | 5 | | | | 9 | 10 | | | | 6 | | 11 | | | 8 | | | | | 39 |
| 1 | 2 | 3 | 7 | 4 | 5 | | | | 9 | 10 | | | | 6 | | 11 | | | 8 | | | | | 40 |
| 1 | 2 | 3 | 7 | 12 | 4 | 5 | | | 9 | 10 | | | | 6 | | 11* | | | 8 | | | | | 41 |
| 1 | 2 | 3 | 7 | 4 | 5 | | | | 9 | 10 | | | | 6 | | 11 | | | 8 | | | | | 42 |
| 19 | 30 | 34 | 37 | 25 | 36 | 20 | 18 | 5 | 30 | 37 | 19 | 8 | 23 | 36 | 6 | 35 | 2 | 17 | 13 | 6 | 3 | 3 | — | |
| | | | +1s | +2s | +2s | +2s | | | +9s | +2s | | | | | | | | +3s | +5s | | | +4s | | |

## SUNDERLAND

| | Ht | Wt | Birthplace | Clubs | League App. | League Gls |
|---|---|---|---|---|---|---|
| **Goalkeepers** | | | | | | |
| Barry Siddall* | 6 0½ | 14 3½ | Ellesmere Port | Bolton W | 137 | — |
| | | | | Sunderland | 167 | — |
| | | | | Darlington (on loan) | 8 | — |
| Chris Turner | 5 10½ | 11 11 | Sheffield | Sheffield W | 91 | — |
| | | | | Lincoln C (on loan) | 5 | — |
| | | | | Sunderland | 76 | — |
| Jim Montgomery* | 5 10 | 11 9 | Sunderland | Sunderland | 537 | — |
| | | | | Southampton (on loan) | 5 | — |
| | | | | Birmingham C | 66 | — |
| | | | | Nottingham F | — | — |
| | | | | Sunderland | — | — |
| Mark Prudhoe | | | Durham | Sunderland | — | — |
| **Defenders** | | | | | | |
| Jeff Clarke* | 6 0½ | 13 8 | Pontefract | Manchester C | 13 | — |
| | | | | Sunderland | 181 | 6 |
| Joe Hinnigan | 6 0½ | 12 10 | Liverpool | Wigan Ath | 66 | 10 |
| | | | | Sunderland | 60 | 4 |
| Rob Hindmarch | 6 1½ | 13 4½ | Stannington | Sunderland | 88 | 2 |
| Gordon Chisholm | 6 0¾ | 12 0 | Glasgow | Sunderland | 96 | 4 |
| Paul Brown* | 5 11½ | 11 10 | Blackhill | Sunderland | — | — |
| Iain Munro | 5 7½ | 10 5 | Uddingston | St Mirren | 104 | 16 |
| (Scotland) | | | | Hibernian | 61 | 11 |
| | | | | Rangers | 5 | — |
| | | | | St Mirren | 90 | 3 |
| | | | | Stoke C | 32 | 1 |
| | | | | Sunderland | 34 | — |
| Nick Pickering | | | Newcastle | Sunderland | 37 | 3 |
| Shaun Elliott | 6 0 | 11 6½ | Haydon Bridge | Sunderland | 204 | 10 |
| **Midfield** | | | | | | |
| Kevin Arnott* | 5 10 | 11 12 | Bensham | Sunderland | 133 | 16 |
| | | | | Blackburn R (on loan) | 17 | 2 |
| Mike Buckley | 5 6 | 10 7 | Manchester | Everton | 135 | 10 |
| | | | | Sunderland | 101 | 6 |
| Stan Cummins | 5 6 | 9 1 | Durham | Middlesbrough | 44 | 9 |
| | | | | Sunderland | 103 | 25 |
| Ally McCoist | 5 9 | 10 6 | Glasgow | St Johnstone | 57 | 22 |
| | | | | Sunderland | 28 | 2 |
| John McGinley* | | | | Sunderland | 3 | — |
| Barry Venison | | | Stanley | Sunderland | 20 | 1 |
| **Forwards** | | | | | | |
| Colin West | 6 1½ | 13 2 | Wallsend | Sunderland | 18 | 6 |
| Gary Rowell | 5 10 | 11 3 | Seaham | Sunderland | 185 | 64 |
| Alan Brown | 5 11½ | 12 10½ | Easington | Sunderland | 113 | 21 |
| | | | | Newcastle U (on loan) | 5 | 3 |
| Colin Crawford | 5 7 | 11 4 | Doagh, | Bangor | — | — |
| (Transferred to Linfield Oct 1981) | | | Co Antrim | Sunderland | — | — |
| John Cooke | 5 8 | 11 0 | Salford | Sunderland | 31 | 3 |
| Mike Whitfield | | | Sunderland | Sunderland | — | — |
| Tom Ritchie | 5 11 | 12 8 | Scotland | Bristol C | 321 | 77 |
| | | | | Sunderland | 35 | 8 |
| | | | | Carlisle U (on loan) | 15 | — |
| Barry Wardrobe | 5 8½ | 11 4 | Newcastle | Sunderland | — | — |
| Pat O'Donnell | | | Newcastle | Sunderland | — | — |
| Simon Tait | | | Morpeth | Sunderland | — | — |

# SWANSEA CITY

# Division 1

*Joint President:* P. E. Holden, I. C. Pursey.

*Chairman:* M. Struel.

*Vice-Chairman:* T. J. Phillips.

*Directors:* E. P. Walters, P. L. W. Owen, R. G. Jones, W. C. Floyd, D. W. A. Rees, D. G. Sharpe.

*Team Manager:* John Toshack.

*Assistant Manager:* Phil Boersma.

*General Secretary:* G. J. Daniels FAAI.

*Football Secretary:* T. A. Howard.

*Year Formed:* About 1900. *Turned Professional:* 1911.

*Limited Company:* 1912.

*Previous Name:* Swansea Town until Feb 1970.

**Football League Record:**
1920 Original Member of Division 3; 1921–25 Division 3(S); 1925–47 Division 2; 1947–49 Division 3(S); 1949–65 Division 2; 1965–67 Division 3; 1967–70 Division 4; 1970–73 Division 3; 1973–78 Division 4; 1978–79 Division 3; 1979–81 Division 2; 1981– Division 1.

**Honours:** *Football League:* Division 2 – Promoted 1980–81 (3rd); Division 3(S) – Champions 1924–25, 1948–49; Division 3 – Promoted 1978–79 (3rd); Division 4 – Promoted 1969–70 (3rd), 1977–78 (3rd). *FA Cup:* semi-finals 1926, 1964. *Football League Cup* best season: 4th rd, 1964–65, 1976–77. *Welsh Cup:* Winners 5 times. **European Competition:** *European Cup-Winners' Cup*; 1961–62, 1966–67, 1981–82.

*Record Victory:* 8-0 v Hartlepool U, Division 4, 1 April, 1978.

*Record Defeat:* 1-8 v Fulham, Division 2, 22 Jan, 1938.

*Most League Points:* 62, Division 3(S), 1948–49. *Three points win:* 69, Division 1, 1981–82.

*Most League Goals:* 90, Division 2, 1956–57.

*Highest League Scorer in Season:* Cyril Pearce, 35, Division 2, 1931–32.

*Most League Goals in Total Aggregate:* Ivor Allchurch, 166, 1949–58, 1965–68.

*Most Capped Player:* Ivor Allchurch, 42 (68), Wales.

*Most League Appearances:* Wilfred Milne, 585, 1919–37.

*Record Transfer Fee Received:* £370,000 from Leeds U for Alan Curtis, May 1979.

*Record Transfer Fee Paid:* £340,000 to Liverpool for Colin Irwin, Aug 1981.

*Previous Managers since the War:* Bill McCandless, Ron Burgess, Trevor Morris, Glyn Davies, Bill Lucas, Roy Bentley, Harry Gregg, Harry Griffiths.

*Address of Supporters Club:* Vetch Field, Swansea.

---

**Vetch Field, Swansea.** Telephone Swansea 474114. Ticket office: 474102. *Ground capacity:* 26,496. *Record attendance:* 32,796 v Arsenal, FA Cup 4th rd, 17 Feb, 1968. *Record receipts:* £33,141 v Manchester U, Division 1, 30 Jan, 1982. *Pitch measurements:* 110yd×70yd.

*How to get there:* 5 minutes' walk from bus depot. South Wales Transport Co Ltd services from High Street General station to Lower Oxford Street. Parking facilities available at the Quadrant.

*Match tickets:* Tickets on sale at the ticket office, Vetch Field, Swansea approx. one month before the match.

*Car parking:* Car park 200 yards from the ground in The Kingsway. Side-street parking available.

*Entertainments/catering facilities:* Disc jockey programme prior to the match. Licensed bar and refreshment kiosk inside the ground.

*Club shop:* Situated in William Street; sells all types of souvenirs. Tel: 462584.

*Handbooks/programmes:* No handbook. Programmes can be obtained from the Secretary by sending remittance and sae.

*Club Colours:* All white with black trim.

*Change Colours:* All blue.

*First Team Coach:* Doug Livermore.

*Youth Team Coach:* Les Chappell.

*Youth Development:* Terry Medwin.

*Club Nickname:* Swans.

## SWANSEA CITY 1981–82 LEAGUE RECORD

| Match No. | Date | Venue | Opponents | Result | H/T Score | Goalscorers | Attendance |
|---|---|---|---|---|---|---|---|
| 1 | Aug 29 | H | Leeds U | W 5-1 | 1-1 | Charles, Latchford 3, Curtis | 23,489 |
| 2 | Sept 1 | A | Brighton & HA | W 2-1 | 2-1 | James L., Latchford | 19,885 |
| 3 | 5 | A | WBA | L 1-4 | 0-1 | Robinson | 18,063 |
| 4 | 12 | H | Notts Co | W 3-2 | 2-0 | Curtis, James L., Latchford | 14,391 |
| 5 | 19 | A | Manchester U | L 0-1 | 0-1 | | 47,309 |
| 6 | 22 | H | Tottenham H | W 2-1 | 0-0 | James R., Curtis | 22,206 |
| 7 | 26 | H | Sunderland | W 2-0 | 0-0 | Curtis, James L. (pen) | 17,826 |
| 8 | Oct 3 | A | Liverpool | D 2-2 | 1-0 | James L. (pen), Latchford | 48,645 |
| 9 | 10 | H | Arsenal | W 2-0 | 1-0 | James L., Thompson | 20,600 |
| 10 | 17 | A | Stoke C | W 2-1 | 0-1 | Stanley, Latchford | 14,665 |
| 11 | 24 | A | Coventry C | L 1-3 | 0-2 | Curtis | 14,050 |
| 12 | 31 | H | Wolverhampton W | D 0-0 | 0-0 | | 17,750 |
| 13 | Nov 7 | A | Ipswich T | W 3-2 | 1-0 | Curtis, Latchford, Stanley | 24,190 |
| 14 | 21 | A | Manchester C | L 0-4 | 0-1 | | 34,744 |
| 15 | 24 | H | Brighton & HA | D 0-0 | 0-0 | | 14,459 |
| 16 | 28 | H | Birmingham C | W 1-0 | 0-0 | James R. | 15,097 |
| 17 | Dec 5 | A | Everton | L 1-3 | 0-0 | Latchford | 23,860 |
| 18 | 12 | H | Nottingham F | L 1-2 | 1-0 | James R. | 17,550 |
| 19 | 15 | H | Aston Villa | W 2-1 | 2-1 | James R. 2 | 15,191 |
| 20 | 28 | A | Southampton | L 1-3 | 1-1 | Rajkovic | 22,703 |
| 21 | Jan 16 | A | Leeds U | L 0-2 | 0-1 | | 18,709 |
| 22 | 30 | H | Manchester U | W 2-0 | 0-0 | Curtis, James R. | 23,900 |
| 23 | Feb 6 | A | Notts Co | W 1-0 | 1-0 | James L. (pen) | 10,070 |
| 24 | 13 | A | Middlesbrough | D 1-1 | 1-0 | Kennedy | 11,209 |
| 25 | 16 | H | Liverpool | W 2-0 | 0-0 | James L., Curtis | 22,604 |
| 26 | 20 | A | Sunderland | W 1-0 | 1-0 | James L. | 13,163 |
| 27 | 27 | A | Arsenal | W 2-0 | 1-0 | Kennedy, James R. (pen) | 29,724 |
| 28 | Mar 6 | H | Stoke C | W 3-0 | 1-0 | James R. 2, Charles | 11,811 |
| 29 | 13 | H | Coventry C | D 0-0 | 0-0 | | 16,425 |
| 30 | 20 | A | Wolverhampton W | W 1-0 | 1-0 | Walsh | 14,158 |
| 31 | 27 | H | Ipswich T | L 1-2 | 1-1 | James R. (pen) | 20,750 |
| 32 | 30 | H | West Ham U | L 0-1 | 0-1 | | 20,272 |
| 33 | Apr 6 | A | WBA | W 3-1 | 0-1 | Marustik, Curtis, Latchford | 15,744 |
| 34 | 10 | A | West Ham U | D 1-1 | 1-0 | James R. | 26,566 |
| 35 | 13 | H | Southampton | W 1-0 | 1-0 | Curtis | 23,771 |
| 36 | 17 | H | Manchester C | W 2-0 | 2-0 | Stanley, Latchford | 19,212 |
| 37 | 24 | A | Birmingham C | L 1-2 | 0-1 | Walsh | 14,973 |
| 38 | May 1 | H | Everton | L 1-3 | 0-1 | James R | 16,243 |
| 39 | 5 | A | Tottenham H | L 1-2 | 0-1 | James L. | 36,348 |
| 40 | 8 | A | Nottingham F | W 2-0 | 1-0 | James R. 2 | 15,037 |
| 41 | 15 | H | Middlesbrough | L 1-2 | 0-0 | Latchford | 12,961 |
| 42 | 21 | A | Aston Villa | L 0-3 | 0-2 | | 18,294 |

**Final League Position: 6**

**Goalscorers**

*League* (58): James R. 14 (2 pens), Latchford 12, Curtis 10, James L. 9 (3 pens), Stanley 3, Charles 2, Kennedy 2, Walsh 2, Marustik 1, Rajkovic 1, Robinson 1, Thompson 1.
*League Cup* (3): Curtis 1, Irwin 1, James L. 1 (pen).
*FA Cup* (0).

| | | | | |
|---|---|---|---|---|
| League Cup | Second Round | Barnsley (a) | | 0-2 |
| | | (h) | | 3-2 |
| FA Cup | Third Round | Liverpool (h) | | 0-4 |

| Davies | Robinson | Hadziabdic | Rajkovic | Irwin | Mahoney | Curtis | James R | James L | Charles | Latchford | Attley | Thompson | Giles | Stanley | Marustik | Stevenson | Kennedy | Walsh | Evans | Sander | Richards | Lewis | Gale | Loveridge | Match No. |
|---|---|---|---|---|---|---|---|---|---|---|---|---|---|---|---|---|---|---|---|---|---|---|---|---|---|
| 1 | 2 | 3 | 4 | 5 | 6 | 7 | 8 | 9 | 10 | 11 | | | | | | | | | | | | | | | 1 |
| 1 | 2 | 3 | 4 | 5 | 6 | 7 | 8 | 9* | 10 | 11 | 12 | | | | | | | | | | | | | | 2 |
| 1 | 2 | 3 | 4 | 5 | 6 | 7 | 8 | 9 | 10* | 11 | 12 | | | | | | | | | | | | | | 3 |
| 1 | 2 | 3 | 4 | 5 | 6 | 7 | 8 | 9 | | 11 | | 10 | | | | | | | | | | | | | 4 |
| 1 | 2 | 3 | 4 | 5 | 6 | 7 | 8 | | | 11* | | 9 | | 10 | 12 | | | | | | | | | | 5 |
| 1 | 2 | 3* | 4 | 5 | 6 | 7 | 8 | 9 | 12 | 11 | | 10 | | | | | | | | | | | | | 6 |
| 1 | 2 | 3 | 4 | 5 | 6 | 7 | 8 | 9 | 10* | 11 | | 12 | | | | | | | | | | | | | 7 |
| 1 | 2 | 3* | 4 | 5 | 6 | 7 | 8 | 9 | 12 | 11 | | 10 | | | | | | | | | | | | | 8 |
| 1 | 2 | 3 | 4 | 5 | 6 | 7 | 8 | 9 | 12 | 11* | | 10 | | | | | | | | | | | | | 9 |
| 1 | 2 | 3 | 4 | 5 | 6 | 7 | 8 | 9* | | 11 | | 10 | | 12 | | | | | | | | | | | 10 |
| 1 | 2 | | 4 | 5 | 6 | 7 | 8 | 9 | | 11 | | 10* | | 3 | 12 | | | | | | | | | | 11 |
| 1 | | | 4 | 5 | 6 | 7 | 8 | 9 | | 11 | | | | 2 | 3 | 10 | | | | | | | | | 12 |
| 1 | 2 | | 4 | 5 | 10 | 7 | 8 | 9 | | 11 | | | | | 3 | 6 | | | | | | | | | 13 |
| 1 | | 2* | 4 | 5 | 10 | 7 | 8 | 9 | | 11 | | | | 12 | 3 | 6 | | | | | | | | | 14 |
| 1 | | 3 | 4* | 5 | 6 | 7 | 8 | 9 | 12 | 11 | | 10 | | 2 | | | | | | | | | | | 15 |
| 1 | 2 | 12 | | 5 | 4 | 7 | 8 | 9 | | 11 | | 10 | | | 3* | 6 | | | | | | | | | 16 |
| 1 | 2 | 3 | 4 | 5 | 6 | 7 | 8 | 9 | | 11 | | 10* | | 12 | | | | | | | | | | | 17 |
| 1 | 2 | | 4 | 5 | 6 | 7 | 8 | 9 | | 11 | | 10 | | | 3 | | | | | | | | | | 18 |
| 1 | | | 4 | | 6 | 7 | 8 | 9 | | 11 | | 10 | | 2 | 3 | | 5 | | | | | | | | 19 |
| 1 | | 3* | 4 | 5 | 6 | 7 | 8 | 9 | | 11 | | 10 | | 2 | 12 | | | | | | | | | | 20 |
| 1 | 9 | | 4 | 5 | 6 | 7 | 8 | 12 | | 11 | | 10* | | 2 | 3 | | | | | | | | | | 21 |
| 1 | 11* | | 6 | 4 | | 7 | 8 | 12 | | 9 | | 10 | | 2 | 3 | | 5 | | | | | | | | 22 |
| 1 | 11 | | 6 | 4 | | 7 | 8 | | | 9 | | 10 | | 2 | 3 | | 5 | | | | | | | | 23 |
| 1 | 12 | 3 | 6* | 4 | | 7 | 8 | 9 | | 11 | | | | 2 | | 10 | 5 | | | | | | | | 24 |
| 1 | | | 6 | 4 | | 7 | 8 | 9 | | 11 | | | | 2 | 3 | 10 | 5 | | | | | | | | 25 |
| 1 | | | 6 | 4 | | 7 | 8 | 9 | | 11 | | | | 2 | 3 | 10 | 5 | | | | | | | | 26 |
| 1 | 11 | | 6 | 4 | | 7 | 8 | 9* | | | | | | 2 | 3 | 10 | 5 | 12 | | | | | | | 27 |
| 1 | 2 | | 6 | 4 | | 7 | 8 | 9 | | 11 | | | | | 3 | 10 | 5 | | | | | | | | 28 |
| 1 | 2 | | 6 | 4 | | 7 | 8 | 9 | | 11* | | | | 12 | 3 | 10 | 5 | | | | | | | | 29 |
| 1 | 11 | 3 | 6 | 4 | | 7 | 8 | | | | | | | 2 | | 10 | 5 | 9 | | | | | | | 30 |
| 1 | | | | 4 | 11 | 7 | 8 | 9 | | | | 10 | | 2 | 3 | 6 | 5 | | | | | | | | 31 |
| 1 | 2 | 3* | 6 | 4 | | 7 | 8 | 9 | | 11 | | | | 12 | | 10 | 5 | | | | | | | | 32 |
| 1 | | 3 | 6 | 4 | | 7 | 8 | 12 | | 11 | | 9* | | 2 | | 10 | 5 | | | | | | | | 33 |
| 1 | 12 | 3 | 6 | 4 | | 7 | 8 | | | 11 | | 9 | | 2* | | 10 | 5 | | | | | | | | 34 |
| 1 | 2 | 3 | 6 | 4 | | 7 | 8 | 9 | | 11* | | | | 12 | | 10 | 5 | | | | | | | | 35 |
| 1 | | 2 | 6 | | | 7 | 8 | 9 | | 11 | | | | 4 | 3 | 10 | 5 | | | | | | | | 36 |
| 1 | | 3 | 6 | 4* | | 7 | 8 | 9 | | 11 | | | | 2 | | 10 | 5 | 12 | | | | | | | 37 |
| 1 | | 3 | 6 | 4 | | 7 | 8 | 12 | | 11 | | 9 | | 2 | | 10 | 5* | | | | | | | | 38 |
| 1 | 2 | | 6 | 5 | | 7 | 8 | 9 | | | | | | 12 | 3 | 10 | | 11 | 4* | | | | | | 39 |
| 1 | 2 | 3 | 6 | 5 | | 7 | 8 | 9 | | 11* | | | | 4 | 12 | 10 | | | | | | | | | 40 |
| 1 | | 3 | 6 | | | | 8 | 9 | | 11 | | 4 | | 2 | 12 | 10 | 5 | 7* | | | | | | | 41 |
| | 2 | | 6 | 5* | 9 | | 8 | | | 11 | | | | | | 10 | | | 1 | 3 | 4 | 12 | | 7 | 42 |
| 41 | 27 | 25 | 40 | 37 | 25 | 40 | 42 | 34 | 9 | 31 | 2 | 22 | — | 22 | 19 | 20 | 18 | 3 | 1 | 1 | 1 | 1 | — | 1 | |
| +2s | +1s | | | | | +4s | +4s | | | | | +2s | +1s | +2s | +7s | +3s | | +2s | | | | +1s | | | |

## SWANSEA CITY

| | Ht | Wt | Birthplace | Clubs | League App. | League Gls |
|---|---|---|---|---|---|---|
| **Goalkeepers** | | | | | | |
| David Stewart* (Scotland) | 6 1½ | 13 0 | Glasgow | Ayr U | 157 | — |
| | | | | Leeds U | 55 | — |
| | | | | WBA | — | — |
| | | | | Swansea C | 57 | — |
| Chris Sander | 5 11 | 10 4 | Swansea | Swansea C | 1 | — |
| Dai Davies (Wales) | 6 1 | 13 3½ | Ammanford | Swansea C | 9 | — |
| | | | | Everton | 82 | — |
| | | | | Swansea C (on loan) | 6 | — |
| | | | | Wrexham | 144 | — |
| | | | | Swansea C | 41 | — |
| **Defenders** | | | | | | |
| Wyndham Evans | 5 9½ | 13 0 | Llanelli | Swansea C | 348 | 19 |
| Nigel Stevenson (Wales) | 6 2 | 12 10 | Swansea | Swansea C | 135 | 10 |
| Neil Robinson | 5 8 | 10 6 | Liverpool | Everton | 16 | 1 |
| | | | | Swansea C | 81 | 7 |
| Dudley Lewis | 5 10¼ | 10 9 | Swansea | Swansea C | 13 | — |
| Dzemal Hadziabdic (Yugoslavia) | 5 8¼ | 10 11 | Yugoslavia | Velez Mostar | (not known) | |
| | | | | Swansea C | 64 | 1 |
| Colin Irwin | 6 1 | 12 13½ | Liverpool | Liverpool | 29 | 3 |
| | | | | Swansea C | 37 | — |
| Gary Richards | 5 8½ | 11 1½ | Swansea | Swansea C | 1 | — |
| Max Thompson | 6 2½ | 14 0 | Liverpool | Liverpool | 1 | — |
| | | | | Blackpool | 99 | 6 |
| | | | | Swansea C | 23 | 1 |
| Chris Marustik (Wales) | 5 8¼ | 11 5½ | Swansea | Swansea C | 41 | 1 |
| **Midfield** | | | | | | |
| Leslie Chappell (Contract cancelled April 1982) | 5 8 | 10 5 | Nottingham | Rotherham U | 111 | 36 |
| | | | | Blackburn R | 7 | — |
| | | | | Reading | 201 | 81 |
| | | | | Doncaster R | 58 | 10 |
| | | | | Swansea C | 67 | 5 |
| John Mahoney (Wales) | 5 8 | 11 3½ | Cardiff | Crewe Alex | 18 | 5 |
| | | | | Stoke C | 284 | 25 |
| | | | | Middlesbrough | 77 | 1 |
| | | | | Swansea C | 86 | 1 |
| Neil Henson* | | | Swansea | Swansea C | — | — |
| Ante Rajkovic (Yugoslavia) | 5 11¼ | 12 13½ | Yugoslavia | Sarajevo | (not known) | |
| | | | | Swansea C | 42 | 1 |
| Huw Lake | 5 8¾ | 10 8½ | Swansea | Swansea C | — | — |
| Tony Guard | 5 6½ | 9 3 | Swansea | Swansea C | — | — |
| Gary Stanley | 5 9 | 12 6 | Burton-on-Trent | Chelsea | 109 | 15 |
| | | | | Everton | 52 | 1 |
| | | | | Swansea C | 29 | 3 |
| Ray Kennedy (England) | 5 11 | 13 4 | Seaton Delaval | Arsenal | 158 | 53 |
| | | | | Liverpool | 275 | 51 |
| | | | | Swansea C | 18 | 2 |
| **Forwards** | | | | | | |
| Bob Latchford (England) | 6 0 | 13 6 | Birmingham | Birmingham C | 159 | 68 |
| | | | | Everton | 236 | 106 |
| | | | | Swansea C | 31 | 12 |
| Ian Walsh (Wales) | 5 9½ | 11 6 | St David's, Pembroke | Crystal Palace | 117 | 23 |
| | | | | Swansea C | 5 | 2 |
| Robbie James (Wales) | 5 11 | 13 0½ | Swansea | Swansea C | 354 | 90 |
| Jeremy Charles (Wales) | 6 1¼ | 13 8½ | Swansea | Swansea C | 205 | 51 |
| John Toshack (Wales) | 6 1 | 12 0 | Cardiff | Cardiff C | 162 | 75 |
| | | | | Liverpool | 172 | 74 |
| | | | | Swansea C | 60 | 24 |
| Leighton James (Wales) | 5 9½ | 12 5½ | Liwchwr, Glam. | Burnley | 181 | 44 |
| | | | | Derby Co | 68 | 15 |
| | | | | QPR | 28 | 4 |
| | | | | Burnley | 76 | 9 |
| | | | | Swansea C | 79 | 25 |
| Jimmy Loveridge | 5 8¼ | 11 1½ | Swansea | Swansea C | 4 | — |
| Pat McQuillan* | | | Belfast | Pembroke B | (not known) | |
| | | | | Swansea C | — | — |
| Darren Gale | 5 10½ | 12 13 | Port Talbot | Swansea C | 1 | — |
| Alan Curtis (Wales) | 5 11 | 12 7½ | Rhondda | Swansea C | 248 | 72 |
| | | | | Leeds U | 28 | 5 |
| | | | | Swansea C | 60 | 16 |

Free transfer: Bryan Cokely*

# SWINDON TOWN

## Division 4

*President:* W. H. Castle.   *Chairman:* C. J. Green.
*Directors:* C. Cowley, T. J. R. Kearsley, R. Stephenson, M.
W. Earle, W. H. Dore, L. Smart, G. Whittock, G. P. Heath.
*Team Manager:* John Trollope.
*Admin Manager/Secretary:* R. Jefferies.
*Finance Manager:* R. A. Morse.
*Year Formed:* 1881.   *Turned Professional:* 1894.
*Limited Company:* 1894.   *Previous Ground:* 1881–96, The Croft.

**Football League Record:**
1920 Original Member of Division 3; 1921–58 Division 3(S);
1958–63 Division 3; 1963–65 Division 2; 1965–69 Division 3;
1969–74 Division 2; 1974–82 Division 3; 1982– Division 4.

**Honours:** *Football League:* Division 2 best season: 5th, 1969–70. Division 3 – Runners-up 1962–63,
1968–69. *FA Cup:* semi-finals 1910, 1912. *Football League Cup:* Winners 1968–69. *Anglo-Italian Cup:*
Winners 1970.

*Record Victory:* 10-1 v Farnham United Breweries, FA Cup 1st rd, 28 Nov, 1925.

*Record Defeat:* 1-10 v Manchester C, FA Cup 4th rd replay, 25 Jan, 1930.

*Most League Points:* 64, Division 3, 1968–69.

*Most League Goals:* 100, Division 3(S), 1926–27.

*Highest League Scorer in Season:* Harry Morris, 47, Division 3(S), 1926–27.

*Most League Goals in Total Aggregate:* Harry Morris, 216, 1926–33.

*Most Capped Player:* Rod Thomas, 30 (50), Wales.

*Most League Appearances:* John Trollope, 770, 1960–80.

*Record Transfer Fee Received:* £175,000 from Chelsea for Alan Mayes, Dec 1980.

*Record Transfer Fee Paid:* £150,000 to Southampton for David Peach, March 1980.

*Previous Managers since the War:* Louis Page, Maurice Lindley, Bert Head, Danny Williams, Fred
Ford, Dave Mackay, Les Allen, Danny Williams, Bob Smith.

*Address of Supporters Club:* Swindon Town Supporters Club, County Ground, Swindon, Wilts.

*Address of the Club Shop or Boutique:* Souvenir and Sports Shop, Swindon Town FC, County Ground,
Swindon.

---

**County Ground, Swindon, Wiltshire.** Telephone Swindon 22118. *Ground capacity:* 26,000 (6500 seats).
*Record attendance:* 32,000 v Arsenal, FA Cup 3rd rd, 15 Jan, 1972. *Record receipts:* £56,024 v Totten-
ham H, FA Cup 4th rd, 26 Jan, 1980. *Pitch measurements:* 114yd×72yd.
*How to get there:* Both Swindon bus and railway stations are half a mile from the ground.
*Match tickets:* Available 3 weeks in advance.
*Car parking:* Corporation car park adjacent to the west end of the ground, off County Road.
*Entertainments/catering facilities:* The Supporters' Club Rendezvous Club and Squash Club in the North Stand. Refresh-
ment kiosks in all parts of the ground. No licensed bars on terraces or stands.
*Club shop:* Postal enquiries welcome. All types of souvenirs are stocked.
*Handbooks/programmes:* Programmes available by postal application, or subscription.
*Extra information:* Harold Fleming of Swindon Town played 11 times for England before World War I when the club
were still a non-League side. Separate terrace enclosure available for adults and accompanied children only.
*Club Colours:* Red shirts with white trimmings, white shorts, red stockings.
*Change Colours:* Yellow shirts, blue shorts, yellow stockings.
*Club Coach:* Ken Beamish.
*Club Nickname:* Robins.

## SWINDON TOWN 1981–82 LEAGUE RECORD

| Match No. | Date | Venue | Opponents | Result | | H/T Score | Goalscorers | Atten- dance |
|---|---|---|---|---|---|---|---|---|
| 1 | Aug 29 | H | Wimbledon | W | 4-1 | 1-0 | Carter R., Graham, Hughes, Greenwood | 5632 |
| 2 | Sept 5 | A | Chester | D | 0-0 | 0-0 | | 1798 |
| 3 | 12 | H | Preston NE | W | 4-0 | 2-0 | Rowland 2, Carter R. 2 | 5695 |
| 4 | 19 | A | Exeter C | W | 2-1 | 1-0 | Williams, Carter R. | 4372 |
| 5 | 21 | A | Southend U | D | 0-0 | 0-0 | | 4578 |
| 6 | 26 | H | Reading | L | 0-2 | 0-1 | | 9316 |
| 7 | 29 | H | Chesterfield | L | 1-2 | 1-1 | Hughes | 5365 |
| 8 | Oct 3 | A | Burnley | W | 2-0 | 2-0 | Rowland, Greenwood | 3359 |
| 9 | 10 | H | Carlisle U | W | 2-1 | 0-1 | Rideout, Hughes | 5265 |
| 10 | 17 | A | Bristol R | W | 4-1 | 2-0 | Rowland 2, Henry, Rideout | 8779 |
| 11 | 20 | A | Walsall | L | 0-5 | 0-2 | | 6010 |
| 12 | 24 | H | Doncaster R | D | 2-2 | 1-0 | Carter R., Williams | 6750 |
| 13 | 31 | A | Gillingham | L | 0-1 | 0-0 | | 8410 |
| 14 | Nov 3 | H | Brentford | L | 0-3 | 0-2 | | 6369 |
| 15 | 7 | H | Millwall | L | 1-2 | 1-1 | Rowland | 5710 |
| 16 | 14 | A | Huddersfield T | L | 0-3 | 0-1 | | 7802 |
| 17 | 28 | A | Lincoln C | L | 0-2 | 0-0 | | 3132 |
| 18 | Dec 5 | H | Bristol C | D | 0-0 | 0-0 | | 6949 |
| 19 | 26 | A | Plymouth Arg | L | 1-2 | 0-2 | Rowland | 8185 |
| 20 | 30 | H | Fulham | L | 1-4 | 0-2 | Rideout | 5641 |
| 21 | Jan 23 | A | Wimbledon | D | 1-1 | 0-1 | Rideout | 2084 |
| 22 | 31 | H | Exeter C | W | 3-2 | 1-1 | Rideout, Carter R., Baddeley | 5656 |
| 23 | Feb 6 | A | Preston NE | D | 0-0 | 0-0 | | 5606 |
| 24 | 9 | H | Southend U | D | 0-0 | 0-0 | | 4472 |
| 25 | 13 | H | Burnley | L | 1-2 | 1-2 | Henry | 4838 |
| 26 | 20 | A | Reading | D | 1-1 | 0-0 | Court (og) | 4130 |
| 27 | 23 | H | Portsmouth | W | 2-0 | 1-0 | Carter R. (pen), Williams | 4860 |
| 28 | 27 | A | Carlisle U | D | 1-1 | 1-1 | Rideout | 4633 |
| 29 | Mar 6 | H | Bristol R | W | 5-2 | 1-1 | Hughes, Rideout 2, Carter R., Henry (pen) | 6689 |
| 30 | 9 | H | Walsall | D | 2-2 | 1-1 | Greenwood, Lewis | 4446 |
| 31 | 12 | A | Doncaster R | D | 0-0 | 0-0 | | 3532 |
| 32 | 20 | H | Gillingham | L | 0-1 | 0-1 | | 4908 |
| 33 | 28 | A | Millwall | D | 0-0 | 0-0 | | 4381 |
| 34 | Apr 3 | H | Huddersfield T | L | 1-5 | 1-1 | Rideout | 3872 |
| 35 | 7 | A | Oxford U | L | 0-5 | 0-2 | | 7354 |
| 36 | 10 | H | Plymouth Arg | L | 0-2 | 0-0 | | 4056 |
| 37 | 13 | A | Fulham | L | 0-2 | 0-2 | | 6665 |
| 38 | 17 | A | Bristol C | W | 3-0 | 1-0 | Pritchard, Emmanuel 2 | 6524 |
| 39 | 19 | A | Brentford | L | 2-4 | 0-2 | Carter R. 2 (2 pens) | 5374 |
| 40 | 24 | H | Lincoln C | W | 1-0 | 0-0 | Rowland | 3981 |
| 41 | 27 | H | Chester | W | 3-0 | 1-0 | Rideout 3 | 3848 |
| 42 | May 1 | A | Chesterfield | L | 1-2 | 0-2 | Carter R. | 2028 |
| 43 | 4 | H | Oxford U | W | 3-2 | 0-0 | Rideout 2, Carter R. | 7880 |
| 44 | 8 | H | Newport Co | D | 1-1 | 1-1 | Carter R. (pen) | 5676 |
| 45 | 15 | A | Portsmouth | L | 0-3 | 0-2 | | 6372 |
| 46 | 18 | A | Newport Co | L | 0-1 | 0-0 | | 5906 |

**Final League Position: 22**

### Goalscorers

*League* (55): Rideout 14, Carter R. 13, Rowland 8, Hughes 4, Greenwood 3, Henry 3 (1 pen), Williams 3, Emmanuel 2, Baddeley 1, Graham 1, Lewis 1, Pritchard 1, own goal 1.
*League Cup* (2): Baddeley 1, Carter R. 1 (pen).
*FA Cup* (5): Pritchard 3, Carter R. 1, Emmanuel 1.

| **League Cup** | First Round | Wrexham (a) | 2-3 |
|---|---|---|---|
| | | (h) | 0-2 |
| **FA Cup** | First Round | Taunton T (a) | 2-1 (at Swindon) |
| | Second Round | Sutton U (h) | 2-1 |
| | Third Round | Luton T (a) | 1-2 |

| Allan | Henry | Williams | Hughes | Lewis | Graham | Carter R. | Emmanuel | Rowland | Greenwood | Moores | Abbley | Rideout | Baddeley | Pritchard | Peach | Stroud | Beamish | Quinn | Carter M. | Bailie | Match No. |
|---|---|---|---|---|---|---|---|---|---|---|---|---|---|---|---|---|---|---|---|---|---|
| 1 | 2 | 3 | 4 | 5 | 6 | 7 | 8 | 9 | 10 | 11 | | | | | | | | | | | 1 |
| 1 | 2 | 3 | 4 | 5 | 6 | 11 | 8 | 9 | | | 7 | 10 | | | | | | | | | 2 |
| 1 | 2 | 3 | 4 | 5 | 6 | 11 | 8 | 9 | | | 7 | 10 | | | | | | | | | 3 |
| 1 | 2 | 3 | 4 | 5 | 6 | 11 | 8 | 9 | 10 | | | | 7 | | | | | | | | 4 |
| 1 | 2 | 11 | 4 | 5 | 6 | 7 | 8 | 9 | 10 | | | | 3 | | | | | | | | 5 |
| 1 | 2 | | 4 | 5 | 6 | 7 | 8 | 9 | 10 | | 11 | | 3 | | | | | | | | 6 |
| 1 | 2 | 8 | 4 | 5 | 6 | 7 | | 9 | 10 | | 11 | | 3* | 12 | | | | | | | 7 |
| 1 | 2 | 11 | 4 | 5 | 6 | 7 | 8 | 9 | 10 | | | | 3 | | | | | | | | 8 |
| 1 | 2 | 11 | 4 | 5 | 6 | 7 | 8 | 9 | 10* | | 12 | | 3 | | | | | | | | 9 |
| 1 | 2 | 11 | 4 | 5 | 6 | 7 | 8 | 9 | | | | 10 | 3 | | | | | | | | 10 |
| 1 | 2 | 11 | 4 | 5 | 6 | 7 | 8 | 9 | | | | 10 | 3 | | | | | | | | 11 |
| 1 | 2 | 11 | 4 | 5 | 6 | 7 | 8 | 9 | | | 12 | 10 | 3* | | | | | | | | 12 |
| 1 | 2 | 11 | 4 | 5 | 6* | 7 | 8 | 9 | | | 12 | 10 | 3 | | | | | | | | 13 |
| 1 | 2 | 11 | 4 | 5 | 6 | 7 | 8 | 9 | | | 12 | 10* | 3 | | | | | | | | 14 |
| 1 | 2 | | 4 | 5 | 6 | 10 | 8 | 9 | | | 7 | | | | 3 | 11 | | | | | 15 |
| 1 | 2 | | 4 | 5 | 6 | 8 | | 9 | 10 | | 7 | | 12 | | 3 | 11* | | | | | 16 |
| 1 | 2 | | 4 | 5 | | 8 | 7 | 9 | 10 | | | | 11 | | 3 | 6 | | | | | 17 |
| 1 | | 3 | 4 | 5 | 6 | 8 | 7 | 9 | | | | 10 | | | 2 | 11 | | | | | 18 |
| 1 | | 3 | 4 | 5 | 6 | 8 | 7 | 9 | | | | 10 | | | 2 | 11 | | | | | 19 |
| 1 | | 3 | 4* | 5 | | 8 | 7 | 9 | | | 12 | 10 | | | 2 | 11 | 6 | | | | 20 |
| 1 | 2 | | 4 | 5 | | 8 | 7 | | 10 | | | 9 | 3 | 11 | | 6 | | | | | 21 |
| 1 | 2 | | 4 | 5 | | 8 | 7 | | 10 | | | 9 | 3 | 11 | | 6 | | | | | 22 |
| 1 | 2 | | 4 | 5 | | 8 | 7 | | 10 | | | 9 | 3 | 11 | | 6 | | | | | 23 |
| 1 | 2 | | 4 | 8 | 5 | | 7 | | | 10* | 12 | 9 | 3 | 11 | | 6 | | | | | 24 |
| 1 | 2 | 4* | 10 | 5 | | 8 | 7 | | | | | 9 | 3 | 11 | | 6 | | 12 | | | 25 |
| 1 | 2 | | 4 | 5 | | 8 | | | 12 | | 7 | 9 | 3 | 11 | | 6 | | 10* | | | 26 |
| 1 | 2 | | 4 | 7 | 5 | 8 | | | 10 | | | 9 | 3 | 11 | | 6 | | | | | 27 |
| 1 | 2 | | 4 | 7 | 5 | 8 | | | 10 | | | 9 | 3 | 11 | | 6 | | | | | 28 |
| 1 | 2 | | 4 | 7 | 5 | 8 | | | 10 | | | 9 | 3 | 11 | | 6 | | | | | 29 |
| 1 | 2 | | 4 | 7 | 5 | 8 | | | 10 | | | 9 | 3* | 11 | | 6 | 12 | | | | 30 |
| 1 | 2 | 3 | 7 | 5 | | 8 | 4 | | 10 | | | 9 | | 11 | | 6 | | | | | 31 |
| 1 | 2 | 3 | 7 | 5 | | 8 | 4* | | 10 | | | 9 | | 11 | | 6 | | | 12 | | 32 |
| 1 | 2 | 3 | 7 | 5 | | 8 | 4 | | | | | 9 | | 11 | | 6 | | | 10 | | 33 |
| 1 | 2 | | 4 | 7 | | 5 | 8 | | | | 12 | 9 | 3 | 11* | | 6 | | | 10 | | 34 |
| 1 | 2 | | 4 | | 5 | 11 | 8 | | | | 7 | | | | | 6 | | 9 | 10 | 3 | 35 |
| 1 | 2 | 4* | | | 5 | 11 | 8 | 12 | | | 7 | | 3 | | | 6 | | 9 | 10 | | 36 |
| 1 | 2 | | | | 5 | 11 | 8 | 4 | 10 | | 7 | 9 | 3 | | | 6 | | | | | 37 |
| 1 | 2* | | | | 5 | 11 | 8 | 4 | 10 | | | 9 | 3 | 7 | | 6 | | | 12 | | 38 |
| 1 | | 3 | | | 5 | 11 | 8 | 4 | 10 | | | 9 | 2 | 7 | | 6 | | | | | 39 |
| 1 | 2 | | | | 5 | 11 | 8 | 4 | 10 | | | 9 | 3 | 7 | | 6 | | | | | 40 |
| 1 | 5 | 11 | | | 2 | 8 | 4 | | 10 | | | 9 | 3 | 7 | | 6 | | | | | 41 |
| 1 | 5 | 12 | 11 | | 2 | 8 | 4 | | 10 | | | 9 | 3* | 7 | | 6 | | | | | 42 |
| 1 | 2 | 7 | | | 5 | 11 | 8 | 4 | 10 | | | 9 | 3 | | | 6 | | | | | 43 |
| 1 | 2 | 7 | | | 5 | 11 | 8 | 4 | 10 | | | 9 | 3 | 12 | | 6* | | | | | 44 |
| 1 | 2 | 7* | | | 5 | 11 | 8 | 4 | 10 | | | 9 | 3 | 12 | | 6 | | | | | 45 |
| 1 | 2 | 3 | 7 | | 5 | 8 | 4 | | 10 | | | 9 | 11 | | | 6 | | | | | 46 |
| 46 | 42 | 37 | 33 | 43 | 30 | 45 | 36 | 27 | 22 | 1 | 10 | 34 | 28 | 24 | 10 | 30 | 1 | 2 | 4 | 1 | |
| | | | | +1s | | | | +1s | +1s | | +1s | +1s | +5s | +1s | +4s | | +1s | +2s | +1s | | |

# SWINDON TOWN

| | Ht | Wt | Birthplace | Clubs | League App. | League Gls |
|---|---|---|---|---|---|---|
| **Goalkeepers** | | | | | | |
| Jim Allan | 6 0 | 12 0 | Inverness | Swindon T | 318 | — |
| Mark Stevens | 6 1½ | 13 4 | Bristol | Bristol R | — | — |
| | | | | Swindon T | — | — |
| **Defenders** | | | | | | |
| Russell Lewis | 5 10½ | 13 3 | Neath | Swindon T | 138 | 6 |
| Ken Stroud | 5 11 | 12 0 | London | Swindon T | 311 | 16 |
| Colin Barrett | 5 11 | 11 7 | Stockport | Manchester C | 53 | — |
| (Contract cancelled May 1981) | | | | Nottingham F | 69 | 4 |
| | | | | Swindon T | 3 | — |
| Charlie Henry | 5 11 | 12 8 | Acton | Swindon T | 74 | 3 |
| Kevin Baddeley | 5 9½ | 12 1 | York | Bristol C | 1 | — |
| | | | | Swindon T | 28 | 1 |
| Gary Williams | 5 9½ | 11 8 | Nantwich | Tranmere R | 1 | — |
| | | | | Djurgaarden | (not known) | — |
| | | | | Blackpool | 31 | 2 |
| | | | | Swindon T | 38 | 3 |
| Ray Baverstock | 5 8 | 11 4 | Southall | Swindon T | — | — |
| Colin Bailie | 5 11 | 10 11 | Belfast | Swindon T | 1 | — |
| David Round | 6 2 | 13 0 | Sedgley | Swindon T | — | — |
| **Midfield** | | | | | | |
| Roy Carter | 6 0½ | 11 7 | Torpoint | Hereford U | 71 | 9 |
| | | | | Swindon T | 197 | 33 |
| Martin Blackler | 5 10 | 11 6 | Swindon | Swindon T | — | — |
| Gary Emmanuel | 5 9 | 11 3 | Swansea | Birmingham C | 71 | 6 |
| | | | | Bristol R | 65 | 2 |
| | | | | Swindon T | 37 | 2 |
| Michael Graham | 5 9½ | 11 7 | Lancaster | Bolton W | 46 | — |
| | | | | Swindon T | 30 | 1 |
| Paul Short* | | | | Swindon T | — | — |
| Paul Batty | 5 7 | 10 11 | Edlington | Swindon T | — | — |
| Brian Hughes | 5 11 | 10 9 | Ludgershall | Swindon T | 52 | 5 |
| **Forwards** | | | | | | |
| Andy Rowland | 5 10½ | 12 1 | Derby | Derby Co | — | — |
| | | | | Bury | 174 | 58 |
| | | | | Swindon T | 141 | 53 |
| Steve Abbley* | 5 11 | 10 8 | Liverpool | Swindon T | 23 | — |
| Roy Greenwood* | 5 9 | 10 3 | Leeds | Hull C | 124 | 24 |
| | | | | Sunderland | 56 | 9 |
| | | | | Derby Co | 31 | 1 |
| | | | | Swindon T | 53 | 7 |
| Paul Rideout | 5 11½ | 12 1 | Bournemouth | Swindon T | 51 | 18 |
| James Quinn | 6 1 | 11 12 | Belfast | Oswestry | (not known) | — |
| | | | | Swindon T | 4 | — |
| Craig Moores | 5 6½ | 10 0 | Macclesfield | Bolton W | 1 | — |
| | | | | Swindon T | 2 | — |
| Ken Beamish | 6 0 | 11 11 | Birkenhead | Tranmere R | 177 | 49 |
| | | | | Brighton | 96 | 27 |
| | | | | Blackburn R | 86 | 18 |
| | | | | Port Vale | 85 | 29 |
| | | | | Bury | 49 | 20 |
| | | | | Tranmere R | 59 | 15 |
| | | | | Swindon T | 2 | — |
| Howard Pritchard | 5 10 | 12 7 | Cardiff | Bristol C | 38 | 2 |
| | | | | Swindon T | 28 | 1 |

# TORQUAY UNITED Division 4

*Chairman:* A. J. Boyce.

*Vice-Chairman:* M. C. Spedding.

*Directors:* D. C. Hair MRCVS, J. H. Perry, Lt-Col W. J. Elliot MBE, FCIS, L. W. Leppington ERD, L. W. Pope, W. W. Rogers, J. Farrell OBE, G. Harvey.

*General Manager:* Frank O'Farrell. *Secretary:* D. J. Easton.

*Team Manager:* Bruce Rioch.

*Year Formed:* 1898. *Turned Professional:* 1921.

*Limited Company:* 1921.

*Previous Name:* 1910, Torquay Town; 1921, Torquay United.

*Previous Grounds:* 1898, Teignmouth Road; 1901, Torquay Recreation Ground; 1905, Cricket Field Road; 1907, Torquay Cricket Ground; 1910, Plainmoor.

**Football League Record:**
1927 Elected to Division 3(S); 1958–60 Division 4; 1960–62 Division 3; 1962–66 Division 4; 1966–72 Division 3; 1972– Division 4.

**Honours:** *Football League:* Division 3 best season: 4th, 1967–68. Division 3(S) – Runners-up 1956–57; Division 4 – Promoted 1959–60 (3rd), 1965–66 (3rd). *FA Cup* best season: 4th rd, 1949, 1955, 1971. *Football League Cup:* never past 3rd rd.

*Record Victory:* 9-0 v Swindon T, Division 3(S), 8 March, 1952.

*Record Defeat:* 2-10 v Fulham, Division 3(S), 7 Sept, 1931 and v Luton T, Division 3(S), 2 Sept, 1933.

*Most League Points:* 60, Division 4, 1959–60.

*Most League Goals:* 89, Division 3(S), 1956–57.

*Highest League Scorer in Season:* Sammy Collins, 40, Division 3(S), 1955–56.

*Most League Goals in Total Aggregate:* Sammy Collins, 204, 1948–58.

*Most Capped Player:* None.

*Most League Appearances:* Dennis Lewis, 443, 1947–59.

*Record Transfer Fee Received:* £80,000 from Tottenham H for Colin Lee, Oct 1977.

*Record Transfer Fee Paid:* £25,000 to Exeter C for Vince O'Keefe, March 1980.

*Previous Managers since the War:* Jack Butler, John McNeil, Bob John, Alex Massie, Eric Webber, Frank O'Farrell, Allan Brown, Jack Edwards, Malcolm Musgrove, Frank O'Farrell, Mike Green, Frank O'Farrell.

*Address of Supporters Association:* Plainmoor, Torquay, Devon.

*Address of Club Shop:* The Gull Shop, Torquay United Supporters Association, Plainmoor, Torquay, Devon.

---

**Plainmoor Ground, Torquay, Devon TQ1 3PS.** Telephone Torquay (0803) 38666/7. *Ground capacity:* 22,000. *Record attendance:* 21,908 v Huddersfield T, FA Cup 4th rd, 29 Jan, 1955. *Record receipts:* £10,326 v Tottenham H, FL Cup 3rd rd, 6 Oct, 1971. *Pitch measurements:* 112yd×74yd.

*How to get there:* Train to Torquay railway station. Bus 30 runs every 12 minutes from the station to the ground.

*Match tickets:* Stand seats available a fortnight before the match. Postal applications accepted provided correct remittance and sae are enclosed.

*Car parking:* Some street parking. Coaches park at Lymington Road coach station.

*Entertainments/catering facilities:* 200 Club – a match day venue luxury club – membership £6 (48 hours notice required for membership). Supporters' Social Club – open all week – now completely up-dated with luxury furnishings – membership £1, OAPs 50p (48 hours notice required).

*Club shop:* Sells all types of souvenirs.

*Handbooks/programmes:* For programmes contact the club shop.

*Extra information:* Running commentaries of home matches to local hospitals. Twelve free seats supplied to members of the local Rehabilitation Centre of the Royal National Institute for the Blind who can listen to the hospital commentary while experiencing the match atmosphere.

*Club Colours:* White shirts with blue and yellow vertical stripes on sleeve, blue shorts with yellow and white stripes on side, white stockings with blue and yellow ring on turnover.

*Change Colours:* Yellow shirts with blue and white vertical stripes on sleeve, yellow shorts with blue and white stripes on side, yellow stockings with blue turnover and yellow ring on turnover.

*Club Captain:* Albert Larmour. *Team Captain:* Tommy Sermanni.

*Player-Coach:*

*Club Nickname:* Gulls.

## TORQUAY UNITED 1981–82 LEAGUE RECORD

| Match No. | Date | Venue | Opponents | Result | H/T Score | Goalscorers | Attendance |
|---|---|---|---|---|---|---|---|
| 1 | Aug 29 | H | Hull C | W 2-1 | 0-0 | Hodge, Cooper | 2651 |
| 2 | Sept 6 | A | Crewe Alex | W 1-0 | 1-0 | Scott (og) | 2054 |
| 3 | 12 | H | Scunthorpe U | W 1-0 | 0-0 | Cooper | 2033 |
| 4 | 18 | A | Colchester U | L 0-3 | 0-1 | | 2820 |
| 5 | 23 | A | Hereford U | W 3-0 | 3-0 | Sermanni, Weston, Lawrence | 2408 |
| 6 | 26 | H | York C | W 3-2 | 2-2 | Larmour (pen), Cooper, Sermanni | 2853 |
| 7 | 30 | H | Mansfield T | W 2-0 | 1-0 | Rioch, Bowker | 3100 |
| 8 | Oct 3 | A | Wigan Ath | L 0-1 | 0-1 | | 4876 |
| 9 | 10 | A | Blackpool | L 1-2 | 0-1 | Lawrence | 6716 |
| 10 | 17 | H | Tranmere R | L 1-2 | 0-0 | Lawrence | 3022 |
| 11 | 21 | H | Northampton T | D 2-2 | 1-0 | Rioch, Bowker | 2414 |
| 12 | 24 | A | Hartlepool U | D 0-0 | 0-0 | | 2099 |
| 13 | 31 | H | Bradford C | W 2-0 | 2-0 | Cooper 2 | 3144 |
| 14 | Nov 3 | A | Halifax T | W 2-1 | 0-0 | Brown, Bourne | 1523 |
| 15 | 8 | A | Rochdale | L 0-1 | 0-0 | | 1790 |
| 16 | 14 | H | Sheffield U | D 1-1 | 0-0 | Cooper | 4952 |
| 17 | 28 | A | Stockport Co | L 1-2 | 0-2 | Cox | 1800 |
| 18 | Dec 5 | H | Bury | D 1-1 | 1-0 | Brown | 2386 |
| 19 | 19 | H | Port Vale | L 0-1 | 0-1 | | 1880 |
| 20 | 28 | H | AFC Bournemouth | L 1-2 | 0-1 | Lawrence | 2831 |
| 21 | Jan 3 | A | Aldershot | D 1-1 | 0-1 | Brown | 2260 |
| 22 | 23 | A | Hull C | L 0-1 | 0-0 | | 3003 |
| 23 | 30 | H | Colchester U | W 1-0 | 0-0 | Sermanni | 2037 |
| 24 | Feb 6 | A | Scunthorpe U | W 2-0 | 1-0 | Cooper, Wilson | 1802 |
| 25 | 10 | H | Hereford U | L 1-2 | 1-0 | Winn | 1914 |
| 26 | 13 | H | Wigan Ath | D 0-0 | 0-0 | | 2524 |
| 27 | 19 | A | York C | D 1-1 | 1-1 | Rodgers | 1660 |
| 28 | 24 | H | Crewe Alex | D 1-1 | 0-1 | Winn | 1601 |
| 29 | 27 | H | Blackpool | D 1-1 | 1-1 | Jones | 2177 |
| 30 | Mar 6 | A | Tranmere R | D 1-1 | 0-0 | Brown | 1187 |
| 31 | 9 | A | Northampton T | L 0-2 | 0-1 | | 1959 |
| 32 | 13 | H | Hartlepool U | D 1-1 | 0-1 | Lawrence | 1619 |
| 33 | 21 | A | Bradford C | L 0-3 | 0-2 | | 4774 |
| 34 | 24 | A | Peterborough U | L 0-1 | 0-1 | | 4045 |
| 35 | 27 | H | Rochdale | W 2-1 | 1-1 | Cox, Cooper | 1554 |
| 36 | Apr 3 | A | Sheffield U | L 1-4 | 0-4 | Brown | 14,992 |
| 37 | 10 | H | Peterborough U | L 1-2 | 0-1 | Brown | 1989 |
| 38 | 13 | A | AFC Bournemouth | L 0-4 | 0-1 | | 6398 |
| 39 | 17 | A | Bury | W 1-0 | 1-0 | Brown | 2346 |
| 40 | 24 | H | Stockport Co | W 1-0 | 0-0 | Brown | 1619 |
| 41 | 27 | H | Halifax T | D 2-2 | 2-1 | Brown, Jones | 1331 |
| 42 | May 1 | A | Mansfield T | L 1-3 | 0-1 | Cox | 1392 |
| 43 | 5 | H | Darlington | L 1-2 | 0-2 | Brown | 1278 |
| 44 | 8 | H | Aldershot | W 2-1 | 1-1 | Tainton, Brown | 1447 |
| 45 | 15 | A | Port Vale | L 0-2 | 0-1 | | 2007 |
| 46 | 18 | A | Darlington | D 1-1 | 0-0 | Jones (pen) | 1283 |

**Final League Position: 15**

### Goalscorers

*League* (47): Brown 11, Cooper 8, Lawrence 5, Cox 3, Jones 3 (1 pen), Sermanni 3, Bowker 2, Rioch 2, Winn 2, Bourne 1, Hodge 1, Larmour 1 (pen), Rodgers 1, Tainton 1, Weston 1, Wilson 1, own goal 1.
*League Cup* (2): Cooper 1, Fell 1.
*FA Cup* (1): Lawrence 1.

| League Cup | First Round | Newport Co (h) | 2-3 |
|---|---|---|---|
| | | (a) | 0-0 |
| FA Cup | First Round | Bristol C (a) | 0-0 |
| | | (h) | 1-2 |

| O'Keefe | Jones | Pendrey | Bowker | Wilson | Larmour | Fell | Lawrence | Cooper | Hodge | Weston | Sermanni | Rioch | Cox | Pethard | Johnson | Young | Brown | Bourne | Butler | Murphy | Wheldon | Winn | Tainton | Rodgers | Keeley | Smith | Musgrove | Match No. |
|---|---|---|---|---|---|---|---|---|---|---|---|---|---|---|---|---|---|---|---|---|---|---|---|---|---|---|---|---|
| 1 | 2 | 3 | 4 | 5 | 6 | 7 | 8 | 9 | 10 | 11 | | | | | | | | | | | | | | | | | | 1 |
| 1 | 2 | 3 | 8 | 5 | 6 | | | 9 | 7 | 11* | 4 | 10 | 12 | | | | | | | | | | | | | | | 2 |
| 1 | 2 | 3 | 11 | 5 | 6 | 7 | 8 | 9 | 12 | | 4* | 10 | | | | | | | | | | | | | | | | 3 |
| 1 | 2 | 3 | 4 | 5 | 6 | 7 | 8 | 9 | | | | 10 | 11 | | | | | | | | | | | | | | | 4 |
| 1 | 4 | 3 | 7 | 5 | 6 | | 8 | 9 | 11 | 10 | | | 2 | | | | | | | | | | | | | | | 5 |
| 1 | 2 | 3 | 4 | 5 | 6 | | 8 | 9 | | | | 7 | 10 | | 11 | | | | | | | | | | | | | 6 |
| 1 | 2 | 3 | 4 | 5 | 6 | | 8 | 9 | | | | 7 | 10 | | 11 | | | | | | | | | | | | | 7 |
| 1 | 2 | 3 | 4 | 5 | 6 | | 8* | 9 | | 11 | | 7 | 10 | 12 | | | | | | | | | | | | | | 8 |
| 1 | 4 | 3 | | 5 | 6 | | 8 | 9 | | | | 7 | 10 | 2 | 11 | | | | | | | | | | | | | 9 |
| 1 | 2 | 3 | 10 | 5 | | 7 | 8 | 9 | | | | 6 | | | | 11 | 4 | | | | | | | | | | | 10 |
| 1 | 2 | 3 | 10* | 5 | 12 | 7 | 8 | 9 | | | | 6 | | | | 11 | 4 | | | | | | | | | | | 11 |
| 1 | 2 | 3 | | 5 | 6 | | 8 | 9 | | | | 7 | 10 | | | 11 | 4 | | | | | | | | | | | 12 |
| 1 | 2 | | | 5 | 6 | | | 9 | | | 3 | 7 | 10 | 8 | | 11 | 4 | | | | | | | | | | | 13 |
| 1 | 2 | | | 5 | 6 | | | 9 | | | 3 | 7 | 10 | 8* | | 11 | 4 | 12 | | | | | | | | | | 14 |
| 1 | 2 | | | 5* | 6 | | | 9 | | | 3 | 7 | 10 | 8 | | 11 | 4 | 12 | | | | | | | | | | 15 |
| 1 | 2 | | | 5 | 6 | 7 | 12 | 9 | | | 3 | 8 | 10* | | | 11 | 4 | | | | | | | | | | | 16 |
| 1 | 2 | | | 5 | 6 | | 8 | 9* | | | 3 | 7 | 10 | 12 | | 11 | 4 | | | | | | | | | | | 17 |
| 1 | 2 | | | 5 | 6 | | 8 | 12 | | | 3 | 10 | 9* | | | 11 | 4 | | 7 | | | | | | | | | 18 |
| 1 | 2 | | 4 | | | | | 9 | | | 3 | 12 | | 5 | | 6 | 7 | 10 | 11 | 8* | | | | | | | | 19 |
| 1 | 2 | 3 | | 5 | 6 | | 8 | | | | | 7 | 10 | | | 11 | 4* | 9 | 12 | | | | | | | | | 20 |
| 1 | 2 | 12 | | 5 | 6 | | | | | | 3 | 7 | 10 | 8 | | 11 | 4 | 9* | | | | | | | | | | 21 |
| 1 | 2 | 10 | | 5 | 6 | | | 9 | | | 3 | 7 | | 8* | | 11 | 4 | 12 | | | | | | | | | | 22 |
| 1 | 8 | | | 5 | 6 | | | 9 | | | 3 | 7 | 12 | 2 | | 11 | 4 | 10* | | | | | | | | | | 23 |
| 1 | 8 | | | 5 | 6 | | | 9 | | | 3 | 7 | | 2 | | 11 | 4 | | | | | 10 | | | | | | 24 |
| 1 | 8 | | | 5 | 6* | | | 9 | | | 3 | 7 | 12 | 2 | | 11 | 4 | | | | | 10 | | | | | | 25 |
| 1 | 7 | | | | 6 | | 8 | 9 | | | 3 | | 12 | 2 | | 11 | 4 | | | | | 10* | 5 | | | | | 26 |
| 1 | 2 | | | | 6 | | 8 | 9 | | | 3 | 7 | | | | 11 | 4* | | | | | 12 | 10 | 5 | | | | 27 |
| 1 | 2 | | | | 6 | | 8 | | | | 3 | 7 | 12 | | | 11 | 4 | 9 | | | | | 10 | 5* | | | | 28 |
| 1 | 2 | | | 5 | 6 | | | 9 | | | 3 | 7 | 10 | | | 11 | 4 | | | | | | 8 | | | | | 29 |
| 1 | 2 | | | | 6 | | 8 | 12 | | | 3 | 10 | | | | 11 | 4 | 7 | | | | 9* | | 5 | | | | 30 |
| 1 | 2 | | | | 6 | | 8 | 12 | | | 3 | 11 | 9 | | | 10* | 4 | 7 | | | | | | 5 | | | | 31 |
| 1 | 2 | | | | 6 | | 8 | 9 | | | 3 | 7 | 10 | 12 | | 11* | 4 | | | | | | | 5 | | | | 32 |
| 1 | 2 | 3 | | 5 | 6 | | 8 | 9* | | | | 7 | 10 | | | 11 | 4 | | | | 12 | | | | | | | 33 |
| 1 | 2* | | | 5 | 6 | | 8 | 12 | | | 3 | 7 | 10 | | | 11 | 4 | 9 | | | | | | | | | | 34 |
| 1 | 2 | 3 | | 5 | 6 | | 8 | | | | | 4 | 10 | | 11* | | | | | | | 12 | 7 | 9 | | | | 35 |
| 1 | 2 | 3 | | 5 | 6 | | 8 | 9 | | | | 4 | | | 11* | | | | | | | 12 | 7 | 10 | | | | 36 |
| 1 | | 3 | | 5 | 6 | | 8 | 9 | | | | 4* | | | 7 | 11 | | | | | | 12 | 10 | | | 2 | | 37 |
| 1 | 8 | 3 | | 5 | 6 | | | 9 | | | | 4 | | | 7 | 11 | | | | | | | 10 | | | 2 | | 38 |
| 1 | 8 | 3 | | 5 | 6 | | | 9 | | | | 4* | | | 7 | 11 | | | | | | 12 | 11*10 | | | 2 | | 39 |
| 1 | 4 | 3 | | 5 | 6 | | 8 | 9 | | | | 7 | | | | 12 | | | | | | | 11*10 | | | 2 | | 40 |
| 1 | 4 | 3 | | 5 | 6 | | 8 | 9 | | | | 7 | | | 11 | | | | | | | | 10 | | | 2 | | 41 |
| 1 | 4 | 3 | | 5 | 6 | | 8 | 9 | | | | 7 | | | | 11 | | | | | | | 10 | | | 2 | | 42 |
| 1 | 4 | 3 | | 5 | 6 | | 8 | 9 | | | | 7 | | | 11 | | | | | | | | 10 | | | 2 | | 43 |
| 1 | 4 | 3 | | 5 | 6 | | 8 | 9 | | | | 7 | | | 11 | | | | | | | | 10 | | | 2 | | 44 |
| 1 | 4 | | | 5 | 6 | | 8 | 9 | | | | 7 | | | 11 | | | | | | | 10 | | | 12 | 2 | 3* | 45 |
| 1 | 2 | | | 5 | | | 8 | 9 | | | 3 | 7 | 10 | | | 4 | | | | | | | | 11 | 6 | | | 46 |
| 46 | 45 | 12 | 12 | 43 | 21 | 6 | 41 | 40 | 3 | 3 | 35 | 35 | 23 | 19 | 2 | 26 | 34 | — | 5 | 2 | 5 | 12 | 19 | 5 | 1 | 10 | 1 | |
| | +1s | | | +1s | | | +1s +3s +1s | | | | +1s +1s +8s | | | | | | | | +2s +1s +1s +3s +2s | | | | | | +2s +1s | | | |

# TORQUAY UNITED

| | Ht | Wt | Birthplace | Clubs | League App. | League Gls |
|---|---|---|---|---|---|---|
| **Goalkeepers** | | | | | | |
| Vince O'Keefe | 6 0 | 11 0 | Birmingham | Birmingham C | — | — |
| | | | | Peterborough U (on loan) | — | — |
| | | | | Walsall | — | — |
| | | | | AP Leamington | (not known) | |
| | | | | Exeter C | 53 | — |
| | | | | Torquay U | 108 | — |
| **Defenders** | | | | | | |
| Richard Bourne* | 6 0 | 12 0 | Colchester | Colchester U | 4 | — |
| | | | | Bath C | (not known) | |
| | | | | Torquay U | 68 | 7 |
| Freddie Pethard | 5 9 | 11 0 | Glasgow | Celtic | — | — |
| (Contract cancelled March 1982) | | | | Cardiff C | 171 | — |
| | | | | Torquay U | 105 | — |
| Brian Wilson | 5 9 | 10 5 | Newcastle | Blackpool | 31 | 6 |
| | | | | Torquay U | 98 | 4 |
| Albert Larmour* | 5 10 | 10 7 | Belfast | Linfield | (not known) | |
| | | | | Cardiff C | 154 | — |
| | | | | Torquay U | 50 | 4 |
| Graham Jones | 6 0 | 13 0 | Worsley | Luton T | 39 | — |
| | | | | Torquay U | 95 | 6 |
| Mark Smith (Non-contract) | | | | Torquay U | 10 | — |
| Tom Wheeldon (Non-contract) | | | | Torquay U | 8 | — |
| **Midfield** | | | | | | |
| Tommy Sermanni* | 5 8 | 11 2 | Glasgow | Albion R | 151 | 38 |
| | | | | Blackpool | 10 | — |
| | | | | Torquay U | 86 | 12 |
| Bruce Rioch (Scotland) | 5 11 | 12 5 | Aldershot | Luton T | 149 | 47 |
| | | | | Aston V | 156 | 34 |
| | | | | Derby Co | 106 | 34 |
| | | | | Everton | 30 | 3 |
| | | | | Birmingham C (on loan) | 3 | — |
| | | | | Sheffield U (on loan) | 8 | 1 |
| | | | | Derby Co | 41 | 4 |
| | | | | Torquay U | 51 | 4 |
| Bobby Hodge (Contract cancelled) | 5 9½ | 11 0 | Exeter | Exeter C | 128 | 18 |
| | | | | Colchester U | 92 | 14 |
| | | | | Torquay U | 4 | 1 |
| Martin Musgrove (Non-contract) | | | | Torquay U | 2 | — |
| Willie Young | 5 7 | 11 7 | Glasgow | Aston V | 3 | — |
| | | | | Torquay U | 26 | — |
| Trevor Tainton (Contract cancelled) | 5 8 | 11 7 | Bristol | Bristol C | 487 | 24 |
| | | | | Torquay U | 19 | 1 |
| **Forwards** | | | | | | |
| Les Lawrence* | 6 3 | 11 0 | Wolverhampton | Shrewsbury T | 14 | 2 |
| | | | | Torquay U | 189 | 46 |
| Steve Cooper | 5 11 | 11 0 | Stourbridge | Torquay U | 164 | 53 |
| Maurice Cox* | 5 10 | 10 7 | Torquay | Torquay U | 62 | 13 |
| Keith Bowker (Contract cancelled Feb 1982) | 5 10 | 11 5 | West Bromwich | Birmingham C | 21 | 5 |
| | | | | Exeter C | 110 | 38 |
| | | | | Cambridge U | 17 | 1 |
| | | | | Northampton T (on loan) | 4 | — |
| | | | | Exeter C | 102 | 28 |
| | | | | Torquay U | 53 | 9 |
| Tony Brown (England) | 5 7 | 11 2 | Oldham | WBA | 574 | 218 |
| | | | | Jackstonville TM | (not known) | |
| | | | | Torquay U | 34 | 11 |
| Ashley Griffiths (Contract cancelled Aug 1981) | 5 9 | 10 6 | Barry | Bristol R | 7 | — |
| | | | | Torquay U | — | — |
| Damian Keeley (Non-contract) | | | | Torquay U | 3 | — |
| David Butler (Contract cancelled Feb 1982) | 5 11 | 12 0 | West Midlands | Wolverhampton W | — | — |
| | | | | Torquay U | 6 | — |
| Steve Winn* | 5 10 | 11 13½ | Thornaby | Rotherham U | 24 | 3 |
| | | | | Torquay U | 14 | 2 |

# TOTTENHAM HOTSPUR  Division 1

*Chairman:* A. Richardson.

*Vice-Chairman:* G. A. Richardson.

*Directors:* D. W. Kennard, D. A. Alexiou, F. P. Sinclair.

*Manager:* Keith Burkinshaw.

*Financial and Administration Controller:* J. Prentice.

*Assistant Secretary:* P. Day.

*Assistant Manager:* P. Shreeves.

*Year Formed:* 1882.  *Turned Professional:* 1895.

*Limited Company:* 1898.

*Previous Grounds:* 1882, Tottenham Marshes; 1885, Northumberland Park; 1898, White Hart Lane.

*Previous Name:* 1882–85, Hotspur Football Club.

**Football League Record:**
1908 Elected to Division 2; 1909–15 Division 1; 1919–20 Division 2; 1920–28 Division 1; 1928–33 Division 2; 1933–35 Division 1; 1935–50 Division 2; 1950–77 Division 1; 1977–78 Division 2; 1978– Division 1.

**Honours:** *Football League:* Division 1 – Champions 1950–51, 1960–61; Runners-up 1921–22, 1951–52, 1956–57, 1962–63; Division 2 – Champions 1919–20, 1949–50; Runners-up 1908–09, 1932–33; Promoted 1977–78 (3rd). *FA Cup:* Winners 1901 (as non-League club), 1921, 1961, 1962, 1967, 1981, 1982. *Football League Cup:* Winners 1970–71, 1972–73, 1981–82. **European Competitions:** *European Cup:* 1961–62; *European Cup-Winners' Cup:* 1962–63 (winners), 1963–64, 1967–68, 1981–82 (runners-up); *UEFA Cup:* 1971–72 (winners), 1972–73, 1973–74 (runners-up).

*Record Victory:* 13-2 v Crewe Alex, FA Cup 4th rd replay, 3 Feb, 1960.

*Record Defeat:* 0-7 v Liverpool, Division 1, 2 Sept, 1978.

*Most League Points:* 70, Division 2, 1919–20 *Three points win:* 71, Division 1, 1981–82.

*Most League Goals:* 115, Division 1, 1960–61.

*Highest League Scorer in Season:* Jimmy Greaves, 37, Division 1, 1962–63.

*Most League Goals in Total Aggregate:* Jimmy Greaves, 220, 1961–70.

*Most Capped Player:* Pat Jennings, 66 (95), Northern Ireland.

*Most League Appearances:* Steve Perryman, 516, 1969–82.

*Record Transfer Fee Received:* £250,000 for Neil McNab from Bolton W, Nov 1978.

*Record Transfer Fee Paid:* £800,000 to Aberdeen for Steve Archibald, May 1980.

*Previous Managers since the War:* Joe Hulme, Arthur Rowe, Jimmy Anderson, Bill Nicholson, Terry Neill.

*Address of Supporters Club:* 744 High Road, N17.

---

**748 High Rd, Tottenham, London, N17.** Telephone 01-801 3411. *Ground capacity:* 50,000. *Record attendance:* 75,038 v Sunderland, FA Cup 6th rd, 5 March, 1938. *Record receipts:* £136,407.70 v WBA, League Cup semi-final 2nd leg, 10 Feb, 1982. *Pitch measurements:* 110yd×73yd.

*How to get there:* Underground to Manor House (Piccadilly line), or Seven Sisters (Victoria line). From Manor House, buses 279, 259; from Seven Sisters 67, 149, 171, 243, 259, 123, 279. White Hart Lane station is three minutes' walk from the ground and is served by trains from Liverpool St.

*Match tickets:* For League matches, seats can be booked not earlier than 21 days before the match. At the Park Lane and Paxton Road ends, there are seats available at the turnstiles.

*Car parking:* No street parking within a ¼ mile radius of the ground.

*Entertainments/catering facilities:* Hot food available at snack bars in the ground.

*Club shop:* There are shops on the corner of Park Lane and High Road, and Paxton Road and High Road.

*Handbooks/programmes:* Programmes available on subscription to shop.

*Extra information:* Supporters' Club with a present membership of over 7000 is open to new members; information from the Secretary, Mr D. Smith (Tel: 808 7430).

*Club Colours:* White shirts, navy shorts, white stockings.

*Change Colours:* All sky blue.

*Club Captain:* Steve Perryman.

*Club Nickname:* Spurs.

## TOTTENHAM HOTSPUR 1981–82 LEAGUE RECORD

| Match No. | Date | Venue | Opponents | Result | H/T Score | Goalscorers | Atten-dance |
|---|---|---|---|---|---|---|---|
| 1 | Aug 29 | A | Middlesbrough | W 3-1 | 2-1 | Falco, Hoddle, Villa | 20,464 |
| 2 | Sept 2 | H | West Ham U | L 0-4 | 0-1 | | 41,200 |
| 3 | 5 | H | Aston Villa | L 1-3 | 0-3 | Villa | 31,265 |
| 4 | 12 | A | Wolverhampton W | W 1-0 | 0-0 | Galvin | 18,675 |
| 5 | 19 | H | Everton | W 3-0 | 0-0 | Roberts, Hughton, Hoddle (pen) | 31,219 |
| 6 | 22 | A | Swansea C | L 1-2 | 0-0 | Hoddle (pen) | 22,206 |
| 7 | 26 | A | Manchester C | W 1-0 | 0-0 | Falco | 39,085 |
| 8 | Oct 3 | H | Nottingham F | W 3-0 | 1-0 | Falco 2, Hazard | 34,870 |
| 9 | 10 | H | Stoke C | W 2-0 | 0-0 | Ardiles, Crooks | 30,520 |
| 10 | 17 | A | Sunderland | W 2-0 | 1-0 | Archibald, Hazard | 25,317 |
| 11 | 24 | H | Brighton & HA | L 0-1 | 0-0 | | 37,294 |
| 12 | 31 | A | Southampton | W 2-1 | 1-1 | Roberts, Corbett | 24,131 |
| 13 | Nov 7 | H | WBA | L 1-2 | 1-2 | Crooks | 32,436 |
| 14 | 21 | H | Manchester U | W 3-1 | 2-1 | Hazard, Roberts, Archibald | 35,534 |
| 15 | 28 | A | Notts Co | D 2-2 | 1-1 | Crooks 2 | 15,572 |
| 16 | Dec 5 | H | Coventry C | L 1-2 | 1-1 | Hazard | 28,073 |
| 17 | 12 | A | Leeds U | D 0-0 | 0-0 | | 28,780 |
| 18 | Jan 27 | H | Middlesbrough | W 1-0 | 0-0 | Crooks | 22,819 |
| 19 | 30 | A | Everton | D 1-1 | 0-1 | Villa | 30,717 |
| 20 | Feb 6 | H | Wolverhampton W | W 6-1 | 2-1 | Hoddle (pen), Villa 3, Crooks, Falco | 29,960 |
| 21 | 17 | A | Aston Villa | D 1-1 | 0-0 | Crooks | 23,877 |
| 22 | 20 | H | Manchester C | W 2-0 | 0-0 | Hoddle 2 (1 pen) | 46,181 |
| 23 | 27 | A | Stoke C | W 2-0 | 0-0 | Crooks 2 | 20,592 |
| 24 | Mar 9 | A | Brighton & HA | W 3-1 | 1-0 | Ardiles, Crooks, Archibald | 27,090 |
| 25 | 20 | H | Southampton | W 3-2 | 2-0 | Roberts 3 | 46,827 |
| 26 | 23 | H | Birmingham C | D 0-0 | 0-0 | | 17,708 |
| 27 | 27 | A | WBA | L 0-1 | 0-0 | | 20,275 |
| 28 | 29 | H | Arsenal | D 2-2 | 0-2 | Archibald, Hughton | 40,940 |
| 29 | Apr 10 | H | Ipswich T | W 1-0 | 0-0 | Hoddle | 45,215 |
| 30 | 12 | A | Arsenal | W 3-1 | 1-0 | Hazard, Crooks 2 | 48,897 |
| 31 | 14 | H | Sunderland | D 2-2 | 2-0 | Galvin, Hoddle | 39,898 |
| 32 | 17 | A | Manchester U | L 0-2 | 0-0 | | 50,724 |
| 33 | 24 | H | Notts Co | W 3-1 | 2-1 | Galvin, Villa, Archibald | 38,017 |
| 34 | 28 | H | Birmingham C | D 1-1 | 0-1 | Villa | 25,470 |
| 35 | May 1 | A | Coventry C | D 0-0 | 0-0 | | 15,431 |
| 36 | 3 | H | Liverpool | D 2-2 | 2-0 | Perryman, Archibald | 38,091 |
| 37 | 5 | H | Swansea C | W 2-1 | 1-0 | Brooke 2 (1 pen) | 36,348 |
| 38 | 8 | H | Leeds U | W 2-1 | 1-0 | Burns (og), Brooke | 35,020 |
| 39 | 10 | A | West Ham U | D 2-2 | 1-0 | Hoddle (pen), Brooke | 27,667 |
| 40 | 12 | A | Nottingham F | L 0-2 | 0-1 | | 15,189 |
| 41 | 15 | A | Liverpool | L 1-3 | 1-0 | Hoddle | 48,122 |
| 42 | 17 | A | Ipswich T | L 1-2 | 0-1 | Crooks | 20,764 |

**Final League Position: 4**

### Goalscorers

*League* (67): Crooks 13, Hoddle 10 (5 pens), Villa 8, Archibald 6, Roberts 6, Falco 5, Hazard 5, Brooke 4 (1 pen), Galvin 3, Ardiles 2, Hughton 2, Corbett 1, Perryman 1, own goal 1.
*League Cup* (8): Hazard 3, Archibald 2, Ardiles 1, Hoddle 1, Hughton 1.
*FA Cup* (10): Crooks 3, Hoddle 3 (1 pen), Archibald 1, Falco 1, Hazard 1, own goal 1.

| | | | |
|---|---|---|---|
| **League Cup** | Second Round | Manchester U (h) | 1-0 |
| | | (a) | 1-0 |
| | Third Round | Wrexham (h) | 2-0 |
| | Fourth Round | Fulham (h) | 1-0 |
| | Fifth Round | Nottingham F (h) | 1-0 |
| | Semi-final | WBA (a) | 0-0 |
| | | (h) | 1-0 |
| | Final | Liverpool | 1-3 (at Wembley) |
| **FA Cup** | Third Round | Arsenal (h) | 1-0 |
| | Fourth Round | Leeds U (h) | 1-0 |
| | Fifth Round | Aston Villa (h) | 1-0 |
| | Sixth Round | Chelsea (a) | 3-2 |
| | Semi-final | Leicester C | 2-0 (at Villa Park) |
| | Final | QPR | 1-1 (at Wembley) |
| | Replay | | 1-0 (at Wembley) |

| Clemence | Hughton | Miller | Price | Villa | Perryman | Ardiles | Brooke | Galvin | Hoddle | Falco | Roberts | Smith | Hazard | Lacy | Jones | Archibald | Crooks | Corbett | Dick | Gibson | O'Reilly | Aleksic | Crook | Parks | Match No. |
|---|---|---|---|---|---|---|---|---|---|---|---|---|---|---|---|---|---|---|---|---|---|---|---|---|---|
| 1 | 2 | 3 | 4 | 5 | 6 | 7 | 8 | 9 | 10 | 11 |  |  |  |  |  |  |  |  |  |  |  |  |  |  | 1 |
| 1 |  | 3 | 4* | 5 | 6 |  | 8 | 9 | 10 | 11 | 2 | 12 | 7 |  |  |  |  |  |  |  |  |  |  |  | 2 |
| 1 |  | 3* |  | 5 | 6 | 7 | 8 |  | 10 | 11 | 2 |  | 4 | 12 | 9 |  |  |  |  |  |  |  |  |  | 3 |
| 1 | 2 | 3 |  | 5 | 6 | 7 | 8* | 9 | 10 | 11 | 4 |  |  | 12 |  |  |  |  |  |  |  |  |  |  | 4 |
| 1 | 2 | 3 |  | 5 | 6 | 7 |  | 9 | 10 | 11 | 4 |  |  |  |  | 8 |  |  |  |  |  |  |  |  | 5 |
| 1 | 2 | 3 |  | 5 | 6 | 7 |  | 9 | 10 | 11 | 4 |  |  |  |  | 8 |  |  |  |  |  |  |  |  | 6 |
| 1 | 2 | 3 |  | 5 | 6 | 7 |  | 9 | 10 | 11 | 4 |  |  |  |  | 8 |  |  |  |  |  |  |  |  | 7 |
| 1 | 2 | 3 |  |  | 6 | 7 |  | 9 | 10 | 11 | 4 |  | 5 |  |  | 8 |  |  |  |  |  |  |  |  | 8 |
| 1 | 2 | 3 | 5* |  | 6 | 7 |  | 9 | 10 |  | 4 |  | 12 |  |  | 8 | 11 |  |  |  |  |  |  |  | 9 |
| 1 | 2 | 3 |  |  | 6 | 7 |  | 9 | 10 |  | 4 |  | 5* | 12 |  | 8 | 11 |  |  |  |  |  |  |  | 10 |
| 1 | 2 | 3 |  |  | 6 | 7 |  | 9 | 10 |  | 4 |  | 5 |  |  | 8 | 11 |  |  |  |  |  |  |  | 11 |
| 1 | 2 | 3 |  |  | 6 | 7 |  | 9 | 10 |  | 4 |  | 5 |  |  | 8 | 11* | 12 |  |  |  |  |  |  | 12 |
| 1 | 2 | 3 | 10 |  | 6 | 7* |  | 9 |  |  | 4 |  | 5 | 12 |  | 8 | 11 |  |  |  |  |  |  |  | 13 |
| 1 | 2 | 3 |  |  | 6 | 7 |  | 9 | 10 |  | 4 |  | 5 |  |  | 8 | 11 |  |  |  |  |  |  |  | 14 |
| 1 | 2 | 3 |  |  | 6 | 7 |  | 9 | 10 |  | 4 |  | 5 |  |  | 8 | 11 |  |  |  |  |  |  |  | 15 |
| 1 | 2* | 3 | 12 |  | 6 | 7 |  | 9 | 10 |  | 4 |  | 5 |  |  | 8 | 11 |  |  |  |  |  |  |  | 16 |
| 1 | 2 | 3 | 8 |  | 6 | 7 |  | 9 | 10 |  | 4 |  | 5* | 12 |  |  | 11 |  |  |  |  |  |  |  | 17 |
| 1 | 2 | 3 |  | 5 | 6 | 7 |  | 9 | 10 | 8 | 4 |  |  |  |  |  | 11 |  |  |  |  |  |  |  | 18 |
| 1 | 2 | 3 | 4 | 5 | 6 | 7 | 12 | 9 | 10 | 8* |  |  |  |  |  |  | 11 |  |  |  |  |  |  |  | 19 |
| 1 | 2 | 3 | 4 | 5 | 6 | 7 |  | 9 | 10 | 8 |  |  | 12 |  |  |  | 11* |  |  |  |  |  |  |  | 20 |
| 1 | 2 | 3 | 9 |  | 6 | 7 |  |  | 10 | 8 | 4* |  | 5 | 12 |  |  | 11 |  |  |  |  |  |  |  | 21 |
| 1 | 2 | 3 | 4 |  | 6 | 7 |  |  | 10 |  | 12 |  | 5 |  |  | 8 | 11 | 9* |  |  |  |  |  |  | 22 |
| 1 | 2 | 3 | 4 |  | 6 | 7* |  | 9 | 10 |  | 12 |  | 5 |  |  | 8 | 11 |  |  |  |  |  |  |  | 23 |
| 1 | 2 | 3 | 4 |  | 6 | 7 |  | 9 | 10 |  |  |  | 5 |  |  | 8 | 11 |  |  |  |  |  |  |  | 24 |
| 1 | 2 | 3 | 4 | 11 | 6 |  |  | 9 | 10 |  | 7 |  | 5 |  |  | 8 |  |  |  |  |  |  |  |  | 25 |
| 1 | 2 | 3 | 11 |  | 6 | 7 |  | 9 | 10 |  | 4 |  | 5 | 12 |  | 8* |  |  |  |  |  |  |  |  | 26 |
| 1 | 2 | 3 | 5 | 11 | 6 | 7 | 12 | 9 | 10* |  | 4 |  |  |  |  | 8 |  |  |  |  |  |  |  |  | 27 |
| 1 | 2 |  | 4 | 5 | 6 | 7 |  | 9 | 10 |  | 3 |  | 11 |  |  | 8 |  |  |  |  |  |  |  |  | 28 |
| 1 | 2 | 3 | 7 |  | 6 |  | 12 | 9 | 10 |  | 4 |  | 5 |  |  | 8* | 11 |  |  |  |  |  |  |  | 29 |
| 1 |  | 3 | 4 | 7 | 6 |  |  | 9 | 10 |  | 2 |  | 5 |  |  | 8 | 11 |  |  |  |  |  |  |  | 30 |
| 1 |  | 3 | 4 | 7 | 6 |  | 12 | 9* | 10 |  | 2 |  | 5 |  |  | 8 | 11 |  |  |  |  |  |  |  | 31 |
| 1 | 2 | 3* | 12 | 7 | 6 |  |  | 9 | 10 |  | 4 |  | 5 |  |  | 8 | 11 |  |  |  |  |  |  |  | 32 |
| 1 | 2 | 3 |  | 7 | 6 |  |  | 9 | 10 |  | 4 |  | 5 |  |  | 8 | 11 |  |  |  |  |  |  |  | 33 |
| 1 | 2 | 3 |  | 7 | 6 |  |  | 9 |  |  | 4 |  | 10 | 5 |  | 8 | 11 |  |  |  |  |  |  |  | 34 |
| 1 | 2 |  |  | 7 | 6 |  | 11 | 9* | 10 |  | 4 |  | 5 |  |  | 8 |  |  |  |  | 3 |  | 12 |  | 35 |
|  | 2 | 3 |  |  | 6 |  | 10 | 9 |  |  |  |  | 4* | 5 | 12 | 8 |  |  |  |  | 7 | 1 | 11 |  | 36 |
|  | 2 |  |  |  | 6 |  | 10 | 9 |  |  |  |  | 4 | 5 | 12 | 8 |  | 3 |  |  | 7 | 1 | 11* |  | 37 |
| 1 | 2 |  |  |  | 6 | 4 | 10 | 9 |  |  |  |  |  | 5 | 12 | 8 |  |  |  |  | 7 |  | 8* |  | 38 |
|  |  | 3 | 4 |  | 6 |  | 8 | 10 | 9 |  | 7 |  | 5 |  |  | 11 |  | 2* |  |  | 12 |  |  | 1 | 39 |
| 1 | 2 | 3 | 9 |  | 6 | 7 |  |  | 10 | 8 | 4 |  | 5 |  |  |  | 11 |  |  |  |  |  |  |  | 40 |
| 1 | 2 | 3 | 12 | 9 | 6 | 7 |  |  | 10 | 8 | 4 |  | 5 |  |  |  | 11* |  |  |  |  |  |  |  | 41 |
|  | 2 | 3 | 12 | 9 | 6 | 7 |  |  | 10* |  | 4 |  | 5 |  |  | 8 | 11 |  |  |  |  |  |  | 1 | 42 |
| **38** | **37** | **35** | **18** | **26** | **42** | **26** | **12** | **32** | **34** | **21** | **35** | **1** | **26** | **7** | **3** | **26** | **27** | **3** | **1** | **1** | **4** | **2** | **3** | **2** |  |
|  |  | +3s | +1s |  | +4s |  |  |  |  |  |  |  | +2s | +1s | +2s | +5s | +4s | +1s |  |  | +1s | +1s |  |  |  |

## TOTTENHAM HOTSPUR

| | Ht | Wt | Birthplace | Clubs | League App. | League Gls |
|---|---|---|---|---|---|---|
| **Goalkeepers** | | | | | | |
| Barry Daines | 5 11½ | 11 8 | Whitham | Tottenham H | 146 | — |
| (Released to Hong Kong) | | | | | | |
| Milija Aleksic* | 6 0 | 13 11 | Stafford | Plymouth Arg | 32 | — |
| | | | | Ipswich T (on loan) | — | — |
| | | | | Oxford U (on loan) | — | — |
| | | | | Luton T | 77 | — |
| | | | | Tottenham H | 25 | — |
| | | | | Sheffield U (on loan) | — | — |
| | | | | Luton T (on loan) | 4 | — |
| Tony Parks | 5 10½ | 10 8 | Hackney | Tottenham H | 2 | — |
| Mark Hughes* | 6 0 | 11 0 | West Ham | Tottenham H | — | — |
| Ray Clemence | 5 11½ | 12 9 | Skegness | Scunthorpe U | 48 | — |
| (England) | | | | Liverpool | 470 | — |
| | | | | Tottenham H | 38 | — |
| **Defenders** | | | | | | |
| Chris Hughton | 5 7¾ | 11 5 | West Ham | Tottenham H | 110 | 4 |
| (Eire) | | | | | | |
| John Lacy | 6 1 | 12 4 | Liverpool | Fulham | 168 | 7 |
| | | | | Tottenham H | 82 | 2 |
| Gordon Smith* | 5 9 | 12 1 | Glasgow | St Johnstone | 118 | 11 |
| | | | | Aston V | 79 | — |
| | | | | Tottenham H | 38 | 1 |
| Giorgio Mazzon | 5 10 | 11 9 | London | Tottenham H | 2 | — |
| Peter Southey | 5 9 | 11 0 | Putney | Tottenham H | 1 | — |
| John Cooper* | 5 11 | 11 0 | London | Tottenham H | — | — |
| Paul Miller | 6 1 | 12 2 | London | Tottenham H | 94 | 4 |
| Graham Roberts | 5 10 | 12 12 | Southampton | Weymouth | (not known) | |
| | | | | Tottenham H | 61 | 6 |
| Pat Corbett | 6 0 | 11 0 | Hackney | Tottenham H | 4 | 1 |
| Paul Price | 5 11 | 12 0 | St Albans | Luton T | 207 | 8 |
| (Wales) | | | | Tottenham H | 21 | — |
| Ken Dixon | 5 7 | 9 0 | Hornsey | Tottenham H | — | — |
| Simon Webster | 6 0 | 11 7 | Hinckley | Tottenham H | — | — |
| **Midfield** | | | | | | |
| Steve Perryman | 5 8 | 10 10 | Ealing | Tottenham H | 516 | 27 |
| (England) | | | | | | |
| Glenn Hoddle | 6 0 | 11 6 | Hayes | Tottenham H | 235 | 65 |
| (England) | | | | | | |
| Mike Hazard | 5 7 | 10 5 | Sunderland | Tottenham H | 35 | 5 |
| Osvaldo Ardiles | 5 6 | 9 10 | Cordoba | Huracan | (not known) | |
| (Argentina) | | | | Tottenham H | 140 | 13 |
| Ricardo Villa | 6 0 | 12 5 | Buenos Aires | Racing | (not known) | |
| (Argentina) | | | | Tottenham H | 110 | 16 |
| Gary O'Reilly | 5 11 | | Isleworth | Tottenham H | 7 | — |
| Ian Crook | 5 8 | 10 6 | Romford | Tottenham H | 4 | — |
| Allan Cockram | 5 7 | 10 6 | Kensington | Tottenham H | — | — |
| Gary Brooke | 5 6 | 10 5 | Bethnal Green | Tottenham H | 34 | 7 |
| Mark Bowen | | | Neath | Tottenham H | — | — |
| **Forwards** | | | | | | |
| Tony Galvin | 5 9 | 11 5 | Huddersfield | Tottenham H | 60 | 8 |
| Chris Jones* | 5 11 | 10 7 | Jersey | Tottenham H | 164 | 37 |
| Mark Falco | 6 0 | 12 0 | Hackney | Tottenham H | 34 | 9 |
| Terry Gibson | 5 5 | 10 0 | London | Tottenham H | 2 | — |
| Steve Archibald | 5 10 | 11 2 | Scotland | Clyde | 65 | 7 |
| (Scotland) | | | | Aberdeen | 76 | 29 |
| | | | | Tottenham H | 68 | 26 |
| Garth Crooks | 5 8 | 11 6 | Stoke | Stoke C | 147 | 48 |
| | | | | Tottenham H | 67 | 29 |
| Alistair Dick | 5 9 | 10 7 | Stirling | Tottenham H | 1 | — |

# TRANMERE ROVERS    Division 4

*Chairman:* H. B. Thomas.

*Directors:* H. A. Bainbridge FCA, G. A. Gould FCA, G. T. H. Kemp. A. J. Adams.

*General Manager/Secretary:* Jack Butterfield.

*Team Manager:* Bryan Hamilton.

*Year Formed:* 1883. *Turned Professional:* 1912.

*Limited Company:* 1920.

*Commercial Department:* 051-608 3677/4194.

**Football League Record:**
1921 Original Member of Division 3(N); 1938–39 Division 2; 1946–58 Division 3(N); 1958–61 Division 3; 1961–67 Division 4; 1967–75 Division 3; 1975–76 Division 4; 1976–79 Division 3; 1979– Division 4.

**Honours:** *Football League:* Division 2 best season: 22nd, 1938–39; Division 3(N) – Champions 1937–38; Promotion to 3rd Division: 1966–67, 1975–76. *FA Cup* best season: 5th rd, 1967–68. *Football League Cup* best season: 4th rd, 1961, 1982. *Welsh Cup:* Winners 1935.

*Record Victory:* 13-4 v Oldham Ath, Division 3(N), 26 Dec, 1935.

*Record Defeat:* 1-9 v Tottenham H, FA Cup 3rd rd replay, 14 Jan, 1953.

*Most League Points:* 60, Division 4, 1964–65. *Three points win:* 60, Division 4, 1981–82.

*Most League Goals:* 111, Division 3(N), 1930–31.

*Highest League Scorer in Season:* Bunny Bell, 35, Division 3(N), 1933–34.

*Most League Goals in Total Aggregate:* Bunny Bell, 104, 1931–36.

*Most Capped Player:* Albert Gray, 3 (23), Wales.

*Most League Appearances:* Harold Bell, 595, 1946–64 (including League record of 401 consecutive appearances).

*Record Transfer Fee Received:* £120,000 from Cardiff C for Ronnie Moore, Feb 1979.

*Record Transfer Fee Paid:* £20,000 to Charlton Ath for Hugh McAuley, Aug 1978.

*Previous Managers since the War:* Ernie Blackburn, Noel Kelly, Peter Farrell, Walter Galbraith, Dave Russell, Jackie Wright, Ron Yeats, John King.

*Address of Supporters Club:* Supporters Assn, Prenton Park, Birkenhead.

---

**Prenton Park, Prenton Road West, Birkenhead.** Telephone 051-608 3677/4194. *Ground capacity:* 18,000. *Record attendance:* 24,424 v Stoke C, FA Cup 4th rd, 5 Feb, 1972. *Record receipts:* £8982 v Stoke C, FA Cup 4th rd, 5 Feb, 1972. *Pitch measurements:* 112yd×74yd.

*How to get there:* Special buses from railway stations, Hamilton Square and Rock Ferry. Mersey Railway Liverpool, to Hamilton Square, then buses 80 to 90 or 64.

*Match tickets:* Not available in advance.

*Car parking:* Large car park at the back of the stand.

*Entertainments/catering facilities:* Snack bars in ground.

*Club shop:* Prenton Road West.

*Handbooks/programmes:* Programmes available on subscription.

*Extra information:* Tranmere's record victory equals the highest score in a League game; in the 13-4 win over Oldham, centre-forward Bunny Bell scored nine goals and missed a penalty.

*Club Colours:* Royal blue shirts, white collar and cuffs, white shorts, royal blue stockings.

*Change Colours:* All yellow.

*First Team Player/Coach:* Roy Mathias.

*Club Nickname:* Rovers.

## TRANMERE ROVERS 1981–82 LEAGUE RECORD

| Match No. | Date | Venue | Opponents | Result | H/T Score | Goalscorers | Attendance |
|---|---|---|---|---|---|---|---|
| 1 | Aug 29 | H | York C | L 0-2 | 0-1 | | 1850 |
| 2 | Sept 4 | A | Colchester U | L 0-4 | 0-2 | | 2474 |
| 3 | 12 | H | Hereford U | D 0-0 | 0-0 | | 1413 |
| 4 | 19 | A | Scunthorpe U | L 1-2 | 0-0 | Mungall | 1592 |
| 5 | 22 | A | Halifax T | W 2-0 | 2-0 | Bramhall, Brown | 1943 |
| 6 | 26 | H | Wigan Ath | D 0-0 | 0-0 | | 2774 |
| 7 | 29 | H | Darlington | D 1-1 | 0-0 | Williams | 1345 |
| 8 | Oct 3 | A | Hull C | W 2-1 | 2-0 | Mountfield, Williams | 3087 |
| 9 | 10 | H | Bury | L 1-3 | 0-1 | Hamilton | 1985 |
| 10 | 17 | A | Torquay U | W 2-1 | 0-0 | Brown 2 | 3022 |
| 11 | 20 | H | Hartlepool U | W 1-0 | 1-0 | Brown | 1431 |
| 12 | 24 | A | Northampton T | L 2-3 | 2-0 | Morley, Brown | 1722 |
| 13 | 31 | H | AFC Bournemouth | L 0-1 | 0-1 | | 1730 |
| 14 | Nov 3 | A | Rochdale | D 0-0 | 0-0 | | 1663 |
| 15 | 7 | A | Sheffield U | L 0-2 | 0-1 | | 13,454 |
| 16 | 14 | H | Bradford C | D 1-1 | 0-1 | Brown | 3218 |
| 17 | 28 | A | Aldershot | L 1-2 | 0-2 | Brown | 1878 |
| 18 | Dec 5 | H | Mansfield T | D 2-2 | 1-0 | Hutchinson, Hamilton | 1317 |
| 19 | Jan 5 | A | Wigan Ath | D 0-0 | 0-0 | | 4133 |
| 20 | 13 | A | Blackpool | W 2-1 | 0-1 | Williams, Hutchinson | 3329 |
| 21 | 19 | H | Crewe Alex | W 3-0 | 1-0 | Kerr 2, Craven | 1609 |
| 22 | 23 | A | York C | W 3-1 | 0-0 | Hutchinson, Kerr, Williams | 1594 |
| 23 | 25 | A | Port Vale | D 0-0 | 0-0 | | 4355 |
| 24 | 30 | H | Scunthorpe U | L 0-1 | 0-1 | | 1520 |
| 25 | Feb 6 | A | Hereford U | D 1-1 | 1-0 | Kerr | 2071 |
| 26 | 9 | H | Halifax T | D 1-1 | 0-0 | Bramhall | 1454 |
| 27 | 13 | H | Hull C | D 2-2 | 0-1 | Craven, Kerr | 1737 |
| 28 | 15 | A | Stockport Co | D 1-1 | 1-0 | Bramhall | 1934 |
| 29 | 23 | H | Peterborough U | L 1-2 | 1-1 | Kerr | 1185 |
| 30 | 27 | A | Bury | L 0-4 | 0-3 | | 3295 |
| 31 | Mar 2 | H | Colchester U | W 2-1 | 2-0 | Craven, Kerr | 1252 |
| 32 | 6 | A | Torquay U | D 1-1 | 0-0 | Kerr | 1187 |
| 33 | 10 | A | Hartlepool U | D 0-0 | 0-0 | | 1633 |
| 34 | 13 | H | Northampton T | L 0-2 | 0-1 | | 1193 |
| 35 | 16 | H | Rochdale | W 2-0 | 0-0 | Kerr 2 | 1131 |
| 36 | 20 | A | AFC Bournemouth | D 1-1 | 0-0 | Williams | 5302 |
| 37 | 27 | H | Sheffield U | D 2-2 | 1-1 | Kerr 2 | 4661 |
| 38 | Apr 3 | A | Bradford C | D 1-1 | 1-0 | Griffiths | 4489 |
| 39 | 10 | H | Blackpool | W 3-1 | 2-0 | Kerr, Craven, Burgess (pen) | 1828 |
| 40 | 12 | A | Crewe Alex | D 1-1 | 0-0 | Craven | 2015 |
| 41 | 17 | A | Mansfield T | L 0-3 | 0-1 | | 1995 |
| 42 | 24 | H | Aldershot | W 1-0 | 1-0 | Williams | 1242 |
| 43 | 30 | A | Darlington | W 2-1 | 0-0 | Ferguson, Craven | 1612 |
| 44 | May 4 | A | Stockport Co | W 2-0 | 2-0 | Hutchinson, Brown | 1212 |
| 45 | 8 | H | Port Vale | L 1-2 | 0-2 | Morley | 1521 |
| 46 | 15 | A | Peterborough U | W 2-1 | 2-0 | Craven 2 | 1897 |

**Final League Position: 11**

**Goalscorers**

*League* (51): Kerr 13, Brown 8, Craven 8, Williams 6, Hutchinson 4, Bramhall 3, Hamilton 2, Morley 2, Burgess 1 (pen), Ferguson 1, Griffiths 1, Mountfield 1, Mungall 1.
*League Cup* (12): Brown 5, Kerr 3, Hutchinson 2, Kelly 1, own goal 1.
*FA Cup* (2): Brown 1, Williams 1.

| | | | |
|---|---|---|---|
| **League Cup** | First Round | Burnley (h) | 4-2 |
| | | (a) | 3-3 |
| | Second Round | Port Vale (h) | 2-0 |
| | | (a) | 2-1 |
| | Third Round | Colchester U (h) | 1-0 |
| | Fourth Round | Nottingham F (a) | 0-2 |
| **FA Cup** | First Round | Bury (h) | 1-1 |
| | | (a) | 1-3 |

| Johnson | Mathias | Burgess | Bramhall | Parry | Williams | Kelly | Hutchinson | Griffiths | Kerr | Brown | Powell | Morley | Mungall | Endersby | Craven | Hamilton | Mountfield | Ferguson | Match No. |
|---|---|---|---|---|---|---|---|---|---|---|---|---|---|---|---|---|---|---|---|
| 1 | 2 | 3 | 4 | 5 | 6 | 7 | 8 | 9 | 10* | 11 | 12 | | | | | | | | 1 |
| 1 | | 2 | 5 | 4 | 6 | 7 | 8 | 11 | 9 | 10 | | 3* | 12 | | | | | | 2 |
| | | 3 | 5 | 4 | 6 | | 8 | 11* | 9 | 10 | | | 2 | 1 | 7 | 12 | | | 3 |
| | | 3 | 5 | 2 | 6* | 7 | | 11 | 9 | 10 | | | | 1 | 8 | 12 | 4 | | 4 |
| | | 3 | 5 | | 6 | 7 | | 11 | 9 | 10 | | | 2 | 1 | 8 | | 4 | | 5 |
| | | 3 | 5 | | 6 | 7 | | 11 | 9 | 10 | | | 2 | 1 | 8 | | 4 | | 6 |
| | | 3 | 5 | | 6 | 7 | 12 | 11 | 9 | 10 | | | 2 | 1 | 8* | | 4 | | 7 |
| | | 3 | 5 | | 6 | 7 | 8 | 11 | 9 | 10* | | | 2 | 1 | 12 | | 4 | | 8 |
| | | 3 | 5 | 4 | 6 | | 8 | 11 | 9* | 10 | | | 2 | 1 | 7 | 12 | | | 9 |
| | | 3 | 5 | | 6 | | | 11 | 9 | 10 | 8 | | 2 | 1 | 4 | 7 | | | 10 |
| | | 3 | 5 | | 6 | | | 11 | 9 | 10 | 8 | | 2 | 1 | 4 | 7 | | | 11 |
| | | 3 | 5 | | 6 | | 12 | 11 | 9 | 10 | 8* | | 2 | 1 | 4 | 7 | | | 12 |
| | | 3 | 5 | | 6 | | 8 | 11 | 9* | 10 | 12 | | 2 | 1 | 4 | 7 | | | 13 |
| | | 3 | 5 | | 6 | | 8 | | 9 | 10 | | | 2 | 1 | 4 | 7 | | 11 | 14 |
| | | 3 | 5 | | 6 | | | 9 | 11 | 10 | 8 | | 2 | 1 | 4 | 7 | | | 15 |
| | | 3 | 5 | | 6 | | | 9 | 11 | 10 | 8 | | 2 | 1 | 4 | 7 | | | 16 |
| | | 3 | 5 | | 6 | | 8 | | 9* | 10 | 11 | | 2 | 1 | 12 | 7 | 4 | | 17 |
| 1 | | 3 | 5 | | 6 | | 8 | 11 | 9 | 10 | | | 2 | | 7 | | 4 | | 18 |
| | | 3 | 5 | 4 | 6 | | 8 | | 9 | 10 | | | 2 | 1 | 11 | 7 | | | 19 |
| | | 3 | 5 | 4 | 6 | | 8 | | 9 | 10 | | | 2 | 1 | 11 | 7 | | | 20 |
| | | 3 | 5 | | 6 | | 8 | | 9 | 10 | | | 2 | 1 | 11 | 7 | 4 | | 21 |
| | | 3 | 5 | 4 | 6 | | 8 | | 9 | 10 | | | 2 | 1 | 11 | 7 | | | 22 |
| | | 3 | 5 | 4 | 6 | | 8 | 12 | 9 | 10 | | | 2 | 1 | 11* | 7 | | | 23 |
| | | 3 | 5 | 4 | 6 | | 8 | 10 | 9 | 12 | | | 2 | 1 | 11* | 7 | | | 24 |
| | | 3 | 5 | 4 | 6 | | 8* | 9 | 10 | 11 | 12 | | 2 | 1 | 7 | | | | 25 |
| | | 3 | 5 | 4 | 6 | | | 9 | 11 | 10 | | | 2 | 1 | 7 | 8* | 12 | | 26 |
| | | 3 | 5 | 4 | 6 | | 8 | 11 | 9 | 10 | | | 2 | 1 | | 7 | | | 27 |
| | | 3 | 5 | 4 | 6 | | 8 | 11 | 9 | 10 | 12 | | 2 | 1 | | 7* | | | 28 |
| | | 3 | 5 | 4 | 6* | | 8 | 11 | 9 | 10 | 12 | | 2 | 1 | | 7 | | | 29 |
| | | 3 | 5* | 4 | 6 | | 8 | | 9 | 10 | 12 | | 2 | 1 | | 7 | | 11 | 30 |
| | | 3 | 5 | 4 | 6 | | 8 | 11 | 9 | 10 | | | 2 | 1 | | 7 | | | 31 |
| | | 3 | 5 | 4 | 6 | | 8 | 11 | 9 | 10* | 12 | | 2 | 1 | | 7 | | | 32 |
| | | 3 | 5 | 4 | 6 | | 8 | 11 | 9 | 10 | 12 | | 2 | 1 | | 7* | | | 33 |
| | | 3 | 5 | 4 | 6* | | 8 | 11 | 9 | 10 | 12 | | 2 | 1 | | 7 | | | 34 |
| | | 3 | 5 | 4 | 6 | | 8 | 11* | 9 | 10 | 12 | | 2 | 1 | | 7 | | | 35 |
| | | 3 | 5 | 4 | 6 | | 8 | 11* | 9 | 10 | 12 | | 2 | 1 | | 7 | | | 36 |
| | | 3 | 5 | 4 | 6 | | 8* | 11 | 9 | 10 | 12 | | 2 | 1 | | 7 | | | 37 |
| | | 3 | 5 | 4 | 6 | | 8 | 11 | 9 | 10 | 12 | | 2 | 1 | | 7* | | | 38 |
| | | 3 | 5 | 4 | 6 | | 8 | 11 | 9 | 10 | | | 2 | 1 | | 7 | | | 39 |
| | | 3 | 5 | 4 | 6 | | 8 | 11 | 9 | 10 | | | 2 | 1 | | 7 | | | 40 |
| | | 3 | 5 | 4 | 6 | | 8 | 11 | 9 | 10* | 12 | | 2 | 1 | | 7 | | | 41 |
| | | 3 | 5 | 4 | 6 | | 8 | 11* | 9 | 10 | 12 | | 2 | 1 | | 7 | | | 42 |
| | | 3 | 5 | 4 | 6 | | 8 | | 9 | 10 | | | 2 | 1 | | 7 | | 11 | 43 |
| | | 3 | 5 | 4 | 6 | | 8 | 11 | 9* | 10 | 12 | | 2 | 1 | | 7 | | | 44 |
| | | 3 | 5 | 4 | 6 | | 8 | 11* | 9 | 10 | 12 | | 2 | 1 | | 7 | | | 45 |
| | | 3 | 5 | 4 | 6 | | 8 | | 9 | 10 | 12 | | 2 | 1 | | 7 | | 11* | 46 |
| 3 | 1 | 46 | 35 | 28 | 44 | 7 | 26 | 36 | 40 | 29 | 19 | 10 | 43 | 43 | 36 | 35 | 21 | 4 | |
| | | | +1s | | +3s | +2s | | +8s | +1s | +6s | 1s | | | | +3s | +3s | +1s | | |

## TRANMERE ROVERS

| | Ht | Wt | Birthplace | Clubs | League App. | League Gls |
|---|---|---|---|---|---|---|
| **Goalkeepers** | | | | | | |
| Dickie Johnson* | 6 1 | 12 10 | Liverpool | Tranmere R | 355 | — |
| Scott Endersby | 5 10 | 12 11 | Lewisham | Ipswich T | — | — |
| | | | | Tranmere R | 43 | — |
| **Defenders** | | | | | | |
| Ray Mathias | 5 9 | 11 4 | Liverpool | Tranmere R | 542 | 5 |
| Les Parry | 5 11 | 11 0 | Wallasey | Tranmere R | 239 | 4 |
| Steve Mungall | 5 8 | 10 2 | Bellshill | Motherwell | 20 | — |
| | | | | Tranmere R | 106 | 4 |
| Derek Mountfield | 6 1 | 12 7 | Liverpool | Tranmere R | 26 | 1 |
| Brian Morley* | 5 7 | 11 3 | Fleetwood | Blackburn R | 20 | — |
| | | | | Tranmere R | 16 | 2 |
| Dave Burgess | 5 10 | 11 2 | | Tranmere R | 46 | 1 |
| John Williams | 6 2 | 13 6 | Liverpool | Tranmere R | 75 | 8 |
| **Midfield** | | | | | | |
| Steve Craven* | 5 10 | 11 0 | Birkenhead | Tranmere R | 114 | 17 |
| Ian Griffiths | 5 5 | 10 7 | Birkenhead | Tranmere R | 73 | 1 |
| Bryan Hamilton | 5 8 | 11 2 | Belfast | Ipswich T | 153 | 43 |
| (N Ireland) | | | | Everton | 41 | 5 |
| | | | | Millwall | 49 | 6 |
| | | | | Swindon T | 24 | 1 |
| | | | | Tranmere R | 70 | 2 |
| **Forwards** | | | | | | |
| John Kerr | 5 11 | 12 5 | Birkenhead | Tranmere R | 121 | 30 |
| Neville Powell | 5 8 | 10 1 | Flint | Tranmere R | 26 | 1 |
| Owen Brown* | 5 10¼ | 11 10 | Liverpool | Liverpool | — | — |
| | | | | Carlisle U | 4 | 2 |
| | | | | Tranmere R | 37 | 8 |
| Bobby Hutchinson | 5 9 | 11 4 | Glasgow | Montrose | 41 | 8 |
| | | | | Dundee | 88 | 25 |
| | | | | Hibernian | 67 | 13 |
| | | | | Wigan Ath | 35 | 3 |
| | | | | Tranmere R | 29 | 4 |
| Mark Ferguson | | | | Tranmere R | 5 | 1 |
| (Non-contract) | | | | | | |

# WALSALL Division 3

*Chairman:* K. E. Wheldon.

*Directors:* J. A. Harris, S. E. Boler, R. Homden, B. E. Bradnack.

*Player-Manager:* Alan Buckley.

*Secretary:* H. J. Westmancoat FAAI.

*Year Formed:* 1888.

*Turned Professional:* 1888.

*Limited Company:* 1921.

*Previous Names:* Walsall Swifts (Founded 1877) and Walsall Town (Founded 1879) amalgamated in 1888 and were known as Walsall Town Swifts until 1895.

**Football League Record:**
1892 Elected to Division 2; 1895 failed re-election; 1896–1901 Division 2; 1901 failed re-election; 1921 Original Member of Division 3(N); 1927–31 Division 3(S); 1931–36 Division 3(N); 1936–58 Division 3(S); 1958–60 Division 4; 1960–61 Division 3; 1961–63 Division 2; 1963–79 Division 3; 1979–80 Division 4; 1980– Division 3.

**Honours:** *Football League:* Division 2 best season: 6th, 1898–99; Division 3 – Runners-up 1960–61; Division 4 – Champions 1959–60; Runners-up 1979–80. *FA Cup* best season: 5th rd, 1939, 1975, 1978, and last 16 1888–89. *Football League Cup* best season: 4th rd, 1966–67.

*Record Victory:* 10-0 v Darwen, Division 2, 4 Mar, 1899.

*Record Defeat:* 0-12 v Small Heath, 17 Dec, 1892 and v Darwen, 26 Dec, 1896, both Division 2.

*Most League Points:* 65, Division 4, 1959–60.

*Most League Goals:* 102, Division 4, 1959–60.

*Highest League Scorer in Season:* Gilbert Alsop, 40, Division 3(N), 1933–34 and 1934–35.

*Most League Goals in Total Aggregate:* Tony Richards, 184, 1954–63, and Colin Taylor, 184, 1958–63, 1964–68, 1969–73.

*Most Capped Player:* Mick Kearns, 15 (17), Eire.

*Most League Appearances:* Colin Harrison, 467, 1964–82.

*Record Transfer Fee Received:* £175,000 from Birmingham C for Alan Buckley, Oct 1978.

*Record Transfer Fee Paid:* £175,000 to Birmingham C for Alan Buckley, June 1979.

*Previous Managers since the War:* Harry Hibbs, Tony McPhee, Brough Fletcher, Major Buckley, John Love, Billy Moore, Alf Wood, Ray Shaw, Ron Lewin, Dick Graham, Billy Moore, John Smith, Ronnie Allen, Doug Fraser, Dave Mackay, Alan Ashman, Frank Sibley, Alan Buckley, Neil Martin.

*Address of Supporters Club:* Saddlers Club, Wallows Lane, Walsall, Staffs.

---

**Fellows Park, Walsall.** Telephone 0922 22791. *Telegraphic address:* 'Walsall FC, Walsall'. *Ground capacity:* 24,100. *Record attendance:* 25,453 v Newcastle U, Division 2, 29 Aug, 1961. *Record receipts:* £12,775.35 v Newcastle U, FA Cup 4th rd, 25 Jan, 1975. *Pitch measurements:* 113yd×73yd.

*How to get there:* Corporation specials from Bradford Place. Buses 237 and 238 within walking distance of the ground. Nearest railway stations, Bescot (10 minutes' walk from ground) and Walsall.

*Match tickets:* Seats can be booked at any time by postal, personal, or telephone application to the ticket office; tel: 0922 22791.

*Car parking:* Car park in Hillary Street for 100 cars. Side-street parking available.

*Entertainments/catering facilities:* Tea bars and licensed bars inside the ground.

*Club shop:* The Boutique, is open on match days.

*Extra information:* In 1947, Walsall set a Division 3(S) record by winning 8-0 away at Northampton.

*Club Colours:* Red shirts, white shorts, red stockings with two white bands on turnover.

*Change Colours:* Blue shirts, black trim, black shorts, black stockings.

*Club Captain:* Peter Hart.

*Club Nickname:* Saddlers.

378

## WALSALL 1981-82 LEAGUE RECORD

| Match No. | Date | Venue | Opponents | Result | H/T Score | Goalscorers | Attendance |
|---|---|---|---|---|---|---|---|
| 1 | Aug 29 | H | Southend U | L 0-1 | 0-1 | | 3419 |
| 2 | Sept 5 | A | Brentford | D 0-0 | 0-0 | | 5315 |
| 3 | 12 | H | Chesterfield | D 1-1 | 1-0 | Waddington S. | 3280 |
| 4 | 19 | A | Oxford U | W 1-0 | 0-0 | Caswell | 3685 |
| 5 | 23 | A | Chester | D 0-0 | 0-0 | | 1978 |
| 6 | 26 | H | Wimbledon | W 1-0 | 0-0 | Penn | 3027 |
| 7 | 29 | H | Lincoln C | W 2-1 | 0-1 | Buckley, Penn | 3653 |
| 8 | Oct 3 | A | Bristol C | W 1-0 | 1-0 | Penn | 6033 |
| 9 | 11 | A | Millwall | L 0-2 | 0-1 | | 6289 |
| 10 | 17 | H | Portsmouth | W 3-1 | 1-0 | Beech, Serella, Buckley | 4408 |
| 11 | 20 | H | Swindon T | W 5-0 | 2-0 | Buckley 2 (1 pen), Loveridge, Rees 2 | 6010 |
| 12 | 24 | A | Carlisle U | L 1-2 | 0-1 | Loveridge | 3956 |
| 13 | 31 | H | Plymouth Arg | L 0-1 | 0-1 | | 4549 |
| 14 | Nov 4 | A | Reading | D 0-0 | 0-0 | | 4057 |
| 15 | 7 | H | Newport Co | W 3-1 | 2-0 | O'Kelly 3 (1 pen) | 4169 |
| 16 | 14 | A | Fulham | D 1-1 | 1-1 | Penn | 6168 |
| 17 | 28 | H | Bristol R | W 2-1 | 1-1 | Rees 2 | 4311 |
| 18 | Dec 5 | A | Gillingham | W 4-1 | 1-0 | O'Kelly 2, Penn, Rees | 5845 |
| 19 | Jan 16 | A | Exeter C | L 0-2 | 0-0 | | 3118 |
| 20 | 19 | H | Brentford | W 3-0 | 2-0 | O'Kelly, Penn, Round | 3853 |
| 21 | 23 | A | Southend U | L 2-3 | 0-3 | Horne, Caswell | 4684 |
| 22 | 30 | H | Oxford U | L 1-3 | 0-3 | Penn | 4573 |
| 23 | Feb 6 | A | Chesterfield | L 0-1 | 0-0 | | 5989 |
| 24 | 9 | H | Chester | W 2-1 | 2-1 | Lowery, Buckley | 3668 |
| 25 | 13 | H | Bristol C | L 0-1 | 0-1 | | 4020 |
| 26 | 16 | H | Huddersfield T | D 1-1 | 0-0 | Waddington S. | 3362 |
| 27 | 20 | A | Lincoln C | D 1-1 | 0-0 | Hart | 3243 |
| 28 | 27 | H | Millwall | D 1-1 | 0-0 | Penn | 3731 |
| 29 | Mar 2 | H | Burnley | D 1-1 | 0-0 | Round | 4196 |
| 30 | 6 | A | Portsmouth | L 0-1 | 0-1 | | 7133 |
| 31 | 9 | A | Swindon T | D 2-2 | 1-1 | Penn (pen), Caswell | 4446 |
| 32 | 13 | H | Carlisle U | D 1-1 | 0-0 | Beech | 3507 |
| 33 | 16 | H | Reading | L 1-2 | 1-0 | Buckley | 2789 |
| 34 | 20 | A | Plymouth Arg | L 1-4 | 0-3 | Penn | 5134 |
| 35 | 27 | A | Newport Co | D 2-2 | 2-2 | Penn 2 | 3484 |
| 36 | Apr 3 | H | Fulham | D 1-1 | 0-0 | Buckley (pen) | 3120 |
| 37 | 10 | A | Huddersfield T | L 1-2 | 0-0 | Teasdale | 6572 |
| 38 | 13 | H | Preston NE | L 0-3 | 0-2 | | 3507 |
| 39 | 17 | H | Gillingham | W 1-0 | 0-0 | Serella | 2684 |
| 40 | 20 | A | Doncaster R | L 0-1 | 0-0 | | 3903 |
| 41 | 24 | A | Bristol R | L 1-2 | 1-0 | Baines | 3677 |
| 42 | 27 | A | Preston NE | L 0-1 | 0-1 | | 4930 |
| 43 | May 1 | H | Exeter C | W 2-1 | 1-0 | Penn 2 | 2487 |
| 44 | 4 | A | Wimbledon | L 0-2 | 0-1 | | 1503 |
| 45 | 8 | A | Burnley | L 1-2 | 0-1 | Rees | 8543 |
| 46 | 15 | H | Doncaster R | D 0-0 | 0-0 | | 3799 |

**Final League Position: 20**

### Goalscorers

*League* (51): Penn 14 (1 pen), Buckley 7 (2 pens), O'Kelly 6 (1 pen), Rees 6, Caswell 3, Beech 2, Loveridge 2, Round 2, Serella 2, Waddington S. 2, Baines 1, Hart 1, Horne 1, Lowery 1, Teasdale 1.
*League Cup* (1): Penn 1.
*FA Cup* (3): Caswell 1, Macken 1, own goal 1.

| League Cup | First Round | Bristol C (a) | 0-2 |
| | | (h) | 1-0 |
| FA Cup | First Round | Blyth Spartans (a) | 2-1 |
| | Second Round | Peterborough U (a) | 1-2 |

| Green | Macken | Caswell | Beech | Serella | Hart | Rees | O'Kelly | Penn | Buckley | Preece | Waddington P. | Loveridge | Waddington S. | Harrison | Round | Mower | Smith | Horne | Lowery | Sinnott | Teasdale | Baines | Match No. |
|---|---|---|---|---|---|---|---|---|---|---|---|---|---|---|---|---|---|---|---|---|---|---|---|
| 1 | 2 | 3 | 4 | 5 | 6 | 7 | 8* | 9 | 10 | 11 | 12 | | | | | | | | | | | | 1 |
| 1 | 2 | 3 | 4 | 5 | 6 | 7 | | 9 | 10 | 11 | | 8*12 | | | | | | | | | | | 2 |
| 1 | 2 | 11 | 4 | 5 | 6 | | | 9 | 10* | | 12 | 8 | | | 3 | 7 | | | | | | | 3 |
| 1 | 2 | 11 | 4 | 5 | 6 | 7 | | 9*10 | | | | 8 | 12 | | | 3 | | | | | | | 4 |
| 1 | 2 | 11 | 4 | 5 | 6 | 7 | | 9 | 10 | | | 8 | | | | 3 | | | | | | | 5 |
| 1 | 2 | 11 | 4 | 5 | 6 | 7 | | 9 | 10* | | | 8 | 12 | | | 3 | | | | | | | 6 |
| 1 | 2 | 11 | 4 | 5 | 6 | 7 | | 9 | 10 | | | 8 | | | | 3 | | | | | | | 7 |
| 1 | 2 | 11 | 4 | 5 | 6* | 7 | | 9 | 10 | | 12 | 8 | | | | 3 | | | | | | | 8 |
| 1 | 2 | 11 | 4 | 5 | 6 | 7 | | 9 | 10 | | 12 | 8 | | | | 3* | | | | | | | 9 |
| 1 | 2 | 3 | 4 | 5 | 6 | 7 | 12 | 9 | 10 | | | 8*11 | | | | | | | | | | | 10 |
| 1 | 2 | 3 | 4 | 5 | 6 | 7 | 12 | 9 | 10 | | | 8 | 11* | | | | | | | | | | 11 |
| 1 | 2 | 3 | 4 | 5 | 6 | 7*12 | | 9 | 10 | | | 8 | 11 | | | | | | | | | | 12 |
| 1 | 2 | 3 | 4 | 5 | 6 | | 12 | 9 | 10 | | | 8 | 11 | | 7* | | | | | | | | 13 |
| 1 | 2 | 10 | 4 | 5 | 6 | 7 | | 9 | | | | 8 | 11 | | | 3 | | | | | | | 14 |
| 1 | 2 | 10 | 4 | 5 | 6 | 7 | | 9 | 12 | | | 8 | 11* | | | 3 | | | | | | | 15 |
| 1 | 2 | 10 | 4 | 5 | 6 | 7 | | 9 | | | | 8 | 11 | | | 3 | | | | | | | 16 |
| 1 | 2 | 10 | 4 | 5 | 6 | 7 | 11 | 9 | | | | 8 | | | | 3 | | | | | | | 17 |
| 1 | 2 | 10 | 4 | 5 | 6 | 7 | 11 | 9 | | | | 8 | | | | 3 | | | | | | | 18 |
| 1 | 2 | 10 | 4 | 5 | 6 | 7 | 11 | 9 | 12 | | | 8* | | | | 3 | | | | | | | 19 |
| 1 | | 10* | 4 | 5 | 6 | 7 | 11 | 9 | | | | 8 | 12 | | | 3 | | | 2 | | | | 20 |
| 1 | 2 | 10 | 4 | 5 | 6 | 7 | | 9 | 11* | | | 8 | | | | 3 | | | 12 | | | | 21 |
| 1 | 2 | 10 | 4 | 5 | 6 | 7 | 11 | 9 | 12 | | | | | | 3* | 8 | | | | | | | 22 |
| 1 | 2 | 11 | 4 | 5 | 6 | 7 | | 9*10 | | | | | | | | 3 | | 8 | | | | | 23 |
| 1 | 2 | 11 | 4 | 5 | 6 | 7 | | 9 | 10 | | | | | | | 3 | | 8 | | | | | 24 |
| 1 | 2*11 | | 4 | 5 | 6 | 7 | | 9 | 10 | | | | | | | 3 | | 8 | | | | | 25 |
| 1 | 2 | 11 | 4 | 5 | 6 | 7 | | | 10 | | 12 | | | | 9 | 3 | | 8* | | | | | 26 |
| 1 | 2 | 11 | 4 | 5 | 6 | 7 | | 9 | 10 | | | 8 | | | | 3 | | | | | | | 27 |
| 1 | 2 | 8* | 4 | 5 | 6 | 7 | | 9 | 10 | | | 11 | | | | 3 | | | 12 | | | | 28 |
| 1 | 2 | | 4 | 5 | 6 | 7 | 9 | | | | | 8 | 11 | 10 | 3* | | | | 12 | | | | 29 |
| 1 | 2 | | 4 | 5 | 6 | 11 | | 9 | 8 | 12 | | | | 7 | 10* | | | | | 3 | | | 30 |
| 1 | 2 | 11 | 4 | 5 | 6 | 7 | 10* | 9 | 12 | | | 8 | | | | | | | | 3 | | | 31 |
| 1 | 2 | 11 | 4 | 5 | 6 | 7 | 12 | 9 | 10* | | | 8 | | | | | | | | 3 | | | 32 |
| 1 | 2 | 3 | 4 | 5 | 6 | 7 | 11*9 | | 10 | | | 8 | 12 | | | | | | | | | | 33 |
| 1 | | 8 | 4* | 5 | 6 | 7 | 10 | 9 | | | 12 | 11 | | | | 2 | | | | 3 | | | 34 |
| 1 | 2 | 11 | | 5 | 6 | 7 | 12 | 9 | 10 | 4* | | | | | | 3 | | | | | 8 | | 35 |
| 1 | 4 | | | 5 | | | 9 | 10 | 11 | 7 | | 12 | | 3 | | 2 | | | | | 8* | 6 | 36 |
| 1 | 2 | | | 5 | 4 | 7 | 12 | 10 | 11* | 8 | | | | 3 | | | | | | | 9 | 6 | 37 |
| 1 | 2 | | | 5 | 4 | 12 | 11*9 | | 10 | 7 | | | | 3 | | | | | | | 8 | 6 | 38 |
| 1 | | 8 | 4 | 5 | 2 | 7 | 11 | | 10 | | | | | 3 | | | | | | | 9 | 6 | 39 |
| 1 | | 8 | 4 | 5 | 2 | 7 | 11*12 | | 10 | | | | | 3 | | | | | | | 9 | 6 | 40 |
| 1 | | 8 | 4 | 5 | 2 | 11 | 12 | 9 | | | | 7 | | 3 | | | | | | | 10* | 6 | 41 |
| 1 | | 8 | 4 | 5 | 2 | 7 | | 10 | | | | 11 | | 3 | | | | | | | 9 | 6 | 42 |
| 1 | 2 | 8 | | 5 | 6 | 7 | | 9 | 10 | 11* | | 4 | | 12 | 3 | | | | | | | | 43 |
| 1 | 2 | 8 | | 5 | 6 | 7 | 12 | | 10 | | | 11 | | 9* | 3 | | | | | | | 4 | 44 |
| 1 | 2 | 8 | | 5 | 6 | 7 | | 9 | 10 | | | 11 | | | 3 | | | | | | | 4 | 45 |
| 1 | 2 | 8*12 | | 5 | 6 | 7 | | 10 | 9 | | | 11 | | | 3 | | | | | | | 4 | 46 |
| 46 | 40 | 41 | 38 | 46 | 45 | 38 | 21 | 38 | 30 | 6 | — | 23 | 24 | 1 | 4 | 34 | 1 | 4 | 4 | 4 | 8 | 10 | |
| | | + | | | + | + | + | + | + | + | + | | | | + | | | | + | + | | | |
| | | 1s | | | 1s | 8s | 2s | 3s | 2s | 2s | 3s | 2s | | | 8s | | | | 1s | 2s | | | |

# WALSALL

| | Ht | Wt | Birthplace | Clubs | League App. | League Gls |
|---|---|---|---|---|---|---|
| **Goalkeepers** | | | | | | |
| Ron Green | 6 2 | 12 10 | Birmingham | Walsall | 111 | — |
| Ian Turner | 6 0 | 12 0 | Middlesbrough | Huddersfield T | — | — |
| (Contract cancelled March 1982) | | | | Grimsby T | 26 | — |
| | | | | Walsall (on loan) | 3 | — |
| | | | | Southampton | 77 | — |
| | | | | Newport Co (on loan) | 7 | — |
| | | | | Lincoln C (on loan) | 7 | — |
| | | | | Luton T (on loan) | — | — |
| | | | | Halifax T (on loan) | 5 | — |
| | | | | Walsall | 39 | — |
| Martin Conneally | 6 0 | 12 0 | Lichfield | Walsall | 3 | — |
| **Defenders** | | | | | | |
| Tony Macken* | 5 8 | 12 6 | Waterford | Derby Co | 23 | 1 |
| (Éire) | | | | Portsmouth (on loan) | 10 | 1 |
| | | | | Walsall | 190 | 1 |
| Colin Harrison* | 5 10 | 11 8 | Pelsall | Walsall | 467 | 33 |
| Dave Serella* | 5 9 | 10 10 | King's Lynn | Nottingham F | 68 | — |
| | | | | Walsall | 267 | 12 |
| Brian Caswell | 5 10 | 10 7 | Wednesbury | Walsall | 294 | 17 |
| Ian Paul | 5 9 | 11 0 | Wolverhampton | Walsall | 70 | 9 |
| (Contract cancelled July 1981, registration retained) | | | | | | |
| Kenny Mower | 6 0¾ | 11 11 | Walsall | Walsall | 112 | 3 |
| John Horne* | 6 0 | 11 6 | Netherton | Walsall | 16 | 1 |
| Stephen Baines | 6 0 | 12 12 | Newark | Nottingham F | 2 | — |
| | | | | Huddersfield T | 114 | 10 |
| | | | | Bradford C | 99 | 17 |
| | | | | Walsall | 48 | 5 |
| | | | | Bury (on loan) | 7 | — |
| Tony Hadland | 5 10 | 11 5 | Birmingham | WBA | — | — |
| (Contract cancelled Sept 1981) | | | | Walsall | — | — |
| Lee Sinnott | | | | Walsall | 4 | — |
| (Apprentice) | | | | | | |
| Peter Hart | 5 10 | 12 7 | Mexborough | Huddersfield T | 210 | 7 |
| | | | | Walsall | 90 | 6 |
| **Midfield** | | | | | | |
| Steve Waddington* | 5 4 | 9 3 | Crewe | Stoke C | 52 | 5 |
| | | | | Walsall | 130 | 13 |
| Richard O'Kelly | 5 10 | 11 0 | West Bromwich | Walsall | 67 | 13 |
| David Preece | 5 5 | 9 0 | Bridgnorth | Walsall | 16 | — |
| Ken Beech | 5 7 | 10 2 | Stoke | Port Vale | 175 | 17 |
| | | | | Walsall | 39 | 2 |
| John Loveridge* | 5 7 | 10 10 | Wolverhampton | WBA | — | — |
| | | | | Walsall | 26 | 2 |
| **Forwards** | | | | | | |
| Don Penn | 5 10 | 12 0 | Smethwick | Walsall | 136 | 51 |
| Paul Waddington | 5 8 | 9 12 | Oldbury | Walsall | 19 | — |
| (Contract cancelled Feb 1982) | | | | | | |
| Mark Rees | 5 10 | 11 10 | Smethwick | Walsall | 92 | 15 |
| Alan Buckley | 5 6 | 10 9 | Mansfield | Nottingham F | 18 | 1 |
| | | | | Walsall | 241 | 125 |
| | | | | Birmingham C | 28 | 8 |
| | | | | Walsall | 117 | 34 |
| Steve Round | 6 1 | 12 2 | Bridgnorth | Walsall | 12 | 2 |
| Steve Smith* | 5 10 | 11 6 | Birmingham | Bromsgrove R | (not known) | |
| | | | | Walsall | 19 | 3 |
| Craig Shakespeare | 5 10 | 10 5 | Birmingham | Walsall | — | — |
| Andrew Parkes | | | | Walsall | — | — |
| (Contract cancelled March 1982) | | | | | | |
| Chris Wilson | | | | Walsall | — | — |
| (Contract cancelled Feb 1982) | | | | | | |
| John Teasdale | 5 9 | 10 7 | Glasgow | Nairn | (not known) | |
| | | | | Wolverhampton W | 8 | — |
| | | | | Walsall | 8 | 1 |

# WATFORD
# Division 1

*Chairman:* E. John.

*Directors:* J. Harrowell, Bertie Mee, J. Reid, G. A. Smith, H. M. Stratford.

*Chief Executive & Company Secretary:* Eddie Plumley FAAI.

*General Manager:* Graham Taylor.

*Marketing Manager:* Caroline Gillies M INST M, MIPR.

*Year Formed:* 1891.  *Turned Professional:* 1897.

*Limited Company:* 1909.

*Previous Grounds:* 1899, Cassio Road; 1919, Vicarage Road.

**Football League Record:**
1920 Original Member of Division 3; 1921–58 Division 3(S); 1958–60 Division 4; 1960–69 Division 3; 1969–72 Division 2; 1972–75 Division 3; 1975–78 Division 4; 1978–79 Division 3; 1979–82 Division 2; 1982– Division 1.

**Honours:** *Football League:* Division 2 Runners-up 1981–82; Division 3 – Champions 1968–69, Runners-up 1978–79; Division 4 – Champions 1977–78; Promoted 1959–60 (4th). *FA Cup:* semi-final 1970. *Football League Cup:* semi-final 1978–79. *FA Youth Cup:* Winners 1981–82.

*Record Victory:* 10-1 v Lowestoft Town, FA Cup 1st rd, 27 Nov, 1926.

*Record Defeat:* 0-10 v Wolverhampton W, FA Cup 1st rd replay, 13 Jan, 1912.

*Most League Points:* 71, Division 4, 1977–78. *Three points win:* 80, Division 2, 1981–82.

*Most League Goals:* 92, Division 4, 1959–60.

*Highest League Scorer in Season:* Cliff Holton, 42, Division 4, 1959–60.

*Most League Goals in Total Aggregate:* Tom Barnett, 144, 1928–39.

*Most Capped Player:* Gerry Armstrong, 15 (42), Northern Ireland.

*Most League Appearances:* Duncan Welbourne, 411, 1963–74.

*Record Transfer Fee Received:* £110,00 from West Ham U for Billy Jennings, Sept 1974.

*Record Transfer Fee Paid:* £250,000 to Tottenham H for Gerry Armstrong, Nov 1980.

*Previous Managers since the War:* Jack Bray, Eddie Hapgood, Haydn Green, Ron Gray, Len Goulden, Neil McBain, Ron Burgess, Bill McGarry, Ken Furphy, George Kirby, Mike Keen.

*Address of Supporters Club:* Watford FC Supporters Club, Vicarage Road, Watford.

*Address of Club Shop:* 85 Vicarage Road, Watford.

---

**Vicarage Road Stadium, Watford WD1 8ER.** Telephone Watford 49747–9. *Ground capacity:* 28,000. *Record attendance:* 34,099 v Manchester U, FA Cup 4th rd, 3 Feb, 1969. *Record receipts:* £61,684 v West Ham U, FA Cup 4th rd, 23 Jan, 1982. *Pitch measurements:* 113yd×73yd.

*How to get there:* Buses 321 and 327 from Watford Junction. This and Watford High Street Station are both within walking distance from the ground. Trains from London leave Euston Station.

*Match tickets:* Stand seats bookable 10 days before each League match. Visiting terrace supporters will be guided by Police to special visitors enclosure (admission £2.50).

*Car parking:* Parking for season ticket holders only at the ground, but several multi-storey car parks a few minutes away.

*Entertainments/catering facilities:* Pre-match entertainment at all League and Cup games by Radio Hornet. Tea kiosks and hot dog stands inside the ground.

*Club shop:* Shops on the ground and 'Hornet Shop' at 85 Vicarage Road Precinct, Watford sell all type of souvenirs and programmes.

*Handbooks/programmes:* Programmes are available on subscription. Price 40p, plus postage. Handbook, £1, will be available for season 1982–83 with full statistics and interesting information and action pictures.

*Extra information:* Answerphone Service – Watford 44930 for information. In 1968–69 Watford conceded only 34 goals, a record for the Third Division.

*Club Colours:* Yellow shirts with black-red facings, red shorts, red stockings with black and yellow tops.

*Change Colours:* White shirts, black shorts, black stockings with red and yellow tops.

---

# WATFORD 1981-82 LEAGUE RECORD

| Match No. | Date | | Venue | Opponents | Result | | H/T Score | Goalscorers | Attendance |
|---|---|---|---|---|---|---|---|---|---|
| 1 | Aug | 29 | A | Newcastle U | W | 1-0 | 1-0 | Callaghan | 19,376 |
| 2 | Sept | 1 | H | Grimsby T | L | 0-2 | 0-0 | | 11,257 |
| 3 | | 5 | H | Oldham Ath | D | 1-1 | 0-0 | Armstrong | 9018 |
| 4 | | 12 | A | Chelsea | W | 3-1 | 1-1 | Callaghan, Rostron, Armstrong | 20,036 |
| 5 | | 19 | H | Rotherham U | W | 1-0 | 0-0 | Armstrong | 10,644 |
| 6 | | 22 | A | Wrexham | W | 1-0 | 1-0 | Taylor | 3911 |
| 7 | | 26 | A | Luton T | L | 1-4 | 0-3 | Bolton | 12,839 |
| 8 | Oct | 3 | H | Barnsley | W | 3-1 | 2-1 | Poskett, Barnes, Jackett | 10,803 |
| 9 | | 10 | H | Orient | W | 3-0 | 0-0 | Terry, Barnes 2 | 10,052 |
| 10 | | 17 | A | Cambridge U | W | 2-1 | 1-0 | Blissett 2 | 7239 |
| 11 | | 24 | H | Norwich C | W | 3-0 | 2-0 | Bolton, Barnes, Blissett | 14,463 |
| 12 | | 31 | A | Shrewsbury T | W | 2-0 | 2-0 | Jenkins, Barnes | 5672 |
| 13 | Nov | 7 | A | Bolton W | L | 0-2 | 0-1 | | 7066 |
| 14 | | 14 | H | Cardiff C | D | 0-0 | 0-0 | | 13,907 |
| 15 | | 21 | H | Blackburn R | W | 3-2 | 2-0 | Jenkins 2, Jackett | 11,822 |
| 16 | | 28 | A | Sheffield W | L | 1-3 | 0-2 | Armstrong | 15,990 |
| 17 | Dec | 5 | H | Charlton Ath | D | 2-2 | 2-0 | Lohman, Taylor | 12,113 |
| 18 | | 12 | A | Leicester C | D | 1-1 | 1-1 | Jenkins | 10,340 |
| 19 | Jan | 9 | A | Oldham Ath | D | 1-1 | 0-0 | Jenkins | 7409 |
| 20 | | 16 | H | Newcastle U | L | 2-3 | 0-1 | Jenkins, Terry | 12,333 |
| 21 | | 26 | H | Derby Co | W | 6-1 | 3-0 | Armstrong 2, Blissett, Bolton, Barnes, Callaghan | 12,643 |
| 22 | | 30 | A | Rotherham U | W | 2-1 | 0-1 | Bolton, Barnes | 8129 |
| 23 | Feb | 6 | H | Chelsea | W | 1-0 | 0-0 | Blissett (pen) | 17,101 |
| 24 | | 9 | A | Barnsley | D | 0-0 | 0-0 | | 17,070 |
| 25 | | 20 | H | Luton T | D | 1-1 | 1-1 | Rostron | 22,580 |
| 26 | | 27 | A | Orient | W | 3-1 | 2-1 | Blissett 2 (1 pen), Jenkins | 6595 |
| 27 | Mar | 6 | H | Cambridge U | D | 0-0 | 0-0 | | 11,804 |
| 28 | | 9 | H | QPR | W | 4-0 | 2-0 | Howe (og), Taylor, Jenkins, Blissett | 16,862 |
| 29 | | 13 | A | Norwich C | L | 2-4 | 2-1 | Barnes, Taylor | 15,534 |
| 30 | | 16 | A | Grimsby T | W | 2-0 | 0-0 | Jenkins, Barnes | 6146 |
| 31 | | 20 | H | Shrewsbury T | W | 3-1 | 1-0 | Jenkins, Blissett 2 (1 pen) | 11,780 |
| 32 | | 27 | H | Bolton W | W | 3-0 | 1-0 | Lohman, Blissett 2 (1 pen) | 12,937 |
| 33 | Apr | 3 | A | Cardiff C | L | 0-2 | 0-0 | | 6734 |
| 34 | | 9 | H | Crystal Palace | D | 1-1 | 0-1 | Barnes | 18,224 |
| 35 | | 12 | A | QPR | D | 0-0 | 0-0 | | 22,091 |
| 36 | | 17 | A | Blackburn R | W | 2-1 | 0-1 | Callaghan, Blissett (pen) | 7284 |
| 37 | | 24 | H | Sheffield W | W | 4-0 | 4-0 | Callaghan, Barnes, Blissett 2 | 23,987 |
| 38 | | 27 | A | Crystal Palace | W | 3-0 | 1-0 | Blissett 2 (2 pens), Armstrong | 12,355 |
| 39 | May | 1 | A | Charlton Ath | D | 1-1 | 0-1 | Jenkins | 9747 |
| 40 | | 4 | H | Wrexham | W | 2-0 | 1-0 | Jenkins 2 | 20,028 |
| 41 | | 8 | H | Leicester C | W | 3-1 | 3-0 | Barnes 2, Blissett | 20,859 |
| 42 | | 15 | A | Derby Co | L | 2-3 | 0-1 | Blissett (pen), Bolton | 14,946 |

**Final League Position: 2**

### Goalscorers

League (76): Blissett 19 (9 pens), Barnes 13, Jenkins 13, Armstrong 7, Bolton 5, Callaghan 5, Taylor 4, Jackett 2, Lohman 2, Rostron 2, Terry 2, Poskett 1, own goal 1.

League Cup (13): Blissett 3 (1 pen), Jenkins 2, Taylor 2, Armstrong 1, Barnes 1, Jackett 1, Pritchett 1, Rostron 1, Terry 1.

FA Cup (3): Armstrong 1, Callaghan 1, Lohman 1.

| League Cup | Second Round | Grimsby T (a) | 0-1 |
|---|---|---|---|
| | | (h) | 3-1 |
| | Third Round | Lincoln C (h) | 2-2 |
| | | (a) | 3-2 |
| | Fourth Round | QPR (h) | 4-1 |
| | Fifth Round | Ipswich T (a) | 1-2 |
| FA Cup | Third Round | Manchester U (h) | 1-0 |
| | Fourth Round | West Ham U (h) | 2-0 |
| | Fifth Round | Leicester C (a) | 0-2 |

| Sherwood | Rice | Henderson | Taylor | Sims | Bolton | Callaghan | Blissett | Armstrong | Jackett | Poskett | Rostron | Pritchett | Barnes | Jenkins | Gilligan | Terry | Lohman | Steele | Johnson | Match No. |
|---|---|---|---|---|---|---|---|---|---|---|---|---|---|---|---|---|---|---|---|---|
| 1 | 2 | 3 | 4 | 5 | 6 | 7 | 8 | 9 | 10 | 11 | | | | | | | | | | 1 |
| 1 | 2 | 3 | 4* | 5 | 6 | 7 | 8 | 9 | 10 | 11 | 12 | | | | | | | | | 2 |
| 1 | 2 | | 4 | 5 | 6 | 7 | 8 | 9 | 10 | 11* | | 3 | 12 | | | | | | | 3 |
| 1 | 2 | | 4 | 5 | 6 | 7 | 8 | 9 | 10 | | | 3 | 11 | | | | | | | 4 |
| 1 | 2 | | 4 | 5 | 6 | 7 | 8 | 9 | 10 | | | 3 | 11 | | | | | | | 5 |
| 1 | 2 | | 4 | 5 | 6 | 7 | 8 | 9 | 10 | | | 3 | 11 | | | | | | | 6 |
| 1 | 2 | | 4 | 5 | 6 | 7 | 8* | 9 | 10 | | 12 | 3 | 11 | | | | | | | 7 |
| 1 | 2 | | 4 | 5 | 6 | 7 | 8* | 9 | 10 | | 12 | 3 | 11 | | | | | | | 8 |
| 1 | 2 | | 4 | | 6 | 7 | 8 | 9 | 10 | | | 3 | 11 | | | 5 | | | | 9 |
| 1 | 2 | | 4 | | 6 | 7 | 8 | | 10 | | | 3 | 11 | 9 | | 5 | | | | 10 |
| 1 | 2 | | 4 | | 6 | 7 | 8 | | 10 | | 12 | 3 | 11 | 9* | | 5 | | | | 11 |
| 1 | 2 | | 4 | 5 | 6 | 7 | 8* | | 10 | | 12 | 3 | 11 | 9 | | | | | | 12 |
| 1 | 2 | | 4 | 5 | 6 | 7 | 8 | | 10 | | 12 | 3 | 11 | 9* | | | | | | 13 |
| 1 | 2 | | 4 | | 6 | 7 | 8 | | 10 | | 12 | 3* | 11 | 9 | | 5 | | | | 14 |
| 1 | 2 | | 4 | | 6 | 7 | 8 | | 10 | | 12 | 3 | 11* | 9 | | 5 | | | | 15 |
| 1 | 2 | | 4 | | 6 | 7 | 8 | 9 | 10 | | 12 | 3 | 11* | | | 5 | | | | 16 |
| 1 | 2 | | 4 | | 6 | 7 | 8 | | 10 | | | 3 | | 9 | | 5 | 11 | | | 17 |
| 1 | 2 | | 4 | | 6 | 7 | 8 | | 10 | | 12 | 3 | | 9* | | 5 | 11 | | | 18 |
| 1 | 2 | | 4 | | 6 | 7 | 8 | | | | 12 | 3 | 10 | 9 | | 5 | 11* | | | 19 |
| 1 | 2 | | 4 | | 6 | 7 | 8 | | | | 12 | 3 | 10 | 9 | | 5 | 11* | | | 20 |
| 1 | 2 | | 4 | | 6 | 7 | 8 | | | | 12 | 3* | 11 | 9 | | 5 | 10 | | | 21 |
| 1 | 2 | 3 | 4 | | 6 | 7 | 8 | | | | 12 | | 11 | 9 | | 5 | 10* | | | 22 |
| 1 | 2 | | 4 | | 6 | 7 | 8 | | | | | 3 | 11 | 9 | | 5 | 10 | | | 23 |
| 1 | 2 | | 4 | | 6 | 7 | 8* | | | | 12 | 3 | 11 | 9 | | 5 | 10 | | | 24 |
| 1 | 2 | | 4 | | 6 | 7 | 8* | | | | 12 | 3 | 11 | 9 | | 5 | 10 | | | 25 |
| 1 | 2 | | 4 | | 6 | 7* | 8 | | | | 12 | 3 | 11 | 9 | | 5 | 10 | | | 26 |
| 1 | 2 | | 4 | | 6 | 7 | 8 | | | | 12 | 3 | 11* | 9 | | 5 | 10 | | | 27 |
| 1 | 2 | | 4 | | 6 | 7 | 8 | | | | | 3 | 11 | 9 | | 5 | 10 | | | 28 |
| 1 | 2 | | 4 | | 6 | 7* | 8 | | | | 12 | 3 | 11 | 9 | | 5 | 10 | | | 29 |
| 1 | 2 | | 4 | | 6 | 7 | 8 | | | | | 3 | 11 | 9 | | 5 | 10 | | | 30 |
| 1 | 2 | | 4 | | 6 | 7 | 8 | | | | 12 | 3* | 11 | 9 | | 5 | 10 | | | 31 |
| | 2 | | 4 | | 6 | 7* | 8 | | | | 12 | 3 | 11 | 9 | | 5 | 10 | 1 | | 32 |
| 1 | 2 | | 4 | | 6 | 7 | 8 | | | | 12 | 3 | 11 | 9 | | 5 | 10* | | | 33 |
| 1 | 2 | | 4 | | 6 | 7 | 8 | | | | 12 | 3 | 11 | 9* | | 5 | 10 | | | 34 |
| 1 | 2 | | 4 | 5 | 6 | 7* | 8 | 9 | | | 12 | 3 | 11 | | | | 10 | | | 35 |
| 1 | 2 | | 4 | | 6 | 7 | 8 | 9 | | | 12 | 3 | 11 | | | 5* | 10 | | | 36 |
| 1 | 2 | | 4 | 5 | 6 | 7 | 8 | | | | | 3 | 11 | 9 | | | 10 | | | 37 |
| 1 | 2 | | 4 | 5 | 6 | 7 | 8 | 9 | | | 12 | 3 | 11* | | | | 10 | | | 38 |
| 1 | 2 | | 4 | 5 | 6 | 7 | 8 | | | | | 3 | 11 | 9 | | | 10 | | | 39 |
| 1 | 2 | | 4 | 5 | 6 | 7 | 8 | | | | | 3 | 11 | 9 | | | 10 | | | 40 |
| 1 | 2 | | 4 | 5 | 6 | 7 | 8 | | | | 12 | 3 | 11 | 9* | | | 10 | | | 41 |
| 1 | 2 | | 4 | | 6 | 7 | 8 | 9 | | | 12 | 3 | 11 | | | 5 | 10* | | | 42 |
| 41 | 41 | 4 | 42 | 16 | 42 | 34 | 40 | 18 | 18 | 4 | 24 | 18 | 35 | 32 | — | 26 | 26 | 1 | — | |

Substitute appearances (+Ns): Sims +1s; Callaghan +3s; Rostron +15s; Pritchett +3s, Barnes +3s; Jenkins +1s, Gilligan +1s, Terry +1s; Steele +1s.

# WATFORD

| | Ht | Wt | Birthplace | Clubs | League App. | League Gls |
|---|---|---|---|---|---|---|
| **Goalkeepers** | | | | | | |
| Steve Sherwood | 6 4 | 14 7 | Selby | Chelsea | 16 | — |
| | | | | Brighton (on loan) | — | — |
| | | | | Millwall (on loan) | 1 | — |
| | | | | Brentford (on loan) | 62 | — |
| | | | | Watford | 107 | — |
| Eric Steele | 6 0 | 12 8½ | Newcastle | Newcastle U | — | — |
| | | | | Peterborough U | 124 | — |
| | | | | Brighton | 87 | — |
| | | | | Watford | 49 | — |
| **Defenders** | | | | | | |
| Keith Pritchett | 5 9¼ | 11 5 | Glasgow | Wolverhampton W | — | — |
| | | | | Doncaster R | 6 | — |
| | | | | QPR | 4 | — |
| | | | | Brentford | 11 | 1 |
| | | | | Watford | 140 | 9 |
| Steve Sims | 6 1½ | 13 9 | Lincoln | Leicester C | 79 | 3 |
| | | | | Watford | 102 | 4 |
| Ian Bolton | 6 1½ | 12 7 | Leicester | Notts Co | 70 | 4 |
| | | | | Lincoln C (on loan) | 1 | — |
| | | | | Watford | 189 | 28 |
| Steve Terry | 6 1½ | 13 3 | Enfield | Watford | 33 | 2 |
| Kenny Jackett | 5 10½ | 11 3 | Watford | Watford | 62 | 5 |
| Pat Rice | 5 9½ | 12 7 | Belfast | Arsenal | 397 | 11 |
| (N Ireland) | | | | Watford | 66 | — |
| Charlie Palmer | 5 11 | 11 9 | Aylesbury | Watford | — | — |
| Paul Franklin | 6 0 | 11 8 | Ilford | Watford | — | — |
| Neil Price | | | Hemel Hempstead | Watford | — | — |
| Colin Hull* | 5 11 | 11 4 | Hitchin | Watford | — | — |
| **Midfield** | | | | | | |
| Martin Patching | 6 0 | 12 9½ | Rotherham | Wolverhampton W | 90 | 10 |
| | | | | Watford | 21 | 2 |
| Les Taylor | 5 8 | 11 7 | North Shields | Oxford U | 219 | 15 |
| | | | | Watford | 66 | 5 |
| Nigel Callaghan | 5 9 | 10 9 | Singapore | Watford | 59 | 7 |
| **Forwards** | | | | | | |
| Wilf Rostron | 5 7 | 11 1½ | Sunderland | Arsenal | 17 | 2 |
| | | | | Sunderland | 76 | 17 |
| | | | | Watford | 85 | 6 |
| Ross Jenkins | 6 2 | 12 2 | Kensington | Crystal Palace | 15 | 2 |
| | | | | Watford | 319 | 113 |
| Luther Blissett | 5 10½ | 11 13½ | Jamaica | Watford | 205 | 68 |
| Malcolm Poskett | 6 0 | 11 7 | Middlesbrough | Middlesbrough | 1 | — |
| | | | | Whitby T | (not known) | |
| | | | | Hartlepool U | 51 | 20 |
| | | | | Brighton | 45 | 16 |
| | | | | Watford | 63 | 17 |
| Gerry Armstrong | 5 11¾ | 13 0 | Belfast | Tottenham H | 84 | 10 |
| (N Ireland) | | | | Watford | 57 | 10 |
| John Barnes | | | Jamaica | Watford | 36 | 13 |
| Ian Richardson | | | Ely | Watford | — | — |
| Jimmy Gilligan | 6 2 | 11 7 | London | Watford | 1 | — |
| Jan Lohman | | | Dussen | Holland | (not known) | |
| | | | | Watford | 26 | 2 |
| David Johnson | | | Gloucester | Watford | 1 | — |

# WEST BROMWICH ALBION     Division 1

*President:* J. W. Gaunt.
*Vice-President:* F. T. D. Hall.
*Chairman:* F. A. Millichip.
*Vice-Chairman:* J. Gordon.
*Directors:* C. I. Edwards, D. B. Boundy, J. S. Lucas, A. Everiss.
*Manager:* Ron Wylie.   *Secretary:* A. E. Rance.
*Assistant Secretary:* Ray Fairfax.
*Statistician:* Tony Matthews.
*Year Formed:* 1879.   *Turned Professional:* 1885.
*Limited Company:* 1892.
*Previous Grounds:* 1879, Coopers Hill; 1879, Dartmouth Park;
1881, Bunns Field, Walsall Street; 1882, Four Acres (Dart-
mouth Cricket Club); 1885, Stoney Lane; 1900, The Haw-
thorns.   *Previous Name:* 1879–81, West Bromwich Strollers.

**Football League Record:**
1888 Founder Member of Football League; 1901–02 Division 2;
1902–04 Division 1; 1904–11 Division 2; 1911–27 Division 1; 1927–31 Division 2; 1931–38 Division 1;
1938–49 Division 2; 1949–73 Division 1; 1973–76 Division 2; 1976– Division 1.
**Honours:** *Football League:* Division 1 – Champions 1919–20; Runners-up 1924–25, 1953–54. Division
2 – Champions 1901–02, 1910–11; Runners-up 1930–31, 1948–49; Promoted to Division 1 1975–76
(3rd). *FA Cup:* Winners 1888, 1892, 1931, 1954, 1968; Runners-up 1886, 1887, 1895, 1912, 1935.
*Football League Cup:* Winners 1965–66; Runners-up 1966–67, 1969–70. **European Competitions:**
*European Cup-Winners' Cup:* 1968–69; *European Fairs Cup:* 1966–67; *UEFA Cup:* 1978–79, 1979–80,
1981–82.
*Record Victory:* 12-0 v Darwen, Division 1, 4 April, 1892.
*Record Defeat:* 3-10 v Stoke C, Division 1, 4 Feb, 1937.
*Most League Points:* 60, Division 1, 1919–20.
*Most League Goals:* 105, Division 2, 1929–30.
*Highest League Scorer in Season:* William 'Ginger' Richardson, 39, Division 1, 1935–36.
*Most League Goals in Total Aggregate:* Tony Brown, 218, 1963–79.
*Most Capped Player:* Stuart Williams, 33 (43), Wales.
*Most League Appearances:* Tony Brown, 574, 1963–80.
*Record Transfer Fee Received:* £995,000 from Real Madrid for Laurie Cunningham, June 1979.
*Record Transfer Fee Paid:* £748,000 to Manchester C for Peter Barnes, July 1979.
*Previous Managers since the War:* Jack Smith, Vic Buckingham, Gordon Clark, Archie Macaulay,
Jimmy Hagan, Alan Ashman, Don Howe, John Giles, Ronnie Allen, Ron Atkinson, Ronnie Allen.
*Address of Supporters Club:* Throstle Club, Birmingham Road, West Bromwich, Staffs.
*Address of the Club Shop or Boutique:* Albion Club Shop, same address as club.

---

**The Hawthorns, West Bromwich B71 4LF.** Telephone 021-525 8888. Box Office 021-553 5472. *Ground
capacity:* 38,600 (seats 12,500). *Record attendance:* 64,815 v Arsenal, FA Cup 6th rd, 6 Mar, 1937.
*Record receipts:* £79,494.76 v Tottenham H, League Cup semi-final, 3 Feb, 1982. *Pitch measurements:*
115yd×75yd.
*How to get there:* Buses 72, 74, 75, and 79 from outside Birmingham New Street station run directly to the ground. A
special bus service from the centre of West Bromwich to the ground runs every three minutes on match days.
*Match tickets:* Advance bookings for Centre and Wing Stands accepted six weeks in advance by post including remittance
and sae. Telephone bookings are accepted but not before two days prior to the match; tickets reserved by telephone
must be collected at least 30 minutes before kick-off. A limited number of unreserved seats in the Paddock is available
at Door E1 on the day of the match.
*Car parking:* Street parking permitted in certain areas, all within 10 minutes' walk of the ground.
*Entertainments/catering facilities:* Post-match entertainment in the Supporters Club adjoining the ground; several restau-
rants within walking distance of the ground. Snack bars in the ground. Excellent facilities at The Hawthorns Throstle
Club alongside the ground include a full-course lunch.
*Club shop:* Situated in the Pools Office on Birmingham Rd, and open from 9–5 Mon–Sat. Stocks over 200 different
articles. Excellent mailing service. Price list available on request.
*Handbooks/programmes:* Handbook and programmes available on subscription.
*Extra information:* There are 3 Throstle Clubs in the surrounding areas, and the club runs a Junior Throstle Club for the
under-15s.
*Club Colours:* Navy blue and white striped shirts, white shorts and white stockings.
*Change Colours:* Yellow and green striped shirts, green shorts, yellow stockings.
*Club Nickname:* Baggies, Throstles and Albion.

## WEST BROMWICH ALBION 1981–82 LEAGUE RECORD

| Match No. | Date | Venue | Opponents | Result | | H/T Score | Goalscorers | Attendance* |
|---|---|---|---|---|---|---|---|---|
| 1 | Aug 29 | A | Manchester C | L | 1-2 | 0-2 | Mills (pen) | 36,187 |
| 2 | Sept 2 | H | Arsenal | L | 0-2 | 0-2 | | 17,104 |
| 3 | 5 | H | Swansea C | W | 4-1 | 1-0 | Regis 3, MacKenzie | 18,063 |
| 4 | 12 | A | Nottingham F | D | 0-0 | 0-0 | | 22,618 |
| 5 | 19 | H | West Ham U | D | 0-0 | 0-0 | | 19,516 |
| 6 | 22 | A | Ipswich T | L | 0-1 | 0-0 | | 20,524 |
| 7 | 26 | A | Everton | L | 0-1 | 0-0 | | 23,871 |
| 8 | Oct 3 | H | Middlesbrough | W | 2-0 | 0-0 | Summerfield, Regis | 12,840 |
| 9 | 10 | H | Brighton & HA | D | 0-0 | 0-0 | | 13,704 |
| 10 | 17 | A | Leeds U | L | 1-3 | 0-0 | Mills | 19,164 |
| 11 | 24 | H | Southampton | D | 1-1 | 1-1 | Brown | 15,730 |
| 12 | 31 | A | Birmingham C | D | 3-3 | 2-1 | Regis 3 | 21,301 |
| 13 | Nov 7 | A | Tottenham H | W | 2-1 | 2-1 | Hughton (og), Jol | 32,436 |
| 14 | 14 | H | Stoke C | L | 1-2 | 1-2 | Smith (og) | 15,787 |
| 15 | 21 | H | Liverpool | D | 1-1 | 0-0 | Regis | 20,871 |
| 16 | 28 | A | Sunderland | W | 2-1 | 0-1 | Brown, Regis | 15,867 |
| 17 | Dec 5 | H | Wolverhampton W | W | 3-0 | 0-0 | Regis 2, Whitehead | 22,378 |
| 18 | 26 | A | Coventry C | W | 2-0 | 1-0 | Owen, Regis | 15,033 |
| 19 | Jan 30 | A | West Ham U | L | 1-3 | 0-1 | King | 24,423 |
| 20 | Feb 6 | H | Nottingham F | W | 2-1 | 1-0 | Bennett, Summerfield | 15,006 |
| 21 | 20 | H | Everton | D | 0-0 | 0-0 | | 14,819 |
| 22 | 27 | A | Brighton & HA | D | 2-2 | 0-1 | Cross, Bennett | 14,553 |
| 23 | Mar 9 | A | Middlesbrough | L | 0-1 | 0-1 | | 9884 |
| 24 | 13 | A | Southampton | D | 0-0 | 0-0 | | 21,376 |
| 25 | 16 | A | Arsenal | D | 2-2 | 1-0 | King, Cross | 15,799 |
| 26 | 20 | H | Birmingham C | D | 1-1 | 0-0 | Robertson | 21,160 |
| 27 | 24 | H | Notts Co | L | 2-4 | 1-0 | Regis, King | 12,759 |
| 28 | 27 | H | Tottenham H | W | 1-0 | 0-0 | Regis | 20,275 |
| 29 | 30 | A | Aston Villa | L | 1-2 | 1-0 | King | 28,440 |
| 30 | Apr 6 | A | Swansea C | L | 1-3 | 1-0 | MacKenzie | 15,744 |
| 31 | 10 | H | Coventry C | L | 1-2 | 1-1 | MacKenzie | 12,718 |
| 32 | 12 | A | Manchester U | L | 0-1 | 0-0 | | 38,717 |
| 33 | 17 | A | Liverpool | L | 0-1 | 0-0 | | 34,286 |
| 34 | 21 | H | Manchester C | L | 0-1 | 0-1 | | 11,073 |
| 35 | 24 | H | Sunderland | L | 2-3 | 1-2 | Brown, Owen (pen) | 13,268 |
| 36 | May 1 | A | Wolverhampton W | W | 2-1 | 1-0 | Regis, Monaghan | 19,813 |
| 37 | 5 | H | Ipswich T | L | 1-2 | 0-1 | Owen | 12,564 |
| 38 | 8 | H | Aston Villa | L | 0-1 | 0-0 | | 19,615 |
| 39 | 12 | H | Manchester U | L | 0-3 | 0-2 | | 19,772 |
| 40 | 15 | A | Notts Co | W | 2-1 | 1-0 | MacKenzie, Regis | 8734 |
| 41 | 18 | H | Leeds U | W | 2-0 | 0-0 | Regis, MacKenzie | 23,118 |
| 42 | 20 | A | Stoke C | L | 0-3 | 0-2 | | 19,698 |

**Final League Position: 17**

### Goalscorers

*League* (46): Regis 17, MacKenzie 5, King 4, Brown 3, Owen 3 (1 pen), Bennett 2, Cross 2, Mills 2 (1 pen), Summerfield 2, Jol 1, Monaghan 1, Robertson 1, Whitehead 1, own goals 2.
*League Cup* (13): Regis 6, Brown 1, Cross 1, King 1, MacKenzie 1, Monaghan 1, Owen 1, Statham 1.
*FA Cup* (7): Regis 2, King 1 (pen), MacKenzie 1, Owen 1, Statham 1, Whitehead 1.

| League Cup | Second Round | Shrewsbury T (a) | 3-3 |
|---|---|---|---|
| | | (h) | 2-1 |
| | Third Round | West Ham U (a) | 2-2 |
| | | (h) | 1-1 |
| | | (a) | 1-0 |
| | Fourth Round | Crystal Palace (a) | 3-1 |
| | Fifth Round | Aston Villa (a) | 1-0 |
| | Semi-final | Tottenham H (h) | 0-0 |
| | | (a) | 0-1 |
| FA Cup | Third Round | Blackburn R (h) | 3-2 |
| | Fourth Round | Gillingham (a) | 1-0 |
| | Fifth Round | Norwich C (h) | 1-0 |
| | Sixth Round | Coventry C (h) | 2-0 |
| | Semi-final | QPR | 0-1 (at Highbury) |

| Godden | Batson | Statham | Moses | Wile | Bennett | Robson | Mills | Deehan | Lowery | MacKenzie | Cross | Robertson | Owen | Regis | Brown | King | Summerfield | Jol | Grew | Whitehead | Monaghan | Lewis | Arthur | Childs | Zondervan | Webb | Cowdrill | Match No. |
|---|---|---|---|---|---|---|---|---|---|---|---|---|---|---|---|---|---|---|---|---|---|---|---|---|---|---|---|---|
| 1 | 2 | 3 | 4 | 5 | 6 | 7 | 8 | 9 | 10* | 11 | 12 | | | | | | | | | | | | | | | | | 1 |
| 1 | 2 | 3 | 4* | 5 | | 7 | 8 | 9 | | 11 | 12 | | 6 | 10 | | | | | | | | | | | | | | 2 |
| 1 | 2 | 3 | 4 | 5 | | 7 | 8 | | | 11 | | | 6 | 10 | 9 | | | | | | | | | | | | | 3 |
| 1 | 2 | 3 | 4 | 5 | | 7 | 8 | | | 11 | | | 6 | 10 | 9 | | | | | | | | | | | | | 4 |
| 1 | 2 | 3 | | 5 | | 7 | 8 | | | 11 | 12 | | 6 | 10 | 9 | 4* | | | | | | | | | | | | 5 |
| 1 | 2 | 3 | | 5 | | 7 | 8 | | | 11 | | 10 | 6* | | 9 | 4 | | | | | | | | | 12 | | | 6 |
| 1 | 2 | 3 | | 5 | | 7 | 8 | | | 11 | | | 6 | 10 | 9 | 4 | | | | | | | | | | | | 7 |
| 1 | 2 | 3 | | 5 | | | | | | 11 | | 7 | 6 | 10 | 9 | 4 | 8 | | | | | | | | | | | 8 |
| 1 | 2 | 3 | | 5 | | | 12 | | | 11 | | 7* | 6 | 10 | 9 | 4 | 8 | | | | | | | | | | | 9 |
| 1 | 2 | 3 | | 5 | | 7 | | | | 11 | | | 6 | 10 | 9 | 4 | 8 | | | | | | | | | | | 10 |
| 1 | 2 | 3 | | 5 | | | 12 | | | 11 | | | 6 | 10 | 9 | 8 | 4* | 7 | | | | | | | | | | 11 |
| 1 | 2 | 3 | | 5 | | | 4 | | | 11 | | | 6 | 10 | 9 | 8 | | 7 | | | | | | | | | | 12 |
| | 2* | 3 | | 5 | | | | | | 11 | | | 6 | 10 | 9 | 8 | 12 | 7 | 1 | 4 | | | | | | | | 13 |
| | 2* | 3 | | 5 | | | | | | 11 | | | 6 | 10 | 9 | 8 | 12 | 7 | 1 | 4 | | | | | | | | 14 |
| | 2 | 3 | | 5 | | | | | | 11 | | | 6 | 10 | 9 | 8* | 12 | 7 | 1 | 4 | | | | | | | | 15 |
| | 2 | 3 | | 5 | | | | | | 11 | | | 6 | 10 | 9 | 8 | | 7 | 1 | 4 | | | | | | | | 16 |
| | 2 | 3 | | 5 | | | | | | 11 | | | 6 | 10 | 9 | 8 | 12 | 7* | 1 | 4 | | | | | | | | 17 |
| | 2 | 3 | | 5 | | | | | | 11 | | | 6 | 10* | 9 | 4 | | | 1 | 7 | 8 | 12 | | | | | | 18 |
| | 2 | 3 | | 5 | | | | | | 11 | 12 | | 6 | 10 | 9 | 4 | | 7 | 1 | 8* | | | | | | | | 19 |
| | 2 | | | 5 | 6 | | | | | 11 | | | | 10 | 9 | 8 | | | 1 | 7 | 4 | 3 | | | | | | 20 |
| | 2 | 3 | | 5 | | | | | | 11 | 12 | | 6 | 10 | 9 | 8* | | | 1 | 4 | 7 | | | | | | | 21 |
| | | 3 | | 5 | 6 | | | | | 11 | 12 | | | 10 | 9 | 8 | | | 1 | 4* | 7 | 2 | | | | | | 22 |
| | 2 | 3 | 4 | 5 | | | | | | 11 | | | 6 | 10* | 9 | 7 | 8 | | 1 | | | | | | 12 | | | 23 |
| | 2 | | 4 | 5 | | | | | | 11 | | | 6 | 10 | 9 | 7 | 8 | | 1 | | | | | | 3 | | | 24 |
| | 2* | 3 | 4 | 5 | | | | | | | 12 | | 6 | 10 | | 7 | 8 | | 1 | 9 | | | | | 11 | | | 25 |
| | 2 | 3 | 4 | 5 | | | | | | | | 7 | 6 | 10 | 9 | 8 | | | 1 | | | | | | 11 | | | 26 |
| | 2 | 3* | 4 | 5 | | | | | | | | 7 | 6 | 10 | 9 | 12 | 8 | | 1 | | | | | | 11 | | | 27 |
| | 2 | | 4 | 5 | | | | | | | | 7 | 6 | 10 | 9 | 8 | | | 1 | | | | | | 11 | 3 | | 28 |
| | 2 | | 4* | 5 | | | | | | 11 | | 7 | 6 | 10 | 9 | 8 | | | 1 | | | | | | | 3 | | 29 |
| | | 3 | 4* | 5 | | | | | | 11 | | 8 | 6 | 10 | 9 | 12 | | | 1 | | | | 2 | 7 | | | | 30 |
| | 2 | 3 | 4 | 5 | | | | | | 11 | | 8* | 6 | 10 | 9 | 12 | | | 1 | | | | | 7 | | | | 31 |
| | 2 | 3 | | 5 | | | | | | 11 | 12 | | 6 | 10 | 9 | 8 | 4 | | 1 | | | | | 7* | | | | 32 |
| | 2 | 3 | | 5 | | 7 | | | | 11 | 12 | | 6* | 9 | 8 | 10 | | | 1 | | | | | | | | 4 | 33 |
| | 2 | 3 | | 5 | | | | | | 11 | | | 6 | 10* | 9 | 8 | 4 | | 1 | | | | | 7 | 12 | | | 34 |
| | 2 | 3 | | 5 | 6 | | | | | 11* | | | | 10 | 9 | 4 | 8 | | 1 | | | | | 12 | 7 | | | 35 |
| 1 | 2 | | 4 | 5 | | | | | | 11 | | | 6 | 10 | 9 | 8 | | | | | | | | | 12 | 7* | 3 | 36 |
| 1 | 2 | | 4 | 5 | | | | | | 11* | | | 6 | 10 | 9 | 8 | | | | | | | | | 12 | 7 | 3 | 37 |
| 1 | 2 | 3 | 4 | 5 | | | | | | | | | 6 | 10 | 9 | 8 | | | | | | | | | 11 | 7 | | 38 |
| 1 | 2 | 3 | 4 | 5 | | | | | | | | 7 | 12 | 10 | 9 | 8* | | | | | | | | | 11 | | 6 | 39 |
| 1 | 2 | 3 | 4 | 5 | | | | | | | | 7 | 12 | 10 | 9 | | | | | | | | | | 11* | 6 | 8 | 40 |
| 1 | 2 | 3 | 4 | 5 | | | | | | 11 | | | | 10 | 9 | 8 | | | | | | | | | | 6 | 7 | 41 |
| 1 | 2 | 3 | 4 | 5 | | | | | | | | 7 | 9 | 10 | 11 | 8 | | | | | | | | | | 6* | 12 | 42 |
| 19 | 39 | 35 | 4 | 42 | 23 | 5 | 9 | 4 | 1 | 37 | 11 | 33 | 39 | 37 | 22 | 21 | 4 | 9 | 23 | 8 | 5 | 3 | 2 | 2 | 13 | 6 | 6 | |
| | | | +2s | | | | | | | | +11s | | | +3s | +4s | | | | +3s | +1s | +1s | | | +1s | | | +2s | |

## WEST BROMWICH ALBION

| | Ht | Wt | Birthplace | Clubs | League App. | League Gls |
|---|---|---|---|---|---|---|
| **Goalkeepers** | | | | | | |
| Tony Godden | 6 0½ | 13 0 | Gillingham | Gillingham | — | — |
| | | | | Ashford T | (not known) | |
| | | | | Preston NE (on loan) | — | — |
| | | | | WBA | 193 | — |
| Mark Grew | 5 10 | 11 2 | Bilston | WBA | 23 | — |
| | | | | Notts Co (on loan) | — | — |
| | | | | Wigan Ath (on loan) | 4 | — |
| David Carlisle | 5 10 | 11 6 | Birmingham | WBA | — | — |
| **Defenders** | | | | | | |
| Alistair Robertson | 5 9½ | 12 2 | Philipstoun | WBA | 406 | 6 |
| David Arthur* | 5 8 | 11 1 | Bushbury | WBA | 3 | — |
| John Wile | 6 1½ | 12 0 | Sherburn | Sunderland | — | — |
| | | | | Peterborough U | 118 | 7 |
| | | | | WBA | 469 | 24 |
| Derek Statham | 5 5½ | 11 1 | Wolverhampton | WBA | 177 | 2 |
| Brendon Batson | 5 10 | 11 7 | Grenada | Arsenal | 10 | — |
| | | | | Cambridge U | 163 | 6 |
| | | | | WBA | 160 | 1 |
| Martyn Bennett | 6 0 | 12 12 | Birmingham | WBA | 44 | 3 |
| Alan Webb | 5 9 | 12 0 | Wrockwardine | WBA | 6 | — |
| Barry Cowdrill | 5 11 | 11 4 | Birmingham | Sutton Coldfield T | (not known) | |
| | | | | WBA | 27 | — |
| John Snape | 5 10 | 11 4 | West Bromwich | WBA | — | — |
| John Smith | 5 11 | 11 7 | Northfield | WBA | — | — |
| Noel Luke | 5 9½ | 11 10 | Birmingham | WBA | — | — |
| Wayne Ebanks | 5 10 | 12 0 | Birmingham | WBA | — | — |
| **Midfield** | | | | | | |
| Romeo Zondervan | 5 9 | 11 2 | Surinam | Den Haag | (not known) | |
| | | | | Twente | (not known) | |
| | | | | WBA | 14 | — |
| David Mills | 5 8 | 11 0 | Whitby | Middlesbrough | 295 | 76 |
| | | | | Newcastle U (on loan) | 23 | 4 |
| | | | | WBA | 56 | 5 |
| Gary Owen | 5 9 | 11 2 | St Helens | Manchester C | 103 | 19 |
| | | | | WBA | 110 | 14 |
| Tony Lowery | 5 8 | 11 9 | Wallsend | Ashington | (not known) | |
| | | | | Walsall (on loan) | 6 | 1 |
| | | | | WBA | 1 | — |
| Gary Childs | 5 6 | 11 0 | Birmingham | WBA | 2 | — |
| Steve MacKenzie | 5 10 | 11 3 | Romford | Crystal Palace | — | — |
| | | | | Manchester C | 58 | 8 |
| | | | | WBA | 37 | 5 |
| Micky Lewis | 5 6½ | 11 2 | Birmingham | WBA | 4 | — |
| Andy King | 5 9½ | 10 13 | Luton | Luton T | 33 | 9 |
| | | | | Everton | 151 | 38 |
| | | | | QPR | 30 | 9 |
| | | | | WBA | 25 | 4 |
| Martin Jol | 6 0½ | 11 7 | The Hague | Den Haag | (not known) | |
| | | | | Bayern Munich | (not known) | |
| | | | | Twente | (not known) | |
| | | | | WBA | 9 | 1 |
| Clive Whitehead | 5 9 | 10 7 | Birmingham | Bristol C | 229 | 10 |
| | | | | WBA | 8 | 1 |
| **Forwards** | | | | | | |
| Alistair Brown | 6 0 | 11 0 | Musselburgh | Leicester C | 101 | 31 |
| | | | | WBA | 262 | 67 |
| Kevin Summerfield* | 5 11 | 11 0 | Walsall | WBA | 9 | 4 |
| Derek Monaghan | 5 9 | 11 2 | Bromsgrove | WBA | 16 | 1 |
| Cyrille Regis | 6 0 | 13 0 | French Guyana | Hayes | (not known) | |
| (England) | | | | WBA | 174 | 62 |
| Nicky Cross | 5 9 | 11 0 | Birmingham | WBA | 24 | 3 |
| Colin Jones | 5 10 | 11 7 | Birmingham | WBA | — | — |
| Peter Frain | 5 8 | 10 13 | Birmingham | WBA | — | — |
| Mick Perry | 5 10 | 11 4 | Wimbledon | WBA | — | — |

# WEST HAM UNITED Division 1

*President:* R. H. Pratt.

*Chairman:* L. C. Cearns.

*Directors:* W. F. Cearns, B. R. Cearns FCIS, J. Petchey, M. W. Cearns AIB.

*Manager:* John Lyall.

*Chief Executive and Secretary:* Eddie Chapman FAAI.

*PRO:* Jack Helliar. *Year Formed:* 1900.

*Turned Professional:* 1900. *Limited Company:* 1900.

*Previous Grounds:* Memorial Recreation Ground, Canning Town; 1904 Boleyn Ground.

**Football League Record:**
1919 Elected to Division 2; 1923–32 Division 1; 1932–58 Division 2; 1958–78 Division 1; 1978–81 Division 2; 1981– Division 1.

**Honours:** *Football League:* Division 1 best season: 6th, 1926–27, 1958–59, 1972–73. Division 2 – Champions 1957–58, 1980–81; Runners-up 1922–23. *FA Cup:* Winners 1964, 1975, 1980; Runners-up 1922–23. *Football League Cup:* Runners-up 1966, 1981. **European Competition:** *European Cup-Winners' Cup:* 1964–65 (winners), 1965–66, 1975–76 (runners-up), 1980–81.

*Record Victory:* 8-0 v Rotherham U, Division 2, 8 Mar, 1958 and v Sunderland, Division 1, 19 Oct, 1968.

*Record Defeat:* 2-8 v Blackburn R, Division 1, 26 Dec, 1963.

*Most League Points:* 66, Division 2, 1980–81.

*Most League Goals:* 101, Division 2, 1957–58.

*Highest League Scorer in Season:* Vic Watson, 41, Division 1, 1929–30.

*Most League Goals in Total Aggregate:* Vic Watson, 306, 1920–35.

*Most Capped Player:* Bobby Moore, 108, England.

*Most League Appearances:* Bobby Moore, 544, 1958–74.

*Record Transfer Fee Received:* £225,000 from Birmingham C for Alan Curbishley, June 1979.

*Record Transfer Fee Paid:* £800,000 (nett) to QPR for Paul Goddard, Aug 1980.

*Previous Managers since the War:* Charlie Paynter, Ted Fenton, Ron Greenwood.

*Address of Supporters Club:* Castle Street, Upton Park, E13.

*Address of the Club Shop or Boutique:* Hammers Shop, Boleyn Ground, Green Street, Upton Park, London E13.

---

**Boleyn Ground, Green Street, Upton Park, London E13.** Telephone 01-472 2740. Answerphone 01-470 1325. *Ground capacity:* 35,500. *Record attendance:* 42,322 v Tottenham H, Division 1, 17 Oct, 1970. *Record receipts:* £71,455 v Aston Villa, FA Cup 6th rd, 8 Mar, 1980. *Pitch measurements:* 110yd×72yd. *How to get there:* Nearest station Upton Park (Underground, District Line) – five minutes' walk. Buses from Barking Road, Romford Road and Green Street.

*Match tickets:* Advance booking, by personal application or by post 21 days prior to League matches.

*Car parking:* Ample side-street parking available.

*Entertainments/catering facilities:* Refreshment points around the ground.

*Club shop:* Situated on the ground; sells all types of souvenirs.

*Handbooks/programmes:* Programmes and handbook available by post from either Sales Service c/o West Ham United FC or from Helliar & Sons, 237 Barking Road, London E13 8EQ.

*Extra information:* Vic Watson's 306 League goals for West Ham is the fourth highest total scored with one club in the history of the competition.

*Club Colours:* Claret shirts with blue sleeves and three claret stripes down sleeves, white shorts with three claret stripes, white stockings.

*Change Colours:* White shirts with three claret stripes down sleeves, blue shorts with three claret stripes, blue stockings.

*Club Captain:* Billy Bonds.

*Physiotherapist:* Rob Jenkins.

*Club Nickname:* Hammers.

## WEST HAM UNITED 1981−82 LEAGUE RECORD

| Match No. | Date | Venue | Opponents | Result | H/T Score | Goalscorers | Atten-dance |
|---|---|---|---|---|---|---|---|
| 1 | Aug 29 | H | Brighton & HA | D | 1-1 | 0-0 | Stewart (pen) | 30,468 |
| 2 | Sept 2 | A | Tottenham H | W | 4-0 | 1-0 | Cross 4 | 41,200 |
| 3 | 5 | A | Sunderland | W | 2-0 | 1-0 | Goddard, Cross | 28,347 |
| 4 | 12 | H | Stoke C | W | 3-2 | 1-1 | Goddard 2, Stewart (pen) | 28,774 |
| 5 | 19 | A | WBA | D | 0-0 | 0-0 | | 19,516 |
| 6 | 22 | H | Southampton | W | 4-2 | 2-1 | Goddard 3, Pike | 34,026 |
| 7 | 26 | H | Liverpool | D | 1-1 | 1-0 | Pike | 30,802 |
| 8 | Oct 3 | A | Birmingham C | D | 2-2 | 1-1 | Cross 2 | 22,290 |
| 9 | 10 | H | Everton | D | 1-1 | 1-1 | Martin | 31,608 |
| 10 | 17 | A | Aston Villa | L | 2-3 | 1-3 | Brooking, Cross | 32,064 |
| 11 | 24 | A | Notts Co | D | 1-1 | 0-0 | Brooking | 12,505 |
| 12 | 31 | H | Middlesbrough | W | 3-2 | 2-0 | Neighbour, Goddard, Stewart (pen) | 27,604 |
| 13 | Nov 7 | A | Nottingham F | D | 0-0 | 0-0 | | 26,327 |
| 14 | 21 | H | Coventry C | W | 5-2 | 2-1 | Brooking, Neighbour, Martin 2, Stewart (pen) | 26,065 |
| 15 | 28 | A | Leeds U | D | 3-3 | 0-1 | Brooking 2, Cross | 25,637 |
| 16 | Dec 5 | A | Arsenal | L | 1-2 | 0-2 | Pearson | 33,833 |
| 17 | Jan 5 | A | Liverpool | L | 0-3 | 0-2 | | 28,427 |
| 18 | 16 | A | Brighton & HA | L | 0-1 | 0-0 | | 22,620 |
| 19 | 27 | A | Manchester U | L | 0-1 | 0-0 | | 41,291 |
| 20 | 30 | H | WBA | W | 3-1 | 1-0 | Goddard, Cross 2 | 24,423 |
| 21 | Feb 2 | H | Manchester C | D | 1-1 | 0-0 | Bonds | 26,552 |
| 22 | 6 | A | Stoke C | L | 1-2 | 0-1 | Van der Elst | 11,987 |
| 23 | 13 | H | Birmingham C | D | 2-2 | 0-1 | Orr, Stewart (pen) | 22,512 |
| 24 | 20 | A | Southampton | L | 1-2 | 1-2 | Stewart (pen) | 24.026 |
| 25 | 27 | A | Everton | D | 0-0 | 0-0 | | 28,618 |
| 26 | Mar 2 | H | Ipswich T | W | 2-0 | 1-0 | Devonshire, Van der Elst | 24,846 |
| 27 | 6 | H | Aston Villa | D | 2-2 | 1-1 | Stewart (pen), Van der Elst | 26,894 |
| 28 | 13 | H | Notts Co | W | 1-0 | 0-0 | Stewart (pen) | 22,145 |
| 29 | 20 | A | Middlesbrough | W | 3-2 | 2-0 | Van der Elst, Goddard 2 | 12,134 |
| 30 | 27 | H | Nottingham F | L | 0-1 | 0-1 | | 24,633 |
| 31 | 30 | A | Swansea C | W | 1-0 | 1-0 | Van der Elst | 20,272 |
| 32 | Apr 3 | A | Manchester C | W | 1-0 | 0-0 | Goddard | 30,875 |
| 33 | 6 | H | Wolverhampton W | W | 3-1 | 0-1 | Martin, Goddard 2 | 20,651 |
| 34 | 10 | H | Swansea C | D | 1-1 | 0-1 | Goddard | 26,566 |
| 35 | 13 | A | Ipswich T | L | 2-3 | 1-2 | Cross 2 | 28,767 |
| 36 | 17 | A | Coventry C | L | 0-1 | 0-1 | | 13,398 |
| 37 | 24 | H | Leeds U | W | 4-3 | 0-2 | Cross, Brooking 2, Stewart (pen) | 24,748 |
| 38 | May 1 | A | Arsenal | L | 0-2 | 0-2 | | 34,977 |
| 39 | 4 | H | Sunderland | D | 1-1 | 0-1 | Stewart (pen) | 17,130 |
| 40 | 8 | H | Manchester U | D | 1-1 | 0-0 | Cross | 26,337 |
| 41 | 10 | H | Tottenham H | D | 2-2 | 0-1 | Brooking, Goddard | 27,667 |
| 42 | 15 | A | Wolverhampton W | L | 1-2 | 1-2 | Cross | 13,283 |

**Final League Position: 9**

### Goalscorers

*League* (66): Cross 16, Goddard 15, Stewart 10 (10 pens), Brooking 8, Van der Elst 5, Martin 4, Neighbour 2, Pike 2, Bonds 1, Devonshire 1, Orr 1, Pearson 1.
*League Cup* (8): Stewart 3 (3 pens), Cross 2, Goddard 2, Brooking 1.
*FA Cup* (2): Bonds 1, Cross 1.

| League Cup | Second Round | Derby Co (a) | 3-2 |
|---|---|---|---|
| | | (h) | 2-0 |
| | Third Round | WBA (h) | 2-2 |
| | | (a) | 1-1 |
| | | (h) | 0-1 |
| FA Cup | Third Round | Everton (h) | 2-1 |
| | Fourth Round | Watford (a) | 0-2 |

| Parkes | Stewart | Lampard | Bonds | Martin | Devonshire | Neighbour | Goddard | Cross | Allen | Pike | Pearson | McAlister | Brooking | Brush | Barnes | Banton | Van der Elst | Orr | Cowie | Laronde | Houghton | Match No. |
|---|---|---|---|---|---|---|---|---|---|---|---|---|---|---|---|---|---|---|---|---|---|---|
| 1 | 2 | 3 | 4 | 5 | 6 | 7 | 8 | 9 | 10 | 11 | | | | | | | | | | | | 1 |
| 1 | 2 | 3 | 4 | 5 | 6 | 7 | 8 | 9 | 10 | 11 | | | | | | | | | | | | 2 |
| 1 | 2 | 3 | 4 | 5 | 6 | 7 | 8* | 9 | 10 | 11 | 12 | | | | | | | | | | | 3 |
| 1 | 2 | 3 | 4 | 5 | 6 | 7 | 8 | 9 | 10 | 11 | | | | | | | | | | | | 4 |
| 1 | 2 | 3 | 4 | 5 | 6 | 7 | 8 | 9 | 10 | 11 | | | | | | | | | | | | 5 |
| 1 | 2 | 3 | 4 | 5 | 6 | 7 | 8 | 9 | 10 | 11 | | | | | | | | | | | | 6 |
| 1 | 2 | 3 | 4 | 5 | 6 | 7 | 8 | 9 | 10 | 11 | | | | | | | | | | | | 7 |
| | 2 | 3 | 4 | 5 | 6 | 7 | 8 | 9 | | 11 | | 1 | 10 | | | | | | | | | 8 |
| | 2 | 3 | 4 | 5 | 6 | 7 | 8 | 9 | | 11 | | 1 | 10 | | | | | | | | | 9 |
| | 2 | 3 | 4 | 5 | 6 | 7* | 8 | 9 | | 11 | | 1 | 10 | 12 | | | | | | | | 10 |
| 1 | 2 | 3 | 4 | 5 | 6 | | 8 | 9 | | 11 | | | 10 | 7 | | | | | | | | 11 |
| 1 | 2 | 3 | 4 | 5 | 6 | 7 | 8 | 9 | | 11 | | | 10 | | | | | | | | | 12 |
| 1 | 2 | 3 | | 5 | 6 | 7 | 8 | 9 | 4* | 11 | | | 10 | 12 | | | | | | | | 13 |
| 1 | 2 | 3 | 4 | 5 | 6 | 7 | 8 | 9 | | 11 | | | 10 | | | | | | | | | 14 |
| 1 | 2 | 3 | 4 | 5 | 6 | 7* | 8 | 9 | 12 | 11 | | | 10 | | | | | | | | | 15 |
| 1 | 2 | 3 | 4 | 5 | 6 | | | 9 | | 11 | | 8 | 10 | | 7* | 12 | | | | | | 16 |
| 1 | 2 | 3 | 4 | 5 | 6* | 7 | | 9 | | 11 | | 8 | 10 | 12 | | | | | | | | 17 |
| 1 | 2 | 3 | 4 | 5 | 6* | 7 | 8 | 9 | | 11 | | | 10 | | | | 12 | | | | | 18 |
| 1 | 8 | 3* | 4 | 5 | | 12 | | 9 | | 11 | | | 10 | 2 | | | 7 | 6 | | | | 19 |
| 1 | 2 | | 4 | 5 | | | 8 | 9 | | 11 | | | 10 | 3 | | | 6 | 7 | | | | 20 |
| 1 | 2 | | 4 | 5 | | | 8 | 9 | | 11 | 12 | | 10 | 3* | | | 7 | 6 | | | | 21 |
| 1 | 2 | | 4 | 5 | | | 8 | 9 | | 11 | | | 10 | 3 | | | 7 | 6 | | | | 22 |
| 1 | 5 | 2 | 4 | | | 12 | 8 | 9 | | 11 | | | 10 | 3* | | | 7 | 6 | | | | 23 |
| 1 | 2 | | 4 | | | 7 | 8 | 9 | | 11 | | | 10 | 3 | | | 6 | 5 | | | | 24 |
| 1 | 2 | 12 | 4 | | | 7* | 8 | 6 | | 11 | | | 10 | 3 | | | 9 | 5 | | | | 25 |
| 1 | 2 | | 4 | | 6 | | 8 | 7 | | 11 | | | 10 | 3 | | | 9 | 5 | | | | 26 |
| 1 | 2 | | 4 | | 6 | | 8 | 7 | | 11 | | | 10 | 3 | | | 9 | 5 | | | | 27 |
| 1 | 2 | 3 | 4 | | 6 | | 8 | 9 | 7 | 11 | | | 10 | | | | | 5 | | | | 28 |
| 1 | 2 | 3 | 4 | | 6 | 12 | 8 | 7 | | 11* | | | 10 | | | | 9 | 5 | | | | 29 |
| 1 | 2 | 3 | 4 | | 6 | 12 | 8 | 9 | | 11* | | | 10 | | | | 7 | 5 | | | | 30 |
| 1 | 2 | 3 | | 5 | 6 | | 8 | 9 | | 11 | | | 10 | | | | 7 | 4 | | | | 31 |
| 1 | 2 | 3 | | 5 | 6 | | 8 | 9 | | 11 | | | 10 | | | | 7 | 4 | | | | 32 |
| 1 | 2 | 3 | | 5 | 6 | | 8 | 9 | | 11 | | | 10 | | | | 7 | 4 | | | | 33 |
| 1 | 2 | 3* | | 5 | 6 | 12 | 8 | 9 | | 11 | | | 10 | | | | 7 | 4 | | | | 34 |
| 1 | 2 | | 5 | | 6 | 11* | 8 | 9 | 3 | | | | 10 | | | | 7 | 4 | 12 | | | 35 |
| 1 | 2 | | 5* | | 6 | | 8 | 9 | 11 | | | | 10 | | | | 7 | 4 | 12 | 3 | | 36 |
| 1 | 2 | | | | 6 | | 8 | 9 | 4 | 11 | | | 10 | | | | 7 | 5 | | 3 | | 37 |
| 1 | 2 | | | | 6 | | | 9 | 4 | 11 | | | 10 | | | | 7 | 5 | 8* | 3 | 12 | 38 |
| 1 | 2 | | | | 6 | | 8 | 9 | 4 | 11 | | | 10 | | | | 7 | 5 | | 3 | | 39 |
| 1 | 2 | | | | 6 | | 8 | 9 | 4 | 11 | | | 10 | | | | 5 | 7 | | 3 | | 40 |
| 1 | 2 | | | | 6 | | 8 | 9 | 4 | 11 | | | 10 | 12 | | | 5 | 7* | | 3 | | 41 |
| 1 | 2 | | | | 6 | | 8 | 9* | 4 | 11 | | | 10 | 12 | | | 5 | 7 | | 3 | | 42 |
| 39 | 42 | 27 | 29 | 28 | 35 | 19 | 38 | 38 | 27 | 34 | 2 | 3 | 34 | 10 | 1 | — | 21 | 24 | 5 | 6 | — | |

Substitute appearances:

| | + | | | | + + | | | + | | + | | | + + + | | | | + + + | | | |
| | 1s | | | | 4s 1s | | | 1s | | 2s | | | 3s 2s 1s 1s | | | | 1s 1s 1s | | | |

## WEST HAM UNITED

| | Ht | Wt | Birthplace | Clubs | League App. | League Gls |
|---|---|---|---|---|---|---|
| **Goalkeepers** | | | | | | |
| Phil Parkes | 6 3 | 14 9 | Sedgeley | Walsall | 52 | — |
| (England) | | | | QPR | 344 | — |
| | | | | West Ham U | 139 | — |
| Tom McAlister | 6 0 | 11 1 | Clydebank | Sheffield U | 63 | — |
| | | | | Rotherham U | 159 | — |
| | | | | Blackpool | 16 | — |
| | | | | Bristol R (on loan) | 13 | — |
| | | | | Swindon T | 1 | — |
| | | | | West Ham U | 3 | — |
| | | | | | | |
| **Defenders** | | | | | | |
| Frank Lampard | 5 11 | 12 9 | West Ham | West Ham U | 496 | 16 |
| (England) | | | | | | |
| Paul Brush | 5 11 | 11 12 | London | West Ham U | 117 | — |
| Alvin Martin | 6 1 | 13 0 | Bootle | West Ham U | 138 | 9 |
| (England) | | | | | | |
| Ray Stewart | 5 11 | 12 0 | Stanley | Dundee U | 44 | 5 |
| (Scotland) | | | | West Ham U | 121 | 25 |
| Mark Smith* | 5 7 | 11 0 | West Ham | West Ham U | 1 | — |
| Billy Bonds | 6 0½ | 13 2 | Woolwich | Charlton Ath | 95 | 1 |
| | | | | West Ham U | 541 | 42 |
| Adrian Keith* | 6 0 | 11 0 | Colchester | West Ham U | — | — |
| Everald Laronde | 5 9 | 10 12 | East Ham | West Ham U | 7 | — |
| Neil Orr | 5 10 | 10 7 | Greenock | Morton | 186 | 1 |
| | | | | West Ham U | 24 | 1 |
| | | | | | | |
| **Midfield** | | | | | | |
| Mike McGiven | 6 0 | 11 13 | Newcastle | Sunderland | 113 | 9 |
| | | | | West Ham U | 48 | — |
| Trevor Brooking | 6 0½ | 13 0 | Barking | West Ham U | 492 | 81 |
| (England) | | | | | | |
| Geoff Pike | 5 6 | 11 3 | Clapton | West Ham U | 172 | 22 |
| George Cowie | 5 9 | 11 0 | Findochty | Buckie R | (not known) | |
| | | | | West Ham U | 6 | — |
| Dale Banton* | 5 10 | 10 5 | Kensington | West Ham U | 5 | — |
| Paul Allen | 5 7 | 9 12 | Averley | West Ham U | 62 | 3 |
| Ray Houghton* | 5 7 | 10 10 | Scotland | West Ham U | 1 | — |
| Bobby Barnes | 5 7 | 10 8 | Kingston | West Ham U | 9 | 1 |
| Glen Burvill | 5 9 | 10 5 | Canning Town | West Ham U | — | — |
| Chris Ampofo | | | Paddington | West Ham U | — | — |
| Bobby Wall* | | | West Ham | West Ham U | — | — |
| François Van der Elst | | | Opwyk | Anderlecht | (not known) | |
| (Belgium) | | | | New York C | (not known) | |
| | | | | West Ham U | 22 | 5 |
| | | | | | | |
| **Forwards** | | | | | | |
| Nicky Morgan | 5 10 | 12 8 | East Ham | West Ham U | 14 | 2 |
| Alan Devonshire | 5 10½ | 11 0 | London | West Ham U | 211 | 20 |
| (England) | | | | | | |
| Pat Holland | 5 10 | 11 7 | Poplar | West Ham U | 245 | 23 |
| | | | | Bournemouth (on loan) | 10 | — |
| Jimmy Neighbour | 5 7½ | 10 8 | Chingford | Tottenham H | 119 | 8 |
| | | | | Norwich C | 106 | 5 |
| | | | | West Ham U | 70 | 5 |
| Stuart Pearson* | 5 8½ | 11 12 | Hull | Hull C | 129 | 44 |
| (England) | | | | Manchester U | 139 | 55 |
| | | | | West Ham U | 34 | 6 |
| David Cross | 6 1 | 12 2 | Bury | Rochdale | 59 | 21 |
| | | | | Norwich C | 84 | 21 |
| | | | | Coventry C | 91 | 29 |
| | | | | WBA | 38 | 18 |
| | | | | West Ham U | 179 | 78 |
| Paul Goddard | 5 9½ | 11 5 | Harlington | QPR | 70 | 23 |
| (England) | | | | West Ham U | 76 | 32 |
| Steve Milton* | 5 11 | 11 9 | Fulham | West Ham U | — | — |
| Keith McPherson | | | Greenwich | West Ham U | — | — |
| Mark Schiavi | | | London | West Ham U | — | — |

# WIGAN ATHLETIC Division 3

*Chairman:* F. Pye.

*Vice-Chairman:*

*Directors:* J. Albert Eckersley, R. Kay, A. Muir, R. Charlton OBE, E. Barnes JP, F. Summers, A. O. Horrocks (President).

*Company Secretary:* Colin Burke.

*Vice-Presidents:* J. H. Farrimond and A. Fitch.

*Asst Secretary:* J. H. Farrimond.

*Player-Manager:* Larry Lloyd.

*Year Formed:* 1932.

**Football League Record:**
1978 Elected to Division 4; 1982– Division 3.

**Honours:** *Northern Premier League:* Champions 1970–71, 1974–75. *Northern Premier Cup:* Winners 1971–72. *Northern Premier Shield:* Winners 1972–73, 1973–74, 1975–76. *Cheshire League:* Champions 1933–34, 1934–35, 1935–36, 1964–65. *Lancashire Combination:* Champions 1947–48, 1950–51, 1952–53, 1953–54. *FA Cup* best season: 4th rd, 1979–80. *Football League Cup* best season: 4th rd, 1981–82.

*Record Victory:* 7-2 v Scunthorpe U, Division 4, 12 Mar, 1982.

*Record Defeat:* 0-4 v Huddersfield T, Division 4, 9 Oct, 1979 and 0-4 v Lincoln C, Division 4, 29 Feb, 1980.

*Most League Points:* 55, Division 4, 1978–79 and 1979–80. *Three points win:* 91, Division 4, 1981–82.

*Most League Goals:* 80, Division 4, 1981–82.

*Highest League Scorer in Season:* Les Bradd, 19, Division 4, 1981–82.

*Most League Goals in Total Aggregate:* Peter Houghton, 49, 1978–82.

*Most Capped Player:* None.

*Most League Appearances:* Jeff Wright, 143, 1978–82.

*Record Transfer Fee Received:* £135,000 from Sunderland for Joe Hinnigan, February 1980.

*Previous Managers of Note:* Ted Goodier, Allan Brown, Gordon Milne, Ian McNeill.

*Address of Social Club:* Springfield Park, Wigan.

---

**Springfield Park, Wigan.** Telephone: 0942 44433. *Telegraphic address:* Springfield, Wigan. *Ground capacity:* 30,000. *Record attendance:* 27,500 v Hereford U, 12 Dec, 1953. *Record receipts:* £29,169 v Aston Villa, League Cup 4th rd, 1 Dec, 1981. *Pitch measurements:* 117yd×73yd.

*How to get there:* Wigan Wallgate and Wigan North West Railway Stations. Wigan is served by three motorways, the M6, the M61 and the M62, with convenient access and exit points. Wigan also enjoys the facilities of the main London to Scotland railway line.

*Match tickets:* Stand – available 14 days prior to game.

*Car parking:* On ground and within close proximity to ground.

*Entertainments/catering facilities:* Licensed bar and tea bar in Main Stand, tea bars on ground, Social Club on ground.

*Extra information:* Springfield Park covers approximately nine acres and is owned by Wigan Athletic AFC Ltd. The ground will hold over 30,000 spectators with seating accommodation for 1069 and additional covered standing accommodation for 10,000. A new Executive Lounge, seating 60, has now been constructed.

There are terraces on all four sides of the excellent playing area, surrounded by four 114 feet high pylons with 36 lights on each.

The dressing rooms are equipped with plunge baths, slipper baths, showers and medical and physiotherapy equipment. There are parking facilities for 200 cars.

A lively Social Club and a productive Development Association office are located on the ground.

Wigan has a population of over 300,000 within a radius of 5 miles from the town centre. The actual town population is 89,000.

*Club Colours:* Blue and white striped shirts, blue shorts, white stockings.

*Change Colours:* White shirts, blue shorts, red stockings.

*First Team Trainer:* Ken Banks.

*Club Captain:* Colin Methven.

*Club Nickname:* The Latics.

## WIGAN ATHLETIC 1981–82 LEAGUE RECORD

| Match No. | Date | Venue | Opponents | Result | H/T Score | Goalscorers | Attendance |
|---|---|---|---|---|---|---|---|
| 1 | Aug 29 | A | Bradford C | D 3-3 | 3-2 | Evans 2, Bradd | 4229 |
| 2 | Sept 5 | H | Sheffield U | L 0-1 | 0-1 | | 8001 |
| 3 | 12 | A | Hartlepool U | L 1-2 | 0-0 | Houghton | 1715 |
| 4 | 19 | H | Northampton T | W 3-1 | 0-0 | Glenn, Houghton, Quinn M. | 3996 |
| 5 | 23 | H | Port Vale | W 2-0 | 1-0 | McMahon, Sheldon | 4525 |
| 6 | 26 | A | Tranmere R | D 0-0 | 0-0 | | 2774 |
| 7 | 29 | A | AFC Bournemouth | D 0-0 | 0-0 | | 4952 |
| 8 | Oct 3 | H | Torquay U | W 1-0 | 1-0 | Houghton | 4876 |
| 9 | 10 | H | Stockport Co | W 2-1 | 0-1 | Houghton, Methven | 4873 |
| 10 | 17 | A | Hull C | W 2-0 | 1-0 | Houghton 2 | 3600 |
| 11 | 20 | A | Bury | L 3-5 | 1-1 | Bradd, Barrow, Methven | 6249 |
| 12 | 24 | H | Scunthorpe U | W 2-1 | 2-1 | McMahon, Barrow | 4553 |
| 13 | 30 | A | Colchester U | W 2-1 | 2-0 | McMahon, Houghton | 3882 |
| 14 | Nov 4 | H | Darlington | W 2-1 | 0-1 | Barrow, Weston | 4512 |
| 15 | 7 | H | Hereford U | D 1-1 | 0-1 | Barrow | 4715 |
| 16 | 14 | A | York C | D 0-0 | 0-0 | | 2780 |
| 17 | 28 | A | Rochdale | D 1-1 | 1-1 | Bradd | 2765 |
| 18 | Dec 5 | H | Halifax T | W 2-0 | 0-0 | Houghton, Bradd | 4022 |
| 19 | Jan 2 | A | Mansfield T | W 2-1 | 1-1 | Lloyd, Bradd | 2173 |
| 20 | 5 | H | Tranmere R | D 0-0 | 0-0 | | 4133 |
| 21 | 19 | H | Peterborough U | W 5-0 | 2-0 | Methven, Bradd 2, Houghton, Barrow | 4111 |
| 22 | 23 | H | Bradford C | W 4-1 | 2-1 | Bradd, Quinn M., Houghton 2 | 7107 |
| 23 | 26 | A | Crewe Alex | W 1-0 | 1-0 | Methven | 3874 |
| 24 | 30 | A | Northampton T | W 3-2 | 1-2 | Lloyd, O'Keefe, Bradd | 2418 |
| 25 | Feb 6 | H | Hartlepool U | D 1-1 | 1-0 | Quinn M. | 6315 |
| 26 | 8 | A | Port Vale | D 1-1 | 1-0 | Barrow | 8775 |
| 27 | 13 | A | Torquay U | D 0-0 | 0-0 | | 2524 |
| 28 | 17 | H | Aldershot | W 1-0 | 0-0 | O'Keefe (pen) | 5120 |
| 29 | 26 | A | Stockport Co | W 1-0 | 0-0 | Quinn M. (pen) | 5084 |
| 30 | Mar 6 | H | Hull C | W 2-1 | 1-1 | Bradd 2 | 6008 |
| 31 | 9 | H | Bury | W 3-2 | 0-1 | Barrow, Methven, O'Keefe | 7508 |
| 32 | 12 | A | Scunthorpe U | W 7-2 | 3-0 | Bradd 3, Houghton 2, Methven, Barrow | 2511 |
| 33 | 16 | A | Darlington | L 1-3 | 0-1 | Glenn | 2147 |
| 34 | 20 | H | Colchester U | W 3-2 | 2-0 | Barrow 2, Bradd | 6747 |
| 35 | 23 | A | Sheffield U | L 0-1 | 0-0 | | 22,336 |
| 36 | 27 | A | Hereford U | L 0-3 | 0-1 | | 4191 |
| 37 | 30 | H | Blackpool | W 2-1 | 2-0 | Bradd, Methven | 7329 |
| 38 | Apr 2 | H | York C | W 4-2 | 1-1 | Barrow, McMahon, Methven 2 | 6029 |
| 39 | 9 | A | Blackpool | W 2-1 | 0-0 | Houghton, Bradd | 9439 |
| 40 | 10 | H | Crewe Alex | W 3-0 | 1-0 | O'Keefe 3 (1 pen) | 6142 |
| 41 | 17 | A | Halifax T | D 0-0 | 0-0 | | 3660 |
| 42 | 24 | H | Rochdale | D 1-1 | 0-1 | Houghton | 6153 |
| 43 | May 1 | A | Peterborough U | W 3-0 | 2-0 | Barrow, Bradd 2 | 6229 |
| 44 | 4 | H | AFC Bournemouth | D 0-0 | 0-0 | | 9021 |
| 45 | 8 | H | Mansfield T | W 3-1 | 2-1 | O'Keefe 3 (1 pen) | 8517 |
| 46 | 15 | A | Aldershot | L 0-2 | 0-0 | | 2493 |

**Final League Position: 3**

### Goalscorers

*League* (80): Bradd 19, Houghton 15, Barrow 12, Methven 9, O'Keefe 9 (3 pens), McMahon 4, Quinn M. 4 (1 pen), Evans 2, Glenn 2, Lloyd 2, Sheldon 1, Weston 1.
*League Cup* (13): Barrow 3, Houghton 2, Lloyd 2, Wignall 2, Bradd 1, Evans 1, Methven 1, Quinn M. 1.
*FA Cup* (2): Methven 1, Quinn M. 1

| | | | |
|---|---|---|---|
| **League Cup** First Round | Stockport Co (h) | 3-0 | |
| | (a) | 2-1 | |
| Second Round | Aldershot (a) | 2-2 | |
| | (h) | 1-0 | |
| Third Round | Chelsea (h) | 4-2 | |
| Fourth Round | Aston Villa (h) | 1-2 | |
| **FA Cup** First Round | Hartlepool U (h) | 2-2 | |
| | (a) | 0-1 | |

| Brown | McMahon | Glenn | Cribley | Lloyd | Methven | Sheldon | Barrow | Bradd | Quinn M. | Evans | Houghton | Wright | McAdam | Ward | Langley | Weston | Wignall | Tunks | O'Keefe | Taylor | Butler | Match No. |
|---|---|---|---|---|---|---|---|---|---|---|---|---|---|---|---|---|---|---|---|---|---|---|
| 1 | 2 | 3 | 4 | 5 | 6 | 7* | 8 | 9 | 10 | 11 | 12 | | | | | | | | | | | 1 |
| 1 | 2 | 3 | 4* | 5 | 6 | 7 | 8 | | | 10 | 11 | 9 | 12 | | | | | | | | | 2 |
| 1 | 2 | | 4 | 5 | 6 | 7 | 8 | | | 10 | 11 | 9 | 12 | 3* | | | | | | | | 3 |
| | 2 | 3 | 12 | 5 | 6 | 7 | | | | 10 | 11 | 9 | 4 | 1 | 8* | | | | | | | 4 |
| | 2 | 3 | | 5 | 6 | 7 | 12 | 8 | | 10*| 11 | 9 | 4 | 1 | | | | | | | | 5 |
| | 2 | 3 | | 5 | 6 | 7 | | 8* | | 10 | 11 | 9 | 4 | 1 | 12 | | | | | | | 6 |
| | 2 | | | 5 | 6 | 7 | 8 | | | 10 | 11 | 9 | 4 | 1 | | 3 | | | | | | 7 |
| | 2 | | | 5 | 6 | 7 | 8 | | | 10 | 11 | 9 | 4 | 1 | | 3 | | | | | | 8 |
| | 2 | | | 5 | 6 | 7 | 8 | 9 | | 11 | 10 | | | 1 | | 3 | 4 | | | | | 9 |
| | 2 | | | 5 | 6 | 7 | 8 | 9 | | 11 | 10 | | | 1 | | 3 | 4 | | | | | 10 |
| | 2 | 12 | | 5* | 6 | 7 | 8 | 9 | | 11 | 10 | | | 1 | | 3 | 4 | | | | | 11 |
| | 2 | | | 5 | 6 | 7 | 8 | 9* | 12 | 11 | 10 | | | 1 | | 3 | 4 | | | | | 12 |
| 1 | 2 | 7 | 3 | 5 | 6 | | 8 | 9 | | | 10 | | | | | 11 | 4 | | | | | 13 |
| 1 | 2 | 7 | 3 | 5 | 6 | | 8 | 9 | | | 10 | | | | | 11 | 4 | | | | | 14 |
| | 2 | 7* | 3 | 5 | 6 | | 8 | 9 | | 12 | 10 | | | | | 11 | 4 | 1 | | | | 15 |
| | 2 | | | 5 | 6 | 7 | 8 | 9 | | 11 | 10 | | | | | 3 | 4 | 1 | | | | 16 |
| 1 | 2 | 3 | | | 6 | 7 | 8 | 5 | 9 | 11 | 10 | | | | | 4 | | | | | | 17 |
| | 2 | 3 | | 5 | | 7 | 8 | 4 | 9 | 11 | 10* | 12 | | | | 6 | | 1 | | | | 18 |
| | 2 | 3 | | 5 | 6 | | 8 | 9 | | 11 | 10 | | | | | 7 | 4 | 1 | | | | 19 |
| | 2 | 3 | | 5 | 6 | | 8 | 9 | 12 | 11 | 10 | | | | | 7* | 4 | 1 | | | | 20 |
| | 2* | 3 | | 5 | 6 | | 8 | 9 | 7 | 11 | 10 | | | | | 12 | 4 | 1 | | | | 21 |
| | | 3 | | 5 | 6 | | 8 | 9 | 7 | 11 | 10 | 4 | | | | 2 | | 1 | | | | 22 |
| | 2 | | | 5 | 6 | | 8 | 9 | 7 | 11 | 10 | 4 | | | | 3 | | 1 | | | | 23 |
| | 2 | 3 | | 5 | 6 | | 8 | 9 | 7 | | 10 | 4 | | | | | | 1 | 11 | | | 24 |
| | 2 | 3 | | 5 | 6 | | 8 | 9 | 7 | | 10 | 4 | | | | | | 1 | 11 | | | 25 |
| | 2 | 3 | | 5 | 6 | | 8 | 9 | 7 | | 10 | | | | | 4 | | 1 | 11 | | | 26 |
| | 2 | 3 | | 5* | 6 | | 8 | 9 | 7 | 12 | 10 | | | | | 4 | | 1 | 11 | | | 27 |
| | 2 | 3 | | | 6 | | 8 | 5 | 7* | 11 | 10 | | | | | 12 | 4 | 1 | 9 | | | 28 |
| | 2 | 3 | | 5* | 6 | | | 9 | 7 | 11 | 10 | | | | | 12 | 4 | 1 | 8 | | | 29 |
| | 2 | | | 5 | 6 | | | 9 | 7 | 11 | 10* | 12 | | | | 3 | 4 | 1 | 8 | | | 30 |
| | 2 | 3 | | 5 | 6 | | 8 | 9 | 12 | 11 | 10* | | | | | | 4 | 1 | 7 | | | 31 |
| | 2 | 3 | | 5 | 6 | | 8 | 9 | | 11 | 10 | | | | | | 4 | 1 | 7 | | | 32 |
| | 2 | 3 | | 5 | 6 | | 8 | 9 | 12 | 11 | 10 | | | | | | 4* | 1 | 7 | | | 33 |
| | 2 | 3 | 4 | 5 | 6 | | 8 | 9 | | 11 | 10 | | | | | | | 1 | 7 | | | 34 |
| | 2 | | 4 | 5 | 6 | | 8 | 9* | 12 | 11 | 10 | | | 3 | | | | 1 | 7 | | | 35 |
| | 2 | 3 | | 5 | 6 | | 8 | 9 | 12 | 11* | 10 | | | | | | | 1 | 7 | 4 | | 36 |
| | 2 | 3 | | 5 | 6 | | 8 | 9 | | | 10 | | | | | 11 | | 1 | 7 | 4 | | 37 |
| | 2 | 3 | | 5 | 6 | | 8 | 9 | 12 | | 10* | | | | | 11 | | 1 | 7 | 4 | | 38 |
| | 2 | 3 | | 5 | 6 | | 8 | 9 | | | 10 | | | | | 11 | | 1 | 7 | 4 | | 39 |
| | 2 | 3 | | 5 | | 6 | 8 | 9* | 12 | | 10 | | | | | 11 | | 1 | 7 | 4 | | 40 |
| | 2 | 3 | 4 | 5 | 6 | | 8 | 9 | | | 10 | | | | | 11 | | 1 | 7 | | | 41 |
| | 2 | 3* | 7 | 4 | 5 | | 8 | 9 | 12 | | 10 | | | | | | | 1 | | 11 | 6 | 42 |
| | 2 | 3 | 4 | 5 | 6 | | 8 | 9 | | | 10 | | | | | | 11 | 1 | 7 | | | 43 |
| | 2 | 3 | 4 | 5 | 6 | | 8 | 9 | | | 10 | | | | | | 11 | 1 | 7 | | | 44 |
| | 2 | 3 | 4 | 5* | 6 | | 8 | 9 | | | 10 | | | | | | 11 | 1 | 7 | 12 | | 45 |
| | 2 | 3 | 4 | | 6 | | | 9 | 12 | | 10 | | | | 5 | | 11 | 1 | 7 | 8* | | 46 |
| 6 | 36 | 35 | 29 | 36 | 46 | 15 | 40 | 41 | 20 | 29 | 45 | 9 | 1 | 9 | 1 | 22 | 25 | 31 | 22 | 7 | 1 | |

Substitute appearances: Glenn +2s; Barrow +1s; Bradd +9s; Quinn M. +3s; Evans +1s; Houghton +4s; Weston +1s; Wignall +3s; O'Keefe +1s.

*Players continued from following page.*

| | | | | |
|---|---|---|---|---|
| Les Bradd | 6 1 | 13 0 | Buxton | Rotherham U — 3 — |
| | | | | Notts Co — 398 — 125 |
| | | | | Stockport Co — 117 — 31 |
| | | | | Wigan Ath — 41 — 19 |
| Eamon O'Keefe (Eire) | 5 7 | 11 5 | Manchester | Stalybridge C — (not known) |
| | | | | Plymouth Arg — (not known) — |
| | | | | Hyde U — (not known) |
| | | | | Saudi Arabia — (not known) |
| | | | | Mossley — (not known) |
| | | | | Everton — 40 — 6 |
| | | | | Wigan Ath — 22 — 9 |

## WIGAN ATHLETIC

| | Ht | Wt | Birthplace | Clubs | League App. | League Gls |
|---|---|---|---|---|---|---|
| **Goalkeepers** | | | | | | |
| John Brown* | 5 11 | 12 7 | Bradford | Preston NE | 67 | — |
| | | | | Stockport Co | 41 | — |
| | | | | Wigan Ath | 93 | — |
| Bob Ward | 6 1 | 12 0 | West Bromwich | WBA | 9 | — |
| | | | | Northampton T (on loan) | 8 | — |
| | | | | Blackpool | 41 | — |
| | | | | Wigan Ath | 46 | — |
| Roy Tunks | 6 1 | 13 11 | Wuppertall | Rotherham U | 138 | — |
| | | | | York C (on loan) | 4 | — |
| | | | | Ipswich T (on loan) | — | — |
| | | | | Newcastle U (on loan) | — | — |
| | | | | Preston NE | 277 | — |
| | | | | Wigan Ath | 31 | — |
| **Defenders** | | | | | | |
| Larry Lloyd | 6 2 | 13 7 | Bristol | Bristol R | 43 | 1 |
| (England) | | | | Liverpool | 150 | 4 |
| | | | | Coventry C | 50 | 5 |
| | | | | Nottingham F | 148 | 6 |
| | | | | Wigan Ath | 45 | 2 |
| John Curtis | 5 8 | 10 0 | Poulton | Blackpool | 102 | — |
| (Contract cancelled Oct 1981) | | | | Blackburn R | 10 | — |
| | | | | Wigan Ath | 32 | — |
| Noel Ward | 6 2½ | 12 10 | Londonderry | Portadown | — | — |
| (Retired, injury) | | | | Aberdeen | 7 | — |
| | | | | Wigan Ath | 48 | 4 |
| Neil Davids* | 6 0¾ | 13 9 | Bingley | Leeds U | — | — |
| | | | | Norwich C | 2 | — |
| | | | | Northampton T (on loan) | 9 | — |
| | | | | Stockport Co (on loan) | 5 | 1 |
| | | | | Swansea C | 9 | — |
| | | | | Wigan Ath | 68 | 1 |
| Colin Methven | 6 2 | 12 7 | Kirkcaldy | East Fife | 154 | 15 |
| | | | | Wigan Ath | 127 | 13 |
| Brian Kettle | 5 9 | 12 13 | Prescot | Liverpool | 3 | — |
| (Contract cancelled Oct 1981) | | | | Wigan Ath | 14 | 1 |
| Alex Cribley | 5 11¼ | 12 9 | Liverpool | Liverpool | — | — |
| | | | | Wigan Ath | 61 | — |
| Steven McAdam* | 6 0½ | 11 2 | Portadown | Portadown | (not known) | — |
| | | | | Burnley | 5 | — |
| | | | | Oldham Ath | — | — |
| | | | | Barnsley | — | — |
| | | | | Wigan Ath | 26 | — |
| John McMahon | 5 9 | 11 2 | Manchester | Preston NE | 257 | 7 |
| | | | | Southend U (on loan) | 3 | — |
| | | | | Chesterfield (on loan) | 1 | — |
| | | | | Crewe Alex | 67 | 2 |
| | | | | Wigan Ath | 36 | 4 |
| John Butler | | | | Preston Cables | (not known) | — |
| | | | | Wigan Ath | 1 | — |
| David Glenn | 5 10 | 10 10 | Wigan | Wigan Ath | 46 | 4 |
| **Midfield** | | | | | | |
| Jeff Wright* | 5 11 | 11 7 | Alston | Wigan Ath | 143 | 19 |
| Frank Corrigan | 5 10 | 11 7 | Liverpool | Blackpool | — | — |
| (Contract cancelled Aug 1981) | | | | Walsall | 1 | — |
| | | | | Wigan Ath | 116 | 12 |
| Mark Wignall | 5 6 | 10 7 | Preston | Wigan Ath | 34 | — |
| Graham Barrow | 6 2 | 13 7 | Chorley | Altrincham | (not known) | — |
| | | | | Wigan Ath | 41 | 12 |
| Jimmy Weston | 5 9 | 11 0 | Liverpool | Blackpool | 105 | 8 |
| | | | | Torquay U | 38 | 1 |
| | | | | Wigan Ath | 25 | 1 |
| Clive Evans | 5 10 | 10 9 | Birkenhead | Tranmere R | 178 | 27 |
| | | | | Wigan Ath | 32 | 2 |
| Kevin Sheldon | 5 5½ | 9 4 | Stoke | Stoke C | 15 | — |
| | | | | Wigan Ath | 15 | 1 |
| Kevin Langley | 6 1 | 9 0 | | Wigan Ath | 2 | — |
| (Apprentice) | | | | | | |
| **Forwards** | | | | | | |
| Peter Houghton | 5 11 | 12 7 | Liverpool | Wigan Ath | 145 | 49 |
| Tony Quinn | 5 9½ | 10 7 | Liverpool | Wigan Ath | 43 | 14 |
| (Contract cancelled Dec 1981) | | | | | | |
| Mike Quinn | 5 10½ | 11 0 | Liverpool | Wigan Ath | 69 | 19 |
| George Urquhart | 5 11 | 12 0 | Glasgow | Wigan Ath | 68 | 6 |
| (Contract cancelled March 1982) | | | | | | |
| Billy Urquhart | 5 10 | 12 0 | Inverness | Inverness Caley | (not known) | — |
| (Contract cancelled Aug 1981) | | | | Rangers | 14 | 6 |
| | | | | Wigan Ath | 10 | 2 |

*Note: Players continued on previous page.*

# WIMBLEDON Division 4

*President:* Rt Hon Sir Michael Havers QC, MP.

*Chairman:* B. Reynolds.

*Vice-Chairman:* W. Unwin.

*Directors:* S. Hammam, P. Cork, M. Dell, E. C. Gush, J. J. McElligott, Q. Spicer.

*Manager:* Dave Bassett.

*Secretary:* Adrian Cook.

*Year Formed:* 1889. *Turned Semi-Professional:* 1964.

*Limited Company:* 1964. *Previous Name:* Wimbledon Old Centrals 1899–1905.

**Football League Record:**
1977–79 Division 4; 1979–80 Division 3; 1980–81 Division 4; 1981– Division 3.

**Honours:** *Southern League:* Champions 1974–75, 1975–76, 1976–77. *Southern League Cup:* Winners 1969–70, 1975–76. Division 4: Promoted 1978–79 (3rd), 1980–81 (4th). *FA Cup* best season: 4th rd, 1974–75. *Football League Cup* best season: 4th rd, 1979–80. *League Group Cup:* Runners-up 1981–82.

*Record Victory:* 15-2 v Polytechnic, FA Cup Preliminary rd, 7 Feb, 1929.

*Record Defeat:* 0-8 v Everton, League Cup 2nd rd, 29 Aug, 1978.

*Most League Points:* 61, Division 4, 1978–79.

*Most League Goals:* 78, Division 4, 1978–79.

*Highest League Scorer in Season:* Alan Cork, 23, 1980–81.

*Most League Goals in Total Aggregate:* John Leslie, 64, 1977–82.

*Most Capped Player:* None.

*Most League Appearances:* John Leslie, 211, 1977–82.

*Record Transfer Fee Received:* £70,000 from Crystal Palace for Steve Galliers, Oct 1981.

*Record Transfer Fee Paid:* £45,000 to QPR for Tommy Cunningham, Mar 1979.

*Previous Managers since 1955:* Les Henley, Mike Everitt, Dick Graham, Allen Batsford, Dario Gradi.

*Address of Supporters Club and Club Shop:* Plough Lane Ground, Durnsford Road.

---

**Plough Lane Ground, Durnsford Road, Wimbledon, London SW19** (first used in 1912). Telephone: 01-946 6311. *Ground capacity:* 15,000. *Record attendance:* 18,000 v HMS Victory in FA Amateur Cup 3rd rd, 1934–35. *Record receipts:* £30,600 v Leeds U, FA Cup 4th rd replay at Crystal Palace, 1974–75. *Pitch measurements:* 110yd×85yd.

*How to get there:* Nearest station Wimbledon or Haydons Road (SR), South Wimbledon Underground. Buses: 77a from Wimbledon, 189 from Tooting.

*Match tickets:* Available 14 days prior to game for important matches.

*Car parking:* On ground and in streets quarter mile from ground.

*Entertainments/catering facilities:* Four licensed bars and two tea bars in main stand. Sportsman Public House adjacent to ground and owned by club.

*Club shop:* Two shops, one in Durnsford Road open weekdays, one in ground open matchdays. Sell all types of souvenirs.

*Handbooks/programmes:* Supporters Club Handbook published annually. Programmes available on subscription.

*Club Colours:* Blue shirts with yellow trim, blue shorts with yellow trim, blue stockings.

*Change Colours:* Yellow shirts with blue trim, yellow shorts with blue trim, yellow stockings.

*Club Captain:*

*Club Nickname:* The Dons.

# WIMBLEDON 1981–82 LEAGUE RECORD

| Match No. | Date | Venue | Opponents | Result | H/T Score | Goalscorers | Attendance |
|---|---|---|---|---|---|---|---|
| 1 | Aug 29 | A | Swindon T | L 1-4 | 0-1 | Ketteridge | 5632 |
| 2 | Sept 5 | H | Millwall | L 1-3 | 0-1 | Joseph | 5102 |
| 3 | 12 | A | Huddersfield T | D 1-1 | 0-0 | Leslie | 7326 |
| 4 | 19 | H | Doncaster R | L 0-1 | 0-0 | | 2364 |
| 5 | 22 | H | Fulham | L 1-3 | 0-1 | Leslie | 5554 |
| 6 | 26 | A | Walsall | L 0-1 | 0-0 | | 3027 |
| 7 | 29 | A | Bristol R | D 2-2 | 0-0 | Hubbick 2 | 5364 |
| 8 | Oct 3 | H | Gillingham | L 0-2 | 0-1 | | 2510 |
| 9 | 10 | A | Lincoln C | L 1-5 | 1-2 | Leslie | 3168 |
| 10 | 17 | H | Chester | W 1-0 | 1-0 | Lazarus | 1659 |
| 11 | 20 | H | Plymouth Arg | W 2-1 | 0-0 | Joseph, Boyle | 2114 |
| 12 | 24 | A | Reading | L 1-2 | 0-2 | Brown (pen) | 3732 |
| 13 | 31 | H | Exeter C | D 1-1 | 1-0 | Lazarus | 2152 |
| 14 | Nov 3 | A | Portsmouth | L 0-1 | 0-0 | | 9063 |
| 15 | 7 | A | Burnley | D 2-2 | 0-1 | Lazarus, Clement | 4231 |
| 16 | 14 | H | Preston NE | W 3-2 | 1-2 | Leslie 2, Belfield | 2428 |
| 17 | 28 | A | Chesterfield | L 0-2 | 0-2 | | 4604 |
| 18 | Dec 5 | H | Newport Co | L 2-3 | 0-2 | Clement, Lazarus | 2056 |
| 19 | Jan 2 | A | Bristol C | W 3-1 | 1-1 | Ketteridge, Lazarus 2 | 4660 |
| 20 | 23 | H | Swindon T | D 1-1 | 1-0 | Ketteridge | 2084 |
| 21 | 29 | A | Doncaster R | W 3-1 | 2-1 | Blochel, Leslie 2 | 5849 |
| 22 | Feb 6 | H | Huddersfield T | W 2-0 | 1-0 | Ketteridge 2 | 2499 |
| 23 | 9 | A | Fulham | L 1-4 | 0-1 | Ketteridge | 7802 |
| 24 | 13 | A | Gillingham | L 1-6 | 1-3 | Ketteridge (pen) | 4214 |
| 25 | 20 | H | Bristol R | W 1-0 | 0-0 | Smith | 2408 |
| 26 | 24 | A | Millwall | L 1-2 | 0-0 | Fishenden | 4072 |
| 27 | 27 | H | Lincoln C | D 1-1 | 1-0 | Gage | 2094 |
| 28 | Mar 13 | H | Reading | D 0-0 | 0-0 | | 2551 |
| 29 | 20 | A | Exeter C | L 1-2 | 1-2 | Joseph | 3002 |
| 30 | 23 | H | Southend U | W 3-0 | 2-0 | Smith, Evans, Joseph | 2051 |
| 31 | 27 | H | Burnley | D 0-0 | 0-0 | | 2641 |
| 32 | 31 | A | Chester | D 1-1 | 0-0 | Joseph | 1359 |
| 33 | Apr 3 | A | Preston NE | L 2-3 | 0-1 | Leslie, Brown | 4964 |
| 34 | 9 | A | Southend U | L 0-2 | 0-2 | | 4779 |
| 35 | 12 | H | Brentford | L 1-2 | 1-0 | Joseph | 4513 |
| 36 | 14 | A | Plymouth Arg | L 0-2 | 0-0 | | 4748 |
| 37 | 17 | A | Newport Co | D 0-0 | 0-0 | | 3900 |
| 38 | 20 | H | Oxford U | L 2-3 | 2-1 | Evans, Joseph | 2903 |
| 39 | 24 | H | Chesterfield | W 3-1 | 1-0 | Belfield 2, Hodges | 2138 |
| 40 | 26 | A | Brentford | W 3-2 | 0-2 | Joseph 2, Belfield | 6612 |
| 41 | May 1 | A | Carlisle U | L 1-2 | 1-0 | Hodges | 4466 |
| 42 | 4 | H | Walsall | W 2-0 | 1-0 | Serella (og), Evans | 1503 |
| 43 | 8 | H | Bristol C | D 0-0 | 0-0 | | 2114 |
| 44 | 11 | H | Carlisle U | W 3-1 | 1-0 | Evans, Joseph 2 | 2022 |
| 45 | 15 | A | Oxford U | W 3-0 | 0-0 | Elliott, Joseph, Brown | 4319 |
| 46 | 18 | H | Portsmouth | W 3-2 | 1-1 | Morris, Joseph, Leslie | 2642 |

**Final League Position: 21**

**Goalscorers**

*League* (61): Joseph 13, Leslie 9, Ketteridge 7 (1 pen), Lazarus 6, Belfield 4, Evans 4, Brown 3 (1 pen), Clement 2, Hodges 2, Hubbick 2, Smith 2, Blochel 1, Boyle 1, Elliott 1, Fishenden 1, Gage 1, Morris 1, own goal 1.
*League Cup* (1): Cork 1 (pen).
*FA Cup* (3): Brown 1 (pen), Ketteridge 1, Suddaby 1.

| | | | |
|---|---|---|---|
| **League Cup** | First Round | Aldershot (a) | 0-0 |
| | | (h) | 1-3 |
| **FA Cup** | First Round | Bedford T (a) | 2-0 |
| | Second Round | Enfield (a) | 1-4 |

| Beasant | Brown | Armstrong | Galliers | Smith | Jones | Ketteridge | Joseph | Leslie | Cork | Hodges | Gage | Cunningham | Downes | Hubbick | Thomas | Lazarus | Boyle | Suddaby | Clement | Morris | Geddes | Fishenden | Belfield | Blochel | Elliott | Evans | Hughes | Match No. |
|---|---|---|---|---|---|---|---|---|---|---|---|---|---|---|---|---|---|---|---|---|---|---|---|---|---|---|---|---|
| 1 | 2 | 3 | 4 | 5 | 6 | 7 | 8 | 9 | 10 | 11*| 12 | | | | | | | | | | | | | | | | | 1 |
| 1 | | 3 | 4 | 5 | 2 | 7 | 8 | 9 | 10 | | | | 6 | 11 | | | | | | | | | | | | | | 2 |
| 1 | | 3 | 4 | 5 | 2 | 7 | 8 | 9 | 10 | | | | 6 | 11 | | | | | | | | | | | | | | 3 |
| 1 | | 3 | 4 | 5 | 2 | 7*| | 9 | 10 | 11 | 8 | | 6 | | 12 | | | | | | | | | | | | | 4 |
| 1 | | 3 | 4 | 5 | 2 | 7 | | 9 | 10 | 11 | 8*| | 6 | | 12 | | | | | | | | | | | | | 5 |
| 1 | 2 | | 4 | 5 | 3 | 7 | 11 | 9 | 10*| 8 | 12 | | 6 | | | | | | | | | | | | | | | 6 |
| 1 | 2 | 8 | 4 | 5 | 6 | 7 | 12 | | | 11 | | | 10 | | 9* | 3 | | | | | | | | | | | | 7 |
| 1 | 11 | | 4 | 5 | 2 | 7 | | | | 8 | | | 10 | | 9 | 3* | 12 | 6 | | | | | | | | | | 8 |
| 1 | | | 4 | 5 | 2 | 7 | | 9 | | 8 | | | 10 | | 3 | 11 | 6 | | | | | | | | | | | 9 |
| 1 | 2 | | 4 | 5 | 3 | | 7 | | | 8 | | | 10 | | 9 | 6 | 11 | | | | | | | | | | | 10 |
| 1 | 2 | | 4 | 5 | 3* | 12 | 8 | | 11 | | | | 10 | | 9 | 7 | 6 | | | | | | | | | | | 11 |
| 1 | 2 | | | 5 | | 8 | 3 | 7 | | 11*| 12 | | 10 | | 9 | 4 | 6 | | | | | | | | | | | 12 |
| 1 | 3 | | | 5 | | 8 | 11 | 7* | | 12 | 4 | | 10 | | 9 | | 2 | 6 | | | | | | | | | | 13 |
| 1 | 3 | | | 5 | | 8 | 11 | 7* | | | 4 | | 10 | | 9 | | 2 | 5 | 6 | 12 | | | | | | | | 14 |
| 1 | 3 | | | 5 | | 8 | 11 | 7 | | | 4 | | 10 | | 9 | | 2 | 5 | 6 | | | | | | | | | 15 |
| 1 | 3 | | | 5 | | 8 | 11*| 7 | | 4 | | | 10 | | 9 | | 6 | 2 | 5 | | | 12 | | | | | | 16 |
| 1 | 7 | 3 | | | | 11 | 8 | 9 | 4* | | | | 10 | | | | 6 | 2 | 5 | | | 12 | | | | | | 17 |
| 1 | 7 | 3 | | | | 11 | 8 | | | 10 | | | | | 9 | 6 | 2 | 5 | 4 | | | | | | | | | 18 |
| 1 | | | 4 | | | 7 | 11 | 8 | 10 | | | | 6 | 3 | 9 | | 2 | 5 | | | | | | | | | | 19 |
| 1 | | | 4 | | | 7 | 11 | 8 | 10 | | | | 6 | 3 | | | 2 | 5 | | | | 9 | | | | | | 20 |
| 1 | | | 4 | | | 7*| 11 | 8 | 10 | 12 | | | 6 | 3 | | | 2 | 5 | | | | 9 | | | | | | 21 |
| 1 | 2 | 10 | 4 | | | 7 | 11 | 8 | | | | | 6 | 3 | | | | 5 | | | | 9 | | | | | | 22 |
| 1 | 2 | 10 | 4 | | | 7 | 11 | | | | | | 6 | 3 | 8 | | | 5 | | | | 9 | | | | | | 23 |
| 1 | 2 | 10 | 4 | | | 7 | 11 | 12 | | | | | 6 | 3* | 8 | | | 5 | | | | 9 | | | | | | 24 |
| 1 | 3 | | 4 | | | 7 | 11 | 10 | 2 | | | | 6 | | 8 | | | 5 | | | | 9 | | | | | | 25 |
| 1 | 6 | 3 | 4 | | | 7 | 11 | 10 | 2 | | | | | | 8 | | | 5 | 9 | | | | | | | | | 26 |
| 1 | 5 | 3 | 4 | | | 7 | 11 | 12 | 10 | 2 | | | 6 | | 8 | | | | 9* | | | | | | | | | 27 |
| 1 | 2 | 3 | 4 | | | 7 | 11 | 9* | 10 | | | | 6 | | 8 | | | 5 | | | | | 12 | | | | | 28 |
| 1 | 2 | 3 | 4* | | | 7 | 8 | 12 | 10 | | | | 6 | | | | | 5 | | | | | | | 11 | 9 | | 29 |
| 1 | 2 | 3 | 4 | | | 7 | 8 | 12 | 10*| | | | 6 | | | | | 5 | | | | | | | 11 | 9 | | 30 |
| 1 | 2 | 3 | 4 | | | 7 | 8 | 10*| | | | | 6 | | | | | 5 | | | | 12 | | | 11 | 9 | | 31 |
| 1 | 2 | 3 | 4 | | | 7 | 8 | 10 | | | | | 6 | | | | | 5 | | | | 12 | | | 11*| 9 | | 32 |
| 1 | 2 | 3 | 4 | | | 7 | 8 | 12 | 10 | | | | 6 | | | | | 5 | | | | 11*| | | | 9 | | 33 |
| 1 | 2 | 3 | 4 | | | | 8 | 10 | 7 | | | | 6 | | 11*| | | 5 | | | | | 12 | | | 9 | | 34 |
| 1 | 2 | 3 | 4 | | | | 8 | 10 | 7* | | | | 6 | | | | | 5 | | | | 12 | 11 | | | 9 | | 35 |
| 1 | | 3 | 4 | | 11 | 9 | 12 | | | | | | 2 | | | | | 5 | | | 6 | | | | 7 | 10 | 8* | 36 |
| 1 | | 3 | 4 | 12 | 8 | | | | | | | | 2 | | | | | 5 | 10 | 6 | | | 11 | 9 | | | 7* | 37 |
| 1 | | 3 | 4 | 7 | 8 | 2 | 9 | | | | | | 6 | | | | | 5 | | | | | 11 | | | 10 | | 38 |
| 1 | | 3 | 4 | 7 | 8 | 2 | 9 | | | | | | 6 | | | | | 5 | | | | | 11 | | | 10 | | 39 |
| 1 | | 3 | 4 | | 8 | 2 | 9 | 12 | | | | | 6* | | 7 | | | 5 | | | | | 11 | | | 10 | | 40 |
| 1 | | 3 | 4 | | 8 | 2 | 9 | | | | | | 6 | | 7 | | | 5 | | | | | 11 | | | 10 | | 41 |
| 1 | | 3 | 4 | | 8 | 2 | 9 | | | | | | 6 | | 7 | | | 5 | | | | | 11 | | | 10 | | 42 |
| 1 | | 3 | 4 | 12 | 9 | 2 | 8 | | | | | | 6 | | 7 | | | 5 | | | | | 11*| | | 10 | | 43 |
| 1 | | | 4 | 11 | 8 | 2 | 9 | 3 | | | | | 6 | | 7 | | | 5 | | | | | | | | 10 | | 44 |
| 1 | 4 | | | 7 | 8 | 2 | 9*| 11 | | | | | 6 | | 3 | | | 5 | | | | | 12 | | | 10 | | 45 |
| 1 | 4 | | | 7 | 8 | 2 | 9*| 11 | | | | | 6 | | 3 | | | 5 | | | | | 12 | | | 10 | | 46 |
| 46 | 27 | 31 | 11 | 39 | 11 | 34 | 38 | 34 | 6 | 32 | 15 | 2 | 42 | 2 | 18 | 17 | 5 | 6 | 9 | 33 | 2 | 4 | 9 | 6 | 7 | 18 | 2 | |

Substitutes: Galliers +2s, Smith +2s, Jones +4s, Ketteridge +2s, Joseph +6s, Cork +2s, Hodges +1s, Clement +1s, Morris +5s, Fishenden +4s

## WIMBLEDON

| | Ht | Wt | Birthplace | Clubs | League App. | League Gls |
|---|---|---|---|---|---|---|
| **Goalkeepers** | | | | | | |
| Dave Beasant | 6 4 | 13 0 | Willesden | Wimbledon | 82 | — |
| **Defenders** | | | | | | |
| Gary Armstrong* | 5 8 | 10 7 | London | Gillingham | 86 | 2 |
| | | | | Wimbledon | 71 | — |
| Mick Smith | 6 0½ | 11 9 | Sunderland | Lincoln C | 25 | — |
| | | | | Wimbledon | 104 | 4 |
| Steve Jones | 6 1 | 12 1 | Eastbourne | QPR | — | — |
| | | | | Walsall | 15 | — |
| | | | | Wimbledon | 76 | — |
| Wally Downes | 5 10 | 10 11 | London | Wimbledon | 105 | 8 |
| Peter Brown* | 5 10 | 11 0 | Hemel Hempstead | Chelsea | — | — |
| | | | | Wimbledon | 55 | 3 |
| Dean Thomas | 5 9 | 11 8 | Bedworth | Nuneaton B | (not known) | |
| | | | | Wimbledon | 18 | — |
| Dave Clement | 6 0 | 12 5 | Battersea | QPR | 405 | 22 |
| (England) (Deceased) | | | | Bolton W | 33 | — |
| | | | | Fulham | 18 | — |
| | | | | Wimbledon | 9 | 2 |
| Peter Suddaby* | 5 11 | 12 2 | Stockport | Blackpool | 332 | 9 |
| | | | | Brighton | 23 | — |
| | | | | Wimbledon | 6 | — |
| Mark Morris | 6 0 | 11 10 | Morden | Wimbledon | 33 | 1 |
| **Midfield** | | | | | | |
| Paul Denny | 5 9 | 10 8 | Croydon | Southend U | 9 | 2 |
| (Contract cancelled Aug 1981) | | | | Wimbledon | 103 | 11 |
| Steve Ketteridge | 5 8½ | 10 7 | Stevenage | Derby Co | — | — |
| | | | | Wimbledon | 126 | 15 |
| Kevin Gage | 5 9 | 11 2 | Chiswick | Wimbledon | 22 | 1 |
| Glyn Hodges | 6 0 | 12 3 | Streatham | Wimbledon | 64 | 7 |
| David Kempton | | | | Wimbledon | — | — |
| (Contract cancelled March 1982) | | | | | | |
| Billy Hughes | 5 10 | 10 8 | Folkestone | Gillingham | 126 | 8 |
| (Contract cancelled) | | | | Crystal Palace | 7 | — |
| | | | | Wimbledon | 2 | — |
| Paul Geddes | 6 1½ | 12 2 | Paisley | Leicester C | — | — |
| (Contract cancelled) | | | | Hibernian | — | — |
| | | | | Wimbledon | 2 | — |
| Mick Belfield | 5 9 | 10 7 | London | Wimbledon | 16 | 4 |
| **Forwards** | | | | | | |
| Alan Cork | 6 0 | 12 0 | Derby | Derby Co | — | — |
| | | | | Lincoln C (on loan) | 5 | — |
| | | | | Wimbledon | 151 | 60 |
| John Leslie | 5 8 | 11 2 | London | Charlton Ath | — | — |
| | | | | Wimbledon | 211 | 64 |
| Dave Hubbick | 5 7 | 10 7 | South Shields | Ipswich T | — | — |
| (Contract cancelled April 1982) | | | | Wimbledon | 26 | 6 |
| Francis Joseph | 5 10 | 12 0 | London | Hillingdon B | (not known) | |
| | | | | Wimbledon | 51 | 14 |
| Keith Fear | 5 7 | 10 8 | Bristol | Bristol C | 151 | 33 |
| (Contract cancelled) | | | | Blackburn R (on loan) | 5 | 2 |
| | | | | Hereford U (on loan) | 6 | — |
| | | | | Plymouth Arg | 45 | 9 |
| | | | | Brentford (on loan) | 8 | 2 |
| | | | | Chester | 44 | 3 |
| | | | | Wimbledon | — | — |
| Paul Lazarus | 5 10 | 11 8 | London | Charlton Ath | 2 | 1 |
| (Contract cancelled April 1982) | | | | Wimbledon | 18 | 6 |
| Paul Fishenden | 6 0 | 10 12 | Hillingdon | Wimbledon | 5 | 1 |
| (Contract cancelled April 1982) | | | | | | |
| Stewart Evans | 6 4 | 11 5 | Rotherham | Rotherham U | — | — |
| | | | | Gainsborough T | (not known) | |
| | | | | Sheffield U | — | — |
| | | | | Wimbledon | 18 | 4 |
| Richard Elliott | | | | Brighton | 3 | — |
| (Non-contract) | | | | Cardiff C | 7 | — |
| | | | | Bournemouth (on loan) | 4 | — |
| | | | | Wimbledon | 11 | 1 |

# WOLVERHAMPTON WANDERERS

## Division 2

*President:* J. R. Ireland.

*Chairman/Chief Executive:* Derek Dougan.

*Vice-Chairman:* D. Hope.

*Manager:* Graham Hawkins.

*Secretary:* P. A. Shaw.

*Year Formed:* 1877. *Turned Professional:* 1888.

*Limited Company:* 1923.

*Previous Grounds:* 1877, Goldthorn Hill; 1884, Dudley Road; 1889, Molineux.

*Previous Name:* 1880, St Luke's, Blakenhall combined with The Wanderers to become Wolverhampton Wanderers.

**Football League Record:**
1888 Founder Members of Football League; 1906–23 Division 2; 1923–24 Division 3(N); 1924–32 Division 2; 1932–65 Division 1; 1965–67 Division 2; 1967–76 Division 1; 1976–77 Division 2; 1977–82 Division 1; 1982– Division 2.

**Honours:** *Football League:* Division 1 – Champions 1953–54, 1957–58, 1958–59; Runners-up 1937–38, 1938–39, 1949–50, 1954–55, 1959–60; Division 2 – Champions 1931–32, 1976–77; Runners-up 1966–67; Division 3(N) – Champions 1923–24. *FA Cup:* Winners 1893, 1908, 1949, 1960; Runners-up 1889, 1896, 1921, 1939. *Football League Cup:* Winners 1973–74, 1979–80. *Texaco Cup:* 1970–71. **European Competitions:** *European Cup:* 1958–59, 1959–60. *European Cup-Winners' Cup:* 1960–61. *UEFA Cup:* 1971–72 (runners-up), 1973–74, 1974–75, 1980–81.

*Record Victory:* 14-0 v Crosswell's Brewery, FA Cup 2nd rd, 1886–87.

*Record Defeat:* 1-10 v Newton Heath, Division 1, 15 Oct, 1892.

*Most League Points:* 64, Division 1, 1957–58.

*Most League Goals:* 115, Division 2, 1931–32.

*Highest League Scorer in Season:* Dennis Westcott, 37, Division 1, 1946–47.

*Most League Goals in Total Aggregate:* Bill Hartill, 164, 1928–35.

*Most Capped Player:* Billy Wright, 105, England (70 consecutive).

*Most League Appearances:* Billy Wright, 491, 1946–59.

*Record Transfer Fee Received:* £1,150,000 from Manchester C for Steve Daley, Sept 1979.

*Record Transfer Fee Paid:* £1,175,000 to Aston Villa for Andy Gray, Sept 1979.

*Previous Managers since the War:* Ted Vizard, Stan Cullis, Andy Beattie, Ron Allen, Bill McGarry, Sammy Chung, John Barnwell, Ian Greaves.

*Address of the Club Shop or Boutique:* 'The Lair', Wolverhampton W FC, Molineux Grounds, Wolverhampton, West Midlands.

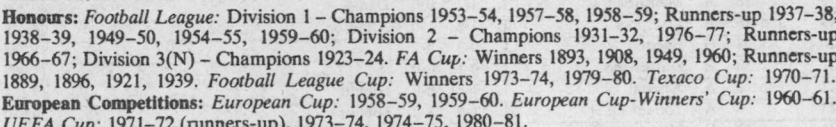

**Molineux Grounds, Wolverhampton WV1 4QR.** Telephone Admin office – Wolverhampton 712181; Ticket office – 711457/711432. *Telegraphic address:* 'Wanderers, Wolverhampton'. *Ground capacity:* 41,074. *Record attendance:* 61,315 v Liverpool, FA Cup 5th rd, 11 Feb, 1939. *Record receipts:* £80,839 v Swindon T, League Cup semi-final, 12 Feb, 1980. *Pitch measurements:* 115yd×72yd.
*How to get there:* The ground is within easy walking distance of both Wolverhampton High Level railway station and the town centre. For this reason the local bus company does not operate special services on match days.
*Match tickets:* Seats are bookable by post one month before the match.
*Car parking:* Parking is available around 'The West Park', in various side streets, and at the Molineux Hotel.
*Entertainments/catering facilities:* Entertainment at the Wolves Sporting Club a few yards from the ground. Bars are provided all around the ground.
*Club shop:* The club shop is situated on the official car park at the ground.
*Handbooks/programmes:* No handbook. Programmes available on subscription.
*Extra information:* Wolves scored over 100 First Division goals in four successive seasons (1957–58 to 1960–61).
*Club Colours:* Old gold shirts, black collar and cuffs, black shorts, old gold stockings.
*Change Colours:* White shirts, white shorts, white stockings.
*Club Captain:* John Richards.
*Club Nickname:* Wolves.

## WOLVERHAMPTON WANDERERS 1981–82 LEAGUE RECORD

| Match No. | Date | Venue | Opponents | Result | | H/T Score | Goalscorers | Attendance |
|---|---|---|---|---|---|---|---|---|
| 1 | Aug 29 | H | Liverpool | W | 1-0 | 0-0 | Matthews | 28,001 |
| 2 | Sept 1 | A | Southampton | L | 1-4 | 0-1 | Clarke | 21,315 |
| 3 | 5 | A | Leeds U | L | 0-3 | 0-1 | | 20,216 |
| 4 | 12 | H | Tottenham H | L | 0-1 | 0-0 | | 18,675 |
| 5 | 19 | A | Sunderland | D | 0-0 | 0-0 | | 22,061 |
| 6 | 22 | H | Brighton & HA | L | 0-1 | 0-1 | | 12,586 |
| 7 | 26 | H | Notts Co | W | 3-2 | 1-1 | Eves 2, Daniel | 11,594 |
| 8 | Oct 3 | A | Manchester U | L | 0-5 | 0-2 | | 46,837 |
| 9 | 10 | A | Ipswich T | L | 0-1 | 0-1 | | 20,498 |
| 10 | 17 | H | Middlesbrough | D | 0-0 | 0-0 | | 12,061 |
| 11 | 24 | H | Aston Villa | L | 0-3 | 0-2 | | 19,942 |
| 12 | 31 | A | Swansea C | D | 0-0 | 0-0 | | 17,750 |
| 13 | Nov 7 | H | Coventry C | W | 1-0 | 0-0 | Eves | 13,193 |
| 14 | 21 | A | Birmingham C | W | 3-0 | 1-0 | Richards, Gray, Brazier | 18,223 |
| 15 | 24 | H | Southampton | D | 0-0 | 0-0 | | 15,438 |
| 16 | 28 | H | Stoke C | W | 2-0 | 1-0 | Palmer (pen), Matthews | 15,314 |
| 17 | Dec 5 | A | WBA | L | 0-3 | 0-0 | | 22,378 |
| 18 | 28 | A | Manchester C | L | 1-2 | 0-0 | Daniel | 40,298 |
| 19 | Jan 16 | A | Liverpool | L | 1-2 | 1-0 | Atkinson | 26,438 |
| 20 | 23 | H | Everton | L | 0-3 | 0-2 | | 11,784 |
| 21 | 30 | H | Sunderland | L | 0-1 | 0-0 | | 11,099 |
| 22 | Feb 2 | A | Arsenal | L | 1-2 | 0-0 | Hibbitt | 15,163 |
| 23 | 6 | A | Tottenham H | L | 1-6 | 1-2 | Hibbitt | 29,960 |
| 24 | 13 | H | Manchester U | L | 0-1 | 0-1 | | 22,481 |
| 25 | 16 | H | Nottingham F | D | 0-0 | 0-0 | | 11,195 |
| 26 | 20 | A | Notts Co | L | 0-4 | 0-1 | | 10,173 |
| 27 | 27 | H | Ipswich T | W | 2-1 | 2-1 | Clarke 2 | 12,439 |
| 28 | Mar 6 | A | Middlesbrough | D | 0-0 | 0-0 | | 10,155 |
| 29 | 13 | A | Aston Villa | L | 1-3 | 1-2 | Clarke | 26,790 |
| 30 | 16 | H | Leeds U | W | 1-0 | 1-0 | Eves | 11,729 |
| 31 | 20 | H | Swansea C | L | 0-1 | 0-1 | | 14,158 |
| 32 | 27 | A | Coventry C | D | 0-0 | 0-0 | | 11,514 |
| 33 | Apr 3 | H | Arsenal | D | 1-1 | 0-0 | Eves | 11,532 |
| 34 | 6 | A | West Ham U | L | 1-3 | 1-0 | Richards | 20,651 |
| 35 | 10 | A | Nottingham F | W | 1-0 | 0-0 | Gray | 15,691 |
| 36 | 12 | H | Manchester C | W | 4-1 | 4-0 | Gray, Clarke, Hibbitt, Eves | 14,891 |
| 37 | 17 | H | Birmingham C | D | 1-1 | 0-0 | Gray | 18,964 |
| 38 | 24 | A | Stoke C | L | 1-2 | 1-1 | Hibbitt | 13,797 |
| 39 | May 1 | H | WBA | L | 1-2 | 0-1 | Gray | 19,813 |
| 40 | 4 | A | Brighton & HA | L | 0-2 | 0-2 | | 10,429 |
| 41 | 8 | A | Everton | D | 1-1 | 1-1 | Clarke | 20,124 |
| 42 | 15 | H | West Ham U | W | 2-1 | 2-1 | Eves, Richards | 13,283 |

**Final League Position: 21**

**Goalscorers**

*League* (32): Eves 7, Clarke 6, Gray 5, Hibbitt 4, Richards 3, Daniel 2, Matthews 2, Atkinson 1, Brazier 1, Palmer 1 (pen).
*League Cup* (3): Gallagher 1, Gray 1, Richards 1.
*FA Cup* (1): Gray 1.

| **League Cup** | Second Round | Aston Villa (a) | 2-3 |
|---|---|---|---|
| | | (h) | 1-2 |
| **FA Cup** | Third Round | Leeds U (h) | 1-3 |

| Bradshaw | Palmer | Parkin | Daniel | Gallagher | Villazan | Birch | Hibbitt | Gray | Clarke | Matthews | Bell | Richards | Humphrey | Berry | Coy | Carr | Eves | Atkinson | Brazier | Hollifield | Teasdale | Moss | Pender | Kernan | Match No. |
|---|---|---|---|---|---|---|---|---|---|---|---|---|---|---|---|---|---|---|---|---|---|---|---|---|---|
| 1 | 2 | 3 | 4 | 5 | 6 | 7 | 8* | 9 | 10 | 11 | 12 |  |  |  |  |  |  |  |  |  |  |  |  |  | 1 |
| 1 | 2 | 3 | 4 | 5 | 6 | 7* | 8 | 9 | 10 | 11 |  | 12 |  |  |  |  |  |  |  |  |  |  |  |  | 2 |
| 1 | 2 | 3 | 4 | 5* | 6 | 7 | 8 | 9 | 10 | 11 |  | 12 |  |  |  |  |  |  |  |  |  |  |  |  | 3 |
| 1 | 12 | 3 | 4* |  | 11 | 7 |  | 9 | 8 | 2 | 5 | 6 | 10 |  |  |  |  |  |  |  |  |  |  |  | 4 |
| 1 |  | 3 | 4 | 5 |  | 11 | 7 |  | 8 | 10* | 9 | 12 | 2 | 6 |  |  |  |  |  |  |  |  |  |  | 5 |
| 1 |  | 3 | 4 | 5 |  | 7 | 8 | 9 | 10 | 11* |  | 12 | 2 | 6 |  |  |  |  |  |  |  |  |  |  | 6 |
| 1 | 2 | 3 | 4 | 5 |  | 8 | 7* | 9 |  | 11 |  | 12 |  |  | 6 |  |  | 10 |  |  |  |  |  |  | 7 |
| 1 | 2 | 3 | 4 | 5 |  | 8* | 7 | 9 |  | 11 |  | 10 |  |  | 6 |  |  | 12 |  |  |  |  |  |  | 8 |
| 1 | 2 | 3 |  | 5 | 6 |  | 7 | 9 | 8 | 11* |  | 10 |  |  |  |  |  | 4 | 12 |  |  |  |  |  | 9 |
| 1 | 2 | 3 |  | 5 | 6 | 11 | 7 | 9 | 12 | 4 |  | 10 |  |  | 8* |  |  |  |  |  |  |  |  |  | 10 |
| 1 | 2 | 3 |  | 5 | 6 | 7 |  | 8 | 4 |  |  | 11 | 9 |  |  |  |  | 10 |  |  |  |  |  |  | 11 |
| 1 | 2 | 3 | 4 |  |  | 7* |  | 12 | 11 |  |  | 10 |  |  | 6 |  | 9 | 8 | 5 |  |  |  |  |  | 12 |
| 1 | 2 | 3 | 8 |  |  | 7 |  | 4 |  | 10 |  | 5 |  |  |  |  | 9 | 11 | 6 |  |  |  |  |  | 13 |
| 1 | 2 | 3 | 4 | 5 |  |  | 9 |  | 7 | 10 |  | 6 |  |  | 11 |  | 8 |  |  |  |  |  |  |  | 14 |
| 1 | 2 | 3 | 4 | 5 | 12 |  | 9 |  | 7* | 10 |  | 6 |  |  | 8 |  | 11 |  |  |  |  |  |  |  | 15 |
| 1 | 2 | 3 | 4 | 5 |  |  | 9 |  | 7 | 10 |  | 6 |  |  | 8 |  | 11 |  |  |  |  |  |  |  | 16 |
| 1 | 2 |  | 4 | 5 | 12 |  | 9 |  | 7 |  |  | 10 | 3* | 6 | 8 |  | 11 |  |  |  |  |  |  |  | 17 |
| 1 | 2 | 3 | 4 | 5 |  | 7* |  | 9 | 12 | 10 |  | 6 |  |  | 8 |  | 11 |  |  |  |  |  |  |  | 18 |
| 1 | 2 | 3 | 4 | 5 |  |  | 9 | 8 | 7 | 10 |  | 6 |  |  |  |  | 11 |  |  |  |  |  |  |  | 19 |
| 1 | 2 |  | 4 | 5 |  | 8 |  | 7 |  | 10 |  | 6* |  |  |  |  | 12 | 3 | 9 | 11 |  |  |  |  | 20 |
| 1 | 2 |  |  | 5* | 12 | 7 | 9 |  | 10 | 3 |  | 6 |  |  |  |  | 8 | 4 | 11 |  |  |  |  |  | 21 |
| 1 | 2 |  |  | 5 | 12 | 7 | 9 |  | 10 | 3 |  | 6 |  |  |  |  | 8* | 4 | 11 |  |  |  |  |  | 22 |
| 1 | 2 |  |  | 5 |  | 7 | 9 | 12 | 10 | 3 |  | 6 |  |  |  |  | 8 | 4 | 11* |  |  |  |  |  | 23 |
| 1 | 2 | 8 |  |  |  | 7 | 9 | 12 | 10 | 3 |  | 6 |  |  |  | 5 | 11* | 4 |  |  |  |  |  |  | 24 |
| 1 | 2 | 8 | 5 |  |  | 7 | 9 | 11 |  | 10 |  | 3 |  |  | 6 |  | 4 |  |  |  |  |  |  |  | 25 |
| 1 | 2 | 8 | 5 |  |  | 7 | 9 | 11 |  | 10 |  | 3 |  |  | 6 |  |  | 12 | 4* |  |  |  |  |  | 26 |
| 1 | 2 | 3 |  | 5 |  | 7 | 9 | 11 | 4 |  |  | 10 |  |  |  | 6 | 8 |  |  |  |  |  |  |  | 27 |
| 1 | 2 | 3 |  | 5 |  | 7 | 9 | 11 | 4 |  |  | 10 |  |  |  | 6 | 8 |  |  |  |  |  |  |  | 28 |
| 1 | 2 | 3 |  | 5 | 4 |  | 7 |  | 11 | 12 | 10* |  |  |  |  | 6 | 8 | 9 |  |  |  |  |  |  | 29 |
| 1 |  | 3 |  | 5 | 4 |  | 7 |  | 11 | 10 |  | 2 |  |  |  | 6 | 8 | 9 |  |  |  |  |  |  | 30 |
| 1 |  | 3 |  |  |  | 7 | 9 | 11 | 4 |  |  | 2 |  |  |  | 6 | 8 | 10 |  |  |  |  | 5 |  | 31 |
| 1 |  | 3 |  |  |  | 7 | 9 |  | 4 |  |  | 2 |  |  |  | 6 | 8 | 10 |  |  |  |  | 5 | 11 | 32 |
| 1 |  | 3 |  |  |  | 7 |  | 11 | 4 | 9 |  | 2 |  |  |  | 6 | 8 | 10 |  |  |  |  | 5 |  | 33 |
| 1 |  | 3 |  |  |  | 7 |  | 11 | 4 | 9 |  | 2 |  |  |  | 6 | 8 | 10 |  |  |  |  | 5 |  | 34 |
| 1 |  | 3 |  | 4* |  | 7 | 12 | 11 |  | 9 |  | 2 |  |  |  | 6 | 8 | 10 |  |  |  |  | 5 |  | 35 |
| 1 |  |  |  |  |  | 7 | 9 | 11 |  | 10 |  | 2 |  |  |  | 6 | 8 | 4 | 3 |  |  |  | 5 |  | 36 |
| 1 |  | 3 |  |  |  | 7 | 9 | 11 |  | 10 |  | 2 |  |  |  | 6 | 8 | 4 |  |  |  |  | 5 |  | 37 |
| 1 |  |  |  |  |  | 7 | 9 | 11 | 12 | 10* |  | 2 | 5 | 6 | 8 | 4 |  |  | 3 |  |  |  |  |  | 38 |
| 1 |  |  |  |  |  | 7 | 9 | 11 | 10 |  |  | 2 | 5 | 6 | 8 | 4 |  |  | 3 |  |  |  |  |  | 39 |
| 1 |  |  |  |  |  | 7 |  | 11 | 9 | 10 |  | 2 |  |  |  | 6 | 8 | 4 | 12 | 3* |  |  | 5 |  | 40 |
| 1 |  | 5 |  |  |  | 7 |  | 11 | 9 | 10 |  | 2 |  |  |  | 6 | 8 | 4 | 3 |  |  |  |  |  | 41 |
| 1 |  | 5 |  |  |  | 7 |  | 11 | 9 | 10 |  | 2 |  |  |  | 6 | 8 | 4 | 3 |  |  |  |  |  | 42 |
| 42 | 33 | 21 | 20 | 28 | 9 | 13 | 33 | 28 | 25 | 29 | 3 | 30 | 23 | 20 | 20 | 19 | 26 | 13 | 11 | 5 | 1 | 1 | 8 | 1 | |

Substitute appearances:
+ 1s (Bradshaw); + 2s (Gallagher); + 2s (Villazan); + 1s (Hibbitt); + 4s (Gray); + 3s (Clarke); + 2s (Matthews); + 4s (Bell); + 1s; + 3s; + 1s

## WOLVERHAMPTON WANDERERS

| | Ht | Wt | Birthplace | Clubs | League App. | League Gls |
|---|---|---|---|---|---|---|
| **Goalkeepers** | | | | | | |
| Paul Bradshaw | 6 2½ | 12 1 | Altrincham | Blackburn R | 78 | — |
| | | | | Wolverhampton W | 190 | — |
| Mick Kearns* | 6 4½ | 14 0 | Banbury | Oxford U | 67 | — |
| (Eire) | | | | Plymouth Arg (on loan) | 1 | — |
| | | | | Charlton Ath (on loan) | 4 | — |
| | | | | Walsall | 249 | — |
| | | | | Wolverhampton W | 9 | — |
| Stephen Lowe* | 6 0 | 11 13 | West Bromwich | Aston V | — | — |
| | | | | Wolverhampton W | — | — |
| **Defenders** | | | | | | |
| Geoff Palmer | 5 10 | 10 5 | Cannock | Wolverhampton W | 315 | 7 |
| George Berry* | 6 0¾ | 11 12 | Germany | Ipswich T | — | — |
| (Wales) | | | | Wolverhampton W | 124 | 4 |
| Colin Brazier | 6 1½ | 10 13 | Birmingham | Wolverhampton W | 78 | 2 |
| (Contract cancelled April 1982) | | | | | | |
| Peter Daniel | 5 8½ | 11 3 | Hull | Hull C | 113 | 9 |
| | | | | Wolverhampton W | 125 | 13 |
| John Humphrey | 5 9½ | 10 13 | Wembley | Wolverhampton W | 37 | — |
| Robert Coy | 5 11 | 11 12 | Birmingham | Wolverhampton W | 20 | — |
| Rafael Villazan* | 5 10 | 12 3 | Montevideo | Huelva | (not known) | |
| (Uruguay) | | | | Wolverhampton W | 23 | — |
| Ian Ross | 5 10 | 12 0 | Glasgow | Liverpool | 46 | 2 |
| (Contract cancelled Aug 1981) | | | | Aston V | 175 | 3 |
| | | | | Peterborough U (on loan) | 21 | — |
| | | | | Northampton T (on loan) | 2 | — |
| | | | | Notts Co (on loan) | 4 | 1 |
| | | | | Peterborough U | 91 | 1 |
| | | | | Wolverhampton W | — | — |
| Mike Hollifield | 5 10½ | 11 0 | Middlesbrough | Wolverhampton W | 21 | — |
| Joe Gallagher | 6 1 | 12 10 | Liverpool | Birmingham C | 286 | 17 |
| | | | | Wolverhampton W | 28 | — |
| John Pender | 6 0½ | 12 3 | Luton | Wolverhampton W | 8 | — |
| **Midfield** | | | | | | |
| Willie Carr | 5 6¾ | 10 7½ | Glasgow | Coventry C | 252 | 32 |
| (Scotland) | | | | Wolverhampton W | 237 | 21 |
| Kenny Hibbitt | 5 10 | 12 0 | Bradford | Bradford PA | 15 | — |
| | | | | Wolverhampton W | 411 | 86 |
| Hugh Atkinson | 6 0 | 11 9 | Dublin | Wolverhampton W | 46 | 3 |
| Anthony Kernan | 5 8 | 9 13 | Letterkenny, | Wolverhampton W | 1 | — |
| | | | Co Donegal | | | |
| Dale Rudge | 5 8 | 10 6 | Wolverhampton | Wolverhampton W | — | — |
| David Beattie | | | Belfast | Wolverhampton W | — | — |
| **Forwards** | | | | | | |
| Michael Matthews | 5 7½ | 10 12 | Hull | Wolverhampton W | 33 | 2 |
| John Richards | 5 9 | 11 1 | Warrington | Wolverhampton W | 381 | 144 |
| (England) | | | | | | |
| Mel Eves | 5 10½ | 10 1 | Wednesbury | Wolverhampton W | 125 | 23 |
| Wayne Clarke | 5 11¼ | 10 6¼ | Wolverhampton | Wolverhampton W | 78 | 12 |
| Craig Moss* | 5 7½ | 10 8 | Birmingham | Wolverhampton W | 4 | — |
| Andy Gray | 5 11 | 11 7 | Glasgow | Dundee U | 62 | 36 |
| (Scotland) | | | | Aston V | 113 | 54 |
| | | | | Wolverhampton W | 91 | 26 |
| William MacLaren | | | Inverness | Wolverhampton W | — | — |

Free transfer: Peter Knowles*.

# WREXHAM

# Division 3

*President:* F. Wellum.

*Chairman:* R. E. A. Clark.

*Vice-Chairman:* W. P. Griffiths.

*Directors:* F. J. Tomlinson, G. Mytton, W. Jones, N. Dickens, S. Freudmann, B. Williams.

*Manager:* Bobby Roberts.   *Asst Manager:*

*General Secretary:* C. N. Wilson FAAI.

*Year Formed:* 1873 (oldest Club in Wales).

*Turned Professional:* 1912.   *Limited Company:* 1912.

*Previous Ground:* Acton Park.

**Football League Record:**
1921 Original Members of Division 3(N); 1958–60 Division 3; 1960–62 Division 4; 1962–64 Division 3; 1964–70 Division 4; 1970–78 Division 3; 1978–82 Division 2; 1982– Division 3.

**Honours:** *Football League:* Division 2 best season: 15th, 1978–79; Division 3 – Champions 1977–78; Division 3(N) – Runners-up 1932–33; Division 4 – Runners-up 1969–70. *FA Cup* best season: 6th rd, 1973–74, 1977–78. *Football League Cup* best season: 5th rd, 1961, 1978. *Welsh Cup:* Winners 21 times.

**European Competition:** *European Cup-Winners' Cup:* 1972–73, 1975–76, 1978–79, 1979–80.

*Record Victory:* 10-1 v Hartlepools U, Division 4, 3 Mar, 1962.

*Record Defeat:* 0-9 v Brentford, Division 3, 15 Oct, 1963.

*Most League Points:* 61, Division 4, 1969–70, Division 3, 1977–78.

*Most League Goals:* 106, Division 3(N), 1932–33.

*Highest League Scorer in Season:* Tom Bamford, 44, Division 3(N), 1933–34.

*Most League Goals in Total Aggregate:* Tom Bamford, 175, 1928–34.

*Most Capped Player:* Dai Davies, 28 (51), Wales.

*Most League Appearances:* Arfon Griffiths, 592, 1959–61; 1962–79.

*Record Transfer Fee Received:* £300,000 from Manchester U for Mickey Thomas, Nov 1978 and £300,000 from Manchester C for Bobby Shinton, July 1979.

*Record Transfer Fee Paid:* £210,000 to Liverpool for Joey Jones, Oct 1978.

*Previous Managers since the War:* Tom Williams, Les McDowell, Peter Jackson, Cliff Lloyd, John Love, Bill Morris, Ken Barnes, Bill Morris, Jack Rowley, Alvan Williams, John Neal, Arfon Griffiths MBE, Mel Sutton.

*Address of Supporters Club:* Secretary, Lyn Williams, c/o Centre Spot, Mold Rd, Wrexham.

---

**Racecourse Ground, Mold Road, Wrexham.** Telephone Wrexham (0978) 262129. *Telegraphic address:* 'Football, Wrexham'. *Ground capacity:* 30,000 (18,000 covered). *Record attendance:* 34,445 v Manchester U, FA Cup 4th rd, 26 Jan, 1957. *Record receipts:* £25,107 v Anderlecht, European Cup-Winners' Cup quarter-final, 17 Mar, 1976. *Pitch measurements:* 117yd×75yd.

*How to get there:* Wrexham General railway station is only 200 yards from the ground. Trains run from Chester and Shrewsbury. Bus services from outlying districts to town.

*Match tickets:* Stand tickets bookable in advance.

*Car parking:* Berse Field Main Car Park plus parking grounds at St Marks, Bodhyfryd Square, Eagles Meadows, Old Guild Hall, Hill Street, Holt Street, and Town Hill, Hill Street.

*Entertainments/catering facilities:* A social club and four catering kiosks at the ground.

*Club shop:* Situated on Mold Road.

*Handbooks/programmes:* Programmes available on subscription.

*Extra information:* Season tickets available for all parts of the ground and all stands.

*Club Colours:* Red shirts with white facings, white shorts with red stripe, red stockings.

*Change Colours:* White shirts, red trim, black shorts, black stockings with white/red tops.

*Club Captain:* Dixie McNeil.

*Club Nickname:* The Robins.

## WREXHAM 1981–82 LEAGUE RECORD

| Match No. | Date | Venue | Opponents | Result | H/T Score | Goalscorers | Attendance |
|---|---|---|---|---|---|---|---|
| 1 | Aug 29 | H | QPR | L 1-3 | 1-2 | Edwards | 4661 |
| 2 | Sept 5 | A | Leicester C | L 0-1 | 0-0 | | 12,905 |
| 3 | 12 | H | Norwich C | L 2-3 | 0-1 | Vinter, McNeil (pen) | 4007 |
| 4 | 19 | A | Orient | D 0-0 | 0-0 | | 2899 |
| 5 | 22 | H | Watford | L 0-1 | 0-1 | | 3911 |
| 6 | 26 | H | Charlton Ath | W 1-0 | 0-0 | McNeil (pen) | 3076 |
| 7 | Oct 3 | A | Sheffield W | W 3-0 | 1-0 | McNeil 2 (1 pen), Hunt | 18,526 |
| 8 | 10 | A | Chelsea | L 0-2 | 0-0 | | 14,170 |
| 9 | 17 | H | Crystal Palace | L 0-1 | 0-0 | | 4795 |
| 10 | 24 | H | Luton T | L 0-2 | 0-2 | | 4069 |
| 11 | 31 | A | Blackburn R | D 0-0 | 0-0 | | 8159 |
| 12 | Nov 4 | A | Cardiff C | L 2-3 | 1-1 | Maddy (og), Carrodus | 4625 |
| 13 | 7 | H | Grimsby T | W 2-0 | 0-0 | McNeil 2 (1 pen) | 3351 |
| 14 | 14 | A | Derby Co | L 1-2 | 0-1 | Edwards | 10,956 |
| 15 | 21 | A | Barnsley | D 2-2 | 1-2 | Buxton, Carrodus | 14,544 |
| 16 | 24 | H | Cardiff C | W 3-1 | 0-0 | Hunt, Buxton 2 | 3635 |
| 17 | 28 | H | Oldham Ath | L 0-3 | 0-2 | | 4330 |
| 18 | Dec 5 | A | Cambridge U | W 3-2 | 0-2 | Edwards 2, Vinter | 3172 |
| 19 | Jan 16 | A | QPR | D 1-1 | 1-0 | Edwards | 10,066 |
| 20 | 30 | H | Orient | L 0-1 | 0-0 | | 4221 |
| 21 | Feb 6 | A | Norwich C | L 0-4 | 0-2 | | 12,300 |
| 22 | 13 | H | Sheffield W | L 0-1 | 0-0 | | 4907 |
| 23 | 20 | A | Charlton Ath | L 0-1 | 0-0 | | 4561 |
| 24 | 23 | A | Rotherham U | L 0-2 | 0-0 | | 9158 |
| 25 | 27 | H | Chelsea | W 1-0 | 0-0 | Carrodus | 3935 |
| 26 | Mar 9 | H | Bolton W | W 2-1 | 2-1 | Edwards 2 | 3202 |
| 27 | 12 | A | Luton T | D 0-0 | 0-0 | | 10,880 |
| 28 | 16 | A | Shrewsbury T | D 1-1 | 0-1 | Edwards | 4741 |
| 29 | 20 | H | Blackburn R | W 1-0 | 1-0 | Leman | 5780 |
| 30 | 27 | A | Grimsby T | D 1-1 | 0-0 | Fox | 6216 |
| 31 | Apr 3 | H | Derby Co | D 1-1 | 0-1 | McNeil | 4073 |
| 32 | 6 | H | Newcastle U | W 4-2 | 1-1 | Edwards 2, McNeil, Ronson | 4517 |
| 33 | 10 | A | Bolton W | L 0-2 | 0-0 | | 6221 |
| 34 | 12 | H | Shrewsbury T | W 1-0 | 0-0 | Carrodus | 6506 |
| 35 | 17 | H | Barnsley | D 0-0 | 0-0 | | 4860 |
| 36 | 20 | H | Leicester C | D 0-0 | 0-0 | | 4913 |
| 37 | 24 | A | Oldham Ath | L 1-2 | 0-0 | McNeil | 3755 |
| 38 | May 1 | H | Cambridge U | D 0-0 | 0-0 | | 3351 |
| 39 | 4 | A | Watford | L 0-2 | 0-1 | | 20,028 |
| 40 | 8 | A | Newcastle U | L 2-4 | 0-2 | Edwards, Hill | 9447 |
| 41 | 11 | A | Crystal Palace | L 1-2 | 0-2 | Bater (pen) | 7272 |
| 42 | 15 | H | Rotherham U | W 3-2 | 1-2 | Vinter 3 | 3350 |

**Final League Position: 21**

### Goalscorers

*League* (40): Edwards 11, McNeil 9 (4 pens), Vinter 5, Carrodus 4, Buxton 3, Hunt 2, Bater 1 (pen), Fox 1, Hill 1, Leman 1, Ronson 1, own goal 1.
*League Cup* (7): Vinter 3, Edwards 2, Davis 1, Hunt 1.
*FA Cup* (5): McNeil 2, Vinter 2, Dowman 1.

| | | | |
|---|---|---|---|
| League Cup | First Round | Swindon T (h) | 3-2 |
| | | (a) | 2-0 |
| | Second Round | Luton T (a) | 2-0 |
| | | (h) | 0-1 |
| | Third Round | Tottenham H (a) | 0-2 |
| FA Cup | Third Round | Nottingham F (a) | 3-1 |
| | Fourth Round | Chelsea (a) | 0-0 |
| | | (h) | 1-1 |
| | | (h) | 1-2 |

| Niedzwiecki | Hill | Jones J. | Davis | Cegielski | Cartwright | Fox | McNeil | Edwards | Vinter | Carrodus | Buxton | Dowman | Hunt | Bater | Ronson | Jones S. | Leman | Arkwright | Match No. |
|---|---|---|---|---|---|---|---|---|---|---|---|---|---|---|---|---|---|---|---|
| 1 | 2 | 3 | 4 | 5 | 6* | 7 | 8 | 9 | 10 | 11 | 12 |  |  |  |  |  |  |  | 1 |
| 1 | 6 | 3 | 4 | 5 |  | 7 | 8 | 9 |  | 11 | 10* | 2 | 12 |  |  |  |  |  | 2 |
| 1 | 6* | 2 |  | 5 |  | 7 | 8 | 9 | 10 | 11 |  | 4 | 12 | 3 |  |  |  |  | 3 |
| 1 | 6 | 2 |  | 5 |  | 7 |  | 9 | 10 | 11 |  | 4 | 8 | 3 |  |  |  |  | 4 |
| 1 | 6 | 2 |  | 5 |  | 7 |  | 9 | 10 | 11 |  | 3 | 8 | 4 |  |  |  |  | 5 |
| 1 |  | 2 |  | 5 |  | 7 | 8 | 9 | 10 | 11 |  | 4 |  | 6 | 3 |  |  |  | 6 |
| 1 |  | 2 |  | 5 |  | 7 | 8 | 9 | 10 | 11 |  | 4 |  | 6 | 3 |  |  |  | 7 |
| 1 |  | 2 |  | 5 |  | 7* | 8 | 9 | 10 | 11 |  | 4 |  | 6 | 3 | 12 |  |  | 8 |
| 1 |  | 2 |  | 5 |  | 7 | 8 | 9 | 10 | 11 |  | 4 |  | 3 | 6 |  |  |  | 9 |
| 1 |  | 2 |  | 5 |  | 7 | 8 | 9 | 10* | 11 |  | 4 | 12 | 3 | 6 |  |  |  | 10 |
| 1 |  | 2 |  | 5 |  |  | 8 | 9 | 10 | 11 |  | 4 | 7 | 3 | 6 |  |  |  | 11 |
| 1 |  | 2 |  | 5 |  |  | 8 | 9 | 10 | 11 |  | 4 | 7 | 3 | 6 |  |  |  | 12 |
| 1 |  | 2 |  | 5 |  |  | 8* | 9 | 10 | 11 | 12 | 4 | 7 | 3 | 6 |  |  |  | 13 |
| 1 |  | 2 |  | 5 |  |  | 8 | 9 | 10 | 11 |  | 4 | 7 | 3 | 6 |  |  |  | 14 |
| 1 | 2 | 3*12 |  | 5 |  | 7 |  |  | 10 | 11 |  | 4 | 8 |  | 6 | 9 |  |  | 15 |
| 1 | 3 | 4 | 2 |  |  | 7 |  | 9 | 10 | 11 |  | 5 | 8 |  | 6 |  |  |  | 16 |
| 1 | 12 | 4 | 3* |  |  | 7 |  | 9 | 10 | 11 |  | 5 | 8 | 2 | 6 |  |  |  | 17 |
| 1 | 8 | 2 |  | 5 |  | 7 |  | 9 | 10 | 11 |  | 4 |  | 3 | 6 |  |  |  | 18 |
| 1 |  | 2 |  | 5 |  | 7 | 8 | 9 | 10 | 11 |  | 4 |  | 3 | 6 |  |  |  | 19 |
| 1 |  | 2 |  | 5 |  | 7 | 8 | 9 | 10 | 11* |  | 4 | 12 | 3 | 6 |  |  |  | 20 |
| 1 |  | 2 |  | 5 |  | 7 | 8 | 9* | 10 | 11 |  | 4 | 12 | 3 | 6 |  |  |  | 21 |
| 1 | 2* | 3 |  | 5 |  | 7 |  | 9 | 10 | 11 |  | 4 | 8 |  | 6 |  | 12 |  | 22 |
| 1 | 12 | 2 |  | 5* |  | 7 |  |  | 10 | 11 |  | 4 | 8 | 3 | 9 |  | 6 |  | 23 |
| 1 | 8 | 2 | 4 |  | 12 | 7 |  | 9 | 10 | 11 |  | 5 |  | 3* | 6 |  |  |  | 24 |
| 1 | 12 | 2 | 4 |  |  |  | 8 | 9 | 10* | 11 |  | 5 |  | 3 | 6 |  | 7 |  | 25 |
| 1 |  | 2 | 4 | 5 |  | 10 | 8 | 9 |  | 11 |  |  |  | 3 | 6 |  | 7 |  | 26 |
| 1 |  | 2 |  | 5 |  | 9 | 8 |  | 10 | 11 |  | 4 |  | 3 | 6 |  | 7 |  | 27 |
| 1 |  | 2 |  | 5 |  | 10 | 8 | 9 |  | 11 |  | 4 |  | 3 | 6 |  | 7 |  | 28 |
| 1 |  | 2 |  | 5 |  | 10 | 8 | 9 |  | 11 |  | 4 |  | 3 | 6 |  | 7 |  | 29 |
| 1 |  | 2 | 4 |  |  | 10 | 8 | 9 |  | 11 | 12 | 5 |  | 3* | 6 |  | 7 |  | 30 |
| 1 |  | 2 | 4 |  |  | 10 | 8 | 9 |  | 11 |  | 5 |  | 3 | 6 |  | 7 |  | 31 |
| 1 |  | 2 | 4 |  |  | 10 | 8 | 9 |  | 11 |  | 5 |  | 3 | 6 |  | 7 |  | 32 |
| 1 |  | 2 | 4 |  |  | 10 | 8 | 9 |  | 11* | 12 | 5 |  | 3 | 6 |  | 7 |  | 33 |
| 1 |  | 2 | 4 |  |  | 10 | 8 | 9 |  | 11 |  | 5 |  | 3 | 6 |  | 7 |  | 34 |
| 1 |  | 2 | 4 |  |  | 10 | 8 | 9 |  | 11 | 12 | 5* |  | 3 |  |  | 7 | 6 | 35 |
| 1 |  | 2 | 4 |  |  | 9 | 8 |  | 10 | 11 |  | 5 |  | 3 | 6 |  |  | 7 | 36 |
| 1 |  | 2 |  | 5 |  | 10 | 8 | 9 |  | 11 |  | 4 |  | 3 | 6 |  | 7 |  | 37 |
| 1 |  | 2 | 4* |  |  | 10 | 8 | 9 |  | 11 | 12 | 5 |  | 3 | 6 |  | 7 |  | 38 |
| 1 |  | 2 | 4 |  |  | 10 | 8* | 9 |  | 11 | 12 | 5 |  | 3 | 6 |  | 7 |  | 39 |
| 1 | 2 | 3 | 4 |  |  |  | 8 | 9 | 10 | 11 | 12 | 5 |  |  | 6 |  |  | 7* | 40 |
| 1 | 8* | 2 | 4 |  |  | 10 |  | 9 |  | 11 | 12 | 5 |  | 3 | 6 |  | 7 |  | 41 |
| 1 | 8 | 2 | 4 |  |  | 10 |  | 9 |  | 11 |  | 5 |  | 3 | 6 |  | 7 |  | 42 |
| 42 | 18 | 35 | 13 | 34 | 4 | 38 | 33 | 28 | 24 | 41 | 7 | 40 | 15 | 36 | 31 | 2 | 17 | 4 |  |
| + | + | + | + |  |  | + | + |  | + |  |  |  |  | + | + |  |  |  |  |
| 2s | 1s | 1s | 1s |  |  | 1s | 6s |  | 2s |  |  |  |  | 4s |  |  | 1s | 2s |  |

# WREXHAM

| | Ht | Wt | Birthplace | Clubs | League App. | League Gls |
|---|---|---|---|---|---|---|
| **Goalkeepers** | | | | | | |
| Eddie Niedzwiecki | 6 0 | 11 0 | Wrexham | Wrexham | 69 | — |
| Stuart Parker | 6 1 | 12 9 | Winsford | Wrexham | — | — |
| **Defenders** | | | | | | |
| Gareth Davis | 5 10½ | 11 7 | Bangor | Wrexham | 484 | 9 |
| (Wales) | | | | | | |
| Alan Hill | 5 11 | 11 4 | Chester | Wrexham | 166 | 6 |
| Wayne Cegielski* | 6 0 | 12 0 | Bedwellty | Tottenham H | — | — |
| | | | | Northampton T (on loan) | 11 | — |
| | | | | Wrexham | 123 | — |
| Joey Jones | 5 10 | 11 7 | Llandudno | Wrexham | 98 | 2 |
| (Wales) | | | | Liverpool | 72 | 3 |
| | | | | Wrexham | 139 | 6 |
| Terry Darracott | 5 9 | 11 6 | Liverpool | Everton | 148 | — |
| (Contract cancelled June 1981) | | | | Wrexham | 22 | — |
| Steve Dowman | 5 11 | 12 4 | Manor Park | Colchester U | 154 | 21 |
| | | | | Wrexham | 44 | — |
| Phil Bater | 5 10½ | 12 12 | Cardiff | Bristol R | 212 | 2 |
| | | | | Wrexham | 36 | 1 |
| **Midfield** | | | | | | |
| Mel Sutton* | 5 10 | 10 10 | Birmingham | Cardiff C | 138 | 5 |
| | | | | Wrexham | 360 | 21 |
| Frank Carrodus* | 5 9 | 10 11 | Manchester | Manchester C | 42 | 1 |
| | | | | Aston V | 151 | 7 |
| | | | | Wrexham | 97 | 6 |
| Ian Arkwright | 5 8¼ | 10 8 | Shafton | Wolverhampton W | 4 | — |
| | | | | Wrexham | 31 | — |
| Simon Hunt | 5 6 | 10 1 | Chester | Wrexham | 19 | 2 |
| Billy Ronson | 5 6 | 9 9 | Fleetwood | Blackpool | 128 | 12 |
| | | | | Cardiff C | 90 | 4 |
| | | | | Wrexham | 32 | 1 |
| **Forwards** | | | | | | |
| Dixie McNeil | 5 10 | 11 12 | Melton | Leicester C | — | — |
| | | | Mowbray | Exeter C | 31 | 11 |
| | | | | Northampton T | 86 | 33 |
| | | | | Lincoln C | 97 | 53 |
| | | | | Hereford U | 129 | 85 |
| | | | | Wrexham | 160 | 53 |
| Steve Buxton | 5 5 | 9 8 | Birmingham | Wrexham | 50 | 8 |
| Steve Fox | 5 7¾ | 11 2 | Tamworth | Birmingham C | 29 | 1 |
| | | | | Wrexham | 136 | 10 |
| Ian Edwards* | 6 1 | 12 5 | Wrexham | WBA | 16 | 3 |
| (Wales) | | | | Chester | 104 | 36 |
| | | | | Wrexham | 75 | 20 |
| Mick Vinter | 5 9 | 11 0 | Boston | Notts Co | 166 | 53 |
| | | | | Wrexham | 102 | 25 |
| Steven Jones* | | | Wrexham | Wrexham | 5 | — |
| Mark Jones* | | | | Wrexham | — | — |

# YORK CITY

## Division 4

*President:* F. H. Magson.

*Chairman:* M. D. B. Sinclair.

*Directors:* D. M. Craig JP, BSC, FICE, FI, MUN E, FCI ARB, M CONS E, B. A. Houghton, R. B. Strachan MA, LLB, FCIS, C. Webb, E. B. Swallow.

*Player-Manager:* Denis Smith.

*Club Secretary:* Tom Hughes.

*Sales Executive:* S. B. Winship.

*Medical Officer:* Dr A. I. MacLeod.

*Year Formed:* 1922.   *Turned Professional:* 1922.

*Limited Company:* 1922.

*Previous Grounds:* 1922, Fulfordgate; 1932, Bootham Crescent.

**Football League Record:**
1929 Elected to Division 3(N); 1958–59 Division 4; 1959–60 Division 3; 1960–65 Division 4; 1965–66 Division 3; 1966–71 Division 4; 1971–74 Division 3; 1974–76 Division 2; 1976–77 Division 3; 1977– Division 4.

**Honours:** *Football League:* Division 2 best season: 15th, 1974–75; Division 3 – Promoted 1973–74 (3rd); Division 4 – Promoted 1958–59 (3rd), 1964–65 (3rd), 1970–71 (4th). *FA Cup:* semi-finals 1955, when in Division 3. *Football League Cup* best season: 5th rd, 1962.

*Record Victory:* 9-1 v Southport, Division 3(N), 2 Feb, 1957.

*Record Defeat:* 0-12 v Chester, Division 3(N), 1 Feb, 1936.

*Most League Points:* 62, Division 4, 1964–65.

*Most League Goals:* 92, Division 3(N), 1954–55.

*Highest League Scorer in Season:* Bill Fenton, 31, Division 3(N), 1951–52; Arthur Bottom, 31, Division 3(N), 1955–56.

*Most League Goals in Total Aggregate:* Norman Wilkinson, 125, 1954–66.

*Most Capped Player:* Peter Scott, 7 (10), Northern Ireland.

*Most League Appearances:* Barry Jackson, 481, 1958–70.

*Record Transfer Fee Received:* £100,000 from Carlisle U for Gordon Staniforth, Oct 1979.

*Record Transfer Fee Paid:* £18,000 to AFC Bournemouth for Micky Cave, August 1974.

*Previous Managers since the War:* Tom Mitchell, Dick Duckworth, Charlie Spencer, Jimmy McCormack, Sam Bartram, Tom Lockie, Joe Shaw, Tom Johnston, Wilf McGuinness, Charlie Wright, Barry Lyons.

*Address of Supporters Club:* G. J. Mortimer, Secretary, 2 Plantation Grove, Boroughbridge Road, York.

---

**Bootham Crescent, York.** Telephone: York 24447. *Telegraphic address:* 'City Football, York'. *Ground capacity:* 16,529. *Record attendance:* 28,123 v Huddersfield T, FA Cup 6th rd, 5 Mar, 1938. *Record receipts:* £9856 v Arsenal, FA Cup 3rd rd replay, 7 Jan, 1975. *Pitch measurements:* 115yd×75yd.

*How to get there:* Buses 2, 2a, and 8 every 10 minutes from York railway station to the ground.

*Match tickets:* On sale 14 days prior to match.

*Car parking:* Ample parking in side-streets.

*Entertainments/catering facilities:* Licensed Social Club open to members only. Three tea bars on the ground.

*Club shop:* Selling all types of souvenirs.

*Handbooks/programmes:* Programmes available on subscription, details available from the Secretary. Programme shop at the ground stocking a wide variety of English, Scottish and non-League programmes.

*Extra information:* One of only five Third Division clubs to reach the semi-finals of the FA Cup (in 1954–55).

*Club Colours:* Red shirts with white trim, navy blue shorts, white stockings.

*Change Colours:* Sky blue shirts, white shorts, sky blue stockings.

*Club Captain:* Malcolm Crosby.

*Player-coach:* Viv Busby.

*Youth team coach:* Barry Lyons.

*Physiotherapist:* John Simpson.

*Club Nickname:* Minster Men.

## YORK CITY 1981–82 LEAGUE RECORD

| Match No. | Date | Venue | Opponents | Result | H/T Score | Goalscorers | Atten-dance |
|---|---|---|---|---|---|---|---|
| 1 | Aug 29 | A | Tranmere R | W 2-0 | 1-0 | Walwyn, Hood | 1850 |
| 2 | Sept 4 | H | Northampton T | W 2-1 | 1-0 | Waldron, Walwyn | 2086 |
| 3 | 12 | A | Bradford C | L 2-6 | 1-3 | Walwyn, Byrne | 3601 |
| 4 | 18 | H | Hartlepool U | L 1-2 | 0-1 | Walwyn | 2244 |
| 5 | 22 | H | AFC Bournemouth | L 0-1 | 0-1 | | 2252 |
| 6 | 26 | A | Torquay U | L 2-3 | 2-2 | Walwyn, Pollard | 2853 |
| 7 | 29 | A | Aldershot | W 1-0 | 1-0 | Pollard | 2056 |
| 8 | Oct 3 | H | Sheffield U | L 3-4 | 2-2 | Walwyn, Ford, McDonald (pen) | 5557 |
| 9 | 9 | H | Darlington | D 2-2 | 2-1 | McDonald, Walwyn | 2407 |
| 10 | 16 | A | Colchester U | L 0-4 | 0-2 | | 3139 |
| 11 | 20 | H | Blackpool | L 0-4 | 0-2 | | 2657 |
| 12 | 24 | A | Peterborough U | W 1-0 | 0-0 | Walwyn | 4220 |
| 13 | 31 | H | Hereford U | L 3-4 | 1-2 | Pollard, Ford, Hedley | 1600 |
| 14 | Nov 3 | A | Hull C | L 0-2 | 0-1 | | 3340 |
| 15 | 7 | A | Scunthorpe U | W 3-0 | 2-0 | Ford, Walwyn 2 | 1622 |
| 16 | 14 | H | Wigan Ath | D 0-0 | 0-0 | | 2780 |
| 17 | 28 | A | Crewe Alex | D 1-1 | 0-0 | Walwyn | 1881 |
| 18 | Dec 5 | H | Stockport Co | D 2-2 | 2-2 | Walwyn, Kay | 1762 |
| 19 | Jan 23 | A | Tranmere R | L 1-3 | 0-0 | Senior | 1594 |
| 20 | 30 | A | Hartlepool U | L 2-3 | 0-0 | Crosby 2 | 2291 |
| 21 | Feb 2 | H | Bury | D 0-0 | 0-0 | | 1713 |
| 22 | 6 | H | Bradford C | L 0-3 | 0-2 | | 3093 |
| 23 | 9 | A | AFC Bournemouth | L 1-5 | 1-2 | Hood | 4373 |
| 24 | 13 | A | Sheffield U | L 0-4 | 0-3 | | 12,901 |
| 25 | 19 | H | Torquay U | D 1-1 | 1-1 | Kay | 1660 |
| 26 | 22 | H | Port Vale | W 2-0 | 1-0 | Ford, Hood (pen) | 1938 |
| 27 | 28 | A | Darlington | L 1-3 | 1-1 | Aitken | 3212 |
| 28 | Mar 5 | H | Colchester U | W 3-0 | 1-0 | Hood (pen), Walwyn 2 | 1854 |
| 29 | 10 | A | Blackpool | L 1-3 | 0-2 | Walwyn | 2164 |
| 30 | 13 | H | Peterborough U | W 4-3 | 2-2 | Kay 2, Laverick, Byrne | 2178 |
| 31 | 16 | H | Hull C | L 1-3 | 0-1 | Walwyn | 4771 |
| 32 | 20 | A | Hereford U | L 1-2 | 1-0 | Aitken | 2703 |
| 33 | 23 | A | Northampton T | L 0-5 | 0-3 | | 2452 |
| 34 | 26 | H | Scunthorpe U | W 3-1 | 1-0 | Walwyn, Hood (pen), Dall (og) | 2189 |
| 35 | Apr 2 | A | Wigan Ath | L 2-4 | 1-1 | Byrne, Smith | 6029 |
| 36 | 5 | A | Mansfield T | W 2-0 | 1-0 | Laverick, Ford | 2388 |
| 37 | 10 | H | Mansfield T | W 2-1 | 1-1 | Walwyn, Ford | 2155 |
| 38 | 12 | A | Rochdale | L 0-2 | 0-1 | | 1421 |
| 39 | 16 | A | Stockport Co | L 1-4 | 0-2 | Laverick | 1938 |
| 40 | 23 | H | Crewe Alex | W 6-0 | 3-0 | Laverick, Walwyn 2, Ford, Byrne, Hood (pen) | 1753 |
| 41 | 27 | H | Rochdale | L 1-2 | 0-1 | Walwyn | 2089 |
| 42 | May 1 | A | Port Vale | D 0-0 | 0-0 | | 1924 |
| 43 | 4 | H | Aldershot | W 4-0 | 1-0 | Walwyn, Ford, Byrne, Hood | 1571 |
| 44 | 7 | H | Halifax T | W 4-0 | 1-0 | Davison (og), Walwyn, Byrne, Hood (pen) | 2423 |
| 45 | 11 | A | Halifax T | D 0-0 | 0-0 | | 1903 |
| 46 | 15 | A | Bury | L 1-3 | 0-1 | Bradley (og) | 2002 |

**Final League Position: 17**

**Goalscorers**

*League* (69): Walwyn 23, Ford 8, Hood 8 (5 pens), Byrne 6, Kay 4, Laverick 4, Pollard 3, Aitken 2, Crosby 2, McDonald 2 (1 pen), Hedley 1, Senior 1, Smith D. 1, Waldron 1, own goals 3.
*League Cup* (1): Byrne 1.
*FA Cup* (5): Pollard 2, Walwyn 2, Ford 1.

| **League Cup** | First Round | Sheffield U (a) | 0-1 |
|---|---|---|---|
| | | (h) | 1-1 |
| **FA Cup** | First Round | Stafford R (a) | 2-1 |
| | Second Round | Altrincham (h) | 0-0 |
| | | (a) | 3-4 |

| Blackburn | Kay | Flood | Croft | Waldron | Dawson | Hood | Walwyn | McDonald | Ford | Byrne | Craig | McGhie | Senior | Pollard | Bentham | Smith M. | Stanley | Hedley | Crosby | Czuczman | Laverick | Astbury | Sweeney | Aitken | Fell | Smith D. | Match No. |
|---|---|---|---|---|---|---|---|---|---|---|---|---|---|---|---|---|---|---|---|---|---|---|---|---|---|---|---|
| 1 | 2 | 3 | 4 | 5 | 6 | 7 | 8 | 9 | 10 | 11 | | | | | | | | | | | | | | | | | 1 |
| 1 | 2 | 5 | 4 | 6 | 3 | 7 | 10 | 8 | 9 | 11* | 12 | | | | | | | | | | | | | | | | 2 |
| 1 | 2 | 3 | 5 | 11* | 6 | 4 | 9 | 10 | 7 | 8 | | 12 | | | | | | | | | | | | | | | 3 |
| 1 | 2 | 5 | | | 4 | 7 | 9 | 10 | 8 | 11 | 3 | 6* | 12 | | | | | | | | | | | | | | 4 |
| 1 | 2 | 5 | 4 | | 3 | 7 | 10 | | 11* | | 12 | | 6 | 8 | 9 | | | | | | | | | | | | 5 |
| 1 | 3 | | 5 | | 6 | 4 | 9 | 10 | 8 | | | | 2 | 7 | 11 | | | | | | | | | | | | 6 |
| 1 | 3 | | 5 | | 6 | 4 | 9 | 10 | 8 | | | | 2* | 7 | 11 | 12 | | | | | | | | | | | 7 |
| 1 | 2 | 3 | 5 | | 6 | 4 | 9 | 10 | 8 | | | | | 7 | 11 | | | | | | | | | | | | 8 |
| 1 | 2 | 3 | 5 | | 6 | 4 | 9 | 10 | 8 | | | | | 7 | 11 | | | | | | | | | | | | 9 |
| 1 | 3 | | 5 | | 6 | 2 | 9 | 10 | 8 | | | | | 7 | 11 | | | | | | 4 | | | | | | 10 |
| 1 | 3 | | 5 | | 6 | 2 | 9 | 10 | 12 | 8* | | | | 7 | 11 | | | | | | 4 | | | | | | 11 |
| 1 | 3 | | 5 | | 6 | 2 | 9 | | 8 | | | | | 7 | 11 | | | | | | 4 | | | | | | 12 |
| 1 | 3 | | 5 | | 6 | 2 | 8 | | 9* | 10 | | | 12 | 7 | 11 | | | | | | 4 | | | | | | 13 |
| 1 | 3 | | 5 | | 6 | 8 | | | 10 | | | 4 | 2 | 9 | 11 | | | 7 | | | | | | | | | 14 |
| 1 | 3 | | 5 | | 6 | 8 | 9 | | 10 | | | | 2 | 7 | 11 | | | | | | 4 | | | | | | 15 |
| 1 | 6 | 3 | | | 5 | 9 | 10 | | | | | | 2 | 7 | 11 | | | | 8 | | 4 | | | | | | 16 |
| 1 | 6 | 3 | | | 4 | 9 | 10 | | 12 | | | | 2 | 7 | 11* | | | | 8 | 5 | | | | | | | 17 |
| 1 | 6 | 3 | | | 4 | 9 | 10 | | | | | | 2 | 7 | 11 | | | | 8 | 5 | | | | | | | 18 |
| 1 | 3 | 6 | 5 | | | 9 | 10 | | | | | | 2 | 7 | 11 | | | | 8 | | 4 | | | | | | 19 |
| | 3 | | 5 | | 6 | 9 | 10 | | | | | | 2 | 7 | 11* | | 12 | | 8 | | 4 | 1 | | | | | 20 |
| | 3 | | 5 | | 6 | 9 | 10 | | | | | | 2 | 7 | 11 | | | | 8 | | 4 | 1 | | | | | 21 |
| | 3 | | 5 | | 6 | 9 | 10 | | 7 | | | | 2 | | 11 | | | | 8 | | 4 | 1 | | | | | 22 |
| | 3 | | 5 | | 6 | 9 | 10* | | 7 | | | | 2 | | 11 | | 12 | | 8 | | 4 | 1 | | | | | 23 |
| 1 | 3 | 12 | | | 6 | 4 | 9 | | 7 | 10 | 5 | | 2 | | 11 | | | | 8* | | | | | | | | 24 |
| 1 | 8 | | | | 3 | 4 | 9 | | 10 | | | | | | 11 | | 7 | | 5 | | | | 2 | 6 | | | 25 |
| 1 | 8 | | | | 3 | 4 | 9 | | 10 | | | | | | 7 | | | | 5 | 11 | | | 2 | 6 | | | 26 |
| 1 | 4 | | | | 3 | 2 | 9 | | 10 | | | | | | 7 | | | 8 | 5 | 11 | | | | 6 | | | 27 |
| 1 | | | | | 3 | 4 | 9 | | 10 | | | | | | | | | 8 | 5 | 11 | | | 2 | 6 | 7 | | 28 |
| 1 | 6 | | | | 3 | 4* | 9 | | 10 | 8 | 5 | | | | 12 | | 2 | | | 11 | | | | | | 7 | 29 |
| 1 | 7 | | | | 3 | 4 | 9 | | 10 | 8 | 5 | | | | | | | | | 11 | | 1 | 2* | 6 | 12 | | 30 |
| | 7* | | | | 3 | 4 | 9 | | 10 | 8 | | | | | | | | | | 11 | 1 | 2 | 6 | 12 | | 5 | 31 |
| | 7 | | | | 3 | 4 | 9 | | 10 | 8 | | | | | | | | | | 11 | 1 | 2 | 6 | | | 5 | 32 |
| | 7 | | | | 3 | 5 | 9 | | 8 | | | | | | | | | | 10 | 4*11 | | 1 | 2 | 6 | 12 | | 33 |
| | | | | | 3 | 7 | 11 | | 9 | 10* | | | | | | | | | 12 | 4 | 6 | 1 | 2 | 8 | | 5 | 34 |
| | | | | | 3 | 4 | 9 | | 7 | 10 | | | | | | | | | 12 | 6 | 11* | 1 | 2 | 8 | | 5 | 35 |
| | | | | | 3 | 4 | 9 | | 7 | 10 | | | | | | | | | 12 | 5*11 | | 1 | 2 | 8 | | 6 | 36 |
| | | | | | 3 | 4 | 9 | | 8 | | | | | | 7 | | | | 10 | 11 | 1 | 2 | 6 | | | 5 | 37 |
| | | | | | 3 | 4 | 9 | | 8 | | | | | | 7 | | | | 10 | 11 | 1 | 2 | 6 | | | 5 | 38 |
| | 4 | | | | 5 | 6 | 9 | | 10 | | | | 2 | 7 | 3 | | | | 8 | 11 | 1 | | | | | | 39 |
| 1 | 3 | | | | 2 | 4 | 9 | | 7 | 11 | | | | | | | | | 10 | 5 | 8 | | | 6 | | | 40 |
| 1 | 6 | | | | 2 | 4 | 9 | | 7 | 8 | | | | 12 | 3 | | | | 10 | 5*11 | | | | | | | 41 |
| 1 | 6 | 12 | | | 3 | 4 | 9 | | 10 | 8 | | | | 7 | | | | | 2* | 5 | 11 | | | | | | 42 |
| 1 | 3 | | | | 2 | 4 | 9 | | 10 | 8 | | | | 7 | | | | | | 5 | 11 | | | 6 | | | 43 |
| 1 | 3 | | | | 2 | 4 | 9 | | 10 | 8 | | | | 7 | | | | | | 5 | 11 | | | 6 | | | 44 |
| | 3 | | | | 2 | 4 | 9 | | 10 | 8 | | | | 7 | | | | | | 5 | 11 | 1 | | 6 | | | 45 |
| | 3* | | | | 2 | 4 | 9 | | 10 | 8 | | | | 7 | | | | 12 | | 5 | 11 | 1 | | 6 | | | 46 |
| 31 | 37 | 13 | 14 | 3 | 43 | 46 | 44 | 10 | 40 | 28 | 7 | 1 | 14 | 25 | 22 | 1 | 6 | 5 | 19 | 17 | 26 | 15 | 12 | 18 | 2 | 7 | |
| | | +2s | | | | | | | +1s | +1s | | | +2s | +3s | +1s | +1s | +3s | | +4s | | | | | +3s | | | |

# YORK CITY

| | Ht | Wt | Birthplace | Clubs | League App. | League Gls |
|---|---|---|---|---|---|---|
| **Goalkeepers** | | | | | | |
| Edwin Blackburn | 5 9 | 10 5 | Houghton-le-Spring | Hull C | 68 | — |
| | | | | York C | 76 | — |
| Mike Astbury | 6 0 | 12 8 | Leeds | York C | 16 | — |
| **Defenders** | | | | | | |
| Steve Faulkner | 6 3 | 13 5 | Sheffield | Sheffield U | 15 | — |
| (Contract cancelled May 1981) | | | | Stockport Co (on loan) | 4 | — |
| | | | | York C | 90 | 7 |
| Roy Kay* | 5 9 | 11 0 | Edinburgh | Hearts | 143 | 1 |
| | | | | Celtic | 5 | — |
| | | | | York C | 160 | 8 |
| Derek Hood | 5 10½ | 11 4 | Washington | WBA | — | — |
| | | | | Hull C | 24 | — |
| | | | | York C | 104 | 9 |
| Derek Craig* | 6 0 | 11 9 | Durham | Newcastle U | — | — |
| | | | | Darlington | 187 | 10 |
| | | | | York C | 53 | 1 |
| Richard Dawson | 5 11 | 11 3 | York | York C | 43 | — |
| Steve Senior | 5 10 | 11 4 | Sheffield | York C | 20 | 1 |
| Gerry Sweeney | 5 10 | 10 10 | Glasgow | Celtic | — | — |
| (Contract cancelled) | | | | Morton | 139 | 16 |
| | | | | Bristol C | 406 | 22 |
| | | | | York C | 12 | — |
| Stuart Croft | 5 11 | 11 5 | Ashington | Hull C | 190 | 4 |
| (Contract cancelled Nov 1981) | | | | Portsmouth | 6 | 1 |
| | | | | York C | 14 | — |
| Eddie Flood | 5 7 | 10 0 | Liverpool | Liverpool | — | — |
| | | | | Tranmere R | 315 | 6 |
| | | | | York C | 15 | — |
| Mike Czuczman* | 6 1 | 12 9 | Carlisle | Preston NE | — | — |
| | | | | Grimsby T | 114 | 6 |
| | | | | Scunthorpe U | 116 | 1 |
| | | | | Stockport Co | 36 | 7 |
| | | | | San José E | (not known) | |
| | | | | Grimsby T | 9 | — |
| | | | | York C | 17 | — |
| Alan Waldron | 5 7 | 9 8 | Royton | Bolton W | 140 | 6 |
| (Non-contract) | | | | Blackpool | 23 | 1 |
| | | | | Bury | 34 | — |
| | | | | York C | 3 | 1 |
| Peter Aitken | 5 11 | 12 1 | Penarth | Bristol R | 234 | 3 |
| | | | | Bristol C | 41 | 1 |
| | | | | York C | 18 | 2 |
| John Bentham | 5 7 | 10 8 | Pontefract | York C | 23 | — |
| **Midfield** | | | | | | |
| Tommy Stanley | 5 7 | 10 6 | Hemsworth | York C | 17 | — |
| Gary Ford | 5 9 | 10 7 | York | York C | 146 | 18 |
| Billy McGhie | 5 9 | 11 0 | Lanark | Leeds U | 2 | 1 |
| (Contract cancelled Nov 1981) | | | | York C | 43 | 1 |
| Malcolm Crosby | 5 9 | 11 0 | South Shields | Aldershot | 294 | 23 |
| | | | | York C | 23 | 2 |
| Mick Laverick | 5 9 | 11 0 | Trimdon | Mansfield T | 89 | 13 |
| | | | | Southend U | 110 | 18 |
| | | | | Huddersfield T | 74 | 9 |
| | | | | York C | 26 | 4 |
| **Forwards** | | | | | | |
| Kevin Randall | 5 11 | 12 9 | Ashton under Lyne | Bury | 4 | — |
| (Non-contract) | | | | Chesterfield | 258 | 97 |
| | | | | Notts Co | 121 | 38 |
| | | | | Mansfield T | 66 | 20 |
| | | | | York C | 107 | 27 |
| John Byrne | 5 11 | 11 6 | Manchester | York C | 76 | 14 |
| Malcolm Smith | 5 8 | 11 0 | Stockton | Middlesbrough | 56 | 11 |
| (Contract cancelled Jan 1982) | | | | Bury (on loan) | 5 | 1 |
| | | | | Blackpool (on loan) | 8 | 5 |
| | | | | Burnley | 85 | 17 |
| | | | | York C | 35 | 6 |
| Keith Walwyn | 6 1 | 13 2 | Jamaica | Winterton | (not known) | |
| | | | | Chesterfield | 3 | 2 |
| | | | | York C | 44 | 23 |
| Brian Pollard | 5 8 | 10 6 | York | York C | 163 | 34 |
| | | | | Watford | 71 | 8 |
| | | | | Mansfield T | 54 | 5 |
| | | | | Blackpool | 1 | — |
| | | | | York C | 26 | 3 |
| Gerry Fell | 6 0 | 12 0 | Newark | Brighton | 79 | 19 |
| (Contract cancelled March 1982) | | | | Southend U | 45 | 10 |
| | | | | Torquay U | 50 | 12 |
| | | | | York C | 5 | — |

# FOOTBALL LEAGUE 1981-82

## DIVISION 1

| | | Home | | | | | Away | | | | | |
|---|---|---|---|---|---|---|---|---|---|---|---|---|
| | P | W | D | L | F | A | W | D | L | F | A | Pts |
| 1. Liverpool | 42 | 14 | 3 | 4 | 39 | 14 | 12 | 6 | 3 | 41 | 18 | 87 |
| 2. Ipswich T | 42 | 17 | 1 | 3 | 47 | 25 | 9 | 4 | 8 | 28 | 28 | 83 |
| 3. Manchester U | 42 | 12 | 6 | 3 | 27 | 9 | 10 | 6 | 5 | 32 | 20 | 78 |
| 4. Tottenham H | 42 | 12 | 4 | 5 | 41 | 26 | 8 | 7 | 6 | 26 | 22 | 71 |
| 5. Arsenal | 42 | 13 | 5 | 3 | 27 | 15 | 7 | 6 | 8 | 21 | 22 | 71 |
| 6. Swansea C | 42 | 13 | 3 | 5 | 34 | 16 | 8 | 3 | 10 | 24 | 35 | 69 |
| 7. Southampton | 42 | 15 | 2 | 4 | 49 | 30 | 4 | 7 | 10 | 23 | 37 | 66 |
| 8. Everton | 42 | 11 | 7 | 3 | 33 | 21 | 6 | 6 | 9 | 23 | 29 | 64 |
| 9. West Ham U | 42 | 9 | 10 | 2 | 42 | 29 | 5 | 6 | 10 | 24 | 28 | 58 |
| 10. Manchester C | 42 | 9 | 7 | 5 | 32 | 23 | 6 | 6 | 9 | 17 | 27 | 58 |
| 11. Aston Villa | 42 | 9 | 6 | 6 | 28 | 24 | 6 | 6 | 9 | 27 | 29 | 57 |
| 12. Nottingham F | 42 | 7 | 7 | 7 | 19 | 20 | 8 | 5 | 8 | 23 | 28 | 57 |
| 13. Brighton & HA | 42 | 8 | 7 | 6 | 30 | 24 | 5 | 6 | 10 | 13 | 28 | 52 |
| 14. Coventry C | 42 | 9 | 4 | 8 | 31 | 24 | 4 | 7 | 10 | 25 | 38 | 50 |
| 15. Notts Co | 42 | 8 | 5 | 8 | 32 | 33 | 5 | 3 | 13 | 29 | 36 | 47 |
| 16. Birmingham C | 42 | 8 | 6 | 7 | 29 | 25 | 2 | 8 | 11 | 24 | 36 | 44 |
| 17. WBA | 42 | 6 | 6 | 9 | 24 | 25 | 5 | 5 | 11 | 22 | 32 | 44 |
| 18. Stoke C | 42 | 9 | 2 | 10 | 27 | 28 | 3 | 6 | 12 | 17 | 35 | 44 |
| 19. Sunderland | 42 | 6 | 5 | 10 | 19 | 26 | 5 | 6 | 10 | 19 | 32 | 44 |
| 20. Leeds U | 42 | 6 | 11 | 4 | 23 | 20 | 4 | 1 | 16 | 16 | 41 | 42 |
| 21. Wolverhampton W | 42 | 8 | 5 | 8 | 19 | 20 | 2 | 5 | 14 | 13 | 43 | 40 |
| 22. Middlesbrough | 42 | 5 | 9 | 7 | 20 | 24 | 3 | 6 | 12 | 14 | 28 | 39 |

## DIVISION 2

| | | Home | | | | | Away | | | | | |
|---|---|---|---|---|---|---|---|---|---|---|---|---|
| | P | W | D | L | F | A | W | D | L | F | A | Pts |
| 1. Luton T | 42 | 16 | 3 | 2 | 48 | 19 | 9 | 10 | 2 | 38 | 27 | 88 |
| 2. Watford | 42 | 13 | 6 | 2 | 46 | 16 | 10 | 5 | 6 | 30 | 26 | 80 |
| 3. Norwich C | 42 | 14 | 3 | 4 | 41 | 19 | 8 | 2 | 11 | 23 | 31 | 71 |
| 4. Sheffield W | 42 | 10 | 8 | 3 | 31 | 23 | 10 | 2 | 9 | 24 | 28 | 70 |
| 5. QPR | 42 | 15 | 4 | 2 | 40 | 9 | 6 | 2 | 13 | 25 | 34 | 69 |
| 6. Barnsley | 42 | 13 | 4 | 4 | 33 | 14 | 6 | 6 | 9 | 26 | 27 | 67 |
| 7. Rotherham U | 42 | 13 | 5 | 3 | 42 | 19 | 7 | 2 | 12 | 24 | 35 | 67 |
| 8. Leicester C | 42 | 12 | 5 | 4 | 31 | 19 | 6 | 7 | 8 | 25 | 29 | 66 |
| 9. Newcastle U | 42 | 14 | 4 | 3 | 30 | 14 | 4 | 4 | 13 | 22 | 36 | 62 |
| 10. Blackburn R | 42 | 11 | 4 | 6 | 26 | 15 | 5 | 7 | 9 | 21 | 28 | 59 |
| 11. Oldham Ath | 42 | 9 | 9 | 3 | 28 | 23 | 6 | 5 | 10 | 22 | 28 | 59 |
| 12. Chelsea | 42 | 10 | 5 | 6 | 37 | 30 | 5 | 7 | 9 | 23 | 30 | 57 |
| 13. Charlton Ath | 42 | 11 | 5 | 5 | 33 | 22 | 2 | 7 | 12 | 17 | 43 | 51 |
| 14. Cambridge U | 42 | 11 | 4 | 6 | 31 | 19 | 2 | 5 | 14 | 17 | 34 | 48 |
| 15. Crystal Palace | 42 | 9 | 2 | 10 | 25 | 26 | 4 | 7 | 10 | 9 | 19 | 48 |
| 16. Derby Co | 42 | 9 | 8 | 4 | 32 | 23 | 3 | 4 | 14 | 21 | 45 | 48 |
| 17. Grimsby T | 42 | 5 | 8 | 8 | 29 | 30 | 6 | 5 | 10 | 24 | 35 | 46 |
| 18. Shrewsbury T | 42 | 10 | 6 | 5 | 26 | 19 | 1 | 7 | 13 | 11 | 38 | 46 |
| 19. Bolton W | 42 | 10 | 4 | 7 | 28 | 24 | 3 | 3 | 15 | 11 | 37 | 46 |
| 20. Cardiff C | 42 | 9 | 2 | 10 | 28 | 32 | 3 | 6 | 12 | 17 | 29 | 44 |
| 21. Wrexham | 42 | 9 | 4 | 8 | 22 | 22 | 2 | 7 | 12 | 18 | 34 | 44 |
| 22. Orient | 42 | 6 | 8 | 7 | 23 | 24 | 4 | 1 | 16 | 13 | 37 | 39 |

## DIVISION 3

| | | Home | | | | | Away | | | | | |
|---|---|---|---|---|---|---|---|---|---|---|---|---|
| | P | W | D | L | F | A | W | D | L | F | A | Pts |
| 1. Burnley | 46 | 13 | 7 | 3 | 37 | 20 | 8 | 10 | 5 | 29 | 25 | 80 |
| 2. Carlisle U | 46 | 17 | 4 | 2 | 44 | 21 | 6 | 7 | 10 | 21 | 29 | 80 |
| 3. Fulham | 46 | 12 | 9 | 2 | 44 | 22 | 9 | 6 | 8 | 33 | 29 | 78 |
| 4. Lincoln C | 46 | 13 | 7 | 3 | 40 | 16 | 8 | 7 | 8 | 26 | 24 | 77 |
| 5. Oxford U | 46 | 10 | 8 | 5 | 28 | 18 | 9 | 6 | 8 | 35 | 31 | 71 |
| 6. Gillingham | 46 | 14 | 5 | 4 | 44 | 26 | 6 | 6 | 11 | 20 | 30 | 71 |
| 7. Southend U | 46 | 11 | 7 | 5 | 35 | 23 | 7 | 8 | 8 | 28 | 28 | 69 |
| 8. Brentford | 46 | 8 | 6 | 9 | 28 | 22 | 11 | 5 | 7 | 28 | 25 | 68 |
| 9. Millwall | 46 | 12 | 4 | 7 | 36 | 28 | 6 | 9 | 8 | 26 | 34 | 67 |
| 10. Plymouth Arg | 46 | 12 | 5 | 6 | 37 | 24 | 6 | 6 | 11 | 27 | 32 | 65 |
| 11. Chesterfield | 46 | 12 | 4 | 7 | 33 | 27 | 6 | 6 | 11 | 24 | 31 | 64 |
| 12. Reading | 46 | 11 | 6 | 6 | 43 | 35 | 6 | 5 | 12 | 24 | 40 | 62 |
| 13. Portsmouth | 46 | 11 | 10 | 2 | 33 | 14 | 3 | 9 | 11 | 23 | 37 | 61 |
| 14. Preston NE | 46 | 10 | 7 | 6 | 25 | 22 | 6 | 6 | 11 | 25 | 34 | 61 |
| 15. Bristol R* | 46 | 12 | 4 | 7 | 35 | 28 | 6 | 5 | 12 | 23 | 37 | 61 |
| 16. Newport Co | 46 | 9 | 10 | 4 | 28 | 21 | 5 | 6 | 12 | 26 | 33 | 58 |
| 17. Huddersfield T | 46 | 10 | 5 | 8 | 38 | 25 | 5 | 7 | 11 | 26 | 34 | 57 |
| 18. Exeter C | 46 | 14 | 4 | 5 | 46 | 33 | 2 | 5 | 16 | 25 | 51 | 57 |
| 19. Doncaster R | 46 | 9 | 9 | 5 | 31 | 24 | 4 | 8 | 11 | 24 | 44 | 56 |
| 20. Walsall | 46 | 10 | 7 | 6 | 32 | 23 | 3 | 7 | 13 | 19 | 32 | 53 |
| 21. Wimbledon | 46 | 10 | 6 | 7 | 33 | 27 | 4 | 5 | 14 | 28 | 48 | 53 |
| 22. Swindon T | 46 | 9 | 5 | 9 | 37 | 36 | 4 | 8 | 11 | 18 | 35 | 52 |
| 23. Bristol C | 46 | 7 | 6 | 10 | 24 | 29 | 4 | 7 | 12 | 16 | 36 | 46 |
| 24. Chester | 46 | 2 | 10 | 11 | 16 | 30 | 5 | 1 | 17 | 20 | 48 | 32 |

*Bristol Rovers had 2 points deducted for fielding an unregistered player.*

## DIVISION 4

| | | Home | | | | | Away | | | | | |
|---|---|---|---|---|---|---|---|---|---|---|---|---|
| | P | W | D | L | F | A | W | D | L | F | A | Pts |
| 1. Sheffield U | 46 | 15 | 8 | 0 | 53 | 15 | 12 | 7 | 4 | 41 | 26 | 96 |
| 2. Bradford C | 46 | 14 | 7 | 2 | 52 | 23 | 12 | 6 | 5 | 36 | 22 | 91 |
| 3. Wigan Ath | 46 | 17 | 5 | 1 | 47 | 18 | 9 | 8 | 6 | 33 | 28 | 91 |
| 4. AFC Bournemouth | 46 | 12 | 10 | 1 | 37 | 15 | 11 | 9 | 3 | 25 | 15 | 88 |
| 5. Peterborough U | 46 | 16 | 3 | 4 | 46 | 22 | 8 | 7 | 8 | 25 | 35 | 82 |
| 6. Colchester U | 46 | 12 | 6 | 5 | 47 | 23 | 8 | 6 | 9 | 35 | 34 | 72 |
| 7. Port Vale | 46 | 9 | 12 | 2 | 26 | 17 | 9 | 4 | 10 | 30 | 32 | 70 |
| 8. Hull C | 46 | 14 | 3 | 6 | 36 | 23 | 5 | 9 | 9 | 34 | 38 | 69 |
| 9. Bury | 46 | 13 | 7 | 3 | 53 | 26 | 4 | 10 | 9 | 27 | 33 | 68 |
| 10. Hereford U | 46 | 10 | 9 | 4 | 36 | 25 | 6 | 10 | 7 | 28 | 33 | 67 |
| 11. Tranmere R | 46 | 7 | 9 | 7 | 27 | 25 | 7 | 9 | 7 | 24 | 31 | 60 |
| 12. Blackpool | 46 | 11 | 5 | 7 | 40 | 26 | 4 | 8 | 11 | 26 | 34 | 58 |
| 13. Darlington | 46 | 10 | 5 | 8 | 36 | 28 | 5 | 8 | 10 | 25 | 34 | 58 |
| 14. Hartlepool U | 46 | 9 | 8 | 6 | 39 | 34 | 4 | 8 | 11 | 34 | 50 | 55 |
| 15. Torquay U | 46 | 9 | 8 | 6 | 30 | 25 | 5 | 5 | 13 | 17 | 34 | 55 |
| 16. Aldershot | 46 | 8 | 7 | 8 | 34 | 29 | 5 | 8 | 10 | 23 | 39 | 54 |
| 17. York C | 46 | 9 | 5 | 9 | 45 | 37 | 5 | 3 | 15 | 24 | 54 | 50 |
| 18. Stockport Co | 46 | 10 | 5 | 8 | 34 | 28 | 2 | 8 | 13 | 14 | 39 | 49 |
| 19. Halifax T | 46 | 6 | 11 | 6 | 28 | 30 | 3 | 11 | 9 | 23 | 42 | 49 |
| 20. Mansfield T* | 46 | 8 | 6 | 9 | 39 | 39 | 5 | 4 | 14 | 24 | 42 | 47 |
| 21. Rochdale | 46 | 7 | 9 | 7 | 26 | 22 | 3 | 7 | 13 | 24 | 40 | 46 |
| 22. Northampton | 46 | 9 | 5 | 9 | 32 | 27 | 2 | 4 | 17 | 25 | 57 | 42 |
| 23. Scunthorpe U | 46 | 7 | 9 | 7 | 26 | 35 | 2 | 6 | 15 | 17 | 44 | 42 |
| 24. Crewe Alex | 46 | 3 | 6 | 14 | 19 | 32 | 3 | 3 | 17 | 10 | 52 | 27 |

*Mansfield Town had 2 points deducted for fielding an ineligible player.*

# FOOTBALL LEAGUE 1888–89 to 1981–82

## FOOTBALL LEAGUE

| | First | Pts | Second | Pts | Third | Pts |
|---|---|---|---|---|---|---|
| 1888–89a | Preston NE | 40 | Aston Villa | 29 | Wolverhampton W | 28 |
| 1889–90a | Preston NE | 33 | Everton | 31 | Blackburn R | 27 |
| 1890–91a | Everton | 29 | Preston NE | 27 | Notts Co | 26 |
| 1891–92b | Sunderland | 42 | Preston NE | 37 | Bolton W | 36 |

## FIRST DIVISION

*Maximum points:a 44; b 52; c 60; d 68; e 76; f 84; g 126.*

| | First | Pts | Second | Pts | Third | Pts |
|---|---|---|---|---|---|---|
| 1892–93c | Sunderland | 48 | Preston NE | 37 | Everton | 36 |
| 1893–94c | Aston Villa | 44 | Sunderland | 38 | Derby Co | 36 |
| 1894–95c | Sunderland | 47 | Everton | 42 | Aston Villa | 39 |
| 1895–96c | Aston Villa | 45 | Derby Co | 41 | Everton | 39 |
| 1896–97c | Aston Villa | 47 | Sheffield U | 36 | Derby Co | 36 |
| 1897–98c | Sheffield U | 42 | Sunderland | 37 | Wolverhampton W | 35 |
| 1898–99d | Aston Villa | 45 | Liverpool | 43 | Burnley | 39 |
| 1899–1900d | Aston Villa | 50 | Sheffield U | 48 | Sunderland | 41 |
| 1900–01d | Liverpool | 45 | Sunderland | 43 | Notts Co | 40 |
| 1901–02d | Sunderland | 44 | Everton | 41 | Newcastle U | 37 |
| 1902–03d | The Wednesday | 42 | Aston Villa | 41 | Sunderland | 41 |
| 1903–04d | The Wednesday | 47 | Manchester C | 44 | Everton | 43 |
| 1904–05d | Newcastle U | 48 | Everton | 47 | Manchester C | 46 |
| 1905–06e | Liverpool | 51 | Preston NE | 47 | The Wednesday | 44 |
| 1906–07e | Newcastle U | 51 | Bristol C | 48 | Everton | 45 |
| 1907–08e | Manchester U | 52 | Aston Villa | 43 | Manchester C | 43 |
| 1908–09e | Newcastle U | 53 | Everton | 46 | Sunderland | 44 |
| 1909–10e | Aston Villa | 53 | Liverpool | 48 | Blackburn R | 45 |
| 1910–11e | Manchester U | 52 | Aston Villa | 51 | Sunderland | 45 |
| 1911–12e | Blackburn R | 49 | Everton | 46 | Newcastle U | 44 |
| 1912–13e | Sunderland | 54 | Aston Villa | 50 | Sheffield W | 49 |
| 1913–14e | Blackburn R | 51 | Aston Villa | 44 | Middlesbrough | 43 |
| 1914–15e | Everton | 46 | Oldham Ath | 45 | Blackburn R | 43 |
| 1919–20f | WBA | 60 | Burnley | 51 | Chelsea | 49 |
| 1920–21f | Burnley | 59 | Manchester C | 54 | Bolton W | 52 |
| 1921–22f | Liverpool | 57 | Tottenham H | 51 | Burnley | 49 |
| 1922-23f | Liverpool | 60 | Sunderland | 54 | Huddersfield T | 53 |
| 1923–24f | Huddersfield T* | 57 | Cardiff C | 57 | Sunderland | 53 |
| 1924–25f | Huddersfield T | 58 | WBA | 56 | Bolton W | 55 |
| 1925–26f | Huddersfield T | 57 | Arsenal | 52 | Sunderland | 48 |
| 1926–27f | Newcastle U | 56 | Huddersfield T | 51 | Sunderland | 49 |
| 1927–28f | Everton | 53 | Huddersfield T | 51 | Leicester C | 48 |
| 1928–29f | Sheffield W | 52 | Leicester C | 51 | Aston Villa | 50 |
| 1929–30f | Sheffield W | 60 | Derby Co | 50 | Manchester C | 47 |
| 1930–31f | Arsenal | 66 | Aston Villa | 59 | Sheffield W | 52 |
| 1931–32f | Everton | 56 | Arsenal | 54 | Sheffield W | 50 |
| 1932–33f | Arsenal | 58 | Aston Villa | 54 | Sheffield W | 51 |
| 1933–34f | Arsenal | 59 | Huddersfield T | 56 | Tottenham H | 49 |
| 1934–35f | Arsenal | 58 | Sunderland | 54 | Sheffield W | 49 |
| 1935–36f | Sunderland | 56 | Derby Co | 48 | Huddersfield T | 48 |
| 1936–37f | Manchester C | 57 | Charlton Ath | 54 | Arsenal | 52 |
| 1937–38f | Arsenal | 52 | Wolverhampton W | 51 | Preston NE | 49 |
| 1938–39f | Everton | 59 | Wolverhampton W | 55 | Charlton Ath | 50 |
| 1946–47f | Liverpool | 57 | Manchester U | 56 | Wolverhampton W | 56 |
| 1947–48f | Arsenal | 59 | Manchester U | 52 | Burnley | 52 |
| 1948–49f | Portsmouth | 58 | Manchester U | 53 | Derby Co | 53 |
| 1949–50f | Portsmouth* | 53 | Wolverhampton W | 53 | Sunderland | 52 |
| 1950–51f | Tottenham H | 60 | Manchester U | 56 | Blackpool | 50 |
| 1951–52f | Manchester U | 57 | Tottenham H | 53 | Arsenal | 53 |
| 1952–53f | Arsenal* | 54 | Preston NE | 54 | Wolverhampton W | 51 |
| 1953–54f | Wolverhampton W | 57 | WBA | 53 | Huddersfield T | 51 |
| 1954–55f | Chelsea | 52 | Wolverhampton W | 48 | Portsmouth | 48 |
| 1955–56f | Manchester U | 60 | Blackpool | 49 | Wolverhampton W | 49 |
| 1956–57f | Manchester U | 64 | Tottenham H | 56 | Preston NE | 56 |
| 1957–58f | Wolverhampton W | 64 | Preston NE | 59 | Tottenham H | 51 |
| 1958–59f | Wolverhampton W | 61 | Manchester U | 55 | Arsenal | 50 |

* Won on goal average.

| | First | Pts | Second | Pts | Third | Pts |
|---|---|---|---|---|---|---|
| 1959–60f | Burnley | 55 | Wolverhampton W | 54 | Tottenham H | 53 |
| 1960–61f | Tottenham H | 66 | Sheffield W | 58 | Wolverhampton W | 57 |
| 1961–62f | Ipswich T | 56 | Burnley | 53 | Tottenham H | 52 |
| 1962–63f | Everton | 61 | Tottenham H | 55 | Burnley | 54 |
| 1963–64f | Liverpool | 57 | Manchester U | 53 | Everton | 52 |
| 1964–65f | Manchester U* | 61 | Leeds U | 61 | Chelsea | 56 |
| 1965–66f | Liverpool | 61 | Leeds U | 55 | Burnley | 55 |
| 1966–67f | Manchester U | 60 | Nottingham F | 56 | Tottenham H | 56 |
| 1967–68f | Manchester C | 58 | Manchester U | 56 | Liverpool | 55 |
| 1968–69f | Leeds U | 67 | Liverpool | 61 | Everton | 57 |
| 1969–70f | Everton | 66 | Leeds U | 57 | Chelsea | 55 |
| 1970–71f | Arsenal | 65 | Leeds U | 64 | Tottenham H | 52 |
| 1971–72f | Derby Co | 58 | Leeds U | 57 | Liverpool | 57 |
| 1972–73f | Liverpool | 60 | Arsenal | 57 | Leeds U | 53 |
| 1973–74f | Leeds U | 62 | Liverpool | 57 | Derby Co | 48 |
| 1974–75f | Derby Co | 53 | Liverpool | 51 | Ipswich T | 57 |
| 1975–76f | Liverpool | 60 | QPR | 59 | Manchester U | 56 |
| 1976–77f | Liverpool | 57 | Manchester C | 56 | Ipswich T | 52 |
| 1977–78f | Nottingham F | 64 | Liverpool | 57 | Everton | 55 |
| 1978–79f | Liverpool | 68 | Nottingham F | 60 | WBA | 59 |
| 1979–80f | Liverpool | 60 | Manchester U | 58 | Ipswich T | 53 |
| 1980–81f | Aston Villa | 60 | Ipswich T | 56 | Arsenal | 53 |
| 1981–82g | Liverpool | 87 | Ipswich T | 83 | Manchester U | 78 |

*No competition during 1915–19 and 1939–46.*

## SECOND DIVISION

*Maximum points: a 44; b 56; c 60; d 68; e 76; f 84; g 126.*

| | First | Pts | Second | Pts | Third | Pts |
|---|---|---|---|---|---|---|
| 1892–93a | Small Heath | 36 | Sheffield U | 35 | Darwen | 30 |
| 1893–94b | Liverpool | 50 | Small Heath | 42 | Notts Co | 39 |
| 1894–95c | Bury | 48 | Notts Co | 39 | Newton Heath | 38 |
| 1895–96c | Liverpool* | 46 | Manchester C | 46 | Grimsby T | 42 |
| 1896–97c | Notts Co | 42 | Newton Heath | 39 | Grimsby T | 38 |
| 1897–98c | Burnley | 48 | Newcastle U | 45 | Manchester C | 39 |
| 1898–99d | Manchester C | 52 | Glossop NE | 46 | Leicester Fosse | 45 |
| 1899–1900d | The Wednesday | 54 | Bolton W | 52 | Small Heath | 46 |
| 1900–01d | Grimsby T | 49 | Small Heath | 48 | Burnley | 44 |
| 1901–02d | WBA | 55 | Middlesbrough | 51 | Preston NE | 42 |
| 1902–03d | Manchester C | 54 | Small Heath | 51 | Woolwich A | 48 |
| 1903–04d | Preston NE | 50 | Woolwich A | 49 | Manchester U | 48 |
| 1904–05d | Liverpool | 58 | Bolton W | 56 | Manchester U | 53 |
| 1905–06e | Bristol C | 66 | Manchester U | 62 | Chelsea | 53 |
| 1906–07e | Nottingham F | 60 | Chelsea | 57 | Leicester Fosse | 48 |
| 1907–08e | Bradford C | 54 | Leicester Fosse | 52 | Oldham Ath | 50 |
| 1908–09e | Bolton W | 52 | Tottenham H* | 51 | WBA | 51 |
| 1909–10e | Manchester C | 54 | Oldham Ath* | 53 | Hull C | 53 |
| 1910–11e | WBA | 53 | Bolton W | 51 | Chelsea | 49 |
| 1911–12e | Derby Co* | 54 | Chelsea | 54 | Burnley | 52 |
| 1912–13e | Preston NE | 53 | Burnley | 50 | Birmingham | 46 |
| 1913–14e | Notts Co | 53 | Bradford PA | 49 | Woolwich A | 49 |
| 1914–15e | Derby Co | 53 | Preston NE | 50 | Barnsley | 47 |
| 1919–20f | Tottenham H | 70 | Huddersfield T | 64 | Birmingham | 56 |
| 1920–21f | Birmingham* | 58 | Cardiff C | 58 | Bristol C | 51 |
| 1921–22f | Nottingham F | 56 | Stoke C | 52 | Barnsley | 52 |
| 1922–23f | Notts Co | 53 | West Ham U* | 51 | Leicester C | 51 |
| 1923–24f | Leeds U | 54 | Bury* | 51 | Derby Co | 51 |
| 1924–25f | Leicester C | 59 | Manchester U | 57 | Derby Co | 55 |
| 1925–26f | Sheffield W | 60 | Derby Co | 57 | Chelsea | 52 |
| 1926–27f | Middlesbrough | 62 | Portsmouth* | 54 | Manchester C | 54 |
| 1927–28f | Manchester C | 59 | Leeds U | 57 | Chelsea | 54 |
| 1928–29f | Middlesbrough | 55 | Grimsby T | 53 | Bradford | 48 |
| 1929–30f | Blackpool | 58 | Chelsea | 55 | Oldham Ath | 53 |
| 1930–31f | Everton | 61 | WBA | 54 | Tottenham H | 51 |
| 1931–32f | Wolverhampton W | 56 | Leeds U | 54 | Stoke C | 52 |
| 1932–33f | Stoke C | 56 | Tottenham H | 55 | Fulham | 50 |
| 1933–34f | Grimsby T | 59 | Preston NE | 52 | Bolton W | 51 |
| 1934–35f | Brentford | 61 | Bolton W* | 56 | West Ham U | 56 |
| 1935–36f | Manchester U | 56 | Charlton Ath | 55 | Sheffield U | 52 |
| 1936–37f | Leicester C | 56 | Blackpool | 55 | Bury | 52 |

*\* Won on goal average.*

| | First | Pts | Second | Pts | Third | Pts |
|---|---|---|---|---|---|---|
| 1937–38f | Aston Villa | 57 | Manchester U* | 53 | Sheffield U | 53 |
| 1938–39f | Blackburn R | 55 | Sheffield U | 54 | Sheffield W | 53 |
| 1946–47f | Manchester C | 62 | Burnley | 58 | Birmingham C | 55 |
| 1947–48f | Birmingham C | 59 | Newcastle U | 56 | Southampton | 52 |
| 1948–49f | Fulham | 57 | WBA | 56 | Southampton | 55 |
| 1949–50f | Tottenham H | 61 | Sheffield W* | 52 | Sheffield U | 52 |
| 1950–51f | Preston NE | 57 | Manchester C | 52 | Cardiff C | 50 |
| 1951–52f | Sheffield W | 53 | Cardiff C* | 51 | Birmingham C | 51 |
| 1952–53f | Sheffield U | 60 | Huddersfield T | 58 | Luton T | 52 |
| 1953–54f | Leicester C* | 56 | Everton | 56 | Blackburn R | 55 |
| 1954–55f | Birmingham C* | 54 | Luton T* | 54 | Rotherham U | 54 |
| 1955–56f | Sheffield W | 55 | Leeds U | 52 | Liverpool | 48 |
| 1956–57f | Leicester C | 61 | Nottingham F | 54 | Liverpool | 53 |
| 1957–58f | West Ham U | 57 | Blackburn R | 56 | Charlton Ath | 55 |
| 1958–59f | Sheffield W | 62 | Fulham | 60 | Sheffield U | 53 |
| 1959–60f | Aston Villa | 59 | Cardiff C | 58 | Liverpool | 50 |
| 1960–61f | Ipswich T | 59 | Sheffield U | 58 | Liverpool | 52 |
| 1961–62f | Liverpool | 62 | Leyton O | 54 | Sunderland | 53 |
| 1962–63f | Stoke C | 53 | Chelsea* | 52 | Sunderland | 52 |
| 1963–64f | Leeds U | 63 | Sunderland | 61 | Preston NE | 56 |
| 1964–65f | Newcastle U | 57 | Northampton T | 56 | Bolton W | 50 |
| 1965–66f | Manchester C | 59 | Southampton | 54 | Coventry C | 53 |
| 1966–67f | Coventry C | 59 | Wolverhampton W | 58 | Carlisle U | 52 |
| 1967–68f | Ipswich T | 59 | QPR* | 58 | Blackpool | 58 |
| 1968–69f | Derby Co | 63 | Crystal Palace | 56 | Charlton Ath | 50 |
| 1969–70f | Huddersfield T | 60 | Blackpool | 53 | Leicester C | 51 |
| 1970–71f | Leicester C | 59 | Sheffield U | 56 | Cardiff C | 53 |
| 1971–72f | Norwich C | 57 | Birmingham C | 56 | Millwall | 55 |
| 1972–73f | Burnley | 62 | QPR | 61 | Aston Villa | 50 |
| 1973–74f | Middlesbrough | 65 | Luton T | 50 | Carlisle U | 49 |
| 1974–75f | Manchester U | 61 | Aston Villa | 58 | Norwich C | 53 |
| 1975–76f | Sunderland | 56 | Bristol C | 53 | WBA | 53 |
| 1976–77f | Wolverhampton W | 57 | Chelsea | 55 | Nottingham F | 52 |
| 1977–78f | Bolton W | 58 | Southampton | 57 | Tottenham H | 56 |
| 1978–79f | Crystal Palace | 57 | Brighton | 56 | Stoke C | 56 |
| 1979–80f | Leicester C | 55 | Sunderland | 54 | Birmingham C | 53 |
| 1980–81f | West Ham U | 66 | Notts Co | 53 | Swansea C* | 50 |
| 1981–82g | Luton T | 88 | Watford | 80 | Norwich C | 71 |

*No competition during 1915–19 and 1939–46.*

## THIRD DIVISION
*Maximum points:* 92; 138† from 1981–82

| | First | Pts | Second | Pts | Third | Pts |
|---|---|---|---|---|---|---|
| 1958–59 | Plymouth Arg | 62 | Hull C | 61 | Brentford | 57 |
| 1959–60 | Southampton | 61 | Norwich C | 59 | Shrewsbury T | 52 |
| 1960–61 | Bury | 68 | Walsall | 62 | QPR | 60 |
| 1961–62 | Portsmouth | 65 | Grimsby T | 62 | Bournemouth | 59 |
| 1962–63 | Northampton T | 62 | Swindon T | 58 | Port Vale | 54 |
| 1963–64 | Coventry C* | 60 | Crystal Palace | 60 | Watford | 58 |
| 1964–65 | Carlisle U | 60 | Bristol C* | 59 | Mansfield T | 59 |
| 1965–66 | Hull C | 69 | Millwall | 65 | QPR | 57 |
| 1966–67 | QPR | 67 | Middlesbrough | 55 | Watford | 54 |
| 1967–68 | Oxford U | 57 | Bury | 56 | Shrewsbury T | 55 |
| 1968–69 | Watford* | 64 | Swindon T | 64 | Luton T | 61 |
| 1969–70 | Orient | 62 | Luton T | 60 | Bristol R | 56 |
| 1970–71 | Preston NE | 61 | Fulham | 60 | Halifax T | 56 |
| 1971–72 | Aston Villa | 70 | Brighton | 65 | Bournemouth | 62 |
| 1972–73 | Bolton W | 61 | Notts Co | 57 | Blackburn R | 55 |
| 1973–74 | Oldham Ath | 62 | Bristol R | 61 | York C | 61 |
| 1974–75 | Blackburn R | 60 | Plymouth Arg | 59 | Charlton Ath | 55 |
| 1975–76 | Hereford U | 63 | Cardiff C | 57 | Millwall | 56 |
| 1976–77 | Mansfield T | 64 | Brighton & HA | 61 | Crystal Palace | 59 |
| 1977–78 | Wrexham | 61 | Cambridge U | 58 | Preston NE | 56 |
| 1978–79 | Shrewsbury T | 61 | Watford | 60 | Swansea C | 60 |
| 1979–80 | Grimsby T | 62 | Blackburn R | 59 | Sheffield W | 58 |
| 1980–81 | Rotherham U | 61 | Barnsley* | 59 | Charlton Ath | 59 |
| 1981–82† | Burnley* | 80 | Carlisle U | 80 | Fulham | 78 |

*Won on goal average/goal difference.*

## FOURTH DIVISION

*Maximum points: 92; 138‡ from 1981–82*

| | First | Pts | Second | Pts | Third | Pts | Fourth | Pts |
|---|---|---|---|---|---|---|---|---|
| 1958–59 | Port Vale | 64 | Coventry C | 60 | York C | 60 | Shrewsbury T | 58 |
| 1959–60 | Walsall | 65 | Notts Co | 60 | Torquay U | 60 | Watford | 57 |
| 1960–61 | Peterborough U | 66 | Crystal Palace | 64 | Northampton T | 60 | Bradford PA | 60 |
| 1961–62† | Millwall | 56 | Colchester U | 55 | Wrexham | 53 | Carlisle U | 52 |
| 1962–63 | Brentford | 62 | Oldham Ath | 59 | Crewe Alex | 59 | Mansfield T | 57 |
| 1963–64 | Gillingham* | 60 | Carlisle U | 60 | Workington T | 59 | Exeter C | 58 |
| 1964–65 | Brighton | 63 | Millwall | 62 | York C | 62 | Oxford U | 61 |
| 1965–66 | Doncaster R* | 59 | Darlington | 59 | Torquay U | 58 | Colchester U | 56 |
| 1966–67 | Stockport Co | 64 | Southport | 59 | Barrow | 59 | Tranmere R | 58 |
| 1967–68 | Luton T | 66 | Barnsley | 61 | Hartlepools U | 60 | Crewe Alex | 58 |
| 1968–69 | Doncaster R | 59 | Halifax T | 57 | Rochdale | 56 | Bradford C | 56 |
| 1969–70 | Chesterfield | 64 | Wrexham | 61 | Swansea C | 60 | Port Vale | 59 |
| 1970–71 | Notts Co | 69 | Bournemouth | 60 | Oldham Ath | 59 | York C | 56 |
| 1971–72 | Grimsby T | 63 | Southend U | 60 | Brentford | 59 | Scunthorpe U | 57 |
| 1972–73 | Southport | 62 | Hereford U | 58 | Cambridge U | 57 | Aldershot* | 56 |
| 1973–74 | Peterborough U | 65 | Gillingham | 62 | Colchester U | 60 | Bury | 59 |
| 1974–75 | Mansfield T | 68 | Shrewsbury T | 62 | Rotherham U | 59 | Chester | 57 |
| 1975–76 | Lincoln C | 74 | Northampton T | 68 | Reading | 60 | Tranmere R | 58 |
| 1976–77 | Cambridge U | 65 | Exeter C | 62 | Colchester U | 59 | Bradford C | 59 |
| 1977–78 | Watford | 71 | Southend U | 60 | Swansea C | 56 | Brentford | 56 |
| 1978–79 | Reading | 65 | Grimsby T | 61 | Wimbledon | 61 | Barnsley | 61 |
| 1979–80 | Huddersfield T | 66 | Walsall | 64 | Newport Co | 61 | Portsmouth | 60 |
| 1980–81 | Southend U | 67 | Lincoln C | 65 | Doncaster R | 56 | Wimbledon | 55 |
| 1981–82‡ | Sheffield U | 96 | Bradford C* | 91 | Wigan Ath | 91 | AFC Bournemouth | 88 |

†*Maximum points:* 88 owing to Accrington Stanley's resignation.

## THIRD DIVISION—SOUTH (1921–1958)

*Maximum points: a 84; b 76; c 80; d 92.*

| | First | Pts | Second | Pts | Third | Pts |
|---|---|---|---|---|---|---|
| 1920–21a | Crystal Palace | 59 | Southampton | 54 | QPR | 53 |
| 1921–22a | Southampton* | 61 | Plymouth Arg | 61 | Portsmouth | 53 |
| 1922–23a | Bristol C | 59 | Plymouth Arg | 53 | Swansea T | 53 |
| 1923–24a | Portsmouth | 59 | Plymouth Arg | 55 | Millwall | 54 |
| 1924–25a | Swansea T | 57 | Plymouth Arg | 56 | Bristol C | 53 |
| 1925–26a | Reading | 57 | Plymouth Arg | 56 | Millwall | 53 |
| 1926–27a | Bristol C | 62 | Plymouth Arg | 60 | Millwall | 56 |
| 1927–28a | Millwall | 65 | Northampton T | 55 | Plymouth Arg | 53 |
| 1928–29a | Charlton Ath* | 54 | Crystal Palace | 54 | Northampton T | 52 |
| 1929–30a | Plymouth Arg | 68 | Brentford | 61 | QPR | 51 |
| 1930–31a | Notts Co | 59 | Crystal Palace | 51 | Brentford | 50 |
| 1931–32a | Fulham | 57 | Reading | 55 | Southend U | 53 |
| 1932–33a | Brentford | 62 | Exeter C | 58 | Norwich C | 57 |
| 1933–34a | Norwich C | 61 | Coventry C | 54 | Reading | 54 |
| 1934–35a | Charlton Ath | 61 | Reading | 53 | Coventry C | 51 |
| 1935–36a | Coventry C | 57 | Luton T | 56 | Reading | 54 |
| 1936–37a | Luton T | 58 | Notts Co | 56 | Brighton | 53 |
| 1937–38a | Millwall | 56 | Bristol C | 55 | QPR | 53 |
| 1938–39a | Newport Co | 55 | Crystal Palace | 52 | Brighton | 49 |
| 1939–46 | Competition cancelled owing to war. | | | | | |
| 1946–47a | Cardiff C | 66 | QPR | 57 | Bristol C | 51 |
| 1947–48a | QPR | 61 | Bournemouth | 57 | Walsall | 51 |
| 1948–49a | Swansea T | 62 | Reading | 55 | Bournemouth | 52 |
| 1949–50a | Notts Co | 58 | Northampton T | 51 | Southend U | 51 |
| 1950–51d | Nottingham F | 70 | Norwich C | 64 | Reading | 57 |
| 1951–52d | Plymouth Arg | 66 | Reading | 61 | Norwich C | 61 |
| 1952–53d | Bristol R | 64 | Millwall | 62 | Northampton T | 62 |
| 1953–54d | Ipswich T | 64 | Brighton | 61 | Bristol C | 56 |
| 1954–55d | Bristol C | 70 | Leyton O | 61 | Southampton | 59 |
| 1955–56d | Leyton O | 66 | Brighton | 65 | Ipswich T | 64 |
| 1956–57d | Ipswich T* | 59 | Torquay U | 59 | Colchester U | 58 |
| 1957–58d | Brighton | 60 | Brentford | 58 | Plymouth Arg | 58 |

* *Won on goal average/goal difference.*

## THIRD DIVISION—NORTH (1921–1958)

*Maximum points: a 84; b 76; c 80; d 92.*

| | First | Pts | Second | Pts | Third | Pts |
|---|---|---|---|---|---|---|
| 1921–22b | Stockport Co | 56 | Darlington | 50 | Grimsby T | 50 |
| 1922–23b | Nelson | 51 | Bradford PA | 47 | Walsall | 46 |
| 1923–24a | Wolverhampton W | 63 | Rochdale | 62 | Chesterfield | 54 |
| 1924–25a | Darlington | 58 | Nelson | 53 | New Brighton | 53 |
| 1925–26a | Grimsby T | 61 | Bradford PA | 60 | Rochdale | 59 |
| 1926–27a | Stoke C | 63 | Rochdale | 58 | Bradford PA | 55 |
| 1927–28a | Bradford PA | 63 | Lincoln C | 55 | Stockport Co | 54 |
| 1928–29a | Bradford C | 63 | Stockport Co | 62 | Wrexham | 52 |
| 1929–30a | Port Vale | 67 | Stockport Co | 63 | Darlington | 50 |
| 1930–31a | Chesterfield | 58 | Lincoln C | 57 | Wrexham | 54 |
| 1931–32c | Lincoln C* | 57 | Gateshead | 57 | Chester | 50 |
| 1932–33a | Hull C | 59 | Wrexham | 57 | Stockport Co | 54 |
| 1933–34a | Barnsley | 62 | Chesterfield | 61 | Stockport Co | 59 |
| 1934–35a | Doncaster R | 57 | Halifax T | 55 | Chester | 54 |
| 1935–36a | Chesterfield | 60 | Chester | 55 | Tranmere R | 55 |
| 1936–37a | Stockport Co | 60 | Lincoln C | 57 | Chester | 53 |
| 1937–38a | Tranmere R | 56 | Doncaster R | 54 | Hull C | 53 |
| 1938–39a | Barnsley | 67 | Doncaster R | 56 | Bradford C | 52 |
| 1939–46 | Competition cancelled owing to war. | | | | | |
| 1946–47a | Doncaster R | 72 | Rotherham U | 64 | Chester | 56 |
| 1947–48a | Lincoln C | 60 | Rotherham U | 59 | Wrexham | 50 |
| 1948–49a | Hull C | 65 | Rotherham U | 62 | Doncaster R | 50 |
| 1949–50a | Doncaster R | 55 | Gateshead | 53 | Rochdale | 51 |
| 1950–51d | Rotherham U | 71 | Mansfield T | 64 | Carlisle U | 62 |
| 1951–52d | Lincoln C | 69 | Grimsby T | 66 | Stockport Co | 59 |
| 1952–53d | Oldham Ath | 59 | Port Vale | 58 | Wrexham | 56 |
| 1953–54d | Port Vale | 69 | Barnsley | 58 | Scunthorpe U | 57 |
| 1954–55d | Barnsley | 65 | Accrington S | 61 | Scunthorpe U | 58 |
| 1955–56d | Grimsby T | 68 | Derby Co | 63 | Accrington S | 59 |
| 1956–57d | Derby Co | 63 | Hartlepools U | 59 | Accrington S | 58 |
| 1957–58d | Scunthorpe U | 66 | Accrington S | 59 | Bradford C | 57 |

* *Won on goal average.*

## LEAGUE TITLE WINS

LEAGUE DIVISION 1 – Liverpool 13, Arsenal 8, Manchester U 7, Everton 7, Aston Villa 7, Sunderland 6, Newcastle U 4, Sheffield W 4, Huddersfield T 3, Wolverhampton W 3, Blackburn R 2, Portsmouth 2, Preston NE 2, Burnley 2, Manchester C 2, Tottenham H 2, Leeds U 2, Derby Co 2, Chelsea 1, Sheffield U 1, WBA 1, Ipswich T 1, Nottingham F 1.

LEAGUE DIVISION 2 – Leicester C 6, Manchester C 6, Sheffield W 5, Birmingham C (one as Small Heath) 4, Liverpool 4, Notts Co 3, Preston NE 3, Derby Co 3, Middlesbrough 3, Grimsby T 2, Nottingham F 2, Tottenham H 2, WBA 2, Aston Villa 2, Stoke C 2, Leeds U 2, Ipswich T 2, Burnley 2, Manchester U 2, West Ham U 2, Wolverhampton W 2, Bolton W 2, Huddersfield T 1, Bristol C 1, Brentford 1, Bury 1, Bradford C 1, Everton 1, Fulham 1, Sheffield U 1, Newcastle U 1, Coventry C 1, Blackpool 1, Blackburn R 1, Norwich C 1, Sunderland 1, Crystal Palace 1, Luton T 1.

LEAGUE DIVISION 3 – Plymouth Arg, Southampton, Bury, Portsmouth, Northampton T, Coventry C, Carlisle U, Hull C, QPR, Oxford U, Watford, Leyton O, Preston NE, Aston Villa, Bolton W, Oldham Ath, Blackburn R, Hereford U, Mansfield T, Wrexham, Shrewsbury T, Grimsby T, Burnley 1 each.

LEAGUE DIVISION 4 – Doncaster R 2, Peterborough U 2; Port Vale, Walsall, Millwall, Brentford, Gillingham, Brighton, Stockport Co, Luton T, Chesterfield, Notts Co, Grimsby T, Southport, Mansfield T, Lincoln C, Cambridge U, Watford, Reading, Huddersfield T, Southend U, Sheffield U 1 each.

### To 1957–58

DIVISION 3 (South) – Bristol C 3; Charlton Ath, Ipswich T, Millwall, Notts Co, Plymouth Arg, Swansea T 2; Brentford, Bristol R, Cardiff C, Crystal Palace, Coventry C, Fulham, Leyton O, Luton T, Newport Co, Nottingham F, Norwich C, Portsmouth, QPR, Reading, Southampton, Brighton 1.

DIVISION 3 (North) – Barnsley, Doncaster R, Lincoln C 3; Chesterfield, Grimsby T, Hull C, Port Vale, Stockport Co 2; Bradford PA, Bradford C, Darlington, Derby Co, Nelson, Oldham Ath, Rotherham U, Stoke C, Tranmere R, Wolverhampton W, Scunthorpe U 1.

## RELEGATED CLUBS

1891–92 League extended. Newton Heath, Sheffield W and Nottingham F admitted. *Second Division formed* including Darwen.

1892–93 In Test matches, Sheffield U and Darwen won promotion in place of Notts Co and Accrington S.

1893–94 In Tests, Liverpool and Small Heath won promotion. Newton Heath and Darwen relegated.

1894–95 After Tests, Bury promoted, Liverpool relegated.

1895–96 After Tests, Liverpool promoted, Small Heath relegated.

1896–97 After Tests, Notts Co promoted, Burnley relegated.

1897–98 Test system abolished after success of Stoke C and Burnley. League extended. Blackburn R and Newcastle U elected to First Division. *Automatic promotion and relegation introduced.*

## DIVISION 1 TO DIVISION 2

| | |
|---|---|
| 1898–99 Bolton W and Sheffield W | 1938–39 Birmingham C and Leicester C |
| 1899–1900 Burnley and Glossop | 1946–47 Brentford and Leeds U |
| 1900–01 Preston NE and WBA | 1947–48 Blackburn R and Grimsby T |
| 1901–02 Small Heath and Manchester C | 1948–49 Preston NE and Sheffield U |
| 1902–03 Grimsby T and Bolton W | 1949–50 Manchester C and Birmingham C |
| 1903–04 Liverpool and WBA | 1950–51 Sheffield W and Everton |
| 1904–05 League extended. Bury and Notts Co, two | 1951–52 Huddersfield and Fulham |
|     bottom clubs in First Division, re-elected. | 1952–53 Stoke C and Derby Co |
| 1905–06 Nottingham F and Wolverhampton W | 1953–54 Middlesbrough and Liverpool |
| 1906–07 Derby Co and Stoke C | 1954–55 Leicester C and Sheffield W |
| 1907–08 Bolton W and Birmingham C | 1955–56 Huddersfield and Sheffield U |
| 1908–09 Manchester C and Leicester Fosse | 1956–57 Charlton Ath and Cardiff C |
| 1909–10 Bolton W and Chelsea | 1957–58 Sheffield W and Sunderland |
| 1910–11 Bristol C and Nottingham F | 1958–59 Portsmouth and Aston Villa |
| 1911–12 Preston NE and Bury | 1959–60 Luton T and Leeds U |
| 1912–13 Notts Co and Woolwich Arsenal | 1960–61 Preston NE and Newcastle U |
| 1913–14 Preston NE and Derby Co | 1961–62 Chelsea and Cardiff C |
| 1914–15 Tottenham H and Chelsea* | 1962–63 Manchester C and Leyton O |
| 1919–20 Notts Co and Sheffield W | 1963–64 Bolton W and Ipswich T |
| 1920–21 Derby Co and Bradford | 1964–65 Wolverhampton W and Birmingham C |
| 1921–22 Bradford C and Manchester U | 1965–66 Northampton T and Blackburn R |
| 1922–23 Stoke C and Oldham Ath | 1966–67 Aston Villa and Blackpool |
| 1923–24 Chelsea and Middlesbrough | 1967–68 Fulham and Sheffield U |
| 1924–25 Preston NE and Nottingham F | 1968–69 Leicester C and QPR |
| 1925–26 Manchester C and Notts Co | 1969–70 Sunderland and Sheffield W |
| 1926–27 Leeds U and WBA | 1970–71 Burnley and Blackpool |
| 1927–28 Tottenham H and Middlesbrough | 1971–72 Huddersfield T and Nottingham F |
| 1928–29 Bury and Cardiff C | 1972–73 Crystal.Palace and WBA |
| 1929–30 Burnley and Everton | 1973–74 Southampton, Manchester U, Norwich C |
| 1930–31 Leeds U and Manchester U | 1974–75 Luton T, Chelsea, Carlisle U |
| 1931–32 Grimsby T and West Ham U | 1975–76 Wolverhampton W, Burnley, Sheffield U |
| 1932–33 Bolton W and Blackpool | 1976–77 Sunderland, Stoke C, Tottenham H |
| 1933–34 Newcastle U and Sheffield U | 1977–78 West Ham U, Newcastle U, Leicester C |
| 1934–35 Leicester C and Tottenham H | 1978–79 QPR, Birmingham C, Chelsea |
| 1935–36 Aston Villa and Blackburn R | 1979–80 Bristol C, Derby Co, Bolton W |
| 1936–37 Manchester U and Sheffield W | 1980–81 Norwich C, Leicester C, Crystal Palace |
| 1937–38 Manchester C and WBA | 1981–82 Leeds U, Wolverhampton W, Middlesbrough |

*Subsequently re-elected to Division 1 when League was extended after the War.

## DIVISION 2 TO DIVISION 3

| | |
|---|---|
| 1920–21 Stockport Co | 1955–56 Plymouth Arg and Hull C |
| 1921–22 Bradford and Bristol C | 1956–57 Port Vale and Bury |
| 1922–23 Rotherham C and Wolverhampton W | 1957–58 Doncaster R and Notts Co |
| 1923–24 Nelson and Bristol C | 1958–59 Barnsley and Grimsby T |
| 1924–25 Crystal Palace and Coventry C | 1959–60 Bristol C and Hull C |
| 1925–26 Stoke C and Stockport Co | 1960–61 Lincoln C and Portsmouth |
| 1926–27 Darlington and Bradford C | 1961–62 Brighton and Bristol R |
| 1927–28 Fulham and South Shields | 1962–63 Walsall and Luton T |
| 1928–29 Port Vale and Clapton O | 1963–64 Grimsby T and Scunthorpe U |
| 1929–30 Hull C and Notts Co | 1964–65 Swindon T and Swansea T |
| 1930–31 Reading and Cardiff C | 1965–66 Middlesbrough and Leyton O |
| 1931–32 Barnsley and Bristol C | 1966–67 Northampton T and Bury |
| 1932–33 Chesterfield and Charlton Ath | 1967–68 Plymouth Arg and Rotherham U |
| 1933–34 Millwall and Lincoln C | 1968–69 Fulham and Bury |
| 1934–35 Oldham Ath and Notts Co | 1969–70 Preston NE and Aston Villa |
| 1935–36 Port Vale and Hull C | 1970–71 Blackburn R and Bolton W |
| 1936–37 Doncaster R and Bradford C | 1971–72 Charlton Ath and Watford |
| 1937–38 Barnsley and Stockport Co | 1972–73 Huddersfield T and Brighton |
| 1938–39 Norwich C and Tranmere R | 1973–74 Crystal Palace, Preston NE, Swindon T |
| 1946–47 Swansea T and Newport Co | 1974–75 Millwall, Cardiff C, Sheffield W |
| 1947–48 Doncaster R and Millwall | 1975–76 Oxford U, York C, Portsmouth |
| 1948–49 Nottingham F and Lincoln C | 1976–77 Carlisle U, Plymouth Arg, Hereford U |
| 1949–50 Plymouth Arg and Bradford | 1977–78 Blackpool, Mansfield T, Hull C |
| 1950–51 Grimsby T and Chesterfield | 1978–79 Sheffield U, Millwall, Blackburn R |
| 1951–52 Coventry C and QPR | 1979–80 Fulham, Burnley, Charlton Ath |
| 1952–53 Southampton and Barnsley | 1980–81 Preston NE, Bristol C, Bristol R |
| 1953–54 Brentford and Oldham Ath | 1981–82 Cardiff C, Wrexham, Orient |
| 1954–55 Ipswich T and Derby Co | |

## DIVISION 3 TO DIVISION 4

1958–59  Rochdale, Notts Co, Doncaster R and Stockport Co

1959–60  Accrington S, Wrexham, Mansfield T and York C

1960–61  Chesterfield, Colchester U, Bradford C and Tranmere R

1961–62  Newport Co, Brentford, Lincoln C and Torquay U

1962–63  Bradford, Brighton, Carlisle U and Halifax T

1963–64  Millwall, Crewe Alex, Wrexham and Notts Co

1964–65  Luton T, Port Vale, Colchester U and Barnsley

1965–66  Southend U, Exeter C, Brentford and York C

1966–67  Doncaster R, Workington T, Darlington and Swansea T

1967–68  Scunthorpe U, Colchester U, Grimsby T and Peterborough U (demoted)

1968–69  Oldham Ath, Crewe Alex, Hartlepool and Northampton T

1969–70  Bournemouth, Southport, Barrow, Stockport Co

1970–71  Reading, Bury, Doncaster R, Gillingham

1971–72  Mansfield T, Barnsley, Torquay U, Bradford C

1972–73  Rotherham U, Brentford, Swansea C, Scunthorpe U

1973–74  Cambridge U, Shrewsbury T, Southport, Rochdale

1974–75  AFC Bournemouth, Tranmere R, Watford, Huddersfield T

1975–76  Aldershot, Colchester U, Southend U, Halifax T

1976–77  Reading, Northampton T, Grimsby T, York C

1977–78  Port Vale, Bradford C, Hereford U, Portsmouth

1978–79  Peterborough U, Walsall, Tranmere R, Lincoln C

1979–80  Bury, Southend U, Mansfield T, Wimbledon

1980–81  Sheffield U, Colchester U, Blackpool, Hull C

1981–82  Wimbledon, Swindon T, Bristol C, Chester

## APPLICATIONS FOR RE-ELECTION

### FOURTH DIVISION

**Nine:** Hartlepool.
**Six:** Barrow (lost League place to Hereford U 1972), Southport (lost League place to Wigan Ath 1978), York C, Crewe Alex
**Five:** Darlington, Lincoln C, Workington (lost League place to Wimbledon 1977), Rochdale
**Four:** Bradford PA (lost League place to Cambridge United 1970), Chester, Halifax T, Newport Co, Stockport Co
**Three:** Doncaster R, Northampton T
**Two:** Bradford C, Hereford U, Oldham Ath, Scunthorpe U
**One:** Aldershot, Colchester U, Exeter C, Gateshead (lost League place to Peterborough U 1960), Grimsby T, Swansea C, Tranmere R, Wrexham
Accrington S resigned and Oxford U were elected 1962.
Port Vale were forced to re-apply following expulsion in 1968.

### THIRD DIVISIONS NORTH & SOUTH

**Seven:** Walsall.
**Six:** Exeter C, Halifax T, Newport Co.
**Five:** Accrington S, Barrow, Gillingham, New Brighton, Southport.
**Four:** Rochdale, Norwich C.
**Three:** Crystal Palace, Crewe Alex, Darlington, Hartlepool, Merthyr T, Swindon T.
**Two:** Aberdare Ath, Aldershot, Ashington, Bournemouth, Brentford, Chester, Colchester U, Durham C, Millwall, Nelson, QPR, Rotherham U, Southend U, Tranmere R, Watford, Workington
**One:** Bradford C, Bradford PA, Brighton, Bristol R, Cardiff C, Carlisle U, Charlton Ath, Gateshead, Grimsby T, Mansfield T, Shrewsbury T, Torquay U, York C.

# LEADING GOALSCORERS 1981–82

*Listed in order of League goals scored.*

## DIVISION 1

| | League | League Cup | FA Cup | Total |
|---|---|---|---|---|
| Kevin Keegan (Southampton) | 26 | 1 | 1 | 28 |
| Alan Brazil (Ipswich T) | 22 | 3 | 3 | 28 |
| Mick Harford (Birmingham C) | 20 | 1 | 2 | 23 |
| (inc 11 for Bristol C in League, plus 1 in League Cup and 2 in FA Cup) | | | | |
| John Wark (Ipswich T) | 18 | 3 | 1 | 22 |
| Frank Worthington (Leeds U) | 18 | 1 | 1 | 20 |
| (inc 9 for Birmingham C in League, plus 1 in League Cup and 1 in FA Cup) | | | | |
| Ian Rush (Liverpool) | 17 | 8 | 3 | 28 |
| Cyrille Regis (WBA) | 17 | 6 | 2 | 25 |
| David Cross (West Ham U) | 16 | 2 | 1 | 19 |
| Lee Chapman (Stoke C) | 16 | 1 | – | 17 |
| Iain McCulloch (Notts Co) | 16 | – | – | 16 |
| Paul Goddard (West Ham U) | 15 | 2 | – | 17 |
| Tony Evans (Birmingham C) | 15 | 1 | – | 16 |
| David Armstrong (Southampton) | 15 | – | – | 15 |
| Graeme Sharp (Everton) | 15 | – | – | 15 |
| Terry McDermott (Liverpool) | 14 | 3 | – | 17 |
| Trevor Francis (Manchester C) | 14 | – | 2 | 16 |
| (inc 2 for Nottingham F in League) | | | | |
| Robbie James (Swansea C) | 14 | – | – | 14 |
| Kenny Dalglish (Liverpool) | 13 | 5 | 2 | 20 |
| Mark Hateley (Coventry C) | 13 | 1 | 4 | 18 |
| Garth Crooks (Tottenham H) | 13 | – | 3 | 16 |
| Andy Ritchie (Brighton & HA) | 13 | 1 | – | 14 |
| Trevor Christie (Notts Co) | 13 | – | – | 13 |
| Kevin Reeves (Manchester C) | 13 | – | – | 13 |
| Frank Stapleton (Manchester U) | 13 | – | – | 13 |
| Keith Cassells (Southampton) | 12 | 4 | 7 | 23 |
| (inc 10 for Oxford U in League, plus 4 in League Cup and 7 in FA Cup) | | | | |
| Bob Latchford (Swansea C) | 12 | – | – | 12 |
| Alan Sunderland (Arsenal) | 11 | 1 | – | 12 |
| Garry Birtles (Manchester U) | 11 | – | – | 11 |
| Adrian Heath (Everton) | 11 | – | – | 11 |
| (inc 5 for Stoke C in League) | | | | |
| Mick Robinson (Brighton & HA) | 11 | – | – | 11 |

## DIVISION 2

| | League | League Cup | FA Cup | Total |
|---|---|---|---|---|
| Ronnie Moore (Rotherham U) | 22 | 2 | – | 24 |
| Gary Bannister (Sheffield W) | 21 | 1 | – | 22 |
| Brian Stein (Luton T) | 21 | – | – | 21 |
| Luther Blissett (Watford) | 19 | 3 | – | 22 |
| Keith Houchen (Orient) | 19 | 1 | – | 20 |
| (inc 18 for Hartlepool U in League, plus 1 in League Cup) | | | | |
| Imre Varadi (Newcastle U) | 18 | – | 2 | 20 |
| Steve White (Luton T) | 18 | 1 | – | 19 |
| Simon Stainrod (QPR) | 17 | 2 | 5 | 24 |
| Ian Atkins (Shrewsbury T) | 17 | 2 | – | 19 |
| Gary Lineker (Leicester C) | 17 | – | 2 | 19 |
| Clive Walker (Chelsea) | 16 | 1 | – | 17 |
| Rodger Wylde (Oldham Ath) | 16 | 1 | – | 17 |
| David Moss (Luton T) | 15 | – | 1 | 16 |
| Ian Banks (Barnsley) | 15 | – | – | 15 |
| Simon Garner (Blackburn R) | 14 | 2 | 2 | 18 |
| Clive Allen (QPR) | 13 | 1 | 7 | 21 |
| Rodney Fern (Rotherham U) | 13 | 2 | – | 15 |
| Ross Jenkins (Watford) | 13 | 2 | – | 15 |
| Gary Stevens (Cardiff C) | 13 | 2 | – | 15 |
| John Barnes (Watford) | 13 | 1 | – | 14 |
| Tony Henry (Bolton W) | 13 | – | – | 13 |
| Paul Walsh (Charlton Ath) | 13 | – | – | 13 |
| Alan Mayes (Chelsea) | 12 | – | 4 | 16 |
| Paul Heaton (Oldham Ath) | 12 | 1 | 1 | 14 |
| Chris Thompson (Bolton W) | 12 | 1 | 1 | 14 |
| Keith Bertschin (Norwich C) | 12 | – | – | 12 |
| Trevor Aylott (Barnsley) | 11 | 4 | – | 15 |
| Jim Melrose (Leicester C) | 11 | 1 | 2 | 14 |
| Ian Edwards (Wrexham) | 11 | 2 | – | 13 |
| Derek Hales (Charlton Ath) | 11 | 2 | – | 13 |
| Trevor Whymark (Grimsby T) | 11 | 1 | 1 | 13 |
| Colin Lee (Chelsea) | 11 | – | 1 | 12 |
| Colin Walker (Barnsley) | 11 | 1 | – | 12 |
| Kevin Stonehouse (Blackburn R) | 11 | – | – | 11 |

## DIVISION 3

| | League | League Cup | FA Cup | Total |
|---|---|---|---|---|
| Gordon Davies (Fulham) | 24 | 1 | – | 25 |
| Tony Kellow (Exeter C) | 21 | 1 | – | 22 |
| Steve Phillips (Southend U) | 20 | 1 | 1 | 22 |
| (inc 10 for Northampton T in League, plus 1 in League Cup and 1 in FA Cup) | | | | |
| Alex Bruce (Preston NE) | 18 | 1 | – | 19 |
| John Sims (Plymouth Arg) | 18 | – | – | 18 |
| Billy Rafferty (Portsmouth) | 17 | 2 | – | 19 |
| Jeff Cook (Plymouth Arg) | 16 | – | – | 16 |
| Dean Horrix (Millwall) | 15 | 3 | – | 18 |
| Bryan Robson (Carlisle U) | 15 | – | 3 | 18 |
| Dave Bamber (Blackpool) | 15 | 1 | 1 | 17 |
| Neil Webb (Reading) | 15 | – | – | 15 |
| Andy Thomas (Oxford U) | 14 | 1 | 3 | 18 |
| Phil Bonnyman (Chesterfield) | 14 | – | 2 | 16 |
| Donald Penn (Walsall) | 14 | 1 | – | 15 |
| Paul Rideout (Swindon T) | 14 | – | – | 14 |
| Dean Coney (Fulham) | 13 | 4 | 2 | 19 |
| Roy Carter (Swindon T) | 13 | 1 | 1 | 15 |
| Martin Henderson (Chesterfield) | 13 | – | 1 | 14 |
| Francis Joseph (Wimbledon) | 13 | – | – | 13 |
| Keith Mercer (Southend U) | 13 | – | – | 13 |
| Tommy Tynan (Newport Co) | 13 | – | 3 | 16 |
| Nick Chatterton (Millwall) | 12 | 1 | 3 | 16 |
| Ken Price (Gillingham) | 12 | 1 | 1 | 14 |
| Dean White (Gillingham) | 12 | – | 2 | 14 |
| Roger Brown (Fulham) | 12 | – | – | 12 |
| Kerry Dixon (Reading) | 12 | – | – | 12 |
| Gary Simpson (Chester) | 12 | – | – | 12 |
| Paul Randall (Bristol R) | 12 | – | – | 12 |
| Billy Hamilton (Burnley) | 11 | 1 | 4 | 16 |
| Tony Cunningham (Lincoln C) | 11 | 4 | – | 15 |
| George Shipley (Lincoln C) | 11 | 3 | – | 14 |
| Gordon Staniforth (Carlisle U) | 11 | 1 | 1 | 13 |
| David Williams (Bristol R) | 11 | 1 | 1 | 13 |
| John Aldridge (Newport Co) | 11 | 1 | – | 12 |
| Glenn Cockerill (Lincoln C) | 11 | 1 | – | 12 |
| Archie Stephens (Bristol R) | 11 | 1 | – | 12 |
| Kevin Hodges (Plymouth Arg) | 11 | – | – | 11 |

## DIVISION 4

| | League | League Cup | FA Cup | Total |
|---|---|---|---|---|
| Keith Edwards (Sheffield U) | 36 | – | 1 | 37 |
| (inc 1 for Hull C in League) | | | | |
| Craig Madden (Bury) | 35 | 3 | 4 | 42 |
| Les Mutrie (Hull C) | 27 | – | 1 | 28 |
| Robbie Cooke (Peterborough U) | 24 | 1 | 3 | 28 |
| Bobby Campbell (Bradford C) | 24 | 3 | – | 27 |
| Keith Walwyn (York C) | 23 | – | 2 | 25 |
| Ian Allinson (Colchester U) | 21 | 2 | 3 | 26 |
| Kevin Bremner (Colchester U) | 21 | 3 | – | 24 |
| Bobby Davison (Halifax T) | 20 | 1 | – | 21 |
| Les Bradd (Wigan Ath) | 19 | 1 | – | 20 |
| David McNiven (Bradford C) | 19 | – | – | 19 |
| David Speedie (Darlington) | 17 | – | 1 | 18 |
| Barry Gallagher (Bradford C) | 16 | 2 | – | 18 |
| Tony Funnell (AFC Bournemouth) | 16 | – | 2 | 18 |
| Bob Hatton (Sheffield U) | 15 | 2 | 1 | 18 |
| Bob Newton (Hartlepool U) | 15 | 1 | 2 | 18 |
| Peter Houghton (Wigan Ath) | 15 | 2 | – | 17 |
| Tony Kenworthy (Sheffield U) | 15 | 1 | – | 16 |
| Jim Lumby (Mansfield T) | 14 | 3 | – | 17 |
| Roy McDonough (Colchester U) | 14 | 2 | – | 16 |
| Colin Morris (Sheffield U) | 14 | – | 2 | 16 |
| (inc 10 for Blackpool in League, plus 2 in FA Cup) | | | | |
| Mark Hilditch (Rochdale) | 14 | 1 | – | 15 |
| Ernie Moss (Port Vale) | 13 | 2 | 2 | 17 |
| John Kerr (Tranmere R) | 13 | 3 | – | 16 |
| Steve Johnson (Bury) | 13 | 1 | 2 | 16 |
| Alan Walsh (Darlington) | 13 | 1 | 1 | 15 |
| Trevor Morgan (AFC Bournemouth) | 13 | – | – | 13 |
| (inc 6 for Mansfield T) | | | | |
| Stuart Phillips (Hereford U) | 12 | 1 | 2 | 15 |
| Graham Barrow (Wigan Ath) | 12 | 3 | – | 15 |
| Eamon O'Keefe (Wigan Ath) | 12 | 1 | – | 13 |
| (inc 3 for Everton in League, plus 1 in League Cup) | | | | |
| Brian Marwood (Hull C) | 12 | – | 1 | 13 |
| Mark Palios (Crewe Alex) | 12 | – | – | 12 |
| Barry Wellings (Rochdale) | 11 | 1 | – | 12 |
| Tony Brown (Torquay U) | 11 | – | – | 11 |
| Billy Kellock (Peterborough U) | 11 | – | – | 11 |
| Mark Sanford (Aldershot) | 11 | – | – | 11 |
| Mike Trusson (Sheffield U) | 11 | – | – | 11 |

## LEADING SCORERS IN LEAGUE SINCE 1946−47

### 1946−47

**Division 1**
| | |
|---|---|
| D. Westcott (Wolverhampton W) | 37 |
| D. Reid (Portsmouth) | 29 |
| F. Steele (Stoke C) | 29 |
| R. Lewis (Arsenal) | 28 |
| S. Mortensen (Blackpool) | 28 |

**Division 3 (South)**
| | |
|---|---|
| D. Clark (Bristol C) | 36 |
| M. G. McPhee (Reading) | 31 |
| S. Richards (Cardiff C) | 31 |
| A. Garrett (Northampton T) | 26 |
| J. W. Stephens (Swindon T) | 25 |

**Division 2**
| | |
|---|---|
| C. Wayman (Newcastle U) | 30 |
| D. J. Walsh (WBA) | 28 |
| G. Lowrie (Coventry C) | 26 |
| G. Robledo (Barnsley) | 24 |

**Division 3 (North)**
| | |
|---|---|
| C. Jordan (Doncaster R) | 42 |
| W. Ardron (Rotherham U) | 38 |
| R. Yates (Chester) | 36 |
| P. M. Cheetham (Lincoln C) | 28 |

### 1947−48

**Division 1**
| | |
|---|---|
| a I R. Rooke (Arsenal) | 33 |
| M. Fenton (Middlesbrough) | 28 |
| A. Stubbins (Liverpool) | 26 |
| J. Rowley (Manchester U) | 23 |
| S. Mortensen (Blackpool) | 21 |

**Division 3 (South)**
| | |
|---|---|
| L. Townsend (Bristol C) | 29 |
| D. Milligan (Bournemouth & BA) | 26 |
| D. Massart (Walsall) | 23 |
| C. Hatton (QPR) | 21 |

**Division 2**
| | |
|---|---|
| E. Quigley (Sheffield W) | 23 |
| A. J. Wakefield (Leeds U) | 22 |
| D. J. Walsh (WBA) | 22 |
| J. Milburn (Newcastle U) | 21 |
| J. Downie (Bradford) | 19 |

**Division 3 (North)**
| | |
|---|---|
| J. Hutchinson (Lincoln C) | 32 |
| W. Ardron (Rotherham U) | 27 |
| J. Lindsay (Carlisle U) | 26 |
| T. Wyles (Southport) | 26 |
| W. F. Tunnicliffe (Wrexham) | 20 |

### 1948−49

**Division 1**
| | |
|---|---|
| W. Moir (Bolton W) | 25 |
| F. Bowyer (Stoke C) | 21 |
| R. Bentley (Chelsea) | 20 |
| J. Rowley (Manchester U) | 20 |
| C. Vaughan (Charlton Ath) | 20 |

**Division 3 (South)**
| | |
|---|---|
| D. McGibbon (Bournemouth & BA) | 30 |
| S. Richards (Swansea T) | 26 |
| J. Sewell (Notts County) | 26 |
| P. E. Chapman (Walsall) | 25 |
| W. M. Jones (Swindon T) | 25 |

**Division 2**
| | |
|---|---|
| C. Wayman (Southampton) | 32 |
| T. Briggs (Grimsby T) | 26 |
| D. Massart (Bury) | 25 |
| R. Thomas (Fulham) | 23 |
| D. J. Walsh (WBA) | 23 |

**Division 3 (North)**
| | |
|---|---|
| W. Ardron (Rotherham U) | 29 |
| A. Patrick (York C) | 26 |
| A. Quinn (Darlington) | 23 |
| N. W. Moore (Hull C) | 22 |
| E. Gemmell (Oldham Ath) | 19 |

### 1949−50

**Division 1**
| | |
|---|---|
| D. Davis (Sunderland) | 25 |
| S. Mortensen (Blackpool) | 22 |
| J. Stamps (Derby Co) | 22 |
| H. Goring (Arsenal) | 21 |
| J. Rowley (Manchester U) | 20 |

**Division 3 (South)**
| | |
|---|---|
| T. Lawton (Notts Co) | 31 |
| W. Ardron (Nottingham F) | 25 |
| A. J. Wakefield (Southend U) | 23 |
| R. Blackman (Reading) | 22 |
| J. Devlin (Walsall) | 22 |

**Division 2**
| | |
|---|---|
| T. Briggs (Grimsby T) | 35 |
| C. Wayman (Southampton) | 24 |
| W. Robinson (West Ham U) | 23 |
| J. Lee (Leicester C) | 22 |
| L. Medley (Tottenham H) | 18 |

**Division 3 (North)**
| | |
|---|---|
| P. Doherty (Doncaster R) | 26 |
| R. Phillips, (Crewe Alex) | 26 |
| A. C. Burgess (Chester) | 24 |
| E. Dodds (Lincoln C) | 21 |
| D. Travis (Accrington Stanley) | 20 |

### 1950−51

**Division 1**
| | |
|---|---|
| S. Mortensen (Blackpool) | 30 |
| J. Lee (Derby Co) | 28 |
| N. Lofthouse (Bolton W) | 21 |
| A. McCrae (Middlesbrough) | 21 |
| D. Reid (Portsmouth) | 21 |

**Division 3 (South)**
| | |
|---|---|
| W. Ardron (Nottingham F) | 36 |
| R. Blackman (Reading) | 35 |
| J. Constantine (Millwall) | 27 |
| M. Tadman (Plymouth Arg) | 23 |

**Division 2**
| | |
|---|---|
| J. McCormack (Barnsley) | 33 |
| A. Rowley (Leicester C) | 28 |
| C. Wayman (Preston NE) | 27 |
| W. Robinson (West Ham U) | 26 |

**Division 3 (North)**
| | |
|---|---|
| J. Shaw (Rotherham U) | 37 |
| R. Crosbie (Bradford) | 27 |
| L. E. Wildon (Hartlepools U) | 26 |
| A. Burgess (Chester) | 22 |
| J. Nuttall (Southport) | 22 |

## 1951–52

| Division 1 | | Division 2 | |
|---|---|---|---|
| G. Robledo (Newcastle U) | 33 | D. Dooley (Sheffield W) | 46 |
| R. Allen (WBA) | 32 | A. Rowley (Leicester C) | 38 |
| J. Rowley (Manchester U) | 30 | W. Ardron (Nottingham F) | 29 |
| J. Dixon (Aston Villa) | 26 | W. Grant (Cardiff C) | 26 |
| C. Wayman (Preston NE) | 24 | **Division 3 (North)** | |
| **Division 3 (South)** | | A. Graver (Lincoln C) | 36 |
| R. Blackman (Reading) | 39 | W. Cairns (Grimsby T) | 32 |
| V. Lambden (Bristol R) | 29 | W. Fenton (York C) | 31 |
| M. Tadman (Plymouth Arg) | 27 | E. Gemmell (Oldham Ath) | 28 |
| F. Ramscar (Northampton T) | 24 | D. Frost (Halifax T) | 24 |

## 1952–53

| Division 1 | | Division 2 | |
|---|---|---|---|
| C. Wayman (Preston NE) | 24 | A. Rowley (Leicester C) | 39 |
| P. Harris (Portsmouth) | 23 | B. Jezzard (Fulham) | 34 |
| D. Lishman (Arsenal) | 23 | J. Glazzard (Huddersfield T) | 30 |
| | | J. Charles (Leeds U) | 26 |
| | | J. Pye (Luton T) | 24 |
| **Division 3 (South)** | | **Division 3 (North)** | |
| G. Bradford (Bristol R) | 33 | J. Whitehouse (Carlisle U) | 29 |
| R. Collins (Torquay U) | 27 | J. Connor (Stockport Co) | 26 |
| J. English (Northampton T) | 26 | W. Fenton (York C) | 24 |
| A. W. Rodgers (Bristol C) | 26 | E. Gemmell (Oldham Ath) | 24 |
| W. O'Donnell (Northampton T) | 26 | D. Travis (Chester) | 24 |

## 1953–54

| Division 1 | | Division 2 | |
|---|---|---|---|
| J. Glazzard (Huddersfield T) | 29 | J. Charles (Leeds U) | 42 |
| J. Nicholls (WBA) | 29 | B. Jezzard (Fulham) | 38 |
| R. Allen (WBA) | 25 | T. Briggs (Blackburn R) | 32 |
| J. Hancocks (Wolverhampton W) | 25 | R. Burke (Rotherham U) | 32 |
| D. Wilshaw (Wolverhampton W) | 25 | J. W. Parker (Everton) | 31 |
| **Division 3 (South)** | | **Division 3 (North)** | |
| J. English (Northampton T) | 28 | J. Connor (Stockport Co) | 31 |
| R. Blackman (Reading) | 27 | G. Ashman (Carlisle U) | 30 |
| E. Day (Southampton) | 26 | C. Done (Tranmere R) | 25 |
| L. Graham (Newport Co) | 24 | R. Brown (Barnsley) | 24 |
| J. Atyeo (Bristol C) | 23 | K. Murray (Mansfield T) | 22 |

## 1954–55

| Division 1 | | Division 2 | |
|---|---|---|---|
| R. Allen (WBA) | 27 | T. Briggs (Blackburn R) | 33 |
| J. Glazzard (Huddersfield T) | 26 | G. Turner (Luton T) | 32 |
| E. Firmani (Charlton Ath) | 25 | W. Liddell (Liverpool) | 30 |
| J. Hancocks (Wolverhampton W) | 25 | J. Evans (Liverpool) | 29 |
| | | G. Bradford (Bristol R) | 27 |
| **Division 3 (South)** | | **Division 3 (North)** | |
| E. Morgan (Gillingham) | 31 | A. Bottom (York C) | 30 |
| J. Atyeo (Bristol C) | 28 | J. Connor (Stockport Co) | 30 |
| E. Day (Southampton) | 27 | D. Travis (Oldham Ath) | 30 |
| R. Hollis (Southend U) | 27 | G. Stewart (Accrington S) | 28 |
| | | J. Whitehouse (Carlisle U) | 25 |

## 1955–56

| Division 1 | | Division 2 | |
|---|---|---|---|
| N. Lofthouse (Bolton W) | 33 | W. Gardiner (Leicester C) | 34 |
| C. Fleming (Sunderland) | 28 | R. Shiner (Sheffield W) | 33 |
| V. Keeble (Newcastle U) | 26 | T. Briggs (Blackburn R) | 31 |
| T. Taylor (Manchester U) | 25 | J. Atyeo (Bristol C) | 30 |
| | | J. Charles (Leeds U) | 30 |
| **Division 3 (South)** | | **Division 3 (North)** | |
| R. Collins (Torquay U) | 40 | R. Crosbie (Grimsby T) | 36 |
| R. A. R. Hunt (Norwich C) | 31 | G. Stewart (Accrington S) | 35 |
| T. Parker (Ipswich T) | 30 | W. Sowden (Chesterfield) | 32 |
| K. McCurley (Colchester U) | 29 | A. Bottom (York C) | 31 |
| A. Mundy (Brighton & HA) | 27 | J. Connor (Stockport Co) | 30 |

## 1956–57

| Division 1 | | Division 2 | |
|---|---|---|---|
| J. Charles (Leeds U) | 38 | A. Rowley (Leicester C) | 44 |
| J. Mudie (Blackpool) | 32 | B. Clough (Middlesbrough) | 38 |
| G. Turner (Luton T) | 30 | T. Briggs (Blackburn R) | 32 |
| N. Lofthouse (Bolton W) | 28 | J. Barrett (Nottingham F) | 27 |
| | | T. Johnston (Leyton O) | 27 |
| **Division 3 (South)** | | **Division 3 (North)** | |
| E. Phillips (Ipswich T) | 41 | R. Straw (Derby Co) | 37 |
| R. Collins (Torquay U) | 30 | G. Stewart (Accrington S) | 33 |
| S. Newsham (Bournemouth & BA) | 30 | W. Tulip (Darlington) | 32 |
| T. Dixon (Reading) | 28 | R. Smith (Bradford) | 28 |
| B. Edwards (Swindon T) | 25 | W. Gordon (Barrow) | 27 |

## 1957–58

| Division 1 | | Division 2 | |
|---|---|---|---|
| R. Smith (Tottenham H) | 36 | T. Johnston (Leyton O 35, | |
| T. Thompson (Preston NE) | 34 | plus 8 for Blackburn R) | 43 |
| G. Turner (Luton T) | 33 | B. Clough (Middlesbrough) | 40 |
| J. Murray (Wolverhampton W) | 29 | J. Summers (Charlton Ath) | 28 |
| T. Finney (Preston NE) | 26 | R. Rafferty (Grimsby T) | 26 |
| | | J. Atyeo (Bristol C) | 23 |
| **Division 3 (South)** | | **Division 3 (North)** | |
| S. McCrory (Southend U) | 31 | A. Ackerman (Carlisle U) | 35 |
| D. Reeves (Southampton) | 31 | K. Williams (Tranmere R) | 28 |
| E. Towers (Brentford) | 29 | G. Stewart (Accrington Stanley) | 27 |
| W. Carter (Plymouth Arg) | 26 | B. Jepson (Chester) | 25 |
| T. Dixon (Reading) | 24 | J. Parker (Bury) | 25 |

## 1958–59

| Division 1 | | Division 2 | |
|---|---|---|---|
| J. Greaves (Chelsea) | 32 | B. Clough (Middlesbrough) | 42 |
| R. Smith (Tottenham H) | 32 | R. Shiner (Sheffield W) | 28 |
| R. Charlton (Manchester U) | 29 | R. Froggatt (Sheffield W) | 26 |
| N. Lofthouse (Bolton W) | 29 | D. Pace (Sheffield U) | 26 |
| | | D. Ward (Bristol R) | 26 |
| **Division 3** | | **Division 4** | |
| E. Towers (Brentford) | 32 | A. Rowley (Shrewsbury T) | 37 |
| W. Bradbury (Hull C) | 30 | A. Woan (Northampton T) | 32 |
| J. McCole (Bradford C) | 28 | A. Richards (Walsall) | 28 |
| C. Smith (Hull C) | 26 | E. Calland (Exeter C) | 27 |
| T. Rowley (Tranmere R) | 25 | R. Straw (Coventry C) | 27 |

## 1959–60

| Division 1 | | Division 2 | |
|---|---|---|---|
| D. Viollet (Manchester U) | 32 | B. Clough (Middlesbrough) | 39 |
| J. Greaves (Chelsea) | 29 | E. Phillips (Ipswich T) | 24 |
| J. Murray (Wolverhampton W) | 29 | T. Johnston (Leyton Orient) | 24 |
| L. White (Newcastle U) | 28 | W. Curry (Brighton & HA) | 23 |
| D. Kevan (WBA) | 26 | G. Hitchens (Aston Villa) | 23 |
| **Division 3** | | **Division 4** | |
| D. Reeves (Southampton) | 39 | C. Holton (Watford) | 42 |
| R. Hunt (Grimsby T) | 33 | E. Uphill (Watford) | 30 |
| A. Rowley (Shrewsbury T) | 32 | J. Allan (Bradford) | 27 |
| M. King (Colchester U) | 30 | H. Llewellyn (Crewe Alex) | 25 |
| D. Price (Southend U) | 28 | | |

## 1960–61

| Division 1 | | Division 2 | |
|---|---|---|---|
| J. Greaves (Chelsea) | 41 | R. Crawford (Ipswich T) | 39 |
| D. Herd (Arsenal) | 29 | B. Clough (Middlesbrough) | 34 |
| G. Hitchens (Aston Villa) | 29 | E. Phillips (Ipswich T) | 30 |
| J. Farmer (Wolverhampton W) | 28 | | |
| R. Smith (Tottenham H) | 28 | | |
| **Division 3** | | **Division 4** | |
| A. Richards (Walsall) | 36 | T. Bly (Peterborough U) | 52 |
| B. Bedford (QPR) | 33 | G. Hudson (Accrington Stanley) | 35 |
| C. Taylor (Walsall) | 33 | P. Burridge (Millwall) | 34 |
| C. Holton (Watford) | 32 | J. Byrne (Crystal Palace) | 30 |
| J. Wheeler (Reading) | 31 | R. Summersby (Crystal Palace) | 25 |

## 1961–62

**Division 1**
| | |
|---|---|
| R. Crawford (Ipswich T) | 33 |
| D. Kevan (WBA) | 33 |
| R. Charnley (Blackpool) | 30 |
| E. Phillips (Ipswich T) | 28 |
| T. R. Vernon (Everton) | 28 |

**Division 3**
| | |
|---|---|
| C. Holton (Northampton T 36, plus 1 for Watford) | 37 |
| D. Bedford (QPR) | 36 |
| R. Rafferty (Grimsby T) | 34 |
| T. Bly (Peterborough U) | 30 |
| J. Atyeo (Bristol C) | 26 |

**Division 2**
| | |
|---|---|
| R. Hunt (Liverpool) | 41 |
| B. Thomas (Scunthorpe U) | 31 |
| B. Clough (Sunderland) | 29 |
| G. O'Brien (Southampton) | 28 |
| A. Peacock (Middlesbrough) | 24 |

**Division 4**
| | |
|---|---|
| R. R. Hunt (Colchester U) | 37 |
| D. Layne (Bradford C) | 34 |
| M. King (Colchester U) | 31 |
| F. Lord (Crewe Alex) | 30 |
| J. Weir (York C) | 28 |

## 1962–63

**Division 1**
| | |
|---|---|
| J. Greaves (Tottenham H) | 37 |
| J. Baker (Arsenal) | 29 |
| D. Layne (Sheffield W) | 29 |
| R. Crawford (Ipswich T) | 25 |

**Division 3**
| | |
|---|---|
| G. Hudson (Coventry C) | 30 |
| D. Ward (Watford) | 29 |
| M. King (Colchester U) | 26 |
| A. Ashworth (Northampton T) | 25 |

**Division 2**
| | |
|---|---|
| R. Tambling (Chelsea) | 35 |
| A. Peacock (Middlesbrough) | 31 |
| T. Allcock (Norwich C) | 26 |
| J. Storrie (Leeds U) | 25 |
| B. Clough (Sunderland) | 24 |

**Division 4**
| | |
|---|---|
| K. Wagstaff (Mansfield T) | 34 |
| C. Booth (Doncaster R) | 34 |
| R. Chapman (Mansfield T) | 31 |
| H. Lister (Oldham Ath) | 30 |
| F. Lord (Crewe Alex) | 30 |

## 1963–64

**Division 1**
| | |
|---|---|
| J. Greaves (Tottenham H) | 35 |
| M. McEvoy (Blackburn R) | 32 |
| R. Hunt (Liverpool) | 31 |
| D. Law (Manchester U) | 30 |
| R. Crawford (Wolverhampton W 26, plus 2 for Ipswich T) | 28 |

**Division 3**
| | |
|---|---|
| A. Biggs (Bristol R) | 30 |
| K. Wagstaff (Mansfield T) | 29 |
| D. Coughlin (Bournemouth & BA) | 28 |
| G. Hudson (Coventry C) | 25 |

**Division 2**
| | |
|---|---|
| R. Saunders (Portsmouth) | 33 |
| A. Dawson (Preston NE) | 31 |
| D. Kevan (Manchester C) | 30 |
| R. T. Davies (Norwich C) | 26 |
| J. Crossan (Sunderland) | 22 |

**Division 4**
| | |
|---|---|
| H. McIlmoyle (Carlisle U) | 39 |
| H. Green (Bradford C) | 29 |
| A. Spence (Southport) | 27 |
| J. Dyson (Tranmere R) | 26 |
| J. Bonson (Newport Co) | 25 |

## 1964–65

**Division 1**
| | |
|---|---|
| J. Greaves (Tottenham H) | 29 |
| A. McEvoy (Blackburn R) | 29 |
| D. Law (Manchester U) | 28 |
| F. Pickering (Everton) | 27 |

**Division 3**
| | |
|---|---|
| K. Wagstaff (Mansfield T 8, plus 23 for Hull C) | 31 |
| C. Chilton (Hull C) | 27 |
| J. Atyeo (Bristol C) | 23 |
| B. Bedford (QPR) | 23 |
| A. Clarke (Walsall) | 23 |

**Division 2**
| | |
|---|---|
| G. O'Brien (Southampton) | 34 |
| A. Dawson (Preston NE) | 26 |
| B. Godfrey (Preston NE) | 25 |
| A. Bennett (Rotherham U) | 24 |
| F. Lee (Bolton W) | 23 |

**Division 4**
| | |
|---|---|
| A. Jeffrey (Doncaster R) | 36 |
| T. Harkin (Crewe Alex) | 35 |
| R. Stubbs (Torquay U) | 31 |
| K. Hector (Bradford) | 29 |

## 1965–66

**Division 1**
| | |
|---|---|
| R. Hunt (Liverpool) | 30 |
| W. Irvine (Burnley) | 29 |
| T. Hateley (Aston Villa) | 27 |
| D. Herd (Manchester U) | 24 |
| G. Hurst (West Ham U) | 23 |

**Division 3**
| | |
|---|---|
| L. Allen (QPR) | 30 |
| M. Tees (Grimsby T) | 28 |
| K. Wagstaff (Hull C) | 27 |
| B. Gibbs (Gillingham) | 23 |

**Division 2**
| | |
|---|---|
| M. Chivers (Southampton) | 30 |
| G. Vowden (Birmingham C) | 21 |
| P. Knowles (Wolverhampton W) | 20 |
| J. Atyeo (Bristol C) | 19 |

**Division 4**
| | |
|---|---|
| K. Hector (Bradford) | 44 |
| J. O'Rourke (Luton T) | 32 |
| J. Dyson (Tranmere R) | 29 |
| L. Sheffield (Doncaster R) | 28 |

428

## 1966-67

| Division 1 | | Division 2 | |
|---|---|---|---|
| R. Davies (Southampton) | 37 | R. Gould (Coventry C) | 24 |
| G. Hurst (West Ham U) | 29 | F. Lee (Bolton W) | 22 |
| J. Greaves (Tottenham H) | 25 | R. Crawford (Ipswich T) | 21 |
| A. Clarke (Fulham) | 24 | K. Wagstaff (Hull C) | 21 |
| D. Law (Manchester U) | 23 | E. Hunt (Wolverhampton W) | 20 |
| **Division 3** | | **Division 4** | |
| R. Marsh (QPR) | 30 | E. Phythian (Hartlepools U) | 23 |
| J. O'Rourke (Middlesbrough) | 27 | E. Chapman (Lincoln C) | 20 |
| I. Towers (Oldham Ath) | 27 | J. Mulvaney (Hartlepools U) | 19 |
| D. Rogers (Swindon T) | 25 | R. Smith (Southend U) | 19 |

## 1967-68

| Division 1 | | Division 2 | |
|---|---|---|---|
| G. Best (Manchester U) | 28 | J. Hickton (Middlesbrough) | 24 |
| R. Davies (Southampton) | 28 | B. Bridges (Birmingham C) | 23 |
| J. Astle (WBA) | 25 | K. Hector (Derby Co) | 21 |
| R. Hunt (Liverpool) | 25 | G. Ingram (Blackpool) | 18 |
| J. Greaves (Tottenham H) | 23 | R. Woodruff (Crystal Palace) | 18 |
| **Division 3** | | **Division 4** | |
| D. Rogers (Swindon T) | 25 | R. Chapman (Port Vale) | 25 |
| R. Owen (Bury) | 25 | L. Massie (Halifax T) | 25 |
| J. Fryatt (Torquay U 2 plus 22 | | B. Rioch (Luton T) | 24 |
| for Stockport County) | 24 | E. Loyden (Chester) | 22 |
| K. Napier (Brighton & HA) | 24 | K. Randall (Chesterfield) | 21 |
| G. Yardley (Tranmere R) | 23 | | |

## 1968-69

| Division 1 | | Division 2 | |
|---|---|---|---|
| J. Greaves (Tottenham H) | 27 | J. Toshack (Cardiff C) | 22 |
| G. Hurst (West Ham U) | 25 | K. Wagstaff (Hull C) | 20 |
| J. Royle (Everton) | 22 | J. Hickton (Middlesbrough) | 18 |
| J. Astle (WBA) | 21 | | |
| B. Robson (Newcastle U) | 21 | | |
| **Division 3** | | **Division 4** | |
| B. Lewis (Luton T) | 22 | G. Talbot (Chester) | 22 |
| D. Rogers (Swindon T) | 22 | W. Best (Southend U) | 20 |
| G. Andrews (Southport) | 19 | J. Howarth (Aldershot) | 19 |
| W. Atkins (Stockport Co) | 18 | E. MacDougall (York C) | 19 |

## 1969-70

| Division 1 | | Division 2 | |
|---|---|---|---|
| J. Astle (WBA) | 25 | J. Hickton (Middlesbrough) | 24 |
| P. Osgood (Chelsea) | 23 | B. Bridges (QPR) | 22 |
| J. Royle (Everton) | 23 | J. Byrom (Bolton W) | 20 |
| B. Robson (Newcastle U) | 22 | | |
| H. Curran (Wolverhampton W) | 20 | | |
| **Division 3** | | **Division 4** | |
| G. Jones (Bury) | 26 | A. Kinsey (Wrexham) | 27 |
| M. Macdonald (Luton T) | 25 | S. Brace (Grimsby T) | 25 |
| L. Chappell (Reading) | 24 | J. Hall (Peterborough U) | 24 |
| S. Earle (Fulham) | 22 | | |
| E. MacDougall (Bournemouth & BA) | 21 | | |

## 1970-71

| Division 1 | | Division 2 | |
|---|---|---|---|
| A. Brown (WBA) | 28 | J. Hickton (Middlesbrough) | 25 |
| M. Chivers (Tottenham H) | 21 | M. Macdonald (Luton T) | 24 |
| A. Clarke (Leeds U) | 19 | C. Chilton (Hull C) | 21 |
| R. Kennedy (Arsenal) | 19 | R. Marsh (QPR) | 21 |
| | | R. Hatton (Carlisle U) | 18 |
| **Division 3** | | **Division 4** | |
| G. Ingram (Preston NE) | 22 | E. MacDougall (Bournemouth & BA) | 42 |
| D. Roberts (Mansfield T) | 22 | P. Aimson (York C) | 26 |
| K. Randall (Chesterfield) | 19 | R. Crawford (Colchester U) | 25 |
| | | J. Fryatt (Oldham Ath) | 24 |

## 1971–72

**Division 1**
| | |
|---|---|
| F. Lee (Manchester C) | 33 |
| M. Chivers (Tottenham H) | 25 |
| P. Lorimer (Leeds U) | 23 |
| M. Macdonald (Newcastle U) | 23 |
| P. Osgood (Chelsea) | 19 |

**Division 2**
| | |
|---|---|
| R. Latchford (Birmingham C) | 23 |
| J. Galley (Bristol C) | 22 |
| R. Hatton (Carlisle U 7 plus 15 for Birmingham C) | 22 |
| B. Clark (Cardiff C) | 21 |
| F. Casper (Burnley) | 18 |

**Division 3**
| | |
|---|---|
| E. MacDougall (Bournemouth & BA) | 35 |
| A. Wood (Shrewsbury T) | 35 |
| C. Gilbert (Rotherham U) | 22 |
| L. Bradd (Notts Co) | 21 |
| A. Lochhead (Aston Villa) | 19 |

**Division 4**
| | |
|---|---|
| P. Price (Peterborough U) | 28 |
| R. McNeil (Lincoln C 13 plus 14 for Northampton T) | 27 |
| M. Tees (Grimsby T) | 27 |
| W. Garner (Southend U) | 25 |
| J. O'Mara (Brentford) | 25 |

## 1972–73

**Division 1**
| | |
|---|---|
| B. Robson (West Ham U) | 28 |
| J. Richards (Wolverhampton W) | 27 |
| W. Dearden (Sheffield U) | 20 |
| R. Latchford (Birmingham C) | 19 |

**Division 2**
| | |
|---|---|
| D. Givens (QPR) | 23 |
| G. Bolland (Millwall) | 19 |
| S. Bowles (QPR) | 17 |
| A. Gowling (Huddersfield T) | 17 |
| S. Pearson (Hull C) | 11 |

**Division 3**
| | |
|---|---|
| B. Bannister (Bristol R) | 25 |
| A. Horsfield (Charlton Ath) | 25 |
| J. Byrom (Bolton W) | 20 |
| E. Loyden (Tranmere R) | 19 |
| K. Randall (Notts Co) | 19 |

**Division 4**
| | |
|---|---|
| F. Binney (Exeter C) | 28 |
| J. Hall (Peterborough U) | 21 |
| R. McNeil (Lincoln C) | 21 |
| A. Provan (Southport) | 21 |
| J. Fairbrother (Mansfield T) | 20 |

## 1973–74

**Division 1**
| | |
|---|---|
| M. Channon (Southampton) | 21 |
| F. Worthington (Leicester C) | 20 |
| S. Bowles (QPR) | 19 |
| K. Hector (Derby Co) | 18 |

**Division 2**
| | |
|---|---|
| D. McKenzie (Nottingham F) | 26 |
| A. Wood (Millwall) | 21 |
| T. Brown (WBA) | 19 |
| A. Foggon (Middlesbrough) | 19 |

**Division 3**
| | |
|---|---|
| W. Jennings (Watford) | 26 |
| J. Howarth (Aldershot) | 25 |
| A. Gowling (Huddersfield T) | 24 |
| A. Warboys (Bristol R) | 22 |
| A. Buckley (Walsall) | 21 |

**Division 4**
| | |
|---|---|
| B. Yeo (Gillingham) | 31 |
| F. Binney (Exeter C) | 25 |
| L. Chappell (Reading) | 24 |
| R. Svarc (Colchester U) | 24 |

## 1974–75

**Division 1**
| | |
|---|---|
| M. Macdonald (Newcastle U) | 21 |
| B. Kidd (Arsenal) | 19 |
| F. Worthington (Leicester C) | 18 |
| K. Hibbitt (Wolverhampton W) | 17 |
| R. Latchford (Everton) | 17 |

**Division 2**
| | |
|---|---|
| B. Little (Aston Villa) | 20 |
| M. Channon (Southampton) | 19 |
| R. Graydon (Aston Villa) | 19 |
| B. Robson (Sunderland) | 19 |

**Division 3**
| | |
|---|---|
| R. McNeil (Hereford U) | 31 |
| P. Eastoe (Swindon T) | 26 |
| R. Svarc (Colchester U) | 24 |
| W. Rafferty (Plymouth Arg) | 23 |

**Division 4**
| | |
|---|---|
| R. Clarke (Mansfield T) | 28 |
| R. Habbin (Rotherham U 10 plus 12 for Reading) | 22 |
| R. Haywood (Shrewsbury T) | 21 |
| P. Kitchen (Doncaster R) | 21 |
| E. Woods (Newport County) | 21 |

## 1975–76

**Division 1**
| | |
|---|---|
| E. MacDougall (Norwich C) | 23 |
| J. Duncan (Tottenham H) | 20 |
| M. Macdonald (Newcastle U) | 19 |
| J. Richards (Wolverhampton W) | 17 |
| T. Francis (Birmingham C) | 17 |

**Division 2**
| | |
|---|---|
| D. Hales (Charlton Ath) | 28 |
| M. Channon (Southampton) | 19 |
| T. Ritchie (Bristol C) | 18 |
| M. Walsh (Blackpool) | 17 |
| L. Bradd (Notts Co) | 16 |

**Division 3**
| | |
|---|---|
| R. McNeil (Hereford U) | 35 |
| A. Buckley (Walsall) | 34 |
| R. Clarke (Mansfield T) | 24 |
| F. Binney (Brighton & HA) | 23 |
| T. Evans (Cardiff C) | 21 |

**Division 4**
| | |
|---|---|
| R. Moore (Tranmere R) | 34 |
| J. Ward (Lincoln C) | 24 |
| N. Freeman (Lincoln C) | 23 |

## 1976–77

| Division 1 | | Division 2 | |
|---|---|---|---|
| A. Gray (Aston Villa) | 25 | M. Walsh (Blackpool) | 26 |
| M. Macdonald (Arsenal) | 25 | N. Whatmore (Bolton W) | 25 |
| B. Kidd (Manchester C) | 21 | S. Finnieston (Chelsea) | 24 |
| T. Francis (Birmingham C) | 21 | E. MacDougall (Southampton) | 23 |
| | | M. Flanagan (Charlton Ath) | 23 |
| **Division 3** | | **Division 4** | |
| P. Ward (Brighton & HA) | 32 | B. Joicey (Barnsley) | 25 |
| G. Whittle (Wrexham) | 28 | P. Kitchen (Doncaster R) | 23 |
| A. Bruce (Preston NE) | 24 | J. Charles (Swansea C) | 23 |
| A. Crawford (Rotherham U) | 23 | G. Sweetzer (Brentford) | 23 |

## 1977–78

| Division 1 | | Division 2 | |
|---|---|---|---|
| R. Latchford (Everton) | 30 | R. Hatton (Blackpool) | 22 |
| T. Francis (Birmingham C) | 25 | P. Kitchen (Orient) | 21 |
| K. Dalglish (Liverpool) | 20 | P. Randall (Bristol R) | 20 |
| I. Wallace (Coventry C) | 20 | S. Taylor (Oldham Ath) | 20 |
| R. Hankin (Leeds U) | 20 | | |
| **Division 3** | | **Division 4** | |
| A. Bruce (Preston NE) | 27 | S. Phillips (Brentford) | 32 |
| A. Buckley (Walsall) | 24 | A. Curtis (Swansea C) | 32 |
| A. Biley (Cambridge U) | 21 | J. Dungworth (Aldershot) | 23 |
| J. Lumby (Carlisle U 1, plus 20 for | | A. McCulloch (Brentford) | 22 |
| Scunthorpe U) | 21 | | |

## 1978–79

| Division 1 | | Division 2 | |
|---|---|---|---|
| F. Worthington (Bolton W) | 24 | B. Robson (West Ham U) | 24 |
| K. Dalglish (Liverpool) | 21 | A. Bruce (Preston NE) | 21 |
| A. Brown (WBA) | 18 | G. Rowell (Sunderland) | 21 |
| F. Stapleton (Arsenal) | 17 | A. Biley (Cambridge U) | 20 |
| **Division 3** | | **Division 4** | |
| R. Jenkins (Watford) | 29 | J. Dungworth (Aldershot) | 26 |
| F. Binney (Plymouth Arg) | 26 | A. Cork (Wimbledon) | 22 |
| K. Edwards (Hull C) | 24 | D. Bell (Barnsley 18, plus | |
| L. Blissett (Watford) | 21 | 3 for Halifax T) | 21 |
| | | S. Lee (Stockport Co) | 20 |

## 1979–80

| Division 1 | | Division 2 | |
|---|---|---|---|
| P. Boyer (Southampton) | 23 | C. Allen (QPR) | 28 |
| D. Johnson (Liverpool) | 21 | D. Moss (Luton T) | 24 |
| A. Biley (Derby Co 9, | | B. Robson (Sunderland) | 20 |
| plus 12 for Cambridge U) | 21 | A. Shoulder (Newcastle U) | 20 |
| G. Hoddle (Tottenham H) | 19 | | |
| **Division 3** | | **Division 4** | |
| T. Curran (Sheffield W) | 22 | C. Garwood (Aldershot 10, | |
| A. Rowland (Swindon T) | 20 | plus 17 for Portsmouth) | 27 |
| R. Glavin (Barnsley) | 20 | I. Robins (Huddersfield T) | 25 |
| | | D. Penn (Walsall) | 25 |
| | | W. Kellock (Peterborough U) | 19 |

## 1980–81

| Division 1 | | Division 2 | |
|---|---|---|---|
| S. Archibald (Tottenham H) | 20 | D. Cross (West Ham U) | 22 |
| P. Withe (Aston Villa) | 20 | B. Stein (Luton T) | 18 |
| J. Fashanu (Norwich C) | 19 | A. McCulloch (Sheffield W) | 18 |
| M. Robinson (Brighton & HA) | 19 | P. Goddard (West Ham U) | 17 |
| **Division 3** | | **Division 4** | |
| A. Kellow (Exeter C) | 25 | A. Cork (Wimbledon) | 23 |
| D. Kemp (Plymouth Arg) | 24 | R. Cooke (Peterborough U) | 22 |
| R. Moore (Rotherham U) | 23 | A. Walsh (Darlington) | 22 |
| A. Birch (Chesterfield) | 22 | J. Lumby (Mansfield T 4, | |
| | | plus 18 for Tranmere R) | 22 |

# THE MANAGERS

A directory of Football League managers with biographical details. In some entries information has been at the discretion of individuals.

**ADDISON, Colin.** *Manager:* Hereford U (player-manager), Durban C, Notts Co (assistant), Newport Co, WBA (assistant), Derby Co, Newport Co Feb 1982– . *Honours:* Promotion to Division 3 1973. *Player:* York C, Nottingham F, Arsenal, Sheffield U, Hereford U.

**ANDERSON, Peter.** *Player-Manager:* Millwall Dec 1980– . *Player:* Hendon, Luton T, San Diego, Antwerp, Tampa Bay R, Sheffield U, Millwall.

**APPLETON, Colin.** *Manager:* Hull C June 1982– . Formerly Scarborough. *Player:* Leicester C, Charlton Ath, Barrow.

**ASHURST, Len.** *Manager:* Hartlepool, Gillingham, Sheffield W, Newport Co, Cardiff C Mar 1982– . *Player:* Sunderland 1957–1971; Hartlepool 1971–1973. *Honours:* One Under-23 cap for England. Promotion to Division 3 1980.

**ATKINSON, Ron.** *Manager:* Kettering T, Cambridge U, WBA, Manchester U June 1981– . *Honours:* Division 4 Champions 1977. *Player:* Aston Villa, Oxford U, Kettering T. *Honours:* Promotion to Division 3 1965; Division 3 Championship medal 1968.

**BAILEY, Mike.** *Manager:* Charlton Ath, Brighton & HA June 1981– . *Honours:* Promotion to Division 2, 1981. *Player-Manager:* Hereford U. *Player-Coach:* Minnesota Kicks. *Player:* Charlton Ath, Wolverhampton W. *Honours:* Five Under-23 and two full England caps.

**BARKER, Richie.** *Manager:* Stoke C June 1981– . Formerly assistant-manager Wolverhampton W. *Player:* Derby Co, Notts Co.

**BARLOW, Frank.** *Manager:* Chesterfield 1980– . *Honours:* Anglo-Scottish Cup 1981. *Player:* Sheffield U, Chesterfield. *Coach:* Chesterfield.

**BARTON, Tony.** *Manager:* Aston Villa, March 1982– . Formerly assistant manager. *Honours:* European Cup Winners 1982. *Player:* Fulham (groundstaff), Sutton U, Fulham, Nottingham Forest, Portsmouth. *Coach:* Portsmouth, Aston Villa.

**BASSETT, Dave.** *Manager:* Wimbledon Jan 1981– . *Honours:* Promotion to Division 3 1981. *Player:* Watford, Chelsea, Wimbledon.

**BOAM, Stuart.** *Player-Manager:* Mansfield T July 1981– . *Player:* Mansfield T, Middlesbrough, Newcastle U. *Honours:* Division 2 championship medal 1974.

**BOND, John.** *Manager:* AFC Bournemouth, Norwich C, Manchester C Oct 1980– . *Honours:* AFC Bournemouth, Promotion to Division 3; Norwich C, Promotion to Division 1 1975; Manchester C FA Cup runners-up 1981. *Player:* West Ham U (17 years), Torquay U (3 years). *Honours:* West Ham U Division 2 Championship medal 1958; FA Cup winners medal 1964; Torquay U, Promotion to Division 3 1966.

**BOOTH, Dave.** *Manager:* Grimsby T, Feb 1982– . *Player:* Barnsley, Grimsby T. *Coach:* Grimsby T.

**BREMNER, Billy.** *Manager:* Doncaster R, November 1978– . *Honours:* Promotion to Division 3, 1981. *Player:* Leeds U, Hull C. *Honours:* FA Cup winners medal 1972, runners-up 1965, 1970, 1973. League Cup winners medal 1968; European Cup runners-up medal 1975; UEFA Cup winners medal 1968, 1971; runners-up 1967. Footballer of the Year 1970. Fifty-four full Scottish caps.

**BROWN, Ken.** *Manager:* Norwich C Nov 1980– . Formerly assistant manager. *Honours:* Division 2 promotion 1982. *Player:* West Ham U, Torquay U, Hereford U. Trainer-coach Bournemouth. *Honours:* West Ham U, Division 2 Championship 1958. FA Cup winners medal 1964, European Cup-Winners' Cup winners medal 1965, League Cup runners-up medal 1966.

**BUCKLEY, Alan.** *Player-Manager:* Walsall July 1982– . *Player:* Walsall, Birmingham C, Walsall. *Honours:* Promotion to Division 3 1980.

**BULLOCK, Mickey.** *Manager:* Halifax T July 1981– (formerly Coach). *Player:* Birmingham C, Oxford U, Orient, Halifax T.

**BURKINSHAW, Keith.** *Manager:* Tottenham H July 1976– . *Honours:* Promotion to Division 1 1978; FA Cup winners 1981, 1982; League Cup runners-up 1982. *Coach:* Newcastle U 1968–1975; Tottenham H 1975–1976. *Honours:* FA Cup finalists 1974. *Player:* Liverpool 1954–1958; Workington 1958–1965; Scunthorpe U 1965–1968.

**BUXTON, Mick.** *Manager:* Huddersfield T October 1978– . *Coach:* Huddersfield T, Southend U. *Player:* Burnley, Halifax T. *Honours:* Div 4 Champions 1980.

**CALLAGHAN, Fred.** *Manager:* Woking, Brentford 1980– . *Player:* Fulham. *Coach:* Brentford.

**CAMPBELL, Bobby.** *Manager:* Fulham, Portsmouth March 1982– . *Coach:* QPR, Arsenal, Fulham. *Assistant Manager:* Aldershot, Portsmouth. *Honours:* Division 2 Championship 1977. *Player:* Liverpool, Portsmouth, Aldershot.

**CHARLTON, Jack, OBE.** *Manager:* Middlesbrough, Sheffield W October 1977– . *Honours:* 'Manager of the Year' 1974. *Player:* Leeds U 1952–1973. *Honours:* Division 2 Championship medal 1964; FA Cup runners-up medal 1965; World Cup winners medal 1966; Fairs Cup runners-up medal 1967; 'Footballer of the Year' 1967; League Cup winners medal 1968; Fairs Cup winners medal 1968; Division 1 championship medal 1969; FA Cup runners-up medal 1970; Fairs Cup winners medal 1971; FA Cup winners medal 1972. Promotion Div 2 1980.

**CLOUGH, Brian.** *Manager:* Hartlepool, Derby Co, Brighton & HA, Leeds U, Nottingham F January 1975– . *Honours:* Division 2 Championship 1969; Division 1 Championship 1972; Promotion to Division 1 1977; Division 1 Championship 1978; League Cup winners 1978, 1979; European Cup winners 1979, 1980; Division 1 runners-up 1979. *Player:* Middlesbrough, Sunderland. *Honours:* Three Under-23 caps and two full caps for England.

**COOPER, Terry.** *Manager:* Bristol C May 1982– . *Player-Manager:* Bristol R. *Player:* Leeds U, Bristol R, Doncaster R. *Coach:* Bristol R. *Honours:* 20 full England caps.

**COX, Arthur.** *Manager:* Chesterfield, Newcastle U Sept 1980– . *Coach:* Youth coach Coventry C, chief coach Walsall, Aston Villa, Preston NE, Halifax T. *Assistant Manager:* Sunderland. *Honours:* Preston NE Division 3 Championship; Sunderland Division 2 Championship; FA Cup winners 1973. *Player:* Coventry C 1955–1958 (broken leg ended career at 18). Joined coaching staff.

**CRAGGS, Ken.** *Manager:* Charlton Ath June 1982– . *Assistant-manager:* Charlton Ath, Brighton & HA.

**DOCHERTY, John.** *Manager:* Brentford, Cambridge U January 1978– . *Coach:* Cambridge U. *Player:* Brentford 1959–1961; 1965–1968; 1970–1974; Sheffield U 1961–1965; Reading 1968–1970; QPR player/coach 1974–1975.

**DUNCAN, John.** *Player-Manager* Scunthorpe U June 1981– . *Player:* Dundee, Tottenham H, Derby Co.

**DURBAN, William Alan.** *Manager:* Shrewsbury T, Stoke C, Sunderland June 1981– . *Honours:* Division 4 runners-up 1975. *Player:* Cardiff C 1959–1963; Derby Co 1963–1973; Shrewsbury T 1973–1978. *Honours:* 27 full caps for Wales; Division 2 Championship medal 1969; Division 1 Championship medal 1972; promotion to Division 3 1975; promotion to Division 1 1979.

**ELLIOTT, Billy.** *Manager:* Sunderland, Darlington June 1979– . *Coach:* Brann (Norway), Sunderland. *Player:* Bradford Park Avenue, Burnley, Sunderland. Five full England caps.

**ELLIS, Sam.** *Manager:* Blackpool June 1982– . *Coach:* Watford. *Player:* Sheffield W, Mansfield T, Lincoln C, Watford.

**EVANS, Maurice.** *Manager:* Shrewsbury T 1972–1974; Reading May 1977– . *Coach:* Shrewsbury T 1968–1972; Reading 1974–1977. *Honours:* Promotion to Division 3 1968. *Player:* Reading 1953–1967. *Honours:* Football Combination team 1957; Division 3 South team 1957.

**FERGUSON, Bobby.** *Manager:* Newport Co, Ipswich T July 1982– . Formerly coach. *Player:* Newport Co, Cardiff C, Derby Co, Newcastle U.

**GODFREY, Brian.** *Manager:* Exeter C January 1979– . *Player:* Everton, Scunthorpe U, Preston NE, Aston Villa, Bristol R, Newport Co. *Honours:* One Under-23 and three full Welsh caps.

**GOULD, Bobby.** *Manager:* Bristol R Oct 1981– . *Assistant Manager:* Aldershot Oct 1981. *Player:* Coventry C, Arsenal, Wolverhampton W (two spells), Bristol C, WBA, West Ham U, Bristol R, Hereford U, Wimbledon, Aldershot. *Coach:* Chelsea.

**GRAY, Eddie.** *Player-Manager:* Leeds U July 1982– . *Player:* Leeds U. *Honours:* 12 full caps for Scotland.

**GRIFFITHS, Arfon.** *Manager:* Wrexham (player-manager) 1977–1981 (formerly assistant manager); Crewe Alex Aug 1981– . *Player:* Wrexham, Arsenal, Wrexham (holds club record of League appearances). *Honours:* 17 full caps for Wales.

**HAMILTON, Bryan.** *Manager:* Tranmere Rovers Oct 1980– . *Player:* Linfield, Ipswich T, Everton, Millwall, Swindon T. *Honours:* 50 full Northern Ireland caps.

**HAWKINS, Graham.** *Manager:* Wolverhampton W Aug 1982– . *Assistant Manager:* Shrewsbury T. *Player:* Wolverhampton W, Preston NE, Blackburn R, Port Vale.

**HORNER, Billy.** *Manager:* Darlington, Hartlepool U November 1976– . *Player:* Middlesbrough, Darlington.

**HUGHES, Emlyn.** *Player-Manager* Rotherham U July 1981– . *Player:* Blackpool, Liverpool, Wolverhampton W. *Honours:* Division 1 championship medals 1973, 1976, 1977, 1979. FA Cup winners medal 1974; runners-up medals 1971, 1977. League Cup winners medal 1980; runners-up medal 1978. UEFA Cup winners medals 1973, 1976. European Cup winners medals 1977, 1978. 62 full England caps.

**HUNTER, Allan.** *Player-Manager:* Colchester U May 1982– . *Player:* Coleraine, Oldham Ath, Blackburn R, Ipswich T. *Honours:* 53 Northern Ireland caps.

**HUNTER, Norman.** *Manager:* Barnsley Sept 1980– . *Honours:* Promotion to Division 2 1981. *Player:* Leeds U, Bristol C, Barnsley (player-manager). *Honours:* 1972 FA Cup winners medal; 1965, 1970, 1973 FA Cup runners-up medals; 1968 League Cup winners medal; 1975 European Cup runners-up medal; 1973 European Cup-Winners' Cup runners-up medal; 1968, 1971 UEFA Cup winners medals; 1967 UEFA Cup runners-up medal. Under-23 and 28 full England caps.

**ILEY, Jim.** *Manager:* Peterborough U 1969; Barnsley 1973; Blackburn R, Bury 1980– . *Honours:* Watney Cup entry 1973, 1974. *Player:* Sheffield U 1953–1957; Tottenham H 1958–1959; Nottingham F 1959–1963; Newcastle U 1963–1969; Peterborough U 1969–1973. *Honours:* Football League XI with Sheffield U, Tottenham H. Under-23 cap for England and FA XI representative team.

**KENDALL, Howard.** *Player/Manager:* Blackburn R, Everton May 1981– . *Player:* Preston NE, Everton. While with Preston, he was the youngest player ever to appear in the FA Cup final. *Honours:* Promotion to Div 2 1980.

**KNIGHTON, Ken.** *Manager:* Sunderland 1979–1981; Orient Oct 1981– . *Coach:* Sheffield W, Sunderland. *Player:* Wolverhampton W, Oldham Ath, Preston NE, Blackburn R, Hull C, Sheffield W. *Honours:* Division 1 promotion 1980.

**LEE, Gordon.** *Manager:* Port Vale 1968–1973; Blackburn R 1973–1975; Newcastle U 1975–1977; Everton 1977–1981; Preston NE Dec 1981– . *Honours:* Port Vale Division 3 promotion 1971; Blackburn R Division 3 Champions 1975; Newcastle U League Cup runners-up 1976; Division 3 Manager of the Year 1975. *Player:* Aston Villa 1955–1966; Shrewsbury T 1966–1968. *Honours:* Aston Villa, League Cup winners medal 1961; League Cup runners-up medal 1963.

**LLOYD, Larry.** *Player-Manager:* Wigan Ath March 1981– . *Honours:* Division 4 promotion 1982. *Player:* Bristol R, Liverpool, Coventry C, Nottingham F. *Honours:* 1971 FA Cup runners-up medal; 1973 UEFA Cup winners medal; European Cup winners medals 1979, 1980; League Cup winners medals 1978, 1979. Under 23 and three full England caps.

**LORD, Frank.** *Manager:* Cape Town (South Africa), Hereford U 1980– . *Player:* Rochdale, Blackburn R, Plymouth Arg. *Player/Coach:* Plymouth Arg. *Coach:* Crystal Palace.

**LYALL, John.** *Manager:* West Ham U August 1974– . Previously Assistant Manager 1971. *Honours:* FA Cup winners 1975, 1980; Division 2 champions 1981; League Cup runners-up 1981. *Player:* West Ham U 1957. *Honours:* Youth International.

**MACDONALD, Malcolm.** *Manager:* Fulham Nov 1980– . *Honours:* Division 3 promotion 1982. Formerly Chief Marketing Executive. *Player:* Tonbridge, Fulham, Luton T, Newcastle U, Arsenal. *Honours:* FA Cup runners-up medal 1974, League Cup runners-up medal 1976, FA Cup runners-up medal 1978. Under-23 and 14 full England caps.

**McFARLAND, Roy.** *Player-Manager:* Bradford C May 1981– . *Honours:* Division 4 promotion 1982. *Player:* Tranmere R, Derby Co. *Honours:* Division 2 Championship 1969, Division 1 Championship 1972. Under-23 and 28 full England caps.

**McGOVERN, John.** *Player-Manager:* Bolton W July 1982– . *Player:* Hartlepool U, Derby Co, Leeds U, Nottingham F.

**McGRATH, John.** *Manager:* Southampton youth side 1975–79, Port Vale Dec 1979– . *Coach:* Southampton. *Player:* Bury, Newcastle U, Southampton.

**McMENEMY, Lawrie.** *Manager:* Doncaster R 1968–1971; Grimsby T 1971–1973; Southampton June 1973– . *Honours:* Doncaster R, Division 4 Championship 1969; Grimsby T, Division 4 Championship 1972; Southampton, FA Cup Winners 1976. League Cup runners-up 1979. *Player:* Newcastle U, Gateshead.

**MADDEN, Peter.** *Manager:* Darlington, Rochdale 1980– . *Assistant Manager:* Rochdale. *Player:* Rotherham U 1955–66, Bradford PA 1966–67, Aldershot 1967–68, Skegness 1968–70. *Honours:* Rotherham U League Cup runners-up medal 1961. Two Lincolnshire Cup medals with Skegness.

**MILLER, Brian.** *Manager:* Burnley 1979–    *Honours:* Division 3 Championship 1982. *Player:* Burnley. *Coach:* Burnley.

**MILNE, Gordon.** *Manager:* Leicester C Aug 1982– . Formerly chief executive and manager: Coventry C. *Player:* Preston NE, Liverpool, Blackpool. *Honours:* 14 full caps for England; Liverpool Division 2 championship medals 1964 and 1966; FA Cup winners medal 1965.

**MONCUR, Bobby.** *Manager:* Carlisle U, Hearts, Plymouth Arg June 1981– . *Honours:* Scottish Division 1 championship 1980. *Player:* Newcastle U, Sunderland. *Honours:* One Under-23 and 16 full Scottish caps; UEFA Cup winners medal 1969; FA Cup runners-up medal 1974; Division 2 championship 1965; Anglo-Italian Cup winners medal 1973; Division 2 championship 1976.
land, South Africa (player-coach). *Honours:* Three full Scottish caps.

**MULLERY, Alan.** *Manager:* Brighton & HA, Charlton Ath, Crystal Palace June 1982–
*Honours:* Promotion to Division 2 1977; Promotion to Division 1 1979. *Player:* Fulham 1959–1964; Tottenham H 1964–1972; Fulham 1972–1976. *Honours:* 35 England caps; FA Cup winners medal 1967; FA Cup runners-up medal 1975; League Cup winners medal 1971; UEFA Cup winners medal 1972; Footballer of the Year 1975; Played for Great Britain XI.

**MURDOCH, Bobby.** *Manager:* Middlesbrough May 1981– . Formerly youth team coach. *Player:* Celtic, Middlesbrough. *Honours:* Regular member of Celtic first team squad during eight of their nine successive Scottish League championship successes 1966–1972. Division 2 Championship medal with Middlesbrough 1974. Scottish international 12 caps. European Cup winners medal 1967, runners-up 1970.

**MURPHY, Colin.** *Manager:* Derby Co, Lincoln C November 1978– . *Coach:* Derby Co (reserve team), Nottingham F (reserve team), Notts Co (assistant manager). *Player:* Cork Hibs, Wimbledon, Hastings U, Crystal Palace. *Honours:* Derby Co Central League runners-up 1974–75; Lincoln C Division 4 runners-up 1981.

**NEAL, John.** *Manager:* Wrexham, Middlesbrough, Chelsea May 1981– . *Honours:* Promotion to Division 3 1970; Welsh Cup winners 1972, 1975; Qualified for Cup-Winners' Cup 1973, 1976 (quarter-finalists). *Player:* Hull C 1949–1955; Swindon T 1956–1958; Aston Villa 1959–1963; Southend U 1964–1967. *Honours:* Aston Villa, Division 2 championship medal 1960; League Cup winners medal 1961.

**NEILL, Terry.** *Manager:* Hull C, N Ireland, Tottenham H, 1974–76; Arsenal July 1976– . *Honours:* FA Cup Winners 1979; Runners-up 1978; 1980. *Player:* Arsenal 1959–1970; Hull C 1970–1974. *Honours:* Schoolboy, Youth, Under-23, 'B' and 59 full caps for N Ireland.

**NEWMAN, John.** *Manager:* Exeter C, Grimsby T, Derby Co Mar 1982– . Formerly assistant. *Honours:* Division 4 runners-up 1979. *Player:* Birmingham C, Leicester C, Plymouth Arg, Exeter C. *Honours:* Birmingham C Division 2 championship 1955; FA Cup runners-up 1956. Football League.

**PAISLEY, Robert.** *Manager:* Liverpool July 1974– . *Honours:* Division 1 Champions 1976, 1977, 1979, 1980 and 1982, runners-up 1978; UEFA Cup winners 1976; European Cup winners 1977, 1978; League Cup winners 1982. *Player:* Bishop Auckland 1938–1939; Liverpool 1939–1954. *Honours:* Amateur Cup winners medal 1939; Division 1 Championship medal 1947.

**PEACOCK, Keith.** *Manager:* Gillingham July 1981– . *Assistant Manager:* Tampa Bay Rowdies. *Player:* Charlton Ath.

**PLEAT, David.** *Manager:* Nuneaton B, Luton T January 1978– . *Honours:* Division 2 Champions 1982. *Coach:* Luton T. *Player:* Nottingham F, Luton T, Shrewsbury T, Exeter C, Peterborough U. *Honours:* England schools and youth international.

**PORTERFIELD, Ian.** *Player/Manager:* Rotherham U, Sheffield U June 1981– . *Honours:* Division 3 Championship 1981; Division 4 Championship 1982. *Player:* Raith R, Sunderland, Reading, Sheffield W. Scored the goal for Sunderland which beat Leeds U in the 1973 FA Cup final.

**RIOCH, Bruce.** *Player-Manager:* Torquay U July 1982– . Formerly player-coach. *Player:* Luton T, Aston V, Derby Co, Everton, Derby Co, Torquay U. *Honours:* 24 full caps for Scotland.

**ROBERTS, Bobby.** *Manager:* Colchester U, Wrexham June 1982– . Promotion to Division 3 1977. *Player:* Motherwell, Leicester C, Mansfield T. *Honours:* One Under-23 cap for Scotland; Scottish League.

**ROYLE, Joe.** *Manager:* Oldham Ath July 1982– . *Player:* Everton, Manchester C, Bristol C, Norwich C. *Honours:* Six full caps for England.

**SAUNDERS, Ron.** *Manager:* Yeovil 1967; Oxford U 1969; Norwich C 1969; Manchester C 1973; Aston Villa June 1974–1982; Birmingham C Jan 1982– . *Honours:* Norwich C Champions Division 2 1972; League Cup runners-up 1973; Manchester C League Cup runners-up 1974; Aston Villa League Cup winners 1975 and 1977; Runners-up Division 2 1975, Division 1 Championship 1981; Manager of the Year 1975. *Player:* Everton, Tonbridge, Gillingham, Portsmouth, Watford, Charlton Ath.

**SAXTON, Bobby.** *Manager:* Exeter C (player-manager), Plymouth Arg, Blackburn R May 1981– . *Honours:* Promotion to Division 3 1977. *Player:* Derby Co 1962–1968; Plymouth Arg 1968–1975; Exeter C 1975– . *Honours:* Promotion to Division 2 Plymouth Arg 1975.

**SEAR, Cliff.** *Manager:* Chester June 1982– . Formerly assistant. *Player:* Manchester U.

**SEXTON, David.** *Manager:* Orient 1965–1966; Chelsea 1967–1974; QPR 1974–1977; Manchester U July 1977–April 1981; Coventry C May 1981– . *Honours:* FA Cup winners 1970, runners-up 1979; European Cup-Winners' Cup 1971; League Cup runners-up 1972, 1976. *Player:* Chelmsford 1950–51; Luton T 1951–53; West Ham U 1953–56; Orient 1956–57; Brighton & HA 1957–59; Crystal Palace 1959–61. *Honours:* FA XI v RAF; Third Division South v Third Division North.

**SIRREL, Jimmy.** *Manager:* Brentford 1965–1969; Notts Co 1969–1975; Sheffield U 1975–1977; Notts Co October 1977– . *Honours:* Notts Co, Division 4 Champions 1971; Division 3 runners-up 1973; Division 2 runners-up 1981. *Player:* Glasgow Celtic 1945–1949; Bradford PA 1949–1951; Brighton & HA 1951–1954; Aldershot 1954–1955 (later trainer).

**SMITH, Dave.** *Manager:* Mansfield T 1974–1976; Southend U 1976– . *Honours:* Division 4 Championship 1975, runners-up 1978; Anglo-Scottish Cup semi-finalists 1976; League Cup quarter-finalists 1976, Division 4 Championship 1981. *Coach:* Chief coach Sheffield W 1965–1968; Chief coach Newcastle U 1968–1971; Reserve team manager Arsenal 1971–1974. *Honours:* FA Cup runners-up 1966 Sheffield W; Fairs Cup winners 1969. *Player:* Burnley 1950–1961; Brighton & HA 1961–1962; Bristol C 1962–1963.

**SMITH, Denis.** *Player-Manager:* York C May 1982– . *Player:* Stoke C.

**SMITH, Jimmy.** *Manager:* Boston U 1968–1972; Colchester U 1972–1975; Blackburn R 1975–1978; Birmingham C March 1978–1982; Oxford U March 1982– . *Honours:* Boston U Eastern Professional Floodlight Cup winners; Colchester U promoted from Division 4 1974. Promoted Div 1 1980. *Player:* Sheffield U 1957–1961; Aldershot 1961–1964; Halifax T 1964–1967; Lincoln C 1967–1968; Boston U 1968–1972.

**STOKOE, Bob.** *Manager:* Charlton Ath, Rochdale, Carlisle U, Blackpool, Sunderland, Bury, Blackpool, Rochdale, Carlisle U 1980– . *Honours:* Sunderland FA Cup winners 1973. Division 2 champions 1976; Division 3 promotion 1982. *Player:* Newcastle U (13 years), Bury (player-manager). *Honours:* FA Cup winners medal 1955.

**TAYLOR, Graham.** *Manager:* Lincoln C, Watford June 1977– . *Honours:* Division 4 Championship 1976, 1978; Division 3 runners-up 1979; Division 2 runners-up 1982. *Player:* Grimsby T 1962–1968; Lincoln C 1968–1972.

**TOSHACK, John.** *Player-Manager:* Swansea C February 1978– . *Honours:* Promotion to Division 3 1978, Division 2 1979, Division 1 1981. *Player:* Cardiff C, Liverpool, Swansea C. *Honours:* Three Under-23 and 39 full Welsh caps.

**TROLLOPE, John, MBE.** *Manager:* Swindon T Nov 1980– . *Player:* Swindon T 1960–1980 making record 770 League appearances.

**TURNER, Graham.** *Player-Manager:* Shrewsbury T December 1978– . *Player:* Wrexham, Chester, Shrewsbury T. *Honours:* Promotion 1979.

**VENABLES, Terry.** *Manager:* Crystal Palace June 1976– (formerly coach), QPR Oct 1980– . *Honours:* Promotion to Division 2 1976, Division 2 Championship 1979. *Player:* Chelsea, Tottenham H, QPR, Crystal Palace. *Honours:* capped at all levels by England schools, youth, Amateur, Under-23 and two full honours; Promotion to Division 1 1963 Chelsea; League Cup winners medal 1965 Chelsea; FA Cup winners medal 1967 Tottenham H.

**WALKER, Clive.** *Manager:* Northampton T May 1982– . *Coach:* Northampton T. *Player:* Leicester C, Northampton T, Mansfield T.

**WALKER, Len.** *Manager:* Darlington, Aldershot April 1981– . *Player:* Spennymoor, Middlesbrough, Newcastle U, Aldershot, Darlington (player-coach).

**WEBB, David.** *Manager:* AFC Bournemouth 1980– . *Honours:* Division 4 promotion 1982. Formerly coach. *Player:* Orient, Southampton, Chelsea, QPR, Leicester C, Derby Co, Bournemouth. *Honours:* FA Cup winners medal 1970. League Cup runners-up medal 1972, European Cup-Winners' Cup winners medal 1971.

**WEBSTER, Eric.** *Manager:* Stockport Co April 1982– . Formerly assistant and groundsman.

**WILKINSON, Martin.** *Manager:* Peterborough U June 1982– . Formerly assistant Leeds U, Barnsley.

**WYLIE, Ron.** *Manager:* WBA July 1982– . *Assistant Manager:* Coventry C. *Coach:* Birmingham C, Aston V, Bulova (Hong Kong). *Player:* Birmingham C, Aston V, Notts Co.

# FOOTBALL LEAGUE REFEREES 1982–83

Allison, D. B. (Lancaster)
Ashley N. J. (Nantwich)
Axcell D. J. (Southend)
Baker K. W. (Rugby)
Banks R. A. (Manchester)
Barratt K. P. (Coventry)
Bates S. G. (Bristol)
Bodenham M. J. (Brighton)
Borrett I. J. (Eye)
Bray J. E. (Hinckley, Leics)
Brazier D. H. (Northampton)
Bridges R. (Deeside)
Bune T. G. (Yattendon)
Burden L. F. (Corfe Mullen, Dorset)
Callow V. G. (Solihull)
Chadwick R. (Darwen)
Challinor A. (Rotherham)
Civil D. W. (Birmingham)
Cooper K. (Pontypridd)
Courtney G. (Spennymoor)
Crickmore E. A. (Plymouth)
Daniels B. H. (Brentwood)
Deakin J. C. (Bedford)
Dimblebee M. (Stevenage)
Downey C. (Hounslow)
Fitzharris T. (Bolton)
Glasson A. R. (Salisbury)
Glover N. H. (Chorley)
Grey A. W. (Great Yarmouth)
Gunn A. (Burgess Hill, Sussex)
Guy R. (Kirkby)
Hackett K. S. (Sheffield)
Hamil A. J. (Wolverhampton)
Heath M. J. (Stoke)
Hedges D. A. (Oxford)
Hill B. (Kettering)
Holbrook G. J. (Wolverhampton)
Hough J. D. (Macclesfield)
Hunting J. (Leicester)
Hutchinson D.(Harrogate)
James M. L. (Horsham)
Jones T. A. (Macclesfield)
Key J. M. (Rotherham)
King H. W. (Merthyr Tydfil)
Letts D. (Basingstoke)

Lewis R. S. (Great Bookham, Surrey)
Lloyd D. W. (Fernhill Heath)
Lovatt J. (Crewe)
Martin J. E. (Alton, Hants)
Midgley N. (Salford)
Milford R. G. (Bristol)
Mills T. (Barnsley)
Moules J. A. (Ongar)
Napthine G. J. (Loughborough)
Newsome C. L. (Broseley)
Nixon R. F. (West Kirby)
Owen D. (Wirral)
Peck M. G. (Kendal)
Read E. A. (Bristol)
Redfern K. A. (Whitley Bay)
Reeves D. V. (Uxbridge)
Richardson D. (Blackburn)
Roberts F. (Prestatyn)
Robinson, Alan (Portsmouth)
Robinson, Arthur (Manchester)
Robinson L. M. (Sutton Coldfield)
Salmon K. G. (Barnet)
Saunders A. (Newcastle)
Scales E. J. (Ware)
Scott D. (Burnley)
Scott M. P. (Nottingham)
Seel C. N. (Carlisle)
Seville A. (Birmingham)
Shapter L. C. (Torquay)
Shaw D. (Sandbach)
Spencer T. D. (Salisbury)
Stevens B. T. (Stonehouse)
Taylor H. (Oadby)
Taylor M. J.(Deal)
Thomas C. (Porthcawl)
Tyldesley P. A. (Stockport)
Tyson G. M. (Sunderland)
Vickers D. S. (Ilford)
Walmsley K. (Thornton)
Ward A. W. (London)
White C. B. (Harrow)
Willis P. N. (Meadowfield)
Wilson N. L. (Morecambe)
Worral J. B. (Warrington)

## DEDUCTION OF POINTS

Two clubs each had two points deducted during the 1981–82 season for fielding unregistered players. In both cases the clubs failed to meet the registration deadline when upgrading apprentices to full professionals.

Third Division Bristol Rovers were penalised for playing Steve Bailey at Newport on 16 March (a 1-1 draw), and Fourth Division Mansfield Town for playing Colin Calderwood at Crewe on 13 March (a 2-0 win). It is interesting to note that the net point Mansfield Town achieved from their win at Crewe was eventually just sufficient to save them from the necessity of re-election.

# TRANSFERS 1981–82

*Denotes player involved in exchange deal*

| | From | To | Fee if known |
|---|---|---|---|
| **June 1981** | | | |
| Clive Allen | Crystal Palace | Queen's Park Rangers | £700,000 |
| Kevin Baddeley | Bristol City | Swindon Town | |
| Joe Cooke | Oxford United | Exeter City | £25,000 |
| Tony Fitzpatrick | Bristol City | St Mirren | £170,000 |
| John Gregory | Brighton | Queen's Park Rangers | £300,000 |
| David Hughes | Lincoln City | Scunthorpe United | |
| Tommy Mason | Fulham | Brighton | |
| Ernie Moss | Chesterfield | Port Vale | £16,000 |
| Martin O'Neill | Norwich City | Manchester City | £275,000 |
| Peter O'Sullivan | Brighton | Fulham | |
| Paul Price | Luton Town | Tottenham Hotspur | £250,000 |
| Mark Stevens | Bristol Rovers | Swindon Town | |
| Steve Wicks | Queen's Park Rangers | Crystal Palace | £275,000 |
| Clive Woods | Queen's Park Rangers | Norwich City | £225,000 |
| | | | |
| **July 1981** | | | |
| Ian Bell | Middlesbrough | Mansfield Town | |
| Alan Biley | Derby County | Everton | £350,000 |
| Stuart Boam | Newcastle United | Mansfield Town | |
| Joe Bolton | Sunderland | Middlesbrough | £150,000 |
| Steve Cammack | Scunthorpe United | Lincoln City | £20,000 |
| Colin Clarke | Ipswich Town | Peterborough United | |
| Peter Coffill | Torquay United | Northampton Town | £350,000 |
| Mick Coop | Coventry City | Derby County | |
| Dai Davies | Wrexham | Swansea City | £45,000 |
| Gary Emmanuel | Bristol Rovers | Swindon Town | |
| Clive Evans | Tranmere Rovers | Wigan Athletic | |
| Tony Grealish | Luton Town | Brighton | £100,000 |
| Billy Lansdowne | West Ham United | Charlton Athletic | |
| Tony Larkin | Shrewsbury Town | Carlisle United | |
| Bob Latchford | Everton | Swansea City | £125,000 |
| David McClurg | Distillery | Middlesbrough | |
| Ian MacDonald | Carlisle United | Dundee | |
| Joe Jordan | Manchester United | AC Milan | £170,000 |
| Bill Rodaway | Burnley | Peterborough United | |
| Neville Southall | Bury | Everton | |
| Keith Walwyn | Chesterfield | York City | |
| Alan West | Luton Town | Millwall | £45,000 |
| Brian Williams | Swindon Town | Bristol Rovers | |
| Nigel Worthington | Ballymena United | Notts County | £10,000 |
| | | | |
| **August 1981** | | | |
| Alan Ainscow | Birmingham City | Everton | £250,000 |
| David Armstrong | Middlesbrough | Southampton | £600,000 |
| Jim Arnold | Blackburn Rovers | Everton | £175,000 |
| Jack Ashurst | Blackpool | Carlisle United | |
| Gary Bannister | Coventry City | Sheffield Wednesday | |
| Peter Barnes | West Bromwich Albion | Leeds United | £900,000 |
| Michael Baxter | Preston North End | Middlesbrough | £425,000 |
| Ken Beech | Port Vale | Walsall | £15,000 |
| Keith Bertschin | Birmingham City | Norwich City | £200,000 |
| Alan Birch | Chesterfield | Wolverhampton Wanderers | £200,000 |
| Andy Blair | Coventry City | Aston Villa | £300,000 |
| Richie Bowman | Reading | Gillingham | £25,000 |
| Jimmy Case | Liverpool | Brighton & Hove Albion | £350,000 |
| Glyn Chamberlain | Chesterfield | Halifax Town | |
| John Chiedozie | Orient | Notts County | £600,000 |
| Ray Clemence | Liverpool | Tottenham Hotspur | £300,000 |
| Glen Cockerill | Swindon Town | Lincoln City | |
| Bobby Davison | Huddersfield Town | Halifax Town | £20,000 |
| Justin Fashanu | Norwich City | Nottingham Forest | £1,000,000 |
| Mike Ferguson | Coventry City | Everton | £280,000 |
| Phil Ferns | AFC Bournemouth | Charlton Athletic | |
| Joe Gallagher | Birmingham City | Wolverhampton Wanderers | £350,000 |
| Terry Gennoe | Southampton | Blackburn Rovers | £40,000 |
| John Gidman | Everton | Manchester United | £450,000 |
| Mick Harford | Newcastle United | Bristol City | £160,000 |
| Brian Horton | Brighton & Hove Albion | Luton Town | £100,000 |
| Geoff Hunter | Crewe Alexandra | Port Vale | |
| Colin Irwin | Liverpool | Swansea City | £340,000 |
| Jeff Johnson | Sheffield Wednesday | Newport County | |
| Chris Kamara | Swindon Town | Portsmouth | £50,000 |
| Mark Lawrenson | Brighton & Hove Albion | Liverpool | £900,000 |
| Bob Lee | Bristol Rovers | Carlisle United | |
| Mike Lester | Barnsley | Exeter City | |
| John McAlle | Wolverhampton Wanderers | Sheffield United | £10,000 |

| | | | |
|---|---|---|---|
| Mike McCartney | Southampton | Plymouth Argyle | £50,000 |
| Ally McCoist | St Johnstone | Sunderland | |
| Jim McDonagh | Everton | Bolton Wanderers | |
| Steve MacKenzie | Manchester City | West Bromwich Albion | £500,000 |
| Gary Megson | Everton | Sheffield Wednesday | |
| Ian Miller | Swindon Town | Blackburn Rovers | |
| Ian Munro | Stoke City | Sunderland | |
| Gary Nicholson | Newcastle United | Mansfield Town | |
| Leighton Phillips | Swansea City | Charlton Athletic | |
| Colin Powell | Charlton Athletic | Gillingham | |
| Mark Proctor | Middlesbrough | Nottingham Forest | £425,000 |
| Paul Richardson | Stoke City | Sheffield United | £20,000 |
| Andy Rollings | Swindon Town | Portsmouth | |
| David Rushbury | Swansea City | Carlisle United | £40,000 |
| Gary Simpson | Chesterfield | Chester | |
| Frank Stapleton | Arsenal | Manchester United | £900,000 |
| Micky Thomas* | Manchester United | Everton | £450,000 |
| Dick Tydeman | Charlton Athletic | Gillingham | |
| Imre Varadi | Everton | Newcastle United | £125,000 |
| Mike Walsh* | Bolton Wanderers | Everton | £90,000 |
| Keith Waugh | Peterborough United | Sheffield United | £90,000 |
| Neil Whatmore | Bolton Wanderers | Birmingham City | £340,000 |
| Alan Whitehead | Bury | Brentford | £65,000 |
| Gary Williams | Blackpool | Swindon Town | £40,000 |

*Temporary transfers*

| | | | |
|---|---|---|---|
| David Brown | Oxford United | Bury | |
| Peter Farrell | Port Vale | Doncaster Rovers | |
| Lee Smelt | Nottingham Forest | Peterborough United | |

**September 1981**

| | | | |
|---|---|---|---|
| Sam Allardyce | Sunderland | Millwall | £95,000 |
| Phil Bater | Bristol Rovers | Wrexham | £50,000 |
| Dave Bennett | Manchester City | Cardiff City | |
| David Brown | Oxford United | Bury | |
| John Buchanan | Cardiff City | Northampton Town | £15,000 |
| Tommy Cunningham | Wimbledon | Orient | |
| Keith Edwards | Hull City | Sheffield United | |
| Trevor Francis | Nottingham Forest | Manchester City | £1,200,000 |
| Neil Freeman | Birmingham City | Peterborough United | |
| Tony Funnell | Brentford | AFC Bournemouth | £5000 |
| Steve Gatting | Arsenal | Brighton & Hove Albion | £250,000 |
| John Hawley | Sunderland | Arsenal | £50,000 |
| Martin Henderson | Leicester City | Chesterfield | £70,000 |
| Tony Henry | Manchester City | Bolton Wanderers | £125,000 |
| Andy King | Queen's Park Rangers | West Bromwich Albion | £400,000 |
| Joe Mayo | Orient | Cambridge United | |
| Remi Moses | West Bromwich Albion | Manchester United | £500,000 |
| Sammy Nelson | Arsenal | Brighton & Hove Albion | |
| Keith Robson | Norwich City | Leicester City | £30,000 |
| Barry Silkman | Queen's Park Rangers | Orient | |
| John Sitton | Millwall | Gillingham | £10,000 |
| Max Thompson | Blackpool | Swansea City | £40,000 |
| Bobby Thomson | Morton | Middlesbrough | £175,000 |
| Jimmy Weston | Torquay United | Wigan Athletic | |

*Temporary transfers*

| | | | |
|---|---|---|---|
| Steve Conroy | Sheffield United | Leeds United | |
| Howard Goddard | Newport County | Blackpool | |
| Trevor Hebberd | Southampton | Bolton Wanderers | |
| Peter Henderson | Gillingham | Crewe Alexandra | |
| Brian Johnson | Plymouth Argyle | Torquay United | |
| Billy O'Rourke | Burnley | Newport County | |
| Chris Pearce | Blackburn Rovers | Barnsley | |
| Andy Rogers | Southampton | Plymouth Argyle | |
| Peter Sayer | Preston North End | Cardiff City | |
| Lindsay Smith | Cambridge United | Lincoln City | |

**October 1981**

| | | | |
|---|---|---|---|
| Trevor Ames | Hereford United | Crystal Palace | |
| Tommy Booth | Manchester City | Preston North End | |
| Stan Bowles | Orient | Brentford | £40,000 |
| Tony Brown | West Bromwich Albion | Torquay United | |
| Gary Buckley | Manchester City | Preston North End | |
| Kenny Burns | Nottingham Forest | Leeds United | £400,000 |
| Jeff Chandler | Leeds United | Bolton Wanderers | £40,000 |
| Jeff Cook | Stoke City | Plymouth Argyle | £25,000 |
| Colin Crawford | Sunderland | Linfield | £10,000 |
| David Crown | Brentford | Portsmouth | |
| Barry Dunn | Sunderland | Preston North End | £22,000 |
| Steve Galliers | Wimbledon | Crystal Palace | £70,000 |
| Asa Hartford | Everton | Manchester City | £350,000 |

| | | | |
|---|---|---|---|
| Chris Kamara | Portsmouth | Brentford | |
| John Kelly | Tranmere Rovers | Preston North End | |
| Kevin Mabbutt* | Bristol City | Crystal Palace | £200,000 |
| Steve Nicol | Ayr United | Liverpool | £300,000 |
| Bryan Robson | West Bromwich Albion | Manchester United | £1,500,000 |
| Billy Ronson | Cardiff City | Wrexham | £100,000 |
| Gary Stanley | Everton | Swansea City | £150,000 |
| Steve Whitworth | Sunderland | Bolton Wanderers | £25,000 |
| William Young | Aston Villa | Torquay United | |

*Temporary transfers*

| | | | |
|---|---|---|---|
| Terry Boyle | Crystal Palace | Wimbledon | |
| Terry Boyle | Wimbledon | Crystal Palace | |
| Paul Clark | Brighton & Hove Albion | Reading | |
| John Dungworth | Shrewsbury Town | Hereford United | |
| Steve Elliott | Preston North End | Cambridge United | |
| Peter Farrell | Port Vale | Shrewsbury Town | |
| Graeme Hedley | Middlesbrough | York City | |
| Tony Mahoney | Fulham | Northampton Town | |
| Lee Smelt | Nottingham Forest | Halifax Town | |
| Colin Tartt | Chesterfield | Port Vale | |
| Wayne Turner | Luton Town | Lincoln City | |

**November 1981**

| | | | |
|---|---|---|---|
| David Beavon | Notts County | Lincoln City | |
| Norman Bell | Wolverhampton Wanderers | Blackburn Rovers | £70,000 |
| Andy Crawford | Blackburn Rovers | AFC Bournemouth | £40,000 |
| Gary Donnellan | Watford | Reading | £5000 |
| Robert Mimms | Halifax Town | Rotherham United | £15,000 |
| Trevor Morgan | AFC Bournemouth | Mansfield Town | |
| Gerry Mullan | Everton | Glentoran | £25,000 |
| Andy Rogers | Southampton | Plymouth Argyle | |
| Lee Smelt | Nottingham Forest | Halifax Town | £10,000 |
| Colin Tartt | Chesterfield | Port Vale | £15,000 |
| Micky Thomas | Everton | Brighton & Hove Albion | £400,000 |
| Clive Whitehead | Bristol City | West Bromwich Albion | £100,000 |

*Temporary transfers*

| | | | |
|---|---|---|---|
| Milija Aleksic | Tottenham Hotspur | Luton Town | |
| Tony Arins | Leeds United | Scunthorpe United | |
| Kevin Arnott | Sunderland | Blackburn Rovers | |
| Ian Bailey | Middlesbrough | Bolton Wanderers | |
| Graham Bell | Preston North End | Huddersfield Town | |
| Alan Brown | Sunderland | Newcastle United | |
| Mike Czuczman | Grimsby Town | York City | |
| David Giles | Swansea City | Orient | |
| Trevor Hebberd | Southampton | Leicester City | |
| Graeme Hedley | York City | Middlesbrough | |
| Brian Hornsby | Sheffield Wednesday | Chester | |
| Brian Johnson | Torquay United | Plymouth Argyle | |
| Paul McGee | Preston North End | Burnley | |
| Jimmy Mullen | Rotherham United | Preston North End | |
| Keith Parkinson | Leeds United | Hull City | |
| Peter Shaw | Charlton Athletic | Exeter City | |
| Gary Westwood | Ipswich Town | Charlton Athletic | |

**December 1981**

| | | | |
|---|---|---|---|
| Keith Osgood | Derby County | Orient | |
| Willie Young | Arsenal | Nottingham Forest | £170,000 |

*Temporary transfers*

| | | | |
|---|---|---|---|
| Stephen Baines | Walsall | Bury | |
| John Deehan | West Bromwich Albion | Norwich City | |
| George Foster | Plymouth Argyle | Exeter City | |
| Peter Grotier | Cardiff City | Gillingham | |
| Alan Hay | Bristol City | St Mirren | |
| Martin Hodge | Everton | Preston North End | |
| Dave Kemp | Plymouth Argyle | Gillingham | |
| Richard Money | Liverpool | Derby County | |
| Donal Murphy | Plymouth Argyle | Torquay United | |
| Jimmy Nicholl | Manchester United | Sunderland | |
| Graham Paddon | Norwich City | Millwall | |
| Steve Spooner | Derby County | Halifax Town | |
| Ian Vaughan | Rotherham United | Stockport County | |

**January 1982**

| | | | |
|---|---|---|---|
| Ian Bowyer | Sunderland | Nottingham Forest | £45,000 |
| John Deehan | West Bromwich Albion | Norwich City | £175,000 |
| Mike Doyle | Stoke City | Bolton Wanderers | |
| Gerry Gow | Manchester City | Rotherham United | £75,000 |
| Adrian Heath | Stoke City | Everton | £700,000 |
| Ray Kennedy | Liverpool | Swansea City | £160,000 |

| Player | From | To | Fee |
|---|---|---|---|
| Mick Laverick | Huddersfield Town | York City | £10,000 |
| David Mail | Aston Villa | Blackburn Rovers | |
| Neil Orr | Morton | West Ham United | £400,000 |
| Eamon O'Keefe | Everton | Wigan Athletic | £60,000 |
| John Ryan | Sheffield United | Manchester City | |
| David Watson | Southampton | Stoke City | £50,000 |
| Steve Winn | Rotherham United | Torquay United | |

*Temporary transfers*

| Player | From | To |
|---|---|---|
| Brian Bason | Crystal Palace | Portsmouth |
| Joe Blochel | Southampton | Wimbledon |
| Joe Cooke | Exeter City | Bradford City |
| Gerry Francis | Queen's Park Rangers | Coventry City |
| Dave Gwyther | Newport County | Crewe Alexandra |
| Jimmy Hamilton | Carlisle United | Morton |
| David Mills | West Bromwich Albion | Newcastle United |
| Nigel Walker | Newcastle United | Plymouth Argyle |

## February 1982

| Player | From | To | Fee |
|---|---|---|---|
| Brian Attley | Swansea City | Derby County | £25,000 |
| Alan Birch | Wolverhampton Wanderers | Barnsley | |
| Mike Czuczman | Grimsby Town | York City | |
| Gerry Francis | Queen's Park Rangers | Coventry City | £150,000 |
| Ian Howat | Chester | Crewe Alexandra | |
| Mike Lester | Exeter City | Bradford City | |
| John Lyons | Cambridge United | Colchester United | |
| Sammy McIlroy | Manchester United | Stoke City | £350,000 |
| Steve Massey | Peterborough United | Northampton Town | |
| Colin Morris | Blackpool | Sheffield United | |
| Martin O'Neill | Manchester City | Norwich City | £125,000 |
| Peter Shaw | Charlton Athletic | Gillingham | |
| Steve Spooner | Derby County | Halifax Town | |
| Ian Walsh | Crystal Palace | Swansea City | |

*Temporary transfers*

| Player | From | To |
|---|---|---|
| David Giles | Swansea City | Crystal Palace |
| Roger Jones | Derby County | Birmingham City |
| Pat Kruse | Brentford | Northampton Town |
| Denis Leman | Sheffield Wednesday | Wrexham |
| Tony Lowery | West Bromwich Albion | Walsall |
| John McAlle | Sheffield United | Derby County |
| Alan McKenna | Millwall | Berwick Rangers |
| Graham Paddon | Millwall | Norwich City |
| Stuart Robertson | Burnley | West Bromwich Albion |
| Geoff Scott | Leicester City | Birmingham City |
| Tony Sealy | Queen's Park Rangers | Port Vale |
| Bobby Shinton | Newcastle United | Millwall |
| Bobby Smith | Leicester City | Peterborough United |

## March 1982

| Player | From | To | Fee |
|---|---|---|---|
| John Barton | Everton | Derby County | |
| John Bramhall | Tranmere Rovers | Bury | |
| Steve Bryant | Portsmouth | Northampton Town | |
| Steve Cammack | Lincoln City | Scunthorpe United | |
| Keith Cassells* | Oxford United | Southampton | £230,000 |
| Graham Cawthorne | Grimsby Town | Doncaster Rovers | |
| Joe Cooke | Exeter City | Bradford City | |
| Neil Cooper | Barnsley | Grimsby Town | £35,000 |
| Tommy Craig | Swansea City | Carlisle United | |
| David Giles | Swansea City | Crystal Palace | |
| Peter Grotier | Cardiff City | Grimsby Town | £5000 |
| Mick Harford | Bristol City | Newcastle United | £100,000 |
| Mick Harford | Newcastle United | Birmingham City | £100,000 |
| Trevor Hebberd* | Southampton | Oxford United | £80,000 |
| Keith Houchen | Hartlepool United | Orient | £25,000 |
| David Hughes | Scunthorpe United | Lincoln City | |
| Paul McGee | Preston North End | Burnley | |
| Alan McKenna | Millwall | Berwick Rangers | |
| Lawrie Madden | Charlton Athletic | Millwall | |
| Trevor Morgan | Mansfield Town | AFC Bournemouth | |
| Steve Phillips | Northampton Town | Southend United | |
| Stuart Robertson | Burnley | Exeter City | |
| Geoff Scott | Leicester City | Birmingham City | |
| Bobby Shinton | Newcastle United | Millwall | |
| Byron Stevenson* | Leeds United | Birmingham City | |
| Ray Train | Watford | Oxford United | £10,000 |
| John Ward | Grimsby Town | Lincoln City | |
| Steve Wicks | Crystal Palace | Queen's Park Rangers | £250,000 |
| Frank Worthington* | Birmingham City | Leeds United | |
| Mark Wright* | Oxford United | Southampton | |

*Temporary transfers*

| | | | |
|---|---|---|---|
| Billy Askew | Middlesbrough | Blackburn Rovers | |
| Leigh Barnard | Portsmouth | Peterborough United | |
| Alan Biley | Everton | Stoke City | |
| Noel Blake | Aston Villa | Shrewsbury Town | |
| Ron Burns | Ipswich Town | Ballymena United | |
| Mike Carter | Bolton Wanderers | Swindon Town | |
| Neil Cooper | Barnsley | Grimsby Town | |
| Brian Cox | Sheffield Wednesday | Huddersfield Town | |
| Neil Firm | Leeds United | Oldham Athletic | |
| Brian Flynn | Leeds United | Burnley | |
| Neil Grewcock | Leicester City | Gillingham | |
| Stewart Hamill | Leicester City | Scunthorpe United | |
| David Kemp | Gillingham | Plymouth Argyle | |
| David Kemp | Plymouth Argyle | Brentford | |
| Paul Keys | Luton Town | Halifax Town | |
| George Lawrence | Southampton | Oxford United | |
| Richard Money | Liverpool | Luton Town | |
| Jimmy Mullen | Rotherham United | Cardiff City | |
| Trevor Phillips | Chester | Stockport County | |
| Tom Ritchie | Sunderland | Carlisle United | |
| Gary Shelton | Aston Villa | Sheffield Wednesday | |
| Denis Smith | Stoke City | York City | |
| Brian Taylor | Preston North End | Wigan Athletic | |
| Wayne Turner | Lincoln City | Luton Town | |
| Loek Ursem | Stoke City | Sunderland | |
| Clive Wigginton | Grimsby Town | Doncaster Rovers | |

**April 1982**

| | | | |
|---|---|---|---|
| John McAlle | Sheffield United | Derby County | |
| Paul McGrath | St Patrick's Athletic | Manchester United | |
| Richard Money | Liverpool | Luton Town | £100,000 |
| Gary Shelton | Aston Villa | Sheffield Wednesday | £50,000 |

*Temporary transfers*

| | | |
|---|---|---|
| Joe Blochel | Wimbledon | Southampton |
| Paul McGrath | St Patrick's Athletic | Manchester United |
| Mike Ring | Brighton & Hove Albion | Morton |

**May 1982**

| | | |
|---|---|---|
| Allan Hunter | Ipswich Town | Colchester United |
| Brian Cox | Sheffield Wednesday | Huddersfield Town |

**June 1982**

| | | | |
|---|---|---|---|
| Sandy Clark | Airdrieonians | West Ham United | £200,000 |
| George Foster | Plymouth Argyle | Derby County | |
| Neil Grewcock | Leicester City | Gillingham | |
| Mark Kendall | Aston Villa | Northampton Town | |
| John McGovern | Nottingham Forest | Bolton Wanderers | |
| Derek Mountfield | Tranmere Rovers | Everton | |
| David Speedie | Darlington | Chelsea | £70,000 |

**July 1982**

| | | | |
|---|---|---|---|
| Terry Bullivant | Aston Villa | Charlton Athletic | |
| David Harle | Doncaster Rovers | Exeter City | |
| Carl Harris | Leeds United | Charlton Athletic | |
| Steve Hetzke | Reading | Blackpool | £12,500 |
| Ray Houghton | West Ham United | Fulham | |
| Les Hunter | Chesterfield | Scunthorpe United | |
| Francis Joseph | Wimbledon | Brentford | £40,000 |
| Andy King | West Bromwich Albion | Everton | |
| Billy Kellock | Peterborough United | Luton Town | £25,000 |
| Trevor Phillips | Chester | Stockport County | |
| Paul Walsh* | Charlton Athletic | Luton Town | £400,000 |
| Neil Webb | Reading | Portsmouth | £87,500 |
| Steve White* | Luton Town | Charlton Athletic | £150,000 |

# FOOTBALL LEAGUE ATTENDANCES 1981–82

## FIRST DIVISION

| | Home | Home avge |
|---|---|---|
| Arsenal | 535,370 | 25,493 |
| Aston Villa | 564,388 | 26,875 |
| Birmingham C | 359,453 | 17,116 |
| Brighton & HA | 383,132 | 18,244 |
| Coventry C | 275,099 | 13,099 |
| Everton | 518,147 | 24,673 |
| Ipswich T | 460,435 | 21,925 |
| Leeds U | 464,291 | 22,109 |
| Liverpool | 736,280 | 35,060 |
| Manchester C | 715,332 | 34,063 |
| Manchester U | 935,983 | 44,570 |
| Middlesbrough | 281,668 | 13,412 |
| Nottingham F | 418,686 | 19,937 |
| Notts Co | 244,178 | 11,627 |
| Southampton | 458,537 | 21,835 |
| Stoke C | 307,335 | 14,635 |
| Sunderland | 411,765 | 19,607 |
| Swansea C | 382,745 | 18,225 |
| Tottenham H | 737,096 | 35,099 |
| WBA | 352,499 | 16,785 |
| West Ham U | 558,284 | 26,584 |
| Wolverhampton W | 320,090 | 15,242 |
| **TOTAL** | **10,420,793** | |

## SECOND DIVISION

| | Home | Home avge |
|---|---|---|
| Barnsley | 317,050 | 15,097 |
| Blackburn R | 176,499 | 8404 |
| Bolton W | 159,540 | 7597 |
| Cambridge U | 106,536 | 5073 |
| Cardiff C | 117,049 | 5573 |
| Charlton Ath | 139,619 | 6648 |
| Chelsea | 275,770 | 13,131 |
| Crystal Palace | 217,996 | 10,380 |
| Derby Co | 248,381 | 11,827 |
| Grimsby T | 176,527 | 8406 |
| Leicester C | 297,822 | 14,182 |
| Luton T | 249,497 | 11,880 |
| Newcastle U | 362,797 | 17,276 |
| Norwich C | 297,844 | 14,183 |
| Oldham Ath | 147,481 | 7022 |
| Orient | 92,805 | 4419 |
| QPR | 264,055 | 12,574 |
| Rotherham U | 206,992 | 9856 |
| Sheffield W | 402,571 | 19,170 |
| Shrewsbury T | 95,981 | 4570 |
| Watford | 307,261 | 14,631 |
| Wrexham | 90,390 | 4309 |
| **TOTAL** | **4,750,463** | |

## THIRD DIVISION

| | Home | Home avge |
|---|---|---|
| Brentford | 130,935 | 5692 |
| Bristol C | 149,754 | 6511 |
| Bristol R | 128,794 | 5599 |
| Burnley | 159,535 | 6936 |
| Carlisle U | 101,418 | 4409 |
| Chester | 49,917 | 2170 |
| Chesterfield | 109,304 | 4752 |
| Doncaster R | 120,393 | 5234 |
| Exeter C | 88,729 | 3857 |
| Fulham | 159,572 | 6937 |
| Gillingham | 120,546 | 5241 |
| Huddersfield T | 155,154 | 6745 |
| Lincoln C | 97,113 | 4222 |
| Millwall | 106,387 | 4625 |
| Newport Co | 102,548 | 4458 |
| Oxford U | 134,562 | 5850 |
| Plymouth Arg | 110,219 | 4792 |
| Portsmouth | 196,510 | 8543 |
| Preston NE | 126,425 | 5496 |
| Reading | 92,403 | 4017 |
| Southend U | 116,901 | 5082 |
| Swindon T | 133,972 | 5824 |
| Walsall | 86,122 | 3744 |
| Wimbledon | 59,702 | 2595 |
| **TOTAL** | **2,836,915** | |

## FOURTH DIVISION

| | Home | Home avge |
|---|---|---|
| Aldershot | 49,860 | 2167 |
| AFC Bournemouth | 136,468 | 5933 |
| Blackpool | 97,142 | 4223 |
| Bradford C | 124,004 | 5391 |
| Bury | 81,830 | 3557 |
| Colchester U | 65,767 | 2859 |
| Crewe Alex | 50,517 | 2196 |
| Darlington | 57,720 | 2509 |
| Halifax T | 55,362 | 2407 |
| Hartlepool U | 47,256 | 2054 |
| Hereford U | 59,616 | 2592 |
| Hull C | 91,838 | 3992 |
| Mansfield T | 61,749 | 2684 |
| Northampton T | 53,036 | 2305 |
| Peterborough U | 108,055 | 4698 |
| Port Vale | 83,691 | 3638 |
| Rochdale | 42,259 | 1837 |
| Scunthorpe U | 51,327 | 2231 |
| Sheffield U | 342,505 | 14,891 |
| Stockport Co | 58,583 | 2547 |
| Torquay U | 51,693 | 2247 |
| Tranmere R | 39,916 | 1735 |
| Wigan Ath | 134,313 | 5839 |
| York C | 54,283 | 2360 |
| **TOTAL** | **1,998,790** | |

## ATTENDANCES AT FOOTBALL LEAGUE MATCHES

| Season | Matches | Total | Div. 1 | Div. 2 | Div. 3 (S) | Div. 3 (N) |
|--------|---------|-------|--------|--------|------------|------------|
| 1946–47 | 1848 | 35,604,606 | 15,005,316 | 11,071,572 | 5,664,004 | 3,863,714 |
| 1947–48 | 1848 | 40,259,130 | 16,732,341 | 12,286,350 | 6,653,610 | 4,586,829 |
| 1948–49 | 1848 | 41,271,414 | 17,914,667 | 11,353,237 | 6,998,429 | 5,005,081 |
| 1949–50 | 1848 | 40,517,865 | 17,278,625 | 11,694,158 | 7,104,155 | 4,440,927 |
| 1950–51 | 2028 | 39,584,967 | 16,679,454 | 10,780,580 | 7,367,884 | 4,757,109 |
| 1951–52 | 2028 | 39,015,866 | 16,110,322 | 11,066,189 | 6,958,927 | 4,880,428 |
| 1952–53 | 2028 | 37,149,966 | 16,050,278 | 9,686,654 | 6,704,299 | 4,708,735 |
| 1953–54 | 2028 | 36,174,590 | 16,154,915 | 9,510,053 | 6,311,508 | 4,198,114 |
| 1954–55 | 2028 | 34,133,103 | 15,087,221 | 8,988,794 | 5,996,017 | 4,051,071 |
| 1955–56 | 2028 | 33,150,809 | 14,108,961 | 9,080,002 | 5,692,479 | 4,269,367 |
| 1956–57 | 2028 | 32,744,405 | 13,803,037 | 8,718,162 | 5,622,189 | 4,601,017 |
| 1957–58 | 2028 | 33,562,208 | 14,468,652 | 8,663,712 | 6,097,183 | 4,332,661 |
| | | | | | Div. 3 | Div. 4 |
| 1958–59 | 2028 | 33,610,985 | 14,727,691 | 8,641,997 | 5,946,600 | 4,276,697 |
| 1959–60 | 2028 | 32,538,611 | 14,391,227 | 8,399,627 | 5,739,707 | 4,008,050 |
| 1960–61 | 2028 | 28,619,754 | 12,926,948 | 7,033,936 | 4,784,256 | 3,874,614 |
| 1961–62 | 2015 | 27,979,902 | 12,061,194 | 7,453,089 | 5,199,106 | 3,266,513 |
| 1962–63 | 2028 | 28,885,852 | 12,490,239 | 7,792,770 | 5,341,362 | 3,261,481 |
| 1963–64 | 2028 | 28,535,022 | 12,486,626 | 7,594,158 | 5,419,157 | 3,035,081 |
| 1964–65 | 2028 | 27,641,168 | 12,708,752 | 6,984,104 | 4,436,245 | 3,512,067 |
| 1965–66 | 2028 | 27,206,980 | 12,480,644 | 6,914,757 | 4,779,150 | 3,032,429 |
| 1966–67 | 2028 | 28,902,596 | 14,242,957 | 7,253,819 | 4,421,172 | 2,984,648 |
| 1967–68 | 2028 | 30,107,298 | 15,289,410 | 7,450,410 | 4,013,087 | 3,354,391 |
| 1968–69 | 2028 | 29,382,172 | 14,584,851 | 7,382,390 | 4,339,656 | 3,075,275 |
| 1969–70 | 2028 | 29,600,972 | 14,868,754 | 7,581,728 | 4,223,761 | 2,926,729 |
| 1970–71 | 2028 | 28,194,146 | 13,954,337 | 7,098,265 | 4,377,213 | 2,764,331 |
| 1971–72 | 2028 | 28,700,729 | 14,484,603 | 6,769,308 | 4,697,392 | 2,749,426 |
| 1972–73 | 2028 | 25,448,642 | 13,998,154 | 5,631,730 | 3,737,252 | 2,081,506 |
| 1973–74 | 2027 | 24,982,203 | 13,070,991 | 6,326,108 | 3,421,624 | 2,163,480 |
| 1974–75 | 2028 | 25,577,977 | 12,613,178 | 6,955,970 | 4,086,145 | 1,992,684 |
| 1975–76 | 2028 | 24,896,053 | 13,089,861 | 5,798,405 | 3,948,449 | 2,059,338 |
| 1976–77 | 2028 | 26,182,800 | 13,647,585 | 6,250,597 | 4,152,218 | 2,132,400 |
| 1977–78 | 2028 | 25,392,872 | 13,255,677 | 6,474,763 | 3,332,042 | 2,330,390 |
| 1978–79 | 2028 | 24,540,627 | 12,704,549 | 6,153,223 | 3,374,558 | 2,308,297 |
| 1979–80 | 2028 | 24,623,975 | 12,163,002 | 6,112,025 | 3,999,328 | 2,349,620 |
| 1980–81 | 2028 | 21,907,569 | 11,392,894 | 5,175,442 | 3,637,854 | 1,701,379 |
| 1981–82 | 2028 | 20,006,961 | 10,420,793 | 4,750,463 | 2,836,915 | 1,998,790 |

# FOOTBALL LEAGUE CUP 1981–82

**FIRST ROUND, FIRST LEG**

**31 AUG**

**Wigan Ath (1) 3** *(Lloyd, Quinn, Houghton)*

**Stockport Co (0) 0**                                    5079

*Wigan Ath:* Brown; McMahon, Glenn, Cribley, Lloyd, Methven, Sheldon, Barrow, Bradd (Houghton), Quinn, Evans.
*Stockport Co:* Lloyd; Thorpe, Sherlock, Fowler, Sword, Uzelac, Williams, Wardrobe, Coyle, Park, Stafford.


**1 SEPT**

**Aldershot (0) 0**

**Wimbledon (0) 0**                                    2098

*Aldershot:* Johnson; Edwards, Wooler, Briley, Bennett, Jopling, McGregor, Sanford, Garwood, Crosby, Robinson.
*Wimbledon:* Beasant; Jones, Armstrong, Galliers, Smith, Downes, Ketteridge, Joseph, Leslie, Cork, Hodges.


**AFC Bournemouth (0) 0**

**Fulham (1) 1** *(Davies)*                              3935

*AFC Bournemouth:* Allen; Heffernan, Sulley, Smith, Compton, Impey, Edmunds, Dawtry, Mooney, Morgan, Williams.
*Fulham:* Peyton; Hopkins, Strong, Beck, Brown, Gale, Davies, Wilson, Coney, O'Sullivan, Lewington.


**Bolton W (1) 2** *(Kidd, Thomas)*

**Oldham Ath (0) 1** *(Atkinson)*                        5156

*Bolton W:* McDonagh; Nicholson, Bennett, McElhinney, Jones, Gowling, Thomas, Kidd, Hoggan, Cantello, Reid.
*Oldham Ath:* McDonnell; Hoolickin, Ryan, Keegan, McDonough, Futcher, Wylde, Atkinson, Steel, Palmer, Heaton.


**Bristol C (2) 2** *(Harford, Mann)*

**Walsall (0) 0**                                    3906

*Bristol C:* Moller; Stevens, Merrick, Mann, Rodgers, Marshall, Tainton, Musker, Mabbutt, Harford, Devine.
*Walsall:* Green; Macken, Mower, Beech, Serella, Hart, Waddington S., Caswell, Penn, Buckley, Preece.


**Bury (1) 3** *(Johnson pen, Madden 2)*

**Carlisle U (1) 3** *(Coady, Haigh, Lee)*              2247

*Bury:* Platt; Bradley, Kennedy, Gore, Cruickshank, Howard, Madden, Butler, Johnson, Jakub, Hilton M.
*Carlisle U:* Swinburne; Ashurst, Rushbury, Coady, Houghton, Parker, Haigh, Campbell, Lee, Robson, Crabbe.


**Colchester U (1) 2** *(Bremner, Allinson pen)*

**Gillingham (0) 0**                                    2431

*Colchester U:* Walker; Cook, Packer (Coleman), Leslie, Wignall, Wright, Adcock, Bremner, Longhorn, McDonough, Allinson.
*Gillingham:* Sutton; Sharpe, Ford, Bruce, Weatherly, Bowman, Powell, Duncan, Tydeman, Lee, Price.


**Darlington (0) 1** *(Walsh)*

**Rotherham U (1) 3** *(Smith og, Henson, Fern)*        3042

*Darlington:* Cuff; Kamara, McLean, Smith, Skipper, Mitchell, Ball, Speedie, Stalker, Hamilton, Walsh.
*Rotherham U:* Mountford; Forrest, Taylor, Green, Stancliffe, Mullen, Towner, Seasman, Moore, Fern, Henson.


**Doncaster R (0) 0**

**Chesterfield (0) 0**                                    3801

*Doncaster R:* Boyd; Lally, Dawson, Snodin I., Lister, Dowd, Pugh, Nimmo (Douglas), Warboys, Harle, Mell.
*Chesterfield:* Turner; Bellamy, O'Neill, Wilson, Green, Ridley, Tartt, Crawford, Bonnyman, Kowalski, Walker.


**Halifax T (0) 1** *(Davison)*

**Preston NE (2) 2** *(Clark, Naughton)*                2719

*Halifax T:* Kilner; Ward, Carr, Evans, Ayre, Hendrie, Firth, Davison, Graham, Chamberlain, McIlwraith.
*Preston NE:* Litchfield; Coleman, Westwell, Clark, O'Riordan, Blackley, Houston, Doyle, Elliott (Walsh), Bruce, Naughton.


**Huddersfield T (3) 3** *(Fletcher 2, Wilson)*

**Rochdale (0) 1** *(Cooper)*                            6713

*Huddersfield T:* Rankin; Brown, Burke, Wilson, Sutton, Hanvey, Lillis, Kennedy, Fletcher, Kindon (Austin), Cowling.
*Rochdale:* Poole; Cooper, Snookes, Dolan, Taylor, Burke, Martinez, O'Loughlin, Esser, Wellings, Hilditch.


**Northampton T (1) 2** *(Denyer, Alexander)*

**Hartlepool U (0) 0**                                    1480

*Northampton T:* Poole; Brady, Denyer, Farmer, Gage, Coffill, Carlton, Heeley, Phillips, Bowen, Alexander.
*Hartlepool U:* Burleigh; Brown, Stimpson, Hogan, Fagan, Linighan, Kerr, Sweeney, Staff, Houchen, Harding (Johnson).


**Orient (1) 1** *(Moores)*

**Millwall (1) 1** *(Horrix)*                            4568

*Orient:* Day; Fisher, Roffey, Taylor T., Gray, Margerrison, Godfrey (Mayo), Jennings, Moores, Bowles, Taylor P.
*Millwall:* Gleasure; Roberts (Massey), Warman, Chatterton, Tagg, Martin, Dibble, Anderson, Horrix, Bartley, West.


**Scunthorpe U (0) 0**

**Mansfield T (0) 0**                                    2249

*Scunthorpe U:* Neenan; Davy, Pilling, Keeley, Dall, Oates, Grimes, Hughes, Green, Cowling (Partridge), Stewart.
*Mansfield T:* Arnold; McJannet, Wood, Bell, Boam, Bird, Thomson, Parkinson, Lumby, Caldwell (Mann), Nicholson.


**Sheffield U (0) 1** *(Kenworthy pen)*

**York C (0) 0**                                    6702

*Sheffield U:* Waugh; Ryan, Kenworthy, Tibbott, McPhail, McAlle, Wiggan, Trusson, Neville, Hatton, Charles.
*York C:* Blackburn; Kay, Flood, Hood, Croft, Dawson, Ford, Byrne, Walwyn, McDonald, Waldron.


**Tranmere R (1) 4** *(Stevenson og, Kerr, Brown 2)*

**Burnley (0) 2** *(Potts, Hamilton)*                    2025

*Tranmere R:* Johnson; Mathias (Mungall), Burgess, Parry, Bramhall, Williams, Kelly, Hutchinson, Kerr, Brown, Griffiths.
*Burnley:* Stevenson; Laws, Holt, Young, Phelan, Dobson, Cavener, Taylor, Hamilton, Cassidy, Potts.

**Wrexham (2) 3** *(Vinter, Edwards, Davis)*

**Swindon T (0) 2** *(Baddeley, Carter* pen*)*     2068

*Wrexham:* Niedzwiecki; Dowman, Jones, Davis, Cegielski, Hill, Fox, McNeil, Edwards, Vinter (Buxton), Carrodus.
*Swindon T:* Allan; Henry, Williams, Hughes, Lewis, Graham, Carter, Emmanuel, Rowland, Greenwood (Baddeley), Moores.

## 2 SEPT

**Bradford C (1) 3** *(Gallagher, Campbell, Greenall og)*

**Blackpool (1) 1** *(Bamber)*     3374

*Bradford C:* Smith; Podd, Watson, Ingham, Jackson, Thompson, Gallagher, Black (Staniforth), Campbell, McNiven, Chapman.
*Blackpool:* Hesford; Simmonite, Pashley, Blair (Hart), Greenall, McEwan, Morris, Wann, Bamber, Hockaday, Harrison.

**Cardiff C (1) 2** *(Stevens 2)*

**Exeter C (0) 1** *(Cooke)*     2688

*Cardiff C:* Healey; Jones, Sullivan, Grapes, Pontin, Dwyer, Lewis, Kitchen, Stevens, Ronson, Buchanan.
*Exeter C:* Main; Rogers M., Hatch, Davey, Cooke, Roberts L., Rogers P., Pratt, Kellow, Lester, Pullar (Roberts P.).

**Chester (1) 2** *(Ludlam 2)*

**Plymouth Arg (1) 2** *(Kemp, Sims)*     1759

*Abandoned after 78 min*

**Crewe Alex (1) 1** *(Ricketts)*

**Bristol R (1) 1** *(Mabbutt)*     2137

*Crewe Alex:* Mulhearn; Salathiel, Lewis, Heath, Scott, Haslegrave, Hanlon, Ricketts, Chesters, Palios, Williams.
*Bristol R:* Kite; Gillies, Slatter, McCaffery, Parkin, Williams B., Curlie (Hughes), Williams D., Mabbutt, Randall, Cooper.

**Hereford U (1) 1** *(Phillips)*

**Port Vale (0) 1** *(Moss)*     2817

*Hereford U:* Hughes; Price, Bartley (Showers), Hicks, Overson, Spiring, Harvey, Laidlaw, Phillips, Lane, White.
*Port Vale:* Harrison; Keenan, Deakin, Hunter, Sproson, Bowles, Higgins, Moss, Armstrong, Bromage, Chamberlain M.

**Lincoln C (1) 3** *(Shipley, Hobson, Cunningham)*

**Hull C (0) 0**     3498

*Lincoln C:* Felgate; Thompson T., McVay, Gilbert, Creane, Carr, Shipley, Cockerill, Hobson, Cunningham, Cammack.
*Hull C:* Norman; McNeil, Booth, Richards, Eccleston, Horswill (Whitehurst), Roberts G., Edwards, Deacy, Mutrie, Ferguson.

**Oxford U (1) 1** *(Cassells)*

**Brentford (0) 0**     3621

*Oxford U:* Burton; Doyle, Fogg, Jeffrey, Briggs, Shotton, Jones, Foley, Cassells, Page, Smithers.
*Brentford:* McKellar; Tucker, Hill, Salman, Whitehead, Hurlock, Shrubb, Roberts, Booker, Harris, Crown.

**Peterborough U (1) 2** *(Slack, Cooke)*

**Barnsley (2) 3** *(Glavin 2, Joyce)*     4608

*Peterborough U:* Smelt; Winters, Collins, Gynn, Slack, Rodaway, Quow, Kellock, Cooke, Hodgson (Chard), Clarke.
*Barnsley:* Horn; Joyce, Chambers, Glavin, Banks, McCarthy, Evans, Parker, Aylott, McHale, Barrowclough.

**Reading (0) 2** *(Earles, Hetzke* pen*)*

**Charlton Ath (1) 2** *(Lansdowne, Hales* pen*)*     3622

*Reading:* Fearon; Williams, White (Dixon), Beavon, Hicks, Hetzke, Earles, Kearney, Heale, Sanchez, Webb.
*Charlton Ath:* Johns; Naylor, Harrison, Gritt, McAllister, Phillips, Walker (Robinson), Walsh, Hales, Lansdowne, Ferns.

**Southend U (0) 0**

**Portsmouth (0) 0**     4887

*Southend U:* Cawston; Stead, Dudley, Hadley, Moody, Cusack, Gray (Nelson), Pountney, Spence, Mercer, Otulakowski.
*Portsmouth:* Knight; McLaughlin, Viney, Kamara, Aizlewood, Rollings, Gregory, Doyle, Rafferty, Berry, Rogers.

**Torquay U (0) 2** *(Cooper, Fell)*

**Newport Co (2) 3** *(Aldridge, Oakes, Moore)*     2514

*Torquay U:* O'Keefe; Jones, Pendrey, Sermanni, Wilson, Larmour, Fell, Lawrence (Bowker), Cooper, Rioch, Weston.
*Newport Co:* Kendall; Elsey, Lees, Davies, Oakes, Bailey, Vaughan, Johnson, Gwyther, Aldridge (Waddle), Moore.

## 8 SEPT

**Chester (1) 1** *(Jones)*

**Plymouth Arg (1) 1** *(Storton og)*     1690

*Chester:* Millington; Needham, Raynor, Storton, Cottam, Oakes, Jones, Simpson, Ludlam, Howat, Sutcliffe.
*Plymouth Arg:* Crudgington; Nisbet, McCartney, Harrison, Foster, Cooper, Hodges, Kemp, Sims, Randell, Murphy.

## FIRST ROUND, SECOND LEG

## 14 SEPT

**Mansfield T (1) 2** *(Lumby 2)*

**Scunthorpe U (0) 0**     2258

*Mansfield T won 2-0*

*Mansfield T:* Arnold; McJannet, Wood, Bell, Boam, Bird, Thomson, Mann, Lumby, Caldwell (Woodhead), Nicholson.
*Scunthorpe U:* Neenan; Davy, Lambert, Keeley, Dall, Oates, Grimes, Cowling, Green, Duffy (Partridge), Stewart.

**Port Vale (1) 2** *(Deakin, Moss)*

**Hereford U (0) 0**     3500

*Port Vale won 3-1*

*Port Vale:* Harrison; Keenan, Deakin, Hunter, Sproson, Bowles, Chamberlain N., Moss, Armstrong, Bromage, Chamberlain M.
*Hereford U:* Hughes; Brady, Price, Hicks, Cornes, Spiring, Harvey, Laidlaw, Phillips, Showers, White.

**Stockport Co (1) 1** *(Fowler)*

**Wigan Ath (2) 2** *(Lloyd, Methven)*  2913

*Wigan Ath won 5-1*

*Stockport Co:* Lloyd; Rutter, Sherlock, Fowler, Thorpe, Uzelac, Williams, Wardrobe, Coyle, Park, Stafford.
*Wigan Ath:* Ward; McMahon; Glenn, Wright, Lloyd, Methven, Sheldon, Langley (Cribley), Houghton, Quinn, Evans.

**15 SEPT**

**Barnsley (4) 6** *(Glavin 2, Parker 2, Aylott, Barrowclough)*

**Peterborough U (0) 0**  11,198

*Barnsley won 9-2*

*Barnsley:* Horn; Joyce, Chambers, Glavin, Banks, McCarthy, Evans, Parker, Aylott, McHale, Barrowclough.
*Peterborough U:* Smelt; Winters, Collins, Gynn, Slack, Rodaway, Quow, Kellock, Cooke, Chard, Clarke.

**Brentford (0) 0**

**Oxford U (0) 2** *(Whitehead og, Foley)*  5490

*Oxford won 3-0*

*Brentford:* McKellar; Tucker, Hill, Salman, Whitehead, Hurlock, Walker, Roberts, Booker, Harris, Crown.
*Oxford U:* Burton; Doyle, Fogg, Jeffrey, Briggs, Shotton, Jones, Foley, Cassels, Lythgoe, Smithers.

**Bristol R (0) 1** *aet (Parkin)*

**Crewe Alex (0) 0**  4050

*Bristol R won 2-1*

*Bristol R:* Kite; Gillies, Slatter, Hughes (Cooper), Parkin, McCaffery, Curle, Williams D., Mabbutt, Stephens, Barrett.
*Crewe Alex:* Mulhearn; Salathiel, Lewis, Griffiths, Scott, Haslegrave, Hanlon (Heath), Ricketts, Keighley, Palios, Bowers.

**Burnley (2) 3** *(Holt 2, Cassidy)*

**Tranmere R (3) 3** *(Brown, Kerr, Kelly)*  2375

*Tranmere won 7-5*

*Burnley:* Stevenson; Laws, Holt (Cavener), Scott, Overson, Dobson, Potts, Stevens, Hamilton, Cassidy, Robertson.
*Tranmere R:* Endersby; Mungall, Burgess, Parry, Bramhall, Williams, Kelly, Hutchinson (Craven), Kerr, Brown, Griffiths.

**Carlisle U (0) 2** *aet (Lee, Hilton P. og)*

**Bury (1) 1** *(Madden)*  3392

*Carlisle U won 5-4*

*Carlisle U:* Swinburne; Haigh, Rushbury, Coady, Ashurst, Larkin, Campbell (Coughlin), Beardsley, Lee, Crabbe, Staniforth.
*Bury:* Platt; Howard, Kennedy, Gore, Hilton P., Cruickshank, Madden, Butler (Mullen), Johnson, Jakub, Hilton M.

**Charlton Ath (0) 3** *aet (Elliott, Hales, Robinson)*

**Reading (1) 1** *(Heale)*  4560

*Charlton Ath won 5-3*

*Charlton Ath:* Johns; Naylor, Harrison (Robinson), Gritt, McAllister, Phillips, Elliott, Walsh, Hales, Lansdowne, Ferns.
*Reading:* Fearon; Williams (Beavon), Lewis, Wood, Hicks, Hetzke, Earles, Kearney, Heale, Sanchez, Webb.

**Fulham (0) 2** *(Beck, Wilson)*

**AFC Bournemouth (0) 0**  3583

*Fulham won 3-0*

*Fulham:* Peyton; Hopkins, Strong, Beck, Brown, Gale, Davies, Wilson, Coney, O'Sullivan, Lewington.
*AFC Bournemouth:* Allen; Heffernan, Sulley, Smith, Compton, Impey, Kelly, Dawtry, Mooney, Morgan, Williams.

**Chesterfield (0) 1** *aet (Green)*

**Doncaster R (0) 1** *(Douglas)*  4962

*Aggregate 1-1; Doncaster R won on away goals rule*

*Chesterfield:* Turner; Bellamy, Pollard, Wilson, Green, Ridley, Walker, Henderson, Bonnyman, Kowalski (Windridge), Crawford.
*Doncaster R:* Boyd; Russell, Dawson, Snodin I., Lally, Dowd, Pugh, Harle, Warboys, Lister, Douglas.

**Gillingham (0) 1** *(Price)*

**Colchester U (0) 1** *(Bremner)*  3260

*Colchester won 3-1*

*Gillingham:* Hillyard; Sharpe (White), Ford, Bruce, Weatherly, Bowman, Powell, Duncan, Tydeman, Lee, Price.
*Colchester U:* Walker; Cook, Coleman, Leslie, Wignall, Wright, Adcock, Bremner, Osborne, McDonough, Allinson.

**Hull C (1) 1** *(Ferguson)*

**Lincoln C (1) 1** *(Carr)*  2702

*Lincoln C won 4-1*

*Hull C:* Norman; Hoolickin, Booth, Richards, Eccleston, Horswill, McClaren (Marwood), Edwards, Whitehurst, Mutrie, Ferguson.
*Lincoln C:* Felgate; Thompson T., McVay, Gilbert (Neale), Creane, Carr, Shipley, Cockerill, Hobson, Cunningham, Cammack.

**Newport Co (0) 0**

**Torquay U (0) 0**  4203

*Newport Co won 3-2*

*Newport Co:* Kendall; Elsey, Waddle (Tynan), Davies, Oakes, Bailey, Vaughan, Johnson, Gwyther, Aldridge, Moore.
*Torquay U:* O'Keefe; Jones, Pendrey, Bowker, Wilson, Larmour, Fell, Lawrence, Cooper, Rioch, Hodge.

**Oldham Ath (2) 4** *aet (Palmer 2, Wylde, Heaton)*

**Bolton W (1) 2** *(Thompson, Berry)*  4779

*Oldham Ath won 5-4*

*Oldham Ath:* McDonnell; Hoolickin, Ryan, Keegan, Clements, Futcher, Wylde (Heaton), Atkinson, Steel, Palmer, McDonough.
*Bolton W:* McDonagh; Nicholson, Bennett, Brennan, Jones, Gowling, Nikolic (Berry), Kidd, Hoggan, Thompson, Carter.

**Plymouth Arg (1) 1** *(Dennis pen)*

**Chester (0) 0**  2348

*Plymouth Arg won 2-1*

*Plymouth Arg:* Crudgington; Nisbet, Uzzell, Harrison, Foster, Rowe, Hodges, Kemp, Sims, Randell, Dennis.
*Chester:* Millington; Needham, Raynor, Storton, Cottam, Oakes, Jones, Simpson, Ludlam, Howat (Cooke), Sutcliffe.

**Preston NE (0) 0**

**Halifax T (0) 0**     4090

*Preston NE won 2-1*

*Preston NE:* Litchfield; Westwell, McAteer, Clark, O'Riordan, Bell J., Walsh, Bell G., Bruce, Coleman, McGee.
*Halifax T:* Kilner; Ward, Carr, Evans, Ayre, Hendrie, Firth, Davison, Allatt, Chamberlain, Graham.


**Rochdale (1) 2** *(Wellings, Hilditch)*

**Huddersfield T (1) 4** *(Fletcher 2, Robins, Kindon)*   3735

*Huddersfield T won 7-3*

*Rochdale:* Crawford; Weir, Snookes, O'Loughlin, Taylor (Hamilton), Cooper, Martinez, Esser, Hilditch, Wellings, Goodwin.
*Huddersfield T:* Rankin; Brown, Burke, Robins, Sutton (Austin), Purdie, Lillis, Kennedy, Fletcher, Kindon, Wilson.


**Rotherham U (1) 2** *(Moore 2)*

**Darlington (0) 1** *(Charlton)*     3894

*Rotherham U won 5-2*

*Rotherham U:* Mountford; Forrest, Breckin, Green, Stancliffe, Mullen, Towner, Rhodes, Moore, Fern, Henson.
*Darlington:* Cuff; Kamara, McLean, Smith, Skipper, Mitchell, Hawker, Speedie, Stalker (Charlton), Hamilton, Walsh.


**Swindon T (0) 0**

**Wrexham (0) 2** *(Vinter, Edwards)*     6776

*Wrexham won 5-2*

*Swindon T:* Allan; Henry, Williams, Hughes, Lewis, Graham, Carter, Emmanuel, Rowland, Rideout, Moores (Pritchard).
*Wrexham:* Niedzwiecki; Jones, Bater, Dowman, Cegielski, Hill, Fox, McNeil (Hunt), Edwards, Vinter, Carrodus.


**Walsall (0) 1** *(Penn)*

**Bristol C (0) 0**     2830

*Bristol C won 2-1*

*Walsall:* Green; Macken, Mower (Round), Beech, Serella, Hart, Rees, Waddington S., Penn, Buckley, Caswell.
*Bristol C:* Moller; Stevens, Sweeney, Aitken, Rodgers, Merrick (Devine), Musker, Mann, Mabbutt, Harford, Hay.


**Wimbledon (0) 1** *(Cork pen)*

**Aldershot (1) 3** *(Garwood 2, Crosby)*   2181

*Aldershot won 3-1*

*Wimbledon:* Beasant; Brown (Gage), Armstrong, Galliers, Smith, Downes, Ketteridge, Joseph, Leslie, Cork, Hodges.
*Aldershot:* Johnson; Edwards, Wooler, Briley, Bennett, Jopling, Wanklyn, Sanford, Garwood, Crosby, Brodie (Lucas).


**York C (1) 1** *(Byrne)*

**Sheffield U (0) 1** *(Hatton)*     4750

*Sheffield U won 2-1*

*York C:* Blackburn; Kay, Flood, Hood, Craig, Dawson, Ford, Byrne, Walwyn, McDonald, McGhie.
*Sheffield U:* Waugh; Ryan, Kenworthy, Charles, MacPhail, McAlle, Wiggan, Trusson, Neville, Hatton, Tibbott.


**16 SEPT**

**Blackpool (0) 0**

**Bradford C (0) 0**     5722

*Bradford C won 3-1*

*Blackpool:* Hesford; Simmonite, Pashley, Blair, Hart, McEwan, Morris, Noble, Bamber, Hockaday, Harrison.
*Bradford C:* Smith; Podd, Watson, Ingham, Jackson, McFarland, Gallagher, Thompson, Campbell, McNiven, Chapman.


**Exeter C (1) 3** *(Kellow pen, Fisher, Cooke)*

**Cardiff C (1) 1** *(Sugrue)*     4449

*Exeter C won 4-3*

*Exeter C:* Main; Mitchell, Roberts L., Davey, Cooke, Roberts P., Fisher (Prince), Pratt, Kellow, Lester, Hatch.
*Cardiff C:* Healey; Jones, Sullivan, Grapes (Hughes), Pontin, Dwyer, Lewis, Sugrue, Stevens, Ronson, Buchanan.


**Hartlepool U (1) 2** *(Newton, Houchen)*

**Northampton T (1) 1** *(Denyer)*     1975

*Northampton T won 3-2*

*Hartlepool U:* Burleigh; Sweeney, Stimpson (Linighan), Hogan, Fagan, Brown, Linacre, Newton, Hampton, Houchen, Johnson.
*Northampton T:* Poole; Brady, Denyer, Farmer, Gage, Coffill, Carlton, Sandy, Bowen, Phillips, Alexander.


**Millwall (0) 3** *(Chatterton, Dibble, West)*

**Orient (0) 2** *(Moores, Jennings)*     4784

*Millwall won 4-3*

*Millwall:* Gleasure; Roberts, Warman, Chatterton, Tagg, Martin, Dibble, Anderson, Horrix, Bartley, West.
*Orient:* Day; Fisher, Roffey, Taylor T., Cunningham, Margerrison, Jennings, Godfrey, Moores, Hughton, Taylor P.


**Portsmouth (2) 4** *(Rafferty, Doyle, Berry, Kamara)*

**Southend U (1) 1** *(Spence)*     10,019

*Portsmouth won 4-1*

*Portsmouth:* Knight; McLaughlin, Viney, Kamara, Aizlewood, Ellis (Rogers), Hemmerman, Doyle, Rafferty, Berry, Tait.
*Southend U:* Keeley; Stead, Yates, Nelson, Moody, Cusack, Gray, Pountney, Spence (Dudley), Mercer, Otulakowski,


**SECOND ROUND, FIRST LEG**

**5 OCT**

**Tranmere R (2) 2** *(Brown 2)*

**Port Vale (0) 0**     2711

*Tranmere R:* Endersby; Mungall, Burgess, Mountfield, Bramhall, Williams, Kelly (Craven), Hutchinson, Kerr, Brown, Griffiths.
*Port Vale:* Harrison; Brissett, Deakin, Hunter, Sproson, Bowles, Greenhoff, Moss, Bromage, Bennett, Chamberlain M.


**6 OCT**

**Aldershot (2) 2** *(Lucas, Robinson)*

**Wigan Ath (1) 2** *(Barrow 2)*     1960

*Aldershot:* Johnson; Edwards, Scott, Briley, Bennett, Wooler, Lucas, Crosby, Garwood, Sanford, Brodie (Robinson).
*Wigan Ath:* Ward; McMahon, Cribley, Wignall, Lloyd, Methven, Sheldon, Barrow, Bradd, Houghton, Evans.

**Barnsley (0) 2** *(Riley, Evans)*

**Swansea C (0) 0** 12,793

*Barnsley:* Horn; Joyce, Chambers, Glavin, Banks, McCarthy, Evans, Parker, Riley, McHale, Campbell (Barrowclough).
*Swansea C:* Davies; Robinson, Lewis, Marustik, Irwin, Charles, Curtis, Stanley, James L. (Attley), Thompson, Latchford.

**Birmingham C (1) 2** *(Whatmore, Worthington)*

**Nottingham F (2) 3** *(Wallace 2, Proctor)* 14,330

*Birmingham C:* Wealands; Langan, Dennis, Dillon, Broadhurst, Todd, Brocken, Whatmore, Worthington, Gemmill, Van Mierlo.
*Nottingham F:* Shilton; Anderson, Gray, Gunn (Mills), Burns, Aas, Walsh, Wallace, Fashanu, Proctor, Robertson.

**Bristol R (0) 1** *(Stephens)*

**Northampton T (1) 2** *(Phillips, Sandy)* 4476

*Bristol R:* Kite; Gillies, Cooper, McCaffery, Parkin, Mabbutt, Barrett, Williams D., Stephens, Randall (Williams S.), Williams G.
*Northampton T:* Poole; Taylor, Carlton, Brady, Gage, Coffill, Denyer, Sandy, Heeley, Phillips, Alexander.

**Carlisle U (0) 0**

**Bristol C (0) 0** 4111

*Carlisle U:* Swinburne; Parker, Rushbury, Haigh, Ashurst, Larkin, Coughlin, Beardsley, Lee, Crabbe (Hamilton), Staniforth.
*Bristol C:* Moller; Stevens, Hay, Aitken, Rodgers, Sweeney, Whitehead, Mann, Mabbutt, Harford, Musker.

**Colchester U (1) 3** *(Cook, McDonough 2)*

**Cambridge U (0) 1** *(Gibbins)* 3844

*Colchester U:* Walker; Cook, Coleman, Leslie, Wignall, Wright, Adcock, Bremner, Osborne, McDonough, Allinson.
*Cambridge U:* Webster; Christie, Murray, Reilly, Fallon, O'Neill, Streete, Spriggs, Goldsmith, Gibbins, Finney.

**Doncaster R (1) 1** *(Mell)*

**Crystal Palace (0) 0** 7783

*Doncaster R:* Humphries S.; Russell, Dawson, Lister, Humphries G., Dowd, Pugh, Harle, Mell, Snodin G. (Noteman), Douglas.
*Crystal Palace:* Barron; Bason, Dare (Lovell), Price, Cannon, Gilbert, Brooks, Smillie, Hughes, Langley, Leahy.

**Everton (0) 1** *(Ferguson)*

**Coventry C (0) 1** *(Hateley)* 17,228

*Everton:* Arnold; Stevens, Bailey, Walsh, Lyons, Thomas, McMahon, O'Keefe, Ferguson, Ross, McBride.
*Coventry C:* Blyth; Thomas, Roberts, Jacobs, Dyson, Gillespie, Kaiser, Whitton, Thompson, Gooding, Hateley.

**Grimsby T (0) 1** *(Moore K.)*

**Watford (0) 0** 7044

*Grimsby T:* Batch; Moore D., Crombie, Waters, Wigginton, Moore K., Brolly, Whymark, Drinkell, Mitchell, Cumming (Ford).
*Watford:* Sherwood; Henderson, Pritchett, Taylor, Sims (Gilligan), Bolton, Callaghan, Poskett, Blissett, Jackett, Barnes.

**Huddersfield T (0) 1** *(Austin)*

**Brighton & HA (0) 0** 9803

*Huddersfield T:* Rankin; Brown, Burke, Wilson, Purdie, Hanvey, Lillis, Kennedy, Kindon, Robins, Austin.
*Brighton & HA:* Moseley; Shanks, Williams, Stevens, Foster, Gatting, Case, Ring, Robinson, McNab, Ryan.

**Luton T (0) 0**

**Wrexham (2) 2** *(Vinter, Hunt)* 6146

*Luton T:* Findlay; Stephens, Antic, Horton, Saxby, Donaghy, Hill, Stein, White, Fuccillo, Moss.
*Wrexham:* Niedzwiecki; Jones, Bater, Dowman, Cegielski, Hunt, Fox, McNeil, Edwards, Vinter, Carrodus.

**Middlesbrough (0) 2** *(Ashcroft, Thomson)*

**Plymouth Arg (1) 1** *(Kemp)* 8201

*Middlesbrough:* Platt; Craggs, Bolton, Angus, Baxter, McAndrew, Cochrane, Otto, Ashcroft, Shearer, Thomson.
*Plymouth Arg:* Crudgington; Nisbet, McCartney, Uzzell, Foster, Cooper, Hodges, Kemp, Sims, Randell, Rogers.

**Millwall (0) 3** *(Horrix 2, Dibble)*

**Oxford U (1) 3** *(Thomas, Cassells 2 [1 pen])* 3744

*Millwall:* Gleasure; Roberts, Warman, Chatterton, Allardyce, Slough, Dibble, Anderson, McKenna (Hayes), Horrix, Massey.
*Oxford U:* Burton; Doyle, Fogg, Jeffrey, Briggs, Shotton, Jones, Foley (Kearns), Cassells, Thomas, Smithers.

**Oldham Ath (1) 1** *(Palmer)*

**Newport Co (0) 0** 5075

*Oldham Ath:* McDonnell; Sinclair, Ryan, Keegan, Hoolickin, Futcher, Wylde, Heaton, Steel, Palmer, McDonough.
*Newport Co:* Kendall; Elsey, Waddle, Davies, Oakes, Bailey, Vaughan, Lowndes, Gwyther, Tynan, Moore.

**Preston NE (1) 1** *(Bruce)*

**Leicester C (0) 0** 5382

*Preston NE:* Litchfield; Coleman, McAteer, Clark, Booth, O'Riordan, Buckley, Anderson, Bruce, Farrelly, Dunn.
*Leicester C:* Wallington; Williams, Gibson, Ramsay, May, O'Neill, Lynex, Melrose, Young, Smith, MacDonald.

**QPR (1) 5** *(Ellis og, Gregory 2, Micklewhite 2)*

**Portsmouth (0) 0** 13,502

*QPR:* Burridge; Gregory, Fenwick, Waddock, Hazell, Roeder, Micklewhite, Stainrod, Allen, Currie (Burke), Gillard.
*Portsmouth:* Knight; McLaughlin, Viney, Kamara, Rollings, Ellis, Hemmerman, Doyle, Rafferty, Rogers, Tait.

**Sheffield U (0) 1** *(Hatton)*

**Arsenal (0) 0** 19,101

*Sheffield U:* Waugh; Ryan, Houston, Richardson, McAlle, Kenworthy, Neville, Trusson, Garner, Hatton, Charles.
*Arsenal:* Jennings; Devine, Sansom, Talbot, O'Leary, Young, Hollins, Sunderland, Hawley, Nicholas, Davis.

**Shrewsbury T (0) 3** *(Atkins pen, Biggins, MacLaren)*

**WBA (3) 3** *(Regis, MacKenzie, Cross)* 9291

*Shrewsbury T:* Wardle; Leonard, Johnson, Petts (Cross), Griffin, MacLaren, Tong, McNally, Atkins, Biggins, Bates.
*WBA:* Godden; Batson, Statham, King, Wile, Robertson, Cross, Summerfield, Regis, Owen, MacKenzie.

**Southampton (1) 1** *(Keegan)*

**Chelsea (0) 1** *(Fillery)* 16,901

*Southampton:* Wells; Golac, Holmes (Lawrence), Baker, Watson, Waldron, Keegan, Channon, Moran, Armstrong, Ball.
*Chelsea:* Francis; Locke, Hutchings, Viljoen, Pates, Chivers, Rhoades-Brown, Britton, Lee, Mayes, Fillery.

**7 OCT**

**Aston Villa (0) 3** *(Bremner, Blair, Morley)*

**Wolverhampton W (1) 2** *(Gray, Gallagher)*          26,353

*Aston Villa:* Rimmer; Swain, Gibson, Evans, Ormsby, Mortimer, Bremner, Shaw, Withe (Blair), Cowans, Morley.
*Wolverhampton W:* Bradshaw; Palmer, Hibbitt, Birch (Bell), Parkin, Atkinson, Gallagher, Villazan, Matthews, Gray, Richards.

**Blackburn R (0) 1** *(Garner)*

**Sheffield W (0) 1** *(Taylor)*          7900

*Blackburn R:* Gennoe; Branagan, Rathbone, Speight, Keeley, Fazackerley, Miller, Burke, Lowey, Garner, Brotherston.
*Sheffield W:* Bolder; Blackhall, Williamson, Smith, Shirtliff, Taylor, Megson, Mirocevic, Bannister, McCulloch, Curran (Mellor).

**Bradford C (1) 3** *(Bird og, Campbell, Black pen)*

**Mansfield T (1) 4** *(Lumby, Wood, Bird, Smith og)*          4293

*Bradford C:* Smith; Podd, Watson, Ingham, Jackson, Thompson, Gallagher, Black, Campbell, McNiven, Chapman.
*Mansfield T:* Arnold; McJannet (Wood), Foster, Bell, Burrows, Bird, Thomson, Mann, Lumby, Caldwell, Nicholson.

**Derby Co (1) 2** *(Stewart og, Hector)*

**West Ham U (1) 3** *(Cross, Brooking, Stewart pen)*          13,764

*Derby Co:* Cherry; Coop, Buckley, Powell S., Ramage, Osgood (Clayton), Skivington, Powell B., Hector, Swindlehurst, Emson.
*West Ham U:* McAlister; Stewart, Lampard, Bonds, Martin, Devonshire, Neighbour, Goddard, Cross, Brooking, Pike.

**Leeds U (0) 0**

**Ipswich T (0) 1** *(Gates)*          16,994

*Leeds U:* Lukic; Stevenson, Gray F., Hird, Hart, Cherry, Harris, Graham, Balcombe, Gray E., Barnes.
*Ipswich T:* Cooper; Steggles, McCall, Thijssen, Osman, Butcher, Wark, Muhren, Mariner, Mills, Gates

**Lincoln C (1) 1** *(Peake)*

**Notts Co (1) 1** *(Hooks)*          4943

*Lincoln C:* Felgate; Thompson T., McVay, Cockerill, Peake, Carr, Cammack, Shipley, Hobson, Cunningham, Neale (Bell).
*Notts Co:* Avramovic; Benjamin, O'Brien, Goodwin, Kilcline, Lahtinen, McCulloch, Masson, Christie, Hunt, Hooks.

**Liverpool (3) 5** *(Rush 2, McDermott, Dalglish, Whelan)*

**Exeter C (0) 0**          11,478

*Liverpool:* Grobbelaar; Neal, Kennedy A., Thompson, Lawrenson, Whelan, Dalglish, Lee, Rush, McDermott, Souness.
*Exeter C:* Bond; Rogers M., Sparrow, Davey, Cooke, Roberts L., Prince (Pullar), Rogers P., Kellow, Delve, Lester.

**Manchester C (1) 2** *(Smith og, Hartford)*

**Stoke C (0) 0**          23,146

*Manchester C:* Corrigan; Ranson, Wilson, Reid, Bond, Caton, Tueart, O'Neill, Hutchison, Hartford, Reeves.
*Stoke C:* Fox; Evans, Hampton, Dodd, O'Callaghan, Smith, Ursem, Heath, Chapman, Bracewell, Maguire.

**Newcastle U (0) 1** *(Barton)*

**Fulham (0) 2** *(Wilson, Coney)*          20,247

*Newcastle U:* Carr; Brownlie, Davies, Trewick, Barton, Halliday, Shinton, Martin, Varadi, Wharton (Shoulder), Waddle.
*Fulham:* Peyton; Hopkins, Strong, O'Driscoll, Brown, Gale, Davies, Wilson, Coney, O'Sullivan, Lewington (Lock).

**Norwich C (1) 1** *(Jack)*

**Charlton Ath (0) 0**          9732

*Norwich C:* Chris Woods; Nightingale, Donachie, McGuire, Walford, Hoadley, Barham, Jack, Bertschin, Shepherd (Muzinic), Clive Woods.
*Charlton Ath:* Johns; Naylor, Ferns, Gritt, McAllister, Phillips, Elliott, Walsh, Hales, Lansdowne, Robinson.

**Sunderland (2) 2** *(Rowell pen, Ritchie)*

**Rotherham U (0) 0**          10,450

*Sunderland:* Siddall; Whitworth, Munro, Buckley (Chisholm), Clarke, Elliott, Pickering, McCoist, Ritchie, Rowell, Cummins.
*Rotherham U:* Mountford; Forrest, Breckin, Green, Stancliffe, Mullen, Towner, Rhodes, Moore, Alexander, Henson.

**Tottenham H (0) 1** *(Archibald)*

**Manchester U (0) 0**          39,333

*Tottenham H:* Clemence; Hughton, Miller, Roberts, Villa, Perryman, Ardiles, Archibald, Galvin, Hoddle, Falco (Mazzon).
*Manchester U:* Bailey; Gidman, Albiston, Wilkins, Moran, Buchan, Coppell, Birtles (Duxbury), Stapleton, McIlroy, Robson.

**SECOND ROUND, SECOND LEG**

**26 OCT**

**Mansfield T (0) 0**

**Bradford C (0) 2** *(Black, Campbell)*          3522

*Bradford C won 5-4*

*Mansfield T:* Arnold; McJannet, Wood, Bell (Parkinson), Burrows, Bird, Thomson, Mann, Lumby, Caldwell, Nicholson.
*Bradford C:* Ramsbottom; Podd, Watson, Ingham, Jackson, Wood, Gallagher, Black, Campbell, McNiven, Chapman.

**27 OCT**

**Arsenal (1) 2** *aet (Young, Sunderland)*

**Sheffield U (0) 0**          22,301

*Arsenal won 2-1*

*Arsenal:* Jennings; Hollins, Sansom, Talbot, O'Leary, Young, McDermott, Sunderland, Meade (Vaessen), Nicholas, Rix.
*Sheffield U:* Waugh; Ryan, Houston, Richardson, McAlle, Kenworthy, Neville, Trusson, Wiggan, Hatton, Charles.

**Brighton & HA (0) 2** *(Ritchie, Grealish)*

**Huddersfield T (0) 0**          14,192

*Brighton & HA won 2-1*

*Brighton & HA:* Moseley; Shanks, Nelson, Grealish, Foster, Gatting, Case, Ritchie, Robinson, McNab, Smith.
*Huddersfield T:* Rankin; Brown, Burke, Wilson, Sutton, Hanvey, Lillis, Kennedy (Cowling), Austin, Robins, Fletcher.

**Bristol C (0) 2** *(Rodgers, Mann pen)*
**Carlisle U (1) 1** *(Staniforth pen)* 5220
*Bristol C won 2-1*

*Bristol C:* Moller; Stevens, Tainton, Aitken, Rodgers, Sweeney, Devine, Mann, Mabbutt, Harford, Whitehead.
*Carlisle U:* Swinburne; Parker, Rushbury, Campbell, Ashurst, Larkin, Crabbe, Robson, Lee, Beardsley, Staniforth.

**Cambridge U (1) 3** *aet (Gibbins 2, Reilly)*
**Colchester U (1) 2** *(Allinson, Bremner)* 4672
*Colchester U won 5-4*

*Cambridge U:* Webster; Donaldson, Murray, Turner, Fallon, O'Neill, Streete (Lyons), Spriggs, Reilly, Gibbins, Christie.
*Colchester U:* Walker; Cook, Coleman, Leslie, Wignall, Wright, Adcock (Longhorn), Bremner, Osborne, McDonough, Allinson.

**Coventry C (0) 0**
**Everton (0) 1** *(Ferguson)* 13,770
*Everton won 2-1*

*Coventry C:* Blyth; Thomas, Roberts, Jacobs, Dyson, Gillespie, Kaiser, Whitton, Thompson, Hateley, Hunt.
*Everton:* Arnold; Stevens, Bailey, Higgins, Lyons, Lodge, McMahon, O'Keefe, Ferguson, Ainscow, McBride.

**Crystal Palace (1) 2** *(Cannon pen, Murphy)*
**Doncaster R (0) 0** 7819
*Crystal Palace won 2-1*

*Crystal Palace:* Barron; Bason, Lovell, Murphy, Cannon, Gilbert, Price, Smillie, Leahy (Brooks), Langley, Hilaire.
*Doncaster R:* Humphries S.; Russell (Humphries G.), Dawson, Lister, Mell, Dowd, Pugh, Harles, Warboys, Snodin G., Douglas.

**Fulham (1) 2** *(Lewington pen, Coney)*
**Newcastle U (0) 0** 7210
*Fulham won 4-1*

*Fulham:* Peyton; Hopkins, Strong, O'Driscoll, Brown, Gale, Davies, Wilson, Coney, O'Sullivan, Lewington.
*Newcastle U:* Carr; Brownlie, Davies, Trewick, Barton, Halliday (Shoulder), Shinton, Martin, Varadi, Wharton, Waddle.

**Ipswich T (3) 3** *(Gates, Mariner, Steggles)*
**Leeds U (0) 0** 16,464
*Ipswich T won 4-0*

*Ipswich T:* Cooper; Steggles, McCall, Thijssen, Osman, Butcher, Wark, Muhren, Mariner (Brazil), Mills, Gates.
*Leeds U:* Lukic; Greenhoff, Gray F., Hird (Stevenson), Hart, Gray E., Harris, Graham, Connor, Hamson, Barnes.

**Newport Co (0) 0**
**Oldham Ath (0) 0** 4578
*Oldham Ath won 1-0*

*Newport Co:* Kendall; Walden, Relish, Davies (Lowndes), Oakes, Bailey, Vaughan, Johnson, Gwyther, Goddard, Elsey.
*Oldham Ath:* McDonnell; Hoolickin, Edwards, Keegan, Clements, Futcher, Wylde, Heaton, Steel, Palmer, Atkinson.

**Northampton T (0) 3** *(Heeley, Mahoney, Saxby)*
**Bristol R (0) 1** *(Williams D.)* 3543
*Northampton T won 5-2*

*Northampton T:* Poole; Taylor, Saxby, Gage, Brady, Heeley, Carlton, Sandy, Phillips, Coffill, Mahoney.
*Bristol R:* Kite; Jones (Penny), Gillies, McCaffery, Hughes, Mabbutt, Randall, Williams D., Stephens, Williams B., Barrett.

**Notts Co (1) 2** *(Mair, Masson)*
**Lincoln C (1) 3** *(Cunningham, Cockerill, Shipley)* 6292
*Lincoln C won 4-3*

*Notts Co:* Avramovic; Goodwin, O'Brien, Hunt, Lahtinen, Richards, Benjamin (Christie), Masson, McCulloch, Hooks, Mair.
*Lincoln C:* Felgate; Thompson T. (Creane), McVay, Cockerill, Peake, Carr, Cammack, Shipley, Bell, Cunningham, Gilbert.

**Portsmouth (2) 2** *(Rafferty, Doyle)*
**QPR (1) 2** *(Flanagan, Micklewhite)* 7677
*QPR won 7-2*

*Portsmouth:* Knight; Ellis, Viney, Barnard, Aizlewood, Rollings, Hemmerman, Doyle, Rafferty, Cropley, Tait.
*QPR:* Burridge; Gregory, Fenwick, Waddock, Hazell (Stewart), Roeder, Micklewhite, Flanagan, Burke, Stainrod, Gillard.

**Plymouth Arg (0) 0**
**Middlesbrough (0) 0** 6402
*Middlesbrough won 2-1*

*Plymouth Arg:* Crudgington; Nisbet, McCartney, Harrison, Phillipson-Masters, Cooper (Murphy), Hodges, Cook, Sims, Randell, Rogers.
*Middlesbrough:* Platt; Nattrass, Bolton, Angus, Baxter, McAndrew, Cochrane, Otto, Woof (Shearer), Hodgson, Thomson.

**Rotherham U (0) 3** *(Breckin, Fern, Gooding)*
**Sunderland (1) 3** *(Ritchie 2, Cummins)* 8179
*Sunderland won 5-3*

*Rotherham U:* Mountford; Forrest, Breckin, Rhodes, Stancliffe, Green, Towner, Gooding, Moore, Fern, Henson (Alexander).
*Sunderland:* Siddall; Venison, Munro, Chisholm, Clarke, Elliott, Arnott (Hindmarch), Rowell, Ritchie, Pickering, Cummins.

**Sheffield W (1) 1** *(Bannister)*
**Blackburn R (2) 2** *(Lowey, Garner)* 13,087
*Blackburn R won 3-2*

*Sheffield W:* Bolder; Blackhall, Williamson, Smith, Shirtliff, Taylor (Pearson), Megson, Stirland, Bannister, McCulloch, Curran.
*Blackburn R:* Gennoe; Branagan, Rathbone, Hamilton, Keeley, Fazackerley, Miller, Burke, Lowey, Garner, Brotherston.

**Swansea C (1) 3** *aet (James L. pen, Irwin, Curtis)*
**Barnsley (0) 2** *(Glavin, Cooper)* 9800
*Barnsley won 3-2*

*Swansea C:* Davies; Robinson, Marustik, Rajkovic, Irwin, Mahoney, Curtis, James R., James L., Stanley, Latchford (Stevenson).
*Barnsley:* Horn; Joyce, Chambers, Glavin (Cooper), Banks, McCarthy, Evans, Parker, Aylott, McHale, Campbell.

**Watford (3) 3** *(Jenkins 2, Blissett)*
**Grimsby T (0) 1** *(Whymark)*                           13,213
*Watford won 3-2*

*Watford:* Sherwood; Rice, Pritchett, Taylor, Sims, Bolton, Callaghan, Blissett, Jenkins, Jackett, Barnes.
*Grimsby T:* Batch; Cumming, Crombie, Waters, Wigginton, Moore K., Brolly, Drinkell, Whymark, Mitchell, Kilmore (O'Dell).

**West Ham U (1) 2** *(Goddard 2)*
**Derby Co (0) 0**                                        21,043
*West Ham U won 5-2*

*West Ham U:* Parkes; Stewart, Lampard, Bonds, Martin, Devonshire, Neighbour, Goddard, Cross, Brooking, Pike.
*Derby Co:* Jones; Coop, Buckley, Powell S., Sheridan, Powell B., Hector (Gibson), Reid, Clayton, Swindlehurst, Emson.

**Wigan Ath (0) 1** *(Barrow)*
**Aldershot (0) 0**                                       4926
*Wigan Ath won 3-2*

*Wigan Ath:* Brown; McMahon, Glenn, Wignall, Cribley, Methven, Sheldon, Barrow, Quinn, Houghton, Evans.
*Aldershot:* Johnson; Edwards, Scott, Briley, Bennett, Wooler, Lucas, Crosby, Garwood, Sanford (Brodie), Robinson.

**Wolverhampton W (0) 1** *(Richards)*
**Aston Villa (1) 2** *(Cowans 2 [1 pen])*                19,491
*Aston Villa won 5-3*

*Wolverhampton W:* Bradshaw; Palmer, Parkin, Matthews, Gallagher, Brazier, Birch, Clarke, Eves, Daniel, Carr (Richards).
*Aston Villa:* Rimmer; Williams, Gibson, Evans, Ormsby, Mortimer, Bremner, Shaw, Withe, Cowans, Morley.

**Wrexham (0) 0**
**Luton T (0) 1** *(White)*                               3453
*Wrexham won 2-1*

*Wrexham:* Niedzwiecki; Jones (Fox), Bater, Dowman, Cegielski, Hunt, Hill, McNeil, Edwards, Vinter, Carrodus.
*Luton T:* Findlay; Stephens, Goodyear (Ingham), Horton, Saxby, Donaghy, Hill, White, Stein, Fuccillo, Moss.

## 28 OCT

**Charlton Ath (0) 0**
**Norwich C (0) 1** *(Jack)*                              7366
*Norwich C won 2-0*

*Charlton Ath:* Johns; Naylor, Dickenson, Gritt, McAlister, Phillips, Elliott, Walsh, Hales, Lansdowne (Madden), Robinson.
*Norwich C:* Woods; Symonds, Donachie, McGuire, Walford, Watson, Barham, Haylock, Jack, Mendham, Bennett.

**Chelsea (1) 2** *aet (Walker, Fillery)*
**Southampton (0) 1** *(Moran)*                           27,370
*Chelsea won 3-2*

*Chelsea:* Borota; Locke, Hutchings, Viljoen, Pates, Chivers, Rhoades-Brown, Bumstead, Lee, Walker, Fillery.
*Southampton:* Katalinic; Baker S., Holmes, Williams, Nicholl, Waldron (Moran), Keegan, Channon, Lawrence, Agboola, Puckett.

**Exeter C (0) 0**
**Liverpool (3) 6** *(Rush 2, Dalglish, Neal, Sheedy, Marker og)*                                                 11,740
*Liverpool won 11-0*

*Exeter C:* Bond; Rogers M., Sparrow, Davey (Hatch), Marker, Roberts P., Pullar, Rogers P., Kellow, Delve, Lester.
*Liverpool:* Grobbelaar; Neal, Lawrenson, Thompson, Kennedy R., Hansen, Dalglish, Whelan, Rush, McDermott, Sheedy.

**Leicester C (2) 4** *(Robson, Lynex, O'Riordan og, Melrose)*
**Preston NE (0) 0**                                      7685
*Leicester C won 4-1*

*Leicester C:* Wallington; Williams, Leet, MacDonald, Scott, O'Neill, Lynex, Melrose, Lineker, Wilson (Peake), Robson.
*Preston NE:* Litchfield; Westwell (Farrelly), McAteer, Clark, Anderson, O'Riordan, Buckley, Coleman, Bruce, Doyle, Dunn.

**Manchester U (0) 0**
**Tottenham H (1) 1** *(Hazard)*                          55,890
*Tottenham H won 2-0*

*Manchester U:* Bailey; Gidman, Albiston, Wilkins, Moran, Buchan, Robson, Birtles, Stapleton, Moses, Coppell.
*Tottenham H:* Clemence; Hughton, Miller, Roberts, Hazard, Perryman, Ardiles, Archibald, Galvin, Hoddle, Crooks.

**Nottingham F (1) 2** *(Needham, Robertson)*
**Birmingham C (0) 1** *(Evans)*                          16,316
*Nottingham F won 5-3*

*Nottingham F:* Shilton; Anderson, Gunn, McGovern, Needham, Aas, Gray (Walsh), Wallace, Fashanu, Proctor, Robertson.
*Birmingham C:* Wealands; Van den Hauwe, Hawker, Dillon, Broadhurst, Todd, Brocken (Handysides), Evans, Worthington, Gemmill, Van Mierlo.

**Oxford U (1) 1** *(Cassells)*
**Millwall (0) 0**                                        4811
*Oxford U won 4-3*

*Oxford U:* Burton; Doyle, Fogg, Jeffrey, Briggs, Shotton, Jones, Foley, Cassells (Kearns), Thomas, Smithers.
*Millwall:* Gleasure; Roberts, Warman, Chatterton, Martin, Slough, Hayes, Massey (Dibble), Bartley, Horrix, West.

**Port Vale (0) 1** *(Chamberlain N.)*
**Tranmere R (0) 2** *(Kerr, Hutchinson)*                 2345
*Tranmere R won 4-1*

*Port Vale:* Harrison; Keenan, Deakin (Higgins), Armstrong, Sproson, Bowles, Chamberlain M., Chamberlain N., Greenhoff, Bromage, Shankland.
*Tranmere R:* Endersby; Mungall, Burgess, Craven, Bramhall, Williams, Hamilton, Hutchinson, Kerr, Brown, Griffiths.

**Stoke C (0) 2** *aet (Chapman, Evans)*
**Manchester C (0) 0**                                    17,373
*Aggregate 2-2; Manchester C won 9-8 on penalties*

*Stoke C:* Fox; Evans, Hampton, Dodd, O'Callaghan, Smith, Johnson, Heath, Chapman, Bracewell, Maguire (Griffiths).
*Manchester C:* Corrigan; Ranson, Bond, Reid, Power, Caton, Tueart, O'Neill (Hareide), Hutchison, Hartford, Reeves.

453

**WBA (2) 2** *(Owen, Brown)*
**Shrewsbury T (0) 1** *(Atkins)*      12,598
*WBA won 5-4*
*WBA:* Godden; Batson, Statham, King, Wile, Robertson, Jol, Brown, Regis, Owen, MacKenzie.
*Shrewsbury T:* Wardle; Leonard, Johnson, Petts, Keay, MacLaren, Tong, McNally (Cross), Atkins, Biggins, Bates.

## THIRD ROUND

### 10 NOV

**Arsenal (1) 1** *(Nicholas)*
**Norwich C (0) 0**      19,899
*Arsenal:* Jennings; Hollins, Sansom, Talbot, O'Leary, Whyte, McDermott, Sunderland (Meade), Davis, Nicholas, Rix.
*Norwich C:* Woods; Symonds, Donachie (Muzinic), McGuire, Walford, Watson, Shepherd, Haylock, Jack, Mendham, Bennett.

**Barnsley (2) 4** *(Glavin, McCarthy, Aylott 2)*
**Brighton & HA (1) 1** *(Gatting)*      19,534
*Barnsley:* Horn; Joyce, Chambers, Glavin, Banks, McCarthy, Evans, Parker, Aylott, McHale, Barrowclough.
*Brighton & HA:* Moseley; Shanks, Nelson, Grealish, Foster, Gatting, Case, Ritchie (Stevens), Robinson, McNab, Smith.

**Ipswich T (1) 1** *(Wark)*
**Bradford C (0) 1** *(Watson)*      13,094
*Ipswich T:* Cooper; Burley, Mills, Thijssen, Osman, Butcher, Wark, Muhren, Mariner, Brazil, Gates.
*Bradford C:* Ramsbottom; Podd, Watson, Ingham, Jackson, Wood, Gallagher, Black, Campbell, McNiven, Ellis.

**Liverpool (1) 4** *(Sheedy, Rush, Johnson 2)*
**Middlesbrough (0) 1** *(Shearer)*      16,145
*Liverpool:* Grobbelaar; Neal, Lawrenson, Thompson, Sheedy, Hansen, Dalglish, Johnson, Rush, McDermott (Johnston), Souness.
*Middlesbrough:* Platt; Craggs, Nattrass, Angus, Baxter, McAndrew, Cochrane, Otto, Woof, Shearer, Bolton.

**Oldham Ath (1) 1** *(Steel)*
**Fulham (0) 1** *(Wilson)*      6619
*Oldham Ath:* McDonnell; Hoolickin, Edwards, Keegan, Clements, Futcher, McDonough, Heaton, Steel, Palmer, Atkinson.
*Fulham:* Peyton; Hopkins, Strong, O'Driscoll, Brown, Gale, Davies, Wilson, Coney, O'Sullivan, Lewington.

**QPR (2) 3** *(Flanagan, Stainrod, Allen)*
**Bristol C (0) 0**      9215
*QPR:* Burridge; Gregory, Fenwick, Wilkins, Hazell, Roeder, Micklewhite, Flanagan (Stewart), Allen, Stainrod, Gillard.
*Bristol C:* Moller; Stevens, Williams, Aitken, Rodgers, Boyle, Tainton, Mann, Harford, Devine, Musker.

**Tranmere R (1) 1** *(Hutchinson)*
**Colchester U (0) 0**      2502
*Tranmere R:* Endersby; Mungall, Burgess, Craven, Bramhall, Williams, Hamilton, Morley, Hutchinson, Brown, Griffiths.
*Colchester U:* Walker; Cook, Coleman, Leslie (Adcock), Wignall, Wright, Rowles, Bremner, Osborne, McDonough, Allinson.

**Watford (2) 2** *(Jackett, Blissett pen)*
**Lincoln C (2) 2** *(Turner W., Shipley)*      12,198
*Watford:* Sherwood; Rice, Pritchett, Taylor, Terry, Bolton, Callaghan, Blissett, Armstrong (Rostron), Jackett, Barnes.
*Lincoln C:* Naylor; Turner P., Turner W., Cockerill, Peake, Thompson S., Shipley, Carr, Bell, Cunningham, Gilbert.

**West Ham U (1) 2** *(Stewart pen, Cross)*
**WBA (2) 2** *(Regis, King)*      24,168
*West Ham U:* Parkes; Brush, Lampard, Stewart, Martin, Devonshire, Neighbour, Goddard, Cross, Brooking, Pike.
*WBA:* Grew; Arthur, Statham, King, Wile, Robertson, Jol, Brown, Regis, Owen, MacKenzie.

### 11 NOV

**Blackburn R (0) 0**
**Nottingham F (1) 1** *(Fashanu)*      14,752
*Blackburn R:* Gennoe; Branagan, Rathbone, Stonehouse, Keeley, Fazackerley, Miller, Burke, Lowey, Garner, Brotherston.
*Nottingham F:* Shilton; Anderson, Gunn, McGovern, Needham, Aas, Gray, Ward, Fashanu, Proctor, Robertson.

**Everton (0) 1** *(O'Keefe)*
**Oxford U (0) 0**      14,910
*Everton:* Arnold; Stevens, Bailey, Higgins, Lyons, Lodge, McMahon, O'Keefe, Ferguson (Ainscow), Biley, McBride.
*Oxford U:* Burton; Doyle, Fogg, Jeffrey, Briggs, Shotton, Jones, Foley (Brock), Cassells, Thomas, Smithers.

**Leicester C (0) 0**
**Aston Villa (0) 0**      19,806
*Leicester C:* Wallington; Williams, Leet, MacDonald, Scott, O'Neill, Lynex, Melrose, Lineker, Wilson, Smith.
*Aston Villa:* Rimmer; Swain, Gibson, Evans, Williams, Mortimer (Blair), Bremner, Shaw, Withe, Cowans, Morley.

**Manchester C (1) 3** *(McDonald, Tueart 2)*
**Northampton T (0) 1** *(Mahoney)*      21,139
*Manchester C:* Corrigan; Ranson, McDonald, Reid, Bond, Caton, Tueart, Reeves, Francis, Hartford, O'Neill (Hutchison).
*Northampton T:* Poole; Taylor, Saxby, Brady, Carlton, Gage, Coffill, Sandy (Alexander), Phillips, Mahoney, Saunders.

**Sunderland (0) 0**
**Crystal Palace (0) 1** *(Cannon)*      11,139
*Sunderland:* Siddall; Venison, Munro, Bowyer, Clarke, Elliott, Arnott, Rowell (Buckley), West, Pickering, Cummins.
*Crystal Palace:* Barron; Bason, Lovell, Murphy, Cannon, Gilbert, Price, Smillie, Hughes, Langley, Hilaire.

**Tottenham H (1) 2** *(Hoddle, Hughton)*
**Wrexham (0) 0**      24,084
*Tottenham H:* Clemence; Hughton, Miller, Roberts, Hazard, Perryman, Ardiles, Archibald, Galvin, Hoddle, Crooks.
*Wrexham:* Niedzwiecki; Jones, Bater, Dowman, Cegielski, Hill, Hunt, McNeil, Edwards, Vinter, Carrodus.

**Wigan Ath (3) 4** *(Wignall 2, Evans, Bradd)*
**Chelsea (2) 2** *(Bumstead, Fillery)* 12,063
*Wigan Ath:* Tunks; McMahon, Cribley, Wignall, Lloyd, Methven, Sheldon, Barrow, Bradd, Houghton, Evans.
*Chelsea:* Francis; Wilkins (Droy), Hutchings, Britton, Pates, Chivers, Rhoades-Brown, Bumstead, Lee, Walker, Fillery.


**THIRD ROUND REPLAYS**

**17 NOV**

**Fulham (2) 3** *(Coney 2, Hopkins)*
**Oldham Ath (0) 0** 7085
*Fulham:* Peyton; Hopkins, Strong, O'Driscoll, Lock, Gale, Davies, Wilson, Coney, O'Sullivan, Lewington.
*Oldham Ath:* McDonnell; Sinclair, Ryan, Keegan, Clements, Futcher, Wylde, Heaton, Steel (Nuttall), McDonough, Atkinson.


**24 NOV**

**WBA (0) 1** *aet (Regis)*
**West Ham U (0) 1** *(Stewart pen)* 15,869
*WBA:* Grew; Batson, Statham, King, Wile, Robertson, Jol, Brown, Regis, Owen, MacKenzie.
*West Ham U:* Parkes; Stewart, Lampard, Bonds, Martin, Devonshire, Neighbour, Goddard, Cross, Brooking, Pike.


**25 NOV**

**Aston Villa (2) 2** *(Cowans pen, Withe)*
**Leicester C (0) 0** 23,136
*Aston Villa:* Rimmer; Swain, Gibson, Evans, Williams, Deacy, Bremner, Shaw, Withe, Cowans, Morley.
*Leicester C:* Wallington; Williams, Leet (Smith), Peake, Scott, O'Neill, Lynex, Melrose, Lineker, Wilson, MacDonald.


**Lincoln C (0) 2** *(Cunningham 2)*
**Watford (2) 3** *(Terry, Pritchett, Rostron)* 8773
*Lincoln C:* Naylor; Turner P. (Cammack), Turner W., Cockerill, Peake, Thompson S., Shipley, Carr, Bell, Cunningham, Gilbert.
*Watford:* Sherwood; Henderson, Pritchett, Taylor, Terry, Bolton, Callaghan, Blissett, Armstrong, Jackett, Rostron.


**2 DEC**

**Bradford C (1) 2** *aet (Ingham, Gallagher pen)*
**Ipswich T (1) 3** *(O'Callaghan, Muhren, Turner)* 13,518
*Bradford C:* Ramsbottom; Podd, Watson (Chapman), Ingham, Jackson, Wood, Gallagher, Staniforth, Campbell, McNiven, Ellis.
*Ipswich T:* Cooper; Burley, McCall, Mills, Osman, Butcher, Wark, Muhren, O'Callaghan, Brazil (Turner), D'Avray.


**THIRD ROUND SECOND REPLAY**

**1 DEC**

**West Ham U (0) 0**
**WBA (0) 1** *(Regis)* 24,502
*West Ham U:* Parkes; Stewart, Lampard, Bonds, Martin, Devonshire, Neighbour, Goddard, Cross (Allen), Brooking, Pike.
*WBA:* Grew; Batson, Statham, King, Wile, Robertson, Jol, Brown, Regis, Owen, MacKenzie.


**FOURTH ROUND**

**1 DEC**

**Arsenal (0) 0**
**Liverpool (0) 0** 37,917
*Arsenal:* Jennings; Hollins, Sansom, Talbot, O'Leary, Whyte, McDermott (Hankin), Sunderland, Davis, Nicholas, Rix.
*Liverpool:* Grobbelaar; Neal, Lawrenson, Thompson, Kennedy R., Hansen, Dalglish, Whelan, Rush (Johnson), McDermott, Souness.


**Watford (1) 4** *(Taylor 2, Armstrong, Blissett)*
**QPR (0) 1** *(Stainrod pen)* 18,276
*Watford:* Sherwood; Rice, Pritchett, Taylor, Terry, Bolton, Callaghan, Blissett, Jenkins, Jackett, Barnes (Armstrong).
*QPR:* Burridge; Gregory, Fenwick, Waddock, Howe, Roeder, Hazell (Micklewhite), Flanagan, Sealy, Stainrod, Gillard.


**Wigan Ath (1) 1** *(Houghton)*
**Aston Villa (0) 2** *(Cowans pen, Withe)* 15,362
*Wigan Ath:* Tunks; McMahon, Glenn, Wignall (Wright), Bradd, Methven, Sheldon, Barrow, Quinn, Houghton, Evans.
*Aston Villa:* Rimmer; Swain, Gibson, Evans, Williams, Deacy, Bremner, Shaw, Withe, Cowans, Morley.


**2 DEC**

**Barnsley (0) 1** *(Aylott)*
**Manchester C (0) 0** 33,792
*Barnsley:* Horn; Joyce, Chambers, Glavin, Banks, McCarthy, Evans, Riley, Aylott, McHale, Barrowclough.
*Manchester C:* Corrigan; Ranson, McDonald, Reid, Bond, Caton, Tueart, Reeves, Boyer, Hartford, Hutchison.


**Nottingham F (0) 2** *(Wallace, Rober)*
**Tranmere R (0) 0** 12,244
*Nottingham F:* Shilton; Anderson, Gray, Proctor, Fairclough, Gunn, Rober (Mills), Wallace, Fashanu, Walsh, Robertson.
*Tranmere R:* Endersby; Mungall, Burgess, Mountfield, Bramhall, Morley, Hamilton, Hutchinson, Williams, Brown, Griffiths.


**Tottenham H (1) 1** *(Hazard)*
**Fulham (0) 0** 30,214
*Tottenham H:* Clemence; Hughton, Miller, Roberts, Hazard, Perryman, Ardiles, Archibald, Galvin, Hoddle, Crooks.
*Fulham:* Peyton; Hopkins, Strong, O'Driscoll, Brown, Gale, Davies, Wilson, Coney, O'Sullivan, Lewington.


**15 DEC**

**Crystal Palace (0) 1** *(Langley)*
**WBA (2) 3** *(Monaghan, Regis 2)* 10,311
*Crystal Palace:* Barron; Bason, Boulter, Murphy, Cannon, Lovell, Brooks, Smillie, Langley, Price (Walsh), Hilaire.
*WBA:* Grew; Batson, Bennett, King, Wile, Robertson (Lewis), Arthur, Monaghan, Regis, Owen, MacKenzie.

**Everton (0) 2** *(McMahon 2)*

**Ipswich T (2) 3** *(Gates, Brazil, Wark)* 15,759

*Everton:* Arnold; Stevens, Ratcliffe, Walsh, Lyons, Kendall, McMahon, Ross, Sharp, Biley (Ferguson), O'Keefe.
*Ipswich T:* Cooper; Burley, McCall, Thijssen (O'Callaghan), Osman, Butcher, Wark, Muhren, Mills, Brazil, Gates.

## FOURTH ROUND REPLAY

### 8 DEC

**Liverpool (0) 3** *(Johnston, McDermott pen, Dalglish)*

**Arsenal (0) 0** 21,375

*Liverpool:* Grobbelaar; Neal, Kennedy A., Lawrenson, Kennedy R., Hansen, Dalglish, Lee (Johnston), Rush, McDermott, Souness.
*Arsenal:* Wood; Robson, Sansom, Talbot, O'Leary, Whyte, Hollins, Sunderland, Davis, Nicholas (Hankin), Rix.

## QUARTER-FINALS

### 12 JAN

**Liverpool (0) 0**

**Barnsley (0) 0** 33,707

*Liverpool:* Grobbelaar; Neal, Lawrenson, Thompson, Whelan, Hansen, Dalglish, Kennedy A., Rush, McDermott, Souness.
*Barnsley:* Horn; Joyce, Chambers, Cooper, Banks, McCarthy, Evans, Walker, Aylott, McHale, Barrowclough.

### 18 JAN

**Ipswich T (0) 2** *(Wark, Brazil)*

**Watford (0) 1** *(Barnes)* 20,817

*Ipswich T:* Cooper; Burley, McCall, Mills, Osman, Butcher, Wark, Muhren, Mariner, Brazil, Gates.
*Watford:* Sherwood; Rice, Pritchett, Taylor, Terry, Bolton, Callaghan (Train), Armstrong, Jenkins, Blissett, Barnes.

**Tottenham H (0) 1** *(Ardiles)*

**Nottingham F (0) 0** 31,192

*Tottenham H:* Clemence; Hughton, Miller, Roberts, Villa, Perryman, Ardiles, Falco (Hazard), Galvin, Hoddle, Crooks.
*Nottingham F:* Shilton; Proctor, Gray, Gunn, Needham, Rober, McGovern, Wallace, Ward, Mills, Robertson.

### 19 JAN

**Aston Villa (0) 0**

**WBA (1) 1** *(Statham)* 35,197

*Aston Villa:* Rimmer; Swain, Gibson, Evans, Williams, Mortimer, Bremner, Shaw, Withe, Cowans, Morley.
*WBA:* Grew; Batson, Statham, Brown, Wile, Robertson, Jol, King, Regis, Owen, MacKenzie.

## QUARTER-FINAL REPLAY

### 19 JAN

**Barnsley (1) 1** *(Walker)*

**Liverpool (1) 3** *(Souness, Johnson, Dalglish)* 29,639

*Barnsley:* Horn; Joyce, Chambers, Cooper, Banks (Glavin), McCarthy, Evans, Walker, Aylott, McHale, Barrowclough.
*Liverpool:* Grobbelaar; Neal, Lawrenson, Thompson (Johnson), Whelan, Hansen, Dalglish, Lee, Rush, McDermott, Souness.

## SEMI-FINALS, FIRST LEG

### 2 FEB

**Ipswich T (0) 0**

**Liverpool (0) 2** *(McDermott, Rush)* 26,690

*Ipswich T:* Cooper; Burley, McCall, Mills, Osman (Thijssen), Steggles, Wark, Muhren, Mariner, Brazil, Gates.
*Liverpool:* Grobbelaar; Neal, Lawrenson, Kennedy A., Whelan, Hansen, Dalglish, Lee, Rush, McDermott, Souness.

### 3 FEB

**WBA (0) 0**

**Tottenham H (0) 0** 32,100

*WBA:* Grew; Batson, Statham, King, Wile, Bennett, Jol, Monaghan (Cross), Regis, Owen, MacKenzie.
*Tottenham H:* Clemence; Hughton, Price, Miller, Villa, Perryman, Ardiles, Falco, Galvin, Hoddle, Crooks.

## SEMI-FINALS, SECOND LEG

### 9 FEB

**Liverpool (1) 2** *(Rush, Dalglish)*

**Ipswich T (0) 2** *(Gates, Brazil)* 34,933

*Liverpool won 4-2*

*Liverpool:* Grobbelaar; Neal, Lawrenson, Kennedy A., Whelan, Hansen, Dalglish, Lee, Rush, McDermott, Souness.
*Ipswich T:* Cooper; Burley, McCall, Thijssen (Turner), Hunter, Wark, Mills, Muhren, O'Callaghan, Brazil, Gates.

### 10 FEB

**Tottenham H (0) 1** *(Hazard)*

**WBA (0) 0** 47,241

*Tottenham H won 1-0*

*Tottenham H:* Clemence; Hughton, Miller, Price, Hazard, Perryman, Ardiles, Falco, Galvin, Hoddle, Crooks.
*WBA:* Grew; Arthur, Statham, Robertson, Wile, Bennett, Jol, Summerfield, Regis, Owen (King), MacKenzie.

## FINAL (at Wembley)

### 13 MAR

**Liverpool (0) 3** *aet (Whelan 2, Rush)*

**Tottenham H (1) 1** *(Archibald)* 100,000

*Liverpool:* Grobbelaar; Neal, Kennedy A., Thompson, Whelan, Lawrenson, Dalglish, Lee, Rush, McDermott (Johnson), Souness.
*Tottenham H:* Clemence; Hughton, Miller, Price, Hazard (Villa), Perryman, Ardiles, Archibald, Galvin, Hoddle, Crooks.

# LEAGUE CUP FINALISTS 1961-1981

*R*: Replay; aet: after extra time.

**1960–61** ROTHERHAM UNITED Ironside; Perry, Morgan; Lambert, Madden, Waterhouse; Webster, Weston, Houghton, Kirkman, Bambridge. *Scorers:* Webster, Kirkman.

2-0 ASTON VILLA Sims; Lynn, Lee; Crowe, Dugdale, Deakin; McEwan, Thomson, Brown, Wylie, McParland.

ASTON VILLA Sidebottom; Neal, Lee; Crowe, Dugdale, Deakin; McEwan, O'Neill, McParland, Thomson, Burrows. *Scorers:* O'Neill, Burrows, McParland.

3-0 ROTHERHAM UNITED Ironside; Perry, Morgan; Lambert, Madden, Waterhouse; Webster, Weston, aet Houghton, Kirkman, Bambridge.

**Aston Villa won on aggregate 3–2.**

**1961–62** ROCHDALE Burgin; Milburn, Winton, Bodell, Aspden, Thompson; Wragg, Hepton, Bimpson, Cairns, Whitaker.

0-3 NORWICH CITY Kennon; McCrohan, Ashman; Burton, Butler, Mullett; Mannion, Lythgoe, Scott, Hill, Punton. *Scorers:* Lythgoe 2, Punton.

NORWICH CITY Kennon; McCrohan, Ashman, Burton, Butler, Mullett; Mannion, Lythgoe, Scott, Hill, Punton. *Scorer:* Hill.

1-0 ROCHDALE Burgin; Milburn, Winton; Bodell, Aspden, Thompson; Whyke, Richardson, Bimpson, Cairns, Whitaker.

**Norwich City won on aggregate 4-0.**

**1962–63** BIRMINGHAM CITY Schofield; Lynn, Green, Hennessey, Smith, Beard; Hellawell, Bloomfield, Harris, Leek, Auld. *Scorers:* Leek 2, Bloomfield.

3-1 ASTON VILLA Sims, Fraser, Aitken; Crowe, Sleeuwenhoek, Lee; Baker, Graham, Thomson, Wylie, Burrows. *Scorer:* Thomson.

ASTON VILLA Chatterley took the place of Sleeuwenhoek.

0-0 BIRMINGHAM CITY No change in team.

**Birmingham City won on aggregate 3-1.**

**1963–64** STOKE CITY Leslie; Asprey, Allen; Palmer, Kinnell, Skeels; Dobing, Viollet, Ritchie, McIlroy, Bebbington. *Scorer:* Bebbington.

1-1 LEICESTER CITY Banks; Sjoberg, Appleton; Dougan, King, Cross; Riley, Heath, Keyworth, Gibson, Stringfellow. *Scorer:* Gibson.

LEICESTER CITY Banks; Sjoberg, Norman, Cross, King, Appleton, Riley, Gibson, Keyworth, Sweenie, Stringfellow. *Scorers:* Stringfellow, Gibson, Riley.

3-2 STOKE CITY Irvine; Asprey, Allen, Palmer, Kinnell, Skeels, Dobing, Viollet, Ritchie, McIlroy, Bebbington. *Scorers:* Viollet, Kinnell.

**Leicester City won on aggregate 4-3**

**1964–65** CHELSEA Bonetti; Hinton, Harris; Hollins, Young, Boyle; Murray, Graham, McCreadie, Venables, Tambling. *Scorers:* Tambling, Venables (pen), McCreadie.

3-2 LEICESTER CITY Banks; Sjoberg, Norman; Chalmers, King, Appleton; Hodgson, Cross, Goodfellow, Gibson, Sweenie. *Scorers:* Appleton, Goodfellow.

LEICESTER CITY Banks; Walker, Norman, Roberts, Sjoberg, Appleton, Hodgson, Cross, Goodfellow, Gibson, Stringfellow.

0-0 CHELSEA Bonetti; Hinton, McCreadie, Harris, Mortimore, Upton, Murray, Boyle, Bridges, Venables, Tambling.

**Chelsea won on aggregate 3-2.**

**1965–66** WEST HAM UNITED Standen; Burnett, Burkett, Peters, Brown, Moore, Brabrook, Boyce, Byrne, Hurst, Dear. *Scorers:* Moore, Byrne.

2-1 WEST BROMWICH ALBION Potter; Cram, Fairfax, Fraser, Campbell, Williams, Brown, Astle, Kaye, Lovett, Clark. *Scorer:* Astle.

WEST BROMWICH ALBION Potter; Cram, Fairfax, Fraser, Campbell, Williams, Brown, Astle, Kaye, Hope, Clark. *Scorers:* Kaye, Brown, Clark, Williams.

4-1 WEST HAM UNITED Standen; Burnett, Peters, Bovington, Brown, Moore, Brabrook, Boyce, Byrne, Hurst, Sissons. *Scorer:* Peters.

**West Bromwich Albion won on aggregate 5-3.**

**1966–67** QUEEN'S PARK RANGERS Springett; Hazell, Langley, Sibley, Hunt, Keen, Lazarus, Sanderson, Allen, Marsh, R. Morgan. *Scorers:* R. Morgan, Marsh, Lazarus.

3-2 WEST BROMWICH ALBION Sheppard; Cram, Williams, Collard, D. Clarke, Fraser, Brown, Astle, Kaye, Hope, C. Clark. *Scorer:* C. Clark 2.

**1967–68** LEEDS UNITED Sprake; Reaney, Cooper; Bremner, Charlton, Hunter, Greenhoff, Lorimer, Madeley, Giles, Gray (Belfitt). *Scorer:* Cooper.

1-0 ARSENAL Furnell; Storey, McNab; McLintock, Simpson, Ure, Radford, Jenkins, Graham, Sammels, Armstrong.

**1968–69** SWINDON TOWN Downsborough; Thomas, Trollope; Butler, Burrows, Harland; Heath, Smart, Smith, Noble (Penman), Rogers. *Scorers:* Smart, Rogers 2.

3-1 ARSENAL Wilson; Storey, McNab; McLintock, Ure, Simpson (Graham); Radford, Sammels, Court, Gould, Armstrong. *Scorer:* Gould.

**1969–70** MANCHESTER CITY Corrigan; Book, Mann; Doyle, Booth, Oakes, Heslop, Bell, Summerbee (Bowyer), Lee, Pardoe. *Scorers:* Doyle, Pardoe.

**2–1** WEST BROMWICH ALBION Osborne; Fraser, Wilson, Brown, Talbut, Kaye; Cantello, Suggett, Astle, Hartford (Krzywicki), Hope. *Scorer:* Astle.

**1970–71** TOTTENHAM HOTSPUR Jennings; Kinnear, Knowles; Mullery, Collins, Beal; Gilzean, Perryman, Chivers, Peters, Neighbour. *Scorer:* Chivers 2.

**2–0** ASTON VILLA Dunn; Bradley, Aitken; Godfrey, Turnbull, Tiler; McMahon, Rioch, Lochhead, Hamilton, Anderson.

**1971–72** STOKE CITY Banks; Marsh, Pejic, Bernard, Smith, Bloor, Conroy, Greenhoff (Mahoney), Ritchie, Dobing, Eastham. *Scorers:* Conroy, Eastham.

**2–1** CHELSEA Bonetti; Mulligan (Baldwin), Harris, Hollins, Dempsey, Webb, Cooke, Garland, Osgood, Hudson, Houseman. *Scorer:* Osgood.

**1972–73** TOTTENHAM HOTSPUR Jennings; Kinnear, Knowles, Pratt (Coates), England, Beal, Gilzean, Perryman, Chivers, Peters, Pearce. *Scorer:* Coates.

**1–0** NORWICH CITY Keelan; Payne, Butler, Stringer, Forbes, Briggs, Livermore, Blair (Howard), Cross, Paddon, Anderson.

**1973–74** WOLVERHAMPTON WANDERERS Pierce; Palmer, Parkin, Bailey, Munro, McAlle, Sunderland, Hibbitt, Richards, Dougan, Wagstaffe (Powell). *Scorers:* Hibbitt, Richards.

**2–1** MANCHESTER CITY MacRae; Pardoe, Donachie, Doyle, Booth, Towers, Summerbee, Bell, Lee, Law, Marsh. *Scorer:* Bell.

**1974–75** ASTON VILLA Cumbes; Robson, Aitken, Ross, Nicholl, McDonald, Graydon, Little, Leonard, Hamilton, Carrodus. *Scorer:* Graydon.

**1–0** NORWICH CITY Keelan; Machin, Sullivan, Morris, Forbes, Stringer, Miller, MacDougall, Boyer, Suggett, Powell.

**1975–76** MANCHESTER CITY Corrigan; Keegan, Donachie, Doyle, Watson, Oakes, Barnes, Booth, Royle, Hartford, Tueart. *Scorers:* Barnes, Tueart.

**2–1** NEWCASTLE UNITED Mahoney; Nattrass, Kennedy, Barrowclough, Keeley, Howard, Burns, Cassidy, Macdonald, Gowling, Craig. *Scorer:* Gowling.

**1976–77** ASTON VILLA Burridge; Gidman, Robson, Phillips, Nicholl, Mortimer, Deehan, Little, Gray, Cropley, Carrodus.

**0–0** EVERTON Lawson; Jones, Darracott, Lyons, McNaught, King, Hamilton, Dobson, Latchford, McKenzie, Goodlass.

*First replay (at Hillsborough)*
ASTON VILLA Burridge; Gidman, Robson, Phillips, Nicholl, Mortimer, Deehan, Little, Gray, Cowans, Carrodus. *Scorer:* Kenyon og.

**R: 1–1** EVERTON Lawson; Bernard, Darracott, Lyons, McNaught, King, Hamilton (Pearson), Kenyon, Latch-
**aet** ford, McKenzie, Goodlass. *Scorer:* Latchford.

*Second replay (at Old Trafford, Manchester)*
**R: 3–2** ASTON VILLA Burridge; Gidman (Smith), Robson, Phillips, Nicholl, Mortimer, Graydon, Little, Deehan,
**aet** Cropley, Cowans. *Scorers:* Little 2, Nicholl.
EVERTON Lawson; Robinson, Darracott, Lyons, McNaught, King, Hamilton, Dobson, Latchford, Pearson (Seargeant), Goodlass. *Scorers:* Latchford, Lyons.

**1977–78** NOTTINGHAM FOREST Woods; Anderson, Clark, McGovern (O'Hare), Lloyd, Burns, O'Neill, Bowyer, Withe, Woodcock, Robertson.

**0–0** LIVERPOOL Clemence; Neal, Smith, Thompson, Kennedy (Fairclough), Hughes, Dalglish, Case, Heigh-
**aet** way, McDermott, Callaghan.

*Replay (at Old Trafford, Manchester)*
**R: 1–0** NOTTINGHAM FOREST Woods; Anderson, Clark, O'Hare, Lloyd, Burns, O'Neill, Bowyer, Withe, Woodcock, Robertson. *Scorer:* Robertson (pen).
LIVERPOOL Clemence; Neal, Smith, Thompson, Kennedy, Hughes, Dalglish, Case (Fairclough), Heighway, McDermott, Callaghan.

**1978–79** NOTTINGHAM FOREST Shilton; Barrett, Clark, McGovern, Lloyd, Needham, O'Neill, Gemmill, Birtles, Woodcock, Robertson. *Scorers:* Birtles 2, Woodcock.

**3–2** SOUTHAMPTON Gennoe; Golac, Peach, Williams, Nicholl, Waldron, Ball, Boyer, Hayes (Sealy), Holmes, Curran. *Scorers:* Peach, Holmes.

**1979–80** WOLVERHAMPTON WANDERERS Bradshaw; Palmer, Parkin, Daniel, Berry, Hughes, Carr, Hibbitt, Gray, Richards, Eves. *Scorer:* Gray.

**1–0** NOTTINGHAM FOREST Shilton; Anderson, Gray, McGovern, Needham, Burnes, O'Neill, Bowyer, Birtles, Francis, Robertson.

**1980–81** LIVERPOOL Clemence; Neal, A. Kennedy, Irwin, R. Kennedy, Hansen, Dalglish, Lee, Heighway (Case), McDermott, Souness. *Scorer:* A. Kennedy.

**1–1** WEST HAM UNITED Parkes; Stewart, Lampard, Bonds, Martin, Devonshire, Neighbour, Goddard (Pear-
**aet** son), Cross, Brooking, Pike. *Scorer:* Stewart (pen).

*Replay (at Villa Park)*
**R: 2–1** LIVERPOOL Clemence; Neal, A. Kennedy, Thompson, R. Kennedy, Hansen, Dalglish, Lee, Rush, McDermott, Case. *Scorers:* Dalglish, Hansen.
WEST HAM UNITED Parkes, Stewart, Lampard, Bonds, Martin, Devonshire, Neighbour, Goddard, Cross, Brooking, Pike (Pearson). *Scorer:* Goddard.

# FOOTBALL LEAGUE GROUP CUP 1981–82

**15 AUG**

**Group A**

Burnley (4) 4 *(Hamilton 2, Taylor 2)*

Carlisle U (2) 2 *(Lee 2)*     2305

*Burnley:* Stevenson; Laws, Holt, Scott, Overson, Dobson, Cavener, Taylor, Hamilton, Cassidy, Potts.
*Carlisle U:* Harrison; Haigh, Larkin, Campbell, Ashurst, Holton, Coughlin, Robson, Staniforth, Lee, Bannon.

Preston NE (1) 2 *(Bruce, Houston)*

Blackpool (0) 1 *(Morris)*     6102

*Preston NE:* Litchfield (Tunks); Taylor, Coleman, Clark, Baxter, O'Riordan (Blackley), Houston, Doyle, Elliott, Bruce, Naughton.
*Blackpool:* Hesford; Gardner (Simmonite), Pashley, Blair, Thompson, McEwan, Morris, Entwistle, Bamber (Pollard), Harrison, Morgan.

**Group B**

Bradford C (1) 2 *(Black, Jackson)*

Hull C (1) 1 *(Whitehurst)*     2148

*Bradford C:* Smith; Podd, Wood, Ingham, Jackson, McFarland (Thompson), Gallagher, Black, Campbell, Staniforth (Guy), Chapman.
*Hull C:* Norman; Hoolickin, Booth, Richards, Eccleston, Horswill, Roberts G., Ferguson, Whitehurst, Marwood (Edwards), Norrie.

Hartlepool U (0) 0

Rotherham U (0) 1 *(Green)*     2031

*Hartlepool U:* Burleigh; Brown, Stimpson, Hogan, Bird, Linighan, Kerr, Linacre, Houchen, Hampton, Harding (Howard).
*Rotherham U:* Mountford; Forrest, Taylor, Mullen, Stancliffe, Green, Towner, Seasman, Moore, Fern, Henson.

**Group C**

Grimsby T (0) 1 *(Waters pen)*

Chesterfield (0) 0     1772

*Grimsby T:* Batch; Stone, Crombie, Waters, Wigginton, Czuczman, Brolly, Whymark, Drinkell, Mitchell, Cumming.
*Chesterfield:* Turner; Tartt, O'Neill, Wilson, Green, Ridley, Birch, Crawford, Bonnyman, Salmons, Walker.

Sheffield U (0) 2 *(Charles, Hatton)*

Doncaster R (1) 1 *(Pugh)*     5555

*Sheffield U:* Richardson; Ryan, Garner, Matthews, MacPhail, Kenworthy, Neville, Trusson, Evans (Tibbott), Hatton, Charles.
*Doncaster R:* Boyd; Lally, Russell, Snodin I. (Mell) (Douglas), Lister, Dowd, Pugh, Nimmo, Warboys, Farrell, Dawson.

**Group D**

Lincoln C (1) 1 *(Hobson)*

Notts Co (1) 1 *(Mair)*     2959

*Lincoln C:* Felgate; Thompson T., Keeley (McVay), Turner P., Peake, Carr, Shipley, Cockerill, Hobson, Cunningham, Cammack.

*Notts Co:* Avramovic; Benjamin, O'Brien, Goodwin, Worthington, Richards, McCulloch, Hooks, Christie (Manns), Hunt, Mair.

Norwich C (2) 2 *(Shepherd, McGuire pen)*

Peterborough U (2) 2 *(Cooke, Quow)*     2707

*Norwich C:* Woods; Barham, Downs, McGuire, Hoadley, Walford, Mendham, Fashanu, Shepherd, Paddon (Jack), Bennett.
*Peterborough U:* Waugh; Winters, Collins, Gynn, Slack, Rodaway, Quow, Kellock, Cooke, Hodgson, Massey.

**Group E**

Bolton W (0) 0

Shrewsbury T (2) 2 *(Tong, Cross)*     2513

*Bolton W:* McDonagh; Nicholson, Brennan, Nikolic (Hoggan), Jones, Gowling, Thomas, Whatmore, Foster, Cantello, Reid.
*Shrewsbury T:* Wardle; Leonard, Johnson, Petts, Keay, McLaren, Tong, McNally, Bates, Dungworth (Gibson), Cross.

Bury (0) 1 *(Hilton P.)*

Chester (2) 2 *(Simpson, Jones)*     1504

*Bury:* Brown; Bradley, Kennedy, Gore (Cruickshank), Hilton P., Howard, Mullen, Butler, Madden, Jakub, Hilton M.
*Chester:* Millington; Raynor, Needham, Storton, Zelem, Oakes, Jones, Simpson, Ludlam, Phillips (Howat), Cooke.

**Group F**

Newport Co (0) 0

Torquay U (0) 0     2490

*Newport Co:* Kendall; Walden, Relish, Lees, Oakes, Tynan, Vaughan, Bailey, Goddard, Waddle (Davies), Elsey.
*Torquay U:* O'Keefe; Jones, Pethard, Bowker, Wilson, Larmour, Fell, Lawrence, Cox (Hodge), Rioch, Weston.

Plymouth Arg (0) 0

AFC Bournemouth (0) 0     2707

*Plymouth Arg:* Crudgington; Nisbet, McCartney, Harrison, James, Hodges, Cooper, Kemp, Sims, Randell, Murphy.
*AFC Bournemouth:* Allen; Heffernan, Sulley, Smith, Compton, Impey, Edmunds, Spackman, Mooney, Morgan, Williams.

**Group G**

Oxford U (0) 0

Aldershot (0) 1 *(Wooler)*     1936

*Oxford U:* Burton; Doyle (Kingston), Fogg, Jeffrey, Briggs, Shotton, Jones (Seacole), Foley, Smithers, Cassells, Page.
*Aldershot:* Johnson; Edwards, Wooler, Briley, Bennett, Jopling, Lucas, Crosby, Garwood, Sanford, Robinson.

**Watford (3) 4** *(Poskett 2, Callaghan, Blissett pen)*
**Reading (1) 1** *(Sanchez)* 4409

*Watford:* Sherwood; Rice, Henderson, Taylor (Rostron), Sims, Bolton, Callaghan, Blissett, Armstrong, Jackett (Train), Poskett.
*Reading:* Fearon; Williams, White, Wood (Beavon), Hicks, Hetzke, Earles, Heale, Dixon, Webb, Sanchez.

## Group H

**Orient (0) 2** *(Jennings, Chiedozie)*
**Southend U (0) 0** 1806

*Orient:* Day; Fisher, Roffey, Taylor T., Gray, Moores, Chiedozie, Jennings, Mayo, Bowles, Taylor P.
*Southend U:* Cawston; Stead, Dudley, Hadley, Moody, Cusack, Gray, Nelson, Spence, Mercer, Otulakowski.

**Wimbledon (1) 4** *(Armstrong, Leslie, Smith, Fear)*
**Gillingham (0) 0** 1352

*Wimbledon:* Beasant; Brown, Armstrong (Thomas), Galliers, Smith, Downes, Fear, Joseph, Leslie, Cork, Hodges (Ketteridge).
*Gillingham:* Hillyard; Sharpe, Ford, Bruce, Weatherly, White, Powell, Duncan (Adams), Tydeman, Westwood (Henderson), Lee.

## 18 AUG

## Group A

**Carlisle U (1) 1** *(Robson)*
**Blackpool (0) 0** 2530

*Carlisle U:* Swinburne; Haigh, Larkin, Coughlin, Houghton, Ashurst, Staniforth, Robson, Lee, Crabbe, Hamilton.
*Blackpool:* Hesford; Simmonite, Pashley, Noble, Greenall, McEwan, Blair, Harrison, Morris, Entwistle, Bamber.

**Preston NE (0) 0**
**Burnley (1) 1** *(Hamilton)* 5269

*Preston NE:* Tunks; Taylor, Coleman, Clark, O'Riordan, Blackley, Houston, Doyle, Elliott (McGee), Bruce, Naughton (Walsh).
*Burnley:* Stevenson; Laws, Holt, Scott, Phelan, Dobson, Cavener, Taylor, Hamilton, Cassidy, Cox.

## Group B

**Hull C (0) 0**
**Rotherham U (1) 1** *(Moore)* 2205

*Hull C:* Norman; Hoolickin, Booth, Richards, Eccleston, Horswill, Marwood, Roberts G., Whitehurst (Edwards), Norrie (Deacy), Ferguson.
*Rotherham U:* Mountford; Forrest, Taylor, Mullen, Stancliffe, Green, Towner (Gooding), Seasman, Moore, Fern (Finney), Henson.

## Group C

**Doncaster R (1) 2** *(Russell, Harle)*
**Chesterfield (0) 0** 3572

*Doncaster R:* Boyd (Humphries S.); Russell, Dawson, Lister, Lally, Dowd, Pugh, Nimmo, Warboys (Harle), Farrell, Mell.
*Chesterfield:* Turner; Tartt, O'Neill, Wilson, Green, Ridley, Birch, Crawford, Bonnyman, Salmons (Windridge), Walker.

**Grimsby T (1) 2** *(Whymark, Mitchell)*
**Sheffield U (0) 0** 2314

*Grimsby T:* Batch; Stone, Crombie, Waters, Wigginton, Czuczman (Moore D.), Brolly, Whymark, Drinkell (Ford), Mitchell, Kilmore.
*Sheffield U:* Richardson (Conroy); Ryan, Houston, McPhail, Kenworthy, Tibbott, Trusson, Neville, Hatton, Matthews, Charles.

## Group E

**Bury (2) 2** *(Gore, Hilton M.)*
**Bolton W (1) 2** *(Nikolic, Hoggan)* 2892

*Bury:* Brown; Bradley, Kennedy, Gore, Hilton P., Howard, Mullen, Butler, Madden, Jakub, Hilton M.
*Bolton W:* McDonagh; Berry, Nicholson, Nikolic (Carter), Jones, Gowling, Thomas, Whatmore, Hoggan, Cantello, Reid.

**Shrewsbury T (1) 1** *(Bates)*
**Chester (0) 0** 1567

*Shrewsbury T:* Wardle; Leonard, Johnson, Petts, MacLaren, Griffin, Tong, McNally, Atkins, Dungworth (Bates), Cross.
*Chester:* Millington; Raynor, Needham, Storton, Zelem, Oakes, Jones, Simpson, Ludlam, Phillips (Cottam), Cooke.

## Group F

**AFC Bournemouth (1) 1** *(Heffernan)*
**Torquay U (0) 1** *(Cooper)* 2519

*AFC Bournemouth:* Allen; Heffernan, Sulley, Smith, Compton, Impey, Edmunds, Kelly, Mooney, Morgan (Spackman), Williams.
*Torquay U:* O'Keefe; Jones, Pethard, Bowker, Wilson, Larmour, Fell, Lawrence, Cox (Cooper), Rioch (Hodge), Weston.

**Newport Co (1) 2** *(Waddle, Lees pen)*
**Plymouth Arg (1) 1** *(Sims)* 2316

*Newport Co:* Kendall; Elsey, Vaughan, Davies, Oakes, Tynan (Walden), Lees, Bailey, Goddard (Gwyther), Waddle, Moore.
*Plymouth Arg:* Crudgington; Nisbet, McCartney, Harrison, Phillipson-Masters, Hodges, Cooper, Kemp, Sims, Randell, Murphy.

## Group H

**Orient (0) 0**
**Wimbledon (1) 1** *(Cork)* 1777

*Orient:* Day; Fisher, Roffey, Taylor T., Gray, Moores, Chiedozie, Bowles, Mayo, Jennings, Taylor P.
*Wimbledon:* Beasant; Brown, Armstrong, Galliers (Hodges), Smith, Cunningham, Ketteridge, Joseph, Leslie, Cork, Downes.

**19 AUG**

**Group B**

**Hartlepool U (0) 0**
**Bradford C (1) 1** *(Campbell)* 1221

*Hartlepool U:* Burleigh; Sweeney, Stimpson, Hogan, Bird, Linighan, Brown, Kerr, Houchen, Hampton (Johnson), Howard (Staff).
*Bradford C:* Smith; Podd, Watson, Ingham, Jackson, Thompson, Gallagher, Black, Campbell, McNiven, Chapman.

**Group D**

**Lincoln C (0) 0**
**Norwich C (1) 1** *(Bennett)* 1990

*Lincoln C:* Felgate; Thompson T., Keeley, Turner P. (Creane), McVay (Brown), Carr, Shipley, Cockerill, Hobson, Cunningham, Cammack.
*Norwich C:* Woods; Barham, Muzinic, McGuire, Nightingale, Watson, Mendham, Shepherd, Royle (Robson), Paddon, Bennett.

**Peterborough U (1) 3** *(Cooke 2, Gynn)*
**Notts Co (0) 1** *(Manns)* 2463

*Peterborough U:* Waugh; Winters, Collins, Gynn, Slack, Rodaway, Quow, Kellock, Cooke, Hodgson, Massey (Clarke).
*Notts Co:* Avramovic; Benjamin, O'Brien, Goodwin, Worthington, Richards, McCulloch, Hooks, Manns, Hunt, Mair.

**Group G**

**Oxford U (2) 2** *(Cassells, Fogg pen)*
**Watford (1) 4** *(Callaghan, Bolton, Sims, Blissett)* 2602

*Oxford U:* Burton; Kingston, Fogg, Jeffrey, Briggs, Shotton, Jones (Seacole), Kearns, Smithers, Cassells, Page (Brock).
*Watford:* Sherwood; Rice, Henderson, Taylor, Sims, Bolton, Callaghan, Blissett, Armstrong, Jackett, Poskett.

**Reading (1) 4** *(Hetzke 3 [2 pens], Sanchez)*
**Aldershot (0) 0** 1759

*Reading:* Fearon; Williams, Lewis, Webb, Hicks, Hetzke, Earles, Heale, Dixon, Beavon, Sanchez.
*Aldershot:* Horn; Scott, Wooler, Briley, Bennett, Jopling, McGregor, French, Garwood (Hampshire), Wanklyn, Robinson.

**Group H**

**Gillingham (0) 0**
**Southend U (0) 0** 2000

*Gillingham:* Hillyard; Sharpe, Ford, Bruce, Weatherly, White, Powell, Duncan, Tydeman, Lee, Westwood.
*Southend U:* Cawston; Stead, Dudley, Hadley, Moody, Cusack, Gray, Pountney, Spence, Mercer, Otulakowski.

**21 AUG**

**Group C**

**Chesterfield (0) 1** *(Bonnyman)*
**Sheffield U (0) 1** *(Trusson)* 4923

*Chesterfield:* Turner; Tartt, O'Neill, Wilson, Green,·Ridley, Birch, Crawford, Bonnyman, Windridge (Athersych), Walker.
*Sheffield U:* Conroy; Ryan, Houston, Matthews, MacPhail, Kenworthy, Neville, Trusson, Tibbott, Hatton, Charles.

**Group F**

**Torquay U (1) 1** *(Weston)*
**Plymouth Arg (0) 1** *(Kemp)* 3088

*Torquay U:* O'Keefe; Jones, Pethard, Bowker, Wilson, Larmour, Fell, Lawrence, Cooper (Cox), Hodge, Weston.
*Plymouth Arg:* Crudgington; Nisbet, McCartney, Phillipson-Masters, Foster, Cooper (Collins), Hodges, Kemp, Sims, Randell, Murphy.

**22 AUG**

**Group A**

**Blackpool (0) 0**
**Burnley (0) 0** 3464

*Blackpool:* Hesford; Simmonite, Pashley, Morgan, Greenall, McEwan, Blair, Entwistle (Hockaday), Bamber, Harrison, Pollard.
*Burnley:* Stevenson; Laws, Holt, Scott, Phelan, Dobson, Cavener, Taylor, Hamilton, Cassidy (Overson), Young.

**Carlisle U (0) 3** *(Lee 2, Robson)*
**Preston NE (0) 0** 3026

*Carlisle U:* Swinburne; Ashurst, Larkin, Coady (Coughlin), Houghton, Parker, Campbell, Robson, Bannon (Staniforth), Lee, Crabbe.
*Preston NE:* Litchfield; Westwell, Coleman, Clark, Anderson, O'Riordan, Houston (McGee), Doyle, Elliott (Walsh), Bruce, Naughton.

**Group B**

**Bradford C (0) 3** *(Campbell, Black, Gallagher)*
**Rotherham U (0) 0** 2873

*Bradford C:* Smith; Podd, Watson, Ingham, Jackson, Thompson, Gallagher, Black, Campbell, McNiven, Chapman (Ellis).
*Rotherham U:* Mountford; Forrest, Taylor, Mullen, Stancliffe, Green, Towner, Seasman, Moore, Fern (Finney), Henson (Gooding).

**Hull C (0) 1** *(Edwards)*
**Hartlepool U (0) 0** 1621

*Hull C:* Norman; McNeil, Booth, Richards, Eccleston, Horswill, Roberts G., Deacy (Norrie), Edwards, Whitehurst, Ferguson.
*Hartlepool U:* Burleigh; Brown, Stimpson (Howard), Hogan, Bird, Linighan, Kerr, Staff (Hampton), Houchen, Sweeney, Harding.

**Group C**

**Doncaster R (0) 0**
**Grimsby T (1) 2** *(Moore K., Brolly)* 4067

*Doncaster R:* Boyd; Lally, Russell, Lister, Humphries G., Dowd, Pugh, Nimmo, Dawson, Harle (Douglas), Mell.
*Grimsby T:* Batch; Stone, Crombie, Waters (Ford), Wigginton, Moore K., Brolly (Czuczman), Whymark, Drinkell, Mitchell, Kilmore.

**Group D**

**Norwich C (2) 3** *(Shepherd 2, Bennett)*
**Notts Co (0) 0** 4038

*Norwich C:* Woods; Barham (Symonds), Muzinic, McGuire, Nightingale, Watson, Mendham, Shepherd, Robson, Paddon (Jack), Bennett.
*Notts Co:* Avramovic; Benjamin, O'Brien, Goodwin, Worthington, Richards, McParland (Manns), McCulloch, Hooks, Hunt, Mair.

**Peterborough U (2) 3** *(Gynn, Massey, Kellock pen)*
**Lincoln C (1) 1** *(Shipley)* 2684

*Peterborough U:* Waugh; Winters, Collins, Gynn, Slack, Rodaway, Quow, Kellock, Cooke, Hodgson (Chard), Massey (Clarke).
*Lincoln C:* Felgate; Thompson T., Keeley, McVay, Peake, Carr, Shipley, Cockerill, Hobson, Cunningham, Bell (Cammack).

**Group E**

**Bury (2) 3** *(Gore, Madden, Jakub)*
**Shrewsbury T (1) 2** *(Keay pen, Cross)* 1508

*Bury:* Platt; Bradley, Kennedy, Gore, Hilton P., Cruickshank (Howard), Mullen, Butler, Madden, Jakub, Hilton M.
*Shrewsbury T:* Wardle; Leonard, Johnson, Petts, Keay, Griffin, Tong, McNally, Biggins (Dungworth), Bates, Cross.

**Chester (0) 1** *(Burns)*
**Bolton W (1) 2** *(Hoggan, Thompson)* 1291

*Chester:* Millington; Cottam, Raynor, Storton, Zelam, Oakes, Jones, Needham, Ludlam, Phillips, Burns.
*Bolton W:* McDonagh; Berry (Nicholson), Brennan, Nikolic, McElhinney, Gowling, Thomas, Thompson, Hoggan (Bennett), Cantello, Reid.

**Group F**

**AFC Bournemouth (0) 0**
**Newport Co (0) 0** 2511

*AFC Bournemouth:* Allen; Heffernan, Sulley, Smith, Compton, Impey, Edmunds, Kelly (Dawtry), Mooney (Graham), Morgan, Williams.
*Newport Co:* Kendall; Walden, Relish, Davies, Oakes, Tynan, Bailey (Vaughan), Lees (Elsey), Gwyther, Goddard, Moore.

**Group G**

**Aldershot (0) 1** *(Garwood)*
**Watford (1) 1** *(Gilligan)* 2469

*Aldershot:* Johnson; Edwards, Wooler, Briley, Bennett, Scott, Sanford (McGregor), Brodie, Garwood, Crosby, Robinson.

*Watford:* Sherwood; Rice, Henderson, Train, Sims, Bolton, Callaghan (Donnellan), Blissett, Armstrong, Jackett, Gilligan.

**Reading (1) 2** *(Kearney 2)*
**Oxford U (0) 0** 2261

*Reading:* Fearon; Williams, Lewis, Webb (Joslyn), Hicks, Hetzke, Earles (Dixon), Kearney, Heale, Beavon, Sanchez.
*Oxford U:* Burton; Kingston (Brock), Fogg, Jeffrey, Briggs, Shotton, Jones, Foley, Kearns (Cassells), Page, Smithers.

**Group H**

**Gillingham (0) 1** *(Bruce)*
**Orient (0) 1** *(Moores)* 2234

*Gillingham:* Hillyard (Sutton); Sharpe, Ford, Bruce, Weatherly, White, Powell, Duncan, Tydeman, Lee, Westwood.
*Orient:* Day; Fisher, Roffey, Taylor T., Gray, Margerrison, Godfrey (Hallybone), Jennings (Mayo), Moores, Bowles, Taylor P.

**24 AUG**

**Group H**

**Southend U (0) 1** *(Spence)*
**Wimbledon (1) 2** *(Lazarus 2)* 1780

*Southend U:* Cawston; Stead, Yates, Hadley, Moody, Cusack, Gray, Nelson, Spence, Mercer, Otulakowski.
*Wimbledon:* Beasant; Brown, Thomas, Gage, Smith, Jones, Ketteridge, Joseph, Hubbick, Lazarus, Hodges.

**FINAL TABLES**

| Group A | P | W | D | L | F | A | Pts |
|---|---|---|---|---|---|---|---|
| Burnley | 3 | 2 | 1 | 0 | 5 | 2 | 8 |
| Carlisle U | 3 | 2 | 0 | 1 | 6 | 4 | 7 |
| Preston NE | 3 | 1 | 0 | 2 | 2 | 5 | 3 |
| Blackpool | 3 | 0 | 1 | 2 | 1 | 3 | 1 |

| Group B | P | W | D | L | F | A | Pts |
|---|---|---|---|---|---|---|---|
| Bradford C | 3 | 3 | 0 | 0 | 6 | 1 | 10 |
| Rotherham U | 3 | 2 | 0 | 1 | 2 | 3 | 6 |
| Hull C | 3 | 1 | 0 | 2 | 2 | 3 | 3 |
| Hartlepool U | 3 | 0 | 0 | 3 | 0 | 3 | 0 |

| Group C | P | W | D | L | F | A | Pts |
|---|---|---|---|---|---|---|---|
| Grimsby T | 3 | 3 | 0 | 0 | 5 | 0 | 9 |
| Doncaster R | 3 | 1 | 0 | 2 | 3 | 4 | 3 |
| Sheffield U | 3 | 1 | 1 | 1 | 3 | 4 | 3 |
| Chesterfield | 3 | 0 | 1 | 2 | 1 | 4 | 1 |

| Group D | P | W | D | L | F | A | Pts |
|---|---|---|---|---|---|---|---|
| Peterborough U | 3 | 2 | 1 | 0 | 8 | 4 | 9 |
| Norwich C | 3 | 2 | 1 | 0 | 6 | 2 | 8 |
| Lincoln C | 3 | 0 | 1 | 2 | 2 | 5 | 1 |
| Notts Co | 3 | 0 | 1 | 2 | 2 | 7 | 1 |

| Group E | P | W | D | L | F | A | Pts |
|---|---|---|---|---|---|---|---|
| Shrewsbury T | 3 | 2 | 0 | 1 | 5 | 3 | 6 |
| Bury | 3 | 1 | 1 | 1 | 6 | 6 | 4 |
| Bolton W | 3 | 1 | 1 | 1 | 4 | 5 | 4 |
| Chester | 3 | 1 | 0 | 2 | 3 | 4 | 3 |

| Group F | P | W | D | L | F | A | Pts |
|---|---|---|---|---|---|---|---|
| Newport Co | 3 | 1 | 2 | 0 | 2 | 1 | 5 |
| AFC Bournemouth | 3 | 0 | 3 | 0 | 1 | 1 | 3 |
| Torquay U | 3 | 0 | 2 | 1 | 2 | 2 | 3 |
| Plymouth Arg | 3 | 0 | 2 | 1 | 2 | 3 | 2 |

| Group G | P | W | D | L | F | A | Pts |
|---|---|---|---|---|---|---|---|
| Watford | 3 | 2 | 1 | 0 | 9 | 4 | 9 |
| Reading | 3 | 2 | 0 | 1 | 7 | 4 | 7 |
| Aldershot | 3 | 1 | 1 | 1 | 2 | 5 | 4 |
| Oxford U | 3 | 0 | 0 | 3 | 2 | 7 | 0 |

| Group H | P | W | D | L | F | A | Pts |
|---|---|---|---|---|---|---|---|
| Wimbledon | 3 | 3 | 0 | 0 | 7 | 1 | 10 |
| Orient | 3 | 1 | 1 | 1 | 3 | 2 | 4 |
| Gillingham | 3 | 0 | 2 | 1 | 1 | 5 | 2 |
| Southend U | 3 | 0 | 1 | 2 | 1 | 4 | 1 |

## QUARTER-FINALS

### 8 DEC

**Burnley (2) 2** *(Scott, Holt)*

**Watford (0) 1** *(Blissett)*      2658

*Burnley:* Stevenson; Dixon, Holt, Scott, Overson, Phelan, Cavener, Potts, Taylor, Anderson, Young.
*Watford:* Steele; Palmer, Pritchett (Franklin), Taylor, Sims, Jackett, Callaghan, Blissett, Armstrong, Rostron, Lohman (Johnson).

**Newport Co (0) 0**

**Grimsby T (1) 2** *(Beacock, Drinkell)*      2202

*Newport Co:* Kendall; Johnson, Relish, Davies, Oakes, Bailey, Vaughan, Lowndes, Waddle (Gwyther), Tynan (Bishop), Elsey.
*Grimsby T:* Batch; Moore D., Crombie, Waters, Wigginton, Moore K., Brolly, Whymark (Ward), Drinkell, Beacock (Mitchell), Cumming.

### 9 DEC

**Bradford C (1) 1** *aet (Jackson)*

**Shrewsbury T (0) 1** *(Dungworth)*      2144

*Shrewsbury T won 4-3 on penalties*
*Bradford C:* Ramsbottom; Podd, Watson, Ingham, Jackson, Wood, Gallagher, Staniforth, Campbell, Ellis, Chapman (Black).
*Shrewsbury T:* Wardle; MacLaren, Johnson, Cross (Cooke), Griffin, Leonard, Tong, Dungworth, Atkins, Petts, Bates.

### 3 FEB

**Peterborough U (0) 0** *aet*

**Wimbledon (0) 1** *(Gage)*      1835

*Peterborough U:* Freeman; Butler (Syrett), Collins, Gynn, Smith, Rodaway, Clarke, Kellock, Cooke, Chard, Massey.
*Wimbledon:* Beasant; Gage, Armstrong, Smith, Morris, Downes, Ketteridge, Leslie (Lazarus), Blochel, Hodges (Brown), Joseph.

## SEMI-FINALS

### 19 JAN

**Grimsby T (0) 2** *(Kilmore 2)*

**Shrewsbury T (1) 1** *(Cross)*      3253

*Grimsby T:* Batch; Moore D., Crombie, Waters (Beacock), Czuczman, Moore K., Stone, Kilmore, Whymark, Mitchell, Ford.
*Shrewsbury T:* Wardle; MacLaren, Johnson, Cross, Griffin, Keay, Petts, Dungworth, Atkins, McNally (Biggins), Bates.

### 16 FEB

**Wimbledon (2) 5** *(Lazarus 2, Hodges, Blochel, Joseph)*

**Burnley (0) 0**      1267

*Wimbledon:* Hatcher; Brown (Fishenden), Thomas, Hodges, Morris, Downes, Ketteridge (Kempton), Lazarus, Blochel, Armstrong, Joseph.
*Burnley:* O'Rourke; Miller, Rae, Holt, Dixon, Anderson, Scott, Cavener, Wright (Allen), Potts, Young.

### FINAL (at Grimsby)

### 6 APR

**Grimsby T (2) 3** *(Cumming, Ford 2)*

**Wimbledon (1) 2** *(Elliott, Smith)*      3423

*Grimsby T:* Batch (Grotier); Waters, Crosby, O'Dell, Moore D., Moore K., Steeples (Brolly), Ford, Whymark, Mitchell, Cumming.
*Wimbledon:* Beasant; Brown, Armstrong, Smith, Morris, Downes, Ketteridge (Gage), Joseph, Lazarus, Hodges, Leslie (Elliott).

*Note:* The Football League Group Cup replaces the Anglo-Scottish Cup, which was discontinued when the Scottish clubs withdrew after the 1980–81 competition; despite having won only one of the competitions, they did not consider the Football League representation to be strong enough. Originally under the sponsorship of Texaco, the competition at first embraced teams from Northern Ireland as well as England and Scotland; it became the Anglo-Scottish Cup in 1975–76.

**Previous winners:** *Texaco Cup* – 1971 Wolverhampton Wanderers, 1972 Derby County, 1973 Ipswich Town, 1974 Newcastle United, 1975 Newcastle United; *Anglo-Scottish Cup* – 1976 Middlesbrough, 1977 Nottingham Forest, 1978 Bristol City, 1979 Burnley, 1980 St Mirren, 1981 Chesterfield.

# THE
# FA CUP

### THE FOOTBALL ASSOCIATION OFFICIALS

### Patron: HER MAJESTY THE QUEEN

### President: HRH THE DUKE OF KENT

**Honorary Vice-Presidents**
His Grace the Duke of Marlborough; The Rt Hon
The Earl of Derby MC; Air Vice-Marshal
D. P. Hall CBE, AFC; Lt-General Sir Edward A.
Burgess KCB, OBE; Admiral Sir Anthony Morton
KCB; Right Hon Earl of Harewood LLD;
Sir Stanley Rous CBE; Sir Cyril Hawker;
Sir Walter Winterbottom CBE; Sir Denis
Follows CBE; Rt Hon Lord Westwood FCIS, JP

**Chairman of the Council**
F. A. Millichip (West Bromwich Albion FC)

**Vice-Chairman of the Council**
A. D. McMullen MBE (Bedfordshire FA)

**Life Vice-Presidents**
I. Robinson (Liverpool County FA);
E. D. Smith MBE, JP (Cumberland FA);
Sir Harold Thompson CBE, FRS (Oxford
University);
S. W. Jacobs (Oxfordshire FA);

**Vice-Presidents**
A. D. McMullen MBE (Bedfordshire FA);
W. H. Webster CBE (Cambridge University);
E. Kangley (Sheffield and Hallamshire FA);
E. A. Brown (Suffolk County FA);
R. Wragg (Football League);
R. H. Speake

**Secretary**
E. Croker, 16 Lancaster Gate, London W2 3LW

# FA CUP 1981–82

## QUALIFYING ROUNDS

**Preliminary Round**

| | |
|---|---|
| Peterlee Newtown v South Bank | 0-2 |
| Willington v Eppleton CW | 0-0 |
| Blue Star v Whitley Bay | 0-0 |
| Lancaster City v Percy Main | 3-1 |
| Wallsend Town v Evenwood Town | 1-4 |
| Boldon CA v Tow Law Town | 1-5 |
| Guisborough Town v Shildon | 3-1 |
| Chester-le-Street v West Auckland Town | 1-0 |
| Farsley Celtic v Mexborough Town Athletic | 1-1 |
| Bridlington Town v Thackley | 1-3 |
| Bridlington Trinity v Winterton Rangers | 3-1 |
| Appleby Frodingham v Buxton | 2-2 |
| Clitheroe v Netherfield | 0-1 |
| Accrington Stanley v South Liverpool | 2-1 |
| Marine v Prestwich Heys | 2-0 |
| Witton Albion v Macclesfield Town | 3-1 |
| Horwich RMI v Skelmersdale United | 4-0 |
| Rhyl v Winsford United | 0-1 |
| Telford United v Oswestry Town | 4-0 |
| Congleton Town v Belper Town | 0-2 |
| Prescot Cables v St Helens Town | 4-1 |
| Shifnal Town v New Mills | 5-0 |
| Colwyn Bay v Matlock Town | 3-3 |
| Boston v Holbeach United | 5-0 |
| Alfreton Town v Ashby Institute | 5-0 |
| *(at Matlock Town FC)* | |
| Heanor Town v Worksop Town | 1-3 |
| Eastwood Town v Friar Lane OB | 3-0 |
| Hednesford Town v Moor Green | 3-0 |
| Long Eaton United v Halesowen Town | 1-3 |
| Bilston v Rushall Olympic | 0-0 |
| Gresley Rovers v Redditch United | 2-1 |
| Brereton Social v Tamworth | 0-3 |
| Dudley Town v Stourbridge | 3-0 |
| Blakenall v Desborough Town | 1-1 |
| Tividale v Milton Keynes City | 3-0 |
| Wellingborough Town w.o.; Brierley Hill Alliance withdrew | |
| Gt Yarmouth Town v Saffron Walden Town | 4-0 |
| Bury Town v Spalding United | 2-0 |
| March Town United v Soham Town Rangers | 1-1 |
| Gorleston v Chelmsford City | 2-0 |
| Chatteris Town v Felixstowe Town | 3-1 |
| Bedford Town v Hoddesdon Town | 4-0 |
| Sudbury Town v Epping Town | 3-3 |
| Histon v Leyton-Wingate | 1-4 |
| Irthlingborough Diamonds v Harefield Utd | 2-1 |
| Abingdon Town v Hendon | 1-2 |
| Wootton Blue Cross v Slough Town | 2-2 |
| Didcot Town w.o.; Willesden withdrew | |
| Hounslow v Kingstonian | 1-3 |
| Thame United v Haringey Borough | 1-0 |
| Edgware v Staines Town | 3-1 |
| Erith & Belvedere v Rainham Town | 2-1 |
| Billericay Town v Tiptree United | 1-0 |
| Egham Town v Marlow | 1-1 |
| Burnham v Newbury Town | 3-4 |
| *(at Newbury Town FC)* | |
| Dartford v Redhill | 2-2 |
| Clapton v Whyteleafe | 1-0 |
| Pagham v Waterlooville | 3-0 |
| *(at Waterlooville FC)* | |
| Woking v Newport IOW | 1-0 |
| Arundel v Wick | 1-4 |
| Horsham YMCA v Uxbridge | 1-1 |
| Burgess Hill Town v Moseley | 4-0 |
| Steyning Town v Three Bridges | 0-0 |
| Bognor Regis Town v Haywards Heath | 5-1 |
| Metropolitan Police v Worthing | 1-2 |
| Dorking Town v Basingstoke Town | 0-2 |
| Chertsey Town v Lewes | 2-5 |
| Chatham Town v Hastings United | 1-4 |
| Croydon v Ringmer | 1-0 |
| Southwick v Thanet United | 0-1 |
| Whitstable Town v Sheppey United | 2-2 |
| Eastbourne United v Tonbridge AFC | 0-2 |
| Hungerford Town v Chippenham Town | 4-0 |

| | |
|---|---|
| Chichester City v Poole Town | 1-5 |
| Clandown v Gloucester City | 1-3 |
| Bridgend Town v Paulton Rovers | 6-0 |
| Cinderford Town v Llanelli | 1-2 |
| Barry Town v Ton Pentre | 2-0 |
| Bridport v Ottery St Mary | 5-0 |
| Almondsbury Greenway v Wellington Town | 1-1 |
| Falmouth Town v Penzance | 2-2 |
| Barnstaple Town v Tiverton Town | 3-1 |

**Preliminary Round – Replays**

| | |
|---|---|
| Eppleton CW v Willington | 0-2 |
| Whitley Bay v Blue Star | 3-1 |
| Mexborough Town Athletic v Farsley Celtic | aet 2-1 |
| Buxton v Appleby Frodingham | 3-0 |
| Matlock Town v Colwyn Bay | 2-2 |
| Rushall Olympic v Bilston | 1-3 |
| Desborough Town v Blakenall | 2-6 |
| Soham Town Rangers v March Town United | 0-4 |
| Epping Town v Sudbury Town | 2-4 |
| Slough Town v Wootton Blue Cross | 4-2 |
| Marlow v Egham Town | 1-1 |
| Redhill v Dartford | aet 1-0 |
| Uxbridge v Horsham YMCA | 2-1 |
| Three Bridges v Steyning Town | 1-3 |
| Sheppey United v Whitstable Town | 1-2 |
| Wellington Town v Almondsbury Greenway | 3-0 |
| Penzance v Falmouth Town | 2-2 |

**Preliminary Round – Second Replays**

| | |
|---|---|
| Colwyn Bay v Matlock Town | 1-4 |
| *(at Mossley FC)* | |
| Egham Town v Marlow | aet 7-4 |
| Falmouth Town v Penzance | 1-0 |

**First Round Qualifying**

| | |
|---|---|
| Whitley Bay v Willington | 3-1 |
| Annfield Plain v Durham City | 2-3 |
| Morecambe v Consett | 2-3 |
| South Bank v Barrow | 3-2 |
| Tow Law Town v Evenwood Town | 4-2 |
| Ashington v Crook Town | 4-2 |
| Horden CW v Brandon United | 1-1 |
| Lancaster City v Billingham Synthonia | 1-0 |
| Ferryhill Athletic v Chester-le-Street | 2-2 |
| North Shields v Wingate | 2-1 |
| Gateshead v Spennymoor United | 1-1 |
| Guisborough Town v Seaham CW Red Star | 2-3 |
| Emley v Thackley | 2-1 |
| Frickley Athletic v Whitby Town | 2-0 |
| Bishop Auckland v Ossett Albion | 4-0 |
| Mexborough Town Athletic v Goole Town | 1-6 |
| Barton Town v Buxton | 1-3 |
| Brigg Town v Curzon Ashton | 0-0 |
| Stalybridge Celtic v Yorkshire Amateurs | 2-1 |
| Bridlington Trinity v Denaby United | 2-0 |
| Chorley v Accrington Stanley | 0-0 |
| Droylsden v Southport | 1-0 |
| Penrith v Rossendale United | 2-1 |
| Netherfield v Leyland Motors | 3-2 |
| Horwich RMI v Witton Albion | 2-0 |
| Ashton United v Lytham | 1-1 |
| Fleetwood Town v Hyde United | 1-1 |
| Marine v Formby | 4-0 |
| Belper Town v Telford United | 0-6 |
| Bangor City v Glossop | 6-0 |
| Burscough v Darwen | 4-0 |
| Winsford United v Caernarfon Town | 2-3 |
| Matlock Town v Shifnal Town | 1-1 |
| Armitage v Nantwich Town | 0-2 |
| Runcorn v Leek Town | 3-0 |
| Prescot Cables v Bootle | 3-1 |
| Arnold v Alfreton Town | 1-2 |
| Bourne Town v North Ferriby United | 1-2 |
| Boston United v Sutton Town | 2-1 |

| | |
|---|---|
| Boston v Gainsborough Trinity | 0-0 |
| Grantham v Eastwood Town | 1-0 |
| Ilkeston Town v Hinckley Athletic | 2-0 |
| Corby Town v Enderby Town | 2-1 |
| Worksop Town v Skegness Town | 2-1 |
| Bilston v Halesowen Town | 2-3 |
| Alvechurch v Evesham United | 2-0 |
| Burton Albion v Coventry Sporting | 3-1 |
| Hednesford Town v Bedworth United | 1-1 |
| Darlaston v Tamworth | 1-2 |
| Oldbury United v Willenhall Town | 0-2 |
| Kidderminster Harriers v Shepshed Charterhouse | 1-2 |
| Gresley Rovers v Racing Club Warwick | 1-1 |
| Bromsgrove Rovers v Blakenall | 2-0 |
| Highgate United v Kempston Rovers | 2-2 |
| Sutton Coldfield Town v Buckingham Town | 2-1 |
| Dudley Town v Malvern Town | 0-2 |
| Lye Town v Wellingborough Town | 2-1 |
| VS Rugby v Wolverton Town | 5-0 |
| Nuneaton Borough v Rushden Town | 6-0 |
| Tividale v Walsall Wood | 3-0 |
| Cambridge City v Bury Town | 1-1 |
| Lowestoft Town v Stamford | 1-0 |
| King's Lynn v Thetford Town | 0-0 |
| Gt Yarmouth Town v Parson Drove United | 3-2 |
| Heybridge Swifts v Gorleston | 2-1 |
| Newmarket Town v Letchworth GC | 1-0 |
| Harwich & Parkeston v Wisbech Town | 1-2 |
| March Town United v St Neots Town | 1-0 |
| Potton United v Bedford Town | 1-1 |
| Clacton Town v Ware | 1-0 |
| Barton Rovers v Haverhill Rovers | 1-0 |
| Chatteris Town v Ely City | 3-3 |
| Stowmarket Town v Leyton-Wingate | 2-3 |
| Basildon United v Walthamstow Avenue | 1-2 |
| St Albans City v Grays Athletic | 2-1 |
| Sudbury Town v Dunstable | 1-1 |
| Ampthill Town v Hendon | 0-1 |
| Rothwell Town v Tring Town | 1-3 |
| Banbury United v Hemel Hempstead | 2-1 |
| Irthlingborough Diamonds v Chesham United | 1-0 |
| Witney Town v Didcot Town | 3-0 |
| Bracknell Town v Wokingham Town | 1-2 |
| Hitchin Town v Southall | 1-2 |
| Slough Town v Chalfont St Peter | 2-1 |
| Edgware v Thame United | 1-3 |
| Berkhamsted Town v Hampton | 0-3 |
| Aylesbury United v Feltham | 0-1 |
| Kingstonian v Boreham Wood | 2-0 |
| Cray Wanderers v Billericay Town | 0-4 |
| Hornchurch v Woodford Town | 0-0 |
| Aveley v Welling United | 1-1 |
| Erith & Belvedere v Leytonstone & Ilford | 2-2 |
| Camberley Town v Newbury Town | 0-2 |
| Harrow Borough v Oxford City | 4-2 |
| Wealdstone v Salisbury | 4-0 |
| Egham Town v Maidenhead United | 1-2 |
| Corinthian Casuals v Clapton | 3-3 |
| Finchley v Sittingbourne | 4-3 |
| Hayes v Tilbury | 1-1 |
| Redhill v Hertford Town | 1-2 |
| Wick v Woking | 2-1 |
| Banstead Athletic v Horsham | 2-0 |
| Farnborough Town v Horndean | 5-0 |
| Pagham v Andover | 2-1 |
| (at Andover FC) | |
| Crawley Town v Burgess Hill Town | 0-1 |
| Littlehampton Town v Carshalton Athletic | 0-3 |
| Windsor & Eton v Walton & Hersham | 3-4 |
| Uxbridge v Peacehaven & Telscombe | 2-2 |
| Worthing v Bognor Regis Town | 0-0 |
| Bromley v Fareham Town | 0-5 |
| Addlestone & Weybridge Town v Ruislip Manor | 3-1 |
| Steyning Town v Dulwich Hamlet | 1-1 |
| Cheshunt v Lewes | 2-2 |
| Hillingdon Borough v Tunbridge Wells | 7-2 |
| Wembley v East Grinstead | 2-1 |
| Basingstoke Town v Tooting & Mitcham United | 2-1 |
| Croydon w.o.; Bexhill Town withdrew | |
| Eastbourne Town v Canterbury City | 0-2 |
| Epsom & Ewell v Herne Bay | 2-1 |
| Hastings United v Faversham Town | 5-0 |
| Tonbridge AFC v Whitstable Town | 3-1 |
| Ashford Town v Hastings Town | 1-0 |
| Dover v Folkestone | 4-1 |

| | |
|---|---|
| Thanet United v Deal Town | 2-2 |
| Eastleigh v Poole Town | 2-1 |
| Frome Town v Trowbridge Town | 2-1 |
| Gosport Borough v Melksham Town | 0-1 |
| Hungerford Town v Dorchester Town | 1-2 |
| Calne Town v Bridgend Town | 1-2 |
| Devizes Town v Shepton Mallet Town | 1-0 |
| Worcester City v Moreton Town | 5-2 |
| Gloucester City v Forest Green Rovers | 2-1 |
| Cheltenham Town v Barry Town | 4-0 |
| Clevedon Town v Welton Rovers | 3-1 |
| Bath City v Mangotsfield United | 3-0 |
| Llanelli v Haverfordwest County | 1-2 |
| Bridgwater Town v Wellington Town | 2-0 |
| Glastonbury v Weston-super-Mare | 3-1 |
| Taunton Town v Saltash United | 1-0 |
| Bridport v Liskeard Athletic | 2-2 |
| Chard Town v Barnstaple Town | 1-2 |
| Ilminster Town v Torrington | 0-2 |
| Bideford v St Blazey | 4-1 |
| Falmouth Town v Newquay | 2-0 |

**First Round Qualifying - Replays**

| | |
|---|---|
| Brandon United v Horden CW | 1-3 |
| Chester-le-Street v Ferryhill Athletic | 2-1 |
| Spennymoor United v Gateshead | 3-0 |
| Curzon Ashton v Brigg Town | 4-1 |
| Accrington Stanley v Chorley | 0-0 |
| Lytham v Ashton United | 3-1 |
| Hyde United v Fleetwood Town | 2-1 |
| Shifnal Town v Matlock Town | 2-0 |
| Gainsborough Trinity v Boston | 1-2 |
| Bedworth United v Hednesford Town | 3-0 |
| Racing Club Warwick v Gresley Rovers | 1-3 |
| Kempston Rovers v Highgate United | 1-2 |
| Bury Town v Cambridge City | 1-1 |
| Thetford Town v King's Lynn | 0-1 |
| Bedford Town v Potton United | 4-1 |
| Ely City v Chatteris Town | 2-1 |
| Dunstable v Sudbury Town | 1-1 |
| Woodford Town v Hornchurch | aet 2-1 |
| Welling United v Aveley | 0-0 |
| Leytonstone & Ilford v Erith & Belvedere | 3-0 |
| Clapton v Corinthian Casuals | aet 1-2 |
| Tilbury v Hayes | 0-0 |
| Peacehaven & Telscombe v Uxbridge | 1-3 |
| Bognor Regis Town v Worthing | 1-0 |
| Dulwich Hamlet v Steyning Town | 3-0 |
| Lewes v Cheshunt | 3-3 |
| Deal Town v Thanet United | 2-1 |
| Liskeard Athletic v Bridport | 3-1 |

**First Round Qualifying - Second Replays**

| | |
|---|---|
| Chorley v Accrington Stanley | 2-0 |
| Cambridge City v Bury Town | 1-2 |
| Aveley v Welling United | 0-0 |
| Hayes v Tilbury | 0-0 |
| Cheshunt v Lewes | 0-2 |

**First Round Qualifying - Third Replays**

| | |
|---|---|
| Welling United v Aveley | 3-2 |
| Tilbury v Hayes | 1-1 |

**First Round Qualifying - Fourth Replay**

| | |
|---|---|
| Hayes v Tilbury | 4-0 |

**Second Round Qualifying**

| | |
|---|---|
| Whitley Bay v Consett | 1-0 |
| South Bank v Durham City | 4-1 |
| Tow Law Town v Horden CW | 1-4 |
| Lancaster City v Ashington | 1-3 |
| Chester-le-Street v Spennymoor United | 1-1 |
| Seaham CW Red Star v North Shields | 0-1 |
| Emley v Bishop Auckland | 1-4 |
| Goole Town v Frickley Athletic | 2-3 |
| Buxton v Stalybridge Celtic | 1-0 |
| Bridlington Trinity v Curzon Ashton | 0-1 |
| Chorley v Penrith | 0-1 |
| Netherfield v Droylsden | 1-1 |

| | |
|---|---|
| Horwich RMI v Hyde United | 0-4 |
| Marine v Lytham | 0-0 |
| Telford United v Burscough | 3-0 |
| Caernarfon Town v Bangor City | 3-2 |
| Shifnal Town v Runcorn | 0-3 |
| Prescot Cables v Nantwich Town | 1-1 |
| Alfreton Town v Boston United | 0-2 |
| *(at Boston United FC)* | |
| Boston v North Ferriby United | 1-2 |
| Grantham v Corby Town | 0-1 |
| Worksop Town v Ilkeston Town | 2-3 |
| Halesowen Town v Burton Albion | 0-0 |
| Bedworth United v Alvechurch | 0-1 |
| Tamworth v Shepshed Charterhouse | 2-2 |
| Gresley Rovers v Willenhall Town | 3-3 |
| Bromsgrove Rovers v Sutton Coldfield Town | 1-0 |
| Malvern Town v Highgate United | 2-1 |
| Lye Town v Nuneaton Borough | 1-2 |
| Tividale v VS Rugby | 2-2 |
| Bury Town v King's Lynn | 0-5 |
| Gt Yarmouth Town v Lowestoft Town | 3-1 |
| Heybridge Swifts v Wisbech Town | 2-2 |
| March Town United v Newmarket Town | 5-5 |
| Bedford Town v Barton Rovers | 2-0 |
| Ely City v Clacton Town | 2-1 |
| Leyton-Wingate v St Albans City | 2-2 |
| Dunstable v Walthamstow Avenue | 3-2 |
| Hendon v Banbury United | 2-2 |
| Irthlingborough Diamonds v Tring Town | 1-1 |
| Witney Town v Southall | 4-1 |
| Slough Town v Wokingham Town | 1-5 |
| Thame United v Feltham | 1-1 |
| Kingstonian v Hampton | 1-0 |
| Billericay Town v Welling United | 3-1 |
| Leytonstone & Ilford v Woodford Town | 2-1 |
| Newbury Town v Wealdstone | 1-6 |
| Maidenhead United v Harrow Borough | 0-2 |
| Corinthian Casuals v Hayes | 2-1 |
| Hertford Town v Finchley | 4-3 |
| Wick v Farnborough Town | 2-2 |
| Pagham v Banstead Athletic | 2-2 |
| Burgess Hill Town v Walton & Hersham | 2-1 |
| Uxbridge v Carshalton Athletic | 0-3 |
| Bognor Regis Town v Addlestone & Weybridge Town | 0-0 |
| Dulwich Hamlet v Fareham Town | 1-2 |
| Lewes v Wembley | 1-2 |
| Basingstoke Town v Hillingdon Borough | 4-2 |
| Croydon v Epsom & Ewell | 1-1 |
| Hastings United v Canterbury City | 4-1 |
| Tonbridge AFC v Dover | 2-2 |
| Deal Town v Ashford Town | 1-2 |
| Eastleigh v Melksham Town | 3-1 |
| Dorchester Town v Frome Town | 3-0 |
| Bridgend Town v Worcester City | 1-3 |
| Gloucester City v Devizes Town | 2-4 |
| Cheltenham Town v Bath City | 2-2 |
| Haverfordwest County v Clevedon Town | 3-2 |
| Bridgwater Town v Taunton Town | 1-1 |
| Liskeard Athletic v Glastonbury | 2-0 |
| Barnstaple Town v Bideford | 1-1 |
| Falmouth Town v Torrington | 1-0 |

**Second Round Qualifying - Replays**

| | |
|---|---|
| Spennymoor United v Chester-le-Street | 1-0 |
| Droylsden v Netherfield | aet 3-1 |
| Lytham v Marine | 2-6 |
| Nantwich Town v Prescot Cables | 0-1 |
| Burton Albion v Halesowen Town | 2-0 |
| Shepshed Charterhouse v Tamworth | 3-1 |
| Willenhall Town v Gresley Rovers | 1-0 |
| VS Rugby v Tividale | 0-2 |
| Wisbech Town v Heybridge Swifts | aet 2-1 |
| Newmarket Town v March Town United | 0-2 |
| St Albans City v Leyton-Wingate | 4-1 |
| Banbury United v Hendon | aet 3-4 |
| Tring Town v Irthlingborough Diamonds | 1-1 |
| Feltham v Thame United | aet 1-2 |
| Farnborough Town v Wick | 3-0 |
| Banstead Athletic v Pagham | 7-1 |
| Addlestone & Weybridge Town v Bognor Regis Town | 2-0 |
| Epsom & Ewell v Croydon | 4-0 |
| Dover v Tonbridge AFC | aet 5-2 |
| Bath City v Cheltenham Town | 1-2 |
| Taunton Town v Bridgwater Town | 1-0 |

**Third Round Qualifying**

| | |
|---|---|
| Whitley Bay v South Bank | 0-2 |
| Horden CW v Ashington | 0-0 |
| Spennymoor United v North Shields | 2-2 |
| Bishop Auckland v Frickley Athletic | 3-0 |
| Buxton v Curzon Ashton | 4-1 |
| Penrith v Droylsden | 3-2 |
| Hyde United v Marine | 3-1 |
| Telford United v Caernarfon Town | 1-2 |
| Runcorn v Prescot Cables | 4-1 |
| Boston United v North Ferriby United | 4-0 |
| Corby Town v Ilkeston Town | 8-1 |
| Burton Albion v Alvechurch | 2-0 |
| Shepshed Charterhouse v Willenhall Town | 1-5 |
| Bromsgrove Rovers v Malvern Town | 4-1 |
| Nuneaton Borough v Tividale | 5-2 |
| King's Lynn v Gt Yarmouth Town | 5-1 |
| Wisbech Town v March Town United | 2-1 |
| Bedford Town v Ely City | 1-0 |
| St Albans City v Dunstable | 1-5 |
| Hendon v Tring Town | 4-0 |
| Witney Town v Wokingham Town | 2-0 |
| Thame United v Kingstonian | 1-2 |
| Billericay Town v Leytonstone & Ilford | 0-0 |
| Wealdstone v Harrow Borough | 1-4 |
| Corinthian Casuals v Hertford Town | 2-0 |
| Farnborough Town v Banstead Athletic | 4-0 |
| Burgess Hill Town v Carshalton Athletic | 1-5 |
| Addlestone & Weybridge v Fareham Town | 2-0 |
| Wembley v Basingstoke Town | 5-1 |
| Epsom & Ewell v Hastings United | 2-4 |
| Dover v Ashford Town | 2-1 |
| Eastleigh v Dorchester Town | 2-4 |
| Worcester City v Devizes Town | 4-1 |
| Cheltenham Town v Haverfordwest County | 4-0 |
| Taunton Town v Liskeard Athletic | 2-0 |
| Bideford v Falmouth Town | 1-0 |

**Third Round Qualifying - Replays**

| | |
|---|---|
| Ashington v Horden CW | aet 1-3 |
| North Shields v Spennymoor United | 1-5 |
| Leytonstone & Ilford v Billericay Town | 1-0 |

**Fourth Round Qualifying**

| | |
|---|---|
| Caernarfon Town v Bishop Auckland | 0-2 |
| Workington v Buxton | 4-1 |
| South Bank v Mossley | 0-1 |
| Horden CW v Hyde United | 2-0 |
| Penrith v Northwich Victoria | 1-0 |
| Scarborough v Blyth Spartans | 2-3 |
| Spennymoor United v Runcorn | 0-1 |
| Boston United v Dunstable | 3-1 |
| Nuneaton Borough v Bromsgrove Rovers | 2-1 |
| Harlow Town v Corby Town | 1-0 |
| Kettering Town v King's Lynn | 2-1 |
| Willenhall Town v Burton Albion | 2-1 |
| Stafford Rangers v AP Leamington | 3-0 |
| Bedford Town v Wisbech Town | 3-0 |
| Gravesend & Northfleet v Dagenham | 0-0 |
| Hendon v Harrow Borough | 2-1 |
| Barnet v Corinthian Casuals | 2-0 |
| Hastings United v Wembley | 2-0 |
| Dover v Leatherhead | 1-1 |
| Maidstone United v Barking | 0-1 |
| Leytonstone & Ilford v Carshalton Athletic | 2-0 |
| Weymouth v Farnborough Town | 3-0 |
| Cheltenham Town v Dorchester Town | 1-3 |
| Minehead v Worcester City | 1-0 |
| Witney Town v Wycombe Wanderers | 0-1 |
| Bideford v Kingstonian | 1-0 |
| Addlestone & Weybridge Town v Taunton Town | 2-2 |
| Yeovil Town v Merthyr Tydfil | 3-0 |

**Fourth Round Qualifying - Replays**

| | |
|---|---|
| Dagenham v Gravesend & Northfleet | 6-3 |
| Leatherhead v Dover | 0-1 |
| Taunton Town v Addlestone & Weybridge Town | 0-0 |

**Fourth Round Qualifying - Second Replay**

| | |
|---|---|
| Taunton Town v Addlestone & Weybridge Town | 4-2 |

# FA CUP 1981–82

## FIRST ROUND

### 20 NOV

**Bristol C (0) 0**
**Torquay U (0) 0**                                     5221
*Bristol C:* Moller; Stevens, Williams, Aitken, Rodgers,
Boyle, Tainton, Mann, Harford, Devine, Chandler.
*Torquay U:* O'Keefe; Jones, Pethard, Brown, Wilson,
Larmour, Fell, Lawrence, Cooper, Rioch, Sermanni.

### 21 NOV

**Aldershot (1) 2** *(Garwood 2)*
**Leytonstone & Ilford (0) 0**                          2643
*Aldershot:* Johnson; Edwards, Scott, Briley, Bennett,
Wooler, Lucas, McDonald, Garwood, Brodie, Robinson.
*Leytonstone & Ilford:* Mullett; Jacques, Hayzelden,
Holder, McCayna, Wells, Scott, Powell, Dingwall, Waight
(Cobb), Borland.

**Bedford (0) 0**
**Wimbledon (1) 2** *(Suddaby, Ketteridge)*             3900
*Bedford:* Luff; Platnauer, James, Gould (Kirkup), Good-
eve, Best, Kurila, McGowan, Robinson, Campbell, Fel-
ton.
*Wimbledon:* Beasant; Clement, Brown, Gage, Morris,
Suddaby, Ketteridge (Hodges), Leslie, Lazarus, Downes,
Belfield.

**Bideford (0) 1** *(Brown)*
**Barking (0) 2** *(Hillman, Key)*                      2000
*Bideford:* Robbins; Smythe, Mallett, Menhenick, Berry,
Hore, Brown, Forbes, Edwards, Pearson, Blanche.
*Barking:* Hitchcock; Cooper, Watts, Campbell, Davy,
White (Brennan), Anderson, Makin, Dormer, Key, Hill-
man.

**Bishop Auckland (1) 4** *(Cross 2, Foster, Newton D.)*
**Nuneaton (0) 1** *(Jones)*                            1425
*Bishop Auckland:* Owers; Newton M., Rutherford, Nat-
tress, Hills, Hissett, Richardson, Parnaby, Foster, Newton
D., Cross.
*Nuneaton:* Duliston; Stockley, Sandercock, Dixey,
Glover, Lowe, Jones, Dale, Clayton, Morley, Robson.

**Bishop's Stortford (1) 2** *(Worrell, Clarke)*
**Sutton (2) 2** *(Bradford og, Sunnucks)*              1200
*Bishop's Stortford:* Moore; Lawrence, Baldry, Smith,
Bradford, Avery, Worrell (Brown), Knapman, Radford,
Clarke, Sullivan.
*Sutton:* Collyer; Cooper, Green, Waldon, Rains T., Ste-
phens, Rogers, Pritchard, Joyce, McCombe, Sunnucks.

**Blyth S (0) 1** *(Rafferty)*
**Walsall (1) 2** *(Macken, Caswell)*                   3440
*Blyth S:* Clarke; Cochrane, Walker A., Rafferty, Ander-
son, Dixon, Walker P., Johnson, Mutrie (Barker), Dunn,
Ross.
*Walsall:* Green; Loveridge, Caswell, Beech, Hart, Serella,
Waddington S., Macken, Penn, Mower, O'Kelly (Rees).

**Boston (0) 0**
**Kettering (0) 1** *(Atkins)*                          2826
*Boston:* Blackwell; Adamson, Dulson, Tyler, Annable,
Simpson, Collier, Cox (Hubbard), Allen, Mallender, Bar-
tlett.
*Kettering:* Tingay; McIntosh, Forster, Clarke, Suddards,
Haverson, Phipps, Evans (Shelton), Atkins, Murphy,
Duggan.

**AFC Bournemouth (1) 1** *(Funnell)*
**Reading (0) 0**                                       7376
*AFC Bournemouth:* Leigh; Heffernan, Sulley, Smith,
Brignull, Impey, Dawtry, Crawford, Funnell, Spackman,
Williams.
*Reading:* Fearon; Williams, Cullen (Dixon), Wood,
Hicks, Hetzke, Beavon, Kearney, Heale, Sanchez, Webb.

**Brentford (2) 2** *(Bowen 2)*
**Exeter C (0) 0**                                      6432
*Brentford:* McKellar; Harris, Tucker, McNichol, White-
head, Hurlock, Kamara, Bowen, Johnson, Booker, Rob-
erts.
*Exeter C:* Bond; Davy, Sparrow, Lester, Shaw, Roberts,
Cooke, Rogers P., Kellow, Delve, Pullar (Pratt).

**Bristol R (0) 1** *(Williams D. pen)*
**Fulham (0) 2** *(Coney 2)*                            6497
*Bristol R:* Thomas; Jones, Williams B., McCaffery,
Hughes, Mabbutt, Curle, Gillies (Barrett), Stephens,
Randall, Williams D.
*Fulham:* Peyton; Hopkins, Strong (Lock), O'Driscoll,
Brown, Gale, Davies, Wilson, Coney, O'Sullivan, Lewing-
ton.

**Burnley (0) 0**
**Runcorn (0) 0**                                       6112
*Burnley:* Stevenson; Laws, Wharton, Cassidy, Overson,
Phelan, Potts, Steven, Hamilton, McGee, Young.
*Runcorn:* Parker; Rutter, Roberts, Edwards, Seddon,
Crompton, Smith, Scott, Fraser, Jones, Joel.

**Chesterfield (3) 4** *(Bonnyman 2, Henderson, Walker)*
**Preston NE (0) 1** *(Doyle)*                          5435
*Chesterfield:* Turner; Stirk, O'Neill, Wilson, Green, Pol-
lard, Windridge, Henderson, Bonnyman, Kowalski,
Walker.
*Preston NE:* Litchfield; Clark, McAteer, Doyle, Ander-
son, O'Riordan, Houston, Buckley, Bruce, Naughton,
Dunn.

**Colchester U (0) 2** *(Leslie, Adcock)*
**Newport Co (0) 0**                                    3535
*Colchester U:* Walker; Cook, Coleman, Rowles, Wignall,
Wright, Adcock, Bremner, Osborne, McDonough (Les-
lie), Allinson.
*Newport Co:* Kendall; Lees, Relish, Davies, Oakes, Bai-
ley, Vaughan, Lowndes, Waddle, Aldridge (Tynan),
Elsey.

**Dagenham (0) 2** *(Burton 2)*
**Yeovil (1) 2** *(Green, Brown)*                       1691
*Dagenham:* Huttley; Wade, Scales, Stein, Elley, Howell
(Maycock), Brown, Ragan, Burton, Stewart, Gibson.
*Yeovil:* Langley; Scott, Ritchie, Payne, Giles, Beck, Grif-
fiths, Platt, Green, Bell, Brown.

**Darlington (1) 2** *(Speedie, Walsh)*

**Carlisle (0) 2** *(Staniforth, Robson)*     4005

*Darlington:* Cuff; Kamara, Wilson (Stalker), Smith, Skipper, Speedie, Mitchell, McLean, Wicks, Hamilton, Walsh.
*Carlisle:* Swinburne; Parker, Haigh, Coughlin, Ashurst, Larkin, Crabbe (Bannon), Robson, Lee, Beardsley, Staniforth.


**Dorchester (0) 3** *(Miller, Steele 2)*

**Minehead (0) 3** *(Guscott, Hodgson, Darke)*     822

*Dorchester:* Hobson; Townsend, Flay, Dominey, Poore, Ames, Chutter, Steele, Senior, Miller, Thorne.
*Minehead:* Lee; Twitchin, Impey, Carter, Darke, Durbin, Guscott, Hodgson, Powell (Druce), Brown, Summers.


**Dover (0) 0**

**Oxford U (1) 2** *(Smithers, Thomas)*     3144

*Dover:* Moseley; Norton, Keeley, Brooks (Gregory), Cugley, Fusco, Godak, Wilson, Walter, Jolley, Lloyd.
*Oxford U:* Burton; Doyle, Fogg, Jeffrey, Briggs, Shotton, Jones, Foley, Cassells, Thomas, Smithers.


**Enfield (1) 2** *(Oliver, Ashford)*

**Hastings (0) 0**     1505

*Enfield:* Jacobs; Oliver, Tone, Jennings, Waite, Ironton, Ashford, Taylor, Holmes, Barrett, King (Turner).
*Hastings:* Armstrong; Wallis, Petkovic, Streeter, Crowe, Hamshare, Crush (Peacock), Stock, Glazier, Batten, Cook.


**Halifax T (0) 0**

**Peterborough U (0) 3** *(Cooke 2, Syrett)*     2614

*Halifax T:* Smelt; Ward, Carr, Evans, Ayre, Hendrie, Whiteley, Davison, Allatt, Chamberlain, Graham.
*Peterborough U:* Freeman; Butler, Collins, Gynn, Smith, Phillips, Syrett, Kellock, Cooke, Hodgson, Chard.


**Harlow (0) 0**

**Barnet (0) 0**     1297

*Harlow:* Kitson; Wickenden, Cusenza, Carrington, Clarke, Taylor (Parker), Pask, Gough, McLeod, Mackay, Harding.
*Barnet:* Phillips; Foody, Pearce, Millett, Campbell, Townsend, Robinson, Watson, Sargent, Barnes, Voice.


**Hendon (0) 1** *(Bennett)*

**Wycombe W (1) 1** *(Vircavs)*     1353

*Hendon:* Smart; Bennett, Hand, Deadman, Anderson, Murphy, Drummy, Gough, Folan, Currie, Brannigan.
*Wycombe W:* Lefter; Birdseye, Borg, Toll, Vircavs, West, Dell, Kennedy, Glynn, Long, Jacobs.


**Hereford U (0) 3** *(Harvey, Laidlaw, Phillips)*

**Southend U (0) 1** *(Gray)*     3527

*Hereford U:* Brand; Price, Bray, Hicks, Dobson (Lane), Spiring, Harvey, Laidlaw, Phillips, Showers, White.
*Southend U:* Keeley; Stead, Yates, Pennyfather, Moody, Walker, Gray, Pountney, Spence, Mercer (Greaves), Nelson.


**Horden C (0) 0**

**Blackpool (0) 1** *(Harrison)*     4465

At Hartlepool
*Horden C:* Wilson; Lormer, Cook, Normanton, Cranson, Hather, Honour (Sherwood), Aylesbury, Turner, Evans, Hogan.
*Blackpool:* Hesford; Simmonite, Pashley, Blair, Hart, McEwan, Noble, Morris, Harrison, Bamber, Hockaday.


**Lincoln C (1) 2** *(Thompson S., Cammack)*

**Port Vale (1) 2** *(Chamberlain N., Chamberlain M.)*     3950

*Lincoln C:* Naylor; Turner P., Turner W., Cockerill, Peake, Thompson S., Shipley (Cammack), Carr, Bell, Cunningham, Gilbert.
*Port Vale:* Harrison; Tartt, Bromage, Hunter, Sproson, Bowles, Chamberlain N., Moss, Higgins, Armstrong, Chamberlain M.


**Mansfield T (0) 0**

**Doncaster R (1) 1** *(Douglas)*     5456

*Mansfield T:* Arnold; McJannet, Foster, Bell (Nicholson), Burrows, Wood, Thompson, Morgan, Mann, Caldwell, Parkinson.
*Doncaster R:* Boyd; Russell, Lister, Snodin I., Douglas, Dowd (Harle), Pugh, Nimmo, Warboys, Snodin G., Noteman.


**Penrith (0) 1** *(Fell)*

**Chester (0) 0**     2700

*Penrith:* McMullen; Wilson, Glover, Carruthers A., Carruthers R., Coulthard, Simpson, Sawyers, Fell, Gash, Armstrong.
*Chester:* Millington; Raynor, Burns, Storton, Zelem, Jones, Needham (Howat), Simpson, Ludlam, Phillips, Sutcliffe.


**Plymouth Arg (0) 0**

**Gillingham (0) 0**     5471

*Plymouth Arg:* Crudgington; Nisbet, McCartney, Harrison, Phillipson-Masters, Cooper, Hodges, Cook, Sims, Randell (Phillips), Rogers.
*Gillingham:* Hillyard; Sharpe, Ford, Bruce, Weatherly, Bowman, Powell, Duncan, White, Ovard, Price.


**Portsmouth (1) 1** *(Hemmerman)*

**Millwall (0) 1** *(Chatterton pen)*     10,113

*Portsmouth:* Knight; McLaughlin, Bryant, Doyle, Aizlewood, Rollings, Hemmerman, Tait, Barnard, Cropley, Crown.
*Millwall:* Gleasure; Martin, Warman, Chatterton, Allardyce, Slough, Hayes, Massey, McKenna, Horrix, West.


**Rochdale (0) 2** *(Dolan, Esser)*

**Hull C (1) 2** *(McClaren, Whitehurst)*     2722

*Rochdale:* Poole; Cooper (Esser), Burke, Taylor, Snookes, Dolan, O'Loughlin, Goodwin, Hilditch, Wellings, Martinez.
*Hull C:* Norman; McNeill, Booth, Roberts D., Deacy, Roberts G., Marwood, McClaren, Whitehurst, Mutrie, Swann.


**Scunthorpe U (1) 1** *(Cowling)*

**Bradford C (0) 0**     3339

*Scunthorpe U:* Neenan; Davy, Pilling, Keeley, Dall, Oates, Grimes, O'Berg (Lambert), Cowling, Moss, Stewart.
*Bradford C:* Ramsbottom; Podd, Wood, Ingham, Jackson, McFarland, Gallagher, Black (Ellis), Campbell, McNiven, Chapman.


**Sheffield U (1) 2** *(Edwards, Hatton)*

**Altrincham (0) 2** *(Rogers 2)*     12,433

*Sheffield U:* Waugh; Ryan, Houston, Richardson, McAlle, Kenworthy, Neville, Trusson, Edwards, Hatton, Charles.
*Altrincham:* Connaughton; Allan, Davison, Goulding, Gardner (Owen), King, Heathcote, Whitbread, Johnson, Rogers, Howard.

**Stafford R (1) 1** *(Burr)*

**York C (1) 2** *(Ford, Walwyn)* 2289

*Stafford R:* Dance; Beckett, Peacock, Chapman, Harris, Richardson, Westwood, Nelson, Kabia, Wood, Burr.
*York C:* Blackburn; Senior, Flood, Stanley, Hood, Kay, Pollard, Crosby, Walwyn, Ford, Bentham.


**Stockport Co (1) 3** *(Williams 2, Park)*

**Mossley (0) 1** *(Moore)* 4216

*Stockport Co:* Lloyd; Rutter, Thorpe, Sword, Dwyer (Sunley), Fowler, Park, Sherlock, Williams, Power, Coyle.
*Mossley:* Sherlock; Derbyshire, Garmory, O'Connor, Vaughan, Duff, Szabo, Moore, Hughes, Skeete, Deakin.


**Swindon T (1) 2** *(Pritchard 2)*

**Taunton (1) 1** *(Hains)* 4494

*Swindon T:* Allan; Graham, Peach, Hughes, Henry, Stroud, Abbley, Carter, Rowland, Greenwood, Pritchard.
*Taunton:* Stevens; Lowe, Smith, Aherne, Awcock, Adams, Hains, Ashdon, Edwards T., Payne, Crook (Edwards A.).


**Tranmere R (0) 1** *(Brown)*

**Bury (0) 1** *(Madden)* 3382

*Tranmere R:* Endersby; Mungall, Burgess, Craven, Bramhall, Williams, Hamilton, Morley (Kerr), Hutchinson, Brown, Griffiths.
*Bury:* Brown; Howard, Kennedy, Gore, Hilton P., Cruickshank, Madden, Butler (Mullen), Johnson, Jakub, Hilton M.


**Weymouth (0) 0**

**Northampton T (0) 0** 2005

*Weymouth:* Baker; Lawrence, Morrell, Elliott, Merrick, Arnold, McCafferty, Pearson, Iannone, Dove, Borthwick.
*Northampton T:* Poole; Taylor, Saxby, Brady, Gage, Saunders, Buchanan, Carlton, Heeley (Sandy), Phillips, Mahoney.


**Wigan Ath (1) 2** *(Methven, Quinn)*

**Hartlepool U (0) 2** *(Linacre P., Newton)* 5303

*Wigan Ath:* Tunks; McMahon, Cribley, Wignall, Bradd, Methven, Sheldon, Barrow, Quinn, Houghton, Weston.
*Hartlepool U:* Burleigh; Brown, Stimpson, Hogan (Clarke), Bird, Linighan, Linacre J., Newton, Linacre P., Sweeney, Johnson.


**Willenhall (0) 0**

**Crewe Alex (1) 1** *(Scott)* 3454

*Willenhall:* Sharrard; White (Heath), Glover, Dams, Newell, Fox, Forrester, Price A., Matthews, Price K., Stringer.
*Crewe Alex:* Mulhearn; Lewis, Bowers, Salathiel, Scott, Griffiths, Haslegrave, Callaghan, Ricketts (Chesters), Palios, Williams.


**Workington (1) 1** *(Reach)*

**Huddersfield T (0) 1** *(Brown)* 3101

*Workington:* Fisher; Hill, Kisby, Reach, Roberts, Williams, Diamond, Smith, Gill, Innes, Harris.
*Huddersfield T:* Taylor; Brown, Smith, Lillis, Sutton, Hanvey, Laverick, Purdie, Austin, Robins, Cowling.


**FIRST ROUND REPLAYS**

**23 NOV**

**Altrincham (0) 3** *(Howard 2, Heathcote)*

**Sheffield U (0) 0** 5137

*Altrincham:* Connaughton; Allan, Davison, Goulding, Gardner, King, Heathcote, Whitbread, Johnson, Rogers, Howard.
*Sheffield U:* Waugh; Ryan, Houston, Richardson, McAlle, Kenworthy, Garner, Trusson, Edwards, Matthews, Charles (Neville).


**Minehead (0) 0**

**Dorchester (1) 4** *(Senior 3, Chutter)* 707

*Minehead:* Lee; Twitchin, Impey, Carter (Druce), Darke, Durbin, Guscott, Hodgson, Powell, Brown, Summers.
*Dorchester:* Hobson; Townsend, Flay, Dominey, Poore, Ames, Chutter, Steele, Senior, Miller, Thorne.


**24 NOV**

**Barnet (1) 1** *(Sargent)*

**Harlow (0) 0** 1577

*Barnet:* Phillips; Pittaway, Pearce, Millett, Watson, Campbell, Townsend, Robinson, Sargent, Barnes, Foody.
*Harlow:* Kitson; Pask, Cusenza, Carrington, Clarke, Gough (Aherne), Taylor, Wiles, McLeod, Mackay, Harding.


**Bury (0) 3** *(Madden 2, Johnson)*

**Tranmere R (0) 1** *(Williams)* 4648

*Bury:* Brown; Howard, Kennedy, Gore, Hilton P., Cruickshank, Madden, Butler, Johnson, Jakub, Hilton M. (Mullen).
*Tranmere R:* Endersby; Mungall, Burgess (Craven), Mountfield, Bramhall, Williams, Hamilton, Hutchinson, Kerr, Brown, Griffiths.


**Carlisle U (0) 3** *(Robson, Beardsley, Bannon)*

**Darlington (0) 1** *(Smith)* 4582

*Carlisle U:* Swinburne; Parker, Rushbury, Haigh, Ashurst, Larkin, Crabbe, Robson, Lee, Beardsley, Staniforth (Bannon).
*Darlington:* Cuff; Kamara, Mitchell (Stalker), Smith, Skipper, Speedie, Hawker, McLean, Wicks, Hamilton, Walsh.


**Gillingham (0) 1** *(Bowman)*

**Plymouth Arg (0) 0** 7370

*Gillingham:* Hillyard; Sharpe, Ford, Bruce, Weatherly, Bowman, Powell, Tydeman, White, Lee (Duncan), Price.
*Plymouth Arg:* Crudgington; Nisbet, McCartney, Harrison, Phillipson-Masters, Cooper, Hodges, Cook (Dennis), Sims, Phillips, Rogers.


**Huddersfield T (1) 5** *(Robins, Lillis, Laverick 2, Brown)*

**Workington (0) 0** 7305

*Huddersfield T:* Taylor; Brown, Purdie, Lillis (Fletcher), Sutton, Hanvey, Laverick, Wilson, Austin, Robins, Cowling.
*Workington:* Fisher; Hill, Kisby, Reach, Roberts, Williams, Diamond, Smith, Gill, Innes, Harris (Armstrong).


**Hull C (1) 2** *aet* *(Whitehurst, Swann)*

**Rochdale (0) 2** *(Burke, Esser)* 4063

*Hull C:* Norman; McNeil, Booth, Roberts D., Deacy, Roberts G., Marwood, McClaren, Whitehurst, Mutrie (Norrie), Swann.
*Rochdale:* Poole; Cooper, Snookes, Dolan, Burke, Taylor, Esser, Weir, Hilditch, Wellings, Martinez.

**Northampton T (5) 6** *(Gage 2, Sandy, Carlton, Phillips, Mahoney)*

**Weymouth (0) 2** *(Finnigan 2)*     2613

*Northampton T:* Poole; Taylor, Saxby, Brady, Gage, Sandy, Carlton, Buchanan, Heeley, Phillips, Mahoney.
*Weymouth:* Roberts; Lawrence, Morrell, Elliott, Merrick, Paterson (Finnigan), McCafferty, Pearson, Iannone, Dove, Borthwick.


**Runcorn (1) 1** *(Seddon)*

**Burnley (1) 2** *(McGee 2)*     5500

*Runcorn:* Parker; Rutter, Scott, Edwards, Seddon, Crompton, Smith, Kelly, Fraser, Jones, Joel (Parry).
*Burnley:* Stevenson; Laws, Wharton, Cassidy, Overson, Phelan, Dobson, Steven, Hamilton, McGee, Young.


**Sutton (0) 2** *(Rogers, Rains J.)*

**Bishop's Stortford (1) 1** *(Clarke)*     2100

*Sutton:* Collyer; Cooper, Green, Rains J., Rains T., Stephens, Rogers, Pritchard, Joyce, McCombe, Sunnucks.
*Bishop's Stortford:* Moore; Lawrence, Baldry, Smith, Bradford, Avery, Worrell, Knapman, Radford, Clarke, Sullivan.


**Wycombe W (0) 2** *(Kennedy, Glynn)*

**Hendon (0) 0**     2507

*Wycombe W:* Lester; Birdseye, Borg, Toll, Vircavs, Kennedy, West (Wilson), Dell, Glynn, Long, Jacobs.
*Hendon:* Smart; Brannigan (Simpson), Hand, Deadman, Bennett, Murphy, Sylvester, Gough, Folan, Currie, Drummy.


**25 NOV**

**Hartlepool U (0) 1** *(Newton)*

**Wigan Ath (0) 0**     3739

*Hartlepool U:* Burleigh; Brown, Stimpson, Hogan, Bird, Linighan, Linacre J., Newton, Linacre P. (Houchen), Sweeney, Johnson.
*Wigan Ath:* Tunks; Cribley, Weston, Wignall (Glenn), Methven, Bradd, Sheldon, Barrow, Quinn, Houghton, Evans.


**Millwall (2) 3 aet** *(Allardyce, Chatterton, Hayes)*

**Portsmouth (0) 2** *(Tait, Hemmerman)*     6842

*Millwall:* Gleasure; Martin, Warman, Chatterton, Allardyce, Slough, Hayes, Massey (Dibble), McKenna, Horrix, West.
*Portsmouth:* Knight; McLaughlin, Bryant, Doyle, Aizlewood, Rollings, Hemmerman, Barnard, Cropley (Rodgers), Tait, Crown.


**Torquay U (0) 1** *(Lawrence)*

**Bristol C (0) 2** *(Mann 2)*     4334

*Torquay U:* O'Keefe; Jones, Pethard, Brown, Wilson, Larmour, Bowker, Lawrence, Cooper, Rioch, Sermanni.
*Bristol C:* Moller; Stevens, Williams, Aitken, Rodgers, Boyle, Tainton, Mann, Harford, Devine, Musker.


**Yeovil (0) 0** *aet*

**Dagenham (0) 1** *(Stewart)*     3816

*Yeovil:* Langley; Scott, Ritchie, Payne, Giles, Beck, Griffiths, Platt, Green (Ward), Bell, Brown.
*Dagenham:* Huttley; Wade, Scales, Stein, Dunwell, Stewart, Brown, Ragan (Maycock), Burton, Francis, Gibson.


**30 NOV**

**Port Vale (0) 0** *aet*

**Lincoln C (0) 0**     4769

*Port Vale:* Harrison; Tartt, Bromage, Hunter, Sproson, Bowles, Chamberlain N., Moss, Greenhoff, Armstrong, Chamberlain M.
*Lincoln C:* Felgate; Turner R., Turner W., Cockerill, Peake, Thompson S., Shipley, Carr, Cammack, Cunningham, Gilbert.


## FIRST ROUND SECOND REPLAY

**30 NOV**

**Hull C (0) 1** *aet (McClaren)*

**Rochdale (0) 0**     3628

At Leeds
*Hull C:* Norman; McNeil, Booth, Roberts D., Deacy, Roberts G., Marwood, McClaren, Whitehurst, Mutrie, Swann.
*Rochdale:* Poole; Cooper, Weir, Dolan, Burke, Taylor, Esser, O'Loughlin, Hilditch, Wellings, Martinez.


**2 DEC**

**Port Vale (0) 2** *(Armstrong, Chamberlain N.)*

**Lincoln C (0) 0**     5373

*Port Vale:* Harrison; Tartt, Bromage, Hunter, Sproson, Bowles, Chamberlain N., Moss, Greenhoff, Armstrong, Chamberlain M.
*Lincoln C:* Felgate; Turner P., Turner W., Cockerill, Peake, Thompson S., Shipley, Carr (Hobson), Cammack, Cunningham, Gilbert.


## SECOND ROUND

**12 DEC**

**Chesterfield (0) 0**

**Huddersfield T (1) 1** *(Cowling)*     8609

*Chesterfield:* Turner; Stirk, O'Neill, Wilson, Green, Pollard, Windridge, Henderson, Bonnyman, Kowalski (Salmons), Walker.
*Huddersfield T:* Taylor; Brown, Burke, Lillis, Sutton, Hanvey, Stanton, Kennedy, Fletcher, Robins, Cowling (Purdie).


**Doncaster R (2) 3** *(Warboys 2, Little)*

**Penrith (0) 0**     6282

*Doncaster:* Boyd; Russell, Cooper, Snodin I., Lally, Dowd, Pugh, Douglas (Nimmo), Warboys, Little, Lister.
*Penrith:* Monkhouse; Wilson, Glover (Skelton), Carruthers A., Carruthers R., Coulthard, Simpson, Sawyers, Fell, Gash, Armstrong.


**Dorchester (1) 1** *(Thorne)*

**AFC Bournemouth (0) 1** *(Funnell)*     5200

*Dorchester:* Hobson; Townsend, Flay, Dominey, Poore, Ames, Chutter, Steele, Senior, Miller, Thorne.
*AFC Bournemouth:* Leigh; Heffernan, Sulley, Smith, Compton, Impey, Dawtry, Crawford, Funnell, Spackman, Williams.


**York C (0) 0**

**Altrincham (0) 0**     3786

*York C:* Blackburn; Senior, Czuczman, Kay, Flood, Pollard, Hood, Crosby, Bentham, Walwyn, Ford.
*Altrincham:* Connaughton; Gardner, Davison, Goulding, Owens, Crossley, Heathcote, Whitbread, Johnson, Rogers, Howard.

**15 DEC**

**Aldershot** (1) 2 *(Brodie, McDonald)*

**Oxford U** (2) 2 *(Cassells 2)*                        3123

*Aldershot:* Johnson; Edwards, Wooler, Scott, Bennett, Jopling, Lucas (French), McDonald, Garwood, Brodie, Robinson.
*Oxford U:* Burton; Doyle, Fogg, Jeffrey, Briggs, Shotton, Jones, Foley (Brock), Cassells, Thomas, Smithers.

**Barnet** (1) 2 *(Foody, Barnes)*

**Wycombe W** (0) 0                        2015

*Barnet:* Phillips; Pittaway, Pearce, Millett, Campbell, Townsend, Robinson, Watson, Sargent, Barnes, Foody (Voyce).
*Wycombe W:* Lester; Birdseye, Borg, Toll (Wilson), Vircavs, Jacobs, Kennedy, Davies, Glynn, Long, Dell.

**Bristol C** (1) 3 *(Tainton, Harford 2)*

**Northampton T** (0) 0                        2901

*Bristol C:* Moller; Stevens, Williams, Aitken, Rodgers, Boyle, Tainton, Mann, Chandler, Harford, Devine.
*Northampton T:* Poole; Saunders, Saxby, Brady, Gage, Sandy, Coffill, Buchanan, Heeley, Phillips, Mahoney (Alexander).

**Enfield** (0) 4 *(Turner, Ironton, Oliver, Waite)*

**Wimbledon** (1) 1 *(Brown pen)*                        3000

*Enfield:* Jacobs; Barrett, Tone, Jennings, Waite, Ironton, Ashford, Taylor, Turner, Oliver, King.
*Wimbledon:* Beasant; Clement, Brown, Fishenden, Morris, Suddaby, Ketteridge, Leslie, Lazarus, Downes, Joseph.

**Gillingham** (0) 1 *(White pen)*

**Barking** (0) 1 *(Hillman)*                        4363

*Gillingham:* Hillyard; Bowman, Ford, Sitton, Young, Duncan, Powell, Tydeman, White, Lee (Ovard), Price.
*Barking:* Hitchcock; Anderson, Cooper, Davy, Watt, White, Jacks, Makin, Hillman, Gibbs (Page), Dormer.

**Swindon T** (1) 2 *(Carter, Pritchard)*

**Sutton U** (1) 1 *(Joyce)*                        2890

*Swindon T:* Allan; Baddeley, Williams, Hughes, Lewis, Graham, Emmanuel, Carter, Rowland, Rideout, Pritchard.
*Sutton U:* Collyer; Cooper, Green, Rains J., Rains T., Stephens, Rogers, Pritchard, Joyce, Brindle, Sunnucks.

**16 DEC**

**Brentford** (1) 1 *(Roberts)*

**Colchester U** (1) 1 *(Allinson)*                        5550

*Brentford:* McKellar; Salman, Tucker, McNichol, Whitehead, Hurlock, Kamara, Bowen, Johnson, Bowles, Roberts.
*Colchester U:* Walker; Cook, Coleman, Leslie, Wignall, Wright, Rowles, Bremner, Osborne, McDonough, Allinson.

**30 DEC**

**Dagenham** (1) 1 *(Stein)*

**Millwall** (1) 2 *(Allardyce, Chatterton)*                        4826

*Dagenham:* Danson; Wade, Scales, Dunwell, Elley, Stewart, Francis (Maycock), Kidd, Burton, Stein, Gibson.
*Millwall:* Gleasure; Roberts, Warman, Chatterton, Allardyce, Slough, Dibble, Massey, Bartley, Neal, West.

**2 JAN**

**Bury** (0) 1 *(Madden)*

**Burnley** (0) 1 *(Taylor)*                        9200

*Bury:* Brown; Constantine, Kennedy, Gore, Hilton P., Cruickshank, Madden, Butler, Johnson, Jakub, Hilton M. (Mullen).
*Burnley:* Stevenson; Laws, Wharton, Cassidy, Overson, Dixon, Dobson, Steven, Hamilton, Taylor, Young.

**Carlisle U** (0) 0

**Bishop Auckland** (0) 0                        5656

Abandoned after 69 minutes

**Crewe Alex** (1) 1 *(Haslegrave)*

**Scunthorpe U** (1) 3 *(Cowling, Telfer, Dall)*                        2729

*Crewe Alex:* Mulhearn; Lewis, Bowers, Salathiel, Scott, Griffiths (Keighley), Haslegrave, Callaghan, Chesters, Palios, Williams.
*Scunthorpe U:* Neenan; Davy, Pilling, Keeley, Dall, Oates (Lambert), Telfer, O'Berg, Cowling, Moss, Stewart.

**Hereford U** (1) 1 *(Laidlaw)*

**Fulham** (0) 0                        4617

*Hereford U:* Brand; Price, Bray, Hicks, Dobson, Spiring (McGrellis), Harvey, Laidlaw, Phillips, Showers, White.
*Fulham:* Peyton; Hopkins, Strong, O'Driscoll, Brown, Gale, Davies, Wilson, Coney, O'Sullivan, Lewington.

**Kettering** (0) 0

**Blackpool** (1) 3 *(Harrison, Wann, Morris)*                        4439

*Kettering:* Tingay; McIntosh, Forster, Clarke, Suddards, Haverson, Phipps, Evans, Atkins, Duggan (Murphy), Shelton.
*Blackpool:* Hesford; Simmonite, Pashley, Blair, Wann, McEwan, Morris, Noble, Bamber, Hockaday, Harrison.

**Peterborough U** (1) 2 *(Cooke, Chard)*

**Walsall** (0) 1 *(Butler og)*                        5421

*Peterborough U:* Freeman; Butler, Collins, Gynn, Smith, Rodaway, Syrett, Kellock (Massey), Cooke, Hodgson, Chard.
*Walsall:* Green; Macken, Mower, Beech, Serella, Hart (Buckley), Rees, Loveridge, Penn, Caswell, O'Kelly.

**Port Vale** (0) 4 *(Moss 2, Chamberlain N. 2)*

**Stockport Co** (0) 1 *(Smith)*                        4478

*Port Vale:* Harrison; Tartt, Bromage, Hunter, Sproson, Bowles, Chamberlain N., Moss, Greenhoff, Armstrong, Chamberlain M.
*Stockport Co:* Lloyd; Rutter, Sherlock, Fowler, Thorpe, Vaughan, Williams, Park, Power, Smith, Coyle.

**4 JAN**

**Hull C** (0) 2 *(Marwood, Mutrie)*

**Hartlepool U** (0) 0                        4975

*Hull C:* Norman; Swann, McNeil, Roberts D., Deacy, Booth, McClaren, Marwood, Roberts G., Norrie, Mutrie.
*Hartlepool U:* Burleigh; Sweeney, Brown, Bainbridge, Linacre P., Linighan, Linacre J., Kerr, Houchen, Johnson, Hampton.

**9 JAN**

**Carlisle U (0) 1** *(Lee)*

**Bishop Auckland (0) 0**      4536

At Workington
*Carlisle U:* Swinburne; Parker, Haigh, Beardsley, Ashurst, Larkin, Crabbe, Robson, Lee, Bannon, Staniforth.
*Bishop Auckland:* Owers; Newton M., Rutherford, Gibbon, Hills, Nattress, Parnaby, Richardson, Foster (Collingwood), Newton D., Cross.


**SECOND ROUND REPLAYS**

**15 DEC**

**AFC Bournemouth (1) 2** *aet (Crawford, Williams)*

**Dorchester (1) 1** *(Steele)*      6766

*AFC Bournemouth:* Leigh; Heffernan, Sulley, Smith, Compton, Impey, Dawtry (Dawkins), Crawford, Funnell, Spackman, Williams.
*Dorchester:* Hobson; Townsend, Flay, Dominey, Poore, Ames, Chutter, Steele, Senior, Miller, Thorne.


**30 DEC**

**Colchester U (1) 1** *(McNichol og)*

**Brentford (0) 0**      5532

*Colchester U:* Walker; Cook, Coleman, Leslie, Wignall, Wright, Rowles, Bremner, Osborne, McDonough, Allinson.
*Brentford:* McKellar; Salman, Tucker, McNichol, Whitehead, Hurlock, Kamara, Bowen, Johnson, Bowles, Booker.


**Oxford U (2) 4** *(Cassells 3, Thomas)*

**Aldershot (1) 2** *(Robinson, French)*      5569

*Oxford U:* Burton; Fogg, Smithers, Jeffrey, Briggs, Shotton, Lythgoe, Berry, Cassells, Thomas, Jones.
*Aldershot:* Johnson; Edwards, Wooler, Scott, Bennett, Jopling, Wanklyn (French), McDonald, Garwood, Brodie, Robinson.


**2 JAN**

**Altrincham (2) 4** *(Goulding, Rogers, Whitbread 2)*

**York C (1) 3** *(Pollard 2, Walwyn)*      3088

*Altrincham:* Connaughton; Gardner (Bailey), Davison, Goulding, Owens, Crossley, Heathcote, Whitbread, Johnson, Rogers, Howard.
*York C:* Blackburn; Senior, Flood, Hood, Dawson, Kay, Pollard, Crosby, Walwyn, Ford, Bentham.


**Barking (0) 1** *aet (Anderson)*

**Gillingham (0) 3** *(Bruce, Price, Powell)*      4779

At Gillingham
*Barking:* Hitchcock; Cooper, Watts, Campbell, Davy, Jacks (White), Makin, Anderson, Key, Dormer, Hillman.
*Gillingham:* Hillyard; Sharpe, Adams, Bruce, Weatherly, Duncan, Powell, Tydeman, White, Ovard, Price.


**4 JAN**

**Burnley (1) 2** *aet (Hamilton, Steven)*

**Bury (0) 1** *(Johnson)*      9108

*Burnley:* Stevenson; Laws, Wharton, Cassidy, Overson, Dixon, Dobson, Steven, Hamilton, Taylor, Young.
*Bury:* Brown; Constantine, Kennedy, Gore, Hilton P., Cruickshank, Madden, Butler, Johnson, Jakub, Hilton M. (Mullen).


**THIRD ROUND**

**2 JAN**

**Barnet (0) 0**

**Brighton & HA (0) (0)**      4800

*Barnet:* Phillips; Pittaway, Pearce, Millett, Campbell, Townsend, Robinson, Watson, Sargent, Barnes, Westwood.
*Brighton & HA:* Moseley; Shanks, Nelson, Grealish, Foster, Gatting, Case, Ritchie, Robinson, McNab (Stevens), Thomas.


**Birmingham C (1) 2** *(Worthington pen, Curbishley)*

**Ipswich T (1) 3** *(Brazil 2, Wark)*      17,236

*Birmingham C:* Coton; Langan, Dennis, Curbishley (Handysides), Broadhurst, Todd, Dillon, Worthington, Evans, Gemmill, Van Mierlo.
*Ipswich T:* Cooper; Burley, McCall, Mills, Osman, Steggles, Wark, Muhren, Mariner, Brazil, Gates.


**Bolton W (2) 3** *(Gowling, Foster, Thompson)*

**Derby Co (0) 1** *(Powell B.)*      9534

*Bolton W:* McDonagh; Whitworth, Bennett, Henry, Jones, McElhinney, Chandler, Foster, Gowling, Langley, Thompson.
*Derby Co:* Jones; Coop, Richards, Powell S., Money, Buckley, Dalziel, Powell B., Clayton, Swindlehurst, Gamble (Emson).


**AFC Bournemouth (0) 0**

**Oxford U (0) 2** *(Cassells, Thomas)*      8989

*AFC Bournemouth:* Leigh; Heffernan, Sulley, Dawkins, Brignull (Smith), Impey, Spackman, Crawford, Funnell, Goddard, Williams.
*Oxford U:* Burton; Fogg, Smithers, Jeffrey, Briggs, Shotton, Lythgoe, Berry, Cassells, Thomas, Jones.


**Coventry C (2) 3** *(Hunt 2, Hateley)*

**Sheffield W (1) 1** *(McCulloch)*      14,213

*Coventry C:* Blyth; Thomas, Barnes, Jacobs, Dyson, Gillespie, Bodak, Daly, Hateley, Kaiser (Hormantschuk), Hunt.
*Sheffield W:* Bolder; Sterland, Williamson, Smith, Shirtliff, Taylor (Mellor), Megson, Mirocevic, Bannister, McCulloch, Curran.


**Doncaster R (2) 2** *(Reilly og, Warboys)*

**Cambridge U (1) 1** *(Taylor)*      6741

*Doncaster R:* Boyd; Russell, Cooper, Lister, Swan, Dowd, Pugh, Dawson, Warboys, Lally, Little.
*Cambridge U:* Key; Donaldson, Murray, Christie (Smith), Fallon, Streete, Taylor, Spriggs, Mayo, Reilly, Finney.


**Enfield (1) 2** *(Ironton, Oliver)*

**Crystal Palace (2) 3** *(Price, Hilaire 2)*      3467

*Enfield:* Jacobs; Barrett, Waite, Jennings, Tone, Taylor, Ching, Oliver, Ironton, Ashford, Holmes.
*Crystal Palace:* Barron; Hinshelwood, Cannon, Wicks, Boulter, Murphy, Price, Hilaire, Smillie, Walsh (Lovell), Mabbutt.


**Leicester C (2) 3** *(Young 2, Lineker)*

**Southampton (1) 1** *(Keegan)*      20,589

*Leicester C:* Wallington; Williams, Friar, Peake, May, O'Neill, Lynex, Lineker, Young (Melrose), Wilson, Kelly.
*Southampton:* Katalinic; Golac, Holmes, Williams, Nicholl (Wallace), Waldron, Keegan, Channon, Moran, Armstrong, Ball.

**Luton T (1) 2** *(Moss* pen, *Horton)*

**Swindon T (0) 1** *(Emmanuel)* 9488

*Luton T:* Findlay; Stephens, Aizlewood, Horton, Goodyear, Donaghy, Hill, Stein, White, Fuccillo, Moss.
*Swindon T:* Allan; Baddeley, Williams, Henry, Lewis, Stroud, Emmanuel, Carter, Rowland, Rideout, Pritchard.

**Manchester C (2) 3** *(Francis 2, McDonald)*

**Cardiff C (1) 1** *(Maddy)* 31,547

*Manchester C:* Corrigan; Ranson, McDonald, Reid, Bond, Caton, Gow, Reeves, Francis, Hartford, Hutchison.
*Cardiff C:* Healey; Grapes, Dwyer, Maddy, Pontin, Bennett G., Bennett D., Micallef, Stevens, Hughes (Sugrue), Lewis.

**Nottingham F (1) 1** *(Proctor)*

**Wrexham (0) 3** *(Dowman, Vinter, McNeil)* 15,649

*Nottingham F:* Shilton; Anderson, Gunn, Needham, Young, Walsh, Rober (McGovern), Wallace, Ward, Proctor, Robertson.
*Wrexham:* Niedzwiecki; Jones, Bater, Dowman, Cegielski, Ronson, Fox, McNeil (Hill), Edwards, Vinter, Carrodus.

**Orient (0) 1** *(Moores)*

**Charlton Ath (0) 0** 6511

*Orient:* Day; Hughton, Foster, Taylor, Gray, Fisher, Godfrey, Silkman, Moores, Margerrison, Jennings (Blackhall).
*Charlton Ath:* Johns; Naylor, Ferns, Gritt, McAllister, Phillips, Lansdowne (Elliott), Walsh, Hales, Berry, Robinson.

**QPR (0) 1** *(Stainrod)*

**Middlesbrough (1) 1** *(Thomson)* 12,100

*QPR:* Hucker; Neill, Fenwick, Waddock, Howe, Roeder, Micklewhite, Flanagan, Stewart, Stainrod, Gillard.
*Middlesbrough:* Platt; Nattrass, Bolton, Ross, Baxter, McAndrew, Cochrane, Otto, Hodgson, Shearer, Thomson.

**Rotherham U (0) 1** *(Towner)*

**Sunderland (0) 1** *(Rowell)* 11,649

*Rotherham U:* Mountford; Forrest, Taylor, Rhodes, Stancliffe, Green, Towner, Gooding, Moore, Fern, Henson.
*Sunderland:* Siddall; Hinnigan, Pickering, Hindmarch, Clarke, Elliott, Buckley, McCoist (Venison), Ritchie, Rowell, Cummins.

**Stoke C (0) 0**

**Norwich C (1) 1** *(Jack)* 12,805

*Stoke C:* Fox; Evans, Hampton (Johnson), Dodd, O'Callaghan, Doyle, Griffiths, Heath, Chapman, Bracewell, Ursem.
*Norwich C:* Woods; Symonds, Downs, McGuire, Walford, Watson, Mendham, Jack, Deehan, Bertschin, Bennett.

**Swansea C (0) 0**

**Liverpool (2) 4** *(Hansen, Rush 2, Lawrenson)* 24,179

*Swansea C:* Davies; Stanley, Marustik (Thompson), Rajkovic, Irwin, Stevenson, Curtis, James R., James L., Mahoney, Latchford.
*Liverpool:* Grobbelaar; Neal, Lawrenson, Thompson, Whelan, Hansen, Dalglish, Kennedy, Rush, McDermott, Souness.

**Tottenham H (1) 1** *(Crooks)*

**Arsenal (0) 0** 38,241

*Tottenham H:* Clemence; Hughton, Miller, Perryman, Villa, Roberts, Ardiles, Falco, Galvin, Hoddle, Crooks.
*Arsenal:* Jennings (Meade); Robson, Sansom, Talbot, O'Leary, Whyte, Hollins, Sunderland, Davis, Nicholas, Rix.

**Watford (1) 1** *(Lohman)*

**Manchester U (0) 0** 26,104

*Watford:* Sherwood; Rice (Armstrong), Pritchett, Taylor, Terry, Bolton, Callaghan, Blissett, Jenkins, Barnes, Lohman.
*Manchester U:* Bailey; Gidman, Albiston, Wilkins, Moran, Buchan, Robson, Birtles, Stapleton, Moses (Macari), McIlroy.

**WBA (1) 3** *(MacKenzie, King* pen, *Whitehead)*

**Blackburn R (0) 2** *(Garner 2)* 17,540

*WBA:* Grew; Batson, Statham, Whitehead, Wile, Robertson, Jol, Monaghan, Regis, King, MacKenzie.
*Blackburn R:* Gennoe; Branagan, Rathbone, Arnott, Keeley, Fazackerley, Miller, Stonehouse, Bell, Garner, Brotherston.

**West Ham U (1) 2** *(Bonds, Cross)*

**Everton (0) 1** *(Eastoe)* 24,431

*West Ham U:* Parkes; Stewart, Lampard, Bonds, Martin, Devonshire, Neighbour, Goddard (Pearson), Cross, Brooking, Pike.
*Everton:* Southall; Stevens, Ratcliffe, Higgins, Lyons, Kendall, Richardson, Ross (O'Keefe), Sharp, Eastoe, Lodge.

**Wolverhampton W (1) 1** *(Gray)*

**Leeds U (1) 3** *(Hamson, Hird, Gray E.)* 20,923

*Wolverhampton W:* Bradshaw; Palmer, Parkin, Daniel, Gallagher, Berry, Birch, Eves, Gray, Richards, Brazier.
*Leeds U:* Lukic; Cherry, Gray F., Stevenson, Hart, Burns, Gray E., Graham, Butterworth, Hamson, Hird.

**4 JAN**

**Newcastle U (1) 1** *(Varadi)*

**Colchester U (0) 1** *(Wignall)* 16,977

*Newcastle U:* Carr; Brownlie, Saunders, Trewick (Todd), Carney, Haddock, Shoulder, Martin, Varadi, Wharton, Waddle.
*Colchester U:* Walker; Cook, Coleman (Adcock), Leslie, Wignall, Wright, Rowles, Bremner, Osborne, McDonough, Allinson.

**5 JAN**

**Barnsley (0) 0**

**Blackpool (1) 2** *(Bamber, Morris)* 13,429

*Barnsley:* Horn; Joyce, Chambers, Glavin, Banks, McCarthy, Evans, Riley (Campbell), Aylott, McHale, Barrowclough.
*Blackpool:* Hesford; Simmonite, Pashley, Blair, Wann, McEwan, Morris, Noble, Bamber, Hockaday, Harrison.

**Gillingham (1) 2** *(Kemp, White* pen)

**Oldham Ath (0) 1** *(Heaton* pen) 9476

*Gillingham:* Hillyard; Sharpe, Adams, Bruce, Weatherly (Sitton), Duncan, Powell, Tydeman, White, Kemp, Price.
*Oldham Ath:* McDonnell; Hoolickin (Nuttall), Ryan, Keegan, Clements, Futcher, McDonough, Heaton, Steel, Palmer, Atkinson.

**Millwall (1) 1** *(Neal)*

**Grimsby T (0) 6** *(Cumming 2, Brolly, Drinkell 2, Whymark)* 5823

*Millwall:* Gleasure; Massey, Roberts, Chatterton, Allardyce, Slough, Dibble, Anderson, Bartley, Neal, West.
*Grimsby T:* Batch; Moore D., Crombie, Waters, Wigginton, Moore K., Brolly, Whymark, Drinkell, Mitchell, Cumming (Ford).

**Notts Co (0) 0**

**Aston Villa (4) 6** *(Richards og, Shaw, Geddis 3, Cowans pen)* 12,321

*Notts Co:* Leonard; Benjamin, O'Brien, Hunt, Lahtinen (Christie), Richards, Chiedozie, Masson, Hooks, Goodwin, Mair.
*Aston Villa:* Rimmer; Swain, Gibson, Evans, Williams, Mortimer, Bremner, Shaw, Geddis, Cowans, Morley.

**Shrewsbury T (0) 1** *(Bates)*

**Port Vale (0) 0** 7230

*Shrewsbury T:* Wardle; MacLaren, Johnson, Cross, Griffin, Keay, Tong, Dungworth, Atkins, McNally (Petts), Bates.
*Port Vale:* Harrison; Tartt, Bromage, Hunter, Sproson, Bowles, Chamberlain N., Higgins, Greenhoff, Armstrong, Chamberlain M.

**6 JAN**

**Peterborough U (0) 0**

**Bristol C (0) 1** *(Chandler)* 6811

*Peterborough U:* Freeman; Butler, Collins, Gynn, Smith, Rodaway, Syrett, Kellock, Cooke, Massey (Cliss), Chard.
*Bristol C:* Moller; Stevens, Williams, Aitken, Boyle, Nicholls, Tainton, Mann, Chandler, Harford, Musker.

**Scunthorpe U (0) 1** *(Stewart)*

**Hereford U (1) 1** *(Showers)* 3781

*Scunthorpe U:* Neenan; Davy, Pilling, Keeley, Dall, Oates, Telfer, O'Berg, Cowling, Moss, Stewart.
*Hereford U:* Brand; Price, Sullivan, Hicks, Dobson, McGrellis, Harvey, Laidlaw, Phillips (Lane), Showers, White.

**18 JAN**

**Burnley (1) 6** *(Taylor 2, Steven, Hamilton 3)*

**Altrincham (0) 1** *(Howard)* 10,174

*Burnley:* Stevenson; Laws, Wharton, Cassidy, Overson, Dixon, Dobson, Steven, Hamilton, Taylor, Young.
*Altrincham:* Connaughton; Gardner, Davison, Goulding, Allan, King, Heathcote, Whitbread, Johnson, Crossley, Howard.

**Chelsea (0) 0**

**Hull C (0) 0** 14,899

*Chelsea:* Francis; Wilkins, Hutchings, Hales, Droy, Pates, Mayes (Rhoades-Brown), Bumstead, Lee, Walker, Fillery.
*Hull C:* Davies; McNeil, Booth, Roberts D., Deacy, Roberts G., Marwood, Ferguson, Whitehurst, Mutrie, Swann.

**23 JAN**

**Carlisle U (0) 2** *(Bannon, Robson)*

**Huddersfield T (3) 3** *(Fletcher 3)* 6345

*Carlisle U:* Swinburne; Parker, Rushbury, Houghton, Ashurst, Larkin (Haigh), Coughlin, Robson, Bannon, Beardsley, Staniforth.
*Huddersfield T:* Taylor; Brown, Burke, Stanton, Sutton, Hanvey, Lillis, Kennedy, Fletcher, Austin, Cowling.

**5 JAN**

**Brighton & HA (0) 3** *(Thomas, Case, McNab pen)*

**Barnet (0) 1** *(Sargent)* 15,884

*Brighton & HA:* Moseley; Shanks, Nelson, Grealish, Foster, Gatting, Case, Ritchie, Robinson (Ryan), McNab, Thomas.
*Barnet:* Phillips; Pittaway, Pearce, Phillips, Campbell, Townsend, Robinson (Voyce), Watson, Sargent, Barnes, Westwood.

## THIRD ROUND REPLAYS

**18 JAN**

**Colchester U (1) 3** *aet (Cook, Allinson 2 [2 pens])*

**Newcastle (2) 4** *(Waddle, Saunders, Brownlie, Varadi)* 7505

*Colchester U:* Walker; Cook, Rowles, Leslie (Coleman), Wignall, Wright, Adcock, Bremner, Osborne, McDonough, Allinson.
*Newcastle U:* Carr; Brownlie, Saunders, Trewick, Carney, Haddock, Martin, Todd, Varadi, Wharton, Waddle.

**Middlesbrough (0) 2** *aet (Otto, Thomson pen)*

**QPR (2) 3** *(Stainrod 2, Neill)* 14,819

*Middlesbrough:* Platt; Nattrass, Bolton, Ross, Baxter, McAndrew, Cochrane, Otto, Hodgson, MacDonald (Woof), Thomson.
*QPR:* Hucker; Fenwick, Gillard, Waddock, Howe, Roeder, Allen, Currie (Neill), Flanagan, Stainrod, Gregory.

**Sunderland (0) 1** *(Buckley)*

**Rotherham U (0) 0** 14,863

*Sunderland:* Siddall; Nicholl, Pickering, Hindmarch, Clarke, Elliott, Buckley, McCoist, Ritchie, Rowell, Cummins.
*Rotherham U:* Mountford; Hughes, Taylor, Rhodes, Stancliffe, Green, Towner, Gooding, Moore, Alexander, Henson (McEwan).

**20 JAN**

**Hereford U (1) 4** *(Showers, Harvey, Overson, Phillips)*

**Scunthorpe U (0) 1** *(Grimes)* 4025

*Hereford U:* Brand; Price, Sullivan, Overson, Dobson, McGrellis, Harvey, Laidlaw, Phillips, Showers, White.
*Scunthorpe U:* Neenan; Hughes, Grimes, Keeley, Dall, Oates, Telfer, O'Berg, Cowling, Moss, Stewart (Pilling).

**21 JAN**

**Hull C (0) 0**

**Chelsea (0) 2** *(Mayes, Bumstead)* 13,238

*Hull C:* Davies; McNeil, Booth, Roberts D., Deacy, Roberts G., Marwood, Ferguson, Whitehurst (Flounders), Mutrie, Swann.
*Chelsea:* Francis; Locke, Hutchings, Hales, Chivers, Pates, Mayes, Bumstead, Lee, Walker, Fillery.

**FOURTH ROUND**

**23 JAN**

**Blackpool (0) 0**

**QPR (0) 0** 10,227

*Blackpool:* Hesford; Simmonite (Deary), Pashley, Blair, Wann, McEwan, Morris, Noble, Bamber, Hockaday, Harrison.
*QPR:* Hucker; Fenwick, Gillard, Waddock, Howe, Roeder, Allen, Currie, Flanagan, Stainrod, Gregory.

**Brighton & HA (0) 0**

**Oxford U (2) 3** *(Cassells, Foley 2)* 17,898

*Brighton & HA:* Moseley; Shanks, Nelson, Foster, Gatting, Grealish, Ryan, Ritchie, Smith, McNab, Thomas.
*Oxford U:* Burton; Doyle, Fogg, Jeffrey, Briggs, Shotton, Jones, Foley, Cassells, Thomas, Smithers.

**Bristol C (0) 0**

**Aston Villa (0) 1** *(Shaw)* 20,279

*Bristol C:* Moller; Stevens, Williams, Aitken, Boyle, Sweeney, Tainton, Mann, Garland (Chandler), Harford, Musker.
*Aston Villa:* Rimmer; Swain, Gibson, Evans, Williams, Mortimer, Blair, Shaw, Withe, Cowans, Morley.

**Chelsea (0) 0**

**Wrexham (0) 0** 17,226

*Chelsea:* Francis; Locke, Hutchings, Hales, Chivers, Pates, Mayes, Bumstead, Lee, Walker, Fillery.
*Wrexham:* Niedzwiecki; Jones, Bater, Dowman, Cegielski, Ronson, Fox, McNeil, Buxton, Vinter, Carrodus.

**Crystal Palace (1) 1** *(Cannon pen)*

**Bolton W (0) 0** 9719

*Crystal Palace:* Barron; Hinshelwood, Boulter, Murphy, Wicks, Cannon, Brooks, Smillie, Walsh, Mabbutt, Hilaire.
*Bolton W:* McDonagh; Whitworth, Bennett, Henry, Jones, McElhinney, Chandler, Foster, Gowling, Langley (Hoggan), Thompson.

**Gillingham (0) 0**

**WBA (0) 1** *(Statham)* 16,000

*Gillingham:* Hillyard; Sharpe, Adams, Bruce, Sitton, Duncan, Powell, Tydeman, White, Kemp, Price.
*WBA:* Grew; Batson, Statham, Brown, Wile, Robertson, Jol, Whitehead, Regis, Owen, MacKenzie.

**Hereford U (0) 0**

**Leicester C (1) 1** *(May)* 10,602

*Hereford U:* Brand; Price, Sullivan, Hicks, Dobson, Musial, Harvey, Laidlaw, Phillips, Showers, White.
*Leicester C:* Wallington; Williams, Friar, Peake, May, O'Neill, Lynex, Lineker, Young, Wilson, Robson (Melrose).

**Luton T (0) 0**

**Ipswich T (0) 3** *(Brazil, Gates 2)* 20,188

*Luton T:* Findlay; Stephens, Aizlewood (Antic), Horton, Goodyear, Donaghy, Hill, Stein, White, Fuccillo, Moss.
*Ipswich T:* Cooper; Burley, McCall, Mills, Osman, Butcher (O'Callaghan), Wark, Muhren, Mariner, Brazil, Gates.

**Manchester C (0) 1** *(Bond pen)*

**Coventry C (2) 3** *(Hunt, Hateley, Bodak)* 31,276

*Manchester C:* Corrigan; Gow (Kinsey), McDonald, Reid, Bond, Caton, Hutchison, Reeves, Francis, Hartford, Power.
*Coventry C:* Blyth; Hormantschuk, Barnes, Thomas (Butterworth), Dyson, Gillespie, Bodak, Daly, Thompson, Hateley, Hunt.

**Newcastle U (0) 1** *(Moore K. og)*

**Grimsby T (0) 2** *(Kilmore, Drinkell)* 25,632

*Newcastle U:* Carr; Brownlie, Saunders, Trewick (Shinton), Carney, Haddock, Todd, Martin, Varadi, Wharton, Waddle.
*Grimsby T:* Batch; Moore D., Crombie, Stone, Moore K., Crosby, Ford, Kilmore, Whymark (Drinkell), Mitchell, Beacock.

**Norwich C (1) 2** *(Jack, Watson)*

**Doncaster R (1) 1** *(Dawson)* 17,311

*Norwich C:* Woods; Symonds, Downs, McGuire, Walford, Watson, Mendham, Jack, Deehan, Bertschin, Barham.
*Doncaster:* Humphries; Lally, Cooper, Russell, Lister, Dowd, Pugh, Dawson, Douglas, Snodin G., Little (Snodin I.).

**Shrewsbury T (0) 1** *(Bates)*

**Burnley (0) 0** 7679

*Shrewsbury T:* Wardle; MacLaren, Johnson, Cross (Petts), Griffin, Keay, Tong, Dungworth, Atkins, McNally, Bates.
*Burnley:* Stevenson; Laws, Wharton, Cassidy, Overson, Dixon (Potts), Dobson, Steven, Hamilton, Taylor, Young.

**Sunderland (0) 0**

**Liverpool (2) 3** *(Dalglish 2, Rush)* 28,582

*Sunderland:* Siddall; Nicholl, Pickering, Hindmarch, Clarke (Brown), Elliott, Buckley, McCoist, Ritchie, Rowell, Cummins.
*Liverpool:* Grobbelaar; Neal, Lawrenson, Kennedy A., Whelan, Hansen, Dalglish (Johnson), Lee, Rush, McDermott, Souness.

**Tottenham H (0) 1** *(Crooks)*

**Leeds U (0) 0** 46,126

*Tottenham H:* Clemence; Hughton, Miller, Roberts, Villa, Perryman, Ardiles, Falco (Hazard), Galvin, Hoddle, Crooks.
*Leeds U:* Lukic; Cherry, Gray F., Stevenson (Flynn), Hart, Burns, Gray E., Graham, Butterworth, Hamson, Hird.

**Watford (0) 2** *(Armstrong, Callaghan)*

**West Ham U (0) 0** 27,004

*Watford:* Sherwood; Rice, Pritchett, Blissett, Terry, Bolton, Callaghan, Armstrong, Jenkins (Rostron), Lohman, Barnes.
*West Ham U:* Parkes; Stewart, Lampard, Bonds, Martin, Van der Elst, Neighbour (Pearson), Goddard, Cross, Brooking, Pike.

**26 JAN**

**Huddersfield T (0) 1** *(Austin)*

**Orient (1) 1** *(Moores)* 13,623

*Huddersfield T:* Taylor; Brown, Burke, Stanton, Sutton, Hanvey, Lillis, Kennedy, Fletcher, Austin, Cowling (Purdie).
*Orient:* Day; Foster, Fisher, Taylor, Gray, Osgood, Godfrey, Margerrison, Moores, Silkman, Hallybone.

**FOURTH ROUND REPLAYS**

**26 JAN**

**QPR (2) 5** *(Allen 4, Stainrod pen)*

**Blackpool (0) 1** *(Entwistle)*                    11,712

*QPR:* Hucker; Fenwick, Gillard, Waddock, Howe, Roeder, Allen, Currie, Flanagan (Stewart), Stainrod, Gregory.
*Blackpool:* Hesford; Deary, Pashley, Blair, Wann, Hart, Morris, Noble, Bamber, Hockaday, Harrison (Entwistle).

**Wrexham (0) 1** *aet (McNeil)*

**Chelsea (0) 1** *(Mayes)*                    8655

*Wrexham:* Niedzwiecki; Jones, Bater, Dowman, Cegielski, Ronson, Fox, McNeil, Edwards, Vinter, Carrodus.
*Chelsea:* Francis; Locke, Hutchings, Hales (Rhoades-Brown), Droy, Pates, Mayes, Bumstead, Lee, Walker, Fillery.

**1 FEB**

**Orient (0) 2** *(Foster, Moores)*

**Huddersfield T (0) 0**                    6478

*Orient:* Day; Foster, Fisher, Taylor, Gray, Osgood, Godfrey, Margerrison, Moores, McNeil (Silkman), Hallybone.
*Huddersfield T:* Taylor; Brown, Burke, Stanton (Robins), Sutton, Hanvey, Lillis, Kennedy, Fletcher, Austin, Cowling.

**FOURTH ROUND SECOND REPLAY**

**1 FEB**

**Wrexham (0) 1** *(Vinter)*

**Chelsea (1) 2** *(Droy, Mayes)*                    10,647

*Wrexham:* Niedzwiecki; Jones J., Bater, Dowman, Cegielski, Ronson, Fox, McNeil, Edwards (Jones S.), Vinter, Hunt.
*Chelsea:* Francis; Locke, Hutchings, Nutton, Droy, Pates, Mayes, Bumstead, Lee, Walker, Rhoades-Brown.

**FIFTH ROUND**

**13 FEB**

**Chelsea (1) 2** *(Rhoades-Brown, Lee)*

**Liverpool (0) 0**                    41,422

*Chelsea:* Francis; Locke, Hutchings, Nutton, Droy, Pates, Rhoades-Brown, Hales, Lee, Walker, Fillery.
*Liverpool:* Grobbelaar; Neal, Lawrenson, Kennedy, Whelan, Hansen, Dalglish, Lee, Rush, McDermott (Johnston), Souness.

**Coventry C (1) 4** *(Thompson 2, Hateley 2)*

**Oxford U (0) 0**                    20,251

*Coventry C:* Blyth; Thomas, Barnes, Francis (Jacobs), Dyson, Gillespie, Bodak, Bradford, Hateley, Thompson, Hunt.
*Oxford U:* Burton; Doyle, Fogg, Jeffrey, Briggs, Wright, Brock (Kearns), Foley, Cassells, Thomas, Smithers.

**Crystal Palace (0) 0**

**Orient (0) 0**                    14,501

*Crystal Palace:* Barron; Hinshelwood, Boulter, Murphy, Wicks, Cannon, Brooks, Smillie, Walsh, Hilaire (Langley), Mabbutt.
*Orient:* Day; Foster, Fisher, Taylor, Gray, Osgood, Godfrey, Margerrison, Moores, Silkman, Hughton.

**Leicester C (0) 2** *(O'Neill, Young)*

**Watford (0) 0**                    27,991

*Leicester C:* Wallington; Williams, Friar, May, Peake, O'Neill, Lynex (Melrose), Lineker, Young, Wilson, Kelly.
*Watford:* Sherwood; Rice, Rostron, Taylor, Terry, Bolton. Blissett, Armstrong (Callaghan), Jenkins, Lohman, Barnes.

**QPR (2) 3** *(Stainrod, Allen, Howe)*

**Grimsby T (0) 1** *(Moore K.)*                    13,344

*QPR:* Hucker; Fenwick, Gillard, Waddock (Fereday), Howe, Roeder, Micklewhite, Flanagan, Allen, Stainrod, Gregory.
*Grimsby T:* Batch; Moore D., Crombie, Waters, Wigginton, Moore K., Brolly, Ford, Drinkell, Mitchell (Beacock), Stone.

**Shrewsbury T (2) 2** *(Cross, King)*

**Ipswich T (0) 1** *(D'Avray)*                    13,965

*Shrewsbury T:* Wardle; King, Johnson, Cross, Griffin, Keay, Tong, McNally, Atkins, Biggins (Dungworth), Bates.
*Ipswich T:* Cooper; Burley, McCall, Mills (D'Avray), Osman, Hunter, Wark, Muhren, O'Callaghan, Brazil, Gates.

**Tottenham H (1) 1** *(Falco)*

**Aston Villa (0) 0**                    43,490

*Tottenham H:* Clemence; Hughton, Miller, Price, Roberts, Perryman, Ardiles, Falco, Galvin, Hoddle, Crooks (Archibald).
*Aston Villa:* Rimmer; Swain, Williams, Evans, McNaught, Mortimer, Bremner, Geddis, Withe, Cowans, Morley.

**WBA (1) 1** *(Regis)*

**Norwich C (0) 0**                    18,867

*WBA:* Grew; Bennett, Statham, Lewis, Wile, Robertson, Cross, King, Regis, Owen, MacKenzie.
*Norwich C:* Woods; Symonds, Downs, McGuire, Walford, Watson, Barham (Jack), O'Neill, Deehan, Bertschin, Mendham.

**FIFTH ROUND REPLAY**

**16 FEB**

**Orient (0) 0**

**Crystal Palace (1) 1** *(Smillie)*                    10,067

*Orient:* Day; Foster, Fisher, Taylor, Gray, Hallybone, Godfrey, Margerrison, Moores, Silkman (McNeil), Hughton.
*Crystal Palace:* Barron; Hinshelwood, Boulter, Murphy (Price), Wicks, Cannon, Brooks, Smillie, Langley, Mabbutt, Hilaire.

## SIXTH ROUND

### 6 MAR

**Chelsea (1) 2** *(Fillery, Mayes)*

**Tottenham H (0) 3** *(Archibald, Hoddle, Hazard)*   42,557

*Chelsea:* Francis; Locke, Hutchings, Nutton, Chivers, Pates, Rhoades-Brown, Bumstead, Mayes, Walker (Rofe), Fillery.
*Tottenham H:* Clemence; Hughton, Miller, Price, Hazard, Perryman, Ardiles, Archibald, Galvin, Hoddle, Crooks.

**Leicester C (2) 5** *(May, Cross og, Melrose 2, Lineker)*

**Shrewsbury T (2) 2** *(Bates, Keay)*   29,117

*Leicester C:* Wallington (Melrose); Williams, Friar, Peake, May, O'Neill, Lynex, Lineker, Young, Wilson, Kelly.
*Shrewsbury T:* Wardle; King (Dungworth), Johnson, Cross, Griffin, Keay, Tong, McNally, Atkins, Biggins, Bates.

**QPR (0) 1** *(Allen)*

**Crystal Palace (0) 0**   24,653

*QPR:* Hucker; Neill, Gillard, Waddock, Hazell, Roeder, Currie, Flanagan, Allen, Stainrod, Gregory.
*Crystal Palace:* Barron; Hinshelwood, Boulter, Murphy, Wicks, Gilbert, Giles, Smillie, Cannon, Mabbutt, Hilaire.

**WBA (1) 2** *(Regis, Owen)*

**Coventry C (0) 0**   27,825

*WBA:* Grew; Batson, Statham, Bennett, Wile, Robertson, Brown, King, Regis, Owen, MacKenzie.
*Coventry C:* Blyth; Roberts, Barnes, Francis, Gillespie, Hagan, Bodak, Thomas, Hateley, Thompson, Hunt.

## SEMI-FINALS

### 3 APRIL

**Tottenham H (0) 2** *(Crooks, Wilson og)*

**Leicester C (0) 0**   46,606

At Villa Park
*Tottenham H:* Clemence; Hughton, Roberts (Miller), Price, Hazard, Perryman, Ardiles, Archibald, Galvin, Hoddle, Crooks.
*Leicester C:* Wallington; Williams, Friar, Peake, May, O'Neill, Lynex, Lineker, Young (Melrose), Wilson, Kelly.

**QPR (0) 1** *(Allen)*

**WBA (0) 0**   45,015

At Highbury
*QPR:* Hucker; Fenwick, Gillard, Waddock, Hazell, Roeder, Currie, Flanagan, Allen, Stainrod, Micklewhite.
*WBA:* Grew; Batson, Statham, Zondervan, Wile, Robertson, Bennett, King (Owen), Regis, Cross, MacKenzie.

## FINAL (at Wembley)

### 22 MAY

**QPR (0) 1** *(Fenwick)*

**Tottenham H (0) 1** *aet (Hoddle)*   100,000

*QPR:* Hucker; Fenwick, Gillard, Waddock, Hazell, Roeder, Currie, Flanagan, Allen (Micklewhite), Stainrod, Gregory.
*Tottenham H:* Clemence; Hughton, Miller, Price, Hazard (Brooke), Perryman, Roberts, Archibald, Galvin, Hoddle, Crooks.

## FINAL REPLAY (at Wembley)

### 27 MAY

**QPR (0) 0**

**Tottenham H (1) 1** *(Hoddle pen)*   90,000

*QPR:* Hucker; Fenwick, Gillard, Waddock, Hazell, Neill, Currie, Flanagan, Micklewhite (Burke), Stainrod, Gregory.
*Tottenham H:* Clemence; Hughton, Miller, Price, Hazard (Brooke), Perryman, Roberts, Archibald, Galvin, Hoddle, Crooks.

## PAID DIRECTORS

By 522 votes to 28, an extraordinary general meeting of the Football Association on 19 November 1981 sanctioned a change in Rule 43A(4) to permit clubs to appoint one paid director. A similar proposal had been rejected by the FA in May 1981, but the amended resolution covered all clubs, not just League clubs.

Within minutes of the FA decision, Fulham's chairman, Ernie Clay, made manager Malcolm Macdonald the first paid director of an English Football League club. Although Macdonald was the first manager to gain a seat on the board, he was not the first paid director in the Football League, the Welsh FA having reached a similar decision earlier in the season, when Cardiff put director Ron Jones on their payroll.

# FA CUP FINALS 1872–1982

| | | | |
|---|---|---|---|
| 1872 and 1874–92 | Kennington Oval | 1911 | Replay at Old Trafford |
| 1873 | Lillie Bridge | 1912 | Replay at Bramall Lane |
| 1893 | Fallowfield, Manchester | 1915 | Old Trafford, Manchester |
| 1894 | Everton | 1920–22 | Stamford Bridge |
| 1895–1914 | Crystal Palace | 1923 to date | Wembley |
| 1901 | Replay at Bolton | 1970 | Replay at Old Trafford |
| 1910 | Replay at Everton | 1981 | Replay at Wembley |

| Year | Winners | Runners-up | Score |
|---|---|---|---|
| 1872 | Wanderers | Royal Engineers | 1-0 |
| 1873 | Wanderers | Oxford University | 2-0 |
| 1874 | Oxford University | Royal Engineers | 2-0 |
| 1875 | Royal Engineers | Old Etonians | 2-0 (after 1-1 draw) |
| 1876 | Wanderers | Old Etonians | 3-0 (after 1-1 draw) |
| 1877 | Wanderers | Oxford University | 2-1 (aet) |
| 1878 | Wanderers* | Royal Engineers | 3-1 |
| 1879 | Old Etonians | Clapham R | 1-0 |
| 1880 | Clapham R | Oxford University | 1-0 |
| 1881 | Old Carthusians | Old Etonians | 3-0 |
| 1882 | Old Etonians | Blackburn R | 1-0 |
| 1883 | Blackburn Olympic | Old Etonians | 2-1 (aet) |
| 1884 | Blackburn R | Queen's Park, Glasgow | 2-1 |
| 1885 | Blackburn R | Queen's Park, Glasgow | 2-0 |
| 1886 | Blackburn R† | WBA | 2-0 (after 0-0 draw) |
| 1887 | Aston Villa | WBA | 2-0 |
| 1888 | WBA | Preston NE | 2-1 |
| 1889 | Preston NE | Wolverhampton W | 3-0 |
| 1890 | Blackburn R | Sheffield W | 6-1 |
| 1891 | Blackburn R | Notts Co | 3-1 |
| 1892 | WBA | Aston Villa | 3-0 |
| 1893 | Wolverhampton W | Everton | 1-0 |
| 1894 | Notts Co | Bolton W | 4-1 |
| 1895 | Aston Villa | WBA | 1-0 |
| 1896 | Sheffield W | Wolverhampton W | 2-1 |
| 1897 | Aston Villa | Everton | 3-2 |
| 1898 | Nottingham F | Derby Co | 3-1 |
| 1899 | Sheffield U | Derby Co | 4-1 |
| 1900 | Bury | Southampton | 4-0 |
| 1901 | Tottenham H | Sheffield U | 3-1 (after 2-2 draw) |
| 1902 | Sheffield U | Southampton | 2-1 (after 1-1 draw) |
| 1903 | Bury | Derby Co | 6-0 |
| 1904 | Manchester C | Bolton W | 1-0 |
| 1905 | Aston Villa | Newcastle U | 2-0 |
| 1906 | Everton | Newcastle U | 1-0 |
| 1907 | Sheffield W | Everton | 2-1 |
| 1908 | Wolverhampton W | Newcastle U | 3-1 |
| 1909 | Manchester U | Bristol C | 1-0 |
| 1910 | Newcastle U | Barnsley | 2-0 (after 1-1 draw) |
| 1911 | Bradford C | Newcastle U | 1-0 (after 0-0 draw) |
| 1912 | Barnsley | WBA | 1-0 (aet) |
| 1913 | Aston Villa | Sunderland | 1-0 (after 0-0 draw) |
| 1914 | Burnley | Liverpool | 1-0 |
| 1915 | Sheffield U | Chelsea | 3-0 |
| 1920 | Aston Villa | Huddersfield T | 1-0 (aet) |
| 1921 | Tottenham H | Wolverhampton W | 1-0 |
| 1922 | Huddersfield T | Preston NE | 1-0 |
| 1923 | Bolton W | West Ham U | 2-0 |
| 1924 | Newcastle U | Aston Villa | 2-0 |
| 1925 | Sheffield U | Cardiff C | 1-0 |
| 1926 | Bolton W | Manchester C | 1-0 |
| 1927 | Cardiff C | Arsenal | 1-0 |
| 1928 | Blackburn R | Huddersfield T | 3-1 |
| 1929 | Bolton W | Portsmouth | 2-0 |
| 1930 | Arsenal | Huddersfield T | 2-0 |
| 1931 | WBA | Birmingham | 2-1 |
| 1932 | Newcastle U | Arsenal | 2-1 |
| 1933 | Everton | Manchester C | 3-0 |
| 1934 | Manchester C | Portsmouth | 2-1 |
| 1935 | Sheffield W | WBA | 4-2 |
| 1936 | Arsenal | Sheffield U | 1-0 |
| 1937 | Sunderland | Preston NE | 3-1 |
| 1938 | Preston NE | Huddersfield T | 1-0 (aet) |
| 1939 | Portsmouth | Wolverhampton W | 4-1 |
| 1946 | Derby Co | Charlton Ath | 4-1 (aet) |
| 1947 | Charlton Ath | Burnley | 1-0 (aet) |
| 1948 | Manchester U | Blackpool | 4-2 |
| 1949 | Wolverhampton W | Leicester C | 3-1 |
| 1950 | Arsenal | Liverpool | 2-0 |
| 1951 | Newcastle U | Blackpool | 2-0 |
| 1952 | Newcastle U | Arsenal | 1-0 |

| Year | Winners | Runners-up | Score |
|---|---|---|---|
| 1953 | Blackpool | Bolton W | 4-3 |
| 1954 | WBA | Preston NE | 3-2 |
| 1955 | Newcastle U | Manchester C | 3-1 |
| 1956 | Manchester C | Birmingham C | 3-1 |
| 1957 | Aston Villa | Manchester U | 2-1 |
| 1958 | Bolton W | Manchester U | 2-0 |
| 1959 | Nottingham F | Luton T | 2-1 |
| 1960 | Wolverhampton W | Blackburn R | 3-0 |
| 1961 | Tottenham H | Leicester C | 2-0 |
| 1962 | Tottenham H | Burnley | 3-1 |
| 1963 | Manchester U | Leicester C | 3-1 |
| 1964 | West Ham U | Preston NE | 3-2 |
| 1965 | Liverpool | Leeds U | 2-1 (aet) |
| 1966 | Everton | Sheffield W | 3-2 |
| 1967 | Tottenham H | Chelsea | 2-1 |
| 1968 | WBA | Everton | 1-0 (aet) |
| 1969 | Manchester C | Leicester C | 1-0 |
| 1970 | Chelsea | Leeds U | 2-1 (aet) |

*(after 2-2 draw, after extra time, at Wembley)*

| | | | |
|---|---|---|---|
| 1971 | Arsenal | Liverpool | 2-1 (aet) |
| 1972 | Leeds U | Arsenal | 1-0 |
| 1973 | Sunderland | Leeds U | 1-0 |
| 1974 | Liverpool | Newcastle U | 3-0 |
| 1975 | West Ham U | Fulham | 2-0 |
| 1976 | Southampton | Manchester U | 1-0 |
| 1977 | Manchester U | Liverpool | 2-1 |
| 1978 | Ipswich T | Arsenal | 1-0 |
| 1979 | Arsenal | Manchester U | 3-2 |
| 1980 | West Ham U | Arsenal | 1-0 |
| 1981 | Tottenham H | Manchester C | 3-2 |

*(after 1-1 draw, after extra time, at Wembley)*

| | | | |
|---|---|---|---|
| 1982 | Tottenham H | QPR | 1-0 |

*(after 1-1 draw, after extra time, at Wembley)*

* *Won outright, but restored to the Football Association.*

† *A special trophy was awarded for third consecutive win.*

## FA CUP WINS

Aston Villa 7, Tottenham H 7, Blackburn R 6, Newcastle U 6, Arsenal 5, The Wanderers 5, WBA 5, Sheffield U 4, Bolton W 4, Wolverhampton W 4, Manchester C 4, Manchester U 4, Sheffield W 3, Everton 3, West Ham U 3, Bury 2, Old Etonians 2, Preston NE 2, Nottingham F 2, Sunderland 2, Liverpool 2, Barnsley 1, Blackburn Olympic 1, Blackpool 1, Bradford C 1, Burnley 1, Cardiff C 1, Charlton Ath 1, Chelsea 1, Clapham R 1, Derby Co 1, Huddersfield T 1, Notts Co 1, Old Carthusians 1, Oxford University 1, Portsmouth 1, Royal Engineers 1, Leeds U 1, Southampton 1, Ipswich T 1.

## APPEARANCES IN FINALS

Arsenal 11, Newcastle U 11, WBA 10, Aston Villa 9, Blackburn R 8, Manchester C 8, Manchester U 8, Wolverhampton W 8, Bolton W 7, Preston NE 7, Everton 7, *Tottenham H 7, Liverpool 6, Old Etonians 6, Sheffield U 6, Huddersfield T 5, *The Wanderers 5, Sheffield W 5, Derby Co 4, Oxford University 4, Royal Engineers 4, Leeds U 4, Leicester C 4, West Ham U 4, Blackpool 3, Burnley 3, Chelsea 3, Portsmouth 3, Sunderland 3, Southampton 3, Barnsley 2, Birmingham C 2, *Bury 2, Cardiff C 2, Charlton Ath 2, Clapham R 2, Notts Co 2, Queen's Park (Glasgow) 2, *Nottingham F 2, *Blackburn Olympic 1, *Bradford C 1, Bristol C 1, *Old Carthusians 1, Luton T 1, Fulham 1, *Ipswich T 1, QPR 1.

* *Denotes undefeated.*

## APPEARANCES IN SEMI-FINALS

WBA 19, Everton 18, Aston Villa 17, Blackburn R 16, Arsenal 15, Manchester U 15, Sheffield W 13, Derby Co 13, Liverpool 13, Newcastle U 13, Wolverhampton W 13, Bolton W 12, Tottenham 11, Sunderland 10, Preston NE 10, Manchester C 10, Sheffield U 10, Chelsea 10, Nottingham F 9, Birmingham C 9, Burnley 8, Southampton 8, Huddersfield T 7, Leeds U 7, Leicester C 7, Old Etonians 6, Oxford University 6, The Wanderers 5, Notts Co 5, Fulham 5, West Ham U 5, Portsmouth 4, Queen's Park (Glasgow) 4, Royal Engineers 4, Blackpool 3, Cardiff C 3, Clapham R 3, Millwall 3, Old Carthusians 3, The Swifts 3, Stoke C 3, Ipswich T 3, Barnsley 2, Blackburn Olympic 2, Bristol C 2, Bury 2, Charlton Ath 2, Grimsby T 2, Swansea T 2, Swindon T 2, Crystal Palace 2, Bradford C 1, Cambridge University 1, Crewe Alex 1, Darwen 1, Derby Junction 1, Glasgow R 1, Hull C 1, Marlow 1, Old Harrovians 1, Oldham Ath 1, Port Vale 1, Reading 1, Shropshire W 1, York C 1, Luton T 1, Norwich C 1, Watford 1, Orient 1, QPR 1.

# FA CUP FINALISTS 1872–1981

*Some goalscorers in the early years are not available.*
*R: replay; aet: after extra time.*

**1871–72** THE WANDERERS  R. de C. Welch; C. W. Alcock, M. P. Betts, A. G. Bonsor, E. E. Bowen, W. P. Crake, T. C. Hooman, E. Lubbock, A. C. Thompson, R. W. S. Vidal, C. H. R. Wollaston. (In alphabetical order.) *Scorer:* 'A. H. Chequer' (M. P. Betts).
**1-0** ROYAL ENGINEERS  Capt. Marindin; Capt. Merriman, Lieut. Addison; Lieut. Creswell, Lieut. Mitchell, Lieut. Renny-Tailyour; Lieut. Rich, Lieut. Goodwyn, Lieut. Muirhead, Lieut. Cotter, Lieut. Bogle.
**1872–73** THE WANDERERS  E. E. Bowen; C. M. Thompson, R. de C. Welch; Hon. A. F. Kinnaird, L. S. Howell, C. H. R. Wollaston; J. R. Sturgiss, Rev. H. H. Stewart, W. S. Kenyon-Slaney, R. K. Kingsford, A. G. Bonsor. *Scorers:* Wollaston, Kinnaird.
**2-0** OXFORD UNIVERSITY  A. Kirke-Smith; A. J. Leach, C. C. Mackarness; F. H. Birley, C. J. Longman, F. B. Chappell-Maddison; H. B. Cixon, W. B. Paton, R. W. S. Vidal, W. E. Sumner, C. J. Ottaway.
**1873–74** OXFORD UNIVERSITY  C. E. B. Neapean; C. C. Mackarness, F. H. Birley; F. T. Green, R. W. S. Vidal, C. J. Ottaway; R. H. Benson, F. J. Patton, W. S. Rawson, F. B. Chappell-Maddison, Rev. A. H. Johnson. *Scorers:* Mackarness, Patton.
**2-0** ROYAL ENGINEERS  Capt. Merriman; Major Marindin, Lieut. G. W. Addison; Lieut. G. C. Onslow, Lieut. H. G. Oliver, Lieut. T. Digby; Lieut. H. W. Renny-Tailyour, Lieut. H. E. Rawson, Lieut. J. E. Blackman, Lieut. A. K. Wood, Lieut. P. G. von Donop.
**1874–75** ROYAL ENGINEERS  Capt. Merriman; Lieut. G. H. Sim, Lieut. G. Onslow; Lieut. R. M. Ruck, Lieut. P. G. von Donop, Lieut. C. K. Wood; Lieut. H. E. Rawson, Lieut. R. H. Stafford, Capt. H. W. Renny-Tailyour, Lieut. Mein, Lieut. C. Wingfield Stratford. *Scorer:* (First match) Not known; (Second match) Renny-Tailyour, Stafford.
**1-1** OLD ETONIANS  Capt. E. H. Drummond-Moray; M. Farrer, E. Lubbock; F. H. Wilson, Hon. A. F. Kinnaird, J. H. Stronge; F. J. Patton, C. E. Farmer, A. G. Bonsor, A. Lubbock, T. *R:2-0* Hammond. (C. J. Ottaway, W. S. Kenyon-Slaney, R. H. Benson and A. G. Thompson took part in the first match in place of A. Lubbock, T. Hammond, M. Farrer and Capt. E. H. Drummond-Moray.) *Scorer:* Bonsor.
**1875–76** THE WANDERERS  W. D. O. Greig; A. Stratford, W. Lindsay; F. B. C. Maddison, F. H. Birley, C. H. R. Wollaston; H. Heron, F. Heron, J. H. Edwards, J. Kenrick, T. Hughes. *Scorers:* (First match) Edwards; (Second match) Wollaston, Hughes 2.
**1-1** OLD ETONIANS  Q. Hogg; E. Lubbock, Hon. E. Lyttelton; M. G. Faner, Hon. A. F. Kinnaird, J. H. Stronge; W. S. Kenyon-Slaney, Hon. A. Lyttelton, J. R. Sturgis, A. G. Bonsor, H. P. *R:3-0* Allene. (C. Meysey, A. C. Thompson and J. E. C. Welldon took part in the first match in place of J. H. Stronge, M. G. Faner and E. Lubbock.) *Scorer:* Bonsor.
**1876–77** THE WANDERERS  F. H. Bitley; C. A. Denton, F. T. Green; H. Heron, T. Hughes, J. Kenrick; Hon. A. F. Kinnaird, W. Lindsay, A. Stratford, H. Wace, C. H. R. Wollaston. (In **2-1** alphabetical order.) *Scorers:* Heron, Kenrick.
**aet** OXFORD UNIVERSITY  E. H. Allington; J. Bain, O. R. Dunnell; J. H. Savory, A. H. Todd, E. W. Waddington; P. H. Fernandez, A. F. Hills, H. S. Otter, E. H. Parry, W. S. Rawson. *Scorer:* Kinnaird og.
**1877–78** THE WANDERERS  J. Kirkpatrick; A. Stratford, W. Lindsay; Hon. A. F. Kinnaird, F. T. Green, C. H. R. Wollaston; H. Heron, J. G. Wylie, H. Wace, C. A. Denton, J. Kenrick.
**3-1** ROYAL ENGINEERS  L. B. Friend; J. H. Cowan, W. J. Morris; C. B. Mayne, F. C. Heath, C. E. Haynes; M. Lindsay, R. B. Hedley, F. G. Bond, H. H. Barnet, O. E. Ruck.
**1878–79** OLD ETONIANS  J. P. Hawtrey; E. Christian, L. Bury; Hon. A. F. Kinnaird, E. Lubbock, C. J. Clerke; N. Pares, H. C. Goodhart, H. Whitfield, J. B. T. Chevallier, H. Beaufoy.
**1-0** CLAPHAM ROVERS  R. H. Birkett; R. A. Ogilvie, E. Field; N. C. Bailey, J. F. M. Prinsep, F. L. Rawson; A. J. Stanley, S. W. Scott, H. S. Bevington, E. F. Growse, C. Keith-Falconer.
**1879–80** CLAPHAM ROVERS  R. H. Birkett; R. A. Ogilvie, E. Field; A. Weston, N. C. Bailey, H. Brougham; A. J. Stanley, F. Barry, F. J. Sparks, C. A. Lloyd-Jones, E. A. Ram. *Scorer:* Lloyd-Jones.
**1-0** OXFORD UNIVERSITY  P. C. Parr; C. W. Wilson, C. J. S. King; F. A. H. Phillips, B. Rogers, R. T. Heygate; G. B. Childs, J. Eyre, F. D. Crowdy, E. H. Hill, J. B. Lubbock.
**1880–81** OLD CARTHUSIANS  L. F. Gillett; W. H. Norris, E. G. Colvin; J. F. M. Prinsep, A. J. Vintcent, W. E. Hansell; L. M. Richards, W. R. Page, E. G. Wynyard, E. H. Parry, A. H. Todd.
**3-0** OLD ETONIANS  J. F. P. Rawlinson; C. W. Foley, C. H. French; Hon. A. F. Kinnaird, R. B. Farrer, J. B. T. Chevallier; W. J. Anderson, H. C. Goodhart, R. H. Macaulay, H. Whitfield, P. C. Novelli.
**1881–82** OLD ETONIANS  J. F. P. Rawlinson; T. H. French, P. J. de Paravicini; Hon. A. F. Kinnaird, C. W. Foley, P. C. Novelli; A. T. R. Dunn, R. H. Macaulay, H. C. Goodhart, W. J. Anderson, J. B. T. Chevallier. *Scorer:* Anderson.
**1-0** BLACKBURN ROVERS  R. Howarth; H. McIntyre, F. Suter; H. Sharples, F. W. Hargreaves, J. Duckworth; J. Douglas, T. Strachan, J. Brown, G. Avery, J. Hargreaves.
**1882–83** BLACKBURN OLYMPIC  T. Hacking; J. T. Ward, S. A. Warburton; T. Gibson, W. Astley, J. Hunter; T. Dewhurst, A. Matthews, G. Wilson, J. Costley, J. Yates. *Scorers:* Costley, Matthews.
**2-1** OLD ETONIANS  J. F. P. Rawlinson, T. H. French, P. J. de Paravicini, Hon. A. F. Kinnaird, **aet** C. W. Foley, J. B. T. Chevallier, W. J. Anderson, R. H. Macaulay, H. C. Goodhart, A. T. B. Dunn, H. W. Bainbridge. *Scorer:* Goodhart.
**1883–84** BLACKBURN ROVERS  H. J. Arthur; J. Beverley, F. Suter; H. McIntyre, J. Hargreaves, J. H. Forrest; J. M. Lofthouse, J. Douglas, J. Sowerbutts, J. Inglis, J. Brown. *Scorers:* Brown, Forrest.
**2-1** QUEEN'S PARK  G. Gillespie; W. Arnott, J. MacDonald; C. Campbell, J. J. Gow, W. Anderson; W. W. Watt, Dr Smith, W. Harrower, D. S. Allan, R. M. Christie. *Scorer:* Christie.
**1884–85** BLACKBURN ROVERS  H. J. Arthur; R. G. Turner, F. Suter; H. McIntyre, G. Haworth, J. H. Forrest; J. M. Lofthouse, J. Douglas, J. Brown, H. E. Fecitt, J. Sowerbutts. *Scorers:* Forrest, Brown.
**2-0** QUEEN'S PARK  G. Gillespie; W. Arnott, W. Macleod; C. Campbell, J. MacDonald, A. Hamilton; W. Anderson, W. Sellar, W. Gray, N. McWhannel, D. S. Allan.

Kenny Dalglish (dark shirt) shows the kind of determination that helped Liverpool to their 13th League Championship. (*Colorsport*)

Glenn Hoddle's successful penalty kick for Tottenham Hotspur in the FA Cup final replay against Queen's Park Rangers. (*Colorsport*)

Celtic captain Danny McGrain with the Premier Division Championship trophy – the club's 33rd overall Scottish League title. (*Colorsport*)

Only Gordon Strachan appears to know where he is going in the Scottish Cup final. Aberdeen beat Rangers for the trophy in extra-time. (*Colorsport*)

Dundee United's Davie Dodds (left) and Rangers Derek Johnstone in the
Scottish League Cup final, won 2-1 by Rangers. (*Sportapics*)

In off the post – but they all count! Peter Withe scores for Aston Villa in the European Cup final against Bayern Munich. (*Colorsport*)

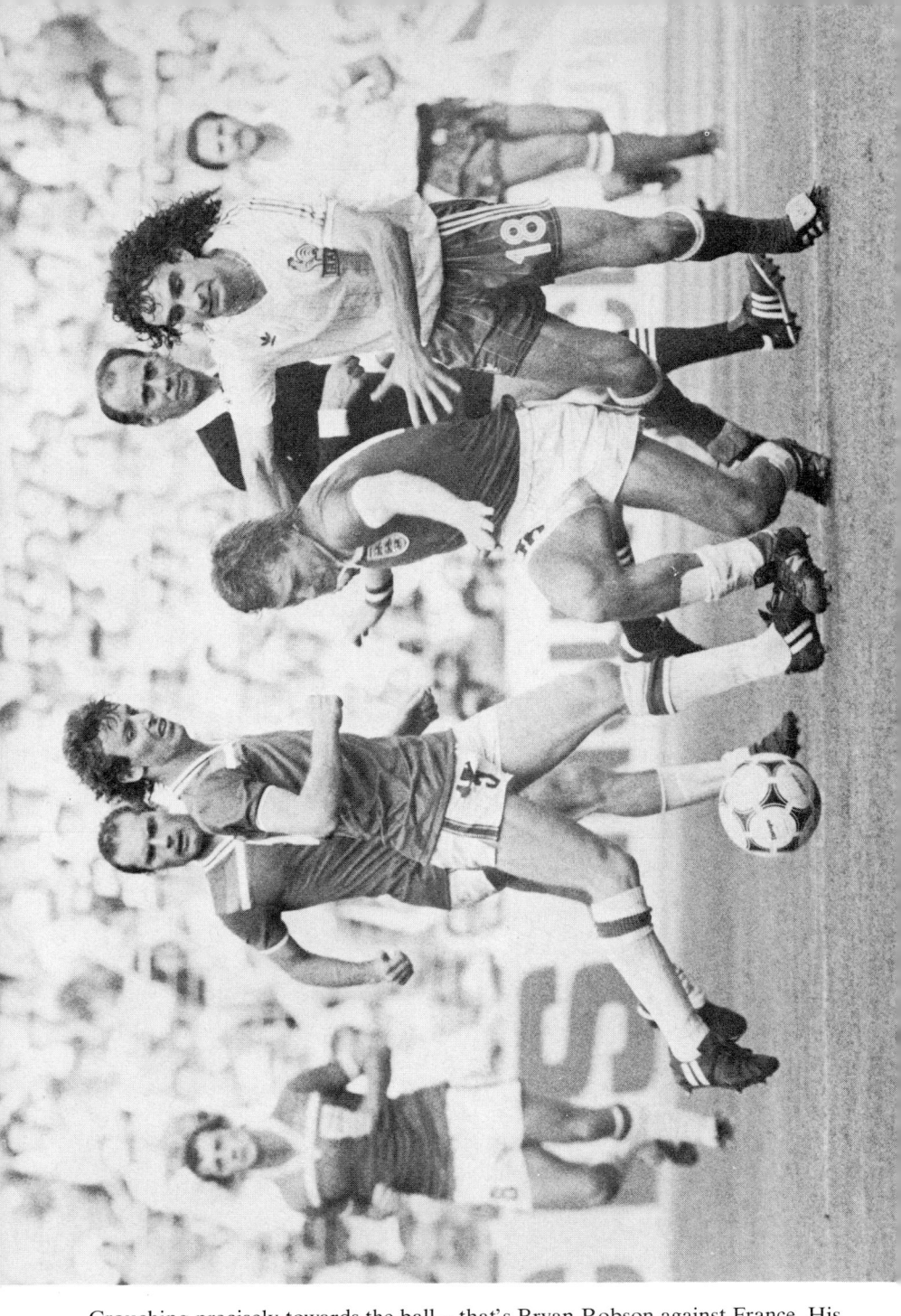

Crouching precisely towards the ball – that's Bryan Robson against France. His 27-seconds goal for England was a tournament record. (*Colorsport*)

Paolo Rossi (dark shirt, left on ground), the top scorer in the 1982 World Cup finals, puts Italy on the way to success against West Germany. (*Colorsport*)

**1885–86** BLACKBURN ROVERS   H. J. Arthur; Turner, Suter; Douglas, Forrest, McIntyre; Walton, Strachan, Brown, Fecitt, J. Sowerbutts. (Heyes played in the first match at the Oval, but Walton
 **0-0**  took his place in the replay.) *Scorers:* Sowerbutts, Brown.
 **R:2-0**  WEST BROMWICH ALBION   Roberts; H. Green, H. Bell; Horton, Perry, Timmins; Woodhall, T. Green, Bayliss, Loach, G. Bell.
**1886–87** ASTON VILLA   Warner; Coulton, Simmonds; Yates, Dawson, Burton; Davis, Brown, Hunter, Vaughton, Hodgetts. *Scorers:* Hodgetts, Hunter.
 **2-0**  WEST BROMWICH ALBION   Roberts; H. Green, Aldridge; Horton, Perry, Timmins; Woodhall, T. Green, Bayliss, Paddock, Pearson.
**1887–88** WEST BROMWICH ALBION   Roberts; Aldridge, Green; Horton, Perry, Timmins; Bassett, Woodhall, Bayliss, Wilson, Pearson. *Scorers:* Bayliss, Woodhall.
 **2-1**  PRESTON NORTH END   Dr R. H. Mills-Roberts; Howarth, N. J. Ross; Holmes, Russell, Graham; Gordon, J. Ross, J. Goodall, F. Dewhurst, Drummond. *Scorer:* Goodall.
**1888–89** PRESTON NORTH END   Dr R. H. Mills-Roberts; Howarth, Holmes; Drummond, Russell, Graham; Gordon, Ross, J. Goodall, F. Dewhurst, Thompson. *Scorers:* Dewhurst, Ross, Thompson.
 **3-0**  WOLVERHAMPTON WANDERERS   Baynton; Baugh, Mason; Fletcher, Allen, Lowder; Hunter, Wykes, Broodie, Wood, Knight.
**1889–90** BLACKBURN ROVERS   J. K. Horne; Southworth (Jas.), Forbes; Barton, Dewar, Forrest; Lofthouse, Campbell, Southworth (John), Walton, Townley. *Scorer:* Dewar, Southworth (John), Lofthouse, Townley 3.
 **6-1**  SHEFFIELD WEDNESDAY   Smith (J.); Brayshaw, H. Morley; Dungworth, Betts, Waller; Ingram, Woodhouse, Bennett, Mumford, Cawley. *Scorer:* Bennett.
**1890–91** BLACKBURN ROVERS   Pennington; Brandon, J. Forbes; Barton, Dewar, Forrest; Lofthouse, Walton, Southworth (John), Hall, Townley. *Scorers:* Dewar, Southworth, Townley.
 **3-1**  NOTTS COUNTY   Thraves; Ferguson, Hendry; H. Osborne, Calderhead, Shelton; A. McGregor, McInnes, Oswald, Locker, H. B. Daft. *Scorer:* Oswald.
**1891–92** WEST BROMWICH ALBION   Reader; Nicholson, McCulloch, Reynolds, Perry, Groves; Bassett, McLeod, Nicholls, Pearson, Geddes. *Scorers:* Geddes, Nicholls, Reynolds.
 **3-0**  ASTON VILLA   Warner; Evans, Cox; H. Devey, Cowan, Baird; Athersmith, J. Devey, Dickson, Campbell, Hodgetts.
**1892–93** WOLVERHAMPTON WANDERERS   Rose; Baugh, Swift; Malpass, Allen, Kinsey; R. Topham, Wykes, Butcher, Wood, Griffin. *Scorer:* Allen.
 **1-0**  EVERTON   Williams; Howarth, Kelso; Stewart, Holt, Boyle; Latta, Gordon, Maxwell, Chadwick, Milward.
**1893–94** NOTTS COUNTY   Toone; Harper, Hendry; Bramley, Calderhead, A. Shelton; Watson, Donnelly, Logan, Bruce, H. B. Daft. *Scorers:* Watson, Logan 3.
 **4-1**  BOLTON WANDERERS   Sutcliffe; Somerville, Jones; Gardiner, Paton, Hughes; Dickinson, Wilson, Tannahill, Bentley, Cassidy. *Scorer:* Cassidy.
**1894–95** ASTON VILLA   Wilkes; Spencer, Welford; Reynolds, Cowan (Jas.), Russell; Athersmith, Chatt, J. Devey, Hodgetts, S. Smith. *Scorer:* Chatt.
 **1-0**  WEST BROMWICH ALBION   Reader; Williams, Horton; Taggart, Higgins, T. Perry; Bassett, McLeod, Richards, Hutchinson, Banks.
**1895–96** SHEFFIELD WEDNESDAY   Massey; Earp, Langley; H. Brandon, Crawshaw, Petrie; Brash, Brady, L. Bell, Davis, Spiksley. *Scorer:* Spiksley 2.
 **2-1**  WOLVERHAMPTON WANDERERS   Tennant; Baugh, Dunn; Owen, Malpass, Griffiths; Tonks, Henderson, Beats, Wood, Black. *Scorer:* Black.
**1896–97** ASTON VILLA   Whitehouse; Spencer, Evans; Reynolds, Cowan (Jas.), Crabtree; Athersmith, J. Devey, Campbell, Wheldon, Cowan (John). *Scorers:* Campbell, Wheldon, Crabtree.
 **3-2**  EVERTON   Menham; Meecham, Storrier; Boyle, Holt, Stewart; Taylor, Bell, Hartley, Chadwick, Milward. *Scorers:* Bell, Boyle.
**1897–98** NOTTINGHAM FOREST   Allsop; Richie, Scott; Forman (Frank), McPherson, Wragg; McInnes, Richards, Benbow, Capes, Spouncer. *Scorers:* Capes 2, McPherson.
 **3-1**  DERBY COUNTY   Fryer; Methven, Leiper; Cox, A. Goodall, Turner; J. Goodall, Bloomer, Boag, Stevenson, McQueen. *Scorer:* Bloomer.
**1898–99** SHEFFIELD UNITED   Foulke; Thickett, Boyle; Johnson, Morren, Needham; Bennett, Beers, Hedley, Almond, Priest. *Scorers:* Bennett, Beers, Almond, Priest.
 **4-1**  DERBY COUNTY   Fryer; Methven, Staley; Cox, Paterson, May; Arkesden, Bloomer, Boag, McDonald, Allen. *Scorer:* Boag.
 **1899–**  BURY   Thompson; Darrock, Davidson; Pray, Leeming, Ross; Richards, Wood, McLuckie, Sagar, Plant.
 **1900**  *Scorers:* McLuckie 2, Wood, Plant.
 **4-0**  SOUTHAMPTON   Robinson; Meehan, Durber; Meston, Chadwick, Petrie; Turner, Yates, Farrell, Wood, Milward.
**1900–01** TOTTENHAM HOTSPUR   Clawley; Erentz, Tait; Norris, Hughes, Jones; Smith, Cameron, Brown, Copeland, Kirwan. *Scorers:* (First match) Brown 2; (Second match), Cameron, Smith, Brown.
 **2-2**  SHEFFIELD UNITED   Foulke; Thickett, Boyle; Johnson, Morren, Needham; Bennett, Field,
 **R:3-1**  Hedley, Priest, Lipsham. *Scorers:* (First match) Bennett, Priest; (Second match) Priest.
**1901–02** SHEFFIELD UNITED   Foulke; Thickett, Boyle; Needham, Wilkinson, Johnson; Barnes, Common, Hedley, Priest, Lipsham. (Bennett was injured in the first match and Barnes took his place in the replay.) *Scorers:* (First match) Common; (Second match) Hedley, Barnes.
 **1-1**  SOUTHAMPTON   Robinson; C. B. Fry, Molyneux; Meston, Bowman, Lee; A. Turner, Wood,
 **R:2-1**  Brown, Chadwick, J. Turner. *Scorers:* (First match) Wood; (Second match) Brown.
**1902–03** BURY   Monteith; Lindsey, McEwen; Johnson, Thorpe, Ross; Richards, Wood, Sagar, Leeming, Plant. *Scorers:* Ross, Sagar, Leeming 2, Wood, Plant.
 **6-0**  DERBY COUNTY   Fryer; Methven, Morris; Warren, A. Goodall, May; Warrington, York, Boag, Richards, Davis.
**1903–04** MANCHESTER CITY   Hillman; McMahon, Burgess; Frost, Hynds, S. B. Ashworth; Meredith, Livingstone, Gillespie, A. Turnbull, Booth. *Scorer:* Meredith.
 **1-0**  BOLTON WANDERERS   D. Davies; Brown, Struthers; Clifford, Greenhaigh, Freebairn; Stokes, Marsh, Yenson, White, Taylor.

**1904–05** ASTON VILLA  George; Spencer, Miles; Pearson, Leake, Windmill; Brawn, Garratty, Hampton, Bache, Hall. *Scorer:* Hampton 2.

**2–0** NEWCASTLE UNITED  Lawrence; McCombie, Carr; Gardner, Aitken, McWilliam; Rutherford, Howie, Appleyard, Veitch, Gosnell.

**1905–06** EVERTON  Scott; W. Balmer, Crelly; Makepeace, Taylor, Abbott; Sharp, Bolton, Young, Settle, H. P. Hardman. *Scorer:* Young.

**1–0** NEWCASTLE UNITED  Lawrence; McCombie, Carr; Gardner, Aitken, McWilliam; Rutherford, Howie, Veitch, Orr, Gosnell.

**1906–07** SHEFFIELD WEDNESDAY  Lyall; Layton, Burton; Brittleton, Crawshaw, Bartlett; Chapman, Bradshaw, Wilson, Stewart, Simpson. *Scorers:* Stewart, Simpson.

**2–1** EVERTON  Scott; W. Balmer, R. Balmer; Makepeace, Taylor, Abbott; Sharp, Bolton, Young, Settle, H. P. Hardman. *Scorer:* Sharp.

**1907–08** WOLVERHAMPTON WANDERERS  Lunn; Jones, Collins; Rev. K. R. G. Hunt, Wooldridge, Bishop; Harrison, Shelton, Hedley, Radford, Pedley. *Scorers:* Hunt, Hedley, Harrison.

**3–1** NEWCASTLE UNITED  Lawrence; McCracken, Pudan; Gardner, Veitch, McWilliam; Rutherford, Howie, Appleyard, Speedie, Wilson. *Scorer:* Howie.

**1908–09** MANCHESTER UNITED  Moger; Stacey, Hayes; Duckworth, Roberts, Bell; Meredith, Halse, J. Turnbull, A. Turnbull, Wall. *Scorer:* A. Turnbull.

**1–0** BRISTOL CITY  Clay; Annan, Cottle; Hanlin, Wedlock, Spear; Staniforth, Hardy, Gilligan, Burton, Hilton.

**1909–10** NEWCASTLE UNITED  Lawrence; McCracken, Carr; Veitch, Low, McWilliam; Rutherford, Howie, Shepherd, Higgins, Wilson. (Whitson was injured in first match and Carr took his place in the replay.) *Scorers:* (First match) Rutherford; (Second match) Shepherd 2 (1 pen.)

**1–1** BARNSLEY  Mearns; Downs, Ness; Glendinning, Boyle, Utley; Bartrop, Gadsby, Lillycrop,
**R:2–0** Tuffnell, Forman. *Scorer:* (First match) Tuffnell.

**1910–11** BRADFORD CITY  Mellors; Campbell, Taylor; Robinson, Torrance, McDonald; Logan, Spiers, O'Rourke, Devine, Thompson. (Gildea played centre-half in the first match.) *Scorer:* Spiers.

**0–0** NEWCASTLE UNITED  Lawrence; McCracken, Whitson; Veitch, Low, Willis; Rutherford,
**R:1–0** Jobey, Stewart, Higgins, Wilson.

**1911–12** BARNSLEY  Cooper; Downs, Taylor; Glendinning, Bratley, Utley; Bartrop, Tuffnell,
**0–0** Lillycrop, Travers, Moore. *Scorer:* Tuffnell.
**R:2–0** WEST BROMWICH ALBION  Pearson; Cook, Pennington; Baddeley, Buck, McNeal;
**aet** Jephcott, Wright, Pailor, Bowser, Shearman.

**1912–13** ASTON VILLA  Hardy; Lyons, Weston; Barber, Harrop, Leach; Wallace, Halse, Hampton, C. Stephenson, Bache. *Scorer:* Barber.

**1–0** SUNDERLAND  Butler; Gladwin, Ness; Cuggy, Thompson, Low; Mordue, Buchan, Richardson, Holley, Martin.

**1913–14** BURNLEY  Sewell; Bamford, Taylor; Halley, Boyle, Watson; Nesbit, Lindley, Freeman, Hodgson, Mosscrop. *Scorer:* Freeman.

**1–0** LIVERPOOL  Campbell; Longworth, Pursell; Fairfoul, Ferguson, McKinlay; Sheldon, Metcalf, Miller, Lacey, Nicholl.

**1914–15** SHEFFIELD UNITED  Gough; Cook, English; Sturgess, Brelsford, Utley; Simmons, Fazackerley, Kitchen, Masterman, Evans. *Scorers:* Simmons, Fazackerley, Kitchen.

**3–0** CHELSEA  Molyneux; Bettridge, Harrow; Taylor, Logan, Walker; Ford, Halse, Thompson, Croal, McNeil.

**1919–20** ASTON VILLA  Hardy; Smart, Weston; Ducat, Barson, Moss; Wallace, Kirton, Walker, C. Stephenson, Dorrell. *Scorer:* Kirton.

**1–0** HUDDERSFIELD TOWN  Mutch; Wood, Bullock; Slade, Wilson, Watson; Richardson,
**aet** Mann, Taylor, Swan, Islip.

**1920–21** TOTTENHAM HOTSPUR  Hunter; Clay, McDonald; Smith, Walters, Grimsdell; Banks, Seed, Cantrell, Bliss, Dimmock. *Scorer:* Dimmock.

**1–0** WOLVERHAMPTON WANDERERS  George; Woodward, Marshall; Gregory, Hodnet, Riley; Lea, Burrill, Edmonds, Potts, Brooks.

**1921–22** HUDDERSFIELD TOWN  Mutch; Wood, Wadsworth; Slade, Wilson, Watson; Richardson, Mann, Islip, Stephenson, W. H. Smith. *Scorer:* Smith (pen).

**1–0** PRESTON NORTH END  J. F. Mitchell; Hamilton, Doolan; Duxbury, McCall, Williamson; Rawlings, Jefferis, Roberts, Woodhouse, Quinn.

**1922–23** BOLTON WANDERERS  Pym; Haworth, Finney; Nuttall, Seddon, Jennings; Butler, Jack, J. R. Smith, J. Smith, Vizard. *Scorers:* Jack, J. R. Smith.

**2–0** WEST HAM UNITED  Hufton; Henderson, Young; Bishop, Kay, Tresadern, Richards, Brown, V. Watson, Moore, Ruffell.

**1923–24** NEWCASTLE UNITED  Bradley; Hampson, Hudspeth; Mooney, Spencer, Gibson; Low, Cowan, Harris, McDonald, Seymour. *Scorers:* Harris, Seymour.

**2–0** ASTON VILLA  Jackson; Smart, Mort; Moss, Dr V. E. Milne, Blackburn; York, Kirton, Capewell, Walker, Dorrell.

**1924–25** SHEFFIELD UNITED  Sutcliffe; Cook, Milton; Pantling, King, Green; Mercer, Boyle, Johnson, Gillespie, Tunstall. *Scorer:* Tunstall.

**1–0** CARDIFF CITY  Farquharson; Nelson, Blair; Wake, Keenor, Hardy; W. Davies; Gill, Nicholson, Beadles, J. Evans.

**1925–26** BOLTON WANDERERS  Pym; Haworth, Greenhalgh; Nuttall, Seddon, Jennings; Butler, Jack, J. R. Smith, J. Smith, Vizard. *Scorer:* Jack.

**1–0** MANCHESTER CITY  Goodchild; Cookson, McCloy; Pringle, Cowan, McMullan; Austin, Browell, Roberts, Johnson, Hicks.

**1926–27** CARDIFF CITY  Farquharson; Nelson, Watson; Keenor, Sloan, Hardy; Curtis, Irving, Ferguson, L. Davies, McLachlan. *Scorer:* Ferguson.

**1–0** ARSENAL  Lewis; Parker, Kennedy; Baker, Butler, John; Hulme, Buchan, Brain, Blyth, Hoar.

**1927–28** BLACKBURN ROVERS  Crawford; Hutton, Jones; Healless, Rankin, Campbell; Thornewell, Puddefoot, Roscamp, McLean, Rigby. *Scorers:* Roscamp 2, McLean.

**3–1** HUDDERSFIELD TOWN  Mercer; Goodall, Barkas; Redfern, Wilson, Steele; A. Jackson, Kelly, Brown, Stephenson, W. H. Smith. *Scorer:* Jackson.

**1928–29** BOLTON WANDERERS Pym; Haworth, Finney; Kean, Seddon, Nuttall; Butler, McClelland, Blackmore, Gibson, W. Cook. *Scorers:* Butler, Blackmore.

**2-0** PORTSMOUTH Gilfillan; Mackie, Bell; Nichol, McIlwaine, Thackeray; Forward, J. Smith, Weddle, Watson, F. Cook.

**1929–30** ARSENAL Preedy; Parker, Hapgood; Baker, Seddon, John; Hulme, Jack, Lambert, James, Bastin. *Scorers:* James, Lambert.

**2-0** HUDDERSFIELD TOWN Turner; Goodall, Spence; Naylor, Wilson, Campbell; A. Jackson, Kelly, Davies, Raw, W. H. Smith.

**1930–31** WEST BROMWICH ALBION Pearson; Shaw, Trentham; Magee, W. Richardson, Edwards; Glidden, Carter, W. G. Richardson, Sandford, Wood. *Scorer:* W. G. Richardson.

**2-1** BIRMINGHAM Hibbs; Liddell, Barkas; Cringan, Morrall, Leslie; Briggs, Crosbie, Bradford, Gregg, Curtis. *Scorer:* Bradford.

**1931–32** NEWCASTLE UNITED McInroy; Nelson, Fairhurst; McKenzie, Davidson, Weaver; Boyd, Richardson, Allen, McMenemy, Lang. *Scorer:* Allen 2.

**2-1** ARSENAL Moss; Parker, Hapgood; C. Jones, Roberts, Male; Hulme, Jack, Lambert, Bastin, John. *Scorer:* John.

**1932–33** EVERTON Sagar; Cook, Cresswell; Britton, White, Thomson; Geldard, Dunn, Dean, Johnson, Stein. *Scorers:* Stein, Dean, Dunn.

**3-0** MANCHESTER CITY Langford; Cann, Dale; Busby, Cowan, Bray; Toseland, Marshall, Herd, McMullan, Brook.

**1933–34** MANCHESTER CITY Swift; Barnett, Dale; Busby, Cowan, Bray; Toseland, Marshall, Tilson, Herd, Brook. *Scorer:* Tilson 2.

**2-1** PORTSMOUTH Gilfillan; Mackie, W. Smith; Nichol, Allen, Thackeray; Worrall, J. Smith, Weddle, Easson, Rutherford. *Scorer:* Rutherford.

**1934–35** SHEFFIELD WEDNESDAY Brown; Nibloe, Catlin; Sharp, Millership, Burrows; Hooper, Surtees, Palethorpe, Starling, Rimmer. *Scorers:* Rimmer 2, Palethorpe, Hooper.

**4-2** WEST BROMWICH ALBION Pearson; Shaw, Trentham; Murphy, W. Richardson, Edwards; Glidden, Carter, W. G. Richardson, Sandford, Boyes. *Scorers:* Boyes, Sandford.

**1935–36** ARSENAL Wilson; Male, Hapgood; Crayston, Robertson, Copping; Hulme, Bowden, Drake, James, Bastin. *Scorer:* Drake.

**1-0** SHEFFIELD UNITED Smith; Hooper, Wilkinson; Jackson, Johnson, McPherson; Barton, Barclay, Dodds, Pickering, Williams.

**1936–37** SUNDERLAND Mapson; Gorman, Hall; Thomson, Johnson, McNab; Duns, Carter, Gurney, Gallacher, Burbanks. *Scorers:* Gurney, Carter, Burbanks.

**3-1** PRESTON NORTH END Burns; Gallimore, A. Beattie; Shankly, Tremelling, Milne; Dougal, Beresford, F. O'Donnell, Fagan, H. O'Donnell. *Scorer:* F. O'Donnell.

**1937–38** PRESTON NORTH END Holdcroft; Gallimore, A. Beattie; Shankly, Smith, Batey; Watmough, Mutch, Maxwell, R. Beattie, H. O'Donnell. *Scorer:* Mutch (pen).

**1-0** HUDDERSFIELD TOWN Hesford; Craig, Mountford; Willingham, Young, Boot; Hulme,
**aet** Isaac, McFadyen, Barclay, Beasley.

**1938–39** PORTSMOUTH Walker; Morgan, Rochford; Guthrie, Rowe, Wharton; Worrall, McAlinden, Anderson, Barlow, Parker. *Scorers:* Parker 2, Barlow, Anderson.

**4-1** WOLVERHAMPTON WANDERERS Scott; Morris, Taylor; Galley, Cullis, Gardiner; Burton, McIntosh, Westcott, Dorsett, Maguire. *Scorer:* Dorsett.

**1945–46** DERBY COUNTY Woodley; Nicholas, Howe; Bullions, Leuty, Musson; Harrison, Carter, Stamps, Doherty, Duncan. *Scorers:* H. Turner og, Doherty, Stamps 2.

**4-1** CHARLTON ATHLETIC Bartram; Phipps, Shreeve; H. Turner, Oakes, Johnson; Fell,
**aet** Brown, A. A. Turner, Welsh, Duffy. *Scorer:* H. Turner.

**1946–47** CHARLTON ATHLETIC Bartram; Crocker, Shreeve; Johnson, Phipps, Whittaker; Hurst, Dawson, W. Robinson, Welsh, Duffy. *Scorer:* Duffy.

**1-0** BURNLEY Strong; Woodruff, Mather; Attwell, Brown, Bray; Chew, Morris, Harrison,
**aet** Potts, F. P. Kippax.

**1947–48** MANCHESTER UNITED Crompton; Carey, Aston; Anderson, Chilton, Cockburn; Delaney, Morris, Rowley, Pearson, Mitten. *Scorers:* Rowley 2, Pearson, Anderson.

**4-2** BLACKPOOL Robinson; Shimwell, Crosland; Johnston, Hayward, Kelly; Matthews, Munro, Mortensen, Dick, Rickett. *Scorers:* Shimwell (pen), Mortensen.

**1948–49** WOLVERHAMPTON WANDERERS Williams; Pritchard, Springthorpe; W. Crook, Shorthouse, Wright; Hancock, Smyth, Pye, Dunn, Mullen. *Scorers:* Pye 2, Smyth.

**3-1** LEICESTER CITY Bradley; Jelly, Scott; W. Harrison, Plummer, King; Griffiths, Lee, J. Harrison, Chisholm, Adam. *Scorer:* Griffiths.

**1949–50** ARSENAL Swindin; Scott, Barnes; Forbes, L. Compton, Mercer; Cox, Logie, Goring, Lewis, D. Compton. *Scorer:* Lewis 2.

**2-0** LIVERPOOL Sidlow; Lambert, Spicer; Taylor, Hughes, Jones; Payne, Baron, Stubbins, Fagan, Liddell.

**1950–51** NEWCASTLE UNITED Fairbrother; Cowell, Corbett; Harvey, Brennan, Crowe; Walker, Taylor, Milburn, G. Robledo, Mitchell. *Scorer:* Milburn 2.

**2-0** BLACKPOOL Farm; Shimwell, Garrett; Johnston, Hayward, Kelly; Matthews, Mudie, Mortensen; W. J. Slater, Perry.

**1951–52** NEWCASTLE UNITED Simpson; Cowell, McMichael; Harvey, Brennan, E. Robledo, Walker, Foulkes, Milburn, G. Robledo, Mitchell. *Scorer:* G. Robledo.

**1-0** ARSENAL Swindin; Barnes, L. Smith; Forbes, Daniel, Mercer; Cox, Logie, Holton, Lishman, Roper.

**1952–53** BLACKPOOL Farm; Shimwell, Garrett; Fenton, Johnston, Robinson; Matthews, Taylor, Mortensen, Mudie, Perry. *Scorers:* Mortensen 3, Perry.

**4-3** BOLTON WANDERERS Hanson; Ball, R. Banks; Wheeler, Barass, Bell; Holden, Moir, Lofthouse, Hassall, Langton. *Scorers:* Lofthouse, Moir, Bell.

**1953–54** WEST BROMWICH ALBION Sanders; Kennedy, Millard; Dudley, Dugdale, Barlow; Griffin, Ryan, Allen, Nicholls, Lee. *Scorers:* Allen 2 (1 pen), Griffin.

**3-2** PRESTON NORTH END Thompson; Cunningham, Walton; Docherty, Marston, Forbes; Finney, Foster, Wayman, Baxter, Morrison. *Scorers:* Morrison, Wayman.

**1954–55** NEWCASTLE UNITED Simpson; Cowell, Batty; Scoular, Stokoe, Casey; White, Milburn, Keeble, Hannah, Mitchell. *Scorers:* Milburn, Mitchell, Hannah.
**3–1** MANCHESTER CITY Trautmann; Meadows, Little; Barnes, Ewing, Paul; Spurdle, Hayes, Revie, Johnstone, Fagan. *Scorer:* Johnstone.
**1955–56** MANCHESTER CITY Trautmann; Leivers, Little; Barnes, Ewing, Paul; Johnstone, Hayes, Revie, Dyson, Clarke. *Scorers:* Hayes, Dyson, Johnstone.
**3–1** BIRMINGHAM CITY Merrick; Hall, Green; Newman, Smith, Boyd; Astall, Kinsey, Brown, Murphy, Govan. *Scorer:* Kinsey.
**1956–57** ASTON VILLA Sims; Lynn, Aldis; Crowther, Dugdale, Saward; Smith, Sewell, Myerscough, Dixon, McParland. *Scorer:* McParland 2.
**2–1** MANCHESTER UNITED Wood; Foulkes, Byrne; Colman, J. Blanchflower, Edwards; Berry, Whelan, T. Taylor, R. Charlton, Pegg. *Scorer:* Taylor.
**1957–58** BOLTON WANDERERS Hopkinson; Hartle, Banks; Hennin, Higgins, Edwards; Birch, Stevens, Lofthouse, Parry, Holden. *Scorer:* Lofthouse 2.
**2–0** MANCHESTER UNITED Gregg; Foulkes, Greaves; Goodwin, Cope, Crowther; Dawson, E. Taylor; R. Charlton, Viollet, Webster.
**1958–59** NOTTINGHAM FOREST Thomson; Whare, McDonald; Whitefoot, McKinlay, Burkitt; Dwight, Quigley, Wilson, Gray, Imlach. *Scorers:* Dwight, Wilson.
**2–1** LUTON TOWN Baynham; McNally, Hawkes; Groves, Owen, Pacey; Bingham, Brown, Morton, Cummins, Gregory. *Scorer:* Pacey.
**1959–60** WOLVERHAMPTON WANDERERS Finlayson; Showell, Harris; Clamp, Slater, Flowers; Deeley, Stobart, Murray, Broadbent, Horne. *Scorers:* McGrath og, Deeley 2.
**3–0** BLACKBURN ROVERS Leyland; Bray, Whelan; Clayton, Woods, McGrath; Bimpson, Dobing, Dougan, Douglas, McLeod.
**1960–61** TOTTENHAM HOTSPUR Brown; Baker, Henry; D. Blanchflower, Norman, Mackay; Jones, White, Smith, Allen, Dyson. *Scorers:* Smith, Dyson.
**2–0** LEICESTER CITY Banks; Chalmers, Norman; McLintock, King, Appleton; Riley, Walsh, McIlmoyle, Keyworth, Cheesebrough.
**1961–62** TOTTENHAM HOTSPUR Brown; Baker, Henry; D. Blanchflower, Norman, Mackay; Medwin, White, Smith, Greaves, Jones. *Scorers:* Greaves, Smith, Blanchflower (pen).
**3–1** BURNLEY Blacklaw; Angus, Elder; Adamson, Cummings, Miller; Connelly, McIlroy, Pointer, Robson, Harris. *Scorer:* Robson.
**1962–63** MANCHESTER UNITED Gaskell; Dunne, Cantwell; Crerand, Foulkes, Setters; Giles, Quixall, Herd, Law, R. Charlton. *Scorers:* Law, Herd 2.
**3–1** LEICESTER CITY Banks; Sjoberg, Norman; McLintock, King, Appleton; Riley, Cross, Keyworth, Gibson, Stringfellow. *Scorer:* Keyworth.
**1963–64** WEST HAM UNITED Standen; Bond, Burkett; Bovington, Brown, Moore; Brabrook, Boyce, Byrne, Hurst, Sissons. *Scorers:* Sissons, Hurst, Boyce.
**3–2** PRESTON NORTH END Kelly; Ross, Smith; Lawton, Singleton, Kendall; Wilson, Ashworth, Dawson, Spavin, Holden. *Scorers:* Holden, Dawson.
**1964–65** LIVERPOOL Lawrence; Lawler, Byrne; Strong, Yeats, Stevenson; Callaghan, Hunt, St John, Smith, Thompson. *Scorers:* Hunt, St John.
**2–1** LEEDS UNITED Sprake; Reaney, Bell; Bremner, J. Charlton, Hunter; Giles, Storrie, Peacock,
**aet** Collins, Johanneson. *Scorer:* Bremner.
**1965–66** EVERTON West; Wright, Wilson; Gabriel, Labone, Harris; Scott, Trebilcock, Young, Harvey, Temple. *Scorers:* Trebilcock 2, Temple.
**3–2** SHEFFIELD WEDNESDAY Springett; Smith, Megson; Eustace, Ellis, Young; Pugh, Fantham, McCalliog, Ford, Quinn. *Scorers:* McCalliog, Ford.
**1966–67** TOTTENHAM HOTSPUR Jennings; Kinnear, Knowles; Mullery, England, Mackay; Robertson, Greaves, Gilzean, Venables, Saul. *Scorers:* Robertson, Saul.
**2–1** CHELSEA Bonetti; A. Harris, McCreadie; Hollins, Hinton, R. Harris; Cooke, Baldwin, Hateley, Tambling, Boyle. *Scorer:* Tambling.
**1967–68** WEST BROMWICH ALBION Osborne; Fraser, Williams; Brown, Talbut, Kaye (Clarke); Lovett, Collard, Astle, Hope, Clark. *Scorer:* Astle.
**1–0** EVERTON West; Wright, Wilson; Kendall, Labone, Harvey; Husband, Ball, Royle, Hurst,
**aet** Morrisey.
**1968–69** MANCHESTER CITY Dowd; Book, Pardoe; Doyle, Booth, Oakes; Summerbee, Bell, Lee, Young, Coleman. *Scorer:* Young.
**1–0** LEICESTER CITY Shilton; Rodrigues, Nish; Roberts, Woollett, Cross; Fern, Gibson, Lochhead, Clarke, Glover (Manley).
**1969–70** CHELSEA Bonetti; Webb, McCreadie; Hollins, Dempsey, R. Harris (Hinton); Baldwin, Houseman, Osgood, Hutchinson, Cooke. *Scorers:* Houseman, Hutchinson.
**2–2** LEEDS UNITED Sprake; Madeley, Cooper; Bremner, J. Charlton, Hunter; Lorimer, Clarke,
**aet** Jones, Giles, E. Gray. *Scorers:* Charlton, Jones.
*Replay (at Old Trafford, Manchester)*
**R:2–1** CHELSEA Bonetti; R. Harris, McCreadie; Hollins, Dempsey, Webb; Baldwin, Cooke, Osgood
**aet** (Hinton), Hutchinson, Houseman. *Scorers:* Osgood, Webb.
LEEDS UNITED Harvey; Madeley, Cooper; Bremner, J. Charlton, Hunter; Lorimer, Clarke, Jones, Giles, E. Gray. *Scorer:* Jones.
**1970–71** ARSENAL Wilson; Rice, McNab; Storey (Kelly), McLintock, Simpson; Armstrong, Graham, Radford, Kennedy, George. *Scorers:* Kelly, George.
**2–1** LIVERPOOL Clemence; Lawler, Lindsay; Smith, Lloyd, Hughes; Callaghan, Evans
**aet** (Thompson), Heighway, Toshack, Hall. *Scorer:* Heighway.
**1971–72** LEEDS UNITED Harvey; Reaney, Madeley; Bremner, J. Charlton, Hunter; Lorimer, Clarke, Jones, Giles, E. Gray. *Scorer:* Clarke.
**1–0** ARSENAL Barnett; Rice, McNab; Storey, McLintock, Simpson; Armstrong, Ball, George, Radford (Kennedy), Graham.

**1972–73** SUNDERLAND Montgomery; Malone, Guthrie; Horswill, Watson, Pitt; Kerr, Hughes, Halom, Porterfield, Tueart. *Scorer:* Porterfield.

**1-0** LEEDS UNITED Harvey; Reaney, Cherry; Bremner, Madeley, Hunter; Lorimer, Clarke, Jones, Giles, E. Gray (Yorath).

**1973–74** LIVERPOOL Clemence; Smith, Lindsay, Thompson, Cormack, Hughes, Keegan, Hall, Heighway, Toshack, Callaghan. *Scorers:* Keegan 2, Heighway.

**3-0** NEWCASTLE UNITED McFaul; Clark, Kennedy, McDermott, Howard, Moncur, Smith (Gibb), Cassidy, Macdonald, Tudor, Hibbitt.

**1974–75** WEST HAM UNITED Day; McDowell, T. Taylor, Lock, Lampard, Bonds, Paddon, Brooking, Jennings, A. Taylor, Holland. *Scorer:* A. Taylor 2.

**2-0** FULHAM Mellor; Cutbush, Lacy, Moore, Fraser, Mullery, Conway, Slough, Mitchell, Busby, Barrett.

**1975–76** SOUTHAMPTON Turner; Rodrigues, Peach; Holmes, Blyth, Steele; Gilchrist, Channon, Osgood, McCalliog, Stokes. *Scorer:* Stokes.

**1-0** MANCHESTER UNITED Stepney; Forsyth, Houston; Daly, Greenhoff, Buchan; Coppell, McIlroy, Pearson, Macari, Hill (McCreery).

**1976–77** MANCHESTER UNITED Stepney; Nicholl, Albiston; McIlroy, B. Greenhoff, Buchan; Coppell, J. Greenhoff, Pearson, Macari, Hill (McCreery). *Scorers:* Pearson, J. Greenhoff.

**2-1** LIVERPOOL Clemence; Neal, Jones; Smith, Kennedy, Hughes; Keegan, Case, Heighway, Johnson (Callaghan), McDermott. *Scorer:* Case.

**1977–78** IPSWICH TOWN Cooper; Burley, Mills; Osborne (Lambert), Hunter, Beattie, Talbot, Wark, Mariner, Geddis, Woods. *Scorer:* Osborne.

**1-0** ARSENAL Jennings; Rice, Nelson, Price, Young, O'Leary, Brady (Rix), Hudson, Macdonald, Stapleton, Sunderland.

**1978–79** ARSENAL Jennings; Rice, Nelson, Talbot, O'Leary, Young, Brady, Sunderland, Stapleton, Price (Walford), Rix. *Scorers:* Talbot, Stapleton, Sunderland.

**3-2** MANCHESTER UNITED Bailey; Nicholl, Albiston, McIlroy, McQueen, Buchan, Coppell, J. Greenhoff, Jordan, Macari, Thomas. *Scorers:* McQueen, McIlroy.

**1979–80** WEST HAM UNITED Parkes; Stewart, Lampard, Bonds, Martin, Devonshire, Allen, Pearson, Cross, Brooking, Pike. *Scorer:* Brooking.

**1-0** ARSENAL Jennings; Rice, Devine (Nelson), Talbot, O'Leary, Young, Brady, Sunderland, Stapleton, Price, Rix

**1980–81** TOTTENHAM HOTSPUR Aleksic; Hughton, Miller, Roberts, Perryman, Villa (Brooke), Ardiles, Archibald, Galvin, Hoddle, Crooks. *Scorer:* Hutchison og.

**1-1** MANCHESTER CITY Corrigan; Ranson, McDonald, Reid, Power, Caton, Bennett, Gow, MacKenzie,
**aet** Hutchison (Henry), Reeves. *Scorer:* Hutchison.

***R*:3-2** TOTTENHAM HOTSPUR Aleksic; Hughton, Miller, Roberts, Perryman, Villa, Ardiles, Archibald, Galvin, Hoddle, Crooks. *Scorers:* Villa 2, Crooks.

MANCHESTER CITY Corrigan; Ranson, McDonald (Tueart), Caton, Reid, Gow, Power, MacKenzie, Reeves, Bennett, Hutchison. *Scorers:* MacKenzie, Reeves (pen).

# FA CHARITY SHIELD WINNERS 1908–81

| Year | Winners | Runners-up | Score |
|------|---------|------------|-------|
| 1908 | Manchester U | QPR | 4-0 after 1-1 draw |
| 1909 | Newcastle U | Northampton T | 2-0 |
| 1910 | Brighton | Aston Villa | 1-0 |
| 1911 | Manchester U | Swindon T | 8-4 |
| 1912 | Blackburn R | QPR | 2-1 |
| 1913 | Professionals | Amateurs | 7-2 |
| 1919 | WBA | Tottenham H | 2-0 |
| 1920 | Tottenham H | Burnley | 2-0 |
| 1921 | Huddersfield | Liverpool | 1-0 |
| 1922 | Not played | | |
| 1923 | Professionals | Amateurs | 2-0 |
| 1924 | Professionals | Amateurs | 3-1 |
| 1925 | Amateurs | Professionals | 6-1 |
| 1926 | Amateurs | Professionals | 6-3 |
| 1927 | Cardiff C | Corinthians | 2-1 |
| 1928 | Everton | Blackburn R | 2-1 |
| 1929 | Professionals | Amateurs | 3-0 |
| 1930 | Arsenal | Sheffield W | 2-1 |
| 1931 | Arsenal | WBA | 1-0 |
| 1932 | Everton | Newcastle U | 5-3 |
| 1933 | Arsenal | Everton | 3-0 |
| 1934 | Arsenal | Manchester C | 4-0 |
| 1935 | Sheffield W | Arsenal | 1-0 |
| 1936 | Sunderland | Arsenal | 2-1 |
| 1937 | Manchester C | Sunderland | 2-0 |
| 1938 | Arsenal | Preston NE | 2-1 |
| 1948 | Arsenal | Manchester U | 4-3 |
| 1949 | Portsmouth | Wolverhampton W | 1-1* |
| 1950 | World Cup Team | Canadian Touring Team | 4-2 |
| 1951 | Tottenham H | Newcastle U | 2-1 |
| 1952 | Manchester U | Newcastle U | 4-2 |
| 1953 | Arsenal | Blackpool | 3-1 |
| 1954 | Wolverhampton W | WBA | 4-4* |
| 1955 | Chelsea | Newcastle U | 3-0 |
| 1956 | Manchester U | Manchester C | 1-0 |
| 1957 | Manchester U | Aston Villa | 4-0 |
| 1958 | Bolton W | Wolverhampton W | 4-1 |
| 1959 | Wolverhampton W | Nottingham F | 3-1 |
| 1960 | Burnley | Wolverhampton W | 2-2* |
| 1961 | Tottenham H | FA XI | 3-2 |
| 1962 | Tottenham H | Ipswich T | 5-1 |
| 1963 | Everton | Manchester U | 4-0 |
| 1964 | Liverpool | West Ham U | 2-2* |
| 1965 | Manchester U | Liverpool | 2-2* |
| 1966 | Liverpool | Everton | 1-0 |
| 1967 | Manchester U | Tottenham H | 3-3* |
| 1968 | Manchester C | WBA | 6-1 |
| 1969 | Leeds U | Manchester C | 2-1 |
| 1970 | Everton | Chelsea | 2-1 |
| 1971 | Leicester C | Liverpool | 1-0 |
| 1972 | Manchester C | Aston Villa | 1-0 |
| 1973 | Burnley | Manchester C | 1-0 |
| 1974 | Liverpool† | Leeds | 1-1 |
| 1975 | Derby Co | West Ham U | 2-0 |
| 1976 | Liverpool | Southampton | 1-0 |
| 1977 | Liverpool | Manchester U | 0-0* |
| 1978 | Nottingham F | Ipswich T | 5-0 |
| 1979 | Liverpool | Arsenal | 3-1 |
| 1980 | Liverpool | West Ham U | 1-0 |

*Each club retained shield for six months.* † *Won on penalties.*

## FA CHARITY SHIELD 1981

**Aston Villa (1) 2 Tottenham H (1) 2**

At Wembley, 22 August, 1981. Attendance 92,500. Receipts £431,000

*Aston Villa:* Rimmer; Swain, Gibson, Evans, McNaught, Mortimer (Blair), Bremner, Geddis, Withe, Cowans, Morley.
*Tottenham H:* Clemence; Hughton, Miller, Roberts, Villa, Perryman, Ardiles, Archibald, Galvin, Hoddle, Falco.
*Scorers:* Aston Villa – Withe 2; Tottenham H – Falco 2.

# THE SCOTTISH SEASON 1981–82

When the time comes to review one season, it is almost time to begin the next. There are plenty who look forward to the start of a new season and we live in high hopes that it will be as interesting as the last; we remember many good matches, notable goals, unusual decisions – and quietly forget those freezing evenings when nothing happened for 90 minutes and we wondered why we had bothered to come out at all.

The League Cup programme opened in 1981–82 at the beginning of August, and interest was immediately aroused when Celtic were defeated on the first day by St Mirren, and subsequently by St Johnstone. From such a start they could not recover, and for the first time in many years they failed to reach the final stages. Notable achievements came from Brechin and Forfar, both of whom won their sections against First Division opposition. The quarter-finals were completed without any upsets, and after the semi-finals, in which Rangers just managed to overcome St Mirren, and Dundee United won a splendid victory at Aberdeen after trailing in the first leg, the final was fought out at Hampden. United missed their chances in a first half which they dominated, and Rangers took over as the game progressed, just managing to edge ahead in the final minutes.

Celtic, smarting from their League Cup rebuff, were at the top of the Premier Division throughout the whole season, winning their first seven games and establishing a seemingly impregnable lead. In the New Year Aberdeen lost to Celtic on 30 January in a game which some, with perhaps more luck than insight, heralded as the championship decider. In February, though, Aberdeen had three no-score draws and a win over Airdrie and in their next sixteen games Aberdeen scored 46 goals whilst only conceding 10. Apart from a stutter when they lost 1-3 to Morton in mid-April, they brushed aside all opposition, and Celtic supporters, sitting comfortably wondering who was going to come second, suddenly found an uncomfortable gale about their necks, relieved only when their team scored the goals which gave them victory and the championship, late in their last match. Rangers were still unconvincing, and in a stage of transition. Dundee United, an exciting team to watch, were going well until the break enforced by the weather; thereafter they showed some uncertainty, but finished with two important wins to regain their place in Europe. Hibernian established themselves nicely in the middle of the table, and proved that they could be difficult to beat, while Morton, with a rather indifferent away record, kept out of trouble but never showed much of a challenge for the lead. The three teams at the bottom spent some time in sorting their final order; although Airdrie looked lost by mid-April, the Thistle challenge went on for longer, and Dundee just managed to hold them off, the final cushion of four points not really indicating the closeness of the final encounters. Dundee were something of an enigma, reported to be playing much better than their league position warranted. None the less, it is the points that count, and it is an indication of the competition aroused by such a small number in the Premier Division that a team like Dundee has no time to re-establish itself on promotion, but must hoard points like gold from the start of the season.

Motherwell, a well-balanced side astutely managed by David Hay, ran away with the First Division; there was a stern battle for the second promotion spot, and Hearts, who had looked favourites for it, came unstuck at the last fence as Kilmarnock, with a vast final victory, went ahead of them. Clydebank and St Johnstone had been up with the others until the last month, but fell away, whilst Ayr, who had looked promotion contenders until February, slipped slowly down the list. East Stirling and Queen of the South were obvious relegation candidates for some time; Dumbarton, after a weak start, drew into safety and Raith Rovers, unable to recapture previous form, were happy to avoid the drop. The other teams, including a Queen's Park side which had a very sound season, were not in serious contention in either direction.

It was almost the same story at the top of the Second Division, for Clyde were quickly ahead of the field, and ran out convincing winners. Again, the contest for the second place was sharp, and five teams were in the hunt until the last moment. Alloa eventually edged ahead of Arbroath on goal difference, but there was tremendous cut-and-thrust between the leaders in the last weeks, and anything could have happened.

The Cup team of the year was Forfar Athletic. They reached the quarter-finals of the League Cup, but went one better in the Scottish Cup, disposing of First Division opponents Hamilton, Hearts and Queen's Park on the way. Then, in the semi-final with Rangers at Hampden, they threatened to cause a cataclysmic upset until Rangers convincingly won the resulting replay. Aberdeen, scoring after only a few seconds in their third-round match against Motherwell, nevertheless found the First Division leaders a handful and that proved to be the only goal of a fascinating and exciting game. If Aberdeen deserved their win, Motherwell at least came away from the encounter with their reputation enhanced. Aberdeen's next-round encounter removed Celtic from the competition, again by just one goal. Eventually Aberdeen were worthy winners in the final, though after extra time and following an early Rangers goal which must have been one of their best in the season.

The Highland League was won by Inverness Caledonian, who displaced Keith from their perch after an imposing run at the top.

In the two top European tournaments, Scottish representatives did not get far, but the UEFA Cup was a different story. The exploits of Dundee United were soon acclaimed furth of Scotland, for they took five away goals against Monaco, another five in a scintillating display against the much-fancied Borussia Moenchengladbach, and yet another five in the next round against Winterslag. Then came that break for the weather, and United failed in the away leg of their Yugoslavian match – a sore disappointment after their magnificent earlier displays. Aberdeen, with a team containing even more Scots than their opponents, had a triumphant encounter with Ipswich Town, then currently at the head of the English league; they swept through the next round, but faltered in the home leg against SV Hamburg, and had an insufficient lead for the away game. Our teams did us well this year, and, with experience in Europe counting for much, it is good to see the same teams again taking the European field in the coming season.

So much has been said and written about our luck in the World Cup draw that it is barely worth further comment. Scotland went out to Spain as underdogs, with the minimum of ballyhoo and the maximum of sensibly expressed comment from the manager. It was so close! Yet, at the end of the day, for all our disappointment, we may well be pleased with our team and with their overall showing. It is also appropriate to congratulate the enormous number of fans who found their way to Spain and gave their team such excellent support. It remains only to congratulate England and Northern Ireland on reaching the secondary stage. Meanwhile, we are already looking forward four years, to next time.

ALAN ELLIOTT

## SCOTTISH LEAGUE REFEREES 1981–82

H. Alexander (Irvine)
R. R. Cuthill (Winchburgh)
M. Delaney (Cleland)
D. S. Downie (Edinburgh)
J. Duncan (Gorebridge)
A. Ferguson (Giffnock)
D. M. Galloway (Pitlessie)
K. J. Hope (Clarkston)
A. N. Huett (Edinburgh)
W. P. Knowles (Inverurie)
A. G. M. McFaull (Knightswood)
B. R. McGinlay (Balfron)
A. McGunnigle (Glasgow)
F. McKenzie (Wishaw)
W. McLeish (Stonehouse)
T. Muirhead (Stenhousemuir)

E. H. Pringle (Edinburgh)
D. Ramsay (Edinburgh)
J. R. S. Renton (Cowdenbeath)
B. Robertson (East Kilbride)
C. C. Sinclair (Forfar)
G. B. Smith (Edinburgh)
K. Stewart (Glasgow)
D. F. T. Syme (Rutherglen)
L. B. Thow (Ayr)
J. J. Timmons (Kilwinning)
R. B. Valentine (Dundee)
A. W. Waddell (Penicuik)
C. J. White (Clarkston)
H. F. Williamson (Renfrew)
H. Young (Larkhall)

# SCOTTISH LEAGUE 1981-82

## PREMIER DIVISION

| | | | Home | | | | | Away | | | | |
|---|---|---|---|---|---|---|---|---|---|---|---|---|
| | P | W | D | L | F | A | W | D | L | F | A | Pts |
| 1. Celtic | 36 | 12 | 5 | 1 | 41 | 16 | 12 | 2 | 4 | 38 | 17 | 55 |
| 2. Aberdeen | 36 | 12 | 4 | 2 | 36 | 15 | 11 | 3 | 4 | 35 | 14 | 53 |
| 3. Rangers | 36 | 10 | 5 | 3 | 34 | 16 | 6 | 6 | 6 | 23 | 29 | 43 |
| 4. Dundee U | 36 | 10 | 4 | 4 | 40 | 14 | 5 | 6 | 7 | 21 | 24 | 40 |
| 5. St Mirren | 36 | 8 | 4 | 6 | 30 | 23 | 6 | 5 | 7 | 19 | 29 | 37 |
| 6. Hibernian | 36 | 8 | 7 | 3 | 23 | 14 | 3 | 7 | 8 | 15 | 26 | 36 |
| 7. Morton | 36 | 9 | 6 | 3 | 20 | 12 | 0 | 6 | 12 | 11 | 42 | 30 |
| 8. Dundee | 36 | 7 | 2 | 9 | 28 | 34 | 4 | 2 | 12 | 18 | 38 | 26 |
| 9. Partick T | 36 | 4 | 5 | 9 | 19 | 23 | 2 | 5 | 11 | 16 | 36 | 22 |
| 10. Airdrieonians | 36 | 5 | 4 | 9 | 24 | 36 | 0 | 4 | 14 | 7 | 40 | 18 |

## FIRST DIVISION

| | | | Home | | | | | Away | | | | |
|---|---|---|---|---|---|---|---|---|---|---|---|---|
| | P | W | D | L | F | A | W | D | L | F | A | Pts |
| 1. Motherwell | 39 | 12 | 7 | 0 | 41 | 17 | 14 | 2 | 4 | 51 | 19 | 61 |
| 2. Kilmarnock | 39 | 6 | 12 | 2 | 25 | 11 | 11 | 5 | 3 | 35 | 18 | 51 |
| 3. Hearts | 39 | 12 | 2 | 5 | 33 | 19 | 9 | 6 | 5 | 32 | 18 | 50 |
| 4. Clydebank | 39 | 12 | 3 | 5 | 33 | 27 | 7 | 5 | 7 | 28 | 26 | 46 |
| 5. St Johnstone | 39 | 12 | 3 | 4 | 44 | 29 | 5 | 5 | 10 | 25 | 31 | 42 |
| 6. Ayr U | 39 | 12 | 6 | 1 | 39 | 20 | 3 | 6 | 11 | 17 | 30 | 42 |
| 7. Hamilton A | 39 | 10 | 3 | 6 | 20 | 16 | 6 | 5 | 9 | 32 | 33 | 40 |
| 8. Queen's Park | 39 | 11 | 5 | 4 | 32 | 17 | 2 | 5 | 12 | 9 | 24 | 36 |
| 9. Falkirk | 39 | 8 | 8 | 4 | 26 | 19 | 3 | 6 | 10 | 23 | 33 | 36 |
| 10. Dunfermline Ath | 39 | 3 | 9 | 7 | 24 | 31 | 8 | 5 | 7 | 22 | 25 | 36 |
| 11. Dumbarton | 39 | 10 | 1 | 9 | 25 | 30 | 3 | 8 | 8 | 24 | 31 | 35 |
| 12. Raith R | 39 | 5 | 2 | 13 | 13 | 32 | 6 | 5 | 8 | 18 | 27 | 29 |
| 13. East Stirling | 39 | 4 | 6 | 9 | 20 | 35 | 3 | 4 | 13 | 18 | 42 | 24 |
| 14. Queen of the S | 39 | 2 | 5 | 13 | 25 | 50 | 2 | 5 | 12 | 19 | 43 | 18 |

## SECOND DIVISION

| | | | Home | | | | | Away | | | | |
|---|---|---|---|---|---|---|---|---|---|---|---|---|
| | P | W | D | L | F | A | W | D | L | F | A | Pts |
| 1. Clyde | 39 | 11 | 6 | 2 | 35 | 16 | 13 | 5 | 2 | 44 | 22 | 59 |
| 2. Alloa | 39 | 9 | 6 | 4 | 33 | 25 | 10 | 6 | 4 | 33 | 17 | 50 |
| 3. Arbroath | 39 | 12 | 5 | 2 | 34 | 16 | 8 | 5 | 7 | 28 | 34 | 50 |
| 4. Berwick R | 39 | 14 | 4 | 2 | 46 | 15 | 6 | 4 | 9 | 20 | 23 | 48 |
| 5. Brechin C | 39 | 9 | 5 | 5 | 28 | 19 | 9 | 5 | 6 | 33 | 24 | 46 |
| 6. Forfar Ath | 39 | 11 | 6 | 3 | 35 | 12 | 4 | 9 | 6 | 24 | 23 | 45 |
| 7. East Fife | 39 | 7 | 5 | 8 | 23 | 24 | 7 | 4 | 8 | 25 | 27 | 37 |
| 8. Stirling Albion | 39 | 9 | 5 | 6 | 25 | 18 | 3 | 6 | 10 | 14 | 26 | 35 |
| 9. Cowdenbeath | 39 | 8 | 6 | 6 | 34 | 26 | 3 | 7 | 9 | 17 | 31 | 35 |
| 10. Montrose | 39 | 8 | 4 | 8 | 28 | 31 | 4 | 4 | 11 | 21 | 43 | 32 |
| 11. Albion R | 39 | 8 | 3 | 8 | 28 | 28 | 5 | 2 | 13 | 24 | 46 | 31 |
| 12. Meadowbank T | 39 | 8 | 6 | 6 | 34 | 29 | 2 | 4 | 13 | 15 | 33 | 30 |
| 13. Stenhousemuir | 39 | 6 | 5 | 8 | 22 | 28 | 5 | 1 | 14 | 19 | 37 | 28 |
| 14. Stranraer | 39 | 5 | 1 | 13 | 22 | 44 | 2 | 5 | 13 | 14 | 41 | 20 |

## HIGHLAND LEAGUE

| | P | W | D | L | F | A | Pts |
|---|---|---|---|---|---|---|---|
| Inverness Caledonian | 30 | 22 | 5 | 3 | 76 | 28 | 49 |
| Peterhead | 30 | 17 | 7 | 6 | 67 | 39 | 41 |
| Keith | 30 | 17 | 6 | 7 | 69 | 28 | 40 |
| Elgin City | 30 | 15 | 7 | 8 | 55 | 37 | 37 |
| Brora Rangers | 30 | 13 | 8 | 9 | 49 | 38 | 34 |
| Ross County | 30 | 12 | 9 | 9 | 61 | 52 | 33 |
| Fraserburgh | 30 | 15 | 3 | 12 | 56 | 48 | 33 |
| Inverness Thistle | 30 | 11 | 9 | 10 | 56 | 55 | 31 |

| | P | W | D | L | F | A | Pts |
|---|---|---|---|---|---|---|---|
| Huntly | 30 | 9 | 11 | 10 | 62 | 71 | 29 |
| Rothes | 30 | 13 | 2 | 15 | 52 | 55 | 28 |
| Deveronvale | 30 | 9 | 9 | 12 | 47 | 47 | 27 |
| Clachnacuddin | 30 | 10 | 6 | 14 | 49 | 59 | 26 |
| Forres Mechanics | 30 | 9 | 5 | 16 | 53 | 84 | 23 |
| Buckie Thistle | 30 | 5 | 9 | 16 | 33 | 62 | 19 |
| Nairn County | 30 | 5 | 6 | 19 | 46 | 85 | 16 |
| Lossiemouth | 30 | 6 | 2 | 22 | 31 | 74 | 14 |

# ABERDEEN Premier Division

*Year Formed:* 1903.
*Ground:* Pittodrie Stadium. *Size:* 110yd×71yd. *Capacity:* 24,000 (all seated and all covered).
*Telephone:* Aberdeen 632328, 633497.
*Manager:* Alec Ferguson. *Assistant-Manager:* Archie Knox.
*Secretary:* I. J. Taggart. *Trainer:* Teddy Scott. *Physiotherapist:* Roland Arnott.
*Club Colours:* Red shirts, red shorts, red stockings.
*Club Nickname:* The Dons.
*Record Attendance:* 45,061 v Hearts, Scottish Cup 4th rd, 13 March, 1954.
(Present Aberdeen FC have had no other home but Pittodrie.)
*Record Transfer Fee Received:* £800,000 from Tottenham H for Steve Archibald, May 1980.
**European Competitions:** *Fairs Cup* 1968–69; *European Cup-Winners' Cup* 1967–68, 1970–71, 1978–79; *UEFA Cup* 1971–72, 1972–73, 1973–74, 1977–78, 1979–80, 1981–82; *European Cup* 1980–81.

## 1981–82 LEAGUE RECORD

| Match No. | Date | Venue | Opponents | Result | H/T Score | League Pos'n | Goalscorers | Attendance |
|---|---|---|---|---|---|---|---|---|
| 1 | Aug 29 | A | Dundee U | L 1-4 | 0-3 | — | McLeish | 10,598 |
| 2 | Sept 5 | H | Celtic | L 1-3 | 1-2 | 10 | Strachan (pen) | 18,825 |
| 3 | 12 | A | Partick T | W 2-0 | 0-0 | 8 | McCall, Cowan | 3606 |
| 4 | 19 | H | Hibernian | W 1-0 | 0-0 | 8 | Simpson | 10,852 |
| 5 | 26 | A | Airdrieonians | W 4-0 | 3-0 | 3 | McLeish, Weir 2, Hewitt | 3000 |
| 6 | Oct 3 | H | Morton | W 2-0 | 0-0 | 2 | Watson, Rougvie | 11,007 |
| 7 | 10 | A | Rangers | D 0-0 | 0-0 | 2 | | 28,000 |
| 8 | 17 | A | St Mirren | W 2-1 | 1-1 | 2 | Watson 2 | 6870 |
| 9 | 24 | H | Dundee | W 2-1 | 2-0 | 2 | McCall, Rougvie | 11,506 |
| 10 | 31 | H | Dundee U | D 1-1 | 1-0 | 2 | Black | 11,035 |
| 11 | Nov 7 | A | Celtic | L 1-2 | 0-1 | 2 | Strachan | 29,326 |
| 12 | 14 | H | Partick T | W 2-1 | 1-0 | 2 | Harrow, Watson | 11,193 |
| 13 | 21 | A | Hibernian | D 1-1 | 0-1 | 2 | Simpson | 7600 |
| 14 | 28 | H | Airdrieonians | D 0-0 | 0-0 | 2 | | 8030 |
| 15 | Dec 5 | A | Morton | L 1-2 | 0-0 | 4 | Hewitt | 3102 |
| 16 | Jan 30 | H | Celtic | L 1-3 | 1-1 | 6 | McMaster | 20,000 |
| 17 | Feb 3 | A | Partick T | D 0-0 | 0-0 | — | | 2317 |
| 18 | 6 | H | Morton | D 0-0 | 0-0 | 6 | | 7217 |
| 19 | 20 | A | Airdrieonians | W 3-0 | 0-0 | 4 | Hewitt, McGhee 2 | 3500 |
| 20 | 27 | H | Dundee | D 0-0 | 0-0 | 4 | | 8961 |
| 21 | Mar 10 | H | Hibernian | W 3-1 | 1-1 | — | Cooper, Jarvie, Strachan (pen) | 8691 |
| 22 | 13 | A | Rangers | W 3-1 | 2-0 | 3 | Cowan, Cooper, Watson | 20,000 |
| 23 | 17 | A | Dundee | W 3-0 | 1-0 | — | Simpson, Cowan, Hewitt | 6126 |
| 24 | 20 | H | Dundee U | W 2-1 | 1-0 | 2 | Hewitt, McLeish | 12,056 |
| 25 | 27 | A | Celtic | W 1-0 | 0-0 | 2 | Kennedy | 30,080 |
| 26 | Apr 10 | A | Hibernian | W 3-0 | 1-0 | 2 | Jarvie, Strachan, McGhee | 8000 |
| 27 | 14 | H | St Mirren | W 4-1 | 0-0 | — | Rougvie 2, Simpson, Strachan | 12,119 |
| 28 | 17 | A | Morton | L 1-2 | 0-1 | 2 | McGhee | 3000 |
| 29 | 21 | H | Rangers | W 3-1 | 0-0 | — | McGhee, Rougvie, Black | 8750 |
| 30 | 24 | H | Airdrieonians | W 2-0 | 0-0 | 2 | McGhee, Black | 8000 |
| 31 | May 1 | A | Dundee | W 5-0 | 2-0 | 2 | McLeish, Bell, Harrow, McCall Glennie (og) | 6415 |
| 32 | 3 | H | Partick T | W 3-1 | 2-1 | — | McCall, Angus, Hewitt | 6000 |
| 33 | 5 | A | Dundee U | W 2-1 | 2-1 | — | Hewitt 2 | 6587 |
| 34 | 8 | H | St Mirren | W 5-1 | 3-1 | 2 | Strachan 2 (1 pen), Cooper, McGhee 2 | 9000 |
| 35 | 12 | A | St Mirren | W 2-0 | 1-0 | — | McLeish, Rougvie | 3942 |
| 36 | 15 | H | Rangers | W 4-0 | 4-0 | 2 | Jackson (og), Hewitt 3 | 18,000 |

**Final League Position: 2**

### Goalscorers
*League* (71): Hewitt 11, McGhee 8, Strachan 7 (3 pens), Rougvie 6, McLeish 5, Watson 5, McCall 4, Simpson 4, Black 3, Cooper 3, Cowan 3, Harrow 2, Jarvie 2, Weir 2, Angus 1, Bell 1, Kennedy 1, McMaster 1, own goals 2.
*League Cup* (21): Strachan 6 (4 pens), McGhee 4, Bell 2, Hewitt 2, Weir 2, Cooper 1, Harrow 1, Kennedy 1, McCall 1, McMaster 1.
*Scottish Cup* (14): Strachan 4 (3 pens), McGhee 3, Hewitt 2, Simpson 2, Cooper 1, McLeish 1, Weir 1.

**Honours**

*Scottish League* – Division 1 Champions 1954–55; Runners-up 1910–11, 1936–37, 1955–56, 1970–71, 1971–72; Premier Division Champions 1979–80; Runners-up 1977–78, 1980–81, 1981–82.
*Scottish Cup* – Winners 1947, 1970, 1982; Runners-up 1937, 1953, 1954, 1959, 1967, 1978.
*Scottish League Cup* – Winners 1955–56, 1976–77; Runners-up 1946–47, 1978–79, 1979–80.
*Drybrough Cup* – Winners 1971.
*Record Victory:* 13-0 v Peterhead, Scottish Cup, 9 Feb, 1923.
*Record Defeat:* 0-8 v Celtic, Division 1, 30 Jan, 1965.
*Most League Points:* 61, Division 1, 1935–36.
*Most Individual League Goals in Season:* Benny Yorston, 38, Division 1, 1929–30.
*Most Capped Player:* Willie Miller, 19, Scotland.

| Leighton J. | Kennedy S. | Rougvie D. | McMaster J. | Cooper N. | Hamilton D. | McLeish A. | Miller W. | Strachan G. | Watson A. | Simpson N. | McGhee M. | Bell D. | Jarvie A. | Black E. | Hewitt J. | Weir P. | Cowan S. | McCall W. | Angus I. | Harrow A. | Mitchell C. B. | Match No. |
|---|---|---|---|---|---|---|---|---|---|---|---|---|---|---|---|---|---|---|---|---|---|---|
| 1 | 2 | 3* | 4 |  |  | 5 | 6 | 7 | 12 |  | 9 | 8† | 13 |  | 10 | 11 |  |  |  |  |  | 1 |
| 1 | 2 | 12 | 3 |  |  | 5 | 6 | 7 | 4 | 9† | 8* |  |  | 11 | 13 | 10 |  |  |  |  |  | 2 |
| 1 | 2 | 10† | 8 |  |  | 5 | 6* | 7 | 4 | 12 |  |  |  | 11 | 13 | 9 |  |  |  |  |  | 3 |
| 1 | 2 | 3 | 4 |  |  | 5 | 6 | 7 | 8* | 12 | 9 |  |  |  | 10† | 11 | 13 |  |  |  |  | 4 |
| 1 | 2 | 3 | 8 |  |  | 5 | 6 | 7 | 4 |  | 9 |  |  |  | 10* | 11 | 12 |  |  |  |  | 5 |
| 1 | 2 | 3 | 12 |  |  | 5* | 6 | 7 | 4 | 8 | 13 |  |  | 11 | 10† | 9 |  |  |  |  |  | 6 |
| 1 | 2 | 3 | 12 | 5 |  |  | 6 | 7 | 8* |  | 9 |  |  |  | 10† | 11 | 13 |  |  |  |  | 7 |
| 1 | 2 | 3 | 12 |  |  | 5 | 6 | 7 | 4 | 8* | 9 |  |  |  | 10 | 11 |  |  |  |  |  | 8 |
| 1 | 2 | 3 | 8* |  |  | 5 | 6 | 7 | 12 | 4 | 9 |  |  |  | 11 | 10 |  |  |  |  |  | 9 |
| 1 | 2 | 3 | 4 |  |  | 5 | 6 | 7 | 12 | 11 | 9* | 8 |  |  | 10 |  |  |  |  |  |  | 10 |
| 1 | 2 | 13 | 3 |  |  | 5 | 6 | 7 | 4* | 8 | 9 |  |  |  | 10† | 12 | 11 |  |  |  |  | 11 |
| 1 | 2 | 3 | 4 |  |  | 5* | 6 | 7 | 12 | 10 | 13 | 8† |  |  | 11 | 9 |  |  |  |  |  | 12 |
| 1 | 2 | 3 | 5* |  |  |  | 6 | 7 | 4 | 10 | 9 | 11 |  |  | 12 | 8† | 13 |  |  |  |  | 13 |
| 1 | 2 | 3 | 8 |  |  | 5 | 6 |  | 4 | 12 | 9 | 7* |  | 13 | 11 | 10† |  |  |  |  |  | 14 |
| 1 | 2 | 3* | 12 |  |  | 5 | 6 | 7 | 4 | 10 | 9† | 8 | 13 |  | 11 |  |  |  |  |  |  | 15 |
| 1 | 2 | 3 | 4 |  |  | 5 | 6 | 7 |  | 9* | 8 | 12 |  |  | 10 | 11 |  |  |  |  |  | 16 |
| 1 | 2 | 3 | 4* |  |  | 5 | 6 | 7 | 12 | 8 | 9† | 10 |  |  | 11 | 13 |  |  |  |  |  | 17 |
| 1 | 2 | 3 | 12 |  |  | 5 | 6 | 7 | 4 | 8* | 9† | 10 |  |  | 11 | 13 |  |  |  |  |  | 18 |
| 1 | 2 | 3 | 4 |  |  | 5 | 6 | 7 | 8 | 9 | 12 |  |  |  | 10 | 11* |  |  |  |  |  | 19 |
| 1 | 2 | 3 | 12 |  |  | 5 | 6 | 7 | 8 | 9 | 4* | 10† |  |  | 11 | 13 |  |  |  |  |  | 20 |
| 1 | 2 | 4 | 8 | 3* |  | 5 | 6 | 7 | 12 | 10† | 9 | 13 |  |  | 11 |  |  |  |  |  |  | 21 |
| 1 | 2 | 3 | 4* | 8 |  | 5 | 6 | 7 | 12 | 10 | 9 | 13 |  |  | 11† |  |  |  |  |  |  | 22 |
| 1 | 2 | 3 | 10 |  |  | 5 | 6* | 7 | 4 | 8 | 9 |  |  |  | 11 | 12 |  |  |  |  |  | 23 |
| 1 | 2 | 3 | 12 | 8 |  | 5 | 6 | 7 | 4* | 10 | 9 |  |  |  | 11† | 13 |  |  |  |  |  | 24 |
| 1 | 2 | 3† | 13 | 8 |  | 5 | 6 | 7 | 4 |  | 9 |  |  |  | 10* | 11 | 12 |  |  |  |  | 25 |
| 1 |  | 3 | 4* |  |  | 5 | 6 | 7 | 8 | 12 | 9 | 10† | 13 |  | 11 |  |  |  |  |  | 2 | 26 |
| 1 | 2 | 3 | 12 |  |  | 5 | 6 | 7 | 4* | 8 | 9 | 13 |  |  | 11 | 10† |  |  |  |  |  | 27 |
| 1 | 2 | 3 | 13 | 4 |  | 5 | 6 | 8† | 12 | 9 | 7* |  |  |  | 10 | 11 |  |  |  |  |  | 28 |
| 1 | 2 | 3 | 12 | 4* |  | 5 | 6 | 8 | 9† | 10 | 13 | 7 |  |  | 11 |  |  |  |  |  |  | 29 |
| 1 | 2 | 3 | 4 |  |  | 5 | 6 | 13 | 8 | 9* | 10† | 12 |  |  | 7 | 11 |  |  |  |  |  | 30 |
| 1 | 2 | 3 | 4 |  |  | 5 | 6 | 12 | 8† | 10 | 7* | 11 |  |  | 13 | 9 |  |  |  |  |  | 31 |
| 1 | 2 | 3 | 12 |  |  | 5 | 6 | 4 | 8 | 7 | 13 | 11† |  |  | 9* | 10 |  |  |  |  |  | 32 |
| 1 | 2 | 3 | 4 | 8 |  | 5 | 6 | 7* | 13 | 10† | 9 |  |  |  | 11 | 12 |  |  |  |  |  | 33 |
| 1 | 2 | 3 | 4 | 8 |  | 5* | 6 | 7 | 10 | 9 | 12 |  |  |  | 11 |  |  |  |  |  |  | 34 |
| 1 | 2 | 3 | 4* | 8 |  | 5 | 6 | 7† | 13 | 10 | 9 |  |  |  | 11 |  |  |  |  |  |  | 35 |
| 1 | 2 | 3 | 13 | 4 |  | 5 | 6 | 7* | 12 | 8 | 9 |  |  |  | 10 | 11† |  |  |  |  |  | 36 |
| 36 | 34 | 28 | 21 | 22 | 1 | 32 | 36 | 30 | 18 | 24 | 29 | 11 | 3 | 10 | 22 | 25 | 3 | 6 | 1 | 3 | 1 |  |
|  |  | + | + |  |  |  |  | + | + | + | + | + | + | + | + | + |  |  |  | + |  |  |
|  |  | 10s | 5s |  |  |  |  | 12s | 5s | 2s | 2s | 7s | 3s | 3s | 10s | 2s |  |  |  | 3s |  |  |

# AIRDRIEONIANS Division 1

*Year Formed:* 1878.
*Ground:* Broomfield Park. *Size:* 112yd×68yd. *Capacity:* 26,000 (2000 seats).
*Telephone:* Airdrie 62067.
*Manager:* William Munro. *Coach:* Jim Storrie. *Second Team:* R. Morrison.
*Secretary:* George W. Peat cA.
*Club Colours:* White shirt with red diamond, white shorts, red stockings and white diamond tops.
*Club Nickname:* Diamonds or Waysiders.
*Record Attendance:* 24,000 v Hearts, Scottish Cup, 8 March, 1952.

## 1981–82 LEAGUE RECORD

| Match No. | Date | Venue | Opponents | Result | H/T Score | League Pos'n | Goalscorers | Atten- dance |
|---|---|---|---|---|---|---|---|---|
| 1 | Aug 29 | A | Celtic | L 2-5 | 1-1 | — | Clark 2 (1 pen) | 21,000 |
| 2 | Sept 5 | H | St Mirren | L 3-4 | 0-0 | 9 | Clark 2 (1 pen), Walker T. | 3000 |
| 3 | 12 | A | Hibernian | D 1-1 | 0-1 | 9 | McKeown | 5020 |
| 4 | 19 | H | Dundee U | W 2-1 | 1-1 | 9 | Clark 2 (1 pen) | 3000 |
| 5 | 26 | H | Aberdeen | L 0-4 | 0-3 | 9 | | 3000 |
| 6 | Oct 3 | A | Rangers | L 1-4 | 1-2 | 9 | Clark (pen) | 12,500 |
| 7 | 10 | H | Dundee | W 4-2 | 1-1 | 8 | Clark 3 (2 pens), Walker T. | 2500 |
| 8 | 17 | A | Morton | L 0-3 | 0-0 | 8 | | 2500 |
| 9 | 24 | H | Partick T | D 1-1 | 1-0 | 8 | McGuire | 3500 |
| 10 | 31 | H | Celtic | L 1-3 | 0-1 | 9 | Clark (pen) | 13,500 |
| 11 | Nov 7 | A | St Mirren | D 1-1 | 0-0 | 10 | Flood | 4575 |
| 12 | 14 | H | Hibernian | W 3-1 | 2-1 | 8 | Clark, Flood, Rodger | 4000 |
| 13 | 21 | A | Dundee U | L 0-4 | 0-2 | 8 | | 6157 |
| 14 | 28 | A | Aberdeen | D 0-0 | 0-0 | 8 | | 8030 |
| 15 | Dec 5 | H | Rangers | D 2-2 | 1-1 | 8 | Anderson N., Gordon | 14,500 |
| 16 | 12 | A | Dundee | L 1-3 | 0-1 | 9 | Rodger | 3988 |
| 17 | Jan 16 | A | Hibernian | L 0-1 | 0-1 | 9 | | 4350 |
| 18 | Feb 9 | H | Dundee U | W 2-0 | 1-0 | — | McDonagh, McKeown | 2000 |
| 19 | 13 | H | Morton | D 1-1 | 0-1 | 8 | Clark | 3200 |
| 20 | 20 | H | Aberdeen | L 0-3 | 0-0 | 9 | | 4000 |
| 21 | 27 | H | Partick T | W 3-1 | 0-0 | 8 | Watson (og), Clark, McGuire | 3600 |
| 22 | Mar 6 | A | Morton | L 0-1 | 0-0 | 8 | | 2000 |
| 23 | 13 | H | Dundee | L 0-2 | 0-0 | 8 | | 2500 |
| 24 | 20 | A | Celtic | L 0-2 | 0-2 | 9 | | 12,000 |
| 25 | 27 | A | St Mirren | L 0-3 | 0-1 | 9 | | 4289 |
| 26 | 31 | A | Rangers | L 0-1 | 0-1 | — | | 3000 |
| 27 | Apr 3 | H | Hibernian | L 0-2 | 0-0 | 9 | | 2500 |
| 28 | 7 | A | Partick T | L 1-4 | 0-1 | — | Thompson | 3000 |
| 29 | 10 | A | Dundee U | L 0-4 | 0-2 | 10 | | 5500 |
| 30 | 14 | H | Celtic | L 1-5 | 1-2 | — | Clark (pen) | 12,000 |
| 31 | 17 | H | Rangers | L 0-1 | 0-0 | 10 | | 8000 |
| 32 | 21 | H | St Mirren | L 0-2 | 0-0 | — | | 2500 |
| 33 | 24 | A | Aberdeen | L 0-2 | 0-0 | 10 | | 8000 |
| 34 | May 1 | A | Partick T | D 0-0 | 0-0 | 10 | | 2000 |
| 35 | 8 | H | Morton | D 1-1 | 0-1 | 10 | Campbell | 2000 |
| 36 | 15 | A | Dundee | L 0-1 | 0-1 | 10 | | 6696 |

**Final League Position: 10**

### Goalscorers
*League* (31): Clark 15 (8 pens), McGuire 2, McKeown 2, Flood 2, Rodger 2, Walker T. 2, Anderson N. 1, Campbell 1, Gordon 1, McDonagh 1, Thompson 1, own goal 1.
*League Cup* (4): Clark 2, Anderson N. 1, Kerr 1.
*Scottish Cup* (1): McCluskey 1.

**Honours**

*Scottish League* – Division 1 Runners-up 1922–23, 1923–24, 1924–25, 1925–26, 1979–80; Division 2 Champions 1902–03, 1954–55, 1973–74; Runners-up 1900–01, 1946–47, 1949–50, 1965–66.
*Scottish Cup* – Winners 1924; Runners-up 1975.
*Scottish League Cup* – None.
*Spring Cup* – Winners 1975–76.
*Record Victory:* 15-1 v Dundee Wanderers, Division 2, 1 Dec, 1894.
*Record Defeat:* 1-11 v Hibernian, Division 1, 24 Oct, 1959.
*Most League Points:* 60, Division 2, 1973–74.
*Most Individual League Goals in Season:* H. G. Yarnall, 45, Division 1, 1916–17.
*Most Capped Player:* Jimmy Crapnell, 9, Scotland.
Highest goalscorers in British league football 1973–74 with 102 goals.

| Martin J. | Davidson A. | Cairney H. | Rodger J. | Anderson G. | McCluskey P. | March J. | Walker T. | Anderson N. | McKeown B. | Gordon I. | Erwin H. | Campbell C. | McGuire W. | Flood J. | Clark A. | Kerr J. | Walker C. | McDonagh J. | Thompson D. | McCafferty T. | Steele W. | Match No. |
|---|---|---|---|---|---|---|---|---|---|---|---|---|---|---|---|---|---|---|---|---|---|---|
| 1 |  |  | 3 | 4 | 5 | 12* | 9 | 7 | 10 | 2 |  | 11 |  |  | 8 | 6* |  |  |  |  |  | 1 |
| 1 |  |  | 3 | 6 | 5 | 4 |  | 7 | 10 | 2 |  | 9 | 11 |  | 8 |  |  |  |  |  |  | 2 |
| 1 |  |  | 3 | 4 | 5 | 6 |  | 7 | 10 | 2 | 12 |  | 9* | 11 | 8 |  |  |  |  |  |  | 3 |
| 1 |  |  | 3 | 6 | 5 | 4 |  | 7 | 10 | 2 | 12 |  | 9 | 11* | 8 |  |  |  |  |  |  | 4 |
| 1 |  |  | 3 | 6 | 5 | 4 | 11 | 7†10 |  | 2 |  | 8 | 9*13 |  |  |  |  | 12 |  |  |  | 5 |
| 1 |  |  | 3 | 6 | 5 | 4 | 9 | 12 | 10 | 2 |  | 11†13 |  |  | 8 |  |  | 7* |  |  |  | 6 |
| 1 |  |  | 3 | 6* | 5 | 2 | 9 | 10 |  |  | 13 | 11† | 7 | 8 | 12 |  |  | 4 |  |  |  | 7 |
| 1 |  |  | 3 | 6 | 5* | 2 | 10 | 11 | 12 |  |  | 9† | 7 | 8 | 13 |  |  | 4 |  |  |  | 8 |
| 1 |  |  | 3† | 5 | 4 | 6 | 12*10 |  | 2 | 13 |  | 11 | 7 | 8 |  |  |  | 9* |  |  |  | 9 |
| 1 |  |  | 3 | 5† | 4 | 6 | 7 | 10 | 2* |  |  | 11 | 9 | 8 | 13 |  |  | 12 |  |  |  | 10 |
| 1 |  |  | 3 | 5 | 4 | 6 | 7 | 10 | 2 |  |  | 11 | 9 | 8 |  |  |  |  |  |  |  | 11 |
| 1 |  |  | 3 | 2 | 5 | 4 | 6 | 7 | 10 |  |  | 11 | 9 | 8 |  |  |  |  |  |  |  | 12 |
| 1 |  |  | 3 | 2 | 5 | 4 | 6 | 7*10 |  |  |  | 11† | 9 | 8 | 13 |  |  | 12 |  |  |  | 13 |
| 1 |  |  | 3 | 6 | 5 | 4 | 9 | 12 | 10 | 2* |  | 7 | 11 | 8 |  |  |  |  |  |  |  | 14 |
| 1 | 2 | 3 | 6* | 5 | 4 | 9 | 12 | 10 |  |  |  | 7 | 11 | 8 |  |  |  |  |  |  |  | 15 |
| 1 | 2 | 3 | 5 | 4† | 6 | 7 | 10 | 11† |  |  |  | 9 | 8 |  |  |  | 12 | 13 |  |  |  | 16 |
| 1 | 2 | 3 | 5 | 4* | 6 | 7 | 10 | 9 |  |  |  | 11†12 | 8 |  |  |  | 13 |  |  |  |  | 17 |
| 1 |  |  | 3 | 5 | 2 | 4 | 6 | 7 | 10 | 12 |  | 11* | 8 |  | 9 |  |  |  |  |  |  | 18 |
| 1 |  |  | 3 | 5 | 2 | 4† | 6 | 7*10 |  | 13 |  | 12 | 11 | 8 |  |  | 9 |  |  |  |  | 19 |
| 1 |  |  | 3 | 5 | 2 | 6 | 7 | 10 | 4 | 12 |  | 11* | 8 |  | 9 |  |  |  |  |  |  | 20 |
| 1 |  |  | 3 | 5 | 2 | 12 | 6 | 7 | 10 | 4 |  | 11 | 9† | 8* | 13 |  |  |  |  |  |  | 21 |
| 1 |  |  | 3 | 2 | 5 | 6 | 7 | 10 | 4 |  |  | 11 | 8*13 | 9†12 |  |  |  |  |  |  |  | 22 |
| 1 | 2 | 3 | 5 | 8 | 6 | 7 | 10 | 4 | 11† |  | 12 | 9*13 |  |  |  |  |  |  |  |  |  | 23 |
| 1 | 2 | 3 | 5 | 12 | 6 | 7 | 10 | 4 | 13 |  | 11*9 | 8† |  |  |  |  |  |  |  |  |  | 24 |
| 1 | 2* | 3 | 5 | 12 | 6 | 7 | 10 | 4 | 11 |  | 8 | 9 |  |  |  |  |  |  |  |  |  | 25 |
| 1 |  |  | 3 | 5 | 2 | 13 | 6 | 7 | 10† | 4 |  | 11 | 8* | 9 |  |  |  | 12 |  |  |  | 26 |
| 1 |  |  | 3 | 2 | 4 | 5 | 6 | 7*12 | 9 | 11 |  | 8 | 10† | 13 |  |  |  |  |  |  |  | 27 |
| 1 |  |  | 3 | 2 | 5 | 4† | 6 | 8 | 11 | 10* | 7 | 9 |  |  |  |  |  | 12 | 13 |  |  | 28 |
| 1 |  |  | 3 | 2 | 5 | 4 | 6 | 8 | 10 | 11 | 7* |  | 9 |  |  |  |  | 12 |  |  |  | 29 |
| 1 |  |  | 3 | 4 | 5 | 2 | 6 | 11 | 10 | 12 | 7* | 8 |  | 9 |  |  |  |  |  |  |  | 30 |
| 1 | 2 | 3 | 4 | 5 | 6*12 | 11 | 10 | 7† |  | 8 | 9 | 13 |  |  |  |  |  |  |  |  |  | 31 |
| 1 | 2 | 3 | 4 | 5 | 6 | 10 | 11 | 9*12 |  | 8 | 7 |  |  |  |  |  |  |  |  |  |  | 32 |
| 1 | 2 | 3 | 4 | 5 | 11 | 6 | 12 | 9* | 10 | 8 | 7 |  |  |  |  |  |  |  |  |  |  | 33 |
| 1 | 2 | 3 | 4 | 5 | 11 | 6 | 9 | 10 | 8 | 7 |  |  |  |  |  |  |  |  |  |  |  | 34 |
| 1 | 2 | 3 | 4 | 5 | 11 | 6 | 9 | 10* | 8 | 7 |  |  |  |  |  | 12 |  |  |  |  |  | 35 |
| 1 | 2 | 4 | 5 | 10 | 3 | 9 | 12 | 8 | 6* | 7 |  |  |  | 11 |  |  |  |  |  |  |  | 36 |
| 27 | 9 | 12 | 35 | 18 | 19 | 28 | 22 | 29 | 30 | 33 | 10 | 20 | 23 | 25 | 30 | 3 | 12 | 5 | 5 | 1 | — |  |

Goals: +2s +3s +5s +2s +1s +5s +7s +3s +5s +1s +3s +11s +1s +1s

# ALBION ROVERS                                        Division 2

*Year Formed:* 1882.   *Ground:* Cliftonhill Park.   *Capacity:* 10,000 (580 seats).   *Size:* 110yd×74yd.
*Telephone:* Coatbridge 32350.
*Manager:* Derek Whiteford.   *Secretary:* David Forrester CA.
*Club Colours:* Primrose shirts with red trim and number, red shorts, primrose stockings.
*Record Attendance:* 27,381 v Rangers, Scottish Cup 2nd rd, 8 Feb, 1936.
*Previous Grounds:* Meadow Park, Whifflet, 1881–1919.
*Club Nickname:* The Wee Rovers.

## 1981–82 LEAGUE RECORD

| Match No. | Date | Venue | Opponents | Result | H/T Score | League Pos'n | Goalscorers | Attendance |
|---|---|---|---|---|---|---|---|---|
| 1 | Aug 29 | H | Cowdenbeath | W 2-0 | 1-0 | — | McDonagh, Hill (pen) | 200 |
| 2 | Sept 5 | A | Montrose | L 2-4 | 2-2 | 5 | Gillespie, Craig | 300 |
| 3 | 8 | A | Meadowbank T | L 2-3 | 1-0 | — | Houston, Gibson | 250 |
| 4 | 12 | H | Stranraer | W 4-0 | 1-0 | 5 | Evans, Craig 2, Gibson (pen) | 200 |
| 5 | 15 | A | Stenhousemuir | D 2-2 | 0-1 | — | Houston, Evans | 380 |
| 6 | 19 | A | East Fife | L 0-3 | 0-1 | 9 |  | 318 |
| 7 | 22 | H | Arbroath | W 2-0 | 2-0 | — | Evans 2 (1 pen) | 221 |
| 8 | 26 | A | Stirling Albion | L 0-1 | 0-0 | 8 |  | 950 |
| 9 | Oct 3 | H | Berwick R | L 1-3 | 0-3 | 9 | Evans (pen) | 844 |
| 10 | 10 | A | Brechin C | L 2-3 | 1-2 | 10 | Shields, Evans | 400 |
| 11 | 17 | H | Forfar Ath | D 3-3 | 1-2 | 9 | Evans 2, Gibson | 426 |
| 12 | 24 | A | Clyde | W 2-1 | 2-0 | 9 | Craig, Gillespie | 500 |
| 13 | 31 | H | Alloa | L 1-5 | 1-2 | 10 | Gillespie | 200 |
| 14 | Nov 7 | H | Montrose | L 0-2 | 0-2 | 11 |  | 200 |
| 15 | 14 | A | Cowdenbeath | L 0-2 | 0-1 | 12 |  | 400 |
| 16 | 21 | H | Stenhousemuir | L 1-4 | 1-1 | 12 | Evans | 300 |
| 17 | 28 | H | Stirling Albion | W 1-0 | 1-0 | 11 | Evans | 250 |
| 18 | Dec 5 | A | Berwick R | L 1-6 | 1-3 | 11 | Burgess | 745 |
| 19 | 19 | A | Arbroath | L 0-4 | 0-2 | 11 |  | 392 |
| 20 | Jan 2 | A | Stranraer | W 1-0 | 1-0 | 11 | Houston | 630 |
| 21 | 23 | H | Brechin C | L 1-2 | 0-0 | 11 | Collins | 390 |
| 22 | Feb 10 | H | Clyde | L 0-1 | 0-1 | — |  | 460 |
| 23 | 17 | A | Alloa | L 0-1 | 0-1 | — |  | 760 |
| 24 | 20 | A | Cowdenbeath | W 3-2 | 1-2 | 12 | Burgess 2, Houston | 287 |
| 25 | 27 | H | Montrose | D 2-2 | 2-1 | 12 | Shields, Evans | 500 |
| 26 | Mar 6 | A | Meadowbank T | W 2-0 | 2-0 | 11 | Burgess, Shields | 200 |
| 27 | 13 | A | Berwick R | L 1-4 | 0-2 | 12 | Evans | 656 |
| 28 | 17 | H | East Fife | W 1-0 | 1-0 | — | Evans (pen) | 725 |
| 29 | 20 | H | Alloa | D 1-1 | 1-1 | 12 | Evans (pen) | 200 |
| 30 | 27 | A | Stranraer | W 4-1 | 3-0 | 12 | Shields, Leishman 2, Burgess | 300 |
| 31 | 31 | H | Meadowbank T | W 2-0 | 1-0 | — | Houston 2 | 600 |
| 32 | Apr 10 | H | Stirling Albion | W 1-0 | 1-0 | 12 | Houston | 400 |
| 33 | 14 | A | Forfar Ath | L 1-3 | 0-2 | — | Gibson | 860 |
| 34 | 17 | H | Brechin C | L 1-2 | 0-2 | 12 | Houston | 200 |
| 35 | 24 | A | Arbroath | L 0-2 | 0-1 | 12 |  | 510 |
| 36 | 28 | A | Forfar Ath | L 0-3 | 0-2 | — |  | 420 |
| 37 | May 1 | H | Clyde | L 2-3 | 1-2 | 12 | Evans 2 | 500 |
| 38 | 8 | A | East Fife | D 1-1 | 0-0 | 12 | Halley (og) | 339 |
| 39 | 15 | H | Stenhousemuir | W 2-0 | 1-0 | 11 | Houston, Sinnett | 700 |

**Final League Position: 11**

### Goalscorers
*League* (52): Evans 16 (4 pens), Houston 9, Burgess 5, Craig 4, Gibson 4 (1 pen), Shields 4, Gillespie 3, Leishman 2, Collins 1, Hill 1 (pen), McDonagh 1, Sinnett 1, own goal 1.
*League Cup* (8): Burgess 3 (1 pen), Campbell 1, Craig 1, Gillespie 1, Hill 1, McDonagh 1.
*Scottish Cup* (4): Houston 3, own goal 1.

**Honours**

*Scottish League* – Division 2 Champions 1933–34; Runners-up 1913–14, 1937–38, 1947–48.
*Scottish Cup* – Runners-up 1920.
*Record Victory:* 12-0 v Airdriehill, Scottish Cup, 3 Sept, 1887.
*Record Defeat:* 1-9 v Motherwell, Division 1, 2 Jan, 1937.
*Most League Points:* 54, Division 2, 1929–30.
*Most Individual League Goals in Season:* Jim Renwick, 41, 1932–33.
*Most Capped Player:* Jock White, 1(2), Scotland.

| Balavage J. | Purdie A. | Allan P. | Lapsley D. | Main D. | Shields D. | Burgess S. | Murray T. | Hamill P. | Gormley J. | Gillespie I. | Hill H. | Houston P. | McDonagh J. | Sinnett J. | Craig J. | Collins G. | Evans S. | Gibson B.D. | Hannigan S. | Ross A. | Sullivan R. | McQueen C. | Leishman W. | Dougan O. | McAlaney W. | Murray D. | Grant F. | Dow R. | Ferry H. | Match No. |
|---|---|---|---|---|---|---|---|---|---|---|---|---|---|---|---|---|---|---|---|---|---|---|---|---|---|---|---|---|---|---|
| 1 | 2 | 13 | 5 |  | 4 |  | 3 | 12 |  | 6 | 7 | 8 |  | 9* |  |  |  |  | 11† |  |  |  |  |  |  |  |  |  |  | 1 |
| 1 | 2 |  | 5 |  | 4 |  | 3 |  |  | 7 | 8 | 9 | 11 | 10 |  | 6 |  |  |  |  |  |  |  |  |  |  |  |  |  | 2 |
| 1 | 2 |  | 5 |  | 4 |  | 12 | 6 |  | 8 | 10 | 9 |  | 7 |  |  | 11 | 3* |  |  |  |  |  |  |  |  |  |  |  | 3 |
| 1 | 2 | 3 |  |  | 5 |  | 12 | 6 |  | 8 | 9 |  |  | 10 |  | 11* | 7 |  |  |  |  | 4 |  |  |  |  |  |  |  | 4 |
| 1* | 2 | 12 | 3 |  | 5 |  | 13 | 7 |  | 8 | 9 |  |  | 6 |  | 10 | 11† |  |  |  |  |  | 4 |  |  |  |  |  |  | 5 |
| 1 | 7 | 13 | 3 |  | 4 | 2* | 12 | 11 |  | 9 |  |  |  | 8 |  | 10 |  | 6† |  |  |  |  | 5 |  |  |  |  |  |  | 6 |
| 1 | 2* |  | 6 |  | 5 | 12 |  | 11 |  | 9 |  |  |  | 7 | 8 | 10 |  | 3 |  |  |  |  | 4 |  |  |  |  |  |  | 7 |
| 1 | 2 | 13 | 8† |  | 4 | 12 |  | 11* |  | 9 |  |  |  | 6 | 7 | 10 |  | 3 |  |  |  |  | 5 |  |  |  |  |  |  | 8 |
| 1 | 3 |  | 6 |  | 5 | 2 |  | 12 |  | 9* |  |  |  | 7 | 8 | 10 | 11 | 4 |  |  |  |  |  |  |  |  |  |  |  | 9 |
| 1 | 6 | 13 |  | 4 | 5 | 2 |  | 12 |  | 9 |  |  |  | 7† |  | 10 | 11* | 3 | 8 |  |  |  |  |  |  |  |  |  |  | 10 |
| 1 | 3 |  |  | 4 | 5 | 2* |  | 11 |  | 9 |  |  |  | 7† | 8 | 10 | 13 | 12 | 6 |  |  |  |  |  |  |  |  |  |  | 11 |
| 1 | 3 | 12 | 4* | 5 | 13 |  |  | 11 |  | 9 |  |  |  | 6 | 8 | 10 | 7† | 2 |  |  |  |  |  |  |  |  |  |  |  | 12 |
| 1 | 3 | 6 | 4* | 5 | 12 | 13 |  | 7 |  | 9 |  |  |  | 11† | 8 | 10 |  | 2 |  |  |  |  |  |  |  |  |  |  |  | 13 |
| 1 | 12 | 3 | 6† |  | 5 | 2 | 4 | 11* |  | 9 |  |  |  | 7 | 8 | 10 | 13 |  |  |  |  |  |  |  |  |  |  |  |  | 14 |
| 1 | 2 | 3 | 6* |  | 5 |  | 4 |  |  | 7 |  |  |  | 9 | 8 | 10 | 11 | 12 |  |  |  |  |  |  |  |  |  |  |  | 15 |
| 1 | 2 | 3 | 4 | 5† |  | 13 |  | 12 |  | 9 |  |  |  | 7 | 8 | 10 | 6 | 11* |  |  |  |  |  |  |  |  |  |  |  | 16 |
| 1 | 2 | 3 | 4 |  | 9 | 5 |  | 12 |  | 8 |  |  |  | 6 | 10 | 7*11 |  |  |  |  |  |  |  |  |  |  |  |  |  | 17 |
| 1 | 2 | 3 | 4† | 5 | 9 |  | 7* | 8 |  | 6 |  |  |  | 10 | 12 | 11 | 13 |  |  |  |  |  |  |  |  |  |  |  |  | 18 |
| 1 | 2 | 3 |  | 5 |  | 11* |  | 8 |  | 6 |  |  |  | 10 | 7 | 12 | 9 | 4 |  |  |  |  |  |  |  |  |  |  |  | 19 |
| 1 | 3 |  | 5 | 2 |  | 11 |  | 6 |  | 8 |  |  |  | 10 | 7 | 9 | 4 |  |  |  |  |  |  |  |  |  |  |  |  | 20 |
| 1 | 3 | 2 | 5 |  | 11 |  | 8 |  |  | 8 | 10 | 7* | 9 | 12 | 4 |  |  |  |  |  |  |  |  |  |  |  |  |  |  | 21 |
| 1 | 2 | 3 |  | 12 |  | 11 |  | 9 |  | 13 | 6 | 10 | 7 |  | 8* | 4† |  | 5 |  |  |  |  |  |  |  |  |  |  |  | 22 |
| 1 | 2 | 3 |  | 5 |  | 12 |  | 8 |  | 7 | 10 | 13 |  | 9 |  | 6 |  |  | 4* | 11† |  |  |  |  |  |  |  |  |  | 23 |
| 1 | 2 | 3 | 9 | 8 |  | 6* | 12 | 11 |  | 5 | 10 | 7 |  |  |  |  |  |  |  |  |  | 4 |  |  |  |  |  |  |  | 24 |
| 1 | 7 | 3 | 9 | 8 |  | 6* | 13 | 11 |  | 5 | 10 |  |  |  |  |  | 12 | 2† | 4 |  |  |  |  |  |  |  |  |  |  | 25 |
| 1 | 2 | 3 | 9 | 8 |  | 6 | 11 |  |  | 5 | 10 | 7 |  |  |  |  |  |  | 4 |  |  |  |  |  |  |  |  |  |  | 26 |
| 1 | 2 | 3 | 9 | 8 |  | 6* | 12 | 11 |  | 5 | 10 | 7 |  |  |  |  |  | 13 | 4† |  |  |  |  |  |  |  |  |  |  | 27 |
| 1 | 2 |  | 8 |  | 6 | 11 |  |  |  | 5 | 10 | 7 | 3 |  |  |  |  | 4 |  |  |  |  |  |  |  |  |  | 9 |  | 28 |
| 1 | 2 | 3 |  | 8 | 12 | 6 |  | 9 |  | 5 | 10 | 7 | 11* |  |  |  |  | 4 |  |  |  |  |  |  |  |  |  |  |  | 29 |
| 1 | 2 | 3 | 11†12 |  | 6 |  | 9 |  |  | 5 | 10 | 7 |  |  | 8* | 4 | 13 |  |  |  |  |  |  |  |  |  |  |  | 30 |
| 1 | 2 | 3 | 9*12 | 6 |  | 13 |  | 11 |  | 5 | 10 | 7 |  |  | 8† | 4 |  |  |  |  |  |  |  |  |  |  |  |  |  | 31 |
| 1 | 2 | 3 | 11* 8 | 6 |  |  | 9 |  |  | 4 | 10 | 7 |  |  | 12 | 5 |  |  |  |  |  |  |  |  |  |  |  |  |  | 32 |
| 1 | 2 | 3 | 11 8 | 12 | 6 |  | 9 |  |  | 5 | 10* | 7 |  |  | 4 |  |  |  |  |  |  |  |  |  |  |  |  |  |  | 33 |
| 1 | 2 | 3 | 11 | 6† | 8* | 9 |  |  |  | 4 | 10 | 13 | 12 | 7 | 5 |  |  |  |  |  |  |  |  |  |  |  |  |  |  | 34 |
| 1 | 2 | 3 | 4 | 6† | 12 | 9 |  |  |  | 8 | 10 | 7 |  | 5 |  | 13 | 11* |  |  |  |  |  |  |  |  |  |  |  |  | 35 |
| 1 | 2* | 3 | 6† | 5 | 13 | 9 |  |  |  | 8 | 10 | 7 |  | 4 | 12 |  |  |  |  |  |  |  | 11 |  |  |  |  |  |  | 36 |
| 1 | 2 | 3 | 5 |  | 11 | 7 |  |  |  | 8 | 10 |  | 9 | 4 |  | 6 |  |  |  |  |  |  |  |  |  |  |  |  |  | 37 |
| 1 | 2 | 3† 6* | 5 |  | 11 | 9 |  |  |  | 8 | 10 | 7 | 13 | 4 |  |  | 12 |  |  |  |  |  |  |  |  |  |  |  | 38 |
| 1 | 2 | 3 6 | 5 |  | 11 | 9 |  |  |  | 8 | 10 | 7 |  | 4 |  |  |  |  |  |  |  |  |  |  |  |  |  |  | 39 |
| 31 | 8 | 33 | 28 | 19 | 14 | 35 | 6 | 12 | — | 26 | 5 | 38 | 3 | 1 | 16 | 32 | 36 | 27 | 15 | 5 | 2 | 11 | 13 | 1 | 2 | 5 | 1 | 2 | 2 |  |

+ + + + + + + + + + + + + + + +
1s 5s 1s 2s 4s 6s 5s 10s 1s 5s 3s 6s 1s 3s 1s

# ALLOA Division 1

*Year Formed:* 1883.   *Ground:* Recreation Ground.   *Size:* 110yd×75yd.   *Capacity:* 9000.
*Telephone:* Alloa 722695.
*Manager:* Alex Totten.   *Secretary:* George Ormiston.
*Club Colours:* Gold with black trim, black shorts, gold socks with black tops.
*Club Nickname:* The Wasps.
*Record Attendance:* 13,000 v Dunfermline Ath, Scottish Cup 3rd rd replay, 26 Feb, 1939.

## 1981–82 LEAGUE RECORD

| Match No. | Date | Venue | Opponents | Result | H/T Score | League Pos'n | Goalscorers | Atten-dance |
|---|---|---|---|---|---|---|---|---|
| 1 | Aug 29 | H | Forfar Ath | L | 1-2 | 0-1 | — | McNab | 619 |
| 2 | Sept 5 | A | Stirling Alb | D | 0-0 | 0-0 | 11 | | 750 |
| 3 | 8 | A | Montrose | L | 0-2 | 0-1 | — | | 400 |
| 4 | 12 | H | Stenhousemuir | W | 1-0 | 1-0 | 10 | Murray | 477 |
| 5 | 16 | A | Cowdenbeath | W | 2-1 | 0-0 | — | McNab, Murray | 300 |
| 6 | 19 | A | Clyde | D | 1-1 | 0-0 | 8 | Purdie | 650 |
| 7 | 23 | H | Stranraer | W | 3-2 | 2-2 | — | Hamilton (og), Purdie, Paterson | 650 |
| 8 | 26 | A | Meadowbank T | D | 1-1 | 1-1 | 6 | Oliver | 660 |
| 9 | Oct 3 | H | Arbroath | W | 2-1 | 0-0 | 5 | Paterson, Murray | 964 |
| 10 | 10 | H | Berwick R | W | 1-0 | 1-0 | 4 | Smith | 575 |
| 11 | 17 | A | East Fife | W | 2-1 | 1-1 | 3 | McNab, Purdie | 415 |
| 12 | 24 | H | Brechin C | L | 1-3 | 0-2 | 5 | Holt (pen) | 780 |
| 13 | 31 | A | Albion R | W | 5-1 | 2-1 | 5 | Murray 4, McNab | 200 |
| 14 | Nov 7 | H | Stirling Albion | D | 0-0 | 0-0 | 5 | | 800 |
| 15 | 14 | A | Forfar Ath | D | 0-0 | 0-0 | 5 | | 980 |
| 16 | 21 | H | Cowdenbeath | W | 3-1 | 0-1 | 5 | Holt (pen), McComb 2 | 623 |
| 17 | 28 | H | Meadowbank T | W | 4-3 | 2-1 | 4 | Holt 2, Grant, McComb | 550 |
| 18 | Dec 5 | A | Arbroath | L | 1-2 | 1-0 | 5 | McComb | 655 |
| 19 | Feb 2 | H | East Fife | L | 1-2 | 0-0 | 5 | Holt | 379 |
| 20 | 6 | A | Brechin C | W | 4-0 | 0-0 | 6 | Grant, McComb, Paterson 2 | 579 |
| 21 | 17 | H | Albion R | W | 1-0 | 1-0 | — | Purdie | 760 |
| 22 | 20 | H | Arbroath | D | 2-2 | 1-0 | 6 | McComb, Murray | 650 |
| 23 | 23 | A | Stranraer | W | 4-0 | 2-0 | — | Grant, Purdie 2 (1 pen), McComb | 572 |
| 24 | 27 | A | Stenhousemuir | D | 2-2 | 1-0 | 5 | Grant, Holt | 500 |
| 25 | Mar 6 | H | Berwick R | D | 1-1 | 1-0 | 5 | Holt | 600 |
| 26 | 13 | A | Brechin C | W | 1-0 | 0-0 | 5 | Holt | 400 |
| 27 | 20 | A | Albion R | D | 1-1 | 1-1 | 5 | Murray | 200 |
| 28 | 22 | H | Montrose | W | 5-0 | 4-0 | — | McComb 3, Murray, Holt | 514 |
| 29 | 27 | H | Clyde | D | 2-2 | 1-0 | 4 | McComb 2 | 1210 |
| 30 | 30 | A | Stenhousemuir | W | 1-0 | 0-0 | — | Holt | 430 |
| 31 | Apr 3 | A | East Fife | W | 2-0 | 2-0 | 2 | Murray, Paterson | 410 |
| 32 | 7 | A | Berwick R | L | 0-2 | 0-0 | — | | 870 |
| 33 | 10 | H | Meadowbank T | W | 2-0 | 1-0 | 2 | Purdie, Paterson | 722 |
| 34 | 17 | A | Montrose | W | 3-0 | 0-0 | 2 | Murray 2, Holt | 450 |
| 35 | 21 | H | Clyde | L | 0-3 | 0-2 | — | | 760 |
| 36 | 24 | A | Stirling Albion | L | 2-3 | 1-2 | 2 | Grant 2 | 1100 |
| 37 | May 1 | H | Stranraer | D | 1-1 | 1-1 | 2 | Wilson | 601 |
| 38 | 8 | H | Cowdenbeath | D | 2-2 | 1-0 | 2 | Murray, McComb | 859 |
| 39 | 15 | A | Forfar Ath | W | 1-0 | 1-0 | 2 | Smith | 1247 |

**Final League Position: 2**

### Goalscorers
*League* (66): Murray 14, McComb 13, Holt 11 (2 pens), Purdie 7 (1 pen), Grant 6, Paterson 6, McNab 4, Smith 2, Oliver 1, Wilson 1, own goal 1.
*League Cup* (8): Grant 6 (2 pens), Holt 1, Smith 1.
*Scottish Cup* (6): Holt 2, Paterson 2, Grant 1, own goal 1.

**Honours**
*Scottish League* – Division 2 Champions 1921–22; Runners-up 1938–39, 1976–77, 1981–82.
*Record Victory:* 9-2 v Forfar, Division 2, 18 March, 1933.
*Record Defeat:* 0-10 v Dundee, Division 2, 8 March, 1947.
*Most League Points:* 60, 1921–22.
*Most Individual League Goals in Season:* Wee Crilley, 49, Division 2, 1931–32.
*Most Capped Player:* Jock Hepburn, 1, Scotland.

| Hunter D. | Ballantine C. | Haggart L. | Wilde A. | MacKenzie A. | Purdie B. | Holt A. | Oliver A. | Stewart J. | Grant A. | Smith I. | McComb L. | Murray S. | Paterson A. | McNab R. | Spence C. | Mitchell R. | Lloyd D. | Wilson J. | Dunn J. | Christie B. | Match No. |
|---|---|---|---|---|---|---|---|---|---|---|---|---|---|---|---|---|---|---|---|---|---|
| 1 | 8 | 2 | 3 | 4 | 5 | 6 | | 7 | | 11† | | | 12 | 9 | 10* | | 13 | | | | 1 |
| 1 | 8 | 2 | 3 | 4 | 5 | 6 | | 7* | | | 11 | | 10 | 9 | | | 12 | | | | 2 |
| 1 | 12 | 8 | 2* | 3 | 4 | 5 | 6 | | | | | 11† | | 10 | 13 | | | 7 | 9 | | 3 |
| 1 | 8† | 2 | 13 | 3 | 4 | 5 | 6 | 11 | | | | 9 | 7* | 10 | | | 12 | | | | 4 |
| 1 | 8 | 2 | | 3 | 4 | 5 | 6 | | 11 | | | 9 | 7 | 10 | | | | | | | 5 |
| 1 | 8 | 2 | | 3* | 4 | 5 | 6 | 12 | 11 | | | 9† | 7 | 10 | 13 | | | | | | 6 |
| 1 | 2 | 3 | 13 | | 4 | 5 | 6 | 11 | 8 | | | 7 | 10† | | 12 | | | 9* | | | 7 |
| 1 | 2 | 3 | | | 4 | 5 | 6 | 11 | 8 | | | 9* | 7 | 10 | 12 | | | | | | 8 |
| 1 | 2 | 3 | | 10 | 4 | 5 | 6 | 11 | 8 | | | 9* | 7 | | 12 | | | | | | 9 |
| 1 | 2 | 3 | | 10† | 4 | 5 | 6 | 11 | 8 | 12 | | 9* | 7 | 13 | | | | | | | 10 |
| 1 | 2 | | 3 | 4 | 5 | 6 | | 11 | 8 | 12 | 9 | 7*10 | | | | | | | | | 11 |
| 1 | 2 | | 3 | 4 | 5 | 6* | | 11 | 8 | 12 | 9 | 7 | 10 | | | | | | | | 12 |
| 1 | 2 | 13 | | 3 | 4 | 5 | | 11 | 8† | 6 | 9 | 7*10 | 12 | | | | | | | | 13 |
| 1 | 2 | 12 | | 3* | 4 | 5 | | | 8 | 6 | 9 | 7 | 10 | 11†13 | | | | | | | 14 |
| 1 | 2 | 3 | | | 4 | 5 | 6 | | 8 | 11 | 9 | 7 | 10 | | | | | | | | 15 |
| 1 | 2 | 3 | | | 4 | 5 | 6† | 12 | 8 | 11 | 9* | 7 | 10 | | | | 13 | | | | 16 |
| 1 | 2 | 3 | | 12 | 4 | 5 | 6* | 9 | 8 | 11 | | 7 | 10 | | | | | | | | 17 |
| 1 | 2 | 13 | | 3† | 4 | 5 | 6* | 9 | 8 | 11 | 12 | 7 | 10 | | | | | | | | 18 |
| 1 | 2 | | | 3 | 4 | 6 | 8† | 5 | 11 | 10 | 9*12 | 7 | | | | | 13 | | | | 19 |
| 1 | 12 | 2 | | 3* | 4 | 6 | 8 | 5 | 11 | 10† | 9 | 7 | | | | | 13 | | | | 20 |
| 1 | 2 | | 3 | 4 | 6†13 | 5 | 11 | 10 | 9*12 | 7 | | | | | | | 8 | | | | 21 |
| 1 | 2 | | 3 | 4 | 6 | 12 | 5 | 7 | 10 | 11 | 9† | 13 | | | | | 8* | | | | 22 |
| 1 | 2 | | 3 | 4 | 6 | 8 | 5 | 9 | 10 | 11 | 12 | 7* | | | | | | | | | 23 |
| 1 | 2 | | 3 | 4 | 6 | 8* | 5 | 9 | 10 | 11 | 7 | | | | | | 12 | | | | 24 |
| 1 | 2 | 3 | | | 4 | 6 | 8 | 5 | 7 | 10 | 11 | 9 | | | | | | | | | 25 |
| 1 | 2 | 3 | | | 4 | 6 | 8 | 5 | 7 | 10 | 11 | 9 | | | | | | | | | 26 |
| 1 | 2 | 3 | 13 | | 4 | | 8 | 5†11 | | | 6 | 9 | 7 | 12 | | | 10* | | | | 27 |
| 1 | 2 | 3 | 13 | | 4† | 6 | 12 | 5 | 11* | | 8 | 9 | 7 | 10 | | | | | | | 28 |
| 1 | 2 | 3 | | | | 6 | | 5 | 11 | 4 | 8 | 9 | 7 | 10* | | | 12 | | | | 29 |
| 1 | 2 | 3 | 10 | | | 6 | | 5 | 11 | 4 | 8 | 9* | 7 | | 12 | | | | | | 30 |
| 1 | 2 | 3 | 10 | | | 6 | | 5 | 11 | 4 | 8 | 9 | 7 | | | | | | | | 31 |
| 1 | 2 | | 3 | 4 | 6 | | | 5 | 11 | 10 | 8 | 9* | 7 | | | | 12 | | | | 32 |
| 1 | 2 | | 3 | 4 | 6 | | | 5 | 11 | 10 | 8 | 9 | 7 | | | | | | | | 33 |
| 1 | 2 | | 3 | 4 | 6 | | | 5 | 11 | 10 | 8 | 9 | 7 | | | | | | | | 34 |
| 1 | 2 | | 3 | 4 | 6*12 | | | 5 | 11 | 10 | 8 | 9 | 7 | | | | | | | | 35 |
| 1 | 12 | 2* | | 3 | 4 | 6 | | 5 | 11 | 10 | 8 | 9 | 7 | | | | | | | | 36 |
| 1 | 2 | 3 | | | 4 | 5 | | 6 | 7 | 10 | 9 | 11 | 12 | | | | 8* | | | | 37 |
| 1 | 2 | 3 | 6* | 4 | 5 | | | | 11 | 8 | 10 | 9 | 7 | | | | 12 | | | | 38 |
| 1 | 2 | 3 | | 6 | 4 | 5 | | | 11 | 8 | 10 | 9 | 7 | | | | | | | | 39 |
| 39 | 24 | 35 | 3 | 28 | 36 | 38 | 23 | 19 | 33 | 34 | 26 | 32 | 31 | 17 | 3 | 1 | — | 4 | 1 | 2 | |
| + | + | + | + | | | + | | + | | | + | + | + | + | + | + | + | + | + | + | |
| 3s | 3s | 2s | 3s | | | 4s | | 2s | | | 3s | 4s | 1s | 4s | 2s | 5s | 2s | 6s | 3s | | |

# ARBROATH
## Division 2

*Year Formed:* 1878.   *Ground:* Gayfield Park.   *Size:* 115yd×73yd.   *Capacity:* 15,000.   *Telephone:* Arbroath 72157.
*Manager:* Ian J. Stewart.   *Trainer:* John Smith.
*Club Colours:* Maroon shirts, white shorts, maroon stockings.
*Club Nickname:* Red Lichties.
*Record Attendance:* 13,510 v Rangers, Scottish Cup 3rd rd, 23 Feb, 1952.
*Record Transfer Fee Received:* £50,000 from Motherwell for Jeo Carson, Jan 1980 and £50,000 from Motherwell for Albert Kidd, Jan 1980.

## 1981–82 LEAGUE RECORD

| Match No. | Date | | Venue | Opponents | Result | H/T Score | League Pos'n | Goalscorers | Atten-dance |
|---|---|---|---|---|---|---|---|---|---|
| 1 | Aug | 29 | H | Meadowbank T | W 3-2 | 2-1 | — | Gavine, Docherty, Robb | 635 |
| 2 | Sept | 5 | A | Stranraer | L 0-4 | 0-1 | 10 | | 630 |
| 3 | | 8 | A | Forfar Ath | L 0-6 | 0-0 | — | | 1444 |
| 4 | | 12 | H | Cowdenbeath | D 1-1 | 0-0 | 11 | Robb | 479 |
| 5 | | 16 | A | Montrose | L 1-2 | 1-0 | — | Robb | 600 |
| 6 | | 19 | H | Brechin C | D 1-1 | 1-1 | 12 | Hyslop | 859 |
| 7 | | 22 | A | Albion R | L 0-2 | 0-2 | — | | 221 |
| 8 | | 26 | H | Stenhousemuir | W 3-0 | 2-0 | 11 | Casey, Robb 2 | 770 |
| 9 | Oct | 3 | A | Alloa | L 1-2 | 0-0 | 11 | Robb | 964 |
| 10 | | 10 | A | Stirling Albion | W 1-0 | 0-0 | 9 | Robb | 450 |
| 11 | | 17 | H | Clyde | L 0-1 | 0-1 | 10 | | 691 |
| 12 | | 24 | H | Berwick R | W 2-1 | 0-0 | 10 | Lees, Shaw | 531 |
| 13 | | 31 | A | East Fife | W 1-0 | 0-0 | 9 | Forsyth | 411 |
| 14 | Nov | 7 | H | Stranraer | W 4-1 | 3-0 | 9 | Yule 2, Robb, Shaw | 488 |
| 15 | | 14 | A | Meadowbank T | W 2-1 | 0-1 | 7 | Yule 2 | 200 |
| 16 | | 21 | H | Montrose | W 1-0 | 1-0 | 6 | Shaw | 400 |
| 17 | | 28 | A | Stenhousemuir | W 3-1 | 2-0 | 6 | Robb, Yule, Shaw | 300 |
| 18 | Dec | 5 | H | Alloa | W 2-1 | 0-1 | 6 | Gavine, Yule | 655 |
| 19 | | 19 | H | Albion R | W 4-0 | 2-0 | 4 | Gavine, Robb, Shaw, Burke | 392 |
| 20 | Jan | 2 | H | Forfar Ath | D 1-1 | 1-0 | 3 | Shaw | 1435 |
| 21 | | 23 | H | Stirling Albion | W 1-0 | 1-0 | — | Yule | 545 |
| 22 | Feb | 6 | A | Berwick R | L 0-3 | 0-0 | 4 | | 500 |
| 23 | | 13 | H | East Fife | W 3-1 | 2-1 | 3 | Robb, Yule, Gavine | 493 |
| 24 | | 17 | A | Brechin C | D 2-2 | 1-0 | — | Robb 2 (1 pen) | 955 |
| 25 | | 20 | A | Alloa | D 2-2 | 0-1 | 3 | Lees, Docherty | 650 |
| 26 | | 27 | H | Cowdenbeath | W 3-0 | 0-0 | 4 | Docherty, Gavine, Robb | 564 |
| 27 | Mar | 13 | H | Montrose | W 2-0 | 2-0 | 4 | Robb 2 | 764 |
| 28 | | 17 | A | Clyde | D 1-1 | 0-1 | — | Yule | 1010 |
| 29 | | 20 | A | Stenhousemuir | W 2-0 | 0-0 | 4 | Docherty, Harley | 500 |
| 30 | | 24 | A | Cowdenbeath | W 2-1 | 2-0 | — | Harley, Robb | 270 |
| 31 | | 27 | H | Meadowbank T | D 0-0 | 0-0 | 2 | | 686 |
| 32 | Apr | 3 | A | Berwick R | D 2-2 | 1-1 | 3 | Gavine, Steele | 350 |
| 33 | | 10 | H | Clyde | I 0-5 | 0-3 | 4 | | 1020 |
| 34 | | 17 | A | Stirling Albion | L 2-3 | 0-2 | 4 | Robb 2 (2 pens) | 400 |
| 35 | | 21 | A | Forfar Ath | D 1-1 | 0-0 | — | Powell | 453 |
| 36 | | 24 | H | Albion R | W 2-0 | 1-0 | 4 | Gavine, Robb | 510 |
| 37 | May | 1 | H | East Fife | D 1-1 | 1-1 | 3 | Robb | 590 |
| 38 | | 8 | A | Brechin C | W 2-0 | 1-0 | 3 | Young, Steele | 750 |
| 39 | | 15 | A | Stranraer | W 3-1 | 2-0 | 3 | Young, Steele, Lees | 350 |

**Final League Position: 3**

### Goalscorers

*League* (62): Robb 21 (3 pens), Yule 9, Gavine 7, Shaw 6, Docherty 4, Lees 3, Steele 3, Harley 2, Young 2, Burke 1, Casey 1, Forsyth 1, Hyslop 1, Powell 1.
*League Cup* (18): Robb 5, Harley 4, Durno 2, Gavine 2, Yule 2, Casey 1, Docherty 1, Lees 1 (pen).
*Scottish Cup* (0).

**Honours**
*Scottish League* – Division 2 Runners-up 1934–35, 1958–59, 1967–68, 1971–72.
*Record Victory:* 36-0 v Bon Accord, Scottish Cup 1st rd, 12 Sept, 1885.
*Record Defeat:* 0-8 v Kilmarnock, Division 2, 3 Jan, 1949.
*Most League Points:* 57, Division 2, 1966–67.
*Most League Goals:* 87, Division 2, 1967–68.
*Most Individual League Goals in Season:* Dave Easson, 45, Division 2, 1958–59.
*Most League Goals in Aggregate:* Jimmy Jack, 120, 1966–71.
*Most Capped Player:* Ned Doig, 2(5), Scotland.

| Lister J. | Robertson D. | Larter D. | Mackenzie A. | Kopel F. | Forsyth S. | Burke N. | Glover S. | Young D. | Casey J. | Gavine W. | Harley I. | Durno D. | Robb D. | Kydd L. | Lees D. | Yule T. | Shaw G. | Docherty B. | Hyslop D. | Powell D. | Duff B. | Hill H. | Steele W. | Match No. |
|---|---|---|---|---|---|---|---|---|---|---|---|---|---|---|---|---|---|---|---|---|---|---|---|---|
| 1 | | 2 | 3 | | 5 | 4 | 6 | 7 | | | | | 9 | | 10 | 13 | 11†12 | | 8* | | | | | 1 |
| 1 | | | 3 | | 5 | 4 | | 7 | 8 | 9 | 6 | | | | | 11*12 | | | 2 | 10 | | | | 2 |
| 1 | 8 | 2 | 3 | | 5 | 6 | | 7* | | 9 | | | 11 | | | | 12 | 4 | 10 | | | | | 3 |
| 1 | | 2 | 3 | | 5 | 4 | 6 | 13 | 8 | 9 | 10†11* | | | | | | 7 | 12 | | | | | | 4 |
| 1 | | 2 | 3 | 5 | | 4 | 6 | 12 | 8 | 9†10 | | | 13 | | | | 7 | 11* | | | | | | 5 |
| 1 | | 2 | 3 | 5 | | 4 | 6 | 7 | 10 | | 11* | | 9 | | | | | 12 | 8 | | | | | 6 |
| 1 | | 2 | 3 | 5 | | 4 | 6 | 12 | 10 | 9 | 11* | | | | | | 7† | 13 | 8 | | | | | 7 |
| 1 | | 2 | 3 | 5 | | 4 | 6 | | 8 | 9 | 12 | | | | | | 7 | 11 | 10* | | | | | 8 |
| 1 | | 2 | 3 | 5 | | 4 | 6 | 13 | 8 | 9 | 12 | | | | | | 7 | 11† | 10* | | | | | 9 |
| 1 | | 2 | 10 | 3 | 5 | 8 | | 7* | 9 | 6 | 11 | | 4 | 12 | | | | | | | | | | 10 |
| 1 | | 2 | 10 | 3 | 5 | | | 7* | 9 | 6†13 | 11 | 12 | 4 | 8 | | | | | | | | | | 11 |
| 1 | | 2 | 10 | 3 | 5 | | | 9 | 6* | 7 | 11 | 12 | 4 | 8 | | | | | | | | | | 12 |
| 1 | | 2 | 10 | 3 | 5 | | 13 | 9 | 6* | 7†11 | 12 | 4 | 8 | | | | | | | | | | | 13 |
| 1 | | 2 | 10* | 3 | 5 | 4 | 13 | 9 | 12 | 7†11 | 6 | | 8 | | | | | | | | | | | 14 |
| 1 | | 2 | | 3 | 5 | | 6 | 12 | 9 | 7*11 | 10 | 4 | 8 | | | | | | | | | | | 15 |
| 1 | | 2 | 13 | 3 | 5 | | 6 | 12 | 9 | 7*11†10 | | 4 | 8 | | | | | | | | | | | 16 |
| 1 | | 2 | 13 | 3 | 5 | | 6 | 7 | 9 | 11†10 | 4 | 8* | | | | | 12 | | | | | | | 17 |
| 1 | | 2 | 12 | 3 | 5 | | 6 | 13 | 9 | 11 | 10† | 4 | 7 | 8* | | | | | | | | | | 18 |
| 1 | 2 | | 12 | 3 | 5 | | 6 | | 9 | 11 | 10 | 4 | 7 | 8* | | | | | | | | | | 19 |
| 1 | 2 | | 12 | 3 | 5 | | 6 | 13 | 9† | 11 | 10 | 4 | 7 | 8* | | | | | | | | | | 20 |
| 1 | 2 | | | 3 | | 5 | 6 | 12 | 9 | 11 | 10 | 4 | 7* | 8 | | | | | | | | | | 21 |
| 1 | 2 | 3 | | 13 | | 5 | 6 | 7 | 9* | 11 | 10 | 4 | 12 | 8† | | | | | | | | | | 22 |
| 1 | | 3 | 2 | | 4 | 5 | 6 | 7 | 9 | 11 | 10 | | | | | | | | 8 | | | | | 23 |
| 1 | | 3 | 2 | 13 | 4 | 5 | 6 | 7* | 9 | 11†10 | | | | | | 8 | 12 | | | | | | | 24 |
| 1 | | 3 | 2†13 | 4 | 5 | 6 | 7 | 9 | 12 | 11*10 | | | | | | 8 | | | | | | | | 25 |
| 1 | 2 | 3 | | 12 | 4 | 5 | 6 | 7* | 9 | 11†13 | 10 | | | | | 8 | | | | | | | | 26 |
| 1 | 2 | 3 | | 13 | 4 | 5 | 6 | 7* | 9 | 11 | 12 | 10† | | | | 8 | | | | | | | | 27 |
| 1 | 2 | 3 | | 12 | 4* | 5 | 6 | 7 | 9 | 11†13 | 10 | | | | | 8 | | | | | | | | 28 |
| 1 | 2 | 3 | | | 4 | 5 | 6 | 7 | 9 | 11 | 10 | | | | | 8 | | | | | | | | 29 |
| 1 | 2 | 3 | | | 4 | 5 | 6 | 7 | 9 | 11*12 | 10 | | | | | 8 | | | | | | | | 30 |
| 1 | 2 | 3 | | | 4 | 5 | 6 | 7* | 9 | 11†13 | 10 | 8 | | | | | | | 12 | | | | | 31 |
| 1 | 2 | 3 | | 4 | | 5 | 6 | 7 | 9 | 11† | 10* | 8 | | | | | | | 12 | 13 | | | | 32 |
| 1 | | 3 | 2 | 10 | 4 | 5* | 6 | 7† | 9 | 12 | 11 | 8 | | | | | | | 13 | | | | | 33 |
| 1 | | 3 | 2 | | 4 | 5 | 6 | 7* | 9 | 11 | 10 | 8 | | | | | | | 12 | | | | | 34 |
| | 1 | 3 | 2 | | 4 | 5 | 6 | | 9 | | 10 | | | | | | | | | 7 | | 8 | 11 | 35 |
| | 1 | 3 | 2 | 13 | 4 | 5 | 6 | | 9† | 12 | 10 | | | | | | | | | | 7* | 8 | 11 | 36 |
| | 1 | 3 | 2 | 10 | 4 | 5 | 13 | 9 | | 12 | 6 | | | | | | | | | | 7* | 8 | 11† | 37 |
| | 1 1 | 2 | 3 | | 2 | 6 | 4 | 5* | 9 | 11 | 10 | | | | | | | | | | | 8 | 7 | 38 |
| | 1 | 3 | 2 | 6 | 4 | 5 | | 9 | | 11* | 10 | 12 | | | | | | | | | | 8 | 7 | 39 |
| 3 | 20 | 16 | 12 | 18 | 27 | 20 | 32 | 34 | 11 | 29 | 20 | 7 | 38 | 8 | 19 | 19 | 25 | 27 | 19 | 4 | 2 | 14 | 5 | |

+ 1s (Robertson D.)   + 12s (Kopel F.)   + 12s (Young D.)   + 3s + 5s + 8s + 5s + 1s + 3s + 1s + 2s + 2s + 4s

# AYR UNITED

## Division 1

*Year Formed:* 1910.
*Ground:* Somerset Park. *Size:* 111yd×75yd. *Capacity:* 18,500 (1500 seats).
*Telephone:* Ayr (0292) 263 435.
*Manager:* Willie McLean. *Asst Manager:* George Caldwell.
*Secretary:* John Robertson.
*Club Colours:* White shirts with black facings, black shorts, white stockings.
*Club Nickname:* The Honest Men.
*Record Attendance:* 25,225 v Rangers, Division 1, 13 Sept, 1969.

## 1981–82 LEAGUE RECORD

| Match No. | Date | Venue | Opponents | Result | H/T Score | League Pos'n | Goalscorers | Attendance |
|---|---|---|---|---|---|---|---|---|
| 1 | Aug 29 | A | Falkirk | W 2-1 | 0-1 | — | Nicol, Ahern | 2500 |
| 2 | Sept 5 | H | Hamilton A | W 2-0 | 2-0 | 1 | Nicol, McAllister | 2429 |
| 3 | 12 | A | Kilmarnock | D 1-1 | 0-0 | 2 | Morris | 5500 |
| 4 | 16 | H | St Johnstone | D 1-1 | 0-1 | — | Frye | 2366 |
| 5 | 19 | A | Queen of the S | W 2-1 | 2-0 | 2 | Morris 2 | 1700 |
| 6 | 23 | H | Hearts | D 0-0 | 0-0 | — | | 3500 |
| 7 | 26 | H | Queen's Park | W 2-0 | 1-0 | 2 | Morris 2 | 2292 |
| 8 | 30 | H | Dumbarton | W 3-2 | 1-2 | — | Christie 2, Kean | 977 |
| 9 | Oct 3 | A | Raith R | W 1-0 | 1-0 | 2 | Frye | 1075 |
| 10 | 10 | A | Motherwell | D 1-1 | 0-0 | 2 | Hendry | 5354 |
| 11 | 17 | H | East Stirling | W 5-1 | 2-1 | 2 | Frye 3, Cashmore, Hendry | 2124 |
| 12 | 24 | H | Dunfermline Ath | D 1-1 | 0-0 | 2 | Morris | 2706 |
| 13 | 31 | A | Clydebank | L 1-2 | 0-1 | 2 | Ahern (pen) | 1000 |
| 14 | Nov 7 | A | Hamilton A | L 0-1 | 0-1 | 2 | | 1579 |
| 15 | 14 | H | Falkirk | W 4-1 | 4-0 | 2 | Frye 2, Hume, Hendry | 2124 |
| 16 | 21 | A | St Johnstone | L 0-2 | 0-1 | 2 | | 1716 |
| 17 | 24 | A | Queen's Park | L 0-2 | 0-1 | — | | 600 |
| 18 | Dec 5 | H | Raith R | W 2-0 | 0-0 | 2 | Morris 2 | 1875 |
| 19 | Jan 26 | H | Queen of the S | W 1-0 | 0-0 | — | Christie | 1500 |
| 20 | Feb 3 | A | Dunfermline Ath | D 0-0 | 0-0 | — | | 1400 |
| 21 | 6 | H | Clydebank | W 2-1 | 2-0 | 2 | Frye, Christie | 724 |
| 22 | 10 | A | East Stirling | L 1-2 | 0-1 | — | Fleeting | 670 |
| 23 | 20 | H | Hearts | L 0-3 | 0-1 | 3 | | 2902 |
| 24 | 27 | A | Kilmarnock | D 1-1 | 0-0 | 3 | Frye | 4041 |
| 25 | Mar 6 | A | Dumbarton | L 1-3 | 1-2 | 4 | Christie | 500 |
| 26 | 13 | H | Motherwell | D 1-1 | 0-0 | 6 | McInally | 3185 |
| 27 | 17 | H | Kilmarnock | D 1-1 | 1-0 | — | McInally | 3663 |
| 28 | 20 | A | St Johnstone | L 2-3 | 1-2 | 6 | Shanks, Frye | 1792 |
| 29 | 27 | H | East Stirling | D 1-1 | 1-0 | 6 | Frye | 1293 |
| 30 | Apr 3 | A | Dunfermline Ath | D 2-2 | 1-1 | 7 | McAllister, McInally | 1600 |
| 31 | 7 | A | Dumbarton | L 1-3 | 1-2 | — | McInally | 282 |
| 32 | 10 | H | Falkirk | W 1-0 | 1-0 | 6 | McInally | 1218 |
| 33 | 14 | H | Motherwell | W 4-3 | 1-0 | — | McInally 2, Ahern, Ward | 2317 |
| 34 | 17 | A | Queen's Park | D 0-0 | 0-0 | 5 | | 784 |
| 35 | 21 | A | Hearts | L 1-2 | 0-0 | — | Shanks | 4675 |
| 36 | 24 | H | Hamilton A | W 3-2 | 2-1 | 5 | McAllister, Ward, Ahern (pen) | 1079 |
| 37 | May 1 | A | Raith R | L 0-1 | 0-0 | 5 | | 900 |
| 38 | 8 | H | Queen of the S | W 5-2 | 1-0 | 5 | Hume, McInally 2, Frye 2 | 863 |
| 39 | 15 | A | Clydebank | L 0-2 | 0-1 | 6 | | 514 |

**Final League Position: 6**

### Goalscorers

*League* (56): Frye 13, McInally 9, Morris 8, Christie 5, Ahern 4 (2 pens), Hendry 3, McAllister 3, Hume 2, Nicol 2, Shanks 2, Ward 2, Cashmore 1, Fleeting 1, Kean 1.
*League Cup* (14): Frye 8, Christie 1, Connor 1, Hendry 1, Kean 1, Nicol 1, own goal 1.
*Scottish Cup* (1): Connor 1.

## Honours

*Scottish League* – Division 2 Champions 1911–12, 1912–13, 1927–28, 1936–37, 1958–59, 1965–66; Runners-up 1910–11, 1955–56, 1968–69.
*Scottish Cup:* None.
*Scottish League Cup* – None.
*Record Victory:* 11-1 v Dumbarton, League Cup, 13 Aug, 1952.
*Record Defeat:* 0-9 v Rangers, Division 1, 16 Nov, 1929; 0-9 v Hearts, Division 1, 28 Feb, 1931.
*Most League Points:* 60, Division 2, 1958–59.
*Most Individual League Goals in Season:* Jimmy Smith, 66, 1927–28.
*Most Capped Player:* Jim Nisbet, 3, Scotland.

| Rennie S. | Brown J. | Shanks M. | Connor R. | Hendry W. | McAllister I. | Fleeting J. | Frye D. | Love A. | McInally A. | Larnach M. | Morris E. | Ahern B. | Christie G. | Hume C. | McSherry J. | Nicol S. | Kean J. | Cashmore I. | Ward J. | Armour D. | Hetherington K. | McCulley R. | McGee L. | Match No. |
|---|---|---|---|---|---|---|---|---|---|---|---|---|---|---|---|---|---|---|---|---|---|---|---|---|
| 1 |  | 3 | 4* | 5 | 6 | 7 | 12 |  | 13 |  | 9 | 10 | 11† |  | 8 | 2 |  |  |  |  |  |  |  | 1 |
| 1 |  | 3 | 5 | 6* | 7 | 4 | 13 | 11 |  |  | 9 | 10 | 12 |  | 8† | 2 |  |  |  |  |  |  |  | 2 |
| 1 |  | 12 | 3 | 6 | 5 | 7 | 4* | 11 |  |  | 9 | 10 |  |  | 8 | 2 |  |  |  |  |  |  |  | 3 |
| 1 |  | 2 | 6 | 4 | 5* | 7 | 13 |  |  |  | 9 | 10 | 11† |  | 8 | 3 | 12 |  |  |  |  |  |  | 4 |
| 1 |  | 2 | 4 | 5 | 6 | 7 | 12 |  |  |  | 9 | 10 | 13 |  | 8* | 3 | 11† |  |  |  |  |  |  | 5 |
| 1 |  | 2 | 4 | 5 | 6 | 7 | 8* |  |  |  | 9 | 10 | 13 |  | 12 | 3 | 11† |  |  |  |  |  |  | 6 |
| 1 |  | 2 | 4 | 5 | 6 | 7 |  |  |  |  | 9 | 10 | 11* |  | 8 | 3 | 12 |  |  |  |  |  |  | 7 |
| 1 |  | 2 | 4* | 5 | 6 | 7 | 12† |  |  |  | 9 | 10 | 11 |  |  | 3 | 8 | 13 |  |  |  |  |  | 8 |
| 1 |  | 2 | 4 | 5 | 6 | 7 |  |  |  |  | 9 | 10 | 11† |  | 13 | 3 | 8* | 12 |  |  |  |  |  | 9 |
| 1 |  | 2 | 4 | 5 | 6 | 7 |  |  |  |  | 9 | 10 | 11 |  |  | 3 | 8* | 12 |  |  |  |  |  | 10 |
| 1 |  | 2 | 4 | 5* | 6 | 7† | 12 |  |  |  | 9 | 10 | 11 |  |  | 3 | 13 | 8 |  |  |  |  |  | 11 |
| 1 |  | 2 | 3 | 4 | 5 | 6 | 7 |  |  |  | 9 | 10 | 11 |  | 12 |  | 8* |  |  |  |  |  |  | 12 |
| 1 |  | 2 | 3 | 4 | 5 | 6 | 7 |  | 12 |  | 9 | 10 | 13 |  | 11† |  | 8* |  |  |  |  |  |  | 13 |
| 1 |  | 2 | 3 | 4 | 5 | 6 | 7* | 12 | 8† | 13 | 9 | 10 | 11 |  |  |  |  |  |  |  |  |  |  | 14 |
| 1 |  | 2 | 3 | 4 | 5 | 6 | 7 | 12 |  |  | 9 | 10 | 11 |  |  |  | 8* |  |  |  |  |  |  | 15 |
| 1 |  | 2* | 3 | 4 | 5 | 6 | 7 | 12 |  |  | 9 | 10† | 11 | 13 |  |  | 8 |  |  |  |  |  |  | 16 |
| 1 |  | 2 | 3 | 4 | 5 | 6 | 7 | 12 |  |  | 9 | 13 | 11 | 10* |  |  | 8† |  |  |  |  |  |  | 17 |
| 1 |  | 2 | 4 | 5 | 6 | 7 | 10 |  |  |  | 9† | 3 | 11 | 13 | 12 |  | 8* |  |  |  |  |  |  | 18 |
| 1 |  | 2 | 10 | 5 | 6 | 7 | 4* |  |  |  | 9 | 3 | 11 |  | 12 |  | 8 |  |  |  |  |  |  | 19 |
| 1 |  | 2 | 10 | 5 | 6 |  |  |  |  |  | 9 | 3 | 11 |  | 12 |  | 8 |  | 7 | 4* |  |  |  | 20 |
| 1 |  | 2 | 10 | 5 | 6 | 7 |  |  |  |  |  | 3 | 11 |  | 12 |  | 8† |  | 9 | 13 | 4* |  |  | 21 |
| 1 |  | 2 | 10 | 5 | 6 | 7 | 12 |  | 8† |  | 9 | 3 | 11 |  |  |  |  |  | 4* | 13 |  |  |  | 22 |
| 1 |  | 2 | 10 | 5 | 6* | 7 | 8† | 12 |  |  | 9 | 3 | 11 |  |  |  |  |  | 13 | 4 |  |  |  | 23 |
| 1 |  | 2 |  |  | 5 | 6 | 12 |  |  |  | 9 | 3 | 11 |  |  |  | 8* |  | 7 | 10 | 4 |  |  | 24 |
| 1 |  | 2 | 12 | 5 | 6* | 7 | 13 |  |  |  | 9 | 3 | 11 |  |  |  | 8 |  | 10† | 4 |  |  |  | 25 |
| 1 |  | 2 | 10 |  | 5 |  | 12 | 7* |  |  | 9 | 3 | 11 |  |  |  | 8 |  |  | 4 | 6 |  |  | 26 |
| 1 |  | 2 | 10 |  | 5 |  | 13 | 12 | 7 |  | 9 | 3 | 11† |  |  |  | 8 |  |  | 4* | 6 |  |  | 27 |
| 1 |  | 2 | 10 |  | 5 | 4* | 13 |  | 7 |  | 9 | 3 | 11† |  |  |  | 8 |  | 12 |  | 6 |  |  | 28 |
| 1 |  | 2 | 10 |  | 5 | 7 | 4* |  |  |  | 9 | 3 | 11† |  | 12 |  | 8 |  | 13 |  | 6 |  |  | 29 |
|  | 1 |  | 10† |  | 5 |  | 12 |  |  |  | 11 | 3* | 13 | 2 |  |  |  |  | 9 | 4 | 6 | 8 |  | 30 |
|  | 1 |  | 10 |  | 5† | 13 | 12 |  |  |  |  | 3 | 11 | 2 |  |  |  |  | 9* | 4 | 6 | 8 |  | 31 |
|  | 1 | 3 | 2 | 6 | 9† | 7 | 4 | 10 | 11* | 13 |  |  |  |  |  |  |  |  | 12 | 5 | 8 |  |  | 32 |
|  | 1 | 2 | 3 |  | 5 | 6 | 7 |  |  |  | 9 | 10 | 12 |  |  |  |  |  | 11 | 4 | 8* |  |  | 33 |
|  | 1 | 2 | 3 |  | 5 | 6 | 7 | 4 |  |  | 9 | 10 |  |  |  |  |  |  | 11 |  | 8 |  |  | 34 |
|  | 1 | 2† | 3 |  | 5 | 6 | 12 | 7 |  |  | 11 | 10 | 13 |  |  |  |  |  | 9 | 4 | 8* |  |  | 35 |
|  | 1 | 2† | 3 |  | 5 | 6 | 8 | 9 | 12 |  | 10 | 7* |  |  |  |  |  |  | 11 | 4 | 13 |  |  | 36 |
|  | 1 | 2 | 3 | 6 | 5 | 12 | 4 | 7 |  |  | 13 | 10 | 11 |  | 8* |  |  |  | 9† |  |  |  |  | 37 |
|  | 1 | 2 | 10 |  | 5 | 6 | 12 | 7 |  |  | 9 | 4 | 11* |  |  |  |  |  |  |  |  | 8 | 3 | 38 |
|  | 1 | 2* | 10 |  | 5 | 12 |  | 7 | 11 |  | 9 | 6 | 4 |  |  |  |  |  | 13 |  |  | 8† | 3 | 39 |
| 29 | 10 | 33 | 29 | 17 | 39 | 31 | 28 | 6 | 15 | 6 | 36 | 36 | 27 | 5 | 12 | 11 | 11 | 5 | 12 | 11 | 10 | 8 | 2 |  |
|  | +1s | +1s |  |  | +4s | +7s | +7s | +2s | +8s | +2s | +1s | +5s | +6s | +4s |  | +4s | +6s | +4s | +2s |  | +1s |  |  |  |

# BERWICK RANGERS　　　　Division 2

*Year Formed:* 1881.　*Ground:* Shielfield Park.　*Size:* 112yd×76yd.　*Capacity:* 10,673 (1473 seats).
*Telephone:* Berwick (0289) 7424/2554.
*Manager:*　　　　　*Commercial Manager:* Ian Davison.
*Secretary:* Dennis McCleary.　*Limited Company:* 1952.
*Club Colours:* Gold shirts with black vertical stripes, black shorts, gold stockings.
*Record Attendance:* 13,365 v Rangers, Scottish Cup 1st rd, 28 Jan, 1967.
*Club Nickname:* The Borderers.

## 1981–82 LEAGUE RECORD

| Match No. | Date | Venue | Opponents | Result | H/T Score | League Pos'n | Goalscorers | Attendance |
|---|---|---|---|---|---|---|---|---|
| 1 | Aug 29 | H | Montrose | W 4-0 | 2-0 | — | Davidson 2, Lawson 2 | 900 |
| 2 | Sept 5 | A | Forfar Ath | L 1-2 | 1-2 | 4 | Lawson | 1141 |
| 3 | 8 | A | Stranraer | W 4-2 | 2-1 | — | Davidson, Moyes, Lawson, McGlinchey | 380 |
| 4 | 12 | H | Meadowbank T | W 3-1 | 0-1 | 3 | McCulloch, McGlinchey, Armstrong | 915 |
| 5 | 16 | A | Stirling Albion | W 1-0 | 1-0 | — | McLeod (og) | 460 |
| 6 | 19 | A | Stenhousemuir | D 1-1 | 0-1 | 2 | Tait | 300 |
| 7 | 26 | H | Cowdenbeath | L 1-2 | 0-1 | 4 | McCulloch | 750 |
| 8 | 30 | H | East Fife | W 2-1 | 1-0 | — | Marshall, Davidson | 480 |
| 9 | Oct 3 | A | Albion R | W 3-1 | 3-0 | 2 | Lawson, Moyes, Dixon | 844 |
| 10 | 10 | A | Alloa | L 0-1 | 0-1 | 3 | | 575 |
| 11 | 17 | H | Brechin C | W 3-1 | 2-0 | 2 | Lawson, Tait 2 | 831 |
| 12 | 24 | A | Arbroath | L 1-2 | 0-0 | 4 | Lawson | 531 |
| 13 | 31 | H | Clyde | W 4-0 | 1-0 | 4 | Davidson 2, McCulloch, Tait | 979 |
| 14 | Nov 7 | H | Forfar Ath | D 1-1 | 1-1 | 4 | Tait | 900 |
| 15 | 14 | A | Montrose | W 2-0 | 1-0 | 2 | Lawson, Davidson | 350 |
| 16 | 21 | H | Stirling Albion | W 1-0 | 0-0 | 2 | Lawson | 400 |
| 17 | 28 | A | Cowdenbeath | L 1-2 | 0-1 | 5 | Lawson | 500 |
| 18 | Dec 5 | H | Albion R | W 6-1 | 3-1 | 2 | Lawson 3, McCulloch, Davidson, McGlynn | 745 |
| 19 | Jan 30 | A | East Fife | W 1-0 | 0-0 | 4 | Tait | 449 |
| 20 | Feb 3 | A | Brechin C | L 0-2 | 0-2 | — | | 400 |
| 21 | 6 | H | Arbroath | W 3-0 | 0-0 | 3 | McKenzie (og), Tait 2 | 500 |
| 22 | 13 | A | Clyde | L 1-3 | 1-0 | 4 | McCulloch | 544 |
| 23 | 17 | H | Stranraer | D 0-0 | 0-0 | — | | 870 |
| 24 | 20 | A | Montrose | D 0-0 | 0-0 | 4 | | 350 |
| 25 | 23 | H | Stenhousemuir | W 1-0 | 0-0 | — | McCulloch | 625 |
| 26 | 27 | H | Meadowbank T | D 2-2 | 2-2 | 3 | McKenna, Davidson | 852 |
| 27 | Mar 6 | A | Alloa | D 1-1 | 0-1 | 3 | Lawson | 600 |
| 28 | 13 | H | Albion R | W 4-1 | 2-0 | 2 | McKenna, Marshall, Armstrong, Davidson | 656 |
| 29 | 17 | A | Meadowbank T | L 1-2 | 0-1 | — | Lawson | 420 |
| 30 | 20 | A | Clyde | W 2-1 | 1-0 | 2 | O'Connor 2 | 580 |
| 31 | 27 | H | East Fife | W 3-0 | 1-0 | 3 | Halley (og), O'Connor, Marshall | 797 |
| 32 | Apr 3 | H | Arbroath | D 2-2 | 1-1 | 4 | Tait, Armstrong | 350 |
| 33 | 7 | H | Alloa | W 2-0 | 0-0 | — | O'Connor 2 | 870 |
| 34 | 10 | A | Cowdenbeath | L 0-2 | 0-1 | 3 | | 468 |
| 35 | 17 | H | Stranraer | W 2-0 | 2-0 | 3 | Lawson, Armstrong (pen) | 814 |
| 36 | 24 | A | Stenhousemuir | L 0-2 | 0-2 | 3 | | 743 |
| 37 | May 1 | A | Brechin C | L 0-1 | 0-1 | 4 | | 300 |
| 38 | 8 | H | Forfar Ath | W 2-1 | 1-1 | 4 | Marshall, O'Connor | 722 |
| 39 | 15 | A | Stirling Albion | D 0-0 | 0-0 | 4 | | 600 |

**Final League Position: 4**

### Goalscorers
*League* (66): Lawson 16, Davidson 10, Tait 9, McCulloch 6, O'Connor 6, Armstrong 4 (1 pen), Marshall 4, McGlinchey 2, McKenna 2, Moyes 2, Dixon 1, McGlynn 1, own goals 3.
*League Cup* (12): Davidson 5, Lawson 4, McGlynn 1, Tait 1, own goal 1.
*Scottish Cup* (6): McGlynn 2, Davidson 1, Lawson 1, McCann 1, Muir 1.

## Honours

*Scottish League* – Division 2 Champions 1978–79.
*East of Scotland FA Shield* – Winners 1981.
*Record Victory:* 8-1 v Forfar Athletic, Division 2, 25 Dec, 1965; 8-1 v Vale of Leithen, Scottish Cup, Dec, 1966.
*Record Defeat:* 1-9 v Hamilton A, Division 2, 9 Aug, 1980.
*Most League Points:* 54, Division 2, 1978–79.
*Most Individual League Goals in Season:* Ken Bowron, 38, Division 2, 1963–64.
*Most League Goals:* 83, Division 2, 1961–62.
*Most League Appearances:* Eric Tait, 334, 1970–82.
*Best Cup Run:* 1963 League Cup semi-final, 1-3 v Rangers (Hampden Park).
*Extra Information:* Only Scottish League club with home ground in England.
*Previous Grounds:* Bull Stob Close, Pier Field, Meadow Field, Union Park and Old Shielfield.

| McDermott M. | Glynn M. | Moyes D. | McCann H. | Black I. | Jefferies J. | Marshall B. | Muir L. | Cameron M. | Dixon S. | McGlynn J. | Romaines S. | Davidson P. | McCulloch W. | Lawson M. | Tait E. | McGlinchey P. | Armstrong G. | O'Connor D. | Thomson A. | Lumsdaine C. | Krawiec S. | McKenna A. | Salton J. | Match No. |
|---|---|---|---|---|---|---|---|---|---|---|---|---|---|---|---|---|---|---|---|---|---|---|---|---|
| 1 | 8 | 2* | 3 | | 6 | | | | 5†13 | | | 7 | 4 | 9 | 10 | 12 | 11 | | | | | | | 1 |
| 1 | 6 | 2 | 3 | | | | | | 5 | 12 | | 4 | 7 | 9 | 10 | 8* | 11 | | | | | | | 2 |
| 1 | 8 | | | 2 | 6 | | | | 5 | | | 4 | 7 | 10 | 11 | 3 | 9 | | | | | | | 3 |
| 1 | 8 | 2 | | | 6 | | | | 5 | | | 4 | 7 | 10 | 11 | 3 | 9 | | | | | | | 4 |
| 1 | 8 | 2 | | | 6 | | | | 5 | 12 | | 7 | 4 | 11 | 10 | 3 | 9* | | | | | | | 5 |
| 1† | 8 | 2 | | | 6 | | 13 | | 5 | 12 | | | 4 | 11 | 10 | 3 | 9 | 7* | | | | | | 6 |
| | 1 | 2 | 3*12 | | 6 | | | | 5 | | | 4 | 7 | 8 | 11 | 10 | 9 | | | | | | | 7 |
| 1 | 4 | | 3 | 5 | 6 | | | | 11 | 13 | | 7 | 8 | 9 | 10* | 2†12 | | | | | | | | 8 |
| 1 | 8 | 2 | 10 | | 6 | | | | 5 | | | 7 | 4 | 9 | | 3 | 11 | | | | | | | 9 |
| 1 | 8 | 2 | 11 | | 6 | | | | 5 | | | 7 | 4 | 9 | 10 | 3 | | | | | | | | 10 |
| 1 | 4 | 12 | 11† | 2* | 6 | | | | 5 | 13 | | 7 | 8 | 9 | 10 | 3 | | | | | | | | 11 |
| 1 | 4 | 2 | 11* | | 6 | | | | 5 | 12 | | 7 | 8 | 9 | 10 | 3 | | | | | | | | 12 |
| 1 | 2 | 3 | | 5 | 6 | | | | 13 | | | 4 | 7 | 8 | 9 | 10* | 11†12 | | | | | | | 13 |
| 1 | 2 | 3 | | 5 | 6 | | | | | | | 4 | 7 | 8 | 9 | 10 | 11 | | | | | | | 14 |
| 1 | 2 | 3 | 4 | | 6 | | | | | | | 7 | 8 | 9 | 10 | 11 | | | | | | | | 15 |
| 1 | 2 | 3 | 4 | | 6 | | | | 5 | | | 7 | 8 | 9 | 10 | | 11 | | | | | | | 16 |
| 1 | 2 | 3 | 4 | | 6 | | | | 5 | | | 7 | 8 | 9 | 10 | 12 | 11* | | | | | | | 17 |
| 1 | 6 | 4 | 2 | | | | | | 5 | 3 | 13 | 7 | 9*11 | | 10 | 8†12 | | | | | | | | 18 |
| 1 | 2 | 3 | 8 | 4 | 5† | 6 | | | 13 | | | 7* | 9 | 11 | 10 | 12 | | | | | | | | 19 |
| 1 | 8 | 2 | 3 | | 6 | | | | 5 | 11 | | 7 | 4 | 9* | 10 | | 12 | | | | | | | 20 |
| 1 | 2 | 3 | 4 | | 6 | | | | 5 | 13 | | 9 | 7* | 8†12 | 10 | 11 | | | | | | | | 21 |
| 1 | 2 | 3 | 4* | | 6 | | | | 5 | 12 | | 9 | 7 | 8 | 10 | 11 | | | | | | | | 22 |
| 1 | 3† | 5 | 2 | | 6 | | | | | | | 4 | 8 | 7 | 12 | 9 | 10* | 11 | 13 | | | | | 23 |
| 1 | 3 | 5 | 2 | | 6 | | | | | | | 4 | 8 | 7 | 12 | 10* | 9 | 11 | | | | | | 24 |
| 1 | 3 | 5 | 2 | | 6 | | | | | | | 4 | 13 | 7 | 12 | 10 | 11 | 8† | | | 9* | | | 25 |
| 1 | 2* | 3 | 11 | 5 | 6 | | | | | | | 4 | 8 | 7 | 10†13 | | 12 | | | | | 9 | | 26 |
| 1 | 2 | 10 | 5* | | 6 | 4 | | | | | | 3† | 7 | 13 | 12 | 8 | 11 | | | | | 9 | | 27 |
| 1 | 3 | 10* | 5 | 2 | 6 | | | | | | | 4 | 7 | 12 | 8 | | 11 | | | | | 9 | | 28 |
| 1 | 3 | 5 | 2 | | 6* | | | | | | | 4 | 7 | 13 | 8†12 | 11 | 10 | | | | | 9 | | 29 |
| 1 | 2* | 6 | 5 | 4 | 3 | | | | | | | 8 | 7 | 12 | 11 | 9 | | | | | | 10 | | 30 |
| 1 | 6 | 2 | 4† | 3 | | | | | | | | 8 | 7 | 12 | 11 | 10 | 13 | 9 | | | | 5* | | 31 |
| 1 | 6 | 2 | 12 | 3 | 4 | | | | | | | | 11 | 10 | 13 | 7 | 9 | | | | | 8* | 5† | 32 |
| 1 | 6 | 5 | 2 | | | | 8 | | | | | 3 | 4 | 11 | 10 | 7 | 9 | | | | | | | 33 |
| 1 | 6 | 10 | 5 | 2 | | | 8* | | | | | 3 | 4 | 11 | 12 | 7 | 9 | | | | | | | 34 |
| 1 | 2 | 6 | 12 | 3 | 5* | | 8 | | | | | 4 | 13 | 11 | 10 | 7† | 9 | | | | | | | 35 |
| 1 | 2 | 6† | 3 | | | | | 12 | | | | 4 | 13 | 11 | 10* | 8 | 9 | | | | | 7 | 5 | 36 |
| 1 | 3 | 6 | 2* | | 8 | | | | | 10 | | 4 | 5 | 7 | 11 | 9 | | | | | | 12 | | 37 |
| 1 | 3 | 5 | 2† | | 6 | | 8 | | | 12 | | 4 | 13 | 10 | 11 | 9 | | | | | | 7* | | 38 |
| 1 | 3 | 5 | 2 | | 6 | | 8* | | | 12 | | 4 | 9 | 10 | 11 | | | | | | | 7 | | 39 |
| 36 | 3 | 27 | 31 | 16 | 22 | 22 | 28 | 14 | 17 | 13 | 26 | 23 | 27 | 35 | 25 | 14 | 26 | 10 | 1 | — | 1 | 9 | 3 | |

Substitute appearances: + 1s, 2s; + 1s; + 1s; + 10s, 6s, 6s, 6s, 3s; + 4s, 7s; + 1s; + 1s.

# BRECHIN CITY

# Division 2

*Year Formed:* 1906. *Ground:* Glebe Park. *Size:* 110yd×67yd. *Capacity:* 7500.
*Telephone:* Brechin 2856.
*Manager:* Doug Houston. *Secretary:* George Johnston.
*Club Colours:* Red shirts, shorts and stockings.
*Club Nickname:* City.
*Record Attendance:* 8123 v Aberdeen, Scottish Cup 3rd rd, 3 Feb, 1973.

## 1981–82 LEAGUE RECORD

| Match No. | Date | Venue | Opponents | Result | H/T Score | League Pos'n | Goalscorers | Attendance |
|---|---|---|---|---|---|---|---|---|
| 1 | Aug 29 | H | Stirling Albion | W 2-1 | 1-0 | — | Lesslie, Paterson | 400 |
| 2 | Sept 5 | A | Meadowbank T | L 0-1 | 0-0 | 7 | | 150 |
| 3 | 8 | A | Stenhousemuir | W 4-0 | 2-0 | — | Lesslie, Campbell I. 2, Henderson | 200 |
| 4 | 12 | H | Montrose | W 3-0 | 1-0 | 4 | Graham 3 (1 pen) | 600 |
| 5 | 19 | A | Arbroath | D 1-1 | 1-1 | 5 | Lorimer | 859 |
| 6 | 26 | A | Stranraer | W 6-0 | 3-0 | 2 | Graham 3, Campbell I., Campbell R., Mackie | 250 |
| 7 | Oct 3 | H | East Fife | W 2-1 | 1-0 | 3 | Graham, Campbell I. (pen) | 1012 |
| 8 | 10 | H | Albion R | W 3-2 | 2-1 | 2 | Cormack, Campbell I. 2 | 400 |
| 9 | 17 | A | Berwick R | L 1-3 | 0-2 | 5 | Lesslie | 831 |
| 10 | 20 | H | Clyde | D 2-2 | 2-2 | — | Henderson, Mackie | 650 |
| 11 | 24 | A | Alloa | W 3-1 | 2-0 | 2 | Campbell I., Henderson, Reid | 780 |
| 12 | 27 | A | Forfar Ath | W 1-0 | 0-0 | — | Stewart | 2000 |
| 13 | 31 | H | Cowdenbeath | L 0-1 | 0-1 | 3 | | 400 |
| 14 | Nov 7 | H | Meadowbank T | W 3-0 | 2-0 | 1 | Campbell I., Mackie, Lesslie | 500 |
| 15 | 14 | A | Stirling Albion | L 0-5 | 0-2 | 4 | | 540 |
| 16 | 21 | H | Forfar Ath | D 0-0 | 0-0 | 4 | | 700 |
| 17 | 28 | H | Stranraer | W 3-0 | 1-0 | 3 | Graham, Elvin, Paterson | 400 |
| 18 | Dec 5 | A | East Fife | D 2-2 | 0-1 | 3 | Mackie, Henderson | 531 |
| 19 | Jan 2 | A | Montrose | D 2-2 | 2-0 | 2 | Paterson, Campbell I. | 780 |
| 20 | 23 | H | Albion R | W 2-1 | 0-0 | 2 | Paterson 2 | 390 |
| 21 | Feb 3 | H | Berwick R | W 2-0 | 2-0 | — | Campbell I. 2 | 400 |
| 22 | 6 | H | Alloa | L 0-4 | 0-0 | 2 | | 579 |
| 23 | 10 | H | Stenhousemuir | D 1-1 | 0-0 | — | Campbell I. | 326 |
| 24 | 13 | A | Cowdenbeath | D 0-0 | 0-0 | 2 | | 300 |
| 25 | 17 | H | Arbroath | D 2-2 | 0-1 | — | Cormack, Elvin (pen) | 955 |
| 26 | 20 | A | Meadowbank T | L 0-2 | 0-0 | 2 | | 200 |
| 27 | 27 | H | Stranraer | W 3-0 | 1-0 | 2 | Paterson, Mackay, Cormack | 400 |
| 28 | Mar 6 | A | Stirling Albion | W 2-0 | 1-0 | 2 | Campbell R., Paterson | 450 |
| 29 | 13 | H | Alloa | L 0-1 | 0-0 | 3 | | 400 |
| 30 | 20 | A | Montrose | W 4-1 | 3-1 | 3 | Campbell I. 2 (1 pen), Mackay, Paterson | 600 |
| 31 | 27 | H | Stenhousemuir | L 0-1 | 0-1 | 5 | | 400 |
| 32 | Apr 3 | A | Clyde | L 1-3 | 0-1 | 5 | Hay (pen) | 450 |
| 33 | 10 | H | East Fife | D 1-1 | 0-1 | 5 | Mackie | 450 |
| 34 | 14 | A | Clyde | L 0-1 | 0-1 | — | | 1210 |
| 35 | 17 | A | Albion R | W 2-1 | 2-0 | 5 | Stewart, Campbell I. | 200 |
| 36 | 24 | A | Forfar Ath | D 0-0 | 0-0 | 6 | | 1307 |
| 37 | May 1 | H | Berwick R | W 1-0 | 1-0 | 6 | Stewart | 300 |
| 38 | 8 | H | Arbroath | L 0-2 | 0-1 | 6 | | 750 |
| 39 | 15 | A | Cowdenbeath | W 2-0 | 1-0 | 5 | Graham, Campbell I. | 300 |

**Final League Position: 5**

### Goalscorers
*League* (61): Campbell I. 16 (2 pens), Graham 9 (1 pen), Paterson 8, Mackie 5, Henderson 4, Lesslie 4, Cormack 3, Stewart 3, Campbell R. 2, Elvin 2, Mackay 2, Hay 1 (pen), Lorimer 1, Reid 1.
*League Cup* (11): Campbell I. 3, Graham 2, Mackie 2, Paterson 2, Mackay 1, own goal 1.
*Scottish Cup* (5): Campbell I. 2, Cormack 1, Lesslie 1, own goal 1.

**Honours**

*Record Victory:* 12-1 v Thornhill, Scottish Cup 1st rd, 28 Jan, 1926.
*Record Defeat:* 1-10 v Dunfermline Ath, Division 2, 14 Dec, 1929.
*Most League Points:* 46, Division 2, 1981–82.
*Most Individual Goals in Season:* Willie McIntosh, 26, 1959–60.
*Highest League Placing:* 4th, Division 2, 1980–81.

| Neilson D. | Watt D. | Reid B. | Lorimer R. | Keating A. | Lesslie G. | Stewart I. | Mackie G. | Campbell R. | Henderson A. | Graham S. | Elvin C. | Cormack R. | Paterson I. | Kyles J. | Mackay H. | Campbell I. | Burnside D. | Hay J. | Millican K. | Cord J. | Match No. |
|---|---|---|---|---|---|---|---|---|---|---|---|---|---|---|---|---|---|---|---|---|---|
| 1 | 12 | 2 | 3 | 6 | | 10 | 4 | | 13 | 8* | 11† | 9 | | | 5 | 7 | | | | | 1 |
| 1 | 6 | 2 | 3 | 5 | | 8 | 4 | | 9† | 10 | 11* | 12 | | | 13 | 7 | | | | | 2 |
| 1 | 2 | 3 | | | 4 | 5 | 8 | 6 | 11* | 10 | 12 | 9 | | | | 7 | | | | | 3 |
| 1 | 2 | 3 | 10 | | 4 | 5 | 8 | 6 | 9* | 11 | 12 | | | | | 7 | | | | | 4 |
| 1 | 2 | 3 | 10* | | 4 | 5 | 8 | 6 | 13 | 11† | | 9 | 12 | | | 7 | | | | | 5 |
| 1 | 2 | 5 | 3 | | 4 | | 8 | 6 | | 9 | 10 | 11 | | | | 7 | | | | | 6 |
| 1 | 2 | 5 | 3 | | 4 | | 8 | 6 | | 9* | 10 | 11 | | | 12 | 7 | | | | | 7 |
| 1 | 2 | 5 | 3 | | 4 | | 8 | 6 | 12 | 9* | 10 | 11 | | | | 7 | | | | | 8 |
| 1 | 2 | 5 | 3 | | 4 | 12 | 8 | 6 | 10* | 11 | | 9 | | | | 7 | | | | | 9 |
| 1 | 2 | 5 | 3 | | 4 | | 8 | 6 | 9* | 10 | 11 | | | | 12 | 7 | | | | | 10 |
| 1 | 2 | 3 | | | 4 | | 8 | 6 | 9* | 10 | 11 | 12 | | | 5 | 7 | | | | | 11 |
| 1 | 2 | 3 | | | 4 | 13 | 8 | 6 | 9* | 10 | 11 | 12 | | | 5† | 7 | | | | | 12 |
| 1 | 2 | 3 | | | 4 | 5* | 8 | 6 | 12 | 10† | 11 | 9 | | | 13 | 7 | | | | | 13 |
| 1 | 2 | 3 | | | 4 | 5 | 6 | 8 | 9 | 10 | 11* | | 12 | | | 7 | | | | | 14 |
| 1 | 2 | 3 | | | 4 | 5 | 8 | 6 | 13 | 9† | 10 | 11* | 12 | | | 7 | | | | | 15 |
| 1 | 2 | 3 | | | 4 | 5 | 6 | 12 | 11* | 10 | 8 | 9 | | | | 7 | | | | | 16 |
| 1 | 2 | 5 | | | 4 | | 3 | 6 | 10 | 8 | 11 | 9 | | | | 7 | | | | | 17 |
| 1 | 2† | 5 | 3 | | | 12 | 4 | 6 | 13 | 10* | 8 | 11 | 9 | | | 7 | | | | | 18 |
| 1 | 2 | 5 | 3 | | 4 | | 6 | | 8 | 10 | 11 | 9 | | | | 7 | | | | | 19 |
| 1 | 2 | 5 | 3 | | 4 | 12 | 6 | | 8* | 10 | 11 | 13 | 9† | | | 7 | | | | | 20 |
| 1 | 2 | 5 | 3 | | 4 | | 6 | 10 | 8 | 12 | 11 | 9 | | | | 7* | | | | | 21 |
| 1 | 2 | 5 | 3 | | 4 | 7* | 6 | 8 | 12 | 10† | 11 | 9 | | | 13 | | | | | | 22 |
| 1 | 2 | 5 | 3 | | 4 | 10 | 6 | | 8† | 12 | 11* | 9 | | | 13 | 7 | | | | | 23 |
| 1 | 2 | 5 | 3 | | 4 | 10 | 6 | | 9 | 13 | 11† | 12 | | | 8 | 7* | | | | | 24 |
| 1 | 2 | 5 | 3* | | 4 | 10 | 6 | | 9† | 12 | 11 | 13 | | | 8 | 7 | | | | | 25 |
| 1 | 2 | 3 | | | 4 | 10 | 6* | 12 | 9 | 11† | 8 | | | | 5 | 7 | 13 | | | | 26 |
| 1 | 2 | 3 | | | 4 | | 6 | 8 | 10 | 11† | 9* | | | | 5 | 7 | 13 | 12 | | | 27 |
| 1 | 2 | 3 | | | 4 | | 8 | | 10 | 11 | 9 | | | | 5 | 7 | 6 | | | | 28 |
| 1 | 2 | 3 | | | 4 | | 8 | 13 | 10 | 11† | 9 | | | | 5 | 12 | 6 | 7* | | | 29 |
| 1 | 2 | 3 | | | 4 | | 8 | | 10 | | 9 | | | | 5 | 7 | 6 | 11 | | | 30 |
| 1 | 2 | 3 | | | 4 | | 8† | 13 | 7* | 12 | 10 | 9 | | | 5 | | 6 | 11 | | | 31 |
| 1 | 12 | 3 | 2 | | 4 | | 8 | 10 | 13 | | 7 | 9† | | | 5* | | 6 | 11 | | | 32 |
| 1 | 5 | 2 | | | 4 | | 8 | | 10 | | 9 | | | | | 7 | 6 | 11 | 3 | | 33 |
| 1 | 2 | 5 | 3 | | 4 | 10 | 8 | 13 | 9 | 12 | | | | | 7† | | 6 | 11* | | | 34 |
| 1 | 2 | 5 | 3 | | 4 | 10 | 6 | 12 | | 8 | 11 | 9* | | | | 7 | | | | | 35 |
| 1 | 2 | 5 | 3 | | 4 | 10 | 6 | | | 8 | 11* | 9 | | | | 7 | | | 12 | | 36 |
| 1 | 2 | 5 | 3 | | 4 | 10 | 6 | | | 9 | 8 | | | | | 7 | | | 11 | | 37 |
| 1 | 2 | 5 | 3 | | 4 | 10† | 6 | | 9* | 8 | 11 | 12 | | | 7 | | | 13 | | | 38 |
| 1 | 2 | 5 | 10 | | 4 | 3 | 7 | | 9* | 11 | 8 | | | | 12 | | | 6 | | | 39 |
| 39 | 35 | 38 | 23 | 4 | 38 | 18 | 38 | 21 | 13 | 21 | 30 | 26 | 23 | — | 12 | 34 | — | 8 | 7 | 1 | |
| +1s | +1s | | +4s | | | +5s | +7s | +5s | +2s | +3s | +7s | +3s | +6s | +2s | +2s | +1s | +2s | | | | |

# CELTIC
# Premier Division

*Year Formed:* 1888. *Ground:* Celtic Park. *Size:* 115yd×75yd. *Capacity:* 67,500/(9000 seats). *Telephone:* 041-554 2710. *Manager:* Billy McNeill. *Secretary:* Desmond White CA. *Asst Manager:* John Clark. *Commercial Manager:* Jack McGinn. *Club Colours:* Green and white hooped shirts, white shorts. *Club Nickname:* The Bhoys. *Record Attendance:* 92,000 v Rangers, Division 1, 1 Jan, 1938.
**European Competitions:** *European Cup* 1966–67 (winners), 1967–68, 1969–70 (finalists), 1970–71, 1971–72, 1972–73, 1973–74, 1974–75, 1976–77, 1979–80, 1981–82; *European Cup-Winners' Cup* 1963–64, 1965–66, 1975–76, 1980–81; *Fairs Cup* 1962–63, 1964–65; *UEFA Cup* 1976–77. *Coronation Cup:* 1953. *Empire Exhibition Cup:* 1938.

## 1981–82 LEAGUE RECORD

| Match No. | Date | Venue | Opponents | Result | H/T Score | League Pos'n | Goalscorers | Attendance |
|---|---|---|---|---|---|---|---|---|
| 1 | Aug 29 | H | Airdrieonians | W 5-2 | 1-1 | — | Burns, McGarvey, McCluskey 2, Nicholas | 21,100 |
| 2 | Sept 5 | A | Aberdeen | W 3-1 | 2-1 | 1 | Burns, McGarvey 2 | 18,825 |
| 3 | 12 | H | Morton | W 2-1 | 0-0 | 1 | MacLeod, McAdam | 19,900 |
| 4 | 19 | A | Rangers | W 2-0 | 1-0 | 1 | McAdam, MacLeod | 45,000 |
| 5 | 26 | H | Partick T | W 2-0 | 0-0 | 1 | Nicholas, Burns | 15,200 |
| 6 | Oct 3 | A | Dundee | W 3-1 | 1-0 | 1 | McCluskey 2, McGarvey | 13,254 |
| 7 | 10 | A | St Mirren | W 2-1 | 2-0 | 1 | Nicholas, McCluskey | 16,411 |
| 8 | 17 | H | Dundee U | D 1-1 | 0-1 | 1 | McCluskey | 23,000 |
| 9 | 24 | A | Hibernian | L 0-1 | 0-1 | 1 | | 18,000 |
| 10 | 31 | A | Airdrieonians | W 3-1 | 1-1 | 1 | Sullivan, McCluskey (pen), Burns | 13,500 |
| 11 | Nov 7 | H | Aberdeen | W 2-1 | 1-0 | 1 | McGarvey, McCluskey | 29,326 |
| 12 | 14 | A | Morton | D 1-1 | 0-0 | 1 | McCluskey | 12,412 |
| 13 | 21 | H | Rangers | D 3-3 | 2-3 | 1 | McAdam, McGarvey, MacLeod | 48,600 |
| 14 | 28 | A | Partick T | W 2-0 | 1-0 | 1 | McCluskey, Provan | 13,073 |
| 15 | Dec 5 | H | Dundee | W 3-1 | 0-0 | 1 | McGarvey 2, Conroy | 14,570 |
| 16 | Jan 9 | A | Rangers | L 0-1 | 0-0 | 1 | | 42,000 |
| 17 | 30 | A | Aberdeen | W 3-1 | 1-1 | 1 | McCluskey (pen), MacLeod, McStay | 20,000 |
| 18 | Feb 2 | H | Hibernian | D 0-0 | 0-0 | — | | 16,700 |
| 19 | 6 | A | Dundee | W 3-1 | 1-0 | 1 | MacLeod 2, McGarvey | 11,377 |
| 20 | 20 | H | Partick T | D 2-2 | 0-0 | 1 | McCluskey, Aitken | 15,200 |
| 21 | 27 | A | Hibernian | L 0-1 | 0-1 | 1 | | 15,914 |
| 22 | Mar 3 | H | Morton | W 1-0 | 0-0 | — | McGarvey | 9000 |
| 23 | 13 | A | St Mirren | W 5-2 | 4-0 | 1 | MacLeod 2, Burns, Sullivan, McCluskey | 17,084 |
| 24 | 20 | H | Airdrieonians | W 2-0 | 2-0 | 1 | Sullivan, Burns | 12,000 |
| 25 | 27 | A | Aberdeen | L 0-1 | 0-0 | 1 | | 30,080 |
| 26 | 31 | A | Dundee U | W 2-0 | 1-0 | — | Burns 2 | 15,143 |
| 27 | Apr 3 | A | Morton | D 1-1 | 1-0 | 1 | Crainie | 10,500 |
| 28 | 10 | H | Rangers | W 2-1 | 1-0 | 1 | Crainie, McAdam | 49,144 |
| 29 | 14 | A | Airdrieonians | W 5-1 | 2-1 | — | Aitken, Provan, Crainie, Reid (pen) McCluskey | 12,000 |
| 30 | 17 | H | Dundee | W 4-2 | 0-1 | 1 | Reid (pen), McCluskey 2, Provan | 14,288 |
| 31 | 21 | H | Dundee U | W 3-1 | 1-0 | — | McCluskey 2, Provan | 14,659 |
| 32 | 24 | A | Partick T | W 3-0 | 0-0 | 1 | Crainie 3 | 14,200 |
| 33 | May 1 | H | Hibernian | W 6-0 | 4-0 | 1 | Burns, Crainie, Aitken, MacLeod 2, McCluskey | 16,064 |
| 34 | 3 | H | St Mirren | D 0-0 | 0-0 | — | | 27,395 |
| 35 | 8 | A | Dundee U | L 0-3 | 0-1 | 1 | | 16,779 |
| 36 | 15 | H | St Mirren | W 3-0 | 0-0 | 1 | McCluskey 2, McAdam | 39,369 |

**Final League Position: 1**

### Goalscorers
*League* (79): McCluskey 21 (2 pens), McGarvey 10, MacLeod 10, Burns 9, Crainie 7, McAdam 5, Provan 4, Aitken 3, Nicholas 3, Sullivan 3, Reid 2 (2 pens), Conroy 1, McStay 1.
*League Cup* (18): MacLeod 5, McGarvey 4, McCluskey 3, Nicholas 3, Provan 2, Sullivan 1.
*Scottish Cup* (4): Halpin 1, McCluskey 1 (pen), McGarvey 1, McGrain 1.

**Honours**

*Scottish League:* Division 1 Champions 1892–93, 1893–94, 1895–96, 1897–98, 1904–05, 1905–06, 1906–07, 1907–08, 1908–09, 1909–10, 1913–14, 1914–15, 1915–16, 1916–17, 1918–19, 1921–22, 1925–26, 1935–36, 1937–38, 1953–54, 1965–66, 1966–67, 1967–68, 1968–69, 1969–70, 1970–71, 1971–72, 1972–73, 1973–74; Runners-up 16 times; Premier Division Champions 1977, 1979, 1981, 1982; Runners-up 1976, 1980. *Scottish Cup:* Winners 1892, 1899, 1900, 1904, 1907, 1908, 1911, 1912, 1914, 1923, 1925, 1927, 1931, 1933, 1937, 1951, 1954, 1965, 1967, 1969, 1971, 1972, 1974, 1975, 1977, 1980; Runners-up 14 times. *Scottish League Cup:* Winners 1956–57, 1957–58, 1965–66, 1966–67, 1967–68, 1968–69, 1969–70, 1974–75; Runners-up 7 times. *Record Victory:* 11-0 v Dundee, Division 1, 26 Oct, 1895. *Record Defeat:* 0-8 v Motherwell, Division 1, 30 Apr, 1937. *Most League Points:* 67, 1915–16, 1921–22. *Most Individual League Goals in Season:* 50, James McGrory, 1935–36. *Most Goals in Total Aggregate:* 397, James McGrory, 1922–39. *Most Capped Player:* Danny McGrain, 62, Scotland.

| Bonner P. | McGrain D. | Reid M. | Moyes D. | Aitken R. | McAdam T. | MacLeod M. | McStay P. | Halpin J. | Conroy M. | Provan D. | Sullivan D. | Burns F. | McGarvey F. | McCluskey G. | Nicholas C. | Crainie D. | Garner W. | Match No. |
|---|---|---|---|---|---|---|---|---|---|---|---|---|---|---|---|---|---|---|
| 1 | 2 | 3 | 5 | 4 |  | 6 |  |  |  | 7 | 8 | 10 | 9* | 11 | 12 |  |  | 1 |
| 1 | 2 | 3 |  | 4 | 5 | 6 |  |  |  | 7 | 8 | 10 | 9 | 11 |  |  |  | 2 |
| 1 | 2 | 3 |  | 4 | 5 | 6 |  |  |  | 7 | 8 | 10 | 9 | 11 |  |  |  | 3 |
| 1 | 2 | 3 |  | 4 | 5 | 6 |  |  |  | 7 | 8 | 10 | 9 | 11 |  |  |  | 4 |
| 1 | 2* | 3 | 12 | 4 | 5 | 6 |  |  |  |  | 8 | 10 | 9 | 11 | 7 |  |  | 5 |
| 1 |  | 3 | 2 | 4 | 5 | 6 |  |  |  |  | 8 | 10 | 9 | 11 | 7 |  |  | 6 |
| 1 | 2 | 3 |  | 4 | 5 | 6 |  |  |  |  | 8 | 10 | 9 | 11 | 7 |  |  | 7 |
| 1 |  | 3 | 2 | 4 | 5 | 6 |  |  |  |  | 8 | 10 | 9 | 11 | 7 |  |  | 8 |
| 1 |  | 3 | 2 | 4 |  | 6 |  |  |  |  | 8 | 10 | 9 | 11 | 7 | 5 |  | 9 |
| 1 |  | 3 | 2 | 4 | 5 | 6 |  |  |  |  | 8 | 10 | 9 | 11 | 7 |  |  | 10 |
| 1 |  | 3 | 2 | 4 | 5 | 6 |  |  | 12 | 7 | 8 | 10* | 9 | 11 |  |  |  | 11 |
| 1 |  | 3 | 2 | 4 | 5 | 6 |  |  | 10 | 7 | 8 |  | 9* | 11 | 12 |  |  | 12 |
| 1 |  | 3 | 2 | 4 | 5 | 6 |  |  | 10 | 7 | 8 |  | 9 | 11 |  |  |  | 13 |
| 1 |  | 3 | 2 | 4 | 5 | 6 |  |  | 10 | 7 | 8* |  | 9 | 11 | 12 |  |  | 14 |
| 1 | 2 | 3 |  | 4 | 5 | 6 |  |  | 8 | 7 |  | 10 | 9 | 11 |  |  |  | 15 |
| 1 | 2 | 3 | 13 | 4 | 5 | 6 |  |  | 8† | 7* |  | 10 | 12 | 11 | 9 |  |  | 16 |
| 1 | 2 | 3 |  | 4 | 5 | 6 |  |  | 10 | 7 | 8 |  | 9 | 11 |  |  |  | 17 |
| 1 | 2 | 3 |  | 4 | 5 | 6 | 8 |  | 12 | 7* |  | 10 | 9 | 11 |  |  |  | 18 |
| 1 | 2 | 3 |  | 4 | 5 | 6 |  |  | 8 | 7 |  | 10 | 9 | 11 |  |  |  | 19 |
| 1 | 2 | 3 |  | 4 | 5 | 6* |  |  | 8 | 7† | 12 | 10 | 9 | 11 | 13 |  |  | 20 |
| 1 | 2 | 3 |  | 4 | 5 | 6 | 7* |  |  |  | 8 | 10 | 9 | 11 | 12 |  |  | 21 |
| 1 | 2 | 3 |  | 4 | 5 | 6 |  |  | 11 | 7 |  | 10 | 9 | 8 |  |  |  | 22 |
| 1 | 2 | 3 |  | 4 | 5 | 6 |  |  | 12 |  | 8 | 10 | 9* | 11 |  | 7 |  | 23 |
| 1 | 2 | 3 | 5 | 4 | 12 | 6 |  |  |  |  | 8 | 10 | 9 | 11 |  | 7 |  | 24 |
| 1 | 2 | 3* | 12 | 4 | 5 | 6 |  |  |  |  | 8 | 10 | 9 | 11 |  | 7 |  | 25 |
| 1 | 2 | 3 |  | 4 | 5 | 6 |  |  | 12 |  | 8 | 10 | 9* | 11 |  | 7 |  | 26 |
| 1 |  | 3 | 2 | 4 | 5 | 6 |  |  | 9 | 12 | 8* | 10 |  | 11 |  | 7 |  | 27 |
| 1 | 2 | 3 | 5 | 4 | 9 | 6 |  |  |  | 7 | 8 | 10 |  | 11 |  |  |  | 28 |
| 1 | 2 | 3 |  | 4 | 5 | 6 |  |  |  | 7 | 8 | 10 | 9 | 11 |  |  |  | 29 |
| 1 | 2 | 3 |  | 4 | 5 | 6 |  |  |  | 7 | 8 | 10 | 9 | 11 |  |  |  | 30 |
| 1 | 2 | 3 |  | 4 | 5 | 6 |  |  |  | 7 | 8 | 10 | 9 | 11 |  |  |  | 31 |
| 1 | 2 | 3 |  | 4 | 5 | 6 |  |  |  | 7 | 8 | 10 | 9 | 11 |  |  |  | 32 |
| 1 | 2 | 3 |  | 4 | 5 | 6 |  |  |  | 7 | 8 | 10 | 11 | 9 |  |  |  | 33 |
| 1 | 2 | 3 |  | 4 | 5 | 6 |  |  |  | 7 | 8 | 10 | 9 | 11 |  |  |  | 34 |
| 1 | 2 | 3 | 13 | 4 | 5 | 6 |  |  | 12 | 7 | 8* | 10 | 9† | 11 |  |  |  | 35 |
| 1 | 2 | 3 |  | 4 | 5 | 6 |  |  | 8 | 7 |  | 10 | 9 | 11 |  |  |  | 36 |
| 36 | 27 | 36 | 15 | 33 | 33 | 36 | 7 | 2 | 6 | 19 | 31 | 33 | 25 | 35 | 7 | 14 | 1 |  |
|  | +4s |  | +1s |  |  | +3s | +1s | +2s | +1s |  | +1s |  |  | +3s | +2s |  |  |  |

# CLYDE

# Division 1

*Year Formed:* 1878.
*Ground:* Shawfield Stadium, Glasgow C5.   *Size:* 110yd×70yd.   *Capacity:* 25,000 (2000 seats).
*Telephone:* 041-647 6329.
*Manager:* Craig Brown BA, DPE.   *Coach:* Rab Thorburn BSC.   *Commercial Manager:* John Donnelly.
*Secretary:* John F. McBeth ARICS.
*Club Colours:* White shirts with red facings, black shorts, red stockings.
*Club Nickname:* The Bully Wee.
*Record Attendance:* 52,000 v Rangers, Division 1, 21 Nov, 1908.

## 1981–82 LEAGUE RECORD

| Match No. | Date | Venue | Opponents | Result | H/T Score | League Pos'n | Goalscorers | Atten- dance |
|---|---|---|---|---|---|---|---|---|
| 1 | Aug 29 | H | Stenhousemuir | W 3-0 | 2-0 | — | Masterton 2, O'Neill | 480 |
| 2 | Sept 5 | A | Cowdenbeath | W 4-0 | 3-0 | 1 | Reilly, O'Neill, Masterton 2 (1 pen) | 435 |
| 3 | 8 | A | Stirling Albion | W 2-1 | 1-1 | — | Reilly, Masterton | 600 |
| 4 | 12 | H | Forfar Ath | D 1-1 | 0-1 | 2 | Nevin | 658 |
| 5 | 16 | A | Stranraer | W 2-0 | 1-0 | — | Brogan, Doherty | 370 |
| 6 | 19 | H | Alloa | D 1-1 | 0-0 | 1 | McCutcheon | 650 |
| 7 | 26 | A | Montrose | W 3-0 | 3-0 | 1 | Masterton, Reilly, Forbes (og) | 670 |
| 8 | Oct 3 | H | Meadowbank T | W 1-0 | 1-0 | 1 | Doherty | 790 |
| 9 | 10 | H | East Fife | W 3-2 | 0-2 | 1 | Masterton 2, Sinclair | 500 |
| 10 | 17 | A | Arbroath | W 1-0 | 1-0 | 1 | Masterton | 691 |
| 11 | 20 | A | Brechin C | D 2-2 | 2-2 | — | Reilly, McCutcheon | 650 |
| 12 | 24 | H | Albion R | L 1-2 | 0-2 | 1 | McCutcheon | 500 |
| 13 | 31 | A | Berwick R | L 0-4 | 0-1 | 1 | | 979 |
| 14 | Nov 7 | H | Cowdenbeath | D 1-1 | 0-1 | 2 | Reilly | 456 |
| 15 | 14 | A | Stenhousemuir | W 3-0 | 1-0 | 1 | McCutcheon, O'Neill, Nevin | 500 |
| 16 | 21 | H | Stranraer | W 3-0 | 1-0 | 1 | Nevin, Masterton, McCutcheon | 800 |
| 17 | 28 | H | Montrose | W 3-0 | 1-0 | 1 | O'Neill, Nevin, Rae | 480 |
| 18 | Dec 5 | A | Meadowbank T | W 3-2 | 2-1 | 1 | Dempsey, Nevin, Hood | 350 |
| 19 | Feb 6 | A | East Fife | D 2-2 | 0-0 | 1 | Nevin, Masterton | 500 |
| 20 | 10 | A | Albion R | W 1-0 | 1-0 | — | Nevin | 460 |
| 21 | 13 | H | Berwick R | W 3-1 | 0-1 | 1 | Doherty, Masterton, O'Neill | 544 |
| 22 | 20 | A | Forfar Ath | D 0-0 | 0-0 | 1 | | 1158 |
| 23 | 27 | H | Stirling Albion | W 2-0 | 1-0 | 1 | Masterton, Hood | 620 |
| 24 | Mar 6 | A | Montrose | L 1-4 | 0-1 | 1 | Nevin | 350 |
| 25 | 13 | H | Stenhousemuir | W 1-0 | 0-0 | 1 | Doherty | 400 |
| 26 | 17 | H | Arbroath | D 1-1 | 1-0 | — | Reilly | 1010 |
| 27 | 20 | H | Berwick R | L 1-2 | 0-1 | 1 | Reilly | 580 |
| 28 | 24 | A | Forfar Ath | W 3-1 | 1-0 | — | Reilly 3 | 1341 |
| 29 | 27 | A | Alloa | D 2-2 | 0-1 | 1 | O'Neill 2 | 1210 |
| 30 | 30 | H | Stirling Albion | D 3-3 | 2-2 | — | Doherty, O'Neill 2 | 700 |
| 31 | Apr 3 | H | Brechin C | W 3-1 | 1-0 | 1 | Masterton, Nevin (pen), McCutcheon | 450 |
| 32 | 10 | A | Arbroath | W 5-0 | 3-0 | 1 | Masterton 4, Nevin (pen) | 1020 |
| 33 | 14 | H | Brechin C | W 1-0 | 1-0 | — | Masterton | 1210 |
| 34 | 17 | H | Cowdenbeath | W 2-0 | 1-0 | 1 | Masterton, Nevin | 550 |
| 35 | 21 | A | Alloa | W 3-0 | 2-0 | — | Doherty, Masterton, O'Neill | 760 |
| 36 | 25 | A | East Fife | D 1-1 | 1-0 | — | O'Neill | 750 |
| 37 | May 1 | A | Albion R | W 3-2 | 2-1 | 1 | Nevin (pen), McCutcheon 2 | 500 |
| 38 | 8 | H | Stranraer | D 1-1 | 0-0 | 1 | Masterton | 622 |
| 39 | 15 | A | Meadowbank T | W 3-1 | 2-1 | 1 | Reilly, Masterton, Doherty | 400 |

**Final League Position: 1**

### Goalscorers

*League* (79): Masterton 23 (1 pen), Nevin 12 (3 pen), O'Neill 11, Reilly 11, McCutcheon 8, Doherty 7, Hood 2, Brogan 1, Dempsey 1, Rae 1, Sinclair 1, own goal 1.
*League Cup* (6): Reilly 2, Doherty 1, Evans 1, McCutcheon 1, Masterton 1.
*Scottish Cup* (9): Doherty 2, Nevin 2, Hood 1, O'Neill 1 (pen), Reilly 1, Sinclair 1, own goal 1.

**Honours**
*Scottish League* – Division 2 Champions 1904–05, 1951–52, 1956–57, 1961–62, 1972–73, 1977–78, 1981–82; Runners-up 1903–04, 1905–06, 1925–26, 1963–64.
*Scottish FA Cup:* Winners 1939, 1955, 1958; Runners-up 1910, 1912, 1949.
*Scottish League Cup:* None.
*Record Victory:* 11-1 v Cowdenbeath, Division 2, 6 Oct, 1951.
*Record Defeat:* 0-11 v Dumbarton, Scottish Cup 4th rd, 22 Nov, 1879; 0-11 v Rangers, Scottish Cup 4th rd, 13 Nov, 1880.
*Most League Points:* 64, Division 2, 1956–57.
*Most Individual League Goals in Season:* 32, Bill Boyd, 1932–33.
*Most Capped Player:* Tommy Ring, 12, Scotland.

| Young G. | Campbell A. | Brogan J. | McQueen T. | Rae D. | McColl W. | Dempsey J. | Sinclair J. | McCutcheon D. | Doherty J. | Reilly R. | O'Neill T. | Hood N. | Masterton D. | Coutts T. | Miller J. | Thorburn R. | Dowie J. | Nevin P. | Match No. |
|---|---|---|---|---|---|---|---|---|---|---|---|---|---|---|---|---|---|---|---|
| 1 |  | 2 | 3 |  | 4 | 5* | 7 | 6 | 11† | 8 | 10 |  | 9 | 12 |  |  | 13 |  | 1 |
| 1 |  | 2 | 3 |  | 4 | 5 | 8 | 6 | 7 | 10* | 11 |  | 9†12 |  |  |  | 13 |  | 2 |
| 1 |  | 2 | 3 |  | 4 | 5 | 8 | 6 | 7 | 10* | 11 |  | 9 | 12 |  |  |  |  | 3 |
| 1 |  | 2 | 3 |  | 4 | 5 | 8 | 6 | 7* |  | 11 |  | 9 | 10 |  |  | 12 |  | 4 |
| 1 |  | 2 | 3 |  | 4 | 5 | 11 |  | 7 | 8 | 10 |  | 9 | 6 |  |  |  |  | 5 |
| 1 |  | 2 | 3 |  | 4 | 5 | 8 | 6 | 7 | 10 | 11 |  | 9 |  |  |  |  |  | 6 |
| 1 |  | 2 | 3 |  | 4 | 5 | 8 | 6 | 7 | 10* | 11 |  | 9† | 13 | 12 |  |  |  | 7 |
| 1 |  | 2 | 3 |  | 4 | 5 | 8 | 6 | 7 | 10* | 11 |  | 9 |  |  |  | 12 |  | 8 |
| 1 |  | 2 | 3 |  | 4 | 5 | 8 | 6 | 7 | 10 | 11 |  | 9 |  |  |  |  |  | 9 |
| 1 |  | 2 | 3 | 12 | 4 | 5 | 8 | 6 | 7 | 10* | 11 |  | 9 |  |  |  |  |  | 10 |
|  | 1 | 2 | 3 | 12 | 4* | 5 | 8 | 6 | 7†10 | 11 |  |  | 9 |  |  |  | 13 |  | 11 |
|  | 1 | 2 | 3 |  | 5 | 8 | 6 | 7 | 10 | 11 |  |  | 9* | 4 |  |  | 12 |  | 12 |
| 1 |  | 2 | 3 | 12 | 4 | 5 | 8 | 6 | 7†10 | 11 |  |  | 9* |  |  |  | 13 |  | 13 |
| 1 |  | 2 | 3 | 6† | 4 | 5 | 8 | 9 |  | 10 | 11*12 | 13 |  |  |  |  | 7 |  | 14 |
| 1 |  | 2 | 3 |  | 4 | 5 | 8 | 6 | 13 | 10*11 | 12 |  | 9 |  |  |  | 7† |  | 15 |
| 1 |  | 2 | 3 |  | 4 | 5 | 8† | 6*13 | 10 | 11 | 12 |  | 9 |  |  |  | 7 |  | 16 |
| 1 |  | 2 | 3 | 13 | 4 | 5 | 8 | 6 | 10† |  | 11 | 12 | 9* |  |  |  | 7 |  | 17 |
| 1 |  | 2 | 3 |  | 4 | 5 | 8 | 6 | 10 |  | 11 | 9 | 12 |  |  |  | 7* |  | 18 |
| 1 |  | 2 | 3 |  | 4 | 5 | 8 | 13 | 7 |  | 10 | 12 | 9* |  |  | 6†11 |  |  | 19 |
| 1 |  | 2 | 3 |  | 4 | 5 | 8 | 6 | 7 | 12 | 10 |  | 9* |  |  | 11 |  |  | 20 |
| 1 |  | 2 | 3 | 4 |  | 5 | 8 | 6 | 7 |  | 10 |  | 9 |  |  | 11 |  |  | 21 |
| 1 |  | 2 | 3 | 4 |  | 5 | 8 | 6* | 7 | 12 | 10 |  | 9 |  |  | 11 |  |  | 22 |
| 1 |  | 3 | 4† | 2 | 5 | 8 | 6 | 7 | 13 | 10 | 12 |  | 9* |  |  | 11 |  |  | 23 |
| 1 | 12 | 3 | 4 | 2 | 5 | 8* | 6 | 7 | 10† |  | 13 | 9 |  |  |  | 11 |  |  | 24 |
| 1 | 2† | 3 | 4 | 8 | 5 |  | 6* | 7 | 13 | 10 | 9 |  |  | 12 | 11 |  |  |  | 25 |
| 1 |  | 3 | 4 | 2 | 5 | 8 |  | 7 |  | 6 | 10 |  | 9 |  |  | 11 |  |  | 26 |
| 1 |  | 3 | 4 | 2 | 5 | 8*13 | 7 |  | 6 | 10 |  | 9† | 12 | 11 |  |  |  |  | 27 |
| 1 |  | 2 | 3 |  | 4 | 5 | 8 | 6 | 7* | 9 | 10 | 13 | 12 | 11† |  |  |  |  | 28 |
| 1 |  | 2 | 3 |  | 4 | 5 | 8 | 6* | 7 |  | 10 | 12 | 9 | 11 |  |  |  |  | 29 |
| 1 |  | 2 | 3 |  | 4 | 5 | 8 | 6* | 7 | 9 | 10 | 12 |  | 11 |  |  |  |  | 30 |
| 1 |  | 2 | 3 |  | 4 | 5 | 8 | 6 | 13 |  | 10 | 12 | 9* |  |  | 7†11 |  |  | 31 |
| 1 |  | 2 | 3 |  | 4 | 5 | 8† | 6 | 7* |  | 10 | 13 | 9 | 12 | 11 |  |  |  | 32 |
| 1 |  | 2 | 3 |  | 4 | 5 | 8 | 6 | 7 |  | 10 |  | 9 |  |  | 11 |  |  | 33 |
| 1 |  | 2 | 3 |  | 4 | 5 | 8 | 6 | 7†13 | 10* |  |  | 9 | 12 | 11 |  |  |  | 34 |
| 1 |  | 2 | 3 |  | 4 | 5 | 8 | 6 | 7 |  | 10 |  | 9 |  |  | 11 |  |  | 35 |
| 1 |  | 2 | 3 |  | 4 | 5 | 8 |  | 7 | 6 | 10 | 12 | 9* |  |  | 11 |  |  | 36 |
| 1 |  | 2 | 3 |  | 4 | 5 | 8 | 6 | 7*12 | 10 |  |  | 9 |  |  | 11 |  |  | 37 |
| 1 |  | 2 | 3 |  | 4 | 5 | 8 |  | 7 | 12 | 10 | 6* | 9 |  |  | 11 |  |  | 38 |
| 1 | 2† | 3 | 5 | 4 |  | 12 |  | 11 | 7 | 10* |  | 9 | 8 |  | 6 | 13 |  |  | 39 |
| 37 | 2 | 35 | 39 | 9 | 36 | 38 | 37 | 32 | 35 | 22 | 38 | 3 | 33 | 3 | 1 | — | 4 | 25 | |

```
      +    +        + + + +        + + +        + + +
     1s   4s       1s 2s 3s 7s    12s 2s 4s    1s 5s 9s
```

# CLYDEBANK

# Division 1

*Year Formed:* 1965. *Ground:* Kilbowie Park. *Size:* 110yd×68yd. *Capacity:* 10,000 (all seated).
*Telephone:* 041-952 2887.
*Secretary:* I. C. Steedman. *Coach:* Sam Henderson.
*Club Colours:* White shirts with red and black vertical stripes on the left breast and red stripe on sleeves, white shorts
with red and black vertical stripe and white stockings with red and black tops.
*Club Nickname:* The Bankies.
*Record Attendance:* 14,900 v Hibernian, Scottish Cup 1st rd, 10 Feb, 1965.

## 1981–82 LEAGUE RECORD

| Match No. | Date | Venue | Opponents | Result | H/T Score | League Pos'n | Goalscorers | Attendance |
|---|---|---|---|---|---|---|---|---|
| 1 | Aug 29 | A | Queen's Park | D 2-2 | 0-1 | — | Fallon, McCabe | 757 |
| 2 | Sept 5 | H | St Johnstone | L 2-3 | 1-0 | 10 | Millar, McGorm | 600 |
| 3 | 8 | H | Kilmarnock | D 0-0 | 0-0 | — | | 1012 |
| 4 | 12 | A | Dumbarton | W 3-1 | 0-1 | 7 | McCabe, McGorm, Millar | 1000 |
| 5 | 16 | H | Dunfermline Ath | W 4-1 | 2-0 | — | McGorm, Millar, McCabe, Fallon | 664 |
| 6 | 19 | A | Hearts | L 0-1 | 0-0 | 5 | | 6000 |
| 7 | 26 | H | Falkirk | D 1-1 | 1-0 | 8 | McLaughlin | 760 |
| 8 | Oct 3 | A | Queen of the S | L 1-2 | 1-2 | 9 | Millar | 1011 |
| 9 | 10 | A | Raith R | W 2-0 | 1-0 | 8 | Coyne, Millar | 1000 |
| 10 | 17 | H | Motherwell | L 1-7 | 1-4 | 9 | Coyne | 1600 |
| 11 | 20 | H | Hamilton A | W 2-1 | 0-1 | — | Coyne, Millar | 450 |
| 12 | 24 | A | East Stirling | D 0-0 | 0-0 | 7 | | 500 |
| 13 | 31 | H | Ayr U | W 2-1 | 1-0 | 6 | Fallon, Given | 1000 |
| 14 | Nov 7 | A | St Johnstone | W 3-1 | 2-0 | 5 | Millar, McKeown, Coyne | 1774 |
| 15 | 14 | H | Queen's Park | W 2-1 | 1-0 | 4 | McKeown, Given | 904 |
| 16 | 21 | A | Dunfermline Ath | W 6-3 | 2-2 | 3 | Millar 4, Ronald, McCabe | 1750 |
| 17 | 28 | A | Falkirk | L 0-3 | 0-1 | 5 | | 1200 |
| 18 | Dec 5 | H | Queen of the S | W 2-1 | 1-0 | 4 | Millar, Coyne | 400 |
| 19 | 12 | A | Hamilton A | W 2-0 | 1-0 | 2 | Coyne, McKeown | 1033 |
| 20 | Jan 19 | A | Motherwell | L 1-3 | 0-1 | — | Millar | 2925 |
| 21 | 30 | H | East Stirling | W 2-1 | 0-1 | 2 | Rennie (og), Coyne | 522 |
| 22 | Feb 3 | H | Raith R | L 0-1 | 0-0 | — | | 500 |
| 23 | 6 | A | Ayr U | L 1-2 | 0-2 | 3 | Ronald | 724 |
| 24 | 17 | H | Dumbarton | W 3-0 | 2-0 | — | Ronald, Given (pen), Millar | 2650 |
| 25 | 20 | A | Hamilton A | L 1-3 | 0-2 | 4 | Given | 1040 |
| 26 | 27 | H | Falkirk | L 0-2 | 0-0 | 5 | | 700 |
| 27 | Mar 10 | H | Queen's Park | W 1-0 | 0-0 | — | Given (pen) | 1400 |
| 28 | 13 | A | Dumbarton | W 2-0 | 0-0 | 4 | Millar, McCabe | 1720 |
| 29 | 20 | H | Queen of the S | W 5-1 | 3-0 | 4 | Millar 3, Coyne, Ronald | 500 |
| 30 | 27 | H | Hearts | W 2-1 | 0-0 | 2 | Hughes, Ronald | 1731 |
| 31 | Apr 3 | A | Kilmarnock | D 0-0 | 0-0 | 4 | | 2100 |
| 32 | 10 | A | East Stirling | W 1-0 | 1-0 | 4 | McCabe | 400 |
| 33 | 14 | H | Hearts | L 1-5 | 1-3 | — | Given (pen) | 960 |
| 34 | 17 | H | Raith R | D 0-0 | 0-0 | 4 | | 520 |
| 35 | 21 | A | Kilmarnock | L 0-2 | 0-1 | — | | 987 |
| 36 | 24 | A | Motherwell | D 0-0 | 0-0 | 4 | | 3689 |
| 37 | May 1 | H | Dunfermline Ath | W 1-0 | 0-0 | 4 | McCabe | 460 |
| 38 | 8 | A | St Johnstone | D 3-3 | 1-2 | 4 | Millar, McCabe, Williamson | 1196 |
| 39 | 15 | H | Ayr U | W 2-0 | 1-0 | 4 | Millar, Coyne | 514 |

**Final League Position: 4**

**Goalscorers**
*League* (61): Millar 20, Coyne 9, McCabe 8, Given 6 (3 pens), Ronald 5, Fallon 3, McGorm 3, McKeown 3, Hughes 1,
McLaughlin 1, Williamson 1, own goal 1.
*League Cup* (8): Millar 2, Ronald 2, Evans 1, Given 1, McCabe 1, McLaughlin 1.
*Scottish Cup* (2): Given 1 (pen), Millar 1.

**Honours**
*Scottish League* – Division 1 Runners-up 1976–77; Division 2 Champions 1975–76.
*Spring Cup* – Runners-up 1975–76.
*Record Victory:* 8-1 v Arbroath, Division 1, 3 Jan, 1977.
*Record Defeat:* 1-9 v Gala Fairydean, Scottish Cup qualifying rd, 15 Sept, 1965.
*Most League Points:* 58, Division 1, 1976–77.
*Most Individual League Goals in Season:* Blair Miller, 28, Division 1, 1978–79.

| Gallacher J. | Sharkey G. | Treanor M. | Gervaise A. | Fallon J. | McGhie W. | Given C. J. | Ronald G. | McKeown C. | Millar B. | Coyne T. | McGorm T. | McCabe G. | McLaughlan G. | Houston D. | Jones D. | Harkins T. | McBride J. | Hughes M. | Sinclair E. | Williamson R. | Lynch F. | Match No. |
|---|---|---|---|---|---|---|---|---|---|---|---|---|---|---|---|---|---|---|---|---|---|---|
| 1 |  | 2 | 3 | 5 | 6 | 7 |  | 9 |  | 11 |  | 4 | 8 | 10*12 |  |  |  |  |  |  |  | 1 |
| 1 |  | 2 | 3 | 5 | 6 | 7 |  | 9 | 12 | 11 |  | 4 | 8 | 10* |  |  |  |  |  |  |  | 2 |
| 1 |  | 2 | 3 | 5 | 6 | 7 |  | 9 | 10 | 11 |  | 4 | 8 |  |  |  |  |  |  |  |  | 3 |
| 1 |  | 2 | 3 | 5 | 6 | 7 | 12 | 9† | 10 | 11 |  | 4 | 13 | 8* |  |  |  |  |  |  |  | 4 |
| 1 |  | 2 | 3 | 5 | 6 | 7 | 8 | 9 | 10 | 11 |  | 4 |  |  |  |  |  |  |  |  |  | 5 |
| 1 |  | 2 | 13 | 3 | 5 | 6 | 8 | 9† | 10 | 11 |  | 4 | 7*12 |  |  |  |  |  |  |  |  | 6 |
| 1 |  | 2 | 3 | 5 | 6 | 7 | 8 | 9 | 10* | 11 |  | 4 | 12 |  |  |  |  |  |  |  |  | 7 |
| 1 |  | 2 | 3 | 5 | 6 | 7 | 8 | 9 | 10 | 11 |  | 4 |  |  |  |  |  |  |  |  |  | 8 |
| 1 |  | 2 | 3 | 5 | 6 | 7 | 8 | 9 | 10 | 11 |  | 4 |  |  |  |  |  |  |  |  |  | 9 |
| 1 |  | 2 | 12 | 3 | 5 | 6 | 7 | 8* | 9 | 10†13 |  | 11 | 4 |  |  |  |  |  |  |  |  | 10 |
| 1 |  | 2 | 5 | 4 | 6 | 7 | 8 | 9 | 10 | 3 |  | 11 |  |  |  |  |  |  |  |  |  | 11 |
| 1 |  | 2 | 3 | 5 | 6 | 7 | 8 | 9 | 10 | 11 |  | 4 |  |  |  |  |  |  |  |  |  | 12 |
| 1 |  | 2 | 3 | 4 | 5 | 6 | 7 | 8* | 9 | 10 |  | 11 | 12 |  |  |  |  |  |  |  |  | 13 |
| 1 |  | 2 | 3 | 4 | 5 | 6 | 7 | 8 | 9 | 10*12 |  | 11 |  |  |  |  |  |  |  |  |  | 14 |
| 1 |  | 2 | 3 | 4 | 5 | 6 | 7 | 8 | 9 | 10 |  | 11 |  |  |  |  |  |  |  |  |  | 15 |
| 1 |  | 2 | 3 | 4 | 5 | 6 | 7 | 8 | 9*10 | 11 |  |  |  |  |  |  |  | 12 |  |  |  | 16 |
| 1 |  | 2 | 3 | 4 | 5 | 6 | 7 | 8* | 9 | 10† |  | 11 | 12 |  |  | 13 |  |  |  |  |  | 17 |
| 1 |  | 2 | 3 | 4 | 5 | 6 | 7 | 8 | 9 | 10 |  | 11 |  |  |  |  |  |  |  |  |  | 18 |
| 1 |  | 2 |  | 4 | 5 | 6 | 7 | 8 | 9 | 10 |  | 11 |  | 3 |  |  |  |  |  |  |  | 19 |
| 1 |  | 2 | 3 | 4 |  | 6 | 7 | 8* | 9 | 10 |  | 11 | 5 | 12 |  |  |  |  |  |  |  | 20 |
| 1 |  | 2 | 3 | 4 | 5 | 6 |  | 8* | 9†10 | 11 |  | 13 | 12 |  |  |  |  |  |  | 7 |  | 21 |
| 1 |  | 2 | 3 | 4 | 5 | 6 | 7 | 8 | 9 | 10 |  | 11 |  |  |  |  |  |  |  |  |  | 22 |
| 1 |  | 2 | 3 | 4 | 5 | 6 | 7 | 9 |  | 11 |  | 10 | 8 |  |  |  |  |  |  |  |  | 23 |
| 1 |  | 2 | 3 | 4 | 5* | 6 | 7 | 8 | 9 | 10† |  | 11 | 12 | 13 |  |  |  |  |  |  |  | 24 |
| 1 |  | 2 | 3 | 5 |  | 6 | 7 | 8 | 9 | 10* |  | 11 | 4 | 12 |  |  |  |  |  |  |  | 25 |
| 1 | 3 | 2 | 4 | 5 | 6 | 7 |  | 9 | 10 | 11 |  |  |  |  |  |  |  | 8 |  |  |  | 26 |
| 1 | 3 | 2 | 4 | 5 | 6 |  |  | 9 | 10 | 11 |  |  |  |  |  |  |  | 8 |  | 7 |  | 27 |
| 1 |  | 3 | 4 | 5 | 6 | 7 |  | 9 | 10 | 11 |  |  |  |  |  |  |  | 8 |  | 2 |  | 28 |
| 1 |  | 2 | 3 | 4 | 5 | 6 | 7 | 9 | 10 | 11 |  |  |  |  |  |  |  | 8 |  |  |  | 29 |
| 1 |  | 3 | 4 | 5 | 6 | 7 |  | 9 | 10* | 11 |  | 12 |  |  |  |  |  | 8 |  | 2 |  | 30 |
| 1 |  | 3 | 4 | 5 | 6 | 7 |  | 9 | 10 | 11 |  |  |  |  |  |  |  | 8 |  | 2 |  | 31 |
| 1 |  | 3 | 4 | 5 | 6 | 7 |  | 9 | 10 | 11 |  |  |  |  |  |  |  | 8 |  | 2 |  | 32 |
| 1 |  | 2 | 3 | 4 | 5 | 6 | 7 | 9 | 12 | 11 |  |  |  |  |  |  |  | 8 |  | 10* |  | 33 |
| 1 |  | 2 | 3 | 4 | 5 | 6 | 7 | 8* | 9 | 10 |  | 11 |  |  |  |  |  | 12 |  |  |  | 34 |
| 1 |  | 2 | 3 | 4 | 5 | 6 | 7 | 8* | 9 | 10† |  | 11 |  |  |  |  |  | 12 |  | 13 |  | 35 |
| 1 |  | 2 | 3 | 4 | 5 | 6 | 7 | 9 | 12 | 11 |  |  |  |  |  |  |  | 8 |  | 10* |  | 36 |
| 1 |  | 2 | 3 |  | 5 | 6 | 7 | 9 |  | 11 |  |  |  |  |  |  |  | 8 |  | 10 | 4 | 37 |
| 1 |  | 2 | 3 | 4 | 5 | 6 | 7†12 | 9 | 10 | 11 |  |  |  |  |  |  |  | 8* |  | 13 |  | 38 |
| 1 |  | 2 | 3 | 4 | 5 | 6 |  | 9 | 10 | 11 |  |  |  |  |  |  |  | 8 |  | 7 |  | 39 |
| 39 | 2 | 35 | 26 | 38 | 35 | 39 | 35 | 23 | 37 | 29 | 7 | 37 | 14 | 5 | 2 | 1 | 1 | 13 | — | 10 | 1 |  |

Substitute appearances:
+ (Treanor) 2s; + (Coyne) 2s; + (McCabe) 2s, (McLaughlan) 3s; + + (Houston) 4s, (Jones) 2s; + + + + + (Harkins) 6s, (McBride) 1s, (Hughes) 3s, (Williamson) 1s, (Lynch) 2s

# COWDENBEATH                                   Division 2

*Year Formed:* 1881.   *Ground:* Central Park.   *Size:* 110yd×70yd.   *Capacity:* 10,000.
*Telephone:* Cowdenbeath 511205.
*Manager:* Hugh Wilson.   *Secretary:* W. Foster.
*Club Colours:* Royal blue shirt, white shorts, white stockings with blue and white tops.
*Club Nickname:* Cowden.
*Record Attendance:* 25,586 v Rangers, League Cup quarter-final, 21 Sept, 1949.
*Previous Grounds:* North End Park, 1881–1917.

## 1981–82 LEAGUE RECORD

| Match No. | Date | Venue | Opponents | Result | | H/T Score | League Pos'n | Goalscorers | Atten- dance |
|---|---|---|---|---|---|---|---|---|---|
| 1 | Aug 29 | A | Albion R | L | 0-2 | 0-1 | — | | 200 |
| 2 | Sept 5 | H | Clyde | L | 0-4 | 0-3 | 14 | | 435 |
| 3 | 8 | H | East Fife | D | 2-2 | 2-2 | — | Liddle 2 | 654 |
| 4 | 12 | A | Arbroath | D | 1-1 | 0-0 | 12 | Marshall | 479 |
| 5 | 16 | H | Alloa | L | 1-2 | 0-0 | — | Steele W. | 300 |
| 6 | 19 | A | Stirling Albion | D | 0-0 | 0-0 | 13 | | 450 |
| 7 | 23 | H | Stenhousemuir | W | 3-1 | 1-0 | — | Liddle 2, Forrest | 380 |
| 8 | 26 | A | Berwick R | W | 2-1 | 1-0 | 9 | Steele W. 2 | 750 |
| 9 | Oct 3 | H | Montrose | W | 6-0 | 3-0 | 6 | Steele W. 3, Forrest 3 | 1250 |
| 10 | 10 | H | Stranraer | D | 1-1 | 0-0 | 7 | Forrest | 400 |
| 11 | 17 | A | Meadowbank T | D | 1-1 | 1-0 | 7 | Forrest | 200 |
| 12 | 24 | H | Forfar Ath | D | 1-1 | 0-0 | 7 | Forrest | 500 |
| 13 | 31 | A | Brechin C | W | 1-0 | 1-0 | 7 | Forrest | 400 |
| 14 | Nov 7 | A | Clyde | D | 1-1 | 1-0 | 7 | McFarlane | 456 |
| 15 | 14 | H | Albion R | W | 2-0 | 1-0 | 6 | Tierney, Forrest | 400 |
| 16 | 21 | A | Alloa | L | 1-3 | 1-0 | 7 | Forrest | 623 |
| 17 | 28 | H | Berwick R | W | 2-1 | 1-0 | 7 | Liddle, Marshall | 500 |
| 18 | Dec 5 | A | Montrose | D | 2-2 | 1-1 | 7 | Forrest (pen), McFarlane | 300 |
| 19 | Jan 2 | A | East Fife | D | 1-1 | 1-1 | 7 | Forrest | 960 |
| 20 | 23 | A | Stranraer | W | 4-1 | 1-0 | — | Steele W., Liddle, Hunter, Forrest (pen) | 250 |
| 21 | Feb 6 | A | Forfar Ath | L | 0-4 | 0-2 | 7 | | 667 |
| 22 | 13 | H | Brechin C | D | 0-0 | 0-0 | 8 | | 300 |
| 23 | 20 | H | Albion R | L | 2-3 | 2-1 | 8 | Forrest (pen), Liddle | 287 |
| 24 | 27 | A | Arbroath | L | 0-3 | 0-0 | 8 | | 564 |
| 25 | Mar 3 | H | Meadowbank T | D | 2-2 | 2-1 | — | Miller, Markey | 636 |
| 26 | 6 | H | East Fife | L | 1-2 | 1-1 | 9 | Scott | 500 |
| 27 | 13 | H | Forfar Ath | W | 3-1 | 2-0 | 8 | Farningham (og), Marshall, Forrest | 440 |
| 28 | 17 | H | Stirling Albion | D | 0-0 | 0-0 | — | | 550 |
| 29 | 20 | A | Meadowbank T | L | 0-1 | 0-1 | 9 | | 200 |
| 30 | 24 | H | Arbroath | L | 1-2 | 0-2 | — | Forrest | 270 |
| 31 | 27 | H | Montrose | W | 3-2 | 2-0 | 7 | Hyslop 2, Liddle | 315 |
| 32 | Apr 3 | A | Stenhousemuir | L | 0-3 | 0-1 | 8 | | 400 |
| 33 | 10 | H | Berwick R | W | 2-0 | 1-0 | 7 | Russell, Hyslop | 468 |
| 34 | 17 | A | Clyde | L | 0-2 | 0-1 | 7 | | 550 |
| 35 | 20 | A | Stenhousemuir | L | 1-2 | 1-1 | — | Gilchrist | 200 |
| 36 | 24 | A | Stranraer | L | 0-1 | 0-0 | 9 | | 250 |
| 37 | May 1 | H | Stirling Albion | W | 2-0 | 1-0 | 7 | McIntosh, Liddle | 300 |
| 38 | 8 | A | Alloa | D | 2-2 | 0-1 | 7 | Russell, Tierney | 859 |
| 39 | 15 | H | Brechin C | L | 0-2 | 0-1 | 9 | | 300 |

**Final League Position: 9**

**Goalscorers**
*League* (51): Forrest 16 (3 pens), Liddle 9, Steele W. 7, Hyslop 3, Marshall 3, McFarlane 2, Russell 2, Tierney 2, Gilchrist 1, Hunter 1, McIntosh 1, Markey 1, Miller 1, Scott 1, own goal 1.
*League Cup* (9): Forrest 3, Liddle 2, Steele W. 2, Allison 1, Mercer 1.
*Scottish Cup* (12): Forrest 5 (1 pen), Liddle 3, McFarlane 1, Marshall 1, Park 1, Steele W. 1.

## Honours

*Scottish League* – Division 2 Champions 1913–14, 1914–15, 1938–39; Runners-up 1921–22, 1923–24, 1969–70.
*Record Victory:* 12-0 v St Johnstone, Scottish Cup 1st rd, 21 Jan, 1928.
*Record Defeat:* 1-11 v Clyde, Division 2, 6 Oct, 1951.
*Most League Points:* 60, Division 2, 1938–39.
*Most Individual League Goals in Season:* Willie Devlin, 40, Division 1, 1925–26.
*Most Capped Player:* Jim Paterson, 3, Scotland.

| Allan R. | Doyle J. | Markey J. | Ferguson K. | Rolland A. | Russell R. | Hunter D. | Tierney G. | McFarlane C. | Park D. | Liddle J. | Marshall J. | Forrest G. | Steele W. | Miekle G. | Kerr G. | Fleming J. | Scott R. | Lewin C. | Marnoch W. | Allison C. | Miller R. | Kydd L. | Hyslop D. | Sinnet J. | Steele T. | Gilchrist A. | Mercer G. | McLean J. | McIntosh C. | Fairley B. | Henderson T. | Match No. |
|---|---|---|---|---|---|---|---|---|---|---|---|---|---|---|---|---|---|---|---|---|---|---|---|---|---|---|---|---|---|---|---|---|
| 1 | | | 2 | 3 | 5 | 6 | 4 | | | 9 | 10 | 11 | 8 | 7* | 12 | | | | | | | | | | | | | | | | | 1 |
| 1 | | | 2 | 10 | 5 | 6 | 4 | | 8 | 9 | | 11 | | 7 | | | 3 | | | | | | | | | | | | | | | 2 |
| 1 | | | 2 | | 5 | 6 | 4 | | 8 | 9 | 10 | 11 | | 7 | | | 3 | | | | | | | | | | | | | | | 3 |
| 1 | | | 2 | 12 | 5 | 6 | 4 | 9 | 8* | | 10 | 11 | | 7 | | | 3 | | | | | | | | | | | | | | | 4 |
| 1 | | | 2 | 13 | 5 | 6 | 4 | | 8† | 9 | 10 | 11 | | 7 | 12 | | 3* | | | | | | | | | | | | | | | 5 |
| 1 | | | 2 | 4 | 5 | 3 | 6 | | 8 | 9 | 10 | 11 | | 7 | | | | | | | | | | | | | | | | | | 6 |
| 1 | | | 2 | 4 | 5 | 3 | 6 | | 8 | 9 | 10 | 11 | | 7 | | | | | | | | | | | | | | | | | | 7 |
| 1 | | | 2 | 4 | 5 | 3 | 6 | | 8 | 9 | 10 | 11 | | 7* | 12 | | | | | | | | | | | | | | | | | 8 |
| 1 | | | 2 | 4 | 5 | 3 | 6 | | 8 | 9 | 10 | 11 | | 7 | | | | | | | | | | | | | | | | | | 9 |
| 1 | | | 2 | 4 | 5 | 3 | 6 | | 8* | 9 | 10 | 11 | | 7 | 12 | | | | | | | | | | | | | | | | | 10 |
| 1 | | | 2 | 4 | 5 | 3 | 6 | | 8 | 9 | 10 | 11 | | 7 | | | | | | | | | | | | | | | | | | 11 |
| 1 | | | 2 | 4 | 5 | 3 | 6 | | 8 | 9 | 10 | 11 | | 7 | | | | | | | | | | | | | | | | | | 12 |
| 1 | | | | 4 | 5 | 3 | 6 | | 7 | 9 | 10 | 11 | 8 | | | 2 | | | | | | | | | | | | | | | | 13 |
| 1* | 2 | | | 4 | 5 | 3 | 6 | 7 | 8 | 9 | 10 | 11 | | | | | | | | | | | 12 | | | | | | | | | 14 |
| | 1 | | 2 | 4 | 5 | 3* | 6 | 12 | 8 | 9 | 10 | 11 | | 7 | | | | | | | | | | | | | | | | | | 15 |
| | 1 | 3 | 2 | 4 | 5 | | 6 | 12 | 8 | 9 | 10 | 11 | | 7* | | | | | | | | | | | | | | | | | | 16 |
| 1 | | | 2 | 4 | 5 | 3 | 6 | | 8 | 9 | 10 | 11 | | 7 | | | | | | | | | | | | | | | | | | 17 |
| 1 | | | 2 | 4 | 5 | 3 | 6 | 12 | 8 | 9 | 10 | 11 | | 7* | | | | | | | | | | | | | | | | | | 18 |
| | 1 | | 2 | 4 | 5 | 3 | 6 | 9 | 8 | | 10 | 11 | | 7 | | | | | | | | | | | | | | | | | | 19 |
| 1 | | | 2 | 4 | 5 | 3 | 6* | 12 | 8 | 9 | 10 | 11 | | 7 | | | | | | | | | | | | | | | | | | 20 |
| 1 | | 3 | 2* | 4 | 5 | 12 | 6 | | 9 | 8 | | 11 | | 7 | | | | 10 | | | | | | | | | | | | | | 21 |
| 1 | | 3 | 2 | | 5 | | 6 | | 8* | 9 | 10 | 11 | | | | | | 4 | 12 | | 7 | | | | | | | | | | | 22 |
| 1 | | | 2 | | 5 | | 6 | | 8 | 9* | 10 | 11 | | | | | | 4 | 12 | 3 | 7 | | | | | | | | | | | 23 |
| 1 | | | 2 | 4 | 5 | | 6 | 12 | | 9* | | 11 | 8 | | | | | 10 | | 3 | 7 | | | | | | | | | | | 24 |
| 1 | | 3 | 2 | | 5 | 4 | 6 | 9 | | 11 | 10 | | 8* | 12 | | | | | | | 7 | | | | | | | | | | | 25 |
| 1 | | 3 | 2 | | 5 | 4 | 6 | 12 | 8 | 9 | 10 | 11 | | | | | | | | | 7* | | | | | | | | | | | 26 |
| 1 | | 3 | 2* | | 5 | 4 | 6 | | 8 | 9 | 10 | 11 | | 12 | | | | | | | 7 | | | | | | | | | | | 27 |
| 1 | | 3 | 2 | | 5 | 4 | 6* | 12 | 8 | 9 | 10 | 7 | | | | | | | | | 11 | | | | | | | | | | | 28 |
| 1 | | 3 | 2* | | 5 | 4 | 6 | 13 | 8† | 9 | 10 | 11 | | | | | 12 | | | | 7 | | | | | | | | | | | 29 |
| 1 | | 3 | 2 | 13 | 5 | 4 | | | 8 | 9 | 10† | 11 | | | | | 12 | | | | 7* | 6 | | | | | | | | | | 30 |
| 1 | | 3 | 2 | | 5 | | | | 8 | 9 | | | | | | | 10 | 4 | | | 7 | 6 | 11 | | | | | | | | | 31 |
| 1 | | 3 | 2 | | 5 | | | | 8 | 9 | 12 | | | | | | 10* | 4 | | | 7 | 6 | 11 | | | | | | | | | 32 |
| 1 | | 3 | 2 | | 5 | 6 | | | | | 12 | | | | | | 10 | 4 | | | 7 | 8 | 11 | 9* | | | | | | | | 33 |
| 1 | | 3 | 2 | | 5 | 6 | | 9 | | | 12 | | | | | | 10 | 4 | | | 7* | 8 | 11 | | | | | | | | | 34 |
| 1 | | 3 | 2 | | 5 | 6* | | 9† | | | 12 | | | | | | 10 | 4 | | | 7 | | 11 | | | 8 | 13 | | | | | 35 |
| 1 | | | 2 | | 5 | 3 | | 9* | | | 12 | | | | | | 10 | 4 | | | 8 | | 11 | | | 6 | | 7 | | | | 36 |
| 1 | | 3 | 2 | | 5 | | | | 8 | 9 | | | | | | | 12 | 4 | | | 10* | | 11 | | | 6 | | 7 | | | | 37 |
| 1 | | | 2 | | 5 | 3 | 6 | | | 9 | 10 | | | | | | | 4 | | | 7 | | 11 | | | | | | | 8 | | 38 |
| 1 | 13 | 2 | | | 5 | 3 | 6 | | 8 | 9 | | | | | | | 4 | | | | 12 | | 11 | | | | | | 10* | | 7† | 39 |
| 34 | 5 | 17 | 36 | 19 | 39 | 28 | 32 | 6 | 27 | 32 | 25 | 30 | 26 | 2 | 1 | 4 | 11 | 14 | — | 2 | 14 | 7 | 9 | 1 | — | 4 | — | 1 | 1 | 1 | 1 | |

Substitute appearances: Doyle +1s, Markey +2s, Ferguson +3s, Rolland +5s, Russell +7s, Scott +1s, Lewin +4s, Miller +2s, Kydd +1s, Hyslop +2s, Allison +2s, Gilchrist +1s, Mercer +1s.

# DUMBARTON Division 1

*Year Formed:* 1872. *Ground:* Boghead Park. *Size:* 112yd×74yd. *Capacity:* 18,000. *Telephone:* Dumbarton 62569.
*Manager:* Billy Lamont.
*Club Colours:* White with gold horizontal band between two black bands, white shorts and stockings.
*Club Nickname:* Sons.
*Record Attendance:* 18,000 v Raith Rovers, Scottish Cup 7th rd, 2 Mar, 1957.
*Previous Name:* Dumbarton Athletic.

## 1981–82 LEAGUE RECORD

| Match No. | Date | Venue | Opponents | Result | H/T Score | League Pos'n | Goalscorers | Attendance |
|---|---|---|---|---|---|---|---|---|
| 1 | Aug 29 | H | East Stirling | L 0-3 | 0-2 | — | | 400 |
| 2 | Sept 5 | A | Queen of the S | W 4-0 | 2-0 | 7 | Coyle J., Blair, Montgomerie, Brown | 1500 |
| 3 | 12 | H | Clydebank | L 1-3 | 1-0 | 11 | Montgomerie | 1000 |
| 4 | 16 | A | Raith R | W 3-1 | 1-1 | — | Brown, Coyle J. 2 | 876 |
| 5 | 19 | H | Motherwell | L 0-6 | 0-3 | 12 | | 1200 |
| 6 | 23 | A | Queen's Park | L 0-3 | 0-2 | — | | 987 |
| 7 | 26 | A | Hearts | L 1-2 | 0-1 | 13 | Blair | 3627 |
| 8 | 30 | A | Ayr U | L 2-3 | 2-1 | — | Coyle J., Dunlop | 977 |
| 9 | Oct 3 | H | St Johnstone | W 2-1 | 1-1 | 12 | McGowan P., Rankin | 500 |
| 10 | 10 | H | Hamilton A | L 1-2 | 1-1 | 13 | Brown | 500 |
| 11 | 17 | A | Dunfermline Ath | D 2-2 | 2-2 | 12 | Blair, Dunlop | 2000 |
| 12 | 24 | H | Kilmarnock | L 0-2 | 0-0 | 13 | | 800 |
| 13 | 31 | A | Falkirk | D 1-1 | 1-0 | 13 | Dunlop | 2500 |
| 14 | Nov 7 | H | Queen of the S | W 1-0 | 0-0 | 12 | McGowan P. | 450 |
| 15 | 14 | A | East Stirling | D 1-1 | 1-1 | 13 | Donnelly (pen) | 300 |
| 16 | 21 | H | Raith R | D 1-1 | 1-0 | 12 | Coyle J. | 450 |
| 17 | 28 | H | Hearts | W 3-1 | 1-0 | 10 | Blair, McGowan P., Dunlop | 1200 |
| 18 | Dec 5 | A | St Johnstone | L 2-5 | 1-2 | 11 | Blair, Kenny (pen) | 1776 |
| 19 | Jan 30 | A | Kilmarnock | D 0-0 | 0-0 | 11 | | 770 |
| 20 | Feb 6 | H | Falkirk | W 3-1 | 1-0 | 11 | Montgomerie, Coyle J., Brown | 400 |
| 21 | 17 | A | Clydebank | L 0-3 | 0-2 | — | | 2650 |
| 22 | 20 | H | St Johnstone | W 2-0 | 0-0 | 12 | Donnelly, Montgomerie | 400 |
| 23 | 23 | H | Dunfermline Ath | L 0-1 | 0-0 | — | | 950 |
| 24 | 27 | A | East Stirling | D 2-2 | 1-1 | 11 | Blair, McGowan M. | 300 |
| 25 | Mar 3 | A | Motherwell | D 1-1 | 1-0 | — | Brown | 3200 |
| 26 | 6 | H | Ayr U | W 3-1 | 2-1 | 10 | Gallacher, Blair, Brown | 500 |
| 27 | 13 | H | Clydebank | L 0-2 | 0-0 | 10 | | 1720 |
| 28 | 20 | A | Dunfermline Ath | D 0-0 | 0-0 | 11 | | 2000 |
| 29 | 27 | A | Queen's Park | L 0-3 | 0-1 | 11 | | 732 |
| 30 | Apr 3 | H | Raith R | L 0-2 | 0-1 | 12 | | 350 |
| 31 | 7 | H | Ayr U | W 3-1 | 2-1 | — | Donnelly 2 (2 pens), Montgomerie | 282 |
| 32 | 10 | A | Motherwell | L 0-1 | 0-0 | 11 | | 2742 |
| 33 | 14 | H | Queen's Park | W 1-0 | 0-0 | — | Craig | 550 |
| 34 | 17 | H | Queen of the S | W 3-1 | 1-0 | 10 | Blair, McNeil, Craig | 350 |
| 35 | 21 | H | Hamilton A | D 0-0 | 0-0 | — | | 1004 |
| 36 | 24 | H | Kilmarnock | L 0-2 | 0-0 | 11 | | 800 |
| 37 | May 1 | A | Hearts | W 5-2 | 1-2 | 11 | Dunlop 3, McGowan P., Blair | 4861 |
| 38 | 8 | H | Falkirk | W 1-0 | 1-0 | 11 | Donnelly (pen) | 500 |
| 39 | 15 | A | Hamilton A | L 0-1 | 0-1 | 11 | | 686 |

**Final League Position: 11**

### Goalscorers

*League* (49): Blair 9, Dunlop 7, Brown 6, Coyle J. 6, Donnelly 5 (4 pens), Montgomerie 5, McGowan P. 4, Craig 2, Gallacher 1, Kenny 1 (pen), McGowan M. 1, McNeil 1, Rankin 1.
*League Cup* (8): Blair 3 (3 pens), Mailer 2, Campbell 1, Gallacher 1, Rankin 1.
*Scottish Cup* (2): Coyle J. 1, Donnelly 1.

## Honours

Original members of Scottish League 1890.

*Scottish League:* Division 1 Champions 1890–91 (shared with Rangers), 1891–92; Division 2 Champions 1910–11, 1971–72; Runners-up 1907–08.

*Scottish Cup:* Winners 1883; Runners-up 1881, 1882, 1887, 1891, 1897.

*Record Victory:* 13-1 v Kirkintilloch Central, Scottish Cup 1st rd, 1 Sept, 1888.

*Record Defeat:* 1-11 v Albion Rovers, Division 2, 30 Jan, 1926; 1-11 v Ayr United, League Cup, 13 August, 1952.

*Most League Points:* 52, Division 2, 1971–72.

*Most Individual League Goals in Season:* Kenny Wilson, 38, Division 2, 1971–72.

*Most Capped Player:* John Lindsay, 8, Scotland; James McAulay, 8, Scotland.

| Carson T. | Craig A. | Sinclair G. | McGowan M. | Gallacher J. | Coyle T. | Rankin M. | McGowan P. | Coyle J. | Dunlop M. | Brown A. | Blair R. | McGeoch D. | Donnelly J. | Clougherty M. | MacLeod A. | Montgomerie R. | Campbell R. | Armstrong S. | McNeil D. | Cameron J. | Mailer J. | Wotherspoon I. | Kenny D. | McRoberts A. | Edmonston A. | Match No. |
|---|---|---|---|---|---|---|---|---|---|---|---|---|---|---|---|---|---|---|---|---|---|---|---|---|---|---|
| 1 | 2 |  | 5 | 6 | 13 | 4 | 12 |  |  | 9 | 11 |  | 10† |  |  | 3 | 7 | 8* |  |  |  |  |  |  |  | 1 |
| 1 |  |  | 5 | 6 |  | 11 | 10 |  |  | 8 | 7 |  |  |  |  | 3 | 9 | 2 | 4*12 |  |  |  |  |  |  |  | 2 |
| 1 | 13 |  | 6 |  |  | 10 |  |  |  | 7 | 11* |  | 8 |  |  | 9 | 3 | 4 | 5 | 2†12 |  |  |  |  |  |  | 3 |
| 1 | 3 |  | 6 |  |  | 8 |  | 4 | 11 | 7*10 |  |  |  |  |  | 9 | 2 |  | 5 |  | 12 |  |  |  |  |  | 4 |
| 1 | 3 | 6 | 7 |  |  | 10 |  | 4 | 11 | 8 |  |  |  |  |  | 9 | 2 |  | 5 |  |  |  |  |  |  |  | 5 |
| 1 | 3 |  | 5 | 12 |  | 8 |  | 13 | 11† | 7 | 10* | 4 |  |  |  | 9 | 2 |  |  |  |  |  |  |  | 6 |  | 6 |
| 1 | 5 |  | 6 | 11 |  | 10 | 9 | 4 | 12 |  | 13 | 2 |  |  |  | 7* | 3 |  |  |  |  |  | 8† |  |  |  | 7 |
| 1 |  |  | 5 | 6 | 7 | 4 | 8 | 9 | 12 | 10 |  |  |  |  |  | 3 | 11* |  | 2 |  |  |  |  |  |  |  | 8 |
| 1 |  |  | 5 | 6 | 7 | 4 | 8 |  | 9 | 11 |  |  | 10 |  |  | 3 |  |  | 2 |  |  |  |  |  |  |  | 9 |
| 1 | 12 |  | 5 | 6* | 7 | 4 | 8 |  | 9†11 |  | 10 | 2 |  |  |  | 13 |  |  | 3 |  |  |  |  |  |  |  | 10 |
| 1 | 2 |  | 5 | 4 |  | 8 | 10 | 9 |  | 11 |  | 12 | 6* |  |  | 7 |  |  | 3 |  |  |  |  |  |  |  | 11 |
| 1 | 2 |  | 5 | 6 | 7* | 4 | 10 | 9 | 12 | 11 |  | 8†13 |  |  |  |  |  |  | 3 |  |  |  |  |  |  |  | 12 |
| 1 | 2 |  | 5 | 6 | 12 | 4 | 11 | 9 |  | 7 |  | 10 | 8 |  |  |  |  |  | 3* |  |  |  |  |  |  |  | 13 |
| 1 | 2 | 3 | 5 | 6 | 7 | 4 | 8 | 9 | 10 | 11 |  |  |  |  |  |  |  |  |  |  |  |  |  |  |  | 14 |
| 1 | 2 | 3 | 5 | 6 | 12 | 4 | 11* | 9 |  | 7 |  | 8 | 10 |  |  |  |  |  |  |  |  |  |  |  |  |  | 15 |
| 1 | 2 | 3 | 5 | 6 |  | 4 | 11* | 9 | 12 | 7 |  | 8 | 10 |  |  |  |  |  |  |  |  |  |  |  |  |  | 16 |
| 1 | 2 | 3 | 5 | 6 | 13 | 8 | 11 | 9 |  | 7 |  | 10† | 4* | 12 |  |  |  |  |  |  |  |  |  |  |  |  | 17 |
| 1 | 2 | 3 | 5 | 6 |  | 8 | 11 | 9* |  | 7 |  | 10† |  | 4 | 12 |  |  |  |  |  |  | 13 |  |  |  |  | 18 |
| 1 | 2 | 3 | 5 | 6 | 13 |  | 10 | 9† |  | 11 |  | 8* | 4 | 7 |  |  |  |  |  |  |  | 12 |  |  |  |  | 19 |
| 1 |  | 3 | 5* | 6 | 7 |  | 10† | 9 | 12 | 11 |  | 4 | 2 | 13 |  |  |  |  |  |  |  | 8 |  |  |  |  | 20 |
| 1 | 8 | 3 |  | 6 | 13 |  | 4 | 9 | 12 | 11 |  | 10 |  | 7† | 5 |  |  |  |  |  |  | 2* |  |  |  |  | 21 |
| 1 |  | 3 | 5 |  |  | 11 | 9 | 4 | 7 |  | 6 | 8 | 10 | 2 |  |  |  |  |  |  |  |  |  |  |  |  | 22 |
| 1 | 12 | 3 |  | 6 | 13 |  | 8† | 9 | 2 | 11 |  | 10 | 4 | 7* | 5 |  |  |  |  |  |  |  |  |  |  |  | 23 |
| 1 | 13 | 2 | 3 | 5† | 6 | 12 |  | 10 | 9 | 7 | 11 |  | 8 |  | 4* |  |  |  |  |  |  |  |  |  |  |  | 24 |
| 1 | 2 | 3 | 5 | 6 |  | 10 | 9 | 7 | 11 |  | 8 |  |  |  |  |  | 4 |  |  |  |  |  |  |  |  |  | 25 |
| 1 | 12 | 2* | 3 | 5 | 6 | 10 | 9 | 11 | 7 |  | 8 |  |  |  |  |  | 4 |  |  |  |  |  |  |  |  |  | 26 |
| 1 | 12 | 2 | 3 | 5 | 6 | 13 | 8 | 9 | 7 | 11† |  | 10* |  |  |  |  | 4 |  |  |  |  |  |  |  |  |  | 27 |
| 1 | 2 | 3 | 5 | 6 | 12 |  | 4 | 9 | 7 | 11 |  | 10 |  | 8* |  |  |  |  |  |  |  |  |  |  |  |  | 28 |
| 1 | 11 | 2 | 3 | 5 | 6 | 7 | 10* | 9 | 8†12 |  |  | 13 |  | 4 |  |  |  |  |  |  |  |  |  |  |  |  | 29 |
| 1 | 8† | 6 | 3 | 5 |  | 7 | 4* | 9 | 12 | 11 |  | 10 |  |  | 2 |  |  |  |  |  |  | 13 |  |  |  |  | 30 |
| 1 |  | 3 | 5 | 6 | 12 | 13 | 9* | 8 | 11 |  | 10 | 4 | 7† | 2 |  |  |  |  |  |  |  |  |  |  |  |  | 31 |
| 1 | 12 |  | 3 | 5 | 6 | 7 |  | 9 |  | 10 | 8 | 11* | 2 | 4 |  |  |  |  |  |  |  |  |  |  |  |  | 32 |
| 1 | 7 | 12 | 5 | 6 | 13 | 9 |  | 11 |  | 10 | 4 |  | 2* | 3 |  |  |  |  |  |  |  |  |  | 8† |  |  | 33 |
| 1 | 7 | 2 | 13 | 5 | 6 | 9 | 8 | 11† |  | 10* | 4 |  | 3 |  |  |  |  |  |  |  |  |  |  | 12 |  |  | 34 |
| 1 | 11 | 2 |  | 5 | 6 | 10 | 9 | 7 | 13 |  | 12 | 4 |  | 3* |  |  |  |  |  |  |  |  |  | 8† |  |  | 35 |
| 1 | 7 | 2 | 3 | 5 | 6 | 12 | 9 | 8*11 |  | 10 | 4 |  |  |  |  |  |  |  |  |  |  |  |  |  |  |  | 36 |
| 1 | 7 | 2 | 3 | 5 | 6 | 8 | 4 | 9 |  | 11 | 10 |  |  |  |  |  |  |  |  |  |  |  |  |  |  |  | 37 |
| 1 | 7* | 2 | 3 | 5 | 6 | 4 |  | 9 | 12 | 11 | 10 | 8 |  |  |  |  |  |  |  |  |  |  |  |  |  |  | 38 |
| 1 | 2 | 3 | 5 | 6 | 12 | 4 | 8 | 9† | 7 | 11* |  | 10 |  |  |  |  |  |  |  |  |  | 13 |  |  |  |  | 39 |
| 39 | 9 | 24 | 26 | 31 | 38 | 11 | 16 | 32 | 30 | 22 | 36 | 2 | 31 | 21 | 2 | 17 | 15 | 2 | 18 | 1 | — | 1 | — | 4 | 1 |  |
|  | + | + | + |  | + |  | + | + |  | + | + |  | + | + |  | + | + | + | + |  |  | + |  | + | + |  |
|  | 4s | 2s | 3s |  | 14s |  | 3s | 8s |  | 3s | 3s |  | 3s | 1s |  | 3s | 1s | 1s | 1s |  |  | 2s |  | 1s | 4s |  |

515

# DUNDEE                     Premier Division

*Year Formed:* 1893.
*Ground:* Dens Park.   *Size:* 113yd×73yd.   *Capacity:* 22,381 (12,130 seats).
*Telephone:* Dundee 826104.
*Manager:* Donald MacKay.   *Coach:* Jocky Scott.
*Secretary:* Ian Gellatly.   *Physiotherapist:* Eric Ferguson.
*Club Colours:* Dark blue shirts with red and white facings on collar and sleeves, white shorts with red facings, red stockings.
*Club Nickname:* Dark Blues or The Dee.
*Record Attendance:* 43,024 v Rangers, Scottish Cup, 1953.
*Previous Name:* East End and Our Boys amalgamated to become Dundee in 1893.
*Previous Ground:* Carolina Port, 1893–98.
*Record Transfer Fee Received:* £210,000 from Rangers for Ian Redford, Feb 1980.
**European Competitions:** *European Cup* 1962–63 (semi-final); *European Cup-Winners' Cup* 1964–65; *Fairs Cup* 1967–68 (semi-final); *UEFA Cup* 1971–72, 1974–75.

## 1981–82 LEAGUE RECORD

| Match No. | Date | Venue | Opponents | Result | H/T Score | League Pos'n | Goalscorers | Attendance |
|---|---|---|---|---|---|---|---|---|
| 1 | Aug 29 | A | Hibernian | L 0-2 | 0-2 | — | | 5738 |
| 2 | Sept 5 | H | Partick T | W 4-2 | 2-1 | 6 | McKinnon (og), Ferguson, Macdonald, Fraser | 4653 |
| 3 | 12 | A | Dundee U | L 2-5 | 1-2 | 7 | Ferguson, Mackie | 16,500 |
| 4 | 19 | H | St Mirren | W 3-0 | 2-0 | 5 | Ferguson 2 (1 pen), Sinclair | 5257 |
| 5 | 26 | A | Morton | L 0-2 | 0-0 | 8 | | 2763 |
| 6 | Oct 3 | H | Celtic | L 1-3 | 0-1 | 8 | McGeachie | 13,254 |
| 7 | 10 | A | Airdrieonians | L 2-4 | 1-1 | 9 | McCluskey (og), Ferguson (pen) | 2500 |
| 8 | 17 | H | Rangers | L 2-3 | 1-1 | 9 | Ferguson, Cameron | 11,956 |
| 9 | 24 | A | Aberdeen | L 1-2 | 0-2 | 10 | Stephen | 11,506 |
| 10 | 31 | H | Hibernian | D 0-0 | 0-0 | 10 | | 6011 |
| 11 | Nov 7 | A | Partick T | W 2-1 | 0-0 | 9 | Mackie 2 | 3337 |
| 12 | 14 | H | Dundee U | L 1-3 | 1-1 | 10 | Ferguson | 15,578 |
| 13 | 21 | A | St Mirren | L 0-4 | 0-3 | 10 | | 3600 |
| 14 | 28 | H | Morton | W 4-1 | 2-1 | 9 | Bell, Mackie, Ferguson, Sinclair | 3598 |
| 15 | Dec 5 | A | Celtic | L 1-3 | 0-0 | 9 | Sinclair | 14,570 |
| 16 | 12 | H | Airdrieonians | W 3-1 | 1-0 | 8 | MacDonald, Sinclair, Fraser | 3988 |
| 17 | 19 | A | Rangers | L 1-2 | 0-1 | 8 | McGeachie | 8500 |
| 18 | Jan 2 | A | Hibernian | L 1-2 | 1-0 | 8 | Sinclair | 8281 |
| 19 | 30 | H | St Mirren | L 0-2 | 0-1 | 8 | | 4628 |
| 20 | Feb 6 | H | Celtic | L 1-3 | 0-1 | 9 | Kidd | 11,377 |
| 21 | 20 | A | Morton | L 0-2 | 0-1 | 10 | | 2000 |
| 22 | 27 | A | Aberdeen | D 0-0 | 0-0 | 10 | | 9000 |
| 23 | Mar 10 | A | Dundee U | D 1-1 | 1-1 | — | Ferguson (pen) | 13,790 |
| 24 | 13 | A | Airdrieonians | W 2-0 | 0-0 | 9 | Fleming, Fraser | 2000 |
| 25 | 17 | H | Aberdeen | L 0-3 | 0-1 | — | | 6126 |
| 26 | 20 | H | Hibernian | D 2-2 | 1-0 | 8 | Fraser, Stephen | 4345 |
| 27 | 27 | A | Partick T | W 2-0 | 2-0 | 8 | Sinclair, Fraser | 2500 |
| 28 | Apr 3 | H | Dundee U | L 0-2 | 0-1 | 8 | | 12,602 |
| 29 | 10 | A | St Mirren | W 1-0 | 1-0 | 8 | Kidd | 3804 |
| 30 | 14 | H | Rangers | W 3-1 | 2-1 | — | Stephen 2, Ferguson | 7975 |
| 31 | 17 | A | Celtic | L 2-4 | 1-0 | 8 | Smith, Ferguson | 14,288 |
| 32 | 21 | H | Partick T | L 1-2 | 1-1 | — | Sinclair | 6463 |
| 33 | 25 | H | Morton | W 2-1 | 1-1 | — | McGeachie, Fraser | 5346 |
| 34 | May 1 | H | Aberdeen | L 0-5 | 0-2 | 8 | | 6415 |
| 35 | 8 | A | Rangers | L 0-4 | 0-1 | 8 | | 8500 |
| 36 | 15 | H | Airdrieonians | W 1-0 | 1-0 | 8 | Ferguson | 6696 |

**Final League Position: 8**

**Goalscorers**
*League* (46): Ferguson 12 (3 pens), Sinclair 7, Fraser 6, Mackie 4, Stephen 4, McGeachie 3, Kidd 2, MacDonald 2, Bell 1, Cameron 1, Fleming 1, Smith 1, own goals 2.
*League Cup* (7): Fleming 4, Cameron 1, MacDonald 1, Stephen 1.
*Scottish Cup* (4): Ferguson 1, Mackie 1, Smith 1, Stephen 1.

**Honours**

*Scottish League* – Division 1 Champions 1961–62, 1978–79; Runners-up 1902–03, 1906–07, 1908–09, 1948–49, 1980–81; Division 2 Champions 1946–47.
*Scottish Cup* – Winners 1910; Runners-up 1925, 1952, 1964.
*Scottish League Cup* – Winners 1951–52, 1952–53, 1973–74; Runners-up 1967–68, 1980–81.
*Record Victory:* 10-0 v Alloa, Division 2, 8 Mar, 1947; 10-0 v Dunfermline Ath, Division 2, 22 Mar, 1947.
*Most League Points:* 55, Division 1, 1978–79.
*Most Individual League Goals in Season:* 38, Dave Halliday, 1923–24.
*Most Capped Player:* Alex Hamilton, 24, Scotland.

| Geddes R. | Blair A. | Barr L. | Cameron D. | McKimmie S. | McLelland C. | Fraser C. | Smith J. | Glennie R. | MacDonald I. | McGeachie G. | Ferguson I. | Bell D. | Sinclair E. | Mackie P. | Kidd A. | Stephen R. | Fleming I. | Murphy J. | Scrimgeour B. | Schaedler E. | Davidson G. | Match No. |
|---|---|---|---|---|---|---|---|---|---|---|---|---|---|---|---|---|---|---|---|---|---|---|
| 1 | 12 | 2 | | | 4* | 5 | 6 | | 7 | 8 | 9† | | 11 | 13 | 10 | | | | 3 | | | 1 |
| 1 | | 2 | 3 | | 4 | 5 | 6 | 11 | 7 | 8 | 9 | | 12 | | 10* | | | | | | | 2 |
| 1 | | 2 | 3 | | 4 | 5 | 6 | 11 | 7 | 8 | 9 | | 12 | | 10* | | | | | | | 3 |
| 1 | | 2 | 3 | | 4 | 5 | 6 | 11* | 7 | 8 | 9 | | 12 | | 10 | | | | | | | 4 |
| 1 | | 2 | 3 | | 4 | 5 | 6 | 11† | 7 | 8 | 9* | 12 | 13 | | 10 | | | | | | | 5 |
| 1 | | 2 | 3 | | 4 | 5 | 6 | 11† | 7 | 8 | 9 | 13 | 10* | 12 | | | | | | | | 6 |
| 1 | | 2 | 3 | | 4* | 5 | 6 | 11 | 7 | 8 | 9† | 13 | 12 | | 10 | | | | | | | 7 |
| 1 | | 2 | 3 | | 4 | 5 | 6 | 11* | 7 | 8 | 9 | | 10 | 12 | | | | | | | | 8 |
| 1 | | 2 | 3 | | 4* | 5 | 6 | 10 | 7 | 8 | 9 | 12 | 11 | | | | | | | | | 9 |
| 1 | | 2 | 3 | | 4* | 5† | 6 | 10 | 7 | 8 | 9 | 12 | 11 | 13 | | | | | | | | 10 |
| 1 | | 2 | 3 | | 4 | 5 | 6 | 10 | 7 | 8 | 9 | 12 | 11* | | | | | | | | | 11 |
| 1 | | 2 | 3 | | 4* | 5 | 6 | 10 | 9 | 8 | 7 | | 11 | 12 | | | | | | | | 12 |
| 1 | | 2 | 3 | 10 | 4 | 5 | 6 | | 7 | 8 | 9 | 12 | 11* | | | | | | | | | 13 |
| 1 | | 2 | 3 | 11 | 4* | 5 | 6† | | 7 | 8 | 9 | | 10 | 12 | 13 | | | | | | | 14 |
| 1 | | 2 | 3 | 11 | 4 | 5* | 6 | | 7 | 8† | 9 | | 10 | 12 | 13 | | | | | | | 15 |
| 1 | | 2 | 3 | 11 | 4 | 5 | 6 | | 7 | 8 | 9 | | 10 | | | | | | | | | 16 |
| 1 | | 2 | 3 | 11 | 4 | 5 | 6 | | 7 | 8 | 9 | | 10 | | | | | | | | | 17 |
| 1 | | 2 | 3 | 11† | 4 | 5 | 6* | | 7 | 8 | 9 | | 10 | 12 | 13 | | | | | | | 18 |
| 1 | | 2 | 3 | | 4* | 5 | 6 | 11 | 7 | 8 | 9 | 12 | 10 | | | | | | | | | 19 |
| 1 | | 2* | 3 | | 4 | 5 | 6 | 11 | 7 | 10 | 9† | 12 | 13 | | | | | | 8 | | | 20 |
| 1 | | 2* | 3 | | 4 | 5 | 6 | 11 | 7 | 8 | 9† | 12 | 13 | | 10 | | | | | | | 21 |
| 1 | 13 | 2 | 3 | | 4 | 5 | 6 | 11 | 7 | 8 | 9* | 12 | 10† | | | | | | | | | 22 |
| 1 | 13 | 2 | 3 | | 4 | 5 | 6 | 11 | 7 | 8* | 9† | 12 | 10 | | | | | | | | | 23 |
| 1 | 12 | 2* | 3 | | 4 | 5 | 6 | 11 | 7 | 8 | 9 | | 10 | | | | | | | | | 24 |
| 1 | | 2 | 3 | | 4 | 5 | 6 | | 7 | 8 | 9 | 12 | 10 | | | | | | 11* | | | 25 |
| 1 | | 2 | 3 | | 4 | 5 | 6 | | 7 | 8* | 9 | 12 | 10 | | | | 11† | | | | 13 | 26 |
| 1 | | 2 | 3 | | 4 | 5 | 6 | | 7 | 8* | 9 | 12 | 10 | | | | 11 | | | | | 27 |
| 1 | | 2* | 3 | | 4 | 5 | 6 | | 7 | | 9 | 12 | 10† | | 13 | | 11 | | 8 | | | 28 |
| 1 | | 2 | 3 | | 4 | 5 | 6 | | 7 | 8* | 9 | 12 | 10 | | | | 11 | | | | | 29 |
| 1 | | 2 | 3 | | 4* | 5 | 6 | | 7† | 8 | 9 | 12 | 13 | | 10 | | 11 | | | | | 30 |
| 1 | | 2 | 3 | | 4 | 5 | 6 | | 7 | 8* | 9 | 13 | 10† | 12 | | | | | | 11 | | 31 |
| 1 | | 2 | 3 | | 4 | 5 | 6 | | 7* | 8 | 9 | | 10† | 12 | | | 11 | | | | 13 | 32 |
| 1 | | 2 | 3 | | 4 | 5 | 6 | | 7 | 8 | 9 | | 10* | 12 | 13 | | 11† | | | | | 33 |
| 1 | | 2 | 3 | | 4 | 5 | 6 | | 7* | 8 | 9 | | 10 | 12 | | | 11 | | | | | 34 |
| 1 | | 2 | 3* | | 4 | 5† | 6 | | 7 | 8 | 9 | | 10 | 13 | | | 11 | | 12 | | | 35 |
| 1 | | 2* | 3 | | 4 | 5 | 6 | | 7 | 8 | 9 | | 10 | 12 | | | 11 | | | | | 36 |
| 28 | 8 | 23 | 25 | 16 | 15 | 31 | 17 | 35 | 17 | 28 | 34 | 15 | 24 | 22 | 21 | 9 | 13 | 7 | 6 | 1 | 1 | |
| | +1s | +3s | | | | | | +1s | | | | | +1s | +1s | +10s | +9s | +15s | +3s | +6s | | +3s | |

# DUNDEE UNITED     Premier Division

*Year Formed:* 1909 as Dundee Hibernians, became Dundee U in October 1923.
*Ground:* Tannadice Park. *Size:* 110yd×74yd. *Capacity:* 18,912 (2204 seats).
*Telephone:* Dundee 86289.
*Manager:* Jim McLean.
*Secretary:* Mrs Helen Lindsay. *Physiotherapist:* Andy Dickson.
*Club Colours:* Tangerine shirts with black trim, black shorts with tangerine trim.
*Club Nickname:* Terrors.
*Record Attendance:* 28,000 v Barcelona, Fairs Cup, 1966.
*Record Transfer Fee Received:* £400,000 from West Ham U for Ray Stewart, Sept 1979.
*Record Transfer Fee Paid:* £165,000 to Chelsea for Eamonn Bannon, Oct 1979.
**European Competitions:** *Fairs Cup* 1966–67, 1969–70, 1970–71; *European Cup-Winners' Cup* 1974–75; *UEFA Cup* 1975–76, 1977–78, 1978–79, 1980–81, 1981–82.

## 1981–82 LEAGUE RECORD

| Match No. | Date | Venue | Opponents | Result | H/T Score | League Pos'n | Goalscorers | Attendance |
|---|---|---|---|---|---|---|---|---|
| 1 | Aug 29 | H | Aberdeen | W 4-1 | 3-0 | — | Sturrock, Pettigrew, Holt, Bannon (pen) | 10,598 |
| 2 | Sept 5 | A | Morton | L 0-1 | 0-0 | 5 | | 3500 |
| 3 | 12 | H | Dundee | W 5-2 | 2-1 | 3 | Kirkwood, Sturrock 2, Milne, Bannon | 16,500 |
| 4 | 19 | A | Airdrieonians | L 1-2 | 1-1 | 3 | Payne | 3100 |
| 5 | Oct 3 | A | Hibernian | D 1-1 | 1-0 | 6 | Dodds | 5000 |
| 6 | 10 | H | Partick T | D 0-0 | 0-0 | 6 | | 5071 |
| 7 | 17 | A | Celtic | D 1-1 | 1-0 | 6 | Milne | 23,000 |
| 8 | 24 | H | St Mirren | L 0-2 | 0-2 | 7 | | 6964 |
| 9 | 31 | A | Aberdeen | D 1-1 | 0-1 | 7 | Milne | 10,000 |
| 10 | Nov 7 | H | Morton | W 3-0 | 0-0 | 5 | Kirkwood, Dodds 2 | 6264 |
| 11 | 11 | H | Rangers | W 2-0 | 1-0 | — | Bannon, Sturrock | 16,138 |
| 12 | 14 | A | Dundee | W 3-1 | 1-1 | 3 | Milne, Sturrock 2 | 15,578 |
| 13 | 21 | H | Airdrieonians | W 4-0 | 2-0 | 3 | Dodds, Sturrock 2, Bannon (pen) | 6157 |
| 14 | Dec 5 | H | Hibernian | W 1-0 | 0-0 | 2 | Bannon (pen) | 7268 |
| 15 | Jan 16 | A | Rangers | L 0-2 | 0-1 | 4 | | 18,000 |
| 16 | Feb 3 | A | St Mirren | L 0-1 | 0-0 | — | | 5198 |
| 17 | 6 | A | Hibernian | W 1-0 | 1-0 | 4 | Bannon (pen) | 6133 |
| 18 | 9 | A | Airdrieonians | L 0-2 | 0-1 | — | | 2000 |
| 19 | 20 | H | Rangers | D 1-1 | 1-0 | 5 | Sturrock | 12,945 |
| 20 | 27 | H | St Mirren | D 1-1 | 0-1 | 6 | Bannon (pen) | 7653 |
| 21 | Mar 10 | H | Dundee | D 1-1 | 1-1 | — | McKimmie (og) | 13,790 |
| 22 | 13 | H | Partick T | W 5-1 | 3-0 | 6 | Dodds 3, Gough, McKinnon (og) | 5465 |
| 23 | 20 | A | Aberdeen | L 1-2 | 0-1 | 6 | Dodds | 14,000 |
| 24 | 27 | H | Morton | W 5-0 | 2-0 | 6 | Sturrock 3, Milne 2 | 5333 |
| 25 | 31 | H | Celtic | L 0-2 | 0-2 | — | | 15,143 |
| 26 | Apr 3 | A | Dundee | W 2-0 | 1-0 | 6 | Bannon, Sturrock | 12,602 |
| 27 | 7 | A | Morton | D 1-1 | 0-0 | — | Milne | 1792 |
| 28 | 10 | H | Airdrieonians | W 4-0 | 2-0 | 4 | Bannon 2, Dodds, Narey | 5416 |
| 29 | 14 | A | Partick T | W 3-2 | 2-1 | — | Dodds 3 | 2890 |
| 30 | 17 | H | Hibernian | L 0-1 | 0-0 | 4 | | 6850 |
| 31 | 21 | A | Celtic | L 1-3 | 0-1 | — | Dodds | 14,659 |
| 32 | 24 | A | Rangers | D 1-1 | 0-1 | 4 | Bannon (pen) | 10,000 |
| 33 | May 1 | A | St Mirren | D 2-2 | 0-1 | 4 | Bannon (pen), Dodds | 3400 |
| 34 | 5 | H | Aberdeen | L 1-2 | 1-2 | — | Hegarty | 6587 |
| 35 | 8 | H | Celtic | W 3-0 | 1-0 | 4 | Hegarty, Sturrock, Milne | 16,779 |
| 36 | 15 | A | Partick T | W 2-1 | 1-1 | 4 | Sturrock, Reilly | 3000 |

**Final League Position: 4**

### Goalscorers
*League* (61): Sturrock 15, Dodds 14, Bannon 12 (7 pens), Milne 8, Hegarty 2, Kirkwood 2, Gough 1, Holt 1, Narey 1, Payne 1, Pettigrew 1, Reilly 1, own goals 2.
*League Cup* (26): Sturrock 6, Bannon 5 (2 pens), Dodds 3, Pettigrew 3, Holt 2, Milne 2, Gough 1, Kirkwood 1, Payne 1, Reilly 1, own goal 1.
*Scottish Cup* (9): Dodds 2, Holt 2, Kirkwood 2, Sturrock 2, Bannon 1 (pen).

**Honours**
*Scottish League:* Division 2 Champions 1924–25, 1928–29; Runners-up 1930–31, 1959–60.
*Scottish Cup:* Runners-up 1973–74, 1980–81.
*Scottish League Cup:* Winners 1979–80, 1980–81; Runners-up 1981–82.
*Summer Cup:* Runners-up 1964–65.
*Scottish Wartime Cup:* Runners-up 1939–40.
*Record Victory:* 14-0 v Nithsdale Wanderers, Scottish Cup 1st rd, 17 Jan, 1931.
*Record Defeat:* 1-12 v Motherwell, Division 2, 23 Jan, 1954.
*Most League Points:* 51, Division 2, 1928–29.
*Most Individual League Goals in Season:* 41, John Coyle, Division 2, 1955–56.
*Most Capped Player:* Dave Narey, 16, Scotland.
*Most League Goals:* 108, Division 2, 1935–36.
*Highest Scorer in Total Aggregate:* Peter McKay, 202.
*Most Appearances:* Doug Smith, 587, 1959–76.

| McAlpine H. | Graham A. | Malpas M. | Holt J. | Stark D. | Kopel F. | Murray D. | Phillip I. | Gough R. | Hegarty P. | Narey D. | Bannon E. | Milne R. | Kirkwood W. | Sturrock P. | Dodds D. | Gibson I. | Reilly J. | Pettigrew W. | Robertson M. | Payne G. | Match No. |
|---|---|---|---|---|---|---|---|---|---|---|---|---|---|---|---|---|---|---|---|---|---|
| 1 |  | 4 | 2 |  | 3 |  | 5 | 6 | 7 | 12 | 8 | 10 | 11 |  |  |  |  | 9* |  |  | 1 |
| 1 |  | 4 | 2* | 3 |  | 8 | 5 | 6 | 7 | 13 | 12 | 10 | 11 |  |  |  |  | 9† |  |  | 2 |
| 1 |  | 2* |  | 3 |  | 4 | 12 | 5 | 6 | 7 | 8 | 9 | 10†| 11 |  |  |  |  | 13 |  | 3 |
| 1 |  | 2* |  | 3 |  | 4 | 12 | 5 | 6 | 7 | 8 | 9 | 10†| 11 |  |  |  |  |  | 13 | 4 |
| 1 |  |  | 2 | 3 |  | 6 | 4 | 5 |  | 7 | 8* | 9 | 10 | 11 |  |  |  |  |  | 12 | 5 |
| 1 |  | 2 | 13 |  | 3 | 4 | 6 | 5 |  | 7 | 8 | 12 |  | 11 | 9* |  |  |  |  | 10†| 6 |
| 1 |  | 10 |  | 2 | 3 | 4 |  | 5 | 6 | 7 | 8 | 9 |  | 11 |  |  |  |  |  |  | 7 |
| 1 |  | 2* | 3 | 4 | 12 | 5 | 6 | 7† | 8 | 9 | 10 | 11 | 13 |  |  |  |  |  |  |  | 8 |
|  | 1 | 2 |  | 3 | 4* | 12 | 5 | 6 | 7 | 8 | 9 | 10 | 11 |  |  |  |  |  |  |  | 9 |
| 1 |  | 2 |  | 3 |  | 4* | 5 | 6 | 7 | 8 | 9 | 10†| 11 | 12 | 13 |  |  |  |  |  | 10 |
| 1 |  | 2 | 12 | 3 |  | 4 | 5 | 6 | 7 | 8 | 9 | 10 | 11 |  |  |  |  |  |  |  | 11 |
| 1 |  | 2 |  | 3* | 12 | 4 | 5 | 6 | 7 | 8 | 9 | 10 | 11 |  |  |  |  |  |  |  | 12 |
| 1 | 3 | 2 |  |  | 4 |  | 5 | 6 | 7 | 8 | 9 | 10 | 11 |  |  |  |  |  |  |  | 13 |
| 1 | 12 | 2 |  | 3 | 4* | 5 | 6 | 7 | 8 | 9 | 10 | 11 |  |  |  |  |  |  |  |  | 14 |
| 1 |  | 2* | 3 | 13 | 4† | 5 | 6 | 7 | 8 | 9 | 10 | 11 | 12 |  |  |  |  |  |  |  | 15 |
| 1 |  | 2 | 3 |  | 4 | 5 | 6 | 7 | 8 | 9 | 10 | 11 |  |  |  |  |  |  |  |  | 16 |
| 1 |  | 2 |  | 3 |  | 4 | 5 | 6 | 7 | 8 | 9 |  | 11 |  |  |  |  | 12 | 10* |  | 17 |
| 1 |  | 2 | 12 |  | 3* | 4 | 5 | 6 | 7 | 8 | 9 |  | 11 |  |  |  |  | 10†| 13 |  | 18 |
| 1 |  | 2 | 3 |  |  | 4 | 5 | 6 | 7 | 8 | 9 | 10 | 11 |  |  |  |  |  |  |  | 19 |
| 1 | 12 | 2 | 3* |  | 4 | 5 | 6 | 7 | 8 | 9 | 10 | 13 |  |  |  |  | 11† |  |  |  | 20 |
| 1 | 3 | 9 | 2 |  | 4 | 5 | 6 | 7 | 8 |  | 10 | 11 |  |  |  |  |  |  |  |  | 21 |
| 1 |  | 2* | 3 |  | 4 | 5 | 6 | 12 | 8 | 9 | 10 | 11 | 7 |  |  |  |  |  |  |  | 22 |
| 1 | 13 | 2* | 3 |  | 4 | 5 | 6 | 7 |  | 9 | 10 | 11 | 8† | 12 |  |  |  |  |  |  | 23 |
| 1 | 3 | 9* | 2 |  | 4 | 5 | 6 | 12 | 8 |  | 10 | 11 | 7 |  |  |  |  |  |  |  | 24 |
| 1 | 3 | 7 | 2 |  | 4* | 5 | 6 | 12 | 8 | 9 | 10 | 11 |  |  |  |  |  |  |  |  | 25 |
| 1 |  | 2 | 3 |  | 4 | 5 | 6 | 7 | 8 | 9 | 10 | 11 |  |  |  |  |  |  |  |  | 26 |
| 1 |  | 2 | 3 |  | 4 | 5 | 6 | 7 | 8 | 9 |  | 11 | 10 |  |  |  |  |  |  |  | 27 |
| 1 | 2 | 8* | 3 |  | 4 | 5 | 6 | 7 | 13 | 12 | 10 | 11 | 9† |  |  |  |  |  |  |  | 28 |
| 1 | 2 |  | 3 |  | 4 | 5 | 6 | 7 | 8 | 9 | 10 | 11 |  |  |  |  |  |  |  |  | 29 |
| 1 | 2 |  | 3 |  | 4 | 5 | 6 | 7 | 8 | 9 | 10 | 11 |  |  |  |  |  |  |  |  | 30 |
| 1 | 2 | 12 |  | 3* | 4 | 5 | 6 | 7 | 8 | 9 | 10 | 11 |  |  |  |  |  |  |  |  | 31 |
| 1 | 3 | 2 |  |  | 4 | 5 | 6 | 7 | 8 | 9 | 10 | 11 |  |  |  |  |  |  |  |  | 32 |
| 1 | 3 | 2 |  |  | 4 | 5 | 6 | 7 | 8 | 9 | 10 | 11 |  |  |  |  |  |  |  |  | 33 |
| 1 | 12 | 2 | 3* |  | 4 | 5 | 6 | 7 | 8 | 9† | 10 | 11 | 13 |  |  |  |  |  |  |  | 34 |
| 1 | 3 | 9 |  | 2 | 4 | 5 | 6 | 7 | 8 |  | 10 | 11 |  |  |  |  |  |  |  |  | 35 |
| 1 | 3 |  | 2 | 4 | 5 | 6 | 7 | 8 |  | 10 | 11* | 9 | 12 |  |  |  |  |  |  |  | 36 |
| 35 | 1 | 15 | 26 | 18 | 6 | 12 | 14 | 26 | 36 | 34 | 33 | 32 | 29 | 31 | 35 | 4 | 3 | 2 | 1 | 3 |  |
|  | + | + | + | + |  | + | + |  |  | + | + | + |  | + | + | + | + | + |  |  |  |
|  | 4s | 2s | 2s | 1s |  | 1s | 4s |  |  | 3s | 3s | 3s |  | 3s | 5s | 1s | 1s | 3s |  |  |  |

# DUNFERMLINE ATHLETIC    Division 1

*Year Formed:* 1885.
*Ground:* East End Park.   *Size:* 114yd×72yd.   *Capacity:* 27,500 (3000 seats).
*Telephone:* Dunfermline 24295.
*Manager:* Pat Stanton.   *Physiotherapist:* Jim Stevenson.
*Secretary:* Jim McColville JP.
*Club Colours:* White and black vertical striped shirts, black shorts.
*Club Nickname:* The Pars.
*Record Attendance:* 27,816 v Celtic, Division 1, 1968.
**European Competitions:** *European Cup-Winners' Cup* 1961–62, 1968–69; *Fairs Cup* 1962–63, 1964–65, 1965–66, 1966–67, 1969–70.

## 1981–82 LEAGUE RECORD

| Match No. | Date | Venue | Opponents | Result | H/T Score | League Pos'n | Goalscorers | Attendance |
|---|---|---|---|---|---|---|---|---|
| 1 | Aug 29 | H | Hearts | D 1-1 | 1-0 | — | Considine | 4300 |
| 2 | Sept 5 | A | East Stirling | W 2-1 | 0-1 | 4 | Jenkins 2 | 885 |
| 3 | 8 | A | Raith R | D 0-0 | 0-0 | — | | 2000 |
| 4 | 12 | H | Queen of the S | D 1-1 | 0-1 | 4 | Hegarty | 1800 |
| 5 | 16 | A | Clydebank | L 1-4 | 0-2 | — | Morrison | 664 |
| 6 | 19 | A | Hamilton A | W 2-0 | 0-0 | 4 | Morrison, McNaughton | 1800 |
| 7 | 23 | H | Falkirk | D 1-1 | 1-1 | — | Morrison | 2700 |
| 8 | 26 | H | Motherwell | L 1-2 | 0-1 | 7 | Jenkins | 3500 |
| 9 | Oct 3 | A | Kilmarnock | W 1-0 | 1-0 | 6 | Jenkins | 2000 |
| 10 | 10 | A | Queen's Park | W 1-0 | 0-0 | 4 | Jenkins | 985 |
| 11 | 17 | H | Dumbarton | D 2-2 | 2-2 | 5 | McNaughton, Considine | 2000 |
| 12 | 24 | A | Ayr U | D 1-1 | 0-0 | 5 | McNaughton | 2706 |
| 13 | 31 | H | St Johnstone | L 1-2 | 1-0 | 7 | Stewart | 2750 |
| 14 | Nov 7 | H | East Stirling | W 2-1 | 0-0 | 6 | McNaughton 2 | 1600 |
| 15 | 14 | A | Hearts | D 1-1 | 0-1 | 6 | McNaughton (pen) | 5570 |
| 16 | 21 | H | Clydebank | L 3-6 | 2-2 | 6 | Jenkins, Hamill, McNaughton | 1750 |
| 17 | 28 | A | Motherwell | L 1-6 | 1-2 | 8 | McNaughton | 3581 |
| 18 | Dec 5 | H | Kilmarnock | L 1-2 | 1-2 | 8 | McNaughton (pen) | 2000 |
| 19 | Feb 3 | H | Ayr U | D 0-0 | 0-0 | — | | 1400 |
| 20 | 6 | H | Raith R | L 2-3 | 1-2 | 9 | Hegarty, McNaughton | 2500 |
| 21 | 10 | H | Hamilton A | L 1-3 | 0-2 | — | McNaughton | 850 |
| 22 | 13 | A | Falkirk | D 0-0 | 0-0 | 11 | | 1200 |
| 23 | 17 | H | Queen's Park | W 2-1 | 1-1 | — | Stewart, McCathie | 980 |
| 24 | 20 | A | Queen of the S | W 3-2 | 1-1 | 9 | McCathie 2, Stewart | 750 |
| 25 | 23 | A | Dumbarton | W 1-0 | 0-0 | — | McNaughton | 950 |
| 26 | 27 | H | Hamilton A | D 1-1 | 1-0 | 9 | McNaughton | 1800 |
| 27 | Mar 10 | A | Kilmarnock | L 0-2 | 0-0 | — | | 1550 |
| 28 | 13 | A | Falkirk | L 0-1 | 0-1 | 9 | | 2000 |
| 29 | 20 | H | Dumbarton | D 0-0 | 0-0 | 9 | | 2000 |
| 30 | 27 | A | Raith R | W 1-0 | 1-0 | 9 | Stewart | 1500 |
| 31 | 31 | A | St Johnstone | L 1-2 | 0-1 | — | Forrest | 1200 |
| 32 | Apr 3 | H | Ayr U | D 2-2 | 1-1 | 9 | Considine, Hegarty | 1600 |
| 33 | 10 | A | Queen's Park | L 1-2 | 1-1 | 9 | Stewart | 830 |
| 34 | 14 | A | Queen of the S | W 3-0 | 2-0 | — | Nicol, Jenkins, Bowie | 370 |
| 35 | 17 | H | St Johnstone | W 1-0 | 1-0 | 8 | Bowie | 1856 |
| 36 | 24 | H | Hearts | L 1-2 | 1-0 | 9 | McCathie | 1620 |
| 37 | May 1 | A | Clydebank | L 0-1 | 0-0 | 9 | | 460 |
| 38 | 8 | A | Motherwell | D 2-2 | 1-1 | 10 | Stewart, Morrison (pen) | 2500 |
| 39 | 15 | H | East Stirling | D 1-1 | 1-1 | 10 | Stewart | 1150 |

**Final League Position: 10**

### Goalscorers

*League* (46): McNaughton 13 (2 pens), Jenkins 7, Stewart 7, McCathie 4, Morrison 4 (1 pen), Considine 3, Hegarty 3, Bowie 2, Forrest 1, Hamill 1, Nicol 1.
*League Cup* (8): Hamill 2, McNaughton 2, Morrison 2, Bowie 1, Forrest 1.
*Scottish Cup* (1): McNaughton 1.

**Honours**
*Scottish League* – Division 2 Champions 1925–26; Runners-up 1912–13, 1933–34, 1954–55, 1957–58, 1972–73, 1978–79.
*Scottish Cup* – Winners 1961, 1968; Runners-up 1965.
*Scottish League Cup* – Runners-up 1949–50.
*Record Victory:* 11-2 v Stenhousemuir, Division 2, 27 Sept, 1930.
*Record Defeat:* 0-10 v Dundee, Division 2, 22 Mar, 1947.
*Most League Points:* 59, Division 2, 1925–26.
*Most Individual League Goals in Season:* Bobby Skinner, 55, Division 2, 1925–26.
*Most Capped Player:* Andy Wilson, 6(12), Scotland.

| Young G. | Whyte H. | Tait G. | Robertson R. | Thomson K. | Leishman W. | Considine D. | Hamill H. | McNaughton A. | Stewart R. | Forrest R. | Morrison S. | Donnelly P. | Jenkins G. R. | Hegarty K. | Nicol G. | Hutt G. | Brown J. | Grant C. | Dunlop R. | Bowie J. | McCathie N. | Mercer B. | Wilcox D. | Dall R. | Match No. |
|---|---|---|---|---|---|---|---|---|---|---|---|---|---|---|---|---|---|---|---|---|---|---|---|---|---|
| 1 | | | 4 | | | 5 | 6 | 7 | | | 9 | | | 11 | 8 | 2 | 3 | | 10 | | | | | | 1 |
| 1 | | | 4 | | | 5 | 6 | 7 | 8 | | 9 | | | 11 | 10 | 2 | 3 | | | | | | | | 2 |
| 1 | | | 4 | | | 5 | 6 | 7 | 8 | | 9 | | | 11 | 10 | 2 | 3 | | | | | | | | 3 |
| 1 | | | 4 | 12 | | 5 | 6* | 7 | 8 | | 9† | 13 | | 11 | 10 | 2 | 3 | | | | | | | | 4 |
| 1 | | | 8 | 12 | 4* | 5 | 6† | 7 | | | 9 | 13 | | 11 | 10 | 2 | 3 | | | | | | | | 5 |
| 1 | | | 4 | 12 | | 5 | 6* | 7 | 13 | | 9 | 8 | | 11† | 10 | 2 | 3 | | | | | | | | 6 |
| 1 | | | 8 | 4 | | 5 | | 7*12 | | | 9 | 10 | | 11 | 6 | 2 | 3 | | | | | | | | 7 |
| 1 | | | 8 | 4 | | 5 | 12 | 7 | | | 9 | 10 | | 11 | 6 | 2* | 3 | | | | | | | | 8 |
| 1 | | | 4 | 2 | | 5 | 6* | 7 | | | 9 | 8 | | 11 | 10 | 12 | 3 | | | | | | | | 9 |
| 1 | | | 4 | 2 | | 5 | 6 | 7 | | | 9 | 8 | | 11 | 10 | | 3 | | | | | | | | 10 |
| 1 | | | 4 | 2 | | 5 | | 7 | 12 | | 9* | 8 | | 11 | 10† | 13 | 3 | | | 6 | | | | | 11 |
| 1 | | | 4 | 2 | | 5 | | 7 | | | 9 | 8 | | 11 | | | 3 | | | 6 | 10 | | | | 12 |
| 1 | | | 4 | 2 | | 5 | | 7 | 11† | | 9 | 6 | 13 | | | 12 | 3* | | | 10 | 8 | | | | 13 |
| 1 | | 2 | 3 | 4 | 5 | 6 | 7 | 8*12 | | | 9 | 10 | 11 | | | | | | | | | | | | 14 |
| 1 | | 2 | 3 | 4* | 5 | 6 | 7 | 8† | | | 9 | 10 | 11 | 12 | 13 | | | | | | | | | | 15 |
| 1 | 8 | 3* | 4 | 5 | 6 | 7 | 13 | | | | 9†10 | 11 | 12 | 2 | | | | | | | | | | | 16 |
| 1 | | 2 | 12 | | | 3 | 6 | 7 | 8* | | 9 | 10 | 11 | | | 4 | | | | | | | | 5 | 17 |
| 1 | | 2 | | | | 6 | 10 | 7 | | 9 | | | 11 | | | 4 | | | | 8 | 5 | 3 | | | 18 |
| 1 | 2 | 4 | | | | | 7 | | | 10 | 11* | 9 | 6 | | | | | | | 8 | 12 | 3 | 5 | | 19 |
| 1 | | 2*12 | | 6 | | | 7 | | | 13 | 10 | 11 | 9 | 4 | | | | | | 8 | | 3 | 5† | | 20 |
| | 1 | 3 | | 4 | | | 7 | | 12 | 9 | 10*11† | 6 | 5 | | | | | | | 8 | 13 | 2 | | | 21 |
| | 1 | 3 | 2 | | | 6 | | 7*13 | | 11† | 12 | 9 | 4 | | | | | | | 8 | 10 | | 5 | | 22 |
| | 1 | 3 | 2 | | | 10 | | 9 | 7 | | 11 | 6 | | | | | | | | 8 | | 4 | 5 | | 23 |
| | 1 | 3 | 2 | | | 12 | 10 | 9 | 7† | | 11 | 6* | | | | | | | | 13 | 8 | 4 | 5 | | 24 |
| | 1 | 3 | 2 | | | 12 | 6* | 7 | 9 | | 11 | 10 | | | | | | | | 8 | | 4 | 5 | | 25 |
| | 1 | 3 | 2 | | | 12 | 6 | 7 | 9 | | 13 | 11†10* | | | | | | | | 8 | | 4 | 5 | | 26 |
| | 1 | 3 | 2 | | | 12 | 10 | 7 | 9 | | 11 | 6 | | | | | | | | 8* | | 4 | 5 | | 27 |
| | 1 | 3 | 8 | | | 10 | | 7*9 | 13 | 12 | 11†6 | 2 | | | | | | | | | | 4 | 5 | | 28 |
| | 1 | 3 | 2 | | | 6 | 8* | 7 | 9 | 11 | 12 | | | | | | | | | 10 | | 4 | 5 | | 29 |
| | 1 | 3 | 2 | | | 10 | 8 | 7 | 9 | 11 | 6 | 12 | | | | | | | | | | 4 | 5* | | 30 |
| | 1 | 3 | 2 | | | 10 | 8 | 7 | 9 | 11 | 6 | | | | | | | | | | | 4 | 5 | | 31 |
| | 1 | 3 | 2 | | | 10 | 8* | 7 | 9 | 11†13 | 6 | 12 | | | | | | | | | | 4 | 5 | | 32 |
| | 1 | 3 | 2 | | | 10 | 8* | | 9 | 11 | 7 | 12 | 6 | | | | | | | | | 4 | 5 | | 33 |
| | 1 | 3 | 2 | | | | 9 | 6 | 7 | 10 | 4 | 11* | | 12 | 8 | | | | | | | | 5 | | 34 |
| | 1 | 2 | | | | | 9 | 6 | 11 | 10 | 4 | | 3 | 7* | 8 | | | | | | | 5 | 12 | | 35 |
| | 1 | 2 | | 13 | 12 | | 9 | 6 | 11 | 10 | 4 | | 3 | 7* | 8† | | | | | | | 5 | | | 36 |
| | 1 | 2 | 4 | 8 | 11* | 9 | | | 12 | 6 | | 3 | 7 | 10 | | | | | | | | | 5 | | 37 |
| | 1 | 2 | 4 | 10 | 11 | 9 | 6 | | | | | 3 | 7 | 8 | | | | | | | | | 5 | | 38 |
| | 1 | 2 | 4 | 8 | 11 | 9 | 10 | | | | | 3 | 7 | 6 | | | | | | | | | 5 | | 39 |
| 20 | 19 | 14 | 38 | 11 | 4 | 30 | 26 | 30 | 21 | 8 | 26 | 18 | 31 | 29 | 11 | 9 | 13 | 5 | 1 | 13 | 17 | 4 | 16 | 15 | |
| | | | + | + | + | + | + | + | + | + | + | + | + | + | | | | | | + | + | | + | | |
| | | | 5s | 4s | 2s | 1s | 5s | 3s | 4s | 2s | 4s | 3s | 2s | 4s | | | | | | 2s | 2s | | 1s | | |

# EAST FIFE

## Division 2

*Year Formed:* 1903.
*Ground:* Bayview Park, Methil, Fife KY8 3AG, Scotland.   *Size:* 110yd×71yd.   *Capacity:* 15,000.
*Telephone:* Leven 26323.
*Manager:* David Clarke.
*Secretary:* Mrs I. McCammon.
*Club Colours:* Black and white striped shirts, white shorts, black stockings.
*Record Attendance:* 22,515 v Raith R, Division 1, 2 Jan, 1950.
*Club Nickname:* The Fifers.

## 1981–82 LEAGUE RECORD

| Match No. | Date | Venue | Opponents | Result | H/T Score | League Pos'n | Goalscorers | Attendance |
|---|---|---|---|---|---|---|---|---|
| 1 | Aug 29 | H | Stranraer | L 0-2 | 0-0 | — | | 480 |
| 2 | Sept 5 | A | Stenhousemuir | L 0-2 | 0-2 | 13 | | 300 |
| 3 | 8 | A | Cowdenbeath | D 2-2 | 2-2 | — | Millar, Caithness | 654 |
| 4 | 12 | H | Stirling Albion | W 3-0 | 2-0 | 9 | Millar, Neilson, O'Brien | 409 |
| 5 | 16 | A | Meadowbank T | D 1-1 | 1-0 | — | Neilson | 150 |
| 6 | 19 | H | Albion R | W 3-0 | 1-0 | 7 | Caithness 2, Burgess (og) | 318 |
| 7 | 26 | H | Forfar Ath | L 0-4 | 0-0 | 10 | | 960 |
| 8 | 30 | A | Berwick R | L 1-2 | 0-1 | — | Scott | 480 |
| 9 | Oct 3 | A | Brechin C | L 1-2 | 0-1 | 10 | Honeyman | 1012 |
| 10 | 10 | A | Clyde | L 2-3 | 2-0 | 11 | Scott, Caithness | 500 |
| 11 | 17 | A | Alloa | L 1-2 | 1-1 | 12 | Scott | 415 |
| 12 | 24 | A | Montrose | W 2-1 | 1-0 | 11 | Caithness 2 | 300 |
| 13 | 31 | H | Arbroath | L 0-1 | 0-0 | 11 | | 411 |
| 14 | Nov 7 | H | Stenhousemuir | W 3-2 | 0-1 | 10 | Scott 2, O'Brien (pen) | 339 |
| 15 | 14 | A | Stranraer | W 3-0 | 0-0 | 10 | Caithness, Scott 2 | 300 |
| 16 | 21 | H | Meadowbank T | W 2-0 | 1-0 | 10 | Scott, McLaren | 300 |
| 17 | 28 | A | Forfar Ath | L 0-1 | 0-1 | 10 | | 908 |
| 18 | Dec 5 | H | Brechin C | D 2-2 | 1-0 | 9 | Caithness, Scott | 531 |
| 19 | Jan 2 | H | Cowdenbeath | D 1-1 | 1-1 | 9 | O'Brien | 960 |
| 20 | 30 | H | Berwick R | L 0-1 | 0-1 | 9 | | 449 |
| 21 | Feb 2 | A | Alloa | W 2-1 | 0-0 | — | O'Brien, Scott | 379 |
| 22 | 6 | H | Clyde | D 2-2 | 0-0 | 9 | Scott, O'Brien (pen) | 500 |
| 23 | 10 | H | Montrose | H 0-1 | 0-1 | — | | 294 |
| 24 | 13 | A | Arbroath | L 1-3 | 1-2 | 9 | Scott | 493 |
| 25 | 20 | A | Stranraer | W 2-1 | 1-0 | 9 | Caithness, Neilson | 479 |
| 26 | 27 | H | Forfar Ath | W 1-0 | 0-0 | 9 | Durie | 527 |
| 27 | Mar 6 | A | Cowdenbeath | W 2-1 | 1-1 | 8 | Caithness 2 | 500 |
| 28 | 13 | H | Meadowbank T | W 1-0 | 0-0 | 9 | Neilson | 468 |
| 29 | 17 | A | Albion R | L 0-1 | 0-1 | — | | 725 |
| 30 | 20 | H | Stirling Albion | L 1-2 | 0-1 | 10 | Caithness | 400 |
| 31 | 27 | A | Berwick R | L 0-3 | 0-1 | 10 | | 797 |
| 32 | Apr 3 | H | Alloa | L 0-2 | 0-2 | 11 | | 410 |
| 33 | 7 | A | Stirling Albion | W 2-0 | 1-0 | — | O'Brien, Scott | 350 |
| 34 | 10 | A | Brechin C | D 1-1 | 1-0 | 9 | O'Brien | 450 |
| 35 | 17 | H | Stenhousemuir | W 1-0 | 0-0 | 8 | Thomson (pen) | 356 |
| 36 | 25 | H | Clyde | D 1-1 | 0-1 | — | Scott | 750 |
| 37 | May 1 | A | Arbroath | D 1-1 | 1-1 | 8 | Caithness | 590 |
| 38 | 8 | H | Albion R | D 1-1 | 1-0 | 8 | Scott | 339 |
| 39 | 15 | A | Montrose | W 2-1 | 1-0 | 7 | O'Brien, Scott | 250 |

**Final League Position: 7**

### Goalscorers

*League* (48): Scott 16, Caithness 13, O'Brien 8 (2 pens), Neilson 4, Millar 2, Durie 1, Honeyman 1, McLaren 1, Thomson 1 (pen), own goal 1.
*League Cup* (8): O'Brien 3, Caithness 1 (pen), Mutch 1, Neilson 1, Scott 1, Tait 1.
*Scottish Cup* (7): Caithness 2, Scott 2, Burt 1, Neilson 1, O'Brien 1.

**Honours**

*Scottish League* – Division 2 Champions 1947–48; Runners-up 1929–30, 1970–71.
*Scottish Cup* – Winners 1938 (only Second Division winners); Runners-up 1927, 1950.
*Scottish League Cup* – Winners 1947–48 (only Second Division winners), 1949–50, 1953–54.
*Record Victory:* 13-2 v Edinburgh City, Division 2, 11 Dec, 1937.
*Record Defeat:* 0-9 v Hearts, Division 1, 5 Oct, 1957.
*Most League Points:* 57, Division 2, 1929–30.
*Most Individual League Goals in a Season:* Henry Morris, 41, Division 2, 1947–48.
*Most Capped Player:* George Aitken, 5 (8), Scotland.

| Gorman D. | Christensen P. | Hamilton S. | Millar D. | McLaren J. | Halley K. | Clarke D. | Cairns D. | O'Brien C. | Neilson G. | Scott G. | Muirhead R. | Caithness M. | Cairns M. | Tait C. | Beveridge G. | Thomson R. | Wedderburn W. | Durie G. | Corrigan D. | Pryde I. | Burt P. | Mutch L. | Honeyman A. | Sokoluk J. | Huskie J. | Match No. |
|---|---|---|---|---|---|---|---|---|---|---|---|---|---|---|---|---|---|---|---|---|---|---|---|---|---|---|
| 1 | 2 | 3 |  | 5 |  |  |  | 7 | 6 | 9 | 4†11 |  |  | 8*13 |  |  |  |  |  |  |  | 10 | 12 |  |  | 1 |
| 1 | 2 | 3 |  | 13 |  |  |  | 7 | 10 | 9 | 5 | 11* |  | 4 | 6† |  |  |  |  |  |  | 8 | 12 |  |  | 2 |
| 1 |  | 3 |  | 4 |  |  |  | 9 | 8 | 7 | 5 | 11 | 10 |  | 2 | 6* |  |  |  |  |  | 12 |  |  |  | 3 |
| 1 | 2 | 3 |  | 4 |  |  |  | 9 | 7 |  | 5 | 11 | 10 | 8 | 6 |  |  |  |  |  |  |  |  |  |  | 4 |
| 1 | 2 |  | 5 | 3 |  |  |  | 7 | 8 | 9 | 4 | 11 | 10 |  | 6 |  |  |  |  |  |  |  |  |  |  | 5 |
| 1 | 2 | 3 |  | 5 |  |  |  | 7 | 8* | 9 | 4 | 11 | 10 | 12 | 6 |  |  |  |  |  |  |  |  |  |  | 6 |
| 1 | 2 | 3 |  | 5 |  |  |  | 7 | 8 | 9 | 4 | 11*10 |  |  | 6 |  |  |  |  |  |  |  | 12 |  |  | 7 |
| 1 | 2 | 3 | 4 | 5 |  |  |  | 7 | 8* | 9 | 12 | 11†10 |  |  | 6 |  |  |  |  |  |  |  | 13 |  |  | 8 |
| 1† | 2 | 3 |  | 5 |  |  |  | 7 | 8* | 9 | 4 | 11 | 10 |  | 6 |  |  |  |  | 12 |  |  | 13 |  |  | 9 |
| 1 | 2 | 3 |  | 5 |  | 4 | 8 | 7 |  | 9 | 10 | 11 |  |  | 6 |  |  |  |  |  |  |  |  |  |  | 10 |
| 1 |  |  | 5 | 3 | 4* | 7 | 8 | 9 | 10 | 11 | 2† |  |  |  | 6 |  |  |  |  |  |  | 13 | 12 |  |  | 11 |
| 1 |  | 3 | 5 | 2 |  |  |  | 8 | 10 | 9 | 4 | 11 | 6 |  | 12 |  |  |  |  |  | 7* |  |  |  |  | 12 |
| 1 | 2 | 3 |  |  |  |  |  | 6 | 8 | 10* | 9 | 4 | 11 | 7†13 |  |  |  |  |  |  |  | 12 |  |  |  | 13 |
| 1 | 2 | 3 | 4 | 5 |  |  |  | 6 | 7 | 8* | 9 | 10 | 11 |  | 12 |  |  |  |  |  |  |  |  |  |  | 14 |
| 1 | 2 | 3 | 4 | 5 |  |  |  | 6 | 7 |  | 9 | 10 | 11 |  | 8 |  |  |  |  |  |  |  |  |  |  | 15 |
| 1 | 2 | 3 | 4 | 5 |  |  |  | 6 | 7 | 12 | 9 | 10 | 11 |  | 8* |  |  |  |  |  |  |  |  |  |  | 16 |
| 1 | 2 | 3 | 4 | 5 |  |  |  | 6† | 7 |  | 9 | 10 | 11 | 13 | 8* | 12 |  |  |  |  |  |  |  |  |  | 17 |
| 1 | 2 | 3 | 4 | 5 |  |  |  | 10* | 7 | 6 | 9 | 8 | 11 |  | 12 |  |  |  |  |  |  |  |  |  |  | 18 |
| 1 | 2 | 3 | 4 | 5 |  |  |  | 7 | 6 | 9 | 8 | 11 |  |  |  |  | 10 |  |  |  |  |  |  |  |  | 19 |
| 1 | 2 | 3† | 4 | 5 |  |  |  | 7 | 12 | 9 | 6*10 | 13 |  |  |  |  | 8 | 11 |  |  |  |  |  |  |  | 20 |
| 1 | 2 | 3 | 4 | 5 |  |  |  | 11* | 6† | 9 | 12 | 10 | 8 |  |  |  | 7 | 13 |  |  |  |  |  |  |  | 21 |
| 1 | 2 | 3 | 4 | 5 |  |  |  | 11 | 6 | 9 |  | 10* | 8 |  |  |  | 7 | 12 |  |  |  |  |  |  |  | 22 |
| 1 | 2 | 3† | 4 | 5 |  |  |  | 11 | 6 | 9 | 13 | 10* | 7 |  |  |  | 8 | 12 |  |  |  |  |  |  |  | 23 |
| 1 | 2 | 3* | 4 | 5 |  |  |  | 7 | 6 | 9 |  | 11 | 10 |  |  |  | 8 | 12 |  |  |  |  |  |  |  | 24 |
|  | 1 | 8 |  | 3 | 5 | 4 |  | 10 | 12 | 7 | 11 | 6 |  |  | 2 |  | 9* |  |  |  |  |  |  |  |  | 25 |
|  | 1 | 8 |  | 4 | 5 | 3 |  | 9 |  | 10 | 11 | 6* |  |  | 2 |  | 7 |  |  |  |  |  | 12 |  |  | 26 |
|  | 1 | 8 |  | 4 | 5 | 3 |  | 9*13 |  | 10 | 11 | 6† |  |  | 2 |  | 7 |  |  |  |  |  | 12 |  |  | 27 |
|  | 1 | 8 |  | 4 | 5 | 10 |  | 9 |  | 6 |  | 2*11 |  |  | 3 |  | 7 |  |  |  |  |  | 12 |  |  | 28 |
|  | 1 | 8 |  | 6 | 5 | 3† |  | 7 | 4* | 9 | 13 |  | 11 |  | 2 |  | 10 |  |  |  |  |  | 12 |  |  | 29 |
|  | 1 | 8 |  | 6 | 5 | 3 |  | 7 | 4* | 9 |  |  | 11 |  | 2 |  | 10 |  |  |  |  |  | 12 |  |  | 30 |
|  | 1 | 8* | 3 |  | 5 | 2 |  | 9 |  | 4 | 6 | 11†12 | 10 |  | 13 |  |  |  |  |  | 7 |  |  |  |  | 31 |
| 1 |  |  | 4 |  | 8 |  |  | 12 | 10† | 9 | 5 | 11 |  |  | 2 | 6 | 13 |  | 7 |  |  |  | 3* |  |  | 32 |
|  | 1 | 8 |  | 2 |  | 4 |  | 7 | 12 | 9 | 5 |  |  |  | 3 | 6 |  |  | 10 |  | 11* |  |  |  |  | 33 |
|  | 1 | 8 |  | 2 |  | 4 |  | 9 | 12 | 7 | 5 | 11† |  |  | 3 | 6 |  |  | 10* |  |  |  | 13 |  |  | 34 |
| 1 | 8 |  | 3 | 12 | 4 |  |  | 9 |  | 7 | 5 | 11* |  |  | 2 | 6 |  |  | 10 |  |  |  |  |  |  | 35 |
| 1 |  |  | 2 | 5 | 3 |  |  | 9†12 | 7 | 8*11 |  |  |  |  | 4 | 6 |  |  | 10 |  |  |  |  |  | 13 | 36 |
| 1 |  |  | 2 | 5 | 3 |  |  | 12 | 7* | 9 | 4 | 11 |  |  |  | 6 |  |  | 10 |  | 8†13 |  |  |  |  | 37 |
| 1 |  |  | 2 | 5 | 3 |  |  | 7 |  | 9 | 4†11 |  |  |  |  | 6 |  |  | 10 |  | 8*12 |  |  |  | 13 | 38 |
| 1 | 8 |  | 2 | 5 | 3 |  |  | 7 |  | 9† | 4 | 11 |  |  |  | 6 |  |  | 10*12 |  |  |  |  |  | 13 | 39 |
| 30 | 9 | 32 | 23 | 26 | 31 | 21 | 9 | 37 | 24 | 34 | 32 | 38 | 13 | 10 | 15 | 18 | 7 | 8 | 5 | — | 3 | 3 | — | 1 | — |  |

```
            +   +     +   +     +     +  +  +     +   +     +  +  +  +  +  +
            1s  1s    2s  7s    4s    3s 5s 2s    1s  5s    3s 9s 2s 6s 1s 1s
```

# EAST STIRLING

## Division 2

*Year Formed:* 1881. *Ground:* Firs Park. *Size:* 112yd×72yd. *Capacity:* 12,000.
*Telephone:* Falkirk 23583. *Secretary:* P. I. McKay. *Manager:* Martin Ferguson.
*Club Colours:* Black and white 1-inch hoops, black shorts, red stockings.
*Club Nickname:* The Shire.
*Record Attendance:* 11,500 v Hibernian, Scottish Cup, 10 Feb, 1969.

### 1981–82 LEAGUE RECORD

| Match No. | Date | Venue | Opponents | Result | | H/T Score | League Pos'n | Goalscorers | Attendance |
|---|---|---|---|---|---|---|---|---|---|
| 1 | Aug 29 | A | Dumbarton | W | 3-0 | 2-0 | — | Howitt, Lamont, Renwick | 400 |
| 2 | Sept 5 | H | Dunfermline Ath | L | 1-2 | 1-0 | 5 | Lamont | 885 |
| 3 | 8 | H | Falkirk | D | 2-2 | 0-0 | — | Lamont, Ashwood | 2000 |
| 4 | 12 | A | Hamilton A | D | 1-1 | 0-0 | 5 | Goodall | 925 |
| 5 | 16 | H | Queen's Park | L | 0-1 | 0-1 | — | | 350 |
| 6 | 19 | A | Raith R | L | 0-1 | 0-0 | 10 | | 1000 |
| 7 | 23 | H | Queen of the S | W | 3-1 | 2-1 | — | Dickson (og), Edgar, McCulley (pen) | 980 |
| 8 | 29 | H | Kilmarnock | W | 2-1 | 2-1 | — | Sharp 2 | 820 |
| 9 | Oct 3 | A | Motherwell | L | 0-3 | 0-1 | 8 | | 2528 |
| 10 | 10 | H | St Johnstone | D | 1-1 | 1-0 | 9 | Howitt | 2000 |
| 11 | 17 | A | Ayr U | L | 1-5 | 1-2 | 10 | Lamont | 2124 |
| 12 | 24 | H | Clydebank | D | 0-0 | 0-0 | 10 | | 500 |
| 13 | 31 | A | Hearts | W | 1-0 | 0-0 | 9 | Howitt | 5093 |
| 14 | Nov 7 | A | Dunfermline Ath | L | 1-2 | 0-0 | 9 | Edgar | 1600 |
| 15 | 14 | H | Dumbarton | D | 1-1 | 1-1 | 9 | McCulley | 300 |
| 16 | 21 | A | Queen's Park | L | 1-2 | 1-1 | 10 | Edgar | 660 |
| 17 | 28 | A | Kilmarnock | L | 0-2 | 0-1 | 11 | | 1400 |
| 18 | Dec 5 | H | Motherwell | L | 0-6 | 0-2 | 12 | | 1000 |
| 19 | Jan 30 | A | Clydebank | L | 1-2 | 1-0 | 13 | Blair | 522 |
| 20 | Feb 6 | H | Hearts | L | 0-1 | 0-1 | 13 | | 1100 |
| 21 | 10 | H | Ayr U | W | 2-1 | 1-0 | — | McCaig, Blair | 670 |
| 22 | 13 | A | Queen of the S | D | 1-1 | 0-0 | 13 | Kettings | 750 |
| 23 | 17 | H | Hamilton A | L | 1-5 | 0-2 | — | Kettings | 231 |
| 24 | 20 | A | Falkirk | L | 0-2 | 0-1 | 13 | | 2000 |
| 25 | 27 | H | Dumbarton | D | 2-2 | 1-1 | 13 | Lowe, Grant | 300 |
| 26 | Mar 3 | H | Raith R | L | 0-1 | 0-0 | — | | 923 |
| 27 | 6 | A | Queen of the S | L | 0-4 | 0-1 | 13 | | 800 |
| 28 | 13 | A | Queen's Park | L | 0-3 | 0-0 | 13 | | 800 |
| 29 | 20 | H | Raith R | D | 1-1 | 0-0 | 13 | Rennie | 300 |
| 30 | 24 | A | St Johnstone | L | 2-3 | 0-2 | — | Blair 2 | 1537 |
| 31 | 27 | A | Ayr U | D | 1-1 | 0-1 | 13 | Grant | 1293 |
| 32 | Apr 3 | H | Motherwell | L | 1-2 | 1-0 | 13 | Grant | 1000 |
| 33 | 7 | A | Falkirk | W | 3-0 | 1-0 | — | McGorm, Kettings, McGall | 1500 |
| 34 | 10 | H | Clydebank | L | 0-1 | 0-1 | 13 | | 400 |
| 35 | 24 | A | St Johnstone | L | 1-7 | 0-3 | 13 | McGorm (pen) | 1069 |
| 36 | 27 | A | Hearts | L | 0-2 | 0-0 | — | | 4300 |
| 37 | May 1 | H | Kilmarnock | L | 1-5 | 0-4 | 13 | McCaig | 300 |
| 38 | 8 | H | Hamilton A | W | 2-1 | 1-1 | 13 | Edgar, Lowe | 250 |
| 39 | 15 | A | Dunfermline Ath | D | 1-1 | 1-1 | 13 | McCaig | 1150 |

**Final League Position: 13**

#### Goalscorers

*League* (38): Blair 4, Edgar 4, Lamont 4, Grant 3, Howitt 3, Kettings 3, McCaig 3, McCulley 2 (1 pen), Lowe 2, McGorm 2 (1 pen), Sharp 2, Ashwood 1, Goodall 1, McGall 1, Rennie 1, Renwick 1, own goal 1.
*League Cup* (2): Hunter 1, McGall 1.
*Scottish Cup* (1): Howitt 1.

**Honours**

*Scottish League* – Division 2 Champions 1931–32; Runners-up 1962–63, 1979–80.
*Record Victory:* 10-1 v Stenhousemuir, Scottish Cup 1st rd, 1 Sept, 1888.
*Record Defeat:* 1-12 v Dundee U, Division 2, 13 Apr, 1936.
*Most League Points:* 55, Division 2, 1931–32.
*Most Individual League Goals in a Season:* Malcolm Morrison, 36, Division 2, 1938–39.
*Most Capped Player:* Humphrey Jones, 5, Wales.

| | McMillan F. | Kelly C. | Pearce B. | McKenna M. | Watt D. | Renwick C. | McGall J. | Sharp R. | Gourlay I. | Lamont P. | Edgar R. | McCaig D. | Howitt W. | Goodall J. | Ashwood K. | McCulley R. | Blair J. | Rennie I. | Ruane B. | Robertson I. | Grant A. | Lowe D. | McGorm T. | Kettings P. | Clifford J. | Hendren R. | Mulloy F. | Scott A. | Ramage D. | Caldwell T. | McElroy J. | Ross J. | McAloon J. | Scott B. |
|---|---|---|---|---|---|---|---|---|---|---|---|---|---|---|---|---|---|---|---|---|---|---|---|---|---|---|---|---|---|---|---|---|---|---|
| 1 | 1 | 13 | 7 | | 2 | 6 | | | 4 | 8* | | | 10 | 12 | | | | 3 | 5 | 9†11 | | | | | | | | | | | | | | |
| 2 | | 1 | 2 | 12 | 4 | 6 | | | 7 | 8† | | | 10 | 13 | 9 | | | 3* | 5 | 11 | | | | | | | | | | | | | | |
| 3 | 1 | | 2 | | 4 | 10 | | | 8 | 7 | | | 9 | | | 11 | 12 | 3 | 5 | 6* | | | | | | | | | | | | | | |
| 4 | 1 | | 2 | | 4* | 6 | | | 7 | 10 | | | 9†13 | 11 | | 8 | | 3 | 5 | 12 | | | | | | | | | | | | | | |
| 5 | 1 | | 2 | | 4 | 6†12 | | | 7 | 10 | | | 9 | 13 | 11 | 8 | | | 5* | 3 | | | | | | | | | | | | | | |
| 6 | 1 | | 2 | 3 | 4 | 6 | 13 | | 7† | | | | 9*10 | | | 11 | 8 | | 5 | 12 | | | | | | | | | | | | | | |
| 7 | 1 | | 2* | 3 | 4 | 12 | 9 | | 10 | 8†13 | | | 7 | | | 5 | 6 | | | 11 | | | | | | | | | | | | | | |
| 8 | 1 | | | 3 | 4 | 11 | 9* | | 7 | 10 | | | 12 | 8 | 2 | 5 | 6 | | | | | | | | | | | | | | | | | |
| 9 | 1 | | | 3 | 4 | 11 | 9† | | 7*10 | 13 | | | 12 | 8 | 2 | 5 | 6 | | | | | | | | | | | | | | | | | |
| 10 | | 1 | | 3 | 4 | 5 | | | 6 | 12 | 9†10 | 13 | 11 | 8* | 2 | | 7 | | | | | | | | | | | | | | | | | |
| 11 | | 1 | 2 | 3 | 4 | 5 | | | 10 | 7 | 13 | 9†12 | 11 | 8* | | 6 | | | | | | | | | | | | | | | | | | |
| 12 | | 1 | 2 | 3 | 4 | 5 | | | 6 | 7 | 13 | 9*12 | 11 | 8 | | 10† | | | | | | | | | | | | | | | | | | |
| 13 | | 1 | 2 | 3 | 4 | 12 | 5 | 6 | 7 | 8 | 13 | 10† | 9*11 | | | | | | | | | | | | | | | | | | | | | |
| 14 | | 1 | 2 | 3 | 4*12 | 5 | 6 | 7 | 8 | 9 | 10†13 | 11 | | | | | | | | | | | | | | | | | | | | | | |
| 15 | | 1 | 2 | 3 | 4 | 10 | | 8 | | 9 | 12 | | 11 | 7 | 5 | | 6* | | | | | | | | | | | | | | | | | |
| 16 | | 1 | 2 | 3 | 4 | 13 | 12 | 10 | 6* | 7† | | 9 | | 11 | 8 | 5 | | | | | | | | | | | | | | | | | | |
| 17 | | 1 | 2 | 3 | 4 | 12 | 9†10 | 6 | 7 | | 13 | | 11 | 8* | 5 | | | | | | | | | | | | | | | | | | | |
| 18 | | 1 | 2* | 3 | 4 | | 9† | 6 | 12 | | 13 | | 11 | 7 | 5 | | 10 | | | | | | | 8 | | | | | | | | | | 8 |
| 19 | | 1 | | 3 | 4 | 12 | 9† | 8 | 6*13 | | 10 | | | 7 | 2 | 5 | | 11 | | | | | | | | | | | | | | | | |
| 20 | | 1 | | 3 | 4 | 13 | | 12 | 7 | | 9 | 13 | | 6 | 2 | 5 | | 10* | 8 | | 11† | | | | | | | | | | | | | |
| 21 | | 1 | | 3 | 4 | 13 | | | 7 | | 9 | 12 | | 6 | 2 | 5 | | 10* | 8 | | 11† | | | | | | | | | | | | | |
| 22 | | 1 | | 3 | 4 | 13 | | | 7 | | 9 | 10* | | 6 | 2 | 5 | | 12 | 8 | | 11† | | | | | | | | | | | | | |
| 23 | 1 | | | 4 | 2 | 3 | | | 6 | | 12 | 9 | 13 | 7 | 5 | | 8*11 | | | 10† | | | | | | | | | | | | | | |
| 24 | | 1 | | | 4 | 3 | 13 | | 6 | | 8 | 9† | | 7 | 2 | 5 | | 12 | 11 | 10* | | | | | | | | | | | | | | |
| 25 | | 1 | | | 3 | 4 | | | 6 | | 8† | 9 | | 7 | 2 | 5* | | 13 | 10 | 12 | 11 | | | | | | | | | | | | | |
| 26 | | 1 | | | 5 | 4 | 12 | | 2 | | 9 | | | 7 | 3 | | | 11†8 | 13 | 6* | 10 | | | | | | | | | | | | | |
| 27 | | 1 | | | 3 | 4 | 6 | | 2 | | 13 | 9* | | 8† | 5 | | | 7 | 10 | 11 | 12 | | | | | | | | | | | | | |
| 28 | | 1 | 2 | 3 | 4 | 6 | | | 8* | | 13 | | | 7 | 5 | | | 12 | 11 | 9 | 10† | | | | | | | | | | | | | |
| 29 | | 1 | 2 | | 4 | | | 8 | | 7†13 | | | 12 | 3 | 5 | | | 10 | 6* | 9 | 11 | | | | | | | | | | | | | |
| 30 | | 1 | 2 | | 4 | 13 | | | 8* | | 11 | | | 7 | 3 | 5 | | 10† | 9 | 6 | | | | | | | | | | | | | | |
| 31 | | 1 | 2* | 6 | 4 | | | | 13 | | 10 | 8 | | 11†7 | 3 | 5 | | 9 | | 12 | | | | | | | | | | | | | | |
| 32 | | 1 | | | 4 | 6 | 13 | | 12 | | 7 | 9 | | | 3 | 5 | | 8 | 2*10†11 | | | | | | | | | | | | | | | |
| 33 | | 1 | 2 | 4 | 6 | 13 | | | 12 | 7 | | | | | 3 | 5 | | 8†10 | 9*11 | | | | | | | | | | | | | | | |
| 34 | | 1 | | | 4 | 6 | 11 | | 7 | | | | | 2 | 5 | | | 9 | 10* | 3 | | | | | | | | | | | | 8 | | |
| 35 | | 1 | 2 | | 4 | | 12 | 6 | 7 | 13 | | | | 3* | 5 | | | 9 | 8†10 | 11 | | | | | | | | | | | | | | |
| 36 | | 1 | 2 | 3 | 4 | 11 | | | 10* | | 7† | 8 | | | 5 | | | 13 | 12 | 9 | 6 | | | | | | | | | | | | | |
| 37 | | 1 | | 12 | 2 | 4* | 6† | | 13 | 7 | 11 | | | | 5 | | | 9 | 8 | 10 | 3 | | | | | | | | | | | | | |
| 38 | | 1 | | 2 | 4 | | 13 | 7 | 10† | | | | | | 5 | | | 12 | 8 | 9 | 3 | | | | | | | | | | | 11* 6 | | |
| 39 | | 1 | | 2 | 4 | 6 | 10 | | 7* | | 12 | 8 | | 9 | 3 | | | 12 | 8 | 9 | 3 | | | | | | | | | | | 5 | 11 | |
| | 1 | 22 | 16 | 23 | 32 | 37 | 16 | 11 | 21 | 14 | 26 | 21 | 14 | 1 | 15 | 25 | 24 | 29 | 9 | 11 | 12 | 14 | 20 | 1 | 2 | 1 | 3 | 1 | 1 | 1 | 2 | 1 | 1 | |
| | | + 1s | + 1s | + 1s | | + 14s | + 4s | + 5s | | | + 6s | + 5s | | | + 8s | + 8s | | + 2s | + 2s | | | + 2s | + 5s | + 1s | + 4s | + 2s | | | | | | | | |

*Note:* The following two players made one appearance each as a substitute – E. Gray v St Johnstone (24 Mar) and P. Tierney v Clydebank (10 Apr).

# FALKIRK

# Division 1

*Year Formed:* 1876.
*Ground:* Brockville Park.  *Size:* 100yd×70yd.  *Capacity:* 22,000 (2750 seats).
*Telephone:* Falkirk 24121.
*Manager:* John Hagart.  *Physiotherapist/Trainer:* Tom Logan.
*Secretary:* R. Shaw.  *PRO:* William McFarlane.
*Club Colours:* Navy blue shirts with white trimmings and white motif, white shorts, red stockings.
*Club Nickname:* The Bairns.
*Record Attendance:* 23,100 v Celtic, Scottish Cup 3rd rd, 21 Feb, 1953.

## 1981–82 LEAGUE RECORD

| Match No. | Date | Venue | Opponents | Result | H/T Score | League Pos'n | Goalscorers | Atten- dance |
|---|---|---|---|---|---|---|---|---|
| 1 | Aug 29 | H | Ayr U | L 1-2 | 1-0 | — | Herd | 2500 |
| 2 | Sept 5 | A | Raith R | W 3-0 | 1-0 | 6 | Herd 2, Smith | 1100 |
| 3 | 8 | A | East Stirling | D 2-2 | 0-0 | — | Brown, Smith | 2000 |
| 4 | 12 | H | Hearts | D 0-0 | 0-0 | 6 | | 6500 |
| 5 | 16 | A | Motherwell | L 2-3 | 1-2 | — | Herd, Hoggan (pen) | 1914 |
| 6 | 19 | H | St Johnstone | W 1-0 | 1-0 | 6 | McIntosh | 2000 |
| 7 | 23 | A | Dunfermline Ath | D 1-1 | 1-1 | — | Hoggan (pen) | 2700 |
| 8 | 26 | A | Clydebank | D 1-1 | 0-1 | 5 | Smith | 760 |
| 9 | Oct 3 | H | Hamilton A | W 3-0 | 0-0 | 3 | Thompson 2, McRoberts | 1300 |
| 10 | 10 | A | Kilmarnock | D 2-2 | 0-1 | 5 | Mackin, McIntosh | 1800 |
| 11 | 17 | H | Queen of the S | D 0-0 | 0-0 | 6 | | 3000 |
| 12 | 24 | A | Queen's Park | D 2-2 | 2-1 | 6 | Smith, Herd | 1045 |
| 13 | 31 | H | Dumbarton | D 1-1 | 0-1 | 5 | Brown | 2500 |
| 14 | Nov 7 | H | Raith R | L 1-2 | 1-1 | 7 | Oliver A. | 2500 |
| 15 | 14 | A | Ayr U | L 1-4 | 0-4 | 7 | McIntosh | 2124 |
| 16 | 21 | H | Motherwell | D 1-1 | 1-0 | 8 | Thompson | 3000 |
| 17 | 28 | H | Clydebank | W 3-0 | 1-0 | 7 | Oliver M., Mackin, Herd | 1200 |
| 18 | Dec 5 | A | Hamilton A | L 0-2 | 0-2 | 7 | | 1296 |
| 19 | Jan 19 | A | Queen of the S | W 4-0 | 3-0 | — | Mackin, Perry, Stevenson, Herd | 600 |
| 20 | 30 | H | Queen's Park | D 0-0 | 0-0 | 7 | | 1200 |
| 21 | Feb 6 | A | Dumbarton | L 1-3 | 0-1 | 7 | Mackin | 400 |
| 22 | 9 | A | Hearts | L 0-3 | 0-2 | — | | 2000 |
| 23 | 13 | H | Dunfermline Ath | D 0-0 | 0-0 | 7 | | 1200 |
| 24 | 17 | H | Kilmarnock | D 2-2 | 1-2 | — | Hoggan (pen), Herd | 2750 |
| 25 | 20 | H | East Stirling | W 2-0 | 1-0 | 8 | Perry, Stevenson | 2000 |
| 26 | 27 | A | Clydebank | W 2-0 | 0-0 | 7 | Smith, Ward | 700 |
| 27 | Mar 6 | A | Hearts | W 3-1 | 1-1 | 5 | Herd, Ward 2 | 2500 |
| 28 | 10 | A | St Johnstone | L 0-2 | 0-1 | — | | 950 |
| 29 | 13 | H | Dunfermline Ath | W 1-0 | 1-0 | 7 | Conn | 2000 |
| 30 | 20 | A | Kilmarnock | L 1-4 | 1-1 | 7 | Stevenson | 1900 |
| 31 | 27 | H | St Johnstone | W 2-1 | 0-0 | 7 | McIntosh, Conn | 2500 |
| 32 | Apr 3 | A | Queen of the S | D 1-1 | 1-1 | 8 | McIntosh | 500 |
| 33 | 7 | H | East Stirling | L 0-3 | 0-1 | — | | 1500 |
| 34 | 10 | A | Ayr U | L 0-1 | 0-1 | 8 | | 1218 |
| 35 | 17 | H | Motherwell | L 1-3 | 1-2 | 9 | Smith | 3000 |
| 36 | 24 | H | Raith R | W 3-2 | 2-0 | 8 | Ward, Smith, Hoggan (pen) | 2000 |
| 37 | May 1 | A | Hamilton A | L 0-1 | 0-0 | 8 | | 830 |
| 38 | 8 | A | Dumbarton | L 0-1 | 0-1 | 9 | | 500 |
| 39 | 15 | H | Queen's Park | D 1-1 | 0-0 | 9 | Herd | 1000 |

**Final League Position: 9**

### Goalscorers

*League* (49): Herd 10, Smith 7, McIntosh 5, Hoggan 4 (4 pens), Mackin 4, Ward 4, Stevenson 3, Thompson 3, Brown 2, Conn 2, Perry 2, McRoberts 1, Oliver A. 1, Oliver M. 1.
*League Cup* (11): Brown 5, Smith 4, Hoggan 1 (pen), McIntosh 1.
*Scottish Cup* (0).

**Honours**
*Scottish League:* Division 1 Runners-up 1907–08, 1909–10; Division 2 Champions 1935–36, 1969–70, 1974–75, 1979–80; Runners-up 1904–05, 1951–52, 1960–61.
*Scottish Cup:* Winners 1913, 1957.   *Scottish League Cup:* Runners-up 1947–48.
*Record Victory:* 12-1 v Laurieston, Scottish Cup 2nd rd, 23 March, 1893.
*Record Defeat:* 1-11 v Airdrieonians, Division 1, 28 Apr, 1951.
*Most League Points:* 59, Division 2, 1935–36.
*Most Individual League Goals in Season:* 43, Evelyn Morrison, Division 1, 1928–29.
*Most Capped Player:* Alec Parker, 14 (15), Scotland.

| Watson G. | Cowan K. | Nicol A. | Burrell A. | Brown B. | Mackin A. | Hay J. | Hogan W. | Thompson G. | Herd W. | Smith G. | Oliver A. | Gillen J. | Conn S. | McIntosh C. | Fowler C. | Perry J. | McRoberts A. | Stevenson W. | Rose A. | Oliver M. | Ward T. | McGivern J. | Lamont P. | Kettings P. | Match No. |
|---|---|---|---|---|---|---|---|---|---|---|---|---|---|---|---|---|---|---|---|---|---|---|---|---|---|
| 1 | 2 | 3 | 4 | 5 | 12† | 6 | 13 | 8 |  |  | 10* |  |  |  |  | 7 | 9 | 11 |  |  |  |  |  |  | 1 |
| 1 | 2 | 3 | 4 | 5 |  | 6 | 12 | 8 | 9 | 10* |  |  |  |  |  | 7 |  |  |  |  |  |  | 11 |  | 2 |
| 1 | 2 | 3 | 4 | 5 |  | 6 | 12 | 8 | 9 | 10 |  |  |  |  |  | 7 |  |  |  |  |  |  |  | 11* | 3 |
| 1 | 2 | 3 | 4 | 5 |  | 6 |  | 8 | 9 | 10* | 11 |  |  |  |  | 7 |  | 12 |  |  |  |  |  |  | 4 |
| 1 | 2 | 3 | 4 | 5 | 12 | 6 |  | 8 | 9† | 10 | 11* |  |  |  |  | 7 |  |  |  | 13 |  |  |  |  | 5 |
| 1 | 2 | 3 | 4 | 5 | 12 | 6 |  |  | 9 | 10 | 11 |  |  | 8* |  | 7 |  |  |  |  |  |  |  |  | 6 |
| 1 | 2 | 3 | 4 | 5 | 12† | 6 |  | 8 |  | 10 | 11* |  | 9 |  |  | 7 |  |  |  | 13 |  |  |  |  | 7 |
| 1 | 2 |  | 4 | 5 |  | 6 | 13 | 8 | 9 | 10* | 11† |  |  |  |  | 7 |  |  | 3 | 12 |  |  |  |  | 8 |
| 1 | 2 | 3 | 4 | 5 |  | 6 | 12 | 8* | 9 | 10 | 11 |  |  |  |  |  | 13 | 7† |  |  |  |  |  |  | 9 |
| 1 | 2 | 3 | 4 | 5 |  | 6 | 12 |  | 9 | 10* | 13 |  |  | 8 |  | 7 |  | 11† |  |  |  |  |  |  | 10 |
| 1 | 2 | 3* | 4 | 5 |  | 6 | 13 | 8 | 9 |  | 11 |  |  |  | 10 | 7† |  |  |  | 12 |  |  |  |  | 11 |
| 1 | 2 |  | 4 | 5 | 6* | 12 |  | 8 | 9 | 10† | 11 |  |  |  |  | 7 | 13 |  | 3 |  |  |  |  |  | 12 |
| 1 | 2 |  | 4 | 5 | 10† | 6 | 13 | 8 | 9 |  | 11 |  |  | 12 |  | 7* |  |  | 3 |  |  |  |  |  | 13 |
| 1 | 2 | 3 | 4 | 5 | 6 | 7* | 12 | 8 | 9 | 10 | 11† | 13 |  |  |  |  |  |  |  |  |  |  |  |  | 14 |
| 1 | 2 | 3† | 4 | 5 |  | 6 | 10 | 8 | 9 | 7* | 11 |  |  | 12 | 13 |  |  |  |  |  |  |  |  |  | 15 |
| 1 |  | 3 | 4 | 5 | 6 | 2 | 7 | 8 | 9 |  |  |  |  |  |  |  | 12 | 11* |  | 10 |  |  |  |  | 16 |
| 1 |  | 3 |  | 5 | 6* | 2 | 7 | 8 | 9† |  |  |  | 12 | 13 | 4 |  | 11 |  |  | 10 |  |  |  |  | 17 |
| 1 |  | 3 |  | 5 | 6* | 2 |  | 8 |  |  |  | 13 | 12 | 9 | 4 | 7† | 11 |  |  | 10 |  |  |  |  | 18 |
| 1 |  | 3 | 4 | 5 | 12 | 2 | 6 | 8 |  |  |  |  | 9 | 13 |  | 7* | 11† |  | 10 |  |  |  |  |  | 19 |
| 1 |  | 3 | 4 | 5 | 12 | 2 | 6 | 8 |  |  | 11* |  | 9 |  |  | 7 |  |  | 10 |  |  |  |  |  | 20 |
| 1 |  | 3 | 4 | 5 |  | 2 | 6 | 8 | 10 | 12 |  |  | 9 |  |  | 7* | 11† | 13 |  |  |  |  |  |  | 21 |
| 1 | 2 |  | 4 | 5 | 12 | 7 | 6 | 8 | 9 | 11† |  |  | 13 | 3 |  |  |  |  |  | 10* |  |  |  |  | 22 |
| 1 |  | 3 | 4 | 6* | 2 |  | 8 | 9 | 11 |  |  |  |  |  |  | 7 |  | 10 |  | 5 | 12 |  |  |  | 23 |
| 1 |  | 3 | 4 | 6 | 2 |  | 8 | 9 | 13 |  |  |  |  | 10* |  | 7 | 11† |  |  | 5 | 12 |  |  |  | 24 |
| 1 |  | 3 | 4 |  | 2 |  | 8 | 9 | 12 | 11 |  |  |  |  |  | 7 |  | 6 |  | 5 | 10* |  |  |  | 25 |
| 1 |  | 3 | 4 |  | 2 |  | 8 | 9 | 12 | 11† |  |  | 13 |  |  | 7 |  | 6 |  | 5 | 10* |  |  |  | 26 |
| 1 |  | 3 | 4 | 5 | 2 |  | 8 | 9 | 11* |  |  |  | 12 |  |  | 7 |  | 6 |  | 10 |  |  |  |  | 27 |
| 1 |  | 3 | 4 | 5 | 2† |  | 8 | 9 | 11* |  |  |  | 12 |  |  | 7 |  | 6 |  | 13 | 10 |  |  |  | 28 |
|  | 1 | 3 | 4 | 5 | 2 |  | 8 | 9 | 11 |  |  |  |  |  |  | 7 |  | 6 |  | 10 |  |  |  |  | 29 |
|  | 1 | 3 | 4 | 5 | 2 |  | 8 | 9 | 12 |  |  |  |  |  |  | 7 |  | 6 |  | 10* |  | 11 |  |  | 30 |
| 1 |  | 3 | 4 | 5 | 2 | 12 | 8 | 9 | 13 | 11 |  |  | 10 |  |  |  |  | 6* |  |  | 7† |  |  |  | 31 |
| 1 |  | 3 | 4 | 5 | 2 |  | 8 | 9 | 12 | 11 |  |  | 7 |  |  |  | 6† |  |  | 13 | 10* |  |  |  | 32 |
| 1 |  | 3 | 4 | 5 | 2 | 12 | 8 | 9* | 10 | 11 |  |  | 13 |  |  |  |  | 6 |  |  | 7† |  |  |  | 33 |
| 1 |  | 3 | 4 |  | 2 |  | 8 | 9 | 13 | 11† | 12 |  |  |  |  | 7 |  | 6 |  | 5 | 10* |  |  |  | 34 |
| 1 |  | 3 | 4 | 5 | 2 |  | 8 | 10 | 11* |  |  |  | 9 |  |  | 7 |  | 6 |  | 12 |  |  |  |  | 35 |
|  | 1 | 3 | 4 | 5 | 2 | 13 | 8 | 9 | 11 |  |  |  |  |  | 6* | 7 |  |  |  | 12 | 10 |  |  |  | 36 |
| 1 |  | 3 | 4 |  | 2 | 11 | 8† |  | 13 |  |  |  |  |  | 6 | 7 | 10* |  |  | 5 | 9 |  | 12 |  | 37 |
| 1 |  | 3 | 4 |  | 2 |  | 8 | 10 | 12 |  |  |  |  |  | 6 | 7* | 11 |  |  | 5 | 9 |  |  |  | 38 |
| 1 |  | 3 | 4 |  | 2 | 6 | 8 | 9 | 12 |  |  |  |  |  |  | 7 |  | 11* |  | 5 | 10 |  |  |  | 39 |
| 36 | 3 | 39 | 12 | 37 | 31 | 7 | 39 | 9 | 37 | 33 | 16 | 18 | 5 | 12 | 7 | 27 | 3 | 23 | 3 | 15 | 12 | — | 3 | 2 | |

```
         +       +        + + + +      +      + + +
        7s      13s     10s 2s 4s 8s 3s   4s   8s 2s 1s 1s
```

# FORFAR ATHLETIC Division 2

*Year Formed:* 1884.   *Ground:* Station Park.   *Size:* 115yd×69yd.   *Capacity:* 9300 (800 seated).
*Telephone:* Forfar 63576 and 62817.
*Manager:* Alex Rae.   *Secretary:* James Robertson.
*Assistant Manager and Trainer-coach:* Alex Carswell.
*Club Colours:* Sky blue shirts with white facings, white shorts, white stockings.
*Club Nickname:* Loons and Sky Blues.
*Record Attendance:* 10,780 v Rangers, Scottish Cup 2nd rd, 2 Feb, 1970.

## 1981−82 LEAGUE RECORD

| Match No. | Date | Venue | Opponents | Result | H/T Score | League Pos'n | Goalscorers | Attendance |
|---|---|---|---|---|---|---|---|---|
| 1 | Aug 29 | A | Alloa | W 2-1 | 1-0 | — | Clark, Hancock | 619 |
| 2 | Sept 5 | H | Berwick R | W 2-1 | 2-1 | 3 | Hancock, Brash (pen) | 1141 |
| 3 | 8 | H | Arbroath | W 6-0 | 0-0 | — | Hancock 2, Brash, Farningham, Rankin, Gallacher | 1444 |
| 4 | 12 | A | Clyde | D 1-1 | 1-0 | 1 | Farningham | 658 |
| 5 | 19 | A | Montrose | L 1-2 | 1-1 | 4 | Farningham | 650 |
| 6 | 26 | A | East Fife | W 4-0 | 0-0 | 3 | Bennett, Hancock, Clark 2 | 960 |
| 7 | Oct 3 | H | Stranraer | W 3-1 | 1-1 | 4 | Farningham, Clark 2 | 430 |
| 8 | 10 | H | Meadowbank T | D 1-1 | 0-0 | 5 | Brash (pen) | 850 |
| 9 | 17 | A | Albion R | D 3-3 | 2-1 | 4 | Hancock, Watt 2 | 426 |
| 10 | 20 | H | Stirling Albion | W 3-1 | 1-0 | — | Craig, Hancock, Allan | 320 |
| 11 | 24 | A | Cowdenbeath | D 1-1 | 0-0 | 3 | Watt | 500 |
| 12 | 27 | H | Brechin C | L 0-1 | 0-0 | — | | 2000 |
| 13 | 31 | H | Stenhousemuir | W 2-0 | 2-0 | 2 | McPhee, Hancock | 937 |
| 14 | Nov 7 | A | Berwick R | D 1-1 | 1-1 | 3 | Craig | 900 |
| 15 | 14 | A | Alloa | D 0-0 | 0-0 | 3 | | 980 |
| 16 | 21 | A | Brechin C | D 0-0 | 0-0 | 3 | | 700 |
| 17 | 28 | H | East Fife | W 1-0 | 1-0 | 2 | McPhee | 908 |
| 18 | Dec 5 | A | Stranraer | L 1-2 | 0-0 | 4 | McPhee | 506 |
| 19 | Jan 2 | A | Arbroath | D 1-1 | 0-1 | 5 | Clark | 1435 |
| 20 | Feb 6 | H | Cowdenbeath | W 4-0 | 2-0 | 5 | Farningham, Bennett, Porter, Hancock | 667 |
| 21 | 17 | A | Stenhousemuir | D 0-0 | 0-0 | — | | 685 |
| 22 | 20 | H | Clyde | D 0-0 | 0-0 | 5 | | 1158 |
| 23 | 23 | A | Meadowbank T | D 1-1 | 1-1 | — | Gallacher | 427 |
| 24 | 27 | A | East Fife | L 0-1 | 0-0 | 6 | | 527 |
| 25 | Mar 10 | A | Stirling Albion | D 0-0 | 0-0 | — | | 647 |
| 26 | 13 | A | Cowdenbeath | L 1-3 | 0-2 | 6 | Brown | 440 |
| 27 | 17 | H | Montrose | W 2-1 | 1-1 | — | McPhee, Alexander | 865 |
| 28 | 20 | H | Stranraer | W 3-0 | 2-0 | 6 | Gallacher, Porter, Leitch | 952 |
| 29 | 24 | H | Clyde | L 1-3 | 0-1 | — | Clark | 1341 |
| 30 | 27 | A | Stirling Albion | L 0-2 | 0-2 | 6 | | 700 |
| 31 | Apr 10 | A | Stenhousemuir | W 1-0 | 0-0 | 6 | Porter | 200 |
| 32 | 14 | A | Albion R | W 3-1 | 2-0 | — | Gallacher, Brash, Allan | 860 |
| 33 | 17 | A | Meadowbank T | W 5-2 | 1-1 | 6 | Allan 2, Clark 2, Porter | 400 |
| 34 | 21 | H | Arbroath | D 1-1 | 0-0 | — | Porter | 453 |
| 35 | 24 | H | Brechin C | D 0-0 | 0-0 | 5 | | 1307 |
| 36 | 28 | H | Albion R | W 3-0 | 2-0 | — | Gallacher 2, Porter | 420 |
| 37 | May 1 | H | Montrose | D 0-0 | 0-0 | 5 | | 875 |
| 38 | 8 | A | Berwick R | L 1-2 | 1-1 | 5 | Gallacher | 722 |
| 39 | 15 | H | Alloa | L 0-1 | 0-1 | 6 | | 1247 |

**Final League Position: 6**

### Goalscorers

*League* (59): Clark 9, Hancock 9, Gallacher 7, Porter 6, Farningham 5, Allan 4, Brash 4 (2 pens), McPhee 4, Watt 3, Bennett 2, Craig 2, Alexander 1, Brown 1, Leitch 1, Rankin 1.
*League Cup* (16): Hancock 4, Morris 3, Allan 2, Clark 2, Rankin 2, Craig 1, Gallacher 1, own goal 1.
*Scottish Cup* (10): Brash 3 (1 pen), Clark 2, Hancock 2, Gallacher 1, Leitch 1, Mitchell 1.

**Honours**
*Scottish League Cup* – Semi-Finalists 1977–78.
*Scottish Cup* – Semi-Finalists 1981–82.
*Forfarshire Cup* – Winners 9 times.
*Record Victory:* 14-1 v Lindertis, Scottish Cup 1st rd, 1 Sept, 1888.
*Record Defeat:* 2-12 v King's Park, Division 2, 2 Jan, 1930.
*Most League Points:* 47, Division 2, 1968–69, 1979–80.
*Most Individual League Goals in Season:* Davie Kilgour, 45, Division 2, 1929–30.

| Kennedy S. | Boardley I. | Gardiner J. | Bennett W. | McPhee I. | Morris R. | Brown K. | Brash A. | Allan J. | Craig C. | Gallacher W. | Farningham R. | Hancock S. | Clark J. | Downie T. | Alexander M. | Watt N. | Leitch G. | Porter J. S. | Redford G. | Mitchell J. | Rankin B. | Match No. |
|---|---|---|---|---|---|---|---|---|---|---|---|---|---|---|---|---|---|---|---|---|---|---|
| 1 |  | 2 | 13 | 11 | 4 |  | 5 | 7 | 8 | 9 | 10* |  |  |  | 12 |  | 6† |  |  |  | 3 | 1 |
| 1 |  | 2 | 11 | 8 | 4 | 5 | 6 | 10 | 7* | 9 | 12 |  |  |  |  |  |  |  |  |  | 3 | 2 |
| 1 |  | 2 | 11 | 8 | 4 | 5 | 6 | 10† | 7* | 9 | 13 | 12 |  |  |  |  |  |  |  |  | 3 | 3 |
| 1 |  | 2 | 11 | 8 | 4 | 5 | 6 | 10 | 7 | 9 |  |  |  |  |  |  |  |  |  |  | 3 | 4 |
| 1 |  | 2 | 8 | 4 | 5 | 6* | 10 | 7 | 9 | 13 | 12 | 11† |  |  |  |  |  |  |  |  | 3 |  | 5 |
| 1 |  | 2 | 8 | 4 | 5 | 3 | 10 | 7 | 9 | 12 | 11* | 6 |  |  |  |  |  |  |  |  |  | 6 |
| 1 | 3 |  | 2 | 4 | 5 | 6 | 12 | 7 | 8 | 9*10 |  | 11 |  |  |  |  |  |  |  |  |  | 7 |
| 1 | 3 |  | 2 | 4 | 5 | 6 | 12 | 7 | 8 | 9 | 10* | 11 |  |  |  |  |  |  |  |  |  | 8 |
| 1 | 3 |  | 2 | 4 | 5 | 6 | 7*12 | 8 | 9 | 13 | 10†11 |  |  |  |  |  |  |  |  |  |  | 9 |
| 1 | 3 |  | 2 | 4 | 5 | 6 | 7 | 12 | 8 | 9 | 10*11 |  |  |  |  |  |  |  |  |  |  | 10 |
| 1 | 3 |  | 2 | 4 | 5 | 6* | 7 | 12 | 8 | 9 | 10 | 11 |  |  |  |  |  |  |  |  |  | 11 |
| 1 | 3 |  | 2 | 4 | 5 | 6 | 7*12 | 8 | 9 | 13 | 10†11 |  |  |  |  |  |  |  |  |  |  | 12 |
| 1 | 3 | 6 | 2 | 4 | 5 | 7 | 11 | 8 | 9 | 12 | 10* |  |  |  |  |  |  |  |  |  |  | 13 |
| 1 | 3 | 6 | 2 | 4 | 5 | 13 | 7*10 | 8 | 9 | 11†12 |  |  |  |  |  |  |  |  |  |  |  | 14 |
| 1 | 3 | 6 | 2 | 4 | 5 | 7*10 | 8 | 9 | 11 |  | 12 |  |  |  |  |  |  |  |  |  |  | 15 |
| 1 |  | 3 | 6 | 2 | 4 | 5 | 10 | 7 | 8 | 9 | 12 | 11* |  |  |  |  |  |  |  |  |  | 16 |
| 1 |  | 3 | 11 | 2 | 4 | 5 | 6 | 12 | 7* | 8 | 9 | 10 |  |  |  |  |  |  |  |  |  | 17 |
| 1 |  | 3 | 11 | 2 | 4 | 5 | 6 | 12 | 7* | 8 | 9 | 10† | 13 |  |  |  |  |  |  |  |  | 18 |
| 1 |  | 3 | 6 | 2 | 4 | 5 | 10 | 7 | 8 | 9†13 | 11* |  | 12 |  |  |  |  |  |  |  |  | 19 |
| 1 |  | 2 | 3 | 4 |  | 5 | 6 |  | 8 | 9 | 11* | 12 | 10 | 7 |  |  |  |  |  |  |  | 20 |
| 1 |  | 2 | 3 | 4 | 7 | 5 | 6 | 13 | 8 | 9 | 11* | 10†12 |  |  |  |  |  |  |  |  |  | 21 |
| 1 |  | 2 | 3 | 4 | 7 | 5 | 12 | 8 | 9*10 |  | 6 | 11 |  |  |  |  |  |  |  |  |  | 22 |
| 1 |  | 2 | 3 | 4 | 7 | 5 | 6† | 10 | 8 | 9*12 | 13 | 11 |  |  |  |  |  |  |  |  |  | 23 |
| 1 |  | 2 | 3 |  | 7 | 5 | 6 | 13 | 10* | 8 | 9†12 | 4 | 11 |  |  |  |  |  |  |  |  | 24 |
| 1 |  | 3 |  | 4 | 5 | 6 | 13 | 7† | 2 | 9 | 11* | 12 | 8 | 10 |  |  |  |  |  |  |  | 25 |
| 1 |  | 2 | 3 | 4 | 5 | 6 |  | 8 | 9 | 11 | 10 | 7 |  |  |  |  |  |  |  |  |  | 26 |
| 1 |  | 2 | 3 | 6† | 4 | 5 | 13 | 12 | 8 | 9* | 7 | 10 | 11 |  |  |  |  |  |  |  |  | 27 |
| 1 |  | 2 | 3 | 4 | 5 | 6 | 13 | 7* | 8 | 12 | 9† | 10 | 11 |  |  |  |  |  |  |  |  | 28 |
| 1 |  | 2 | 3 | 4 | 5 | 6†13 | 7* | 8 | 12 | 9 | 10 | 11 |  |  |  |  |  |  |  |  |  | 29 |
| 1 |  | 3 |  | 4 | 5 | 6 | 9 | 2 | 10†11*13 | 8 | 7 | 12 |  |  |  |  |  |  |  |  |  | 30 |
| 1 |  | 2 | 3 |  | 5 | 12 | 7 | 8 | 9 | 11 | 6 | 10 | 4* |  |  |  |  |  |  |  |  | 31 |
| 1 |  | 2 | 3 |  | 5 | 9 | 7 | 8 | 6 | 4 | 10 | 11 |  |  |  |  |  |  |  |  |  | 32 |
| 1 |  | 2 | 3 | 4 | 5 | 9*13 | 7†8 | 6 | 11 | 10 | 12 |  |  |  |  |  |  |  |  |  |  | 33 |
| 1 |  | 2 | 3 |  | 5 | 13 | 7* | 8 | 6 | 4 | 12 | 9 | 10†11 |  |  |  |  |  |  |  |  | 34 |
| 1 |  | 2 | 3 | 4 | 5 | 9*13 | 7 | 8 | 6†11 | 10 | 12 |  |  |  |  |  |  |  |  |  |  | 35 |
| 1 |  | 2 | 3 | 4 | 5 |  | 6 | 8 | 9 | 7 | 10 | 11 |  |  |  |  |  |  |  |  |  | 36 |
| 1 |  | 2 | 3 | 10 | 4 | 5 | 6 | 8 | 12 | 9* | 7 | 13 | 11† |  |  |  |  |  |  |  |  | 37 |
| 1 |  | 2 | 3 | 4 |  | 5 | 13 | 6 | 8 | 9 | 11 | 12 | 10† | 7* |  |  |  |  |  |  |  | 38 |
| 1 |  | 2 | 3 | 4 |  | 5 | 7* | 6 | 8 | 9 | 13 | 11† | 10 | 12 |  |  |  |  |  |  |  | 39 |
| 17 | 17 | 5 | 37 | 30 | 27 | 33 | 36 | 30 | 8 | 30 | 39 | 33 | 19 | 4 | 7 | 8 | 27 | 16 | 1 | — | 5 |  |

|  |  | + |  |  | + | + | + |  |  |  |  |  | + | + |  | + | + | + | + | + | + |  |
|  |  | 1s |  |  | 3s | 12s | 7s |  |  |  |  |  | 1s | 12s |  | 2s | 8s | 4s | 4s | 1s | 2s |  |

# HAMILTON ACADEMICAL  Division 1

*Year Formed:* 1875.
*Ground:* Douglas Park (since 1888). *Size:* 104yd×72yd. *Capacity:* 14,065 (1065 seated).
*Telephone:* Hamilton 286103.
*Manager:* David McParland.
*Secretary:* Joseph Friel. *PRO:* Alan Dick. *Physiotherapist:* R. Reid. *Coach:* P. Barkey.
*Club Colours:* Red and white hooped shirts, white shorts with white stockings.
*Club Nickname:* The Accies.
*Record Attendance:* 28,690 v Hearts, Scottish Cup 3rd rd, 3 Mar, 1937.
*Previous Grounds:* Bent Farm, South Avenue, South Haugh.
*Record Transfer Fee Received:* £30,000 from Dundee United for Paul Hegarty, Nov 1974.
*Record Transfer Fee Paid:* £15,000 to Motherwell for Bobby Graham, July 1977.

## 1981–82 LEAGUE RECORD

| Match No. | Date | Venue | Opponents | Result | | H/T Score | League Pos'n | Goalscorers | Atten- dance |
|---|---|---|---|---|---|---|---|---|---|
| 1 | Aug 29 | H | Raith R | W | 1-0 | 1-0 | — | Brown | 1348 |
| 2 | Sept 5 | A | Ayr U | L | 0-2 | 0-2 | 8 | | 2429 |
| 3 | 8 | A | Motherwell | D | 2-2 | 2-0 | — | Craig, Howie | 2310 |
| 4 | 12 | H | East Stirling | D | 1-1 | 0-0 | 9 | Donnelly | 925 |
| 5 | 16 | A | Hearts | L | 1-2 | 0-1 | — | Wright | 3500 |
| 6 | 19 | H | Dunfermline Ath | L | 0-2 | 0-0 | 11 | | 1118 |
| 7 | 26 | H | Queen of the S | L | 2-3 | 1-1 | 12 | Fairlie, Howie | 883 |
| 8 | Oct 3 | A | Falkirk | L | 0-3 | 0-0 | 13 | | 1500 |
| 9 | 10 | A | Dumbarton | W | 2-1 | 1-1 | 12 | Craig 2 | 500 |
| 10 | 17 | H | Kilmarnock | L | 1-2 | 0-0 | 13 | Fairlie (pen) | 1747 |
| 11 | 20 | A | Clydebank | L | 1-2 | 1-0 | — | Craig | 590 |
| 12 | 24 | A | St Johnstone | D | 1-1 | 1-0 | 12 | McDowall | 1797 |
| 13 | 31 | A | Queen's Park | W | 2-1 | 0-1 | 11 | McDowall 2 | 1668 |
| 14 | Nov 7 | H | Ayr U | W | 1-0 | 1-0 | 11 | Craig | 1579 |
| 15 | 14 | A | Raith R | L | 0-2 | 0-1 | 11 | | 1500 |
| 16 | 21 | H | Hearts | L | 0-2 | 0-1 | 13 | | 2200 |
| 17 | 28 | A | Queen of the S | W | 4-2 | 1-1 | 12 | Brown 2, Fairlie, Wilson | 1000 |
| 18 | Dec 5 | A | Falkirk | W | 2-0 | 2-0 | 10 | Brown, McDowall | 1296 |
| 19 | 12 | H | Clydebank | L | 0-2 | 0-1 | 10 | | 1033 |
| 20 | Jan 16 | A | Kilmarnock | D | 2-2 | 2-2 | 10 | Donnelly 2 | 1750 |
| 21 | 30 | H | St Johnstone | D | 0-0 | 0-0 | 10 | | 1067 |
| 22 | Feb 6 | A | Queen's Park | L | 0-2 | 0-1 | 12 | | 972 |
| 23 | 10 | A | Dunfermline Ath | W | 3-1 | 2-0 | — | Wright, Donnelly, McDowall | 1500 |
| 24 | 13 | H | Motherwell | W | 1-0 | 0-0 | 8 | Donnelly | 4049 |
| 25 | 17 | A | East Stirling | W | 5-1 | 2-0 | — | Craig, Fairlie 2 (2 pens), Donnelly, Deeney | 231 |
| 26 | 20 | H | Clydebank | W | 3-1 | 2-0 | 6 | McLauchlan (og), Brown, Wilson | 1040 |
| 27 | 27 | A | Dunfermline Ath | D | 1-1 | 0-1 | 8 | Fairlie | 1500 |
| 28 | Mar 6 | A | Raith R | W | 2-1 | 0-1 | 8 | Craig, Wright | 1500 |
| 29 | 13 | H | St Johnstone | W | 2-0 | 1-0 | 8 | Craig, Fairlie | 1277 |
| 30 | 20 | A | Motherwell | L | 2-3 | 1-2 | 8 | Wright, Howie | 4030 |
| 31 | 27 | A | Queen of the S | W | 3-0 | 1-0 | 8 | Fairlie 2 (1 pen), Deeney | 500 |
| 32 | Apr 3 | H | Queen's Park | W | 2-0 | 1-0 | 6 | Donnelly, McAdams | 1056 |
| 33 | 10 | H | Hearts | L | 0-2 | 0-0 | 7 | | 3432 |
| 34 | 17 | A | Kilmarnock | D | 0-0 | 0-0 | 7 | | 1900 |
| 35 | 21 | H | Dumbarton | D | 0-0 | 0-0 | — | | 1004 |
| 36 | 24 | A | Ayr U | L | 2-3 | 1-2 | 7 | Craig, McDowall | 1079 |
| 37 | May 1 | H | Falkirk | W | 1-0 | 0-0 | 7 | Fairlie (pen) | 830 |
| 38 | 8 | A | East Stirling | L | 1-2 | 1-1 | 7 | Wright | 222 |
| 39 | 15 | H | Dumbarton | W | 1-0 | 1-0 | 7 | McGowan M. (og) | 686 |

**Final League Position: 7**

### Goalscorers

*League (52):* Fairlie 10 (5 pens), Craig 9, Donnelly 7, McDowall 6, Brown 5, Wright 5, Howie 3, Deeney 2, Wilson 2, McAdams 1, own goals 2.
*League Cup (14):* Deeney 6, McDowall 3, Paton 2, Callan 1, Donnelly 1, Howie 1.
*Scottish Cup (2):* Fairlie 1, Howie 1.

**Honours**

*Scottish League:* Division 2 Champions 1903–04; Runners-up 1952–53, 1964–65.
*Scottish Cup:* Runners-up 1911, 1935.   *Lanarkshire Cup:* 9 times winners.
*Best Season:* 4th in Division 1, 1934–35.
*Record Victory:* 10-2 v Cowdenbeath, Division 1, 15 Oct, 1932.
*Record Defeat:* 1-11 v Hibernian, Division 1, 6 Nov, 1965.
*Most League Points:* 55, Division 2, 1973–74.
*Most League Goals:* 92, Division 1, 1932–33.
*Most Individual League Goals in a Season:* 34, David Wilson, 1936–37.
*Highest Scorer in Total Aggregate:* 246, David Wilson, 1928–39.
*Most Capped Players:* Jimmy King, 2, Bobby Howe, 2, Scotland.
*Extra Information:* The hat-trick by John Brown v Berwick R, 9 Aug, 1980, is the only one (without the aid of a penalty) by a full-back in Scottish League history.

| Ferguson R. | Moffat J. | Frew J. | Brown J. | Wright B. | McDougall A. | Blackley J. | Fairlie J. | McDowall G. | Craig J. | McAdams P. | Howie N. | Donnelly T. | Mitchell G. | Marshall G. | Deeney J. | Paton W. | Colgan G. | McGrogan J. | Alexander E. | Wilson T. | Anderson P. | Callan G. | Hamill S. | Match No. |
|---|---|---|---|---|---|---|---|---|---|---|---|---|---|---|---|---|---|---|---|---|---|---|---|---|
| 1 | 2 | 3 | 4 | 5 | 6 |  | 8 | 9†| 10 | 11 | | 7* | 12 | | 13 | | | | | | | | | 1 |
| 1 | 2 | 3 | 4 | 5 | 6 | 7 | 8 | 9 | 10 | | 11* | | 12 | | | | | | | | | | | 2 |
| 1 | 2 | 3 | 4 | 5 | 6 | 7 | 8* | 9 | 10 | | 11 | | 12 | | | | | | | | | | | 3 |
| 1 | 2 | 3 | 4 | 5 | 6 | 7 | 8 | 9 | 10* | | 11† | | 12 | | 13 | | | | | | | | | 4 |
| 1 | 2* | 3 | 4 | 5 | 6 | 7 | 8 | 9 | 10 | | 11 | | 12 | | | | | | | | | | | 5 |
| 1 | 2* | 3 | 4 | 5 | 6 | 7 | 8 | 9† | 10 | | 11 | | 12 | | 13 | | | | | | | | | 6 |
| 1 | 2 | 3 | 4 | 5 | 6 | 7 | 8 | 9 | 10* | | 11† | | 12 | | 13 | | | | | | | | | 7 |
| 1 | 2 | 3* | 4 | 5 | 6 | 7 | 8 | 9 | 10 | | 11 | | 12 | | | | | | | | | | | 8 |
| 1 | 2 | 3 | 4 | 5 | 6 | 7 | 8 | 9 | 10* | | 11† | | 12 | | 13 | | | | | | | | | 9 |
| 1 | 2 | 3 | 4 | 5 | 6* | 7 | 8 | 9 | 10† | | 11 | | 12 | | 13 | | | | | | | | | 10 |
| 1 | 2 | 3 | 4 | 5 | 6 | 7 | 8 | 9 | 10 | | 11* | | 12 | | | | | | | | | | | 11 |
| 1 | 2 | 3 | 4 | 5 | 6 | 7 | 8* | 9 | 10 | | 11† | | 12 | | 13 | | | | | | | | | 12 |
| 1 | 2 | 3 | 12 | 5 | 6 | 7 | 8 | 9 | 10 | 13 | 11† | | 4* | | | | | | | | | | | 13 |
| 1 | 2 | 3 | 4 | 5 | 6 | 7 | 8 | 9 | 10 | 11 | | | | | | | | | | | | | | 14 |
| 1 | 2* | 3 | 4 | 5 | 6 | 7 | 8 | 9† | 10 | 11 | | | 12 | | 13 | | | | | | | | | 15 |
| 1 | 2 | 3 | 4 | 5 | 6 | | 8 | 9* | 10 | | 11† | 7 | 12 | | 13 | | | | | | | | | 16 |
| 1 | | | 4 | 5 | 6 | | 8 | 9 | 10 | | 11* | 7 | 12 | | | | 3 | | | 2 | | | | 17 |
| 1 | | | 4 | 5 | 6 | | 8 | 9 | 10 | | 11* | 7 | 12 | | | | 3 | | | 2 | | | | 18 |
| 1 | | | 4 | 5 | 6 | | 8 | 9† | 10 | | 11 | 7 | 12 | | 13 | | 3* | | | 2 | | | | 19 |
| 1 | 2 | 3 | 4 | 5 | 6* | | 8 | 9 | 10 | | | 7 | 12 | | | | | | 11 | | | | | 20 |
| 1 | 2 | 3 | 4 | 5 | 6 | | 8 | 9 | 10 | | | 7 | 12 | | | | | | 11* | | | | | 21 |
| 1 | 2 | 3 | 4 | 5 | 6* | | 8 | 9 | 10 | 11 | | 7† | 12 | | 13 | | | | | | | | | 22 |
| 1 | 2 | 3 | 4 | 5 | 6 | | 8 | 9 | 10 | | | 7* | 12 | | 13 | | | | 11† | | | | | 23 |
| 1 | 2 | 3 | 4 | 5 | 6 | | 8 | 9 | 10 | | | 7 | 12 | | | | | | 11* | | | | | 24 |
| 1 | 2 | 3 | 4 | 5 | 6 | | 8 | 9 | 10 | | | 7* | 12 | | | | | | 11 | | | | | 25 |
| 1 | 2 | 3 | 4 | 5 | 6 | | 8 | 9 | 10 | | | 7* | 12 | | | | | | 11 | | | | | 26 |
| 1 | 2 | 3 | 4 | 5 | 6 | | 8 | 9 | 10 | | | 7 | 12 | | | | | | 11* | | | | | 27 |
| 1 | 2 | 3 | 4 | 5 | 6 | | 8* | 9 | 10 | | | 7 | 12 | | | | | | 11 | | | | | 28 |
| 1 | 2 | 3 | 4 | 5 | 6 | | 8* | 9 | 10 | | | 7 | 12 | | | | | | 11 | | | | | 29 |
| 1 | 2 | 3 | 4 | 5 | 6 | | 8 | 9* | 10 | | | 7 | 12 | | | | | | 11 | | | | | 30 |
| 1 | 2 | 3 | 4 | 5 | 6 | | 8 | 9* | 10 | | | 7 | 12 | | 13 | | | | 11† | | | | | 31 |
| 1 | 2 | | 4 | 5 | 6 | | 8* | 9† | 10 | | | 7 | 12 | | 13 | | 3 | | 11 | | | | | 32 |
| 1 | 2 | | 4 | 5 | 6 | | 8* | 9 | 10 | | | 7 | 12 | | 13 | | 3 | | 11† | | | | | 33 |
| 1 | 2 | | 4 | 5 | 6* | | 8† | 9 | 10 | | | 7 | 12 | | 13 | | 3 | | 11 | | | | | 34 |
| 1 | | | 4 | 5 | 6 | | 8 | 9† | 10 | | | 7* | 12 | | 13 | | 3 | | 11 | 2 | | | | 35 |
| 1 | 2 | | 4 | 5 | 6 | | 8* | 9 | 10 | | | 7 | 12 | | 13 | | 3 | | 11† | | | | | 36 |
| 1 | | | 4 | 5 | 6 | | 8 | 9 | 10 | | | 7 | | | 13 | | 3 | | 11† | 2 | | | | 37 |
| 1 | | | 4 | 5 | 6† | | 8 | 9 | 10 | | | 7 | 12 | | 13 | | 3* | | 11 | 2 | | | | 38 |
| 1 | | 3 | 4 | 5 | 6 | | 8 | 9† | 10 | | | 7* | 12 | | 13 | | | | 11 | 2 | | | | 39 |
| 36 | 3 | 31 | 28 | 36 | 39 | 19 | 33 | 36 | 32 | 10 | 11 | 26 | 32 | 2 | 7 | 2 | 10 | 3 | 10 | 19 | 2 | — | 2 | |

+ 1s (subs): Moffat 1s, Wright 1s, Blackley 1s, McAdams 1s, Howie 3s, Donnelly 12s, Mitchell 6s, Marshall 5s, Deeney 2s, Paton 8s, Colgan 2s, McGrogan 5s, Alexander 3s, Wilson 4s, Anderson 2s, Callan 2s, Hamill 1s

# HEART OF MIDLOTHIAN Division 1

*Year Formed:* 1874.
*Ground:* Tynecastle Park, Gorgie Road, Edinburgh EH11 2NL. *Size:* 110yd×76yd. *Capacity:* 23,450 (7000 seats).
*Telephone:* 031-337 6132.
*Manager:* Alex MacDonald.
*Secretary:* L. W. Porteous. *Trainer:* Andy Stevenson.
*Club Colours:* Maroon shirts, white collar and cuffs, white shorts, maroon stockings with white tops.
*Club Nickname:* Jam Tarts.
*Record Attendance:* 53,496 v Rangers, Scottish Cup 3rd rd, 13 Feb, 1932.
*Previous Grounds:* The Meadows, 1873–78; Powderhall, 1878–81; Tynecastle, 1881–86; Tyneside Park, 1886–
*Record Transfer Fee Received:* £200,000 from Chelsea for Eamonn Bannon, Jan 1979.
*Record Transfer Fee Paid:* £100,000 to Dundee U for Willie Pettigrew, Sept 1981.
**European Competitions:** *European Cup 1958–59, 1960–61; Fairs Cup 1961–62, 1963–64, 1965–66; European Cup-Winners' Cup 1976–77.*

## 1981–82 LEAGUE RECORD

| Match No. | Date | Venue | Opponents | Result | | H/T Score | League Pos'n | Goalscorers | Atten-dance |
|---|---|---|---|---|---|---|---|---|---|
| 1 | Aug 29 | A | Dunfermline Ath | D | 1-1 | 0-1 | — | Liddell G. | 4300 |
| 2 | Sept 5 | H | Kilmarnock | L | 0-1 | 0-1 | 12 | | 4796 |
| 3 | 12 | A | Falkirk | D | 0-0 | 0-0 | 12 | | 6500 |
| 4 | 16 | H | Hamilton A | W | 2-1 | 1-0 | — | Mackay, Hamill | 3500 |
| 5 | 19 | H | Clydebank | W | 1-0 | 0-0 | 7 | O'Connor | 6000 |
| 6 | 23 | A | Ayr U | D | 0-0 | 0-0 | — | | 3500 |
| 7 | 26 | H | Dumbarton | W | 2-1 | 1-0 | 4 | MacDonald R., O'Connor | 3627 |
| 8 | Oct 3 | A | Queen's Park | L | 0-1 | 0-0 | 7 | | 2450 |
| 9 | 7 | H | St Johnstone | W | 3-1 | 1-0 | — | O'Connor 2, Pettigrew | 4077 |
| 10 | 10 | A | Queen of the S | W | 2-1 | 1-0 | 3 | Shields, Addison | 2400 |
| 11 | 17 | H | Raith R | W | 2-1 | 2-0 | 3 | MacDonald R., Liddell G. | 5001 |
| 12 | 24 | A | Motherwell | D | 2-2 | 1-1 | 3 | Pettigrew 2 | 7662 |
| 13 | 31 | H | East Stirling | L | 0-1 | 0-0 | 4 | | 5093 |
| 14 | Nov 7 | A | Kilmarnock | D | 0-0 | 0-0 | 4 | | 3400 |
| 15 | 14 | H | Dunfermline Ath | D | 1-1 | 1-0 | 3 | Robertson C. | 5570 |
| 16 | 21 | A | Hamilton A | W | 2-0 | 1-0 | 4 | Mackay, Addison | 2200 |
| 17 | 28 | A | Dumbarton | L | 1-3 | 0-1 | 4 | Marinello | 1200 |
| 18 | Dec 5 | H | Queen's Park | D | 1-1 | 0-0 | 5 | Pettigrew | 3516 |
| 19 | Jan 30 | H | Motherwell | L | 0-3 | 0-1 | 6 | | 11,054 |
| 20 | Feb 6 | A | East Stirling | W | 1-0 | 1-0 | 6 | Byrne | 1100 |
| 21 | 9 | H | Falkirk | W | 3-0 | 2-0 | — | McCoy, Marinello, Pettigrew | 2000 |
| 22 | 17 | H | Queen of the S | W | 4-1 | 2-1 | — | Robertson C., McCoy, MacDonald R., Pettigrew | 2397 |
| 23 | 20 | A | Ayr U | W | 3-0 | 1-0 | 2 | McCoy, Pettigrew, Byrne | 2902 |
| 24 | 23 | A | St Johnstone | L | 1-2 | 1-0 | — | McCoy | 2300 |
| 25 | 27 | H | Raith R | W | 4-0 | 2-0 | 2 | Robertson C., McCoy 2, Bowman | 4000 |
| 26 | Mar 6 | A | Falkirk | L | 1-3 | 1-1 | 2 | Robertson C. | 2500 |
| 27 | 13 | A | Queen of the S | W | 5-1 | 2-0 | 2 | Pettigrew 3, Addison, Byrne | 2620 |
| 28 | 20 | H | Queen's Park | W | 1-0 | 0-0 | 2 | Byrne | 3777 |
| 29 | 27 | A | Clydebank | L | 1-2 | 0-0 | 3 | Byrne (pen) | 1731 |
| 30 | 31 | H | Raith R | W | 3-0 | 0-0 | — | McCoy 2, MacDonald R. | 2500 |
| 31 | Apr 3 | H | St Johnstone | W | 3-0 | 2-0 | 2 | MacDonald R., Robertson 2 | 4577 |
| 32 | 10 | A | Hamilton A | W | 2-0 | 0-0 | 2 | MacDonald A., Pettigrew | 3432 |
| 33 | 14 | A | Clydebank | W | 5-1 | 3-1 | — | Pettigrew 4, Byrne | 960 |
| 34 | 21 | H | Ayr U | W | 2-1 | 0-0 | — | Hamill, Addison | 4675 |
| 35 | 24 | A | Dunfermline Ath | W | 2-1 | 0-1 | 2 | Robertson C., MacDonald R. | 1620 |
| 36 | 27 | H | East Stirling | W | 2-0 | 0-0 | — | Byrne (pen), McCoy | 4300 |
| 37 | May 1 | H | Dumbarton | L | 2-5 | 2-1 | 2 | Byrne, Pettigrew | 4861 |
| 38 | 8 | A | Kilmarnock | D | 0-0 | 0-0 | 2 | | 10,000 |
| 39 | 15 | H | Motherwell | L | 0-1 | 0-1 | 3 | | 14,709 |

**Final League Position: 3**

**Goalscorers**
*League* (65): Pettigrew 16, McCoy 9, Byrne 8 (2 pens), Robertson C. 7, MacDonald R. 6, Addison 4, O'Connor 4, Hamill 2, Liddell G. 2, Mackay 2, Marinello 2, Bowman 1, MacDonald A. 1, Shields 1.
*League Cup* (5): Liddell G. 2, Robertson C. 2, McCoy 1.
*Scottish Cup* (4): Byrne 1, MacDonald R. 1, Marinello 1, Robertson C. 1.

**Honours**

*Scottish League* – Division 1 Champions 1894–95, 1896–97, 1957–58, 1959–60, 1979–80; Runners-up 1893–94, 1898–99, 1903–04, 1905–06, 1914–15, 1937–38, 1953–54, 1956–57, 1958–59, 1964–65, 1977–78.
*Scottish Cup* – Winners 1891, 1896, 1901, 1906, 1956; Runners-up 1903, 1907, 1968, 1976.
*Scottish League Cup* – Winners 1954–55, 1958–59, 1959–60, 1962–63; Runners-up 1961–62.
*Record Victory:* 15-0 v King's Park, Scottish Cup 2nd rd, 13 Feb, 1937.
*Record Defeat:* 0-7 v Hibernian, Division 1, 1 Jan, 1973.
*Most League Points:* 62, Division 1, 1957–58.
*Most League Goals:* 132, Division 1, 1957–58. (Record for Division 1.)
*Most Individual Goals in Season:* Barney Battles, 44, 1930–31.
*Highest Scorer in Total Aggregate:* Jimmy Wardhaugh, 206, 1946–59.
*Most Capped Player:* Bobby Walker, 29, Scotland.

| Brough J. | Smith H. | Kidd W. | Shields P. | Byrne P. | MacDonald R. | McNeil B. | Liddell G. | Robertson C. | Pettigrew W. | O'Connor D. | Bowman D. | Hamill A. | Addison D. | Mackay G. | Strickland D. | MacLaren S. | McCoy G. | O'Brien P. | MacDonald A. | Marinello P. | More C. | Robertson J. | Gauld S. | Match No. |
|---|---|---|---|---|---|---|---|---|---|---|---|---|---|---|---|---|---|---|---|---|---|---|---|---|
| 1 | 11 | 3 | 4 | 5 | 2 | 9 |  |  |  |  |  | 7 | 10† |  |  | 6 | 8 |  |  |  |  |  |  | 1 |
| 1 | 11 | 3 | 4 | 5 | 2 | 9 |  | 13 |  |  |  | 7* | 10† |  |  | 6 | 8 | 12 |  |  |  |  |  | 2 |
| 1 |  | 3 | 4 | 5 | 2 | 9 | 8* | 12 | 10 | 11 |  |  |  |  |  | 6 | 7 |  |  |  |  |  |  | 3 |
| 1 | 12 | 3 | 4 | 5 | 2 |  | 8* | 9 | 10 | 11 |  |  |  |  |  | 6 | 7 |  |  |  |  |  |  | 4 |
| 1 |  | 3 | 4 | 5 | 2 |  | 8 | 9 | 12 | 10* | 11 |  |  |  |  | 6 | 7 |  |  |  |  |  |  | 5 |
| 1 |  | 3 | 4 | 5 | 2 |  | 8 | 9 | 7 | 11 | 10 |  |  |  |  | 6 |  |  |  |  |  |  |  | 6 |
| 1 |  | 3 | 4 | 5 | 2* |  | 8 | 9 | 11 | 10 | 7 | 12 |  |  |  | 6 |  |  |  |  |  |  |  | 7 |
| 1 | 2 | 3 | 4 | 5 |  |  | 8 | 9 | 11 | 10 | 12 |  |  |  |  | 6 |  |  | 7* |  |  |  |  | 8 |
| 1 | 2 | 3 | 4 | 5 | 11* | 12 | 8 | 9 |  | 10 | 7 |  |  |  |  | 6 |  |  |  |  |  |  |  | 9 |
| 1 | 2 | 3 | 4 | 5 | 11† | 13 | 8 | 9 | 12 | 10 | 7* |  |  |  |  | 6 |  |  |  |  |  |  |  | 10 |
| 1 | 2 | 3 | 4 | 5 | 11 |  | 8 | 9 |  | 10 | 7 |  |  |  |  | 6 |  |  |  |  |  |  |  | 11 |
| 1 | 2* | 3 | 4 | 5 |  | 7 | 8 | 9 | 12 | 10 |  |  |  |  |  | 6 |  |  |  | 11 |  |  |  | 12 |
| 1 | 2* | 3 | 4 | 5 | 12 | 7 | 8 | 9 | 11† | 10 |  |  |  |  |  | 6 |  |  |  |  | 13 |  |  | 13 |
| 1 | 2 | 3 | 4 | 5 | 6 | 7* | 12 | 8 | 9 | 10 | 11 |  |  |  |  |  |  |  |  |  |  |  |  | 14 |
| 1 | 2 | 3 | 4 | 5 | 6 | 7* | 8 | 9 | 11 | 10 | 12 |  |  |  |  |  |  |  |  |  |  |  |  | 15 |
| 1 | 2 | 3 |  | 5 | 6 |  | 7 | 8 |  |  | 4 | 12 | 10 | 9 |  | 11* |  |  |  |  |  |  |  | 16 |
| 1 | 2 | 3 | 4 |  | 6 |  | 7 | 8 |  |  |  |  | 10* | 9 |  | 11 | 12 |  | 5 |  |  |  |  | 17 |
| 1 | 2 | 3 | 4 | 5 | 6 | 12 | 9* | 8 |  |  |  |  | 10 |  |  | 11 | 7 |  |  |  |  |  |  | 18 |
| 1 | 2* | 3 | 4 | 5 | 13 |  |  | 9 | 8 |  |  | 7 | 10† |  |  | 6 | 12 |  | 11 |  |  |  |  | 19 |
| 1 |  | 3 | 4 | 5 | 2 | 13 | 8 |  |  |  | 12 | 7* | 10 |  |  | 6 | 9 |  | 11† |  |  |  |  | 20 |
| 1 |  | 3 | 4 | 5 | 2 | 12 | 8 |  |  |  |  | 7 | 10 |  |  | 6 | 9* |  | 11 |  |  |  |  | 21 |
| 1 | 2 | 3 | 4 | 5 |  |  |  | 11 | 8 |  |  | 7 | 10 |  |  | 6 | 9* |  |  | 12 |  |  |  | 22 |
| 1 | 2 | 3 | 4 | 5 |  |  |  | 11 | 8 |  |  | 7 | 10 |  |  | 6 | 9 |  |  |  |  |  |  | 23 |
| 1 | 2 | 3 | 4 | 5 |  |  |  | 11 | 8 |  |  | 7 | 10 |  |  | 6 | 9 |  |  |  |  |  |  | 24 |
| 1 | 2 | 3 | 4 | 5 |  |  |  | 11† | 8 |  |  | 7 | 10 | 12 |  | 6 | 9* |  | 13 |  |  |  |  | 25 |
| 1 | 2 | 3 | 4 | 5 |  |  |  | 11† | 8 |  |  | 7* | 10 | 12 |  | 6 | 9 |  | 13 |  |  |  |  | 26 |
| 1 | 2 | 3 | 4 | 5 |  |  |  | 11 | 8 |  |  | 7* | 10 |  |  | 6 | 9 |  | 12 |  |  |  |  | 27 |
| 1 | 2 | 3 | 4 | 5 |  |  |  | 11 | 8 |  |  | 7 |  | 9* |  | 6 | 10 |  | 12 |  |  |  |  | 28 |
| 1 | 2 | 3 | 4 | 5 |  |  |  | 11 | 8 |  |  | 7 |  |  |  | 6* | 9 |  | 10 | 12 |  |  |  | 29 |
| 1 | 2 | 3 | 4 | 5 |  |  |  | 9 | 8 |  |  | 7 |  |  |  | 6 | 10 |  | 11 |  |  |  |  | 30 |
| 1 | 2 | 3 | 4 | 5 |  |  |  | 9 | 8 |  |  | 7 |  |  |  | 6 | 10* |  | 11 | 12 |  |  |  | 31 |
| 1 | 2 | 3 | 4 | 5 |  |  |  | 9 | 8 |  |  | 7 |  |  |  | 6 | 10 |  | 11 |  |  |  |  | 32 |
| 1 | 2 |  | 4 | 5 |  |  |  | 9 | 8 | 3 |  | 7 |  |  |  | 6 | 10 |  | 11 |  |  |  |  | 33 |
| 1 | 2 | 3 |  | 5 |  |  |  | 9 | 8 | 4 |  | 7 |  |  |  | 6 | 10 |  | 11 |  |  |  |  | 34 |
| 1 | 2 |  | 4 | 5 |  |  |  | 9 | 8 | 3 |  | 7 |  |  |  | 6 | 12 |  | 10 | 11* |  |  |  | 35 |
| 1 | 2 | 3 | 4 | 5 |  |  |  | 9 | 8 |  |  | 7 |  |  |  | 6 | 10 |  | 11 |  |  |  |  | 36 |
| 1 |  | 3 | 4 |  | 5 |  |  | 9* | 8 | 2 |  | 7 |  |  |  | 6 | 10 |  | 11 | 12 |  |  |  | 37 |
| 1 |  | 3 | 4 |  |  |  |  |  | 8 | 11 | 10 | 12 |  |  |  | 6 | 9 |  | 7* |  | 5 |  | 2 | 38 |
| 1 |  | 3 | 4 |  |  |  |  | 9 | 8 | 11 | 10* | 12 |  |  |  | 6 | 7 |  |  |  | 5 |  | 2 | 39 |
| 6 | 33 | 29 | 37 | 37 | 35 | 15 | 9 | 24 | 35 | 12 | 16 | 16 | 32 | 10 | — | 34 | 19 | — | 15 | 10 | 3 | — | 2 |  |

Substitute appearances: + 1s (Smith H.); + + + 2s 2s 4s (McNeil B., Liddell G., Robertson C.); + 2s (Pettigrew W.); + 4s (Bowman D.); + + 7s 1s (Addison D., Mackay G.); + + + + 2s 1s 1s 8s (MacLaren S., McCoy G., O'Brien P., MacDonald A.); + 1s (Marinello P.)

# HIBERNIAN                                  Premier Division

*Year Formed:* 1875.   *Ground:* Easter Road Park.   *Size:* 112yd×74yd.   *Capacity:* 29,464 (6636 seats).
*Telephone:* 031-661 2159.
*Manager:* Bertie Auld.   *Secretary:* C. F. Graham.   *Assistant Manager:* Pat Quinn.   *Trainer:* John Lambie.
*Club Colours:* Green shirts with white collars and sleeves, white shorts, green and white stockings.
*Club Nickname:* Hi-Bees.
*Record Attendance:* 65,840 v Hearts, Division 1, 2 Jan, 1950.
*Previous Name:* Edinburgh Hibernians.   *Previous Ground:* Mayfield 1875–80.
*Record Transfer Fee Received:* £275,000 from Aston Villa for Des Bremner, Sept 1979.
*Record Transfer Fee Paid:* £120,000 to Everton for Joe Harper, Feb 1974.
**European Competitions:** *European Cup* 1955–56. *European Cup-Winners' Cup* 1972–73; *Fairs Cup* 1960–61, 1961–62, 1962–63, 1965–66, 1967–68, 1968–69; *UEFA Cup* 1973–74, 1974–75, 1975–76, 1976–77, 1978–79.

## 1981–82 LEAGUE RECORD

| Match No. | Date | Venue | Opponents | Result | H/T Score | League Pos'n | Goalscorers | Attendance |
|---|---|---|---|---|---|---|---|---|
| 1 | Aug 29 | H | Dundee | W 2-0 | 2-0 | — | Murray, Rae G. | 6100 |
| 2 | Sept 5 | A | Rangers | D 2-2 | 1-1 | 3 | MacLeod, Rae G. | 25,000 |
| 3 | 12 | H | Airdrieonians | D 1-1 | 1-0 | 4 | Flavell | 5020 |
| 4 | 19 | A | Aberdeen | L 0-1 | 0-0 | 4 | | 10,000 |
| 5 | 26 | A | St Mirren | L 0-1 | 0-0 | 6 | | 2400 |
| 6 | Oct 3 | H | Dundee U | D 1-1 | 0-1 | 7 | Duncan | 5000 |
| 7 | 10 | H | Morton | W 4-0 | 1-0 | 4 | Murray, MacLeod, Flavell, Callachan | 5000 |
| 8 | 17 | A | Partick T | L 0-1 | 0-0 | 7 | | 4000 |
| 9 | 24 | H | Celtic | W 1-0 | 1-0 | 5 | MacLeod (pen) | 18,000 |
| 10 | 31 | A | Dundee | D 0-0 | 0-0 | 4 | | 6011 |
| 11 | Nov 7 | H | Rangers | L 1-2 | 1-1 | 6 | Rae G. | 14,800 |
| 12 | 14 | A | Airdrieonians | L 1-3 | 1-2 | 6 | Rae G. | 4000 |
| 13 | 21 | H | Aberdeen | D 1-1 | 1-0 | 6 | Callachan | 7600 |
| 14 | 28 | H | St Mirren | D 0-0 | 0-0 | 6 | | 4750 |
| 15 | Dec 5 | A | Dundee U | L 0-1 | 0-0 | 7 | | 7268 |
| 16 | 19 | H | Partick T | W 3-0 | 2-0 | 6 | MacLeod 2, Rae G. | 4200 |
| 17 | Jan 2 | H | Dundee | W 2-1 | 0-1 | 6 | Jamieson, MacLeod | 8281 |
| 18 | 16 | H | Airdrieonians | W 1-0 | 1-0 | — | MacLeod | 4350 |
| 19 | 30 | A | Rangers | D 1-1 | 0-1 | 4 | Flavell | 15,000 |
| 20 | Feb 2 | A | Celtic | D 0-0 | 0-0 | — | | 16,700 |
| 21 | 6 | H | Dundee U | L 0-1 | 0-1 | 5 | | 6133 |
| 22 | 20 | A | St Mirren | D 2-2 | 2-1 | 6 | Rae G. 2 | 5138 |
| 23 | 27 | H | Celtic | W 1-0 | 1-0 | 5 | Rae G. | 15,914 |
| 24 | Mar 6 | A | Partick T | W 2-1 | 1-1 | 4 | Rae G., Paterson | 3000 |
| 25 | 10 | A | Aberdeen | L 1-3 | 1-1 | — | Rae G. | 9000 |
| 26 | 13 | H | Morton | D 2-2 | 1-1 | 5 | Rae G., Murray | 5000 |
| 27 | 20 | A | Dundee | D 2-2 | 0-1 | 5 | Callachan 2 | 4345 |
| 28 | 27 | H | Rangers | D 0-0 | 0-0 | 5 | | 12,390 |
| 29 | Apr 3 | A | Airdrieonians | W 2-0 | 0-0 | 5 | Jamieson 2 | 2500 |
| 30 | 10 | H | Aberdeen | L 0-3 | 0-1 | 6 | | 8000 |
| 31 | 14 | A | Morton | L 1-2 | 0-0 | — | Jamieson | 2500 |
| 32 | 17 | A | Dundee U | W 1-0 | 0-0 | 6 | Turnbull | 6850 |
| 33 | 24 | H | St Mirren | W 2-1 | 0-0 | 6 | Jamieson, Murray (pen) | 4070 |
| 34 | May 1 | A | Celtic | L 0-6 | 0-4 | 6 | | 16,064 |
| 35 | 8 | H | Partick T | D 1-1 | 1-0 | 6 | Murray | 4000 |
| 36 | 15 | A | Morton | D 0-0 | 0-0 | 6 | | 1500 |

**Final League Position: 6**

### Goalscorers

*League* (38): Rae G. 11, MacLeod 7 (1 pen), Jamieson 5, Murray 5 (1 pen), Callachan 4, Flavell 3, Duncan 1, Paterson 1, Turnbull 1.
*League Cup* (5): Duncan 1, Flavell 1, Murray 1, Paterson 1, Rodier 1.
*Scottish Cup* (4): Duncan 1, Paterson 1, Rae G. 1, Rodier 1.

**Honours**

*Scottish League* – Division 1 Champions 1902–03, 1947–48, 1950–51, 1951–52, 1980–81; Runners-up 1896–97, 1946–47, 1949–50, 1952–53, 1973–74; Division 2 Champions 1893–94, 1894–95, 1932–33.
*Scottish Cup* – Winners 1887, 1902; Runners-up 1896, 1914, 1923, 1924, 1947, 1958, 1972, 1979.
*Scottish League Cup* – Winners 1972–73; Runners-up 1950–51, 1968–69, 1974–75.
*Drybrough Cup* – Winners 1972–73, 1973–74.
*Record Victory:* 15-1 v Peebles Rovers, Scottish Cup 2nd rd, 11 Feb, 1961.
*Record Defeat:* 1-9 v Dumbarton, Scottish Cup 2nd rd, 27 Sept, 1890.
*Most League Points:* 57, Division 1, 1980–81.
*Most Individual League Goals in Season:* Joe Baker, 42, Division 1, 1959–60.
*Most Capped Player:* Lawrie Reilly, 38, Scotland.

| McArthur J. | Rae R. | Sneddon A. | Schaedler E. | Flavell R. | Brazil A. | Paterson C. | McLaren W. | McNamara J. | Turnbull S. | Callachan R. | Rae G. | MacLeod A. | Jamieson W. | Duncan A. | Murray G. | Rodier D. | Docherty P. | Connolly J. | Rice B. | Hendry I. | Match No. |
|---|---|---|---|---|---|---|---|---|---|---|---|---|---|---|---|---|---|---|---|---|---|
| 1 |  | 2 | 3 | 5 | 6 | 7 | 8 | 10 | 11 | 4 | 9 |  |  |  |  |  |  |  |  |  | 1 |
| 1 |  | 2 | 3 | 5 | 6 | 4 | 12 | 7 | 8 | 9* | 10 | 11 |  |  |  |  |  |  |  |  | 2 |
| 1 |  | 2 | 3 | 5 | 6 | 4 | 7 | 8 | 9* | 10 | 11 | 12 |  |  |  |  |  |  |  |  | 3 |
| 1 |  | 2 | 12 | 3* | 5 | 6 | 4 | 7 | 8 | 9 | 10 | 11 |  |  |  |  |  |  |  |  | 4 |
| 1 |  | 2 | 3 | 5 | 6 | 4 | 7 | 9 | 8 | 11 | 10* | 12 |  |  |  |  |  |  |  |  | 5 |
| 1 |  | 2 | 12 | 3 | 5 | 6 | 4 | 7 | 8 | 9† | 10 | 11* | 13 |  |  |  |  |  |  |  | 6 |
| 1 |  | 12 | 3 | 2 | 5 | 6 | 4* | 7 | 10 | 11 | 9 | 8 |  |  |  |  |  |  |  |  | 7 |
| 1 |  | 12 | 3 | 2 | 5 | 6* | 4 | 7 | 13 | 9 | 10 | 11† | 8 |  |  |  |  |  |  |  | 8 |
| 1 |  | 2 | 10 | 5 | 4 | 3 | 7 | 8 | 11 | 6 | 9 |  |  |  |  |  |  |  |  |  | 9 |
| 1 |  | 2 | 3 | 6 | 12 | 5 | 4 | 7* | 9 | 8 | 11 | 10 |  |  |  |  |  |  |  |  | 10 |
| 1 |  | 2 | 3 | 11 | 4 | 5 | 7 | 6 | 8 | 10 | 9 |  |  |  |  |  |  |  |  |  | 11 |
| 1 |  | 2 | 3 | 6 | 5 | 4 | 7 | 8 | 9* | 11 | 10 | 12 |  |  |  |  |  |  |  |  | 12 |
| 1 |  | 2 | 3 | 11 | 4 | 5 | 12 | 7 | 8 | 9* | 6 | 13 | 10† |  |  |  |  |  |  |  | 13 |
| 1 |  | 2 | 3 | 11* | 4 | 5 | 7 | 8 | 9 | 6 | 10 | 12 |  |  |  |  |  |  |  |  | 14 |
| 1 |  | 2 | 3 | 6 | 5 | 4 | 7 | 8 | 11 | 10 | 9 |  |  |  |  |  |  |  |  |  | 15 |
| 1 |  | 2 | 3 | 12 | 6 | 5 | 4* | 7 | 8 | 9 | 11 | 10 |  |  |  |  |  |  |  |  | 16 |
| 1 |  | 2 | 3 | 11 | 4 | 5 | 7 | 8 | 9 | 10 | 6 |  |  |  |  |  |  |  |  |  | 17 |
| 1 |  | 2 | 3 | 6* | 4 | 5 | 12 | 7 | 8† | 9 | 10 | 11 | 13 |  |  |  |  |  |  |  | 18 |
| 1 |  | 2 | 3 | 8 | 4 | 5 | 13 | 7 | 9† | 12 | 11 | 6* | 10 |  |  |  |  |  |  |  | 19 |
| 1 |  | 2 | 3 | 8 | 4 | 5 | 6 | 7 | 11 | 10* | 12 |  |  |  |  |  |  |  |  |  | 20 |
| 1 |  | 2 | 3* | 8 | 4 | 5 | 6 | 7 | 12 | 9 | 11 | 10 |  |  |  |  |  |  |  |  | 21 |
| 1 |  | 2 | 13 | 3 | 6 | 5 | 4 | 7 | 8* | 11† | 10 | 9 | 12 |  |  |  |  |  |  |  | 22 |
| 1 |  | 2 | 3 | 12 | 4 | 5 | 6 | 7 | 10 | 9 | 11 | 8* |  |  |  |  |  |  |  |  | 23 |
| 1 |  | 2 | 3 | 13 | 4 | 5 | 6 | 7 | 10 | 9† | 11 | 8* |  |  |  |  |  |  | 12 |  | 24 |
| 1 |  | 2 | 11 | 5 | 4 | 6 | 7 | 10 | 9 | 3 | 8 |  |  |  |  |  |  |  |  |  | 25 |
| 1 |  | 2 | 3 | 4 | 5 | 6 | 7 | 10 | 9 | 11 | 8 |  |  |  |  |  |  |  |  |  | 26 |
| 1 |  | 2 | 3 | 6 | 5 | 13 | 4 | 7* | 10 | 9† | 11 | 8 |  |  |  |  |  |  | 12 |  | 27 |
| 1 |  | 2 | 3 | 7 | 4 | 5 | 6 | 10 | 9 | 11 | 8 |  |  |  |  |  |  |  |  |  | 28 |
| 1 |  | 2 | 6 | 3 | 4 | 7 | 5 | 10* | 9 | 8 | 11 | 12 |  |  |  |  |  |  |  |  | 29 |
| 1 |  | 2 | 12 | 3 | 6 | 5 | 7 | 4* | 10 | 9† | 8 | 11 | 13 |  |  |  |  |  |  |  | 30 |
| 1 |  | 2 | 3 | 4 | 5 | 7 | 6 | 10 | 9 | 8 | 11 |  |  |  |  |  |  |  |  |  | 31 |
| 1 |  | 2 | 3 | 11† | 6 | 5 | 7 | 4 | 12 | 9 | 13 | 10* | 8 |  |  |  |  |  |  |  | 32 |
| 1 |  | 2 | 7 | 4 | 5 | 6 | 11 | 12 | 8* | 10 | 9 | 3 |  |  |  |  |  |  |  |  | 33 |
| 1 |  | 2 | 12 | 7 | 6* | 5 | 3 | 4 | 10 | 11† | 13 | 9 | 8 |  |  |  |  |  |  |  | 34 |
| 1 |  | 2 | 3 | 12 | 4 | 5 | 8 | 6 | 7 | 9 | 13 | 10* | 11† |  |  |  |  |  |  |  | 35 |
| 1 |  | 2 | 12 | 4 | 5* | 7 | 6 | 3 | 11 | 9 | 8 | 10† | 13 |  |  |  |  |  |  |  | 36 |
| 33 | 3 | 34 | 23 | 27 | 23 | 36 | 18 | 27 | 4 | 29 | 27 | 33 | 8 | 32 | 27 | 9 | 2 | 1 | — | — | |

+ + + +  + + +  + + +  + +  + + +
2s 5s 5s 1s  2s 2s 2s  2s 1s 4s  1s 10s  1s 1s 1s

# KILMARNOCK                    Premier Division

*Year Founded:* 1869.
*Ground:* Rugby Park.  *Size:* 115yd×75yd.  *Capacity:* 18,500 (4200 seats).
*Telephone:* Kilmarnock 25184.
*Manager:* Jim Clunie.  *Secretary/General Manager:* Walter W. McCrae.
*Trainer/Physiotherapist:* Hugh Allan.
*Club Colours:* Blue and white hoops, blue shorts.
*Club Nickname:* The Killies.
*Record Attendance:* 34,246 v Rangers, League Cup, Aug 1963.
*Record Transfer Fee Received:* £120,000 from Celtic for David Provan, Sept 1978.
**European Competitions:** *European Cup* 1965–66; *Fairs Cup* 1964–65, 1966–67, 1969–70.

## 1981–82 LEAGUE RECORD

| Match No. | Date | Venue | Opponents | Result | H/T Score | League Pos'n | Goalscorers | Attendance |
|---|---|---|---|---|---|---|---|---|
| 1 | Aug 29 | H | Motherwell | W 2-0 | 1-0 | — | Carson (og), Gallagher | 2700 |
| 2 | Sept 5 | A | Hearts | W 1-0 | 1-0 | 2 | Robertson | 4796 |
| 3 | 8 | A | Clydebank | D 0-0 | 0-0 | — | | 1012 |
| 4 | 12 | H | Ayr U | D 1-1 | 0-0 | 1 | Gallagher | 5500 |
| 5 | 16 | A | Queen of the S | D 1-1 | 1-1 | — | Clarke P. | 1500 |
| 6 | 19 | H | Queen's Park | D 0-0 | 0-0 | 3 | | 2400 |
| 7 | 23 | A | St Johnstone | W 2-0 | 2-0 | — | Bourke, Clark J. | 956 |
| 8 | 29 | A | East Stirling | L 1-2 | 1-2 | — | McCready | 820 |
| 9 | Oct 3 | H | Dunfermline Ath | L 0-1 | 0-1 | 4 | | 2000 |
| 10 | 10 | H | Falkirk | D 2-2 | 1-0 | 6 | Eadie 2 | 1800 |
| 11 | 17 | A | Hamilton A | W 2-1 | 0-0 | 4 | Gallagher, Bourke | 1747 |
| 12 | 24 | A | Dumbarton | W 2-0 | 0-0 | 4 | Mauchlen, Clark J. | 800 |
| 13 | 31 | H | Raith R | D 1-1 | 1-0 | 3 | Gallagher | 1900 |
| 14 | Nov 7 | H | Hearts | D 0-0 | 0-0 | 3 | | 3400 |
| 15 | 14 | A | Motherwell | L 0-2 | 0-0 | 5 | | 5068 |
| 16 | 21 | H | Queen of the S | D 0-0 | 0-0 | 5 | | 1600 |
| 17 | 28 | A | East Stirling | W 2-0 | 1-0 | 3 | Eadie, Gallagher | 1400 |
| 18 | Dec 5 | A | Dunfermline Ath | W 2-1 | 2-1 | 3 | McBride, McDicken | 2000 |
| 19 | 12 | H | St Johnstone | L 0-2 | 0-1 | 5 | | 1300 |
| 20 | Jan 16 | H | Hamilton A | D 2-2 | 2-2 | 5 | Mauchlen, Bryson (pen) | 1450 |
| 21 | 30 | H | Dumbarton | D 0-0 | 0-0 | 4 | | 770 |
| 22 | Feb 17 | A | Falkirk | D 2-2 | 2-1 | — | Bourke 2 | 2750 |
| 23 | 20 | A | Queen's Park | W 2-0 | 1-0 | 5 | Clarke P., Gallagher | 1253 |
| 24 | 27 | H | Ayr U | D 1-1 | 0-0 | 4 | McGivern | 4041 |
| 25 | Mar 10 | A | Dunfermline Ath | W 2-0 | 0-0 | — | Bryson (pen), Bourke | 1550 |
| 26 | 13 | A | Raith R | W 3-0 | 1-0 | 3 | Mauchlen, Bourke, McDicken | 1000 |
| 27 | 17 | A | Ayr U | D 1-1 | 0-1 | — | McDicken | 3663 |
| 28 | 20 | H | Falkirk | W 4-1 | 1-1 | 3 | MacLeod, Armstrong, Bourke, McDicken | 1900 |
| 29 | 27 | A | Motherwell | L 0-1 | 0-0 | 4 | | 4816 |
| 30 | 30 | A | Queen's Park | W 3-2 | 1-2 | — | McDicken, Gallagher 2 | 800 |
| 31 | Apr 3 | H | Clydebank | D 0-0 | 0-0 | 3 | | 2100 |
| 32 | 6 | A | Raith R | D 3-3 | 2-3 | — | Bryson, Clarke P., Bourke | 1025 |
| 33 | 10 | A | St Johnstone | W 3-1 | 0-1 | 3 | Mauchlen, Clarke P., Bourke | 2209 |
| 34 | 17 | H | Hamilton A | D 0-0 | 0-0 | 3 | | 1900 |
| 35 | 21 | H | Clydebank | W 2-0 | 1-0 | — | Bourke 2 | 987 |
| 36 | 24 | A | Dumbarton | W 2-0 | 0-0 | 3 | McDicken 2 | 800 |
| 37 | May 1 | A | East Stirling | W 5-1 | 4-0 | 3 | Bourke 2, Robertson, McLean (pen) McGivern | 300 |
| 38 | 8 | H | Hearts | D 0-0 | 0-0 | 3 | | 10,000 |
| 39 | 15 | H | Queen of the S | W 6-0 | 5-0 | 2 | Gallagher 2, McDicken, Robertson G. (og), Bourke, Armstrong | 2400 |

**Final League Position: 2**

**Goalscorers**
*League* (60): Bourke 14, Gallagher 10, McDicken 8, Clarke P. 4, Mauchlen 4, Bryson 3 (2 pens), Eadie 3, Armstrong 2, Clark J. 2, McGivern 2, Robertson 2, McBride 1, McCready 1, McLean 1 (pen), MacLeod 1, own goals 2.
*League Cup* (5): Bourke 2, Clark J. 1, McLean 1 (pen), Wilson 1 (pen).
*Scottish Cup* (6): Bourke 3, McGivern 2, Gallagher 1.

**Honours**

*Scottish League* – Division 1 Champions 1964–65; Runners-up 1959–60, 1960–61, 1962–63, 1963–64, 1975–76, 1978–79, 1981–82; Division 2 Champions 1897–98, 1898–99; Runners-up 1953–54, 1973–74.
*Scottish Cup* – Winners 1920, 1929; Runners-up 1898, 1932, 1938, 1957, 1960.
*Scottish League Cup* – Runners-up 1953, 1961, 1963.
*Record Victory:* 13-2 v Saltcoats Victoria, Scottish Cup 2nd rd, 12 Sept, 1896.
*Record Defeat:* 0-8 v Hibernian, Division 1, 22 Aug, 1925; 0-8 v Rangers, Division 1, 27 Feb, 1937.
*Most League Points:* 58, Division 2, 1973–74.
*Most Individual League Goals in Season:* Peerie Cunningham, 35, Division 1, 1927–28.
*Most Capped Player:* Joe Nibloe, 11, Scotland.

| McCulloch A. | McLean S. | Robertson A. | Cockburn J. | Clark J. | Armstrong K. | McDicken D. | Gallagher B. | Mauchlen A. | Bourke J. | MacLeod A. | Eadie K. | McGivern S. | Clarke P. | McCready G. | McBride J. | Wilson G. | Bryce T. | Bryson I. | Robin K. | Match No. |
|---|---|---|---|---|---|---|---|---|---|---|---|---|---|---|---|---|---|---|---|---|
| 1 | 2 | 3 | 10 | 4 | 5 | | 7 | 8 | 9 | | | 12 | 6 | 11* | | | | | | 1 |
| 1 | 2 | 3 | 10 | 4 | 5 | | 7 | 8 | | | | 9* | 6 | 11 | 12 | | | | | 2 |
| 1 | 2 | 3 | 10 | 4 | 5 | | | 8 | | | | 9 | 12 | 6 | 11 | 7* | | | | 3 |
| 1 | 2 | 12 | 3* | 4 | 5 | | 7 | 8 | 9 | 10 | | | 6 | 11 | | | | | | 4 |
| 1 | 2 | 12 | 3* | 4 | 5 | | 7 | 8 | 9† | 10 | 13 | | 6 | 11 | | | | | | 5 |
| 1 | 2 | 3 | | 4 | 5 | | 7 | 8 | 9 | 10 | | 12 | 6 | 11* | | | | | | 6 |
| 1 | 2 | 3 | | 4 | 5 | | 7 | 8 | 9 | 10 | | | 6 | 11 | | | | | | 7 |
| 1 | 2 | 3 | | 4 | 5 | | 7 | 8 | 9 | 10 | 12 | | 6 | 11* | | | | | | 8 |
| 1 | 2 | 3 | 12 | 4 | 5 | | 7 | 8 | 9 | 10*13 | | | 6 | 11† | | | | | | 9 |
| 1 | 2 | 3 | 4* | 5 | 12 | | 7 | 8 | 9 | 10 | 11 | | 6 | | | | | | | 10 |
| 1 | 2 | 3 | 4* | 5 | 8 | | 7 | 12 | 13 | 10 | 9† | | 6 | 11 | | | | | | 11 |
| 1 | 2 | 3 | 4 | 5 | 8 | | 7 | 12 | 9 | 10*13 | | | 6 | 11† | 12 | | | | | 12 |
| 1 | 2 | 3 | 4 | 5 | 6 | | 7 | 8 | 9 | 10*11 | | | | | | | | | | 13 |
| 1 | 2 | 3 | 4 | 5 | 6 | | 7 | 8 | 9 | 10 | 11*12 | | | | | | | | | 14 |
| 1 | 2 | 3 | 4 | 5 | 6 | | 7 | 8 | 9 | 10 | 11*12 | | | | | | | | | 15 |
| 1 | 12 | 2 | 3 | 4* | 5 | 6 | 7† | 8 | 9 | 10 | 11 | 13 | | | | | | | | 16 |
| 1 | 8 | 2 | 3 | 5 | 4† | 7 | | 10 | 9*11 | 6 | 12 | 13 | | | | | | | | 17 |
| 1 | 8 | 2 | 3 | 5 | 4 | 7 | 13 | 10† | 11* | 6 | 9 | 12 | | | | | | | | 18 |
| 1 | 8 | 2 | 3 | 5 | 4 | 7 | 12 | 10* | 13 | 6 | 11† | 9 | | | | | | | | 19 |
| 1 | 12 | 2 | 3 | 5 | 4* | 7 | 10 | 9 | 8 | 6 | | | | | 11 | | | | | 20 |
| 1 | 12 | 2 | 3 | 5 | 4 | 7 | 10 | 9 | 8 | 13 | 6* | | | | 11† | | | | | 21 |
| 1 | 13 | 2 | 3† | 4 | 5 | 7 | 10 | 9 | 8 | 12 | 6 | | | | 11* | | | | | 22 |
| 1 | 2 | 3 | | 5 | | 7 | 10 | 9 | 8 | 11* | 6 | | | | | | | 4 | 12 | 23 |
| 1 | 2 | 3 | | 4 | 5 | 12 | 7 | 10 | 9 | 8* | 11 | 6 | | | | | | | | 24 |
| 1 | | 2 | 3* | 4 | 5 | 12 | 7†10 | 9 | 8 | 11 | 6 | 13 | | | | | | | | 25 |
| 1 | 2 | 3 | | 4 | 5 | 8 | 10* | 9 | 7 | 11 | 6 | | | | 12 | | | | | 26 |
| 1 | 2 | 3 | | 4* | 5 | 12 | 7 | 10 | 9 | 8 | 11 | 6 | | | | | | | | 27 |
| 1 | 2 | 3 | | | 5 | 4 | 7 | 10 | 9 | 8 | 11 | 6 | | | | | | | | 28 |
| 1 | 2 | 3 | | | 5 | 4 | 7 | 10 | 9 | 8 | 11 | 6 | | | | | | | | 29 |
| 1 | 2 | 3 | | 10 | 5 | 6 | 7 | | 9 | 8 | 11* | 4 | | | 12 | | | | | 30 |
| 1 | 2 | 3 | | 10 | 5 | 6* | 7 | 12 | 9 | 8 | 11† | 4 | | | 13 | | | | | 31 |
| 1 | 2 | 3 | | 10 | 5 | 4* | 7 | 12 | 9 | 8 | 13 | 6 | | | 11† | | | | | 32 |
| 1 | 2 | 3 | | 4 | 5 | | 7 | 8 | 9 | 10 | 11 | 6 | | | | | | | | 33 |
| 1 | 2 | 3 | | 4 | 5 | 12 | | 8 | 9 | 10*13 | 7† | 6 | | | 11 | | | | | 34 |
| 1 | 8 | 2 | 3 | 4* | 5 | 12 | | 10 | 9 | | 7 | 6 | | | 11 | | | | | 35 |
| 1 | 8 | 3 | | 5 | 12 | 13 | 4* | 9 | | 7 | 6 | | | 10†11 | 2 | | | | | 36 |
| 1 | 8 | 3 | | 5 | 4 | 7*10 | 9 | | 11 | 6 | | | | | 12 | 2 | | | | 37 |
| 1 | 8 | 3 | | 5 | 4* | 7 | 10 | 9 | 12 | 11 | 6 | | | | | 2 | | | | 38 |
| 1 | 4 | 3 | 12 | 5 | 2 | 7 | 10* | 9 | 8 | 11† | 6 | | | | 13 | | | | | 39 |
| **39** | **28** | **37** | **20** | **27** | **39** | **20** | **34** | **31** | **33** | **32** | **9** | **18** | **35** | **10** | **5** | **—** | **2** | **7** | **3** | |
| +4s | +2s | +1s | +1s | | | | +7s | +1s | +6s | +1s | +1s | +5s | +10s | | +2s | +1s | | +2s | +7s | |

# MEADOWBANK THISTLE Division 2

*Year Formed:* 1974. (Previously called Ferranti Thistle, founded 1943.)   *Ground:* Meadowbank Stadium.
*Size:* 105yd×72yd.   *Capacity:* 16,000 (at present only main stand, 7500 seats, is used for football).
*Telephone:* (Secretary's office) 031-337 2442, ext 3666.
*Manager:* Terry Christie.   *Secretary:* William L. Mill.
*Club Colours:* Amber with black trim shirts, black shorts, amber stockings.
*Record Attendance:* 4000 v Albion Rovers, Scottish League Cup, 9 Aug, 1974.

## 1981–82 LEAGUE RECORD

| Match No. | Date | Venue | Opponents | Result | H/T Score | League Pos'n | Goalscorers | Attendance |
|---|---|---|---|---|---|---|---|---|
| 1 | Aug 29 | A | Arbroath | L 2-3 | 1-2 | — | McPhee, Jobson | 635 |
| 2 | Sept 5 | H | Brechin C | W 1-0 | 0-0 | 6 | Georgeson | 150 |
| 3 | 8 | H | Albion R | W 3-2 | 0-1 | — | Godfrey 2, Sprott | 250 |
| 4 | 12 | A | Berwick R | L 1-3 | 1-0 | 7 | Jobson | 915 |
| 5 | 16 | H | East Fife | D 1-1 | 0-1 | — | Jobson | 150 |
| 6 | 19 | A | Stranraer | W 1-0 | 1-0 | 6 | Jobson | 350 |
| 7 | 23 | H | Montrose | D 2-2 | 2-0 | — | Sprott, Jobson | 420 |
| 8 | 26 | H | Alloa | D 1-1 | 1-1 | 5 | Jobson | 660 |
| 9 | Oct 3 | A | Clyde | L 0-1 | 0-1 | 7 | | 790 |
| 10 | 10 | A | Forfar Ath | D 1-1 | 0-0 | 8 | Jobson | 850 |
| 11 | 17 | H | Cowdenbeath | D 1-1 | 0-1 | 8 | Georgeson (pen) | 200 |
| 12 | 24 | A | Stenhousemuir | W 2-1 | 0-1 | 6 | Brown, Sprott | 500 |
| 13 | 31 | H | Stirling Albion | W 2-1 | 1-1 | 6 | Georgeson, Hendrie | 300 |
| 14 | Nov 7 | A | Brechin C | L 0-3 | 0-2 | 8 | | 500 |
| 15 | 14 | A | Arbroath | L 1-2 | 1-0 | 9 | Hendrie | 200 |
| 16 | 21 | A | East Fife | L 0-2 | 0-1 | 9 | | 300 |
| 17 | 28 | A | Alloa | L 3-4 | 1-2 | 9 | Conroy, Jobson, McPhee | 550 |
| 18 | Dec 5 | H | Clyde | L 2-3 | 1-2 | 10 | Sprott, Godfrey | 350 |
| 19 | 19 | A | Montrose | L 0-1 | 0-0 | 10 | | 200 |
| 20 | Feb 6 | H | Stenhousemuir | W 6-1 | 2-1 | 10 | Conroy, Godfrey 2, Jobson 2, Sprott | 380 |
| 21 | 17 | A | Stirling Albion | L 0-1 | 0-0 | — | | 570 |
| 22 | 20 | H | Brechin C | W 2-0 | 0-0 | 10 | Sprott, Hendrie | 200 |
| 23 | 23 | H | Forfar Ath | D 1-1 | 1-1 | — | Hendrie | 427 |
| 24 | 27 | A | Berwick R | D 2-2 | 2-2 | 10 | Hendrie, Godfrey | 852 |
| 25 | Mar 3 | A | Cowdenbeath | D 2-2 | 1-2 | — | Sprott, Jobson | 636 |
| 26 | 6 | H | Albion R | L 0-2 | 0-2 | 10 | | 200 |
| 27 | 10 | A | Stranraer | W 4-1 | 0-1 | — | Jobson, Georgeson, Hendrie, Sprott | 460 |
| 28 | 13 | A | East Fife | L 0-1 | 0-0 | 10 | | 468 |
| 29 | 17 | H | Berwick R | W 2-1 | 1-0 | — | Jobson, Georgeson | 420 |
| 30 | 20 | H | Cowdenbeath | W 1-0 | 1-0 | 8 | Leetion | 200 |
| 31 | 27 | A | Arbroath | D 0-0 | 0-0 | 8 | | 686 |
| 32 | 31 | A | Albion R | L 0-2 | 0-1 | — | | 600 |
| 33 | Apr 3 | H | Stranraer | D 1-1 | 0-0 | 7 | Jobson (pen) | 200 |
| 34 | 10 | A | Alloa | L 0-2 | 0-1 | 8 | | 722 |
| 35 | 17 | H | Forfar Ath | L 2-5 | 1-1 | 10 | Sprott, Jobson (pen) | 400 |
| 36 | 24 | A | Montrose | L 0-1 | 0-1 | 11 | | 200 |
| 37 | May 1 | A | Stenhousemuir | L 1-3 | 1-0 | 11 | Hendrie | 300 |
| 38 | 8 | H | Stirling Albion | L 0-1 | 0-1 | 11 | | 250 |
| 39 | 15 | H | Clyde | L 1-3 | 1-2 | 12 | Thomson | 400 |

**Final League Position: 12**

### Goalscorers

*League* (49): Jobson 15 (2 pens), Sprott 9, Hendrie 7, Godfrey 6, Georgeson 5 (1 pen), Conroy 2, McPhee 2, Brown 1, Leetion 1, Thomson 1.
*League Cup* (8): Jobson 3, Boyd 1, Dunn 1, Leetion 1, Masterton 1, Sprott 1.
*Scottish Cup* (10): Boyd 3, Jobson 3 (1 pen), Georgeson 2, Godfrey 1, Hendrie 1.

**Honours**

*East of Scotland Qualifying Cup* – Winners 1963–64.
*Scottish Qualifying Cup (South)* – Winners 1973–74.
*Record Victory:* 4–1 v Forfar Athletic, League Cup, 23 Aug, 1975; v Albion Rovers, Division 2, 17 Jan, 1976; v Clyde, 22 Feb, 1981.
*Record Defeat:* 0–8 v Hamilton A, Division 2, 14 Dec, 1974.
*Most League Points:* 32, Division 2, 1976–77, 1979–80.
*Most Individual League Goals in a Season:* John Jobson, 17, Division 2, 1979–80.

| McKell R. | McQueen J. | Dunn L. | Henderson I. | Conroy D. | Brown D. | Masterton R. | Godfrey P. | Fraser G. | Burrell A. | Skilling A. | Hendrie T. | Georgeson R. | Jobson J. | Boyd W. | Sprott A. | McPhee M. | Leeton M. | Thomson A. | Frizell R. | Nisbet D. | McLeod I. | Williamson S. | Wishart M. | Match No. |
|---|---|---|---|---|---|---|---|---|---|---|---|---|---|---|---|---|---|---|---|---|---|---|---|---|
| 1 | 2 | 3 | 10 |  |  | 4* | 5 |  |  |  | 13 | 12 | 9 | 8 | 11 | 7 | 6† |  |  |  |  |  |  | 1 |
| 1 | 2 | 3 | 10 | 6* | 5 | 4 |  |  |  |  | 8† | 12 | 9 |  | 11 | 7 | 13 |  |  |  |  |  |  | 2 |
| 1 | 2† | 3 | 10 | 13 | 5* | 4 |  |  |  |  | 6 | 8 | 9 |  | 11 | 7 | 12 |  |  |  |  |  |  | 3 |
| 1 | 2 | 3† | 10 | 13 |  | 4 |  |  |  |  | 6* | 8 | 9 | 5 | 11 | 7 | 12 |  |  |  |  |  |  | 4 |
| 1 | 2 | 3 | 10 |  |  | 4 |  |  |  | 13 | 12 | 8 | 9 | 5 | 11 | 7* | 6† |  |  |  |  |  |  | 5 |
| 1 | 2 | 3 | 10 |  |  | 4 |  |  |  |  | 6 | 8 | 9 | 5 | 11 |  | 7 |  |  |  |  |  |  | 6 |
| 1 | 2 | 3 | 10 |  |  | 4 |  |  |  |  | 6 | 8 | 9 | 5 | 11 | 12 | 7* |  |  |  |  |  |  | 7 |
| 1 | 2 | 3 | 13 |  |  | 4 |  |  | 10 |  | 6 | 8† | 9 | 5 | 11 | 12 | 7* |  |  |  |  |  |  | 8 |
| 1 | 2* | 10 | 3† | 7 |  | 4 |  |  |  |  | 6 | 12 | 8 | 9 | 5 | 11 | 13 |  |  |  |  |  |  | 9 |
| 1 | 2 | 10 | 5 | 6* |  | 4 | 3 |  |  |  | 7 | 8 | 9 |  | 11 |  | 12 |  |  |  |  |  |  | 10 |
| 1 | 2 | 10 | 5 | 6* |  | 4 | 3 |  |  |  | 7 | 8 | 9 |  | 11 |  | 12 |  |  |  |  |  |  | 11 |
| 1 | 2 | 10 | 5 |  |  | 4 | 3* |  |  | 13 | 7† | 8 | 9 |  | 11 | 6 | 12 |  |  |  |  |  |  | 12 |
| 1 | 2 | 3 | 4 | 6 | 5 |  |  |  |  |  | 7 | 8 | 9 | 10 | 11 |  |  |  |  |  |  |  |  | 13 |
| 1 | 2 | 3 | 4 | 6 | 5 |  |  |  |  |  | 7* | 8 | 9 | 10 | 11 | 12 |  |  |  |  |  |  |  | 14 |
| 1 | 2 | 3 | 4 | 6 | 5 |  |  |  |  | 13 | 7 | 8* | 9 | 10 | 11† | 12 |  |  |  |  |  |  |  | 15 |
| 1 | 2 | 3 | 4 | 12 | 5 |  |  |  |  | 10 | 6 | 8* | 9 | 13 | 11 | 7† |  |  |  |  |  |  |  | 16 |
| 1 | 2 | 3* | 11 | 10 | 5 |  |  |  |  |  | 6† | 7 | 8 | 9 | 4 | 12 | 13 |  |  |  |  |  |  | 17 |
| 1 |  | 10 | 12 | 6 | 5 | 4* |  |  |  |  | 2 | 7 | 8 | 9 | 3 | 11 |  |  |  |  |  |  |  | 18 |
| 1 |  | 12 |  | 10 | 5 | 4 |  |  |  |  | 2 | 6 | 8† | 9 | 3 | 11 | 7* | 13 |  |  |  |  |  | 19 |
| 1 | 2 | 3* |  | 5 |  | 4 | 6 |  |  |  | 9 | 8† | 12 | 10 | 11 | 7 |  | 13 |  |  |  |  |  | 20 |
| 1 | 2 | 13 | 10 | 5 |  | 4 | 6 | 3† |  |  | 7* |  | 9 | 8 | 11 |  |  | 12 |  |  |  |  |  | 21 |
| 1 | 2 | 10* |  | 5 |  | 4 | 6 | 3 |  |  | 7 |  | 9 |  | 11 | 12 | 8 |  |  |  |  |  |  | 22 |
| 1 | 2 | 10 |  | 5 |  | 4 | 6 | 3* |  |  | 7 |  | 9 | 12 | 11 | 13 |  | 8† |  |  |  |  |  | 23 |
| 1 | 2 | 10 |  | 5 |  | 4 | 6 | 3* |  |  | 7 |  | 9 | 8 | 11 | 12 |  |  |  |  |  |  |  | 24 |
| 1 | 2 | 3 |  | 5 |  | 4 | 6 |  |  |  | 7 | 8* | 9 | 10 | 11 |  | 12 |  |  |  |  |  |  | 25 |
| 1 | 2 | 3 |  | 5 |  | 4 | 6 |  |  |  | 7 | 8* | 9 | 10† | 11 | 13 | 12 |  |  |  |  |  |  | 26 |
| 1† | 2 | 10 |  | 5 |  | 4 |  | 3† |  |  | 7* | 8 | 9 | 6 | 11 | 12 | 13 |  |  |  |  |  |  | 27 |
| 1 | 2 | 10 |  | 5 |  | 4 |  | 3 |  |  | 7 | 8 | 9 | 6* | 11 | 12 |  |  |  |  |  |  |  | 28 |
| 1 | 2 | 10 |  | 5 |  | 4 | 12 | 3* |  |  | 7 | 8 | 9 | 6 | 11 |  |  |  |  |  |  |  |  | 29 |
| 1† | 2 | 3* |  | 5 |  | 4 | 6 |  |  |  | 7 | 8 | 9 | 10 | 11 |  | 12 |  |  |  |  |  |  | 30 |
| 1 | 2 |  |  | 5 |  | 4 | 6 | 3* |  |  | 7 | 8† | 9 | 10 | 11 | 12 | 13 |  |  |  |  |  |  | 31 |
| 1 | 2 | 3 |  | 5 |  | 4 | 6 |  |  |  | 7 | 13 | 9 | 10 | 11* | 12 |  |  | 8† |  |  |  |  | 32 |
| 1 | 2 | 3 |  | 5 |  | 4 | 6 |  |  |  | 7 | 8 | 9 | 10* | 11 | 12 |  |  |  |  |  |  |  | 33 |
| 1 | 2 | 3 |  | 5 |  | 4 | 6 |  |  |  | 7† | 8 | 9 | 10* | 11 | 13 | 12 |  |  |  |  |  |  | 34 |
| 1 | 2 | 3 |  |  | 6 | 4 |  |  |  |  | 8 | 9 | 5 | 11 |  | 7* | 10 | 12 |  |  |  |  |  | 35 |
| 1 | 2 | 3 |  |  |  | 4 | 6 |  |  |  | 7 | 8 | 9 | 5 | 11 |  | 10* | 12 |  |  |  |  |  | 36 |
| 1 | 2 |  |  |  |  | 4 | 6 | 3 |  |  | 7 | 8 |  | 5 | 11† | 10* | 13 | 9 |  |  |  | 12 |  | 37 |
| 1 | 2 |  |  | 5 | 6 |  |  | 3 |  |  | 13 | 8 | 10 | 11* | 12 | 7 | 9† |  |  |  | 4 |  |  | 38 |
| 1 |  | 10 |  | 5 | 6 |  |  | 3* |  |  | 4 | 8 | 11 | 12 | 7 |  | 2† | 9 |  |  |  | 13 |  | 39 |
| 37 | 2 | 37 | 9 | 33 | 23 | 11 | 29 | 30 | 10 | 9 | 35 | 35 | 32 | 36 | 35 | 8 | 11 | 5 | 1 | — | — | 1 | — | |

Substitute appearances:

|  |  | + | + | + | + | + | + |  |  | + | + | + | + | + | + | + | + | + |  | + | + | + |  | |
|---|---|---|---|---|---|---|---|---|---|---|---|---|---|---|---|---|---|---|---|---|---|---|---|---|
|  |  | 1s | 1s | 2s | 3s | 1s | 1s |  |  | 2s | 4s | 3s | 2s | 1s | 4s | 16s | 7s | 9s |  | 1s | 1s | 1s |  | |

# MONTROSE
Division 2

*Year Formed:* 1879. *Ground:* Links Park. *Size:* 114yd×66yd. *Capacity:* 9000. *Telephone:* Montrose 3200.
*Manager:* Steve Murray.
*Secretary:* William Coull.
*Club Colours:* All white.
*Club Nickname:* Gable Endies.
*Record Attendance:* 8983 v Dundee, Scottish Cup 3rd rd, 17 Mar, 1973.
*Record Transfer Fee Received:* £50,000 from Hibernian for Gary Murray, Dec 1980.

## 1981–82 LEAGUE RECORD

| Match No. | Date | Venue | Opponents | Result | H/T Score | League Pos'n | Goalscorers | Atten- dance |
|---|---|---|---|---|---|---|---|---|
| 1 | Aug 29 | A | Berwick R | L 0-4 | 0-2 | — | | 900 |
| 2 | Sept 5 | H | Albion R | W 4-2 | 2-2 | 9 | Turnbull 2 (1 pen), Johnston, Taylor | 300 |
| 3 | 8 | H | Alloa | W 2-0 | 1-0 | — | Taylor 2 | 400 |
| 4 | 12 | A | Brechin C | L 0-3 | 0-1 | 8 | | 600 |
| 5 | 16 | H | Arbroath | W 2-1 | 0-1 | — | Turnbull (pen), Taylor | 600 |
| 6 | 19 | H | Forfar Ath | W 2-1 | 1-1 | 3 | Campbell, Allan | 650 |
| 7 | 23 | A | Meadowbank T | D 2-2 | 0-2 | — | Taylor, Allan | 420 |
| 8 | 26 | H | Clyde | L 0-3 | 0-3 | 7 | | 670 |
| 9 | Oct 3 | A | Cowdenbeath | L 0-6 | 0-3 | 8 | | 1250 |
| 10 | 10 | A | Stenhousemuir | W 4-2 | 1-1 | 6 | Campbell 2, Taylor, McManus | 250 |
| 11 | 17 | H | Stirling Albion | D 1-1 | 0-1 | 6 | Forrest | 200 |
| 12 | 24 | H | East Fife | L 1-2 | 0-1 | 8 | Turnbull | 300 |
| 13 | 31 | A | Stranraer | W 5-3 | 2-2 | 8 | Johnston, Campbell, Milne, Turnbull McManus | 300 |
| 14 | Nov 7 | A | Albion R | W 2-0 | 2-0 | 6 | Allan, Murray (og) | 200 |
| 15 | 14 | H | Berwick R | L 0-2 | 0-1 | 8 | | 350 |
| 16 | 21 | A | Arbroath | L 0-1 | 0-1 | 8 | | 400 |
| 17 | 28 | A | Clyde | L 0-3 | 0-1 | 8 | | 480 |
| 18 | Dec 5 | H | Cowdenbeath | D 2-2 | 1-1 | 8 | Turnbull, Fletcher | 300 |
| 19 | 19 | H | Meadowbank T | W 1-0 | 0-0 | 8 | McManus | 200 |
| 20 | Jan 2 | A | Brechin C | D 2-2 | 0-2 | 8 | Turnbull (pen), Oliver | 780 |
| 21 | 23 | H | Stenhousemuir | W 2-1 | 1-0 | 8 | Campbell, Allan | 620 |
| 22 | 30 | A | Stirling Albion | D 1-1 | 0-1 | 8 | Fletcher (pen) | 720 |
| 23 | Feb 10 | A | East Fife | W 1-0 | 1-0 | — | Allan | 294 |
| 24 | 13 | H | Stranraer | L 1-2 | 1-1 | 7 | Turnbull | 300 |
| 25 | 20 | H | Berwick R | D 0-0 | 0-0 | 7 | | 350 |
| 26 | 27 | A | Albion R | D 2-2 | 1-2 | 7 | Campbell, Sheran | 500 |
| 27 | Mar 6 | H | Clyde | W 4-1 | 1-0 | 7 | Taylor, Oliver, Campbell 2 | 350 |
| 28 | 13 | A | Arbroath | L 0-2 | 0-2 | 7 | | 764 |
| 29 | 17 | A | Forfar Ath | L 1-2 | 1-1 | — | Nicoll | 865 |
| 30 | 20 | H | Brechin C | L 1-4 | 1-3 | 7 | Johnston | 600 |
| 31 | 22 | A | Alloa | L 0-5 | 0-4 | — | | 514 |
| 32 | 27 | A | Cowdenbeath | L 2-3 | 0-2 | 9 | Campbell, Fletcher | 315 |
| 33 | Apr 3 | H | Stirling Albion | L 1-2 | 1-1 | 9 | Johnston | 250 |
| 34 | 10 | A | Stranraer | L 0-2 | 0-1 | 10 | | 300 |
| 35 | 17 | H | Alloa | L 0-3 | 0-0 | 11 | | 450 |
| 36 | 24 | H | Meadowbank T | W 1-0 | 1-0 | 10 | Oliver | 200 |
| 37 | May 1 | A | Forfar Ath | D 0-0 | 0-0 | 10 | | 875 |
| 38 | 8 | A | Stenhousemuir | L 1-2 | 1-0 | 10 | Fletcher | 300 |
| 39 | 15 | H | East Fife | L 1-2 | 0-1 | 10 | Taylor | 250 |

**Final League Position: 10**

**Goalscorers**
*League* (49): Campbell 9, Taylor 8, Turnbull 8 (3 pens), Allan 5, Fletcher 4 (1 pen), Johnston 4, McManus 3, Oliver 3, Forrest 1, Milne 1, Nicoll 1, Sheran 1, own goal 1.
*League Cup* (5): Turnbull 3 (1 pen), McManus 1, Milne 1.
*Scottish Cup* (2): Campbell 1, Johnston 1.

**Honours**
*Record Victory:* 12-0 v Vale of Leithen, Scottish Cup 2nd rd, 4 Jan, 1975.
*Record Defeat:* 0-13 v Aberdeen, 17 Mar, 1951.
*Most League Points:* 53, Division 2, 1974–75.
*Most Capped Player:* Alexander Keillor, 2 (6), Scotland.

| Charles R. | Kelly C. | Forbes N. | Milne M. | Sheran J. | Young A. | Clark G. | Johnston H. | Neill D. | Allan C. | McManus M. | Turnbull M. | Campbell I. | Taylor K. | Forrest A. | Wright A. | Fletcher J. | McDonald I. | Pirie R. | Oliver J. | Nicoll D. | Guyan C. | Gunn M. | Match No. |
|---|---|---|---|---|---|---|---|---|---|---|---|---|---|---|---|---|---|---|---|---|---|---|---|
| 1 | 2 | 3* | 12 | 4 | 6 |  |  |  |  | 7† | 8 | 11 | 5 | 10 | 13 | 9 |  |  |  |  |  |  | 1 |
| 1 | 2† | 11 | 4 | 6 | 5 |  |  |  |  | 12 | 7 | 10 | 8 | 3 | 13 | 9* |  |  |  |  |  |  | 2 |
| 1 | 2 |  | 4 | 6 | 5 |  |  |  |  | 8 | 10 | 9 | 3 | 11* |  | 7 |  |  |  |  | 12 |  | 3 |
| 1 | 2 | 13 | 4 | 6 | 5 |  |  |  |  | 8 | 10 | 9† | 3 | 11* |  | 7 |  |  |  |  | 12 |  | 4 |
| 1 | 2 | 3 | 4 |  | 5 | 11 |  |  |  | 7 | 9 | 8 | 6 |  |  | 10 |  |  |  |  |  |  | 5 |
| 1 | 2 | 3 | 4 |  | 5 | 9 |  |  |  | 10 | 11 | 8 | 6 |  |  | 7 |  |  |  |  |  |  | 6 |
| 1 | 2 | 3 | 4 |  | 5 | 9 |  |  |  | 10 | 11 | 8 | 6 |  |  | 7 |  |  |  |  |  |  | 7 |
| 1 | 2 | 3 | 12 | 4 | 8* |  | 9 | 7†10 | 11 | 5 | 6 | 13 |  |  |  |  |  |  |  |  |  |  | 8 |
| 1 | 2 | 3 | 4 |  | 5 | 9 |  |  |  | 10 | 11 | 8 | 6 | 12† | 7* |  |  |  | 13 |  |  |  | 9 |
| 1 | 2 |  | 4 | 6 | 5 | 12 |  |  |  | 7 | 10 | 9 | 8† | 3 | 11* |  |  |  | 13 |  |  |  | 10 |
| 1 | 2 | 3 | 4 | 6 | 5 |  |  |  |  | 11 | 8 | 9 |  | 10 |  | 7 |  |  |  |  |  |  | 11 |
| 1 | 2 | 3* | 4 | 12 | 6 | 5 | 13 | 7 | 10 | 9† |  | 8 | 11 |  |  |  |  |  |  |  |  |  | 12 |
| 1 | 2 | 12 |  | 8 | 4 | 6 | 5 | 9 | 7†10 | 11 |  | 3*13 |  |  |  |  |  |  |  |  |  |  | 13 |
| 1 | 2 | 3 |  | 8 | 4 | 6 | 5 | 9 |  | 7 | 10 | 11 |  |  |  |  |  |  |  |  |  |  | 14 |
| 1 | 2 | 3* |  | 8 | 4 | 6 | 5 |  | 7 | 11† | 9 | 10 | 12 | 13 |  |  |  |  |  |  |  |  | 15 |
|  | 1 | 2 | 3 | 4 | 13 | 5 | 9 | 7 | 6†11*10 | 12 | 8 |  |  |  |  |  |  |  |  |  |  |  | 16 |
|  | 1 | 2 | 3 | 4 |  | 5 | 9 | 7†8 | 13 | 6 | 12 | 11*10 |  |  |  |  |  |  |  |  |  |  | 17 |
|  | 1 | 2 | 3 | 4 |  | 5 | 10†12 | 11 | 13 | 6 | 7 | 8 | 9* |  |  |  |  |  |  |  |  |  | 18 |
|  | 1 | 2 | 3 | 4 |  | 5 | 7 | 11 | 12 | 6 | 9* | 8 | 10 |  |  |  |  |  |  |  |  |  | 19 |
|  | 1 | 2† | 3 | 4 |  | 5 | 9*11 | 10 | 13 | 6 | 8 | 7 |  |  |  | 12 |  |  |  |  |  |  | 20 |
|  | 1 | 3 |  | 4 |  | 6 | 5 | 9†11*10 | 8 | 2 | 7 |  | 12 |  | 13 |  |  |  |  |  |  |  | 21 |
|  | 1 | 3 |  | 4 | 6 | 5 | 9 | 12 | 10 | 2 | 11 | 8 | 7* |  |  |  |  |  |  |  |  |  | 22 |
|  | 1 | 2 | 3 | 4 | 6 |  | 9 | 11 | 10 | 8 | 5 |  | 7 |  |  |  |  |  |  |  |  |  | 23 |
|  | 1 | 3 |  | 4 | 6 | 5 | 9 | 11 | 10 | 8* | 2†12 | 7 | 13 |  |  |  |  |  |  |  |  |  | 24 |
|  | 1 | 2 | 3 | 5 | 4 | 6 | 8 | 11† | 7*10 | 13 |  | 12 |  |  |  |  | 9 |  |  |  |  |  | 25 |
|  | 1 | 2 | 3 | 5 | 4 | 6 | 8 |  | 10† | 7 |  | 11* |  | 13 | 12 |  | 9 |  |  |  |  |  | 26 |
|  | 1 | 2 | 3 | 5 | 4† | 6 |  | 11*10 | 12 | 8 |  | 7 | 9 |  | 13 |  |  |  |  |  |  |  | 27 |
|  | 1 | 2 | 3 | 5* |  | 7 | 6 | 10 | 13 | 4 | 11 | 9 | 8† |  | 12 |  |  |  |  |  |  |  | 28 |
|  | 1 |  | 3 | 5 | 4 | 6 | 11† | 10 | 2 | 13 | 12 | 8 | 9 | 7* |  |  |  |  |  |  |  |  | 29 |
|  | 1 | 3 |  | 5 | 4 | 6* | 2 | 9 | 12 | 13 | 7 | 10 | 8 | 11† |  |  |  |  |  |  |  |  | 30 |
| 1 | 2 | 3 | 5 | 4 |  |  | 10 | 11 | 6 | 7†13 | 8*12 | 9 |  |  |  |  |  |  |  |  |  |  | 31 |
| 1 | 2 | 3 | 5 | 4 |  | 6† | 7 | 10* | 11 | 12 | 8 | 13 | 9 |  |  |  |  |  |  |  |  |  | 32 |
| 1 | 3 |  | 2 | 4* | 6 | 5 | 7 | 8 | 10† | 13 | 11 | 12 | 9 |  |  |  |  |  |  |  |  |  | 33 |
| 1 | 3 |  | 5 | 6* | 11 | 8 | 13 | 7 | 10 | 2 | 4 | 9†12 |  |  |  |  |  |  |  |  |  |  | 34 |
| 1 | 3 |  | 4 | 6* | 11 | 7 | 12 | 8 | 10 | 2 | 5 | 9 |  |  |  |  |  |  |  |  |  |  | 35 |
| 1 | 2 | 3 | 5 | 13 | 4 | 9 | 11 | 10 | 12 | 6 | 8† | 7* |  |  |  |  |  |  |  |  |  |  | 36 |
| 1 | 2 | 5* | 4 | 12 | 7 | 10 | 11 | 9 | 3 | 6 | 13 | 8† |  |  |  |  |  |  |  |  |  |  | 37 |
| 1 | 2 | 12 |  | 5 | 7 | 4 | 13 | 11 | 10 | 3 | 6 | 9† | 8* |  |  |  |  |  |  |  |  |  | 38 |
| 1 | 2 | 5 |  | 9† | 3 | 13 | 4 | 11*10 | 8 | 6 |  | 7 | 12 |  |  |  |  |  |  |  |  |  | 39 |
| 19 | 20 | 38 | 24 | 14 | 25 | 12 | 25 | 27 | 16 | 24 | 34 | 27 | 24 | 17 | 19 | 15 | 25 | 8 | 10 | 6 | — | — |  |
|  | + | + | + | + | + | + | + | + | + | + | + | + | + | + | + | + | + | + | + | + | + |  |  |
|  | 1s |  | 4s | 1s | 1s | 1s | 2s | 3s | 2s11s | 1s | 4s | 9s | 3s | 4s | 4s | 5s | 3s | 2s | 1s |  |  |  |  |

# MORTON                              Premier Division

*Year Formed:* 1874.   *Limited Company:* 1896.
*Ground:* Cappielow Park, Greenock PA15 2TY.   *Size:* 110yd×71yd.   *Capacity:* 16,400 (6400 seats).
*Telephone:* Greenock 23571.
*Manager:* Benny Rooney.
*Secretaries:* T. Robertson & Co. CA, Greenock.
*Club Colours:* Blue and white hooped shirts, white shorts and stockings.
*Club Nickname:* Ton.
*Record Attendance:* 23,500 v Celtic, Division 1, 1922.
*Record Transfer Fee Received:* £300,000 from West Ham U for Neil Orr, Dec 1981.
**European Competitions:** *Fairs Cup* 1968–69.

## 1981–82 LEAGUE RECORD

| Match No. | Date | Venue | Opponents | Result | H/T Score | League Pos'n | Goalscorers | Atten-dance |
|---|---|---|---|---|---|---|---|---|
| 1 | Aug 29 | A | St Mirren | L 0-2 | 0-0 | — | | 5609 |
| 2 | Sept 5 | H | Dundee U | W 1-0 | 0-0 | 7 | Cochrane | 3331 |
| 3 | 12 | A | Celtic | L 1-2 | 0-0 | 6 | Thomson | 19,900 |
| 4 | 19 | H | Partick T | W 1-0 | 0-0 | 7 | Docherty | 3411 |
| 5 | 26 | H | Dundee | W 2-0 | 0-0 | 4 | McNeil, Houston | 2763 |
| 6 | Oct 3 | A | Aberdeen | L 0-2 | 0-0 | 5 | | 11,007 |
| 7 | 10 | A | Hibernian | L 0-4 | 0-1 | 7 | | 5000 |
| 8 | 17 | H | Airdrieonians | W 3-0 | 0-0 | 5 | Hutchison 2, Ritchie | 2500 |
| 9 | 24 | A | Rangers | D 1-1 | 1-0 | 6 | Rooney | 17,000 |
| 10 | 31 | H | St Mirren | L 0-2 | 0-0 | 6 | | 4500 |
| 11 | Nov 7 | A | Dundee U | L 0-3 | 0-0 | 7 | | 6264 |
| 12 | 14 | H | Celtic | D 1-1 | 0-0 | 7 | Ritchie (pen) | 12,412 |
| 13 | 21 | A | Partick T | D 2-2 | 0-2 | 7 | Houston, McNeil | 2483 |
| 14 | 28 | A | Dundee | L 1-4 | 1-2 | 7 | Hutchison | 3598 |
| 15 | Dec 5 | H | Aberdeen | W 2-1 | 0-0 | 6 | McNeil, Houston | 3102 |
| 16 | Jan 3 | A | St Mirren | L 1-3 | 0-1 | — | Houston | 7078 |
| 17 | 30 | H | Partick T | D 0-0 | 0-0 | 7 | | 2500 |
| 18 | Feb 6 | A | Aberdeen | D 0-0 | 0-0 | 7 | | 7217 |
| 19 | 13 | A | Airdrieonians | D 1-1 | 1-0 | 7 | Slaven | 3200 |
| 20 | 20 | H | Dundee | W 2-0 | 1-0 | 7 | Docherty, Hutchison | 2121 |
| 21 | 27 | A | Rangers | L 0-3 | 0-1 | 7 | | 10,200 |
| 22 | Mar 3 | A | Celtic | L 0-1 | 0-0 | — | | 9000 |
| 23 | 6 | H | Airdrieonians | W 1-0 | 0-0 | 7 | Ritchie (pen) | 2000 |
| 24 | 13 | A | Hibernian | D 2-2 | 1-1 | 7 | McNeil, Ritchie | 5000 |
| 25 | 17 | H | Rangers | D 0-0 | 0-0 | — | | 4579 |
| 26 | 20 | A | St Mirren | L 0-1 | 0-0 | 7 | | 4200 |
| 27 | 27 | A | Dundee U | L 0-5 | 0-2 | 7 | | 5333 |
| 28 | Apr 3 | H | Celtic | D 1-1 | 0-1 | 7 | Ritchie | 10,500 |
| 29 | 7 | H | Dundee U | D 1-1 | 0-0 | — | Rooney | 1792 |
| 30 | 10 | A | Partick T | L 0-4 | 0-2 | 7 | | 2717 |
| 31 | 14 | H | Hibernian | W 2-1 | 0-0 | — | Cochrane, Hutchison | 2500 |
| 32 | 17 | H | Aberdeen | W 2-1 | 1-0 | 7 | McNeil, Rooney | 3000 |
| 33 | 25 | A | Dundee | L 1-2 | 1-1 | — | Rooney | 5346 |
| 34 | May 1 | H | Rangers | L 1-3 | 1-3 | 7 | Docherty | 6500 |
| 35 | 8 | A | Airdrieonians | D 1-1 | 0-0 | 7 | Ritchie | 2000 |
| 36 | 15 | H | Hibernian | D 0-0 | 0-0 | 7 | | 1500 |

**Final League Position: 7**

### Goalscorers

*League* (31): Ritchie 6 (2 pens), Hutchison 5, McNeil 5, Houston 4, Rooney 4, Docherty 3, Cochrane 2, Slaven 1, Thomson 1.
*League Cup* (13): Thomson 4, Busby 2, Hutchison 2, McNeil 2, Rooney 2 (1 pen), Ritchie 1.
*Scottish Cup* (1): Houston 1.

## Honours

*Scottish League* – Division 1 Champions 1977–78; Runners-up 1916–17; Division 2 Champions 1949–50, 1963–64, 1966–67; Runners-up 1899–1900, 1928–29, 1936–37.
*Scottish Cup* – Winners 1922; Runners-up 1948.
*Scottish League Cup* – Runners-up 1964.
*Southern League Cup* – Runners-up 1941–42.
*Renfrewshire Cup:* 39 times winners.
*War Shield winners:* 1914.
*Record Victory:* 11-0 v Carfin Shamrock, Scottish Cup 1st rd, 13 Nov, 1886.
*Record Defeat:* 1-10 v Port Glasgow Ath, Division 2, 5 May, 1894.
*Most League Points:* 69, Division 2, 1966–67.
*Most League Goals:* 135, Division 2, 1963–64.
*Most Individual League Goals in Season:* 41, Allan McGraw, Division 2, 1963–64.
*Most Capped Player:* Jimmy Cowan, 25, Scotland.

| Baines R. | Hayes D. | Holmes J. | Rooney J. | McLaughlin J. | Orr N. | Duffy J. | Houston R. | McNeil J. | Docherty D. | Busby A. | Hutchison R. | Ritchie A. | Slaven B. | Cochrane I. | McNab E. | Marr J. | Thomson R. | Ring M. | Cavigan E. | Match No. |
|---|---|---|---|---|---|---|---|---|---|---|---|---|---|---|---|---|---|---|---|---|
| 1 | 2 | 3 | 4 | 5 | 6* |  | 7 |  |  | 11 | 9 | 10 |  | 12 | 8 |  |  |  |  | 1 |
| 1 | 2 | 3 | 4* | 5 | 6 |  | 7 |  |  | 11 | 8 | 10 |  | 12 | 9 |  |  |  |  | 2 |
| 1 | 2 | 3 | 4 | 5 | 6 |  | 7 |  |  | 11 | 8* | 10 |  | 12 | 9 |  |  |  |  | 3 |
| 1 | 2 | 3 | 4 | 5 | 6 |  | 7 |  |  | 11 | 8 | 10† | 12 | 13 | 9* |  |  |  |  | 4 |
| 1 | 2 | 3 | 4 | 5 | 6 |  | 7 |  | 8 | 11 | 9 | 10 |  |  |  |  |  |  |  | 5 |
| 1 | 2 | 3 | 4 | 5 | 6 |  | 7 |  |  | 11 | 9* | 10 | 8 | 12 |  |  |  |  |  | 6 |
| 1 | 2 | 3 | 4 | 5 | 6 |  | 12 | 7 | 8 | 9 | 10* | 11 |  |  |  |  |  |  |  | 7 |
| 1 | 2 | 3 | 4 | 5 | 6 |  | 7* | 8 | 9 | 10 | 11 | 12 |  |  |  |  |  |  |  | 8 |
| 1 | 2 | 3 | 4 | 5 | 6 |  | 7 | 8 | 9 | 10* | 11† | 13 | 12 |  |  |  |  |  |  | 9 |
| 1 | 2 | 3 | 4 | 5 | 6 |  | 12 | 7 | 8 | 9* | 10 | 11 |  |  |  |  |  |  |  | 10 |
| 1 | 2 | 3 | 4* | 5 | 6 |  | 12 | 7 | 8 | 10 | 11† | 13 | 9 |  |  |  |  |  |  | 11 |
| 1 | 2 | 3 |  | 5 | 6 |  | 12 | 7 | 8 | 10* | 11 | 9 |  | 4 |  |  |  |  |  | 12 |
| 1 |  | 3 |  | 5 | 6 | 2 | 7 | 8 |  | 10 | 11* | 9 |  | 4 | 12 |  |  |  |  | 13 |
| 1 | 2 | 3 |  | 5 | 6 |  | 11 | 7 | 8 | 4 | 10 | 9* |  | 12 |  |  |  |  |  | 14 |
| 1 | 2 | 3 | 4 | 5 | 6 |  | 11 | 7 | 8 | 9 | 10 |  |  |  |  |  |  |  |  | 15 |
| 1 | 2 | 3 | 4 | 5 | 6 |  | 11 | 7* | 8 | 9 | 10† |  | 12 | 13 |  |  |  |  |  | 16 |
| 1 | 2 | 3 | 4 | 5 |  | 6 | 7 | 12 | 8 | 13 | 9 | 11† | 10* |  |  |  |  |  |  | 17 |
| 1 | 2 | 3 | 4 | 5 |  | 6 | 7 | 12 | 8 |  | 9 | 11 | 10* |  |  |  |  |  |  | 18 |
| 1 | 2 | 3 | 4 | 5 |  | 6 | 7* |  | 8 | 12 | 9 | 11 | 10 |  |  |  |  |  |  | 19 |
| 1 | 2 | 3 | 4 | 5 |  | 6 | 7 | 12 | 8 | 13 | 9 | 11† | 10* |  |  |  |  |  |  | 20 |
| 1 | 2 | 3 | 4 | 5 |  | 6 | 7 |  | 8 |  | 9 | 10 | 11 |  |  |  |  |  |  | 21 |
| 1 | 2 | 3 | 4 | 5 |  | 6 | 7 | 12 |  | 9* | 10 | 11 |  | 8 |  |  |  |  |  | 22 |
| 1 | 2 | 3 | 4 | 5 |  | 6 | 7 | 12 |  | 9* | 10 | 11 |  | 8 |  |  |  |  |  | 23 |
| 1 | 2 | 3 | 4 | 5 |  | 6 | 12 | 7* | 13 | 9 | 10 | 11 |  | 8† |  |  |  |  |  | 24 |
| 1 | 2 | 3 | 4 | 5 |  | 6 | 8 | 7 | 12 | 9 | 10* | 11 |  |  |  |  |  |  |  | 25 |
| 1 | 2 | 3 | 4 | 5 |  | 6 | 12 | 7 | 8 | 9* | 10 | 11 |  |  |  |  |  |  |  | 26 |
| 1 | 2 | 3 | 4 | 5 |  | 6 | 11 | 7* | 8 | 10 | 9 |  | 12 |  |  |  |  |  |  | 27 |
| 1 | 2 | 3 | 4 | 5 |  | 6 |  |  | 8 | 10 | 11 | 9 |  |  |  |  | 7 |  |  | 28 |
| 1 | 2 | 3 | 4 | 5 |  | 6 |  |  | 8 | 12 | 10 | 11 | 9* |  |  |  | 7 |  |  | 29 |
| 1 | 2 | 3 | 4 | 5 |  | 6 |  | 12 | 8* | 10 | 11 | 9 |  |  |  |  | 7 |  |  | 30 |
| 1 | 2 | 3 | 4 | 5 |  | 6 |  |  | 8 | 10 | 11 | 9 |  |  |  |  | 7 |  |  | 31 |
| 1 | 2 | 3 | 4 | 5 |  | 6 | 7 |  | 8* | 13 | 10 | 11† | 12 | 9 |  |  |  |  |  | 32 |
| 1 | 2 | 3 | 4 | 5 |  | 6 | 11 | 7 |  | 9 | 10 | 8 |  |  |  |  |  |  |  | 33 |
| 1 | 2 | 3 | 4 | 5 |  | 6 | 7 |  | 8 | 10 | 11 | 9 |  |  |  |  |  |  |  | 34 |
| 1 | 2 | 3 | 4 | 5 |  | 6 | 10 | 13 | 8 | 12 | 11† | 9* |  |  |  |  |  | 7 |  | 35 |
| 1 | 2 |  | 4 | 5 |  | 6 | 3 | 7 | 8 | 10 | 12 | 9 |  |  |  |  |  |  | 11* | 36 |
| 36 | 35 | 35 | 33 | 36 | 16 | 20 | 19 | 22 | 31 | 20 | 35 | 23 | 8 | 14 | 4 | — | 4 | 4 | 1 |  |

```
      +   +   +   +   +   +   +   +   +   +
     6s  5s  4s  5s  1s  2s  5s  6s  3s  1s
```

# MOTHERWELL

## Premier Division

*Year Formed:* 1886.
*Ground:* Fir Park.  *Size:* 110yd×72yd.  *Capacity:* 22,600 (3200 seats).
*Telephone:* Motherwell 61437.
*Manager:* Jock Wallace.
*Secretary:* Jack McGraw.
*Club Colours:* Amber with claret.
*Club Nickname:* Well.
*Record Attendance:* 35,632 v Rangers, Scottish Cup 4th rd replay, 12 Mar, 1952.
*Previous Names:* Club formed following the amalgamation of Alpha and Glencairn, known as Wee Alpha for a year before becoming Motherwell in 1886.
*Previous Grounds:* Roman Park, Dalziel Park.

### 1981–82 LEAGUE RECORD

| Match No. | Date | Venue | Opponents | Result | H/T Score | League Pos'n | Goalscorers | Atten- dance |
|---|---|---|---|---|---|---|---|---|
| 1 | Aug 29 | A | Kilmarnock | L 0-2 | 0-1 | — | | 2700 |
| 2 | Sept 5 | H | Queen's Park | W 1-0 | 0-0 | 9 | Irvine | 1966 |
| 3 | 8 | H | Hamilton A | D 2-2 | 0-2 | — | McLaughlin (pen), Forbes | 2130 |
| 4 | 12 | A | St Johnstone | W 3-1 | 2-0 | 3 | McLaughlin, Cleland, Irvine | 2518 |
| 5 | 16 | H | Falkirk | W 3-2 | 2-1 | — | McLaughlin 2 (2 pens), Irvine | 1914 |
| 6 | 19 | A | Dumbarton | W 6-0 | 3-0 | 1 | Cleland 3, McLaughlin 2 (1 pen), Clinging | 1200 |
| 7 | 23 | H | Raith R | W 3-0 | 3-0 | — | McLaughlin 2, Irvine | 4300 |
| 8 | 26 | A | Dunfermline Ath | W 2-1 | 1-0 | 1 | Irvine, Mills | 3500 |
| 9 | Oct 3 | H | East Stirling | W 3-0 | 1-0 | 1 | McLaughlin, Conn, McLelland | 2528 |
| 10 | 10 | H | Ayr U | D 1-1 | 0-0 | 1 | Gahagan | 5354 |
| 11 | 17 | A | Clydebank | W 7-1 | 4-1 | 1 | Gahagan, Irvine 2, Rafferty 2, Conn, McLelland | 1600 |
| 12 | 24 | H | Hearts | D 2-2 | 1-1 | 1 | McKeever 2 | 7662 |
| 13 | 31 | A | Queen of the S | W 2-0 | 0-0 | 1 | Irvine, McKeever | 2500 |
| 14 | Nov 7 | A | Queen's Park | W 1-0 | 1-0 | 1 | McLaughlin (pen) | 2640 |
| 15 | 14 | H | Kilmarnock | W 2-0 | 0-0 | 1 | Cleland, Irvine | 5068 |
| 16 | 21 | A | Falkirk | D 1-1 | 0-1 | 1 | Gahagan | 3000 |
| 17 | 28 | H | Dunfermline Ath | W 6-1 | 2-1 | 1 | Forbes, Rafferty, Gahagan, McLaughlin, Irvine 2 | 3581 |
| 18 | Dec 5 | A | East Stirling | W 6-0 | 2-0 | 1 | Carson, Forbes, Rafferty, Irvine, McLaughlin (pen), McLelland | 1000 |
| 19 | Jan 19 | H | Clydebank | W 3-1 | 1-0 | — | Rafferty, Gahagan, McLaughlin (pen) | 2925 |
| 20 | 30 | A | Hearts | W 3-0 | 1-0 | 1 | Irvine, Coyne, Clinging | 11,054 |
| 21 | Feb 6 | H | Queen of the S | W 2-1 | 2-0 | 1 | Carson, Cleland | 2946 |
| 22 | 13 | A | Hamilton A | L 0-1 | 0-0 | 1 | | 4039 |
| 23 | 17 | H | St Johnstone | D 2-2 | 0-2 | — | Gahagan, McLaughlin | 4205 |
| 24 | 20 | A | Raith R | W 2-0 | 1-0 | 1 | Irvine, Cleland | 2000 |
| 25 | 27 | H | Queen's Park | W 3-0 | 1-0 | 1 | McLaughlin, Cleland, Irvine | 3325 |
| 26 | Mar 3 | H | Dumbarton | D 1-1 | 0-1 | — | Carson | 3200 |
| 27 | 6 | A | St Johnstone | L 2-3 | 2-1 | 1 | Coyne, Irvine | 2914 |
| 28 | 13 | A | Ayr U | D 1-1 | 0-0 | 1 | Cleland | 3185 |
| 29 | 20 | H | Hamilton A | W 3-2 | 2-1 | 1 | Irvine, McLaughlin, Cleland | 4030 |
| 30 | 27 | H | Kilmarnock | W 1-0 | 0-0 | 1 | McLaughlin | 4816 |
| 31 | Apr 3 | A | East Stirling | W 2-1 | 0-1 | 1 | Forbes, Cleland | 1000 |
| 32 | 10 | H | Dumbarton | W 1-0 | 0-0 | 1 | Cleland | 2742 |
| 33 | 14 | A | Ayr U | L 3-4 | 0-1 | — | Cleland 2, Irvine | 2317 |
| 34 | 17 | A | Falkirk | W 3-1 | 2-1 | 1 | Forbes 2, McClair | 3000 |
| 35 | 21 | A | Raith R | W 1-0 | 0-0 | — | McLaughlin (pen) | 1568 |
| 36 | 24 | H | Clydebank | D 0-0 | 0-0 | 1 | | 3689 |
| 37 | May 1 | A | Queen of the S | W 5-2 | 2-0 | 1 | McClair 2, Irvine, Gahagan, Cleland | 500 |
| 38 | 8 | H | Dunfermline Ath | D 2-2 | 1-1 | 1 | McLaughlin, McClair | 2500 |
| 39 | 15 | A | Hearts | W 1-0 | 1-0 | 1 | Irvine | 14,709 |

**Final League Position: 1**

### Goalscorers

*League* (92): Irvine 20, McLaughlin 19 (8 pens), Cleland 15, Gahagan 7, Forbes 6, Rafferty 5, McClair 4, Carson 3, McKeever 3, McLelland 3, Clinging 2, Conn 2, Coyne 2, Mills 1.
*League Cup* (4): Cleland 1, Clinging 1 (pen), Forbes 1, McLaughlin 1 (pen).
*Scottish Cup* (0).

## Honours

*Scottish League* – Division 1 Champions 1931–32, 1981–82; Runners-up 1926–27, 1929–30, 1932–33, 1933–34; Division 2 Champions 1953–54, 1968–69; Runners-up 1894–95, 1902–03.
*Scottish Cup* – Winners 1952; Runners-up 1931, 1933, 1939, 1951.
*Scottish League Cup* – Winners 1950–51; Runners-up 1954–55.
*Record Victory:* 12-1 v Dundee U, Division 2, 23 Jan, 1954.
*Record Defeat:* 0-8 v Aberdeen, Premier Division, 26 March, 1979.
*Most League Points:* 66, Division 1, 1931–32.
*Most Individual League Goals in Season:* Willie McFadyen, 52, 1931–32.
*Highest Scorer in Total Aggregate:* Hugh Ferguson, 283, 1916–25.
*Most Capped Player:* George Stevenson, 12, Scotland.

| Sproat H. | Samaroff H. | McLeod I. | Wark J. | McLelland S. | Carson J. | Coyne B. | McLaughlin B. | McKeever J. | Cleland B. | Irvine W. | Rafferty S. | Gahagan J. | Forbes G. | Soutar G. | Mills P. | McClair B. | Clinging I. | Conn A. | Mackay J. | O'Hara T. | McAllister G. | Match No. |
|---|---|---|---|---|---|---|---|---|---|---|---|---|---|---|---|---|---|---|---|---|---|---|
| 1 | 2 | 3 |  | 5 |  | 7 |  |  | 8 | 9 |  | 11 | 4 |  |  | 6* | 12 | 10†13 |  |  |  | 1 |
| 1 | 2 | 3 | 4 | 5 |  | 10 | 8 |  |  | 9 |  | 11* | 6 |  |  |  | 7 | 12 |  |  |  | 2 |
| 1 | 2 | 3 | 4 | 5 |  | 7 | 8* | 9 |  | 12 | 6 | 13 | 11 | 10† |  |  |  |  |  |  |  | 3 |
| 1 | 2 | 3 | 4 | 5 |  | 7 |  | 8 | 9 | 11 | 6 |  |  | 12 | 10* |  |  |  |  |  |  | 4 |
| 1 | 2 | 3 | 4 | 5 |  | 7 |  | 8* | 9 | 11 | 6 |  |  | 12 | 10 |  |  |  |  |  |  | 5 |
| 1 | 2 | 3 | 4 | 5 |  | 7 | 8 | 9 |  | 11* | 6 |  |  | 12 | 10 |  |  |  |  |  |  | 6 |
| 1 | 2 | 3 | 4 | 5 |  | 7 | 8 | 9 |  | 11 | 6 |  | 12 | 10* |  |  |  |  |  |  |  | 7 |
| 1 | 2 | 3† | 4 | 5 |  | 7 | 8 | 9 |  | 11* | 6 | 13 | 12 | 10 |  |  |  |  |  |  |  | 8 |
| 1 |  | 3 | 4 | 5 |  | 7 | 8* | 9 |  | 12 |  | 6 | 11 | 10 | 2 |  |  |  |  |  |  | 9 |
| 1 |  | 3 | 4 | 5 |  | 7 | 8* | 9 |  | 11 | 6 |  | 12 | 10 | 2 |  |  |  |  |  |  | 10 |
| 1 |  | 3 | 4 | 5 |  | 7 |  | 9 | 8 | 11 | 6 |  |  | 10 | 2 |  |  |  |  |  |  | 11 |
| 1 |  | 3 | 4·5 |  | 7 | 8 | 9 |  | 11 | 6 | 12 |  | 10* | 2 |  |  |  |  |  |  |  | 12 |
|  | 1 | 3 12 | 4 | 5 |  | 7 | 8 |  | 9 | 13 | 11 | 6 |  | 10† | 2* |  |  |  |  |  |  | 13 |
|  | 1 | 2 | 3 | 4 | 5 6 | 7 | 8 |  | 9*13 | 9 | 10 | 11 |  | 12 | 10† |  |  |  |  |  |  | 14 |
|  | 1 | 2 | 3 | 4 | 5 6 | 7 | 8*12 | 9 | 10 | 11 |  |  |  |  |  |  |  |  |  |  |  | 15 |
|  | 1 | 2 | 3 | 4 | 5 6 | 7 | 8* | 9 | 10†11 |  |  | 12 | 13 |  |  |  |  |  |  |  |  | 16 |
| 1 |  | 2 | 3 | 4 | 5 10 | 7 |  | 9 | 8 | 11 | 6 |  |  |  |  |  |  |  |  |  |  | 17 |
| 1 |  | 2 | 3 | 4 | 5 10 | 7 | 13 | 9† | 8 | 11 | 6* |  | 12 |  |  |  |  |  |  |  |  | 18 |
| 1 |  | 2 | 3 | 4 | 5 10*7 | 13 | 9 | 8†11 | 6 |  |  |  | 12 |  |  |  |  |  |  |  |  | 19 |
| 1 |  | 2 | 3 | 4 | 5 7 |  | 8 | 9 | 11 | 6 |  | 12 | 10* |  |  |  |  |  |  |  |  | 20 |
| 1 |  | 3 | 4 | 5 10 |  | 8* | 9 | 11 | 6 | 12 | 7 |  | 2 12 |  |  |  |  |  |  |  |  | 21 |
| 1 |  | 3 | 4 | 5 10 | 7*13 | 8 | 9† | 11 | 6 |  |  |  | 2 12 |  |  |  |  |  |  |  |  | 22 |
| 1 | 2 | 3 | 4 | 5 10*7 | 8 | 13 | 9† | 11 | 6 |  |  | 12 |  |  |  |  |  |  |  |  |  | 23 |
| 1 | 2 | 3 | 4 | 5 |  | 7 | 8*12 | 9 |  | 11 | 6 |  | 10 |  |  |  |  |  |  |  |  | 24 |
| 1 | 2 | 3* | 4 | 5 |  | 7 |  | 8 | 9 | 12 | 11 | 6 |  | 10 |  |  |  |  |  |  |  | 25 |
| 1 | 2 | 12 | 4 | 5 10*7 | 13 | 9 | 8†11 | 6· |  |  |  | 3 |  |  |  |  |  |  |  |  |  | 26 |
| 1 | 4 | 12 |  | 5 10 | 7 | 8 | 9 | 2*11 | 6 |  |  | 3 |  |  |  |  |  |  |  |  |  | 27 |
| 1 | 2 | 3 | 4 | 5 |  | 7 | 8 | 9 | 11 | 6 |  | 10 |  |  |  |  |  |  |  |  |  | 28 |
| 1 | 2 | 3 | 4 | 5 6* | 7 | 8 | 9 | 12 | 11 | 6 |  | 10 |  |  |  |  |  |  |  |  |  | 29 |
| 1 | 2 | 3 | 4 |  | 6 | 7 | 8 | 9 | 11* | 5 |  | 12 | 10 |  |  |  |  |  |  |  |  | 30 |
| 1 | 2 | 3* | 4 |  | 7 | 8 | 9 | 11 | 5 | 12 | 10 | 6 |  |  |  |  |  |  |  |  |  | 31 |
| 1 | 2 |  | 4 | 5 |  | 7 | 8 | 9 | 11 | 6 |  | 10 | 3 |  |  |  |  |  |  |  |  | 32 |
| 1 | 2 |  | 4 | 5 |  | 7 | 8 | 9 | 11 | 6* | 12 | 10 | 3 |  |  |  |  |  |  |  |  | 33 |
| 1 | 2 | 3* | 4 | 5 7 | 12 | 9 | 11 | 6 | 8 |  | 10 |  |  |  |  |  |  |  |  |  |  | 34 |
| 1 | 2 |  | 4 | 5 7 | 10 | 9 | 11 | 6 | 8 |  | 3 |  |  |  |  |  |  |  |  |  |  | 35 |
| 1 | 2 |  | 4 | 5 7 | 10† | 13 | 9 | 11 | 6* | 8 | 12 | 3 |  |  |  |  |  |  |  |  |  | 36 |
| 1 | 2 |  | 5 |  | 6* 7 | 10 | 9† | 11 | 8 | 12 | 4 | 3 13 |  |  |  |  |  |  |  |  |  | 37 |
| 1 | 4 |  | 5 | 12 7 | 10 | 9 | 11 | 8 | 6* | 2 | 3 |  |  |  |  |  |  |  |  |  |  | 38 |
| 1 | 2 |  | 5 |  | 4 7 | 10 | 9 | 12 | 11 | 8 | 6* | 3 |  |  |  |  |  |  |  |  |  | 39 |
| 35 | 4 | 37 | 25 | 37 | 34 | 19 | 36 | 6 | 25 | 39 | 8 | 37 | 31 | 1 | 1 | 7 | 4 | 17 | 9 | 17 | — | |
|  |  | + |  |  | + | + | + |  | + |  | + | + |  |  |  | + | + | + | + | + | + | |
|  |  | 3s |  |  | 1s | 1s | 2s |  | 6s |  | 5s | 2s |  |  |  | 7s | 4s | 7s | 5s | 3s | 1s | |

# PARTICK THISTLE Division 1

*Year Formed:* 1876. *Address:* Firhill Park, Glasgow, N.W. *Size:* 110yd×71yd. *Capacity:* 36,000 (3500 seated). *Telephone:* 041-946 2673.
*Team Manager:* Peter Cormack. *Admin. Manager:* Scot Symon. *Secretary:* L. J. McIntyre, CA.
*Previous Grounds:* Kelvingrove, 1876–81; Jordanvale Park, 1881–83; Muirpark, 1883–85; Meadowside Park, 1891–1908; Firhill Park, 1909 (1908–9, Ibrox was used by Partick T when they had no ground of their own, but some 'home games' still had to be played away).
*Nickname:* The Jags.
*Colours:* Red and yellow shirts with broad vertical stripes, red shorts, red stockings with black and yellow tops.
*Record Attendance:* 49,838 v Rangers, Division 1, 18 Feb, 1922.
**European Competitions:** *Fairs Cup* 1963–64; *UEFA Cup* 1973–74.

## 1981–82 LEAGUE RECORD

| Match No. | Date | Venue | Opponents | Result | H/T Score | League Pos'n | Goalscorers | Attendance |
|---|---|---|---|---|---|---|---|---|
| 1 | Aug 29 | H | Rangers | L 0-1 | 0-0 | — | | 16,000 |
| 2 | Sept 5 | A | Dundee | L 2-4 | 1-2 | 8 | Gibson, Doyle | 4653 |
| 3 | 12 | H | Aberdeen | L 0-2 | 0-0 | 10 | | 3606 |
| 4 | 19 | A | Morton | L 0-1 | 0-0 | 10 | | 3411 |
| 5 | 26 | A | Celtic | L 0-2 | 0-0 | 10 | | 15,200 |
| 6 | Oct 3 | H | St Mirren | D 1-1 | 1-0 | 10 | Park | 4159 |
| 7 | 10 | A | Dundee U | D 0-0 | 0-0 | 10 | | 5017 |
| 8 | 17 | H | Hibernian | W 1-0 | 0-0 | 10 | Watson (pen) | 4069 |
| 9 | 24 | A | Airdrieonians | D 1-1 | 0-1 | 9 | Clark | 3500 |
| 10 | 31 | A | Rangers | W 2-0 | 1-0 | 8 | Clark, Johnston | 17,000 |
| 11 | Nov 7 | H | Dundee | L 1-2 | 0-0 | 8 | Johnston | 3337 |
| 12 | 14 | A | Aberdeen | L 1-2 | 0-1 | 9 | Clark | 11,193 |
| 13 | 21 | H | Morton | D 2-2 | 2-0 | 9 | Johnston, Clark | 2483 |
| 14 | 28 | H | Celtic | L 0-2 | 0-1 | 10 | | 13,073 |
| 15 | Dec 5 | A | St Mirren | L 1-2 | 0-0 | 10 | Park | 4513 |
| 16 | 19 | A | Hibernian | L 0-3 | 0-2 | 10 | | 4200 |
| 17 | Jan 30 | A | Morton | D 0-0 | 0-0 | 10 | | 2500 |
| 18 | Feb 3 | H | Aberdeen | D 0-0 | 0-0 | — | | 2317 |
| 19 | 6 | H | St Mirren | D 0-0 | 0-0 | 8 | | 3988 |
| 20 | 17 | H | Rangers | W 2-0 | 1-0 | — | Higgins, Johnston | 6513 |
| 21 | 20 | A | Celtic | D 2-2 | 0-0 | 8 | Jardine, Watson (pen) | 15,200 |
| 22 | 27 | A | Airdrieonians | L 1-3 | 0-0 | 9 | Higgins | 3600 |
| 23 | Mar 6 | H | Hibernian | L 1-2 | 1-1 | 9 | Johnston | 2439 |
| 24 | 13 | A | Dundee U | L 1-5 | 0-3 | 10 | O'Hara | 5465 |
| 25 | 20 | A | Rangers | L 1-4 | 0-0 | 10 | Johnston | 8000 |
| 26 | 27 | H | Dundee | L 0-2 | 0-2 | 10 | | 2413 |
| 27 | Apr 7 | H | Airdrieonians | W 4-1 | 1-0 | — | Johnston 2, Watson, O'Hara | 1709 |
| 28 | 10 | H | Morton | W 4-0 | 2-0 | 9 | Park, Johnston, O'Hara, Watson (pen) | 2717 |
| 29 | 14 | H | Dundee U | L 2-3 | 1-2 | — | Jardine, Watson | 2896 |
| 30 | 17 | A | St Mirren | L 0-2 | 0-0 | 9 | | 3593 |
| 31 | 21 | A | Dundee | W 2-1 | 1-1 | — | Park, Jardine | 6463 |
| 32 | 24 | H | Celtic | L 0-3 | 0-0 | 9 | | 14,200 |
| 33 | May 1 | H | Airdrieonians | D 0-0 | 0-0 | 9 | | 2000 |
| 34 | 3 | A | Aberdeen | L 1-3 | 1-2 | — | Doyle | 6000 |
| 35 | 8 | A | Hibernian | D 1-1 | 0-1 | 9 | Jardine | 4000 |
| 36 | 15 | H | Dundee U | L 1-2 | 1-1 | 9 | Park | 3000 |

**Final League Position: 9**

**Goalscorers**
*League* (35): Johnston 9, Park 5, Watson 5 (3 pens), Clark 4, Jardine 4, O'Hara 3, Doyle 2, Higgins 2, Gibson 1.
*League Cup* (5): Higgins 2, Gibson 1 (pen), Johnston 1, O'Hara 1.
*Scottish Cup* (1): Johnston 1.

**Honours**

*Scottish League* – Division 1 Champions 1975–76; Division 2 Champions 1896–97, 1899–1900, 1970–71; Runners-up 1901–02.
*Scottish Cup* – Winners 1921; Runners-up 1930.
*Scottish League Cup* – Winners 1971–72; Runners-up 1953–54, 1956–57, 1958–59.
*Glasgow Cup* – 1980–81.
*Most Capped Player:* Alan Rough, 51, Scotland.
*Most League Points:* 56, Division 2, 1970–71.
*Record Victory:* 16-0 v Royal Albert, Scottish Cup 1st rd, 17 Jan, 1931.
*Record Defeat:* 0-10 v Queen's Park, Scottish Cup 5th rd, 3 Dec, 1881.
*Most Individual League Goals in Season:* Alec Hair, 41, Division 1, 1926–27.

| Rough A. | McKinnon D | Whittaker B. | Lapsley J. | Campbell J. | Anderson A. | Dunlop A. | Watson K. | Park D. | McDonald I. | Higgins A. | Doyle J. | Jardine I. | Johnston M. | O'Hara A. | Clark G. | Kay A. | Gibson W. | Murray J. | Sweeney J. | McDowall K. | Smith K. | Docherty G. | Match No. |
|---|---|---|---|---|---|---|---|---|---|---|---|---|---|---|---|---|---|---|---|---|---|---|---|
| 1 | 2 | 3 | 6 |  |  | 5 | 7 | 8 | 9* | 11 |  | 13 | 10† | 12 | 4 |  |  |  |  |  |  |  | 1 |
| 1 | 2 | 3 | 4 |  | 5 | 6* | 7 | 8 | 13 | 11 | 10 |  | 9† |  |  |  | 12 |  |  |  |  |  | 2 |
| 1 |  | 3 |  |  | 5 | 7 | 10 | 8 | 2 |  |  | 6 | 11 | 4 | 9 |  |  |  |  |  |  |  | 3 |
| 1 | 13 | 3 | 12 |  |  | 5 | 7 | 11 | 8 | 2 |  | 6 |  |  | 4 | 10† |  | 9* |  |  |  |  | 4 |
| 1 | 2* | 3 | 6 |  | 4 | 5 | 11 | 7† | 12 |  | 10 | 8 |  | 13 | 9 |  |  |  |  |  |  |  | 5 |
| 1 | 2 | 3 |  |  | 5 | 4 | 6 | 7 | 8 |  | 10 |  | 9 | 11 |  |  |  |  |  |  |  |  | 6 |
| 1 | 2* | 4 | 3 |  | 5 | 6 | 7 | 8 |  |  | 10 | 12 | 9 | 11 |  |  |  |  |  |  |  |  | 7 |
| 1 | 2 | 3 | 12 |  | 4* | 5 | 6 | 7 | 8 | 13 | 10 |  | 9 | 11† |  |  |  |  |  |  |  |  | 8 |
| 1 | 2 | 3 | 12 |  | 4 | 5 | 6* | 7† | 8 | 13 | 10 |  | 9 | 11 |  |  |  |  |  |  |  |  | 9 |
| 1 |  | 3 | 12 |  | 4 | 5 | 6 | 7 | 8 | 13 | 10 |  | 9* | 11† |  |  |  | 2 |  |  |  |  | 10 |
| 1 |  | 5 | 3 |  | 4 | 6 | 7 | 8 |  |  | 10 |  | 9 | 12 | 11* |  |  | 2 |  |  |  |  | 11 |
| 1 |  | 5 | 3 |  | 4 | 6 | 7 | 8 |  |  | 10 |  | 9* | 12 | 11 |  |  | 2 |  |  |  |  | 12 |
| 1 |  | 3 |  |  | 4 | 5 | 6 | 7* | 8 |  | 10 |  | 9 | 12 | 11 |  |  | 2 |  |  |  |  | 13 |
| 1 |  | 3 | 13 |  | 4 | 5 | 6 | 7* | 8 |  | 10 |  | 9 |  | 11† |  |  | 2 | 12 |  |  |  | 14 |
| 1 |  | 3 |  |  | 5 | 4 | 6 | 7 |  | 11 | 10 | 8 | 9 |  |  |  |  | 2 |  |  |  |  | 15 |
| 1 |  | 5 | 3 |  | 4 | 6 | 7 |  |  | 11 | 2 | 8 | 9 |  | 10 |  |  |  |  |  |  |  | 16 |
| 1 | 2 | 3 |  |  | 4 | 5 | 6 | 13 | 7 |  | 10 | 8 | 9* | 11† |  |  | 12 |  |  |  |  |  | 17 |
| 1 | 2 | 3 |  |  | 4 | 5* | 6 | 12 | 7 | 9 | 10 | 8 | 13 | 11† |  |  |  |  |  |  |  |  | 18 |
| 1 | 2 | 3 |  |  | 4 | 5 | 6 | 7 | 10 | 11† | 8 |  | 9* |  | 12 |  | 13 |  |  |  |  |  | 19 |
| 1 | 2 | 3 |  |  | 4 | 5 | 6 | 7 |  | 11 | 10 | 8 | 9* |  | 12 |  |  |  |  |  |  |  | 20 |
| 1 | 2 | 3 |  |  | 4 | 5 | 6 | 7* | 12 | 11 | 10 | 8 | 9 |  |  |  |  |  |  |  |  |  | 21 |
| 1 | 2 | 3 |  |  | 4 | 5* | 6 | 7† | 12 | 11 | 10 | 8 | 9 | 13 |  |  |  |  |  |  |  |  | 22 |
| 1 | 2 | 3* |  |  | 4† |  | 6 | 7 |  | 11 | 10 | 8 | 9 | 12 | 13 |  |  |  |  |  | 5 |  | 23 |
| 1 | 2 |  | 3 | 5 |  | 6 | 7 | 4 | 11† |  | 8 |  | 9* | 10 | 12 |  | 13 |  |  |  |  |  | 24 |
| 1 | 2 |  | 3 |  |  | 5 | 6 | 7 | 12 | 11† |  | 8 | 9 | 10* |  | 4 | 13 |  |  |  |  |  | 25 |
| 1 | 2 | 3* |  |  |  | 5 | 6 | 7 | 10 | 11† | 4 | 12 | 9 | 8 |  | 13 |  |  |  |  |  |  | 26 |
| 1 | 2 |  | 3 |  | 4 | 5 | 6 | 7* | 12 | 13 | 8 | 11 | 9† | 10 |  |  |  |  |  |  |  |  | 27 |
| 1 | 2 |  | 3 |  | 4 | 5 | 6 | 7* | 13 | 12 | 8 | 11 | 9 | 10† |  |  |  |  |  |  |  |  | 28 |
| 1 | 2 |  | 3 |  | 4 | 5 | 6 | 7 |  | 12 | 8 | 11 | 9 | 10* |  |  |  |  |  |  |  |  | 29 |
| 1 | 2 |  | 3 |  | 4* | 5 | 6 | 7 |  | 12 | 10 | 8 | 9† | 11 | 13 |  |  |  |  |  |  |  | 30 |
| 1 | 2 | 4 | 3 |  |  | 5 | 6 | 7 |  |  | 10 | 8 | 9 | 11* | 12 |  |  |  |  |  |  |  | 31 |
| 1 | 2 | 4 | 3 |  |  | 5 | 6* | 7 | 12 |  | 10 | 8 | 9 | 11† | 13 |  |  |  |  |  |  |  | 32 |
| 1 |  | 4 | 3 |  |  | 5 | 6 | 7 |  | 12 | 10 | 8 | 9 | 11* |  |  |  | 2 |  |  |  |  | 33 |
| 1 |  | 4 | 3 |  |  | 5 | 6* | 7 | 12 |  | 10 | 8 | 9 | 11 |  |  |  | 2 |  |  |  |  | 34 |
| 1 | 12 | 3 |  |  | 4* | 5 |  | 7 | 13 |  | 10 | 8 | 9 | 6 | 11† |  |  | 2 |  |  |  |  | 35 |
| 1 | 2 | 3 |  |  | 4 | 5 |  | 7 | 11 |  | 10 | 8 | 9† | 6* | 13 |  |  |  |  |  |  | 12 | 36 |
| 36 | 24 | 28 | 18 | 2 | 21 | 34 | 31 | 34 | 19 | 14 | 33 | 22 | 30 | 17 | 15 | 4 | 2 | 9 | 2 | — | 1 | — |  |
| +2s | +5s |  |  |  | +2s | +9s | +9s |  |  |  | +2s | +2s | +6s | +9s |  |  |  | +6s | +1s |  | +1s |  |  |

# QUEEN OF THE SOUTH     Division 2

*Year Formed:* 1919.   *Ground:* Palmerston Park.   *Size:* 111yd×73yd.   *Capacity:* 20,000.
*Telephone:* Dumfries 4853.
*Manager:* Drew Busby.   *Secretary:* J. K. Farrell.
*Club Colours:* Royal blue shirts with white facings, white shorts, royal blue stockings with two white hoops on top.
*Club Nickname:* Queens or The Doonhamers.
*Record Attendance:* 24,500 v Hearts, Scottish Cup 3rd rd, 23 Feb, 1952.

## 1981–82 LEAGUE RECORD

| Match No. | Date | Venue | Opponents | Result | H/T Score | League Pos'n | Goalscorers | Attendance |
|---|---|---|---|---|---|---|---|---|
| 1 | Aug 29 | A | St Johnstone | L 0-1 | 0-1 | — | | 1892 |
| 2 | Sept 5 | H | Dumbarton | L 0-4 | 0-2 | 14 | | 1500 |
| 3 | 8 | H | Queen's Park | D 1-1 | 0-0 | — | Cloy (pen) | 1400 |
| 4 | 12 | A | Dunfermline Ath | D 1-1 | 1-0 | 14 | Phillips | 1800 |
| 5 | 16 | H | Kilmarnock | D 1-1 | 1-1 | — | Coughlin | 1500 |
| 6 | 19 | H | Ayr U | L 1-2 | 0-2 | 14 | Roddy | 1700 |
| 7 | 23 | A | East Stirling | L 1-3 | 1-2 | — | McCann | 980 |
| 8 | 26 | A | Hamilton A | W 3-2 | 1-1 | 11 | Phillips 2, Coughlin | 1200 |
| 9 | Oct 3 | H | Clydebank | W 2-1 | 2-1 | 11 | Phillips, Coughlin | 1011 |
| 10 | 10 | H | Hearts | L 1-2 | 0-1 | 11 | McVittie | 2400 |
| 11 | 17 | A | Falkirk | D 0-0 | 0-0 | 11 | | 3000 |
| 12 | 24 | A | Raith R | L 1-2 | 1-0 | 11 | Robertson G. | 1000 |
| 13 | 31 | H | Motherwell | L 0-2 | 0-0 | 12 | | 2500 |
| 14 | Nov 7 | A | Dumbarton | L 0-1 | 0-0 | 14 | | 450 |
| 15 | 14 | H | St Johnstone | D 3-3 | 0-1 | 14 | Phillips 2, McCann | 1500 |
| 16 | 21 | A | Kilmarnock | D 0-0 | 0-0 | 14 | | 1600 |
| 17 | 28 | H | Hamilton A | L 2-4 | 1-1 | 14 | Cloy (pen), Phillips | 1000 |
| 18 | Dec 5 | A | Clydebank | L 1-2 | 0-1 | 14 | McCann | 400 |
| 19 | Jan 19 | H | Falkirk | L 0-4 | 0-3 | — | | 600 |
| 20 | 26 | A | Ayr U | L 0-1 | 0-0 | — | | 1500 |
| 21 | 30 | H | Raith R | L 2-3 | 1-0 | 14 | Cloy (pen), Gordon | 750 |
| 22 | Feb 2 | A | Queen's Park | D 1-1 | 0-1 | — | Cloy (pen) | 450 |
| 23 | 6 | A | Motherwell | L 1-2 | 0-2 | 14 | McLeod | 2946 |
| 24 | 13 | H | East Stirling | D 1-1 | 0-0 | 14 | Alexander | 750 |
| 25 | 17 | A | Hearts | L 1-4 | 1-2 | — | Alexander | 2397 |
| 26 | 20 | H | Dunfermline Ath | L 2-3 | 1-1 | 14 | Alexander, McLeod | 750 |
| 27 | 27 | A | St Johnstone | D 3-3 | 1-1 | 14 | Alexander 2, Clark | 1884 |
| 28 | Mar 6 | H | East Stirling | W 4-0 | 1-0 | 14 | Phillips 3, Alexander | 800 |
| 29 | 13 | H | Hearts | L 1-5 | 0-1 | 14 | Clark | 2620 |
| 30 | 20 | A | Clydebank | L 1-5 | 0-3 | 14 | Phillips | 500 |
| 31 | 27 | H | Hamilton A | L 0-3 | 0-1 | 14 | | 500 |
| 32 | Apr 3 | H | Falkirk | D 1-1 | 1-1 | 14 | Phillips | 500 |
| 33 | 10 | A | Raith R | W 2-1 | 2-1 | 14 | Alexander 2 | 1200 |
| 34 | 14 | H | Dunfermline Ath | L 0-3 | 0-2 | — | | 370 |
| 35 | 17 | A | Dumbarton | L 1-3 | 0-1 | 14 | Alexander | 350 |
| 36 | 24 | H | Queen's Park | L 1-2 | 0-1 | 14 | Alexander | 300 |
| 37 | May 1 | H | Motherwell | L 2-5 | 0-2 | 14 | McLeod, Robertson J. | 500 |
| 38 | 8 | A | Ayr U | L 2-5 | 0-1 | 14 | Alexander, McCann | 863 |
| 39 | 15 | A | Kilmarnock | L 0-6 | 0-5 | 14 | | 2400 |

**Final League Position: 14**

### Goalscorers

*League* (44): Phillips 12, Alexander 11, Cloy 4 (4 pens), McCann 4, Coughlin 3, McLeod 3, Clark 2, Gordon 1, McVittie 1, Robertson G. 1, Robertson J. 1, Roddy 1.
*League Cup* (10): Alexander 5, Robertson J. 2, Clark 1, McVittie 1, Phillips 1.
*Scottish Cup* (0).

**Honours**

*Scottish League* – Division 2 Champions 1950-51; Runners-up 1932-33, 1961-62, 1974-75, 1980-81.
*Record Victory:* 11-1 v Stranraer, Scottish Cup 1st rd, 16 Jan, 1932.
*Record Defeat:* 2-10 v Dundee, Division 1, 1 Dec, 1962.
*Most League Points:* 53, Division 2, 1961-62.
*Most Individual League Goals in Season:* Jimmy Gray, 33, Division 2, 1927-28.
*Most Capped Player:* Billy Houliston, 3, Scotland.

| Ball A. | Boles A. | Roddy J. | Cloy G. | Gordon W. | Clark R. | Malone R. | McVittie G. | Boyd C. | Phillips G. | Robertson G. | Mitchell I. | McCann K. | Robertson J. | Dickson P. | McLeod W. | Alexander R. | Coughlin J. | McChesney I. | Robertson M. | Miller J. | Young W. | Jamieson I. | Findlay A. | McGregor J. | Mason A. | Match No. |
|---|---|---|---|---|---|---|---|---|---|---|---|---|---|---|---|---|---|---|---|---|---|---|---|---|---|---|
| 1 |  | 3 | 8 | 5 | 2* | 7 | 6 |  |  | 4 |  | 11 | 12 |  |  | 9 | 10 |  |  |  |  |  |  |  |  | 1 |
| 1 |  | 3 | 8 | 5 |  | 7 | 6 | 12 |  | 4 |  | 13 | 2 |  | 10† | 9* | 11 |  |  |  |  |  |  |  |  | 2 |
| 1 | 2 | 3 | 4* | 6 |  | 7 | 8 | 9 | 12 |  |  | 11 |  |  | 10 |  |  |  | 5 |  |  |  |  |  |  | 3 |
| 1 | 2 | 3* | 4† | 6 |  | 7 | 8 | 9 | 13 |  |  | 11 |  |  | 10 |  | 12 |  | 5 |  |  |  |  |  |  | 4 |
| 1 | 2 | 3 | 4 | 6 |  | 7 | 8 | 9 |  |  |  | 11 |  |  | 10 |  |  |  | 5 |  |  |  |  |  |  | 5 |
| 1 | 13 | 3 | 4* | 6 | 12 | 7 | 8† | 9 |  |  |  | 11 |  | 2 | 10 |  |  |  | 5 |  |  |  |  |  |  | 6 |
| 1 | 4 | 3 |  | 5 | 6 | 7 | 8 | 9 |  |  |  | 11 |  | 2 | 10 |  |  |  |  |  |  |  |  |  |  | 7 |
| 1 |  | 3* | 4 | 2 | 6 | 7 | 5 | 9 |  |  |  | 11 | 12 |  | 10 |  | 8 |  |  |  |  |  |  |  |  | 8 |
| 1 |  | 3 | 4 | 2 | 6 | 7 | 8 | 9 |  |  |  | 11 |  |  | 10 |  |  |  | 5 |  |  |  |  |  |  | 9 |
| 1 |  | 3 | 4 | 2 | 6 | 7 | 8 | 9 | 12 |  |  | 11 |  |  | 10* |  |  |  | 5 |  |  |  |  |  |  | 10 |
| 1 | 2 | 3 | 4 | 5 | 6 | 7 | 8 | 9 | 12 |  |  | 11 |  |  | 10* |  |  |  |  |  |  |  |  |  |  | 11 |
| 1 | 2 | 3 | 4 | 5 | 6 | 7 | 8 | 9 | 10 |  |  | 11 |  |  |  |  |  |  |  |  |  |  |  |  |  | 12 |
| 1 | 2 | 3 | 4 | 5 | 6 | 7 | 8 | 9 | 10 |  |  |  | 11 |  |  |  |  |  |  |  |  |  |  |  |  | 13 |
| 1 | 2 | 3 | 4 | 5 | 6 | 7 | 8 | 9* | 10† |  |  | 13 | 11 | 12 |  |  |  |  |  |  |  |  |  |  |  | 14 |
| 1 | 2 | 3 | 4 | 5 | 6 | 7 | 8* | 9 | 10† |  |  | 13 | 12 | 11 |  |  |  |  |  |  |  |  |  |  |  | 15 |
| 1 | 12 | 3 | 6 | 4 |  |  | 8 | 11* | 9 |  |  | 5 | 7 |  | 10 | 2 |  |  |  |  |  |  |  |  |  | 16 |
| 1 | 2 | 3 | 8 | 6 |  | 7 | 5 | 9 |  |  |  | 4 |  |  | 10 | 11 |  |  |  |  |  |  |  |  |  | 17 |
| 1 | 2 | 3 | 8† | 4 | 6 | 12 | 5 | 13 |  |  |  | 7* | 10 | 11 |  | 9 |  |  |  |  |  |  |  |  |  | 18 |
| 1 |  |  | 4 | 5 | 6 | 7 | 8 |  |  | 11 |  |  |  |  | 10 | 3 | 9 |  |  | 2 |  |  |  |  |  | 19 |
| 1 |  | 3 | 10 | 4 | 5 |  | 6 | 9 |  |  |  | 11 |  |  | 2 | 7 |  |  |  | 8 |  |  |  |  |  | 20 |
| 1 |  | 3 | 10 | 4 |  | 9 | 6 | 12 |  | 11 |  |  |  |  | 2 | 7 |  |  | 5 | 8* |  |  |  |  |  | 21 |
| 1 |  | 3 | 6 | 4 | 5 |  |  |  |  |  |  | 7 | 10 | 11 | 2 | 9 |  |  |  | 8 |  |  |  |  |  | 22 |
| 1 |  | 3 | 10 | 4 | 5 |  | 6 |  |  | 11* |  |  | 7 |  | 2 | 9 | 12 |  |  | 8 |  |  |  |  |  | 23 |
| 1 | 5 | 3 | 6 | 4 |  |  | 7* |  |  | 13 |  |  | 10† | 11 | 2 | 9 | 12 |  |  | 8 |  |  |  |  |  | 24 |
| 1 | 4 | 3 | 6 | 5 |  |  |  | 10 |  |  |  | 11 |  |  | 2 | 8 | 9 |  |  | 7 |  |  |  |  |  | 25 |
| 1 | 4 | 3 | 6 | 5 |  |  |  | 10 |  |  |  | 7* | 11 | 12 |  | 8 | 9 |  |  | 2 |  |  |  |  |  | 26 |
| 1 | 10 | 3 | 8 | 4 | 5 |  | 6 |  |  |  |  | 11 |  |  |  | 7 | 9 |  |  | 2 |  |  |  |  |  | 27 |
| 1 |  | 3 | 12 | 5 |  |  | 6 | 10 |  | 7 |  | 11 |  |  |  | 8* | 9 |  |  | 2 | 4 |  |  |  |  | 28 |
| 1 |  | 3 |  | 5 |  |  | 6 | 10 |  | 7* | 12 | 11 |  |  |  | 8 | 9 |  |  | 2 | 4 |  |  |  |  | 29 |
| 1 | 2* | 3 | 12 | 4 |  |  | 6 | 10 |  | 7† | 13 | 11 |  |  |  | 8 | 9 |  |  | 5 |  |  |  |  |  | 30 |
| 1 |  | 3 |  | 7 |  |  | 13 | 10 | 12 | 4 |  | 11† |  |  |  | 8 | 9* |  | 5 | 2 | 6 |  |  |  |  | 31 |
| 1 |  | 3 |  | 7 | 5 |  |  | 11 | 8* | 6 |  | 10 |  |  |  | 9 |  |  | 12 | 4 | 2 |  |  |  |  | 32 |
| 1 |  | 3 | 6 | 4 |  |  |  | 7 |  |  |  | 10 |  |  |  | 9 | 8 |  | 5 |  |  | 2 | 11 |  |  | 33 |
| 1 |  | 3 | 6 | 4 |  |  |  | 7 | 11 |  |  |  |  |  |  | 8 | 9 |  | 5 |  |  |  |  | 10 | 2 | 34 |
| 1 |  | 7 | 4 |  | 5 |  | 8 | 10 |  | 11 |  |  |  |  |  | 9 |  |  |  | 2 | 6 |  |  | 3 |  | 35 |
| 1 | 2 |  | 8 | 6 | 5 |  |  | 12 | 10* |  |  | 11 |  |  |  | 7 | 9 |  | 3 | 4 |  |  |  |  |  | 36 |
| 1 | 2 | 3 | 6 | 8 | 5 |  |  | 10 |  |  |  | 11 |  |  |  | 7 | 9 |  |  | 4 |  |  |  |  |  | 37 |
| 1 |  | 3 | 7 | 5 |  |  | 6 | 10 |  |  |  | 11 |  |  |  | 8 | 9 |  |  | 2 | 4 |  |  |  |  | 38 |
| 1 |  | 3 | 8 | 4 | 5 |  | 6 | 10 |  |  |  | 11 |  |  |  | 7 | 9 |  |  | 2 |  |  |  |  |  | 39 |
| 29 | 10 | 18 | 36 | 35 | 38 | 12 | 19 | 30 | 24 | 19 | 9 | 25 | 21 | 11 | 19 | 21 | 11 | — | 11 | 16 | 9 | 2 | 2 | 1 | 1 |  |

+2s +2s +1s 2s +2s 7s 5s 2s +4s 2s +1s 1s

# QUEEN'S PARK

# Division 1

*Year Formed:* 1867.　*Ground:* Hampden Park, Glasgow G42.　*Size:* 115yd×75yd.　*Capacity:* 75,000
*Telephone:* 041-632 1275 (ground).
*Coach:* Eddie Hunter.
*Secretary:* James C. Rutherford.
*Club Colours:* Black and white hooped shirts, white shorts, white stockings with two black hoops on top.
*Club Nickname:* Spiders.
Only amateur club in British senior football.
*Record Attendance:* 97,000 v Rangers, Scottish Cup 2nd rd, 18 Feb, 1933. (Record for ground – 149,547, Scotland v England, 1937).
*Previous Grounds:* Queen's Park Recreation Ground 1867–73; 'First' Hampden (site: approx Florida Ave) 1873–83; 'Second' Hampden (renamed Cathkin Park and used by Third Lanark FC until 1967) 1883–1903.

## 1981–82 LEAGUE RECORD

| Match No. | Date | Venue | Opponents | Result | | H/T Score | League Pos'n | Goalscorers | Atten- dance |
|---|---|---|---|---|---|---|---|---|---|
| 1 | Aug 29 | H | Clydebank | D | 2-2 | 1-0 | — | McGregor, Melrose | 757 |
| 2 | Sept 5 | A | Motherwell | L | 0-1 | 0-0 | 11 | | 1966 |
| 3 | 8 | A | Queen of the S | D | 1-1 | 0-0 | — | McNiven | 1400 |
| 4 | 12 | H | Raith R | D | 0-0 | 0-0 | 10 | | 746 |
| 5 | 16 | A | East Stirling | W | 1-0 | 1-0 | — | Nicholson | 350 |
| 6 | 19 | A | Kilmarnock | D | 0-0 | 0-0 | 8 | | 2400 |
| 7 | 23 | H | Dumbarton | W | 3-0 | 2-0 | — | Gilmour 2, Wood | 987 |
| 8 | 26 | A | Ayr U | L | 0-2 | 0-1 | 6 | | 2292 |
| 9 | Oct 3 | H | Hearts | W | 1-0 | 0-0 | 5 | Gilmour | 2450 |
| 10 | 10 | H | Dunfermline Ath | L | 0-1 | 0-0 | 7 | | 985 |
| 11 | 17 | A | St Johnstone | L | 0-2 | 0-1 | 7 | | 1840 |
| 12 | 24 | H | Falkirk | D | 2-2 | 1-2 | 8 | McGregor, McNiven | 1045 |
| 13 | 31 | A | Hamilton A | L | 1-2 | 1-0 | 10 | Crawley | 1200 |
| 14 | Nov 7 | H | Motherwell | L | 0-1 | 0-1 | 10 | | 2640 |
| 15 | 14 | A | Clydebank | L | 1-2 | 1-1 | 10 | Grant | 904 |
| 16 | 21 | H | East Stirling | W | 2-1 | 1-1 | 9 | Verrechia, Crawley | 660 |
| 17 | 24 | H | Ayr U | W | 2-0 | 1-0 | — | McGregor, Nicholson | 600 |
| 18 | Dec 5 | A | Hearts | D | 1-1 | 0-0 | 9 | Crawley (pen) | 3516 |
| 19 | Jan 30 | A | Falkirk | D | 0-0 | 0-0 | 8 | | 1200 |
| 20 | Feb 2 | H | Queen of the S | D | 1-1 | 1-0 | — | Crawley (pen) | 450 |
| 21 | 6 | H | Hamilton A | W | 2-0 | 1-0 | 8 | Crawley 2 | 972 |
| 22 | 9 | A | Raith R | L | 0-1 | 0-0 | — | | 622 |
| 23 | 17 | A | Dunfermline Ath | L | 1-2 | 1-1 | — | Grant | 980 |
| 24 | 20 | H | Kilmarnock | L | 0-2 | 0-1 | 10 | | 1253 |
| 25 | 27 | A | Motherwell | L | 0-3 | 0-1 | 10 | | 3325 |
| 26 | Mar 10 | A | Clydebank | L | 0-1 | 0-0 | — | | 1400 |
| 27 | 13 | H | East Stirling | W | 3-0 | 0-0 | 11 | Crawley 2 (1 pen), Verrechia | 800 |
| 28 | 16 | H | St Johnstone | W | 3-2 | 2-2 | — | Verrechia, Gilmour, Rutherford (og) | 475 |
| 29 | 20 | A | Hearts | L | 0-1 | 0-0 | 10 | | 3777 |
| 30 | 27 | H | Dumbarton | W | 3-0 | 1-0 | 10 | McNiven, Gilmour, McGregor | 732 |
| 31 | 30 | H | Kilmarnock | L | 2-3 | 2-1 | — | Verrechia, McNiven | 800 |
| 32 | Apr 3 | A | Hamilton A | L | 0-2 | 0-1 | 10 | | 1056 |
| 33 | 10 | H | Dunfermline Ath | W | 2-1 | 1-1 | 10 | Wood, Nicholson | 830 |
| 34 | 14 | A | Dumbarton | L | 0-1 | 0-0 | — | | 550 |
| 35 | 17 | H | Ayr U | D | 0-0 | 0-0 | 11 | | 784 |
| 36 | 24 | A | Queen of the S | W | 2-1 | 1-0 | 10 | Wood, Gilmour | 300 |
| 37 | May 1 | H | St Johnstone | W | 2-1 | 1-0 | 10 | Crawley 2 (1 pen) | 708 |
| 38 | 8 | H | Raith R | W | 2-0 | 1-0 | 8 | Nicholson, Houston (og) | 720 |
| 39 | 15 | A | Falkirk | D | 1-1 | 0-0 | 8 | Gilmour | 1000 |

**Final League Position: 8**

### Goalscorers

*League* (41): Crawley 10 (4 pen), Gilmour 7, McGregor 4, McNiven 4, Nicholson 4, Verrechia 4, Wood 3, Grant 2, Melrose 1, own goals 2.
*League Cup* (8): Nicholson 3, McGregor 2, McNiven 1, Wood 1, own goal 1.
*Scottish Cup* (5): McNiven 3, McFarlane 1, Verrechia 1.

**Honours**
*Scottish League* – Division 2 Champions 1922–23, 1955–56, 1980–81.
*Scottish Cup* – Winners 1874, 1875, 1876, 1880, 1881, 1882, 1884, 1886, 1890, 1893; Runners-up 1892, 1900.
*FA Cup* – Runners-up 1884, 1885.
*Record Victory:* 16-0 v St Peters, Scottish Cup 1st rd, Sept 1885.
*Record Defeat:* 0-9 v Motherwell, Division 1, 26 Apr, 1930.
*Most League Points:* 57, Division 2, 1922–23.
*Most Individual League Goals in Season:* Peter Buchanan, 32, Division 2, 1962–63.
*Most Capped Player:* Watty Arnott, 14, Scotland.

| Atkins D. | Storrie G. | Wilson T. | Dickson R. | Rennie A. | McGregor J. | McFarlane R. | Crawley G. | McNiven J. | Wood D. | Grant A. | Gilmour J. | Cook S. | Nicholson J. | Melrose F. | Verrechia B. | Shearer I. | Woods J. | Cairns W. | Robertson G. | Match No. |
|---|---|---|---|---|---|---|---|---|---|---|---|---|---|---|---|---|---|---|---|---|
| 1 | 2 | 3*12 | 5 | 6 | 7 | 8 | 9 | | | | 4 10 | 11†13 | | | | | | | | 1 |
| 1 | | 3 | 4 | 5 | 6 | 7 | 8 | 9* | | 12 | 2 10 | 11 | | | | | | | | 2 |
| 1 | | 3 | 4 | 5 | 6 | 8 | 7 | 9 | | 12 | 2 10 | 11* | | | | | | | | 3 |
| 1 | | 3 | 4 | 5 | 6 | 8 | 7 | 9 | | 12 | 2 10 | 11* | | | | | | | | 4 |
| 1 | | 3 | 4 | 5 | 6 | 7 | 8 | 9 | | 11 | 2 10 | | | | | | | | | 5 |
| 1 | | 3 | 4 | 5 | 6 | 7 | 8 | 9 | | 11 | 2*10 | 12 | | | | | | | | 6 |
| 1 | 2 | 3 | 4 | 5 | 6 | 7 | 8 | 9†13 | 11 | | 10* | 12 | | | | | | | | 7 |
| 1 | 2 | 3 | 4 | 5 | 6 | 7 | 8 | 9* | 11 | 12 | 10 | | | | | | | | | 8 |
| 1 | 2 | 3 | 4 | 5 | 6 | 7 | 8 | 9 10 12 | | 11* | | | | | | | | | | 9 |
| 1 | 2 | 3 | 4 | 5 | 6 | 7 | 8 | 9 10*11 | | | 12 | | | | | | | | | 10 |
| 1 | 2 | 3 | 4 | 5 | 6 | 7 | 8 | 9 10 12 | | 11* | | | | | | | | | | 11 |
| 1 | 2 | 3 | 4 | 5 | 6 | 7 | 8 | 9 10 12 | | 11* | | | | | | | | | | 12 |
| 1 | 2 | 3 | 4 | 5 | 6 | 7 | 8 | 9 10*11 | | | 12 | | | | | | | | | 13 |
| 1 | 2 | 3 | 4 | 5 | 6 | 7 | 8 | 9*10†11 | | | 12 13 | | | | | | | | | 14 |
| 1 | 2 | 3 | 4 | 5 | 6 | 7 | 8 | 9 10 11 | | | | | | | | | | | | 15 |
| 1 | 2 | 3 | | 5 | 6 | 8 | 7* | 9 10 | | 4 13 | | 11† | 12 | | | | | | | 16 |
| 1 | 2 | 3 | | 5 | 6 | 8 | 7 | 9 10 | | 4 12 | | 11* | | | | | | | | 17 |
| 1 | 2 | 3 | 4 | 5 | 6 | 7 | | 9 10* | | 12 | | 11 | | | | | | | | 18 |
| 1 | 2 | 3 | | 5 | 6 | 8 | 7 | 9 10*12 | 4 | | | 11 | | | | | | | | 19 |
| 1 | 2 | 3 | 4 | 5 | 6 | 8 | 7 | 9 10 12 | | | | 11* | | | | | | | | 20 |
| 1 | 2 | 3 | 4 | | 6 | 8 | 7 | 9 10*12 | 13 | | | 11† | | | 5 | | | | | 21 |
| 1 | 2 | 3 | 4 | | 6 | 8 | 7 | 9 10 12 | | | | 11* | | | 5 | | | | | 22 |
| 1 | 2 | 3 | 4 | 5 | 6 | 8 | 7 | 9 10 | | | | 11* | | 12 | | | | | | 23 |
| 1 | 2 | 3 | 4* | 7 | 6 | | 8 | 9 10†12 | 13 | | | 11 | | | 5 | | | | | 24 |
| 1 | 2 | 3 | | 5 | | 8* | 7 | 9 10 6 | 13 | | | 11† | | | 4 12 | | | | | 25 |
| 1 | 2 | 3 | 4* | 5 | 6 | 8 | 7 | 9 10†13 12 | | | | 11 | | | | | | | | 26 |
| 1 | | 3 | | 5 | 2 | 7 | 6 | 9 | 13 4 | | | 11 12 10† | | | 8* | | | | | 27 |
| 1 | 2 | 3 | | 5 | | 7 | 6* | 11 | 4 10 | | | 9 | 12 | | 8 | | | | | 28 |
| 1 | 2 | 3 | | 5 | | 8 | 6 | 11 | 4 10 | | | 9 | | | 7 | | | | | 29 |
| 1 | | 2 | 3 | 5* | | 7 | 8 | 6 | 11 12 10 | | | 9†13 | | | 4 | | | | | 30 |
| 1 | 2 | 3 | | 5 | 6 | 7 | 8 | 12 11 | 10 | | | 9* | | | 4 | | | | | 31 |
| 1 | 2 | 3 | | 5 | 6 | 7 | 8*13 | 11 12 10† | | | | 9 | | | 4 | | | | | 32 |
| 1 | 2* | 3 | 4 | 5 | 7 | | 8 | 6 | 11 12 10 | | | 9 | | | | | | | | 33 |
| 1 | | 3 | 4 | 5 | 7 | | 8 | 6 | 11 | 2 10 | | 9*12 | | | | | | | | 34 |
| 1 | 2 | 3 | 4 | 7 | 6 | | 8 | 9* | 11 | | | 10† | 13 12 | | 5 | | | | | 35 |
| 1 | 2 | 3 | 4 | 5 | 6 | 7 | 8 | 9 | 11 | | | 10 | | | | | | | | 36 |
| 1 | | 3 | | 5 | 2 | 7 | 8 | 6 10*11 | 4 9 | | | 12 | | | | | | | | 37 |
| 1 | | 3 | 4 | 5 | 2 | 7 | 8 | 6 10*11 | | 9 | | 12 | | | | | | | | 38 |
| | 1 | 3 | 4 | 5 | 2 | 7 | 8 | 6 9 11 | | 10 | | | | | | | | | | 39 |
| 38 | 1 | 30 | 38 | 27 | 37 | 35 | 35 | 38 | 36 | 21 | 21 | 14 20 | 4 | 22 | — | 1 | 9 | 2 | | |
| | + 1s | | | | | | | + 1s | + 2s 13s | + 5s | + 6s | + 1s | + 7s | + 6s | + 2s | + 1s | + 1s | | | |

# RAITH ROVERS Division 1

*Year Formed:* 1883.   *Limited Company:* 1907.   *Ground:* Stark's Park.   *Size:* 113yd×67yd.
*Capacity:* 28,000.   *Telephone:* Kirkcaldy 263514.
*Manager:* Gordon Wallace.   *Club Secretary:* Mrs M. B. Watters.
*Club Colours:* Royal blue, white.
*Record Attendance:* 31,306 v Hearts, Scottish Cup 2nd rd, 7 Feb, 1953.
*Previous Grounds:* Robbie's Park 1883–89.
*Managers since the War:* Bert Herdman, Hugh Shaw, Doug Cowie, George Farm, Tommy Walker, Jimmy Millar, Bill Baxter, George Farm, Bert Paton, Andy Matthew, Willie McLean.

## 1981–82 LEAGUE RECORD

| Match No. | Date | Venue | Opponents | Result | H/T Score | League Pos'n | Goalscorers | Attendance |
|---|---|---|---|---|---|---|---|---|
| 1 | Aug 29 | A | Hamilton A | L 0-1 | 0-1 | — | | 1348 |
| 2 | Sept 5 | H | Falkirk | L 0-3 | 0-0 | 13 | | 1100 |
| 3 | 8 | H | Dunfermline Ath | D 0-0 | 0-0 | — | | 2000 |
| 4 | 12 | A | Queen's Park | D 0-0 | 0-0 | 13 | | 746 |
| 5 | 16 | H | Dumbarton | L 1-3 | 1-1 | — | Ford | 876 |
| 6 | 19 | H | East Stirling | W 1-0 | 0-0 | 13 | Robinson | 1000 |
| 7 | 23 | A | Motherwell | L 0-3 | 0-3 | — | | 4300 |
| 8 | 26 | A | St Johnstone | L 0-2 | 0-1 | 14 | | 1798 |
| 9 | Oct 3 | H | Ayr U | L 0-1 | 0-1 | 14 | | 1075 |
| 10 | 10 | H | Clydebank | L 0-2 | 0-1 | 14 | | 1000 |
| 11 | 17 | A | Hearts | L 1-2 | 0-2 | 14 | Irvine | 5001 |
| 12 | 24 | H | Queen of the S | W 2-1 | 0-1 | 14 | Ballantyne 2 | 1000 |
| 13 | 31 | A | Kilmarnock | D 1-1 | 0-1 | 14 | Irvine | 1900 |
| 14 | Nov 7 | A | Falkirk | W 2-1 | 1-1 | 13 | Robinson, Ballantyne | 2500 |
| 15 | 14 | H | Hamilton A | W 2-0 | 1-0 | 12 | Gibson, Ford | 1000 |
| 16 | 21 | A | Dumbarton | D 1-1 | 0-1 | 11 | Gibson (pen) | 450 |
| 17 | 28 | H | St Johnstone | L 0-4 | 0-2 | 13 | | 1800 |
| 18 | Dec 5 | A | Ayr U | L 0-2 | 0-0 | 13 | | 1875 |
| 19 | Jan 30 | A | Queen of the S | W 3-2 | 0-1 | 12 | Ballantyne 2, Gibson | 750 |
| 20 | Feb 3 | A | Clydebank | W 1-0 | 0-0 | — | Gibson | 500 |
| 21 | 6 | A | Dunfermline Ath | W 3-2 | 2-1 | 10 | Houston, Ford, Gibson | 2500 |
| 22 | 9 | H | Queen's Park | W 1-0 | 0-0 | — | Ballantyne | 622 |
| 23 | 20 | H | Motherwell | L 0-2 | 0-1 | 11 | | 2000 |
| 24 | 27 | A | Hearts | L 0-4 | 0-2 | 12 | | 4000 |
| 25 | Mar 3 | A | East Stirling | W 1-0 | 0-0 | — | Gibson | 923 |
| 26 | 6 | H | Hamilton A | L 1-2 | 1-0 | 11 | Ballantyne | 1500 |
| 27 | 13 | H | Kilmarnock | L 0-3 | 0-1 | 12 | | 1000 |
| 28 | 20 | A | East Stirling | D 1-1 | 0-0 | 12 | Ballantyne | 300 |
| 29 | 27 | H | Dunfermline Ath | L 0-1 | 0-1 | 12 | | 1500 |
| 30 | 31 | H | Hearts | L 0-3 | 0-0 | — | | 2500 |
| 31 | Apr 3 | A | Dumbarton | W 2-0 | 1-0 | 11 | Ballantyne 2 | 350 |
| 32 | 6 | H | Kilmarnock | D 3-3 | 3-2 | — | Ballantyne 2, Gibson | 1025 |
| 33 | 10 | H | Queen of the S | L 1-2 | 1-2 | 12 | Harris | 1200 |
| 34 | 17 | A | Clydebank | D 0-0 | 0-0 | 12 | | 520 |
| 35 | 21 | H | Motherwell | L 0-1 | 0-0 | — | | 1568 |
| 36 | 24 | A | Falkirk | L 2-3 | 0-2 | 12 | Gibson 2 (1 pen) | 2000 |
| 37 | May 1 | H | Ayr U | W 1-0 | 0-0 | 12 | Berry | 900 |
| 38 | 8 | A | Queen's Park | L 0-2 | 0-1 | 12 | | 720 |
| 39 | 15 | H | St Johnstone | L 0-1 | 0-1 | 12 | | 950 |

**Final League Position: 12**

**Goalscorers**

*League* (31): Ballantyne 12, Gibson 9 (2 pens), Ford 3, Irvine 2, Robinson 2, Berry 1, Harris 1, Houston 1.
*League Cup* (7): Russell 4, Ballantyne 2, Forsyth 1.
*Scottish Cup* (0).

**Honours**

*Scottish League* – Division 2 Champions 1907–08, 1909–10 (shared), 1937–38, 1948–49; Runners-up 1908–09, 1926–27, 1966–67, 1975–76, 1977–78.
*Scottish Cup* – Runners-up 1913.
*Scottish League Cup* – Runners-up 1948–49.
*Record Victory:* 10-1 v Coldstream, Scottish Cup 2 rd, 13 Feb, 1954.
*Record Defeat:* 2-11 v Morton, Division 2, 18 March, 1936.
*Most League Points:* 59, Division 2, 1937–38.
*Most Individual League Goals in Season:* Norman Haywood, 38, Division 2, 1937–38.
*Most Capped Player:* Dave Morris, 6, Scotland.
*Most League Goals:* 142, Division 2, 1937–38.
*British Record Goalscorers:* 142 goals in 34 Division 2 matches, 1937–38.

| Donaldson A. | Walker T. | Houston T. | Candlish C. | Ford R. | Forsyth A. | Steen I. | Carroll P. | Steel D. | Ballantyne I. | Berry D. | Gibson W. | Irvine L. | Robinson R. | Harris C. | Urquhart D. | Russell R. | Mitchell J. | McDonough B. | Miller R. | Thomson D. | Robertson C. | Spence C. | Lowe A. | Addison B. | Match No. |
|---|---|---|---|---|---|---|---|---|---|---|---|---|---|---|---|---|---|---|---|---|---|---|---|---|---|
| 1 | 2 | 3 | 13 | 5 | | | 6 | 7 | 10 | | | 4*12 | | 8† | 9 | 11 | | | | | | | | | 1 |
| 1 | 5 | 3 | 4 | | | | 6 | 7*10 | | | 12 | 8 | 9 | | 2 | 11 | | | | | | | | | 2 |
| 1 | 6 | 3 | 4 | 5 | 10 | | 12 | | | | 7 | 8 | 9 | 11* | 2 | | | | | | | | | | 3 |
| 1 | 6 | 3 | 4 | 5 | 10 | | 13 | | | 12 | 7 | 8* | 9†11 | 2 | | | | | | | | | | | 4 |
| 1 | 6 | 3 | 4 | 5 | 10 | | | | | 12 | 7 | 8 | 9 | 11* | 2 | | | | | | | | | | 5 |
| 1 | 5 | 3 | 12 | | 10 | | 6 | 7 | 8* | | 4 | 11 | | 9† | 2 | 13 | | | | | | | | | 6 |
| 1 | 2 | 3 | | 5 | 10 | | 6 | 9 | | | 4 | 11 | 8 | 7 | | | | | | | | | | | 7 |
| 1 | 2 | 3 | | 5 | 10 | | 6 | 9 | 8 | | 4 | 11 | | 7* | 12 | | | | | | | | | | 8 |
| 1 | | 3 | | 5 | 10† | | 6 | 7 | | 8 | 4 | 9*13 | 12 | 2 | 11 | | | | | | | | | | 9 |
| 1 | | 3 | | 5 | 10† | | 6 | 12 | | 9 | 8 | 4 | 7*13 | 2 | 11 | | | | | | | | | | 10 |
| 1 | 2 | 3 | 4 | | | | 6 | 12 | | 9 | 7 | 11* | 8 | 10 | | | | | | | | | | | 11 |
| 1 | | 2 | 3 | 4 | 5 | | 6 | 12 | | 9 | | 12 | 8 | 10* | 7 | | | | | | | | | | 12 |
| 1 | | 2 | 3 | 4 | 5 | | 6 | 7 | | 9 | 10 | 11 | 8 | | | | | | | | | | | | 13 |
| 1 | | 2 | 3 | 4 | 5 | 12 | 6 | 7 | | 9 | 10 | 11 | 8* | | | | | | | | | | | | 14 |
| 1 | | 2 | 3* | 4 | 5 | | 12 | 6 | 7 | 8 | 9 | 10 | 11 | | | | | | | | | | | | 15 |
| 1 | | 2 | | 4 | 5 | | 12 | 6 | 7 | 9 | 10*11 | 8 | | | 3 | | | | | | | | | | 16 |
| 1 | | 2* | | 4 | 5 | | 12 | 6 | 7 | 9 | 10†11 | 13 | 8 | | 3 | | | | | | | | | | 17 |
| 1 | | 2 | | 12 | | 4*10 | 5 | | 9 | | 11 | 8 | 7 | 3 | 6 | | | | | | | | | | 18 |
| 1 | | 6 | | 4 | | 5 | 7 | | 9 | | 11 | 8 | 10 | 3 | | 2 | | | | | | | | | 19 |
| 1 | | 6 | | 4 | | 5 | 7 | | 9 | | 11 | 8 | | 10 | 3 | 2 | | | | | | | | | 20 |
| 1 | | 6 | | 4 | | 12 | 5 | 7* | 9 | | 11 | 8 | 13 | 10* | 3 | 2 | | | | | | | | | 21 |
| 1 | | 6 | | 4 | | 5 | 7 | | 9 | | 11 | 8 | | 10 | 3 | 2 | | | | | | | | | 22 |
| 1 | | 2 | | 4 | 5 | 12 | 6 | 7 | | 9 | | 11 | 8 | | 10 | 3* | | | | | | | | | 23 |
| 1 | | 6 | | 4 | 5 | 13 | | 7 | | 9 | 11†12 | 8 | | 10* | 3 | 2 | | | | | | | | | 24 |
| 1 | | 6 | | 4 | 5 | 10 | | 7 | | 9 | | 8 | 12 | 11* | 3 | 2 | | | | | | | | | 25 |
| 1 | | 6 | | 4 | 5 | 10 | | 7 | | 9 | | 8 | | 3 | 2*12 | 11 | | | | | | | | | 26 |
| 1 | | 6 | 13 | | 10 | 5 | 7* | 9† | | 4 | 8 | | 3 | 2 | 12 | 11 | | | | | | | | | 27 |
| 1 | | 12 | 5 | | 10 | 6 | 7 | | 13 | 4 | 8* | 3 | 2 | 11† | 9 | | | | | | | | | | 28 |
| 1 | | 12 | 5 | | 10 | 6 | 7 | 3 | 13 | | 4† | 8 | | 2*11 | 9 | | | | | | | | | | 29 |
| 1 | | 2 | 5 | | 10 | 6 | 7 | 4 | | 12 | 8 | 3 | | 11* | 9 | | | | | | | | | | 30 |
| | 1 | 2 | 5 | 10 | | 7 | 4 | 9 | | 11 | 8 | 3 | 6 | | | | | | | | | | | | 31 |
| | 1 | 2 | 5 | 10 | | 7 | 4 | 9* | | 11 | 8 | 3 | 6 | 12 | | | | | | | | | | | 32 |
| 1 | 2 | | 5 | 10 | | 7 | 4* | 9† | | 11 | 8 | 13 | 3 | 6 | 12 | | | | | | | | | | 33 |
| 1 | 2 | 13 | 5†10 | | 9 | | 4 | 7 | 8 | 12 | 3 | 6 | 11* | | | | | | | | | | | | 34 |
| 1 | 2 | 13 | 5 | 10† | 9* | 12 | 4 | 7 | 8 | | 3 | 6 | 11 | | | | | | | | | | | | 35 |
| 1 | 2 | 10 | 5 | | 9 | 12 | 4 | 11 | 8 | 7* | 3 | 6 | | | | | | | | | | | | | 36 |
| 1 | 2 | | 5 | | 7* | 8 | 9 | 4 | 11 | 12 | 3 | 6 | 10 | | | | | | | | | | | | 37 |
| 1 | 2 | 3 | 5 | | 7 | 10 | 9 | 4 | | 8 | 13 | 12 | 6† | 11* | | | | | | | | | | | 38 |
| 1 | 6 | 3 | 5 | | 9 | | 4 | 7 | 8 | 12 | 11 | 2 | 10* | | | | | | | | | | | | 39 |
| 18 | 21 | 32 | 15 | 25 | 31 | 14 | 7 | 24 | 32 | 12 | 24 | 8 | 25 | 16 | 32 | 17 | 11 | 28 | 4 | 9 | 11 | 6 | 6 | 1 | |
| | | | | + | | + | + | | + | | + | | + | + | + | + | | + | | | + | | | | |
| | | | | 8s | | 1s | 6s | | 4s | | 3s | | 3s | 6s | 2s | 8s | | 1s | | | 2s | | 4s | | |

# RANGERS                    Premier Division

*Year Formed:* 1873.   *Turned Professional:* 1893.   *Limited Company:* 1899.
*Ground:* Ibrox Stadium, Glasgow G51 2XD.   *Size:* 115yd×75yd.   *Capacity:* 44,000 (19,500 seated).
*Telephone:* 041-427 0159.   *Manager:* John Greig MBE.   *Secretary:* R. C. Ogilvie.
*Club Colours:* Royal blue shirts with white shorts, royal blue stockings.
*Club Nickname:* Blues or Gers.
*Record Attendance:* 118,567 v Celtic, Division 1, 2 Jan, 1939.
*Previous Grounds:* Flesher's Haugh on Glasgow Green was shared with Great Eastern FC: Kinning Park, Burnbank; Ibrox Park since 1887.
*Record Transfer Fee Received:* £140,000 from Coventry C for Colin Stein, Oct 1972.
*Record Transfer Fee Paid:* £100,000 to Hibernian for Colin Stein, Oct 1968.
**European Competitions:** *European Cup* 1956–57, 1957–58, 1959–60, 1961–62, 1963–64, 1964–65, 1975–76, 1976–77; *European Cup-Winners' Cup* 1960–61 (finalists), 1962–63, 1966–67 (finalists), 1969–70, 1971–72 (winners), 1973–74, 1977–78, 1981–82. *Fairs Cup* 1967–68, 1968–69, 1970–71.

## 1981–82 LEAGUE RECORD

| Match No. | Date | Venue | Opponents | Result | H/T Score | League Pos'n | Goalscorers | Atten-dance |
|---|---|---|---|---|---|---|---|---|
| 1 | Aug 29 | A | Partick T | W 1-0 | 0-0 | — | McLean (pen) | 16,000 |
| 2 | Sept 5 | H | Hibernian | D 2-2 | 1-1 | 4 | Bett, Cooper | 25,000 |
| 3 | 12 | A | St Mirren | D 1-1 | 1-0 | 5 | MacDonald | 15,652 |
| 4 | 19 | H | Celtic | L 0-2 | 0-1 | 6 | | 45,000 |
| 5 | Oct 3 | H | Airdrieonians | W 4-1 | 2-1 | 4 | Bett 2, Johnstone, Jardine | 12,500 |
| 6 | 10 | H | Aberdeen | D 0-0 | 0-0 | 5 | | 28,000 |
| 7 | 17 | A | Dundee | W 3-2 | 1-1 | 3 | Russell, MacDonald 2 | 11,956 |
| 8 | 24 | H | Morton | D 1-1 | 0-1 | 3 | Russell | 17,000 |
| 9 | 31 | H | Partick T | L 0-2 | 0-1 | 5 | | 17,000 |
| 10 | Nov 7 | A | Hibernian | W 2-1 | 1-1 | 4 | Bett 2 (1 pen) | 14,800 |
| 11 | 11 | A | Dundee U | L 0-2 | 0-1 | — | | 16,138 |
| 12 | 14 | H | St Mirren | W 4-1 | 1-0 | 4 | Johnstone, Russell, Bett (pen), Cooper | 18,000 |
| 13 | 21 | A | Celtic | D 3-3 | 3-2 | 5 | Dalziel, Bett, MacDonald | 48,600 |
| 14 | Dec 5 | A | Airdrieonians | D 2-2 | 1-1 | 5 | MacDonald, Russell | 14,500 |
| 15 | 19 | H | Dundee | W 2-1 | 1-0 | 5 | Bett (pen), McAdam | 8500 |
| 16 | Jan 9 | H | Celtic | W 1-0 | 0-0 | — | Bett (pen) | 42,000 |
| 17 | 16 | H | Dundee U | W 2-0 | 1-0 | — | Dalziel, Cooper | 18,000 |
| 18 | 30 | H | Hibernian | D 1-1 | 1-0 | 2 | Johnstone | 15,000 |
| 19 | Feb 17 | A | Partick T | L 0-2 | 0-1 | — | | 6513 |
| 20 | 20 | A | Dundee U | D 1-1 | 0-1 | 3 | Dawson | 12,945 |
| 21 | 27 | H | Morton | W 3-0 | 1-0 | 3 | MacDonald, Mackay, Dalziel | 10,200 |
| 22 | Mar 10 | A | St Mirren | W 3-2 | 1-2 | — | Bett (pen), Johnstone 2 | 9000 |
| 23 | 13 | A | Aberdeen | L 1-3 | 0-2 | 2 | Johnstone | 24,000 |
| 24 | 17 | A | Morton | D 0-0 | 0-0 | — | | 4579 |
| 25 | 20 | H | Partick T | W 4-1 | 0-0 | 3 | Johnstone, Russell, Bett (pen) MacDonald | 8000 |
| 26 | 27 | A | Hibernian | D 0-0 | 0-0 | 3 | | 12,390 |
| 27 | 31 | H | Airdrieonians | W 1-0 | 1-0 | — | MacDonald | 3000 |
| 28 | Apr 10 | A | Celtic | L 1-2 | 0-1 | 3 | Johnstone | 49,144 |
| 29 | 14 | A | Dundee | L 1-3 | 1-2 | — | MacDonald | 7975 |
| 30 | 17 | A | Airdrieonians | W 1-0 | 0-0 | 3 | MacDonald | 8000 |
| 31 | 21 | A | Aberdeen | L 1-3 | 0-0 | — | Johnstone | 8750 |
| 32 | 24 | H | Dundee U | D 1-1 | 1-0 | 3 | MacDonald | 10,000 |
| 33 | May 1 | A | Morton | W 3-1 | 3-1 | 3 | Russell, MacDonald 2 | 6500 |
| 34 | 5 | A | St Mirren | W 3-0 | 1-0 | — | MacDonald, McAdam, Redford | 4500 |
| 35 | 8 | H | Dundee | W 4-0 | 1-0 | 3 | Dalziel 3, Redford | 8500 |
| 36 | 15 | A | Aberdeen | L 0-4 | 0-4 | 3 | | 18,000 |

**Final League Position: 3**

### Goalscorers

*League* (57): MacDonald 14, Bett 11 (6 pens), Johnstone 9, Dalziel 6, Russell 6, Cooper 3, McAdam 2, Redford 2, Dawson 1, Jardine 1, Mackay 1, McLean 1 (pen).
*League Cup* (30): Redford 7, MacDonald 5, McAdam 4, Johnstone 3, Russell 3, Bett 1 (pen), Cooper 1, Jackson 1, Jardine 1, McLean 1 (pen), Miller 1, Stevens 1, own goal 1.
*Scottish Cup* (16): Johnstone 4, McAdam 3, Jardine 2, MacDonald 2, Bett 1, Cooper 1, McPherson 1, Redford 1, Russell 1.

## Honours

*Scottish League:* Division 1 Champions 1890–91 (shared with Dumbarton), 1898–99, 1899–1900, 1900–01, 1901–02, 1910–11, 1911–12, 1912–13, 1917–18, 1919–20, 1920–21, 1922–23, 1923–24, 1924–25, 1926–27, 1927–28, 1928–29, 1929–30, 1930–31, 1932–33, 1933–34, 1934–35, 1936–37, 1938–39, 1946–47, 1948–49, 1949–50, 1952–53, 1955–56, 1956–57, 1958–59, 1960–61, 1962–63, 1963–64, 1974–75; Runners-up 21 times; Premier Division Champions 1975–76, 1977–78; Runners-up 1976–77, 1978–79.

*Scottish Cup:* Winners 1894, 1897, 1898, 1903, 1928, 1930, 1932, 1934, 1935, 1936, 1948, 1949, 1950, 1953, 1960, 1962, 1963, 1964, 1966, 1973, 1976, 1978, 1979, 1981; Runners-up 13 times.

*Scottish League Cup:* Winners 1946–47, 1948–49, 1960–61, 1961–62, 1963–64, 1964–65, 1970–71, 1975–76, 1977–78, 1978–79, 1981–82; Runners-up 5 times.

*Record Victory:* 14-2 v Blairgowrie, Scottish Cup 1st rd, 20 Jan, 1934. *Record Defeat:* 2-10 v Airdrieonians, 1886. *Most League Points:* 76, Division 1, 1920–21. *Most Individual League Goals in Season:* 44, Sam English, Division 1, 1931–32. *Highest Scorer in Total Aggregate:* Bob McPhail, 233, 1927–39. *Most Capped Player:* George Young, 53, Scotland. *Most League Appearances:* John Greig, 496, 1962–78.

| McCloy P. | Stewart J. | Jardine W. | Dawson A. | Black K. | Miller A. | Stevens G. | Jackson C. | McClelland J. | Bett J. | Forsyth T. | Redford I. | Cooper D. | Russell R. | Johnstone D. | McAdam C. | Dalziel G. | MacDonald J. | McClean T. | Davies W. | Lyall K. | Mackay W. | McIntyre J. | Johnston W. | Robertson D. | Match No. |
|---|---|---|---|---|---|---|---|---|---|---|---|---|---|---|---|---|---|---|---|---|---|---|---|---|---|
| 1 | 2* |  | 3 | 4 |  |  | 6 |  | 5 | 12 | 7 | 8 | 10 | 9† |  |  | 13 | 11 |  |  |  |  |  |  | 1 |
| 1 | 2 | 3* | 13 | 4 |  |  | 6 |  | 5 | 9† | 7 | 8 |  |  | 10 | 11 |  |  |  | 12 |  |  |  |  | 2 |
| 1 | 2 |  |  | 5 | 3 | 6 | 4 | 10* | 7 | 8 | 9 | 12 |  | 11 |  |  |  |  |  |  |  |  |  |  | 3 |
| 1 | 2* | 3 |  | 6 | 5 |  | 8 | 4 | 10 | 7 |  | 9 | 12 | 13 |  |  |  |  |  |  |  |  | 11† |  | 4 |
| 1 | 2 | 3 |  | 4 |  | 6 | 5 | 12 | 7* | 8 | 9 |  | 10 |  |  | 13 |  |  |  |  |  |  | 11† |  | 5 |
| 1 | 2 | 3 |  | 4 |  | 6 | 5 | 12 | 7 | 8 |  | 9 | 10 |  |  |  |  |  |  |  |  |  | 11* |  | 6 |
| 1 | 2 | 3 |  | 4 |  | 6 | 5 | 12 | 7 | 8 |  | 9 | 10 |  |  |  |  |  |  |  |  |  | 11* |  | 7 |
| 1 | 2 | 3 |  |  | 5 | 6 | 4 | 12 | 7 | 8 |  | 9 | 10 |  |  |  |  |  |  |  |  |  | 11* |  | 8 |
| 1 | 2 | 3 |  | 5* |  | 6 | 4 | 12 | 7 | 8 | 13 | 9 | 10 |  |  |  |  |  |  |  |  |  | 11† |  | 9 |
| 1 | 2 |  | 3 |  | 5 |  | 6 | 4 | 10 | 7 | 8 | 9 |  | 11 |  |  |  |  |  |  |  |  |  |  | 10 |
| 1 | 2* | 3 | 13 |  | 5 |  | 6 | 4 | 10† | 7 | 8 | 9 | 12 | 11 |  |  |  |  |  |  |  |  |  |  | 11 |
| 1 | 2 |  | 3 | 4 |  | 6 | 5 | 10† | 7* | 8 | 9 | 13 | 11 |  |  |  | 12 |  |  |  |  |  |  |  | 12 |
| 1 | 2 |  | 3 | 4 | 5 | 6 | 13 | 7* | 8 | 9 | 10† | 11 |  |  |  |  | 12 |  |  |  |  |  |  |  | 13 |
| 1 | 2 |  | 3* | 4 | 5 | 6 | 12 | 7† | 8 | 9 | 11 | 10 |  |  |  |  | 13 |  |  |  |  |  |  |  | 14 |
| 1 | 2 |  | 3* | 4 | 5 | 6 | 10† | 7 | 8 | 9 | 13 | 11 |  |  |  | 12 |  |  |  |  |  |  |  |  | 15 |
| 1 | 2 | 3 |  | 4 | 5 | 6 | 7* | 8 | 9 | 12 | 10 | 11 |  |  |  |  |  |  |  |  |  |  |  |  | 16 |
| 1 | 2 | 3 |  | 4 |  | 6 | 12 | 7 | 8 | 9 | 5 | 10* | 11 |  |  |  |  |  |  |  |  |  |  |  | 17 |
| 1 | 2 | 3 |  |  | 5 | 6* | 7 | 8 | 9 | 4 | 10 | 11 |  |  |  | 12 |  |  |  |  |  |  |  |  | 18 |
| 1 | 2 |  | 3 | 6 | 5 |  | 7 | 10 | 8 | 4 | 9 | 11 |  |  |  |  |  |  |  |  |  |  |  |  | 19 |
| 1 | 2 | 3 |  | 6 |  | 5 | 10 | 12 | 7* | 8 | 9 | 4 | 11 |  |  |  |  |  |  |  |  |  |  |  | 20 |
| 1 | 2 | 3 | 10† |  | 5 | 6 | 7* | 8 | 9 | 4 | 13 | 11 |  |  |  | 12 |  |  |  |  |  |  |  |  | 21 |
| 1 | 2 | 3 |  | 10 | 5 | 6 | 11 | 7 | 8 | 9 | 4 |  |  |  |  |  |  |  |  |  |  |  |  |  | 22 |
| 1 | 2 | 3 |  | 10* | 5 | 6 | 11 | 7 | 8 | 9 | 4 | 12 |  |  |  |  |  |  |  |  |  |  |  |  | 23 |
| 1 | 2 | 3 |  |  | 5 | 4 | 6 | 10 | 8 | 9 | 11 |  |  |  |  |  |  |  | 7 |  |  |  |  |  | 24 |
| 1 | 2 | 3 | 12 |  | 5* | 4 | 6† | 10 | 8 | 9 | 7 | 11 | 13 |  |  |  |  |  |  |  |  |  |  |  | 25 |
| 1 | 4 | 2 | 3 |  | 5 | 6 | 10* | 8 | 7 | 9 | 12 | 11† |  | 13 |  |  |  |  |  |  |  |  |  |  | 26 |
| 1 | 4 | 2 | 3 |  | 5 | 6 | 12 | 8 | 7 | 10 | 11* | 9 |  |  |  |  |  |  |  |  |  |  |  |  | 27 |
| 1 | 2 | 3 |  | 5 | 4 | 6 | 10* | 7 | 8 | 9 | 12 | 11 |  |  |  |  |  |  |  |  |  |  |  |  | 28 |
| 1 | 2 | 3 |  | 5 | 4 | 6 | 10 | 7 | 8 | 9 | 11 |  |  |  |  |  |  |  |  |  |  |  |  |  | 29 |
| 1 | 4 | 2 | 3 |  | 5 | 6 | 7 | 8 | 9 | 10 | 11 |  |  |  |  |  |  |  |  |  |  |  |  |  | 30 |
| 1 | 4 | 2 | 3 |  | 5 | 6 | 8 | 9 | 12 | 7 | 10 | 11* |  |  |  |  |  |  |  |  |  |  |  |  | 31 |
| 1 | 4 | 2 | 3 |  | 5 | 6* | 12 | 13 | 8 | 9 | 10 | 7† | 11 |  |  |  |  |  |  |  |  |  |  |  | 32 |
| 1 | 2 | 3 |  | 5 | 4 | 6 | 10 | 7 | 8* | 9 | 12 | 11 |  |  |  |  |  |  |  |  |  |  |  |  | 33 |
| 1 | 2 |  | 3 |  | 4 | 6 | 10 | 7 |  | 9 | 5 | 8 | 11 |  |  |  |  |  |  |  |  |  |  |  | 34 |
| 1 | 2* |  | 3 |  | 4 | 6 | 10 | 7 |  | 9 | 5 | 8 | 11† | 13 |  | 12 |  |  |  |  |  |  |  |  | 35 |
| 1 | 2* | 3 |  | 8 |  | 5 | 4 | 6 | 10 | 7 |  | 9 | 11 | 12 |  |  |  |  |  |  |  |  |  |  | 36 |
| 10 | 26 | 36 | 25 | 7 | 14 | 13 | 21 | 14 | 35 | 12 | 20 | 29 | 32 | 27 | 15 | 14 | 32 | 2 | 1 | 3 | 1 | — | 6 | 1 | |
|  |  | + 1s | + 2s |  |  |  |  |  |  |  | + 12s | + 1s |  | + 1s | + 7s | + 3s | + 3s | + 1s | + 3s |  | + 6s | + 1s | + 2s | + 1s | |

# ST JOHNSTONE Division 1

*Year Formed:* 1884.
*Ground:* Muirton Park. *Size:* 109yd×74yd. *Capacity:* 24,950 (2415 seats).
*Telephone:* Perth 26961.
*Manager:* Alec Rennie.
*Secretary:* George Bell. *Coach:* T. G. Fleming.
*Club Colours:* Royal blue with white collar and cuffs, white shorts and white stockings with royal blue tops.
*Club Nickname:* Saints.
*Record Attendance:* 29,972 v Dundee, Scottish Cup 2nd rd, 10 Feb, 1952.
*Previous Ground:* Recreation Ground.
**European Competition:** *UEFA Cup 1971–72.*

## 1981–82 LEAGUE RECORD

| Match No. | Date | Venue | Opponents | Result | H/T Score | League Pos'n | Goalscorers | Atten- dance |
|---|---|---|---|---|---|---|---|---|
| 1 | Aug 29 | H | Queen of the S | W 1-0 | 1-0 | — | Pelosi | 1892 |
| 2 | Sept 5 | A | Clydebank | W 3-2 | 0-1 | 3 | Caldwell, Pelosi, Weir | 600 |
| 3 | 12 | H | Motherwell | L 1-3 | 0-2 | 8 | Docherty | 2518 |
| 4 | 16 | A | Ayr U | D 1-1 | 1-0 | — | Morton | 2366 |
| 5 | 19 | A | Falkirk | L 0-1 | 0-1 | 9 | | 2000 |
| 6 | 23 | H | Kilmarnock | L 0-2 | 0-2 | — | | 956 |
| 7 | 26 | H | Raith R | W 2-0 | 1-0 | 9 | Caldwell, McDonald | 1798 |
| 8 | Oct 3 | A | Dumbarton | L 1-2 | 1-1 | 10 | McDonald | 500 |
| 9 | 7 | A | Hearts | L 1-3 | 0-1 | — | Morton | 4077 |
| 10 | 10 | A | East Stirling | D 1-1 | 1-1 | 10 | Rutherford | 2000 |
| 11 | 17 | H | Queen's Park | W 2-0 | 1-0 | 8 | Brogan, Brannigan | 1840 |
| 12 | 24 | H | Hamilton A | D 1-1 | 0-1 | 9 | Brogan | 1797 |
| 13 | 31 | A | Dunfermline Ath | W 2-1 | 0-1 | 8 | Brannigan 2 | 2750 |
| 14 | Nov 7 | H | Clydebank | L 1-3 | 0-2 | 8 | Morton | 1774 |
| 15 | 14 | A | Queen of the S | D 3-3 | 1-0 | 8 | Brogan, Morton, Brannigan | 1500 |
| 16 | 21 | H | Ayr U | W 2-0 | 1-0 | 7 | Brannigan 2 | 1716 |
| 17 | 28 | A | Raith R | W 4-0 | 2-0 | 6 | Morton, Brogan 3 | 1800 |
| 18 | Dec 5 | H | Dumbarton | W 5-2 | 2-1 | 6 | Weir, Morton 2, Mackay, Brogan | 1776 |
| 19 | 12 | A | Kilmarnock | W 2-0 | 1-0 | 4 | Beedie, Morton | 1300 |
| 20 | Jan 30 | A | Hamilton A | D 0-0 | 0-0 | 5 | | 1067 |
| 21 | Feb 17 | A | Motherwell | D 2-2 | 2-0 | — | Morton, Rutherford | 4205 |
| 22 | 20 | A | Dumbarton | L 0-2 | 0-0 | 7 | | 400 |
| 23 | 23 | H | Hearts | W 2-1 | 0-1 | — | Docherty, Brogan | 2300 |
| 24 | 27 | H | Queen of the S | D 3-3 | 1-1 | 6 | Brannigan 2, Morton (pen) | 1884 |
| 25 | Mar 6 | H | Motherwell | W 3-2 | 1-2 | 3 | Morton 3 | 2914 |
| 26 | 10 | H | Falkirk | W 2-0 | 1-0 | — | Beedie, Brogan | 950 |
| 27 | 13 | A | Hamilton A | L 0-2 | 0-1 | 5 | | 1277 |
| 28 | 16 | A | Queen's Park | L 2-3 | 2-2 | — | Morton, Brogan | 475 |
| 29 | 20 | H | Ayr U | W 3-2 | 2-1 | 5 | Rutherford, Beedie, Morton | 1792 |
| 30 | 24 | H | East Stirling | W 3-2 | 2-0 | — | Brogan 2, Beedie | 1537 |
| 31 | 27 | A | Falkirk | L 1-2 | 0-0 | 5 | Rutherford | 2500 |
| 32 | 31 | H | Dunfermline Ath | W 2-1 | 1-0 | — | Morton 2 (1 pen) | 1200 |
| 33 | Apr 3 | A | Hearts | L 0-3 | 0-2 | 5 | | 4577 |
| 34 | 10 | H | Kilmarnock | L 1-3 | 1-0 | 5 | Brannigan | 2209 |
| 35 | 17 | A | Dunfermline Ath | L 0-1 | 0-1 | 6 | | 1856 |
| 36 | 24 | H | East Stirling | W 7-1 | 3-0 | 6 | Beedie, McNeil 2, Brogan 2, Rutherford 2 | 1069 |
| 37 | May 1 | A | Queen's Park | L 1-2 | 0-1 | 6 | McNeil | 708 |
| 38 | 8 | H | Clydebank | D 3-3 | 2-1 | 6 | Brannigan 2, Brogan | 1196 |
| 39 | 15 | A | Raith R | W 1-0 | 1-0 | 5 | Brogan | 950 |

**Final League Position: 5**

### Goalscorers

*League* (69): Morton 17 (2 pens), Brogan 16, Brannigan 11, Rutherford 6, Beedie 5, McNeil 3, Caldwell 2, Docherty 2, McDonald 2, Pelosi 2, Weir 2, Mackay 1.
*League Cup* (8): McCoist 4, Beedie 1, Brogan 1, McDonald 1, Morton 1 (pen).
*Scottish Cup* (3): Beedie 1, Brogan 1, Morton 1 (pen).

**Honours**

*Scottish League* – Division 2 Champions 1923–24, 1959–60, 1962–63; Runners-up 1931–32.
*Scottish League Cup* – Runners-up 1969–70.
*Record Victory:* 8–1 v Partick T, League Cup, 16 Aug, 1969.
*Record Defeat:* 1–10 v Third Lanark, Scottish Cup 1st rd, 24 Jan, 1903.
*Most League Points:* 56, Division 2, 1923–24.
*Most Individual League Goals in Season:* Jimmy Benson, 36, Division 2, 1931–32.
*Most Capped Player:* Sandy McLaren, 5, Scotland.

| Tulloch G. | McGregor R. | Mackay J. | Kilgour R. | McNeil T. | Weir J. | Rutherford A. | Caldwell A. | Beedie S. | Brogan J. | Fleming G. | Morton J. | Brannigan A. | Docherty J. | Pelosi J. | McDonald K. | McVicar D. | Redford G. | Barron D. | O'Brien P. | Aitchison D. | Reid J. | Match No. |
|---|---|---|---|---|---|---|---|---|---|---|---|---|---|---|---|---|---|---|---|---|---|---|
| 1 | 2 | 3 | 4 | 5 | 6 |  |  |  | 11 | 10 | 8 | 9* | 7 | 12 |  |  |  |  |  |  |  | 1 |
| 1 | 2 |  | 4 | 5 | 6 |  |  | 8 | 11 | 10 | 9 |  | 7 |  |  |  | 3 |  |  |  |  | 2 |
| 1 | 2 | 3 | 4* | 5 | 6 |  |  | 8 | 11 | 10 | 9† | 13 | 7 |  |  | 12 |  |  |  |  |  | 3 |
| 1 | 2 | 3 |  | 5 | 6 |  |  |  | 11 | 10 | 8 | 9 | 7 |  |  |  | 4 |  |  |  |  | 4 |
| 1 | 2 | 3 | 5* | 6† |  |  |  |  | 11 | 10 | 8 | 9 | 7 |  | 13 | 12 | 4 |  |  |  |  | 5 |
| 1 | 2 | 3 |  | 5 | 6 |  |  |  | 11 | 10 | 8* | 9 | 7 | 12 |  |  | 4 |  |  |  |  | 6 |
| 1 | 2 | 3 |  | 5 | 6 |  |  |  | 11 | 10 | 8 | 9 |  |  | 7 |  | 4 |  |  |  |  | 7 |
| 1 | 2 | 3 | 12 | 5 | 6 |  |  | 13 | 11 | 10 | 8 | 9† | 7 |  |  |  | 4* |  |  |  |  | 8 |
| 1 | 2 | 3* |  | 5 | 6 | 11 |  | 8 | 9 | 10 | 12 |  |  |  | 7 |  | 4 |  |  |  |  | 9 |
| 1 | 2 |  |  | 5 | 6 | 11 |  | 8 | 9 | 10 |  |  | 7 |  | 3 |  | 4 |  |  |  |  | 10 |
| 1 | 2 | 3 | 4 | 5 | 6 |  |  | 8 | 9 | 10 | 11 | 7 |  |  |  |  |  |  |  |  |  | 11 |
| 1 | 2 | 3 | 4 | 5 | 6 |  |  | 8 | 9* | 10 | 11 | 7 | 12† | 13 |  |  |  |  |  |  |  | 12 |
| 1 | 2 | 3 | 4 | 5 | 6 |  |  | 8 |  | 10 | 11 | 7 | 9 |  |  |  |  |  |  |  |  | 13 |
| 1 | 2 | 3 | 4 | 5 | 6 | 7* |  | 8 |  | 10 | 11 | 13 | 9† | 12 |  |  |  |  |  |  |  | 14 |
| 1 | 2 | 3 | 4 | 5 | 6* | 7 |  | 8 | 9 | 10 | 11 | 12 |  |  |  |  |  |  |  |  |  | 15 |
| 1 | 6 | 2 | 3 | 4 | 5 |  | 7 | 8 | 9 | 10 | 11 |  |  |  |  |  |  |  |  |  |  | 16 |
| 1 | 6 | 2 | 3 | 4 | 5 |  | 7 | 8 | 9 | 10 | 11 |  |  |  |  |  |  |  |  |  |  | 17 |
| 1 | 6 | 2 | 3 | 4 | 5 |  | 7 | 8 | 9 | 10 | 11 |  |  |  |  |  |  |  |  |  |  | 18 |
| 1 | 6 | 2 | 3 | 4 | 5 |  | 7 | 8 | 9 | 10 | 11 |  |  |  |  |  |  |  |  |  |  | 19 |
| 1 |  | 2 | 3 |  | 5 |  | 7 | 8 | 9 | 10 | 11 | 4* |  |  |  | 6 |  | 12 |  |  |  | 20 |
| 1 |  | 2 | 3 | 4 | 5 |  |  | 8 | 11 | 10 | 9 |  |  |  |  | 6 | 7 |  |  |  |  | 21 |
| 1 |  | 2 | 3 | 4* | 5 |  |  | 8 | 11 | 10 | 13 | 9† |  | 12 |  | 6 | 7 |  |  |  |  | 22 |
| 1 |  | 2 | 3 | 4 | 5 |  | 13 | 8 | 11† | 10 | 12 | 9 |  |  |  | 6 | 7* |  |  |  |  | 23 |
| 1 |  | 2 | 3 | 4* | 5 |  | 7 |  | 11 | 10 | 8 | 9 |  |  |  | 6 |  | 12 |  |  |  | 24 |
| 1 |  | 2 | 3 |  | 5 | 4* |  | 8 | 11 | 10 | 7 | 9 |  |  |  | 6 |  | 12 |  |  |  | 25 |
| 1 |  | 2 | 3 |  | 5 | 4* |  | 8 | 11 | 10 | 7 | 9 |  |  |  | 6 |  | 12 |  |  |  | 26 |
| 1 |  | 2 | 3 | 12 | 5 | 4* |  | 8 | 11 | 10 | 7† | 9 |  |  |  | 6 | 13 |  |  |  |  | 27 |
| 1 |  | 2 | 3 | 13 | 5† | 4 |  | 8 | 11 | 10 | 7 | 9* |  |  |  | 6 |  | 12 |  |  |  | 28 |
| 1 |  | 2 | 3 | 4 | 5* | 6 | 7 | 8 | 11 | 10 | 9 |  |  |  |  | 3 |  | 12 |  |  |  | 29 |
| 1 |  | 2 | 3 | 4 |  | 6 | 7 | 8 | 11 | 10 | 9 |  |  |  |  |  | 5 |  |  |  |  | 30 |
| 1 |  | 2 | 3 | 4 | 5 | 6 | 7 | 8 | 11 | 10 | 9 |  |  |  |  |  |  |  |  |  |  | 31 |
|  | 1 | 2 | 3 | 4 | 5* | 6 | 7 | 8 | 11 | 10 | 9 |  |  |  |  |  | 12 |  |  |  |  | 32 |
|  | 1 | 2 | 3 | 4 |  | 6 | 7 | 8 | 11 | 10 | 9 |  |  |  |  |  | 5 |  |  |  |  | 33 |
| 1 |  | 2 | 3 | 4* | 5 |  | 7 | 8 | 11† | 10 | 9 |  |  |  | 12 |  | 6 | 13 |  |  |  | 34 |
| 1 |  | 2 | 3 | 13 | 5 |  | 7 | 8 | 12 | 10 | 9 |  |  |  |  | 4* | 6 | 11† |  |  |  | 35 |
| 1 |  | 2 | 3 | 4* | 5 | 6† | 7 | 8 | 11 | 10 | 9 | 12 |  |  |  |  |  | 13 |  |  |  | 36 |
| 1 |  | 2 | 3 | 4 | 5 |  | 7 | 8 | 11 |  | 9 | 10* |  |  | 12 |  | 6 |  |  |  |  | 37 |
| 1 |  | 2 | 3 | 4* | 5 |  | 7 | 8 | 11 | 10 | 9 |  |  |  | 12 |  | 6 |  |  |  |  | 38 |
| 1 |  |  | 3 |  | 5 |  | 7 | 8 | 4 | 10 | 6 | 9 |  |  | 11 | 2*/ |  |  | 12 |  |  | 39 |
| 37 | 2 | 13 | 36 | 29 | 25 | 37 | 21 | 25 | 32 | 36 | 38 | 35 | 16 | 9 | 4 | 8 | 7 | 14 | 4 | 1 | — | |

Substitute appearances (included in totals): McGregor 1s, Mackay 3s; Brogan 1s, Fleming 1s, Morton 1s; Docherty 3s, Pelosi 3s; McVicar 5s, Redford 5s, Barron 2s, O'Brien 3s, Aitchison 7s, Reid 1s, 1s.

558

# ST MIRREN — Premier Division

*Year Formed:* 1876. *Ground:* St Mirren Park (also known as Love Street). *Size:* 115yd×74yd. *Capacity:* 25,800.
*Telephone:* 041-889 2558 and 840 1337.
*Manager:* Ricky McFarlane. *Secretary:* A. W. Marshall.
*Club Colours:* Black and white stripes, black shorts and black stockings with three white bands.
*Club Nickname:* The Buddies.
*Record Attendance:* 47,428 v Celtic, Scottish Cup 4th rd, 7 Mar, 1925.
**European Competition:** *UEFA Cup:* 1980–81.

## 1981–82 LEAGUE RECORD

| Match No. | Date | Venue | Opponents | Result | H/T Score | League Pos'n | Goalscorers | Atten- dance |
|---|---|---|---|---|---|---|---|---|
| 1 | Aug 29 | H | Morton | W 2-0 | 0-0 | — | Scanlon 2 (1 pen) | 5609 |
| 2 | Sept 5 | A | Airdrieonians | W 4-3 | 0-0 | 2 | McAvennie 2, Stark 2 | 3000 |
| 3 | 12 | H | Rangers | D 1-1 | 0-1 | 2 | McDougall | 15,652 |
| 4 | 19 | A | Dundee | L 0-3 | 0-2 | 2 | | 5257 |
| 5 | 26 | H | Hibernian | W 1-0 | 0-0 | 2 | Stark (pen) | 2400 |
| 6 | Oct 3 | A | Partick T | D 1-1 | 0-1 | 3 | McDougall | 4159 |
| 7 | 10 | H | Celtic | L 1-2 | 0-2 | 3 | Scanlon (pen) | 16,411 |
| 8 | 17 | H | Aberdeen | L 1-2 | 1-1 | 4 | McAvennie | 6870 |
| 9 | 24 | A | Dundee U | W 2-0 | 2-0 | 4 | Bone 2 | 6964 |
| 10 | 31 | A | Morton | W 2-0 | 0-0 | 3 | Stark, McEachran | 4500 |
| 11 | Nov 7 | H | Airdrieonians | D 1-1 | 0-0 | 3 | Stark | 4575 |
| 12 | 14 | A | Rangers | L 1-4 | 0-1 | 5 | Richardson | 18,000 |
| 13 | 21 | H | Dundee | W 4-0 | 3-0 | 4 | McAvennie 2, Somner, Fitzpatrick | 3600 |
| 14 | 28 | A | Hibernian | D 0-0 | 0-0 | 4 | | 4750 |
| 15 | Dec 5 | H | Partick T | W 2-1 | 0-0 | 3 | Bone, Stark | 4513 |
| 16 | Jan 3 | H | Morton | W 3-1 | 1-0 | — | McAvennie 2, Scanlon | 7078 |
| 17 | 30 | A | Dundee | W 2-0 | 1-0 | 3 | Bone, McAvennie | 4628 |
| 18 | Feb 3 | H | Dundee U | W 1-0 | 0-0 | — | Richardson | 5198 |
| 19 | 6 | A | Partick T | D 0-0 | 0-0 | 2 | | 3988 |
| 20 | 20 | H | Hibernian | D 2-2 | 1-2 | 2 | McAvennie, McDougall | 5138 |
| 21 | 27 | A | Dundee U | D 1-1 | 1-0 | 2 | McDougall | 7653 |
| 22 | Mar 10 | H | Rangers | L 2-3 | 2-1 | — | Richardson, Scanlon (pen) | 9000 |
| 23 | 13 | H | Celtic | L 2-5 | 0-4 | 4 | McDougall 2 | 17,084 |
| 24 | 20 | A | Morton | W 1-0 | 0-0 | 4 | Richardson | 4200 |
| 25 | 27 | H | Airdrieonians | W 3-0 | 1-0 | 4 | Stark, McDougall, McAvennie | 4289 |
| 26 | Apr 10 | A | Dundee | L 0-1 | 0-1 | 5 | | 3804 |
| 27 | 14 | A | Aberdeen | L 1-4 | 0-0 | — | Stark | 12,119 |
| 28 | 17 | H | Partick T | W 2-0 | 0-0 | 5 | Somner, Logan | 3593 |
| 29 | 21 | A | Airdrieonians | W 2-0 | 0-0 | — | McAvennie 2 | 2500 |
| 30 | 24 | A | Hibernian | L 1-2 | 0-0 | 5 | Stark (pen) | 4070 |
| 31 | May 1 | H | Dundee U | D 2-2 | 1-0 | 5 | McAvennie, Stark (pen) | 3404 |
| 32 | 3 | A | Celtic | D 0-0 | 0-0 | — | | 27,395 |
| 33 | 5 | A | Rangers | L 0-3 | 0-1 | — | | 4500 |
| 34 | 8 | A | Aberdeen | L 1-5 | 1-3 | 5 | Speirs | 9000 |
| 35 | 12 | H | Aberdeen | L 0-2 | 0-1 | — | | 3942 |
| 36 | 15 | A | Celtic | L 0-3 | 0-0 | 5 | | 39,369 |

**Final League Position: 5**

### Goalscorers
*League* (49): McAvennie 13, Stark 10 (3 pens), McDougall 7, Scanlon 5 (3 pens), Bone 4, Richardson 4, Somner 2, Fitzpatrick 1, Logan 1, McEachran 1, Speirs 1.
*League Cup* (20): McDougall 6, Scanlon 4 (2 pens), Logan 2, McAvennie 2, Stark 2, McCormack 1, Richardson 1, Somner 1, own goal 1.
*Scottish Cup* (8): McAvennie 2, Abercromby 1, Bone 1, Fitzpatrick 1, McDougall 1, Scanlon 1, Somner 1.

**Honours**

*Scottish League* – Division 1 Champions 1976–77; Division 2 Champions 1967–68; Runners-up 1935–36.
*Scottish Cup* – Winners 1926, 1959; Runners-up 1908, 1934, 1962.
*Victory Cup:* 1919–20.
*Scottish Summer Cup:* 1943–44.
*Scottish League Cup:* Runners-up 1955–56.
*Anglo-Scottish Cup:* Winners 1979–80.
*Record Victory:* 15-0 v Glasgow University, Scottish Cup 1st rd, 30 Jan, 1960.
*Record Defeat:* 2-9 v Dundee, Division 1, 29 Feb, 1964.
*Most League Points:* 62, Division 2, 1967–68; Division 1, 1976–77.
*Most Individual League Goals in Season:* Dunky Walker, 45, Division 1, 1921–22.
*Most Capped Player:* Iain Munro, 7, Scotland.

| Thomson W. | Money C. | Beckett A. | Abercromby W. | Fitzpatrick A. | McCormack J. | Fulton M. | Copland J. | Richardson A. | Bone J. | Stark W. | McDougall F. | Logan A. | McAvennie F. | Scanlon I. | Somner D. | Young J. | Walker D. | McEachran J. | Curran J. | Boag J. | Speirs G. | McAveety P. | Match No. |
|---|---|---|---|---|---|---|---|---|---|---|---|---|---|---|---|---|---|---|---|---|---|---|---|
| 1 |  | 2 | 3 | 4 | 5 | 6 | 10 | 9 | 8 |  | 7 |  | 11 |  |  |  |  |  |  |  |  |  | 1 |
| 1 |  | 2 | 3 |  | 5 | 6 | 4 | 9 | 8 | 12 | 7* | 10 | 11 |  |  |  |  |  |  |  |  |  | 2 |
| 1 |  | 2 | 3 | 4 | 5 | 12 | 6 | 9 | 8 |  | 7 | 10* | 11 |  |  |  |  |  |  |  |  |  | 3 |
| 1 |  | 2 | 3 | 4 | 5 | 6 |  | 9 | 8 | 12 | 7 | 10 | 11 |  |  |  |  |  |  |  |  |  | 4 |
| 1 |  | 2 | 10 | 4 | 5 | 3 | 6 |  | 8 |  | 7 | 12 | 11* | 9 |  |  |  |  |  |  |  |  | 5 |
| 1 |  | 2 | 6 |  | 5 | 3* | 4 | 12 | 8 |  | 7 | 10 | 11 | 9 |  |  |  |  |  |  |  |  | 6 |
| 1 |  | 3 | 10 | 4 | 5 | 6 |  | 9 | 8 | 12 | 7 |  | 11 | 2* |  |  |  |  |  |  |  |  | 7 |
| 1 |  | 3 | 10 | 4 | 5* | 6 |  | 9 | 8 | 12 | 7 |  | 11 | 2 |  |  |  |  |  |  |  |  | 8 |
| 1 |  | 6 |  | 4 | 3 | 5 |  | 9 | 8 | 12 | 10 |  | 11 | 2 | 7* |  |  |  |  |  |  |  | 9 |
| 1 |  | 3 | 6 |  | 4 | 5 |  | 9 | 8 | 7* | 10 |  | 11 | 2 | 12 |  |  |  |  |  |  |  | 10 |
| 1 |  | 3 | 6 |  | 4 | 5 |  | 9 | 8 | 12 | 10 |  | 11 | 2 | 7* |  |  |  |  |  |  |  | 11 |
| 1 |  | 2 | 3 | 4* | 6 | 5 | 10 | 8 | 13 | 12 | 11† | 9 |  |  | 7 |  |  |  |  |  |  |  | 12 |
| 1 |  | 3 | 10 | 4 | 2 | 5 | 6 | 8 | 7* |  | 11 |  | 9 |  | 12 |  |  |  |  |  |  |  | 13 |
| 1 |  | 3 | 10 | 4 | 2 | 5 | 6 | 8* | 7 | 12 | 11 |  | 9 |  |  |  |  |  |  |  |  |  | 14 |
| 1 |  | 3* | 10 | 4 | 2 | 5 | 6 | 13 | 8 | 12 | 7 |  | 11 | 9† |  |  |  |  |  |  |  |  | 15 |
| 1 |  | 3 | 10 | 4 | 2 | 5 | 6 | 9 | 8 |  | 7 |  | 11 |  |  |  |  |  |  |  |  |  | 16 |
| 1 |  | 3 | 10 | 4* | 2 | 5 | 6 | 12 | 9 |  | 7† | 13 | 8 | 11 |  |  |  |  |  |  |  |  | 17 |
| 1 |  | 3 | 10 | 4 | 2 | 5 | 6 | 12 | 9 |  | 8 |  | 11 |  | 7* |  |  |  |  |  |  |  | 18 |
| 1 |  | 3 | 4 | 2 | 5 | 6 | 8 | 9 | 7 |  | 12 | 10 | 11* |  |  |  |  |  |  |  |  |  | 19 |
| 1 |  | 4 | 3 | 5 | 6 | 7 | 13 | 8 | 9 |  | 10 | 11† |  | 2* |  |  |  |  | 12 |  |  |  | 20 |
| 1 |  | 4 | 3 | 5 | 6 |  | 7 | 8 | 9 | 12 | 10 |  |  | 2 | 11* |  |  |  |  |  |  |  | 21 |
| 1 |  | 3 | 4 | 2 | 5 | 6 | 10 | 8 | 9 |  | 11 |  |  |  |  |  |  | 7 |  |  |  |  | 22 |
| 1 |  | 3 | 4 | 2 | 5 | 6 | 10 | 9 | 8 | 12 | 11 |  |  |  |  |  |  | 7* |  |  |  |  | 23 |
| 1 |  | 3 | 4 | 2 | 5 | 6 | 10 | 7 | 8 | 9 |  |  | 11* | 12 |  |  |  |  |  |  |  |  | 24 |
| 1 |  | 2 | 3 |  | 5 | 6 | 4 | 7 | 8 | 9 | 10 |  | 11 |  |  |  |  |  |  |  |  |  | 25 |
| 1 |  | 3 | 4* | 5 | 6 | 13 | 8 | 7 | 10 | 11† | 9 |  |  | 2 | 12 |  |  |  |  |  |  |  | 26 |
|  | 1 | 6 | 4 | 3 | 5 | 12 | 7 |  | 10 | 11 |  |  |  | 2 | 9 | 8* |  |  |  |  |  |  | 27 |
| 1 |  | 10 | 4 | 5 | 6 | 11 | 8† | 12 | 13 | 9 |  |  |  | 2 | 7* | 3 |  |  |  |  |  |  | 28 |
| 1 |  | 3 | 4 | 5 | 6 | 11 | 8 |  | 10 | 9 |  |  |  | 7 | 2 |  |  |  |  |  |  |  | 29 |
| 1 |  | 3* | 4 | 5 | 6 | 7 | 8 | 13 | 10 | 11† | 9 |  |  | 12 | 2 |  |  |  |  |  |  |  | 30 |
| 1 |  | 3 | 4 | 5 | 4 | 8 | 11 | 7 | 10 | 9 |  |  |  | 2 |  |  |  |  |  |  |  |  | 31 |
| 1 |  | 3* | 11 | 5 | 6 | 8 | 9 | 13 | 10† | 12 |  |  |  | 2 | 7 | 4 |  |  |  |  |  |  | 32 |
| 1 |  | 2 | 11 | 4 | 5 | 6 | 8 | 7 | 10 | 9 |  |  |  | 3 |  |  |  |  |  |  |  |  | 33 |
| 1 |  | 3 | 4 | 5 | 6 | 8* | 12 | 2 | 7 | 10 | 9 |  |  | 11 |  |  |  |  |  |  |  |  | 34 |
| 1 |  | 2 | 4 | 5 | 6 | 11 | 9 | 8 | 12 | 10 |  |  |  | 3 | 7* |  |  |  |  |  |  |  | 35 |
| 1 |  | 2 | 4 | 5 | 6 | 11† | 8 | 10* | 12 | 7 | 9 |  |  | 3 |  |  |  | 13 |  |  |  |  | 36 |
| 35 | 1 | 27 | 30 | 24 | 25 | 28 | 36 | 17 | 20 | 32 | 15 | 5 | 29 | 25 | 14 | 5 | 9 | 10 | 5 | 2 | 1 | 1 |  |

Substitute appearances: +1s, +2s, +6s, +1s, +3s, +15s, +2s, +2s, +4s, +2s

# STENHOUSEMUIR Division 2

*Year Formed:* 1884. *Ground:* Ochilview Park. *Size:* 110yd×72yd. *Capacity:* 10,450 (450 seated).
*Telephone:* Larbert (0324) 562992.
*Team Manager:* Jim Black. *Secretary:* Jim Richardson. *Trainer:* W. Williamson.
*Club Colours:* Maroon shirts with white trimmings, white shorts and stockings.
*Change Colours:* Sky blue shirts with white trimmings, white shorts and stockings.
*Club Nickname:* The Warriors.
*Previous Grounds:* South Broomage until 1889, Goschen Park 1889–1890, Ochilview Park from 1890.
*Record Attendance:* 12,500 v East Fife, Scottish Cup 4th rd, 11 Mar, 1950.
*Record Receipts:* £2,800 v Celtic, Scottish League Cup quarter-final 1st leg, 10 Sept, 1975.

## 1981–82 LEAGUE RECORD

| Match No. | Date | Venue | Opponents | Result | H/T Score | League Pos'n | Goalscorers | Atten- dance |
|---|---|---|---|---|---|---|---|---|
| 1 | Aug 29 | A | Clyde | L 0-3 | 0-2 | — | | 480 |
| 2 | Sept 5 | H | East Fife | W 2-0 | 2-0 | 8 | Jack, Murray | 300 |
| 3 | 8 | H | Brechin C | L 0-4 | 0-2 | — | | 200 |
| 4 | 12 | A | Alloa | L 0-1 | 0-1 | 13 | | 477 |
| 5 | 15 | H | Albion R | D 2-2 | 1-0 | — | Campbell, Meakin | 380 |
| 6 | 19 | H | Berwick R | D 1-1 | 1-0 | 11 | Kirkland | 300 |
| 7 | 23 | A | Cowdenbeath | L 1-3 | 0-1 | — | Bremner | 380 |
| 8 | 26 | A | Arbroath | L 0-3 | 0-2 | 14 | | 770 |
| 9 | Oct 3 | H | Stirling Albion | D 0-0 | 0-0 | 13 | | 470 |
| 10 | 10 | H | Montrose | L 2-4 | 1-1 | 14 | Jenkins, Munn | 250 |
| 11 | 17 | A | Stranraer | L 1-2 | 1-1 | 14 | Hamilton (og) | 448 |
| 12 | 24 | H | Meadowbank T | L 1-2 | 1-0 | 14 | Meakin | 500 |
| 13 | 31 | A | Forfar Ath | L 0-2 | 0-2 | 14 | | 937 |
| 14 | Nov 7 | A | East Fife | L 2-3 | 1-0 | 14 | Murray, Meakin (pen) | 339 |
| 15 | 14 | H | Clyde | L 0-3 | 0-1 | 14 | | 500 |
| 16 | 21 | A | Albion R | W 4-1 | 1-1 | 13 | Jenkins 2, Bremner, Harper | 300 |
| 17 | 28 | H | Arbroath | L 1-3 | 0-2 | 13 | Jack | 300 |
| 18 | Dec 5 | A | Stirling Albion | W 3-2 | 1-1 | 13 | Murray 2, Jenkins (pen) | 460 |
| 19 | Jan 23 | A | Montrose | L 1-2 | 0-1 | 13 | Munn | 620 |
| 20 | 30 | H | Stranraer | W 1-0 | 1-0 | 13 | Murray | 300 |
| 21 | Feb 6 | A | Meadowbank T | L 1-6 | 1-2 | 13 | Jack | 380 |
| 22 | 10 | A | Brechin C | D 1-1 | 0-0 | — | Jenkins | 326 |
| 23 | 17 | A | Forfar Ath | D 0-0 | 0-0 | — | | 685 |
| 24 | 20 | A | Stirling Albion | L 1-3 | 1-1 | 13 | Murray | 400 |
| 25 | 23 | A | Berwick R | L 0-1 | 0-0 | — | | 625 |
| 26 | 27 | H | Alloa | D 2-2 | 0-1 | 13 | Murray, Jack | 500 |
| 27 | Mar 6 | A | Stranraer | W 1-0 | 0-0 | 13 | Kirkland | 504 |
| 28 | 13 | A | Clyde | L 0-1 | 0-0 | 13 | | 400 |
| 29 | 20 | H | Arbroath | L 0-2 | 0-0 | 13 | | 500 |
| 30 | 27 | A | Brechin C | W 1-0 | 1-0 | 13 | Meakin | 400 |
| 31 | 30 | H | Alloa | L 0-1 | 0-0 | — | | 430 |
| 32 | Apr 3 | H | Cowdenbeath | W 3-0 | 1-0 | 13 | Buchanan, Munn, Meakin | 400 |
| 33 | 10 | H | Forfar Ath | L 0-1 | 0-0 | 13 | | 200 |
| 34 | 17 | A | East Fife | L 0-1 | 0-0 | 13 | | 356 |
| 35 | 20 | H | Cowdenbeath | W 2-1 | 1-1 | — | Stirling, Munn | 200 |
| 36 | 24 | A | Berwick R | W 2-0 | 2-0 | 13 | Munn, Jenkins | 743 |
| 37 | May 1 | H | Meadowbank T | W 3-1 | 0-1 | 13 | Buchanan, Munn, Jenkins | 300 |
| 38 | 8 | H | Montrose | W 2-1 | 0-1 | 13 | Munn, Jenkins | 300 |
| 39 | 15 | A | Albion R | L 0-2 | 0-1 | 13 | | 700 |

**Final League Position: 13**

### Goalscorers

*League* (41): Jenkins 8 (1 pen), Munn 7, Murray 7, Meakin 5 (1 pen), Jack 4, Bremner 2, Buchanan 2, Kirkland 2, Campbell 1, Harper 1, Stirling 1, own goal 1.
*League Cup* (7): Meakin 2, Munn 2, Murray 2, Jack 1.
*Scottish Cup* (2): Meakin 1, Murray 1.

**Honours**
*Scottish Cup* – 1902–03 (semi-finalists).
*Stirlingshire Cup* – Winners 8 times.
*Scottish Qualifying Cup* – Winners 1900–01, 1901–02.
*Record Victory:* 9-2 v Dundee U, Division 2, 16 Apr, 1937.
*Record Defeat:* 2-11 v Dunfermline Ath, Division 2, 27 Sept, 1930.
*Most League Points:* 50, Division 2, 1960–61.
*Most League Goals:* 99, Division 2, 1960–61.
*Most Individual Goals in Season:* Evelyn Morrison, 31, Division 2, 1927–28 and Robert Murray, 31, Division 2, 1936–37.
*Record Transfer Fee Received:* £11,000 from Forfar Athletic for Stephen Hancock, Aug 1981.

| McLaren I. | Howie B. | Rennie A. | Rose A. | Bremner G. | Evans B. | Black J. | Strain M. | Smith B. | Kirkland B. | Mullen T. | Jack D. | Meakin J. | Murray G. | Munn D. | Harper D. | Jenkins B. | Buchanan G. | McAuley P. | Morrison G. | Frickleton J. | Campbell C. | Stirling J. | Smith K. | Christie B. | Quinn P. | O'Sullivan D. | Mulvaney F. | Black G. | Brown A. | McCusker J. | Fairley B. | Match No. |
|---|---|---|---|---|---|---|---|---|---|---|---|---|---|---|---|---|---|---|---|---|---|---|---|---|---|---|---|---|---|---|---|---|
| 1 | 2 | 12 | 5 | 4 | 3 | 6 |  | 8 | 9 | 10† |  |  |  |  |  |  |  | 7* | 11 | 13 |  |  |  |  |  |  |  |  |  |  |  | 1 |
| 1 | 3 | 7 | 5 | 4 | 11 | 6 | 10 | 8 | 9 |  |  |  |  |  |  |  |  |  |  |  | 2 |  |  |  |  |  |  |  |  |  |  | 2 |
| 1 | 3 | 7* | 5 | 4 |  | 6 | 10 | 9 |  |  |  |  |  |  |  |  |  |  | 11 | 8 | 2 | 12 |  |  |  |  |  |  |  |  |  | 3 |
| 1 | 3 | 7 | 5 |  | 11 | 6 | 8 | 4 | 9 | 10 |  |  |  |  |  |  |  |  | 10 | 2 |  |  |  |  |  |  |  |  |  |  |  | 4 |
| 1 |  |  | 12 | 3 |  | 7 | 4 | 9 |  | 11 |  |  |  |  |  | 10* | 6 |  | 2 |  | 5 | 8 |  |  |  |  |  |  |  |  |  | 5 |
|  | 1 | 3 | 7 | 5 |  | 6 | 11 | 8 | 4 | 9 | 10 |  |  |  |  |  |  |  | 2 |  |  |  |  |  |  |  |  |  |  |  |  | 6 |
|  | 1 | 3 | 12 | 5 |  | 6 | 11 | 7* | 4 | 8 | 10 |  |  |  |  |  |  |  | 2 |  |  | 9 |  |  |  |  |  |  |  |  |  | 7 |
|  | 1 | 3† | 7 | 5* | 6 | 11 | 9 | 4 | 8 | 12 | 10 | 13 |  |  |  |  |  |  | 2 |  |  |  |  |  |  |  |  |  |  |  |  | 8 |
|  | 1 | 3 |  | 5 | 4 | 7 | 6 |  | 9 | 10 | 11 | 8 |  |  |  |  |  |  | 2 |  |  |  |  |  |  |  |  |  |  |  |  | 9 |
|  | 1 | 3 | 7* | 5 | 13 | 6 |  | 4 | 9 | 12 | 10 | 11 | 8† |  |  |  |  |  | 2 |  |  |  |  |  |  |  |  |  |  |  |  | 10 |
|  | 1 | 3 |  | 5 | 11 | 6 | 12 | 4 | 8 | 7* | 10 |  | 9 |  |  |  |  |  | 2 |  |  |  |  |  |  |  |  |  |  |  |  | 11 |
|  | 1 | 3 | 8 | 5 | 12 | 6 | 7 | 4 | 9 | 10* | 11 |  |  |  |  |  |  |  | 2 |  |  |  |  |  |  |  |  |  |  |  |  | 12 |
| 1 |  |  | 4 | 5 | 2 | 3 | 6 | 7 | 8 | 9 | 10 | 12 | 11* |  |  |  |  |  |  |  |  |  |  |  |  |  |  |  |  |  |  | 13 |
| 1 |  |  | 4 | 5 | 2 | 3 | 6 | 7 | 8 | 9 | 10 | 11 |  |  |  |  |  |  |  |  |  |  |  |  |  |  |  |  |  |  |  | 14 |
|  | 1 | 12 |  | 6* | 5 | 2 | 3 | 7 | 4 | 9 | 8†11 | 10 |  |  |  |  |  |  |  |  |  |  |  |  |  |  |  | 13 |  |  |  | 15 |
| 1 |  | 7 | 5 |  | 3 | 6 | 8 | 4 | 9 | 11 | 10 |  |  |  |  |  |  |  | 2 |  |  |  |  |  |  |  |  |  |  |  |  | 16 |
| 1 |  | 4* | 5 | 12 | 3 | 6 | 7 | 8 | 9 | 11 | 10 |  |  |  |  |  |  |  | 2 |  |  |  |  |  |  |  |  |  |  |  |  | 17 |
| 1 |  | 4 | 5 |  | 3 | 6 | 7* | 8 | 9 | 12 | 11 | 10 |  |  |  |  |  |  | 2 |  |  |  |  |  |  |  |  |  |  |  |  | 18 |
| 1 | 2 | 4* | 5 | 12 | 3 | 6 | 8 | 10 | 9 | 7 | 11 |  |  |  |  |  |  |  |  |  |  |  |  |  |  |  |  |  |  |  |  | 19 |
|  | 1 | 2 | 4 | 5 | 3 | 8 | 7 | 10 | 9 | 11 | 6 |  |  |  |  |  |  |  |  |  |  |  |  |  |  |  |  |  |  |  |  | 20 |
| 1 | 2 | 3 | 13 | 5 | 11 | 8† | 7* | 4 | 9 | 12 | 10 | 6 |  |  |  |  |  |  |  |  |  |  |  |  |  |  |  |  |  |  |  | 21 |
|  | 1 | 2 | 3 | 4 | 5 | 8 | 10 | 7 | 9 | 11 | 6 |  |  |  |  |  |  |  |  |  |  |  |  |  |  |  |  |  |  |  |  | 22 |
|  | 1 | 2 | 3 | 4* | 5 | 8 | 12 | 10 | 7 | 9†13 | 11 | 6 |  |  |  |  |  |  |  |  |  |  |  |  |  |  |  |  |  |  |  | 23 |
|  | 1 | 2 | 3 | 12 | 5 | 4*13 | 10 | 8 | 9 | 7† | 11 | 6 |  |  |  |  |  |  |  |  |  |  |  |  |  |  |  |  |  |  |  | 24 |
|  | 1 | 2 | 3 | 4 | 5 | 12 | 10 | 8 | 9 | 11* | 6 |  |  |  |  |  |  |  |  |  |  |  | 7 |  |  |  |  |  |  |  |  | 25 |
|  | 1 | 2 | 3* | 4 | 5 | 11 | 12 | 7 | 8 | 9 | 13 | 10† | 6 |  |  |  |  |  |  |  |  |  |  |  |  |  |  |  |  |  |  | 26 |
| 1 |  | 2 | 3 |  | 4 | 11 | 6 | 7 | 8 | 9 | 10 | 5 |  |  |  |  |  |  |  |  |  |  |  |  |  |  |  |  |  |  |  | 27 |
|  | 1 | 2* | 3 | 12 | 4 | 11† | 6 | 8 | 7 | 13 | 10 | 5 |  |  |  |  |  |  |  |  |  |  |  | 9 |  |  |  |  |  |  |  | 28 |
|  | 1 | 3* | 4 | 13 | 2 | 12 | 6† | 7 | 8 | 9 | 10 | 11 | 5 |  |  |  |  |  |  |  |  |  |  |  |  |  |  |  |  |  |  | 29 |
|  | 1 | 2 | 3 | 5 | 4 | 6 | 10 | 8 | 9 | 7 | 11 |  |  |  |  |  |  |  |  |  |  |  |  |  |  |  |  |  |  |  |  | 30 |
|  | 1 | 2 | 5 | 4 | 3 | 6 | 10 | 9 | 7 | 11 | 8 |  |  |  |  |  |  |  |  |  |  |  |  |  |  |  |  |  |  |  |  | 31 |
|  | 1 | 2 | 5 | 4 | 3 | 6 | 10 | 9 | 7 | 11 | 8 |  |  |  |  |  |  |  |  |  |  |  |  |  |  |  |  |  |  |  |  | 32 |
|  | 1 | 2 | 3 | 5 | 4 | 8* | 6 | 12 | 9 | 7 | 11 | 10 |  |  |  |  |  |  |  |  |  |  |  |  |  |  |  |  |  |  |  | 33 |
|  | 1 | 2 | 3 | 5* | 4 | 12 | 6 | 8 | 7 | 11 | 10 | 9 |  |  |  |  |  |  |  |  |  |  |  |  |  |  |  |  |  | 9 |  | 34 |
| 1 |  | 2 | 3 | 5 | 6* | 8 | 12 | 10 | 11 | 9 | 7 | 4 |  |  |  |  |  |  |  |  |  |  |  |  |  |  |  |  |  |  |  | 35 |
|  | 1 | 2 | 3 | 5 | 4 | 11 | 8 | 9 | 7 | 10 | 6 |  |  |  |  |  |  |  |  |  |  |  |  |  |  |  |  |  |  |  |  | 36 |
|  | 1 | 2 | 3 | 5 | 4 | 8 | 9 | 10 | 11 | 6 | 7 |  |  |  |  |  |  |  |  |  |  |  |  |  |  |  |  |  |  |  |  | 37 |
|  | 1 | 2 | 3 | 5 | 8 | 7 | 9 | 10 | 11 | 6 | 4 |  |  |  |  |  |  |  |  |  |  |  |  |  |  |  |  |  | 4 |  |  | 38 |
|  | 1 | 2 | 3 | 5 | 12 | 8* | 13 | 10 | 7 | 11 | 6 | 4 | 9† |  |  |  |  |  |  |  |  |  |  |  |  |  |  |  | 4 |  |  | 39 |
| 11 | 28 | 31 | 17 | 19 | 17 | 19 | 10 | 17 | 24 | 28 | 25 | 30 | 38 | 19 | 10 | 31 | 19 | 1 | 7 | 2 | 14 | 2 | 1 | 1 | 1 | 1 | — | 1 | 3 | 1 |  |

Substitute appearances: + 1s (Rennie A.); + 5s, + 1s (Bremner G., Evans B.); + 1s, + 3s, + 7s, + 1s, + 3s (Strain M., Smith B., Kirkland B., Mullen T., Jack D.); + 1s, + 6s, + 2s (Munn D., Harper D., Jenkins B.); + 1s (Morrison G.); + 1s (Campbell C.); + 1s (Stirling J.); + 1s (Brown A.).

# STIRLING ALBION Division 2

*Year Formed:* 1945. *Ground:* Annfield Park. *Size:* 110yd×74yd. *Capacity:* 20,000 (900 seated).
*Telephone:* Stirling 3584.
*Manager:* Alex Smith. *Secretary:* Duncan McCallum.
*Club Colours:* Red shirts, socks and shorts.
*Record Attendance:* 26,400 v Celtic, Scottish Cup 4th rd, 14 Mar, 1959.

## 1981–82 LEAGUE RECORD

| Match No. | Date | Venue | Opponents | Result | | H/T Score | League Pos'n | Goalscorers | Attendance |
|---|---|---|---|---|---|---|---|---|---|
| 1 | Aug 29 | A | Brechin C | L | 1-2 | 0-1 | — | Torrance | 400 |
| 2 | Sept 5 | H | Alloa | D | 0-0 | 0-0 | 12 | | 750 |
| 3 | 8 | H | Clyde | L | 1-2 | 1-1 | — | Colquhoun | 600 |
| 4 | 12 | A | East Fife | L | 0-3 | 0-2 | 14 | | 409 |
| 5 | 16 | H | Berwick R | L | 0-1 | 0-1 | — | | 460 |
| 6 | 19 | H | Cowdenbeath | D | 0-0 | 0-0 | 14 | | 450 |
| 7 | 26 | H | Albion R | W | 1-0 | 0-0 | 12 | Colquhoun (pen) | 950 |
| 8 | Oct 3 | A | Stenhousemuir | D | 0-0 | 0-0 | 12 | | 470 |
| 9 | 10 | H | Arbroath | L | 0-1 | 0-0 | 12 | | 450 |
| 10 | 17 | A | Montrose | D | 1-1 | 1-0 | 13 | Torrance | 200 |
| 11 | 20 | A | Forfar Ath | L | 1-3 | 0-1 | — | McNeil | 320 |
| 12 | 24 | H | Stranraer | W | 1-0 | 0-0 | 12 | Torrance | 400 |
| 13 | 31 | A | Meadowbank T | L | 1-2 | 1-1 | 12 | Kennedy A. | 300 |
| 14 | Nov 7 | A | Alloa | D | 0-0 | 0-0 | 12 | | 800 |
| 15 | 14 | H | Brechin C | W | 5-0 | 2-0 | 11 | Philliben, Torrance 2, Colquhoun (pen) Leetion | 540 |
| 16 | 21 | A | Berwick R | L | 0-1 | 0-0 | 11 | | 400 |
| 17 | 28 | A | Albion R | L | 0-1 | 0-1 | 12 | | 250 |
| 18 | Dec 5 | H | Stenhousemuir | L | 2-3 | 1-1 | 12 | Kennedy A., McNeil | 460 |
| 19 | Jan 23 | A | Arbroath | L | 0-1 | 0-1 | 11 | | 545 |
| 20 | 30 | H | Montrose | D | 1-1 | 1-0 | 12 | Moffat | 720 |
| 21 | Feb 6 | A | Stranraer | D | 2-2 | 0-2 | 12 | Hay (og), Cavanagh | 620 |
| 22 | 17 | H | Meadowbank T | W | 1-0 | 0-0 | — | Leetion | 570 |
| 23 | 20 | A | Stenhousemuir | W | 3-1 | 1-1 | 11 | Colquhoun 2, McNeil | 400 |
| 24 | 27 | A | Clyde | L | 0-2 | 0-1 | 11 | | 620 |
| 25 | Mar 6 | H | Brechin C | L | 0-2 | 0-1 | 12 | | 450 |
| 26 | 10 | H | Forfar Ath | D | 0-0 | 0-0 | — | | 647 |
| 27 | 13 | H | Stranraer | W | 2-1 | 1-1 | 11 | Cavanagh, Steele | 400 |
| 28 | 17 | A | Cowdenbeath | D | 0-0 | 0-0 | — | | 550 |
| 29 | 20 | A | East Fife | W | 2-1 | 1-0 | 11 | Leetion, Colquhoun | 400 |
| 30 | 27 | H | Forfar Ath | W | 2-0 | 2-0 | 11 | Steedman, Colquhoun | 700 |
| 31 | 30 | A | Clyde | D | 3-3 | 2-2 | — | Colquhoun, Steele, Torrance | 700 |
| 32 | Apr 3 | A | Montrose | W | 2-1 | 1-1 | 10 | Colquhoun 2 | 250 |
| 33 | 7 | H | East Fife | L | 0-2 | 0-1 | — | | 350 |
| 34 | 10 | A | Albion R | L | 0-1 | 0-1 | 11 | | 400 |
| 35 | 17 | H | Arbroath | W | 3-2 | 2-0 | 9 | Colquhoun 2 (1 pen), Torrance | 400 |
| 36 | 24 | H | Alloa | W | 3-2 | 2-1 | 8 | Colquhoun, Leetion, Stewart (og) | 1100 |
| 37 | May 1 | A | Cowdenbeath | L | 0-2 | 0-1 | 9 | | 300 |
| 38 | 8 | A | Meadowbank T | W | 1-0 | 1-0 | 9 | Steele | 250 |
| 39 | 15 | H | Berwick R | D | 0-0 | 0-0 | 8 | | 600 |

**Final League Position: 8**

### Goalscorers
*League* (39): Colquhoun 13 (3 pens), Torrance 7, Leetion 4, McNeil 3, Steele 3, Cavanagh 2, Kennedy A. 2, Moffat 1, Philliben 1, Steedman 1, own goals 2.
*League Cup* (6): Torrance 2, Colquhoun 1, Gibson 1, Morrison 1, Philliben 1.
*Scottish Cup* (1): Torrance 1.

**Honours**

*Scottish League:* Division 2 Champions 1952–53, 1957–58, 1960–61, 1964–65, 1976–77; Runners-up 1948–49, 1950–51.
*Record Victory:* 7-0 v Albion R, Division 2, 19 Nov, 1947; v Montrose, Division 2, 28 Sept, 1957; v St Mirren, Division 1, 5 March 1960; v Arbroath, Division 2, 11 March 1961.
*Record Defeat:* 0-9 v Dundee United, Division 1, 30 Dec, 1967.
*Most League Points:* 59, Division 2, 1964–65.
*Most Individual League Goals in Season:* Michael Lawson, 26, Division 2, 1975–76.

| Arthur G. | Gordon D. | Kennedy J. | Dawson R. | Steedman D. | McCue A. | Denny J. | Young R. | Philliben J. | Moffat A. | Colquhoun J. | Leeton P. | Steele W. | Gray R. | Torrance R. | Kennedy A. | Cavanagh P. | McNeil C. | McLeod I. | Clarke A. | Beaton R. | Morrison W. | Gibson J. | Fryer J. | Dunlop J. | Perrie B. | Mailer J. | Grant B. | Match No. |
|---|---|---|---|---|---|---|---|---|---|---|---|---|---|---|---|---|---|---|---|---|---|---|---|---|---|---|---|---|
|  | 1 | 3 | 2 | 6 | 5 |  |  | 9 |  |  |  |  |  |  |  |  | 8 | 4* | 7 | 10 | 11† | 12 |  | 13 |  |  |  | 1 |
|  | 1 | 5 | 2 | 6 | 4 |  |  | 9 |  |  |  |  |  |  |  |  | 11 | 3 | 7* | 10 | 8† | 13 | 12 |  |  |  |  | 2 |
|  | 1 | 5 | 4* | 6 | 2 | 11 |  | 9 |  |  |  |  |  |  |  |  | 7† |  | 8 | 10 | 12 | 13 | 3 |  |  |  |  | 3 |
|  | 1 | 5 |  | 6 | 2 | 11 |  | 9 |  |  |  |  |  |  |  |  | 7* | 4 | 10 | 8† | 13 | 12 | 3 |  |  |  |  | 4 |
|  | 1 | 5 | 8 | 6 | 2 | 11 |  | 9 |  |  |  |  |  |  |  |  | 3 | 13 | 4 | 7* | 12 | 10† |  |  |  |  |  | 5 |
| 1 |  | 3 | 12 | 2 | 5 | 6 | 11 | 9 |  |  |  |  |  | 8† | 4 | 7 | 10* | 13 |  |  |  |  |  |  |  |  |  |  | 6 |
| 1 |  | 3 |  | 2 | 4 | 5 | 6 | 11 | 9 |  |  |  |  | 12 | 10 | 8 |  | 7* |  |  |  |  |  |  |  |  |  |  | 7 |
| 1 |  | 3 |  | 2* | 4 | 5 | 6 | 11 | 9 |  |  |  |  | 12 | 10† | 8 | 13 | 7 |  |  |  |  |  |  |  |  |  |  | 8 |
| 1 |  | 3 | 13 | 4 | 2 | 5 | 6 | 11 | 8 |  |  |  |  | 9 | 10† | 12 | 7* |  |  |  |  |  |  |  |  |  |  | 9 |
| 1 |  | 3 |  | 4 | 8 | 5 | 6 | 11 | 9 | 10* | 7† |  |  | 12 |  | 13 | 2 |  |  |  |  |  |  |  |  |  |  |  | 10 |
| 1 |  | 3 | 4 | 8 | 5 | 6 | 11 | 9* | 10 | 7 |  |  |  | 12 |  | 2 |  |  |  |  |  |  |  |  |  |  |  |  | 11 |
| 1 |  | 3 | 8 | 2 | 5 | 6 | 11† | 4 | 9 | 10 | 7* |  |  | 12 |  | 13 |  |  |  |  |  |  |  |  |  |  |  |  | 12 |
| 1 | 5 | 3 | 13 | 2 | 4 | 6 | 7 | 11 | 8 | 9* | 10† | 12 |  |  |  |  |  |  |  |  |  |  |  |  |  |  |  | 13 |
| 1 | 5 | 3 | 12 | 2† | 4 | 6 | 7 | 11 | 8 | 9 | 10* | 13 |  |  |  |  |  |  |  |  |  |  |  |  |  |  |  | 14 |
| 1 | 5 | 3 |  | 2 | 4 | 6 | 7 | 11 | 8* | 9 | 10† | 13 | 12 |  |  |  |  |  |  |  |  |  |  |  |  |  |  | 15 |
| 1 | 5 | 3 |  | 2 | 4 | 6 | 7 | 11 | 8 | 9† | 10* | 13 | 12 |  |  |  |  |  |  |  |  |  |  |  |  |  |  | 16 |
| 1 | 5 | 3 |  | 2 | 4 | 6 | 7 | 11 | 8* | 9 | 12 | 10 |  |  |  |  |  |  |  |  |  |  |  |  |  |  |  | 17 |
| 1 | 5 |  | 12 | 4 | 6 | 7 | 11 | 8† | 9 | 10* | 13 | 3 | 2 |  |  |  |  |  |  |  |  |  |  |  |  |  |  | 18 |
| 1 | 5 | 7* | 4 | 3 | 2 | 6 | 12 | 10 | 13 | 9 | 11 | 8† |  |  |  |  |  |  |  |  |  |  |  |  |  |  |  | 19 |
| 1 | 5 | 12 | 7* | 4† | 3 | 2 | 6 | 8 | 10 | 9 | 11 |  |  |  |  |  |  |  |  | 13 |  |  |  |  |  |  |  | 20 |
| 1 | 5 | 3 |  | 2 | 4 | 6 | 8 | 11 | 12 | 10 | 7 | 9* |  |  |  |  |  |  |  |  |  |  |  |  |  |  |  | 21 |
| 1 | 5 | 2 | 3 |  | 4 | 6 | 7 | 8 | 9 | 11 |  |  |  | 10 |  |  |  |  |  |  |  |  |  |  |  |  |  | 22 |
| 1 | 5 | 2 | 3 |  | 4 | 6 | 7 | 8 | 9* | 11 | 12 | 10† | 13 |  |  |  |  |  |  |  |  |  |  |  |  |  |  | 23 |
| 1 | 5 | 2 | 3 |  | 4 | 6 | 7 | 8 | 9 | 11 | 12 | 10* |  |  |  |  |  |  |  |  |  |  |  |  |  |  |  | 24 |
| 1 |  | 3 | 13 |  | 6 | 7† | 2 | 8 | 9 | 11 | 4* | 12 | 5 | 10 |  |  |  |  |  |  |  |  |  |  |  |  |  | 25 |
| 1 |  | 2 | 3 | 4 | 5 | 6 | 7 | 8 | 9 | 11 |  | 10 |  |  |  |  |  |  |  |  |  |  |  |  |  |  |  | 26 |
| 1 |  | 2 | 3 | 4* | 5 | 6 | 7 | 8 | 9 | 12 | 11 | 10† | 13 |  |  |  |  |  |  |  |  |  |  |  |  |  |  | 27 |
| 1 |  | 2 | 3 | 4 | 5 | 6 | 7† | 8 | 9 | 12 | 11 | 10* | 13 |  |  |  |  |  |  |  |  |  |  |  |  |  |  | 28 |
| 1 |  | 2 | 3 | 4* | 5 | 6 | 7 | 8 | 9 | 12 | 10 | 11 |  |  |  |  |  |  |  |  |  |  |  |  |  |  |  | 29 |
| 1 |  | 2† | 3 | 4 | 5 | 6 | 7 | 8 | 9 | 12 | 10* | 11 | 13 |  |  |  |  |  |  |  |  |  |  |  |  |  |  | 30 |
| 1 |  | 2 | 3 | 4 | 5 | 6 | 7† | 8 | 9 | 12 | 10* | 11 | 13 |  |  |  |  |  |  |  |  |  |  |  |  |  |  | 31 |
| 1 |  | 2 | 3 | 4 | 5 | 6 | 7 | 8 | 9 | 12 | 10* | 11 |  |  |  |  |  |  |  |  |  |  |  |  |  |  |  | 32 |
| 1 |  | 2 | 3 | 4 | 5 | 6 | 7 | 8 | 9 | 12 | 10* | 11† | 13 |  |  |  |  |  |  |  |  |  |  |  |  |  |  | 33 |
| 1 |  | 2 | 3 | 4* | 5 | 6 | 7 | 8 | 9 | 12 |  | 11 |  | 10 |  |  |  |  |  |  |  |  |  |  |  |  |  | 34 |
| 1 |  | 2 | 3 |  | 10† | 5 | 6 | 7 | 8 | 9 | 12 |  | 11 | 13 |  | 4* |  |  |  |  |  |  |  |  |  |  |  | 35 |
| 1 |  | 2 | 3 |  | 4† | 5 | 6 | 7 | 8 | 9 | 12 |  | 11 | 13 |  | 10* |  |  |  |  |  |  |  |  |  |  |  | 36 |
| 1 |  | 2† | 3 |  | 4 | 5 | 6 | 7 | 8 | 9 | 12 |  | 11 | 13 |  | 10* |  |  |  |  |  |  |  |  |  |  |  | 37 |
| 1 |  | 2 | 3 | 4* |  | 5 | 6 | 7 | 8†10 | 9 | 11 | 12 |  |  |  |  |  |  |  |  |  | 13 |  |  |  |  |  | 38 |
| 1 |  | 2 | 3 |  | 5 | 6 | 7 | 8 | 9 | 10 | 11 |  |  |  |  |  |  |  |  |  |  |  | 4* |  |  | 12 |  | 39 |
| 34 | 5 | 12 | 18 | 35 | 9 | 20 | 19 | 37 | 34 | 36 | 26 | 18 | 7 | 23 | 13 | 21 | 10 | 14 | 7 | 13 | 4 | 2 | 6 | 1 | 4 | 1 | — | |

Sub appearances:
| | +1s | +5s | | +1s | +1s | | | | +1s | +9s | +2s | | | +18s | +2s | +2s | +5s | | | | | +2s | +10s | +3s | +1s | +1s | +1s | |

# STRANRAER

# Division 2

*Year Formed:* 1870. *Ground:* Stair Park. *Size:* 110yd×70yd. *Capacity:* 5500.
*Telephone:* Stranraer 3271.
*Manager:* Dave Sneddon. *Secretary:* Graham Rodgers.
*Club Colours:* Royal blue shirts, white shorts, blue stockings with red tops.
*Record Attendance:* 6500 v Rangers, Scottish Cup 1st rd, 24 Jan, 1948.

## 1981–82 LEAGUE RECORD

| Match No. | Date | Venue | Opponents | Result | H/T Score | League Pos'n | Goalscorers | Attendance |
|---|---|---|---|---|---|---|---|---|
| 1 | Aug 29 | A | East Fife | W 2-0 | 0-0 | — | Black, Sweeney | 480 |
| 2 | Sept 5 | H | Arbroath | W 4-0 | 1-0 | 2 | Neil, Devine, Armour, Sweeney | 630 |
| 3 | 8 | H | Berwick R | L 2-4 | 1-2 | — | Sweeney, McIntosh | 380 |
| 4 | 12 | A | Albion R | L 0-4 | 0-1 | 6 | | 200 |
| 5 | 16 | H | Clyde | L 0-2 | 0-1 | — | | 370 |
| 6 | 19 | H | Meadowbank T | L 0-1 | 0-1 | 10 | | 350 |
| 7 | 23 | A | Alloa | L 2-3 | 2-2 | — | Neil, Sweeney | 650 |
| 8 | 26 | H | Brechin C | L 0-6 | 0-3 | 13 | | 250 |
| 9 | Oct 3 | A | Forfar Ath | L 1-3 | 1-1 | 14 | Black | 430 |
| 10 | 10 | A | Cowdenbeath | D 1-1 | 0-0 | 13 | Sweeney | 400 |
| 11 | 17 | H | Stenhousemuir | W 2-1 | 1-1 | 11 | Dolan 2 | 448 |
| 12 | 24 | A | Stirling Albion | L 0-1 | 0-0 | 13 | | 400 |
| 13 | 31 | H | Montrose | L 3-5 | 2-2 | 13 | Dolan 2, McLaughlan | 300 |
| 14 | Nov 7 | A | Arbroath | L 1-4 | 0-3 | 13 | Sweeney | 488 |
| 15 | 14 | H | East Fife | L 0-3 | 0-0 | 13 | | 300 |
| 16 | 21 | A | Clyde | L 0-3 | 0-1 | 14 | | 800 |
| 17 | 28 | A | Brechin C | L 0-3 | 0-1 | 14 | | 400 |
| 18 | Dec 5 | H | Forfar Ath | W 2-1 | 0-0 | 14 | Sweeney, Murphy | 506 |
| 19 | Jan 2 | H | Albion R | L 0-1 | 0-1 | 14 | | 630 |
| 20 | 23 | H | Cowdenbeath | L 1-4 | 0-1 | 14 | McDonald (pen) | 250 |
| 21 | 30 | A | Stenhousemuir | L 0-1 | 0-1 | 14 | | 300 |
| 22 | Feb 6 | H | Stirling Albion | D 2-2 | 2-0 | 14 | Sweeney, Dolan | 620 |
| 23 | 13 | A | Montrose | W 2-1 | 1-1 | 14 | Taylor I., McDonald (pen) | 300 |
| 24 | 17 | A | Berwick R | D 0-0 | 0-0 | — | | 870 |
| 25 | 20 | H | East Fife | L 1-2 | 0-1 | 14 | Sweeney | 479 |
| 26 | 23 | H | Alloa | L 0-4 | 0-2 | — | | 572 |
| 27 | 27 | A | Brechin C | L 0-3 | 0-1 | 14 | | 400 |
| 28 | Mar 6 | H | Stenhousemuir | L 0-1 | 0-0 | 14 | | 504 |
| 29 | 10 | A | Meadowbank T | L 1-4 | 1-0 | — | Taylor I. | 460 |
| 30 | 13 | A | Stirling Albion | L 1-2 | 1-1 | 14 | Sweeney | 400 |
| 31 | 20 | A | Forfar Ath | L 0-3 | 0-2 | 14 | | 952 |
| 32 | 27 | H | Albion R | L 1-4 | 0-3 | 14 | Murdoch (pen) | 300 |
| 33 | Apr 3 | A | Meadowbank T | D 1-1 | 0-0 | 14 | Sweeney | 200 |
| 34 | 10 | H | Montrose | W 2-0 | 1-0 | 14 | Taylor I., Dolan | 300 |
| 35 | 17 | A | Berwick R | L 0-2 | 0-2 | 14 | | 814 |
| 36 | 24 | H | Cowdenbeath | W 1-0 | 0-0 | 14 | Taylor I. | 250 |
| 37 | May 1 | A | Alloa | D 1-1 | 1-1 | 14 | Gibb | 601 |
| 38 | 8 | A | Clyde | D 1-1 | 0-0 | 14 | Dolan | 622 |
| 39 | 15 | H | Arbroath | L 1-3 | 0-2 | 14 | Gibb | 350 |

**Final League Position: 14**

### Goalscorers
*League* (36): Sweeney 11, Dolan 7, Taylor I. 4, Black 2, Gibb 2, McDonald 2 (2 pens), Neil 2, Armour 1, Devine 1, McIntosh 1, McLaughlan 1, Murdoch 1 (pen), Murphy 1.
*League Cup* (7): Neil 3, Hamilton 1, Murphy 1, Sweeney 1, own goal 1.
*Scottish Cup* (2): Harvey 2.

**Honours**

*Record Victory:* 7-0 v Brechin C, Division 2, 6 Feb, 1965.
*Record Defeat:* 1-11 v Queen of the South, Scottish Cup 1st rd, 16 Jan, 1932.
*Most League Points:* 44, Division 2, 1960–61, 1971–72.
*Most Individual Goals in Season:* Derek Frye, 27, Division 2, 1977–78.

| McFall R. | Robinson A. | Traynor C. | Taylor J. | Allan J. | Strachan B. | McDonald D. | Devine T. | Black S. | Hay H. | Hyslop J. | Murdoch H. | Armour W. | Neil M. | Murphy I. | Sweeney S. | Dolan P. | Hamilton G. | Quinn F. | McKie W. | Harvey A. | Hutchison R. | Gibb I. | Taylor I. | McCaig J. | Filson T. | Woods J. | McIntosh G. | Ewing J. | McLaughlin H. | McGuigan I. | Match No. |
|---|---|---|---|---|---|---|---|---|---|---|---|---|---|---|---|---|---|---|---|---|---|---|---|---|---|---|---|---|---|---|---|
| 1 | | | | | | 2 | 3 | 6 | 8 | 4 | 5 | 7 | 11 | 12 | 10 | | | | | | | | | | | | 9* | | | | 1 |
| 1 | | | | | | 8 | 3 | 6 | 10* | 4 | 5 | 2 | 7 | 11 | 9 | | 12 | | | | | | | | | | | | | | 2 |
| 1 | | | | | | 8 | 3 | 6† | | 4 | 5 | 2 | 7 | 10* | 9 | 13 | 12 | | | | | | | | | | 11 | | | | 3 |
| 1 | | | | | | 3 | | 2 | 10† | 4 | 6 | 13 | 7 | | 9 | 11* | 5 | 8 | | 12 | | | | | | | | | | | 4 |
| 1 | | | | | | 2 | 6 | | | 3* | 5 | 12 | 7 | 13 | 9 | 11† | 4 | 8 | | 10 | | | | | | | | | | | 5 |
| 1 | | | | | | 3 | 2 | 6 | 13 | | 5 | 12 | 7 | | 9 | | 4 | 8 | 11* | 10† | | | | | | | | | | | 6 |
| 1 | | | | | | 2 | | 6 | 3 | | 5 | | 7 | | 9 | 11 | 4 | 8 | | 10 | | | | | | | | | | | 7 |
| 1 | | | | | | 2 | | 6 | 3 | | 5 | | 7 | | 9 | | 4 | 8* | | 11†10 | 13 | | | | | | 12 | | | | 8 |
| 1 | | | | | | 3 | | 2 | 4 | | | 7 | | | 12 | 5 | 8 | 9 | 10 | 6*11 | | | | | | | | | | | 9 |
| 1 | | | | | | 4 | 3 | 2 | | | | 7 | | 9 | 12 | 5 | 6 | 11 | 8 | | 10* | | | | | | | | | | 10 |
| 1 | | | | | | 4 | | 2 | 12 | 3 | | 7 | | 9 | 10 | 5 | 6 | 11 | 8* | | | | | | | | | | | | 11 |
| 1 | | | | | | 4 | | 2 | | 3 | | 7 | | 9 | 8 | 5 | 6 | 11 | 10 | | | | | | | | | | | | 12 |
| 1 | | | | | | 4 | | 2*12 | 3 | | | 7 | | 8 | 9 | | 10 | 11† | | 6 | 13 | | | | | | | 5 | | | 13 |
| 1* | | | | | | 3 | 2 | | 4 | 5 | 12 | | 7 | 11 | 9 | | 6 | | 8†10 | 13 | | | | | | | | | | | 14 |
| | | 1 | | | | 3 | 2 | | 4† | 6 | 5 | | 7 | 11 | 9* | | 8 | | 13 | 10 | 12 | | | | | | | | | | 15 |
| | | 1 | | | | 3 | 2* | | 4 | 6 | 5 | 12 | 7 | | 11 | 9 | | 8 | | 10 | | | | | | | | | | | 16 |
| | | | 1 | | | 3 | 2 | | 4 | | 5 | 13 | 7 | | 11*12 | | 6 | | 8 | 10† | 9 | | | | | | | | | | 17 |
| | | | | 1 | | 4 | | | 3 | | 5 | 2 | 7* | 9 | 12 | | 8 | | 10 | 13 | 11 | | | | | | | | 6† | | 18 |
| 1 | | | | | | 3 | | 6 | 4 | | 5 | 2 | 7 | 9* | | 12 | 8 | | 10 | | 11 | | | | | | | | | | 19 |
| | | | | | 1 | 3 | | 6 | 4 | 12 | 5 | 2* | 7 | | | 9 | 8 | | 10 | | 11 | | | | | | | | | | 20 |
| 1 | | | | | | 3 | | 10 | 2 | 4 | 5 | | 7 | 13 | 11 | 9* | 6† | | 8 | 12 | | | | | | | | | | 21 |
| 1 | | | | | | 4 | | 8 | 3 | 2 | 5 | | 12 | | 11 | 7* | 6 | | 10 | | | 9 | | | | | | | | | 22 |
| 1 | | | | | | 4 | | 8 | 3 | 2 | 5 | 7 | | | 11 | | 6 | | 10 | | | 9 | | | | | | | | | 23 |
| 1 | | | | | | 4 | | 8 | 3 | 2 | 5 | 7*13 | | | 11 | | 6 | | 10 | | 12 | 9† | | | | | | | | | 24 |
| 1 | | | | | | 4 | | 8 | 3 | 2 | 5 | | 7* | | 11 | | 6 | | 10 | | 12 | 9 | | | | | | | | | 25 |
| 1 | | | | | | 4 | | 8 | 3 | 2 | 5 | 7 | | | 11 | | 6 | | 10 | | | 9 | | | | | | | | | 26 |
| 1 | | | | | | 4 | | 2 | 3 | | 5 | | 7 | | 11 | | 6 | | 10 | | 8 | 9 | | | | | | | | | 27 |
| 1 | | | | | | 4 | | 2 | 5 | | | 3 | 7 | | 11 | | 6 | 12 | 10* | | 8 | 9 | | | | | | | | | 28 |
| 1 | | | | | | 4 | | 8 | 3 | | | 2* | 7 | | 11 | | 10 | | 12 | | | 9 | 5 | 6 | | | | | | | 29 |
| 1 | | | | | | 4 | | 10† | | | | 3 | 7 | 12 | 11 | | 2 | | 8 | | 13 | 9* | 5 | 6 | | | | | | | 30 |
| | | | | 1 | | 4 | | | | | | 3 | 7 | 11 | | 12 | | 2* | 8 | 6 | | 10 | 9 | 5 | | | | | | | 31 |
| | | 1 | | | | 2 | | | 3 | | 8 | | 7 | 11†13 | 12 | | 10* | | | 4 | 9 | 5 | 6 | | | | | | | 32 |
| | | | | 1 | | 2 | | | 3 | | 8 | 7 | | 11 | 10 | | 4 | | | 12 | 9* | 5 | 6 | | | | | | | 33 |
| | | | | 1 | | 2 | | | 3 | | 8 | 7 | | 11 | 10 | | 4 | | | | 9 | 5 | 6 | | | | | | | 34 |
| | | | | 1 | | 2 | | | 3 | | 8 | 7 | | 11 | 10 | | 4 | | | 12 | 9* | 5 | 6 | | | | | | | 35 |
| | | | | 1 | | 2 | | | 3 | | | 7 | | 11 | 10 | | 4 | 8 | | | 9 | 5 | 6 | | | | | | | 36 |
| | | | | 1 | | 2 | | 4 | 3 | | | | | 9 | 8 | | | | 7 | | 10 | 11 | 5 | 6 | | | | | | | 37 |
| | | | | 1 | | 2 | | 10 | 3 | | | | 7 | 11* | | | 4 | | 8 | | 12 | 9 | 5 | 6 | | | | | | | 38 |
| | | | | 1 | | 2 | | 8† | 3 | | 10 | | 7*11 | | | 4 | | 13 | | 12 | 9 | 5 | 6 | | | | | | | 39 |
| 25 | 1 | 3 | 1 | 1 | | 8 | 38 | 10 | 28 | 30 | 17 | 26 | 13 | 32 | 6 | 33 | 19 | 9 | 35 | 7 | 26 | 7 | 11 | 18 | 11 | 10 | 1 | 1 | — | 1 | 1 |
| | | | | | | + | | + | + | + | + | + | + | + | + | | + | + | + | + | | | | | | | + | | | | |
| | | | | | | 3s | | 1s | 1s | 5s | 5s | 2s | 4s | 2s | 7s | 2s | | 1s | 4s | 1s | 12s | | | | | | | 1s | | | | |

# SCOTTISH LEAGUE 1890–91 to 1981–82

*On goal average/difference. †Held jointly after indecisive play-off. ‡Won on deciding match.
††Held jointly. ¶Two points deducted for fielding ineligible player.
Competition suspended 1940–45 during war. ‡‡Two points deducted for registration irregularities.

## PREMIER DIVISION
### Maximum points: 72

|         | First    | Pts | Second   | Pts | Third      | Pts |
|---------|----------|-----|----------|-----|------------|-----|
| 1975–76 | Rangers  | 54  | Celtic   | 48  | Hibernian  | 43  |
| 1976–77 | Celtic   | 55  | Rangers  | 46  | Aberdeen   | 43  |
| 1977–78 | Rangers  | 55  | Aberdeen | 53  | Dundee U   | 40  |
| 1978–79 | Celtic   | 48  | Rangers  | 45  | Dundee U   | 44  |
| 1979–80 | Aberdeen | 48  | Celtic   | 47  | St Mirren  | 42  |
| 1980–81 | Celtic   | 56  | Aberdeen | 49  | Rangers*   | 44  |
| 1981–82 | Celtic   | 55  | Aberdeen | 53  | Rangers    | 43  |

## FIRST DIVISION
### Maximum points: 52

| 1975–76 | Partick T | 41 | Kilmarnock | 35 | Montrose | 30 |
|---------|-----------|-----|-----------|-----|----------|-----|

### Maximum points: 78

|         | First      | Pts | Second      | Pts | Third        | Pts |
|---------|------------|-----|-------------|-----|--------------|-----|
| 1976–77 | St Mirren  | 62  | Clydebank   | 58  | Dundee       | 51  |
| 1977–78 | Morton*    | 58  | Hearts      | 58  | Dundee       | 57  |
| 1978–79 | Dundee     | 55  | Kilmarnock* | 54  | Clydebank    | 54  |
| 1979–80 | Hearts     | 53  | Airdrieonians | 51 | Ayr U       | 44  |
| 1980–81 | Hibernian  | 57  | Dundee      | 52  | St Johnstone | 51  |
| 1981–82 | Motherwell | 61  | Kilmarnock  | 51  | Hearts       | 50  |

## SECOND DIVISION
### Maximum points: 52

| 1975–76 | Clydebank* | 40 | Raith R | 40 | Alloa | 35 |
|---------|------------|-----|--------|-----|-------|-----|

### Maximum points: 78

|         | First        | Pts | Second          | Pts | Third            | Pts |
|---------|--------------|-----|-----------------|-----|------------------|-----|
| 1976–77 | Stirling A   | 55  | Alloa           | 51  | Dunfermline Ath  | 50  |
| 1977–78 | Clyde*       | 53  | Raith R         | 53  | Dunfermline Ath  | 48  |
| 1978–79 | Berwick R    | 54  | Dunfermline Ath | 52  | Falkirk          | 50  |
| 1979–80 | Falkirk      | 50  | East Stirling   | 49  | Forfar Ath       | 46  |
| 1980–81 | Queen's Park | 50  | Queen of the S  | 46  | Cowdenbeath      | 45  |
| 1981–82 | Clyde        | 59  | Alloa*          | 50  | Arbroath         | 50  |

## FIRST DIVISION to 1974–75
### Maximum points: a 36; b 44; c 40; d 52; e 60; f 68; g 76; h 84.

|           | First        | Pts | Second   | Pts | Third       | Pts |
|-----------|--------------|-----|----------|-----|-------------|-----|
| 1890–91a†† | Dumbarton   | 29  | Rangers  | 29  | Celtic      | 24  |
| 1891–92b  | Dumbarton    | 37  | Celtic   | 35  | Hearts      | 30  |
| 1892–93a  | Celtic       | 29  | Rangers  | 28  | St Mirren   | 23  |
| 1893–94a  | Celtic       | 29  | Hearts   | 26  | St Bernard's | 22 |
| 1894–95a  | Hearts       | 31  | Celtic   | 26  | Rangers     | 21  |
| 1895–96a  | Celtic       | 30  | Rangers  | 26  | Hibernian   | 24  |
| 1896–97a  | Hearts       | 28  | Hibernian | 26 | Rangers     | 25  |
| 1897–98a  | Celtic       | 33  | Rangers  | 29  | Hibernian   | 22  |
| 1898–99a  | Rangers      | 36  | Hearts   | 26  | Celtic      | 24  |
| 1899–1900a | Rangers     | 32  | Celtic   | 25  | Hibernian   | 24  |
| 1900–01c  | Rangers      | 35  | Celtic   | 29  | Hibernian   | 25  |
| 1901–02a  | Rangers      | 28  | Celtic   | 26  | Hearts      | 22  |
| 1902–03b  | Hibernian    | 37  | Dundee   | 31  | Rangers     | 29  |
| 1903–04d  | Third Lanark | 43  | Hearts   | 39  | Rangers*    | 38  |
| 1904–05d  | Celtic‡      | 41  | Rangers  | 41  | Third Lanark | 35 |
| 1905–06e  | Celtic       | 49  | Hearts   | 43  | Airdrieonians | 38 |
| 1906–07f  | Celtic       | 55  | Dundee   | 48  | Rangers     | 45  |
| 1907–08f  | Celtic       | 55  | Falkirk  | 51  | Rangers     | 50  |
| 1908–09f  | Celtic       | 51  | Dundee   | 50  | Clyde       | 48  |
| 1909–10f  | Celtic       | 54  | Falkirk  | 52  | Rangers     | 46  |
| 1910–11f  | Rangers      | 52  | Aberdeen | 48  | Falkirk     | 44  |
| 1911–12f  | Rangers      | 51  | Celtic   | 45  | Clyde       | 42  |
| 1912–13f  | Rangers      | 53  | Celtic   | 49  | Hearts*     | 41  |

| | First | Pts | Second | Pts | Third | Pts |
|---|---|---|---|---|---|---|
| 1913–14g | Celtic | 65 | Rangers | 59 | Hearts* | 54 |
| 1914–15g | Celtic | 65 | Hearts | 61 | Rangers | 50 |
| 1915–16g | Celtic | 67 | Rangers | 56 | Morton | 51 |
| 1916–17g | Celtic | 64 | Morton | 54 | Rangers | 53 |
| 1917–18f | Rangers | 56 | Celtic | 55 | Kilmarnock | 43 |
| 1918–19f | Celtic | 58 | Rangers | 57 | Morton | 47 |
| 1919–20h | Rangers | 71 | Celtic | 68 | Motherwell | 57 |
| 1920–21h | Rangers | 76 | Celtic | 66 | Hearts | 56 |
| 1921–22h | Celtic | 67 | Rangers | 66 | Raith R | 56 |
| 1922–23g | Rangers | 55 | Airdrieonians | 50 | Celtic | 46 |
| 1923–24g | Rangers | 59 | Airdrieonians | 50 | Celtic | 41 |
| 1924–25g | Rangers | 60 | Airdrieonians | 57 | Hibernian | 52 |
| 1925–26g | Celtic | 58 | Airdrieonians* | 50 | Hearts | 50 |
| 1926–27g | Rangers | 56 | Motherwell | 51 | Celtic | 49 |
| 1927–28g | Rangers | 60 | Celtic* | 55 | Motherwell | 55 |
| 1928–29g | Rangers | 67 | Celtic | 51 | Motherwell | 50 |
| 1929–30g | Rangers | 60 | Motherwell | 55 | Aberdeen | 53 |
| 1930–31g | Rangers | 60 | Celtic | 58 | Motherwell | 56 |
| 1931–32g | Motherwell | 66 | Rangers | 61 | Celtic | 48 |
| 1932–33g | Rangers | 62 | Motherwell | 59 | Hearts | 50 |
| 1933–34g | Rangers | 66 | Motherwell | 62 | Celtic | 47 |
| 1934–35g | Rangers | 55 | Celtic | 52 | Hearts | 50 |
| 1935–36g | Celtic | 66 | Rangers* | 61 | Aberdeen | 61 |
| 1936–37g | Rangers | 61 | Aberdeen | 54 | Celtic | 52 |
| 1937–38g | Celtic | 61 | Hearts | 58 | Rangers | 49 |
| 1938–39g | Rangers | 59 | Celtic | 48 | Aberdeen | 46 |
| 1946–47e | Rangers | 46 | Hibernian | 44 | Aberdeen | 39 |
| 1947–48e | Hibernian | 48 | Rangers | 46 | Partick T | 36 |
| 1948–49e | Rangers | 46 | Dundee | 45 | Hibernian | 39 |
| 1949–50e | Rangers | 50 | Hibernian | 49 | Hearts | 43 |
| 1950–51e | Hibernian | 48 | Rangers* | 38 | Dundee | 38 |
| 1951–52e | Hibernian | 45 | Rangers | 41 | East Fife | 37 |
| 1952–53e | Rangers* | 43 | Hibernian | 43 | East Fife | 39 |
| 1953–54e | Celtic | 43 | Hearts | 38 | Partick T | 35 |
| 1954–55e | Aberdeen | 49 | Celtic | 46 | Rangers | 41 |
| 1955–56f | Rangers | 52 | Aberdeen | 46 | Hearts* | 45 |
| 1956–57f | Rangers | 55 | Hearts | 53 | Kilmarnock | 42 |
| 1957–58f | Hearts | 62 | Rangers | 49 | Celtic | 46 |
| 1958–59f | Rangers | 50 | Hearts | 48 | Motherwell | 44 |
| 1959–60f | Hearts | 54 | Kilmarnock | 50 | Rangers* | 42 |
| 1960–61f | Rangers | 51 | Kilmarnock | 50 | Third Lanark | 42 |
| 1961–62f | Dundee | 54 | Rangers | 51 | Celtic | 46 |
| 1962–63f | Rangers | 57 | Kilmarnock | 48 | Partick T | 46 |
| 1963–64f | Rangers | 55 | Kilmarnock | 49 | Celtic* | 47 |
| 1964–65f | Kilmarnock* | 50 | Hearts | 50 | Dunfermline Ath | 49 |
| 1965–66f | Celtic | 57 | Rangers | 55 | Kilmarnock | 45 |
| 1966–67f | Celtic | 58 | Rangers | 55 | Clyde | 46 |
| 1967–68f | Celtic | 63 | Rangers | 61 | Hibernian | 45 |
| 1968–69f | Celtic | 54 | Rangers | 49 | Dunfermline Ath | 45 |
| 1969–70f | Celtic | 57 | Rangers | 45 | Hibernian | 44 |
| 1970–71f | Celtic | 56 | Aberdeen | 54 | St Johnstone | 44 |
| 1971–72f | Celtic | 60 | Aberdeen | 50 | Rangers | 44 |
| 1972–73f | Celtic | 57 | Rangers | 56 | Hibernian | 45 |
| 1973–74f | Celtic | 53 | Hibernian | 49 | Rangers | 48 |
| 1974–75f | Rangers | 56 | Hibernian | 49 | Celtic | 45 |

## SECOND DIVISION to 1974–75

*Maximum points: a 76; b 72; c 68; d 52; e 60; f 36; g 44; h 52.*

| | First | Pts | Second | Pts | Third | Pts |
|---|---|---|---|---|---|---|
| 1893–94f | Hibernian | 29 | Cowlairs | 27 | Clyde | 24 |
| 1894–95f | Hibernian | 30 | Motherwell | 22 | Port Glasgow | 20 |
| 1895–96f | Abercorn | 27 | Leith Ath | 23 | Renton | 21 |
| 1896–97f | Partick T | 31 | Leith Ath | 27 | Kilmarnock | 21 |
| 1897–98f | Kilmarnock | 29 | Port Glasgow | 25 | Morton | 22 |
| 1898–99f | Kilmarnock | 32 | Leith Ath | 27 | Port Glasgow | 25 |
| 1899–1900f | Partick T | 29 | Morton | 26 | Port Glasgow | 20 |
| 1900–01f | St Bernard's | 26 | Airdrieonians | 23 | Abercorn | 21 |
| 1901–02f | Port Glasgow | 32 | Partick T | 31 | Motherwell | 26 |
| 1902–03g | Airdrieonians | 35 | Motherwell | 28 | Ayr U | 27 |
| 1903–04g | Hamilton A | 37 | Clyde | 29 | Ayr U | 28 |
| 1904–05g | Clyde | 32 | Falkirk | 28 | Hamilton A | 27 |

| | First | Pts | Second | Pts | Third | Pts |
|---|---|---|---|---|---|---|
| 1905–06g | Leith Ath | 34 | Clyde | 31 | Albion R | 27 |
| 1906–07g | St Bernard's | 32 | Vale of Leven* | 27 | Arthurlie | 27 |
| 1907–08g | Raith R | 30 | Dumbarton | ‡‡27 | Ayr U | 27 |
| 1908–09g | Abercorn | 31 | Raith R* | 28 | Vale of Leven | 28 |
| 1909–10g‡ | Leith Ath | 33 | Raith R | 33 | St Bernard's | 27 |
| 1910–11g | Dumbarton | 31 | Ayr U | 27 | Albion R | 25 |
| 1911–12g | Ayr U | 35 | Abercorn | 30 | Dumbarton | 27 |
| 1912–13h | Ayr U | 34 | Dunfermline Ath | 33 | East Stirling | 32 |
| 1913–14g | Cowdenbeath | 31 | Albion R | 27 | Dunfermline Ath | 26 |
| 1914–15h | Cowdenbeath* | 37 | St Bernard's* | 37 | Leith Ath | 37 |
| 1921–22a | Alloa | 60 | Cowdenbeath | 47 | Armadale | 45 |
| 1922–23a | Queen's Park | 57 | Clydebank | ¶50 | St Johnstone | ¶45 |
| 1923–24a | St Johnstone | 56 | Cowdenbeath | 55 | Bathgate | 44 |
| 1924–25a | Dundee U | 50 | Clydebank | 48 | Clyde | 47 |
| 1925–26a | Dunfermline Ath | 59 | Clyde | 53 | Ayr U | 52 |
| 1926–27a | Bo'ness | 56 | Raith R | 49 | Clydebank | 45 |
| 1927–28a | Ayr U | 54 | Third Lanark | 45 | King's Park | 44 |
| 1928–29b | Dundee U | 51 | Morton | 50 | Arbroath | 47 |
| 1929–30a | Leith Ath* | 57 | East Fife | 57 | Albion R | 54 |
| 1930–31a | Third Lanark | 61 | Dundee U | 50 | Dunfermline Ath | 47 |
| 1931–32a | East Stirling* | 55 | St Johnstone | 55 | Raith Rovers* | 46 |
| 1932–33c | Hibernian | 54 | Queen of the S | 49 | Dunfermline Ath | 47 |
| 1933–34c | Albion R | 45 | Dunfermline Ath* | 44 | Arbroath | 44 |
| 1934–35c | Third Lanark | 52 | Arbroath | 50 | St Bernard's | 47 |
| 1935–36c | Falkirk | 59 | St Mirren | 52 | Morton | 48 |
| 1936–37c | Ayr U | 54 | Morton | 51 | St Bernard's | 48 |
| 1937–38c | Raith R | 59 | Albion R | 48 | Airdrieonians | 47 |
| 1938–39c | Cowdenbeath | 60 | Alloa* | 48 | East Fife | 48 |
| 1946–47d | Dundee | 45 | Airdrieonians | 42 | East Fife | 31 |
| 1947–48e | East Fife | 53 | Albion R | 42 | Hamilton A | 40 |
| 1948–49e | Raith R* | 42 | Stirling Albion | 42 | Airdrieonians* | 41 |
| 1949–50e | Morton | 47 | Airdrieonians | 44 | St Johnstone* | 36 |
| 1950–51e | Queen of the S* | 45 | Stirling Albion | 45 | Ayr U* | 36 |
| 1951–52e | Clyde | 44 | Falkirk | 43 | Ayr U | 39 |
| 1952–53e | Stirling Albion | 44 | Hamilton A | 43 | Queen's Park | 37 |
| 1953–54e | Motherwell | 45 | Kilmarnock | 42 | Third Lanark* | 36 |
| 1954–55e | Airdrieonians | 46 | Dunfermline Ath | 42 | Hamilton A | 39 |
| 1955–56b | Queen's Park | 54 | Ayr U | 51 | St Johnstone | 49 |
| 1956–57b | Clyde | 64 | Third Lanark | 51 | Cowdenbeath | 45 |
| 1957–58b | Stirling Albion | 55 | Dunfermline Ath | 53 | Arbroath | 47 |
| 1958–59b | Ayr U | 60 | Arbroath | 51 | Stenhousemuir | 40 |
| 1959–60b | St Johnstone | 53 | Dundee U | 50 | Queen of the S | 49 |
| 1960–61b | Stirling Albion | 55 | Falkirk | 54 | Stenhousemuir | 50 |
| 1961–62b | Clyde | 54 | Queen of the S | 53 | Morton | 44 |
| 1962–63b | St Johnstone | 55 | East Stirling | 49 | Morton | 48 |
| 1963–64b | Morton | 67 | Clyde | 53 | Arbroath | 46 |
| 1964–65b | Stirling Albion | 59 | Hamilton A | 50 | Queen of the S | 45 |
| 1965–66b | Ayr U | 53 | Airdrieonians | 50 | Queen of the S | 49 |
| 1966–67b | Morton | 69 | Raith R | 58 | Arbroath | 57 |
| 1967–68b | St Mirren | 62 | Arbroath | 53 | East Fife | 40 |
| 1968–69b | Motherwell | 64 | Ayr U | 53 | East Fife* | 47 |
| 1969–70b | Falkirk | 56 | Cowdenbeath | 55 | Queen of the S | 50 |
| 1970–71b | Partick T | 56 | East Fife | 51 | Arbroath | 46 |
| 1971–72b | Dumbarton* | 52 | Arbroath | 52 | Stirling Albion | 50 |
| 1972–73b | Clyde | 56 | Dunfermline Ath | 52 | Raith R* | 47 |
| 1973–74b | Airdrieonians | 60 | Kilmarnock | 58 | Hamilton A | 55 |
| 1974–75a | Falkirk | 54 | Queen of the S | 53 | Montrose | 53 |

Elected to First Division: 1894 Clyde; 1897 Partick T; 1899 Kilmarnock; 1900 Partick T; 1902 Partick T; 1903 Airdrieonians; 1905 Falkirk, Aberdeen and Hamilton A; 1906 Clyde; 1910 Raith R; 1913 Ayr U.

## RELEGATED FROM PREMIER DIVISION

1975–76 Dundee, St Johnstone
1976–77 Hearts, Kilmarnock
1977–78 Ayr U, Clydebank
1978–79 Hearts, Motherwell
1979–80 Dundee, Hibernian
1980–81 Kilmarnock, Hearts
1981–82 Partick T, Airdrieonians

## RELEGATED FROM DIVISION 1

1975–76 Dunfermline Ath, Clyde
1976–77 Raith R, Falkirk
1977–78 Alloa Ath, East Fife
1978–79 Montrose, Queen of the S
1979–80 Arbroath, Clyde
1980–81 Stirling A, Berwick R
1981–82 East Stirling, Queen of the S

## RELEGATED FROM DIVISION 1 (to 1973–74)

1921–22*Queen's Park, Dumbarton, Clydebank
1922–23 Albion R, Alloa Ath
1923–24 Clyde, Clydebank
1924–25 Third Lanark, Ayr U
1925–26 Raith R, Clydebank
1926–27 Morton, Dundee U
1927–28 Dunfermline Ath, Bo'ness
1928–29 Third Lanark, Raith R
1929–30 St Johnstone, Dundee U
1930–31 Hibernian, East Fife
1931–32 Dundee U, Leith Ath
1932–33 Morton, East Stirling
1933–34 Third Lanark, Cowdenbeath
1934–35 St Mirren, Falkirk
1935–36 Aidrieonians, Ayr U
1936–37 Dunfermline Ath, Albion R
1937–38 Dundee, Morton
1938–39 Queen's Park, Raith R
1946–47 Kilmarnock, Hamilton A
1947–48 Airdrieonians, Queen's Park
1948–49 Morton, Albion R
1949–50 Queen of the S, Stirling Albion
1950–51 Clyde, Falkirk

1951–52 Morton, Stirling Albion
1952–53 Motherwell, Third Lanark
1953–54 Airdrieonians, Hamilton A
1954–55 No clubs relegated
1955–56 Stirling Albion, Clyde
1956–57 Dunfermline Ath, Ayr U
1957–58 East Fife, Queen's Park
1958–59 Queen of the S, Falkirk
1959–60 Arbroath, Stirling Albion
1960–61 Ayr U, Clyde
1961–62 St Johnstone, Stirling Albion
1962–63 Clyde, Raith R
1963–64 Queen of the S, East Stirling
1964–65 Airdrieonians, Third Lanark
1965–66 Morton, Hamilton A
1966–67 St Mirren, Ayr U
1967–68 Motherwell, Stirling Albion
1968–69 Falkirk, Arbroath
1969–70 Raith R, Partick T
1970–71 St Mirren, Cowdenbeath
1971–72 Clyde, Dunfermline Ath
1972–73 Kilmarnock, Airdrieonians
1973–74 East Fife, Falkirk

*Season 1921–22 – only 1 club promoted, 3 clubs relegated.
*The Scottish Football League was reconstructed into three divisions at the end of the 1974–75 season, so the usual relegation statistics do not apply.*

# SCOTTISH FA CUP FINALS 1874–1982

| Year | Winners | Runners-up | Score |
|------|---------|------------|-------|
| 1874 | Queen's Park | Clydesdale | 2-0 |
| 1875 | Queen's Park | Renton | 3-0 |
| 1876 | Queen's Park | Third Lanark | 2-0 after 1-1 draw |
| 1877 | Vale of Leven | Rangers | 3-2 after 0-0 and 1-1 draws |
| 1878 | Vale of Leven | Third Lanark | 1-0 |
| 1879 | Vale of Leven* | Rangers | |
| 1880 | Queen's Park | Thornlibank | 3-0 |
| 1881 | Queen's Park† | Dumbarton | 3-1 |
| 1882 | Queen's Park | Dumbarton | 4-1 after 2-2 draw |
| 1883 | Dumbarton | Vale of Leven | 2-1 after 2-2 draw |
| 1884 | Queen's Park‡ | Vale of Leven | |
| 1885 | Renton | Vale of Leven | 3-1 after 0-0 draw |
| 1886 | Queen's Park | Renton | 3-1 |
| 1887 | Hibernian | Dumbarton | 2-1 |
| 1888 | Renton | Cambuslang | 6-1 |
| 1889 | Third Lanark§ | Celtic | 2-1 |
| 1890 | Queen's Park | Vale of Leven | 2-1 after 1-1 draw |
| 1891 | Hearts | Dumbarton | 1-0 |
| 1892 | Celtic¶ | Queen's Park | 5-1 |
| 1893 | Queen's Park | Celtic | 2-1 |
| 1894 | Rangers | Celtic | 3-1 |
| 1895 | St Bernard's | Renton | 2-1 |
| 1896 | Hearts | Hibernian | 3-1 |
| 1897 | Rangers | Dumbarton | 5-1 |
| 1898 | Rangers | Kilmarnock | 2-0 |
| 1899 | Celtic | Rangers | 2-0 |
| 1900 | Celtic | Queen's Park | 4-3 |
| 1901 | Hearts | Celtic | 4-3 |
| 1902 | Hibernian | Celtic | 1-0 |
| 1903 | Rangers | Hearts | 2-0 after 1-1 and 0-0 draws |
| 1904 | Celtic | Rangers | 3-2 |
| 1905 | Third Lanark | Rangers | 3-1 after 0-0 draw |
| 1906 | Hearts | Third Lanark | 1-0 |
| 1907 | Celtic | Hearts | 3-0 |
| 1908 | Celtic | St Mirren | 5-1 |
| 1909 | •• | | |
| 1910 | Dundee | Clyde | 2-1 after 2-2 and 0-0 draws |
| 1911 | Celtic | Hamilton A | 2-0 after 0-0 draw |
| 1912 | Celtic | Clyde | 2-0 |
| 1913 | Falkirk | Raith R | 2-0 |
| 1914 | Celtic | Hibernian | 4-1 after 0-0 draw |
| 1920 | Kilmarnock | Albion R | 3-2 |
| 1921 | Partick T | Rangers | 1-0 |
| 1922 | Morton | Rangers | 1-0 |
| 1923 | Celtic | Hibernian | 1-0 |
| 1924 | Airdrieonians | Hibernian | 2-0 |
| 1925 | Celtic | Dundee | 2-1 |
| 1926 | St Mirren | Celtic | 2-0 |
| 1927 | Celtic | East Fife | 3-1 |
| 1928 | Rangers | Celtic | 4-0 |
| 1929 | Kilmarnock | Rangers | 2-0 |
| 1930 | Rangers | Partick T | 2-1 after 0-0 draw |
| 1931 | Celtic | Motherwell | 4-2 after 2-2 draw |
| 1932 | Rangers | Kilmarnock | 3-0 after 1-1 draw |
| 1933 | Celtic | Motherwell | 1-0 |
| 1934 | Rangers | St Mirren | 5-0 |
| 1935 | Rangers | Hamilton A | 2-1 |
| 1936 | Rangers | Third Lanark | 1-0 |
| 1937 | Celtic | Aberdeen | 2-1 |
| 1938 | East Fife | Kilmarnock | 4-2 after 1-1 draw |
| 1939 | Clyde | Motherwell | 4-0 |
| 1947 | Aberdeen | Hibernian | 2-1 |
| 1948 | Rangers | Morton | 1-0 after 1-1 draw |
| 1949 | Rangers | Clyde | 4-1 |
| 1950 | Rangers | East Fife | 3-0 |
| 1951 | Celtic | Motherwell | 1-0 |
| 1952 | Motherwell | Dundee | 4-0 |

| Year | Winners | Runners-up | Score |
|------|---------|------------|-------|
| 1953 | Rangers | Aberdeen | 1-0 after 1-1 draw |
| 1954 | Celtic | Aberdeen | 2-1 |
| 1955 | Clyde | Celtic | 1-0 after 1-1 draw |
| 1956 | Hearts | Celtic | 3-1 |
| 1957 | Falkirk | Kilmarnock | 2-1 after 1-1 draw |
| 1958 | Clyde | Hibernian | 1-0 |
| 1959 | St Mirren | Aberdeen | 3-1 |
| 1960 | Rangers | Kilmarnock | 2-0 |
| 1961 | Dunfermline Ath | Celtic | 2-0 after 0-0 draw |
| 1962 | Rangers | St Mirren | 2-0 |
| 1963 | Rangers | Celtic | 3-0 after 1-1 draw |
| 1964 | Rangers | Dundee | 3-1 |
| 1965 | Celtic | Dunfermline Ath | 3-2 |
| 1966 | Rangers | Celtic | 1-0 after 0-0 draw |
| 1967 | Celtic | Aberdeen | 2-0 |
| 1968 | Dunfermline Ath | Hearts | 3-1 |
| 1969 | Celtic | Rangers | 4-0 |
| 1970 | Aberdeen | Celtic | 3-1 |
| 1971 | Celtic | Rangers | 2-1 after 1-1 draw |
| 1972 | Celtic | Hibernian | 6-1 |
| 1973 | Rangers | Celtic | 3-2 |
| 1974 | Celtic | Dundee U | 3-0 |
| 1975 | Celtic | Airdrieonians | 3-1 |
| 1976 | Rangers | Heai . | 3-1 |
| 1977 | Celtic | Rangers | 1-0 |
| 1978 | Rangers | Aberdeen | 2-1 |
| 1979 | Rangers | Hibernian | 3-2 after 0-0 and 0-0 draws |
| 1980 | Celtic | Rangers | 1-0 |
| 1981 | Rangers | Dundee U | 4-1 after 0-0 draw |
| 1982 | Aberdeen | Rangers | 4-1 (aet) |

*Vale of Leven awarded cup, Rangers failed to appear for replay after 1-1 draw.
†After Dumbarton protested the first game, which Queen's Park won 2-1.
‡Queen's Park awarded cup, Vale of Leven failing to appear.
§Replay by order of Scottish FA because of playing conditions in first match, won 3-0 by Third Lanark.
¶After mutual protested game which Celtic won 1-0.
•• Owing to riot, the cup was withheld after two drawn games – Celtic 2-1, Rangers 2-1.

# SCOTTISH LEAGUE CUP FINALS 1946–82

| Season | Winners | Runners-up | Score |
|---|---|---|---|
| 1946–47 | Rangers | Aberdeen | 4-0 |
| 1947–48 | East Fife | Falkirk | 4-1 after 0-0 draw |
| 1948–49 | Rangers | Raith R | 2-0 |
| 1949–50 | East Fife | Dunfermline Ath | 3-0 |
| 1950–51 | Motherwell | Hibernian | 3-0 |
| 1951–52 | Dundee | Rangers | 3-2 |
| 1952–53 | Dundee | Kilmarnock | 2-0 |
| 1953–54 | East Fife | Partick T | 3-2 |
| 1954–55 | Hearts | Motherwell | 4-2 |
| 1955–56 | Aberdeen | St Mirren | 2-1 |
| 1956–57 | Celtic | Partick T | 3-0 after 0-0 draw |
| 1957–58 | Celtic | Rangers | 7-1 |
| 1958–59 | Hearts | Partick T | 5-1 |
| 1959–60 | Hearts | Third Lanark | 2-1 |
| 1960–61 | Rangers | Kilmarnock | 2-0 |
| 1961–62 | Rangers | Hearts | 3-1 after 1-1 draw |
| 1962–63 | Hearts | Kilmarnock | 1-0 |
| 1963–64 | Rangers | Morton | 5-0 |
| 1964–65 | Rangers | Celtic | 2-1 |
| 1965–66 | Celtic | Rangers | 2-1 |
| 1966–67 | Celtic | Rangers | 1-0 |
| 1967–68 | Celtic | Dundee | 5-3 |
| 1968–69 | Celtic | Hibernian | 6-2 |
| 1969–70 | Celtic | St Johnstone | 1-0 |
| 1970–71 | Rangers | Celtic | 1-0 |
| 1971–72 | Partick T | Celtic | 4-1 |
| 1972–73 | Hibernian | Celtic | 2-1 |
| 1973–74 | Dundee | Celtic | 1-0 |
| 1974–75 | Celtic | Hibernian | 6-3 |
| 1975–76 | Rangers | Celtic | 1-0 |
| 1976–77 | Aberdeen | Celtic | 2-1 |
| 1977–78 | Rangers | Celtic | 2-1 |
| 1978–79 | Rangers | Aberdeen | 2-1 |
| 1979–80 | Dundee U | Aberdeen | 3-0 after 0-0 draw |
| 1980–81 | Dundee U | Dundee | 3-0 |
| 1981–82 | Rangers | Dundee U | 2-1 |

# SCOTTISH LEAGUE CUP 1981–82

## SECTION 1

### 8 AUG

**Celtic (1) 1** *(McGarvey)*

**St Mirren (1) 3** *(McDougall, Garner og, McCormack)* 26,100

*Celtic:* Bonner; McGrain, Reid, Aitken, Garner, MacLeod (Conroy), Provan, Sullivan, McGarvey, Burns, Nicholas (McCluskey).
*St Mirren:* Thomson; Beckett, Abercromby, Fitzpatrick, McCormack, Copland, McDougall (Logan), Stark, Bone, Richardson, Scanlon.

**Hibernian (1) 1** *(Murray)*

**St Johnstone (1) 2** *(McCoist, Beedie)* 5654

*Hibernian:* Donaldson; Flavell, Turnbull, McNamara, McLaren (Rodier), Rice, Callachan, Rae, Murray, MacLeod, Duncan.
*St Johnstone:* Tulloch; Kilgour, McNeil, Weir, Rutherford, Caldwell, Pelosi, McCoist, Beedie, Fleming, Brogan.

**Dundee (1) 1** *(Fleming)*

**Raith R (1) 2** *(Russell 2)* 5362

*Dundee:* Geddes; Barr, McKimmie, Fraser (McGeachie), Glennie, MacDonald, Murphy, Kidd, Sinclair (Stephen), Fleming, Scrimgeour.
*Raith R:* Walker; Ford, Candlish, Robinson, Houston, Steel, Ballantyne, Urquhart, Russell, Carroll (Steen), Mitchell (Harris).

**Morton (1) 1** *(Hutchison)*

**Rangers (1) 1** *(McAdam)* 14,000

*Morton:* Baines; Hayes, Holmes, Rooney, McLaughlin, Orr, McNeil, Marr (Houston), Busby, Hutchison, Ritchie.
*Rangers:* Stewart; Jardine, Miller, Bett, Stevens, Redford, Cooper, Russell, McAdam (Jackson), Johnstone D., Johnston W.

**Aberdeen (2) 3** *(McGhee 2, Kennedy)*

**Kilmarnock (0) 0** 9000

*Aberdeen:* Leighton; Kennedy, McMaster, Cooper, McLeish, Miller, Strachan, Bell, McGhee, Harrow, Weir.
*Kilmarnock:* McCulloch; McLean, Cockburn, Clark (McBride), Armstrong, McDicken, Gallagher, Mauchlen, Bourke, Bryce, McCready.

**Airdrieonians (0) 0**

**Hearts (1) 1** *(Robertson)* 6000

*Airdrieonians:* Martin; Walker, Rodger, McCluskey, March, Anderson, McKeown (McGuire), Flood, Campbell (Kerr), Gordon, Clark.
*Hearts:* Smith; More, Shields (Liddell F.), Byrne, MacDonald R., MacLaren, Mackay, Robertson, Liddell G., Bowman, Hamill.

**Ayr U (3) 3** *(Connor, Nicol, Frye)*

**Dundee U (1) 4** *(Bannon 3 [1 pen], Sturrock)* 3341

*Ayr U:* Rennie; Shanks, Nicol, Hendry, McAllister, Fleeting, Kean, Ahern, Morris (Christie), Connor, Frye.
*Dundee U:* McAlpine; Holt, Kopel, Phillip, Stark, Narey, Bannon, Addison, Reilly (Pettigrew), Sturrock, Kirkwood.

**Partick T (1) 2** *(Higgins, Gibson pen)*

**Motherwell (0) 0** 3172

*Partick T:* Rough; McKinnon, Whittaker, Campbell (O'Hara), Anderson, Watson (McDonald), Park, Jardine, Gibson, Doyle, Higgins.
*Motherwell:* Sproat; More, McLeod, McLelland, Carson, Forbes (Cleland), Clinging, McLaughlin, Irvine, Soutar, Gahagan.

**Cowdenbeath (1) 2** *(Allison, Mercer)*

**Dumbarton (0) 0** 368

*Cowdenbeath:* Allan; Rolland, Allison, Tierney, Russell, Hunter, Park, Steele, Liddle, McFarlane, Duncan (Mercer).
*Dumbarton:* Carson; Sinclair, McLeod, McGowan (Clougherty), Gallacher, Coyle T., Donnelly, Campbell (Rankin), Blair, Coyle J., Brown.

**Queen of the S (0) 1** *(Phillips)*

**Brechin C (0) 3** *(Mackie, Campbell I., Dickson og)* 850

*Queen of the S:* Ball; Dickson, Cloy, Gordon, Clark, Malone, Phillips, Boyd, Alexander, Coughlin, Robertson J.
*Brechin C:* Neilson; Watt, Lorimer, Lesslie, Stewart (Campbell R.), Reid, Campbell I., Mackie, Henderson, Elvin (Graham), Burnside.

**Falkirk (1) 4** *(Smith, Brown 2, McIntosh)*

**Stirling Albion (1) 1** *(Torrance)* 1500

*Falkirk:* Watson; Hoggan, Rose, Thompson, Brown, Hay, Perry, Herd (Oliver M.), McIntosh, Smith, McRoberts.
*Stirling Albion:* Arthur; Clarke (Morrison), Young, Denny, Steedman, Moffat, McNeil, Gray, Torrance, McLeod, Colquhoun.

**Forfar Ath (4) 4** *(Morris, Craig, Hancock 2)*

**Alloa (1) 1** *(Smith)* 1076

*Forfar Ath:* Boardley; Morris, Rankin, Brown, Allan, Leitch, Craig, Farningham, Hancock, Gallacher, Downie.
*Alloa:* McGowan; Haggart, McKenzie, Purdie, Stewart, Holt, Grant, Smith, McComb, McNab, Murray.

**Berwick R (1) 2** *(Davidson, Coutts og)*

**Clyde (1) 1** *(Evans)* 817

*Berwick R:* McDonald; McGlinchey, McCann, McCulloch, Dixon, Muir, Davidson, McGlynn, Lawson, Tait, Armstrong.
*Clyde:* Young; Brogan, McQueen, McColl, Dempsey, Rae, McCutcheon, Reilly, Masterton, O'Neill (Coutts), Evans.

**Queen's Park (0) 1** *(McNiven)*

**Clydebank (0) 0** 800

*Queen's Park:* Atkins; Wilson, Dickson, Cook, McGregor, McFarlane, McNiven, Crawley, Melrose, Grant, Nicholson.
*Clydebank:* Gallacher; Gervaise, Sharkey, McLaughlin, Evans, Given, Ronald, McKeown, Miller, McGorm, McCabe.

**Hamilton A (0) 2** *(McDowall, Deeney)*

**Dunfermline Ath (0) 0** 1250

*Hamilton A:* Ferguson; Frew, Brown, Wright, McDougall, Marshall, Howie, McDowall, Craig, Deeney, McAdams.
*Dunfermline Ath:* Whyte; Robertson, Brown, Thomson, Hutt, Hamill (Dunlop), Jenkins, Bowie, Morrison, Donnelly, Forrest.

**Montrose (0) 1** *(Turnbull)*

**East Stirling (0) 0** 450

*Montrose:* Charles; Forbes, Milne, Clark, Taylor, Johnston, McDonald, Turnbull, McManus (Nicoll), Forrest, Wright.

574

*East Stirling:* Kelly; Blair, Renwick, Watt, Rennie, Gourlay, McCulley, Hunter (McCall), Sharp (Goodall), Robertson, Ashwood.

**Arbroath (2) 3** *(Durno, Robb 2)*
**Stenhousemuir (0) 0**                                   613
*Arbroath:* Lister; Forsyth, Burke, Casey, Young, Gavine, Harley, Durno, Robb, Kydd, Lees.
*Stenhousemuir:* McLaren; Frickleton, Rennie, McAuley, Smith, Mullen, Jack, Meakin, Murray, Munn, Bremner.

**Meadowbank T (0) 2** *(Jobson, Dunn)*
**Albion R (0) 2** *(Gillespie, Hill)*                   250
*Meadowbank T:* McKell; Henderson, Skilling, Fraser, Godfrey, Dunn, McPhee, Leetion, Jobson, Conroy, Boyd.
*Albion R:* Balavage; Murray, Main, Burgess, Hamill, Gormley, Gillespie, Hill, Houston, McDonagh, Campbell.

**Stranraer (0) 1** *(Sweeney)*
**East Fife (1) 3** *(Scott, Tait, O'Brien)*            350
*Stranraer:* McFall; McDonald, Hyslop, Hamilton, Murdoch, Black, Neil, Dolan, Sweeney, Armour, Murphy.
*East Fife:* Gorman; Muirhead, Miller, Beveridge, MacLaren, O'Brien, Neilson, Clarke, Scott, Tait, Wedderburn.

## SECTION 2

### 12 AUG

**St Johnstone (1) 2** *(McCoist, Morton pen)*
**Celtic (0) 0**                                       10,406
*St Johnstone:* Tulloch; Mackay, Kilgour, Weir, Rutherford, Caldwell, Pelosi, McCoist, Beedie (Morton), Fleming, Brogan.
*Celtic:* Bonner; McGrain, McAdam, Aitken, Garner, MacLeod, Provan, Sullivan, McGarvey, Burns, McCluskey.

**St Mirren (0) 0**
**Hibernian (0) 0**                                     5912
*St Mirren:* Thomson; Beckett, Abercromby, Fitzpatrick, McCormack, Copland, McDougall, Stark, Bone, Richardson, Scanlon.
*Hibernian:* Donaldson; Sneddon, Turnbull, MacLaren, Flavell, McNamara, Callachan, MacLeod, Murray (Jamieson), Rae, Duncan.

**Raith R (2) 2** *(Ballantyne, Forsyth)*
**Morton (2) 5** *(Ritchie, Rooney, Busby, Hutchison, McNeil)*                                         3000
*Raith R:* Walker, Ford, Candlish, Robinson, Forsyth, Steel, Ballantyne, Urquhart, Russell (Harris), Carroll, Mitchell.
*Morton:* Baines; Hayes, Holmes, Rooney, McLaughlin, Orr, McNeil, Marr (Houston), Busby, Hutchison, Ritchie.

**Rangers (1) 4** *(MacDonald, Miller, Johnstone, McAdam)*
**Dundee (1) 1** *(Fleming)*                          13,500
*Rangers:* Stewart; Bett (MacDonald), Miller, Stevens, Jackson, Redford, Cooper, Russell, McAdam (Johnston), Johnstone, McLean.
*Dundee:* Geddes; Barr (Stephen), McKimmie, Kidd, Glennie, MacDonald, Murphy, McGeachie, Sinclair, Fleming, Scrimgeour (Mackie).

**Hearts (0) 1** *(Robertson)*
**Aberdeen (0) 0**                                     10,423
*Hearts:* Smith; More, Shields, Byrne, MacDonald R., MacLaren, Robertson, Liddell, Bowman, Hamill, MacDonald A.
*Aberdeen:* Leighton; Kennedy, McMaster, Cooper, McLeish, Miller, Strachan, Bell, McGhee, Harrow (Jarvie), Weir.

**Kilmarnock (0) 1** *(Bourke)*
**Airdrieonians (0) 1** *(Clark)*                       1950
*Kilmarnock:* McCulloch; McLean, Cockburn, Clark, Armstrong, McDicken, Gallagher, Mauchlen, Bourke, Bryce (McBride), McCready.
*Airdrieonians:* Martin; Walker, Rodger, McCluskey, March, Anderson, McKeown (Kerr), Clark, Campbell (McGuire), Gordon, Flood.

**Dundee U (0) 2** *(Pettigrew, Sturrock)*
**Partick T (0) 0**                                     5926
*Dundee U:* McAlpine; Holt, Kopel, Phillip, Stark, Narey, Bannon, Payne, Pettigrew (Gough), Sturrock, Dodds.
*Partick T:* Rough; McKinnon, Whittaker, Campbell, Anderson, Doyle, Park, Jardine, Gibson (McDonald), O'Hara, Higgins.

**Motherwell (1) 2** *(Cleland, Clinging pen)*
**Ayr U (1) 3** *(Carson og, Hendry, Frye)*            1970
*Motherwell:* Sproat; Wark, MacLeod, McLelland, Carson, Forbes (Mills), Clinging, McClair, Irvine (Conn), Cleland, Gahagan.
*Ayr U:* Rennie; Shanks, Nicol, Hendry, McAllister, Fleeting, Kean, McSherry, Morris, Ahern, Frye.

**Brechin C (2) 2** *(Mackay, Graham)*
**Cowdenbeath (0) 0**                                    500
*Brechin C:* Neilson; Watt, Reid, Lesslie, Mackay, Campbell R., Campbell I., Elvin, Graham, Lorimer, Burnside.
*Cowdenbeath:* Allan; Rolland, Allison, Tierney, Russell, Hunter, Park, Meikle, McFarlane, Steele, Mercer.

**Dumbarton (0) 1** *(Blair pen)*
**Queen of the S (0) 0**                                 980
*Dumbarton:* Carson; Sinclair, MacLeod, McGowan P., Gallacher, Coyle T., Rankin, Campbell (Donnelly), Brown, Coyle J., Blair.
*Queen of the S:* Ball; Dickson, Cloy, Gordon (Robertson G.), Clark, Malone, Phillips, Boyd, Alexander, Coughlin, Robertson J.

**Alloa (1) 1** *(Holt)*
**Falkirk (0) 1** *(Brown)*                             1280
*Alloa:* McGowan; Haggart, McKenzie, Purdie, Stewart, Holt, Grant, Oliver A., McComb, Spence, Smith.
*Falkirk:* Watson; Hoggan, Rose, Thompson, Oliver M. (Stevenson), Brown, Perry, Herd, McIntosh, Smith, McRoberts.

**Stirling Albion (0) 0**
**Forfar Ath (1) 1** *(Allan)*                         1100
*Stirling Albion:* Arthur; Clarke, McLeod, Gray, Philliben, Denny (Morrison), McNeil (Gibson), McCue, Torrance, Dunlop, Colquhoun.
*Forfar Ath:* Boardley; Morris, Rankin, Brown, Allan, Leitch, Craig (Clark), Farningham, Hancock, Gallacher, Downie.

**Clyde (0) 0**
**Queen's Park (1) 3** *(Nicholson 2, Wood)*            870
*Clyde:* Young; Brogan, McQueen, McColl, Dempsey, Miller, McCutcheon, Reilly, Masterton, O'Neill, Evans.
*Queen's Park:* Atkins; Wilson (Wood), Dickson, Cook, McGregor, McFarlane, McNiven, Crawley, Melrose, Grant (Verrechia), Nicholson.

**Clydebank (1) 2** *(McLaughlin, Evans)*

**Berwick R (1) 2** *(Davidson, Lawson)* 350

*Clydebank:* Gallacher; Gervaise (Treanor), Fallon, McLaughlin, Sharkey, Given, Ronald (McGorm), McKeown, Evans, Millar, McCabe.
*Berwick R:* McDonald; Marshall, McCann, MuCulloch, Dixon, Muir, Davidson, McGlinchey, Lawson, Tait, Armstrong.

**Dunfermline Ath (2) 2** *(McNaughton, Hamill)*

**Montrose (0) 1** *(Turnbull)* 2200

*Dunfermline Ath:* Young; Robertson, Brown, Dall R., Thomson, Hamill, McNaughton, Bowie, Morrison, Donnelly, Forrest.
*Montrose:* Charles; Forbes, Milne, Clark, Taylor, Johnston, McDonald, Forrest, McManus, Turnbull, Wright.

**East Stirling (0) 0**

**Hamilton A (1) 2** *(Deeney 2)* 350

*East Stirling:* Kelly; Renwick (Lamont), Blair, Watt, Rennie, Gourlay, Hunter, McCulley, Sharp, Robertson, McGall (Goodall).
*Hamilton A:* Ferguson; Frew, Brown, Wright, McDougall, Marshall, Howie, McDowall (Mitchell), Craig, Deeney, McAdams (Donnelly).

**Meadowbank T (1) 2** *(Jobson)*

**Arbroath (0) 3** *(Yule 2, Gavine)* 250

*Meadowbank T:* McKell; Henderson, Brown, Fraser, Godfrey, Dunn, McPhee, Leetion, Jobson, Conroy, Boyd.
*Arbroath:* Lister; Forsyth, Burke, Casey, Young, Gavine, Harley, Durno, Robb, Kydd (Shaw), Lees (Yule).

**Stenhousemuir (2) 2** *(Munn, Jack)*

**Stranraer (2) 3** *(Neil, Murphy, Bremner og)* 475

*Stenhousemuir:* Howie; Rennie, Kirkland, Bremner, Smith, Mullen, Jack, Meakin, Murray, Munn, Morrison.
*Stranraer:* McFall; McDonald, Hyslop, Hamilton, Murdoch, Black, Neil (Dolan), Harley, Sweeney, Armour (Devine), Murphy.

**13 AUG**

**Albion R (0) 1** *(Craig)*

**East Fife (0) 1** *(O'Brien)* 760

*Albion R:* Balavage; Murray, Main, Craig, Burgess, Hamill, Gillespie (Gormley), Hill, Houston, McDonagh, Campbell.
*East Fife:* Gorman; Hamilton, Millar, Muirhead, Beveridge, Neilson, Tait, O'Brien, Scott (Honeyman), Clarke, Wedderburn.

**SECTION 3**

**15 AUG**

**Celtic (2) 4** *(MacLeod 2, Nicholas 2)*

**Hibernian (0) 1** *(Duncan)* 19,200

*Celtic:* Bonner; McGrain, Reid, Aitken, McAdams (Moyes), MacLeod, Provan, Sullivan, McGarvey, Burns, Nicholas.
*Hibernian:* Donaldson; Sneddon, Turnbull, MacLaren, Paterson, McNamara, MacLeod (Murray), Flavell, Connolly, Rae, Duncan.

**St Johnstone (1) 2** *(McCoist, Brogan)*

**St Mirren (1) 3** *(McDougall 2, Richardson)* 4662

*St Johnstone:* Tulloch; Mackay, Kilgour (Docherty), Weir,

Rutherford, Caldwell, Pelosi, McCoist, Fleming, Morton, Brogan.
*St Mirren:* Thomson; Beckett, Abercromby, Fitzpatrick, McCormack, Copland, McDougall, Stark, Bone (Logan), Richardson, Scanlon.

**Dundee (1) 1** *(Fleming)*

**Morton (1) 2** *(McNeil, Thomson)* 4710

*Dundee:* Geddes; McGeachie, McKimmie, Fraser (Mackie), Glennie, MacDonald, Bell, Kidd (Scrimgeour), Sinclair, Fleming, Stephen.
*Morton:* Baines; Hayes, Holmes, Rooney, McLaughlin, Orr, McNeil, Thomson, Busby, Hutchison, Ritchie.

**Rangers (4) 8** *(Jardine, Russell 2, McAdam, Redford 4)*

**Raith R (1) 1** *(Russell)* 16,000

*Rangers:* Stewart; Jardine, Miller (Johnston), Stevens, Forsyth, Redford, Cooper, Russell, McAdam (MacDonald), Johnstone, McLean.
*Raith R:* Walker; Houston, Candlish, Robinson, Forsyth, Steel, Ford, Urquhart (Steen), Russell, Carroll, Ballantyne.

**Aberdeen (2) 3** *(Hewitt, Weir, Strachan pen)*

**Airdrieonians (0) 0** 8000

*Aberdeen:* Leighton; Kennedy, Hamilton, Cooper, McLeish, Miller, Strachan, Bell (Jarvie), McGhee (Cowan), Hewitt, Weir.
*Airdrieonians:* Martin; Walker, Rodger, McCluskey, March, Anderson, Kerr (McGuire), Clark, Campbell (Erwin), Gordon, Flood.

**Hearts (1) 1** *(Liddell)*

**Kilmarnock (0) 1** *(Wilson pen)* 7746

*Hearts:* Smith; More, Shields, Byrne, MacDonald R., MacLaren, Bowman, Robertson, Liddell G., MacDonald A., Hamill.
*Kilmarnock:* McCulloch; McLean, Cockburn, Clark, Armstrong, McDicken, Gallagher, Mauchlen, Bourke, Wilson, McBride (McCready).

**Ayr U (1) 1** *(Kean)*

**Partick T (0) 0** 3093

*Ayr U:* Rennie; Shanks (Connor), Nicol, Hendry, McAllister, Fleeting, Kean, McSherry, Morris, Ahern, Frye.
*Partick T:* Rough; McKinnon, Lapsley, Campbell, Whittaker, Watson (Jardine), Park, O'Hara, Gibson, Doyle, Higgins.

**Motherwell (1) 1** *(McLaughlin pen)*

**Dundee U (1) 2** *(Pettigrew, Gough)* 2884

*Motherwell:* Sproat; Wark, MacLeod, McLelland, Carson, McLaughlin (Irvine), Clinging, Forbes, Cleland, Conn (Soutar), Gahagan.
*Dundee U:* McAlpine; Holt, Kopel, Phillip, Stark, Narey, Bannon, Payne (Gough), Pettigrew, Sturrock, Dodds.

**Brechin C (0) 2** *(Graham, Campbell I.)*

**Dumbarton (0) 1** *(Blair pen)* 500

*Brechin C:* Neilson; Watt, Reid, Lesslie, Campbell R., Mackie, Campbell I., Elvin, Graham, Lorimer, Burnside (Paterson).
*Dumbarton:* Carson; Sinclair, MacLeod, McGowan P., Gallacher, Coyle T., Rankin (McNeil), Campbell (Donnelly), Brown, Coyle J., Blair.

**Cowdenbeath (0) 1** *(Liddle)*

**Queen of the S (1) 2** *(Robertson J. 2)* 539

*Cowdenbeath:* Allan; Rolland, Fleming, Tierney, Russell, Hunter, Meikle, Steele, Liddle, McFarlane (Adamson), Mercer.

*Queen of the S:* Ball; Dickson, Cloy, Clark, Boyd, Robertson G., McVitie, Gordon, Alexander, Coughlin, Robertson J.

**Alloa (2) 4** *(Grant 4* [1 pen])
**Stirling Albion (1) 3** *(Gibson, Colquhoun, Morrison)* 657

*Alloa:* McGowan; Haggart, McKenzie, Purdie, Stewart, Holt (Mitchell), Grant, Oliver, McComb (Wilde), Spence, Smith.
*Stirling Albion:* Gordon; Philliben, McLeod, Young, Steedman (Clarke), Moffat (McNeil), Gibson, Gray, Torrance, Morrison, Colquhoun.

**Falkirk (0) 1** *(Smith)*
**Forfar Ath (0) 0** 2000

*Falkirk:* Watson; Hoggan, Burrell, Brown, Mackin, Thompson, Perry, Herd, McIntosh, Smith, McRoberts (Stevenson).
*Forfar Ath:* Boardley; Brash, McPhee, Brown, Allan, Leitch, Craig (Clark), Farningham, Hancock, Gallacher, Rankin (Bennett).

**Clyde (1) 3** *(Reilly 2, Masterton)*
**Clydebank (0) 0** 450

*Clyde:* Young; Brogan (McAlpine), McQueen, Docherty, Dempsey, Miller, McCutcheon, Reilly, Masterton (Nevin), Coutts, O'Neill.
*Clydebank:* Gallacher; Treanor, Fallon, McLaughlin, Sharkey, Given, McKeown (McGorm), Houston, Evans (Ronald), Miller, McCabe.

**Queen's Park (1) 2** *(McGregor 2)*
**Berwick R (0) 0** 656

*Queen's Park:* Atkins; Wilson, Dickson, Cook, McGregor, McFarlane, McNiven, Crawley, Melrose (Wood), Grant (Verrechia), Nicholson.
*Berwick R:* Glynn; Marshall, McCann, McCulloch (McGlynn), Dixon, Muir, Davidson, McGlinchey (Black), Lawson, Tait, Armstrong.

**Dunfermline Ath (1) 2** *(Forrest, Bowie)*
**East Stirling (1) 1** *(McCall)* 1500

*Dunfermline Ath:* Whyte; Robertson, Thomson, Brown, Dall R., Hamill, McNaughton (Hegarty), Bowie, Morrison, Donnelly, Forrest (Jenkins).
*East Stirling:* Kelly; Blair, Renwick, Watt, Rennie, Gourlay, Hunter (Lamont), McCulley, Sharp (McCaig), Robertson, McCall.

**Montrose (1) 1** *(Turnbull pen)*
**Hamilton A (1) 2** *(Deeney 2)* 600

*Montrose:* Charles; Forbes, Milne, Clark, Taylor, Johnston, McDonald (Young), Turnbull, Allan (McManus), Forrest, Wright.
*Hamilton A:* Ferguson; Frew, Brown, Wright, McDougall, Marshall, Howie, McDowall, Craig, Deeney, Donnelly (Alexander).

**Albion R (3) 5** *(Burgess 3* [1 pen], *McDonagh, Campbell)*
**Stenhousemuir (0) 2** *(Murray 2)* 674

*Albion R:* Balavage; Murray, Main (Gormley), Craig (Lapsley), Burgess, Hamill, Gillespie, Hill, Houston, McDonagh, Campbell.
*Stenhousemuir:* McLaren; Rennie, Kirkland, McAuley (Frickleton), Smith, Mullen, Jack (Bremner), Meakin, Murray, Munn, Morrison.

**Arbroath (2) 4** *(Robb, Harley 2, Durno)*
**Stranraer (0) 0** 551

*Arbroath:* Lister; Forsyth, Burke, Casey, Young, Gavine, Harley, Durno, Robb (Lees), Kydd, Yule.

*Stranraer:* McFall; McDonald (Hay), Devine, Hyslop, Murdoch, Black, Neil (Dolan), Hamilton, Harvey, Armour, Murphy.

**East Fife (0) 0**
**Meadowbank T (0) 1** *(Boyd)* 586

*East Fife:* Gorman; Hamilton, Millar, Clarke, Muirhead, Beveridge, Neilson, O'Brien, Scott, Tait (Honeyman), Wedderburn (Sokoluk).
*Meadowbank T:* McKell; Dunn, Henderson, Fraser, Godfrey, Leetion, McPhee, Boyd, Jobson, Conroy (Skilling), Sprott.

## SECTION 4

**19 AUG**

**Celtic (2) 4** *(McGarvey, Provan 2, Nicholas)*
**St Johnstone (0) 1** *(McCoist)* 14,600

*Celtic:* Bonner; McGrain, Reid, Aitken, Moyes, MacLeod, Provan, Sullivan, McGarvey, Burns, Nicholas.
*St Johnstone:* Tulloch; Mackay, Kilgour, Weir, Rutherford, Caldwell, Pelosi, McCoist, Fleming, Morton (Brannigan), Brogan.

**Hibernian (0) 0**
**St Mirren (0) 1** *(McDougall)* 4000

*Hibernian:* Donaldson; Sneddon, Turnbull, MacLaren, Paterson, McNamara, Flavell, Rae, Connolly, Jamieson, Duncan.
*St Mirren:* Thomson; Beckett, Abercromby, Fitzpatrick, McCormack, Copland, McDougall, Stark, Bone, Richardson, Scanlon.

**Dundee (0) 1** *(MacDonald)*
**Rangers (0) 2** *(McGeachie og, Stevens)* 9124

*Dundee:* Geddes; McGeachie, McKimmie (Scrimgeour), Fraser, Glennie, MacDonald, Bell, Kidd, Sinclair, Fleming, Stephen (Mackie).
*Rangers:* Stewart; Jardine, Miller, Stevens, Forsyth, Redford, Cooper, Bett, McAdam (Johnston), Johnstone, McLean (MacDonald).

**Morton (1) 2** *(Thomson, Rooney pen)*
**Raith R (0) 0** 2500

*Morton:* Baines; Hayes, Holmes, Rooney, McLaughlin, Orr, McNeil, Thomson, Busby, Hutchison, Ritchie.
*Raith R:* Walker; Houston, Candlish, Robinson, Forsyth, Steel, Ballantyne, Urquhart, Russell, Berry, Mitchell.

**Aberdeen (1) 3** *(Bell, Hewitt, Strachan pen)*
**Hearts (0) 0** 8000

*Aberdeen:* Leighton; Kennedy, McMaster (Watson), Cooper, McLeish, Miller, Strachan, Bell (McCall), McGhee, Hewitt, Weir.
*Hearts:* Smith; More, Shields, Byrne (Kidd), MacDonald R., MacLaren, Bowman (O'Connor), Robertson, McCoy, MacDonald A., Hamill.

**Airdrieonians (0) 0**
**Kilmarnock (1) 1** *(Bourke)* 2000

*Airdrieonians:* Martin; Cairney (McKeown), Rodger (Flood), Walker, Richardson, McCluskey, Campbell, Clark, Anderson, Gordon, Kerr.
*Kilmarnock:* McCulloch; McLean, Cockburn, Clark, Armstrong, McDicken, Gallacher, Cramond, Bourke, Wilson, McCready.

**Ayr U (1) 1** *(Frye)*
**Motherwell (0) 0** 2202

*Ayr U:* Rennie; Nicol, Connor, Hendry, McAllister, Fleeting, Kean (Christie), McSherry, Morris, Ahern, Frye.

*Motherwell:* Sproat; Wark, MacLeod, McLelland, Carson, McLaughlin, Clinging, McClair (Irvine), Cleland, Conn, Gahagan.

**Partick T (0) 1** *(Johnstone)*

**Dundee U (2) 2** *(Sturrock, Bannon)*  1760

*Partick T:* Rough; McKinnon, Lapsley, Campbell, Whittaker, Watson, Higgins, Jardine (Johnstone), O'Hara (McDonald), Doyle, Clark.
*Dundee U:* McAlpine; Holt, Kopel, Phillip, Stark, Narey, Bannon, Milne, Pettigrew (Dodds), Sturrock, Gough.

**Cowdenbeath (3) 4** *(Steele 2, Forrest, Liddle)*

**Brechin C (0) 0**  450

*Cowdenbeath:* Allan; Rolland, Fleming, Tierney, Russell, Hunter, Meikle, Park, Liddle, Steele, Forrest.
*Brechin C:* Neilson; Watt, Reid, Lesslie, Campbell R. (Keating), Mackie, Campbell I., Elvin, Graham, Lorimer, Burnside.

**Queen of the S (1) 3** *(Alexander 2, McVitie)*

**Dumbarton (0) 2** *(Mailer, Campbell)*  567

*Queen of the S:* Ball; Dickson, Cloy, Robertson G., Clark, Boyd, McVitie, Gordon, Alexander, Coughlin, Robertson J.
*Dumbarton:* Carson; Sinclair, MacLeod, Coyle T., Gallacher, McNeil, Donnelly, Brown, Blair (Campbell), Coyle J., Rankin (Mailer).

**Falkirk (0) 3** *(Brown 2, Smith)*

**Alloa (0) 0**  1500

*Falkirk:* Watson; Rose, Burrell, Brown, Mackin, Thompson, Perry (Oliver A.), Herd, McIntosh, Smith, Stevenson.
*Alloa:* McGowan; Haggart, McKenzie, Purdie, Stewart, Holt, Grant, Oliver (Dunn), Spence, McNab, Smith.

**Forfar Ath (0) 1** *(Hancock)*

**Stirling Albion (0) 0**  943

*Forfar Ath:* Boardley; Bennett, Rankin, Brown, Allan, McPhee, Craig, Farningham, Hancock, Gallacher, Morris (Leitch).
*Stirling Albion:* Gordon; Clarke, McLeod, Beaton, Philliben, Young, Gibson, McNeil, Torrance, Gray (Fryer), McCue.

**Berwick R (1) 3** *(Davidson 2, Lawson)*

**Clydebank (0) 1** *(Miller)*  685

*Berwick R:* Glynn; McCann, Black, McCulloch, Marshall, Muir, Davidson, McGlinchey (Romaines), Lawson, Tait, Armstrong.
*Clydebank:* Gallacher; Treanor, Given, McLaughlan, Fallon, McCabe, McGorm, Houston, Millar, Jones (Harkins), McBride.

**Queen's Park (0) 1** *(Nicholson)*

**Clyde (0) 0**  769

*Queen's Park:* Atkins; Wilson, Cook, Rennie, McGregor, McFarlane, McNiven, Crawley, Wood (Verrechia), Grant (Melrose), Nicholson.
*Clyde:* Young; Brogan, McQueen, McColl, Dempsey, Coutts, Doherty (Evans), Miller, Reilly, O'Neill, McCutcheon (Nevin).

**Hamilton A (0) 1** *(McDowall)*

**East Stirling (0) 0**  998

*Hamilton A:* Ferguson; Frew, Brown, Wright, McDougall, Marshall (Alexander), Howie, McDowall, Craig (Donnelly), Deeney, McAdams.
*East Stirling:* Kelly; Renwick, Blair, Watt, Rennie, Gourlay, McCulley, Lamont, Howitt, Robertson, McGall.

**Montrose (0) 0**

**Dunfermline Ath (1) 1** *(Hamill)*  450

*Montrose:* Charles; Forbes, Milne, Clark, Taylor, Johnston, McManus (Pirie), Turnbull, McDonald, Forrest (Young), Wright.
*Dunfermline Ath:* Whyte; Hutt, Brown, Robertson, Thomson, Hamill, McNaughton, Hegarty, Morrison, Donnelly (Dunlop), Forrest.

**East Fife (0) 1** *(Caithness pen)*

**Arbroath (0) 1** *(Robb)*  745

*East Fife:* Gorman; Hamilton, Millar, Tait (Muirhead), Halley, Beveridge, Neilson, O'Brien, Scott (Honeyman), Mutch, Caithness.
*Arbroath:* Lister; Forsyth, Burke, Casey, Docherty, Gavine, Harley (Lees), Durno, Robb, Kydd, Yule.

**Meadowbank T (0) 1** *(Sprott)*

**Stenhousemuir (0) 1** *(Meakin)*  349

*Meadowbank T:* McKell; Dunn, Henderson, Fraser, Godfrey, Leetion, McPhee, Boyd, Jobson, Conroy, Sprott.
*Stenhousemuir:* Howie; McCraw, Kirkland, Smith, Black, Mullen, Bremner, Meakin, Murray, Munn, Morrison (Rennie).

**Stranraer (1) 2** *(Neil 2)*

**Albion R (0) 0**  325

*Stranraer:* McFall; Hamilton, Devine, McDonald, Murdoch, Hyslop, Black, Harvey, Sweeney, Murphy, Neil.
*Albion R:* Balavage; Murray, Main, Craig, Burgess, Hamill, Gillespie, Hill, Houston, McDonagh, Campbell.

## SECTION 5

**22 AUG**

**St Johnstone (0) 1** *(MacDonald)*

**Hibernian (1) 2** *(Flavell, Rodier)*  3430

*St Johnstone:* Tulloch; Mackay, Kilgour (MacDonald), Weir, Rutherford, Caldwell, Brannigan (Docherty), McCoist, Morton, Fleming, Brogan.
*Hibernian:* Donaldson; Sneddon, Flavell, McLaren, Paterson, McNamara (Docherty), Callachan, Rae, Rodier, Murray, Duncan.

**St Mirren (1) 1** *(Stark pen)*

**Celtic (2) 5** *(MacLeod 2, McCluskey 3)*  18,065

*St Mirren:* Thomson; Young, Abercromby, Fitzpatrick, McCormack, Copland, McDougall (Logan), Stark, Bone, Richardson, Scanlon.
*Celtic:* Bonner; McGrain, Reid, Aitken, Moyes, MacLeod, Provan, Sullivan, McGarvey, Burns, McCluskey.

**Raith R (0) 1** *(Ballantyne)*

**Dundee (1) 1** *(Stephen)*  1800

*Raith R:* Walker; Houston, Candlish, Robinson, Forsyth (Irvine), Steel, Ballantyne, Urquhart, Russell, Berry, Mitchell (Miller).
*Dundee:* Blair; McGeachie, McLelland (Scrimgeour), Kidd, Glennie, MacDonald, Mackie, Stephen, Fleming, Bell, Murphy (Ferguson).

**Rangers (0) 1** *(Johnstone)*

**Morton (0) 0**  23,000

*Rangers:* Stewart; Jardine, Miller, Stevens, Forsyth, Redford, Cooper, Bett, McAdam, Johnstone, McLean (MacDonald).
*Morton:* Baines; Hayes, Holmes, Rooney, McLaughlin, Orr, McNeil, Busby, Thomson, Hutchison, Ritchie (Houston).

**Hearts (0) 2** *(McCoy, Liddell)*

**Airdrieonians (2) 3** *(Anderson, Clark, Kerr)*  4881

*Hearts:* Smith; Kidd, McNeil, Bowman, More, MacLaren, O'Brien, McCoy, Liddell G., Hamill, MacDonald A. (Robertson).
*Airdrieonians:* Martin; Erwin, Gordon, McCluskey, Richardson, Kerr, Thomson (Flood), Clark, Anderson, McGuire, McKeown (Cairney).


**Kilmarnock (0) 0**

**Aberdeen (2) 3** *(Strachan 2 [1 pen], McGhee)*  3100

*Kilmarnock:* McCulloch; McLean, Cockburn, Clark, Armstrong, McDicken, Gallagher, Mauchlen, Bourke, Cramond (McBride), McCready.
*Aberdeen:* Leighton; Kennedy, Rougvie (McMaster), Cooper, McLeish, Miller, Strachan, Bell (Watson), McGhee, Hewitt, Weir.


**Dundee U (0) 2** *(Holt, Fleeting og)*

**Ayr U (0) 1** *(Frye)*  5847

*Dundee U:* McAlpine; Holt, Kopel, Phillip, Stark, Narey, Bannon, Milne, Gough (Hegarty), Sturrock, Dodds.
*Ayr U:* Rennie; Nicol, Connor, Love, McAllister, Fleeting, Christie, McSherry (Larnach), Morris, Ahern (Cashmore), Frye.


**Motherwell (0) 0**

**Partick T (0) 1** *(O'Hara)*  2098

*Motherwell:* Sproat; MacLeod, Wark, McLelland, Carson (Irvine), McLaughlin, Clinging, McClair, Cleland, Conn, Gahagan.
*Partick T:* Rough; McKinnon, Whittaker, Campbell, Anderson, Watson, McDonald, Doyle, Johnstone (Lapsley), O'Hara, Clark.


**Brechin C (1) 1** *(Mackie)*

**Queen of the S (1) 2** *(Alexander 2)*  450

*Brechin C:* Neilson; Watt, Keating, Lesslie, Reid, Mackie, Campbell I., Elvin, Graham, Lorimer, Cormack.
*Queen of the S:* Ball; Dickson, Cloy, Robertson G., Clark, Boyd, McVitie, Gordon, Alexander, Coughlin, Robertson J.


**Dumbarton (2) 3** *(Blair pen, Mailer, Rankin)*

**Cowdenbeath (0) 0**  500

*Dumbarton:* Carson; Sinclair, MacLeod, Clougherty, Gallacher, Coyle T., Brown (Donnelly), Campbell (Rankin), Mailer, Coyle J., Blair.
*Cowdenbeath:* Allan; Rolland, Allison, Tierney, Russell, Hunter, Meikle, Park, Liddle, Mercer, Forrest.


**Alloa (0) 0**

**Forfar Ath (1) 2** *(Allan, Gallacher)*  525

*Alloa:* McGowan; Haggart (McNab), McKenzie, Purdie, Holt, Stewart, Grant, Oliver, Spence (Murray), Smith, Dunn.
*Forfar Ath:* Boardley; Bennett, Rankin, Brown, Allan, Leitch, Gallacher, Farningham, Hancock, Alexander (Clark), Morris.


**Stirling Albion (0) 0**

**Falkirk (0) 0**  1377

*Stirling Albion:* Gordon; Clarke, McLeod, Gray, Philliben, Young, Gibson, McCue (McNeil), Torrance, Beaton, Fryer.
*Falkirk:* Watson; Rose, Burrell, Brown, Mackin, Thompson, Perry, Herd, McIntosh (Oliver A.), Smith (Hoggan), Stevenson.


**Clyde (0) 2** *(McCutcheon, Doherty)*

**Berwick R (2) 2** *(Davidson, McGlynn)*  406

*Clyde:* Young; Brogan, McQueen, McColl, Dempsey, Miller, O'Neill, Reilly, Masterton, McCutcheon, Doherty.
*Berwick R:* McDermott; McCann, Black, McCulloch (Moyes), Dixon, Muir (Romaines), Davidson, McGlynn, Lawson, Tait, Armstrong.


**Clydebank (1) 4** *(Miller, McCabe, Ronald, Given)*

**Queen's Park (1) 1** *(McLaughlan og)*  450

*Clydebank:* Gallacher; Treanor, Fallon, McLaughlan, McGhie, Given, Ronald, Houston, Miller, Jones, McCabe.
*Queen's Park:* Atkins; Cook (McSkimming), Dickson, Rennie, McGregor, McFarlane, McNiven, Crawley, Melrose, Grant, Nicholson (Verrechia).


**Dunfermline Ath (2) 2** *(McNaughton, Morrison)*

**Hamilton A (0) 3** *(McDowall, Deeney, Donnelly)*  3000

*Dunfermline Ath:* Whyte; Hutt, Brown, Robertson, Thomson, Hamill, McNaughton, Hegarty, Morrison, Dunlop (Forrest), Jenkins.
*Hamilton A:* Ferguson; Frew, Brown, Wright, McDougall, Alexander, Howie, McDowall, Craig, Deeney, McAdams (Donnelly).


**East Stirling (0) 1** *(Hunter)*

**Montrose (0) 2** *(McManus, Milne)*  200

*East Stirling:* Kelly; Renwick, Blair, Lamont, Rennie, Gourlay, Hunter, Goodall, Howitt, Robertson, McCall.
*Montrose:* Charles; Forbes, Milne, Clark, Taylor, Johnston, McManus (Forrest), MacDonald, Turnbull, Young, Wright (Nicol).


**Arbroath (2) 4** *(Casey, Harley, Lees pen, Robb)*

**Albion R (0) 0**  531

*Arbroath:* Lister; Forsyth, Burke, Casey, Young, Gavine, Harley, Docherty, Robb, Shaw, Lees.
*Albion R:* Purdie; Murray, Lapsley, Main, Burgess, Craig, Hill, Gormley, Campbell, Ross, McDonagh.


**Stenhousemuir (0) 2** *(Meakin, Munn)*

**East Fife (3) 3** *(Neilson, O'Brien, Mutch)*  200

*Stenhousemuir:* McLaren; McCraw, Rennie, Smith, Black, Mullen, Bremner, Meakin, Murray, Munn, Kirkland.
*East Fife:* Gorman; Hamilton, Millar, Muirhead, Halley, Neilson, O'Brien, Tait, Scott, Mutch, Caithness.


**Stranraer (0) 1** *(Hamilton)*

**Meadowbank T (0) 2** *(Masterton, Leetion)*  500

*Stranraer:* McFall; Hamilton, Devine, McDonald, Murdoch, Hyslop, Black, Harvey (Armour), Sweeney, Murphy (Dolan), Neil.
*Meadowbank T:* McKell; Dunn, Henderson, Fraser, Godfrey, Conroy, McPhee, Boyd, Jobson, Masterton, Sprott.


## SECTION 6

### 26 AUG

**Hibernian (0) 1** *(Paterson)*

**Celtic (0) 4** *(McGarvey 2, Sullivan, MacLeod)*  13,685

*Hibernian:* Donaldson; Sneddon, Flavell, McLaren, Docherty, Paterson, McNamara, Callachan, Rae, Rodier, Duncan.
*Celtic:* Bonner; McGrain, Reid, Aitken, Moyes, MacLeod, Provan, Sullivan, McGarvey, Burns, McCluskey.

**St Mirren (0) 2** *(Scanlon 2 [1 pen])*

**St Johnstone (0) 0**    7080

*St Mirren:* Thomson; Beckett, Abercromby, Fitzpatrick, McCormack, Copland, McDougall, Stark, Bone (Logan), Richardson, Scanlon.
*St Johnstone:* Tulloch; Mackay, Kilgour, Weir, Rutherford, Caldwell, Pelosi, Brogan, Docherty (MacDonald), Morton, Fleming.

**Morton (2) 3** *(Thomson 2, Busby)*

**Dundee (0) 2** *(Fleming, Cameron)*    2500

*Morton:* Baines; Hayes, Holmes, Rooney, McLaughlin, Orr, McNeil, Thomson, Busby, Hutchison, Docherty.
*Dundee:* Blair; Cameron, Schaedler, Fraser, Glennie, MacDonald, Ferguson, Bell, Sinclair, Fleming, Kidd.

**Raith R (1) 1** *(Russell)*

**Rangers (0) 3** *(Redford, Johnstone, MacDonald)*    6000

*Raith R:* Walker; Houston, Candlish, Robinson, Forsyth, Steel, Ballantyne, Urquhart (Harris), Russell, Berry, Mitchell (Ford).
*Rangers:* McCloy; Jardine (Dawson), McLelland, Bett, Stevens, Redford, Cooper, Russell, Johnstone, MacDonald, Johnston (Miller).

**Airdrieonians (0) 0**

**Aberdeen (0) 0**    3000

*Airdrieonians:* Martin; Gordon, Rodger, McCluskey, Erwin, Kerr, Flood, Clark, Anderson, McGuire, McKeown.
*Aberdeen:* Leighton, Rougvie, Angus, Watson, McLeish, Miller, Harrow, Bell (Jarvie), McCall, McMaster, Weir.

**Kilmarnock (2) 2** *(Clark, McLean pen)*

**Hearts (0) 0**    1400

*Kilmarnock:* McCulloch; McLean, Robertson, Clark, Armstrong, McDicken (Wilson), Gallagher, Mauchlen, Bourke, Cockburn, McCready (McGivern).
*Hearts:* Smith; More, McNeill, Kidd, Liddell F., MacLaren, McCoy, Robertson, Liddell G., Mackay, Hamill.

**Partick T (1) 1** *(Higgins)*

**Ayr U (3) 5** *(Frye 4, Christie)*    1286

*Partick T:* Rough; McKinnon, Lapsley, Anderson, Campbell, Watson, Park, Doyle, Higgins, O'Hara, Clark.
*Ayr U:* Rennie; Larnach, Nicol, Love, McAllister, Fleeting, Frye, Morris, McInally, Ahern, Christie.

**Dundee U (0) 1** *(Pettigrew)*

**Motherwell (1) 1** *(Forbes)*    4484

*Dundee U:* McAlpine; Nicol (Kopel), Holt, Kirkwood, Hegarty, Narey, Bannon, Milne, Pettigrew, Sturrock, Payne (Taylor).
*Motherwell:* Sproat; MacLeod, Wark, McLelland, Carson, Forbes, McLaughlin (Clinging), McClair, Irvine, Soutar, Gahagan.

**Dumbarton (0) 1** *(Gallacher)*

**Brechin C (2) 3** *(Paterson 2, Campbell)*    400

*Dumbarton:* Carson; Sinclair, MacLeod, Campbell (Donnelly), Gallacher, Coyle T., Rankin, Brown, Mailer (Armstrong), Coyle J., Blair.
*Brechin C:* Neilson; Lorimer, Keating, Lesslie, Mackay, Reid, Campbell I., Elvin, Graham (Cormack), Mackie, Paterson.

**Queen of the S (1) 2** *(Alexander, Clark)*

**Cowdenbeath (0) 2** *(Forrest 2)*    1800

*Queen of the S:* Ball, Dickson, Cloy, Robertson G., Clark,

Boyd, McVitie, Gordon, Alexander, Coughlin, Robertson J.
*Cowdenbeath:* Allan; Ferguson, Allison, Tierney, Russell, Hunter, Meikle, Park, Liddle, Mercer, Forrest.

**Forfar Ath (2) 3** *(Clark, Morris, Hancock)*

**Falkirk (1) 2** *(Hoggan pen, Smith)*    1561

*Forfar Ath:* Boardley; Bennett, Rankin, Brown, Allan, McPhee (Leitch), Gallacher, Farningham, Hancock, Clark, Morris.
*Falkirk:* Watson, Rose, Burrell, Brown, Mackin, Hay (McRoberts), Hoggan, Herd, McIntosh (Oliver A.), Smith, Thompson.

**Stirling Albion (1) 2** *(Torrance, Philliben)*

**Alloa (1) 2** *(Grant 2 [1 pen])*    700

*Stirling Albion:* Gordon; Clarke, McLeod, Gray (Perrie), Philliben, Young, Gibson (McCue), McNeil, Torrance, Beaton, Fryer.
*Alloa:* McGowan; Wilde, McKenzie, Purdie, Holt, Stewart (McNab), Grant, Haggart, Mitchell, Murray (Spence), Smith.

**Berwick R (1) 3** *(Lawson 2, Tait)*

**Queen's Park (0) 0**    1194

*Berwick R:* McDermott, McCann, Black (McGlynn), McCulloch, Dixon, Muir, Davidson, Moyes, Lawson, Tait, Armstrong.
*Queen's Park:* Atkins; Wilson, Dickson, Cook, McGregor, McFarlane, McNiven (Melrose), Crawley, Wood, Verrechia (Rennie), Nicholson.

**Clydebank (0) 1** *(Ronald)*

**Clyde (0) 0**    320

*Clydebank:* Gallacher; Treanor, Fallon, McLaughlan, McGhie, Given, Ronald, Houston, Millar, Jones (Harkins), McCabe.
*Clyde:* Young; Brogan, McQueen, McColl, Dempsey, Sinclair (Miller), Doherty, Reilly, Masterton (Evans), O'Neill, McCutcheon.

**East Stirling (0) 0**

**Dunfermline Ath (0) 1** *(Morrison)*    450

*East Stirling:* Pearce; Renwick, Blair, Lamont, Rennie, Gourlay, Robertson, Goodall, Kelly, Howitt, McGall.
*Dunfermline Ath:* Whyte; Hutt, Brown, Robertson, Thomson, Hamill, McNaughton, Hegarty, Morrison, Dunlop, Jenkins.

**Hamilton A (2) 4** *(Paton 2, Callan, Howie)*

**Montrose (1) 2** *(Johnston, Taylor)*    1250

*Hamilton A:* Moffat; Alexander (Howie), Brown, Dailly, McDougall, Marshall, Donnelly (Deeney), Callan, Paton, McAdams, Mitchell.
*Montrose:* Charles; Forbes, Milne, Clark, Taylor, Johnston, Wright (Forrest), Young, MacDonald, Turnbull (Pirie), McManus.

## SECTIONAL PLAY-OFF, FIRST LEG

### 31 AUG

**Arbroath (0) 1** *(Docherty)*

**Forfar Ath (0) 2** *(Clark, Rankin)*    680

*Arbroath:* Lister; Forsyth, Burke, Casey, Young, Gavine, Harley, Docherty, Robb, Kydd (Durno), Yule (Lees).
*Forfar Ath:* Boardley; Bennett, Rankin, Brown, Allan, McPhee, Gallacher, Farningham, Hancock, Clark (Watt), Morris.

## SECTIONAL PLAY-OFF, SECOND LEG

**2 SEPT**

**Forfar Ath (1) 2** *aet (Docherty og, Rankin)*
**Arbroath (0) 2** *(Gavine, Harley)*     1922

*Forfar Ath:* Boardley; Bennett, Rankin, Brown, Allan, McPhee, Gallacher, Farningham, Alexander (Brash), Clark (Watt), Morris.
*Arbroath:* Lister; Forsyth, Burke, McKenzie (Harley) (Kydd), Young, Gavine, Hyslop, Docherty, Robb, Durno, Lees.

## QUARTER-FINALS, FIRST LEG

**2 SEPT**

**Aberdeen (4) 5** *(Cooper, Strachan 2 [1 pen], Bell, McCall)*
**Berwick R (0) 0**     5000

*Aberdeen:* Leighton; Kennedy, McMaster, Cooper (Jarvie), McLeish, Miller, Strachan, Bell, McGhee, Hewitt, Weir (McCall).
*Berwick R:* McDermott; McCann, Black (McGlinchey), McCulloch, Dixon, Muir, Davidson, Moyes, Lawson, Tait (Romaines), Armstrong.

**Brechin C (0) 0**
**Rangers (2) 4** *(Russell, Jackson, McLean* pen, *Redford)*     7000

*Brechin C:* Neilson; Reid, Keating, Lesslie, Mackay (Cormack), Campbell R., Campbell I., Mackie, Graham, Lorimer, Paterson.
*Rangers:* McCloy; McLelland, Dawson, Forsyth, Jackson, Bett, Cooper, Russell, Redford, MacDonald, McLean (Johnston).

**Hamilton A (0) 0**
**Dundee U (2) 4** *(Holt, Bannon* pen, *Dodds 2)*     4600

*Hamilton A:* Ferguson; Frew, Brown, Wright, McDougall, Marshall (Mitchell), Howie, McDowall, Craig, Deeney, McAdams.
*Dundee U:* McAlpine; Stark, Phillip, Holt, Hegarty, Narey, Bannon, Kirkwood, Pettigrew, Sturrock, Dodds.

**16 SEPT**

**Forfar Ath (0) 1** *(Morris)*
**St Mirren (0) 1** *(McAvennie)*     3200

*Forfar Ath:* Boardley; Bennett, Rankin, Brown, Brash, Allan (Leitch), Farningham, Morris, Hancock, Gallacher, McPhee.
*St Mirren:* Thomson; Beckett, Abercromby, Fitzpatrick, McCormack, Copland, McDougall (Somner), Stark, Bone, McAvennie, Scanlon.

## QUARTER-FINALS, SECOND LEG

**23 SEPT**

**Berwick R (0) 0**
**Aberdeen (2) 3** *(McMaster, McGhee, Harrow)*     2000

*Berwick R:* Glynn; Moyes, McCann, Marshall, Dixon, Muir, Romaines, Lawson (Krawiec), Armstrong, Tait, Black.
*Aberdeen:* Leighton; Kennedy, Rougvie, Watson, McLeish, Miller, Simpson, McCall, McGhee (Harrow), McMaster (Jarvie), Weir.

**Dundee U (2) 5** *(Payne, Reilly, Sturrock, Dodds, Kirkwood)*
**Hamilton A (0) 0**     4200

*Dundee U:* Graham; Holt, Phillip (Kirkwood), Gough, Hegarty, Narey, Bannon, Payne, Reilly, Sturrock (Milne), Dodds.
*Hamilton A:* Moffat; Frew, Brown, Wright, McDougall, Mitchell, Fairlie, McDowall, Deeney, Craig, McAdams (Howie).

**Rangers (0) 1** *(MacDonald)*
**Brechin C (0) 0**     2000

*Rangers:* Stewart; McLelland, Dawson, Forsyth, McPherson, Redford, Cooper, Russell (Davies), Dalziel, MacDonald, McLean (Mackay).
*Brechin C:* Neilson; Watt, Keating, Lesslie, Stewart, Reid, Henderson, Mackie (Campbell I.), Paterson (Lorimer), Elvin, Cormack.

**St Mirren (2) 6** *(McDougall 2, Logan 2, Somner, Stark)*
**Forfar Ath (0) 0**     3101

*St Mirren:* Thomson; Beckett, Abercromby, Fitzpatrick, McCormack, Copland, McDougall, Stark, Somner, McAvennie, Scanlon (Logan).
*Forfar Ath:* Boardley; Bennett, Rankin (Watt), Brown, Allan, Clark (Leitch), Farningham, Morris, Hancock, Gallacher, McPhee.

## SEMI-FINALS, FIRST LEG

**7 OCT**

**Dundee U (0) 0**
**Aberdeen (1) 1** *(Weir)*     13,824

*Dundee U:* McAlpine; Stark (Gough), Kopel, Phillip, Hegarty, Narey, Bannon, Milne, Kirkwood, Sturrock, Dodds.
*Aberdeen:* Leighton; Kennedy, Rougvie, Watson, Cooper, Miller, Strachan, Simpson (McMaster), McGhee, Hewitt, Weir.

**St Mirren (0) 2** *(McAvennie, Scanlon)*
**Rangers (1) 2** *(McAdam, MacDonald)*     14,058

*St Mirren:* Thomson; Beckett, Fulton, Copland, McCormack, Abercromby, McDougall (Bone), Stark, Somner, McAvennie, Scanlon.
*Rangers:* Stewart; Jardine, Dawson, Stevens, Forsyth, Bett, Cooper, Russell, McAdam, MacDonald, Johnston.

## SEMI-FINALS, SECOND LEG

**28 OCT**

**Aberdeen (0) 0**
**Dundee U (2) 3** *(Milne, Sturrock 2)*     20,137

*Aberdeen:* Leighton; Kennedy, Rougvie, Watson, Cooper, Miller, Strachan, Simpson, McGhee, Hewitt, Weir (McCall).
*Dundee U:* McAlpine; Holt, Murray, Phillip, Hegarty, Narey, Bannon, Milne, Kirkwood, Sturrock, Dodds.

**Rangers (0) 2** *(Bett* pen, *MacDonald)*
**St Mirren (1) 1** *(Scanlon* pen*)*     17,000

*Rangers:* Stewart; Jardine, Dawson (Johnstone), Forsyth, Jackson, Bett, Cooper, Russell, McAdam, MacDonald, Johnston.
*St Mirren:* Thomson; Young, Fulton, McCormack, Copland, Abercromby, Richardson (Logan), Stark, Bone, McAvennie, Scanlon.

## FINAL (at Hampden Park)

**28 NOV**

**Dundee U (0) 1** *(Milne)*
**Rangers (0) 2** *(Cooper, Redford)*     53,777

*Dundee U:* McAlpine; Holt, Stark, Narey, Hegarty, Phillip, Bannon, Milne, Kirkwood, Sturrock, Dodds.
*Rangers:* Stewart; Jardine, Miller, Stevens, Jackson, Bett, Cooper, Johnstone, Russell, MacDonald, Dalziel (Redford).

# SCOTTISH CUP 1981−82

## FIRST ROUND

### 12 DEC

**Arbroath (0) 0**

**Meadowbank T (0) 2** *(Jobson 2)*     592

*Arbroath:* Robertson; Forsyth, Glover, Docherty, Young, Gavine, Hyslop, Hill (Harley), Robb, Burke (Lees), Yule.
*Meadowbank T:* McKell; Skilling, Boyd, Fraser, Godfrey, Hendrie, McPhee (Henderson), Georgeson, Jobson, Masterton, Sprott.

### 23 DEC

**Stranraer (0) 1** *(Harvey)*

**East Fife (0) 1** *(Burt)*     600

*Stranraer:* McFall; Armour, McDonald, Hay, Murdoch, Gibb, Neil, Quinn, Murphy, Harvey, Sweeney.
*East Fife:* Gorman; Hamilton, Millar, McLaren, Halley, Neilson, O'Brien, Muirhead, Burt, Cairns R., Caithness.

### 30 DEC

**Fraserburgh (0) 1** *(Gibson)*

**Clachnacuddin (0) 1** *(Shearer)*     950

*Fraserburgh:* Clark; Scott, Sim, Mackenzie, Slavin, Crawford, Adams, Oxley, Gibson, Grant, Beagrie (Shand).
*Clachnacuddin:* Arris; Flannigan, Dennison, Dingwall, Shearer, Cowie, Watt, Davidson, Kenny, Masson, Stevenson.

### 20 JAN

**Stirling Albion (0) 1** *(Torrance)*

**Clyde (1) 2** *(Sinclair, Hood)*     700

*Stirling Albion:* Arthur; Philliben, Young, Denny, Kennedy J., Moffat, Leetion, Gray, Torrance, Kennedy A., Colquhoun.
*Clyde:* Young; Brogan, McQueen, McColl, Dempsey, McCutcheon, Nevin, Sinclair, Masterton, Doherty (Hood), O'Neill.

### 21 JAN

**Civil Service Strollers (2) 3** *(Clapperton 2, Spence 1)*

**Cowdenbeath (1) 3** *(Liddle 2, Forrest)*     260

*Civil Service Strollers:* Gordon; Darling, Davidson, Cruickshanks, Crookston, Wight, Rogers, Callaghan, Ashton, Boyle, Clapperton (Spence).
*Cowdenbeath:* Doyle; Ferguson, Hunter, Rolland, Russell, Tierney, Steele, Park, Liddle, Marshall, Forrest.

**Stenhousemuir (1) 2** *(Meakin, Murray)*

**Berwick R (1) 5** *(Lawson, Muir, McGlynn, McCann, Davidson)*     375

*Stenhousemuir:* Howie; Rennie, Kirkland, Bremner, Evans, Mullen, Munn, Jack, Murray, Meakin, Jenkins.
*Berwick R:* McDermott; McCann, McGlynn, Jefferies, Marshall, Muir, Davidson, Moyes, McCulloch, Tait, Lawson.

## FIRST ROUND REPLAYS

### 4 JAN

**East Fife (4) 4** *(Neilson, Caithness 2, O'Brien)*

**Stranraer (0) 1** *(Harvey)*     661

*East Fife:* Gorman; Hamilton, Millar, Burt (Tait), Halley, McLaren, O'Brien, Muirhead, Scott, Neilson (Cairns), Caithness.
*Stranraer:* McFall; Armour, McDonald, Hay, Murdoch, Black, Neil, Quinn, Murphy, Harvey, Gibb.

### 25 JAN

**Clachnacuddin (0) 3** *aet (Cowie 2, Davidson)*

**Fraserburgh (0) 2** *(Robertson, Oxley)*     200

*Clachnacuddin:* Mackay; Flannigan, Dennison, Dingwall, Shearer, Cowie, Watt, Davidson, Kenny, Masson, Stevenson.
*Fraserburgh:* Clark; Shand, Sim, Scott, Slavin, Gibson, Mackenzie, Adams, Oxley, Robertson, Grant.

**Cowdenbeath (3) 6** *(Forrest 3 [1 pen], Park, Steele, Marshall)*

**Civil Service Strollers (0) 1** *(Ashton)*     210

*Cowdenbeath:* Allan; Ferguson, Hunter, Rolland, Russell, Tierney, Steele, Park, Liddle, Marshall, Forrest.
*Civil Service Strollers:* Gordon; Darling, Davidson, McLelland, Wight, Boyle, Clapperton, Rogers, Ashton, Cruickshanks, Callaghan.

## SECOND ROUND

### 18 JAN

**East Fife (1) 2** *(Caithness, Neilson)*

**Forfar Ath (1) 3** *(Mitchell, Clark, Brash)*     760

*East Fife:* Gorman; Hamilton, Millar, Burt, Halley, McLaren, O'Brien, Muirhead, Scott, Caithness, Neilson.
*Forfar Ath:* Kennedy; Bennett, McPhee, Morris, Brash, Allan, Craig, Farningham, Clark, Leitch, Mitchell.

### 20 JAN

**Montrose (0) 0**

**Elgin City (0) 0**     450

*Montrose:* Kelly; Forbes, Milne, Young, Neil, Forrest (Wright), McManus, McDonald, Oliver, Turnbull, Fletcher (Taylor).
*Elgin City:* Morrison; Brown, Buchan, McAndrew, McHardy, Armstrong, Kellas, Massin, Blacklaw, Cumming (Mackay), Drews.

### 23 JAN

**Alloa (0) 4** *(Inglis og, Paterson, Holt, Grant)*

**Hawick Royal Albert (1) 1** *(McConnell)*     900

*Alloa:* Hunter; Ballantyne, Mackenzie, Purdie, Stewart, Holt, Paterson (Murray), Oliver, McComb, McNab (Wilson), Grant.
*Hawick Royal Albert:* Nichol; McLean (Oliver), Robertson, Rutherford, Colville, Tait K., Welsh, Tait M. (Laughran), Brown, McConnell, Inglis.

**Clyde (0) 0**

**Berwick R (0) 0**     358

*Clyde:* Young; Brogan, McQueen, McColl, Dempsey, McCutcheon, Nevin, Sinclair, Masterton, Doherty, O'Neill.

*Berwick R:* McDermott; McCann, McGlynn, Jefferies, Marshall, Muir, Davidson, Moyes, McCulloch, Tait, Lawson.

### Coldstream (0) 0

**Meadowbank T (1) 2** *(Boyd, Jobson* pen)  400

*Coldstream:* Kelly; Oliver, Roughead, Anderson, Waddell, Renton A., Brydon, Stewart, Haigh, Chisolm, Hutchison.
*Meadowbank T:* McKell; Dunn, Henderson, Godfrey (Sprott), Brown, Fraser, Hendrie, Georgeson (McPhee), Jobson, Boyd, Conroy.

### 24 JAN

**Inverness Caledonian (1) 1** *(Urquhart)*

**Brechin C (1) 3** *(Campbell 2, Lesslie)*  2000

*Inverness Caledonian:* McDonald; Davidson, Mann, Lisle, Summers, Corbett, Baxter, McIntosh, Urquhart, McIntosh, Robertson.
*Brechin C:* Neilson; Watt, Lorimer, Lesslie, Reid, Mackie, Campbell I., Henderson, Paterson, Stewart, Cormack.

### 30 JAN

**Albion R (1) 2** *(Houston, Dennison og)*

**Clachnacuddin (0) 1** *(Kenny)*  1400

*Albion R:* Purdie; Allan, Lapsley, Hamill, Burgess, Collins, Gibson, Houston, Hannigan, Evans, Gillespie.
*Clachnacuddin:* Mackay; Flanagan, Dennison, Dingwall, Shearer, Cowie, Stevenson, Davidson, Kenny, Masson, Watt.

### Cowdenbeath (0) 1 *(Liddle)*

**Gala Fairydean (0) 1** *(Frizzell)*  397

*Cowdenbeath:* Allan; Ferguson, Hunter, Rolland, Russell, Tierney, Steele, Park, Liddle, Marshall, Forrest.
*Gala Fairydean:* McNulty; Mann, Nicol, Frizzell, Stewart, McLaren, Notman, Dick, Lothian, Mather, Thompson.

### SECOND ROUND REPLAYS

### 25 JAN

### Elgin City (0) 0

**Montrose (0) 0**  300

*Elgin City:* Morrison; Brown, Buchan, McAndrew, McHardy, Armstrong, Kellas, Masson, Blacklaw, Mackay, Drews.
*Montrose:* Kelly; Taylor, Forbes, Young, Neill, Johnston, Wright, Campbell, Allan, Turnbull, McManus (McDonald).

### 26 JAN

**Berwick R (0) 1** *(McGlynn)*

**Clyde (2) 3** *(Marshall og, Nevin, Reilly)*  984

*Berwick R:* McDermott; McCann, Black, Jefferies, Marshall, Muir, Davidson, Moyes, McCulloch, McGlynn, Lawson.
*Clyde:* Young; Brogan, McQueen, McColl, Dempsey, McCutcheon, Nevin, Sinclair, Reilly, Doherty, O'Neill.

### 3 FEB

**Gala Fairydean (2) 3** *(Russell og, Notman, Lothian)*

**Cowdenbeath (1) 2** *(Forrest* pen, *McFarlane)*  1320

*Gala Fairydean:* McNulty; Mann, Nicol, Frizzell, Stewart, McLaren, Notman, Dick, Lothian, Mather, Thompson.
*Cowdenbeath:* Allan; Ferguson, Hunter, Rolland, Russell, Tierney, Steele, Park (McFarlane), Liddle, Marshall, Forrest.

### SECOND ROUND SECOND REPLAY

### 1 FEB

**Montrose (1) 2** *aet (Johnston, Campbell)*

**Elgin City (0) 1** *(McHardy)*  1252

(At Kynoch Park, Keith)
*Montrose:* Kelly; Taylor, Forbes, Young, Neill, Johnston, McManus, Campbell, Allan, Turnbull, Wright (McDonald).
*Elgin City:* Morrison; Brown, Buchan, McAndrew, McHardy, Drews, Kellas, Masson, Blacklaw, Mackay, Armstrong (Bruce).

### THIRD ROUND

### 23 JAN

**Airdrieonians (1) 1** *(McCluskey)*

**Queen's Park (1) 2** *(McNiven 2)*  2150

*Airdrieonians:* Martin; Erwin, Kerr, Walker T., March, McCluskey, McGuire (Steele), Clark, Anderson, Gordon, McDonagh.
*Queen's Park:* Atkins; Wilson, Dickson, Rennie, McGregor, McFarlane, Cook, McNiven, Nicholson (Gilmour), Grant, Verrechia.

### Celtic (3) 4 *(McGarvey, McGrain, McCluskey* pen, *Halpin)*

**Queen of the S (0) 0**  11,281

*Celtic:* Bonner; McGrain, Reid, Aitken, McAdam, MacLeod, Halpin, McStay, McGarvey, Burns, McCluskey.
*Queen of the S:* Ball; Dickson, Cloy, Clark, Boyd, Robertson G., Robertson J., Miller, Phillips, Alexander, McCann.

### Clydebank (0) 2 *(Given* pen, *Millar)*

**Dunfermline Ath (0) 1** *(McNaughton)*  911

*Clydebank:* Gallacher; Treanor (McLaughlan), Gervaise, Fallon, McGhie, Given, Ronald (Houston), McKeown, Millar, Coyne, McCube.
*Dunfermline Ath:* Young; Tait, Thomson, Nicol, Robertson, Considine, McNaughton, Hamill, Hegarty, Donnelly, Jenkins.

### Dundee (0) 1 *(Stephen)*

**Raith R (0) 0**  5474

*Dundee:* Blair; Scrimgeour (Kidd), McLelland, Fraser, Glennie, McGeachie, Ferguson, Bell (Stephen), Sinclair, Mackie, Cameron.
*Raith R:* Donaldson; Robertson, McDonough, Ford (Mitchell), Steel, Houston, Russell (Ballantyne), Urquhart, Gibson, Carroll, Robinson.

**Hamilton A (0) 0**

**Forfar Ath (0) 0** 898

*Hamilton A:* Ferguson; Frew, Brown, Alexander, McDougall, Blackley, Donnelly (Mitchell) (Wright), Fairlie, Craig, McDowall, Wilson.
*Forfar Ath:* Kennedy; Bennett, McPhee, Morris, Brash, Allan, Gallacher, Farningham, Clark, Leitch, Mitchell.

**Hibernian (0) 2** *(Rodier, Duncan)*

**Falkirk (0) 0** 5082

*Hibernian:* McArthur; Sneddon, Schaedler (McNamara), Brazil, Paterson, Duncan, Callachan, Jamieson (Murray), MacLeod, Rodier, Flavell.
*Falkirk:* Watson; Hoggan, Fowler, Brown, Mackin, Thomson, Perry, Herd, McIntosh, Oliver M., Stevenson (Burrell).

**Motherwell (0) 0**

**Aberdeen (1) 1** *(Hewitt)* 12,679

*Motherwell:* Sproat; McLeod (Coyne), Wark, McLelland, Carson, Forbes, McLaughlin, Rafferty (Cleland), Irvine, O'Hara, Gahagan.
*Aberdeen:* Leighton; Kennedy, Rougvie, Cooper, McLeish, Miller, Strachan (McMaster), Bell, McGhee (Black), Hewitt, Weir.

**St Mirren (0) 2** *(Bone, Abercromby)*

**Morton (1) 1** *(Houston)* 6984

*St Mirren:* Thomson; McCormack, Bennett, Fitzpatrick, Fulton, Copland, McAvennie, Stark (Bone), McDougall, Abercromby, Scanlon.
*Morton:* Baines; Hayes, Holmes, Rooney, McLaughlin, Hutchison, Houston, Docherty, Busby, Slaven (McNeil), Ritchie (Cochrane).

**24 JAN**

**Partick T (1) 1** *(Johnston)*

**Dumbarton (2) 2** *(Coyle J., Donnelly)* 2908

*Partick T:* Rough; McKinnon, Whittaker, Anderson, Dunlop, Watson, Park, Jardine, Johnston, Doyle, Clark (Sweeney).
*Dumbarton:* Carson; Sinclair, McGowan M., McGowan P., Gallacher, Coyle T., Blair, Clougherty, Dunlop, Donnelly, Coyle J.

**27 JAN**

**East Stirling (1) 1** *(Howitt)*

**Hearts (3) 4** *(MacDonald, Robertson, Marinello, Byrne)* 3000

*East Stirling:* Pearce; Blair, Watt, Renwick, Rennie, Gourlay, Lamont, McGall, Edgar, Howitt, Sharp.
*Hearts:* Smith; Kidd, Shields, Byrne, MacDonald R., MacLaren, Bowman, Pettigrew, Robertson, Addison, Marinello.

**30 JAN**

**Alloa (1) 2** *(Paterson, Holt)*

**Ayr U (0) 1** *(Connor)* 1136

*Alloa:* Hunter; Ballantyne, MacKenzie, Purdie, Stewart, Holt, Paterson, Smith, McComb, Oliver, Grant.
*Ayr U:* Rennie; Shanks, Ahern, Hume, McAllister, Fleeting, Frye, Kean, Morris, Connor, Christie.

**Brechin C (1) 2** *(Cormack, Holt og)*

**Dundee U (1) 4** *(Sturrock 2, Dodds, Kirkwood)* 4348

*Brechin C:* Neilson; Watt, Lorimer, Lesslie, Reid, Mackie, Campbell I. (Graham), Henderson (Campbell R.), Paterson, Stewart, Cormack.
*Dundee U:* McAlpine; Malpas, Murray (Holt), Stark, Hegarty, Narey, Bannon, Milne, Kirkwood, Sturrock, Dodds.

**Clyde (0) 2** *(O'Neill pen, Doherty)*

**Meadowbank T (0) 2** *(Boyd, Godfrey)* 610

*Clyde:* Young; Brogan, McQueen, McColl, Dempsey, McCutcheon, Nevin, Sinclair, Reilly, Doherty, O'Neill.
*Meadowbank T:* McKell; Dunn, Conroy, Godfrey, Brown, Fraser, McPhee, Georgeson, Hendrie, Boyd, Sprott.

**6 FEB**

**Gala Fairydean (1) 1** *(Dick)*

**St Johnstone (1) 2** *(Beedie, Morton pen)* 1500

*Gala Fairydean:* McNulty; Mann, Nicol, Frizzell, Stewart, McLaren, Notman, Dick, Lothian, Mather, Thompson.
*St Johnstone:* Tulloch; Kilgour, McNeil, McVicar (O'Brien), Rutherford, Barron, Beedie, Brogan, Fleming, Morton, Brannigan.

**Kilmarnock (0) 1** *(Bourke)*

**Montrose (0) 0** 1441

*Kilmarnock:* McCulloch; Robertson, Cockburn, McLean, Armstrong, McDicken, Gallagher, MacLeod (Bryce), Bourke, Mauchlen (Bryson), McGivern.
*Montrose:* Kelly; Forbes, Milne (Fletcher), Young, Neill (Forrest), Johnston, Campbell, Taylor, Allan, Turnbull, McManus.

**Rangers (3) 6** *(Johnstone, Russell, MacDonald, McAdam, McPherson pen, Redford)*

**Albion R (0) 2** *(Houston 2)* 10,000

*Rangers:* Stewart; Jardine (Miller), Dawson, McPherson, Jackson (Dalziel), McAdam, Cooper, Russell, Johnstone, Redford, MacDonald.
*Albion R:* Purdie; Allan, Lapsley, Hamill, Burgess, Collins, Gibson (Craig), Houston, Hannigan, Evans, Gillespie (Ross).

**THIRD ROUND REPLAYS**

**27 JAN**

**Forfar Ath (2) 3** *(Clark, Brash, Gallacher)*

**Hamilton A (1) 2** *(Fairlie, Howie)* 970

*Forfar Ath:* Kennedy; Bennett, McPhee, Morris, Brash, Allan, Gallacher, Farningham, Clark, Leitch, Mitchell (Hancock).
*Hamilton A:* Ferguson; Frew, Brown, Alexander (Howie), McDougall, Blackley, Wright, Fairlie, Craig (Donnelly), McDowall, Wilson.

**3 FEB**

**Meadowbank T (0) 4** *(Boyd, Hendrie, Georgeson 2)*

**Clyde (0) 2** *(Nevin, Doherty)* 700

*Meadowbank T:* McKell; Dunn, Conroy, Godfrey, Brown, Fraser, McPhee, Georgeson, Hendrie, Boyd, Sprott.
*Clyde:* Young; Brogan, McQueen, McColl, Dempsey, McCutcheon, Nevin, Sinclair, Reilly, Doherty, O'Neill.

## FOURTH ROUND

**13 FEB**

**Aberdeen (1) 1** *(Hewitt)*

**Celtic (0) 0** 24,000

*Aberdeen:* Leighton; Kennedy, Rougvie, McMaster, McLeish, Miller, Strachan, Simpson (Bell), McGhee, Hewitt, Weir.
*Celtic:* Bonner; McGrain, Reid, Aitken, McAdam, MacLeod, Sullivan (Halpin), McStay, McGarvey, Burns, McCluskey.

**Clydebank (0) 0**

**St Mirren (2) 2** *(Scanlon, McAvennie)* 5088

*Clydebank:* Gallacher; Treanor, Gervaise, Fallon, McGhie, Given, Ronald, McKeown (Houston), Millar, Coyne, McCabe.
*St Mirren:* Thomson; Walker, McCormack, Fitzpatrick, Fulton, Copland, Richardson, Stark, Bone (Logan), McAvennie, Scanlon.

**Dundee U (1) 1** *(Holt)*

**Hibernian (0) 1** *(Rae)* 10,735

*Dundee U:* McAlpine; Malpas, Holt, Gough, Hegarty, Narey, Bannon, Milne (Payne), Kirkwood, Sturrock, Dodds.
*Hibernian:* McArthur; Sneddon, Flavell, McNamara, Paterson, Brazil, Callachan, Murray (Rodier), Duncan, Rae, MacLeod.

**Hearts (0) 0**

**Forfar Ath (0) 1** *(Hancock)* 5671

*Hearts:* Smith; Kidd, Shields, Byrne, MacDonald, MacLaren, Bowman (Robertson), Pettigrew, McCoy, Addison, Marinello (Mackay).
*Forfar Ath:* Kennedy; Bennett, McPhee, Morris, Brash, Allan, Brown, Farningham, Hancock, Leitch, Clark.

**Kilmarnock (1) 3** *(McGivern, Bourke 2)*

**St Johnstone (0) 1** *(Brogan)* 2693

*Kilmarnock:* McCulloch; Robertson, Cockburn, Clark J., Armstrong, Clarke P., Gallagher (McGivern), McLeod, Bourke, Mauchlen, Bryson.
*St Johnstone:* Tulloch; Kilgour, McNeil, Weir, Rutherford, Barron (O'Brien), Beedie, Brogan, Fleming, Morton, Brannigan (Docherty).

**Queen's Park (1) 2** *(McNiven, Verrechia)*

**Alloa (0) 0** 1753

*Queen's Park:* Atkins; Wilson, Dickson, Cairns, McGregor, McFarlane, McNiven, Crawley, Wood, Grant (Gilmour), Verrechia.
*Alloa:* Hunter; Haggart, MacKenzie, Purdie, Stewart, McComb, Paterson, Oliver, Murray (Holt), Smith, Grant.

**Rangers (0) 4** *(Jardine 2, McAdam, Johnstone)*

**Dumbarton (0) 0** 12,000

*Rangers:* Stewart; Jardine, Dawson (Miller), McAdam, Jackson, Bett, Cooper, Russell, Johnstone, Redford, MacDonald (Dalziel).
*Dumbarton:* Carson; Sinclair, Campbell, Clougherty (Montgomerie), Gallacher, Coyle T., Coyle J., McRoberts (Rankin), Dunlop, Donnelly, Blair.

**14 FEB**

**Dundee (1) 3** *(Ferguson, Smith, Mackie)*

**Meadowbank T (0) 0** 4453

*Dundee:* Geddes; McKimmie, McLelland, Kidd, Smith, Glennie, Ferguson, McGeachie, Fleming, Cameron, Murphy.
*Meadowbank T:* McKell; Dunn, Conroy, Godfrey, Brown, Fraser, McPhee, Georgeson (Thomson), Hendrie, Boyd, Sprott.

## FOURTH ROUND REPLAY

**17 FEB**

**Hibernian (0) 1** *aet (Paterson)*

**Dundee U (0) 1** *(Kirkwood)* 11,039

*Hibernian:* McArthur; Sneddon, Flavell, McNamara, Paterson, Brazil, Callachan (Schaedler), Jamieson (Rodier), Duncan, Rae, MacLeod.
*Dundee U:* McAlpine; Malpas (Stark), Holt, Gough, Hegarty, Narey, Bannon, Milne, Kirkwood, Sturrock, Dodds.

## FOURTH ROUND SECOND REPLAY

**22 FEB**

**Hibernian (0) 0**

**Dundee U (0) 3** *(Holt, Dodds, Bannon pen)* 13,759

(At Easter Road)
*Hibernian:* McArthur; Sneddon, Flavell, McNamara, Paterson, Brazil, Callachan, Rae, Duncan, Murray, MacLeod (Schaedler).
*Dundee U:* McAlpine; Holt, Stark, Gough, Hegarty, Narey, Bannon, Milne, Kirkwood, Sturrock, Dodds.

## QUARTER-FINALS

**6 MAR**

**Aberdeen (2) 4** *(McGhee, Simpson, Strachan 2 [2 pens])*

**Kilmarnock (2) 2** *(McGivern, Gallagher)* 9000

*Aberdeen:* Leighton; Kennedy, Hamilton, McMaster, McLeish, Miller, Strachan, Cooper, McGhee, Simpson, Hewitt.
*Kilmarnock:* McCulloch; McLean, Robertson, Clark J., Armstrong, Clarke P., Gallagher, McLeod, Bourke, Mauchlen, McGivern.

**Queen's Park (0) 1** *(McFarlane)*

**Forfar Ath (0) 2** *(Hancock, Leitch)* 2643

*Queen's Park:* Atkins; Wilson, Dickson, Cook, Cairns, McFarlane, McNiven, Crawley, Grant (Gilmour), Wood, Nicholson (Verrechia).
*Forfar Ath:* Kennedy; Bennett, McPhee, Brash, Brown, Farningham, Allan (Morris), Leitch, Gallacher, Clark, Porter (Hancock).

**Rangers (0) 2** *(Johnstone, McAdam)*

**Dundee (0) 0** 16,500

*Rangers:* Stewart; Jardine, Dawson, McAdam, Jackson, Bett, Russell, Miller (Redford), Johnstone, MacDonald, Cooper (Mackay).
*Dundee:* Geddes; McKimmie, McLelland, Glennie, Smith, Kidd (Cameron), Fraser, McGeachie, Ferguson, Fleming (Stephen), Mackie.

**St Mirren (0) 1** *(Fitzpatrick)*

**Dundee U (0) 0**             9425

*St Mirren:* Thomson; McCormack, Beckett, Fulton, Copland, Fitzpatrick, Stark, McAvennie (Richardson), Bone, McDougall, Scanlon.
*Dundee U:* McAlpine; Stark, Gough (Phillip), Holt, Hegarty, Narey, Malpas, Bannon, Kirkwood, Sturrock, Dodds.

## SEMI-FINALS
## 3 APRIL

**Aberdeen (0) 1** *(Strachan* pen*)*

**St Mirren (0) 1** *(McDougall)*       16,782

(At Celtic Park)
*Aberdeen:* Leighton; Kennedy, Rougvie (Bell), McMaster, McLeish, Miller, Strachan, Cooper, McGhee, Simpson, Hewitt (Jarvie).
*St Mirren:* Thomson; Beckett, Abercromby, Richardson, McCormack, Copland, Bone, Stark, McDougall, McAvennie, Scanlon.

**Forfar Ath (0) 0**

**Rangers (0) 0**             15,878

(At Hampden Park)
*Forfar Ath:* Kennedy; Bennett, McPhee, Brown, Brash, Allan (Porter), Gallacher, Farningham, Hancock, Leitch, Clark (Watt).
*Rangers:* Stewart; Dawson, Black, Jardine, McClelland, Bett, Dalziel (Davies), Russell, McAdam (Robertson), Redford, MacDonald.

## SEMI-FINAL REPLAYS

### 6 APRIL

**Forfar Ath (1) 1** *(Brash* pen*)*

**Rangers (2) 3** *(Johnstone, Bett, Cooper)*    11,864

(At Hampden Park)
*Forfar Ath:* Kennedy; Bennett, McPhee, Brown, Brash, Allan, Gallacher, Farningham, Hancock, Leitch (Watt), Clark (Porter).
*Rangers:* Stewart; Jardine, Dawson, McClelland, Jackson, Bett, Cooper, Russell, Johnstone, Redford, MacDonald.

### 7 APRIL

**Aberdeen (2) 3** *(McGhee, Simpson, Weir)*

**St Mirren (1) 2** *(McAvennie, Somner)*    15,633

(At Dens Park)
*Aberdeen:* Leighton; Rougvie, McMaster, Cooper, McLeish, Miller, Strachan, Simpson, McGhee, Hewitt, Weir.
*St Mirren:* Thomson; Beckett, McCormack, Richardson, Fulton (Fitzpatrick), Copland, McDougall, Stark (Bone), Somner, McAvennie, Scanlon.

### FINAL (At Hampden Park)

### 22 MAY

**Aberdeen (1) 4** *aet (McLeish, McGhee, Strachan, Cooper)*

**Rangers (1) 1** *(MacDonald)*       53,788

*Aberdeen:* Leighton; Kennedy, Rougvie, McMaster (Bell), McLeish, Miller, Strachan, Cooper, McGhee, Simpson, Hewitt (Black).
*Rangers:* Stewart; Jardine (McAdam), Dawson, McClelland, Jackson, Bett, Cooper, Russell, Dalziel (McLean), Miller, MacDonald.
*Referee:* Mr B. R. McGinlay (Balfron)

# BRITISH HOME INTERNATIONALS

## INTERNATIONAL CHAMPIONSHIP 1883–1982

| Year | Champions | Pts | Year | Champions | Pts | Year | Champions | Pts |
|---|---|---|---|---|---|---|---|---|
| 1883–84 | Scotland | 6 | 1920–21 | Scotland | 6 | 1956–57 | England | 5 |
| 1884–85 | Scotland | 5 | 1921–22 | Scotland | 4 | 1957–58 | England | 4 |
| 1885–86 | England | 5 | 1922–23 | Scotland | 5 | | Ireland | 4 |
| | Scotland | 5 | 1923–24 | Wales | 6 | 1958–59 | Ireland | 4 |
| 1886–87 | Scotland | 6 | 1924–25 | Scotland | 6 | | England | 4 |
| 1887–88 | England | 6 | 1925–26 | Scotland | 6 | 1959–60 | England | 4 |
| 1888–89 | Scotland | 5 | 1926–27 | Scotland | 4 | | Scotland | 4 |
| 1889–90 | Scotland | 5 | | England | 4 | | Wales | 4 |
| | England | 5 | 1927–28 | Wales | 5 | 1960–61 | England | 6 |
| 1890–91 | England | 6 | 1928–29 | Scotland | 6 | 1961–62 | Scotland | 6 |
| 1891–92 | England | 6 | 1929–30 | England | 6 | 1962–63 | Scotland | 6 |
| 1892–93 | England | 6 | 1930–31 | Scotland | 4 | 1963–64 | Scotland | 4 |
| 1893–94 | Scotland | 5 | | England | 4 | | England | 4 |
| 1894–95 | England | 5 | 1931–32 | England | 6 | | Ireland | 4 |
| 1895–96 | Scotland | 5 | 1932–33 | Wales | 5 | 1964–65 | England | 5 |
| 1896–97 | Scotland | 5 | 1933–34 | Wales | 5 | 1965–66 | England | 5 |
| 1897–98 | England | 6 | 1934–35 | England | 4 | 1966–67 | Scotland | 5 |
| 1898–99 | England | 6 | | Scotland | 4 | 1967–68 | England | 5 |
| 1899–1900 | Scotland | 6 | 1935–36 | Scotland | 4 | 1968–69 | England | 6 |
| 1900–01 | England | 5 | 1936–37 | Wales | 6 | 1969–70 | England | 4 |
| 1901–02 | Scotland | 5 | 1937–38 | England | 4 | | Scotland | 4 |
| 1902–03 | England | 4 | | England | 4 | | Wales | 4 |
| | Ireland | 4 | 1938–39 | Scotland | 4 | 1970–71 | England | 5 |
| | Scotland | 4 | | Wales | 4 | 1971–72 | England | 4 |
| 1903–04 | England | 5 | 1946–47 | England | 5 | | Scotland | 4 |
| 1904–05 | England | 5 | 1947–48 | England | 5 | 1972–73 | England | 6 |
| 1905–06 | England | 4 | 1948–49 | Scotland | 6 | 1973–74 | England | 4 |
| | Scotland | 4 | 1949–50 | England | 6 | | Scotland | 4 |
| 1906–07 | Wales | 5 | 1950–51 | Scotland | 6 | 1974–75 | England | 4 |
| 1907–08 | Scotland | 5 | 1951–52 | Wales | 5 | 1975–76 | Scotland | 6 |
| | England | 5 | | England | 5 | 1976–77 | Scotland | 5 |
| 1908–09 | England | 6 | 1952–53 | England | 4 | 1977–78 | England | 6 |
| 1909–10 | Scotland | 4 | | Scotland | 4 | 1978–79 | England | 5 |
| 1910–11 | England | 5 | 1953–54 | England | 6 | 1979–80 | Ireland | 5 |
| 1911–12 | England | 5 | 1954–55 | England | 6 | 1980–81 | Not completed | |
| | Scotland | 5 | | England | 3 | 1981–82 | England | 6 |
| 1912–13 | England | 4 | 1955–56 | Scotland | 3 | | | |
| 1913–14 | Ireland | 5 | | Wales | 3 | | | |
| 1919–20 | Wales | 4 | | Ireland | 3 | | | |

*Note:* In the results that follow, wc = World Cup, ec = European Championship.

### ENGLAND v SCOTLAND

*Played:* 100; England won 39, Scotland won 39, Drawn 22. *Goals:* England 180, Scotland 165.

| | E | S | | E | S | | E | S |
|---|---|---|---|---|---|---|---|---|
| 1872 Glasgow | 0 | 0 | 1890 Glasgow | 1 | 1 | 1908 Glasgow | 1 | 1 |
| 1873 Kennington Oval | 4 | 2 | 1891 Blackburn | 2 | 1 | 1909 Crystal Palace | 2 | 0 |
| 1874 Glasgow | 1 | 2 | 1892 Glasgow | 4 | 1 | 1910 Glasgow | 0 | 2 |
| 1875 Kennington Oval | 2 | 2 | 1893 Richmond | 5 | 2 | 1911 Everton | 1 | 1 |
| 1876 Glasgow | 0 | 3 | 1894 Glasgow | 2 | 2 | 1912 Glasgow | 1 | 1 |
| 1877 Kennington Oval | 1 | 3 | 1895 Everton | 3 | 0 | 1913 Chelsea | 1 | 0 |
| 1878 Glasgow | 2 | 7 | 1896 Glasgow | 1 | 2 | 1914 Glasgow | 1 | 3 |
| 1879 Kennington Oval | 5 | 4 | 1897 Crystal Palace | 1 | 2 | 1920 Sheffield | 5 | 4 |
| 1880 Glasgow | 4 | 5 | 1898 Glasgow | 3 | 1 | 1921 Glasgow | 0 | 3 |
| 1881 Kennington Oval | 1 | 6 | 1899 Birmingham | 2 | 1 | 1922 Aston Villa | 0 | 1 |
| 1882 Glasgow | 1 | 5 | 1900 Glasgow | 1 | 4 | 1923 Glasgow | 2 | 2 |
| 1883 Sheffield | 2 | 3 | 1901 Crystal Palace | 2 | 2 | 1924 Wembley | 1 | 1 |
| 1884 Glasgow | 0 | 1 | 1902 Birmingham | 2 | 2 | 1925 Glasgow | 0 | 2 |
| 1885 Kennington Oval | 1 | 1 | 1903 Sheffield | 1 | 2 | 1926 Manchester | 0 | 1 |
| 1886 Glasgow | 1 | 1 | 1904 Glasgow | 1 | 0 | 1927 Glasgow | 2 | 1 |
| 1887 Blackburn | 2 | 3 | 1905 Crystal Palace | 1 | 0 | 1928 Wembley | 1 | 5 |
| 1888 Glasgow | 5 | 0 | 1906 Glasgow | 1 | 2 | 1929 Glasgow | 0 | 1 |
| 1889 Kennington Oval | 2 | 3 | 1907 Newcastle | 1 | 1 | 1930 Wembley | 5 | 2 |

| | E | S | | E | S | | E | S |
|---|---|---|---|---|---|---|---|---|
| 1931 Glasgow | 0 | 2 | wc1954 Glasgow | 4 | 2 | 1970 Glasgow | 0 | 0 |
| 1932 Wembley | 3 | 0 | 1955 Wembley | 7 | 2 | 1971 Wembley | 3 | 1 |
| 1933 Glasgow | 1 | 2 | 1956 Glasgow | 1 | 1 | 1972 Glasgow | 1 | 0 |
| 1934 Wembley | 3 | 0 | 1957 Wembley | 2 | 1 | 1973 Glasgow | 5 | 0 |
| 1935 Glasgow | 0 | 2 | 1958 Glasgow | 4 | 0 | 1973 Wembley | 1 | 0 |
| 1936 Wembley | 1 | 1 | 1959 Wembley | 1 | 0 | 1974 Glasgow | 0 | 2 |
| 1937 Glasgow | 1 | 3 | 1960 Glasgow | 1 | 1 | 1975 Wembley | 5 | 1 |
| 1938 Wembley | 0 | 1 | 1961 Wembley | 9 | 3 | 1976 Glasgow | 1 | 2 |
| 1939 Glasgow | 2 | 1 | 1962 Glasgow | 0 | 2 | 1977 Wembley | 1 | 2 |
| 1947 Wembley | 1 | 1 | 1963 Wembley | 1 | 2 | 1978 Glasgow | 1 | 0 |
| 1948 Glasgow | 2 | 0 | 1964 Glasgow | 0 | 1 | 1979 Wembley | 3 | 1 |
| 1949 Wembley | 1 | 3 | 1965 Wembley | 2 | 2 | 1980 Glasgow | 2 | 0 |
| wc1950 Glasgow | 1 | 0 | 1966 Glasgow | 4 | 3 | 1981 Wembley | 0 | 1 |
| 1951 Wembley | 2 | 3 | EC1967 Wembley | 2 | 3 | 1982 Glasgow | 1 | 0 |
| 1952 Glasgow | 2 | 1 | EC1968 Glasgow | 1 | 1 | | | |
| 1953 Wembley | 2 | 2 | 1969 Wembley | 4 | 1 | | | |

## ENGLAND v WALES

*Played:* 95; England won 61, Wales won 13, Drawn 21. *Goals:* England 237, Wales 88.

| | E | W | | E | W | | E | W |
|---|---|---|---|---|---|---|---|---|
| 1879 Kennington Oval | 2 | 1 | 1910 Cardiff | 1 | 0 | wc1953 Cardiff | 4 | 1 |
| 1880 Wrexham | 3 | 2 | 1911 Millwall | 3 | 0 | 1954 Wembley | 3 | 2 |
| 1881 Blackburn | 0 | 1 | 1912 Wrexham | 2 | 0 | 1955 Cardiff | 1 | 2 |
| 1882 Wrexham | 3 | 5 | 1913 Bristol | 4 | 3 | 1956 Wembley | 3 | 1 |
| 1883 Kennington Oval | 5 | 0 | 1914 Cardiff | 2 | 0 | 1957 Cardiff | 4 | 0 |
| 1884 Wrexham | 4 | 0 | 1920 Highbury | 1 | 2 | 1958 Aston Villa | 2 | 2 |
| 1885 Blackburn | 1 | 1 | 1921 Cardiff | 0 | 0 | 1959 Cardiff | 1 | 1 |
| 1886 Wrexham | 3 | 1 | 1922 Liverpool | 1 | 0 | 1960 Wembley | 5 | 1 |
| 1887 Kennington Oval | 4 | 0 | 1923 Cardiff | 2 | 2 | 1961 Cardiff | 1 | 1 |
| 1888 Crewe | 5 | 1 | 1924 Blackburn | 1 | 2 | 1962 Wembley | 4 | 0 |
| 1889 Stoke | 4 | 1 | 1925 Swansea | 2 | 1 | 1963 Cardiff | 4 | 0 |
| 1890 Wrexham | 3 | 1 | 1926 Crystal Palace | 1 | 3 | 1964 Wembley | 2 | 1 |
| 1891 Sunderland | 4 | 1 | 1927 Wrexham | 3 | 3 | 1965 Cardiff | 0 | 0 |
| 1892 Wrexham | 2 | 0 | 1927 Burnley | 1 | 2 | EC1966 Wembley | 5 | 1 |
| 1893 Stoke | 6 | 0 | 1928 Swansea | 3 | 2 | EC1967 Cardiff | 3 | 0 |
| 1894 Wrexham | 5 | 1 | 1929 Chelsea | 6 | 0 | 1969 Wembley | 2 | 1 |
| 1894 Queen's Club, | | | 1930 Wrexham | 4 | 0 | 1970 Cardiff | 1 | 1 |
| Kensington | 1 | 1 | 1931 Liverpool | 3 | 1 | 1971 Wembley | 0 | 0 |
| 1896 Cardiff | 9 | 1 | 1932 Wrexham | 0 | 0 | 1972 Cardiff | 3 | 0 |
| 1897 Sheffield | 4 | 0 | 1933 Newcastle | 1 | 2 | wc1972 Cardiff | 1 | 0 |
| 1898 Wrexham | 3 | 0 | 1934 Cardiff | 4 | 0 | wc1973 Wembley | 1 | 1 |
| 1899 Bristol | 4 | 0 | 1935 Wolverhampton | 1 | 2 | 1973 Wembley | 3 | 0 |
| 1900 Cardiff | 1 | 1 | 1936 Cardiff | 1 | 2 | 1974 Cardiff | 2 | 0 |
| 1901 Newcastle | 6 | 0 | 1937 Middlesbrough | 2 | 1 | 1975 Wembley | 2 | 2 |
| 1902 Wrexham | 0 | 0 | 1938 Cardiff | 2 | 4 | 1976 Wrexham | 2 | 1 |
| 1903 Portsmouth | 2 | 1 | 1946 Manchester | 3 | 0 | 1976 Cardiff | 1 | 0 |
| 1904 Wrexham | 2 | 2 | 1947 Cardiff | 3 | 0 | 1977 Wembley | 0 | 1 |
| 1905 Liverpool | 3 | 1 | 1948 Aston Villa | 1 | 0 | 1978 Cardiff | 3 | 1 |
| 1906 Cardiff | 1 | 0 | wc1949 Cardiff | 4 | 1 | 1979 Wembley | 0 | 0 |
| 1907 Fulham | 1 | 1 | 1950 Sunderland | 4 | 2 | 1980 Wrexham | 1 | 4 |
| 1908 Wrexham | 7 | 1 | 1951 Cardiff | 1 | 1 | 1981 Wembley | 0 | 0 |
| 1909 Nottingham | 2 | 0 | 1952 Wembley | 5 | 2 | 1982 Cardiff | 1 | 0 |

## ENGLAND v IRELAND

*Played:* 90; England won 70, Ireland won 6, Drawn 14. *Goals:* England 312, Ireland 80.

| | E | I | | E | I | | E | I |
|---|---|---|---|---|---|---|---|---|
| 1882 Belfast | 13 | 0 | 1895 Derby | 9 | 0 | 1908 Belfast | 3 | 1 |
| 1883 Liverpool | 7 | 0 | 1896 Belfast | 2 | 0 | 1909 Bradford | 4 | 0 |
| 1884 Belfast | 8 | 1 | 1897 Nottingham | 6 | 0 | 1910 Belfast | 1 | 1 |
| 1885 Manchester | 4 | 0 | 1898 Belfast | 3 | 2 | 1911 Derby | 2 | 1 |
| 1886 Belfast | 6 | 1 | 1899 Sunderland | 13 | 2 | 1912 Dublin | 6 | 1 |
| 1887 Sheffield | 7 | 0 | 1900 Dublin | 2 | 0 | 1913 Belfast | 1 | 2 |
| 1888 Belfast | 5 | 1 | 1901 Southampton | 3 | 0 | 1914 Middlesbrough | 0 | 3 |
| 1889 Everton | 6 | 1 | 1902 Belfast | 1 | 0 | 1919 Belfast | 1 | 1 |
| 1890 Belfast | 9 | 1 | 1903 Wolverhampton | 4 | 0 | 1920 Sunderland | 2 | 0 |
| 1891 Wolverhampton | 6 | 1 | 1904 Belfast | 3 | 1 | 1921 Belfast | 1 | 1 |
| 1892 Belfast | 2 | 0 | 1905 Middlesbrough | 1 | 1 | 1922 West Bromwich | 2 | 0 |
| 1893 Birmingham | 6 | 1 | 1906 Belfast | 5 | 0 | 1923 Belfast' | 1 | 2 |
| 1894 Belfast | 2 | 2 | 1907 Everton | 1 | 0 | 1924 Everton | 3 | 1 |

| | E | I | | | E | I | | | E | I |
|---|---|---|---|---|---|---|---|---|---|---|
| 1925 Belfast | 0 | 0 | wc1949 Manchester | 9 | 2 | BC1966 Belfast | 2 | 0 |
| 1926 Liverpool | 3 | 3 | 1950 Belfast | 4 | 1 | BC1967 Wembley | 2 | 0 |
| 1927 Belfast | 0 | 2 | 1951 Aston Villa | 2 | 0 | 1969 Belfast | 3 | 1 |
| 1928 Everton | 2 | 1 | 1952 Belfast | 2 | 2 | 1970 Wembley | 3 | 1 |
| 1929 Belfast | 3 | 0 | wc1953 Everton | 3 | 1 | 1971 Belfast | 1 | 0 |
| 1930 Sheffield | 5 | 1 | 1954 Belfast | 2 | 0 | 1972 Wembley | 0 | 1 |
| 1931 Belfast | 6 | 2 | 1955 Wembley | 3 | 0 | 1973 Everton | 2 | 1 |
| 1932 Blackpool | 1 | 0 | 1956 Belfast | 1 | 1 | 1974 Wembley | 1 | 0 |
| 1933 Belfast | 3 | 0 | 1957 Wembley | 2 | 3 | 1975 Belfast | 0 | 0 |
| 1935 Everton | 2 | 1 | 1958 Belfast | 3 | 3 | 1976 Wembley | 4 | 0 |
| 1935 Belfast | 3 | 1 | 1959 Wembley | 2 | 1 | 1977 Belfast | 2 | 1 |
| 1936 Stoke | 3 | 1 | 1960 Belfast | 5 | 2 | 1978 Wembley | 1 | 0 |
| 1937 Belfast | 5 | 1 | 1961 Wembley | 1 | 1 | EC1979 Wembley | 4 | 0 |
| 1938 Manchester | 7 | 0 | 1962 Belfast | 3 | 1 | 1979 Belfast | 2 | 0 |
| 1946 Belfast | 7 | 2 | 1963 Wembley | 8 | 3 | BC1979 Belfast | 5 | 1 |
| 1947 Everton | 2 | 2 | 1964 Belfast | 4 | 3 | 1980 Wembley | 1 | 1 |
| 1948 Belfast | 6 | 2 | 1965 Wembley | 2 | 1 | 1982 Wembley | 4 | 0 |

## SCOTLAND v WALES

*Played:* 97; Scotland won 58, Wales won 17, Drawn 22. *Goals:* Scotland 233, Wales 108.

| | S | W | | | S | W | | | S | W |
|---|---|---|---|---|---|---|---|---|---|---|
| 1876 Glasgow | 4 | 0 | 1909 Wrexham | 2 | 3 | 1953 Glasgow | 3 | 3 |
| 1877 Wrexham | 2 | 0 | 1910 Kilmarnock | 1 | 0 | 1954 Cardiff | 1 | 0 |
| 1878 Glasgow | 9 | 0 | 1911 Cardiff | 2 | 2 | 1955 Glasgow | 2 | 0 |
| 1879 Wrexham | 3 | 0 | 1912 Tynecastle | 1 | 0 | 1956 Cardiff | 2 | 2 |
| 1880 Glasgow | 5 | 1 | 1913 Wrexham | 0 | 0 | 1957 Glasgow | 1 | 1 |
| 1881 Wrexham | 5 | 1 | 1914 Glasgow | 0 | 0 | 1958 Cardiff | 3 | 0 |
| 1882 Glasgow | 5 | 0 | 1920 Cardiff | 1 | 1 | 1959 Glasgow | 1 | 1 |
| 1883 Wrexham | 4 | 1 | 1921 Aberdeen | 2 | 1 | 1960 Cardiff | 0 | 2 |
| 1884 Glasgow | 4 | 1 | 1922 Wrexham | 1 | 2 | 1961 Glasgow | 2 | 0 |
| 1885 Wrexham | 8 | 1 | 1923 Paisley | 2 | 0 | 1962 Cardiff | 3 | 2 |
| 1886 Glasgow | 4 | 1 | 1924 Cardiff | 0 | 2 | 1963 Glasgow | 2 | 1 |
| 1887 Wrexham | 2 | 0 | 1925 Tynecastle | 3 | 1 | 1964 Cardiff | 2 | 3 |
| 1888 Edinburgh | 5 | 1 | 1926 Cardiff | 3 | 0 | EC1965 Glasgow | 4 | 1 |
| 1889 Wrexham | 0 | 0 | 1927 Glasgow | 3 | 0 | EC1966 Cardiff | 1 | 1 |
| 1890 Paisley | 5 | 0 | 1928 Wrexham | 2 | 2 | 1967 Glasgow | 3 | 2 |
| 1891 Wrexham | 4 | 3 | 1929 Glasgow | 4 | 2 | 1969 Wrexham | 5 | 3 |
| 1892 Edinburgh | 6 | 1 | 1930 Cardiff | 4 | 2 | 1970 Glasgow | 0 | 0 |
| 1893 Wrexham | 8 | 0 | 1931 Glasgow | 1 | 1 | 1971 Cardiff | 0 | 0 |
| 1894 Kilmarnock | 5 | 2 | 1932 Wrexham | 3 | 2 | 1972 Glasgow | 1 | 0 |
| 1895 Wrexham | 2 | 2 | 1933 Edinburgh | 2 | 5 | 1973 Wrexham | 2 | 0 |
| 1896 Dundee | 4 | 0 | 1934 Cardiff | 2 | 3 | 1974 Glasgow | 2 | 0 |
| 1897 Wrexham | 2 | 2 | 1935 Aberdeen | 3 | 2 | 1975 Cardiff | 2 | 2 |
| 1898 Motherwell | 5 | 2 | 1936 Cardiff | 1 | 1 | 1976 Glasgow | 3 | 1 |
| 1899 Wrexham | 6 | 0 | 1937 Dundee | 1 | 2 | wc1977 Glasgow | 1 | 0 |
| 1900 Aberdeen | 5 | 2 | 1938 Cardiff | 1 | 2 | 1977 Wrexham | 0 | 0 |
| 1901 Wrexham | 1 | 1 | 1939 Edinburgh | 3 | 2 | wc1977 Liverpool | 2 | 0 |
| 1902 Greenock | 5 | 1 | 1946 Wrexham | 1 | 3 | 1978 Glasgow | 1 | 1 |
| 1903 Cardiff | 1 | 0 | 1947 Glasgow | 1 | 2 | 1979 Cardiff | 0 | 3 |
| 1904 Dundee | 1 | 1 | wc1948 Cardiff | 3 | 1 | 1980 Glasgow | 1 | 0 |
| 1905 Wrexham | 1 | 3 | 1949 Glasgow | 2 | 0 | 1981 Swansea | 0 | 2 |
| 1906 Edinburgh | 0 | 2 | 1950 Cardiff | 3 | 1 | 1982 Glasgow | 1 | 0 |
| 1907 Wrexham | 0 | 1 | 1951 Glasgow | 0 | 1 | | | |
| 1908 Dundee | 2 | 1 | wc1952 Cardiff | 2 | 1 | | | |

## SCOTLAND v IRELAND

*Played:* 89; Scotland won 60, Ireland won 14, Drawn 15. *Goals:* Scotland 253, Ireland 79.

| | S | I | | | S | I | | | S | I |
|---|---|---|---|---|---|---|---|---|---|---|
| 1884 Belfast | 5 | 0 | 1895 Glasgow | 3 | 1 | 1906 Dublin | 1 | 0 |
| 1885 Glasgow | 8 | 2 | 1896 Belfast | 3 | 3 | 1907 Glasgow | 3 | 0 |
| 1886 Belfast | 7 | 2 | 1897 Glasgow | 5 | 1 | 1908 Dublin | 5 | 0 |
| 1887 Glasgow | 4 | 1 | 1898 Belfast | 3 | 0 | 1909 Glasgow | 5 | 0 |
| 1888 Belfast | 10 | 2 | 1899 Glasgow | 9 | 1 | 1910 Belfast | 0 | 1 |
| 1889 Glasgow | 7 | 0 | 1900 Belfast | 3 | 0 | 1911 Glasgow | 2 | 0 |
| 1890 Belfast | 4 | 1 | 1901 Glasgow | 11 | 0 | 1912 Belfast | 4 | 1 |
| 1891 Glasgow | 2 | 1 | 1902 Belfast | 5 | 1 | 1913 Dublin | 2 | 1 |
| 1892 Belfast | 3 | 2 | 1903 Glasgow | 0 | 2 | 1914 Belfast | 1 | 1 |
| 1893 Glasgow | 6 | 1 | 1904 Dublin | 1 | 1 | 1920 Glasgow | 3 | 0 |
| 1894 Belfast | 2 | 1 | 1905 Glasgow | 4 | 0 | 1921 Belfast | 2 | 0 |

| | S | I | | | S | I | | | S | I |
|---|---|---|---|---|---|---|---|---|---|---|
| 1922 Glasgow | 2 | 1 | 1947 Belfast | | 0 | 2 | 1966 Glasgow | | 2 | 1 |
| 1923 Belfast | 1 | 0 | 1948 Glasgow | | 3 | 2 | 1967 Belfast | | 0 | 1 |
| 1924 Glasgow | 2 | 0 | 1949 Belfast | | 8 | 2 | 1969 Glasgow | | 1 | 1 |
| 1925 Belfast | 3 | 0 | 1950 Glasgow | | 6 | 1 | 1970 Belfast | | 1 | 0 |
| 1926 Glasgow | 4 | 0 | 1951 Belfast | | 3 | 0 | 1971 Glasgow | | 0 | 1 |
| 1927 Belfast | 2 | 0 | 1952 Glasgow | | 1 | 1 | 1972 Glasgow | | 2 | 0 |
| 1928 Glasgow | 0 | 1 | 1953 Belfast | | 3 | 1 | 1973 Glasgow | | 1 | 2 |
| 1929 Belfast | 7 | 3 | 1954 Glasgow | | 2 | 2 | 1974 Glasgow | | 0 | 1 |
| 1930 Glasgow | 3 | 1 | 1955 Belfast | | 1 | 2 | 1975 Glasgow | | 3 | 0 |
| 1931 Belfast | 0 | 0 | 1956 Glasgow | | 1 | 0 | 1976 Glasgow | | 3 | 0 |
| 193? Glasgow | 3 | 1 | 1957 Belfast | | 1 | 1 | 1977 Glasgow | | 3 | 0 |
| 1933 Belfast | 4 | 0 | 1958 Glasgow | | 2 | 2 | 1978 Glasgow | | 1 | 1 |
| 1934 Glasgow | 1 | 2 | 1959 Belfast | | 4 | 0 | 1979 Glasgow | | 1 | 0 |
| 1935 Belfast | 1 | 2 | 1960 Glasgow | | 5 | 2 | 1980 Belfast | | 0 | 1 |
| 1936 Edinburgh | 2 | 1 | 1961 Belfast | | 6 | 1 | wc1981 Glasgow | | 1 | 1 |
| 1937 Belfast | 3 | 1 | 1962 Glasgow | | 5 | 1 | 1981 Glasgow | | 2 | 0 |
| 1938 Aberdeen | 1 | 1 | 1963 Belfast | | 1 | 2 | wc1981 Belfast | | 0 | 0 |
| 1939 Belfast | 2 | 0 | 1964 Glasgow | | 3 | 2 | 1982 Belfast | | 1 | 1 |
| 1946 Glasgow | 0 | 0 | 1965 Belfast | | 2 | 3 | | | | |

## WALES v IRELAND

*Played:* 88; Wales won 41, Ireland won 27, Drawn 20. *Goals:* Wales 179, Ireland 125.

| | W | I | | | W | I | | | W | I |
|---|---|---|---|---|---|---|---|---|---|---|
| 1882 Wrexham | 7 | 1 | 1912 Cardiff | | 2 | 3 | wc1954 Wrexham | | 1 | 2 |
| 1883 Belfast | 1 | 1 | 1913 Belfast | | 1 | 0 | 1955 Belfast | | 3 | 2 |
| 1884 Wrexham | 6 | 0 | 1914 Wrexham | | 1 | 2 | 1956 Cardiff | | 1 | 1 |
| 1885 Belfast | 8 | 2 | 1920 Belfast | | 2 | 2 | 1957 Cardiff | | 0 | 0 |
| 1886 Wrexham | 5 | 0 | 1921 Swansea | | 2 | 1 | 1958 Cardiff | | 1 | 1 |
| 1887 Belfast | 1 | 4 | 1922 Belfast | | 1 | 1 | 1959 Belfast | | 1 | 4 |
| 1888 Wrexham | 11 | 0 | 1923 Wrexham | | 0 | 3 | 1960 Wrexham | | 3 | 2 |
| 1889 Belfast | 3 | 1 | 1924 Belfast | | 1 | 0 | 1961 Belfast | | 5 | 1 |
| 1890 Shrewsbury | 5 | 2 | 1925 Wrexham | | 0 | 0 | 1962 Cardiff | | 4 | 0 |
| 1891 Belfast | 2 | 7 | 1926 Belfast | | 0 | 3 | 1963 Belfast | | 4 | 1 |
| 1892 Bangor | 1 | 1 | 1927 Cardiff | | 2 | 2 | 1964 Cardiff | | 2 | 3 |
| 1893 Belfast | 3 | 4 | 1928 Belfast | | 2 | 1 | 1965 Belfast | | 5 | 0 |
| 1894 Swansea | 4 | 1 | 1929 Wrexham | | 2 | 2 | 1966 Cardiff | | 1 | 4 |
| 1895 Belfast | 2 | 2 | 1930 Belfast | | 0 | 7 | EC1967 Belfast | | 0 | 0 |
| 1896 Wrexham | 6 | 1 | 1931 Wrexham | | 3 | 2 | EC1968 Wrexham | | 2 | 0 |
| 1897 Belfast | 3 | 4 | 1932 Belfast | | 0 | 4 | 1969 Belfast | | 0 | 0 |
| 1898 Llandudno | 0 | 1 | 1933 Wrexham | | 4 | 1 | 1970 Swansea | | 1 | 0 |
| 1899 Belfast | 0 | 1 | 1934 Belfast | | 1 | 1 | 1971 Belfast | | 0 | 1 |
| 1900 Llandudno | 2 | 0 | 1935 Wrexham | | 3 | 1 | 1972 Wrexham | | 0 | 0 |
| 1901 Belfast | 1 | 0 | 1936 Belfast | | 2 | 3 | 1973 Everton | | 0 | 1 |
| 1902 Cardiff | 0 | 3 | 1937 Wrexham | | 4 | 1 | 1974 Wrexham | | 1 | 0 |
| 1903 Belfast | 0 | 2 | 1938 Belfast | | 0 | 1 | 1975 Belfast | | 0 | 1 |
| 1904 Bangor | 0 | 1 | 1939 Wrexham | | 3 | 1 | 1976 Swansea | | 1 | 0 |
| 1905 Belfast | 2 | 2 | 1947 Belfast | | 1 | 2 | 1977 Belfast | | 1 | 0 |
| 1906 Wrexham | 4 | 4 | 1948 Wrexham | | 2 | 0 | 1978 Wrexham | | 1 | 0 |
| 1907 Belfast | 3 | 2 | 1949 Belfast | | 2 | 0 | 1979 Belfast | | 1 | 1 |
| 1908 Aberdare | 0 | 1 | wc1950 Wrexham | | 0 | 0 | 1980 Cardiff | | 0 | 1 |
| 1909 Belfast | 3 | 2 | 1951 Belfast | | 2 | 1 | 1982 Wrexham | | 3 | 0 |
| 1910 Wrexham | 4 | 1 | 1952 Swansea | | 3 | 0 | | | | |
| 1911 Belfast | 2 | 1 | 1953 Belfast | | 3 | 2 | | | | |

## OTHER BRITISH INTERNATIONAL RESULTS 1908–1982

### ENGLAND

| v ARGENTINA | | E | A | | v AUSTRIA | | E | A |
|---|---|---|---|---|---|---|---|---|
| 1951 | 9 May | Wembley | 2 | 1 | 1908 | 6 June | Vienna | 6 | 1 |
| 1953 | 17 May | Buenos Aires | 0 | 0 | 1908 | 8 June | Vienna | 11 | 1 |
| | (abandoned after 21 mins) | | | | 1909 | 1 June | Vienna | 8 | 1 |
| wc1962 | 2 June | Rancagua | 3 | 1 | 1930 | 14 May | Vienna | 0 | 0 |
| 1964 | 6 June | Rio de Janeiro | 0 | 1 | 1932 | 7 Dec | Chelsea | 4 | 3 |
| wc1966 | 23 July | Wembley | 1 | 0 | 1936 | 6 May | Vienna | 1 | 2 |
| 1974 | 22 May | Wembley | 2 | 2 | 1951 | 28 Nov | Wembley | 2 | 2 |
| 1977 | 12 June | Buenos Aires | 1 | 1 | 1952 | 25 May | Vienna | 3 | 2 |
| 1980 | 13 May | Wembley | 3 | 1 | wc1958 | 15 June | Boras | 2 | 2 |
| | | | | | 1961 | 27 May | Vienna | 1 | 3 |
| | | | | | 1962 | 4 Apr | Wembley | 3 | 1 |
| | | | | | 1965 | 20 Oct | Wembley | 2 | 3 |
| v AUSTRALIA | | E | A | | 1967 | 27 May | Vienna | 1 | 0 |
| | | | | | 1973 | 26 Sept | Wembley | 7 | 0 |
| 1980 | 31 May | Sydney | 2 | 1 | 1979 | 13 June | Vienna | 3 | 4 |

## v BELGIUM

| | | | E | B |
|---|---|---|---|---|
| 1921 | 21 May | Brussels | 2 | 0 |
| 1923 | 19 Mar | Highbury | 6 | 1 |
| 1923 | 1 Nov | Antwerp | 2 | 2 |
| 1924 | 8 Dec | West Bromwich | 4 | 0 |
| 1926 | 24 May | Antwerp | 5 | 3 |
| 1927 | 11 May | Brussels | 9 | 1 |
| 1928 | 19 May | Antwerp | 3 | 1 |
| 1929 | 11 May | Brussels | 5 | 1 |
| 1931 | 16 May | Brussels | 4 | 1 |
| 1936 | 9 May | Brussels | 2 | 3 |
| 1947 | 21 Sept | Brussels | 5 | 2 |
| 1950 | 18 May | Brussels | 4 | 1 |
| 1952 | 26 Nov | Wembley | 5 | 0 |
| wc1954 | 17 June | Basle | 4 | 4* |
| 1964 | 21 Oct | Wembley | 2 | 2 |
| 1970 | 25 Feb | Brussels | 3 | 1 |
| EC1980 | 12 June | Turin | 1 | 1 |

*After extra time.

## v BOHEMIA

| | | | E | B |
|---|---|---|---|---|
| 1908 | 13 June | Prague | 4 | 0 |

## v BRAZIL

| | | | E | B |
|---|---|---|---|---|
| 1956 | 9 May | Wembley | 4 | 2 |
| wc1958 | 11 June | Gothenburg | 0 | 0 |
| 1959 | 13 May | Rio de Janeiro | 0 | 2 |
| wc1962 | 10 June | Vina del Mar | 1 | 3 |
| 1963 | 8 May | Wembley | 1 | 1 |
| 1964 | 30 May | Rio de Janeiro | 1 | 5 |
| 1969 | 12 June | Rio de Juneiro | 1 | 2 |
| wc1970 | 7 June | Guadalajara | 0 | 1 |
| 1976 | 23 May | Los Angeles | 0 | 1 |
| 1977 | 8 June | Rio de Janeiro | 0 | 0 |
| 1978 | 19 Apr | Wembley | 1 | 1 |
| 1981 | 12 May | Wembley | 0 | 1 |

## v BULGARIA

| | | | E | B |
|---|---|---|---|---|
| wc1962 | 7 June | Rancagua | 0 | 0 |
| 1968 | 11 Dec | Wembley | 1 | 1 |
| 1974 | 1 June | Sofia | 1 | 0 |
| EC1979 | 6 June | Sofia | 3 | 0 |
| EC1979 | 22 Nov | Wembley | 2 | 0 |

## v CHILE

| | | | E | C |
|---|---|---|---|---|
| wc1950 | 25 June | Rio de Janeiro | 2 | 0 |
| 1953 | 24 May | Santiago | 2 | 1 |

## v COLOMBIA

| | | | E | C |
|---|---|---|---|---|
| 1970 | 20 May | Bogota | 4 | 0 |

## v CYPRUS

| | | | E | C |
|---|---|---|---|---|
| EC1975 | 16 Apr | Wembley | 5 | 0 |
| EC1975 | 11 May | Limassol | 1 | 0 |

## v CZECHOSLOVAKIA

| | | | E | C |
|---|---|---|---|---|
| 1934 | 16 May | Prague | 1 | 2 |
| 1937 | 1 Dec | Tottenham | 5 | 4 |
| 1963 | 29 May | Bratislava | 4 | 2 |
| 1966 | 2 Nov | Wembley | 0 | 0 |
| wc1970 | 11 June | Guadalajara | 1 | 0 |
| 1973 | 27 May | Prague | 1 | 1 |
| EC1974 | 30 Oct | Wembley | 3 | 0 |
| EC1975 | 30 Oct | Bratislava | 1 | 2 |
| 1978 | 29 Nov | Wembley | 1 | 0 |
| wc1982 | 20 June | Bilbao | 2 | 0 |

## v DENMARK

| | | | E | D |
|---|---|---|---|---|
| 1948 | 26 Sept | Copenhagen | 0 | 0 |
| 1955 | 2 Oct | Copenhagen | 5 | 1 |
| wc1956 | 5 Dec | Wolverhampton | 5 | 2 |
| wc1957 | 15 May | Copenhagen | 4 | 1 |
| 1966 | 3 July | Copenhagen | 2 | 0 |
| EC1978 | 20 Sept | Copenhagen | 4 | 3 |
| EC1979 | 12 Sept | Wembley | 1 | 0 |

## v ECUADOR

| | | | E | Ec |
|---|---|---|---|---|
| 1970 | 24 May | Quito | 2 | 0 |

## v FIFA

| | | | E | FIFA |
|---|---|---|---|---|
| 1938 | 26 Oct | Highbury | 3 | 0 |
| 1953 | 21 Oct | Wembley | 4 | 4 |
| 1963 | 23 Oct | Wembley | 2 | 1 |

## v FINLAND

| | | | E | F |
|---|---|---|---|---|
| 1937 | 20 May | Helsinki | 8 | 0 |
| 1956 | 20 May | Helsinki | 5 | 1 |
| 1966 | 26 June | Helsinki | 3 | 0 |
| wc1976 | 13 June | Helsinki | 4 | 1 |
| wc1976 | 13 Oct | Wembley | 2 | 1 |
| 1982 | 3 June | Helsinki | 4 | 1 |

## v FRANCE

| | | | E | F |
|---|---|---|---|---|
| 1923 | 10 May | Paris | 4 | 1 |
| 1924 | 17 May | Paris | 3 | 1 |
| 1925 | 21 May | Paris | 3 | 2 |
| 1927 | 26 May | Paris | 6 | 0 |
| 1928 | 17 May | Paris | 5 | 1 |
| 1929 | 9 May | Paris | 4 | 1 |
| 1931 | 14 May | Paris | 2 | 5 |
| 1933 | 6 Dec | Tottenham | 4 | 1 |
| 1938 | 26 May | Paris | 4 | 2 |
| 1947 | 3 May | Highbury | 3 | 0 |
| 1949 | 22 May | Paris | 3 | 1 |
| 1951 | 3 Oct | Highbury | 2 | 2 |
| 1955 | 15 May | Paris | 0 | 1 |
| 1957 | 27 Nov | Wembley | 4 | 0 |
| EC1962 | 3 Oct | Sheffield | 1 | 1 |
| EC1963 | 27 Feb | Paris | 2 | 5 |
| wc1966 | 20 July | Wembley | 2 | 0 |
| 1969 | 12 Mar | Wembley | 5 | 0 |
| wc1982 | 16 June | Bilbao | 3 | 1 |

## v GERMANY

| | | | E | G |
|---|---|---|---|---|
| 1930 | 10 May | Berlin | 3 | 3 |
| 1935 | 4 Dec | Tottenham | 3 | 0 |
| 1938 | 14 May | Berlin | 6 | 3 |

## v EAST GERMANY

| | | | E | EG |
|---|---|---|---|---|
| 1963 | 2 June | Leipzig | 2 | 1 |
| 1970 | 25 Nov | Wembley | 3 | 1 |
| 1974 | 29 May | Leipzig | 1 | 1 |

## WEST GERMANY

| | | | E | WG |
|---|---|---|---|---|
| 1954 | 1 Dec | Wembley | 3 | 1 |
| 1956 | 26 May | Berlin | 3 | 1 |
| 1965 | 12 May | Nuremberg | 1 | 0 |
| 1966 | 23 Feb | Wembley | 1 | 0 |
| wc1966 | 30 July | Wembley | 4 | 2* |
| 1968 | 1 June | Hanover | 0 | 1 |
| wc1970 | 14 June | Leon | 2 | 3* |
| EC1972 | 29 Apr | Wembley | 1 | 3 |
| EC1972 | 13 May | Berlin | 0 | 0 |
| 1975 | 12 Mar | Wembley | 2 | 0 |
| 1978 | 22 Feb | Munich | 1 | 2 |
| wc1982 | 29 June | Madrid | 0 | 0 |

*After extra time.

## v GREECE

| | | | E | G |
|---|---|---|---|---|
| EC1971 | 21 Apr | Wembley | 3 | 0 |
| EC1971 | 1 Dec | Athens | 2 | 0 |

## v HUNGARY

| | | | E | H |
|---|---|---|---|---|
| 1908 | 10 June | Budapest | 7 | 0 |
| 1909 | 29 May | Budapest | 4 | 2 |
| 1909 | 31 May | Budapest | 8 | 2 |
| 1934 | 10 May | Budapest | 1 | 2 |
| 1936 | 2 Dec | Highbury | 6 | 2 |
| 1953 | 25 Nov | Wembley | 3 | 6 |
| 1954 | 23 May | Budapest | 1 | 7 |
| 1960 | 22 May | Budapest | 0 | 2 |
| wc1962 | 31 May | Rancagua | 1 | 2 |

| | | | E | |
|---|---|---|---|---|
| 1965 | 5 May | Wembley | 1 | 0 |
| 1978 | 24 May | Wembley | 4 | 1 |
| wc1981 | 6 June | Budapest | 3 | 1 |
| wc1982 | 18 Nov | Wembley | 1 | 0 |

### v ICELAND

| | | | E | I |
|---|---|---|---|---|
| 1982 | 2 June | Reykjavik | 1 | 1 |

### v REPUBLIC OF IRELAND

| | | | E | RI |
|---|---|---|---|---|
| 1946 | 30 Sept | Dublin | 1 | 0 |
| 1949 | 21 Sept | Everton | 0 | 2 |
| wc1957 | 8 May | Wembley | 5 | 1 |
| wc1957 | 19 May | Dublin | 1 | 1 |
| 1964 | 24 May | Dublin | 3 | 1 |
| 1976 | 8 Sept | Wembley | 1 | 1 |
| EC1978 | 25 Oct | Dublin | 1 | 1 |
| EC1980 | 6 Feb | Wembley | 2 | 0 |

### v ITALY

| | | | E | I |
|---|---|---|---|---|
| 1933 | 13 May | Rome | 1 | 1 |
| 1934 | 14 Nov | Highbury | 3 | 2 |
| 1939 | 13 May | Milan | 2 | 2 |
| 1948 | 16 May | Turin | 4 | 0 |
| 1949 | 30 Nov | Tottenham | 2 | 0 |
| 1952 | 18 May | Florence | 1 | 1 |
| 1959 | 6 May | Wembley | 2 | 2 |
| 1961 | 24 May | Rome | 3 | 2 |
| 1973 | 14 June | Turin | 0 | 2 |
| 1973 | 14 Nov | Wembley | 0 | 1 |
| 1976 | 28 May | New York | 3 | 2 |
| wc1976 | 17 Nov | Rome | 0 | 2 |
| wc1977 | 16 Nov | Wembley | 2 | 0 |
| EC1980 | 15 June | Turin | 0 | 1 |

### v KUWAIT

| | | | E | K |
|---|---|---|---|---|
| wc1982 | 25 June | Bilbao | 1 | 0 |

### v LUXEMBOURG

| | | | E | L |
|---|---|---|---|---|
| 1927 | 21 May | Luxembourg | 5 | 2 |
| wc1960 | 19 Oct | Luxembourg | 9 | 0 |
| wc1961 | 28 Sept | Highbury | 4 | 1 |
| wc1977 | 30 Mar | Wembley | 5 | 0 |
| wc1977 | 12 Oct | Luxembourg | 2 | 0 |

### v MALTA

| | | | E | M |
|---|---|---|---|---|
| EC1971 | 3 Feb | Valletta | 1 | 0 |
| EC1971 | 12 May | Wembley | 5 | 0 |

### v MEXICO

| | | | E | M |
|---|---|---|---|---|
| 1959 | 24 May | Mexico City | 1 | 2 |
| 1961 | 10 May | Wembley | 8 | 0 |
| wc1966 | 16 July | Wembley | 2 | 0 |
| 1969 | 1 June | Mexico City | 0 | 0 |

### v NETHERLANDS

| | | | E | N |
|---|---|---|---|---|
| 1935 | 18 May | Amsterdam | 1 | 0 |
| 1946 | 27 Nov | Huddersfield | 8 | 2 |
| 1964 | 9 Dec | Amsterdam | 1 | 1 |
| 1969 | 5 Nov | Amsterdam | 1 | 0 |
| 1970 | 14 Jan | Wembley | 0 | 0 |
| 1977 | 9 Feb | Wembley | 0 | 2 |
| 1982 | 25 May | Wembley | 2 | 0 |

### v NORWAY

| | | | E | N |
|---|---|---|---|---|
| 1937 | 14 May | Oslo | 6 | 0 |
| 1938 | 9 Nov | Newcastle | 4 | 0 |
| 1949 | 18 May | Oslo | 4 | 1 |
| 1966 | 29 June | Oslo | 6 | 1 |
| wc1980 | 10 Sept | Wembley | 4 | 0 |
| wc1981 | 9 Sept | Oslo | 1 | 2 |

### v PERU

| | | | E | P |
|---|---|---|---|---|
| 1959 | 17 May | Lima | 1 | 4 |
| 1962 | 20 May | Lima | 4 | 0 |

### v POLAND

| | | | E | P |
|---|---|---|---|---|
| 1966 | 5 Jan | Everton | 1 | 1 |
| 1966 | 5 July | Chorzow | 1 | 0 |
| wc1973 | 6 June | Chorzow | 0 | 2 |
| wc1973 | 17 Oct | Wembley | 1 | 1 |

### v PORTUGAL

| | | | E | P |
|---|---|---|---|---|
| 1947 | 25 May | Lisbon | 10 | 0 |
| 1950 | 14 May | Lisbon | 5 | 3 |
| 1951 | 19 May | Everton | 5 | 2 |
| 1955 | 22 May | Oporto | 1 | 3 |
| 1958 | 7 May | Wembley | 2 | 1 |
| wc1961 | 21 May | Lisbon | 1 | 1 |
| wc1961 | 25 Oct | Wembley | 2 | 0 |
| 1964 | 17 May | Lisbon | 4 | 3 |
| 1964 | 4 June | São Paulo | 1 | 1 |
| wc1966 | 26 July | Wembley | 2 | 1 |
| 1969 | 10 Dec | Wembley | 1 | 0 |
| 1974 | 3 Apr | Lisbon | 0 | 0 |
| EC1974 | 20 Nov | Wembley | 0 | 0 |
| EC1975 | 19 Nov | Lisbon | 1 | 1 |

### v RUMANIA

| | | | E | R |
|---|---|---|---|---|
| 1939 | 24 May | Bucharest | 2 | 0 |
| 1968 | 6 Nov | Bucharest | 0 | 0 |
| 1969 | 15 Jan | Wembley | 1 | 1 |
| wc1970 | 2 June | Guadalajara | 1 | 0 |
| wc1980 | 15 Oct | Bucharest | 1 | 2 |
| wc1981 | 29 April | Wembley | 0 | 0 |

### v SPAIN

| | | | E | S |
|---|---|---|---|---|
| 1929 | 15 May | Madrid | 3 | 4 |
| 1931 | 9 Dec | Highbury | 7 | 1 |
| wc1950 | 2 July | Rio de Janeiro | 0 | 1 |
| 1955 | 18 May | Madrid | 1 | 1 |
| 1955 | 30 Nov | Wembley | 4 | 1 |
| 1960 | 15 May | Madrid | 0 | 3 |
| 1960 | 26 Oct | Wembley | 4 | 2 |
| 1965 | 8 Dec | Madrid | 2 | 0 |
| 1967 | 24 May | Wembley | 2 | 0 |
| EC1968 | 3 Apr | Wembley | 1 | 0 |
| EC1968 | 8 May | Madrid | 2 | 1 |
| 1980 | 26 Mar | Barcelona | 2 | 0 |
| EC1980 | 18 June | Naples | 2 | 1 |
| 1981 | 25 Mar | Wembley | 1 | 2 |
| wc1982 | 5 July | Madrid | 0 | 0 |

### v SWEDEN

| | | | E | S |
|---|---|---|---|---|
| 1923 | 21 May | Stockholm | 4 | 2 |
| 1923 | 24 May | Stockholm | 3 | 1 |
| 1937 | 17 May | Stockholm | 4 | 0 |
| 1947 | 19 Nov | Highbury | 4 | 2 |
| 1949 | 13 May | Stockholm | 1 | 3 |
| 1956 | 16 May | Stockholm | 0 | 0 |
| 1959 | 28 Oct | Wembley | 2 | 3 |
| 1965 | 16 May | Gothenburg | 2 | 1 |
| 1968 | 22 May | Wembley | 3 | 1 |
| 1979 | 10 June | Stockholm | 0 | 0 |

### v SWITZERLAND

| | | | E | S |
|---|---|---|---|---|
| 1933 | 20 May | Berne | 4 | 0 |
| 1938 | 21 May | Zurich | 1 | 2 |
| 1947 | 18 May | Zurich | 0 | 1 |
| 1948 | 2 Dec | Highbury | 6 | 0 |
| 1952 | 28 May | Zurich | 3 | 0 |
| wc1954 | 20 June | Berne | 2 | 0 |
| 1962 | 9 May | Wembley | 3 | 1 |
| 1963 | 5 June | Basle | 8 | 1 |
| EC1971 | 13 Oct | Basle | 3 | 2 |
| EC1971 | 10 Nov | Wembley | 1 | 1 |

| 1975 | 3 Sept | Basle | 2 | 1 |
|------|--------|-------|---|---|
| 1977 | 7 Sept | Wembley | 0 | 0 |
| wc1980 | 19 Nov | Wembley | 2 | 1 |
| wc1981 | 30 May | Basle | 1 | 2 |

### v USA

| | | | E | USA |
|------|--------|-------|---|-----|
| wc1950 | 29 June | Belo Horizonte | 0 | 1 |
| 1953 | 8 June | New York | 6 | 3 |
| 1959 | 28 May | Los Angeles | 8 | 1 |
| 1964 | 27 May | New York | 10 | 0 |

### v URUGUAY

| | | | E | U |
|------|--------|-------|---|---|
| 1953 | 31 May | Montevideo | 1 | 2 |
| wc1954 | 26 June | Basle | 2 | 4 |
| 1964 | 6 May | Wembley | 2 | 1 |
| wc1966 | 11 July | Wembley | 0 | 0 |
| 1969 | 8 June | Montevideo | 2 | 1 |
| 1977 | 15 June | Montevideo | 0 | 0 |

### v USSR

| | | | E | USSR |
|------|--------|-------|---|------|
| 1958 | 18 May | Moscow | 1 | 1 |
| wc1958 | 8 June | Gothenburg | 2 | 2 |
| wc1958 | 17 June | Gothenburg | 0 | 1 |
| 1958 | 22 Oct | Wembley | 5 | 0 |
| 1967 | 6 Dec | Wembley | 2 | 2 |
| EC1968 | 8 June | Rome | 2 | 0 |
| 1973 | 10 June | Moscow | 2 | 1 |

### v YUGOSLAVIA

| | | | E | Y |
|------|--------|-------|---|---|
| 1939 | 18 May | Belgrade | 1 | 2 |
| 1950 | 22 Nov | Highbury | 2 | 2 |
| 1954 | 16 May | Belgrade | 0 | 1 |
| 1956 | 28 Nov | Wembley | 3 | 0 |
| 1958 | 11 May | Belgrade | 0 | 5 |
| 1960 | 11 May | Wembley | 3 | 3 |
| 1965 | 9 May | Belgrade | 1 | 1 |
| 1966 | 4 May | Wembley | 2 | 0 |
| EC1968 | 5 June | Florence | 0 | 1 |
| 1972 | 11 Oct | Wembley | 1 | 1 |
| 1974 | 5 June | Belgrade | 2 | 2 |

## SCOTLAND

### v ARGENTINA

| | | | S | A |
|------|--------|-------|---|---|
| 1977 | 18 June | Buenos Aires | 1 | 1 |
| 1979 | 2 June | Glasgow | 1 | 3 |

### v AUSTRIA

| | | | S | A |
|------|--------|-------|---|---|
| 1931 | 16 May | Vienna | 0 | 5 |
| 1933 | 29 Nov | Glasgow | 2 | 2 |
| 1937 | 9 May | Vienna | 1 | 1 |
| 1950 | 13 Dec | Glasgow | 0 | 1 |
| 1951 | 27 May | Vienna | 0 | 4 |
| wc1954 | 16 June | Zurich | 0 | 1 |
| 1955 | 19 May | Vienna | 4 | 1 |
| 1956 | 2 May | Glasgow | 1 | 1 |
| 1960 | 29 May | Vienna | 1 | 4 |
| 1963 | 8 May | Glasgow | 4 | 1 |

*(abandoned after 79 mins)*

| wc1968 | 6 Nov | Glasgow | 2 | 1 |
|------|--------|-------|---|---|
| wc1969 | 5 Nov | Vienna | 0 | 2 |
| EC1978 | 20 Sept | Vienna | 2 | 3 |
| EC1979 | 17 Oct | Glasgow | 1 | 1 |

### v BELGIUM

| | | | S | B |
|------|--------|-------|---|---|
| 1947 | 18 May | Brussels | 1 | 2 |
| 1948 | 28 Apr | Glasgow | 2 | 0 |
| 1951 | 20 May | Brussels | 5 | 0 |
| EC1971 | 3 Feb | Liège | 0 | 3 |
| EC1971 | 10 Nov | Aberdeen | 1 | 0 |
| 1974 | 2 June | Brussels | 1 | 2 |
| EC1979 | 21 Nov | Brussels | 0 | 2 |
| EC1979 | 19 Dec | Glasgow | 1 | 3 |

### v BRAZIL

| | | | S | B |
|------|--------|-------|---|---|
| 1966 | 25 June | Glasgow | 1 | 1 |
| 1972 | 5 July | Rio de Janeiro | 0 | 1 |
| 1973 | 30 June | Glasgow | 0 | 1 |
| wc1974 | 18 June | Frankfurt | 0 | 0 |
| 1977 | 23 June | Rio de Janeiro | 0 | 2 |
| wc1982 | 18 June | Seville | 1 | 4 |

### v BULGARIA

| | | | S | B |
|------|--------|-------|---|---|
| 1978 | 22 Feb | Glasgow | 2 | 1 |

### v CHILE

| | | | S | C |
|------|--------|-------|---|---|
| 1977 | 15 June | Santiago | 4 | 2 |

### v CYPRUS

| | | | S | C |
|------|--------|-------|---|---|
| wc1968 | 17 Dec | Nicosia | 5 | 0 |
| wc1969 | 11 May | Glasgow | 8 | 0 |

### v CZECHOSLOVAKIA

| | | | S | C |
|------|--------|-------|---|---|
| 1937 | 22 May | Prague | 3 | 1 |
| 1937 | 8 Dec | Glasgow | 5 | 0 |
| wc1961 | 14 May | Bratislava | 0 | 4 |
| wc1961 | 26 Sept | Glasgow | 3 | 2 |
| wc1961 | 29 Nov | Brussels | 2 | 4* |
| 1972 | 2 July | Porto Alegre | 0 | 0 |
| wc1973 | 26 Sept | Glasgow | 2 | 1 |
| wc1973 | 17 Oct | Prague | 0 | 1 |
| wc1976 | 13 Oct | Prague | 0 | 2 |
| wc1977 | 21 Sept | Glasgow | 3 | 1 |

*After extra time.*

### v DENMARK

| | | | S | D |
|------|--------|-------|---|---|
| 1951 | 12 May | Glasgow | 3 | 1 |
| 1952 | 25 May | Copenhagen | 2 | 1 |
| 1968 | 16 Oct | Copenhagen | 1 | 0 |
| EC1970 | 11 Nov | Glasgow | 1 | 0 |
| EC1971 | 9 June | Copenhagen | 0 | 1 |
| wc1972 | 18 Oct | Copenhagen | 4 | 1 |
| wc1972 | 15 Nov | Glasgow | 2 | 0 |
| EC1975 | 3 Sept | Copenhagen | 1 | 0 |
| EC1975 | 29 Oct | Glasgow | 3 | 1 |

### v FINLAND

| | | | S | F |
|------|--------|-------|---|---|
| 1954 | 25 May | Helsinki | 2 | 1 |
| wc1964 | 21 Oct | Glasgow | 3 | 1 |
| wc1965 | 27 May | Helsinki | 2 | 1 |
| 1976 | 8 Sept | Glasgow | 6 | 0 |

### v FRANCE

| | | | S | F |
|------|--------|-------|---|---|
| 1930 | 18 May | Paris | 2 | 0 |
| 1932 | 8 May | Paris | 3 | 1 |
| 1948 | 23 May | Paris | 0 | 3 |
| 1949 | 27 Apr | Glasgow | 2 | 0 |
| 1950 | 27 May | Paris | 1 | 0 |
| 1951 | 16 May | Glasgow | 1 | 0 |
| wc1958 | 15 June | Orebro | 1 | 2 |

### v GERMANY

| | | | S | G |
|------|--------|-------|---|---|
| 1929 | 1 June | Berlin | 1 | 1 |
| 1936 | 14 Oct | Glasgow | 2 | 0 |

### v EAST GERMANY

| | | | S | EG |
|------|--------|-------|---|----|
| 1974 | 30 Oct | Glasgow | 3 | 0 |
| 1977 | 7 Sept | East Berlin | 0 | 1 |

### v WEST GERMANY

|  |  |  | S | WG |
|---|---|---|---|---|
| 1957 | 22 May | Stuttgart | 3 | 1 |
| 1959 | 6 May | Glasgow | 3 | 2 |
| 1964 | 12 May | Hanover | 2 | 2 |
| wc1969 | 16 Apr | Glasgow | 1 | 1 |
| wc1969 | 22 Oct | Hamburg | 2 | 3 |
| 1973 | 14 Nov | Glasgow | 1 | 1 |
| 1974 | 27 Mar | Frankfurt | 1 | 2 |

### v HUNGARY

|  |  |  | S | H |
|---|---|---|---|---|
| 1938 | 7 Dec | Glasgow | 3 | 1 |
| 1954 | 8 Dec | Glasgow | 2 | 4 |
| 1955 | 29 May | Budapest | 1 | 3 |
| 1958 | 7 May | Glasgow | 1 | 1 |
| 1960 | 5 June | Budapest | 3 | 3 |
| 1980 | 31 May | Budapest | 1 | 3 |

### v IRAN

|  |  |  | S | I |
|---|---|---|---|---|
| wc1978 | 7 June | Cordoba | 1 | 1 |

### v REPUBLIC OF IRELAND

|  |  |  | S | RI |
|---|---|---|---|---|
| wc1961 | 3 May | Glasgow | 4 | 1 |
| wc1961 | 7 May | Dublin | 3 | 0 |
| 1963 | 9 June | Dublin | 0 | 1 |
| 1969 | 21 Sept | Dublin | 1 | 1 |

### v ISRAEL

|  |  |  | S | I |
|---|---|---|---|---|
| wc1981 | 25 Feb | Tel Aviv | 1 | 0 |
| wc1981 | 28 Apr | Glasgow | 3 | 1 |

### v ITALY

|  |  |  | S | I |
|---|---|---|---|---|
| 1931 | 20 May | Rome | 0 | 3 |
| wc1965 | 9 Nov | Glasgow | 1 | 0 |
| wc1965 | 7 Dec | Naples | 0 | 3 |

### v LUXEMBOURG

|  |  |  | S | L |
|---|---|---|---|---|
| 1947 | 24 May | Luxembourg | 6 | 0 |

### v NETHERLANDS

|  |  |  | S | N |
|---|---|---|---|---|
| 1929 | 4 June | Amsterdam | 2 | 0 |
| 1938 | 21 May | Amsterdam | 3 | 1 |
| 1959 | 27 May | Amsterdam | 2 | 1 |
| 1966 | 11 May | Glasgow | 0 | 3 |
| 1968 | 30 May | Amsterdam | 0 | 0 |
| 1971 | 1 Dec | Rotterdam | 1 | 2 |
| wc1978 | 11 June | Mendoza | 3 | 2 |
| 1982 | 23 Mar | Glasgow | 2 | 1 |

### v NEW ZEALAND

|  |  |  | S | NZ |
|---|---|---|---|---|
| wc1982 | 15 June | Malaga | 5 | 2 |

### v NORWAY

|  |  |  | S | N |
|---|---|---|---|---|
| 1929 | 28 May | Oslo | 7 | 3 |
| 1954 | 5 May | Glasgow | 1 | 0 |
| 1954 | 19 May | Oslo | 1 | 1 |
| 1963 | 4 June | Bergen | 3 | 4 |
| 1963 | 7 Nov | Glasgow | 6 | 1 |
| 1974 | 6 June | Oslo | 2 | 1 |
| EC1978 | 25 Oct | Glasgow | 3 | 2 |
| EC1979 | 7 June | Oslo | 4 | 0 |

### v PARAGUAY

|  |  |  | S | P |
|---|---|---|---|---|
| wc1958 | 11 June | Norrkoping | 2 | 3 |

### v PERU

|  |  |  | S | P |
|---|---|---|---|---|
| 1972 | 26 Apr | Glasgow | 2 | 0 |
| wc1978 | 3 June | Cordoba | 1 | 3 |
| 1979 | 12 Sept | Glasgow | 1 | 1 |

### v POLAND

|  |  |  | S | P |
|---|---|---|---|---|
| 1958 | 1 June | Warsaw | 2 | 1 |
| 1960 | 4 May | Glasgow | 2 | 3 |
| wc1965 | 23 May | Chorzow | 1 | 1 |
| wc1965 | 13 Oct | Glasgow | 1 | 2 |
| 1980 | 28 May | Poznan | 0 | 1 |

### v PORTUGAL

|  |  |  | S | P |
|---|---|---|---|---|
| 1950 | 21 May | Lisbon | 2 | 2 |
| 1955 | 4 May | Glasgow | 3 | 0 |
| 1959 | 3 June | Lisbon | 0 | 1 |
| 1966 | 18 June | Glasgow | 0 | 1 |
| EC1971 | 21 Apr | Lisbon | 0 | 2 |
| EC1971 | 13 Oct | Glasgow | 2 | 1 |
| 1975 | 13 May | Glasgow | 1 | 0 |
| EC1978 | 29 Nov | Lisbon | 0 | 1 |
| EC1980 | 26 Mar | Glasgow | 4 | 1 |
| wc1980 | 15 Oct | Glasgow | 0 | 0 |
| wc1981 | 18 Nov | Lisbon | 1 | 2 |

### v RUMANIA

|  |  |  | S | R |
|---|---|---|---|---|
| EC1975 | 1 June | Bucharest | 1 | 1 |
| EC1975 | 17 Dec | Glasgow | 1 | 1 |

### v SPAIN

|  |  |  | S | Sp |
|---|---|---|---|---|
| wc1957 | 8 May | Glasgow | 4 | 2 |
| wc1957 | 26 May | Madrid | 1 | 4 |
| 1963 | 13 June | Madrid | 6 | 2 |
| 1965 | 8 May | Glasgow | 0 | 0 |
| EC1974 | 20 Nov | Glasgow | 1 | 2 |
| EC1975 | 5 Feb | Valencia | 1 | 1 |
| 1982 | 24 Feb | Valencia | 0 | 3 |

### v SWEDEN

|  |  |  | S | Sw |
|---|---|---|---|---|
| 1952 | 30 May | Stockholm | 1 | 3 |
| 1953 | 6 May | Glasgow | 1 | 2 |
| 1975 | 16 Apr | Gothenburg | 1 | 1 |
| 1977 | 27 Apr | Glasgow | 3 | 1 |
| wc1980 | 10 Sept | Stockholm | 1 | 0 |
| wc1981 | 9 Sept | Glasgow | 2 | 0 |

### v SWITZERLAND

|  |  |  | S | Sw |
|---|---|---|---|---|
| 1931 | 24 May | Geneva | 3 | 2 |
| 1948 | 17 May | Berne | 1 | 2 |
| 1950 | 26 Apr | Glasgow | 3 | 1 |
| wc1957 | 19 May | Basle | 2 | 1 |
| wc1957 | 6 Nov | Glasgow | 3 | 2 |
| 1973 | 22 June | Berne | 0 | 1 |
| 1976 | 7 Apr | Glasgow | 1 | 0 |

### v TURKEY

|  |  |  | S | T |
|---|---|---|---|---|
| 1960 | 8 June | Ankara | 2 | 4 |

### v URUGUAY

|  |  |  | S | U |
|---|---|---|---|---|
| wc1954 | 19 June | Basle | 0 | 7 |
| 1962 | 2 May | Glasgow | 2 | 3 |

### v USA

|  |  |  | S | USA |
|---|---|---|---|---|
| 1952 | 30 Apr | Glasgow | 6 | 0 |

### v USSR

|  |  |  | S | USSR |
|---|---|---|---|---|
| 1967 | 10 May | Glasgow | 0 | 2 |
| 1971 | 14 June | Moscow | 0 | 1 |
| wc1982 | 22 June | Malaga | 2 | 2 |

### v YUGOSLAVIA

|  |  |  | S | Y |
|---|---|---|---|---|
| 1955 | 15 May | Belgrade | 2 | 2 |
| 1956 | 21 Nov | Glasgow | 2 | 0 |
| wc1958 | 8 June | Vasteras | 1 | 1 |
| 1972 | 29 June | Belo Horizonte | 2 | 1 |
| wc1974 | 22 June | Frankfurt | 1 | 1 |

### v ZAIRE

|  |  |  | S | Z |
|---|---|---|---|---|
| wc1974 | 14 June | Dortmund | 2 | 0 |

# WALES

<table>
<tr><td colspan="5">v AUSTRIA</td></tr>
<tr><td></td><td></td><td></td><td>W</td><td>A</td></tr>
<tr><td>1954</td><td>9 May</td><td>Vienna</td><td>0</td><td>2</td></tr>
<tr><td>EC1955</td><td>23 Nov</td><td>Wrexham</td><td>1</td><td>2</td></tr>
<tr><td>EC1974</td><td>4 Sept</td><td>Vienna</td><td>1</td><td>2</td></tr>
<tr><td>1975</td><td>19 Nov</td><td>Wrexham</td><td>1</td><td>0</td></tr>
<tr><td colspan="5">v BELGIUM</td></tr>
<tr><td></td><td></td><td></td><td>W</td><td>B</td></tr>
<tr><td>1949</td><td>22 May</td><td>Liège</td><td>1</td><td>3</td></tr>
<tr><td>1949</td><td>23 Nov</td><td>Cardiff</td><td>5</td><td>1</td></tr>
<tr><td colspan="5">v BRAZIL</td></tr>
<tr><td></td><td></td><td></td><td>W</td><td>B</td></tr>
<tr><td>wc1958</td><td>19 June</td><td>Gothenburg</td><td>0</td><td>1</td></tr>
<tr><td>1962</td><td>12 May</td><td>Rio de Janeiro</td><td>1</td><td>3</td></tr>
<tr><td>1962</td><td>16 May</td><td>São Paulo</td><td>1</td><td>3</td></tr>
<tr><td>1966</td><td>14 May</td><td>Rio de Janeiro</td><td>1</td><td>3</td></tr>
<tr><td>1966</td><td>18 May</td><td>Belo Horizonte</td><td>0</td><td>1</td></tr>
<tr><td colspan="5">v CHILE</td></tr>
<tr><td></td><td></td><td></td><td>W</td><td>C</td></tr>
<tr><td>1966</td><td>22 May</td><td>Santiago</td><td>0</td><td>2</td></tr>
<tr><td colspan="5">v CZECHOSLOVAKIA</td></tr>
<tr><td></td><td></td><td></td><td>W</td><td>C</td></tr>
<tr><td>wc1957</td><td>1 May</td><td>Cardiff</td><td>1</td><td>0</td></tr>
<tr><td>wc1957</td><td>26 May</td><td>Prague</td><td>0</td><td>2</td></tr>
<tr><td>EC1971</td><td>21 Apr</td><td>Swansea</td><td>1</td><td>3</td></tr>
<tr><td>EC1971</td><td>27 Oct</td><td>Prague</td><td>0</td><td>1</td></tr>
<tr><td>wc1977</td><td>30 Mar</td><td>Wrexham</td><td>3</td><td>0</td></tr>
<tr><td>wc1977</td><td>16 Nov</td><td>Prague</td><td>0</td><td>1</td></tr>
<tr><td>wc1980</td><td>19 Nov</td><td>Cardiff</td><td>1</td><td>0</td></tr>
<tr><td>wc1981</td><td>9 Sept</td><td>Prague</td><td>0</td><td>2</td></tr>
<tr><td colspan="5">v DENMARK</td></tr>
<tr><td></td><td></td><td></td><td>W</td><td>D</td></tr>
<tr><td>wc1964</td><td>21 Oct</td><td>Copenhagen</td><td>0</td><td>1</td></tr>
<tr><td>wc1965</td><td>1 Dec</td><td>Wrexham</td><td>4</td><td>2</td></tr>
<tr><td colspan="5">v FINLAND</td></tr>
<tr><td></td><td></td><td></td><td>W</td><td>F</td></tr>
<tr><td>EC1971</td><td>26 May</td><td>Helsinki</td><td>1</td><td>0</td></tr>
<tr><td>EC1971</td><td>13 Oct</td><td>Swansea</td><td>3</td><td>0</td></tr>
<tr><td colspan="5">v FRANCE</td></tr>
<tr><td></td><td></td><td></td><td>W</td><td>F</td></tr>
<tr><td>1933</td><td>25 May</td><td>Paris</td><td>1</td><td>1</td></tr>
<tr><td>1939</td><td>20 May</td><td>Paris</td><td>1</td><td>2</td></tr>
<tr><td>1953</td><td>14 May</td><td>Paris</td><td>1</td><td>6</td></tr>
<tr><td>1982</td><td>2 June</td><td>Toulouse</td><td>1</td><td>0</td></tr>
<tr><td colspan="5">v EAST GERMANY</td></tr>
<tr><td></td><td></td><td></td><td>W</td><td>EG</td></tr>
<tr><td>wc1957</td><td>19 May</td><td>Leipzig</td><td>1</td><td>2</td></tr>
<tr><td>wc1957</td><td>25 Sept</td><td>Cardiff</td><td>4</td><td>1</td></tr>
<tr><td>wc1969</td><td>16 Apr</td><td>Dresden</td><td>1</td><td>2</td></tr>
<tr><td>wc1969</td><td>22 Oct</td><td>Cardiff</td><td>1</td><td>3</td></tr>
<tr><td colspan="5">v WEST GERMANY</td></tr>
<tr><td></td><td></td><td></td><td>W</td><td>WG</td></tr>
<tr><td>1968</td><td>8 May</td><td>Cardiff</td><td>1</td><td>1</td></tr>
<tr><td>1969</td><td>26 Mar</td><td>Frankfurt</td><td>1</td><td>1</td></tr>
<tr><td>1976</td><td>6 Oct</td><td>Cardiff</td><td>0</td><td>2</td></tr>
<tr><td>1977</td><td>14 Dec</td><td>Dortmund</td><td>1</td><td>1</td></tr>
<tr><td>EC1979</td><td>2 May</td><td>Wrexham</td><td>0</td><td>2</td></tr>
<tr><td>EC1979</td><td>17 Oct</td><td>Cologne</td><td>1</td><td>5</td></tr>
<tr><td colspan="5">v GREECE</td></tr>
<tr><td></td><td></td><td></td><td>W</td><td>G</td></tr>
<tr><td>wc1964</td><td>9 Dec</td><td>Athens</td><td>0</td><td>2</td></tr>
<tr><td>wc1965</td><td>17 Mar</td><td>Cardiff</td><td>4</td><td>1</td></tr>
<tr><td colspan="5">v HUNGARY</td></tr>
<tr><td></td><td></td><td></td><td>W</td><td>H</td></tr>
<tr><td>wc1958</td><td>8 June</td><td>Sanviken</td><td>1</td><td>1</td></tr>
<tr><td>wc1958</td><td>17 June</td><td>Stockholm</td><td>2</td><td>1</td></tr>
<tr><td>1961</td><td>28 May</td><td>Budapest</td><td>2</td><td>3</td></tr>
<tr><td>EC1962</td><td>7 Nov</td><td>Budapest</td><td>1</td><td>3</td></tr>
</table>

<table>
<tr><td>EC1963</td><td>20 Mar</td><td>Cardiff</td><td>1</td><td>1</td></tr>
<tr><td>EC1974</td><td>30 Oct</td><td>Cardiff</td><td>2</td><td>0</td></tr>
<tr><td>EC1975</td><td>16 Apr</td><td>Budapest</td><td>2</td><td>1</td></tr>
<tr><td colspan="5">v ICELAND</td></tr>
<tr><td></td><td></td><td></td><td>W</td><td>I</td></tr>
<tr><td>wc1980</td><td>2 June</td><td>Reykjavik</td><td>4</td><td>0</td></tr>
<tr><td>wc1981</td><td>14 Oct</td><td>Swansea</td><td>2</td><td>2</td></tr>
<tr><td colspan="5">v IRAN</td></tr>
<tr><td></td><td></td><td></td><td>W</td><td>I</td></tr>
<tr><td>1978</td><td>18 Apr</td><td>Teheran</td><td>1</td><td>0</td></tr>
<tr><td colspan="5">v REPUBLIC OF IRELAND</td></tr>
<tr><td></td><td></td><td></td><td>W</td><td>RI</td></tr>
<tr><td>1960</td><td>28 Sept</td><td>Dublin</td><td>3</td><td>2</td></tr>
<tr><td>1979</td><td>11 Sept</td><td>Swansea</td><td>2</td><td>1</td></tr>
<tr><td>1981</td><td>24 Feb</td><td>Dublin</td><td>3</td><td>1</td></tr>
<tr><td colspan="5">v ISRAEL</td></tr>
<tr><td></td><td></td><td></td><td>W</td><td>I</td></tr>
<tr><td>wc1958</td><td>15 Jan</td><td>Tel Aviv</td><td>2</td><td>0</td></tr>
<tr><td>wc1958</td><td>5 Feb</td><td>Cardiff</td><td>2</td><td>0</td></tr>
<tr><td colspan="5">v ITALY</td></tr>
<tr><td></td><td></td><td></td><td>W</td><td>I</td></tr>
<tr><td>1965</td><td>1 May</td><td>Florence</td><td>1</td><td>4</td></tr>
<tr><td>wc1968</td><td>23 Oct</td><td>Cardiff</td><td>0</td><td>1</td></tr>
<tr><td>wc1969</td><td>4 Nov</td><td>Rome</td><td>1</td><td>4</td></tr>
<tr><td colspan="5">v KUWAIT</td></tr>
<tr><td></td><td></td><td></td><td>W</td><td>K</td></tr>
<tr><td>1977</td><td>6 Sept</td><td>Wrexham</td><td>0</td><td>0</td></tr>
<tr><td>1977</td><td>20 Sept</td><td>Kuwait</td><td>0</td><td>0</td></tr>
<tr><td colspan="5">v LUXEMBOURG</td></tr>
<tr><td></td><td></td><td></td><td>W</td><td>L</td></tr>
<tr><td>EC1974</td><td>20 Nov</td><td>Swansea</td><td>5</td><td>0</td></tr>
<tr><td>EC1975</td><td>1 May</td><td>Luxembourg</td><td>3</td><td>1</td></tr>
<tr><td colspan="5">v MALTA</td></tr>
<tr><td></td><td></td><td></td><td>W</td><td>M</td></tr>
<tr><td>EC1978</td><td>25 Oct</td><td>Wrexham</td><td>7</td><td>0</td></tr>
<tr><td>EC1979</td><td>2 June</td><td>Valletta</td><td>2</td><td>0</td></tr>
<tr><td colspan="5">v MEXICO</td></tr>
<tr><td></td><td></td><td></td><td>W</td><td>M</td></tr>
<tr><td>wc1958</td><td>11 June</td><td>Stockholm</td><td>1</td><td>1</td></tr>
<tr><td>1962</td><td>22 May</td><td>Mexico City</td><td>1</td><td>2</td></tr>
<tr><td colspan="5">v POLAND</td></tr>
<tr><td></td><td></td><td></td><td>W</td><td>P</td></tr>
<tr><td>wc1973</td><td>28 Mar</td><td>Cardiff</td><td>2</td><td>0</td></tr>
<tr><td>wc1973</td><td>26 Sept</td><td>Katowice</td><td>0</td><td>3</td></tr>
<tr><td colspan="5">v PORTUGAL</td></tr>
<tr><td></td><td></td><td></td><td>W</td><td>P</td></tr>
<tr><td>1949</td><td>15 May</td><td>Lisbon</td><td>2</td><td>3</td></tr>
<tr><td>1951</td><td>12 May</td><td>Cardiff</td><td>2</td><td>1</td></tr>
<tr><td colspan="5">v RUMANIA</td></tr>
<tr><td></td><td></td><td></td><td>W</td><td>R</td></tr>
<tr><td>EC1970</td><td>11 Nov</td><td>Cardiff</td><td>0</td><td>0</td></tr>
<tr><td>EC1971</td><td>24 Nov</td><td>Bucharest</td><td>0</td><td>2</td></tr>
<tr><td colspan="5">v SPAIN</td></tr>
<tr><td></td><td></td><td></td><td>W</td><td>S</td></tr>
<tr><td>wc1961</td><td>19 Apr</td><td>Cardiff</td><td>1</td><td>2</td></tr>
<tr><td>wc1961</td><td>18 May</td><td>Madrid</td><td>1</td><td>1</td></tr>
<tr><td>1982</td><td>24 Mar</td><td>Valencia</td><td>1</td><td>1</td></tr>
<tr><td colspan="5">v SWEDEN</td></tr>
<tr><td></td><td></td><td></td><td>W</td><td>S</td></tr>
<tr><td>wc1958</td><td>15 June</td><td>Stockholm</td><td>0</td><td>0</td></tr>
</table>

### v SWITZERLAND

| | | | W | S |
|---|---|---|---|---|
| 1949 | 26 May | Berne | 0 | 4 |
| 1951 | 16 May | Wrexham | 3 | 2 |

### v TURKEY

| | | | W | T |
|---|---|---|---|---|
| EC1978 | 29 Nov | Wrexham | 1 | 0 |
| EC1979 | 21 Nov | Izmir | 0 | 1 |
| wc1980 | 15 Oct | Cardiff | 4 | 0 |
| wc1981 | 25 Mar | Ankara | 1 | 0 |

### v REST OF UNITED KINGDOM

| | | | W | UK |
|---|---|---|---|---|
| 1951 | 5 Dec | Cardiff | 3 | 2 |
| 1969 | 28 July | Cardiff | 0 | 1 |

### v USSR

| | | | W | USSR |
|---|---|---|---|---|
| wc1965 | 30 May | Moscow | 1 | 2 |
| wc1965 | 27 Oct | Cardiff | 2 | 1 |
| wc1981 | 30 May | Wrexham | 0 | 0 |
| wc1981 | 18 Nov | Tbilisi | 0 | 3 |

### v YUGOSLAVIA

| | | | W | Y |
|---|---|---|---|---|
| 1953 | 21 May | Belgrade | 2 | 5 |
| 1954 | 22 Nov | Cardiff | 1 | 3 |
| EC1976 | 24 Apr | Zagreb | 0 | 2 |
| EC1976 | 22 May | Cardiff | 1 | 1 |

# NORTHERN IRELAND

### v ALBANIA

| | | | NI | A |
|---|---|---|---|---|
| wc1965 | 7 May | Belfast | 4 | 1 |
| wc1965 | 24 Nov | Tirana | 1 | 1 |

### v ARGENTINA

| | | | NI | A |
|---|---|---|---|---|
| wc1958 | 11 June | Halmstad | 1 | 3 |

### v AUSTRIA

| | | | NI | A |
|---|---|---|---|---|
| wc1982 | 1 July | Madrid | 2 | 2 |

### v AUSTRALIA

| | | | NI | A |
|---|---|---|---|---|
| 1980 | 11 June | Sydney | 2 | 1 |
| 1980 | 15 June | Melbourne | 1 | 1 |
| 1980 | 18 June | Adelaide | 2 | 1 |

### v BELGIUM

| | | | NI | B |
|---|---|---|---|---|
| wc1976 | 10 Nov | Liège | 0 | 2 |
| wc1977 | 16 Nov | Belfast | 3 | 0 |

### v BULGARIA

| | | | NI | B |
|---|---|---|---|---|
| wc1972 | 18 Oct | Sofia | 0 | 3 |
| wc1973 | 26 Sept | Sheffield | 0 | 0 |
| EC1978 | 29 Nov | Sofia | 2 | 0 |
| EC1979 | 2 May | Belfast | 2 | 0 |

### v CYPRUS

| | | | NI | C |
|---|---|---|---|---|
| EC1971 | 3 Feb | Nicosia | 3 | 0 |
| EC1971 | 21 Apr | Belfast | 5 | 0 |
| wc1973 | 14 Feb | Nicosia | 0 | 1 |
| wc1973 | 8 May | London | 3 | 0 |

### v CZECHOSLOVAKIA

| | | | NI | C |
|---|---|---|---|---|
| wc1958 | 8 June | Halmstad | 1 | 0 |
| wc1958 | 17 June | Malmo | 2 | 1* |

*After extra time

### v DENMARK

| | | | NI | D |
|---|---|---|---|---|
| EC1978 | 25 Oct | Belfast | 2 | 1 |
| EC1979 | 6 June | Copenhagen | 0 | 4 |

### v FRANCE

| | | | NI | F |
|---|---|---|---|---|
| 1951 | 12 May | Belfast | 2 | 2 |
| 1952 | 11 Nov | Paris | 1 | 3 |
| wc1958 | 19 June | Norrkoping | 0 | 4 |
| 1982 | 24 Mar | Paris | 0 | 4 |
| wc1982 | 4 July | Madrid | 1 | 4 |

### v WEST GERMANY

| | | | NI | WG |
|---|---|---|---|---|
| wc1958 | 15 June | Malmo | 2 | 2 |
| wc1960 | 26 Oct | Belfast | 3 | 4 |
| wc1961 | 10 May | Hamburg | 1 | 2 |
| 1966 | 7 May | Belfast | 0 | 2 |
| 1977 | 27 Apr | Cologne | 0 | 5 |

### v GREECE

| | | | NI | G |
|---|---|---|---|---|
| wc1961 | 3 May | Athens | 1 | 2 |
| wc1961 | 17 Oct | Belfast | 2 | 0 |

### v HONDURAS

| | | | NI | H |
|---|---|---|---|---|
| wc1982 | 21 June | Zaragoza | 1 | 1 |

### v ICELAND

| | | | NI | I |
|---|---|---|---|---|
| wc1977 | 11 June | Reykjavik | 0 | 1 |
| wc1977 | 21 Sept | Belfast | 2 | 0 |

### v REPUBLIC OF IRELAND

| | | | NI | RI |
|---|---|---|---|---|
| EC1978 | 20 Sept | Dublin | 0 | 0 |
| EC1979 | 21 Nov | Belfast | 1 | 0 |

### v ISRAEL

| | | | NI | I |
|---|---|---|---|---|
| 1968 | 10 Sept | Jaffa | 3 | 2 |
| 1976 | 3 Mar | Tel Aviv | 1 | 1 |
| wc1980 | 26 Mar | Tel Aviv | 0 | 0 |
| wc1981 | 18 Nov | Belfast | 1 | 0 |

### v ITALY

| | | | NI | I |
|---|---|---|---|---|
| wc1957 | 25 Apr | Rome | 0 | 1 |
| 1957 | 4 Dec | Belfast | 2 | 2 |
| wc1958 | 15 Jan | Belfast | 2 | 1 |
| 1961 | 25 Apr | Bologna | 2 | 3 |

### v MEXICO

| | | | NI | M |
|---|---|---|---|---|
| 1966 | 22 June | Belfast | 4 | 1 |

### v NETHERLANDS

| | | | NI | N |
|---|---|---|---|---|
| 1962 | 9 May | Rotterdam | 0 | 4 |
| wc1965 | 17 Mar | Belfast | 2 | 1 |
| wc1965 | 7 Apr | Rotterdam | 0 | 0 |
| wc1976 | 13 Oct | Rotterdam | 2 | 2 |
| wc1977 | 12 Oct | Belfast | 0 | 1 |

### v NORWAY

| | | | NI | N |
|---|---|---|---|---|
| EC1974 | 4 Sept | Oslo | 1 | 2 |
| EC1975 | 29 Oct | Belfast | 3 | 0 |

## v POLAND

| | | | NI | P |
|---|---|---|---|---|
| EC1962 | 10 Oct | Katowice | 2 | 0 |
| EC1962 | 28 Nov | Belfast | 2 | 0 |

## v PORTUGAL

| | | | NI | P |
|---|---|---|---|---|
| wc1957 | 16 Jan | Lisbon | 1 | 1 |
| wc1957 | 1 May | Belfast | 3 | 0 |
| wc1973 | 28 Mar | Coventry | 1 | 1 |
| wc1973 | 14 Nov | Lisbon | 1 | 1 |
| wc1980 | 19 Nov | Lisbon | 0 | 1 |
| wc1981 | 29 Apr | Belfast | 1 | 0 |

## v SPAIN

| | | | NI | S |
|---|---|---|---|---|
| 1958 | 15 Oct | Madrid | 2 | 6 |
| 1963 | 30 May | Bilbao | 1 | 1 |
| 1963 | 30 Oct | Belfast | 0 | 1 |
| EC1970 | 11 Nov | Seville | 0 | 3 |
| EC1972 | 16 Feb | Hull | 1 | 1 |
| wc1982 | 25 June | Valencia | 1 | 0 |

## v SWEDEN

| | | | NI | S |
|---|---|---|---|---|
| EC1974 | 30 Oct | Solna | 2 | 0 |
| EC1975 | 3 Sept | Belfast | 1 | 2 |
| wc1980 | 15 Oct | Belfast | 3 | 0 |
| wc1981 | 3 June | Solna | 0 | 1 |

## v SWITZERLAND

| | | | NI | S |
|---|---|---|---|---|
| wc1964 | 14 Oct | Belfast | 1 | 0 |
| wc1964 | 14 Nov | Lausanne | 1 | 2 |

## v TURKEY

| | | | NI | T |
|---|---|---|---|---|
| wc1968 | 23 Oct | Belfast | 4 | 1 |
| wc1968 | 11 Dec | Istanbul | 3 | 0 |

## v URUGUAY

| | | | NI | U |
|---|---|---|---|---|
| 1964 | 29 Apr | Belfast | 3 | 0 |

## v USSR

| | | | NI | USSR |
|---|---|---|---|---|
| wc1969 | 10 Sept | Belfast | 0 | 0 |
| wc1969 | 22 Oct | Moscow | 0 | 2 |
| EC1971 | 22 Sept | Moscow | 0 | 1 |
| EC1971 | 13 Oct | Belfast | 1 | 1 |

## v YUGOSLAVIA

| | | | NI | Y |
|---|---|---|---|---|
| EC1975 | 16 Mar | Belfast | 1 | 0 |
| EC1975 | 19 Nov | Belgrade | 0 | 1 |
| wc1982 | 17 June | Zaragoza | 0 | 0 |

# REPUBLIC OF IRELAND

## v ALGERIA

| | | | RI | A |
|---|---|---|---|---|
| 1982 | 28 Apr | Algiers | 0 | 2 |

## v ARGENTINA

| | | | RI | A |
|---|---|---|---|---|
| 1951 | 13 May | Dublin | 0 | 1 |
| 1979 | 29 May | Dublin | 0 | 0 |
| 1980 | 16 May | Dublin | 0 | 1 |

## v AUSTRIA

| | | | RI | A |
|---|---|---|---|---|
| 1952 | 7 May | Vienna | 0 | 6 |
| 1953 | 25 Mar | Dublin | 4 | 0 |
| 1958 | 14 Mar | Vienna | 1 | 3 |
| 1962 | 8 Apr | Dublin | 2 | 3 |
| EC1963 | 25 Sept | Vienna | 0 | 0 |
| EC1963 | 13 Oct | Dublin | 3 | 2 |
| 1966 | 22 May | Vienna | 0 | 1 |
| 1968 | 10 Nov | Dublin | 2 | 2 |
| EC1971 | 30 May | Dublin | 1 | 4 |
| EC1971 | 10 Oct | Linz | 0 | 6 |

## v BELGIUM

| | | | RI | B |
|---|---|---|---|---|
| 1928 | 12 Feb | Liège | 4 | 2 |
| 1929 | 30 Apr | Dublin | 4 | 0 |
| 1930 | 11 May | Brussels | 3 | 1 |
| wc1934 | 25 Feb | Dublin | 4 | 4 |
| 1949 | 24 Apr | Dublin | 0 | 2 |
| 1950 | 10 May | Brussels | 1 | 5 |
| 1965 | 24 Mar | Dublin | 0 | 2 |
| 1966 | 25 May | Liège | 3 | 2 |
| wc1980 | 15 Oct | Dublin | 1 | 1 |
| wc1981 | 25 Mar | Brussels | 0 | 1 |

## v BRAZIL

| | | | RI | B |
|---|---|---|---|---|
| 1974 | 5 May | Rio de Janeiro | 1 | 2 |
| 1982 | 27 May | Uberlandia | 0 | 7 |

## v BULGARIA

| | | | RI | B |
|---|---|---|---|---|
| wc1977 | 1 June | Sofia | 1 | 2 |
| wc1977 | 12 Oct | Dublin | 0 | 0 |
| EC1979 | 19 May | Sofia | 0 | 1 |
| EC1979 | 17 Oct | Dublin | 3 | 0 |

## v CHILE

| | | | RI | C |
|---|---|---|---|---|
| 1960 | 30 Mar | Dublin | 2 | 0 |
| 1972 | 21 June | Recife | 1 | 2 |
| 1974 | 12 May | Santiago | 2 | 1 |
| 1982 | 22 May | Santiago | 0 | 1 |

## v CYPRUS

| | | | RI | C |
|---|---|---|---|---|
| wc1980 | 26 Mar | Nicosia | 3 | 2 |
| wc1980 | 19 Nov | Dublin | 6 | 0 |

## v CZECHOSLOVAKIA

| | | | RI | C |
|---|---|---|---|---|
| 1938 | 18 May | Prague | 2 | 2 |
| EC1959 | 5 Apr | Dublin | 2 | 0 |
| EC1959 | 10 May | Bratislava | 0 | 4 |
| wc1961 | 8 Oct | Dublin | 1 | 3 |
| 1979 | 26 Sept | Prague | 1 | 4 |
| wc1961 | 29 Oct | Prague | 1 | 7 |
| EC1967 | 21 May | Dublin | 0 | 2 |
| EC1967 | 22 Nov | Prague | 2 | 1 |
| wc1969 | 4 May | Dublin | 1 | 2 |
| wc1969 | 7 Oct | Prague | 0 | 3 |
| 1981 | 29 Apr | Dublin | 3 | 1 |

## v DENMARK

| | | | RI | D |
|---|---|---|---|---|
| wc1956 | 3 Oct | Dublin | 2 | 1 |
| wc1957 | 2 Oct | Copenhagen | 2 | 0 |
| wc1968 | 4 Dec | Dublin | 1 | 1 |

*(abandoned after 51 mins)*

| | | | | |
|---|---|---|---|---|
| wc1969 | 27 May | Copenhagen | 0 | 2 |
| wc1969 | 15 Oct | Dublin | 1 | 1 |
| EC1978 | 24 May | Copenhagen | 3 | 3 |
| EC1979 | 2 May | Dublin | 2 | 0 |

## v ECUADOR

| | | | RI | E |
|---|---|---|---|---|
| 1972 | 19 June | Natal | 3 | 2 |

## v FINLAND

| | | | RI | F |
|---|---|---|---|---|
| wc1949 | 8 Sept | Dublin | 3 | 0 |
| wc1949 | 9 Oct | Helsinki | 1 | 1 |

## v FRANCE

| | | | RI | F |
|---|---|---|---|---|
| 1937 | 23 May | Paris | 2 | 0 |
| 1952 | 16 Nov | Dublin | 1 | 1 |
| wc1953 | 4 Oct | Dublin | 3 | 5 |
| wc1953 | 25 Nov | Paris | 0 | 1 |
| wc1972 | 15 Nov | Dublin | 2 | 1 |
| wc1973 | 19 May | Paris | 1 | 1 |
| wc1976 | 17 Nov | Paris | 0 | 2 |
| wc1977 | 30 Mar | Dublin | 1 | 0 |
| wc1980 | 28 Oct | Paris | 0 | 2 |
| wc1981 | 14 Oct | Dublin | 3 | 2 |

## v GERMANY

| | | | RI | G |
|---|---|---|---|---|
| 1935 | 8 May | Dortmund | 1 | 3 |
| 1936 | 17 Oct | Dublin | 5 | 2 |
| 1939 | 23 May | Bremen | 1 | 1 |

## v WEST GERMANY

| | | | RI | WG |
|---|---|---|---|---|
| 1951 | 17 Oct | Dublin | 3 | 2 |
| 1952 | 4 May | Cologne | 0 | 3 |
| 1955 | 28 May | Hamburg | 1 | 2 |
| 1956 | 25 Nov | Dublin | 3 | 0 |
| 1960 | 11 May | Dusseldorf | 1 | 0 |
| 1966 | 4 May | Dublin | 0 | 4 |
| 1970 | 9 May | Berlin | 1 | 2 |
| 1979 | 22 May | Dublin | 1 | 3 |
| 1981 | 21 May | Bremen | 0 | 3† |

†v West Germany 'B'

## v HUNGARY

| | | | RI | H |
|---|---|---|---|---|
| 1934 | 15 Dec | Dublin | 2 | 4 |
| 1936 | 3 May | Budapest | 3 | 3 |
| 1936 | 6 Dec | Dublin | 2 | 3 |
| 1939 | 19 Mar | Cork | 2 | 2 |
| 1939 | 18 May | Budapest | 2 | 2 |
| wc1969 | 8 June | Dublin | 1 | 2 |
| wc1969 | 5 Nov | Budapest | 0 | 4 |

## v ICELAND

| | | | RI | I |
|---|---|---|---|---|
| EC1962 | 12 Aug | Dublin | 4 | 2 |
| EC1962 | 2 Sept | Reykjavik | 1 | 1 |

## v LUXEMBOURG

| | | | RI | L |
|---|---|---|---|---|
| 1936 | 9 May | Luxembourg | 5 | 1 |
| wc1953 | 28 Oct | Dublin | 4 | 0 |
| wc1954 | 7 Mar | Luxembourg | 1 | 0 |

## v IRAN

| | | | RI | I |
|---|---|---|---|---|
| 1972 | 18 June | Recife | 2 | 1 |

## v N IRELAND

| | | | RI | NI |
|---|---|---|---|---|
| EC1978 | 20 Sept | Dublin | 0 | 0 |
| EC1979 | 21 Nov | Belfast | 0 | 1 |

## v ITALY

| | | | RI | I |
|---|---|---|---|---|
| 1926 | 21 Mar | Turin | 0 | 3 |
| 1927 | 23 Apr | Dublin | 1 | 2 |
| EC1970 | 8 Dec | Rome | 0 | 3 |
| EC1971 | 10 May | Dublin | 1 | 2 |

## v NETHERLANDS

| | | | RI | N |
|---|---|---|---|---|
| 1932 | 8 May | Amsterdam | 2 | 0 |
| 1934 | 8 Apr | Amsterdam | 2 | 5 |
| 1935 | 8 Dec | Dublin | 3 | 5 |
| 1955 | 1 May | Dublin | 1 | 0 |
| 1956 | 10 May | Rotterdam | 4 | 1 |
| wc1980 | 10 Sept | Dublin | 2 | 1 |
| wc1981 | 9 Sept | Rotterdam | 2 | 2 |

## v NORWAY

| | | | RI | N |
|---|---|---|---|---|
| wc1937 | 10 Oct | Oslo | 2 | 3 |
| wc1937 | 7 Nov | Dublin | 3 | 3 |
| 1950 | 26 Nov | Dublin | 2 | 2 |
| 1951 | 30 May | Oslo | 3 | 2 |
| 1954 | 8 Nov | Dublin | 2 | 1 |
| 1955 | 25 May | Oslo | 3 | 1 |
| 1960 | 6 Nov | Dublin | 3 | 1 |
| 1964 | 13 May | Oslo | 4 | 1 |
| 1973 | 6 June | Oslo | 1 | 1 |
| 1976 | 24 Mar | Dublin | 3 | 0 |
| 1978 | 21 May | Oslo | 0 | 0 |

## v POLAND

| | | | RI | P |
|---|---|---|---|---|
| 1938 | 22 May | Warsaw | 0 | 6 |
| 1938 | 13 Nov | Dublin | 3 | 2 |
| 1958 | 11 May | Katowice | 2 | 2 |
| 1958 | 5 Oct | Dublin | 2 | 2 |
| 1964 | 10 May | Cracow | 1 | 3 |
| 1964 | 25 Oct | Dublin | 3 | 2 |
| 1968 | 15 May | Dublin | 2 | 2 |
| 1968 | 30 Oct | Katowice | 0 | 1 |
| 1970 | 6 May | Dublin | 1 | 2 |
| 1970 | 23 Sept | Dublin | 0 | 2 |
| 1973 | 16 May | Wroclaw | 0 | 2 |
| 1973 | 21 Oct | Dublin | 1 | 0 |
| 1976 | 26 May | Posnan | 2 | 0 |
| 1977 | 24 Apr | Dublin | 0 | 0 |
| 1978 | 12 Apr | Lodz | 0 | 3 |
| 1981 | 23 May | Bydgoszcz | 0 | 3 |

## v PORTUGAL

| | | | RI | P |
|---|---|---|---|---|
| 1946 | 16 June | Lisbon | 1 | 3 |
| 1947 | 4 May | Dublin | 0 | 2 |
| 1948 | 23 May | Lisbon | 0 | 2 |
| 1949 | 22 May | Dublin | 1 | 0 |
| 1972 | 25 June | Recife | 1 | 2 |

## v SCOTLAND

| | | | RI | S |
|---|---|---|---|---|
| wc1961 | 3 May | Glasgow | 1 | 4 |
| wc1961 | 7 May | Dublin | 0 | 3 |
| 1963 | 9 June | Dublin | 1 | 0 |
| 1969 | 21 Sept | Dublin | 1 | 1 |

## v SPAIN

| | | | RI | S |
|---|---|---|---|---|
| 1931 | 26 Apr | Barcelona | 1 | 1 |
| 1931 | 13 Dec | Dublin | 0 | 5 |
| 1946 | 23 June | Madrid | 1 | 0 |
| 1947 | 2 Mar | Dublin | 3 | 2 |
| 1948 | 30 May | Barcelona | 1 | 2 |
| 1949 | 12 June | Dublin | 1 | 4 |
| 1952 | 1 June | Madrid | 0 | 6 |
| 1955 | 27 Nov | Dublin | 2 | 2 |
| EC1964 | 11 Mar | Seville | 1 | 5 |
| EC1964 | 8 Apr | Dublin | 0 | 2 |
| wc1965 | 5 May | Dublin | 1 | 0 |
| wc1965 | 27 Oct | Seville | 1 | 4 |
| wc1965 | 10 Nov | Paris | 0 | 1 |
| EC1966 | 23 Oct | Dublin | 0 | 0 |
| EC1966 | 7 Dec | Valencia | 0 | 2 |
| 1977 | 9 Feb | Dublin | 0 | 1 |

## v SWEDEN

| | | | RI | S |
|---|---|---|---|---|
| wc1949 | 2 June | Stockholm | 1 | 3 |
| wc1949 | 13 Nov | Dublin | 1 | 3 |
| 1959 | 1 Nov | Dublin | 3 | 2 |
| 1960 | 18 May | Malmo | 1 | 4 |
| EC1970 | 14 Oct | Dublin | 1 | 1 |
| EC1970 | 28 Oct | Malmo | 0 | 1 |

**v SWITZERLAND**

| | | | RI | S |
|---|---|---|---|---|
| 1935 | 5 May | Basle | 0 | 1 |
| 1936 | 17 Mar | Dublin | 1 | 0 |
| 1937 | 17 May | Berne | 1 | 0 |
| 1938 | 18 Sept | Dublin | 4 | 0 |
| 1948 | 5 Dec | Dublin | 0 | 1 |
| EC1975 | 11 May | Dublin | 2 | 1 |
| EC1975 | 21 May | Berne | 0 | 1 |
| 1980 | 30 Apr | Dublin | 2 | 0 |

**v TURKEY**

| | | | RI | T |
|---|---|---|---|---|
| EC1966 | 16 Nov | Dublin | 2 | 1 |
| EC1967 | 22 Feb | Ankara | 1 | 2 |
| EC1974 | 20 Nov | Izmir | 1 | 1 |
| EC1975 | 29 Oct | Dublin | 4 | 0 |
| 1976 | 13 Oct | Ankara | 3 | 3 |
| 1978 | 5 Apr | Dublin | 4 | 2 |

**v TRINIDAD & TOBAGO**

| | | | RI | TT |
|---|---|---|---|---|
| 1982 | 30 May | Port of Spain | 1 | 2 |

**v URUGUAY**

| | | | RI | U |
|---|---|---|---|---|
| 1974 | 8 May | Montevideo | 0 | 2 |

**v USA**

| | | | RI | USA |
|---|---|---|---|---|
| 1979 | 29 Oct | Dublin | 3 | 2 |

**v USSR**

| | | | RI | USSR |
|---|---|---|---|---|
| wc1972 | 18 Oct | Dublin | 1 | 2 |
| wc1973 | 13 May | Moscow | 0 | 1 |
| EC1974 | 30 Oct | Dublin | 3 | 0 |
| EC1975 | 18 May | Kiev | 1 | 2 |

**v WALES**

| | | | RI | W |
|---|---|---|---|---|
| 1960 | 28 Sept | Dublin | 2 | 3 |
| 1979 | 11 Sept | Swansea | 1 | 2 |
| 1981 | 24 Feb | Dublin | 1 | 3 |

**v YUGOSLAVIA**

| | | | RI | Y |
|---|---|---|---|---|
| 1955 | 19 Sept | Dublin | 1 | 4 |

## ENGLAND v YOUNG ENGLAND

| | | | E | YE | | | | | E | YE |
|---|---|---|---|---|---|---|---|---|---|---|
| 1954 | 30 April | Highbury | 2 | 1 | | 1963 | 24 May | Highbury | 3 | 2 |
| 1955 | 6 May | Highbury | 5 | 0 | | 1964 | 1 May | Stamford Bridge | 3 | 0 |
| 1957 | 3 May | Highbury | 1 | 2 | | 1965 | 30 April | Highbury | 2 | 2 |
| 1958 | 2 May | Stamford Bridge | 4 | 1 | | 1966 | 13 May | Stamford Bridge | 1 | 1 |
| 1959 | 1 May | Highbury | 3 | 3 | | 1967 | 19 May | Highbury | 0 | 5 |
| 1960 | 6 May | Highbury | 2 | 1 | | 1968 | 17 May | Highbury | 1 | 4 |
| 1961 | 5 May | Stamford Bridge | 1 | 1 | | 1969 | 25 April | Stamford Bridge | 0 | 0 |
| 1962 | 4 May | Highbury | 3 | 2 | | | | | | |

## FOOTBALL LEAGUE MEETING

At an extraordinary general meeting of the Football League, held on 11 June 1982, the clubs agreed in principle the proposals put forward by the Busby Advisory Committee, and recommended that the FA be asked to put those requiring Law changes to the International Football Association Board.

Although there was no intent expressed to 'go it alone' if FIFA refused permission to experiment, it was agreed that many of the proposals could be implemented by instructing referees on the interpretation of the Laws (as had been done before, for example, in the case of the 'tackle from behind'). Thus 'pinching' ground at a throw-in could be eliminated by treating it as a foul throw (i.e. a ball not thrown in from the point where it crossed the line would be treated as a ball improperly thrown in). And if the proposal suggesting penalty awards against 'professional fouls' were rejected, referees could be instructed to send off the offender, again as provided for in the Laws (presumably for 'serious' foul play).

Other resolutions passed at the meeting included the following:

*Transfer fees* – half to be paid immediately, half within a year.

*Transfers* – ban on buying back a player within a year (to curtail 'temporary' transfers to American clubs for the summer).

*Poaching* – 'gentleman's agreement' on inducing managers or other club employees to break their contract now written into the League rules.

*Loans* – number of players a club can sign on loan during the season increased from two to five, but not more than two at a time.

*Artificial pitches* – may not be installed without the agreement of the League Management Committee and all the clubs (not, however, to affect QPR's three-year trial).

# BRITISH INTERNATIONAL MATCHES 1981–82

**World Cup matches appear on pages 777–793**

**Drammen, 8 Sept, 1981**

### UNDER-21 INTERNATIONAL

**Norway (0) 0**

**England (0) 0**     5200

*Norway:* Hansen; Iversen, Eggen, Kojedal, Roed (Hagen), Steinsholt (Johanssen), Herlovsen, Erlandsen, Soler, Hellevik, Raum (Husby).
*England:* Bailey; Fenwick, Gibson, MacKenzie, Duxbury (Gilbert), Caton, Mills (Moses), Fashanu (Goddard), Thompson (Moran), Heath, Proctor (Owen).

**Easter Road, 8 Sept, 1981**

### UEFA UNDER-21 CHAMPIONSHIP

**Scotland (1) 4** *(Blair, Brazil, MacDonald, Sturrock)*

**Sweden (0) 0**     7000

*Scotland:* Geddes; Nicol, Connor, Blair, McLaughlin, Gillespie, Sturrock, Bett, Nicholas (MacDonald), Brazil (Milne), Redford.
*Sweden:* Ljung; Marko, Hansson, Engvist, Kullberg, Prytz, Stromberg (Kinnvall), Andersson, Nilsson, Trudsson, Palmer (Holmqvist).

**Maceio, 24 Sept, 1981**

**Brazil (2) 6** *(Zico 4, Eder, Roberto)*

**League of Ireland (0) 0**     54,000

*Brazil:* Valdir Peres; Perivaldo (Leandro), Oscar, Edinho, Junior, Cerezo, Renato, Zico, Paulo Isidoro (Robertinho), Roberto, Eder (Mario Sergio).
*League of Ireland:* Blackmore; McConville, Fenink, Nolan, Lawlor, O'Connor, Flanagan, Devlin, Buckley, Fairclough, Eviston (Murray).

**Aarhus, 13 Oct, 1981**

### UEFA UNDER-21 CHAMPIONSHIP

**Denmark (1) 1** *(Eriksen)*

**Scotland (0) 1** *(Blair)*     2000

*Denmark:* Rasmussen; Olczyk, Weber, Molby, Hansen, Helt, Birkedal, Frimann, Brylle, Eriksen, Olsen.
*Scotland:* Geddes; Cooper, Nicol, Gillespie, McLaughlin, Watson (MacDonald), Blair, Bett, McGarvey, Redford, McCluskey.

**Newport, 13 Oct, 1981**

### UNDER-21 INTERNATIONAL

**Wales (0) 2** *(Micallef 2)*

**France (0) 0**     1305

*Wales:* Wilmot; Jones, Boyle, Lewis, Jackett, Pugh, Davies, Marustik, Vaughan, Giles, Micallef.
*France:* Fuffier; Ayache, Dreossi, Zambelli, Marsiglia, Martinez (Marin), Amoros, Henry, Picot (Buscher), Stopyra, Zenier.

**Nottingham, 17 Nov, 1981**

### UEFA UNDER-21 CHAMPIONSHIP

**England (1) 2** *(Thompson, Fashanu)*

**Hungary (0) 0**     8734

*England:* Lukic; Fenwick, McCall, Reid, Gilbert (Caton), Owen, Moses, Fashanu, Thompson, Shaw, Heath.
*Hungary:* Disztl; Kerepeczky, Szucs, Vadasz, Kardos, Komjati, Kiprich (Fecscy), Roth, Poloskei, Rixer, Hajszan (Melis).

**Wembley, 23 Feb, 1982**

### BRITISH INTERNATIONAL CHAMPIONSHIP

**England (1) 4** *(Robson, Keegan, Wilkins, Hoddle)*

**Northern Ireland (0) 0**     54,900

*England:* Clemence; Anderson, Sansom, Wilkins, Watson, Foster, Keegan, Robson, Francis (Regis), Hoddle, Morley (Woodcock).
*Northern Ireland:* Jennings; Nicholl J., Nelson, Donaghy, Nicholl C., O'Neill J., Brotherston (Cochrane), O'Neill M. (McCreery), Armstrong, McIlroy, Hamilton.

**Catanzaro, 23 Feb, 1982**

### UEFA UNDER-21 CHAMPIONSHIP

**Italy (0) 0**

**Scotland (1) 1** *(McAvennie)*

*Italy:* Zinetti; Bergomi, Nela, Baresi, Tassotti, Celestini, Mauro, Battistini, Borghi, Romano, Bivi (Galderisi).
*Scotland:* Leighton; Stewart, Nicol, Simpson, McLaughlin, Gillespie, Bett, McAvennie, McCluskey, Redford, McDonald (Doyle).

**Valencia, 24 Feb, 1982**

**Spain (1) 3** *(Victor, Quini pen, Gallego)*

**Scotland (0) 0**     30,000

*Spain:* Arconada; Camacho, Gordillo, Alonso, Tendillo, Alesanco, Saura, Sanchez, Satrustegui (Quini), Victor (Gallego), Lopez Ufarte.
*Scotland:* Rough; McGrain, Gray F., Strachan (Archibald), McLeish, Hansen, Brazil, Wark, Dalglish, Hartford, Souness.

**Troyes, 24 Feb, 1982**

### UNDER-21 INTERNATIONAL

**France (0) 0**

**Wales (0) 0**     4811

*France:* Ruffier (D'Angelo); Dreossi, Le Roux, Martin, Marsiglia (Puel) (Martinez), Lemoult, Fernandez, Zanon, Anziani (Ferratge), N'Gom, Toure.
*Wales:* Wilmot; Jones (Hopkins), Nicholas, Stevenson N., Ratcliffe, Lewis, Davies, Marustik, Pugh, Rush, Giles (Balcombe).

**Warsaw, 17 March, 1982**

### UEFA UNDER-21 CHAMPIONSHIP

**Poland (0) 1** *(Buda)*

**England (1) 2** *(Goddard, Hodgson)*     4000

*Poland:* Famula; Chojnacki, Geszlecht, Kubicki, Skrobowski, Buda, Matysik, Ciolek, Dziekanowski (Palasz), Iwan, Okonski.
*England:* Hesford; Ranson, Caton, Reid, Mabbutt, McMahon, Gale, Heath, Hodgson, Fashanu, Goddard.

**Hampden Park, 23 March, 1982**

**Scotland (2) 2** *(Gray pen, Dalglish)*

**Netherlands (1) 1** *(Kieft)*     71,848

*Scotland:* Rough; McGrain, Gray F., Narey, Evans, Miller, Dalglish (Brazil), Archibald (Burns T.), Jordan (Strachan), Bett, Wark.
*Netherlands:* Van Breukelen; Spelbos, Krol, Van der Korput, Metgod, Hovenkamp, Rijkaard, Peters, Kieft, Muhren, Tahamata.

**Wrexham, 23 March, 1982**

UNDER-21 INTERNATIONAL

**Wales** (1) 2 *(Davies, Rutten og)*

**Netherlands** (2) 2 *(Koolhof 2)*                   530

*Wales:* Wilmot; Jones, Hopkins, Lewis, Stevenson N.,
Maddy, Davies, Vaughan, Micallef, Loveridge, Giles.
*Netherlands:* Storm; Rutten, Andriessen, Blind, Koeman
R., Steinman, Gaasbeek, Adelaar, Van der Gijp, Koeman
E., Koolhof.

**Bilbao, 23 March, 1982**

**Athletic Bilbao** (0) 1 *(Sarabia)*

**England XI** (1) 1 *(Keegan)*                   40,000

*Athletic Bilbao:* Zubizarreta; Urquiaga, de la Fuente
(Purroy), Liceranzu, Giocoechba, Gallego, Nosiga, Sola
(Merayo), Sarabia, Rojo, Argote.
*England:* Corrigan; Mills, Thompson, Foster, Sansom,
Robson, Brooking, Coppell, Regis (Withe), Keegan, Mor-
ley.

**Paris, 24 March, 1982**

**France** (2) 4 *(Zenier, Couriol, Larios pen, Genghini)*

**Northern Ireland** (0) 0                   34,000

*France:* Castaneda; Amoros (Battiston), Lopez, Tresor,
Bossis, Larios, Genghini, Giresse (Girard), Couriol
(Soler), Bellone, Zenier.
*Northern Ireland:* Platt; Nicholl J., O'Neill J., Nicholl C.,
Donaghy, McCreery (Caskey), O'Neill M., McIlroy
(Spence), Brotherston, Armstrong, Cochrane (Stewart).

**Valencia, 24 March, 1982**

**Spain** (1) 1 *(Satrustegui)*

**Wales** (0) 1 *(James)*                   20,000

*Spain:* Arconada; Camacho, Alesanco, Tendillo, Gor-
dillo, Sanchez, Gallego, Estella, Saura, Satrustegui, Lopez
Ufarte.
*Wales:* Davies D.; Marustik, Jones, Price, Ratcliffe,
Nicholas, James R., Thomas (Giles), Stevenson B., Walsh
(Davies G.), Curtis.

**Aberdeen, 24 March, 1982**

UEFA UNDER-21 CHAMPIONSHIP

**Scotland** (0) 0

**Italy** (0) 0

*Scotland:* Leighton; Stewart, Nicol, Blair (Watson),
Paterson, Gillespie, MacDonald, Simpson, Sturrock, Redford, Hewitt.
*Italy:* Zinetti; Bergomi, Tassotti, Baresi, Pin, Nela (Con-
tratto), Galderisi, Mauro (Bivi), Virdis, Bonini, Massaro.

**Upton Park, 7 April, 1982**

UEFA UNDER-21 CHAMPIONSHIP

**England** (2) 2 *(Hateley 2)*

**Poland** (0) 2 *(Biernat, Baran)*                   6680

*England:* Hesford; Ranson, Mabbutt, Reid, Proctor,
Caton, Peake, Ritchie, Hateley, Bannister (Hilaire),
Davis (Smith).
*Poland:* Stawarz; Kabicki, Geszlecht, Frankowski,
Matysik, Biernat, Turowski, Ciolek, Buda, Palasz, Baran.

**Hampden Park, 19 April, 1982**

UEFA UNDER-21 CHAMPIONSHIP

**Scotland** (0) 0

**England** (1) 1 *(Thompson)*                   16,130

*Scotland:* Geddes; Stewart, Nicol, Cooper, McLaughlin,
Gillespie, McCulloch, Bett, Sturrock, McAvennie, Red-
ford (MacDonald).
*England:* Hesford; Ranson, Fenwick, Reid, Wicks,
Whyte, Mabbutt, MacKenzie, Hateley, Thompson, Davis.

**Ninian Park, 27 April, 1982**

BRITISH INTERNATIONAL CHAMPIONSHIP

**Wales** (0) 0

**England** (0) 1 *(Francis)*                   23,000

*Wales:* Davies; Marustik, Ratcliffe, Nicholas, Stevenson
N., Jones, Curtis, Flynn (Harris), Rush, Thomas (James
L.), James R.
*England:* Corrigan; Neal, Sansom, Thompson, Butcher,
Robson, Wilkins, Francis (Regis), Withe, Hoddle
(McDermott), Morley.

**Gibraltar, 27 April, 1982**

**Gibraltar** (1) 2

**England Semi-Professionals** (0) 3 *(Ashford, Stephens, og)*

*England Semi-Professionals:* Phillips; Barrett, Davison,
Jennings, Waite, Sellers, Stephens, Johnson, Ashford
(Howard), Rogers, Smith.

**Windsor Park, 28 April, 1982**

BRITISH INTERNATIONAL CHAMPIONSHIP

**Northern Ireland** (0) 1 *(McIlroy)*

**Scotland** (1) 1 *(Wark)*                   20,000

*Northern Ireland:* Platt; Donaghy, Nelson, O'Neill J.,
McClelland, Cleary, Brotherston, O'Neill M., Campbell,
McIlroy, Healy.
*Scotland:* Wood; McGrain, Albiston, Wark, McLeish
(Hansen), Evans, Provan, Brazil, Dalglish, Hartford,
Robertson (Sturrock).

**Maine Road, 28 April, 1982**

UEFA UNDER-21 CHAMPIONSHIP

**England** (1) 1 *(Heath)*

**Scotland** (1) 1 *(Sharp)*                   8212

*England:* Hesford; Fenwick, McCall, Reid, Lee, Caton,
Heath (Whyte), MacKenzie, Shaw, Goddard, Fashanu.
*Scotland:* Geddes; Nicol, Reid (MacDonald), Simpson,
McLaughlin, Cooper, McCulloch, Bett, Sharp, Burns T.,
McAvennie (McGarvey).

**Algiers, 28 April, 1982**

**Algeria** (1) 2 *(Assad, Madjer)*

**Eire** (0) 0                   60,000

*Algeria:* Cerbah; Guendouz, Merzekane (Kouici), Kour-
ichi, Medjadi, Mansouri, Maroc, Belloumi (Bensheik),
Tiemcani (Madjer), Assad, Bourebbou (Chebel).
*Eire:* Bonnar; Devine, Moran (Deacy), Martin, Grimes,
Grealish, Waddock, Daly, O'Callaghan K. (Ryan), Sta-
pleton, Robinson (Mickey Walsh [FC Porto]).

**Santiago, 22 May, 1982**

**Chile** (1) 1 *(Gamboa)*

**Eire** (0) 0                   25,000

*Chile:* Osben; Garrido (Galindo), Valenzuela, Figueroa,
Bigorra, Rivas, Dubo, Soto, Yanez, Gamboa (Letelier),
Moscoso.
*Eire:* McDonagh; Deacy, Martin, Anderson, Walsh M.,
Brady, Driscoll (Fairclough), Grealish, Daly, Robinson
(Ryan), O'Callaghan K.

**Hampden Park, 24 May, 1982**

BRITISH INTERNATIONAL CHAMPIONSHIP

Scotland (1) 1 *(Hartford)*

Wales (0) 0                                                      25,284

*Scotland:* Rough; Stewart (Burley), Gray E., Souness, Hansen, Narey, Dalglish, Brazil, Jordan (Sturrock), Burns T., Hartford.

*Wales:* Davies; Marustik, Jones, Nicholas, Stevenson N., Stevenson B., Curtis (Walsh), James R., Rush, Flynn (Thomas), James L.


**Wembley, 25 May, 1982**

England (0) 2 *(Woodcock, Mariner)*

Netherlands (0) 0                                               69,000

*England:* Shilton; Neal, Sansom, Thompson, Foster, Robson, Wilkins, Devonshire (Rix), Mariner (Barnes), McDermott, Woodcock.

*Netherlands:* Van Breukelen; Ophof, Van de Korput, Krol, Metgod (Rijkaard), Boeve, Peters (Van de Kerkhof R.), Muhren, La Ling (Van Kooten), Kieft, Tahamata.


**Wrexham, 27 May, 1982**

BRITISH INTERNATIONAL CHAMPIONSHIP

Wales (1) 3 *(Curtis, Rush, Nicholas)*

Northern Ireland (0) 0                                          2315

*Wales:* Southall; Marustik, Jones, Nicholas, Stevenson N., Stevenson B., Curtis (Walsh), James R., Rush, Flynn, James L. (Thomas).

*Northern Ireland:* Jennings (Platt); Nicholl J., Donaghy, McClelland, Nicholl C., Cleary (Campbell), Brotherston, Healy, Armstrong, McIlroy, Hamilton.


**Uberlandia, 27 May, 1982**

Brazil (1) 7 *(Falcao, Socrates 2, Serginho 2, Luizinho, Zico)*

Eire (0) 0                                                      60,000

*Brazil:* Valdir Peres (Paulo Sergio); Leandro, Oscar, Luizinho, Junior, Falcao, Socrates, Zico, Paulo Isidoro (Cerezo), Careca (Serginho), Eder (Dirceu).

*Eire:* McDonagh; Deacy, Martin, Anderson, Walsh M., Brady, Grealish, O'Driscoll, Daly, O'Callaghan B., O'Callaghan K.


**Hampden Park, 29 May, 1982**

BRITISH INTERNATIONAL CHAMPIONSHIP

Scotland (0) 0

England (1) 1 *(Mariner)*                                       80,529

*Scotland:* Rough; Burley, McGrain, Hansen, Evans, Narey, Dalglish, Souness, Jordan (Sturrock), Hartford (Robertson), Brazil.

*England:* Shilton; Mills, Sansom, Thompson, Butcher, Robson, Keegan (McDermott), Coppell, Mariner (Francis), Brooking, Wilkins.


**Port of Spain, 30 May, 1982**

Trinidad & Tobago (0) 2

Eire (0) 1 *(Brady)*

*Eire:* Peyton; Deacy (O'Callaghan K.), Walsh M., Anderson, Martin, Grealish, Walsh J., O'Callaghan B. (O'Driscoll), Daly, Brady, Ryan (Fairclough).


**Port of Spain, 1 June, 1982**

ASL (0) 1

Eire (0) 3 *(O'Driscoll, O'Callaghan, Ryan)*

*Eire:* Peyton; Deacy, Martin, Anderson, Walsh M., Grealish, Brady (O'Driscoll), O'Callaghan K., Walsh J., Ryan, Daly.


**Reykjavik, 2 June, 1982**

Iceland (1) 1 *(Gudjohnson)*

England (0) 1 *(Goddard)*                                       11,000

*Iceland:* Baldursson; Askarsson, Giersson, Jonsson, Haraldsson, Thordarsson K., Gudjohnson, Gudlaugsson, Edvaldsson, Thordarsson P., Gudmundsson.

*England:* Corrigan; Anderson, Watson, Osman, Neal, McDermott, Hoddle, Devonshire (Perryman), Withe, Regis (Goddard), Morley.


**Toulouse, 2 June, 1982**

France (0) 0

Wales (0) 1 *(Rush)*                                            35,000

*France:* Castaneda; Battiston, Lopez, Tresor (Mahut), Bossis, Larios (Tigana), Giresse, Platini, Couriol, Soler, Six (Bellone).

*Wales:* Davies D.; Marustik, Price, Stevenson B., Jones, Nicholas, James R., Flynn, Walsh (Davies G.), Rush, James L.


**Helsinki, 3 June, 1982**

Finland (0) 1 *(Haaskivi pen)*

England (1) 4 *(Mariner 2, Robson 2)*                           21,421

*Finland:* Alaja (Hurrunen); Lahtinen, Iraelaeinen, Granskog, Pekonen, Turunen (Kymaelainen), Haaskivi, Rautiainen, Himanka, Ismael, Nieminen (Valvee).

*England:* Clemence; Mills, Thompson, Martin, Sansom, Coppell (Francis), Robson (Rix), Wilkins, Brooking (Woodcock), Keegan, Mariner.


## BRITISH INTERNATIONAL CHAMPIONSHIP
### Final Table

|                  | P | W | D | L | F | A | Pts |
|------------------|---|---|---|---|---|---|-----|
| England          | 3 | 3 | 0 | 0 | 6 | 0 | 6   |
| Scotland         | 3 | 1 | 1 | 1 | 2 | 2 | 3   |
| Wales            | 3 | 1 | 0 | 2 | 3 | 2 | 2   |
| Northern Ireland | 3 | 0 | 1 | 2 | 1 | 8 | 1   |


## LEAGUE OF IRELAND TOUR

Auckland, 8 May, 1982
New Zealand (0) 1 *(Turner G.)*
League of Ireland (0) 0

Rotorua, 9 May, 1982
New Zealand (0) 1 *(Rufer)*
League of Ireland (0) 0

Gisborne, 12 May, 1982
New Zealand (0) 0
League of Ireland (0) 0

Dunedin, 16 May, 1982
New Zealand (0) 1 *(McClure pen)*
League of Ireland (2) 3
*(Byrne, Clarke)*

Invercargill, 19 May, 1982
New Zealand (1) 1 *(Rufer)*
League of Ireland (0) 0

# INTERNATIONAL APPEARANCES

This is a list of full international appearances by Englishmen, Irishmen, Scotsmen and Welshmen in matches against the Home Countries and against foreign nations. It does not include unofficial matches against Commonwealth and Empire countries. The year indicated refers to the season; ie 1982 is the 1981-82 season.

Explanatory code for matches played by all five countries: A represents Austria; Alb, Albania; Alg, Algeria; Arg, Argentina; Aus, Australia; B, Bohemia; Bel, Belgium; Br, Brazil; Bul, Bulgaria; Ch, Chile; Co, Colombia; Cy, Cyprus; Cz, Czechoslovakia; D, Denmark; Ec, Ecuador; Ei, Eire; EG, East Germany; F, France; Fi, Finland; G, Germany (pre-war); Gr, Greece; H, Hungary; Ho, Holland; Hon, Honduras; I, Italy; Ic, Iceland; Ir, Iran; Is, Israel; K, Kuwait; L, Luxembourg; M, Mexico; Ma, Malta; N, Norway; Ni, Northern Ireland; Nz, New Zealand; P, Portugal; Par, Paraguay; Pe, Peru; Pol, Poland; R, Rumania; R of E, Rest of Europe; R of W, Rest of World; S, Scotland; Se, Sweden; Sp, Spain; Sw, Switzerland; T, Turkey; Tr, Trinidad & Tobago; U, Uruguay; UK, Rest of United Kingdom; US, United States of America; USSR; W, Wales; WG, West Germany; Y, Yugoslavia.

(Note: For purposes of this code, and in order to distinguish from Eire, Northern Ireland is given throughout the series as Ni).

## ENGLAND

Abbott, W. (Everton), 1902 v W (1)

A'Court, A. (Liverpool), 1958 v Ni, Br, A, USSR; 1959 v W (5)

Adcock, H. (Leicester C), 1929 v F, Bel, Sp; 1930 v Ni, W (5)

Alcock, C. W. (Wanderers), 1875 v S (1)

Alderson, J. T. (C Palace), 1923 v F (1)

Aldridge, A. (WBA), 1888 v Ni; (with Walsall Town Swifts), 1889 v Ni (2)

Allen, A. (Stoke C) 1960 v Se, W, Ni (3)

Allen, A. (Aston Villa), 1888 v Ni (1)

Allen, H. (Wolverhampton W), 1888 v S, W, Ni; 1889 v S; 1890 v S (5)

Allen, J. P. (Portsmouth), 1934 v Ni, W (2)

Allen, R. (WBA), 1952 v Sw; 1954 v Y, S; 1955 v WG, W (5)

Alsford, W. J. (Tottenham H), 1935 v S (1)

Amos, A. (Old Carthusians), 1885 v S; 1886 v W (2)

Anderson, R. D. (Old Etonians), 1879 v W (1)

Anderson, S. (Sunderland), 1962, v A, S (2)

Anderson, V. (Nottingham F), 1979 v Cz, Se; 1980 v Bul, Sp; 1981 v N, R, W, S; 1982 v Ni, Ic (10)

Angus, J. (Burnley), 1961 v A (1)

Armfield, J. C. (Blackpool), 1959 v Br, Pe, M, US; 1960 v Y, Sp, H, S; 1961 v L, P, Sp, M, L, A, W, Ni, S; 1962 v A, Sw, Pe, W, Ni, S, L, P, H, Arg, Bul, Br; 1963 v F (2), Br, EG, Sw, Ni, W, S; 1964 v R of W, Ni, S; 1966 v Y, Fi (43)

Armitage, G. H. (Charlton Ath), 1926 v Ni (1)

Armstrong, D. (Middlesbrough), 1980 v Aus (1)

Armstrong, K. (Chelsea), 1955 v S (1)

Arnold, J. (Fulham), 1933 v S (1)

Arthur, J. W. H. (Blackburn R), 1885 v S, W, Ni; 1886 v S, W; 1887 v W, Ni (7)

Ashcroft, J. (Woolwich Arsenal), 1906 v Ni, W, S (3)

Ashmore, G. S. (WBA), 1926 v Bel (1)

Ashton, C. T. (Corinthians), 1926 v Ni (1)

Ashurst, W. (Notts Co), 1923 v Se (2); 1925 v S, W, Bel (5)

Astall, G. (Birmingham C), 1956 v Fi, WG (2)

Astle, J. (WBA), 1969 v W; 1970 v S, P, Br (sub), Cz (5)

Aston, J. (Manchester U), 1949 v S, W, D, Sw, Se, N, F; 1950 v S, W, Ni, Ei, I, P, Bel, Ch, US; 1951 v Ni (17)

Athersmith, W. C. (Aston Villa), 1892 v Ni, 1897 v S, W, Ni; 1898 v S, W, Ni; 1899 v S, W, Ni; 1900 v S, W (12)

Atyeo, P. J. W. (Bristol C), 1956 v Br, Se, Sp; 1957 v D, Ei (2) (6)

Austin, S. W. (Manchester C), 1926 v Ni (1)

Bach, P. (Sunderland), 1899 v Ni (1)

Bache, J. W. (Aston Villa), 1903 v W; 1904 v W, Ni; 1905 v S; 1907 v Ni; 1910 v Ni; 1911 v S (7)

Baddeley, T. (Wolverhampton W), 1903 v S, Ni; 1904 v S, W, Ni (5)

Bagshaw, J. J. (Derby Co), 1920 v Ni (1)

Bailey, H. P. (Leicester Fosse), 1908 v W, A (2), H, B (5)

Bailey, M. A. (Charlton Ath), 1964 v US; 1965 v W (2)

Bailey, N. C. (Clapham Rovers), 1878 v S; 1879 v S, W; 1880 v S; 1881 v S; 1882 v S, W; 1883 v S, W; 1884 v S, W, Ni; 1885 v S, W, Ni; 1886 v S, W; 1887 v S, W (19)

Baily, E. F. (Tottenham H), 1950 v Sp; 1951 v Y, Ni, W; 1952 v A (2), Sw, W; 1953 v Ni (9)

Bain, J. (Oxford University), 1887 v S (1)

Baker, A. (Arsenal), 1928 v W (1)

Baker, B. H. (Everton), 1921 v Bel; (with Chelsea), 1926 v Ni (2)

Baker, J. H. (Hibernian), 1960 v Y, Sp, H, Ni, S; (with Arsenal) 1966 v Sp, Pol, Ni (8)

Ball, A. J. (Blackpool), 1965 v Y, WG, Se; 1966 v S, Sp, Fi, D, U, Arg, P, WG (2), Pol (2); (with Everton), 1967 v W, S, Ni, A, Cz, Sp; 1968 v W, S, USSR, Sp (2), Y, WG; 1969 v Ni, W, S, R (2), M, Br, U; 1970 v P, Co, Ec, R, Br, Cz (sub), WG, W, S, Bel; 1971 v Ma, EG, Gr, Ma (sub), Ni, S; 1972 v Sw, Gr; (with Arsenal) WG (2), S; 1973 v W (3), Y, S (2), Cz, Ni, Pol; 1974 v P (sub); 1975 v WG, Cy (2), Ni, W, S (72)

Ball, J. (Bury), 1928 v Ni (1)

Balmer, W. (Everton), 1905 v Ni (1)

Bamber, J. (Liverpool), 1921 v W (1)

Bambridge, A. L. (Swifts), 1881 v W; 1883 v W; 1884 v Ni (3)

Bambridge, E. C. (Swifts), 1879 v S; 1880 v S; 1881 v S; 1882 v S, W, Ni; 1883 v W; 1884 v S, W, Ni; 1885 v S, W, Ni; 1886 v S, W; 1887 v S, W, Ni (18)

Bambridge, E. H. (Swifts), 1876 v S (1)

Banks, G. (Leicester C), 1963 v S, Br, Cz, EG; 1964 v W, Ni, S, R of W, U P (2), US, Arg; 1965 v Ni, S, H, Y, WG, Se; 1966 v Ni, S, Sp, Pol (2), WG (2), Y, Fi, U, M, F, Arg, P; 1967 v Ni, W, S, Cz; (with Stoke C), 1968 v W, Ni, S, USSR (2), Sp, WG, Y; 1969 v Ni, S, R (2), F, U, Br; 1970 v W, Ni, S, Ho, Bel, Co, Ec, R, Br, Cz; 1971 v Gr, Ma (2), Ni, S; 1972 v Sw, Gr, WG (2), W, S (73)

Banks, H. E. (Millwall), 1901 v Ni (1)

Banks, T. (Bolton W), 1958 v USSR (3), Br, A; 1959 v Ni (6)

Bannister, W. (Burnley), 1901 v W; (with Bolton W), 1902 v Ni (2)

Barclay, R. (Sheffield W), 1932 v S; 1933 v Ni; 1936 v S (3)

Barkas, S. (Manchester C), 1936 v Bel; 1937 v S; 1938 v W, Ni, Cz (5)

Barker, J. (Derby Co), 1935 v I, Ho, S, W, Ni; 1936 v G, A, S, W, Ni; 1937 v W (11)

Barker, R. (Herts Rangers), 1872 v S (1)

Barker, R. R. (Casuals), 1895 v W (1)

Barlow, R. J. (WBA), 1955 v Ni (1)

Barnes, P. S. (Manchester C), 1978 v I, WG, Br, W, S, H; 1979 v D, Ei, Cz, Ni (2), S, Bul, A; (with WBA), 1980 v D, W; 1981 v Sp (sub), Br, W, Sw (sub); (with Leeds U), 1982 v N (sub), Ho (sub) (22)

Barnet, H. H. (Royal Engineers), 1882 v Ni (1)
Barrass, M. W. (Bolton W), 1952 v W, Ni; 1953 v S (3)
Barrett, A. F. (Fulham), 1930 v Ni (1)
Barrett, J. W. (West Ham U), 1929 v Ni (1)
Barry, L. (Leicester C), 1928 v F, Bel; 1929 v F, Bel, Sp (5)
Barson, F. (Aston Villa), 1920 v W (1)
Barton, J. (Blackburn R), 1890 v Ni (1)
Barton, P. H. (Birmingham), 1921 v Bel; 1922 v Ni; 1923 v F; 1924 v Bel, S, W; 1925 v Ni (7)
Bassett, W. I. (WBA), 1888 v Ni, 1889 v S, W; 1890 v S, W; 1891 v S, Ni; 1892 v S; 1893 v S, W; 1894 v S; 1895 v S, Ni; 1896 v S, W, Ni (16)
Bastard, S. R. (Upton Park), 1880 v S (1)
Bastin, C. S. (Arsenal), 1932 v W; 1933 v I, Sw; 1934 v S, Ni, W, H, Cz; 1935 v S, Ni, I; 1936 v S, W, G, A; 1937 v W, Ni; 1938 v S, G, Sw, F (21)
Baugh, R. (Stafford Road), 1886 v Ni; (with Wolverhampton W) 1890 v Ni (2)
Bayliss, A. E. J. M. (WBA), 1891 v Ni (1)
Baynham, R. L. (Luton T), 1956 v Ni, D, Sp (3)
Beasley, A. (Huddersfield T), 1939 v S (1)
Beats, W. E. (Wolverhampton W), 1901 v W; 1902 v S (2)
Beattie, T. K. (Ipswich T), 1975 v Cy (2), S; 1976 v Sw, P; 1977 v Fi, I (sub), Ho; 1978 v L (sub) (9)
Becton, F. (Preston NE), 1895 v Ni; (with Liverpool), 1897 v W (2)
Bedford, H. (Blackpool), 1923 v Se; 1925 v Ni (2)
Bell, C. (Manchester C), 1968 v Se, WG; 1969 v W, Bul, F, U, Br; 1970 v Ni (sub), Ho (2), P, Br (sub), Cz, WG (sub); 1972 v Gr, WG (2), W, Ni, S; 1973 v W (3), Y, S (2), Ni, Cz, Pol; 1974 v A, Pol, I, W, Ni, S, Arg, EG, Bul, Y; 1975 v Cz, P, WG, Cy (2), Ni, S; 1976 v Sw, Cy (48)
Bennett, W. (Sheffield U), 1901 v S, W (2)
Benson, R. W. (Sheffield U), 1913 v Ni (1)
Bentley, R. T. F. (Chelsea), 1949 v Se; 1950 v S, P, Bel, Ch, USA; 1953 v W, Bel; 1955 v W, WG, Sp, P (12)
Beresford, J. (Aston Villa), 1934 v Cz (1)
Berry, A. (Oxford University), 1909 v Ni (1)
Berry, J. J. (Manchester U), 1953 v Arg, Ch, U; 1956 v Se (4)
Bestall, J. G. (Grimsby T), 1935 v Ni (1)
Betmead, H. A. (Grimsby T), 1937 v Fi (1)
Betts, M. P. (Old Harrovians), 1877 v S (1)
Betts, W. (Sheffield W), 1889 v W (1)
Beverley, J. (Blackburn R), 1884 v S, W, Ni (3)
Birkett, R. H. (Clapham Rovers), 1879 v S (1)
Birkett, R. J. E. (Middlesbrough), 1936 v Ni (1)
Birley, F. H. (Oxford University), 1874 v S; (with Wanderers), 1875 v S (2)
Birtles, G. (Nottingham F), 1980 v Arg (sub), I; 1981 v R (3)
Bishop, S. M. (Leicester C), 1927 v S, Bel, L, F (4)
Blackburn, F. (Blackburn R), 1901 v S; 1902 v Ni; 1904 v S (3)
Blackburn, G. F. (Aston Villa), 1924 v F (1)
Blenkinsop, E. (Sheffield W), 1928 v F, Bel; 1929 v S, W, Ni, F, Bel, Sp; 1930 v S, W, Ni, G, A; 1931 v S, W, Ni, F, Bel; 1932 v S, W, Ni, Sp; 1933 v S, W, Ni, A (26)
Bliss, H. (Tottenham H), 1921 v S (1)
Blockley, J. P. (Arsenal), 1973 v Y (1)
Bloomer, S. (Derby Co), 1895 v S, Ni; 1896 v W, Ni; 1897 v S, W, Ni; 1898 v S; 1899 v S, W, Ni; 1900 v S; 1901 v S, W; 1902 v S, W, Ni; 1904 v S; 1905 v S, W, Ni; (with Middlesbrough), 1907 v S, W (23)
Blunstone, F. (Chelsea), 1955 v W, S, F, P; 1957 v Y (5)
Bond, R. (Preston NE), 1905 v Ni, W; 1906 v S, W, Ni; (with Bradford C), 1910 v S, W, Ni (8)
Bonetti, P. P. (Chelsea), 1966 v D; 1967 v Sp, A; 1968 v Sp; 1970 v Ho, P, WG (7)
Bonsor, A. G. (Wanderers), 1873 v S; 1875 v S (2)

Booth, F. (Manchester C), 1905 v Ni (1)
Booth, T. (Blackburn R.), 1898 v W; (with Everton), 1903 v S (2)
Bowden, E. R. (Arsenal), 1935 v W, I; 1936 v W, Ni, A; 1937 v H (6)
Bower, A. G. (Corinthians), 1924 v Ni, Bel; 1925 v W, Bel; 1927 v W (5)
Bowers, J. W. (Derby Co), 1934 v S, Ni, W (3)
Bowles, S. (QPR), 1974 v P, W, Ni; 1977 v I, Ho (5)
Bowser, S. (WBA), 1920 v Ni (1)
Boyer, P. J. (Norwich C), 1976 v W (1)
Boyes, W. (WBA), 1935 v Ho; (with Everton), 1939 v W, R of E (3)
Boyle, T. W. (Burnley), 1913 v Ni (1)
Brabrook, P. (Chelsea), 1958 v USSR; 1959 v Ni; 1960 v Sp (3)
Bradford, G. R. W. (Bristol R), 1956 v D (1)
Bradford, J. (Birmingham), 1924 v Ni; 1925 v Bel; 1928 v S; 1929 v Ni, W, F, Sp; 1930 v S, Ni, G, A; 1931 v W (12)
Bradley, W. (Manchester U), 1959 v I, US, M (sub) (3)
Bradshaw, F. (Sheffield W), 1908 v A (1)
Bradshaw, T. H. (Liverpool), 1897 v Ni (1)
Bradshaw, W. (Blackburn R), 1910 v W, Ni; 1912 v Ni; 1913 v W (4)
Brann, G. (Swifts), 1886 v S, W; 1891 v W (3)
Brawn, W. F. (Aston Villa), 1904 v W, Ni (2)
Bray, J. (Manchester C), 1935 v W; 1936 v S, W, Ni, G; 1937 v S (6)
Brayshaw, E. (Sheffield W), 1887 v Ni (1)
Bridges, B. J. (Chelsea), 1965 v S, H, Y; 1966 v A (4)
Bridgett, A. (Sunderland), 1905 v S; 1908 v S, A (2), H, B; 1909 v Ni, W, H (2), A (11)
Brindle, T. (Darwen), 1880 v S, W (2)
Brittleton, J. T. (Sheffield W), 1912 v S, W, Ni; 1913 v S; 1914 v W (5)
Britton, C. S. (Everton), 1935 v S, W, Ni, I; 1937 v S, Ni, H, N, Se (9)
Broadbent, P. F. (Wolverhampton W), 1958 v USSR; 1959 v S, W, Ni, I, Br; 1960 v S (7)
Broadis, I. A. (Manchester C), 1952 v S, A, I; 1953 v S, Arg, Ch, U, US; (with Newcastle U), 1954 v S, H, Y, Bel, Sw, U (14)
Brockbank, J. (Cambridge University), 1872 v S (1)
Brodie, J. B. (Wolverhampton W), 1889 v S, Ni; 1891 v Ni (3)
Bromilow, T. G. (Liverpool), 1921 v W; 1922 v S, W; 1923 v Bel; 1926 v Ni (5)
Bromley-Davenport, W. E. (Oxford University), 1884 v S, W (2)
Brook, E. F. (Manchester C), 1930 v Ni; 1933 v Sw; 1934 v S, W, Ni, F, H, Cz; 1935 v S, W, Ni, I; 1936 v S, W, Ni; 1937 v H; 1938 v W, Ni (18)
Brooking, T. D. (West Ham U), 1974 v P, Arg, EG, Bul, Y; 1975 v Cz (sub), P; 1976 v P, W, Br, I, Fi; 1977 v Ei, Fi, I, Ho, Ni, W; 1978 v I, WG, W, S (sub), H; 1979 v D, Ei, Ni, W (sub), S, Bul, Se (sub), A; 1980 v D, Ni, Arg (sub), W, Ni, S, Bel, Sp; 1981 v Sw, Sp, R, H; 1982 v H, S, Fi, Sp (sub) (47)
Brooks, J. (Tottenham H), 1957 v W, Y, D (3)
Broome, F. H. (Aston Villa), 1938 v G, Sw, F; 1939 v N, I, R, Y (7)
Brown, A. (Aston Villa), 1882 v S, W, Ni (3)
Brown, A. S. (Sheffield U), 1904 v W; 1906 v Ni (2)
Brown, A. (WBA), 1971 v W (1)
Brown, G. (Huddersfield T), 1927 v S, W, Ni, Bel, L, F; 1928 v W; 1929 v S; (with Aston Villa), 1933 v W (9)
Brown, J. (Blackburn R), 1881 v W; 1882 v Ni; 1885 v S, W, Ni (5)
Brown, J. H. (Sheffield W), 1927 v S, W, Bel, L, F; 1930 v Ni (6)
Brown, K. (West Ham U), 1960 v Ni (1)

Brown, W. (West Ham U), 1924 v Bel (1)

Bruton, J. (Burnley), 1928 v F, Bel; 1929 v S (3)

Bryant, W. I. (Clapton), 1925 v F (1)

Buchan, C. M. (Sunderland), 1913 v Ni; 1920 v W; 1921 v W, Bel; 1923 v F; 1924 v S (6)

Buchanan, W. S. (Clapham R), 1876 v S (1)

Buckley, F. C. (Derby Co), 1914 v Ni (1)

Bullock, F. E. (Huddersfield T), 1921 v Ni (1)

Bullock, N. (Bury), 1923 v Bel; 1926 v W; 1927 v Ni (3)

Burgess, H. (Manchester C), 1904 v S, W, Ni; 1906 v S (4)

Burgess, H. (Sheffield W), 1931 v S, Ni, F, Bel (4)

Burnup, C. J. (Cambridge University), 1896 v S (1)

Burrows, H. (Sheffield W), 1934 v H, Cz; 1935 v Ho (3)

Burton, F. E. (Nottingham F), 1889 v Ni (1)

Bury, L. (Cambridge University), 1877 v S; (with Old Etonians), 1879 v W (2)

Butcher, T. (Ipswich T), 1980 v Aus; 1981 v Sp; 1982 v W, S, F, Cz, WG, Sp (8)

Butler, J. D. (Arsenal), 1925 v Bel (1)

Butler, W. (Bolton W), 1924 v S (1)

Byrne, G. (Liverpool), 1963 v S; 1966 v N (2)

Byrne, J. J. (C Palace), 1962 v Ni; (with West Ham U), 1963 v Sw; 1964 v S, U, P (2), Ei, Br, Arg; 1965 v W, S (11)

Byrne, R. W. (Manchester U), 1954 v S, H, Y, Bel, Sw, U; 1955 v S, W, Ni, WG, F, Sp, P; 1956 v S, W, Ni, Br, Se, Fi, WG, D, Sp; 1957 v S, W, Ni, Y, D (2), Ei (2); 1958 v W, Ni, F (33)

Callaghan, I. R. (Liverpool), 1966 v Fi, F; 1978 v Sw, L (4)

Calvey, J. (Nottingham F), 1902 v Ni (1)

Campbell, A. F. (Blackburn R), 1929 v W, Ni; (with Huddersfield T), 1931 v W, S, Ni; 1932 v W, Ni, Sp (8)·

Camsell, G. H. (Middlesbrough), 1929 v F, Bel; 1930 v Ni, W; 1934 v F; 1936 v S, G, A, Bel (9)

Capes, A. J. (Stoke C), 1903 v S (1)

Carr, J. (Middlesbrough), 1920 v Ni; 1923 v W (2)

Carr, J. (Newcastle U), 1905 v Ni; 1907 v Ni (2)

Carr, W. H. (Owlerton, Sheffield), 1875 v S (1)

Carter, H. S. (Sunderland), 1934 v S, H; 1936 v G; 1937 v S, Ni, H; (with Derby Co), 1947 v S, W, Ni, Ei, Ho, F, Sw (13)

Carter, J. H. (WBA), 1926 v Bel; 1929 v Bel, Sp (3)

Catlin, A. E. (Sheffield W), 1937 v W, Ni, H, N, Se (5)

Chadwick, A. (Southampton), 1900 v S, W (2)

Chadwick, E. (Everton), 1891 v S, W; 1892 v S; 1893 v S; 1894 v S; 1896 v Ni; 1897 v S (7)

Chambers, H. (Liverpool), 1921 v S, W, Bel; 1923 v S, W, Ni, Bel; 1924 v Ni (8)

Channon, M. R. (Southampton), 1973 v Y, S (2), Ni, W, Cz, USSR, I; 1974 v A, Pol, I, P, W, Ni, S, Arg, EG, Bul, Y; 1975 v Cz, P, WG, Cy (2), Ni (sub), W, S; 1976 v Sw, Cz, P, W, Ni, S, Br, I, Fi; 1977 v Fi, I, L, Ni, W, S, Br (sub), Arg, U; (with Manchester C), 1978 v Sw (46)

Charlton, J. (Leeds U), 1965 v S, H, Y, WG, Se; 1966 v W, Ni, S, A, Sp, Pol (2), WG (2), Y, Fi, D, U, M, F, Arg, P; 1967 v W, S, Ni, Cz; 1968 v W, Sp; 1969 v W, R, F; 1970 v Ho (2), P, Cz (35)

Charlton, R. (Manchester U), 1958 v S, P, Y; 1959 v S, W, Ni, USSR, I, Br, Pe, M, US; 1960 v W, S, Se, Y, Sp, H; 1961 v Ni, W, S, L, P, Sp, M, I, A; 1962 v W, Ni, S, A, Sw, Pe, L, P, H, Arg, Bul, Br; 1963 v S, F, Br, Cz, EG, Sw; 1964 v S, W, Ni, R of W, U, P, Ei, Br, Arg, US (sub); 1965 v Ni, S, Ho; 1966 v W, Ni, S, A, Sp, WG (2), Y, Fi, N, Pol, U, M, F, Arg, P; 1967 v Ni, W, S, Cz; 1968 v W, Ni, S, USSR (2), Sp (2), Se, Y; 1969 v S, W, Ni, R (2), Bul, M, Br; 1970 v W, Ni, Ho (2), P, Co, Ec, Cz, R, Br, WG (106)

Charnley, R. O. (Blackpool), 1963 v F (1)

Charsley, C. C. (Small Heath), 1893 v Ni (1)

Chedgzoy, S. (Everton), 1920 v W; 1921 v W, S, Ni; 1922 v Ni; 1923 v S; 1924 v W; 1925 v Ni (8)

Chenery, C. J. (C Palace), 1872 v S; 1873 v S; 1874 v S (3)

Cherry, T. J. (Leeds U), 1976 v W, S (sub), Br, Fi; 1977 v Ei, I, L, Ni, S (sub), Br, Arg, U; 1978 v Sw, L, I, Br, W; 1979 v Cz, W, Se; 1980 v Ei, Arg (sub), W, Ni, S, Aus, Sp (sub) (27)

Chilton, A. (Manchester U), 1951 v Ni; 1952 v F (2)

Chippendale, H. (Blackburn R), 1894 v Ni (1)

Chivers, M. (Tottenham H), 1971 v Ma (2), Gr, Ni, S; 1972 v Sw (1+1 sub), Gr, WG (2), Ni (sub), S; 1973 v W (3), S (2), Ni, Cz, Pol, USSR, I; 1974 v A, Pol (24)

Christian, E. (Old Etonians), 1879 v S (1)

Clamp, E. (Wolverhampton W), 1958 v USSR (2), Br, A (4)

Clapton, D. R. (Arsenal), 1959 v W (1)

Clare, T. (Stoke C), 1889 v Ni; 1892 v Ni; 1893 v W; 1894 v S (4)

Clarke, A. J. (Leeds U), 1970 v Cz; 1971 v EG, Ma, Ni, W (sub), S (sub); 1973 v S (2), W, Cz, Pol, USSR, I; 1974 v A, Pol, I; 1975 v P; 1976 v Cz, P (sub) (19)

Clarke, H. A. (Tottenham H), 1954 v S (1)

Clay, T. (Tottenham H), 1920 v W; 1922 v W, S, Ni (4)

Clayton, R. (Blackburn R), 1956 v Ni, Br, Se, Fi, WG, Sp; 1957 v S, W, Ni, Y, D (2), Ei (2); 1958 v S, W, Ni, F, P, Y, USSR; 1959 v S, W, Ni, USSR, I, Br, Pe, M, US; 1960 v W, Ni, S, Se, Y (35)

Clegg, J. C. (Sheffield W), 1872 v S (1)

Clegg, W. E. (Sheffield W), 1873 v S; (with Sheffield Albion), 1879 v W (2)

Clemence, R. N. (Liverpool), 1973 v W (2); 1974 v EG, Bul, Y; 1975 v Cz, P, WG, Cy, Ni, W, S; 1976 v Sw, Cz, P, W (2), Ni, S, Br, Fi; 1977 v Ei, Fi, I, Ho, L, S, Br, Arg, U; 1978 v Sw, L, I, WG, Ni, S; 1979 v D, Ei, Ni (2), S, Bul, A (sub); 1980 v D, Bul, Ei, Arg, W, S, Bel, Sp; 1981 v R, Sp, Br, Sw, H; (with Tottenham H), 1982 v N, Ni, Fi (59)

Clement, D. T. (QPR), 1976 v W (sub), W, I; 1977 v I, Ho (5)

Clough, B. H. (Middlesbrough), 1960 v W, Se (2)

Coates, R. (Burnley), 1970 v Ni; 1971 v Gr (sub); (with Tottenham H), Ma, W (4)

Cobbold, W. N. (Cambridge University), 1883 v S, Ni; 1885 v S, Ni; 1886 v S, W; (with Old Carthusians), 1887 v S, W, Ni (9)

Cock, J. G. (Huddersfield T), 1920 v Ni; (with Chelsea), v S (2)

Cockburn, H. (Manchester U), 1947 v W, Ni, Ei; 1948 v S, I; 1949 v S, Ni, D, Sw, Se; 1951 v Arg, P; 1952 v F (13)

Cohen, G. R. (Fulham), 1964 v U, P, Ei, US, Br; 1965 v W, S, Ni, Bel, H, Ho, Y, WG, Se; 1966 v W, S, Ni, A, Sp, Pol (2), WG (2), N, D, U, M, F, Arg, P; 1967 v W, S, Ni, Cz, Sp; 1968 v W, Ni (37)

Coleclough, H. (C Palace), 1914 v W (1)

Coleman, E. H. (Dulwich Hamlet), 1921 v W (1)

Coleman, J. (Woolwich Arsenal), 1907 v Ni (1)

Common, A. (Sheffield U), 1904 v W, Ni; (with Middlesbrough), 1906 v W (3)

Compton, L. H. (Arsenal), 1951 v W, Y (2)

Conlin, J. (Bradford C), 1906 v S (1)

Connelly, J. M. (Burnley), 1960 v W, N, S, Se; 1962 v W, A, Sw, P; 1963 v W, F; (with Manchester U), 1965 v H, Y, Se; 1966 v W, Ni, S, A, N, D, U (20)

Cook, T. E. R. (Brighton), 1925 v W (1)

Cooper, N. C. (Cambridge University), 1893 v Ni (1)

Cooper, T. (Derby Co), 1928 v Ni; 1929 v W, Ni, S, F, Bel, Sp; 1931 v F; 1932 v W, Sp; 1933 v S; 1934 v S, H, Cz; 1935 v W (15)

Cooper, T. (Leeds U), 1969 v W, S, F, M; 1970 v Ho, Bel, Co, Ec, R, Cz, Br, WG; 1971 v EG, Ma, Ni, W, S; 1972 v Sw (2); 1975 v P (20)

Coppell, S. J. (Manchester U), 1978 v I, WG, Br, W, Ni, S, H; 1979 v D, Ei, Cz, Ni (2), W (sub), S, Bul, A; 1980 v D, Ni, Ei (sub), Sp, Arg, W, S, Bel, I; 1981 v R (sub), Sw, R, Br, W, S, Sw, H; 1982 v H, S, Fi, F, Cz, K, WG (40)

Copping, W. (Leeds U), 1933 v I, Sw; 1934 v S, Ni, W, F; (with Arsenal), 1935 v Ni, I; 1936 v A, Bel; 1937 v N, Se, Fi; 1938 v S, W, Ni, Cz; 1939 v W, R of E; (with Leeds U), R (20)

Corbett, B. O. (Corinthians), 1901 v W (1)

Corbett, R. (Old Malvernians), 1903 v W (1)

Corbett, W. S. (Birmingham), 1908 v A, H, B (3)

Corrigan, J. T. (Manchester C), 1976 v I (sub), Br; 1979 v W; 1980 v Ni, Aus; 1981 v W, S; 1982 v W, Ic (9)

Cotterill, G. H. (Cambridge University), 1891 v Ni; (with Old Brightonians), 1892 v W; 1893 v S, Ni (4)

Cottle, J. R. (Bristol C), 1909 v Ni (1)

Cowan, S. (Manchester C), 1926 v Bel; 1930 v A; 1931 v Bel (3)

Cowell, A. (Blackburn R), 1910 v Ni (1)

Cox, J. (Liverpool), 1901 v Ni; 1902 v S; 1903 v S (3)

Cox, J. D. (Derby Co), 1892 v Ni (1)

Crabtree, J. W. (Burnley), 1894 v Ni; 1895 v Ni, S; (with Aston Villa), 1896 v W, S, Ni; 1899 v S, W, Ni; 1900 v S, W, Ni; 1901 v W; 1902 v W (14)

Crawford, J. F. (Chelsea), 1931 v S (1)

Crawford, R. (Ipswich T), 1962 v Ni, A (2)

Crawshaw, T. H. (Sheffield W), 1895 v Ni; 1896 v S, W, Ni; 1897 v S, W, Ni; 1901 v Ni; 1904 v W, Ni (10)

Crayston, W. J. (Arsenal), 1936 v S, W, G, A, Bel; 1938 v W, Ni, Cz (8)

Creek, F. N. S. (Corinthians), 1923 v F (1)

Cresswell, W. (South Shields), 1921 v W; (with Sunderland), 1923 v F; 1924 v Bel; 1925 v Ni; 1926 v W; 1927 v Ni; (with Everton), 1930 v Ni (7)

Crompton, R. (Blackburn R), 1902 v S, W, Ni; 1903 v S, W; 1904 v S, W, Ni; 1906 v S, W, Ni; 1907 v S, W, Ni; 1908 v S, W, Ni, A (2), H, B; 1909 v S, W, Ni, H (2), A; 1910 v S, W; 1911 v S, W, Ni; 1912 v S, W, Ni; 1913 v S, W, Ni; 1914 v S, W, Ni (41)

Crooks, S. D. (Derby Co), 1930 v S, G, A; 1931 v S, W, Ni, F, Bel; 1932 v S, W, Ni, Sp; 1933 v Ni, W, A; 1934 v S, Ni, W, F, H, Cz; 1935 v Ni; 1936 v S, W; 1937 v W, H (26)

Crowe, C. (Wolverhampton W), 1963 v F (1)

Cuggy, F. (Sunderland), 1913 v Ni; 1914 v Ni (2)

Cullis, S. (Wolverhampton W), 1938 v S, W, Ni, F, Cz; 1939 v S, Ni, R of E, N, I, R, Y (12)

Cunliffe, A. (Blackburn R), 1933 v Ni, W (2)

Cunliffe, D. (Portsmouth), 1900 v Ni (1)

Cunliffe, J. N. (Everton), 1936 v Bel (1)

Cunningham, L. (WBA), 1979 v W, Se, A (sub); (with Real Madrid), 1980 v Ei, Sp (sub); 1981 v R (sub) (6)

Currey, E. S. (Oxford University), 1890 v S, W (2)

Currie, A. W. (Sheffield U), 1972 v Ni; 1973 v USSR, I; 1974 v A, Pol, I; 1976 v Sw; (with Leeds U), 1978 v Br, W (sub), Ni, S, H (sub); 1979 v Cz, Ni (2), W, Se (17)

Cursham, A. W. (Notts Co), 1876 v S; 1877 v S; 1878 v S; 1879 v W; 1883 v S, W (6)

Cursham, H. A. (Notts Co), 1880 v W; 1882 v S, W, Ni; 1883 v S, W, Ni; 1884 v Ni (8)

Daft, H. B. (Notts Co), 1889 v Ni; 1890 v S, W; 1891 v Ni; 1892 v Ni (5)

Danks, T. (Nottingham F), 1885 v S (1)

Davenport, J. K. (Bolton W), 1885 v W; 1890 v Ni (2)

Davis, G. (Derby Co), 1904 v W, Ni (2)

Davis, H. (Sheffield W), 1903 v S, W, Ni (3)

Davison, J. E. (Sheffield W), 1922 v W (1)

Dawson, J. (Burnley), 1922 v S, Ni (2)

Day, S. H. (Old Malvernians), 1906 v Ni, W, S (3)

Dean, W. R. (Everton), 1927 v S, W, F, Bel, L; 1928 v S, W, Ni, F, Bel; 1929 v S, W, Ni; 1931 v S; 1932 v Sp; 1933 v Ni (16)

Deeley, N. V. (Wolverhampton W), 1959 v Br, Pe (2)

Devey, J. H. G. (Aston Villa), 1892 v Ni; 1894 v Ni (2)

Devonshire, A. (West Ham U), 1980 v Aus (sub), Ni; 1982 v Ho, Ic (4)

Dewhurst, F. (Preston NE), 1886 v W, Ni; 1887 v S, W, Ni; 1888 v S, W, Ni; 1889 v W (9)

Dewhurst, G. P. (Liverpool Ramblers), 1895 v W (1)

Dickinson, J. W. (Portsmouth), 1949 v N, F; 1950 v S, W, Ei, P, Bel, Ch, US, Sp; 1951 v Ni, W, Y; 1952 v W, Ni, S, A (2), I, Sw; 1953 v W, Ni, S, Bel, Arg, Ch, U, US; 1954 v W, Ni, S, R of E, H (2), Y, Bel, Sw, U; 1955 v Sp, P; 1956 v W, Ni, S, D, Sp; 1957 v W, Y, D (48)

Dimmock, J. H. (Tottenham H), 1921 v S; 1926 v W, Bel (3)

Ditchburn, E. G. (Tottenham H), 1949 v Sw, Se; 1953 v US; 1957 v W, Y, D (6)

Dix, R. W. (Derby Co), 1939 v N (1)

Dixon, J. A. (Notts Co), 1885 v W (1)

Dobson, A. T. C. (Notts Co), 1882 v Ni; 1884 v S, W, Ni (4)

Dobson, C. F. (Notts Co), 1886 v Ni (1)

Dobson, J. M. (Burnley), 1974 v P, EG, Bul, Y; (with Everton), 1975 v Cz (5)

Doggart, A. G. (Corinthians), 1924 v Bel (1)

Dorrell, A. R. (Aston Villa), 1925 v W, Bel, F; 1926 v Ni (4)

Douglas, B. (Blackburn R), 1958 v S, W, Ni, F, P, Y, USSR (2), Br, A; 1959 v S, USSR; 1960 v Y, H; 1961 v Ni, W, S, L, P, Sp, M, I, A; 1962 v W, Ni, S, Pe, L, P, H, Arg, Bul, Br; 1963 v S, Br, Sw (36)

Downs, R. W. (Everton), 1921 v Ni (1)

Doyle, M. (Manchester C), 1976 v W, S (sub), Br, I; 1977 v Ho (5)

Drake, E. J. (Arsenal), 1935 v Ni, I; 1936 v W; 1937 v H; 1938 v F (5)

Ducat, A. (Woolwich Arsenal), 1910 v S, W, Ni; (with Aston Villa), 1920 v S, W; 1921 v Ni (6)

Dunn, A. T. B. (Cambridge University), 1883 v Ni; 1884 v Ni; (with Old Etonians), 1892 v S, W (4)

Earle, S. G. J. (Clapton), 1924 v F; (with West Ham U), 1928 v Ni (2)

Eastham, G. (Arsenal), 1963 v Br, Cz, EG; 1964 v W, Ni, S, R of W, U, P, Ei, US, Br, Arg; 1965 v H, WG, Se; 1966 v Sp, Pol, D (19)

Eastham, G. R. (Bolton W), 1935 v Ho (1)

Eckersley, W. (Blackburn R), 1950 v Sp; 1951 v S, Y, Arg, P; 1952 v A (2), Sw; 1953 v Ni, Arg, Ch, U, US; 1954 v W, Ni, R of E, H (17)

Edwards, D. (Manchester U), 1955 v S, F, Sp, P; 1956 v S, Br, Se, Fi, WG; 1957 v S, Ni, Ei (2), D (2); 1958 v W, Ni, F (18)

Edwards, J. H. (Shropshire Wanderers), 1874 v S (1)

Edwards, W. (Leeds U), 1926 v S, W; 1927 v W, Ni, S, F, Bel, L; 1928 v S, F, Bel; 1929 v S, W, Ni; 1930 v W, Ni (16)

Ellerington, W. (Southampton), 1949 v N, F (2)

Elliott, G. W. (Middlesbrough), 1913 v Ni; 1914 v Ni; 1920 v W (3)

Elliott, W. H. (Burnley), 1952 v I, A; 1953 v Ni, W, Bel (5)

Evans, R. E. (Sheffield U), 1911 v S, W, Ni; 1912 v W (4)

Ewer, F. H. (Casuals), 1924 v F; 1925 v Bel (2)

Fairclough, P. (Old Foresters), 1878 v S (1)

Fairhurst, D. (Newcastle U), 1934 v F (1)

Fantham, J. (Sheffield W), 1962 v L (1)

Felton, W. (Sheffield W), 1925 v F (1)

Fenton, M. (Middlesbrough), 1938 v S (1)

Field, E. (Clapham Rovers), 1876 v S; 1881 v S (2)

Finney, T. (Preston NE), 1947 v W, Ni, Ei, Ho, F, P; 1948 v S, W, Ni, Bel, Se, I; 1949 v S, W, Ni, Se, N, F; 1950 v S, W, Ni, Ei, I, P, Bel, Ch, US, Sp; 1951 v W, S, Arg, P; 1952 v W, Ni, S, F, I, Sw, A; 1953 v W, Ni, S, Bel, Arg, Ch, U, US; 1954 v W, S, Bel, Sw, U, H, Y; 1955 v WG; 1956 v S, W, Ni, D, Sp; 1957 v S, W, Y, D (2), Ei (2); 1958 v W, S, F, P, Y, USSR (2); 1959 v Ni, USSR (76)

Fleming, H. J. (Swindon T), 1909 v S, H (2); 1910 v W, Ni; 1911 v W, Ni; 1912 v Ni; 1913 v S, W; 1914 v S (11)

Fletcher, A. (Wolverhampton W), 1889 v W; 1890 v W (2)

Flowers, R. (Wolverhampton W), 1955 v F; 1959 v S, W, I, Br, Pe, US, M (sub); 1960 v W, Ni, S, Se, Y, Sp, H; 1961 v Ni, W, S, L, P, Sp, M, I, A; 1962 v W, Ni, S, A, Sw, Pe, L, P, H, Arg, Bul, Br; 1963 v Ni, W, S, F (2), Sw; 1964 v Ei, US, P; 1965 v Ni, W, Ho, WG; 1966 v N (49)

Forman, Frank (Nottingham F), 1898 v S, Ni; 1899 v S, W, Ni; 1901 v S; 1902 v S, Ni; 1903 v W (9)

Forman, F. R. (Nottingham F), 1899 v S, W, Ni (3)

Forrest, J. H. (Blackburn R), 1884 v W; 1885 v S, W, Ni; 1886 v S, W; 1887 v S, W, Ni; 1889 v S; 1890 v Ni (11)

Fort, J. (Millwall), 1921 v Bel (1)

Foster, R. E. (Oxford University), 1900 v W; (with Corinthians), 1901 v W, Ni, S; 1902 v W (5)

Foster, S. (Brighton & HA), 1982 v Ni, Ho, K (3)

Foulke, W. J. (Sheffield U), 1897 v W (1)

Foulkes, W. A. (Manchester U), 1955 v Ni (1)

Fox, F. S. (Gillingham), 1925 v F (1)

Francis, G. C. J. (QPR), 1975 v Cz, P, W, S; 1976 v Sw, Cz, P, W, Ni, S, Br, Fi (12)

Francis, T. (Birmingham C), 1977 v Ho, L, S, Br; 1978 v Sw, L, I (sub), WG (sub), Br, W, S, H; (with Nottingham F), 1979 v Bul (sub), Se, A (sub); 1980 v Ni, Bul, Sp; 1981 v Sp, R, S (sub), Sw; (with Manchester C), 1982 v N, Ni, W, S (sub), Fi (sub), F, Cz, K, WG, Sp (32)

Franklin, C. F. (Stoke C), 1947 v S, W, Ni, Ei, Ho, F, Sw, P; 1948 v S, W, Ni, Bel, Se, I; 1949 v S, W, Ni, D, Sw, N, F, Se; 1950 v W, S, Ni, Ei, I (27)

Freeman, B. C. (Everton), 1909 v S, W; (with Burnley), 1912 v S, W, Ni (5)

Froggatt, J. (Portsmouth), 1950 v Ni, I; 1951 v S; 1952 v S, A (2), I, Sw; 1953 v Ni, W, S, Bel, US (13)

Froggatt, R. (Sheffield W), 1953 v W, S, Bel, US (4)

Fry, C. B. (Corinthians), 1901 v Ni (1)

Furness, W. I. (Leeds U), 1933 v I (1)

Galley, T. (Wolverhampton W), 1937 v N, Se (2)

Gardner, T. (Aston Villa), 1934 v Cz; 1935 v Ho (2)

Garfield, B. (WBA), 1898 v Ni (1)

Garratty, W. (Aston Villa), 1903 v W (1)

Garrett, T. (Blackpool), 1952 v S, I; 1954 v W (3)

Gates, E. (Ipswich T), 1981 v N, R (2)

Gay, L. H. (Cambridge University), 1893 v S; (with Old Brightonians), 1894 v S, W (3)

Geary, F. (Everton), 1890 v Ni; 1891 v S (2)

Geaves, R. L. (Clapham Rovers), 1875 v S (1)

Gee, C. W. (Everton), 1932 v W, Sp; 1937 v Ni (3)

Geldard, A. (Everton), 1933 v I, Sw; 1935 v S; 1938 v Ni (4)

George, C. (Derby Co), 1977 v Ei (1)

George, W. (Aston Villa), 1902 v S, W, Ni (3)

Gibbins, W. V. T. (Clapton), 1924 v F; 1925 v F (2)

Gidman, J. (Aston Villa), 1977 v L (1)

Gillard, I. T. (QPR), 1975 v WG, W; 1976 v Cz (3)

Gilliat, W. E. (Old Carthusians), 1893 v Ni (1)

Goddard, P. (West Ham U), 1982 v Ic (sub) (1)

Goodall, F. R. (Huddersfield T), 1926 v S; 1927 v S, F, Bel, L; 1928 v S, W, F, Bel; 1930 v S, G, A; 1931 v S, W, Ni, Bel; 1932 v Ni; 1933 v W, Ni, A, I, Sw; 1934 v W, Ni, F (25)

Goodall, J. (Preston NE), 1888 v S, W; 1889 v S, W; (with Derby Co), 1891 v S, W; 1892 v S; 1893 v W; 1894 v S; 1895 v S, Ni; 1896 v S, W; 1898 v W (14)

Goodhart, H. C. (Old Etonians), 1883 v S, W, Ni (3)

Goodwyn, A. G. (Royal Engineers), 1873 v S (1)

Goodyer, A. C.(Nottingham F), 1879 v S (1)

Gosling, R. C. (Old Etonians), 1892 v W; 1893 v S; 1894 v W; 1895 v W, S (5)

Gosnell, A. A. (Newcastle U), 1906 v Ni (1)

Gough, H. C. (Sheffield U), 1921 v S (1)

Goulden, L. A. (West Ham U), 1937 v Se, N; 1938 v W, Ni, Cz, G, Sw, F; 1939 v S, W, R of E, I, R, Y (14)

Graham, L. (Millwall), 1925 v S, W (2)

Graham, T. (Nottingham F), 1931 v F; 1932 v Ni (2)

Grainger, C. (Sheffield U), 1956 v Br, Se, Fi, WG; 1957 v W, Ni; (with Sunderland), 1957 v S (7)

Greaves, J. (Chelsea), 1959 v Pe, M, US; 1960 v W, Se, Y, Sp; 1961 v Ni, W, S, L, P, Sp, I, A; (with Tottenham H), 1962 v S, Sw, Pe, H, Arg, Bul, Br; 1963 v Ni, W, S, F (2), Br, Cz, Sw; 1964 v W, Ni, R of W, P (2), Ei, Br, U, Arg; 1965 v Ni, S, Bel, Ho, H, Y; 1966 v W, A, Y, N, D, Pol, U, M, F; 1967 v S, Sp, A (57)

Green, F. T. (Wanderers), 1876 v S (1)

Green, G. H. (Sheffield U), 1925 v F; 1926 v S, Bel, W; 1927 v W; 1928 v F, Bel (8)

Greenhalgh, E. H. (Notts Co), 1872 v S; 1873 v S (2)

Greenhoff, B. (Manchester U), 1976 v W, Ni; 1977 v Ei, Fi, I, Ho, Ni, W, S, Br, Arg, U; 1978 v Br, W, Ni, S (sub), H (sub); (with Leeds U), 1980 v Aus (sub) (18)

Greenwood, D. H. (Blackburn R), 1882 v S, Ni (2)

Grimsdell, A. (Tottenham H), 1920 v S, W; 1921 v S, Ni; 1923 v W, Ni (6)

Grosvenor, A. T. (Birmingham), 1934 v Ni, W, F (3)

Gunn, W. (Notts Co), 1884 v S, W (2)

Gurney, R. (Sunderland), 1935 v S (1)

Hacking, J. (Oldham Ath), 1929 v S, W, Ni (3)

Hadley, N. (WBA), 1903 v Ni (1)

Hagan, J. (Sheffield U), 1949 v D (1)

Haines, J. T. W. (WBA), 1949 v Sw (1)

Hall, A. E. (Aston Villa), 1910 v Ni (1)

Hall, G. W. (Tottenham H), 1934 v F; 1938 v S, W, Ni, Cz; 1939 v S, Ni, R of E, I, Y (10)

Hall, J. (Birmingham C), 1956 v S, W, Ni, Br, Se, Fi, WG, D, Sp; 1957 v S, W, Ni, Y, D (2), Ei (2) (17)

Halse, H. J. (Manchester U), 1909 v A (1)

Hammond, H. E. D. (Oxford University), 1889 v S (1)

Hampson, J. (Blackpool), 1931 v Ni, W; 1933 v A (3)

Hampton, H. (Aston Villa), 1913 v S, W; 1914 v S, W (4)

Hancocks, J. (Wolverhampton W), 1949 v Sw; 1950 v W; 1951 v Y (3)

Hapgood, E. (Arsenal), 1933 v I, Sw; 1934 v S, Ni, W, H, Cz; 1935 v S, Ni, W, I, Ho; 1936 v S, Ni, W, G, A, Bel; 1937 v Fi; 1938 v S, G, Sw, F; 1939 v S, W, Ni, R of E, N, I, Y (30)

Hardinge, H. T. W. (Sheffield U), 1910 v S (1)

Hardman, H. P. (Everton), 1905 v W; 1907 v S, Ni; 1908 v W (4)

Hardwick, G. F. M. (Middlesbrough), 1947 v S, W, Ni, Ei, Ho, F, Sw, P; 1948 v S, W, Ni, Bel, Se (13)

Hardy, H. (Stockport Co), 1925 v Bel (1)

Hardy, S. (Liverpool), 1907 v S, W, Ni; 1908 v S; 1909 v S, W, Ni, H (2), A; 1910 v S, W, Ni; 1912 v Ni; (with Aston Villa), 1913 v S; 1914 v Ni, W, S; 1920 v S, W, Ni (21)

Hargreaves, F. W. (Blackburn R), 1880 v W; 1881 v W; 1882 v Ni (3)

Hargreaves, J. (Blackburn R), 1881 v S, W (2)

Harper, E. C. (Blackburn R), 1926 v S (1)

Harris, G. (Burnley), 1966 v Pol (1)

Harris, P. P. (Portsmouth), 1950 v Ei; 1954 v H (2)

Harris, S. S. (Cambridge University), 1904 v S; (with Old Westminsters), 1905 v Ni, W; 1906 v S, W, Ni (6)

Harrison, A. H. (Old Westminsters), 1893 v S, Ni (2)

Harrison, G. (Everton), 1921 v Bel; 1922 v Ni (2)

Harrow, J. H. (Chelsea), 1923 v Ni, Se (2)

Hart, E. (Leeds U), 1929 v W; 1930 v W, Ni; 1933 v S, A; 1934 v S, H, Cz (8)

Hartley, F. (Oxford C), 1923 v F (1)

Harvey, A. (Wednesbury Strollers), 1881 v W (1)

Harvey, J. C. (Everton), 1971 v Ma (1)

Hassall,!H. W. (Huddersfield T), 1951 v S, Arg, P; 1952 v F; (with Bolton W), 1954 v Ni (5)

Haworth, G. (Accrington), 1887 v Ni, W, S; 1888 v S; 1890 v S (5)

Hawtrey, J. P. (Old Etonians), 1881 v S, W (2)

Hawkes, R. M. (Luton T), 1907 v Ni; 1908 v A (2), H, B (5)

Haygarth, E. B. (Swifts), 1875 v S (1)

Haynes, J. N. (Fulham), 1955 v Ni; 1956 v S, Ni, Br, Se, Fi, WG, Sp; 1957 v W, Y, D, Ei (2); 1958 v W, Ni, S, F, P, Y, USSR (3), Br, A; 1959 v S, Ni, USSR, I, Br, Pe, M, US; 1960 v Ni, Y, Sp, H; 1961 v Ni, W, S, L, P, Sp, M, I, A; 1962 v W, Ni, S, A, Sw, Pe, P, H, Arg, Bul, Br (56)

Healless, H. (Blackburn R), 1925 v Ni; 1928 v S (2)

Hector, K. J. (Derby Co), 1974 v Pol (sub), I (sub), (2)

Hedley, G. A. (Sheffield U), 1901 v Ni (1)

Hegan, K. E. (Corinthians), 1923 v Bel, F; 1924 v Ni, Bel (4)

Hellawell, M. S. (Birmingham C), 1963 v Ni, F (2)

Henfrey, A. G. (Cambridge University), 1891 v Ni; (with Corinthians), 1892 v W; 1895 v W; 1896 v S, W (5)

Henry, R. P. (Tottenham H), 1963 v F (1)

Heron, F. (Wanderers), 1876 v S (1)

Heron, G. H. H. (Uxbridge), 1873 v S; 1874 v S; (with Wanderers), 1875 v S; 1876 v S; 1878 v S (5)

Hibbert, W. (Bury), 1910 v S (1)

Hibbs, H. E. (Birmingham), 1930 v S, W, A, G; 1931 v S, W, Ni; 1932 v W, Ni, Sp; 1933 v S, W, Ni, A, I, Sw; 1934 v Ni, W, F; 1935 v S, W, Ni, Ho; 1936 v G, W (25)

Hill, F. (Bolton W), 1963 v Ni, W (2)

Hill, J. H. (Burnley), 1925 v W; 1926 v S; 1927 v S, Ni, Bel, F; 1928 v Ni, W; 1929 v F, Bel, Sp (11)

Hill, G. A. (Manchester U), 1976 v I; 1977 v Ei (sub), Fi (sub), L; 1978 v Sw (sub), L (6)

Hill, R. H. (Millwall), 1926 v Bel (1)

Hillman, J. (Burnley), 1899 v Ni (1)

Hills, A. F. (Old Harrovians), 1879 v S (1)

Hilsdon, G. R. (Chelsea), 1907 v Ni; 1908 v S, W, Ni, A, H, B; 1909 v Ni (8)

Hine, E. W. (Leicester C), 1929 v W, Ni; 1930 v W, Ni; 1932 v W, Ni (6)

Hinton, A. T. (Wolverhampton W), 1963 v F; (with Nottingham F), 1965 v W, Bel (3)

Hitchens, G. A. (Aston Villa), 1961 v M, I, A; (with Inter-Milan), 1962 v Sw, Pe, H, Br (7)

Hobbis, H. H. F. (Charlton Ath), 1936 v A, Bel (2)

Hoddle, G. (Tottenham H), 1980 v Bul, W, Aus, Sp; 1981 v Sp, W, S; 1982 v N, Ni, W, Ic, Cz (sub), K (13)

Hodgetts, D. (Aston Villa), 1888 v S, W, Ni; 1892 v S, Ni; 1894 v Ni (6)

Hodgkinson, A. (Sheffield U), 1957 v S, Ei (2), D; 1961 v W (5)

Hodgson, G. (Liverpool), 1931 v S, Ni, W (3)

Hodkinson, J. (Blackburn R), 1913 v W, S; 1920 v Ni (3)

Hogg, W. (Sunderland), 1902 v S, W, Ni (3)

Holdcroft, G. H. (Preston NE), 1937 v W, Ni (2)

Holden, A. D. (Bolton W), 1959 v S, I, Br, Pe, M (5)

Holden, G. H. (Wednesday OA), 1881 v S; 1884 v S, W, Ni (4)

Holden-White, C. (Corinthians), 1888 v W, S (2)

Holford, T. (Stoke), 1903 v Ni (1)

Holley, G. H. (Sunderland), 1909 v S, W, H (2), A; 1910 v W; 1912 v S, W, NI; 1913 v S (10)

Holliday, E. (Middlesbrough), 1960 v W, Ni, Se (3)

Hollins, J. W. (Chelsea), 1967 v Sp (1)

Holmes, R. (Preston NE), 1888 v Ni; 1891 v S; 1892 v S; 1893 v S, W; 1894 v Ni; 1895 v Ni (7)

Holt, J. (Everton), 1890 v W; 1891 v S, W; 1892 v S, Ni; 1893 v S; 1894 v S, Ni; 1895 v S; (with Reading), 1900 v Ni (10)

Hopkinson, E. (Bolton W), 1958 v W, Ni, S, F, P, Y; 1959 v S, I, Br, Pe, M, US; 1960 v W, Se (14)

Hossack, A. H. (Corinthians), 1892 v W; 1894 v W (2)

Houghton, W. E. (Aston Villa), 1931 v Ni, W, F, Bel; 1932 v S, Ni; 1933 v A (7)

Houlker, A. E. (Blackburn R), 1902 v S; (with Portsmouth), 1903 v S, W; (with Southampton), 1906 v W, Ni (5)

Howarth, R. H. (Preston NE), 1887 v Ni; 1888 v S, W; 1891 v S; (with Everton), 1894 v Ni (5)

Howe, D. (WBA), 1958 v S, W, Ni, F, P, Y, USSR (3), Br, A; 1959 v S, W, Ni, USSR, I, Br, Pe, M, US; 1960 v W, Ni, Se (23)

Howe, J. R. (Derby Co), 1948 v I; 1949 v S, Ni (3)

Howell, L. S. (Wanderers), 1873 v S (1)

Howell, R. (Sheffield U), 1895 v Ni; (with Liverpool) 1899 v S (2)

Hudson, A. A. (Stoke C), 1975 v WG, Cy (2)

Hudson, J. (Sheffield), 1883 v Ni (1)

Hudspeth, F. C. (Newcastle U), 1926 v Ni (1)

Hufton, A. E. (West Ham U), 1924 v Bel; 1928 v S, Ni; 1929 v F, Bel, Sp (6)

Hughes, E. W. (Liverpool), 1970 v W, Ni, S, Ho, P, Bel; 1971 v EG, Ma (2), Gr, W; 1972 v Sw, Gr, Wg (2), W, Ni, S; 1973 v W (3), S (2), Pol, USSR, I; 1974 v A, Pol, I, W, Ni, S, Arg, EG, Bul, Y; 1975 v Cz, P, Cy (sub), Ni; 1977 v I, L, W, S, Br, Arg, U; 1978 v Sw, L, I, WG, Ni, S, H; 1979 v D, Ei, Ni, W, Se; (with Wolverhampton W), 1980 v Sp (sub), Ni, S (sub) (62)

Hughes, L. (Liverpool), 1950 v Ch, US, Sp (3)

Hulme, J. H. A. (Arsenal), 1927 v S, Bel, F; 1928 v S, Ni, W; 1929 v Ni, W; 1933 v S (9)

Humphreys, P. (Notts Co), 1903 v S (1)

Hunt, G. S. (Tottenham H), 1933 v I, Sw, S (3)

Hunt, Rev K. R. G. (Leyton), 1911 v S, W (2)

Hunt, R. (Liverpool), 1962 v A; 1963 v EG; 1964 v S, US, P; 1965 v W; 1966 v S, Sp, Pol (2), WG (2), Fi, N, U, M, F, Arg, P; 1967 v Ni, W, Cz, Sp, A; 1968 v W, Ni, USSR (2), Sp (2), Se, Y; 1969 v R (2) (34)

Hunter, J. (Sheffield Heeley), 1878 v S; 1880 v S, W; 1881 v S, W; 1882 v S, W (7)

Hunter, N. (Leeds U), 1966 v WG, Y, Fi, Sp (sub); 1967 v A; 1968 v Sp, Se, Y, WG, USSR; 1969 v R, W; 1970 v Ho, WG (sub); 1971 v Ma; 1972 v WG (2), W, Ni, S; 1973 v W (2) USSR (sub); 1974 v A, Pol, Ni (sub), S; 1975 v Cz (28)

Hurst, G. C. (West Ham U), 1966 v S, WG (2), Y, Fi, D, Arg, P; 1967 v Ni, W, S, Cz, Sp, A; 1968 v W, Ni, S, Se (sub), WG, USSR (2); 1969 v Ni, S, R (2), Bul, F, M, U, Br; 1970 v W, Ni, S, Ho (1 + 1 sub), Bel, Co, Ec, R, Br, WG; 1971 v EG, Gr, W, S; 1972 v Sw (2), Gr, WG (49)

Iremonger, J. (Nottingham F), 1901 v S; 1902 v Ni (2)

Jack, D. N. B. (Bolton W), 1924 v S, W; 1928 v F, Bel; (with Arsenal), 1930 v S, G, A; 1933 v W, A (9)

Jackson, B. (Oxford University), 1891 v W (1)

Jarrett, B. G. (Cambridge University), 1876 v S; 1877 v S; 1878 v S (3)

Jefferis, F. (Everton), 1912 v S, W (2)

Jezzard, B. A. G. (Fulham), 1954 v H; 1956 v Ni (2)

Johnson, D. E. (Ipswich T), 1975 v W, S; 1976 v Sw; (with Liverpool), 1980 v Ei, Arg, Ni, S, Bel (8)

Johnson, E. (Saltley College), 1880 v W; (with Stoke C), 1884 v Ni (2)

Johnson, J. A. (Stoke C), 1937 v N, Se, Fi, S, Ni (5)

Johnson, T. C. F. (Manchester C), 1926 v Bel; 1930 v W; (with Everton), 1932 v S, Sp; 1933 v Ni (5)

Johnson, W. H. (Sheffield U), 1900 v S, W, Ni; 1903 v S, W, Ni (6)

Johnston, H. (Blackpool), 1947 v S, Ho; 1951 v S; 1953 v Arg, Ch, U, US; 1954 v W, Ni, H (10)

Jones, A. (Walsall Town Swifts), 1882 v S, W; (with Great Lever), 1883 v S (3)

Jones, H. (Blackburn R), 1927 v S, Bel, L, F; 1928 v S, Ni (6)

Jones, H. (Nottingham F), 1923 v F (1)

Jones, M. D. (Sheffield U), 1965 v WG, Se; (with Leeds U), 1970 v Ho (3)

Jones, W. (Bristol C), 1901 v Ni (1)

Jones, W. H. (Liverpool), 1950 v P, Bel (2)

Joy, B. (Casuals), 1936 v Bel (1)

Kail, E. I. L. (Dulwich Hamlet), 1929 v F, Bel, Sp (3)

Kay, A. H. (Everton), 1963 v Sw (1)

Kean, F. W. (Sheffield W), 1923 v S, Bel; 1924 v W; 1925 v Ni; 1926 v Ni, Bel; 1927 v L; (with Bolton W), 1929 v F, Sp (9)

Keegan, J. K. (Liverpool), 1973 v W (2); 1974 v W, Ni, Arg, EG, Bul, Y; 1975 v Cz, WG, Cy (2), Ni, S; 1976 v Sw, Cz, P, W (2), Ni, S, Br, Fi; 1977 v Ei, Fi, I, Ho, L; (with SV Hamburg), W, Br, Arg, U; 1978 v Sw, I, WG, Br, H; 1979 v D, Ei, Cz, Ni, W, S, Bul, Se, A; 1980 v D, Ni, Ei, Sp (2), Arg, Bel, I; (with Southampton), 1981 v Sp, Sw, H; 1982 v N, H, Ni, S, Fi, Sp (sub) (63)

Keen, E. R. L. (Derby Co), 1933 v A; 1937 v W, Ni, H (4)

Kelly, R. (Burnley), 1920 v S; 1921 v S, W, Ni; 1922 v S, W; 1923 v S; 1924 v Ni; 1925 v W, Ni, S; (with Sunderland), 1926 v W; (with Huddersfield T), 1927 v L; 1928 v S (14)

Kennedy, R. (Liverpool), 1976 v W (2), Ni, S; 1977 v L, W, S, Br (sub), Arg (sub); 1978 v Sw, L; 1980 v Bul, Sp, Arg, W, Bel (sub), I (17)

Kenyon-Slaney, W. S. (Wanderers), 1873 v S (1)

Kevan, D. T. (WBA), 1957 v S; 1958 v W, Ni, S, P, Y, USSR (3), Br, A; 1959 v M, US; 1961 v M (14)

Kidd, B. (Manchester U), 1970 v Ni, Ec (sub) (2)

King, R. S. (Oxford University), 1882 v Ni (1)

Kingsford, R. K. (Wanderers), 1874 v S (1)

Kingsley, M. (Newcastle U), 1901 v W (1)

Kinsey, G. (Wolverhampton W), 1892 v W; 1893 v S; (with Derby Co), 1896 v W, Ni (4)

Kirchen, A. J. (Arsenal), 1937 v N, Se, Fi (3)

Kirton, W. J. (Aston Villa), 1922 v Ni (1)

Knight, A. E. (Portsmouth), 1920 v Ni (1)

Knowles, C. (Tottenham H), 1968 v USSR, Sp, Se, WG (4)

Labone, B. L. (Everton), 1963 v Ni, W, F; 1967 v Sp, A; 1968 v S, Sp, Se, Y, USSR, Wg; 1969 v Ni, S, R, Bul, M, U, Br; 1970 v S, W, Bel, Co, Ec, R, Br, WG (26)

Lampard, F. R. G. (West Ham U), 1973 v Y; 1980 v Aus (2)

Langley, E. J. (Fulham), 1958 v S, P, Y (3)

Langton, R. (Blackburn R), 1947 v W, Ni, Ei, Ho, F, Sw; 1948 v Se; (with Preston NE), 1949 v D, Se; (with Bolton W), 1950 v S; 1951 v Ni (11)

Latchford, R. D. (Everton), 1978 v I, Br, W; 1979 v D, Ei, Cz (sub), Ni (2), W, S, Bul, A (12)

Latheron, E. G. (Blackburn R), 1913 v W; 1914 v Ni (2)

Lawler, C. (Liverpool), 1971 v Ma, W, S; 1972 v Sw (4)

Lawton, T. (Everton), 1939 v S, W, Ni, R of E, N, I, R, Y; (with Chelsea), 1947 v S, W, Ni, Ei, Ho, F, Sw, P; 1948 v W, Ni, Bel; (with Notts Co), 1948 v S, Se, I; 1949 v D (23)

Leach, T. (Sheffield W), 1931 v W, Ni (2)

Leake, A. (Aston Villa), 1904 v S, Ni; 1905 v S, W, Ni (5)

Lee, E. A. (Southampton), 1904 v W (1)

Lee, F. H. (Manchester C), 1969 v Ni, W, S, Bul, F, M, U; 1970 v Ho (2), P, Bel, Co, Ec, R, Br, WG; 1971 v EG, Gr, Ma, Ni, W, S; 1972 v Sw (2), Gr, WG (27)

Lee, J. (Derby Co), 1951 v Ni (1)

Leighton, J. E. (Nottingham F), 1886 v Ni (1)

Lilley, H. E. (Sheffield U), 1892 v W (1)

Linacre, H. J. (Nottingham F), 1905 v W, S (2)

Lindley, T. (Cambridge University), 1886 v S, W, Ni, 1887 v S, W, Ni; 1888 v S, W, Ni; (with Nottingham F), 1889 v S; 1890 v S, W; 1891 v Ni (13)

Lindsay, A. (Liverpool), 1974 v Arg, EG, Bul, Y (4)

Lindsay, W. (Wanderers), 1877 v S (1)

Lintott, E. H. (QPR), 1908 v S, W, Ni; (with Bradford C), 1909 v S, Ni, H (2) (7)

Lipsham, H. B. (Sheffield U), 1902 v W (1)

Little, B. (Aston Villa), 1975 v W (sub) (1)

Lloyd, L. V. (Liverpool), 1971 v W; 1972 v Sw, Ni; (with Nottingham F), 1980 v W (4)

Lockett, A. (Stoke C), 1903 v Ni (1)

Lodge, L. V. (Cambridge University), 1894 v W; 1895 v S, W; (with Corinthians), 1896 v S, Ni (5)

Lofthouse, J. M. (Blackburn R), 1885 v S, W, Ni; 1887 v S, W; (with Accrington), 1889 v Ni; (with Blackburn R), 1890 v Ni (7)

Lofthouse, N. (Bolton W), 1951 v Y; 1952 v W, Ni, S, A (2), I, Sw; 1953 v W, Ni, S, Bel, Arg, Ch, U, US; 1954 v W, Ni, R of E, Bel, U; 1955 v Ni, S, F, Sp, P; 1956 v W, S, Sp, D, Fi (sub); 1959 v W, USSR (33)

Longworth, E. (Liverpool), 1920 v S; 1921 v Bel; 1923 v S, W, Bel (5)

Lowder, A. (Wolverhampton W), 1889 v W (1)

Lowe, E. (Aston Villa), 1947 v F, Sw, P (3)

Lucas, T. (Liverpool), 1922 v Ni; 1924 v F; 1926 v Bel (3)

Luntley, E. (Nottingham F), 1880 v S, W (2)

Lyttelton, Hon. A. (Cambridge University), 1877 v S (1)

Lyttelton, Hon. E. (Cambridge University), 1878 v S (1)

McCall, J. (Preston NE), 1913 v S, W; 1914 v S; 1920 v S; 1921 v Ni (5)

McDermott, T. (Liverpool), 1978 v Sw, L; 1979 v Ni, W, Se; 1980 v D, Ni (sub), Ei, Ni, S, Bel (sub), Sp; 1981 v N, R, Sw, R (sub), Br, Sw (sub), H; 1982 v N, H, W (sub), Ho, S (sub), Ic (25)

McDonald, C. A. (Burnley), 1958 v USSR (3), Br, A; 1959 v W, Ni, USSR (8)

McFarland, R. L. (Derby Co), 1971 v Gr, Ma (2), Ni, S; 1972 v Sw, Gr, WG, W, S; 1973 v W (3), Ni, S, Cz, Pol, USSR, I; 1974 v A, Pol, I, W, Ni; 1976 v Cz, S; 1977 v Ei, I (28)

McGarry, W. H. (Huddersfield T), 1954 v Sw, U; 1956 v W, D (4)

McGuinness, W. (Manchester U), 1959 v Ni, M (2)

McInroy, A. (Sunderland), 1927 v Ni (1)

McNab, R. (Arsenal), 1969 v Ni, Bul, R (1 + 1 sub) (4)

McNeal, R. (WBA), 1914 v S, W (2)

McNeil, M. (Middlesbrough), 1961 v W, Ni, S, L, P, Sp, M, I; 1962 v L (9)

Macaulay, R. H. (Cambridge University), 1881 v S (1)

Macdonald, M. (Newcastle U), 1972 v W, Ni, S (sub); 1973 v USSR (sub); 1974 v P, S (sub), Y (sub); 1975 v WG, Cy (2), Ni; 1976 v Sw (sub), Cz, P (14)

Macrae, S. (Notts Co), 1883 v S, W, Ni; 1884 v S, W, Ni (6)

Maddison, F. B. (Oxford University), 1872 v S (1)

Oakley, W. J. (Oxford University), 1895 v W; 1896 v S, W, Ni; (with Corinthians), 1897 v S, W, Ni; 1898 v S, W, Ni; 1900 v S, W, Ni; 1901 v S, W, Ni (16)
O'Dowd, J. P. (Chelsea), 1932 v S; 1933 v Ni, Sw (3)
O'Grady, M. (Huddersfield T), 1963 v Ni; (with Leeds U), 1969 v F (2)
Ogilvie, R. A. M. M. (Clapham R), 1874 v S (1)
Oliver, L. F. (Fulham), 1929 v Bel (1)
Olney, B. A. (Aston Villa), 1928 v F, Bel (2)
Osborne, F. R. (Fulham), 1923 v Ni, F; (with Tottenham H), 1925 v Bel; 1926 v Bel (4)
Osborne, R. (Leicester C), 1928 v W (1)
Osgood, P. L. (Chelsea), 1970 v Bel, R (sub), Cz (sub), 1974 v I (4)
Osman, R. (Ipswich T), 1980 v Aus; 1981 v Sp, R, Sw; 1982 v N, Ic (6)
Ottaway, C. J. (Oxford University), 1872 v S; 1874 v S (2)
Owen, J. R. B. (Sheffield), 1874 v S (1)
Owen, S. W. (Luton T), 1954 v H, Y, Bel (3)

Page, L. A. (Burnley), 1927 v S, W, Bel, L, F; 1928 v W, Ni (7)
Paine, T. L. (Southampton), 1963 v Cz, EG; 1964 v W, Ni, S, R of W, U, US, P; 1965 v Ni, H, Y, WG, Se; 1966 v W, A, Y, N, M (19)
Pantling, H. H. (Sheffield U), 1924 v Ni (1)
Paravacini, P. J. de (Cambridge University), 1883 v S, W, Ni (3)
Parker, T. R. (Southampton), 1925 v F (1)
Parkes, P. B. (QPR), 1974 v P (1)
Parkinson, J. (Liverpool), 1910 v S, W (2)
Parr, P. C. (Oxford University), 1882 v W (1)
Parry, E. H. (Old Carthusians), 1879 v W; 1882 v W, S (3)
Parry, R. A. (Bolton W), 1960 v Ni, S (2)
Patchitt, B. C. A. (Corinthians), 1923 v Se (2)
Pawson, F. W. (Cambridge University), 1883 v Ni; (with Swifts), 1885 v Ni (2)
Payne, J. (Luton T), 1937 v Fi (1)
Peacock, A. (Middlesbrough), 1962 v Arg, Bul; 1963 v Ni, W; (with Leeds U), 1966 v W, Ni (6)
Peacock, J. (Middlesbrough), 1929 v F, Bel, Sp (3)
Pearson, H. F. (WBA), 1932 v S (1)
Pearson, J. H. (Crewe Alex), 1892 v Ni (1)
Pearson, J. S. (Manchester U), 1976 v W, Ni, S, Br, Fi; 1977 v Ei, Ho (sub), W, S, Br, Arg, U; 1978 v I (sub), WG, Ni (15)
Pearson, S. C. (Manchester U), 1948 v S; 1949 v S, Ni; 1950 v Ni, I; 1951 v P; 1952 v S, I (8)
Pease, W. H. (Middlesbrough), 1927 v W (1)
Pegg, D. (Manchester U), 1957 v Ei (1)
Pejic, M. (Stoke C), 1974 v P, W, Ni, S (4)
Pelly, F. R. (Old Foresters), 1893 v Ni; 1894 v S, W (3)
Pennington, J. (WBA), 1907 v S, W; 1908 v S, W, Ni, A; 1909 v S, W, H (2), A; 1910 v S, W; 1911 v S, W, Ni; 1912 v S, W, Ni; 1913 v S, W; 1914 v S, Ni; 1920 v S, W (25)
Pentland, F. B. (Middlesbrough), 1909 v S, W, H (2), A (5)
Perry, C. (WBA), 1890 v Ni; 1891 v Ni; 1893 v W (3)
Perry, T. (WBA), 1898 v W (1)
Perry, W. (Blackpool), 1956 v Ni, S, Sp (3)
Perryman, S. (Tottenham H), 1982 v Ic (sub) (1)
Peters, M. (West Ham U), 1966 v Y, Fi, Pol, M, F, Arg, P, WG; 1967 v Ni, W, S, Cz; 1968 v W, Ni, S, USSR (2), Sp (2), Se, Y; 1969 v Ni, S, R, Bul, F, M, U, Br; 1970 v Ho (2), P (sub), Bel; (with Tottenham H), W, Ni, S, Co, Ec, R, Br, Cz, WG; 1971 v EG, Gr, Ma (2), Ni, W, S; 1972 v Sw, Gr, WG (1 + 1 sub) Ni (sub) 1973 v S (2), Ni, W, Cz, Pol, USSR, I; 1974 v A, Pol, I, P, S (67)

Phillips, L. H. (Portsmouth), 1952 v Ni; 1955 v W, WG (3)
Pickering, F. (Everton), 1964 v US; 1965 v Ni, Bel (3)
Pickering, J. (Sheffield U), 1933 v S (1)
Pike, T. M. (Cambridge University), 1886 v Ni (1)
Pilkington, B. (Burnley), 1955 v Ni (1)
Plant, J. (Bury), 1900 v S (1)
Plum, S. L. (Charlton Ath), 1923 v F (1)
Pointer, R. (Burnley), 1962 v W, L, P (3)
Porteous, T. S. (Sunderland), 1891 v W (1)
Priest, A. E. (Sheffield U), 1900 v Ni (1)
Prinsep, J. F. M. (Clapham Rovers), 1879 v S (1)
Puddefoot, S. C. (Blackburn R), 1926 v S, Ni (2)
Pye, J. (Wolverhampton W), 1950 v Ei (1)
Pym, R. H. (Bolton W), 1925 v S, W; 1926 v W (3)

Quantrill, A. (Derby Co), 1920 v S, W; 1921 v W, Ni (4)
Quixall, A. (Sheffield W), 1954 v W, Ni, R of E; 1955 v Sp, P (sub) (5)

Radford, J. (Arsenal), 1969 v R; 1972 v Sw (sub) (2)
Raikes, G. B. (Oxford University), 1895 v W; 1896 v W, Ni, S (4)
Ramsey, A. E. (Southampton), 1949 v Sw; (with Tottenham H), 1950 v S, I, P, Bel, Ch, US, Sp; 1951 v S, Ni, W, Y, Arg, P; 1952 v S, W, Ni, F, A (2), I, Sw; 1953 v Ni, W, S, Bel, Arg, Ch, U, US; 1954 v R of E, H (32)
Rawlings, A. (Preston NE), 1921 v Bel (1)
Rawlings, W. E. (Southampton), 1922 v S, W (2)
Rawlinson, J. F. P. (Cambridge University), 1882 v Ni (1)
Rawson, H. E. (Royal Engineers), 1875 v S (1)
Rawson, W. S. (Oxford University), 1875 v S; 1877 v S (2)
Read, A. (Tufnell Park), 1921 v Bel (1)
Reader, J. (WBA), 1894 v Ni (1)
Reaney, P. (Leeds U), 1969 v Bul (sub); 1970 v P; 1971 v Ma (3)
Reeves, K. (Norwich C), 1980 v Bul; (with Manchester C), Ni (2)
Regis, C. (WBA), 1982 v Ni (sub), W (sub), Ic (3)
Revie, D. G. (Manchester C), 1955 v Ni, S, F; 1956 v W, D; 1957 v Ni (6)
Reynolds, J. (WBA), 1892 v S; 1893 v S, W; (with Aston Villa), 1894 v S, Ni; 1895 v S; 1897 v S, W (8)
Richards, C. H. (Nottingham F), 1898 v Ni (1)
Richards, G. H. (Derby Co), 1909 v A (1)
Richards, J. P. (Wolverhampton W), 1973 v Ni (1)
Richardson, J. R. (Newcastle U), 1933 v I, Sw (2)
Richardson, W. G. (WBA), 1935 v Ho (1)
Rickaby, S. (WBA), 1954 v Ni (1)
Rigby, A. (Blackburn R), 1927 v S, Bel, L, F; 1928 v W (5)
Rimmer, E. J. (Sheffield W), 1930 v S, G, A; 1932 v Sp (4)
Rimmer, J. J. (Arsenal), 1976 v I (1)
Rix, G. (Arsenal), 1981 v N, R, Sw (sub), Br, W, S; 1982 v Ho (sub), Fi (sub), F, Cz, K, WG, Sp (13)
Robb, G. (Tottenham H), 1954 v H (1)
Roberts, C. (Manchester U), 1905 v Ni, W, S (3)
Roberts, F. (Manchester C), 1925 v S, W, Bel, F (4)
Roberts, H. (Arsenal), 1931 v S (1)
Roberts, H. (Millwall), 1931 v Bel (1)
Roberts, R. (WBA), 1887 v S; 1888 v Ni; 1890 v Ni (3)
Roberts, W. T. (Preston NE), 1924 v W, Bel (2)
Robinson, J. (Sheffield W), 1937 v Fi; 1938 v G, Sw; 1939 v W (4)
Robinson, J. W. (Derby Co), 1897 v S, Ni; (with New Brighton Tower), 1898 v S, W, Ni; (with Southampton), 1899 v W, S; 1900 v S, W, Ni; 1901 v Ni (11)
Robson, B. (WBA), 1980 v Ei, Aus; 1981 v N, R, Sw, Sp, R, Br, W, S, Sw, H; 1982 v N (with Manchester U), H, Ni, W, Ho, S, Fi, F, Cz, WG, Sp (23)

Robson, R. (WBA), 1958 v F, USSR (2), Br, A; 1960 v Sp, H; 1961 v Ni, W, S, L, P, Sp, M, I; 1962 v W, Ni, Sw, L, P (20)

Rose, W. C. (Wolverhampton W), 1884 v S, W, Ni; (with Preston NE), 1886 v Ni; (with Wolverhampton W), 1891 v Ni (5)

Rostron, T. (Darwen), 1881 v S, W (2)

Rowe, A. (Tottenham H), 1934 v F (1)

Rowley, J. F. (Manchester U), 1949 v Sw, Se, F; 1950 v Ni, I; 1952 v S (6)

Rowley, W. (Stoke C), 1889 v Ni; 1892 v Ni (2)

Royle, J. (Everton), 1971 v Ma; 1973 v Y; (with Manchester C), 1976 v Ni (sub), I; 1977 v Fi, L (6)

Ruddlesdin, H. (Sheffield W), 1904 v W, Ni; 1905 v S (3)

Ruffell, J. W. (West Ham U), 1926 v S; 1927 v Ni; 1929 v S, W, Ni; 1930 v W (6)

Russell, B. B. (Royal Engineers), 1883 v W (1)

Rutherford, J. (Newcastle U), 1904 v S; 1907 v S, Ni, W; 1908 v S, Ni, W, A (2), H, B (11)


Sadler, D. (Manchester U), 1968 v Ni, USSR; 1970 v Ec (sub); 1971 v EG (4)

Sagar, C. (Bury), 1900 v Ni; 1902 v W (2)

Sagar, E. (Everton), 1936 v S, Ni, A, Bel (4)

Sandford, E. A. (WBA), 1933 v W (1)

Sandilands, R. R. (Old Westminsters), 1892 v W; 1893 v Ni; 1894 v W; 1895 v W; 1896 v W (5)

Sands, J. (Nottingham F), 1880 v W (1)

Sansom, K. (C Palace), 1979 v W; 1980 v Bul, Ei, Arg, W (sub), Ni, S, Bel, I; (with Arsenal), 1981 v N, R, Sw, Sp, R, Br, W, S, Sw; 1982 v Ni, W, Ho, S, Fi, F, Cz, WG, Sp (27)

Saunders, F. E. (Swifts), 1888 v W (1)

Savage, A. H. (C Palace), 1876 v S (1)

Sayer, J. (Stoke C), 1887 v Ni (1)

Scattergood, E. (Derby Co), 1913 v W (1)

Schofield, J. (Stoke C), 1892 v W; 1893 v W; 1895 v Ni (3)

Scott, L. (Arsenal), 1947 v S, W, Ni, Ei, Ho, F, Sw, P; 1948 v S, W, Ni, Bel, Se, I; 1949 v W, Ni, D (17)

Scott, W. R. (Brentford), 1937 v W (1)

Seddon, J. (Bolton W), 1923 v F, Se (2); 1924 v Bel; 1927 v W; 1929 v S (6)

Seed, J. M. (Tottenham H), 1921 v Bel: 1923 v W, Ni, Bel; 1925 v S (5)

Settle, J. (Bury), 1899 v S, W, Ni; (with Everton), 1902 v S, Ni; 1903 v Ni (6)

Sewell, J. (Sheffield W), 1952 v Ni, A, Sw; 1953 v Ni; 1954 v H (2) (6)

Sewell, W. R. (Blackburn R), 1924 v W (1)

Shackleton, L. F. (Sunderland), 1949 v W, D; 1950 v W; 1955 v W, WG (5)

Sharp, J. (Everton), 1903 v Ni; 1905 v S (2)

Shaw, G. E. (WBA), 1932 v S (1)

Shaw, G. L. (Sheffield U), 1959 v S, W, USSR, I; 1963 v W (5)

Shea, D. (Blackburn R), 1914 v W, Ni (2)

Shellito, K. J. (Chelsea), 1963 v Cz (1)

Shelton A. (Notts Co), 1889 v Ni; 1890 v S, W; 1891 v S, W; 1892 v S (6)

Shelton, C. (Notts Rangers), 1888 v Ni (1)

Shepherd, A. (Bolton W), 1906 v S; (with Newcastle U), 1911 v Ni (2)

Shilton, P. L. (Leicester C), 1971 v EG, W; 1972 v Sw, Ni; 1973 v Y, S (2), Ni, W, Cz, Pol, USSR, I; 1974 v A, Pol, I, W, Ni, S, Arg; (with Stoke C), 1975 v Cy; 1977 v Ni, W; (with Nottingham F), 1978 v W, H; 1979 v Cz, Se, A; 1980 v Ni, Sp, I; 1981 v N, Sw, R; 1982 v H, Ho, S, F, Cz, K, WG, Sp (42)

Shimwell, E. (Blackpool), 1949 v Se (1)

Shutt, G. (Stoke C), 1886 v Ni (1)

Silcock, J. (Manchester U), 1921 v S, W; 1923 v Se (3)

Sillett, R. P. (Chelsea), 1955 v F, Sp, P (3)

Simms, E. (Luton T), 1922 v Ni (1)

Simpson, J. (Blackburn R), 1911 v S, W, Ni; 1912 v S, W, Ni; 1913 v S; 1914 v W (8)

Slater, W. J. (Wolverhampton W), 1955 v W, WG; 1958 v S, P, Y, USSR (3), Br, A; 1959 v USSR; 1960 v S (12)

Smalley, T. (Wolverhampton W), 1937 v W (1)

Smart, T. (Aston Villa), 1921 v S; 1924 v S, W; 1926 v Ni; 1930 v W (5)

Smith, A. (Nottingham F), 1891 v S, W; 1893 v Ni (3)

Smith, A. K. (Oxford University), 1872 v S (1)

Smith, B. (Tottenham H), 1921 v S; 1922 v W (2)

Smith, C. E. (C Palace), 1876 v S (1)

Smith, G. O. (Oxford University), 1893 v Ni; 1894 v W, S; 1895 v W; 1896 v Ni, W, S; (with Old Carthusians), 1897 v Ni, W, S; 1898 v Ni, W, S; (with Corinthians), 1899 v Ni, W, S; 1899 v Ni, W, S; 1901 v S (20)

Smith, H. (Reading), 1905 v W, S; 1906 v W, Ni (4)

Smith, J. (WBA), 1920 v Ni; 1923 v Ni (2)

Smith, Joe (Bolton W), 1913 v Ni; 1914 v S, W; 1920 v W, Ni (5)

Smith, J. C. R. (Millwall), 1939 v Ni, N (2)

Smith, J. W. (Portsmouth), 1932 v Ni, W, Sp (3)

Smith, Leslie (Brentford), 1939 v R (1)

Smith, Lionel (Arsenal), 1951 v W; 1952 v W, Ni; 1953 v W, S, Bel (6)

Smith, R. A. (Tottenham H), 1961 v Ni, W, S, L, P, Sp; 1962 v S; 1963 v S, F, Br, Cz, EG; 1964 v W, Ni, R of W (15)

Smith, S. (Aston Villa), 1895 v S (1)

Smith, S. C. (Leicester C), 1936 v Ni (1)

Smith, T. (Birmingham C), 1960 v W, Se (2)

Smith, T. (Liverpool), 1971 v W (1)

Smith, W. H. (Huddersfield T), 1922 v W, S; 1928 v S (3)

Sorby, T. H. (Thursday Wanderers, Sheffield), 1879 v W (1)

Southworth, J. (Blackburn R), 1889 v W; 1891 v W; 1892 v S (3)

Sparks, F. J. (Herts Rangers), 1879 v S; (with Clapham Rovers), 1880 v S, W (3)

Spence, J. W. (Manchester U), 1926 v Bel; 1927 v Ni (2)

Spence, R. (Chelsea), 1936 v A, Bel (2)

Spencer, C. W. (Newcastle U), 1924 v S; 1925 v W (2)

Spencer, H. (Aston Villa), 1897 v S, W; 1900 v W; 1903 v Ni; 1905 v W, S (6)

Spiksley, F. (Sheffield W), 1893 v S, W; 1894 v S, Ni; 1896 v Ni; 1898 v S, W (7)

Spilsbury, B. W. (Cambridge University), 1885 v Ni; 1886 v Ni, S (3)

Spouncer, W. A. (Nottingham F), 1900 v W (1)

Springett, R. D. G. (Sheffield W), 1960 v Ni, S, Y, Sp, H; 1961 v Ni, S, L, P, Sp, M, I, A; 1962 v W, Ni, S, A, Sw, Pe, L, P, H, Arg, Bul, Br; 1963 v Ni, W, F (2), Sw; 1966 v W, A, N (33)

Sproston, B. (Leeds U), 1937 v W; 1938 v S, W, Ni, Cz, G, Sw, F; (with Tottenham H), 1939 v W, R of E; (with Manchester C), N (11)

Squire, R. T. (Cambridge University), 1886 v S, W, Ni (3)

Stanbrough, M. H. (Old Carthusians), 1895 v W (1)

Staniforth, R. (Huddersfield T), 1954 v S, H, Y, Bel, Sw, U; 1955 v W, WG (8)

Starling, R. W. (Sheffield W), 1933 v S; (with Aston Villa), 1937 v S (2)

Steele, F. C. (Stoke C), 1937 v S, W, Ni, N, Se, Fi (6)

Stephenson, C. (Huddersfield T), 1924 v W (1)

Stephenson, G. T. (Derby Co), 1928 v F, Bel; (with Sheffield W), 1931 v F (3)

Stephenson, J. E. (Leeds U), 1938 v S; 1939 v Ni (2)

Stepney, A. C. (Manchester U), 1968 v Se (1)

Stewart, J. (Sheffield W), 1907 v S, W; (with Newcastle U), 1911 v S (3)

Stiles, N. P. (Manchester U), 1965 v S, H, Y, Se; 1966 v W, Ni, S, A, Sp, Pol (2), WG (2), N, D, U, M, F, Arg, P; 1967 v Ni, W, S, Cz; 1968 v USSR; 1969 v R; 1970 v Ni, S (28)

Stoker, J. (Birmingham), 1933 v W; 1934 v S, H (3)

Storer, H. (Derby Co), 1924 v F; 1928 v Ni (2)

Storey, P. E. (Arsenal), 1971 v Gr, Ni, S; 1972 v Sw, WG, W, Ni, S; 1973 v W (3), Y, S (2), Ni, Cz, Pol, USSR, I (19)

Storey-Moore, I. (Nottingham F), 1970 v Ho (1)

Strange, A. H. (Sheffield W), 1930 v S, A, G; 1931 v S, W, Ni, F, Bel; 1932 v S, W, Ni, Sp; 1933 v S, Ni, A, I, Sw; 1934 v Ni, W, F (20)

Stratford, A. H. (Wanderers), 1874 v S (1)

Streten, B. (Luton T), 1950 v Ni (1)

Sturgess, A. (Sheffield U), 1911 v Ni; 1914 v S (2)

Summerbee, M. G. (Manchester C), 1968 v S, Sp, WG; 1972 v Sw, WG (sub), W, Ni; 1973 v USSR (sub) (8)

Sunderland, A. (Arsenal), 1980 v Aus (1)

Sutcliffe, J. W. (Bolton W), 1893 v W; 1895 v S, Ni; 1901 v S; (with Millwall), 1903 v W (5)

Swan, P. (Sheffield W), 1960 v Y, Sp, H; 1961 v Ni, W, S, L, P, Sp, M, I, A; 1962 v W, Ni, S, A, Sw, L, P (19)

Swepstone, H. A. (Pilgrims), 1880 v S; 1882 v S, W; 1883 v S, W, Ni (6)

Swift, F. V. (Manchester C), 1947, v S, W, Ni, Ei, Ho, F, Sw, P; 1948 v S, W, Ni, Bel, Se, I; 1949 v S, W, Ni, D, N (19)


Tait, G. (Birmingham Excelsior), 1881 v W (1)

Talbot, B. (Ipswich T), 1977 v Ni (sub), S, Br, Arg, U; (with Arsenal), 1980 v Aus (6)

Tambling, R. V. (Chelsea), 1963 v W, F; 1966 v Y (3)

Tate, J. T. (Aston Villa), 1931 v F, Bel; 1933 v W (3)

Taylor, E. (Blackpool), 1954 v H (1)

Taylor, E. H. (Huddersfield T), 1923 v S, W, Ni, Bel; 1924 v S, Ni, F; 1926 v S (8)

Taylor, J. G. (Fulham), 1951 v Arg, P (2)

Taylor, P. J. (C Palace), 1976 v W (sub), W, Ni, S (4)

Taylor, P. H. (Liverpool), 1948 v W, Ni, Se (3)

Taylor, T. (Manchester U), 1953 v Arg, Ch, U; 1954 v Bel, Sw; 1956 v S, Br, Se, Fi, WG; 1957 v Ni, Y (sub), D (2), Ei (2); 1958 v W, Ni, F (19)

Temple, D. W. (Everton), 1965 v WG (1)

Thickett, H. (Sheffield U), 1899 v S, W (2)

Thomas, D. (QPR), 1975 v Cz (sub), P, Cy (sub + 1), W, S (sub); 1976 v Cz (sub), P (sub) (8)

Thompson, P. (Liverpool), 1964 v P (2), Ei, US, Br, Arg; 1965 v Ni, W, S, Bel, Ho; 1966 v Ni; 1968 v Ni, WG; 1970 v S, Ho (sub) (16)

Thompson, P. B. (Liverpool), 1976 v W (2), Ni, S, Br, I, Fi; 1977 v Fi; 1979 v Ei (sub), Cz, Ni, S, Bul, Se (sub), A; 1980 v D, Ni, Bul, Ei, Sp (2), Arg, W, S, Bel, I; 1981 v N, R, H; 1982 v N, H, W, Ho, S, Fi, F, Cz, K, WG, Sp (40)

Thompson, T. (Aston Villa), 1952 v W; (with Preston NE), 1957 v S (2)

Thomson, R. A. (Wolverhampton W), 1964 v Ni, US, P, Arg; 1965 v Bel, Ho, Ni, W (8)

Thornewell, G. (Derby Co), 1923 v Se (2); 1924 v F; 1925 v F (4)

Thornley, I. (Manchester C), 1907 v W (1)

Tilson, S. F. (Manchester C), 1934 v H, Cz; 1935 v W; 1936 v Ni (4)

Titmuss, F. (Southampton), 1922 v W; 1923 v W (2)

Todd, C. (Derby Co), 1972 v Ni; 1974 v P, W, Ni, S, Arg, EG, Bul, Y; 1975 v P (sub), WG, Cy (2), Ni, W, S; 1976 v Sw, Cz, P, Ni, S, Br, Fi; 1977 v Ei, Fi, Ho (sub), Ni (27)

Toone, G. (Notts Co), 1892 v S, W (2)

Topham, A. G. (Casuals), 1894 v W (1)

Topham, R. (Wolverhampton W), 1893 v Ni; (with Casuals) 1894 v W (2)

Towers, M. A. (Sunderland), 1976 v W, Ni (sub), I (3)

Townley, W. J. (Blackburn R), 1889 v W; 1890 v Ni (2)

Townrow, J. E. (Clapton Orient), 1925 v S; 1926 v W (2)

Tremelling, D. R. (Birmingham), 1928 v W (1)

Tresadern, J. (West Ham U), 1923 v S, Se (2)

Tueart, D. (Manchester C), 1975 v Cy (sub), Ni; 1977 v Fi, Ni, W (sub), S (sub) (6)

Tunstall, F. E. (Sheffield U), 1923 v S; 1924 v S, W, Ni, F; 1925 v Ni, S (7)

Turnbull, R. J. (Bradford), 1920 v Ni (1)

Turner, A. (Southampton), 1900 v Ni; 1901 v Ni (2)

Turner, H. (Huddersfield T), 1931 v F, Bel (2)

Turner, J. A. (Bolton W), 1893 v W; (with Stoke C) 1895 v Ni; (with Derby Co) 1898 v Ni (3)

Tweedy, G. J. (Grimsby T), 1937 v H (1)


Ufton, D. G. (Charlton Ath), 1954 v R of E (1)

Underwood A. (Stoke C), 1891 v Ni; 1892 v Ni (2)

Urwin, T. (Middlesbrough), 1923 v Se (2); (with Newcastle U) 1924 v Bel; 1926 v W (4)

Utley, G. (Barnsley), 1913 v Ni (1)


Vaughton, O. H. (Aston Villa), 1882 v S, W, Ni; 1884 v S, W (5)

Veitch, C. C. M. (Newcastle U), 1906 v S, W, Ni; 1907 v S, W; 1909 v W (6)

Veitch, J. G. (Old Westminsters), 1894 v W (1)

Venables, T. F. (Chelsea), 1965 v Ho, Bel (2)

Vidal, R. W. S. (Oxford University), 1873 v S (1)

Viljoen, C. (Ipswich T), 1975 v Ni, W (2)

Viollet, D. S. (Manchester U), 1960 v H; 1962 v L (2)

Von Donop (Royal Engineers), 1873 v S; 1875 v S (2)


Wace, H. (Wanderers), 1878 v S; 1879 v S, W (3)

Wadsworth, S. J. (Huddersfield T), 1922 v S; 1923 v S, Bel; 1924 v S, Ni; 1925 v S, Ni; 1926 v W; 1927 v Ni (9)

Wainscoat, W. R. (Leeds U), 1929 v S (1)

Waiters, A. K. (Blackpool), 1964 v Ei, Br; 1965 v W, Bel, Ho (5)

Walden, F. I. (Tottenham H), 1914 v S; 1922 v W (2)

Walker, W. H. (Aston Villa), 1921 v Ni; 1922 v Ni, W, S; 1923 v Se (2); 1924 v S; 1925 v Ni, W, S, Bel, F; 1926 v Ni, W, S; 1927 v Ni, W; 1933 v A (18)

Wall, G. (Manchester U), 1907 v W; 1908 v Ni; 1909 v S; 1910 v W, S; 1912 v S; 1913 v Ni (7)

Wallace, C. W. (Aston Villa), 1913 v W; 1914 v Ni; 1920 v S (3)

Walters, A. M. (Cambridge University), 1885 v S, N; 1886 v S; 1887 v S, W; (with Old Carthusians) 1889 v S, W; 1890 v S, W (9)

Walters, P. M. (Oxford University), 1885 v S, Ni; (with Old Carthusians), 1886 v S, W, Ni; 1887 v S, W; 1888 v S, Ni; 1889 v S, W; 1890 v S, W (13)

Walton, N. (Blackburn R) 1890 v Ni (1)

Ward, J. T. (Blackburn Olympic), 1885 v W (1)

Ward, P. (Brighton & HA), 1980 v Aus (sub) (1)

Ward, T. V. (Derby Co), 1948 v Bel; 1949 v W (2)

Waring, T. (Aston Villa), 1931 v F, Bel; 1932 v S, W, Ni (5)

Warner, C. (Upton Park), 1878 v S (1)

Warren, B. (Derby Co), 1906 v S, W, Ni; 1907 v S, W, Ni; 1908 v S, W, Ni, A (2), H, B; 1909 v S, Ni, W, H (2), A; 1911 v S, Ni, W (22)

Waterfield, G. S. (Burnley), 1927 v W (1)

Watson, D. V. (Sunderland), 1974 v P, S (sub), Arg, EG, Bul, Y; 1975 v Cz, P, WG, Cy (2), Ni, W, S; (with

Manchester C) 1976 v Sw, Cz (sub), P; 1977 v Ho, L, Ni, W, S, Br, Arg, U; 1978 v Sw, L, I, WG, Br, W, Ni, S, H; 1979 v D, Ei, Cz, Ni (2), W, S, Bul, Se, A; (with Werder Bremen), 1980 v D; (with Southampton) Ni, Bul, Ei, Sp (2), Arg, Ni, S, Bel, I; 1981 v N, R, Sw, R, W, S, Sw, H; (with Stoke C), 1982 v Ni, Ic (65)

Watson, V. M. (West Ham U), 1923 v W, S; 1930 v S, G, A (5)

Watson, W. (Burnley), 1913 v S; 1914 v Ni; 1920 v Ni (3)

Watson, W. (Sunderland), 1950 v Ni, I; 1951 v W, Y (4)

Weaver, S. (Newcastle U), 1932 v S, 1933 v S, Ni (3)

Webb, G. W. (West Ham U), 1911 v S, W (2)

Webster, M. (Middlesbrough), 1930 v S, A, G (3)

Wedlock, W. J. (Bristol C), 1907 v S, Ni, W; 1908 v S, Ni, W, A (2), H, B; 1909 v S, W, Ni, H (2), A; 1910 v S, W, Ni; 1911 v S, W, Nj; 1912 v S, W, Ni; 1914 v W (26)

Weir, D. (Bolton W), 1889 v S, Ni (2)

Welch, R. de C. (Wanderers), 1872 v S; (with Harrow Chequers) 1874 v S (2)

Weller, K. (Leicester C), 1974 v W, Ni, S, Arg (4)

Welsh, D. (Charlton Ath), 1938 v G, Sw; 1939 v R (3)

West, G. (Everton), 1969 v W, Bul, M (3)

Westwood, R. W. (Bolton W), 1935 v S, W, Ho; 1936 v Ni, G; 1937 v W (6)

Whateley, O. (Aston Villa), 1883 v S, Ni (2)

Wheeler, J. E. (Bolton W), 1955 v Ni (1)

Wheldon, G. F. (Aston Villa), 1897 v Ni; 1898 v S, W, Ni (4)

White, T. A. (Everton), 1933 v I (1)

Whitehead, J. (Accrington), 1893 v W; (with Blackburn R) 1894 v Ni (2)

Whitfeld, H. (Old Etonians), 1879 v W (1)

Whitham, M. (Sheffield U), 1892 v Ni (1)

Whitworth, S. (Leicester C), 1975 v WG, Cy, Ni, W, S; 1976 v Sw, P (7)

Whymark, T. J. (Ipswich T), 1978 v L (sub) (1)

Widdowson, S. W. (Nottingham F), 1880 v S (1)

Wignall, F. (Nottingham F), 1965 v W, Ho (2)

Wilkes, A. (Aston Villa), 1901 v S, W; 1902 v S, W, Ni (5)

Wilkins, R. G. (Chelsea), 1976 v I; 1977 v Ei, Fi, Ni, Br, Arg, U; 1978 v Sw (sub), L, I, WG, W, Ni, S, H; 1979 v D, Ei, Cz, Ni, W, S, Bul, Se (sub), A; (with Manchester U) 1980 v D, Ni, Bul, Sp (2), Arg, W (sub), Ni, S, Bel, I; 1981 v Sp (sub), R, Br, W, S, Sw, H (sub); 1982 v Ni, W, Ho, S, Fi, F, Cz, K, WG, Sp (52)

Wilkinson, B. (Sheffield U), 1904 v S (1)

Wilkinson, L. R. (Oxford University), 1891 v W (1)

Williams, B. F. (Wolverhampton W), 1949 v F; 1950 v S, W, Ei, I, P, Bel, Ch, US, Sp; 1951 v Ni, W, S, Y, Arg, P; 1952 v W, F; 1955 v S, WG, F, Sp, P; 1956 v W (24)

Williams, O. (Clapton Orient), 1923 v W, Ni (2)

Williams, W. (WBA), 1897 v Ni; 1898 v W, Ni, S; 1899 v W, Ni (6)

Williamson, E. C. (Arsenal), 1923 v Se (2) (2)

Williamson, R. G. (Middlesbrough), 1905 v Ni; 1911 v Ni, S, W; 1912 v S, W; 1913 v Ni (7)

Willingham, C. K. (Huddersfield T), 1937 v Fi; 1938 v S, G, Sw, F; 1939 v S, W, Ni, R of E, N, I, Y (12)

Willis, A. (Tottenham H), 1952 v F (1)

Wilshaw, D. J. (Wolverhampton W), 1954 v W, Sw, U; 1955 v S, F, Sp, P; 1956 v W, Ni, Fi, WG; 1957 v Ni (12)

Wilson, C. P. (Hendon), 1884 v S, W (2)

Wilson, C. W. (Oxford University), 1879 v W; 1881 v S (2)

Wilson, G. (Sheffield W), 1921 v S, W, Bel; 1922 v S, Ni; 1923 v S, W, Ni, Bel; 1924 v W, Ni, F (12)

Wilson, G. P. (Corinthians), 1900 v S, W (2)

Wilson, R. (Huddersfield T), 1960 v S, Y, Sp, H; 1962 v W, Ni, S, A, Sw, Pe, P, H, Arg, Bul, Br; 1963 v Ni, F, Br, Cz, EG, Sw; 1964 v W, S, R of W, U, P (2), Ei, Br, Arg; (with Everton), 1965 v S, H, Y, WG, Se; 1966 v WG (sub), W, Ni, A, Sp, Pol (2), Y, Fi, D, U, M, F, Arg, P, WG; 1967 v Ni, W, S, Cz, A; 1968 v Ni, S, USSR (2), Sp (2), Y (63)

Wilson, T. (Huddersfield T), 1928 v S (1)

Winckworth, W. N. (Old Westminsters), 1892 v W; 1893 v Ni (2)

Windridge, J. E. (Chelsea), 1908 v S, W, Ni, A (2), H, B; 1909 v Ni (8)

Wingfield-Stratford, C. V. (Royal Engineers), 1877 v S (1)

Withe, P. (Aston Villa), 1981 v Br, W, S; 1982 v N (sub), W, Ic (6)

Wollaston, C. H. R. (Wanderers), 1874 v S; 1875 v S; 1877 v S; 1880 v S (4)

Wolstenholme, S. (Everton), 1904 v S; (with Blackburn R), 1905 v W, Ni (3)

Wood, H. (Wolverhampton W), 1890 v S, W; 1896 v S (3)

Wood, R. E. (Manchester U), 1955 v Ni, W; 1956 v Fi (3)

Woodcock, T. (Nottingham F), 1978 v Ni; 1979 v Ei (sub), Cz, Bul (sub), Se; 1980 v Ni; (with Cologne), Bul, Ei, Sp (2), Arg, Bel, I; 1981 v N, R, Sw, R, W (sub), S; 1982 v Ni (sub), Ho, Fi (sub), WG (sub), Sp (24)

Woodger, G. (Oldham Ath), 1911 v Ni (1)

Woodhall, G. (WBA), 1888 v S, W (2)

Woodley, V. R. (Chelsea), 1937 v S, N, Se, Fi; 1938 v S, W, Ni, Cz, G, Sw, F; 1939 v S, W, Ni, R of E, N, I, R, Y (19)

Woodward, V. J. (Tottenham H), 1903 v S, W, Ni; 1904 v S, Ni; 1905 v S, W, Ni; 1907 v S; 1908 v S, W, Ni, A (2), H, B; 1909 v W, Ni, H (2), A; (with Chelsea), 1910 v Ni; 1911 v W (23)

Woosnam, M. (Manchester C), 1922 v W (1)

Worrall, F. (Portsmouth), 1935 v Ho; 1937 v Ni (2)

Worthington, F. S. (Leicester C), 1974 v Ni (sub), S, Arg, EG, Bul, Y; 1975 v Cz, P (sub) (8)

Wreford-Brown, C. (Oxford University), 1889 v Ni; (with Old Carthusians), 1894 v W; 1895 v W; 1898 v S (4)

Wright, E, G. D. (Cambridge University), 1906 v W (1)

Wright, J. D. (Newcastle U), 1939 v N (1)

Wright, T. J. (Everton), 1968 v USSR; 1969 v R (2), M (sub), U, Br; 1970 v W, Ho, Bel, R (sub), Br (11)

Wright, W. A. (Wolverhampton W), 1947 v S, W, Ni, Ei, Ho, F, Sw, P; 1948 v S, W, Ni, Bel, Se, I; 1949 v S, W, Ni, D, Sw, Se, N, F; 1950 v S, W, Ni, Ei, I, P, Bel, Ch, US, Sp; 1951 v Ni, S, Arg; 1952 v W, Ni, S, F, A (2), I, Sw; 1953 v Ni, W, S, Bel, Arg, Ch, U, US; 1954 v W, Ni, S, R of E, H (2), Y, Bel, Sw, U; 1955 v W, Ni, S, WG, F, Sp, P; 1956 v Ni, W, S, Br, Se, Fi, WG, D, Sp; 1957 v S, W, Ni, Y, D (2), Ei (2); 1958 v W, Ni, S, P, Y, USSR (3), Br, A, F; 1959 v W, Ni, S, USSR, I, Br, Pe, M, US (105)

Wylie, J. G. (Wanderers), 1878 v S (1)

Yates, J. (Burnley), 1889 v Ni (1)

York, R. E. (Aston Villa), 1922 v S; 1926 v S (2)

Young, A. (Huddersfield T), 1933 v W; 1937 v S, H, N, Se; 1938 v G, Sw, F; 1939 v W (9)

Young, G. M. (Sheffield W), 1965 v W (1)

R. E. Evans also played for Wales against E, Ni, S; J. Reynolds also played for Ireland against E, W, S.


# NORTHERN IRELAND

Aherne, T. (Belfast C), 1947 v E; 1948 v S; 1949 v W; (with Luton T), 1950 v W (4)

Alexander, A. (Cliftonville), 1895 v S (1)

Allen, C. A. (Cliftonville), 1936 v E (1)

Allen, J. (Limavady), 1887 v E (1)

Anderson, T. (Manchester U), 1973 v Cy, E, S, W; 1974 v Bul, P; (with Swindon T), 1975 v S (sub); 1976 v Is; 1977 v Ho, Bel, WG, E, S, W, Ic; 1978 v Ic, Ho, Bel; (with Peterborough U), S, E, W; 1979 v D (22)

Anderson, W. (Linfield), 1898 v W, E, S; 1899 v S (4)

Andrews, W. (Glentoran), 1908 v S; (with Grimsby T), 1913 v E, S (3)

Armstrong, G. (Tottenham H), 1977 v WG, E, W (sub), Ic (sub); 1978 v Bel, S, E, W; 1979 v Ei, D, Bul, E, Bul, E, S, W, D; 1980 v E, Ei, Is, S, E, W, Aus (3); 1981 v Se; (with Watford), P, S, P, S, Se; 1982 v S, Is, E, F, W, Y, Hon, Sp, A, F (42)

Baird, G. (Distillery), 1896 v S, E, W (3)
Baird, H. (Huddersfield T), 1939 v E (1)
Balfe, J. (Shelbourne), 1909 v E; 1910 v W (2)
Bambrick, J. (Linfield), 1929 v W, S, E; 1930 v W, S, E; 1932 v W; (with Chelsea), 1935 v W; 1936 v E, S; 1938 v W (11)
Banks, S. J. (Cliftonville), 1937 v W (1)
Barr, H. H. (Linfield), 1962 v E; (with Coventry C), 1963 v E, Pol (3)
Barron, H. (Cliftonville), 1894 v E, W, S; 1895 v S; 1896 v S; 1897 v E, W (7)
Barry, H. (Bohemians), 1900 v S (1)
Baxter, R. A. (Cliftonville), 1887 v S, W (2)
Bennett, L. V. (Dublin University), 1889 v W (1)
Berry, J. (Cliftonville), 1888 v S, W; 1889 v E (3)
Best, G. (Manchester U), 1964 v W, U; 1965 v E, Ho (2), S, Sw (2), Alb; 1966 v S, E, Alb; 1967 v E; 1968 v S; 1969 v E, S, W, T; 1970 v S, E, W, USSR; 1971 v Cy (2), Sp, E, S, W; 1972 v USSR, Sp; 1973 v Bul; 1974 v P; (with Fulham), 1977 v Ho, Bel, WG; 1978 v Ic, Ho (37)
Bingham, W. L. (Sunderland), 1951 v F; 1952 v E, S, W; 1953 v E, S, F, W; 1954 v E, S, W; 1955 v E, S, W; 1956 v E, S, W; 1957 v E, S, W, P (2), I; 1958 v S, E, W, I (2), Arg, Cz (2), WG, F; (with Luton T), 1959 v E, S, W, Sp; 1960 v S, E, W; (with Everton), 1961 v E, S, WG (2), Gr, I; 1962 v E, Gr; 1963 v E, S, Pol (2), Sp; (with Port Vale), 1964 v S, E, Sp (56)
Black, J. (Glentoran), 1901 v E (1)
Blair, H. (Portadown), 1931 v S; 1932 v S; (with Swansea), 1934 v S (3)
Blair, J. (Cliftonville), 1907 v W, E, S; 1908 v E, S (5)
Blair, R. V. (Oldham Ath), 1975 v Se (sub), S (sub), W; 1976 v Se, Is (5)
Blanchflower, R. D. (Barnsley), 1950 v S, W; 1951 v E, S; (with Aston Villa), F; 1952 v W; 1953 v E, S, W, F; 1954 v E, S, W; (with Tottenham H), 1955 v E, S, W; 1956 v E, S, W; 1957 v E, S, W, I, P (2); 1958 v E, S, W, I (2), Cz (2), Arg, F, WG; 1959 v E, S, W, Sp; 1960 v E, S, W; 1961 v E, S, W, WG (2); 1962 v E, S, W, Gr, Ho; 1963 v E, S, Pol (2) (56)
Blanchflower, J. (Manchester U), 1954 v W; 1955 v E, S; 1956 v S, W; 1957 v S, E, P; 1958 v S, E, I (2) (12)
Bookman, L. O. (Bradford C), 1914 v W; (with Luton T), 1921 v S, W; 1922 v E (4)
Bothwell, A. W. (Ards), 1926 v S, E, W; 1927 v E, W (5)
Bowler, G. C. (Hull C), 1950 v E, S, W (3)
Boyle, P. (Sheffield U), 1901 v E; 1902 v E; 1903 v S, W; 1904 v E (5)
Braithwaite, R. S. (Linfield), 1962 v W; 1963 v P, Sp; (with Middlesbrough), 1964 v W, U; 1965 v E, S, Sw (2), Ho (10)
Breen, T. (Belfast C), 1935 v E, W; 1937 v E, S; (with Manchester U), 1937 v W; 1938 v E, S; 1939 v W, S (9)
Brennan, B. (Bohemians), 1912 v W (1)
Brennan, R. A. (Luton T), 1949 v W; (with Birmingham C), 1950 v E, S, W; (with Fulham), 1951 v E (5)
Briggs, W. R. (Manchester U), 1962 v W; (with Swansea T), 1965 v Ho (2)
Brisby, D. (Distillery), 1891 v S (1)
Brolly, T. (Millwall), 1937 v W; 1938 v W; 1939 v E, W (4)
Brookes, E. A. (Shelbourne), 1920 v S (1)
Brotherston, N. (Blackburn R), 1980 v S, E, W, Aus (3); 1981 v Se, P; 1982 v S, Is, E, F, S, W, Hon (sub), A (sub) (16)

Brown, J. (Glenavon), 1921 v W; (with Tranmere R), 1924 v E, W (3)
Brown, J. (Wolverhampton W), 1935 v E, W; 1936 v E; (with Coventry C), 1937 v E, W; 1938 v S, W; (with Birmingham C), 1939 v E, S, W (10)
Brown, W. G. (Glenavon), 1926 v W (1)
Brown, W. M. (Limavady), 1887 v E (1)
Browne, F. (Cliftonville), 1887 v E, S, W; 1888 v E, S (5)
Browne, R. J. (Leeds U), 1936 v E, W; 1938 v E, W; 1939 v E, S (6)
Bruce, W. (Glentoran), 1961 v S; 1967 v W (2)
Buckle, H. (Cliftonville), 1882 v E (1)
Buckle, H. R. (Sunderland), 1904 v E; (with Bristol R), 1908 v W (2)
Burnett, J. (Distillery), 1894 v E, W, S; (with Glentoran), 1895 v E, W (5)
Burnison, J. (Distillery), 1901 v E, W (2)
Burnison, S. (Distillery), 1908 v E; 1910 v E, S; (with Bradford), 1911 v E, S, W; (with Distillery), 1912 v E; 1913 v W (8)
Burns, J. (Glenavon), 1923 v E (1)
Butler, M. P. (Blackpool), 1939 v W (1)

Campbell, A. C. (Crusaders), 1963 v W; 1965 v Sw (2)
Campbell, J. (Cliftonville), 1896 v W; 1897 v E, S, W; (with Distillery), 1898 v E, S, W; (with Cliftonville), 1899 v E; 1900 v E, S; 1901 v S, W; 1902 v S; 1903 v E; 1904 v S (15)
Campbell, J. P. (Fulham), 1951 v E, S (2)
Campbell, R. (Bradford C), 1982 v S, W (sub) (2)
Campbell, W. G. (Dundee), 1968 v S, E; 1969 v T; 1970 v S, W, USSR (6)
Carey, J. J. (Manchester U), 1947 v E, S, W; 1948 v E; 1949 v E, S, W (7)
Carroll, E. (Glenavon), 1925 v S (1)
Casey, T. (Newcastle U), 1955 v W; 1956 v W; 1957 v E, S, W, I, P (2); 1958 v WG, F; (with Portsmouth), 1959 v E, Sp (12)
Cashin, M. (Cliftonville), 1898 v S (1)
Caskey, W. (Derby Co), 1979 v Bul, E, Bul, E, D (sub); 1980 v E (sub); (with Tulsa R), 1982 v F (sub) (7)
Cassidy, T. (Newcastle U), 1971 v E (sub); 1972 v USSR (sub); 1974 v Bul (sub), S, E, W; 1975 v N; 1976 v S, E, W; 1977 v WG (sub); 1980 v E, Ei (sub), Is, S, E, W, Aus (3); (with Burnley), 1981 v Se, P; 1982 v Is, Sp (sub) (24)
Chambers, J. (Distillery), 1921 v W; (with Bury), 1928 v E, S, W; 1929 v E, S, W; 1930 v S, W; (with Nottingham F), 1932 v E, S, W (12)
Chatton, H. A. (Partick T), 1925 v E, S; 1926 v E (3)
Christian, J. (Linfield), 1889 v S (1)
Clarke, R. (Belfast C), 1901 v E, S (2)
Cleary, J. (Glentoran), 1982 v S, W (2)
Clements, D. (Coventry C), 1965 v W, Ho; 1966 v M; 1967 v S, W; 1968 v S, E; 1969 v T (2), S, W; 1970 v S, E, W, USSR (2); 1971 v Sp, E, S, W, Cy; (with Sheffield W), 1972 v USSR (2), Sp, E, S, W; 1973 v Bul, Cy (2), P, E, S, W; (with Everton), 1974 v Bul, P, S, E, W; 1975 v N, Y, E, S, W; 1976 v Se, Y; (with New York Cosmos), E, W (48)
Clugston, J. (Cliftonville), 1888 v W; 1889 v W, S, E; 1890 v E, S; 1891 v E, W; 1892 v E, S, W; 1893 v E, S, W (14)
Cochrane, D. (Leeds U), 1939 v E, W; 1947 v E, S, W; 1948 v E, S, W; 1949 v S, W; 1950 v S, E (12)
Cochrane, M. (Distillery), 1898 v S, W, E; 1899 v E; 1900 v E, S, W; (with Leicester Fosse), 1901 v S (8)
Cochrane, T. (Coleraine), 1976 v N; (with Burnley), 1978 v S (sub), E (sub), W (sub); 1979 v Ei (sub); (with Middlesbrough), D, Bul, E, Bul, E; 1980 v Is, E (sub), W (sub), Aus (1+2 sub); 1981 v Se (sub), P (sub), S, P, S, Se; 1982 v E (sub), F (24)

Collins, F. (Glasgow C), 1922 v S (1)

Condy, J. (Distillery), 1882 v W; 1886 v E, S (3)

Connell, T. (Manchester U), 1978 v W (sub) (1)

Connor, J. (Glentoran), 1901 v S, E; (with Belfast C), 1905 v E, S, W; 1907 v E, S; 1908 v E, S; 1909 v W; 1911 v S, E, W (13)

Connor, M. J. (Brentford), 1903 v S, W; (with Fulham), 1904 v E (3)

Cook, W. (Celtic), 1933 v E, W, S; (with Everton), 1935 v E; 1936 v S, W; 1937 v E, S, W; 1938 v E, S, W; 1939 v E, S, W (15)

Cooke, S. (Belfast YMCA), 1889 v E; (with Cliftonville), 1890 v E, S (3)

Coulter, J. (Belfast C), 1934 v E, S, W; (with Everton), 1935 v E, S, W; 1937 v S, W; (with Grimsby T), 1938 v S, W; (with Chelmsford C), 1939 v S (11)

Cowan, J. (Newcastle U), 1970 v E (sub) (1)

Cowan, T. S. (Queen's Island), 1925 v W (1)

Coyle, F. (Coleraine), 1956 v E, S; 1957 v P (with Nottingham F), 1958 v Arg (4)

Coyle, R. I. (Sheffield W), 1973 v P, Cy (sub), W (sub); 1974 v Bul (sub), P (sub) (5)

Craig, A. B. (Rangers), 1908 v E, S, W; 1909 v S; (with Morton), 1912 v S, W; 1914 v E, S, W (9)

Craig, D. J. (Newcastle U), 1967 v W; 1968 v W; 1969 v T (2), E, S, W; 1970 v E, S, W, USSR; 1971 v Cy (2), S, S (sub); 1972 v USSR, S (sub); 1973 v Cy (2), E, S, W; 1974 v Bul, P; 1975 v N (25)

Crawford, S. (Distillery), 1889 v E, W; (with Cliftonville), 1891 v E, S, W; 1893 v E, W (7)

Croft, T. (Queen's Island), 1924 v E (1)

Crone, R. (Distillery), 1889 v S; 1890 v E, S, W (4)

Crone, W. (Distillery), 1882 v W; 1884 v E, S, W; 1886 v E, S, W; 1887 v E; 1888 v E, W; 1889 v S; 1890 v W (12)

Crooks, W. (Manchester U), 1922 v W (1)

Crossan, E. (Blackburn R), 1950 v S; 1951 v E; 1955 v W (3)

Crossan, J. A. (Sparta-Rotterdam), 1960 v E; (with Sunderland), 1963 v W, P, Sp; 1964 v E, S, W, U, Sp; 1965 v E, S, Sw (2); (with Manchester C), W, Ho (2), Alb; 1966 v S, E, Alb, WG; 1967 v E, S; (with Middlesbrough), 1968 v S (24)

Crothers, C. (Distillery), 1907 v W (1)

Cumming, L. (Huddersfield T), 1929 v W, S; (with Oldham Ath), 1930 v E (3)

Cunningham, R. (Ulster), 1892 v S, E, W; 1893 v E (4)

Cunningham, W. E. (St Mirren), 1951 v W; 1953 v E; 1954 v S; 1955 v S; (with Leicester C), 1956 v E, S, W; 1957 v E, S, W, I, P (2); 1958 v S, W, I, Cz (2), Arg, WG, F; 1959 v E, S, W; 1960 v E, S, W; (with Dunfermline Ath), 1961 v W; 1962 v W, Ho (30)

Curran, S. (Belfast C), 1926 v S, W; 1928 v S (3)

Curran, J. J. (Glenavon), 1922 v W; (with Pontypridd), 1923 v E, S; (with Glenavon), 1924 v E (4)

Cush, W. W. (Glenavon), 1951 v E, S; 1954 v S; E; 1957 v W, I, P (2); (with Leeds U), 1958 v I (2), W, Cz (2), Arg, WG, F; 1959 v E, S, W, Sp; 1960 v E, S, W; (with Portadown), 1961 v WG, Gr; 1962 v Gr (26)

Dalton, W. (YMCA), 1888 v S; (with Linfield), 1890 v S, W; 1891 v S, W; 1892 v E, S, W; 1894 v E, S, W (11)

D'Arcy, S. D. (Chelsea), 1952 v W; 1953 v E; (with Brentford), 1953 v S, W, F (5)

Darling, J. (Linfield), 1897 v E, S; 1900 v S; 1902 v E, S, W; 1903 v E, S, W; 1905 v E, S, W; 1906 v E, S, W; 1908 v W; 1909 v E; 1910 v E, S, W; 1912 v S (21)

Davey, H. H. (Reading), 1926 v E; 1927 v E, S; 1928 v E; (with Portsmouth), 1928 v W (5)

Davis, T. L. (Oldham Ath), 1937 v E (1)

Davison, J. R. (Cliftonville), 1882 v E, W; 1883 v E, W; 1884 v E, W, S; 1885 v E (8)

Devine, W. (Limavady), 1886 v E, W; 1887 v W; 1888 v W (4)

Dickson, D. (Coleraine), 1970 v S (sub), W; 1973 v Cy, P (4)

Dickson, T. A. (Linfield), 1957 v S (1)

Dickson, W. (Chelsea), 1951 v W, F; 1952 v E, S, W; 1953 v E, S, W, F; (with Arsenal), 1954 v E, W; 1955 v E (12)

Diffin, W. (Belfast C), 1931 v W (1)

Dill, A. H. (Knock and Down Ath), 1882 v E, W; (with Cliftonville), 1883 v W; 1884 v E, S, W; 1885 v E, S, W (9)

Doherty, I. (Belfast C), 1901 v E (1)

Doherty, J. (Cliftonville), 1933 v E, W (2)

Doherty, M. (Derry C), 1938 v S (1)

Doherty, P. D. (Blackpool), 1935 v E, W; 1936 v E, S; (with Manchester C), 1937 v E, W; 1938 v E, S; 1939 v E, W; (with Derby Co), 1947 v E; (with Huddersfield T), 1947 v W; 1948 v E, W; 1949 v S; (with Doncaster R), 1951 v S (16)

Donaghy, M. (Luton T), 1980 v S, E, W; 1981 v Se, P, S (sub); 1982 v S, Is, E, F, S, W, Y, Hon, Sp, F (16)

Donnelly, L. (Distillery), 1913 v W (1)

Doran, J. F. (Brighton), 1921 v E; 1922 v E, W (3)

Dougan, A. D. (Portsmouth), 1958 v Cz; (with Blackburn R), 1960 v S; 1961 v E, W, I, Gr; (with Aston Villa), 1963 v S, P (2); (with Leicester C), 1966 v S, E, W, M, Alb, WG; 1967 v E, S; (with Wolverhampton W), 1967 v W; 1968 v S, W, Is; 1969 v T (2), E, S, W; 1970 v S, E, USSR (2); 1971 v Cy (2), Sp, E, S, W; 1972 v USSR (2), E, S, W; 1973 v Bul, Cy (43)

Douglas, J. P. (Belfast C), 1947 v E (1)

Dowd, H. O. (Glenavon), 1974 v W; 1975 v N (sub), Se (3)

Duggan, H. A. (Leeds U), 1930 v E; 1931 v E, W; 1933 v E; 1934 v E; 1935 v S, W; 1936 v S (8)

Dunne, J. (Sheffield U), 1928 v W; 1931 v W, E; 1932 v E, S; 1933 v E, W (7)

Eames, W. L. E. (Dublin U), 1885 v E, S, W (3)

Eglington, T. J. (Everton), 1947 v S, W; 1948 v E, S, W; 1949 v E (6)

Elder, A. R. (Burnley), 1960 v W; 1961 v S, E, W, WG (2), Gr; 1962 v E, S, Gr; 1963 v E, S, W, P (2), Sp; 1964 v W, U; 1965 v E, S, W, Sw (2), Ho (2), Alb; 1966 v E, S, W, M, Alb; 1967 v E, S, W; (with Stoke C), 1968 v E, W; 1969 v E (sub), S, W; 1970 v USSR (40)

Elleman, A. R. (Cliftonville), 1889 v W; 1890 v E (2)

Elwood, J. H. (Bradford), 1929 v W; 1930 v E (2)

Emerson, W. (Glentoran), 1920 v E, S, W; 1921 v E; 1922 v E, S; (with Burnley), 1922 v W; 1923 v E, S, W; 1924 v E (11)

English, S. (Glasgow R), 1933 v W, S (2)

Enright, J. (Leeds C), 1912 v S (1)

Falloon, E. (Aberdeen), 1931 v S; 1933 v S (2)

Farquharson, T. G. (Cardiff C), 1923 v S, W; 1924 v E, S, W; 1925 v E, S (7)

Farrell, P. (Distillery), 1901 v S, W (2)

Farrell, P. (Hibernian), 1938 v W (1)

Farrell, P. D. (Everton), 1947 v S, W; 1948 v E, S, W; 1949 v E, W (7)

Feeney, J. M. (Linfield), 1947 v S; (with Swansea T), 1950 v E (2)

Feeney, W. (Glentoran), 1976 v Is (1)

Ferguson, W. (Linfield), 1966 v M; 1967 v E (2)

Ferris, J. (Belfast Celtic), 1920 v E, W; (with Chelsea), 1921 v S, E; (with Belfast C), 1928 v S (5)

Ferris, R. O. (Birmingham), 1950 v S; 1951 v F; 1952 v S (3)

Finney, T. (Sunderland), 1975 v N, E (sub), S, W; 1976 v N, Y, S; (with Cambridge U), 1980 v E, Is, S, E, W, Aus (2) (14)

Fitzpatrick, J. C. (Bohemians), 1896 v E, S (2)

Flack, H. (Burnley), 1929 v S (1)

Forbes, G. (Limavady), 1888 v W; (with Distillery), 1891 v E, S (3)

Forde, J. T. (Ards), 1959 v Sp; 1961 v E, S, WG (4)

Foreman, T. A. (Cliftonville), 1899 v S (1)

Forsyth, J. (YMCA), 1888 v E, S (2)

Fox, W. (Ulster), 1887 v E, S (2)

Fulton, R. P. (Belfast C), 1930 v W; 1931 v E, S, W; 1932 v W, E; 1933 v E, S; 1934 v E, W, S; 1935 v E, W, S; 1936 v S, W; 1937 v E, S, W; 1938 v W (20)

Gaffikin, J. (Linfield Ath), 1890 v S, W; 1891 v S, W; 1892 v E, S, W; 1893 v E, S, W; 1894 v E, S, W; 1895 v E, W (15)

Galbraith, W. (Distillery), 1890 v W (1)

Gallagher, P. (Celtic), 1920 v E, S; 1922 v S; 1923 v S, W; 1924 v S, W; 1925 v S, W, E; (with Falkirk), 1927 v S (11)

Gallogly, C. (Huddersfield T), 1951 v E, S (2)

Gara, A. (Preston NE), 1902 v E, S, W (3)

Gardiner, A. (Cliftonville), 1930 v S, W; 1931 v S; 1932 v E, S (5)

Garrett, J. (Distillery), 1925 v W (1)

Gaston, R. (Oxford U), 1969 v Is (sub) (1)

Gaukrodger, G. (Linfield), 1895 v W (1)

Gaussen, A. W. (Moyola Park), 1884 v E, S; 1888 v E, W; 1889 v E, W (6)

Geary, J. (Glentoran), 1931 v S; 1932 v S (2)

Gibb, J. T. (Wellington Park) 1884 v S, W; 1885 v S, E, W; 1886 v S; 1887 v S, E, W; 1889 v S (10)

Gibb, T. J. (Cliftonville), 1936 v W (1)

Gibson W. K. (Cliftonville), 1894 v S, W, E; 1895 v S; 1897 v W; 1898 v S, W, E; 1901 v S, W, E; 1902 v S, W (13)

Gillespie, R. (Hertford), 1886 v E, S, W; 1887 v E, S, W (6)

Gillespie, W. (Sheffield U), 1913 v E, S; 1914 v E, W; 1920 v S, W; 1921 v E; 1922 v E, S, W; 1923 v E, S, W; 1924 v E, S, W; 1925 v E, S; 1926 v S, W; 1927 v E, W; 1928 v E; 1929 v E; 1931 v E (25)

Gillespie, W. (West Down), 1889 v W (1)

Goodall, A. L. (Derby Co), 1899 v S, W; 1900 v E, W; 1901 v E; 1902 v S; 1903 v E, W; (with Glossop), 1904 v E, W (10)

Goodbody, M. F. (Dublin University), 1889 v E; 1891 v W (2)

Gordon, H. (Linfield), 1891 v S; 1892 v E, S, W; 1893 v E, S, W; 1895 v E, W; 1896 v E, S (11)

Gordon, T. (Linfield), 1894 v W; 1895 v E (2)

Gorman, W. C. (Brentford), 1947 v E, S, W; 1948 v W (4)

Gowdy, J. (Glentoran), 1920 v E; (with Queen's Island), 1924 v W; (with Falkirk), 1926 v E, S; 1927 v E, S (6)

Gowdy, W. A. (Hull C), 1932 v S; (with Sheffield W), 1933 v S; (with Linfield), 1935 v E, S, W; (with Hibernian), 1936 v W (6)

Graham, W. G. L. (Doncaster R), 1951 v W, F; 1952 v E, S, W; 1953 v S, F; 1954 v E, W; 1955 v S, W; 1956 v E, S; 1959 v E (14)

Greer, W. (QPR), 1909 v E, S, W (3)

Gregg, H. (Doncaster R), 1954 v W; 1957 v E, S, W, I, P (2); 1958 v E, I; (with Manchester U), 1958 v Cz, Arg, WG, F, W; 1959 v E, W; 1960 v S, E, W; 1961 v E, S; 1962 v S, Gr; 1964 v S, E (25)

Hall, G. (Distillery), 1897 v E (1)

Halligan, W. (Derby Co), 1911 v W; (with Wolverhampton W), 1912 v E (2)

Hamill, M. (Manchester U), 1912 v E; 1914 v E, S; (with Belfast C), 1920 v E, S, W; (with Manchester C), 1921 v S (7)

Hamilton, B. (Linfield), 1969 v T; 1971 v Cy (2), E, S, W; (with Ipswich T), 1972 v USSR (1+1 sub), Sp; 1973 v Bul, Cy (2), P, E, S, W; 1974 v Bul, S, E, W; 1975 v N, Se, Y, E; 1976 v Se, N, Y; (with Everton), Is, S, E, W; 1977 v Ho, Bel, WG, E, S, W, Ic; (with Millwall), 1978 v S, E, W; 1979 v Ei (sub); (with Swindon T), Bul (2), E, S, W, D; 1980 v Aus (2 sub) (50)

Hamilton, J. (Knock), 1882 v E, W (2)

Hamilton, R. (Distillery), 1908 v W (1)

Hamilton, R. (Glasgow R), 1928 v S; 1929 v E; 1930 v S, E; 1932 v S (5)

Hamilton, W. (QPR), 1978 v S (sub); (with Burnley), 1980 v S, E, W, Aus (2); 1981 v Se, P, S, P, S, Se; 1982 v S, Is, E, W, Y, Hon, Sp, A, F (21)

Hamilton, W. D. (Dublin Association), 1885 v W (1)

Hamilton, W. J. (Dublin Association), 1885 v W (1)

Hampton, H. (Bradford C), 1911 v E, S, W; 1912 v E, W; 1913 v E, S, W; 1914 v E (9)

Hanna, D. R. A. (Portsmouth), 1899 v W (1)

Hanna, J. (Nottingham F), 1912 v S, W (2)

Hannon, D. J. (Bohemian), 1908 v E, S; 1911 v E, S; 1912 v W; 1913 v E (6)

Harkin, J. T. (Southport), 1968 v W; 1969 v T; (with Shrewsbury T), W (sub); 1970 v USSR; 1971 v Sp (5)

Harland, A. I. (Linfield), 1923 v E (1)

Harris, J. (Cliftonville), 1921 v W (1)

Harris, V. (Shelbourne), 1906 v E; 1907 v E, W; 1908 v E, W, S; (with Everton), 1909 v E, W, S; 1910 v E, S, W; 1911 v E, S, W; 1912 v E; 1913 v E, S; 1914 v S, W (20)

Harvey, M. (Sunderland), 1961 v I; 1962 v Ho; 1963 v W, Sp; 1964 v S, E, W, U, Sp; 1965 v E, S, W, Sw (2), Ho (2), Alb; 1966 v S, E, W, M, Alb, WG; 1967 v E, S; 1968 v E, W; 1969 v Is, T (2), E; 1970 v USSR; 1971 v Cy, W (sub) (33)

Hastings, J. (Knock), 1882 v E, W; (with Ulster), 1883 v W; 1884 v E, S; 1886 v E, S (7)

Hatton, S. (Linfield), 1963 v S, Pol (2)

Hayes, W. E. (Huddersfield T), 1938 v E, S; 1939 v E, S (4)

Healy, F. (Coleraine), 1982 v S, W, Hon (sub) (3)

Hegan, D. (WBA), 1970 v USSR; (with Wolverhampton W), 1972 v USSR, E, S, W; 1973 v Bul, Cy (7)

Henderson, A. W. (Ulster), 1885 v E, S, W (3)

Hewison, G. (Moyola Park), 1885 v E, S (2)

Hill, M. J. (Norwich C), 1959 v W; 1960 v W; 1961 v WG; 1962 v S; (with Everton), 1964 v S, E, Sp (7)

Hinton, E. (Fulham), 1947 v S, W; 1948 v S, E, W; (with Millwall), 1951 v W, F (7)

Hopkins, J. (Brighton), 1926 v E (1)

Houston, J. (Linfield), 1912 v S, W; 1913 v W; (with Everton), 1913 v E, S; 1914 v S (6)

Houston, W. (Linfield), 1933 v W (1)

Houston, W. G. (Moyola Park), 1885 v E, S (2)

Hughes, W. (Bolton W), 1951 v W (1)

Humphries, W. (Ards), 1962 v W; (with Coventry C), 1962 v Ho; 1963 v E, S, W, Pol, Sp; 1964 v S, E, Sp; 1965 v S; (with Swansea T), 1965 v W, Ho, Alb (14)

Hunter, A. (Blackburn R), 1970 v USSR; 1971 v Cy (2), E, S, W; (with Ipswich T), 1972 v USSR (2), Sp, E, S, W; 1973 v Bul, Cy (2), P, E, S, W; 1974 v Bul, S, E, W; 1975 v N, Se, Y, E, S, W; 1976 v Se, N, Y, Is, S, E, W; 1977 v Ho, Bel, WG, E, S, W, Ic; 1978 v Ic, Ho, Bel; 1979 v Ei, D, S, W, D; 1980 v E, Ei (53)

Hunter, A. (Distillery), 1905 v W; 1906 v W, E, S; (with Belfast C), 1908 v W; 1909 v W, E, S (8)

Hunter, R. J. (Cliftonville), 1884 v E, S, W (3)

Hunter, V. (Coleraine), 1962 v E; 1964 v Sp (2)

Irvine, R. W. (Everton), 1922 v S; 1923 v E, W; 1924 v E, S; 1925 v E; 1926 v E; 1927 v E, W; 1928 v E, S; (with Portsmouth), 1929 v E; 1930 v S; (with Connah's Quay), 1931 v E; (with Derry C), 1932 v W (15)

Irvine, R. J. (Linfield), 1962 v Ho; 1963 v E, S, W, Pol (2), Sp; (with Stoke C), 1965 v W (8)

Irvine, W. J. (Burnley), 1963 v W, Sp; 1965 v S, W, Sw, Ho (2), Alb; 1966 v S, E, W, M, Alb; 1967 v E, S; 1968 v E, W; (with Preston NE), 1969 v Is, T, E; (with Brighton), 1972 v E, S, W (23)

Irving, S, J. (Dundee), 1923 v S, W; 1924 v S, E, W; 1925 v S, E, W; 1926 v S, W; (with Cardiff C), 1927 v S, E, W; 1928 v S, E, W; (with Chelsea), 1929 v E; 1931 v W (18)

Jackson, T. (Everton), 1969 v Is, E, S, W; 1970 v USSR (1+1 sub); (with Nottingham F), 1971 v Sp; 1972 v E, S, W; 1973 v Cy, E, S, W; 1974 v Bul, P, S (sub), E (sub), W (sub); 1975 v N (sub), Se, Y, E, S, W; (with Manchester U); 1976 v Se, N, Y; 1977 v Ho, Bel, WG, E, S, W, Ic (35)

Jamison, J. (Glentoran), 1976 v N (1)

Jennings, P. A. (Watford), 1964 v W, U; (with Tottenham H), 1965 v E, S, Sw (2), Ho, Alb; 1966 v S, E, W, Alb, WG; 1967 v E, S; 1968 v S, E, W; 1969 v Is, T (2), E, S, W; 1970 v S, E, USSR (2); 1971 v Cy (2), E, S, W; 1972 v USSR, Sp, S, E, W; 1973 v Bul, Cy, P, E, S, W; 1974 v P, S, E, W; 1975 v N, Se, Y, E, S, W; 1976 v Se, N, Y, Is, S, E, W; 1977 v Ho, Bel, WG, E, S, W, Ic; (with Arsenal), 1978 v Ic, Ho, Bel; 1979 v Ei, D, Bul, E, Bul, E, S, W, D; 1980 v E, Ei, Is; 1981 v S, P, S, Se; 1982 v S, Is, E, W, Y, Hon, Sp, F (95)

Johnston, H. (Portadown), 1927 v W (1)

Johnston, R. (Old Park), 1885 v S, W (2)

Johnston, S. (Distillery), 1882 v W; 1884 v E; 1886 v E, S (4)

Johnston, S. (Linfield), 1890 v W; 1893 v S, W; 1894 v E (4)

Johnston, S. (Distillery), 1905 v W (1)

Johnston, W. C. (Glenavon), 1962 v W; (with Oldham Ath), 1966 v M (sub) (2)

Jones, J. (Linfield), 1930 v S, W; 1931 v S, W, E; 1932 v S, E; 1933 v S, E, W; 1934 v S, E, W; 1935 v S, E, W; 1936 v E, S; (with Hibernian), 1936 v W; 1937 v E, W, S; (with Glenavon), 1938 v E (23)

Jones, J. (Glenavon), 1956 v W; 1957 v E, W (3)

Jones, S. (Distillery), 1934 v E; (with Blackpool), 1934 v W (2)

Jordan, T. (Linfield), 1895 v E, W (2)

Kavanagh, P. J. (Glasgow C), 1930 v E (1)

Keane, T. R. (Swansea T), 1949 v S (1)

Kearns, A. (Distillery), 1900 v E, S, W; 1902 v E, S, W (6)

Keith, R, M. (Newcastle U), 1958 v E, W, Cz (2), Arg, I, WG, F; 1959 v E, S, W, Sp; 1960 v S, E; 1961 v S, E, W, I, WG (2), Gr; 1962 v W, Ho (23)

Kelly, H. R. (Fulham), 1950 v E, W; (with Southampton), 1951 v E, S (4)

Kelly, J. (Glentoran), 1896 v E (1)

Kelly, J. (Derry C), 1932 v E, W; 1933 v E, W, S; 1934 v W; 1936 v E, S, W; 1937 v S, E (11)

Kelly, P. (Manchester C), 1921 v E (1)

Kelly, P. M. (Barnsley), 1950 v S (1)

Kennedy, A. L. (Arsenal), 1923 v W; 1925 v E (2)

Kernaghan, N. (Belfast C), 1936 v W; 1937 v S; 1938 v E (3)

Kirkwood, H. (Cliftonville), 1904 v W (1)

Kirwan, J. (Tottenham H), 1900 v W; 1902 v E, W; 1903 v E, S, W; 1904 v E, S, W; 1905 v E, S, W; (with Chelsea), 1906 v E, S, W; 1907 v W; (with Clyde), 1909 v S (17)

Lacey, W. (Everton), 1909 v E, S, W; 1910 v E, S, W; 1911 v E, S, W; 1912 v E; (with Liverpool), 1913 v W; 1914 v E, S, W; 1920 v E, S, W; 1921 v E, S, W; 1922 v E, S; (with New Brighton), 1925 v E (23)

Lawther, W. I. (Sunderland), 1960 v W; 1961 v I; (with Blackburn R), 1962 v S, Ho (4)

Leatham, J. (Belfast C), 1939 v W (1)

Ledwidge, J. J. (Shelbourne), 1906 v S, W (2)

Lemon, J. (Glentoran), 1886 v W; 1888 v S; (with Belfast YMCA), 1889 v W (3)

Leslie, W. (YMCA), 1887 v E (1)

Lewis, J. (Glentoran), 1899 v S, E, W; (with Distillery), 1900 v S (4)

Little, J. (Glentoran), 1898 v W (1)

Lockhart, H. (Rossall School), 1884 v W (1)

Lockhart, N. (Linfield), 1947 v E; (with Coventry C), 1950 v W; 1951 v W; 1952 v W; (with Aston Villa), 1954 v S, E; 1955 v W; 1956 v W (8)

Lowther, R. (Glentoran), 1888 v E, S (2)

Loyal, J. (Clarence), 1891 v S (1)

Lutton, R. J. (Wolverhampton W), 1970 v S, E; (with West Ham U), 1973 v Cy (sub), S (sub), W (sub); 1974 v P (6)

Lyner, D. (Glentoran), 1920 v E, W; 1922 v S, W; (with Manchester U), 1923 v E; (with Kilmarnock), 1923 v W (6)

McAdams, W. J. (Manchester C), 1954 v W; 1955 v S; 1957 v E; 1958 v S, I; (with Bolton W), 1961 v E, S, W, I, WG (2), Gr; 1962 v E, Gr; (with Leeds U), Ho (15)

McAlery, J. M. (Cliftonville), 1882 v E, W (2)

McAlinden, J. (Belfast C), 1938 v S; 1939 v S; (with Portsmouth), 1947 v E; (with Southend U), 1949 v E (4)

McAllen, J. (Linfield), 1898 v E; 1899 v E, S, W; 1900 v E, S, W; 1901 v W; 1902 v S (9)

McAlpine, W. J. (Cliftonville), 1901 v S (1)

McArthur, A. (Distillery), 1886 v W (1)

McAuley, J. L. (Huddersfield T), 1911 v E, W; 1912 v E, S; 1913 v E, S (6)

McAuley, P. (Belfast C), 1900 v S (1)

McCabe, J. J. (Leeds U), 1949 v S, W; 1950 v E; 1951 v W; 1953 v W; 1954 v S (6)

McCabe, W. (Ulster), 1891 v E (1)

McCambridge, J. (Ballymena), 1930 v S, W; (with Cardiff C), 1931 v W; 1932 v E (4)

McCandless, J. (Bradford), 1912 v W; 1913 v W; 1920 v W, S; 1921 v E (5)

McCandless, W. (Linfield), 1920 v E, W; 1921 v E; (with Rangers), 1921 v W; 1922 v S; 1924 v W, S; 1925 v S; 1929 v W (9)

McCann, P. (Belfast C), 1910 v E, S, W; 1911 v E; (with Glentoran), 1911 v S; 1912 v E; 1913 v W (7)

McCashin, J. (Cliftonville), 1896 v W; 1898 v S, W; 1899 v S (4)

McCavana, W. T. (Coleraine), 1955 v S; 1956 v E, S (3)

McCaw, D. (Distillery), 1882 v E (1)

McCaw, J. H. (Linfield), 1927 v W; 1930 v S; 1931 v E, S, W (5)

McClatchey, J. (Distillery), 1886 v E, S, W (3)

McClatchey, R. (Distillery), 1895 v S (1)

McCleary, J. W. (Cliftonville), 1955 v W (1)

McCleery, W. (Cliftonville), 1922 v N; 1930 v E, W; 1931 v E, S, W; 1932 v S, W; 1933 v E, W (10)

McClelland, J. (Arsenal), 1961 v W, I, WG (2), Gr; (with Fulham), 1967 v M (6)

McClelland, J. (Mansfield T), 1980 v S (sub), Aus (3); 1981 v Se, S (with Rangers), S, Se; 1982 v S, W, Y, Hon, Sp, A, F (15)

McCluggage, A. (Bradford), 1924 v E; (with Burnley), 1927 v S, W; 1928 v S, E, W; 1929 v S, E, W; 1930 v W; 1931 v E, W (14)

McClure, G. (Cliftonville), 1907 v S, W; 1908 v E; (with Distillery), 1909 v E (4)

McConnell, E. (Cliftonville), 1904 v S, W; (with Glentoran), 1905 v S; (with Sunderland), 1906 v E; 1907 v E; 1908 v S, W; (with Sheffield W), 1909 v S, W; 1910 v S, W, E (12)

McConnell, P. (Doncaster R), 1928 v W; (with Southport), 1932 v E (2)

McConnell, W. G. (Bohemians), 1912 v W; 1913 v E, S; 1914 v E, S, W (6)

McConnell, W. H. (Reading), 1925 v W; 1926 v E, W; 1927 v E, S, W; 1928 v E, W (8)

McCourt, F. J. (Manchester C), 1952 v E, W; 1953 v E, S, W, F (6)

McCoy, J. (Distillery), 1896 v W (1)

McCracken, R. (C Palace), 1921 v E; 1922 v E, S, W (4)

McCracken, W. (Distillery), 1902 v E, W; 1903 v E; 1904 v E, S, W; (with Newcastle U), 1905 v E, S, W; 1907 v E; 1920 v E; 1922 v E, S, W; (with Hull C), 1923 v S (15)

McCreery, D. (Manchester U), 1976 v S (sub), E, W; 1977 v Ho, Bel, WG, E, S, W, Ic; 1978 v Ic, Ho, Bel, S, E, W; 1979 v Ei, D, Bul, E, Bul, W, D; (with QPR), 1980 v E, Ei, S (sub), E (sub), W (sub), Aus (1+ sub); 1981 v Se (sub), P (sub); (with Tulsa R), S, P, Se; 1982 v S, Is, E (sub), F, Y, Hon, Sp, A, F (44)

McCrory, S. (Southend U), 1958 v E (1)

McCullough, K. (Belfast C), 1935 v W; 1936 v E; (with Manchester C), 1936 v S; 1937 v E, S (5)

McCullough, W. J. (Arsenal), 1961 v I; 1963 v Sp; 1964 v S, E, W, U, Sp; 1965 v E, Sw; (with Millwall), 1967 v E (10)

McCurdy, C. (Linfield), 1980 v Aus (sub) (1)

McDonald, R. (Glasgow R), 1930 v S; 1932 v E (2)

McDonnell, J. (Bohemians), 1911 v E, S; 1912 v W; 1913 v W (4)

McFaul, W. S. (Linfield), 1967 v E (sub); (with Newcastle U), 1970 v W; 1971 v Sp; 1972 v USSR; 1973 v Cy; 1974 v Bul (6)

McGarry, J. K. (Cliftonville), 1951 v W, F, S (3)

McGee, G. (Wellington Park), 1885 v E, S, W (3)

McGrath, R. C. (Tottenham H), 1974 v S, E, W; 1975 v N; 1976 v Is (sub); (with Manchester U), 1977 v Ho, Bel, WG, E, S, W, Ic; 1978 v Ic, Ho, Bel, S, E, W; 1979 v Bul (sub), E (sub), E (sub) (21)

McGregor, S. (Glentoran), 1921 v S (1)

McGrillen, J. (Clyde), 1924 v S; (with Belfast C), 1927 v S (2)

McGuire, E. (Distillery), 1907 v S (1)

McIlroy, H. (Cliftonville), 1906 v E (1)

McIlroy, J. (Burnley), 1952 v E, S, W; 1953 v E, S, W; 1954 v E, S, W; 1955 v E, S, W; 1956 v E, S, W; 1957 v E, S, W, I, P (2); 1958 v E, S, W, I (2), Cz (2), Arg, WG, F; 1959 v E, S, W, Sp; 1960 v E, S, W; 1961 v E, W, WG (2), Gr; 1962 v E, S, Gr, Ho; 1963 v E, S, Pol (2); (with Stoke C), 1963 v W; 1966 v S, E, Alb (55)

McIlroy, S. B. (Manchester U), 1972 v Sp, S (sub); 1974 v S, E, W; 1975 v N, Se, Y, E, S, W; 1976 v Se, N, Y, S, E, W; 1977 v Ho, Bel, E, S, W, Ic; 1978 v Ic, Ho, Bel, S, E, W; 1979 v Ei, D, Bul, E, Bul, E, S, W, D; 1980 v E, Ei, Is, S, E, W; 1981 v Se, P, S, P, S, Se; 1982 v S, Is; (with Stoke C), E, F, S, W, Y, Hon, Sp, A, F (61)

McIlvenny, J. (Distillery), 1890 v E; 1891 v E (2)

McIlvenny, P. (Distillery), 1924 v W (1)

McKeag, W. (Glentoran), 1968 v S, W (2)

McKee, F. W. (Cliftonville), 1906 v S, W; (with Belfast C), 1914 v E, S, W (5)

McKelvie, H. (Glentoran), 1901 v W (1)

McKenna, J. (Huddersfield), 1950 v E, S, W; 1951 v E, S, F; 1952 v E (7)

McKenzie, H. (Distillery), 1923 v S (1)

McKenzie, R. (Airdrie), 1967 v W (1)

McKeown, H. (Linfield), 1892 v E, S, W; 1893 v S, W; 1894 v S, W (7)

McKie, H. (Cliftonville), 1895 v E, S, W (3)

McKinney, D. (Hull C), 1921 v S; (with Bradford C), 1924 v S (2)

McKinney, V. J. (Falkirk), 1966 v WG (1)

McKnight, J. (Preston NE), 1912 v S; (with Glentoran), 1913 v S (2)

McLaughlin, J. C. (Shrewsbury T), 1962 v E, S, W, Gr; 1963 v W; (with Swansea T), 1964 v W, U; 1965 v E, W, Sw (2); 1966 v W (12)

McLean, T. (Limavady), 1885 v S (1)

McMahon, J. (Bohemians), 1934 v S (1)

McMaster, G. (Glentoran), 1897 v E, S, W (3)

McMichael, A. (Newcastle U), 1950 v E, S; 1951 v E, S, F; 1952 v E, S, W; 1953 v E, S, W, F; 1954 v E, S, W; 1955 v E, W; 1956 v W; 1957 v E, S, W, I, P (2); 1958 v E, S, W, I (2), Cz (2), Arg, WG, F; 1959 v S, W, Sp; 1960 v E, S, W (40)

McMillan, G. (Distillery), 1903 v E; 1905 v W (2)

McMillan, S. (Manchester U), 1963 v E, S (2)

McMillen, W. S. (Manchester U), 1934 v E; 1935 v S; 1937 v S; (with Chesterfield), 1938 v S, W; 1939 v E, S (7)

McMordie, A. S. (Middlesbrough), 1969 v Is, T (2), E, S, W; 1970 v E, S, W, USSR; 1971 v Cy (2), E, S, W; 1972 v USSR, Sp, E, S, W; 1973 v Bul (21)

McMorran, E. J. (Belfast C), 1947 v E; (with Barnsley), 1951 v E, S, W; 1952 v E, S, W; 1953 v E, S, F; (with Doncaster R), 1953 v W; 1954 v E; 1956 v W; 1957 v I, P (15)

McMullan, D. (Liverpool), 1926 v E, W; 1927 v S (3)

McNinch, J. (Ballymena), 1931 v S; 1932 v S, W (3)

McParland, P. J. (Aston Villa), 1954 v W; 1955 v E, S; 1956 v E, S; 1957 v E, S, W, P; 1958 v E, S, W, I (2), Cz (2), Arg, WG, F; 1959 v E, S, W, Sp; 1960 v E, S; 1961 v E, S, W, I, WG (2), Gr; (with Wolverhampton W), 1962 v Ho (34)

McShane, J. (Cliftonville), 1899 v S; 1900 v E, S, W (4)

McVickers, J. (Glentoran), 1888 v E; 1889 v S (2)

McWha, W. B. R. (Knock), 1882 v E, W; (with Cliftonville), 1883 v E, W; 1884 v E; 1885 v E, W (7)

Macartney, A. (Ulster), 1903 v S, W; (with Linfield), 1904 v S, W; (with Everton), 1905 v E, S; (with Belfast C), 1907 v E, S, W; 1908 v E, S, W; (with Glentoran), 1909 v E, S, W (15)

Mackie, J. (Arsenal), 1923 v W; (with Portsmouth), 1935 v S, W (3)

Madden, O. (Norwich C), 1938 v E (1)

Magill, E. J. (Arsenal), 1962 v E, S, Gr; 1963 v E, S, W, Pol (2), Sp; 1964 v E, S, W, U, Sp; 1965 v E, S, Sw (2), Ho, Alb; 1966 v S, Alb; (with Brighton), 1966 v E, W, WG, M (26)

Maginnis, H. (Linfield), 1900 v E, S, W; 1903 v S, W; 1904 v E, S, W (8)

Maguire, E. (Distillery), 1907 v S (1)

Mahood, J. (Belfast C), 1926 v S; 1928 v E, S, W; 1929 v E, S, W; 1930 v W; (with Ballymena), 1934 v S (9)

Manderson, R. (Glasgow R), 1920 v W, S; 1925 v S, E; 1926 v S (5)

Mansfield, J. (Dublin Freebooters), 1901 v E (1)

Martin, C. J. (Glentoran), 1947 v S; (with Leeds U), 1948 v E, S, W; (with Aston Villa), 1949 v E; 1950 v W (6)

Martin, D. (Bo'ness), 1925 v S (1)

Martin, D. C. (Cliftonville), 1882 v E, W; 1883 v E (3)

Martin, D. K. (Belfast C), 1934 v E, S, W; 1935 v S; (with Wolverhampton W), 1935 v E; 1936 v W; (with Nottingham F), 1937 v S; 1938 v E, S; 1939 v S (10)

Mathieson, A. (Luton T), 1921 v W; 1922 v E (2)

Maxwell, J. (Linfield), 1902 v W; 1903 v W, E; (with Glentoran), 1905 v W, S; (with Belfast C), 1906 v W; 1907 v S (7)

Meek, H. L. (Glentoran), 1925 v W (1)
Mehaffy, J. A. C. (Queen's Island), 1922 v W (1)
Meldon, J. (Dublin Freebooters), 1899 v S, W (2)
Mercer, H. V. A. (Linfield), 1908 v E (1)
Mercer, J. T. (Distillery), 1898 v E, S, W; 1899 v E; (with Linfield), 1902 v E, W; (with Distillery), 1903 v S, W; (with Derby Co), 1904 v E, W; 1905 v S (11)
Millar, W. (Barrow), 1932 v W; 1933 v S (2)
Miller, J. (Middlesbrough), 1929 v W, S; 1930 v E (3)
Milligan, D. (Chesterfield), 1939 v W (1)
Milne, R. G. (Linfield), 1894 v E, S, W; 1895 v E, W; 1896 v E, S, W; 1897 v E, S; 1898 v E, S, W; 1899 v E, W; 1901 v W; 1902 v E, S, W; 1903 v E, S; 1904 v E, S, W; 1906 v E, S, W (27)
Mitchell, C. (Glentoran), 1934 v W (1)
Mitchell, E. J. (Cliftonville), 1933 v S (1)
Mitchell, W. (Distillery), 1932 v E, W; 1933 v E, W; (with Chelsea), 1934 v W, S; 1935 v S, E; 1936 v S, E; 1937 v E, S, W; 1938 v E, S (15)
Molyneux, T. B. (Ligoniel), 1883 v E, W; (with Cliftonville), 1884 v E, W, S; 1885 v E, W; 1886 v E, W, S; 1888 v S (11)
Montgomery, F. J. (Coleraine), 1955 v E (1)
Moore, C. (Glentoran), 1949 v W (1)
Moore, J. (Linfield Ath), 1891 v E, S, W (3)
Moore, P. (Aberdeen), 1933 v E (1)
Moore, T. (Ulster), 1887 v S, W (2)
Moore, W. (Falkirk), 1923 v S (1)
Moorhead, F. W. (Dublin University), 1885 v E (1)
Moorhead, G. (Linfield), 1923 v S; 1928 v S; 1929 v S (3)
Moran, J. (Leeds C), 1912 v S (1)
Moreland, V. (Derby Co), 1979 v Bul (sub), Bul (sub), E, S; 1980 v E, Ei (6)
Morgan, F. G. (Linfield), 1923 v E; (with Nottingham F), 1924 v S; 1927 v E; 1928 v E, S, W; 1929 v E (7)
Morgan, S. (Port Vale), 1972 v Sp; 1973 v Bul (sub), P, Cy, E, S, W; (with Aston Villa), 1974 v Bul, P, S, E; 1975 v Se; 1976 v Se (sub), N, Y; (with Brighton & HA), S, W (sub); (with Sparta Rotterdam), 1979 v D (18)
Morrison, J. (Linfield Ath), 1891 v E, W (2)
Morrison, T. (Glentoran), 1895 v E, S, W; (with Burnley), 1899 v W; 1900 v W; 1902 v E, S (7)
Morrogh, E. (Bohemians), 1896 v S (1)
Morrow, W. J. (Moyola Park), 1883 v E, W; 1884 v S (3)
Muir, R. (Oldpark), 1885 v S, W (2)
Mulholland, S. (Celtic), 1906 v S, E (2)
Mulligan, J. (Manchester C), 1921 v S (1)
Murphy, J. (Bradford C), 1910 v E, S, W (3)
Murphy, N. (QPR), 1905 v E, S, W (3)
Murray, J. M. (Motherwell), 1910 v E, S; (with Sheffield W), 1910 v W (3)

Napier, R. J. (Bolton W), 1966 v WG (1)
Neill, W. J. T. (Arsenal), 1961 v I, Gr, WG; 1962 v E, S, W, Gr; 1963 v E, W, Pol, Sp; 1964 v S, E, W, U, Sp; 1965 v E, S, W, Sw, Ho (2), Alb; 1966 v S, E, W, Alb, WG, M; 1967 v S, W; 1968 v S, E; 1969 v E, S, W, Is, T (2); 1970 v S, E, W, USSR (2); (with Hull C), 1971 v Cy, Sp; 1972 v USSR (2), Sp, S, E, W; 1973 v Bul, Cy (2), P, E, S, W (59)
Nelis, P. (Nottingham F), 1923 v E (1)
Nelson, S. (Arsenal), 1970 v W, E (sub); 1971 v Cy, Sp, E, S, W; 1972 v USSR (2), Sp, E, S, W; 1973 v Bul, Cy, P; 1974 v S, E; 1975 v Se, Y; 1976 v Se, N, Is, E; 1977 v Bel (sub), WG, W, Ic; 1978 v Ic, Ho, Bel; 1979 v Ei, D, Bul, E, Bul, E, S, W, D; 1980 v E, Ei, Is; 1981 v S, P, S, Se; (with Brighton & HA), 1982 v E, S, Sp (sub), A (51)
Nicholl, C. J. (Aston Villa), 1975 v Se, Y, E, S, W; 1976 v Se, N, Y, S, E, W; 1977 v W; (with Southampton),

1978 v Bel (sub), S, E, W; 1979 v Ei, Bul, E, Bul, E, W; 1980 v Ei, Is, S, E, W, Aus (3); 1981 v Se, P, S, P, S, Se; 1982 v S, Is, E, F, W, Y, Hon, Sp, A, F (46)
Nicholl, H. (Belfast C), 1902 v E, W; 1905 v E (3)
Nicholl, J. M. (Manchester U), 1976 v Is, W (sub); 1977 v Ho, Bel, E, S, W, Ic; 1978 v Ic, Ho, Bel, S, E, W; 1979 v Ei, D, Bul, E, Bul, E, S, W, D; 1980 v E, Ei, Is, S, E, W, Aus (3); 1981 v Se, P, S, P, S, Se; 1982 v S, Is, E; (with Toronto B), F, W, Y, Hon, Sp, A, F (48)
Nicholson, J. J. (Manchester U), 1961 v S, W; 1962 v E, W, Gr, Ho; 1963 v E, S, Pol (2); (with Huddersfield T), 1965 v W, Ho (2), Alb; 1966 v S, E, W, Alb, M; 1967 v S, W; 1968 v S, E, W; 1969 v S, E, W, T (2); 1970 v S, E, W, USSR (2); 1971 v Cy (2), E, S, W; 1972 v USSR (2) (41)
Nixon, R. (Linfield), 1914 v S (1)
Nolan-Whelan, J. V. (Dublin Freebooters), 1901 v E, W; 1902 v S, W (4)


O'Brien, M. T. (QPR), 1921 v S; (with Leicester C), 1922 v S, W; 1924 v S, W; (with Hull C), 1925 v S, E, W; 1926 v W; (with Derby Co), 1927 v W (10)
O'Connell, P. (Sheffield W), 1912 v E, S; (with Hull C), 1914 v S, E, W (5)
O'Doherty, A. (Coleraine), 1970 v E, W (sub) (2)
O'Driscoll, J. F. (Swansea T), 1949 v E, S, W (3)
O'Hagan, C. (Tottenham H), 1905 v S, W; 1906 v S, W, E; (with Aberdeen), 1907 v E, S, W; 1908 v S, W; 1909 v E (11)
O'Hagan, W. (St Mirren), 1920 v E, W (2)
O'Hehir, J. C. (Bohemians), 1910 v W (1)
O'Kane, W. J. (Nottingham F), 1970 v E, W, S (sub); 1971 v Sp, E, S, W; 1972 v USSR (2); 1973 v P, Cy; 1974 v Bul, P, S, E, W; 1975 v N, Se, E, S (20)
O'Mahoney, M. T. (Bristol R), 1939 v S (1)
O'Neill, J. (Leicester C), 1980 v Is, S, E, W, Aus (3); 1981 v P, S, P, S, Se; 1982 v S, Is, E, F, S, F (sub) (18)
O'Neill, J. (Sunderland), 1962 v W (1)
O'Neill, M. H. (Distillery), 1972 v USSR (sub), (with Nottingham F), Sp (sub), W (sub); 1973 v P, Cy, E, S, W; 1974 v Bul, P, E (sub), W; 1975 v Se, Y, E, S; 1976 v Y; 1977 v E (sub), S; 1978 v Ic, Ho, S, E, W; 1979 v Ei, D, Bul, E, Bul, D; 1980 v Ei, Is, Aus (3); 1981 v Se, P (with Norwich C), P, S, Se; (with Manchester C), 1982 v S (with Norwich C), E, F, S, Y, Hon, Sp, A, F (49)
O'Reilly, H. (Dublin Freebooters), 1901 v S, W; 1904 v S (3)


Parke, J. (Linfield), 1964 v S; (with Hibernian), 1964 v E, Sp; (with Sunderland), 1965 v Sw, S, W, Ho (2), Alb; 1966 v WG; 1967 v E, S; 1968 v S, E (14)
Peacock, R. (Celtic), 1952 v S; 1953 v F; 1954 v W; 1955 v E, S; 1956 v E, S; 1957 v W, I, P; 1958 v S, E, W, I (2), Arg, Cz (2), WG; 1959 v E, S, W; 1960 v S, E; 1961 v E, S, I, WG (2), Gr; (with Coleraine), 1962 v S (31)
Peden, J. (Linfield), 1887 v S, W; 1888 v W, E; 1889 v S, E; 1890 v W, S; 1891 v W, E; 1892 v W, E; 1893 v E, S, W; (with Distillery), 1896 v W, E, S; 1897 v W, S; 1898 v W, E, S; (with Linfield), 1899 v W (24)
Percy, J. C. (Belfast YMCA), 1889 v W (1)
Platt, J. A. (Middlesbrough), 1976 v Is (sub); 1978 v S, E, W; 1980 v S, E, W, Aus (3); 1981 v Se, P; 1982 v F, S, W (sub), A (16)
Ponsonby, J. (Distillery), 1895 v S; 1896 v E, S, W; 1897 v E, S, W; 1899 v E (8)
Potts, R. M. C. (Cliftonville), 1883 v E, W (2)
Priestley, T. J. (Coleraine), 1933 v S; (with Chelsea), 1934 v E (2)
Pyper, Jas. (Cliftonville), 1897 v S, W; 1898 v S, E, W; 1899 v S; 1900 v E (7)

Pyper, John (Cliftonville), 1897 v E, S, W; 1899 v E, W; 1900 v E, W, S; 1902 v S (9)
Pyper, M. (Linfield), 1932 v W (1)

Rafferty, P. (Linfield), 1980 v E (sub) (1)
Rankine, J. (Alexander), 1883 v E, W (2)
Raper, E. O. (Dublin University), 1886 v W (1)
Rattray, D. (Avoniel), 1882 v E; 1883 v E, W (3)
Rea, B. (Glentoran), 1901 v E (1)
Redmond, J. (Cliftonville), 1884 v W (1)
Reid, G. H. (Cardiff C), 1923 v S (1)
Reid, J. (Ulster), 1883 v E; 1884 v W; 1887 v S; 1889 v W; 1890 v S, W (6)
Reid, S. E. (Derby Co), 1934 v E, W; 1936 v E (3)
Reid, W. (Hearts), 1931 v E (1)
Reilly, J. (Portsmouth), 1900 v E; 1902 v E (2)
Renneville, W. T. (Leyton), 1910 v S, E, W; (with Aston Villa), 1911 v W (4)
Reynolds, J. (Distillery), 1890 v E, W; (with Ulster), 1891 v E, S, W (5)
Reynolds, R. (Bohemians), 1905 v W (1)
Rice, P. J. (Arsenal), 1969 v Is; 1970 v USSR; 1971 v E, S, W; 1972 v USSR, Sp, E, S, W; 1973 v Bul, Cy, E, S, W; 1974 v Bul, P, S, E, W; 1975 v N, Y, E, S, W; 1976 v Se, N, Y, Is, S, E, W; 1977 v Ho, Bel, WG, E, S, Ic; 1978 v Ic, Ho, Bel; 1979 v Ei, D, E (2), S, W, D; 1980 v E (49)
Roberts, F. C. (Glentoran), 1931 v S (1)
Robinson, P. (Distillery), 1920 v S; (with Blackburn R), 1921 v W (2)
Rollo, D. (Linfield), 1912 v W; 1913 v W; 1914 v W, E; (with Blackburn R), 1920 v S, W; 1921 v E, S, W; 1922 v E; 1923 v E; 1924 v S, W; 1925 v W; 1926 v E; 1927 v E (16)
Rosbotham, A. (Cliftonville), 1887 v E, S, W; 1888 v E, S, W; 1889 v E (7)
Ross, W. E. (Newcastle U), 1969 v Is (1)
Rowley, R. W. M. (Southampton), 1929 v S, W; 1930 v W, E; (with Tottenham H), 1931 v W; 1932 v S (6)
Russell, A. (Linfield), 1947 v E (1)
Russell, S. R. (Bradford C), 1930 v E, S; (with Derry C), 1932 v E (3)
Ryan, R. A. (WBA), 1950 v W (1)

Scott, E. (Liverpool), 1920 v S; 1921 v E, S, W; 1922 v E; 1925 v W; 1926 v E, S, W; 1927 v E, S, W; 1928 v E, S, W; 1929 v E, S, W; 1930 v E; 1931 v E; 1932 v W; 1933 v E, S, W; 1934 v E, S, W; (with Belfast C), 1935 v S; 1936 v E, S, W (30)
Scott, J. (Grimsby), 1958 v Cz, F (2)
Scott, J. E. (Cliftonville), 1901 v S (1)
Scott, L. J. (Dublin University), 1895 v S, W (2)
Scott, P. W. (Everton), 1975 v W; 1976 v Y; (with York C), Is, S, E (sub); 1978 v S, E, W; (with Aldershot), 1979 v S (sub) (10)
Scott, T. (Cliftonville), 1894 v E, S; 1895 v S, W; 1896 v S, E, W; 1897 v E, W; 1898 v E, S, W; 1900 v W (13)
Scott, W. (Linfield), 1903 v E, S, W; 1904 v E, S, W; (with Everton), 1905 v E, S; 1907 v E, S; 1908 v E, S, W; 1909 v E, S, W; 1910 v E, S; 1911 v E, S, W; 1912 v E; (with Leeds City), 1913 v E, S, W (25)
Scraggs, M. J. (Glentoran), 1921 v W; 1922 v E (2)
Seymour, H. C. (Bohemians), 1914 v W (1)
Seymour, J. (Cliftonville), 1907 v W; 1909 v W (2)
Shanks, T. (Woolwich Arsenal), 1903 v S; 1904 v W; (with Brentford), 1905 v E (3)
Sharkey, P. (Ipswich T), 1976 v S (1)
Sheehan, Dr G. (Bohemians), 1899 v S; 1900 v E, W (3)
Sheridan, J. (Everton), 1903 v W, E, S; 1904 v E, S; (with Stoke C), 1905 v E (6)

Sherrard, J. (Limavady), 1885 v S; 1887 v W; 1888 v W (3)
Sherrard, W. (Cliftonville), 1895 v E, W, S (3)
Sherry, J. J. (Bohemians), 1906 v E; 1907 v W (2)
Shields, J. (Southampton), 1957 v S (1)
Silo, M. (Belfast YMCA), 1888 v E (1)
Simpson, W. J. (Glasgow R), 1951 v W, F; 1954 v E, S; 1955 v E; 1957 v I, P; 1958 v S, E, W, I; 1959 v S (12)
Sinclair, J. (Knock), 1882 v E, W (2)
Slemin, J. C. (Bohemians), 1909 v W (1)
Sloan, A. S. (London Caledonians), 1925 v W (1)
Sloan, D. (Oxford U), 1969 v Is; 1971 v Sp (2)
Sloan, H. A. de B. (Bohemians), 1903 v E; 1904 v S; 1905 v E; 1906 v W; 1907 v E, W; 1908 v W; 1909 v S (8)
Sloan, J. W. (Arsenal), 1947 v W (1)
Sloan, T. (Cardiff C), 1926 v S, W, E; 1927 v W, S; 1928 v E, W; 1929 v E; (with Linfield), 1930 v W, S; 1931 v S (11)
Sloan, T. (Manchester U), 1979 v S, W (sub), D (sub) (3)
Small, J. (Clarence), 1887 v E (1)
Small, J. M. (Cliftonville), 1893 v E, S, W (3)
Smith, E. E. (Cardiff C), 1921 v S; 1923 v W, E; 1924 v E (4)
Smith, J. (Distillery), 1901 v S, W (2)
Smyth, R. H. (Dublin University), 1886 v W (1)
Smyth, S. (Wolverhampton W), 1948 v E, S, W; 1949 v S, W; 1950 v E, S, W; (with Stoke C), 1952 v E (9)
Smyth, W. (Distillery), 1949 v E, S; 1954 v S, E (4)
Snape, A. (Airdrie), 1920 v E (1)
Spence, D. W. (Bury), 1975 v Y, E, S, W; 1976 v Se, Is, E, W, S (sub); (with Blackpool), 1977 v Ho (sub), WG (sub), E (sub), S (sub), W (sub), Ic (sub); 1979 v Ei, D (sub), E (sub), Bul (sub), E (sub), S, W, D; 1980 v Ei; (with Southend U), Is (sub), Aus (sub); 1981 v S (sub), Se (sub); 1982 v F (sub) (29)
Spencer, S. (Distillery), 1890 v E, S; 1892 v E, S, W; 1893 v E (6)
Spiller, E. A. (Cliftonville), 1883 v E, W; 1884 v E, W, S (5)
Stanfield, O. M. (Distillery), 1887 v E, S, W; 1888 v E, S, W; 1889 v E, S, W; 1890 v E, S; 1891 v E, S, W; 1892 v E, S, W; 1893 v E, W; 1894 v E, S, W; 1895 v E, S; 1896 v E, S, W; 1897 v E, S, W (30)
Steele, A. (Charlton Ath), 1926 v W, S; (with Fulham), 1929 v W, S (4)
Stevenson, A. E. (Rangers), 1934 v E, S, W; (with Everton), 1935 v E, S; 1936 v S, W; 1937 v E, W; 1938 v E, W; 1939 v E, S, W; 1947 v S, W; 1948 v S (17)
Stewart, A. (Glentoran), 1967 v W; 1968 v S, E; (with Derby Co), 1968 v W; 1969 v Is, T (1+1 sub) (7)
Stewart, D. C. (Hull C), 1978 v Bel (1)
Stewart, I. (QPR), 1982 v F (sub) (1)
Stewart, R. H. (St Columb's Court), 1890 v E, S, W; (with Cliftonville), 1892 v E, S, W; 1893 v E, W; 1894 v E, S, W (11)
Stewart, T. C. (Linfield), 1961 v W (1)
Swan, S. (Linfield), 1899 v S (1)

Taggart, J. (Walsall), 1899 v W (1)
Thompson, F. W. (Cliftonville), 1910 v E, S, W; (with Bradford C), 1911 v E; (with Linfield), v W; 1912 v E, W; 1913 v E, S, W; (with Clyde), 1914 v E, S (12)
Thompson, J. (Distillery), 1897 v S (1)
Thompson, J. (Belfast Ath), 1889 v S (1)
Thunder, P. J. (Bohemians), 1911 v W (1)
Todd, S. J. (Burnley), 1966 v M (sub); 1967 v E; 1968 v W; 1969 v E, S, W; 1970 v S, USSR; (with Sheffield W), 1971 v Cy (2), Sp (sub) (11)
Toner, J. (Arsenal), 1922 v W; 1923 v W; 1924 v W, E; 1925 v E, S; (with St Johnstone), 1927 v E, S (8)
Torrans, R. (Linfield), 1893 v S (1)

Torrans, S. (Linfield), 1889 v S; 1890 v S, W; 1891 v S, W; 1892 v E, S, W; 1893 v E, S; 1894 v E, S, W; 1895 v E; 1896 v E, S, W; 1897 v E, S, W; 1898 v E, S; 1899 v E, W; 1901 v S, W (26)

Trainor, D. (Crusaders), 1967 v W (1)

Tully, C. P. (Glasgow C), 1949 v E; 1950 v E; 1952 v S; 1953 v E, S, W, F; 1954 v S; 1956 v E; 1959 v Sp (10)

Turner, E. (Cliftonville), 1896 v E, W (2)

Turner, W. (Cliftonville), 1886 v E; 1886 v S; 1888 v S (3)

Twoomey, J. F. (Leeds U), 1938 v W; 1939 v E (2)

Uprichard, W. N. M. C. (Swindon T), 1952 v E, S, W; 1953 v E, S; (with Portsmouth), 1953 v W, F; 1955 v E, S, W; 1956 v E, S, W; 1958 v S, I, Cz; 1959 v S, Sp (18)

Vernon, J. (Belfast C), 1947 v E, S; (with WBA), 1947 v W; 1948 v E, S, W; 1949 v E, S, W; 1950 v E, S; 1951 v E, S, W, F; 1952 v S, E (17)

Waddell, T. M. R. (Cliftonville), 1906 v S (1)

Walker, J. (Doncaster R), 1955 v W (1)

Walker, T. (Bury), 1911 v S (1)

Walsh, D. J. (WBA), 1947 v S, W; 1948 v E, S, W; 1949 v E, S, W; 1950 v W (9)

Walsh, W. (Manchester C), 1948 v E, S, W; 1949 v E, S (5)

Waring, R. (Distillery), 1899 v E (1)

Warren, P. (Shelbourne), 1913 v E, S (2)

Watson, J. (Ulster), 1883 v E, W; 1886 v E, S, W; 1887 v S, W; 1889 v E, W (9)

Watson, P. (Distillery), 1971 v Cy (sub) (1)

Watson, T. (Cardiff C), 1926 v S (1)

Wattle, J. (Distillery), 1899 v E (1)

Webb, C. G. (Brighton), 1909 v S, W; 1911 v S (3)

Weir, E. (Clyde), 1939 v W (1)

Welsh, E. (Carlisle U), 1966 v W, WG, M; 1967 v W (4)

Whiteside, N. (Manchester U), 1982 v Y, Hon, Sp, A, F (5)

Whiteside, T. (Distillery), 1891 v E (1)

Whitfield, E. R. (Dublin University), 1886 v W (1)

Williams, J. R. (Ulster), 1886 v E, S (2)

Williamson, J. (Cliftonville), 1890 v E; 1892 v S; 1893 v S (3)

Willigham, T. (Burnley), 1933 v W; 1934 v S (2)

Willis, G. (Linfield), 1906 v S, W; 1907 v S; 1912 v S (4)

Wilson, H. (Linfield), 1925 v W (1)

Wilson, M. (Distillery), 1884 v E, S, W (3)

Wilson, R. (Cliftonville), 1888 v S (1)

Wilson, S. J. (Glenavon), 1962 v S; 1964 v S; (with Falkirk), 1964 v E, W, U, Sp; 1965 v E, Sw; (with Dundee), 1966 v W, WG; 1967 v S; 1968 v E (12)

Wilton, J. M. (St Columb's Court), 1888 v E, W; 1889 v S, E; (with Cliftonville), 1890 v E; (with St Columb's Court), 1892 v W; 1893 v S (7)

Wright, J. (Cliftonville), 1906 v E, S, W; 1907 v E, S, W (6)

Young, S. (Linfield), 1907 v E, S; 1908 v E, S; (with Airdrie), 1909 v E; 1912 v S; (with Linfield), 1914 v E, S, W (9)

# SCOTLAND

Adams, J. (Hearts), 1889 v Ni; 1892 v W; 1893 v Ni (3)

Agnew, W. B. (Kilmarnock), 1907 v Ni; 1908 v W, Ni (3)

Aird, J. (Burnley), 1954 v N (2), A, U (4)

Aitken, A. (Newcastle U), 1901 v E; 1902 v E; 1903 v E, W; 1904 v E; 1905 v E, W; 1906 v E; (with Middlesbrough), 1907 v E, W; 1908 v E; (with Leicester Fosse), 1910 v E; 1911 v E, Ni (14)

Aitken, G. G. (East Fife), 1949 v E, F; 1950 v W, Ni, Sw; (with Sunderland), 1953 v W, Ni; 1954 v E (8)

Aitken, R. (Dumbarton), 1886 v E; 1888 v Ni (2)

Aitken, R. (Celtic), 1980 v Pe (sub), Bel, W (sub), E, Pol (5)

Aitkenhead, W. A. C. (Blackburn R), 1912 v Ni (1)

Albiston, A. (Manchester U), 1982 v Ni (1)

Alexander, D. (East Stirlingshire), 1894 v W, Ni (2)

Allan, D. S. (Queen's Park), 1885 v E, W; 1886 v W (3)

Allan, G. (Liverpool), 1897 v E (1)

Allan, H. (Hearts), 1902 v W (1)

Allan, J. (Queen's Park), 1887 v E, W (2)

Allan, T. (Dundee), 1974 v WG, N (2)

Ancell, R. F. D. (Newcastle U), 1937 v W, Ni (2)

Anderson, A. (Hearts), 1933 v E; 1934 v A, E, W, Ni; 1935 v E, W, Ni; 1936 v E, W, Ni; 1937 v G, E, W, Ni, A; 1938 v E, W, Ni, Cz, Ho; 1939 v W, H (23)

Anderson, F. (Clydesdale), 1874 v E (1)

Anderson, G. (Kilmarnock), 1901 v Ni (1)

Anderson, H. A. (Raith R), 1914 v W (1)

Anderson, J. (Leicester C), 1954 v Fi (1)

Anderson, K. (Queen's Park), 1896 v Ni; 1898 v E, Ni (3)

Anderson, W. (Queen's Park), 1882 v E; 1883 v E, W; 1884 v E; 1885 v E, W (6)

Andrews, P. (Eastern), 1875 v E (1)

Archibald, A. (Rangers), 1921 v W; 1922 v W, E; 1923 v Ni; 1924 v E, W; 1931 v E; 1932 v E (8)

Archibald, S. (Aberdeen), 1980 v P (sub); (with Tottenham H), Ni, Pol, H; 1981 v Se (sub), Is, Ni, Is, Ni, E; 1982 v Ni, P, Sp (sub), Ho, Nz (sub), Br, USSR (17)

Armstrong, M. W. (Aberdeen), 1936 v W, Ni; 1937 v G (3)

Arnott, W. (Queen's Park), 1883 v W; 1884 v E, Ni; 1885 v E, W; 1886 v E; 1887 v E, W; 1888 v E; 1889 v E; 1890 v E; 1891 v E; 1892 v E; 1893 v E (14)

Auld, J. R. (Third Lanark), 1887 v E, W; 1889 v W (3)

Auld, R. (Celtic), 1959 v H, P; 1960 v W (3)

Baird, A. (Queen's Park), 1892 v Ni; 1894 v W (2)

Baird, D. (Hearts), 1890 v Ni; 1891 v E; 1892 v W (3)

Baird, H. (Airdrie), 1956 v A (1)

Baird, J. C. (Vale of Leven), 1876 v E; 1878 v W; 1880 v E (3)

Baird, S. (Rangers), 1957 v Y, Sp (2), Sw, WG; 1958 v F, Ni (7)

Baird, W. U. (St Bernard), 1897 v Ni (1)

Bannon, E. (Dundee U), 1980 v Bel (1)

Barbour, A. (Renton), 1885 v Ni (1)

Barker, J. B. (Rangers), 1893 v W; 1894 v W (2)

Barrett, F. (Dundee), 1894 v Ni; 1895 v W (2)

Battles, B. (Celtic), 1901 v E, W, Ni (3)

Battles, B. jun. (Hearts), 1931 v W (1)

Bauld, W. (Hearts), 1950 v E, Sw, P (3)

Baxter, J. C. (Rangers), 1961 v Ni, Ei (2), Cz; 1962 v Ni, W, E, Cz (2), U; 1963 v W, Ni, E, A, N, Ei, Sp; 1964 v W, E, N, WG; 1965 v W, Ni, Fi; (with Sunderland), 1966 v P, Br, Ni, W, E, I; 1967 v W, E, USSR; 1968 v W (34)

Baxter, R. D. (Middlesbrough), 1939 v E, W, H (3)

Beattie, A. (Preston NE), 1937 v E, A, Cz; 1938 v E; 1939 v W, Ni, H (7)

Beattie, R. (Preston NE), 1939 v W (1)

Begbie, I. (Hearts), 1890 v Ni; 1891 v E; 1892 v W; 1894 v E (4)

Bell, A. (Manchester U), 1912 v Ni (1)

Bell, J. (Dumbarton), 1890 v Ni; 1892 v E; (with Everton), 1896 v E; 1897 v E; 1898 v E; (with Celtic), 1899 v E, W, Ni; 1900 v E, W (10)

Bell, M. (Hearts), 1901 v W (1)

Bell, W. J. (Leeds U), 1966 v P, Br (2)

Bennett, A. (Celtic), 1904 v W; 1907 v Ni; 1908 v W; (with Rangers), 1909 v W, Ni, E; 1910 v E, W; 1911 v E, W; 1913 v Ni (11)

Bennie, R. (Airdrieonians), 1925 v W, Ni; 1926 v Ni (3)

Berry, D. (Queen's Park), 1894 v W; 1899 v W, Ni (3)

Berry, W. H. (Queen's Park), 1888 v E; 1889 v E; 1890 v E; 1891 v E (4)

Bett, J. (Rangers), 1982 v Ho (1)

Beveridge, W. W. (Glasgow University), 1879 v E, W; 1880 v W (3)

Black, A. (Hearts), 1938 v Cz, Ho; 1939 v H (3)

Black, D. (Hurlford), 1889 v Ni (1)

Black, I. H. (Southampton), 1948 v E (1)

Blackburn, J. E. (Royal Engineers), 1873 v E (1)

Blacklaw, A. S. (Burnley), 1963 v N, Sp; 1966 v I (3)

Blackley, J. (Hibernian), 1974 v Cz, E, Bel, Z; 1976 v Sw; 1977 v W, Se (7)

Blair, D. (Clyde), 1929 v W, Ni; 1931 v E, A, I; 1932 v W, Ni; (with Aston Villa), 1933 v W (8)

Blair, J. (Sheffield W), 1920 v E, Ni; (with Cardiff C), 1921 v E; 1922 v E; 1923 v E, W, Ni; 1924 v W (8)

Blair, J. (Motherwell), 1934 v W (1)

Blair, J. A. (Blackpool), 1947 v W (1)

Blair, W. (Third Lanark), 1896 v W (1)

Blessington J. (Celtic), 1894 v E, Ni; 1896 v E, Ni (4)

Blyth, J. A. (Coventry C), 1978 v Bul, W (2)

Bone, J. (Norwich C), 1972 v Y (sub); 1973 v D (2)

Bowie, J. (Rangers), 1920 v E, Ni (2)

Bowie, W. (Linthouse), 1891 v Ni (1)

Bowman, G. A. (Montrose), 1892 v Ni (1)

Boyd, J. M. (Newcastle U), 1934 v Ni (1)

Boyd, R. (Mossend Swifts), 1889 v Ni; 1891 v W (2)

Boyd, W. G. (Clyde), 1931 v I, Sw (2)

Brackenbridge, T. (Hearts), 1888 v Ni (1)

Bradshaw, T. (Bury), 1928 v E (1)

Brand, R. (Rangers), 1961 v Ni, Cz, Ei (2); 1962 v Ni, W, Cz, U (8)

Branden, T. (Blackburn R), 1896 v E (1)

Brazil, A. (Ipswich T), 1980 v Pol (sub), H; 1982 v Sp, Ho (sub), Ni, W, E, Nz, USSR (sub) (9)

Bremner, D. (Hibernian), 1976 v Sw (sub) (1)

Bremner, W. J. (Leeds U), 1965 v Sp; 1966 v E, Pol, P, Br, I (2); 1967 v W, Ni, E; 1968 v W, E; 1969 v W, E, Ni, D, A, WG, Cy (2); 1970 v Ei, WG, A; 1971 v W, E; 1972 v P, Bel, Ho, Ni, W, E, Y, Cz, Br; 1973 v D (2), E (2), Ni (sub), Sw, Br; 1974 v Cz, WG, Ni, W, E, Bel, N, Z, Br, Y; 1975 v Sp (2); 1976 v D (54)

Brennan, F. (Newcastle U), 1947 v W, Ni; 1953 v W, Ni, E; 1954 v Ni, E (7)

Breslin, B. (Hibernian), 1897 v W (1)

Brewster, G. (Everton), 1921 v E (1)

Brogan, J. (Celtic), 1971 v W, Ni, P, E (4)

Brown, A. (Middlesbrough), 1904 v E (1)

Brown, A. (St Mirren), 1890 v W; 1891 v W (2)

Brown, A. D. (East Fife), 1950 v Sw, P, F; (with Blackpool), 1952 v USA, D, Se; 1953 v W; 1954 v W, E, N (2), Fi, A, U (14)

Brown, G. C. P. (Rangers), 1931 v W; 1932 v E, W, Ni; 1933 v E; 1935 v A, E, W; 1936 v E, W; 1937 v G, E, W, Ni, Cz; 1938 v E, W, Cz, Ho (19)

Brown, H. (Partick T), 1947 v W, Bel, L (3)

Brown, J. (Cambuslang), 1890 v W (1)

Brown, J. B. (Clyde), 1939 v W (1)

Brown, J. G. (Sheffield U), 1975 v R (1)

Brown, R. (Dumbarton), 1884 v W, Ni (2)

Brown, R. (Rangers), 1947 v Ni; 1949 v Ni; 1952 v E (3)

Brown, R. jun. (Dumbarton), 1885 v W (1)

Brown, W. D. F. (Dundee), 1958 v F; 1959 v E, W, Ni; (with Tottenham H), 1960 v W, Ni, Pol, A, H, T; 1962 v Ni, W, E, Cz; 1963 v W, Ni, E, A; 1964 v Ni, W, N; 1965 v E, Fi, Pol, Sp; 1966 v Ni, Pol, I (28)

Browning, J. (Celtic), 1914 v W (1)

Brownie, J. (Hibernian), 1971 v USSR; 1972 v Pe, Ni, E; 1973 v D (2); 1976 v R (7)

Brownlie, J. (Third Lanark), 1909 v E, Ni; 1910 v E, W, Ni; 1911 v W, Ni; 1912 v W, Ni, E; 1913 v W, Ni, E; 1914 v W, Ni, E (16)

Bruce, D. (Vale of Leven), 1890 v W (1)

Bruce, R. F. (Middlesbrough), 1934 v A (1)

Buchan, M. M. (Aberdeen), 1972 v P (sub), Bel; (with Manchester U), W, Y, Cz, Br; 1973 v D (2), E; 1974 v WG, Ni, W, N, Br, Y; 1975 v EG, Sp, P; 1976 v D, R; 1977 v Fi, Cz, Ch, Arg, Br; 1978 v EG, W (sub), Ni, Pe, Ir, Ho; 1979 v A, N, P (34)

Buchanan, J. (Cambuslang), 1889 v Ni (1)

Buchanan, J. (Rangers), 1929 v E; 1930 v E (2)

Buchanan, P. S. (Chelsea), 1938 v Cz (1)

Buchanan, R. (Abercorn), 1891 v W (1)

Buckley, P. (Aberdeen), 1954 v N; 1955 v W, Ni (3)

Buick, A. (Hearts), 1902 v W, Ni (2)

Burley, G. (Ipswich T), 1979 v W, Ni, E, Arg, N; 1980 v P, Ni, E (sub), Pol; 1982 v W (sub), E (11)

Burns, F. (Manchester U), 1970 v A (1)

Burns, K. (Birmingham C), 1974 v WG; 1975 v EG (sub), Sp (2); 1977 v Cz (sub), W, Se, W (sub); (with Nottingham F), 1978 v Ni (sub), W, E, Pe, Ir; 1979 v N; 1980 v Pe, A, Bel; 1981 v Is, Ni, W (20)

Burns, T. (Celtic), 1981 v Ni; 1982 v Ho (sub), W (3)

Busby, M. W. (Manchester C), 1934 v W (1)

Cairns, T. (Rangers), 1920 v W; 1922 v E; 1923 v E, W; 1924 v Ni; 1925 v W, E, Ni (8)

Calderhead, D. (Queen of the South), 1889 v Ni (1)

Calderwood, R. (Cartvale), 1885 v Ni, E, W (3)

Caldow, E. (Rangers), 1957 v Sp (2), Sw, WG, E; 1958 v Ni, W, Sw, Par, H, Pol, Y, F; 1959 v E, W, Ni, WG, Ho, P; 1960 v E, W, Ni, A, H, T; 1961 v E, W, Ni, Ei (2), Cz; 1962 v Ni, W, E, Cz (2), U; 1963 v W, Ni, E (40)

Callaghan, P. (Hibernian), 1900 v Ni (1)

Callaghan, W. (Dunfermline Ath), 1970 v Ei (sub), W (2)

Cameron, J. (St Mirren), 1904 v Ni; (with Chelsea), 1909 v E (2)

Cameron, J. (Queen's Park), 1896 v Ni (1)

Cameron, J. (Rangers), 1886 v Ni (1)

Campbell, C. (Queen's Park), 1874 v E; 1876 v W; 1877 v E, W; 1878 v E; 1879 v E; 1880 v E; 1881 v E; 1882 v E, W; 1884 v E; 1885 v E; 1886 v E (13)

Campbell, H. (Renton), 1889 v W (1)

Campbell, Jas. (Sheffield W), 1913 v W (1)

Campbell, J. (South Western), 1880 v W (1)

Campbell, J. (Kilmarnock), 1891 v Ni; 1892 v W (2)

Campbell, John (Celtic), 1893 v E, Ni; 1898 v E, Ni; 1900 v E, Ni; 1901 v E, W, Ni; 1902 v W, Ni; 1903 v W (12)

Campbell, John (Rangers), 1899 v E, W, Ni; 1901 v Ni (4)

Campbell, K. (Liverpool), 1920 v E, W, Ni; (with Partick T), 1921 v W, Ni; 1922 v W, Ni, E (8)

Campbell, P. (Rangers), 1878 v W; 1879 v W (2)

Campbell, P. (Morton), 1898 v W (1)

Campbell, R. (Chelsea), 1947 v Bel, L; 1950 v Sw, P, F (5)

Campbell, W. (Morton), 1947 v Ni; 1948 v E, Bel, Sw, F (5)

Carabine, J. (Third Lanark), 1938 v Ho; 1939 v E, Ni (3)

Carr, W. M. (Coventry C), 1970 v Ni, W, E; 1971 v D; 1972 v Pe; 1973 v D (sub) (6)

Cassidy, J. (Celtic), 1921 v W, Ni; 1923 v Ni; 1924 v W (4)

Chalmers, S. (Celtic), 1965 v W, Fi; 1966 v P (sub), Br; 1967 v Ni (5)

Chalmers, W. (Rangers), 1885 v Ni (1)

Chalmers, W. S. (Queen's Park), 1929 v Ni (1)

Chambers, T. (Hearts), 1894 v W (1)

Chaplin, G. D. (Dundee), 1908 v W (1)

Drummond, J. (Falkirk), 1892 v Ni; (with Rangers), 1894 v Ni; 1895 v Ni, E; 1896 v E, Ni; 1897 v Ni; 1898 v E; 1900 v E; 1901 v E; 1902 v E, W, Ni; 1903 v Ni (14)

Dunbar, M. (Cartvale), 1886 v Ni (1)

Duncan, A. (Hibernian), 1975 v P (sub), W, Ni, E, R; 1976 v D (6)

Duncan, D. (Derby Co), 1933 v E, W; 1934 v A, W; 1935 v E, W; 1936 v E, W, Ni; 1937 v G, E, W, Ni; 1938 v W (14)

Duncan, D. M. (East Fife), 1948 v Bel, Sw, F (3)

Duncan, J. (Alexandra Ath), 1878 v W; 1882 v W (2)

Duncan, J. (Leicester C), 1926 v W (1)

Duncanson, J. (Rangers), 1947 v Ni (1)

Dunlop, J. (St Mirren), 1890 v W (1)

Dunlop, W. (Liverpool), 1906 v E (1)

Dunn, J. (Hibernian), 1925 v W, Ni; 1927 v Ni; 1928 v Ni, E; (with Everton), 1929 v W (6)

Dykes, J. (Hearts), 1938 v Ho; 1939 v Ni (2)


Easson, J. F. (Portsmouth), 1931 v A, Sw; 1934 v W (3)

Ellis, J. (Mossend Swifts), 1892 v Ni (1)

Evans, A. (Aston Villa), 1982 v Ho, Ni, E, Nz (4)

Evans, R. (Celtic), 1949 v E, W, Ni, F; 1950 v W, Ni, Sw, P; 1951 v E, A; 1952 v Ni; 1953 v Se; 1954 v Ni, W, E, N, Fi; 1955 v Ni, P, Y, A, H; 1956 v E, Ni, W, A; 1957 v WG, Sp; 1958 v Ni, W, E, Sw, H, Pol, Y, Par, F; 1959 v E, WG, Ho, P; 1960 v E, Ni, W, Pol; (with Chelsea), 1960 v A, H, T (48)

Ewart, J. (Bradford C), 1921 v E (1)

Ewing, T. (Partick T), 1958 v W, E (2)


Farm, G. N. (Blackpool), 1953 v W, Ni, E, Se; 1954 v Ni, W, E; 1959 v WG, Ho, P (10)

Ferguson, J. (Vale of Leven), 1874 v E; 1876 v E, W; 1877 v E, W; 1878 v W (6)

Ferguson, R. (Kilmarnock), 1966 v W, E, Ho, P, Br; 1967 v W, Ni (7)

Fernie, W. (Celtic), 1954 v Fi, A, U; 1955 v W, Ni; 1957 v E, Ni, W, Y; 1958 v W, Sw, Par (12)

Findlay, R. (Kilmarnock), 1898 v W (1)

Fitchie, T. T. (Woolwich Arsenal), 1905 v W; 1906 v W, Ni; (with Queen's Park), 1907 v W (4)

Flavell, R. (Airdrieonians), 1947 v Bel, L (2)

Fleming, C. (East Fife), 1954 v Ni (1)

Fleming, J. W. (Rangers), 1929 v G, Ho; 1930 v E (3)

Fleming, R. (Morton), 1886 v Ni (1)

Forbes, A. R. (Sheffield U), 1947 v Bel, L, E; 1948 v W, Ni; (with Arsenal), 1950 v E, P, F; 1951 v W, Ni, A; 1952 v W, D, Se (14)

Forbes, J. (Vale of Leven), 1884 v E, W, Ni; 1887 v W, E (5)

Ford, D. (Hearts), 1974 v Cz (sub), WG (sub), W (3)

Forrest, J. (Rangers), 1966 v W, I; (with Aberdeen), 1971 v Bel (sub), D, USSR (5)

Forrest, J. (Motherwell), 1958 v E (1)

Forsyth, A. (Partick T), 1972 v Y, Cz, Br; 1973 v D; (with Manchester U), E; 1975 v Sp, Ni (sub), R, EG; 1976 v D (10)

Forsyth, C. (Kilmarnock), 1964 v E; 1965 v W, Ni, Fi (4)

Forsyth, T. (Motherwell), 1971 v D; (with Rangers), 1974 v Cz; 1976 v Sw, Ni, W, E; 1977 v Fi, Se, W, Ni, E, Ch, Arg, Br; 1978 v Cz, W, Ni, W (sub), E, Pe, Ir (sub), Ho (22)

Foyers, R. (St Bernards), 1893 v W; 1894 v W (2)

Fraser, D. M. (WBA), 1968 v Ho; 1969 v Cy (2)

Fraser, J. (Moffat), 1891 v Ni (1)

Fraser, M. J. E. (Queen's Park), 1880 v W; 1882 v W, E; 1883 v W, E (5)

Fraser, J. (Dundee), 1907 v Ni (1)

Fraser, W. (Sunderland), 1955 v W, Ni (2)

Fulton, W. (Abercorn), 1884 v Ni (1)

Fyfe, J. H. (Third Lanark), 1895 v W (1)


Gabriel, J. (Everton), 1961 v W; 1964 v N (sub) (2)

Gallacher, H. K. (Airdrieonians), 1924 v Ni; 1925 v E, W, Ni; 1926 v W; (with Newcastle U), 1926 v E, Ni; 1927 v E, W, Ni; 1928 v E, W; 1929 v E, W, Ni; 1930 v W, Ni, F; (with Chelsea), 1934 v E; (with Derby Co), 1935 v E (20)

Gallacher, P. (Sunderland), 1935 v Ni (1)

Galt, J. H. (Rangers), 1908 v W, Ni (2)

Gardiner, I. (Motherwell), 1958 v W (1)

Gardner, D. R. (Third Lanark), 1897 v W (1)

Gardner, R. (Queen's Park), 1872 v E; 1873 v E; (with Clydesdale), 1874 v E; 1875 v E; 1878 v E (5)

Gemmell, T. (St Mirren), 1955 v P, Y (2)

Gemmell, T. (Celtic), 1966 v E; 1967 v W, Ni, E, USSR; 1968 v Ni, E; 1969 v W, Ni, E, D, A, WG, Cy; 1970 v E, Ei, WG; 1971 v Bel (18)

Gemmill, A. (Derby Co), 1971 v Bel; 1972 v P, Ho, Pe, Ni, W, E; 1976 v D, R, Ni, W, E; 1977 v Fi, Cz, W (2), Ni (sub), E (sub), Ch (sub), Arg, Br; 1978 v EG (sub); (with Nottingham F), Bul, Ni, W, E (sub), Pe (sub), Ir, Ho; 1979 v A, N, P, N; (with Birmingham C), 1980 v A, P, Ni, W, E, H; 1981 v Se, P, Is, Ni (43)

Gibb, W. (Clydesdale), 1873 v E (1)

Gibson, D. W. (Leicester C), 1963 v A, N, Ei, Sp; 1964 v Ni; 1965 v W, Fi (7)

Gibson, J. D. (Partick T), 1926 v E; 1927 v E, W, Ni; (with Aston Villa), 1928 v E, W; 1930 v W, Ni (8)

Gibson, N. (Rangers), 1895 v E, Ni; 1896 v E, Ni; 1897 v E, Ni; 1898 v E; 1899 v E, W, Ni; 1900 v E, Ni; 1901 v W; (with Partick T), 1905 v Ni (14)

Gilchrist, J. E. (Celtic), 1922 v E (1)

Gilhooley, M. (Hull C), 1922 v W (1)

Gillespie, G. (Rangers), 1880 v W; 1881 v E, W; 1882 v E; (with Queen's Park), 1886 v W; 1890 v W; 1891 v Ni (7)

Gillespie, Jas. (Third Lanark), 1898 v W (1)

Gillespie, John. (Queen's Park), 1896 v W (1)

Gillespie, R. (Queen's Park), 1927 v W; 1931 v W; 1932 v F; 1933 v E (4)

Gillick, T. (Everton), 1937 v A, Cz; 1939 v W, Ni, H (5)

Gilmour, J. (Dundee), 1931 v W (1)

Gilzean, A. J. (Dundee), 1964 v W, E, N, WG; 1965 v Ni, (with Tottenham H), Sp; 1966 v Ni, W, Pol, I; 1968 v W; 1969 v W, E, WG, Cy (2), A (sub); 1970 v Ni, E (sub), WG, A; 1971 v P (22)

Glavin, R. (Celtic), 1977 v Se (1)

Glen, A. (Aberdeen), 1956 v E, Ni (2)

Glen, R. (Renton), 1895 v W; 1896 v W; (with Hibernian), 1900 v Ni (3)

Gordon, J. E. (Rangers), 1912 v E, Ni; 1913 v E, Ni, W; 1914 v E, Ni; 1920 v W, E, Ni (10)

Gossland, J. (Rangers), 1884 v Ni (1)

Goudie, J. (Abercorn), 1884 v Ni (1)

Gourlay, J. (Cambuslang), 1886 v Ni; 1888 v W (2)

Govan, J. (Hibernian), 1948 v E, W, Bel, Sw, F; 1949 v Ni (6)

Gow, D. R. (Rangers), 1888 v E (1)

Gow, J. J. (Queen's Park), 1885 v E (1)

Gow, J. R. (Rangers), 1888 v Ni (1)

Graham, A. (Leeds U), 1978 v EG (sub); 1979 v A (sub), N, W, Ni, E, Arg, N; 1980 v A; 1981 v W (10)

Graham, G. (Arsenal), 1972 v P, Ho, Ni, Y, Cz, Br; 1973 v D (2); (with Manchester U), E, W, Ni, Br (sub) (12)

Graham, J. (Annbank), 1884 v Ni (1)

Graham, J. A. (Arsenal), 1921 v Ni (1)

Grant, J. (Hibernian), 1959 v W, Ni (2)

Gray, A. (Hibernian), 1903 v Ni (1)

Gray, A. M. (Aston Villa), 1976 v R, Sw; 1977 v Fi, Cz; 1979 v A, N; (with Wolverhampton W), 1980 v P, E (sub); 1981 v Se, P, Is (sub), Ni; 1982 v Se (sub), Ni (sub) (14)

Gray, D. (Rangers), 1929 v W, Ni, G, Ho; 1930 v W, E, Ni; 1931 v W; 1933 v W, Ni (10)

Gray, E. (Leeds U), 1969 v E, Cy; 1970 v WG, A; 1971 v W, Ni; 1972 v Bel, Ho; 1976 v W, E; 1977 v Fi, W (12)

Gray, F. T. (Leeds U), 1976 v Sw; 1979 v N, P, W, Ni, E, Arg (sub); (with Nottingham F) 1980 v Bel (sub); 1981 v Se, P, Is, Ni, Is, W, (with Leeds U) Ni, E; 1982 v Se, Ni, P, Sp, Ho, W, Nz, Br, USSR (25)

Gray, W. (Pollokshields Ath), 1886 v E (1)

Green, A. (Blackpool), 1971 v Bel (sub), P (sub), Ni, E; 1972 v W, E (sub) (6)

Greig, J. (Rangers), 1964 v E, WG; 1965 v W, Ni, E, Fi (2), Sp, Pol; 1966 v Ni, W, E, Pol, I (2), P, Ho, Br; 1967 v W, Ni, E; 1968 v Ni, W, E, Ho; 1969 v W, Ni, E, D, A, WG, Cy (2); 1970 v W, E, Ei, WG, A; 1971 v D, Bel, W (sub), Ni, E; 1976 v D (44)

Groves, W. (Hibernian), 1888 v W; (with Celtic), 1889 v Ni; 1890 v E (3)

Guilliland, W. (Queen's Park), 1891 v W; 1892 v Ni; 1894 v E; 1895 v E (4)

Haddock, H. (Clyde), 1955 v E, H (2), P, Y; 1958 v E (6)

Haddow, D. (Rangers), 1894 v E (1)

Haffey, F. (Celtic), 1960 v E; 1961 v E (2)

Hamilton, A. (Queen's Park), 1885 v E, W; 1886 v E; 1888 v E (4)

Hamilton, A. W. (Dundee), 1962 v Cz, U, W, E; 1963 v W, Ni, E, A, N, Ei; 1964 v Ni, W, E, N, WG; 1965 v Ni, W, E, Fi (2), Pol, Sp; 1966 v Pol, Ni (24)

Hamilton, G. (Aberdeen), 1947 v Ni; 1951 v Bel, A; 1954 v N (2) (5)

Hamilton, G. (Port Glasgow Ath), 1906 v Ni (1)

Hamilton, J. (Queen's Park), 1892 v W; 1893 v E, Ni (3)

Hamilton, J. (St Mirren), 1924 v Ni (1)

Hamilton, R. C. (Rangers), 1899 v E, W, Ni; 1900 v W; 1901 v E, Ni; 1902 v W, Ni; 1903 v E; 1904 v Ni; (with Dundee), 1911 v W (11)

Hamilton, T. (Hurlford), 1891 v Ni (1)

Hamilton, T. (Rangers), 1932 v E (1)

Hamilton, W. M. (Hibernian), 1965 v Fi (1)

Hannah, A. B. (Renton), 1888 v W (1)

Hannah, J. (Third Lanark), 1889 v W (1)

Hansen, A. D. (Liverpool), 1979 v W, Arg; 1980 v Bel, P: 1981 v Se, P, Is; 1982 v Se, Ni, P, Sp, Ni (sub), W, E, Nz, Br, USSR (17)

Hansen, J. (Partick T), 1972 v Bel (sub), Y (sub) (2)

Harkness, J. D. (Queen's Park), 1927 v E, Ni; 1928 v E; (with Hearts), 1929 v W, E, Ni; 1930 v E, W; 1932 v W, F; 1934 v Ni (11)

Harper, J. M. (Aberdeen), 1973 v D (1 + 1 sub); (with Hibernian), 1976 v D; (with Aberdeen), 1978 v Ir (sub) (4)

Harper, W. (Hibernian), 1923 v E, Ni, W; 1924 v E, Ni, W; 1925 v E, Ni, W; (with Arsenal), 1926 v E, Ni (11)

Harris, J. (Partick T), 1921 v W, Ni (2)

Harris, N. (Newcastle U), 1924 v E (1)

Harrower, W. (Queen's Park), 1882 v E; 1884 v Ni; 1886 v W (3)

Hartford, R. A. (WBA), 1972 v Pe, W (sub), E, Y, Cz, Br; (with Manchester C), 1976 v D, R, Ni (sub); 1977 v Cz (sub), W (sub), Se, W, Ni, E, Ch, Arg, Br; 1978 v EG, Cz, W, Bul, W, E, Pe, Ir, Ho; 1979 v A, N, P, W, Ni, E, Arg, N; (with Everton), 1980 v Pe, Bel; 1981 v Ni (sub), Is, W, Ni, E; 1982 v Se; (with Manchester C), Ni, P, Sp, Ni, W, E, Br (50)

Harvey, D. (Leeds U), 1973 v D; 1974 v Cz, WG, Ni, W, E, Bel, Z, Br, Y; 1975 v EG, Sp (2); 1976 v D (2); 1977 v Fi (sub) (16)

Hastings, A. C. (Sunderland), 1936 v Ni; 1938 v Ni (2)

Haughney, M. (Celtic), 1954 v E (1)

Hay, D. (Celtic), 1970 v Ni, W, E; 1971 v D, Bel, W, P, Ni; 1972 v P, Bel, Ho; 1973 v W, Ni, E, Sw, Br; 1974 v Cz (2), WG, Ni, W, E, Bel, N, Z, Br, Y (27)

Hay, J. (Celtic), 1905 v Ni; 1909 v Ni; 1910 v W, Ni, E; 1911 v Ni, E; (with Newcastle U), 1912 v E, W; 1914 v E, Ni (11)

Hegarty, P. (Dundee U), 1979 v W, Ni, E, Arg, N (sub); 1980 v W, E (7)

Heggie, C. (Rangers), 1886 v Ni (1)

Henderson, G. H. (Rangers), 1904 v Ni (1)

Henderson, J. G. (Portsmouth), 1953 v Se; 1954 v Ni, E, N; 1956 v W; (with Arsenal), 1959 v W, Ni (7)

Henderson, W. (Rangers), 1963 v W, Ni, E, A, N, Ei, Sp; 1964 v W, Ni, E, N, WG; 1965 v Fi, Pol, E, Sp; 1966 v Ni, W, Pol, I, Ho; 1967 v W, Ni; 1968 v Ho; 1969 v Ni, E, Cy; 1970 v Ei; 1971 v P (29)

Hepburn, J. (Alloa Ath), 1891 v W (1)

Hepburn, R. (Ayr U), 1932 v Ni (1)

Herd, A. C. (Hearts), 1935 v Ni (1)

Herd, D. G. (Arsenal), 1959 v E, W, Ni; 1961 v E, Cz (5)

Herd, G. (Clyde), 1958 v E; 1960 v H, T; 1961 v W, Ni (5)

Herriot, J. (Birmingham C), 1969 v Ni, E, D, Cy (2), W (sub); 1970 v Ei (sub), WG (8)

Hewie, J. D. (Charlton Ath), 1956 v E, A; 1957 v E, Ni, W, Y, Sp (2), Sw, WG; 1958 v Pol, Y, F; 1959 v Ho, P; 1960 v Ni, W, Pol (18)

Higgins, A. (Kilmarnock), 1885 v Ni (1)

Higgins, A. (Newcastle U), 1910 v E, Ni; 1911 v E, Ni (4)

Highet, T. C. (Queen's Park), 1875 v E; 1876 v E, W; 1878 v E (4)

Hill, D. (Rangers), 1881 v E, W; 1882 v W (3)

Hill, D. A. (Third Lanark), 1906 v Ni (1)

Hill, F. R. (Aberdeen), 1930 v F; 1931 v W, Ni (3)

Hill, J. (Hearts), 1891 v E; 1892 v W (2)

Hogg, G (Hearts), 1896 v E, Ni (2)

Hogg, J. (Ayr U), 1922 v Ni (1)

Hogg, R. M. (Celtic), 1937 v Cz (1)

Holm, A. H. (Queen's Park), 1882 v W; 1883 v E, W (3)

Holt, D. D. (Hearts), 1963 v A, N, Ei, Sp; 1964 v WG (sub) (5)

Holton, J. A. (Manchester U), 1973 v W, Ni, E, Sw, Br; 1974 v Cz, WG, Ni, W, E, N, Z, Br, Y; 1975 v EG (15)

Hope, R. (WBA), 1968 v Ho; 1969 v D (2)

Houliston, W. (Queen of the South), 1949 v E, Ni, F (3)

Houston, S. M. (Manchester U), 1976 v D (1)

Howden, W. (Partick T), 1905 v Ni (1)

Howe, R. (Hamilton A), 1929 v N, Ho (2)

Howie, J. (Newcastle U), 1905 v E; 1906 v E; 1908 v E (3)

Howie, H. (Hibernian), 1949 v W (1)

Howieson, J. (St Mirren), 1927 v Ni (1)

Hughes, J. (Celtic), 1965 v Pol, Sp; 1966 v Ni, I (2); 1968 v E; 1969 v A; 1970 v Ei (8)

Hughes, W. (Sunderland), 1975 v Se (sub) (1)

Humphries, W. (Motherwell), 1952 v Se (1)

Hunter, A. (Kilmarnock), 1972 v Pe, Y; (with Celtic), 1973 v E; 1974 v Cz (4)

Hunter, J. (Dundee), 1909 v Ni (1)

Hunter, J. (Third Lanark), 1874 v E; (with Eastern), 1875 v E; (with Third Lanark), 1876 v E; 1877 v W (4)

Hunter, R. (St Mirren), 1890 v Ni (1)

Hunter, W. (Motherwell), 1960 v H, T; 1961 v W (3)

Husband, J. (Partick T), 1947 v W (1)

Hutchison, T. (Coventry C), 1974 v Cz (2), WG (2), Ni, W, Bel (sub), N, Z (sub), Y (sub); 1975 v EG, Sp (2), P, E (sub), R (sub); 1976 v D (17)

Hutton, J. (Aberdeen), 1923 v E, W, Ni; 1924 v Ni; 1926 v W, E, Ni; (with Blackburn R), 1927 v Ni; 1928 v W, Ni (10)

Hutton, J. (St Bernards), 1887 v Ni (1)

Hyslop, T. (Stoke C), 1896 v E; (with Rangers), 1897 v E (2)

Imlach, J. J. S. (Nottingham F), 1958 v H, Pol, Y, F (4)

Imrie, W. N. (St Johnstone), 1929 v N, G (2)

Inglis, J. (Kilmarnock Ath), 1884 v Ni (1)

Inglis, J. (Rangers), 1883 v E, W (2)

Irons, J. H. (Queen's Park), 1900 v W (1)

Low, T. P. (Rangers), 1897 v Ni (1)
Low, W. L. (Newcastle U), 1911 v E, W; 1912 v Ni; 1920 v E, Ni (5)
Lowe, J. (Cambuslang), 1891 v Ni (1)
Lowe, J. (St Bernards), 1887 v Ni (1)
Lundie, J. (Hibernian), 1886 v W (1)
Lyall, J. (Sheffield W), 1905 v E (1)

McAdam, J. (Third Lanark), 1880 v W (1)
McArthur, D. (Celtic), 1895 v E, Ni; 1899 v W (3)
McAtee, A. (Celtic), 1913 v W (1)
McAulay, J. (Dumbarton), 1882 v W; (with Arthurlie), 1884 v Ni (2)
McAulay, J. (Dumbarton), 1883 v E, W; 1884 v E; 1885 v E, W; 1886 v E; 1887 v E, W (8)
McAuley, R. (Rangers), 1932 v Ni, W (2)
McBain, E. (St Mirren), 1894 v W (1)
McBain, N. (Manchester U), 1922 v E; (with Everton), 1923 v Ni; 1924 v W (3)
McBride, J. (Celtic), 1967 v W, Ni (2)
McBride, P. (Preston NE), 1904 v E; 1906 v E; 1907 v E, W; 1908 v E; 1909 v W (6)
McCall, J. (Renton), 1886 v W; 1887 v E, W; 1888 v E; 1890 v E (5)
McCalliog, J. (Sheffield W), 1967 v E, USSR; 1968 v Ni; 1969 v D; (with Wolverhampton W), 1971 v P (5)
McCallum, N. (Renton), 1888 v Ni (1)
McCann, R. J. (Motherwell), 1959 v WG; 1960 v E, Ni, W; 1961 v E (5)
McCartney, W. (Hibernian), 1902 v Ni (1)
McClory, A. (Motherwell), 1927 v W; 1928 v Ni; 1935 v W (3)
McCloy, P. (Ayr U), 1924 v E; 1925 v E (2)
McCloy, P. (Rangers), 1973 v W, Ni, Sw, Br (4)
McColl, A. (Renton), 1888 v Ni (1)
McColl, I. M. (Rangers), 1950 v E, F; 1951 v W, Ni, Bel; 1957 v E, Ni, W, Y, Sp, Sw, WG; 1958 v Ni, E (14)
McColl, R. S. (Queen's Park), 1896 v W, Ni; 1897 v Ni; 1898 v Ni; 1899 v Ni, E, W; 1900 v E, W; 1901 v E, W; (with Newcastle U), 1902 v E; (with Queen's Park), 1908 v Ni (13)
McColl, W. (Renton), 1895 v W (1)
McCombie, A. (Sunderland), 1903 v E, W; (with Newcastle U), 1905 v E, W (4)
McCorkindale, J. (Partick T), 1891 v W (1)
McCormick, R. (Abercorn), 1886 v W (1)
McCrae, D. (St Mirren), 1929 v N, G (2)
McCreadie, A. (Rangers), 1893 v W; 1894 v E (2)
McCreadie, E. G. (Chelsea), 1965 v E, Sp, Fi, Pol; 1966 v P, Ni, W, Pol, I; 1967 v E, USSR; 1968 v Ni, W, E, Ho; 1969 v W, Ni, E, D, A, WG, Cy (2) (23)
McCulloch, D. (Hearts), 1935 v W; (with Brentford), 1936 v E; 1937 v W, Ni; 1938 v Cz; (with Derby Co), 1939 v H, W (7)
MacDonald, A. (Rangers), 1976 v Sw (1)
McDonald, J. (Edinburgh University), 1886 v E (1)
McDonald, J. (Sunderland), 1956 v W, Ni (2)
MacDougall, E. J. (Norwich C) 1975 v Se, P, W, Ni, E; 1976 v D, R (7)
McDougall, J. (Liverpool), 1931 v I, A (2)
McDougall, J. (Airdrieonians), 1926 v Ni (1)
McDougall, J. (Vale of Leven), 1877 v E, W; 1878 v E; 1879 v E, W (5)
McFadyen, W. (Motherwell), 1934 v A, W (2)
Macfarlane, A. (Dundee), 1904 v W; 1906 v W; 1908 v W; 1909 v Ni; 1911 v W (5)
McFarlane, R. (Greenock Morton), 1896 v W (1)
Macfarlane, W. (Hearts), 1947 v L (1)
McGarr, E. (Aberdeen), 1970 v Ei, A (2)
McGarvey, F. P. (Liverpool), 1979 v Ni (sub), Arg (2)
McGeoch, A. (Dumbreck), 1876 v E, W; 1877 v E, W (4)

McGhee, J. (Hibernian), 1886 v W (1)
McGonagle, W. (Celtic), 1933 v E; 1934 v A, E, Ni; 1935 v Ni, W (6)
McGrain, D. (Celtic), 1973 v W, Ni, E, Sw, Br; 1974 v Cz (2), WG, W (sub), E, Bel, N, Z, Br, Y; 1975 v Sp, Se, P, W, Ni, E, R; 1976 v D (2), Sw, Ni, W, E; 1977 v Fi, Cz, W (2), Se, Ni, E, Ch, Arg, Br; 1978 v EG, Cz; 1980 v Bel, P, Ni, W, E, Pol, H; 1981 v Se, P, Is, Ni, Is, W (sub), Ni, E; 1982 v Se, Sp, Ho, Ni, E, Nz, USSR (sub) (62)
McGregor, J. C. (Vale of Leven), 1877 v E, W; 1878 v E; 1880 v E (4)
McGrory, J. E. (Kilmarnock), 1965 v Ni, Fi; 1966 v P (3)
McGrory, J. (Celtic), 1928 v Ni; 1931 v E; 1932 v Ni, W; 1933 v E, Ni; 1934 v Ni (7)
McGuire, W. (Beith), 1881 v E, W (2)
McGurk, F. (Birmingham), 1934 v W (1)
McHardy, H. (Rangers), 1885 v Ni (1)
McInally, T. B. (Celtic), 1926 v Ni; 1927 v W (2)
McInnes, T. (Cowlairs), 1889 v Ni (1)
McIntosh, W. (Third Lanark), 1905 v Ni (1)
McIntyre, A. (Vale of Leven), 1878 v E; 1882 v E (2)
McIntyre, H. (Rangers), 1880 v W (1)
McIntyre, J. (Rangers), 1884 v W (1)
McKay, D. (Celtic), 1959 v E, WG, Ho, P; 1960 v E, Pol, A, H, T; 1961 v W, Ni; 1962 v Ni, Cz, U (sub) (14)
Mackay, D. C. (Hearts), 1957 v Sp; 1958 v F; 1959 v W, Ni; (with Tottenham H), 1959 v WG, E; 1960 v W, Ni, A, Pol, H, T; 1961 v W, Ni, E; 1963 v E, A, N; 1964 v Ni, W, N; 1966 v Ni (22)
McKay, J. (Blackburn R), 1924 v W (1)
McKay, R. (Newcastle U), 1928 v W (1)
McKean, R. (Rangers), 1976 v Sw (1)
McKenzie, D. (Brentford), 1938 v Ni (1)
Mackenzie, J. A. (Partick T), 1954 v W, E, N, Fi, A, U; 1955 v E, H; 1956 v A (9)
McKeown, M. (Celtic), 1889 v Ni; 1890 v E (2)
McKie, J. (East Stirling), 1898 v W (1)
McKillop, T. R. (Rangers), 1938 v Ho (1)
McKinlay, D. (Liverpool), 1922 v W, Ni (2)
McKinnon, A. (Queen's Park), 1874 v E (1)
McKinnon, R. (Rangers), 1966 v W, E, I (2), Ho, Br; 1967 v W, Ni, E; 1968 v Ni, W, E, Ho; 1969 v D, A, WG, Cy; 1970 v Ni, W, E, Ei, WG, A; 1971 v D, Bel, P, USSR, D (28)
MacKinnon, W. (Dumbarton), 1883 v E, W; 1884 v E, W (4)
McKinnon, W. W. (Queen's Park), 1872 v E; 1873 v E; 1874 v E; 1875 v E; 1876 v E, W; 1877 v E; 1878 v E; 1879 v E (9)
McLaren, A. (St Johnstone), 1929 v N, G, Ho; 1933 v W, Ni (5)
McLaren, A. (Preston NE), 1947 v E, Bel, L; 1948 v W (4)
McLaren, J. (Hibernian), 1888 v W; (with Celtic), 1889 v E; 1890 v E (3)
McLean, A. (Celtic), 1926 v W, Ni; 1927 v W, E (4)
McLean, D. (St Bernards), 1896 v W; 1897 v Ni (2)
McLean, D. (Sheffield W), 1912 v E (1)
McLean, G. (Dundee), 1968 v Ho (1)
McLean, T. (Kilmarnock), 1969 v D, Cy, W; 1970 v Ni, W; 1971 v D (6)
McLeish, A. (Aberdeen), 1980 v F, Ni, W, E, Pol, H; 1981 v Se, Is, Ni, Is, Ni, E; 1982 v Se, Sp, Ni, Br (sub) (16)
McLeod, D. (Celtic), 1905 v Ni; 1906 v E, W, Ni (4)
McLeod, J. (Dumbarton), 1888 v Ni; 1889 v Ni; 1890 v Ni; 1892 v E; 1893 v W (5)
MacLeod, J. M. (Hibernian), 1961 v E, Ei (2), Cz (4)
McLeod, W. (Cowlairs), 1886 v Ni (1)
McLintock, A. (Vale of Leven), 1875 v E; 1876 v E; 1880 v E (3)
McLintock, F. (Leicester C), 1963 v N (sub), Ei, Sp; (with Arsenal), 1965 v Ni; 1967 v USSR; 1970 v Ni; 1971 v W, Ni, E (9)
McLuckie, J. S. (Manchester C), 1934 v W (1)

McMahon, A. (Celtic), 1892 v E; 1893 v E, Ni; 1894 v E; 1901 v Ni; 1902 v W (6)

McMenemy, J. (Celtic), 1905 v Ni; 1909 v Ni; 1910 v E, W; 1911 v Ni, W, E; 1912 v W; 1914 v W, Ni, E; 1920 v Ni (12)

McMenemy, J. (Motherwell), 1934 v W (1)

McMillan, J. (St Bernards), 1897 v W (1)

McMillan, I. L. (Airdrieonians), 1952 v E, USA, D; 1955 v E; 1956 v E; (with Rangers), 1961 v Cz (6)

McMillan, T. (Dumbarton), 1887 v Ni (1)

McMullan, J. (Partick T), 1920 v W; 1921 v W, Ni, E; 1924 v E, Ni; 1925 v E; 1926 v W; (with Manchester C), 1926 v E; 1927 v E, W; 1928 v E, W; 1929 v W, E, Ni (16)

McNab, A. (Morton), 1921 v E, Ni (2)

McNab, A. (Sunderland), 1937 v A; (with WBA), 1939 v E (2)

McNab, C. D. (Dundee), 1931 v E, W, A, I, Sw; 1932 v E (6)

McNab, J. S. (Liverpool), 1923 v W (1)

McNair, A. (Celtic), 1906 v W; 1907 v Ni; 1908 v E, W; 1909 v E; 1910 v W; 1912 v E, W, Ni; 1913 v E; 1914 v E, Ni; 1920 v E, W, Ni (15)

McNaught, W. (Raith R), 1951 v A, W, Ni; 1952 v E; 1955 v Ni (5)

McNeil, H. (Queen's Park), 1874 v E; 1875 v E; 1876 v E, W; 1877 v W; 1878 v E; 1879 v E, W; 1881 v E, W (10)

McNeil, M. (Rangers), 1876 v W; 1880 v E (2)

McNeill, W. (Celtic), 1961 v E, Ei (2), Cz; 1962 v Ni, E, Cz, U; 1963 v Ei, Sp; 1964 v W, E, WG; 1965 v E, Fi, Pol, Sp; 1966 v Ni, Pol; 1967 v USSR; 1968 v E; 1969 v Cy, W, E, Cy (sub); 1970 v WG; 1972 v Ni, W, E (29)

McPhail, J. (Celtic), 1950 v W; 1951 v W, Ni, A; 1954 v Ni (5)

McPhail, R. (Airdrieonians), 1927 v E; (with Rangers), 1929 v W; 1931 v E, Ni; 1932 v W, Ni, F; 1933 v E, Ni; 1934 v A, Ni; 1935 v E; 1937 v G, E, Cz; 1938 v W, Ni (17)

McPherson, D. (Kilmarnock), 1892 v Ni (1)

McPherson, J. (Kilmarnock), 1888 v W; (with Cowlairs), 1889 v E; 1890 v Ni, E; (with Rangers), 1892 v W; 1894 v E; 1895 v E, Ni; 1897 v Ni (9)

McPherson, J. (Clydesdale), 1875 v E (1)

McPherson, J. (Vale of Leven), 1879 v E, W; 1880 v E; 1881 v W; 1883 v E, W; 1884 v E; 1885 v N (8)

McPherson, J. (Hearts), 1891 v E (1)

McPherson, R. (Arthurlie), 1882 v E (1)

McQueen, G. (Leeds U), 1974 v Bel; 1975 v Sp (2), P, W, Ni, E, R; 1976 v D; 1977 v Cz, W (2), Ni, E; 1978 v EG, Cz, W; (with Manchester U), Bul, Ni, W; 1979 v A, N, P, Ni, E, N; 1980 v Pe, A, Bel; 1981 v W (30)

McQueen, M. (Leith Ath), 1890 v W; 1891 v W (2)

McRorie, D. M. (Morton), 1931 v W (1)

McSpadyen, A. (Partick T), 1939 v E, H (2)

McStay, W. (Celtic), 1921 v W, Ni; 1925 v E, Ni, W; 1926 v E, Ni, W; 1927 v E, Ni, W; 1928 v W, Ni (13)

McTavish, J. (Falkirk), 1910 v Ni (1)

McWhattie, G. C. (Queen's Park), 1901 v W, Ni (2)

McWilliam, P. (Newcastle U) 1905 v E; 1906 v E; 1907 v E, W; 1909 v E, W; 1910 v E; 1911 v W (8)

Macari, L. (Celtic), 1972 v W (sub), E, Y, Cz, Br; 1973 v D; (with Manchester U), E (2), W (sub), Ni (sub); 1975 v Se, P (sub), W, E (sub), R; 1977 v Ni (sub), E (sub), Ch, Arg; 1978 v EG, W, Bul, Pe (sub), Ir (24)

Macauley, A. R. (Brentford), 1947 v E; (with Arsenal ), 1948 v E, W, Ni, Bel, Sw, F (7)

Madden, J. (Celtic), 1893 v W; 1895 v W (2)

Main, F. R. (Rangers), 1938 v W (1)

Main, J. (Hibernian), 1909 v Ni (1)

Maley, W. (Celtic), 1893 v E, Ni (2)

Marshall, H. (Celtic), 1899 v W; 1900 v Ni (2)

Marshall, J. (Rangers), 1932 v E; 1933 v E; 1934 v E (3)

Marshall, J. (Middlesbrough), 1921 v E, W, Ni; 1922 v E, W, Ni; (with Llanelly), 1924 v W (7)

Marshall, J. (Third Lanark), 1885 v Ni; 1886 v W; 1887 v E, W (4)

Marshall, R. W. (Rangers), 1892 v Ni; 1894 v Ni (2)

Martin, F. (Aberdeen), 1954 v N (2), A, U; 1955 v E, H (6)

Martin, N. (Hibernian), 1965 v Fi, Pol; (with Sunderland), 1966 v I (3)

Martis, J. (Motherwell), 1961 v W (1)

Mason, J. (Third Lanark), 1949 v E, W, Ni; 1950 v Ni; 1951 v Ni, Bel, A (7)

Massie, A. (Hearts), 1932 v Ni, W, F; 1933 v Ni; 1934 v E, Ni; 1935 v E, Ni, W; 1936 v W, Ni; (with Aston Villa), 1936 v E; 1937 v G, E, W, Ni, A; 1938 v W (18)

Masson, D. S. (QPR), 1976 v Ni, W, E; 1977 v Fi, Cz, W, Ni, E, Ch, Arg, Br; 1978 v EG, Cz, W; (with Derby Co), Ni, E, Pe (17)

Mathers, D. (Partick T), 1954 v Fi (1)

Maxwell, W. S. (Stoke C), 1898 v E (1)

May, J. (Rangers), 1906 v W, Ni; 1908 v E, Ni; 1909 v W (5)

Meechan, P. (Celtic), 1896 v Ni (1)

Meiklejohn, D. D. (Rangers), 1922 v W; 1924 v W; 1925 v W, Ni, E; 1928 v W, Ni; 1929 v E, Ni; 1930 v E, Ni; 1931 v E; 1932 v W, Ni; 1934 v A (15)

Menzies, A. (Hearts), 1906 v E (1)

Mercer, R. (Hearts), 1912 v W; 1913 v Ni (2)

Middleton, R. (Cowdenbeath), 1930 v Ni (1)

Millar, J. (Rangers), 1897 v E; 1898 v E, W (3)

Millar, J. (Rangers), 1963 v A, Ei (2)

Millar, A. (Hearts), 1939 v W (1)

Miller, J. (St Mirren), 1931 v E, I, Sw; 1932 v F; 1934 v E (5)

Miller, P. (Dumbarton), 1882 v E; 1883 v E, W (3)

Miller, T. (Liverpool), 1920 v E; (with Manchester U), 1921 v E, Ni (3)

Miller, W. (Third Lanark), 1876 v E (1)

Miller, W. (Celtic), 1947 v E, W, Bel, L; 1948 v W, Ni (6)

Miller, W. (Aberdeen), 1975 v R; 1978 v Bul; 1980 v Bel, W, E, Pol, H; 1981 v Se, P, Is (sub), Ni, W, Ni, E; 1982 v Ni, P, Ho, Br, USSR (19)

Mills, W. (Aberdeen), 1936 v W, Ni; 1937 v W (3)

Milne, J. V. (Middlesbrough), 1938 v E; 1939 v E (2)

Mitchell, D. (Rangers), 1890 v Ni; 1892 v E; 1893 v E, Ni; 1894 v E (5)

Mitchell, J. (Kilmarnock), 1908 v Ni; 1910 v Ni, W (3)

Mitchell, R. C. (Newcastle U), 1951 v D, F (2)

Mochan, N. (Celtic), 1954 v N, A, U (3)

Moir, W. (Bolton W), 1950 v E (1)

Moncur, R. (Newcastle U), 1968 v Ho; 1970 v Ni, W, E, Ei; 1971 v D, Bel, W, P, Ni, E, D; 1972 v Pe, Ni, W, E (16)

Morgan, H. (St Mirren), 1898 v W; (with Liverpool), 1899 v E (2)

Morgan, W. (Burnley), 1968 v Ni; (with Manchester U) 1972 v Pe, Y, Cz, Br; 1973 v D (2), E (2), W, Ni, Sw, Br; 1974 v Cz (2), WG (2), Ni, Bel (sub), Br, Y (21)

Morris, D. (Raith R), 1923 v Ni; 1924 v E, Ni; 1925 v E, W, Ni (6)

Morris, H. (East Fife), 1950 v Ni (1)

Morrison, T. (St Mirren), 1927 v E (1)

Morton, A. L. (Queen's Park), 1920 v W, Ni; (with Rangers), 1921 v E; 1922 v E, W; 1923 v E, W, Ni; 1924 v E, W, Ni; 1925 v E, W, Ni; 1927 v E, Ni; 1928 v E, W, Ni; 1929 v E, W, Ni; 1930 v E, W, Ni; 1931 v E, W, Ni; 1932 v E, W, F (31)

Morton, H. A. (Kilmarnock), 1929 v G, Ho (2)

Mudie, J. K. (Blackpool), 1957 v W, Ni, E, Y, Sw, Sp (2), WG; 1958 v Ni, E, W, Sw, H, Pol, Y, Par, F (17)

Muir, W. (Dundee), 1907 v Ni (1)

Muirhead, T. A. (Rangers), 1922 v Ni; 1923 v E; 1924 v W; 1927 v Ni; 1928 v Ni; 1929 v W, Ni; 1930 v W (8)

Mulhall, G. (Aberdeen), 1960 v Ni; (with Sunderland), 1963 v Ni; 1964 v Ni (3)

Munro, A. D. (Hearts), 1937 v W, Ni; (with Blackpool), 1938 v Ho (3)

Munro, F. M. (Wolverhampton W), 1971 v Ni (sub), E (sub), D, USSR; 1975 v Se, W (sub), Ni, E, R (9)

Munro, I. (St Mirren), 1979 v Arg, N; 1980 v Pe, A, Bel, W, E (7)

Munro, N. (Abercorn), 1888 v W; 1889 v E (2)

Murdoch, J. (Motherwell), 1931 v Ni (1)

Murdoch, R. (Celtic), 1966 v W, E, I (2); 1967 v Ni; 1968 v Ni; 1969 v W, Ni, E, WG, Cy; 1970 v A (12)

Murphy, F. (Celtic), 1938 v Ho (1)

Murray, J. (Renton), 1895 v W (1)

Murray, J. (Hearts), 1958 v E, H, Pol, Y, F (5)

Murray, J. W. (Vale of Leven), 1890 v W (1)

Murray, P. (Hibernian), 1896 v Ni; 1897 v W (2)

Murray, S. (Aberdeen), 1972 v Bel (1)

Mutch, G. (Preston NE), 1938 v E (1)

Napier, C. E. (Celtic), 1932 v E; 1935 v E, W; (with Derby Co), 1937 v Ni, A (5)

Narey, D. (Dundee U), 1977 v Se (sub); 1979 v P, Ni (sub), Arg; 1980 v P, Ni, Pol, H; 1981 v W, E (sub); 1982 v Ho, W, E, Nz (sub), Br, USSR (16)

Neil, R. G. (Hibernian), 1896 v W; (with Rangers), 1900 v W (2)

Neill, R. W. (Queen's Park), 1876 v W; 1877 v E, W; 1878 v W; 1880 v E (5)

Neilles, P. (Hearts), 1914 v W, Ni (2)

Nelson, J. (Cardiff C), 1925 v W, Ni; 1928 v E; 1930 v F (4)

Niblo, T. D. (Aston Villa), 1904 v E (1)

Nibloe, J. (Kilmarnock), 1929 v E, N, Ho; 1930 v W; 1931 v E, Ni, A, I, Sw; 1932 v E, F (11)

Nisbet, J. (Ayr U), 1929 v N, G, Ho (3)

Niven, J. B. (Moffatt), 1885 v Ni (1)

O'Donnell, F. (Preston NE), 1937 v E, A, Cz; 1938 v E, W; (with Blackpool), Ho (6)

Ogilvie, D. H. (Motherwell), 1934 v A (1)

O'Hare, J. (Derby Co), 1970 v W, Ni, E; 1971 v D, Bel, W, Ni; 1972 v P, Bel, Ho (sub), Pe, Ni, W (13)

Ormond, W. E. (Hibernian), 1954 v E, N, Fi, A, U; 1959 v E (6)

O'Rourke, F. (Airdrieonians), 1907 v Ni (1)

Orr, J. (Kilmarnock), 1892 v W (1)

Orr, R. (Newcastle U), 1902 v E; 1904 v E (2)

Orr, T. (Morton), 1952 v Ni, W (2)

Orr, W. (Celtic), 1900 v Ni; 1903 v Ni; 1904 v W (3)

Orrock, R. (Falkirk), 1913 v W (1)

Oswald, J. (Third Lanark), 1889 v E; (with St Bernards), 1895 v E; (with Rangers), 1897 v W (3)

Parker, A. H. (Falkirk), 1955 v P, Y, A; 1956 v E, Ni, W, A; 1957 v Ni, W, Y; 1958 v Ni, W, E, Sw; (with Everton), Par (15)

Parlane, D. (Rangers), 1973 v W, Sw, Br; 1975 v Sp (sub), Se, P, W, Ni, E, R; 1976 v D (sub); 1977 v W (12)

Parlane, R. (Vale of Leven), 1878 v W; 1879 v E, W (3)

Paterson, G. D. (Celtic), 1939 v Ni (1)

Paterson, J. (Leicester C), 1920 v E (1)

Paterson, J. (Cowdenbeath), 1931 v A, I, Sw (3)

Paton, A. (Motherwell), 1952 v D, Se (2)

Paton, D. (St Bernards), 1896 v W (1)

Paton, M. (Dumbarton), 1883 v E; 1884 v W; 1885 v W, E; 1886 v E (5)

Paton, R. (Vale of Leven), 1879 v E, W (2)

Patrick, J. (St Mirren), 1897 v E, W (2)

Paul, H. McD. (Queen's Park), 1909 v E, W, Ni (3)

Paul, W. (Partick T), 1888 v W; 1889 v W; 1890 v W (3)

Paul, W. (Dykebar), 1891 v Ni (1)

Pearson, T. (Newcastle U), 1947 v E, Bel (2)

Penman, A. (Dundee), 1966 v Ho (1)

Pettigrew, W. (Motherwell), 1976 v Sw, Ni, W; 1977 v W (sub), Se (5)

Phillips, J. (Queen's Park), 1877 v E, W; 1878 v W (3)

Plenderleith, J. B. (Manchester C), 1961 v Ni (1)

Porteous, W. (Hearts), 1903 v Ni (1)

Pringle, C. (St Mirren), 1921 v W (1)

Provan, D. (Rangers), 1964 v Ni, N; 1966 v I (2), Ho (5)

Provan, D. (Celtic), 1980 v Bel (2 sub), P (sub), Ni (sub); 1981 v Is, W, E; 1982 v Se, P, Ni (10)

Pursell, P. (Queen's Park), 1914 v W (1)

Quinn, J. (Celtic), 1905 v Ni; 1906 v Ni, W; 1908 v Ni, E; 1909 v E; 1910 v E, Ni, W; 1912 v E, W (11)

Quinn, P. (Motherwell), 1961 v E, Ei (2); 1962 v U (4)

Rae, J. (Third Lanark), 1889 v W; 1890 v Ni (2)

Raeside, J. S. (Third Lanark), 1906 v W (1)

Raisbeck, A. G. (Liverpool), 1900 v E; 1901 v E; 1902 v E; 1903 v E, W; 1904 v E; 1906 v E; 1907 v E (8)

Rankin, G. (Vale of Leven), 1890 v Ni; 1891 v E (2)

Rankin, R. (St Mirren), 1929 v N, G, Ho (3)

Redpath, W. (Motherwell), 1949 v W, Ni; 1951 v E, D, F, Bel, A; 1952 v Ni, E (9)

Reid, J. G. (Airdrieonians), 1914 v W; 1920 v W; 1924 v Ni (3)

Reid, R. (Brentford), 1938 v E, Ni (2)

Reid, W. (Rangers), 1911 v E, W, Ni; 1912 v Ni; 1913 v E, W, Ni; 1914 v E, Ni (9)

Reilly, L. (Hibernian), 1949 v E, W, F; 1950 v W, Ni, Sw, F; 1951 v W, E, D, F, Bel, A; 1952 v Ni, W, E, USA, D, Se; 1953 v Ni, W, E, Se; 1954 v W; 1955 v H (2), P, Y, A, E; 1956 v E, W, Ni, A; 1957 v E, Ni, W, Y (38)

Rennie, H. G. (Hearts), 1900 v E, Ni; (with Hibernian), 1901 v E; 1902 v E, Ni, W; 1903 v Ni, W; 1904 v Ni; 1905 v W; 1906 v Ni; 1908 v Ni, W (13)

Renny-Tailyour, H. W. (Royal Engineers), 1873 v E (1)

Rhind, A. (Queen's Park), 1872 v E (1)

Richmond, A. (Queen's Park), 1906 v W (1)

Richmond, J. T. (Clydesdale), 1877 v E; (with Queen's Park), 1878 v E; 1882 v W (3)

Ring, T. (Clyde), 1953 v Se; 1955 v W, Ni, E, H; 1957 v E, Sp (2), Sw, WG; 1958 v Ni, Sw (12)

Rioch, B. D. (Derby Co), 1975 v P, W, Ni, E, R; 1976 v D (2), R, Ni, W, E; 1977 v Fi, Cz, W; (with Everton), W, Ni, E, Ch, Br; 1978 v Cz; (with Derby Co), Ni, E, Pe, Ho (24)

Ritchie, A. (East Stirlingshire), 1891 v W (1)

Ritchie, H. (Hibernian), 1923 v W; 1928 v Ni (2)

Ritchie, J. (Queen's Park), 1897 v W (1)

Ritchie, W. (Rangers), 1962 v U (sub) (1)

Robb, D. T. (Aberdeen), 1971 v W, E, P, D (sub), USSR (5)

Robb, W. (Rangers), 1926 v W; (with Hibernian), 1928 v W (2)

Robertson, A. (Clyde), 1955 v P, A, H; 1958 v Sw, Par (5)

Robertson, G. (Motherwell), 1910 v W; (with Sheffield W), 1912 v W; 1913 v E, Ni (4)

Robertson, G. (Kilmarnock), 1938 v Cz (1)

Robertson, H. (Dundee), 1962 v Cz (1)

Robertson, J. (Dundee), 1931 v A, I (2)

Robertson, J. (Nottingham F), 1978 v Ni, Ir; 1979 v P, N; 1980 v Pe, A, Bel (2), P; 1981 v Se, P, Is, Ni, Is, Ni, E; 1982 v Se, Ni (2), E (sub), Nz, Br, USSR (23)

Robertson, J. G. (Tottenham H), 1965 v W (1)

Robertson, J. T. (Everton), 1898 v E; (with Southampton), 1899 v E; (with Rangers), 1900 v E, W; 1901 v W, Ni, E; 1902 v W, Ni, E; 1903 v E, W; 1904 v E, W, Ni; 1905 v W (16)

Robertson, P. (Dundee), 1903 v Ni (1)

Robertson, T. (Queen's Park), 1889 v Ni; 1890 v E; 1891 v W; 1892 v Ni (4)

Robertson, T. (Hearts), 1898 v Ni (1)

Robertson, W. (Dumbarton), 1887 v E, W (2)

Robinson, R. (Dundee), 1974 v WG (sub); 1975 v Se, Ni, R (sub) (4)

Rough, A. (Partick T), 1976 v Sw, Ni, W, E; 1977 v Fi, Cz, W (2), Se, Ni, E, Ch, Arg, Br; 1978 v Cz, W, Ni, E, Pe, Ir, Ho; 1979 v A, P, W, Arg, N; 1980 v Pe, A,

Bel (2), P, W, E, Pol, H; 1981 v Se, P, Is, Ni, Is, W, E; 1982 v Se, Ni, Sp, Ho, W, E, Nz, Br, USSR (51)

Rowan, A. (Caledonian), 1880 v E; (with Queen's Park), 1882 v W (2)

Russell, D. (Hearts), 1895 v E, Ni; (with Celtic), 1897 v W; 1898 v Ni; 1901 v W, Ni (6)

Russell, J. (Cambuslang), 1890 v Ni (1)

Russell, W. F. (Airdrieonians), 1924 v W; 1925 v E (2)

Rutherford, E. (Rangers), 1948 v F (1)


St John, I. (Motherwell), 1959 v WG; 1960 v E, Ni, W, Pol, A; 1961 v E; (with Liverpool), 1962 v Ni, W, E, Cz (2), U; 1963 v W, Ni, E, N, Ei (sub), Sp; 1964 v Ni; 1965 v E (21)

Sawers, W. (Dundee), 1895 v W (1)

Scarff, P. (Celtic), 1931 v Ni (1)

Schaedler, E. (Hibernian), 1974 v WG (1)

Scott, A. S. (Rangers), 1957 v Ni, Y, WG; 1958 v W, Sw; 1959 v P; 1962 v Ni, W, E, Cz, U; (with Everton), 1964 v W, N; 1965 v Fi; 1966 v P, Br (16)

Scott, J. (Hibernian), 1966 v Ho (1)

Scott, J. (Dundee), 1971 v D (sub), USSR (2)

Scott, M. (Airdrieonians), 1898 v W (1)

Scott, R. (Airdrieonians), 1894 v Ni (1)

Scoular, J. (Portsmouth), 1951 v D, F, A; 1952 v E, USA, D, Se; 1953 v W, Ni (9)

Sellar, W. (Battlefield), 1885 v E; 1886 v E; 1887 v E, W; 1888 v E; (with Queen's Park), 1891 v E; 1892 v E; 1893 v E, Ni (9)

Semple, W. (Cambuslang), 1886 v W (1)

Shankly, W. (Preston NE), 1938 v E; 1939 v E, W, Ni, H (5)

Sharp, J. (Dundee), 1904 v W; (with Woolwich Arsenal), 1907 v W, E; 1908 v E; (with Fulham), 1909 v W (5)

Shaw, D. (Hibernian), 1947 v W, Ni; 1948 v E, Bel, Sw, F; 1949 v W, Ni (8)

Shaw, F. W. (Pollokshields Ath), 1884 v E, W (2)

Shaw, J. (Rangers), 1947 v E, Bel, L; 1948 v Ni (4)

Shearer, R. (Rangers), 1961 v E, Ei (2), Cz (4)

Sillars, D. C. (Queen's Park), 1891 v Ni; 1892 v E; 1893 v W; 1894 v E; 1895 v W (5)

Simpson, J. (Third Lanark), 1895 v E, W, Ni (3)

Simpson, J. (Rangers), 1935 v E, W, Ni; 1936 v E, W, Ni; 1937 v G, E, W, Ni, A, Cz; 1938 v W, Ni (14)

Simpson, R. C. (Celtic), 1967 v E, USSR; 1968 v Ni, E; 1969 v A (5)

Sinclair, G. L. (Hearts), 1910 v Ni; 1912 v W, Ni (3)

Sinclair, J. W. E. (Leicester C), 1966 v P (1)

Skene, L. H. (Queen's Park), 1904 v W (1)

Sloan, T. (Third Lanark), 1904 v W (1)

Smellie, R. (Queen's Park), 1887 v Ni; 1888 v W; 1889 v E; 1891 v E; 1893 v E, Ni (6)

Smith, A. (Rangers), 1898 v E; 1900 v E, Ni, W; 1901 v E, Ni, W; 1902 v E, Ni, W; 1903 v E, Ni, W; 1904 v Ni; 1905 v W; 1906 v E, Ni; 1907 v W; 1911 v E, Ni (20)

Smith, D. (Aberdeen), 1966 v Ho; (with Rangers), 1968 v Ho (2)

Smith, G. (Hibernian), 1947 v E, Ni; 1948 v W, Bel, Sw, F; 1952 v E, USA; 1955 v P, Y, A, H; 1956 v E, Ni, W; 1957 v Sp (2), Sw (18)

Smith, J. (Rangers), 1935 v Ni; 1938 v Ni (2)

Smith, J. (Ayr U), 1924 v E (1)

Smith, J. (Aberdeen), 1968 v Ho (sub); (with Newcastle U), 1974 v WG, Ni (sub), W (sub) (4)

Smith, J. E. (Celtic), 1959 v H, P (2)

Smith, Jas. (Queen's Park), 1872 v E (1)

Smith, John. (Mauchline), 1877 v E, W; 1879 v E, W; (with Edinburgh University), 1880 v E; (with Queen's Park), 1881 v W, E; 1883 v E, W; 1884 v E (10)

Smith, N. (Rangers), 1897 v E; 1898 v W; 1899 v E, W, Ni; 1900 v E, W, Ni; 1901 v Ni, W; 1902 v E, Ni (12)

Smith, R. (Queen's Park), 1872 v E; 1873 v E (2)

Smith, T. M. (Kilmarnock), 1934 v E; (with Preston NE), 1938 v E (2)

Somers, P. (Celtic), 1905 v E, Ni; 1907 v Ni; 1909 v W (4)

Somers, W. S. (Third Lanark), 1879 v E, W; (with Queen's Park), 1880 v W (3)

Somerville, G. (Queen's Park), 1886 v E (1)

Souness, G. J. (Middlesbrough), 1975 v EG, Sp, Se; (with Liverpool), 1978 v Bul, W, E (sub), Ho; 1979 v A, N, W, Ni, E; 1980 v Pe, A, Bel, P, Ni; 1981 v P, Is (2); 1982 v Ni, P, Sp, W, E, Nz, Br, USSR (28)

Speedie, F. (Rangers), 1903 v E, W, Ni (3)

Speirs, J. H. (Rangers), 1908 v W (1)

Stanton, P. (Hibernian), 1966 v Ho; 1969 v Ni; 1970 v Ei, A; 1971 v D, Bel, P, USSR, D; 1972 v P, Bel, Ho, W; 1973 v W, Ni; 1974 v WG (16)

Stark, J. (Rangers), 1909 v E, Ni (2)

Steel, W. (Morton), 1947 v E, Bel, L; (with Derby Co), 1948 v F, E, W, Ni; 1949 v E, W, Ni, F; 1950 v E, W, Ni, Sw, P, F; (with Dundee), 1951 v W, Ni, E, A (2), D, F, Bel; 1952 v W; 1953 v W, E, Ni, Se (30)

Steele, D. M. (Huddersfield), 1923 v E, W, Ni (3)

Stein, C. (Rangers), 1969 v W, Ni, D, E, Cy (2); 1970 v A (sub), Ni (sub), W, E, Ei, WG; 1971 v D, USSR, Bel, D; 1972 v Cz (sub); (with Coventry C), 1973 v E (2 sub), W (sub), Ni (21)

Stephen, J. F. (Bradford), 1947 v W; 1948 v W (2)

Stevenson, G. (Motherwell), 1928 v W, Ni; 1930 v Ni, E, F; 1931 v E, W; 1932 v W, Ni; 1933 v Ni; 1934 v E; 1935 v Ni (12)

Stewart, A. (Queen's Park), 1888 v Ni; 1889 v W (2)

Stewart, A. (Third Lanark), 1894 v W (1)

Stewart, D. (Dumbarton), 1888 v Ni (1)

Stewart, D. (Queen's Park), 1893 v W; 1894 v Ni; 1897 v Ni (3)

Stewart, D. S. (Leeds U), 1978 v EG (1)

Stewart, G. (Hibernian), 1906 v W, E; (with Manchester C), 1907 v E, W (4)

Stewart, J. (Kilmarnock), 1977 v Ch (sub); (with Middlesbrough), 1979 v N (2)

Stewart, R. (West Ham U), 1981 v W, Ni, E; 1982 v Ni, P, W (6)

Stewart, W. E. (Queen's Park), 1898 v Ni; 1900 v Ni (2)

Storrier, D. (Celtic), 1899 v E, W, Ni (3)

Strachan, G. (Aberdeen), 1980 v Ni, W, E, Pol, H (sub); 1981 v Se, P; 1982 v Ni, P, Sp, Ho (sub), Nz, Br, USSR (14)

Sturrock, P. (Dundee U), 1981 v W (sub), Ni, E (sub); 1982 v P, Ni (sub), W (sub), E (sub) (7)

Summers, W. (St Mirren), 1926 v E (1)

Symon, J. S. (Rangers), 1939 v H (1)


Tait, T. S. (Sunderland), 1911 v W (1)

Taylor, J. (Queen's Park), 1872 v E; 1873 v E; 1874 v E; 1875 v E; 1876 v E, W (6)

Taylor, J. D. (Dumbarton), 1892 v W; 1893 v W; 1894 v Ni; (with St Mirren), 1895 v Ni (4)

Taylor, W. (Hearts), 1892 v E (1)

Telfer, W. (Motherwell), 1933 v Ni; 1934 v Ni (2)

Telfer, W. D. (St Mirren), 1954 v W (1)

Templeton, R. (Aston Villa), 1902 v E; (with Newcastle U), 1903 v E, W; 1904 v E; (with Woolwich Arsenal), 1905 v W; (with Kilmarnock), 1908 v Ni; 1910 v E, Ni; 1912 v E, Ni; 1913 v W (11)

Thomson, A. (Arthurlie), 1886 v Ni (1)

Thomson, A. (Airdrieonians), 1909 v Ni (1)

Thomson, A. (Celtic), 1926 v E; 1932 v F; 1933 v W (3)

Thomson, A. (Third Lanark), 1889 v W (1)

Thomson, C. (Hearts), 1904 v Ni; 1905 v E, Ni, W; 1906 v W, Ni; 1907 v E, W, Ni; 1908 v E, W, Ni; (with Sunderland), 1909 v W; 1910 v E; 1911 v Ni; 1912 v E, W; 1913 v E, W; 1914 v E, Ni (21)

Thomson, C. (Sunderland), 1937 v Cz (1)

Thomson, D. (Dundee), 1920 v W (1)

Thomson, J. (Celtic), 1930 v F; 1931 v E, W, Ni (4)

Thomson, J. J. (Queen's Park), 1872 v E; 1873 v E; 1874 v E (3)

Thomson, J. R. (Everton), 1933 v W (1)

Thomson, R. (Celtic), 1932 v W (1)

Thomson, R. W. (Falkirk), 1927 v E (1)

Thomson, S. (Rangers), 1884 v W, Ni (2)

Thomson, W. (Dumbarton), 1892 v W; 1893 v W; 1898 v Ni, W (4)

Thomson, W. (Dundee), 1896 v W (1)

Thomson, W. (St Mirren), 1980 v Ni; 1981 v Ni (sub), Ni; 1982 v P (4)

Thornton, W. (Rangers), 1947 v W, Ni; 1948 v E, Ni; 1949 v F; 1952 v D, Se (7)

Toner, W. (Kilmarnock), 1959 v W, Ni (2)

Townsley, T. (Falkirk), 1926 v W (1)

Troup, A. (Dundee), 1920 v E; 1921 v W, Ni; 1922 v Ni; (with Everton), 1926 v E (5)

Turnbull, E. (Hibernian), 1948 v Bel, Sw; 1951 v A; 1958 v H, Pol, Y, Par, F (8)

Turner, T. (Arthurlie), 1884 v W (1)

Turner, W. (Pollokshields), 1885 v Ni; 1886 v Ni (2)


Ure, J. F. (Dundee), 1962 v W, Cz; 1963 v W, Ni, E, A, N, Sp; (with Arsenal), 1964 v Ni, N; 1968 v Ni (11)

Urquhart, D. (Hibernian), 1934 v W (1)


Vallance, T. (Rangers), 1877 v E, W; 1878 v E; 1879 v E, W; 1881 v E, W (7)

Venters, A. (Cowdenbeath), 1934 v Ni; (with Rangers), 1936 v E; 1939 v E (3)


Waddell, T. S. (Queen's Park), 1891 v Ni; 1892 v E; 1893 v E, Ni; 1895 v E, Ni (6)

Waddell, W. (Rangers), 1947 v W; 1949 v E, W, Ni, F; 1950 v E, Ni; 1951 v E, D, F, Bel, A; 1952 v Ni, W; 1954 v Ni; 1955 v W, Ni (17)

Wales, H. M. (Motherwell), 1933 v W (1)

Walker, F. (Third Lanark), 1922 v W (1)

Walker, G. (St Mirren), 1930 v F; 1931 v Ni, A, Sw (4)

Walker, J. (Hearts), 1895 v Ni; 1897 v W; 1898 v Ni; (with Rangers), 1904 v W, Ni (5)

Walker, J. (Swindon T), 1911 v E, W, Ni; 1912 v E, W, Ni; 1913 v E, W, Ni (9)

Walker, R. (Hearts), 1900 v E, Ni; 1901 v E, W; 1902 v E, W, Ni; 1903 v E, W, Ni; 1904 v E, W, Ni; 1905 v E, W, Ni; 1906 v Ni; 1907 v E, Ni; 1908 v E, W, Ni; 1909 v E, W; 1912 v E, W, Ni; 1913 v E, W (29)

Walker, T. (Hearts), 1935 v E, W; 1936 v E, W, Ni; 1937 v G, E, W, Ni, A, Cz; 1938 v E, W, Ni, Cz, Ho; 1939 v E, W, Ni, H (20)

Walker, W. (Clyde), 1909 v Ni; 1910 v Ni (2)

Wallace, I. A. (Coventry C), 1978 v Bul (sub); 1979 v P (sub), W (3)

Wallace, W. S. B. (Hearts), 1965 v Ni; 1966 v E, Ho; (with Celtic), 1967 v E, USSR (sub); 1968 v Ni; 1969 v E (sub) (7)

Wardhaugh, J. (Hearts), 1955 v H; 1957 v Ni (2)

Wark, J. (Ipswich T), 1979 v W, Ni, E, Arg, N (sub); 1980 v Pe, A, Bel (2); 1981 v Is, Ni; 1982 v Se, Sp, Ho, Ni, Nz, Br, USSR (18)

Watson, A. (Queen's Park), 1881 v E, W; 1882 v E (3)

Watson, J. (Sunderland), 1903 v E, W; 1904 v E; 1905 v E; (with Middlesbrough), 1909 v E, Ni (6)

Watson, J. (Motherwell), 1948 v Ni; (with Huddersfield T), 1954 v Ni (2)

Watson, J. A. K. (Rangers), 1878 v W (1)

Watson, P. R. (Blackpool), 1934 v A (1)

Watson, R. (Motherwell), 1971 v USSR (1)

Watson, W. (Falkirk), 1898 v W (1)

Watt, F. (Kilbirnie), 1889 v W, Ni; 1890 v W; 1891 v E (4)

Watt, W. W. (Queen's Park), 1887 v Ni (1)

Waugh, W. (Hearts), 1938 v Cz (1)

Weir, A. (Motherwell), 1959 v WG; 1960 v E, P, A, H, T (6)

Weir, J. (Third Lanark), 1887 v Ni (1)

Weir, J. B. (Queen's Park), 1872 v E; 1874 v E; 1875 v E; 1878 v W (4)

Weir, P. (St Mirren), 1980 v N (sub), W, Pol (sub), H (4)

White, John (Albion R), 1922 v W; (with Hearts), 1923 v Ni (2)

White, J. A. (Falkirk), 1959 v WG, Ho, P; 1960 v Ni; (with Tottenham H), 1960 v W, Pol, A, T; 1961 v W; 1962 v Ni, W, E, Cz (2); 1963 v W, Ni, E; 1964 v Ni, W, E, N, WG (22)

White, W. (Bolton W), 1907 v E; 1908 v E (2)

Whitelaw, A. (Vale of Leven), 1887 v Ni; 1890 v W (2)

Wilson, A. (Sheffield W), 1907 v E; 1908 v E; 1912 v E; 1913 v E, W; 1914 v Ni (6)

Wilson, A. (Portsmouth), 1954 v Fi (1)

Wilson, A. N. (Dunfermline), 1920 v E, W, Ni; 1921 v E, W, Ni; (with Middlesbrough), 1922 v E, W, Ni; 1923 v E, W, Ni (12)

Wilson, D. (Queen's Park), 1900 v W (1)

Wilson, D. (Oldham Ath), 1913 v E (1)

Wilson, D. (Rangers), 1961 v E, W, Ni, Ei (2), Cz; 1962 v Ni, W, E, Cz, U; 1963 v W, E, A, N, Ei, Sp; 1964 v E, WG; 1965 v Ni, E, Fi (22)

Wilson, G. W. (Hearts), 1904 v W; 1905 v E, Ni; 1906 v W; (with Everton), 1907 v E; (with Newcastle U), 1909 v E (6)

Wilson, Hugh, (Newmilns), 1890 v W; (with Sunderland), 1897 v E; (with Third Lanark), 1902 v W; 1904 v Ni (4)

Wilson, J. (Vale of Leven), 1888 v W; 1889 v E; 1890 v E; 1891 v E (4)

Wilson, P. (Celtic), 1926 v Ni; 1930 v F; 1931 v Ni; 1933 v E (4)

Wilson, P. (Celtic), 1975 v Sp (sub) (1)

Wilson, R. P. (Arsenal), 1972 v P, Ho (2)

Wiseman, W. (Queen's Park), 1927 v W; 1930 v Ni (2)

Wood, G. (Everton), 1979 v Ni, E, Arg (sub); (with Arsenal), 1982 v Ni (4)

Woodburn, W. A. (Rangers), 1947 v E, Bel, L; 1948 v W, Ni; 1949 v E, F; 1950 v E, W, Ni, P, F; 1951 v E, W, Ni, A (2), D, F, Bel; 1952 v E, W, Ni, USA (24)

Wotherspoon, D. N. (Queen's Park), 1872 v E; 1873 v E (2)

Wright, T. (Sunderland), 1953 v W, Ni, E (3)

Wylie, T. G. (Rangers), 1890 v Ni (1)


Yeats, R. (Liverpool), 1965 v W; 1966 v I (2)

Yorston, B. C. (Aberdeen), 1931 v Ni (1)

Yorston, H. (Aberdeen), 1955 v W (1)

Young, A. (Hearts), 1960 v E, A (sub), H, T; 1961 v W, Ni; (with Everton), Ei; 1966 v P (8)

Young, A. (Everton), 1905 v E; 1907 v W (2)

Young, G. L. (Rangers), 1947 v E, Ni, Bel, L; 1948 v E, Ni, Bel, Sw, F; 1949 v E, W, Ni, F; 1950 v E, W, Ni, Sw, P, F; 1951 v E, W, Ni, A (2), D, F, Bel; 1952 v E, W, Ni, USA, D, Se; 1953 v W, E, Ni, Se; 1954 v Ni, W; 1955 v W, Ni, P, Y; 1956 v Ni, W, E, A; 1957 v E, Ni, W, Y, Sp, Sw (53)

Young, J. (Celtic), 1906 v Ni (1)

Younger, T. (Hibernian), 1955 v P, Y, A, H; 1956 v E, Ni, W, A; (with Liverpool), 1957 v E, Ni, W, Y, Sp (2), Sw, WG; 1958 v Ni, W, E, Sw, H, Pol, Y, Par (24)


## WALES

Adams, H. (Berwyn R), 1882 v Ni, E; (with Druids), 1883 v Ni, E (4)

Allchurch, I. J. (Swansea T), 1951 v E, Ni, P, Sw; 1952 v E, S, Ni, R of UK; 1953 v S, E, Ni, F, Y; 1954 v S, E, Ni, A; 1955 v S, E, Ni, Y; 1956 v E, S, Ni, A; 1957 v E, S; 1958 v Ni, Is (2), H (2), M, Sw, Br; (with Newcastle U), 1959 v E, S, Ni; 1960 v E, S; 1961 v Ni, H, Sp (2); 1962 v E, S, Br (2), M; (with Cardiff C), 1963 v S, E, Ni, H (2); 1964 v E; 1965 v S, E, Ni, Gr, I, USSR; 1966 (with Swansea T), v USSR, E, S, D, Br (2), Ch (68)

Allchurch, L. (Swansea T), 1955 v Ni; 1956 v A; 1958 v S, Ni, EG, Is; 1959 v S; (with Sheffield U), 1962 v S, Ni, Br; 1964 v E (11)

Allen, B. W. (Coventry C), 1951 v S, E (2)

Arridge, S. (Bootle), 1892 v S, Ni; (with Everton), 1894 v Ni; 1895 v Ni; 1896 v E; (with New Brighton Tower), 1898 v E, Ni; 1899 v E (8)

Astley, D. J. (Charlton Ath), 1931 v Ni; (with Aston Villa), 1932 v E; 1933 v E, S, Ni; 1934 v E, S; 1935 v S; 1936 v E, Ni; (with Derby Co), 1939 v E, S; (with Blackpool), F (13)

Atherton, R. W. (Hibernian), 1899 v E, Ni; 1903 v E, S, Ni; (with Middlesbrough), 1904 v E, S, Ni; 1905 v Ni (9)

Bailiff, W. E. (Llanelly), 1913 v E, S, Ni; 1920 v Ni (4)

Baker, C. W. (Cardiff C), 1958 v M; 1960 v S, Ni; 1961 v S, E, Ei; 1962 v S (7)

Baker, W. G. (Cardiff C), 1948 v Ni (1)

Bamford, T. (Wrexham), 1931 v E, S, Ni; 1932 v Ni; 1933 v F (5)

Barnes, W. (Arsenal), 1948 v E, S, Ni; 1949 v E, S, Ni; 1950 v E, S, Ni, Bel; 1951 v E, S, Ni, P; 1952 v E, S, Ni, R of UK; 1954 v E, S; 1955 v S, Y (22)

Bartley, T. (Glossop NE), 1898 v E (1)

Beadles, G. H. (Cardiff C), 1925 v E, S (2)

Bell, W. S. (Shrewsbury Engineers), 1881 v E, S; (with Crewe Alex), 1886 v E, S, Ni (5)

Bennion, S. R. (Manchester U), 1926 v S; 1927 v S; 1928 v S, E, Ni; 1929 v S, E, Ni; 1930 v S; 1932 v Ni (10)

Berry, G. F. (Wolverhampton W), 1979 v WG; 1980 v Ei, WG (sub), T (4)

Blew, H. (Wrexham), 1899 v E, S, Ni; 1902 v S, Ni; 1903 v E, S; 1904 v E, S, Ni; 1905 v S, Ni; 1906 v E, S, Ni; 1907 v S; 1908 v E, S, Ni; 1909 v E, S; 1910 v E (22)

Boden, T. (Wrexham), 1880 v E (1)

Bostock, A. M. (Shrewsbury), 1892 v Ni (1)

Boulter, L. M. (Brentford), 1939 v Ni (1)

Bowdler, H. E. (Shrewsbury), 1893 v S (1)

Bowdler, J. C. H. (Shrewsbury), 1890 v Ni; (with Wolverhampton W), 1891 v S; 1892 v Ni; (with Shrewsbury), 1894 v E (4)

Bowen, D. L. (Arsenal), 1955 v S, Y; 1957 v Ni, Cz, EG; 1958 v E, S, Ni, EG, Is (2), H (2), M, Se, Br; 1959 v E, S, Ni (19)

Bowen, E. (Druids), 1880 v S; 1883 v S (2)

Bowsher, S. J. (Burnley), 1929 v Ni (1)

Boyle, T. (C Palace), 1981 v Ei, S (sub) (2)

Britten, T. J. (Parkgrove), 1878 v S; (with Presteigne), 1880 v S (2)

Brookes, S. J. (Llandudno), 1900 v E, Ni (2)

Brown, A. I. (Aberdare Ath), 1926 v Ni (1)

Bryan, T. (Oswestry), 1886 v E, Ni (2)

Buckland, T. (Bangor), 1899 v E (1)

Burgess, W. A. R. (Tottenham H), 1947 v E, S, Ni; 1948 v E, S; 1949 v E, S, Ni, P, Bel, Sw; 1950 v E, S, Ni, Bel; 1951 v S, Ni, P, Sw; 1952 v E, S, Ni, R of UK; 1953 v S, E, Ni, F, Y; 1954 v S v E, S, Ni, A (32)

Burke, T. (Wrexham), 1883 v E; 1884 v S; 1885 v E, S, Ni; (with Newton Heath), 1887 v E, S; 1888 v S (8)

Burnett, T. B. (Ruabon), 1877 v S (1)

Burton, A. D. (Norwich C), 1963 v Ni, H; (with Newcastle U), 1964 v E; 1969 v S, E, Ni, I, EG; 1972 v Cz (9)

Butler, A. (Druids), 1900 v S, Ni (2)

Butler, J. (Chirk), 1893 v E, S, Ni (3)

Cartwright, L. (Coventry C), 1974 v E (sub), S, Ni; 1976 v S (sub); 1977 v WG (sub); (with Wrexham), 1978 v Ir (sub); 1979 v Ma (7)

Carty, T. (Wrexham), 1889 v Ni (1)

Challen, J. B. (Corinthians), 1887 v E, S; 1888 v E; (with Wellingborough GS), 1890 v E (4)

Chapman, T. (Newtown), 1894 v E, S, Ni; 1895 v S, Ni; (with Manchester C), 1896 v E; 1897 v E (7)

Charles, J. (Swansea C), 1981 v Cz, T (sub), S (sub), USSR (sub); 1982 v Ic (5)

Charles, M. (Swansea T), 1955 v Ni; 1956 v E, S, A; 1957 v E, Ni, Cz (2), EG; 1958 v E, S, EG, Is (2), H (2), M, Se, Br; 1959 v E, S; (with Arsenal), 1961 v Ni, H, Sp (2); 1962 v E, S; (with Cardiff C), 1962 v Br, Ni; 1963 v S, H (31)

Charles, W. J. (Leeds U), 1950 v Ni; 1951 v Sw; 1953 v Ni, F, Y; 1954 v E, S, Ni, A; 1955 v S, E, Ni, Y; 1956 v E, S, A, Ni; 1957 v E, S, Ni, Cz (2), EG; (with Juventus), 1958 v Is (2), H (2) M, Se; 1960 v S; 1962 v E, Br (2), M; (with Leeds U), 1963 v S; (with Cardiff C), 1964 v S; 1965 v S, USSR (38)

Clarke, R. J. (Manchester C), 1949 v E; 1950 v S, Ni, Bel; 1951 v E, S, Ni, P, Sw; 1952 v S, E, Ni, R of UK; 1953 v S, E; 1954 v E, S, Ni; 1955 v Y, S, E; 1956 v Ni (22)

Collier, D. J. (Grimsby T), 1921 v S (1)

Collins, W. S. (Llanelly), 1931 v S (1)

Conde, C. (Chirk), 1884 v E, S, Ni (3)

Cook, F. C. (Newport Co), 1925 v E, S; (with Portsmouth), 1928 v E, S; 1930 v E, S, Ni; 1932 v E (8)

Crompton, W. (Wrexham), 1931 v E, S, Ni (3)

Cross, E. A. (Wrexham), 1876 v S; 1877 v S (2)

Cross, K. (Druids), 1879 v S; 1881 v E, S (3)

Crowe, V. H. (Aston Villa), 1959 v E, Ni; 1960 v E, Ni; 1961 v S, E, Ni, Ei, H, Sp (2); 1962 v E, S, Br, M; 1963 v H (16)

Cumner, R. H. (Arsenal), 1939 v E, S, Ni (3)

Curtis, A. (Swansea C), 1976 v E, Y (sub), S, Ni, Y (sub), E; 1977 v WG, S (sub), Ni (sub); 1978 v WG, E, S; 1979 v WG, S; (with Leeds U), E, Ni, Ma; 1980 v Ei, WG, T; (with Swansea C), 1982 v Cz, Ic, USSR, Sp, E, S, Ni (27)

Curtis, E. R. (Cardiff C), 1928 v S; (with Birmingham), 1932 v S; 1934 v Ni (3)

Daniel, R. W. (Arsenal), 1951 v E, Ni, P; 1952 v E, S, Ni, R of UK; 1953 v S, E, Ni, F, Y; (with Sunderland), 1954 v E, S, Ni; 1955 v E, Ni; 1957 v S, E, Ni, Cz (21)

Darvell, S. (Oxford University), 1897 v S, Ni (2)

Davies, A. (Wrexham), 1876 v S; 1877 v S (2)

Davies, A. (Shrewsbury), 1891 v Ni (1)

Davies, A. (Druids), 1904 v S; (with Middlesbrough), 1905 v S (2)

Davies, A. O. (Barmouth), 1885 v Ni; 1886 v E, S; (with Swifts), 1887 v E, S; 1888 v E, Ni; (with Wrexham), 1889 v S; (with Crewe Alex), 1890 v E (9)

Davies, C. (Brecon), 1899 v Ni; (with Hereford), 1900 v Ni (2)

Davies, C. (Charlton Ath), 1972 v R (sub) (1)

Davies, D. (Bolton W), 1904 v S, Ni; 1908 v E (sub) (3)

Davies, D. W. (Treharris), 1912 v Ni; (with Oldham Ath), 1913 v Ni (2)

Davies, E. Lloyd, (Stoke C), 1904 v E; 1907 v E, S, Ni; (with Northampton T), 1908 v S; 1909 v Ni; 1910 v Ni; 1911 v E, S; 1912 v E, S; 1913 v E, S; 1914 v Ni, E, S (16)

Davies, E. R. (Newcastle U), 1953 v S, E; 1954 v E, S; 1958 v E, EG (6)

Davies, G. (Fulham), 1980 v T, Ic; 1982 v Sp (sub), F (sub) (4)

Davies, Rev. H. (Wrexham), 1928 v Ni (1)
Davies, Idwal (Liverpool Marine), 1923 v S (1)
Davies, J. E. (Oswestry), 1885 v E (1)
Davies, Jas. (Wrexham), 1878 v S (1)
Davies, John. (Wrexham), 1879 v S (1)
Davies, Jos. (Everton), 1889 v S, Ni; (with Chirk), 1891 v Ni; (with Ardwick), v E, S; (with Sheffield U), 1895 v E, S, Ni; (with Manchester C), 1896 v E; (with Millwall), 1897 v E; (with Reading), 1900 v E (11)
Davies, Jos. (Newton Heath), 1888 v E, S, Ni; 1889 v S; 1890 v E; (with Wolverhampton W), 1892 v E; 1893 v E (7)
Davies, J. P. (Druids), 1883 v E, Ni (2)
Davies, Ll. (Wrexham), 1907 v Ni; 1910 v Ni, S, E; (with Everton), 1911 v S, Ni; 1912 v Ni, S, E; 1913 v Ni, S, E; 1914 v Ni (13)
Davies, L. S. (Cardiff C), 1922 v E, S, Ni; 1923 v E, S, Ni; 1924 v E, S, Ni; 1925 v S, Ni; 1926 v E, Ni; 1927 v E, Ni; 1928 v S, Ni, E; 1929 v S, Ni, E; 1930 v E, S (23)
Davies, O. (Wrexham), 1890 v S (1)
Davies, R. (Wrexham), 1883 v Ni; 1884 v Ni; 1885 v Ni (3)
Davies, R. (Druids), 1885 v E (1)
Davies, R. L. (Wrexham), 1892 v Ni (1)
Davies, R. O. (Wrexham), 1892 v Ni, E (2)
Davies, R. T. (Norwich C), 1964 v Ni; 1965 v E; 1966 v Br (2), Ch; (with Southampton), 1967 v S, E, Ni; 1968 v S, Ni, WG; 1969 v S, E, Ni, I, WG, R of UK; 1970 v E, S, Ni; 1971 v Cz, S, E, Ni; 1972 v R, E, S, N; (with Portsmouth), 1974 v E (29)
Davies, R. W. (Bolton W), 1964 v E; 1965 v E, S, Ni, D, Gr, USSR; 1966 v E, S, Ni, USSR, D, Br (2), Ch (sub); 1967 v S; (with Newcastle U), E; 1968 v S, Ni, WG; 1969 v S, E, Ni, I; 1970 v EG; 1971 v R, Cz; (with Manchester C), 1972 v E, S, Ni; (with Manchester U), 1973 v E, S (sub), Ni; (with Blackpool), 1974 v Pol (34)
Davies, Stanley (Preston NE), 1920 v E, S, Ni; (with Everton), 1921 v E, S, Ni; (with WBA), 1922 v E, S, Ni; 1923 v S; 1925 v S, Ni; 1926 v S, E, Ni; 1927 v S; 1928 v S; (with Rotherham U), 1930 v Ni (18)
Davies, T. (Oswestry), 1886 v E (1)
Davies, T. (Druids), 1903 v E, Ni, S; 1904 v S (4)
Davies, W. (Swansea T), 1924 v E, S, Ni; (with Cardiff C), 1925 v E, S, Ni; 1926 v E, S, Ni; 1927 v S; 1928 v Ni; (with Notts Co), 1929 v E, S, Ni; 1930 v E, S, Ni (17)
Davies, W. (Wrexham), 1884 v Ni (1)
Davies, William (Wrexham), 1903 v Ni; 1905 v Ni; (with Blackburn R), 1908 v E, S; 1909 v E, S, Ni; 1911 v E, S, Ni; 1912 v Ni (11)
Davies, W. C. (C Palace), 1908 v S; (with WBA), 1909 v E; 1910 v S; (with C Palace), 1914 v E (4)
Davies, W. D. (Everton), 1975 v H, L, S, E, Ni; 1976 v Y (2), E, Ni; 1977 v WG, S (2), Cz, E, Ni; 1978 v K; (with Wrexham), S, Cz, WG, Ir, E, S, Ni; 1979 v Ma, T, WG S, E, Ni, Ma; 1980 v Ei, WG, T, E, S, Ni, Ic; 1981 v T, Cz, Ei, T, S, E, USSR; (with Swansea C), 1982 v Cz, Ic, USSR, Sp, E, S, F (51)
Davies, W. H. (Oswestry), 1876 v S; 1877 v S; 1879 v E; 1880 v E (4)
Davies, W. O. (Millwall Ath), 1913 v E, S, Ni; 1914 v S, Ni (5)
Davis, G. (Wrexham), 1978 v Ir, E (sub), Ni (3)
Day, A. (Tottenham H), 1934 v Ni (1)
Deacy, N. (PSV Eindhoven), 1977 v Cz, S, E, Ni; 1978 v K (sub), S (sub), Cz (sub), WG, Ir, S (sub), Ni; (with Beringen), 1979 v T (12)
Dearson, D. J. (Birmingham), 1939 v S, Ni, F (3)
Derrett, S. C. (Cardiff C), 1969 v S, WG; 1970 v I; 1971 v Fi (4)
Dewey, F. T. (Cardiff Corinthians), 1931 v E, S (2)
Doughty, J. (Druids), 1886 v S; (with Newton Heath), 1887 v S, Ni; 1888 v E, S, Ni; 1889 v S (7)

Doughty, R. (Newton Heath and Druids), 1888 v S, Ni; 1890 v E (3)
Durban, A. (Derby Co), 1966 v Br (sub); 1967 v Ni; 1968 v E, S, Ni, WG; 1969 v EG, S, E, Ni, WG; 1970 v E, S, Ni, EG, I; 1971 v R, S, E, Ni, Cz, Fi; 1972 v Fi, Cz, E, S, Ni (27)
Dwyer, P. (Cardiff C), 1978 v Ir, E, S, Ni; 1979 v T, S, E, Ni, Ma (sub); 1980 v WG (10)

Edwards, C. (Wrexham), 1878 v S (1)
Edwards, G. (Birmingham C), 1947 v E, S, Ni; 1948 v E, S, Ni; (with Cardiff C), 1949 v Ni, P, Bel, Sw; 1950 v E, S (12)
Edwards, H. (Wrexham Civil Service), 1878 v S; 1880 v E; 1882 v E, S; 1883 v S; 1884 v Ni; 1887 v Ni (7)
Edwards, R. I. (Chester), 1978 v K (sub); 1979 v Ma, WG; (with Wrexham), 1980 v T (sub) (4)
Edwards, J. H. (Oswestry), 1895 v Ni; 1897 v E, Ni; (with Aberystwyth), 1898 v Ni (4)
Edwards, J. H. (Wanderers), 1876 v S (1)
Edwards, L. T. (Charlton Ath), 1957 v Ni, EG (2)
Edwards, T. (Linfield), 1932 v S (1)
Egan, W. (Chirk), 1892 v S (1)
Ellis, B. (Motherwell), 1932 v E; 1933 v E, S; 1934 v S; 1936 v E; 1937 v S (6)
Ellis, E. (Nunhead), 1931 v E; (with Oswestry), S; 1932 v Ni (3)
Emanuel, W. J. (Bristol C), 1973 v E (sub), Ni (sub) (2)
England, H. M. (Blackburn R), 1962 v Ni, Br, M; 1963 v Ni, H; 1964 v E, S, Ni; 1965 v E, D, Gr (2), USSR, Ni, I; 1966 v E, S, Ni, USSR, D; (with Tottenham H), 1967 v S, E; 1968 v E, Ni, WG; 1969 v EG; 1970 v R of UK, EG, E, S, Ni, I; 1971 v R; 1972 v Fi, E, S, Ni; 1973 v E (3), S; 1974 v Pol; 1975 v H, L (44)
Evans, B. C. (Swansea C), 1972 v Fi, Cz; 1973 v E (2), Pol, S; (with Hereford U), 1974 v Pol (7)
Evans, D. G. (Reading), 1926 v Ni; 1927 v Ni, E; (with Huddersfield T), 1929 v S (4)
Evans, H. P. (Cardiff C), 1922 v E, S, Ni; 1924 v E, S, Ni (6)
Evans, I. (Crystal Palace), 1976 v A, E, Y (2), E, Ni; 1977 v WG, S (2), Cz, E, Ni; 1978 v K (13)
Evans, J. (Cardiff C), 1912 v Ni; 1913 v Ni; 1914 v S; 1920 v S, Ni; 1922 v Ni; 1923 v E, Ni (8)
Evans, J. (Oswestry), 1893 v Ni; 1894 v E, Ni (3)
Evans, J. H. (Southend U), 1922 v E, S, Ni; 1923 v S (4)
Evans, Len (Cardiff C), 1931 v E, S; (with Birmingham), 1934 v Ni (3)
Evans, L. H. (Aberdare Ath), 1927 v Ni (1)
Evans, M. (Oswestry), 1884 v E (1)
Evans, R. (Clapton), 1902 v Ni (1)
Evans, R. E. (Wrexham), 1906 v E, S; (with Aston Villa), Ni; 1907 v E; 1908 v E, S; (with Sheffield U), 1909 v S; 1910 v E, S, Ni (10)
Evans, R. O. (Wrexham), 1902 v Ni; 1903 v E, S, Ni; (with Blackburn R), 1908 v Ni; (with Coventry C), 1911 v E, Ni; 1912 v E, S, Ni (10)
Evans, R. S. (Swansea T), 1964 v Ni (1)
Evans T. J. (Clapton Orient), 1927 v S; 1928 v E, S; (with Newcastle U), Ni (4)
Evans, W. (Tottenham H), 1933 v Ni; 1934 v E, S; 1935 v E; 1936 v E, Ni (6)
Evans, W. A. W. (Oxford University), 1876 v S; 1877 v S (2)
Evans, W. G. (Bootle), 1890 v E; 1891 v E; (with Aston Villa), 1892 v E (3)
Evelyn, E. C. (Crusaders), 1887 v E (1)
Eyton-Jones, J. A. (Wrexham), 1883 v Ni; 1884 v Ni, E, S (4)

Farmer, G. (Oswestry), 1885 v E, S (2)
Finnigan, R. J. (Wrexham), 1930 v Ni (1)

Flynn, B. (Burnley), 1975 v L (2 sub), H (sub), S, E, Ni; 1976 v A, E, Y (2), E, Ni; 1977 v WG (sub), S (2), Cz, E, Ni; 1978 v K (2), S; (with Leeds U), Cz, WG, Ir (sub), E, S, Ni; 1979 v Ma, T, S, E, Ni, Ma; 1980 v Ei, WG, E, S, Ni, Ic; 1981 v T, Cz, Ei, T, S, E, USSR; 1982 v Cz, USSR, E, S, Ni, F (52)

Ford, T. (Swansea T), 1947 v S; (with Aston Villa), 1947 v Ni; 1948 v S, Ni; 1949 v E, S, Ni, P, Bel, Sw; 1950 v E, S, Ni, Bel; 1951 v S; (with Sunderland), 1951 v E, Ni, P, Sw; 1952 v E, S, Ni, R of UK; 1953 v S, E, Ni, F, Y; (with Cardiff C), 1954 v A; 1955 v S, E, Ni, Y; 1956 v S, Ni, E, A; 1957 v S (38)

Foulkes, H. E. (WBA), 1932 v Ni (1)

Foulkes, W. I. (Newcastle U), 1952 v E, S, Ni, R of UK; 1953 v E, S, F, Y; 1954 v E, S, Ni (11)

Foulkes, W. T. (Oswestry), 1884 v Ni; 1885 v S (2)

Fowler, J. (Swansea T), 1925 v E; 1926 v E, Ni; 1927 v S; 1928 v S; 1929 v E (6)

Garner, J. (Aberystwyth), 1896 v S (1)

Giles, D. (Swansea C), 1980 v E, S, Ni, Ic; 1981 v T, Cz, T (sub), E (sub), USSR (sub); (with C Palace), 1982 v Sp (sub) (10)

Gillam, S. G. (Wrexham), 1889 v S, Ni; (with Shrewsbury), 1890 v E, Ni; (with Clapton), 1894 v S (5)

Glascodine, G. (Wrexham), 1879 v E (1)

Glover, E. M. (Grimsby T), 1932 v S; 1934 v Ni; 1936 v S; 1937 v E, S, Ni; 1939 v Ni (7)

Godding, G. (Wrexham), 1923 v S, Ni (2)

Godfrey, B. C. (Preston NE), 1964 v Ni; 1965 v D, I (3)

Goodwin, U. (Ruthin), 1881 v E (1)

Gough, R. T. (Oswestry White Star), 1883 v S (1)

Gray, A. (Oldham Ath), 1924 v E, S, Ni; 1925 v E, S, Ni; 1926 v E, S; 1927 v S; (with Manchester C), 1928 v E, S; 1929 v E, S, Ni; (with Manchester Central), 1930 v S; (with Tranmere R), 1932 v E, S, Ni; (with Chester), 1937 v E, S, Ni; 1938 v E, S, Ni (24)

Green, A. W. (Aston Villa), 1901 v Ni; (with Notts Co), 1903 v E; 1904 v S, Ni; 1906 v Ni, E; (with Nottingham F), 1907 v E; 1908 v S (8)

Green, C. R. (Birmingham C), 1965 v USSR, I; 1966 v E, S, USSR, Br (2); 1967 v E; 1968 v E, S, Ni, WG; 1969 v S, I, Ni (sub) (15)

Green, G. H. (Charlton Ath), 1938 v Ni; 1939 v E, Ni, F (4)

Grey, Dr W. (Druids), 1876 v S; 1878 v S (2)

Griffiths, A. T. (Wrexham), 1971 v Cz (sub); 1975 v A, H (2), L (2), E, Ni; 1976 v A, E, S, E (sub), Ni, Y (2); 1977 v WG, S (17)

Griffiths, F. J. (Blackpool), 1900 v E, S (2)

Griffiths, G. (Chirk), 1887 v Ni (1)

Griffiths, J. H. (Swansea T), 1953 v Ni (1)

Griffiths, M. W. (Leicester C), 1947 v Ni; 1949 v P, Bel; 1950 v E, S, Bel; 1951 v E, Ni, P, Sw; 1954 v A (11)

Griffiths, P. (Chirk), 1884 v E, Ni; 1888 v E; 1890 v S, Ni; 1891 v Ni (6)

Griffiths, S. (Wrexham), 1902 v S (1)

Griffiths, T. P. (Everton), 1927 v E, Ni; 1929 v E; 1930 v E; 1931 v Ni; 1932 v Ni, S, E; (with Bolton W), 1933 v F, E, S, Ni; (with Middlesbrough), 1934 v E, S; 1935 v E, Ni; 1936 v S; (with Aston Villa), Ni; 1937 v E, S, Ni (21)

Hallam, J. (Oswestry), 1889 v E (1)

Hanford, H. (Swansea T), 1934 v Ni; 1935 v S; 1936 v E; (with Sheffield W), 1936 v Ni; 1938 v E, S; 1939 v F (7)

Harrington, A. C. (Cardiff C), 1956 v Ni; 1957 v E, S; 1958 v S, Ni, Is (2); 1961 v S, E; 1962 v E, S (11)

Harris, C. S. (Leeds U), 1976 v E, S; 1978 v WG, Ir, E, S, Ni; 1979 v Ma, T, WG, E (sub), Ma; 1980 v Ni (sub), Ic (sub); 1981 v T, Cz (sub), Ei, T, S, E, USSR; 1982 v Cz, Ic, E (sub) (24)

Harris, W. C. (Middlesbrough), 1954 v A; 1957 v EG, Cz; 1958 v E, S, EG (6)

Harrison, W. C. (Wrexham), 1899 v E; 1900 v E, S, Ni; 1901 v Ni (5)

Hayes, A. (Wrexham), 1890 v Ni; 1894 v Ni (2)

Hennessey, W. T. (Birmingham C), 1962 v Ni, Br (2); 1963 v S, E, H (2); 1964 v E, S; 1965 v S, E, D, Gr, USSR; 1966 v E, USSR; (with Nottingham F), 1966 v S, Ni, D, Br (2), Ch; 1967 v S, E; 1968 v E, S, Ni; 1969 v WG, EG, R of UK, EG; (with Derby Co), 1970 v E, S, Ni; 1972 v Fi, Cz, E, S; 1973 v E (39)

Hersee, A. M. (Bangor), 1886 v S, Ni (2)

Hersee, R. (Llandudno), 1886 v Ni (1)

Hewitt, R. (Cardiff C), 1958 v Ni, Is, Se, H, Br (5)

Hewitt, T. J. (Wrexham), 1911 v E, S, Ni; (with Chelsea), 1913 v E, S, Ni; (with South Liverpool), 1914 v E, S (8)

Heywood, D. (Druids), 1879 v E (1)

Hibbott, H. (Newtown Excelsior), 1880 v E, S (2)

Hibbott, R. (Newtown), 1885 v S (1)

Higham, G. G. (Oswestry), 1878 v S; 1879 v E (2)

Hill, M. R. (Ipswich T), 1972 v Cz, R (2)

Hockey, T. (Sheffield U), 1972 v Fi, R; 1973 v E (2); (with Norwich C), Pol, S, E, Ni; (with Aston Villa), 1974 v Pol (9)

Hoddinott, T. F. (Watford), 1921 v E, S (2)

Hodgkinson, A. V. (Southampton), 1908 v Ni (1)

Hole, B. G. (Cardiff C), 1963 v Ni; 1964 v Ni; 1965 v S, E, Ni, D, Gr (2), USSR, I; 1966 v E, S, Ni, USSR, D, Br (2), Ch; (with Blackburn R), 1967 v S, E, Ni; 1968 v E, S, Ni, WG; (with Aston Villa), 1969 v I, WG, EG; 1970 v I; (with Swansea C), 1971 v R (30)

Hole, W. J. (Swansea T), 1921 v Ni; 1922 v E; 1923 v E, Ni; 1928 v E, S, Ni; 1929 v E, S (9)

Hollins, D. M. (Newcastle U), 1962 v Br (sub), M; 1963 v Ni, H; 1964 v E; 1965 v Ni, Gr, I; 1966 v S, D, Br (11)

Hopkins, I. J. (Brentford), 1935 v S, Ni; 1936 v E, Ni; 1937 v E, S, Ni; 1938 v Ni; 1939 v E, S, Ni (12)

Hopkins, M. (Tottenham H), 1956 v Ni; 1957 v Ni, S, E, Cz (2), EG; 1958 v E, S, Ni, EG, Is (2), H (2), M, Se, Br; 1959 v E, S, Ni; 1960 v E, S; 1961 v Ni, H, Sp (2); 1962 v Ni, Br (2), M; 1963 v S, Ni, H (34)

Howell, E. G. (Builth), 1888 v Ni; 1890 v E; 1891 v E (3)

Howells, R. G. (Cardiff C), 1954 v E, S (2)

Hugh, A. R. (Newport Co), 1930 v Ni (1)

Hughes, A. (Rhos), 1894 v E, S (2)

Hughes, A. (Chirk), 1907 v Ni (1)

Hughes, A. J. (Aberystwyth), 1879 v S (1)

Hughes, E. (Everton), 1899 v S, Ni; (with Tottenham H), 1901 v E, S; 1902 v Ni; 1904 v E, Ni, S; 1905 v E, Ni, S; 1906 v E, Ni; 1907 v E (14)

Hughes, E. (Wrexham), 1906 v S; (with Nottingham F), 1906 v Ni; 1908 v S, E; 1910 v Ni, E, S; 1911 v Ni, E, S; (with Wrexham), 1912 v Ni, E, S; (with Manchester C), 1913 v E, S; 1914 v N (16)

Hughes, F. W. (Northwich Victoria), 1882 v E, Ni; 1883 v E, Ni, S; 1884 v S (6)

Hughes, I. (Luton T), 1951 v E, Ni, P, Sw (4)

Hughes, J. (Cambridge University), 1877 v S (1)

Hughes, J. (Liverpool), 1905 v E, S, Ni (3)

Hughes, J. I. (Blackburn R), 1935 v Ni (1)

Hughes, P. W. (Bangor), 1887 v Ni; 1889 v Ni, E (3)

Hughes, W. (Bootle), 1891 v E; 1892 v S, Ni (3)

Hughes, W. A. (Blackburn R), 1949 v E, Ni, P, Bel, Sw (5)

Hughes, W. M. (Birmingham), 1938 v E, Ni, S; 1939 v E, Ni, S, F; 1947 v E, S, Ni (10)

Humphreys, J. V. (Everton), 1947 v Ni (1)

Humphreys, R. (Druids), 1888 v Ni (1)

Hunter, W. H. (North End, Belfast), 1887 v Ni (1)

Jackson, W. (St Helens Rec), 1899 v Ni (1)

James, E. (Chirk), 1893 v E, Ni; 1894 v E, S, Ni; 1898 v E; 1899 v Ni (7)

James, E. G. (Blackpool), 1966 v Br (2), Ch; 1967 v Ni; 1968 v S; 1971 v Cz, S, E, Ni (9)

James, L. (Burnley), 1972 v Cz, R, S (sub); 1973 v E (3), Pol, S, Ni; 1974 v Pol, E, S, Ni; 1975 v A, H (2), L (2), S, E, Ni; 1976 v A; (with Derby Co), S, E, Y (2), Ni; 1977 v WG, S (2), Cz, E, Ni; 1978 v K (2); (with QPR), WG; (with Burnley) 1979 v T; 1980 (with Swansea C), v E, S, Ni, Ic; 1981 v T, Ei, T, S, E; 1982 v Cz, Ic, USSR, E (sub), S, Ni, F (53)

James, R. (Swansea C), 1979 v Ma, WG (sub), S, E, Ni, Ma; 1980 v WG; 1982 v Cz (sub), Ic, Sp, E, S, Ni, F (14)

James, W. (West Ham U), 1931 v Ni; 1932 v Ni (2)

Jarrett, R. H. (Ruthin), 1889 v Ni; 1890 v S (2)

Jarvis, A. L. (Hull C), 1967 v S, E, Ni (3)

Jenkins, E. (Lovell's Ath), 1925 v E (1)

Jenkins, J. (Brighton), 1924 v Ni, E, S; 1925 v S, Ni; 1926 v E, S; 1927 v S (8)

Jenkins, R. W. (Rhyl), 1902 v Ni (1)

Jenkyns, C. A. L. (Small Heath), 1892 v E, S, Ni; 1895 v E; (with Woolwich Arsenal), 1896 v S; (with Newton Heath), 1897 v Ni; (with Walsall), 1898 v S, E (8)

Jennings, W. (Bolton W), 1914 v E, S; 1920 v S; 1923 v Ni, E; 1924 v E, S, Ni; 1927 v S, Ni; 1929 v S (11)

John, R. F. (Arsenal), 1923 v S, Ni; 1925 v Ni; 1926 v E; 1927 v E; 1928 v E, Ni; 1930 v E, S; 1932 v E; 1933 v F, Ni; 1935 v Ni; 1936 v S; 1937 v E (15)

John, W. R. (Walsall), 1931 v Ni; (with Stoke C), 1933 v E, S, Ni, F; 1934 v E, S; (with Preston NE), 1935 v E, S; (with Sheffield U), 1936 v E, S, Ni; (with Swansea T), 1939 v E, S (14)

Johnson, M. G. (Swansea T), 1964 v Ni (1)

Jones, A. F. (Oxford University), 1877 v S (1)

Jones, A. T. (Nottingham F), 1905 v E; (with Notts Co), 1906 v E (2)

Jones, Bryn (Wolverhampton W), 1935 v Ni; 1936 v E, S, Ni; 1937 v E, S, Ni; 1938 v E, S, Ni; (with Arsenal), 1939 v E, S, Ni; 1947 v S, Ni; 1948 v E; 1949 v S (17)

Jones, B. S. (Swansea T), 1963 v E, Ni, H (2); 1964 v S, Ni; (with Plymouth Arg), 1965 v D; (with Cardiff C), 1969 v S, E, Ni, I (sub), WG, EG, R of UK (15)

Jones, Charlie (Nottingham F), 1926 v E; 1927 v S, Ni; 1928 v E; (with Arsenal), 1930 v E, S; 1932 v E; 1933 v F (7)

Jones, Cliff (Swansea T), 1954 v A; 1956 v E, Ni, S, A; 1957 v E, S, Ni, Cz (2), EG; 1958 v EG, E, S, Is (2); (with Tottenham H), 1958 v Ni, H (2), M, Se, Br; 1959 v Ni; 1960 v E, S, Ni; 1961 v S, E, Ni, Sp, H, Ei; 1962 v E, Ni, S, Br (2), M; 1963 v S, Ni, H; 1964 v E, S, Ni; 1965 v E, S, Ni, D, Gr (2), USSR, I; 1967 v S, E; 1968 v E, S, WG; (with Fulham), 1969 v I, R of UK (59)

Jones, C. W. (Birmingham), 1935 v Ni; 1939 v F (2)

Jones, D. (Chirk), 1888 v S, Ni; (with Bolton W), 1889 v E, S, Ni; 1890 v E, Ni; 1891 v S; 1892 v Ni; 1893 v E; 1894 v E; 1895 v E; 1898 v S; (with Manchester C), 1900 v E, Ni (15)

Jones, D. E. (Norwich C), 1976 v S, E (sub); 1978 v S, Cz, WG, Ir, E; 1980 v E (8)

Jones, D. O. (Leicester C), 1934 v E, Ni; 1935 v E, S; 1936 v E, Ni; 1937 v Ni (7)

Jones, Evan (Chelsea), 1910 v S, Ni; (with Oldham Ath), 1911 v E, S; 1912 v E, S; (with Bolton W), 1914 v Ni (7)

Jones, F. R. (Bangor), 1885 v E, Ni; 1886 v S (3)

Jones, F. W. (Small Heath), 1893 v S (1)

Jones, G. P. (Wrexham), 1907 v S, Ni (2)

Jones, H. (Aberaman), 1902 v Ni (1)

Jones, Humphrey (Bangor), 1885 v E, Ni, S; 1886 v E, Ni, S; (with Queen's Park), 1887 v E; (with East Stirlingshire), 1889 v E, Ni; 1890 v E, S, Ni; (with Queen's Park), 1891 v E, S (14)

Jones, Ivor (Swansea T), 1920 v S, Ni; 1921 v Ni, E; 1922 v S, Ni; (with WBA), 1923 v E, Ni; 1924 v S; 1926 v Ni (10)

Jones, J. (Druids), 1876 v S (1)

Jones, J. (Berwyn Rangers), 1883 v S, Ni; 1884 v S (3)

Jones, J. (Wrexham), 1925 v Ni (1)

Jones, Jeffrey (Llandrindod Wells), 1908 v Ni; 1909 v Ni; 1910 v S (3)

Jones, J. L. (Sheffield U), 1895 v E, S, Ni; 1896 v Ni, S, E; 1897 v Ni, S, E; (with Tottenham H), 1898 v Ni, E, S; 1899 v S, Ni; 1900 v S; 1902 v E, S, Ni; 1904 v E, S, Ni (21)

Jones, J. Love (Stoke C), 1906 v S; (with Middlesbrough), 1910 v Ni (2)

Jones, J. O. (Bangor), 1901 v S, Ni (2)

Jones, J. P. (Liverpool), 1976 v A, E, S; 1977 v WG, S (2), Cz, E, Ni; 1978 v K (2), S, Cz, WG, Ir, E, S, Ni; (with Wrexham), 1979 v Ma, T, WG, S, E, Ni, Ma; 1980 v Ei, WG, T, E, S, Ni, Ic; 1981 v T, Ei, T, S, E, USSR; 1982 v Cz, Ic, USSR, Sp, E, S, Ni, F (46)

Jones, J. T. (Stoke C), 1912 v E, S, Ni; 1913 v E, Ni; 1914 v S, Ni; 1920 v E, S, Ni; (with C Palace), 1921 v E, S; 1922 v E, S, Ni (15)

Jones, K. (Aston Villa), 1950 v S (1)

Jones, Leslie J. (Cardiff C), 1933 v F; (with Coventry C), 1935 v Ni; 1936 v S; 1937 v E, S, Ni; (with Arsenal), 1938 v E, S, Ni; 1939 v E, S (11)

Jones, P. W. (Bristol R), 1971 v Fi (1)

Jones, R. (Bangor), 1887 v S; 1889 v E; (with Crewe Alex), 1890 v E (3)

Jones, R. (Bangor), 1900 v S, Ni (2)

Jones, R. (Druids), 1899 v S; (with Millwall), 1906 v S, Ni (3)

Jones, R. A. (Druids), 1884 v E, Ni, S; 1885 v S (4)

Jones, R. S. (Everton), 1894 v Ni; (with Leicester Fosse), 1898 v S (2)

Jones, S. (Wrexham), 1887 v Ni; (with Chester), 1890 v S (2)

Jones, S. (Wrexham), 1893 v S, Ni; (with Burton Swifts), 1895 v S; 1896 v E, Ni (5)

Jones, T. (Manchester U), 1926 v Ni; 1927 v E, Ni; 1930 v Ni (4)

Jones, T. D. (Aberdare), 1908 v Ni (1)

Jones, T. G. (Everton), 1938 v Ni; 1939 v E, S, Ni; 1947 v E, S; 1948 v E, S, Ni; 1949 v E, Ni, P, Bel, Sw; 1950 v E, S, Bel (17)

Jones, T. J. Sheffield W), 1932 v Ni; 1933 v F (2)

Jones, W. (Druids), 1899 v E (1)

Jones, W. E. A. (Swansea T), 1947 v E, S; (with Tottenham H), 1949 v E, S (4)

Jones, W. J. (Aberdare), 1901 v E, S; (with West Ham U), 1902 v S, E (4)

Jones, W. Lot (Manchester C), 1905 v E, Ni; 1906 v E, S, Ni; 1907 v E, S, Ni; 1908 v S; 1909 v E, S, Ni; 1910 v E; 1911 v E; 1913 v E, S; 1914 v S, Ni; (with Southend U), 1920 v E, Ni (20)

Jones, W. P. (Druids), 1889 v E, Ni; (with Wynstay), 1890 v S, Ni (4)

Jones, W. R. (Aberystwyth), 1897 v S (1)


Keenor, F. C. (Cardiff C), 1920 v E, Ni; 1921 v E, Ni, S; 1922 v Ni; 1923 v E, Ni, S; 1924 v E, Ni, S; 1925 v E, Ni, S; 1926 v S; 1927 v E, Ni, S; 1928 v E, Ni, S; 1929 v E, Ni, S; 1930 v E, Ni, S; 1931 v E, Ni, S; (with Crewe Alex), 1933 v S (32)

Kelly, F. C. (Wrexham), 1899 v S, Ni; (with Druids), 1902 v Ni (3)

Kelsey, A. J. (Arsenal), 1954 v Ni, A; 1955 v S, Ni, Y; 1956 v E, Ni, S, A; 1957 v E, Ni, S, Cz (2), EG; 1958 v E, S, Ni, Is (2), H (2), M, Se, Br; 1959 v E, S; 1960 v E, Ni, S; 1961 v E, Ni, S, H, Sp (2); 1962 v E, S, Ni, Br (2) (41)

Kenrick, S. L. (Druids), 1876 v S; 1877 v S; (with Oswestry), 1879 v E, S; (with Shropshire Wanderers), 1881 v E (5)

Ketley, C. F. (Druids), 1882 v Ni (1)

King, J. (Swansea T), 1955 v E (1)

Kinsey, N. (Norwich C), 1951 v Ni, P, Sw; 1952 v E; (with Birmingham C), 1954 v Ni; 1956 v E, S (7)

Krzywicki, R. L. (Huddersfield T), 1970 v E, S; (with WBA), Ni, EG, I; 1971 v R, Fi; 1972 v Cz (sub) (8)

Lambert, R. (Liverpool), 1947 v S; 1948 v E; 1949 v P, Bel, Sw (5)

Lathom, G. (Liverpool), 1905 v E, S; 1906 v S; 1907 v E, S, Ni; 1908 v E; 1909 v Ni; (with Southport Central), 1910 v E; (with Cardiff C), 1913 v Ni (10)

Lawrence, E. (Clapton Orient), 1930 v Ni; (with Notts Co), 1932 v S (2)

Lawrence, S. (Swansea T), 1932 v Ni; 1933 v F; 1934 v S, E, Ni; 1935 v E, S; 1936 v S (8)

Lea, A. (Wrexham), 1889 v E; 1891 v S, Ni; 1893 v Ni (4)

Lea, C. (Ipswich T), 1965 v Ni, I (2)

Leary, P. (Bangor), 1889 v Ni (1)

Leek, K. (Leicester C), 1961 v S, E, Ni, H, Sp (2); (with Newcastle U), 1962 v S; (with Birmingham C), v Br (sub), M; 1963 v E; 1965 v S, Gr; (with Northampton T), 1965 v Gr (13)

Lever, A. R. (Leicester C), 1953 v S (1)

Lewis, B. (Wrexham), 1891 v Ni; 1892 v S, E, Ni; (with Middlesbrough), 1893 v S, E; (with Wrexham), 1894 v S, E, Ni; 1895 v S (10)

Lewis, D. (Arsenal), 1927 v E; 1928 v Ni; 1930 v E (3)

Lewis, D. J. (Swansea T), 1933 v E, S (2)

Lewis, J. (Bristol R), 1906 v E (1)

Lewis, J. (Cardiff C), 1926 v S (1)

Lewis, T. (Wrexham), 1881 v E, S (2)

Lewis, W. L. (Swansea T), 1927 v E, Ni; 1928 v E, Ni; 1929 v S; (with Huddersfield T), 1930 v E (6)

Lewis, W. (Bangor), 1885 v E; 1886 v E, S; 1887 v E, S; 1888 v E; 1889 v E, Ni, S; (with Crewe Alex), 1890 v E, Ni, S; 1891 v E, Ni, S; 1892 v E, S, Ni; 1894 v E, S, Ni; (with Chester), 1895 v S, Ni, E; 1896 v E, S, Ni; (with Manchester C), 1897 v E, S; (with Chester), 1898 v Ni (30)

Lloyd, B. W. (Wrexham), 1976 v A, E, S (3)

Lloyd, J. W. (Wrexham), 1879 v S; (with Newtown), 1885 v S (2)

Lloyd, R. A. (Ruthin), 1891 v Ni; 1895 v S (2)

Lockley, A. (Chirk), 1898 v Ni (1)

Lovell, S. (C Palace), 1982 v USSR (sub) (1)

Lowrie, G. (Coventry C), 1948 v E, S, Ni; (with Newcastle U), 1949 v P (4)

Lucas, P. M. (Leyton Orient), 1962 v Ni, M; 1963 v S, E (4)

Lucas, W. H. (Swansea T), 1949 v S, Ni, P, Bel, Sw; 1950 v E; 1951 v E (7)

Lumberg, A. (Wrexham), 1929 v Ni; 1930 v E, S; (with Wolverhampton W), 1932 v S (4)

McMillan, R. (Shrewsbury Engineers), 1881 v E, S (2)

Mahoney, J. F. (Stoke C), 1968 v E; 1969 v EG; 1971 v Cz; 1973 v E (3), Pol, S, Ni; 1974 v Pol, E, S, Ni; 1975 v A, H (2), L (2), S, E, Ni; 1976 v A, Y (2), E, Ni; 1977 v WG, Cz, S, E, Ni; (with Middlesbrough), 1978 v K (2), S, Cz, Ir, E (sub), S, Ni; 1979 v WG, S, E, Ni, Ma; (with Swansea C), 1980 v Ei, WG, T (sub); 1982 v Ic, USSR (49)

Martin, T. J. (Newport Co), 1930 v Ni (1)

Marustik, C. (Swansea C), 1982 v Sp, E, S, Ni, F (5)

Mates, J. (Chirk), 1891 v Ni; 1897 v E, S (3)

Mathews, R. W. (Liverpool), 1921 v Ni; (with Bristol C), 1923 v E; (with Bradford), 1926 v Ni (3)

Matthews, W. (Chester), 1905 v Ni; 1908 v E (2)

Matthias, J. S. (Brymbo), 1896 v S, Ni; (with Shrewsbury), 1897 v E, S; (with Wolverhampton W), 1899 v S (5)

Matthias, T. J. (Wrexham), 1914 v S, E; 1920 v Ni, S, E; 1921 v S, E, Ni; 1922 v S, E, Ni; 1923 v S (12)

Mays, A. W. (Wrexham), 1929 v Ni (1)

Medwin, T. C. (Swansea T), 1953 v Ni, F, Y; (with Tottenham H), 1957 v E, S, Ni, Cz (2), EG; 1958 v E, S, Ni, Is (2), H (2), M, Br; 1959 v E, S, Ni; 1960 v E, S, Ni; 1961 v S, Ei, Sp; 1963 v E, H (30)

Meredith, S. (Chirk), 1900 v S; 1901 v S, E, Ni; (with Stoke C), 1902 v E; 1903 v Ni; 1904 v E; (with Leyton), 1907 v E (8)

Meredith, W. H. (Manchester C), 1895 v E, Ni; 1896 v E, Ni; 1897 v E, Ni, S; 1898 v E, Ni; 1899 v E; 1900 v E, Ni; 1901 v E, Ni; 1902 v E, S; 1903 v E, S, Ni; 1904 v E; 1905 v E, S; (with Manchester U), 1907 v E, S, Ni; 1908 v E, Ni; 1909 v E, S, Ni; 1910 v E, S, Ni; 1911 v E, S, Ni; 1912 v E, S, Ni; 1913 v E, S, Ni; 1914 v E, S, Ni; 1920 v E, S, Ni (48)

Mielczarek, R. (Rotherham U), 1971 v Fi (1)

Millership, H. (Rotherham Co), 1920 v E, S, Ni; 1921 v E, S, Ni (6)

Millington, A. H. (WBA), 1963 v S, E, H; (with C Palace), 1965 v E, USSR; (with Peterborough U), 1966 v Ch, Br; 1967 v E, Ni; 1968 v Ni, WG; 1969 v I, EG; (with Swansea) 1970 v E, S, Ni; 1971 v Cz, Fi; 1972 v Fi (sub), Cz, R (21)

Mills, T. J. (Clapton Orient), 1934 v E, Ni; (with Leicester C), 1935 v E, S (4)

Mills-Roberts, R. H. (St Thomas' Hospital), 1885 v E, S, Ni; 1886 v E; 1887 v E; (with Preston NE), 1888 v E, Ni; (with Llanberis), 1892 v E (8)

Moore, G. (Cardiff C), 1960 v E, S, Ni; 1961 v Ei, Sp; (with Chelsea), 1962 v Br; 1963 v Ni, H; (with Manchester U), 1964 v S, Ni; (with Northampton T), 1966 v Ni, Ch; (with Charlton Ath), 1969 v S, E, Ni, R of UK; 1970 v E, S, Ni, I; 1971 v R (21)

Morgan, J. R. (Cambridge University), 1877 v S; (with Swansea), 1879 v S; (with Derby School Staff), 1880 v E, S; 1881 v E, S; 1882 v E, S, Ni; (with Swansea), 1883 v E (10)

Morgan, J. T. (Wrexham), 1905 v Ni (1)

Morgan-Owen, H. (Oxford University), 1901 v E, S; 1902 v S; 1906 v E, Ni; (with Welshpool), 1907 v S (6)

Morgan-Owen, M. M. (Oxford University), 1897 v S, Ni; 1898 v E, S; 1899 v S; 1900 v E; (with Corinthians), 1903 v S; 1906 v S, E, Ni; 1907 v E (11)

Morley, E. J. (Swansea T), 1925 v E; (with Clapton Orient), 1929 v E, S, Ni (4)

Morris, A. G. (Aberystwyth), 1896 v E, Ni, S; (with Swindon T), 1897 v E; 1898 v S; (with Nottingham F), 1899 v E, S; 1903 v E, S; 1905 v E, S; 1907 v E, S; 1908 v E; 1910 v E, S, Ni; 1911 v E, S, Ni; 1912 v E (21)

Morris, C. (Chirk), 1900 v E, S, Ni; (with Derby Co), 1901 v E, S, Ni; 1902 v E, S; 1903 v E, S, Ni; 1904 v Ni; 1905 v E, S, Ni; 1906 v S; 1907 v S; 1908 v E, S; 1909 v E, S, Ni; 1910 v E, S, Ni; (with Huddersfield T), 1911 v E, S, Ni (28)

Morris, E. (Chirk), 1893 v E, S, Ni (3)

Morris, H. (Sheffield U), 1894 v S; (with Manchester C), 1896 v E; (with Grimsby T), 1897 v E (3)

Morris, J. (Oswestry), 1887 v S (1)

Morris, J. (Chirk), 1898 v Ni (1)

Morris, R. (Chirk), 1900 v E, Ni; 1901 v Ni; 1902 v S; (with Shrewsbury T), 1903 v E, Ni (6)

Morris, R. (Druids), 1902 v E, S; (with Newtown), 1902 v Ni; (with Liverpool), 1903 v S, Ni; 1904 v E, S, Ni; (with Leeds C), 1906 v S; (with Grimsby T), 1907 v Ni; (with Plymouth Arg), 1908 v Ni (11)

Morris, S. (Birmingham), 1937 v E, S; 1938 v E, S; 1939 v F (5)

Morris, W. (Burnley), 1947 v Ni; 1949 v E; 1952 v S, Ni, R of UK (5)

Moulsdale, J. R. B. (Corinthians), 1925 v Ni (1)

Murphy, J. P. (WBA), 1933 v F, E, Ni; 1934 v E, S; 1935 v E, S, Ni; 1936 v E, S, Ni; 1937 v S, Ni; 1938 v E, S (15)

Nardiello, D. (Coventry C), 1978 v Cz, WG (sub) (2)

Neal, J. E. (Colwyn Bay), 1931 v E, S (2)

Newnes, J. (Nelson), 1926 v Ni (1)

Newton, L. F. (Cardiff Corinthians), 1912 v Ni (1)

Nicholas, D. S. (Stoke C), 1923 v S; (with Swansea T), 1927 v E, Ni (3)

Nicholas, P. (C Palace), 1979 v S (sub), Ni (sub), Ma; 1980 v Ei, WG, T, E, S, Ni, Ic; 1981 v T, Cz, E; (with Arsenal), T, S, E, USSR; 1982 v Cz, Ic, USSR, Sp, E, S, Ni, F (25)

Nicholls, J. (Newport Co), 1924 v E, Ni; (with Cardiff C), 1925 v E, S (4)

Nock, W. (Newtown), 1897 v Ni (1)

Nurse, M. T. G. (Swansea T), 1960 v E, Ni; 1961 v S, E, H, Ni, Ei, Sp (2); (with Middlesbrough), 1963 v E, H; 1964 v S (12)

O'Callaghan, E. (Tottenham H), 1929 v Ni; 1930 v S; 1932 v S, E; 1933 v Ni, S, E; 1934 v Ni, S, E; 1935 v E (11)

Oliver, A. (Blackburn R), 1905 v E; (with Bangor), S (2)

O'Sullivan, P. A. (Brighton), 1973 v S (sub); 1976 v S; 1979 v Ma (sub) (3)

Owen, D. (Oswestry), 1879 v E (1)

Owen, E. (Ruthin Grammar School), 1884 v E, Ni, S (3)

Owen, G. (Chirk), 1888 v S; (with Newton Heath), 1889 v S, Ni; 1892 v E; 1893 v Ni (5)

Owen, T (Oswestry), 1879 v E (1)

Owen, Trevor (Crewe Alex), 1899 v E, S (2)

Owen, W. (Chirk), 1884 v E; 1885 v Ni; 1887 v E; 1888 v E; 1889 v E, Ni, S; 1890 v S, Ni; 1891 v E, S, Ni; 1892 v E, S; 1893 v S, Ni (16)

Owen, W. P. (Ruthin), 1880 v E, S; 1881 v E, S; 1882 v E, S, Ni; 1883 v E, S; 1884 v E, S, Ni (12)

Owens, J. (Wrexham), 1902 v S (1)

Page, M. E. (Birmingham C), 1971 v Fi; 1972 v S, Ni; 1973 v E (1 + 1 sub), Ni; 1974 v S, Ni; 1975 v H, L, S, E, Ni; 1976 v E, Y (2), E, Ni; 1977 v WG, S; 1978 v K (sub + 1), WG, Ir, E, S; 1979 v Ma, WG (28)

Palmer, D. (Swansea T), 1957 v Cz; 1958 v E, EG (3)

Parris, J. E. (Bradford), 1932 v Ni (1)

Parry, B. J. (Swansea T), 1951 v S (1)

Parry, C. (Everton), 1891 v E, S; 1893 v E; 1894 v E; 1895 v E, S; (with Newtown), 1896 v E, S, Ni; 1897 v Ni; 1898 v E, S, Ni (13)

Parry, E. (Liverpool), 1922 v S; 1923 v E, Ni; 1925 v Ni; 1926 v Ni (5)

Parry, H. (Newtown), 1895 v Ni (1)

Parry, M. (Liverpool), 1901 v E, S, Ni; 1902 v E, S, Ni; 1903 v E, S; 1904 v E, Ni; 1906 v E; 1908 v E, S, Ni; 1909 v E, S (16)

Parry, T. D. (Oswestry), 1900 v E, S, Ni; 1901 v E, S, Ni; 1902 v E (7)

Paul, R. (Swansea T), 1949 v E, S, Ni, P, Sw; 1950 v E, S, Ni, Bel; (with Manchester C), 1951 v S, E, Ni, P, Sw; 1952 v E, S, Ni, R of UK; 1953 v S, E, Ni, H, F, Y; 1954 v E, S, Ni; 1955 v S, E, Y; 1956 v E, Ni, S, A (33)

Peake, E. (Aberystwyth), 1908 v Ni; (with Liverpool), 1909 v Ni, S, E; 1910 v S, Ni; 1911 v Ni; 1912 v E; 1913 v E, Ni; 1914 v Ni (11)

Peers, E. J. (Wolverhampton W), 1914 v Ni, S, E; 1920 v E, S; 1921 v S, Ni, E; (with Port Vale), 1922 v E, S, Ni; 1923 v E (12)

Perry, E. (Doncaster R), 1938 v E, S, Ni (3)

Phennah, E. (Civil Service), 1878 v S (1)

Phillips, C. (Wolverhampton W), 1931 v Ni; 1932 v E; 1933 v S; 1934 v E, S, Ni; 1935 v E, S, Ni; 1936 v S; (with Aston Villa), 1936 v E, Ni; 1938 v S (13)

Phillips, L. (Cardiff C), 1971 v Cz, S, E, Ni; 1972 v Cz, R, S, Ni; 1973 v E; 1974 v Pol (sub), Ni; 1975 v A; (with Aston Villa), H (2), L (2), S, E, Ni; 1976 v A, E, Y (2), E, Ni; 1977 v WG, S (2), Cz, E; 1978 v K (2), S, Cz, WG, E, S; 1979 v Ma; (Swansea C), T, WG, S, E, Ni, Ma; 1980 v Ei, WG, T, S (sub), Ni, Ic; 1981 v T, Cz, T, S, E, USSR; (with Charlton Ath), 1982 v Cz, USSR (58)

Phillips, T. J. S. (Chelsea), 1973 v E; 1974 v E; 1975 v H (sub); 1978 v K (4)

Phoenix, H. (Wrexham), 1882 v S (1)

Poland, G. (Wrexham), 1939 v Ni, F (2)

Pontin, K. (Cardiff C), 1980 v E (sub), S (2)

Powell, A. (Leeds U), 1947 v E, S; 1948 v E, S, Ni; (with Everton), 1949 v E; 1950 v Bel; (with Birmingham C), 1951 v S (8)

Powell, D. (Wrexham), 1968 v WG; (with Sheffield U), 1969 v S, E, Ni, I, WG; 1970 v E, S, Ni, EG; 1971 v R (11)

Powell, I. V. (QPR), 1947 v E; 1948 v E, S, Ni; (with Aston Villa), 1949 v Bel; 1950 v S, Bel; 1951 v S (8)

Powell, J. (Druids), 1878 v S; 1880 v E, S; 1882 v E, S, Ni; 1883 v E, S, Ni; (with Bolton W), 1884 v E; (with Newton Heath), 1887 v E, S; 1888 v E, S, Ni (15)

Powell, Seth (WBA), 1885 v S; 1886 v E, Ni; 1891 v E, S; 1892 v E, S (7)

Price, H. (Aston Villa), 1907 v S; (with Burton U), 1908 v Ni; (with Wrexham), 1909 v S, E, Ni (5)

Price, J. (Wrexham), 1877 v S; 1878 v S; 1879 v E; 1880 v E, S; 1881 v E, S; (with Druids), 1882 v S, E, Ni; 1883 v S, Ni (12)

Price, P. (Luton T), 1980 v E, S, Ni, Ic; 1981 v T, Cz, Ei, T, S, E, USSR; (with Tottenham H), 1982 v USSR, Sp, F (14)

Pring, K. D. (Rotherham U), 1966 v Ch, D; 1967 v Ni (3)

Pryce-Jones, A. W. (Newtown), 1895 v E (1)

Pryce-Jones, W. E. (Cambridge University), 1887 v S; 1888 v S, E, Ni; 1890 v Ni (5)

Pugh, A. (Rhostyllen), 1889 v S (sub) (1)

Pugh, D. H. (Wrexham), 1896 v S, Ni; 1897 v S, Ni; (with Lincoln C), 1900 v S; 1901 v S, E (7)

Pugsley, J. (Charlton Ath), 1930 v Ni (1)

Pullen, W. J. (Plymouth Arg), 1926 v E (1)

Rankmore, F. E. J. (Peterborough), 1966 v Ch (sub) (1)

Ratcliffe, K. (Everton), 1981 v Cz, Ei, T, S, E, USSR; 1982 v Cz, Ic, USSR, Sp, E (11)

Rea, J. C. (Aberystwyth), 1894 v Ni, S, E; 1895 v S; 1896 v S, Ni; 1897 v S, Ni; 1898 v Ni (9)

Reece, G. I. (Sheffield U), 1966 v E, S, Ni, USSR; 1967 v S; 1969 v R of UK (sub); 1970 v I (sub); 1971 v S, E, Ni, Fi; 1972 v Fi, R, E (sub), S, Ni; (with Cardiff C), 1973 v E (sub), Ni; 1974 v Pol (sub), E, S, Ni; 1975 v A, H (2), L (2), S, Ni (29)

Reed, W. G. (Ipswich T), 1955 v S, Y (2)

Rees, R. R. (Coventry C), 1965 v S, E, Ni, D, Gr (2), I, R; 1966 v E, S, Ni, R, D, Br (2), Ch; 1967 v E, Ni; 1968 v E, S, Ni; (with WBA), WG; 1969 v I; (with Nottingham F), 1969 v WG, EG, S (sub), R of UK; 1970 v E, S, Ni, EG, I; 1971 v Cz, R, E (sub), Ni (sub), Fi; 1972 v Cz (sub), R (39)

Rees, W. (Cardiff C), 1949 v Ni, Bel, Sw; (with Tottenham H), 1950 v Ni (4)

Richards, A. (Barnsley), 1932 v S (1)

Richards, D. (Wolverhampton W), 1931 v Ni; 1933 v E, S, Ni; 1934 v E, S, Ni; 1935 v E, S, Ni; 1936 v S; (with Brentford), 1936 v E, Ni; 1937 v S, E; (with Birmingham), 1937 v Ni; 1938 v E, S, Ni; 1939 v E, S (21)

Richards, G. (Druids), 1899 v E, S, Ni; (with Oswestry), 1903 v Ni; (with Shrewsbury), 1904 v S; 1905 v Ni (6)

Richards, R. W. (Wolverhampton W), 1920 v E, S; 1921 v Ni; 1922 v E, S; (with West Ham U), 1924 v E, S, Ni; (with Mold), 1926 v S (9)

Richards, S. V. (Cardiff C), 1947 v E (1)

Richards, W. E. (Fulham), 1933 v Ni (1)

Roach, J. (Oswestry), 1885 v Ni (1)

Robbins, W. W. (Cardiff C), 1931 v E, S; 1932 v Ni, E, S; (with WBA), 1933 v F, E, S, Ni; 1934 v S; 1936 v S (11)

Roberts, D. F. (Oxford U), 1973 v Pol, E (sub), Ni; 1974 v E, S; 1975 v A; (with Hull C), L, Ni; 1976 v S, Ni, Y; 1977 v E (sub), Ni; 1978 v K (1 + sub), S, Ni (18)

Roberts, J. G. (Arsenal), 1971 v S, E, Ni, Fi; 1972 v Fi, E, Ni; (with Birmingham C), 1973 v E (2), Pol, S, Ni; 1974 v Pol, E, S, Ni; 1975 v A, H, S, E; 1976 v E, S (22)

Roberts, J. H. (Bolton), 1949 v Bel (1)

Roberts, J. (Corwen), 1879 v S; 1880 v E, S; 1882 v E, S, Ni; (with Berwyn R), 1883 v E (7)

Roberts, J. (Ruthin), 1881 v S; 1882 v S (2)
Roberts, J. (Bradford C), 1906 v Ni; 1907 v Ni (2)
Roberts, Jas. (Chirk), 1898 v S (1)
Roberts, Jas (Wrexham), 1913 v S, Ni (2)
Roberts, P. S. (Portsmouth), 1974 v E; 1975 v A, H, L (4)
Roberts, R. (Rhos), 1891 v Ni; (with Crewe Alex), 1893 v E (2)
Roberts, R. (Druids), 1884 v S; (with Bolton W), 1887 v S; 1888 v S, E; 1889 v S, E; 1890 v S; 1892 v Ni; (with PNE), S (9)
Roberts, R. (Wrexham), 1886 v Ni; 1887 v Ni; 1891 v Ni (3)
Roberts, W. (Llangollen), 1879 v E, S; 1880 v E, S; (with Berwyn R), 1881 v S; 1883 v E, S (7)
Roberts, W. (Wrexham), 1886 v E, S, Ni; 1887 v Ni (4)
Roberts, W. H. (Ruthin), 1882 v E, S; 1883 v E, S, Ni; (with Rhyl), 1884 v S (6)
Rodrigues, P. J. (Cardiff C), 1965 v Ni, Gr (2); 1966 v USSR, E, S, D; (with Leicester C), v Ni, Br (2), Ch; 1967 v S; 1968 v E, S, Ni; 1969 v E, Ni, EG, R of UK; 1970 v E, S, Ni, EG; (with Sheffield W), 1971 v R, E, S, Cz, Ni; 1972 v Fi, Cz, R, E, Ni (sub); 1973 v E (3), Pol, S, Ni; 1974 v Pol (40)
Rogers, J. P. (Wrexham), 1896 v E, S, Ni (3)
Rogers, W. (Wrexham), 1931 v E, S (2)
Roose, L. R. (Aberystwyth), 1900 v Ni; (with London Welsh), 1901 v E, S, Ni; (with Stoke C), 1902 v E, S; 1904 v E; (with Everton), 1905 v S, E; (with Stoke C), 1906 v E, S, Ni; 1907 v E, S, Ni; (with Sunderland), 1908 v E, S; 1909 v E, S, Ni; 1910 v E, S, Ni; 1911 v S (24)
Rouse, R. V. (C Palace), 1959 v Ni (1)
Rowlands, A. C. (Tranmere R), 1914 v E (1)
Rowley, T. (Tranmere R), 1959 v Ni (1)
Rush, I. (Liverpool), 1980 v S (sub), Ni; 1981 v E (sub); 1982 v Ic (sub), USSR, E, S, Ni, F (9)
Russell, M. R. (Merthyr T), 1912 v S, Ni; 1914 v E; (with Plymouth Arg), 1920 v E, S, Ni; 1921 v E, S, Ni; 1922 v E, Ni; 1923 v E, S, Ni; 1924 v E, S, Ni; 1925 v E, S; 1926 v E, S; 1928 v S; 1929 v E (23)


Sabine, H. W. (Oswestry), 1887 v Ni (1)
Savin, G. (Oswestry), 1878 v S (1)
Sayer, P. (Cardiff C), 1977 v Cz, S, E, Ni; 1978 v K (2), S (7)
Scrine, F. H. (Swansea T), 1950 v E, Ni (2)
Sear, C. R. (Manchester C), 1963 v E (1)
Shaw, E. G. (Oswestry), 1882 v Ni; 1884 v S, Ni (3)
Sherwood, A. T. (Cardiff C), 1947 v E, Ni; 1948 v S, Ni; 1949 v E, S, Ni, P, Sw; 1950 v E, S, Ni, Bel; 1951 v E, S, Ni, P, Sw; 1952 v E, S, Ni, R of UK; 1953 v S, E, Ni, F, Y; 1954 v E, S, Ni, A; 1955 v S, E, Y, Ni; 1956 v E, S, Ni, A; (with Newport Co), 1957 v E, S (41)
Shone, W. W. (Oswestry), 1879 v E (1)
Shortt, W. W. (Plymouth Arg), 1947 v Ni; 1950 v Ni, Bel; 1952 v E, S, Ni, R of UK; 1953 v S, E, Ni, F, Y (12)
Showers, D. (Cardiff C), 1975 v E (sub), Ni (2)
Sidlow, C. (Liverpool), 1947 v E, S; 1948 v E, S, Ni; 1949 v S; 1950 v E (7)
Sisson, H. (Wrexham Olympic), 1885 v Ni; 1886 v S, Ni (3)
Smallman, D. P. (Wrexham), 1974 v E (sub), S (sub), Ni; (with Everton), 1975 v H (sub), E, Ni (sub); 1976 v A (7)
Southall, N. (Everton), 1982 v Ni (1)
Sprake, G. (Leeds U), 1964 v S, Ni; 1965 v S, D, Gr; 1966 v E, Ni, USSR; 1967 v S; 1968 v E, S; 1969 v S, E, Ni, WG, R of UK; 1970 v EG, I; 1971 v R, S, E, Ni; 1972 v Fi, E, S, Ni; 1973 v E (2), Pol, S, Ni; 1974 v Pol; (with Birmingham C), S, Ni; 1975 v A, H, L (37)
Stansfield, F. (Cardiff C), 1949 v S (1)
Stevenson, B. (Leeds U), 1978 v Ni; 1979 v Ma, T, S, E, Ni, Ma; 1980 v WG, T, Ic (sub); 1982 v Cz; (with Birmingham C), Sp, S, Ni, F (15)
Stevenson, N. (Swansea C), 1982 v E, S, Ni (3)
Stitfall, R. F. (Cardiff C), 1953 v E; 1957 v Cz(2)

Sullivan, D. (Cardiff C), 1953 v Ni, F, Y; 1954 v Ni; 1955 v E, Ni; 1957 v E, S; 1958 v Ni, H (2), Se, Br; 1959 v S, Ni; 1960 v E, S (17)

Tapscott, D. R. (Arsenal), 1954 v A; 1955 v S, E, Ni, Y; 1956 v E, Ni, S, A; 1957 v Ni, Cz, EG; (with Cardiff C), 1959 v E, Ni (14)
Taylor, J. (Wrexham), 1898 v E (1)
Taylor, O. D. S. (Newtown), 1893 v S, Ni; 1894 v S, Ni (4)
Thomas, C. (Druids), 1899 v Ni; 1900 v S (2)
Thomas, D. A. (Swansea T), 1957 v Cz; 1958 v EG (2)
Thomas, D. S. (Fulham), 1948 v E, S, Ni; 1949 v S (4)
Thomas, E. (Cardiff Corinthians), 1925 v E (1)
Thomas, G. (Wrexham), 1885 v E, S (2)
Thomas, H. (Manchester U), 1927 v E (1)
Thomas, M. (Wrexham), 1977 v WG, S (1 + 1 sub), Ni (sub); 1978 v K (sub), S, Cz, Ir, E, Ni (sub); 1979 v Ma; (with Manchester U), T, WG, Ma (sub); 1980 v Ei, WG (sub), T, E, S, Ni; 1981 v Cz, S, E, USSR; (with Everton), 1982 v Cz; (with Brighton & HA), USSR (sub), Sp, E, S (sub), Ni (sub) (30)
Thomas, R. J. (Swindon T), 1967 v Ni; 1968 v WG; 1969 v E, Ni, I, WG, R of UK; 1970 v E, S, Ni, EG, I; 1971 v S, E, Ni, R, Cz; 1972 v Fi, Cz, R, E, S, Ni; 1973 v E (3), Pol, S, Ni; 1974 v Pol; (with Derby Co), E, S, Ni; 1975 v H (2), L (2), S, E, Ni; 1976 v A, Y, E; 1977 v Cz, S, E, Ni; 1978 v K, S; (with Cardiff C), Cz (50)
Thomas, T. (Bangor), 1898 v S, Ni (2)
Thomas, W. R. (Newport Co), 1931 v E, S (2)
Thomson, D. (Druids), 1876 v S (1)
Thomson, G. F. (Druids), 1876 v S; 1877 v S (2)
Toshack, J. B. (Cardiff C), 1969 v S, E, Ni, WG, EG, R of UK; 1970 v EG, I; (with Liverpool), 1971 v S, E, Ni, Fi; 1972 v Fi, E; 1973 v E (3), Pol, S; 1975 v A, H (2), L (2), S, E; 1976 v Y (2), E; 1977 v S; 1978 v K (2), S, Cz; (Swansea C), 1979 v WG (sub), S, E, Ni, Ma; 1980 v WG (40)
Townsend, W. (Newtown), 1887 v Ni; 1893 v Ni (2)
Trainer, H. (Wrexham), 1895 v E, S, Ni (3)
Trainer, J. (Bolton W), 1887 v S; (with Preston NE), 1888 v S; 1889 v E; 1890 v S; 1891 v S; 1892 v Ni, S; 1893 v E; 1894 v Ni, E; 1895 v Ni, E; 1896 v S; 1897 v Ni, S, E; 1898 v S, E; 1899 v Ni, S (20)
Turner, H. G. (Charlton Ath), 1937 v E, S, Ni; 1938 v E, S, Ni; 1939 v Ni, F (8)
Turner, J. (Wrexham), 1892 v E (1)
Turner, R. E. (Wrexham), 1891 v E, Ni (2)
Turner, W. H. (Wrexham), 1887 v E, Ni; 1890 v S; 1891 v E, S (5)

Vaughan, Jas (Druids), 1893 v E, S, Ni; 1899 v E (4)
Vaughan, John (Oswestry), 1879 v S; 1880 v S; 1881 v E, S; 1882 v E, S, Ni; 1883 v E, S, Ni; (with Bolton W), 1884 v E (11)
Vaughan, J. O. (Rhyl), 1885 v Ni; 1886 v Ni, E, S (4)
Vaughan, T. (Rhyl), 1885 v E (1)
Vearncombe, G. (Cardiff C), 1958 v EG; 1961 v Ei (2)
Vernon, T. R. (Blackburn R), 1957 v Ni, Cz (2), EG; 1958 v E, S, EG, Se; 1959 v S; (with Everton), 1960 v Ni; 1961 v S, E, Ei; 1962 v Ni, Br (2), M; 1963 v S, E, H; 1964 v E, S; (with Stoke C), 1965 v Ni, Gr, I; 1966 v E, S, Ni, USSR, D; 1967 v Ni; 1968 v E (32)
Villars, A. K. (Cardiff C), 1974 v E, S, Ni (sub) (3)
Vizard, E. T. (Bolton W), 1911 v E, S, Ni; 1912 v E, S; 1913 v S; 1914 v E, Ni; 1920 v E; 1921 v E, S, Ni; 1922 v E, S; 1923 v E, Ni; 1924 v E, S, Ni; 1926 v E, S; 1927 v S (22)

Walley, J. T. (Watford), 1971 v Cz (1)
Walsh, I. (C Palace), 1980 v Ei, T, E, S, Ic; 1981 v T, Cz, Ei, T, S, E, USSR; 1982 v Cz (sub), Ic; (with Swansea C), Sp, S (sub), Ni (sub), F (18)
Ward, D. (Bristol R), 1959 v E; (with Cardiff C), 1962 v E (2)

Warner, J. (Swansea T), 1937 v E; (with Manchester U), 1939 v F (2)

Warren, F. W. (Cardiff C), 1929 v Ni; (with Middlesbrough), 1931 v Ni; 1933 v F, E; (with Hearts), 1937 v Ni; 1938 v Ni (6)

Watkins, A. E. (Leicester Fosse), 1898 v E, S; (with Aston Villa), 1900 v E, S; (with Millwall), 1904 v Ni (5)

Watkins, W. M. (Stoke C), 1902 v E; 1903 v E, S; (with Aston Villa); 1904 v E, S, Ni; (with Sunderland), 1905 v E, S, Ni; (with Stoke C), 1908 v Ni (10)

Webster, C (Manchester U), 1957 v Cz; 1958 v H, M, Br (4)

Whatley, W. J. (Tottenham H), 1939 v E, S (2)

White, P. F. (London Welsh), 1896 v Ni (1)

Wilcocks, A. R. (Oswestry), 1890 v Ni (1)

Wilding, J. (Wrexham O), 1885 v E, S, Ni; 1886 v E, Ni; (with Bootle), 1887 v E; 1888 v S, Ni; (with Wrexham), 1892 v S (9)

Williams, A. L. (Wrexham), 1931 v E (1)

Williams, B. D. (Swansea T), 1928 v Ni, E; 1930 v E, S; (with Everton), 1931 v Ni; 1932 v E; 1933 v E, S, Ni; 1935 v Ni (10)

Williams, B. (Bristol C), 1930 v Ni (1)

Williams, D. R. (Merthyr T), 1921 v E, S; (with Sheffield W), 1923 v S; 1926 v S; 1927 v E, Ni; (with Manchester U), 1929 v E, S (8)

Williams, E. (Crewe Alex), 1893 v E, S (2)

Williams, E. (Druids), 1901 v E, Ni, S; 1902 v E, Ni (5)

Williams, G. (Chirk), 1893 v S; 1894 v S; 1895 v E, S, Ni; 1898 v Ni (6)

Williams, G. E. (WBA), 1960 v Ni; 1961 v S, E, Ei; 1963 v Ni, H; 1964 v E, S, Ni; 1965 v S, E, Ni, D, Gr (2), USSR, I; 1966 v Ni, Br (2), Ch; 1967 v S, E, Ni; 1968 v Ni; 1969 v I (26)

Williams, G. G. (Swansea T), 1961 v Ni, H, Sp (2); 1962 v E (5)

Williams, G. J. J. (Cardiff C), 1951 v Sw (1)

Williams, G. O. (Wrexham), 1907 v Ni (1)

Williams, H. J. (Swansea), 1965 v Gr (2); 1972 v R (3)

Williams, H. T. (Newport Co), 1949 v Ni, Sw; (with Leeds U), 1950 v Ni; 1951 v S (4)

Williams, J. H. (Oswestry), 1884 v E (1)

Williams, J. T. (Wrexham), 1939 v F (1)

Williams J. T. (Middlesbrough), 1925 v Ni (1)

Williams, J. W. (C Palace), 1912 v S, Ni (2)

Williams, R. (Newcastle U), 1935 v S, E (2)

Williams, R. P. (Caernarvon), 1886 v S (1)

Williams, S. G. (WBA), 1954 v A; 1955 v E, Ni; 1956 v E, S, A; 1958 v E, S, Ni, Is (2), H (2), M, Se, Br; 1959 v E, S, Ni; 1960 v E, S, Ni; 1961 v Ni, Ei, H, Sp (2); 1962 v E, S, Ni, Br (2), M; (with Southampton), 1963 v S, E, H (2); 1964 v E, S; 1965 v S, E, D; 1966 v D (43)

Williams, W. (Druids), 1876 v S; 1878 v S; (with Oswestry), 1879 v E, S; (with Druids), 1880 v E, S; 1881 v E, S; 1882 v E, S, Ni; 1883 v Ni (12)

Williams, W. (Northampton T), 1925 v S (1)

Witcomb, D. F. (WBA), 1947 v E, S; (with Sheffield W), 1947 v Ni (3)

Woosnam, A. P. (Leyton Orient), 1959 v S; (with West Ham U), v E; 1960 v E, S, Ni; 1961 v S, E, Ni, Ei, Sp, H; 1962 v E, S, Ni, Br; (with Aston Villa), 1963 v Ni, H (17)

Woosnam, G. (Newton White Star), 1879 v S (1)

Worthington, T. (Newtown), 1894 v S (1)

Wynn, G. A. (Chirk), 1903 v Ni; (with Wrexham), 1909 v E, S, Ni; (with Manchester C), 1910 v E; 1911 v Ni; 1912 v E, S; 1913 v E, S; 1914 v E, S (12)

Yorath, T. C. (Leeds U), 1970 v I; 1971 v S, E, Ni; 1972 v Cz, E, S, Ni; 1973 v E, Pol, S; 1974 v Pol, E, S, Ni; 1975 v A, H (2), L (2), S; 1976 v A, E, S, Y (2), E, Ni; (with Coventry C), 1977 v WG, S (2), Cz, E, Ni; 1978 v K (2), S, Cz, WG, Ir, E, S, Ni; 1979 v T, WG, S, E, Ni; (with Tottenham H),

1980 v Ei, T, E, S, Ni, Ic; 1981 v T, Cz; (with Vancouver W), Ei, T, USSR (59)


# REPUBLIC OF IRELAND

Aherne, T. (Belfast Celtic), 1946 v P, Sp; (with Luton T), 1950 v Fi, E, Fi, Se, Bel; 1951 v N, Arg, N; 1952 v WG (2), A, Sp; 1953 v F; 1954 v F (16)

Ambrose, P. (Shamrock R), 1955 v N, Ho; 1964 v Pol, N, E (5)

Anderson, J. (Preston NE), 1980 v Cz (sub), US (sub); 1982 v Ch, Br, Tr (5)

Andrews, P. (Bohemians), 1936 v Ho (1)

Arrigan, T. (Waterford), 1938 v N (1)

Bailham, E. (Shamrock R), 1964 v E (1)

Barber, E. (Shelbourne), 1966 v Sp; (with Birmingham C), 1966 v Bel (2)

Barry, P. (Fordsons), 1928 v Bel; 1929 v Bel (2)

Bermingham, J. (Bohemians), 1929 v Bel (1)

Bermingham, P. (St James' Gate), 1935 v H (1)

Braddish, S. (Dundalk), 1978 v Pol (1)

Bonner, P. (Celtic), 1981 v Pol; 1982 v Alg (2)

Bradshaw, P. (St James' Gate), 1939 v Sw, Pol, H (2), G (5)

Brady, F. (Fordsons), 1926 v I; 1927 v I (2)

Brady, T. R. (QPR), 1964 v A (2), Sp (2), Pol, N (6)

Brady, W. L. (Arsenal), 1975 v USSR, T, Sw, USSR, Sw; 1976 v T, N, Pol; 1977 v E, T, F (2), Sp, Bul; 1978 v Bul, N; 1979 v Ni, E, D, Bul, WG, Arg; 1980 v W, Bul, E, Cy; (with Juventus), 1981 v Ho, Bel, F, Cy, Bel; 1982 v Ho, F, Ch, Br, Tr (36)

Breen, T. (Manchester U), 1937 v Sw, F; (with Shamrock R), 1947 v E, Sp, P (5)

Brennan, F. (Drumcondra), 1965 v Bel (1)

Brennan, S. A. (Manchester U), 1965 v Sp; 1966 v Sp, A, Bel; 1967 v Sp, T, Sp; 1969 v Cz, D, H; 1970 v S, Cz, D, H, Pol (sub), WG; (with Waterford), 1971 v Pol, Se, I (19)

Brown, J. (Coventry C), 1937 v Sw, F (2)

Browne, W. (Bohemians), 1964 v A, Sp, E (3)

Burke, F. (Cork), 1934 v Bel (1)

Burke, F. (Cork Ath), 1952 v WG (1)

Burke, J. (Shamrock R), 1929 v Bel (1)

Byrne, A. B. (Southampton), 1970 v D, Pol, WG; 1971 v Pol, Se (2), I (2), A; 1973 v F, USSR (sub), F, N; 1974 v Pol (14)

Byrne, D. (Shelbourne), 1929 v Bel; (with Shamrock R), 1932 v Sp; (with Coleraine), 1934 v Bel (3)

Byrne, J. (Bray Unknowns), 1928 v Bel (1)

Byrne, P. (Shelbourne), 1931 v Sp; 1932 v Ho; (with Drumcondra), 1934 v Ho (3)

Byrne, S. (Bohemians), 1931 v Sp (1)

Campbell, N. (St Patrick's Ath), 1971 v A (sub); (with Fortuna, Cologne), 1972 v Ir, Ec, Ch, P; 1973 v USSR, F (sub); 1976 v N; 1977 v Sp, Bul (sub) (10)

Cannon, H. (Bohemians), 1926 v I; 1928 v Bel (2)

Cantwell, N. (West Ham U), 1954 v L; 1956 v Sp, Ho; 1957 v D, WG, E (2); 1958 v D, Pol, A; 1959 v Pol, Cz (2); 1960 v Se, Ch, Se; 1961 v N; (with Manchester U), 1961 v S (2); 1962 v Cz (2), A; 1963 v Ic (2), S; 1964 v A, Sp, E; 1965 v Pol, Sp; 1966 v Sp (2), A, Bel; 1967 v Sp, T (36)

Carey, J. J. (Manchester U), 1938 v N, Cz, Pol; 1939 v Sw, Pol, H (2), G; 1946 v P, Sp; 1947 v E, Sp, P; 1948 v P, Sp; 1949 v Sw, Bel, P, Se, Sp; 1950 v Fi, E, Fi, Se; 1951 v N, Arg, N; 1953 v F, A (29)

Carolan, J. (Manchester U), 1960 v Se, Ch (2)

Carroll, B. (Shelbourne), 1949 v Bel; 1950 v Fi (2)

Flood, J. J. (Shamrock R), 1926 v I; 1929 v Bel; 1930 v Bel; 1931 v Sp; 1932 v Sp (5)

Fogarty, A. (Sunderland), 1960 v WG, Se; 1961 v S; 1962 v Cz (2); 1963 v Ic (2), S (sub); 1964 v A (2); (with Hartlepools U), Sp (11)

Foley, J. (Cork), 1934 v Bel, Ho; (with Celtic), 1935 v H, Sw, G; 1937 v G, H (7)

Foley, M. (Shelbourne), 1926 v I (1)

Foley, T. C. (Northampton T), 1964 v Sp, Pol, N; 1965 v Pol, Bel; 1966 v Sp (2), WG; 1967 v Cz (9)

Foy, T. (Shamrock R), 1938 v N; 1939 v H (2)

Fullam, J. (Preston NE), 1961 v N; (with Shamrock R), 1964 v Sp, Pol, N; 1966 v A, Bel; 1968 v Pol; 1969 v Pol, A, D; 1970 v Cz (sub) (11)

Fullam, R. (Shamrock R), 1926 v I; 1927 v I (2)


Gallagher, C. (Celtic), 1967 v T, Cz (2)

Gallagher, M. (Hibernian), 1954 v L (1)

Gallagher, P. (Falkirk), 1932 v Sp (1)

Gannon, E. (Notts Co), 1949 v Sw; (with Sheffield W), 1949 v Bel, P, Se, Sp; 1950 v Fi; 1951 v N; 1952 v G, A; 1954 v L, F; 1955 v N; (with Shelbourne), 1955 v N, WG (14)

Gannon, M. (Shelbourne), 1972 v A (1)

Gaskins, P. (Shamrock R), 1934 v Bel, Ho; 1935 v H, Sw, G; (with St James' Gate), 1938 v Cz, Pol (7)

Gavin, J. T. (Norwich C), 1950 v Fi (2); 1953 v F; 1954 v L; (with Tottenham H), 1955 v Ho, WG; (with Norwich C), 1957 v D (7)

Geoghegan, M. (St James' Gate), 1937 v G; 1938 v N (2)

Gibbons, A. (St Patrick's Ath), 1952 v WG; 1954 v L; 1956 v Y, Sp (4)

Gilbert, R. (Shamrock R), 1966 v WG (1)

Giles, C. (Doncaster R), 1951 v N (1)

Giles, M. J. (Manchester U), 1960 v Se, Ch; 1961 v W, N, S (2); 1962 v Cz (2), A; 1963 v Ic, S; (with Leeds U), 1964 v A (2), Sp (2), Pol, N, E; 1965 v Sp; 1966 v Sp (2), A, Bel; 1967 v Sp, T (2); 1969 v A, D, Cz; 1970 v S, Pol, WG; 1971 v I; 1973 v F, USSR; 1974 v Br, U, Ch; 1975 v USSR, T, Sw, USSR, Sw; (with WBA), 1976 v T; 1977 v E, T, F (2), Pol, Bul; (with Shamrock R), 1978 v Bul, T, Pol, N, D; 1979 v Ni, D, Bul, WG, Arg (60)

Givens, D. J. (Manchester U), 1969 v D, H; 1970 v S, Cz, D, H; (with Luton T), 1970 v Pol, WG; 1971 v Se, I (2), A; 1972 v Ir, Ec, P; (with QPR), 1973 v F, USSR, Pol, F, N; 1974 v Pol, Br, U, Cb; 1975 v USSR, T, Sw, USSR, Sw; 1976 v T, N, Pol; 1977 v E, T, F (2), Sp, Bul; 1978 v Bul, N, D; (with Birmingham C), 1979 v Ni (sub), E, D, Bul, WG, Arg; 1980 v US (sub), Ni (sub), Sw, Arg; 1981 v Ho, Bel, Cy (sub), W; (with Neuchatel X), 1982 v F (sub) (56)

Glen, W. (Shamrock R), 1927 v I; 1929 v Bel; 1930 v Bel; 1932 v Sp; 1936 v Ho, Sw, H, L (8)

Glynn, D. (Drumcondra), 1952 v WG; 1955 v N (2)

Godwin, T. F. (Shamrock R), 1949 v P, Se, Sp; 1950 v Fi, E; (with Leicester C), 1950 v Fi, Se, Bel; 1951 v N; (with Bournemouth & Boscombe Ath), 1956 v Ho; 1957 v E; 1958 v D, Pol (13)

Golding, L. (Shamrock R), 1928 v Bel; 1930 v Bel (2)

Gorman, W. C. (Bury), 1936 v Sw, H, L; 1937 v G, H; 1938 v N, Cz, Pol; 1939 v Sw, Pol, H; (with Brentford), 1947 v E, P (13)

Grace, J. (Drumcondra), 1926 v I (1)

Grealish, A. (Orient), 1976 v N, Pol, N, D; 1979 v Ni, E, WG, Arg; (with Luton T), 1980 v W, Cz, Bul, US, Ni, E, Cy, Sw, Arg; 1981 v Ho, Bel, F, Cy, W, Bel, WG 'B', Pol; (with Brighton & HA), 1982 v Ho, Alg, Ch, Br, Tr (30)

Gregg, E. (Bohemians), 1978 v Pol, D (sub); 1979 v E (sub), D, Bul, WG, Arg; 1980 v W, Cz (9)

Griffith, R. (Walsall), 1935 v H (1)

Grimes, A. A. (Manchester U), 1978 v T, Pol, N (sub); 1980 v Bul, US, Ni, E, Cy; 1981 v Cz, WG 'B' (sub), Pol; 1982 v Alg (12)


Hale, A. (Aston Villa), 1962 v A; (with Doncaster R), 1963 v Ic; 1964 v Sp (2); (with Waterford), 1967 v Sp; 1968 v Pol (sub); 1969 v Pol, A, D; 1970 v S, Cz; 1971 v Pol (sub); 1972 v A (sub) (13)

Hamilton, T. (Shamrock R), 1959 v Cz (2) (2)

Hand, E. K. (Portsmouth), 1969 v Cz (sub); 1970 v Pol, WG; 1971 v Pol, A; 1973 v USSR, F, USSR, Pol, F; 1974 v Pol, Br, U, Ch; 1975 v T, Sw, USSR, Sw; 1976 v T (19)

Harrington, W. (Cork), 1936 v Ho, Sw, H, L (4)

Hartnett, J. B. (Middlesbrough), 1949 v Sp; 1954 v L (2)

Haverty, J. (Arsenal), 1956 v Ho; 1957 v D, WG, E (2); 1958 v D, Pol, A; 1959 v Pol; 1960 v Se, Ch; 1961 v W, N, S (2); (with Blackburn R), 1962 v Cz (2); (with Millwall), 1963 v S; 1964 v A, Sp, Pol, N, E; (with Celtic), 1965 v Pol; (with Bristol R), 1965 v Sp; (with Shelbourne), 1966 v Sp (2), WG, A, Bel; 1967 v T, Sp (32)

Hayes, A. W. P. (Southampton), 1979 v D (1)

Hayes, W. E. (Huddersfield T), 1947 v E, P (2)

Hayes, W. J. (Limerick), 1949 v Bel (1)

Healey, R. (Cardiff C), 1977 v Pol; 1980 v E (sub) (2)

Heighway, S. D. (Liverpool), 1971 v Pol, Se (2), I, A; 1973 v USSR: 1975 v USSR, T, USSR; 1976 v T, N; 1977 v E, F (2), Sp, Bul; 1978 v Bul, N, D; 1979 v Ni, Bul; 1980 v Bul, US, Ni, E, Cy, Arg; 1981 v Bel, F, Cy, W, Bel; (with Minnesota K), 1982 v Ho (33)

Henderson, B. (Drumcondra), 1948 v P, Sp (2)

Hennessy, J. (Shelbourne), 1956 v Pol, B, Sp; 1966 v WG; (with St Patrick's Ath), 1969 v A (5)

Herrick, J. (Cork Hibernians), 1972 v A, Ch (sub); (with Shamrock R), 1973 v F (sub) (3)

Higgins, J. (Birmingham C), 1951 v Arg (1)

Holmes, J. (Coventry C), 1971 v A (sub); 1973 v F, USSR, Pol, F, N; 1974 v Pol, Br; 1975 v USSR, Sw; 1976 v T, N, Pol; 1977 v E, T, F, Sp; (with Tottenham H), F, Pol, Bul; 1978 v Bul, T, Pol, N, D; 1979 v Ni, E, D, Bul; 1981 (with Vancouver W), v W (30)

Horlecher, A. F. (Bohemians), 1930 v Bel; 1932 v Sp, Ho; 1935 v H; 1936 v Ho, Sw (6)

Hoy, M. (Dundalk), 1938 v N; 1939 v Sw, Pol, H (2), G (6)

Hughton, C. (Tottenham H), 1980 v US, E, Sw, Arg; 1981 v Ho, Bel, F, Cy, W, Bel, Pol; 1982 v F (12)

Hurley, C. J. (Millwall), 1957 v E; 1958 v D, Pol, A; (with Sunderland), 1959 v Cz (2); 1960 v Se, Ch,WG, Se; 1961 v W, N, S (2); 1962 v Cz (2), A; 1963 v Ic (2), S; 1964 v A (2), Sp (2), Pol, N; 1965 v Sp; 1966 v WG, A, Bel; 1967 v T, Sp, T, Cz; 1968 v Cz, Pol (2); (with Bolton W), 1969 v D, Cz, H (40)

Hutchinson, F. (Drumcondra), 1935 v Sw, G (2)


Jordan, D. (Wolverhampton W), 1937 v Sw, F (2)

Jordan, W. (Bohemians), 1934 v Ho; 1938 v N (2)


Kavanagh, P. J. (Celtic), 1931 v Sp; 1932 v Sp (2)

Keane, T. R. (Swansea T), 1949 v Sw, P, Se, Sp (4)

Kearin, M. (Shamrock R), 1972 v A (1)

Kearns, F. T. (West Ham U), 1954 v L (1)

Kearns, M. (Oxford U), 1970 v Pol (sub); (with Walsall), 1974 v Pol (sub), U, Ch; 1976 v N, Pol; 1977 v E, T, F (2), Sp, Bul; 1978 v N, D; 1979 v Ni, E; (with Wolverhampton W), 1980 v US, Ni (18)

Kelly, J. (Derry C), 1932 v Ho; 1934 v Bel; 1936 v Sw, L (4)

Kelly, J. A. (Drumcondra), 1957 v WG, E; (with Preston NE), 1962 v A; 1963 v Ic (2), S; 1964 v A (2), Sp (2),

Pol; 1965 v Bel; 1966 v A, Bel; 1967 v Sp (2), T, Cz (2), Pol; 1968 v Pol, A, D, Cz, D, H; 1970 v S, D, H, Pol, WG; 1971 v Pol, Se (2), I (2), A; 1972 v Ir, Ec, Ch, P; 1973 v USSR, F, USSR, Pol, F, N (47)

Kelly, J. P. V. (Wolverhampton W), 1961 v W, N, S; 1962 v Cz (2) (5)

Kelly, N. (Nottingham F), 1954 v L (1)

Kendrick, J. (Everton), 1927 v I; 1934 v Bel, Ho; 1936 v Ho (4)

Kennedy, W. (St James' Gate), 1932 v Ho; 1934 v Bel, Ho (3)

Keogh, J. (Shamrock R), 1966 v WG (sub) (1)

Keogh, S. (Shamrock R), 1959 v Pol (1)

Kiernan, F. W. (Shamrock R), 1951 v Arg, N; (with Southampton), 1952 v WG (2), A (5)

Kinnear, J. P. (Tottenham H), 1967 v T; 1968 v Cz, Pol; 1969 v A; 1970 v Cz, D, H, Pol; 1971 v Se (sub), I; 1972 v Ir, Ec, Ch, P; 1973 v USSR, F; 1974 v Pol, Br, U, Ch; 1975 v USSR, T, Sw, USSR; (with Brighton), 1976 v T (sub) (25)

Kinsella, J. (Shelbourne), 1928 v Bel (1)

Kinsella, P. (Shamrock R), 1932 v Ho; 1938 v N (2)

Kirkland, A. (Shamrock R), 1927 v I (1)

Lacey, W. (Shelbourne), 1927 v I; 1928 v Bel; 1930 v Bel (3)

Langan, D. (Derby Co), 1978 v T, N; 1980 v Sw, Arg; (with Birmingham C), 1981 v Ho, Bel, F, Cy, W, Bel, Cz, WG 'B', Pol; 1982 v Ho, F (15)

Lawler, J. F. (Fulham), 1953 v A; 1954 v L, F; 1955 v N, H, N, WG; 1956 v Y (8)

Lawlor, J. C. (Drumcondra), 1949 v Bel; (with Doncaster R), 1951 v N, Arg (3)

Lawlor, M. (Shamrock R), 1971 v Pol, Se (2), I (sub); 1973 v Pol (5)

Lawrenson, M. (Preston NE), 1977 v Pol; (with Brighton), 1978 v Bul, Pol, N (sub); 1979 v Ni, E; 1980 v E, Cy, Sw; 1981 v Ho, Bel, F, Cy, Pol; (with Liverpool), 1982 v Ho, F (16)

Leech, M. (Shamrock R), 1969 v Cz, D, H; 1972 v A, Ir, Ec, P; 1973 v USSR (sub) (8)

Lennon, C. (St James' Gate), 1935 v H, Sw, G (3)

Lennox, G. (Dolphin), 1931 v Sp; 1932 v Sp (2)

Lowry, D. (St Patrick's Ath), 1962 v A (sub) (1)

Lunn, R. (Dundalk), 1939 v Sw, Pol (2)

Lynch, J. (Cork Bohemians), 1934 v Bel (1)

McAlinden, J. (Portsmouth), 1946 v P, Sp (2)

McCann, J. (Shamrock R), 1957 v WG (1)

McCarthy, J. (Bohemians), 1926 v I; 1928 v Bel; 1930 v Bel (3)

McCarthy, M. (Shamrock R), 1932 v Ho (1)

McConville, T. (Dundalk), 1972 v A; (with Waterford), 1973 v USSR, F, USSR, Pol, F (6)

McDonagh, J. (Everton), 1981 v W, Bel, Cz, WG 'B'; (with Bolton W), 1982 v Ho, F, Ch, Br (8)

McEvoy, M. A. (Blackburn R), 1961 v S (2); 1963 v S; 1964 v A, Sp (2), Pol, N, E; 1965 v Pol, Bel, Sp; 1966 v Sp (2); 1967 v Sp, T, Cz (17)

McGee, P. (QPR), 1978 v T, N (sub), D (sub); 1979 v Ni, E, D (sub), Bul (sub), Arg (sub); 1980 v Cz, Bul; (with Preston NE), US, Ni, Cy, Sw, Arg; 1981 v Bel (sub) (16)

McGowan, D. (West Ham U), 1949 v P, Se, Sp (3)

McGowan, J. (Cork U), 1947 v Sp (1)

McGrath, M. (Blackburn R), 1958 v A; 1959 v Pol, Cz (2); 1960 v Se, WG, Se; 1961 v W; 1962 v C (2); 1963 v S; 1964 v A (2), E; 1965 v Pol, Bel, Sp; 1966 v Sp; (with Bradford), 1966 v WG, A, Bel; 1967 v T (22)

McGuire, W. (Bohemians), 1936 v Ho (1)

McKenzie, G. (Southend U), 1938 v N (2), Cz, Pol; 1939 v Sw, Pol, H (2), G (9)

Mackey, G. (Shamrock R), 1957 v D, WG, E (3)

McLoughlin, F. (Fordsons), 1930 v Bel; (with Cork), 1932 v Sp (2)

McMillan, W. (Belfast Celtic), 1946 v P, Sp (2)

McNally, J. B. (Luton T), 1959 v Cz; 1961 v Sp; 1963 v Ic (3)

Macken, A. (Derby Co), 1977 v Sp (1)

Madden, O. (Cork), 1936 v H (1)

Maguire, J. (Shamrock R), 1929 v Bel (1)

Malone, G. (Shelbourne), 1949 v Bel (1)

Mancini, T. J. (QPR), 1974 v Pol, Br, U, Ch; (with Arsenal), 1975 v USSR (5)

Martin, C. (Bo'ness), 1927 v I (1)

Martin, C. J. (Glentoran), 1946 v P (sub), Sp; 1947 v E; (with Leeds U), 1947 v Sp; 1948 v P, Sp; (with Aston Villa), 1949 v Sw, Bel, P, Se, Sp; 1950 v Fi, E, Fi, Se, Bel; 1951 v Arg; 1952 v WG, A, Sp; 1954 v F (2), L; 1955 v N, Ho, N, WG; 1956 v Y, Sp, Ho (30)

Martin, M. P. (Bohemians), 1972 v A, Ir, Ec, Ch, P; 1973 v USSR; (with Manchester U), 1973 v USSR, Pol, F, N; 1974 v Pol, Br, U, Ch; 1975 v USSR, T, Sw, USSR, Sw; (with WBA), 1976 v T, N, Pol; 1977 v E, T, F (2), Sp, Pol, Bul; (with Newcastle U), 1979 v D, Bul, WG, Arg; 1980 v W, Cz, Bul, US, Ni; 1981 v F, Bel, Cz, WG 'B'; 1982 v Ho, F, Alg, Ch, Br, Tr (48)

Meagan, M. K. (Everton), 1961 v S; 1962 v A; 1963 v Ic; 1964 v Sp; (with Huddersfield T), 1965 v Bel; 1966 v Sp (2), A, Bel; 1967 v Sp, T, Sp, T, Cz; 1968 v Cz, Pol; (with Drogheda), 1970 v S (17)

Meehan, P. (Drumcondra), 1934 v Ho (1)

Monahan, P. (Sligo R), 1935 v Sw, G (2)

Mooney, J. (Shamrock R), 1965 v Pol, Bel (2)

Moore, P. (Shamrock R), 1931 v Sp; 1932 v Ho; (with Aberdeen), 1934 v Bel, Ho; 1935 v H, G; (with Shamrock R), 1936 v Ho; 1937 v G, H (9)

Moran, K. (Manchester U), 1980 v Sw, Arg; 1981 v Bel, F, Cy, W (sub), Bel, Cz, WG 'B', Pol; 1982 v F, Alg (12)

Moroney, T. (West Ham U), 1948 v Sp; 1949 v P, Se, Sp; 1950 v Fi, E, Fi, Bel; 1951 v N (2); 1952 v WG; 1954 v F (12)

Moulson, C. (Lincoln C), 1936 v H, L; (with Notts Co), 1937 v H, Sw, F (5)

Moulson, G. B. (Lincoln C), 1948 v P, Sp; 1949 v Sw (3)

Mucklan, C. (Drogheda U), 1978 v Pol (1)

Muldoon, T. (Aston Villa), 1927 v I (1)

Mulligan, P. M. (Shamrock R), 1969 v Cz, D, H; 1970 v S, Cz, D; (with Chelsea), 1970 v H, Pol, WG; 1971 v Pol, Se, I; 1972 v A, Ir, Ec, Ch, P; 1973 v F, USSR, Pol, F, N; 1974 v Pol, Br, U, Ch; 1975 v USSR, T, Sw, USSR, Sw; (with WBA), 1976 v T, Pol; 1977 v E, T, F (2), Pol, Bul; 1978 v Bul, N, D; 1979 v E, D, Bul (sub), WG, Arg; (with Shamrock R) 1980 v W, Cz, Bul, US (sub) (51)

Munroe, L. (Shamrock R), 1954 v L (1)

Murphy, A. (Clyde), 1956 v Y (1)

Murphy, J. (C. Palace), 1980 v W, US, Cy (3)

Murray, T. (Dundalk), 1950 v Bel (1)

Newman, W. (Shelbourne), 1969 v D (1)

Nolan, R. (Shamrock R), 1957 v D, WG, E; 1958 v Pol; 1960 v Ch, WG, Se; 1962 v Cz (2); 1963 v Ic (10)

O'Brien, F. (Philadelphia F), 1980 v Cz, E, Cy (sub), Arg (4)

O'Brien, M. T. (Derby Co), 1927 v I; (with Walsall), 1929 v Bel; (with Norwich C), 1930 v Bel; (with Watford), 1932 v Ho (4)

O'Brien, R. (Notts Co), 1976 v N, Pol; 1977 v Sp, Pol (4)

O'Byrne, L. B. (Shamrock R), 1949 v Bel (1)

O'Callaghan, B. R. (Stoke C), 1979 v WG (sub), Arg (sub); 1980 v W, US; 1981 v W; 1982 v Br, Tr (7)

## EUROPEAN FOOTBALL CHAMPIONSHIP 1982–84 – FIXTURE LIST

**Preliminary Round**

**Group 1**

*Belgium, East Germany, Scotland, Switzerland*

| | |
|---|---|
| 6.10.82 | Belgium v Switzerland |
| 13.10.82 | Scotland v East Germany |
| 17.11.82 | Switzerland v Scotland |
| 15.12.82 | Belgium v Scotland |
| 30.3.83 | Scotland v Switzerland |
| 30.3.83 | East Germany v Belgium |
| 27.4.83 | Belgium v East Germany |
| 14.5.83 | Switzerland v East Germany |
| 12.10.83 | Scotland v Belgium |
| 12.10.83 | East Germany v Switzerland |
| 9.11.83 | Switzerland v Belgium |
| 16.11.83 | East Germany v Scotland |

**Group 2**

*Poland, USSR, Portugal, Finland*

| | |
|---|---|
| 8.9.82 | Finland v Poland |
| 22.9.82 | Finland v Portugal |
| 10.10.82 | Portugal v Poland |
| 13.10.82 | USSR v Finland |
| 17.4.83 | Poland v Finland |
| 22.5.83 | Poland v USSR |
| 1.6.83 | Finland v USSR |
| 21.9.83 | Portugal v Finland |
| 9.10.83 | USSR v Poland |
| 28.10.83 | Poland v Portugal |

**Group 3**

*England, Hungary, Greece, Denmark, Luxembourg*

| | |
|---|---|
| 22.9.82 | Denmark v England |
| 9.10.82 | Luxembourg v Greece |
| 10.11.82 | Luxembourg v Denmark |
| 17.11.82 | Greece v England |
| 15.12.82 | England v Luxembourg |
| 27.3.83 | Luxembourg v Hungary |
| 30.3.83 | England v Greece |
| 16.4.83 | Hungary v Luxembourg |
| 27.4.83 | England v Hungary |
| 27.4.83 | Denmark v Greece |
| 15.5.83 | Hungary v Greece |
| 1.6.83 | Denmark v Hungary |
| 21.9.83 | England v Denmark |
| 12.10.83 | Hungary v England |
| 12.10.83 | Denmark v Luxembourg |
| 26.10.83 | Hungary v Denmark |
| 16.11.83 | Greece v Denmark |
| 16.11.83 | Luxembourg v England |
| 3.12.83 | Greece v Hungary |
| 14.12.83 | Greece v Luxembourg |

**Group 4**

*Yugoslavia, Wales, Bulgaria, Norway*

| | |
|---|---|
| 22.9.82 | Wales v Norway |
| 13.10.82 | Norway v Yugoslavia |
| 27.10.82 | Bulgaria v Norway |
| 17.11.82 | Bulgaria v Yugoslavia |
| 15.12.82 | Yugoslavia v Wales |
| 27.4.83 | Wales v Bulgaria |
| 7.9.83 | Norway v Bulgaria |
| 21.9.83 | Norway v Wales |
| 12.10.83 | Yugoslavia v Norway |
| 16.11.83 | Bulgaria v Wales |
| 14.12.83 | Wales v Yugoslavia |
| 21.12.83 | Yugoslavia v Bulgaria |

**Group 5**

*Italy, Czechoslovakia, Rumania, Sweden, Cyprus*

| | |
|---|---|
| 1.5.82 | Rumania v Cyprus |
| 8.9.82 | Rumania v Sweden |
| 6.10.82 | Czechoslovakia v Sweden |
| 13.11.82 | Italy v Czechoslovakia |
| 13.11.82 | Cyprus v Sweden |
| 4.12.82 | Italy v Rumania |
| 12.2.83 | Cyprus v Italy |
| 27.3.83 | Cyprus v Czechoslovakia |
| 16.4.83 | Rumania v Italy |
| 16.4.83 | Czechoslovakia v Cyprus |
| 15.5.83 | Sweden v Cyprus |
| 15.5.83 | Rumania v Czechoslovakia |
| 26.5.83 | Sweden v Italy |
| 9.6.83 | Sweden v Rumania |
| 21.9.83 | Sweden v Czechoslovakia |
| 15.10.83 | Italy v Sweden |
| 12.11.83 | Cyprus v Rumania |
| 16.11.83 | Czechoslovakia v Italy |
| 30.11.83 | Czechoslovakia v Rumania |
| 22.12.83 | Italy v Cyprus |

**Group 6**

*West Germany, Austria, Northern Ireland, Turkey, Albania*

| | |
|---|---|
| 13.10.82 | Austria v Northern Ireland |
| 27.10.82 | Turkey v Albania |
| 17.11.82 | Northern Ireland v West Germany |
| 17.11.82 | Austria v Turkey |
| 15.12.82 | Albania v Northern Ireland |
| 30.3.83 | Northern Ireland v Turkey |
| 30.3.83 | Albania v West Germany |
| 23.4.83 | Turkey v West Germany |
| 27.4.83 | Austria v West Germany |
| 27.4.83 | Northern Ireland v Albania |
| 12.5.83 | Albania v Turkey |
| 21.9.83 | Northern Ireland v Austria |
| 5.10.83 | West Germany v Austria |
| 12.10.83 | Turkey v Northern Ireland |
| 26.10.83 | West Germany v Turkey |
| 16.11.83 | West Germany v Northern Ireland |
| 16.11.83 | Turkey v Austria |
| 20.11.83 | West Germany v Albania |

**Group 7**

*Spain, Netherlands, Eire, Iceland, Malta*

| | |
|---|---|
| 1.9.82 | Iceland v Netherlands |
| 22.9.82 | Netherlands v Eire |
| 13.10.82 | Eire v Iceland |
| 27.10.82 | Spain v Iceland |
| 17.11.82 | Eire v Spain |
| 19.12.82 | Malta v Netherlands |
| 16.2.83 | Spain v Netherlands |
| 27.4.83 | Spain v Eire |
| 15.5.83 | Malta v Spain |
| 29.5.83 | Iceland v Spain |
| 7.9.83 | Netherlands v Iceland |
| 21.9.83 | Iceland v Eire |
| 12.10.83 | Eire v Netherlands |
| 16.11.83 | Netherlands v Spain |
| 18.12.83 | Netherlands v Malta |
| 21.12.83 | Spain v Malta |

# ENGLAND INTERNATIONAL TEAMS
## 1872–1981
### Substitute in brackets † World Cup final stages

| 1872 Scotland | 1873 Scotland | 1874 Scotland | 1875 Scotland | 1876 Scotland |
|---|---|---|---|---|
| 1 Maynard | 1 Morton | 1 Welch | 1 Carr | 1 Savage |
| 2 Greenhalgh | 2 Greenhalgh | 2 Ogilvie | 2 Haygarth | 2 Green |
| 3 Welch | 3 Howell | 3 Stratford | 3 Rawson | 3 Field |
| 4 Maddison | 4 Goodwyn | 4 Ottaway | 4 Birley | 4 Bambridge E.H. |
| 5 Barker | 5 Vidal | 5 Birley | 5 von Donop | 5 Jarrett |
| 6 Brockbank | 6 von Donop | 6 Wollaston | 6 Wollaston | 6 Heron H. |
| 7 Clegg J.C. | 7 Chenery | 7 Kingsford | 7 Alcock | 7 Cursham A.W. |
| 8 Smith A.K. | 8 Clegg W.E. | 8 Edwards | 8 Rawson | 8 Heron F. |
| 9 Ottaway | 9 Bonsor | 9 Chenery | 9 Bonsor | 9 Smith C.E. |
| 10 Chenery | 10 Capt Kenyon-Slaney | 10 Heron | 10 Heron | 10 Buchanan |
| 11 Morice | 11 Heron | 11 Owen | 11 Geaves | 11 Maynard |

| Glasgow Nov 30: 0-0 | Kennington Oval Mar 8: 4-2 *Kenyon-Slaney 2, Bonsor, Chenery* | Glasgow Mar 7: 1-2 *Kingsford* | Kennington Oval Mar 6: 2-2 *Wollaston, Alcock* | Glasgow Mar 4: 0-3 |
|---|---|---|---|---|

| 1877 Scotland | 1878 Scotland | 1879 Wales | 1879 Scotland | 1880 Scotland |
|---|---|---|---|---|
| 1 Betts | 1 Warner | 1 Anderson | 1 Birkett | 1 Swepstone |
| 2 Lindsay | 2 Hon E. Lyttelton | 2 Bury | 2 Morse | 2 Brindle |
| 3 Bury | 3 Hunter | 3 Wilson | 3 Christian | 3 Luntley |
| 4 Rawson | 4 Bailey | 4 Bailey | 4 Bailey | 4 Bailey |
| 5 Jarrett | 5 Jarrett | 5 Clegg W.E. | 5 Prinsep | 5 Hunter |
| 6 Wollaston | 6 Cursham A.W. | 6 Parry | 6 Hills | 6 Wollaston |
| 7 Cursham A.W. | 7 Fairclough | 7 Sorby | 7 Goodyer | 7 Bastard |
| 8 Hon A. Lyttelton | 8 Wace | 8 Cursham A.W. | 8 Wace | 8 Sparks |
| 9 Wingfield-Stratford | 9 Wylie | 9 Wace | 9 Sparks | 9 Widdowson |
| 10 Bain | 10 Heron H. | 10 Mosforth | 10 Bambridge E.C. | 10 Mosforth |
| 11 Mosforth | 11 Mosforth | 11 Whitfield | 11 Mosforth | 11 Bambridge E.C. |

| Kennington Oval Mar 3: 1-3 *Lyttelton* | Glasgow Mar 2: 2-7 *Wylie, Cursham* | Kennington Oval Jan 18: 2-1 *Sorby, Whitfield* | Kennington Oval April 5: 5-4 *Mosforth, Bambridge 2, Goodyer, Bailey* | Glasgow Mar 13: 4-5 *Mosforth, Bambridge 2, Sparks* |
|---|---|---|---|---|

| 1880 Wales | 1881 Wales | 1881 Scotland | 1882 Ireland | 1882 Scotland |
|---|---|---|---|---|
| 1 Sands | 1 Hawtrey | 1 Hawtrey | 1 Rawlinson | 1 Swepstone |
| 2 Luntley | 2 Harvey | 2 Field | 2 Dobson | 2 Greenwood |
| 3 Brindle | 3 Bambridge A.L. | 3 Wilson | 3 Greenwood | 3 Jones A. |
| 4 Hunter | 4 Hunter | 4 Bailey | 4 Hargreaves | 4 Bailey |
| 5 Hargreaves | 5 Hargreaves | 5 Hunter | 5 King | 5 Hunter |
| 6 Marshall | 6 Marshall | 6 Holden | 6 Bambridge E.C. | 6 Cursham H.A. |
| 7 Cursham H.A. | 7 Rostron | 7 Rostron | 7 Barnet | 7 Parry |
| 8 Sparks | 8 Brown J. | 8 Macauley | 8 Brown A. | 8 Brown A. |
| 9 Mitchell | 9 Tait | 9 Mitchell | 9 Brown J. | 9 Vaughton |
| 10 Johnson | 10 Hargreaves | 10 Bambridge E.C. | 10 Vaughton | 10 Mosforth |
| 11 Mosforth | 11 Mosforth | 11 Hargreaves | 11 Cursham H.A. | 11 Bambridge E.C. |

| Wrexham Mar 15: 3-2 *Sparks 2, Brindle* | Blackburn Feb 26: 0-1 | Kennington Oval Mar 12: 1-6 *Bambridge* | Belfast Feb 18: 13-0 *Vaughton 5, Brown A. 4, Brown J. 2, Cursham, Bambridge* | Glasgow Mar 11: 1-5 *Vaughton* |
|---|---|---|---|---|

646

| 1882 Wales | 1883 Wales | 1883 Ireland | 1883 Scotland | 1884 Ireland |
|---|---|---|---|---|
| 1 Swepstone | 1 Swepstone | 1 Swepstone | 1 Swepstone | 1 Rose |
| 2 Hunter | 2 Paravacini | 2 Paravacini | 2 Paravacini | 2 Dobson |
| 3 Jones A. | 3 Russell | 3 Moore | 3 Jones A. | 3 Beverley |
| 4 Bailey | 4 Bailey | 4 Hudson | 4 Bailey | 4 Bailey |
| 5 Bambridge E.C. | 5 Macrae | 5 Macrae | 5 Macrae | 5 Macrae |
| 6 Parry | 6 Cursham A.W. | 6 Whateley | 6 Cursham H.A. | 6 Johnson |
| 7 Cursham H.A. | 7 Bambridge A.L. | 7 Pawson | 7 Cobbold | 7 Holden |
| 8 Parr | 8 Mitchell | 8 Goodhart | 8 Mitchell | 8 Bambridge A.L. |
| 9 Brown A. | 9 Goodhart | 9 Dunn | 9 Goodhart | 9 Dunn |
| 10 Vaughton | 10 Cursham H.A. | 10 Cobbold | 10 Cursham A.W. | 10 Bambridge E.C. |
| 11 Mosforth | 11 Bambridge E.C. | 11 Cursham H.A. | 11 Whateley | 11 Cursham H.A. |

| | | | | |
|---|---|---|---|---|
| Wrexham Mar 13: 3-5 *Mosforth, Parry, Cursham* | Kennington Oval Feb 3: 5-0 *Mitchell 3, Cursham A.W., Bambridge E.C.* | Liverpool Feb 24: 7-0 *Cobbold 2, Dunn 2, Whateley 2, Pawson* | Sheffield Mar 10: 2-3 *Mitchell, Cobbold* | Belfast Feb 25: 8-1 *Johnson 2, Bambridge E. C. 2, Cursham 3, Bambridge A.L.* |

| 1884 Scotland | 1884 Wales | 1885 Ireland | 1885 Wales | 1885 Scotland |
|---|---|---|---|---|
| 1 Rose | 1 Rose | 1 Arthur | 1 Arthur | 1 Arthur |
| 2 Dobson | 2 Dobson | 2 Walters P.M. | 2 Moore | 2 Walters P.M. |
| 3 Beverley | 3 Beverley | 3 Walters A.M. | 3 Ward | 3 Walters A.M. |
| 4 Bailey | 4 Bailey | 4 Bailey | 4 Bailey | 4 Bailey |
| 5 Macrae | 5 Forrest | 5 Forrest | 5 Forrest | 5 Forrest |
| 6 Wilson C.P. | 6 Wilson C.P. | 6 Lofthouse | 6 Lofthouse | 6 Amos |
| 7 Bromley-Davenport | 7 Holden | 7 Spilsbury | 7 Davenport | 7 Brown J. |
| 8 Gunn | 8 Vaughton | 8 Brown J. | 8 Brown J. | 8 Lofthouse |
| 9 Bambridge E.C. | 9 Bromley-Davenport | 9 Pawson | 9 Mitchell | 9 Danks |
| 10 Vaughton | 10 Gunn | 10 Cobbold | 10 Dixon | 10 Bambridge E.C. |
| 11 Holden | 11 Bambridge E.C. | 11 Bambridge E.C. | 11 Bambridge E.C. | 11 Cobbold |

| | | | | |
|---|---|---|---|---|
| Glasgow Mar 15: 0-1 | Wrexham Mar 17: 4-0 *Bromley-Davenport 2, Gunn, Bailey* | Manchester Feb 28: 4-0 *Bambridge E.C., Spilsbury, Brown, Lofthouse* | Blackburn Mar 14: 1-1 *Mitchell* | Kennington Oval Mar 21: 1-1 *Bambridge* |

| 1886 Ireland | 1886 Wales | 1886 Scotland | 1887 Ireland | 1887 Wales |
|---|---|---|---|---|
| 1 Rose | 1 Arthur | 1 Arthur | 1 Arthur | 1 Arthur |
| 2 Walters P.M. | 2 Squire | 2 Walters A.M. | 2 Howarth R. | 2 Walters P.M. |
| 3 Baugh | 3 Walters P.M. | 3 Walters P.M. | 3 Mason | 3 Walters A.M. |
| 4 Shutt | 4 Bailey | 4 Bailey | 4 Haworth G. | 4 Haworth G. |
| 5 Squire | 5 Amos | 5 Squire | 5 Brayshaw | 5 Bailey |
| 6 Dobson | 6 Forrest | 6 Forrest | 6 Forrest | 6 Forrest |
| 7 Leighton | 7 Dewhurst | 7 Cobbold | 7 Sayer | 7 Lofthouse |
| 8 Dewhurst | 8 Brann | 8 Bambridge E.C. | 8 Dewhurst | 8 Dewhurst |
| 9 Lindley | 9 Lindley | 9 Lindley | 9 Lindley | 9 Lindley |
| 10 Spilsbury | 10 Cobbold | 10 Spilsbury | 10 Cobbold | 10 Cobbold |
| 11 Pike | 11 Bambridge E.C. | 11 Brann | 11 Bambridge E.C. | 11 Bambridge E.C. |

| | | | | |
|---|---|---|---|---|
| Belfast Mar 13: 6-1 *Spilsbury 4, Dewhurst, Lindley* | Wrexham Mar 29: 3-1 *Dewhurst, Bambridge, Lindley* | Glasgow Mar 31: 1-1 *Lindley* | Sheffield Feb 5: 7-0 *Cobbold 2, Lindley 3, Dewhurst 2* | Kennington Oval Feb 26: 4-0 *Cobbold 2, Lindley 2* |

| 1887 Scotland | 1888 Wales | 1888 Scotland | 1888 Ireland | 1889 Wales |
|---|---|---|---|---|
| 1 Roberts | 1 Moon | 1 Moon | 1 Roberts | 1 Moon |
| 2 Walters A.M. | 2 Howarth R. | 2 Howarth R. | 2 Aldridge | 2 Walters A.M. |
| 3 Walters P.M. | 3 Mason | 3 Walters P.M. | 3 Walters P.M. | 3 Walters P.M. |
| 4 Bailey | 4 Saunders | 4 Allen H. | 4 Holmes | 4 Fletcher |
| 5 Haworth G. | 5 Allen H. | 5 Haworth G. | 5 Allen H. | 5 Lowder |
| 6 Forrest | 6 Holden-White | 6 Holden-White | 6 Shelton | 6 Betts |
| 7 Bambridge E.C. | 7 Woodhall | 7 Woodhall | 7 Bassett | 7 Bassett |
| 8 Cobbold | 8 Goodall | 8 Goodall | 8 Dewhurst | 8 Goodall |
| 9 Lofthouse | 9 Lindley | 9 Lindley | 9 Lindley | 9 Southworth |
| 10 Dewhurst | 10 Dewhurst | 10 Hodgetts | 10 Allen A. | 10 Dewhurst |
| 11 Lindley | 11 Hodgetts | 11 Dewhurst | 11 Hodgetts | 11 Townley |

| | | | | |
|---|---|---|---|---|
| Blackburn Mar 19: 2-3 *Dewhurst, Lindley* | Crewe Feb 4: 5-1 *Dewhurst 2, Woodhall, Goodall, Lindley* | Glasgow Mar 17: 5-0 *Lindley, Hodgetts, Dewhurst 2, Goodall* | Belfast Mar 31: 5-1 *Dewhurst, Allen A. 3, Lindley* | Stoke Feb 23: 4-1 *Bassett, Goodall, Southworth, Dewhurst* |

| 1889 Ireland | 1889 Scotland | 1890 Wales | 1890 Ireland | 1890 Scotland |
|---|---|---|---|---|
| 1 Rowley | 1 Moon | 1 Moon | 1 Roberts | 1 Moon |
| 2 Clare | 2 Walters A.M. | 2 Walters A.M. | 2 Baugh | 2 Walters A.M. |
| 3 Aldridge | 3 Walters P.M. | 3 Walters P.M. | 3 Mason | 3 Walters P.M. |
| 4 Wreford-Brown | 4 Hammond | 4 Fletcher | 4 Barton | 4 Haworth G. |
| 5 Weir | 5 Allen | 5 Holt | 5 Perry | 5 Allen |
| 6 Shelton | 6 Forrest | 6 Shelton | 6 Forrest | 6 Shelton |
| 7 Lofthouse | 7 Brodie | 7 Bassett | 7 Lofthouse | 7 Bassett |
| 8 Burton | 8 Goodall | 8 Currey | 8 Davenport | 8 Currey |
| 9 Brodie | 9 Bassett | 9 Lindley | 9 Geary | 9 Lindley |
| 10 Daft | 10 Weir | 10 Daft | 10 Walton | 10 Wood |
| 11 Yates | 11 Lindley | 11 Wood | 11 Townley | 11 Daft |

| | | | | |
|---|---|---|---|---|
| Everton Mar 2: 6-1 *Weir, Yates 3, Lofthouse, Brodie* | Kennington Oval April 13: 2-3 *Bassett, Weir* | Wrexham Mar 15: 3-1 *Currey 2, Lindley* | Belfast Mar 15: 9-1 *Townley 2, Davenport 2, Geary 3, Lofthouse, Barton* | Glasgow April 5: 1-1 *Wood* |

| 1891 Wales | 1891 Ireland | 1891 Scotland | 1892 Wales | 1892 Ireland |
|---|---|---|---|---|
| 1 Wilkinson | 1 Rose | 1 Moon | 1 Toone | 1 Rowley |
| 2 Porteous | 2 Marsden | 2 Howarth | 2 Dunn | 2 Underwood |
| 3 Jackson | 3 Underwood | 3 Holmes | 3 Lilley | 3 Clare |
| 4 Smith A. | 4 Bayliss | 4 Smith A. | 4 Hossack | 4 Cox |
| 5 Holt | 5 Perry | 5 Holt | 5 Winckworth | 5 Holt |
| 6 Shelton | 6 Brodie | 6 Shelton | 6 Kinsey | 6 Whitham |
| 7 Brann | 7 Bassett | 7 Bassett | 7 Gosling | 7 Athersmith |
| 8 Goodall | 8 Cotterill | 8 Goodall | 8 Cotterill | 8 Pearson |
| 9 Southworth | 9 Lindley | 9 Geary | 9 Henfrey | 9 Devey |
| 10 Milward | 10 Henfrey | 10 Chadwick | 10 Schofield | 10 Daft |
| 11 Chadwick | 11 Daft | 11 Milward | 11 Sandilands | 11 Hodgetts |

| | | | | |
|---|---|---|---|---|
| Sunderland Mar 7: 4-1 *Goodall, Southworth, Chadwick, Milward* | Wolverhampton Mar 7: 6-1 *Cotterill, Daft, Henfrey, Lindley 2, Bassett* | Blackburn April 6: 2-1 *Goodall, Chadwick* | Wrexham Mar 5: 2-0 *Henfrey, Sandilands* | Belfast Mar 5: 2-0 *Daft 2* |

| 1892 Scotland | 1893 Ireland | 1893 Wales | 1893 Scotland | 1894 Ireland |
|---|---|---|---|---|
| 1 Toone | 1 Charsley | 1 Sutcliffe | 1 Gay | 1 Reader |
| 2 Dunn | 2 Harrison | 2 Clare | 2 Harrison | 2 Howarth |
| 3 Holmes | 3 Pelly | 3 Holmes | 3 Holmes | 3 Holmes |
| 4 Holt | 4 Smith A. | 4 Reynolds | 4 Reynolds | 4 Reynolds |
| 5 Reynolds | 5 Winckworth | 5 Perry | 5 Holt | 5 Holt |
| 6 Shelton | 6 Cooper | 6 Turner | 6 Kingsley | 6 Crabtree |
| 7 Bassett | 7 Topham | 7 Bassett | 7 Bassett | 7 Chippendale |
| 8 Goodall | 8 Smith G.O. | 8 Whitehead | 8 Gosling | 8 Whitehead |
| 9 Chadwick | 9 Cotterill | 9 Goodall | 9 Cotterill | 9 Devey |
| 10 Hodgetts | 10 Gilliatt | 10 Schofield | 10 Chadwick | 10 Hodgetts |
| 11 Southworth | 11 Sandilands | 11 Spiksley | 11 Spiksley | 11 Spiksley |

| | | | | |
|---|---|---|---|---|
| Glasgow | Birmingham | Stoke | Richmond | Belfast |
| April 2: 4-1 | Feb 25: 6-1 | Mar 13: 6-0 | April 1: 5-2 | Mar 1: 2-2 |
| *Southworth,* | *Sandilands,* | *Spiksley 2, Goodall,* | *Spiksley 2,* | *Devey, Spiksley* |
| *Goodall 2, Chadwick* | *Gilliatt 3,* | *Bassett, Schofield,* | *Gosling, Cotterill,* | |
| | *Winckworth,* | *Reynolds* | *Reynolds* | |
| | *Smith G.O.* | | | |


| 1894 Wales | 1894 Scotland | 1895 Ireland | 1895 Wales | 1895 Scotland |
|---|---|---|---|---|
| 1 Gay | 1 Gay | 1 Sutcliffe | 1 Raikes | 1 Sutcliffe |
| 2 Lodge | 2 Clare | 2 Crabtree | 2 Lodge | 2 Crabtree |
| 3 Pelly | 3 Pelly | 3 Holmes | 3 Oakley | 3 Lodge |
| 4 Hossack | 4 Reynolds | 4 Howell | 4 Henfrey | 4 Needham |
| 5 Wreford-Brown | 5 Holt | 5 Crawshaw | 5 Wreford-Brown | 5 Holt |
| 6 Topham A.G. | 6 Needham | 6 Turner | 6 Barker | 6 Reynolds |
| 7 Topham R. | 7 Bassett | 7 Bassett | 7 Stanbrough | 7 Gosling |
| 8 Gosling | 8 Smith G.O. | 8 Bloomer | 8 Dewhurst | 8 Smith S. |
| 9 Smith G.O. | 9 Goodall | 9 Goodall | 9 Smith G.O. | 9 Goodall |
| 10 Veitch | 10 Chadwick | 10 Becton | 10 Gosling | 10 Bassett |
| 11 Sandilands | 11 Spiksley | 11 Schofield | 11 Sandilands | 11 Bloomer |

| | | | | |
|---|---|---|---|---|
| Wrexham | Glasgow | Derby | Queen's Club | Goodison Park |
| Mar 12: 5-1 | April 7: 2-2 | Mar 9: 9-0 | Mar 18: 1-1 | April 6: 3-0 |
| *Veitch 3, Gosling,* | *Goodall, Reynolds* | *Bloomer 2,* | *Smith* | *Bloomer, Smith,* |
| *1 og* | | *Goodall 2, Bassett,* | | *Gibson og* |
| | | *Howell, Becton 2,* | | |
| | | *1 og* | | |


| 1896 Ireland | 1896 Wales | 1896 Scotland | 1897 Ireland | 1897 Wales |
|---|---|---|---|---|
| 1 Raikes | 1 Raikes | 1 Raikes | 1 Robinson | 1 Foulke |
| 2 Lodge | 2 Oakley | 2 Lodge | 2 Oakley | 2 Oakley |
| 3 Oakley | 3 Crabtree | 3 Oakley | 3 Williams | 3 Spencer |
| 4 Crabtree | 4 Henfrey | 4 Crabtree | 4 Middleditch | 4 Reynolds |
| 5 Crawshaw | 5 Crawshaw | 5 Crawshaw | 5 Crawshaw | 5 Crawshaw |
| 6 Kinsey | 6 Kinsey | 6 Henfrey | 6 Needham | 6 Needham |
| 7 Bassett | 7 Bassett | 7 Goodall | 7 Athersmith | 7 Athersmith |
| 8 Bloomer | 8 Bloomer | 8 Bassett | 8 Bloomer | 8 Bloomer |
| 9 Smith G.O. | 9 Smith G.O. | 9 Smith G.O. | 9 Smith G.O. | 9 Smith G.O. |
| 10 Chadwick | 10 Goodall | 10 Wood | 10 Wheldon | 10 Beeton |
| 11 Spiksley | 11 Sandilands | 11 Burnup | 11 Bradshaw | 11 Milward |

| | | | | |
|---|---|---|---|---|
| Belfast | Cardiff | Glasgow | Nottingham | Sheffield |
| Mar 7: 2-0 | Mar 16: 9-1 | April 4: 1-2 | Feb 20: 6-0 | Mar 29: 4-0 |
| *Bloomer, Smith* | *Bloomer 5,* | *Bassett* | *Bloomer 2,* | *Bloomer, Needham,* |
| | *Smith 2,* | | *Wheldon 3,* | *Milward 2* |
| | *Goodall, Bassett* | | *Athersmith* | |

| 1897 Scotland | 1898 Ireland | 1898 Wales | 1898 Scotland | 1899 Ireland |
|---|---|---|---|---|
| 1 Robinson | 1 Robinson | 1 Robinson | 1 Robinson | 1 Hillman |
| 2 Oakley | 2 Oakley | 2 Oakley | 2 Williams | 2 Bach |
| 3 Spencer | 3 Williams | 3 Williams | 3 Oakley | 3 Williams |
| 4 Reynolds | 4 Forman, Frank | 4 Perry | 4 Needham | 4 Forman, Frank |
| 5 Crawshaw | 5 Morren | 5 Booth | 5 Wreford-Brown | 5 Crabtree |
| 6 Needham | 6 Turner | 6 Needham | 6 Forman, Frank | 6 Needham |
| 7 Athersmith | 7 Athersmith | 7 Athersmith | 7 Spiksley | 7 Athersmith |
| 8 Bloomer | 8 Richards | 8 Goodall | 8 Wheldon | 8 Bloomer |
| 9 Smith G.O. | 9 Smith G.O. | 9 Smith G.O. | 9 Smith G.O. | 9 Smith G.O. |
| 10 Chadwick | 10 Garfield | 10 Wheldon | 10 Bloomer | 10 Settle |
| 11 Milward | 11 Wheldon | 11 Spiksley | 11 Athersmith | 11 Forman, Fred |

| | | | | |
|---|---|---|---|---|
| Crystal Palace April 3: 1-2 *Bloomer* | Belfast Mar 5: 3-2 *Morren, Athersmith, Smith* | Wrexham Mar 28: 3-0 *Smith, Wheldon 2* | Glasgow April 2: 3-1 *Bloomer 2, Wheldon* | Sunderland Feb 18: 13-2 *Frank Forman, Bloomer 2, Athersmith, Settle 3, Smith 4, Fred Forman 2* |

| 1899 Wales | 1899 Scotland | 1900 Ireland | 1900 Wales | 1900 Scotland |
|---|---|---|---|---|
| 1 Robinson | 1 Robinson | 1 Robinson | 1 Robinson | 1 Robinson |
| 2 Thickett | 2 Thickett | 2 Oakley | 2 Spencer | 2 Oakley |
| 3 Williams | 3 Crabtree | 3 Crabtree | 3 Oakley | 3 Crabtree |
| 4 Needham | 4 Forman, Frank | 4 Johnson | 4 Johnson | 4 Johnson |
| 5 Crabtree | 5 Howell | 5 Holt | 5 Chadwick A. | 5 Chadwick A. |
| 6 Forman, Frank | 6 Needham | 6 Needham | 6 Crabtree | 6 Needham |
| 7 Athersmith | 7 Athersmith | 7 Turner | 7 Athersmith | 7 Athersmith |
| 8 Bloomer | 8 Bloomer | 8 Cunliffe | 8 Foster | 8 Bloomer |
| 9 Smith G.O. | 9 Smith G.O. | 9 Smith G.O. | 9 Smith G.O. | 9 Smith G.O. |
| 10 Settle | 10 Settle | 10 Sagar | 10 Wilson | 10 Wilson |
| 11 Forman, Fred | 11 Forman, Fred | 11 Priest | 11 Spouncer | 11 Plant |

| | | | | |
|---|---|---|---|---|
| Bristol Mar 20: 4-0 *Bloomer 2, Fred Forman, Needham* | Birmingham April 8: 2-1 *Smith, Settle* | Dublin Mar 17: 2-0 *Johnson, Sagar* | Cardiff Mar 26: 1-1 *Wilson* | Glasgow April 7: 1-4 *Bloomer* |

| 1901 Ireland | 1901 Wales | 1901 Scotland | 1902 Wales | 1902 Ireland |
|---|---|---|---|---|
| 1 Robinson | 1 Kingsley | 1 Sutcliffe | 1 George | 1 George |
| 2 Fry | 2 Crabtree | 2 Iremonger | 2 Crompton | 2 Crompton |
| 3 Oakley | 3 Oakley | 3 Oakley | 3 Crabtree | 3 Iremonger |
| 4 Jones W. | 4 Wilkes | 4 Wilkes | 4 Wilkes | 4 Wilkes |
| 5 Crawshaw | 5 Bannister | 5 Forman, Frank | 5 Abbott | 5 Bannister |
| 6 Needham | 6 Needham | 6 Needham | 6 Needham | 6 Forman, Frank |
| 7 Turner | 7 Bennett | 7 Bennett | 7 Hogg | 7 Hogg |
| 8 Foster | 8 Bloomer | 8 Bloomer | 8 Bloomer | 8 Bloomer |
| 9 Hedley | 9 Beats | 9 Smith G.O. | 9 Sagar | 9 Calvey |
| 10 Banks | 10 Foster | 10 Foster | 10 Foster | 10 Settle |
| 11 Cox | 11 Corbett | 11 Blackburn | 11 Lipsham | 11 Blackburn |

| | | | | |
|---|---|---|---|---|
| Southampton Mar 9: 3-0 *Foster 2, Crawshaw* | Newcastle Mar 18: 6-0 *Bloomer 4, Foster, Needham* | Crystal Palace Mar 30: 2-2 *Blackburn, Bloomer* | Wrexham Mar 3: 0-0 | Belfast Mar 22: 1-0 *Settle* |

650

<table>
<tr><td>1902<br>Scotland</td><td>1903<br>Ireland</td><td>1903<br>Wales</td><td>1903<br>Scotland</td><td>1904<br>Wales</td></tr>
<tr><td>1 George</td><td>1 Baddeley</td><td>1 Sutcliffe</td><td>1 Baddeley</td><td>1 Baddeley</td></tr>
<tr><td>2 Crompton</td><td>2 Spencer</td><td>2 Crompton</td><td>2 Crompton</td><td>2 Crompton</td></tr>
<tr><td>3 Molyneux</td><td>3 Molyneux</td><td>3 Molyneux</td><td>3 Molyneux</td><td>3 Burgess</td></tr>
<tr><td>4 Wilkes</td><td>4 Johnson</td><td>4 Johnson</td><td>4 Johnson</td><td>4 Lee</td></tr>
<tr><td>5 Forman, Frank</td><td>5 Holford</td><td>5 Forman, Frank</td><td>5 Booth</td><td>5 Crawshaw</td></tr>
<tr><td>6 Houlker</td><td>6 Hadley</td><td>6 Houlker</td><td>6 Houlker</td><td>6 Ruddlesdin</td></tr>
<tr><td>7 Hogg</td><td>7 Davis</td><td>7 Davis</td><td>7 Davis</td><td>7 Brawn</td></tr>
<tr><td>8 Bloomer</td><td>8 Sharp</td><td>8 Garraty</td><td>8 Humphreys</td><td>8 Common</td></tr>
<tr><td>9 Beats</td><td>9 Woodward</td><td>9 Woodward</td><td>9 Woodward</td><td>9 Brown A.</td></tr>
<tr><td>10 Settle</td><td>10 Settle</td><td>10 Bache</td><td>10 Capes</td><td>10 Bache</td></tr>
<tr><td>11 Cox</td><td>11 Lockett</td><td>11 Corbett</td><td>11 Cox</td><td>11 Davis</td></tr>
<tr><td>Birmingham<br>May 3: 2-2<br>*Wilkes, Settle*</td><td>Wolverhampton<br>Feb 14: 4-0<br>*Sharp, Davis,<br>Woodward 2*</td><td>Portsmouth<br>Mar 2: 2-1<br>*Bache, Woodward*</td><td>Sheffield<br>April 4: 1-2<br>*Woodward*</td><td>Wrexham<br>Feb 29: 2-2<br>*Common, Bache*</td></tr>
</table>

<table>
<tr><td>1904<br>Ireland</td><td>1904<br>Scotland</td><td>1905<br>Ireland</td><td>1905<br>Wales</td><td>1905<br>Scotland</td></tr>
<tr><td>1 Baddeley</td><td>1 Baddeley</td><td>1 Williamson</td><td>1 Linacre</td><td>1 Linacre</td></tr>
<tr><td>2 Crompton</td><td>2 Crompton</td><td>2 Balmer</td><td>2 Spencer</td><td>2 Spencer</td></tr>
<tr><td>3 Burgess</td><td>3 Burgess</td><td>3 Carr</td><td>3 Smith H.</td><td>3 Smith H.</td></tr>
<tr><td>4 Ruddlesdin</td><td>4 Wolstenholme</td><td>4 Wolstenholme</td><td>4 Wolstenholme</td><td>4 Ruddlesdin</td></tr>
<tr><td>5 Crawshaw</td><td>5 Wilkinson</td><td>5 Roberts</td><td>5 Roberts</td><td>5 Roberts</td></tr>
<tr><td>6 Leake</td><td>6 Leake</td><td>6 Leake</td><td>6 Leake</td><td>6 Leake</td></tr>
<tr><td>7 Brawn</td><td>7 Rutherford</td><td>7 Bond</td><td>7 Bond</td><td>7 Sharp</td></tr>
<tr><td>8 Common</td><td>8 Bloomer</td><td>8 Bloomer</td><td>8 Bloomer</td><td>8 Bloomer</td></tr>
<tr><td>9 Woodward</td><td>9 Woodward</td><td>9 Woodward</td><td>9 Woodward</td><td>9 Woodward</td></tr>
<tr><td>10 Bache</td><td>10 Harris</td><td>10 Harris</td><td>10 Harris</td><td>10 Bache</td></tr>
<tr><td>11 Davis</td><td>11 Blackburn</td><td>11 Booth</td><td>11 Hardman</td><td>11 Bridgett</td></tr>
<tr><td>Belfast<br>Mar 12: 3-1<br>*Common, Bache,<br>Davis*</td><td>Glasgow<br>April 9: 1-0<br>*Bloomer*</td><td>Middlesbrough<br>Feb 25: 1-1<br>*Bloomer*</td><td>Liverpool<br>Mar 27: 3-1<br>*Woodward 2,<br>Harris*</td><td>Crystal Palace<br>April 1: 1-0<br>*Bache*</td></tr>
</table>

<table>
<tr><td>1906<br>Ireland</td><td>1906<br>Wales</td><td>1906<br>Scotland</td><td>1907<br>Ireland</td><td>1907<br>Wales</td></tr>
<tr><td>1 Ashcroft</td><td>1 Ashcroft</td><td>1 Ashcroft</td><td>1 Hardy</td><td>1 Hardy</td></tr>
<tr><td>2 Crompton</td><td>2 Crompton</td><td>2 Crompton</td><td>2 Crompton</td><td>2 Crompton</td></tr>
<tr><td>3 Smith H.</td><td>3 Smith H.</td><td>3 Burgess</td><td>3 Carr</td><td>3 Pennington</td></tr>
<tr><td>4 Warren</td><td>4 Warren</td><td>4 Warren</td><td>4 Warren</td><td>4 Warren</td></tr>
<tr><td>5 Veitch</td><td>5 Veitch</td><td>5 Veitch</td><td>5 Wedlock</td><td>5 Wedlock</td></tr>
<tr><td>6 Houlker</td><td>6 Houlker</td><td>6 Makepeace</td><td>6 Hawkes</td><td>6 Veitch</td></tr>
<tr><td>7 Bond</td><td>7 Bond</td><td>7 Bond</td><td>7 Rutherford</td><td>7 Rutherford</td></tr>
<tr><td>8 Day</td><td>8 Day</td><td>8 Day</td><td>8 Coleman</td><td>8 Bloomer</td></tr>
<tr><td>9 Brown A.</td><td>9 Common</td><td>9 Shepherd</td><td>9 Hilsdon</td><td>9 Thornley</td></tr>
<tr><td>10 Harris</td><td>10 Harris</td><td>10 Harris</td><td>10 Bache</td><td>10 Stewart</td></tr>
<tr><td>11 Gosnell</td><td>11 Wright</td><td>11 Conlin</td><td>11 Hardman</td><td>11 Wall</td></tr>
<tr><td>Belfast<br>Feb 17: 5-0<br>*Bond 2, Day,<br>Harris, Brown*</td><td>Cardiff<br>Mar 19: 1-0<br>*Day*</td><td>Glasgow<br>April 7: 1-2<br>*Shepherd*</td><td>Everton<br>Feb 16: 1-0<br>*Hardman*</td><td>Fulham<br>Mar 18: 1-1<br>*Stewart*</td></tr>
</table>

| 1907 Scotland | 1908 Ireland | 1908 Wales | 1908 Scotland | 1908 Austria |
|---|---|---|---|---|
| 1 Hardy | 1 Maskrey | 1 Bailey | 1 Hardy | 1 Bailey |
| 2 Crompton | 2 Crompton | 2 Crompton | 2 Crompton | 2 Crompton |
| 3 Pennington | 3 Pennington | 3 Pennington | 3 Pennington | 3 Corbett |
| 4 Warren | 4 Warren | 4 Warren | 4 Warren | 4 Warren |
| 5 Wedlock | 5 Wedlock | 5 Wedlock | 5 Wedlock | 5 Wedlock |
| 6 Veitch | 6 Lintott | 6 Lintott | 6 Lintott | 6 Hawkes |
| 7 Rutherford | 7 Rutherford | 7 Rutherford | 7 Rutherford | 7 Rutherford |
| 8 Bloomer | 8 Woodward | 8 Woodward | 8 Woodward | 8 Woodward |
| 9 Woodward | 9 Hilsdon | 9 Hilsdon | 9 Hilsdon | 9 Hilsdon |
| 10 Stewart | 10 Windridge | 10 Windridge | 10 Windridge | 10 Windridge |
| 11 Hardman | 11 Wall | 11 Hardman | 11 Bridgett | 11 Bridgett |

| Newcastle April 6: 1-1 *Bloomer* | Belfast Feb 15: 3-1 *Woodward, Hilsdon 2* | Wrexham Mar 16: 7-1 *Wedlock, Windridge Hilsdon 2, Woodward 3* | Glasgow April 4: 1-1 *Windridge* | Vienna June 6: 6-1 *Hilsdon 2, Windridge 2, Bridgett, Woodward* |
|---|---|---|---|---|

| 1908 Austria | 1908 Hungary | 1908 Bohemia | 1909 Ireland | 1909 Wales |
|---|---|---|---|---|
| 1 Bailey | 1 Bailey | 1 Bailey | 1 Hardy | 1 Hardy |
| 2 Crompton | 2 Crompton | 2 Crompton | 2 Crompton | 2 Crompton |
| 3 Pennington | 3 Corbett | 3 Corbett | 3 Cottle | 3 Pennington |
| 4 Warren | 4 Warren | 4 Warren | 4 Warren | 4 Warren |
| 5 Wedlock | 5 Wedlock | 5 Wedlock | 5 Wedlock | 5 Wedlock |
| 6 Hawkes | 6 Hawkes | 6 Hawkes | 6 Lintott | 6 Veitch |
| 7 Rutherford | 7 Rutherford | 7 Rutherford | 7 Berry | 7 Pentland |
| 8 Woodward | 8 Woodward | 8 Woodward | 8 Woodward | 8 Woodward |
| 9 Bradshaw | 9 Hilsdon | 9 Hilsdon | 9 Hilsdon | 9 Freeman |
| 10 Windridge | 10 Windridge | 10 Windridge | 10 Windridge | 10 Holley |
| 11 Bridgett | 11 Bridgett | 11 Bridgett | 11 Bridgett | 11 Bridgett |

| Vienna June 8: 11-1 *Woodward 4, Bridgett, Bradshaw 3, Warren, Rutherford, Windridge* | Budapest June 10: 7-0 *Hilsdon 2, Windridge, Woodward, Rutherford* | Prague June 13: 4-0 *Hilsdon 2, Windridge, Rutherford* | Bradford Feb 13: 4-0 *Hilsdon 2, Woodward 2* | Nottingham Mar 15: 2-0 *Holley, Freeman* |
|---|---|---|---|---|

| 1909 Scotland | 1909 Hungary | 1909 Hungary | 1909 Austria | 1910 Ireland |
|---|---|---|---|---|
| 1 Hardy | 1 Hardy | 1 Hardy | 1 Hardy | 1 Hardy |
| 2 Crompton | 2 Crompton | 2 Crompton | 2 Crompton | 2 Morley |
| 3 Pennington | 3 Pennington | 3 Pennington | 3 Pennington | 3 Cowell |
| 4 Warren | 4 Warren | 4 Warren | 4 Warren | 4 Ducat |
| 5 Wedlock | 5 Wedlock | 5 Wedlock | 5 Wedlock | 5 Wedlock |
| 6 Lintott | 6 Lintott | 6 Lintott | 6 Richards | 6 Bradshaw |
| 7 Pentland | 7 Pentland | 7 Pentland | 7 Pentland | 7 Bond |
| 8 Fleming | 8 Fleming | 8 Fleming | 8 Halse | 8 Fleming |
| 9 Freeman | 9 Woodward | 9 Woodward | 9 Woodward | 9 Woodward |
| 10 Holley | 10 Holley | 10 Holley | 10 Holley | 10 Bache |
| 11 Wall | 11 Bridgett | 11 Bridgett | 11 Bridgett | 11 Hall |

| Crystal Palace April 3: 2-0 *Wall 2* | Budapest May 29: 4-2 *Woodward 2, Fleming, Bridgett* | Budapest May 31: 8-2 *Woodward 4, Fleming 2, Holley 2* | Vienna June 1: 8-1 *Woodward 3, Warren, Halse 2, Holley 2* | Belfast Feb 12: 1-1 *Fleming* |
|---|---|---|---|---|

| 1910 Wales | 1910 Scotland | 1911 Ireland | 1911 Wales | 1911 Scotland |
|---|---|---|---|---|
| 1 Hardy | 1 Hardy | 1 Williamson | 1 Williamson | 1 Williamson |
| 2 Crompton | 2 Crompton | 2 Crompton | 2 Crompton | 2 Crompton |
| 3 Pennington | 3 Pennington | 3 Pennington | 3 Pennington | 3 Pennington |
| 4 Ducat | 4 Ducat | 4 Warren | 4 Warren | 4 Warren |
| 5 Wedlock | 5 Wedlock | 5 Wedlock | 5 Wedlock | 5 Wedlock |
| 6 Bradshaw | 6 Makepeace | 6 Sturgess | 6 Rev Hunt | 6 Rev Hunt |
| 7 Bond | 7 Bond | 7 Simpson | 7 Simpson | 7 Simpson |
| 8 Fleming | 8 Hibbett | 8 Fleming | 8 Fleming | 8 Stewart |
| 9 Parkinson | 9 Parkinson | 9 Shepherd | 9 Webb | 9 Webb |
| 10 Holley | 10 Hardinge | 10 Woodger | 10 Woodward | 10 Bache |
| 11 Wall | 11 Wall | 11 Evans | 11 Evans | 11 Evans |
| Cardiff | Glasgow | Derby | Millwall | Everton |
| Mar 14: 1-0 | April 2: 0-2 | Feb 11: 2-1 | Mar 13: 3-0 | April 1: 1-1 |
| *Ducat* | | *Shepherd, Evans* | *Woodward 2, Webb* | *Stewart* |

| 1912 Ireland | 1912 Wales | 1912 Scotland | 1913 Ireland | 1913 Wales |
|---|---|---|---|---|
| 1 Hardy | 1 Williamson | 1 Williamson | 1 Williamson | 1 Scattergood |
| 2 Crompton | 2 Crompton | 2 Crompton | 2 Crompton | 2 Crompton |
| 3 Pennington | 3 Pennington | 3 Pennington | 3 Benson | 3 Pennington |
| 4 Brittleton | 4 Brittleton | 4 Brittleton | 4 Cuggy | 4 Moffatt |
| 5 Wedlock | 5 Wedlock | 5 Wedlock | 5 Boyle | 5 McCall |
| 6 Bradshaw | 6 Makepeace | 6 Makepeace | 6 Utley | 6 Bradshaw |
| 7 Simpson | 7 Simpson | 7 Simpson | 7 Mordue | 7 Wallace |
| 8 Fleming | 8 Jefferis | 8 Jefferis | 8 Buchan | 8 Fleming |
| 9 Freeman | 9 Freeman | 9 Freeman | 9 Elliott | 9 Hampton |
| 10 Holley | 10 Holley | 10 Holley | 10 Smith, Joe | 10 Latheron |
| 11 Mordue | 11 Evans | 11 Wall | 11 Wall | 11 Hodkinson |
| Dublin | Wrexham | Glasgow | Belfast | Bristol |
| Feb 10: 6-1 | Mar 11: 2-0 | Mar 23: 1-1 | Feb 15: 1-2 | Mar 17: 4-3 |
| *Fleming 3, Freeman, Holley, Simpson* | *Holley, Freeman* | *Holley* | *Buchan* | *Fleming, McCall, Latheron, Hampton* |

| 1913 Scotland | 1914 Ireland | 1914 Wales | 1914 Scotland | 1919 Ireland |
|---|---|---|---|---|
| 1 Hardy | 1 Hardy | 1 Hardy | 1 Hardy | 1 Hardy |
| 2 Crompton | 2 Crompton | 2 Crompton | 2 Crompton | 2 Smith, Joe (WBA) |
| 3 Pennington | 3 Pennington | 3 Colclough | 3 Pennington | 3 Knight |
| 4 Brittleton | 4 Cuggy | 4 Brittleton | 4 Sturgess | 4 Bagshaw |
| 5 McCall | 5 Buckley | 5 Wedlock | 5 McCall | 5 Bowser |
| 6 Watson | 6 Watson | 6 McNeal | 6 McNeal | 6 Watson |
| 7 Simpson | 7 Wallace | 7 Simpson | 7 Walden | 7 Turnbull |
| 8 Fleming | 8 Shea | 8 Shea | 8 Fleming | 8 Carr |
| 9 Hampton | 9 Elliott | 9 Hampton | 9 Hampton | 9 Cock |
| 10 Holley | 10 Latheron | 10 Smith, Joe | 10 Smith, Joe | 10 Smith, Joe (Bolton W) |
| 11 Hodkinson | 11 Martin | 11 Mosscrop | 11 Mosscrop | 11 Hodkinson |
| Chelsea | Middlesbrough | Cardiff | Glasgow | Belfast |
| April 5: 1-0 | Feb 14: 0-3 | Mar 16: 2-0 | April 4: 1-3 | Oct 25: 1-1 |
| *Hampton* | | *Smith, Wedlock* | *Fleming* | *Cock* |

| 1920 Wales | 1920 Scotland | 1920 Ireland | 1921 Wales | 1921 Scotland |
|---|---|---|---|---|
| 1 Hardy | 1 Hardy | 1 Mew | 1 Coleman | 1 Gough |
| 2 Clay | 2 Longworth | 2 Downs | 2 Cresswell | 2 Smart |
| 3 Pennington | 3 Pennington | 3 Bullock | 3 Silcock | 3 Silcock |
| 4 Ducat | 4 Ducat | 4 Ducat | 4 Bamber | 4 Smith B. |
| 5 Barson | 5 McCall | 5 McCall | 5 Wilson | 5 Wilson |
| 6 Grimsdell | 6 Grimsdell | 6 Grimsdell | 6 Bromilow | 6 Grimsdell |
| 7 Chedgzoy | 7 Wallace | 7 Chedgzoy | 7 Chedgzoy | 7 Chedgzoy |
| 8 Buchan | 8 Kelly | 8 Kelly | 8 Kelly | 8 Kelly |
| 9 Elliott | 9 Cock | 9 Walker | 9 Buchan | 9 Chambers |
| 10 Smith, Joe | 10 Morris | 10 Morris | 10 Chambers | 10 Bliss |
| 11 Quantrill | 11 Quantrill | 11 Quantrill | 11 Quantrill | 11 Dimmock |
| Arsenal Mar 15: 1-2 *Buchan* | Sheffield April 10: 5-4 *Kelly 2, Cock, Morris, Quantrill* | Sunderland Oct 23: 2-0 *Kelly, Walker* | Cardiff Mar 14: 0-0 | Glasgow April 9: 0-3 |

| 1921 Belgium | 1921 Ireland | 1922 Wales | 1922 Scotland | 1922 Ireland |
|---|---|---|---|---|
| 1 Baker H. | 1 Dawson | 1 Davison | 1 Dawson | 1 Taylor |
| 2 Fort | 2 Clay | 2 Clay | 2 Clay | 2 Smith, Joe (WBA) |
| 3 Longworth | 3 Lucas | 3 Titmuss | 3 Wadsworth | 3 Harrow |
| 4 Read | 4 Moss | 4 Smith B. | 4 Moss | 4 Moss |
| 5 Wilson | 5 Wilson | 5 Woosnam | 5 Wilson | 5 Wilson |
| 6 Barton | 6 Barton | 6 Bromilow | 6 Bromilow | 6 Grimsdell |
| 7 Rawlings | 7 Chedgzoy | 7 Walden | 7 York | 7 Mercer |
| 8 Seed | 8 Kirton | 8 Kelly | 8 Kelly | 8 Seed |
| 9 Buchan | 9 Simms | 9 Rawlings | 9 Rawlings | 9 Osborne |
| 10 Chambers | 10 Walker | 10 Walker | 10 Walker | 10 Chambers |
| 11 Harrison | 11 Harrison | 11 Smith W.H. | 11 Smith W.H. | 11 Williams |
| Brussels May 21: 2-0 *Buchan, Chambers* | Belfast Oct 22: 1-1 *Kirton* | Liverpool Mar 13: 1-0 *Kelly* | Birmingham April 8: 0-1 | West Bromwich Oct 21: 2-0 *Chambers 2* |

| 1923 Wales | 1923 Belgium | 1923 Scotland | 1923 France | 1923 Sweden |
|---|---|---|---|---|
| 1 Taylor | 1 Taylor | 1 Taylor | 1 Alderson | 1 Williamson |
| 2 Longworth | 2 Longworth | 2 Longworth | 2 Cresswell | 2 Ashurst |
| 3 Titmuss | 3 Wadsworth | 3 Wadsworth | 3 Jones H. | 3 Harrow |
| 4 Magee | 4 Kean | 4 Kean | 4 Plum | 4 Patchitt |
| 5 Wilson | 5 Wilson | 5 Wilson | 5 Seddon | 5 Seddon |
| 6 Grimsdell | 6 Bromilow | 6 Tresadern | 6 Barton | 6 Tresadern |
| 7 Carr | 7 Mercer | 7 Chedgzoy | 7 Osborne | 7 Thornewell |
| 8 Seed | 8 Seed | 8 Kelly | 8 Buchan | 8 Moore |
| 9 Watson | 9 Bullock | 9 Watson | 9 Creek | 9 Bedford |
| 10 Chambers | 10 Chambers | 10 Chambers | 10 Hartley | 10 Walker |
| 11 Williams | 11 Hegan | 11 Tunstall | 11 Hegan | 11 Urwin |
| Cardiff Mar 5: 2-2 *Chambers, Watson* | Arsenal Mar 19: 6-1 *Hegan 2, Chambers, Mercer, Seed, Bullock* | Glasgow April 14: 2-2 *Kelly, Watson* | Paris May 10: 4-1 *Hegan 2, Buchan, Creek* | Stockholm May 21: 4-2 *Walker 2, Moore, Thornewell* |

| 1923 Sweden | 1923 Ireland | 1923 Belgium | 1924 Wales | 1924 Scotland |
|---|---|---|---|---|
| 1 Williamson | 1 Taylor | 1 Hufton | 1 Sewell | 1 Taylor |
| 2 Ashurst | 2 Bower | 2 Cresswell | 2 Smart | 2 Smart |
| 3 Silcock | 3 Wadsworth | 3 Bower | 3 Mort | 3 Wadsworth |
| 4 Magee | 4 Pantling | 4 Moss | 4 Kean | 4 Moss |
| 5 Seddon | 5 Wilson | 5 Seddon | 5 Wilson | 5 Spencer |
| 6 Patchitt | 6 Meehan | 6 Barton | 6 Barton | 6 Barton |
| 7 Thornewell | 7 Hegan | 7 Hegan | 7 Chedgzoy | 7 Butler |
| 8 Moore | 8 Kelly | 8 Brown W. | 8 Jack | 8 Jack |
| 9 Walker | 9 Bradford | 9 Roberts | 9 Roberts | 9 Buchan |
| 10 Miller | 10 Chambers | 10 Doggart | 10 Stephenson | 10 Walker |
| 11 Urwin | 11 Tunstall | 11 Urwin | 11 Tunstall | 11 Tunstall |
| Stockholm | Belfast | Antwerp | Blackburn | Wembley |
| May 24: 3-1 | Oct 20: 1-2 | Nov 1: 2-2 | Mar 3: 1-2 | April 12: 1-1 |
| *Moore 2, Miller* | *Bradford* | *Brown, Roberts* | *Roberts* | *Walker* |

| 1924 France | 1924 Ireland | 1924 Belgium | 1925 Wales | 1925 Scotland |
|---|---|---|---|---|
| 1 Taylor | 1 Mitchell | 1 Hardy | 1 Pym | 1 Pym |
| 2 Lucas | 2 Cresswell | 2 Ashurst | 2 Ashurst | 2 Ashurst |
| 3 Mort | 3 Wadsworth | 3 Bower | 3 Bower | 3 Wadsworth |
| 4 Ewer | 4 Keen | 4 Magee | 4 Hill | 4 Magee |
| 5 Wilson | 5 Healless | 5 Butler | 5 Spencer | 5 Townrow |
| 6 Blackburn | 6 Barton | 6 Ewer | 6 Graham | 6 Graham |
| 7 Thornewell | 7 Chedgzoy | 7 Osborne | 7 Kelly | 7 Kelly |
| 8 Earle | 8 Kelly | 8 Roberts | 8 Roberts | 8 Seed |
| 9 Gibbins | 9 Bedford | 9 Bradford | 9 Cook | 9 Roberts |
| 10 Storer | 10 Walker | 10 Walker | 10 Walker | 10 Walker |
| 11 Tunstall | 11 Tunstall | 11 Dorrell | 11 Dorrell | 11 Tunstall |
| Paris | Everton | West Bromwich | Swansea | Glasgow |
| May 17: 3-1 | Oct 22: 3-1 | Dec 8: 4-0 | Feb 28: 2-1 | April 4: 0-2 |
| *Gibbins 2, Storer* | *Kelly, Bedford,* | *Bradford 2,* | *Roberts 2* | |
| | *Walker* | *Walker 2* | | |

| 1925 France | 1925 Ireland | 1926 Wales | 1926 Scotland | 1926 Belgium |
|---|---|---|---|---|
| 1 Fox | 1 Baker H. | 1 Pym | 1 Taylor | 1 Ashmore |
| 2 Parker | 2 Smart | 2 Cresswell | 2 Goodall | 2 Lucas |
| 3 Felton | 3 Hudspeth | 3 Wadsworth | 3 Mort | 3 Hill R.H. |
| 4 Magee | 4 Kean | 4 Edwards | 4 Edwards | 4 Kean |
| 5 Bryant | 5 Armitage | 5 Townrow | 5 Hill | 5 Cowan |
| 6 Green | 6 Bromilow | 6 Green | 6 Green | 6 Green |
| 7 Thornewell | 7 Austin | 7 Urwin | 7 York | 7 Spence |
| 8 Roberts | 8 Puddefoot | 8 Kelly | 8 Puddefoot | 8 Carter J.H. |
| 9 Gibbins | 9 Ashton | 9 Bullock | 9 Harper | 9 Osborne |
| 10 Walker | 10 Walker | 10 Walker | 10 Walker | 10 Johnson |
| 11 Dorrell | 11 Dorrell | 11 Dimmock | 11 Ruffell | 11 Dimmock |
| Paris | Belfast | Selhurst | Manchester | Antwerp |
| May 21: 3-2 | Oct 24: 0-0 | Mar 1: 1-3 | April 17: 0-1 | May 24: 5-3 |
| *Gibbins, Dorrell, 1 og* | | *Walker* | | *Osborne 3, Carter,* |
| | | | | *Johnson* |

| 1926 Ireland | 1927 Wales | 1927 Scotland | 1927 Belgium | 1927 Luxembourg |
|---|---|---|---|---|
| 1 McInroy | 1 Brown J. | 1 Brown J. | 1 Brown J. | 1 Brown J. |
| 2 Cresswell | 2 Bower | 2 Goodall | 2 Goodall | 2 Goodall |
| 3 Wadsworth | 3 Waterfield | 3 Jones H. | 3 Jones H. | 3 Jones H. |
| 4 Edwards | 4 Edwards | 4 Edwards | 4 Edwards | 4 Edwards |
| 5 Hill | 5 Seddon | 5 Hill | 5 Hill | 5 Kean |
| 6 Green | 6 Green | 6 Bishop | 6 Bishop | 6 Bishop |
| 7 Spence | 7 Pease | 7 Hulme | 7 Hulme | 7 Kelly |
| 8 Brown G. | 8 Brown G. | 8 Brown G. | 8 Brown G. | 8 Brown G. |
| 9 Bullock | 9 Dean | 9 Dean | 9 Dean | 9 Dean |
| 10 Walker | 10 Walker | 10 Rigby | 10 Rigby | 10 Rigby |
| 11 Ruffell | 11 Page | 11 Page | 11 Page | 11 Page |
| Liverpool Oct 20: 3-3 *Brown, Spence, Bullock* | Wrexham Feb 12: 3-3 *Dean 2, Walker* | Glasgow April 2: 2-1 *Dean 2* | Brussels May 11: 9-1 *Dean 3, Brown 2, Rigby 2, Page, Hulme* | Luxembourg May 21: 5-2 *Dean 3, Kelly, Bishop.* |

| 1927 France | 1927 Ireland | 1927 Wales | 1928 Scotland | 1928 France |
|---|---|---|---|---|
| 1 Brown J. | 1 Hufton | 1 Tremelling | 1 Hufton | 1 Olney |
| 2 Goodall | 2 Cooper | 2 Goodall | 2 Goodall | 2 Goodall |
| 3 Jones H. | 3 Jones H. | 3 Osborne | 3 Jones H. | 3 Blenkinsop |
| 4 Edwards | 4 Nuttall | 4 Baker | 4 Edwards | 4 Edwards |
| 5 Hill | 5 Hill | 5 Hill | 5 Wilson | 5 Matthews |
| 6 Bishop | 6 Storer | 6 Nuttall | 6 Healless | 6 Green |
| 7 Hulme | 7 Hulme | 7 Hulme | 7 Hulme | 7 Bruton |
| 8 Brown G. | 8 Earle | 8 Brown G. | 8 Kelly | 8 Jack |
| 9 Dean | 9 Dean | 9 Dean | 9 Dean | 9 Dean |
| 10 Rigby | 10 Ball | 10 Rigby | 10 Bradford | 10 Stephenson |
| 11 Page | 11 Page | 11 Page | 11 Smith W.H. | 11 Barry |
| Paris May 26: 6-0 *Dean 2, Brown 2, Rigby, Rollet og* | Belfast Oct 22: 0-2 | Burnley Nov 28: 1-2 *Keenor og* | Wembley Mar 31: 1-5 *Kelly* | Paris May 17: 5-1 *Stephenson 2, Dean 2, Jack* |

| 1928 Belgium | 1928 Ireland | 1928 Wales | 1929 Scotland | 1929 France |
|---|---|---|---|---|
| 1 Olney | 1 Hacking | 1 Hacking | 1 Hacking | 1 Hufton |
| 2 Goodall | 2 Cooper | 2 Cooper | 2 Cooper | 2 Blenkinsop |
| 3 Blenkinsop | 3 Blenkinsop | 3 Blenkinsop | 3 Blenkinsop | 3 Cooper |
| 4 Edwards | 4 Edwards | 4 Edwards | 4 Edwards | 4 Kean |
| 5 Matthews | 5 Barrett J. | 5 Hart | 5 Seddon | 5 Hill |
| 6 Green | 6 Campbell | 6 Campbell | 6 Nuttall | 6 Peacock |
| 7 Bruton | 7 Hulme | 7 Hulme | 7 Bruton | 7 Adcock |
| 8 Jack | 8 Hine | 8 Hine | 8 Brown G. | 8 Kail |
| 9 Dean | 9 Dean | 9 Dean | 9 Dean | 9 Camsell |
| 10 Stephenson | 10 Bradford | 10 Bradford | 10 Wainscoat | 10 Bradford |
| 11 Barry | 11 Ruffell | 11 Ruffell | 11 Ruffell | 11 Barry |
| Antwerp May 19: 3-1 *Dean 2, Matthews* | Everton Oct 22: 2-1 *Hulme, Dean* | Swansea Nov 17: 3-2 *Hulme 2, Hine* | Glasgow April 13: 0-1 | Paris May 9: 4-1 *Kail 2, Camsell 2* |

| 1929 Belgium | 1929 Spain | 1929 Ireland | 1929 Wales | 1930 Scotland |
|---|---|---|---|---|
| 1 Hufton | 1 Hufton | 1 Brown J. | 1 Hibbs | 1 Hibbs |
| 2 Cooper | 2 Cooper | 2 Cresswell | 2 Smart | 2 Goodall |
| 3 Blenkinsop | 3 Blenkinsop | 3 Blenkinsop | 3 Blenkinsop | 3 Blenkinsop |
| 4 Oliver | 4 Kean | 4 Edwards | 4 Edwards | 4 Strange |
| 5 Hill | 5 Hill | 5 Hart | 5 Hart | 5 Webster |
| 6 Peacock | 6 Peacock | 6 Barrett A. | 6 Marsden | 6 Marsden |
| 7 Adcock | 7 Adcock | 7 Adcock | 7 Adcock | 7 Crooks |
| 8 Kail | 8 Kail | 8 Hine | 8 Hine | 8 Jack |
| 9 Camsell | 9 Bradford | 9 Camsell | 9 Camsell | 9 Watson |
| 10 Carter J.H. | 10 Carter J.H. | 10 Bradford | 10 Johnson | 10 Bradford |
| 11 Barry | 11 Barry | 11 Brook | 11 Ruffell | 11 Rimmer |
| Brussels | Madrid | Belfast | Chelsea | Wembley |
| May 11: 5-1 | May 15: 3-4 | Oct 19: 3-0 | Nov 20: 6-0 | April 5: 5-2 |
| *Camsell 4, Carter* | *Carter 2, Bradford* | *Camsell 2, Hine* | *Adcock, Camsell 3, Johnson 2* | *Jack, Watson 2, Rimmer 2* |

| 1930 Germany | 1930 Austria | 1930 Ireland | 1930 Wales | 1931 Scotland |
|---|---|---|---|---|
| 1 Hibbs | 1 Hibbs | 1 Hibbs | 1 Hibbs | 1 Hibbs |
| 2 Goodall | 2 Goodall | 2 Goodall | 2 Goodall | 2 Goodall |
| 3 Blenkinsop | 3 Blenkinsop | 3 Blenkinsop | 3 Blenkinsop | 3 Blenkinsop |
| 4 Strange | 4 Strange | 4 Strange | 4 Strange | 4 Strange |
| 5 Webster | 5 Webster | 5 Leach | 5 Leach | 5 Roberts |
| 6 Marsden | 6 Cowan | 6 Campbell | 6 Campbell | 6 Campbell |
| 7 Crooks | 7 Crooks | 7 Crooks | 7 Crooks | 7 Crooks |
| 8 Jack | 8 Jack | 8 Hodgson | 8 Hodgson | 8 Hodgson |
| 9 Watson | 9 Watson | 9 Hampson | 9 Hampson | 9 Dean |
| 10 Bradford | 10 Bradford | 10 Burgess | 10 Bradford | 10 Burgess |
| 11 Rimmer | 11 Rimmer | 11 Houghton | 11 Houghton | 11 Crawford |
| Berlin | Vienna | Sheffield | Wrexham | Glasgow |
| May 10: 3-3 | May 14: 0-0 | Oct 20: 5-1 | Nov 22: 4-0 | Mar 28: 0-2 |
| *Bradford 2, Jack* | | *Burgess 2, Crooks, Hampson, Houghton* | *Hodgson, Bradford, Hampson 2* | |

| 1931 France | 1931 Belgium | 1931 Ireland | 1931 Wales | 1931 Spain |
|---|---|---|---|---|
| 1 Turner | 1 Turner | 1 Hibbs | 1 Hibbs | 1 Hibbs |
| 2 Cooper | 2 Goodall | 2 Goodall | 2 Cooper | 2 Cooper |
| 3 Blenkinsop | 3 Blenkinsop | 3 Blenkinsop | 3 Blenkinsop | 3 Blenkinsop |
| 4 Strange | 4 Strange | 4 Strange | 4 Strange | 4 Strange |
| 5 Graham | 5 Cowan | 5 Graham | 5 Gee | 5 Gee |
| 6 Tate | 6 Tate | 6 Campbell | 6 Campbell | 6 Campbell |
| 7 Crooks | 7 Crooks | 7 Crooks | 7 Crooks | 7 Crooks |
| 8 Stephenson | 8 Roberts | 8 Smith J. | 8 Smith J. | 8 Smith J. |
| 9 Waring | 9 Waring | 9 Waring | 9 Waring | 9 Dean |
| 10 Burgess | 10 Burgess | 10 Hine | 10 Hine | 10 Johnson |
| 11 Houghton | 11 Houghton | 11 Houghton | 11 Bastin | 11 Rimmer |
| Paris | Brussels | Belfast | Liverpool | Arsenal |
| May 14: 2-5 | May 16: 4-1 | Oct 17: 6-2 | Nov 18: 3-1 | Dec 9: 7-1 |
| *Crooks, Waring* | *Burgess 2, Houghton, Roberts* | *Waring 2, Smith, Hine, Houghton 2* | *Smith, Crooks, Hine* | *Smith 2, Johnson 2, Crooks 2, Dean* |

| 1932 Scotland | 1932 Ireland | 1932 Wales | 1932 Austria | 1933 Scotland |
|---|---|---|---|---|
| 1 Pearson | 1 Hibbs | 1 Hibbs | 1 Hibbs | 1 Hibbs |
| 2 Shaw | 2 Goodall | 2 Goodall | 2 Goodall | 2 Cooper |
| 3 Blenkinsop | 3 Blenkinsop | 3 Blenkinsop | 3 Blenkinsop | 3 Blenkinsop |
| 4 Strange | 4 Strange | 4 Stoker | 4 Strange | 4 Strange |
| 5 O'Dowd | 5 O'Dowd | 5 Young | 5 Hart | 5 Hart |
| 6 Weaver | 6 Weaver | 6 Tate | 6 Keen | 6 Weaver |
| 7 Crooks | 7 Crooks | 7 Crooks | 7 Crooks | 7 Hulme |
| 8 Barclay | 8 Barclay | 8 Jack | 8 Jack | 8 Starling |
| 9 Waring | 9 Dean | 9 Brown G. | 9 Hampson | 9 Hunt |
| 10 Johnson | 10 Johnson | 10 Sandford | 10 Walker | 10 Pickering |
| 11 Houghton | 11 Cunliffe | 11 Cunliffe | 11 Houghton | 11 Arnold |
| Wembley | Blackpool | Wrexham | Chelsea | Glasgow |
| April 9: 3-0 | Oct 17: 1-0 | Nov 16: 0-0 | Dec 7: 4-3 | April 1: 1-2 |
| *Waring, Crooks* | *Barclay* | | *Hampson 2,* | *Hunt* |
| *Barclay* | | | *Houghton, Crooks* | |

| 1933 Italy | 1933 Switzerland | 1933 Ireland | 1933 Wales | 1933 France |
|---|---|---|---|---|
| 1 Hibbs | 1 Hibbs | 1 Hibbs | 1 Hibbs | 1 Hibbs |
| 2 Goodall | 2 Goodall | 2 Goodall | 2 Goodall | 2 Goodall |
| 3 Hapgood | 3 Hapgood | 3 Hapgood | 3 Hapgood | 3 Fairhurst |
| 4 Strange | 4 Strange | 4 Strange | 4 Strange | 4 Strange |
| 5 White | 5 O'Dowd | 5 Allen | 5 Allen | 5 Rowe |
| 6 Copping | 6 Copping | 6 Copping | 6 Copping | 6 Copping |
| 7 Geldard | 7 Geldard | 7 Crooks | 7 Crooks | 7 Crooks |
| 8 Richardson J.R. | 8 Richardson J.R. | 8 Grosvenor | 8 Grosvenor | 8 Grosvenor |
| 9 Hunt | 9 Hunt | 9 Bowers | 9 Bowers | 9 Camsell |
| 10 Furness | 10 Bastin | 10 Bastin | 10 Bastin | 10 Hall |
| 11 Bastin | 11 Brook | 11 Brook | 11 Brook | 11 Brook |
| Rome | Berne | Belfast | Newcastle | Tottenham |
| May 13: 1-1 | May 20: 4-0 | Oct 14: 3-0 | Nov 15: 1-2 | Dec 6: 4-1 |
| *Bastin* | *Bastin 2,* | *Brook, Grosvenor* | *Brook* | *Camsell 2, Brook,* |
| | *Richardson 2* | *Bowers* | | *Grosvenor* |

| 1934 Scotland | 1934 Hungary | 1934 Czechoslovakia | 1934 Wales | 1934 Italy |
|---|---|---|---|---|
| 1 Moss | 1 Moss | 1 Moss | 1 Hibbs | 1 Moss |
| 2 Cooper | 2 Cooper | 2 Cooper | 2 Cooper | 2 Male |
| 3 Hapgood | 3 Hapgood | 3 Hapgood | 3 Hapgood | 3 Hapgood |
| 4 Stoker | 4 Stoker | 4 Gardner | 4 Britton | 4 Britton |
| 5 Hart | 5 Hart | 5 Hart | 5 Barker | 5 Barker |
| 6 Copping | 6 Burrows | 6 Burrows | 6 Bray | 6 Copping |
| 7 Crooks | 7 Crooks | 7 Crooks | 7 Matthews | 7 Matthews |
| 8 Carter H.S. | 8 Carter H.S. | 8 Beresford | 8 Bowden | 8 Bowden |
| 9 Bowers | 9 Tilson | 9 Tilson | 9 Tilson | 9 Drake |
| 10 Bastin | 10 Bastin | 10 Bastin | 10 Westwood | 10 Bastin |
| 11 Brook | 11 Brook | 11 Brook | 11 Brook | 11 Brook |
| Wembley | Budapest | Prague | Cardiff | Arsenal |
| April 14: 3-0 | May 10: 1-2 | May 16: 1-2 | Sept 29: 4-0 | Nov 14: 3-2 |
| *Brook, Bastin,* | *Tilson* | *Tilson* | *Tilson 2, Brook,* | *Brook 2, Drake* |
| *Bowers* | | | *Matthews* | |

| 1935 Ireland | 1935 Scotland | 1935 Holland | 1935 Ireland | 1935 Germany |
|---|---|---|---|---|
| 1 Hibbs | 1 Hibbs | 1 Hibbs | 1 Sagar | 1 Hibbs |
| 2 Male | 2 Male | 2 Male | 2 Male | 2 Male |
| 3 Hapgood | 3 Hapgood | 3 Hapgood | 3 Hapgood | 3 Hapgood |
| 4 Britton | 4 Britton | 4 Gardner | 4 Smith S. | 4 Crayston |
| 5 Barker | 5 Barker | 5 Barker | 5 Barker | 5 Barker |
| 6 Copping | 6 Alsford | 6 Burrows | 6 Bray | 6 Bray |
| 7 Crooks | 7 Geldard | 7 Worrall | 7 Birkett | 7 Matthews |
| 8 Bestall | 8 Bastin | 8 Eastham | 8 Bowden | 8 Carter H.S. |
| 9 Drake | 9 Gurney | 9 Richardson W.G. | 9 Tilson | 9 Camsell |
| 10 Bastin | 10 Westwood | 10 Westwood | 10 Westwood | 10 Westwood |
| 11 Brook | 11 Brook | 11 Boyes | 11 Brook | 11 Bastin |
| Everton | Glasgow | Amsterdam | Belfast | Tottenham |
| Feb 6: 2-1 | April 6: 0-2 | May 18: 1-0 | Oct 19: 3-1 | Dec 4: 3-0 |
| *Bastin 2* | | *Worrall* | *Tilson 2, Brook* | *Camsell 2, Bastin* |

| 1936 Wales | 1936 Scotland | 1936 Austria | 1936 Belgium | 1936 Wales |
|---|---|---|---|---|
| 1 Hibbs | 1 Sagar | 1 Sagar | 1 Sagar | 1 Holdcroft |
| 2 Male | 2 Male | 2 Male | 2 Male | 2 Sproston |
| 3 Hapgood | 3 Hapgood | 3 Hapgood | 3 Hapgood | 3 Catlin |
| 4 Crayston | 4 Crayston | 4 Crayston | 4 Crayston | 4 Smalley |
| 5 Barker | 5 Barker | 5 Barker | 5 Joy | 5 Barker |
| 6 Bray | 6 Bray | 6 Copping | 6 Copping | 6 Keen |
| 7 Crooks | 7 Crooks | 7 Spence | 7 Spence | 7 Crooks |
| 8 Bowden | 8 Barclay | 8 Bowden | 8 Barkas | 8 Scott |
| 9 Drake | 9 Camsell | 9 Camsell | 9 Camsell | 9 Steele |
| 10 Bastin | 10 Bastin | 10 Bastin | 10 Cunliffe | 10 Westwood |
| 11 Brook | 11 Brook | 11 Hobbis | 11 Hobbis | 11 Bastin |
| Wolverhampton | Wembley | Vienna | Brussels | Cardiff |
| Feb 5: 1-2 | April 4: 1-1 | May 6: 1-2 | May 9: 2-3 | Oct 17: 1-2 |
| *Bowden* | *Camsell* | *Camsell* | *Camsell, Hobbis* | *Bastin* |

| 1936 Ireland | 1936 Hungary | 1937 Scotland | 1937 Norway | 1937 Sweden |
|---|---|---|---|---|
| 1 Holdcroft | 1 Tweedy | 1 Woodley | 1 Woodley | 1 Woodley |
| 2 Male | 2 Male | 2 Male | 2 Male | 2 Male |
| 3 Catlin | 3 Catlin | 3 Barkas | 3 Catlin | 3 Catlin |
| 4 Britton | 4 Britton | 4 Britton | 4 Britton | 4 Britton |
| 5 Gee | 5 Young | 5 Young | 5 Young | 5 Young |
| 6 Keen | 6 Keen | 6 Bray | 6 Copping | 6 Copping |
| 7 Worrall | 7 Crooks | 7 Matthews | 7 Kirchen | 7 Kirchen |
| 8 Carter H.S. | 8 Bowden | 8 Carter H.S. | 8 Galley | 8 Galley |
| 9 Steele | 9 Drake | 9 Steele | 9 Steele | 9 Steele |
| 10 Bastin | 10 Carter H.S. | 10 Starling | 10 Goulden | 10 Goulden |
| 11 Johnson | 11 Brook | 11 Johnson | 11 Johnson | 11 Johnson |
| Stoke | Arsenal | Glasgow | Oslo | Stockholm |
| Nov 18: 3-1 | Dec 2: 6-2 | April 17: 1-3 | May 14: 6-0 | May 17: 4-0 |
| *Carter, Bastin, Worrall* | *Drake 3, Brook, Britton, Carter* | *Steele* | *Steele 2, Kirchen, Galley, Goulden, Holmsen og* | *Steele 3, Johnson* |

| 1937 Finland | 1937 Ireland | 1937 Wales | 1937 Czechoslovakia | 1938 Scotland |
|---|---|---|---|---|
| 1 Woodley | 1 Woodley | 1 Woodley | 1 Woodley | 1 Woodley |
| 2 Male | 2 Sproston | 2 Sproston | 2 Sproston | 2 Sproston |
| 3 Hapgood | 3 Barkas | 3 Barkas | 3 Barkas | 3 Hapgood |
| 4 Willingham | 4 Crayston | 4 Crayston | 4 Crayston | 4 Willingham |
| 5 Betmead | 5 Cullis | 5 Cullis | 5 Cullis | 5 Cullis |
| 6 Copping | 6 Copping | 6 Copping | 6 Copping | 6 Copping |
| 7 Kirchen | 7 Geldard | 7 Matthews | 7 Matthews | 7 Matthews |
| 8 Robinson | 8 Hall | 8 Hall | 8 Hall | 8 Hall |
| 9 Payne | 9 Mills | 9 Mills | 9 Mills | 9 Fenton |
| 10 Steele | 10 Goulden | 10 Goulden | 10 Goulden | 10 Stephenson |
| 11 Johnson | 11 Brook | 11 Brook | 11 Morton | 11 Bastin |

| Helsinki May 20: 8-0 *Payne 2, Steele 2, Kirchen, Willingham, Johnson, Robinson* | Belfast Oct 23: 5-1 *Mills 3, Hall, Brook* | Middlesbrough Nov 17: 2-1 *Matthews, Hall* | Tottenham Dec 1: 5-4 *Crayston, Morton, Matthews 3* | Wembley April 9: 0-1 |
|---|---|---|---|---|

| 1938 Germany | 1938 Switzerland | 1938 France | 1938 Wales | 1938 FIFA |
|---|---|---|---|---|
| 1 Woodley | 1 Woodley | 1 Woodley | 1 Woodley | 1 Woodley |
| 2 Sproston | 2 Sproston | 2 Sproston | 2 Sproston | 2 Sproston |
| 3 Hapgood | 3 Hapgood | 3 Hapgood | 3 Hapgood | 3 Hapgood |
| 4 Willingham | 4 Willingham | 4 Willingham | 4 Willingham | 4 Willingham |
| 5 Young | 5 Young | 5 Young | 5 Young | 5 Cullis |
| 6 Welsh | 6 Welsh | 6 Cullis | 6 Copping | 6 Copping |
| 7 Matthews | 7 Matthews | 7 Broome | 7 Matthews | 7 Matthews |
| 8 Robinson | 8 Robinson | 8 Matthews | 8 Robinson | 8 Hall |
| 9 Broome | 9 Broome | 9 Drake | 9 Lawton | 9 Lawton |
| 10 Goulden | 10 Goulden | 10 Goulden | 10 Goulden | 10 Goulden |
| 11 Bastin | 11 Bastin | 11 Bastin | 11 Boyes | 11 Boyes |

| Berlin May 14: 6-3 *Robinson 2, Bastin, Broome, Matthews, Goulden* | Zurich May 21: 1-2 *Bastin* | Paris May 26: 4-2 *Drake 2, Broome, Bastin* | Cardiff Oct 22: 2-4 *Lawton, Matthews* | Arsenal Oct 26: 3-0 *Hall, Lawton, Goulden* |
|---|---|---|---|---|

| 1938 Norway | 1938 Ireland | 1939 Scotland | 1939 Italy | 1939 Yugoslavia |
|---|---|---|---|---|
| 1 Woodley | 1 Woodley | 1 Woodley | 1 Woodley | 1 Woodley |
| 2 Sproston | 2 Morris | 2 Morris | 2 Male | 2 Male |
| 3 Hapgood | 3 Hapgood | 3 Hapgood | 3 Hapgood | 3 Hapgood |
| 4 Willingham | 4 Willingham | 4 Willingham | 4 Willingham | 4 Willingham |
| 5 Cullis | 5 Cullis | 5 Cullis | 5 Cullis | 5 Cullis |
| 6 Wright D. | 6 Mercer | 6 Mercer | 6 Mercer | 6 Mercer |
| 7 Matthews | 7 Matthews | 7 Matthews | 7 Matthews | 7 Matthews |
| 8 Broome | 8 Hall | 8 Hall | 8 Hall | 8 Hall |
| 9 Lawton | 9 Lawton | 9 Lawton | 9 Lawton | 9 Lawton |
| 10 Dix | 10 Stephenson | 10 Goulden | 10 Goulden | 10 Goulden |
| 11 Smith J.R. | 11 Smith J.R. | 11 Beasley | 11 Broome | 11 Broome |

| Newcastle Nov 9: 4-0 *Smith 2, Dix, Lawton* | Manchester Nov 16: 7-0 *Hall 5, Lawton, Matthews* | Glasgow April 15: 2-1 *Beasley, Lawton* | Milan May 13: 2-2 *Lawton, Hall* | Belgrade May 18: 1-2 *Broome* |
|---|---|---|---|---|

| | 1939 Rumania | 1946 N Ireland | 1946 Rep of Ireland | 1946 Wales | 1946 Netherlands |
|---|---|---|---|---|---|
| 1 | Woodley | Swift | Swift | Swift | Swift |
| 2 | Male | Scott | Scott | Scott | Scott |
| 3 | Morris | Hardwick | Hardwick | Hardwick | Hardwick |
| 4 | Mercer | Wright W. | Wright W. | Wright W. | Wright W. |
| 5 | Cullis | Franklin | Franklin | Franklin | Franklin |
| 6 | Copping | Cockburn | Cockburn | Cockburn | Johnston |
| 7 | Broome | Finney | Finney | Finney | Finney |
| 8 | Goulden | Carter | Carter | Carter | Carter |
| 9 | Lawton | Lawton | Lawton | Lawton | Lawton |
| 10 | Welsh | Mannion | Mannion | Mannion | Mannion |
| 11 | Smith L.C. | Langton | Langton | Langton | Langton |
| | Bucharest May 24: 2-0 *Goulden, Welsh* | Belfast Sept 28: 7-2 *Carter, Mannion 3, Finney, Lawton, Langton* | Dublin Sept 30: 1-0 *Finney* | Maine Road Oct 19: 3-0 *Mannion 2, Lawton* | Huddersfield Nov 27: 8-2 *Lawton 4, Carter 2, Mannion, Finney* |

| | 1947 Scotland | 1947 France | 1947 Switzerland | 1947 Portugal | 1947 Belgium |
|---|---|---|---|---|---|
| 1 | Swift | Swift | Swift | Swift | Swift |
| 2 | Scott | Scott | Scott | Scott | Scott |
| 3 | Hardwick | Hardwick | Hardwick | Hardwick | Hardwick |
| 4 | Wright W. | Wright W. | Wright W. | Wright W. | Ward |
| 5 | Franklin | Franklin | Franklin | Franklin | Franklin |
| 6 | Johnston | Lowe | Lowe | Lowe | Wright W. |
| 7 | Matthews S. | Finney | Matthews S. | Matthews S. | Matthews S. |
| 8 | Carter | Carter | Carter | Mortensen | Mortensen |
| 9 | Lawton | Lawton | Lawton | Lawton | Lawton |
| 10 | Mannion | Mannion | Mannion | Mannion | Mannion |
| 11 | Mullen | Langton | Langton | Finney | Finney |
| | Wembley April 12: 1-1 *Carter* | Highbury May 3: 3-0 *Finney, Mannion, Carter* | Zurich May 18: 0-1 | Lisbon May 27: 10-0 *Lawton 4, Mortensen 4, Finney, Matthews* | Brussels Sept 21: 5-2 *Lawton 2, Mortensen, Finney 2* |

| | 1947 Wales | 1947 N Ireland | 1947 Sweden | 1948 Scotland | 1948 Italy |
|---|---|---|---|---|---|
| 1 | Swift | Swift | Swift | Swift | Swift |
| 2 | Scott | Scott | Scott | Scott | Scott |
| 3 | Hardwick | Hardwick | Hardwick | Hardwick | Howe J. |
| 4 | Taylor P. | Taylor P. | Taylor P. | Wright W. | Wright W. |
| 5 | Franklin | Franklin | Franklin | Franklin | Franklin |
| 6 | Wright W. | Wright W. | Wright W. | Cockburn | Cockburn |
| 7 | Matthews S. | Matthews S. | Finney | Matthews S. | Matthews S. |
| 8 | Mortensen | Mortensen | Mortensen | Mortensen | Mortensen |
| 9 | Lawton | Lawton | Lawton | Lawton | Lawton |
| 10 | Mannion | Mannion | Mannion | Pearson | Mannion |
| 11 | Finney | Finney | Langton | Finney | Finney |
| | Cardiff Oct 18: 3-0 *Finney, Mortensen, Lawton* | Everton Nov 5: 2-2 *Mannion, Lawton* | Highbury Nov 19: 4-2 *Mortensen 3, Lawton (pen)* | Glasgow April 10: 2-0 *Finney, Mortensen* | Turin May 16: 4-0 *Mortensen, Lawton, Finney 2* |

| **1948**<br>**Denmark** | **1948**<br>**N Ireland** | **1948**<br>**Wales** | **1948**<br>**Switzerland** | **1948**<br>**Scotland** |
|---|---|---|---|---|
| 1 Swift | 1 Swift | 1 Swift | 1 Ditchburn | 1 Swift |
| 2 Scott | 2 Scott | 2 Scott | 2 Ramsey | 2 Aston |
| 3 Aston | 3 Howe J. | 3 Aston | 3 Aston | 3 Howe J. |
| 4 Wright W. | 4 Wright W. | 4 Ward | 4 Wright W. | 4 Wright W. |
| 5 Franklin | 5 Franklin | 5 Franklin | 5 Franklin | 5 Franklin |
| 6 Cockburn | 6 Cockburn | 6 Wright W. | 6 Cockburn | 6 Cockburn |
| 7 Matthews S. | 7 Matthews S. | 7 Matthews S. | 7 Matthews S. | 7 Matthews S. |
| 8 Hagan | 8 Mortensen | 8 Mortensen | 8 Rowley J. | 8 Mortensen |
| 9 Lawton | 9 Milburn | 9 Milburn | 9 Milburn | 9 Milburn |
| 10 Shackleton | 10 Pearson | 10 Shackleton | 10 Haines | 10 Pearson |
| 11 Langton | 11 Finney | 11 Finney | 11 Hancocks | 11 Finney |

| Copenhagen<br>Sept 26: 0-0 | Belfast<br>Oct 9: 6-2<br>*Matthews S,*<br>*Mortensen 3,*<br>*Milburn, Pearson* | Villa Park<br>Nov 10: 1-0<br>*Finney* | Highbury<br>Dec 1: 6-0<br>*Haines 2,*<br>*Hancocks 2*<br>*Rowley, Milburn* | Wembley<br>April 9: 1-3<br>*Milburn* |
|---|---|---|---|---|

| **1949**<br>**Sweden** | **1949**<br>**Norway** | **1949**<br>**France** | **1949**<br>**Rep of Ireland** | **1949**<br>**Wales** |
|---|---|---|---|---|
| 1 Ditchburn | 1 Swift | 1 Williams | 1 Williams | 1 Williams |
| 2 Shinwell | 2 Ellerington | 2 Ellerington | 2 Mozley | 2 Mozley |
| 3 Aston | 3 Aston | 3 Aston | 3 Aston | 3 Aston |
| 4 Wright W. | 4 Wright W. | 4 Wright W. | 4 Wright W. | 4 Wright W. |
| 5 Franklin | 5 Franklin | 5 Franklin | 5 Franklin | 5 Franklin |
| 6 Cockburn | 6 Dickinson | 6 Dickinson | 6 Dickinson | 6 Dickinson |
| 7 Finney | 7 Finney | 7 Finney | 7 Harris P. | 7 Finney |
| 8 Mortensen | 8 Morris | 8 Morris | 8 Morris | 8 Mortensen |
| 9 Bentley | 9 Mortensen | 9 Rowley J. | 9 Pye | 9 Milburn |
| 10 Rowley J. | 10 Mannion | 10 Mannion | 10 Mannion | 10 Shackleton |
| 11 Langton | 11 Mullen | 11 Mullen | 11 Finney | 11 Hancocks |

| Stockholm<br>May 13: 1-3<br>*Finney* | Oslo<br>May 18: 4-1<br>*Mullen, Finney,*<br>*Spydevolde og,*<br>*Morris* | Paris<br>May 22: 3-1<br>*Morris 2*<br>*Wright* | Goodison Park<br>Sept 21: 0-2 | Cardiff<br>Oct 15: 4-1<br>*Mortensen,*<br>*Milburn 3* |
|---|---|---|---|---|

| **1949**<br>**N Ireland** | **1949**<br>**Italy** | **1950**<br>**Scotland** | **1950**<br>**Portugal** | **1950**<br>**Belgium** |
|---|---|---|---|---|
| 1 Streten | 1 Williams | 1 Williams | 1 Williams | 1 Williams |
| 2 Mozley | 2 Ramsey | 2 Ramsey | 2 Ramsey | 2 Ramsey |
| 3 Aston | 3 Aston | 3 Aston | 3 Aston | 3 Aston |
| 4 Watson | 4 Watson | 4 Wright W. | 4 Wright W. | 4 Wright W. |
| 5 Franklin | 5 Franklin | 5 Franklin | 5 Jones W.H. | 5 Jones W.H. |
| 6 Wright W. | 6 Wright W. | 6 Dickinson | 6 Dickinson | 6 Dickinson |
| 7 Finney | 7 Finney | 7 Finney | 7 Milburn | 7 Milburn |
| | | | | (Mullen) |
| 8 Mortensen | 8 Mortensen | 8 Mannion | 8 Mortensen | 8 Mortensen |
| 9 Rowley J. | 9 Rowley J. | 9 Mortensen | 9 Bentley | 9 Bentley |
| 10 Pearson | 10 Pearson | 10 Bentley | 10 Mannion | 10 Mannion |
| 11 Froggatt J. | 11 Froggatt J. | 11 Langton | 11 Finney | 11 Finney |

| Maine Road<br>Nov 16: 9-2<br>*Rowley 4,*<br>*Froggatt, Pearson 2,*<br>*Mortensen 2* | Tottenham<br>Nov 30: 2-0<br>*Rowley, Wright* | Glasgow<br>April 15: 1-0<br>*Bentley* | Luton<br>May 14: 5-3<br>*Finney 4 (2 pens),*<br>*Mortensen* | Brussels<br>May 18: 4-1<br>*Mullen,*<br>*Mortensen, Mannion,*<br>*Bentley* |
|---|---|---|---|---|

| 1950 Chile † | 1950 USA † | 1950 Spain † | 1950 N Ireland | 1950 Wales |
|---|---|---|---|---|
| 1 Williams | 1 Williams | 1 Williams | 1 Williams | 1 Williams |
| 2 Ramsey | 2 Ramsey | 2 Ramsey | 2 Ramsey | 2 Ramsey |
| 3 Aston | 3 Aston | 3 Eckersley | 3 Aston | 3 Smith L. |
| 4 Wright W. | 4 Wright W. | 4 Wright W. | 4 Wright W. | 4 Watson |
| 5 Hughes L. | 5 Hughes L. | 5 Hughes L. | 5 Chilton | 5 Compton L. |
| 6 Dickinson | 6 Dickinson | 6 Dickinson | 6 Dickinson | 6 Dickinson |
| 7 Finney | 7 Finney | 7 Matthews S. | 7 Matthews S. | 7 Finney |
| 8 Mannion | 8 Mannion | 8 Mortensen | 8 Mannion | 8 Mannion |
| 9 Bentley | 9 Bentley | 9 Milburn | 9 Lee J. | 9 Milburn |
| 10 Mortensen | 10 Mortensen | 10 Baily E. | 10 Baily E. | 10 Baily E. |
| 11 Mullen | 11 Mullen | 11 Finney | 11 Langton | 11 Medley |
| Rio de Janeiro | Belo Horizonte | Rio de Janeiro | Belfast | Sunderland |
| June 15: 2-0 | June 29: 0-1 | July 2: 0-1 | Oct 7: 4-1 | Nov 15: 4-2 |
| *Mortensen, Mannion* | | | *Baily 2, Lee, Wright* | *Baily 2, Mannion, Milburn* |

| 1950 Yugoslavia | 1951 Scotland | 1951 Argentina | 1951 Portugal | 1951 France |
|---|---|---|---|---|
| 1 Williams | 1 Williams | 1 Williams | 1 Williams | 1 Williams |
| 2 Ramsey | 2 Ramsey | 2 Ramsey | 2 Ramsey | 2 Ramsey |
| 3 Eckersley | 3 Eckersley | 3 Eckersley | 3 Eckersley | 3 Willis |
| 4 Watson | 4 Johnston | 4 Wright W. | 4 Nicholson | 4 Wright W. |
| 5 Compton L. | 5 Froggatt J. | 5 Taylor J. | 5 Taylor J. | 5 Chilton |
| 6 Dickinson | 6 Wright W. | 6 Cockburn | 6 Cockburn | 6 Cockburn |
| 7 Hancocks | 7 Matthews S. | 7 Finney | 7 Finney | 7 Finney |
| 8 Mannion | 8 Mannion | 8 Mortensen | 8 Pearson | 8 Mannion |
| 9 Lofthouse | 9 Mortensen | 9 Milburn | 9 Milburn | 9 Milburn |
| 10 Baily E. | 10 Hassall | 10 Hassall | 10 Hassall | 10 Hassall |
| 11 Medley | 11 Finney | 11 Metcalfe | 11 Metcalfe | 11 Medley |
| Highbury | Wembley | Wembley | Goodison Park | Highbury |
| Nov 22: 2-2 | April 14: 2-3 | May 9: 2-1 | May 19: 5-2 | Oct 3: 2-2 |
| *Lofthouse 2* | *Hassall, Finney* | *Mortensen 2* | *Nicholson, Milburn 2, Finney, Hassall* | *Firoud og, Medley* |

| 1951 Wales | 1951 N Ireland | 1951 Austria | 1952 Scotland | 1952 Italy |
|---|---|---|---|---|
| 1 Williams | 1 Merrick | 1 Merrick | 1 Merrick | 1 Merrick |
| 2 Ramsey | 2 Ramsey | 2 Ramsey | 2 Ramsey | 2 Ramsey |
| 3 Smith L. | 3 Smith L. | 3 Eckersley | 3 Garrett | 3 Garrett |
| 4 Wright W. | 4 Wright W. | 4 Wright W. | 4 Wright W. | 4 Wright W. |
| 5 Barrass | 5 Barrass | 5 Froggatt J. | 5 Froggatt J. | 5 Froggatt J. |
| 6 Dickinson | 6 Dickinson | 6 Dickinson | 6 Dickinson | 6 Dickinson |
| 7 Finney | 7 Finney | 7 Milton | 7 Finney | 7 Finney |
| 8 Thompson T. | 8 Sewell | 8 Broadis | 8 Broadis | 8 Broadis |
| 9 Lofthouse | 9 Lofthouse | 9 Lofthouse | 9 Lofthouse | 9 Lofthouse |
| 10 Baily E. | 10 Phillips | 10 Baily E. | 10 Pearson | 10 Pearson |
| 11 Medley | 11 Medley | 11 Medley | 11 Rowley J. | 11 Elliott |
| Cardiff | Villa Park | Wembley | Glasgow | Florence |
| Oct 20: 1-1 | Nov 14: 2-0 | Nov 28: 2-2 | April 5: 2-1 | May 18: 1-1 |
| *Baily* | *Lofthouse 2* | *Ramsey (pen), Lofthouse* | *Pearson 2* | *Broadis* |

| 1952 Austria | 1952 Switzerland | 1952 N Ireland | 1952 Wales | 1952 Belgium |
|---|---|---|---|---|
| 1 Merrick | 1 Merrick | 1 Merrick | 1 Merrick | 1 Merrick |
| 2 Ramsey | 2 Ramsey | 2 Ramsey | 2 Ramsey | 2 Ramsey |
| 3 Eckersley | 3 Eckersley | 3 Eckersley | 3 Smith L. | 3 Smith L. |
| 4 Wright W. | 4 Wright W. | 4 Wright W. | 4 Wright W. | 4 Wright W. |
| 5 Froggatt J. | 5 Froggatt J. | 5 Froggatt J. | 5 Froggatt J. | 5 Froggatt J. |
| 6 Dickinson | 6 Dickinson | 6 Dickinson | 6 Dickinson | 6 Dickinson |
| 7 Finney | 7 Allen R. | 7 Finney | 7 Finney | 7 Finney |
| 8 Sewell | 8 Sewell | 8 Sewell | 8 Froggatt R. | 8 Bentley |
| 9 Lofthouse | 9 Lofthouse | 9 Lofthouse | 9 Lofthouse | 9 Lofthouse |
| 10 Baily E. | 10 Baily E. | 10 Baily E. | 10 Bentley | 10 Froggatt R. |
| 11 Elliott | 11 Finney | 11 Elliott | 11 Elliott | 11 Elliott |
| Vienna May 25: 3-2 *Lofthouse 2, Sewell* | Zurich May 28: 3-0 *Sewell, Lofthouse 2* | Belfast Oct 4: 2-2 *Lofthouse, Elliott* | Wembley Nov 12: 5-2 *Finney, Lofthouse 2, Froggatt J., Bentley* | Wembley Nov 26: 5-0 *Elliott 2, Lofthouse 2, Froggatt R.* |

| 1953 Scotland | 1953 Argentina | 1953 Chile | 1953 Uruguay | 1953 USA |
|---|---|---|---|---|
| 1 Merrick | 1 Merrick | 1 Merrick | 1 Merrick | 1 Ditchburn |
| 2 Ramsey | 2 Ramsey | 2 Ramsey | 2 Ramsey | 2 Ramsey |
| 3 Smith L. | 3 Eckersley | 3 Eckersley | 3 Eckersley | 3 Eckersley |
| 4 Wright W. | 4 Wright W. | 4 Wright W. | 4 Wright W. | 4 Wright W. |
| 5 Barrass | 5 Johnston | 5 Johnston | 5 Johnston | 5 Johnston |
| 6 Dickinson | 6 Dickinson | 6 Dickinson | 6 Dickinson | 6 Dickinson |
| 7 Finney | 7 Finney | 7 Finney | 7 Finney | 7 Finney |
| 8 Broadis | 8 Broadis | 8 Broadis | 8 Broadis | 8 Broadis |
| 9 Lofthouse | 9 Lofthouse | 9 Lofthouse | 9 Lofthouse | 9 Lofthouse |
| 10 Froggatt R. | 10 Taylor T. | 10 Taylor T. | 10 Taylor T. | 10 Froggatt R. |
| 11 Froggatt J. | 11 Berry | 11 Berry | 11 Berry | 11 Froggatt J. |
| Wembley April 18: 2-2 *Broadis 2* | Buenos Aires May 17: 0-0 *(abandoned after 23 min.)* | Santiago May 24: 2-1 *Taylor, Lofthouse* | Montevideo May 31: 1-2 *Taylor* | New York June 8: 6-3 *Broadis, Finney 2, Lofthouse 2, Froggatt R.* |

| 1953 Wales | 1953 Rest of Europe | 1953 N Ireland | 1953 Hungary | 1954 Scotland |
|---|---|---|---|---|
| 1 Merrick | 1 Merrick | 1 Merrick | 1 Merrick | 1 Merrick |
| 2 Garrett | 2 Ramsey | 2 Rickaby | 2 Ramsey | 2 Staniforth |
| 3 Eckersley | 3 Eckersley | 3 Eckersley | 3 Eckersley | 3 Byrne R. |
| 4 Wright W. | 4 Wright W. | 4 Wright W. | 4 Wright W. | 4 Wright W. |
| 5 Johnston | 5 Ufton | 5 Johnston | 5 Johnston | 5 Clarke H. |
| 6 Dickinson | 6 Dickinson | 6 Dickinson | 6 Dickinson | 6 Dickinson |
| 7 Finney | 7 Matthews S. | 7 Matthews S. | 7 Matthews S. | 7 Finney |
| 8 Quixall | 8 Mortensen | 8 Quixall | 8 Taylor E. | 8 Broadis |
| 9 Lofthouse | 9 Lofthouse | 9 Lofthouse | 9 Mortensen | 9 Allen R. |
| 10 Wilshaw | 10 Quixall | 10 Hassall | 10 Sewell | 10 Nicholls |
| 11 Mullen | 11 Mullen | 11 Mullen | 11 Robb | 11 Mullen |
| Cardiff Oct 10: 4-1 *Wilshaw 2, Lofthouse 2* | Wembley Oct 21: 4-4 *Mullen 2, Mortensen, Ramsey (pen)* | Goodison Park Nov 11: 3-1 *Hassall 2, Lofthouse* | Wembley Nov 25: 3-6 *Sewell, Mortensen, Ramsey (pen)* | Glasgow April 3: 4-2 *Broadis, Nicholls, Allen, Mullen* |

| 1954 Yugoslavia | 1954 Hungary | 1954 Belgium † | 1954 Switzerland † | 1954 Uruguay † |
|---|---|---|---|---|
| 1 Merrick | 1 Merrick | 1 Merrick | 1 Merrick | 1 Merrick |
| 2 Staniforth | 2 Staniforth | 2 Staniforth | 2 Staniforth | 2 Staniforth |
| 3 Byrne R. | 3 Byrne R. | 3 Byrne R. | 3 Byrne R. | 3 Byrne R. |
| 4 Wright W. | 4 Wright W. | 4 Wright W. | 4 McGarry | 4 McGarry |
| 5 Owen | 5 Owen | 5 Owen | 5 Wright W. | 5 Wright W. |
| 6 Dickinson | 6 Dickinson | 6 Dickinson | 6 Dickinson | 6 Dickinson |
| 7 Finney | 7 Harris P. | 7 Matthews S. | 7 Finney | 7 Matthews S. |
| 8 Broadis | 8 Broadis | 8 Broadis | 8 Broadis | 8 Broadis |
| 9 Allen R. | 9 Jezzard | 9 Lofthouse | 9 Taylor T. | 9 Lofthouse |
| 10 Nicholls | 10 Broadis | 10 Taylor T. | 10 Wilshaw | 10 Wilshaw |
| 11 Mullen | 11 Finney | 11 Finney | 11 Mullen | 11 Finney |
| Belgrade May 16: 0-1 | Budapest May 23: 1-7 *Broadis* | Basle June 17: 4-4 (aet) *Broadis 2, Lofthouse 2* | Berne June 20: 2-0 *Wilshaw, Mullen* | Basle June 26: 2-4 *Lofthouse, Finney* |

| 1954 N Ireland | 1954 Wales | 1954 W Germany | 1955 Scotland | 1955 France |
|---|---|---|---|---|
| 1 Wood | 1 Wood | 1 Williams | 1 Williams | 1 Williams |
| 2 Foulkes | 2 Staniforth | 2 Meadows | 2 Meadows | 2 Sillett P. |
| 3 Byrne R. | 3 Byrne R. | 3 Byrne R. | 3 Byrne R. | 3 Byrne R. |
| 4 Wheeler | 4 Phillips | 4 Phillips | 4 Armstrong | 4 Flowers |
| 5 Wright W. | 5 Wright W. | 5 Wright W. | 5 Wright W. | 5 Wright W. |
| 6 Barlow | 6 Slater | 6 Slater | 6 Edwards | 6 Edwards |
| 7 Matthews S. | 7 Matthews S. | 7 Matthews S. | 7 Matthews S. | 7 Matthews S. |
| 8 Revie | 8 Bentley | 8 Bentley | 8 Revie | 8 Revie |
| 9 Lofthouse | 9 Allen R. | 9 Allen R. | 9 Lofthouse | 9 Lofthouse |
| 10 Haynes | 10 Shackleton | 10 Shackleton | 10 Wilshaw | 10 Wilshaw |
| 11 Pilkington | 11 Blunstone | 11 Finney | 11 Blunstone | 11 Blunstone |
| Belfast Oct 2: 2-0 *Haynes, Revie* | Wembley Nov 10: 3-2 *Bentley 3* | Wembley Dec 1: 3-1 *Bentley, Allen, Shackleton* | Wembley April 1: 7-2 *Wilshaw 4, Lofthouse 2, Revie* | Paris May 18: 0-1 |

| 1955 Spain | 1955 Portugal | 1955 Denmark | 1955 Wales | 1955 N Ireland |
|---|---|---|---|---|
| 1 Williams | 1 Williams | 1 Baynham | 1 Williams | 1 Baynham |
| 2 Sillet P. | 2 Sillett P. | 2 Hall | 2 Hall | 2 Hall |
| 3 Byrne R. | 3 Byrne R. | 3 Byrne R. | 3 Byrne R. | 3 Byrne R. |
| 4 Dickinson | 4 Dickinson | 4 McGarry | 4 McGarry | 4 Clayton |
| 5 Wright W. | 5 Wright W. | 5 Wright W. | 5 Wright W. | 5 Wright W. |
| 6 Edwards | 6 Edwards | 6 Dickinson | 6 Dickinson | 6 Dickinson |
| 7 Matthews S. | 7 Matthews S. | 7 Milburn | 7 Matthews S. | 7 Finney |
| 8 Bentley | 8 Bentley | 8 Revie | 8 Revie | 8 Haynes |
| 9 Lofthouse | 9 Lofthouse (Quixall) | 9 Lofthouse | 9 Lofthouse | 9 Jezzard |
| 10 Quixall | 10 Wilshaw | 10 Bradford | 10 Wilshaw | 10 Wilshaw |
| 11 Wilshaw | 11 Blunstone | 11 Finney | 11 Finney | 11 Perry |
| Madrid May 18: 1-1 *Bentley* | Oporto May 22: 1-3 *Bentley* | Copenhagen Oct 2: 5-1 *Revie 2 (1 pen), Lofthouse 2, Bradford* | Cardiff Oct 22: 1-1 *Charles J. og* | Wembley Nov 2: 3-0 *Wilshaw 2, Finney* |

| 1955 Spain | 1956 Scotland | 1956 Brazil | 1956 Sweden | 1956 Finland |
|---|---|---|---|---|
| 1 Baynham | 1 Matthews R. | 1 Matthews R. | 1 Matthews R. | 1 Wood |
| 2 Hall | 2 Hall | 2 Hall | 2 Hall | 2 Hall |
| 3 Byrne R. | 3 Byrne R. | 3 Byrne R. | 3 Byrne R. | 3 Byrne R. |
| 4 Clayton | 4 Dickinson | 4 Clayton | 4 Clayton | 4 Clayton |
| 5 Wright W. | 5 Wright W. | 5 Wright W. | 5 Wright W. | 5 Wright W. |
| 6 Dickinson | 6 Edwards | 6 Edwards | 6 Edwards | 6 Edwards |
| 7 Finney | 7 Finney | 7 Matthews S. | 7 Berry | 7 Astall |
| 8 Atyeo | 8 Taylor T. | 8 Atyeo | 8 Atyeo | 8 Haynes |
| 9 Lofthouse | 9 Lofthouse | 9 Taylor T. | 9 Taylor T. | 9 Taylor T. (Lofthouse) |
| 10 Haynes | 10 Haynes | 10 Haynes | 10 Haynes | 10 Wilshaw |
| 11 Perry | 11 Perry | 11 Grainger | 11 Grainger | 11 Grainger |

| | | | | |
|---|---|---|---|---|
| Wembley | Glasgow | Wembley | Stockholm | Helsinki |
| Nov 30: 4-1 | April 14: 1-1 | May 9: 4-2 | May 16: 0-0 | May 20: 5-1 |
| *Atyeo, Perry 2, Finney* | *Haynes* | *Taylor 2, Grainger 2* | | *Wilshaw, Haynes, Astall, Lofthouse 2* |

| 1956 W Germany | 1956 N Ireland | 1956 Wales | 1956 Yugoslavia | 1956 Denmark |
|---|---|---|---|---|
| 1 Matthews R. | 1 Matthews R. | 1 Ditchburn | 1 Ditchburn | 1 Ditchburn |
| 2 Hall | 2 Hall | 2 Hall | 2 Hall | 2 Hall |
| 3 Byrne R. | 3 Byrne R. | 3 Byrne R. | 3 Byrne R. | 3 Byrne R. |
| 4 Clayton | 4 Clayton | 4 Clayton | 4 Clayton | 4 Clayton |
| 5 Wright W. | 5 Wright W. | 5 Wright W. | 5 Wright W. | 5 Wright W. |
| 6 Edwards | 6 Edwards | 6 Dickinson | 6 Dickinson | 6 Dickinson |
| 7 Astall | 7 Matthews S. | 7 Matthews S. | 7 Matthews S. | 7 Matthews S. |
| 8 Haynes | 8 Revie | 8 Brooks | 8 Brooks | 8 Brooks |
| 9 Taylor T. | 9 Taylor T. | 9 Finney | 9 Finney | 9 Taylor T. |
| 10 Wilshaw | 10 Wilshaw | 10 Haynes | 10 Haynes (Taylor T.) | 10 Edwards |
| 11 Grainger | 11 Grainger | 11 Grainger | 11 Blunstone | 11 Finney |

| | | | | |
|---|---|---|---|---|
| Berlin | Belfast | Wembley | Wembley | Wolverhampton |
| May 26: 3-1 | Oct 6: 1-1 | Nov 14: 3-1 | Nov 28: 3-0 | Dec 5: 5-2 |
| *Edwards, Grainger, Haynes* | *Matthews S.* | *Haynes, Brooks, Finney* | *Brooks, Taylor 2* | *Taylor 3, Edwards 2* |

| 1957 Scotland | 1957 Rep of Ireland | 1957 Denmark | 1957 Rep of Ireland | 1957 Wales |
|---|---|---|---|---|
| 1 Hodgkinson | 1 Hodgkinson | 1 Hodgkinson | 1 Hodgkinson | 1 Hopkinson |
| 2 Hall | 2 Hall | 2 Hall | 2 Hall | 2 Howe D. |
| 3 Byrne R. | 3 Byrne R. | 3 Byrne R. | 3 Byrne R. | 3 Byrne R. |
| 4 Clayton | 4 Clayton | 4 Clayton | 4 Clayton | 4 Clayton |
| 5 Wright W. | 5 Wright W. | 5 Wright W. | 5 Wright W. | 5 Wright W. |
| 6 Edwards | 6 Edwards | 6 Edwards | 6 Edwards | 6 Edwards |
| 7 Matthews S. | 7 Matthews S. | 7 Matthews S. | 7 Finney | 7 Douglas |
| 8 Thompson T. | 8 Atyeo | 8 Atyeo | 8 Atyeo | 8 Kevan |
| 9 Finney | 9 Taylor T. | 9 Taylor T. | 9 Taylor T. | 9 Taylor T. |
| 10 Kevan | 10 Haynes | 10 Haynes | 10 Haynes | 10 Haynes |
| 11 Grainger | 11 Finney | 11 Finney | 11 Pegg | 11 Finney |

| | | | | |
|---|---|---|---|---|
| Wembley | Wembley | Copenhagen | Dublin | Cardiff |
| April 6: 2-1 | May 8: 5-1 | May 15: 4-1 | May 19: 1-1 | Oct 19: 4-0 |
| *Kevan, Edwards* | *Taylor 3, Atyeo 2* | *Haynes, Taylor 2, Atyeo* | *Atyeo* | *Hopkins og, Haynes 2, Finney* |

| 1957<br>N Ireland | 1957<br>France | 1958<br>Scotland | 1958<br>Portugal | 1958<br>Yugoslavia |
|---|---|---|---|---|
| 1 Hopkinson | 1 Hopkinson | 1 Hopkinson | 1 Hopkinson | 1 Hopkinson |
| 2 Howe D. | 2 Howe D. | 2 Howe D. | 2 Howe D. | 2 Howe D. |
| 3 Byrne R. | 3 Byrne R. | 3 Langley | 3 Langley | 3 Langley |
| 4 Clayton | 4 Clayton | 4 Clayton | 4 Clayton | 4 Clayton |
| 5 Wright W. | 5 Wright W. | 5 Wright W. | 5 Wright W. | 5 Wright W. |
| 6 Edwards | 6 Edwards | 6 Slater | 6 Slater | 6 Slater |
| 7 Douglas | 7 Douglas | 7 Douglas | 7 Douglas | 7 Douglas |
| 8 Kevan | 8 Robson R. | 8 Charlton R. | 8 Charlton R. | 8 Charlton R. |
| 9 Taylor T. | 9 Taylor T. | 9 Kevan | 9 Kevan | 9 Kevan |
| 10 Haynes | 10 Haynes | 10 Haynes | 10 Haynes | 10 Haynes |
| 11 A'Court | 11 Finney | 11 Finney | 11 Finney | 11 Finney |
| Wembley<br>Nov 6: 2-3<br>*A'Court, Edwards* | Wembley<br>Nov 27: 4-0<br>*Taylor 2,*<br>*Robson 2* | Glasgow<br>April 19: 4-0<br>*Douglas, Kevan 2,*<br>*Charlton* | Wembley<br>May 7: 2-1<br>*Charlton 2* | Belgrade<br>May 11: 0-5 |

| 1958<br>USSR | 1958<br>USSR † | 1958<br>Brazil † | 1958<br>Austria † | 1958<br>USSR † |
|---|---|---|---|---|
| 1 McDonald | 1 McDonald | 1 McDonald | 1 McDonald | 1 McDonald |
| 2 Howe D. | 2 Howe D. | 2 Howe D. | 2 Howe D. | 2 Howe D. |
| 3 Banks T. | 3 Banks T. | 3 Banks T. | 3 Banks T. | 3 Banks T. |
| 4 Clamp | 4 Clamp | 4 Clamp | 4 Clamp | 4 Clayton |
| 5 Wright W. | 5 Wright W. | 5 Wright W. | 5 Wright W. | 5 Wright W. |
| 6 Slater | 6 Slater | 6 Slater | 6 Slater | 6 Slater |
| 7 Douglas | 7 Douglas | 7 Douglas | 7 Douglas | 7 Brabrook |
| 8 Robson R. | 8 Robson R. | 8 Robson R. | 8 Robson R. | 8 Broadbent |
| 9 Kevan | 9 Kevan | 9 Kevan | 9 Kevan | 9 Kevan |
| 10 Haynes | 10 Haynes | 10 Haynes | 10 Haynes | 10 Haynes |
| 11 Finney | 11 Finney | 11 A'Court | 11 A'Court | 11 A'Court |
| Moscow<br>May 18: 1-1<br>*Kevan* | Gothenburg<br>June 8: 2-2<br>*Kevan, Finney (pen)* | Gothenburg<br>June 11: 0-0 | Boras<br>June 15: 2-2<br>*Haynes, Kevan* | Gothenburg<br>June 17: 0-1 |

| 1958<br>N Ireland | 1958<br>USSR | 1958<br>Wales | 1959<br>Scotland | 1959<br>Italy |
|---|---|---|---|---|
| 1 McDonald | 1 McDonald | 1 McDonald | 1 Hopkinson | 1 Hopkinson |
| 2 Howe D. | 2 Howe D. | 2 Howe D. | 2 Howe D. | 2 Howe D. |
| 3 Banks T. | 3 Shaw G. | 3 Shaw G. | 3 Shaw G. | 3 Shaw G. |
| 4 Clayton | 4 Clayton | 4 Clayton | 4 Clayton | 4 Clayton |
| 5 Wright W. | 5 Wright W. | 5 Wright W. | 5 Wright W. | 5 Wright W. |
| 6 McGuinness | 6 Slater | 6 Flowers | 6 Flowers | 6 Flowers |
| 7 Brabrook | 7 Douglas | 7 Clapton | 7 Douglas | 7 Bradley |
| 8 Broadbent | 8 Charlton R. | 8 Broadbent | 8 Broadbent | 8 Broadbent |
| 9 Charlton R. | 9 Lofthouse | 9 Lofthouse | 9 Charlton R. | 9 Charlton R. |
| 10 Haynes | 10 Haynes | 10 Charlton R. | 10 Haynes | 10 Haynes |
| 11 Finney | 11 Finney | 11 A'Court | 11 Holden | 11 Holden |
| Belfast<br>Oct 4: 3-3<br>*Charlton 2,*<br>*Finney* | Wembley<br>Oct 22: 5-0<br>*Haynes 3*<br>*Charlton (pen),*<br>*Lofthouse* | Villa Park<br>Nov 26: 2-2<br>*Broadbent 2* | Wembley<br>April 11: 1-0<br>*Charlton* | Wembley<br>May 6: 2-2<br>*Charlton,*<br>*Bradley* |

| 1959 Brazil | 1959 Peru | 1959 Mexico | 1959 USA | 1959 Wales |
|---|---|---|---|---|
| 1 Hopkinson | 1 Hopkinson | 1 Hopkinson | 1 Hopkinson | 1 Hopkinson |
| 2 Howe D. | 2 Howe D. | 2 Howe D. | 2 Howe D. | 2 Howe D. |
| 3 Armfield | 3 Armfield | 3 Armfield | 3 Armfield | 3 Allen A. |
| 4 Clayton | 4 Clayton | 4 Clayton | 4 Clayton | 4 Clayton |
| 5 Wright W. | 5 Wright W. | 5 Wright W. | 5 Wright W. | 5 Smith T. |
| 6 Flowers | 6 Flowers | 6 McGuinness (Flowers) | 6 Flowers | 6 Flowers |
| 7 Deeley | 7 Deeley | 7 Holden (Bradley) | 7 Bradley | 7 Connelly |
| 8 Broadbent | 8 Greaves | 8 Greaves | 8 Greaves | 8 Greaves |
| 9 Charlton R. | 9 Charlton R. | 9 Kevan | 9 Kevan | 9 Clough |
| 10 Haynes | 10 Haynes | 10 Haynes | 10 Haynes | 10 Charlton R. |
| 11 Holden | 11 Holden | 11 Charlton R. | 11 Charlton R. | 11 Holliday |
| Rio de Janeiro May 13: 0-2 | Lima May 17: 1-4 *Greaves* | Mexico City May 24: 1-2 *Kevan* | Los Angeles May 28: 8-1 *Charlton 3, Flowers 2, Bradley, Kevan, Haynes* | Cardiff Oct 17: 1-1 *Greaves* |

| 1959 Sweden | 1959 N Ireland | 1960 Scotland | 1960 Yugoslavia | 1960 Spain |
|---|---|---|---|---|
| 1 Hopkinson | 1 Springett R. | 1 Springett R. | 1 Springett R. | 1 Springett R. |
| 2 Howe D. | 2 Howe D. | 2 Armfield | 2 Armfield | 2 Armfield |
| 3 Allen A. | 3 Allen A. | 3 Wilson | 3 Wilson | 3 Wilson |
| 4 Clayton | 4 Clayton | 4 Clayton | 4 Clayton | 4 Robson R. |
| 5 Smith T. | 5 Brown | 5 Slater | 5 Swan | 5 Swan |
| 6 Flowers | 6 Flowers | 6 Flowers | 6 Flowers | 6 Flowers |
| 7 Connelly | 7 Connelly | 7 Connelly | 7 Douglas | 7 Brabrook |
| 8 Greaves | 8 Haynes | 8 Broadbent | 8 Haynes | 8 Haynes |
| 9 Clough | 9 Baker | 9 Baker | 9 Baker | 9 Baker |
| 10 Charlton R. | 10 Parry | 10 Parry | 10 Greaves | 10 Greaves |
| 11 Holliday | 11 Holliday | 11 Charlton R. | 11 Charlton R. | 11 Charlton R. |
| Wembley Oct 28: 2-3 *Connelly, Charlton* | Wembley Nov 18: 2-1 *Baker, Parry* | Glasgow April 19: 1-1 *Charlton (pen)* | Wembley May 11: 3-3 *Douglas, Greaves, Baker* | Madrid May 15: 0-3 |

| 1960 Hungary | 1960 N Ireland | 1960 Luxembourg | 1960 Spain | 1960 Wales |
|---|---|---|---|---|
| 1 Springett R. | 1 Springett R. | 1 Springett R. | 1 Springett R. | 1 Hodgkinson |
| 2 Armfield | 2 Armfield | 2 Armfield | 2 Armfield | 2 Armfield |
| 3 Wilson | 3 McNeil | 3 McNeil | 3 McNeil | 3 McNeil |
| 4 Robson R. | 4 Robson R. | 4 Robson R. | 4 Robson R. | 4 Robson R. |
| 5 Swan | 5 Swan | 5 Swan | 5 Swan | 5 Swan |
| 6 Flowers | 6 Flowers | 6 Flowers | 6 Flowers | 6 Flowers |
| 7 Douglas | 7 Douglas | 7 Douglas | 7 Douglas | 7 Douglas |
| 8 Haynes | 8 Greaves | 8 Greaves | 8 Greaves | 8 Greaves |
| 9 Baker | 9 Smith R. | 9 Smith R. | 9 Smith R. | 9 Smith R. |
| 10 Viollet | 10 Haynes | 10 Haynes | 10 Haynes | 10 Haynes |
| 11 Charlton R. | 11 Charlton R. | 11 Charlton R. | 11 Charlton R. | 11 Charlton R. |
| Budapest May 22: 0-2 | Belfast Oct 8: 5-2 *Smith, Greaves 2, Charlton Douglas* | Luxembourg Oct 19: 9-0 *Greaves 3, Charlton 3, Smith 2, Haynes* | Wembley Oct 26: 4-2 *Greaves, Douglas, Smith 2* | Wembley Nov 23: 5-1 *Greaves 2, Charlton, Smith, Haynes* |

| 1961 Scotland | 1961 Mexico | 1961 Portugal | 1961 Italy | 1961 Austria |
|---|---|---|---|---|
| 1 Springett R. | 1 Springett R. | 1 Springett R. | 1 Springett R. | 1 Springett R. |
| 2 Armfield | 2 Armfield | 2 Armfield | 2 Armfield | 2 Armfield |
| 3 McNeil | 3 McNeil | 3 McNeil | 3 McNeil | 3 Angus |
| 4 Robson R. | 4 Robson R. | 4 Robson R. | 4 Robson R. | 4 Miller |
| 5 Swan | 5 Swan | 5 Swan | 5 Swan | 5 Swan |
| 6 Flowers | 6 Flowers | 6 Flowers | 6 Flowers | 6 Flowers |
| 7 Douglas | 7 Douglas | 7 Douglas | 7 Douglas | 7 Douglas |
| 8 Greaves | 8 Greaves | 8 Greaves | 8 Greaves | 8 Greaves |
| 9 Smith R. | 9 Hitchens | 9 Smith R. | 9 Hitchens | 9 Hitchens |
| 10 Haynes | 10 Haynes | 10 Haynes | 10 Haynes | 10 Haynes |
| 11 Charlton R. | 11 Charlton R. | 11 Charlton R. | 11 Charlton R. | 11 Charlton R. |

| Wembley | Wembley | Lisbon | Rome | Vienna |
|---|---|---|---|---|
| April 15: 9-3 | May 10: 8-0 | May 21: 1-1 | May 24: 3-2 | May 27: 1-3 |
| *Robson, Greaves 3, Douglas, Smith 2, Haynes 2* | *Hitchens, Charlton 3, Robson, Douglas 2, Flowers (pen)* | *Flowers* | *Hitchens 2, Greaves* | *Greaves* |

| 1961 Luxembourg | 1961 Wales | 1961 Portugal | 1961 N Ireland | 1962 Austria |
|---|---|---|---|---|
| 1 Springett R. | 1 Springett R. | 1 Springett R. | 1 Springett R. | 1 Springett R. |
| 2 Armfield | 2 Armfield | 2 Armfield | 2 Armfield | 2 Armfield |
| 3 McNeil | 3 Wilson | 3 Wilson | 3 Wilson | 3 Wilson |
| 4 Robson R. | 4 Robson R. | 4 Robson R. | 4 Robson R. | 4 Anderson |
| 5 Swan | 5 Swan | 5 Swan | 5 Swan | 5 Swan |
| 6 Flowers | 6 Flowers | 6 Flowers | 6 Flowers | 6 Flowers |
| 7 Douglas | 7 Connelly | 7 Connelly | 7 Douglas | 7 Connelly |
| 8 Fantham | 8 Douglas | 8 Douglas | 8 Byrne J. | 8 Hunt |
| 9 Pointer | 9 Pointer | 9 Pointer | 9 Crawford | 9 Crawford |
| 10 Viollet | 10 Haynes | 10 Haynes | 10 Haynes | 10 Haynes |
| 11 Charlton R. | 11 Charlton R. | 11 Charlton R. | 11 Charlton R. | 11 Charlton R. |

| Highbury | Cardiff | Wembley | Wembley | Wembley |
|---|---|---|---|---|
| Sept 28: 4-1 | Oct 14: 1-1 | Oct 25: 2-0 | Nov 22: 1-1 | April 4: 3-1 |
| *Pointer, Viollet, Charlton 2* | *Douglas* | *Connelly, Pointer* | *Charlton* | *Crawford, Flowers (pen), Hunt* |

| 1962 Scotland | 1962 Switzerland | 1962 Peru | 1962 Hungary † | 1962 Argentina † |
|---|---|---|---|---|
| 1 Springett R. | 1 Springett R. | 1 Springett R. | 1 Springett R. | 1 Springett R. |
| 2 Armfield | 2 Armfield | 2 Armfield | 2 Armfield | 2 Armfield |
| 3 Wilson | 3 Wilson | 3 Wilson | 3 Wilson | 3 Wilson |
| 4 Anderson | 4 Robson R. | 4 Moore | 4 Moore | 4 Moore |
| 5 Swan | 5 Swan | 5 Norman | 5 Norman | 5 Norman |
| 6 Flowers | 6 Flowers | 6 Flowers | 6 Flowers | 6 Flowers |
| 7 Douglas | 7 Connelly | 7 Douglas | 7 Douglas | 7 Douglas |
| 8 Greaves | 8 Greaves | 8 Greaves | 8 Greaves | 8 Greaves |
| 9 Smith R. | 9 Hitchens | 9 Hitchens | 9 Hitchens | 9 Peacock |
| 10 Haynes | 10 Haynes | 10 Haynes | 10 Haynes | 10 Haynes |
| 11 Charlton R. | 11 Charlton R. | 11 Charlton R. | 11 Charlton R. | 11 Charlton R. |

| Glasgow | Wembley | Lima | Rancagua | Rancagua |
|---|---|---|---|---|
| April 14: 0-2 | May 9: 3-1 | May 20: 4-0 | May 31: 1-2 | June 2: 3-1 |
| | *Flowers, Hitchens, Connelly* | *Flowers (pen), Greaves 3* | *Flowers (pen)* | *Flowers (pen), Charlton, Greaves* |

| 1962 Bulgaria † | 1962 Brazil † | 1962 France | 1962 N Ireland | 1962 Wales |
|---|---|---|---|---|
| 1 Springett R. | 1 Springett R. | 1 Springett R. | 1 Springett R. | 1 Springett R. |
| 2 Armfield | 2 Armfield | 2 Armfield | 2 Armfield | 2 Armfield |
| 3 Wilson | 3 Wilson | 3 Wilson | 3 Wilson | 3 Shaw G. |
| 4 Moore | 4 Moore | 4 Moore | 4 Moore | 4 Moore |
| 5 Norman | 5 Norman | 5 Norman | 5 Labone | 5 Labone |
| 6 Flowers | 6 Flowers | 6 Flowers | 6 Flowers | 6 Flowers |
| 7 Douglas | 7 Douglas | 7 Hellawell | 7 Hellawell | 7 Connelly |
| 8 Greaves | 8 Greaves | 8 Crowe | 8 Hill F. | 8 Hill F. |
| 9 Peacock | 9 Hitchens | 9 Charnley | 9 Peacock | 9 Peacock |
| 10 Haynes | 10 Haynes | 10 Greaves | 10 Greaves | 10 Greaves |
| 11 Charlton R. | 11 Charlton R. | 11 Hinton A. | 11 O'Grady | 11 Tambling |
| Rancagua | Vina del Mar | Hillsborough | Belfast | Wembley |
| June 7: 0-0 | June 10: 1-3 | Oct 3: 1-1 | Oct 20: 3-1 | Nov 21: 4-0 |
| | *Hitchens* | *Flowers (pen)* | *Greaves, O'Grady 2* | *Connelly, Peacock 2, Greaves* |

| 1963 France | 1963 Scotland | 1963 Brazil | 1963 Czechoslovakia | 1963 E Germany |
|---|---|---|---|---|
| 1 Springett R. | 1 Banks G. | 1 Banks G. | 1 Banks G. | 1 Banks G. |
| 2 Armfield | 2 Armfield | 2 Armfield | 2 Shellito | 2 Armfield |
| 3 Henry | 3 Byrne G. | 3 Wilson | 3 Wilson | 3 Wilson |
| 4 Moore | 4 Moore | 4 Milne | 4 Milne | 4 Milne |
| 5 Labone | 5 Norman | 5 Norman | 5 Norman | 5 Norman |
| 6 Flowers | 6 Flowers | 6 Moore | 6 Moore | 6 Moore |
| 7 Connelly | 7 Douglas | 7 Douglas | 7 Paine | 7 Paine |
| 8 Tambling | 8 Greaves | 8 Greaves | 8 Greaves | 8 Hunt |
| 9 Smith R. | 9 Smith R. | 9 Smith R. | 9 Smith R. | 9 Smith R. |
| 10 Greaves | 10 Melia | 10 Eastham | 10 Eastham | 10 Eastham |
| 11 Charlton R. | 11 Charlton R. | 11 Charlton R. | 11 Charlton R. | 11 Charlton R. |
| Paris | Wembley | Wembley | Bratislava | Leipzig |
| Feb 27: 2-5 | April 6: 1-2 | May 8: 1-1 | May 20: 4-2 | June 2: 2-1 |
| *Smith, Tambling* | *Douglas* | *Douglas* | *Greaves 2, Smith, Charlton* | *Hunt, Charlton* |

| 1963 Switzerland | 1963 Wales | 1963 Rest of World | 1963 N Ireland | 1964 Scotland |
|---|---|---|---|---|
| 1 Springett R. | 1 Banks G. | 1 Banks G. | 1 Banks G. | 1 Banks G. |
| 2 Armfield | 2 Armfield | 2 Armfield | 2 Armfield | 2 Armfield |
| 3 Wilson | 3 Wilson | 3 Wilson | 3 Thomson R. | 3 Wilson |
| 4 Kay | 4 Milne | 4 Milne | 4 Milne | 4 Milne |
| 5 Moore | 5 Norman | 5 Norman | 5 Norman | 5 Norman |
| 6 Flowers | 6 Moore | 6 Moore | 6 Moore | 6 Moore |
| 7 Douglas | 7 Paine | 7 Paine | 7 Paine | 7 Paine |
| 8 Greaves | 8 Greaves | 8 Greaves | 8 Greaves | 8 Hunt |
| 9 Byrne J. | 9 Smith R. | 9 Smith R. | 9 Smith R. | 9 Byrne J. |
| 10 Melia | 10 Eastham | 10 Eastham | 10 Eastham | 10 Eastham |
| 11 Charlton R. | 11 Charlton R. | 11 Charlton R. | 11 Charlton R. | 11 Charlton R. |
| Basle | Cardiff | Wembley | Wembley (first | Glasgow |
| June 5: 8-1 | Oct 12: 4-0 | Oct 23: 2-1 | by floodlight) | April 11: 0-1 |
| *Charlton 3,* | *Smith 2, Greaves,* | *Paine, Greaves* | Nov 20: 8-3 | |
| *Byrne 2, Douglas,* | *Charlton* | | *Greaves 4, Paine 3,* | |
| *Kay, Melia* | | | *Smith* | |

| 1964 Uruguay | 1964 Portugal | 1964 Rep of Ireland | 1964 USA | 1964 Brazil |
|---|---|---|---|---|
| 1 Banks G. | 1 Banks G. | 1 Waiters | 1 Banks G. | 1 Waiters |
| 2 Cohen | 2 Cohen | 2 Cohen | 2 Cohen | 2 Cohen |
| 3 Wilson | 3 Wilson | 3 Wilson | 3 Thomson R. | 3 Wilson |
| 4 Milne | 4 Milne | 4 Milne | 4 Bailey M. | 4 Milne |
| 5 Norman | 5 Norman | 5 Flowers | 5 Norman | 5 Norman |
| 6 Moore | 6 Moore | 6 Moore | 6 Flowers | 6 Moore |
| 7 Paine | 7 Thompson P. | 7 Thompson P. | 7 Paine | 7 Thompson P. |
| 8 Greaves | 8 Greaves | 8 Greaves | 8 Hunt | 8 Greaves |
| 9 Byrne J. | 9 Byrne J. | 9 Byrne J. | 9 Pickering | 9 Byrne J. |
| 10 Eastham | 10 Eastham | 10 Eastham | 10 Eastham (Charlton R.) | 10 Eastham |
| 11 Charlton R. | 11 Charlton R. | 11 Charlton R. | 11 Thompson P. | 11 Charlton R. |
| Wembley | Lisbon | Dublin | New York | Rio de Janeiro |
| May 6: 2-1 | May 17: 4-3 | May 24: 3-1 | May 27: 10-0 | May 30: 1-5 |
| *Byrne 2* | *Byrne 3, Charlton* | *Eastham, Byrne, Greaves* | *Hunt 4, Pickering 3, Paine 2, Charlton* | *Greaves* |

| 1964 Portugal | 1964 Argentina | 1964 N Ireland | 1964 Belgium | 1964 Wales |
|---|---|---|---|---|
| 1 Banks G. | 1 Banks G. | 1 Banks G. | 1 Waiters | 1 Waiters |
| 2 Thomson R. | 2 Thomson R. | 2 Cohen | 2 Cohen | 2 Cohen |
| 3 Wilson | 3 Wilson | 3 Thomson R. | 3 Thomson R. | 3 Thomson R. |
| 4 Flowers | 4 Milne | 4 Milne | 4 Milne | 4 Bailey M. |
| 5 Norman | 5 Norman | 5 Norman | 5 Norman | 5 Flowers |
| 6 Moore | 6 Moore | 6 Moore | 6 Moore | 6 Young |
| 7 Paine | 7 Thompson P. | 7 Paine | 7 Thompson P. | 7 Thompson P. |
| 8 Greaves | 8 Greaves | 8 Greaves | 8 Greaves | 8 Hunt |
| 9 Byrne J. | 9 Byrne J. | 9 Pickering | 9 Pickering | 9 Wignall |
| 10 Hunt | 10 Eastham | 10 Charlton R. | 10 Venables | 10 Byrne J. |
| 11 Thompson P. | 11 Charlton R. | 11 Thompson P. | 11 Hinton A. | 11 Hinton A. |
| Sao Paulo | Rio de Janeiro | Belfast | Wembley | Wembley |
| June 4: 1-1 | June 6: 0-1 | Oct 3: 4-3 | Oct 21: 2-2 | Nov 18: 2-1 |
| *Hunt* | | *Pickering, Greaves 3* | *Pickering, Hinton* | *Wignall 2* |

| 1964 Netherlands | 1965 Scotland | 1965 Hungary | 1965 Yugoslavia | 1965 W Germany |
|---|---|---|---|---|
| 1 Waiters | 1 Banks G. | 1 Banks G. | 1 Banks G. | 1 Banks G. |
| 2 Cohen | 2 Cohen | 2 Cohen | 2 Cohen | 2 Cohen |
| 3 Thomson R. | 3 Wilson | 3 Wilson | 3 Wilson | 3 Wilson |
| 4 Mullery | 4 Stiles | 4 Stiles | 4 Stiles | 4 Flowers |
| 5 Norman | 5 Charlton J. | 5 Charlton J. | 5 Charlton J. | 5 Charlton J. |
| 6 Flowers | 6 Moore | 6 Moore | 6 Moore | 6 Moore |
| 7 Thompson P. | 7 Thompson P. | 7 Paine | 7 Paine | 7 Paine |
| 8 Greaves | 8 Greaves | 8 Greaves | 8 Greaves | 8 Ball |
| 9 Wignall | 9 Bridges | 9 Bridges | 9 Bridges | 9 Jones M. |
| 10 Venables | 10 Byrne J. | 10 Eastham | 10 Ball | 10 Eastham |
| 11 Charlton R. | 11 Charlton R. | 11 Connelly | 11 Connelly | 11 Temple |
| Amsterdam | Wembley | Wembley | Belgrade | Nuremberg |
| Dec 9: 1-1 | April 10: 2-2 | May 5: 1-0 | May 9: 1-1 | May 12: 1-0 |
| *Greaves* | *Charlton R., Greaves* | *Greaves* | *Bridges* | *Paine* |

| 1965 Sweden | 1965 Wales | 1965 Austria | 1965 N Ireland | 1965 Spain |
|---|---|---|---|---|
| 1 Banks G. | 1 Springett R. | 1 Springett R. | 1 Banks G. | 1 Banks G. |
| 2 Cohen | 2 Cohen | 2 Cohen | 2 Cohen | 2 Cohen |
| 3 Wilson | 3 Wilson | 3 Wilson | 3 Wilson | 3 Wilson |
| 4 Stiles | 4 Stiles | 4 Stiles | 4 Stiles | 4 Stiles |
| 5 Charlton J. | 5 Charlton J. | 5 Charlton J. | 5 Charlton J. | 5 Charlton J. |
| 6 Moore | 6 Moore | 6 Moore | 6 Moore | 6 Moore |
| 7 Paine | 7 Paine | 7 Paine | 7 Thompson P. | 7 Ball |
| 8 Ball | 8 Greaves | 8 Greaves | 8 Baker | 8 Hunt |
| 9 Jones M. | 9 Peacock | 9 Bridges | 9 Peacock | 9 Baker (Hunter) |
| 10 Eastham | 10 Charlton R. | 10 Charlton R. | 10 Charlton R. | 10 Eastham |
| 11 Connelly | 11 Connelly | 11 Connelly | 11 Connelly | 11 Charlton R. |
| Gothenburg | Cardiff | Wembley | Wembley | Madrid |
| May 16: 2-1 | Oct 2: 0-0 | Oct 20: 2-3 | Nov 10: 2-1 | Dec 8: 2-0 |
| *Ball, Connelly* | | *Charlton R., Connelly* | *Baker, Peacock* | *Baker, Hunt* |

| 1966 Poland | 1966 W Germany | 1966 Scotland | 1966 Yugoslavia | 1966 Finland |
|---|---|---|---|---|
| 1 Banks G. | 1 Banks G. | 1 Banks G. | 1 Banks G. | 1 Banks G. |
| 2 Cohen | 2 Cohen | 2 Cohen | 2 Armfield | 2 Armfield |
| 3 Wilson | 3 Newton K. (Wilson) | 3 Newton K. | 3 Wilson | 3 Wilson |
| 4 Stiles | 4 Moore | 4 Stiles | 4 Peters | 4 Peters |
| 5 Charlton J. | 5 Charlton J. | 5 Charlton J. | 5 Charlton J. | 5 Charlton J. |
| 6 Moore | 6 Hunter | 6 Moore | 6 Hunter | 6 Hunter |
| 7 Ball | 7 Ball | 7 Ball | 7 Paine | 7 Callaghan |
| 8 Hunt | 8 Hunt | 8 Hunt | 8 Greaves | 8 Hunt |
| 9 Baker | 9 Stiles | 9 Charlton R. | 9 Charlton R. | 9 Charlton R. |
| 10 Eastham | 10 Hurst G. | 10 Hurst G. | 10 Hurst G. | 10 Hurst G. |
| 11 Harris G. | 11 Charlton R. | 11 Connelly | 11 Tambling | 11 Ball |
| Liverpool | Wembley | Glasgow | Wembley | Helsinki |
| Jan 5: 1-1 | Feb 23: 1-0 | April 2: 4-3 | May 4: 2-0 | June 26: 3-0 |
| *Moore* | *Stiles* | *Hurst, Hunt 2, Charlton R.* | *Greaves, Charlton R.* | *Peters, Hunt, Charlton J.* |

| 1966 Norway | 1966 Denmark | 1966 Poland | 1966 Uruguay † | 1966 Mexico † |
|---|---|---|---|---|
| 1 Springett R. | 1 Bonetti | 1 Banks G. | 1 Banks G. | 1 Banks G. |
| 2 Cohen | 2 Cohen | 2 Cohen | 2 Cohen | 2 Cohen |
| 3 Byrne G. | 3 Wilson | 3 Wilson | 3 Wilson | 3 Wilson |
| 4 Stiles | 4 Stiles | 4 Stiles | 4 Stiles | 4 Stiles |
| 5 Flowers | 5 Charlton J. | 5 Charlton J. | 5 Charlton J. | 5 Charlton J. |
| 6 Moore | 6 Moore | 6 Moore | 6 Moore | 6 Moore |
| 7 Paine | 7 Ball | 7 Ball | 7 Ball | 7 Paine |
| 8 Greaves | 8 Greaves | 8 Greaves | 8 Greaves | 8 Greaves |
| 9 Charlton R. | 9 Hurst G. | 9 Charlton R. | 9 Charlton R. | 9 Charlton R. |
| 10 Hunt | 10 Eastham | 10 Hunt | 10 Hunt | 10 Hunt |
| 11 Connelly | 11 Connelly | 11 Peters | 11 Connelly | 11 Peters |
| Oslo | Copenhagen | Chorzow | Wembley | Wembley |
| June 29: 6-1 | July 3: 2-0 | July 5: 1-0 | July 11: 0-0 | July 16: 2-0 |
| *Greaves 4, Connelly, Moore* | *Charlton, Eastham* | *Hunt* | | *Charlton R., Hunt* |

672

| 1966 France † | 1966 Argentina † | 1966 Portugal † | 1966 W Germany † | 1966 N Ireland |
|---|---|---|---|---|
| 1 Banks G. | 1 Banks G. | 1 Banks G. | 1 Banks G. | 1 Banks G. |
| 2 Cohen | 2 Cohen | 2 Cohen | 2 Cohen | 2 Cohen |
| 3 Wilson | 3 Wilson | 3 Wilson | 3 Wilson | 3 Wilson |
| 4 Stiles | 4 Stiles | 4 Stiles | 4 Stiles | 4 Stiles |
| 5 Charlton J. | 5 Charlton J. | 5 Charlton J. | 5 Charlton J. | 5 Charlton J. |
| 6 Moore | 6 Moore | 6 Moore | 6 Moore | 6 Moore |
| 7 Callaghan | 7 Ball | 7 Ball | 7 Ball | 7 Ball |
| 8 Greaves | 8 Hurst G. | 8 Hurst G. | 8 Hurst G. | 8 Hurst G. |
| 9 Charlton R. | 9 Charlton R. | 9 Charlton R. | 9 Charlton R. | 9 Charlton R. |
| 10 Hunt | 10 Hunt | 10 Hunt | 10 Hunt | 10 Hunt |
| 11 Peters | 11 Peters | 11 Peters | 11 Peters | 11 Peters |
| Wembley | Wembley | Wembley | Wembley | Belfast |
| July 20: 2-0 | July 23: 1-0 | July 26: 2-1 | (*World Cup Final*) | Oct 22: 2-0 |
| *Hunt 2* | *Hurst* | *Charlton R. 2* | July 30: 4-2 (aet) | *Hunt, Peters* |
| | | | *Hurst 3, Peters* | |

| 1966 Czechoslovakia | 1966 Wales | 1967 Scotland | 1967 Spain | 1967 Austria |
|---|---|---|---|---|
| 1 Banks G. | 1 Banks G. | 1 Banks G. | 1 Bonetti | 1 Bonetti |
| 2 Cohen | 2 Cohen | 2 Cohen | 2 Cohen | 2 Newton K. |
| 3 Wilson | 3 Wilson | 3 Wilson | 3 Newton K. | 3 Wilson |
| 4 Stiles | 4 Stiles | 4 Stiles | 4 Mullery | 4 Mullery |
| 5 Charlton J. | 5 Charlton J. | 5 Charlton J. | 5 Labone | 5 Labone |
| 6 Moore | 6 Moore | 6 Moore | 6 Moore | 6 Moore |
| 7 Ball | 7 Ball | 7 Ball | 7 Ball | 7 Ball |
| 8 Hurst G. | 8 Hurst G. | 8 Greaves | 8 Greaves | 8 Greaves |
| 9 Charlton R. | 9 Charlton R. | 9 Charlton R. | 9 Hurst G. | 9 Hurst G. |
| 10 Hunt | 10 Hunt | 10 Hurst G. | 10 Hunt | 10 Hunt |
| 11 Peters | 11 Peters | 11 Peters | 11 Hollins | 11 Hunter |
| Wembley | Wembley | Wembley | Wembley | Vienna |
| Nov 2: 0-0 | Nov 16: 5-1 | April 15: 2-3 | May 24: 2-0 | May 27: 1-0 |
| | *Hurst 2,* | *Charlton J., Hurst* | *Greaves, Hunt* | *Ball* |
| | *Charlton R.,* | | | |
| | *Charlton J.,* | | | |
| | *Hennessy og* | | | |

| 1967 Wales | 1967 N Ireland | 1967 USSR | 1968 Scotland | 1968 Spain |
|---|---|---|---|---|
| 1 Banks G. | 1 Banks G. | 1 Banks G. | 1 Banks G. | 1 Banks G. |
| 2 Cohen | 2 Cohen | 2 Knowles C. | 2 Newton K. | 2 Knowles C. |
| 3 Newton K. | 3 Wilson | 3 Wilson | 3 Wilson | 3 Wilson |
| 4 Mullery | 4 Mullery | 4 Mullery | 4 Mullery | 4 Mullery |
| 5 Charlton J. | 5 Sadler | 5 Sadler | 5 Labone | 5 Charlton J. |
| 6 Moore | 6 Moore | 6 Moore | 6 Moore | 6 Moore |
| 7 Ball | 7 Thompson P. | 7 Ball | 7 Ball | 7 Ball |
| 8 Hunt | 8 Hunt | 8 Hunt | 8 Hurst G. | 8 Hunt |
| 9 Charlton R. | 9 Charlton R. | 9 Charlton R. | 9 Summerbee | 9 Summerbee |
| 10 Hurst G. | 10 Hurst G. | 10 Hurst G. | 10 Charlton R. | 10 Charlton R. |
| 11 Peters | 11 Peters | 11 Peters | 11 Peters | 11 Peters |
| Cardiff | Wembley | Wembley | Glasgow | Wembley |
| Oct 21: 3-0 | Nov 22: 2-0 | Dec 6: 2-2 | Feb 24: 1-1 | April 3: 1-0 |
| *Peters, Charlton R.,* | *Hurst, Charlton* | *Ball, Peters* | *Peters* | *Charlton R.* |
| *Ball* | | | | |

| 1968 Spain | 1968 Sweden | 1968 W Germany | 1968 Yugoslavia | 1968 USSR |
|---|---|---|---|---|
| 1 Bonetti | 1 Stepney | 1 Banks G. | 1 Banks G. | 1 Banks G. |
| 2 Newton K. | 2 Newton K. | 2 Newton K. | 2 Newton K. | 2 Wright T. |
| 3 Wilson | 3 Knowles C. | 3 Knowles C. | 3 Wilson | 3 Wilson |
| 4 Mullery | 4 Mullery | 4 Hunter | 4 Mullery | 4 Stiles |
| 5 Labone | 5 Labone | 5 Labone | 5 Labone | 5 Labone |
| 6 Moore | 6 Moore | 6 Moore | 6 Moore | 6 Moore |
| 7 Ball | 7 Bell | 7 Ball | 7 Ball | 7 Hunter |
| 8 Peters | 8 Peters | 8 Bell | 8 Peters | 8 Hunt |
| 9 Charlton R. | 9 Charlton R. (Hurst G.) | 9 Summerbee | 9 Charlton R. | 9 Charlton R. |
| 10 Hunt | 10 Hunt | 10 Hurst G. | 10 Hunt | 10 Hurst G. |
| 11 Hunter | 11 Hunter | 11 Thompson P. | 11 Hunter | 11 Peters |
| Madrid May 8: 2-1 *Peters, Hunter* | Wembley May 22: 3-1 *Peters, Charlton, Hunt* | Hanover June 1: 0-1 | Florence June 5: 0-1 | Rome June 8: 2-0 *Charlton, Hurst* |

| 1968 Rumania | 1968 Bulgaria | 1969 Rumania | 1969 France | 1969 N Ireland |
|---|---|---|---|---|
| 1 Banks G. | 1 West | 1 Banks G. | 1 Banks G. | 1 Banks G. |
| 2 Wright T. (McNab) | 2 Newton K. (Reaney) | 2 Wright T. | 2 Newton K. | 2 Newton K. |
| 3 Newton K. | 3 McNab | 3 McNab | 3 Cooper | 3 McNab |
| 4 Mullery | 4 Mullery | 4 Stiles | 4 Mullery | 4 Mullery |
| 5 Labone | 5 Labone | 5 Charlton J. | 5 Charlton J. | 5 Labone |
| 6 Moore | 6 Moore | 6 Hunter | 6 Moore | 6 Moore |
| 7 Ball | 7 Lee F. | 7 Radford | 7 Lee F. | 7 Ball |
| 8 Hunt | 8 Bell | 8 Hunt | 8 Bell | 8 Lee F. |
| 9 Charlton R. | 9 Charlton R. | 9 Charlton R. | 9 Hurst G. | 9 Charlton R. |
| 10 Hurst G. | 10 Hurst G. | 10 Hurst G. | 10 Peters | 10 Hurst G. |
| 11 Peters | 11 Peters | 11 Ball | 11 O'Grady | 11 Peters |
| Bucharest Nov 6: 0-0 | Wembley Dec 11: 1-1 *Hurst* | Wembley Jan 15: 1-1 *Charlton J.* | Wembley Mar 12: 5-0 *Hurst 3, O'Grady, Lee* | Belfast May 3: 3-1 *Peters, Lee, Hurst* (pen) |

| 1969 Wales | 1969 Scotland | 1969 Mexico | 1969 Uruguay | 1969 Brazil |
|---|---|---|---|---|
| 1 West | 1 Banks G. | 1 West | 1 Banks G. | 1 Banks G. |
| 2 Newton K. | 2 Newton K. | 2 Newton K. (Wright T.) | 2 Wright T. | 2 Wright T. |
| 3 Cooper | 3 Cooper | 3 Cooper | 3 Newton K. | 3 Newton K. |
| 4 Moore | 4 Mullery | 4 Mullery | 4 Mullery | 4 Mullery |
| 5 Charlton J. | 5 Labone | 5 Labone | 5 Labone | 5 Labone |
| 6 Hunter | 6 Moore | 6 Moore | 6 Moore | 6 Moore |
| 7 Lee F. | 7 Lee F. | 7 Lee F. | 7 Lee F. | 7 Ball |
| 8 Bell | 8 Ball | 8 Ball | 8 Bell | 8 Bell |
| 9 Astle | 9 Charlton R. | 9 Charlton R. | 9 Hurst G. | 9 Charlton R. |
| 10 Charlton R. | 10 Hurst G. | 10 Hurst G. | 10 Ball | 10 Hurst G. |
| 11 Ball | 11 Peters | 11 Peters | 11 Peters | 11 Peters |
| Wembley May 7: 2-1 *Charlton R., Lee* | Wembley May 10: 4-1 *Peters 2, Hurst 2* (1 pen) | Mexico City June 1: 0-0 | Montevideo June 8: 2-1 *Lee, Hurst* | Rio de Janeiro June 12: 1-2 *Bell* |

674

| 1969 Netherlands | 1969 Portugal | 1970 Netherlands | 1970 Belgium | 1970 Wales |
|---|---|---|---|---|
| 1 Bonetti | 1 Bonetti | 1 Banks G. | 1 Banks G. | 1 Banks G. |
| 2 Wright T. | 2 Reaney | 2 Newton K. | 2 Wright T. | 2 Wright T. |
| 3 Hughes E. | 3 Hughes E. | 3 Cooper | 3 Cooper | 3 Hughes E. |
| 4 Mullery | 4 Mullery | 4 Peters | 4 Moore | 4 Mullery |
| 5 Charlton J. | 5 Charlton J. | 5 Charlton J. | 5 Labone | 5 Labone |
| 6 Moore | 6 Moore | 6 Hunter | 6 Hughes E. | 6 Moore |
| 7 Lee F. | 7 Lee F. | 7 Lee F. | 7 Lee F. | 7 Lee F. |
| (Thompson P.) | | (Mullery) | | |
| 8 Bell | 8 Bell | 8 Bell | 8 Ball | 8 Ball |
| | (Peters) | | | |
| 9 Charlton R. | 9 Astle | 9 Jones M. | 9 Osgood | 9 Charlton R. |
| | | (Hurst G.) | | |
| 10 Hurst G. | 10 Charlton R. | 10 Charlton R. | 10 Hurst G. | 10 Hurst G. |
| 11 Peters | 11 Ball | 11 Moore I. | 11 Peters | 11 Peters |

| Amsterdam | Wembley | Wembley | Brussels | Cardiff |
|---|---|---|---|---|
| Nov 5: 1-0 | Dec 10: 1-0 | Jan 14: 0-0 | Feb 25: 3-1 | April 18: 1-1 |
| *Bell* | *Charlton J.* | | *Ball 2, Hurst* | *Lee* |

| 1970 N Ireland | 1970 Scotland | 1970 Colombia | 1970 Ecuador | 1970 Rumania † |
|---|---|---|---|---|
| 1 Banks G. | 1 Banks G. | 1 Banks G. | 1 Banks G. | 1 Banks G. |
| 2 Newton K. | 2 Newton K. | 2 Newton K. | 2 Newton K. | 2 Newton K. |
| (Bell) | | | | (Wright T.) |
| 3 Hughes E. | 3 Hughes E. | 3 Cooper | 3 Cooper | 3 Cooper |
| 4 Mullery | 4 Stiles | 4 Mullery | 4 Mullery | 4 Mullery |
| 5 Moore | 5 Labone | 5 Labone | 5 Labone | 5 Labone |
| 6 Stiles | 6 Moore | 6 Moore | 6 Moore | 6 Moore |
| 7 Coates | 7 Thompson P. | 7 Lee F. | 7 Lee F. | 7 Lee F. |
| | (Mullery) | | (Kidd) | (Osgood) |
| 8 Kidd | 8 Ball | 8 Ball | 8 Ball | 8 Ball |
| 9 Charlton R. | 9 Astle | 9 Charlton R. | 9 Charlton R. | 9 Charlton R. |
| | | | (Sadler) | |
| 10 Hurst G. | 10 Hurst G. | 10 Hurst G. | 10 Hurst G. | 10 Hurst G. |
| 11 Peters | 11 Peters | 11 Peters | 11 Peters | 11 Peters |

| Wembley | Glasgow | Bogota | Quito | Guadalajara |
|---|---|---|---|---|
| April 21: 3-1 | April 25: 0-0 | May 20: 4-0 | May 24: 2-0 | June 2: 1-0 |
| *Peters, Hurst,* | | *Peters 2, Charlton,* | *Lee, Kidd* | *Hurst* |
| *Charlton* | | *Ball* | | |

| 1970 Brazil † | 1970 Czechoslovakia † | 1970 W Germany † | 1970 E Germany | 1971 Malta |
|---|---|---|---|---|
| 1 Banks G. | 1 Banks G. | 1 Bonetti | 1 Shilton | 1 Banks G. |
| 2 Wright T. | 2 Newton K. | 2 Newton K. | 2 Hughes | 2 Reaney |
| 3 Cooper | 3 Cooper | 3 Cooper | 3 Cooper | 3 Hughes |
| 4 Mullery | 4 Mullery | 4 Mullery | 4 Mullery | 4 Mullery |
| 5 Labone | 5 Charlton J. | 5 Labone | 5 Sadler | 5 McFarland |
| 6 Moore | 6 Moore | 6 Moore | 6 Moore | 6 Hunter |
| 7 Lee F. | 7 Bell | 7 Lee F. | 7 Lee F. | 7 Ball |
| (Astle) | | | | |
| 8 Ball | 8 Charlton R. | 8 Ball | 8 Ball | 8 Chivers |
| | (Ball) | | | |
| 9 Charlton R. | 9 Astle | 9 Charlton R. | 9 Hurst G. | 9 Royle |
| (Bell) | (Osgood) | (Bell) | | |
| 10 Hurst G. | 10 Clarke A. | 10 Hurst G. | 10 Clarke A. | 10 Harvey |
| 11 Peters | 11 Peters | 11 Peters | 11 Peters | 11 Peters |
| | | (Hunter) | | |

| Guadalajara | Guadalajara | Leon | Wembley | Valletta |
|---|---|---|---|---|
| June 7: 0-1 | June 11: 1-0 | June 14: 2-3 (aet) | Nov 25: 3-1 | Feb 3: 1-0 |
| | *Clarke* (pen) | *Mullery, Peters* | *Lee, Peters,* | *Peters* |
| | | | *Clarke* | |

| 1971 Greece | 1971 Malta | 1971 N Ireland | 1971 Wales | 1971 Scotland |
|---|---|---|---|---|
| 1 Banks G. | 1 Banks G. | 1 Banks G. | 1 Shilton | 1 Banks G. |
| 2 Storey | 2 Lawler | 2 Madeley | 2 Lawler | 2 Lawler |
| 3 Hughes | 3 Cooper | 3 Cooper | 3 Cooper | 3 Cooper |
| 4 Mullery | 4 Moore | 4 Storey | 4 Smith | 4 Storey |
| 5 McFarland | 5 McFarland | 5 McFarland | 5 Lloyd | 5 McFarland |
| 6 Moore | 6 Hughes | 6 Moore | 6 Hughes | 6 Moore |
| 7 Lee F. | 7 Lee F. | 7 Lee F. | 7 Lee F. | 7 Lee F. (Clarke) |
| 8 Ball (Coates) | 8 Coates | 8 Ball | 8 Coates (Clarke) | 8 Ball |
| 9 Chivers | 9 Chivers | 9 Chivers | 9 Hurst G. | 9 Chivers |
| 10 Hurst G. | 10 Clarke | 10 Clarke | 10 Brown A. | 10 Hurst G. |
| 11 Peters | 11 Peters (Ball) | 11 Peters | 11 Peters | 11 Peters |
| Wembley April 21: 3-0 *Chivers, Hurst, Lee* | Wembley May 12: 5-0 *Chivers 2, Lee, Clarke (pen), Lawler* | Belfast May 15: 1-0 *Clarke* | Wembley May 19: 0-0 | Wembley May 22: 3-1 *Peters, Chivers 2* |

| 1971 Switzerland | 1971 Switzerland | 1971 Greece | 1972 W Germany | 1972 W Germany |
|---|---|---|---|---|
| 1 Banks G. | 1 Shilton | 1 Banks G. | 1 Banks G. | 1 Banks G. |
| 2 Lawler | 2 Madeley | 2 Madeley | 2 Madeley | 2 Madeley |
| 3 Cooper | 3 Cooper | 3 Hughes | 3 Hughes | 3 Hughes |
| 4 Mullery | 4 Storey | 4 Bell | 4 Bell | 4 Storey |
| 5 McFarland | 5 Lloyd | 5 McFarland | 5 Moore | 5 McFarland |
| 6 Moore | 6 Moore | 6 Moore | 6 Hunter | 6 Moore |
| 7 Lee F. | 7 Summerbee (Chivers) | 7 Lee F. | 7 Lee F. | 7 Ball |
| 8 Madeley | 8 Ball | 8 Ball | 8 Ball | 8 Bell |
| 9 Chivers | 9 Hurst G. | 9 Chivers | 9 Chivers | 9 Chivers |
| 10 Hurst G. (Radford) | 10 Lee F. (Marsh) | 10 Hurst G. | 10 Hurst G. (Marsh) | 10 Marsh (Summerbee) |
| 11 Peters | 11 Hughes | 11 Peters | 11 Peters | 11 Hunter (Peters) |
| Basle Oct 13: 3-2 *Hurst, Chivers, Weibel og* | Wembley Nov 10: 1-1 *Summerbee* | Athens Dec 1: 2-0 *Hurst, Chivers* | Wembley April 29: 1-3 *Lee* | Berlin May 13: 0-0 |

| 1972 Wales | 1972 N Ireland | 1972 Scotland | 1972 Yugoslavia | 1972 Wales |
|---|---|---|---|---|
| 1 Banks G. | 1 Shilton | 1 Banks G. | 1 Shilton | 1 Clemence |
| 2 Madeley | 2 Todd | 2 Madeley | 2 Mills | 2 Storey |
| 3 Hughes | 3 Hughes | 3 Hughes | 3 Lampard | 3 Hughes |
| 4 Storey | 4 Storey | 4 Storey | 4 Storey | 4 Hunter |
| 5 McFarland | 5 Lloyd | 5 McFarland | 5 Blockley | 5 McFarland |
| 6 Moore | 6 Hunter | 6 Moore | 6 Moore | 6 Moore |
| 7 Summerbee | 7 Summerbee | 7 Ball | 7 Ball | 7 Keegan |
| 8 Bell | 8 Bell | 8 Bell | 8 Channon | 8 Chivers |
| 9 Macdonald | 9 Macdonald (Chivers) | 9 Chivers | 9 Royle | 9 Marsh |
| 10 Marsh | 10 Marsh | 10 Marsh (Macdonald) | 10 Bell | 10 Bell |
| 11 Hunter | 11 Currie (Peters) | 11 Hunter | 11 Marsh | 11 Ball |
| Cardiff May 20: 3-0 *Hughes, Bell, Marsh* | Wembley May 23: 0-1 | Glasgow May 27: 1-0 *Ball* | Wembley Oct 11: 1-1 *Royle* | Cardiff Nov 15: 1-0 *Bell* |

| 1973 Wales | 1973 Scotland | 1973 N Ireland | 1973 Wales | 1973 Scotland |
|---|---|---|---|---|
| 1 Clemence | 1 Shilton | 1 Shilton | 1 Shilton | 1 Shilton |
| 2 Storey | 2 Storey | 2 Storey | 2 Storey | 2 Storey |
| 3 Hughes | 3 Hughes | 3 Nish | 3 Hughes | 3 Hughes |
| 4 Hunter | 4 Bell | 4 Bell | 4 Bell | 4 Bell |
| 5 McFarland | 5 Madeley | 5 McFarland | 5 McFarland | 5 McFarland |
| 6 Moore | 6 Moore | 6 Moore | 6 Moore | 6 Moore |
| 7 Keegan | 7 Ball | 7 Ball | 7 Ball | 7 Ball |
| 8 Bell | 8 Channon | 8 Channon | 8 Channon | 8 Channon |
| 9 Chivers | 9 Chivers | 9 Chivers | 9 Chivers | 9 Chivers |
| 10 Marsh | 10 Clarke | 10 Richards | 10 Clarke | 10 Clarke |
| 11 Ball | 11 Peters | 11 Peters | 11 Peters | 11 Peters |
| Wembley | Glasgow | Goodison Park | Wembley | Wembley |
| Jan 24: 1-1 | Feb 14: 5-0 | May 12: 2-1 | May 15: 3-0 | May 19: 1-0 |
| *Hunter* | *Lorimer og, Clarke 2, Channon, Chivers* | *Chivers 2* | *Chivers, Channon, Peters* | *Peters* |

| 1973 Czechoslovakia | 1973 Poland | 1973 USSR | 1973 Italy | 1973 Austria |
|---|---|---|---|---|
| 1 Shilton | 1 Shilton | 1 Shilton | 1 Shilton | 1 Shilton |
| 2 Madeley | 2 Madeley | 2 Madeley | 2 Madeley | 2 Madeley |
| 3 Storey | 3 Hughes | 3 Hughes | 3 Hughes | 3 Hughes |
| 4 Bell | 4 Storey | 4 Storey | 4 Storey | 4 Bell |
| 5 McFarland | 5 McFarland | 5 McFarland | 5 McFarland | 5 McFarland |
| 6 Moore | 6 Moore | 6 Moore | 6 Moore | 6 Hunter |
| 7 Ball | 7 Ball | 7 Currie | 7 Currie | 7 Currie |
| 8 Channon | 8 Bell | 8 Channon (Summerbee) | 8 Channon | 8 Channon |
| 9 Chivers | 9 Chivers | 9 Chivers | 9 Chivers | 9 Chivers |
| 10 Clarke | 10 Clarke | 10 Clarke (Macdonald) | 10 Clarke | 10 Clarke |
| 11 Peters | 11 Peters | 11 Peters (Hunter) | 11 Peters | 11 Peters |
| Prague | Chorzow | Moscow | Turin | Wembley |
| May 27: 1-1 | June 6: 0-2 | June 10: 2-1 | June 14: 0-2 | Sept 26: 7-0 |
| *Clarke* | | *Chivers, Khurtislava og* | | *Channon 2, Clarke 2, Chivers, Currie, Bell* |

| 1973 Poland | 1973 Italy | 1974 Portugal | 1974 Wales | 1974 N Ireland |
|---|---|---|---|---|
| 1 Shilton | 1 Shilton | 1 Parkes | 1 Shilton | 1 Shilton |
| 2 Madeley | 2 Madeley | 2 Nish | 2 Nish | 2 Nish |
| 3 Hughes | 3 Hughes | 3 Pejic | 3 Pejic | 3 Pejic |
| 4 Bell | 4 Bell | 4 Dobson | 4 Hughes | 4 Hughes |
| 5 McFarland | 5 McFarland | 5 Watson | 5 McFarland | 5 McFarland (Hunter) |
| 6 Hunter | 6 Moore | 6 Todd | 6 Todd | 6 Todd |
| 7 Currie | 7 Currie | 7 Bowles | 7 Keegan | 7 Keegan |
| 8 Channon | 8 Channon | 8 Channon | 8 Bell | 8 Weller |
| 9 Chivers (Hector) | 9 Osgood | 9 Macdonald (Ball) | 9 Channon | 9 Channon |
| 10 Clarke | 10 Clarke (Hector) | 10 Brooking | 10 Weller | 10 Bell |
| 11 Peters | 11 Peters | 11 Peters | 11 Bowles | 11 Bowles (Worthington) |
| Wembley | Wembley | Lisbon | Cardiff | Wembley |
| Oct 17: 1-1 | Nov 14: 0-1 | April 3: 0-0 | May 11: 2-0 | May 15: 1-0 |
| *Clarke* (pen) | | | *Bowles, Keegan* | *Weller* |

| 1974 Scotland | 1974 Argentina | 1974 E Germany | 1974 Bulgaria | 1974 Yugoslavia |
|---|---|---|---|---|
| 1 Shilton | 1 Shilton | 1 Clemence | 1 Clemence | 1 Clemence |
| 2 Nish | 2 Hughes | 2 Hughes | 2 Hughes | 2 Hughes |
| 3 Pejic | 3 Lindsay | 3 Lindsay | 3 Todd | 3 Lindsay |
| 4 Hughes | 4 Todd | 4 Todd | 4 Watson | 4 Todd |
| 5 Hunter (Watson) | 5 Watson | 5 Watson | 5 Lindsay | 5 Watson |
| 6 Todd | 6 Bell | 6 Dobson | 6 Dobson | 6 Dobson |
| 7 Channon | 7 Keegan | 7 Keegan | 7 Brooking | 7 Keegan |
| 8 Bell | 8 Channon | 8 Channon | 8 Bell | 8 Channon |
| 9 Worthington (Macdonald) | 9 Worthington | 9 Worthington | 9 Keegan | 9 Worthington (Macdonald) |
| 10 Weller | 10 Weller | 10 Bell | 10 Channon | 10 Bell |
| 11 Peters | 11 Brooking | 11 Brooking | 11 Worthington | 11 Brooking |
| Glasgow May 18: 0-2 | Wembley May 22: 2-2 *Channon, Worthington* | Leipzig May 29: 1-1 *Channon* | Sofia June 1: 1-0 *Worthington* | Belgrade June 5: 2-2 *Channon, Keegan* |

| 1974 Czechoslovakia | 1974 Portugal | 1975 W Germany | 1975 Cyprus | 1975 Cyprus |
|---|---|---|---|---|
| 1 Clemence | 1 Clemence | 1 Clemence | 1 Shilton | 1 Clemence |
| 2 Madeley | 2 Madeley | 2 Whitworth | 2 Madeley | 2 Whitworth |
| 3 Hughes | 3 Watson | 3 Gillard | 3 Watson | 3 Beattie (Hughes) |
| 4 Dobson (Brooking) | 4 Hughes | 4 Bell | 4 Todd | 4 Watson |
| 5 Watson | 5 Cooper (Todd) | 5 Watson | 5 Beattie | 5 Todd |
| 6 Hunter | 6 Brooking | 6 Todd | 6 Bell | 6 Bell |
| 7 Bell | 7 Francis G. | 7 Ball | 7 Ball | 7 Thomas |
| 8 Francis G. | 8 Bell | 8 Macdonald | 8 Hudson | 8 Ball |
| 9 Worthington (Thomas) | 9 Thomas | 9 Channon | 9 Channon (Thomas) | 9 Channon |
| 10 Channon | 10 Channon | 10 Hudson | 10 Macdonald | 10 Macdonald |
| 11 Keegan | 11 Clarke (Worthington) | 11 Keegan | 11 Keegan | 11 Keegan (Tueart) |
| Wembley Oct 30: 3-0 *Channon, Bell 2* | Wembley Nov 20: 0-0 | Wembley Mar 12: 2-0 *Bell, Macdonald* | Wembley April 16: 5-0 *Macdonald 5* | Limassol May 11: 1-0 *Keegan* |

| 1975 N Ireland | 1975 Wales | 1975 Scotland | 1975 Switzerland | 1975 Czechoslovakia |
|---|---|---|---|---|
| 1 Clemence | 1 Clemence | 1 Clemence | 1 Clemence | 1 Clemence |
| 2 Whitworth | 2 Whitworth | 2 Whitworth | 2 Whitworth | 2 Madeley |
| 3 Hughes | 3 Gillard | 3 Beattie | 3 Todd | 3 Gillard |
| 4 Bell | 4 Francis G. | 4 Bell | 4 Watson | 4 Francis G. |
| 5 Watson | 5 Watson | 5 Watson | 5 Beattie | 5 McFarland (Watson) |
| 6 Todd | 6 Todd | 6 Todd | 6 Bell | 6 Todd |
| 7 Ball | 7 Ball | 7 Ball | 7 Currie | 7 Keegan |
| 8 Viljoen | 8 Channon (Little) | 8 Channon | 8 Francis G. | 8 Channon (Thomas) |
| 9 Macdonald (Channon) | 9 Johnson | 9 Johnson | 9 Channon | 9 Macdonald |
| 10 Keegan | 10 Viljoen | 10 Francis G. | 10 Johnson (Macdonald) | 10 Clarke |
| 11 Tueart | 11 Thomas | 11 Keegan (Thomas) | 11 Keegan | 11 Bell |
| Belfast May 17: 0-0 | Wembley May 21: 2-2 *Johnson 2* | Wembley May 24: 5-1 *Francis 2, Beattie, Bell, Johnson* | Basle Sept 3: 2-1 *Keegan, Channon* | Bratislava Oct 30: 1-2 *Channon* |

| 1975 Portugal | 1976 Wales | 1976 Wales | 1976 N Ireland | 1976 Scotland |
|---|---|---|---|---|
| 1 Clemence | 1 Clemence | 1 Clemence | 1 Clemence | 1 Clemence |
| 2 Whitworth | 2 Cherry (Clement) | 2 Clement | 2 Todd | 2 Todd |
| 3 Beattie | 3 Mills | 3 Mills | 3 Mills | 3 Mills |
| 4 Francis G. | 4 Neal | 4 Towers | 4 Thompson | 4 Thompson |
| 5 Watson | 5 Thompson | 5 Greenhoff | 5 Greenhoff | 5 McFarland (Doyle) |
| 6 Todd | 6 Doyle | 6 Thompson | 6 Kennedy | 6 Kennedy |
| 7 Keegan | 7 Keegan | 7 Keegan | 7 Keegan (Royle) | 7 Keegan |
| 8 Channon | 8 Channon (Taylor) | 8 Francis G. | 8 Francis G. | 8 Francis G. |
| 9 Macdonald (Thomas) | 9 Boyer | 9 Pearson | 9 Pearson | 9 Pearson (Cherry) |
| 10 Brooking | 10 Brooking | 10 Kennedy | 10 Channon | 10 Channon |
| 11 Madeley (Clarke) | 11 Kennedy | 11 Taylor | 11 Taylor (Towers) | 11 Taylor |
| Lisbon Nov 19: 1-1 *Channon* | Wrexham Mar 24: 2-1 *Kennedy, Taylor* | Cardiff May 8: 1-0 *Taylor* | Wembley May 11: 4-0 *Francis, Channon 2 (1 pen), Pearson* | Glasgow May 15: 1-2 *Channon* |

| 1976 Brazil | 1976 Italy | 1976 Finland | 1976 Rep of Ireland | 1976 Finland |
|---|---|---|---|---|
| 1 Clemence | 1 Rimmer (Corrigan) | 1 Clemence | 1 Clemence | 1 Clemence |
| 2 Todd | 2 Clement | 2 Todd | 2 Todd | 2 Todd |
| 3 Doyle | 3 Neal (Mills) | 3 Mills | 3 Madeley | 3 Beattie |
| 4 Thompson | 4 Thompson | 4 Thompson | 4 Cherry | 4 Thompson |
| 5 Mills | 5 Doyle | 5 Madeley | 5 McFarland | 5 Greenhoff |
| 6 Francis G. | 6 Towers | 6 Cherry | 6 Greenhoff | 6 Wilkins |
| 7 Cherry | 7 Wilkins | 7 Keegan | 7 Keegan | 7 Keegan |
| 8 Brooking | 8 Brooking | 8 Channon | 8 Wilkins | 8 Channon |
| 9 Keegan | 9 Royle | 9 Pearson | 9 Pearson | 9 Royle |
| 10 Pearson | 10 Channon | 10 Brooking | 10 Brooking | 10 Brooking (Mills) |
| 11 Channon | 11 Hill | 11 Francis G. | 11 George (Hill) | 11 Tueart (Hill) |
| Los Angeles May 23: 0-1 | New York May 28: 3-2 *Channon 2, Thompson* | Helsinki June 13: 4-1 *Keegan 2, Channon, Pearson* | Wembley Sept 8: 1-1 *Pearson* | Wembley Oct 13: 2-1 *Tueart, Royle* |

| 1976 Italy | 1977 Netherlands | 1977 Luxembourg | 1977 N Ireland | 1977 Wales |
|---|---|---|---|---|
| 1 Clemence | 1 Clemence | 1 Clemence | 1 Shilton | 1 Shilton |
| 2 Clement (Beattie) | 2 Clement | 2 Gidman | 2 Cherry | 2 Neal |
| 3 Mills | 3 Beattie | 3 Cherry | 3 Mills | 3 Mills |
| 4 Greenhoff | 4 Doyle | 4 Kennedy | 4 Greenhoff | 4 Greenhoff |
| 5 McFarland | 5 Watson | 5 Watson | 5 Watson | 5 Watson |
| 6 Hughes | 6 Madeley (Pearson) | 6 Hughes | 6 Todd | 6 Hughes |
| 7 Keegan | 7 Keegan | 7 Keegan | 7 Wilkins (Talbot) | 7 Keegan |
| 8 Channon | 8 Greenhoff (Todd) | 8 Channon | 8 Channon | 8 Channon |
| 9 Bowles | 9 Francis T. | 9 Royle (Mariner) | 9 Mariner | 9 Pearson |
| 10 Cherry | 10 Bowles | 10 Francis T. | 10 Brooking | 10 Brooking (Tueart) |
| 11 Brooking | 11 Brooking | 11 Hill | 11 Tueart | 11 Kennedy |
| Rome Nov 17: 0-2 | Wembley Feb 9: 0-2 | Wembley Mar 30: 5-0 *Keegan, Francis, Kennedy, Channon 2 (1 pen)* | Belfast May 28: 2-1 *Channon, Tueart* | Wembley May 31: 0-1 |

| 1977 Scotland | 1977 Brazil | 1977 Argentina | 1977 Uruguay | 1977 Switzerland |
|---|---|---|---|---|
| 1 Clemence | 1 Clemence | 1 Clemence | 1 Clemence | 1 Clemence |
| 2 Neal | 2 Neal | 2 Neal | 2 Neal | 2 Neal |
| 3 Mills | 3 Cherry | 3 Cherry | 3 Cherry | 3 Cherry |
| 4 Greenhoff (Cherry) | 4 Greenhoff | 4 Greenhoff (Kennedy) | 4 Greenhoff | 4 McDermott |
| 5 Watson | 5 Watson | 5 Watson | 5 Watson | 5 Watson |
| 6 Hughes | 6 Hughes | 6 Hughes | 6 Hughes | 6 Hughes |
| 7 Francis T. | 7 Keegan | 7 Keegan | 7 Keegan | 7 Keegan |
| 8 Channon | 8 Francis T. | 8 Channon | 8 Channon | 8 Channon (Hill) |
| 9 Pearson | 9 Pearson (Channon) | 9 Pearson | 9 Pearson | 9 Francis T. |
| 10 Talbot | 10 Wilkins (Kennedy) | 10 Wilkins | 10 Wilkins | 10 Kennedy |
| 11 Kennedy (Tueart) | 11 Talbot | 11 Talbot | 11 Talbot | 11 Callaghan (Wilkins) |
| Wembley June 4: 1-2 *Channon* (pen) | Rio de Janeiro June 8: 0-0 | Buenos Aires June 12: 1-1 *Pearson* | Montevideo June 15: 0-0 | Wembley Sept 7: 0-0 |

| 1977 Luxembourg | 1977 Italy | 1978 W Germany | 1978 Brazil | 1978 Wales |
|---|---|---|---|---|
| 1 Clemence | 1 Clemence | 1 Clemence | 1 Corrigan | 1 Shilton |
| 2 Cherry | 2 Neal | 2 Neal | 2 Mills | 2 Mills |
| 3 Watson (Beattie) | 3 Cherry | 3 Mills | 3 Cherry | 3 Cherry (Currie) |
| 4 Hughes | 4 Wilkins | 4 Wilkins | 4 Greenhoff | 4 Greenhoff |
| 5 Kennedy | 5 Watson | 5 Watson | 5 Watson | 5 Watson |
| 6 Callaghan | 6 Hughes | 6 Hughes | 6 Currie | 6 Wilkins |
| 7 McDermott (Whymark) | 7 Keegan (Francis T.) | 7 Keegan (Francis T.) | 7 Keegan | 7 Coppell |
| 8 Wilkins | 8 Coppell | 8 Coppell | 8 Coppell | 8 Francis T. |
| 9 Francis T. | 9 Latchford (Pearson) | 9 Pearson | 9 Latchford | 9 Latchford (Mariner) |
| 10 Mariner | 10 Brooking | 10 Brooking | 10 Francis T. | 10 Brooking |
| 11 Hill | 11 Barnes | 11 Barnes | 11 Barnes | 11 Barnes |
| Luxembourg Oct 12: 2-0 *Kennedy, Mariner* | Wembley Nov 16: 2-0 *Keegan, Brooking* | Munich Feb 22: 1-2 *Pearson* | Wembley April 19: 1-1 *Keegan* | Cardiff May 13: 3-1 *Latchford, Currie, Barnes* |

| 1978 N Ireland | 1978 Scotland | 1978 Hungary | 1978 Denmark | 1978 Rep of Ireland |
|---|---|---|---|---|
| 1 Clemence | 1 Clemence | 1 Shilton | 1 Clemence | 1 Clemence |
| 2 Neal | 2 Neal | 2 Neal | 2 Neal | 2 Neal |
| 3 Mills | 3 Mills | 3 Mills | 3 Mills | 3 Mills |
| 4 Wilkins | 4 Currie | 4 Wilkins | 4 Wilkins | 4 Wilkins |
| 5 Watson | 5 Watson | 5 Watson (Greenhoff) | 5 Watson | 5 Watson (Thompson) |
| 6 Hughes | 6 Hughes (Greenhoff) | 6 Hughes | 6 Hughes | 6 Hughes |
| 7 Currie | 7 Wilkins | 7 Keegan | 7 Keegan | 7 Keegan |
| 8 Coppell | 8 Coppell | 8 Coppell | 8 Coppell | 8 Coppell |
| 9 Pearson | 9 Mariner (Brooking) | 9 Francis T. | 9 Latchford | 9 Latchford |
| 10 Woodcock | 10 Francis T. | 10 Brooking (Currie) | 10 Brooking | 10 Brooking |
| 11 Greenhoff | 11 Barnes | 11 Barnes | 11 Barnes | 11 Barnes (Woodcock) |
| Wembley May 16: 1-0 *Neal* | Glasgow May 20: 1-0 *Coppell* | Wembley May 24: 4-1 *Barnes, Neal* (pen), *Francis, Currie* | Copenhagen Sept 20: 4-3 *Keegan 2, Latchford, Neal* | Dublin Oct 25: 1-1 *Latchford* |

680

| 1978 Czechoslovakia | 1979 N Ireland | 1979 N Ireland | 1979 Wales | 1979 Scotland |
|---|---|---|---|---|
| 1 Shilton | 1 Clemence | 1 Clemence | 1 Corrigan | 1 Clemence |
| 2 Anderson | 2 Neal | 2 Neal | 2 Cherry | 2 Neal |
| 3 Cherry | 3 Mills | 3 Mills | 3 Sansom | 3 Mills |
| 4 Thompson | 4 Currie | 4 Thompson | 4 Wilkins (Brooking) | 4 Thompson |
| 5 Watson | 5 Watson | 5 Watson | 5 Watson | 5 Watson |
| 6 Wilkins | 6 Hughes | 6 Wilkins | 6 Hughes | 6 Wilkins |
| 7 Keegan | 7 Keegan | 7 Coppell | 7 Keegan (Coppell) | 7 Keegan |
| 8 Coppell | 8 Coppell | 8 McDermott | 8 Currie | 8 Coppell |
| 9 Woodcock (Latchford) | 9 Latchford | 9 Latchford | 9 Latchford | 9 Latchford |
| 10 Currie | 10 Brooking | 10 Currie | 10 McDermott | 10 Brooking |
| 11 Barnes | 11 Barnes | 11 Barnes | 11 Cunningham | 11 Barnes |
| Wembley Nov 29: 1-0 *Coppell* | Wembley Feb 7: 4-0 *Keegan, Latchford 2, Watson* | Belfast May 19: 2-0 *Watson, Coppell* | Wembley May 23: 0-0 | Wembley May 26: 3-1 *Barnes, Coppell, Keegan* |

| 1979 Bulgaria | 1979 Sweden | 1979 Austria | 1979 Denmark | 1979 N Ireland |
|---|---|---|---|---|
| 1 Clemence | 1 Shilton | 1 Shilton (Clemence) | 1 Clemence | 1 Shilton |
| 2 Neal | 2 Anderson | 2 Neal | 2 Neal | 2 Neal |
| 3 Mills | 3 Cherry | 3 Mills | 3 Mills | 3 Mills |
| 4 Thompson | 4 McDermott (Wilkins) | 4 Thompson | 4 Thompson | 4 Thompson |
| 5 Watson | 5 Watson | 5 Watson | 5 Watson | 5 Watson |
| 6 Wilkins | 6 Hughes | 6 Wilkins | 6 Wilkins | 6 Wilkins |
| 7 Keegan | 7 Keegan | 7 Keegan | 7 Coppell | 7 Keegan |
| 8 Coppell | 8 Currie (Brooking) | 8 Coppell | 8 McDermott | 8 Coppell |
| 9 Latchford (Francis T.) | 9 Francis T. | 9 Latchford (Francis T.) | 9 Keegan | 9 Francis T. |
| 10 Brooking | 10 Woodcock | 10 Brooking | 10 Brooking | 10 Brooking (McDermott) |
| 11 Barnes (Woodcock) | 11 Cunningham | 11 Barnes (Cunningham) | 11 Barnes | 11 Woodcock |
| Sofia June 6: 3-0 *Keegan, Watson, Barnes* | Stockholm June 10: 0-0 | Vienna June 13: 3-4 *Keegan, Coppell, Wilkins* | Wembley Sept 9: 1-0 *Keegan* | Belfast Oct 17: 5-1 *Francis 2, Woodcock 2, Nicholl og* |

| 1979 Bulgaria | 1980 Rep of Ireland | 1980 Spain | 1980 Argentina | 1980 Wales |
|---|---|---|---|---|
| 1 Clemence | 1 Clemence | 1 Shilton | 1 Clemence | 1 Clemence |
| 2 Anderson | 2 Cherry | 2 Neal (Hughes) | 2 Neal (Cherry) | 2 Neal (Sansom) |
| 3 Sansom | 3 Sansom | 3 Mills | 3 Sansom | 3 Cherry |
| 4 Thompson | 4 Thompson | 4 Thompson | 4 Thompson | 4 Thompson |
| 5 Watson | 5 Watson | 5 Watson | 5 Watson | 5 Lloyd (Wilkins) |
| 6 Wilkins | 6 Robson | 6 Wilkins | 6 Wilkins | 6 Kennedy |
| 7 Reeves | 7 Keegan | 7 Keegan | 7 Keegan | 7 Coppell |
| 8 Hoddle | 8 McDermott | 8 Coppell | 8 Coppell | 8 Hoddle |
| 9 Francis T. | 9 Johnson (Coppell) | 9 Francis T. (Cunningham) | 9 Johnson (Birtles) | 9 Mariner |
| 10 Kennedy | 10 Woodcock | 10 Kennedy | 10 Woodcock | 10 Brooking |
| 11 Woodcock | 11 Cunningham | 11 Woodcock | 11 Kennedy (Brooking) | 11 Barnes |
| Wembley Nov 22: 2-0 *Watson, Hoddle* | Wembley Feb 6: 2-0 *Keegan 2* | Barcelona March 26: 2-0 *Woodcock, Francis* | Wembley May 13: 3-1 *Johnson 2, Keegan* | Wrexham May 17: 1-4 *Mariner* |

| 1980 N Ireland | 1980 Scotland | 1980 Australia | 1980 Belgium | 1980 Italy |
|---|---|---|---|---|
| 1 Corrigan | 1 Clemence | 1 Corrigan | 1 Clemence | 1 Shilton |
| 2 Cherry | 2 Cherry | 2 Cherry | 2 Neal | 2 Neal |
| 3 Sansom | 3 Sansom | 3 Lampard | 3 Sansom | 3 Sansom |
| 4 Hughes | 4 Thompson | 4 Talbot | 4 Thompson | 4 Thompson |
| 5 Watson | 5 Watson | 5 Osman | 5 Watson | 5 Watson |
| 6 Wilkins | 6 Wilkins | 6 Butcher | 6 Wilkins | 6 Wilkins |
| 7 Reeves (Mariner) | 7 Coppell | 7 Robson (Greenhoff) | 7 Keegan | 7 Keegan |
| 8 McDermott | 8 McDermott | 8 Sunderland (Ward) | 8 Coppell (McDermott) | 8 Coppell |
| 9 Johnson | 9 Johnson | 9 Mariner | 9 Johnson (Kennedy) | 9 Birtles (Mariner) |
| 10 Brooking | 10 Mariner (Hughes) | 10 Hoddle | 10 Woodcock | 10 Kennedy |
| 11 Devonshire | 11 Brooking | 11 Armstrong (Devonshire) | 11 Brooking | 11 Woodcock |

| Wembley May 20: 1-1 *Brotherston og* | Glasgow May 24: 2-0 *Brooking, Coppell* | Sydney May 31: 2-1 *Hoddle, Mariner* | Turin June 12: 1-1 *Wilkins* | Turin June 15: 0-1 |
|---|---|---|---|---|

| 1980 Spain | 1980 Norway | 1980 Rumania | 1980 Switzerland | 1981 Spain |
|---|---|---|---|---|
| 1 Clemence | 1 Shilton | 1 Clemence | 1 Shilton | 1 Clemence |
| 2 Anderson (Cherry) | 2 Anderson | 2 Neal | 2 Neal | 2 Neal |
| 3 Mills | 3 Sansom | 3 Sansom | 3 Sansom | 3 Sansom |
| 4 Thompson | 4 Thompson | 4 Thompson | 4 Robson | 4 Robson |
| 5 Watson | 5 Watson | 5 Watson | 5 Watson | 5 Butcher |
| 6 Wilkins | 6 Robson | 6 Robson | 6 Mills | 6 Osman |
| 7 McDermott | 7 Gates | 7 Rix | 7 Coppell | 7 Keegan |
| 8 Hoddle (Mariner) | 8 McDermott | 8 McDermott | 8 McDermott | 8 Francis (Barnes) |
| 9 Keegan | 9 Mariner | 9 Birtles (Cunningham) | 9 Mariner | 9 Mariner |
| 10 Woodcock | 10 Woodcock | 10 Woodcock | 10 Brooking (Rix) | 10 Brooking (Wilkins) |
| 11 Brooking | 11 Rix | 11 Gates (Coppell) | 11 Woodcock | 11 Hoddle |

| Naples June 18: 2-1 *Brooking, Woodcock* | Wembley Sept 10: 4-0 *McDermott 2 (1 pen), Woodcock, Mariner* | Bucharest Oct 15: 1-2 *Woodcock* | Wembley Nov 19: 2-1 *Tanner og, Mariner* | Wembley Mar 25: 1-2 *Hoddle* |
|---|---|---|---|---|

| 1981 Rumania | 1981 Brazil | 1981 Wales | 1981 Scotland | 1981 Switzerland |
|---|---|---|---|---|
| 1 Shilton | 1 Clemence | 1 Corrigan | 1 Corrigan | 1 Clemence |
| 2 Anderson | 2 Neal | 2 Anderson | 2 Anderson | 2 Mills |
| 3 Sansom | 3 Sansom | 3 Sansom | 3 Sansom | 3 Sansom |
| 4 Robson | 4 Robson | 4 Robson | 4 Wilkins | 4 Wilkins |
| 5 Watson | 5 Martin | 5 Watson | 5 Watson (Martin) | 5 Watson (Barnes) |
| 6 Osman | 6 Wilkins | 6 Wilkins | 6 Robson | 6 Osman |
| 7 Wilkins | 7 Coppell | 7 Coppell | 7 Coppell | 7 Coppell |
| 8 Brooking (McDermott) | 8 McDermott | 8 Hoddle | 8 Hoddle | 8 Robson |
| 9 Coppell | 9 Withe | 9 Withe (Woodcock) | 9 Withe | 9 Keegan |
| 10 Francis | 10 Rix | 10 Rix | 10 Rix | 10 Mariner |
| 11 Woodcock | 11 Barnes | 11 Barnes | 11 Woodcock (Francis) | 11 Francis (McDermott) |

| Wembley April 29: 0-0 | Wembley May 12: 0-1 | Wembley May 20: 0-0 | Wembley May 23: 0-1 | Basle May 30: 1-2 *McDermott* |
|---|---|---|---|---|

**1981**
**Hungary**

1 Clemence
2 Neal
3 Mills
4 Thompson
5 Watson
6 Robson
7 Coppell
8 McDermott
9 Mariner
10 Brooking
   (Wilkins)
11 Keegan

Budapest
June 6: 3-1
*Brooking 2,*
*Keegan* (pen)

## INTERNATIONAL FOOTBALL ASSOCIATION BOARD 1982

The annual meeting of the International Football Association Board was held in Madrid on 6 July. One change was made in the actual Laws. In Law XII, Fouls and Misconduct, paragraph 5(a) in the section dealing with offences punishable by an indirect free-kick has been changed. It now reads (changes italicised):

'A player committing any of the five following offences:–
. . . 5. When playing as goalkeeper *and within his own penalty area*
   (a) *from the moment the ball comes under his control, he takes more than four steps without releasing the ball into play and – having released it – he touches the ball again before it has been touched or played by another player* . . .
shall be penalised by the award of an indirect free-kick . . .'

Apart from the fact that the new paragraph does not fit in with the construction of the section as a whole, it opens up another area of uncertain interpretation. What is the meaning of 'under his control'? If the ball is in the goalkeeper's hands, it is obviously under his control. But there are grey areas. If, for example, a 'keeper just parries the ball with his hands and allows it to drop to his feet, may he then dribble the ball to the edge of the penalty-area, pick it up, and kick it from hand? And what is to stop him rolling the ball to a team-mate, making ground, and then picking the ball up again?

After the meeting of the International Board, there was an extraordinary general meeting in which the Football Association put forward, on the behalf of the Football League, a request for permission to try out three experimental Laws: (i) making it an offence to play the ball to your own 'keeper from outside the penalty-area, (ii) no off-side when receiving the ball from your own 'keeper if he played it from his own penalty-area, and (iii) making the 'cynical foul' punishable by a penalty-kick even when committed outside the penalty-area. The League were refused permission to make these experiments because it would 'confuse the rest of the world'.

*Comment:* While it is understandable that FIFA should not want individual countries experimenting with the Laws, their continuing expressed satisfaction with the Laws as they stand is unpardonable. The following two quotes say it all:

'Soccer has been perfect since it was born 100 years ago . . . Anybody can enjoy soccer because the rules are so simple.'

*João Havelange, President of FIFA*

'If a player taking a goal-kick plays the ball a second time after it has passed beyond the penalty-area, but before it has touched or been played by another player, an indirect free-kick shall be awarded to the opposing team, to be taken from the place where the infringement occurred, unless the offence is committed by a player in his opponents' goal area, in which case, the free-kick shall be taken from a point anywhere within that half of the goal-area in which the offence occurred.'

*Typical extract from the Laws of the Game*

# IRELAND INTERNATIONAL TEAMS 1882-1981

### Substitutes in brackets †World Cup final stages

| 1882 England | 1882 Wales | 1883 England | 1883 Wales | 1884 Scotland |
|---|---|---|---|---|
| 1 Hamilton | 1 Hamilton | 1 Rankine | 1 Rankine | 1 Hunter |
| 2 McAlery | 2 Crone W. | 2 Watson | 2 Watson | 2 Wilson |
| 3 Rattray | 3 McAlery | 3 Rattray | 3 Rattray | 3 Crone W. |
| 4 Martin | 4 Martin | 4 Molyneux | 4 Molyneux | 4 Hastings |
| 5 Hastings | 5 Hastings | 5 Martin | 5 Hastings | 5 Molyneux |
| 6 Buckle | 6 Davison | 6 Morrow | 6 Morrow | 6 Dill |
| 7 McWha | 7 McWha | 7 Potts | 7 Potts | 7 Spiller |
| 8 Davison | 8 Gibb | 8 McWha | 8 McWha | 8 Gibb |
| 9 Sinclair | 9 Sinclair | 9 Davison | 9 Davison | 9 Morrow |
| 10 Dill | 10 Dill | 10 Reid | 10 Spiller | 10 Davison |
| 11 McCaw | 11 Johnston | 11 Spiller | 11 Dill | 11 Gaussen |
| Belfast Feb 18: 0-13 | Wrexham Feb 25: 1-7 *Johnston* | Liverpool Feb 24: 0-7 | Belfast Mar 17: 1-1 *Morrow* | Belfast Jan 26: 0-5 |

| 1884 Wales | 1884 England | 1885 England | 1885 Scotland | 1885 Wales |
|---|---|---|---|---|
| 1 Hunter | 1 Hunter | 1 Henderson | 1 Henderson | 1 Henderson |
| 2 Wilson | 2 Wilson | 2 Hewison | 2 Hewison | 2 Johnston |
| 3 Crone W. | 3 Crone W. | 3 Moorhead | 3 Johnston | 3 Eames |
| 4 Molyneux | 4 Hastings | 4 Molyneux | 4 Muir | 4 Molyneux |
| 5 Lockhart | 5 Molyneux | 5 Houston | 5 Houston | 5 Muir |
| 6 Redmond | 6 Dill | 6 Eames | 6 Eames | 6 McWha |
| 7 Davison | 7 Spiller | 7 McWha | 7 McLean | 7 Hamilton W.J. |
| 8 Gibb | 8 McWha | 8 Davison | 8 Sherrard | 8 Hamilton W.D. |
| 9 Reid | 9 Johnston | 9 Gibb | 9 Gibb | 9 Gibb |
| 10 Spiller | 10 Davison | 10 McGee | 10 McGee | 10 McGee |
| 11 Dill | 11 Gaussen | 11 Dill | 11 Dill | 11 Dill |
| Wrexham Feb 9: 0-6 | Belfast Feb 23: 1-8 *McWha* | Manchester Feb 28: 0-4 | Glasgow Mar 14: 2-8 *Gibb 2* | Belfast April 11: 2-8 *Molyneux, Dill* |

| 1886 Wales | 1886 England | 1886 Scotland | 1887 England | 1887 Scotland |
|---|---|---|---|---|
| 1 Gillespie | 1 Gillespie | 1 Gillespie | 1 Gillespie | 1 Gillespie |
| 2 Watson | 2 Watson | 2 Watson | 2 Browne | 2 Fox |
| 3 Devine | 3 Devine | 3 Crone W. | 3 Fox | 3 Watson |
| 4 Molyneux | 4 Molyneux | 4 Molyneux | 4 Rosbotham | 4 Moore |
| 5 Crone W. | 5 Crone W. | 5 Williams | 5 Leslie | 5 Rosbotham |
| 6 McArthur | 6 Hastings | 6 Hastings | 6 Crone W. | 6 Baxter |
| 7 McClatchey | 7 Turner | 7 McClatchey | 7 Allen | 7 Reid |
| 8 Smyth | 8 Condy | 8 Johnston | 8 Gibb | 8 Stanfield |
| 9 Whitfield | 9 Johnston | 9 Gibb | 9 Stanfield | 9 Browne |
| 10 Lemon | 10 McClatchey | 10 Condy | 10 Small | 10 Peden |
| 11 Raper | 11 Williams | 11 Turner | 11 Brown W.M. | 11 Gibb |
| Wrexham Feb 27: 0-5 | Belfast Mar 13: 1-6 *Williams* | Belfast Mar 20: 2-7 *Condy, Johnston* | Sheffield Feb 5: 0-7 | Glasgow Feb 19: 1-4 *Browne* |

| 1887 Wales | 1888 Wales | 1888 Scotland | 1888 England | 1889 England |
|---|---|---|---|---|
| 1 Gillespie | 1 Clugston | 1 Lowther | 1 Lowther | 1 Clugston |
| 2 Browne | 2 Forbes | 2 Wilson | 2 McVickers | 2 Goodbody |
| 3 Watson | 3 Crone W. | 3 Browne | 3 Browne | 3 Watson |
| 4 Sherrard | 4 Sherrard | 4 Forsyth | 4 Forsyth | 4 Crawford |
| 5 Rosbotham | 5 Rosbotham | 5 Rosbotham | 5 Rosbotham | 5 Rosbotham |
| 6 Devine | 6 Devine | 6 Molyneux | 6 Crone W. | 6 Cooke |
| 7 Moore | 7 Gaussen | 7 Dalton | 7 Gaussen | 7 Gaussen |
| 8 Baxter | 8 Stanfield | 8 Stanfield | 8 Stanfield | 8 Stanfield |
| 9 Gibb | 9 Berry | 9 Berry | 9 Silo | 9 Berry |
| 10 Stanfield | 10 Wilton | 10 Lemon | 10 Wilton | 10 Wilton |
| 11 Peden | 11 Peden | 11 Turner | 11 Peden | 11 Peden |

| Belfast | Wrexham | Belfast | Belfast | Everton |
|---|---|---|---|---|
| Mar 12: 4-1 | Mar 3: 0-11 | Mar 24: 2-10 | April 7: 1-5 | Mar 2: 1-6 |
| *Stanfield, Browne, Peden, Sherrard* | | *Lemon, Dalton* | *Crone* | *Wilton* |

| 1889 Scotland | 1889 Wales | 1890 Wales | 1890 England | 1890 Scotland |
|---|---|---|---|---|
| 1 Clugston | 1 Clugston | 1 Galbraith | 1 Clugston | 1 Clugston |
| 2 McVickers | 2 Elleman | 2 Crone R. | 2 Stewart | 2 Stewart |
| 3 Crone R. | 3 Watson | 3 Stewart | 3 Crone R. | 3 Crone R. |
| 4 Thompson | 4 Crawford | 4 Crone W. | 4 Williamson | 4 Reid |
| 5 Christian | 5 Bennett | 5 Reynolds | 5 Spencer | 5 Spencer |
| 6 Crone W. | 6 Reid | 6 Reid | 6 Cooke | 6 Cooke |
| 7 Torrans S. | 7 Gaussen | 7 Dalton | 7 Elleman | 7 Dalton |
| 8 Stanfield | 8 Stanfield | 8 Gaffikin | 8 Stanfield | 8 Gaffikin |
| 9 Gibb | 9 Percy | 9 Johnston | 9 Wilton | 9 Stanfield |
| 10 Wilton | 10 Lemon | 10 Torrans S. | 10 McIlvenny | 10 Torrans S. |
| 11 Peden | 11 Gillespie | 11 Peden | 11 Reynolds | 11 Peden |

| Glasgow | Belfast | Shrewsbury | Belfast | Belfast |
|---|---|---|---|---|
| Mar 9: 0-7 | April 27: 1-3 | Feb 8: 2-5 | Mar 15: 1-9 | Mar 29: 1-4 |
| | *Lemon* | *Dalton 2* | *Reynolds* | *Peden* |

| 1891 Wales | 1891 England | 1891 Scotland | 1892 Wales | 1892 England |
|---|---|---|---|---|
| 1 Clugston | 1 Clugston | 1 Loyal | 1 Clugston | 1 Clugston |
| 2 Goodbody | 2 Forbes | 2 Gordon H. | 2 Gordon H. | 2 Gordon H. |
| 3 Morrison | 3 Morrison | 3 Forbes | 3 Stewart | 3 Stewart |
| 4 Crawford | 4 Crawford | 4 Crawford | 4 McKeown | 4 McKeown |
| 5 Reynolds | 5 Reynolds | 5 Reynolds | 5 Spencer | 5 Spencer |
| 6 Moore | 6 Moore | 6 Moore | 6 Cunningham | 6 Cunningham |
| 7 Dalton | 7 Whiteside | 7 Dalton | 7 Dalton | 7 Dalton |
| 8 Gaffikin | 8 Stanfield | 8 Gaffikin | 8 Gaffikin | 8 Gaffikin |
| 9 Stanfield | 9 McCabe | 9 Stanfield | 9 Stanfield | 9 Stanfield |
| 10 Torrans S. | 10 McIlvenny | 10 Brisby | 10 Torrans S. | 10 Torrans S. |
| 11 Peden | 11 Peden | 11 Torrans S. | 11 Peden | 11 Peden |

| Belfast | Wolverhampton | Glasgow | Bangor | Belfast |
|---|---|---|---|---|
| Feb 7: 7-2 | Mar 7: 1-6 | Mar 28: 1-2 | Feb 27: 1-1 | Mar 5: 0-2 |
| *Dalton 3, Stanfield 2, Gaffikin 2* | *Whiteside* | *Stanfield* | *Stanfield* | |

| 1892 Scotland | 1893 England | 1893 Scotland | 1893 Wales | 1894 Wales |
|---|---|---|---|---|
| 1 Clugston | 1 Clugston | 1 Clugston | 1 Clugston | 1 Gordon T. |
| 2 Gordon H. | 2 Gordon H. | 2 Gordon H. | 2 Gordon H. | 2 Stewart |
| 3 Stewart | 3 Stewart | 3 Torrans R. | 3 Stewart | 3 Torrans S. |
| 4 McKeown | 4 Crawford | 4 McKeown | 4 Crawford | 4 McKeown |
| 5 Spencer | 5 Spencer | 5 Johnston | 5 McKeown | 5 Burnett |
| 6 Cunningham | 6 Cunningham | 6 Torrans S. | 6 Johnston | 6 Milne |
| 7 Dalton | 7 Small | 7 Small | 7 Small | 7 Dalton |
| 8 Gaffikin | 8 Gaffikin | 8 Gaffikin | 8 Gaffikin | 8 Gaffikin |
| 9 Williamson | 9 Stanfield | 9 Williamson | 9 Stanfield | 9 Stanfield |
| 10 Stanfield | 10 Torrans S. | 10 Wilton | 10 Wilton | 10 Gibson |
| 11 Torrans S. | 11 Peden | 11 Peden | 11 Peden | 11 Barron |

| Belfast | Birmingham | Glasgow | Belfast | Swansea |
| Mar 19: 2-3 | Feb 25: 1-6 | Mar 25: 1-6 | April 5: 4-3 | Feb 24: 1-4 |
| *Williamson, Gaffikin* | *Gaffikin* | *Gaffikin* | *Peden 3, Wilton* | *Stanfield* |

| 1894 England | 1894 Scotland | 1895 England | 1895 Wales | 1895 Scotland |
|---|---|---|---|---|
| 1 Scott T. | 1 Scott T. | 1 Gordon T. | 1 Scott T. | 1 Scott T. |
| 2 Stewart | 2 Stewart | 2 Gordon H. | 2 Gordon H. | 2 Ponsonby |
| 3 Torrans S. | 3 Torrans S. | 3 Torrans S. | 3 Scott L.J. | 3 Scott L.J. |
| 4 Johnston | 4 McKeown | 4 McKie | 4 McKie | 4 McKie |
| 5 Burnett | 5 Burnett | 5 Milne | 5 Milne | 5 Alexander |
| 6 Milne | 6 Milne | 6 Burnett | 6 Burnett | 6 McClatchey |
| 7 Dalton | 7 Dalton | 7 Morrison | 7 Morrison | 7 Morrison |
| 8 Gaffikin | 8 Gaffikin | 8 Gaffikin | 8 Sherrard | 8 Sherrard |
| 9 Stanfield | 9 Stanfield | 9 Stanfield | 9 Jordan | 9 Stanfield |
| 10 Gibson | 10 Gibson | 10 Sherrard | 10 Gawkrodger | 10 Gibson |
| 11 Barron | 11 Barron | 11 Jordan | 11 Gaffikin | 11 Barron |

| Belfast | Belfast | Derby | Belfast | Glasgow |
| Mar 3: 2-2 | Mar 31: 1-2 | Mar 9: 0-9 | Mar 16: 2-2 | Mar 30: 1-3 |
| *Stanfield, Gibson* | *Stanfield* | | *Gawkrodger, Sherrard* | *Sherrard* |

| 1896 Wales | 1896 England | 1896 Scotland | 1897 England | 1897 Wales |
|---|---|---|---|---|
| 1 Scott T. | 1 Scott T. | 1 Scott T. | 1 Scott T. | 1 Scott T. |
| 2 Ponsonby | 2 Ponsonby | 2 Ponsonby | 2 Ponsonby | 2 Gibson |
| 3 Torrans S. | 3 Torrans S. | 3 Torrans S. | 3 Torrans S. | 3 Torrans S. |
| 4 McCoy | 4 Fitzpatrick | 4 Gordon H. | 4 Pyper, John | 4 Pyper, John |
| 5 Milne | 5 Milne | 5 Milne | 5 Milne | 5 Ponsonby |
| 6 Campbell | 6 Gordon H. | 6 Fitzpatrick | 6 McMaster | 6 McMaster |
| 7 Turner | 7 Baird | 7 Baird | 7 Campbell | 7 Campbell |
| 8 Kelly | 8 Kelly | 8 Morrogh | 8 Hall | 8 Stanfield |
| 9 Stanfield | 9 Stanfield | 9 Stanfield | 9 Stanfield | 9 Pyper, James |
| 10 McCashin | 10 Turner | 10 Barron | 10 Darling | 10 Peden |
| 11 Peden | 11 Peden | 11 Peden | 11 Barron | 11 Barron |

| Wrexham | Belfast | Belfast | Nottingham | Belfast |
| Feb 29: 1-6 | Mar 7: 0-2 | Mar 28: 3-3 | Feb 20: 0-6 | Mar 6: 4-3 |
| *Turner* | | *Barron 2, Milne (pen)* | | *Barron, Stanfield, John Pyper, Peden* |

| 1897 Scotland | 1898 Wales | 1898 England | 1898 Scotland | 1899 England |
|---|---|---|---|---|
| 1 Thompson | 1 Scott T. | 1 Scott T. | 1 Scott T. | 1 Lewis |
| 2 Ponsonby | 2 Gibson | 2 Gibson | 2 Gibson | 2 Pyper, John |
| 3 Torrans S. | 3 Cochrane | 3 Torrans S. | 3 Torrans S. | 3 Torrans S. |
| 4 Pyper, John | 4 Anderson | 4 Anderson | 4 Anderson | 4 Ponsonby |
| 5 Milne | 5 Milne | 5 Milne | 5 Milne | 5 Milne |
| 6 McMaster | 6 Little | 6 Cochrane | 6 Cochrane | 6 Cochrane |
| 7 Campbell | 7 Campbell | 7 Campbell | 7 Campbell | 7 Campbell |
| 8 Stanfield | 8 Mercer | 8 Mercer | 8 Mercer | 8 Mercer |
| 9 Pyper, James | 9 Pyper, James | 9 Pyper, James | 9 Pyper, James | 9 Waring |
| 10 Darling | 10 McCashin | 10 Peden | 10 McCashin | 10 Wattie |
| 11 Peden | 11 Peden | 11 McAllen | 11 Peden | 11 McAllen |

| Glasgow | Llandudno | Belfast | Belfast | Sunderland |
|---|---|---|---|---|
| Mar 27: 1-5' | Feb 19: 1-0 | Mar 5: 2-3 | Mar 26: 0-3 | Feb 18: 2-13 |
| *James Pyper* | *Peden* | *Pyper, Mercer* | | *McAllen, Campbell* |


| 1899 Wales | 1899 Scotland | 1900 Wales | 1900 Scotland | 1900 England |
|---|---|---|---|---|
| 1 Lewis | 1 Lewis | 1 Scott T. | 1 Lewis | 1 Reilly |
| 2 Pyper, John | 2 Swan | 2 Pyper, John | 2 Pyper, John | 2 Pyper, John |
| 3 Torrans S. | 3 Foreman | 3 Cochrane | 3 Cochrane | 3 Cochrane |
| 4 Goodall | 4 Anderson | 4 McShane | 4 McShane | 4 McShane |
| 5 Milne | 5 Goodall | 5 Goodall | 5 Barry | 5 Goodall |
| 6 Taggart | 6 McShane | 6 Maginnis | 6 Maginnis | 6 Maginnis |
| 7 Morrison | 7 Sheehan | 7 Sheehan | 7 Campbell | 7 Sheehan |
| 8 Meldon | 8 Meldon | 8 Morrison | 8 Darling | 8 Campbell |
| 9 Hanna | 9 Pyer, James | 9 Kirwan | 9 McAuley | 9 Pyper, James |
| 10 McAllen | 10 McCashin | 10 Kearns | 10 McAllen | 10 McAllen |
| 11 Peden | 11 McAllen | 11 McAllen | 11 Kearns | 11 Kearns |

| Belfast | Glasgow | Llandudno | Belfast | Dublin |
|---|---|---|---|---|
| Mar 4: 1-0 | Mar 25: 1-9 | Feb 24: 0-2 | Mar 3: 0-3 | Mar 17: 0-2 |
| *Meldon* | *Goodall* | | | |


| 1901 Scotland | 1901 England | 1901 Wales | 1902 Wales | 1902 Scotland |
|---|---|---|---|---|
| 1 McAlpine | 1 Nolan-Whelan | 1 Nolan-Whelan | 1 Nolan-Whelan | 1 Nolan-Whelan |
| 2 Gibson | 2 Gibson | 2 Gibson | 2 Gibson | 2 Gibson |
| 3 Torrans S. | 3 Boyle | 3 Torrans S. | 3 McCracken W. | 3 Pyper, John |
| 4 Farrell | 4 Connor | 4 Farrell | 4 Darling | 4 Darling |
| 5 Connor | 5 Goodall | 5 Milne | 5 Milne | 5 Goodall |
| 6 Cochrane | 6 Burnison | 6 Burnison | 6 Nicholl | 6 Milne |
| 7 Scott J. | 7 Black | 7 Campbell | 7 Mercer | 7 Campbell |
| 8 Smith J. | 8 Rea | 8 Smith J. | 8 Maxwell | 8 Morrison |
| 9 Campbell | 9 Mansfield | 9 McKelvie | 9 Gara | 9 Gara |
| 10 O'Reilly | 10 Doherty | 10 O'Reilly | 10 Kearns | 10 Kearns |
| 11 Clarke | 11 Clarke | 11 McAllen | 11 Kirwan | 11 McAllen |

| Glasgow | Southampton | Belfast | Cardiff | Belfast |
|---|---|---|---|---|
| Feb 23: 0-11 | Mar 9: 0-3 | Mar 23: 0-1 | Feb 22: 3-0 | Mar 1: 1-3 |
| | | | *Gara 3* | *Milne* |

| 1902 England | 1903 England | 1903 Scotland | 1903 Wales | 1904 England |
|---|---|---|---|---|
| 1 Reilly | 1 Scott W. | 1 Scott W. | 1 Scott W. | 1 Scott W. |
| 2 McCracken W. | 2 McCracken W. | 2 McCartney | 2 McCartney | 2 McCracken W. |
| 3 Boyle | 3 McMillan | 3 Boyle | 3 Boyle | 3 Boyle |
| 4 Darling | 4 Darling | 4 Darling | 4 Darling | 4 Milne |
| 5 Milne | 5 Milne | 5 Milne | 5 Goodall | 5 Goodall |
| 6 Nicholl | 6 Goodall | 6 Maginnis | 6 Maginnis | 6 Maginnis |
| 7 Mercer | 7 Campbell | 7 Mercer | 7 Mercer | 7 Mercer |
| 8 Morrison | 8 Maxwell | 8 Sheridan | 8 Maxwell | 8 Sheridan |
| 9 Gara | 9 Sheridan | 9 Connor | 9 Connor | 9 Connor |
| 10 Kearns | 10 Sloan | 10 Shanks | 10 Sheridan | 10 Kirwan |
| 11 Kirwan | 11 Kirwan | 11 Kirwan | 11 Kirwan | 11 Buckle |
| Belfast Mar 22: 0-1 | Wolverhampton Feb 14: 0-4 | Glasgow Mar 21: 2-0 *Connor, Kirwan* | Belfast Mar 28: 2-0 *Goodall, Sheridan* | Belfast Mar 12: 1-3 *Kirwan* |

| 1904 Wales | 1904 Scotland | 1905 England | 1905 Scotland | 1905 Wales |
|---|---|---|---|---|
| 1 Scott W. | 1 Scott W. | 1 Scott W. | 1 Scott W. | 1 Reynolds |
| 2 McCracken W. | 2 McCracken W. | 2 McCracken W. | 2 McCartney | 2 McCracken W. |
| 3 McCartney | 3 McCartney | 3 McCartney | 3 McCracken W. | 3 McMillan |
| 4 McConnell E. | 4 McConnell E. | 4 Darling | 4 Darling | 4 Darling |
| 5 Milne | 5 Milne | 5 Connor | 5 Connor | 5 Connor |
| 6 Maginnis | 6 Maginnis | 6 Nicholl | 6 McConnell E. | 6 Johnston |
| 7 Mercer | 7 Campbell | 7 Sloan | 7 Mercer | 7 Hunter |
| 8 Shanks | 8 Sheridan | 8 Sheridan | 8 Maxwell | 8 Maxwell |
| 9 Goodall | 9 O'Reilly | 9 Murphy | 9 Murphy | 9 Murphy |
| 10 Kirkwood | 10 Sloan | 10 Shanks | 10 O'Hagan | 10 O'Hagan |
| 11 Kirwan | 11 Kirwan | 11 Kirwan | 11 Kirwan | 11 Kirwan |
| Bangor Mar 21: 1-0 *McCracken (pen)* | Dublin Mar 26: 1-1 *Sheridan* | Middlesbrough Feb 25: 1-1 *Williamson og* | Glasgow Mar 18: 0-4 | Belfast April 8: 2-2 *Murphy, O'Hagan* |

| 1906 England | 1906 Scotland | 1906 Wales | 1907 England | 1907 Wales |
|---|---|---|---|---|
| 1 Sherry | 1 McKee | 1 McKee | 1 Scott W. | 1 Sherry |
| 2 Darling | 2 Willis | 2 Willis | 2 McCracken W. | 2 Seymour |
| 3 McIlroy | 3 Darling | 3 Darling | 3 McCartney | 3 McCartney |
| 4 Wright | 4 Wright | 4 Wright | 4 Wright | 4 Wright |
| 5 Milne | 5 Milne | 5 Milne | 5 Connor | 5 Crothers |
| 6 McConnell E. | 6 Ledwidge | 6 Ledwidge | 6 McConnell E. | 6 McClure |
| 7 Hunter | 7 Hunter | 7 Hunter | 7 Blair | 7 Blair |
| 8 Mulholland | 8 Mulholland | 8 Maxwell | 8 Harris | 8 Harris |
| 9 Harris | 9 Waddell | 9 O'Hagan | 9 Sloan | 9 Sloan |
| 10 O'Hagan | 10 O'Hagan | 10 Sloan | 10 O'Hagan | 10 O'Hagan |
| 11 Kirwan | 11 Kirwan | 11 Kirwan | 11 Young | 11 Kirwan |
| Belfast Feb 17: 0-5 | Dublin Mar 17: 0-1 | Wrexham April 2: 4-4 *Maxwell 2, Sloan 2* | Everton Feb 16: 0-1 | Belfast Feb 23: 2-3 *O'Hagan, Sloan* |

| 1907 Scotland | 1908 England | 1908 Scotland | 1908 Wales | 1909 England |
|---|---|---|---|---|
| 1 Scott W. | 1 Scott W. | 1 Scott W. | 1 Scott W. | 1 Scott W. |
| 2 Willis | 2 Craig | 2 Craig | 2 Craig | 2 Balfe |
| 3 McCartney | 3 McCartney | 3 McCartney | 3 McCartney | 3 McCartney |
| 4 Wright | 4 Harris | 4 Harris | 4 Darling | 4 Harris |
| 5 Connor | 5 Connor | 5 Connor | 5 McConnell E. | 5 Darling |
| 6 McClure | 6 McClure | 6 McConnell E. | 6 Harris | 6 McClure |
| 7 Blair | 7 Blair | 7 Blair | 7 Hunter | 7 Hunter |
| 8 Maxwell | 8 Hannon | 8 Hannon | 8 Hamilton | 8 Lacey |
| 9 McGuire | 9 Mercer | 9 Andrews | 9 Sloan | 9 Greer |
| 10 O'Hagan | 10 Burnison | 10 O'Hagan | 10 O'Hagan | 10 O'Hagan |
| 11 Young | 11 Young | 11 Young | 11 Buckle | 11 Young |
| Glasgow Mar 16: 0-3 | Belfast Feb 15: 1-3 *Hannon* | Dublin Mar 14: 0-5 | Aberdare April 11: 1-0 *Sloan* | Bradford Feb 13: 0-4 |

| 1909 Scotland | 1909 Wales | 1910 England | 1910 Scotland | 1910 Wales |
|---|---|---|---|---|
| 1 Scott W. | 1 Scott W. | 1 Scott W. | 1 Scott W. | 1 O'Hehir |
| 2 Craig | 2 Seymour | 2 Burnison | 2 Burnison | 2 Balfe |
| 3 McCartney | 3 McCartney | 3 McCann | 3 McCann | 3 McCann |
| 4 Harris | 4 Harris | 4 Harris | 4 Harris | 4 Harris |
| 5 McConnell E. | 5 Connor | 5 McConnell E. | 5 McConnell E. | 5 McConnell E. |
| 6 Sloan | 6 McConnell E. | 6 Darling | 6 Darling | 6 Darling |
| 7 Hunter | 7 Hunter | 7 Renneville | 7 Renneville | 7 Renneville |
| 8 Lacey | 8 Lacey | 8 Lacey | 8 Lacey | 8 Lacey |
| 9 Greer | 9 Greer | 9 Murray | 9 Murray | 9 Murray |
| 10 Webb | 10 Webb | 10 Murphy | 10 Murphy | 10 Murphy |
| 11 Kirwan | 11 Slemin | 11 Thompson | 11 Thompson | 11 Thompson |
| Glasgow Mar 15: 0-5 | Belfast Mar 20: 2-3 *Lacey, Hunter* | Belfast Feb 12: 1-1 *Thompson* | Belfast Mar 19: 1-0 *Thompson* | Wrexham April 11: 1-4 *Darling* (pen) |

| 1911 Wales | 1911 England | 1911 Scotland | 1912 England | 1912 Scotland |
|---|---|---|---|---|
| 1 Scott W. | 1 Scott W. | 1 Scott W. | 1 Scott W. | 1 Hanna |
| 2 Burnison | 2 Burnison | 2 Burnison | 2 Burnison | 2 Willis |
| 3 Thunder | 3 McCann | 3 McCann | 3 McCann | 3 Craig |
| 4 Harris | 4 Harris | 4 Harris | 4 Harris | 4 Darling |
| 5 Connor | 5 Connor | 5 Connor | 5 O'Connell | 5 O'Connell |
| 6 Hampton | 6 Hampton | 6 Hampton | 6 Hampton | 6 Moran |
| 7 Renneville | 7 Lacey | 7 Lacey | 7 Lacey | 7 Houston |
| 8 Lacey | 8 Hannon | 8 Hannon | 8 Hamill | 8 McKnight |
| 9 Halligan | 9 McDonnell | 9 McDonnell | 9 Halligan | 9 McAuley |
| 10 McAuley | 10 McAuley | 10 Webb | 10 McAuley | 10 Enright |
| 11 Thompson | 11 Thompson | 11 Walker | 11 Thompson | 11 Young |
| Belfast Jan 28: 1-2 *Halligan* | Derby Feb 11: 1-2 *McAuley* | Glasgow Mar 18: 0-2 | Dublin Feb 10: 1-6 *Hamill* | Belfast Mar 16: 1-4 *McKnight* (pen) |

689

| 1912 Wales | 1913 Wales | 1913 England | 1913 Scotland | 1914 Wales |
|---|---|---|---|---|
| 1 Hanna | 1 Scott W. | 1 Scott W. | 1 Scott W. | 1 McKee |
| 2 Craig | 2 Burnison | 2 McConnell W.G. | 2 McConnell W.G. | 2 McConnell W.G. |
| 3 McConnell W.G. | 3 McCann | 3 Warren | 3 Warren | 3 Craig |
| 4 Hampton | 4 Rollo | 4 Hampton | 4 Andrews | 4 Harris |
| 5 Brennan | 5 Donnelly | 5 Harris | 5 Harris | 5 O'Connell |
| 6 Rollo | 6 Hampton | 6 Andrews | 6 Hampton | 6 Rollo |
| 7 Houston | 7 Houston | 7 Houston | 7 Houston | 7 Seymour |
| 8 Hannon | 8 Lacey | 8 Hannon | 8 McKnight | 8 Young |
| 9 McDonnell | 9 McDonnell | 9 Gillespie | 9 Gillespie | 9 Gillespie |
| 10 McCandless J. | 10 McCandless J. | 10 McAuley | 10 McAuley | 10 Lacey |
| 11 Thompson | 11 Thompson | 11 Thompson | 11 Thompson | 11 Bookman |

| Cardiff | Belfast | Belfast | Dublin | Wrexham |
|---|---|---|---|---|
| April 13: 3-2 | Jan 18: 0-1 | Feb 15: 2-1 | Mar 15: 1-2 | Jan 19: 2-1 |
| *McCandless 2, Brennan* | | *Gillespie 2* | *McKnight* | *Young, Gillespie* |

| 1914 England | 1914 Scotland | 1919 England | 1920 Wales | 1920 Scotland |
|---|---|---|---|---|
| 1 McKee | 1 McKee | 1 O'Hagan | 1 O'Hagan | 1 Scott E. |
| 2 McConnell W.G. | 2 McConnell W.G. | 2 McCandless W. | 2 Manderson | 2 Manderson |
| 3 Craig | 3 Craig | 3 McCracken W. | 3 Rollo | 3 Rollo |
| 4 Hampton | 4 Harris | 4 Emerson | 4 McCandless W. | 4 Hamill |
| 5 O'Connell | 5 O'Connell | 5 Hamill | 5 Hamill | 5 Lacey |
| 6 Hamill | 6 Hamill | 6 Lacey | 6 Emerson | 6 Emerson |
| 7 Rollo | 7 Houston | 7 Ferris | 7 Lyner | 7 Robinson |
| 8 Young | 8 Nixon | 8 Snape | 8 Lacey | 8 Gallagher |
| 9 Gillespie | 9 Young | 9 Gowdy | 9 Gillespie | 9 Brookes |
| 10 Lacey | 10 Lacey | 10 Gallagher | 10 Ferris | 10 Gillespie |
| 11 Thompson | 11 Thompson | 11 Lyner | 11 McCandless J. | 11 McCandless J. |

| Middlesbrough | Belfast | Belfast | Belfast | Glasgow |
|---|---|---|---|---|
| Feb 14: 3-0 | Mar 14: 1-1 | Oct 25: 1-1 | Feb 14: 2-2 | Mar 13: 0-3 |
| *Lacey 2, Gillespie* | *Young* | *Ferris* | *McCandless J. Emerson* | |

| 1920 England | 1921 Scotland | 1921 Wales | 1921 England | 1922 Scotland |
|---|---|---|---|---|
| 1 Scott E. | 1 Scott E. | 1 Scott E. | 1 Scott E. | 1 Collins |
| 2 Rollo | 2 Mulligan | 2 Rollo | 2 McCracken W. | 2 McCracken W. |
| 3 McCandless W. | 3 Rollo | 3 McCandless W. | 3 Rollo | 3 McCandless W. |
| 4 McCracken R. | 4 Lacey | 4 Lacey | 4 McCracken R. | 4 McCracken R. |
| 5 Lacey | 5 Smith E.E. | 5 Scraggs | 5 Scraggs | 5 O'Brien |
| 6 Emerson | 6 O'Brien | 6 Harris J. | 6 Emerson | 6 Emerson |
| 7 Kelly | 7 McGregor | 7 Robinson | 7 Lacey | 7 Lacey |
| 8 Ferris | 8 Ferris | 8 Brown J. | 8 Gillespie | 8 Gallagher |
| 9 Doran | 9 McKinney | 9 Chambers | 9 Doran | 9 Irvine |
| 10 Gillespie | 10 Hamill | 10 Mathieson | 10 Mathieson | 10 Gillespie |
| 11 McCandless J. | 11 Bookman | 11 Bookman | 11 Bookman | 11 Lyner |

| Sunderland | Belfast | Swansea | Belfast | Glasgow |
|---|---|---|---|---|
| Oct 23: 0-2 | Feb 26: 0-2 | April 9: 1-2 | Oct 22: 1-1 | Mar 4: 1-2 |
| | | *Chambers* | *Gillespie* | *Gillespie* |

| 1922 Wales | 1922 England | 1923 Scotland | 1923 Wales | 1923 England |
|---|---|---|---|---|
| 1 Mehaffy | 1 Harland | 1 Farquharson | 1 Farquharson | 1 Farquharson |
| 2 McCracken W. | 2 Rollo | 2 McCracken W. | 2 Mackie | 2 McCluggage |
| 3 Curran | 3 Curran | 3 Curran | 3 Kennedy | 3 Curran |
| 4 McCracken R. | 4 Emerson | 4 Irving | 4 Irving | 4 Irving |
| 5 O'Brien | 5 Smith E.E. | 5 Moorhead | 5 Smith E.E. | 5 Smith E.E. |
| 6 Emerson | 6 Morgan | 6 Emerson | 6 Emerson | 6 Emerson |
| 7 Lyner | 7 Lyner | 7 McKenzie | 7 Lyner | 7 Brown J. |
| 8 Crooks | 8 Irvine | 8 Gallagher | 8 Gallagher | 8 Croft |
| 9 Doran | 9 Nelis | 9 Reid | 9 Irvine | 9 Irvine |
| 10 Gillespie | 10 Gillespie | 10 Gillespie | 10 Gillespie | 10 Gillespie |
| 11 Toner | 11 Burns | 11 Moore | 11 Toner | 11 Toner |

| Belfast April 1: 1-1 *Gillespie* | West Bromwich Oct 21: 0-2 | Belfast Mar 3: 0-1 | Wrexham April 14: 3-0 *Irvine 2, Gillespie* | Belfast Oct 20: 2-1 *Gillespie, Croft* |
|---|---|---|---|---|

| 1924 Scotland | 1924 Wales | 1924 England | 1925 Scotland | 1925 Wales |
|---|---|---|---|---|
| 1 Farquharson | 1 Farquharson | 1 Farquharson | 1 Farquharson | 1 Scott E. |
| 2 Rollo | 2 Rollo | 2 Manderson | 2 Manderson | 2 Rollo |
| 3 McCandless W. | 3 McCandless W. | 3 Kennedy | 3 McCandless W. | 3 McConnell W.H. |
| 4 Irving | 4 Gowdy | 4 Chatton | 4 Chatton | 4 Garrett |
| 5 O'Brien | 5 O'Brien | 5 O'Brien | 5 O'Brien | 5 O'Brien |
| 6 Morgan | 6 Irving | 6 Irving | 6 Irving | 6 Irving |
| 7 McKinney | 7 Brown J. | 7 Lacey | 7 Martin | 7 Cowan |
| 8 Gallagher | 8 Gallagher | 8 Gallagher | 8 Gallagher | 8 Gallagher |
| 9 Irvine | 9 McIlvenny | 9 Irvine | 9 Carroll | 9 Sloan |
| 10 Gillespie | 10 Gillespie | 10 Gillespie | 10 Gillespie | 10 Meek |
| 11 McGrillen | 11 Toner | 11 Toner | 11 Toner | 11 Wilson |

| Glasgow Mar 1: 0-2 | Belfast Mar 15: 0-1 | Everton Oct 22: 1-3 *Gillespie* | Belfast Feb 28: 0-3 | Wrexham April 18: 0-0 |
|---|---|---|---|---|

| 1925 England | 1926 Wales | 1926 Scotland | 1926 England | 1927 Scotland |
|---|---|---|---|---|
| 1 Scott E. | 1 Scott E. | 1 Scott E. | 1 Scott E. | 1 Scott E. |
| 2 Rollo | 2 Brown W.G. | 2 Manderson | 2 Rollo | 2 McCluggage |
| 3 McConnell W.H. | 3 McConnell W.H. | 3 Watson | 3 McConnell W.H. | 3 McConnell W.H. |
| 4 Gowdy | 4 Irving | 4 Irving | 4 Gowdy | 4 Gowdy |
| 5 Chatton | 5 O'Brien | 5 Gowdy | 5 Morgan | 5 Sloan |
| 6 Sloan | 6 Sloan | 6 Sloan | 6 Irving | 6 McMullan |
| 7 Bothwell | 7 Bothwell | 7 Bothwell | 7 Bothwell | 7 McGrillen |
| 8 Irvine | 8 Steele | 8 Steele | 8 Irvine | 8 Gallagher |
| 9 Davey | 9 Curran | 9 Curran | 9 Davey | 9 Davey |
| 10 Hopkins | 10 Gillespie | 10 Gillespie | 10 Gillespie | 10 Irving |
| 11 McMullan | 11 McMullan | 11 Mahood | 11 Toner | 11 Toner |

| Belfast Oct 24: 0-0 | Belfast Feb 13: 3-0 *Gillespie, Curran 2* | Glasgow Feb 27: 0-4 | Liverpool Oct 20: 3-3 *Gillespie, Davey, Irvine* | Belfast Feb 26: 0-2 |
|---|---|---|---|---|

| 1927 Wales | 1927 England | 1928 Wales | 1928 Scotland | 1928 England |
|---|---|---|---|---|
| 1 Scott E. | 1 Scott E. | 1 Scott E. | 1 Scott E. | 1 Scott E. |
| 2 McCluggage | 2 McCluggage | 2 McCluggage | 2 McCluggage | 2 McCluggage |
| 3 McConnell W.H. | 3 McConnell W.H. | 3 McConnell W.H. | 3 Hamilton | 3 Hamilton |
| 4 Irving | 4 Irving | 4 Irving | 4 Irving | 4 Irving |
| 5 Sloan | 5 Morgan | 5 Morgan | 5 Moorhead | 5 Sloan |
| 6 O'Brien | 6 Sloan | 6 Sloan | 6 Morgan | 6 Morgan |
| 7 Bothwell | 7 Chambers | 7 Chambers | 7 Chambers | 7 Chambers |
| 8 Irvine | 8 Irvine | 8 Dunne | 8 Irvine | 8 Irvine |
| 9 Johnston | 9 Davey | 9 Davey | 9 Curran | 9 Bambrick |
| 10 Gillespie | 10 Gillespie | 10 McConnell P. | 10 Ferris | 10 Gillespie |
| 11 McCaw | 11 Mahood | 11 Mahood | 11 Mahood | 11 Mahood |

| Cardiff | Belfast | Belfast | Glasgow | Everton |
|---|---|---|---|---|
| April 9: 2-2 | Oct 22: 2-0 | Feb 4: 1-2 | Feb 25: 1-0 | Oct 22: 1-2 |
| *Johnston 2* | *Jones og, Mahood* | *Chambers* | *Chambers* | *Bambrick* |

| 1929 Wales | 1929 Scotland | 1929 England | 1930 Wales | 1930 Scotland |
|---|---|---|---|---|
| 1 Scott E. | 1 Scott E. | 1 Scott E. | 1 Gardiner | 1 Gardiner |
| 2 McCluggage | 2 McCluggage | 2 Russell | 2 McCluggage | 2 Russell |
| 3 McCandless W. | 3 Flack | 3 Hamilton | 3 Fulton | 3 Hamilton |
| 4 Miller | 4 Miller | 4 Miller | 4 McCleery | 4 McDonald |
| 5 Elwood | 5 Moorhead | 5 Elwood | 5 Cpl J. Jones | 5 Cpl J. Jones |
| 6 Steele | 6 Steele | 6 McCleery | 6 Sloan | 6 Sloan |
| 7 Chambers | 7 Chambers | 7 Duggan | 7 Chambers | 7 Chambers |
| 8 Rowley | 8 Rowley | 8 Rowley | 8 Rowley | 8 Irvine |
| 9 Bambrick | 9 Bambrick | 9 Bambrick | 9 Bambrick | 9 Bambrick |
| 10 Cumming | 10 Cumming | 10 Cumming | 10 McCambridge | 10 McCambridge |
| 11 Mahood | 11 Mahood | 11 Kavanagh | 11 Mahood | 11 McCaw |

| Wrexham | Belfast | Belfast | Belfast | Glasgow |
|---|---|---|---|---|
| Feb 2: 2-2 | Feb 23: 3-7 | Oct 19: 0-3 | Feb 1: 7-0 | Feb 22: 1-3 |
| *Mahood, McCluggage (pen)* | *Bambrick 2, Rowley* | | *Bambrick 6, McCluggage* | *McCaw* |

| 1930 England | 1931 Scotland | 1931 Wales | 1931 Scotland | 1931 England |
|---|---|---|---|---|
| 1 Scott E. | 1 Gardiner | 1 Diffin | 1 Gardiner | 1 Gardiner |
| 2 McCluggage | 2 McNinch | 2 McCluggage | 2 McNinch | 2 Russell |
| 3 Fulton | 3 Fulton | 3 Fulton | 3 Hamilton R. | 3 Fulton |
| 4 Jones J. | 4 McCleery | 4 Irving | 4 McCleery | 4 McDonald |
| 5 Reid | 5 Jones J. | 5 Jones J. | 5 Jones J. | 5 Jones J. |
| 6 McCleery | 6 Sloan | 6 McCleery | 6 Gowdy | 6 Mitchell |
| 7 Duggan | 7 Blair | 7 Duggan | 7 Blair | 7 Chambers |
| 8 Irvine | 8 Falloon | 8 Rowley | 8 Rowley | 8 McConnell P. |
| 9 Dunne | 9 Roberts | 9 Dunne | 9 Dunne | 9 Dunne |
| 10 Gillespie | 10 Geary | 10 McCambridge | 10 Geary | 10 McCambridge |
| 11 McCaw | 11 McCaw | 11 McCaw | 11 Chambers | 11 Kelly |

| Sheffield | Belfast | Wrexham | Glasgow | Belfast |
|---|---|---|---|---|
| Oct 20: 1-5 | Feb 21: 0-0 | April 22: 2-3 | Sept 19: 1-3 | Oct 17: 2-6 |
| *Dunne* | | *Dunne, Rowley* | *Dunne* | *Dunne, Kelly* |

| 1931 Wales | 1932 Scotland | 1932 England | 1932 Wales | 1933 Scotland |
|---|---|---|---|---|
| 1 Scott E. | 1 Scott E. | 1 Scott E. | 1 Scott E. | 1 Scott E. |
| 2 McNinch | 2 Cook | 2 Cook | 2 Cook | 2 Willingham |
| 3 Fulton | 3 Fulton | 3 Fulton | 3 Willingham | 3 Fulton |
| 4 McCleery | 4 Falloon | 4 Mitchell W. | 4 Mitchell W. | 4 McMahon |
| 5 Pyper | 5 Jones J. | 5 Jones J. | 5 Jones J. | 5 Jones J. |
| 6 Mitchell W. | 6 Gowdy | 6 McCleery | 6 McCleery | 6 Mitchell W. |
| 7 Chambers | 7 Mitchell E. | 7 Duggan | 7 Houston | 7 Blair |
| 8 Irvine | 8 Priestley | 8 Moore | 8 English | 8 Stevenson |
| 9 Bambrick | 9 Millar | 9 Dunne | 9 Dunne | 9 Martin |
| 10 Millar | 10 English | 10 Doherty J. | 10 Doherty J. | 10 Coulter |
| 11 Kelly | 11 Kelly | 11 Kelly | 11 Kelly | 11 Mahood |

| Belfast | Belfast | Blackpool | Wrexham | Glasgow |
|---|---|---|---|---|
| Dec 5: 4-0 | Sept 12: 0-4 | Oct 17: 0-1 | Dec 7: 1-4 | Sept 16: 2-1 |
| *Kelly 2, Millar, Bambrick* | | | *English* | *Martin 2* |

| 1933 England | 1933 Wales | 1934 Scotland | 1935 England | 1935 Wales |
|---|---|---|---|---|
| 1 Scott E. | 1 Scott E. | 1 Scott E. | 1 Breen | 1 Breen |
| 2 Reid | 2 Reid | 2 Mackie | 2 Cook | 2 Mackie |
| 3 Fulton | 3 Fulton | 3 Fulton | 3 Fulton | 3 Fulton |
| 4 McMillen | 4 Mitchell W. | 4 McMillen | 4 Gowdy | 4 McCullough |
| 5 Jones J. | 5 Jones J. | 5 Jones J. | 5 Jones J. | 5 Jones J. |
| 6 Jones S. | 6 Jones S. | 6 Mitchell W. | 6 Mitchell W. | 6 Gowdy |
| 7 Duggan | 7 Mitchell C. | 7 Duggan | 7 Brown J. | 7 Duggan |
| 8 Stevenson | 8 Stevenson | 8 Gowdy | 8 Doherty P. | 8 Brown J. |
| 9 Martin | 9 Martin | 9 Martin | 9 Martin | 9 Bambrick |
| 10 Coulter | 10 Coulter | 10 Stevenson | 10 Stevenson | 10 Doherty P. |
| 11 Priestley | 11 Kelly | 11 Coulter | 11 Coulter | 11 Coulter |

| Belfast | Belfast | Belfast | Everton | Wrexham |
|---|---|---|---|---|
| Oct 14: 0-3 | Nov 4: 1-1 | Oct 20: 2-1 | Feb 6: 1-2 | Mar 27: 1-3 |
| | *Jones S.* | *Martin, Coulter* | *Stevenson* | *Bambrick* |

| 1935 England | 1935 Scotland | 1936 Wales | 1936 Scotland | 1936 England |
|---|---|---|---|---|
| 1 Scott E. | 1 Scott E. | 1 Scott E. | 1 Breen | 1 Breen |
| 2 Reid | 2 Cook | 2 Cook | 2 Cook | 2 Cook |
| 3 Allen | 3 Fulton | 3 Fulton | 3 Fulton | 3 Fulton |
| 4 Mitchell W. | 4 McCullough | 4 Gowdy | 4 McMillen | 4 McCullough |
| 5 Jones J. | 5 Jones J. | 5 Jones J. | 5 Jones J. | 5 Jones J. |
| 6 Browne R. | 6 Mitchell W. | 6 Browne R. | 6 Mitchell W. | 6 Mitchell W. |
| 7 Brown J. | 7 Duggan | 7 Kernaghan | 7 Kernaghan | 7 Brown J. |
| 8 McCullough | 8 Stevenson | 8 Gibb | 8 McCullough | 8 Stevenson |
| 9 Bambrick | 9 Bambrick | 9 Martin | 9 Martin | 9 Davis |
| 10 Doherty P. | 10 Doherty P. | 10 Stevenson | 10 Coulter | 10 Doherty P. |
| 11 Kelly | 11 Kelly | 11 Kelly | 11 Kelly | 11 Kelly |

| Belfast | Edinburgh | Belfast | Belfast | Stoke |
|---|---|---|---|---|
| Oct 19: 1-3 | Nov 13: 1-2 | Mar 11: 3-2 | Oct 31: 1-3 | Nov 18: 1-3 |
| *Brown* | *Kelly* | *Gibb, Stevenson, Kernaghan* | *Kernaghan* | *Davis* |

| 1937 Wales | 1937 England | 1937 Scotland | 1938 Wales | 1938 Scotland |
|---|---|---|---|---|
| 1 Breen | 1 Breen | 1 Breen | 1 Twoomey | 1 Breen |
| 2 Cook | 2 Hayes | 2 Hayes | 2 Cook | 2 Hayes |
| 3 Fulton | 3 Cook | 3 Cook | 3 Fulton | 3 Cook |
| 4 Brolly | 4 Mitchell W. | 4 Doherty M. | 4 Brolly | 4 McMillen |
| 5 Jones J. | 5 Jones J. | 5 McMillen | 5 McMillen | 5 O'Mahoney |
| 6 Mitchell W. | 6 Browne R. | 6 Mitchell W. | 6 Browne R. | 6 Browne R. |
| 7 Brown J. | 7 Kernaghan | 7 Brown J. | 7 Brown J. | 7 Brown J. |
| 8 Doherty P. | 8 Stevenson | 8 McAlinden | 8 Farrell | 8 McAlinden |
| 9 Banks | 9 Martin | 9 Martin | 9 Bambrick | 9 Martin |
| 10 Stevenson | 10 Doherty P. | 10 Doherty P. | 10 Stevenson | 10 Stevenson |
| 11 Coulter | 11 Madden | 11 Coulter | 11 Coulter | 11 Coulter |

| Wrexham Mar 17: 1-4 *Stevenson* | Belfast Oct 23: 1-5 *Stevenson* | Aberdeen Nov 10: 1-1 *Doherty P.* | Belfast Mar 16: 1-0 *Bambrick* | Belfast Oct 8: 0-2 |
|---|---|---|---|---|

| 1938 England | 1939 Wales | 1946 England | 1946 Scotland | 1947 Wales |
|---|---|---|---|---|
| 1 Twoomey | 1 Breen | 1 Russell | 1 Hinton | 1 Hinton |
| 2 Hayes | 2 Cook | 2 Gorman | 2 Gorman | 2 Gorman |
| 3 Cook | 3 Butler | 3 Ahearne | 3 Feeney | 3 Carey |
| 4 Brolly | 4 Brolly | 4 Carey | 4 Martin | 4 Sloan |
| 5 McMillen | 5 Leatham | 5 Vernon | 5 Vernon | 5 Vernon |
| 6 Browne R. | 6 Weir | 6 Douglas | 6 Farrell | 6 Farrell |
| 7 Cochrane | 7 Cochrane | 7 Cochrane | 7 Cochrane | 7 Cochrane |
| 8 Stevenson | 8 Stevenson | 8 McAlinden | 8 Carey | 8 Stevenson |
| 9 Baird | 9 Milligan | 9 McMorran | 9 Walsh D. | 9 Walsh D. |
| 10 Doherty P. | 10 Doherty P. | 10 Doherty P. | 10 Stevenson | 10 Doherty P. |
| 11 Brown J. | 11 Brown J. | 11 Lockhart | 11 Eglington | 11 Eglington |

| Manchester Nov 16: 0-7 | Wrexham Mar 15: 1-3 *Milligan* | Belfast Sept 28: 2-7 *Lockhart 2* | Hampden Nov 27: 0-0 | Belfast April 16: 2-1 *Stevenson, Doherty* |
|---|---|---|---|---|

| 1947 Scotland | 1947 England | 1948 Wales | 1948 England | 1948 Scotland |
|---|---|---|---|---|
| 1 Hinton | 1 Hinton | 1 Hinton | 1 Smyth W. | 1 Smyth W. |
| 2 Martin | 2 Martin | 2 Martin | 2 Carey | 2 Carey |
| 3 Aherne | 3 Carey | 3 Gorman | 3 Martin | 3 Keane |
| 4 Walsh W. | 4 Walsh W. | 4 Walsh W. | 4 Walsh W. | 4 McCabe |
| 5 Vernon | 5 Vernon | 5 Vernon | 5 Vernon | 5 Vernon |
| 6 Farrell | 6 Farrell | 6 Farrell | 6 Farrell | 6 Walsh W. |
| 7 Cochrane | 7 Cochrane | 7 Cochrane | 7 O'Driscoll | 7 Cochrane |
| 8 Smyth S. | 8 Smyth S. | 8 Smyth S. | 8 McAlinden | 8 Smyth S. |
| 9 Walsh D. | 9 Walsh D. | 9 Walsh D. | 9 Walsh D. | 9 Walsh D. |
| 10 Stevenson | 10 Doherty P. | 10 Doherty P. | 10 Tully | 10 Doherty P. |
| 11 Eglington | 11 Eglington | 11 Eglington | 11 Eglington | 11 O'Driscoll |

| Belfast Oct 4: 2-0 *Smyth 2* | Everton Nov 5: 2-2 *Doherty, Walsh D.* | Wrexham Mar 10: 0-2 | Belfast Oct 9: 2-6 *Walsh D. 2* | Hampden Nov 17: 2-3 *Walsh D. 2* |
|---|---|---|---|---|

| 1949 Wales | 1949 Scotland | 1949 England | 1950 Wales | 1950 England |
|---|---|---|---|---|
| 1 Moore | 1 Kelly P.M | 1 Kelly H. | 1 Kelly H. | 1 Kelly H. |
| 2 Carey | 2 Bowler | 2 Feeney | 2 Bowler | 2 Gallogly |
| 3 Aherne | 3 McMichael | 3 McMichael | 3 Aherne | 3 McMichael |
| 4 McCabe | 4 Blanchflower D. | 4 Bowler | 4 Blanchflower D. | 4 Blanchflower D. |
| 5 Vernon | 5 Vernon | 5 Vernon | 5 Martin | 5 Vernon |
| 6 Farrell | 6 Ferris | 6 McCabe | 6 Ryan | 6 Cush |
| 7 Cochrane | 7 Cochrane | 7 Cochrane | 7 McKenna | 7 Campbell |
| 8 Smyth S. | 8 Smyth S. | 8 Smyth S. | 8 Smyth S. | 8 Crossan |
| 9 Walsh D. | 9 Brennan | 9 Brennan | 9 Walsh D. | 9 McMorran |
| 10 Brennan | 10 Crossan | 10 Tully | 10 Brennan | 10 Brennan |
| 11 O'Driscoll | 11 McKenna | 11 McKenna | 11 Lockhart | 11 McKenna |
| Belfast | Belfast | Maine Road | Wrexham | Belfast |
| Mar 9: 0-2 | Oct 1: 2-8 | Nov 6: 2-9 | Mar 8: 0-0 | Oct 7: 1-4 |
| | *Smyth 2* | *Smyth, Brennan* | | *McMorran* |

| 1950 Scotland | 1951 Wales | 1951 France | 1951 Scotland | 1951 England |
|---|---|---|---|---|
| 1 Kelly H. | 1 Hinton | 1 Hinton | 1 Uprichard | 1 Uprichard |
| 2 Gallogly | 2 Graham | 2 Graham | 2 Graham | 2 Graham |
| 3 McMichael | 3 Cunningham | 3 McMichael | 3 McMichael | 3 McMichael |
| 4 Blanchflower D. | 4 McCabe | 4 Blanchflower D. | 4 Dickson | 4 Dickson |
| 5 Vernon | 5 Vernon | 5 Vernon | 5 Vernon | 5 Vernon |
| 6 Cush | 6 Dickson | 6 Ferris | 6 Ferris | 6 McCourt |
| 7 Campbell | 7 Hughes | 7 Bingham | 7 Bingham | 7 Bingham |
| 8 McGarry | 8 McMorran | 8 McGarry | 8 McIlroy | 8 Smyth S. |
| 9 McMorran | 9 Simpson | 9 Simpson | 9 McMorran | 9 McMorran |
| 10 Doherty P. | 10 McGarry | 10 Dickson | 10 Peacock | 10 McIlroy |
| 11 McKenna | 11 Lockhart | 11 McKenna | 11 Tully | 11 McKenna |
| Hampden | Belfast | Belfast | Belfast | Villa Park |
| Nov 1: 1-6 | Mar 7: 1-2 | May 12: 2-2 | Oct 6: 0-3 | Nov 20: 0-2 |
| *McGarry* | *Simpson* | *Ferris, Simpson* | | |

| 1952 Wales | 1952 England | 1952 Scotland | 1952 France | 1953 Wales |
|---|---|---|---|---|
| 1 Uprichard | 1 Uprichard | 1 Uprichard | 1 Uprichard | 1 Uprichard |
| 2 Graham | 2 Cunningham | 2 Graham | 2 Graham | 2 McCabe |
| 3 McMichael | 3 McMichael | 3 McMichael | 3 McMichael | 3 McMichael |
| 4 Blanchflower D. | 4 Blanchflower D. | 4 Blanchflower D. | 4 Blanchflower D. | 4 Blanchflower D. |
| 5 Dickson | 5 Dickson | 5 Dickson | 5 Dickson | 5 Dickson |
| 6 McCourt | 6 McCourt | 6 McCourt | 6 McCourt | 6 McCourt |
| 7 Bingham | 7 Bingham | 7 Bingham | 7 Bingham | 7 Bingham |
| 8 D'Arcy | 8 D'Arcy | 8 D'Arcy | 8 D'Arcy | 8 McIlroy |
| 9 McMorran | 9 McMorran | 9 McMorran | 9 McMorran | 9 McMorran |
| 10 McIlroy | 10 McIlroy | 10 McIlroy | 10 Peacock | 10 D'Arcy |
| 11 Lockhart | 11 Tully | 11 Tully | 11 Tully | 11 Tully |
| Swansea | Belfast | Hampden | Paris | Belfast |
| Mar 19: 0-3 | Oct 4: 2-2 | Nov 5: 1-1 | Nov 11: 1-3 | April 15: 2-3 |
| | *Tully 2* | *D'Arcy* | *Tully* | *McMorran 2* |

| 1953 Scotland | 1953 England | 1954 Wales | 1954 England | 1954 Scotland |
|---|---|---|---|---|
| 1 Smyth W. | 1 Smyth W. | 1 Gregg | 1 Uprichard | 1 Uprichard |
| 2 Cunningham | 2 Graham | 2 Graham | 2 Montgomery | 2 Graham |
| 3 McMichael | 3 McMichael | 3 McMichael | 3 McMichael | 3 Cunningham |
| 4 Blanchflower D. | 4 Blanchflower D. | 4 Blanchflower D. | 4 Blanchflower D. | 4 Blanchflower D. |
| 5 McCabe | 5 Dickson | 5 Dickson | 5 Dickson | 5 McCavana |
| 6 Cush | 6 Cush | 6 Peacock | 6 Peacock | 6 Peacock |
| 7 Bingham | 7 Bingham | 7 Bingham | 7 Bingham | 7 Bingham |
| 8 McIlroy | 8 McIlroy | 8 Blanchflower J. | 8 Blanchflower J. | 8 Blanchflower J. |
| 9 Simpson | 9 Simpson | 9 McAdams | 9 Simpson | 9 McAdams |
| 10 Tully | 10 McMorran | 10 McIlroy | 10 McIlroy | 10 McIlroy |
| 11 Lockhart | 11 Lockhart | 11 McParland | 11 McParland | 11 McParland |
| Belfast Oct 3: 1-3 *Lockhart* | Everton Nov 11: 1-3 *McMorran* | Wrexham Mar 31: 2-1 *McParland 2* | Belfast Oct 2: 0-2 | Hampden Nov 3: 2-2 *Bingham, McAdams* |

| 1955 Wales | 1955 Scotland | 1955 England | 1956 Wales | 1956 England |
|---|---|---|---|---|
| 1 Uprichard | 1 Uprichard | 1 Uprichard | 1 Uprichard | 1 Gregg |
| 2 Graham | 2 Graham | 2 Cunningham | 2 Cunningham | 2 Cunningham |
| 3 McMichael | 3 Cunningham | 3 Graham | 3 McMichael | 3 McMichael |
| 4 Blanchflower D. | 4 Blanchflower D. | 4 Blanchflower D. | 4 Blanchflower D. | 4 Blanchflower D. |
| 5 McCleary | 5 McCavana | 5 McCavana | 5 Blanchflower J. | 5 Blanchflower J. |
| 6 Casey | 6 Peacock | 6 Peacock | 6 Casey | 6 Casey |
| 7 Bingham | 7 Bingham | 7 Bingham | 7 Bingham | 7 Bingham |
| 8 Crossan | 8 Blanchflower J. | 8 McIlroy | 8 McIlroy | 8 McIlroy |
| 9 Walker | 9 Coyle | 9 Coyle | 9 Jones J. | 9 Jones J. |
| 10 McIlroy | 10 McIlroy | 10 Tully | 10 McMorran | 10 McAdams |
| 11 Lockhart | 11 McParland | 11 McParland | 11 Lockhart | 11 McParland |
| Belfast April 20: 2-3 *Crossan, Walker* | Belfast Oct 8: 2-1 *Blanchflower J., Bingham* | Wembley Nov 2: 0-3 | Cardiff April 11: 1-1 *Jones* | Belfast Oct 6: 1-1 *McIlroy* |

| 1956 Scotland | 1957 Portugal | 1957 Wales | 1957 Italy | 1957 Portugal |
|---|---|---|---|---|
| 1 Gregg | 1 Gregg | 1 Gregg | 1 Gregg | 1 Gregg |
| 2 Cunningham | 2 Cunningham | 2 Cunningham | 2 Cunningham | 2 Cunningham |
| 3 McMichael | 3 McMichael | 3 McMichael | 3 McMichael | 3 McMichael |
| 4 Blanchflower D. | 4 Blanchflower D. | 4 Blanchflower D. | 4 Blanchflower D. | 4 Blanchflower D. |
| 5 Blanchflower J. | 5 Blanchflower J. | 5 Cush | 5 Cush | 5 Cush |
| 6 Casey | 6 Casey | 6 Peacock | 6 Casey | 6 Casey |
| 7 Bingham | 7 Bingham | 7 Bingham | 7 Bingham | 7 Bingham |
| 8 McIlroy | 8 McIlroy | 8 McIlroy | 8 Simpson | 8 Simpson |
| 9 Shields | 9 Coyle | 9 Jones | 9 McMorran | 9 McMorran |
| 10 Dickson | 10 Cush | 10 Casey | 10 McIlroy | 10 McIlroy |
| 11 McParland | 11 McParland | 11 McParland | 11 Peacock | 11 Peacock |
| Hampden Nov 7: 0-1 | Lisbon Jan 16: 1-1 *Bingham* | Belfast April 10: 0-0 | Rome April 25: 0-1 | Belfast May 1: 3-0 *Simpson, McIlroy, Casey* |

| 1957 Scotland | 1957 England | 1957 Italy | 1958 Italy | 1958 Wales |
|---|---|---|---|---|
| 1 Uprichard | 1 Gregg | 1 Gregg | 1 Uprichard | 1 Gregg |
| 2 Cunningham | 2 Keith | 2 Keith | 2 Cunningham | 2 Cunningham |
| 3 McMichael | 3 McMichael | 3 McMichael | 3 McMichael | 3 McMichael |
| 4 Blanchflower D. | 4 Blanchflower D. | 4 Blanchflower D. | 4 Blanchflower D. | 4 Blanchflower D. |
| 5 Blanchflower J. | 5 Blanchflower J. | 5 Blanchflower J. | 5 Blanchflower J. | 5 Keith |
| 6 Peacock | 6 Peacock | 6 Peacock | 6 Peacock | 6 Peacock |
| 7 Bingham | 7 Bingham | 7 Bingham | 7 Bingham | 7 Bingham |
| 8 Simpson | 8 McCrory | 8 McIlroy | 8 Cush | 8 Cush |
| 9 McAdams | 9 Simpson | 9 McAdams | 9 Simpson | 9 Simpson |
| 10 McIlroy | 10 McIlroy | 10 Cush | 10 McIlroy | 10 McIlroy |
| 11 McParland | 11 McParland | 11 McParland | 11 McParland | 11 McParland |

| | | | | |
|---|---|---|---|---|
| Belfast | Wembley | Belfast | Belfast | Cardiff |
| Oct 5: 1-1 | Nov 6: 3-2 | Dec 4: 2-2 | Jan 15: 2-1 | April 16: 1-1 |
| *Bingham* | *McIlroy, McCrory, Simpson* | *Cush 2* | *McIlroy, Cush* | *Simpson* |

| 1958 Czechoslovakia † | 1958 Argentina † | 1958 W Germany † | 1958 Czechoslovakia † | 1958 France † |
|---|---|---|---|---|
| 1 Gregg | 1 Gregg | 1 Gregg | 1 Uprichard | 1 Gregg |
| 2 Keith | 2 Keith | 2 Keith | 2 Keith | 2 Keith |
| 3 McMichael | 3 McMichael | 3 McMichael | 3 McMichael | 3 McMichael |
| 4 Blanchflower D. | 4 Blanchflower D. | 4 Blanchflower D. | 4 Blanchflower D. | 4 Blanchflower D. |
| 5 Cunningham | 5 Cunningham | 5 Cunningham | 5 Cunningham | 5 Cunningham |
| 6 Peacock | 6 Peacock | 6 Peacock | 6 Peacock | 6 Cush |
| 7 Bingham | 7 Bingham | 7 Bingham | 7 Bingham | 7 Bingham |
| 8 Cush | 8 Cush | 8 Cush | 8 Cush | 8 Casey |
| 9 Dougan | 9 Coyle | 9 Casey | 9 Scott | 9 Scott |
| 10 McIlroy | 10 McIlroy | 10 McIlroy | 10 McIlroy | 10 McIlroy |
| 11 McParland | 11 McParland | 11 McParland | 11 McParland | 11 McParland |

| | | | | |
|---|---|---|---|---|
| Halmstad | Halmstad | Malmo | Malmo | Norrkoping |
| June 8: 1-0 | June 11: 1-3 | June 15: 2-2 | June 17: 2-1 | June 19: 0-4 |
| *Cush* | *McParland* | *McParland 2* | *McParland 2* | |

| 1958 England | 1958 Spain | 1958 Scotland | 1959 Wales | 1959 Scotland |
|---|---|---|---|---|
| 1 Gregg | 1 Uprichard | 1 Uprichard | 1 Gregg | 1 Gregg |
| 2 Keith | 2 Keith | 2 Keith | 2 Keith | 2 Keith |
| 3 Graham | 3 McMichael | 3 McMichael | 3 McMichael | 3 McMichael |
| 4 Blanchflower D. | 4 Blanchflower D. | 4 Blanchflower D. | 4 Blanchflower D. | 4 Blanchflower D. |
| 5 Cunningham | 5 Forde | 5 Cunningham | 5 Cunningham | 5 Cunningham |
| 6 Peacock | 6 Casey | 6 Peacock | 6 Peacock | 6 Peacock |
| 7 Bingham | 7 Bingham | 7 Bingham | 7 Bingham | 7 Bingham |
| 8 Cush | 8 Cush | 8 Cush | 8 McIlroy | 8 Cush |
| 9 Casey | 9 McParland | 9 Simpson | 9 Cush | 9 Dougan |
| 10 McIlroy | 10 McIlroy | 10 McIlroy | 10 Hill | 10 McIlroy |
| 11 McParland | 11 Tully | 11 McParland | 11 McParland | 11 McParland |

| | | | | |
|---|---|---|---|---|
| Belfast | Madrid | Hampden | Belfast | Belfast |
| Oct 4: 3-3 | Oct 15: 2-6 | Nov 5: 2-2 | April 22: 4-1 | Oct 3: 0-4 |
| *Cush, Peacock, Casey* | *Bingham, McIlroy* | *1 og, McIlroy* | *McParland 2, Peacock, McIlroy* | |

## 1959 England | 1960 Wales | 1960 England | 1960 W Germany | 1960 Scotland

| 1959 England | 1960 Wales | 1960 England | 1960 W Germany | 1960 Scotland |
|---|---|---|---|---|
| 1 Gregg | 1 Gregg | 1 Gregg | 1 McClelland | 1 Gregg |
| 2 Keith | 2 Elder | 2 Keith | 2 Keith | 2 Keith |
| 3 McMichael | 3 McMichael | 3 Elder | 3 Elder | 3 Elder |
| 4 Blanchflower D. | 4 Blanchflower D. | 4 Blanchflower D. | 4 Blanchflower D. | 4 Blanchflower D. |
| 5 Cunningham | 5 Cunningham | 5 Forde | 5 Forde | 5 Forde |
| 6 Peacock | 6 Cush | 6 Peacock | 6 Peacock | 6 Peacock |
| 7 Bingham | 7 Bingham | 7 Bingham | 7 Bingham | 7 Bingham |
| 8 Crossan | 8 McIlroy | 8 McIlroy | 8 McIlroy | 8 Bruce |
| 9 Cush | 9 Lawther | 9 McAdams | 9 McAdams | 9 McAdams |
| 10 McIlroy | 10 Hill | 10 Dougan | 10 Hill | 10 Nicholson |
| 11 McParland | 11 McParland | 11 McParland | 11 McParland | 11 McParland |
| Wembley | Wrexham | Belfast | Belfast | Hampden |
| Nov 18: 1-2 | April 6: 2-3 | Oct 8: 2-5 | Oct 26: 3-4 | Nov 9: 2-5 |
| *Bingham* | *Bingham, Blanchflower* | *McAdams 2* | *McAdams 3* | *Blanchflower, McParland* |

| 1961 Wales | 1961 Italy | 1961 Greece | 1961 W Germany | 1961 Scotland |
|---|---|---|---|---|
| 1 McClelland | 1 McClelland | 1 McClelland | 1 McClelland | 1 Gregg |
| 2 Keith | 2 Keith | 2 Keith | 2 Keith | 2 Magill |
| 3 Elder | 3 McCullough | 3 Elder | 3 Elder | 3 Elder |
| 4 Blanchflower D. | 4 Harvey | 4 Cush | 4 Blanchflower D. | 4 Blanchflower D. |
| 5 Cunningham | 5 Neill | 5 Neill | 5 Neill | 5 Neill |
| 6 Nicholson | 6 Peacock | 6 Peacock | 6 Peacock | 6 Peacock |
| 7 Stewart | 7 Bingham | 7 Bingham | 7 Bingham | 7 Wilson |
| 8 Dougan | 8 Dougan | 8 McIlroy | 8 Cush | 8 McIlroy |
| 9 McAdams | 9 Lawther | 9 McAdams | 9 McAdams | 9 Lawther |
| 10 McIlroy | 10 McAdams | 10 Dougan | 10 McIlroy | 10 Hill |
| 11 McParland | 11 McParland | 11 McParland | 11 McParland | 11 McLaughlin |
| Belfast | Bologna | Athens | Berlin | Belfast |
| April 12: 1-5 | April 25: 2-3 | May 3: 1-2 | May 10: 1-2 | Oct 7: 1-6 |
| *Dougan* | *Dougan, McAdams* | *McIlroy* | *McIlroy* | *McLaughlin* |

| 1961 Greece | 1961 England | 1962 Wales | 1962 Netherlands | 1962 Poland |
|---|---|---|---|---|
| 1 Gregg | 1 Hunter | 1 Briggs | 1 Irvine R. | 1 Irvine R. |
| 2 Magill | 2 Magill | 2 Keith | 2 Keith | 2 Magill |
| 3 Elder | 3 Elder | 3 Cunningham | 3 Cunningham | 3 Elder |
| 4 Blanchflower D. | 4 Blanchflower D. | 4 Blanchflower D. | 4 Harvey | 4 Blanchflower D. |
| 5 Neill | 5 Neill | 5 Neill | 5 Blanchflower D. | 5 Hatton |
| 6 Nicholson | 6 Nicholson | 6 Nicholson | 6 Nicholson | 6 Nicholson |
| 7 Bingham | 7 Bingham | 7 Humphries | 7 Humphries | 7 Humphries |
| 8 McIlroy | 8 Barr | 8 Johnston W. | 8 Lawther | 8 Barr |
| 9 McAdams | 9 McAdams | 9 O'Neill | 9 McAdams | 9 Dougan |
| 10 Cush | 10 McIlroy | 10 McLaughlin | 10 McIlroy | 10 McIlroy |
| 11 McLaughlin | 11 McLaughlin | 11 Braithwaite | 11 McParland | 11 Bingham |
| Belfast | Wembley | Cardiff | Rotterdam | Katowice |
| Oct 17: 2-0 | Nov 22: 1-1 | April 11: 0-4 | May 9: 0-4 | Oct 10: 2-0 |
| *McLaughlin 2* | *McIlroy* | | | *Dougan, Humphries* |

| 1962 England | 1962 Scotland | 1962 Poland | 1963 Wales | 1963 Spain |
|---|---|---|---|---|
| 1 Irvine R. | 1 Irvine R. | 1 Irvine R. | 1 Irvine R. | 1 Irvine R. |
| 2 Magill | 2 Magill | 2 Magill | 2 Magill | 2 Magill |
| 3 Elder | 3 Elder | 3 Elder | 3 Elder | 3 Elder |
| 4 Blanchflower D. | 4 Blanchflower D. | 4 Blanchflower D. | 4 Harvey | 4 Harvey |
| 5 Neill | 5 Hatton | 5 Neill | 5 Campbell | 5 Neill |
| 6 Nicholson | 6 Nicholson | 6 Nicholson | 6 Neill | 6 McCullough |
| 7 Humphries | 7 Humphries | 7 Bingham | 7 Humphries | 7 Bingham |
| 8 Barr | 8 McMillan | 8 Crossan | 8 Crossan | 8 Humphries |
| 9 McMillan | 9 Dougan | 9 Dougan | 9 Irvine W. | 9 Irvine W. |
| 10 McIlroy | 10 McIlroy | 10 McIlroy | 10 McIlroy | 10 Crossan |
| 11 Bingham | 11 Bingham | 11 Braithwaite | 11 McLaughlin | 11 Braithwaite |

| | | | | |
|---|---|---|---|---|
| Belfast | Hampden | Belfast | Belfast | Bilbao |
| Oct 20: 1-3 | Nov 7: 1-5 | Nov 28: 2-0 | April 3: 1-4 | May 30: 1-1 |
| *Barr* | *Bingham* | *Crossan, Bingham* | *Harvey* | *Irvine W.* |

| 1963 Scotland | 1963 Spain | 1963 England | 1964 Wales | 1964 Uruguay |
|---|---|---|---|---|
| 1 Gregg | 1 Hunter | 1 Gregg | 1 Jennings | 1 Jennings |
| 2 Magill | 2 Magill | 2 Magill | 2 Magill | 2 Magill |
| 3 Parke | 3 Parke | 3 Parke | 3 Elder | 3 Elder |
| 4 Harvey | 4 Harvey | 4 Harvey | 4 Harvey | 4 Harvey |
| 5 Neill | 5 Neill | 5 Neill | 5 Neill | 5 Neill |
| 6 McCullough | 6 McCullough | 6 McCullough | 6 McCullough | 6 McCullough |
| 7 Bingham | 7 Bingham | 7 Bingham | 7 Best | 7 Best |
| 8 Humphries | 8 Humphries | 8 Humphries | 8 Crossan | 8 Crossan |
| 9 Wilson | 9 Wilson | 9 Wilson | 9 Wilson | 9 Wilson |
| 10 Crossan | 10 Crossan | 10 Crossan | 10 McLaughlin | 10 McLaughlin |
| 11 Hill | 11 Hill | 11 Hill | 11 Braithwaite | 11 Braithwaite |

| | | | | |
|---|---|---|---|---|
| Belfast | Belfast | Wembley | Swansea | Belfast |
| Oct 12: 2-1 | Oct 30: 0-1 | Nov 20: 3-8 | April 15: 3-2 | April 29: 3-0 |
| *Bingham, Wilson* | | *Crossan, Wilson 2* | *McLaughlin, Wilson, Harvey* | *Crossan 2, Wilson* |

| 1964 England | 1964 Switzerland | 1964 Switzerland | 1964 Scotland | 1965 Netherlands |
|---|---|---|---|---|
| 1 Jennings | 1 Jennings | 1 Jennings | 1 Jennings | 1 Briggs |
| 2 Magill | 2 Magill | 2 Magill | 2 Magill | 2 Parke |
| 3 Elder | 3 Elder | 3 Elder | 3 Elder | 3 Elder |
| 4 Harvey | 4 Harvey | 4 Harvey | 4 Harvey | 4 Harvey |
| 5 Neill | 5 Neill | 5 Campbell | 5 Neill | 5 Neill |
| 6 McCullough | 6 McCullough | 6 Parke | 6 Parke | 6 Nicholson |
| 7 Best | 7 Best | 7 Best | 7 Best | 7 Humphries |
| 8 Crossan | 8 Crossan | 8 Crossan | 8 Humphries | 8 Crossan |
| 9 Wilson | 9 Wilson | 9 Irvine W. | 9 Irvine W. | 9 Irvine W. |
| 10 McLaughlin | 10 McLaughlin | 10 McLaughlin | 10 Crossan | 10 Clements |
| 11 Braithwaite | 11 Braithwaite | 11 Braithwaite | 11 Braithwaite | 11 Best |

| | | | | |
|---|---|---|---|---|
| Belfast | Belfast | Lausanne | Hampden | Belfast |
| Oct 3: 3-4 | Oct 14: 1-0 | Nov 14: 1-2 | Nov 25: 2-3 | Mar 17: 2-1 |
| *Wilson, McLaughlin 2* | *Crossan* | *Best* | *Best, Irvine* | *Crossan, Neill* |

| 1965 Wales | 1965 Netherlands | 1965 Albania | 1965 Scotland | 1965 England |
|---|---|---|---|---|
| 1 Irvine R. | 1 Jennings | 1 Jennings | 1 Jennings | 1 Jennings |
| 2 Parke | 2 Magill | 2 Magill | 2 Magill | 2 Magill |
| 3 Elder | 3 Elder | 3 Elder | 3 Elder | 3 Elder |
| 4 Harvey | 4 Harvey | 4 Harvey | 4 Harvey | 4 Harvey |
| 5 Neill | 5 Neill | 5 Neill | 5 Neill | 5 Neill |
| 6 Nicholson | 6 Parke | 6 Parke | 6 Nicholson | 6 Nicholson |
| 7 Humphries | 7 Best | 7 Humphries | 7 McIlroy | 7 McIlroy |
| 8 Crossan | 8 Crossan | 8 Crossan | 8 Crossan | 8 Crossan |
| 9 Irvine W. | 9 Irvine W. | 9 Irvine W. | 9 Irvine W. | 9 Irvine W. |
| 10 McLaughlin | 10 Nicholson | 10 Nicholson | 10 Dougan | 10 Dougan |
| 11 Clements | 11 Braithwaite | 11 Best | 11 Best | 11 Best |
| Belfast | Rotterdam | Belfast | Belfast | Wembley |
| March 31: 0-5 | April 7: 0-0 | May 7: 4-1 | Oct 2: 3-2 | Nov 10: 1-2 |
| | | *Crossan 3, Best* | *Dougan, Crossan, Irvine* | *Irvine* |

| 1965 Albania | 1966 Wales | 1966 W Germany | 1966 Mexico | 1966 England |
|---|---|---|---|---|
| 1 Jennings | 1 Jennings | 1 Jennings | 1 McClelland | 1 Jennings (McFaul) |
| 2 Magill | 2 Magill | 2 Magill | 2 Magill | 2 Parke |
| 3 Elder | 3 Elder | 3 Parke | 3 Elder | 3 Elder |
| 4 Harvey | 4 Harvey | 4 Harvey | 4 Harvey | 4 Todd |
| 5 Neill | 5 Neill | 5 Napier | 5 Neill | 5 Harvey |
| 6 Nicholson | 6 Nicholson | 6 Neill | 6 Nicholson | 6 McCullough |
| 7 McIlroy | 7 Welsh | 7 Welsh | 7 Welsh | 7 Ferguson |
| 8 Crossan | 8 Wilson | 8 Crossan | 8 Ferguson | 8 Crossan |
| 9 Irvine W. | 9 Irvine W. | 9 Wilson | 9 Irvine W. (Johnston) | 9 Irvine W. |
| 10 Dougan | 10 Dougan | 10 Dougan | 10 Dougan | 10 Dougan |
| 11 Best | 11 McLaughlin | 11 McKinney | 11 Clements (Todd) | 11 Best |
| Tirana | Cardiff | Belfast | Belfast | Belfast |
| Nov 24: 1-1 | Mar 30: 4-1 | May 7: 0-2 | June 22: 4-1 | Oct 22: 0-2 |
| *Irvine* | *Irvine, Wilson, Welsh, Harvey* | | *Johnston, Elder, Nicholson, Ferguson* | |

| 1966 Scotland | 1967 Wales | 1967 Scotland | 1967 England | 1968 Wales |
|---|---|---|---|---|
| 1 Jennings | 1 McKenzie | 1 Jennings | 1 Jennings | 1 Jennings |
| 2 Parke | 2 Craig | 2 McKeag | 2 Parke | 2 Craig |
| 3 Elder | 3 Elder | 3 Parke | 3 Elder | 3 Elder |
| 4 Harvey | 4 Stewart | 4 Stewart | 4 Stewart | 4 Harvey |
| 5 Neill | 5 Neill | 5 Neill | 5 Neill | 5 Todd |
| 6 Nicholson | 6 Nicholson | 6 Clements | 6 Harvey | 6 McKeag |
| 7 Wilson | 7 Welsh | 7 Campbell | 7 Campbell | 7 Irvine |
| 8 Crossan | 8 Trainor | 8 Crossan | 8 Irvine W. | 8 Stewart |
| 9 Irvine W. | 9 Dougan | 9 Dougan | 9 Wilson | 9 Dougan |
| 10 Dougan | 10 Bruce | 10 Nicholson | 10 Nicholson | 10 Nicholson |
| 11 Clements | 11 Clements | 11 Best | 11 Clements | 11 Harkin |
| Hampden | Belfast | Belfast | Wembley | Wrexham |
| Nov 16: 1-2 | April 12: 0-0 | Oct 21: 1-0 | Nov 22: 0-2 | Feb 28: 0-2 |
| *Nicholson* | | *Clements* | | |

| 1968 Israel | 1968 Turkey | 1968 Turkey | 1969 England | 1969 Scotland |
|---|---|---|---|---|
| 1 Jennings | 1 Jennings | 1 Jennings | 1 Jennings | 1 Jennings |
| 2 Rice | 2 Craig (Stewart) | 2 Craig | 2 Craig | 2 Craig |
| 3 Jackson | 3 Harvey | 3 Harvey | 3 Harvey (Elder) | 3 Elder |
| 4 Stewart | 4 Nicholson | 4 Nicholson | 4 Todd | 4 Todd |
| 5 Neill | 5 Neill | 5 Neill | 5 Neill | 5 Neill |
| 6 Harvey | 6 Clements | 6 Stewart | 6 Nicholson | 6 Nicholson |
| 7 Sloan | 7 Campbell | 7 Hamilton | 7 McMordie | 7 Best |
| 8 McMordie | 8 McMordie | 8 McMordie | 8 Jackson | 8 McMordie |
| 9 Dougan (Gaston) | 9 Dougan | 9 Dougan | 9 Dougan | 9 Dougan |
| 10 Irvine W. | 10 Irvine W. | 10 Harkin | 10 Irvine W. | 10 Jackson |
| 11 Ross | 11 Best | 11 Clements | 11 Best | 11 Clements |
| Jaffa Sept 10: 3-2 *Irvine 2, Dougan* | Belfast Oct 23: 4-1 *Best, McMordie, Dougan, Campbell* | Istanbul Dec 11: 3-0 *Harkin 2, Nicholson* | Belfast May 3: 1-3 *McMordie* | Hampden May 6: 1-1 *McMordie* |

| 1969 Wales | 1969 USSR | 1969 USSR | 1970 Scotland | 1970 England |
|---|---|---|---|---|
| 1 Jennings | 1 Jennings | 1 Jennings | 1 Jennings | 1 Jennings |
| 2 Craig | 2 Rice | 2 Craig | 2 Craig | 2 Craig |
| 3 Elder | 3 Elder | 3 Harvey | 3 Clements | 3 Clements |
| 4 Todd | 4 Todd | 4 Hunter | 4 Todd (O'Kane) | 4 O'Kane |
| 5 Neill | 5 Neill | 5 Neill | 5 Neill | 5 Neill |
| 6 Nicholson | 6 Nicholson | 6 Nicholson | 6 Nicholson | 6 Nicholson |
| 7 Best | 7 Campbell | 7 Hegan | 7 Campbell (Dickson) | 7 McMordie |
| 8 McMordie | 8 McMordie | 8 Jackson | 8 Lutton | 8 Best |
| 9 Dougan | 9 Dougan | 9 Dougan | 9 Dougan | 9 Dougan |
| 10 Jackson | 10 Clements (Jackson) | 10 Harkin | 10 McMordie | 10 O'Doherty (Nelson) |
| 11 Clements (Harkin) | 11 Best | 11 Clements | 11 Best | 11 Lutton (Cowan) |
| Belfast May 10: 0-0 | Belfast Sept 10: 0-0 | Moscow Oct 22: 0-2 | Belfast April 18: 0-1 | Wembley April 21: 1-3 *Best* |

| 1970 Wales | 1970 Spain | 1971 Cyprus | 1971 Cyprus | 1971 England |
|---|---|---|---|---|
| 1 McFaul | 1 McFaul | 1 Jennings | 1 Jennings | 1 Jennings |
| 2 Craig | 2 Craig | 2 Craig | 2 Craig | 2 Rice |
| 3 Nelson | 3 Nelson | 3 Nelson | 3 Clements | 3 Nelson |
| 4 O'Kane | 4 Jackson | 4 Hunter | 4 Harvey | 4 O'Kane |
| 5 Neill | 5 Neill | 5 Neill | 5 Hunter | 5 Hunter |
| 6 Nicholson | 6 O'Kane | 6 Todd | 6 Todd (Watson) | 6 Nicholson |
| 7 Campbell (O'Doherty) | 7 Sloan | 7 Hamilton | 7 Hamilton | 7 Hamilton |
| 8 Best | 8 Best | 8 McMordie | 8 McMordie | 8 McMordie (Cassidy) |
| 9 Dickson | 9 Dougan (Todd) | 9 Dougan | 9 Dougan | 9 Dougan |
| 10 McMordie | 10 Harkin | 10 Nicholson | 10 Nicholson | 10 Clements |
| 11 Clements | 11 Clements | 11 Best | 11 Best | 11 Best |
| Swansea April 25: 0-1 | Seville Nov 11: 0-3 | Nicosia Feb 3: 3-0 *Nicholson, Dougan, Best* | Belfast April 21: 5-0 *Dougan, Best 3, Nicholson* | Belfast May 15: 0-1 |

| 1971 Scotland | 1971 Wales | 1971 USSR | 1971 USSR | 1972 Spain |
|---|---|---|---|---|
| 1 Jennings | 1 Jennings | 1 McFaul | 1 Jennings | 1 Jennings |
| 2 Rice | 2 Rice | 2 Craig (Hamilton) | 2 Rice | 2 Rice |
| 3 Nelson | 3 Nelson | 3 Neill | 3 Nelson | 3 Nelson |
| 4 O'Kane | 4 O'Kane | 4 Hunter | 4 Nicholson | 4 Neill |
| 5 Hunter | 5 Hunter | 5 Nelson | 5 Hunter | 5 Hunter |
| 6 Nicholson | 6 Nicholson (Harvey) | 6 Hegan | 6 O'Kane | 6 Clements |
| 7 Hamilton | 7 Hamilton | 7 Clements | 7 McMordie | 7 Hamilton (O'Neill) |
| 8 McMordie (Craig) | 8 McMordie | 8 Nicholson | 8 Hamilton (O'Neill) | 8 McMordie |
| 9 Dougan | 9 Dougan | 9 O'Kane | 9 Neill | 9 Morgan |
| 10 Clements | 10 Clements | 10 Dougan | 10 Dougan (Cassidy) | 10 McIlroy |
| 11 Best | 11 Best | 11 Best | 11 Clements | 11 Best |
| Hampden May 18: 1-0 *1 og* | Belfast May 22: 1-0 *Hamilton* | Moscow Sept 22: 0-1 | Belfast Oct 13: 1-1 *Nicholson* | Hull Feb 16: 1-1 *Morgan* |

| 1972 Scotland | 1972 England | 1972 Wales | 1972 Bulgaria | 1973 Cyprus |
|---|---|---|---|---|
| 1 Jennings | 1 Jennings | 1 Jennings | 1 Jennings | 1 Jennings |
| 2 Rice | 2 Rice | 2 Rice | 2 Rice | 2 Rice |
| 3 Nelson | 3 Nelson | 3 Nelson | 3 Nelson | 3 Neill |
| 4 Neill | 4 Neill | 4 Neill | 4 Hunter | 4 Hunter |
| 5 Hunter | 5 Hunter | 5 Hunter | 5 Neill | 5 Craig |
| 6 Clements (Craig) | 6 Clements | 6 Clements | 6 Clements | 6 Hegan |
| 7 Hegan | 7 Hegan | 7 Hegan | 7 Hamilton (Morgan) | 7 Clements |
| 8 McMordie (McIlroy) | 8 McMordie | 8 McMordie | 8 Hegan | 8 Hamilton |
| 9 Dougan | 9 Dougan | 9 Dougan (O'Neill) | 9 McMordie | 9 Dickson |
| 10 Irvine W. | 10 Irvine W. | 10 Irvine W. | 10 Dougan | 10 Dougan |
| 11 Jackson | 11 Jackson | 11 Jackson | 11 Best | 11 Nelson |
| Hampden May 20: 0-2 | Wembley May 23: 1-0 *Neill* | Wrexham May 27: 0-0 | Sofia Oct 18: 0-3 | Nicosia Feb 14: 0-1 |

| 1973 Portugal | 1973 Cyprus | 1973 England | 1973 Scotland | 1973 Wales |
|---|---|---|---|---|
| 1 Jennings | 1 McFaul | 1 Jennings | 1 Jennings | 1 Jennings |
| 2 O'Kane | 2 O'Kane | 2 Rice | 2 Rice | 2 Rice |
| 3 Nelson | 3 Hunter (Coyle) | 3 Craig | 3 Craig | 3 Craig |
| 4 Neill | 4 Neill | 4 Neill | 4 Neill | 4 Neill |
| 5 Hunter | 5 Craig | 5 Hunter | 5 Hunter | 5 Hunter |
| 6 Clements | 6 Hamilton (Lutton) | 6 Clements | 6 Clements | 6 Clements |
| 7 Hamilton | 7 Jackson | 7 Hamilton | 7 Hamilton | 7 Hamilton (Lutton) |
| 8 Coyle | 8 Clements | 8 Jackson | 8 Jackson | 8 Jackson |
| 9 Morgan | 9 Morgan | 9 Morgan | 9 Morgan | 9 Morgan |
| 10 Dickson | 10 O'Neill | 10 O'Neill | 10 O'Neill | 10 O'Neill |
| 11 O'Neill | 11 Anderson | 11 Anderson | 11 Anderson (Lutton) | 11 Anderson (Coyle) |
| Coventry Mar 28: 1-1 *O'Neill* | London May 8: 3-0 *Morgan, Anderson 2* | Everton May 12: 1-2 *Clements* (pen) | Glasgow May 16: 2-1 *O'Neill, Anderson* | Everton May 19: 1-0 *Hamilton* |

| 1973 Bulgaria | 1973 Portugal | 1974 Scotland | 1974 England | 1974 Wales |
|---|---|---|---|---|
| 1 McFaul | 1 Jennings | 1 Jennings | 1 Jennings | 1 Jennings |
| 2 Rice | 2 Rice | 2 Rice | 2 Rice | 2 Rice |
| 3 Craig | 3 Craig | 3 Nelson | 3 Nelson (Jackson) | 3 Dowd |
| 4 O'Kane | 4 Lutton | 4 O'Kane | 4 O'Kane | 4 O'Kane |
| 5 Hunter | 5 O'Kane | 5 Hunter | 5 Hunter | 5 Hunter |
| 6 Clements | 6 Clements | 6 Clements | 6 Clements | 6 Clements |
| 7 Hamilton | 7 Jackson (Coyle) | 7 Hamilton (Jackson) | 7 Hamilton (O'Neill) | 7 Hamilton (Jackson) |
| 8 Jackson (Coyle) | 8 O'Neill | 8 Cassidy | 8 Cassidy | 8 Cassidy |
| 9 Morgan | 9 Morgan | 9 Morgan | 9 Morgan | 9 McIlroy |
| 10 Anderson | 10 Anderson | 10 McIlroy | 10 McIlroy | 10 McGrath |
| 11 O'Neill (Cassidy) | 11 Best | 11 McGrath | 11 McGrath | 11 O'Neill |
| Hillsborough Sept 26: 0-0 | Lisbon Nov 14: 1-1 *O'Kane* | Hampden May 11: 1-0 *Cassidy* | Wembley May 15: 0-1 | Wrexham May 18: 0-1 |

| 1974 Norway | 1974 Sweden | 1975 Yugoslavia | 1975 England | 1975 Scotland |
|---|---|---|---|---|
| 1 Jennings | 1 Jennings | 1 Jennings | 1 Jennings | 1 Jennings |
| 2 Rice | 2 O'Kane | 2 Rice | 2 Rice | 2 Rice |
| 3 Craig (Dowd) | 3 Nelson (Blair) | 3 Nelson | 3 O'Kane | 3 O'Kane |
| 4 O'Kane | 4 Dowd | 4 Nicholl C. | 4 Nicholl C. | 4 Nicholl C. |
| 5 Hunter | 5 Hunter | 5 Hunter | 5 Hunter | 5 Hunter (Blair) |
| 6 Clements | 6 Nicholl C. | 6 Clements | 6 Clements | 6 Clements |
| 7 Hamilton | 7 Jackson | 7 Hamilton | 7 Hamilton (Finney) | 7 Finney |
| 8 Cassidy | 8 O'Neill | 8 O'Neill | 8 O'Neill | 8 O'Neill (Anderson) |
| 9 Finney | 9 Morgan | 9 Spence | 9 Spence | 9 Spence |
| 10 McIlroy | 10 McIlroy | 10 McIlroy | 10 McIlroy | 10 McIlroy |
| 11 McGrath (Jackson) | 11 Hamilton | 11 Jackson | 11 Jackson | 11 Jackson |
| Oslo Sept 4: 1-2 *Finney* | Solna Oct 30: 2-0 *O'Neill, Nicholl* | Belfast March 16: 1-0 *Hamilton* | Belfast May 17: 0-0 | Hampden May 20: 0-3 |

| 1975 Wales | 1975 Sweden | 1975 Norway | 1975 Yugoslavia | 1976 Israel |
|---|---|---|---|---|
| 1 Jennings | 1 Jennings | 1 Jennings | 1 Jennings | 1 Jennings (Platt) |
| 2 Scott | 2 Rice | 2 Rice | 2 Rice | 2 Scott |
| 3 Rice | 3 Nelson | 3 Nelson | 3 Scott | 3 Nicholl J. |
| 4 Nicholl C. | 4 Clements | 4 Nicholl C. | 4 Nicholl C. | 4 Hunter |
| 5 Hunter | 5 Hunter | 5 Hunter | 5 Hunter | 5 Rice |
| 6 Clements | 6 Nicholl C. | 6 Jackson | 6 Clements | 6 Blair |
| 7 Blair | 7 Blair | 7 Hamilton | 7 Hamilton | 7 Nelson |
| 8 Jackson | 8 Hamilton (Morgan) | 8 McIlroy | 8 McIlroy | 8 Hamilton |
| 9 Spence | 9 Spence | 9 Morgan (Cochrane) | 9 Morgan | 9 Anderson (McGrath) |
| 10 McIlroy | 10 McIlroy | 10 Jamison | 10 Jackson (O'Neill) | 10 Spence |
| 11 Finney | 11 Jackson | 11 Finney | 11 Finney | 11 Finney |
| Belfast May 23: 1-0 *Finney* | Belfast Sept 3: 1-2 *Hunter* | Belfast Oct 29: 3-0 *Morgan, McIlroy, Hamilton* | Belgrade Nov 19: 0-1 | Tel Aviv Mar 24: 1-1 *Lev og* |

| 1976 Scotland | 1976 England | 1976 Wales | 1976 Netherlands | 1976 Belgium |
|---|---|---|---|---|
| 1 Jennings | 1 Jennings | 1 Jennings | 1 Jennings | 1 Jennings |
| 2 Scott | 2 Rice | 2 Scott | 2 Nicholl J. | 2 Nicholl J. |
| 3 Nicholl C. | 3 Nelson (Scott) | 3 Rice | 3 Jackson | 3 Rice (Nelson) |
| 4 Hunter | 4 Clements | 4 Nicholl C. | 4 Rice | 4 Jackson |
| 5 Rice | 5 Hunter | 5 Hunter | 5 Hunter | 5 Hunter |
| 6 Hamilton B. | 6 Nicholl C. | 6 Clements | 6 Hamilton B. | 6 Hamilton B. |
| 7 Cassidy | 7 Hamilton B. | 7 Hamilton B. | 7 Best | 7 Best |
| 8 Sharkey (McCreery) | 8 Cassidy | 8 McIlroy | 8 McIlroy | 8 McIlroy |
| 9 McIlroy | 9 McCreery | 9 Spence (Morgan) | 9 McGrath (Spence) | 9 McGrath |
| 10 Morgan (Spence) | 10 Spence | 10 Cassidy (Nicholl J.) | 10 McCreery | 10 McCreery |
| 11 Finney | 11 McIlroy | 11 McCreery | 11 Anderson | 11 Anderson |
| Hampden May 8: 0-3 | Wembley May 11: 0-4 | Swansea May 14: 0-1 | Rotterdam Oct 13: 2-2 McGrath, Spence | Liège Nov 10: 0-2 |

| 1977 W Germany | 1977 England | 1977 Scotland | 1977 Wales | 1977 Iceland |
|---|---|---|---|---|
| 1 Jennings | 1 Jennings | 1 Jennings | 1 Jennings | 1 Jennings |
| 2 Rice | 2 Nicholl J. | 2 Nicholl J. | 2 Nicholl J. | 2 Rice |
| 3 Nelson | 3 Rice | 3 Rice | 3 Nelson | 3 Nelson |
| 4 Jackson | 4 Jackson | 4 Jackson | 4 Nicholl C. | 4 Nicholl J. |
| 5 Hunter | 5 Hunter | 5 Hunter | 5 Hunter | 5 Hunter |
| 6 McCreery (Cassidy) | 6 Hamilton B. | 6 Hamilton B. | 6 Hamilton B. | 6 Hamilton B. |
| 7 Hamilton B. | 7 McGrath | 7 McGrath | 7 McGrath | 7 McGrath |
| 8 Best | 8 McIlroy | 8 McIlroy | 8 McIlroy | 8 McIlroy |
| 9 Armstrong (Spence) | 9 Armstrong (O'Neill) | 9 O'Neill (Spence) | 9 Jackson | 9 Jackson (Spence) |
| 10 McGrath | 10 McCreery | 10 McCreery | 10 McCreery (Armstrong) | 10 McCreery |
| 11 Anderson | 11 Anderson (Spence) | 11 Anderson | 11 Anderson (Spence) | 11 Anderson (Armstrong) |
| Cologne April 27: 0-5 | Belfast May 28: 1-2 McGrath | Hampden June 1: 0-2 | Belfast June 3: 1-1 Nelson | Reykjavik June 11: 0-1 |

| 1977 Iceland | 1977 Netherlands | 1977 Belgium | 1978 Scotland | 1978 England |
|---|---|---|---|---|
| 1 Jennings | 1 Jennings | 1 Jennings | 1 Platt | 1 Platt |
| 2 Rice | 2 Rice | 2 Rice | 2 Hamilton B. | 2 Hamilton B. |
| 3 Nicholl J. | 3 Nelson | 3 Nelson | 3 Scott | 3 Scott |
| 4 Nelson | 4 Nicholl J. | 4 Nicholl J. | 4 Nicholl C. | 4 Nicholl C. |
| 5 Hunter | 5 Hunter | 5 Hunter (Nicholl C.) | 5 Nicholl J. | 5 Nicholl J. |
| 6 McCreery | 6 O'Neill | 6 McIlroy | 6 McIlroy | 6 McIlroy |
| 7 McGrath | 7 McIlroy | 7 McGrath | 7 McCreery | 7 McCreery |
| 8 Best | 8 Best | 8 McCreery | 8 O'Neill | 8 O'Neill |
| 9 McIlroy | 9 McCreery | 9 Armstrong | 9 Anderson (Hamilton W.) | 9 Anderson |
| 10 O'Neill | 10 McGrath | 10 Stewart | 10 Armstrong | 10 Armstrong |
| 11 Anderson | 11 Anderson | 11 Anderson | 11 McGrath (Cochrane) | 11 McGrath (Cochrane) |
| Belfast Sept 21: 2-0 McGrath, McIlroy | Belfast Oct 12: 0-1 | Belfast Nov 16: 3-0 Armstrong 2, McGrath | Hampden May 13: 1-1 O'Neill | Wembley May 16: 0-1 |

| 1978 Wales | 1978 Rep of Ireland | 1978 Denmark | 1978 Bulgaria | 1979 England |
|---|---|---|---|---|
| 1 Platt | 1 Jennings | 1 Jennings | 1 Jennings | 1 Jennings |
| 2 Hamilton B. | 2 Rice | 2 Rice | 2 Hamilton B. | 2 Rice |
| 3 Scott (Connell) | 3 Nelson | 3 Nelson | 3 Nelson | 3 Nelson |
| 4 Nicholl C. | 4 Nicholl C. | 4 Nicholl J. | 4 Nicholl C. | 4 Nicholl C. |
| 5 Nicholl J. | 5 Hunter (Hamilton B.) | 5 Hunter | 5 Nicholl J. | 5 Nicholl J. |
| 6 O'Neill | 6 Nicholl J. | 6 McCreery | 6 McCreery | 6 McCreery |
| 7 McCreery | 7 O'Neill | 7 O'Neill | 7 O'Neill | 7 O'Neill |
| 8 McIlroy | 8 McCreery | 8 McIlroy | 8 McIlroy (Moreland) | 8 McIlroy |
| 9 Anderson (Cochrane) | 9 Armstrong | 9 Armstrong | 9 Armstrong | 9 Armstrong |
| 10 Armstrong | 10 McIlroy | 10 Morgan (Spence) (Anderson) | 10 Caskey | 10 Caskey (Spence) |
| 11 McGrath | 11 Spence (Cochrane) | 11 Cochrane | 11 Cochrane (McGrath) | 11 Cochrane (McGrath) |
| Wrexham May 19: 0-1 | Dublin Sept 20: 0-0 | Belfast Oct 25: 2-1 *Spence, Anderson* | Sofia Nov 29: 2-0 *Armstrong, Caskey* | Wembley Feb 7: 0-4 |

| 1979 Bulgaria | 1979 England | 1979 Scotland | 1979 Wales | 1979 Denmark |
|---|---|---|---|---|
| 1 Jennings | 1 Jennings | 1 Jennings | 1 Jennings | 1 Jennings |
| 2 Hamilton B. | 2 Rice | 2 Rice | 2 Rice | 2 Rice |
| 3 Nelson | 3 Nelson | 3 Nelson | 3 Nelson | 3 Nelson |
| 4 Nicholl C. (Moreland) | 4 Nicholl C. | 4 Nicholl J. | 4 Nicholl C. | 4 Nicholl J. |
| 5 Nicholl J. | 5 Nicholl J. | 5 Hunter | 5 Hunter | 5 Hunter |
| 6 McCreery | 6 Moreland (McGrath) | 6 Moreland | 6 Nicholl J. | 6 McCreery |
| 7 O'Neill | 7 Hamilton B. | 7 Hamilton B. | 7 McCreery | 7 O'Neill |
| 8 McIlroy | 8 McIlroy | 8 McIlroy (Scott) | 8 McIlroy | 8 McIlroy |
| 9 Armstrong | 9 Armstrong | 9 Armstrong | 9 Armstrong | 9 Armstrong |
| 10 Caskey (Spence) | 10 Caskey | 10 Sloan | 10 Spence (Sloan) | 10 Spence |
| 11 Cochrane | 11 Cochrane (Spence) | 11 Spence | 11 Hamilton B. | 11 Hamilton B. |
| Belfast May 2: 2-0 *Nicholl C., Armstrong* | Belfast May 19: 0-2 | Hampden May 22: 0-1 | Belfast May 25: 1-1 *Spence* | Copenhagen June 6: 0-4 |

| 1979 England | 1979 Rep of Ireland | 1980 Israel | 1980 Scotland | 1980 England |
|---|---|---|---|---|
| 1 Jennings | 1 Jennings | 1 Jennings | 1 Platt | 1 Platt |
| 2 Rice | 2 Nicholl J. | 2 Nicholl J. | 2 Nicholl J. | 2 Nicholl J. |
| 3 Nelson | 3 Nelson | 3 Nelson | 3 Donaghy | 3 Donaghy |
| 4 Nicholl J. | 4 Nicholl C. | 4 Nicholl C. | 4 Nicholl C. | 4 Nicholl C. |
| 5 Hunter (Rafferty) | 5 Hunter | 5 O'Neill J. | 5 O'Neill J. | 5 O'Neill J. |
| 6 McCreery | 6 McCreery | 6 O'Neill M. | 6 Cassidy (McCreery) | 6 Cassidy (McCreery) |
| 7 Cassidy | 7 O'Neill M. (Cassidy) | 7 McIlroy | 7 McIlroy | 7 McIlroy |
| 8 McIlroy | 8 McIlroy | 8 Cassidy | 8 Hamilton W. (McClelland) | 8 Hamilton W. (Cochrane) |
| 9 Armstrong | 9 Armstrong | 9 Armstrong | 9 Armstrong | 9 Armstrong |
| 10 Finney (Caskey) | 10 Spence | 10 Finney (Spence) | 10 Finney | 10 Finney |
| 11 Moreland | 11 Moreland | 11 Cochrane | 11 Brotherston | 11 Brotherston |
| Belfast Oct 17: 1-5 *Moreland* (pen) | Belfast Nov 21: 1-0 *Armstrong* | Tel Aviv Mar 26: 0-0 | Belfast May 16: 1-0 *Hamilton* | Wembley May 20: 1-1 *Cochrane* |

| 1980 Wales | 1980 Australia | 1980 Australia | 1980 Australia | 1980 Sweden |
|---|---|---|---|---|
| 1 Platt | 1 Platt | 1 Platt | 1 Platt | 1 Platt |
| 2 Nicholl J. | 2 Nicholl J. | 2 Nicholl J. | 2 Nicholl J. | 2 Nicholl J. |
| 3 Donaghy | 3 Nicholl C. | 3 Nicholl C. | 3 Nicholl C. | 3 Donaghy |
| 4 Nicholl C. | 4 O'Neill J. | 4 O'Neill J. | 4 O'Neill J. | 4 Cassidy (McCreery) |
| 5 O'Neill J. | 5 McClelland | 5 McClelland | 5 McClelland | 5 Nicholl C. |
| 6 Cassidy (McCreery) | 6 Cassidy (McCreery) | 6 Cassidy | 6 Cassidy (Hamilton B.) | 6 McClelland |
| 7 McIlroy | 7 Brotherston | 7 Brotherston | 7 Cochrane | 7 Brotherston |
| 8 Hamilton W. (Cochrane) | 8 Hamilton W. | 8 McCreery (Cochrane) | 8 Hamilton W. (McCurdy) | 8 O'Neill M. |
| 9 Armstrong | 9 Armstrong | 9 Armstrong | 9 Armstrong | 9 Hamilton (Cochrane) |
| 10 Finney | 10 Finney (Hamilton B.) | 10 Finney | 10 O'Neill M. | 10 Armstrong |
| 11 Brotherston | 11 O'Neill M. | 11 O'Neill M. | 11 Brotherston | 11 McIlroy |
| Cardiff May 23: 1-0 *Brotherston* | Sydney June 11: 2-1 *Nicholl C., O'Neill M.* | Melbourne June 15: 1-1 *O'Neill M.* | Adelaide June 18: 2-1 *Brotherston, McCurdy* | Belfast Oct 15: 3-0 *Brotherston, McIlroy, Nicholl J.* |

| 1980 Portugal | 1981 Scotland | 1981 Portugal | 1981 Scotland | 1981 Sweden |
|---|---|---|---|---|
| 1 Platt | 1 Jennings | 1 Jennings | 1 Jennings | 1 Jennings |
| 2 Nicholl J. | 2 Nicholl J. | 2 Nicholl J. | 2 Nicholl J. | 2 Nicholl J. (McClelland) |
| 3 Donaghy | 3 Nelson | 3 Nelson | 3 Nelson (Donaghy) | 3 Nelson |
| 4 Cassidy (McCreery) | 4 McClelland | 4 McCreery | 4 McClelland | 4 McCreery |
| 5 Nicholl C. | 5 Nicholl C. | 5 Nicholl C. | 5 Nicholl C. | 5 Nicholl C. |
| 6 O'Neill J. | 6 O'Neill J. | 6 O'Neill J. | 6 O'Neill J. | 6 O'Neill J. |
| 7 Brotherston | 7 Cochrane | 7 Cochrane | 7 Cochrane | 7 Cochrane |
| 8 O'Neill M. | 8 McCreery | 8 O'Neill M. | 8 O'Neill M. | 8 O'Neill M. |
| 9 Hamilton (Cochrane) | 9 Hamilton (Spence) | 9 Hamilton | 9 Armstrong | 9 Hamilton (Spence) |
| 10 Armstrong | 10 Armstrong | 10 Armstrong | 10 McIlroy | 10 Armstrong |
| 11 McIlroy | 11 McIlroy | 11 McIlroy | 11 Hamilton | 11 McIlroy |
| Lisbon Nov 19: 0-1 | Glasgow Mar 25: 1-1 *Hamilton* | Belfast April 29: 1-0 *Armstrong* | Glasgow May 19: 0-2 | Stockholm June 3: 0-1 |

# SCOTLAND INTERNATIONAL TEAMS
# 1872–1981

Substitutes in brackets   †World Cup final stages

| 1872 England | 1873 England | 1874 England | 1875 England | 1876 England |
|---|---|---|---|---|
| 1 Gardner | 1 Gardner | 1 Gardner | 1 Gardner | 1 McGeoch |
| 2 Ker | 2 Ker | 2 Hunter | 2 Hunter | 2 Hunter |
| 3 Taylor | 3 Taylor | 3 Taylor | 3 Taylor | 3 Taylor |
| 4 Thomson | 4 Gibb | 4 Thomson | 4 McLintock | 4 McLintock |
| 5 Smith, James | 5 Smith, Robert | 5 Campbell C. | 5 Kennedy | 5 Kennedy |
| 6 Smith, Robert | 6 Wotherspoon | 6 Weir | 6 Weir | 6 McNeil H. |
| 7 Leckie | 7 Renny-Tailyour | 7 McKinnon W.W. | 7 McKinnon W.W. | 7 Highet |
| 8 Rhind | 8 Kinnaird | 8 Ferguson | 8 Highet | 8 McKinnon W.W. |
| 9 McKinnon W.W. | 9 Blackburn | 9 McKinnon A. | 9 McNeil H. | 9 Miller |
| 10 Weir | 10 Thomson | 10 McNeil H. | 10 Andrews | 10 Ferguson |
| 11 Wotherspoon | 11 McKinnon W.W. | 11 Anderson | 11 McPherson | 11 Baird |
| Glasgow Nov 30: 0-0 | London Mar 8: 2-4 *Renny-Tailyour, Gibb* | Glasgow Mar 7: 2-1 *McKinnon A., Anderson* | London Mar 6: 2-2 *McNeil, Andrews* | Glasgow Mar 4: 3-0 *McKinnon, McNeil Highet* |

| 1876 Wales | 1877 England | 1877 Wales | 1878 England | 1878 Wales |
|---|---|---|---|---|
| 1 McGeoch | 1 McGeoch | 1 McGeoch | 1 Gardner | 1 Parlane |
| 2 Taylor | 2 Neill | 2 Neill | 2 McIntyre | 2 Neill |
| 3 Neill | 3 Vallance | 3 Vallance | 3 Vallance | 3 Duncan |
| 4 Kennedy | 4 Campbell C. | 4 Phillips | 4 Campbell C. | 4 Phillips |
| 5 Campbell C. | 5 Phillips | 5 Campbell C. | 5 Kennedy | 5 Davidson |
| 6 Highet | 6 Richmond | 6 Smith J. | 6 Richmond | 6 Lang |
| 7 Ferguson | 7 McKinnon W.W. | 7 McGregor | 7 McKinnon W.W. | 7 Weir |
| 8 Lang | 8 McGregor | 8 Ferguson | 8 McGregor | 8 Watson |
| 9 McKinnon W.W. | 9 McDougall | 9 McDougall | 9 McDougall | 9 Campbell P. |
| 10 McNeil M. | 10 Smith J. | 10 McNeil H. | 10 Highet | 10 Ferguson |
| 11 McNeil H. | 11 Ferguson | 11 Hunter | 11 McNeil H. | 11 Baird |
| Glasgow Mar 25: 4-0 *Ferguson, Lang, McKinnon, McNeil H.* | London Mar 3: 3-1 *Ferguson 2 Richmond* | Wrexham Mar 5: 2-0 *Campbell, Powell og* | Glasgow Mar 2: 7-2 *McDougall 3, McGregor, McNeil 2, McKinnon* | Glasgow Mar 23: 9-0 *Campbell, Weir 2, Ferguson 3, Baird, Watson and one other* |

| 1879 Wales | 1879 England | 1880 England | 1880 Wales | 1881 England |
|---|---|---|---|---|
| 1 Parlane | 1 Parlane | 1 Rowan | 1 Gillespie | 1 Gillespie |
| 2 Vallance | 2 Somers | 2 Neill | 2 Somers | 2 Watson |
| 3 Somers | 3 Vallance | 3 McLintock | 3 Lang | 3 Vallance |
| 4 McPherson | 4 Campbell C. | 4 Campbell C. | 4 Davidson | 4 Campbell C. |
| 5 Davidson | 5 McPherson | 5 McPherson | 5 McIntyre | 5 Davidson |
| 6 McNeil H. | 6 Beveridge | 6 Smith J. | 6 Douglas | 6 McGuire |
| 7 McDougall | 7 Smith J. | 7 McNeil M. | 7 McAdam | 7 Hill |
| 8 Campbell P. | 8 McDougall | 8 Ker | 8 Frazer | 8 Ker |
| 9 Paton | 9 Paton | 9 McGregor | 9 Lindsay | 9 Lindsay |
| 10 Beveridge | 10 McKinnon W.W. | 10 Baird | 10 Campbell J. | 10 McNeil H. |
| 11 Smith J. | 11 McNeil H. | 11 Kay | 11 Beveridge | 11 Smith J. |
| Wrexham April 7: 3-0 *Campbell, Smith 2* | London April 5: 4-5 *McKinnon 2, McDougall, Smith* | Glasgow Mar 13: 5-4 *Ker 3, Baird, Kay* | Glasgow Mar 27: 5-1 *Davidson, Beveridge, Lindsay, McAdam, Campbell* | London Mar 12: 6-1 *Smith 3, Ker 2, McGuire* |

| 1881 Wales | 1882 England | 1882 Wales | 1883 England | 1883 Wales |
|---|---|---|---|---|
| 1 Gillespie | 1 Gillespie | 1 Rowan | 1 McAulay (Dumbarton) | 1 McAulay (Dumbarton) |
| 2 Vallance | 2 Watson | 2 Holm | 2 Holm | 2 Arnott |
| 3 Watson | 3 McIntyre | 3 Duncan | 3 Paton | 3 Holm |
| 4 McPherson | 4 Campbell C. | 4 Kennedy | 4 Miller | 4 Miller |
| 5 Davidson | 5 Miller | 5 Campbell C. | 5 McPherson | 5 McPherson |
| 6 Smith J. | 6 Fraser | 6 Fraser | 6 Fraser | 6 Smith Dr J. |
| 7 McNeil H. | 7 Anderson | 7 Hill | 7 Anderson | 7 Inglis |
| 8 Lindsay | 8 Ker | 8 Ker | 8 Smith Dr J. | 8 Mackinnon W. |
| 9 McGuire | 9 Harrower | 9 McAulay (Dumbarton) | 9 Inglis | 9 Anderson |
| 10 Ker | 10 Kay | 10 Kay | 10 Kay | 10 Kay |
| 11 Hill | 11 McPherson | 11 Richmond | 11 Mackinnon W. | 11 Fraser |
| Wrexham Mar 14: 5-1 *Smith 2, Ker 2, Lindsay* | Glasgow Mar 11: 5-1 *Harrower, Ker 2, Kay, McPherson* | Glasgow Mar 25: 5-0 *Kay, Ker, Fraser 2, McAulay* | Sheffield Mar 10: 3-2 *Smith 2, Fraser* | Wrexham Mar 12, 3-0 *Smith, Fraser, Anderson* |

| 1884 Ireland | 1884 England | 1884 Wales | 1885 Ireland | 1885 England |
|---|---|---|---|---|
| 1 Inglis | 1 McAulay (Dumbarton) | 1 Turner | 1 Chalmers | 1 McAulay (Dumbarton) |
| 2 Forbes | 2 Arnott | 2 Forbes | 2 Niven | 2 Arnott |
| 3 Arnott | 3 Forbes | 3 Paton | 3 McHardy | 3 Paton |
| 4 Graham | 4 Campbell C. | 4 Kennedy | 4 McPherson | 4 Campbell C. |
| 5 Fulton | 5 McPherson | 5 McIntyre | 5 Kelso | 5 Gow |
| 6 Brown R. | 6 Shaw | 6 Kay | 6 Turner | 6 Anderson |
| 7 Thomson | 7 Anderson | 7 Lindsay | 7 Lamont | 7 Hamilton |
| 8 Gossland | 8 Lindsay | 8 Shaw | 8 Barbour | 8 Sellar |
| 9 Goudie | 9 Smith Dr J. | 9 Mackinnon W. | 9 Calderwood | 9 Lindsay |
| 10 Harrower | 10 Christie | 10 Thomson | 10 Marshall | 10 Allan |
| 11 McAulay (Arthurlie) | 11 Mackinnon W. | 11 Brown R. | 11 Higgins | 11 Calderwood |
| Belfast Jan 26: 5-0 *Goudie, Harrower 2, Gossland 2* | Glasgow Mar 15: 1-0 *Smith* | Glasgow Mar 29: 4-1 *Kay 2, Lindsay, Shaw* | Glasgow Mar 14: 8-2 *Higgins 4, Kelso, Barbour, McPherson, Calderwood* | London Mar 21: 1-1 *Lindsay* |

| 1885 Wales | 1886 Ireland | 1886 England | 1886 Wales | 1887 Ireland |
|---|---|---|---|---|
| 1 McAulay (Dumbarton) | 1 Connor | 1 McAulay (Dumbarton) | 1 Gillespie | 1 Doig |
| 2 Arnott | 2 McLeod | 2 Arnott | 2 Lundie | 2 Whitelaw |
| 3 Paton | 3 Thomson | 3 Paton | 3 Semple | 3 Smellie |
| 4 Kelso | 4 Keir | 4 Campbell C. | 4 Kelso | 4 Weir |
| 5 Keir | 5 Cameron | 5 McDonald | 5 McCall | 5 McMillan |
| 6 Hamilton | 6 Turner | 6 Sellar | 6 Jackson | 6 Hutton |
| 7 Anderson | 7 Heggie | 7 Hamilton | 7 McCormack | 7 Jenkinson |
| 8 Lindsay | 8 Dunbar | 8 Somerville | 8 Marshall | 8 Lambie |
| 9 Calderwood | 9 Fleming | 9 Lindsay | 9 Harrower | 9 Watt |
| 10 Brown R. jun | 10 Lambie J. | 10 Gray | 10 McGhee | 10 Lowe |
| 11 Allan | 11 Gourlay | 11 Aitken | 11 Allan | 11 Johnstone |
| Wrexham Mar 23: 8-1 *Anderson 3, Lindsay 2, Allan 2, Calderwood* | Belfast Mar 20: 7-2 *Heggie 5, Dunbar, Gourlay* | Glasgow Mar 31: 1-1 *Somerville* | Glasgow April 10: 4-1 *Harrower 2, Allan 2* | Glasgow Feb 19: 4-1 *Watt, Jenkinson, Johnstone, Lowe* |

| 1887 England | 1887 Wales | 1888 Wales | 1888 England | 1888 Ireland |
|---|---|---|---|---|
| 1 McAulay (*Dumbarton*) | 1 McAulay (*Dumbarton*) | 1 Wilson | 1 Lindsay | 1 McLeod |
| 2 Arnott | 2 Arnott | 2 Hannah | 2 Arnott | 2 Jackson |
| 3 Forbes | 3 Forbes | 3 Smellie | 3 Gow | 3 Stewart D. |
| 4 Kelso | 4 Keir | 4 Gourlay | 4 Kelso | 4 Stewart A. |
| 5 Auld | 5 Auld | 5 Johnston J. | 5 Kelly | 5 Dewar |
| 6 Keir | 6 Kelso | 6 McLaren | 6 Keir | 6 Kelso |
| 7 Marshall | 7 Robertson | 7 Latta | 7 Hamilton | 7 Gow |
| 8 Robertson | 8 McCall | 8 McPherson | 8 Berry | 8 Brackenridge |
| 9 Sellar | 9 Allan | 9 Groves | 9 Sellar | 9 Dickson |
| 10 Allan | 10 Marshall | 10 Paul | 10 McCall | 10 Aitken |
| 11 McCall | 11 Sellar | 11 Munro | 11 Lambie | 11 McCallum |

| Blackburn Mar 19: 3-2 *McCall, Allan 2* | Wrexham Mar 21: 2-0 *Robertson, Marshall* | Edinburgh Mar 10: 5-1 *Paul 2, McPherson 2, Groves* | Glasgow Mar 17: 0-5 | Belfast Mar 24: 10-2 *Dewar, Dickson, Aitken, McCallum, Brackenridge, Wilson og and 4 others* |

| 1889 Ireland | 1889 England | 1889 Wales | 1890 Wales | 1890 Ireland |
|---|---|---|---|---|
| 1 Doig | 1 Wilson | 1 McLeod | 1 Gillespie | 1 McLeod |
| 2 Adams | 2 Arnott | 2 Thomson | 2 Whitelaw | 2 Hunter |
| 3 McKeown | 3 Smellie | 3 Rae | 3 Murray | 3 Rae |
| 4 Robertson | 4 Kelly | 4 Stewart | 4 McQueen | 4 Russell |
| 5 Calderhead | 5 Dewar | 5 Auld | 5 Brown A. | 5 Begbie |
| 6 Buchanan | 6 McLaren | 6 Lochead | 6 Wilson | 6 Mitchell |
| 7 Watt | 7 Latta | 7 Watt | 7 Watt | 7 Wylie |
| 8 McInnes | 8 Berry | 8 Campbell H. | 8 Brown J. | 8 Rankin |
| 9 Groves | 9 Oswald | 9 Paul | 9 Paul | 9 McPherson |
| 10 Boyd | 10 McPherson | 10 Johnstone | 10 Dunlop | 10 Bell |
| 11 Black | 11 Munro | 11 Hannah | 11 Bruce | 11 Baird |

| Glasgow Mar 9: 7-0 *Watt, McInnes 2, Black, Groves 3* | London April 13: 3-2 *McLaren, Oswald, Munro* | Wrexham April 15: 0-0 | Glasgow Mar 22: 5-0 *Paul 4, Wilson* | Belfast Mar 29: 4-1 *Wylie, Rankin 2, McPherson* |

| 1890 England | 1891 Wales | 1891 Ireland | 1891 England | 1892 Ireland |
|---|---|---|---|---|
| 1 Wilson | 1 McCorkindale | 1 Gillespie | 1 Wilson | 1 Baird |
| 2 Arnott | 2 Ritchie | 2 Sillars | 2 Arnott | 2 Bowman |
| 3 McKeown | 3 Hepburn | 3 Paul | 3 Smellie | 3 Drummond |
| 4 Robertson | 4 McQueen | 4 Hamilton | 4 Begbie | 4 Marshall |
| 5 Kelly | 5 Brown A. | 5 Cleland | 5 McPherson | 5 Robertson |
| 6 McLaren | 6 Robertson | 6 Campbell (*Kilm'k*) | 6 Hill | 6 Dowds |
| 7 Groves | 7 Gulliland | 7 Lowe | 7 Rankin | 7 Gulliland |
| 8 Berry | 8 Buchanan | 8 Bowie | 8 Watt | 8 McPherson |
| 9 Johnstone W. | 9 Boyd | 9 Fraser | 9 Sellar | 9 Ellis |
| 10 McPherson | 10 Logan | 10 Clements | 10 Berry | 10 Keillor |
| 11 McCall | 11 Keillor | 11 Waddell | 11 Baird | 11 Lambie |

| Glasgow April 5: 1-1 *McPherson* | Wrexham Mar 21: 4-3 *Logan, Buchanan, Boyd 2* | Glasgow Mar 28: 2-1 *Waddell, Lowe* | Blackburn April 6: 1-2 *Watt* | Belfast Mar 19: 3-2 *Keillor, Lambie, Ellis* |

| 1892 Wales | 1892 England | 1893 Wales | 1893 Ireland | 1893 England |
|---|---|---|---|---|
| 1 Downie | 1 McLeod | 1 McLeod | 1 Lindsay | 1 Lindsay |
| 2 Adams | 2 Doyle | 2 Doyle | 2 Adams | 2 Arnott |
| 3 Orr | 3 Arnott | 3 Foyers | 3 Smellie | 3 Smellie |
| 4 Begbie | 4 Kelly | 4 Sillars | 4 Maley | 4 Maley |
| 5 Campbell (*Kilm'k*) | 5 Sillars | 5 McCreadie | 5 Kelly | 5 Kelly |
| 6 Hill | 6 Mitchell | 6 Stewart | 6 Mitchell | 6 Mitchell |
| 7 Taylor | 7 Sellar | 7 Taylor | 7 Waddell | 7 Sellar |
| 8 Thomson | 8 Taylor | 8 Thomson | 8 Campbell (*Celtic*) | 8 Waddell |
| 9 Hamilton | 9 Waddell | 9 Madden | 9 Hamilton | 9 Hamilton |
| 10 McPherson | 10 McMahon | 10 Lambie | 10 Sellar | 10 McMahon |
| 11 Baird | 11 Bell | 11 Barker | 11 McMahon | 11 Campbell (*Celtic*) |

Edinburgh
Mar 26: 6-1
*Thomson, Hamilton 2, McPherson, Baird 2*

Glasgow
April 2: 1-4
*Bell*

Wrexham
Mar 18: 8-0
*Madden 4, Barker 3, Lambie*

Glasgow
Mar 25: 6-1
*Sellar 2, Kelly, McMahon, Hamilton, 1 og*

Richmond
April 1: 2-5
*Sellar 2*

| 1894 Wales | 1894 Ireland | 1894 England | 1895 Wales | 1895 Ireland |
|---|---|---|---|---|
| 1 Baird | 1 Barrett | 1 Haddow | 1 Barrett | 1 McArthur |
| 2 Crawford | 2 Crawford | 2 Sillars | 2 Sillars | 2 Doyle |
| 3 Foyers | 3 Drummond | 3 Doyle | 3 Glen | 3 Drummond |
| 4 Johnstone | 4 Marshall | 4 Begbie | 4 Simpson | 4 Simpson |
| 5 Kelly | 5 Stewart | 5 McCreadie | 5 McColl | 5 Russell |
| 6 McBain | 6 Longair | 6 Mitchell | 6 Keillor | 6 Gibson |
| 7 Chalmers | 7 Taylor | 7 Gulliland | 7 Fyfe | 7 Taylor |
| 8 Stewart | 8 Blessington | 8 Blessington | 8 Murray | 8 Waddell |
| 9 Alexander | 9 Alexander | 9 McMahon | 9 Madden | 9 McPherson |
| 10 Berry | 10 Scott | 10 McPherson | 10 Sawers | 10 Walker J. |
| 11 Barker | 11 Keillor | 11 Lambie | 11 Divers | 11 Lambie |

Kilmarnock
Mar 24: 5-2
*Berry, Barker, Chalmers, Alexander, Johnstone*

Belfast
Mar 31: 2-1
*Taylor, Torrans og*

Glasgow
April 7: 2-2
*Lambie, McMahon*

Wrexham
Mar 23: 2-2
*Madden, Divers*

Glasgow
Mar 30: 3-1
*Lambie, Walker 2*

| 1895 England | 1896 Wales | 1896 Ireland | 1896 England | 1897 Wales |
|---|---|---|---|---|
| 1 McArthur | 1 McFarlane | 1 Anderson | 1 Doig | 1 Patrick |
| 2 Drummond | 2 McLean | 2 Meechan | 2 Brandon | 2 Ritchie |
| 3 Doyle | 3 Glen | 3 Drummond | 3 Drummond | 3 Gardner |
| 4 Russell | 4 Gillespie | 4 Gibson | 4 Gibson | 4 Breslin |
| 5 Simpson | 5 Neil | 5 Kelly | 5 Cowan | 5 Russell |
| 6 Gibson | 6 Blair | 6 Hogg | 6 Hogg | 6 Keillor |
| 7 Lambie | 7 Thomson | 7 Murray | 7 Bell | 7 Kennedy |
| 8 McPherson | 8 Paton | 8 Blessington | 8 Blessington | 8 Murray |
| 9 Oswald | 9 McColl | 9 McColl | 9 Hyslop | 9 Oswald |
| 10 Waddell | 10 King | 10 Cameron | 10 King | 10 McMillan |
| 11 Gulliland | 11 Keillor | 11 Lambie | 11 Lambie | 11 Walker J. |

Liverpool
April 6: 0-3

Dundee
Mar 21: 4-0
*Neil 2, Keillor 2*

Belfast
Mar 28: 3-3
*McColl 2, Drummond*

Glasgow
April 4: 2-1
*Lambie, Bell*

Wrexham
Mar 20: 2-2
*Ritchie (pen), Jones og*

| 1897 Ireland | 1897 England | 1898 Wales | 1898 Ireland | 1898 England |
|---|---|---|---|---|
| 1 Dickie | 1 Patrick | 1 Watson | 1 Anderson | 1 Anderson |
| 2 McLean | 2 Smith N. | 2 Smith N. | 2 Kelso | 2 Drummond |
| 3 Drummond | 3 Doyle | 3 Scott | 3 Doyle | 3 Doyle |
| 4 Gibson | 4 Gibson | 4 Thomson | 4 Thomson | 4 Gibson |
| 5 Stewart | 5 Cowan | 5 Christie | 5 Russell | 5 Cowan |
| 6 Baird | 6 Wilson | 6 Campbell P. | 6 King | 6 Robertson |
| 7 Low | 7 Bell | 7 Gillespie | 7 Stewart | 7 Bell |
| 8 King | 8 Miller | 8 Miller | 8 Campbell (*Celtic*) | 8 Campbell (*Celtic*) |
| 9 McColl | 9 Allan | 9 McKie | 9 McColl | 9 Maxwell |
| 10 McPherson | 10 Hyslop | 10 Morgan | 10 Walker J. | 10 Miller |
| 11 Lambie | 11 Lambie | 11 Findlay | 11 Robertson | 11 Smith A. |

| Glasgow Mar 27: 5-1 *McPherson 2, Gibson, McColl, King* | London April 3: 2-1 *Hyslop, Miller* | Motherwell Mar 19: 5-2 *Gillespie 3, McKie 2* | Belfast Mar 26: 3-0 *Robertson, McColl, Stewart* | Glasgow April 2: 1-3 *Miller* |
|---|---|---|---|---|

| 1899 Wales | 1899 Ireland | 1899 England | 1900 Wales | 1900 Ireland |
|---|---|---|---|---|
| 1 McArthur | 1 Dickie | 1 Doig | 1 Dickie | 1 Rennie |
| 2 Smith N. | 2 Smith N. | 2 Smith N. | 2 Smith N. | 2 Smith N. |
| 3 Storrier | 3 Storrier | 3 Storrier | 3 Crawford | 3 Glen |
| 4 Gibson | 4 Gibson | 4 Gibson | 4 Irons | 4 Marshall |
| 5 Marshall | 5 Christie | 5 Christie | 5 Neil | 5 Orr |
| 6 King | 6 King | 6 Robertson | 6 Robertson | 6 Gibson |
| 7 Campbell (*Rangers*) | 7 Campbell (*Rangers*) | 7 Campbell (*Rangers*) | 7 Bell | 7 Stewart |
| 8 Hamilton | 8 Hamilton | 8 Hamilton | 8 Wilson | 8 Walker R. |
| 9 McColl | 9 McColl | 9 McColl | 9 McColl | 9 Campbell (*Celtic*) |
| 10 Bell | 10 Bell | 10 Morgan | 10 Hamilton | 10 Callaghan |
| 11 Berry | 11 Berry | 11 Bell | 11 Smith A. | 11 Smith A. |

| Wrexham Mar 18: 6-0 *Campbell 2, McColl 3, Marshall* | Glasgow Mar 25: 9-1 *McColl 3, Hamilton 2, Campbell 2, Bell, Christie* | Birmingham April 8: 1-2 *Hamilton* | Aberdeen Feb 3: 5-2 *Bell, Wilson 2, Hamilton, Smith A.* | Belfast Mar 3: 3-0 *Campbell 2, Smith A.* |
|---|---|---|---|---|

| 1900 England | 1901 Ireland | 1901 Wales | 1901 England | 1902 Ireland |
|---|---|---|---|---|
| 1 Rennie | 1 McWhattie | 1 McWhattie | 1 Rennie | 1 Rennie |
| 2 Smith N. | 2 Smith N. | 2 Smith N. | 2 Battles | 2 Smith N. |
| 3 Drummond | 3 Battles | 3 Battles | 3 Drummond | 3 Drummond |
| 4 Gibson | 4 Russell | 4 Gibson | 4 Aitken | 4 Key |
| 5 Raisbeck | 5 Anderson | 5 Russell | 5 Raisbeck | 5 Buick |
| 6 Robertson | 6 Robertson | 6 Robertson | 6 Robertson | 6 Robertson |
| 7 Walker R. | 7 Campbell (*Rangers*) | 7 Bell | 7 Walker R. | 7 McCartney |
| 8 Campbell (*Celtic*) | 8 Campbell (*Celtic*) | 8 Walker R. | 8 Campbell (*Celtic*) | 8 Walker R. |
| 9 McColl | 9 Hamilton | 9 McColl | 9 McColl | 9 Hamilton |
| 10 Bell | 10 McMahon | 10 Campbell (*Celtic*) | 10 Hamilton | 10 Campbell (*Celtic*) |
| 11 Smith A. | 11 Smith A. | 11 Smith A. | 11 Smith A. | 11 Smith A. |

| Glasgow April 7: 4-1 *McColl 3, Bell* | Glasgow Feb 23: 11-0 *Campbell (Celtic) 2, McMahon 4, Hamilton 4, Russell* | Wrexham Mar 2: 1-1 *Robertson* | London Mar 30: 2-2 *Campbell, Hamilton* | Belfast Mar 1: 5-1 *Hamilton 3, Buick, Walker* |
|---|---|---|---|---|

| 1902 Wales | 1902 England | 1903 Wales | 1903 Ireland | 1903 England |
|---|---|---|---|---|
| 1 Rennie | 1 Rennie | 1 Rennie | 1 Rennie | 1 Doig |
| 2 Allan | 2 Smith N. | 2 McCombie | 2 Gray | 2 McCombie |
| 3 Drummond | 3 Drummond | 3 Watson | 3 Drummond | 3 Watson |
| 4 Wilson | 4 Aitken | 4 Aitken | 4 Cross | 4 Aitken |
| 5 Buick | 5 Raisbeck | 5 Raisbeck | 5 Robertson | 5 Raisbeck |
| 6 Robertson | 6 Robertson | 6 Robertson | 6 Orr | 6 Robertson |
| 7 Campbell (*Celtic*) | 7 Templeton | 7 Templeton | 7 Lindsay | 7 Templeton |
| 8 Walker R. | 8 Walker R. | 8 Walker R. | 8 Walker R. | 8 Walker R. |
| 9 Hamilton | 9 McColl | 9 Campbell (*Celtic*) | 9 Porteous | 9 Hamilton |
| 10 McMahon | 10 Orr | 10 Speedie | 10 Speedie | 10 Speedie |
| 11 Smith A. | 11 Smith A. | 11 Smith A. | 11 Smith A. | 11 Smith A. |

| Greenock | Birmingham | Cardiff | Glasgow | Sheffield |
|---|---|---|---|---|
| Mar 15: 5-1 | May 3: 2-2 | Mar 9: 1-0 | Mar 21: 0-2 | April 4: 2-1 |
| *Smith 3, Buick,* | *Templeton, Orr* | *Speedie* | | *Speedie, Walker* |
| *Drummond* | | | | |

| 1904 Wales | 1904 Ireland | 1904 England | 1905 Wales | 1905 Ireland |
|---|---|---|---|---|
| 1 Skene | 1 Rennie | 1 McBride | 1 Rennie | 1 Howden |
| 2 Jackson | 2 Jackson | 2 Jackson | 2 McCombie | 2 McLeod |
| 3 Sharp | 3 Cameron | 3 Watson | 3 Jackson | 3 McIntosh |
| 4 Orr | 4 Henderson | 4 Aitken | 4 Aitken | 4 Gibson |
| 5 Sloan | 5 Thomson | 5 Raisbeck | 5 Thomson | 5 Thomson |
| 6 Robertson | 6 Robertson | 6 Robertson | 6 Robertson | 6 Hay |
| 7 Walker J. | 7 Walker J. | 7 Niblo | 7 Templeton | 7 McMenemy |
| 8 Walker R. | 8 Walker R. | 8 Walker R. | 8 Walker R. | 8 Walker R. |
| 9 Bennett | 9 Hamilton | 9 Brown A. | 9 Kennedy | 9 Quinn |
| 10 McFarlane | 10 Wilson | 10 Orr | 10 Fitchie | 10 Somers |
| 11 Wilson | 11 Smith A. | 11 Templeton | 11 Smith A. | 11 Wilson |

| Dundee | Dublin | Glasgow | Wrexham | Glasgow |
|---|---|---|---|---|
| Mar 12: 1-1 | Mar 26: 1-1 | April 9: 0-1 | Mar 6: 1-3 | Mar 18: 4-0 |
| *Walker R.* | *Hamilton* | | *Robertson* | *Thomas 2 (2 pens),* |
| | | | | *Walker, Quinn* |

| 1905 England | 1906 Wales | 1906 Ireland | 1906 England | 1907 Wales |
|---|---|---|---|---|
| 1 Lyall | 1 Raeside | 1 Rennie | 1 McBride | 1 McBride |
| 2 McCombie | 2 McLeod | 2 McLeod | 2 McLeod | 2 Jackson |
| 3 Watson | 3 Richmond | 3 Hill | 3 Dunlop | 3 Sharp |
| 4 Aitken | 4 McNair | 4 Young | 4 Aitken | 4 Aitken |
| 5 Thomson | 5 Thomson | 5 Thomson | 5 Raisbeck | 5 Thomson |
| 6 McWilliam | 6 Hay | 6 Hay | 6 McWilliam | 6 McWilliam |
| 7 Walker R. | 7 Stewart | 7 Hamilton | 7 Stewart | 7 Stewart |
| 8 Howie | 8 McFarlane | 8 Walker R. | 8 Howie | 8 Livingstone |
| 9 Young | 9 Quinn | 9 Quinn | 9 Menzies | 9 Young |
| 10 Somers | 10 Fitchie | 10 Fitchie | 10 Livingstone | 10 Fitchie |
| 11 Wilson | 11 Wilson | 11 Smith A. | 11 Smith A. | 11 Smith A. |

| London | Edinburgh | Dublin | Glasgow | Wrexham |
|---|---|---|---|---|
| April 1: 0-1 | Mar 3: 0-2 | Mar 17: 1-0 | April 7: 2-1 | Mar 4: 0-1 |
| | | *Fitchie* | *Howie 2* | |

| 1907 Ireland | 1907 England | 1908 Wales | 1908 Ireland | 1908 England |
|---|---|---|---|---|
| 1 Muir | 1 McBride | 1 Rennie | 1 Rennie | 1 McBride |
| 2 Jackson | 2 Thomson | 2 Agnew | 2 Mitchell | 2 McNair |
| 3 Agnew | 3 Sharp | 3 Chaplin | 3 Agnew | 3 Sharp |
| 4 Key | 4 Aitken | 4 McNair | 4 May | 4 Aitken |
| 5 Thomson | 5 Raisbeck | 5 Thomson | 5 Thomson | 5 Thomson |
| 6 McNair | 6 McWilliam | 6 Galt | 6 Galt | 6 May |
| 7 Bennett | 7 Stewart | 7 Bennett | 7 Templeton | 7 Howie |
| 8 Walker R. | 8 Walker R. | 8 Walker R. | 8 Walker R. | 8 Walker R. |
| 9 O'Rourke | 9 Wilson A. | 9 Spiers | 9 Quinn | 9 Wilson A. |
| 10 Somers | 10 White | 10 McFarlane | 10 McColl | 10 White |
| 11 Fraser | 11 Wilson G. | 11 Lennie | 11 Lennie | 11 Quinn |

| Glasgow | Newcastle | Dundee | Dublin | Glasgow |
|---|---|---|---|---|
| Mar 16: 3-0 | April 6: 1-1 | Mar 7: 2-1 | Mar 14: 5-0 | April 4: 1-1 |
| *O'Rourke, Walker, Thomson* (pen) | *Crompton og* | *Bennett, Lennie* | *Quinn 4, Galt* | *Wilson* |

| 1909 Wales | 1909 Ireland | 1909 England | 1910 Wales | 1910 Ireland |
|---|---|---|---|---|
| 1 McBride | 1 Brownlie | 1 Brownlie | 1 Brownlie | 1 Brownlie |
| 2 Collins | 2 Main | 2 Cameron | 2 Law | 2 Law |
| 3 Sharp | 3 Watson | 3 Watson | 3 Mitchell | 3 Mitchell |
| 4 May | 4 Walker W. | 4 McNair | 4 McNair | 4 Walker W. |
| 5 Thomson | 5 Stark | 5 Stark | 5 Loney | 5 Loney |
| 6 McWilliam | 6 Hay | 6 McWilliam | 6 Hay | 6 Hay |
| 7 Bennett | 7 Bennett | 7 Bennett | 7 Bennett | 7 Sinclair |
| 8 Hunter | 8 McMenemy | 8 Walker R. | 8 McMenemy | 8 McTavish |
| 9 Walker R. | 9 Thomson | 9 Quinn | 9 Quinn | 9 Quinn |
| 10 Somers | 10 McFarlane | 10 Wilson G. | 10 Devine | 10 Higgins |
| 11 Paul | 11 Paul | 11 Paul | 11 Robertson | 11 Templeton |

| Wrexham | Glasgow | London | Kilmarnock | Belfast |
|---|---|---|---|---|
| Mar 1: 2-3 | Mar 15: 5-0 | April 3: 0-2 | Mar 5: 1-0 | Mar 19: 0-1 |
| *Walker, Paul* | *McMenemy 2, McFarlane, Thomson, Paul* | | *Devine* | |

| 1910 England | 1911 Wales | 1911 Ireland | 1911 England | 1912 Wales |
|---|---|---|---|---|
| 1 Brownlie | 1 Brownlie | 1 Brownlie | 1 Lawrence | 1 Brownlie |
| 2 Law | 2 Colman | 2 Colman | 2 Colman | 2 McNair |
| 3 Hay | 3 Walker J. | 3 Walker J. | 3 Walker J. | 3 Walker J. |
| 4 Aitken | 4 Tait | 4 Aitken | 4 Aitken | 4 Mercer |
| 5 Thomson | 5 Low | 5 Thomson | 5 Low | 5 Thomson |
| 6 McWilliam | 6 McWilliam | 6 Hay | 6 Hay | 6 Hay |
| 7 Bennett | 7 Bennett | 7 Douglas | 7 Bennett | 7 Sinclair |
| 8 McMenemy | 8 McMenemy | 8 McMenemy | 8 McMenemy | 8 McMenemy |
| 9 Quinn | 9 Reid | 9 Reid | 9 Reid | 9 Quinn |
| 10 Higgins | 10 McFarlane | 10 Higgins | 10 Higgins | 10 Walker R. |
| 11 Templeton | 11 Hamilton | 11 Smith A. | 11 Smith A. | 11 Robertson |

| Glasgow | Cardiff | Glasgow | Liverpool | Edinburgh |
|---|---|---|---|---|
| April 2: 2-0 | Mar 6: 2-2 | Mar 18: 2-0 | April 1: 1-1 | Mar 2: 1-0 |
| *McMenemy, Quinn* | *Hamilton 2* | *Reid, McMenemy* | *Higgins* | *Quinn* |

| 1912 Ireland | 1912 England | 1913 Wales | 1913 Ireland | 1913 England |
|---|---|---|---|---|
| 1 Brownlie | 1 Brownlie | 1 Brownlie | 1 Brownlie | 1 Brownlie |
| 2 McNair | 2 McNair | 2 Orrock | 2 Colman | 2 McNair |
| 3 Walker J. | 3 Walker J. | 3 Walker J. | 3 Walker J. | 3 Walker J. |
| 4 Gordon | 4 Gordon | 4 Gordon | 4 Mercer | 4 Gordon |
| 5 Low | 5 Thomson | 5 Thomson | 5 Logan | 5 Thomson |
| 6 Bell | 6 Hay | 6 Campbell | 6 Nellies | 6 Wilson D. |
| 7 Sinclair | 7 Templeton | 7 McAtee | 7 Bennett | 7 Donnachie |
| 8 Walker R. | 8 Walker R. | 8 Walker R. | 8 Gordon | 8 Walker R. |
| 9 Reid | 9 McLean | 9 Reid | 9 Reid | 9 Reid |
| 10 Aitkenhead | 10 Wilson A. | 10 Wilson A. | 10 Croal | 10 Wilson A. |
| 11 Templeton | 11 Quinn | 11 Templeton | 11 Robertson | 11 Robertson |

| Belfast | Glasgow | Wrexham | Dublin | Stamford Bridge |
|---|---|---|---|---|
| Mar 16: 4-1 | Mar 23: 1-1 | Mar 3: 0-0 | Mar 15: 2-1 | April 5: 0-1 |
| *Aitkenhead 2,* | *Wilson* | | *Reid, Bennett* | |
| *Reid, Walker R.* | | | | |

| 1914 Wales | 1914 Ireland | 1914 England | 1920 Wales | 1920 Ireland |
|---|---|---|---|---|
| 1 Brownlie | 1 Brownlie | 1 Brownlie | 1 Campbell | 1 Campbell |
| 2 Kelso | 2 Dodds | 2 McNair | 2 McNair | 2 McNair |
| 3 Dodds | 3 McNair | 3 Dodds | 3 Thomson | 3 Blair |
| 4 Nellies | 4 Gordon | 4 Gordon | 4 Gordon | 4 Bowie |
| 5 Pursell | 5 Thomson | 5 Thomson | 5 Cringen | 5 Low |
| 6 Anderson | 6 Hay | 6 Hay | 6 McMullan | 6 Gordon |
| 7 Donaldson | 7 Donaldson | 7 Donaldson | 7 Reid | 7 Donaldson |
| 8 McMenemy | 8 McMenemy | 8 McMenemy | 8 Crosby | 8 McMenemy |
| 9 Reid | 9 Reid | 9 Reid | 9 Wilson A.N. | 9 Wilson A.N. |
| 10 Croal | 10 Wilson A. | 10 Croal | 10 Cairns | 10 Cunningham |
| 11 Browning | 11 Donnachie | 11 Donnachie | 11 Morton | 11 Morton |

| Glasgow | Belfast | Glasgow | Cardiff | Glasgow |
|---|---|---|---|---|
| Feb 28: 0-0 | Mar 14: 1-1 | April 4: 3-1 | Feb 26: 1-1 | Mar 13: 3-0 |
| | *Donnachie* | *Thomson,* | *Cairns* | *Wilson, Morton,* |
| | | *McMenemy, Reid* | | *Cunningham* |

| 1920 England | 1921 Wales | 1921 Ireland | 1921 England | 1922 Wales |
|---|---|---|---|---|
| 1 Campbell | 1 Campbell | 1 Campbell | 1 Ewart | 1 Campbell |
| 2 McNair | 2 Marshall | 2 Marshall | 2 Marshall | 2 Marshall |
| 3 Blair | 3 McStay | 3 McStay | 3 Blair | 3 McKinlay |
| 4 Bowie | 4 Harris | 4 Harris | 4 Davidson | 4 Meiklejohn |
| 5 Low | 5 Pringle | 5 Graham | 5 Brewster | 5 Gilhooley |
| 6 Gordon | 6 McMullan | 6 McMullan | 6 McMullan | 6 Collier |
| 7 Donaldson | 7 Archibald | 7 McNab | 7 McNab | 7 Archibald |
| 8 Miller | 8 Cunningham | 8 Miller | 8 Miller | 8 White |
| 9 Wilson A.N. | 9 Wilson A.N. | 9 Wilson A.N. | 9 Wilson A.N. | 9 Wilson A.N. |
| 10 Paterson | 10 Cassidy | 10 Cassidy | 10 Cunningham | 10 Walker F. |
| 11 Troup | 11 Troup | 11 Troup | 11 Morton | 11 Morton |

| Sheffield | Aberdeen | Belfast | Glasgow | Wrexham |
|---|---|---|---|---|
| April 10: 4-5 | Feb 12: 2-1 | Feb 26: 2-0 | April 9: 3-0 | Feb 4: 1-2 |
| *Miller 2, Wilson,* | *Wilson 2* | *Wilson (pen),* | *Wilson, Morton,* | *Archibald* |
| *Donaldson* | | *Cassidy* | *Cunningham* | |

| 1922 Ireland | 1922 England | 1923 Ireland | 1923 Wales | 1923 England |
|---|---|---|---|---|
| 1 Campbell | 1 Campbell | 1 Harper | 1 Harper | 1 Harper |
| 2 Marshall | 2 Hutton | 2 Hutton | 2 Hutton | 2 Hutton |
| 3 McKinlay | 3 Blair | 3 Blair | 3 Blair | 3 Blair |
| 4 Hogg | 4 Gilchrist | 4 Steele | 4 McNab | 4 Steele |
| 5 Cringan | 5 Cringan | 5 Morris | 5 Cringan | 5 Cringan |
| 6 Muirhead | 6 McBain | 6 McBain | 6 Steele | 6 Muirhead |
| 7 Donaldson | 7 Archibald | 7 Archibald | 7 Ritchie | 7 Lawson |
| 8 Kinloch | 8 Crosbie | 8 White | 8 Cunningham | 8 Cunningham |
| 9 Wilson A.N. | 9 Wilson A.N. | 9 Wilson A.N. | 9 Wilson A.N. | 9 Wilson A.N. |
| 10 Cunningham | 10 Cairns | 10 Cassidy | 10 Cairns | 10 Cairns |
| 11 Troup | 11 Morton | 11 Morton | 11 Morton | 11 Morton |

| Glasgow Mar 4: 2-1 *Wilson 2* | Birmingham April 8: 1-0 *Wilson* | Belfast Mar 3: 1-0 *Wilson* | Glasgow Mar 17: 2-0 *Wilson 2* | Glasgow April 14: 2-2 *Cunningham, Wilson* |

| 1924 Wales | 1924 Ireland | 1924 England | 1925 Wales | 1925 Ireland |
|---|---|---|---|---|
| 1 Harper | 1 Harper | 1 Harper | 1 Harper | 1 Harper |
| 2 Marshall | 2 Hutton | 2 Smith J. | 2 Nelson | 2 Nelson |
| 3 Blair | 3 Hamilton | 3 McCloy | 3 McStay | 3 McStay |
| 4 Meiklejohn | 4 Kerr | 4 Clunas | 4 Meiklejohn | 4 Meiklejohn |
| 5 McBain | 5 Morris | 5 Morris | 5 Morris | 5 Morris |
| 6 Muirhead | 6 McMullan | 6 McMullan | 6 Bennie | 6 Bennie |
| 7 Archibald | 7 Reid | 7 Archibald | 7 Jackson | 7 Jackson |
| 8 Russell | 8 Cunningham | 8 Cowan | 8 Dunn | 8 Dunn |
| 9 Cassidy | 9 Gallacher | 9 Harris | 9 Gallacher | 9 Gallacher |
| 10 McKay | 10 Cairns | 10 Cunningham | 10 Cairns | 10 Cairns |
| 11 Morton | 11 Morton | 11 Morton | 11 Morton | 11 Morton |

| Cardiff Feb 16: 0-2 | Glasgow Mar 1: 2-0 *Cunningham, Morris* | Wembley April 12: 1-1 *Taylor og* | Edinburgh Feb 14: 3-1 *Meiklejohn, Gallacher 2* | Belfast Feb 28: 3-0 *Meiklejohn, Gallacher, Dunn* |

| 1925 England | 1925 Wales | 1926 Ireland | 1926 England | 1926 Wales |
|---|---|---|---|---|
| 1 Harper | 1 Robb | 1 Harper | 1 Harper | 1 McClory |
| 2 McStay | 2 Hutton | 2 Hutton | 2 Hutton | 2 McStay |
| 3 McCloy | 3 McStay | 3 McStay | 3 McStay | 3 Wiseman |
| 4 Meiklejohn | 4 Clunas | 4 Wilson | 4 Gibson | 4 Gibson |
| 5 Morris | 5 Townsley | 5 McDougall | 5 Summers | 5 Gillespie |
| 6 McMullan | 6 McMullan | 6 Bennie | 6 McMullan | 6 McMullan |
| 7 Jackson | 7 Jackson | 7 Jackson | 7 Jackson | 7 Jackson |
| 8 Russell | 8 Duncan | 8 Cunningham | 8 Thomson | 8 Cunningham |
| 9 Gallacher | 9 Gallacher | 9 Gallacher | 9 Gallacher | 9 Gallacher |
| 10 Cairns | 10 James | 10 McInally | 10 Cunningham | 10 McInally |
| 11 Morton | 11 McLean | 11 McLean | 11 Troup | 11 McLean |

| Glasgow April 4: 2-0 *Gallacher 2* | Cardiff Oct 31: 3-0 *Duncan, McLean, Clunas* | Glasgow Feb 27: 4-0 *Gallacher 3, Cunningham* | Manchester April 17: 1-0 *Jackson* | Glasgow Oct 30: 3-0 *Gallacher, Jackson 2* |

| 1927 Ireland | 1927 England | 1927 Wales | 1928 Ireland | 1928 England |
|---|---|---|---|---|
| 1 Harkness | 1 Harkness | 1 Robb | 1 McClory | 1 Harkness |
| 2 Hutton | 2 McStay | 2 Hutton | 2 Hutton | 2 Nelson |
| 3 McStay | 3 Thomson | 3 McStay | 3 McStay | 3 Law |
| 4 Muirhead | 4 Morrison | 4 Meiklejohn | 4 Muirhead | 4 Gibson |
| 5 Gibson | 5 Gibson | 5 Gibson | 5 Meiklejohn | 5 Bradshaw |
| 6 Craig | 6 McMullan | 6 McMullan | 6 Craig | 6 McMullan |
| 7 Jackson | 7 McLean | 7 Jackson | 7 Ritchie | 7 Jackson |
| 8 Dunn | 8 Cunningham | 8 McKay | 8 Dunn | 8 Dunn |
| 9 Gallacher | 9 Gallacher | 9 Gallacher | 9 McGrory | 9 Gallacher |
| 10 Howieson | 10 McPhail | 10 Stevenson | 10 Stevenson | 10 James |
| 11 Morton | 11 Morton | 11 Morton | 11 Morton | 11 Morton |
| Belfast Feb 26: 2-0 *Morton 2* | Glasgow April 2: 1-2 *Morton* | Wrexham Oct 29: 2-2 *Gallacher, Hutton (pen)* | Glasgow Feb 25: 0-1 | Wembley Mar 31: 5-1 *Jackson 3, James, Gibson* |

| 1928 Wales | 1929 Ireland | 1929 England | 1929 Norway | 1929 Germany |
|---|---|---|---|---|
| 1 Harkness | 1 Harkness | 1 Harkness | 1 McLaren | 1 McLaren |
| 2 Gray | 2 Gray | 2 Crapnell | 2 Crapnell | 2 Gray |
| 3 Blair | 3 Blair | 3 Nibloe | 3 Nibloe | 3 Crapnell |
| 4 Muirhead | 4 Muirhead | 4 Buchanan | 4 Imrie | 4 Morton H. |
| 5 King | 5 Meiklejohn | 5 Meiklejohn | 5 Craig A. | 5 Imrie |
| 6 McMullan | 6 McMullan | 6 McMullan | 6 Craig T. | 6 Craig T. |
| 7 Jackson | 7 Jackson | 7 Jackson | 7 Nisbet | 7 Nisbet |
| 8 Dunn | 8 Chalmers | 8 Cheyne | 8 Cheyne | 8 Cheyne |
| 9 Gallacher | 9 Gallacher | 9 Gallacher | 9 McCrae | 9 McCrae |
| 10 McPhail | 10 James | 10 James | 10 Rankin | 10 Rankin |
| 11 Morton | 11 Morton | 11 Morton | 11 Howe | 11 Fleming |
| Glasgow Oct 27: 4-2 *Gallacher 3, Dunn* | Belfast Feb 23: 7-3 *Gallacher 4, Jackson 2, James* | Glasgow April 13: 1-0 *Cheyne* | Bergen May 26: 7-3 *Cheyne 3, Nisbet 2, Craig T., Rankin* | Berlin June 1: 1-1 *Imrie* |

| 1929 Netherlands | 1929 Wales | 1930 Ireland | 1930 England | 1930 France |
|---|---|---|---|---|
| 1 McClaren | 1 Harkness | 1 Middleton | 1 Harkness | 1 Thomson |
| 2 Gray | 2 Gray | 2 Gray | 2 Gray | 2 Nelson |
| 3 Nibloe | 3 Nibloe | 3 Wiseman | 3 Law | 3 Crapnell |
| 4 Morton H. | 4 Gibson | 4 Gibson | 4 Buchanan | 4 Wilson |
| 5 Craig A. | 5 Johnstone | 5 Meiklejohn | 5 Meiklejohn | 5 Walker G. |
| 6 Craig T. | 6 Craig T. | 6 Craig T. | 6 Craig T. | 6 Hill |
| 7 Nisbet | 7 Jackson | 7 Jackson | 7 Jackson | 7 Jackson |
| 8 Cheyne | 8 Muirhead | 8 Stevenson | 8 James | 8 Cheyne |
| 9 Fleming | 9 Gallacher | 9 Gallacher | 9 Fleming | 9 Gallacher |
| 10 Rankin | 10 James | 10 James | 10 Stevenson | 10 Stevenson |
| 11 Howe | 11 Morton | 11 Morton | 11 Morton | 11 Connor |
| Amsterdam June 4: 2-0 *Fleming, Rankin* | Cardiff Oct 26: 4-2 *Gallacher 2, James, Gibson* | Glasgow Feb 22: 3-1 *Gallacher 2, Stevenson* | Wembley April 5: 2-5 *Fleming 2* | Paris May 18: 2-0 *Gallacher 2* |

| 1930 Wales | 1931 Ireland | 1931 England | 1931 Austria | 1931 Italy |
|---|---|---|---|---|
| 1 Thomson | 1 Thomson | 1 Thomson | 1 Jackson | 1 Jackson |
| 2 Gray | 2 Crapnell | 2 Blair | 2 Blair | 2 Blair |
| 3 Gilmour | 3 Nibloe | 3 Nibloe | 3 Nibloe | 3 Nibloe |
| 4 McNab | 4 Wilson P. | 4 McNab | 4 McNab | 4 McNab |
| 5 Gillespie | 5 Walker G. | 5 Meiklejohn | 5 McDougall | 5 McDougall |
| 6 Hill | 6 Hill | 6 Miller | 6 Walker G. | 6 Miller |
| 7 McRorie | 7 Murdoch | 7 Archibald | 7 Love | 7 Love |
| 8 Brown G. | 8 Scarff | 8 Stevenson | 8 Paterson | 8 Paterson |
| 9 Battles | 9 Yorston | 9 McGrory | 9 Easson | 9 Boyd |
| 10 Stevenson | 10 McPhail | 10 McPhail | 10 Robertson | 10 Robertson |
| 11 Morton | 11 Morton | 11 Morton | 11 Liddell D. | 11 Liddell D. |
| Glasgow Oct 25: 1-1 *Battles* | Belfast Feb 21: 0-0 | Glasgow Mar 28: 2-0 *Stevenson, McGrory* | Vienna May 16: 0-5 | Rome May 20: 0-3 |

| 1931 Switzerland | 1931 Ireland | 1931 Wales | 1932 England | 1932 France |
|---|---|---|---|---|
| 1 Jackson | 1 Hepburn | 1 Harkness | 1 Hamilton T. | 1 Harkness |
| 2 Crapnell | 2 Blair | 2 Blair | 2 Crapnell | 2 Crapnell |
| 3 Nibloe | 3 McAulay | 3 McAulay | 3 Nibloe | 3 Nibloe |
| 4 McNab | 4 Massie | 4 Massie | 4 McNab | 4 Massie |
| 5 Walker G. | 5 Meiklejohn | 5 Meiklejohn | 5 Craig A. | 5 Gillespie |
| 6 Miller | 6 Brown G. | 6 Brown G. | 6 Brown G. | 6 Miller |
| 7 Love | 7 Crawford | 7 Thomson R. | 7 Archibald | 7 Crawford |
| 8 Paterson | 8 Stevenson | 8 Stevenson | 8 Marshall | 8 Thomson A. |
| 9 Boyd | 9 McGrory | 9 McGrory | 9 Dewar | 9 Dewar |
| 10 Easson | 10 McPhail | 10 McPhail | 10 Napier | 10 McPhail |
| 11 Liddell D. | 11 Connor | 11 Morton | 11 Morton | 11 Morton |
| Geneva May 24: 3-2 *Easson, Boyd, Love* | Glasgow Sept 19: 3-1 *Stevenson, McGrory, McPhail* | Wrexham Oct 31: 3-2 *Stevenson, Thomson, McGrory* | Wembley April 9: 0-3 | Paris May 8: 3-1 *Dewar 3* |

| 1932 Ireland | 1932 Wales | 1933 England | 1933 Ireland | 1933 Wales |
|---|---|---|---|---|
| 1 McLaren | 1 McLaren | 1 Jackson | 1 Harkness | 1 Kennaway |
| 2 Gray | 2 Gray | 2 Anderson | 2 Anderson | 2 Anderson |
| 3 Crapnell | 3 Blair | 3 McGonagle | 3 McGonagle | 3 Urquhart |
| 4 Massie | 4 Wales | 4 Wilson P. | 4 Massie | 4 Busby |
| 5 Johnstone | 5 Johnstone | 5 Gillespie | 5 Lowe | 5 Blair |
| 6 Telfer | 6 Thomson J. | 6 Brown G. | 6 Telfer | 6 McLuckie |
| 7 Crawford | 7 Crawford | 7 Crawford | 7 Boyd | 7 McGurk |
| 8 Stevenson | 8 Thomson A. | 8 Marshall | 8 Venters | 8 McMenemy |
| 9 McGrory | 9 Dewar | 9 McGrory | 9 McGrory | 9 McFadyen |
| 10 McPhail | 10 James | 10 McPhail | 10 McPhail | 10 Easson |
| 11 King | 11 Duncan | 11 Duncan | 11 King | 11 Duncan |
| Belfast Sept 19: 4-0 *McPhail 2, King, McGrory* | Edinburgh Oct 26: 2-5 *Dewar, Duncan* | Glasgow April 1: 2-1 *McGrory 2* | Glasgow Sept 16: 1-2 *McPhail* | Cardiff Oct 4: 2-3 *Duncan, McFadyen* |

| 1933 Austria | 1934 England | 1934 Ireland | 1934 Wales | 1935 England |
|---|---|---|---|---|
| 1 Kennaway | 1 Jackson | 1 Dawson | 1 McClory | 1 Jackson |
| 2 Anderson | 2 Anderson | 2 Anderson | 2 Anderson | 2 Anderson |
| 3 McGonagle | 3 McGonagle | 3 McGonagle | 3 McGonagle | 3 Cummings |
| 4 Meiklejohn | 4 Massie | 4 Massie | 4 Massie | 4 Massie |
| 5 Watson P. | 5 Smith T. | 5 Simpson | 5 Simpson | 5 Simpson |
| 6 Brown G. | 6 Miller | 6 Herd | 6 Brown G. | 6 Brown G. |
| 7 Ogilvie | 7 Cook | 7 Cook | 7 Cook | 7 Napier |
| 8 Bruce | 8 Marshall | 8 Stevenson | 8 Walker T. | 8 Walker T. |
| 9 McFadyen | 9 Gallacher | 9 Smith J. | 9 McCulloch | 9 Gallacher |
| 10 McPhail | 10 Stevenson | 10 Gallacher | 10 Napier | 10 McPhail |
| 11 Duncan | 11 Connor | 11 Connor | 11 Duncan | 11 Duncan |
| Glasgow Nov 29: 2-2 *Meiklejohn, McFadyen* | Wembley April 14: 0-3 | Belfast Oct 20: 1-2 *Gallacher* | Aberdeen Nov 21: 3-2 *Duncan, Napier 2* | Glasgow April 6: 2-0 *Duncan 2* |


| 1935 Wales | 1935 Ireland | 1936 England | 1936 Germany | 1936 Ireland |
|---|---|---|---|---|
| 1 Jackson | 1 Jackson | 1 Dawson | 1 Dawson | 1 Dawson |
| 2 Anderson | 2 Anderson | 2 Anderson | 2 Anderson | 2 Anderson |
| 3 Cummings | 3 Cummings | 3 Cummings | 3 Cummings | 3 Ancell |
| 4 Massie | 4 Massie | 4 Massie | 4 Massie | 4 Massie |
| 5 Simpson | 5 Simpson | 5 Simpson | 5 Simpson | 5 Simpson |
| 6 Brown G. | 6 Hastings | 6 Brown G. | 6 Brown G. | 6 Brown G. |
| 7 Delaney | 7 Delaney | 7 Crum | 7 Delaney | 7 Munro |
| 8 Walker T. | 8 Walker T. | 8 Walker T. | 8 Walker T. | 8 Walker T. |
| 9 Armstrong | 9 Armstrong | 9 McCulloch | 9 Armstrong | 9 McCulloch |
| 10 Mills | 10 Mills | 10 Venters | 10 McPhail | 10 Napier |
| 11 Duncan | 11 Duncan | 11 Duncan | 11 Duncan | 11 Duncan |
| Cardiff Oct 5: 1-1 *Duncan* | Edinburgh Nov 13: 2-1 *Walker, Duncan* | Wembley April 4: 1-1 *Walker* | Glasgow Oct 14: 2-0 *Delaney 2* | Belfast Oct 31: 3-1 *Napier, Munro, McCulloch* |


| 1936 Wales | 1937 England | 1937 Austria | 1937 Czechoslovakia | 1937 Wales |
|---|---|---|---|---|
| 1 Dawson | 1 Dawson | 1 Dawson | 1 Dawson | 1 Dawson |
| 2 Anderson | 2 Anderson | 2 Anderson | 2 Hogg | 2 Anderson |
| 3 Ancell | 3 Beattie A. | 3 Beattie A. | 3 Beattie A. | 3 Cummings |
| 4 Massie | 4 Massie | 4 Massie | 4 Thomson | 4 Massie |
| 5 Simpson | 5 Simpson | 5 Simpson | 5 Simpson | 5 Simpson |
| 6 Brown G. | 6 Brown G. | 6 McNab | 6 Brown G. | 6 Brown G. |
| 7 Munro | 7 Delaney | 7 Delaney | 7 Delaney | 7 Main |
| 8 Walker T. | 8 Walker T. | 8 Walker T. | 8 Walker T. | 8 Walker T. |
| 9 McCulloch | 9 O'Donnell F. | 9 O'Donnell F. | 9 O'Donnell F. | 9 O'Donnell F. |
| 10 Mills | 10 McPhail | 10 Napier | 10 McPhail | 10 McPhail |
| 11 Duncan | 11 Duncan | 11 Gillick | 11 Gillick | 11 Duncan |
| Dundee Dec 2: 1-2 *Walker* | Glasgow April 17: 3-1 *O'Donnell, McPhail 2* | Vienna May 9: 1-1 *O'Donnell* | Prague May 22: 3-1 *Simpson, McPhail, Gillick* | Cardiff Oct 30: 1-2 *Massie* |

| 1937 Ireland | 1937 Czechoslovakia | 1938 England | 1938 Netherlands | 1938 Ireland |
|---|---|---|---|---|
| 1 Dawson | 1 Waugh | 1 Cumming | 1 Dawson | 1 Dawson |
| 2 Anderson | 2 Anderson | 2 Anderson | 2 Anderson | 2 Carabine |
| 3 Cummings | 3 Cummings | 3 Beattie A. | 3 Carabine | 3 Beattie A. |
| 4 McKenzie | 4 Robertson | 4 Shankly | 4 McKillop | 4 Shankly |
| 5 Simpson | 5 Johnston | 5 Smith T. | 5 Dykes | 5 Dykes |
| 6 Hastings | 6 Brown G. | 6 Brown G. | 6 Brown G. | 6 Paterson |
| 7 Delaney | 7 Buchanan | 7 Milne | 7 Munro | 7 Delaney |
| 8 Walker T. | 8 Walker T. | 8 Walker T. | 8 Walker T. | 8 Walker T. |
| 9 Smith J. | 9 McCulloch | 9 O'Donnell F. | 9 O'Donnell F. | 9 Crum |
| 10 McPhail | 10 Black | 10 Mutch | 10 Black | 10 Divers |
| 11 Reid | 11 Kinnear | 11 Reid | 11 Murphy | 11 Gillick |

| Aberdeen Nov 10: 1-1 *Smith* | Glasgow Dec 8: 5-0 *McCulloch 2, Black, Buchanan, Kinnear* | Wembley April 9: 1-0 *Walker* | Amsterdam May 21: 3-1 *Black, Murphy, Walker* | Belfast Oct 8: 2-0 *Delaney, Walker* |
|---|---|---|---|---|

| 1938 Wales | 1938 Hungary | 1939 England | 1946 Wales | 1946 N Ireland |
|---|---|---|---|---|
| 1 Brown J. | 1 Dawson | 1 Dawson | 1 Miller | 1 Brown R. |
| 2 Anderson | 2 Anderson | 2 Carabine | 2 Stephen | 2 Young |
| 3 Beattie A. | 3 Beattie A. | 3 Cummings | 3 Shaw D. | 3 Shaw D. |
| 4 Shankly | 4 Shankly | 4 Shankly | 4 Brown | 4 Campbell |
| 5 Baxter | 5 Baxter | 5 Baxter | 5 Brennan | 5 Brennan |
| 6 Miller | 6 Symon | 6 McNab | 6 Husband | 6 Long |
| 7 Delaney | 7 McSpadyen | 7 McSpadyen | 7 Waddell | 7 Smith |
| 8 Walker T. | 8 Walker T. | 8 Walker T. | 8 Dougall | 8 Hamilton |
| 9 McCulloch | 9 McCulloch | 9 Dougall | 9 Thornton | 9 Thornton |
| 10 Beattie R. | 10 Black | 10 Venters | 10 Blair | 10 Duncanson |
| 11 Gillick | 11 Gillick | 11 Milne | 11 Liddell | 11 Liddell |

| Edinburgh Nov 9: 3-2 *Walker 2, Gillick* | Glasgow Dec 7: 3-1 *Black, Walker, Gillick* | Glasgow April 15: 1-2 *Dougall* | Wrexham Oct 19: 1-3 *Waddell* | Hampden Nov 27: 0-0 |
|---|---|---|---|---|

| 1947 England | 1947 Belgium | 1947 Luxembourg | 1947 N Ireland | 1947 Wales |
|---|---|---|---|---|
| 1 Miller | 1 Miller | 1 Miller | 1 Miller | 1 Miller |
| 2 Young | 2 Young | 2 Young | 2 Young | 2 Govan |
| 3 Shaw J. | 3 Shaw J. | 3 Shaw J. | 3 Shaw J. | 3 Stephen |
| 4 Macaulay | 4 Brown | 4 Brown | 4 Macaulay | 4 Macaulay |
| 5 Woodburn | 5 Woodburn | 5 Woodburn | 5 Woodburn | 5 Woodburn |
| 6 Forbes | 6 Forbes | 6 Forbes | 6 Forbes | 6 Forbes |
| 7 Smith | 7 Campbell | 7 McFarlane | 7 Delaney | 7 Smith |
| 8 McLaren | 8 McLaren | 8 McLaren | 8 Watson | 8 McLaren |
| 9 Delaney | 9 Flavell | 9 Flavell | 9 Thornton | 9 Delaney |
| 10 Steel | 10 Steel | 10 Steel | 10 Steel | 10 Steel |
| 11 Pearson | 11 Pearson | 11 Campbell | 11 Liddell | 11 Liddell |

| Wembley April 12: 1-1 *McLaren* | Brussels May 18: 1-2 *Steel* | Luxembourg May 24: 6-0 *McLaren 2, Steel 2, Flavell 2* | Belfast Oct 4: 0-2 | Hampden Nov 12: 1-2 *McLaren* |
|---|---|---|---|---|

| 1948 England | 1948 Belgium | 1948 Switzerland | 1948 France | 1948 Wales |
|---|---|---|---|---|
| 1 Black | 1 Cowan | 1 Cowan | 1 Cowan | 1 Cowan |
| 2 Govan | 2 Govan | 2 Govan | 2 Govan | 2 Howie |
| 3 Shaw D. | 3 Shaw D. | 3 Shaw D. | 3 Shaw D. | 3 Shaw D. |
| 4 Campbell | 4 Campbell | 4 Campbell | 4 Campbell | 4 Evans |
| 5 Young | 5 Young | 5 Young | 5 Young | 5 Young |
| 6 Macaulay | 6 Macaulay | 6 Macaulay | 6 Macaulay | 6 Redpath |
| 7 Delaney | 7 Smith | 7 Smith | 7 Rutherford | 7 Waddell |
| 8 Combe | 8 Combe | 8 Combe | 8 Steel | 8 Mason |
| 9 Thornton | 9 Johnstone | 9 Johnstone | 9 Smith | 9 Reilly |
| 10 Steel | 10 Turnbull | 10 Turnbull | 10 Cox | 10 Steel |
| 11 Liddell | 11 Duncan | 11 Duncan | 11 Duncan | 11 Kelly |
| Hampden April 10: 0-2 | Hampden April 28: 2-0 *Combe, Duncan* | Berne May 17: 1-2 *Johnstone* | Paris May 23: 0-3 | Cardiff Oct 23: 3-1 *Howie, Waddell 2* |

| 1948 N Ireland | 1949 England | 1949 France | 1949 N Ireland | 1949 Wales |
|---|---|---|---|---|
| 1 Brown R. | 1 Cowan | 1 Cowan | 1 Cowan | 1 Cowan |
| 2 Govan | 2 Young | 2 Young | 2 Young | 2 Young |
| 3 Shaw D. | 3 Cox | 3 Cox | 3 Cox | 3 Cox |
| 4 Evans | 4 Evans | 4 Evans | 4 Evans | 4 Evans |
| 5 Young | 5 Woodburn | 5 Woodburn | 5 Woodburn | 5 Woodburn |
| 6 Redpath | 6 Aitken | 6 Aitken | 6 Aitken | 6 Aitken |
| 7 Waddell | 7 Waddell | 7 Waddell | 7 Waddell | 7 Liddell |
| 8 Mason | 8 Mason | 8 Thornton | 8 Mason | 8 McPhail |
| 9 Houliston | 9 Houliston | 9 Houliston | 9 Morris | 9 Linwood |
| 10 Steel | 10 Steel | 10 Steel | 10 Steel | 10 Steel |
| 11 Kelly | 11 Reilly | 11 Reilly | 11 Reilly | 11 Reilly |
| Hampden Nov 17: 3-2 *Houliston 2, Mason* | Wembley April 9: 3-1 *Mason, Steel Reilly* | Hampden April 27: 2-0 *Steel 2* | Belfast Oct 1: 8-2 *Morris 3, Waddell 2, Steel, Reilly, Mason* | Hampden Nov 9: 2-0 *McPhail, Linwood* |

| 1950 England | 1950 Switzerland | 1950 Portugal | 1950 France | 1950 Wales |
|---|---|---|---|---|
| 1 Cowan | 1 Cowan | 1 Cowan | 1 Cowan | 1 Cowan |
| 2 Young | 2 Young | 2 Young | 2 Young | 2 Young |
| 3 Cox | 3 Cox | 3 Cox | 3 Cox | 3 McNaught |
| 4 McColl | 4 Evans | 4 Evans | 4 McColl | 4 McColl |
| 5 Woodburn | 5 Dougan | 5 Woodburn | 5 Woodburn | 5 Woodburn |
| 6 Forbes | 6 Aitken | 6 Forbes | 6 Forbes | 6 Forbes |
| 7 Waddell | 7 Campbell | 7 Campbell | 7 Campbell | 7 Collins |
| 8 Moir | 8 Brown | 8 Brown | 8 Brown | 8 McPhail |
| 9 Bauld | 9 Bauld | 9 Bauld | 9 Reilly | 9 Reilly |
| 10 Steel | 10 Steel | 10 Steel | 10 Steel | 10 Steel |
| 11 Liddell | 11 Reilly | 11 Liddell | 11 Liddell | 11 Liddell |
| Hampden April 15: 0-1 | Hampden April 26: 3-1 *Bauld, Campbell, Brown* | Lisbon May 25: 2-2 *Brown, Bauld* | Paris May 27: 1-0 *Brown* | Cardiff Oct 21: 3-1 *Reilly 2, Liddell* |

| 1950 N Ireland | 1950 Austria | 1951 England | 1951 Denmark | 1951 France |
|---|---|---|---|---|
| 1 Cowan | 1 Cowan | 1 Cowan | 1 Cowan | 1 Cowan |
| 2 Young | 2 Young | 2 Young | 2 Young | 2 Young |
| 3 McNaught | 3 McNaught | 3 Cox | 3 Cox | 3 Cox |
| 4 McColl | 4 Evans | 4 Evans | 4 Scoular | 4 Scoular |
| 5 Woodburn | 5 Woodburn | 5 Woodburn | 5 Woodburn | 5 Woodburn |
| 6 Forbes | 6 Forbes | 6 Redpath | 6 Redpath | 6 Redpath |
| 7 Collins | 7 Collins | 7 Waddell | 7 Waddell | 7 Waddell |
| 8 Mason | ‹8 Turnbull | 8 Johnstone | 8 Johnstone | 8 Johnstone |
| 9 McPhail | 9 McPhail | 9 Reilly | 9 Reilly | 9 Reilly |
| 10 Steel | 10 Steel | 10 Steel | 10 Steel | 10 Steel |
| 11 Liddell | 11 Liddell | 11 Liddell | 11 Mitchell | 11 Mitchell |
| Hampden | Hampden | Wembley | Hampden | Hampden |
| Nov 1: 6-1 | Dec 13: 0-1 | April 14: 3-2 | May 12: 3-1 | May 16: 1-0 |
| *McPhail 2, Steel 4* | | *Johnstone, Reilly, Liddell* | *Steel, Reilly, Mitchell* | *Reilly* |

| 1951 Belgium | 1951 Austria | 1951 N Ireland | 1951 Wales | 1952 England |
|---|---|---|---|---|
| 1 Cowan | 1 Cowan | 1 Cowan | 1 Cowan | 1 Brown R. |
| 2 Young | 2 Young | 2 Young | 2 Young | 2 Young |
| 3 Cox | 3 Cox | 3 Cox | 3 Cox | 3 McNaught |
| 4 McColl | 4 Scoular | 4 Evans | 4 Docherty | 4 Scoular |
| 5 Woodburn | 5 Woodburn | 5 Woodburn | 5 Woodburn | 5 Woodburn |
| 6 Redpath | 6 Redpath | 6 Redpath | 6 Forbes | 6 Redpath |
| 7 Waddell | 7 Waddell | 7 Waddell | 7 Waddell | 7 Smith |
| 8 Mason | 8 Mason | 8 Johnstone | 8 Orr | 8 Johnstone |
| 9 Hamilton | 9 Hamilton | 9 Reilly | 9 Reilly | 9 Reilly |
| 10 Steel | 10 Steel | 10 Orr | 10 Steel | 10 McMillan |
| 11 Reilly | 11 Reilly | 11 Liddell | 11 Liddell | 11 Liddell |
| Brussels | Vienna | Belfast | Hampden | Hampden |
| May 20: 5-0 | May 27: 0-4 | Oct 6: 3-0 | Nov 28: 0-1 | April 5: 1-2 |
| *Hamilton 3, Mason, Waddell* | | *Johnstone 2, Orr* | | *Reilly* |

| 1952 USA | 1952 Denmark | 1952 Sweden | 1952 Wales | 1952 N Ireland |
|---|---|---|---|---|
| 1 Cowan | 1 Cowan | 1 Cowan | 1 Farm | 1 Farm |
| 2 Young | 2 Young | 2 Young | 2 Young | 2 Young |
| 3 Cox | 3 Cox | 3 Cox | 3 Cox | 3 Cox |
| 4 Scoular | 4 Scoular | 4 Scoular | 4 Scoular | 4 Scoular |
| 5 Woodburn | 5 Paton | 5 Paton | 5 Brennan | 5 Brennan |
| 6 Kelly | 6 Forbes | 6 Forbes | 6 Aitken | 6 Aitken |
| 7 Smith | 7 Reilly | 7 Reilly | 7 Wright T. | 7 Wright T. |
| 8 McMillan | 8 McMillan | 8 Humphries | 8 Brown | 8 Logie |
| 9 Reilly | 9 Thornton | 9 Thornton | 9 Reilly | 9 Reilly |
| 10 Brown | 10 Brown | 10 Brown | 10 Steel | 10 Steel |
| 11 Liddell | 11 Liddell | 11 Liddell | 11 Liddell | 11 Liddell |
| Hampden | Copenhagen | Stockholm | Cardiff | Hampden |
| April 30: 6-0 | May 25: 2-1 | May 30: 1-3 | Oct 15: 2-1 | Nov 5: 1-1 |
| *Reilly 3, McMillan 2, 1 og* | *Thornton, Reilly* | *Liddell* | *Brown, Liddell* | *Reilly* |

| 1953 England | 1953 Sweden | 1953 N Ireland | 1953 Wales | 1954 England |
|---|---|---|---|---|
| 1 Farm | 1 Farm | 1 Farm | 1 Farm | 1 Farm |
| 2 Young | 2 Young | 2 Young | 2 Young | 2 Haughney |
| 3 Cox | 3 Little | 3 Cox | 3 Cox | 3 Cox |
| 4 Docherty | 4 Evans | 4 Evans | 4 Evans | 4 Evans |
| 5 Brennan | 5 Cowie | 5 Brennan | 5 Telfer | 5 Brennan |
| 6 Cowie | 6 Docherty | 6 Cowie | 6 Cowie | 6 Aitken |
| 7 Wright T. | 7 Henderson | 7 Waddell | 7 McKenzie | 7 McKenzie |
| 8 Johnstone | 8 Johnstone | 8 Fleming | 8 Johnstone | 8 Johnstone |
| 9 Reilly | 9 Reilly | 9 McPhail | 9 Reilly | 9 Henderson |
| 10 Steel | 10 Steel | 10 Watson | 10 Brown | 10 Brown |
| 11 Liddell | 11 Ring | 11 Henderson | 11 Liddell | 11 Ormond |

| Wembley | Hampden | Belfast | Hampden | Hampden |
|---|---|---|---|---|
| April 18: 2-2 | May 6: 1-2 | Oct 3: 3-1 | Nov 4: 3-3 | April 3: 2-4 |
| *Reilly 2* | *Johnstone* | *Fleming 2,* | *Brown, Johnstone,* | *Brown,* |
| | | *Henderson* | *Reilly* | *1 og* |

| 1954 Norway | 1954 Norway | 1954 Finland | 1954 Austria † | 1954 Uruguay † |
|---|---|---|---|---|
| 1 Martin | 1 Martin | 1 Anderson | 1 Martin | 1 Martin |
| 2 Cunningham | 2 Cunningham | 2 Wilson | 2 Cunningham | 2 Cunningham |
| 3 Aird | 3 Aird | 3 Cunningham | 3 Aird | 3 Aird |
| 4 Docherty | 4 Docherty | 4 Evans | 4 Docherty | 4 Docherty |
| 5 Davidson | 5 Davidson | 5 Cowie | 5 Davidson | 5 Davidson |
| 6 Evans | 6 Cowie | 6 Mathers | 6 Cowie | 6 Cowie |
| 7 Johnstone | 7 McKenzie | 7 McKenzie | 7 McKenzie | 7 McKenzie |
| 8 Hamilton | 8 Hamilton | 8 Johnstone | 8 Fernie | 8 Fernie |
| 9 Buckley | 9 Henderson | 9 Brown | 9 Mochan | 9 Mochan |
| 10 Brown | 10 Brown | 10 Fernie | 10 Brown | 10 Brown |
| 11 Ormond | 11 Mochan | 11 Ormond | 11 Ormond | 11 Ormond |

| Hampden | Oslo | Helsinki | Zurich | Basle |
|---|---|---|---|---|
| May 5: 1-0 | May 19: 1-1 | May 25: 2-1 | June 16: 0-1 | June 19: 0-7 |
| *Hamilton* | *McKenzie* | *Ormond, Johnstone* | | |

| 1954 Wales | 1954 N Ireland | 1954 Hungary | 1955 England | 1955 Portugal |
|---|---|---|---|---|
| 1 Fraser | 1 Fraser | 1 Martin | 1 Martin | 1 Younger |
| 2 Young | 2 Young | 2 Cunningham | 2 Cunningham | 2 Parker |
| 3 Cunningham | 3 McNaught | 3 Haddock | 3 Haddock | 3 Haddock |
| 4 Docherty | 4 Evans | 4 Docherty | 4 Docherty | 4 Evans |
| 5 Davidson | 5 Davidson | 5 Davidson | 5 Davidson | 5 Young |
| 6 Cowie | 6 Cowie | 6 Cumming | 6 Cumming | 6 Cumming |
| 7 Waddell | 7 Waddell | 7 McKenzie | 7 McKenzie | 7 Smith |
| 8 Yorston | 8 Johnstone | 8 Johnstone | 8 Johnstone | 8 Robertson |
| 9 Buckley | 9 Buckley | 9 Reilly | 9 Reilly | 9 Reilly |
| 10 Fernie | 10 Fernie | 10 Wardhaugh | 10 McMillan | 10 Gemmell |
| 11 Ring | 11 Ring | 11 Ring | 11 Ring | 11 Liddell |

| Cardiff | Hampden | Hampden | Wembley | Hampden |
|---|---|---|---|---|
| Oct 16: 1-0 | Nov 3: 2-2 | Dec 8: 2-4 | April 2: 2-7 | May 16: 3-0 |
| *Buckley* | *Davidson,* | *Ring, Johnstone* | *Reilly, Docherty* | *Reilly, Gemmell,* |
| | *Johnstone* | | | *Liddell* |

| 1955 Yugoslavia | 1955 Austria | 1955 Hungary | 1955 N Ireland | 1955 Wales |
|---|---|---|---|---|
| 1 Younger | 1 Younger | 1 Younger | 1 Younger | 1 Younger |
| 2 Parker | 2 Parker | 2 Kerr | 2 Parker | 2 Parker |
| 3 Haddock | 3 Kerr | 3 Haddock | 3 McDonald | 3 McDonald |
| 4 Evans | 4 Docherty | 4 Docherty | 4 Evans | 4 Evans |
| 5 Young | 5 Evans | 5 Evans | 5 Young | 5 Young |
| 6 Cumming | 6 Cowie | 6 Cowie | 6 Glen | 6 Cowie |
| 7 Smith | 7 Smith | 7 Smith | 7 Smith | 7 Smith |
| 8 Collins | 8 Collins | 8 Collins | 8 Collins | 8 Johnstone |
| 9 Reilly | 9 Reilly | 9 Reilly | 9 Reilly | 9 Reilly |
| 10 Gemmell | 10 Robertson | 10 Robertson | 10 Johnstone | 10 Collins |
| 11 Liddell | 11 Liddell | 11 Liddell | 11 Liddell | 11 Henderson |

| Belgrade | Vienna | Budapest | Belfast | Hampden |
|---|---|---|---|---|
| May 15: 2-2 | May 19: 4-1 | May 29: 1-3 | Oct 8: 1-2 | Nov 9: 2-0 |
| *Reilly, Smith* | *Robertson, Smith, Liddell, Reilly* | *Smith* | *Reilly* | *Johnstone 2* |

| 1956 England | 1956 Austria | 1956 Wales | 1956 N Ireland | 1956 Yugoslavia |
|---|---|---|---|---|
| 1 Younger | 1 Younger | 1 Younger | 1 Younger | 1 Younger |
| 2 Parker | 2 Parker | 2 Parker | 2 Parker | 2 Parker |
| 3 Hewie | 3 Hewie | 3 Hewie | 3 Hewie | 3 Hewie |
| 4 Evans | 4 Evans | 4 McColl | 4 McColl | 4 McColl |
| 5 Young | 5 Young | 5 Young | 5 Young | 5 Young |
| 6 Glen | 6 Cowie | 6 Cowie | 6 Cowie | 6 Docherty |
| 7 Leggat | 7 McKenzie | 7 Leggat | 7 Scott | 7 Scott |
| 8 Johnstone | 8 Conn | 8 Mudie | 8 Mudie | 8 Mudie |
| 9 Reilly | 9 Reilly | 9 Reilly | 9 Reilly | 9 Reilly |
| 10 McMillan | 10 Baird | 10 Collins | 10 Wardhaugh | 10 Baird |
| 11 Smith | 11 Cullen | 11 Fernie | 11 Fernie | 11 Fernie |

| Hampden | Hampden | Cardiff | Hampden | Hampden |
|---|---|---|---|---|
| April 14: 1-1 | May 2: 1-1 | Oct 20: 2-2 | Nov 7: 1-0 | Nov 21: 2-0 |
| *Leggat* | *Conn* | *Fernie, Reilly* | *Scott* | *Mudie, Baird* |

| 1957 England | 1957 Spain | 1957 Switzerland | 1957 W Germany | 1957 Spain |
|---|---|---|---|---|
| 1 Younger | 1 Younger | 1 Younger | 1 Younger | 1 Younger |
| 2 Caldow | 2 Caldow | 2 Caldow | 2 Caldow | 2 Caldow |
| 3 Hewie | 3 Hewie | 3 Hewie | 3 Hewie | 3 Hewie |
| 4 McColl | 4 McColl | 4 McColl | 4 McColl | 4 Mackay |
| 5 Young | 5 Young | 5 Young | 5 Evans | 5 Evans |
| 6 Docherty | 6 Docherty | 6 Docherty | 6 Docherty | 6 Docherty |
| 7 Collins | 7 Smith | 7 Smith | 7 Scott | 7 Smith |
| 8 Fernie | 8 Collins | 8 Collins | 8 Collins | 8 Collins |
| 9 Reilly | 9 Mudie | 9 Mudie | 9 Mudie | 9 Mudie |
| 10 Mudie | 10 Baird | 10 Baird | 10 Baird | 10 Baird |
| 11 Ring | 11 Ring | 11 Ring | 11 Ring | 11 Ring |

| Wembley | Hampden | Basle | Stuttgart | Madrid |
|---|---|---|---|---|
| April 6: 1-2 | May 8: 4-2 | May 19: 2-1 | May 22: 3-1 | May 26: 1-4 |
| *Ring* | *Mudie 3, Hewie (pen)* | *Mudie, Collins* | *Collins 2, Mudie* | *Smith* |

| 1957 N Ireland | 1957 Switzerland | 1957 Wales | 1958 England | 1958 Hungary |
|---|---|---|---|---|
| 1 Younger | 1 Younger | 1 Younger | 1 Younger | 1 Younger |
| 2 Parker | 2 Parker | 2 Parker | 2 Parker | 2 Caldow |
| 3 Caldow | 3 Caldow | 3 Caldow | 3 Haddock | 3 Hewie |
| 4 McColl | 4 Fernie | 4 Docherty | 4 McColl | 4 Turnbull |
| 5 Evans | 5 Evans | 5 Evans | 5 Evans | 5 Evans |
| 6 Docherty | 6 Docherty | 6 Fernie | 6 Docherty | 6 Cowie |
| 7 Leggat | 7 Scott | 7 Scott | 7 Herd | 7 Leggat |
| 8 Collins | 8 Collins | 8 Collins | 8 Murray | 8 Murray |
| 9 Mudie | 9 Mudie | 9 Gardiner | 9 Mudie | 9 Mudie |
| 10 Baird | 10 Robertson | 10 Mudie | 10 Forrest | 10 Collins |
| 11 Ring | 11 Ring | 11 Ewing | 11 Ewing | 11 Imlach |

| Belfast Oct 5: 1-1 *Leggat* | Hampden Nov 6: 3-2 *Robertson, Mudie, Scott* | Hampden Nov 13: 1-1 *Collins* | Hampden April 19: 0-4 | Hampden May 7: 1-1 *Mudie* |
|---|---|---|---|---|

| 1958 Poland | 1958 Yugoslavia † | 1958 Paraguay † | 1958 France † | 1958 Wales |
|---|---|---|---|---|
| 1 Younger | 1 Younger | 1 Younger | 1 Brown | 1 Brown |
| 2 Caldow | 2 Caldow | 2 Parker | 2 Caldow | 2 Grant |
| 3 Hewie | 3 Hewie | 3 Caldow | 3 Hewie | 3 Caldow |
| 4 Turnbull | 4 Turnbull | 4 Turnbull | 4 Turnbull | 4 Mackay |
| 5 Evans | 5 Evans | 5 Evans | 5 Evans | 5 Toner |
| 6 Cowie | 6 Cowie | 6 Cowie | 6 Mackay | 6 Docherty |
| 7 Leggat | 7 Leggat | 7 Leggat | 7 Collins | 7 Leggat |
| 8 Murray | 8 Murray | 8 Collins | 8 Murray | 8 Collins |
| 9 Mudie | 9 Mudie | 9 Mudie | 9 Mudie | 9 Herd |
| 10 Collins | 10 Collins | 10 Robertson | 10 Baird | 10 Law |
| 11 Imlach | 11 Imlach | 11 Fernie | 11 Imlach | 11 Henderson |

| Warsaw June 1: 2-1 *Collins 2* | Vasteraas June 8: 1-1 *Murray* | Norrkoping June 11: 2-3 *Mudie, Collins* | Orebro June 15: 1-2 *Baird* | Cardiff Oct 18: 3-0 *Leggat, Law, Collins* |
|---|---|---|---|---|

| 1958 N Ireland | 1959 England | 1959 W Germany | 1959 Netherlands | 1959 Portugal |
|---|---|---|---|---|
| 1 Brown | 1 Brown | 1 Farm | 1 Farm | 1 Farm |
| 2 Grant | 2 McKay | 2 McKay | 2 McKay | 2 McKay |
| 3 Caldow | 3 Caldow | 3 Caldow | 3 Caldow | 3 Caldow |
| 4 Mackay | 4 Docherty | 4 Mackay | 4 Smith | 4 Smith |
| 5 Toner | 5 Evans | 5 Evans | 5 Evans | 5 Evans |
| 6 Docherty | 6 Mackay | 6 McCann | 6 Hewie | 6 Hewie |
| 7 Leggat | 7 Leggat | 7 Leggat | 7 Leggat | 7 Scott |
| 8 Collins | 8 Collins | 8 White | 8 Collins | 8 Collins |
| 9 Herd | 9 Herd | 9 St John | 9 White | 9 White |
| 10 Law | 10 Dick | 10 Collins | 10 Law | 10 Law |
| 11 Henderson | 11 Ormond | 11 Weir | 11 Auld | 11 Auld |

| Hampden Nov 5: 2-2 *Herd, Collins* | Wembley April 11: 0-1 | Hampden May 6: 3-2 *White, Weir, Leggat* | Amsterdam May 27: 2-1 *Collins, Leggat* | Lisbon June 3: 0-1 |
|---|---|---|---|---|

| 1959<br>N Ireland | 1959<br>Wales | 1960<br>England | 1960<br>Poland | 1960<br>Austria |
|---|---|---|---|---|
| 1 Brown | 1 Brown | 1 Haffey | 1 Brown | 1 Brown |
| 2 Caldow | 2 Caldow | 2 McKay | 2 McKay | 2 McKay |
| 3 Hewie | 3 Mackay | 3 Caldow | 3 Hewie | 3 Caldow |
| 4 Mackay | 4 Hewie | 4 Cumming | 4 Mackay | 4 Mackay |
| 5 Evans | 5 Evans | 5 Evans | 5 Evans | 5 Evans |
| 6 McCann | 6 McCann | 6 McCann | 6 Cumming | 6 Cumming |
| 7 Leggat | 7 Leggat | 7 Leggat | 7 Leggat | 7 Leggat |
| 8 White | 8 White | 8 Young | 8 White | 8 White |
| 9 St John | 9 St John | 9 St John | 9 St John | 9 St John |
| 10 Law | 10 Law | 10 Law | 10 Law | 10 Law<br>(Young) |
| 11 Mulhall | 11 Auld | 11 Weir | 11 Weir | 11 Weir |

| Belfast<br>Oct 3: 4-0<br>*Leggat, Hewie,*<br>*White, Mulhall* | Hampden<br>Nov 14: 1-1<br>*Leggat* | Hampden<br>April 9: 1-1<br>*Leggat* | Hampden<br>May 4: 2-3<br>*Law, St John* | Vienna<br>May 29: 1-4<br>*Mackay* |
|---|---|---|---|---|

| 1960<br>Hungary | 1960<br>Turkey | 1960<br>Wales | 1960<br>N Ireland | 1961<br>England |
|---|---|---|---|---|
| 1 Brown | 1 Brown | 1 Leslie | 1 Leslie | 1 Haffey |
| 2 McKay | 2 McKay | 2 McKay | 2 McKay | 2 Shearer |
| 3 Caldow | 3 Caldow | 3 Caldow | 3 Caldow | 3 Caldow |
| 4 Cumming | 4 Mackay | 4 Gabriel | 4 Mackay | 4 Mackay |
| 5 Evans | 5 Evans | 5 Martins | 5 Plenderleith | 5 McNeill |
| 6 Mackay | 6 Cumming | 6 Mackay | 6 Baxter | 6 McCann |
| 7 Leggat | 7 White | 7 Herd | 7 Herd | 7 McLeod |
| 8 Herd | 8 Herd | 8 White | 8 Law | 8 Law |
| 9 Young | 9 Young | 9 Young | 9 Young | 9 St John |
| 10 Hunter | 10 Hunter | 10 Hunter | 10 Brand | 10 Quinn |
| 11 Weir | 11 Weir | 11 Wilson | 11 Wilson | 11 Wilson |

| Budapest<br>June 5: 3-3<br>*Hunter, Herd,*<br>*Young* | Ankara<br>June 8: 2-4<br>*Caldow, Young* | Cardiff<br>Oct 22: 0-2 | Hampden<br>Nov 9: 5-2<br>*Law, Caldow,*<br>*Young, Brand 2* | Wembley<br>April 15: 3-9<br>*Mackay, Wilson,*<br>*Quinn* |
|---|---|---|---|---|

| 1961<br>Rep of Ireland | 1961<br>Rep of Ireland | 1961<br>Czechoslovakia | 1961<br>Czechoslovakia | 1961<br>N Ireland |
|---|---|---|---|---|
| 1 Leslie | 1 Leslie | 1 Leslie | 1 Brown | 1 Brown |
| 2 Shearer | 2 Shearer | 2 Shearer | 2 McKay | 2 McKay |
| 3 Caldow | 3 Crerand | 3 Caldow | 3 Caldow | 3 Caldow |
| 4 Crerand | 4 Caldow | 4 Crerand | 4 Crerand | 4 Crerand |
| 5 McNeill | 5 McNeill | 5 McNeill | 5 McNeill | 5 McNeill |
| 6 Baxter | 6 Baxter | 6 Baxter | 6 Baxter | 6 Baxter |
| 7 McLeod | 7 McLeod | 7 McLeod | 7 Scott | 7 Scott |
| 8 Quinn | 8 Quinn | 8 McMillan | 8 White | 8 White |
| 9 Herd | 9 Young | 9 Herd | 9 St John | 9 St John |
| 10 Brand | 10 Brand | 10 Brand | 10 Law | 10 Brand |
| 11 Wilson | 11 Wilson | 11 Wilson | 11 Wilson | 11 Wilson |

| Hampden<br>May 3: 4-1<br>*Brand 2, Herd 2* | Dublin<br>May 7: 3-0<br>*Young 2, Brand* | Bratislava<br>May 14: 0-4 | Hampden<br>Sept 26: 3-2<br>*St John, Law 2* | Belfast<br>Oct 7: 6-1<br>*Wilson, Scott 3*<br>*Brand 2* |
|---|---|---|---|---|

| 1961 Wales | 1961 Czechoslovakia | 1962 England | 1962 Uruguay | 1962 Wales |
|---|---|---|---|---|
| 1 Brown | 1 Connachan | 1 Brown | 1 Connachan (Ritchie) | 1 Brown |
| 2 Hamilton | 2 Hamilton | 2 Hamilton | 2 Hamilton | 2 Hamilton |
| 3 Caldow | 3 Caldow | 3 Caldow | 3 Caldow | 3 Caldow |
| 4 Crerand | 4 Crerand | 4 Crerand | 4 Crerand (McKay) | 4 Crerand |
| 5 Ure | 5 Ure | 5 McNeill | 5 McNeill | 5 Ure |
| 6 Baxter | 6 Baxter | 6 Baxter | 6 Baxter | 6 Baxter |
| 7 Scott | 7 Brand | 7 Scott | 7 Scott | 7 Henderson |
| 8 White | 8 White | 8 White | 8 Quinn | 8 White |
| 9 St John | 9 St John | 9 St John | 9 St John | 9 St John |
| 10 Brand | 10 Law | 10 Law | 10 Brand | 10 Law |
| 11 Wilson | 11 Robertson | 11 Wilson | 11 Wilson | 11 Wilson |
| Hampden Nov 8: 2-0 *St John 2* | Brussels Nov 29: 2-4 *St John 2* | Hampden April 14: 2-0 *Wilson, Caldow* | Hampden May 2: 2-3 *Baxter, Brand* | Cardiff Oct 20: 3-2 *Caldow, Law Henderson* |

| 1962 N Ireland | 1963 England | 1963 Austria | 1963 Norway | 1963 Rep of Ireland |
|---|---|---|---|---|
| 1 Brown | 1 Brown | 1 Brown | 1 Blacklaw | 1 Lawrence |
| 2 Hamilton | 2 Hamilton | 2 Hamilton | 2 Hamilton | 2 Hamilton |
| 3 Caldow | 3 Caldow | 3 Holt | 3 Holt | 3 Holt |
| 4 Crerand | 4 Mackay | 4 Mackay | 4 Mackay (McLintock) | 4 McLintock |
| 5 Ure | 5 Ure | 5 Ure | 5 Ure | 5 McNeill |
| 6 Baxter | 6 Baxter | 6 Baxter | 6 Baxter | 6 Baxter |
| 7 Henderson | 7 Henderson | 7 Henderson | 7 Henderson | 7 Henderson |
| 8 White | 8 White | 8 Gibson | 8 Gibson | 8 Gibson |
| 9 St John | 9 St John | 9 Millar | 9 St John | 9 Millar (St John) |
| 10 Law | 10 Law | 10 Law | 10 Law | 10 Law |
| 11 Mulhall | 11 Wilson | 11 Wilson | 11 Wilson | 11 Wilson |
| Hampden Nov 7: 5-1 *Law 4, Henderson* | Wembley April 6: 2-1 *Baxter 2* | Hampden May 8: 4-1 *Wilson 2, Law 2 (abandoned after 79 min.)* | Bergen June 4: 3-4 *Law 3* | Dublin June 9: 0-1 |

| 1963 Spain | 1963 N Ireland | 1963 Norway | 1963 Wales | 1964 England |
|---|---|---|---|---|
| 1 Blacklaw | 1 Brown | 1 Brown | 1 Brown | 1 Forsyth |
| 2 McNeill | 2 Hamilton | 2 Hamilton | 2 Hamilton | 2 Hamilton |
| 3 Holt | 3 Provan | 3 Provan | 3 Kennedy | 3 Kennedy |
| 4 McLintock | 4 Crerand | 4 Mackay | 4 Mackay | 4 Greig |
| 5 Ure | 5 Ure | 5 Ure | 5 McNeill | 5 McNeill |
| 6 Baxter | 6 Mackay | 6 Baxter (Gabriel) | 6 Baxter | 6 Baxter |
| 7 Henderson | 7 Henderson | 7 Scott | 7 Henderson | 7 Henderson |
| 8 Gibson | 8 White | 8 White | 8 White | 8 White |
| 9 St John | 9 St John | 9 Gilzean | 9 Gilzean | 9 Gilzean |
| 10 Law | 10 Gibson | 10 Law | 10 Law | 10 Law |
| 11 Wilson | 11 Mulhall | 11 Henderson | 11 Scott | 11 Wilson |
| Madrid June 13: 6-2 *St John, Wilson, Law, Henderson, Gibson, McLintock* | Belfast Oct 12: 1-2 *St John* | Hampden Nov 7: 6-1 *Law 4, Mackay 2* | Hampden Nov 20: 2-1 *White, Law* | Hampden April 11: 1-0 *Gilzean* |

| 1964 W Germany | 1964 Wales | 1964 Finland | 1964 N Ireland | 1965 England |
|---|---|---|---|---|
| 1 Cruickshank | 1 Forsyth | 1 Forsyth | 1 Forsyth | 1 Brown |
| 2 Hamilton (Holt) | 2 Hamilton | 2 Hamilton | 2 Hamilton | 2 Hamilton |
| 3 Kennedy | 3 Kennedy | 3 Kennedy | 3 Kennedy | 3 McCreadie |
| 4 Greig | 4 Greig | 4 Greig | 4 Greig | 4 Crerand |
| 5 McNeill | 5 Yeats | 5 McGrory | 5 McGrory | 5 McNeill |
| 6 Baxter | 6 Baxter | 6 Baxter | 6 McLintock | 6 Greig |
| 7 Henderson | 7 Johnstone | 7 Johnstone | 7 Wallace | 7 Henderson |
| 8 White | 8 Gibson | 8 Gibson | 8 Law | 8 Collins |
| 9 Gilzean | 9 Chalmers | 9 Chalmers | 9 Gilzean | 9 St John |
| 10 Law | 10 Law | 10 Law | 10 Baxter | 10 Law |
| 11 Wilson | 11 Robertson | 11 Scott | 11 Wilson | 11 Wilson |
| | | | | |
| Hanover | Cardiff | Hampden | Hampden | Wembley |
| May 12: 2-2 | Oct 3: 2-3 | Oct 21: 3-1 | Nov 25: 3-2 | April 10: 2-2 |
| *Gilzean 2* | *Chalmers, Gibson* | *Law, Chalmers, Gibson* | *Wilson 2, Gilzean* | *Law, St John* |

| 1965 Spain | 1965 Poland | 1965 Finland | 1965 N Ireland | 1965 Poland |
|---|---|---|---|---|
| 1 Brown | 1 Brown | 1 Brown | 1 Brown | 1 Brown |
| 2 Hamilton | 2 Hamilton | 2 Hamilton | 2 Hamilton | 2 Hamilton |
| 3 McCreadie | 3 McCreadie | 3 McCreadie | 3 McCreadie | 3 McCreadie |
| 4 Bremner | 4 Greig | 4 Crerand | 4 Mackay | 4 Crerand |
| 5 McNeill | 5 McNeill | 5 McNeill | 5 McNeill | 5 McNeill |
| 6 Greig | 6 Crerand | 6 Greig | 6 Greig | 6 Greig |
| 7 Henderson | 7 Henderson | 7 Henderson | 7 Henderson | 7 Henderson |
| 8 Collins | 8 Collins | 8 Law | 8 Law | 8 Bremner |
| 9 Law | 9 Martin | 9 Martin | 9 Gilzean | 9 Gilzean |
| 10 Gilzean | 10 Law | 10 Hamilton | 10 Baxter | 10 Law |
| 11 Hughes | 11 Hughes | 11 Wilson | 11 Hughes | 11 Johnston |
| | | | | |
| Hampden | Chorzow | Helsinki | Belfast | Hampden |
| May 8: 0-0 | May 23: 1-1 | May 27: 2-1 | Oct 2: 2-3 | Oct 13: 1-2 |
| | *Law* | *Wilson, Greig* | *Gilzean 2* | *McNeill* |

| 1965 Italy | 1965 Wales | 1965 Italy | 1966 England | 1966 Netherlands |
|---|---|---|---|---|
| 1 Brown | 1 Ferguson | 1 Blacklaw | 1 Ferguson | 1 Ferguson |
| 2 Greig | 2 Greig | 2 Provan | 2 Greig | 2 Greig |
| 3 Provan | 3 McCreadie | 3 McCreadie | 3 Gemmell | 3 Provan |
| 4 Murdoch | 4 Murdoch | 4 Murdoch | 4 Murdoch | 4 Stanton |
| 5 McKinnon | 5 McKinnon | 5 McKinnon | 5 McKinnon | 5 McKinnon |
| 6 Baxter | 6 Baxter | 6 Greig | 6 Baxter | 6 Smith |
| 7 Henderson | 7 Henderson | 7 Forrest | 7 Johnstone | 7 Henderson |
| 8 Bremner | 8 Cooke | 8 Bremner | 8 Law | 8 Penman |
| 9 Gilzean | 9 Forrest | 9 Yeats | 9 Wallace | 9 Scott |
| 10 Martin | 10 Gilzean | 10 Cooke | 10 Bremner | 10 Wallace |
| 11 Hughes | 11 Johnston | 11 Hughes | 11 Johnston | 11 Johnston |
| | | | | |
| Hampden | Hampden | Naples | Hampden | Hampden |
| Nov 9: 1-0 | Nov 24: 4-1 | Dec 7: 0-3 | April 2: 3-4 | May 11: 0-3 |
| *Greig* | *Murdoch 2, Henderson, Greig* | | *Law, Johnston 2* | |

| 1966 Portugal | 1966 Brazil | 1966 Wales | 1966 N Ireland | 1967 England |
|---|---|---|---|---|
| 1 Ferguson | 1 Ferguson | 1 Ferguson | 1 Ferguson | 1 Simpson |
| 2 Bell | 2 Greig | 2 Greig | 2 Greig | 2 Gemmell |
| 3 McCreadie | 3 Bell | 3 Gemmell | 3 Gemmell | 3 McCreadie |
| 4 Greig | 4 Bremner | 4 Bremner | 4 Bremner | 4 Greig |
| 5 McGrory | 5 McKinnon | 5 McKinnon | 5 McKinnon | 5 McKinnon |
| 6 Bremner | 6 Clark | 6 Clark | 6 Clark | 6 Bremner |
| 7 Scott | 7 Scott | 7 Johnstone | 7 Henderson | 7 McCalliog |
| 8 Cooke | 8 Cooke | 8 Law | 8 Murdoch | 8 Law |
| 9 Young (Chalmers) | 9 Chalmers | 9 McBride | 9 McBride | 9 Wallace |
| 10 Baxter | 10 Baxter | 10 Baxter | 10 Chalmers | 10 Baxter |
| 11 Sinclair | 11 Cormack | 11 Henderson | 11 Lennox | 11 Lennox |
| Hampden June 18: 0-1 | Hampden June 25: 1-1 *Chalmers* | Cardiff Oct 22: 1-1 *Law* | Hampden Nov 16: 2-1 *Murdoch, Lennox* | Wembley April 15: 3-2 *Law, Lennox, McCalliog* |

| 1967 USSR | 1967 N Ireland | 1967 Wales | 1968 England | 1968 Netherlands |
|---|---|---|---|---|
| 1 Simpson | 1 Simpson | 1 Clark | 1 Simpson | 1 Clark |
| 2 Gemmell | 2 Gemmell | 2 Craig | 2 Gemmell | 2 Fraser |
| 3 McCreadie | 3 McCreadie | 3 McCreadie | 3 McCreadie | 3 McCreadie |
| 4 Clark | 4 Greig | 4 Greig | 4 McNeill | 4 Moncur |
| 5 McNeill | 5 McKinnon | 5 McKinnon | 5 McKinnon | 5 McKinnon |
| 6 Baxter | 6 Ure | 6 Baxter | 6 Greig | 6 Smith D. |
| 7 Johnstone | 7 Wallace | 7 Johnstone | 7 Cooke | 7 Henderson |
| 8 McLintock | 8 Murdoch | 8 Bremner | 8 Bremner | 8 Hope (Smith J.) |
| 9 McCalliog | 9 McCalliog | 9 Gilzean | 9 Hughes | 9 McLean |
| 10 Law (Wallace) | 10 Law | 10 Johnston | 10 Johnston | 10 Greig |
| 11 Lennox | 11 Morgan | 11 Lennox | 11 Lennox | 11 Cooke |
| Hampden May 10: 0-2 | Belfast Oct 21: 0-1 | Hampden Nov 22: 3-2 *Gilzean 2, McKinnon* | Hampden Feb 24: 1-1 *Hughes* | Amsterdam May 30: 0-0 |

| 1968 Denmark | 1968 Austria | 1968 Cyprus | 1969 W Germany | 1969 Wales |
|---|---|---|---|---|
| 1 Herriot | 1 Simpson | 1 Herriot | 1 Lawrence | 1 Lawrence (Herriot) |
| 2 Gemmell | 2 Gemmell | 2 Fraser | 2 Gemmell | 2 Gemmell |
| 3 McCreadie | 3 McCreadie | 3 McCreadie | 3 McCreadie | 3 McCreadie |
| 4 Bremner | 4 Bremner | 4 Bremner | 4 Murdoch | 4 Bremner |
| 5 McKinnon | 5 McKinnon | 5 McKinnon (McNeill) | 5 McKinnon | 5 McNeill |
| 6 Greig | 6 Greig | 6 Greig | 6 Greig | 6 Greig |
| 7 McLean | 7 Johnstone | 7 McLean | 7 Johnstone | 7 McLean |
| 8 McCalliog (Cormack) | 8 Cooke | 8 Murdoch | 8 Bremner | 8 Murdoch |
| 9 Stein | 9 Hughes | 9 Stein | 9 Law | 9 Stein |
| 10 Hope | 10 Law (Gilzean) | 10 Gilzean | 10 Gilzean | 10 Gilzean |
| 11 Lennox | 11 Lennox | 11 Cooke (Lennox) | 11 Lennox (Cooke) | 11 Cooke |
| Copenhagen Oct 16: 1-0 *Lennox* | Hampden Nov 6: 2-1 *Law, Bremner* | Nicosia Dec 11: 5-0 *Gilzean 2, Stein 2, Murdoch* | Hampden April 16: 1-1 *Murdoch* | Wrexham May 3: 5-3 *McNeill, Stein, Gilzean, Bremner, McLean* |

| 1969 N Ireland | 1969 England | 1969 Cyprus | 1969 Rep of Ireland | 1969 W Germany |
|---|---|---|---|---|
| 1 Herriot | 1 Herriot | 1 Herriot | 1 McGarr (Herriot) | 1 Herriot |
| 2 McCreadie | 2 McCreadie | 2 McCreadie | 2 Greig | 2 Greig |
| 3 Gemmell | 3 Gemmell | 3 Gemmell | 3 Gemmell (Callaghan) | 3 Gemmell |
| 4 Bremner | 4 Murdoch | 4 Bremner | 4 Stanton | 4 Bremner |
| 5 Greig | 5 McNeill | 5 McNeill | 5 McKinnon | 5 McKinnon |
| 6 Stanton | 6 Greig | 6 Greig | 6 Moncur | 6 McNeill |
| 7 Henderson | 7 Henderson | 7 Henderson | 7 Henderson | 7 Johnstone |
| 8 Murdoch | 8 Bremner | 8 Cooke | 8 Bremner | 8 Cormack |
| 9 Stein | 9 Stein | 9 Stein | 9 Stein | 9 Gilzean |
| 10 Law | 10 Gilzean (Wallace) | 10 Gilzean | 10 Cormack | 10 Gray |
| 11 Cooke (Johnston) | 11 Gray | 11 Gray | 11 Hughes | 11 Stein |

| Hampden May 6: 1-1 *Stein* | Wembley May 10: 1-4 *Stein* | Hampden May 12: 8-0 *Gray, McNeill, Stein 4, Henderson, Gemmell* | Dublin Sept 21: 1-1 *Stein* | Hamburg Oct 22: 2-3 *Johnstone, Gilzean* |
|---|---|---|---|---|

| 1969 Austria | 1970 N Ireland | 1970 Wales | 1970 England | 1970 Denmark |
|---|---|---|---|---|
| 1 McGarr | 1 Clark | 1 Cruickshank | 1 Cruickshank | 1 Cruickshank |
| 2 Greig | 2 Hay | 2 Callaghan | 2 Gemmell | 2 Hay (Jardine) |
| 3 Burns | 3 Dickson | 3 Dickson | 3 Dickson | 3 Greig |
| 4 Murdoch | 4 McLintock | 4 Greig | 4 Greig | 4 Stanton |
| 5 McKinnon | 5 McKinnon | 5 McKinnon | 5 McKinnon | 5 McKinnon |
| 6 Stanton | 6 Moncur | 6 Moncur | 6 Moncur (Gilzean) | 6 Moncur |
| 7 Cooke (Stein) | 7 McLean | 7 McLean (Lennox) | 7 Johnstone | 7 Johnstone |
| 8 Bremner | 8 Carr | 8 Hay | 8 Hay | 8 Carr |
| 9 Gilzean | 9 O'Hare | 9 O'Hare | 9 Stein | 9 Stein |
| 10 Curran (Lorimer) | 10 Gilzean (Stein) | 10 Stein | 10 O'Hare | 10 O'Hare (Cormack) |
| 11 Gray | 11 Johnston | 11 Carr | 11 Carr | 11 Johnston |

| Vienna Nov 5: 0-2 | Belfast April 18: 1-0 *O'Hare* | Hampden April 22: 0-0 | Hampden April 25: 0-0 | Hampden Nov 11: 1-0 *O'Hare* |
|---|---|---|---|---|

| 1971 Belgium | 1971 Portugal | 1971 Wales | 1971 N Ireland | 1971 England |
|---|---|---|---|---|
| 1 Cruickshank | 1 Clark | 1 Clark | 1 Clark | 1 Clark |
| 2 Hay | 2 Hay | 2 Hay | 2 Hay | 2 Greig |
| 3 Gemmell | 3 Brogan | 3 Brogan | 3 Brogan | 3 Brogan |
| 4 Stanton (Green) | 4 Stanton (Green) | 4 Bremner (Greig) | 4 Greig | 4 Bremner |
| 5 McKinnon | 5 McKinnon | 5 McLintock | 5 McLintock (Munro) | 5 McLintock |
| 6 Moncur | 6 Moncur | 6 Moncur | 6 Moncur | 6 Moncur |
| 7 Gemmill | 7 Henderson | 7 Lorimer | 7 Lorimer | 7 Johnstone |
| 8 Greig | 8 McCalliog (Jarvie) | 8 Robb | 8 Green | 8 Robb |
| 9 Stein (Forrest) | 9 Robb | 9 O'Hare | 9 O'Hare (Jarvie) | 9 Curran (Munro) |
| 10 O'Hare | 10 Cormack | 10 Cormack | 10 Curran | 10 Green (Jarvie) |
| 11 Cooke | 11 Gilzean | 11 Gray | 11 Gray | 11 Cormack |

| Liège Feb 3: 0-3 | Lisbon April 21: 0-2 | Cardiff May 15: 0-0 | Hampden May 18: 0-1 | Wembley May 22: 1-3 *Curran* |
|---|---|---|---|---|

| 1971 Denmark | 1971 USSR | 1971 Portugal | 1971 Belgium | 1971 Netherlands |
|---|---|---|---|---|
| 1 Clark | 1 Clark | 1 Wilson | 1 Clark | 1 Wilson |
| 2 Munro | 2 Brownlie | 2 Jardine | 2 Jardine | 2 Jardine |
| 3 Dickson | 3 Dickson | 3 Colquhoun (Buchan) | 3 Hay | 3 Hay |
| 4 Stanton | 4 Munro | 4 Stanton | 4 Bremner | 4 Bremner |
| 5 McKinnon | 5 McKinnon | 5 Hay | 5 Buchan | 5 Colquhoun |
| 6 Moncur | 6 Stanton | 6 Bremner | 6 Stanton | 6 Stanton |
| 7 McLean | 7 Forrest | 7 Cropley | 7 Johnstone (Hansen) | 7 Johnstone (O'Hare) |
| 8 Forsyth (Robb) | 8 Watson | 8 Graham | 8 Murray | 8 Gemmill |
| 9 Stein | 9 Stein (Curran) | 9 Johnstone | 9 O'Hare | 9 Dalglish |
| 10 Curran | 10 Robb | 10 O'Hare | 10 Gray | 10 Graham |
| 11 Forrest (Scott) | 11 Scott | 11 Gemmill | 11 Cropley (Dalglish) | 11 Gray (Cormack) |
| Copenhagen June 9: 0-1 | Moscow June 14: 0-1 | Hampden Oct 13: 2-1 *O'Hare, Gemmill* | Aberdeen Nov 10: 1-0 *O'Hare* | Amsterdam Dec 1: 1-2 *Graham* |

| 1972 Peru | 1972 N Ireland | 1972 Wales | 1972 England | 1972 Yugoslavia |
|---|---|---|---|---|
| 1 Hunter | 1 Clark | 1 Clark | 1 Clark | 1 Hunter |
| 2 Brownlie | 2 Brownlie | 2 Stanton | 2 Brownlie | 2 Forsyth A. (Hansen) |
| 3 Donachie | 3 Donachie | 3 Buchan | 3 Donachie (Green) | 3 Buchan |
| 4 Carr | 4 Bremner | 4 Bremner | 4 Bremner | 4 Colquhoun |
| 5 Colquhoun | 5 McNeill | 5 McNeill | 5 McNeill | 5 Donachie |
| 6 Moncur | 6 Moncur | 6 Moncur | 6 Moncur | 6 Bremner |
| 7 Morgan | 7 Johnstone (Lorimer) | 7 Lorimer | 7 Gemmill (Johnstone) | 7 Hartford |
| 8 Hartford | 8 Gemmill | 8 Green | 8 Hartford | 8 Graham |
| 9 O'Hare | 9 O'Hare | 9 O'Hare (Macari) | 9 Lorimer | 9 Morgan |
| 10 Law | 10 Law | 10 Law | 10 Macari | 10 Law (Bone) |
| 11 Gemmill | 11 Graham | 11 Gemmill (Hartford) | 11 Law | 11 Macari |
| Hampden April 26: 2-0 *O'Hare, Law* | Hampden May 20: 2-0 *Law, Lorimer* | Hampden May 24: 1-0 *Lorimer* | Hampden May 27: 0-1 | Belo Horizonte June 29: 2-2 *Macari 2* |

| 1972 Czechoslovakia | 1972 Brazil | 1972 Denmark | 1972 Denmark | 1973 England |
|---|---|---|---|---|
| 1 Clark | 1 Clark | 1 Clark | 1 Harvey | 1 Clark |
| 2 Forsyth A. | 2 Forsyth A. | 2 Brownlie | 2 Brownlie | 2 Forsyth A. |
| 3 Colquhoun | 3 Colquhoun | 3 Forsyth A. | 3 Donachie | 3 Donachie |
| 4 Buchan | 4 Buchan | 4 Bremner | 4 Bremner | 4 Bremner |
| 5 Donachie | 5 Donachie | 5 Colquhoun | 5 Colquhoun | 5 Colquhoun |
| 6 Bremner | 6 Bremner | 6 Buchan | 6 Buchan | 6 Buchan |
| 7 Graham | 7 Graham | 7 Lorimer | 7 Lorimer | 7 Lorimer |
| 8 Law (Stein) | 8 Hartford | 8 Macari (Dalglish) | 8 Dalglish (Carr) | 8 Dalglish |
| 9 Hartford | 9 Morgan | 9 Bone (Harper) | 9 Harper | 9 Macari |
| 10 Morgan | 10 Law | 10 Graham | 10 Graham | 10 Graham |
| 11 Macari | 11 Macari | 11 Morgan | 11 Morgan | 11 Morgan (Stein) |
| Porto Alegre July 2: 0-0 | Rio de Janeiro July 5: 0-1 | Copenhagen Oct 18: 4-1 *Macari, Bone, Harper, Morgan* | Glasgow Nov 15: 2-0 *Dalglish, Lorimer* | Glasgow Feb 14: 0-5 |

| 1973 Wales | 1973 N Ireland | 1973 England | 1973 Switzerland | 1973 Brazil |
|---|---|---|---|---|
| 1 McCloy | 1 McCloy | 1 Hunter | 1 McCloy | 1 McCloy |
| 2 McGrain | 2 McGrain | 2 Jardine | 2 Jardine | 2 Jardine |
| 3 Donachie | 3 Donachie | 3 McGrain | 3 McGrain | 3 McGrain |
| 4 Graham | 4 Graham (Macari) | 4 Bremner | 4 Bremner | 4 Bremner |
| 5 Holton | 5 Holton | 5 Holton | 5 Holton | 5 Holton |
| 6 Johnstone D. | 6 Johnstone D. | 6 Johnstone D. | 6 Johnstone D. | 6 Johnstone D. |
| 7 Dalglish (Macari) | 7 Dalglish | 7 Morgan | 7 Dalglish | 7 Morgan |
| 8 Stanton | 8 Stanton (Bremner) | 8 Macari (Jordan) | 8 Hay | 8 Hay |
| 9 Parlane (Stein) | 9 Stein | 9 Dalglish | 9 Parlane | 9 Parlane |
| 10 Hay | 10 Hay | 10 Hay | 10 Connolly (Jordan) | 10 Jordan |
| 11 Morgan | 11 Morgan | 11 Lorimer (Stein) | 11 Morgan | 11 Dalglish (Graham) |
| Wrexham May 12: 2-0 *Graham 2* | Glasgow May 16: 1-2 *Dalglish* | Wembley May 19: 0-1 | Berne June 22: 0-1 | Glasgow June 30: 0-1 |

| 1973 Czechoslovakia | 1973 Czechoslovakia | 1973 W Germany | 1974 W Germany | 1974 N Ireland |
|---|---|---|---|---|
| 1 Hunter | 1 Harvey | 1 Harvey | 1 Allan | 1 Harvey |
| 2 Jardine | 2 Jardine | 2 Jardine | 2 Jardine | 2 Jardine |
| 3 McGrain | 3 McGrain | 3 McGrain | 3 Schaedler | 3 Donachie (Smith) |
| 4 Bremner | 4 Forsyth T. | 4 Bremner | 4 Hay | 4 Bremner |
| 5 Holton | 5 Blackley | 5 Holton | 5 Buchan | 5 Holton |
| 6 Connolly | 6 Hay | 6 Connolly | 6 Stanton | 6 Buchan |
| 7 Hay | 7 Morgan | 7 Morgan | 7 Morgan | 7 Morgan |
| 8 Law | 8 Jordan | 8 Smith (Lorimer) | 8 Dalglish | 8 Hay |
| 9 Morgan | 9 Law (Ford) | 9 Law (Jordan) | 9 Law (Ford) | 9 Law (Jordan) |
| 10 Dalglish (Jordan) | 10 Dalglish | 10 Dalglish | 10 Hutchison | 10 Dalglish |
| 11 Hutchison | 11 Hutchison | 11 Hutchison | 11 Burns (Robinson) | 11 Hutchison |
| Hampden Sept 26: 2-1 *Holton, Jordan* | Bratislava Oct 17: 0-1 | Hampden Nov 14: 1-1 *Holton* | Frankfurt March 27: 1-2 *Dalglish* | Hampden May 11: 0-1 |

| 1974 Wales | 1974 England | 1974 Belgium | 1974 Norway | 1974 Zaire † |
|---|---|---|---|---|
| 1 Harvey | 1 Harvey | 1 Harvey | 1 Allan | 1 Harvey |
| 2 Jardine | 2 Jardine | 2 Jardine | 2 Jardine | 2 Jardine |
| 3 Hay | 3 McGrain | 3 McGrain | 3 McGrain | 3 McGrain |
| 4 Bremner | 4 Bremner | 4 Bremner | 4 Bremner | 4 Bremner |
| 5 Holton | 5 Holton | 5 McQueen | 5 Holton | 5 Holton |
| 6 Buchan (McGrain) | 6 Blackley | 6 Blackley | 6 Buchan | 6 Blackley |
| 7 Johnstone J. | 7 Lorimer | 7 Johnstone J. (Morgan) | 7 Johnstone J. (Dalglish) | 7 Dalglish (Hutchison) |
| 8 Dalglish | 8 Johnstone J. | 8 Dalglish (Hutchison) | 8 Lorimer | 8 Hay |
| 9 Ford | 9 Jordan | 9 Jordan | 9 Jordan | 9 Lorimer |
| 10 Jordan | 10 Dalglish | 10 Hay | 10 Hay | 10 Jordan |
| 11 Hutchison (Smith) | 11 Hay | 11 Lorimer | 11 Hutchison | 11 Law |
| Hampden May 14: 2-0 *Dalglish, Jardine* | Hampden May 18: 2-0 *Jordan, Todd og* | Bruges June 1: 1-2 *Johnstone* | Oslo June 6: 2-1 *Jordan, Dalglish* | Dortmund June 14: 2-0 *Lorimer, Jordan* |

| 1974 Brazil † | 1974 Yugoslavia † | 1974 E Germany | 1974 Spain | 1975 Spain |
|---|---|---|---|---|
| 1 Harvey | 1 Harvey | 1 Harvey | 1 Harvey | 1 Harvey |
| 2 Jardine | 2 Jardine | 2 Jardine | 2 Jardine | 2 Jardine |
| 3 McGrain | 3 McGrain | 3 Forsyth A. | 3 Forsyth A. | 3 McQueen |
| 4 Holton | 4 Holton | 4 Souness | 4 McQueen | 4 Buchan |
| 5 Buchan | 5 Buchan | 5 Holton (Burns) | 5 Burns | 5 McGrain |
| 6 Bremner | 6 Bremner | 6 Buchan | 6 Bremner | 6 Bremner |
| 7 Hay | 7 Dalglish (Hutchison) | 7 Johnstone J. | 7 Souness | 7 Cooke |
| 8 Dalglish | 8 Hay | 8 Dalglish (Johnstone D.) | 8 Hutchison (Dalglish) | 8 Hutchison |
| 9 Morgan | 9 Morgan | 9 Deans | 9 Johnstone J. | 9 Dalglish |
| 10 Jordan | 10 Jordan | 10 Jordan | 10 Deans (Lorimer) | 10 Jordan (Parlane) |
| 11 Lorimer | 11 Lorimer | 11 Hutchison | 11 Jordan | 11 Burns (Wilson) |
| Frankfurt June 18: 0-0 | Frankfurt June 22: 1-1 *Jordan* | Hampden Oct 30: 3-0 *Hutchison (pen), Burns, Dalglish* | Hampden Nov 20: 1-2 *Bremner* | Valencia Feb 5: 1-1 *Jordan* |

| 1975 Sweden | 1975 Portugal | 1975 Wales | 1975 N Ireland | 1975 England |
|---|---|---|---|---|
| 1 Kennedy | 1 Kennedy | 1 Kennedy | 1 Kennedy | 1 Kennedy |
| 2 Jardine | 2 Jardine | 2 Jardine | 2 Jardine (Forsyth A.) | 2 Jardine |
| 3 McGrain | 3 McGrain | 3 McGrain | 3 McGrain | 3 McGrain |
| 4 Munro | 4 Buchan (Jackson) | 4 Jackson (Munro) | 4 Munro | 4 Munro |
| 5 Jackson | 5 McQueen | 5 McQueen | 5 McQueen | 5 McQueen |
| 6 Robinson | 6 Rioch | 6 Rioch | 6 Rioch | 6 Rioch |
| 7 Dalglish | 7 Cooke (Macari) | 7 Macari | 7 Dalglish | 7 Dalglish |
| 8 Souness (Johnstone D.) | 8 Dalglish | 8 Dalglish | 8 Robinson (Conn) | 8 Conn |
| 9 Parlane | 9 Parlane | 9 Parlane | 9 Parlane | 9 Parlane |
| 10 MacDougall | 10 MacDougall | 10 MacDougall | 10 MacDougall | 10 MacDougall (Macari) |
| 11 Macari (Hughes) | 11 Hutchison (Duncan) | 11 Duncan | 11 Duncan | 11 Duncan (Hutchison) |
| Gothenburg April 16: 1-1 *MacDougall* | Hampden May 13: 1-0 *Artur og* | Cardiff May 17: 2-2 *Jackson, Rioch* | Hampden May 20: 3-0 *MacDougall, Dalglish, Parlane* | Wembley May 24: 1-5 *Rioch (pen)* |

| 1975 Rumania | 1975 Denmark | 1975 Denmark | 1975 Rumania | 1976 Switzerland |
|---|---|---|---|---|
| 1 Brown | 1 Harvey | 1 Harvey | 1 Cruickshank | 1 Rough |
| 2 McGrain | 2 McGrain | 2 McGrain | 2 Brownlie | 2 McGrain |
| 3 Forsyth A. | 3 Forsyth A. | 3 Houston | 3 Donachie | 3 Gray F. |
| 4 Munro | 4 Bremner | 4 Greig | 4 Buchan | 4 Forsyth T. |
| 5 McQueen | 5 McQueen | 5 Jackson | 5 Jackson | 5 Blackley |
| 6 Rioch (Hutchison) | 6 Buchan | 6 Rioch | 6 Rioch | 6 Craig |
| 7 Dalglish | 7 Lorimer | 7 Lorimer | 7 Doyle (Lorimer) | 7 Dalglish (Bremner D.) |
| 8 Miller | 8 Dalglish | 8 Dalglish | 8 Hartford | 8 Pettigrew (McKean) |
| 9 Parlane | 9 Harper | 9 MacDougall (Parlane) | 9 Gray A. | 9 Gray A. |
| 10 Macari (Robinson) | 10 Rioch | 10 Hartford | 10 Dalglish (MacDougall) | 10 MacDonald |
| 11 Duncan | 11 Hutchison (Duncan) | 11 Gemmill | 11 Gemmill | 11 Johnstone D. |
| Bucharest June 1: 1-1 *McQueen* | Copenhagen Sept 3: 1-0 *Harper* | Glasgow Oct 29: 3-1 *Dalglish, Rioch, MacDougall* | Glasgow Dec 17: 1-1 *Rioch* | Glasgow April 7: 1-0 *Pettigrew* |

| 1976 Wales | 1976 N Ireland | 1976 England | 1976 Finland | 1976 Czechoslovakia |
|---|---|---|---|---|
| 1 Rough | 1 Rough | 1 Rough | 1 Rough (Harvey) | 1 Rough |
| 2 McGrain | 2 McGrain | 2 McGrain | 2 McGrain | 2 McGrain |
| 3 Donachie | 3 Donachie | 3 Donachie | 3 Donachie | 3 Donachie |
| 4 Forsyth T. | 4 Forsyth T. | 4 Forsyth T. | 4 Rioch | 4 Buchan |
| 5 Jackson | 5 Jackson | 5 Jackson | 5 Forsyth T. | 5 McQueen |
| 6 Rioch | 6 Rioch (Hartford) | 6 Rioch | 6 Buchan | 6 Rioch |
| 7 Pettigrew | 7 Masson | 7 Masson | 7 Dalglish | 7 Dalglish (Burns) |
| 8 Masson | 8 Gemmill | 8 Gemmill | 8 Gemmill | 8 Masson (Hartford) |
| 9 Jordan | 9 Pettigrew (Johnstone D.) | 9 Dalglish | 9 Gray A. | 9 Jordan |
| 10 Gemmill | 10 Jordan | 10 Jordan | 10 Masson | 10 Gray A. |
| 11 Gray E. | 11 Dalglish | 11 Grey E. (Johnstone D.) | 11 Gray E. | 11 Gemmill |
| Glasgow May 6: 3-1 *Pettigrew, Rioch, Gray* | Glasgow May 8: 3-0 *Gemmill, Masson, Dalglish* | Glasgow May 15: 2-1 *Masson, Dalglish* | Glasgow Sept 8: 6-0 *Rioch, Masson (pen), Dalglish, Gray A. 2, Gray E.* | Prague Oct 13: 0-2 |

| 1976 Wales | 1977 Sweden | 1977 Wales | 1977 N Ireland | 1977 England |
|---|---|---|---|---|
| 1 Rough | 1 Rough | 1 Rough | 1 Rough | 1 Rough |
| 2 McGrain | 2 McGrain | 2 McGrain | 2 McGrain | 2 McGrain |
| 3 Donachie | 3 Forsyth T. | 3 Donachie | 3 Donachie | 3 Donachie |
| 4 Blackley | 4 Blackley (Narey) | 4 Rioch (Johnston) | 4 Forsyth T. | 4 Forsyth T. |
| 5 McQueen | 5 Donachie | 5 McQueen | 5 McQueen | 5 McQueen |
| 6 Rioch (Hartford) | 6 Glavin (Jardine) | 6 Forsyth T. | 6 Rioch | 6 Rioch |
| 7 Burns | 7 Dalglish | 7 Masson | 7 Masson | 7 Masson (Gemmill) |
| 8 Dalglish | 8 Hartford | 8 Gemmill | 8 Hartford | 8 Dalglish |
| 9 Jordan | 9 Burns (Craig J.) | 9 Parlane (Burns) | 9 Jordan (Macari) | 9 Jordan (Macari) |
| 10 Gemmill | 10 Pettigrew | 10 Dalglish | 10 Dalglish | 10 Hartford |
| 11 Gray E. (Pettigrew) | 11 Johnston | 11 Hartford | 11 Johnston (Gemmill) | 11 Johnston |
| Glasgow Nov 17: 1-0 *Evans og* | Glasgow April 27: 3-1 *Hartford, Dalglish, Craig* | Wrexham May 28: 0-0 | Glasgow June 1: 3-0 *Dalglish 2, McQueen* | Wembley June 4: 2-0 *McQueen, Dalglish* |

| 1977 Chile | 1977 Argentina | 1977 Brazil | 1977 E Germany | 1977 Czechoslovakia |
|---|---|---|---|---|
| 1 Rough (Stewart) | 1 Rough | 1 Rough | 1 Stewart | 1 Rough |
| 2 McGrain | 2 McGrain | 2 McGrain | 2 McGrain | 2 Jardine |
| 3 Donachie | 3 Donachie | 3 Donachie | 3 Donachie | 3 McGrain |
| 4 Buchan | 4 Gemmill | 4 Rioch | 4 Masson | 4 Forsyth T. |
| 5 Forsyth T. | 5 Forsyth T. | 5 Forsyth T. | 5 McQueen | 5 McQueen |
| 6 Rioch (Gemmill) | 6 Buchan | 6 Buchan | 6 Buchan | 6 Rioch |
| 7 Masson | 7 Masson | 7 Masson | 7 Dalglish | 7 Dalglish |
| 8 Dalglish | 8 Dalglish | 8 Gemmill | 8 Hartford (Gemmill) | 8 Masson |
| 9 Macari | 9 Macari | 9 Dalglish | 9 Jordan | 9 Jordan |
| 10 Hartford (Jardine) | 10 Hartford | 10 Hartford | 10 Macari | 10 Hartford |
| 11 Johnston | 11 Johnston | 11 Johnston (Jardine) | 11 Johnston (Graham) | 11 Johnston |
| Santiago June 15: 4-2 *Dalglish, Macari 2, Hartford* | Buenos Aires June 18: 1-1 *Masson (pen)* | Rio de Janeiro June 23: 0-2 | East Berlin Sept 7: 0-1 | Glasgow Sept 21: 3-1 *Jordan, Hartford, Dalglish* |

| 1977 Wales | 1978 Bulgaria | 1978 N Ireland | 1978 Wales | 1978 England |
|---|---|---|---|---|
| 1 Rough | 1 Blyth | 1 Rough | 1 Blyth | 1 Rough |
| 2 Jardine (Buchan) | 2 Kennedy | 2 Jardine | 2 Kennedy | 2 Kennedy |
| 3 Donachie | 3 Donachie | 3 Buchan (Burns) | 3 Donachie | 3 Burns |
| 4 Masson | 4 Souness | 4 Forsyth T. | 4 Burns | 4 Forsyth T. |
| 5 McQueen | 5 McQueen | 5 McQueen | 5 McQueen (Forsyth T.) | 5 Donachie |
| 6 Forsyth T. | 6 Miller | 6 Rioch | 6 Gemmill | 6 Rioch (Souness) |
| 7 Dalglish | 7 Dalglish (Wallace) | 7 Masson | 7 Souness | 7 Masson (Gemmill) |
| 8 Hartford | 8 Hartford | 8 Gemmill | 8 Hartford | 8 Hartford |
| 9 Jordan | 9 Jordan (Johnstone D.) | 9 Jordan (Dalglish) | 9 Johnstone D. | 9 Dalglish |
| 10 Macari | 10 Macari | 10 Johnstone D. | 10 Dalglish | 10 Jordan |
| 11 Johnston | 11 Gemmill | 11 Robertson | 11 Johnston (Robertson) | 11 Johnston |
| Liverpool | Glasgow | Glasgow | Glasgow | Glasgow |
| Oct 12: 2-0 | Feb 22: 2-1 | May 13: 1-1 | May 17: 1-1 | May 20: 0-1 |
| *Masson* (pen), *Dalglish* | *Gemmill* (pen), *Wallace* | *Johnstone* | *Johnstone* | |

| 1978 Peru † | 1978 Iran † | 1978 Netherlands † | 1978 Austria | 1978 Norway |
|---|---|---|---|---|
| 1 Rough | 1 Rough | 1 Rough | 1 Rough | 1 Stewart |
| 2 Burns | 2 Buchan (Forsyth T.) | 2 Donachie | 2 Kennedy | 2 Donachie |
| 3 Kennedy | 3 Jardine | 3 Buchan | 3 Donachie | 3 Gray F. |
| 4 Forsyth T. | 4 Burns | 4 Kennedy | 4 Gemmill | 4 Souness |
| 5 Buchan | 5 Donachie | 5 Forsyth T. | 5 McQueen | 5 McQueen |
| 6 Rioch (Macari) | 6 Macari | 6 Rioch | 6 Buchan | 6 Buchan |
| 7 Masson (Gemmill) | 7 Gemmill | 7 Hartford | 7 Dalglish | 7 Dalglish |
| 8 Hartford | 8 Hartford | 8 Gemmill | 8 Hartford | 8 Gemmill |
| 9 Dalglish | 9 Jordan | 9 Souness | 9 Jordan (Graham) | 9 Gray A. |
| 10 Jordan | 10 Dalglish (Harper) | 10 Dalglish | 10 Gray A. | 10 Hartford |
| 11 Johnston | 11 Robertson | 11 Jordan | 11 Souness | 11 Graham |
| Cordoba | Cordoba | Mendoza | Vienna | Glasgow |
| June 3: 1-3 | June 7: 1-1 | June 11: 3-2 | Sept 20: 2-3 | Oct 25: 3-2 |
| *Jordan* | *Eskandarian og* | *Dalglish, Gemmill 2 (1 pen)* | *McQueen, Gray* | *Dalglish 2, Gemmill* (pen) |

| 1978 Portugal | 1979 Wales | 1979 N Ireland | 1979 England | 1979 Argentina |
|---|---|---|---|---|
| 1 Rough | 1 Rough | 1 Wood | 1 Wood | 1 Rough (Wood) |
| 2 Kennedy | 2 Burley | 2 Burley | 2 Burley | 2 Burley |
| 3 Gray F. (Donachie) | 3 Gray F. | 3 Gray F. | 3 Gray F. | 3 Munro |
| 4 Narey | 4 Wark | 4 Wark (Narey) | 4 Wark | 4 Narey |
| 5 McQueen | 5 Hegarty | 5 McQueen | 5 McQueen | 5 Hegarty |
| 6 Buchan | 6 Hansen | 6 Souness | 6 Hegarty | 6 Hansen |
| 7 Dalglish | 7 Dalglish | 7 Dalglish | 7 Dalglish | 7 McGarvey |
| 8 Hartford | 8 Hartford | 8 Hartford | 8 Souness | 8 Wark |
| 9 Jordan (Wallace) | 9 Wallace (Jordan) | 9 Jordan | 9 Jordan | 9 Dalglish |
| 10 Gemmill | 10 Souness | 10 Hegarty | 10 Hartford | 10 Hartford (Gray F.) |
| 11 Robertson | 11 Graham | 11 Graham (McGarvey) | 11 Graham | 11 Graham |
| Lisbon | Cardiff | Glasgow | Wembley | Glasgow |
| Nov 29: 0-1 | May 19: 0-3 | May 22: 1-0 | May 26: 1-3 | June 2: 1-3 |
| | | *Graham* | *Wark* | *Graham* |

| 1979 Norway | 1979 Peru | 1979 Austria | 1979 Belgium | 1979 Belgium |
|---|---|---|---|---|
| 1 Rough | 1 Rough | 1 Rough | 1 Rough | 1 Rough |
| 2 Burley (Hegarty) (Wark) | 2 Jardine | 2 Jardine | 2 Jardine | 2 Jardine |
| 3 Munro | 3 Munro | 3 Munro | 3 Munro (Gray F.) | 3 McGrain |
| 4 Burns | 4 Souness | 4 Souness | 4 Wark | 4 Wark |
| 5 McQueen | 5 McQueen | 5 McQueen | 5 Hansen | 5 McQueen |
| 6 Gemmill | 6 Burns | 6 Burns | 6 Miller | 6 Burns |
| 7 Graham | 7 Cooper (Wark) | 7 Wark | 7 Dalglish | 7 Dalglish |
| 8 Dalglish | 8 Aitken | 8 Gemmill | 8 Souness | 8 Aitken |
| 9 Jordan | 9 Dalglish | 9 Dalglish | 9 Jordan (Provan) | 9 Johnstone D. |
| 10 Hartford | 10 Hartford | 10 Graham (Cooper) | 10 Hartford | 10 Bannon (Provan) |
| 11 Robertson | 11 Robertson | 11 Robertson | 11 Robertson | 11 Robertson |
| Oslo June 7: 4-0 *Jordan, Dalglish, Robertson, McQueen* | Hampden Sept 12: 1-1 *Olaechea og* | Hampden Oct 17: 1-1 *Gemmill* | Brussels Nov 21: 0-2 | Hampden Dec 19: 1-3 *Robertson* |

| 1980 Portugal | 1980 N Ireland | 1980 Wales | 1980 England | 1980 Poland |
|---|---|---|---|---|
| 1 Rough | 1 Thomson | 1 Rough | 1 Rough | 1 Rough |
| 2 Burley | 2 Burley | 2 McGrain | 2 McGrain | 2 Burley (Dawson) |
| 3 McGrain | 3 McGrain | 3 Munro | 3 Munro (Burley) | 3 McGrain |
| 4 Narey | 4 Narey | 4 Hegarty | 4 Hegarty | 4 Narey |
| 5 McLeish | 5 McLeish | 5 McLeish | 5 McLeish | 5 McLeish |
| 6 Hansen | 6 Souness (Jordan) | 6 Miller | 6 Miller | 6 Miller |
| 7 Dalglish (Archibald) | 7 Strachan | 7 Strachan | 7 Strachan | 7 Strachan |
| 8 Souness | 8 Archibald | 8 Gemmill | 8 Aitken (Gray A.) | 8 Aitken |
| 9 Gray A. | 9 Dalglish | 9 Dalglish | 9 Dalglish | 9 Dalglish (Weir) |
| 10 Gemmill | 10 Gemmill | 10 Jordan | 10 Jordan | 10 Archibald |
| 11 Robertson (Provan) | 11 Weir (Provan) | 11 Weir (Aitken) | 11 Gemmill | 11 Jordan (Brazil) |
| Hampden March 26: 4-1 *Dalglish, Gray, Archibald, Gemmill* (pen) | Belfast May 16: 0-1 | Hampden May 21: 1-0 *Miller* | Hampden May 24: 0-2 | Poznan May 28: 0-1 |

| 1980 Hungary | 1980 Sweden | 1980 Portugal | 1981 Israel | 1981 N Ireland |
|---|---|---|---|---|
| 1 Rough | 1 Rough | 1 Rough | 1 Rough | 1 Rough (Thomson) |
| 2 McGrain | 2 McGrain | 2 McGrain | 2 McGrain | 2 McGrain |
| 3 Dawson | 3 Gray F. | 3 Gray F. | 3 Gray F. | 3 Gray F. |
| 4 Narey | 4 Miller | 4 Souness | 4 Souness | 4 Burns K. (Hartford) |
| 5 McLeish | 5 McLeish | 5 Hansen | 5 McLeish | 5 McLeish |
| 6 Miller | 6 Hansen | 6 Miller | 6 Burns K. | 6 Miller |
| 7 Brazil (Strachan) | 7 Dalglish (Archibald) | 7 Strachan | 7 Wark (Miller) | 7 Wark |
| 8 Archibald | 8 Strachan | 8 Dalglish | 8 Dalglish (Gray A.) | 8 Archibald |
| 9 Dalglish | 9 Gray A. | 9 Gray A. | 9 Archibald | 9 Gray A. |
| 10 Gemmill | 10 Gemmill | 10 Gemmill | 10 Gemmill | 10 Gemmill |
| 11 Weir | 11 Robertson | 11 Robertson | 11 Robertson | 11 Robertson |
| Budapest May 31: 1-3 *Archibald* | Stockholm Sept 10: 1-0 *Strachan* | Glasgow Oct 15: 0-0 | Tel Aviv Feb 25: 1-0 *Dalglish* | Glasgow Mar 25: 1-1 *Wark* |

| 1981 Israel | 1981 Wales | 1981 N Ireland | 1981 England |
|---|---|---|---|
| 1 Rough | 1 Rough | 1 Thomson | 1 Rough |
| 2 McGrain | 2 Burns | 2 McGrain | 2 Stewart |
| 3 Gray F. | 3 Stewart | 3 Gray F. | 3 Gray F. |
| 4 Hansen | 4 Gray F. (McGrain) | 4 Stewart | 4 McGrain |
| 5 McLeish | 5 McQueen | 5 McLeish | 5 McLeish |
| 6 Souness | 6 Miller | 6 Miller | 6 Miller |
| 7 Provan | 7 Hartford | 7 Hartford | 7 Provan (Sturrock) |
| 8 Archibald | 8 Narey | 8 Sturrock | 8 Archibald |
| 9 Jordan | 9 Jordan | 9 Archibald | 9 Jordan |
| 10 Hartford | 10 Provan | 10 Burns T. | 10 Hartford (Narey) |
| 11 Robertson | 11 Graham (Sturrock) | 11 Robertson | 11 Robertson |
| Glasgow April 28: 3-1 Robertson 2 (2 pens), Provan | Swansea May 16: 0-2 | Glasgow May 19: 2-0 Stewart, Archibald | Wembley May 23: 1-0 Robertson (pen) |

# WORLD CLUB CHAMPIONSHIP

Played annually up to 1974 and intermittently since then between the winners of the European Cup and the winners of the South American Champions Cup – known as the Copa Libertadores. In 1980 the winners were decided by one match arranged on neutral territory in February 1981 and the venue was the same in December 1981.

1960 Real Madrid beat Penarol 0-0, 5-1
1961 Penarol beat Benfica 0-1, 5-0, 2-1
1962 Santos beat Benfica 3-2, 5-2
1963 Santos beat AC Milan 2-4, 4-2, 1-0
1964 Inter-Milan beat Independiente 0-1, 2-0, 1-0
1965 Inter-Milan beat Independiente 3-0, 0-0
1966 Penarol beat Real Madrid 2-0, 2-0
1967 Racing Club beat Celtic 0-1, 2-1, 1-0
1968 Estudiantes beat Manchester United 1-0, 1-1
1969 AC Milan beat Estudiantes 3-0,1-2
1970 Feyenoord beat Estudiantes 2-2, 1-0
1971 Nacional beat Panathinaikos 1-1, 2-1
1972 Ajax beat Independiente 1-1, 3-0
1973 Independiente beat Juventus 1-0
1974 Atlético Madrid beat Independiente 0-1, 2-0
1975 Independiente and Bayern Munich could not agree dates; no matches.
1976 Bayern Munich beat Cruzeiro 2-0, 0-0
1977 Boca Juniors beat Borussia Moenchengladbach 2-2, 3-0
1978 Not played
1979 Olimpia beat Malmö 1-0, 2-1
1980 Nacional beat Nottingham Forest 1-0

**13 Dec 1981**
**Tokyo** (National Stadium)

**Flamengo (Brazil) (3) 3** (*Nunes 2, Adilio*)
**Liverpool (0) 0**                                                                 62,000

*Flamengo:* Raul; Leandro, Junior, Mozer, Marinho, Adilio, Tita, Andrade, Nunes, Zico, Lico.

*Liverpool:* Grobbelaar; Neal, Lawrenson, Thompson, Kennedy R., Hansen, Dalglish, Lee, Johnston, McDermott (Johnson), Souness.

# WALES INTERNATIONAL TEAMS 1876-1981

Substitutes in brackets    †World Cup final stages

| 1876 Scotland | 1877 Scotland | 1878 Scotland | 1879 England | 1879 Scotland |
|---|---|---|---|---|
| 1 Thompson | 1 Burnett | 1 Phennah | 1 Glascodine | 1 Davies, John |
| 2 Evans W.A.W. | 2 Evans W.A.W. | 2 Higham | 2 Kenrick | 2 Kenrick |
| 3 Kenrick | 3 Kenrick | 3 Powell | 3 Higham | 3 Morgan J.R. |
| 4 Cross | 4 Morgan J.R. | 4 Edwards H. | 4 Williams W. | 4 Cross |
| 5 Williams W. | 5 Cross | 5 Williams W. | 5 Owen T. | 5 Williams W. |
| 6 Dr Gray | 6 Davies W.H. | 6 Savin | 6 Davies W.H. | 6 Lloyd J.W. |
| 7 Davies W.H. | 7 Davies A. | 7 Davies, James | 7 Shone | 7 Woosnam |
| 8 Thomson | 8 Price | 8 Dr Gray | 8 Heywood | 8 Hughes A.J. |
| 9 Edwards J.H. | 9 Jones A.F. | 9 Britten | 9 Price | 9 Roberts J. |
| 10 Jones J. | 10 Hughes J. | 10 Price | 10 Owen D. | 10 Roberts W. |
| 11 Davies A. | 11 Thomson | 11 Edwards C. | 11 Roberts W. | 11 Vaughan |
| Glasgow Mar 25: 0-4 | Wrexham Mar 5: 0-2 | Glasgow Mar 23: 0-9 | London Jan 18: 1-2 *Davies* | Wrexham April 7: 0-3 |

| 1880 England | 1880 Scotland | 1881 England | 1881 Scotland | 1882 Ireland |
|---|---|---|---|---|
| 1 Hibbott | 1 Hibbott | 1 McMillan | 1 McMillan | 1 Adams |
| 2 Morgan J.R. | 2 Morgan J.R. | 2 Morgan J.R. | 2 Morgan J.R. | 2 Morgan J.R. |
| 3 Powell | 3 Powell | 3 Kenrick | 3 Roberts J. *(Ruthin)* | 3 Powell |
| 4 Edwards H. | 4 Bowen | 4 Williams W. | 4 Williams W. | 4 Hughes F.W. |
| 5 Williams W. | 5 Bell | 5 Bell | 5 Bell | 5 Williams W. |
| 6 Owen W.P. | 6 Owen W.P. | 6 Owen W.P. | 6 Owen W.P. | 6 Owen W.P. |
| 7 Davies W.H. | 7 Roberts W. | 7 Lewis T. | 7 Lewis T. | 7 Shaw |
| 8 Boden | 8 Roberts J. | 8 Cross | 8 Price | 8 Ketley |
| 9 Price | 9 Price | 9 Price | 9 Cross | 9 Price |
| 10 Roberts J. | 10 Britten | 10 Goodwin | 10 Roberts W. | 10 Roberts J. |
| 11 Roberts W. | 11 Vaughan | 11 Vaughan | 11 Vaughan | 11 Vaughan |
| Wrexham Mar 15: 2-3 *Roberts J., Roberts W.* | Glasgow Mar 27: 1-5 *Roberts W.* | Blackburn Feb 26: 1-0 *Vaughan* | Wrexham Mar 14: 1-5 *Cross* | Wrexham Feb 25: 7-1 *Price 4, Morgan, Owen 2* |

| 1882 England | 1882 Scotland | 1883 England | 1883 Scotland | 1883 Ireland |
|---|---|---|---|---|
| 1 Adams | 1 Phoenix | 1 Adams | 1 Gough | 1 Adams |
| 2 Morgan J.R. | 2 Morgan J.R. | 2 Powell | 2 Powell | 2 Powell |
| 3 Powell | 3 Powell | 3 Morgan J.R. | 3 Hughes F.W. | 3 Hughes F.W. |
| 4 Edwards H. | 4 Edwards H. | 4 Hughes F.W. | 4 Bowen | 4 Jones J. |
| 5 Hughes F.W. | 5 Williams W. | 5 Burke | 5 Jones J. | 5 Williams W. |
| 6 Williams W. | 6 Roberts J. *(Ruthin)* | 6 Roberts W.H. | 6 Edwards H. | 6 Eyton-Jones |
| 7 Owen W.P. | 7 Owen W.P. | 7 Owen W.P. | 7 Price | 7 Price |
| 8 Roberts W.H. | 8 Roberts W.H. | 8 Davies J.P. | 8 Owen W.P. | 8 Vaughan |
| 9 Price | 9 Price | 9 Roberts W. | 9 Roberts W.H. | 9 Roberts W.H. |
| 10 Roberts J. | 10 Roberts J. | 10 Roberts J. | 10 Vaughan | 10 Davies J.P. |
| 11 Vaughan | 11 Vaughan | 11 Vaughan | 11 Roberts W. | 11 Davies R. |
| Wrexham Mar 13: 5-3 *Owen 2, Morgan, Vaughan, 1 og* | Glasgow Mar 25: 0-5 | London Feb 3: 0-5 | Wrexham Mar 12: 0-3 | Belfast Mar 17: 1-1 *Roberts* |

| 1884 Ireland | 1884 England | 1884 Scotland | 1885 England | 1885 Scotland |
|---|---|---|---|---|
| 1 Owen E. | 1 Owen E. | 1 Owen E. | 1 Mills-Roberts | 1 Mills-Roberts |
| 2 Conde | 2 Powell | 2 Roberts R. | 2 Jones F.R. | 2 Powell |
| 3 Davies W. | 3 Conde | 3 Conde | 3 Thomas G. | 3 Thomas G. |
| 4 Foulkes | 4 Evans M. | 4 Hughes F.W. | 4 Davies R. | 4 Burke |
| 5 Griffiths | 5 Williams J.H. | 5 Burke | 5 Jones H. | 5 Jones H. |
| 6 Edwards H. | 6 Griffiths | 6 Jones J. | 6 Davies J.E. | 6 Foulkes |
| 7 Owen W.P. | 7 Owen W.P. | 7 Owen W.P. | 7 Vaughan | 7 Hibbott |
| 8 Davies R. | 8 Owen W. | 8 Roberts W.H. | 8 Farmer | 8 Farmer |
| 9 Shaw | 9 Vaughan | 9 Shaw | 9 Lewis W. | 9 Lloyd |
| 10 Eyton-Jones | 10 Eyton-Jones | 10 Eyton-Jones | 10 Burke | 10 Jones R.A. |
| 11 Jones R.A. | 11 Jones R.A. | 11 Jones R.A. | 11 Wilding | 11 Wilding |

| Wrexham Feb 9: 6-0 *Shaw 2, Owen W.P. 2, Jones, Eyton-Jones* | Wrexham Mar 17: 0-4 | Glasgow Mar 29: 1-4 *Roberts R.* | Blackburn Mar 14: 1-1 *Wilding* | Wrexham Mar 23: 1-8 *Jones R.A.* |
|---|---|---|---|---|

| 1885 Ireland | 1886 Ireland | 1886 England | 1886 Scotland | 1887 England |
|---|---|---|---|---|
| 1 Mills-Roberts | 1 Hersee M. | 1 Mills-Roberts | 1 Hersee M. | 1 Mills-Roberts |
| 2 Jones F.R. | 2 Roberts R. (*Wrexham*) | 2 Davies A.O. | 2 Davies A.O. | 2 Davies A.O. |
| 3 Davies A.O. | 3 Powell | 3 Powell | 3 Jones F.R. | 3 Powell |
| 4 Burke | 4 Vaughan | 4 Vaughan | 4 Vaughan | 4 Jones H. |
| 5 Vaughan | 5 Bell | 5 Bell | 5 Bell | 5 Burke |
| 6 Jones H. | 6 Jones H. | 6 Jones H. | 6 Jones H. | 6 Evelyn |
| 7 Davies R. | 7 Wilding | 7 Wilding | 7 Williams R.P. | 7 Challen |
| 8 Owen W. | 8 Roberts W. | 8 Roberts W. | 8 Roberts W. | 8 Owen W. |
| 9 Wilding | 9 Sisson | 9 Davies T. | 9 Sisson | 9 Wilding |
| 10 Sisson | 10 Bryan | 10 Bryan | 10 Lewis W. | 10 Turner W.H. |
| 11 Roach | 11 Hersee R. | 11 Lewis W. | 11 Doughty J. | 11 Lewis W. |

| Belfast April 11: 8-2 *Owen, Burke, Sisson 3, Roach 2, Jones H.* | Wrexham Feb 27: 5-0 *Roberts, W., Wilding, Hersee R., Sisson, Bryan* | Wrexham Mar 29: 1-3 *Lewis* | Glasgow April 10: 1-4 *Lundie og* | London Feb 26: 0-4 |
|---|---|---|---|---|

| 1887 Ireland | 1887 Scotland | 1888 England | 1888 Ireland | 1888 Scotland |
|---|---|---|---|---|
| 1 Roberts R. (*Wrexham*) | 1 Trainer | 1 Mills-Roberts | 1 Mills-Roberts | 1 Trainer |
| 2 Townsend | 2 Davies A.O. | 2 Davies A.O. | 2 Davies A.O. | 2 Jones D. |
| 3 Jones S. | 3 Powell | 3 Roberts R. | 3 Powell | 3 Powell |
| 4 Hughes P.W. | 4 Morris | 4 Powell | 4 Jones D. | 4 Burke |
| 5 Hunter | 5 Burke | 5 Griffiths | 5 Humphreys | 5 Davies J. (*N Heath*) |
| 6 Edwards H. | 6 Roberts R. | 6 Davies J. (*N Heath*) | 6 Davies J. (*N Heath*) | 6 Roberts R. |
| 7 Sabine | 7 Challen | 7 Challen | 7 Doughty J. | 7 Doughty J. |
| 8 Doughty J. | 8 Doughty J. | 8 Doughty J. | 8 Howell | 8 Doughty R. |
| 9 Turner W.H. | 9 Lewis W. | 9 Lewis W. | 9 Pryce-Jones | 9 Pryce-Jones |
| 10 Roberts W. | 10 Pryce-Jones | 10 Pryce-Jones | 10 Doughty R. | 10 Owen G. |
| 11 Griffiths | 11 Jones R. | 11 Owen W. | 11 Wilding | 11 Wilding |

| Belfast Mar 12: 1-4 *Sabine* | Wrexham Mar 21: 0-2 | Crewe Feb 4: 1-5 *Doughty J.* | Wrexham Mar 3: 11-0 *Wilding 2, Doughty J. 4, Howell 2, Doughty R. 2, Pryce-Jones* | Edinburgh Mar 10: 1-5 *Doughty J.* |
|---|---|---|---|---|

| 1889 England | 1889 Scotland | 1889 Ireland | 1890 Ireland | 1890 England |
|---|---|---|---|---|
| 1 Trainer | 1 Gillam (Pugh) | 1 Gillam | 1 Gillam | 1 Gillam |
| 2 Jones W.P. | 2 Davies A.O. | 2 Jones W.P. | 2 Jones D. | 2 Davies A.O. |
| 3 Jones D. | 3 Jones D. | 3 Jones D. | 3 Jones W.P. | 3 Jones D. |
| 4 Hughes P.W. | 4 Roberts R. | 4 Hughes P.W. | 4 Griffiths | 4 Davies J. (N Heath) |
| 5 Jones H. | 5 Davies J. (N Heath) | 5 Carty | 5 Hayes | 5 Jones H. |
| 6 Roberts R. | 6 Jones H. | 6 Leary | 6 Jones H. | 6 Evans W.G. |
| 7 Hallam | 7 Davies Jos | 7 Davies Jos | 7 Bowdler J.C.H. | 7 Challen |
| 8 Jones R. | 8 Owen W. | 8 Owen W. | 8 Willcocks | 8 Jones R. |
| 9 Lewis W. | 9 Doughty J. | 9 Owen G. | 9 Pryce-Jones | 9 Doughty R. |
| 10 Lea | 10 Owen G. | 10 Jarrett | 10 Owen W. | 10 Howell |
| 11 Owen W. | 11 Lewis W. | 11 Lewis W. | 11 Lewis W. | 11 Lewis W. |
| Stoke Feb 23: 1-4 *Owen* | Wrexham April 15: 0-0 | Belfast April 27: 3-1 *Jarrett 3* | Shrewsbury Feb 8: 5-2 *Lewis 2, Pryce-Jones 2, Owen* | Wrexham Mar 15: 1-3 *Lewis* |

| 1890 Scotland | 1891 Ireland | 1891 England | 1891 Scotland | 1892 Ireland |
|---|---|---|---|---|
| 1 Trainer | 1 Turner R.E. | 1 Turner R.E. | 1 Trainer | 1 Trainer |
| 2 Jones W.P. | 2 Roberts R. (Wrexham) | 2 Evans W.G. | 2 Powell | 2 Arridge |
| 3 Jones S. | 3 Lloyd | 3 Powell | 3 Jones D. | 3 Jones D. |
| 4 Griffiths | 4 Griffiths | 4 Hughes W. | 4 Lea | 4 Hughes W. |
| 5 Jones H. | 5 Mates | 5 Jones H. | 5 Jones H. | 5 Jenkyns |
| 6 Roberts R. | 6 Lea | 6 Parry | 6 Parry | 6 Roberts R. |
| 7 Lewis W. | 7 Davies Jos | 7 Davies Jos | 7 Davies Jos | 7 Davies R.O. |
| 8 Davies O. | 8 Owen W. | 8 Owen W. | 8 Owen W. | 8 Bostock |
| 9 Owen W. | 9 Davies A. | 9 Turner W.H. | 9 Turner W.H. | 9 Lewis B. |
| 10 Jarrett | 10 Roberts R. (Rhos) | 10 Howell | 10 Bowdler J.C.H. | 10 Bowdler J.C.H. |
| 11 Turner W.H. | 11 Lewis W. | 11 Lewis W. | 11 Lewis W. | 11 Lewis W. |
| Glasgow Mar 22: 0-5 | Belfast Feb 7: 2-7 *Lewis 2* | Sunderland Mar 7: 1-4 *Howell* | Wrexham Mar 21: 3-4 *Bowdler 2, Owen* | Bangor Feb 27: 1-1 *Lewis B.* |

| 1892 England | 1892 Scotland | 1893 England | 1893 Scotland | 1893 Ireland |
|---|---|---|---|---|
| 1 Mills-Roberts | 1 Trainer | 1 Trainer | 1 Jones S. | 1 Jones S. |
| 2 Evans | 2 Arridge | 2 Jones D. | 2 Taylor | 2 Townsend |
| 3 Powell | 3 Powell | 3 Parry | 3 Jones F.W. | 3 Taylor |
| 4 Davies J. (Wolves) | 4 Hughes W. | 4 Williams E. | 4 Williams G. | 4 Lea |
| 5 Jenkyns | 5 Jenkyns | 5 Davies J. (Wolves) | 5 Williams E. | 5 Evans J. |
| 6 Owen G. | 6 Roberts R. | 6 Morris E. | 6 Morris E. | 6 Morris E. |
| 7 Owen W. | 7 Wilding | 7 Butler | 7 Vaughan | 7 Vaughan |
| 8 Turner J. | 8 Owen W. | 8 Vaughan | 8 Butler | 8 Owen W. |
| 9 Lewis B. | 9 Lewis B. | 9 James | 9 Owen W. | 9 Butler |
| 10 Davies R.O. | 10 Egan | 10 Lewis B. | 10 Lewis B. | 10 Owen G. |
| 11 Lewis W. | 11 Lewis W. | 11 Roberts R. (Crewe Alex) | 11 Bowdler H.E. | 11 James |
| Wrexham Mar 5: 0-2 | Edinburgh Mar 26: 1-6 *Lewis B.* | Stoke Mar 13: 0-6 | Wrexham Mar 18: 0-8 | Belfast April 5: 3-4 *Owen G. 2, Stewart og* |

| 1894 Ireland | 1894 England | 1894 Scotland | 1895 Ireland | 1895 England |
|---|---|---|---|---|
| 1 Trainer | 1 Trainer | 1 Gillam | 1 Trainer J. | 1 Trainer J. |
| 2 Arridge | 2 Parry | 2 Taylor | 2 Arridge | 2 Parry |
| 3 Taylor | 3 Jones D. | 3 Hughes A. | 3 Edwards | 3 Jones D. |
| 4 Jones R.S. | 4 Evans J. | 4 Williams G. | 4 Williams G. | 4 Williams G. |
| 5 Chapman | 5 Chapman | 5 Chapman | 5 Chapman | 5 Jenkyns |
| 6 Hayes | 6 Hughes A. | 6 Worthington | 6 Jones J.L. | 6 Jones J.L. |
| 7 Evans J. | 7 James | 7 Morris H. | 7 Meredith W. | 7 Meredith W. |
| 8 Lewis B. | 8 Lewis B. | 8 Lewis B. | 8 Davies Jos | 8 Davies Jos |
| 9 Lewis W. | 9 Lewis W. | 9 Lewis W. | 9 Trainer H. | 9 Trainer H. |
| 10 Rea | 10 Rea | 10 Rea | 10 Parry | 10 Pryce-Jones |
| 11 James | 11 Bowdler J.C.H. | 11 James | 11 Lewis W. | 11 Lewis W. |

| Swansea | Wrexham | Kilmarnock | Belfast | London |
|---|---|---|---|---|
| Feb 24: 4-1 | Mar 12: 1-5 | Mar 24: 2-5 | Mar 16: 2-2 | Mar 18: 1-1 |
| *Lewis W. 2, James 2* | *Bowdler* | *Morris 2* | *Trainer H. 2* | *Lewis* |

| 1895 Scotland | 1896 Ireland | 1896 England | 1896 Scotland | 1897 Ireland |
|---|---|---|---|---|
| 1 Jones S. | 1 Jones S. | 1 Jones S. | 1 Trainer | 1 Trainer |
| 2 Lloyd | 2 Parry | 2 Arridge | 2 Parry | 2 Edwards |
| 3 Parry | 3 Matthias | 3 Parry | 3 Matthias | 3 Parry |
| 4 Williams G. | 4 Rogers | 4 Rogers | 4 Rogers | 4 Darvell |
| 5 Chapman | 5 White | 5 Chapman | 5 Jenkyns | 5 Jenkyns |
| 6 Jones J.L. | 6 Jones J.L. | 6 Jones J.L. | 6 Jones J.L. | 6 Jones J.L. |
| 7 Davies Jos | 7 Meredith W. | 7 Meredith W. | 7 Pugh | 7 Meredith W. |
| 8 Lewis B. | 8 Pugh | 8 Davies Jos | 8 Garner | 8 Pugh |
| 9 Trainer H. | 9 Morris A.G. | 9 Morris A.G. | 9 Morris A.G. | 9 Morgan-Owen |
| 10 Lewis W. | 10 Rea | 10 Morris H. | 10 Lewis W. | 10 Rea |
| 11 Rea | 11 Lewis W. | 11 Lewis W. | 11 Rea | 11 Nock |

| Wrexham | Wrexham | Cardiff | Dundee | Belfast |
|---|---|---|---|---|
| Mar 23: 2-2 | Feb 29: 6-1 | Mar 16: 1-9 | Mar 21: 0-4 | Mar 6: 3-4 |
| *Lewis W., Chapman* | *Lewis 2, Meredith 2, Pugh, Morris* | *Chapman* | | *Meredith 2, Jenkyns* |

| 1897 Scotland | 1897 England | 1898 Ireland | 1898 Scotland | 1898 England |
|---|---|---|---|---|
| 1 Trainer | 1 Trainer | 1 Morris J. | 1 Trainer | 1 Trainer |
| 2 Jones W.R. | 2 Matthias | 2 Parry | 2 Parry | 2 Parry |
| 3 Matthias | 3 Edwards | 3 Arridge | 3 Jones D. | 3 Arridge |
| 4 Darvell | 4 Chapman | 4 Williams G. | 4 Jones R.S. | 4 Taylor |
| 5 Mates | 5 Mates | 5 Edwards | 5 Jenkyns | 5 Jenkyns |
| 6 Jones J.L. | 6 Jones J.L. | 6 Jones J.L. | 6 Jones J.L. | 6 Jones J.L. |
| 7 Meredith W. | 7 Meredith W. | 7 Meredith W. | 7 Roberts J. (Chirk) | 7 Meredith W. |
| 8 Pugh | 8 Davies Jos | 8 Thomas | 8 Thomas | 8 Bartley |
| 9 Morgan-Owen | 9 Morris A.G. | 9 Lewis W. | 9 Morgan-Owen | 9 Morgan-Owen |
| 10 Rea | 10 Morris H. | 10 Lockley | 10 Morris A.G. | 10 Watkins |
| 11 Lewis W. | 11 Lewis W. | 11 Rea | 11 Watkins | 11 James |

| Wrexham | Sheffield | Llandudno | Motherwell | Wrexham |
|---|---|---|---|---|
| Mar 20: 2-2 | Mar 29: 0-4 | Feb 19: 0-1 | Mar 19: 2-5 | Mar 28: 0-3 |
| *Pugh, Morgan-Owen* | | | *Thomas, Morgan-Owen* | |

| 1899 Ireland | 1899 Scotland | 1899 England | 1900 Scotland | 1900 Ireland |
|---|---|---|---|---|
| 1 Trainer | 1 Trainer | 1 Jones W. | 1 Griffiths | 1 Roose |
| 2 Blew | 2 Matthias | 2 Thomas | 2 Thomas | 2 Jones D. |
| 3 Thomas | 3 Blew | 3 Arridge | 3 Morris C. | 3 Morris C. |
| 4 Richards | 4 Richards | 4 Richards | 4 Meredith S. | 4 Brookes |
| 5 Jones J.L. | 5 Jones J.L. | 5 Buckland | 5 Jones J.L. | 5 Morris R. (*Chirk*) |
| 6 Hughes E. | 6 Hughes E. | 6 Harrison | 6 Harrison | 6 Harrison |
| 7 Kelly | 7 Kelly | 7 Vaughan | 7 Pugh | 7 Meredith W. |
| 8 Atherton | 8 Owen T. | 8 Meredith W. | 8 Butler | 8 Butler |
| 9 James | 9 Morgan-Owen | 9 Owen T. | 9 Jones R. | 9 Jones R. |
| 10 Davies C. | 10 Jones R. | 10 Morris A.G. | 10 Parry T.D. | 10 Parry T.D. |
| 11 Jackson | 11 Morris A.G. | 11 Atherton | 11 Watkins | 11 Davies C. |
| Belfast Mar 4: 0-1 | Wrexham Mar 18: 0-6 | Bristol Mar 20: 0-4 | Aberdeen Feb 3: 2-5 *Butler, Parry* | Llandudno Feb 24: 2-0 *Parry, Meredith* (pen) |

| 1900 England | 1901 Scotland | 1901 England | 1901 Ireland | 1902 Ireland |
|---|---|---|---|---|
| 1 Griffiths | 1 Roose | 1 Roose | 1 Roose | 1 Evans R.O. |
| 2 Jones D. | 2 Meredith S. | 2 Meredith S. | 2 Meredith S. | 2 Blew |
| 3 Morris C. | 3 Morris C. | 3 Morris C. | 3 Morris C. | 3 Jones H. |
| 4 Brookes | 4 Parry M. | 4 Parry M. | 4 Parry M. | 4 Parry M. |
| 5 Morris R. (*Chirk*) | 5 Jones W.J. | 5 Jones W.J. | 5 Morris R. (*Chirk*) | 5 Hughes E. |
| 6 Harrison | 6 Hughes E. | 6 Hughes E. | 6 Harrison | 6 Jones J.L. |
| 7 Meredith W. | 7 Pugh | 7 Meredith W. | 7 Meredith W. | 7 Kelly |
| 8 Davies Jos | 8 Jones J.O. | 8 Pugh | 8 Jones J.O. | 8 Jenkins |
| 9 Morgan-Owen | 9 Morgan-Owen | 9 Morgan-Owen | 9 Green | 9 Evans R. |
| 10 Watkins | 10 Parry T.D. | 10 Parry T.D. | 10 Parry T.D. | 10 Williams E. |
| 11 Parry T.D. | 11 Williams E. | 11 Williams E. | 11 Williams E. | 11 Morris R. |
| Cardiff Mar 26: 1-1 *Meredith* | Wrexham Mar 2: 1-1 *Parry* | Newcastle Mar 18: 0-6 | Belfast Mar 23: 1-0 *Jones* | Cardiff Feb 22: 0-3 |

| 1902 England | 1902 Scotland | 1903 England | 1903 Scotland | 1903 Ireland |
|---|---|---|---|---|
| 1 Roose | 1 Roose | 1 Evans R.O. | 1 Evans R.O. | 1 Evans R.O. |
| 2 Meredith S. | 2 Blew | 2 Blew | 2 Blew | 2 Meredith S. |
| 3 Morris C. | 3 Morris R. (*Chirk*) | 3 Morris C. | 3 Morris C. | 3 Morris C. |
| 4 Parry M. | 4 Parry M. | 4 Parry M. | 4 Parry M. | 4 Richards |
| 5 Jones J.L. | 5 Jones J.L. | 5 Morris R. (*Shrewsbury T*) | 5 Morgan-Owen | 5 Morris R. (*Shrewsbury T*) |
| 6 Jones W.J. | 6 Jones W.J. | 6 Davies T. | 6 Davies T. | 6 Davies T. |
| 7 Meredith W. | 7 Meredith W. | 7 Meredith W. | 7 Meredith W. | 7 Meredith W. |
| 8 Watkins W.M. | 8 Griffiths | 8 Watkins W.M. | 8 Watkins W.M. | 8 Wynn |
| 9 Parry T.D. | 9 Morgan-Owen | 9 Green | 9 Morris A.G. | 9 Davies W. |
| 10 Williams E. | 10 Morris R. | 10 Morris A.G. | 10 Morris R. | 10 Morris R. |
| 11 Morris R. | 11 Owens J. | 11 Atherton | 11 Atherton | 11 Atherton |
| Wrexham Mar 3: 0-0 | Greenock Mar 15: 1-5 *Meredith* | Portsmouth Mar 2: 1-2 *Watkins* | Cardiff Mar 9: 0-1 | Belfast Mar 28: 0-2 |

| 1904 England | 1904 Scotland | 1904 Ireland | 1905 Scotland | 1905 England |
|---|---|---|---|---|
| 1 Roose | 1 Davies D. | 1 Davies D. | 1 Roose | 1 Roose |
| 2 Meredith S. | 2 Blew | 2 Blew | 2 Blew | 2 Jones A.T. |
| 3 Blew | 3 Davies T. | 3 Morris C. | 3 Morris C. | 3 Morris C. |
| 4 Parry M. | 4 Richards | 4 Parry M. | 4 Lathom | 4 Lathom |
| 5 Hughes E. | 5 Hughes E. | 5 Hughes E. | 5 Hughes E. | 5 Hughes E. |
| 6 Jones J.L. | 6 Jones J.L. | 6 Jones J.L. | 6 Hughes J. | 6 Hughes J. |
| 7 Meredith W. | 7 Davies A. | 7 Watkins A.E. | 7 Meredith W. | 7 Meredith W. |
| 8 Atherton | 8 Watkins W.M. | 8 Watkins W.M. | 8 Davies A. | 8 Jones W.L. |
| 9 Watkins W.M. | 9 Green | 9 Green | 9 Watkins M. | 9 Watkins M. |
| 10 Morris R. | 10 Morris R. | 10 Atherton | 10 Morris A.G. | 10 Morris A.G. |
| 11 Davies Lloyd | 11 Atherton | 11 Morris R. | 11 Oliver | 11 Oliver |
| Wrexham | Dundee | Bangor | Wrexham | Liverpool |
| Feb 29: 2-2 | Mar 12: 1-1 | Mar 21: 0-1 | Mar 6: 3-1 | Mar 27: 1-5 |
| *Watkins, Davies* | *Atherton* | | *Morris A.G., Meredith, Watkins* | *Morris A.G.* |

| 1905 Ireland | 1906 Scotland | 1906 England | 1906 Ireland | 1907 Ireland |
|---|---|---|---|---|
| 1 Morgan | 1 Roose | 1 Roose | 1 Roose | 1 Roose |
| 2 Blew | 2 Blew | 2 Jones A.T. | 2 Blew | 2 Roberts |
| 3 Morris C. | 3 Morris C. | 3 Blew | 3 Roberts | 3 Davies Lloyd |
| 4 Richards | 4 Hughes E. (*Wrexham*) | 4 Parry M. | 4 Hughes E. (*N Forest*) | 4 Lathom |
| 5 Hughes E. | 5 Morgan-Owen M.M. | 5 Morgan-Owen M.M. | 5 Morgan-Owen M.M. | 5 Williams G.O. |
| 6 Hughes J. | 6 Lathom | 6 Hughes E. | 6 Hughes E. | 6 Davies Llew |
| 7 Matthews | 7 Jones W.L. | 7 Jones W.L. | 7 Jones W.L. | 7 Meredith W. |
| 8 Watkins | 8 Morris R. | 8 Morgan-Owen H. | 8 Morgan-Owen H. | 8 Jones W.L. |
| 9 Davies W. | 9 Jones J.L. | 9 Green | 9 Green | 9 Hughes A. |
| 10 Jones W.L. | 10 Jones R. | 10 Lewis | 10 Jones R. | 10 Morris R. |
| 11 Atherton | 11 Evans R. | 11 Evans R. | 11 Evans R. | 11 Jones G.P. |
| Belfast | Edinburgh | Cardiff | Wrexham | Belfast |
| April 8: 2-2 | Mar 3: 2-0 | Mar 19: 0-1 | April 2: 4-4 | Feb 23: 3-2 |
| *Watkins, Atherton* | *Jones W.L., Jones J.L.* | | *Green 3, Morgan-Owen H.* | *Morris, Meredith, Jones W.L.* |

| 1907 Scotland | 1907 England | 1908 Scotland | 1908 England | 1908 Ireland |
|---|---|---|---|---|
| 1 Roose | 1 Roose | 1 Roose | 1 Roose (Davies D.) | 1 Evans R.O. |
| 2 Blew | 2 Davies Lloyd | 2 Blew | 2 Blew | 2 Blew |
| 3 Morris C. | 3 Meredith S. | 3 Morris C. | 3 Morris C. | 3 Jones J. |
| 4 Lathom | 4 Hughes E. | 4 Hughes E. (*N Forest*) | 4 Hughes E. (*N Forest*) | 4 Peake |
| 5 Davies Lloyd | 5 Morgan-Owen M.M. | 5 Parry M. | 5 Parry M. | 5 Parry M. |
| 6 Price | 6 Lathom | 6 Davies Lloyd | 6 Lathom | 6 Price |
| 7 Meredith W. | 7 Meredith W. | 7 Davies W.C. | 7 Meredith W. | 7 Meredith W. |
| 8 Jones W.L. | 8 Jones W.L. | 8 Jones W.L. | 8 Matthews | 8 Morris R. |
| 9 Morgan-Owen H. | 9 Green | 9 Davies W. | 9 Davies W. | 9 Watkins W.M. |
| 10 Morris A.G. | 10 Morris A.G. | 10 Green | 10 Morris A.G. | 10 Hodgkinson |
| 11 Jones G.P. | 11 Evans R. | 11 Evans R. | 11 Evans R. | 11 Jones T.D. |
| Wrexham | Fulham | Dundee | Wrexham | Aberdare |
| Mar 4: 1-0 | Mar 18: 1-1 | Mar 7: 1-2 | Mar 16:1-7 | April 11: 0-1 |
| *Morris A.G.* | *Jones* | *Jones* | *Davies W.* | |

| 1909 Scotland | 1909 England | 1909 Ireland | 1910 Scotland | 1910 England |
|---|---|---|---|---|
| 1 Roose | 1 Roose | 1 Roose | 1 Roose | 1 Roose |
| 2 Blew | 2 Blew | 2 Morris C. | 2 Jones J. | 2 Blew |
| 3 Morris C. | 3 Morris C. | 3 Jones J. | 3 Morris C. | 3 Morris C. |
| 4 Parry M. | 4 Parry M. | 4 Lathom | 4 Hughes E. (N Forest) | 4 Hughes E. (N Forest) |
| 5 Peake | 5 Peake | 5 Peake | 5 Peake | 5 Lathom |
| 6 Price | 6 Price | 6 Davies Lloyd | 6 Davies Llew | 6 Davies Llew |
| 7 Meredith W. | 7 Meredith W. | 7 Meredith W. | 7 Meredith W. | 7 Meredith W. |
| 8 Wynn | 8 Wynn | 8 Wynn | 8 Davies W.C. | 8 Wynn |
| 9 Davies W. | 9 Davies W. | 9 Davies W. | 9 Jones E. | 9 Jones W.L. |
| 10 Jones W.L. | 10 Jones W.L. | 10 Jones W.L. | 10 Morris A.G. | 10 Morris A.G. |
| 11 Evans R. | 11 Davies W.C. | 11 Price | 11 Evans R. | 11 Evans R. |
| Wrexham Mar 1: 3-2 *Davies 2, Jones* | Nottingham Mar 15: 0-2 | Belfast Mar 20: 3-2 *Jones W.L., Wynn, Meredith* | Kilmarnock Mar 5: 0-1 | Cardiff Mar 14: 0-1 |

| 1910 Ireland | 1911 Ireland | 1911 Scotland | 1911 England | 1912 Scotland |
|---|---|---|---|---|
| 1 Roose | 1 Evans R.O. | 1 Roose | 1 Evans R.O. | 1 Evans R.O. |
| 2 Davies Lloyd | 2 Hewitt | 2 Morris C. | 2 Morris C. | 2 Davies Llew |
| 3 Morris C. | 3 Morris C. | 3 Hewitt | 3 Hewitt | 3 Davies Lloyd |
| 4 Hughes E. (N Forest) | 4 Hughes E. (N Forest) | 4 Hughes E. (N Forest) | 4 Hughes E. (N Forest) | 4 Jones J.T. |
| 5 Peake | 5 Peake | 5 Davies Lloyd | 5 Davies Lloyd | 5 Hughes E. (Wrexham) |
| 6 Davies Llew | 6 Davies Llew | 6 Davies LLew | 6 Jones W.L. | 6 Russell |
| 7 Meredith W. | 7 Meredith W. | 7 Meredith W. | 7 Meredith W. | 7 Meredith W. |
| 8 Jones J.L. | 8 Wynn | 8 Jones E. | 8 Jones E. | 8 Wynn |
| 9 Jones E. | 9 Davies W. | 9 Davies W. | 9 Davies W. | 9 Jones E. |
| 10 Morris A.G. | 10 Morris A.G. | 10 Morris A.G. | 10 Morris A.G. | 10 Williams J.W. |
| 11 Evans R. | 11 Vizard | 11 Vizard | 11 Vizard | 11 Vizard |
| Wrexham April 11: 4-1 *Evans 2, Morris A.G. 2* | Belfast Jan 28: 2-1 *Davies W., Morris A.G.* | Cardiff Mar 6: 2-2 *Morris A.G.2* | London Mar 13: 0-3 | Edinburgh Mar 2: 0-1 |

| 1912 England | 1912 Ireland | 1913 Ireland | 1913 Scotland | 1913 England |
|---|---|---|---|---|
| 1 Evans R.O. | 1 Evans R.O. | 1 Bailiff | 1 Bailiff | 1 Bailiff |
| 2 Davies Llew | 2 Davies Llew | 2 Hewitt | 2 Hewitt | 2 Hewitt |
| 3 Davies Lloyd | 3 Russell | 3 Davies Llew | 3 Davies Llew | 3 Davies Lloyd |
| 4 Hughes E. (Wrexham) | 4 Hughes E. (Wrexham) | 4 Lathom | 4 Hughes E. (Man City) | 4 Hughes E. (Man City) |
| 5 Newton | 5 Newton | 5 Peake | 5 Davies Lloyd | 5 Peake |
| 6 Jones J.T. | 6 Jones J.T. | 6 Jones J.T. | 6 Jones W.L. | 6 Jones J.T. |
| 7 Meredith W. | 7 Meredith W. | 7 Meredith W. | 7 Meredith W. | 7 Meredith W. |
| 8 Wynn | 8 Williams J.W. | 8 Davies D.W. | 8 Wynn | 8 Wynn |
| 9 Jones E. | 9 Davies W. | 9 Davies W. | 9 Davies W. | 9 Davies W. |
| 10 Morris A.G. | 10 Davies D.W. | 10 Roberts | 10 Roberts | 10 Jones W.L. |
| 11 Vizard | 11 Evans J. | 11 Evans J. | 11 Vizard | 11 Davies Llew |
| Wrexham Mar 11: 0-2 | Cardiff April 13: 2-3 *Davies W., Davies D.W.* | Belfast Jan 18: 1-0 *Roberts* | Wrexham Mar 3: 0-0 | Bristol Mar 17: 3-4 *Davies W., Meredith, Peake* |

| 1914 Ireland | 1914 Scotland | 1914 England | 1920 Ireland | 1920 Scotland |
|---|---|---|---|---|
| 1 Peers | 1 Peers | 1 Peers | 1 Bailiff | 1 Peers |
| 2 Davies Llew | 2 Hewitt | 2 Hewitt | 2 Millership | 2 Millership |
| 3 Davies Lloyd | 3 Jennings | 3 Russell | 3 Russell | 3 Russell |
| 4 Hughes E. (*Man City*) | 4 Matthias | 4 Matthias | 4 Matthias | 4 Matthias |
| 5 Peake | 5 Davies Lloyd | 5 Davies Lloyd | 5 Jones J.T. | 5 Jones J.T. |
| 6 Jones J.T. | 6 Jones J.T. | 6 Jennings | 6 Keenor | 6 Jennings |
| 7 Meredith W. | 7 Meredith W. | 7 Meredith W. | 7 Meredith W. | 7 Meredith W. |
| 8 Jones E. | 8 Wynn | 8 Wynn | 8 Jones W.L. | 8 Jones I. |
| 9 Davies W. | 9 Davies W. | 9 Rowlands | 9 Davies S. | 9 Davies S. |
| 10 Jones W.L. | 10 Jones W.L. | 10 Davies W.C. | 10 Jones I. | 10 Richards |
| 11 Vizard | 11 Evans J. | 11 Vizard | 11 Evans J. | 11 Evans J. |

| Wrexham Jan 19: 1-2 *Jones E.* (pen) | Glasgow Feb 28: 0-0 | Cardiff Mar 16: 0-2 | Belfast Feb 14: 2-2 *Davies 2* | Cardiff Feb 26: 1-1 *Evans* |
|---|---|---|---|---|


| 1920 England | 1921 Scotland | 1921 England | 1921 Ireland | 1922 Scotland |
|---|---|---|---|---|
| 1 Peers | 1 Peers | 1 Peers | 1 Peers | 1 Peers |
| 2 Millership | 2 Millership | 2 Millership | 2 Russell | 2 Parry |
| 3 Russell | 3 Russell | 3 Russell | 3 Millership | 3 Evans J.H. |
| 4 Matthias | 4 Keenor | 4 Keenor | 4 Keenor | 4 Evans H.P. |
| 5 Jones J.T. | 5 Jones J.T. | 5 Jones J.T. | 5 Matthews | 5 Jones J.T. |
| 6 Keenor | 6 Matthias | 6 Matthias | 6 Matthias | 6 Matthias |
| 7 Meredith W. | 7 Williams R. | 7 Williams R. | 7 Hole | 7 Davies S. |
| 8 Jones W.L. | 8 Collier | 8 Jones I. | 8 Jones I. | 8 Jones I. |
| 9 Davies S. | 9 Hoddinott | 9 Hoddinott | 9 Davies S. | 9 Davies L. |
| 10 Richards | 10 Davies S. | 10 Davies S. | 10 Richards | 10 Richards |
| 11 Vizard | 11 Vizard | 11 Vizard | 11 Vizard | 11 Vizard |

| London Mar 15: 2-1 *Davies* (pen), *Richards* | Aberdeen Feb 12: 1-2 *Collier* | Cardiff Mar 16: 0-0 | Swansea April 9: 2-1 *Hole, Davies* | Wrexham Feb 4: 2-1 *Davies L., Davies S.* |
|---|---|---|---|---|


| 1922 England | 1922 Ireland | 1923 England | 1923 Scotland | 1923 Ireland |
|---|---|---|---|---|
| 1 Peers | 1 Peers | 1 Peers | 1 Godding | 1 Godding |
| 2 Russell | 2 Russell | 2 Parry | 2 Russell | 2 Russell |
| 3 Evans J.H. | 3 Evans J.H. | 3 Russell | 3 Evans J.H. | 3 Parry |
| 4 Evans H.P. | 4 Evans H.P. | 4 Keenor | 4 Matthias | 4 John |
| 5 Jones J.T. | 5 Jones J.T. | 5 Matthews | 5 Keenor | 5 Keenor |
| 6 Matthias | 6 Matthias | 6 Jennings | 6 John | 6 Jennings |
| 7 Hole | 7 Davies S. | 7 Hole | 7 Williams R. | 7 Hole |
| 8 Davies S. | 8 Keenor | 8 Jones I. | 8 Davies I. | 8 Jones I. |
| 9 Davies L. | 9 Davies L. | 9 Davies L. | 9 Davies S. | 9 Davies L. |
| 10 Richards | 10 Jones I. | 10 Vizard | 10 Davies L. | 10 Vizard |
| 11 Vizard | 11 Evans J. | 11 Evans J. | 11 Nicholas | 11 Evans J. |

| Liverpool Mar 13: 0-1 | Belfast April 1: 1-1 *Davies L.* | Cardiff Mar 5: 2-2 *Keenor, Jones* | Glasgow Mar 17: 0-2 | Wrexham April 14: 0-3 |
|---|---|---|---|---|

L.

| 1924 Scotland | 1924 England | 1924 Ireland | 1925 Scotland | 1925 England |
|---|---|---|---|---|
| 1 Gray | 1 Gray | 1 Gray | 1 Gray | 1 Gray |
| 2 Russell | 2 Russell | 2 Russell | 2 Jenkins | 2 Morley |
| 3 Jenkins | 3 Jenkins | 3 Jenkins | 3 Russell | 3 Russell |
| 4 Evans H.P. | 4 Evans J.P. | 4 Evans H.P. | 4 Davies S. | 4 Jenkins E. |
| 5 Keenor | 5 Keenor | 5 Keenor | 5 Keenor | 5 Keenor |
| 6 Jennings | 6 Jennings | 6 Jennings | 6 Williams W. | 6 Thomas E. |
| 7 Davies W. | 7 Davies W. | 7 Davies W. | 7 Davies W. | 7 Davies W. |
| 8 Jones I. | 8 Nicholls | 8 Nicholls | 8 Nicholls | 8 Nicholls |
| 9 Davies L. | 9 Davies L. | 9 Davies L. | 9 Davies L. | 9 Fowler |
| 10 Richards | 10 Richards | 10 Richards | 10 Beadles | 10 Beadles |
| 11 Vizard | 11 Vizard | 11 Vizard | 11 Cook | 11 Cook |
| Cardiff Feb 16: 2-0 *Davies W., Davies L.* | Blackburn Mar 3: 2-1 *Davies W., Vizard* | Belfast Mar 15: 1-0 *Russell (pen)* | Edinburgh Feb 14: 1-3 *Williams* | Swansea Feb 28: 1-2 *Bower og* |

| 1925 Ireland | 1925 Scotland | 1926 Ireland | 1926 England | 1926 Scotland |
|---|---|---|---|---|
| 1 Gray | 1 Gray | 1 Brown | 1 Gray | 1 Gray |
| 2 Parry | 2 Russell | 2 Parry | 2 Russell | 2 Evans T.J. |
| 3 Jenkins | 3 Jenkins | 3 Jones T. | 3 Jenkins | 3 Jenkins |
| 4 Mousdale | 4 Bennion | 4 Newnes | 4 Davies S. | 4 Bennion |
| 5 Keenor | 5 Keenor | 5 Matthews | 5 Pullen | 5 Keenor |
| 6 Lewis | 6 Lewis | 6 Evans D. | 6 John | 6 Jennings |
| 7 Davies W. | 7 Williams R. | 7 Davies W. | 7 Davies W. | 7 Davies W. |
| 8 Davies S. | 8 Davies W. | 8 Davies L. | 8 Davies L. | 8 Davies S. |
| 9 Jones J. | 9 Davies S. | 9 Fowler | 9 Fowler | 9 Fowler |
| 10 Davies L. | 10 Richards | 10 Davies S. | 10 Jones C. | 10 Jones C. |
| 11 Williams J. | 11 Vizard | 11 Jones I. | 11 Vizard | 11 Vizard |
| Wrexham April 18: 0-0 | Cardiff Oct 31: 0-3 | Belfast Feb 13: 0-3 | London Mar 1: 3-1 *Fowler 2, Davies W.* | Glasgow Oct 30: 0-3 |

| 1927 England | 1927 Ireland | 1927 Scotland | 1927 England | 1928 Ireland |
|---|---|---|---|---|
| 1 Lewis D. | 1 Evans L. | 1 Gray | 1 Gray | 1 Lewis D. |
| 2 Jones T. | 2 Jones T. | 2 Russell | 2 Williams B. | 2 Williams B. |
| 3 John | 3 Jennings | 3 Evans T.J. | 3 Evans T.J. | 3 Evans T.J. |
| 4 Keenor | 4 Keenor | 4 Bennion | 4 Bennion | 4 Bennion |
| 5 Griffiths T. | 5 Griffiths T. | 5 Keenor | 5 Keenor | 5 Keenor |
| 6 Evans D. | 6 Evans D. | 6 Davies S. | 6 John | 6 John |
| 7 Williams R. | 7 Williams R. | 7 Hole | 7 Hole | 7 Hole |
| 8 Lewis | 8 Lewis | 8 Davies L. | 8 Davies L. | 8 Davies W. |
| 9 Davies L. | 9 Davies L. | 9 Fowler | 9 Lewis | 9 Lewis |
| 10 Nicholas | 10 Jones C. | 10 Curtis | 10 Jones C. | 10 Davies L. |
| 11 Thomas | 11 Nicholas | 11 Cook | 11 Cook | 11 Rev H. Davies |
| Wrexham Feb 14: 3-3 *Davies L. 2, Lewis* | Cardiff April 9: 2-2 *Williams 2* | Wrexham Oct 29: 2-2 *Curtis, Gibson og* | Burnley Nov 28: 2-1 *Lewis, Hill og* | Belfast Feb 4: 2-1 *Davies W., Lewis* |

| 1928 Scotland | 1928 England | 1929 Ireland | 1929 Scotland | 1929 England |
|---|---|---|---|---|
| 1 Gray | 1 Gray | 1 Gray | 1 Gray | 1 Lewis D. |
| 2 Morley | 2 Morley | 2 Morley | 2 Williams B. | 2 Williams B. |
| 3 Jennings | 3 Russell | 3 Lumberg | 3 Lumberg | 3 Lumberg |
| 4 Bennion | 4 Griffiths T. | 4 Bennion | 4 Bennion | 4 Keenor |
| 5 Keenor | 5 Keenor | 5 Keenor | 5 Keenor | 5 Griffiths T. |
| 6 Evans D. | 6 Bennion | 6 Bowsher | 6 John | 6 John |
| 7 Hole | 7 Hole | 7 Davies W. | 7 Davies W. | 7 Davies W. |
| 8 Davies W. | 8 Davies W. | 8 O'Callaghan | 8 O'Callaghan | 8 Davies L. |
| 9 Lewis | 9 Fowler | 9 Mays | 9 Davies L. | 9 Lewis |
| 10 Davies L. | 10 Davies L. | 10 Davies L. | 10 Jones C. | 10 Jones C. |
| 11 Williams R. | 11 Williams R. | 11 Warren | 11 Cook | 11 Cook |

| | | | | |
|---|---|---|---|---|
| Glasgow | Swansea | Wrexham | Cardiff | London |
| Oct 27: 2-4 | Nov 17: 2-3 | Feb 2: 2-2 | Oct 26: 2-4 | Nov 20: 0-6 |
| *Davies W. 2* | *Fowler, Keenor* | *Mays, Warren* | *O'Callaghan* | |
| | | | *Davies L.* | |

| 1930 Ireland | 1930 Scotland | 1930 England | 1931 Ireland | 1931 Scotland |
|---|---|---|---|---|
| 1 Finnigan | 1 Evans L. | 1 Evans L. | 1 John W. | 1 Gray |
| 2 Hugh | 2 Dewey | 2 Dewey | 2 Williams B. | 2 Richards |
| 3 Jones T. | 3 Crompton | 3 Crompton | 3 Crompton | 3 Lumberg |
| 4 Lawrence | 4 Rogers | 4 Rogers | 4 Keenor | 4 Edwards |
| 5 Keenor | 5 Keenor | 5 Keenor | 5 Griffiths T. | 5 Griffiths T. |
| 6 Pugsley | 6 Ellis | 6 Ellis | 6 Richards | 6 Lawrence |
| 7 Davies W. | 7 Collins | 7 Williams L. | 7 Phillips | 7 Griffiths T.P. |
| 8 Williams B. | 8 Neal | 8 Neal | 8 Astley | 8 O'Callaghan |
| 9 Martin | 9 Bamford | 9 Bamford | 9 Bamford | 9 Glover |
| 10 Davies S. | 10 Robbins | 10 Robbins | 10 James | 10 Robbins |
| 11 Cook | 11 Thomas | 11 Thomas | 11 Warren | 11 Curtis |

| | | | | |
|---|---|---|---|---|
| Belfast | Glasgow | Wrexham | Wrexham | Wrexham |
| Feb 1: 0-7 | Oct 25: 1-1 | Nov 22: 0-4 | April 22: 3-2 | Oct 31: 2-3 |
| | *Bamford* | | *Phillips, Griffiths,* | *Curtis 2* |
| | | | *Warren* | |

| 1931 England | 1931 Ireland | 1932 Scotland | 1932 England | 1932 Ireland |
|---|---|---|---|---|
| 1 Gray | 1 Gray | 1 John W. | 1 John W. | 1 John W. |
| 2 Williams B. | 2 Lawrence | 2 Williams B. | 2 Williams B. | 2 Williams B. |
| 3 Ellis | 3 Foulkes | 3 Ellis | 3 Ellis | 3 John |
| 4 Jones C. | 4 Bennion | 4 Keenor | 4 Murphy | 4 Murphy |
| 5 Griffiths T. | 5 Griffiths T. | 5 Griffiths T. | 5 Griffiths T. | 5 Griffiths T. |
| 6 John | 6 Ellis | 6 Richards | 6 Richards | 6 Richards |
| 7 Phillips | 7 Jones T.J. | 7 Phillips | 7 Warren | 7 Richards W. |
| 8 O'Callaghan | 8 James | 8 O'Callaghan | 8 O'Callaghan | 8 O'Callaghan |
| 9 Astley | 9 Bamford | 9 Astley | 9 Astley | 9 Astley |
| 10 Robbins | 10 Robbins | 10 Robbins | 10 Robbins | 10 Robbins |
| 11 Cook | 11 Parris | 11 Lewis D.J. | 11 Lewis D.J. | 11 Evans W. |

| | | | | |
|---|---|---|---|---|
| Liverpool | Belfast | Edinburgh | Wrexham | Wrexham |
| Nov 18: 1-3 | Dec 5: 0-4 | Oct 26: 5-2 | Nov 16: 0-0 | Dec 7: 4-1 |
| *Robbins* | | *O'Callaghan 2,* | | *Astley 2,* |
| | | *Griffiths, Astley* | | *Robbins 2* |
| | | *Thomson J. og* | | |

| 1933 France | 1933 Scotland | 1933 Ireland | 1933 England | 1934 England |
|---|---|---|---|---|
| 1 John W. | 1 John W. | 1 Evans L. | 1 John W. | 1 John W. |
| 2 John | 2 Lawrence | 2 Lawrence | 2 Lawrence | 2 Lawrence |
| 3 Lawrence | 3 Ellis | 3 Jones D.O. | 3 Jones D.O. | 3 Jones D.O. |
| 4 Murphy | 4 Murphy | 4 Day | 4 Murphy | 4 Murphy |
| 5 Griffiths T. | 5 Griffiths T. | 5 Hanford | 5 Griffiths T. | 5 Griffiths T. |
| 6 Jones C. | 6 Richards | 6 Richards | 6 Richards | 6 Richards |
| 7 Jones T. | 7 Phillips | 7 Phillips | 7 Phillips | 7 Phillips |
| 8 Jones L. | 8 O'Callaghan | 8 O'Callaghan | 8 O'Callaghan | 8 O'Callaghan |
| 9 Bamford | 9 Astley | 9 Glover | 9 Astley | 9 Williams R. |
| 10 Robbins | 10 Robbins | 10 Mills | 10 Mills | 10 Mills |
| 11 Warren | 11 Evans W. | 11 Curtis | 11 Evans W. | 11 Evans W. |

| Paris | Cardiff | Belfast | Newcastle | Cardiff |
|---|---|---|---|---|
| May 25: 1-1 | Oct 4: 3-2 | Nov 4: 1-1 | Nov 15: 2-1 | Sept 29: 0-4 |
| *Griffiths* | *Evans, Robbins, Astley* | *Glover* | *Mills, Astley* | |

| 1934 Scotland | 1935 Ireland | 1935 Scotland | 1936 England | 1936 Ireland |
|---|---|---|---|---|
| 1 John W. | 1 Hughes J.I. | 1 John W. | 1 John W. | 1 John W. |
| 2 Lawrence | 2 Williams B. | 2 Lawrence | 2 Jones D.O. | 2 Griffiths T. |
| 3 Jones D.O. | 3 John | 3 John | 3 Ellis | 3 Jones D.O. |
| 4 Murphy | 4 Murphy | 4 Murphy | 4 Murphy | 4 Murphy |
| 5 Hanford | 5 Griffiths T. | 5 Griffiths T. | 5 Hanford | 5 Hanford |
| 6 Richards | 6 Richards | 6 Richards | 6 Richards | 6 Richards |
| 7 Hopkins | 7 Hopkins | 7 Phillips | 7 Hopkins | 7 Hopkins |
| 8 Williams R. | 8 Jones L. | 8 Jones B. | 8 Phillips | 8 Phillips |
| 9 Astley | 9 Jones C.W. | 9 Glover | 9 Astley | 9 Astley |
| 10 Mills | 10 Jones B. | 10 Jones L. | 10 Jones B. | 10 Jones B. |
| 11 Phillips | 11 Phillips | 11 Robbins | 11 Evans W. | 11 Evans W. |

| Aberdeen | Wrexham | Cardiff | Wolverhampton | Belfast |
|---|---|---|---|---|
| Nov 21: 2-3 | Mar 27: 3-1 | Oct 5: 1-1 | Feb 5: 2-1 | Mar 11: 2-3 |
| *Phillips, Astley* | *Jones C.W., Phillips, Hopkins* | *Phillips* | *Astley, Jones B.* | *Astley, Phillips* |

| 1936 England | 1936 Scotland | 1937 Ireland | 1937 Scotland | 1937 England |
|---|---|---|---|---|
| 1 Gray | 1 Gray | 1 Gray | 1 Gray | 1 Gray |
| 2 Turner | 2 Turner | 2 Turner | 2 Turner | 2 Turner |
| 3 John | 3 Ellis | 3 Jones D. | 3 Hughes | 3 Hughes |
| 4 Warner | 4 Murphy | 4 Murphy | 4 Murphy | 4 Murphy |
| 5 Griffiths T. | 5 Griffiths T. | 5 Griffiths T. | 5 Hanford | 5 Hanford |
| 6 Richards | 6 Richards | 6 Richards | 6 Richards | 6 Richards |
| 7 Hopkins | 7 Hopkins | 7 Hopkins | 7 Phillips | 7 Hopkins |
| 8 Jones B. | 8 Jones B. | 8 Jones B. | 8 Jones L. | 8 Jones L. |
| 9 Glover | 9 Glover | 9 Glover | 9 Perry | 9 Perry |
| 10 Jones L. | 10 Jones L. | 10 Jones L. | 10 Jones B. | 10 Jones B. |
| 11 Morris | 11 Morris | 11 Warren | 11 Morris | 11 Morris |

| Cardiff | Dundee | Wrexham | Cardiff | Middlesbrough |
|---|---|---|---|---|
| Oct 17: 2-1 | Dec 2: 2-1 | Mar 17: 4-1 | Oct 30: 2-1 | Nov 17: 1-2 |
| *Morris, Glover* | *Glover 2* | *Glover 2, Jones B., Warren* | *Jones B., Morris* | *Perry* |

| 1938 Ireland | 1938 England | 1938 Scotland | 1939 Ireland | 1939 France |
|---|---|---|---|---|
| 1 Gray | 1 John W. | 1 John W. | 1 Poland | 1 Poland |
| 2 Turner | 2 Whatley | 2 Whatley | 2 Turner | 2 Turner |
| 3 Hughes | 3 Hughes | 3 Hughes | 3 Hughes | 3 Hughes |
| 4 Green | 4 Green | 4 Dearson | 4 Green | 4 Green |
| 5 Jones T.G. | 5 Jones T.G. | 5 Jones T.G. | 5 Jones T.G. | 5 Hanford |
| 6 Richards | 6 Richards | 6 Richards | 6 Dearson | 6 Warner |
| 7 Hopkins | 7 Hopkins | 7 Hopkins | 7 Hopkins | 7 Williams J. |
| 8 Jones L. | 8 Jones L. | 8 Jones L. | 8 Boulter | 8 Astley |
| 9 Perry | 9 Astley | 9 Astley | 9 Glover | 9 Jones W. |
| 10 Jones B. | 10 Jones B. | 10 Jones B. | 10 Jones B. | 10 Dearson |
| 11 Warren | 11 Cumner | 11 Cumner | 11 Cumner | 11 Morris |
| Belfast Mar 16: 0-1 | Cardiff Oct 22: 4-2 *Astley 2, Hopkins, Jones B.* | Edinburgh Nov 9: 2-3 *Astley, Jones L.* | Wrexham Mar 15: 3-1 *Cumner, Glover, Boulter* | Paris May 20: 1-2 *Astley* |

| 1946 Scotland | 1946 England | 1947 N Ireland | 1947 England | 1947 Scotland |
|---|---|---|---|---|
| 1 Sidlow | 1 Sidlow | 1 Shortt | 1 Sidlow | 1 Sidlow |
| 2 Lambert | 2 Sherwood | 2 Sherwood | 2 Lambert | 2 Sherwood |
| 3 Hughes | 3 Hughes | 3 Hughes | 3 Barnes | 3 Barnes |
| 4 Witcomb | 4 Witcomb | 4 Whitcomb | 4 Powell I. | 4 Powell I. |
| 5 Jones T.G. | 5 Jones T.G. | 5 Humphreys | 5 Jones T.G. | 5 Jones T.G. |
| 6 Burgess | 6 Burgess | 6 Burgess | 6 Burgess | 6 Burgess |
| 7 Jones E. | 7 Jones E. | 7 Griffiths | 7 Thomas S. | 7 Thomas S. |
| 8 Powell A. | 8 Powell A. | 8 Morris | 8 Powell A. | 8 Powell A. |
| 9 Ford | 9 Richards | 9 Ford | 9 Lowrie | 9 Ford |
| 10 Jones B. | 10 Powell I. | 10 Jones B. | 10 Jones B. | 10 Lowrie |
| 11 Edwards | 11 Edwards | 11 Edwards | 11 Edwards | 11 Edwards |
| Wrexham Oct 19: 3-1 *Jones B., Ford, Stephen og* | Maine Road Nov 13: 0-3 | Belfast April 16: 1-2 *Ford* | Cardiff Oct 18: 0-3 | Hampden Nov 12: 2-1 *Ford, Lowrie* |

| 1948 N Ireland | 1948 Scotland | 1948 England | 1949 N Ireland | 1949 Portugal |
|---|---|---|---|---|
| 1 Sidlow | 1 Sidlow | 1 Hughes W.A. | 1 Hughes W.A. | 1 Hughes W.A. |
| 2 Sherwood | 2 Sherwood | 2 Barnes | 2 Barnes | 2 Sherwood |
| 3 Barnes | 3 Barnes | 3 Sherwood | 3 Sherwood | 3 Lambert |
| 4 Powell I. | 4 Paul | 4 Paul | 4 Paul | 4 Paul |
| 5 Jones T.G. | 5 Stansfield | 5 Jones T.G. | 5 Jones T.G. | 5 Jones T.G. |
| 6 Baker | 6 Burgess | 6 Burgess | 6 Burgess | 6 Burgess |
| 7 Thomas S. | 7 Thomas S. | 7 Jones E. | 7 Williams H.T. | 7 Griffiths |
| 8 Powell A. | 8 Lucas | 8 Powell A. | 8 Rees | 8 Lucas |
| 9 Ford | 9 Ford | 9 Ford | 9 Ford | 9 Ford |
| 10 Lowrie | 10 Jones B. | 10 Morris | 10 Lucas | 10 Lowrie |
| 11 Edwards | 11 Jones E. | 11 Clarke | 11 Edwards | 11 Edwards |
| Wrexham Mar 10: 2-0 *Lowrie, Edwards* | Cardiff Oct 23: 1-3 *Jones B.* | Villa Park Nov 10: 0-1 | Belfast Mar 9: 2-0 *Edwards, Ford* | Lisbon May 15: 2-3 *Ford 2* |

748

| 1949 Belgium | 1949 Switzerland | 1949 England | 1949 Scotland | 1949 Belgium |
|---|---|---|---|---|
| 1 Hughes W.A. | 1 Hughes W.A. | 1 Sidlow | 1 Jones K.B. | 1 Shortt |
| 2 Roberts | 2 Sherwood | 2 Barnes | 2 Barnes | 2 Barnes |
| 3 Lambert | 3 Lambert | 3 Sherwood | 3 Sherwood | 3 Sherwood |
| 4 Powell I. | 4 Paul | 4 Paul | 4 Powell I. | 4 Powell I. |
| 5 Jones T.G. | 5 Jones T.G. | 5 Jones T.G. | 5 Jones T.G. | 5 Jones T.G. |
| 6 Burgess | 6 Burgess | 6 Burgess | 6 Burgess | 6 Burgess |
| 7 Griffiths | 7 Williams H.T. | 7 Griffiths | 7 Griffiths | 7 Griffiths |
| 8 Rees | 8 Rees | 8 Lucas | 8 Paul | 8 Paul |
| 9 Ford | 9 Ford | 9 Ford | 9 Ford | 9 Ford |
| 10 Lucas | 10 Lucas | 10 Scrine | 10 Clarke | 10 Powell A. |
| 11 Edwards | 11 Edwards | 11 Edwards | 11 Edwards | 11 Clarke |
| Liège May 23: 1-3 Ford | Berne May 26: 0-4 | Cardiff Oct 15: 1-4 Griffiths | Hampden Nov 9: 0-2 | Cardiff Nov 23: 5-1 Clarke, Paul, Ford 3 |

| 1950 N Ireland | 1950 Scotland | 1950 England | 1951 N Ireland | 1951 Portugal |
|---|---|---|---|---|
| 1 Shortt | 1 Parry | 1 Hughes I. | 1 Hughes I. | 1 Hughes I. |
| 2 Barnes | 2 Barnes | 2 Barnes | 2 Barnes | 2 Barnes |
| 3 Sherwood | 3 Sherwood | 3 Sherwood | 3 Sherwood | 3 Sherwood |
| 4 Paul | 4 Powell I. | 4 Paul | 4 Paul | 4 Paul . |
| 5 Charles J. | 5 Paul | 5 Daniel | 5 Daniel | 5 Daniel |
| 6 Burgess | 6 Burgess | 6 Lucas | 6 Burgess | 6 Burgess |
| 7 Williams H.T. | 7 Williams H.T. | 7 Griffiths | 7 Griffiths | 7 Griffiths |
| 8 Rees | 8 Allen | 8 Allen | 8 Kinsey | 8 Kinsey |
| 9 Ford | 9 Ford | 9 Ford | 9 Ford | 9 Ford |
| 10 Scrine | 10 Powell A. | 10 Allchurch I. | 10 Allchurch I. | 10 Allchurch I. |
| 11 Clarke | 11 Clarke | 11 Clarke | 11 Clarke | 11 Clarke |
| Wrexham Mar 8: 0-0 | Cardiff Oct 21: 1-3 Powell A. | Sunderland Nov 15: 2-4 Ford 2 | Belfast Mar 7: 2-1 Clarke 2 | Cardiff May 12: 2-1 Griffiths, Ford |

| 1951 Switzerland | 1951 England | 1951 Scotland | 1951 Rest of UK | 1952 N Ireland |
|---|---|---|---|---|
| 1 Hughes I. | 1 Shortt | 1 Shortt | 1 Shortt | 1 Shortt |
| 2 Williams G. J. | 2 Barnes | 2 Barnes | 2 Barnes | 2 Barnes |
| 3 Sherwood | 3 Sherwood | 3 Sherwood | 3 Sherwood | 3 Sherwood |
| 4 Paul | 4 Paul | 4 Paul | 4 Paul | 4 Paul |
| 5 Charles J. | 5 Daniel | 5 Daniel | 5 Daniel | 5 Daniel |
| 6 Burgess | 6 Burgess | 6 Burgess | 6 Burgess | 6 Burgess |
| 7 Griffiths | 7 Foulkes | 7 Foulkes | 7 Foulkes | 7 Foulkes |
| 8 Kinsey | 8 Kinsey | 8 Morris | 8 Morris | 8 Morris |
| 9 Ford | 9 Ford | 9 Ford | 9 Ford | 9 Ford |
| 10 Allchurch I. | 10 Allchurch I. | 10 Allchurch I. | 10 Allchurch I. | 10 Allchurch I. |
| 11 Clarke | 11 Clarke | 11 Clarke | 11 Clarke | 11 Clarke |
| Wrexham May 16: 3-2 Ford 2, Burgess | Cardiff Oct 20: 1-1 Foulkes | Hampden Nov 20: 1-0 Allchurch | Cardiff Dec 5: 3-2 Allchurch 2, Ford | Swansea Mar 19: 3-0 Barnes, Allchurch, Clarke |

| 1952 Scotland | 1952 England | 1953 N Ireland | 1953 France | 1953 Yugoslavia |
|---|---|---|---|---|
| 1 Shortt | 1 Shortt | 1 Shortt | 1 Shortt | 1 Shortt |
| 2 Lever | 2 Stitfall | 2 Sullivan | 2 Sullivan | 2 Sullivan |
| 3 Sherwood | 3 Sherwood | 3 Sherwood | 3 Sherwood | 3 Sherwood |
| 4 Paul | 4 Paul | 4 Paul | 4 Paul | 4 Paul |
| 5 Daniel | 5 Daniel | 5 Daniel | 5 Daniel | 5 Daniel |
| 6 Burgess | 6 Burgess | 6 Burgess | 6 Burgess | 6 Burgess |
| 7 Foulkes | 7 Foulkes | 7 Medwin | 7 Medwin | 7 Medwin |
| 8 Davies R. | 8 Davies R. | 8 Charles J. | 8 Charles J. | 8 Charles J. |
| 9 Ford | 9 Ford | 9 Ford | 9 Ford | 9 Ford |
| 10 Allchurch I. | 10 Allchurch I. | 10 Allchurch I. | 10 Allchurch I. | 10 Allchurch I. |
| 11 Clarke | 11 Clarke | 11 Griffiths J.H. | 11 Foulkes | 11 Foulkes |

| Cardiff | Wembley | Belfast | Paris | Belgrade |
|---|---|---|---|---|
| Oct 18: 1-2 | Nov 12: 2-5 | April 15: 3-2 | May 14: 1-6 | May 21: 2-5 |
| *Ford* | *Ford 2* | *Charles 2, Ford* | *Allchurch* | *Ford 2* |

| 1953 England | 1953 Scotland | 1954 N Ireland | 1954 Austria | 1954 Yugoslavia |
|---|---|---|---|---|
| 1 Howells | 1 Howells | 1 Kelsey | 1 Kelsey | 1 Kelsey |
| 2 Barnes | 2 Barnes | 2 Sullivan | 2 Williams S. | 2 Barnes |
| 3 Sherwood | 3 Sherwood | 3 Sherwood | 3 Sherwood | 3 Sherwood |
| 4 Paul | 4 Paul | 4 Paul | 4 Harris | 4 Paul |
| 5 Daniel | 5 Daniel | 5 Daniel | 5 Charles J. | 5 Charles J. |
| 6 Burgess | 6 Burgess | 6 Burgess | 6 Burgess | 6 Bowen |
| 7 Foulkes | 7 Foulkes | 7 Foulkes | 7 Griffiths | 7 Reed |
| 8 Davies R. | 8 Davies R. | 8 Kinsey | 8 Tapscott | 8 Tapscott |
| 9 Charles J. | 9 Charles J. | 9 Charles J. | 9 Ford | 9 Ford |
| 10 Allchurch I. | 10 Allchurch I. | 10 Allchurch I. | 10 Allchurch I. | 10 Allchurch I. |
| 11 Clarke | 11 Clarke | 11 Clarke | 11 Jones C. | 11 Clarke |

| Cardiff | Hampden | Wrexham | Vienna | Cardiff |
|---|---|---|---|---|
| Oct 10: 1-4 | Nov 4: 3-3 | Mar 31: 1-2 | May 9: 0-2 | Sept 22: 1-3 |
| *Allchurch* | *Charles 2,* | *Charles* | | *Allchurch* |
| | *Allchurch* | | | |

| 1954 Scotland | 1954 England | 1955 N Ireland | 1955 England | 1955 Scotland |
|---|---|---|---|---|
| 1 Kelsey | 1 King | 1 Kelsey | 1 Kelsey | 1 Kelsey |
| 2 Barnes | 2 Williams S. | 2 Williams S. | 2 Williams S. | 2 Williams S. |
| 3 Sherwood | 3 Sherwood | 3 Sherwood | 3 Sherwood | 3 Sherwood |
| 4 Paul | 4 Paul | 4 Charles M. | 4 Charles M. | 4 Charles M. |
| 5 Charles J. | 5 Daniel | 5 Daniel | 5 Charles J. | 5 Charles J. |
| 6 Bowen | 6 Sullivan | 6 Sullivan | 6 Paul | 6 Paul |
| 7 Reed | 7 Tapscott | 7 Tapscott | 7 Tapscott | 7 Tapscott |
| 8 Tapscott | 8 Ford | 8 Ford | 8 Kinsey | 8 Kinsey |
| 9 Ford | 9 Charles J. | 9 Charles J. | 9 Ford | 9 Ford |
| 10 Allchurch I. | 10 Allchurch I. | 10 Allchurch I. | 10 Allchurch I. | 10 Allchurch I. |
| 11 Clarke | 11 Clarke | 11 Allchurch L. | 11 Jones C. | 11 Jones C. |

| Cardiff | Wembley | Belfast | Cardiff | Hampden |
|---|---|---|---|---|
| Oct 16: 0-1 | Nov 10: 2-3 | April 20: 3-2 | Oct 22: 2-1 | Nov 9: 0-2 |
| | *Charles 2* | *Charles J. 3* | *Tapscott, Jones* | |

750

| 1955 Austria | 1956 N Ireland | 1956 Scotland | 1956 England | 1957 N Ireland |
|---|---|---|---|---|
| 1 Kelsey | 1 Kelsey | 1 Kelsey | 1 Kelsey | 1 Kelsey |
| 2 Williams S. | 2 Sherwood | 2 Sherwood | 2 Sherwood | 2 Edwards |
| 3 Sherwood | 3 Hopkins | 3 Hopkins | 3 Hopkins | 3 Hopkins |
| 4 Charles M. | 4 Harrington | 4 Harrington | 4 Harrington | 4 Charles M. |
| 5 Charles J. | 5 Charles J. | 5 Daniel | 5 Daniel | 5 Daniel |
| 6 Paul | 6 Paul | 6 Sullivan | 6 Sullivan | 6 Bowen |
| 7 Allchurch L. | 7 Jones C. | 7 Medwin | 7 Medwin | 7 Medwin |
| 8 Tapscott | 8 Tapscott | 8 Charles J. | 8 Charles M. | 8 Tapscott |
| 9 Ford | 9 Ford | 9 Ford | 9 Charles J. | 9 Charles J. |
| 10 Allchurch I. | 10 Allchurch I. | 10 Allchurch I. | 10 Allchurch I. | 10 Vernon |
| 11 Jones C. | 11 Clarke | 11 Jones C. | 11 Jones C. | 11 Jones C. |
| Wrexham Nov 23: 1-2 *Tapscott* | Cardiff April 11: 1-1 *Clarke* | Cardiff Oct 20: 2-2 *Ford, Medwin* | Wembley Nov 14: 1-3 *Charles J.* | Belfast April 10: 0-0 |

| 1957 Czechoslovakia | 1957 E Germany | 1957 Czechoslovakia | 1957 E Germany | 1957 England |
|---|---|---|---|---|
| 1 Kelsey | 1 Kelsey | 1 Kelsey | 1 Vearncombe | 1 Kelsey |
| 2 Stitfall | 2 Edwards | 2 Thomas | 2 Thomas | 2 Williams S. |
| 3 Hopkins | 3 Hopkins | 3 Hopkins | 3 Hopkins | 3 Hopkins |
| 4 Charles M. | 4 Harris | 4 Charles M. | 4 Harris | 4 Harris |
| 5 Charles J. | 5 Charles J. | 5 Daniel | 5 Charles M. | 5 Charles M. |
| 6 Bowen | 6 Bowen | 6 Harris | 6 Bowen | 6 Bowen |
| 7 Medwin | 7 Medwin | 7 Medwin | 7 Allchurch L. | 7 Medwin |
| 8 Tapscott | 8 Tapscott | 8 Palmer | 8 Davies R. | 8 Davies R. |
| 9 Webster | 9 Charles M. | 9 Charles J. | 9 Palmer | 9 Palmer |
| 10 Vernon | 10 Vernon | 10 Vernon | 10 Vernon | 10 Vernon |
| 11 Jones C. | 11 Jones C. | 11 Jones C. | 11 Jones C. | 11 Jones C. |
| Cardiff May 1: 1-0 *Vernon* | Leipzig May 19: 1-2 *Charles M.* | Prague May 26: 0-2 | Cardiff Sept 25: 4-1 *Palmer 3, Jones* | Cardiff Oct 19: 0-4 |

| 1957 Scotland | 1958 Israel | 1958 Israel | 1958 N Ireland | 1958 Hungary † |
|---|---|---|---|---|
| 1 Kelsey | 1 Kelsey | 1 Kelsey | 1 Kelsey | 1 Kelsey |
| 2 Williams S. | 2 Williams S. | 2 Williams S. | 2 Williams S. | 2 Williams S. |
| 3 Hopkins | 3 Hopkins | 3 Hopkins | 3 Hopkins | 3 Hopkins |
| 4 Harrington | 4 Harrington | 4 Harrington | 4 Harrington | 4 Sullivan |
| 5 Charles M. | 5 Charles M. | 5 Charles M. | 5 Sullivan | 5 Charles M. |
| 6 Bowen | 6 Bowen | 6 Bowen | 6 Bowen | 6 Bowen |
| 7 Allchurch L. | 7 Allchurch L. | 7 Medwin | 7 Allchurch L. | 7 Webster |
| 8 Harris | 8 Charles J. | 8 Hewitt | 8 Hewitt | 8 Medwin |
| 9 Medwin | 9 Medwin | 9 Charles J. | 9 Medwin | 9 Charles J. |
| 10 Vernon | 10 Allchurch I. | 10 Allchurch I. | 10 Allchurch I. | 10 Allchurch I. |
| 11 Jones C. | 11 Jones C. | 11 Jones C. | 11 Jones C. | 11 Jones C. |
| Hampden Nov 13: 1-1 *Medwin* | Tel Aviv Jan 15: 2-0 *Allchurch I., Bowen* | Cardiff Feb 5: 2-0 *Allchurch, Jones* | Cardiff April 16: 1-1 *Hewitt* | Sandviken June 8: 1-1 *Charles* |

| 1958 Mexico † | 1958 Sweden † | 1958 Hungary † | 1958 Brazil † | 1958 Scotland |
|---|---|---|---|---|
| 1 Kelsey | 1 Kelsey | 1 Kelsey | 1 Kelsey | 1 Kelsey |
| 2 Williams S. | 2 Williams S. | 2 Williams S. | 2 Williams S. | 2 Williams S. |
| 3 Hopkins | 3 Hopkins | 3 Hopkins | 3 Hopkins | 3 Hopkins |
| 4 Baker | 4 Sullivan | 4 Sullivan | 4 Sullivan | 4 Sullivan |
| 5 Charles M. | 5 Charles M. | 5 Charles M. | 5 Charles M. | 5 Charles M. |
| 6 Bowen | 6 Bowen | 6 Bowen | 6 Bowen | 6 Bowen |
| 7 Webster | 7 Vernon | 7 Medwin | 7 Medwin | 7 Allchurch L. |
| 8 Medwin | 8 Hewitt | 8 Hewitt | 8 Hewitt | 8 Vernon |
| 9 Charles J. | 9 Charles J. | 9 Charles J. | 9 Webster | 9 Medwin |
| 10 Allchurch I. | 10 Allchurch I. | 10 Allchurch I. | 10 Allchurch I. | 10 Allchurch I. |
| 11 Jones C. | 11 Jones C. | 11 Jones C. | 11 Jones C. | 11 Woosnam |
| Stockholm June 11: 1-1 *Allchurch* | Stockholm June 15: 0-0 | Stockholm June 17: 2-1 *Allchurch, Medwin* | Gothenburg June 19:0-1 | Cardiff Oct 18: 0-3 |

| 1958 England | 1959 N Ireland | 1959 England | 1959 Scotland | 1960 N Ireland |
|---|---|---|---|---|
| 1 Kelsey | 1 Rouse | 1 Kelsey | 1 Kelsey | 1 Kelsey |
| 2 Williams S. | 2 Williams S. | 2 Williams S. | 2 Williams S. | 2 Williams S. |
| 3 Hopkins | 3 Hopkins | 3 Hopkins | 3 Hopkins | 3 Williams G. |
| 4 Crowe | 4 Crowe | 4 Crowe | 4 Sullivan | 4 Crowe |
| 5 Charles M. | 5 Sullivan | 5 Nurse | 5 Charles J. | 5 Nurse |
| 6 Bowen | 6 Bowen | 6 Sullivan | 6 Baker | 6 Baker |
| 7 Medwin | 7 Medwin | 7 Medwin | 7 Medwin | 7 Medwin |
| 8 Ward | 8 Tapscott | 8 Woosnam | 8 Woosnam | 8 Woosnam |
| 9 Tapscott | 9 Rowley | 9 Moore | 9 Moore | 9 Moore |
| 10 Allchurch I. | 10 Allchurch I. | 10 Allchurch I. | 10 Allchurch I. | 10 Vernon |
| 11 Woosnam | 11 Jones C. | 11 Jones C. | 11 Jones C. | 11 Jones C. |
| Villa Park Nov 26: 2-2 *Tapscott, Allchurch* | Belfast April 22: 1-4 *Tapscott* | Cardiff Oct 17: 1-1 *Moore* | Hampden Nov 4: 1-1 *Charles* | Wrexham April 6: 3-2 *Medwin 2, Woosnam* |

| 1960 Rep of Ireland | 1960 Scotland | 1960 England | 1961 N Ireland | 1961 Spain |
|---|---|---|---|---|
| 1 Vearncombe | 1 Kelsey | 1 Kelsey | 1 Kelsey | 1 Kelsey |
| 2 Williams S. | 2 Harrington | 2 Harrington | 2 Williams S. | 2 Williams S. |
| 3 Williams G. | 3 Williams G. | 3 Williams G. | 3 Hopkins | 3 Hopkins |
| 4 Crowe | 4 Crowe | 4 Crowe | 4 Charles M. | 4 Charles M. |
| 5 Nurse | 5 Nurse | 5 Nurse | 5 Nurse | 5 Nurse |
| 6 Baker | 6 Baker | 6 Baker | 6 Crowe | 6 Crowe |
| 7 Medwin | 7 Medwin | 7 Medwin | 7 Jones C. | 7 Medwin |
| 8 Woosnam | 8 Woosnam | 8 Woosnam | 8 Woosnam | 8 Woosnam |
| 9 Moore | 9 Leek | 9 Leek | 9 Leek | 9 Leek |
| 10 Vernon | 10 Vernon | 10 Vernon | 10 Allchurch I. | 10 Allchurch I. |
| 11 Jones C. | 11 Jones C. | 11 Jones C. | 11 Williams G. | 11 Williams G. |
| Dublin Sept 28: 3-2 *Jones 2, Woosnam* | Cardiff Oct 22: 2-0 *Vernon, Jones* | Wembley Nov 23: 1-5 *Leek* | Belfast April 12: 5-1 *Charles, Jones 2, Allchurch, Leek* | Cardiff April 19: 1-2 *Woosnam* |

| 1961 Spain | 1961 Hungary | 1961 England | 1961 Scotland | 1962 N Ireland |
|---|---|---|---|---|
| 1 Kelsey | 1 Kelsey | 1 Kelsey | 1 Kelsey | 1 Kelsey |
| 2 Williams S. | 2 Williams S. | 2 Harrington | 2 Harrington | 2 Williams S. |
| 3 Hopkins | 3 Hopkins | 3 Williams S. | 3 Williams S. | 3 Hopkins |
| 4 Charles M. | 4 Charles M. | 4 Charles M. | 4 Crowe | 4 Lucas |
| 5 Nurse | 5 Nurse | 5 Charles J. | 5 Charles M. | 5 England |
| 6 Crowe | 6 Crowe | 6 Crowe | 6 Baker | 6 Hennessey |
| 7 Jones C. | 7 Jones C. | 7 Jones C. | 7 Allchurch L. | 7 Allchurch L. |
| 8 Moore | 8 Woosnam | 8 Woosnam | 8 Woosnam | 8 Woosnam |
| 9 Leek | 9 Leek | 9 Ward | 9 Leek | 9 Charles M. |
| 10 Allchurch I. | 10 Allchurch I. | 10 Allchurch I. | 10 Allchurch I. | 10 Vernon |
| 11 Williams G. | 11 Williams G. | 11 Williams G. | 11 Jones C. | 11 Jones C. |

| | | | | |
|---|---|---|---|---|
| Madrid | Budapest | Cardiff | Hampden | Cardiff |
| May 18: 1-1 | May 28: 2-3 | Oct 14: 1-1 | Nov 8: 0-2 | April 11: 4-0 |
| *Allchurch* | *Allchurch, Jones* | *Williams G.* | | *Charles 4* |

| 1962 Brazil | 1962 Brazil | 1962 Mexico | 1962 Scotland | 1962 Hungary |
|---|---|---|---|---|
| 1 Kelsey | 1 Kelsey (Hollins) | 1 Hollins | 1 Millington | 1 Millington |
| 2 Williams S. | 2 Williams S. | 2 Williams S. | 2 Williams S. | 2 Williams S. |
| 3 Hopkins | 3 Hopkins | 3 Hopkins | 3 Hopkins | 3 Hopkins |
| 4 Hennessey | 4 England | 4 Lucas | 4 Hennessey | 4 Hennessey |
| 5 Charles J. | 5 Charles J. | 5 England | 5 Charles J. | 5 Nurse |
| 6 Crowe | 6 Hennessey | 6 Crowe | 6 Lucas | 6 Crowe |
| 7 Allchurch L. | 7 Woosnam | 7 Vernon | 7 Jones B. | 7 Medwin |
| 8 Vernon | 8 Vernon | 8 Allchurch I. | 8 Allchurch I. | 8 Allchurch I. |
| 9 Charles M. | 9 Moore (Leek) | 9 Charles J. | 9 Charles M. | 9 Charles M. |
| 10 Allchurch I. | 10 Allchurch I. | 10 Leek | 10 Vernon | 10 Vernon |
| 11 Jones C. | 11 Jones C. | 11 Jones C. | 11 Jones C. | 11 Jones B. |

| | | | | |
|---|---|---|---|---|
| Rio de Janeiro | Sao Paulo | Mexico City | Cardiff | Budapest |
| May 12: 1-3 | May 16: 1-3 | May 22: 1-2 | Oct 20: 2-3 | Nov 7: 1-3 |
| *Allchurch I.* | *Leek* | *Charles* | *Allchurch, Charles J.* | *Medwin* |

| 1962 England | 1963 Hungary | 1963 N Ireland | 1963 England | 1963 Scotland |
|---|---|---|---|---|
| 1 Millington | 1 Hollins | 1 Hollins | 1 Hollins | 1 Sprake |
| 2 Williams S. | 2 Williams S. | 2 Hopkins | 2 Williams S. | 2 Williams S. |
| 3 Sear | 3 Williams G. | 3 Williams G. | 3 Williams G. | 3 Williams G. |
| 4 Hennessey | 4 Hennessey | 4 Burton | 4 Hennessey | 4 Hennessey |
| 5 Nurse | 5 England | 5 England | 5 England | 5 England |
| 6 Lucas | 6 Burton | 6 Hole | 6 Burton | 6 Nurse |
| 7 Jones B. | 7 Jones B. | 7 Jones B. | 7 Allchurch L. | 7 Jones B. |
| 8 Allchurch I. | 8 Woosnam | 8 Woosnam | 8 Vernon | 8 Moore |
| 9 Leek | 9 Moore | 9 Moore | 9 Davies W. | 9 Charles J. |
| 10 Vernon | 10 Allchurch I. | 10 Allchurch I. | 10 Allchurch I. | 10 Vernon |
| 11 Medwin | 11 Jones C. | 11 Jones C. | 11 Jones C. | 11 Jones C. |

| | | | | |
|---|---|---|---|---|
| Wembley | Cardiff | Belfast | Cardiff | Hampden |
| Nov 21: 0-4 | Mar 20: 1-1 | April 3: 4-1 | Oct 12: 0-4 | Nov 20: 1-2 |
| | *Jones C.* | *Woosnam, Jones C. 3* | | *Jones B.* |

753

| 1964 N Ireland | 1964 Scotland | 1964 Denmark | 1964 England | 1964 Greece |
|---|---|---|---|---|
| 1 Sprake | 1 Sprake | 1 Sprake | 1 Millington | 1 Sprake |
| 2 Evans R. | 2 Williams S. | 2 Williams S. | 2 Williams S. | 2 Rodrigues |
| 3 Williams G. | 3 Williams G. | 3 Williams G. | 3 Williams G. | 3 Williams G. |
| 4 Johnson | 4 Hole | 4 Hennessey | 4 Hennessey | 4 Hennessey |
| 5 England | 5 Charles J. | 5 England | 5 England | 5 England |
| 6 Hole | 6 Hennessey | 6 Hole | 6 Hole | 6 Hole |
| 7 Jones B. | 7 Jones C. | 7 Jones B. | 7 Rees | 7 Rees |
| 8 Moore | 8 Leek | 8 Godfrey | 8 Davies R. | 8 Leek |
| 9 Davies R. | 9 Davies W. | 9 Davies W. | 9 Davies W. | 9 Davies W. |
| 10 Godfrey | 10 Allchurch I. | 10 Jones C. | 10 Allchurch I. | 10 Williams H. |
| 11 Jones C. | 11 Rees | 11 Rees | 11 Jones C. | 11 Jones C. |

Swansea April 15: 2-3 *Godfrey, Davies* — Cardiff Oct 3: 3-2 *Davies, Leek 2* — Copenhagen Oct 21: 0-1 — Wembley Nov 18: 1-2 *Jones* — Athens Dec 9: 0-2

| 1965 Greece | 1965 N Ireland | 1965 Italy | 1965 USSR | 1965 England |
|---|---|---|---|---|
| 1 Hollins | 1 Hollins | 1 Hollins | 1 Millington | 1 Sprake |
| 2 Rodrigues | 2 Rodrigues | 2 Green | 2 Green | 2 Rodrigues |
| 3 Williams G. | 3 Williams G. | 3 Williams G. | 3 Williams G. | 3 Green |
| 4 Williams H. | 4 Lea | 4 Lea | 4 Hennessey | 4 Hennessey |
| 5 England | 5 England | 5 England | 5 England | 5 England |
| 6 Hole | 6 Hole | 6 Hole | 6 Hole | 6 Hole |
| 7 Jones C. | 7 Jones C. | 7 Jones C. | 7 Jones C. | 7 Rees |
| 8 Allchurch I. | 8 Allchurch I. | 8 Allchurch I. | 8 Allchurch I. | 8 Vernon |
| 9 Leek | 9 Davies W. | 9 Godfrey | 9 Davies W, | 9 Davies W. |
| 10 Vernon | 10 Vernon | 10 Vernon | 10 Charles J. | 10 Allchurch I. |
| 11 Rees | 11 Rees | 11 Rees | 11 Rees | 11 Reece |

Cardiff May 17: 4-1 *Allchurch 2, England, Vernon* — Belfast Mar 31: 5-0 *Vernon 2, Jones, Williams, Allchurch* — Florence May 1: 1-4 *Godfrey* — Moscow May 30: 1-2 *Davies* — Cardiff Oct 2: 0-0

| 1965 USSR | 1965 Scotland | 1965 Denmark | 1966 N Ireland | 1966 Brazil |
|---|---|---|---|---|
| 1 Sprake | 1 Hollins | 1 Hollins | 1 Sprake | 1 Hollins |
| 2 Rodrigues | 2 Rodrigues | 2 Rodrigues | 2 Rodrigues | 2 Green |
| 3 Green | 3 Green | 3 Williams S. | 3 Williams G. | 3 Rodrigues |
| 4 Hennessey | 4 Hennessey | 4 Hennessey | 4 Hennessey | 4 Hennessey |
| 5 England | 5 England | 5 England | 5 England | 5 James |
| 6 Hole | 6 Hole | 6 Hole | 6 Hole | 6 Hole |
| 7 Rees | 7 Rees | 7 Rees | 7 Rees | 7 Rees |
| 8 Vernon | 8 Vernon | 8 Vernon | 8 Vernon | 8 Davies R. |
| 9 Davies W. | 9 Davies W. | 9 Davies W. | 9 Davies W. | 9 Davies W. |
| 10 Allchurch I. | 10 Allchurch I. | 10 Allchurch I. | 10 Moore | 10 Allchurch I. |
| 11 Reece | 11 Reece | 11 Pring | 11 Reece | 11 Williams G. |

Cardiff Oct 27: 2-1 *Vernon, Allchurch* — Hampden Nov 24: 1-4 *Allchurch* — Wrexham Dec 1: 4-2 *Vernon 2, Davies, Rees* — Cardiff Mar 30: 1-4 *Davies* — Rio de Janeiro May 14: 1-3 *Davies R.*

| 1966 Brazil | 1966 Chile | 1966 Scotland | 1966 England | 1967 N Ireland |
|---|---|---|---|---|
| 1 Millington | 1 Millington | 1 Sprake | 1 Millington | 1 Millington |
| 2 Green | 2 Rodrigues | 2 Rodrigues | 2 Green | 2 Thomas |
| 3 Rodrigues | 3 Williams G. | 3 Williams G. | 3 Williams G. | 3 Williams G. |
| 4 Hennessey | 4 Hennessey | 4 Hennessey | 4 Hennessey | 4 Jarvis |
| 5 James E.G. | 5 James E.G. (Rankmore) | 5 England | 5 England | 5 James E.G. |
| 6 Hole | 6 Hole | 6 Hole | 6 Hole | 6 Hole |
| 7 Rees (Durban) | 7 Rees | 7 Reece | 7 Rees | 7 Rees |
| 8 Davies R. | 8 Moore | 8 Davies W. | 8 Davies W. | 8 Durban |
| 9 Davies W. | 9 Davies R. | 9 Davies R. | 9 Davies R. | 9 Davies R. |
| 10 Allchurch I. | 10 Allchurch I. | 10 Jones C. | 10 Jones C. | 10 Vernon |
| 11 Williams G. | 11 Pring (Davies W.) | 11 Jarvis | 11 Jarvis | 11 Pring |
| Belo Horizonte May 18: 0-1 | Santiago May 22: 0:2 | Cardiff Oct 22: 1-1 *Davies R.* | Wembley Nov 16: 1-5 *Davies W.* | Belfast April 12: 0-0 |

| 1967 England | 1967 Scotland | 1968 N Ireland | 1968 W Germany | 1968 Italy |
|---|---|---|---|---|
| 1 Sprake | 1 Sprake | 1 Millington | 1 Millington | 1 Millington |
| 2 Rodrigues | 2 Rodrigues | 2 Rodrigues | 2 Thomas | 2 Thomas |
| 3 Green | 3 Green | 3 Green | 3 Green | 3 Williams G. |
| 4 Hennessey | 4 Hennessey | 4 Hennessey | 4 Powell | 4 Burton |
| 5 England | 5 James E.G. | 5 England | 5 England | 5 Powell |
| 6 Hole | 6 Hole | 6 Hole | 6 Hole | 6 Hole |
| 7 Rees | 7 Rees | 7 Rees | 7 Rees | 7 Rees |
| 8 Durban | 8 Davies W. | 8 Davies W. | 8 Davies W. | 8 Davies W. |
| 9 Mahoney | 9 Davies R. | 9 Davies R. | 9 Davies R. | 9 Davies R. |
| 10 Vernon | 10 Durban | 10 Durban | 10 Durban | 10 Green (Jones B.) |
| 11 Jones C. | 11 Jones C. | 11 Williams G. | 11 Jones C. | 11 Jones C. |
| Cardiff Oct 21: 0-3 | Hampden Nov 22: 2-3 *Davies R., Durban* | Wrexham Feb 28: 2-0 *Rees, Davies W.* | Cardiff May 8: 1-1 *Davies W.* | Cardiff Oct 23: 0-1 |

| 1969 W Germany | 1969 E Germany | 1969 Scotland | 1969 England | 1969 N Ireland |
|---|---|---|---|---|
| 1 Sprake | 1 Millington | 1 Sprake | 1 Sprake | 1 Sprake |
| 2 Thomas | 2 Rodrigues | 2 Derrett (Rees) | 2 Rodrigues | 2 Rodrigues (Green) |
| 3 Derrett | 3 Burton | 3 Green | 3 Thomas | 3 Thomas |
| 4 Powell | 4 Hennessey | 4 Durban | 4 Durban | 4 Durban |
| 5 Hennessey | 5 England | 5 Burton | 5 Powell | 5 Powell |
| 6 Hole | 6 Hole | 6 Powell | 6 Burton | 6 Burton |
| 7 Jones B. | 7 Jones B. | 7 Moore | 7 Jones B. | 7 Jones B. |
| 8 Durban | 8 Durban | 8 Toshack | 8 Davies R. | 8 Davies R. |
| 9 Davies R. | 9 Toshack | 9 Davies R. | 9 Toshack | 9 Toshack |
| 10 Toshack | 10 Mahoney | 10 Davies W. | 10 Davies W. | 10 Davies W. |
| 11 Rees | 11 Rees | 11 Jones B. | 11 Moore | 11 Moore |
| Frankfurt Mar 26: 1-1 *Jones* | Dresden April 16: 1-2 *Toshack* | Wrexham May 3: 3-5 *Davies R. 2, Toshack* | Wembley May 7: 1-2 *Davies R.* | Belfast May 10: 0-0 |

| 1969 Rest of UK | 1969 E Germany | 1969 Italy | 1970 England | 1970 Scotland |
|---|---|---|---|---|
| 1 Sprake | 1 Sprake | 1 Sprake | 1 Millington | 1 Millington |
| 2 Rodrigues | 2 Rodrigues | 2 Thomas | 2 Rodrigues | 2 Rodrigues |
| 3 Thomas | 3 Thomas | 3 Derrett | 3 Thomas | 3 Thomas |
| 4 Hennessey | 4 Hennessey | 4 Durban | 4 Hennessey | 4 Hennessey |
| 5 England | 5 England | 5 England | 5 England | 5 England |
| 6 Moore | 6 Powell | 6 Moore | 6 Powell | 6 Powell |
| 7 Jones B. | 7 Durban | 7 Yorath | 7 Krzywicki | 7 Krzywicki |
| 8 Jones C. | 8 Krzywicki | 8 Toshack | 8 Durban | 8 Durban |
| 9 Davies R. | 9 Davies W. | 9 Hole | 9 Davies R. | 9 Davies R. |
| 10 Toshack | 10 Toshack | 10 Krzywicki | 10 Moore | 10 Moore |
| 11 Rees (Reece) | 11 Rees | 11 Rees (Reece) | 11 Rees | 11 Rees |
| Cardiff July 28: 0-1 | Cardiff Oct 22: 1-3 *Powell* | Rome Nov 4: 1-4 *England* | Cardiff April 18: 1-1 *Krzywicki* | Hampden April 22: 0-0 |

| 1970 N Ireland | 1970 Rumania | 1971 Czechoslovakia | 1971 Scotland | 1971 England |
|---|---|---|---|---|
| 1 Millington | 1 Sprake | 1 Millington | 1 Sprake | 1 Sprake |
| 2 Rodrigues | 2 Rodrigues | 2 Rodrigues | 2 Rodrigues | 2 Rodrigues |
| 3 Thomas | 3 Thomas | 3 Thomas | 3 Thomas | 3 Thomas |
| 4 Hennessey | 4 Powell | 4 Phillips | 4 James E.G. | 4 James E.G. |
| 5 England | 5 England | 5 James E.G. | 5 Roberts J. | 5 Roberts J. |
| 6 Powell | 6 Hole | 6 Walley | 6 Yorath | 6 Yorath |
| 7 Krzywicki | 7 Krzywicki | 7 Rees | 7 Phillips | 7 Phillips |
| 8 Durban | 8 Durban | 8 Durban | 8 Durban | 8 Durban |
| 9 Davies R. | 9 Davies W. | 9 Davies R. | 9 Davies R. | 9 Davies R. |
| 10 Moore | 10 Moore | 10 Davies W. | 10 Toshack | 10 Toshack |
| 11 Rees | 11 Rees | 11 Mahoney (Griffiths) | 11 Reece | 11 Reece (Rees) |
| Swansea April 25: 1-0 *Rees* | Cardiff Nov 11: 0-0 | Swansea April 21: 1-3 *Davies R.* | Cardiff May 15: 0-0 | Wembley May 18: 0-0 |

| 1971 N Ireland | 1971 Finland | 1971 Finland | 1971 Czechoslovakia | 1971 Rumania |
|---|---|---|---|---|
| 1 Sprake | 1 Millington | 1 Sprake (Millington) | 1 Millington | 1 Millington |
| 2 Rodrigues | 2 Page | 2 Rodrigues | 2 Rodrigues | 2 Rodrigues |
| 3 Thomas | 3 Derrett | 3 Thomas | 3 Phillips | 3 Thomas |
| 4 James E.G. | 4 Durban | 4 Roberts J. | 4 Burton | 4 Phillips |
| 5 Roberts J. | 5 Roberts J. | 5 England | 5 Thomas | 5 Williams H. |
| 6 Yorath | 6 Mielczarek | 6 Hennessey | 6 Yorath | 6 Hockey |
| 7 Phillips (Rees) | 7 Krzywicki | 7 Evans | 7 Hennessey (Rees) | 7 James |
| 8 Durban | 8 Jones W. | 8 Reece | 8 Durban | 8 Hill (Davies C.) |
| 9 Davies R. | 9 Rees | 9 Toshack | 9 Evans (Krzywicki) | 9 Davies R. |
| 10 Toshack | 10 Toshack | 10 Durban | 10 Hill | 10 Reece |
| 11 Reece | 11 Reece | 11 Hockey | 11 James | 11 Rees |
| Belfast May 22: 0-1 | Helsinki May 26: 1-0 *Toshack* | Swansea Oct 13: 3-0 *Durban, Toshack, Reece* | Prague Oct 27: 0-1 | Bucharest Nov 24: 0-2 |

| 1972 England | 1972 Scotland | 1972 N Ireland | 1972 England | 1973 England |
|---|---|---|---|---|
| 1 Sprake | 1 Sprake | 1 Sprake | 1 Sprake | 1 Sprake |
| 2 Rodrigues | 2 Page | 2 Page | 2 Rodrigues (Reece) | 2 Rodrigues (Page) |
| 3 Thomas | 3 Thomas | 3 Thomas | 3 Thomas | 3 Thomas |
| 4 Hennessey | 4 Hennessey (James) | 4 Yorath (Rodrigues) | 4 Hennessey | 4 Hockey |
| 5 England | 5 England | 5 England | 5 England | 5 England |
| 6 Roberts J. (Reece) | 6 Yorath | 6 Roberts J. | 6 Hockey | 6 Roberts J. |
| 7 Yorath | 7 Durban | 7 Durban | 7 Phillips | 7 Evans |
| 8 Davies R. | 8 Davies W. | 8 Davies W. | 8 Mahoney | 8 Mahoney |
| 9 Davies W. | 9 Reece | 9 Reece | 9 Davies W. | 9 Toshack |
| 10 Toshack | 10 Davies R. | 10 Davies R. | 10 Toshack | 10 Yorath |
| 11 Durban | 11 Phillips | 11 Phillips | 11 James | 11 James |
| Cardiff May 20: 0-3 | Hampden May 24: 0-1 | Wrexham May 27: 0-0 | Cardiff Nov 15: 0-1 | Wembley Jan 24: 1-1 *Toshack* |

| 1973 Poland | 1973 Scotland | 1973 England | 1973 N Ireland | 1973 Poland |
|---|---|---|---|---|
| 1 Sprake | 1 Sprake | 1 Phillips J. | 1 Sprake | 1 Sprake |
| 2 Rodrigues | 2 Rodrigues | 2 Rodrigues | 2 Rodrigues | 2 Rodrigues |
| 3 Thomas | 3 Thomas | 3 Thomas | 3 Thomas | 3 Thomas |
| 4 Roberts D. | 4 Hockey | 4 Hockey | 4 Hockey (Emanuel) | 4 Mahoney (Phillips) |
| 5 Roberts J. | 5 England | 5 England (Roberts D.) | 5 Roberts D. | 5 England |
| 6 Hockey | 6 Roberts J. | 6 Roberts J. | 6 Roberts J. | 6 Roberts J. |
| 7 James | 7 James | 7 James | 7 James | 7 Evans (Reece) |
| 8 Yorath | 8 Mahoney | 8 Mahoney | 8 Mahoney | 8 Yorath |
| 9 Toshack | 9 Toshack | 9 Toshack | 9 Reece | 9 Davies W. |
| 10 Mahoney | 10 Yorath (Davies W.) | 10 Page (Emanuel) | 10 Page | 10 Hockey |
| 11 Evans | 11 Evans (O'Sullivan) | 11 Evans | 11 Davies W. | 11 James |
| Cardiff Mar 28: 2-0 *James, Hockey* | Wrexham May 12: 0-2 | Wembley May 15: 0-3 | Everton May 19: 0-1 | Chorzow Sept 26: 0-3 |

| 1974 England | 1974 Scotland | 1974 N Ireland | 1974 Austria | 1974 Hungary |
|---|---|---|---|---|
| 1 Phillips | 1 Sprake | 1 Sprake | 1 Sprake | 1 Sprake (Phillips J.) |
| 2 Roberts P. (Cartwright) | 2 Thomas | 2 Page | 2 Roberts P. | 2 Thomas |
| 3 Thomas | 3 Page | 3 Thomas | 3 Phillips | 3 Roberts P. |
| 4 Mahoney | 4 Mahoney | 4 Mahoney | 4 Roberts D. | 4 Mahoney |
| 5 Roberts J. | 5 Roberts J. | 5 Roberts J. | 5 Roberts J. | 5 England |
| 6 Roberts D. | 6 Roberts D. | 6 Reece | 6 Yorath | 6 Phillips |
| 7 Reece | 7 Reece (Smallman) | 7 Yorath | 7 Mahoney | 7 Griffiths |
| 8 Villars | 8 Villars | 8 James | 8 Griffiths | 8 Yorath |
| 9 Davies R. (Smallman) | 9 Yorath | 9 Smallman (Villars) | 9 Reece | 9 Reece |
| 10 Yorath | 10 Cartwright | 10 Phillips | 10 Toshack | 10 Toshack |
| 11 James | 11 James | 11 Cartwright | 11 James | 11 James |
| Cardiff May 11: 0-2 | Hampden May 14: 0-2 | Wrexham May 18: 1-0 *Smallman* | Vienna Sept 4: 1-2 *Griffiths* | Cardiff Oct 30: 2-0 *Griffiths, Toshack* |

| 1974 Luxembourg | 1975 Hungary | 1975 Luxembourg | 1975 Scotland | 1975 England |
|---|---|---|---|---|
| 1 Sprake | 1 Davies | 1 Davies | 1 Davies | 1 Davies |
| 2 Thomas | 2 Thomas | 2 Page | 2 Thomas | 2 Thomas |
| 3 England | 3 Page | 3 Yorath | 3 Page | 3 Page |
| 4 Roberts P. | 4 Phillips | 4 Thomas | 4 Yorath | 4 Mahoney |
| 5 Phillips | 5 Roberts J. | 5 Roberts D. | 5 Roberts J. | 5 Roberts J. |
| 6 Mahoney (Flynn) | 6 Yorath | 6 Mahoney | 6 Phillips | 6 Phillips |
| 7 Yorath | 7 Mahoney | 7 Phillips | 7 Mahoney | 7 Griffiths |
| 8 Griffiths | 8 Griffiths | 8 Griffiths (Flynn) | 8 Flynn | 8 Flynn |
| 9 James | 9 Reece (Smallman) | 9 Reece | 9 Reece | 9 Smallman (Showers) |
| 10 Reece | 10 Toshack | 10 Toshack | 10 Toshack | 10 Toshack |
| 11 Toshack | 11 James (Flynn) | 11 James | 11 James | 11 James |

Swansea
Nov 20: 5-0
*Toshack, England, Roberts P., Griffiths, Yorath*

Budapest
April 16: 2-1
*Toshack, Mahoney*

Luxembourg
May 1: 3-1
*Reece, James 2 (1 pen)*

Cardiff
May 17: 2-2
*Toshack, Flynn*

Wembley
May 21: 2-2
*Toshack, Griffiths*


| 1975 N Ireland | 1975 Austria | 1976 England | 1976 Yugoslavia | 1976 Scotland |
|---|---|---|---|---|
| 1 Davies | 1 Lloyd | 1 Lloyd | 1 Davies | 1 Lloyd |
| 2 Thomas | 2 Thomas | 2 Page | 2 Thomas | 2 Jones D. |
| 3 Page | 3 Jones J. | 3 Jones J. | 3 Page | 3 Jones J. |
| 4 Mahoney | 4 Mahoney | 4 Yorath | 4 Mahoney | 4 Roberts D. |
| 5 Roberts D. | 5 Evans | 5 Phillips | 5 Phillips | 5 Roberts J. |
| 6 Phillips | 6 Phillips | 6 Evans | 6 Phillips | 6 Yorath |
| 7 Griffiths | 7 Griffiths | 7 Harris | 7 James (Curtis) | 7 Griffiths |
| 8 Flynn | 8 Flynn | 8 Flynn | 8 Flynn | 8 Harris (Cartwright) |
| 9 Reece (Smallman) | 9 Yorath | 9 Curtis | 9 Yorath | 9 Curtis |
| 10 Showers | 10 Smallman | 10 Roberts J. | 10 Toshack | 10 O'Sullivan |
| 11 James | 11 James | 11 Griffiths | 11 Griffiths | 11 James |

Belfast
May 23: 0-1

Wrexham
Nov 19: 1-0
*Griffiths*

Wrexham
Mar 24: 1-2
*Curtis*

Zagreb
April 24: 0-2

Glasgow
May 6: 1-3
*Griffiths* (pen)


| 1976 England | 1976 N Ireland | 1976 Yugoslavia | 1976 W Germany | 1976 Scotland |
|---|---|---|---|---|
| 1 Davies | 1 Davies | 1 Davies | 1 Davies | 1 Davies |
| 2 Thomas (Jones D.) | 2 Phillips | 2 Phillips | 2 Page (Cartwright) | 2 Page |
| 3 Page | 3 Page | 3 Roberts D. | 3 Jones J. | 3 Jones J. |
| 4 Mahoney | 4 Mahoney | 4 Evans | 4 Mahoney | 4 Phillips |
| 5 Phillips | 5 Roberts D. | 5 Page | 5 Phillips | 5 Evans |
| 6 Evans | 6 Evans | 6 Griffiths (Curtis) | 6 Evans | 6 Griffiths |
| 7 Yorath | 7 Griffiths | 7 Yorath | 7 James | 7 Thomas M. |
| 8 Flynn | 8 Flynn | 8 Mahoney | 8 Yorath | 8 Flynn |
| 9 Curtis (Griffiths) | 9 Yorath | 9 Flynn | 9 Curtis | 9 Yorath |
| 10 Toshack | 10 Curtis | 10 Toshack | 10 Thomas M. | 10 Toshack |
| 11 James | 11 James | 11 James | 11 Griffiths (Flynn) | 11 James (Curtis) |

Cardiff
May 8: 0-1

Swansea
May 14: 1-0
*James*

Cardiff
May 22: 1-1
*Evans*

Cardiff
Oct 6: 0-2

Glasgow
Nov 17: 0-1

758

| 1977 Czechoslovakia | 1977 Scotland | 1977 England | 1977 N Ireland | 1977 Kuwait |
|---|---|---|---|---|
| 1 Davies | 1 Davies | 1 Davies | 1 Davies | 1 Davies |
| 2 Thomas | 2 Thomas | 2 Thomas | 2 Thomas | 2 Thomas (Page) |
| 3 Jones J. | 3 Jones J. | 3 Jones J. | 3 Jones J. | 3 Jones J. |
| 4 Mahoney | 4 Mahoney | 4 Mahoney | 4 Mahoney | 4 Mahoney |
| 5 Phillips | 5 Phillips | 5 Phillips (Roberts D.) | 5 Roberts D. | 5 Phillips |
| 6 Evans | 6 Evans | 6 Evans | 6 Evans | 6 Roberts D. |
| 7 Sayer | 7 Sayer | 7 Sayer | 7 Sayer (Curtis) | 7 Sayer (Deacy) |
| 8 Flynn | 8 Flynn | 8 Flynn | 8 Flynn | 8 Flynn |
| 9 Yorath | 9 Yorath | 9 Yorath | 9 Yorath | 9 Yorath |
| 10 Deacy | 10 Deacy | 10 Deacy | 10 Deacy | 10 Toshack |
| 11 James | 11 James (Thomas M.) | 11 James | 11 James (Thomas M.) | 11 James |
| Wrexham | Wrexham | Wembley | Belfast | Wrexham |
| Mar 30: 3-0 | May 28: 0-0 | May 31: 1-0 | June 3: 1-1 | Sept 6: 0-0 |
| *James 2, Deacy* | | *James (pen)* | *Deacy* | |

| 1977 Kuwait | 1977 Scotland | 1977 Czechoslovakia | 1977 W Germany | 1978 Iran |
|---|---|---|---|---|
| 1 Phillips J. | 1 Davies | 1 Davies | 1 Davies | 1 Davies |
| 2 Page | 2 Thomas | 2 Thomas | 2 Page | 2 Page |
| 3 Jones J. | 3 Jones J. | 3 Jones J. | 3 Jones J. | 3 Jones J. |
| 4 Mahoney | 4 Mahoney | 4 Mahoney | 4 Jones D. | 4 Davis |
| 5 Phillips | 5 Jones D. | 5 Jones D. | 5 Phillips | 5 Jones D. |
| 6 Evans | 6 Phillips | 6 Phillips | 6 Harris | 6 Mahoney (Flynn) |
| 7 Sayer | 7 Flynn | 7 Nardiello | 7 Flynn | 7 Harris (Cartwright) |
| 8 Flynn | 8 Sayer | 8 Flynn | 8 Yorath | 8 Yorath |
| 9 Yorath (Roberts D.) | 9 Yorath | 9 Yorath | 9 Deacy | 9 Dwyer |
| 10 Toshack (Edwards) | 10 Toshack | 10 Toshack | 10 James | 10 Deacy |
| 11 James (Thomas M.) | 11 Thomas M. | 11 Thomas M. (Deacy) | 11 Curtis (Nardiello) | 11 Thomas M. |
| Kuwait | Liverpool | Prague | Dortmund | Teheran |
| Sept 20: 0-0 | Oct 12: 0-2 | Nov 16: 0-1 | Dec 14: 1-1 | April 18: 1-0 |
| | | | *Jones D.* | *Dwyer* |

| 1978 England | 1978 Scotland | 1978 N Ireland | 1978 Malta | 1978 Turkey |
|---|---|---|---|---|
| 1 Davies | 1 Davies | 1 Davies | 1 Davies | 1 Davies |
| 2 Page | 2 Page (Deacy) | 2 Jones J. | 2 Stevenson | 2 Stevenson |
| 3 Jones J. | 3 Jones J. | 3 Stevenson | 3 Jones J. | 3 Jones J. |
| 4 Phillips | 4 Roberts D. | 4 Roberts D. | 4 Phillips | 4 Phillips |
| 5 Jones D. (Davis) | 5 Phillips | 5 Davis | 5 Page | 5 Yorath |
| 6 Yorath (Mahoney) | 6 Yorath | 6 Mahoney | 6 Thomas M. | 6 Thomas M. |
| 7 Harris | 7 Mahoney | 7 Yorath (Thomas M.) | 7 Harris | 7 Harris |
| 8 Flynn | 8 Flynn | 8 Flynn | 8 Flynn | 8 Flynn |
| 9 Curtis | 9 Harris | 9 Harris | 9 Edwards | 9 Deacy |
| 10 Dwyer | 10 Dwyer | 10 Dwyer | 10 James R. | 10 Dwyer |
| 11 Thomas M. | 11 Curtis | 11 Deacy | 11 Cartwright (O'Sullivan) | 11 James |
| Cardiff | Glasgow | Wrexham | Wrexham | Wrexham |
| May 13: 1-3 | May 17: 1-1 | May 19: 1-0 | Oct 25: 7-0 | Nov 29: 1-0 |
| *Dwyer* | *Donachie og* | *Deacy (pen)* | *Edwards 4, O'Sullivan, Thomas, Flynn* | *Deacy* |

| 1979 W Germany | 1979 Scotland | 1979 England | 1979 N Ireland | 1979 Malta |
|---|---|---|---|---|
| 1 Davies | 1 Davies | 1 Davies | 1 Davies | 1 Davies |
| 2 Page | 2 Stevenson | 2 Stevenson | 2 Stevenson | 2 Stevenson |
| 3 Jones J. | 3 Jones J. | 3 Jones J. | 3 Jones J. | 3 Jones J. |
| 4 Phillips | 4 Phillips | 4 Phillips | 4 Phillips | 4 Phillips |
| 5 Berry | 5 Dwyer | 5 Dwyer | 5 Dwyer | 5 Nicholas |
| 6 Mahoney | 6 Mahoney | 6 Mahoney | 6 Mahoney | 6 Mahoney |
| 7 Yorath (James R.) | 7 Yorath (Nicholas) | 7 Yorath | 7 Yorath | 7 Harris (Thomas M.) |
| 8 Harris | 8 Flynn | 8 Flynn | 8 Flynn | 8 Flynn (Dwyer) |
| 9 Edwards (Toshack) | 9 James R. | 9 James R. | 9 James R. | 9 James R. |
| 10 Curtis | 10 Toshack | 10 Toshack | 10 Toshack | 10 Toshack |
| 11 Thomas M. | 11 Curtis | 11 Curtis | 11 Curtis (Nicholas) | 11 Curtis |
| Wrexham May 2: 0-2 | Cardiff May 19: 3-0 *Toshack 3* | Wembley May 23: 0-0 | Belfast May 25: 1-1 *James* | Valetta June 2: 2-0 *Nicholas, Flynn* |

| 1979 Rep of Ireland | 1979 W Germany | 1979 Turkey | 1980 England | 1980 Scotland |
|---|---|---|---|---|
| 1 Davies | 1 Davies | 1 Davies | 1 Davies | 1 Davies |
| 2 Nicholas | 2 Stevenson | 2 Stevenson | 2 Nicholas | 2 Nicholas |
| 3 Jones J. | 3 Jones J. (Berry) | 3 Jones J. | 3 Jones J. | 3 Jones J. |
| 4 Mahoney | 4 Mahoney | 4 Yorath | 4 Yorath | 4 Yorath |
| 5 Berry | 5 Phillips | 5 Berry | 5 Jones D. (Pontin) | 5 Pontin (Phillips) |
| 6 Phillips | 6 Dwyer | 6 Phillips | 6 Price | 6 Price |
| 7 Yorath | 7 Nicholas | 7 Davies G. (Mahoney) | 7 Giles | 7 Giles |
| 8 Flynn | 8 Flynn | 8 Nicholas | 8 Flynn | 8 Flynn |
| 9 Walsh | 9 Curtis | 9 Curtis | 9 Walsh | 9 Walsh (Rush) |
| 10 Curtis | 10 Toshack (Thomas M.) | 10 Walsh (Edwards) | 10 James | 10 James |
| 11 Thomas M. | 11 James R. | 11 Thomas M. | 11 Thomas M. | 11 Thomas M. |
| Swansea Sept 11: 2-1 *Walsh, Curtis* | Cologne Oct 17: 1-5 *Curtis* | Izmir Nov 21: 0-1 | Wrexham May 17: 4-1 *Thomas, Walsh, James, Thompson og* | Hampden May 21: 0-1 |

| 1980 N Ireland | 1980 Iceland | 1980 Turkey | 1980 Czechoslovakia | 1981 Rep of Ireland |
|---|---|---|---|---|
| 1 Davies | 1 Davies | 1 Davies | 1 Davies | 1 Davies |
| 2 Nicholas | 2 Nicholas | 2 Nicholas | 2 Price | 2 Nicholas |
| 3 Jones J. | 3 Jones J. | 3 Jones J. | 3 Ratcliffe | 3 Ratcliffe |
| 4 Yorath | 4 Yorath (Stevenson) | 4 Phillips | 4 Nicholas | 4 Price |
| 5 Phillips | 5 Phillips | 5 Price | 5 Yorath | 5 Boyle |
| 6 Price | 6 Price | 6 Yorath | 6 Phillips | 6 Jones J. |
| 7 Giles | 7 Giles | 7 Flynn | 7 Thomas | 7 Harris |
| 8 Flynn (Harris) | 8 Flynn | 8 Giles | 8 Flynn | 8 Yorath |
| 9 Rush | 9 Walsh | 9 Harris | 9 Walsh | 9 Walsh |
| 10 James | 10 James | 10 Walsh | 10 Giles (Harris) | 10 Yorath |
| 11 Thomas M. | 11 Davies G. (Harris) | 11 James L. | 11 Charles | 11 James L. |
| Cardiff May 23: 0-1 | Reykjavik June 2: 4-0 *Walsh 2, Giles, Flynn (pen)* | Cardiff Oct 15: 4-0 *Flynn, James L. 2 (1 pen), Walsh* | Cardiff Nov 19: 1-0 *Giles* | Dublin Feb 24: 3-1 *Price, Boyle, Yorath* |

| 1981<br>Turkey | 1981<br>Scotland | 1981<br>England | 1981<br>USSR |
|---|---|---|---|
| 1 Davies | 1 Davies | 1 Davies | 1 Davies |
| 2 Jones J. | 2 Jones J.<br>(Boyle) | 2 Jones J. | 2 Jones J. |
| 3 Ratcliffe | 3 Ratcliffe | 3 Ratcliffe | 3 Ratcliffe |
| 4 Nicholas | 4 Nicholas | 4 Nicholas | 4 Flynn |
| 5 Phillips | 5 Price | 5 Phillips | 5 Price |
| 6 Price | 6 Phillips | 6 Price | 6 Phillips |
| 7 Harris<br>(Giles) | 7 Harris | 7 Harris<br>(Giles) | 7 Nicholas |
| 8 Walsh<br>(Charles) | 8 Flynn | 8 Flynn | 8 Yorath |
| 9 James L. | 9 Walsh<br>(Charles) | 9 Walsh | 9 Walsh<br>(Charles) |
| 10 Flynn | 10 James L. | 10 Thomas M. | 10 Thomas M. |
| 11 Yorath | 11 Thomas M. | 11 James L.<br>(Rush) | 11 Harris<br>(Giles) |

| Ankara<br>Mar 25: 1-0<br>*Harris* | Swansea<br>May 16: 2-0<br>*Walsh 2* | Wembley<br>May 20: 0-0 | Wrexham<br>May 30: 0-0 |
|---|---|---|---|

# OLYMPIC FOOTBALL 1908–1980

## LONDON 1908
**Third Place Final:** Holland v Sweden*  2-1
**Final:** Gt Britain v Denmark  2-0
*Sweden were nominated for the third-place final in preference to France 'A', who had been awarded a bye into the semi-finals.*

## STOCKHOLM 1912
**Third Place Final:** Holland v Finland  9-0
**Final:** Gt Britain v Denmark  4-2

## ANTWERP 1920
**Play-off for Second and Third Places**
Spain v Holland  2-0
**Final:** Belgium v Czechoslovakia  3-1
*Czechoslovakia were disqualified for walking off during the final. Placings: Belgium – Olympic champions; Spain – Second; Holland – Third, France – Fourth.*

## PARIS 1924
**Third Place Final:** Sweden v Holland  1-1, 3-1
**Final:** Uruguay v Switzerland  3-0

## AMSTERDAM 1928
**Third Place Final:** Italy v Egypt  11-3
**Final:** Uruguay v Argentina  1-1, 2-1

## BERLIN 1936
**Third Place Final:** Norway v Poland  3-2
**Final:** Italy v Austria  aet 2-1

## LONDON 1948
**Third Place Final:** Denmark v Gt Britain  5-3
**Final:** Sweden v Yugoslavia  3-1

## HELSINKI 1952
**Third Place Final:** Sweden v West Germany  2-0
**Final:** Hungary v Yugoslavia  2-0

## MELBOURNE 1956
**Third Place Final:** Bulgaria v India  3-0
**Final:** USSR v Yugoslavia  1-0

## ROME 1960
**Third Place Final:** Italy v Hungary  2-1
**Final:** Yugoslavia v Denmark  3-1

## TOKYO 1964
**Third Place Final:** East Germany v UAR  3-1
**Final:** Hungary v Czechoslovakia  2-1

## MEXICO CITY 1968
**Third Place Final:** Japan v Mexico  2-0
**Final:** Hungary v Bulgaria  4-1

## MUNICH 1972
**Third Place Final:** USSR v East Germany  2-2
**Final:** Poland v Hungary  2-1

## MONTREAL 1976
**Third Place Final:** USSR v Brazil  2-0
**Final:** East Germany v Poland  3-1

## MOSCOW 1980
**Third Place Final:** USSR v Yugoslavia  2-0
**Final:** Czechoslovakia v East Germany  1-0

# UNDER-21 APPEARANCES 1976–1982

## ENGLAND

Allen, C. (QPR), 1980 v EG (sub); 1981 (with C Palace) v N, R (3)

Anderson, V. A. (Nottingham F), 1978 v I (1)

Bailey, G. R. (Manchester U), 1979 v W, Bul; 1980 v D, S (2), EG; 1982 v N (7)

Baker, G. E. (Southampton), 1981 v N, R (2)

Bannister, G. (Sheffield W), 1982 v Pol (1)

Barnes, P. S. (Manchester C), 1977 v W (sub), S, Fi, N; 1978 v N, Fi, I (2), Y (9)

Bertschin, K. E. (Birmingham C), 1977 v S; 1978 v Y (2) (3)

Birtles, G. (Nottingham F), 1980 v Bul, EG (sub) (2)

Blissett, L. L. (Watford), 1979 v W, Bul (sub), Se; 1980 v D (4)

Bradshaw, P. W. (Wolverhampton W), 1977 v W, S; 1978 v Fi, Y (4)

Butcher, T. I. (Ipswich T), 1979 v Se; 1980 v D, Bul, S (2), EG (2) (7)

Caton, T. (Manchester C), 1982 v N, H (sub), Pol (2), S (5)

Chapman, L. (Stoke C), 1981 v Ei (1)

Corrigan, J. T. (Manchester C), 1978 v I (2), Y (3)

Cowans, G. S. (Aston Villa), 1979 v W, Se; 1980 v Bul, EG; 1981 v R (5)

Crooks, G. (Stoke C), 1980 v Bul, S (2), EG (sub) (4)

Cunningham, L. (WBA), 1977 v S, Fi, N (sub); 1978 v N, Fi, I (6)

Curbishley, L. C. (Birmingham C), 1981 v Sw (1)

Daniel, P. W. (Hull C), 1977 v S, Fi, N; 1978 v Fi, I, Y (2) (7)

Davis, P. (Arsenal), 1982 v Pol, S (2)

Deehan, J. M. (Aston Villa), 1977 v N; 1978 v N, Fi, I; 1979 v Bul, Se (sub); 1980 v D (7)

Dennis, M. E. (Birmingham C), 1980 v Bul; 1981 v N, R (3)

Dillon, K. P. (Birmingham C), 1981 v R (1)

Duxbury, M. (Manchester U), 1981 v Sw (sub), Ei (sub), R (sub), Sw; 1982 v N (5)

Dyson, P. I. (Coventry C), 1981 v N, R, Sw, Ei (4)

Fairclough, D. (Liverpool), 1977 v W (1)

Fashanu, J. (Norwich C), 1980 v EG; 1981 v N (sub), R, Sw, Ei (sub), H; (with Nottingham F), 1982 v N, H, Pol, S (10)

Fenwick, T. W. (C Palace), 1981 v N, R, Sw, Ei, (with QPR), R; 1982 v N, H, S (2) (9)

Foster, S. (Brighton & HA), 1980 v EG (sub) (1)

Futcher, P. (Luton T), 1977 v W, S, Fi, N; (with Manchester C), 1978 v N, Fi, I (2), Y (2); 1979 v D (11)

Gale, A. (Fulham), 1982 v Pol (1)

Gibson, C. (Aston Villa), 1982 v N (1)

Gilbert, W. A. (C Palace), 1979 v W, Bul; 1980 v Bul; 1981 v N, R, Sw, R, Sw, H; 1982 v N (sub), H (11)

Goddard, P. (West Ham U), 1981 v N, Sw, Ei (sub); 1982 v N (sub), Pol, S (6)

Haigh, P. (Hull C), 1977 v N (sub) (1)

Hateley, M. (Coventry C), 1982 v Pol, S (2)

Hazell, R. J. (Wolverhampton W), 1979 v D (1)

Heath, A. (Stoke C), 1981 v R, Sw, H; 1982 v N, H, (with Everton), Pol, S (7)

Hesford, I. (Blackpool), 1981 v Ei (sub), Pol (2), S (2) (5)

Hilaire, V. (C Palace), 1980 v Bul, S (1+sub) EG (2); 1981 v N, R, Sw (sub); 1982 v Pol (sub) (9)

Hinshelwood, P. A. (C Palace), 1978 v N; 1980 v EG (2)

Hoddle, G. (Tottenham H), 1977 v W (sub); 1978 v Fi (sub), I (2), Y; 1979 v D, W, Bul; 1980 v S (2), EG (2) (12)

Hodgson, D. J. (Middlesbrough), 1981 v N, R (sub), Sw, Ei; 1982 v Pol (5)

Johnston, C. P. (Middlesbrough), 1981 v N, Ei (2)

Jones, D. R. (Everton), 1977 v W (1)

Jones, C. H. (Tottenham H), 1978 v Y (sub) (1)

Keegan, G. A. (Manchester C), 1977 v W (1)

King, A. E. (Everton), 1977 v W; 1978 v Y (2)

Langley, T. W. (Chelsea), 1978 v I (sub) (1)

Lee, S. (Liverpool), 1981 v R, Sw, H; 1982 v S (4)

Lukic, J. (Leeds U), 1981 v N, R, Ei, R, Sw, H; 1982 v H (7)

Mabbutt, G. (Bristol R), 1982 v Pol (2), S (3)

McCall, S. H. (Ipswich T), 1981 v Sw, H; 1982 v H, S (4)

MacKenzie, S. (WBA), 1982 v N, S (2) (3)

McMahon, S. (Everton), 1981 v Ei; 1982 v Pol (2)

Middleton, J. (Nottingham F), 1977 v Fi, N; (with Derby Co), 1978 v N (3)

Mills, G. R. (Nottingham F), 1981 v R; 1982 v N (2)

Moran, S. (Southampton), 1982 v N (sub) (1)

Moses, R. M. (WBA), 1981 v N (sub), Sw, Ei, R, Sw, H; 1982 v N (sub), (with Manchester U), H (8)

Osman R. C. (Ipswich T), 1979 v W (sub), Se; 1980 v D, S (2), EG (2) (7)

Owen, G. A. (Manchester C), 1977 v S, Fi, N; 1978 v N, Fi, I (2), Y; 1979 v D, W; (with WBA), Bul, Se (sub); 1980 v D, S (2), EG; 1981 v Sw, R; 1982 v N (sub), H (20)

Parkes, P. B. F. (QPR), 1979 v D (1)

Peach, D. S. (Southampton), 1977 v S, Fi, N; 1978 v N, I (2), Y (2) (8)

Peake, A. (Leicester C), 1982 v Pol (1)

Proctor, M. (Middlesbrough), 1981 v Ei (sub), Sw; 1982 (with Nottingham F) v N, Pol (4)

Ranson, R. (Manchester C), 1980 v Bul, EG; 1981 v R (sub), R, Sw, Sw (sub), H, Pol (2), S (10)

Reeves, K. P. (Norwich C), 1978 v I, Y (2); 1979 v N, W, Bul, Se; 1980 v D, S; (with Manchester C), EG (10)

Regis, C. (WBA), 1979 v D, Bul, Se; 1980 v S, EG (5)

Reid, N. S. (Manchester C), 1981 v H (sub); 1982 v H, Pol (2), S (2) (6)

Reid, P. (Bolton W), 1977 v S, Fi, N; 1978 v Fi, I, Y (6)

Richards, J. P. (Wolverhampton W), 1977 v Fi, N (2)

Ritchie, A. (Brighton & HA), 1982 v Pol (1)

Rix, G. (Arsenal), 1978 v Fi (sub), Y; 1979 v D, Se; 1980 v D (sub), Bul, S (7)

Robson, B. (WBA), 1979 v W, Bul (sub), Se; 1980 v D, Bul, S (2) (7)

Rowell, G. (Sunderland), 1977 v Fi (1)

Sansom, K. G. (C Palace), 1979 v D, W, Bul, Se; 1980 v S (2), EG (2) (8)

Shaw, G. R. (Aston Villa), 1981 v Ei, Sw, H; 1982 v H, S (5)

Sims, S. (Leicester C), 1977 v W, S, Fi, N; 1978 v N, Fi, I (2), Y (2) (10)

Smith. M. (Sheffield W), 1981 v Ei, R, Sw, H; 1982 v Pol (sub) (5)

Statham, D. J. (WBA), 1978 v Fi; 1979 v W, Bul, Se; 1980 v D (5)

Sunderland, A. (Wolverhampton W), 1977 v W (1)

Swindlehurst, D. (C Palace), 1977 v W (1)

Talbot, B. (Ipswich T), 1977 v W (1)

Thomas, D. (Coventry C), 1981 v Ei (1)

Thompson, G. L. (Coventry C), 1981 v R, Sw, H; 1982 v N, H, S (6)

Ward, P. D. (Brighton & HA), 1978 v N; 1980 v EG (2)

Whyte, C. (Arsenal), 1982 v S (1+sub) (2)

Wicks, S. (QPR), 1982 v S (1)

Wilkins, R. C. (Chelsea), 1977 v W (1)

Williams, S. C. (Southampton), 1977 v S, Fi, N; 1978 v N, I (sub), I, Y (2); 1979 v D, Bul, Se (sub); 1980 v D, EG (2) (14)

Woodcock, A. S. (Nottingham F), 1978 v Fi, I (2)

Woods, C. C. E. (Nottingham F), 1979 v W (sub), Se; (with QPR), 1980 v Bul, EG; 1981 v Sw (5)

Wright, W. (Everton), 1979 v D, W, Bul; 1980 v D, S (2) (6)

## SCOTLAND

Aitken, R. (Celtic), 1977 v Cz, W, Sw; 1978 v Cz, W; 1979 v P, N (2); 1980 v B, E (10)

Albiston A. (Manchester U), 1977 v Cz, W, Sw; 1978 v Sw, Cz (5)

Archibald, S. (Aberdeen), 1980 v B, E (2), WG; (with Tottenham H), 1981 v D (5)

Bannon, E. J. P. (Hearts), 1979 v US, (with Chelsea), P, N (2); (with Dundee U), 1980 v B, WG, E (7)

Bell, D. (Aberdeen), 1981 v D (1)

Bett, J. (Rangers), 1981 v Se, D; 1982 v Se, D, I, E (2) (7)

Blair, A. (Coventry C), 1980 v E; 1981 v Se, (with Aston Villa), 1982 v Se, D, I (5)

Brazil, A. (Hibernian), 1978 v W (1)
Brazil, A. (Ipswich T), 1979 v N; 1980 v B (2), E (2), WG; 1981 v Se; 1982 v Se (8)
Brough, J. (Hearts), 1981 v D (1)
Burley, G. E. (Ipswich T), 1977 v Cz, W, Sw; 1978 v Sw, Cz (5)
Burns, T. (Celtic), 1977 v Cz, W, E; 1978 v Sw; 1982 v E (5)
Casey, J. (Celtic), 1978 v W (1)
Clark, R. (Aberdeen), 1977 v Cz, W, Sw (3)
Connor, R. (Ayr U), 1981 v Se; 1982 v Se (2)
Cooper, D. (Clyde), 1977 v Cz, W, Sw, E; (with Rangers), 1978 v Sw, Cz (6)
Cooper, N. (Aberdeen), 1982 v D, E (2) (3)
Craig, T. (Newcastle U), 1977 v E (1)
Dawson, A. (Rangers), 1979 v P, N (2); 1980 v B (2), E (2) WG (8)
Dodds, D. (Dundee U), 1978 v W (1)
Doyle, J. (Partick T), 1981 v D, I (sub) (2)
Ferguson, R. (Hamilton A), 1977 v E (1)
Fitzpatrick, A. (St Mirren), 1977 v W (sub), Sw (sub), E; 1978 v Sw, Cz (5)
Fulton, M. (St Mirren), 1980 v B, WG, E; 1981 v Se, D (sub) (5)
Geddes, R. (Dundee), 1982 v Se, D, E (2) (4)
Gillespie, G. (Coventry C), 1979 v US; 1980 v E; 1981 v D; 1982 v Se, D, I (2), E (8)
Hartford, R. A. (Manchester C), 1977 v Sw (1)
Hewitt, J. (Aberdeen), 1982 v I (1)
Jardine, I. (Kilmarnock), 1979 v US (1)
Leighton, J. (Aberdeen), 1982 v I (1)
Lindsey, J. (Motherwell), 1979 v US (1)
McAvennie, F. (St Mirren), 1982 v I, E (2)
McBride, J. (Everton), 1981 v D (1)
McCluskey, G. (Celtic), 1979 v US, P; 1980 v B (2); 1982 v D, I (6)
McCulloch, A. (Kilmarnock), 1981 v Se (1)
McCulloch, I. (Notts Co), 1982 v E (2)
MacDonald, J. (Rangers), 1980 v WG (sub); 1981 v Se; 1982 v Se (sub), L, I (2), E (2 sub) (7)
McGarvey, F. (St Mirren), 1977 v E; 1978 v Cz; (with Celtic), 1982 v D (3)
McGarvey, S. (Manchester U), 1982 v E (sub) (1)
McGhee, M. (Aberdeen), 1981 v D (1)
McLaughlin, J. (Morton), 1981 v D; 1982 v Se, D, I, E (2) (6)
McLeish, A. (Aberdeen), 1978 v W; 1979 v US; 1980 v B, E (2) (5)
MacLeod, A. (Hibernian), 1979 v P, N (2) (3)
MacLeod, M. (Dumbarton), 1979 v US; (with Celtic), P (sub), N (2); 1980 v B (5)
McNab, N. (Tottenham H), 1978 v W (1)
McNichol, J. (Brentford), 1979 v P, N (2); 1980 v B (2), WG, E (7)
McNiven, D. (Leeds U), 1977 v Cz, W (sub), Sw (sub) (3)
Melrose, J. (Partick T), 1977 v Sw; 1979 v US, P, N (2); 1980 v B (sub), WG, E (8)
Miller, W. (Aberdeen), 1978 v Sw, Cz (2)
Milne, R. (Dundee U), 1982 v Se (sub) (1)
Muir, L. (Hibernian), 1977 v Cz (sub) (1)
Narey, D. (Dundee U), 1977 v Cz, Sw; 1978 v Sw, Cz (4)
Nicholas, C. (Celtic), 1981 v Se; 1982 v Se (2)
Nicol, S. (Ayr U), 1981 v Se; 1982 v Se, D; (with Liverpool), 1982 v I (2), E (2) (7)
Orr, N. (Morton), 1978 v W (sub); 1979 v US, P, N (2); 1980 v B, E (6)
Parlane, D. (Rangers), 1977 v W (1)
Paterson, C. (Hibernian), 1981 v Se; 1982 v I (2)
Payne, G. (Dundee U), 1978 v Sw, Cz, W (3)
Provan, D. (Kilmarnock), 1977 v Cz (sub) (1)
Redford, I. (Rangers), 1981 v Se (sub); 1982 v Se, D, I (2), E (6)
Reid, M. (Celtic), 1982 v E (1)
Reid, R. (St Mirren), 1977 v W, Sw, E (3)
Richardson, L. (St Mirren), 1980 v WG, E (sub) (2)
Ritchie, A. (Morton), 1980 v B (1)
Robertson, C. (Rangers), 1977 v E (sub) (1)
Ross, T. W. (Arsenal), 1977 v W (1)
Russell, R. (Rangers), 1978 v W; 1980 v B (2)
Sharp, G. (Everton), 1982 v E (1)
Simpson, N. (Aberdeen), 1982 v I (2), E (3)
Sinclair, G. (Dumbarton), 1977 v E (1)

Smith, G. (Rangers), 1978 v W (1)
Sneddon, A. (Celtic), 1979 v US (1)
Stanton, P. (Hibernian), 1977 v Cz (1)
Stevens, G. (Motherwell), 1977 v E (1)
Stewart, J. (Kilmarnock), 1978 v Sw, Cz; (with Middlesbrough), 1979 v P (3)
Stewart, R. (Dundee U), 1979 v P, N (2); (with West Ham U), 1980 v B (2), E (2), WG; 1981 v D; 1982 v I (2), E (12)
Strachan, G. (Aberdeen), 1980 v B (1)
Sturrock, P. (Dundee U), 1977 v Cz, W, Sw, E; 1978 v Sw, Cz; 1982 v Se, I, E (9)
Thomson, W. (Partick T), 1977 v E (sub); 1978 v W; (with St Mirren), 1979 v US, N (2); 1980 v B (2), E (2), WG (10)
Tolmie, J. (Morton), 1980 v B (sub) (1)
Wallace, I. (Coventry C), 1978 v Sw (1)
Wark, J. (Ipswich T), 1977 v Cz, W, Sw; 1978 v W; 1979 v P; 1980 v E (2), WG (8)
Watson, A. (Aberdeen), 1981 v Se, D; 1982 v D, I (sub) (4)
Watson, K. (Rangers), 1977 v E; 1978 v Sw (sub) (2)

## WALES

Aizlewood, M. (Luton T), 1979 v E; 1981 v Ho (2)
Balcombe, S. (Leeds U), 1982 v F (sub) (1)
Bater, P. T. (Bristol R), 1977 v E, S (2)
Boyle, T. (Crystal Palace), 1982 v F (1)
Cegielski, W. (Wrexham), 1977 v E (sub), S (2)
Charles, J. M. (Swansea C), 1979 v E; 1981 v Ho (2)
Clark, J. (Manchester U), 1978 v S; (with Derby Co), 1979 v E (2)
Curtis, A. T. (Swansea C), 1977 v E (1)
Davies, A. (Manchester U), 1982 v F, Ho (3)
Davies, I. C. (Norwich C), 1978 v S (sub) (1)
Deacy, N. (PSV Eindhoven), 1977 v S (1)
Doyle, S. C. (Preston NE), 1979 v E (sub) (1)
Dwyer, P. J. (Cardiff C), 1979 v E (1)
Edwards, R. I. (Chester), 1977 v S; 1978 v W (2)
Evans, A. (Bristol R), 1977 v E (1)
Giles, D. C. (Cardiff C), 1977 v S; 1978 v S; 1981 (with Swansea C), v Ho (3)
Giles, P. (Cardiff C), 1982 v F, Ho (3)
Hopkins, J. (Fulham), 1982 v F (sub), Ho (2)
Hughes, W. (WBA), 1977 v E, S; 1978 v S (3)
Jackett, K. (Watford), 1981 v Ho; 1982 v F (2)
James, R. M. (Swansea C), 1977 v E, S; 1978 v S (3)
Jones, F. (Wrexham), 1981 v Ho (1)
Jones, L. (Cardiff C), 1982 v F, Ho (2)
Jones, V. (Bristol R), 1979 v E; 1981 v Ho (2)
Kendall, M. (Tottenham H), 1978 v S (1)
Letheran, G. (Leeds U), 1977 v E, S (2)
Lewis, D. (Swansea C), 1982 v F, Ho (3)
Loveridge, J. (Swansea C), 1982 v Ho (1)
Lowndes, S. R. (Newport Co), 1979 v E; 1981 v Ho (2)
Maddy, P. (Cardiff C), 1982 v Ho (1)
Marustik, C. (Swansea C), 1982 v F (2) (2)
Micallef, C. (Cardiff C), 1982 v F, Ho (2)
Nardiello, D. (Coventry C), 1978 v S (1)
Nicholas, P. (C Palace), 1978 v S; 1979 v E; (with Arsenal), 1982 v F (3)
Phillips, L. (Swansea C), 1979 v E (1)
Pontin, K. (Cardiff C), 1978 v S (1)
Price, P. (Luton T), 1981 v Ho (1)
Pugh, D. (Doncaster R), 1982 v F (2) (2)
Ratcliffe, K. (Everton), 1981 v Ho; 1982 v F (2)
Roberts, J. G. (Wrexham), 1977 v E (1)
Rush, I. (Liverpool), 1981 v Ho; 1982 v F (2)
Sayer, P. A. (Cardiff C), 1977 v E, S (2)
Stevenson, N. (Swansea C), 1982 v F, Ho (2)
Stevenson, W. B. (Leeds U), 1977 v E, S; 1978 v S (3)
Thomas, Martin R. (Bristol R), 1979 v E; 1981 v Ho (2)
Thomas, Mickey R. (Wrexham), 1977 v E; 1978 v S (2)
Thomas, D. G. (Leeds U), 1977 v E; 1979 v E (2)
Tibbott, L. (Ipswich T), 1977 v E, S (2)
Vaughan, N. (Newport Co), 1982 v F, Ho (2)
Walsh, I. P. (C Palace), 1979 v E (1)
Wilmot, R. (Arsenal), 1982 v F, Ho (3)

## ENGLAND 'B' INTERNATIONAL MATCHES

### v AUSTRALIA

| | | | E | A |
|---|---|---|---|---|
| 1980 | 17 Nov | Birmingham | 1 | 0 |

### v AUSTRIA

| | | | E | A |
|---|---|---|---|---|
| *1979 | 12 June | Klagenfurt | 1 | 0 |

*Abandoned after an hour's play.

### v CZECHOSLOVAKIA

| | | | E | C |
|---|---|---|---|---|
| 1978 | 28 Nov | Prague | 1 | 0 |

### v FINLAND

| | | | E | F |
|---|---|---|---|---|
| 1949 | 15 May | Helsinki | 4 | 0 |

### v FRANCE

| | | | E | F |
|---|---|---|---|---|
| 1952 | 22 May | Le Havre | 1 | 7 |

### v WEST GERMANY

| | | | E | WG |
|---|---|---|---|---|
| 1954 | 24 Mar | Gelsenkirchen | 4 | 0 |
| 1955 | 23 Mar | Sheffield | 1 | 1 |
| 1978 | 21 Feb | Augsburg | 1 | 2 |

### v ITALY

| | | | E | I |
|---|---|---|---|---|
| 1950 | 11 May | Milan | 0 | 5 |

### v LUXEMBOURG

| | | | E | L |
|---|---|---|---|---|
| 1950 | 21 May | Luxembourg | 2 | 1 |

### v MALAYSIA

| | | | E | M |
|---|---|---|---|---|
| 1978 | 30 May | Kuala Lumpur | 1 | 1 |

### v THE NETHERLANDS

| | | | E | N |
|---|---|---|---|---|
| 1949 | 18 May | Amsterdam | 4 | 0 |
| 1950 | 22 Feb | Newcastle | 1 | 0 |
| 1950 | 17 Mar | Amsterdam | 0 | 3 |
| 1952 | 26 Mar | Amsterdam | 1 | 0 |

### v NEW ZEALAND

| | | | E | NZ |
|---|---|---|---|---|
| 1978 | 7 June | Christchurch | 4 | 0 |
| 1978 | 11 June | Wellington | 3 | 1 |
| 1978 | 14 June | Auckland | 4 | 0 |
| 1979 | 17 Oct | Auckland | 4 | 1 |

### v SCOTLAND

| | | | E | S |
|---|---|---|---|---|
| 1953 | 11 Mar | Edinburgh | 2 | 2 |
| 1954 | 3 Mar | Sunderland | 1 | 1 |
| 1956 | 29 Feb | Dundee | 2 | 2 |
| 1957 | 6 Feb | Birmingham | 4 | 1 |

### v SPAIN

| | | | E | S |
|---|---|---|---|---|
| 1980 | 26 Mar | Sunderland | 1 | 0 |
| 1981 | 25 Mar | Granada | 2 | 3 |

### v SWITZERLAND

| | | | E | S |
|---|---|---|---|---|
| 1950 | 18 Jan | Sheffield | 5 | 0 |
| 1954 | 22 May | Basle | 0 | 2 |
| 1956 | 21 Mar | Southampton | 4 | 1 |

### v USA

| | | | E | USA |
|---|---|---|---|---|
| 1980 | 14 Oct | Manchester | 1 | 0 |

### v YUGOSLAVIA

| | | | E | Y |
|---|---|---|---|---|
| 1954 | 16 May | Lubljana | 1 | 2 |
| 1955 | 19 Oct | Manchester | 5 | 1 |

## ENGLAND UNOFFICIAL INTERNATIONAL MATCHES

### v SCOTLAND

| | | | E | S |
|---|---|---|---|---|
| D1902 | 5 Apr | Glasgow | 1 | 1 |
| †1919 | 26 Apr | Everton | 2 | 2 |
| †1919 | 3 May | Glasgow | 4 | 3 |
| J1935 | 21 Aug | Glasgow | 2 | 4 |
| *1939 | 2 Dec | Newcastle | 2 | 1 |
| *1940 | 11 May | Glasgow | 1 | 1 |
| *1941 | 8 Feb | Newcastle | 2 | 3 |
| *1941 | 3 May | Glasgow | 3 | 1 |
| *1941 | 4 Oct | Wembley | 2 | 0 |
| *1942 | 17 Jan | Wembley | 3 | 0 |
| *1942 | 18 Apr | Glasgow | 4 | 5 |
| *1942 | 10 Oct | Wembley | 0 | 0 |
| *1943 | 17 Apr | Glasgow | 4 | 0 |
| *1943 | 16 Oct | Manchester | 8 | 0 |
| *1944 | 19 Feb | Wembley | 6 | 2 |
| *1944 | 22 Apr | Glasgow | 3 | 2 |
| *1944 | 14 Oct | Wembley | 6 | 2 |
| *1945 | 3 Feb | Aston Villa | 3 | 2 |
| *1945 | 14 April | Glasgow | 6 | 1 |
| †1946 | 13 Apr | Glasgow | 0 | 1 |

### v SWITZERLAND

| | | | E | S |
|---|---|---|---|---|
| †1946 | 11 May | Chelsea | 4 | 1 |

### v FRANCE

| | | | E | F |
|---|---|---|---|---|
| *1945 | 26 May | Wembley | 2 | 2 |

### v WALES

| | | | E | W |
|---|---|---|---|---|
| †1919 | 11 Oct | Cardiff | 1 | 2 |
| †1919 | 18 Oct | Stoke | 2 | 0 |
| *1939 | 11 Nov | Cardiff | 1 | 1 |
| *1939 | 18 Nov | Wrexham | 3 | 2 |
| *1940 | 13 Apr | Wembley | 0 | 1 |
| *1941 | 26 Apr | Nottingham | 4 | 1 |
| *1941 | 7 June | Cardiff | 3 | 2 |
| *1941 | 25 Oct | Birmingham | 2 | 1 |
| *1942 | 9 May | Cardiff | 0 | 1 |
| *1942 | 24 Oct | Wolverhampton | 1 | 2 |
| *1943 | 27 Feb | Wembley | 5 | 3 |
| *1943 | 8 May | Cardiff | 1 | 1 |
| *1943 | 25 Sept | Wembley | 8 | 3 |
| *1944 | 6 May | Cardiff | 2 | 0 |
| *1944 | 16 Sept | Liverpool | 2 | 2 |
| *1945 | 5 May | Cardiff | 3 | 2 |
| †1945 | 20 Oct | West Bromwich | 0 | 1 |

### v IRELAND

| | | | E | I |
|---|---|---|---|---|
| †1945 | 15 Sept | Belfast | 1 | 0 |

### v BELGIUM

| | | | E | B |
|---|---|---|---|---|
| †1946 | 19 Jan | Wembley | 2 | 0 |

### v TEAM AMERICA

| | | | E | TA |
|---|---|---|---|---|
| B1976 | 30 May | Philadelphia | 3 | 1 |

DDeclared unofficial owing to disaster at ground.   †Victory matches.   JJubilee match.   *War-time matches.   BAmerican Bicentennial Tournament.

# IRISH FOOTBALL 1981-82

By Malcolm Brodie

Northern Ireland's qualification for the World Cup finals, for the first time since 1958, was the highlight of the season and earned for manager Billy Bingham the Personality of the Year award in the Province, as well as many other accolades.

Domestically Linfield triumphed, winning the Irish League championship, the Irish Cup, Gold Cup and the County Antrim Shield. Only the Ulster Cup eluded the Blues in a remarkable season which began with a series of indifferent results. However, Roy Coyle, ex-Northern Ireland and Grimsby Town half-back, guided them through the crisis to earn himself the Manager of the Year award. Sadly, part of Linfield history was lost when fire destroyed the unreserved stand at Windsor Park, Northern Ireland's international headquarters; but with financial backing from the Government, Football Grounds Improvement Trust and the Irish FA, a new multi-million-pound cantilever stand is to be constructed on the site.

Glentoran, celebrating their centenary, looked set to make a decisive impact after winning the Ulster Cup, but they collapsed in January, struggled for six weeks and ended with a late but unavailing flourish.

Sponsorship again played a vital part in Northern Ireland soccer competitions with all but the County Antrim Shield commercially backed. In addition there was a Fair Play League award, Player of the Month scheme for the League championship and a personality prize in each round of the Irish Cup.

Felix Healy, Coleraine and ex-Port Vale striker, took the individual honours, winning the Ulster Footballer of the Year award from the Castlereagh Glentoran Supporters Club, the Football Writers Trophy and that from the Northern Ireland Players Association, who obtained freedom of contract negotiations with the Irish FA. They, too, became affiliated to the General and Municipal Workers Union.

For B Division RUC it was a season of triumph. They won the British Police championship, celebrating their diamond jubilee with a victory over the Metropolitan Police in the final at Selhurst Park.

Football lost many personalities, including Wilbur Cush, Jackie Vernon, Jimmy McCune, Bertie Fulton and Mickey McColgan, for many years a legendary figure in the Irish FA Council.

## SMIRNOFF IRISH LEAGUE CHAMPIONSHIP

*Winners – £5000; Runners-up – £2500; Third – £1000; Fourth – £500. Irish League £1000*

|  | P | W | D | L | F | A | Pts |
|---|---|---|---|---|---|---|---|
| Linfield | 22 | 17 | 3 | 2 | 59 | 19 | 37 |
| Glentoran | 22 | 16 | 1 | 5 | 61 | 22 | 33 |
| Coleraine | 22 | 14 | 3 | 5 | 63 | 31 | 31 |
| Crusaders | 22 | 11 | 4 | 7 | 36 | 31 | 26 |
| Cliftonville | 22 | 9 | 6 | 7 | 33 | 28 | 24 |
| Portadown | 22 | 11 | 2 | 9 | 29 | 29 | 24 |
| Ballymena Utd | 22 | 6 | 8 | 8 | 25 | 30 | 20 |
| Distillery | 22 | 7 | 4 | 11 | 30 | 44 | 18 |
| Glenavon | 22 | 4 | 7 | 11 | 30 | 52 | 15 |
| Ards | 22 | 5 | 4 | 13 | 18 | 47 | 14 |
| Larne | 22 | 5 | 3 | 14 | 27 | 42 | 13 |
| Bangor | 22 | 3 | 3 | 16 | 20 | 56 | 9 |

## GUINNESS PLAYER OF THE MONTH

| September | Gary Blackledge (Glentoran) |
|---|---|
| October | Dennis Matthews (Ballymena Utd) |
| November | Kevin Mahon (Coleraine) |
| December | Peter Dornan (Linfield) |
| January | Pat Mullan (Coleraine) |
| February | Felix Healy (Coleraine) |
| March | Martin McGaughey (Linfield) |
| April | Roy Walsh (Linfield) |

## SMIRNOFF FAIR PLAY LEAGUE

*£200 per month*

| December | Glenavon/Larne (shared) |
|---|---|
| January | Ballymena Utd |
| February | Portadown |
| March | Coleraine |
| April | Glenavon |
| Overall Winner | Glenavon |

## IRISH LEAGUE CHAMPIONSHIP WINNERS

| | | | | | | | |
|---|---|---|---|---|---|---|---|
| 1891 | Linfield | 1912 | Glentoran | 1936 | Belfast Celtic | 1963 | Distillery |
| 1892 | Linfield | 1913 | Glentoran | 1937 | Belfast Celtic | 1964 | Glentoran |
| 1893 | Linfield | 1914 | Linfield | 1938 | Belfast Celtic | 1965 | Derry City |
| 1894 | Glentoran | 1915 | Belfast Celtic | 1939 | Belfast Celtic | 1966 | Linfield |
| 1895 | Linfield | 1920 | Belfast Celtic | 1940 | Belfast Celtic | 1967 | Glentoran |
| 1896 | Distillery | 1921 | Glentoran | 1948 | Belfast Celtic | 1968 | Glentoran |
| 1897 | Glentoran | 1922 | Linfield | 1949 | Linfield | 1969 | Linfield |
| 1898 | Linfield | 1923 | Linfield | 1950 | Linfield | 1970 | Glentoran |
| 1899 | Distillery | 1924 | Queen's Island | 1951 | Glentoran | 1971 | Linfield |
| 1900 | Belfast Celtic | 1925 | Glentoran | 1952 | Glenavon | 1972 | Glentoran |
| 1901 | Distillery | 1926 | Belfast Celtic | 1953 | Glentoran | 1973 | Crusaders |
| 1902 | Linfield | 1927 | Belfast Celtic | 1954 | Linfield | 1974 | Coleraine |
| 1903 | Distillery | 1928 | Belfast Celtic | 1955 | Linfield | 1975 | Linfield |
| 1904 | Linfield | 1929 | Belfast Celtic | 1956 | Linfield | 1976 | Crusaders |
| 1905 | Glentoran | 1930 | Linfield | 1957 | Glentoran | 1977 | Glentoran |
| 1906 | Cliftonville/Dist | 1931 | Glentoran | 1958 | Ards | 1978 | Linfield |
| 1907 | Linfield | 1932 | Linfield | 1959 | Linfield | 1979 | Linfield |
| 1908 | Linfield | 1933 | Belfast Celtic | 1960 | Glenavon | 1980 | Linfield |
| 1909 | Linfield | 1934 | Linfield | 1961 | Linfield | 1981 | Glentoran |
| 1910 | Cliftonville | 1935 | Linfield | 1962 | Linfield | 1982 | Linfield |
| 1911 | Linfield | | | | | | |

## MORANS ULSTER CUP

*Winners – £1000; Runners-up – £600; Third – £400; Fourth – £300; Fifth – £200.*

| | P | W | D | L | F | A | Pts |
|---|---|---|---|---|---|---|---|
| Glentoran | 11 | 8 | 3 | 0 | 28 | 9 | 19 |
| Coleraine | 11 | 7 | 3 | 1 | 25 | 15 | 17 |
| Cliftonville | 11 | 6 | 4 | 1 | 20 | 11 | 16 |
| Portadown | 11 | 6 | 2 | 3 | 19 | 11 | 14 |
| Glenavon | 11 | 5 | 3 | 3 | 22 | 20 | 13 |
| Linfield | 11 | 4 | 4 | 3 | 18 | 18 | 12 |
| Crusaders | 11 | 4 | 2 | 5 | 16 | 14 | 10 |
| Ards | 11 | 3 | 3 | 5 | 18 | 21 | 9 |
| Ballymena Utd | 11 | 3 | 1 | 7 | 12 | 19 | 7 |
| Larne | 11 | 3 | 1 | 7 | 10 | 21 | 7 |
| Distillery | 11 | 2 | 1 | 8 | 12 | 28 | 5 |
| Bangor | 11 | 1 | 1 | 9 | 8 | 21 | 3 |

### Winners

| | | | | | | | |
|---|---|---|---|---|---|---|---|
| 1949 | Linfield | 1958 | Distillery | 1966 | Glentoran | 1974 | Linfield |
| 1950 | Larne | 1959 | Glenavon | 1967 | Linfield | 1975 | Coleraine |
| 1951 | Glentoran | 1960 | Linfield | 1968 | Coleraine | 1976 | Glentoran |
| 1952 | | 1961 | Ballymena Utd | 1969 | Coleraine | 1977 | Linfield |
| 1953 | Glentoran | 1962 | Linfield | 1970 | Linfield | 1978 | Linfield |
| 1954 | Crusaders | 1963 | Crusaders | 1971 | Linfield | 1979 | Linfield |
| 1955 | Glenavon | 1964 | Linfield | 1972 | Coleraine | 1980 | Ballymena Utd |
| 1956 | Linfield | 1965 | Coleraine | 1973 | Ards | 1981 | Glentoran |
| 1957 | Linfield | | | | | | |

## HENNESSY GOLD CUP

*Winners – £1200; Runners-up – £700; Second in Sections – £400; Third in Sections – £300.*

**Section A**

| | P | W | D | L | F | A | Pts |
|---|---|---|---|---|---|---|---|
| Linfield | 5 | 4 | 0 | 1 | 13 | 2 | 8 |
| Portadown | 5 | 4 | 0 | 1 | 10 | 5 | 8 |
| Glenavon | 5 | 3 | 0 | 2 | 7 | 5 | 6 |
| Distillery | 5 | 2 | 0 | 3 | 4 | 8 | 4 |
| Ards | 5 | 1 | 0 | 4 | 4 | 10 | 2 |
| Bangor | 5 | 1 | 0 | 4 | 5 | 13 | 2 |

**Section B**

| | P | W | D | L | F | A | Pts |
|---|---|---|---|---|---|---|---|
| Ballymena Utd | 5 | 3 | 2 | 0 | 7 | 3 | 8 |
| Coleraine | 5 | 2 | 2 | 1 | 8 | 5 | 6 |
| Crusaders | 5 | 1 | 3 | 1 | 6 | 5 | 5 |
| Cliftonville | 5 | 1 | 2 | 2 | 6 | 6 | 4 |
| Larne | 5 | 2 | 0 | 3 | 5 | 8 | 4 |
| Glentoran | 5 | 1 | 1 | 3 | 4 | 9 | 3 |

**Play-off** (*at The Oval, 8 December 1981. Attendance 6000*)
**Ballymena Utd (0) 1** (*Malone*), **Linfield (0) 1** (*McGaughey*) aet
*Linfield won 5-4 on pens*

*Ballymena Utd:* Matthews; Beattie, McAuley, Gracey, McCullough, McGuigan, Neill, Sloan, Guy, Malone, McCusker (Sub: McQuiston, 76 min).
*Linfield:* Dunlop; Mooney, McCartney, Walsh, Rafferty, Dornan, McKee, Hayes (Sub: Crawford, 71 min), McGaughey, Murray, Anderson.

*Manager of Tournament:* Roy Coyle (Linfield)
*Player of Final:* Ray McGuigan (Ballymena Utd)

## OTHER IRISH TROPHIES AND COMPETITIONS

|  | *Winners* | *Runners-up* |
|---|---|---|
| **County Antrim Shield** | Linfield | Distillery |
| **Irish League B Division** | | |
| *Section 1* | Dundela | RUC |
| *Section 2* | Larne Oly | Crusaders Res |
| **George Wilson Cup** | Distillery 11 | Glenavon Res |
| **Steel Cup** | Ballyclare Coms | Killyleagh |
| **Irish Intermediate Cup** | Chimney Corner | Institute |
| **IFA Junior Cup** | Oxford Utd | Rathfriland |
| **IFA Youth Cup** | Glentoran Colts | Linfield Rangers |

**Ulster Footballer of the Year** (Promoted by Castlereagh Glentoran Supporters Club): Felix Healy (Coleraine)
**Northern Ireland Footballer of the Year** (FWA): Felix Healy (Coleraine)
**Young Footballer of the Year:** Peter Dunlop (Cliftonville)
**Ulster Personality of the Year:** Billy Bingham (Northern Ireland team Manager)
**NIPFA Player of the Year:** Felix Healy (Coleraine)
**Most Promising Newcomer:** Peter Dunlop (Cliftonville)
**Mullan-Stewart Award for Meritorious Service:** Bob Bishop (Manchester U Northern Ireland Representative)
**Manager of the Year** (Coaches Association): Roy Coyle (Linfield)

## BASS IRISH CUP 1981–82

*Winners* – £3000; *Runners-up* – £2000; *Defeated semi-finalists* – £1000 each; *Personality of each round* – £250 (First Round – Gary McCartney [RUC]; Second Round – Peter Rafferty [Linfield]; Semi-Finals – Dessie Dickson [Coleraine]; Final – George Gibson [Linfield])

**First Round** (30 January)
| Portadown v Crusaders | 0-0, 1-2 |
|---|---|
| Ards v Chimney Corner | 2-2, 1-1, 1-0 |
| Linfield v Bangor | 5-0 |
| Distillery v Ballymena Utd | 3-2 |
| Cliftonville v Glentoran | 1-0 |
| Coleraine v Derry Inst | 2-1 |
| Glenavon v Limavady Utd | 1-2 |
| Larne v RUC | 2-4 |

**Second Round** (20 February)
| Distillery v Ards | 2-2, 0-0, 2-0 |
|---|---|
| Limavady Utd v Coleraine | 0-2 |
| Cliftonville v RUC | 3-2 |
| Portadown v Linfield | 0-1 |

**Semi-Finals** (20 March)
| Coleraine v Cliftonville (*at Ballymena*) | 1-0 |
|---|---|
| Linfield v Ards (*at The Oval*) | 2-1 |

**Final** (*at The Oval, 24 April. Attendance 12,000*)
**Linfield 2** (*McKeown, Murray* pen), **Coleraine 1** (*Healy*)

*Linfield:* Dunlop; Mooney, Hayes, Walsh, Gibson, Dornan (Sub: Rafferty, 61 min), McKee, McKeown, McGaughey, Murray, Anderson.
*Coleraine:* Magee; McDowell, McNutt, O'Kane, Shannon, Mullan, Mahon, Healy, McManus, Dickson, Henry.
*Referee:* O. Donnelly.

## IRISH CUP FINALS (from 1946–47)

| | | | |
|---|---|---|---|
| 1946–47 | Belfast Celtic 1, Glentoran 0 | 1964–65 | Coleraine 2, Glenavon 1 |
| 1947–48 | Linfield 3, Coleraine 0 | 1965–66 | Glentoran 2, Linfield 0 |
| 1948–49 | Derry City 3, Glentoran 1 | 1966–67 | Crusaders 3, Glentoran 1 |
| 1949–50 | Linfield 2, Distillery 1 | 1967–68 | Crusaders 2, Linfield 0 |
| 1950–51 | Glentoran 3, Ballymena Utd 1 | 1968–69 | Ards 4, Distillery 2 |
| 1951–52 | Ards 1, Glentoran 0 | 1969–70 | Linfield 2, Ballymena Utd 1 |
| 1952–53 | Linfield 5, Coleraine 0 | 1970–71 | Distillery 3, Derry City 0 |
| 1953–54 | Derry City 1, Glentoran 0 | 1971–72 | Coleraine 2, Portadown 1 |
| 1954–55 | Dundela 3, Glenavon 0 | 1972–73 | Glentoran 3, Linfield 2 |
| 1955–56 | Distillery 1, Glentoran 0 | 1973–74 | Ards 2, Ballymena Utd 1 |
| 1956–57 | Glenavon 2, Derry City 0 | 1974–75 | Coleraine 1:0:1, Linfield 1:0:0 |
| 1957–58 | Ballymena Utd 2, Linfield 0 | 1975–76 | Carrick Rangers 2, Linfield 1 |
| 1958–59 | Glenavon 2, Ballymena Utd 0 | 1976–77 | Coleraine 4, Linfield 1 |
| 1959–60 | Linfield 5, Ards 1 | 1977–78 | Linfield 3, Ballymena Utd 1 |
| 1960–61 | Glenavon 5, Linfield 1 | 1978–79 | Cliftonville 3, Portadown 2 |
| 1961–62 | Linfield 4, Portadown 0 | 1979–80 | Linfield 2, Crusaders 0 |
| 1962–63 | Linfield 2, Distillery 1 | 1980–81 | Ballymena Utd 1, Glenavon 0 |
| 1963–64 | Derry City 2, Glentoran 0 | 1981–82 | Linfield 2, Coleraine 1 |

# WELSH FOOTBALL 1981–82

## WELSH FOOTBALL LEAGUE

### PREMIER DIVISION

| | P | W | D | L | F | A | Pts |
|---|---|---|---|---|---|---|---|
| Ton Pentre | 34 | 21 | 7 | 6 | 84 | 46 | 70 |
| Cardiff Cor | 34 | 20 | 5 | 9 | 67 | 44 | 65 |
| Caerleon | 34 | 20 | 3 | 11 | 59 | 46 | 63 |
| Haverfordwest Co | 34 | 19 | 3 | 12 | 60 | 42 | 60 |
| Milford U | 34 | 17 | 8 | 9 | 56 | 39 | 59 |
| Sully | 34 | 14 | 12 | 8 | 55 | 41 | 54 |
| Ammanford T | 34 | 16 | 5 | 13 | 38 | 39 | 53 |
| Maesteg Park | 34 | 15 | 5 | 14 | 56 | 43 | 50 |
| Merthyr Tydfil | 34 | 14 | 6 | 14 | 43 | 42 | 48 |
| Pembroke Bor | 34 | 12 | 10 | 12 | 54 | 52 | 46 |
| Pontllanfraith | 34 | 13 | 7 | 14 | 49 | 56 | 46 |
| Newport YMCA | 34 | 12 | 9 | 13 | 43 | 52 | 45 |
| Barry Town | 34 | 13 | 5 | 16 | 67 | 60 | 44 |
| Lake United | 34 | 12 | 6 | 16 | 47 | 51 | 42 |
| Llanelli | 34 | 11 | 6 | 17 | 38 | 54 | 39 |
| Bridgend T | 34 | 7 | 10 | 17 | 44 | 60 | 31 |
| Briton Ferry Ath | 34 | 7 | 6 | 21 | 34 | 62 | 27 |
| Pontlottyn | 34 | 4 | 5 | 25 | 31 | 96 | 17 |

### DIVISION ONE

| | P | W | D | L | F | A | Pts |
|---|---|---|---|---|---|---|---|
| Brecon Cor | 34 | 26 | 4 | 4 | 74 | 30 | 82 |
| Pontardawe Ath | 34 | 22 | 8 | 4 | 75 | 36 | 74 |
| Blaenrhondda | 34 | 21 | 10 | 3 | 74 | 27 | 73 |
| Treharris Ath | 34 | 21 | 9 | 4 | 87 | 39 | 72 |
| Spencer Works | 34 | 19 | 6 | 9 | 74 | 40 | 63 |
| BP (Llandarcy) | 34 | 15 | 8 | 11 | 58 | 41 | 53 |
| Abercynon Ath | 34 | 13 | 10 | 11 | 61 | 48 | 49 |
| Clydach United | 34 | 13 | 7 | 14 | 48 | 53 | 46 |
| South Glamorgan Inst | 34 | 12 | 8 | 14 | 53 | 53 | 44 |
| Caerau | 34 | 11 | 10 | 13 | 59 | 50 | 43 |
| Morriston T | 34 | 10 | 10 | 14 | 53 | 48 | 40 |
| Trelewis | 34 | 10 | 10 | 14 | 55 | 64 | 40 |
| Afan Lido | 34 | 9 | 11 | 14 | 48 | 46 | 38 |
| Taffs Well | 34 | 10 | 5 | 19 | 43 | 63 | 35 |
| Tredomen Works | 34 | 9 | 4 | 21 | 40 | 92 | 31 |
| Carmarthen T | 34 | 5 | 11 | 18 | 28 | 69 | 26 |
| Aberaman | 34 | 7 | 5 | 22 | 34 | 91 | 26 |
| Pontyclun | 34 | 3 | 4 | 27 | 28 | 102 | 13 |

### DIVISION TWO

| | P | W | D | L | F | A | Pts |
|---|---|---|---|---|---|---|---|
| Ferndale Ath | 32 | 22 | 5 | 5 | 81 | 39 | 71 |
| Cwmbran T | 32 | 20 | 8 | 4 | 77 | 27 | 68 |
| Ebbw Vale | 32 | 20 | 6 | 6 | 78 | 35 | 66 |
| Tondu Robins | 32 | 19 | 6 | 7 | 78 | 33 | 63 |
| Abergavenny Thursdays | 32 | 19 | 4 | 9 | 88 | 36 | 61 |
| Tonyrefail Welfare | 32 | 20 | 1 | 11 | 79 | 47 | 61 |
| Port Talbot Ath | 32 | 16 | 7 | 9 | 56 | 37 | 55 |
| Blaenavon Blues | 32 | 15 | 8 | 9 | 64 | 46 | 53 |
| Seven Sisters | 32 | 14 | 7 | 11 | 75 | 59 | 49 |
| Garw | 32 | 12 | 8 | 12 | 68 | 57 | 44 |
| Swansea Univ | 32 | 9 | 6 | 17 | 42 | 75 | 33 |
| Skewen Ath | 32 | 8 | 6 | 18 | 40 | 68 | 30 |
| Panteg | 32 | 8 | 5 | 19 | 44 | 68 | 29 |
| Blaina West Side | 32 | 7 | 3 | 22 | 37 | 98 | 24 |
| Ynysybwl | 32 | 7 | 2 | 23 | 35 | 96 | 23 |
| Tynte Rovers | 32 | 7 | 0 | 25 | 48 | 104 | 21 |
| Lewistown | 32 | 4 | 8 | 20 | 37 | 102 | 20 |

## WELSH FOOTBALL LEAGUE (NORTH)

### DIVISION ONE

| | P | W | D | L | F | A | Pts |
|---|---|---|---|---|---|---|---|
| Greenfield | 26 | 19 | 3 | 4 | 81 | 31 | 41 |
| Blaenau Ffestiniog | 26 | 17 | 6 | 3 | 68 | 33 | 40 |
| Colwyn Bay | 26 | 18 | 3 | 5 | 70 | 36 | 39 |
| Conwy United | 26 | 15 | 5 | 6 | 41 | 30 | 35 |
| Llandudno Amat | 26 | 9 | 10 | 7 | 49 | 45 | 28 |
| Flint Town Utd | 26 | 7 | 9 | 10 | 49 | 54 | 23 |
| Pwllheli & Dist | 26 | 8 | 6 | 12 | 35 | 42 | 22 |
| UCNW (Bangor) | 26 | 9 | 4 | 13 | 39 | 46 | 22 |
| Caernarfon Town | 26 | 8 | 6 | 12 | 43 | 59 | 22 |
| Bangor City | 26 | 7 | 6 | 13 | 50 | 59 | 20 |
| Porthmadog | 26 | 8 | 4 | 14 | 54 | 65 | 20 |
| Menai Bridge (T) | 26 | 5 | 9 | 12 | 30 | 47 | 19 |
| Rhyl | 26 | 5 | 7 | 14 | 30 | 57 | 17 |
| Holyhead Utd (J) | 26 | 5 | 6 | 15 | 31 | 66 | 16 |

### HONOURS LIST

**League Champions:** Colwyn Bay
**Cookson Cup Winners:** Colwyn Bay
**Alves Cup Winners:** Colwyn Bay
**Barritt Cup Winners:** Colwyn Bay

## OTHER WELSH HONOURS

**Welsh National League (Wrexham):** Brymbo Steel Works (*Champions and League Cup winners*)
**Welsh National League (Central Wales):** Newtown (*Champions and League Cup winners*)
**Welsh Youth Cup winners:** Abergavenny Thursdays
**North Wales Coast FA Challenge Cup winners:** Colwyn Bay
**North East Wales FA Challenge Cup winners:** Brymbo Steel Works
**Central Wales FA Challenge Cup winners:** Aberystwyth Town
**South Wales FA Senior Cup winners:** Sully
**West Wales FA Senior Cup winners:** Haverfordwest County
**Gwent County FA Senior Cup winners:** Girlings (Cwmbran)

# WELSH CUP 1981–82

**First Round**

| | |
|---|---|
| Menai Bridge Tigers v Conwy U | 0-4 |
| Greenfield v Flint Town U | 0-0, 1-0 |
| Porthmadog v UCNW Bangor | 2-1 |
| Druids U v Gresford Ath | 1-0 |
| Bala T v Ruthin | 3-2 |
| St Mary's (Ruabon) v Denbigh T | 2-0 |
| Bargod Rangers v Llandrindod Wells | 3-1 |
| Montgomery T v Caersws | 1-9 |
| (at Caersws) | |
| Cheltenham T v Oswestry T | 0-2 |
| Stafford R v Kidderminster H | 2-1 |
| Sully v Garw | 1-0 |
| Spencer Works v Milford U | 4-2 |
| Briton Ferry Ath v Aberaman | 8-0 |
| Lake U v Ebbw Vale | 2-0 |
| Abergavenny Thursdays v Carmarthen T | 3-2 |
| Pontlottyn v Newport YMCA | 1-1, 0-2 |

**Second Round**

| | |
|---|---|
| Conwy U v Bangor C | 0-0, 1-8 |
| Newtown v Porthmadog | 5-0 |
| Caernarfon T v Llandudno Amateurs | 4-2 |
| Knighton T v Presteigne St Andrews | 1-3 |
| Caersws v Connah's Quay Nomads | 1-2 |
| Bargod Rangers v Stourbridge | 0-5 |
| Rhyl v Colwyn Bay | 0-1 |
| Bala T v Greenfield | 2-5 |
| Towyn v Druids U | 1-0 |
| Blaenau Ffestiniog v Aberystwyth T | 7-2 |
| St Mary's (Ruabon) v Oswestry T | 0-2 |
| (at Oswestry) | |
| Llanidloes T v Welshpool | 4-0 |
| Pwllheli & District v Brymbo Steelworks | 1-0 |
| Llanelli v Briton Ferry Ath | 3-0 |
| Spencer Works v Haverfordwest Co | 1-2 |
| Lake U v Worcester C | 2-2, 1-2 |
| (both matches at Worcester) | |
| Sully v Cardiff Cor | 2-2,0-1 |
| South Glamorgan Inst v BP Llandarcy | 1-2 |
| Taffs Well v Ton Pentre | 3-1 |
| Ammanford T v Abercynon Ath | 4-1 |
| Abergavenny Thursdays v Bridgend T | 0-3 |
| Pontllanfraith v Pembroke Borough | 4-0 |
| Caerleon v Newport YMCA | 2-0 |
| Stafford R v Merthyr Tydfil | 1-0 |

| | |
|---|---|
| Ferndale Ath v Barry T | 0-3 |
| Maesteg Park v Pontardawe Ath | 0-1 |

**Third Round**

| | |
|---|---|
| Towyn v Hereford U | 0-8 |
| (at Hereford) | |
| Llanidloes v Colwyn Bay | 0-2 |
| Greenfield v Presteigne St Andrews | 2-1 |
| Caernarfon T v Blaenau Ffestiniog | 4-2 |
| Connah's Quay Nomads v Pwllheli & District | 1-0 |
| Shrewsbury T v Oswestry T | 4-1 |
| Stourbridge v Wrexham | 2-4 |
| Bangor C v Newtown | 4-2 |
| Stafford R v Swansea C | 0-4 |
| Taffs Well v Newport Co | 0-5 |
| Barry T v Caerleon | 5-0 |
| Llanelli v Worcester C | 1-1, 1-5 |
| Ammanford T v Haverfordwest Co | 1-1, 4-0 |
| Pontllanfraith v BP Llandarcy | 2-1 |
| Bridgend T v Cardiff C | 1-4 |
| Cardiff Cor v Pontardawe Ath | 0-1 |

**Fourth Round**

| | |
|---|---|
| Cardiff C v Newport Co | 3-1 |
| Swansea C v Worcester C | 6-0 |
| Caernarfon T v Shrewsbury T | 1-8 |
| Bangor C v Ammanford T | 1-0 |
| Greenfield v Connah's Quay Nomads | 3-0 |
| Pontllanfraith v Colwyn Bay | 0-2 |
| Pontardawe Ath v Wrexham | 1-5 |
| Hereford U v Barry T | 3-1 |

**Fifth Round**

| | |
|---|---|
| Cardiff C v Wrexham | 4-1 |
| Bangor C v Shrewsbury T | 2-1 |
| Swansea C v Colwyn Bay | 2-2, 3-0 |
| (both matches at Swansea) | |
| Greenfield v Hereford U | 1-2 |
| (at Hereford) | |

**Semi-finals**

| | |
|---|---|
| Bangor C v Swansea C | 1-2, 0-0 |
| Hereford U v Cardiff C | 0-0, 1-2 |

## Final, First Leg: Cardiff C 0, Swansea C 0

(At Cardiff, 11 May, 1982)

*Cardiff C:* Dibble; Jones L., Henderson, Pontin, Micallef, Mullen, Lythgoe, Gilbert, Bennett G., Bennett D., Stevens.
*Swansea C:* Davies· Marustik, Hadziabdic, Thompson, Kennedy, Rajkovic, Curtis, James R., James L., Stevenson, Latchford.

## Final, Second Leg: Swansea C 2, Cardiff C 1

(At Swansea, 19 May, 1982)

*Swansea C:* Davies; Robinson, Hadziabdic, Stanley, Kennedy, Rajkovic, Curtis, James R., James L., Stevenson, Latchford.
*Cardiff C:* Dibble; Jones L., Henderson, Pontin, Micallef, Mullen, Lythgoe, Gilbert, Bennett G., McEwan, Bennett D.
*Scorers:* Swansea C – Latchford 2; Cardiff C – Bennett G.

# WELSH INTERMEDIATE CUP 1981–82

**First Round**

| | |
|---|---|
| Pilkingtons v UCNW Bangor | 4-3 |
| Pwllheli & District v Porthmadog | 3-0 |
| St Mary's (Ruabon) v Castell Alun C | 3-0 |
| Llangedwyn v Guilsfield | 5-3 |
| Merlins Bridge v Newcastle Emlyn | 3-2 |
| BP Llandarcy v Pontllanfraith | 2-0 |
| Hirwaun Welfare v Pontyclun | 3-3, 4-2 |
| Tondu Robins v Caerau | 3-8 |

**Second Round**

| | |
|---|---|
| Greenfield v Holywell T | 2-0 |
| Pilkingtons v Holyhead U Jnrs | 3-1 |
| Pwllheli & District v Menai Bridge Tigers | 5-1 |
| St Mary's (Ruabon) v Rhos Aelwyd | 1-2 |
| Lex XI v Rhostyllen Villa | 4-1 |
| Bow Street Barmouth v Dyffryn | 0-2 |
| Llangedwyn v Llanfair Caereinion | 1-0 |
| Aberaeron T v Bont | 1-0 |
| Bargod Rangers v Merlins Bridge | 3-2 |
| Caldicot T v Caerau | 2-1 |
| Pontardulais T v Newport Cor | 0-0, 0-2 |
| Llanelli Steel v Hirwaun Welfare | 2-2, 0-4 |
| Cardiff Cosmos v Cwmbran Celtic | 0-1 |
| Coedffranc v BP Llandarcy | 1-2 |

**Third Round**

| | |
|---|---|
| Llandudno Amateurs v Abergele U | 5-1 |
| Pwllheli & District v Connah's Quay N | 1-1, 0-1 |
| Pilkingtons v Flint Town U | 1-5 |
| Greenfield v Hawarden Rangers | 3-2 |
| Llanberis Ath v Conwy U | 1-4 |
| Harlech T v Blaenau Ffestiniog | 1-5 |
| Ruthin v Chirk AAA | 2-0 |
| Rhos Aelwyd v Denbigh T | 1-3 |
| Llay Welfare v Llangollen | 0-3 |
| Gresford Ath v Mold Alex | 2-5 |
| Brymbo Steelworks v Lex XI | 0-0, 4-5 |
| *(after penalty kicks, following extra time)* | |
| Buckley v Cefn Albion | 2-3 |
| Bala T v Druids U | 3-3, 4-2 |
| Llanidloes T v Barmouth & Dyffryn | 6-1 |
| Welshpool v Dolgellau Ath | 13-1 |
| Aberaeron T v Aberystwyth T | 1-4 |
| Newtown v Llangedwyn | 9-0 |
| Llanfyllin v Towyn | 1-7 |
| Llandrindod Wells v Caersws | 1-2 |
| Rhayader T v Presteigne St Andrews | 2-1 |
| Bargod Rangers v Montgomery T | 2-2, 0-2 |
| Blaenrhondda v Cardiff Cor | 1-0 |
| Brecon Cor v Treharris Ath | 2-1 |
| Alcan v Llantwit Major | 1-2 |
| Bryntirion Ath v Fields Park | 2-1 |
| Newport YMCA v Hirwaun Welfare | 3-2 |
| *(at Hirwaun Welfare)* | |

| | |
|---|---|
| Taffs Well v Afan Lido | 1-0 |
| BP Llandarcy v Dafen Welfare | 2-1 |
| Newport Cor v Abergavenny Thursdays | 2-0 |
| South Glamorgan Inst v Carmarthen T | 7-0 |
| Aberaman v Caldicot T | 0-0, 1-2 |
| Tonyrefail Welfare v Cwmbran Celtic | 5-0 |

**Fourth Round**

| | |
|---|---|
| Conwy U v Cefn Albion | 2-1 |
| Newtown v Welshpool | 1-0 |
| Greenfield v Llanidloes T | 2-0 |
| Ruthin v Mold Alexandra | 1-0 |
| Denbigh T v Connah's Quay Nomads | 0-4 |
| Bala T v Lex XI | 2-3 |
| Llandudno Amateurs v Flint T U | 1-6 |
| Blaenau Ffestiniog v Towyn | 3-1 |
| Llangollen v Montgomery T | 3-1 |
| Newport Cor v Taffs Well | 1-0 |
| Caldicot T v BP Llandarcy | 0-2 |
| Blaenrhondda v South Glamorgan Inst | 2-1 |
| Brecon Cor v Tonyrefail Welfare | 3-1 |
| Rhayader T v Caersws | 2-3 |
| Llantwit Major v Newport YMCA | 3-2 |
| Aberystwyth T v Bryntirion Ath | 1-1, 2-0 |

**Fifth Round**

| | |
|---|---|
| Caersws v Connah's Quay Nomads | 3-2 |
| Blaenau Ffestiniog v Greenfield | 2-0 |
| Conwy U v Newport Cor | 5-1 |
| Aberystwyth T v Blaenrhondda | 1-3 |
| Lex XI v Llangollen | 1-1, 3-1 |
| Flint Town U v Brecon Cor | 1-5 |
| Ruthin v Newtown | 0-2 |
| BP Llandarcy v Llantwit Major | 0-0, 3-2 |

**Sixth Round**

| | |
|---|---|
| Lex XI v Newtown | 2-2, 0-1 |
| Blaenrhondda v Caersws | 4-1 |
| BP Llandarcy v Blaenau Ffestiniog | 0-1 |
| Brecon Cor v Conwy U | 1-1, 0-1 |

**Semi-finals**

| | |
|---|---|
| Blaenau Ffestiniog v Blaenrhondda | 2-2, 2-0 |
| *(at Llanidloes)* | |
| Conwy U v Newtown | 2-1 |
| *(at Bala)* | |

**Final**

| | |
|---|---|
| Blaenau Ffestiniog v Conwy U | 0-1 |
| *(at Bangor)* | |

## WELSH INTERMEDIATE CUP 1975–81

(replacing Welsh Amateur Cup)

| | |
|---|---|
| 1975–76 | Cardiff Coll of Ed 2, Shifnal T 1 |
| 1976–77 | Welshpool 4, Whitchurch Alport 1 |
| 1977–78 | Caernarvon T 1, Llanidloes T 0 |
| 1978–79 | Flint Town U 0, Pontllanfraith 1 |
| 1979–80 | Blaenau Ffestiniog 3:1, Brymbo Steelworks 3:0 |
| 1980–81 | Connah's Quay Nomads 1, Newport YMCA 0 |

# THE WORLD CUP 1930–1982

## URUGUAY 1930

**Pool 1**

France 4, Mexico 1
Argentina 1, France 0
Chile 3, Mexico 0
Chile 1, France 0
Argentina 6, Mexico 3
Argentina 3, Chile 1

|  | P | W | D | L | F | A | Pts |
|---|---|---|---|---|---|---|---|
| Argentina | 3 | 3 | 0 | 0 | 10 | 4 | 6 |
| Chile | 3 | 2 | 0 | 1 | 5 | 3 | 4 |
| France | 3 | 1 | 0 | 2 | 4 | 3 | 2 |
| Mexico | 3 | 0 | 0 | 3 | 4 | 13 | 0 |

**Pool 2**

Yugoslavia 2, Brazil 1
Yugoslavia 4, Bolivia 0
Brazil 4, Bolivia 0

|  | P | W | D | L | F | A | Pts |
|---|---|---|---|---|---|---|---|
| Yugoslavia | 2 | 2 | 0 | 0 | 6 | 1 | 4 |
| Brazil | 2 | 1 | 0 | 1 | 5 | 2 | 2 |
| Bolivia | 2 | 0 | 0 | 2 | 0 | 8 | 0 |

**Pool 3**

Rumania 3, Peru 1
Uruguay 1, Peru 0
Uruguay 4, Rumania 0

|  | P | W | D | L | F | A | Pts |
|---|---|---|---|---|---|---|---|
| Uruguay | 2 | 2 | 0 | 0 | 5 | 0 | 4 |
| Rumania | 2 | 1 | 0 | 1 | 3 | 5 | 2 |
| Peru | 2 | 0 | 0 | 2 | 1 | 4 | 0 |

**Pool 4**

United States 3, Belgium 0
United States 3, Paraguay 0
Paraguay 1, Belgium 0

|  | P | W | D | L | F | A | Pts |
|---|---|---|---|---|---|---|---|
| United States | 2 | 2 | 0 | 0 | 6 | 0 | 4 |
| Paraguay | 2 | 1 | 0 | 1 | 1 | 3 | 2 |
| Belgium | 2 | 0 | 0 | 2 | 0 | 4 | 0 |

**Semi-Finals**

Argentina 6, United States 1
Uruguay 6, Yugoslavia 1

**Final** (Montevideo, 30 July, 1930)

Uruguay (1) 4, Argentina (2) 2
*Uruguay:* Ballesteros; Nasazzi (capt), Mascheroni, Andrade, Fernandez, Gestido, Dorado, Scarone, Castro, Cea, Iriarte.
*Argentina:* Botasso; Della Torre, Paternoster, Evaristo J., Monti, Suarez, Peucelle, Varallo, Stabile, Ferreira (capt), Evaristo M.
*Scorers:* Dorado, Cea, Iriarte, Castro for Uruguay; Peucelle, Stabile for Argentina.
*Leading scorer:* Stabile (Argentina) 8.

## ITALY 1934

**First Round**

Italy 7, United States 1
Czechoslovakia 2, Rumania 1
Germany 5, Belgium 2
Austria 3, France 2
Spain 3, Brazil 1

Switzerland 3, Holland 2
Sweden 3, Argentina 2
Hungary 4, Egypt 2

**Second Round**

Germany 2, Sweden 1
Austria 2, Hungary 1
Italy 1, Spain 1
Italy 1, Spain 0 *replay*
Czechoslovakia 3, Switzerland 2

**Semi-Finals**

Czechoslovakia 3, Germany 1 (in Rome)
Italy 1, Austria 0 (in Milan)

**Third Place Match** (Naples)

Germany 3, Austria 2

**Final** (Rome, 10 June, 1934)

Italy (0) (1) 2, Czechoslovakia (0) (1) 1 aet
*Italy:* Combi (capt); Monzeglio, Allemandi; Ferraris IV, Monti, Bertolini, Guaita, Meazza, Schiavio, Ferrari, Orsi.
*Czechoslovakia:* Planicka (capt); Zenisek, Ctyroky, Kostalek, Cambal, Krcil; Junek, Svoboda, Sobotka, Nejedly, Puc.
*Scorers:* Orsi, Schiavio for Italy; Puc for Czechoslovakia.
*Leading scorers:* Schiavio (Italy), Nejedly (Czechoslovakia), Conen (Germany) 4 each.

## FRANCE 1938

**First Round**

Switzerland 1, Germany 1
Switzerland 4, Germany 2 *replay*
Cuba 3, Rumania 3
Cuba 2, Rumania 1 *replay*
Hungary 6, Dutch East Indies 0
France 3, Belgium 1
Czechoslovakia 3, Holland 0
Brazil 6, Poland 5
Italy 2, Norway 1

**Second Round**

Sweden 8, Cuba 0
Hungary 2, Switzerland 0
Italy 3, France 1
Brazil 1, Czechoslovakia 1
Brazil 2, Czechoslovakia 1 *replay*

**Semi-Finals**

Italy 2, Brazil 1 (in Marseilles)
Hungary 5, Sweden 1 (in Paris)

**Third Place Match** (Bordeaux)

Brazil 4, Sweden 2

**Final** (Paris, 19 June, 1938)

Italy (3) 4, Hungary (1) 2
*Italy:* Olivieri; Foni, Rava; Serantoni, Andreolo, Locatelli; Biavati, Meazza (capt), Piola, Ferrari, Colaussi.
*Hungary:* Szabo; Polgar, Biro; Szalay, Szucs, Lazar; Sas, Vincze, Sarosi (capt), Szengeller, Titkos.
*Scorers:* Colaussi 2, Piola 2 for Italy; Titkos, Sarosi for Hungary.
*Leading Scorer:* Leonidas (Brazil) 8.

# BRAZIL 1950

**Pool 1**

Brazil 4, Mexico 0
Yugoslavia 3, Switzerland 0
Yugoslavia 4, Mexico 1
Brazil 2, Switzerland 2
Brazil 2, Yugoslavia 0
Switzerland 2, Mexico 1

|  | P | W | D | L | F | A | Pts |
|---|---|---|---|---|---|---|---|
| Brazil | 3 | 2 | 1 | 0 | 8 | 2 | 5 |
| Yugoslavia | 3 | 2 | 0 | 1 | 7 | 3 | 4 |
| Switzerland | 3 | 1 | 1 | 1 | 4 | 6 | 3 |
| Mexico | 3 | 0 | 0 | 3 | 2 | 10 | 0 |

**Pool 2**

Spain 3, United States 1
England 2, Chile 0
United States 1, England 0
Spain 2, Chile 0
Spain 1, England 0
Chile 5, United States 2

|  | P | W | D | L | F | A | Pts |
|---|---|---|---|---|---|---|---|
| Spain | 3 | 3 | 0 | 0 | 6 | 1 | 6 |
| England | 3 | 1 | 0 | 2 | 2 | 2 | 2 |
| Chile | 3 | 1 | 0 | 2 | 5 | 6 | 2 |
| United States | 3 | 1 | 0 | 2 | 4 | 8 | 2 |

**Pool 3**

Sweden 3, Italy 2
Sweden 2, Paraguay 2
Italy 2, Paraguay 0

|  | P | W | D | L | F | A | Pts |
|---|---|---|---|---|---|---|---|
| Sweden | 2 | 1 | 1 | 0 | 5 | 4 | 3 |
| Italy | 2 | 1 | 0 | 1 | 4 | 3 | 2 |
| Paraguay | 2 | 0 | 1 | 1 | 2 | 4 | 1 |

**Pool 4**

Uruguay 8, Bolivia 0

|  | P | W | D | L | F | A | Pts |
|---|---|---|---|---|---|---|---|
| Uruguay | 1 | 1 | 0 | 0 | 8 | 0 | 2 |
| Bolivia | 1 | 0 | 0 | 1 | 0 | 8 | 0 |

**Final Pool**

Final pool replaced knockout system.

Uruguay 2, Spain 2
Brazil 7, Sweden 1
Uruguay 3, Sweden 2
Brazil 6, Spain 1
Sweden 3, Spain 1
Uruguay (0) 2, Brazil (0) 1 (Rio de Janeiro, 16 July, 1950)
*Uruguay:* Maspoli; Matthias, Gonzales, Tejera; Gambetta, Varela (capt), Andrade; Ghiggia, Perez, Miguez, Schiaffino, Moran.
*Brazil:* Barbosa; Augusto (capt), Juvenal; Bauer, Danilo, Bigode; Friaça, Zizinho, Ademir, Jair, Chico.
*Scorers:* Schiffino, Ghiggia for Uruguay; Friaça for Brazil.

|  | P | W | D | L | F | A | Pts |
|---|---|---|---|---|---|---|---|
| Uruguay | 3 | 2 | 1 | 0 | 7 | 5 | 5 |
| Brazil | 3 | 2 | 0 | 1 | 14 | 4 | 4 |
| Sweden | 3 | 1 | 0 | 2 | 6 | 11 | 2 |
| Spain | 3 | 0 | 1 | 2 | 4 | 11 | 1 |

*Leading Scorer:* Ademir (Brazil) 7


# SWITZERLAND 1954

**Group 1**

Yugoslavia 1, France 0
Brazil 5, Mexico 0
France 3, Mexico 2
Brazil 1, Yugoslavia 1

|  | P | W | D | L | F | A | Pts |
|---|---|---|---|---|---|---|---|
| Brazil | 2 | 1 | 1 | 0 | 6 | 1 | 3 |
| Yugoslavia | 2 | 1 | 1 | 0 | 2 | 1 | 3 |
| France | 2 | 1 | 0 | 1 | 3 | 3 | 2 |
| Mexico | 2 | 0 | 0 | 2 | 2 | 8 | 0 |

**Group 2**

Hungary 9, Korea 0
West Germany 4, Turkey 1
Hungary 8, West Germany 3
Turkey 7, Korea 0

|  | P | W | D | L | F | A | Pts |
|---|---|---|---|---|---|---|---|
| Hungary | 2 | 2 | 0 | 0 | 17 | 3 | 4 |
| West Germany | 2 | 1 | 0 | 1 | 7 | 9 | 2 |
| Turkey | 2 | 1 | 0 | 1 | 8 | 4 | 2 |
| Korea | 2 | 0 | 0 | 2 | 0 | 16 | 0 |

*Play-off:* West Germany 7, Turkey 2

**Group 3**

Austria 1, Scotland 0
Uruguay 2, Czechoslovakia 0
Austria 5, Czechoslovakia 0
Uruguay 7, Scotland 0

|  | P | W | D | L | F | A | Pts |
|---|---|---|---|---|---|---|---|
| Uruguay | 2 | 2 | 0 | 0 | 9 | 0 | 4 |
| Austria | 2 | 2 | 0 | 0 | 6 | 0 | 4 |
| Czechoslovakia | 2 | 0 | 0 | 2 | 0 | 7 | 0 |
| Scotland | 2 | 0 | 0 | 2 | 0 | 8 | 0 |

**Group 4**

England 4, Belgium 4
England 2, Switzerland 0
Switzerland 2, Italy 1
Italy 4, Belgium 1

|  | P | W | D | L | F | A | Pts |
|---|---|---|---|---|---|---|---|
| England | 2 | 1 | 1 | 0 | 6 | 4 | 3 |
| Italy | 2 | 1 | 0 | 1 | 5 | 3 | 2 |
| Switzerland | 2 | 1 | 0 | 1 | 2 | 3 | 2 |
| Belgium | 2 | 0 | 1 | 1 | 5 | 8 | 1 |

*Play-off:* Switzerland 4, Italy 1

**Quarter-Finals**

West Germany 2, Yugoslavia 0
Hungary 4, Brazil 2
Austria 7, Switzerland 5
Uruguay 4, England 2

**Semi-Finals**

West Germany 6, Austria 1 (in Basle)
Hungary 4, Uruguay 2 (in Lausanne)

**Third Place Match** (Zurich)

Austria 3, Uruguay 1

**Final** (Berne, 4 July, 1954)

West Germany (2) 3, Hungary (2) 2
*West Germany:* Turek; Posipal, Kohlmeyer; Eckel, Liebrich, Mai; Rahn, Morlock, Walter O., Walter F. (capt), Schaefer.
*Hungary:* Grosics; Buzansky, Lantos; Bozsik, Lorant, Zakarias; Czibor, Kocsis, Hidegkuti, Puskas (capt), Toth J.
*Scorers:* Morlock, Rahn 2 for West Germany; Puskas, Czibor for Hungary.
*Leading Scorer:* Kocsis (Hungary) 11.

## SWEDEN 1958

### Group 1

West Germany 3, Argentina 1
Northern Ireland 1, Czechoslovakia 0
West Germany 2, Czechoslovakia 2
Argentina 3, Northern Ireland 1
West Germany 2, Northern Ireland 2
Czechoslovakia 6, Argentina 1

|  | P | W | D | L | F | A | Pts |
|---|---|---|---|---|---|---|---|
| West Germany | 3 | 1 | 2 | 0 | 7 | 5 | 4 |
| Czechoslovakia | 3 | 1 | 1 | 1 | 8 | 4 | 3 |
| Ireland | 3 | 1 | 1 | 1 | 4 | 5 | 3 |
| Argentina | 3 | 1 | 0 | 2 | 5 | 10 | 2 |

*Play-off:* Northern Ireland 2, Czechoslovakia 1

### Group 2

France 7, Paraguay 3
Yugoslavia 1, Scotland 1
Yugoslavia 3, France 2
Paraguay 3, Scotland 2
France 2, Scotland 1
Yugoslavia 3, Paraguay 3

|  | P | W | D | L | F | A | Pts |
|---|---|---|---|---|---|---|---|
| France | 3 | 2 | 0 | 1 | 11 | 7 | 4 |
| Yugoslavia | 3 | 1 | 2 | 0 | 7 | 6 | 4 |
| Paraguay | 3 | 1 | 1 | 1 | 9 | 12 | 3 |
| Scotland | 3 | 0 | 1 | 2 | 4 | 6 | 1 |

### Group 3

Sweden 3, Mexico 0
Hungary 1, Wales 1
Wales 1, Mexico 1
Sweden 2, Hungary 1
Sweden 0, Wales 0
Hungary 4, Mexico 0

|  | P | W | D | L | F | A | Pts |
|---|---|---|---|---|---|---|---|
| Sweden | 3 | 2 | 1 | 0 | 5 | 1 | 5 |
| Hungary | 3 | 1 | 1 | 1 | 6 | 3 | 3 |
| Wales | 3 | 0 | 3 | 0 | 2 | 2 | 3 |
| Mexico | 3 | 0 | 1 | 2 | 1 | 8 | 1 |

*Play-off:* Wales 2, Hungary 1

### Group 4

England 2, USSR 2
Brazil 3, Austria 0
England 0, Brazil 0
USSR 2, Austria 0
Brazil 2, USSR 0
England 2, Austria 2

|  | P | W | D | L | F | A | Pts |
|---|---|---|---|---|---|---|---|
| Brazil | 3 | 2 | 1 | 0 | 5 | 0 | 5 |
| England | 3 | 0 | 3 | 0 | 4 | 4 | 3 |
| USSR | 3 | 1 | 1 | 1 | 4 | 4 | 3 |
| Austria | 3 | 0 | 1 | 2 | 2 | 7 | 1 |

*Play-off:* USSR 1, England 0

### Quarter-Finals

France 4, Ireland 0
West Germany 1, Yugoslavia 0
Sweden 2, USSR 0
Brazil 1, Wales 0

### Semi-Finals

Brazil 5, France 2 (in Stockholm)
Sweden 3, West Germany 1 (in Gothenburg)

### Third Place Match (Gothenburg)

France 6, West Germany 3

**Final** (Stockholm, 29 June, 1958)

Brazil (2) 5, Sweden (1) 2

*Brazil:* Gilmar; Santos D., Santos N.; Zito, Bellini, Orlando, Garrincha, Didi, Vavà, Pelé, Zagalo.

*Sweden:* Svensson; Bergmark, Axbom; Boerjesson, Gustavsson, Parliag, Hamrin, Gren, Simonsson, Liedholm, Skoglund.

*Scorers:* Vavà 2, Pelé 2, Zagalo for Brazil; Liedholm, Simonsson for Sweden.

*Leading Scorer:* Fontaine (France) 13 (present record total).

## CHILE 1962

### Group 1

Uruguay 2, Colombia 1
USSR 2, Yugoslavia 0
Yugoslavia 3, Uruguay 1
USSR 4, Colombia 4
USSR 2, Uruguay 1
Yugoslavia 5, Colombia 0

|  | P | W | D | L | F | A | Pts |
|---|---|---|---|---|---|---|---|
| USSR | 3 | 2 | 1 | 0 | 8 | 5 | 5 |
| Yugoslavia | 3 | 2 | 0 | 1 | 8 | 3 | 4 |
| Uruguay | 3 | 1 | 0 | 2 | 4 | 6 | 2 |
| Colombia | 3 | 0 | 1 | 2 | 5 | 11 | 1 |

### Group 2

Chile 3, Switzerland 1
West Germany 0, Italy 0
Chile 2, Italy 0
West Germany 2, Switzerland 1
West Germany 2, Chile 0
Italy 3, Switzerland 0

|  | P | W | D | L | F | A | Pts |
|---|---|---|---|---|---|---|---|
| West Germany | 3 | 2 | 1 | 0 | 4 | 1 | 5 |
| Chile | 3 | 2 | 0 | 1 | 5 | 3 | 4 |
| Italy | 3 | 1 | 1 | 1 | 3 | 2 | 3 |
| Switzerland | 3 | 0 | 0 | 3 | 2 | 8 | 0 |

### Group 3

Brazil 2, Mexico 0
Czechoslovakia 1, Spain 0
Brazil 0, Czechoslovakia 0
Spain 1, Mexico 0
Brazil 2, Spain 1
Mexico 3, Czechoslovakia 1

|  | P | W | D | L | F | A | Pts |
|---|---|---|---|---|---|---|---|
| Brazil | 3 | 2 | 1 | 0 | 4 | 1 | 5 |
| Czechoslovakia | 3 | 1 | 1 | 1 | 2 | 3 | 3 |
| Mexico | 3 | 1 | 0 | 2 | 3 | 4 | 2 |
| Spain | 3 | 1 | 0 | 2 | 2 | 3 | 2 |

### Group 4

Argentina 1, Bulgaria 0
Hungary 2, England 1
England 3, Argentina 1
Hungary 6, Bulgaria 1
Argentina 0, Hungary 0
England 0, Bulgaria 0

|  | P | W | D | L | F | A | Pts |
|---|---|---|---|---|---|---|---|
| Hungary | 3 | 2 | 1 | 0 | 8 | 2 | 5 |
| England | 3 | 1 | 1 | 1 | 4 | 3 | 3 |
| Argentina | 3 | 1 | 1 | 1 | 2 | 3 | 3 |
| Bulgaria | 3 | 0 | 1 | 2 | 1 | 7 | 1 |

### Quarter-Finals

Yugoslavia 1, West Germany 0
Brazil 3, England 1
Chile 2, USSR 1
Czechoslovakia 1, Hungary 0

## Semi-Finals

Brazil 4, Chile 2 (in Santiago)
Czechoslovakia 3, Yugoslavia 1 (in Viña del Mar)

**Third Place Match** (Santiago)

Chile 1, Yugoslavia 0

**Final** (Santiago, 17 June, 1962)

Brazil (1) 3, Czechoslovakia (1) 1

*Brazil:* Gilmar; Santos D., Mauro, Zozimo, Santos N.; Zito, Didi; Garrincha, Vavà, Amarildo, Zagalo.

*Czechoslovakia:* Schroiff; Tichy, Novak; Pluskal, Popluhar, Masopust, Pospichal, Scherer, Kvasniak, Kadraba, Jelinek.

*Scorers:* Amarildo, Zito, Vavà for Brazil; Masopust for Czechoslovakia.

*Leading Scorer:* Jerkovic (Yugoslavia) 5.

# ENGLAND 1966

### Group 1

England 0, Uruguay 0
France 1, Mexico 1
Uruguay 2, France 1
England 2, Mexico 0
Uruguay 0, Mexico 0
England 2, France 0

|  | P | W | D | L | F | A | Pts |
|---|---|---|---|---|---|---|---|
| England | 3 | 2 | 1 | 0 | 4 | 0 | 5 |
| Uruguay | 3 | 1 | 2 | 0 | 2 | 1 | 4 |
| Mexico | 3 | 0 | 2 | 1 | 1 | 3 | 2 |
| France | 3 | 0 | 1 | 2 | 2 | 5 | 1 |

### Group 2

West Germany 5, Switzerland 0
Argentina 2, Spain 1
Spain 2, Switzerland 1
Argentina 0, West Germany 0
Argentina 2, Switzerland 0
West Germany 2, Spain 1

|  | P | W | D | L | F | A | Pts |
|---|---|---|---|---|---|---|---|
| West Germany | 3 | 2 | 1 | 0 | 7 | 1 | 5 |
| Argentina | 3 | 2 | 1 | 0 | 4 | 1 | 5 |
| Spain | 3 | 1 | 0 | 2 | 4 | 5 | 2 |
| Switzerland | 3 | 0 | 0 | 3 | 1 | 9 | 0 |

### Group 3

Brazil 2, Bulgaria 0
Portugal 3, Hungary 1
Hungary 3, Brazil 1
Portugal 3, Bulgaria 0
Portugal 3, Brazil 1
Hungary 3, Bulgaria 1

|  | P | W | D | L | F | A | Pts |
|---|---|---|---|---|---|---|---|
| Portugal | 3 | 3 | 0 | 0 | 9 | 2 | 6 |
| Hungary | 3 | 2 | 0 | 1 | 7 | 5 | 4 |
| Brazil | 3 | 1 | 0 | 2 | 4 | 6 | 2 |
| Bulgaria | 3 | 0 | 0 | 3 | 1 | 8 | 0 |

### Group 4

USSR 3, North Korea 0
Italy 2, Chile 0
Chile 1, North Korea 1
USSR 1, Italy 0
North Korea 1, Italy 0
USSR 2, Chile 1

|  | P | W | D | L | F | A | Pts |
|---|---|---|---|---|---|---|---|
| USSR | 3 | 3 | 0 | 0 | 6 | 1 | 6 |
| North Korea | 3 | 1 | 1 | 1 | 2 | 4 | 3 |
| Italy | 3 | 1 | 0 | 2 | 2 | 2 | 2 |
| Chile | 3 | 0 | 1 | 2 | 2 | 5 | 1 |

## Quarter-Finals

England 1, Argentina 0
West Germany 4, Uruguay 0
Portugal 5, North Korea 3
USSR 2, Hungary 1

## Semi-Finals

West Germany 2, USSR 1 (at Goodison Park)
England 2, Portugal 1 (at Wembley)

**Third Place Match** (Wembley)

Portugal 2, USSR 1

**Final** (Wembley, 30 July, 1966)

England (1) (2) 4, West Germany (1) (2) 2 aet

*England:* Banks; Cohen, Wilson; Stiles, Charlton J., Moore; Ball, Hurst, Hunt, Charlton R., Peters.

*West Germany:* Tilkowski; Hottges, Schulz, Weber, Schnellinger; Haller, Beckenbauer; Overath, Seeler, Held, Emmerich.

*Scorers:* Hurst 3, Peters for England; Haller, Weber for West Germany.

*Leading Scorer:* Eusebio (Portugal) 9.

# MEXICO 1970

### Group A

Mexico 0, USSR 0
Belgium 3, El Salvador 0
USSR 4, Belgium 1
Mexico 4, El Salvador 0
USSR 2, El Salvador 0
Belgium 0, Mexico 1

|  | P | W | D | L | F | A | Pts |
|---|---|---|---|---|---|---|---|
| USSR | 3 | 2 | 1 | 0 | 6 | 1 | 5 |
| Mexico | 3 | 2 | 1 | 0 | 5 | 0 | 5 |
| Belgium | 3 | 1 | 0 | 2 | 4 | 5 | 2 |
| El Salvador | 3 | 0 | 0 | 3 | 0 | 9 | 0 |

### Group B

Uruguay 2, Israel 0
Italy 1, Sweden 0
Uruguay 0, Italy 0
Israel 1, Sweden 1
Sweden 1, Uruguay 0
Israel 0, Italy 0

|  | P | W | D | L | F | A | Pts |
|---|---|---|---|---|---|---|---|
| Italy | 3 | 1 | 2 | 0 | 1 | 0 | 4 |
| Uruguay | 3 | 1 | 1 | 1 | 2 | 1 | 3 |
| Sweden | 3 | 1 | 1 | 1 | 2 | 2 | 3 |
| Israel | 3 | 0 | 2 | 1 | 1 | 3 | 2 |

### Group C

England 1, Rumania 0
Brazil 4, Czechoslovakia 1
Rumania 2, Czechoslovakia 1
Brazil 1, England 0
Brazil 3, Rumania 2
England 1, Czechoslovakia 0

|  | P | W | D | L | F | A | Pts |
|---|---|---|---|---|---|---|---|
| Brazil | 3 | 3 | 0 | 0 | 8 | 3 | 6 |
| England | 3 | 2 | 0 | 1 | 2 | 1 | 4 |
| Rumania | 3 | 1 | 0 | 2 | 4 | 5 | 2 |
| Czechoslovakia | 3 | 0 | 0 | 3 | 2 | 7 | 0 |

## Group D

Peru 3, Bulgaria 2
West Germany 2, Morocco 1
Peru 3, Morocco 0
West Germany 5, Bulgaria 2
West Germany 3, Peru 1
Bulgaria 1, Morocco 1

|  | P | W | D | L | F | A | Pts |
|---|---|---|---|---|---|---|---|
| West Germany | 3 | 3 | 0 | 0 | 10 | 4 | 6 |
| Peru | 3 | 2 | 0 | 1 | 7 | 5 | 4 |
| Bulgaria | 3 | 0 | 1 | 2 | 5 | 9 | 1 |
| Morocco | 3 | 0 | 1 | 2 | 2 | 6 | 1 |

### Quarter-Finals

Uruguay 1, USSR 0
Italy 4, Mexico 1
Brazil 4, Peru 2
West Germany 3, England 2

### Semi-Finals

Italy 4, West Germany 3 (in Mexico City)
Brazil 3, Uruguay 1 (in Guadalajara)

### Third Place Match (Mexico City)

West Germany 1, Uruguay 0

### Final (Mexico City, 21 June, 1970)

Brazil (1) 4, Italy (1) 1

*Brazil:* Felix; Carlos Alberto, Brito, Piazza, Everaldo; Gerson, Clodoaldo; Jairzinho, Pelé, Tostão, Rivelino.

*Italy:* Albertosi; Burgnich, Cera, Rosato, Facchetti; Bertini (Juliano), Riva; Domenghini, Mazzola, De Sisti, Boninsegna (Rivera).

*Scorers:* Pelé, Gerson, Jairzinho, Carlos Alberto for Brazil; Boninsegna for Italy.

*Leading Scorer:* Müller (West Germany) 10.

# WEST GERMANY 1974

## Group 1

West Germany 1, Chile 0
East Germany 2, Australia 0
West Germany 3, Australia 0
East Germany 1, Chile 1
East Germany 1, West Germany 0
Chile 0, Australia 0

|  | P | W | D | L | F | A | Pts |
|---|---|---|---|---|---|---|---|
| East Germany | 3 | 2 | 1 | 0 | 4 | 1 | 5 |
| West Germany | 3 | 2 | 0 | 1 | 4 | 1 | 4 |
| Chile | 3 | 0 | 2 | 1 | 1 | 2 | 2 |
| Australia | 3 | 0 | 1 | 2 | 0 | 5 | 1 |

## Group 2

Brazil 0, Yugoslavia 0
Scotland 2, Zaire 0
Brazil 0, Scotland 0
Yugoslavia 9, Zaire 0
Scotland 1, Yugoslavia 1
Brazil 3, Zaire 0

|  | P | W | D | L | F | A | Pts |
|---|---|---|---|---|---|---|---|
| Yugoslavia | 3 | 1 | 2 | 0 | 10 | 1 | 4 |
| Brazil | 3 | 1 | 2 | 0 | 3 | 0 | 4 |
| Scotland | 3 | 1 | 2 | 0 | 3 | 1 | 4 |
| Zaire | 3 | 0 | 0 | 3 | 0 | 14 | 0 |

## Group 3

Holland 2, Uruguay 0
Sweden 0, Bulgaria 0
Holland 0, Sweden 0
Bulgaria 1, Uruguay 1
Holland 4, Bulgaria 1
Sweden 3, Uruguay 0

|  | P | W | D | L | F | A | Pts |
|---|---|---|---|---|---|---|---|
| Holland | 3 | 2 | 1 | 0 | 6 | 1 | 5 |
| Sweden | 3 | 1 | 2 | 0 | 3 | 0 | 4 |
| Bulgaria | 3 | 0 | 2 | 1 | 2 | 5 | 2 |
| Uruguay | 3 | 0 | 1 | 2 | 1 | 6 | 1 |

## Group 4

Italy 3, Haiti 1
Poland 3, Argentina 2
Argentina 1, Italy 1
Poland 7, Haiti 0
Argentina 4, Haiti 1
Poland 2, Italy 1

|  | P | W | D | L | F | A | Pts |
|---|---|---|---|---|---|---|---|
| Poland | 3 | 3 | 0 | 0 | 12 | 3 | 6 |
| Argentina | 3 | 1 | 1 | 1 | 7 | 5 | 3 |
| Italy | 3 | 1 | 1 | 1 | 5 | 4 | 3 |
| Haiti | 3 | 0 | 0 | 3 | 2 | 14 | 0 |

## Group A

Brazil 1, East Germany 0
Holland 4, Argentina 0
Holland 2, East Germany 0
Brazil 2, Argentina 1
Holland 2, Brazil 0
Argentina 1, East Germany 1

|  | P | W | D | L | F | A | Pts |
|---|---|---|---|---|---|---|---|
| Holland | 3 | 3 | 0 | 0 | 8 | 0 | 6 |
| Brazil | 3 | 2 | 0 | 1 | 3 | 3 | 4 |
| East Germany | 3 | 0 | 1 | 2 | 1 | 4 | 1 |
| Argentina | 3 | 0 | 1 | 2 | 2 | 7 | 1 |

## Group B

Poland 1, Sweden 0
West Germany 2, Yugoslavia 0
Poland 2, Yugoslavia 1
West Germany 4, Sweden 2
Sweden 2, Yugoslavia 1
West Germany 1, Poland 0

|  | P | W | D | L | F | A | Pts |
|---|---|---|---|---|---|---|---|
| West Germany | 3 | 3 | 0 | 0 | 7 | 2 | 6 |
| Poland | 3 | 2 | 0 | 1 | 3 | 2 | 4 |
| Sweden | 3 | 1 | 0 | 2 | 4 | 6 | 2 |
| Yugoslavia | 3 | 0 | 0 | 3 | 2 | 6 | 0 |

### Third Place Match (Munich)

Poland 1, Brazil 0

### Final (Munich, 7 July, 1974)

West Germany (2) 2, Holland (1) 1

*West Germany:* Maier; Vogts, Schwarzenbeck, Beckenbauer, Breitner, Bonhof, Hoeness, Overath, Grabowski, Müller, Holzenbein.

*Holland:* Jongbloed; Suurbier, Rijsbergen (De Jong), Haan, Krol, Jansen, Van Hanegem, Neeskens, Rep, Cruyff, Rensenbrink (Van der Kerkhof R).

*Scorers:* Breitner (*pen*), Müller for West Germany; Neeskens (*pen*) for Holland.

*Leading Scorer:* Lato (Poland) 7.

# ARGENTINA 1978

|        | P | W | D | L | F | A | Pts |
|--------|---|---|---|---|---|---|-----|
| Peru     | 3 | 2 | 1 | 0 | 7 | 2 | 5 |
| Holland  | 3 | 1 | 1 | 1 | 5 | 3 | 3 |
| Scotland | 3 | 1 | 1 | 1 | 5 | 6 | 3 |
| Iran     | 3 | 0 | 1 | 2 | 2 | 8 | 1 |

## Group 1

Italy 2, France 1
Argentina 2, Hungary 1
Italy 3, Hungary 1
Argentina 2, France 1
France 3, Hungary 1
Italy 1, Argentina 0

|           | P | W | D | L | F | A | Pts |
|-----------|---|---|---|---|---|---|-----|
| Italy     | 3 | 3 | 0 | 0 | 6 | 2 | 6 |
| Argentina | 3 | 2 | 0 | 1 | 4 | 3 | 4 |
| France    | 3 | 1 | 0 | 2 | 5 | 5 | 2 |
| Hungary   | 3 | 0 | 0 | 3 | 3 | 8 | 0 |

## Group 2

West Germany 0, Poland 0
Tunisia 3, Mexico 1
Poland 1, Tunisia 0
West Germany 6, Mexico 0
Poland 3, Mexico 1
West Germany 0, Tunisia 0

|              | P | W | D | L | F | A  | Pts |
|--------------|---|---|---|---|---|----|-----|
| Poland       | 3 | 2 | 1 | 0 | 4 | 1  | 5 |
| West Germany | 3 | 1 | 2 | 0 | 6 | 0  | 4 |
| Tunisia      | 3 | 1 | 1 | 1 | 3 | 2  | 3 |
| Mexico       | 3 | 0 | 0 | 3 | 2 | 12 | 0 |

## Group 3

Austria 2, Spain 1
Brazil 1, Sweden 1
Austria 1, Sweden 0
Brazil 0, Spain 0
Spain 1, Sweden 0
Brazil 1, Austria 0

|         | P | W | D | L | F | A | Pts |
|---------|---|---|---|---|---|---|-----|
| Austria | 3 | 2 | 0 | 1 | 3 | 2 | 4 |
| Brazil  | 3 | 1 | 2 | 0 | 2 | 1 | 4 |
| Spain   | 3 | 1 | 1 | 1 | 2 | 2 | 3 |
| Sweden  | 3 | 0 | 1 | 2 | 1 | 3 | 1 |

## Group 4

Peru 3, Scotland 1
Holland 3, Iran 0
Scotland 1, Iran 1
Holland 0, Peru 0
Peru 4, Iran 1
Scotland 3, Holland 2

## Group A

West Germany 0, Italy 0
Holland 5, Austria 1
Italy 1, Austria 0
Holland 2, West Germany 2
Holland 2, Italy 1
Austria 3, West Germany 2

|              | P | W | D | L | F | A | Pts |
|--------------|---|---|---|---|---|---|-----|
| Holland      | 3 | 2 | 1 | 0 | 9 | 4 | 5 |
| Italy        | 3 | 1 | 1 | 1 | 2 | 2 | 3 |
| West Germany | 3 | 0 | 2 | 1 | 4 | 5 | 2 |
| Austria      | 3 | 1 | 0 | 2 | 4 | 8 | 2 |

## Group B

Brazil 3, Peru 0
Argentina 2, Poland 0
Poland 1, Peru 0
Argentina 0, Brazil 0
Brazil 3, Poland 1
Argentina 6, Peru 0

|           | P | W | D | L | F | A  | Pts |
|-----------|---|---|---|---|---|----|-----|
| Argentina | 3 | 2 | 1 | 0 | 8 | 0  | 5 |
| Brazil    | 3 | 2 | 1 | 0 | 6 | 1  | 5 |
| Poland    | 3 | 1 | 0 | 2 | 2 | 5  | 2 |
| Peru      | 3 | 0 | 0 | 3 | 0 | 10 | 0 |

## Third Place Match (Buenos Aires)

Brazil 2, Italy 1

## Final (Buenos Aires, 25 June, 1978)

Argentina (1) (1) 3, Holland (0) (1) 1 aet

*Argentina:* Fillol; Passarella, Olquin, Galvan L., Tarantini, Ardiles (Larrosa), Gallego, Ortiz (Houseman), Bertoni, Luque, Kempes.

*Holland:* Jongbloed; Krol, Poortvliet, Brandts, Jansen (Suurbier), Haan, Neeskens, Van der Kerkhof W., Rep (Nanninga), Van der Kerkhof R., Resenbrink.

*Scorers:* Kempes 2, Bertoni for Argentina; Nanninga for Holland.

*Leading Scorer:* Kempes (Argentina) 6.

# GOALSCORING AND ATTENDANCES IN WORLD CUP FINAL ROUNDS

|                      | Matches | Goals (avge) | Attendance (avge)    |
|----------------------|---------|--------------|----------------------|
| 1930, Uruguay        | 18      | 70 (3.8)     | 434,500 (24,138)     |
| 1934, Italy          | 17      | 70 (4.1)     | 395,000 (23,235)     |
| 1938, France         | 18      | 84 (4.6)     | 483,000 (26,833)     |
| 1950, Brazil         | 22      | 88 (4.0)     | 1,337,000 (60,772)   |
| 1954, Switzerland    | 26      | 140 (5.3)    | 943,000 (36,270)     |
| 1958, Sweden         | 35      | 126 (3.6)    | 868,000 (24,800)     |
| 1962, Chile          | 32      | 89 (2.7)     | 776,000 (24,250)     |
| 1966, England        | 32      | 89 (2.7)     | 1,614,677 (50,458)   |
| 1970, Mexico         | 32      | 95 (2.9)     | 1,673,975 (52,311)   |
| 1974, West Germany   | 38      | 97 (2.5)     | 1,774,022 (46,684)   |
| 1978, Argentina      | 38      | 102 (2.6)    | 1,610,215 (42,374)   |
| 1982, Spain          | 52      | 146 (2.8)    | 1,766,277 (33,967)   |

# WORLD CUP 1982

Italy deservedly won the 1982 World Cup, and if there were reservations about their overall performance in Spain, there was no denying that they were the most improved team over the tournament. Even by their own standards their record in the opening group matches was abysmally negative. They failed to win a match, drawing all three of their games – as did the modest Cameroon, who retired undefeated from the fray – and progressed to the next stage by virtue of their superior goalscoring: two goals to Cameroon's one!

Paolo Rossi, the prodigal son of Italy, returned from a two-year suspension after the bribes scandal, struggled to find his form in those early encounters, but became transformed in the second round to finish as the tournament's leading goalscorer with six goals.

The Italians physically dealt with the holders, Argentina, in the first half, then beat them fairly and squarely after the break. Not content with that, they three times took the lead against Brazil, which was once too often for the South Americans, who had been the outstanding team both for the quality of their football and for entertainment value. Indeed, the contrast in styles of this match provided the second-most memorable encounter of the World Cup, the top game unquestionably being the pulsating, end to end semi-final between West Germany and France. All square at 3-3 after extra-time, the emotionally and physically drained players were called upon to settle the matter by penalty kicks. It was the first time that this unsatisfactory system had been used in the World Cup, but sadly, in a competition covering 52 games, there was no margin for a play-off.

The Germans, two down at one stage, in fact salvaged part of their reputation against the French, who were only slightly inferior to Brazil in terms of attractiveness. However, there were less savoury aspects of German play. Humiliated by one of the outsiders, Algeria, the Germans gave a miserly display on other occasions. They descended to the feigning of injury which oddly enough helped them reach the 1966 final against England, and a blatant foul on French substitute Patrick Battiston by goalkeeper Harald Schumacher at a crucial moment disrupted the French rhythm and yet went unpunished. Just as disturbing was the furore caused by the apparent arrangement between the Germans and Austria which prevented Algeria from going into the second round.

The Germans could claim that Karl-Heinz Rummenigge, easily their most gifted player, was handicapped throughout by injury. Indeed, he seemed to be either coming on or going off late to preserve his fitness. Yet the Italians were hit more seriously, in the final alone having to start without Giancarlo Antognoni and losing Francesco Graziani in the early stages.

Italy's success was a triumph for manager Enzo Bearzot, whose endeavours to unfetter his international players from the strictures of Italian domestic football had invariably foundered in the past. This time they were technically right, professional and clinical in their finishing. Another to savour the fruits of success after many campaigns was their goalkeeper and captain Dino Zoff, at 40 the oldest player in the finals. His display against Brazil belied both his years and ageing reflexes.

The youngest player of the tournament was 17-year-old Norman Whiteside of a Northern Ireland side who were one of few teams to play above themselves. They reached a peak against their dismally disappointing Spanish hosts, beating them 1-0 despite having to play for the greater part of the second half with 10 men following the sending-off of Mal Donaghy. Yet their defence never once faltered or allowed itself to be drawn into rash tackles that would inevitably have led to howls for a Spanish penalty. Such fears were understandable, for two of Spain's three previous goals had come from the spot.

The refereeing was of no greater standard than the play overall, and, despite the increase in goalscoring, this was in many respects the most unenterprising World Cup of all time. Forwards were scarce; those of above-average ability were almost non-existent. Rossi was one of the few successful orthodox leaders. Most teams packed the midfield, but whereas those like Brazil and France used the midfield as a springboard to attack from all angles, too many others relied on the mistakes of the opposition to goad them on to the offensive.

England could rightly claim to have been forced out of the competition by the vagaries of its system, for they remained unbeaten. However, just how much of the euphoria which surrounded their performances was borne of Bryan Robson scoring after 27 seconds of the first game and of catching the French on their worst day is debatable. For the Scots, in a difficult group, defensive errors proved costly when they had revealed imagination and skill in combating sides of differing quality in Brazil and the rather over-rated USSR.

The minnows certainly enlivened Spain. Honduras, Algeria and even Kuwait had their moments. New Zealand played better than their results suggest, and El Salvador shored up their defence after conceding 10 goals to Hungary.

Generally, though, the Eastern Europeans were dreadfully dull and stereotyped, especially Yugoslavia and Czechoslovakia. Poland, for whom Grzegorz Lato equalled Kazimierz Deyna's 102 caps, operated fitfully, despite their third place.

Few of the top stars enhanced their reputations. Diego Maradona, in spite of his multi-million pound rating, was a big disappointment, as indeed was the Argentine side generally. Chile and Peru failed to excite, and even the admirable Brazilians would have been better rewarded with more accomplished performers at centre-forward and in goal.

France, with Marius Tresor, Michel Platini, Jean Tigana and Alain Giresse outstanding; Zico, Falcao, Socrates and Junior memorable for Brazil; Rossi, Bruno Conti and Gaetano Scirea in the blue of Italy; these were among those to be affectionately recalled. But there were many others who faded into obscurity – as did some 50 matches, including the final.

# QUALIFYING COMPETITION

## EUROPE

### GROUP 1
West Germany, Austria, Bulgaria, Finland, Albania

**Helsinki, 4 June, 1980**

**Finland (0) 0**

**Bulgaria (1) 2** *(Markov, Kostadinov)*     7800

*Finland:* Sairanen (Nurmio); Lampi, Tolsa, Houtsonen, Ranta, Ronkainen (Ismail), Pyykko, Toivola, Rautianen, Hakala, Nieminen.
*Bulgaria:* Christov; Zafirov, Kolev, Maldjanski, Karakolev, Dimitrov G., Kostadinov, Markov (Tsvetkov P.), Jeliazkov, Kostov, Tsvetkov C. (Iliev).

**Tirana, 3 September, 1980**

**Albania (2) 2** *(Braho, Baci)*

**Finland (0) 0**     30,000

*Albania:* Kaci; Baci, Hysi, Turgaj, Berisha, Ragami, Zeri, Lleshi, Marko, Minga, Braho.
*Finland:* Isoaho; Lahtinen, Helin (Rajaniemi), Tolsa, Ahonen, Pyykko, Dahllund, Virtanen, Pulliainen (Turunen), Himanka, Hakala.

**Helsinki, 24 September, 1980**

**Finland (0) 0**

**Austria (1) 2** *(Jara, Welzl)*     8099

*Finland:* Isoaho; Lahtinen, Tolsa, Houtsonen, Ranta, Virtanen, Pyykko, Dahllund, Ronkainen (Turunen), Tissari, Rajaniemi (Jakosaari).
*Austria:* Koncilia; Obermayer, Pregesbauer, Pezzey, Zuenelli, Wartinger (Welzl), Hattenberger, Prohaska, Jara, Schachner, Krankl.

**Sofia, 19 October, 1980**

**Bulgaria (1) 2** *(Jeliazkov, Slavkov)*

**Albania (0) 1** *(Pernaska)*     20,000

*Bulgaria:* Christov; Zafirov, Dimitrov B., Maldjanski, Blangev, Slavkov, Markov (Iliev), Kerimov, Dimitrov G., Kostadinov, Jeliazkov.
*Albania:* Kaci; Baci, Hysi, Turgaj, Berisha, Cipi, Ballgjini H., Lleshi (Bajazidi), Zeri, Pernaska, Braho.

**Vienna, 15 November, 1980**

**Austria (3) 5** *(Pezzey, Schachner 2, Welzl, Krankl)*

**Albania (0) 0**     30,000

*Austria:* Feurer; Dihanich, Obermayer, Pezzey, Mirnegg, Prohaska, Hattenberger, Jara, Welzl, Krankl, Schachner (Keglevits).
*Albania:* Kaci; Baci, Berisha, Hysi, Targaj, Cipi, Ballgjini H., Pernaska, Lleshi, Braho (Bregu), Bajazidi.

**Sofia, 3 December, 1980**

**Bulgaria (0) 1** *(Yonchev)*

**West Germany (2) 3** *(Kaltz 2* [1 pen],
*Rummenigge)*     45,000

*Bulgaria:* Christov; Dimitrov G. (Slavkov), Zafirov, Rangelov, Vassilev, Iliev, Markov, Jeliazkov, Zdravkov (Kerimov), Djevizov, Yonchev.
*West Germany:* Schumacher; Kaltz, Stielike, Forster K. H., Dietz, Briegel, Magath (Votava), Muller H., Allofs K. (Borchers), Hrubesch, Rummenigge.

**Tirana, 6 December, 1980**

**Albania (0) 0**

**Austria (1) 1** *(Welzl)*     30,000

*Albania:* Kaci; Baci, Hysi, Berisha, Targaj, Ragami, Zeri, Lleshi, Marko (Lame), Pernaska, Braho (Kola).
*Austria:* Feurer; Weber, Obermayer, Pezzey, Mirnegg, Hattenberger, Prohaska, Jara, Welzl, Gasselich (Baumeister), Schachner (Jurtin).

**Tirana, 1 April, 1981**

**Albania (0) 0**

**West Germany (1) 2** *(Schuster 2)*     30,000

*Albania:* Kaci; Targaj, Berisha, Hysi, Cocoli, Xhafa, Lame, Ballgjini H. (Baci), Pernaska, Minga, Lleshi.
*West Germany:* Schumacher; Kaltz, Stielike, Forster K. H. (Hannes), Dietz, Magath, Schuster, Muller H., Allofs K., Rummenigge, Hrubesch.

**Hamburg, 29 April, 1981**

**West Germany (2) 2** *(Krauss og, Fischer)*

**Austria (0) 0**     60,000

*West Germany:* Schumacher; Kaltz, Stielike, Forster K. H., Briegel, Schuster, Magath, Breitner, Muller H., Rummenigge, Fischer (Allgower).
*Austria:* Koncilia; Krauss, Obermayer, Pezzey, Mirnegg, Hattenberger (Weber), Prohaska, Hintermaier (Baumeister), Jara, Krankl, Welzl.

**Sofia, 13 May, 1981**

**Bulgaria (1) 4** *(Slavkov 2, Kostadinov, Tsvetkov C.)*

**Finland (0) 0**     10,000

*Bulgaria:* Velinov; Vassilev, Balevski, Bonev, Dimitrov G., Grigorov, Tsvetkov P. (Yonchev), Slavkov (Zdravkov), Kostadinov, Jeliazkov, Tsvetkov C.
*Finland:* Isoaho; Lahtinen, Tolsa, Vaittainen, Pekonen (Bergqvist), Houtsonen, Dahllund (Jakosaari), Ikalainen, Pyykko, Ismail, Valvee.

**Lahti, 24 May, 1981**

**Finland (0) 0**

**West Germany (3) 4** *(Briegel, Fischer 2, Kaltz)*     10,000

*Finland:* Isoaho; Houtsonen, Tolsa (Helin), Vaittinen, Lahtinen, Kupiainen, Ikalainen, Virtanen, Pyykko, Kousa, Valvee (Ismail).
*West Germany:* Schumacher; Kaltz, Hannes, Forster K. H., Briegel, Dremmler, Breitner, Magath (Borchers), Muller H. (Allgower), Rummenigge, Fischer.

**Vienna, 28 May, 1981**

**Austria (1) 2** *(Krankl pen, Jara)*

**Bulgaria (0) 0**     60,000

*Austria:* Feurer; Dihanich, Weber, Pezzey, Mirnegg, Prohaska, Hattenberger, Jara, Welzl, Krankl, Keglevits (Schachner).
*Bulgaria:* Christov; Sabatinov, Balevski, Maldjanski, Vassilev, Zdravkov (Kostadinov), Dimitrov G., Jeliazkov, Grigorov (Markov), Slavkov, Tsvetkov C.

**Linz, 17 June, 1981**

**Austria (3) 5** *(Prohaska 2, Krankl, Welzl, Jurtin)*

**Finland (0) 1** *(Valvee)*     27,500

*Austria:* Feurer; Dihanich, Pezzey, Weber, Mirnegg, Hattenberger, Prohaska (Kreuz), Jara, Welzl (Schachner), Krankl, Jurtin.
*Finland:* Huttunen; Helin, Lahtinen, Vaittinen, Houtsonen, Ikalainen, Virtanen, Kousa (Rajaniemi), Turunen, Dahllund, Valvee.

**Kotka, 2 September, 1981**

**Finland (0) 2** *(Houtsonen, Kousa)*

**Albania (0) 1** *(Targaj pen)*     6830

*Finland:* Isoaho; Lahtinen, Dahllund, Vaittinen, Pekonen, Turunen, Houtsonen, Pyykko (Ronkainen), Utrainen, Kousa, Jakosaari.
*Albania:* Musta; Targaj, Hysi, Cocoli, Berisha, Lleshi, Pernaska (Minga), Lame, Luci (Ragami), Ballgjini H., Ballgjini S.

**Bochum, 23 September, 1981**

**West Germany (2) 7** *(Fischer, Rummenigge 3, Breitner 2, Dremmler)*

**Finland (1) 1** *(Turunen)* 45,000

*West Germany:* Schumacher; Kaltz, Stielike, Forster B., Briegel, Dremmler, Magath, Breitner, Borchers, Fischer, Rummenigge.
*Finland:* Isoaho; Pekonen, Dahllund, Lahtinen, Turunen, Houtsonen, Ikalainen (Ronkainen), Pyykko, Kousa, Utrainen, Jakosaari (Nieminen).

**Tirana, 14 October, 1981**

**Albania (0) 0**

**Bulgaria (0) 2** *(Slavkov, Mladenov)* 30,000

*Albania:* Musta; Baci, Cocoli, Targaj, Berisha, Ragami, Minga, Lame, Zeri (Seiti), Ballgjini S., Kola.
*Bulgaria:* Velinov; Nikolov, Balevski, Blangev, Dimitrov G., Lubomirov, Slavkov, Tsvetkov P. (Markov), Jeliazkov (Sabotinov), Kostadinov, Mladenov.

**Vienna, 14 October, 1981**

**Austria (1) 1** *(Schachner)*

**West Germany (2) 3** *(Littbarski 2, Magath)* 70,000

*Austria:* Koncilia; Dihanich, Weber, Pezzey, Mirnegg, Prohaska, Hintermaier (Hagmayr), Hattenberger, Jara, Krankl, Schachner.
*West Germany:* Schumacher; Kaltz, Forster K. H., Stielike, Briegel, Dremmler, Breitner, Magath, Littbarski, Fischer, Rummenigge.

**Sofia, 11 November, 1981**

**Bulgaria (0) 0**

**Austria (0) 0** 30,000

*Bulgaria:* Velinov; Nikolov, Balevski, Dimitrov G., Blangev, Slavkov (Yonchev), Lubomirov, Jeliazkov (Markov), Kostadinov, Mladenov, Tsvetkov C.
*Austria:* Feurer; Krauss, Pezzey, Weber, Mirnegg (Dihanich), Hattenberger, Prohaska, Jara, Hintermaier, Schachner, Krankl (Hagmayr).

**Dortmund, 18 November, 1981**

**West Germany (5) 8** *(Rummenigge 3, Fischer 2, Kaltz, Littbarski, Breitner pen)*

**Albania (0) 0** 45,000

*West Germany:* Immel; Kaltz (Matthaus), Briegel, Dremmler, Forster K. H., Stielike, Littbarski, Breitner, Fischer, Magath, Rummenigge (Milewski).
*Albania:* Musta (Lurasi); Targaj, Berisha, Kola, Lleshi, Ragami, Ballgjini H., Braho, Popantuci, Hysi, Luci.

**Düsseldorf, 22 November, 1981**

**West Germany (1) 4** *(Fischer, Rummenigge 2, Kaltz pen)*

**Bulgaria (0) 0** 55,000

*West Germany:* Schumacher; Kaltz, Forster K. H., Hannes, Briegel, Dremmler, Breitner, Magath (Allofs K.), Rummenigge, Hrubesch, Fischer.
*Bulgaria:* Velinov; Balevski, Nikolov, Dimitrov G., Bonev, Iliev, Kostadinov, Markov (Lubomirov), Zdravkov, Yonchev, Mladenov.

|  | P | W | D | L | F | A | Pts |
|---|---|---|---|---|---|---|---|
| West Germany | 8 | 8 | 0 | 0 | 33 | 3 | 16 |
| Austria | 8 | 5 | 1 | 2 | 16 | 6 | 11 |
| Bulgaria | 8 | 4 | 1 | 3 | 11 | 10 | 9 |
| Albania | 8 | 1 | 0 | 7 | 4 | 22 | 2 |
| Finland | 8 | 1 | 0 | 7 | 4 | 27 | 2 |

**GROUP 2**
*Netherlands, France, Belgium, Eire, Cyprus*

**Nicosia, 26 March, 1980**

**Cyprus (1) 2** *(Pantzarias, Kaiafas pen)*

**Eire (3) 3** *(McGee 2, Lawrenson)* 10,000

*Cyprus:* Stylianou; Papakostas, Neofitou, Papadopoulos, Lysandrou, Pantzarias N., Demetriou (Tsingis), Mavroudis, Kaiafas, Kissonergis, Kanaris (Theofanos).
*Eire:* Peyton; Grealish, Grimes, Lawrenson, O'Leary D., Brady, Daly, Murphy (O'Brien F.), Heighway (Ryan), Stapleton, McGee.

**Dublin, 10 September, 1980**

**Eire (0) 2** *(Daly, Lawrenson)*

**Netherlands (0) 1** *(Tahamata)* 32,000

*Eire:* Peyton; Langan, O'Leary D., O'Leary P., Hughton, Lawrenson, Daly, Grealish, Brady, Stapleton, Givens.
*Netherlands:* Hiele; Wijnstekers, Spelbos, Van de Korput (Metgod), Brandts, Thijssen, Schoenaker (Van de Kerkhov W.), Peters, Van Deinsen, Van Mierlo, Tahamata.

**Limassol, 11 October, 1980**

**Cyprus (0) 0**

**France (4) 7** *(Lacombe, Platini 2, Larios 2 [2 pens], Six, Zimako)* 15,000

*Cyprus:* Pantzarias G.; Papakostas, Kizas, Erotokritou, Papadopoulos, Pantzarias N., Tsingis (Lysandrou), Omirou, Kaiafas (Theofanos), Mavroudis, Kissonergis.
*France:* Dropsy; Battiston, Bossis, Specht, Michel, Larios, Baronchelli (Zimako), Tigana (Petit), Lacombe, Platini, Six.

**Dublin, 15 October, 1980**

**Eire (1) 1** *(Grealish)*

**Belgium (1) 1** *(Cluytens)* 40,000

*Eire:* Peyton; Langan, Moran, Lawrenson, Hughton, Brady, Daly, Grealish, Stapleton, Heighway, Givens (McGee).
*Belgium:* Pfaff; Gerets, Millecamps L. (De Wolf), Meeuws, Renquin, Cluytens, Vandereycken, Van Moer (Heyligen), Van den Bergh, Coeck, Ceulemans.

**Paris, 28 October, 1980**

**France (1) 2** *(Platini, Zimako)*

**Eire (0) 0** 46,300

*France:* Dropsy; Battiston, Specht, Lopez, Bossis, Larios, Tigana, Platini (Petit), Rocheteau, Lacombe (Zimako), Six.
*Eire:* Peyton; Langan, Lawrenson, Moran, Hughton, Martin (Ryan), Brady, Grealish, Heighway, Stapleton, Robinson.

**Brussels, 19 November, 1980**

**Belgium (0) 1** *(Van den Bergh pen)*

**Netherlands (0) 0** 60,000

*Belgium:* Pfaff; Gerets, Millecamps L., Meeuws, Renquin, Coeck, Vandereycken, Van Moer, Cluytens, Van den Bergh, Ceulemans.
*Netherlands:* Doesburg; Wijnstekers (Metgod), Krol, Brandts, Hovenkamp, Van de Korput, Van de Kerkhof W., Peters, Kist, Tol (Van de Kerkhof R.), Tahamata.

**Dublin, 19 November, 1980**

**Eire (4) 6** *(Daly 2 [1 pen], Grealish, Robinson, Stapleton, Hughton)*

**Cyprus (0) 0** 25,000

*Eire:* Peyton; Langan, Hughton, Lawrenson, Moran, Daly, Grealish, Brady, Stapleton, Heighway, Robinson (Givens).
*Cyprus:* Konstantinou; Kalotheou, Louka, Lysandrou, Pantzarias N., Erotokritou, Theofanos, Yiagudakis, Kaiafas (Laetios), Tsingis, Miamialitis A. (Mavroudis).

**Nicosia, 20 December, 1980**

Cyprus (0) 0

Belgium (1) 2 *(Van den Bergh, Ceulemans)*  10,000

*Cyprus:* Konstantinou; Louka, Erotokritou, Pantzarias N., Lysandrou, Kalotheou, Yiagudakis, Tsingis, Theofanos, Kaiafas, Mavroudis.
*Belgium:* Pfaff; Gerets, Millecamps L., Meeuws, De Wolf, Van Moer, Vandereycken, Coeck, Cluytens, Van den Bergh, Ceulemans.


**Brussels, 18 February, 1981**

Belgium (2) 3 *(Plessers, Van den Bergh, Ceulemans)*

Cyprus (1) 2 *(Lysandrou, Vrahimis)*  20,000

*Belgium:* Pfaff; Gerets, Coeck, Renquin, Plessers (Vercauteren), Cluytens (Voordeckers), Vandereycken, Mommens, Wellens, Van den Bergh, Ceulemans.
*Cyprus:* Konstantinou; Louka, Toumazou, Erotokritou, Lysandrou, Demetriou, Miamialitis A., Pantzarias N., Vrahimis, Yiagudakis, Theofanos (Kyriatou).


**Groningen, 22 February, 1981**

Netherlands (1) 3 *(Hovenkamp, Schapendonck, Nanninga)*

Cyprus (0) 0  17,500

*Netherlands:* Doesburg; Zondervan, Metgod, Spelbos, Hovenkamp, Arntz (Nanninga), Peters, Thijssen, Jonker, Schapendonck, Tol (Vermeulen).
*Cyprus:* Konstantinou; Louka, Erotokritou, Lysandrou, Toumazou, Demetriou, Miamialitis A. (Tsingis), Pantzarias N., Vrahimis (Lakos), Theofanos, Yiagudakis.


**Brussels, 25 March, 1981**

Belgium (0) 1 *(Ceulemans)*

Eire (0) 0  46,000

*Belgium:* Preud'homme; Gerets, Millecamps L., Meeuws, Renquin, Mommens (Vercauteren), Vandereycken, Coeck (Wellens), Cluytens, Van den Bergh, Ceulemans.
*Eire:* McDonagh; Langan, Martin, Moran, Hughton, Daly, Grealish, Brady, Robinson, Stapleton (Walsh), Heighway.


**Rotterdam, 25 March, 1981**

Netherlands (0) 1 *(Muhren)*

France (0) 0  65,000

*Netherlands:* Schrijvers; Poortvliet, Krol, Ophof, Hovenkamp (La Ling), Van de Kerkhof W., Thijssen, Muhren, Peters (Stevens), Van de Kerkhof R., Rep.
*France:* Dropsy; Janvion, Lopez, Specht, Bossis, Moizan (Christophe), Larios, Giresse, Rocheteau, Lacombe (Zimako), Six.


**Paris, 29 April, 1981**

France (3) 3 *(Soler 2, Six)*

Belgium (1) 2 *(Van den Bergh, Ceulemans)*  44,594

*France:* Dropsy; Janvion, Tresor, Lopez, Bossis, Tigana, Giresse, Genghini, Soler (Zimako), Rocheteau, Six.
*Belgium:* Preud'homme; Gerets, Millecamps L. (De Wolf), Meeuws, Renquin, Vercauteren (Verheyen), Vandereycken, Van Moer, Cluytens, Van den Bergh, Ceulemans.


**Nicosia, 29 April, 1981**

Cyprus (0) 0

Netherlands (1) 1 *(Van Kooten)*  7500

*Cyprus:* Pantzarias G.; Louka, Kalotheou, Papadopoulos, Erotokritou, Pantzarias N., Kunas (Theofanos) (Lakos), Demetriou, Vrahimis, Yiagudakis, Mavroudis.
*Netherlands:* Schrijvers; Wijnstekers, Stevens, Krol, Hovenkamp, Van de Kerkhof W., Metgod, Muhren, La Ling, Van Kooten, Rep (Tahamata).


**Brussels, 9 September, 1981**

Belgium (1) 2 *(Czerniatynski, Van den Bergh)*

France (0) 0  52,500

*Belgium:* Pfaff; Renquin, Millecamps L., Meeuws, Baecke, Van Moer (Millecamps M.), Coeck, Vercauteren, Czerniatynski, Van den Bergh, Ceulemans.
*France:* Hiard; Janvion, Mahut, Lopez, Bossis, Moizan (Stopyra), Giresse, Larios, Zimako, Platini, Six.


**Rotterdam, 9 September, 1981**

Netherlands (1) 2 *(Thijssen, Muhren pen)*

Eire (1) 2 *(Robinson, Stapleton)*  46,000

*Netherlands:* Schrijvers; Wijnstekers, Krol, Van de Korput, Brandts, Thijssen, Muhren, La Ling (Van de Kerkhof R.), Van Kooten, Geels (Peters), Rep.
*Eire:* McDonagh; Langan, Devine, Lawrenson, O'Leary D., Brady, Martin (Whelan), Grealish, Heighway (Ryan), Stapleton, Robinson.


**Rotterdam, 14 October, 1981**

Netherlands (2) 3 *(Metgod, Van Kooten, Geels)*

Belgium (0) 0  65,000

*Netherlands:* Van Breukelen; Van de Korput, Metgod, Krol, Hovenkamp, Thijssen, Neeskens, Muhren, La Ling, Van Kooten (Geels), Rep.
*Belgium:* Pfaff; Gerets, Millecamps L., Meeuws, Renquin, Snelders (Plessers), Millecamps M., Vandereycken, Vercauteren, Czerniatynski, Voordeckers (Cluytens).


**Dublin, 14 October, 1981**

Eire (3) 3 *(Mahut og, Stapleton, Robinson)*

France (1) 2 *(Bellone, Platini)*  53,000

*Eire:* McDonagh; Langan, O'Leary D., Moran, Hughton, Whelan, Martin, Lawrenson, Brady, Stapleton (Givens), Robinson.
*France:* Castaneda; Janvion, Mahut (Bracci), Lopez, Bossis, Christophe, Girard, Larios, Platini, Couriol, Bellone (Six).


**Paris, 18 November, 1981**

France (0) 2 *(Platini, Six)*

Netherlands (0) 0  50,000

*France:* Castaneda; Janvion, Lopez, Tresor, Bossis, Giresse, Platini (Tigana), Genghini, Rocheteau, Lacombe (Zimako), Six.
*Netherlands:* Van Breukelen; Wijnstekers, Van de Korput (La Ling), Krol, Poortvliet, Metgod (Tahamata), Peters, Neeskens, Muhren, Van Kooten, Rep.


**Paris, 5 December, 1981**

France (2) 4 *(Rocheteau, Lacombe 2, Genghini)*

Cyprus (0) 0  40,000

*France:* Castaneda; Janvion, Lopez, Tresor, Bossis, Tigana, Giresse, Genghini, Rocheteau, Lacombe, Six (Bellone).
*Cyprus:* Stylianou; Miamialitis C., Erotokritou, Lysandrou, Kezos, Demetriou, Pantzarias N., Theofanos, Yiagudakis, Mavroudis, Vrahimis.

|  | P | W | D | L | F | A | Pts |
|---|---|---|---|---|---|---|---|
| Belgium | 8 | 5 | 1 | 2 | 12 | 9 | 11 |
| France | 8 | 5 | 0 | 3 | 20 | 8 | 10 |
| Eire | 8 | 4 | 2 | 2 | 17 | 11 | 10 |
| Netherlands | 8 | 4 | 1 | 3 | 11 | 7 | 9 |
| Cyprus | 8 | 0 | 0 | 8 | 4 | 29 | 0 |

**GROUP 3**
*Czechoslovakia, USSR, Wales, Turkey, Iceland*

**Reykjavik, 2 June, 1980**

**Iceland (0) 0**

**Wales (1) 4** *(Walsh 2, Giles, Flynn pen)*       13,000

*Iceland:* Olafsson; Gudjohnsson, Edvaldsson, Gudlaugsson, Thordarsson, Thorbjornsson, Geirsson, Jonsson (Sveinsson), Petursson J., Haraldsson, Halldorsson S. (Gudmundsson).
*Wales:* Davies D.; Jones, Flynn, Nicholas, Price, Yorath (Stevenson), Giles, Phillips, Walsh, James L., Davies G. (Harris).

**Reykjavik, 3 September, 1980**

**Iceland (0) 1** *(Sveinsson)*

**USSR (1) 2** *(Gavrilov, Andreyev)*       7000

*Iceland:* Bjarnasson; Gudmundsson, Sveinsson, Thorbjornsson, Bergs, Geirsson, Halldorsson V., Ormslev (Gretarsson), Oskarsson, Thorleifsson (Olgeirsson), Halldorsson S.
*USSR:* Dasayev; Chivadze, Khidiatulin, Romantsev, Bessonov, Shavlo (Ognesian), Gavrilov, Andreyev, Buryak, Sulakvelidze, Blokhin (Rodionov).

**Izmir, 24 September, 1980**

**Turkey (0) 1** *(Fatih pen)*

**Iceland (1) 3** *(Gudlaugsson, Gudmundsson, Thordarsson)*       20,000

*Turkey:* Senol G.; Turgay A., Erol, Fatih, Cem, Sedat, Mustafa K. (Volkan), Sendar, Necdet, Sadullah (Ayhan), Mustafa B.
*Iceland:* Bjarnsson; Halldorsson V., Halldorsson S., Haraldsson, Giersson, Gudlaugsson, Gudmundsson, Edvaldsson, Thordarsson, Sigurvinsson, Thorleifsson (Gretarsson).

**Moscow, 15 October, 1980**

**USSR (2) 5** *(Andreyev 2, Oganesian 2, Bessonov)*

**Iceland (0) 0**       31,000

*USSR:* Dasayev; Sulakvelidze, Chivadze, Khidialutin (Mirzoyan), Baltacha, Shavlo (Yevtushenko), Andreyev, Bessonov, Gavrilov, Tarkhanov, Oganesian.
*Iceland:* Bjarnasson; Oskarsson, Haraldsson, Halldorsson V., Geirsson, Halldorsson S., Thorbjornsson, Gudlaugsson (Thorleifsson), Thordarsson, Sigurvinsson, Gudmundsson (Sveinsson).

**Cardiff, 15 October, 1980**

**Wales (2) 4** *(Flynn, James L. 2 [1 pen], Walsh)*

**Turkey (0) 0**       11,770

*Wales:* Davies D.; Nicholas, Jones, Phillips, Price, Yorath, Flynn, Giles, Harris, Walsh, James L.
*Turkey:* Senol G.; Turgay A., Cem, Husnu, Fatih, Erhan, Necdet (Serrdar); Gungor, Tuncay, Sedat, Ibrahim.

**Cardiff, 19 November, 1980**

**Wales (1) 1** *(Giles)*

**Czechoslovakia (0) 0**       20,175

*Wales:* Davies D.; Price, Charles, Phillips, Ratcliffe, Flynn, Yorath, Nicholas, Giles (Harris), Walsh, Thomas.
*Czechoslovakia:* Hruska; Barmos, Vojacek, Jurkemik (Janecka), Macela, Radimec, Kozak, Panenka, Vizek, Masny, Nehoda.

**Prague, 3 December, 1980**

**Czechoslovakia (2) 2** *(Nehoda 2)*

**Turkey (0) 0**       8000

*Czechoslovakia:* Hruska; Barmos, Vojacek, Jurkemik, Macela, Kozak, Panenka, Bicovsky, Janecka, Nehoda, Vizek.
*Turkey:* Senol G.; Turgay A., Necati, Zafer, Onur, Sedat, Gungor, Iskender, Mustafa B., Ibrahim, Bahtiyar.

**Ankara, 25 March, 1981**

**Turkey (0) 0**

**Wales (0) 1** *(Harris)*       35,000

*Turkey:* Senol G.; Onur, Necati, Husnu, Gelik-Sedat, Gungor, Sedat, Volkan, Necdet, Tuncay, Ibrahim (Sinan).
*Wales:* Davies D.; Jones, Price, Phillips, Ratcliffe, Flynn, Nicholas, Yorath, James L., Harris (Giles), Walsh (Charles).

**Istanbul, 15 April, 1981**

**Turkey (0) 0**

**Czechoslovakia (0) 3** *(Janecka, Kozak, Vizek)*       40,000

*Turkey:* Senol G.; Fatih, Zafer, Onal, Gelik-Sedat, Tufekci, Ibrahim (Necdat), Bahtiyar, Tuncay (Oksi), Sedat, Onur.
*Czechoslovakia:* Seman; Jakubec, Barmos, Macela, Radimec, Kozak, Berger, Nemec (Masny), Vizek, Janecka, Nehoda.

**Bratislava, 27 May, 1981**

**Czechoslovakia (2) 6** *(Vizek, Panenka pen, Nehoda, Kozak 2, Janecka)*

**Iceland (0) 1** *(Bergs)*       22,000

*Czechoslovakia:* Seman; Jakubec, Radimec, Macela, Barmos, Kozak, Berger, Panenka (Janecka), Masny, Nehoda, Vizek.
*Iceland:* Bjarnasson; Tharaisson, Gudlaugsson, Halldorsson V., Haraldsson, Gudjohnsson, Bergs, Sigurvinsson, Petursson P., Edvaldsson, Sveinsson.

**Wrexham, 30 May, 1981**

**Wales (0) 0**

**USSR (0) 0**       29,366

*Wales:* Davies D.; Ratcliffe, Price, Phillips, Jones, Yorath, Thomas, Nicholas, Flynn, Walsh (Charles), Harris (Giles).
*USSR:* Dasayev; Sulakvelidze, Chivadze, Baltacha, Burovsky, Buryak, Kipiani (Gavrilov), Bessonov, Oganesian, Andreyev, Blokhin.

**Reykjavik, 9 September, 1981**

**Iceland (1) 2** *(Gudmundsson, Edvaldsson)*

**Turkey (0) 0**       6000

*Iceland:* Baldursson; Halldorsson S., Oskarsson, Ormslev, Geirsson, Jonsson, Sveinsson (Larvsson), Edvaldsson, Petursson P., Gudmundsson, Bergs.
*Turkey:* Senol G.; Onur, Fatih, Zafer, Engin (Riza), Sedat, Ceyhun, Ibrahim (Husnu), Turgay A., Bahtiyar, Tufekci.

**Prague, 9 September, 1981**

**Czechoslovakia (1) 2** *(Davies og, Licka)*

**Wales (0) 0**       41,500

*Czechoslovakia:* Seman; Bicovsky, Vojacek, Radimec, Barmos, Kozak, Berger, Jurkemik, Panenka (Licka), Vizek, Nehoda.
*Wales:* Davies D.; Stevenson, Jones, Phillips (Walsh), Ratcliffe, Flynn, Nicholas, Thomas (James R.), James L., Harris, Curtis.

Moscow, 23 September, 1981

USSR (3) 4 (Chivadze, Demyanenko, Blokhin, Shengelia)

Turkey (0) 0                                          41,500

USSR: Dasayev; Chivadze, Gavrilov, Baltacha, Demyanenko, Shengelia, Daraselia, Bessonov, Lozinsky, Buryak (Oganesian), Blokhin (Andreyev).
Turkey: Senol G.; Turgay A., Gungor, Fatih, Turgay K. (Sadik), Necati, Ceyhun, Sedat, Mustafa B., Bahtiyar, Senol K.


Reykjavik, 23 September, 1981

Iceland (1) 1 (Ormslev)

Czechoslovakia (0) 1 (Kozak)                         9000

Iceland: Baldursson; Oskarsson, Halldorsson V., Geirsson, Bergs (Larvsson), Gudlaugsson, Jonsson, Edvaldsson, Sigurvinsson, Ormslev (Margeirsson), Gudjohnsson.
Czechoslovakia: Seman; Barmos, Bicovsky, Radimec, Vojacek, Kozak, Panenka (Nemec), Berger, Nehoda, Licka (Masny), Vizek.


Izmir, 7 October, 1981

Turkey (0) 0

USSR (2) 3 (Shengelia, Blokhin 2)                    6215

Turkey: Senol G. (Yasar); Erhan, Necati, Husnu, Suleyman, Coney T., Fatih, Sedat, Selcuk, Bora, Sadik (Isa).
USSR: Dasayev; Demyanenko, Chivadze, Lozinsky, Baltacha (Susloparov), Daraselia, Bessonov, Buryak, Shengelia (Andreyev), Gavrilov, Blokhin.


Swansea, 14 October, 1981

Wales (1) 2 (James R., Curtis)

Iceland (0) 2 (Sigurvinsson 2)                       20,000

Wales: Davies D.; Ratcliffe, Jones, Nicholas, Mahoney, Curtis, James R., Walsh, Charles, Harris (Rush), James L.
Iceland: Baldursson; Halldorsson V., Oskarsson, Ormslev, Geirsson, Jonsson, Gudlaugsson, Edvaldsson, Gudjohnsson, Sigurvinsson, Bergs.


Tbilisi, 28 October, 1981

USSR (1) 2 (Shengelia 2)

Czechoslovakia (0) 0                                 75,000

USSR: Dasayev; Sulakvelidze, Chivadze (Susloparov), Baltacha, Borovsky, Daraselia (Shavlo), Buryak, Bessonov, Shengelia, Gavrilov, Blokhin.
Czechoslovakia: Seman; Barmos, Vojacek, Jurkemik, Radimec, Bicovsky, Berger, Kozak, Vizek (Licka), Kriz, Nehoda.


Tbilisi, 18 November, 1981

USSR (2) 3 (Daraselia, Blokhin, Shengelia)

Wales (0) 0                                          80,000

USSR: Dasayev; Burovsky, Susloparov, Demyanenko, Baltacha, Daraselia, Shengelia, Sulakvelidze, Gavrilov (Gutsayev), Buryak, Blokhin.
Wales: Davies D.; Ratcliffe, Jones (Lovell), Nicholas, Phillips, Price, Curtis, Flynn, Rush, Mahoney (Thomas), James L.


Bratislava, 29 November, 1981

Czechoslovakia (1) 1 (Vojacek)

USSR (1) 1 (Blokhin)                                 47,000

Czechoslovakia: Hruska; Jakubec, Vojacek, Fiala, Barmos, Kozak, Bicovsky, Panenka, Masny, Nehoda, Kriz (Vizek).
USSR: Dasayev; Burovsky, Sulakvelidze, Susloparov, Demyanenko, Buryak, Daraselia, Bal, Shengelia (Andreyev), Gavrilov, Blokhin.


| | P | W | D | L | F | A | Pts |
|---|---|---|---|---|---|---|---|
| USSR | 8 | 6 | 2 | 0 | 20 | 2 | 14 |
| Czechoslovakia | 8 | 4 | 2 | 2 | 15 | 6 | 10 |
| Wales | 8 | 4 | 2 | 2 | 12 | 7 | 10 |
| Iceland | 8 | 2 | 2 | 4 | 10 | 21 | 6 |
| Turkey | 8 | 0 | 0 | 8 | 1 | 22 | 0 |


## GROUP 4
England, Hungary, Switzerland, Rumania, Norway

Wembley, 10 September, 1980

England (1) 4 (McDermott 2 [1 pen], Woodcock, Mariner)

Norway (0) 0                                         48,000

England: Shilton, Anderson, Sansom, Thompson, Watson, Robson, Gates, McDermott, Mariner, Woodcock, Rix.
Norway: Jacobsen T. R.; Berntsen, Kordahl, Aas, Grondalen, Albertsen, Hareide, Dokken, Larsen-Okland, Jacobsen P., Erlandsen (Ottesen).


Oslo, 24 September, 1980

Norway (1) 1 (Hareide)

Rumania (1) 1 (Iordanescu)                           23,000

Norway: Jacobsen T. R.; Berntsen, Aas, Kordahl, Grondalen, Hareide, Ottesen, Dokken, Larsen-Okland, Jacobsen P., Thoresen.
Rumania: Iordache; Negrila, Munteanu, Sames, Stefanescu (Nicolae), Beldeanu, Crisan, Iordanescu, Camataru, Ticleanu (Balaci), Radacanu.


Bucharest, 15 October, 1980

Rumania (1) 2 (Radacanu, Iordanescu pen)

England (0) 1 (Woodcock)                             75,000

Rumania: Iordache; Negrila, Sames, Stefanescu, Munteanu, Ticleanu (Dumitru), Beldeanu, Iordanescu, Crisan, Camataru, Radacanu.
England: Clemence; Neal, Sansom, Thompson, Watson, Robson, Gates (Coppell), McDermott, Birtles (Cunningham), Woodcock, Rix.


Berne, 29 October, 1980

Switzerland (0) 1 (Barberis)

Norway (1) 2 (Hareide, Mathisen)                     14,000

Switzerland: Engel; Wehrli, Stohler, Ludi, Heinz Hermann, Barberis, Zappa (Elsener), Botteron, Marti, Schonenberger, Tanner.
Norway: Jacobsen T. R.; Berntsen, Aas, Kordahl, Grondalen, Albertsen, Hareide, Ottesen (Vinje), Dokken (Mathisen), Jacobsen P., Thoresen.


Wembley, 19 November, 1980

England (2) 2 (Tanner og, Mariner)

Switzerland (0) 1 (Pfister)                          70,000

England: Shilton; Neal, Sansom, Mills, Watson, Robson, Coppell, McDermott, Mariner, Brooking (Rix), Woodcock.
Switzerland: Bergener; Wehrli, Heinz Hermann, Ludi, Geiger, Barberis, Pfister, Tanner (Egli), Botteron, Elsener, Schonenberger (Marti).


Lucerne, 28 April, 1981

Switzerland (1) 2 (Sulser 2)

Hungary (1) 2 (Balint, Muller pen)                   17,000

Switzerland: Burgener; Herbert Hermann, Zappa, Egli, Heinz Hermann, Wehrli, Barberis, Botteron, Scheiwiler (Zwicker), Elsener, Sulser.
Hungary: Meszaros; Martos, Balint, Garaba, Toth J., Csapo (Szanto), Muller (Warga), Mucha, Fazekas, Torocsik, Kiss.

**Wembley, 29 April, 1981**

**England (0) 0**

**Rumania (0) 0**                                              68,500

*England:* Shilton; Anderson, Sansom, Wilkins, Watson, Osman, Coppell, Robson, Francis, Brooking (McDermott), Woodcock.
*Rumania:* Iordache; Negrila, Sames, Stefanescu, Munteanu, Beldeanu, Iordanescu, Stoica, Crisan, Camataru, Balaci.

**Budapest, 13 May, 1981**

**Hungary (1) 1** *(Fazekas)*

**Rumania (0) 0**                                              60,000

*Hungary:* Katzirz; Martos, Balint, Garaba, Toth J., Muller (Szanto), Nyilasi, Varga, Fazekas, Kiss (Bodonyi), Torocsik.
*Rumania:* Iordache; Negrila, Tilihoi, Stefanescu, Munteanu, Balaci, Beldeanu, Iordanescu (Radacanu), Stoica, Crisan, Camataru.

**Oslo, 20 May, 1981**

**Norway (0) 1** *(Thoresen)*

**Hungary (0) 2** *(Kiss 2)*                                   28,000

*Norway:* Abrahamsen; Berntsen (Mathisen), Kordahl, Aas, Pedersen, Hareide (Davidsen), Giske, Lund, Jacobsen P., Larsen-Okland, Thoresen.
*Hungary:* Katzirz; Martos, Karekes A., Garaba, Toth J., Muller, Nyilasi, Varga, Fazekas, Kiss, Torocsik (Bodonyi).

**Basle, 30 May, 1981**

**Switzerland (2) 2** *(Scheiwiler, Sulser)*

**England (0) 1** *(McDermott)*                               40,000

*Switzerland:* Burgener; Herbert Hermann (Weber), Zappa, Egli, Ludi, Wehrli, Barberis, Botteron, Scheiwiler, Sulser, Elsener (Maissen).
*England:* Clemence; Mills, Sansom, Wilkins, Watson (Barnes), Osman, Coppell, Keegan, Mariner, Francis (McDermott), Robson.

**Bucharest, 3 June, 1981**

**Rumania (0) 1** *(Ticleanu)*

**Norway (0) 0**                                              50,000

*Rumania:* Cristian; Negrila, Sames, Stefanescu, Munteanu, Ticleanu, Beldeanu, Balaci (Talnar), Crisan, Camataru (Mircea Sandu), Radacanu.
*Norway:* Amundsen; Kordahl, Aas, Pedersen, Grondalen, Hansen, Berntsen, Giske (Brandhaug), Dokken, Mathisen, Larsen-Okland (Davidsen).

**Budapest, 6 June, 1981**

**Hungary (1) 1** *(Garaba)*

**England (1) 3** *(Brooking 2, Keegan pen)*                  62,000

*Hungary:* Katzirz; Martos, Balint, Garaba, Varga, Muller (Komjati), Nyilasi, Mucha, Fazekas (Bodonyi), Kiss, Torocsik.
*England:* Clemence; Neal, Mills, Thompson, Watson, Robson, Keegan, Coppell, Mariner, Brooking (Wilkins), McDermott.

**Oslo, 17 June, 1981**

**Norway (0) 1** *(Davidsen)*

**Switzerland (0) 1** *(Barberis)*                            18,000

*Norway:* Amundsen; Pedersen, Aas, Kordahl, Grondalen, Hareide (Mathisen), Giske, Hansen (Davidsen), Jacobsen P., Larsen-Okland, Lund.
*Switzerland:* Burgener; Ludi, Zappa, Egli, Herbert Hermann, Wehrli, Botteron, Scheiwiler, Elsener (Zwicker), Barberis (Maissen), Sulser.

**Oslo, 9 September, 1981**

**Norway (2) 2** *(Albertsen, Thoresen)*

**England (1) 1** *(Robson)*                                  28,000

*Norway:* Antonsen; Berntsen, Aas, Hereide, Grondalen, Thoresen, Albertsen, Giske, Jacobsen P., Lund (Dokken), Larsen-Okland (Pedersen).
*England:* Clemence; Neal, Mills, Thompson, Osman, Robson, Keegan, McDermott, Mariner (Withe), Francis, Hoddle (Barnes).

**Bucharest, 23 September, 1981**

**Rumania (0) 0**

**Hungary (0) 0**                                             80,000

*Rumania:* Cristian; Negrila, Sames, Stefanescu, Munteanu, Beldeanu (Ticleanu), Iordanescu, Stoica, Crisan (Cimpeanu), Camataru, Balaci.
*Hungary:* Meszaros; Martos, Balint, Garaba, Toth J., Sallai, Nyilasi, Rab, Fazekas, Torocsik (Csapo), Kiss (Muller).

**Bucharest, 10 October, 1981**

**Rumania (0) 1** *(Balaci)*

**Switzerland (0) 2** *(Zappa, Luthi)*                        55,000

*Rumania:* Cristian; Negrila, Sames, Stefanescu, Munteanu, Ticleanu (Augustin), Stoica, Iordanescu, Talnar, Georgescu, Balaci.
*Switzerland:* Burgener; Ludi, Zappa, Egli, Herbert Hermann, Wehrli (Luthi), Botteron, Barberis, Heinz Hermann, Elsener (Elia), Sulser.

**Budapest, 14 October, 1981**

**Hungary (1) 3** *(Nyilasi 2, Fazekas)*

**Switzerland (0) 0**                                         70,000

*Hungary:* Meszaros; Szanto, Kerekes A., Garaba, Toth J., Muller, Nyilasi, Sallai, Fazekas, Torocsik, Kiss (Kerekes G.).
*Switzerland:* Burgener; Ludi, Zappa, Egli, Herbert Hermann, Wehrli, Barberis (Luthi), Botteron, Heinz Hermann, Sulser, Elsener (Elia).

**Budapest, 31 October, 1981**

**Hungary (1) 4** *(Balint, Kiss 2, Fazekas)*

**Norway (1) 1** *(Lund)*                                     68,000

*Hungary:* Meszaros; Martos, Garaba, Balint, Toth J., Muller (Csapo), Nyilasi, Sallai, Fazekas, Torocsik, Kiss.
*Norway:* Antonsen; Pedersen, Berntsen, Gronlund, Grondalen, Davidsen, Jacobsen T., Giske (Mathisen), Lund, Jacobsen P., Refvik.

**Berne, 11 November, 1981**

**Switzerland (0) 0**

**Rumania (0) 0**                                             16,000

*Switzerland:* Burgener (Engel); Egli, Zappa, Herbert Hermann (Elia), Wehrli, Botteron, Ludi, Favre, Elsener, Barberis, Sulser.
*Rumania:* Moraru; Rednic, Stefanescu, Iorgulescu, Stanescu, Ticleanu (Andone), Balaci, Augustin, Klein, Gabor, Mircea Sandu (Boloni).

**Wembley, 18 November, 1981**

**England (1) 1** *(Mariner)*

**Hungary (0) 0**                                             92,000

*England:* Shilton; Neal, Mills, Thompson, Martin, Robson, Keegan, Coppell (Morley), Mariner, McDermott, Brooking.
*Hungary:* Meszaros; Martos, Balint, Garaba, Toth J., Sallai, Muller, Csapo (Szanto), Fazekas (Kerekes G.), Torocsik, Kiss.

| | P | W | D | L | F | A | Pts |
|---|---|---|---|---|---|---|---|
| Hungary | 8 | 4 | 2 | 2 | 13 | 8 | 10 |
| England | 8 | 4 | 1 | 3 | 13 | 8 | 9 |
| Rumania | 8 | 2 | 4 | 2 | 5 | 5 | 8 |
| Switzerland | 8 | 2 | 3 | 3 | 9 | 12 | 7 |
| Norway | 8 | 2 | 2 | 4 | 8 | 15 | 6 |

## GROUP 5
*Italy, Yugoslavia, Greece, Denmark, Luxembourg*

**Luxembourg, 10 September, 1980**

**Luxembourg (0) 0**

**Yugoslavia (0) 5** *(Susic, Zlatko Vujovic 2, Petrovic, Buljan)* 5000

*Luxembourg:* Moes; Girres, Zuang, Dax (Bossi), Meunier, Wagner (Hoscheid), Dresch, Di Domenico, Weis, Langers, Reiter.
*Yugoslavia:* Pantelic; Zoran Vujovic (Gudelj), Klincarski, Buljan, Jovanovic, Slijvo, Petrovic, Sestic (Surjak), Zlatko Vujovic, Susic, Secerbegovic.

**Ljubljana, 27 September, 1980**

**Yugoslavia (2) 2** *(Pantelic pen, Zoran Vujovic)*

**Denmark (1) 1** *(Arnesen pen)* 20,000

*Yugoslavia:* Pantelic; Zoran Vujovic, Hrstic, Jovanovic, Primorac, Buljan (Mustadanic), Petrovic, Jerolimov, Zlatko Vujovic, Susic, Secerbegovic (Klincarski).
*Denmark:* Qvist; Rasmussen, Ziegler, Steffensen, Rontved, Lerby, Bertelsen, Arnesen, Jensen (Nielsen B.), Elkjaer, Bastrup.

**Luxembourg, 11 October, 1980**

**Luxembourg (0) 0**

**Italy (1) 2** *(Collovati, Bettega)* 10,000

*Luxembourg:* Moes; Dax, Rohmann, Bossi (Schreiner), Meunier, Weis, Philipp (Wagner), Dresch, Di Domenico, Reiter, Langers.
*Italy:* Zoff; Gentile, Baresi G., Oriali, Collovati, Scirea, Causio, Tardelli (Sala P.), Altobelli (Conti), Antognoni, Bettega.

**Copenhagen, 15 October, 1980**

**Denmark (0) 0**

**Greece (0) 1** *(Kouis)* 50,000

*Denmark:* Qvist; Rasmussen, Ziegler, Steffensen, Olsen, Bertelsen (Nielsen B.), Arnesen, Lerby, Simonsen, Jensen (Bastrup), Elkjaer.
*Greece:* Sarganis; Kyrastas, Firos, Kapsis, Iosifidis, Livanthinos, Kouis, Delikaris (Paraskos), Ardizoglou, Kostikos (Mitropoulos), Mavros.

**Rome, 1 November, 1980**

**Italy (1) 2** *(Graziani 2)*

**Denmark (0) 0** 50,000

*Italy:* Zoff; Gentile, Collovati, Scirea, Cabrini, Marini, Tardelli, Bettega, Conti, Graziani, Altobelli.
*Denmark:* Kjaer; Rasmussen, Steffensen, Rontved, Lerby, Olsen, Bertelsen, Jensen, Arnesen, Elkjaer, Bastrup.

**Turin, 15 November, 1980**

**Italy (1) 2** *(Cabrini pen, Conti)*

**Yugoslavia (0) 0** 50,000

*Italy:* Zoff; Gentile, Collovati, Scirea, Cabrini, Marini, Tardelli, Antognoni (Zaccarelli), Conti, Graziani, Bettega.
*Yugoslavia:* Pantelic; Zoran Vujovic, Krmpotic, Sinonovic, Primorac, Jerolimov (Petrovic), Sestic (Halilhodzic), Slijvo, Zlatko Vujovic, Salov, Secerbegovic.

**Copenhagen, 19 November, 1980**

**Denmark (2) 4** *(Arnesen 2 [1 pen], Elkjaer, Simonsen)*

**Luxembourg (0) 0** 10,500

*Denmark:* Kjaer; Rasmussen, Rontved, Nielsen I., Steffensen, Bertelsen, Lerby, Arnesen, Simonsen, Bastrup (Brylle), Elkjaer.
*Luxembourg:* Moes; Dax (Bianchini), Philipp, Bossi, Meunier, Girres, Weis, Dresch, Di Domenico, Reiter (Michaux), Langers.

**Athens, 6 December, 1980**

**Greece (0) 0**

**Italy (1) 2** *(Antognoni, Scirea)* 25,000

*Greece:* Sarganis; Kyrastas, Firos, Kapsis, Iosifidis, Livanthinos (Galakos), Delikaris, Kouis, Ardizoglou, Kostikos (Charalambidis), Mavros.
*Italy:* Zoff; Gentile, Collovati, Scirea, Cabrini, Marini, Tardelli, Antognoni (Oriali), Conti, Graziani, Altobelli.

**Salonika, 28 January, 1981**

**Greece (2) 2** *(Kouis, Kostikos)*

**Luxembourg (0) 0** 14,000

*Greece:* Sarganis; Kyrastas, Iosifidis, Kapsis, Ravoussis, Damanakis, Kouis, Koussoulakis (Delikaris), Anastopoulos (Charalambidis), Kostikos, Galakos.
*Luxembourg:* Moes; Dax (Bossi), Philipp, Rohmann, Wagner, Girres, Dresch, Reiter (Langers), Meunier, Zuang, Di Domenico.

**Luxembourg, 11 March, 1981**

**Luxembourg (0) 0**

**Greece (1) 2** *(Kouis, Mavros pen)* 6750

*Luxembourg:* Moes; Dax, Philipp, Rohmann, Wagner (Meunier), Girres, Weis, Dresch, Reiter, Langers, Di Domenico.
*Greece:* Sarganis; Kyrastas, Kapsis, Firos, Iosifidis, Kouis, Koussoulakis (Anastopoulos), Galakos (Vanvakoulos), Kostikos, Mavros, Livanthinos.

**Split, 29 April, 1981**

**Yugoslavia (3) 5** *(Slijvo, Halilhodzic, Pantelic pen, Zlatko Vujovic 2)*

**Greece (0) 1** *(Kostikos)* 50,000

*Yugoslavia:* Pantelic; Krmpotic, Hrstic (Jerolimov), Zajec, Stojkovic, Buljan, Zlatko Vujovic, Sliskovic (Sestic), Halilhodzic, Slijvo, Pasic.
*Greece:* Sarganis; Gounaris, Iosifidis, Firos, Kapsis, Livanthinos (Koudas), Koussoulakis, Kouis, Kostikos, Ballis, Ardizoglou.

**Luxembourg, 1 May, 1981**

**Luxembourg (1) 1** *(Nuremberg)*

**Denmark (1) 2** *Elkjaer, Arnesen)* 2844

*Luxembourg:* Moes; Meunier (Schreiner), Philipp, Dax, Wagner, Langers, Weis, Nuremberg, Girres, Di Domenico, Schreitler (Back).
*Denmark:* Qvist; Rasmussen, Rontved, Busk, Eigenbrod (Simonsen), Bertelsen, Lerby, Arnesen, Olsen, Eriksen, Elkjaer.

**Copenhagen, 3 June, 1981**

**Denmark (0) 3** *(Rontved, Arnesen, Bastrup)*

**Italy (0) 1** *(Graziani)* 35,600

*Denmark:* Qvist; Rasmussen, Rontved, Busk, Lerby, Olsen (Eigenbrod), Bertelsen, Arnesen, Simonsen, Bastrup, Elkjaer.
*Italy:* Zoff; Gentile, Collovati, Scirea, Cabrini, Marini (Dossena), Tardelli, Antognoni, Conti, Graziani, Bettega (Ancelotti).

**Copenhagen, 9 September, 1981**

**Denmark (0) 1** *(Elkjaer)*

**Yugoslavia (0) 2** *(Zlatko Vujovic, Petrovic)*     48,000

*Denmark:* Qvist; Rasmussen, Madsen, Rontved, Ziegler, Lerby, Bertelsen, Arnesen, Simonsen, Bastrup, Elkjaer.
*Yugoslavia:* Pantelic; Krmpotic, Hrstic, Zajec, Stojkovic, Gudelj, Zlatko Vujovic, Petrovic, Halilhodzic, Slijvo, Surjak.

**Salonika, 14 October, 1981**

**Greece (0) 2** *(Anastopoulos, Kouis)*

**Denmark (2) 3** *(Lerby, Arnesen, Elkjaer)*     20,000

*Greece:* Constantinou; Gounaris (Karoulias), Papazoglou, Firos, Iosifidis, Livanthinos, Kouis, Delikaris (Kostikos), Anastopoulos, Mitropoulos, Koudas.
*Denmark:* Qvist; Rasmussen, Nielsen I., Rontved, Lerby, Bertelsen, Olsen, Arnesen (Ziegler), Simonsen, Bastrup, Elkjaer.

**Belgrade, 17 October, 1981**

**Yugoslavia (1) 1** *(Zlatko Vujovic)*

**Italy (1) 1** *(Bettega)*     70,000

*Yugoslavia:* Pantelic; Stojkovic, Buljan, Zajec, Gudelj, Surjak, Zlatko Vujovic (Zoran Vujovic), Petrovic, Slijvo, Halilhodzic, Pasic.
*Italy:* Zoff; Gentile, Cabrini, Dossena, Collovati, Scirea, Conti, Tardelli, Altobelli, Antognoni (Oriali), Bettega.

**Turin, 14 November, 1981**

**Italy (0) 1** *(Conti)*

**Greece (0) 1** *(Kouis)*     40,000

*Italy:* Zoff; Gentile, Collovati, Scirea, Cabrini, Marini, Dossena, Antognoni (Oriali), Conti (Pruzzo), Graziani, Selvaggi.
*Greece:* Pantelis; Karoulias, Kapsis, Firos, Iosifidis, Damanakis, Kouis, Vanvakoulos, Ardizoglou (Zindros), Mitropoulos (Kostikos), Anastopoulos.

**Novi Sad, 21 November, 1981**

**Yugoslavia (2) 5** *(Halilhodzic 2, Surjak, Pasic, Zlatko Vujovic)*

**Luxembourg (0) 0**     23,000

*Yugoslavia:* Pantelic; Krmpotic, Stojkovic, Zajec, Buljan, Gudelj, Zlatko Vujovic, Petrovic, Halilhodzic (Jerolimov), Susic, Surjak (Pasic).
*Luxembourg:* Moes; Dax (Schreiner), Bossi, Rohmann, Clemens, Girres, Weis, Dresch, Di Domenico (Wagner), Langers, Reiter.

**Athens, 29 November, 1981**

**Greece (1) 1** *(Mavros)*

**Yugoslavia (2) 2** *(Surjak, Jerkovic)*     12,000

*Greece:* Pantelis (Davkos); Karoulias, Iosifidis (Kostikos), Vanvakoulos, Ravoussis, Kapsis, Anastopoulos, Livanthinos, Mitropoulos, Kouis, Mavros.
*Yugoslavia:* Pantelic; Buljan, Zoran Vujovic (Pasic), Gudelj, Stojkovic, Zajec, Zlatko Vujovic (Hrstic), Petrovic, Jerkovic, Surjak, Susic.

**Naples, 5 December, 1981**

**Italy (1) 1** *(Collovati)*

**Luxembourg (0) 0**     60,000

*Italy:* Zoff; Gentile, Collovati, Scirea, Cabrini, Oriali, Tardelli, Marocchino, Dossena, Pruzzo, Graziani.
*Luxembourg:* Moes; Meunier, Bossi, Rohmann, Clemens, Weis, Wagner (Schreiner), Dresch, Langers, Reiter (Girres), Di Domenico.

| | P | W | D | L | F | A | Pts |
|---|---|---|---|---|---|---|---|
| Yugoslavia | 8 | 6 | 1 | 1 | 22 | 7 | 13 |
| Italy | 8 | 5 | 2 | 1 | 12 | 5 | 12 |
| Denmark | 8 | 4 | 0 | 4 | 14 | 11 | 8 |
| Greece | 8 | 3 | 1 | 4 | 10 | 13 | 7 |
| Luxembourg | 8 | 0 | 0 | 8 | 1 | 23 | 0 |

**GROUP 6**
*Scotland, Sweden, Portugal, Northern Ireland, Israel*

**Tel Aviv, 26 March, 1980**

**Israel (0) 0**

**Northern Ireland (0) 0**     45,000

*Israel:* Haviv; Machness G., Shum, Bar, Cohen A., Turk, Spiegel, Cohen Y., Gariani (Machness O.), Damti, Peretz.
*Northern Ireland:* Jennings; Nicholl J., Nelson, Nicholl C., O'Neill J., O'Neill M., McIlroy, Cassidy, Finney (Spence), Armstrong, Cochrane.

**Stockholm, 18 June, 1980**

**Sweden (1) 1** *(Ramberg)*

**Israel (0) 1** *(Damti)*     24,711

*Sweden:* Moller; Borg, Gustavsson, Arvidsson, Erlandsson, Holmgren, Ramberg (Nilsson P.), Sjoberg, Nordgren, Backe, Edstrom.
*Israel:* Mizrahi; Machness G., Bar, Shum, Cohen Y., Turk (Ekhois), Spiegel (Fogel), Cohen A., Gariani, Peretz, Damti.

**Stockholm, 10 September, 1980**

**Sweden (0) 0**

**Scotland (0) 1** *(Strachan)*     39,831

*Sweden:* Hellstrom; Gustavsson, Borg, Bild, Arvidsson, Erlandsson (Nilsson P.), Ramberg, Nordgren, Thomas Nilsson, Sjoberg, Ohlsson.
*Scotland:* Rough; McGrain, McLeish, Hansen, Gray F., Miller, Strachan, Gemmill, Dalglish (Archibald), Gray A., Robertson.

**Belfast, 15 October, 1980**

**Northern Ireland (3) 3** *(Brotherston, McIlroy, Nicholl J.)*

**Sweden (0) 0**     20,000

*Northern Ireland:* Platt; Nicholl J., Nicholl C., McClelland, Donaghy, Cassidy (McCreery), Hamilton (Cochrane), O'Neill M., McIlroy, Armstrong, Brotherston.
*Sweden:* Moller; Arvidsson, Borg, Borjesson B., Holmgren, Larsson, Ramberg (Erlandsson), Nilsson P., Thomas Nilsson, Edstrom, Ohlsson (Sjoberg).

**Hampden Park, 15 October, 1980**

**Scotland (0) 0**

**Portugal (0) 0**     50,000

*Scotland:* Rough; McGrain, Hansen, Miller, Gray F., Souness, Strachan, Gemmill, Dalglish, Gray A., Robertson.
*Portugal:* Bento; Gabriel, Pietra, Simoes (Sheu), Laranjeira, Fernandes, Eurico, Costa, Chalana, Do Santos, Jordao (Nene).

**Tel Aviv, 12 November, 1980**

**Israel (0) 0**

**Sweden (0) 0**     42,000

*Israel:* Mizrahi; Cohen A., Shum, Bar, Cohen Y., Ekhois, Turk (Cohen N.), Gariani, Damti, Spiegel, Peretz (Machness O.).
*Sweden:* Wernersson; Fredriksson, Arvidsson, Borjesson B., Erlandsson, Larsson, Prytz (Nilsson P.), Holmgren, Thomas Nilsson (Ravelli A.), Edstrom, Ohlsson.

**Lisbon, 19 November, 1980**

**Portugal (0) 1** *(Jordao)*

**Northern Ireland (0) 0**     60,000

*Portugal:* Bento; Gabriel, Simoes, Laranjeira, Pietra, Sheu, Carlos Manuel (Nene), Alves (Teixeira), Costa, Jordao, Chalana.
*Northern Ireland:* Platt; Nicholl J., Nicholl C., O'Neill J., Donaghy, McIlroy, O'Neill M., Cassidy (McCreery), Hamilton (Cochrane), Brotherston, Armstrong.

**Lisbon, 17 December, 1980**

**Portugal (2) 3** *(Humberto 2, Jordao)*

**Israel (0) 0** 55,000

*Portugal:* Bento; Gabriel, Humberto, Laranjeira (Simoes), Pietra, Carlos Manuel (Fernandes), Alves, Sheu, Chalana, Nene, Jordao.
*Israel:* Mizrahi; Kirat, Bar, Shum, Cohen Y., Einstein, Ekhois, Turk, Gariani (Schwartz), Damti, Peretz (Cohen N.).

**Tel Aviv, 25 February, 1981**

**Israel (0) 0**

**Scotland (0) 1** *(Dalglish)* 40,000

*Israel:* Mizrahi; Machness G., Cohen A., Bar, Cohen Y., Ekhois, Shum, Sinai, Cohen N., Damti, Tabak.
*Scotland:* Rough; McGrain, McLeish, Burns, Gray F., Souness, Wark (Miller), Gemmill, Dalglish (Gray A.), Archibald, Robertson.

**Hampden Park, 25 March, 1981**

**Scotland (0) 1** *(Wark)*

**Northern Ireland (0) 1** *(Hamilton)* 68,000

*Scotland:* Rough (Thomson); McGrain, Miller, McLeish, Gray F., Burns (Hartford), Wark, Gemmill, Archibald, Gray A., Robertson.
*Northern Ireland:* Jennings; Nicholl J., Nicholl C., O'Neill J., Nelson, McCreery, McIlroy, Cochrane, McClelland, Armstrong, Hamilton (Spence).

**Hampden Park, 28 April, 1981**

**Scotland (2) 3** *(Robertson 2 [2 pens], Provan)*

**Israel (0) 1** *(Sinai)* 61,489

*Scotland:* Rough; McGrain, McLeish, Hansen, Gray F., Souness, Provan, Hartford, Archibald, Jordan, Robertson.
*Israel:* Mizrahi; Machness G., Cohen Y., Ekhois, Cohen A., Bar, Shum, Zeitouni, Sinai, Damti, Tabak.

**Belfast, 29 April, 1981**

**Northern Ireland (0) 1** *(Armstrong)*

**Portugal (0) 0** 25,000

*Northern Ireland:* Jennings; Nicholl J., Nicholl C., O'Neill J., Nelson, O'Neill M., McCreery, McIlroy, Cochrane, Armstrong, Hamilton.
*Portugal:* Bento; Gabriel, Humberto, Simoes, Pietra, Carlos Manuel, Sheu, Alves, Costa, Oliveira (Nene), Jordao.

**Stockholm, 3 June, 1981**

**Sweden (0) 1** *(Borg pen)*

**Northern Ireland (0) 0** 21,431

*Sweden:* Ravelli T.; Fredriksson, Hysen, Borjesson B., Erlandsson, Persson, Borg, Nilsson P., Thomas Nilsson (Torbjorn Nilsson), Sjoberg, Svensson (Ravelli A.).
*Northern Ireland:* Jennings; Nicholl J. (McClelland), Nicholl C., O'Neill J., Nelson, O'Neill M., McCreery, McIlroy, Cochrane, Armstrong, Hamilton (Spence).

**Stockholm, 24 June, 1981**

**Sweden (1) 3** *(Borjesson, Hysen, Svensson)*

**Portugal (0) 0** 34,531

*Sweden:* Ravelli T.; Fredriksson, Erlandsson, Borjesson B., Hysen, Nilsson P., Bjorklund, Ravelli A. (Hallen), Sjoberg, Persson (Thomas Nilsson), Svensson.
*Portugal:* Bento; Simoes, Gabriel, Pietra, Eurico, Sheu, Carlos Manuel, Costa, Alves (Sousa), Nene, Fernandes (Chalana).

**Hampden Park, 9 September, 1981**

**Scotland (1) 2** *(Jordan, Robertson pen)*

**Sweden (0) 0** 80,000

*Scotland:* Rough; McGrain, McLeish, Hansen, Gray F., Wark, Provan, Hartford, Dalglish (Gray A.), Jordan, Robertson.
*Sweden:* Ravelli T.; Erlandsson, Fredriksson (Hallen), Borg, Hysen, Borjesson B., Ravelli A., Bjorklund, Larsson, Sjoberg, Svensson (Tommy Holmgren).

**Belfast, 14 October, 1981**

**Northern Ireland (0) 0**

**Scotland (0) 0** 35,000

*Northern Ireland:* Jennings; Nicholl J., Nicholl C., O'Neill J., Donaghy, O'Neill M., McIlroy, McCreery, Armstrong, Hamilton, Brotherston.
*Scotland:* Rough; Stewart, Hansen, Miller, Gray F., Strachan (Gray A.), Souness, Hartford, Dalglish, Archibald, Robertson.

**Lisbon, 14 October, 1981**

**Portugal (0) 1** *(Pietra)*

**Sweden (0) 2** *(Larsson, Persson)* 70,000

*Portugal:* Bento (Amaral); Gabriel, Humberto, Eurico, Pietra, Carlos Manuel, Nene, Sheu, Romeu, Chalana (Costa), Jordao.
*Sweden:* Ravelli T.; Hysen, Hallen, Borjesson B., Erlandsson, Borg, Ravelli A. (Persson), Bjorklund, Larsson, Tommy Holmgren, Borjesson S. (Nilsson P.).

**Tel Aviv, 28 October, 1981**

**Israel (4) 4** *(Tabak 3, Damti)*

**Portugal (1) 1** *(Jordao)* 20,000

*Israel:* Mizrahi (Haviv); Machness G., Cohen A., Bar, Cohen Y., Ekhois, Shum, Malmillian (Turk), Tabak, Damti, Gariani.
*Portugal:* Amaral; Gabriel, Eurico, Humberto (Dito), Teixeira, Rodolfo, Sousa, Fernandes, Freire (Nene), Romeu, Jordao.

**Belfast, 18 November, 1981**

**Northern Ireland (1) 1** *(Armstrong)*

**Israel (0) 0** 40,000

*Northern Ireland:* Jennings; Nicholl J., Nicholl C., O'Neill J., Donaghy, McCreery, Cassidy, McIlroy, Armstrong, Hamilton, Brotherston.
*Israel:* Haviv; Machness G., Bar, Cohen A., Shum, Ekhois, Cohen Y., Malmillian, Lamm (Sinai), Damti, Tabak.

**Lisbon, 18 November, 1981**

**Portugal (1) 2** *(Fernandes 2)*

**Scotland (1) 1** *(Sturrock)* 15,000

*Portugal:* Bento; Freixo (Veloso), Simoes, Eurico, Teixeira, Oliveira, Dito, Romeu, Jaime (Diamantino), Fernandes, Costa.
*Scotland:* Thomson; Stewart, Hansen, Miller, Gray F. (Kennedy), Provan, Souness, Strachan, Hartford, Archibald (Dalglish), Sturrock.

| | P | W | D | L | F | A | Pts |
|---|---|---|---|---|---|---|---|
| Scotland | 8 | 4 | 3 | 1 | 9 | 4 | 11 |
| Northern Ireland | 8 | 3 | 3 | 2 | 6 | 3 | 9 |
| Sweden | 8 | 3 | 2 | 3 | 7 | 8 | 8 |
| Portugal | 8 | 3 | 1 | 4 | 8 | 11 | 7 |
| Israel | 8 | 1 | 3 | 4 | 6 | 10 | 5 |

## GROUP 7
*Poland, East Germany, Malta*

**Valletta, 7 December, 1980**

**Malta (0) 0**

**Poland (0) 2** *(Smolarek, Lipka)*     10,000

*(abandoned after 77 minutes)*
*Malta:* Bonello; Em. Farrugia, Ed. Farrugia, Holland, Buttigieg, Fabri, Curmi (Farrugia L.), Fenech, Spiteri-Gonzi, Xuereb J., Xuereb G.
*Poland:* Mowlik; Majewski, Janas, Rudy, Skrobowski, Dziuba, Palasz, Lipka, Iwan, Ciolek, Smolarek.

**Valletta, 4 April, 1981**

**Malta (1) 1** *(Fabri)*

**East Germany (2) 2** *(Schnuphase* pen, *Hafner)*   5000

*Malta:* Bonello; Ed. Farrugia, Mizzi (Xuereb R.), Holland, Buttigieg, Fabri, Xuereb G., Em. Farrugia, Xuereb J., De Giorgio, Spiteri-Gonzi.
*East Germany:* Grapenthin; Noack, Dorner, Ulrich (Strozniak), Liebers, Schnuphase, Hafner, Steinbach, Streich, Netz, Hoffman.

**Chorzow, 2 May, 1981**

**Poland (0) 1** *(Buncol)*

**East Germany (0) 0**     75,000

*Poland:* Tomaszewski; Dziuba, Janas, Zmuda, Jalocha, Lato, Kupcewicz, Buncol, Iwan (Skrobowski), Szarmach, Smolarek.
*East Germany:* Grapenthin; Stronzniak, Dorner, Schmuck, Kurbjuweit, Hafner, Schnuphase, Steinbach, Riediger, Streich (Liebers), Hoffman (Bielau).

**Leipzig, 10 October, 1981**

**East Germany (0) 2** *(Schnuphase* pen, *Streich)*

**Poland (2) 3** *(Szarmach, Smolarek 2)*   80,000

*East Germany:* Grapenthin; Weise, Schnuphase, Dorner, Baum, Pommerenke (Steinbach), Kurbjuweit, Liebers, Riediger, Streich, Trocha.
*Poland:* Mlynarczyk; Dziuba (Wojcicki), Zmuda, Janas, Jalocha, Matysik, Majewski, Boniek, Lato, Szarmach (Iwan), Smolarek.

**Jena, 11 November, 1981**

**East Germany (2) 5** *(Krause, Streich, Hein, Liebers, Spiteri-Gonzi og)*

**Malta (1) 1** *(Spiteri-Gonzi)*     2000

*East Germany:* Rudwaleit; Ulrich, Schnuphase, Troppa, Baum, Liebers, Krause, Steinbach (Ernst), Bielau (Hein), Streich, Trocha.
*Malta:* Bonello; Consiglio (Farrugia M.), Ed. Farrugia, Holland, Buttigieg, Fabri, Em. Farrugia, Xuereb J., Spiteri-Gonzi, Xuereb R., Fenech (De Giorgio).

**Wroclaw, 15 November, 1981**

**Poland (1) 6** *(Iwan, Smolarek 2, Majewski, Dziekanowski, Boniek)*

**Malta (0) 0**     25,000

*Poland:* Mowlik; Majewski, Zmuda, Dolny, Jalocha, Matysik (Palasz), Boniek, Buncol, Okonski, Iwan, Smolarek (Dziekanowski).
*Malta:* Sciberras; Em. Farrugia, Ed. Farrugia, Holland, Buttigieg, Fabri, Spiteri-Gonzi, Farrugia M., Xuereb J., Xuereb R., Fenech.

| | P | W | D | L | F | A | Pts |
|---|---|---|---|---|---|---|---|
| Poland | 4 | 4 | 0 | 0 | 12 | 2 | 8 |
| East Germany | 4 | 2 | 0 | 2 | 9 | 6 | 4 |
| Malta | 4 | 0 | 0 | 4 | 2 | 15 | 0 |

## SOUTH AMERICA

### GROUP 1
*Brazil, Bolivia, Venezuela*

**Caracas, 8 February, 1981**

**Venezuela (0) 0**

**Brazil (0) 1** *(Zico* pen)     30,000

*Venezuela:* Vega; Ochoa, Castro (Simonelli), Acosta, Campos, Marin, Echenausi, Torres, Scarpeccio, Garcia, Hernandez (Castillo A.).
*Brazil:* Valdir Peres; Edevaldo, Oscar, Luisinho, Junior, Batista, Cerezo, Zico, Paulo Isidoro, Serginho, Ze Sergio.

**La Paz, 15 February, 1981**

**Bolivia (1) 3** *(Aguilar, Aragones, Reynaldo)*

**Venezuela (0) 0**     40,000

*Bolivia:* Jimenez; Trigo, Espinoza, Vaca, Del Llano, Angulo, Romero, Aragones, Borja, Taborga (Reynaldo), Aguilar.
*Venezuela:* Vega; Ochoa, Castro, Acosta, Campos, Torres, Scarpeccio (Aguirre), Sanchez, Castillo A., Garcia, Castillo W. (Flores).

**La Paz, 22 February, 1981**

**Bolivia (1) 1** *(Aragones)*

**Brazil (1) 2** *(Socrates, Reinaldo)*   50,000

*Bolivia:* Jimenez; Trigo, Espinoza (Rojas), Vaca, Del Llano, Romero, Villaruel (Fierro), Aragones, Borja, Reynaldo, Aguilar.
*Brazil:* Valdir Peres; Oscar, Edevaldo, Luisinho (Edinho), Junior, Cerezo, Socrates, Zico, Eder, Reinaldo, Tita.

**Caracas, 15 March, 1981**

**Venezuela (1) 1** *(Acosta)*

**Bolivia (0) 0**     25,000

*Venezuela:* Vega; Salles, Acosta, Castro, Campos, Marin (Aguirre), Filomeno, Gutierrez, Garcia, Febles, Bosetti (Castillo W.).
*Bolivia:* Jimenez; Vaca, Espinoza, Trigo, Del Llano, Borja, Villaruel, Romero, Aragones (Melgar), Taborga, Aguilar.

**Rio de Janeiro, 22 March, 1981**

**Brazil (1) 3** *(Zico 3* [1 pen])

**Bolivia (0) 1** *(Aragones)*     122,000

*Brazil:* Valdir Peres; Edevaldo, Oscar, Luisinho, Junior, Batista, Socrates, Zico, Tita (Ze Sergio), Reinaldo, Eder.
*Bolivia:* Jimenez; Trigo, Vaca, Espinoza, Del Llano, Romero, Villaruel, Aragones, Gonzalez (Borja), Taborda, Aguilar.

**Goiania, 29 March, 1981**

**Brazil (1) 5** *(Tita 2, Socrates, Zico* pen, *Junior)*

**Venezuela (0) 0**     35,000

*Brazil:* Valdir Peres; Getulio, Oscar, Junior, Batista, Socrates, Zico, Tita, Reinaldo (Serginho), Eder (Ze Sergio).
*Venezuela:* Vega; Ochoa, Castro, Acosta, Salles, Torres, Filomeno, Carrero, Garcia, Febles, Gutierrez (Castillo A.).

| | P | W | D | L | F | A | Pts |
|---|---|---|---|---|---|---|---|
| Brazil | 4 | 4 | 0 | 0 | 11 | 2 | 8 |
| Bolivia | 4 | 1 | 0 | 3 | 5 | 6 | 2 |
| Venezuela | 4 | 1 | 0 | 3 | 1 | 9 | 2 |

## GROUP 2
*Peru, Uruguay, Colombia*

**Bogota, 26 July, 1981**

**Colombia (0) 1** *(Herrera)*

**Peru (0) 1** *(La Rosa)*     60,000

*Colombia:* Zape; Porras, Romero, Maturana, Castro, Caicedo, Valverde (Agudelo), Otero (Torres), Ortiz, Vilarete, Herrera.
*Peru:* Quiroga; Rojas R., Diaz, Chumpitaz, Duarte, Cueto, Velasquez (Olaechea), Uribe (La Rosa), Oblitas, Cubillas, Barbadillo.

**Montevideo, 9 August, 1981**

**Uruguay (1) 3** *(Paz, Morales 2 [1 pen])*

**Colombia (1) 2** *(Sarmiento, Herrera)*     71,000

*Uruguay:* Rodriguez, Moreira, Blanco, De Leon, Martinez, De la Pena (Barrios), Krasowski, Paz, Vargas, Victorino, Morales.
*Colombia:* Zape; Porras, Romero, Maturana, Castro, Valverde, Otero (Caicedo), Sarmiento, Herrera, Ortiz (Umana), Torres.

**Lima, 16 August, 1981**

**Peru (1) 2** *(Barbadillo, Uribe pen)*

**Colombia (0) 0**     45,000

*Peru:* Quiroga; Duarte, Diaz, Chumpitaz, Rojas R., Velasquez (Olaechea), Cueto, Uribe, Barbadillo, La Rosa, Oblitas.
*Colombia:* Zape; Porras, Reyes, Maturana, Castro, Otero (Caicedo), Valverde, Sarmiento (Vilarete), Herrera, Ortiz, Torres.

**Montevideo, 23 August, 1981**

**Uruguay (0) 1** *(Victorino)*

**Peru (1) 2** *(La Rasa, Uribe)*     75,000

*Uruguay:* Rodriguez; Moreira, Blanco, De Leon, Martinez, Barrios (De la Pena), Krasowsky, Paz, Vargas (Bueno), Victorino, Morales.
*Peru:* Quiroga; Duarte, Diaz, Chumpitaz, Rojas R., Velasquez, Cueto, Uribe, Barbadillo, La Rosa (Olaechea), Oblitas.

**Lima, 6 September, 1981**

**Peru (0) 0**

**Uruguay (0) 0**     45,000

*Peru:* Quiroga; Duarte, Diaz, Chumpitaz, Rojas R., Cueto, Velasquez, Uribe, Barbadillo, La Rosa, Oblitas (Olaechea).
*Uruguay:* Rodriguez; Moreira, Blanco, De Leon, Martinez, Agresta (Krasowski), De la Pena, Barrios (Morales), Bueno, Victorino, Paz.

**Bogota, 13 September, 1981**

**Colombia (1) 1** *(Herrera pen)*

**Uruguay (1) 1** *(Victorino)*     10,000

*Colombia:* Valencia; Gonzalez, Prince, Reyes (Morales), Castro, Sarmiento (Caicedo), Valverde, Umana, Torres, Agudelo, Herrera.
*Uruguay:* Rodriguez; Moreira, Blanco, Marcenaro, Martinez (Gonzalez), Barrios, Krasowski (Russo), Paz, Bueno, Victorino, Vargas.

| | P | W | D | L | F | A | Pts |
|---|---|---|---|---|---|---|---|
| Peru | 4 | 2 | 2 | 0 | 5 | 2 | 6 |
| Uruguay | 4 | 1 | 2 | 1 | 5 | 5 | 4 |
| Colombia | 4 | 0 | 2 | 2 | 3 | 6 | 2 |

## GROUP 3
*Chile, Ecuador, Paraguay*

**Guayaquil, 17 May, 1981**

**Ecuador (0) 1** *(Klinger)*

**Paraguay (0) 0**     55,000

*Ecuador:* Delgado; Perlaza, Figueroa (Klinger), Paez, Valenzia, Villafuerte, Parraga, Carrera (Burbano), Tenorio, Quinones, Nieves.
*Paraguay:* Almeida; Solalinde, Paredes, Sosa, Torales, Florentin (Kiese), Benitez, Romero, Isasi, Diarte, Aquino (Diaz).

**Guayaquil, 24 May, 1981**

**Ecuador (0) 0**

**Chile (0) 0**     50,000

*Ecuador:* Delgado; Perlaza, Klinger, Paez, Valenzia, Parraga, Villafuerte, Carrera (Revello), Tenorio, Quinones, Nieves (Paz).
*Chile:* Osben; Garrido, Valenzuela, Soto, Bigorra, Rivas, Rojas (Neira), Bonvallet, Yanez, Caszely, Moscoso.

**Asuncion, 31 May, 1981**

**Paraguay (0) 3** *(Michelagnoli, Morel, Romero)*

**Ecuador (0) 1** *(Figueroa)*     37,000

*Paraguay:* Almeida; Espinola, Paredes, Aifuch, Torales, Florentin, Benitez, Romero, Isasi, Diarte (Michelagnoli), Morel.
*Ecuador:* Delgado; Perlaza, Paez, Figueroa, Valenzia, Tenorio (Burbano), Klinger, Parraga, Quinones, Carrera, Nieves.

**Asuncion, 7 June, 1981**

**Paraguay (0) 0**

**Chile (0) 1** *(Yanez)*     50,000

*Paraguay:* Almeida; Espinola, Paredes, Aifuch, Torales, Florentin, Benitez, Romero, Isasi, Michelagnoli (Diarte), Morel (Cabanas).
*Chile:* Osben; Garrido, Figueroa, Valenzuela, Bigorra, Bonvallet (Neira), Soto, Dubo, Moscoso, Castec, Yanez (Rojas).

**Santiago, 14 June, 1981**

**Chile (1) 2** *(Rivas, Caszely)*

**Ecuador (0) 0**     80,000

*Chile:* Osben; Garrido, Valenzuela, Figueroa, Bigorra, Rojrs, Rivas, Castec (Dubo), Yanez (Herrera), Caszely, Moscoso.
*Ecuador:* Delgado; Perlaza, Klinger, Parraga, Paez, Valenzia, Parraga, Villafuerte, Tenorio, Quinones, Nieves.

**Santiago, 21 June, 1981**

**Chile (3) 3** *(Caszely, Yanez, Neira)*

**Paraguay (0) 0**     75,000

*Chile:* Osben; Garrido, Soto, Valenzuela, Bigorra, Dubo (Mondaca), Rojas, Neira, Yanez (Herrera), Caszely, Moscoso.
*Paraguay:* Almeida; Solalinde, Paredes, Aifuch, Torales, Benitez (Chepini), Isasi, Kiese, Rivera (Aquino), Florentin, Michelagnoli.

| | P | W | D | L | F | A | Pts |
|---|---|---|---|---|---|---|---|
| Chile | 4 | 3 | 1 | 0 | 6 | 0 | 7 |
| Ecuador | 4 | 1 | 1 | 2 | 2 | 5 | 3 |
| Paraguay | 4 | 1 | 0 | 3 | 3 | 3 | 2 |

# AFRICA

## First Round

*Results:* Senegal v Morocco 0-1, 0-0; Zaire v Mozambique 5-2, 2-1; Cameroon v Malawi 3-0, 1-1; Guinea v Lesotho 3-1, 1-1; Tunisia v Nigeria 2-0, 0-2 (Nigeria won 4-3 on pens); Libya v Gambia 2-1, 0-0; Ethiopia v Zambia 0-0, 0-4; Niger v Somalia 0-0, 1-0; Sierra Leone v Algeria 2-2, 1-3; Kenya v Tanzania 3-1, 0-5; Egypt w.o. v Ghana (scr); Madagascar w.o. v Uganda (scr).

## Second Round

*Results:* Algeria v Sudan 2-0, 1-1; Niger v Togo 0-1, 2-1 (Niger won on away goals); Liberia v Guinea 0-0, 0-1; Cameroon v Zimbabwe 2-0, 0-1; Morocco v Zambia 2-0, 0-2 (Morocco won 5-4 on pens); Nigeria v Tanzania 1-1, 2-0; Madagascar v Zaire 1-1, 2-3; Egypt w.o. v Libya (scr).

## Third Round

*Results:* Algeria v Niger 4-0, 0-1; Guinea v Nigeria 1-1, 0-1; Morocco v Egypt 1-0, 0-0; Zaire v Cameroon 1-0, 1-6.

## Final Round

**Lagos, 10 October, 1981**

**Nigeria (0) 0**

**Algeria (2) 2** *(Belloumi, Zidane)*                    100,000

*Nigeria:* Best; Opkala, Bamidele, Chekwu (Kachi), Isima, Banjo, Muda, Andrew, Odegdami, Usugnan, Owolabi (Nwokocho).
*Algeria:* Cerbah; Larbes, Kourichi, Guendouz, Mansouri, Kaci-Said, Belloumi, Fergani, Chebel (Assad), Zidane, Gamouh (Kouici).

**Constantine, 30 October, 1981**

**Algeria (1) 2** *(Belloumi, Madjer)*

**Nigeria (1) 1** *(Isima)*                    60,000

*Algeria:* Cerbah; Larbes, Kourichi, Guendouz, Mansouri, Kaci-Said, Mahyouz, Belloumi, Madjer, Zidane (Dahleb), Gamouh.
*Nigeria:* Best; Opkala, Fregene (Fataie), Boateng, Owolabi, Isima, Lawal, Bamidele, Odegdami, Nwosu, Chiedozie.

**Kenitra, 15 November, 1981**

**Morocco (0) 0**

**Cameroon (2) 2** *(Aoudou* pen, *Tokoto)*                    16,000

*Morocco:* Raounek; Dolmi, Mouh, Jawad, Filali, Abdelatif, Chicha, Amanallah (Houcine), Aziz, Jamal (Safari), Boussati.
*Cameroon:* N'Kono; Kaham, Aoudou, N'Doumbe Lea, M'Bom, Kunde, Abega, Tokoto, Bahoken (Bengue), Milla, N'Guea.

**Yaounde, 29 November, 1981**

**Cameroon (1) 2** *(Aoudou* pen, *Milla)*

**Morocco (1) 1** *(Mustapha* pen*)*                    120,000

*Cameroon:* N'Kono; Kaham, Aoudou, N'Doumbe Lea, M'Bom, M'Bida, Abega, Tokoto, Bahoken, Milla, Maya.
*Morocco:* Raounek; Houcine, Jawad, Bouyahyaoui, Filali, Abdelatif, Mustapha, Amanallah (Dousati), Aziz, Krimau, Tissir.

# NORTH AND CENTRAL AMERICA (CONCACAF)

## Northern Zone

*Results:* Canada 1, Mexico 1; USA 0, Canada 0; Canada 2, USA 1; Mexico 5, USA 1; Mexico 1, Canada 1; USA 2, Mexico 1.

|        | P | W | D | L | F | A | Pts |
|--------|---|---|---|---|---|---|-----|
| Canada | 4 | 1 | 3 | 0 | 4 | 3 | 5 |
| Mexico | 4 | 1 | 2 | 1 | 8 | 5 | 4 |
| USA    | 4 | 1 | 1 | 2 | 4 | 8 | 3 |

## Central Zone

*Results:* Panama 0, Guatemala 2; Panama 0, Honduras 2; Panama 1, Costa Rica 1; Panama 1, El Salvador 3; Costa Rica 2, Honduras 3; El Salvador 4, Panama 1; Guatemala 0, Costa Rica 0; Honduras 0, Guatemala 0; El Salvador v Costa Rica awarded to El Salvador 2-0 when Costa Rica refused to play in El Salvador for security reasons; Costa Rica 2, Panama 0; Guatemala 0, El Salvador 0; Guatemala 5, Panama 0; Honduras 1, Costa Rica 1; El Salvador 2, Honduras 1; Costa Rica 0, Guatemala 3; Honduras 2, El Salvador 0; Guatemala 0, Honduras 1; Costa Rica 0, El Salvador 0; Honduras 5, Panama 0; El Salvador 1, Guatemala 0.

|             | P | W | D | L | F  | A  | Pts |
|-------------|---|---|---|---|----|----|-----|
| Honduras    | 8 | 5 | 2 | 1 | 15 | 5  | 12 |
| El Salvador | 8 | 5 | 2 | 1 | 12 | 5  | 12 |
| Guatemala   | 8 | 3 | 3 | 2 | 10 | 2  | 9 |
| Costa Rica  | 8 | 1 | 4 | 3 | 6  | 10 | 6 |
| Panama      | 8 | 0 | 1 | 7 | 3  | 24 | 1 |

# CARIBBEAN ZONE

## Extra Preliminary Round

Guyana 5, Grenada 2; Grenada 2, Guyana 3.

## Group A

*Results:* Cuba 3, Surinam 0; Surinam 0, Cuba 0; Guyana 0, Surinam 1; Surinam 4, Guyana 0; Cuba 1, Guyana 0; Guyana 0, Cuba 3.

|         | P | W | D | L | F | A | Pts |
|---------|---|---|---|---|---|---|-----|
| Cuba    | 4 | 3 | 1 | 0 | 7 | 0 | 7 |
| Surinam | 4 | 2 | 1 | 1 | 5 | 3 | 5 |
| Guyana  | 4 | 0 | 0 | 4 | 0 | 9 | 0 |

## Group B

*Results:* Haiti 2, Trinidad-Tobago 0; Trinidad-Tobago 1, Haiti 0; Haiti 1, Netherlands Antilles 0; Trinidad-Tobago 0, Netherlands Antilles 0; Netherlands Antilles 0, Trinidad-Tobago 0; Netherlands Antilles 1, Haiti 1.

|                     | P | W | D | L | F | A | Pts |
|---------------------|---|---|---|---|---|---|-----|
| Haiti               | 4 | 2 | 1 | 1 | 4 | 2 | 5 |
| Trinidad-Tobago     | 4 | 1 | 2 | 1 | 2 | 1 | 4 |
| Netherlands Antilles| 4 | 0 | 3 | 1 | 1 | 2 | 3 |

## Final Tournament *(in Honduras)*

*Results:* Mexico 4, Cuba 0; Canada 1, El Salvador 0; Honduras 4, Haiti 0; Haiti 1, Canada 1; Mexico 0, El Salvador 1; Honduras 2, Cuba 0; El Salvador 0, Cuba 0; Mexico 1, Haiti 1; Honduras 2, Canada 1; Haiti 0, Cuba 2; Mexico 1, Canada 1.

## Honduras 0, El Salvador 0

*Honduras:* Arzu; Gutierrez, Villegas, Bulnes, Costly A., Maradiaga, Toledo, Figueroa, Costly J. (Urquia), Caballero, Bernardez.
*El Salvador:* Mora; Jovel, Rodriguez, Recinos, Osorto, Quinteros, Huezo, Rugamas (Gonzalez G.), Gonzalez J., Hernandez, Romeo (Quintanilla).
Haiti 0, El Salvador 1; Cuba 2, Canada 2; Honduras 0, Mexico 0.

| | P | W | D | L | F | A | Pts |
|---|---|---|---|---|---|---|---|
| Honduras | 5 | 3 | 2 | 0 | 8 | 1 | 8 |
| El Salvador | 5 | 2 | 2 | 1 | 2 | 1 | 6 |
| Mexico | 5 | 1 | 3 | 1 | 6 | 3 | 5 |
| Canada | 5 | 1 | 3 | 1 | 6 | 6 | 5 |
| Cuba | 5 | 1 | 2 | 2 | 4 | 8 | 4 |
| Haiti | 5 | 0 | 2 | 3 | 2 | 9 | 2 |

## ASIA/OCEANIA

### Group 1

*Results:* New Zealand 3, Australia 3; Fiji 0, New Zealand 4; Taiwan 0, New Zealand 0; Indonesia 0, New Zealand 2; Australia 0, New Zealand 2; Australia 2, Indonesia 0; New Zealand 5, Indonesia 0; New Zealand 2, Taiwan 0; Fiji 0, Indonesia 0; Fiji 2, Taiwan 1; Australia 3, Taiwan 2; Indonesia 1, Taiwan 0; Taiwan 2, Indonesia 0; Fiji 1, Australia 4; Taiwan 0, Fiji 0; Indonesia 3, Fiji 3; Australia 10, Fiji 0; New Zealand 13, Fiji 0; Indonesia 1, Australia 0; Taiwan 0, Australia 0.

| | P | W | D | L | F | A | Pts |
|---|---|---|---|---|---|---|---|
| New Zealand | 8 | 6 | 2 | 0 | 31 | 3 | 14 |
| Australia | 8 | 4 | 2 | 2 | 22 | 9 | 10 |
| Indonesia | 8 | 2 | 2 | 4 | 5 | 14 | 6 |
| Taiwan | 8 | 1 | 3 | 4 | 5 | 8 | 5 |
| Fiji | 8 | 1 | 3 | 4 | 6 | 35 | 5 |

### Group 2 *(in Saudi Arabia)*

*Results:* Qatar 0, Iraq 1; Syria 0, Bahrain 1; Iraq 0, Saudi Arabia 1; Qatar 3, Bahrain 0; Syria 0, Saudi Arabia 2; Iraq 2, Bahrain 0; Qatar 2, Syria 1; Bahrain 0, Saudi Arabia 1; Iraq 2, Syria 1; Qatar 0, Saudi Arabia 1.

| | P | W | D | L | F | A | Pts |
|---|---|---|---|---|---|---|---|
| Saudi Arabia | 4 | 4 | 0 | 0 | 5 | 0 | 8 |
| Iraq | 4 | 3 | 0 | 1 | 5 | 2 | 6 |
| Qatar | 4 | 2 | 0 | 2 | 5 | 3 | 4 |
| Bahrain | 4 | 1 | 0 | 3 | 1 | 6 | 2 |
| Syria | 4 | 0 | 0 | 4 | 2 | 7 | 0 |

### Group 3 *(in Kuwait)*

*Results:* Malaysia 1, South Korea 2; Kuwait 6, Thailand 0; South Korea 5, Thailand 1; Kuwait 4, Malaysia 0; Malaysia 2, Thailand 2; Kuwait 2, South Korea 0.

| | P | W | D | L | F | A | Pts |
|---|---|---|---|---|---|---|---|
| Kuwait | 3 | 3 | 0 | 0 | 12 | 0 | 6 |
| South Korea | 3 | 2 | 0 | 1 | 7 | 4 | 4 |
| Malaysia | 3 | 0 | 1 | 2 | 3 | 8 | 1 |
| Thailand | 3 | 0 | 1 | 2 | 3 | 13 | 1 |

Iran withdrew

### Group 4 *(in Hong Kong)*

**Play-off matches**

*Results:* Hong Kong 0, China 1; North Korea 3, Macao 0; Singapore 0, Japan 1.

### Group A

*Results:* China 3, Macao 0; China 1, Japan 0; Japan 3, Macao 0.

### Group B

*Results:* Hong Kong 1, Singapore 1; Singapore 0, North Korea 1; Hong Kong 2, North Korea 2.

**Semi-finals**

North Korea 1, Japan 0; China 0, Hong Kong 0 (China won 5-4 on pens).

**Final**

China 4, North Korea 2 *aet.*

**Final Tournament**

*Results:* China 0, New Zealand 0; New Zealand 1, China 0; New Zealand 1, Kuwait 2; China 3, Kuwait 0; Saudi Arabia 0, Kuwait 1; Saudi Arabia 2, China 4; China 2, Saudi Arabia 0; New Zealand 2, Saudi Arabia 2; Kuwait 1, China 0; Kuwait 2, Saudi Arabia 0.

**Kuwait, 14 December, 1981**

**Kuwait (1) 2** *(Fatih Kameel, Al Hashash)*

**New Zealand (0) 2** *(Sumner, Rufer)*                    25,000

*Kuwait:* Tarabulsi; Naeem, Al Hashash, Mahboud, Waleed, Al Ghanem, Buloushi, Ahmed (Suwayyed), Fatih Kameel, Al Dakheel, Al Anbari.
*New Zealand:* Wilson; Dods, Herbert, Almond, Elrick, Turner B., Wooddin, Sumner, Cole, Rufer, Turner G.
Saudi Arabia 0, New Zealand 5.

| | P | W | D | L | F | A | Pts |
|---|---|---|---|---|---|---|---|
| Kuwait | 6 | 4 | 1 | 1 | 8 | 6 | 9 |
| New Zealand | 6 | 2 | 3 | 1 | 11 | 6 | 7 |
| China | 6 | 3 | 1 | 2 | 9 | 4 | 7 |
| Saudi Arabia | 6 | 0 | 1 | 5 | 4 | 16 | 1 |

**Play-off**

**Singapore, 10 January, 1982**

**New Zealand (1) 2** *(Wooddin, Rufer)*

**China (0) 1** *(Huang Xiangdong)*                    60,000

*New Zealand:* Wilson; Dods, Herbert, Almond, Elrick, Boath (Simonsen), Sumner, Cole, Turner G., Rufer (Adam), Wooddin.
*China:* Li Fusheng; Cai Jinbiao, Chi Shangbin, Lin Luofeng, Huang Xiangdong, Zang Cailing, Zuo Shusheng (Yang Yumin), Gu Guangmin (Liu Chender), Rong Zhihang, Chen Xurong, Wu Yuhua.

# FINAL TOURNAMENT

## Group 1

*Poland, Italy, Cameroon, Peru*

### Vigo, 14 June

**Italy (0) 0**

**Poland (0) 0**      27,000

*Italy:* Zoff; Gentile, Scirea, Collovati, Cabrini, Marini, Antognoni, Tardelli, Conti, Rossi, Graziani.
*Poland:* Mlynarczyk; Jalocha, Majewski, Zmuda, Janas, Buncol, Lato, Boniek, Matysik, Iwan (Kusto), Smolarek.

### La Coruna, 15 June

**Peru (0) 0**

**Cameroon (0) 0**      11,000

*Peru:* Quiroga; Duarte, Gonzales, Diaz, Olaechea, Uribe, Cueto, Velasquez, Leguia (La Rosa), Cubillas (Barbadillo), Oblitas.
*Cameroon:* N'Kono; M'Bom, Aoudou, Onana, Kaham, Abega, M'Bida, Kunde, Milla (Tokoto), N'Djeya, N'Guea (Bahoken).

### Vigo, 18 June

**Italy (1) 1** *(Conti)*

**Peru (0) 1** *(Diaz)*      31,000

*Italy:* Zoff; Cabrini, Collovati, Gentile, Scirea, Antognoni, Marini, Tardelli, Conti, Graziani, Rossi (Causio).
*Peru:* Quiroga; Duarte, Diaz, Salguero, Olaechea, Cueto, Velasquez (La Rosa), Cubillas, Uribe, Oblitas, Barbadillo (Leguia).

### La Coruna, 19 June

**Poland (0) 0**

**Cameroon (0) 0**      15,000

*Poland:* Mlynarczyk; Majewski, Janas, Zmuda, Jalocha, Lato, Buncol, Boniek, Iwan (Szarmach), Palasz (Kusto), Smolarek.
*Cameroon:* N'Kono; Kaham, Onana, N'Djeya, M'Bom, Aoudou, Abega, Kunde, M'Bida, Milla, N'Guea (Tokoto).

### La Coruna, 22 June

**Poland (0) 5** *(Smolarek, Lato, Boniek, Buncol, Ciolek)*

**Peru (0) 1** *(La Rosa)*      25,000

*Poland:* Mlynarczyk; Majewski, Janas, Zmuda, Jalocha, Buncol, Matysik, Kupcewicz, Lato, Boniek, Smolarek (Ciolek).
*Peru:* Quiroga; Duarte, Diaz, Salguero, Olaechea, Cubillas (Uribe), Velasquez, Cueto, Leguia, La Rosa, Oblitas (Barbadillo).

### Vigo, 23 June

**Italy (0) 1** *(Graziani)*

**Cameroon (0) 1** *(M'Bida)*      31,000

*Italy:* Zoff; Gentile, Collovati, Scirea, Cabrini, Oriali, Tardelli, Antognoni, Conti, Rossi, Graziani.
*Cameroon:* N'Kono; Kaham, N'Djeya, Onana, M'Bom, Aoudou, Kunde, M'Bida, Abega, Milla, Tokoto.

## Group 2

*West Germany, Austria, Algeria, Chile*

### Gijon, 16 June

**Algeria (0) 2** *(Madjer, Belloumi)*

**West Germany (0) 1** *(Rummenigge)*      42,000

*Algeria:* Cerbah; Guendouz, Kourichi, Merzekane, Mansouri, Belloumi, Dhaleb, Fergani, Madjer (Larbes), Zidane (Bensaoula), Assad.
*West Germany:* Schumacher; Kaltz, Stielike, Forster K. H., Briegel, Breitner, Magath (Fischer), Dremmler, Rummenigge, Hrubesch, Littbarski.

### Oviedo, 17 June

**Austria (1) 1** *(Schachner)*

**Chile (0) 0**      22,500

*Austria:* Koncilia; Krauss, Obermayer, Pezzey, Degeorgi (Baumeister), Hattenberger, Hintermaier, Weber (Jurtin), Prohaska, Krankl, Schachner.
*Chile:* Osben; Garrido, Figueroa, Valenzuela, Bigorra, Bonvallet, Dubo, Neira (Manuel Rojas), Moscoso (Gamboa), Yanez, Caszely.

### Gijon, 20 June

**West Germany (1) 4** *(Rummenigge 3, Reinders)*

**Chile (0) 1** *(Moscoso)*      30,000

*West Germany:* Schumacher; Kaltz, Stielike, Forster K. H., Briegel, Dremmler, Breitner (Matthaus), Magath, Littbarski (Reinders), Hrubesch, Rummenigge.
*Chile:* Osben; Garrido, Figueroa, Valenzuela, Bigorra, Dubo, Bonvallet, Soto (Letelier), Moscoso, Yanez, Gamboa (Neira).

### Oviedo, 21 June

**Algeria (0) 0**

**Austria (0) 2** *(Schachner, Krankl)*      22,000

*Algeria:* Cerbah; Guendouz, Kourichi, Marzekane, Mansouri, Belloumi (Bensaoula), Dhaleb (Tiemcani), Fergani, Madjer, Zidane, Assad.
*Austria:* Koncilia; Krauss, Obermayer, Degeorgi, Pezzey, Hattenberger, Hintermaier, Baumeister (Welzl), Prohaska (Weber), Krankl, Schachner.

### Oviedo, 24 June

**Algeria (3) 3** *(Assad 2, Bensaoula)*

**Chile (0) 2** *(Neira pen, Letelier)*      18,500

*Algeria:* Cerbah; Kourichi, Marzekane, Guendouz, Larbes, Mansouri (Dhaleb), Fergani, Assad, Bensaoula, Bourebbou (Yahi), Madjer.
*Chile:* Osben; Galindo, Valenzuela, Figueroa, Bigorra, Bonvallet (Soto), Dubo, Neira, Yanez, Caszely (Letelier), Moscoso.

### Gijon, 25 June

**West Germany (1) 1** *(Hrubesch)*

**Austria (0) 0**      41,000

*West Germany:* Schumacher; Kaltz, Stielike, Forster K. H., Briegel, Dremmler, Breitner, Magath, Littbarski, Hrubesch (Fischer), Rummenigge (Matthaus).
*Austria:* Koncilia; Krauss, Pezzey, Obermayer, Degeorgi, Hattenberger, Prohaska, Hintermaier, Weber, Schachner, Krankl.

| | P | W | D | L | F | A | Pts |
|---|---|---|---|---|---|---|---|
| Poland | 3 | 1 | 2 | 0 | 5 | 1 | 4 |
| Italy | 3 | 0 | 3 | 0 | 2 | 2 | 3 |
| Cameroon | 3 | 0 | 3 | 0 | 1 | 1 | 3 |
| Peru | 3 | 0 | 2 | 1 | 2 | 6 | 2 |

| | P | W | D | L | F | A | Pts |
|---|---|---|---|---|---|---|---|
| West Germany | 3 | 2 | 0 | 1 | 6 | 3 | 4 |
| Austria | 3 | 2 | 0 | 1 | 3 | 1 | 4 |
| Algeria | 3 | 2 | 0 | 1 | 5 | 5 | 4 |
| Chile | 3 | 0 | 0 | 3 | 3 | 8 | 0 |

## Group 3

*Belgium, Argentina, Hungary, El Salvador*

### Barcelona, 13 June

**Argentina (0) 0**

**Belgium (0) 1** *(Van den Bergh)*                     85,000

*Argentina:* Fillol; Olguin, Galvan, Passarella, Tarantini, Ardiles, Gallego, Maradona, Bertoni, Diaz (Valdano), Kempes.
*Belgium:* Pfaff; Gerets, Millecamps L., de Schrijver, Baecke, Coeck, Vercauteren, Vandersmissen, Czerniatynski, Van den Bergh, Ceulemans.

### Elche, 15 June

**Hungary (3) 10** *(Nyilasi 2, Poloskei, Fazekas 2, Toth, Kiss 3, Szentes)*

**El Salvador (0) 1** *(Zapata)*                     19,750

*Hungary:* Meszaros; Martos, Balint, Toth, Garaba, Muller (Szentes), Nyilasi, Sallai, Fazekas, Torocsik (Kiss), Poloskei.
*El Salvador:* Mora; Castillo, Jovel, Rodriguez, Recinos, Rugamas (Zapata), Ventura, Huezo, Hernandez F., Gonzalez, Rivas.

### Alicante, 18 June

**Argentina (2) 4** *(Bertoni, Maradona 2, Ardiles)*

**Hungary (0) 1** *(Poloskei)*                     32,000

*Argentina:* Fillol; Olguin, Galvan, Passarella, Tarantini (Barbas), Ardiles, Gallego, Maradona, Bertoni, Valdano (Calderon), Kempes.
*Hungary:* Meszaros; Martos (Fazekas), Balint, Toth, Varga, Garaba, Nyilasi, Sallai, Rab, Kiss (Szentes), Poloskei.

### Elche, 19 June

**Belgium (1) 1** *(Coeck)*

**El Salvador (0) 0**                     15,000

*Belgium:* Pfaff; Gerets, Meeuws, Baecke, Millecamps L., Vandersmissen (Van der Elst), Coeck, Vercauteren, Ceulemans (Van Moer), Van den Bergh, Czerniatynski.
*El Savador:* Mora; Osorto (Diaz), Jovel, Rodriguez, Recinos, Fagoaga, Ventura, Huezo, Zapata, Gonzalez, Rivas.

### Elche, 22 June

**Belgium (0) 1** *(Czerniatynski)*

**Hungary (1) 1** *(Varga)*                     30,000

*Belgium:* Pfaff; Gerets (Plessers), Millecamps L., Meeuws, Baecke, Coeck, Vercauteren, Vandersmissen (Van Moer), Czerniatynski, Van den Bergh, Ceulemans.
*Hungary:* Meszaros; Martos, Kerekes (Sallai), Garaba, Varga, Nyilasi, Muller, Fazekas, Torocsik, Kiss (Csongradi), Poloskei.

### Alicante, 23 June

**Argentina (1) 2** *(Passarella pen, Bertoni)*

**El Salvador (0) 0**                     28,000

*Argentina:* Fillol; Olguin, Galvan, Passarella, Tarantini, Ardiles, Gallego, Kempes, Bertoni (Diaz), Maradona, Calderon (Santamaria).
*El Salvador:* Mora; Osorto (Arevalo), Jovel, Rodriguez, Ortiz, Fagoaga, Ventura (Alfaro), Huezo, Zapata, Gonzalez, Rivas.

|           | P | W | D | L | F  | A  | Pts |
|-----------|---|---|---|---|----|----|-----|
| Belgium   | 3 | 2 | 1 | 0 | 3  | 1  | 5   |
| Argentina | 3 | 2 | 0 | 1 | 6  | 2  | 4   |
| Hungary   | 3 | 1 | 1 | 1 | 12 | 6  | 3   |
| El Salvador | 3 | 0 | 0 | 3 | 1  | 13 | 0   |

## Group 4

*England, France, Czechoslovakia, Kuwait*

### Bilbao, 16 June

**England (1) 3** *(Robson 2, Mariner)*

**France (1) 1** *(Soler)*                     45,000

*England:* Shilton; Mills, Sansom (Neal), Thompson, Butcher, Robson, Coppell, Wilkins, Mariner, Francis, Rix.
*France:* Ettori; Battiston, Bossis, Tresor, Lopez, Larios (Tigana), Girard, Giresse, Rocheteau (Six), Platini, Soler.

### Valladolid, 17 June

**Czechoslovakia (1) 1** *(Panenka pen)*

**Kuwait (0) 1** *(Al Dakheel)*                     25,000

*Czechoslovakia:* Hruska; Barmos, Jurkemik, Fiala, Kukucka, Panenka, Berger, Kriz (Bicovsky), Janecka (Petrzela), Nehoda, Vizek.
*Kuwait:* Al Tarabulsi; Naeem Saed, Mayoof, Mahboub, Waleed Jasem, Al Bouloushi, Saed Al Houti, Karam (Fathi Kameel), Al Dakheel, Jasem Yacoub, Al Anbari.

### Bilbao, 20 June

**England (0) 2** *(Francis, Mariner)*

**Czechoslovakia (0) 0**                     42,000

*England:* Shilton; Mills, Thompson, Butcher, Sansom, Coppell, Robson (Hoddle), Wilkins, Francis, Mariner, Rix.
*Czechoslovakia:* Seman (Stromsik); Barmos, Fiala, Radimec, Vojacek, Jurkemik, Chaloupka, Vizek, Berger, Janecka (Masny), Nehoda.

### Valladolid, 21 June

**France (2) 4** *(Genghini, Platini, Six, Bossis)*

**Kuwait (0) 1** *(Al Buloushi)*                     18,000

*France:* Ettori; Amoros, Tresor, Janvion, Bossis, Giresse, Platini (Girard), Genghini, Soler, Lacombe, Six.
*Kuwait:* Al Tarabulsi; Naeem Saed, Mayoof, Mahboub, Waleed Jasem (Al Shemmari), Al Buloushi, Saed Al Houti, Karam (Fathi Kameel), Al Dakheel, Jasem Yacoub, Al Anbari.

### Valladolid, 24 June

**France (0) 1** *(Six)*

**Czechoslovakia (0) 1** *(Panenka pen)*                     25,000

*France:* Ettori; Amoros, Tresor, Janvion, Bossis, Giresse, Platini, Genghini, Soler (Girard), Lacombe (Couriol), Six.
*Czechoslovakia:* Stromsik; Barmos, Fiala, Stambacher, Vojacek, Jurkemik, Kriz (Masny), Bicovsky, Vizek, Janecka (Panenka), Nehoda.

### Bilbao, 25 June

**England (1) 1** *(Francis)*

**Kuwait (0) 0**                     39,700

*England:* Shilton; Neal, Thompson, Foster, Mills, Coppell, Hoddle, Wilkins, Rix, Mariner, Francis.
*Kuwait:* Al Tarabulsi; Naeem Saed, Mahboub, Mayoof, Waleek Jasem (Al Shemmari), Saed Al Houti, Al Buloushi, Al Suwayed, Fathi Kameel, Al Dakheel, Al Anbari.

|               | P | W | D | L | F | A | Pts |
|---------------|---|---|---|---|---|---|-----|
| England       | 3 | 3 | 0 | 0 | 6 | 1 | 6   |
| France        | 3 | 1 | 1 | 1 | 6 | 5 | 3   |
| Czechoslovakia | 3 | 0 | 2 | 1 | 2 | 4 | 2   |
| Kuwait        | 3 | 0 | 1 | 2 | 2 | 6 | 1   |

## Group 5

*Northern Ireland, Spain, Yugoslavia, Honduras*

**Valencia, 16 June**

**Spain (0) 1** *(Lopez Ufarte pen)*

**Honduras (1) 1** *(Zelaya)*                     50,000

*Spain:* Arconada; Gordillo, Camacho, Alonso, Alesanco, Tendillo, Juanito (Saura), Joaquim (Sanchez), Satrustegui, Zamora, Lopez Ufarte.
*Honduras:* Arzu; Guitierrez, Costly, Villegas, Bulnes, Zelaya, Gilberto, Maradiaga, Norales (Caballero), Betancourt, Figueroa.

**Zaragoza, 17 June**

**Northern Ireland (0) 0**

**Yugoslavia (0) 0**                     25,000

*Northern Ireland:* Jennings; Nicholl J., Nicholl C., McClelland, Donaghy, McIlroy, O'Neill M., McCreery, Armstrong, Hamilton, Whiteside.
*Yugoslavia:* Pantelic; Gudelj, Zajec, Stojkovic, Petrovic, Sljivo, Zlatko Vujovic, Susic, Jovanovic, Hrstic, Surjak.

**Valencia, 20 June**

**Spain (1) 2** *(Juanito pen, Saura)*

**Yugoslavia (1) 1** *(Gudelj)*                     47,500

*Spain:* Arconada; Camacho, Tendillo, Alesanco, Gordillo, Alonso, Sanchez (Saura), Zamora, Juanito, Satrustegui (Quini), Lopez Ufarte.
*Yugoslavia:* Pantelic; Krmpotic, Zajec, Stojkovic, Jovanovic (Halilhodzic), Gudelj, Petrovic, Sljivo, Zlatko Vujovic (Sestic), Surjak, Susic.

**Zaragoza, 21 June**

**Honduras (0) 1** *(Laing)*

**Northern Ireland (1) 1** *(Armstrong)*                     20,000

*Honduras:* Arzu; Gutierrez, Villegas, Cruz, Costly, Maradiaga, Gilberto, Zelaya, Norales (Laing), Betancourt, Figueroa.
*Northern Ireland:* Jennings; Nicholl J., Nicholl C., McClelland, Donaghy, O'Neill M. (Healy), McCreery, McIlroy, Whiteside (Brotherston), Armstrong, Hamilton.

**Zaragoza, 24 June**

**Honduras (0) 0**

**Yugoslavia (0) 1** *(Petrovic pen)*                     12,000

*Honduras:* Arzu; Droumond, Villegas, Costly, Bulnes, Zelaya, Gilberto, Maradiaga, Murillo (Laing), Betancourt, Figueroa.
*Yugoslavia:* Patelic; Krmpotic, Stojkovic, Zajec, Jovanovic (Halilhodzic), Sljivo, Gudelj, Surjak, Zlatko Vujovic (Sestic), Susic, Petrovic.

**Valencia, 25 June**

**Northern Ireland (0) 1** *(Armstrong)*

**Spain (0) 0**                     49,562

*Northern Ireland:* Jennings; Nicholl J., Nicholl C., McClelland, Donaghy, O'Neill M., McCreery, McIlroy (Cassidy), Armstrong, Hamilton, Whiteside (Nelson).
*Spain:* Arconada; Camacho, Tendillo, Alesanco, Gordillo, Sanchez, Alonso, Saura, Juanito, Satrustegui (Quini), Lopez Ufarte (Gallego).

## Group 6

*Brazil, USSR, Scotland, New Zealand*

**Seville, 14 June**

**Brazil (0) 2** *(Socrates, Eder)*

**USSR (1) 1** *(Bal)*                     50,000

*Brazil:* Valdir Peres; Leandro, Oscar, Luizinho, Junior, Socrates, Serginho, Zico, Eder, Falcao, Dirceu (Paulo Isidoro).
*USSR:* Dasachan; Sulakvelidze, Chivadze, Baltacha, Demyanenko, Shengelia (Andreyev), Bessonov, Gavrilov (Susloparov), Blokhin, Bal, Daraselia.

**Malaga, 15 June**

**Scotland (3) 5** *(Dalglish, Wark 2, Robertson, Archibald)*

**New Zealand (0) 2** *(Sumner, Wooddin)*                     25,000

*Scotland:* Rough; McGrain, Gray F., Hansen, Evans, Souness, Strachan (Narey), Dalglish, Wark, Brazil (Archibald), Robertson.
*New Zealand:* Van Hattum; Elrick, Hill, Malcolmson (Cole), Almond (Herbert), Sumner, Mackay, Cresswell, Boath, Rufer W., Wooddin.

**Seville, 18 June**

**Brazil (1) 4** *(Zico, Oscar, Eder, Falcao)*

**Scotland (1) 1** *(Narey)*                     47,000

*Brazil:* Valdir Peres; Leandro, Oscar, Luizinho, Junior, Cerezo, Falcao, Socrates, Serginho (Paulo Isidoro), Zico, Eder.
*Scotland:* Rough; Narey, Gray F., Souness, Hansen, Miller, Strachan (Dalglish), Hartford (McLeish), Archibald, Wark, Robertson.

**Malaga, 19 June**

**USSR (1) 3** *(Gavrilov, Blokhin, Baltacha)*

**New Zealand (0) 0**                     20,000

*USSR:* Dasayev; Sulakvelidze, Chivadze, Baltacha, Demyanenko, Shengelia, Bessonov, Bal, Daraselia (Oganesian), Gavrilov (Rodionov), Blokhin.
*New Zealand:* Van Hattum; Dods, Herbert, Elrick, Boath, Cole, Sumner, Mackay, Cresswell, Rufer W., Wooddin.

**Malaga, 22 June**

**Scotland (1) 2** *(Jordan, Souness)*

**USSR (0) 2** *(Chivadze, Shengelia)*                     38,000

*Scotland:* Rough; Narey, Gray F., Souness, Hansen, Miller, Strachan (McGrain), Archibald, Jordan (Brazil), Wark, Robertson.
*USSR:* Dasayev; Sulakvelidze, Chivadze, Baltacha, Demyanenko, Borovsky, Shengelia (Andreyev), Bessonov, Gavrilov, Bal, Blokhin.

**Seville, 23 June**

**Brazil (2) 4** *(Zico 2, Falcao, Serginho)*

**New Zealand (0) 0**                     45,000

*Brazil:* Valdir Peres; Leandro, Oscar (Edinho), Luizinho, Junior, Cerezo, Socrates, Zico, Falcao, Serginho (Paulo Isidoro), Eder.
*New Zealand:* Van Hattum; Dods, Herbert, Elrick, Boath, Sumner, Mackay, Cresswell (Turner B.), Almond, Rufer W. (Cole), Wooddin.

| | P | W | D | L | F | A | Pts |
|---|---|---|---|---|---|---|---|
| Northern Ireland | 3 | 1 | 2 | 0 | 2 | 1 | 4 |
| Spain | 3 | 1 | 1 | 1 | 3 | 3 | 3 |
| Yugoslavia | 3 | 1 | 1 | 1 | 2 | 2 | 3 |
| Honduras | 3 | 0 | 2 | 1 | 2 | 3 | 2 |

| | P | W | D | L | F | A | Pts |
|---|---|---|---|---|---|---|---|
| Brazil | 3 | 3 | 0 | 0 | 10 | 2 | 6 |
| USSR | 3 | 1 | 1 | 1 | 6 | 4 | 3 |
| Scotland | 3 | 1 | 1 | 1 | 8 | 8 | 3 |
| New Zealand | 3 | 0 | 0 | 3 | 2 | 12 | 0 |

## Group A

*Poland, USSR, Belgium*

**Barcelona, 28 June**

**Poland (2) 3** *(Boniek 3)*

**Belgium (0) 0**                                           20,000

*Poland:* Mlynarczyk; Dziuba, Zmuda, Janas, Majewski, Kupcewicz (Ciolek), Buncol, Matysik, Lato, Boniek, Smolarek.
*Belgium:* Custers; Renquin, Millecamps L., Meeuws, Plessers (Baecke), Van Moer (Van der Elst), Coeck, Vercauteren, Czerniatynski, Van den Bergh, Ceulemans.

**Barcelona, 1 July**

**Belgium (0) 0**

**USSR (0) 1** *(Oganesian)*                                25,000

*Belgium:* Munaron; Renquin, Millecamps L., Meeuws, de Schrijver (Millecamps M.), Verheyen, Coeck, Vercauteren, Vandersmissen (Czerniatynski), Van den Bergh, Ceulemans.
*USSR:* Dasayev; Borovsky, Chivadze, Baltacha, Demyanenko, Bal (Daraselia), Oganesian, Bessonov, Shengelia (Rodionov), Gavrilov, Blokhin.

**Barcelona, 4 July**

**Poland (0) 0**

**USSR (0) 0**                                              40,000

*Poland:* Mlynarczyk; Dziuba, Zmuda, Janas, Majewski, Kupcewicz (Ciolek), Buncol, Matysik, Lato, Boniek, Smolarek.
*USSR:* Dasayev; Sulakvelidze, Chivadze, Baltacha, Demyanenko, Borovsky, Oganesian, Bessonov, Shengelia (Andreyev), Gavrilov (Daraselia), Blokhin.

|          | P | W | D | L | F | A | Pts |
|----------|---|---|---|---|---|---|-----|
| Poland   | 2 | 1 | 1 | 0 | 3 | 0 | 3   |
| USSR     | 2 | 1 | 1 | 0 | 1 | 0 | 3   |
| Belgium  | 2 | 0 | 0 | 2 | 0 | 4 | 0   |

## Group B

*West Germany, England, Spain*

**Madrid, 29 June**

**West Germany (0) 0**

**England (0) 0**                                           75,000

*West Germany:* Schumacher; Kaltz, Forster K. H., Stielike, Forster B., Muller (Fischer), Breitner, Dremmler, Briegel, Rummenigge, Reinders (Littbarski).
*England:* Shilton; Mills, Thompson, Butcher, Sansom, Coppell, Wilkins, Robson, Rix, Francis (Woodcock), Mariner.

**Madrid, 2 July**

**Spain (0) 1** *(Zamora)*

**West Germany (0) 2** *(Littbarski, Fischer)*             98,000

*Spain:* Arconada; Camacho, Gordillo, Alonso, Tendillo, Alesanco, Juanito (Lopez Ufarte), Zamora, Urquiaga, Santillana, Quini (Sanchez).
*West Germany:* Schumacher; Kaltz, Forster K. H., Stielike, Forster B., Breitner, Briegel, Dremmler, Littbarski, Fischer, Rummenigge (Reinders).

**Madrid, 5 July**

**England (0) 0**

**Spain (0) 0**                                             75,000

*England:* Shilton; Mills, Thompson, Butcher, Sansom, Wilkins, Robson, Rix (Brooking), Francis, Mariner, Woodcock (Keegan).
*Spain:* Arconada; Camacho, Gordillo, Alonso, Tendillo (Macedo), Alesanco, Satrustegui, Zamora, Urquiaga, Saura (Uralde), Santillana.

|              | P | W | D | L | F | A | Pts |
|--------------|---|---|---|---|---|---|-----|
| West Germany | 2 | 1 | 1 | 0 | 2 | 1 | 3   |
| England      | 2 | 0 | 2 | 0 | 0 | 0 | 2   |
| Spain        | 2 | 0 | 1 | 1 | 1 | 2 | 1   |

## Group C

*Italy, Brazil, Argentina*

**Barcelona, 29 June**

**Italy (0) 2** *(Tardelli, Cabrini)*

**Argentina (0) 1** *(Passarella)*                         39,150

*Italy:* Zoff; Gentile, Collovati, Scirea, Cabrini, Oriali (Marini), Tardelli, Antognoni, Conti, Rossi (Altobelli), Graziani.
*Argentina:* Fillol; Olguin, Passarella, Galvan, Tarantini, Ardiles, Gallego, Maradona, Bertoni, Diaz (Calderon), Kempes (Valencia).

**Barcelona, 2 July**

**Brazil (1) 3** *(Zico, Serginho, Junior)*

**Argentina (0) 1** *(Diaz)*                               44,000

*Brazil:* Valdir Peres; Leandro (Edevaldo), Oscar, Luizinho, Junior, Cerezo, Falcao, Socrates, Serginho, Zico (Batista), Eder.
*Argentina:* Fillol; Olguin, Barbas, Passarella, Tarantini, Ardiles, Galvan, Maradona, Bertoni (Santamaria), Calderon, Kempes (Diaz).

**Barcelona, 5 July**

**Italy (2) 3** *(Rossi 3)*

**Brazil (1) 2** *(Socrates, Falcao)*                      44,000

*Italy:* Zoff; Collovati (Bergomi), Gentile, Scirea, Cabrini, Oriali, Antognoni, Tardelli (Marini), Conti, Graziani, Rossi.
*Brazil:* Valdir Peres; Leandro, Oscar, Luizinho, Junior, Cerezo, Falcao, Socrates, Zico, Serginho (Paulo Isidoro), Eder.

|           | P | W | D | L | F | A | Pts |
|-----------|---|---|---|---|---|---|-----|
| Italy     | 2 | 2 | 0 | 0 | 5 | 3 | 4   |
| Brazil    | 2 | 1 | 0 | 1 | 5 | 4 | 2   |
| Argentina | 2 | 0 | 0 | 2 | 2 | 5 | 0   |

## Group D

*France, Austria, Northern Ireland*

**Madrid, 28 June**

**France (1) 1** *(Genghini)*

**Austria (0) 0**                                           37,000

*France:* Ettori; Battiston, Janvion, Tresor, Bossis, Giresse, Genghini (Girard), Tigana, Soler, Lacombe (Rocheteau), Six.
*Austria:* Koncilia; Krauss, Obermayer, Pezzey, Degeorgi (Baumeister), Hattenberger, Hintermaier, Jara (Welzl), Schachner, Prohaska, Krankl.

**Madrid, 1 July**

**Northern Ireland (1) 2** *(Hamilton 2)*

**Austria (0) 2** *(Pezzey, Hintermaier)*        24,000

*Northern Ireland:* Platt; Nicholl J., Nicholl C., McClelland, Nelson, McCreery, O'Neill M., McIlroy, Armstrong, Hamilton, Whiteside (Brotherston).
*Austria:* Koncilia; Krauss, Obermayer, Pezzey, Schachner, Prohaska, Pichler, Hagmayr (Welzl), Baumeister, Pregesbauer (Hintermaier), Jurtin.

**Madrid, 4 July**

**Northern Ireland (0) 1** *(Armstrong)*

**France (1) 4** *(Giresse 2, Rocheteau 2)*        26,000

*Northern Ireland:* Jennings; Nicholl J., Nicholl C., McClelland, Donaghy, McIlroy, McCreery (O'Neill J.), O'Neill M., Armstrong, Hamilton, Whiteside.
*France:* Ettori; Amoros, Janvion, Tresor, Bossis, Giresse, Genghini, Tigana, Platini, Soler (Six), Rocheteau (Couriol).

|                  | P | W | D | L | F | A | Pts |
|------------------|---|---|---|---|---|---|-----|
| France           | 2 | 2 | 0 | 0 | 5 | 1 | 4   |
| Austria          | 2 | 0 | 1 | 1 | 2 | 3 | 1   |
| Northern Ireland | 2 | 0 | 1 | 1 | 3 | 6 | 1   |

## SEMI-FINALS

**Barcelona, 8 July**

**Poland (0) 0**

**Italy (1) 2** *(Rossi 2)*        75,000

*Poland:* Mlynarczyk; Dziuba, Zmuda, Janas, Majewski, Kupcewicz, Buncol, Matysik, Lato, Ciolek (Palasz), Smolarek (Kusto).
*Italy:* Zoff; Bergomi, Collovati, Scirea, Cabrini, Oriali, Antognoni (Marini), Tardelli, Conti, Rossi, Graziani (Altobelli).

**Seville, 8 July**

**West Germany (1) 3** *aet (Littbarski, Rummenigge, Fischer)*

**France (1) 3** *(Platini* pen, *Tresor, Giresse)*        70,500

*West Germany* won 5-4 on pens: Kaltz, Breitner, Littbarski, Rummenigge and Hrubesch scored for West Germany: Stielike's shot was saved; Giresse, Amoros, Rocheteau and Platini scored for France: shots by Six and Bossis were saved.
*West Germany:* Schumacher; Kaltz, Forster K. H., Stielike, Forster B., Briegel (Rummenigge), Dremmler, Breitner, Littbarski, Fischer, Magath (Hrubesch).
*France:* Ettori; Amoros, Janvion, Tresor, Bossis, Genghini (Battiston) (Lopez), Platini, Giresse, Rocheteau, Six, Tigana.

## THIRD PLACE MATCH

**Alicante, 10 July**

**France (1) 2** *(Girard, Couriol)*

**Poland (2) 3** *(Szarmach, Majewski, Kupcewicz)*        25,000

*France:* Castaneda; Amoros, Mahut, Tresor, Janvion (Lopez), Tigana (Six), Girard, Larios, Couriol, Soler, Bellone.
*Poland:* Mlynarczyk; Dziuba, Janas, Zmuda, Majewski, Matysik (Wojcicki), Kupcewicz, Buncol, Lato, Szarmach, Boniek.

## FINAL

**Madrid, 11 July**

**West Germany (0) 1** *(Breitner)*

**Italy (0) 3** *(Rossi, Tardelli, Altobelli)*        90,089

*West Germany:* Schumacher; Kaltz, Forster K. H., Stielike, Forster B., Breitner, Dremmler (Hrubesch), Littbarski, Briegel, Fischer (Muller).
*Italy:* Zoff; Bergomi, Cabrini, Collovati, Scirea, Gentile, Oriali, Tardelli, Conti, Graziani (Altobelli) (Causio), Rossi.

## WORLD CUP 1930—82 FINAL SERIES

| | P | W | D | L | F | A |
|---|---|---|---|---|---|---|
| Brazil | 57 | 37 | 10 | 10 | 134 | 62 |
| West Germany | 54 | 31 | 11 | 12 | 122 | 78 |
| Italy | 43 | 24 | 9 | 10 | 74 | 46 |
| Argentina | 34 | 16 | 5 | 13 | 63 | 50 |
| England | 29 | 13 | 8 | 8 | 40 | 29 |
| Uruguay | 29 | 14 | 5 | 10 | 57 | 39 |
| Hungary | 29 | 14 | 3 | 12 | 85 | 48 |
| USSR | 24 | 12 | 5 | 7 | 37 | 25 |
| Poland | 21 | 12 | 4 | 5 | 38 | 22 |
| Yugoslavia | 28 | 12 | 4 | 12 | 47 | 36 |
| Sweden | 28 | 11 | 6 | 11 | 48 | 46 |
| France | 27 | 11 | 3 | 13 | 59 | 50 |
| Austria | 23 | 11 | 2 | 10 | 38 | 40 |
| Spain | 23 | 8 | 5 | 10 | 26 | 30 |
| Czechoslovakia | 25 | 8 | 5 | 12 | 34 | 40 |
| Holland | 16 | 8 | 3 | 5 | 32 | 19 |
| Chile | 21 | 7 | 3 | 11 | 26 | 32 |
| Switzerland | 18 | 5 | 2 | 11 | 28 | 44 |
| Scotland | 14 | 3 | 5 | 6 | 20 | 29 |
| Peru | 15 | 4 | 3 | 8 | 19 | 31 |
| Portugal | 6 | 5 | 0 | 1 | 17 | 8 |
| Norway | 10 | 3 | 4 | 3 | 11 | 17 |
| Mexico | 24 | 3 | 4 | 17 | 21 | 62 |
| Belgium | 14 | 3 | 2 | 9 | 15 | 30 |
| East Germany | 6 | 2 | 2 | 2 | 5 | 5 |
| Paraguay | 7 | 2 | 3 | 2 | 12 | 19 |

| | P | W | D | L | F | A |
|---|---|---|---|---|---|---|
| USA | 7 | 3 | 0 | 4 | 12 | 21 |
| Wales | 5 | 1 | 3 | 1 | 4 | 4 |
| Rumania | 8 | 2 | 1 | 5 | 12 | 17 |
| Algeria | 3 | 2 | 0 | 1 | 5 | 5 |
| Bulgaria | 12 | 0 | 4 | 8 | 9 | 29 |
| Tunisia | 3 | 1 | 1 | 1 | 3 | 2 |
| Cameroon | 3 | 0 | 3 | 0 | 1 | 1 |
| Cuba | 3 | 1 | 1 | 1 | 5 | 12 |
| North Korea | 4 | 1 | 1 | 2 | 5 | 9 |
| Turkey | 3 | 1 | 0 | 2 | 10 | 11 |
| Honduras | 3 | 0 | 2 | 1 | 2 | 3 |
| Israel | 3 | 1 | 0 | 2 | 1 | 3 |
| Kuwait | 3 | 0 | 1 | 2 | 2 | 6 |
| Morocco | 3 | 0 | -1 | 2 | 2 | 6 |
| Australia | 3 | 0 | 1 | 2 | 0 | 5 |
| Colombia | 3 | 0 | 1 | 2 | 5 | 11 |
| Iran | 3 | 0 | 1 | 2 | 2 | 8 |
| Norway | 1 | 0 | 0 | 1 | 1 | 2 |
| Egypt | 1 | 0 | 1 | 0 | 2 | 4 |
| Dutch East Indies | 1 | 0 | 0 | 1 | 0 | 6 |
| South Korea | 2 | 0 | 0 | 2 | 0 | 16 |
| New Zealand | 3 | 0 | 0 | 3 | 2 | 12 |
| Haiti | 3 | 0 | 0 | 3 | 2 | 14 |
| Zaire | 3 | 0 | 0 | 3 | 0 | 14 |
| Bolivia | 3 | 0 | 0 | 3 | 0 | 16 |
| El Salvador | 6 | 0 | 0 | 6 | 1 | 22 |

# SOUTH AMERICAN CHAMPIONSHIPS

| | | | | | |
|---|---|---|---|---|---|
| 1916 | Uruguay | 1929 | Argentina | 1955 | Argentina |
| 1917 | Uruguay | 1935 | Uruguay | 1956 | Uruguay |
| 1919 | Brazil | 1937 | Argentina | 1957 | *rgentina |
| 1920 | Uruguay | 1939 | Peru | 1959 | Argentina |
| 1921 | Argentina | 1941 | Argentina | 1959 | Uruguay |
| 1922 | Brazil | 1942 | Uruguay | 1963 | Bolivia |
| 1923 | Uruguay | 1945 | Argentina | 1967 | Uruguay |
| 1924 | Uruguay | 1946 | Argentina | 1975 | Peru |
| 1925 | Argentina | 1947 | Argentina | 1979 | Paraguay |
| 1926 | Uruguay | 1949 | Brazil | | |
| 1927 | Argentina | 1953 | Paraguay | | |

## CHAMPIONSHIP RECORD 1917–1979

| | P | W | D | L | F | A |
|---|---|---|---|---|---|---|
| Argentina | 91 | 62 | 12 | 17 | 250 | 90 |
| Uruguay | 96 | 57 | 9 | 30 | 235 | 127 |
| Brazil | 82 | 45 | 11 | 26 | 210 | 115 |
| Paraguay | 97 | 46 | 13 | 38 | 177 | 182 |
| Peru | 75 | 31 | 14 | 30 | 124 | 127 |
| Chile | 90 | 27 | 18 | 45 | 142 | 186 |
| Bolivia | 52 | 13 | 6 | 33 | 60 | 164 |
| Colombia | 39 | 10 | 6 | 23 | 42 | 93 |
| Ecuador | 55 | 3 | 9 | 43 | 52 | 170 |
| Venezuela | 13 | 1 | 2 | 10 | 9 | 54 |

*Table includes only 23 championships considered as 'official' tournaments.*

# COPA LIBERTADORES (South American Cup)

| Year | Winners | Year | Winners | Year | Winners |
|---|---|---|---|---|---|
| 1960 | Penarol (Uruguay) | 1967 | Racing (Argentina) | 1974 | Independiente |
| 1961 | Penarol | 1968 | Estudiantes | 1975 | Independiente |
| 1962 | Santos (Brazil) | | (Argentina) | 1976 | Cruzeiro (Brazil) |
| 1963 | Santos | 1969 | Estudiantes | 1977 | Boca Juniors (Argentina) |
| 1964 | Independiente | 1970 | Estudiantes | 1978 | Boca Juniors |
| | (Argentina) | 1971 | Nacional (Uruguay) | 1979 | Olimpia (Paraguay) |
| 1965 | Independiente | 1972 | Independiente | 1980 | Nacional (Uruguay) |
| 1966 | Penarol | 1973 | Independiente | 1981 | Flamengo (Brazil) |

# MUNDIALITO

Played in Montevideo, Uruguay, from December 1980 to January 1981 to celebrate the 50th anniversary of the first World Cup.

**Group A**

Uruguay 2, Holland 0
Uruguay 2, Italy 0
Holland 1, Italy 1

**Group B**

Argentina 2, West Germany 1
Argentina 1, Brazil 1
Brazil 4, West Germany 1

**Final** (attendance 71,000)

Uruguay 2, Brazil 1

# NORTH AMERICAN SOCCER LEAGUE

**Winners**

| | | | | | |
|---|---|---|---|---|---|
| 1967 | Oakland Clippers* | 1972 | New York Cosmos | 1977 | New York Cosmos |
| 1968 | Atlanta Chiefs | 1973 | Philadelphia Atoms | 1978 | New York Cosmos |
| 1969 | Kansas City Spurs | 1974 | Los Angeles Aztecs | 1979 | Vancouver Whitecaps |
| 1970 | Rochester Lancers | 1975 | Tampa Bay Rowdies | 1980 | New York Cosmos |
| 1971 | Dallas Tornado | 1976 | Toronto Metro-Croatia | 1981 | Chicago Sting |

* National Professional Soccer League.

# EUROPEAN FOOTBALL CHAMPIONSHIP
## (formerly EUROPEAN NATIONS' CUP)

| Year | Winners | | Runners-up | | Venue |
|------|---------|---|------------|---|-------|
| 1960 | USSR | 2 | Yugoslavia | 1 | Paris |
| 1964 | Spain | 2 | USSR | 1 | Madrid |
| 1968 | Italy | 2 | Yugoslavia | 0 | Rome |
| | | | After 1-1 draw | | |
| 1972 | West Germany | 3 | USSR | 0 | Brussels |
| 1976 | Czechoslovakia | 2 | West Germany | 2 | Belgrade |
| | Czechoslovakia won on penalties | | | | |
| 1980 | West Germany | 2 | Belgium | 1 | Rome |

## EUROPEAN NATIONS' CUP 1958—60

### Preliminary Round

Eire 2, Czechoslovakia 0
Czechoslovakia 4, Eire 0

### First Round

France 7, Greece 1
Greece 1, France 1
USSR 3, Hungary 1
Hungary 0, USSR 1
Rumania 3, Turkey 0
Turkey 2, Rumania 0
Norway 0, Austria 1
Austria 5, Norway 2
Yugoslavia 2, Bulgaria 0
Bulgaria 1, Yugoslavia 1
Portugal 3, East Germany 2
East Germany 0, Portugal 2
Denmark 2, Czechoslovakia 2
Czechoslovakia 5, Denmark 1
Poland 2, Spain 4
Spain 3, Poland 0

### Quarter-Finals

Portugal 2, Yugoslavia 1
Yugoslavia 5, Portugal 1
France 5, Austria 2
Austria 2, France 4
Rumania 0, Czechoslovakia 2
Czechoslovakia 3, Rumania 0
Russia w.o. Spain withdrew

### Semi-Finals

Yugoslavia 5, France 4 (in Paris)
USSR 3, Czechoslovakia 0 (in Marseilles)

### Third Place Match (Marseilles)

Czechoslovakia 2, France 0

### Final (Paris, 10 July, 1960)

USSR (0) 2, Yugoslavia (1) 1 after extra time
*USSR:* Yachin; Tchekeli, Kroutikov; Voinov, Maslenkin, Netto; Metreveli, Ivanov, Ponedelnik, Bubukin, Meshki.
*Yugoslavia:* Vidinic; Durkovic, Jusufi; Zanetic, Miladinovic, Perusic; Sekularac, Jerkovic, Galic, Matus, Kostic.
*Scorers:* Metreveli, Ponedelnik for USSR; Netto og for Yugoslavia.

## EUROPEAN NATIONS' CUP 1962—64

### First Round

Spain 6, Rumania 0
Rumania 3, Spain 1
Poland 0, Northern Ireland 2

Northern Ireland 2, Poland 0
Denmark 6, Malta 1
Malta 1, Denmark 3
Eire 4, Iceland 2
Iceland 1, Eire 1
Greece withdrew against Albania
East Germany 2, Czechoslovakia 1
Czechoslovakia 1, East Germany 1
Hungary 3, Wales 1
Wales 1, Hungary 1
Italy 6, Turkey 0
Turkey 0, Italy 1
Holland 3, Switzerland 1
Switzerland 1, Holland 1
Norway 0, Sweden 2
Sweden 1, Norway 1
Yugoslavia 3, Belgium 2
Belgium 0, Yugoslavia 1
Bulgaria 3, Portugal 1
Portugal 3, Bulgaria 1
Bulgaria 1, Portugal 0
England 1, France 1
France 5, England 2

### Second Round

Spain 1, Northern Ireland 1
Northern Ireland 0, Spain 1
Denmark 4, Albania 0
Albania 1, Denmark 0
Austria 0, Eire 0
Eire 3, Austria 2
East Germany 1, Hungary 2
Hungary 3, East Germany 3
USSR 2, Italy 0
Italy 1, USSR 1
Holland 1, Luxembourg 1
Luxembourg 2, Holland 1
Yugoslavia 0, Sweden 0
Sweden 3, Yugoslavia 2
Bulgaria 1, France 0
France 3, Bulgaria 1

### Quarter-Finals

Luxembourg 2, Denmark 2
Denmark 3, Luxembourg 3
Denmark 1, Luxembourg 0
Spain 5, Eire 1
Eire 0, Spain 2
France 1, Hungary 3
Hungary 2, France 1
Sweden 1, USSR 1
USSR 3, Sweden 1

### Semi-Finals

USSR 3, Denmark 0 (in Barcelona)
Spain 2, Hungary 1 (in Madrid)

### Third Place Match (Barcelona)

Hungary 3, Denmark 1 after extra time

### Final (Madrid, 21 June, 1964)

Spain (1) 2, USSR (1) 1

*Spain:* Iribar; Rivilla, Calleja; Fuste, Olivella, Zoco; Amancio, Pereda, Marcellino, Suarez, Lapetra.
*USSR:* Yachin; Chustikov, Mudrik, Voronin, Shesternjev, Anitchkin; Chislenko, Ivanov, Ponedelnik, Kornaev, Khusainov.
*Scorers:* Pereda, Marcellino for Spain; Khusainov for USSR.

# EUROPEAN CHAMPIONSHIP 1966–68

## Group 1

Eire 0, Spain 0
Eire 2, Turkey 1
Spain 2, Eire 0
Turkey 0, Spain 0
Turkey 2, Eire 1
Eire 0, Czechoslovakia 2
Spain 2, Turkey 0
Czechoslovakia 1, Spain 0
Spain 2, Czechoslovakia 1
Czechoslovakia 3, Turkey 0
Turkey 0, Czechoslovakia 0
Czechoslovakia 1, Eire 2

## Group 2

Norway 0, Bulgaria 0
Portugal 1, Sweden 2
Bulgaria 4, Norway 2
Sweden 1, Portugal 1
Norway 1, Portugal 2
Sweden 0, Bulgaria 2
Norway 3, Sweden 1
Sweden 5, Norway 2
Bulgaria 3, Sweden 0
Portugal 2, Norway 1
Bulgaria 1, Portugal 0
Portugal 0, Bulgaria 0

## Group 3

Finland 0, Austria 0
Austria 2, Finland 1
Greece 2, Finland 1
Greece 4, Austria 1
Finland 1, Greece 1
Austria 1, USSR 0
USSR 4, Austria 3
Greece 0, USSR 1
USSR 2, Finland 0
Austria 1, Greece 1
Finland 2, USSR 5
USSR 4, Greece 0

## Group 4

Albania 0, Yugoslavia 2
West Germany 6, Albania 0
Yugoslavia 1, West Germany 0
West Germany 3, Yugoslavia 1
Yugoslavia 4, Albania 0
Albania 0, West Germany 0

## Group 5

Holland 2, Hungary 2
Hungary 6, Denmark 0
Holland 2, Denmark 0
East Germany 4, Holland 3
Hungary 2, Holland 1
Denmark 0, Hungary 2
Denmark 1, East Germany 1
Holland 1, East Germany 0
Hungary 3, East Germany 1
Denmark 3, Holland 2
East Germany 3, Denmark 2
East Germany 1, Hungary 0

## Group 6

Cyprus 1, Rumania 5
Rumania 4, Switzerland 2
Italy 3, Rumania 1
Cyprus 0, Italy 2
Rumania 7, Cyprus 0

Switzerland 7, Rumania 1
Italy 5, Cyprus 0
Switzerland 5, Cyprus 0
Switzerland 2, Italy 2
Italy 4, Switzerland 0
Cyprus 2, Switzerland 1
Rumania 0, Italy 1

## Group 7

Poland 4, Luxembourg 0
France 2, Poland 1
Luxembourg 0, France 3
Luxembourg 0, Belgium 5
Luxembourg 0, Poland 0
Poland 3, Belgium 1
Belgium 2, France 1
Poland 1, France 4
Belgium 2, Poland 4
France 1, Belgium 1
Belgium 3, Luxembourg 0
France 3, Luxembourg 1

## Group 8

Northern Ireland 0, England 2
Wales 1, Scotland 1
England 5, Wales 1
Scotland 2, Northern Ireland 1
Northern Ireland 0, Wales 0
England 2, Scotland 3
Wales 0, England 3
Northern Ireland 1, Scotland 0
England 2, Northern Ireland 0
Scotland 3, Wales 2
Scotland 1, England 1
Wales 2, Northern Ireland 0

## Quarter-Finals

England 1, Spain 0
Spain 1, England 2
Bulgaria 3, Italy 2
Italy 2, Bulgaria 0
France 1, Yugoslavia 1
Yugoslavia 5, France 1
Hungary 2, USSR 0
USSR 3, Hungary 0

## Semi-Finals

Yugoslavia 1, England 0 (in Florence)
Italy 0, USSR 0 (Italy won toss) (in Naples)

## Third Place Match (Rome)

England 2, USSR 0

## Final (Rome, 8 June, 1968)

Italy (0) 1, Yugoslavia (1) 1

*Italy:* Zoff; Burgnich, Facchetti; Ferrini, Guarneri, Castano; Domenghini, Juliano, Anastasi, Lodetti, Prati.
*Yugoslavia:* Pantelic; Fazlagic, Damjanovic; Pavlovic, Paunovic, Holcer; Petkovic, Acimovic, Musemic, Trivic, Dzajic.
*Scorers:* Domenghini for Italy; Dzajic for Yugoslavia.

## Replayed Final (Rome, 10 June, 1968)

Italy (2) 2, Yugoslavia (0) 0

*Italy:* Zoff; Burgnich, Facchetti; Rosato, Guarneri, Salvadore; Domenghini, Mazzola, Anastasi, De Sisti, Riva.
*Yugoslavia:* Pantelic; Fazlagic, Damjanovic, Pavlovic, Paunovic, Holcer; Hosic, Acimovic, Musemic, Trivic, Dzajic.
*Scorers:* Riva, Anastasi for Italy.

## EUROPEAN CHAMPIONSHIP 1970-72

### Group 1

Czechoslovakia 1, Finland 1
Rumania 3, Finland 0
Wales 0, Rumania 0
Wales 1, Czechoslovakia 3
Finland 0, Wales 1
Czechoslovakia 1, Rumania 0
Finland 0, Czechoslovakia 4
Finland 0, Rumania 4
Wales 3, Finland 0
Czechoslovakia 1, Wales 0
Rumania 2, Czechoslovakia 1
Rumania 2, Wales 0

### Group 2

Norway 1, Hungary 3
France 3, Norway 1
Bulgaria 1, Norway 1
Hungary 1, France 1
Bulgaria 3, Hungary 0
Norway 1, Bulgaria 4
Norway 1, France 3
Hungary 2, Bulgaria 0
France 0, Hungary 2
Hungary 4, Norway 0
France 2, Bulgaria 1
Bulgaria 2, France 1

### Group 3

Greece 0, Switzerland 1
Malta 1, Switzerland 2
Malta 0, England 1
England 3, Greece 0
Switzerland 5, Malta 0
England 5, Malta 0
Malta 1, Greece 1
Switzerland 1, Greece 0
Greece 2, Malta 0
Switzerland 2, England 3
England 1, Switzerland 1
Greece 0, England 2

### Group 4

Spain 3, Northern Ireland 0
Cyprus 0, Northern Ireland 3
Northern Ireland 5, Cyprus 0
Cyprus 1, USSR 3
Cyprus 0, Spain 2
USSR 2, Spain 1
USSR 6, Cyprus 1
USSR 1, Northern Ireland 0
Northern Ireland 1, USSR 1
Spain 0, USSR 0
Spain 7, Cyprus 0
Northern Ireland 1, Spain 1

### Group 5

Denmark 0, Portugal 1
Scotland 1, Denmark 0
Belgium 2, Denmark 0
Belgium 3, Scotland 0
Belgium 3, Portugal 0
Portugal 2, Scotland 0
Denmark 1, Scotland 0
Portugal 5, Denmark 0
Denmark 1, Belgium 2
Scotland 2, Portugal 1
Scotland 1, Belgium 0
Portugal 1, Belgium 1

### Group 6

Eire 1, Sweden 1
Sweden 1, Eire 0

Austria 1, Italy 2
Italy 3, Eire 0
Eire 1, Italy 2
Eire 1, Austria 4
Sweden 1, Austria 0
Sweden 0, Italy 0
Austria 1, Sweden 0
Italy 3, Sweden 0
Austria 6, Eire 0
Italy 2, Austria 2

### Group 7

Holland 1, Yugoslavia 1
East Germany 1, Holland 0
Luxembourg 0, East Germany 5
Yugoslavia 2, Holland 0
East Germany 2, Luxembourg 1
Luxembourg 0, Yugoslavia 2
Holland 6, Luxembourg 0
East Germany 1, Yugoslavia 2
Holland 3, East Germany 2
Yugoslavia 0, East Germany 0
Yugoslavia 0, Luxembourg 0
Luxembourg 0, Holland 8

### Group 8

Poland 3, Albania 0
West Germany 1, Turkey 1
Turkey 2, Albania 1
Albania 0, West Germany 1
Turkey 0, West Germany 3
Albania 1, Poland 1
West Germany 2, Albania 0
Poland 5, Turkey 1
Poland 1, West Germany 3
Albania 3, Turkey 0
West Germany 0, Poland 0
Turkey 1, Poland 0

### Quarter-Finals

England 1, West Germany 3
Italy 0, Belgium 0
Hungary 1, Rumania 1
Yugoslavia 0, USSR 0
West Germany 0, England 0
Belgium 2, Italy 1
USSR 3, Yugoslavia 0
Rumania 2, Hungary 2
Play-off: Hungary 2, Rumania 1

### Semi-Finals

USSR 1, Hungary 0 (in Brussels)
West Germany 2, Belgium 1 (in Antwerp)

### Third Place Match (Liège)

Belgium 2, Hungary 1

### Final (Brussels, 18 June, 1972)

West Germany (1) 3, USSR (0) 0

*West Germany:* Maier, Hottges, Schwarzenbeck, Beckenbauer, Breitner, Hoeness, Wimmer, Netzer, Heynkes, Müller, Kremers.
*USSR:* Rudakov, Dzodzuashvili, Khurtsilava, Kaplichny, Istomin, Troshkin, Kolotov, Baidachni, Konkov (Dolmatov), Banishevski (Kozinkievits), Onishenko.
*Scorers:* Müller 2, Wimmer for West Germany.

## EUROPEAN CHAMPIONSHIP 1974-76

### Group 1

England 3, Czechoslovakia 0
England 0, Portugal 0
England 5, Cyprus 0
Czechoslovakia 4, Cyprus 0

Czechoslovakia 5, Portugal 0
Cyprus 0, England 1
Cyprus 0, Portugal 2
Czechoslovakia 2, England 1
Portugal 1, Czechoslovakia 1
Portugal 1, England 1
Cyprus 0, Czechoslovakia 3
Portugal 1, Cyprus 0

## Group 2

Austria 2, Wales 1
Luxembourg 2, Hungary 4
Wales 2, Hungary 0
Wales 5, Luxembourg 0
Luxembourg 1, Austria 2
Austria 0, Hungary 0
Hungary 1, Wales 2
Luxembourg 1, Wales 3
Hungary 2, Austria 1
Austria 6, Luxembourg 2
Hungary 8, Luxembourg 1
Wales 1, Austria 0

## Group 3

Norway 2, Northern Ireland 1
Yugoslavia 3, Norway 1
Sweden 0, Northern Ireland 2
Northern Ireland 1, Yugoslavia 0
Sweden 1, Yugoslavia 2
Norway 1, Yugoslavia 3
Sweden 3, Norway 1
Norway 0, Sweden 2
Northern Ireland 1, Sweden 2
Yugoslavia 3, Sweden 0
Northern Ireland 3, Norway 0
Yugoslavia 1, Northern Ireland 0

## Group 4

Denmark 1, Spain 2
Denmark 0, Rumania 0
Scotland 1, Spain 2
Spain 1, Scotland 1
Spain 1, Rumania 1
Rumania 6, Denmark 1
Rumania 1, Scotland 1
Denmark 0, Scotland 1
Spain 2, Denmark 0
Scotland 3, Denmark 1
Rumania 2, Spain 2
Scotland 1, Rumania 1

## Group 5

Finland 1, Poland 2
Finland 1, Holland 3
Poland 3, Finland 0
Holland 3, Italy 1
Italy 0, Poland 0
Finland 0, Italy 1
Holland 4, Finland 1
Poland 4, Holland 1
Italy 0, Finland 0
Holland 3, Poland 0
Poland 0, Italy 0
Italy 1, Holland 0

## Group 6

Eire 3, USSR 0
Turkey 1, Eire 1
Turkey 2, Switzerland 1
USSR 3, Turkey 0
Switzerland 1, Turkey 1
Eire 2, Switzerland 1
USSR 2, Eire 1

Switzerland 1, Eire 0
Switzerland 0, USSR 1
Eire 4, Turkey 0
USSR 4, Switzerland 1
Turkey 1, USSR 0

## Group 7

Iceland 0, Belgium 2
East Germany 1, Iceland 1
Belgium 2, France 1
France 2, East Germany 2
East Germany 0, Belgium 0
Iceland 0, France 0
Iceland 2, East Germany 1
France 3, Iceland 0
Belgium 1, Iceland 0
Belgium 1, East Germany 2
East Germany 2, France 1
France 0, Belgium 0

## Group 8

Bulgaria 3, Greece 3
Greece 2, West Germany 2
Greece 2, Bulgaria 1
Malta 0, West Germany 1
Malta 2, Greece 0
Bulgaria 1, West Germany 1
Greece 4, Malta 0
Bulgaria 5, Malta 0
West Germany 1, Greece 1
West Germany 1, Bulgaria 0
Malta 0, Bulgaria 2
West Germany 8, Malta 0

## Quarter-Finals

Spain 1, West Germany 1
Yugoslavia 2, Wales 0
Czechoslovakia 2, USSR 0
Holland 5, Belgium 0
West Germany 2, Spain 0
USSR 2, Czechoslovakia 2
Wales 1, Yugoslavia 1
Belgium 1, Holland 2

## Semi-Finals

Czechoslovakia 3, Holland 1 after extra time
(in Zagreb)
West Germany 4, Yugoslavia 2 after extra time
(in Belgrade)

## Third Place Match (Zagreb)

Holland 3, Yugoslavia 2 after extra time

## Final (Belgrade, 20 June, 1976)

Czechoslovakia (2) 2, West Germany (1) 2 (aet)
(*Czechoslovakia won 5-3 on penalties*)

*Czechoslovakia:* Viktor; Dobias (Vesely F.), Pivarnik,
Ondrus, Capkovic, Gogh, Moder, Panenka, Svehlic (Jur-
kemik), Masny, Nehoda.
*West Germany:* Maier; Vogts, Beckenbauer, Schwarzen-
beck, Dietz, Bonhof, Wimmer (Flohe), Müller D., Beer
(Bongartz), Hoeness, Holzenbein.
*Scorers:* Svehlic, Dobias for Czechoslovakia; Müller, Hol-
zenbein for West Germany.

# EUROPEAN CHAMPIONSHIP 1978–80

## Group 1

Denmark 3, Eire 3
Denmark 3, England 4
Eire 0, Northern Ireland 0

Denmark 2, Bulgaria 2
Eire 1, England 1
Northern Ireland 2, Denmark 1
Bulgaria 0, Northern Ireland 2
England 4, Northern Ireland 0
Northern Ireland 2, Bulgaria 0
Eire 2, Denmark 0
Bulgaria 1, Eire 0
Denmark 4, Northern Ireland 0
Bulgaria 0, England 3
England 1, Denmark 0
Eire 3, Bulgaria 0
Northern Ireland 1, England 5
Bulgaria 3, Denmark 0
Northern Ireland 1, Eire 0
England 2, Bulgaria 0
England 2, Eire 0

## Group 2
Norway 0, Austria 2
Belgium 1, Norway 1
Austria 3, Scotland 2
Portugal 1, Belgium 1
Scotland 3, Norway 2
Austria 1, Portugal 2
Portugal 1, Scotland 0
Belgium 1, Austria 1
Austria 0, Belgium 0
Norway 0, Portugal 1
Norway 0, Scotland 4
Austria 4, Norway 0
Norway 1, Belgium 2
Belgium 2, Portugal 0
Scotland 1, Austria 1
Portugal 3, Norway 1
Belgium 2, Scotland 0
Portugal 1, Austria 2
Scotland 1, Belgium 3
Scotland 4, Portugal 1

## Group 3
Yugoslavia 1, Spain 2
Rumania 3, Yugoslavia 2
Spain 1, Rumania 0
Spain 5, Cyprus 0
Cyprus 0, Yugoslavia 3
Rumania 2, Spain 2
Cyprus 1, Rumania 1
Spain 0, Yugoslavia 1
Yugoslavia 2, Rumania 1
Yugoslavia 5, Cyprus 0
Rumania 2, Cyprus 0
Cyprus 1, Spain 3

## Group 4
Iceland 0, Poland 2
Holland 3, Iceland 0
East Germany 3, Iceland 1
Switzerland 1, Holland 3
Holland 3, East Germany 0
Poland 2, Switzerland 0
Holland 3, Switzerland 0
East Germany 2, Poland 1
Poland 2, Holland 0
Switzerland 0, East Germany 2
Switzerland 2, Iceland 0
Iceland 1, Switzerland 2
Iceland 0, Holland 4
Switzerland 0, Poland 2
Iceland 0, East Germany 3
Poland 1, East Germany 1
Poland 2, Iceland 0
East Germany 5, Switzerland 2
Holland 1, Poland 1
East Germany 2, Holland 3

## Group 5
France 2, Sweden 2
Sweden 1, Czechoslovakia 3
Luxembourg 1, France 3
France 3, Luxembourg 0
Czechoslovakia 2, France 0
Luxembourg 0, Czechoslovakia 3
Sweden 3, Luxembourg 0
Sweden 1, France 3
Czechoslovakia 4, Sweden 1
Luxembourg 1, Sweden 1
France 2, Czechoslovakia 0
Czechoslovakia 4, Luxembourg 0

## Group 6
Finland 3, Greece 0
Finland 2, Hungary 1
USSR 2, Greece 0
Hungary 2, USSR 0
Greece 8, Finland 1
Greece 4, Hungary 1
Hungary 0, Greece 0
USSR 2, Hungary 2
Finland 1, USSR 1
Greece 1, USSR 0
Hungary 3, Finland 1
USSR 2, Finland 2

## Group 7
Wales 7, Malta 0
Wales 1, Turkey 0
Malta 0, West Germany 0
Turkey 2, Malta 1
Turkey 0, West Germany 0
Wales 0, West Germany 2
Malta 0, Wales 2
West Germany 5, Wales 1
Malta 1, Turkey 2
Turkey 1, Wales 0
West Germany 2, Turkey 0
West Germany 8, Malta 0

## Final Tournament
### Group 1
West Germany 1, Czechoslovakia 0
Greece 0, Holland 1
West Germany 3, Holland 2
Czechoslovakia 3, Greece 1
Czechoslovakia 1, Holland 1
West Germany 0, Greece 0

### Group 2
Belgium 1, England 1
Spain 0, Italy 0
Spain 1, Belgium 2
Italy 1, England 0
England 2, Spain 1
Italy 0, Belgium 0

### Third Place Match (Naples)
Italy 1, Czechoslovakia 1
(*Czechoslovakia won 9-8 on penalties*)

### Final (Rome, 22 June, 1980)
West Germany (1) 2, Belgium (0) 1

*West Germany:* Schumacher; Briegel, Forster K., Dietz, Schuster, Rummenigge, Hrubesch, Müller, Aloffs, Stielike, Kaltz.
*Belgium:* Pfaff; Gerets, Millecamps, Meeuws, Renquin, Cools, Van der Eycken, Van Moer, Mommens, Van der Elst, Ceulemans.
*Scorers:* Hrubesch 2 for West Germany; Van der Eychen for Belgium.

## EUROPEAN UNDER-21 CHAMPIONSHIP 1980–82

### Group 1
*Results:* Finland 0, Bulgaria 1; Finland 1, Austria 2; Bulgaria 1, West Germany 0; West Germany 4, Austria 0; Bulgaria 1, Finland 0; Finland 1, West Germany 2; Austria 1, Bulgaria 2; Austria 0, Finland 0; West Germany 4, Finland 2; Austria 0, West Germany 1; Bulgaria 1, Austria 0; West Germany 4, Bulgaria 1.

|              | P | W | D | L | F  | A  | Pts |
|--------------|---|---|---|---|----|----|-----|
| West Germany | 6 | 5 | 0 | 1 | 15 | 5  | 10  |
| Bulgaria     | 6 | 5 | 0 | 1 | 7  | 5  | 10  |
| Austria      | 6 | 1 | 1 | 4 | 3  | 9  | 3   |
| Finland      | 6 | 0 | 1 | 5 | 4  | 10 | 1   |

### Group 2
*Results:* France 3, Cyprus 1; Belgium 2, Cyprus 1; Cyprus 0, Belgium 1; France 1, Belgium 0; Belgium 1, France 2; Cyprus 2, France 1.

|         | P | W | D | L | F | A | Pts |
|---------|---|---|---|---|---|---|-----|
| France  | 4 | 3 | 0 | 1 | 7 | 4 | 6   |
| Belgium | 4 | 2 | 0 | 2 | 4 | 4 | 4   |
| Cyprus  | 4 | 1 | 0 | 3 | 4 | 7 | 2   |

### Group 3
*Results:* Czechoslovakia 3, Turkey 0; Turkey 2, Czechoslovakia 1; USSR 1, Turkey 0; Turkey 0, USSR 0; USSR 0, Czechoslovakia 0; Czechoslovakia 0, USSR 0.

|                | P | W | D | L | F | A | Pts |
|----------------|---|---|---|---|---|---|-----|
| USSR           | 4 | 1 | 3 | 0 | 1 | 0 | 5   |
| Czechoslovakia | 4 | 1 | 2 | 1 | 4 | 2 | 4   |
| Turkey         | 4 | 1 | 1 | 2 | 2 | 5 | 3   |

### Group 4
*Results:* Rumania 4, England 0; England 5, Switzerland 0; England 3, Rumania 0; Switzerland 0, Hungary 1; Hungary 4, Rumania 2; Switzerland 0, England 0; Hungary 1, England 2; Rumania 2, Hungary 1; Rumania 1, Switzerland 1; Hungary 5, Switzerland 1; Switzerland 3, Rumania 0; England 2, Hungary 0.

|             | P | W | D | L | F  | A  | Pts |
|-------------|---|---|---|---|----|----|-----|
| England     | 6 | 4 | 1 | 1 | 12 | 5  | 9   |
| Hungary     | 6 | 3 | 0 | 3 | 12 | 9  | 6   |
| Rumania     | 6 | 2 | 1 | 3 | 9  | 12 | 5   |
| Switzerland | 6 | 1 | 2 | 3 | 5  | 12 | 4   |

### Group 5
*Results:* Italy 1, Yugoslavia 0; Greece 1, Italy 3; Yugoslavia 1, Greece 1; Yugoslavia 1, Italy 0; Italy 1, Greece 0; Greece 0, Yugoslavia 2.

|            | P | W | D | L | F | A | Pts |
|------------|---|---|---|---|---|---|-----|
| Italy      | 4 | 3 | 0 | 1 | 5 | 2 | 6   |
| Yugoslavia | 4 | 2 | 1 | 1 | 4 | 2 | 5   |
| Greece     | 4 | 0 | 1 | 3 | 2 | 7 | 1   |

### Group 6
*Results:* Sweden 2, Scotland 0; Denmark 2, Sweden 1; Scotland 2, Denmark 1; Sweden 0, Denmark 0; Scotland 4, Sweden 0; Denmark 1, Scotland 1.

|          | P | W | D | L | F | A | Pts |
|----------|---|---|---|---|---|---|-----|
| Scotland | 4 | 2 | 1 | 1 | 7 | 4 | 5   |
| Denmark  | 4 | 1 | 2 | 1 | 4 | 4 | 4   |
| Sweden   | 4 | 1 | 1 | 2 | 3 | 6 | 3   |

### Group 7
*Results:* Norway 0, Poland 1; East Germany 0, Norway 4; East Germany 2, Poland 3; Norway 1, East Germany 1; Poland 3, East Germany 1; Poland 4, Norway 0.

|              | P | W | D | L | F  | A  | Pts |
|--------------|---|---|---|---|----|----|-----|
| Poland       | 4 | 4 | 0 | 0 | 11 | 3  | 8   |
| Norway       | 4 | 1 | 1 | 2 | 5  | 6  | 3   |
| East Germany | 4 | 0 | 1 | 3 | 4  | 11 | 1   |

### Group 8
*Results:* Netherlands 0, Spain 2; Spain 4, Luxembourg 1; Netherlands 1, Luxembourg 0; Luxembourg 1, Spain 5; Luxembourg 0, Netherlands 2; Spain 2, Netherlands 1.

|             | P | W | D | L | F  | A  | Pts |
|-------------|---|---|---|---|----|----|-----|
| Spain       | 4 | 4 | 0 | 0 | 13 | 3  | 8   |
| Netherlands | 4 | 2 | 0 | 2 | 4  | 4  | 4   |
| Luxembourg  | 4 | 0 | 0 | 4 | 2  | 12 | 0   |

### Quarter-Finals
France 0, USSR 0; USSR 4, France 2; Spain 1, West Germany 0; West Germany 2, Spain 0; Poland 1, England 2; England 2, Poland 2; Italy 0, Scotland 1; Scotland 0, Italy 0.

### Semi-Finals
Scotland 0, England 1; England 1, Scotland 1; USSR 3, West Germany 4; West Germany 5, USSR 0.

**Final dates:** 21.9.82 England v West Germany; 12.10.82 West Germany v England

### Draw for European Under-21 Championship 1982–84
*Group 1:* Belgium, East Germany, Scotland, Switzerland; *Group 2:* Poland, USSR, Portugal, Finland; *Group 3:* England, Hungary, Greece, Denmark; *Group 4:* Yugoslavia, Wales, Bulgaria, Norway; *Group 5:* Italy, Czechoslovakia, Rumania, Cyprus; *Group 6:* West Germany, Austria, Turkey, Albania; *Group 7:* Spain, Netherlands, Iceland; *Group 8:* France, Luxembourg, Sweden.

## WHEN THE KISSING HAS TO STOP
In September 1981, after discussing 'the influence of the players' attitude on the field on the behaviour of spectators', FIFA's Technical Committee expressed their concern about the 'excessive demonstrative attitude of some players and teams when a goal is scored'.

The Technical Committee felt that 'the scorer should be congratulated by the team captain or the player who made the pass, but the exultant outbursts of several players at once jumping on top of each other, kissing and embracing . . . should be banned from the football pitch'. They recommended that National Associations be encouraged to curb such exaggerated behaviour with disciplinary action.

# EUROPEAN NATIONS SECTION

Details have been listed for all European footballing nations but unfortunately owing to some countries' seasons finishing at different times from the British season, not all league champions and cup winners are known for the current season. Total number of championship and cup wins is given with winners' present names, with previous names in brackets. In the tables of league champions and cup winners, contemporary names are used.

## ALBANIA

*President:* Zyber Konci.
*Secretary:* Skender Begeja.
*Address of Association:* Federation Albanaise de Football, Rruga, Kongresi I Permetit, 41 Tirana.
*Telephone:* 7256, 7984.
*Cable:* Albsport Tirana.
*Telex:* 2142.
*Area:* 11,100 square miles.
*Population:* 2,671,300. *Number of Clubs:* 42.
*Teams:* 219.
*Number of Players:* 5,038.
*Year of Formation:* 1932.
*National Colours:* Red shirts, black shorts, red stockings.
*Second Choice of Colours:* White shirts, white shorts, white stockings.
*Name, Address and Capacity of National Stadium:* Qemal Stafa, Tirana, 30,000.
*Names and Capacity of Other Principal Football Grounds:* Dinamo, 15,000; Shkodra, 13,000; Durresi, 15,000; Korca, 13,000; Fier, 10,000; Vlora, 13,000.
*Season:* September–May.

### International matches 1981

1 April, Tirana: v West Germany (h) lost 0-2
2 Sept, Kotka: v Finland (a) lost 1-2 (*Targaj*)
14 Oct, Tirana: v Bulgaria (h) lost 0-2
18 Nov, Dortmund: v West Germany (a) lost 0-8

### League Championship wins (1945–82)

Dinamo Tirana 15; Partizan Tirana 12; 17 Nendori 6; Vlaznia 4.

### Cup wins (1948–82)

Dinamo Tirana 13; Partizan Tirana 9; 17 Nendori 4; Vlaznia 3; Besa 1; Labinoti 1.

| League Champions | Cup Winners |
|---|---|
| 1945 Vlaznia | |
| 1946 Vlaznia | |
| 1947 Partizan Tirana | |
| 1948 Partizan Tirana | Partizan Tirana |
| 1949 Partizan Tirana | Partizan Tirana |
| 1950 Dinamo Tirana | Dinamo Tirana |

| | |
|---|---|
| 1951 Dinamo Tirana | Dinamo Tirana |
| 1952 Dinamo Tirana | Dinamo Tirana |
| 1953 Dinamo Tirana | Dinamo Tirana |
| 1954 Partizan Tirana | Dinamo Tirana |
| 1955 Dinamo Tirana | *No competition* |
| 1956 Dinamo Tirana | *No competition* |
| 1957 Partizan Tirana | Partizan Tirana |
| 1958 Partizan Tirana | Partizan Tirana |
| 1959 Partizan Tirana | *No competition* |
| 1960 Dinamo Tirana | Dinamo Tirana |
| 1961 Partizan Tirana | Partizan Tirana |
| 1963*Dinamo Tirana | 17 Nendori |
| 1964 Partizan Tirana | Partizan Tirana |
| 1965 17 Nendori | Dinamo Tirana |
| 1966 17 Nendori | Dinamo Tirana |
| 1967 Dinamo Tirana | Vlaznia |
| 1968 17 Nendori | Dinamo Tirana |
| 1969 17 Nendori | 17 Nendori |
| 1970 17 Nendori | Partizan Tirana |
| 1971 Partizan Tirana | Dinamo Tirana |
| 1972 Vlaznia | Besa |
| 1973 Dinamo Tirana | Partizan Tirana |
| 1974 Vlaznia | Dinamo Tirana |
| 1975 Dinamo Tirana | Labinoti |
| 1976 Dinamo Tirana | 17 Nendori |
| 1977 Dinamo Tirana | 17 Nendori |
| 1978 Dinamo Tirana | Dinamo Tirana |
| 1979 Partizan Tirana | Vlaznia |
| 1980 Dinamo Tirana | Partizan Tirana |
| 1981 Partizan Tirana | Vlaznia |
| 1982 17 Nendori | Dinamo Tirana |

* *Changed from calendar season to overlapping season from autumn to spring.*

### Final League Table 1981–82

| | P | W | D | L | F | A | Pts |
|---|---|---|---|---|---|---|---|
| 17 Nendori | 26 | 15 | 7 | 4 | 42 | 15 | 37 |
| Flamurtari | 26 | 13 | 7 | 6 | 26 | 12 | 33 |
| Dinamo Tirana | 26 | 14 | 4 | 8 | 33 | 19 | 32 |
| Partizani | 26 | 11 | 9 | 6 | 31 | 18 | 31 |
| Vlaznia | 26 | 11 | 8 | 7 | 39 | 26 | 30 |
| Tomori | 26 | 10 | 6 | 10 | 21 | 18 | 26 |
| Beselidhija | 26 | 9 | 7 | 10 | 22 | 27 | 25 |
| Besa | 26 | 9 | 7 | 10 | 20 | 28 | 25 |
| Lokomotiva | 26 | 8 | 8 | 10 | 18 | 25 | 24 |
| Luftetari | 26 | 8 | 7 | 11 | 22 | 23 | 23 |
| Naftetari | 26 | 5 | 13 | 8 | 23 | 26 | 23 |
| Labinoti | 26 | 9 | 4 | 13 | 17 | 27 | 22 |
| 31 Korriku | 26 | 5 | 10 | 11 | 22 | 37 | 20 |
| 24 Maji | 26 | 4 | 5 | 17 | 9 | 44 | 13 |

# AUSTRIA

*President:* Karl Sekanina.
*Secretary:* Otto Demuth.
*Address of Association:* Oesterreichischer Fussball-Bund, Mariahilferstrasse 99, Postfach 161, Wien A-1061.
*Telephone:* 57-15-36.
*Cable:* Football Wien.
*Telex:* 11919oefb a.
*Area:* 32,374 square miles.
*Population:* 7,457,000.
*Number of Clubs:* 1,971.   *Teams:* 8,223.
*Number of Players:* 287,000.
*Year of Formation:* 1904.
*National Colours:* White shirt, black shorts, black stockings.
*Second Choice of Colours:* Red shirts, white shorts, red stockings.
*Name, Address and Capacity of National Stadium:* Wiener Stadion, Prater, Vienna, 70,714.
*Names, Addresses and Capacities of Other Principal Football Grounds:* Linzer Stadion, Linz, 22,000; Stadion Salzburger, Bundesstadion Liebenau, Graz, 19,000; Tivoli Stadion, Innsbruck, 14,400; Stadion, Wiener Neustadt, 12,600; Bodenseestadion, Bregenz, 12,000; Stadion Klagenfurt, Klagenfurt, 11,000; Hohe Warte, Vienna Weststadion, Vienna, 20,000; Bundesstadion Sudstadt, Maria Enzersdorf, 15,600.
*Season:* August–December; February–June.

## Principal Honours

Olympic Games: *runners-up* 1936.
European Cup-Winners' Cup: *runners-up* Austria/WAC (1978).

## International matches 1981

5 Feb, Tel Aviv: v Israel (a) lost 0-1
29 April, Hamburg: v West Germany (a) lost 0-2
28 May, Vienna: v Bulgaria (h) won 2-0 (*Krankl* pen, *Jara*)
17 June Linz: v Finland (h) won 5-1 (*Prohaska 2, Krankl, Welzl, Jurtin*)
23 Sept, Vienna: v Spain (h) drew 0-0
14 Oct, Vienna: v West Germany (h) lost 1-3 (*Schachner*)
11 Nov, Sofia: v Bulgaria (a) drew 0-0

## League Championship wins (1912–82)

Rapid Vienna 26; Austria/Vienna (prev. Austria/WAC, FK Austria and WAC) 16; Admira-Energie-Wacker (prev. Sportklub Admira & Admira-Energie) 8; First Vienna 6; Tirol-Svarowski-Innsbruck (prev. Wacker Innsbruck) 5; Wiener Sportklub 3; FAC 1; Hakoah 1; Linz ASK 1; Wacker Vienna 1; WAF 1; Voest Linz 1.

## Cup wins (1919–82)

Austria/WAC 21; Rapid Vienna 9; Admira-Energie-Wacker (prev. Sportklub Admira & Admira-Energie) 5; TS Innsbruck (prev. Wacker Innsbruck) 5; First Vienna 3; Linz ASK 1; Wacker Vienna 1; WAF 1; Wiener Sportklub 1, Graz AK 1.

| | League Champions | Cup Winners |
|---|---|---|
| 1946 | Rapid Vienna | Rapid Vienna |
| 1947 | Wacker Vienna | Wacker Vienna |
| 1948 | Rapid Vienna | FK Austria |
| 1949 | FK Austria | FK Austria |
| 1950 | FK Austria | *No competition* |
| 1951 | Rapid Vienna | *No competition* |
| 1952 | Rapid Vienna | *No competition* |
| 1953 | FK Austria | *No competition* |
| 1954 | Rapid Vienna | *No competition* |
| 1955 | First Vienna | *No competition* |
| 1956 | Rapid Vienna | *No competition* |
| 1957 | Rapid Vienna | *No competition* |
| 1958 | Wiener Sportklub | *No competition* |
| 1959 | Wiener Sportklub | Wiener AC |
| 1960 | Rapid Vienna | FK Austria |
| 1961 | FK Austria | Rapid Vienna |
| 1962 | FK Austria | FK Austria |
| 1963 | FK Austria | FK Austria |
| 1964 | Rapid Vienna | Admira-Energie |
| 1965 | Linz ASK | Linz ASK |
| 1966 | Admira-Energie | Admira-Energie |
| 1967 | Rapid Vienna | FK Austria |
| 1968 | Rapid Vienna | Rapid Vienna |
| 1969 | FK Austria | Rapid Vienna |
| 1970 | FK Austria | Wacker Innsbruck |
| 1971 | Wacker Innsbruck | FK Austria |
| 1972 | TS Innsbruck | Rapid Vienna |
| 1973 | TS Innsbruck | TS Innsbruck |
| 1974 | Voest Linz | Austria/WAC |
| 1975 | TS Innsbruck | TS Innsbruck |
| 1976 | Austria/WAC | Rapid Vienna |
| 1977 | TS Innsbruck | Austria/WAC |
| 1978 | Austria/WAC | TS Innsbruck |
| 1979 | Austria/WAC | TS Innsbruck |
| 1980 | Austria/WAC | Austria/WAC |
| 1981 | Austria/Vienna | Graz AK |
| 1982 | Rapid Vienna | Austria/Vienna |

### Final League Table 1981–82

| | P | W | D | L | F | A | Pts |
|---|---|---|---|---|---|---|---|
| Rapid Vienna | 36 | 18 | 11 | 7 | 69 | 43 | 47 |
| Austria/Vienna | 36 | 18 | 8 | 10 | 54 | 32 | 44 |
| Graz AK | 36 | 16 | 6 | 14 | 40 | 47 | 38 |
| Admira Wacker | 36 | 14 | 8 | 14 | 52 | 39 | 36 |
| SW Innsbruck | 36 | 14 | 7 | 15 | 60 | 52 | 35 |
| Sturm Graz | 36 | 14 | 5 | 17 | 53 | 62 | 33 |
| Wiener SK | 36 | 12 | 9 | 15 | 49 | 61 | 33 |
| Voest Linz | 36 | 12 | 8 | 16 | 38 | 41 | 32 |
| Austria Salzburg | 36 | 11 | 9 | 16 | 48 | 55 | 31 |
| Linz ASK | 36 | 12 | 7 | 17 | 36 | 47 | 31 |

# BELGIUM

*President:* M. Louis Wouters.
*Secretary:* Albert Roosens.
*Address of Association:* Union Royale Belge des Sociétés de Football Association, Rue de la Loi 43, B-1040 Bruxelles.
*Telephone:* 02/230.07.30.
*Telex:* 23257 bvbfbfb.
*Cable:* UBSFA Bruxelles.
*Area:* 11,779 square miles.
*Population:* 9,863,374.
*Number of Clubs:* 3,320.  *Teams:* 14,400.
*Number of Players:* 283,960.
*Year of Formation:* 1895.
*National Colours:* Red shirts with tricoloured (black-yellow-red) collar and cuffs, red shorts, red stockings with tricoloured (black-yellow-red) tops.
*Second Choice of Colours:* All white.
*Name, Address and Capacity of National Stadium:* Centenary Stadium, Marathon Avenue, Brussels (Heysel), 70,000.
*Names, Addresses and Capacities of Other Principal Football Grounds:* R. Antwerp FC-Bosuilbaan, at Deurne (Antwerp), 62,000; RFC Liégeois-Chaussée de Tongres, at Rocourt (Liège), 43,000; R. Standard C. Liégeois-2, rue de la Centrale at Sclessin (Liège), 43,000; RSC Anderlechtois-2, avenue Théo Verbeeck, Anderlecht (Brussels), 38,000.
*Season:* September–May.

## Principal Honours

Olympic Games: *winners* 1920
European Championship: *runners-up* 1980
European Champions Cup: *runners-up* FC Bruges (1978)
European Cup-Winners' Cup: *winners* Anderlecht (1976, 1978); *runners-up* Anderlecht (1977), Standard Liège (1982)
Fairs Cup: *runners-up* Anderlecht (1970)
UEFA Cup: *runners-up* FC Bruges (1976)
Super Cup: Anderlecht (1978)

## International matches 1981

18 Feb, Brussels: v Cyprus (h) won 3-2 (*Plessers, Van den Bergh, Ceulemans*)
25 March, Brussels: v Eire (h) won 1-0 (*Ceulemans*)
29 April, Paris: v France (a) lost 2-3 (*Van den Bergh, Ceulemans*)
9 Sept, Brussels: v France (h) won 2-0 (*Czerniatynski, Van den Bergh*)
14 Oct, Rotterdam: v Holland (a) lost 0-3
16 Dec, Valencia v Spain (a) lost 0-2

## League Championship wins (1896–1982)

Anderlecht 17; Union St Gilloise 11; Beerschot 7; Standard Liège 7; FC Bruges 6; RC Brussels 6; FC Liège 5; Daring Brussels 5; Antwerp 4; Lierse SK 3; Malines 3; CS Bruges 3; RWD Molenbeek 1, Beveren 1.

## Cup wins (1954–82)

Anderlecht 5; Standard Liège 4; FC Bruges 3; Beerschot 2; Waterschei 2; Antwerp 1; La Gantoise 1; Lierse SK 1; Tournai 1; Waregem 1; Beveren 1.

| League Champions | Cup Winners |
|---|---|
| 1946 Malines | |
| 1947 Anderlecht | |
| 1948 Malines | |
| 1949 Anderlecht | |
| 1950 Anderlecht | |
| 1951 Anderlecht | |
| 1952 FC Liège | |
| 1953 FC Liège | |
| 1954 Anderlecht | Standard Liège |
| 1955 Anderlecht | Antwerp |
| 1956 Anderlecht | Tournai |
| 1957 Antwerp | *No competition* |
| 1958 Standard Liège | *No competition* |
| 1959 Anderlecht | *No competition* |
| 1960 Lierse SK | *No competition* |
| 1961 Standard Liège | *No competition* |
| 1962 Anderlecht | *No competition* |
| 1963 Standard Liège | *No competition* |
| 1964 Anderlecht | La Gantoise |
| 1965 Anderlecht | Anderlecht |
| 1966 Anderlecht | Standard Liège |
| 1967 Anderlecht | Standard Liège |
| 1968 Anderlecht | FC Bruges |
| 1969 Standard Liège | Lierse SK |
| 1970 Standard Liège | FC Bruges |
| 1971 Standard Liège | Beerschot |
| 1972 Anderlecht | Anderlecht |
| 1973 FC Bruges | Anderlecht |
| 1974 Anderlecht | Waregem |
| 1975 RWD Molenbeek | Anderlecht |
| 1976 FC Bruges | Anderlecht |
| 1977 FC Bruges | FC Bruges |
| 1978 FC Bruges | Beveren |
| 1979 Beveren | Beerschot |
| 1980 FC Bruges | Waterschei |
| 1981 Anderlecht | Standard Liège |
| 1982 Standard Liège | Waterschei |

**Final League Table 1981–82**

| | P | W | D | L | F | A | Pts |
|---|---|---|---|---|---|---|---|
| Standard Liège | 34 | 19 | 10 | 5 | 59 | 23 | 48 |
| Anderlecht | 34 | 19 | 8 | 7 | 56 | 31 | 46 |
| La Gantoise | 34 | 16 | 13 | 5 | 36 | 21 | 45 |
| Lokeren | 34 | 17 | 10 | 7 | 56 | 32 | 44 |
| Antwerp | 34 | 17 | 9 | 8 | 45 | 23 | 43 |
| Kortryk | 34 | 14 | 10 | 10 | 39 | 35 | 38 |
| Beveren | 34 | 14 | 9 | 11 | 45 | 33 | 37 |
| Lierse | 34 | 14 | 8 | 12 | 49 | 51 | 36 |
| Waterschei | 34 | 11 | 8 | 15 | 44 | 55 | 30 |
| Tongeren | 34 | 11 | 8 | 15 | 40 | 54 | 30 |
| RWD Molenbeek | 34 | 11 | 7 | 16 | 41 | 50 | 29 |
| Waregem | 34 | 10 | 9 | 15 | 30 | 34 | 29 |
| Winterslag | 34 | 10 | 9 | 15 | 24 | 49 | 29 |
| FC Bruges | 34 | 10 | 8 | 16 | 46 | 46 | 28 |
| CS Bruges | 34 | 10 | 8 | 16 | 57 | 61 | 28 |
| FC Liège | 34 | 10 | 8 | 16 | 36 | 50 | 28 |
| Beringen | 34 | 9 | 9 | 16 | 33 | 50 | 27 |
| FC Mechelen | 34 | 6 | 5 | 23 | 28 | 65 | 17 |

# BULGARIA

President: Kroum Vassiltchev.
Secretary: Kostadin Stoytcheyski.
Address of Association: Federation Bulgare de Football, Boul. Tolboukhin 18, Sofia.
Telephone: 877490, 874725.
Cable: Besefese Sofia.
Telex: 22723, 22724 csbsfs bg.
Area: 42,830 square miles.
Population: 9,000,000.
Number of Clubs: 4,336.   Teams: 5,781.
Number of Players: 117,940.
Year of Formation: 1923.
National Colours: White shirts, green shorts, red stockings.
Second Choice of Colours: Red shirts, green shorts, white stockings.
Name, Address and Capacity of National Stadium: 'Vassil Levski', Sofia, 55,000.
Names, Addresses and Capacities of Other Principal Football Grounds: Stade Narodna Armia, Parc de la Liberté, Sofia, 43,000; Levski-Gerena, Sofia, 40,000; Stade Slavia, Ovtcha Koupel, Sofia, 35,000; Stade Rakovski, quartier Ivan Vasoc, Sofia, 29,000; Stade Guerena, quartier Podouene, Sofia, 33,000; Stade 9 Septembre, Plovdiv, 40,000; Stade Christo Botev, Plovdiv, 30,000; Stade Yuri Gagarine, Varna, 40,000; Stade de la ville de Rousse, 20,000; Stade 9 Septembre, Bourgass, 15,000.
Season: August–December; March–June.

## Principal Honours

Olympic Games: runners-up 1968

## International matches 1981

20 Jan, Mexico City: v Mexico (a) drew 1-1 (Kostadinov pen)
27 Jan, Quito: v Ecuador (a) won 3-1 (Slavkov, Tzvetkov C., Kostadinov)
1 Feb, La Paz: v Bolivia (a) won 3-1 (Slavkov, Tzvetkov C., Kostadinov)
11 Feb, Lima: v Peru (a) won 2-1 (Zetlinski, Tzvetkov C.)
25 March, Subotica: v Yugoslavia (a) lost 1-2 (Slavkov)
17 April, Oporto: v Portugal (a) drew 1-1 (Tzvetkov C.)
29 April, Pleven: v Norway (h) won 1-0 (Tzvetkov P.)
13 May, Sofia: v Finland (h) won 4-0 (Slavkov 2, Kostadinov, Tzvetkov C.)
28 May, Vienna: v Austria (a) lost 0-2
12 Aug, Uddevalla: v Sweden (a) lost 0-1
9 Sept, Bucharest: v Rumania (a) won 2-1 (Yonchev, Kostadinov)
23 Sept, Bologna: v Italy (a) lost 2-3 (Mladenov, Dossen og)
14 Oct, Tirana: v Albania (a) won 2-0 (Slavkov, Mladenov)
28 Oct, Porto Alegre: v Brazil (a) lost 0-3
11 Nov, Sofia: v Austria (h) drew 0-0
22 Nov, Düsseldorf: v West Germany (a) lost 0-4
16 Dec, Haskovo: v Portugal (h) won 5-2 (Yonchev 2, Zdravkov 2 [1 pen], Bento og)

## League Championship wins (1925–82)

CSKA Sofia (prev. CDNA) 22; Levski Spartak (prev. Levski Sofia) 13; Slavia Sofia 6; Vladislav Varna 3; Lokomotiv Sofia 3; AS 23 Sofia 1; Botev Plovdiv 1; SC Sofia 1; Sokol Varna 1; Spartak Plovdiv 1; Tichka Varan 1; Trakia Plovdiv 1; ZSK Sofia 1.

## Cup wins (1946–82)

Levski Spartak (prev. Levski Sofia) 13; CSKA Sofia (prev. CDNA) 10; Slavia Sofia 6; Lokomotiv Sofia 3; Botev Plovdiv 1; Spartak Plovdiv 1; Spartak Sofia 1; Marek Stanke 1, Trakia Plovdiv 1.

| League Champions | Cup Winners |
| --- | --- |
| 1946 Levski Sofia | Levski Sofia |
| 1947 Levski Sofia | Levski Sofia |
| 1948 CDNA Sofia | Lokomotiv Sofia |
| 1949 Levski Sofia | Levski Sofia |
| 1950 Levski Sofia | Levski Sofia |
| 1951 CDNA Sofia | CDNA Sofia |
| 1952 CDNA Sofia | Slavia Sofia |
| 1953 Levski Sofia | Lokomotiv Sofia |
| 1954 CDNA Sofia | CDNA Sofia |
| 1955 CDNA Sofia | CDNA Sofia |
| 1956 CDNA Sofia | Levski Sofia |
| 1957 CDNA Sofia | Levski Sofia |
| 1958 CDNA Sofia | Spartak Plovdiv |
| 1959 CDNA Sofia | Levski Sofia |
| 1960 CDNA Sofia | CDNA Sofia |
| 1961 CDNA Sofia | CDNA Sofia |
| 1962 CDNA Sofia | Botev Plovdiv |
| 1963 Spartak Plovdiv | Slavia Sofia |
| 1964 Lokomotiv Sofia | Slavia Sofia |
| 1965 Levski Sofia | CSKA Sofia |
| 1966 CSKA Sofia | Slavia Sofia |
| 1967 Trakia Plovdiv | Levski Sofia |
| 1968 Levski Sofia | Spartak Sofia |
| 1969 CSKA Sofia | CSKA Sofia |
| 1970 Levski Spartak | Levski Spartak |
| 1971 CSKA Sofia | Levski Spartak |
| 1972 CSKA Sofia | CSKA Sofia |
| 1973 CSKA Sofia | CSKA Sofia |
| 1974 Levski Spartak | CSKA Sofia |
| 1975 CSKA Sofia | Slavia Sofia |
| 1976 CSKA Sofia | Levski Spartak |
| 1977 Levski Spartak | Levski Spartak |
| 1978 Lokomotiv Sofia | Marek Stanke |
| 1979 Levski Spartak | Levski Spartak |
| 1980 CSKA Sofia | Slavia Sofia |
| 1981 CSKA Sofia | Trakia Plovdiv |
| 1982 CSKA Sofia | Lokomotiv Sofia |

### Final League Table 1981–82

| | P | W | D | L | F | A | Pts |
| --- | --- | --- | --- | --- | --- | --- | --- |
| CSKA Sofia | 30 | 22 | 3 | 5 | 73 | 27 | 47 |
| Levski Spartak | 30 | 20 | 6 | 4 | 61 | 32 | 46 |
| Slavia Sofia | 30 | 15 | 5 | 10 | 35 | 33 | 35 |
| Tschernomore | 30 | 14 | 5 | 11 | 41 | 37 | 33 |
| Lokomotiv Sofia | 30 | 13 | 6 | 11 | 41 | 37 | 32 |
| Tschernomoretz | 30 | 14 | 4 | 12 | 48 | 44 | 32 |
| Trakia Plovdiv | 30 | 13 | 4 | 13 | 46 | 42 | 30 |
| Haskovo | 30 | 12 | 6 | 12 | 34 | 37 | 30 |
| Spartak Pleven | 30 | 13 | 3 | 14 | 40 | 40 | 29 |
| Etar Tirnovo | 30 | 9 | 10 | 11 | 46 | 48 | 28 |
| Sliven | 30 | 10 | 7 | 13 | 38 | 40 | 27 |
| Belasitsa | 30 | 11 | 5 | 14 | 32 | 43 | 27 |
| Marek Stanke | 30 | 9 | 8 | 13 | 23 | 40 | 26 |
| Botev Vratza | 30 | 7 | 8 | 15 | 23 | 41 | 22 |
| Beroe | 30 | 7 | 5 | 18 | 33 | 51 | 19 |
| Akademik | 30 | 6 | 5 | 19 | 33 | 55 | 17 |

# CYPRUS

*President:* Michalakis Kyprianou.
*General Secretary:* Demetrakis Stephanides.
*Address of Association:* Cyprus Football Association, Stasinos Street 1, Engomi 114, PO Box 5071, Nicosia.
*Telephone:* 45341, 45342.
*Telex:* 3880 football cy.
*Cable:* Football Nicosia.
*Area:* 3,572 square miles.
*Population:* 630,000.
*Number of Clubs:* 42. *Teams:* 56.
*Number of Players:* 16,000.
*Year of Formation:* 1934.
*National Colours:* Sky blue shirts, white shorts, blue and white stockings.
*Second Choice of Colours:* White shirts, blue shorts, white stockings.
*Name, Address and Capacity of National Stadium:* GSP, Nicosia, 12,000.
*Names, Addresses and Capacities of Other Principal Football Grounds:* Tsition, Limassol, 20,000; GSE, Famagusta, 10,000; GSO Limassol, 10,000; GSj, Larnaca, 8,000.
*Season:* October–June.
All players are amateurs.

## International matches 1981

18 Feb, Brussels: v Belgium (a) lost 2-3
  (*Lysandrou, Firos*)
22 Feb, Groningen: v Holland (a) lost 0-3
15 April, Nicosia: v Greece (h) lost 0-1
29 April, Nicosia: v Holland (h) lost 0-1
5 Dec, Paris: v France (a) lost 0-4

## League Championship wins (1935–82)

Apoel 12; Omonia 11; Anorthosis 6; AEL 5; EPA 3; Olympiakos 3; Chetin Kayal 1; Pezoporikos 1; Trast 1.

## Cup wins (1935–82)

Apoel 10; EPA 5; Omonia 5; AEL 3; Trast 3; Chetin Kaya 2; Apollon 2; Pezoporikos 2; Anorthosis 2; Paralimni 1; Olympiakos 1.

| League Champions | Cup Winners |
|---|---|
| 1946 EPA | EPA |
| 1947 Apoel | Apoel |
| 1948 Apoel | AEL |
| 1949 Apoel | Anorthosis |
| 1950 Anorthosis | EPA |
| 1951 Chetin Kaya | Apoel |
| 1952 Apoel | Chetin Kaya |
| 1953 AEL | EPA |
| 1954 Pezoporikos | Chetin Kaya |
| 1955 AEL | EPA |
| 1956 AEL | *No competition* |
| 1957 Anorthosis | *No competition* |
| 1958 Anorthosis | *No competition* |
| 1959 *No competition* | *No competition* |
| 1960 Anorthosis | *No competition* |
| 1961 Omonia | *No competition* |
| 1962 Anorthosis | Anorthosis |
| 1963 Anorthosis | Apoel |
| 1964 *No competition* | *No competition* |
| 1965 Apoel | Omonia |
| 1966 Omonia | Apollon |
| 1967 Olympiakos | Apollon |
| 1968 AEL | Apoel |
| 1969 Olympiakos | Apoel |
| 1970 EPA | Pezoporikos |
| 1971 Olympiakos | Anorthosis |
| 1972 Omonia | Omonia |
| 1973 Apoel | Pezoporikos |
| 1974 Omonia | Paralimni |
| 1975 Omonia | Anorthosis |
| 1976 Omonia | Apoel |
| 1977 Omonia | Olympiakos |
| 1978 Omonia | Apoel |
| 1979 Omonia | Apoel |
| 1980 Apoel | Omonia |
| 1981 Omonia | Omonia |
| 1982 Omonia | Omonia |

### Final League Table 1981–82

| | P | W | D | L | F | A | Pts |
|---|---|---|---|---|---|---|---|
| Omonia Nicosia | 26 | 20 | 4 | 2 | 61 | 9 | 44 |
| Pezoporikos | 26 | 13 | 8 | 5 | 38 | 17 | 34 |
| Apoel | 26 | 10 | 14 | 2 | 29 | 14 | 34 |
| Apollon | 26 | 13 | 8 | 5 | 34 | 23 | 34 |
| AEL | 26 | 9 | 10 | 7 | 29 | 22 | 28 |
| NEA Salamis | 26 | 8 | 9 | 9 | 34 | 30 | 25 |
| Omonia Aradippou | 26 | 8 | 9 | 9 | 27 | 33 | 25 |
| Athletic Union of Paralimni | 26 | 8 | 7 | 11 | 25 | 32 | 23 |
| Anorthosis | 26 | 8 | 6 | 12 | 23 | 34 | 22 |
| Olympiakos | 26 | 7 | 8 | 11 | 26 | 40 | 22 |
| EPA | 26 | 6 | 10 | 10 | 24 | 41 | 22 |
| APOP | 26 | 5 | 9 | 12 | 24 | 35 | 19 |
| Keravnos | 26 | 7 | 5 | 14 | 22 | 37 | 19 |
| Evagoras | 26 | 2 | 9 | 15 | 18 | 47 | 13 |

*President:* Jaromir Tomanek.
*Secretary:* Ing. Rudolf Bata.
*Address of Association:* Czechoslovak Football, 12, Na Porící, 11530 Prague, 1.
*Telephone:* 24 98 41, 22 58 36.
*Cable:* Sportsvaz Praha.
*Telex:* 122650 cstv c.
*Area:* 49,370 square miles.
*Population:* 16,000,000.
*Number of Clubs:* 5,919.   *Teams:* 5,366.
*Number of Players:* 541,379.
*Year of Formation:* 1906.
*National Colours:* Red shirts, white shorts, blue stockings.
*Second Choice of Colours:* White shirts, white shorts, white stockings.
*Name, Address and Capacity of National Stadium:* Stadion Ceskoslovenské Armády, Praha-Strahov, 60,000.
*Names, Addresses and Capacities of Other Principal Football Grounds:* Slovan Bratislava, Bratislava-Tehelné Pole, 63,000; Zbrojovka Brno, Brno, 70,000; Slavia Prague, Prague, 43,000; International, Bratislava, 40,000; Sparta Praha, Prague, 38,000.
*Season:* August–November; February–June.

**Principal Honours**

World Cup: *runners-up* 1934, 1962
European Championship: *winners* 1976
Olympic Games: *runners-up* 1964
European Cup-Winners' Cup: *winners* Slovan Bratislava (1969)

**International matches 1981**

25 Jan, La Paz: v Bolivia (a) lost 1-2 (*Janecka*)
30 Jan, Santa Cruz: v Bolivia (a) won 5-2 (*Daneska, Nehoda 2, Kozak, Vizek* pen)
4 Feb, Lima: v Peru (a) won 3-1 (*Vizek 2, Jakubec*)
24 March, Bratislava: v Switzerland (h) lost 0-1
15 April, Ankara: v Turkey (a) won 3-0 (*Janecka, Kozak, Vizek*)
29 April, Dublin: v Eire (a) lost 1-3 (*Masny*)
27 May, Bratislava: v Iceland (h) won 6-1 (*Vizek, Panenka* pen, *Nehoda, Kozak 2, Janecka*)
18 Aug, Prague: v European XI (h) won 4-0 (*Kozak 2, Nehoda 2*)
9 Sept, Prague: v Wales (h) won 2-0 (*Stevenson* og, *Licka*)
23 Sept, Reykjavik: v Iceland (a) drew 1-1 (*Kozak*)
28 Oct, Tbilisi: v USSR (a) lost 0-2
11 Nov, Buenos Aires: v Argentina (a) drew 1-1 (*Valek*)
29 Nov, Bratislava: v USSR (h) drew 1-1 (*Vojacek*)

**League Championship wins (1926–82)**

Sparta Prague 13; Slavia Prague 12; Dukla Prague (prev. UDA) 11; Slovan Bratislava 6; Spartak Trnava 5; Banik Ostrava 3; Inter-Bratislava 1; Spartak Hradec Kralove 1; Viktoria Zizkov 1; Zbrojovka Brno 1.

**Cup wins (1961–82)**

Dukla Prague 5; Slovan Bratislava 5; Sparta Prague 4; Spartak Trnava 3; Banik Ostrava 2; Lokomotiv Kosice 2; TJ Gottwaldov 1.

| League Champions | Cup Winners |
|---|---|
| 1946 Sparta Prague | |
| 1947 Slavia Prague | |
| 1948 Sparta Prague | |
| 1949 Slovan Bratislava | |
| 1950 Slovan Bratislava | |
| 1951 Slovan Bratislava | |
| 1952 Sparta Prague | |
| 1953 Dukla Prague | |
| 1954 Sparta Prague | |
| 1955 Slovan Bratislava | |
| 1956 Dukla Prague | |
| 1957 *No competition* | |
| 1958 Dukla Prague | |
| 1959 Inter-Bratislava | |
| 1960 Hradec Kralove | |
| 1961 Dukla Prague | Dukla Prague |
| 1962 Dukla Prague | Slovan Bratislava |
| 1963 Dukla Prague | Slovan Bratislava |
| 1964 Dukla Prague | Sparta Prague |
| 1965 Sparta Prague | Dukla Prague |
| 1966 Dukla Prague | Dukla Prague |
| 1967 Sparta Prague | Sparta Trnava |
| 1968 Spartak Trnava | Slovan Bratislava |
| 1969 Spartak Trnava | Dukla Prague |
| 1970 Slovan Bratislava | TJ Gottwaldov |
| 1971 Spartak Trnava | Spartak Trnava |
| 1972 Spartak Trnava | Sparta Prague |
| 1973 Spartak Trnava | Banik Ostrava |
| 1974 Slovan Bratislava | Slovan Bratislava |
| 1975 Slovan Bratislava | Spartak Trnava |
| 1976 Banik Ostrava | Sparta Prague |
| 1977 Dukla Prague | Lokomotiv Kosice |
| 1978 Zbrojovka Brno | Banik Ostrava |
| 1979 Dukla Prague | Lokomotiv Kosice |
| 1980 Banik Ostrava | Sparta Prague |
| 1981 Banik Ostrava | Dukla Prague |
| 1982 Dukla Prague | Slovan Bratislava |

**Final League Table 1981–82**

| | P | W | D | L | F | A | Pts |
|---|---|---|---|---|---|---|---|
| Dukla Prague | 30 | 18 | 6 | 6 | 54 | 20 | 42 |
| Banik Ostrava | 30 | 15 | 8 | 7 | 53 | 24 | 38 |
| Bohemians | 30 | 15 | 8 | 7 | 41 | 22 | 38 |
| Plastika | 30 | 14 | 8 | 8 | 35 | 26 | 36 |
| Lokomotiv Kosice | 30 | 12 | 8 | 10 | 36 | 34 | 32 |
| Sparta Prague | 30 | 11 | 9 | 10 | 40 | 35 | 31 |
| Slavia Prague | 30 | 10 | 10 | 10 | 44 | 41 | 30 |
| Inter Bratislava | 30 | 11 | 8 | 11 | 29 | 29 | 30 |
| Vitkovice | 30 | 11 | 8 | 11 | 33 | 41 | 30 |
| Slovan Bratislava | 30 | 11 | 7 | 12 | 42 | 47 | 29 |
| Zbrojovka Brno | 30 | 11 | 6 | 13 | 32 | 38 | 28 |
| Tatran Presov | 30 | 10 | 8 | 12 | 28 | 40 | 28 |
| RH Cheb | 30 | 8 | 9 | 13 | 36 | 45 | 25 |
| Spartak Trnava | 30 | 10 | 4 | 16 | 31 | 41 | 24 |
| Petrzalka | 30 | 8 | 6 | 16 | 26 | 43 | 22 |
| Bystrica | 30 | 5 | 7 | 18 | 29 | 63 | 17 |

# DENMARK

*President:* Carl Nielsen.
*Secretary:* Erik Hyldstrup.
*Address of Association:* Dansk Boldspil – Union PW Ligns Alle 4, Copenhagen, 2100.
*Telephone:* 424540.
*Cable:* Danksboldspil.
*Telex:* 15545 dbu dk.
*Area:* 17,159 square miles.
*Population:* 4,750,000.
*Number of Clubs:* 1,479.   *Teams:* 7,400.
*Number of Players:* 208,350.
*Year of Formation:* 1889.
*National Colours:* Red shirts, white shorts, red stockings.
*Second Choice of Colours:* White shirts, red shorts, white stockings.
*Name, Address and Capacity of National Stadium:* Kobenhavns Idraetspark, PH-Lings-Alle 2, 50,000.
*Names, Addresses and Capacities of Other Principal Football Grounds:* Odense stadium, Odense, 20,000; Aarhus stadium, Aarhus, 24,000; Aalborg stadium, Aalborg, 22,000; Esbjerg stadium, Esbjerg, 18,000; Vejle stadium, Vejle, 18,000.
*Season:* April–November.

## Principal Honours

Olympic Games: *runners-up* 1908, 1912, 1960

## International matches 1981

15 April, Copenhagen: v Rumania (h) won 2-1 (*Simonsen* pen, *Bastrup*)
1 May, Luxembourg: v Luxembourg (a) won 2-1 (*Elkjaer, Arnesen*)
14 May, Malmo: v Sweden (a) won 2-1 (*Bastrup, Elkjaer*)
3 June, Copenhagen: v Italy (h) won 3-1 (*Roentved, Arnesen, Bastrup*)
12 Aug, Tammerfors: v Finland (a) won 2-1 (*Madsen, Eigenbrod*)
26 Aug, Copenhagen: v Iceland (h) 3-0 (*Lundqvist, Simonsen 2*)
9 Sept, Copenhagen: v Yugoslavia (h) lost 1-2 (*Elkjaer*)
23 Sept, Copenhagen: v Norway (h) won 2-1 (*Elkjaer, Arnesen*)
14 Oct, Salonika: v Greece (a) won 3-2 (*Lerby, Arnesen, Elkjaer*)

## League Championship wins (1913–81)

KB Copenhagen 15; B 93 Copenhagen 9; AB (Akademisk) 9; B 1903 Copenhagen 7; Frem 6; Esbjergs BK 5; AGF Aarhus 4; Vejle BK 4; Hvidovre 3; B 1909 Odense 2; Koge BK 2; Odense BK 1.

## Cup wins (1955–82)

Vejle BK 6; Aarhus GF 5; BK 09 Odense 3; Randers Freja 3; Aalborg BK 2; Esbjerg BK 2; Frem 2; KB Copenhagen 1; Vanlose 1; B 1903 Copenhagen 1; Hvidovre 1; B93 Copenhagen 1.

| League Champions | Cup Winners |
|---|---|
| 1946 BK 93 | |
| 1947 Akademisk | |
| 1948 KB Copenhagen | |
| 1949 KB Copenhagen | |
| 1950 KB Copenhagen | |
| 1951 Akademisk | |
| 1952 Akademisk | |
| 1953 KB Copenhagen | |
| 1954 Koge BK | |
| 1955 Aarhus GF | Aarhus GF |
| 1956 Aarhus GF | Frem |
| 1957 Aarhus GF | Aarhus GF |
| 1958 Vejle | Vejle |
| 1959 BK 09 Odense | Vejle |
| 1960 Aarhus GF | Aarhus GF |
| 1961 Esbjerg BK | Aarhus GF |
| 1962 Esbjerg BK | BK Odense 09 |
| 1963 Esbjerg BK | BK Odense 09 |
| 1964 BK 09 Odense | Esbjerg |
| 1965 Esbjerg BK | Aarhus GF |
| 1966 Hvidovre | Aalborg BK |
| 1967 Akademisk | Randers Freja |
| 1968 KB Copenhagen | Randers Freja |
| 1969 BK 03 Copenhagen | KB Copenhagen |
| 1970 BK 03 Copenhagen | Aalborg BK |
| 1971 Vejle | BK 09 Odense |
| 1972 Vejle | Vejle |
| 1973 Hvidovre | Randers Freja |
| 1974 KB Copenhagen | Vanlose |
| 1975 Koge BK | Vejle |
| 1976 BK 03 Copenhagen | Esbjerg |
| 1977 Odense BK | Vejle |
| 1978 Vejle | Frem |
| 1979 Esbjerg BK | B 1903 Copenhagen |
| 1980 KB Copenhagen | Hvidovre |
| 1981 Hvidovre | Vejle |
| 1982 | B 93 Copenhagen |

### Final League Table 1981

| | P | W | D | L | F | A | Pts |
|---|---|---|---|---|---|---|---|
| Hvidovre | 30 | 15 | 10 | 5 | 42 | 25 | 40 |
| Lyngby | 30 | 16 | 7 | 7 | 54 | 34 | 39 |
| Naestved | 30 | 13 | 12 | 5 | 51 | 36 | 38 |
| Aarhus | 30 | 14 | 10 | 6 | 47 | 33 | 38 |
| Esbjerg | 30 | 13 | 10 | 7 | 46 | 38 | 36 |
| Odense | 30 | 13 | 8 | 9 | 53 | 40 | 34 |
| KB Copenhagen | 30 | 13 | 6 | 11 | 62 | 58 | 32 |
| B 1901 | 30 | 13 | 6 | 11 | 51 | 50 | 32 |
| Vejle | 30 | 7 | 15 | 8 | 51 | 48 | 29 |
| Koge | 30 | 9 | 11 | 10 | 38 | 45 | 29 |
| B 93 | 30 | 9 | 10 | 11 | 39 | 48 | 28 |
| Ikast | 30 | 10 | 6 | 14 | 46 | 49 | 26 |
| B 1903 | 30 | 5 | 13 | 12 | 28 | 39 | 23 |
| Kastrup | 30 | 6 | 11 | 13 | 30 | 42 | 23 |
| Herfolge | 30 | 6 | 6 | 18 | 33 | 57 | 18 |
| Viborg | 30 | 5 | 5 | 20 | 33 | 62 | 15 |

# FINLAND

*President:* Jouko Loikkanen.
*Secretary:* Karl Salonen.
*Address of Association:* Suomen Palloliitto – Finlands Bollförbund, Stadion, 00250 Helsinki 25.
*Telephone:* 44 12 81.
*Cable:* Suomifotboll.
*Telex:* 123186 spl sf.
*Area:* 130,119 square miles.
*Population:* 4,792,000.
*Number of Clubs:* 987.   *Teams:* 2,325.
*Number of Players:* 49,662.
*Year of Formation:* 1907.
*National Colours:* White shirts, blue shorts, white stockings.
*Second Choice of Colours:* Blue shirts, white shorts, blue stockings.
*Name, Address and Capacity of National Stadium:* Olympiastadion, Helsinki, 50,000.
*Names, Addresses and Capacities of Other Principal Football Grounds:* Ratina, Tampere, 25,000; Urhei Lukeskus Kotka, 14,500; Kupittaa, Turku, 11,000; Vaino Lanniemi, Kuopio, 10,100.
All amateur players.
*Season:* April–October.

**International matches 1981**

13 May, Sofia: v Bulgaria (a) lost 0–4
24 May, Lahtis: v West Germany (h) lost 0–4
17 June, Linz: v Austria (a) lost 1–5 (*Valvee*)
2 July, Helsingfors: v Norway (h) won 3–1
    (*Kousa, Rajaniemi, Turunen*)
29 July, Halmstad: v Sweden (a) lost 0–1
12 Aug, Tammerfors: v Denmark (h) lost 1–2
    (*Valvee*)
2 Sept, Kotka: v Albania (h) won 2–1
    (*Houtsonen, Kousa*)
23 Sept, Bochum: v West Germany (a) lost 1–7
    (*Turunen*)

**Championship wins (1949–81)**

Turun Palloseura 5; Kupion Palloseura 5; Helsinki JK 4; Valkeakosken Haka 4; Lahden Reipas 3; IF Kamraterna 2; Kotkan TP 2; OPS Oulu 2; Turun Pyrkivä 1; IF Kronohagens 1; Helsinki PS 1; Ilves-Kissat 1; Kokkolan PV 1; IF Kamraterna I Vasa 1.

**Cup wins (1955–81)**

Lahden Reipas 7; Valkeakosken Haka 6; Kotkan TP 4; Mikkelin 2; Helsinki JK 2; IFK Abo 1; Drott 1; Helsinki PS 1; Kuopion Palloseura 1; Pallo-Peikot 1; Ilves Tampere 1.

| League Champions | Cup Winners |
| --- | --- |
| 1949 Turun Palloseura | |
| 1950 Ilves-Kissat | |
| 1951 Kotkan TP | |
| 1952 Kotkan TP | |
| 1953 IF Kamraterna I | |
| 1954 Turun Pyrkivä | |
| 1955 IF Kronohagens | Valkaekosken Haka |
| 1956 Kuopion Palloseura | Pallo-Peikot |
| 1957 Helsinki PS | Drott |
| 1958 Kuopion Palloseura | Kotkan TP |
| 1959 IF Kamraterna | Valkeakosken Haka |
| 1960 Valkeakosken Haka | Valkeakosken Haka |
| 1961 IF Kamraterna | Kotkan TP |
| 1962 Valkeakosken Haka | Helsinki PS |
| 1963 Lahden Reipas | Valkeakosken Haka |
| 1964 Helsinki JK | Lahden Reipas |
| 1965 Valkeakosken Haka | IFK Abo |
| 1966 Kuopion Palloseura | Helsinki JK |
| 1967 Lahden Reipas | Kotkan TP |
| 1968 Turun Palloseura | Kuopion Palloseura |
| 1969 Kokkolan PV | Valkeakosken Haka |
| 1970 Lahden Reipas | Mikkelin |
| 1971 Turun Palloseura | Mikkelin |
| 1972 Turun Palloseura | Lahden Reipas |
| 1973 Helsinki JK | Lahden Reipas |
| 1974 Kuopion Palloseura | Lahden Reipas |
| 1975 Turun Palloseura | Lahden Reipas |
| 1976 Kuopion Palloseura | Lahden Reipas |
| 1977 Valkeakosken Haka | Valkeakosken Haka |
| 1978 Helsinki JK | Lahden Reipas |
| 1979 OPS Oulu | Ilves |
| 1980 OPS Oulu | Kotkan TP |
| 1981 Helsinki JK | Helsinki JK |

**Qualifying series**

| | P | W | D | L | F | A | Pts |
| --- | --- | --- | --- | --- | --- | --- | --- |
| KPT Kuopion | 22 | 11 | 9 | 2 | 45 | 22 | 31 |
| HJK Helsinki | 22 | 12 | 4 | 6 | 40 | 24 | 28 |
| TPS Turun | 22 | 11 | 6 | 5 | 36 | 22 | 28 |
| Haka Valkeakosken | 22 | 11 | 5 | 6 | 42 | 24 | 27 |
| KTP Kotkan | 22 | 11 | 4 | 7 | 33 | 26 | 26 |
| Oulun Palloseura | 22 | 9 | 7 | 6 | 43 | 34 | 25 |
| Ilves | 22 | 9 | 6 | 7 | 44 | 28 | 24 |
| KuPS | 22 | 10 | 3 | 9 | 34 | 37 | 23 |
| Sepsi-78 | 22 | 8 | 4 | 10 | 21 | 30 | 20 |
| RoPS | 22 | 5 | 3 | 14 | 27 | 44 | 13 |
| MP | 22 | 4 | 3 | 15 | 17 | 50 | 11 |
| MiPK | 22 | 2 | 4 | 16 | 22 | 63 | 8 |

**Championship**

| | P | W | D | L | F | A | Group Pts | Total |
| --- | --- | --- | --- | --- | --- | --- | --- | --- |
| HJK Helsinki | 7 | 5 | 1 | 1 | 57 | 32 | 14  +11 | 25 |
| KPT Kuopion | 7 | 2 | 3 | 2 | 56 | 28 | 16  + 7 | 23 |
| Haka Valkeakosken | 7 | 4 | 1 | 2 | 54 | 34 | 14  + 9 | 23 |
| TPS Turun | 7 | 2 | 4 | 1 | 46 | 27 | 14  + 8 | 22 |
| Ilves | 7 | 3 | 1 | 3 | 59 | 46 | 12  + 7 | 19 |
| KTP Kotkan | 7 | 1 | 3 | 3 | 38 | 36 | 13  + 5 | 18 |
| KuPS | 7 | 1 | 4 | 2 | 46 | 50 | 12  + 6 | 18 |
| Oulon Palloseura | 7 | 1 | 1 | 5 | 55 | 58 | 13  + 3 | 16 |

**Promotion/Relegation series**

| | P | W | D | L | F | A | Group Pts | Total |
| --- | --- | --- | --- | --- | --- | --- | --- | --- |
| Kuusysi | 7 | 4 | 2 | 1 | 17 | 8 | 4  +10 | 14 |
| Kuopion Elo | 7 | 5 | 1 | 1 | 12 | 4 | 2  +11 | 13 |
| KPV | 7 | 4 | 1 | 2 | 16 | 10 | 3  + 9 | 12 |
| Sepsi-78 | 7 | 3 | 2 | 2 | 16 | 11 | 4  + 8 | 12 |
| RoPS | 7 | 4 | 1 | 2 | 16 | 13 | 3  + 9 | 12 |
| MP | 7 | 0 | 3 | 4 | 7 | 18 | 2  + 3 | 5 |
| Espoon Esbo | 7 | 1 | 1 | 5 | 7 | 16 | 1  + 3 | 4 |
| MiPK | 7 | 1 | 1 | 5 | 8 | 19 | 1  + 3 | 4 |

# FRANCE

*President:* Fernand Sastre.
*Secretary:* Michel Cagnion (Dir Gen).
*Address of Association:* Fédération Française de Football, 60 bis, Avenue d'Iena, Paris 16e.
*Telephone:* 720 65–40.
*Cable:* Cefi Paris 034.
*Telex:* Fedfoot 620837 f.
*Area:* 209,454 square miles.
*Population:* 52,000,000.
*Number of Clubs:* 20,938.   *Teams:* 52,000.
*Number of Players:* 1,430,679.
*Year of Formation:* 1919.
*National Colours:* Blue shirts, white shorts, red stockings.
*Second Choice of Colours:* White shirts, blue shorts, red stockings.
*Name, Address and Capacity of National Stadium:* Stade du Parc des Princes, 24 rue du Commandant Guilbaud, 75, Paris 16ème, 50,000.
*Names, Addresses and Capacities of Other Principal Football Grounds:* Stade Vélodrome Jean Bouin, Marseilles, 45,000; Stade Municipal de Bordeaux, Avenue de la Côte d'Argent, 33, Bordeaux, 30,000; Stade Municipal de Gerland, Lyon, 45,000; Stade Geoffroy Guichard Saint Etienne, 42,000; Stade Marcel Saupin, Nantes, 33,000; Stade de la Meinau, Strasbourg, 30,000; Stadium Municipal de Toulouse, Parc des Sports, 31 Toulouse, 30,000.
*Season:* August–June.

**Principal Honours**

European Champions Cup: *runners-up* Stade de Reims (1956, 1959); St Etienne (1976)
UEFA Cup: *runners-up* Bastia (1978)

**International matches 1981**

18 Feb, Madrid: v Spain (a) lost 0-1
25 March, Rotterdam: v Holland (a) lost 0-1
29 April, Paris: v Belgium (h) won 3-2 (*Soler 2, Six*)
15 May, Paris: v Brazil (h) lost 1-3 (*Six*)
9 Sept, Brussels: v Belgium (a) lost 0-2
14 Oct, Dublin: v Eire (a) lost 2-3 (*Bellone, Platini*)
18 Nov, Paris: v Holland (h) won 2-0 (*Platini, Six*)
5 Dec, Paris: v Cyprus (h) won 4-0 (*Rocheteau, Lacombe 2, Genghini*)

**League Championship wins (1933–82)**

Saint Etienne 10; Stade de Reims 6; Nantes 5; AS Monaco 4; OGC Nice 4; Olympique Marseilles 4; Lille OSC 3; FC Sete 2; Sochaux 2; Racing Club Paris 1; Roubaix-Tourcoing 1; Girondins Bordeaux 1; Strasbourg 1.

**Cup wins (1918–82)**

Olympique Marseilles 9; Saint Etienne 6; Lille OSC 5; Racing Club Paris 5; Red Star 5; AS Monaco 3; Olympique Lyon 3; CAS Genereaux 2; Nancy 2; OGC Nice 2; Racing Club Strasbourg 2; Sedan 2; FC Sete 2; Stade de Reims 2; Stade Rennes 2; AS Cannes 1; Club Français 1; Excelsior Roubaix 1; Girondins Bordeaux 1; Le Havre 1; SO Montpelier 1; Olympique de Pantin 1; CA Paris 1; Sochaux 1; Toulouse 1; Bastia 1; Nantes 1; Paris St Germain 1.

| Year | League Champions | Cup Winners |
|---|---|---|
| 1946 | Lille OSC | Lille OSC |
| 1947 | Roubaix-Tourcoing | Lille OSC |
| 1948 | Ol Marseilles | Lille OSC |
| 1949 | Stade de Reims | Racing Paris |
| 1950 | Girondins Bordeaux | Stade de Reims |
| 1951 | OGC Nice | Racing Strasbourg |
| 1952 | OGC Nice | OGC Nice |
| 1953 | Stade de Reims | Lille OSC |
| 1954 | Lille OSC | OGC Nice |
| 1955 | Stade de Reims | Lille OSC |
| 1956 | OGC Nice | Sedan |
| 1957 | Saint Etienne | Toulouse |
| 1958 | Stade de Reims | Stade de Reims |
| 1959 | OGC Nice | Le Havre |
| 1960 | Stade de Reims | AS Monaco |
| 1961 | AS Monaco | Sedan |
| 1962 | Stade de Reims | Saint Etienne |
| 1963 | AS Monaco | AS Monaco |
| 1964 | Saint Etienne | Ol Lyon |
| 1965 | Nantes | Stade Rennes |
| 1966 | Nantes | Racing Club Strasbourg |
| 1967 | Saint Etienne | Ol Lyon |
| 1968 | Saint Etienne | Saint Etienne |
| 1969 | Saint Etienne | Ol Marseilles |
| 1970 | Saint Etienne | Saint Etienne |
| 1971 | Ol Marseilles | Stade Rennes |
| 1972 | Ol Marseilles | Ol Marseilles |
| 1973 | Nantes | Ol Lyon |
| 1974 | Saint Etienne | Saint Etienne |
| 1975 | Saint Etienne | Saint Etienne |
| 1976 | Saint Etienne | Ol Marseilles |
| 1977 | Nantes | Saint Etienne |
| 1978 | Monaco | Nancy |
| 1979 | Strasbourg | Nantes |
| 1980 | Nantes | Monaco |
| 1981 | Saint Etienne | Bastia |
| 1982 | Monaco | Paris St Germain |

**Final League Table 1981–82**

| | P | W | D | L | F | A | Pts |
|---|---|---|---|---|---|---|---|
| Monaco | 38 | 24 | 7 | 7 | 70 | 29 | 55 |
| St Etienne | 38 | 22 | 10 | 6 | 74 | 31 | 54 |
| Sochaux | 38 | 20 | 9 | 9 | 59 | 43 | 49 |
| Bordeaux | 38 | 19 | 10 | 9 | 55 | 45 | 48 |
| Laval | 38 | 16 | 12 | 10 | 49 | 40 | 44 |
| Nantes | 38 | 19 | 5 | 14 | 64 | 34 | 43 |
| Paris SG | 38 | 17 | 9 | 12 | 58 | 45 | 43 |
| Nancy | 38 | 13 | 13 | 12 | 50 | 52 | 39 |
| Brest | 38 | 14 | 10 | 14 | 48 | 57 | 38 |
| Strasbourg | 38 | 12 | 12 | 14 | 41 | 41 | 36 |
| Tours | 38 | 14 | 7 | 17 | 61 | 59 | 35 |
| Bastia | 38 | 12 | 11 | 15 | 43 | 65 | 35 |
| Lens | 38 | 12 | 10 | 16 | 44 | 51 | 34 |
| Lille | 38 | 13 | 8 | 17 | 46 | 54 | 34 |
| Auxerre | 38 | 11 | 12 | 15 | 43 | 58 | 34 |
| Lyon | 38 | 13 | 6 | 19 | 38 | 46 | 32 |
| Metz | 38 | 8 | 16 | 14 | 35 | 49 | 32 |
| Valenciennes | 38 | 10 | 10 | 18 | 40 | 59 | 30 |
| Nice | 38 | 7 | 9 | 22 | 34 | 57 | 23 |
| Montpellier | 38 | 7 | 8 | 23 | 30 | 67 | 22 |

# EAST GERMANY

*President:* Gunter Schneider.
*Secretary:* Werner Lempert.
*Address of Association:* Deutscher Fussball-Verband, Storkower Strasse 118, 1055 Berlin.
*Telephone:* 438 43 88/91, 438 44 75.
*Cable:* Fussball Verband Berlin.
*Telex:* 0112119.   *Area:* 41,802 square miles.
*Population:* 17,000,000.
*Number of Clubs:* 5,488.   *Teams:* 28,025.
*Number of Players:* 557,106.
*Year of Formation:* 1948.
*National Colours:* White shirts, blue shorts, white stockings.
*Second Choice of Colours:* Blue shirts, white shorts, blue stockings.
*Name, Address and Capacity of National Stadium:* Sportforum-Leipzig, 95,000.
*Names, Addresses and Capacities of Other Principal Football Grounds:* Festival Stadion, Berlin; Dynamo-Stadion, Dresden, 37,000; Ernst-Thälmann-Stadion, Karl-Marx-Stadt, 45,000; Georg-Dimitroff-Stadion, Erfurt, 50,000; Kurt-Wabbel-Stadion, Halle, 32,000; Ernest-Abbe-Stadion, Jena, 25,000; Ostsee-Stadion, Rostock, 30,000; Friedrich-Ludwig-Jahn-Sportpark, Berlin, 25,000; Ernest-Grube-Stadion, Magdeburg, 45,000.
*Season:* August–June (with winter break).

## Principal Honours

Olympic Games: *winners* 1976
European Cup-Winners' Cup: *winners* FC Magdeburg (1974); *runners-up* Carl Zeiss Jena (1981)

## International matches 1981

11 March, Braila: v Rumania (a) lost 1-2 (*Schnuphase* pen)
4 April, Valletta: v Malta (a) won 2-1 (*Schnuphase* pen, *Hafner*)
19 April, Udinese: v Italy (a) drew 0-0
2 May, Chorzow: v Poland (a) lost 0-1
19 May, Senftenberg: v Cuba (h) won 5-0 (*Heun 2, Schnuphase, Streich, Hernandez og*)
10 Oct, Leipzig: v Poland (h) lost 2-3 (*Schnuphase* pen, *Streich*)
11 Nov, Jena: v Malta (h) won 5-1 (*Krause, Streich, Heun, Liebers, Spiteri-Gonzi og*)

## League Championship wins (1950–82)

ASK Vorwaerts 6; Dynamo Dresden 5; Dynamo Berlin 4; Wismut Karl-Marx-Stadt 4; FC Magdeburg 4; Carl Zeiss Jena (prev. Motor Jena) 3; Chemie Leipzig 2; Turbine Erfurt 2; Turbine Halle 1; Zwickau Horch 1; Empor Rostock 1.

## Cup wins (1949–82)

Carl Zeiss Jena (prev. Motor Jena) 5; Dynamo Dresden 4; FC Magdeburg 3; Lokomotiv Leipzig 3; Chemie Leipzig 2; Magdeburg Aufbau 2; Motor Zwickau 2; ASK Vorwaerts 2; Dresden Einheit SC 1; Dresden VP 1; Dynamo Berlin 1; Halle Chemie SC 1; North Dessau Waggonworks 1; Thale EHW 1; Union East Berlin 1; Wismut Karl-Marx-Stadt 1; Sachsenring Zwickau 1.

| League Champions | Cup Winners |
|---|---|
| 1949 | North Dessau Waggonworks |
| 1950 Zwickau Horch | Thale EHW |
| 1951 Chemie Leipzig | *No competition* |
| 1952 Halle Turbine | Dresden VP |
| 1953 Dynamo Dresden | *No competition* |
| 1954 Turbine Erfurt | ASK Vorwaerts |
| 1955 Turbine Erfurt | Wismut Karl-Marx-Stadt |
| 1956 Wismut Karl-Marx-Stadt | Chemie Leipzig |
| 1957 Wismut Karl-Marx-Stadt | Lokomotiv Leipzig |
| 1958 ASK Vorwaerts | Dresden Einheit SC |
| 1959 Wismut Karl-Marx-Stadt | Dynamo Berlin |
| 1960 ASK Vorwaerts | Motor Jena |
| 1961 Empor Rostock | Motor Jena |
| 1962 ASK Vorwaerts | Halle Chemie SC |
| 1963 Motor Jena | Motor Zwickau |
| 1964 Leipzig Chemie | Magdeburg Aufbau |
| 1965 ASK Vorwaerts | Magdeburg Aufbau |
| 1966 ASK Vorwaerts | Chemie Leipzig |
| 1967 Wismut Karl-Marx-Stadt | Motor Zwickau |
| 1968 Carl Zeiss Jena | Union East Berlin |
| 1969 ASK Vorwaerts | FC Magdeburg |
| 1970 Carl Zeiss Jena | ASK Vorwaerts |
| 1971 Dynamo Dresden | Dynamo Dresden |
| 1972 FC Magdeburg | Carl Zeiss Jena |
| 1973 Dynamo Dresden | FC Magdeburg |
| 1974 FC Magdeburg | Carl Zeiss Jena |
| 1975 FC Magdeburg | Sachsenring Zwickau |
| 1976 Dynamo Dresden | Lokomotiv Leipzig |
| 1977 Dynamo Dresden | Dynamo Dresden |
| 1978 FC Magdeburg | Dynamo Dresden |
| 1979 Dynamo Berlin | FC Magdeburg |
| 1980 Dynamo Berlin | Carl Zeiss Jena |
| 1981 Dynamo Berlin | Lokomotiv Leipzig |
| 1982 Dynamo Berlin | Dynamo Dresden |

### Final League Table 1981–82

| | P | W | D | L | F | A | Pts |
|---|---|---|---|---|---|---|---|
| Dynamo Berlin | 26 | 18 | 5 | 3 | 73 | 27 | 41 |
| Dynamo Dresden | 26 | 15 | 4 | 7 | 50 | 24 | 34 |
| Lokomotiv Leipzig | 26 | 13 | 7 | 6 | 53 | 29 | 33 |
| Vorwaerts Frankfurt | 26 | 14 | 5 | 7 | 57 | 40 | 33 |
| Carl Zeiss Jena | 26 | 14 | 4 | 8 | 49 | 27 | 32 |
| Magdeburg | 26 | 13 | 6 | 7 | 49 | 42 | 32 |
| Rot-Weiss Erfurt | 26 | 10 | 8 | 8 | 55 | 44 | 28 |
| Rostock | 26 | 9 | 7 | 10 | 37 | 40 | 25 |
| Karl-Marx-Stadt | 26 | 9 | 6 | 11 | 50 | 38 | 24 |
| Aue | 26 | 8 | 7 | 11 | 33 | 48 | 23 |
| Halle | 26 | 8 | 7 | 11 | 28 | 46 | 23 |
| Zwickau | 26 | 4 | 6 | 16 | 25 | 58 | 14 |
| Cottbus | 26 | 3 | 5 | 18 | 21 | 62 | 11 |
| Schkopau | 26 | 3 | 5 | 18 | 21 | 77 | 11 |

# WEST GERMANY

*President:* Hermann Neuberger.
*Secretary:* Hans Passlack.
*Address of Association:* Deutscher Fussball-Bund, Otto-Fleck-Schneise 6, Frankfurt (Main) 71.
*Telephone:* (0611) 63161.
*Cable:* Fussball, Frankfurt.
*Telex:* 41 6815 dfb d.
*Area:* 95,097 square miles.
*Population:* 63,300,000.
*Number of Clubs:* 18,957.   *Teams:* 122,345.
*Number of Players:* 4,020,240.
*Year of Formation:* 1900.
*National Colours:* White shirts, black shorts, white stockings.
*Second Choice of Colours:* Green shirts, white shorts, white stockings.
*Name, Address and Capacity of National Stadium:* There is no stadium which could be considered as the National Stadium.
*Names, Addresses and Capacities of Principal Football Grounds:* Olympiastadion Berlin, 80,000 (61,800 seats); Olympiastadion München, 75,600 (44,200 seats); Neckarstadion Stuttgart, 72,200 (34,400 seats); Parkstadion Gelsenkirchen, 70,000 (36,000 seats); Rheinstadion Düsseldorf, 69,600 (31,800 seats); Waldstadion Frankfurt 61,000 (29,900 seats); Volksparkstadion Hamburg; 61,400 (27,800 seats); Niedersachsenstadion Hannover, 60,500 (39,000 seats); Westfalen Stadion Dortmund, 53,600 (16,600 seats); Müngersdorfer Stadion, Cologne 60,000 (28,000 seats).
*Season:* August–June.

## Principal Honours

World Cup: *winners* 1954, 1974; *runners-up* 1966, 1982
European Championship: *winners* 1972, 1980; *runners-up* (1976)
World Club Champions: Bayern Munich (1976)
European Champions Cup: *winners* Bayern Munich (1974, 1975, 1976); *runners-up* Eintracht Frankfurt (1960), Borussia Moenchengladbach (1977), SV Hamburg (1980), Bayern Munich (1982)
European Cup-Winners' Cup: *winners* Borussia Dortmund (1966), Bayern Munich (1967), SV Hamburg (1977); *runners-up* Munich 1860 (1965), SV Hamburg (1968), Fortuna Düsseldorf (1979)
UEFA Cup: *winners* Borussia Moenchengladbach (1975, 1979), Eintracht Frankfurt (1980); *runners-up* Borussia Moenchengladbach (1973, 1980), SV Hamburg (1982)

## International matches 1981

1 Jan, Montevideo: v Argentina (a) lost 1-2 (*Hrubesch*)
7 Jan, Montevideo: v Brazil (a) lost 1-4 (*Klaus Allofs*)
1 April, Tirana: v Albania (a) won 2-0 (*Schuster 2*)
29 April, Hamburg: v Austria (h) won 2-0 (*Fischer, Kraus og*)
19 May, Stuttgart: v Brazil (h) lost 1-2 (*Fischer*)
24 May, Lahtis: v Finland (a) won 4-0 (*Fischer 2, Kaltz, Briegel*)
2 Sept, Chorzow: v Poland (a) won 2-0 (*Fischer, Rummenigge*)
23 Sept, Bochum: v Finland (h) won 7-1 (*Rummenigge 3, Breitner 2, Fischer, Dremmler*)
14 Oct, Vienna: v Austria (a) won 3-1 (*Littbarski 2, Magath*)
18 Nov, Dortmund: v Albania (h) won 8-0 (*Rummenigge 3, Fischer 2, Kaltz, Breitner, Littbarski*)
22 Nov, Düsseldorf: v Bulgaria (h) won 4-0 (*Fischer, Rummenigge 2, Kaltz*)

## League Championship wins (1903–82)

IFC Nuremberg 9; Schalke 04 7; Bayern Munich 7; Borussia Moenchengladbach 5; SV Hamburg 5; VfB Leipzig 3; Sp Vgg Fürth 3; Borussia Dortmund 3; IFC Cologne 3; Viktoria Berlin 2; Hertha Berlin 2; Hanover 96 2; Dresden SC 2; VfB Stuttgart 2; IFC Kaiserslautern 2; Munich 1860 1; SV Werder Bremen 1; Union Berlin 1; FC Freibourg 1; Phoenix Karlsruhe 1; Karlsruher FV 1; Holstein Kiel 1; Fortuna Düsseldorf 1; Rapid Vienna 1; VfR Mannheim 1; Rot-Weiss Essen 1; Eintracht Frankfurt 1; Eintracht Brunswick 1.

## Cup wins (1935–82)

Bayern Munich 6; IFC Nuremberg 3; IFC Cologne 3; Eintracht Frankfurt 3; Dresden SC 2; Fortuna Düsseldorf 2; Karlsruhe SC 2; Munich 1860 2; Schalke 04 2; VfB Stuttgart 2; Borussia Moenchengladbach 2; SV Hamburg 2; Borussia Dortmund 1; First Vienna 1; VfB Leipzig 1; Kickers Offenbach 1; Rapid Vienna 1; Rot-Weiss Essen 1; SW Essen 1; Werder Bremen 1.

| League Champions | Cup Winners |
|---|---|
| 1948 IFC Nuremberg | |
| 1949 VfR Mannheim | |
| 1950 VfB Stuttgart | |
| 1951 IFC Kaiserslautern | |
| 1952 VfB Stuttgart | |
| 1953 IFC Kaiserslautern | Rot-Weiss Essen |
| 1954 Hanover 96 | VfB Stuttgart |
| 1955 Rot-Weiss Essen | Karlsruhe SC |
| 1956 Borussia Dortmund | Karlsruhe SC |
| 1957 Borussia Dortmund | Bayern Munich |
| 1958 Schalke 04 | VfB Stuttgart |
| 1959 Eintracht Frankfurt | SW Essen |
| 1960 SV Hamburg | Borussia Moenchengladbach |

| | | | |
|---|---|---|---|
| 1961 | IFC Nuremberg | Werder Bremen | |
| 1962 | IFC Cologne | IFC Nuremberg | |
| 1963 | Borussia Dortmund | SV Hamburg | |
| 1964 | IFC Cologne | Munich 1860 | |
| 1965 | Werder Bremen | Borussia Dortmund | |
| 1966 | Munich 1860 | Bayern Munich | |
| 1967 | Eintracht Brunswick | Bayern Munich | |
| 1968 | IFC Nuremberg | IFC Cologne | |
| 1969 | Bayern Munich | Bayern Munich | |
| 1970 | Borussia Moenchengladbach | Kickers Offenbach | |
| 1971 | Borussia Moenchengladbach | Bayern Munich | |
| 1972 | Bayern Munich | Schalke 04 | |
| 1973 | Bayern Munich | Borussia Moenchengladbach | |
| 1974 | Bayern Munich | Eintracht Frankfurt | |
| 1975 | Borussia Moenchengladbach | Eintracht Frankfurt | |
| 1976 | Borussia Moenchengladbach | SV Hamburg | |
| 1977 | Borussia Moenchengladbach | IFC Cologne | |
| 1978 | Cologne | Cologne | |
| 1979 | SV Hamburg | Fortuna Düsseldorf | |
| 1980 | Bayern Munich | Fortuna Düsseldorf | |
| 1981 | Bayern Munich | Eintracht Frankfurt | |
| 1982 | SV Hamburg | Bayern Munich | |

**Final League Table 1981–82**

| | P | W | D | L | F | A | Pts |
|---|---|---|---|---|---|---|---|
| SV Hamburg | 34 | 18 | 12 | 4 | 95 | 45 | 48 |
| IFC Cologne | 34 | 18 | 9 | 7 | 72 | 38 | 45 |
| Bayern Munich | 34 | 20 | 3 | 11 | 77 | 56 | 43 |
| IFC Kaiserslautern | 34 | 16 | 10 | 6 | 70 | 61 | 42 |
| Werder Bremen | 34 | 17 | 8 | 9 | 61 | 52 | 42 |
| Borussia Dortmund | 34 | 18 | 5 | 11 | 59 | 40 | 41 |
| Borussia Moenchengladbach | 34 | 15 | 10 | 9 | 61 | 51 | 40 |
| Eintracht Frankfurt | 34 | 17 | 3 | 14 | 83 | 72 | 37 |
| VfB Stuttgart | 34 | 13 | 9 | 12 | 62 | 55 | 35 |
| VfL Bochum | 34 | 12 | 8 | 14 | 52 | 51 | 32 |
| Eintracht Brunswick | 34 | 14 | 4 | 16 | 61 | 66 | 32 |
| Arminia Bielefeld | 34 | 12 | 8 | 16 | 46 | 50 | 30 |
| IFC Nuremberg | 34 | 11 | 6 | 17 | 53 | 72 | 28 |
| Fortuna Düsseldorf | 34 | 6 | 13 | 15 | 48 | 73 | 25 |
| Bayer Leverkusen | 34 | 9 | 7 | 18 | 45 | 72 | 25 |
| Darmstadt 98 | 34 | 5 | 11 | 18 | 48 | 82 | 21 |
| MSV Duisburg | 34 | 8 | 3 | 23 | 40 | 77 | 19 |

## BUSBY ADVISORY COMMITTEE

At their Solihull seminar in February, the League's chairmen set up a committee under the chairmanship of Sir Matt Busby to formulate proposals for Law changes that would eliminate the tactical and unsportsmanlike trends that are stifling soccer.

The committee, which included Bobby Charlton and Jimmy Hill, came up with a series of revolutionary and far-reaching proposals three months later, the chief of which were:

The cynical, or so-called 'professional' or 'tactical', foul to be punishable by a penalty-kick even if the offence occurs outside the penalty-area, if a goal is considered likely. (*Comment:* A long overdue reform that would eliminate this canker from the game.)

No off-side when a player receives the ball from his goalkeeper directly from the penalty-area. (*Comment:* Worth an experiment, but must be coupled with changes limiting a goalkeeper's movement with the ball.)

Foul throw to be ruled if a player throws in from the wrong place. (*Comment:* An obvious and long overdue interpretation of the Law that would eliminate this form of cheating at a stroke.)

Deliberate pass to goalkeeper from outside the penalty-area to be punished by indirect free-kick. (*Comment:* Not thought through sufficiently. The Law should be framed so as to prevent a goalkeeper *handling* the ball if it is played to him by a team-mate from a move originating outside the penalty-area.)

Unharassed goalkeepers who hold the ball for more than four seconds to concede an indirect free-kick. (*Comment:* Many referees cannot count steps – as Dino Zoff well knows – let alone seconds. Nevertheless, something has to be done to limit the time a goalkeeper can hold up the game.)

Other recommendations included the following: referees to ensure that an off-side player is seeking to gain an advantage or is interfering with play before penalising his side; clubs to formulate schemes for fining their own players for dissent; more contact with referees and discussions with them on the Laws of the Game; and the elimination of 'inflammatory' time-wasting such as keeping the ball near the corner flag.

*Comment:* On the whole, the committee's findings constitute a praiseworthy effort to save the game. The only way to get them agreed and implemented is to edit the suggestions into concrete proposals for Law changes, and then lobby the four Home FAs and the FIFA Referees' Committee by December, so that they stand a chance of being formerly proposed at the annual meeting of the International Football Association Board in the summer of 1983.

N.S.B.

# GREECE

*President:* Dr Basile Hadzijannis.
*Secretary:* Charalambos David.
*Address of Association:* Federation Hellenique de Football Association, Singrou Avenue 137, Athenes.
*Telephone:* 933 4922.
*Cable:* Football Athenes.
*Telex:* 215328.
*Area:* 50,547 square miles.
*Population:* 9,850,000.
*Number of Clubs:* 2,624.
*Teams:* 1,936.
*Number of Players:* 163,470.
*Year of Formation:* 1926.
*National Colours:* White shirts, blue shorts, white stockings.
*Second Choice of Colours:* Blue shirts, white shorts, blue stockings.
*Name, Address and Capacity of National Stadium:* Karaïskaki, Neon Faliron, 42,000.
*Names, Addresses and Capacities of Other Principal Football Grounds:* Kaftatzoglion, Salonika, 47,000; AEK, Athens, 35,000; Panathinaikos, Athenes, 25,000; PAOK, Salonika, 40,000; Aris, Salonika, 30,000.

## Principal Honours

European Champions Cup: *runners-up*
Panathinaikos (1971)

## International matches 1981

28 Jan, Salonika: v Luxembourg (h) won 2-0 (*Kouis, Kostikos*)
11 March, Luxembourg: v Luxembourg (a) won 2-0 (*Kouis, Mavros* pen)
15 April, Nicosia: v Cyprus (a) won 1-0 (*Iosifidis*)
29 April, Split: v Yugoslavia (a) lost 1-5 (*Kostikos*)
23 Sept, Salonika: v Sweden (h) won 2-1 (*Anastopoulos, Kouis*)
14 Oct, Salonika: v Denmark (h) lost 2-3 (*Anastopoulos, Kouis*)
14 Nov, Turin: v Italy (a) drew 1-1 (*Kouis*)
29 Nov, Athens: v Yugoslavia (h) lost 1-2 (*Mavros*)

## League Championship wins (1928–82)

Olympiakos 23; Panathinaikos 12; AEK Athens 7; Aris Salonika 3; PAOK Salonika 1.

## Cup wins (1932–82)

Olympiakos 18; AEK Athens 8; Panathinaikos 7; PAOK Salonika 2; Aris Salonika 1; Ethnikos 1; Iraklis 1; Panionios 1; Kastoria 1.

| League Champions | | Cup Winners |
|---|---|---|
| 1946 | Aris Salonika | |
| 1947 | Olympiakos | Olympiakos |
| 1948 | Olympiakos | Panathinaikos |
| 1949 | *No competition* | AEK Athens |
| 1950 | Panathinaikos | AEK Athens |
| 1951 | Olympiakos | Olympiakos |
| 1952 | *No competition* | Olympiakos |
| 1953 | Panathinaikos | Olympiakos |
| 1954 | Olympiakos | Olympiakos |
| 1955 | Olympiakos | Panathinaikos |
| 1956 | Olympiakos | AEK Athens |
| 1957 | Olympiakos | Olympiakos |
| 1958 | Olympiakos | Olympiakos |
| 1959 | Olympiakos | Olympiakos |
| 1960 | Panathinaikos | Olympiakos |
| 1961 | Panathinaikos | Olympiakos |
| 1962 | Panathinaikos | Olympiakos |
| 1963 | AEK Athens | Olympiakos |
| 1964 | Panathinaikos | AEK Athens |
| 1965 | Panathinaikos | Olympiakos |
| 1966 | Olympiakos | AEK Athens |
| 1967 | Olympiakos | Panathinaikos |
| 1968 | AEK Athens | Olympiakos |
| 1969 | Panathinaikos | Panathinaikos |
| 1970 | Panathinaikos | Aris Salonika |
| 1971 | AEK Athens | Olympiakos |
| 1972 | Panathinaikos | PAOK Salonika |
| 1973 | Olympiakos | Olympiakos |
| 1974 | Olympiakos | PAOK Salonika |
| 1975 | Olympiakos | Olympiakos |
| 1976 | PAOK Salonika | Iraklis |
| 1977 | Panathinaikos | Panathinaikos |
| 1978 | AEK Athens | AEK Athens |
| 1979 | AEK Athens | Panionios |
| 1980 | Olympiakos | Kastoria |
| 1981 | Olympiakos | Olympiakos |
| 1982 | Olympiakos | Panathinaikos |

### Final League Table 1981–82

| | P | W | D | L | F | A | Pts |
|---|---|---|---|---|---|---|---|
| Olympiakos* | 34 | 19 | 12 | 3 | 58 | 28 | 50 |
| Panathinaikos | 34 | 18 | 14 | 2 | 46 | 21 | 50 |
| PAOK Salonika | 34 | 18 | 10 | 6 | 55 | 22 | 48 |
| AEK Athens | 34 | 17 | 11 | 6 | 54 | 36 | 45 |
| Aris Salonika | 34 | 15 | 11 | 8 | 56 | 30 | 41 |
| Iraklis | 34 | 15 | 10 | 9 | 52 | 38 | 40 |
| Panionios | 34 | 14 | 8 | 12 | 39 | 31 | 36 |
| Kastoria | 34 | 13 | 8 | 13 | 38 | 43 | 34 |
| Ofi | 34 | 11 | 11 | 12 | 38 | 36 | 33 |
| Doxa | 34 | 10 | 11 | 13 | 38 | 46 | 32 |
| Larissa | 34 | 12 | 7 | 15 | 40 | 38 | 31 |
| Rhodos | 34 | 11 | 9 | 14 | 37 | 46 | 31 |
| Ethnikos | 34 | 10 | 10 | 14 | 30 | 38 | 30 |
| Iannina | 34 | 9 | 10 | 15 | 32 | 48 | 28 |
| Apollon | 34 | 9 | 9 | 16 | 27 | 42 | 27 |
| Panseraikos | 34 | 8 | 9 | 17 | 26 | 45 | 25 |
| Kavala | 34 | 8 | 8 | 18 | 19 | 58 | 25 |
| Korinthos | 34 | 6 | 4 | 24 | 24 | 63 | 16 |

*Olympiakos beat Panathinaikos 2-1 in play-off.

President: Gyorgy Szepesi.

Secretary: Jozsef Krizsan.

Address of Association: Fédération Hongroise de Football, Népköztársaság utja 47, 1061 Budapest VI.

Telephone: 22 58 17, 42 13 16.

Cable: Misz-Budapest.

Telex: 225782 misz h.

Area: 35,919 square miles.

Population: 10,713,000.

Year of Formation: 1901.

Number of Clubs: 2,503. Teams: 5,424.

Number of Players: 143,675.

National Colours: Red shirts, white shorts, green stockings.

Second Choice of Colours: All white.

Name, Address and Capacity of National Stadium: Népstadion Budapest XIV, István Mezei ut 3/5, 80,000.

Names, Addresses and Capacities of Other Principal Football Grounds: Ferencvaros, Budapest IX Ullöi-ut, 30,000; Bp Vasas SC Budapest XIII, Fay-u 58, 20,000; Ujpesti Dozsa SE Budapest IV, Mergyeri ut 13, 25,000; MTK-VM Budapest VIII, Hungaria krt 6, 20,000; Csepel SE Budapest XXI, Béke tér, 22,000; Györi Raba ETO Györ, 20,000; Pécs MSC, Pécs, 25,000; Szegedi Egyetemi OL Szeged, 25,000; Diösgyöri VTK, Diösgyör, 25,000; Bp Honved, Budapest, 30,000.

Season: September–December; March–June.

**Principal Honours**

World Cup: runners-up 1938, 1954

Olympic Games: winners 1952, 1964, 1968; runners-up 1972

European Cup-Winners' Cup: runners-up MTK Budapest (1964); Ferencvaros (1975)

Fairs Cup: winners Ferencvaros (1965); runners-up Ferencvaros (1968), Ujpest Dozsa (1969)

**International matches 1981**

15 April, Valencia: v Spain (a) won 3-0 (Kiss, Bodony, Nyilasi)

28 April, Lucerne: v Switzerland (a) drew 2-2 (Balint, Muller pen)

13 May, Budapest: v Rumania (h) won 1-0 (Fazekas)

20 May, Oslo: v Norway (a) won 2-1 (Kiss 2)

6 June, Budapest: v England (h) lost 1-3 (Garaba)

19 Aug, Budapest: v Kuwait (h) won 1-0 (Kiss)

23 Sept, Bucharest: v Rumania (a) drew 0-0

14 Oct, Budapest: v Switzerland (h) won 3-0 (Nyilasi 2, Fazekas)

31 Oct, Budapest: v Norway (h) won 4-1 (Balint, Kiss 2, Fazekas)

18 Nov, Wembley: v England (a) lost 0-1

**League Championship wins (1901–82)**

Ferencvaros (prev. FTC) 23; MTK-VM Budapest (prev. Hungaria, Bastay and Vörös Lobogo) 18; Ujpest Dozsa 18; Vasas Budapest 6; Honved 6; Csepel 4; BTC 2; Raba Györ (prev. Vasas Györ) 2; Nagyvarad 1.

**Cup wins (1910–82)\***

Ferencvaros (prev. FTC) 14; MTK-VM Budapest (prev. Hungaria, Bastya and Vörös Lobogo) 9; Ujpest Dozsa 5; Raba Györ (prev. Vasas Györ) 4; Diösgyör 2; Vasas Budapest 2; Bocskai 1; Honved 1; III Ker 1; Kispesti AC 1; Soroksar 1; Szolnoki MAV 1.

\* Cup not held regularly until 1964

| League Champions | Cup Winners |
|---|---|
| 1946 Ujpest Dozsa | |
| 1947 Ujpest Dozsa | |
| 1948 Vasas Csepel | |
| 1949 Ferencvaros | |
| 1950 Honved | |
| 1950\*Honved | |
| 1951 Bastya | |
| 1952 Honved | Bastya |
| 1953 Vörös Lobogo | |
| 1954 Honved | |
| 1955 Honved | Vasas Budapest |
| 1956 Champ. abandoned | |
| 1957 Vasas Budapest | |
| 1958 MTK Budapest | Ferencvaros |
| 1959 Vasas Csepel | |
| 1960 Ujpest Dozsa | |
| 1961 Vasas Budapest | |
| 1962 Vasas Budapest | |
| 1963 Ferencvaros | |
| 1963\*Vasas Györ | |
| 1964 Ferencvaros | Honved |
| 1965 Vasas Budapest | Vasas Györ |
| 1966 Vasas Budapest | Vasas Györ |
| 1967 Ferencvaros | Vasas Györ |
| 1968 Ferencvaros | MTK Budapest |
| 1969 Ujpest Dozsa | Ujpest Dozsa |
| 1970 Ujpest Dozsa | Ujpest Dozsa |
| 1971 Ujpest Dozsa | Ujpest Dozsa |
| 1972 Ujpest Dozsa | Ferencvaros |
| 1973 Ujpest Dozsa | Vasas Budapest |
| 1974 Ujpest Dozsa | Ferencvaros |
| 1975 Ujpest Dozsa | Ujpest Dozsa |
| 1976 Ferencvaros | Ferencvaros |
| 1977 Vasas Budapest | Diösgyör |
| 1978 Ujpest Dozsa | Ferencvaros |
| 1979 Ujpest Dozsa | Raba Györ |
| 1980 Honved | Diösgyör |
| 1981 Ferencvaros | Vasas Budapest |
| 1982 Raba Györ | Ujpest Dozsa |

\* Short season.

**Final League Table 1981–82**

| | P | W | D | L | F | A | Pts |
|---|---|---|---|---|---|---|---|
| Raba Györ | 34 | 21 | 7 | 6 | 102 | 50 | 49 |
| Ferencvaros | 34 | 20 | 4 | 10 | 76 | 46 | 44 |
| Tatabanya | 34 | 15 | 13 | 6 | 58 | 43 | 43 |
| Videoton | 34 | 18 | 5 | 11 | 49 | 44 | 41 |
| Ujpest Dozsa | 34 | 14 | 12 | 8 | 49 | 37 | 40 |
| Honved | 34 | 15 | 9 | 10 | 54 | 40 | 39 |
| Csepel | 34 | 11 | 14 | 9 | 37 | 34 | 36 |
| Pecs | 34 | 15 | 5 | 14 | 51 | 45 | 35 |
| Haladas | 34 | 13 | 9 | 12 | 46 | 42 | 35 |
| Spartakus | 34 | 11 | 13 | 10 | 44 | 44 | 35 |
| Debrecen | 34 | 13 | 8 | 13 | 46 | 55 | 34 |
| Vasas | 34 | 12 | 8 | 14 | 57 | 54 | 32 |
| Zalaegerszeg | 34 | 9 | 14 | 11 | 33 | 47 | 32 |
| Diösgyör | 34 | 9 | 11 | 14 | 48 | 62 | 29 |
| Nyireghaza | 34 | 8 | 12 | 14 | 35 | 51 | 28 |
| Volan | 34 | 5 | 11 | 18 | 43 | 61 | 21 |
| Szeged | 34 | 8 | 4 | 22 | 35 | 74 | 20 |
| Ozd | 34 | 7 | 5 | 22 | 41 | 75 | 19 |

# ICELAND

*President:* Ellert B. Schram.
*Secretary:* K. T. Sigurdsson.
*Address of Association:* Football Association of Iceland, PO Box 1011, Reykjavik.
*Telephone:* 84 44.   *Cable:* KSI Reykjavik.
*Telex:* 2314 isi is, or 2110 (att. E. Schram).
*Area:* 39,768 square miles.
*Population:* 229,187.   *Number of Clubs:* 67.
*Teams:* 460.   *Number of Players:* 17,534.
*Year of Formation:* 1929.
*National Colours:* Blue shirts, white shorts and blue stockings.
*Second Choice of Colours:* White shirts, blue shorts, white stockings.
*Name, Address and Capacity of National Stadium:* Laugardalsvöllur, Reykjavik, 14,800.
*Names and Addresses of Other Principal Football Grounds:* Melavöllur, Reykjavik; Ibróttavöllu-rinn, Akureyri; Ibróttavöllurinn, Akranesi; Ibróttavöllurinn, Keflavik, 10,000.
*Season:* April–October.

## International matches 1981

27 May, Bratislava: v Czechoslovakia (a) lost 1-6 (*Berg*)
22 Aug, Reykjavik: v Nigeria (h) won 3-0 (*Sveinsson, Geirsson, Gudmundsson*)
26 Aug, Copenhagen: v Denmark (a) lost 0-3
9 Sept, Reykjavik: v Turkey (h) won 2-0 (*Gudmundsson, Edvaldsson*)
23 Sept, Reykjavik: v Czechoslovakia (h) drew 1-1 (*Ormslev*)
14 Oct, Swansea: v Wales (a) drew 2-2 (*Sigurvinsson 2*)

## League Championship wins (1912–81)

KR 20; Valur 17; Fram 15; IA Akranes 10; IBK Keflavik 3; Vikingur 3; IBV Vestmann 2.

## Cup wins (1960–81)

KR 7; Valur 4; Fram 4; IBV Vestmann 3; IBA Akureyri 1; Vikingur 1; IBK Keflavik 1; IA Akranes 1.

| League Champions | Cup Winners |
|---|---|
| 1946 Fram | |
| 1947 Fram | |
| 1948 KR | |
| 1949 KR | |
| 1950 KR | |
| 1951 IA Akranes | |
| 1952 KR | |
| 1953 IA Akranes | |
| 1954 IA Akranes | |
| 1955 KR | |
| 1956 Valur | |
| 1957 IA Akranes | |
| 1958 IA Akranes | |
| 1959 KR | |
| 1960 IA Akranes | KR |
| 1961 KR | KR |
| 1962 Fram | KR |
| 1963 KR | KR |
| 1964 IBK Keflavik | KR |
| 1965 KR | Valur |
| 1966 Valur | KR |
| 1967 Valur | KR |
| 1968 KR | IBV Vestmann |
| 1969 IBK Keflavik | IBV Akureyri |
| 1970 IA Akranes | Fram |
| 1971 IBV Vestmann | Vikingur |
| 1972 Fram | IBV Vestmann |
| 1973 IBK Keflavik | Fram |
| 1974 IA Akranes | Valur |
| 1975 IA Akranes | IBV Keflavik |
| 1976 Valur | Valur |
| 1977 IA Akranes | Valur |
| 1978 Valur | IA Akranes |
| 1979 IBV Vestmann | Fram |
| 1980 Valur | Fram |
| 1981 Vikingur | IBV Vestmann |

### Final League Table 1981

| | P | W | D | L | F | A | Pts |
|---|---|---|---|---|---|---|---|
| Vikingur | 18 | 11 | 3 | 4 | 30 | 23 | 25 |
| Fram | 18 | 7 | 9 | 2 | 24 | 17 | 23 |
| IB Akranes | 18 | 8 | 6 | 4 | 29 | 17 | 22 |
| UBK | 18 | 7 | 8 | 3 | 27 | 20 | 22 |
| Valur | 18 | 8 | 4 | 6 | 30 | 24 | 20 |
| IBV Vestmann | 18 | 8 | 3 | 7 | 29 | 21 | 19 |
| KA | 18 | 7 | 4 | 7 | 22 | 18 | 18 |
| KR | 18 | 3 | 6 | 9 | 13 | 25 | 12 |
| IT | 18 | 3 | 6 | 9 | 18 | 35 | 12 |
| FH | 18 | 2 | 3 | 13 | 20 | 42 | 7 |

# REPUBLIC OF IRELAND

*President:* Dr B. Menton.
*Secretary:* P. J. O'Driscoll PC.
*Address of Association:* The Football Association of Ireland, 80 Merrion Square, Dublin 2.
*Telephone:* 76 68 64.
*Cable:* Soccer Dublin.
*Telex:* 30498.
*Population:* 4,000,000.
*Year of Formation:* 1921.
*Number of Clubs:* 3,503.  *Teams:* 3,028.
*Number of Players:* 62,701.
*National Colours:* Green shirts, white shorts, green stockings.
*Second Choice of Colours:* White.
*Name, Address and Capacity of National Stadium:* Dalymount Park, Dublin, 45,000; and Lansdowne Road, Dublin, 48,000.
*Names, Addresses and Capacities of Other Principal Football Grounds:* Glenmalure Park, Milltown, Dublin, 25,000; Flower Lodge, Cork, 25,000; Lourdes Stadium, Drogheda, 25,000; Tolka Park, Dublin, 20,000; Oriel Park, Dundalk, 15,000; Richmond Park, Dublin, 10,000; Markeis Field, Limerick, 10,000; Kilcohan Park, Waterford, 15,000.
*Season:* August–May.

## International matches 1981

24 Feb, Dublin: v Wales (h) lost 1-2 (*Grealish*)
25 March, Brussels: v Belgium (a) lost 0-1
29 April, Dublin: v Czechoslovakia (h) won 3-1 (*Moran 2, Stapleton*)
24 May, Bydgoszcz: v Poland (a) lost 0-3
9 Sept, Rotterdam: v Holland (a) drew 2-2 (*Robinson, Stapleton*)
14 Oct, Dublin: v France (h) won 3-2 (*Mahut og, Stapleton, Robinson*)

## League Championship wins (1922–82)

Shamrock Rovers 10; Shelbourne 7; Bohemians 7; Dundalk 6; Waterford 6; Cork United 5; Drumcondra 5; St Patrick's Athletic 3; St James's Gate 2; Cork Athletic 2; Sligo Rovers 2; Limerick 2; Dolphin 1; Cork Hibernians 1; Cork Celtic 1; Athlone Town 1.

## Cup wins (1922–82)

Shamrock Rovers 21; Dundalk 7; Drumcondra 5; Bohemians 4; Shelbourne 3; Cork Athletic 2; Cork United 2; St James's Gate 2; St Patrick's Athletic 2; Cork Hibernians 2; Limerick 2; Waterford 2; Alton United 1; Athlone Town 1; Cork 1; Fordsons 1; Transport 1; Finn Harps 1; Home Farm 1.

| League Champions | | Cup Winners |
|---|---|---|
| 1946 | Cork United | Drumcondra |
| 1947 | Shelbourne | Cork United |
| 1948 | Drumcondra | Shamrock Rovers |
| 1949 | Drumcondra | Dundalk |
| 1950 | Cork Athletic | Transport |
| 1951 | Cork Athletic | Cork Athletic |
| 1952 | St Patrick's Ath | Dundalk |
| 1953 | Shelbourne | Cork Athletic |
| 1954 | Shamrock Rovers | Drumcondra |
| 1955 | St Patrick's Ath | Shamrock Rovers |
| 1956 | St Patrick's Ath | Shamrock Rovers |
| 1957 | Shamrock Rovers | Drumcondra |
| 1958 | Drumcondra | Dundalk |
| 1959 | Shamrock Rovers | St Patrick's Ath |
| 1960 | Limerick | Shelbourne |
| 1961 | Drumcondra | St Patrick's Ath |
| 1962 | Shelbourne | Shamrock Rovers |
| 1963 | Dundalk | Shelbourne |
| 1964 | Shamrock Rovers | Shamrock Rovers |
| 1965 | Drumcondra | Shamrock Rovers |
| 1966 | Waterford | Shamrock Rovers |
| 1967 | Dundalk | Shamrock Rovers |
| 1968 | Waterford | Shamrock Rovers |
| 1969 | Waterford | Shamrock Rovers |
| 1970 | Waterford | Bohemians |
| 1971 | Cork Hibernians | Limerick |
| 1972 | Waterford | Cork Hibernians |
| 1973 | Waterford | Cork Hibernians |
| 1974 | Cork Celtic | Finn Harps |
| 1975 | Bohemians | Home Farm |
| 1976 | Dundalk | Bohemians |
| 1977 | Sligo Rovers | Dundalk |
| 1978 | Bohemians | Shamrock Rovers |
| 1979 | Dundalk | Dundalk |
| 1980 | Limerick | Waterford |
| 1981 | Athlone Town | Dundalk |
| 1982 | Dundalk | Limerick |

**Final League Table 1981–82**

| | P | W | D | L | F | A | Pts |
|---|---|---|---|---|---|---|---|
| Dundalk | 30 | 20 | 6 | 4 | 61 | 24 | 80 |
| Shamrock Rovers | 30 | 21 | 3 | 6 | 50 | 23 | 76 |
| Bohemians | 30 | 17 | 9 | 4 | 50 | 18 | 72 |
| Athlone Town | 30 | 18 | 3 | 9 | 70 | 42 | 67 |
| Sligo Rovers | 30 | 16 | 5 | 9 | 55 | 45 | 62 |
| Limerick United | 30 | 13 | 9 | 8 | 56 | 34 | 58 |
| St Patrick's Athletic | 30 | 14 | 6 | 10 | 49 | 39 | 56 |
| Waterford | 30 | 12 | 4 | 14 | 39 | 46 | 47 |
| Shelbourne | 30 | 10 | 7 | 13 | 44 | 46 | 45 |
| Cork United | 30 | 10 | 6 | 14 | 41 | 50 | 42 |
| Drogheda United | 30 | 8 | 10 | 12 | 45 | 50 | 41 |
| Home Farm | 30 | 8 | 7 | 15 | 34 | 48 | 40 |
| UCD | 30 | 7 | 10 | 13 | 30 | 41 | 37 |
| Finn Harps | 30 | 7 | 4 | 19 | 42 | 61 | 31 |
| Galway United | 30 | 5 | 8 | 17 | 30 | 62 | 29 |
| Thurles Town | 30 | 3 | 5 | 22 | 29 | 96 | 18 |

## ITALY

*President d'honneur:* Dr Artemio Franchi.
*President:* Avv. Federico Sordillo.
*Secretary:* Dr Dario Borgogno.
*Address of Association:* Federazione Italiana Giuoco Calcio, via Gregorio Allegri 14, CP 2450, 00198 Rome.
*Telephone:* 84 911.
*Cable:* Federcalcio Roma.
*Telex:* 611483 calcio.
*Area:* 97,068 square miles.
*Population:* 54,134,846.
*Number of Clubs:* 19,084.   *Teams:* 30,618.
*Number of Players:* 1,022,030.
*Year of Formation:* 1898.
*National Colours:* Blue shirts, white shorts, blue stockings with white tops.
*Second Choice of Colours:* White shirts with light blue stripe, blue shorts and blue stockings.
*Name, Address and Capacity of National Stadium:* Stadio Olimpico, Roma, 90,000.
*Names, Addresses and Capacities of Other Principal Football Grounds:* Bologna, Stadio Comunale, Via A. Costa 176, 50,000; Firenze, Stadio Comunale, Viale M. Fanti 4/6, 67,000; Milano, Stadio Comunale San Siro, Via Fetonte, 85,000; Torino, Stadio Comunale, Corso Sebatopoli 123, 71,000; Napoli, Stadio S. Paolo, Fuorigrotta, 82,000; Genova, Stadio Luigi, Ferraris, Via del Piano, 64,000.
*Season:* September–June.

### Principal Honours

World Cup: *winners* 1934, 1938, 1982; *runners-up* 1970
European Championship: *winners* 1968
Olympic Games: *winners* 1936
World Club Champions: Inter-Milan (1964, 1965), AC Milan (1969)
European Champions Cup: *winners* AC Milan (1963, 1969), Inter-Milan (1964, 1965); *runners-up* Fiorentina (1957), AC Milan (1958), Inter-Milan (1967, 1972), Juventus (1973)
European Cup-Winners' Cup: *winners* Fiorentina (1961), AC Milan (1968, 1973); *runners-up* Fiorentina (1962), AC Milan (1974)
Fairs Cup: *winners* AS Roma (1961); *runners-up* Juventus (1965, 1971)
UEFA Cup: *winners* Juventus (1977)

### International matches 1981

3 Jan, Montevideo: v Uruguay (a) lost 0-2
6 Jan, Montevideo: v Netherlands (a) drew 1-1 (*Ancelotti*)
25 Feb, Rome: v European Selection (h) lost 0-3
19 April, Udinese: v East Germany (h) drew 0-0
3 June, Copenhagen: v Denmark (a) lost 1-3 (*Graziani*)
23 Sept, Bologna: v Bulgaria (h) won 3-2 (*Graziani 2, Dossena*)
17 Oct, Belgrade: v Yugoslavia (a) drew 1-1 (*Bettega*)
14 Nov, Turin: v Greece (h) drew 1-1 (*Conti B.*)
5 Dec, Naples: v Luxembourg (h) won 1-0 (*Collovati*)

### League Championship wins (1898–1982)

Juventus 20; Inter-Milan 12; AC Milan 10; Genoa 9; Torino 8; Pro Vercelli 7; Bologna 7; Fiorentina 2; Casale 1; Novese 1; AS Roma 1; Cagliari 1; Lazio 1.

### Cup wins (1922–82)

Juventus 6; Torino 4; Fiorentina 4; AC Milan 4; AS Roma 4; Inter-Milan 3; Napoli 2; Bologna 2; Atalanta 1; Genoa 1; Lazio 1; Vado 1; Venezia 1.

| | League Champions | Cup Winners |
|---|---|---|
| 1946 | Torino | |
| 1947 | Torino | |
| 1948 | Torino | |
| 1949 | Torino | |
| 1950 | Juventus | |
| 1951 | AC Milan | |
| 1952 | Juventus | |
| 1953 | Inter-Milan | |
| 1954 | Inter-Milan | |
| 1955 | AC Milan | |
| 1956 | Fiorentina | |
| 1957 | AC Milan | |
| 1958 | Juventus | Lazio |
| 1959 | AC Milan | Juventus |
| 1960 | Juventus | Juventus |
| 1961 | Juventus | Fiorentina |
| 1962 | AC Milan | Napoli |
| 1963 | Inter-Milan | Atalanta |
| 1964 | Bologna | AS Roma |
| 1965 | Inter-Milan | Juventus |
| 1966 | Inter-Milan | Fiorentina |
| 1967 | Juventus | AC Milan |
| 1968 | AC Milan | Torino |
| 1969 | Fiorentina | AS Roma |
| 1970 | Cagliari | Bologna |
| 1971 | Inter-Milan | Torino |
| 1972 | Juventus | AC Milan |
| 1973 | Juventus | AC Milan |
| 1974 | Lazio | Bologna |
| 1975 | Juventus | Fiorentina |
| 1976 | Torino | Napoli |
| 1977 | Juventus | AC Milan |
| 1978 | Juventus | Inter-Milan |
| 1979 | AC Milan | Juventus |
| 1980 | Inter-Milan | AS Roma |
| 1981 | Juventus | AS Roma |
| 1982 | Juventus | Inter-Milan |

### Final League Table 1981–82

| | P | W | D | L | F | A | Pts |
|---|---|---|---|---|---|---|---|
| Juventus | 30 | 19 | 8 | 3 | 48 | 14 | 46 |
| Fiorentina | 30 | 17 | 11 | 2 | 36 | 17 | 45 |
| Roma | 30 | 15 | 8 | 7 | 40 | 29 | 38 |
| Napoli | 30 | 10 | 15 | 5 | 31 | 21 | 35 |
| Internazionale | 30 | 11 | 13 | 6 | 39 | 34 | 35 |
| Ascoli | 30 | 9 | 14 | 7 | 26 | 21 | 32 |
| Catanzaro | 30 | 9 | 10 | 11 | 25 | 29 | 28 |
| Avellino | 30 | 9 | 9 | 12 | 22 | 26 | 27 |
| Torino | 30 | 8 | 11 | 11 | 25 | 30 | 27 |
| Cesena | 30 | 8 | 11 | 11 | 34 | 41 | 27 |
| Udinese | 30 | 9 | 8 | 13 | 27 | 37 | 26 |
| Cagliari | 30 | 7 | 11 | 12 | 33 | 36 | 25 |
| Genoa | 30 | 6 | 13 | 11 | 24 | 29 | 25 |
| AC Milan | 30 | 7 | 10 | 13 | 21 | 31 | 24 |
| Bologna | 30 | 6 | 11 | 13 | 25 | 37 | 23 |
| Como | 30 | 3 | 11 | 16 | 18 | 42 | 17 |

# LIECHTENSTEIN

*President:* David Vogt.
*Secretary:* Dr Werner Ospelt.
*Address of Association:* Liechtensteiner Fussball-Verband, Postfach 165, 9490 Vaduz.
*Telephone:* 27128, 66251.
*Year of Formation:* 1933.
*National Colours:* Blue/red shirts, red shorts, blue stockings.
*Second Choice of Colours:* Yellow/red shirts, red shorts, yellow stockings.
*Name, Address and Capacity of National Stadium:* Landessportplatz, Vaduz, 10,000.

*Population:* 25,000.
*Number of Clubs:* 7. *Teams:* 64.
*Number of Players:* 1,200.
Liechtenstein has no national league. Teams compete in Swiss regional leagues.
*Season:* August–July.

**International matches 1981**

14 June, Seoul: v Malta (a) drew 1-1
16 June, Seoul: v Thailand (a) lost 0-2
22 June, Seoul: v Indonesia (a) won 3-2
6 Oct, Balzers: v Malaysia (h) won 1-0

# LUXEMBOURG

*President:* M. Remy Wagner.
*Secretary:* Mlle Eliane Cremona.
*Address of Association:* Fédération Luxembourgeoise de Football, 50 Rue de Strasbourg, L-2560 Luxembourg.
*Telephone:* 48–86–65.
*Area:* 999 square miles.
*Population:* 350,000.
*Number of Clubs:* 216. *Teams:* 646.
*Number of Players:* 22,029.
*Year of Formation:* 1908.
*National Colours:* Red shirts, white shorts, blue stockings.
*Second Choice of Colours:* Blue/white shirts, white shorts, blue/white stockings.
*Name, Address and Capacity of National Stadium:* City Stadium Luxembourg, 15,100.
*Names, Addresses and Capacities of Other Principal Football Grounds:* Stade Emile Mayrisch, Esch-sur-Alzette, 11,000; Stade Municipal, Differdange, 10,000.
*Season:* August–June.

**International matches 1981**

28 Jan, Salonika: v Greece (a) lost 0-2
11 March, Luxembourg: v Greece (h) lost 0-2
1 May, Luxembourg: v Denmark (h) lost 1-2 (*Nuremberg*)
14 Oct, Valencia: v Spain (a) lost 0-3
21 Nov, Novi Sad: v Yugoslavia (a) lost 0-5
5 Dec, Naples: v Italy (a) lost 0-1

**League Championship wins (1910–82)**

Jeunesse Esch 17; Spora Luxembourg 10; Stade Dudelange 10; Red Boys Differdange 6; US Hollerich-Bonnevoie 5; Fola Esch 5; US Luxembourg 3; Aris Bonnevoie 3; Progres Niedercorn 2; Avenir Beggen 2; Sporting Luxembourg 2; Racing Luxembourg 1; National Schiffige 1.

**Cup wins (1922–82)**

Red Boys Differdange 15; Spora Luxembourg 8; Jeunesse Esch 8; US Luxembourg 6; Stade Dudelange 4; Progres Niedercorn 4; Fola Esch 3; Alliance Dudelange 2; US Rumelange 2; Aris Bonnevoie 1; US Dudelange 1; Jeunesse Hautcharage 1; National Schiffige 1; Racing Luxembourg 1; SC Tetange 1.

| | League Champions | Cup Winners |
|---|---|---|
| 1946 | Stade Dudelange | Jeunesse Esch |
| 1947 | Stade Dudelange | US Luxembourg |
| 1948 | Stade Dudelange | Stade Dudelange |
| 1949 | Spora Luxembourg | Stade Dudelange |
| 1950 | Stade Dudelange | Spora Luxembourg |
| 1951 | Jeunesse Esch | SC Tetange |
| 1952 | National Schiffige | Red Boys Differdange |
| 1953 | Progres Niedercorn | Red Boys Differdange |
| 1954 | Jeunesse Esch | Jeunesse Esch |
| 1955 | Stade Dudelange | Fola Esch |
| 1956 | Spora Luxembourg | Stade Dudelange |
| 1957 | Stade Dudelange | Spora Luxembourg |
| 1958 | Jeunesse Esch | Red Boys Differdange |
| 1959 | Jeunesse Esch | US Luxembourg |
| 1960 | Jeunesse Esch | National Schiffige |
| 1961 | Spora Luxembourg | Alliance Dudelange |
| 1962 | US Luxembourg | Alliance Dudelange |
| 1963 | Jeunesse Esch | US Luxembourg |
| 1964 | Aris Bonnevoie | US Luxembourg |
| 1965 | Stade Dudelange | Spora Luxembourg |
| 1966 | Aris Bonnevoie | Spora Luxembourg |
| 1967 | Jeunesse Esch | Aris Bonnevoie |
| 1968 | Jeunesse Esch | US Rumelange |
| 1969 | Avenir Beggen | US Luxembourg |
| 1970 | Jeunesse Esch | US Luxembourg |
| 1971 | US Luxembourg | Jeunesse Hautcharage |
| 1972 | Aris Bonnevoie | Red Boys Differdange |
| 1973 | Jeunesse Esch | Jeunesse Esch |
| 1974 | Jeunesse Esch | Jeunesse Esch |
| 1975 | Jeunesse Esch | US Rumelange |
| 1976 | Jeunesse Esch | Jeunesse Esch |
| 1977 | Jeunesse Esch | Progres Niedercorn |
| 1978 | Progres Niedercorn | Progres Niedercorn |
| 1979 | Red Boys Differdange | Red Boys Differdange |
| 1980 | Jeunesse Esch | Spora Luxembourg |
| 1981 | Progres Niedercorn | Jeunesse Esch |
| 1982 | Avenir Beggen | Red Boys Differdange |

**Final League Table 1981–82**

| | P | W | D | L | F | A | Pts |
|---|---|---|---|---|---|---|---|
| Avenir Beggen | 22 | 17 | 2 | 3 | 59 | 16 | 36 |
| Progres Niedercorn | 22 | 13 | 6 | 3 | 41 | 19 | 32 |
| Jeunesse Esch | 22 | 11 | 7 | 4 | 55 | 33 | 29 |
| Red Boys Differdange | 22 | 12 | 3 | 7 | 45 | 29 | 27 |
| Union | 22 | 11 | 4 | 7 | 38 | 38 | 26 |
| Alliance | 22 | 10 | 5 | 7 | 41 | 36 | 25 |
| Wiltz | 22 | 8 | 5 | 9 | 32 | 30 | 21 |
| Grevenmacher | 22 | 8 | 3 | 11 | 21 | 32 | 19 |
| Aris Bonnevoie | 22 | 4 | 7 | 11 | 23 | 44 | 15 |
| Eischen | 22 | 5 | 4 | 13 | 22 | 41 | 14 |
| Hautcharage | 22 | 3 | 4 | 15 | 20 | 48 | 10 |
| Spora Luxembourg | 22 | 2 | 6 | 14 | 18 | 49 | 10 |

# MALTA

*President:* Dr Giuseppe Mifsud Bonnici LL.D.
*Secretary:* Frank Attard.
*Address of Association:* Malta Football Association, 84 Old Mint Street, Valletta, Malta.
*Telephone:* 22697, 67 43 72.
*Cable:* Football Malta Valletta.
*Telex:* 673 Merlin MW or 477 Madafa MW. Attn. MFA.
*Area:* 122 square miles.
*Population:* 300,000.
*Number of Clubs:* 157.
*Number of Players:* 7,644.   *Teams:* 320.
*Year of Formation:* 1900.
*National Colours:* Red shirts, white shorts, red stockings.
*Second Choice of Colours:* White shirts, white shorts, red stockings.
*Name, Address and Capacity of National Stadium:* The Stadium, Gzira, 30,000.
*Name, Address and Capacity of Other Principal Football Grounds:* Schreiber Sports Ground, Paola, 8,000; Manoel Island Upper Ground, 10,000.
*Season:* September–May.

**International matches 1981**

4 April, Valletta: v East Germany (h) lost 1-2 (*Fabbri*)
11 Nov, Jena: v East Germany (a) lost 1-5 (*Spiteri-Gonzi*)
15 Nov, Wroclaw: v Poland (a) lost 0-6
14 June, Seoul: v Liechtenstein (a) drew 1-1
23 June, Seoul: v Indonesia (a) won 1-0
27 June, Seoul: v Thailand (a) won 2-0
23 Oct, Tunis: v Tunisia (a) won 1-0 (*Tortello*)

**League Championship wins (1910–82)**

Floriana 24; Sliema Wanderers 21; Valletta 11; Hibernians 6; Hamrun Spartans 3; St George's 1; KOMR 1.

**Cup wins (1935–82)**

Sliema Wanderers 16; Floriana 15; Valletta 5; Hibernians 5; Gzira United 1; Melita 1.

| League Champions | | Cup Winners |
|---|---|---|
| 1946 | Valletta | Sliema W |
| 1947 | Hamrun Spart | Floriana |
| 1948 | Valletta | Sliema W |
| 1949 | Sliema W | Floriana |
| 1950 | Floriana | Floriana |
| 1951 | Floriana | Sliema W |
| 1952 | Floriana | Sliema W |
| 1953 | Floriana | Floriana |
| 1954 | Sliema W | Floriana |
| 1955 | Floriana | Floriana |
| 1956 | Sliema W | Sliema W |
| 1957 | Sliema W | Floriana |
| 1958 | Floriana | Floriana |
| 1959 | Valletta | Sliema W |
| 1960 | Valletta | Valletta |
| 1961 | Hibernians | Floriana |
| 1962 | Floriana | Hibernians |
| 1963 | Valletta | Sliema W |
| 1964 | Sliema W | Valletta |
| 1965 | Sliema W | Sliema W |
| 1966 | Sliema W | Floriana |
| 1967 | Hibernians | Floriana |
| 1968 | Floriana | Sliema W |
| 1969 | Hibernians | Sliema W |
| 1970 | Floriana | Hibernians |
| 1971 | Sliema W | Hibernians |
| 1972 | Sliema W | Floriana |
| 1973 | Floriana | Gzira |
| 1974 | Valletta | Sliema W |
| 1975 | Floriana | Valletta |
| 1976 | Sliema W | Floriana |
| 1977 | Floriana | Valletta |
| 1978 | Valletta | Valletta |
| 1979 | Hibernians | Sliema W |
| 1980 | Valletta | Hibernians |
| 1981 | Hibernians | Floriana |
| 1982 | Hibernians | Hibernians |

**Final League Table 1981–82**

| | P | W | D | L | F | A | Pts |
|---|---|---|---|---|---|---|---|
| Hibernians | 14 | 12 | 2 | 0 | 36 | 7 | 25 |
| Sliema | 14 | 8 | 2 | 4 | 24 | 20 | 18 |
| Zurrieq | 14 | 7 | 2 | 5 | 20 | 13 | 16 |
| Floriana | 14 | 7 | 2 | 5 | 23 | 16 | 16 |
| Valletta | 14 | 5 | 3 | 6 | 17 | 18 | 13 |
| Hamrun | 14 | 5 | 2 | 7 | 19 | 23 | 12 |
| Senglea | 14 | 4 | 2 | 8 | 13 | 26 | 10 |
| Gzira | 14 | 0 | 1 | 13 | 7 | 34 | 1 |

# NETHERLANDS

*President:* J. W. van Marle.
*Secretary/Treasurer:* Drs E. J. van Eijk.
*Address of Association:* Koninklijke Nederlandsche Voetbalbond, (KNVB) Woudenbergseweg 56–58, Postbus 615, 3700 Am., Zeist, Netherlands.
*Telephone:* (0031) 3439 1922.
*Cable:* Voetbal Zeist.
*Telex:* 40497.
*Area:* 12,616 square miles.
*Population:* 14,000,000.

*Number of Clubs:* 7,866.   *Teams:* 57,222.
*Number of Players:* 1,112,616.
*Year of Formation:* 1889.
*National Colours:* Orange shirts, white shorts, orange stockings.
*Second Choice of Colours:* All white.
*Name, Address and Capacity of National Stadium:* Olympisch Stadion, Stadionplein, 20, Amsterdam, 67,000.
*Names, Addresses and Capacities of Other Principal Football Grounds:* Stadion Feijenoord,

Olympiaweg 50, Rotterdam, 67,000; Ground of Sparta, Spartastraat 5, Rotterdam, 30,000; Stadium De Goffert, Nijmegen, 30,000; Sportpark Diekman, J. J. van Deinselaan 30, Enschede, 27,564; PSV Eindhoven, Eindhoven, 27,500; Ajax Middemweg, Amsterdam, 29,000; AZ Alkmaar Dehout, 23,000.

*Season:* August–June.

### Principal Honours

World Cup: *runners-up* 1974, 1978
World Club Champions: Feyenoord (1970), Ajax Amsterdam (1972)
European Champions Cup: *winners* Feyenoord (1970), Ajax Amsterdam (1971, 1972, 1973); *runners-up* Ajax Amsterdam (1969)
UEFA Cup: *winners* Feyenoord (1974), PSV Eindhoven (1978); *runners-up* Twente Enschede (1975); AZ 67 Alkmaar (1981)
Super Cup: Ajax Amsterdam (1972, 1973)

### International matches 1981

6 Jan, Montevideo: v Italy (a) drew 1-1 (*Peters*)
22 Feb, Groningen: v Cyprus (h) won 3-0 (*Hovenkamp, Schapendonk, Nanninga*)
25 March, Rotterdam: v France (h) won 1-0 (*Muhren A.*)
29 April, Nicosia: v Cyprus (a) won 1-0 (*Van Kooten*)
1 Sept, Zurich: v Switzerland (a) lost 1-2 (*Metgod*)
9 Sept, Rotterdam: v Eire (h) drew 2-2 (*Thijssen, Muhren A.* pen)
14 Oct, Rotterdam: v Belgium (h) won 3-0 (*Metgod, Van Kooten, Geels*)
18 Nov, Paris: v France (a) lost 0-2

### League Championship wins (1898–1982)

Ajax Amsterdam 20; Feyenoord 12; HVV The Hague 8; PSV Eindhoven 7; Sparta Rotterdam 6; Go Ahead Deventer 4; HBS The Hague 3; Willem II Tilburg 3; RCH Haarlem 2; RAP 2; Heracles 2; ADO The Hague 2; Quick The Hague 1; BVV Scheidam 1; NAC Breda 1; Eindhoven 1; Enschede 1; Volewijckers Amsterdam 1; Limburgia 1; Rapid JC Haarlem 1; DOS Utrecht 1; DWS Amsterdam 1; Haarlem 1; Be Quick Groningen 1; SVV Scheidam 1; AZ 67 Alkmaar 1.

### Cup wins (1899–1982)

Ajax Amsterdam 8; Feyenoord 5; Quick The Hague 4; PSV Eindhoven 4; AZ 67 Alkmaar 3; HEC 3; Sparta Rotterdam 3; DFC 2; Fortuna Geleen 2; Haarlem 2; HBS The Hague 2; RCH 2; VOC 2; Wageningen 2; Willem II Tilburg 2; FC Den Haag 2; Concordia Rotterdam 1; CVV 1; Eindhoven 1; HVV The Hague 1; Longa 1; Quick Njimegen 1; RAP 1; Roermond 1; Schoten 1; Velocitas Breda 1; Velocitas

Groningen 1; VSV 1; VUC 1; VVV Groningen 1; ZFC 1; NAC Breda 1; Twente Enschede 1.

| League Champions | Cup Winners |
|---|---|
| 1946 Haarlem | |
| 1947 Ajax Amsterdam | |
| 1948 BVV Scheidam | Wageningen |
| 1949 SVV Scheidam | Quick Njimegen |
| 1950 Limburgia | PSV Eindhoven |
| 1951 PSV Eindhoven | *No competition* |
| 1952 Willem II Tilburg | *No competition* |
| 1953 RCH Haarlem | *No competition* |
| 1954 Eindhoven | *No competition* |
| 1955 Willem II Tilburg | *No competition* |
| 1956 Rapid JC Haarlem | *No competition* |
| 1957 Ajax Amsterdam | Fortuna Geleen |
| 1958 DOS Utrecht | Sparta Rotterdam |
| 1959 Sparta Rotterdam | VVV Groningen |
| 1960 Ajax Amsterdam | *No competition* |
| 1961 Feyenoord | Ajax Amsterdam |
| 1962 Feyenoord | Sparta Rotterdam |
| 1963 PSV Eindhoven | Willem II Tilburg |
| 1964 DWS Amsterdam | Fortuna Geleen |
| 1965 Feyenoord | Feyenoord |
| 1966 Ajax Amsterdam | Sparta Rotterdam |
| 1967 Ajax Amsterdam | Ajax Amsterdam |
| 1968 Ajax Amsterdam | ADO The Hague |
| 1969 Feyenoord | Feyenoord |
| 1970 Ajax Amsterdam | Ajax Amsterdam |
| 1971 Feyenoord | Ajax Amsterdam |
| 1972 Ajax Amsterdam | Ajax Amsterdam |
| 1973 Ajax Amsterdam | NAC Breda |
| 1974 Feyenoord | PSV Eindhoven |
| 1975 PSV Eindhoven | FC Den Haag |
| 1976 PSV Eindhoven | PSV Eindhoven |
| 1977 Ajax Amsterdam | Twente Enschede |
| 1978 PSV Eindhoven | AZ 67 Alkmaar |
| 1979 Ajax Amsterdam | Ajax Amsterdam |
| 1980 Ajax Amsterdam | Feyenoord |
| 1981 AZ 67 Alkmaar | AZ 67 Alkmaar |
| 1982 Ajax Amsterdam | AZ 67 Alkmaar |

### Final League Table 1981–82

| | P | W | D | L | F | A | Pts |
|---|---|---|---|---|---|---|---|
| Ajax Amsterdam | 34 | 26 | 4 | 4 | 117 | 42 | 56 |
| PSV Eindhoven | 34 | 24 | 3 | 7 | 81 | 38 | 51 |
| AZ 67 Alkmaar | 34 | 21 | 5 | 8 | 74 | 40 | 47 |
| Haarlem | 34 | 17 | 8 | 9 | 57 | 41 | 42 |
| Utrecht | 34 | 17 | 5 | 12 | 56 | 38 | 39 |
| Feyenoord | 34 | 13 | 12 | 9 | 61 | 59 | 38 |
| Groningen | 34 | 14 | 9 | 11 | 56 | 38 | 37 |
| Sparta | 34 | 13 | 10 | 11 | 61 | 48 | 36 |
| Roda | 34 | 15 | 6 | 13 | 60 | 53 | 36 |
| Go Ahead | 34 | 13 | 9 | 12 | 58 | 49 | 35 |
| NAC Breda | 34 | 12 | 9 | 13 | 41 | 47 | 33 |
| Twente | 34 | 13 | 5 | 16 | 50 | 58 | 31 |
| NEC Nijmegen | 34 | 11 | 8 | 15 | 41 | 62 | 30 |
| Willem II | 34 | 10 | 7 | 17 | 50 | 64 | 27 |
| PEC Zwolle | 34 | 8 | 10 | 16 | 45 | 69 | 26 |
| MVV Maastricht | 34 | 6 | 11 | 17 | 35 | 70 | 23 |
| Den Haag | 34 | 4 | 5 | 25 | 29 | 82 | 13 |
| De Graafschap | 34 | 3 | 6 | 25 | 29 | 95 | 12 |

# NORWAY

*President:* Eldar Hansen.
*Secretary:* Nicolai Johansen.
*Address of Association:* Norges Fotballforbund, Ullevaal Stadium, Postboks 3823, Ullevål Hageby, Oslo 8.
*Telephone:* 46.98.30.   *Telex:* 71722 nff n.
*Cable:* Fotballforbund Oslo.
*Area:* 125,064 square miles.
*Population:* 4,000,000.
*Number of Clubs:* 3,400.   *Teams:* 9,700.
*Number of Players:* 177,000.
*Year of Formation:* 1902.
*National Colours:* Red shirts, white shorts, blue and white stockings.
*Second Choice of Colours:* Blue shirts, white shorts, blue stockings.
*Name, Address and Capacity of National Stadium:* Ulleval Stadium, Sognsveien 75, Oslo, 24,500.
*Names, Addresses and Capacities of Other Principal Football Grounds:* Bislet Stadium, Oslo, 24,000; Brann Stadium, Bergen, 26,000; Lerkendal Stadium, Trondheim, 30,000; Stavanger Stadium, Stavanger, 19,800.
*Season:* April–November.

## International matches 1981

29 April, Pleven: v Bulgaria (a) lost 0–1
20 May, Oslo: v Hungary (h) lost 1–2 (*Thoresen*)
3 June, Bucharest: v Rumania (a) lost 0–1
17 June, Oslo: v Switzerland (h) drew 1–1 (*Davidsen*)
2 July, Helsingfors: v Finland (a) lost 1–3 (*Davidsen*)
12 Aug, Oslo: v Nigeria (h) drew 2–2 (*Jacobsen, Lund*)
9 Sept, Oslo: v England (h) won 2–1 (*Albertsen, Thoresen*)
23 Sept, Copenhagen: v Denmark (a) lost 1–2 (*Krujedal*)
31 Oct, Budapest: v Hungary (a) lost 1–4 (*Lund*)

## League Championship wins (1938–81)

Fredrikstad 9; Viking Stavanger 6; Rosenborg Trondheim 3; Larvik Turn 3; Lillestroem 3; Brann Bergen 2; Lyn Oslo 2; IK Start 2; Valerengen 2; Friedig 1; Fram 1; Skeid Oslo 1; Strömgodset Drammen 1.

## Cup wins (1902–81)

Odds Bk, Skien 11; Fredrikstads 9; Lyn Oslo 8; Skeid Oslo 8; Sarpsborg FK 6; Orn F Horten 4; Brann Bergen 4; Mjondalens F 4; Lillestroem 3; Rosenborg Trondheim 3; Strömgodset Drammen 3; Viking Stavanger 3; Mercantile 2; Grane Nordstrand 1; Kvik Halden 1; Sparta 1; Gjovik 1; Bodo-Glimt 1; Valerengen 1.
(*Until 1937 the cup-winners were regarded as champions.*)

| League Champions | | Cup Winners |
|---|---|---|
| 1946 | | Lyn Oslo |
| 1947 | | Skeid Oslo |
| 1948 | Freidig | Sarpsborg FK |
| 1949 | Fredrikstad | Sarpsborg FK |
| 1950 | Fram | Fredrikstad |
| 1951 | Fredrikstad | Sarpsborg FK |
| 1952 | Fredrikstad | Sparta Sarpsborg |
| 1953 | Larvik Turn | Viking Stav |
| 1954 | Fredrikstad | Skeid Oslo |
| 1955 | Larvik Turn | Skeid Oslo |
| 1956 | Larvik Turn | Skeid Oslo |
| 1957 | Fredrikstad | Fredrikstad |
| 1958 | Viking Stav | Skeid Oslo |
| 1959 | Lillestroem | Viking Stav |
| 1960 | Fredrikstad | Rosenborg Tr |
| 1961 | Fredrikstad | Fredrikstad |
| 1962 | Brann Bergen | Gjovik Lyn |
| 1963 | Brann Bergen | Skeid Oslo |
| 1964 | Lyn Oslo | Rosenborg Tr |
| 1965 | Valerengen | Skeid Oslo |
| 1966 | Skeid Oslo | Fredrikstad |
| 1967 | Rosenborg Tr | Lyn Oslo |
| 1968 | Lyn Oslo | Lyn Oslo |
| 1969 | Rosenborg Tr | Strömgodset Dr |
| 1970 | Strömgodset Dr | Strömgodset Dr |
| 1971 | Rosenborg Tr | Rosenborg Tr |
| 1972 | Viking Stav | Brann Bergen |
| 1973 | Viking Stav | Strömgodset Dr |
| 1974 | Viking Stav | Skeid Oslo |
| 1975 | Viking Stav | Bodo-Glim |
| 1976 | Lillestroem | Brann Bergen |
| 1977 | Lillestroem | Lillestroem |
| 1978 | IK Start | Lillestroem |
| 1979 | Viking Stav | Viking Stav |
| 1980 | IK Start | Valerengen |
| 1981 | Valerengen | Lillestroem |

### Final League Table 1981

| | P | W | D | L | F | A | Pts |
|---|---|---|---|---|---|---|---|
| Valerengen | 22 | 9 | 11 | 2 | 44 | 27 | 29 |
| Viking Stavanger | 22 | 11 | 6 | 5 | 32 | 30 | 28 |
| Rosenborg Trondheim | 22 | 9 | 8 | 5 | 35 | 24 | 26 |
| Fredrikstad | 22 | 9 | 7 | 6 | 45 | 26 | 25 |
| Moss | 22 | 8 | 8 | 6 | 27 | 27 | 24 |
| Hamarkameratene | 22 | 8 | 6 | 8 | 25 | 21 | 22 |
| Lillestroem | 22 | 6 | 10 | 6 | 26 | 25 | 22 |
| IK Start | 22 | 8 | 5 | 9 | 36 | 38 | 21 |
| Bryne | 22 | 6 | 9 | 7 | 29 | 34 | 21 |
| Brann | 22 | 5 | 7 | 10 | 26 | 40 | 17 |
| Haugar | 22 | 2 | 12 | 8 | 20 | 38 | 16 |
| Lyn Oslo | 22 | 4 | 5 | 13 | 22 | 37 | 13 |

# POLAND

*President:* Dr Wlodzimierz Reczek.
*General-Secretary:* Zbigniew Kalinski.
*Address of Association:* Polish Football Association, Al. Ujazdowskie 22, 00-478 Warszawa.
*Telephone:* 28-93-44, 29-24-89, 21-91-75.
*Area:* 120,359 square miles.
*Population:* 36,000,000.
*Number of Clubs:* 5,334.   *Teams:* 11,343.
*Number of Players:* 234,052.
*Year of Formation:* 1923.
*National Colours:* White shirts, red shorts, white and red stockings.
*Second Choice of Colours:* Red shirts, white shorts, red stockings.
*Name, Address and Capacity of National Stadium:* Stadium of the X Anniversary, Warszawa, 87,000.
*Names, Addresses and Capacities of Other Principal Football Grounds:* Stadium Slaski, Chorzow, 93,000; Stadium Warta, Poznan, 45,000; Stadium Olimpijski, Wroclaw, 72,000; Stadium Wisla Kraków, 45,000; Stadium Ruch, Chorzów, 40,000; Stadium Legia, Warszawa, 35,000; Stadium Piast, Gliwice, 55,000; Stadium Pgoon, Szczecin, 36,000; Stadium Polonia, Bytom, 35,000; Stade KS Zawisza, Bydgoszcz, 55,000.
*Season:* August–November; March–June.

## Principal Honours

Olympic Games: *winners* 1972; *runners-up* 1976
European Cup-Winners' Cup: *runners-up* Gornik Zabrze (1970)

## International matches 1981

24 Jan, Tokyo: v Japan (a) won 2-0 (*Buda, Novicki*)
27 Jan, Tokushima: v Japan (a) won 4-2 (*Kairis, Ianikovski 2, Baran*)
30 Jan, Nagoya: v Japan (a) won 4-1 (*Walczak, Kazimierz, Baran, Rzepka*)
1 Feb, Tokyo: v Japan (a) won 3-0 (*Pekala, Okonski, opponent og*)
25 March, Bucharest: v Rumania (a) lost 0-2
2 May, Chorzow: v East Germany (h) won 1-0 (*Buncol*)
24 May, Bydgoszcz: v Eire (h) won 3-0 (*Iwan, O'Leary og, Ogaza*)
2 Sept, Chorzow: v West Germany (h) lost 0-2
23 Sept, Lisbon: v Portugal (a) lost 0-2
10 Oct, Leipzig: v East Germany (a) won 3-2 (*Szarmach, Smolarek 2*)
28 Oct, Buenos Aires: v Argentina (a) won 2-1 (*Smolarek, Boniek*)
15 Nov, Wroclaw: v Malta (h) won 6-0 (*Iwan, Smolarek 2, Majewski, Dziebanowski, Boniek*)
18 Nov, Lodz: v Spain (h) lost 2-3 (*Palasz, Boniek*)

## League Championship wins (1921–82)

Ruch Chorzow 12; Gornik Zabrze 10; Wisla Krakow 6; Cracovia 5; Pogon Lwow 4; Legia Warsaw 4; Warta Poznan 2; Polonia Bytom 2; Stal Mielec 2; Widzew Lodz 2; Garbarnia Krakow 1; Polonia Warsaw 1; LKS Lodz 1; Slask Wroclaw 1; Szombierki Bytom 1.

## Cup wins (1951–82)

Legia Warsaw 7; Gornik Zabrze 6; Zaglebie Sosnowiec 4; Ruch Chorzow 2; Gwardia Warsaw 1; LKS Lodz 1; Polonia Warsaw 1; Wisla Krakow 1; Stal Rzeszow 1; Slask Wroclaw 1; Arka Gdynia 1; Lech Poznan.

| League Champions | Cup Winners |
|---|---|
| 1946 Polonia Warsaw | |
| 1947 Warta Poznan | |
| 1948 Cracovia | |
| 1949 Wisla Krakow | |
| 1950 Wisla Krakow | |
| 1951 Wisla Krakow | Ruch Chorzow |
| 1952 Ruch Chorzow | Polonia Warsaw |
| 1953 Ruch Chorzow | *No competition* |
| 1954 Polonia Bytom | Gwardia Warsaw |
| 1955 Legia Warsaw | Legia Warsaw |
| 1956 Legia Warsaw | Legia Warsaw |
| 1957 Gornik Zabrze | LKS Lodz |
| 1958 LKS Lodz | *No competition* |
| 1959 Gornik Zabrze | *No competition* |
| 1960 Ruch Chorzow | *No competition* |
| 1961 Gornik Zabrze | *No competition* |
| 1962 Polonia Bytom | Zaglebie Sosnowiec |
| 1963 Gornik Zabrze | Zaglebie Sosnowiec |
| 1964 Gornik Zabrze | Legia Warsaw |
| 1965 Gornik Zabrze | Gornik Zabrze |
| 1966 Gornik Zabrze | Legia Warsaw |
| 1967 Gornik Zabrze | Wisla Krakow |
| 1968 Ruch Chorzow | Gornik Zabrze |
| 1969 Legia Warsaw | Gornik Zabrze |
| 1970 Legia Warsaw | Gornik Zabrze |
| 1971 Gornik Zabrze | Gornik Zabrze |
| 1972 Gornik Zabrze | Gornik Zabrze |
| 1973 Stal Mielec | Legia Warsaw |
| 1974 Ruch Chorzow | Ruch Chorzow |
| 1975 Ruch Chorzow | Stal Rzeszow |
| 1976 Stal Mielec | Slask Wroclaw |
| 1977 Slask Wroclaw | Zaglebie Sosnowiec |
| 1979 Ruch Chorzow | Arka Gdynia |
| 1980 Szombierki Bytom | Legia Warsaw |
| 1981 Widzew Lodz | Legia Warsaw |
| 1982 Widzew Lodz | Lech Poznan |

**Final League Table 1981–82**

| | P | W | D | L | F | A | Pts |
|---|---|---|---|---|---|---|---|
| Widzew Lodz | 30 | 14 | 11 | 5 | 44 | 31 | 39 |
| Slask Wroclaw | 30 | 16 | 7 | 7 | 40 | 22 | 39 |
| Legia Warsaw | 30 | 11 | 13 | 6 | 39 | 29 | 35 |
| Stal Mielec | 30 | 10 | 13 | 7 | 33 | 26 | 35 |
| Gornik Zabrze | 30 | 13 | 7 | 10 | 34 | 27 | 33 |
| Pogon | 30 | 13 | 7 | 10 | 44 | 43 | 33 |
| Gwardia Warsaw | 30 | 12 | 8 | 10 | 36 | 34 | 32 |
| Wisla Krakow | 30 | 9 | 11 | 10 | 41 | 32 | 29 |
| Zaglebie | 30 | 8 | 13 | 9 | 24 | 30 | 29 |
| Szombierki | 30 | 10 | 8 | 12 | 38 | 30 | 28 |
| Lech Poznan | 30 | 11 | 6 | 13 | 25 | 25 | 28 |
| LKS Lodz | 30 | 12 | 4 | 14 | 30 | 39 | 28 |
| Baltyk | 30 | 9 | 8 | 13 | 24 | 36 | 26 |
| Ruch Chorzow | 30 | 9 | 7 | 14 | 29 | 35 | 25 |
| Arka Gdynia | 30 | 7 | 8 | 15 | 16 | 37 | 22 |
| Motor Lublin | 30 | 6 | 7 | 17 | 34 | 57 | 19 |

# PORTUGAL

*President:* Romao Martins.
*Secretary:* Cesar Gracio.
*Address of Association:* Federação Portuguesa de Futebol, Praça de Alegria 25, Apartado 21.000, 1128 Lisboa Codex.
*Telephone:* 32 82 07/08/09, 32 82 00.
*Cable:* Futebol Lisboa.
*Telex:* 13 489 fpfp.
*Area:* 34,139 square miles.
*Population:* 10,000,000.
*Number of Clubs:* 1,251.   *Teams:* 224.
*Number of Players:* 60,056.
*Year of Formation:* 1914.
*National Colours:* Red shirts, white shorts, red stockings.
*Second Choice of Colours:* All white.
*Name, Address and Capacity of National Stadium:* National Stadium, Lisbon, 51,000.
*Names, Addresses and Capacities of Other Principal Football Grounds:* Estadio de Luz, Lisbon, 69,000; Estadio Jose Alvalade, Lisbon, 47,000; Estadio do Restelo, Lisbon, 35,000; Estadio das Antas, Porto, 40,000; Estadio 28 de Maio, Braga, 30,000; Estadio Bonfim, Setubal, 20,000; Estadio Alfredo da Silva, 23,000; Estadio Municipal, Coimbra, 25,000; Estadio Municipal, Guimaraes, 25,000.
*Season:* September–July.

## Principal Honours

European Champions Cup: *winners* Benfica (1961, 1962); *runners-up* Benfica (1963, 1965, 1968)
European Cup-Winners' Cup: *winners* Sporting Lisbon (1964)

## International matches 1981

17 April, Oporto: v Bulgaria (h) drew 1-1 (*Oliveira*)
29 April, Belfast: v Northern Ireland (a) lost 0-1
20 June, Oporto: v Spain (h) won 2-0 (*Nene, Noguera*)
24 June, Solna: v Sweden (a) lost 0-3
23 Sept, Lisbon: v Poland (h) won 2-0 (*Nene, Sheu*)
14 Oct, Lisbon: v Sweden (h) lost 1-2 (*Pietra*)
28 Oct, Tel Aviv: v Israel (a) lost 1-4 (*Jordao*)
18 Nov, Lisbon: v Scotland (h) won 2-1 (*Manuel Fernandez, Oliveira*)
16 Dec, Haskovo: v Bulgaria (a) lost 2-5 (*Oliveira 2*)

## League Championship wins (1935–82)

Benfica 24; Sporting Lisbon 16; FC Porto 7; Belenenses 1.

## Cup wins (1939–82)

Benfica 17; Sporting Lisbon 10; FC Porto 4; Boavista 3; Belenenses 2; Vitoria Setubal 2; Academica Coimbra 1; Leixoes Porto 1; Sporting Braga 1.

| | League Champions | Cup Winners |
|---|---|---|
| 1946 | Belenenses | Sporting Lisbon |
| 1947 | Sporting Lisbon | *No competition* |
| 1948 | Sporting Lisbon | Sporting Lisbon |
| 1949 | Sporting Lisbon | Benfica |
| 1950 | Benfica | *No competition* |
| 1951 | Sporting Lisbon | Benfica |
| 1952 | Sporting Lisbon | Benfica |
| 1953 | Sporting Lisbon | Benfica |
| 1954 | Sporting Lisbon | Sporting Lisbon |
| 1955 | Benfica | Benfica |
| 1956 | FC Porto | FC Porto |
| 1957 | Benfica | Benfica |
| 1958 | Sporting Lisbon | FC Porto |
| 1959 | FC Porto | Benfica |
| 1960 | Benfica | Belenenses |
| 1961 | Benfica | Leixoes |
| 1962 | Sporting Lisbon | Benfica |
| 1963 | Benfica | Sporting Lisbon |
| 1964 | Benfica | Benfica |
| 1965 | Benfica | Vitoria Setubal |
| 1966 | Sporting Lisbon | Sporting Braga |
| 1967 | Benfica | Vitoria Setubal |
| 1968 | Benfica | FC Porto |
| 1969 | Benfica | Benfica |
| 1970 | Sporting Lisbon | Benfica |
| 1971 | Benfica | Sporting Lisbon |
| 1972 | Benfica | Benfica |
| 1973 | Benfica | Sporting Lisbon |
| 1974 | Sporting Lisbon | Sporting Lisbon |
| 1975 | Benfica | Boavista |
| 1976 | Benfica | Boavista |
| 1977 | Benfica | FC Porto |
| 1978 | FC Porto | Sporting Lisbon |
| 1979 | FC Porto | Boavista |
| 1980 | Sporting Lisbon | Benfica |
| 1981 | Benfica | Benfica |
| 1982 | Sporting Lisbon | Sporting Lisbon |

### Final League Table 1981–82

| | P | W | D | L | F | A | Pts |
|---|---|---|---|---|---|---|---|
| Sporting Lisbon | 30 | 19 | 8 | 3 | 63 | 25 | 46 |
| Benfica | 30 | 20 | 4 | 6 | 60 | 22 | 44 |
| Porto | 30 | 17 | 9 | 4 | 46 | 17 | 43 |
| Guimaraes | 30 | 13 | 12 | 5 | 42 | 22 | 38 |
| Rio Ave | 30 | 13 | 8 | 9 | 26 | 31 | 34 |
| Portimonense | 30 | 12 | 8 | 10 | 35 | 24 | 32 |
| Braga | 30 | 11 | 8 | 11 | 34 | 42 | 30 |
| Vitoria Setubal | 30 | 9 | 10 | 11 | 30 | 35 | 28 |
| Boavista | 30 | 10 | 6 | 14 | 36 | 37 | 26 |
| Espinho | 30 | 7 | 11 | 12 | 32 | 42 | 25 |
| Amora | 30 | 6 | 12 | 12 | 29 | 37 | 24 |
| Estoril | 30 | 7 | 10 | 13 | 30 | 41 | 24 |
| Penafiel | 30 | 9 | 5 | 16 | 20 | 37 | 23 |
| Viseu | 30 | 9 | 5 | 16 | 24 | 51 | 23 |
| Belenenses | 30 | 5 | 10 | 15 | 29 | 48 | 20 |
| Leiria | 30 | 8 | 4 | 18 | 25 | 50 | 20 |

# RUMANIA

*President:* Ing. Andrei Radulescu.
*Secretary:* Florian Dumitrescu.
*Address of Association:* Federatia Romana de Fotbal, Vasile Conta 16, Bucharest 6.
*Telephone:* 12–10–60, 11–97–87. *Cable:* Sportrom Bucaresti. *Telex:* 11180 Bucaresti.
*Area:* 91,699 square miles. *Population:* 23,000,000. *Number of Clubs:* 5,453. *Teams:* 5,777. *Number of Players:* 179,987.
*Year of Formation:* 1908.
*National Colours:* Yellow shirts, blue shorts, red stockings.
*Second Choice of Colours:* Blue shirts, yellow shorts, red stockings.
*Name, Address and Capacity of National Stadium:* 23 August, Bucharest, 95,000.
*Names, Addresses and Capacities of Other Principal Football Grounds:* Republicii, Bucharest, 37,000; Giulesti, Bucharest, 20,000; Municipal, Cluj, 40,000; 1 Mai, Timisoara, 30,000; 23 August, Iasi, 20,000; 1 Mai, Constanta, 20,000; Petrolul, Ploiesti, 20,000; 1 Mai, Pitesti, 20,000; Stade Central Craiova, 40,000.
*Season:* August–July (with winter break).

## International matches 1981

8 Feb, La Paz: v Bolivia (a) drew 1-1 (*Gabor*)
11 March, Braila: v East Germany (h) won 2-1 (*Balaci, Beldeanu* pen)
25 March, Bucharest: v Poland (h) won 2-0 (*Camataru, Iordanescu*)
8 April, Tel Aviv: v Israel (a) lost 1-2 (*M. Sandu*)
15 April, Copenhagen: v Denmark (a) lost 1-2 (*Camataru*)
29 April, Wembley: v England (a) drew 0-0
13 May, Budapest: v Hungary (a) lost 0-1
3 June, Bucharest: v Norway (h) won 1-0 (*Ticleanu*)
9 Sept, Bucharest: v Bulgaria (h) lost 1-2 (*Balaci*)
23 Sept, Bucharest: v Hungary (h) drew 0-0
10 Oct, Bucharest: v Switzerland (h) lost 1-2 (*Balaci*)
11 Nov, Berne: v Switzerland (a) drew 0-0

## League Championship wins (1910–82)

Dynamo Bucharest 10; Steaua Bucharest (prev. CCA) 9; Venus Bucharest 7; CSC Temesvar 6; UT Arad 6; Rapid Bucharest 4; Uni Craiova 3; Ripensia Temesvar 3; Petrolul Ploesti 3; Olimpia Bucharest 2; CAC Bucharest 2; Arges Pitesti 2; Soc RA Bucharest 1; Prahova Ploesti 1; CSC Brasov 1; Juventius Bucharest 1; SSUD Reita 1; Craiova Bucharest 1; Progresul 1; Ploesti United 1.

## Cup wins (1934–82)

Steaua Bucharest (prev. CCA) 13; Rapid Bucharest 7; Dynamo Bucharest 4; Uni Craiova 3; UT Arad 2; CFR Bucharest 2; Progresul 2; RIP Timisoara 2; ICO Oradeo 1; Metal Ochimia Resita 1; Petrolul Ploesti 1; Stinta Cluj 1; Stinta Timisoara 1; Turnu Severin 1; Chimia Ramnicu 1; Jiul Petroseni 1; Poli Timisoara 1.

| League Champions | Cup Winners |
|---|---|
| 1947 UT Arad | *No competition* |
| 1948 UT Arad | UT Arad |
| 1949 Progresul | CCA Bucharest |
| 1950 UT Arad | CCA Bucharest |
| 1951 CCA Bucharest | CCA Bucharest |
| 1952 CCA Bucharest | CCA Bucharest |
| 1953 CCA Bucharest | UT Arad |
| 1954 UT Arad | Metal Och, Resitta |
| 1955 Dynamo Bucharest | CCA Bucharest |
| 1956 CCA Bucharest | ICO Oradea |
| 1957 *No competition* | *No competition* |
| 1958 Petrolul Ploesti | Stinta Timisoara |
| 1959 Petrolul Ploesti | Dynamo Bucharest |
| 1960 CCA Bucharest | Progresul |
| 1961 CCA Bucharest | Progresul |
| 1962 Dynamo Bucharest | Steaua Bucharest |
| 1963 Dynamo Bucharest | Petrolul Ploesti |
| 1964 Dynamo Bucharest | Dynamo Bucharest |
| 1965 Dynamo Bucharest | Stinta Cluj |
| 1966 Petrolul Ploesti | Steaua Bucharest |
| 1967 Rapid Bucharest | Steaua Bucharest |
| 1968 Steaua Bucharest | Dynamo Bucharest |
| 1969 UT Arad | Steaua Bucharest |
| 1970 UT Arad | Steaua Bucharest |
| 1971 Dynamo Bucharest | Steaua Bucharest |
| 1972 Arges Pitesti | Rapid Bucharest |
| 1973 Dynamo Bucharest | Chimia Ramnicu |
| 1974 Uni Craiova | Jiul Petroseni |
| 1975 Dynamo Bucharest | Rapid Bucharest |
| 1976 Steaua Bucharest | Steaua Bucharest |
| 1977 Dynamo Bucharest | Uni Craiova |
| 1978 Steaua Bucharest | Uni Craiova |
| 1979 Arges Pitesti | Steaua Bucharest |
| 1980 Uni Craiova | Poli Timisoara |
| 1981 Uni Craiova | Uni Craiova |
| 1982 Dynamo Bucharest | Dynamo Bucharest |

## Final League Table 1981–82

| | P | W | D | L | F | A | Pts |
|---|---|---|---|---|---|---|---|
| Dynamo Bucharest | 34 | 20 | 7 | 7 | 62 | 31 | 47 |
| Craiova | 34 | 20 | 5 | 9 | 67 | 28 | 45 |
| Corvinul | 34 | 15 | 9 | 10 | 64 | 42 | 39 |
| Olt | 34 | 17 | 5 | 12 | 48 | 41 | 39 |
| Sportul | 34 | 12 | 14 | 8 | 36 | 36 | 38 |
| Steaua Bucharest | 34 | 14 | 9 | 11 | 41 | 33 | 37 |
| SC Bacau | 34 | 11 | 11 | 12 | 40 | 47 | 33 |
| Chimia RM Valcea | 34 | 12 | 9 | 13 | 37 | 48 | 33 |
| Tirgoviste | 34 | 12 | 9 | 13 | 30 | 43 | 33 |
| Arges Pitesti | 34 | 11 | 10 | 13 | 36 | 34 | 32 |
| Poli Timisoara | 34 | 12 | 8 | 14 | 40 | 41 | 32 |
| Jiul Petroseni | 34 | 11 | 10 | 13 | 40 | 43 | 32 |
| Brasov | 34 | 13 | 6 | 15 | 31 | 40 | 32 |
| Constanta | 34 | 10 | 11 | 13 | 38 | 46 | 31 |
| ASA | 34 | 14 | 4 | 16 | 45 | 47 | 30 |
| UTA | 34 | 10 | 9 | 15 | 33 | 40 | 30 |
| Stinta Cluj | 34 | 11 | 8 | 15 | 34 | 49 | 30 |
| Progresul | 34 | 7 | 6 | 21 | 29 | 62 | 20 |

# SPAIN

*President:* Pablo Porta Bussoms.
*Secretary:* Augustin Dominguez.
*Address of Association:* Real Federación Española de Futbol, Calle Alberto Bosch 13, Apartado Postal 347, Madrid 14.
*Telephone:* 2391000, 2391008, 2391009.
*Cable:* Futbol. *Telex:* 42420 rfgf.
*Area:* 190,115 square miles.
*Population:* 35,400,000.
*Number of Clubs:* 7,581. *Teams:* 7,581.
*Number of Players:* 318,392.
*Year of Formation:* 1913.
*National Colours:* Red shirts, dark blue shorts, black with yellow border stockings.
*Second Choice of Colours:* Blue shirts, dark blue shorts, black stockings. *No National Stadium.*
*Names, Addresses and Capacities of Principal Football Grounds:* Santiago Bernabeu, Madrid, 101,663; Campo Nuevo, Barcelona, 120,000; Manzanares, Madrid, 70,000; Luis Casanova, Valencia, 53,436; Sánchez Pizjuan, Sevilla, 68,110; San Mamés, Bilbao, 46,273; Sarriá, Barcelona, 40,400; Riazor, La Coruña, 35,860; La Romareda, Zaragoza, 32,416.
*Season:* September–June.

## Principal Honours

European Nations Cup: *winners* 1964
Olympic Games: *runners-up* 1920
European Champions Cup: *winners* Real Madrid (1956, 1957, 1958, 1959, 1960, 1966); *runners-up* Real Madrid (1962, 1964, 1981), Barcelona (1961), Atlético Madrid (1974)
World Club Champions: Real Madrid (1960), Atlético Madrid (1975)
European Cup-Winners' Cup: *winners* Atlético Madrid (1962), Barcelona (1979, 1982), Valencia (1980); *runners-up* Atlético Madrid (1963), Barcelona (1969), Real Madrid (1971)
Fairs Cup: *winners* Barcelona (1958, 1960, 1966), Valencia (1962, 1963), Zaragoza (1964); *runners-up* Barcelona (1962), Valencia (1964), Zaragoza (1966)
UEFA Cup: *runners-up* Athletic Bilbao (1977)
Super Cup: *winners* Valencia (1981)

## International matches 1981

18 Feb, Madrid: v France (h) won 1-0 (*Juanito* pen)
25 March, Wembley: v England (a) won 2-1 (*Satrustegui, Zamora*)
15 April, Valencia: v Hungary (h) lost 0-3
20 June, Oporto: v Portugal (a) lost 0-2
23 June, Mexico City: v Mexico (a) won 3-1 (*Juanito 2, Zamora*)
28 June, Caracas: v Venezuela (a) won 2-0 (*Juanito, Satrustegui* pen)
2 July, Bogota: v Columbia (a) drew 1-1 (*Alesanco*)
5 July, Santiago: v Chile (a) drew 1-1 (*Satrustegui*)
8 July, Salvador: v Brazil (a) lost 0-1
23 Sept, Vienna: v Austria (a) drew 0-0
14 Oct, Valencia: v Luxembourg (h) won 3-0 (*Lopez-Ufarte 2, Saura*)
18 Nov, Lodz: v Poland (a) won 3-2 (*Lopez-Ufarte, Alesanco, Alonso*)
16 Dec, Valencia: v Belgium (h) won 2-0 (*Satrustegui 2*)

## League Championship wins (1929–82)

Real Madrid 20; Barcelona 9; Atlético Madrid 8; Atlético Bilbao 6; Valencia 4; Real Sociedad 2; Real Betis 1; Seville 1.

## Cup wins (1902–82)

Atlético Bilbao 22; Barcelona 19; Real Madrid 15; Atlético Madrid 5; Valencia 5; Real Union de Irun 3; Seville 3; Espanol 2; Real Zaragoza 2; Arenas 1; Ciclista Sebastian 1; Racing de Irun 1; Vizcaya Bilbao 1; Real Betis 1.

| League Champions | | Cup Winners |
|---|---|---|
| 1946 | Seville | Real Madrid |
| 1947 | Valencia | Real Madrid |
| 1948 | Barcelona | Seville |
| 1949 | Barcelona | Valencia |
| 1950 | Atlético Madrid | Atlético Bilbao |
| 1951 | Atlético Madrid | Barcelona |
| 1952 | Barcelona | Barcelona |
| 1953 | Barcelona | Barcelona |
| 1954 | Real Madrid | Valencia |
| 1955 | Real Madrid | Atlético Bilbao |
| 1956 | Atlético Bilbao | Atlético Bilbao |
| 1957 | Real Madrid | Barcelona |
| 1958 | Real Madrid | Atlético Bilbao |
| 1959 | Barcelona | Barcelona |
| 1960 | Barcelona | Atlético Madrid |
| 1961 | Real Madrid | Atlético Madrid |
| 1962 | Real Madrid | Real Madrid |
| 1963 | Real Madrid | Barcelona |
| 1964 | Real Madrid | Real Zaragoza |
| 1965 | Real Madrid | Atlético Madrid |
| 1966 | Atlético Madrid | Real Zaragoza |
| 1967 | Real Madrid | Valencia |
| 1968 | Real Madrid | Barcelona |
| 1969 | Real Madrid | Atlético Bilbao |
| 1970 | Atlético Madrid | Real Madrid |
| 1971 | Valencia | Barcelona |
| 1972 | Real Madrid | Atlético Madrid |
| 1973 | Atlético Madrid | Atlético Bilbao |
| 1974 | Barcelona | Real Madrid |
| 1975 | Real Madrid | Real Madrid |
| 1976 | Real Madrid | Atlético Madrid |
| 1977 | Atlético Madrid | Real Betis |
| 1978 | Real Madrid | Barcelona |
| 1979 | Real Madrid | Valencia |
| 1980 | Real Madrid | Real Madrid |
| 1981 | Real Sociedad | Barcelona |
| 1982 | Real Sociedad | Real Madrid |

## Final League Table 1981–82

| | P | W | D | L | F | A | Pts |
|---|---|---|---|---|---|---|---|
| Real Sociedad | 34 | 20 | 7 | 7 | 58 | 33 | 47 |
| Barcelona | 34 | 19 | 7 | 8 | 75 | 40 | 45 |
| Real Madrid | 34 | 18 | 8 | 8 | 57 | 34 | 44 |
| Athletic Bilbao | 34 | 18 | 4 | 12 | 63 | 41 | 40 |
| Valencia | 34 | 17 | 5 | 12 | 54 | 46 | 39 |
| Betis | 34 | 15 | 6 | 13 | 53 | 44 | 36 |
| Seville | 34 | 15 | 5 | 14 | 52 | 39 | 35 |
| Atlético Madrid | 34 | 15 | 4 | 15 | 38 | 37 | 34 |
| Osasuna | 34 | 14 | 6 | 14 | 45 | 45 | 34 |
| Real Zaragoza | 34 | 13 | 8 | 13 | 45 | 56 | 34 |
| Valladolid | 34 | 13 | 8 | 13 | 40 | 53 | 34 |
| Espanol | 34 | 13 | 6 | 15 | 48 | 55 | 32 |
| Santander | 34 | 12 | 8 | 14 | 41 | 52 | 32 |
| Gijon | 34 | 10 | 9 | 15 | 38 | 44 | 29 |
| Las Palmas | 34 | 11 | 7 | 16 | 41 | 53 | 29 |
| Cadiz | 34 | 13 | 3 | 18 | 31 | 47 | 29 |
| Hercules | 34 | 11 | 5 | 18 | 41 | 52 | 27 |
| Castellon | 34 | 3 | 6 | 25 | 33 | 82 | 12 |

# SWEDEN

*President:* Tore Brodd.
*Secretary:* Robert Hernadi.
*Address of Association:* Svenska Fotbollförbundet, Box 1216 S-171 23, Solna.
*Telephone:* 08/27 25 00..
*Cable:* Fotball, Solna. *Telex:* 17711 fotball s.
*Area:* 173,665 square miles.
*Population:* 8,323,765.
*Number of Clubs:* 3,346. *Teams:* 8,082.
*Number of Players:* 170,821.
*Year of Formation:* 1904.
*National Colours:* Yellow shirts, blue shorts, yellow and blue stockings.
*Second Choice of Colours:* Blue shirts, white shorts, yellow stockings.
*Name, Address and Capacity of National Stadium:* Fotbollstadion, Solna, 52,000.
*Names, Addresses and Capacities of Other Principal Football Grounds:* Nya Ullevi, Göteborg, 52,000; Malmö Stadion, Malmö, 35,000; Idrottsparken, Norrköping, 35,000; Olympia, Helsingborg, 25,000; Stadion, Stockholm, 25,000.
*Season:* April–October.

## Principal Honours

Olympic Games: *winners* 1948
World Cup: *runners-up* 1958
European Champions Cup: *runners-up* Malmö FF (1979)
UEFA Cup: *winners* IFK Gothenburg (1982)

## International matches 1981

14 May, Malmö: v Denmark (h) lost 1-2 (*Borjesson*)
3 June, Solna: v Northern Ireland (h) won 1-0 (*Borg* pen)
24 June, Solna: v Portugal (h) won 3-0 (*Borjesson, Hysen, Svensson*)
29 July, Halmstad: v Finland (h) won 1-0 (*Bjoerklund*)
12 Aug, Uddevalla: v Bulgaria (h) won 1-0 (*Sjoberg*)
9 Sept, Glasgow: v Scotland (a) lost 0-2
23 Sept, Salonika: v Greece (a) lost 1-2 (*Larsson*)
14 Oct, Lisbon: v Portugal (a) won 2-1 (*Larsson, Nilsson*)
28 Oct, Riyadh: v Saudi Arabia (a) won 2-1 (*Larsson 2*)

## League Championship wins (1896–1981)

Oergryte IS Gothenburg 13; Malmö FF 12; IFK Norrköping 11; Djurgaarden 8; IFK Gothenburg 8; AIK Stockholm 8; GAIS Gothenburg 4; Boras IF Elfsborg 4; Oster Vaxjo 4; IF Halsingborg 3; Halmstad 2; Atvidaberg 2; IFK Ekilstune 1; IF Gavle Brynas 1; IF Gothenburg 1; Fassbergs 1; Norrköping IK Sleipner 1.

## Cup wins (1941–82)

Malmö FF 11; IFK Norrköping 3; AIK Stockholm 3; Atvidaberg 2; IFK Gothenburg 2; GAIS Gothenburg 1; IFK Halsingborg 1; Raa 1; Landskrona 1; Kalmar 1; Oster Vaxjo 1.

| | League Champions | Cup Winners |
|---|---|---|
| 1946 | IFK Norrköping | Malmö FF |
| 1947 | IFK Norrköping | Malmö FF |
| 1948 | IFK Norrköping | Raa |
| 1949 | Malmö FF | AIK Stockholm |
| 1950 | Malmö FF | AIK Stockholm |
| 1951 | Malmö FF | Malmö FF |
| 1952 | IFK Norrköping | *No competition* |
| 1953 | Malmö FF | Malmö FF |
| 1954 | GAIS Gothenburg | *No competition* |
| 1955 | Djurgaarden | *No competition* |
| 1956 | IFK Norrköping | *No competition* |
| 1957 | IFK Norrköping | *No competition* |
| 1958 | IFK Gothenburg | *No competition* |
| 1959 | Djurgaarden | *No competition* |
| 1960 | IFK Norrköping | *No competition* |
| 1961 | Boras Elfsborg | *No competition* |
| 1962 | IFK Norrköping | *No competition* |
| 1963 | IFK Norrköping | *No competition* |
| 1964 | Djurgaarden | *No competition* |
| 1965 | Malmö FF | *No competition* |
| 1966 | Djurgaarden | *No competition* |
| 1967 | Malmö FF | Malmö FF |
| 1968 | Oster Vaxjo | *No competition* |
| 1969 | IFK Gothenburg | IFK Norrköping |
| 1970 | Malmö FF | Atvidaberg |
| 1971 | Malmö FF | Atvidaberg |
| 1972 | Atvidaberg | Landskrona |
| 1973 | Atvidaberg | Malmö FF |
| 1974 | Malmö FF | Malmö FF |
| 1975 | Malmö FF | Malmö FF |
| 1976 | Halmstad BK | AIK Stockholm |
| 1977 | Malmö FF | Malmö FF |
| 1978 | Oster Vaxjo | Oster Vaxjo |
| 1979 | Halmstad BK | IFK Gothenburg |
| 1980 | Oster Vaxjo | Malmö FF |
| 1981 | Oster Vaxjo | Kalmar |
| 1982 | | IFK Gothenburg |

### Final League Table 1981

| | P | W | D | L | F | A | Pts |
|---|---|---|---|---|---|---|---|
| Oster Vaxjo | 26 | 19 | 2 | 5 | 57 | 20 | 40 |
| IFK Gothenburg | 26 | 15 | 6 | 5 | 60 | 24 | 36 |
| IFK Norrköping | 26 | 12 | 8 | 6 | 40 | 30 | 32 |
| Brage | 26 | 11 | 8 | 7 | 34 | 27 | 30 |
| Malmö | 26 | 11 | 5 | 10 | 48 | 44 | 27 |
| Orgryte | 26 | 12 | 3 | 11 | 45 | 49 | 27 |
| Hammarby | 26 | 9 | 7 | 10 | 48 | 46 | 25 |
| AIK | 26 | 8 | 8 | 10 | 35 | 34 | 24 |
| Halmstad | 26 | 11 | 2 | 13 | 35 | 44 | 24 |
| Atvidaberg | 26 | 8 | 6 | 12 | 28 | 35 | 22 |
| Elfsborg Boras | 26 | 7 | 8 | 11 | 27 | 38 | 22 |
| Kalmar | 26 | 9 | 3 | 14 | 28 | 38 | 21 |
| Sundsvall | 26 | 6 | 6 | 14 | 24 | 58 | 18 |
| Djurgaarden | 26 | 6 | 4 | 16 | 25 | 47 | 16 |

# SWITZERLAND

*President:* Walter Baumann.
*Secretary:* Edgar Obertufer.
*Address of Association:* Schweizerischer Fuss-
ballverband, Laubeggstrasse 70 BP 24, 3000
Berne 32.
*Telephone:* (031) 44–62–23.
*Cable:* Fussballverband Berne.
*Telex:* 33582 sfv ch.
*Area:* 15,941 square miles.
*Population:* 6,000,000.
*Number of Clubs:* 1,419.  *Teams:* 8,174.
*Number of Players:* 163,477.
*Year of Formation:* 1895.
*National Colours:* Red jersey, white shorts, red
stockings.
*Second Choice of Colours:* White jersey, white
shorts, red stockings.
*Name, Address and Capacity of National Sta-
dium:* Wankdorf Stadium, Berne, 60,000.
*Names, Addresses and Capacities of Other Prin-
cipal Football Grounds:* St Jakob Stadium, Basle,
60,000; Stade Olympique, Lausanne, 45,000; Parc
des Sports des Charmilles, Genève, 38,800; Sport-
platz Hardturm; Zurich, 37,200.
*Season:* September–May.

## Principal Honours

Olympic Games: *runners-up* 1924

## International matches 1981

24 March, Bratislava: v Czechoslovakia (a) won
1-0 (*Botteron* pen)
28 April, Lucerne: v Hungary (h) drew 2-2
(*Sulser 2*)
30 May, Basle: v England (h) won 2-1
(*Schweiwiler, Sulser*)
17 June, Oslo: v Norway (a) drew 1-1 (*Barberis*)
1 Sept, Zurich: v Netherlands (h) won 2-1
(*Fàvre, Elia*)
10 Oct, Bucharest: v Rumania (a) won 2-1
(*Zappa, Luthi*)
14 Oct, Budapest: v Hungary (a) lost 0-3
11 Nov, Berne: v Rumania (h) drew 0-0

## League Championship wins (1898–1982)

Grasshoppers 18; Servette 14; Young Boys
Berne 10; FC Zurich 9; FC Basle 8; Lausanne 7;
La Chaux-de-Fonds 3; FC Lugano 3; Winterthur
3; FC Aarau 2; FC Anglo-Americans 1; St
Gallen 1; FC Brühl 1; Cantonal-Neuchatel 1;
Biel 1; Bellinzona 1; FC Etoile La Chaux-de-
Fonds 1.

## Cup wins (1926–82)

Grasshoppers 13; Lausanne 7; La Chaux-de-
Fonds 6; FC Basle 5; FC Zurich 5; Young Boys
Berne 5; Servette 5; FC Sion 4; FC Lugano 2;
FC Granges 1; Lucerne 1; St Gallen 1; Urania
Geneva 1; Young Fellows Zurich 1.

| League Champions | | Cup Winners |
|---|---|---|
| 1946 | Servette | Grasshoppers |
| 1947 | Biel | FC Basle |
| 1948 | Bellinzona | La Chaux-de-Fonds |
| 1949 | FC Lugano | Servette |
| 1950 | Servette | Lausanne |
| 1951 | Lausanne | La Chaux-de-Fonds |
| 1952 | Grasshoppers | Grasshoppers |
| 1953 | FC Basle | Young Boys |
| 1954 | La Chaux-de-Fonds | La Chaux-de-Fonds |
| 1955 | La Chaux-de-Fonds | La Chaux-de-Fonds |
| 1956 | Grasshoppers | Grasshoppers |
| 1957 | Young Boys | La Chaux-de-Fonds |
| 1958 | Young Boys | Young Boys |
| 1959 | Young Boys | FC Granges |
| 1960 | Young Boys | Lucerne |
| 1961 | Servette | La Chaux-de-Fonds |
| 1962 | Servette | Lausanne |
| 1963 | FC Zurich | FC Basle |
| 1964 | La Chaux-de-Fonds | Lausanne |
| 1965 | Lausanne | FC Sion |
| 1966 | FC Zurich | FC Zurich |
| 1967 | FC Basle | FC Basle |
| 1968 | FC Zurich | FC Lugano |
| 1969 | FC Basle | St Gallen |
| 1970 | FC Basle | FC Zurich |
| 1971 | Grasshoppers | Servette |
| 1972 | FC Basle | FC Zurich |
| 1973 | FC Basle | FC Zurich |
| 1974 | FC Zurich | FC Sion |
| 1975 | FC Zurich | FC Basle |
| 1976 | FC Zurich | FC Zurich |
| 1977 | FC Basle | Young Boys |
| 1978 | Grasshoppers | Servette |
| 1979 | Servette | Servette |
| 1980 | FC Basle | FC Sion |
| 1981 | FC Zurich | Lausanne |
| 1982 | Grasshoppers | FC Sion |

**Final League Table 1981–82**

| | P | W | D | L | F | A | Pts |
|---|---|---|---|---|---|---|---|
| Grasshoppers | 30 | 21 | 7 | 2 | 72 | 24 | 49 |
| Servette | 30 | 20 | 6 | 4 | 76 | 32 | 46 |
| Zurich | 30 | 18 | 10 | 2 | 62 | 25 | 46 |
| Neuchatel Xamax | 30 | 18 | 9 | 3 | 67 | 30 | 45 |
| Young Boys | 30 | 15 | 9 | 6 | 52 | 40 | 39 |
| Sion | 30 | 12 | 7 | 11 | 51 | 46 | 31 |
| Aarau | 30 | 10 | 8 | 12 | 51 | 55 | 28 |
| Basle | 30 | 11 | 6 | 13 | 47 | 51 | 28 |
| Lucerne | 30 | 10 | 7 | 13 | 54 | 59 | 27 |
| St Gallen | 30 | 10 | 5 | 15 | 40 | 45 | 25 |
| Vevey | 30 | 6 | 11 | 13 | 44 | 57 | 23 |
| Bellinzona | 30 | 7 | 7 | 16 | 34 | 66 | 21 |
| Lausanne | 30 | 6 | 8 | 16 | 39 | 52 | 20 |
| Bulle | 30 | 5 | 9 | 16 | 29 | 58 | 19 |
| Nordstern | 30 | 6 | 5 | 19 | 29 | 69 | 17 |
| Chiasso | 30 | 4 | 8 | 18 | 25 | 63 | 16 |

# TURKEY

*President:* Yilmaz Tokatli.
*Secretary General:* Ayhan Sarman.
*Address of Association:* Federation Turque de Football, Ulus 15 Hani, A Blok Kat 4, Ankara.
*Telephone:* 24 39 34/5.
*Cable:* Futbolspor Ankara.
*Telex:* 42251 tff tr.
*Area:* 296,185 square miles.
*Population:* 45,000,000.
*Number of Clubs:* 1,793.   *Teams:* 3,586.
*Number of Players:* 71,273.
*Year of Formation:* 1923.
*National Colours:* White shirts with white crescent and star on red hoop, white shorts, red and white stockings.
*Second Choice of Colours:* Red shirts, white shorts, red and white stockings.
*Name, Address and Capacity of National Stadium:* Stade 19, Mayis, Ankara, 35,000.
*Names, Addresses and Capacities of Other Principal Football Grounds:* Stade Ali Sam, Yen Istanbul, 40,000; Stade Mithatpasat, Istanbul, 45,000; Stade Alsancak, Izmiri, 30,000; Stade d'Ataturk, Eskisehir, 35,000; Stade d'Ataturk, Adana, 30,000; Stade de Ville, Kayseri, 25,000; Stade d'Ataturk, Izmir, 70,000.
*Season:* September–June.

| League Champions | | Cup Winners |
| --- | --- | --- |
| 1960 | Besiktas | |
| 1961 | *No competition* | |
| 1962 | Fenerbahce | |
| 1963 | Galatasaray | Galatasaray |
| 1964 | Fenerbahce | Galatasaray |
| 1965 | Fenerbahce | Galatasaray |
| 1966 | Besiktas | Galatasaray |
| 1967 | Besiktas | Altay Izmir |
| 1968 | Fenerbahce | Fenerbahce |
| 1969 | Galatasaray | Goztepe Izmir |
| 1970 | Fenerbahce | Goztepe Izmir |
| 1971 | Galatasaray | Eskisehirspor |
| 1972 | Galatasaray | Ankaragücü |
| 1973 | Galatasaray | Galatasaray |
| 1974 | Fenerbahce | Fenerbahce |
| 1975 | Fenerbahce | Besiktas |
| 1976 | Trabzonspor | Galatasaray |
| 1977 | Trabzonspor | Trabzonspor |
| 1978 | Fenerbahce | Trabzonspor |
| 1979 | Trabzonspor | Fenerbahce |
| 1980 | Trabzonspor | Altay Izmir |
| 1981 | Trabzonspor | Ankaragücü |
| 1982 | Besiktas | Galatasaray |

## International matches 1981

25 March, Ankara: v Wales (h) lost 0-1
15 April, Ankara: v Czechoslovakia (h) lost 0-3
9 Sept, Reykjavik: v Iceland (a) lost 0-2
23 Sept, Moscow: v USSR (a) lost 0-4
7 Oct, Izmir: v USSR (h) lost 0-3

## League Championship wins (1960–1982)

Fenerbahce 8; Galatasaray 5; Trabzonspor 5; Besiktas 4.

## Cup wins (1963–82)

Galatasaray 7; Fenerbahce 3; Trabzonspor 2; Goztepe Izmir 2; Altay Izmir 2; Ankaragücü 2; Eskisehirspor 1; Besiktas 1.

**Final League Table 1981–82**

| | P | W | D | L | F | A | Pts |
| --- | --- | --- | --- | --- | --- | --- | --- |
| Besiktas | 32 | 14 | 16 | 2 | 37 | 18 | 44 |
| Trabzonspor | 32 | 14 | 15 | 3 | 26 | 11 | 43 |
| Fenerbahce | 32 | 15 | 11 | 6 | 48 | 26 | 41 |
| Zonguldakspor | 32 | 12 | 13 | 7 | 30 | 26 | 37 |
| Sakariaspor | 32 | 14 | 8 | 10 | 36 | 28 | 36 |
| Adana Demirspor | 32 | 10 | 13 | 9 | 30 | 23 | 33 |
| Ankaragucu | 32 | 14 | 5 | 13 | 31 | 28 | 33 |
| Adanaspor | 32 | 11 | 11 | 10 | 24 | 27 | 33 |
| Altay Izmir | 32 | 8 | 16 | 8 | 37 | 27 | 32 |
| Kocaelispor | 32 | 10 | 12 | 10 | 36 | 31 | 32 |
| Galatasaray | 32 | 10 | 12 | 10 | 26 | 26 | 32 |
| Boluspor | 32 | 7 | 17 | 8 | 24 | 24 | 31 |
| Bursaspor | 32 | 11 | 9 | 12 | 25 | 26 | 31 |
| Gaziantpsor | 32 | 9 | 12 | 11 | 30 | 35 | 30 |
| Eskisehirspor | 32 | 10 | 9 | 13 | 17 | 26 | 29 |
| Goztepe Izmir | 32 | 4 | 8 | 20 | 17 | 53 | 16 |
| Diyarbakirspor | 32 | 2 | 7 | 23 | 16 | 55 | 11 |

*President:* Dr Boris Topornin.
*Secretary:* Anatoly Chetirko.
*Address of Association:* USSR Football Federation, Luzhnetskaya Naberezhnaja 8, 119270 Moscow.
*Telephone:* 201 0834.
*Cable:* Sportkomitet SSSR Moscow.
*Area:* 8,598,678 square miles.
*Population:* 266,560,000.
*Number of Clubs:* 51,299.  *Teams:* 199 (teams in national championship).
*Number of Players:* 4,372,000.  *Year of Formation:* 1912.  *National Colours:* Red shirts, white shorts, red stockings.
*Second Choice of Colours:* White.
*Name, Address and Capacity of National Stadium:* Lenin Stadium, Moscow, 102,000.
*Names, Addresses and Capacities of Other Principal Football Grounds:* Kirov Stadium, Victory Park, Leningrad, 84,000; Pakhtakov Central Stadium, Tashkent, Socialism Street 23, 60,000; Ukraine Republic Stadium, Kiev, Krasnoarmeiskaya Street 51, 100,000; Dynamo Stadium, Moscow, Leningrad Prospect 36, 54,000; Dynamo Stadium, Tbilisi, Tseretely Street 2, 75,000.
*Season:* South: March–December;
       Central: April–October;
       North: May–September.

**Principal Honours**

Olympic Games: *winners* 1956
European Nations Cup: *winners* 1960; *runners-up* 1964
European Championship: *runners-up* 1972
European Cup-Winners' Cup: *winners* Dynamo Kiev (1975), Dynamo Tbilisi (1981); *runners-up* Dynamo Moscow (1972)
Super Cup: Dynamo Kiev (1975)

**International matches 1981**

1 Feb, Merida: v Venezuela (a) drew 1-1 (*Rogovsky*)
30 May, Wrexham: v Wales (a) drew 0-0
23 Sept, Moscow: v Turkey (h) won 4-0 (*Chivadze, Demyanenko, Blokhin, Shengelia*)
7 Oct, Izmir: v Turkey (a) won 3-0 (*Shengelia, Blokhin 2*)
28 Oct, Tbilisi: v Czechoslovakia (h) won 2-0 (*Shengelia 2*)
18 Nov, Tbilisi: v Wales (h) won 3-0 (*Daraselia, Blokhin, Shengelia*)
29 Nov, Bratislava: v Czechoslovakia (a) drew 1-1 (*Blokhin*)

**League Championship wins (1936–81)**

Dynamo Moscow 11; Dynamo Kiev 10; Spartak Moscow 10; CSKA Moscow 6; Torpedo Moscow 3; Dynamo Tbilisi 2; Saria Voroshilovgrad 1; Ararat Erevan 1.

**Cup wins (1936–81)**
Spartak Moscow 9; Torpedo Moscow 5; Dynamo Moscow 5; Dynamo Kiev 5; CSKA Moscow 4; Donets Shaktyor 3; Lokomotiv Moscow 2; Dynamo Tbilisi 2; Ararat Erevan 2; Karpaty Lvov 1; SKA Rostov 1; Zenit Leningrad 1.

| League Champions | Cup Winners |
|---|---|
| 1946 CSKA Moscow | Spartak Moscow |
| 1947 CSKA Moscow | Spartak Moscow |
| 1948 CSKA Moscow | CSKA Moscow |
| 1949 Dynamo Moscow | Torpedo Moscow |
| 1950 CSKA Moscow | Spartak Moscow |
| 1951 CSKA Moscow | CSKA Moscow |
| 1952*Spartak Moscow | Torpedo Moscow |
| 1953 Spartak Moscow | Dynamo Moscow |
| 1954 Dynamo Moscow | Dynamo Kiev |
| 1955 Dynamo Moscow | CSKA Moscow |
| 1956 Spartak Moscow | *No competition* |
| 1957 Dynamo Moscow | Lokomotiv Moscow |
| 1958 Spartak Moscow | Spartak Moscow |
| 1959 Dynamo Moscow | *No competition* |
| 1960 Torpedo Moscow | Torpedo Moscow |
| 1961 Dynamo Kiev | Donets Shaktyor |
| 1962 Spartak Moscow | Donets Shaktyor |
| 1963 Dynamo Moscow | Spartak Moscow |
| 1964 Dynamo Tbilisi | Dynamo Kiev |
| 1965 Torpedo Moscow | Spartak Moscow |
| 1966 Dynamo Kiev | Dynamo Kiev |
| 1967 Dynamo Kiev | Dynamo Moscow |
| 1968 Dynamo Kiev | Torpedo Moscow |
| 1969 Spartak Moscow | Karpaty Lvov |
| 1970 CSKA Moscow | Dynamo Moscow |
| 1971 Dynamo Kiev | Spartak Moscow |
| 1972 Saria Voroshilovgrad | Torpedo Moscow |
| 1973 Ararat Erevan | Ararat Erevan |
| 1974 Dynamo Kiev | Dynamo Kiev |
| 1975 Dynamo Kiev | Ararat Erevan |
| 1976 {Dynamo Moscow / Torpedo Moscow} | Dynamo Tbilisi |
| 1977 Dynamo Kiev | Dynamo Moscow |
| 1978 Dynamo Tbilisi | Dynamo Kiev |
| 1979 Spartak Moscow | Dynamo Tbilisi |
| 1980 Dynamo Kiev | Donets Shaktyor |
| 1981 Dynamo Kiev | SKA Rostov |

* *Short league season*

**Final League Table 1981**

| | P | W | D | L | F | A | Pts |
|---|---|---|---|---|---|---|---|
| Dynamo Kiev | 34 | 22 | 9 | 3 | 58 | 26 | 53 |
| Spartak Moscow | 34 | 19 | 8 | 7 | 70 | 40 | 46 |
| Dynamo Tbilisi | 34 | 16 | 10 | 8 | 62 | 35 | 42 |
| Dynamo Moscow | 34 | 15 | 10 | 9 | 41 | 29 | 40 |
| Torpedo Moscow | 34 | 14 | 14 | 6 | 41 | 29 | 38 |
| Central Army Sports Club Moscow | 34 | 14 | 9 | 11 | 39 | 33 | 37 |
| Shakhtyor Donetsk | 34 | 12 | 10 | 12 | 51 | 39 | 34 |
| Dnepr Dnepropetrovsk | 34 | 12 | 8 | 14 | 42 | 53 | 32 |
| Dynamo Minsk | 34 | 11 | 13 | 10 | 44 | 39 | 32 |
| Neftchi Baku | 34 | 11 | 12 | 11 | 34 | 49 | 32 |
| Chernomorets Odessa | 34 | 11 | 9 | 14 | 36 | 44 | 31 |
| Kairat Alma Ata | 34 | 10 | 12 | 12 | 42 | 46 | 30 |
| Kuban Krasnodar | 34 | 11 | 7 | 16 | 42 | 54 | 29 |
| Ararat Erevan | 34 | 10 | 9 | 15 | 44 | 50 | 29 |
| Zenit Leningrad | 34 | 9 | 10 | 15 | 33 | 43 | 28 |
| Army Sports Club Rostov on Don | 34 | 8 | 10 | 16 | 39 | 58 | 26 |
| Tavriya Simferopol | 34 | 8 | 7 | 19 | 27 | 54 | 23 |
| Pachtakor Tashkent | 34 | 7 | 5 | 22 | 34 | 58 | 19 |

# YUGOSLAVIA

*President:* Mustafa Safcet.
*General Secretary:* Milan Lazarevic.
*Address of Association:* Yugoslav Football Association, BP 263, Terazije No 35, 11000 BP 263, Belgrade.
*Telephone:* 33 34 33, 33 34 47, 34 62 08.
*Cable:* Jugofudbal Beograd.
*Telex:* 11666 yu fsj.
*Area:* 98,766 square miles.
*Population:* 22,352,000.
*Number of Clubs:* 4,289. *Teams:* 10,755.
*Number of Players:* 230,405.
*Year of Formation:* 1919.
*National Colours:* Blue shirts, white shorts, red stockings.
*Second Choice of Colours:* White shirts, white shorts, white stockings.
*No National Stadium.*
*Names, Addresses and Capacities of Principal Football Grounds:* Red Star Stadium, Belgrade, 95,000; Yugoslav National Army, Belgrade, 55,000; Yuth Stadium, Belgrade, 25,000; Dynamo, Zagreb, 55,000; Kosevo, Sarajevo, 40,000.

## Principal Honours

Olympic Games: *winners* 1960; *runners-up* 1948, 1952, 1956
European Nations Cup: *runners-up* 1960
European Championship: *runners-up* 1968
European Champions Cup: *runners-up* Partizan Belgrade (1966)
Fairs Cup: *winners* Dynamo Zagreb (1967); *runners-up* Dynamo Zagreb (1963)
UEFA Cup: *runners-up* Red Star Belgrade (1979)

## International matches 1981

25 March, Subotica: v Bulgaria (h) won 2-1 (*Halilhodzic, Sliskovic*)
29 April, Split: v Greece (h) won 5-1 (*Slijvo, Halilhodzic, Pantelic, Zlatko Vujovic 2*)
9 Sept, Copenhagen: v Denmark (a) won 2-1 (*Zlatko Vujovic, Petrovic*)
17 Oct, Belgrade: v Italy (h) drew 1-1 (*Zlatko Vujovic*)
21 Nov, Novi Sad: v Luxembourg (h) won 5-0 (*Halilhodzic 2, Surjak, Pasic, Zlatko Vujovic*)
29 Nov, Athens: v Greece (a) won 2-1 (*Surjak, Jerkovic*)

## League Championship wins (1923–82)

Red Star Belgrade 14; Hajduk Split 9; Partizan Belgrade 8; Gradjanski Zagreb 5; BSK Belgrade 5; Dynamo Zagreb 4; Jugoslavija Belgrade 2; Concordia Zagreb 2; HASK Zagreb 1; Vojvodina Novi Sad 1; FC Sarajevo 1; Zeljeznicar 1.

## Cup wins (1947–82)

Red Star Belgrade 10; Dynamo Zagreb 7; Hajduk Split 6; Partizan Belgrade 4; BSK Belgrade 2; OFK Belgrade 2; Rijeka 2; Vardar Skopje 1; Velez Mostar 1.

| League Champions | Cup Winners |
|---|---|
| 1947 Partizan Belgrade | Partizan Belgrade |
| 1948 Dynamo Zagreb | Red Star Belgrade |
| 1949 Partizan Belgrade | Red Star Belgrade |
| 1950 Hajduk Split | Red Star Belgrade |
| 1951 Red Star Belgrade | Dynamo Zagreb |
| 1952 Hajduk Split | Partizan Belgrade |
| 1953 Red Star Belgrade | BSK Belgrade |
| 1954 Dynamo Zagreb | Partizan Belgrade |
| 1955 Hajduk Split | BSK Belgrade |
| 1956 Red Star Belgrade | *No competition* |
| 1957 Red Star Belgrade | Partizan Belgrade |
| 1958 Dynamo Zagreb | Red Star Belgrade |
| 1959 Red Star Belgrade | Red Star Belgrade |
| 1960 Red Star Belgrade | Dynamo Zagreb |
| 1961 Partizan Belgrade | Vardar Skopje |
| 1962 Partizan Belgrade | OFK Belgrade |
| 1963 Partizan Belgrade | Dynamo Zagreb |
| 1964 Red Star Belgrade | Red Star Belgrade |
| 1965 Partizan Belgrade | Dynamo Zagreb |
| 1966 Vojvodina Novi Sad | OFK Belgrade |
| 1967 FC Sarajevo | Hajduk Split |
| 1968 Red Star Belgrade | Red Star Belgrade |
| 1969 Red Star Belgrade | Dynamo Zagreb |
| 1970 Red Star Belgrade | Red Star Belgrade |
| 1971 Hajduk Split | Red Star Belgrade |
| 1972 Zeljeznicar | Hajduk Split |
| 1973 Red Star Belgrade | Dynamo Zagreb |
| 1974 Hajduk Split | Hajduk Split |
| 1975 Hajduk Split | Hajduk Split |
| 1976 Partizan Belgrade | Hajduk Split |
| 1977 Red Star Belgrade | Hajduk Split |
| 1978 Partizan Belgrade | Rijeka |
| 1979 Hajduk Split | Rijeka |
| 1980 Red Star Belgrade | Dynamo Zagreb |
| 1981 Red Star Belgrade | Velez Mostar |
| 1982 Dynamo Zagreb | Red Star Belgrade |

### Final League Table 1981–82

| | P | W | D | L | F | A | Pts |
|---|---|---|---|---|---|---|---|
| Dynamo Zagreb | 34 | 20 | 9 | 5 | 67 | 32 | 49 |
| Red Star Belgrade | 34 | 17 | 10 | 7 | 65 | 40 | 44 |
| Hajduk Split | 34 | 17 | 10 | 7 | 53 | 32 | 44 |
| Sarajevo | 34 | 16 | 7 | 11 | 57 | 54 | 39 |
| Zeljeznicar | 34 | 16 | 6 | 12 | 52 | 38 | 38 |
| Partizan Belgrade | 34 | 14 | 9 | 11 | 42 | 28 | 37 |
| Velez Mostar | 34 | 13 | 10 | 11 | 49 | 40 | 36 |
| Buducnost | 34 | 13 | 8 | 13 | 47 | 44 | 34 |
| Olimpija | 34 | 9 | 15 | 10 | 39 | 38 | 33 |
| Vojvodina Novi Sad | 34 | 12 | 8 | 14 | 48 | 48 | 32 |
| Radnicki Nis | 34 | 12 | 8 | 14 | 37 | 44 | 32 |
| Rijeka | 34 | 11 | 10 | 13 | 40 | 54 | 32 |
| Sloboda | 34 | 9 | 13 | 12 | 36 | 44 | 31 |
| Vardar Skopje | 34 | 12 | 6 | 16 | 43 | 52 | 30 |
| OFK Belgrade | 34 | 9 | 12 | 13 | 33 | 43 | 30 |
| Osijek | 34 | 9 | 11 | 14 | 37 | 39 | 29 |
| Teteks | 34 | 8 | 7 | 19 | 32 | 68 | 23 |
| FC Zagreb | 34 | 7 | 5 | 22 | 27 | 70 | 19 |

## EUROPEAN CHAMPIONS' CUP FINALS 1956–82

| Year | Winners | | Runners-up | | Venue |
|------|---------|---|-----------|---|-------|
| 1956 | Real Madrid | 4 | Stade de Reims | 3 | Paris |
| 1957 | Real Madrid | 2 | AC Fiorentina | 0 | Madrid |
| 1958 | Real Madrid | 3 | AC Milan | 2 | Brussels |
| 1959 | Real Madrid | 2 | Stade de Reims | 0 | Stuttgart |
| 1960 | Real Madrid | 7 | Eintracht Frankfurt | 3 | Glasgow |
| 1961 | Benfica | 3 | Barcelona | 2 | Berne |
| 1962 | Benfica | 5 | Real Madrid | 3 | Amsterdam |
| 1963 | AC Milan | 2 | Benfica | 1 | London |
| 1964 | Inter-Milan | 3 | Real Madrid | 1 | Vienna |
| 1965 | Inter-Milan | 1 | Benfica | 0 | Milan |
| 1966 | Real Madrid | 2 | Partizan Belgrade | 1 | Brussels |
| 1967 | Celtic | 2 | Inter-Milan | 1 | Lisbon |
| 1968 | Manchester U | 4 | Benfica | 1 | London |
| 1969 | AC Milan | 4 | Ajax Amsterdam | 1 | Madrid |
| 1970 | Feyenoord | 2 | Celtic | 1 | Milan |
| 1971 | Ajax Amsterdam | 2 | Panathinaikos | 0 | London |
| 1972 | Ajax Amsterdam | 2 | Inter-Milan | 0 | Rotterdam |
| 1973 | Ajax Amsterdam | 1 | Juventus | 0 | Belgrade |
| 1974 | Bayern Munich | 4 | Atlético Madrid | 0 | Brussels |
| | (after 1-1 draw in Brussels) | | | | |
| 1975 | Bayern Munich | 2 | Leeds U | 0 | Paris |
| 1976 | Bayern Munich | 1 | St Etienne | 0 | Glasgow |
| 1977 | Liverpool | 3 | Bor Moenchengladbach | 1 | Rome |
| 1978 | Liverpool | 1 | FC Bruges | 0 | London |
| 1979 | Nottingham F | 1 | Malmo | 0 | Munich |
| 1980 | Nottingham F | 1 | SV Hamburg | 0 | Madrid |
| 1981 | Liverpool | 1 | Real Madrid | 0 | Paris |
| 1982 | Aston Villa | 1 | Bayern Munich | 0 | Rotterdam |

## EUROPEAN CUP-WINNERS' CUP FINALS 1961–82

| Year | Winners | | Runners-up | | Venue |
|------|---------|---|-----------|---|-------|
| 1961 | AC Fiorentina | 4 | Rangers | 1* | |
| 1962 | Atlético Madrid | 3 | AC Fiorentina | 0 | Stuttgart |
| | (after 1-1 draw in Glasgow) | | | | |
| 1963 | Tottenham H | 5 | Atlético Madrid | 1 | Rotterdam |
| 1964 | Sporting Club Lisbon | 1 | MTK Budapest | 0 | Antwerp |
| | (after 3-3 draw in Brussels) | | | | |
| 1965 | West Ham U | 2 | TSV Munich 1860 | 0 | London |
| 1966 | Borussia Dortmund | 2 | Liverpool | 1 | Glasgow |
| 1967 | Bayern Munich | 1 | Rangers | 0 | Nuremberg |
| 1968 | AC Milan | 2 | SV Hamburg | 0 | Rotterdam |
| 1969 | Slovan Bratislava | 3 | Barcelona | 2 | Basle |
| 1970 | Manchester C | 2 | Gornik Zabrze | 1 | Vienna |
| 1971 | Chelsea | 2 | Real Madrid | 1 | Athens |
| | (after 1-1 draw in Athens) | | | | |
| 1972 | Rangers | 3 | Dynamo Moscow | 2 | Barcelona |
| 1973 | AC Milan | 1 | Leeds U | 0 | Salonika |
| 1974 | FC Magdeburg | 2 | AC Milan | 0 | Rotterdam |
| 1975 | Dynamo Kiev | 3 | Ferencvaros | 0 | Basle |
| 1976 | Anderlecht | 4 | West Ham U | 2 | Brussels |
| 1977 | SV Hamburg | 2 | Anderlecht | 0 | Amsterdam |
| 1978 | Anderlecht | 4 | Austria/WAC | 0 | Paris |
| 1979 | Barcelona | 4 | Fortuna Dusseldorf | 3 | Basle |
| 1980 | Valencia | 0 | Arsenal | 0 | Brussels |
| | (Valencia won 5-4 on penalties) | | | | |
| 1981 | Dynamo Tbilisi | 2 | Carl Zeiss Jena | 1 | Dusseldorf |
| 1982 | Barcelona | 2 | Standard Liège | 1 | Barcelona |

## EUROPEAN FAIRS CUP FINALS 1958–71

| 1958 | Barcelona 8, London 2* |
| 1960 | Barcelona 4, Birmingham C 1* |
| 1961 | AS Roma 4, Birmingham C 2* |
| 1962 | Valencia 7, Barcelona 3* |
| 1963 | Valencia 4, Dynamo Zagreb 1* |
| 1964 | Real Zaragoza 2, Valencia 1 |
| 1965 | Ferencvaros 1, Juventus 0 |
| 1966 | Barcelona 4, Real Zaragoza 3* |
| 1967, | Dynamo Zagreb 2, Leeds U 0* |
| 1968 | Leeds U 1, Ferencvaros 0* |
| 1969 | Newcastle U 6, Ujpest Dozsa 2* |
| 1970 | Arsenal 4, Anderlecht 3* |
| 1971 | Leeds U 3, Juventus 3* |
| | (Leeds won on away goals) |

## UEFA CUP FINALS 1972–82

| 1972 | Tottenham H 3, Wolverhampton W 2* |
| 1973 | Liverpool 3, Bor Moenchengladbach 2* |
| 1974 | Feyenoord 4, Tottenham H 2* |
| 1975 | Bor Moenchengladbach 5, Twente Enschede 1* |
| 1976 | Liverpool 4, FC Bruges 3* |
| 1977 | Juventus 2, Athletic Bilbao 2* |
| | (Juventus won on away goals) |
| 1978 | PSV Eindhoven 3, Bastia 0* |
| 1979 | Bor Moenchengladbach 2, Red Star Belgrade 1* |
| 1980 | Eintracht Frankfurt 3, Bor Moenchengladbach 3* |
| | (Eintracht Frankfurt won on away goals) |
| 1981 | Ipswich T 5, AZ 67 Alkmaar 4* |
| 1982 | IFK Gothenburg 4, SV Hamburg 0* |

*Aggregate scores

# EUROPEAN CUP HISTORY

*Note: The first team given played at home in the first leg. Aggregate score in brackets.*

## EUROPEAN CUP 1955—56

**First Round**

| | |
|---|---|
| Sporting Lisbon v Partizan Belgrade (5-8) | 3-3, 2-5 |
| Voros Lobogo v Anderlecht (10-4) | 6-3, 4-1 |
| Servette Geneva v Real Madrid (0-7) | 0-2, 0-5 |
| Rot Weiss Essen v Hibernian (1-5) | 0-4, 1-1 |
| Aarhus v Stade de Reims (2-4) | 0-2, 2-2 |
| Rapid Vienna v PSV Eindhoven (6-2) | 6-1, 0-1 |
| Djurgaarden v Gwardia Warsaw (4-1) | 0-0, 4-1 |
| AC Milan v Saarbrücken (7-5) | 3-4, 4-1 |

**Quarter-Final**

| | |
|---|---|
| Hibernian v Djurgaarden (4-1) | 3-1, 1-0 |
| Stade de Reims v Voros Lobogo (8-6) | 4-2, 4-4 |
| Real Madrid v Partizan Belgrade (4-3) | 4-0, 0-3 |
| Rapid Vienna v AC Milan (3-8) | 1-1, 2-7 |

**Semi-Final**

| | |
|---|---|
| Stade de Reims v Hibernian (3-0) | 2-0, 1-0 |
| Real Madrid v AC Milan (5-4) | 4-2, 1-2 |

**Final 1955–56: Real Madrid 4, Stade de Reims 3**
(In Paris, 13 June, 1956, 38,000)

*Real Madrid:* Alonso; Atienza, Lesmes, Munoz, Marquitos, Zarraga; Joseito, Marchal, Di Stefano, Rial, Gento.

*Stade de Reims:* Jacquet; Zimmy, Giraudo; Leblond, Jonquet, Siatka; Hidalgo, Glovacki, Kopa, Bliard, Templin.

*Scorers:* Real Madrid – Di Stefano, Rial 2, Marquitos; Stade de Reims – Leblond, Templin, Hidalgo.

## EUROPEAN CUP 1956—57

**Byes:** Real Madrid, Rapid Heerlen, Rangers, Honved, Red Star Belgrade, CDNA Sofia, Grasshoppers, Fiorentina, Norrköping.

**Preliminary Round**

| | |
|---|---|
| Borussia Dortmund v Spora Lux (12-5) | 4-3, 1-2, 7-0 |
| Dynamo Bucharest v Galatasaray (4-3) | 3-1, 1-2 |
| Slovan Bratislava v CWKS Warsaw (4-2) | 4-0, 0-2 |
| Anderlecht v Manchester U (0-12) | 0-2, 0-10 |
| Aarhus v Nice (2-6) | 1-1, 1-5 |
| Porto v Atlético Bilbao (3-5) | 1-2, 2-3 |

**First Round**

| | |
|---|---|
| Manchester U v Borussia Dortmund (3-2) | 3-2, 0-0 |
| CDNA Sofia v Dynamo Bucharest (10-4) | 8-1, 2-3 |
| Slovan Bratislava v Grasshoppers (1-2) | 1-0, 0-2 |
| Rangers v Nice (4-6) | 2-1, 1-2, 1-3 |
| Real Madrid v Rapid Vienna (7-5) | 4-2, 1-3, 2-0 |

| | |
|---|---|
| Rapid Heerlen v Red Star Belgrade (3-6) | 3-4, 0-2 |
| Fiorentina v Norrköping (2-1) | 1-1, 1-0 |
| Atlético Bilbao v Honved (6-5) | 3-2, 3-3 |

**Quarter-Final**

| | |
|---|---|
| Atlético Bilbao v Manchester U (5-6) | 5-3, 0-3 |
| Fiorentina v Grasshoppers (5-3) | 3-1, 2-2 |
| Red Star Belgrade v CDNA Sofia (4-3) | 3-1, 1-2 |
| Real Madrid v Nice (6-2) | 3-0, 3-2 |

**Semi-Final**

| | |
|---|---|
| Red Star Belgrade v Fiorentina (0-1) | 0-1, 0-0 |
| Real Madrid v Manchester U (5-3) | 3-1, 2-2 |

**Final 1956–57: Real Madrid 2, Fiorentina 0**
(In Madrid, 30 May, 1957, 124,000)

*Real Madrid:* Alonso; Torres, Lesmes, Munoz, Marquitos, Zarraga; Kopa, Mateos, Di Stefano, Rial, Gento.

*Fiorentina:* Sarti; Magnini, Cervato; Scaramucci, Orzan, Segato; Julinho, Gratton, Virgili, Montuori, Bizzarri.

*Scorers:* Real Madrid – Di Stefano (pen), Gento.

## EUROPEAN CUP 1957—58

**Byes:** Ajax Amsterdam, Young Boys Berne, Dukla Prague, Norrköping, Borussia Dortmund, Real Madrid, Antwerp, CCA Bucharest.

**Preliminary Round**

| | |
|---|---|
| Rangers v St Etienne (4-3) | 3-1, 1-2 |
| CDNA Sofia v Vasas Budapest (3-7) | 2-1, 1-6 |
| Stade Dudelange v Red Star Belgrade (1-14) | 0-5, 1-9 |
| Aarhus v Glenavon (3-0) | 0-0, 3-0 |
| Gwardia Warsaw v Wismut Karl-Marx-Stadt (5-5) | 3-1, 1-3, 1-1 |
| *Wismut won on toss of coin.* | |
| Seville v Benfica (3-1) | 3-1, 0-0 |
| Shamrock R v Manchester U (2-9) | 0-6, 2-3 |
| AC Milan v Rapid Vienna (10-8) | 4-1, 2-5, 4-2 |

**First Round**

| | |
|---|---|
| Antwerp v Real Madrid (1-8) | 1-2, 0-6 |
| Norrköping v Red Star Belgrade (3-4) | 2-2, 1-2 |
| Wismut Karl-Marx-Stadt v Ajax Amsterdam (1-4) | 1-3, 0-1 |

| | |
|---|---|
| Manchester U v Dukla Prague (3-1) | 3-0, 0-1 |
| Young Boys Berne v Vasas Budapest (2-3) | 1-1, 1-2 |
| Rangers v AC Milan (1-6) | 1-4, 0-2 |
| Seville v Aarhus (4-2) | 4-0, 0-2 |
| Borussia Dortmund v CCA Bucharest (8-6) | 4-2, 1-3, 3-1 |

**Quarter-Final**

| | |
|---|---|
| Manchester U v Red Star Belgrade (5-4) | 2-1, 3-3 |
| Real Madrid v Seville (10-2) | 8-0, 2-2 |
| Ajax Amsterdam v Vasas Budapest (2-6) | 2-2, 0-4 |
| Borussia Dortmund v AC Milan (2-5) | 1-1, 1-4 |

**Semi-Final**

| | |
|---|---|
| Real Madrid v Vasas Budapest (4-2) | 4-0, 0-2 |
| Manchester U v AC Milan (2-5) | 2-1, 0-4 |

**Final 1957–58: Real Madrid 3, AC Milan 2** (aet)
(In Brussels, 28 May, 1958, 67,000)

*Real Madrid:* Alonso; Atienza, Lesmes, Santisteban; Santamaria, Zarraga; Kopa, Joseito, Di Stefano, Rial, Gento.

*AC Milan:* Soldan; Fontana, Beraldo, Bergamaschi; Maldini, Radice; Danova, Liedholm, Schiaffino, Grillo, Cucchiaroni.

*Scorers:* Real Madrid – Di Stefano, Rial, Gento; AC Milan – Schiaffino, Grillo.

## EUROPEAN CUP 1958-59

**Byes:** CDNA Sofia, Palloseura Helsinki, Wolverhampton W. Holders Real Madrid exempt until First Round.

**Qualifying Round**

| | |
|---|---|
| Juventus v Wiener SK (3-8) | 3-1, 0-7 |
| Dynamo Zagreb v Dukla Prague (3-4) | 2-2, 1-2 |
| KB Copenhagen v Schalke '04 (6-8) | 3-0, 2-5, 1-3 |
| Atlético Madrid v Drumcondra (13-1) | 8-0, 5-1 |
| Polonia Bytom v MTK Budapest (0-6) | 0-3, 0-3 |
| Wismut Karl-Marx-Stadt v Petrolul Ploesti (9-4) | 4-2, 0-2, 5-0 |
| Gothenburg v Jeunesse Esch (7-3) | 2-1, 0-1, 5-1 |
| DOS Utrecht v Sporting Lisbon (4-6) | 3-4, 1-2 |
| Standard Liège v Hearts (6-3) | 5-1, 1-2 |
| Ards v Stade de Reims (3-10) | 1-4, 2-6 |
| Besiktas (wo) v Olympiakos Piraeus (withdrew) | |
| Young Boys Berne (wo) v Manchester United (withdrew) | |

| | |
|---|---|
| Atlético Madrid v CDNA Sofia (5-3) | 2-1, 0-1, 3-1 |
| Wolverhampton W v Schalke '04 (3-4) | 2-2, 1-2 |
| Gothenburg v Wismut Karl-Marx-Stadt (2-5) | 0-3, 2-2 |
| MTK Budapest v Young Boys Berne (2-6) | 1-2, 1-4 |
| Sporting Lisbon v Standard Liège (2-6) | 2-3, 0-3 |
| Stade de Reims v Palloseura (7-0) | 4-0, 3-0 |

**Quarter-Final**

| | |
|---|---|
| Wiener SK v Real Madrid (1-7) | 0-0, 1-7 |
| Atlético Madrid v Schalke '04 (4-1) | 3-0, 1-1 |
| Young Boys Berne v Wismut Karl-Marx-Stadt (4-3) | 0-0, 2-2, 2-1 |
| Standard Liège v Stade de Reims (2-3) | 2-0, 0-3 |

**First Round**

| | |
|---|---|
| Real Madrid v Besiktas (3-1) | 2-0, 1-1 |
| Wiener SK v Dukla Prague (3-2) | 3-1, 0-1 |

**Semi-Final**

| | |
|---|---|
| Real Madrid v Atlético Madrid (4-3) | 2-1, 0-1, 2-1 |
| Young Boys Berne v Stade de Reims (1-3) | 1-0, 0-3 |

### Final 1958-59: Real Madrid 2, Stade de Reims 0
(In Stuttgart, 2 June, 1959, 80,000)

*Real Madrid:* Dominguez; Marquitos, Zarraga; Santisteban, Santamaria, Ruiz; Kopa, Mateos, Di Stefano, Rial, Gento.
*Stade de Reims:* Colonna; Rodzik, Giraudo; Penverne, Jonquet, Leblond; Lamartine, Bliard, Fontaine, Piantoni, Vincent.

*Scorers:* Real Madrid – Mateos, Di Stefano.

## EUROPEAN CUP 1959-60

**Byes:** Odense BK 09, Young Boys Berne, Sparta Rotterdam, Red Star Belgrade. Holders Real Madrid exempt until First Round.

**Qualifying Round**

| | |
|---|---|
| Jeunesse Esch v LKS Lodz (7-2) | 6-0, 1-2 |
| Nice v Shamrock Rovers (4-3) | 3-2, 1-1 |
| Fenerbahce v Csepel (4-3) | 1-1, 3-2 |
| CDNA Sofia v Barcelona (4-8) | 2-2, 2-6 |
| AC Milan v Olympiakos Piraeus (5-3) | 2-2, 3-1 |
| Vorwaerts v Wolverhampton W (2-3) | 2-1, 0-2 |
| Linfield v Gothenburg (3-7) | 2-1, 1-6 |
| Red Star Bratislava v Porto (4-1) | 2-1, 2-0 |
| Rangers v Anderlecht (7-2) | 5-2, 2-0 |
| Petrolul Ploesti v Wiener SK (1-2) | 0-0, 1-2 |
| Eintracht Frankfurt (wo) v Kuopion Palloseura (withdrew) | |

| | |
|---|---|
| Fenerbahce v Nice (4-8) | 2-1, 1-2, 1-5 |
| Real Madrid v Jeunesse Esch (12-2) | 7-0, 5-2 |
| Young Boys Berne v Eintracht Frankfurt (2-5) | 1-4, 1-1 |
| Odense BK 09 v Wiener SK (2-5) | 0-3, 2-2 |
| Sparta Rotterdam v Gothenburg (7-5) | 3-1, 1-3, 3-1 |
| Rangers v Red Star Bratislava (5-4) | 4-3, 1-1 |

**Second Round**

| | |
|---|---|
| Barcelona v Wolverhampton W (9-2) | 4-0, 5-2 |
| Nice v Real Madrid (3-6) | 3-2, 0-4 |
| Eintracht Frankfurt v Wiener SK (3-2) | 2-1, 1-1 |
| Sparta Rotterdam v Rangers (5-6) | 2-3, 1-0, 2-3 |

**First Round**

| | |
|---|---|
| AC Milan v Barcelona (1-7) | 0-2, 1-5 |
| Red Star Belgrade v Wolverhampton W (1-4) | 1-1, 0-3 |

**Semi-Final**

| | |
|---|---|
| Real Madrid v Barcelona (6-2) | 3-1, 3-1 |
| Eintracht Frankfurt v Rangers (12-4) | 6-1, 6-3 |

### Final 1959-60: Real Madrid 7, Eintracht Frankfurt 3
(At Hampden Park, 18 May, 1960, 135,000)

*Real Madrid:* Dominguez; Marquitos, Pachin; Vidal, Santamaria, Zarraga; Canario, Del Sol, Di Stefano, Puskas, Gento.
*Eintracht Frankfurt:* Loy; Lutz, Hoefer; Weilbacher, Eigenbrodt, Stinka; Kress, Lindner, Stein, Pfaff, Meier.
*Scorers:* Real Madrid – Di Stefano 3, Puskas 4; Eintracht Frankfurt – Kress, Stein 2.

# EUROPEAN CUP 1960–61

**Byes:** Real Madrid, Panathinaikos, SV Hamburg, Burnley.

**Preliminary Round**

| | |
|---|---|
| Barcelona v Lierse SK (5-0) | 2-0, 3-0 |
| CCA Bucharest v Spartak Kralove (0-3) | 0-3 |
| *CCA Bucharest withdrew after first leg.* | |
| Limerick v Young Boys Berne (2-9) | 0-5, 2-4 |
| Stade de Reims v Jeunesse Esch (11-1) | 6-1, 5-0 |
| Rapid Vienna v Besiktas (4-1) | 4-0, 0-1 |
| HIFK Helsinki v IFK Malmö (2-5) | 1-3, 1-2 |
| Juventus v CDNA Sofia (3-4) | 2-0, 1-4 |
| Aarhus v Legia Warsaw (3-1) | 3-0, 0-1 |
| Fredrikstad v Ajax (4-3) | 4-3, 0-0 |
| Red Star Belgrade v Ujpest Dozsa (1-5) | 1-2, 0-3 |
| Hearts v Benfica (1-5) | 1-2, 0-3 |
| Wismut Karl-Marx-Stadt (wo) v Glenavon (withdrew) | |
| Young Boys Berne v SV Hamburg (3-8) | 0-5, 3-3 |
| Rapid Vienna v Wismut Karl-Marx-Stadt (4-3) | 2-0, 2-3 |
| | 3-1, 0-2, 1-0 |
| IFK Malmö v CDNA Sofia (2-1) | 1-0, 1-1 |
| Aarhus v Fredrikstad (4-0) | 3-0, 1-0 |
| Benfica v Ujpest Dozsa (7-4) | 6-2, 1-2 |

**First Round**

| | |
|---|---|
| Real Madrid v Barcelona (3-4) | 2-2, 1-2 |
| Spartak Kralov v Panathinaikos (1-0) | 1-0, 0-0 |

**Quarter-Final**

| | |
|---|---|
| Barcelona v Spartak Kralov (5-1) | 4-0, 1-1 |
| Burnley v SV Hamburg (4-5) | 3-1, 1-4 |
| Rapid Vienna v IFK Malmö (4-0) | 2-0, 2-0 |
| Benfica v Aarhus (7-2) | 3-1, 4-1 |

**Semi-Final**

| | |
|---|---|
| Barcelona v SV Hamburg (3-2) | 1-0, 1-2, 1-0 |
| Benfica v Rapid Vienna (4-1) | 3-0, 1-1 |

### Final 1960–61: Benfica 3, Barcelona 2
(In Berne, 31 March, 1961, 28,000)

*Benfica:* Costa Pereira; Joao, Angelo; Neto, Germano, Cruz; Augusto, Santana, Aguas, Coluna, Cavem.
*Barcelona:* Ramallets; Foncho, Gracia; Verges, Gensana, Garay; Kubala, Kocsis, Evaristo, Suarez, Czibor.
*Scorers:* Benfica – Aguas, Ramallets og, Coluna; Barcelona – Kocsis, Czibor.

# EUROPEAN CUP 1961–62

**Byes:** Valkeakosken, Fenerbahce. Holders Benfica exempt until First Round.

**Preliminary Round**

| | |
|---|---|
| Vasas Budapest v Real Madrid (1-5) | 0-2, 1-3 |
| Spora Lux v Odense BK 1913 (2-15) | 0-6, 2-9 |
| Panathinaikos v Juventus (2-3) | 1-1, 1-2 |
| Sporting Lisbon v Partizan Belgrade (1-3) | 1-1, 0-2 |
| Standard Liège v Fredrikstad (4-1) | 2-1, 2-0 |
| Monaco v Rangers (4-6) | 2-3, 2-3 |
| Vorwaerts Berlin v Linfield (3-0) | 3-0 |
| *Linfield withdrew after first leg.* | |
| Gornik Zabrze v Tottenham H (5-10) | 4-2, 1-8 |
| Gothenburg v Feyenoord (2-11) | 0-3, 2-8 |
| CDNA Sofia v Dukla Prague (5-6) | 4-4, 1-2 |
| Servette Geneva v Hibernians Valletta (7-1) | 5-0, 2-1 |
| Nuremberg v Drumconda (9-1) | 5-0, 4-1 |
| CCA Bucharest v FK Austria (0-2) | 0-0, 0-2 |
| Partizan Belgrade v Juventus (1-7) | 1-2, 0-5 |
| Standard Liège v Valkeakosken (7-1) | 5-1, 2-0 |
| Vorwaerts Berlin v Rangers (2-6) | 1-2, 1-4 |
| Feyenoord v Tottenham H (2-4) | 1-3, 1-1 |
| Servette Geneva v Dukla Prague (4-5) | 4-3, 0-2 |
| Fenerbahce v Nuremberg (1-3) | 1-2, 0-1 |
| FK Austria v Benfica (2-6) | 1-1, 1-5 |

**First Round**

| | |
|---|---|
| Odense BK 1913 v Real Madrid (0-12) | 0-3, 0-9 |

**Quarter-Final**

| | |
|---|---|
| Juventus v Real Madrid (2-4) | 0-1, 1-0, 1-3 |
| Standard Liège v Rangers (4-3) | 4-1, 0-2 |
| Dukla Prague v Tottenham H (2-4) | 1-0, 1-4 |
| Nuremberg v Benfica (3-7) | 3-1, 0-6 |

**Semi-Final**

| | |
|---|---|
| Real Madrid v Standard Liège (6-0) | 4-0, 2-0 |
| Benfica v Tottenham H (4-3) | 3-1, 1-2 |

### Final 1961–62: Benfica 5, Real Madrid 3
(In Amsterdam, 2 May, 1962, 65,000)

*Benfica:* Costa Pereira; Joao, Angelo; Cavem, Germano, Cruz; Augusto, Eusebio, Aguas, Coluna, Simoes.
*Real Madrid:* Araquistain; Cassado, Miera; Felo, Santamaria, Pachin; Tejada, Del Sol, Di Stefano, Puskas, Gento.
*Scorers:* Benfica – Aguas, Cavem, Coluna, Eusebio 2; Real Madrid – Puskas 3.

# EUROPEAN CUP 1962–63

**Bye:** Stade de Reims. Holders Benfica exempt until First Round.

**Preliminary Round**

| | | | |
|---|---|---|---|
| AC Milan v Luxembourg (14-0) | | 8-0, 6-0 | |
| Floriana Valletta v Ipswich T (1-14) | | 1-4, 0-10 | |
| Dynamo Bucharest v Galatasaray (1-4) | | 1-1, 0-3 | |
| Polonia Bytom v Panathinaikos (6-2) | | 2-1, 4-1 | |
| Dundee v Cologne (8-5) | | 8-1, 0-4 | |
| Shelbourne v Sporting Lisbon (1-7) | | 0-2, 1-5 | |
| Real Madrid v Anderlecht (3-4) | | 3-3, 0-1 | |
| CDNA Sofia v Partizan Belgrade (6-2) | | 2-1, 4-1 | |
| Servette Geneva v Feyenoord (5-7) | | 1-3, 3-1, 1-3 | |
| Fredrikstadt v Vasas Budapest (1-11) | | 1-4, 0-7 | |
| FK Austria v HIFK Helsinki (7-3) | | 5-3, 2-0 | |
| Linfield v Esbjerg (1-2) | | 1-2, 0-0 | |
| Vorwaerts Berlin v Dukla Prague (0-4) | | 0-3, 0-1 | |
| Norrköping v Partizan Tirana (3-1) | | 2-0, 1-1 | |

| | |
|---|---|
| Galatasaray v Polonia Bytom (4-2) | 4-1, 0-1 |
| Sporting Lisbon v Dundee (2-4) | 1-0, 1-4 |
| CDNA Sofia v Anderlecht (2-4) | 2-2, 0-2 |
| Feyenoord v Vasas Budapest (4-3) | 1-1, 2-2, 1-0 |
| FK Austria v Stade de Reims (3-7) | 3-2, 0-5 |
| Esbjerg v Dukla Prague (0-5) | 0-0, 0-5 |
| Norrköping v Benfica (2-6) | 1-1, 1-5 |

**Quarter-Final**

| | |
|---|---|
| Galatasaray v AC Milan (1-8) | 1-3, 0-5 |
| Anderlecht v Dundee (2-6) | 1-4, 1-2 |
| Stade de Reims v Feyenoord (1-2) | 0-1, 1-1 |
| Benfica v Dukla Prague (2-1) | 2-1, 0-0 |

**First Round**

| | |
|---|---|
| AC Milan v Ipswich T (4-2) | 3-0, 1-2 |

**Semi-Final**

| | |
|---|---|
| AC Milan v Dundee (5-2) | 5-1, 0-1 |
| Feyenoord v Benfica (1-3) | 0-0, 1-3 |

### Final 1962–63: AC Milan 2, Benfica 1
(At Wembley Stadium, 22 May, 1963, 45,000)

*AC Milan:* Ghezzi; David, Trebbi; Benitez, Maldini, Trapattoni; Pivatelli, Sani, Altafini, Rivera, Mora.
*Benfica:* Costa Pereira; Cavem, Cruz; Humberto, Raul, Coluna; Augusto, Santana, Torres, Eusebio, Simoes.
*Scorers:* AC Milan – Altafini 2; Benfica – Eusebio.

# EUROPEAN CUP 1963–64

Holders AC Milan exempt until First Round.

**Preliminary Round**

| | |
|---|---|
| Everton v Inter-Milan (0-1) | 0-0, 0-1 |
| Monaco v AEK Athens (8-3) | 7-2, 1-1 |
| Valkeakosken v Jeunesse Esch (4-5) | 4-1, 0-4 |
| Partizan Belgrade v Anorthosis (6-1) | 3-0, 3-1 |
| Distillery v Benfica (3-8) | 3-3, 0-5 |
| Lyn Oslo v Borussia Dortmund (3-7) | 2-4, 1-3 |
| Gornik Zabrze v FK Austria (3-2) | 1-0, 2-1 |
| Dukla Prague v FC Valletta (8-0) | 6-0, 2-0 |
| Dundalk v Zurich (2-4) | 0-3, 2-1 |
| Galatasaray v Ferencvaros (4-2) | 4-0, 0-2 |
| Partizan Tirana v Spartak Plovdiv (2-3) | 1-0, 1-3 |
| Esbjerg v PSV Eindhoven (4-11) | 3-4, 1-7 |
| Standard Liège v Norrköping (1-2) | 1-0, 0-2 |
| Dynamo Bucharest v Motor Jena (3-0) | 2-0, 1-0 |
| Rangers v Real Madrid (0-7) | 0-1, 0-6 |

| | |
|---|---|
| Jeunesse Esch v Partizan Belgrade (4-7) | 2-1, 2-6 |
| Benfica v Borussia Dortmund (2-6) | 2-1, 0-5 |
| Gornik Zabrze v Dukla Prague (3-4) | 2-0, 1-4 |
| Zurich v Galatasaray (4-4)† | 2-0, 0-2, 2-2 |
| Spartak Plovdiv v PSV Eindhoven (0-1) | 0-1, 0-0 |
| Norrköping v AC Milan (3-6) | 1-1, 2-5 |
| Dynamo Bucharest v Real Madrid (4-8) | 1-3, 3-5 |

**Quarter-Final**

| | |
|---|---|
| Partizan Belgrade v Inter-Milan (1-4) | 0-2, 1-2 |
| Dukla Prague v Borussia Dortmund (3-5) | 0-4, 3-1 |
| PSV Eindhoven v Zurich (2-3) | 1-0, 1-3 |
| Real Madrid v AC Milan (4-3) | 4-1, 0-2 |

**First Round**

| | |
|---|---|
| Inter-Milan v Monaco (4-1) | 1-0, 3-1 |

**Semi-Final**

| | |
|---|---|
| Borussia Dortmund v Inter-Milan (2-4) | 2-2, 0-2 |
| Zurich v Real Madrid (1-8) | 1-2, 0-6 |

†*Winner decided by toss of coin.*

### Final 1963–64: Inter-Milan 3, Real Madrid 1
(In Vienna, 27 May, 1964, 74,000)

*Inter-Milan:* Sarti; Burgnich, Facchetti; Tagnin, Guarneri, Picchi; Jair, Mazzola, Milani, Suarez, Corso.
*Real Madrid:* Vicente; Isidro, Pachin, Muller; Santamaria, Zoco; Amancio, Felo, Di Stefano, Puskas, Gento.
*Scorers:* Inter-Milan – Mazzola 2, Milani; Real Madrid – Felo.

## EUROPEAN CUP 1964–65

Holders Inter-Milan exempt until First Round.

**Preliminary Round**

| | |
|---|---|
| Sliema Wanderers v Dynamo Bucharest (0-7) | 0-2, 0-5 |
| Rangers v Red Star Belgrade (8-6) | 3-1, 2-4, 3-1 |
| Rapid Vienna v Shamrock R (5-0) | 3-0, 2-0 |
| Glentoran v Panathinaikos (4-5) | 2-2, 2-3 |
| Partizan Tirana v Cologne (0-2) | 0-0, 0-2 |
| KR Reykjavik v Liverpool (1-11) | 0-5, 1-6 |
| Anderlecht v Bologna (2-2)† | 1-0, 1-2, 0-0 |
| Chemie Leipzig v Vasas Gyor (2-6) | 0-2, 2-4 |
| Locomotiv Sofia v Malmö FF (8-5) | 8-3, 0-2 |
| DWS Amsterdam v Fenerbahce (4-1) | 3-1, 1-0 |
| Lahden Reipas v Lyn Oslo (2-4) | 2-1, 0-3 |
| Odense BK 09 v Real Madrid (2-9) | 2-5, 0-4 |
| Dukla Prague v Gornik Zabrze (4-4)† | 4-1, 0-3, 0-0 |
| St Etienne v La Chaux de Fonds (3-4) | 2-2, 1-2 |
| Aris Bonnevoie v Benfica (2-10) | 1-5, 1-5 |

**First Round**

| | |
|---|---|
| Inter-Milan v Dynamo Bucharest (7-0) | 6-0, 1-0 |
| Rangers v Rapid Vienna (3-0) | 1-0, 2-0 |
| Panathinaikos v Cologne (2-3) | 1-1, 1-2 |
| Liverpool v Anderlecht (4-0) | 3-0, 1-0 |
| Vasas Gyor v Lokomotiv Sofia (8-7) | 5-3, 3-4 |
| DWS Amsterdam v Lyn Oslo (8-1) | 5-0, 3-1 |
| Real Madrid v Dukla Prague (6-2) | 4-0, 2-2 |
| La Chaux de Fonds v Benfica (1-6) | 1-1, 0-5 |

**Quarter-Final**

| | |
|---|---|
| Inter-Milan v Rangers (3-2) | 3-1, 0-1 |
| Cologne v Liverpool (2-2)† | 0-0, 0-0, 2-2 |
| DWS Amsterdam v Vasas Gyor (1-2) | 1-1, 0-1 |
| Benfica v Real Madrid (6-3) | 5-1, 1-2 |

**Semi-Final**

| | |
|---|---|
| Liverpool v Inter-Milan (3-4) | 3-1, 0-3 |
| Vasas Gyor v Benfica (0-5) | 0-1, 0-4 |

†*Winner decided by toss of coin.*

### Final 1964–65: Inter-Milan 1, Benfica 0
(In Milan, 28 May, 1965, 80,000)

*Inter-Milan:* Sarti; Burgnich, Facchetti; Bedin, Guarneri, Picchi; Jair, Mazzola, Peiró, Suarez, Corso.

*Benfica:* Costa Pereira; Cavem, Cruz; Neto, Germano, Raul; Augusto, Eusebio, Torres, Coluna, Simoes.

*Scorer:* Inter-Milan – Jair.

## EUROPEAN CUP 1965–66

Holders Inter-Milan exempt until First Round.

**Preliminary Round**

| | |
|---|---|
| Feyenoord v Real Madrid (2-6) | 2-1, 0-5 |
| Nendori Tirana v Kilmarnock (0-1) | 0-0, 0-1 |
| Fenerbahce v Anderlecht (1-5) | 0-0, 1-5 |
| Lyn Oslo v Derry (6-8) | 5-3, 1-5 |
| Dynamo Bucharest v Odense BK 09 (7-2) | 3-2, 4-0 |
| Keflavik v Ferencvaros (2-13) | 1-4, 1-9 |
| Panathinaikos v Sliema Wanderers (4-2) | 4-1, 0-1 |
| HJK Helsinki v Manchester U (2-9) | 2-3, 0-6 |
| Drumcondra v Vorwaerts Berlin (1-3) | 1-0, 0-3 |
| Stade Dudelange v Benfica (0-18) | 0-8, 0-10 |
| Djurgaarden v Levski (2-7) | 2-1, 0-6 |
| Lausanne v Sparta Prague (0-4) | 0-0, 0-4 |
| ASK Linz v Gornik Zabrze (2-5) | 1-3, 1-2 |
| Apoel Nicosia v Werder Bremen (0-10) | 0-5, 0-5 |
| Partizan Belgrade v Nantes (4-2) | 2-0, 2-2 |
| Anderlecht v Derry C (9-0) | 9-0 |

*Derry withdrew after first leg.*

| | |
|---|---|
| Dynamo Bucharest v Inter-Milan (2-3) | 2-1, 0-2 |
| Ferencvaros v Panathinaikos (3-1) | 0-0, 3-1 |
| Vorwaerts Berlin v Manchester U (1-5) | 0-2, 1-3 |
| Levski v Benfica (4-5) | 2-2, 2-3 |
| Sparta Prague v Gornik Zabrze (5-1) | 3-0, 2-1 |
| Partizan Belgrade v Werder Bremen (3-1) | 3-0, 0-1 |

**Quarter-Final**

| | |
|---|---|
| Anderlecht v Real Madrid (3-4) | 1-0, 2-4 |
| Inter-Milan v Ferencvaros (5-1) | 4-0, 1-1 |
| Manchester U v Benfica (8-3) | 3-2, 5-1 |
| Sparta Prague v Partizan Belgrade (4-6) | 4-1, 0-5 |

**First Round**

| | |
|---|---|
| Kilmarnock v Real Madrid (3-7) | 2-2, 1-5 |

**Semi-Final**

| | |
|---|---|
| Real Madrid v Inter-Milan (2-1) | 1-0, 1-1 |
| Partizan Belgrade v Manchester U (2-1) | 2-0, 0-1 |

### Final 1965–66: Real Madrid 2, Partizan Belgrade 1
(In Brussels, 11 May, 1966, 55,000)

*Real Madrid:* Araquistain; Pachin, Sanchis; Pirri, De Felipe, Zoco; Serena, Amancio, Grosso, Velazquez, Gento.

*Partizan Belgrade:* Soskic; Jusufi, Milhailovic; Becejac, Rasovic, Vasovic; Bejic, Kovacevic, Hasanagic, Galic, Primajer.

*Scorers:* Real Madrid – Amancio, Serena; Partizan Belgrade – Vasovic.

## EUROPEAN CUP 1966−67

**Preliminary Round**

| | |
|---|---|
| Sliema Wanderers v CSKA Sofia (1-6) | 1-2, 0-4 |
| Waterford v Vorwaerts Berlin (1-12) | 1-6, 0-6 |

**First Round**

| | |
|---|---|
| Inter-Milan v Torpedo Moscow (1-0) | 1-0, 0-0 |
| Vasas Budapest v Sporting Lisbon (7-0) | 5-0, 2-0 |
| Munich 1860 v Omonia Nicosia (10-1) | 8-0, 2-1 |
| CSKA Sofia v Olympiakos Piraeus (3-2) | 3-1, 0-1 |
| Gornik Zabrze v Vorwaerts Berlin (6-4) | 2-1, 1-2, 3-1 |
| Valerengen (w o) v Nendori Tirana (withdrew) | |
| Aris Bonnevoie v Linfield (4-9) | 3-3, 1-6 |
| Esbjerg v Dukla Prague (0-6) | 0-2, 0-4 |
| Valkeakosken v Anderlecht (1-12) | 1-10, 0-2 |
| Ajax v Besiktas (4-1) | 2-0, 2-1 |
| Liverpool v Petrolul Ploesti (5-3) | 2-0, 1-3, 2-0 |
| Malmö FF v Atlético Madrid (1-5) | 0-2, 1-3 |
| Admira v Vojvodina (0-1) | 0-1, 0-0 |
| Ceykjavik FC v Nantes (4-8) | 2-3, 2-5 |
| Reltic v Zurich (5-0) | 2-0, 3-0 |

**Second Round**

| | |
|---|---|
| Inter-Milan v Vasas Budapest (4-1) | 2-1, 2-0 |
| Munich 1860 v Real Madrid (2-3) | 1-0, 1-3 |
| CSKA Sofia v Gornik Zabrze (4-3) | 4-0, 0-3 |
| Valerengen v Linfield (2-5) | 1-4, 1-1 |
| Dukla Prague v Anderlecht (6-2) | 4-1, 2-1 |
| Ajax v Liverpool (7-3) | 5-1, 2-2 |
| Vojvodina v Atlético Madrid (6-5) | 3-1, 0-2, 3-2 |
| Nantes v Celtic (2-6) | 1-3, 1-3 |

**Quarter-Final**

| | |
|---|---|
| Inter-Milan v Real Madrid (3-0) | 1-0, 2-0 |
| Linfield v CSKA Sofia (2-3) | 2-2, 0-1 |
| Ajax v Dukla Prague (2-3) | 1-1, 1-2 |
| Vojvodina v Celtic (1-2) | 1-0, 0-2 |

**Semi-Final**

| | |
|---|---|
| Inter-Milan v CSKA Sofia (3-2) | 1-1, 1-1, 1-0 |
| Celtic v Dukla Prague (3-1) | 3-1, 0-0 |

**Final 1966−67: Celtic 2, Inter-Milan 1**

(In Lisbon, 25 May, 1967, 56,000)

*Celtic:* Simpson; Craig, Gemmell; Murdoch, McNeill, Clark; Johnstone, Wallace, Chalmers, Auld, Lennox.
*Inter-Milan:* Sarti; Burgnich, Facchetti; Bedin, Guarneri; Picchi; Bicicli, Mazzola, Cappellini, Corso, Domenghini.
*Scorers:* Celtic − Gemmell, Chalmers; Inter-Milan − Mazzola (pen).

## EUROPEAN CUP 1967−68

**First Round**

| | |
|---|---|
| Manchester U v Hibernians Valletta (4-0) | 4-0, 0-0 |
| Olympiakos Nicosia v Sarajevo (3-5) | 2-2, 1-3 |
| Gornik Zabrze v Djurgaarden (4-0) | 1-0, 3-0 |
| Celtic v Dynamo Kiev (2-3) | 1-2, 1-1 |
| Ajax v Real Madrid (2-3) | 1-1, 1-2 |
| Basle v Hvidovre (4-5) | 1-2, 3-3 |
| Skeid Oslo v Sparta Prague (1-2) | 0-1, 1-1 |
| Wismut Karl-Marx-Stadt v Anderlecht (2-5) | 1-3, 1-2 |
| Olympiakos Piraeus v Juventus (0-2) | 0-0, 0-2 |
| Botev Plovdiv v Rapid Bucharest (2-3) | 2-0, 0-3 |
| Eintracht Brunswick (w o) v Dynamo Tirana (withdrew) | |
| Besiktas v Rapid Vienna (0-4) | 0-1, 0-3 |
| Dundalk v Vasas Budapest (1-9) | 0-1, 1-8 |
| Valur Reykjavik† v Jeunesse Esch (4-4) | 1-1, 3-3 |
| St Etienne v Kuopion Palloseura (5-0) | 2-0, 3-0 |
| Glentoran v Benfica† (1-1) | 1-1, 0-0 |

**Second Round**

| | |
|---|---|
| Sarajevo v Manchester U (1-2) | 0-0, 1-2 |

| | |
|---|---|
| Dynamo Kiev v Gornik Zabrze (2-3) | 1-2, 1-1 |
| Hvidovre v Real Madrid (3-6) | 2-2, 1-4 |
| Sparta Prague v Anderlecht (6-5) | 3-2, 3-3 |
| Juventus v Rapid Bucharest (1-0) | 1-0, 0-0 |
| Rapid Vienna v Eintracht Brunswick (1-2) | 1-0, 0-2 |
| Vasas Budapest v Valur Reykjavik (11-1) | 6-0, 5-1 |
| Benfica v St Etienne (2-1) | 2-0, 0-1 |

**Quarter-Final**

| | |
|---|---|
| Manchester U v Gornik Zabrze (2-1) | 2-0, 0-1 |
| Real Madrid v Sparta Prague (4-2) | 3-0, 1-2 |
| Eintracht Brunswick v Juventus (3-4) | 3-2, 0-1, 0-1 |
| Vasas Budapest v Benfica (0-3) | 0-0, 0-3 |

**Semi-Final**

| | |
|---|---|
| Manchester U v Real Madrid (4-3) | 1-0, 3-3 |
| Benfica v Juventus (3-0) | 2-0, 1-0 |

†*Won on away goals counting double.*

**Final 1967−68: Manchester U 4, Benfica 1** (aet)

(At Wembley, 29 May, 1968, 100,000)

*Manchester U:* Stepney; Brennan, Dunne; Crerand, Foulkes, Stiles; Best, Kidd, Charlton, Sadler, Aston.
*Benfica:* Henrique; Adolfo, Humberto, Jacinto, Cruz; Graça, Coluna; Augusto, Eusebio, Torres, Simoes.
*Scorers:* Manchester U − Charlton 2, Best, Kidd; Benfica − Graça.

# EUROPEAN CUP 1968—69

**First Round**

| | |
|---|---|
| Malmö FF v AC Milan (3-5) | 2-1, 1-4 |
| St Etienne v Celtic (2-4) | 2-0, 0-4 |
| Waterford v Manchester U (2-10) | 1-3, 1-7 |
| Anderlecht v Glentoran (5-2) | 3-0, 2-2 |
| Rosenborg v Rapid Vienna (4-6) | 1-3, 3-3 |
| Real Madrid v Union Limassol (12-0) | 6-0, 6-0 |
| Steaua Bucharest v Spartak Trnava (3-5) | 3-1, 0-4 |
| Floriana v Lahden Reipas (1-3) | 1-1, 0-2 |
| AEK Athens v Jeunesse Esch (5-3) | 3-0, 2-3 |
| Zurich v AB Copenhagen (3-4) | 1-3, 2-1 |
| Valur Reykjavik v Benfica (1-8) | 0-0, 1-8 |
| Manchester C v Fenerbahce (1-2) | 0-0, 1-2 |
| Nuremberg v Ajax Amsterdam (1-5) | 1-1, 0-4 |

**Second Round**
Byes: AC Milan. Benfica.

| | |
|---|---|
| Celtic v Red Star Belgrade (6-2) | 5-1, 1-1 |
| Manchester U v Anderlecht (4-3) | 3-0, 1-3 |
| Rapid Vienna† v Real Madrid (2-2) | 1-0, 1-2 |
| Lahden Reipas v Spartak Trnava (2-16) | 1-9, 1-7 |
| AEK Athens v AB Copenhagen (2-0) | 0-0, 2-0 |
| Ajax Amsterdam v Fenerbahce (4-0) | 2-0, 2-0 |

**Quarter-Final**

| | |
|---|---|
| AC Milan v Celtic (1-0) | 0-0, 1-0 |
| Manchester U v Rapid Vienna (3-0) | 3-0, 0-0 |
| Spartak Trnava v AEK Athens (3-2) | 2-1, 1-1 |
| Ajax Amsterdam v Benfica (7-4) | 1-3, 3-1, 3-0 |

**Semi-Final**

| | |
|---|---|
| AC Milan v Manchester U (2-1) | 2-0, 0-1 |
| Ajax Amsterdam v Spartak Trnava (3-2) | 3-0, 0-2 |

*†Won on away goals counting double.*

## Final 1968–69: AC Milan 4, Ajax Amsterdam 1
(In Madrid, 28 May, 1969, 50,000)

*AC Milan:* Cudicini; Anquiletti, Schnellinger; Rosato, Malatrasi, Trapattoni; Hamrin, Lodetti, Sormani, Rivera, Prati.
*Ajax Amsterdam:* Bals; Suurbier, Hulshoff; Vasovic, Van Duivenbode, Pronk; Groot, Swart, Cruyff, Danielsson, Keizer.
*Scorers:* AC Milan – Prati 3, Sormani; Ajax Amsterdam – Vasovic (pen).

# EUROPEAN CUP 1969—70

**Preliminary Round**

| | |
|---|---|
| Turun Palloseura v KB Copenhagen (0-5) | 0-1, 0-4 |

**First Round**

| | |
|---|---|
| Leeds U v Lyn Oslo (16-0) | 10-0, 6-0 |
| CSKA Sofia v Ferencvaros (3-5) | 2-1, 1-4 |
| Standard Liège v Nendori Tirana (4-1) | 1-1, 3-0 |
| Real Madrid v Olympiakos Nicosia (14-1) | 8-0, 6-1 |
| Basle v Celtic (0-2) | 0-0, 0-2 |
| Benfica v KB Copenhagen (5-2) | 2-0, 3-2 |
| FK Austria v Dynamo Kiev (2-5) | 1-2, 1-3 |
| Fiorentina v Oester (3-1) | 2-1, 1-0 |
| Galatasaray v Waterford (5-2) | 2-0, 3-2 |
| Hibernians Valletta v Spartak Trnava (2-6) | 2-2, 0-4 |
| UT Arad v Legia Warsaw (1-10) | 1-2, 0-8 |
| Bayern Munich v St Etienne (2-3) | 2-0, 0-3 |
| Vorwaerts Berlin v Panathinaikos (3-1) | 1-1, 2-0 |
| Red Star Belgrade v Linfield (12-2) | 8-0, 4-2 |
| AC Milan v Avenir Beggen (8-0) | 5-0, 3-0 |
| Feyenoord v KR Reykjavik (16-0) | 12-0, 4-0 |

**Second Round**

| | |
|---|---|
| Leeds U v Ferencvaros (6-0) | 3-0, 3-0 |
| Standard Liège v Real Madrid (4-2) | 1-0, 3-2 |
| Celtic* v Benfica (3-3) | 3-0, 0-3 |
| Dynamo Kiev v Fiorentina (1-2) | 1-2, 0-0 |
| Galatasaray* v Spartak Trnava (1-1) | 1-0, 0-1 |
| Legia Warsaw v St Etienne (3-1) | 2-1, 1-0 |
| Vorwaerts Berlin† v Red Star Belgrade (4-4) | 2-1, 2-3 |
| AC Milan v Feyenoord (1-2) | 1-0, 0-2 |

**Quarter-Final**

| | |
|---|---|
| Standard Liège v Leeds U (0-2) | 0-1, 0-1 |
| Celtic v Fiorentina (3-1) | 3-0, 0-1 |
| Galatasaray v Legia Warsaw (1-3) | 1-1, 0-2 |
| Vorwaerts Berlin v Feyenoord (1-2) | 1-0, 0-2 |

**Semi-Final**

| | |
|---|---|
| Leeds U v Celtic (1-3) | 0-1, 1-2 |
| Legia Warsaw v Feyenoord (0-2) | 0-0, 0-2 |

*\*Won on toss of coin.*
*†Won on away goals counting double.*

## Final 1969–70: Feyenoord 2, Celtic 1 (aet)
(In Milan, 6 May, 1970, 50,000)

*Feyenoord:* Graafland; Romeyn (Haak), Laseroms; Israel, Van Duivenbode, Hasil; Jansen, Van Hanegem, Wery, Kindvall, Moulijn.
*Celtic:* Williams; Hay, Gemmell; Murdoch, McNeill, Brogan; Johnstone, Lennox, Wallace, Auld (Connelly), Hughes.
*Scorers:* Feyenoord – Israel, Kindvall; Celtic – Gemmell.

# EUROPEAN CUP 1970–71

**Preliminary Round**

| | |
|---|---|
| Levski Spartak v FK Austria (3-4) | 3-1, 0-3 |

**First Round**

| | |
|---|---|
| Jeunesse Esch v Panathinaikos (1-7) | 1-2, 0-5 |
| Slovan Bratislava v BK 1903 Copenhagen (4-3) | 2-1, 2-2 |
| Everton v Keflavik (9-2) | 6-2, 3-0 |
| Bor Moenchengladbach v EPA Larnaca (16-0) | 6-0, 10-0 |
| Fenerbahce v Carl Zeiss Jena (0-5) | 0-4, 0-1 |
| Sporting Lisbon v Floriana (9-0) | 5-0, 4-0 |
| Ujpest Dozsa v Red Star Belgrade (2-4) | 2-0, 0-4 |
| Feyenoord† v UT Arad (1-1) | 1-1, 0-0 |
| Atlético Madrid v FK Austria (4-1) | 2-0, 2-1 |
| Cagliari v St Etienne (3-1) | 3-0, 0-1 |
| Gothenburg v Legia Warsaw (1-6) | 0-4, 1-2 |
| Rosenborg v Standard Liège (0-7) | 0-2, 0-5 |
| Celtic v KPV Kokkola (14-0) | 9-0, 5-0 |
| Glentoran v Waterford (1-4) | 1-3, 0-1 |
| Moscow Spartak v Basle† (4-4) | 3-2, 1-2 |
| Nendori Tirana v Ajax Amsterdam (2-4) | 2-2, 0-2 |

**Second Round**

| | |
|---|---|
| Panathinaikos v Slovan Bratislava (4-2) | 3-0, 1-2 |
| Bor Moenchengladbach v Everton* (2-2) | 1-1, 1-1 |
| Carl Zeiss Jena v Sporting Lisbon (4-2) | 2-1, 2-1 |
| Red Star Belgrade v UT Arad (6-1) | 3-0, 3-1 |
| Cagliari v Atlético Madrid (2-4) | 2-1, 0-3 |
| Standard Liège v Legia Warsaw (1-2) | 1-0, 0-2 |
| Waterford v Celtic (2-10) | 0-7, 2-3 |
| Ajax Amsterdam v Basle (5-1) | 3-0, 2-1 |

**Quarter-Final**

| | |
|---|---|
| Everton v Panathinaikos† (1-1) | 1-1, 0-0 |
| Carl Zeiss Jena v Red Star Belgrade (3-6) | 3-2, 0-4 |
| Atlético Madrid† v Legia Warsaw (2-2) | 1-0, 1-2 |
| Ajax Amsterdam v Celtic (3-1) | 3-0, 0-1 |

**Semi-Final**

| | |
|---|---|
| Red Star Belgrade v Panathinaikos† (4-4) | 4-1, 0-3 |
| Atlético Madrid v Ajax Amsterdam (1-3) | 1-0, 0-3 |

*Won on penalties.
†Won on away goals counting double.

### Final 1970–71: Ajax Amsterdam 2, Panathinaikos 0
(At Wembley, 2 June, 1971, 90,000)

*Ajax Amsterdam:* Stuy; Vasovic, Suurbier; Hulshoff, Rijnders (Haan), Neeskens; Swart (Blankenburg), Muhren, Keizer, Van Dijk, Cruyff.

*Panathinaikos:* Economopoulos; Tomaros, Vlahos; Elefterakis, Kamaras, Sourpis; Grammos, Filokouris, Antoniadis, Domazos, Kapsis.

*Scorers:* Ajax Amsterdam – Van Dijk, Kapsis og.

# EUROPEAN CUP 1971–72

**Preliminary Round**

| | |
|---|---|
| Valencia v US Luxembourg (4-1) | 3-1, 1-0 |

**First Round**

| | |
|---|---|
| Galatasaray v CSKA Moscow (1-4) | 1-1, 0-3 |
| Standard Liège v Linfield (5-2) | 2-0, 3-2 |
| BK 1903 Copenhagen v Celtic (2-4) | 2-1, 0-3 |
| Feyenoord v Olympiakos Nicosia (17-0) | 8-0, 9-0 |
| Inter-Milan v AEK Athens (6-4) | 4-1, 2-3 |
| Ujpest Dozsa v Malmö FF (4-1) | 4-0, 0-1 |
| Valencia* v Hajduk Split (1-1) | 0-0, 1-1 |
| Cork Hibs v Bor Moenchengladbach (1-7) | 0-5, 1-2 |
| Wacker Innsbruck v Benfica (1-7) | 0-4, 1-3 |
| Ajax Amsterdam v Dynamo Dresden (2-0) | 2-0, 0-0 |
| Stromsgodset v Arsenal (1-7) | 1-3, 0-4 |
| Dynamo Bucharest* v Spartak Trnava (2-2) | 0-0, 2-2 |
| Marseille v Gornik Zabrze (3-2) | 2-1, 1-1 |
| CSKA Sofia v Partizan Tirana (4-0) | 3-0, 1-0 |
| Lahden Reipas v Grasshoppers (1-9) | 1-1, 0-8 |
| Akranes v Sliema Wanderers (0-4) | 0-4, 0-0 |

**Second Round**

| | |
|---|---|
| CSKA Moscow v Standard Liège (1-2) | 1-0, 0-2 |
| Dynamo Bucharest v Feyenoord (0-5) | 0-3, 0-2 |
| Valencia v Ujpest Dozsa (1-3) | 0-1, 1-2 |
| Inter-Milan v Bor Moenchengladbach (4-2) | 4-2, 0-0 |
| Benfica v CSKA Sofia (2-1) | 2-1, 0-0 |
| Grasshoppers v Arsenal (0-5) | 0-2, 0-3 |
| Marseille v Ajax Amsterdam (2-6) | 1-2, 1-4 |
| Celtic v Sliema Wanderers (7-1) | 5-0, 2-1 |

**Quarter-Final**

| | |
|---|---|
| Ajax Amsterdam v Arsenal (3-1) | 2-1, 1-0 |
| Feyenoord v Benfica (2-5) | 1-0, 1-5 |
| Ujpest Dozsa v Celtic (2-3) | 1-2, 1-1 |
| Inter-Milan* v Standard Liège (2-2) | 1-0, 1-2 |

**Semi-Final**

| | |
|---|---|
| Ajax Amsterdam v Benfica (1-0) | 1-0, 0-0 |
| Inter-Milan† v Celtic (0-0) | 0-0, 0-0 |

*Won on away goals rule.
†Won on penalty kicks after extra time.

### Final 1971–72: Ajax Amsterdam 2, Inter-Milan 0
(In Rotterdam, 31 May, 1972, 67,000)

*Ajax Amsterdam:* Stuy; Suurbier, Blankenburg, Hulshoff, Krol, Neeskens, Haan, Muhren G., Swart, Cruyff, Keizer.

*Inter-Milan:* Bordon; Burgnich, Bellugi, Oriali, Facchetti, Bedin, Mazzola, Giubertoni (Bertini), Jair (Pellizzaro), Boninsegna, Frustalupi.

*Scorers:* Ajax Amsterdam – Cruyff 2.

## EUROPEAN CUP 1972–73

**Byes:** Ajax Amsterdam, Spartak Trnava.

| First Round | | | |
|---|---|---|---|
| Real Madrid v Keflavik (4-0) | 3-0, 1-0 | Spartak Trnava v Anderlecht (2-0) | 1-0, 1-0 |
| Anderlecht v Vejle (7-2) | 4-2, 3-0 | Derby Co v Benfica (3-0) | 3-0, 0-0 |
| Ujpest Dozsa v Basle (4-3) | 2-0, 2-3 | Celtic v Ujpest Dozsa (2-4) | 2-1, 0-3 |
| Celtic v Rosenborg (5-2) | 2-1, 3-1 | Dynamo Kiev v Gornik Zabrze (3-2) | 2-0, 1-2 |
| Galatasaray v Bayern Munich (1-7) | 1-1, 0-6 | Juventus v FC Magdeburg (2-0) | 1-0, 1-0 |
| Marseille v Juventus (1-3) | 1-0, 0-3 | Arges Pitesti v Real Madrid (3-4) | 2-1, 1-3 |
| Malmö FF v Benfica (2-4) | 1-0, 1-4 | CSKA Sofia v Ajax Amsterdam (1-6) | 1-3, 0-3 |
| TS Innsbruck v Dynamo Kiev (0-3) | 0-1, 0-2 | | |
| CSKA Sofia v Panathinaikos (4-1) | 2-1, 2-0 | **Quarter-Final** | |
| Sliema Wand v Gornik Zabrze (0-10) | 0-5, 0-5 | Juventus* v Ujpest Dozsa (2-2) | 0-0, 2-2 |
| FC Magdeburg v Turun Palloreura (9-1) | 6-0, 3-1 | Spartak Trnava v Derby Co (1-2) | 1-0, 0-2 |
| Aris Bonnevoie v Arges Pitesti (0-6) | 0-2, 0-4 | Dynamo Kiev v Real Madrid (0-3) | 0-0, 0-3 |
| Derby Co v Zeljeznicar (4-1) | 2-0, 2-1 | Ajax Amsterdam v Bayern Munich (5-2) | 4-0, 1-2 |
| Waterford v Omonia Nicosia (2-3) | 2-1, 0-2 | | |
| | | **Semi-Final** | |
| **Second Round** | | Juventus v Derby Co (3-1) | 3-1, 0-0 |
| Omonia Nicosia v Bayern Munich (0-13) | 0-9, 0-4 | Ajax Amsterdam v Real Madrid (3-1) | 2-1, 1-0 |

*Won on away goals rule.*

### Final 1972–73: Ajax Amsterdam 1, Juventus 0
(In Belgrade, 30 May, 1973, 93,500)

*Ajax Amsterdam:* Stuy; Suurbier, Krol, Neeskens, Hulshoff, Blankenburg, Rep, Haan, Cruyff, Muhren G., Keizer.

*Juventus:* Zoff; Longobucco, Marchetti, Furino, Morini, Salvadore, Altafini, Causio (Cuccureddu), Anastasi, Capello, Bettega (Haller).

*Scorer:* Ajax Amsterdam – Rep.

## EUROPEAN CUP 1973–74

**Bye:** Ajax Amsterdam

| First Round | | | |
|---|---|---|---|
| Waterford v Ujpest Dozsa (2-6) | 2-3, 0-3 | Celtic v Vejle (1-0) | 0-0, 1-0 |
| Bayern Munich v Atvidaberg (4-4) | 3-1, 1-3 | Spartak Trnava v Sarja Voroshilovgrad (1-0) | 0-0, 1-0 |
| Benfica v Olympiakos Piraeus (2-0) | 1-0, 1-0 | Red Star Belgrade v Liverpool (4-2) | 2-1, 2-1 |
| Turku v Celtic (1-9) | 1-6, 0-3 | Bruges v Basle (6-7) | 2-1, 4-6 |
| Dynamo Dresden v Juventus (4-3) | 2-0, 2-3 | Dinamo Bucharest v Atlético Madrid (2-4) | 0-2, 2-2 |
| Sarja Voroshilovgrad v Apoel Nicosia (3-0) | 2-0, 1-0 | Ajax Amsterdam v CSKA Sofia (1-2) | 1-0, 0-2 |
| Red Star Belgrade v Stal Mielec (3-1) | 2-1, 1-0 | Bayern Munich v Dynamo Dresden (7-6) | 4-3, 3-3 |
| Bruges v Floriana (10-0) | 8-0, 2-0 | | |
| Jeunesse D'Esch v Liverpool (1-3) | 1-1, 0-2 | **Quarter-Final** | |
| Atlético Madrid v Galatasaray (1-0) | 0-0, 1-0 | Spartak Trnava† v Ujpest Dozsa (2-2) | 1-1, 1-1 |
| Viking Stavanger v Spartak Trnava (1-3) | 1-2, 0-1 | Bayern Munich v CSKA Sofia (5-3) | 4-1, 1-2 |
| Vejle v Nantes (3-2) | 2-2, 1-0 | Red Star Belgrade v Atlético Madrid (0-2) | 0-2, 0-0 |
| CSKA Sofia v SW Innsbruck (4-0) | 3-0, 1-0 | Basle v Celtic (5-6) | 3-2, 2-4 |
| Frem Reykjavik v Basle (2-11) | 0-5, 2-6 | | |
| Crusaders v Dinamo Bucharest (0-12) | 0-1, 0-11 | **Semi-Final** | |
| | | Ujpest Dozsa v Bayern Munich (1-4) | 1-1, 0-3 |
| **Second Round** | | Celtic v Atlético Madrid (0-2) | 0-0, 0-2 |
| Benfica v Ujpest Dozsa (1-3) | 1-1, 0-2 | | |

†*Won on penalty kicks.*

### Final 1973–74: Bayern Munich 1, Atlético Madrid 1
(In Brussels, 15 May, 1974, 65,000)

*Bayern Munich:* Maier; Hansen, Breitner, Schwarzenbeck, Beckenbauer, Roth, Torstensson (Durnberger), Zobel, Müller, Hoeness, Kappelmann.

*Atlético Madrid:* Reina; Melo, Capon, Adelardo, Heredia, Eusebio, Ufarte (Becerra), Luis, Garate, Irureta, Salcedo (Alberto).

*Scorers:* Bayern Munich – Schwarzenbech; Atlético Madrid – Luis.

### Replay: Bayern Munich 4, Atlético Madrid 0
(In Brussels, 17 May, 1974, 65,000)

*Bayern Munich:* Maier; Hansen, Breitner; Schwarzenbeck, Beckenbauer, Roth, Torstensson, Zobel, Müller, Hoeness, Kappelmann.

*Atlético Madrid:* Reina; Melo, Capon, Adelardo (Benegas), Heredia, Eusebio, Luis, Garate, Salcedo, Alberto, Ufarte (Becerra).

*Scorers:* Bayern Munich – Müller 2, Hoeness 2.

# EUROPEAN CUP 1974–75

**First Round, First Leg**

Leeds U 4 (*Lorimer pen, Clarke 2, Jordan*), Zurich 1 (*Katic*)
Celtic 1 (*Wilson*), Olympiakos Piraeus 1 (*Viera*)
Uni Craiova 2 (*Oblemenco 2*), Atvidaberg 1 (*Bo Augustsson*)
Valletta 1 (*Magro*), HJK Helsinki 0
Levski Spartak 0, Ujpest Dozsa 3 (*Horvath, Bene, Antal Dunai*)
Jeunesse D'Esch 2 (*Mond, Guiliani*), Fenerbahce 3 (*Osman, Cemel, Ender*)
Viking Stavanger 0, Ararat Erevan 2 (*Markarov 2*)
Hvidovre 0, Ruch Chorzow 0
Slovan Bratislava 4 (*Novotny, Masny 2, Svehlik*), Anderlecht 2 (*Coeck, Van Himst*)
Feyenoord 7 (*Schoenmaker, Kreuz 3, Van Hanegem 2, Ressel*), Coleraine 0
St Etienne 2 (*Herve Revelli, Bereta*), Sporting Lisbon 0
VOEST Linz 0, Barcelona 0
Hajduk Split 7 (*Zungul 2, Surjak 2, Jerkovic, Buljan, Boljat*), Keflavik 1 (*Jonsson*)

**First Round, Second Leg**

Zurich 2 (*Katic, Rutschmann pen*), Leeds U 1 (*Clarke*)
Olympiakos Piraeus 2 (*Kritikopoulos, Stravropoulos*), Celtic 0
Atvidaberg 3 (*Andersson, Almqvist 2*), Uni Craiova 1 (*Badin*)
HJK Helsinki 4 (*Rahja, Peltonen, Hamalainen, Forsell*), Valletta 1 (*Gigilo*)
Ujpest Dozsa 4 (*Bene 2, Antal Dunai 2*), Levski Spartak 1 (*Voinov*)
Fenerbahce 2 (*Cemil, Yilmaz*), Jeunesse D'Esch 0
Ararat Erevan 4 (*Markarov 3, Bondarenko*), Viking Stavanger 2
Ruch Chorzow 2 (*Bula 2*), Hvidovre 1 (*Pedersen B.*)
Anderlecht 3 (*Van Himst, Coeck, Thijssen*), Slovan Bratislava 1(*Masny*)
Coleraine 1 (*Simpson*), Feyenoord 4 (*Schoenmaker 3, Kreuz*)
Sporting Lisbon 1 (*Yazalde*), St Etienne 1 (*Herve Revelli*)
Barcelona 5 (*Clares 2, Asensi, Juan Carlos, Cruyff*), VOEST Linz 0
Keflavik 0, Hajduk Split 2 (*Dzoni, Mijac*)
Bayern Munich and Magdeburg received byes; Cork Celtic had a walkover when Omonia Nicosia withdrew.

**Second Round, First Leg**

Ujpest Dozsa 1 (*Fazekas pen*), Leeds U 2 (*Lorimer, McQueen*)
Bayern Munich 3 (*Müller 2, Wunder*), Magdeburg 2 (*Hoffmann, Sparwasser*)

Hajduk Split 4 (*Jerkovic 2, Zungul, Mijac*), St Etienne 1 (*Herve Revelli*)
Feyenoord 0, Barcelona 0
Cork Celtic 1 (*Tambling*), Ararat Erevan 2 (*Zanazanyan, Kazaryan*)
Ruch Chorzow 2 (*Kopicera, Beniger*), Fenerbahce 1 (*Niazi*)
HJK Helsinki 0, Atvidaberg 3 (*Almqvist 2, Hasselberg*)
Anderlecht 5 (*Rensenbrink 3 [2 pens], Ladinszky, Van der Elst*), Olympiakos Piraeus 1 (*Persides pen*)

**Second Round, Second Leg**

Leeds U 3 (*McQueen, Yorath, Bremner*), Ujpest Dozsa 1
Magdeburg 1 (*Sparwasser*), Bayern Munich 2 (*Müller 2*)
St Etienne 5 (*Triantafilos 2, Bathenay, Synaeghel, Larque*), Hajduk Split 1 (*Jovanic*)
Barcelona 3 (*Rexach 3*), Feyenoord 0
Ararat Erevan 5 (*Markarov 2, Andriassian, Kazaryan 2*), Cork Celtic 0
Fenerbahce 0, Ruch Chorzow 2 (*Kopicera, Chojnacki*)
Atvidaberg 1 (*Almqvist*), HJK Helsinki 0
Olympiakos Piraeus 3 (*Galakos 3*), Anderlecht 0

**Quarter-Final, First Leg**

Bayern Munich (0) 2 (*Hoeness, Torstensson*), Ararat Erevan (0) 0
Leeds U (2) 3 (*Jordan, McQueen, Lorimer*), Anderlecht (0) 0
Ruch Chorzow (2) 3 (*Maszczyk, Beniger, Bula pen*), St Etienne (0) 2 (*Larque, Triantafilos*)
Barcelona (1) 2 (*Mario Marinho, Clares*), Atvidaberg (0) 0

**Quarter-Final, Second Leg**

Atvidaberg (0) 0, Barcelona (1) 3 (*Gallego, Asensi, Neeskens*)
St Etienne (1) 2 (*Janvion, Herve, Revelli pen*), Ruch Chorzow (0) 0
Ararat Erevan (1) 1 (*Andriassian*), Bayern Munich (0) 0
Anderlecht (0) 0, Leeds U (0) 1 (*Bremner*)

**Semi-Final, First Leg**

St Etienne (0) 0, Bayern Munich (0) 0
Leeds U (1) 2 (*Bremner, Clarke*), Barcelona (0) 1 (*Asensi*)

**Semi-Final, Second Leg**

Bayern Munich (1) 2 (*Beckenbauer, Durnberger*), St Etienne (0) 0
Barcelona (0) 1 (*Clares*), Leeds U (1) 1 (*Lorimer*)

## Final 1974–75: Bayern Munich 2, Leeds U 0

(In Paris, 28 May, 1975, 50,000)

*Bayern Munich:* Maier; Durnberger, Andersson (Weiss), Schwarzenbeck, Beckenbauer, Roth, Torstensson, Zobel, Müller, Hoeness (Wunder), Kapellmann.

*Leeds U:* Stewart; Reaney, Gray F., Bremner, Madeley, Hunter, Lorimer, Clarke, Jordan, Giles, Yorath (Gray E.).

*Scorers:* Bayern Munich – Roth, Müller.

# EUROPEAN CUP 1975-76

**First Round, First Leg**
Benfica 7 (*Sheu, Nene 3, Jordao 3*), Fenerbahce 0
Borussia Moenchengladbach 1 (*Simonsen pen*), Swarowski Innsbruck 1 (*Welzl*)
KB Copenhagen 0, St Etienne 2 (*P. Revelli, Larque*)
CSKA Sofia 2 (*Denev, Marashliev*), Juventus 1 (*Anastasi*)
Floriana 0, Hajduk Split 5 (Zungul 3, Buljan, Surjak)
Jeunesse D'Esch 0, Bayern Munich 5 (*Wunder, Schuster 2, Rummenigge 2*)
Linfield 1 (*P. Malone*), PSV Eindhoven 2 (*Rene Van der Kerkhof, Edstrom*)
Malmö 2 (*Cervin, Bo Larsson*), Magdeburg 1 (*Hoffmann*)
Olympiakos 2 (*Kritikopoulos, Aidiniou*), Dynamo Kiev 2 (*Kolotov, Burjak*)
Rangers 4 (*Fyfe, Burge og, O'Hara, Johnstone*), Bohemians 1 (*Flanagan*)
Real Madrid 4 (*Santillana 2, Roberto Martinez, Netzer*), Dinamo Bucharest 1 (*Lucescu*)
Ruch Chorzow 5 (*Marx 2, Bula, Beniger, Kopicera*), Kuopion Palloseura 0
Slovan Bratislava 1 (*Masny*), Derby Co 0
Ujpest Dozsa 4 (*Fazekas, Dunai, Toth pen, Keleman*), Zurich 0
RWD Molenbeek 3 (*Boskamp, Teugals, Wellens*), Viking Stavanger 2 (*Johansson, Kvia*)
Omonia Nicosia 2 (*Philippou 2*), Akranes 1 (*Alfredsson*)

**First Round, Second Leg**
Akranes 4 (*M. Hallgrimsson 2, T. Thordarson, K. Thordarson*), Omonia Nicosia 0
Viking Stavanger 0, RWD Molenbeek 1 (*Neilsen*)
Bayern Munich 3 (*Schuster 3*), Jeunesse D'Esch 1 (*Zwally*)
Bohemians 1 (*T. O'Connor*), Rangers 1 (*Johnstone*)
Derby Co 3 (*Bourne, Lee 2*), Slovan Bratislava 0
Dinamo Bucharest 1 (*Satmareanu*), Real Madrid 0
Dynamo Kiev 1 (*Onischenko*), Olympiakos 0
Fenerbahce 1 (*Engin*), Benfica 0
Hajduk Split 3 (*Buljan, Djordjevic, Salvov*), Floriana 0
Juventus 2 (*Furino, Anastasi*), CSKA Sofia 0
Kuopion Palloseura 2 (*Toernroos, Heiskanen*), Ruch Chorzow 2 (*Chojnacki, Faber*)
Magdeburg 2 (*Hoffmann, Streich*), Malmö 1 (*Andersson*)
PSV Eindhoven 8 (*Lubse 2, Dahlqvist, Willy Van der Kerkhof, Van der Kuylen, Edstrom, Deacy 2*), Linfield 0
St Etienne 3 (*Rocheteau, Patrick Revelli, Larque*), KB Copenhagen 1 (*Petersen*)
Swarowski Innsbruck 6 (*Stielike, Simonsen, Heynckes 4*), Borussia Moenchengladbach 1 (*Flindt*)
Zurich 5 (*Katic, Risi 3, Kuhn*), Ujpest Dozsa 1 (*Nagy*)

**Second Round, First Leg**
Benfica 5 (*Moinhos, Sheu, Vitor Baptista 2, Toni*), Ujpest Dozsa 2 (*Dunai A., Fazekas*)

Borussia Moenchengladbach 2 (*Heynckes, Simonsen*), Juventus 0
Derby Co 4 (*George 3 [2 pens], Nish*), Real Madrid 1 (*Pirri*)
Dynamo Kiev 3 (*Burjak 2, Blokhin*), Akranes 0
Hajduk Split 4 (*Zungul, Rozic, Surjak, Mijac*), RWD Molenbeek 0
Malmö 1 (*Andersson T.*), Bayern Munich 0
Ruch Chorzow 1 (*Bula*), PSV Eindhoven 3 (*Lubse, Edstrom, Rene Van der Kerkhof*)
St Etienne 2 (*Patrick Revelli, Bathenay*), Rangers 0

**Second Round, Second Leg**
Akranes 0, Dynamo Kiev 2 (*Onischenko, Gunnlaugsson og*)
Bayern Munich 2 (*Durnberger pen, Torstensson*), Malmö 0
Juventus 2 (*Gori, Bettega*), Borussia Moenchengladbach 2 (*Danner, Simonsen*)
PSV Eindhoven 4 (*Rene Van der Kerkhof, Van der Kuylen 2, Lubse*), Ruch Chorzow 0
Rangers 1 (*MacDonald*), St Etienne 2 (*Rocheteau, Herve Revelli*)
Real Madrid 5 (*Roberto Martinez 2, Santillana 2, Pirri pen*), Derby Co 1 (*George*)
RWD Molenbeek 2 (*Teugels, Nielsen pen*), Hajduk Split 3 (*Surjak, Zungul, Jovanic*)
Ujpest Dozsa 3 (*Bene 2, Nagy L.*), Benfica 1 (*Nene*)

**Quarter-Final, First Leg**
Benfica 0, Bayern Munich 0
Borussia Moenchengladbach 2 (*Jensen, Wittkamp*), Real Madrid 2 (*Roberto Martinez, Pirri*)
Dynamo Kiev 2 (*Konkov, Blokhin*), St Etienne 0
Hajduk Split 2 (*Mijac, Surjak*), PSV Eindhoven 0

**Quarter-Final, Second Leg**
Bayern Munich 5 (*Durnberger 2, Rummenigge, Müller 2*), Benfica 1 (*Barros*)
PSV Eindhoven 3 (*Dahlqvist, Lubse, Van der Kuylen*), Hajduk Split 0
Real Madrid 1 (*Santillana*), Borussia Moenchengladbach 1 (*Heynckes*)
St Etienne 3 (*Herve Revelli, Larque, Rocheteau*), Dynamo Kiev 0 (*after extra time*)

**Semi-Final, First Leg**
Real Madrid 1 (*Roberto Martinez*), Bayern Munich 1 (*Müller*)
St Etienne 1 (*Larque*), PSV Eindhoven 0

**Semi-Final, Second Leg**
Bayern Munich 2 (*Müller 2*), Real Madrid 0
PSV Eindhoven 0, St Etienne 0

## Final 1975-76: Bayern Munich 1, St Etienne 0
(At Hampden Park, 12 May, 1976, 54,864)

*Bayern Munich:* Maier; Hansen, Schwarzenbeck, Beckenbauer, Horsmann, Roth, Durnberger, Kapellmann, Rummenigge, Müller, Hoeness.

*St Etienne:* Curkovic; Repellini, Piazza, Lopez, Janvion, Bathenay, Santini, Larque, Patrick Revelli, Herve Revelli, Sarramagna (Rocheteau).

*Scorer:* Bayern Munich – Roth.

# EUROPEAN CUP 1976–77

**First Round, First Leg**

Akranes 1 (*Sveinsson*), Trabzonspor 3 (*Perikli, Ali Kemal 2*)

Austria/WAC 1 (*Daxbacher*), Borussia Moenchengladbach 0

FC Bruges 2 (*Davies pen, Verbeeke*), Steaua Bucharest 1 (*Troi*)

CSKA Sofia 0, St Etienne 0

Dynamo Dresden 2 (*Kotte pen, Riedel*), Benfica 0

Dundalk 1 (*McDowell*), PSV Eindhoven 1 (*Van der Kuylen*)

Ferencvaros 5 (*Nyilasi 2, Magyar, Onhaus, Ebedli*), Jeunesse D'Esch 1 (*Giuliani*)

Dynamo Kiev 3 (*Onischenko, Troshkin, Blokhin pen*), Partizan Belgrade 0

Omonia Nicosia 0, PAOK Salonika 2 (*Koudas, Sarafis*)

Rangers 1 (*Parlane*), Zurich 1 (*Cucinotta*)

Stal Mielec 1 (*Sekulski*), Real Madrid 2 (*Santillani, Del Bosque*)

Viking Stavanger 2 (*Valen, Johanessen*), Banik Ostrava 1 (*Slany*)

Torino 2 (*Mozzini, Graziani*), Malmö 1 (*Jonsson*)

Liverpool 2 (*Neal pen, Toshack*), Crusaders 0

Koge 0, Bayern Munich 5 (*Torstensson 2, Müller 2, Durnberger*)

Sliema Wanderers 2 (*E. Aquilina 2*), Turun Palloseura 1 (*Mannien*)

**First Round, Second Leg**

Turun Palloseura 1 (*Suhonen*), Sliema Wanderers 0

Crusaders 0, Liverpool 5 (*Keegan, Johnson 2, McDermott, Heighway*)

Banik Ostrava 2 (*Vojacek 2*), Viking Stavanger 0

Bayern Munich 2 (*Beckenbauer, Torstensson*), Koge 1 (*Poulsen*)

Borussia Moenchengladbach 3 (*Stielike, Bonhof pen, Heynckes*), Austria/WAC 0

Jeunesse D'Esch 2 (*Zwallay 2*), Ferencvaros 6 (*Nyilasi 2 [1 pen], Pusztai 2, Szabo 2 [1 pen]*)

Malmö 1 (*Ljungberg pen*), Torino 1 (*Claudio Sala*)

PAOK Salonika 1 (*Sarafis*), Omonia Nicosia 1 (*Philippos pen*)

Partizan Belgrade 0, Dynamo Kiev 2 (*Muntian pen, Slobodan*)

PSV Eindhoven 6 (*Van der Kuylen, Postuma, Rene Van der Kerkhof 4*), Dundalk 0

St Etienne 1 (*Piazza*), CSKA Sofia 0

Steaua Bucharest 1 (*Vigu*), FC Bruges 1 (*Lambert*)

Trabzonspor 3 (*Huseyin 2, Engin*), Akranes 2 (*Pogarson 2 [1 pen]*)

Zurich 1 (*Martinelli*), Rangers 0

Real Madrid 1 (*Pirri*), Stal Mielec 0

Benfica 0, Dynamo Dresden 0

**Second Round, First Leg**

Dynamo Kiev 4 (*Burjak 2, Kolotov, Slobodan*), PAOK Salonika 0

Ferencvaros 1 (*Onhaus*), Dynamo Dresden 0

Real Madrid 0, FC Bruges 0

St Etienne 1 (*Piazza*), PSV Eindhoven 0

Torino 1 (*Wittkamp og*), Borussia Moenchengladbach 2 (*Vogts, Klinkhammer*)

Trabzonspor 1 (*Cemil pen*), Liverpool 0

Zurich 2 (*Cucinottā, Scheiwiler*), Turun Palloseura 0

Banik Ostrava 2 (*Lorenc, Licka*), Bayern Munich 1 (*Müller*)

**Second Round, Second Leg**

Bayern Munich 5 (*Müller 2, Rummenigge, Kapellmann, Torstensson*), Banik Ostrava 0

Borussia Moenchengladbach 0, Torino 0

FC Bruges 2 (*Le Fevre, Camacho og*), Real Madrid 0

Dynamo Dresden 4 (*Heidler, Schmuck, Riedel, Kotte*), Ferencvaros 0

Liverpool 3 (*Heighway, Johnson, Keegan*), Trabzonspor 0

Turun Palloseura 0, Zurich 1 (*Cucinotta*)

PAOK Salonika 0, Dynamo Kiev 2 (*Kolotov, Blokhin*)

PSV Eindhoven 0, St Etienne 0

**Quarter-Final, First Leg**

Bayern Munich 1 (*Kunkel*), Dynamo Kiev 0

Borussia Moenchengladbach 2 (*Kulik, Simonsen*), FC Bruges 2 (*Cools, Courant*)

St Etienne 1 (*Bathenay*), Liverpool 0

Zurich 2 (*Cucinotta, Risi*), Dynamo Dresden 1 (*Kreische*)

**Quarter-Final, Second Leg**

FC Bruges 0, Borussia Moenchengladbach 1 (*Hannes*)

Dynamo Dresden 3 (*Schade pen, Kreische 2*), Zurich 2 (*Cucinotta, Risi*)

Dynamo Kiev 2 (*Burjak pen, Slobodan*), Bayern Munich 0

Liverpool 3 (*Keegan, Kennedy, Fairclough*), St Etienne 1 (*Bathenay*)

**Semi-Final, First Leg**

Dynamo Kiev 1 (*Onischenko*), Borussia Moenchengladbach 0

Zurich 1 (*Risi pen*), Liverpool 3 (*Neal 2 [1 pen], Heighway*)

**Semi-Final, Second Leg**

Borussia Moenchengladbach 2 (*Bonhof pen, Wittkamp*), Dynamo Kiev 0

Liverpool 1 (*Case 2, Keegan*), Zurich 0

### Final 1976–77: Liverpool 3, Borussia Moenchengladbach 1
(In Rome, 25 May, 1977, 57,000)

*Liverpool:* Clemence; Neal, Jones, Smith, Kennedy, Hughes, Keegan, Case, Heighway, Callaghan, McDermott.

*Borussia Moenchengladbach:* Kneib; Vogts, Klinkhammer, Wittkamp, Bonhof, Wohlers (Hannes), Simonsen, Wimmer (Kulik), Stielike, Schaffer, Heynckes.

*Scorers:* Liverpool – McDermott, Smith, Neal (pen); Borussia Moenchengladbach – Simonsen.

## EUROPEAN CUP 1977—78

**First Round, First Leg**
Basle 1 (*Von Wartburg*), SW Innsbruck 3 (*Welzl 2 [1 pen], Constantini*)
Celtic 5 (*McDonald, Wilson, Craig 2, McLaughlin*), Jeunesse Esch 0
Benfica 0, Moscow Torpedo 0
Dynamo Dresden 2 (*Heidler, Schade*), Halmstad 0
Dukla Prague 1 (*Vizek*), Nantes 1 (*Amisse*)
Floriana 1 (*George Xuereb*), Panathinaikos 1 (*Aslanidis*)
Kuopion Palloseura 0, FC Bruges 4 (*Van der Eycken, Cools, Lambert, Davies*)
Levsky Spartak 3 (*Panov, Milanov 2*), Slask Wroclaw 0
Lillestrom 2 (*Lonsdal, Johansen*), Ajax Amsterdam 0
Omonia 0 Juventus 3 (*Bettega, Fanna, Virdis*)
Red Star Belgrade 3 (*Dzajic 2, Filipovic*), Sligo Rovers 0
Trabzonspor 1 (*Necdet*), BK 03 Copenhagen 0
Vasas 0, Borussia Moenchengladbach 3 (*Schaefer, Simonsen, Wohlers*)
Valur 1 (*Magnus Bergs*), Glentoran 0
Dinamo Bucharest 2 (*Vrinceanu, Georgescu*), Atlético Madrid 1 (*Luis Pereira*)

**First Round, Second Leg**
Ajax Amsterdam 4 (*Birkelund og, Geels, La Ling 2*), Lillestrom 0
Atlético Madrid 2 (*Benegas, Ruben Cano*), Dinamo Bucharest 0
BK 03 Copenhagen 2 (*Francker 2*), Trabzonspor 0
Borussia Moenchengladbach 1 (*Simonsen*), Vasas 1 (*Izso*)
FC Bruges 5 (*Davies 2, Van der Eycken, Simoen, Maes*), Kuopion Palloseura 2 (*Rissanen, Laikonen*)
Halmstad 2 (Johansson, Larsson), Dynamo Dresden 1 (Heidler)
Jeunesse Esch 1 (*Giuliano*), Celtic 6 (*Lennox 2, Glavin, McLaughlin, Edvaldsson 2*)
Juventus 2 (Boninsegna, Virdis), Omonia 0
Nantes 0, Dukla Prague 0
Panathinaikos 4 (*Alvarez, Antoniadis 2 [1 pen], Gonios*), Floriana 0
Slask Wroclaw 2 (*Pawlowsky, Kopycky*), Levski Spartak 2 (*Panov 2*)
Sligo Rovers 0, Red Star Belgrade 3 (*Filipovic 2, Jovanovic*)
SW Innsbruck 0, Basle 1 (*Miessen*)
Moscow Torpedo 0, Benfica 0
*Benfica won 4-1 on penalties.*
Glentoran 2 (*Robson, Jamison*), Valur 0

**Second Round, First Leg**
Benfica 1 (*Pietra pen*), BK 03 Copenhagen 0
FC Bruges 2 (*Davies pen, Cools*), Panathinaikos 0
Celtic 2 (*Craig, Burns*), SW Innsbruck 1 (*Kriess*)

Glentoran 0, Juventus 1 (*Causio*)
Levski Spartak 1 (*Voinov pen*), Ajax Amsterdam 2 (*Geels, Erkens*)
Liverpool 5 (*Hansen, Case 2, Neal pen, Kennedy*), Dynamo Dresden 1 (*Hafner*)
Nantes 1 (*Lacombe*), Atlético Madrid 1 (*Marcial*)
Red Star Belgrade 0, Borussia Moenchengladbach 3 (*Schaffer, Heynckes, Simonsen*)

**Second Round, Second Leg**
Ajax Amsterdam 2 (*Lerby, Geels*), Levski Spartak 1 (*Milanov*)
Atlético Madrid 2 (*Ruben Cano, Luis Pereira*), Nantes 1 (*Lacombe*)
Borussia Moenchengladbach 5 (*Simonsen 2, Heynckes, Nikolic og, Wittkamp*), Red Star Belgrade 1 (*Susic*)
BK 03 Copenhagen 0, Benfica 1 (*Pietra*)
Dynamo Dresden 2 (*Kotte, Sachse*), Liverpool 1 (*Heighway*)
SW Innsbruck 3 (*Welzl, Stering, Oberacher*), Celtic 0
Juventus 5 (Virdis 2, Boninsegna, Fanna, Benetti), Glentoran 0
Panathinaikos 1 (*Gonios*), FC Bruges 0

**Quarter-Final, First Leg**
Benfica 1 (*Nene*), Liverpool 2 (*Case, Hughes*)
Ajax Amsterdam 1 (*Van Dord*), Juventus 1 (*Causio*)
FC Bruges 2 (*Courant, De Cubber*), Atlético Madrid 0
SW Innsbruck 3 (*Peter Koncilia, Kriess, Werner Schwarz*), Borussia Moenchengladbach 1 (*Heynckes*)

**Quarter-Final, Second Leg**
Juventus 1 (*Tardelli*), Ajax Amsterdam 1 (*La Ling*)
*Juventus won 3-0 on penalties.*
Atlético Madrid 3 (*Benegas, Marcial 2*), FC Bruges 2 (*Cools, Lambert*)
Liverpool 4 (*Callaghan, Dalglish, McDermott, Neal*), Benfica 1 (*Nene*)
Borussia Moenchengladbach 2 (*Bonhof pen, Heynckes*), SW Innsbruck 0

**Semi-Final, First Leg**
Borussia Moenchengladbach 2 (*Hannes, Bonhof*), Liverpool 1 (*Johnson*)
Juventus 1 (*Bettega*), FC Bruges 0

**Semi-Final, Second Leg**
Liverpool 3 (*Kennedy, Dalglish, Case*), Borussia Moenchengladbach 0
FC Bruges 2 (*Bastijns, Van der Eycken*), Juventus 0

---

**Final 1977—78: Liverpool 1, FC Bruges 0**
(At Wembley, 10 May, 1978, 92,000)

*Liverpool:* Clemence; Neal, Thompson, Hansen, Hughes, McDermott, Kennedy, Souness, Case (Heighway), Fairclough, Dalglish.

*FC Bruges:* Jensen; Bastijns, Krieger, Leekens, Maes (Volders), Cools, De Cubber, Van der Eycken, Ku (Sanders), Simoen, Sorensen.

*Scorer:* Liverpool – Dalglish.

## EUROPEAN CUP 1978–79

**Preliminary Round, First Leg**
Monaco 3 (Onnis, Zorzetto, Nogues), Steaua 0

**Preliminary Round, Second Leg**
Steaua 2 (Troi 2), Monaco 0

**First Round, First Leg**
Juventus 1 (Virdis), Rangers 0
Real Madrid 5 (Jensen, Juanito 2, Del Bosque, Wolff), Progress Niedercorn 0
AEK Athens 6 (Bajevic 2, Ardizoglou, Tassos, Nikolau, Mavros), Porto 1 (Oliveira)
Fenerbahce 2 (Rasit, Cemil), PSV Eindhoven 1 (Brandts)
Nottingham F 2 (Birtles, Barrett), Liverpool 0
Vllaznia 2 (Zhega, Ballgijni), Austria/WAC 0
Malmö 0, Monaco 0
Linfield 0, Lillestrom 0
Cologne 4 (Littbarski, Neumann 2, Konopka), Akranes 1 (Hallgrimsson)
Zbrojovka Brno 2 (Kroupa, Janecka), Ujpest Dozsa 2 (Fekete, Torocsik)
Partizan Belgrade 2 (Prekazi, Djurovic), Dynamo Dresden 0
Grasshoppers 8 (Sulser 5, Ponte 2, Wehrli), Valletta 0
Bruges 2 (Cuelemans, Cools), Wisla Krakow 1 (Kapka)
Odense 2 (Jensen M. 2), Lokomotiv Sofia 2 (Kolev, Veliotzkov)
Valkeakosken 0, Dynamo Kiev 1 (Boltatsha)
Omonia 2 (Kanaris, Gootkrtou), Bohemians 1 (O'Connor)

**First Round, Second Leg**
Rangers 2 (MacDonald, Smith), Juventus 0
Progress Niedercorn 0, Real Madrid 7 (Pirri, Jensen, Stielike, Santillana 2, Hernandez, Bossi og)
Porto 4 (Vital 2, Teixeira, Gomes), AEK Athens 1 (Bajevic)
PSV Eindhoven 6 (Van der Kuylen 4, Deykers 2), Fenerbahce 1 (Rasit)
Liverpool 0, Nottingham F 0
Austria/WAC 4 (Parits, Schachner 2, Robert Sara), Vllaznia 1 (Hafizi)
Monaco 0, Malmö 1 (Kinnvall)
Lillestrom 1 (Lonstad), Linfield 0
Akranes 1 (Hein og), Cologne 1 (Van Gool)
Ujpest Dozsa 0, Zbrojovka Brno 2 (Dosek, Kroupa)
Dynamo Dresden 2 (Dorner, Weber), Partizan Belgrade 0
Valletta 3 (Seychell, Agius, Farrugia), Grasshoppers 5 (Sulser, Ponte, Heinz Hermann, Traber 2)
Wisla Krakow 3 (Kmiecik, Lipka, Krupinski), Bruges 1 (Van der Eycken)
Lokomotiv Sofia 2 (Mihailov, Kostov), Odense 1 (Erikson)

Dynamo Kiev 3 (Veremeev, Khapsalis, Buriak), Valkeakosken 1 (Ronkainen)
Bohemians 1 (Joyce), Omonia 0

**Second Round, First Leg**
Real Madrid 3 (Juanito, Garcia, Santillana), Grasshoppers 1 (Sulser)
AEK Athens 1 (Mavros), Nottingham F 2 (McGovern, Birtles)
Dynamo Kiev 0, Malmö 0
Lokomotiv Sofia 0, Cologne 1 (Zimmermann)
Bohemians 0, Dynamo Dresden 0
Austria/WAC 4 (Gasselich 2, Robert Sara, Schachner), Lillestrom 1 (Dokker)
Rangers 0, PSV Eindhoven 0
Zbrojovka Brno 2 (Pesice, Kroupa), Wisla Krakow 2 (Kmiecik, Maculewicz)

**Second Round, Second Leg**
Grasshoppers 2 (Sulser 2), Real Madrid 0
Nottingham F 5 (Needham, Woodcock, Anderson, Birtles 2), AEK Athens 1 (Bajevic)
Malmö 2 (Kinnvall, Cervin), Dynamo Kiev 0
Cologne 4 (Dieter Muller 2, Van Gool, Glowacz), Lokomotiv Sofia 0
Dynamo Dresden 6 (Trautmann 2, Dorner, Schmuch, Riedl, Kotte), Bohemians 0
Lillestrom 0, Austria/WAC 0
PSV Eindhoven 2 (Lubse, Deykers), Rangers 3 (MacDonald, Watson, Johnstone)
Wisla Krakow 1 (Kapka), Zbrojovka Brno 1 (Dosek)

**Quarter-Final, First Leg**
Nottingham F 4 (Birtles, Robertson pen, Gemmill, Lloyd), Grasshoppers 1 (Sulser)
Cologne 1 (Dieter Muller), Rangers 0
Wisla Krakow 2 (Nawalka, Kmiecik), Malmö 1 (Hansson)
Austria/WAC 3 (Schachner 2, Zach), Dynamo Dresden 1 (Weber)

**Quarter-Final, Second Leg**
Grasshoppers 1 (Sulser pen), Nottingham F 1 (O'Neill)
Rangers 1 (McLean), Cologne 1 (Dieter Muller)
Malmö 4 (Ljungberg 3 [2 pens], Cervin), Wisla Krakow 1 (Kmiecik)
Dynamo 1 (Riedl pen), Austria/WAC 0

**Semi-Final, First Leg**
Nottingham F 3 (Birtles, Bowyer, Robertson), Cologne 3 (Van Gool, Dieter Muller, Okudera)
Austria/WAC 0, Malmö 0

**Semi-Final, Second Leg**
Cologne 0, Nottingham F 1 (Bowyer)
Malmö 1 (Hansson), Austria/WAC 0

**Final 1978–79: Nottingham F 1, Malmö 0**
(In Munich, 30 May, 1979, 57,500)

*Nottingham F:* Shilton; Anderson, Lloyd, Burns, Clark, Francis, McGovern, Bowyer, Robertson, Woodcock, Birtles.
*Malmö:* Moller; Roland Andersson, Jonsson, Magnus Andersson, Erlandsson, Tapper (Malmberg), Ljungberg, Prytz, Kinnvall, Hansson (Tommy Andersson), Cervin.
*Scorer:* Nottingham F – Francis.

# EUROPEAN CUP 1979–80

**Preliminary Round, First Leg**
Dundalk 1 (*Devine*), Linfield 1 (*Feeney*)

**Preliminary Round, Second Leg**
Linfield 0, Dundalk 2 (*Muckian 2*)

**First Round, First Leg**
AC Milan 0, Porto 0
Liverpool 2 (*Johnson, Case*), Dinamo Tbilisi 1 (*Chivadze*)
Arges Pitesti 3 (*Nicolae 2, Radu*), AEK Athens 0
Partizan Tirana 1 (*Murati*), Celtic 0
Levski Spartak 0, Real Madrid 1 (*Martinez*)
Ujpest Dozsa 3 (*Sarlos, Nagy, Fazekas pen*), Dukla Prague 2 (*Gajdusek, Nehoda*)
Start Kristiansand 1 (*Ervik*), Strasbourg 2 (*Piasecki 2*)
HJK Helsinki 1 (*Rautiainen pen*), Ajax Amsterdam 8 (*Lerby 2, Tahamata 2, Arnesen 2, Krol pen, La Ling*)
Valur Reykjavik 0, SV Hamburg 3 (*Hrubesch 2, Buljan*)
Nottingham F 2 (*Bowyer 2*), Oester Vaxjo 0
Hajduk Split 1 (*Primorac*), Trabzonspor 0
Dinamo Berlin 4 (*Netz, Pelka 2, Riediger*), Ruch Chorzow 1 (*Wycislik*)
Vejle BK 3 (*Andersen, Rasmussen, Sorensen pen*), Austria Vienna 2 (*Baumeister, Schachner*)
Dundalk 2 (*Carlisle, Devine*), Hibernian Malta 0
Red Boys Differdange 3 (*Di Domenico pen, Wagner*), Omonia Nicosia 1 (*Patikis*)
Servette Geneva 3 (*Van Genechtem og, Koutas, Hamberg*), Beveren 1 (*Janssens*)

**First Round, Second Leg**
Porto 1 (*Duda*), AC Milan 0
Dinamo Tbilisi 3 (*Gutsayev, Shengelya, Chivadze pen*), Liverpool 0
AEK Athens 2 (*Ivan og, Vladic*), Arges Pitesti 0
Celtic 4 (*McDonald, Aitken, Davidson, McCluskey*), Partizan Tirana 1 (*Sneddon og*)
Real Madrid 2 (*Del Bosque, Cunningham pen*), Levski Spartak 0
Dukla Prague 2 (*Vizek, Nehoda*), Ujpest Dozsa 0
Strasbourg 4 (*Bianchi 3, Decastel*), Start Kristiansand 0
Ajax Amsterdam 8 (*Blanker 4, Krol 2, Everse, Lerby*), HJK Helsinki 1 (*Toivola*)
SV Hamburg 2 (Hrubesch, Wehmeyer), Valur Reykjavik 1 (*Edvaldsson*)
Oester Vaxjo 1 (*Nordgren*), Nottingham F 1 (*Woodcock*)
Trabzonspor 0, Hajduk Split 1 (*Djordjevic*)
Ruch Chorzow 0, Dinamo Berlin 0
Austria Vienna 1 (*Gasselich*), Vejle BK 1 (*Brylle*)
Hibernian Malta 1 (*Vella*), Dundalk 0
Omonia Nicosia 6 (*Kaiafas 4, Kanaris, Filippos*), Red Boys Differdange 1 (*Muller*)
Beveren 1 (*Albert pen*), Servette Geneva 1 (*Barberis*)

**Second Round, First Leg**
Nottingham F 2 (*Woodcock, Birtles*), Arges Pitesti 0
Vejle BK 0, Hajduk Split 3 (*Surjak, Jujowicz, Salov*)
SV Hamburg 3 (*Muchiri og, Keegan, Hartwig*), Dinamo Tbilisi 1 (*Kipiani*)
Celtic 3 (*McDonald, McCluskey, Burns*), Dundalk 2 (*Muckian, Lawlor*)
Ajax 10 (*Lerby 5, Krol pen, Arnesen, Blanker 3*), Omonia Nicosia 0
Dinamo Berlin 2 (*Pelka, Netz*), Servette Geneva 1 (*Cucinotta*)
Dukla Prague 1 (*Vizek pen*), Strasbourg 0
Porto 2 (*Gomes 2* [*1 pen*]), Real Madrid 1 (*Cunningham*)

**Second Round, Second Leg**
Arges Pitesti 1 (*Barbulescu pen*), Nottingham F 2 (*Bowyer, Birtles*)
Hajduk Split 1 (*Vujovic*), Vejle BK 2 (*Brille, Ostersen*)
Dinamo Tbilisi 2 (*Gutsayev, Kipiani*), SV Hamburg 3 (*Keegan, Hrubesch, Buljan*)
Dundalk 0, Celtic 0
Omonia Nicosia 4 (*Tsikkos, Demetrios, Kaiafas 2*), Ajax Amsterdam 0
Servette Geneva 2 (*Hamberg, Barberis*), Dinamo Berlin 2 (*Noak, Terletzki*)
Strasbourg 2 (*Piasecki, Decastel*), Dukla Prague 0
Real Madrid 1 (*Benito*), Porto 0

**Quarter-Final, First Leg**
Nottingham F 0, Dinamo Berlin 1 (*Riediger*)
SV Hamburg 1 (*Reimann*), Hajduk Split 0
Celtic 2 (*McCluskey, Doyle*), Real Madrid 0
Strasbourg 0, Ajax Amsterdam 0

**Quarter-Final, Second Leg**
Dinamo Berlin 1 (*Terletzki pen*), Nottingham F 3 (*Francis 2, Robertson pen*)
Hajduk Split 3 (*Vujovic 2, Primorac*), SV Hamburg 2 (*Hrubesch, Hieronymus*)
Real Madrid 3 (*Santillana, Stielike, Juanito*), Celtic 0
Ajax Amsterdam 4 (*Schoenmaker, Arnesen, Lerby, La Ling*), Strasbourg 0

**Semi-Final, First Leg**
Nottingham F 2 (*Francis, Robertson pen*), Ajax Amsterdam 0
Real Madrid 2 (*Santillana 2*), SV Hamburg 0

**Semi-Final, Second Leg**
Ajax Amsterdam 1 (*Lerby*), Nottingham F 0
SV Hamburg 5 (*Kaltz 2* [*1 pen*], *Hrubesch 2, Memering*), Real Madrid 1 (*Cunningham*)

**Final 1979–80: Nottingham F 1, SV Hamburg 0**
(In Madrid, 28 May, 1980, 50,000)

*Nottingham F:* Shilton; Anderson, Gray (Gunn), McGovern, Lloyd, Burns, O'Neill, Bowyer, Birtles, Mills (O'Hare), Robertson.

*SV Hamburg:* Kargus; Kaltz, Nogly, Jakobs, Buljan, Hieronymus (Hrubesch), Keegan, Memering, Milewski, Magath, Reimann.

*Scorer:* Nottingham F – Robertson.

# EUROPEAN CUP 1980–81

**Preliminary Round**
Honved 8 (*Bodonyi, Garaba, Esterhazy, Kocsis, Dajka 2, Varga 2 [1 pen]*), Valletta 0
Valletta 0, Honved 3 (*Esterhazy 2, Bodonyi*)

**First Round, First Leg**
Linfield 0, Nantes 1 (*Amisse*)
Aberdeen 1 (*McGhee*), Austria Vienna 0
FC Bruges 0, Basle 1 (*Maissen*)
CSKA Sofia 1 (*Yonchev*), Nottingham F 0
Dynamo Berlin 3 (*Terletzki, Trieloff, Schulz*), Apoel 0
Dynamo Tirana 0, Ajax 2 (*Arnesen 2*)
Inter-Milan 2 (*Altobelli 2 [1 pen]*), Uni Craiova 0
Jeunesse Esch 0, Moscow Spartak 5 (*Gavrilov 3, Khidiatulin, Yartsev*)
Limerick 1 (*Kennedy*), Real Madrid 2 (*Juanito pen, Pineda*)
Olympiakos 2 (*Galakos, Ahlstrom*), Bayern Munich 4 (*Dremmler 2, Rummenigge, Kraus*)
OPS Oulu 1 (*Puotiniemi*), Liverpool 1 (*McDermott*)
Sporting Club 0, Honved 2 (*Bodonyi, Nagy*)
Trabzonspor 2 (*Sinan, Tuncay*), Szombierki Bytom 1 (*Wazniewsky*)
Viking Stavanger 2 (*Svendsen, Sabo*), Red Star Belgrade 3 (*Petrovic, Brekke og, Repcic*)
IBV Vestmannayjar 1 (*Thorleifsson*), Banik Ostrava 1 (*Danek*)
Halmstad 0, Esbjerg 0

**First Round, Second Leg**
Nantes 2 (*Rampillon, Trossero E.*), Linfield 0
Honved 1 (*Dajka*), Sporting Club 0
Red Star Belgrade 4 (*Djurovski, Janjanin, Petrovic, Stamenkovic*), Viking Stavanger 1 (*Brekke*)
Uni Craiova 1 (*Beldeanu*), Inter-Milan 1 (*Muraro*)
Szombierki Bytom 3 (*Bys, Ogaza, Srodka pen*), Tranzonspor 0
Banik Ostrava 1 (*Vojacek*), IBV Vestmannayjar 0
Real Madrid 5 (*Santillana, Juanito 2, Cunningham, Pineda*), Limerick 1 (*Kennedy*)
Moscow Spartak 4 (*Pigat og, Rodionov, Gavrilov, Yartsev*), Jeunesse Esch 0
Nottingham Forest 0, CSKA Sofia 1 (*Kerimov*)
Bayern Munich 3 (*Hoeness, Rummenigge, Janzon pen*), Olympiakos 0
Basle 4 (*Tanner, Stohler pen, Von Wartburg, Gaisser*), FC Bruges 1 (*Ceulemans*)
Esbjerg 3 (*Iversen, Lauridsen, Nielsen*), Halmstad 2 (*Johansson, Larsson*)
Ajax 1 (*Lerby pen*), Dynamo Tirana 0
Austria Vienna 0, Aberdeen 0
Apoel 2 (*Hailis, Petrou*), Dynamo Berlin 1 (*Schnuphase*)

Liverpool 10 (*Souness 3, McDermott 2, Dalglish, Lee, Kennedy R., Fairclough 2*), OPS Oulu 1 (*Armstrong*)

**Second Round, First Leg**
Nantes 1 (*Rio pen*), Inter-Milan 2 (*Altobelli, Prohaska*)
Real Madrid 1 (*Santillana*), Honved 0
Bayern Munich 5 (*Durnberger, Rummenigge 2, Hoeness 2*), Ajax 1 (*Arnesen*)
Aberdeen 0, Liverpool 1 (*McDermott*)
CSKA Sofia 4 (*Yonchev 3, Zdranov*), Szombierki Bytom 0
Banik Ostrava 0, Dynamo Berlin 0
Moscow Spartak 3 (*Khidiatulin 2, Shavio*), Esbjerg 0
Basle 1 (*Lauscher*), Red Star Belgrade 0

**Second Round, Second Leg**
Honved 0, Real Madrid 2 (*Cunningham, Garcia Hernandez*)
Inter-Milan 1 (*Altobelli*), Nantes 1 (*Amisse*)
Ajax 2 (*Wiggemansen, Rijkaart*), Bayern Munich 1 (*Rummenigge*)
Red Star Belgrade 2 (*Repcic, Janjanin*), Basle 0
Liverpool 4 (*Miller og, Neal, Dalglish, Hansen*), Aberdeen 0
Dynamo Berlin 1 (*Troppa pen*), Banik Ostrava 1 (*Knapp pen*)
Esbjerg 2 (*Lauridsen, Iversen*), Moscow Spartak 0
Szombierki Bytom 0, CSKA Sofia 1 (*Djevisov*)

**Quarter-Final, First Leg**
Liverpool 5 (*Souness 3, Lee, McDermott*), CSKA Sofia 1 (*Yonchev*)
Bayern Munich 2 (*Janzon, Breitner pen*), Banik Ostrava 0
Inter-Milan 1 (*Caso*), Red Star Belgrade 1 (*Repcic*)
Moscow Spartak 0, Real Madrid 0

**Quarter-Final, Second Leg**
CSKA Sofia 0, Liverpool 1 (*Johnson*)
Banik Ostrava 2 (*Nemec, Licka*), Bayern Munich 4 (*Hoeness, Kraus, Rober, Durnberger*)
Red Star Belgrade 0, Inter-Milan 1 (*Muraro*)
Real Madrid 2 (*Isidro 2*), Moscow Spartak 0

**Semi-Final, First Leg**
Liverpool 0, Bayern Munich 0
Real Madrid 2 (*Santillana, Juanito*), Inter-Milan 0

**Semi-Final, Second Leg**
Bayern Munich 1 (*Rummenigge*), Liverpool 1 (*Kennedy R.*)
Inter-Milan 1 (*Bini*), Real Madrid 0

## Final 1980–81: Liverpool (0) 1, Real Madrid (0) 0
(In Paris, 27 May 1981, 48,360)

*Liverpool:* Clemence; Neal, Kennedy A., Thompson, Kennedy R., Hansen, Dalglish (Case), Lee, Johnson, McDermott, Souness.

*Real Madrid:* Rodriguez; Garcia Cortes, Camacho, Ştielike, Sabido (Pineda), Del Bosque, Juanito, De Los Santos, Santillana, Navajas, Cunningham.

*Scorer:* Liverpool – Kennedy A.

# CUP-WINNERS' CUP HISTORY

## EUROPEAN CUP-WINNERS' CUP 1960–61

**Qualifying Round**

| | | | |
|---|---|---|---|
| Vorwaerts Berlin v Red Brno (2-3) | 2-1, 0-2 | | |
| Rangers v Ferencvaros (5-4) | 4-2, 1-2 | | |

| | |
|---|---|
| Borussia Moenchengladbach v Rangers (0-11) | 0-3, 0-8 |
| Lucerne v Fiorentina (2-9) | 0-3, 2-6 |

**Quarter-Final**

| | |
|---|---|
| Red Star Brno v Dynamo Zagreb (0-2) | 0-0, 0-2 |
| FK Austria v Wolverhampton W (2-5) | 2-0, 0-5 |

**Semi-Final**

| | |
|---|---|
| Fiorentina v Dynamo Zagreb (4-2) | 3-0. 1-2 |
| Rangers v Wolverhampton W (3-1) | 2-0, 1-1 |

**Final 1960–61: Rangers 0, Fiorentina 2**
(First leg, Glasgow, 17 May, 1961)

*Rangers:* Ritchie; Shearer, Caldow; Davis, Paterson, Baxter, Wilson, McMillan, Scott, Brand, Hume.
*Fiorentina:* Albertosi; Robotti, Castelletti; Gonfiantini, Orzan, Rimbaldo; Hamrin, Micheli, Da Costa, Milan, Petris.
*Scorer:* Fiorentina – Milan 2.

**Fiorentina 2, Rangers 1**
(Second leg, Florence, 27 May, 1961)

*Fiorentina:* Albertosi; Robotti, Castelletti; Gonfiantini, Orzan, Rimbaldo; Hamrin, Micheli, Da Costa, Milan, Petris.
*Rangers:* Ritchie; Shearer, Caldow; Davis, Paterson, Baxter; Scott, McMillan, Millar, Brand, Wilson.
*Scorers:* Fiorentina – Milan, Hamrin; Rangers – Scott.

## EUROPEAN CUP-WINNERS' CUP 1961–62

*Byes:* Ajax Amsterdam, Werder, Aarhus, Dudelange, Progresul, Vardar, Zilina, Olympiakos. Holders Fiorentina exempt until Second Round.

**First Round**

| | |
|---|---|
| Glenavon v Leicester C (2-7) | 1-4, 1-3 |
| Dunfermline Ath v St Patrick's Ath (8-1) | 4-1, 4-0 |
| Swansea T v Motor Jena (3-7) | 2-2, 1-5 |
| La Chaux de Fonds v Leixoes (6-7) | 6-2, 0-5 |
| Sedan v Atlético Madrid (3-7) | 2-3, 1-4 |
| Rapid Vienna v Spartak Varna (5-2) | 0-0, 5-2 |
| Floriana v Ujpest (4-15) | 2-5, 2-10 |

**Second Round**

| | |
|---|---|
| Fiorentina v Rapid Vienna (9-3) | 3-1, 6-2 |
| Leicester C v Atlético Madrid (1-3) | 1-1, 0-2 |
| Dunfermline Ath v Vardar Skoplje (5-2) | 5-0, 0-2 |
| Werder Bremen v Aarhus (5-2) | 2-0, 3-2 |

| | |
|---|---|
| Ajax Amsterdam v Ujpest (3-4) | 2-1, 1-3 |
| Olympiakos Piraeus v Dynamo Zilina (2-4) | 2-3, 0-1 |
| Leixos v Progresul (2-1) | 1-1, 1-0 |
| Motor Jena v Alliance Dudelange (9-2) | 7-0, 2-2 |

**Quarter-Final**

| | |
|---|---|
| Werder Bremen v Atlético Madrid (2-4) | 1-3, 1-1 |
| Ujpest v Dunfermline Ath (5-3) | 4-3, 1-0 |
| Dynamo Zilina v Fiorentina (3-4) | 3-2, 0-2 |
| Motor Jena v Leixoes (4-2) | 1-1, 3-1 |

**Semi-Final**

| | |
|---|---|
| Fiorentina v Ujpest (3-0) | 2-0, 1-0 |
| Motor Jena v Atlético Madrid (0-5) | 0-1, 0-4 |

**Final 1961–62: Fiorentina 1, Atlético Madrid 1**
(In Glasgow, 10 May, 1962)

*Fiorentina:* Albertosi; Robotti, Castelletti; Malatrasi, Orzan, Marchesi; Hamrin, Ferretti, Milan, Dell'Angelo, Petris.
*Atlético Madrid:* Madinabeytia; Rivilla, Calleja, Ramirez, Griffa, Glaria; Jones, Adelardo, Mendonça, Peirò, Collar.
*Scorers:* Fiorentina – Hamrin; Atlético Madrid – Peirò.

**Replay: Atlético Madrid 3, Fiorentina 0**
(In Stuttgart, 5 September, 1962)

No change in teams. *Scorers:* Atlético Madrid – Jones, Mendonça, Peirò

## EUROPEAN CUP-WINNERS' CUP 1962–63

*Byes:* Graz, Nuremberg, Portadown, Shamrock R, Slovan, Tottenham H. Holders Atlético Madrid exempt until Second Round.

**First Round**

| | |
|---|---|
| Lausanne v Sparta Rotterdam (5-4) | 3-0, 2-4 |
| St Etienne v Vitoria Setubal (4-1) | 1-1, 3-0 |
| Alliance Dudelange v Odense BK 09 (2-9) | 1-1, 1-8 |
| Rangers v Seville (4-2) | 4-0, 0-2 |
| OFK Belgrade v Chemie Halle (5-3) | 2-0, 3-3 |
| Steaua Bucharest v Botev Plovdiv (4-7) | 3-2, 1-5 |
| Ujpest v Zaglebie Sosnowiec (5-0) | 5-0, 0-0 |
| Bangor C v Napoli (4-5) | 2-0, 1-3, 1-2 |

**Second Round**

| | |
|---|---|
| St Etienne v Nuremberg (0-3) | 0-0, 0-3 |
| Atlético Madrid v Hibernians Valletta (5-0) | 4-0, 1-0 |
| Shamrock R v Botev Plovdiv (0-5) | 0-4, 0-1 |

| | |
|---|---|
| Sturm Graz v Odense BK 09 (4-6) | 1-1, 3-5 |
| Tottenham H v Rangers (8-4) | 5-2, 3-2 |
| OFK Belgrade v Portadown (7-4) | 5-1, 2-3 |
| Lausanne v Slovan Bratislava (1-2) | 1-1, 0-1 |
| Ujpest v Napoli (3-5) | 1-1, 1-1, 1-3 |

**Quarter-Final**

| | |
|---|---|
| Slovan Bratislava v Tottenham H (2-6) | 2-0, 0-6 |
| Odense BK 09 v Nuremberg (0-7) | 0-1, 0-6 |
| Botev Plovdiv v Atlético Madrid (1-5) | 1-1, 0-4 |
| OFK Belgrade v Napoli (6-4) | 2-0, 1-3, 3-1 |

**Semi-Final**

| | |
|---|---|
| OFK Belgrade v Tottenham H (2-5) | 1-2, 1-3 |
| Nuremberg v Atlético Madrid (2-3) | 2-1, 0-2 |

**Final 1962–63: Tottenham H 5, Atlético Madrid 1**
(In Rotterdam, 15 May, 1963)

*Tottenham H:* Brown; Baker, Henry, Blanchflower, Norman, Marchi; Jones, White, Smith, Greaves, Dyson.
*Atlético Madrid:* Madinabeytia; Rivilla, Rodrigues; Ramiro, Griffa, Glaria; Jones, Adelardo, Chuzo, Mendonça, Collar.
*Scorers:* Tottenham H – Greaves 2, White, Dyson 2; Atlético Madrid – Collar (pen).

## EUROPEAN CUP-WINNERS' CUP 1963—64

*Byes:* Linfield, Zwickau. Holders Tottenham H exempt until Second Round.

**First Round**

| | |
|---|---|
| Fenerbahce v Petrolul Ploesti (4-2) | 4-1, 0-1 |
| Basle v Celtic (1-10) | 1-5, 0-5 |
| Tilburg Willem II v Manchester U (2-7) | 1-1, 1-6 |
| SV Hamburg v US Luxembourg (7-2) | 4-0, 3-2 |
| Olympiakos Piraeus v Zaglebie Sosnowiec (4-2) | 2-1, 0-1, 2-0 |
| Shelbourne v Barcelona (1-5) | 0-2, 1-3 |
| Lyon v Odense BK 09 (6-2) | 3-1, 3-1 |
| MTK Budapest v Slavia Sofia (2-1) | 1-0, 1-1 |
| ASK Linz v Dynamo Zagreb (2-2) | 1-0, 0-1, 1-1 |
| *Linz lost on toss of coin.* | |
| Sliema Wanderers v Borough U (0-2) | 0-0, 0-2 |
| Atlanta v Sporting Lisbon (4-6) | 2-0, 1-3, 1-3 |
| Apoel Nicosia v Gjoevik Lyn (6-1) | 6-0, 0-1 |
| Helsinki Palloseura v Slovan Bratislava (2-12) | 1-4, 1-8 |

**Second Round**

| | |
|---|---|
| Tottenham H v Manchester U (3-4) | 2-0, 1-4 |

| | |
|---|---|
| Fenerbahce v Linfield (4-3) | 4-1, 0-2 |
| Barcelona v SV Hamburg (6-7) | 4-4, 0-0, 2-3 |
| Sporting Lisbon v Apoel Nicosia (18-1) | 16-1, 2-0 |
| Lyon v Olympiakos Piraeus (5-3) | 4-1, 1-2 |
| Motor Zwickau v MTK Budapest (1-2) | 1-0, 0-2 |
| Celtic v Dynamo Zagreb (4-2) | 3-0, 1-2 |
| Borough U v Slovan Bratislava (0-4) | 0-1, 0-3 |

**Quarter-Final**

| | |
|---|---|
| Manchester U v Sporting Lisbon (4-6) | 4-1, 0-5 |
| SV Hamburg v Lyon (1-3) | 1-1, 0-2 |
| Celtic v Slovan Bratislava (2-0) | 1-0, 1-0 |
| MTK Budapest v Fenerbahce (4-3) | 2-0, 1-3, 1-0 |

**Semi-Final**

| | |
|---|---|
| Celtic v MTK Budapest (3-4) | 3-0, 0-4 |
| Lyon v Sporting Lisbon (1-2) | 0-0, 1-1, 0-1 |

**Final 1963—64: MTK Budapest 3, Sporting Lisbon 3 (aet)**
(In Brussels, 13 May, 1964)

*MTK Budapest:* Kovalik; Keszei, Dansky, Jenei, Nagy, Kovacs; Sandor, Vasas, Kuti, Bodor, Halapi.

*Sporting Lisbon:* Carvalho; Gomez, Perdis; Battista, Carlos, Geo; Mendes, Oswaldo, Mascarenhas, Figueiredo, Morais.

*Scorers:* MTK Budapest – Sandor 2, Kuti; Sporting Lisbon – Figueiredo 2, Dansky og.

**Replay 1963—64: Sporting Lisbon 1, MTK Budapest 0**
(In Antwerp, 15 May, 1964)

Teams unchanged. *Scorer:* Sporting Lisbon – Mendes.

## EUROPEAN CUP-WINNERS' CUP 1964—65

*Bye:* Dundee. Holders Sporting Lisbon exempt until Second Round.

**First Round**

| | |
|---|---|
| Admira Vienna v Legia Warsaw (1-4) | 1-3, 0-1 |
| Lausanne v Honved (2-1) | 2-0, 0-1 |
| US Luxembourg v Munich 1860 (0-10) | 0-4, 0-6 |
| Valletta v Real Zaragoza (1-8) | 0-3, 1-5 |
| AEK Athens v Dynamo Zagreb (2-3) | 2-0, 0-3 |
| Steaua Bucharest v Derry C (5-0) | 3-0, 2-0 |
| Magdeburg v Galatasaray (3-3) | 1-1, 1-1, 1-1 |
| *Galatasaray won on toss of coin.* | |
| Esbjerg v Cardiff C (0-1) | 0-0, 0-1 |
| Skeid Oslo v Valkeakosken (1-2) | 1-0, 0-2 |
| Porto v Lyon (4-0) | 3-0, 1-0 |
| Sparta Prague v Anorthosis (16-0) | 10-0, 6-0 |
| La Gantoise v West Ham U (1-2) | 0-1, 1-1 |
| Torino v Fortuna Geelen (5-3) | 3-1, 2-2 |
| Slavia Sofia v Cork Celtic (3-1) | 1-1, 2-0 |

**Second Round**

| | |
|---|---|
| Dundee v Real Zaragoza (3-4) | 2-2, 1-2 |

| | |
|---|---|
| Slavia Sofia v Lausanne (4-5) | 1-0, 1-2, 2-3 |
| Legia Warsaw v Galatasaray (3-2) | 2-1, 0-1, 1-0 |
| West Ham U v Sparta Prague (3-2) | 2-0, 1-2 |
| Porto v Munich 1860 (1-2) | 0-1, 1-1 |
| Steaua Bucharest v Dynamo Zagreb (1-5) | 1-3, 0-2 |
| Sporting Lisbon v Cardiff C (1-2) | 1-2, 0-0 |
| Torino v Valkeakosken (6-0) | 5-0, 1-0 |

**Quarter-Final**

| | |
|---|---|
| Real Zaragoza v Cardiff C (3-2) | 2-2, 1-0 |
| Legia Warsaw v Munich 1860 (0-4) | 0-4, 0-0 |
| Torino v Dynamo Zagreb (3-2) | 1-1, 2-1 |
| Lausanne v West Ham U (4-6) | 1-2, 3-4 |

**Semi-Final**

| | |
|---|---|
| West Ham U v Real Zaragoza (3-2) | 2-1, 1-1 |
| Torino v Munich 1860 (3-5) | 2-0, 1-3, 0-2 |

**Final 1964—65: West Ham U 2, Munich 1860 0**
(At Wembley, 19 May, 1965)

*West Ham U:* Standen; Kirkup, Burkett; Peters, Brown, Moore; Sealey, Boyce, Hurst, Dear, Sissons.

*Munich 1860:* Radenkovic; Wagner, Kohlars; Bena, Reich, Luttrop; Heiss, Kuppers, Brunnenmeier, Grosser, Rebele.

*Scorer:* West Ham U – Sealey 2.

## EUROPEAN CUP-WINNERS' CUP 1965—66

Holders West Ham U exempt until Second Round.

**First Round**

| | |
|---|---|
| Juventus v Liverpool (1-2) | 1-0, 0-2 |
| Cardiff C v Standard Liège (1-3) | 1-2, 0-1 |
| Lahden Reipas v Honved (2-16) | 2-10, 0-6 |
| Dukla Prague v Stade Rennes (2-0) | 2-0, 0-0 |
| Go Ahead Deventer v Celtic (0-7) | 0-6, 0-1 |
| Aarhus v Vitoria Setubal (4-2) | 2-1, 2-1 |
| Coleraine v Dynamo Kiev (1-10) | 1-6, 0-4 |

| | |
|---|---|
| KR Rekyjavik v Rosenborg (2-6) | 1-3, 1-3 |
| Omonia Nicosia v Olympiakos Piraeus (1-2) | 0-1, 1-1 |
| Magdeburg v Spora Luxembourg (3-0) | 1-0, 2-0 |
| Sion v Galatasaray (6-3) | 5-1, 1-2 |
| Atlético Madrid v Dynamo Zagreb (5-0) | 1-0, 4-0 |
| Wiener Neustadt v Stinta Cluj (0-3) | 0-1, 0-2 |
| Limerick v CSKA Sofia (1-4) | 1-2, 0-2 |
| Fioriana v Borussia Dortmund (1-13) | 1-5, 0-8 |

**Second Round**

| | |
|---|---|
| Liverpool v Standard Liège (5-2) | 3-1, 2-1 |
| Dukla Prague v Honved (4-4) | 3-2, 1-2 |
| *Honved won on away goals rule.* | |
| Aarhus v Celtic (0-3) | 0-1, 0-2 |
| Rosenborg v Dynamo Kiev (1-6) | 1-4, 0-2 |
| West Ham U v Olympiakos Piraeus (6-2) | 4-0, 2-2 |
| Magdeburg v Sion (10-3) | 8-1, 2-2 |
| Stinta Cluj v Atlético Madrid (0-6) | 0-2, 0-4 |
| Borussia Dortmund v CSKA Sofia (5-4) | 3-0, 2-4 |

**Quarter-Final**

| | |
|---|---|
| Honved v Liverpool (0-2) | 0-0, 0-2 |
| Celtic v Dynamo Kiev (4-1) | 3-0, 1-1 |
| West Ham U v Magdeburg (2-1) | 1-0, 1-1 |
| Atlético Madrid v Borussia Dortmund (1-2) | 1-1, 0-1 |

**Semi-Final**

| | |
|---|---|
| Celtic v Liverpool (1-2) | 1-0, 0-2 |
| West Ham U v Borussia Dortmund (2-5) | 1-2, 1-3 |

**Final 1965–66: Borussia Dortmund 2, Liverpool 1 (aet)**
(In Glasgow, 5 May, 1966)
*Borussia Dortmund:* Tilkowski; Cyliax, Redder; Kurrat, Paul, Assauer; Libuda, Schmidt, Held, Sturm, Emmerich.
*Liverpool:* Lawrence; Lawler, Byrne; Milne, Yeats, Stevenson; Callaghan, Hunt, St John, Smith, Thompson.
*Scorers:* Borussia Dortmund – Held, Yeats og; Liverpool – Hunt.

# EUROPEAN CUP-WINNERS' CUP 1966–67

Holders Borussia Dortmund exempt until Second Round.

**Preliminary Round**

| | |
|---|---|
| Valur Reykjavik v Standard Liège (2-9) | 1-1, 1-8 |

**First Round**

| | |
|---|---|
| Tatran Presov v Bayern Munich (3-4) | 1-1, 2-3 |
| Shamrock R v Spora Luxembourg (8-2) | 4-1, 4-1 |
| OFK Belgrade v Spartak Moscow (1-6) | 1-3, 0-3 |
| Rapid Vienna v Galatasaray (9-3) | 4-0, 5-3 |
| Fiorentina v Vasas Gyor (3-4) | 1-0, 2-4 |
| AEK Athens v Sporting Braga (2-4) | 0-1, 2-3 |
| Chemie Leipzig v Legia Warsaw (5-2) | 3-0, 2-2 |
| Standard Liège v Apollon Limassol (6-1) | 5-1, 1-0 |
| Servette Geneva v Kamraterna (3-2) | 1-1, 2-1 |
| Floriana v Sparta Rotterdam (1-7) | 1-1, 0-6 |
| Swansea T v Slavia Sofia (1-5) | 1-1, 0-4 |
| Strasbourg v Steaua Bucharest (2-1) | 1-0, 1-1 |
| Skeid Oslo v Real Zaragoza (4-5) | 3-2, 1-3 |
| Aalborg v Everton (1-2) | 0-0, 1-2 |
| Glentoran v Rangers (1-5) | 1-1, 0-4 |

**Second Round**

| | |
|---|---|
| Shamrock R v Bayern Munich (3-4) | 1-1, 2-3 |
| Spartak Moscow v Rapid Vienna (1-2) | 1-1, 0-1 |
| Vasas Gyor v Sporting Braga (3-2) | 3-0, 0-2 |
| Chemie Leipzig v Standard Liège† (2-2) | 2-1, 0-1 |
| Servette Geneva v Sparta Rotterdam (2-1) | 2-0, 0-1 |
| Strasbourg v Slavia Sofia (1-2) | 1-0, 0-2 |
| Real Zaragoza v Everton (2-1) | 2-0, 0-1 |
| Rangers v Borussia Dortmund (2-1) | 2-1, 0-0 |

**Quarter-Final**

| | |
|---|---|
| Rapid Vienna v Bayern Munich (1-2) | 1-0, 0-2 |
| Vasas Gyor v Standard Liège (2-3) | 2-1, 0-2 |
| Servette Geneva v Slavia Sofia (1-3) | 1-0, 0-3 |
| Rangers* v Real Zaragoza (2-2) | 2-0, 0-2 |

**Semi-Final**

| | |
|---|---|
| Bayern Munich v Standard Liège (5-1) | 2-0, 3-1 |
| Slavia Sofia v Rangers (0-2) | 0-1, 0-1 |

*\*Won on toss of a disc.* †*Won on away goals counting double.*

**Final 1966–67: Bayern Munich 1, Rangers 0 (aet)**
(At Nuremberg, 31 May, 1967)
*Bayern Munich:* Maier; Nowak, Kupferschmidt; Roth, Beckenbauer, Olk; Nafziger, Ohlhauser, Müller, Koulmann, Brenninger.
*Rangers:* Martin; Johansen, Provan; Jardine, McKinnon, Greig; Henderson, Smith A., Hynd, Smith D., Johnston.
*Scorer:* Bayern Munich – Roth.

# EUROPEAN CUP-WINNERS' CUP 1967–68

**First Round**

| | |
|---|---|
| AC Milan v Levski Sofia (6-2) | 5-1, 1-1 |
| Vasas Gyor v Apollon Limassol (9-0) | 5-0, 4-0 |
| Altay Izmir v Standard Liège (2-3) | 2-3, 0-0 |
| Aberdeen v KR Reykjavik (14-1) | 10-0, 4-1 |
| Bayern Munich v Panathinaikos (7-1) | 5-0, 2-1 |
| Frederikstad v Vitoria Setubal (2-7) | 1-5, 1-2 |
| Valencia v Crusaders (8-2) | 4-0, 4-2 |
| FK Austria v Steaua Bucharest (1-4) | 0-2, 1-2 |
| Shamrock R v Cardiff C (1-3) | 1-1, 0-2 |
| Floriana v NAC Breda (1-3) | 1-2, 0-1 |
| Moscow Torpedo v Motor Zwickau (1-0) | 0-0, 1-0 |
| Lausanne v Spartak Trnava (3-4) | 3-2, 0-2 |
| Aris Bonneweg v Lyon (1-5) | 0-3, 1-2 |
| Hajduk Split v Tottenham H (3-6) | 0-2, 3-4 |
| HJK Helsinki v Wisla Krakow (1-8) | 1-4, 0-4 |
| SV Hamburg v Randers Freja (7-3) | 5-3, 2-0 |

**Second Round**

| | |
|---|---|
| Vasas Gyor v AC Milan* (3-3) | 2-2, 1-1 |

| | |
|---|---|
| Standard Liège v Aberdeen (3-2) | 3-0, 0-2 |
| Bayern Munich v Vitoria Setubal (7-3) | 6-2, 1-1 |
| Valencia v Steaua Bucharest (3-1) | 3-0, 0-1 |
| NAC Breda v Cardiff C (2-5) | 1-1, 1-4 |
| Moscow Torpedo v Spartak Trnava (6-1) | 3-0, 3-1 |
| Lyon* v Tottenham H (4-4) | 1-0, 3-4 |
| Wisla Krakow v SV Hamburg (0-5) | 0-1, 0-4 |

**Quarter-Final**

| | |
|---|---|
| Standard Liège v AC Milan (2-4) | 1-1, 1-1, 0-2 |
| Valencia v Bayern Munich (1-2) | 1-1, 0-1 |
| Cardiff C v Moscow Torpedo (2-1) | 1-0, 0-1, 1-0 |
| SV Hamburg v Lyon (4-2) | 2-0, 0-2, 2-0 |

**Semi-Final**

| | |
|---|---|
| AC Milan v Bayern Munich (2-0) | 2-0, 0-0 |
| SV Hamburg v Cardiff C (4-3) | 1-1, 3-2 |

*\*Won on away goals counting double.*

**Final 1967–68: AC Milan 2, SV Hamburg 0**
(In Rotterdam, 23 May, 1968)
*AC Milan:* Cudicini; Anquilletti, Schnellinger; Trappatoni, Rosato, Scala; Hamrin, Lodetti, Sormani, Rivera, Prati.
*SV Hamburg:* Ozcan; Sondemann, Kurbjohn; Dieckemann, Horst, Schulz H., Dorfel II, Kramer, Seeler, Hornig, Dorfel
*Scorer:* AC Milan – Hamrin 2.

## EUROPEAN CUP-WINNERS' CUP 1968—69

**First Round**
| | |
|---|---|
| Slovan Bratislava v Bor (3-2) | 3-0, 0-2 |
| Cardiff C v Porto (3-4) | 2-2, 1-2 |
| Partizan Tirana v Torino (2-3) | 1-3, 1-0 |
| Dunfermline Ath v Apoel Nicosia (12-1) | 10-1, 2-0 |
| Olympiakos Piraeus v Fram Reykjavik (4-0) | 2-0, 2-0 |
| Bruges v WBA* (3-3) | 3-1, 0-2 |
| Bordeaux v Cologne (2-4) | 2-1, 0-3 |
| AK Graz v ADO The Hague (1-6) | 1-4, 0-2 |
| Randers Freja v Shamrock R (3-1) | 1-0, 2-1 |
| Rumelange v Sliema Wanderers* (2-2) | 2-1, 0-1 |
| Altay Izmir v Lyn Oslo (4-5) | 3-1, 1-4 |
| Crusaders v Norrköping (3-6) | 2-2, 1-4 |
| Lugano v Barcelona (0-4) | 0-1, 0-3 |

**Second Round**
*Byes:* Torino, Barcelona

| | |
|---|---|
| Porto v Slovan Bratislava (1-4) | 1-0, 0-4 |
| Dunfermline Ath v Olympiakos Piraeus (4-3) | 4-0, 0-3 |
| Dynamo Bucharest v WBA (1-5) | 1-1, 0-4 |
| ADO The Hague v Cologne (0-4) | 0-1, 0-3 |
| Randers Freja v Sliema Wanderers (8-0) | 6-0, 2-0 |
| Lyn Oslo v Norrköping (4-3) | 2-0, 2-3 |

**Quarter-Final**
| | |
|---|---|
| Torino v Slovan Bratislava (1-3) | 0-1, 1-2 |
| Dunfermline Ath v WBA (1-0) | 0-0, 1-0 |
| Cologne v Randers Freja (5-1) | 2-1, 3-0 |
| Barcelona v Lyn Oslo (5-4) | 3-2, 2-2 |

**Semi-Final**
| | |
|---|---|
| Dunfermline Ath v Slovan Bratislava (1-2) | 1-1, 0-1 |
| Cologne v Barcelona (3-6) | 2-2, 1-4 |

*Won on away goals counting double.*

### Final 1968—69: Slovan Bratislava 3, Barcelona 2
(In Basle, 21 May, 1969, 40,000)

*Slovan Bratislava:* Vencel; Filo, Hrivnak; Jan Zlocha, Horvath, Hrdlicka, Cvetler; Moder, Josef Capkovic, Jokl, Jan Capkovic.

*Barcelona:* Sadurni; Franch (Pereda), Eladio; Rife, Olivella, Zabalza; Pellicer, Castro (Mendoca), Zaluda, Fuste, Rexach.

*Scorers:* Slovan Bratislava – Cvetler, Hrivnak, Jan Capkovic; Barcelona – Zaluda, Rexach.

## EUROPEAN CUP-WINNERS' CUP 1969—70

**Preliminary Round**
| | |
|---|---|
| Rapid Vienna* v Moscow Torpedo (1-1) | 0-0, 1-1 |

**First Round**
| | |
|---|---|
| Olympiakos Piraeus v Gornik Zabrze (2-7) | 2-2, 0-5 |
| Rangers v Steaua Bucharest (2-0) | 2-0, 0-0 |
| IBV Reykjavik v Levski Sofia (0-8) | 0-4, 0-4 |
| Frem Copenhagen v St Gallen* (2-2) | 2-1, 0-1 |
| Ards v AS Roma (1-3) | 0-0, 1-3 |
| Rapid Vienna v PSV Eindhoven (3-6) | 2-4, 1-2 |
| Goztepe Izmir v US Luxembourg (6-2) | 3-0, 3-2 |
| Mjoendalen v Cardiff C (2-12) | 1-7, 1-5 |
| Shamrock R v Schalke 04 (2-4) | 2-1, 0-3 |
| Norrköping v Sliema Wanderers (5-2) | 5-1, 0-1 |
| Dukla Prague v Marseille (1-2) | 1-0, 0-2 |
| Dynamo Zagreb v Slovan Bratislava (3-0) | 3-0, 0-0 |
| Magdeburg v MTK Budapest (2-1) | 1-1, 1-0 |
| Academica Coimbra v Kuopion Pallo (1-0) | 0-0, 1-0 |
| Lierse v Apoel Nicosia (11-1) | 10-1, 1-0 |
| Atlético Bilbao v Manchester C (3-6) | 3-3, 0-3 |

| | |
|---|---|
| **Second Round** | |
| Gornik Zabrze v Rangers (6-2) | 3-1, 3-1 |
| Levski Sofia v St Gallen (4-0) | 4-0, 0-0 |
| AS Roma† v PSV Eindhoven (1-1) | 1-0, 0-1 |
| Goztepe Izmir v Cardiff C (3-1) | 3-0, 0-1 |
| Norrköping v Schalke 04 (0-1) | 0-0, 0-1 |
| Marseille v Dynamo Zagreb (1-3) | 1-1, 0-2 |
| Magdeburg v Academica Coimbra (1-2) | 1-0, 0-2 |
| Lierse v Manchester C (0-8) | 0-3, 0-5 |

**Quarter-Final**
| | |
|---|---|
| Levski Sofia v Gornik Zabrze* (4-4) | 3-2, 1-2 |
| AS Roma v Goztepe Izmir (2-0) | 2-0, 0-0 |
| Dynamo Zagreb v Schalke 04 (1-4) | 1-3, 0-1 |
| Academica Coimbra v Manchester C (0-1) | 0-0, 0-1 |

**Semi-Final**
| | |
|---|---|
| AS Roma v Gornik Zabrze† (4-4) | 1-1, 2-2, 1-1 |
| Schalke 04 v Manchester C (2-5) | 1-0, 1-5 |

*Won on away goals counting double.*     †*Won on toss of coin after extra time.*

### Final 1969—70: Manchester C 2, Gornik Zabrze 1
(In Vienna, 20 April, 1970, 10,000)

*Manchester C:* Corrigan; Book, Pardoe; Doyle (Bowyer), Booth, Oakes, Heslop, Bell, Lee, Young, Towers.

*Gornik Zabrze:* Kostka; Gorgan, Ozlizlo; Latogha, Forenski, Szoltysik; Wilczek, Olek, Banas, Lubanski, Szaryniski.

*Scorers:* Manchester C – Young, Lee (pen); Gornik Zabrze – Ozlizlo.

## EUROPEAN CUP-WINNERS' CUP 1970–71

**Preliminary Round**

| | |
|---|---|
| Atvidaberg v Partizan Tirana (1-3) | 0-2, 1-1 |
| Bohemians v Gottwaldov (3-4) | 1-2, 2-2 |

**First Round**

| | |
|---|---|
| Manchester C* v Linfield (2-2) | 1-0, 1-2 |
| Olympija Ljubljana v Benfica (2-9) | 1-1, 1-8 |
| Akureyri v Zurich (1-14) | 1-7, 0-7 |
| Cardiff C v Pezoporikos (8-0) | 8-0, 0-0 |
| Offenbach Kickers v Bruges (2-3) | 2-1, 0-2 |
| Hibernians Valletta v Real Madrid (0-5) | 0-0, 0-5 |
| Vorwaerts Berlin* v Bologna (1-1) | 0-0, 1-1 |
| Steaua Bucharest v Karpaty Lvov (4-3) | 3-3, 1-0 |
| CSKA Sofia v Valkeakosken (11-1) | 9-0, 2-1 |
| Aberdeen v Honved† (4-4) | 1-3, 3-1 |
| Stromsgodset v Nantes (3-7) | 0-5, 3-2 |
| Aalborg v Gornik Zabrze (1-9) | 0-1, 1-8 |
| Goztepe Izmir v US Luxembourg (5-1) | 5-0, 0-1 |
| Wacker Innsbruck v Partizan Tirana (5-3) | 3-2, 2-1 |
| Gottwaldov v PSV Eindhoven* (2-2) | 2-1, 0-1 |
| Aris Salonika v Chelsea (2-6) | 1-1, 1-5 |

**Second Round**

| | |
|---|---|
| CSKA Sofia v Chelsea (0-2) | 0-1, 0-1 |
| Honved v Manchester C (0-3) | 0-1, 0-2 |
| Cardiff C v Nantes (7-2) | 5-1, 2-1 |
| Bruges v Zurich (4-3) | 2-0, 2-3 |
| PSV Eindhoven v Steaua Bucharest (7-0) | 4-0, 3-0 |
| Goztepe Izmir v Gornik Zabrze (0-4) | 0-1, 0-3 |
| Real Madrid v Wacker Innsbruck (2-1) | 0-1, 2-0 |
| Benfica v Vorwaerts Berlin† (2-2) | 2-0, 0-2 |

**Quarter-Final**

| | |
|---|---|
| Manchester C v Gornik Zabrze (5-3) | 2-0, 0-2, 3-1 |
| PSV Eindhoven v Vorwaerts Berlin (2-1) | 2-0, 0-1 |
| Cardiff C v Real Madrid (1-2) | 1-0, 0-2 |
| Bruges v Chelsea (2-4) | 2-0, 0-4 |

**Semi-Final**

| | |
|---|---|
| Chelsea v Manchester C (2-0) | 1-0, 1-0 |
| PSV Eindhoven v Real Madrid (1-2) | 0-0, 1-2 |

*Won on away goals counting double.*     †*Won on penalty kicks.*

### Final 1970–71: Chelsea 2, Real Madrid 1
(after 1-1 draw aet, both games in Athens)
(First game, 19 May, 1971, 42,000)

*Chelsea:* Bonetti; Boyle, Harris; Hollins, Dempsey, Webb; Weller, Hudson, Osgood, Cooke, Houseman.
*Real Madrid:* Borja; Luis, Zunzunegui; Pirri, Benito, Zoco; Perez, Amancio, Grosso, Velazquez, Gento.
*Scorers:* Chelsea – Osgood; Real Madrid – Zoco.

(Second game, 21 May, 1971, 24,000)

*Chelsea:* Bonetti; Boyle, Harris; Cooke, Dempsey, Webb; Weller, Baldwin, Osgood (Smethurst), Hudson, Houseman.
*Real Madrid:* Borja; Luis, Zunzunegui; Pirri, Benito, Zoco; Fleitas, Amancio, Grosso, Velazquez (Gento), Bueno (Grande).
*Scorers:* Chelsea – Dempsey, Osgood; Real Madrid – Fleitas.

## EUROPEAN CUP-WINNERS' CUP 1971–72

**Preliminary Round**

| | |
|---|---|
| Odense BK 09 v FK Austria* (4-4) | 4-2, 0-2 |
| Hibernians Valletta v Fram Reykjavik (3-2) | 3-0, 0-2 |

**First Round**

| | |
|---|---|
| Servette Geneva v Liverpool (2-3) | 2-1, 0-2 |
| Distillery v Barcelona (1-7) | 1-3, 0-4 |
| Dynamo Berlin† v Cardiff C (2-2) | 1-1, 1-1 |
| Jeunesse Hautcharage v Chelsea (0-21) | 0-8, 0-13 |
| Limerick v Torino (0-5) | 0-1, 0-4 |
| Dynamo Tirana v FK Austria (1-2) | 1-1, 0-1 |
| Rennes v Rangers (1-2) | 1-1, 0-1 |
| Hibernians Valletta v Steaua Bucharest (0-1) | 0-0, 0-1 |
| Sporting Lisbon v Lyn Oslo (7-0) | 3-0, 4-0 |
| Skoda Pilzen v Bayern Munich (1-7) | 0-1, 1-6 |
| Komlo Banyasi v Red Star Belgrade (4-8) | 2-7, 2-1 |
| Olympiakos Piraeus v Dynamo Moscow (2-3) | 0-2, 2-1 |
| Levski Sofia v Sparta Rotterdam (1-3) | 1-1, 0-2 |
| Zaglebie Sosnowiec v Atvidaberg (4-5) | 3-4, 1-1 |
| Mikkeli v Eskisehirspor (0-4) | 0-0, 0-4 |
| Beerschot v Famagusta (8-0) | 7-0, 1-0 |

**Second Round**

| | |
|---|---|
| Liverpool v Bayern Munich (1-3) | 0-0, 1-3 |
| Atvidaberg* v Chelsea (1-1) | 0-0, 1-1 |
| Torino v FK Austria (1-0) | 1-0, 0-0 |
| Rangers† v Sporting Lisbon (6-6) | 3-2, 3-4 |
| Beerschot v Dynamo Berlin (2-6) | 1-3, 1-3 |
| Sparta Rotterdam v Red Star Belgrade (2-3) | 1-1, 1-2 |
| Barcelona v Steaua Bucharest (1-3) | 0-1, 1-2 |
| Eskisehirspor v Dynamo Moscow (0-2) | 0-1, 0-1 |

**Quarter-Final**

| | |
|---|---|
| Torino v Rangers (1-2) | 1-1, 0-1 |
| Steaua Bucharest v Bayern Munich* (1-1) | 1-1, 0-0 |
| Atvidaberg v Dynamo Berlin (2-4) | 0-2, 2-2 |
| Red Star Belgrade v Dynamo Moscow (2-3) | 1-2, 1-1 |

**Semi-Final**

| | |
|---|---|
| Bayern Munich v Rangers (1-3) | 1-1, 0-2 |
| Dynamo Berlin v Dynamo Moscow† (2-2) | 1-1, 1-1 |

*Won on away goals rule.*     †*Won on penalty kicks.*

### Final 1971-72: Rangers 3, Dynamo Moscow 2
(In Barcelona, 24 May, 1972, 35,000)

*Rangers:* McCloy; Jardine, Mathieson, Greig, Johnstone, Smith, McLean, Conn, Stein, MacDonald, Johnston.
*Dynamo Moscow:* Pilgui; Basalev, Dolmatov, Zykov, Dobbonosov (Gerschkovitch), Zhukov, Baidatchini, Jakubik (Estrekov), Sabo, Makovikov, Evryuzhikhin.
*Scorers:* Rangers – Stein, Johnston 2; Dynamo Moscow – Estrekov, Makovikov.

## EUROPEAN CUP-WINNERS' CUP 1972–73

**First Round**

| | |
|---|---|
| Bastia v Atlético Madrid (1-2) | 0-0, 1-2 |
| Floriana Valletta v Ferencvaros (1-6) | 1-0, 0-6 |
| Schalke 04 v Slavia Sofia (5-2) | 2-1, 3-1 |
| Standard Liège v Sparta Prague (3-4) | 1-0, 2-4 |
| Spartak Moscow v FC Den Haag (1-0) | 1-0, 0-0 |
| Vikingur Reykjavik v Legia Warsaw (0-11) | 0-2, 0-9 |
| Ankaragucu v Leeds U (1-2) | 1-1, 0-1 |
| Hajduk Split v Fredrikstad (2-0) | 1-0, 1-0 |
| Rapid Vienna* v PAOK Saloniki (2-2) | 0-0, 2-2 |
| Zurich v Wrexham (2-3) | 1-1, 1-2 |
| Sporting Lisbon v Hibernian (3-7) | 2-1, 1-6 |
| Rapid Bucharest v Landskrona (3-1) | 3-0, 0-1 |
| Pezoporikos v Cork Hibs (2-6) | 1-2, 1-4 |
| Fremad Amager v Besa* (1-1) | 1-1, 0-0 |
| Carl Zeiss Jena v Mikkeli (8-4) | 6-1, 2-3 |
| Red Boys Differdingen v AC Milan (1-7) | 1-4, 0-3 |

**Second Round**

| | |
|---|---|
| Rapid Vienna v Rapid Bucharest (2-4) | 1-1, 1-3 |

| | |
|---|---|
| Carl Zeiss Jena v Leeds U (0-2) | 0-0, 0-2 |
| Wrexham v Hajduk Split* (3-3) | 3-1, 0-2 |
| Cork Hibs v Schalke 04 (0-3) | 0-0, 0-3 |
| Atlético Madrid v Spartak Moscow* (5-5) | 3-4, 2-1 |
| Hibernian v Besa (8-2) | 7-1, 1-1 |
| Ferencvaros v Sparta Prague (3-4) | 2-0, 1-4 |
| Legia Warsaw v AC Milan (2-3) | 1-1, 1-2 |

**Quarter-Final**

| | |
|---|---|
| Leeds U v Rapid Bucharest (8-1) | 5-0, 3-1 |
| Hibernian v Hajduk Split (4-5) | 4-2, 0-3 |
| Schalke 04 v Sparta Prague (2-4) | 2-1, 0-3 |
| Spartak Moscow v AC Milan (1-2) | 0-1, 1-1 |

**Semi-Final**

| | |
|---|---|
| Leeds U v Hajduk Split (1-0) | 1-0, 0-0 |
| AC Milan v Sparta Prague (2-0) | 1-0, 1-0 |

*Won on away goals rule.*

### Final 1972–73: AC Milan 1, Leeds U 0
(In Salonika, 16 May, 1973, 45,000)

*AC Milan:* Vecchi; Sabadini, Zigno, Anquilletti, Turone, Rosato (Dolci), Sogliano, Benetti, Bigon, Rivera, Chiarugi.
*Leeds U:* Harvey; Reaney, Cherry, Bates, Madeley, Hunter, Lorimer, Jordan, Jones, Gray E., Yorath (McQueen).
*Scorer:* AC Milan – Chiarugi.

## EUROPEAN CUP-WINNERS' CUP 1973–74

**First Round**

| | |
|---|---|
| Legia Warsaw v PAOK Salonika (1-2) | 1-1, 0-1 |
| Anderlecht v Zurich* (3-3) | 3-2, 0-1 |
| Vestmannajar v Bor Moenchengladbach (1-16) | 0-7, 1-9 |
| Vasas Budapest v Sunderland (0-3) | 0-2, 0-1 |
| Ankaragucu v Rangers (0-6) | 0-2, 0-4 |
| AC Milan v Dynamo Zagreb (4-1) | 3-1, 1-0 |
| Torpedo Moscow v Atlético Bilbao (0-2) | 0-0, 0-2 |
| Gzira v Brann Bergen (0-9) | 0-2, 0-7 |
| NAC v Magdeburg (0-2) | 0-0, 0-2 |
| Randers Freja v Rapid Vienna (1-2) | 0-0, 1-2 |
| Chimia Ramnicu v Glentoran (2-4) | 2-2, 0-2 |
| Larnaca v Malmo (0-11) | 0-0, 0-11 |
| Fola Esch v Beroe Stara (1-11) | 0-7, 1-4 |
| Banik Ostrava v Cork Hibs (3-1) | 1-0, 2-1 |
| Reipas Lahti v Lyon (0-2) | 0-0, 0-2 |
| Cardiff C v Sporting Lisbon (1-2) | 0-0, 1-2 |

**Second Round**

| | |
|---|---|
| Lyon v PAOK Salonika (3-7) | 3-3, 0-4 |

| | |
|---|---|
| Bor Moenchengladbach v Rangers (5-3) | 3-0, 2-3 |
| Brann Bergen v Glentoran (2-4) | 1-1, 1-3 |
| Banik Ostrava v Magdeburg (2-3) | 2-0, 0-3 |
| Zurich* v Malmo (1-1) | 0-0, 1-1 |
| Beroe Stara v Atlético Bilbao (3-1) | 3-0, 0-1 |
| Sunderland v Sporting Lisbon (2-3) | 2-1, 0-2 |
| AC Milan v Rapid Vienna (2-0) | 0-0, 2-0 |

**Quarter Final**

| | |
|---|---|
| Magdeburg v Beroe Stara (3-1) | 2-0, 1-1 |
| Glentoran v Bor Moenchengladbach (0-7) | 0-2, 0-5 |
| Sporting Lisbon v Zurich (4-1) | 3-0, 1-1 |
| AC Milan v PAOK Salonika (5-2) | 3-0, 2-2 |

**Semi-Final**

| | |
|---|---|
| AC Milan v Bor Moenchengladbach (2-1) | 2-0, 0-1 |
| Sporting Lisbon v Magdeburg (2-3) | 1-1, 1-2 |

*Won on away goals rule.*

### Final 1973–74: FC Magdeburg 2, AC Milan 0
(In Rotterdam, 8 May, 1974, 5000)

*FC Magdeburg:* Schultz; Enge, Zapf, Gaube, Abraham, Tyll, Pommerenke, Seguin, Raugust, Sparwasser, Hoffman.
*AC Milan:* Pizzaballa; Anquilletti, Sabadini, Lanzi, Schnellinger, Maldera, Tresoldi, Benetti, Bigon, Rivera, Bergamaschi.
*Scorers:* FC Magdeburg – Lanzi og, Seguin.

## EUROPEAN CUP-WINNERS' CUP 1974-75

**First Round, First Leg**
Liverpool 11 (*Lindsay pen, Boersma 2, Thompson 2, Heighway, Cormack, Hughes, Callaghan, Smith, Kennedy*), Stromsgodset 0
Dundee United 3 (*Narey, Copland, Gardener*), Jiul Petrosani 0
Ferencvaros 2 (*Nyilasi, Szabo*), Cardiff City 0
Bursapor 4 (*Turan 2, Ali, Sinan pen*), Finn Harps 2 (*Ferry, Bradley*)
Sliema Wanderers 2 (*Camilleri 2*), Reipas Lahti 0
Dynamo Kiev 1 (*Blokhin*), CSKA Sofia 0
Malmö 1 (*Cervin*), Sion 0
Gwardia Warsaw 2 (*Sroka, Kraska*), Bologna 1 (*Savoldi*)
Slavia Prague 1 (*Herda*), Carl Zeiss Jena 0
Waregem 2 (*Delesie 2*), Austria/WAC 1 (*Pirkner*)
PAOK Salonika 1 (*Terzanides*), Red Star Belgrade 0
PSV Eindhoven 10 (*Van der Kuylen 3, Lubse 3, Kemper, Deykers, Edstrom, Van Kraay*), Ards 0
Fram Reykjavik 0, Real Madrid 2 (*Roberto Martinez 2*)
Benfica 4 (*Jordao 2, Humberto, Nene*), Vanlose 0
Eintracht Frankfurt 3 (*Holzenbein 2, Rohrbach*), Monaco 0

**First Round, Second Leg**
Stromsgodset 0, Liverpool 1 (*Kennedy*)
Jiul Petrosani 2 (*Rosnai, Tonca*), Dundee United 0
Cardiff City 1 (*Dwyer*), Ferencvaros 4 (*Takacs, Szabo, Pusztai, Mate*)
Finn Harps 0, Bursaspor 0
Reipas Lahti 4 (*Salonen, Lahtanen, Sandberg 2*), Sliema Wanderers 1 (*Aquilina*)
CSKA Sofia 0, Dynamo Kiev 1 (*Blokhin*)
Sion 1 (*Suiza*), Malmö 0
Bologna 2 (*Savoldi 2*), Gwardia Warsaw 1 (*Terlecki*)
Carl Zeiss Jena 1 (*Stein*), Slavia Prague 0
Austria/WAC 4 (*Pirkner, Weigel, Fiala*), Waregem 1 (*Koudijzer*)
Red Star Belgrade 2 (*Petrovic V., Savic*), PAOK Salonika 0
Ards 1 (*Guy*), PSV Eindhoven 4 (*Van der Kuylen, Edstrom, Dahlqvist 2*)
Real Madrid 6 (*Pirri 2, Santillana, Netzer, Macanas, Aguilar*), Fram Reykjavik 0
Vanlose 1 (*Petersen*), Benfica 4 (*Nene, Jordao 2, Barros*)
Monaco 2 (*Onnis, Petit*), Eintracht Frankfurt 2 (*Beverungen, Nickel*)
Avenir Beggen had a walkover when Paralimni withdrew.

**Second Round, First Leg**
Liverpool 1 (*Keegan*), Ferencvaros 1 (*Mate*)
Dundee United 0, Bursaspor 0

Real Madrid 3 (*Krieger og, Santillana, Roberto Martinez*), Austria/WAC 0
Gwardia Warsaw 1 (*Malkiewicz*), PSV Eindhoven 5 (*Willy Van der Kerkhof, Kialak og, Deykers, Lubse, Van der Kuylen*)
Carl Zeiss Jena 1 (*Vogel*), Benfica 1 (*Nene*)
Red Star Belgrade 6 (*Sestic 3, Filipovic 2, Rajkovic*), Avenir Beggen 1 (*Sinner*)
Malmö 3 (*Larsson 2, Sjoberg*), Reipas Lahti 1 (*Kautonen*)
Eintracht Frankfurt 2 (*Nickel, Koerbel*), Dynamo Kiev 3 (*Kolotov, Blokhin, Muntian*)

**Second Round, Second Leg**
Ferencvaros 0, Liverpool 0
Bursaspor 1 (*Vahit*), Dundee United 0
Austria/WAC 2 (*Pirkner, Fiala*), Real Madrid 2 (*Roberto Martinez, Netzer*)
PSV Eindhoven 3 (*Van der Kuylen 2 [1 pen], Lubse*), Gwardia Warsaw 0
Benfica 0, Carl Zeiss Jena 0
Avenir Beggen 1 (*Dresch*), Red Star Belgrade 5 (*Rajkovic 2, Filipovic, Sestic, Savic*)
Reipas Lahti 0, Malmö 0
Dynamo Kiev 2 (*Onischenko 2*), Eintracht Frankfurt 1 (*Rohrbach*)

**Quarter-Finals, First Leg**
Real Madrid 2 (*Santillana, Netzer pen*), Red Star Belgrade 0
PSV Eindhoven 0, Benfica 0
Malmö 1 (*Sjoberg*), Ferencvaros 3 (*Nyilasi, Magyar, Mate*)
Bursaspor 0, Dynamo Kiev 1 (*Onischenko*)

**Quarter-Finals, Second Leg**
Benfica 1 (*Humberto*), PSV Eindhoven 2 (*Willy Van der Kerkhof, Quaars*)
Ferencvaros 1 (*Mate*), Malmö 1 (*Sjoberg*)
Dynamo Kiev 2 (*Kolotov pen, Muntian*), Bursaspor 0
Red Star Belgrade 2 (*Dzajic, Petrovic O. pen*), Real Madrid 0
Red Star Belgrade won on penalties.

**Semi-Finals, First Leg**
Ferencvaros 2 (*Branikovits, Magyar*), Red Star Belgrade 1 (*Savic*)
Dynamo Kiev 3 (*Kolotov, Onischenko, Blokhin*), PSV Eindhoven 0

**Semi-Finals, Second Leg**
Red Star Belgrade 2 (*Keri, Filipovic*), Ferencvaros 2 (*Pusztai, Megyesi pen*)
PSV Eindhoven 2 (*Edstrom 2*), Dynamo Kiev 1 (*Burjak*)

### Final 1974–75: Dynamo Kiev 3, Ferencvaros 0
(at Basle, 14 May, 1975, 13,000)

*Dynamo Kiev:* Rudakov; Fomenko, Troshkin, Reshko, Matvienko, Muntian, Konkov, Burjak, Kolotov, Onischenko, Blokhin.
*Ferencvaros:* Geczi; Pataki, Martos, Rab, Megyesi, Nyilasi (Onhaus), Juhasz, Mucha, Szabo, Mate, Magyar.
*Scorers:* Dynamo Kiev – Onischenko 2, Blokhin.

# EUROPEAN CUP-WINNERS' CUP 1975–76

**First Round, First Leg**
Ararat Erevan 9 (*Markarov 5 [1 pen], Oganiesian 2, Petrosian S., Bondarenko*), Anorthosis 0
Basle 1 (*Schoenberger*), Atlético Madrid 2 (*Garate, Ayala*)
Besiktas 0, Fiorentina 3 (*Caso 2, Casarsa*)
Borac Banja Luka 9 (*Cetina 3, Ibrahimbegovic 5, Jurkovic*), US Rumelange 0
Eintracht Frankfurt 5 (*Korbel, Beverungen, Holzenbein, Nickel 2*), Coleraine 1 (*Cochrane*)
Haladas Szombathely 7 (*Fedor 2, Horath 2, Frakas og, Halmosi*), Valletta 0
Home Farm 1 (*Brophy*), Lens 1 (*Hopquin*)
Lahden Reipas 2 (*Lindholm, Tupasela*), West Ham U 2 (*Brooking, Bonds*)
Panathinaikos 0, Sachsenring Zwickau 0
Rapid Bucharest 1 (*Thissen og*), Anderlecht 0
Spartak Trnava 0, Boavista 0
Skeid Oslo 1 (*Skjoensberg B.*), Stal Rzeszow 4 (*Kozierski 2, Curylo, Krawczyk*)
Sturm Graz 3 (*Stendal 2 pens, Kulmer*), Slavia Sofia 1 (*Kostov*)
Valur Reykjavik 0, Celtic 2 (*Dalglish, McDonald*)
Vejle 0, Den Haag 2 (*Jol, Van Leeuwen*)
Wrexham 2 (*Griffiths, Davis*), Djurgaardens 1 (*Krantz*)

**First Round, Second Leg**
Anderlecht 2 (*Van Binst, Rensenbrink*), Rapid Bucharest 0
Anorthosis 1 (*Fivos pen*), Ararat Erevan 1 (*Bondarenko*)
Atlético Madrid 1 (*Becerra*), Basle 1 (*Demarmels*)
Boavista 3 (*Mane, Celse, Salvador*), Spartak Trnava 0
Celtic 7 (*Edvaldsson, Dalglish, McCluskey pen, Hood 2, Deans, Callaghan*), Valur 0
Den Haag 2 (*Perazic, Mansveld*), Vejle 0
Djurgaarden 1 (*Lovfors*), Wrexham 1 (*Whittle*)
Lens 6 (*Northeaux, Mujica pen, Kaiser 3, Llorens*), Home Farm 0
Sachsenring Zwickau 2 (*Schykowski, Dietzsch pen*), Panathinaikos 0
Slavia Sofia 1 (*Kostov*), Sturm Graz 0
West Ham U 3 (*Robson 2, Jennings*), Reipas Landen 0
US Rumelange 1 (*Rohmann*), Borac Banja Luka 5 (*Smilevski, Reso, Kovahevic, Vidacek, Marjonaovic*)
Coleraine 2 (*McCurdy, Cochrane*), Eintracht Frankfurt 6 (*Grabowski 3, Nickel, Lorenz, Holzenbein*)
Valletta 1 (*Giglio*), Haladas Szombathely 1 (*Karaci*)
Fiorentina 3 (*Caso 2, Casarsa*), Besiktas 0
Stal Rzeszow 4 (*Kozierski, Miler, Krawczyk, Napieracz*), Skeid Oslo 0

**Second Round, First Leg**
Anderlecht 3 (*Rensenbrink 2, Coeck*), Borac Banja Luka 0

Ararat Erevan 1 (*Petrosian S.*), West Ham U 1 (*Taylor A.*)
Atlético Madrid 1 (*Bacerra*), Eintracht Frankfurt 2 (*Holzenbein 2*)
Boavista 0, Celtic 0
Den Haag 3 (*Schoenmaker, Van Vliet, Van Leeawen*), Lens 2 (*Zuraszek, Janovic*)
Fiorentina 1 (*Speggiorin*), Sachsenring Zwickau 0
Sturm Graz 2 (*Stendal, Stenier pen*), Haladas Szombathely 0
Wrexham 2 (*Ashcroft 2*), Stal Rzeszow 0

**Second Round, Second Leg**
Borac Banja Luka 1 (*Ibrahimbegovic*), Anderlecht 0
Celtic 3, (*Dalglish, Edvaldsson, Deans*), Boavista 1 (*Mane*)
Eintracht Frankfurt 1 (*Reichel*), Atlético Madrid 0
Haladas Szombathely 1 (*Horvath*), Sturm Graz 1 (*Jurtin*)
Lens 1 (*Mujica pen*), Den Haag 3 (*Shoenmaker 2, Van Leeuwen*)
Sachsenring Zwickau 1 (*Schykowski J.*), Fiorentina 0
Stal Rzeszow 1 (*Kozierski*), Wrexham 1 (*Sutton*)
West Ham U 3 (*Paddon, Robson, Taylor A.*), Ararat Erevan 1 (*Petrosian N.*)

**Quarter-Finals, First Leg**
Anderlecht 1 (*Van Binst*), Wrexham 0
Celtic 1 (*Dalglish*), Sachsenring Zwickau 1 (*Blank*)
Den Haag 4 (*Mansveld 3 [2 pens], Schoenmaker*), West Ham U 2 (*Jennings 2*)
Sturm Graz 0, Eintracht Frankfurt 2 (*Holzenbein, Wenzel*)

**Quarter-Finals, Second Leg**
Eintracht Frankfurt 1 (*Holzenbein*), Sturm Graz 0
Sachsenring Zwickau 1 (*Blank*), Celtic 0
West Ham U 3 (*Taylor A., Lampard, Bonds pen*), Den Haag 1 (*Schoenmaker*)
Wrexham 1 (*Lee*), Anderlecht 1 (*Rensenbrink*)

**Semi-Finals, First Leg**
Eintracht Frankfurt 2 (*Neuberger, Kraus*), West Ham U 1 (*Paddon*)
Sachsenring Zwickau 0, Anderlecht 3 (*Van der Elst 2, Rensenbrink*)

**Semi-Finals, Second Leg**
Anderlecht 2 (*Rensenbrink, Van der Elst*), Sachsenring Zwickau 0
West Ham U 3 (*Brooking 2, Robson*), Eintracht Frankfurt 1 (*Beverungen*)

**Final 1976–76: Anderlecht 4, West Ham U 2**
(At Heysel Stadium, Brussels, 5 May, 1976, 58,000)

*Anderlecht:* Ruiter; Lomme, Broos, Van Binst, Thissen, Dockx, Coeck (Vercauteren), Van der Elst, Ressel, Haan, Rensenbrink.

*West Ham U:* Day; Coleman, Bonds, Taylor T., Lampard (Taylor A.), McDowell, Brooking, Paddon, Holland, Jennings, Robson.

*Scorers:* Anderlecht – Rensenbrink 2 (1 pen), Van der Elst 2; West Ham U – Holland, Robson.

## EUROPEAN CUP-WINNERS' CUP 1976-77

**Preliminary Round, First Leg**
Cardiff City 1 (*Evans*), Servette 0

**Preliminary Round, Second Leg**
Servette 2 (*Bizzini, Pfister*), Cardiff City 1 (*Showers*)

**First Round, First Leg**
Lierse 1 (*Ceulemans*), Hajduk Split 0
MTK Budapest 3 (*Kunszt, Kovacs, Borso*), Sparta Prague 1 (*Cermak*)
AIK Stockholm 1 (*Wallgren*), Galatasaray 2 (*Gokmen, Nehmet*)
Anderlecht 2 (*Van der Elst, Rensenbrink*), Roda JC 1 (*Toonstra*)
Bodo Glimt 0, Napoli 2 (*Speggiorin 2*)
Bohemians 2 (*Ryan, Hansen B. og*), Esbjerg 1 (*Nielsen H.*)
Cardiff City 1 (*Alston*), Dynamo Tbilisi 0
Carrick Rangers 3 (*Prenter 2, Connor*), Aris Bonnevoie 1 (*Pissinger*)
Hamburg 3 (*Zaczyk, Reimann, Hidien*), Keflavik 0
Iraklis 0, Apoel Nicosia 0
Lokomotive Leipzig 2 (*Sekora, Fritsche*), Hearts 0
Southampton 4 (*Waldron, Channon 2 [1 pen], Osgood*), Marseille 0
Levski Spartak 12 (*Yordanov 2, Milanov 6, Panov 2, Spassov 2*), Reipas Lahden 2 (*Sandberg, Tupasela*)
Floriana 1 (*Vassallo*), Slask Wroclaw 4 (*Gavslovski 2, Kwiatkowski, Farrugia og*)
Rapid Vienna 1 (*Krankl*), Atlético Madrid 2 (*Cano, Ayala*)
CSÚ Galati 2 (*Simionescu, Holzer*), Boavista 3 (*Mane 2, Salvador*)

**First Round, Second Leg**
Apoel Nicosia 2 (*Marcou 2*), Iraklis 0
Atlético Madrid 1 (*Leivinha*), Rapid Vienna 1 (*Krejcirik*)
Boavista 2 (*Mane 2*), CSU Galati 0
Esbjerg 0, Bohemians 1 (*Mitten*)
Galatasaray 1 (*Gokmen*), AIK Stockholm 1 (*Wallgren*)
Hajduk Split 3 (*Zungul 2, Jerkovic*), Lierse 0
Hearts 5 (*Kay, Gibson 2, Brown, Busby*), Lokomotive Leipzig 1 (*Fritsche*)
Keflavik 1 (*Johansson S.*), Hamburg 1 (*Hidien*)
Reipas Lahden 1 (*Sandberg*), Levski Spartak 7 (*Panov, Milanov 4 [2 pens], Spassov, Krastanov*)
Marseille 2 (*Nogues, Emon*), Southampton 1 (*Peach*)
Napoli 1 (*Massa*), Bodo Glimt 0
Roda JC 2 (*Vermeulen, Van der Lem pen*), Anderlecht 3 (*Rensenbrink, Van der Elst 2*)
Slask Wroclaw 2 (*Pawlowski, Ehrlich*), Floriana 0
Sparta Prague 1 (*Urban*), MTK Budapest 1 (*Kunszt*)

Dynamo Tbilisi 3 (*Gutsaev, Kipiani, Kandeladze pen*), Cardiff City 0
Aris Bonnevoie 2 (*Werner, Langers*), Carrick Rangers 1 (*Irwin*)

**Second Round, First Leg**
Anderlecht 5 (*Coeck, Vercauteren, Rensenbrink 2 [1 pen]*), Galatasaray 1 (*Ozdewak*)
Apoel Nicosia 1 (*Leonidas*), Napoli 1 (*Savoldi pen*)
Atlético Madrid 1 (*Cano*), Hajduk Split 0
Boavista 3 (*Celso 2, Mane*), Levski Spartak 1 (*Milanov*)
Carrick Rangers 2 (*Irwin, Prenter*), Southampton 5 (*Channon 2, Stokes, McCalliog, Osgood*)
Hamburg 4 (*Bjornmose, Eigl, Reimann, Gallacher og*), Hearts 2 (*Busby, Park*)
Dynamo Tbilisi 1 (*Macheidze*), MTK Budapest 4 (*Shyloshi, Takach 2, Kish*)
Slask Wroclaw 3 (*Kwiatkowski, Sybis 2*), Bohemians 0

**Second Round, Second Leg**
Bohemians 0, Slask Wroclaw 1 (*Pawlowski*)
Galatasaray 1 (*Gokmen*), Anderlecht 5 (*Rensenbrink 2, Haan, Ressel, Coeck*)
Hearts 1 (*Gibson*), Hamburg 4 (*Eigl 2, Magath 2*)
Levski Spartak 2 (*Panov, Milanov*), Boavista 0
MTK Budapest 1 (*Koritar*), Dynamo Tbilisi 0
Southampton 4 (*Williams, Hayes 2, Stokes*), Carrick Rangers 1 (*Reid*)
Napoli 2 (*Speggiorin, Massa*), Apoel Nicosia 0
Hajduk Split 1 (*Zungul*), Atlético Madrid 2 (*Ayala, Leal*)

**Quarter-Finals, First Leg**
Anderlecht 2 (*Ressel, Rensenbrink*), Southampton 0
Levski Spartak 2 (*Tsvetkov, Milanov*), Atlético Madrid 1 (*Ayala*)
MTK Budapest 1 (*Borso*), Hamburg 1 (*Volkert*)
Slask Wroclaw 0, Napoli 0

**Quarter-Finals, Second Leg**
Atlético Madrid 2 (*Ayala 2 pens*), Levski Spartak 0
Hamburg 4 (*Reimann 2, Kaltz pen, Zaczyk*), MTK Budapest 1 (*Siklosi*)
Napoli 2 (*Massa, Chiarugi*), Slask Wroclaw 0
Southampton 2 (*Peach pen, MacDougall*), Anderlecht 1 (*Van der Elst*)

**Semi-Finals, First Leg**
Napoli 1 (*Bruscolotti*), Anderlecht 0
Atlético Madrid 3 (*Cano 2, Leal*), Hamburg 1 (*Magath*)

**Semi-Finals, Second Leg**
Hamburg 3 (*Capon og, Reimann, Keller*), Atlético Madrid 0
Anderlecht 2 (*Thissen, Van der Elst*), Napoli 0

---

**Final 1976-77: Hamburg 2, Anderlecht 0**
(In Amsterdam, 11 May, 1977, 65,000)

*Hamburg:* Kargus; Kaltz, Ripp, Nogly, Hidien, Steffenhagen, Keller, Reimann, Memering, Magath, Volkert.

*Anderlecht:* Ruiter; Van Binst, Van den Daele, Broos, Thissen, Van der Elst, Coeck, Haan, Dockx (Van Poucke), Ressel, Rensenbrink.

*Scorers:* Hamburg – Volkert (pen), Magath.

858

# EUROPEAN CUP-WINNERS' CUP 1977-78

**Preliminary Round, First Leg**
Rangers 1 (*Greig*), Young Boys 0

**Preliminary Round, Second Leg**
Young Boys 2 (*Jackson og, Leuzinger*), Rangers 2 (*Johnstone, Smith*)

**First Round, First Leg**
Lokomotiv Sofia 1 (*Kolev*), Anderlecht 6 (*Van der Elst 4 [1 pen], Nielsen, Van Poucke*)
Besiktas 2 (*Zeferiya Burth, Paunovic*), Diosgyor 0
Betis 2 (*Garcia Soriano, Eulate*), AC Milan 0
Brann Bergen 1 (*Aase*), IA Akranes 0
Cardiff City 0, Austria/WAC 0
Coleraine 1 (*Tweed*), Lokomotiv Leipzig 4 (*Eichhorn, Kuhn, Lowe 2*)
Dundalk 1 (*Flanagan*), Hajduk Split 0
Hamburg 8 (*Keller 4, Volkert pen, Buljan, Steffenhagen, Reimann*), Lahden Reipas 1 (*Riotto*)
FC Cologne 2 (*Lohr, Muller*), Porto 2 (*Gabriel, Octavio*)
Lokomotiv Kosice 0, Oster Vaxjo 0
PAOK Salonika 2 (*Pelios, Anastasiadis*), Zaglebie Sosnowiec 0
Progres Niedercorn 0, Vejle 1 (*Steen Tychosen*)
Rangers 0, Twente 0
St Etienne 1 (*Synaeghel*), Manchester U 1 (*Hill*)
Olympiakos Nicosia 1 (*Aristidou*), Uni Craiova 6 (*Balaci 2, Girtsu, Marcu, Crisan, Irinescu*)
Valletta 0, Moscow Dynamo 2 (*Kazachenok, Maximenkov*)

**First Round, Second Leg**
IA Akranes 0, Brann Bergen 4 (*Aase 2, Dahlhaug, Tronstad*)
Anderlecht 2 (*Van der Elst, Bouvy*), Lokomotiv Sofia 0
Austria/WAC 1 (*Baumeister*), Cardiff City 0
Diosgyor 5 (*Fuko, Olah 2 [1 pen], Fekete 2*), Besiktas 0
Hajduk Split 4 (*Vujovic, McManus og, Rukljac, McConville og*), Dundalk 0
Lahden Reipas 2 (*Riotto 2*), Hamburg 5 (*Volkert pen, Keegan, Magath, Keller, Steffenhagen*)
Lokomotiv Leipzig 2 (*Altmann, Fritschepen*), Coleraine 2 (*Guy 2*)
AC Milan 2 (*Tosetto,·Capello*), Betis 1 (*Lopez*)
Oster Vaxjo 2 (*Bild, Evesson*), Lokomotiv Kosice 2 (*Jozsa, Dobrovic*)
Porto 1 (*Murca*), FC Cologne 0
Twente 3 (*Gritter, Arnold Muhren, Van der Vall*), Rangers 0
Uni Craiova 2 (*Marcu, Cirtu*), Olympiakos Nicosia 0
Vejle 9 (*Sorensen, Ostergaard 2, Eg, Norgaard 3, Schacke, Tychosen*), Progres Niedercorn 0
Zaglebie Sosnowiec 0, PAOK Salonika 2 (*Kermanidis, Damanikis*)

**Second Round, First Leg**
Austria/WAC 0, Lokomotiv Kosice 0
Diosgyor 2 (*Tatar, Varadi*), Hajduk Split 1 (*Muzinic*)
Hamburg 1 (*Keller*), Anderlecht 2 (*Coeck, Rensenbrink*)
Lokomotiv Leipzig 1 (*Grobner*), Betis 1 (*Lopez*)
Moscow Dynamo 2 (*Kazachenov, Minaev*), Uni Craiova 0
Twente 2 (*Gritter 2*), Brann Bergen 0
Vejle 3 (*Eg, Jaquet, Ostergaard*), PAOK Salonika 0
Porto 4 (*Duda 3, Oliveira*), Manchester U 0

**Second Round, Second Leg**
Anderlecht 1 (*Van der Elst*), Hamburg 1 (*Keegan*)
Betis 2 (*Garcia Soriano 2*), Lokomotiv Leipzig 1 (*Liebers*)
Brann Bergen 1 (*Tronstad*), Twente 2 (*Gritter, Thoresen*)
Uni Craiova 2 (*Cirtu, Beideanu*), Moscow Dynamo 0
*Dynamo won 3-0 on penalties*
Hajduk Split 2 (*Vujovic, Rukljac pen*) Diosgyor 1 (*Tatar*)
*Hajduk Split won 4-3 on penalties*
Lokomotiv Kosice 1 (*Farkas pen*), Austria/WAC 1 (*Morales*)
Manchester U 5 (*Coppell 2, Murca 2 og, Nicholl*), Porto 2 (*Seninho 2*)
PAOK Salonika 2 (*Orfanos, Kermanides*), Vejle 1 (*Jaquet*)

**Quarter-Finals, First Leg**
Vejle 0, Twente 3 (*Arnold Muhren, Gritter, Thijssen*)
Austria/WAC 1 (*Parits*), Hajduk Split 1 (*Surjak*)
Betis 0, Moscow Dynamo 0
Porto 1 (*Gomes*), Anderlecht 0

**Quarter-Finals, Second Leg**
Hajduk Split 1 (*Cop*), Austria/WAC 1 (*Daxbacher*)
*Austria/WAC won 3-0 on penalties.*
Moscow Dynamo 3 (*Gershkovich, Kazachenov, Maximenkov*), Betis 0
Anderlecht 3 (*Rensenbrink pen, Nielsen, Vercauteren*), Porto 0
Twente 4 (*Thijssen, Overweg, Gritter, Van der Vall*), Vejle 0

**Semi-Finals, First Leg**
Moscow Dynamo 2 (*Tseretli, Gershkovich*), Austria/WAC 1 (*Baumeister*)
Twente 0, Anderlecht 1 (*Nielsen*)

**Semi-Finals, Second Leg**
Anderlecht 2 (*Haan, Rensenbrink pen*), Twente 0
Austria/WAC 2 (*Pirkner pen, Morales*), Moscow Dynamo 1 (*Yakubik*)

## Final 1977-78: Anderlecht 4, Austria/WAC 0
(In Paris, 3 May, 1978, 48,679)

*Anderlecht:* De Bree; Van Binst, Broos, Dusbaba, Thissen, Van der Elst, Haan, Nielsen, Coeck, Vercauteren (Dockx), Rensenbrink.

*Austria/WAC:* Baumgartner; Robert Sara, Josef Sara, Obermayer, Baumeister, Prohaska, Daxbacher (Martinez), Gasselich, Morales (Drazen), Pirkner, Parits.

*Scorers:* Anderlecht – Rensenbrink 2, Van Binst 2.

## EUROPEAN CUP-WINNERS' CUP 1978-79

**First Round, First Leg**
Floriana 1 (*Xuereb R.*), Inter-Milan 3 (*Altobelli 3*)
Valur 1 (*Albertsson*), Magdeburg 1 (*Steinbach*)
Sporting Lisbon 0, Banik Ostrava 1 (*Antalik*)
Beveren 3 (*Albert, Stevens, Schonberger*), Ballymena 0
Ferencvaros 2 (*Nyilasi, Major*), Kalmar 0
Marek Stanke Dimitrov 3 (*Petrov V., Petrov I. 2*), Aberdeen 2 (*Jarvie, Harper*)
Barcelona 3 (*Krankl 2, Sanchez*), Shakhtor 0
PAOK Salonika 2 (*Karmanides, Sarafis*), Servette 0
Uni Craiova 3 (*Camataru 2, Crisan*), Fortuna Dusseldorf 4 (*Fanz 2, Allofs, Zimmermann*)
Zaglebie Sosnowiec 2 (*Zarichta, Starinskj*), SW Innsbruck 3 (*Peter Koncilia, Oberacher, Brasoler*)
AZ 67 0, Ipswich T 0
Apoel 0
Shamrock Rovers 2 (*Giles, Lynex*)
Rijeka 3 (*Tomic, Durkalic, Curkov*), Wrexham 0
Bodo Glimt 4 (*Solhang 2, Berg, Hanssen*), Union Luxembourg 1 (*Teitgen*)
Frem 2 (*Jacobsen, Hansen*), Nancy 0

**First Round, Second Leg**
Inter-Milan 5 (*Muraro 2, Fedele 2, Chierico*), Floriana 0
Magdeburg 4 (*Seguin, Steinbach, Hoffmann, Streich*), Valur 0
Banik Ostrava 1 (*Licka*), Sporting Lisbon 0
Ballymena 0, Beveren 3 (*Jansen 2, Wissmann*)
Kalmar 2 (*Magnusson, Nyberg*), Ferencvaros 2 (*Ebedli, Szokolai*)
Aberdeen 3 (*Strachan, Jarvie, Harper*), Marek Stanke Dimitrov 0
Shakhtor 1 (*Resnik*), Barcelona 1 (*Krankl*)
Servette 4 (*Pfister, Hamberg, Elia 2*), PAOK Salonika 0
Fortuna Dusseldorf 1 (*Bommer*), Uni Craiova 1 (*Marcu*)
SW Innsbruck 1 (*Koterva og*), Zaglebie Sosnowiec 1 (*Dvorczik*)
Ipswich T 2 (*Mariner, Wark*), AZ 67 0
Shamrock Rovers 1 (*Lynex*), Apoel 0
Wrexham 2 (*McNeil, Cartwright*), Rijeka 0
Union Luxembourg 1 (*Teitgen*), Bodo Glimt 0
Nancy 4 (*Curbelo, Jeannol 2, Zenier*), Frem 0

**Second Round, First Leg**
Servette 2 (*Hamberg, Barberis*), Nancy 1 (*Robio*)

Banik Ostrava 3 (*Knapp, Radimec, Rygel*), Shamrock Rovers 0
Ipswich T 1 (*Wark*), SW Innsbruck 0
Anderlecht 3 (*Van der Elst 2, Coeck*), Barcelona 0
Inter-Milan 5 (*Beccalossi, Altobelli 3, Muraro*), Bodo Glimt 0
Fortuna Dusseldorf 3 (*Gunther 2, Zimmermann*), Aberdeen 0
Rijeka 0, Beveren 0
Magdeburg 1 (*Streich*), Ferencvaros 0

**Second Round, Second Leg**
Nancy 2 (*Zenier, Umpierrez*), Servette 2 (*Elia, Schnyder*)
Shamrock Rovers 1 (*Giles*), Banik Ostrava 3 (*Licka 2, Albrecht*)
SW Innsbruck 1 (*Oberacher*), Ipswich T 1 (*Burley*)
Barcelona 3 (*Krankl, Heredia, Zuviria*), Anderlecht 0
Bodo Glimt 1 (*Hansen*), Inter-Milan 2 (*Altobelli, Scanziani*)
Aberdeen 2 (*McLelland, Jarvie*), Fortuna Dusseldorf 0
Beveren 2 (*Baecke 2*), Rijeka 0
Ferencvaros 2 (*Pusztai, Szokolai*), Magdeburg 1 (*Stachmann*)

**Quarter-Finals, First Leg**
Inter-Milan 0, Beveren 0
Fortuna Dusseldorf 0, Servette 0
Ipswich T 2 (*Gates 2*), Barcelona 1 (*Esteban*)
Magdeburg 2 (*Streich 2*), Banik Ostrava 1 (*Antalik*)

**Quarter-Finals, Second Leg**
Beveren 1 (*Stevens*), Inter-Milan 0
Servette 1 (*Andrey*), Fortuna Dusseldorf 1 (*Bommer*)
Barcelona 1 (*Migueli*), Ipswich T 0
Banik Ostrava 4 (*Rygel 2, Albrecht, Nemec*), Magdeburg 2 (*Sparwasser, Pommerenke*)

**Semi-Finals, First Leg**
Fortuna Dusseldorf 3 (*Klaus Allofs 2, Thomas Allofs*), Banik Ostrava 1 (*Nemec*)
Barcelona 1 (*Rexach pen*), Beveren 0

**Semi-Finals, Second Leg**
Banik Ostrava 2 (*Licka, Antalik*), Fortuna Dusseldorf 1 (*Zewe*)
Beveren 0, Barcelona 1 (*Krankl pen*)

### Final 1978-79: Barcelona 4, Fortuna Dusseldorf 3 aet
(In Basle, 16 May, 1979)

*Barcelona:* Artola; Zuviria, Migueli, Costas (Martinez), Albaladejo (De la Cruz), Sanchez, Neeskens, Asensi, Rexach, Krankl, Carrasco.

*Fortuna Dusseldorf:* Daniel; Baltes, Zewe, Zimmermann (Lund), Brei (Weikl), Kohnen, Bommer, Schmitz, Thomas Allofs, Klaus Allofs, Seel.

*Scorers:* Barcelona – Sanchez, Asensi, Rexach, Krankl; Fortuna Dusseldorf – Klaus Allofs, Seel 2.

# EUROPEAN CUP-WINNERS' CUP 1979–80

**Preliminary Round, First Leg**
Rangers 1 (*Smith*), Lillestrom 0
B 1903 6 (*Haarby, Larsen, Kristiansen 2, Thygesen 2*),
  Apoel 0

**Preliminary Round, Second Leg**
Lillestrom 0, Rangers 2 (*MacDonald A., Johnstone*)
Apoel 0, B 1903 1 (*Larsen*)

**First Round, First Leg**
Juventus 2 (*Pozsgai og, Cabrini*), Raba Gyor 0
Reipas Lahti 0, Aris Bonnevoi 1 (*Schlitz*)
Arka Gdynia 3 (*Kwiatkovski, Kornynt 2*), Stara Zagora 2
  (*Petkov, Lipenski*)
Panionios 4 (*Liolios 2, Pafiakakis, Anastopoulos*), Twente
  Enschede 0
Innsbruck 1 (*Poell pen*), Lokomotiv Kosice 2 (*Strapek,
  Jacko*)
Rangers 2 (*MacDonald, McLean*), Fortuna Dusseldorf 1
  (*Wenzel*)
Arsenal 2 (*Sunderland, Young*), Fenerbahce 0
B 1903 2 (*Thycosen, Hansen*), Valencia 2 (*Arias, Castel-
  lanos*)
Wrexham 3 (*McNeil, Fox, Buxton*), Magdeburg 2
  (*Streich, Steinbach*)
IFK Gothenburg 1 (*Holmgren*), Waterford 0
Beerschot 0, Rijeka Fiume 0
Young Boys Berne 2 (*Zwygart, Schoenenberger*), Steaua
  Bucharest 2 (*Soica, Jordanescu*)
Sliema Wanderers 2 (*Tortell 2 pens*), Boavista 1 (*Eliseu*)
Cliftonville 0, Nantes 1 (*Rampillon*)
IA Akranes 0, Barcelona 1 (*Rexach*)

**First Round, Second Leg**
Raba Gyor 2 (*Furino og, Poczik*), Juventus 1 (*Causio*)
Aris Bonnevoi 1 (*Colling*), Reipas Lahti 0
Stara Zagora 2 (*Stoyanov, Petkov*), Arka Gdynia 0
Twente Enschede 3 (*Bos pen, Linstadt, Otto*), Panionios
  1 (*Anastopoulos*)
Lokomotiv Kosice 1 (*Kozak*), Innsbruck 0
Fortuna Dusseldorf 0, Rangers 0
Fenerbahce 0, Arsenal 0
Valencia 4 (*Felman, Kempes 2, Saura*), B 1903 0
Magdeburg 5 (*Hoffman 2, Newes, Steinbach pen, Streich*),
  Wrexham 2 (*Vinter, Hill*)
Waterford 1 (*Keane*), IFK Gothenburg 1 (*Holmgren*)
Rijeka Fiume 2 (*Radovic 2*), Beerschot 1 (*Demushel*)
Steaua Bucharest 6 (*Mitu, Sames 2, Aelenei, Raducanu,
  Zahlu*), Young Boys Berne 0
Boavista 8 (*Ailten, Julio 3, Moinhos, Salvador, Folha,
  Oscar*), Sliema Wanderers 0
Nantes 7 (*Pecout 3, Trossero 2, Rampillon, Rio*), Clifton-
  ville 0

Barcelona 5 (*Krankl, Simonsen, Rexach, Carrasco,
  Asensi*), IA Akranes 0

**Second Round, First Leg**
Stara Zagora 1 (*Stojanov pen*), Juventus 0
Panionios 1 (*Anastopoulos*), IFK Gothenburg 0
Lokomotiv Kosice 2 (*Kozak 2*), Rijeka Fiume 0
Valencia 1 (*Kempes*), Rangers 1 (*McLean*)
Nantes 3 (*Pecout 2, Toure*), Steaua Bucharest 2 (*Radu-
  canu 2 [1 pen]*)
Arsenal 2 (*Young, Sunderland*), Magdeburg 1 (*Pommer-
  enke*)
Aris Bonnevoi 1 (*Mattes*), Barcelona 4 (*Simonsen 3, Rex-
  ach*)
Dynamo Moscow 0, Boavista 0

**Second Round, Second Leg**
Juventus 3 (*Scirea, Causio, Verza*), Stara Zagora 0
IFK Gothenburg 2 (*Nordin, Holmgren*), Panionios 0
Rijeka Fiume 3 (*Desnica 3*), Lokomotiv Kosice 0
Rangers 1 (*Johnstone*), Valencia 3 (*Bonhof, Kempes2*)
Steaua Bucharest 1 (*Jordanescu*), Nantes 2 (*Pecout,
  Amisse*)
Magdeburg 2 (*Streich, Stahmann*), Arsenal 2 (*Rice,
  Brady*)
Barcelona 7 (*Krankl 3, Heredia 2, Carrasco, Canito*), Aris
  Bonnevoi 1 (*Tuliuv*)
Boavista 1 (*Moinhos*), Dynamo Moscow 1 (*Minaev*)

**Quarter-Finals, First Leg**
Rijeka Fiume 0, Juventus 0
Arsenal 5 (*Sunderland 2, Price, Brady, Young*), IFK
  Gothenburg 1 (*Nilsson*)
Barcelona 0, Valencia 1 (*Pablo*)
Dynamo Moscow 0, Nantes 2 (*Tusseau, Pecout*)

**Quarter-Finals, Second Leg**
Juventus 2 (*Causio, Bettega*), Rijeka Fiume 0
IFK Gothenburg 0, Arsenal 0
Valencia 4 (*Saura 2, Bonhof, Kempes pen*), Barcelona 3
  (*Canito 2, Landaburu*)
Nantes 2 (*Michel, Toure*), Dynamo Moscow 3 (*Minaev,
  Gatzaiev, Kolessov*)

**Semi-Finals, First Leg**
Arsenal 1 (*Bettega og*), Juventus 1 (*Cabrini*)
Nantes 2 (*Baronchelli 2*), Valencia 1 (*Kempes*)

**Semi-Finals, Second Leg**
Juventus 0, Arsenal 1 (*Vaessen*)
Valencia 4 (*Bonhof, Michel og, Kempes 2 [1 pen]*), Nantes

**Final 1979–80: Valencia 0, Arsenal 0 (aet)**
*Valencia won 5-4 on penalties.*
(In Brussels, 14 May, 1980, 40,000)

*Valencia:* Pereira; Carrette, Botubot, Arias, Tendillo, Solsona, Saura, Bonhof, Kempes, Subirates (Castellanos), Pablo.
*Arsenal:* Jennings; Rice, Nelson, Talbot, O'Leary, Young, Brady, Sunderland, Stapleton, Price (Hollins), Rix.

## EUROPEAN CUP-WINNERS' CUP 1980—81

**Preliminary Round**
Celtic 6 (*McGarvey 2, McCluskey 2, Nedder og, Sullivan*), Diosgyor 0
Diosgyor 2 (*Gorgey 2*), Celtic 1 (*Nicholas*)
Altay Izmir 0, Benfica 0
Benfica 4 (*Chalana, Humberto, Nene, Cesar*), Altay Izmir 0

**First Round, First Leg**
Newport Co 4 (*Gwyther, Moore, Aldridge, Bruton*), Crusaders 0
Spora Luxembourg 0, Sparta Prague 6 (*Berger 2, Kotek, Chalana, Chaloupka 2*)
Slavia Sofia 3 (*Tsvetkov pen, Velichkov 2*), Legia Warsaw 1 (*Miloszewisz*)
Castilla 3 (*Paco, Balin, Cidon*), West Ham U 1 (*Cross*)
Celtic 2 (*Nicholas 2*), Poli Timisoara 1 (*Adrian*)
Dynamo Zagreb 0, Benfica 0
Fortuna Dusseldorf 5 (*Kohnen 2, Wenzel, Klaus Allofs, Theis*), Austria Salzburg 0
Hibernians Malta 1 (*Xuereb P.*), Waterford 0
Ilves Tampere 1 (*Uimonen*), Feyenoord 3 (*Notten pen, Van Deinsen, Troost*)
Hvidovre 1 (*Steen Hansen pen*), Fram Reykjavik 0
Kastoria 0, Dynamo Tbilisi 0
Malmö 1 (*McKinnon*), Partizan Tirana 0
Omonia Nicosia 1 (*Kanaris*), Waterschei 3 (*Van Pouche, Janssen, Meds*)
Roma 3 (*Pruzzo, Ancelotti, Falcao*), Carl Zeiss Jena 0
Sion 1 (*Brigger*), Haugar 1 (*Osborne*)
Valencia 2 (*Kempes, Morena pen*), Monaco 0

**First Round, Second Leg**
Monaco 3 (*Petit 2, Barberis*), Valencia 3 (*Morena, Kempes, Felman*)
Benfica 2 (*Nene, Cesar*), Dynamo Zagreb 0
Haugar 2 (*Nilsen, Kristophersen pen*), Sion 0
Partizan Tirana 0, Malmö 0
Poli Timisoara 1 (*Paltinisan*), Celtic 0
Waterford 4 (*Kirk 2, Finucane, Fitzpatrick*), Hibernians Malta 0
Sparta Prague 6 (*Pospisil, Slany, Jarohm 2, Berger, Horvath*), Spora Luxembourg 0
Dynamo Tbilisi 2 (*Shengelia, Gutsayev*), Kastoria 0
Legia Warsaw 1 (*Okonski pen*), Slavia Sofia 0
Austria Salzburg 0, Fortuna Dusseldorf 3 (*Thomas Allofs, Dusend*)
West Ham U 5 (*Pike, Cross 3, Goddard*), Castilla 1 (*Bernal*)
Feyenoord 4 (*Vermaulen, Nielsen, Troost, Notten*), Ilves Tampere 2 (*Prinen pen, Wacklin*)
Waterschei 4 (*Janssen, Plessers pen, Van Poucke, Grundel*), Omonia Nicosia 0

Fram Reykjavik 0, Hvidovre 2 (*Ambrose, Hansen*)
Crusaders 0, Newport Co 0
Carl Zeiss Jena 4 (*Krause, Lindeman, Bielau 2*) Roma 0

**Second Round, First Leg**
Carl Zeiss Jena 3 (*Sengewald, Schnuphase pen, Trocha*), Valencia 1 (*Morena*)
Malmö 1 (*Andersson M.*), Benfica 0
Waterschei 0, Fortuna Dusseldorf 0
Feyenoord 2 (*Wijnstekers, Bouwens*), Hvidovre 1 (*Mannicke*)
Sparta Prague 2 (*Vkovjak 2*), Slavia Sofia 0
Waterford 0, Dynamo Tbilisi 1 (*Shengelia*)
Haugar 0, Newport Co 0
West Ham U 4 (*Bonds, Goddard, Stewart pen, Cross*), Poli Timisoara 0

**Second Round, Second Leg**
Newport Co 6 (*Gwyther, Lowndes, Aldridge, Tynan 2, Moore*), Haugar 0
Valencia 1 (*Botubot*), Carl Zeiss Jena 0
Poli Timisoara 1 (*Paltinisan*), West Ham U 0
Dynamo Tbilisi 4 (*Daraselia 2, Chivadze, Chilaia*), Waterford 0
Fortuna Dusseldorf 1 (*Bansemer*), Waterschei 0
Feyenoord 1 (*Nielsen*), Hvidovre 0
Slavia Sofia 3 (*Velitchkov, Jeliazkov, Tsvetkov*), Sparta Prague 0
Benfica 2 (*Nene 2*), Malmö 0

**Quarter-Final, First Leg**
West Ham U 1 (*Cross*), Dynamo Tbilisi 4 (*Chivadze, Gutsayev, Shengelia 2*)
Carl Zeiss Jena 2 (*Raab 2*), Newport Co 2 (*Tynan 2*)
Slavia Sofia 3 (*Tsvetkov 2 [1 pen], Aliev*), Feyenoord 2 (*Nielsen, Vermeulen pen*)
Fortuna Dusseldorf 2 (*Wenzel, Dusend*), Benfica 2 (*Carlos Manuel, Humberto*)

**Quarter-Final, Second Leg**
Feyenoord 4 (*Notten, Van Deinsen, Vermeulen, Bouwens*), Slavia Sofia 0
Benfica 1 (*Chalana*), Fortuna Dusseldorf 0
Dynamo Tbilisi 0, West Ham U 1 (*Pearson*)
Newport Co 0, Carl Zeiss Jena 1 (*Kurbjuweit*)

**Semi-Final, First Leg**
Carl Zeiss Jena 2 (*Bielau, Raab*), Benfica 0
Dynamo Tbilisi 3 (*Sulakvelidze 2, Gutsayev*), Feyenoord 0

**Semi-Final, Second Leg**
Benfica 1 (*Reinaldo*), Carl Zeiss Jena 0
Feyenoord 2 (*Bouwens, Notten pen*), Dynamo Tbilisi 0

---

**Final 1980—81: Dynamo Tbilisi (0) 2, Carl Zeiss Jena (0) 1**
(In Dusseldorf, 13 May, 1981, 9000)

*Dynamo Tbilisi:* Gabelia; Kostava, Chivadze, Khisanishvili, Tavadze, Svanadze (Kakilashvili), Sulakvelidze, Daraselia, Gutsayev, Kipiani, Shengelia.

*Carl Zeiss Jena:* Grapenthin; Brauer, Kurbjuweit, Schnuphase, Schilling, Hoppe (Overmann), Krause, Lindemann, Bielau (Topfer), Raab, Vogel.

*Scorers:* Dynamo Tbilisi – Gutsayev, Daraselia; Carl Zeiss Jena – Hoppe.

# FAIRS & UEFA CUP HISTORY

## FAIRS CUP 1955−58

**Group A**
Barcelona 6, Copenhagen 2
Copenhagen 1, Barcelona 1
Vienna withdrew

|            | P | W | D | L | F | A | Pts |
|------------|---|---|---|---|---|---|-----|
| Barcelona  | 2 | 1 | 1 | 0 | 7 | 3 | 3   |
| Copenhagen | 2 | 0 | 1 | 1 | 3 | 7 | 1   |

**Group B**
Inter-Milan 0, Birmingham C 0
Zagreb 0, Birmingham C 1
Zagreb 0, Inter-Milan 1
Birmingham C 3, Zagreb 0
Inter-Milan 4, Zagreb 0
Birmingham C 2, Inter-Milan 1

|             | P | W | D | L | F | A | Pts |
|-------------|---|---|---|---|---|---|-----|
| Birmingham C| 4 | 3 | 1 | 0 | 6 | 1 | 7   |
| Inter-Milan | 4 | 2 | 1 | 1 | 6 | 2 | 5   |
| Zagreb      | 4 | 0 | 0 | 4 | 0 | 9 | 0   |

**Group C**
Leipzig 6, Lausanne 3
Lausanne 7, Leipzig 3
Cologne withdrew

|          | P | W | D | L | F  | A  | Pts |
|----------|---|---|---|---|----|----|-----|
| Lausanne | 2 | 1 | 0 | 1 | 10 | 9  | 2   |
| Leipzig  | 2 | 1 | 0 | 1 | 9  | 10 | 2   |

**Group D**
Basle 0, London 5
London 3, Frankfurt 2
London 1, Basle 0
Frankfurt 5, Basle 1
Frankfurt 1, London 0
Basle 6, Frankfurt 2

|           | P | W | D | L | F  | A  | Pts |
|-----------|---|---|---|---|----|----|-----|
| London    | 4 | 3 | 0 | 1 | 9  | 3  | 6   |
| Frankfurt | 4 | 2 | 0 | 2 | 10 | 10 | 4   |
| Basle     | 4 | 1 | 0 | 3 | 7  | 13 | 2   |

**Semi-Final**

| | |
|---|---|
| Birmingham C v Barcelona (5-6) | 4-3, 0-1, 1-2 |
| Lausanne v London (2-3) | 2-1, 0-2 |

**Final**

| | |
|---|---|
| **London v Barcelona (2-8)** | **2-2, 0-6** |

## FAIRS CUP 1958−60

**First Round**

| | |
|---|---|
| Basle v Barcelona (3-7) | 1-2, 2-5 |
| Inter-Milan v Lyon (8-1) | 7-0, 1-1 |
| Belgrade v Lausanne (11-4) | 6-1, 5-3 |
| Frem Copenhagen v Chelsea (2-7) | 1-3, 1-4 |
| Union St Gilloise v Leipzig (6-1) | 6-0, 0-1 |
| Hanover 96 v AS Roma (2-4) | 1-3, 1-1 |
| Zagreb v Ujpest Dozsa (4-3) | 4-2, 0-1 |
| Cologne v Birmingham C (2-4) | 2-2, 0-2 |
| Chelsea v Belgrade (2-4) | 1-0, 1-4 |
| Union St Gilloise v AS Roma (3-1) | 2-0, 1-1 |
| Birmingham C v Zagreb (4-3) | 1-0, 3-3 |

**Quarter-Final**

| | |
|---|---|
| Barcelona v Inter-Milan (8-2) | 4-0, 4-2 |

**Semi-Final**

| | |
|---|---|
| Belgrade v Barcelona (2-4) | 1-1, 1-3 |
| Union St Gilloise v Birmingham C (4-8) | 2-4, 2-4 |

**Final**

| | |
|---|---|
| **Birmingham C v Barcelona (1-4)** | **0-0, 1-4** |

## FAIRS CUP 1960−61

**First Round**

| | |
|---|---|
| Union St Gilloise v AS Roma (1-4) | 0-0, 1-4 |
| Lyon v Cologne (3-4) | 1-3, 2-1 |
| Lausanne v Hibernian (0-2) | 0-2 |
| *Lausanne withdrew after first leg.* | |
| Zagreb v Barcelona (4-5) | 1-1, 3-4 |
| Leipzig v Belgrade (6-8) | 5-2, 1-4, 0-2 |
| Inter-Milan v Hanover 96 (14-3) | 8-2, 6-1 |
| Copenhagen v Basle (11-4) | 8-1, 3-3 |
| Birmingham C v Ujpest Dozsa (5-3) | 3-2, 2-1 |
| Barcelona v Hibernian (6-7) | 4-4, 2-3 |
| Inter-Milan v Belgrade (5-1) | 5-0, 0-1 |
| Copenhagen v Birmingham C (4-9) | 4-4, 0-5 |

**Semi-Final**

| | |
|---|---|
| Hibernian v AS Roma (5-11) | 2-2, 3-3, 0-6 |
| Inter-Milan v Birmingham C (2-4) | 1-2, 1-2 |

**Quarter-Final**

| | |
|---|---|
| Cologne v AS Roma (3-6) | 0-2, 2-0, 1-4 |

**Final**

| | |
|---|---|
| **Birmingham C v AS Roma (2-4)** | **2-2, 0-2** |

# FAIRS CUP 1961-62

**First Round**

| | |
|---|---|
| Valencia v Nottingham F (7-1) | 2-0, 5-1 |
| Lausanne | bye |
| Cologne v Inter-Milan (7-9) | 4-2, 0-2, 3-5 |
| Union St Gilloise v Hearts (1-5) | 1-3, 0-2 |
| Spartak Brno v Leipzig (3-6) | 2-2, 1-4 |
| Strasbourg v MTK Budapest (3-13) | 1-3, 2-10 |
| AC Milan v Novisad (0-2) | 0-0, 0-2 |
| Iraklis Salonika | bye |
| Basle v Red Star Belgrade (2-5) | 1-1, 1-4 |
| Hibernian v Belenenses (6-4) | 3-3, 3-1 |
| Hanover 96 v Espanol (0-3) | 0-1, 0-2 |
| Birmingham C | bye |
| Lyon v Sheffield W (6-7) | 4-2, 2-5 |
| AS Roma | bye |
| Copenhagen v Dynamo Zagreb (4-9) | 2-7, 2-2 |
| West Berlin v Barcelona (1-3) | 1-0, 0-3 |

**Second Round**

| | |
|---|---|
| Lausanne v Valencia (3-4) | 3-4 |

*Second leg not played.*

| | |
|---|---|
| Hearts v Inter-Milan (0-5) | 0-1, 0-4 |
| MTK Budapest v Leipzig (5-3) | 3-0, 0-3, 2-0 |
| Iraklis Salonika v Novisad (3-10) | 2-1, 1-9 |
| Red Star Belgrade v Hibernian (5-0) | 4-0, 1-0 |
| Espanol v Birmingham C (5-3) | 5-2, 0-1 |
| Sheffield W v AS Roma (4-1) | 4-0, 0-1 |
| Barcelona v Dynamo Zagreb (7-3) | 5-1, 2-2 |

**Quarter-Final**

| | |
|---|---|
| Valencia v Inter-Milan (5-3) | 2-0, 3-3 |
| Novisad v MTK Budapest (2-6) | 1-4, 1-2 |
| Espanol v Red Star Belgrade (2-6) | 2-1, 0-5 |
| Sheffield W v Barcelona (3-4) | 3-2, 0-2 |

**Semi-Final**

| | |
|---|---|
| Valencia v MTK Budapest (10-3) | 3-0, 7-3 |
| Red Star Belgrade v Barcelona (1-6) | 0-2, 1-4 |

**Final**

| | |
|---|---|
| **Valencia v Barcelona (7-3)** | **6-2, 1-1** |

# FAIRS CUP 1962-63

**First Round**

| | |
|---|---|
| Valencia v Celtic (6-4) | 4-2, 2-2 |
| Everton v Dunfermline Ath (1-2) | 1-0, 0-2 |
| Hibernian v Copenhagen (7-2) | 4-0, 3-2 |
| DOS Utrecht v Tasmania Berlin (5-3) | 3-2, 2-1 |
| Altay Izmir v AS Roma (3-13) | 2-3, 1-10 |
| Glentoran v Real Zaragoza (2-8) | 0-2, 2-6 |
| Rapid Vienna v Red Star Belgrade (1-2) | 1-1, 0-1 |
| Barcelona v Belenenses (5-4) | 1-1, 1-1, 3-2 |
| Viktoria Cologne v Ferencvaros (5-7) | 4-3, 1-4 |
| Sampdoria v Aris Luxembourg (3-0) | 1-0, 2-0 |
| Petrolul Ploesti v Spartak Brno (4-3) | 2-2, 0-1 |
| Vojvodina v Leipzig (1-2) | 1-0, 0-2 |
| Basle v Bayern Munich (0-3) | 0-3 |

*Second leg not played.*

| | |
|---|---|
| Drumcondra v Odense BK 09 (6-5) | 4-1, 2-4 |
| Marseille v Union St Gilloise (3-4) | 1-0, 2-4 |
| Porto v Dynamo Zagreb (1-2) | 1-2, 0-0 |

**Second Round**

| | |
|---|---|
| Valencia v Dunfermline Ath (7-6) | 4-0, 2-6, 1-0 |

| | |
|---|---|
| DOS Utrecht v Hibernian (1-3) | 0-1, 1-2 |
| Real Zaragoza v AS Roma (3-6) | 2-4, 1-2 |
| Red Star Belgrade v Barcelona (4-3) | 3-2, 0-1, 1-0 |
| Sampdoria v Ferencvaros (1-6) | 1-0, 0-6 |
| Petrolul Ploesti v Leipzig (2-1) | 1-0, 0-1, 1-0 |
| Bayern Munich v Drumcondra (6-1) | 6-0, 0-1 |
| Dynamo Zagreb v Union St Gilloise (5-4) | 2-1, 0-1, 3-2 |

**Quarter-Final**

| | |
|---|---|
| Valencia v Hibernian (6-2) | 5-0, 1-2 |
| AS Roma v Red Star Belgrade (3-2) | 3-0, 0-2 |
| Ferencvaros v Petrolul Ploesti (2-1) | 2-0, 0-1 |
| Bayern Munich v Dynamo Zagreb (1-4) | 1-4, 0-0 |

**Semi-Final**

| | |
|---|---|
| Valencia v AS Roma (3-1) | 3-0, 0-1 |
| Ferencvaros v Dynamo Zagreb (1-3) | 0-1, 1-2 |

**Final**

| | |
|---|---|
| **Dynamo Zagreb v Valencia (1-4)** | **1-2, 0-2** |

# FAIRS CUP 1963-64

**First Round**

| | |
|---|---|
| Real Zaragoza v Iraklis Salonika (9-1) | 3-0, 6-1 |
| Lausanne v Hearts (9-8) | 2-2, 4-4, 3-2 |
| Atlético Madrid v Porto (2-1) | 2-1, 0-0 |
| Juventus v OFK Belgrade (4-3) | 2-1, 1-2, 1-0 |
| Aris Luxembourg v Liège (0-2) | 0-2, 0-0 |
| Staevnet Copenhagen v Arsenal (4-9) | 1-7, 3-2 |
| Glentoran v Partick T (1-7) | 1-4, 0-3 |
| Spartak Brno v Servette Geneva (7-1) | 5-0, 2-1 |
| Cologne v La Gantoise (4-2) | 3-1, 1-1 |
| DOS Utrecht v Sheffield W (2-8) | 1-4, 1-4 |
| Hertha Berlin v AS Roma (1-5) | 1-3, 0-2 |
| Tresnjevka Zagreb v Belenenses (1-4) | 0-2, 1-2 |
| Ujpest Dozsa v Lokomotiv Leipzig (3-2) | 0-0, 3-2 |
| Red Flag Brasov v Lokomotiv Plovdiv (2-5) | 1-3, 1-2 |
| Rapid Vienna v Racing Club de Paris (4-2) | 1-0, 3-2 |
| Shamrock Rovers v Valencia (2-3) | 0-1, 2-2 |

**Second Round**

| | |
|---|---|
| Lausanne v Real Zaragoza (1-5) | 1-2, 0-3 |

| | |
|---|---|
| Juventus v Atlético Madrid (3-1) | 1-0, 2-1 |
| Arsenal v Liège (2-4) | 1-1, 1-3 |
| Partick T v Spartak Brno (3-6) | 3-2, 0-4 |
| Cologne v Sheffield W (5-3) | 3-2, 2-1 |
| AS Roma v Belenenses (3-1) | 2-1, 1-0 |
| Ujpest Dozsa v Lokomotiv Plovdiv (3-1) | 0-0, 3-1 |
| Rapid Vienna v Valencia (2-3) | 0-0, 2-3 |

**Quarter-Final**

| | |
|---|---|
| Real Zaragoza v Juventus (3-2) | 3-2, 0-0 |
| Liège v Spartak Brno (3-2) | 2-0, 0-2, 1-0 |
| AS Roma v Cologne (3-5) | 3-1, 0-4 |
| Valencia v Ujpest Dozsa (6-5) | 5-2, 1-3 |

**Semi-Final**

| | |
|---|---|
| Liège v Real Zaragoza (2-4) | 1-0, 1-2, 0-2 |
| Valencia v Cologne (4-3) | 4-1, 0-2 |

**Final** (at Barcelona)

| | |
|---|---|
| **Real Zaragoza v Valencia** | **2-1** |

## FAIRS CUP 1964–65

**First Round**

| | |
|---|---|
| Union St Gilloise v Juventus (0-2) | 0-1, 0-1 |
| Betis v Stade Français (1-3) | 1-1, 0-2 |
| Goztepe Izmir v Petrolul Ploesti (1-3) | 1-2, 0-1 |
| Vojvodina v Lokomotiv Plovdiv (2-4) | 1-1, 1-1, 0-2 |
| KB Copenhagen v DOS Utrecht (4-6) | 3-4, 1-2 |
| Valencia v Liège (2-4) | 1-1, 1-3 |
| Belenenses v Shelbourne (2-3) | 1-1, 0-0, 1-2 |
| Servette Geneva v Atlético Madrid (3-8) | 2-2, 1-6 |
| Basle v Spora Luxembourg (2-1) | 2-0, 0-1 |
| Strasbourg v AC Milan (2-1) | 2-0, 0-1 |
| Barcelona v Fiorentina (2-1) | 0-1, 2-0 |
| Leixoes v Celtic (1-4) | 1-1, 0-3 |
| Borussia Dortmund v Bordeaux (4-3) | 4-1, 0-2 |
| Manchester U v Djurgaarden (7-2) | 1-1, 6-1 |
| Eintracht Frankfurt v Kilmarnock (4-5) | 3-0, 1-5 |
| Valerengen v Everton (4-9) | 2-5, 2-4 |
| Atlético Bilbao v OFK Belgrade (4-2) | 2-2, 2-0 |
| Hertha Berlin v Antwerp (2-3) | 2-1, 0-2 |
| Odense BK 13 v Stuttgart (1-4) | 1-3, 0-1 |
| Dunfermline Ath v Oergryte (4-2) | 4-2, 0-0 |
| Dynamo Zagreb v Graz (3-9) | 3-2, 6-0 |
| Aris Salonika v AS Roma (0-3) | 0-0, 0-3 |
| Wiener SK v Lokomotiv Leipzig (3-1) | 2-1, 1-0 |
| Ferencvaros v Spartak Brno (2-1) | 2-0, 0-1 |

**Second Round**

| | |
|---|---|
| Stade Français v Juventus (0-1) | 0-0, 0-1 |
| Petrolul Ploesti v Lokomotiv Plovdiv (1-2) | 1-0, 0-2 |
| DOS Utrecht v Liège (0-4) | 0-2, 0-2 |

| | |
|---|---|
| Shelbourne v Atlético Madrid (0-2) | 0-1, 0-1 |
| Basle v Strasbourg (2-6) | 0-1, 2-5 |
| Barcelona v Celtic (3-1) | 3-1, 0-0 |
| Borussia Dortmund v Manchester U (1-10) | 1-6, 0-4 |
| Kilmarnock v Everton (1-6) | 0-2, 1-4 |
| Atlético Bilbao v Antwerp (3-0) | 2-0, 1-0 |
| Dunfermline Ath v Stuttgart (1-0) | 1-0, 0-0 |
| Dynamo Zagreb v AS Roma (1-2) | 1-1, 0-1 |
| Ferencvaros v Wiener SK (4-2) | 0-1, 2-1, 2-0 |

**Third Round**

| | |
|---|---|
| Juventus v Lokomotiv Plovdiv (4-3) | 1-1, 1-1, 2-1 |
| Liège v Atlético Madrid (1-2) | 1-0, 0-2 |
| Strasbourg v Barcelona (2-2) | 0-0, 2-2, 0-0 |
| *Strasbourg won on toss of coin.* | |
| Manchester U v Everton (3-2) | 1-1, 2-1 |
| Atlético Bilbao v Dunfermline Ath (3-2) | 1-0, 0-1, 2-1 |
| AS Roma v Ferencvaros (1-3) | 1-2, 0-1 |

**Quarter-Final**

*Byes: Juventus, Atlético Madrid*

| | |
|---|---|
| Strasbourg v Manchester U (0-5) | 0-5, 0-0 |
| Ferencvaros v Atlético Bilbao (5-2) | 1-0, 1-2, 3-0 |

**Semi-Final**

| | |
|---|---|
| Atlético Madrid v Juventus (5-7) | 3-1, 1-3, 1-3 |
| Manchester U v Ferencvaros (4-5) | 3-2, 0-1, 1-2 |

**Final (in Turin)**

| | |
|---|---|
| **Juventus v Ferencvaros** | **0-1** |

## FAIRS CUP 1965–66

**First Round**

*Byes:* Hanover 96, Espanol, Red Flag Brasov, Goztepe Izmir, Servette Geneva, CUF, Lokomotiv Leipzig, Basle, Aris Salonika, Ujpest Dozsa, Dunfermline Ath, KB Copenhagen, Hearts, Valerengen, Shamrock Rovers, Real Zaragoza.

| | |
|---|---|
| DOS Utrecht v Barcelona (1-7) | 0-0, 1-7 |
| Antwerp v Glentoran (4-3) | 1-0, 3-3 |
| Stade Français v Porto (0-1) | 0-0, 0-1 |
| Bordeaux v Sporting Lisbon (1-10) | 0-4, 1-6 |
| Liège v Dynamo Zagreb (1-2) | 1-0, 0-2 |
| Munich 1860 v Malmö FF (7-1) | 4-1, 3-0 |
| AIK Stockholm v Daring (3-1) | 3-1, 0-0 |
| AC Milan* v Strasbourg (3-3) | 1-0, 1-2, 1-1 |
| Wiener SK v PAOK Salonika (7-2) | 6-0, 1-2 |
| Chelsea v AS Roma (4-1) | 4-1, 0-0 |
| Leeds U v Torino (2-1) | 2-1, 0-0 |
| Hibernian v Valencia (2-5) | 2-0, 0-2, 0-3 |
| US Luxembourg v Cologne (0-17) | 0-4, 0-13 |
| Nuremberg v Everton (1-2) | 1-1, 0-1 |
| Red Star Belgrade v Fiorentina (1-7) | 0-4, 1-3 |
| Spartak Brno v Lokomotiv Plovdiv (2-1) | 2-0, 0-1 |

**Second Round**

| | |
|---|---|
| Antwerp v Barcelona (2-3) | 2-1, 0-2 |
| Hanover 96 v Porto (6-2) | 5-0, 1-2 |
| Sporting Lisbon v Espanol (6-7) | 2-1, 3-4, 1-2 |
| Dynamo Zagreb v Red Flag Brasov (2-3) | 2-2, 0-1 |
| Goztepe Izmir v Munich 1860 (3-10) | 2-1, 1-9 |
| AIK Stockholm v Servette Geneva (3-5) | 2-1, 1-4 |
| CUF v AC Milan (2-3) | 2-0, 0-2, 0-1 |
| Wiener SK v Chelsea (1-2) | 1-0, 0-2 |

| | |
|---|---|
| Lokomotiv Leipzig v Leeds U (1-2) | 1-2, 0-0 |
| Basle v Valencia (2-8) | 1-3, 1-5 |
| Aris Salonika v Cologne (2-3) | 2-1, 0-2 |
| Ujpest Dozsa v Everton (4-2) | 3-0, 1-2 |
| Dunfermline Ath v KB Copenhagen (9-2) | 5-0, 4-2 |
| Fiorentina v Spartak Brno (2-4) | 2-0, 0-4 |
| Hearts v Valerengen (4-1) | 1-0, 3-1 |
| Shamrock Rovers v Real Zaragoza (2-3) | 1-1, 1-2 |

**Third Round**

| | |
|---|---|
| Hanover 96 v Barcelona* (3-3) | 2-1, 0-1, 1-1 |
| Espanol v Red Flag Brasov (6-5) | 3-1, 2-4, 1-0 |
| Servette Geneva v Munich 1860 (2-5) | 1-1, 1-4 |
| AC Milan v Chelsea* (4-4) | 2-1, 1-2, 1-1 |
| Leeds U v Valencia (2-1) | 1-1, 1-0 |
| Cologne v Ujpest Dozsa (3-6) | 3-2, 0-4 |
| Dunfermline Ath v Spartak Brno (2-0) | 2-0, 0-0 |
| Hearts v Real Zaragoza (5-6) | 3-3, 2-2, 0-1 |

**Quarter-Final**

| | |
|---|---|
| Barcelona v Espanol (2-0) | 1-0, 1-0 |
| Munich 1860 v Chelsea (2-3) | 2-2, 0-1 |
| Leeds U v Ujpest Dozsa (5-2) | 4-1, 1-1 |
| Dunfermline Ath v Real Zaragoza (3-4) | 1-0, 2-4 |

**Semi-Final**

| | |
|---|---|
| Barcelona v Chelsea (7-2) | 2-0, 0-2, 5-0 |
| Real Zaragoza v Leeds U (5-3) | 1-0, 1-2, 3-1 |

**Final**

| | |
|---|---|
| **Barcelona v Real Zaragoza (4-3)** | **0-1, 4-2** |

*Won on toss after extra time.*

# EUROPEAN FAIRS CUP 1966–67

**First Round**
*Byes:* Leeds U, DWS Amsterdam, WBA, Sparta Prague, Liège, Benfica, Spartak Plovdiv, Kilmarnock, La Gantoise, Hvidovre, Lausanne, Odense BK 09, Vitoria Setubal, Dundee U, Barcelona, Toulouse.

| | |
|---|---|
| Nuremberg v Valencia (1-4) | 1-2, 0-2 |
| Red Star Belgrade v Atlético Bilbao (5-2) | 5-0, 0-2 |
| DOS Utrecht v Basle (4-3) | 2-1, 2-2 |
| Bologna v Goztepe Izmir (5-2) | 2-1, 3-1 |
| Djurgaarden v Lokomotiv Leipzig (2-5) | 1-3, 1-2 |
| US Luxembourg v Antwerp (0-2) | 0-1, 0-1 |
| Porto v Bordeaux* (3-3) | 2-1, 1-2 |
| Drumcondra v Eintracht Frankfurt (1-8) | 0-2, 1-6 |
| Nice v Oergryte (3-4) | 2-2, 1-2 |
| Olympia Ljubljana v Ferencvaros (3-6) | 3-3, 0-3 |
| Stuttgart v Burnley (1-3) | 1-1, 0-2 |
| Wiener SK v Napoli (2-5) | 1-2, 1-3 |
| Juventus v Aris Salonika (7-0) | 5-0, 2-0 |
| Dynamo Pitesti v Seville (4-2) | 2-0, 2-2 |
| Frigg Oslo v Dunfermline Ath (2-6) | 1-3, 1-3 |
| Spartak Brno v Dynamo Zagreb* (2-2) | 0-2, 2-0 |

**Second Round**

| | |
|---|---|
| DWS Amsterdam v Leeds U (2-8) | 1-3, 1-5 |
| Valencia v Red Star Belgrade (3-1) | 1-0, 2-1 |
| WBA v DOS Utrecht (6-3) | 5-2, 1-1 |
| Sparta Prague v Bologna (3-4) | 2-2, 1-2 |
| Liège v Lokomotiv Leipzig (1-2) | 0-0, 1-2 |
| Spartak Plovdiv v Benfica (1-4) | 1-1, 0-3 |
| Antwerp v Kilmarnock (2-8) | 0-1, 2-7 |
| La Gantoise v Bordeaux (1-0) | 1-0, 0-0 |

| | |
|---|---|
| Eintracht Frankfurt v Hvidovre (7-3) | 5-1, 2-2 |
| Oergryte v Ferencvaros (1-7) | 0-0, 1-7 |
| Lausanne v Burnley (1-8) | 1-3, 0-5 |
| Odense BK 09 v Napoli (2-6) | 1-4, 1-2 |
| Juventus v Vitoria Setubal (5-1) | 3-1, 2-0 |
| Barcelona v Dundee U (1-4) | 1-2, 0-2 |
| Toulouse v Dynamo Pitesti (4-5) | 3-0, 1-5 |
| Dunfermline Ath v Dynamo Zagreb† (4-4) | .4-2, 0-2 |

**Third Round**

| | |
|---|---|
| Leeds U v Valencia (3-1) | 1-1, 2-0 |
| Bologna v WBA (6-1) | 3-0, 3-1 |
| Lokomotiv Leipzig v Benfica (4-3) | 3-1, 1-2 |
| Kilmarnock v La Gantoise (3-1) | 1-0, 2-1 |
| Eintracht Frankfurt v Ferencvaros (5-3) | 4-1, 1-2 |
| Burnley v Napoli (3-0) | 3-0, 0-0 |
| Juventus v Dundee U (3-1) | 3-0, 0-1 |
| Dynamo Pitesti v Dynamo Zagreb (0-1) | 0-1, 0-0 |

**Quarter-Final**

| | |
|---|---|
| Bologna v Leeds U* (1-1) | 1-0, 0-1 |
| Lokomotiv Leipzig v Kilmarnock (1-2) | 1-0, 0-2 |
| Eintracht Frankfurt v Burnley (3-2) | 1-1, 2-1 |
| Juventus v Dynamo Zagreb (2-5) | 2-2, 0-3 |

**Semi-Final**

| | |
|---|---|
| Leeds U v Kilmarnock (4-2) | 4-2, 0-0 |
| Eintracht Frankfurt v Dynamo Zagreb (3-4) | 3-0, 0-4 |

**Final**

| | |
|---|---|
| **Dynamo Zagreb v Leeds U (2-0)** | **2-0, 0-0** |

*Won on toss of coin.     †Won on away goals rule.*

# EUROPEAN FAIRS CUP 1967–68

**First Round**

| | |
|---|---|
| Spora Luxembourg v Leeds U (0-16) | 0-9, 0-7 |
| PAOK Salonika v Liège (2-5) | 0-2, 2-3 |
| Wiener SK v Atlético Madrid (3-7) | 2-5, 1-2 |
| St Patrick's Athletic v Bordeaux (4-9) | 1-3, 3-6 |
| DOS Utrecht v Real Zaragoza (4-5) | 3-2, 1-3 |
| Napoli v Hanover 96 (5-1) | 4-0, 1-1 |
| Bologna v Lyn Oslo (2-0) | 2-0, 0-0 |
| Nice v Fiorentina (0-5) | 0-1, 0-4 |
| Dynamo Dresden v Rangers (2-3) | 1-1, 1-2 |
| Servette Geneva v Munich 1860 (2-6) | 2-2, 0-4 |
| Argesul Pitesti v Ferencvaros (3-5) | 3-1, 0-4 |
| Malmö FF v Liverpool (1-4) | 0-2, 1-2 |
| Hibernian v Porto (4-3) | 3-0, 1-3 |
| Eintracht Frankfurt v Nottingham F (0-5) | 0-1, 0-4 |
| Dynamo Zagreb v Petrolul Ploesti (5-2) | 5-0, 0-2 |
| Bruges v Sporting Lisbon (1-2) | 0-0, 1-2 |
| Frem Copenhagen v Atlético Bilbao (2-4) | 0-1, 2-3 |
| Zurich v Barcelona (3-2) | 3-1, 0-1 |
| Lokomotiv Leipzig v Linfield (5-2) | 5-1, 0-1 |
| DWS Amsterdam v Dundee (2-4) | 2-1, 0-3 |
| Partizan Belgrade v Lokomotiv Plovdiv (6-2) | 5-1, 1-1 |
| Vojvodina v CUF (4-1) | 1-0, 3-1 |
| Cologne v Slavia Prague (4-2) | 2-0, 2-2 |
| Antwerp v Goztepe Izmir (1-2) | 1-2, 0-0 |

**Second Round**

| | |
|---|---|
| Nottingham F v Zurich (2-2) | 2-1, 0-1 |
| *Zurich won on away goals rule.* | |
| Bordeaux v Atlético Bilbao (1-4) | 1-3, 0-1 |

| | |
|---|---|
| Dundee v Liège (7-2) | 3-1, 4-1 |
| Vojvodina v Lokomotiv Leipzig (2-0) | 0-0, 2-0 |
| Real Zaragoza v Ferencvaros (2-4) | 2-1, 0-3 |
| Liverpool v Munich 1860 (9-2) | 8-0, 1-2 |
| Rangers v Cologne (4-3) | 3-0, 1-3 |
| Bologna v Dynamo Zagreb (2-1) | 0-0, 2-1 |
| Napoli v Hibernian (4-6) | 4-1, 0-5 |
| Partizan Belgrade v Leeds U (2-3) | 1-2, 1-1 |
| Fiorentina v Sporting Lisbon (2-3) | 1-1, 1-2 |
| Atlético Madrid v Goztepe Izmir (2-3) | 2-0, 0-3 |

**Third Round**
*Byes:* Atlético Bilbao, Bologna, Dundee, Rangers

| | |
|---|---|
| Ferencvaros v Liverpool (2-0) | 1-0, 1-0 |
| Leeds U v Hibernian (2-1) | 1-0, 1-1 |
| Vojvodina v Goztepe Izmir (2-0) | 1-0, 1-0 |
| Zurich v Sporting Lisbon (3-1) | 3-0, 0-1 |

**Quarter-Final**

| | |
|---|---|
| Ferencvaros v Atlético Bilbao (4-2) | 2-1, 2-1 |
| Rangers v Leeds U (0-2) | 0-0, 0-2 |
| Dundee v Zurich (2-0) | 1-0, 1-0 |
| Bologna v Vojvodina (2-0) | 0-0, 2-0 |

**Semi-Final**

| | |
|---|---|
| Dundee v Leeds U (1-2) | 1-1, 0-1 |
| Ferencvaros v Bologna (5-4) | 3-2, 2-2 |

**Final**

| | |
|---|---|
| **Leeds U v Ferencvaros (1-0)** | **1-0, 0-0** |

# EUROPEAN FAIRS CUP 1968-69

**First Round**
*Byes:* Argesul, Leipzig, Ujpest

| | |
|---|---|
| Chelsea v Morton (9-3) | 5-0, 4-3 |
| Newcastle U v Feyenoord (4-2) | 4-0, 0-2 |
| Atlético Bilbao* v Liverpool (3-3) | 2-1, 1-2 |
| Rangers v Vojvodina (2-1) | 2-0, 0-1 |
| Ljubljana v Hibernian (1-5) | 0-3, 1-2 |
| Rapid Bucharest v OFK Belgrade (4-7) | 3-1, 1-6 |
| Wiener SK v Slavia Prague (1-5) | 1-0, 0-5 |
| Skeid Oslo v AIK Stockholm (2-3) | 1-1, 1-2 |
| Trakia Plovdiv v Real Zaragoza† (3-3) | 3-1, 0-2 |
| Dynamo Zagreb v Fiorentina (2-3) | 1-1, 1-2 |
| Legia Warsaw v Munich 1860 (9-2) | 6-0, 3-2 |
| Daring v Panathinaikos (2-3) | 2-1, 0-2 |
| Wacker Innsbruck v Eintracht Frankfurt (2-5) | 2-2, 0-3 |
| Sporting Lisbon v Valencia (5-4) | 4-0, 1-4 |
| Bologna v Basle (6-2) | 4-1, 2-1 |
| Aris Salonika v Hibernians Valletta (7-0) | 1-0, 6-0 |
| DOS Utrecht v Dundalk (2-3) | 1-1, 1-2 |
| Atlético Madrid v Waregem* (2-2) | 2-1, 0-1 |
| Hansa Rostock v Nice (4-2) | 3-0, 1-2 |
| Goztepe Izmir* v Marseille (2-2) | 2-0, 0-2 |
| Metz v SV Hamburg (3-7) | 1-4, 2-3 |
| Lyon* v Academica Coimbra (1-1) | 1-0, 0-1 |
| Lausanne v Juventus (0-4) | 0-2, 0-2 |
| Beerschot v DWS Amsterdam (2-3) | 1-1, 1-2 |
| Hanover 96 v Odense BK 09 (4-2) | 3-2, 1-0 |
| Vitoria Setubal v Linfield (6-1) | 3-0, 3-1 |
| Standard Liège v Leeds U (2-3) | 0-0, 2-3 |
| Napoli v Grasshoppers (3-2) | 3-1, 0-1 |
| Slavia Sofia v Aberdeen (0-2) | 0-0, 0-2 |

**Second Round**

| | |
|---|---|
| Hibernian v Lokomotiv Leipzig (4-1) | 3-1, 1-0 |
| Leeds U* v Napoli (2-2) | 2-0, 0-2 |
| Rangers v Dundalk (9-1) | 6-1, 3-0 |

*Won on toss of coin.*

| | |
|---|---|
| Aberdeen v Real Zaragoza (2-4) | 2-1, 0-3 |
| Chelsea v DWS Amsterdam* (0-0) | 0-0, 0-0 |
| Sporting Lisbon v Newcastle U (1-2) | 1-1, 0-1 |
| Vitoria Setubal v Lyon (7-1) | 5-0, 2-1 |
| Goztepe Izmir v Argesul Pitesti (5-3) | 3-0, 2-3 |
| Hansa Rostock v Fiorentina† (4-4) | 3-2, 1-2 |
| SV Hamburg v Slavia Prague (5-4) | 4-1, 1-3 |
| Panathinaikos v Atlético Bilbao (0-1) | 0-0, 0-1 |
| OFK Belgrade v Bologna (2-1) | 1-0, 1-1 |
| Aris Salonika v Ujpest Dozsa (2-11) | 1-2, 1-9 |
| AIK Stockholm v Hanover 96 (6-7) | 4-2, 2-5 |
| Waregem v Legia Warsaw (1-2) | 1-0, 0-2 |
| Juventus v Eintracht Frankfurt (0-1) | 0-0, 0-1 |

**Third Round**

| | |
|---|---|
| Leeds U v Hanover 96 (7-2) | 5-1, 2-1 |
| SV Hamburg† v Hibernian (2-2) | 1-0, 1-2 |
| Legia Warsaw v Ujpest Dozsa (2-3) | 0-1, 2-2 |
| Real Zaragoza v Newcastle U† (4-4) | 3-2, 1-2 |
| OFK Belgrade v Goztepe Izmir† (3-3) | 3-1, 0-2 |
| Eintracht Frankfurt v Atlético Bilbao (1-2) | 1-1, 0-1 |
| DWS Amsterdam v Rangers (1-4) | 0-2, 1-2 |
| Vitoria Setubal v Fiorentina (4-2) | 3-0, 1-2 |

**Quarter-Final**

| | |
|---|---|
| Newcastle U v Vitoria Setubal (6-4) | 5-1, 1-3 |
| Rangers v Atlético Bilbao (4-3) | 4-1, 0-2 |
| Leeds U v Ujpest Dozsa (0-3) | 0-1, 0-2 |
| Goztepe Izmir v SV Hamburg *Hamburg withdrew* | |

**Semi-Final**

| | |
|---|---|
| Goztepe Izmir v Ujpest Dozsa (1-8) | 1-4, 0-4 |
| Rangers v Newcastle U (0-2) | 0-0, 0-2 |

**Final**

| | |
|---|---|
| **Newcastle U v Ujpest Dozsa (6-2)** | **3-0, 3-2** |

†*Won on away goals rule*

---

# EUROPEAN FAIRS CUP 1969-70

**First Round**

| | |
|---|---|
| Arsenal v Glentoran (3-1) | 3-0, 0-1 |
| Dundee U v Newcastle U (1-3) | 1-2, 0-1 |
| Liverpool v Dundalk (14-0) | 10-0, 4-0 |
| Partizan Belgrade v Ujpest Dozsa (2-3) | 2-1, 0-2 |
| Sabadell v Bruges (3-5) | 2-0, 1-5 |
| Las Palmas v Hertha Berlin (0-1) | 0-0, 0-1 |
| Wiener SK v Ruch Chorzow (5-6) | 4-2, 1-4 |
| Rouen v Twente (2-0) | 2-0, 0-1 |
| Vitoria Guimaraes v Banik Ostrava (2-1) | 1-0, 1-1 |
| Sporting Lisbon v ASK Linz (6-2) | 4-0, 2-2 |
| Carl Zeiss Jena v Altay Izmir (1-0) | 1-0, 0-0 |
| Lausanne v Vasas Gyor (2-4) | 1-2, 1-2 |
| Rosenborg v Southampton (1-2) | 1-0, 0-2 |
| Hansa Rostock v Panionios (3-2) | 3-0, 0-2 |
| Dynamo Bacau v Floriana (7-0) | 6-0, 1-0 |
| Slavia Sofia v Valencia (3-1) | 2-0, 1-1 |
| Inter-Milan v Sparta Prague (4-0) | 3-0, 1-0 |
| Juventus v Lokomotiv Plovdiv (5-2) | 3-1, 2-1 |
| Stuttgart v Malmö FF (4-1) | 3-0, 1-1 |
| Hanover 96 v Ajax (2-4) | 2-1, 0-3 |
| Aris Salonika v Cagliari (1-4) | 1-1, 0-3 |
| Metz v Napoli (2-3) | 1-1, 1-2 |
| Barcelona v Odense BK 09 (6-0) | 4-0, 2-0 |
| Gwardia Warsaw v Vojvodina (2-1) | 1-0, 1-1 |
| Dunfermline Ath v Bordeaux (4-2) | 4-0, 0-2 |
| Zurich v Kilmarnock (4-5) | 3-2, 1-3 |
| Munich 1860 v Skeid Oslo (3-4) | 2-2, 1-2 |
| Valur Reykjavik v Anderlecht (0-8) | 0-6, 0-2 |
| SC Charleroi v ZNK Zagreb (5-2) | 2-1, 3-1 |
| Hvidovre v Porto (1-4) | 1-2, 0-2 |
| Jeunesse Esch v Coleraine (3-6) | 3-2, 0-4 |
| Vitoria Setubal v Rapid Bucharest (7-2) | 3-1, 4-1 |

**Second Round**

| | |
|---|---|
| Sporting Lisbon v Arsenal (0-3) | 0-0, 0-3 |

| | |
|---|---|
| SC Charleroi v Rouen† (3-3) | 3-1, 0-2 |
| Skeid Oslo v Dynamo Bacau (0-2) | 0-0, 0-2 |
| Kilmarnock v Slavia Sofia (4-3) | 4-1, 0-2 |
| Ajax v Ruch Chorzow (9-1) | 7-0, 2-1 |
| Stuttgart v Napoli (0-1) | 0-0, 0-1 |
| Carl Zeiss Jena v Cagliari (3-0) | 2-0, 1-0 |
| Bruges v Ujpest Dozsa† (5-5) | 5-2, 0-3 |
| Hansa Rostock v Inter-Milan (2-4) | 2-1, 0-3 |
| Vasas Gyor v Barcelona (2-5) | 2-3, 0-2 |
| Hertha Berlin v Juventus (3-1) | 3-1, 0-0 |
| Vitoria Setubal† v Liverpool (3-3) | 1-0, 2-3 |
| Porto v Newcastle U (0-1) | 0-0, 0-1 |
| Vitoria Guimaraes v Southampton (4-8) | 3-3, 1-5 |
| Dunfermline Ath v Gwardia Warsaw (3-1) | 2-1, 1-0 |
| Anderlecht v Coleraine (13-4) | 6-1, 7-3 |

**Third Round**

| | |
|---|---|
| Rouen v Arsenal (0-1) | 0-0, 0-1 |
| Kilmarnock v Dynamo Bacau (1-3) | 1-1, 0-2 |
| Napoli v Ajax (1-4) | 1-0, 0-4 |
| Carl Zeiss Jena v Ujpest Dozsa (4-0) | 1-0, 3-0 |
| Barcelona v Inter-Milan (2-3) | 1-2, 1-1 |
| Vitoria Setubal v Hertha Berlin (1-2) | 1-1, 0-1 |
| Newcastle U† v Southampton (1-1) | 0-0, 1-1 |
| Anderlecht† v Dunfermline Ath (3-3) | 1-0, 2-3 |

**Quarter-Final**

| | |
|---|---|
| Dynamo Bacau v Arsenal (1-9) | 0-2, 1-7 |
| Carl Zeiss Jena v Ajax (4-6) | 3-1, 1-5 |
| Hertha Berlin v Inter-Milan (1-2) | 1-0, 0-2 |
| Anderlecht† v Newcastle U (3-3) | 2-0, 1-3 |

**Semi-Final**

| | |
|---|---|
| Arsenal v Ajax (3-1) | 3-0, 0-1 |
| Anderlecht v Inter-Milan (2-1) | 0-1, 2-0 |

† *Won on away goals counting double.*

### Final 1969–70: Anderlecht 3, Arsenal 1
(At Brussels, 22 April, 1970, 37,000)

*Anderlecht:* Trappeniers; Heylens, Velkeneers; Nordahl, Kialunda, Cornelis (Peeters); Desanghere, Devrindt, Mulder, Van Himst, Puis.
*Arsenal:* Wilson; Storey, McNab; Kelly, McLintock, Simpson; Armstrong, Sammels, Radford, George (Kennedy), Graham.
*Scorers:* Anderlecht – Devrindt, Mulder 2; Arsenal – Kennedy.

### Arsenal 3, Anderlecht 0
(At Highbury, 28 April, 1970, 51,612)

*Arsenal:* Wilson; Storey, McNab; Kelly, McLintock, Simpson; Armstrong, Sammels, Radford, George, Graham.
*Anderlecht:* Trappeniers; Heylens, Maartens; Nordahl, Velkeneers, Kialunda; Desanghere, Devrindt, Mulder, Van Himst, Puis.
*Scorers:* Arsenal – Kelly, Radford, Sammels.

## EUROPEAN FAIRS CUP 1970–71

**First Round**

| | |
|---|---|
| AEK Athens v Twente (0-4) | 0-1, 0-3 |
| Zeljeznicar v Anderlecht (7-9) | 4-5, 3-4 |
| La Gantoise v SV Hamburg (1-8) | 0-1, 1-7 |
| Seville v Eskisehirspor (2-3) | 1-0, 1-3 |
| Coleraine v Kilmarnock (4-3) | 1-1, 3-2 |
| Dundee U v Grasshoppers (3-2) | 3-2, 0-0 |
| Sarpsborg v Leeds U (0-6) | 0-1, 0-5 |
| Spartak Trnava* v Marseille (2-2) | 2-0, 0-2 |
| Cologne v Sedan (5-2) | 5-1, 0-1 |
| Lausanne v Vitoria Setubal (1-4) | 0-2, 1-2 |
| Hibernian v Malmo FF (9-2) | 6-0, 3-2 |
| Liverpool v Ferencvaros (2-1) | 1-0, 1-1 |
| Trakia Plovdiv v Coventry C (1-6) | 1-4, 0-2 |
| Lazio v Arsenal (2-4) | 2-2, 0-2 |
| Bayern Munich v Rangers (2-1) | 1-0, 1-1 |
| Dynamo Bucharest v PAOK Salonika (5-1) | 5-0, 0-1 |
| Uni Craiova v Pecs Dozsa (2-4) | 2-1, 0-3 |
| Katowice v Barcelona (2-4) | 0-1, 2-3 |
| Wiener SK v Beveren (0-5) | 0-2, 0-3 |
| Ilves Kissat v Sturm Graz (4-5) | 4-2, 0-3 |
| Barreirense v Dynamo Zagreb (3-6) | 2-0, 1-6 |
| Hajduk Split v Slavia Sofia (3-1) | 3-0, 0-1 |
| Cork Hibs v Valencia (1-6) | 0-3, 1-3 |
| Sparta Prague v Atletico Bilbao (3-1) | 2-0, 1-1 |
| Partizan Belgrade v Dynamo Dresden (0-6) | 0-0, 0-6 |
| AB Copenhagen v Sliema Wanderers (10-2) | 7-0, 3-2 |
| Juventus v Rumelange (11-0) | 7-0, 4-0 |
| Nykoping v Hertha Berlin (3-8) | 2-4, 1-4 |
| Ruch Chorzow v Fiorentina (1-3) | 1-1, 0-2 |
| Inter-Milan v Newcastle U (1-3) | 1-1, 0-2 |
| Sparta Rotterdam v Akranes (15-0) | 6-0, 9-0 |
| Vitoria Guimaraes v Angouleme (4-3) | 3-0, 1-3 |

**Second Round**

| | |
|---|---|
| Hibernian v Vitoria Guimaraes (3-2) | 2-0, 1-2 |

| | |
|---|---|
| Sparta Rotterdam v Coleraine (4-1) | 2-0, 2-1 |
| Bayern Munich v Coventry C (7-3) | 6-1, 1-2 |
| Barcelona v Juventus (2-4) | 1-2, 1-2 |
| Fiorentina v Cologne (1-3) | 1-2, 0-1 |
| Sturm Graz v Arsenal (1-2) | 1-0, 0-2 |
| Leeds U† v Dynamo Dresden (2-2) | 1-0, 1-2 |
| Liverpool v Dynamo Bucharest (4-1) | 3-0, 1-1 |
| AB Copenhagen v Anderlecht (1-7) | 1-3, 0-4 |
| Newcastle U v Pecs Dozsa* (2-2) | 2-0, 0-2 |
| Sparta Prague v Dundee U (3-2) | 3-1, 0-1 |
| Hertha Berlin v Spartak Trnava (2-3) | 1-0, 1-3 |
| Dynamo Zagreb v Hamburg (4-1) | 4-0, 0-1 |
| Vitoria Setubal v Hajduk Split (3-2) | 2-0, 1-2 |
| Valencia v Beveren (1-2) | 0-1, 1-1 |
| Eskisehir v Twente (4-8) | 3-2, 1-6 |

**Third Round**

| | |
|---|---|
| Spartak Trnava v Cologne (0-4) | 0-1, 0-3 |
| Bayern Munich v Sparta Rotterdam (5-2) | 2-1, 3-1 |
| Leeds U v Sparta Prague (9-2) | 6-0, 3-2 |
| Arsenal v Beveren (4-0) | 4-0, 0-0 |
| Pecs Dozsa v Juventus (0-3) | 0-1, 0-2 |
| Dynamo Zagreb v Twente (2-3) | 2-2, 0-1 |
| Anderlecht v Vitoria Setubal (3-4) | 2-1, 1-3 |
| Hibernian v Liverpool (0-3) | 0-1, 0-2 |

**Quarter-Final**

| | |
|---|---|
| Juventus v Twente (4-2) | 2-0, 2-2 |
| Arsenal v Cologne† (2-2) | 2-1, 0-1 |
| Leeds U v Setubal (3-2) | 2-1, 1-1 |
| Liverpool v Bayern Munich (4-1) | 3-0, 1-1 |

**Semi-Final**

| | |
|---|---|
| Liverpool v Leeds U (0-1) | 0-1, 0-0 |
| Cologne v Juventus (1-3) | 1-1, 0-2 |

*\* Won on penalty kicks.  † Won on away goals rule.*

### Final 1970–71: Juventus 2, Leeds U 2
(In Turin, 29 May, 1971, 45,000)

*Juventus:* Piloni; Spinosi, Marchetti, Furino, Morini, Salvadore, Haller, Causio, Anastasi (Novellini), Capello, Bettega.
*Leeds U:* Sprake; Reaney, Cooper, Bremner, Charlton, Hunter, Lorimer, Clarke, Jones (Bates), Giles, Madeley.
*Scorers:* Juventus – Bettega, Capello; Leeds U – Madeley, Bates.

### Leeds U 1, Juventus 1
(At Leeds, 2 June, 1971, 42,483)

*Leeds U:* Sprake; Reaney, Cooper, Bremner, Charlton, Hunter, Lorimer, Clarke, Jones, Giles, Madeley (Bates).
*Juventus:* Tancredi; Spinosi, Marchetti, Furino, Morini, Salvadore, Haller, Causio, Anastasi, Capello, Bettega.
*Scorers:* Leeds U – Clarke; Juventus – Anastasi.
*Leeds U won on away goals rule.*

# UEFA CUP 1971–72

**First Round**

| | |
|---|---|
| Hertha Berlin v Elfsborg (7-2) | 4-1, 3-1 |
| Dundee v Akademisk Copenhagen (5-2) | 4-2, 1-0 |
| Rosenborg v IFK Helsinki (4-0) | 3-0, 1-0 |
| Vasas Budapest v Shelbourne (2-1) | 1-0, 1-1 |
| Glentoran v Eintracht Brunswick (1-7) | 0-1, 1-6 |
| Keflavik v Tottenham H (1-15) | 1-6, 0-9 |
| Celta Vigo v Aberdeen (0-3) | 0-2, 0-1 |
| FC Den Haag v Aris Luxembourg (6-1) | 5-0, 1-1 |
| Wolverhampton W v Academica Coimbra (7-1) | 4-1, 3-0 |
| St Etienne v Cologne (2-3) | 1-1, 1-2 |
| Lugano v Legia Warsaw (1-3) | 1-3, 0-0 |
| Porto v Nantes (1-3) | 0-2, 1-1 |
| SV Hamburg v St Johnstone (2-4) | 2-1, 0-3 |
| Southampton v Atlético Bilbao (2-3) | 2-1, 0-2 |
| Bologna v Anderlecht (3-1) | 2-0, 1-1 |
| Napoli v Rapid Bucharest (1-2) | 1-0, 0-2 |
| Vitoria Setubal v Nîmes (2-2) | 1-0, 1-2 |
| Atlético Madrid v Panionios* (2-2) | 2-1, 0-1 |
| Carl Zeiss Jena v Lokomotiv Plovdiv (4-3) | 3-0, 1-3 |
| Basle v Real Madrid (2-4) | 1-2, 1-2 |
| Marsa v Juventus (0-11) | 0-6, 0-5 |
| Dynamo Zagreb v Botev Vratza (8-2) | 6-1, 2-1 |
| UT Arad v Austria Salzburg (5-4) | 4-1, 1-3 |
| Fenerbahce v Ferencvaros (2-4) | 1-1, 1-3 |
| AC Milan v Dighenis (7-0) | 4-0, 3-0 |
| Spartak Moscow v VSS Kosice (3-2) | 1-2, 2-0 |
| OFK Belgrade v Djurgaarden (6-3) | 2-2, 4-1 |
| Rapid Vienna | Bye |
| Zeljeznicar v Bruges (4-3) | 3-0, 1-3 |
| Chemie Halle (withdrew) v PSV Eindhoven (0-0) | 0-0, – |
| Zaglebie Walbrzych v Union Teplice (4-2) | 1-0, 3-2 |
| Lierse v Leeds U (4-2) | 0-2, 4-0 |

**Second Round**

| | |
|---|---|
| Rosenborg v Lierse* (4-4) | 4-1, 0-3 |

| | |
|---|---|
| Rapid Bucharest v Legia Warsaw (4-2) | 4-0, 0-2 |
| Cologne v Dundee (4-5) | 2-1, 2-4 |
| FC Den Haag v Wolverhampton W (1-7) | 1-3, 0-4 |
| Zeljeznicar* v Bologna (3-3) | 1-1, 2-2 |
| Nantes v Tottenham H (0-1) | 0-0, 0-1 |
| Eintracht Brunswick v Atlético Bilbao (4-3) | 2-1, 2-2 |
| St Johnstone v Vasas Budapest (2-1) | 2-0, 0-1 |
| Spartak Moscow v Vitoria Setubal (0-4) | 0-0, 0-4 |
| Hertha Berlin v AC Milan (4-5) | 2-1, 2-4 |
| OFK Belgrade v Carl Zeiss Jena (1-5) | 1-1, 0-4 |
| Zaglebie Walbrzych v UT Arad (2-3) | 1-1, 1-2 |
| Dynamo Zagreb v Rapid Vienna* (2-2) | 2-2, 0-0 |
| Real Madrid v PSV Eindhoven* (3-3) | 3-1, 0-2 |
| Juventus v Aberdeen (3-1) | 2-0, 1-1 |
| Ferencvaros v Panionios (6-0) | 6-0, – |
| *Panionios disqualified* | |

**Third Round**

| | |
|---|---|
| AC Milan v Dundee (3-2) | 3-0, 0-2 |
| Carl Zeiss Jena v Wolverhampton W (0-4) | 0-1, 0-3 |
| Eintracht Brunswick v Ferencvaros (3-6) | 1-1, 2-5 |
| PSV Eindhoven v Lierse (1-4) | 1-0, 0-4 |
| Rapid Vienna v Juventus (1-5) | 0-1, 1-4 |
| St Johnstone v Zeljeznicar (2-5) | 1-0, 1-5 |
| Tottenham H v Rapid Bucharest (5-0) | 3-0, 2-0 |
| UT Arad v Vitoria Setubal (3-1) | 3-0, 0-1 |

**Quarter-Final**

| | |
|---|---|
| AC Milan v Lierse (3-1) | 2-0, 1-1 |
| UT Arad v Tottenham H (1-3) | 0-2, 1-1 |
| Ferencvaros† v Zeljeznicar (3-3) | 1-2, 2-1 |
| Juventus v Wolverhampton W (2-3) | 1-1, 1-2 |

**Semi-Final**

| | |
|---|---|
| Tottenham H v AC Milan (3-2) | 2-1, 1-1 |
| Ferencvaros v Wolverhampton W (3-4) | 2-2, 1-2 |

*\* Won on away goals rule. † Won on penalty kicks.*

---

**Final 1971–72: Wolverhampton W 1, Tottenham H 2**

(At Wolverhampton, 3 May, 1972, 45,000)

*Wolverhampton W:* Parkes; Shaw, Taylor, Hegan, Munro, McAlle, McCalliog, Hibbitt, Richards, Dougan, Wagstaffe.

*Tottenham H:* Jennings; Kinnear, Knowles, Mullery, England, Beal, Coates (Pratt), Perryman, Chivers, Peters, Gilzean.

*Scorers:* Wolverhampton W – McCalliog; Tottenham H – Chivers 2.

**Tottenham H 1, Wolverhampton W 1**

(At White Hart Lane, 17 May, 1972)

*Tottenham H:* Jennings; Kinnear, Knowles, Mullery, England, Beal, Coates, Perryman, Chivers, Peters, Gilzean.

*Wolverhampton W:* Parkes; Shaw, Taylor, Hegan, Munro, McAlle, McCalliog, Hibbitt (Bailey), Richards, Dougan (Curran), Wagstaffe.

*Scorers:* Tottenham H – Mullery; Wolverhampton W – Wagstaffe.

---

# UEFA CUP 1972–73

**First Round**

| | |
|---|---|
| Aberdeen v Bor Moenchengladbach (5-9) | 2-3, 3-6 |
| Atvidaberg v Bruges (5-6) | 3-5, 2-1 |
| Manchester C v Valencia (3-4) | 2-2, 1-2 |
| Lyn Oslo v Tottenham H (3-12) | 3-6, 0-6 |
| Cologne v Bohemians (5-1) | 2-1, 3-0 |
| Honved v Partick T (4-0) | 1-0, 3-0 |
| Viking Stavanger v IBV Vastmannejar (1-0) | 1-0, 0-0 |
| Feyenoord v US Rumelange (21-0) | 9-0, 12-0 |
| Liverpool v Eintracht Frankfurt (2-0) | 2-0, 0-0 |
| Grasshoppers v Nîmes (4-2) | 2-1, 2-1 |
| Vitoria Setubal v Zaglebie Sosnowiec (6-2) | 6-1, 0-1 |
| Stoke C v Kaiserslautern (3-5) | 3-1, 0-4 |
| Racing White v CUF Barrierense (0-3) | 0-1, 0-2 |
| Torino v Las Palmas (2-4) | 2-0, 0-4 |
| Sochaux v Frem Copenhagen (2-5) | 1-3, 1-2 |
| Olympiakos Piraeus v Cagliari (3-1) | 2-1, 1-0 |
| Angers v Dynamo Berlin (2-3) | 1-1, 1-2 |
| Porto v Barcelona (4-1) | 3-1, 1-0 |
| Univ Cluj v Levski Sofia (5-6) | 4-1, 1-5 |
| Red Star Belgrade v Lausanne (7-4) | 5-1, 2-3 |
| Inter-Milan v FC Valetta (7-1) | 6-1, 1-0 |
| Beroe Stara v FK Austria (10-1) | 7-0, 3-1 |

| | |
|---|---|
| UT Arad v Norrköping (1-4) | 1-2, 0-2 |
| EPA Larna v Ararat Erevan (0-2) | 0-1, 0-1 |
| AEK Athens v Salgotarjan (4-2) | 3-1, 1-1 |
| Eskisehirspor v Fiorentina (1-5) | 1-2, 0-3 |
| Dukla Prague v OFK Belgrade (3-5) | 2-2, 1-3 |
| Slovan Bratislava v Vojvodina (8-1) | 6-0, 2-1 |
| Dynamo Tbilisi v FC Twente (3-4) | 3-2, 0-2 |
| Ruch Chorzow v Fenerbahce (3-1) | 3-0, 0-1 |
| Dynamo Dresden v Voest Linz (4-2) | 2-0, 2-2 |
| Hvidovre Copenhagen | bye |

**Second Round**

| | |
|---|---|
| Dynamo Berlin v Levski Sofia (3-2) | 3-0, 0-2 |
| Bor Moenchengladbach v Hvidovre Copenhagen (6-1) | 3-0, 3-1 |
| Porto v Bruges (5-3) | 3-0, 2-3 |
| Tottenham H v Olympiakos Piraeus (4-1) | 4-0, 0-1 |
| Red Star Belgrade v Valencia (4-1) | 3-1, 1-0 |
| Inter-Milan v Norrköping (4-2) | 2-2, 2-0 |
| Viking Stavanger v Cologne (2-9) | 1-0, 1-9 |
| Beroe Stara v Honved (3-1) | 3-0, 0-1 |
| Feyenoord v OFK Belgrade* (5-5) | 4-3, 1-2 |
| Liverpool v AEK Athens (6-1) | 3-0, 3-1 |

Vitoria Setubal* v Fiorentina (2-2)   1-0, 1-2
Grasshoppers v Ararat Erevan (3-7)   1-3, 2-4
CUF Barreirense v Kaiserslautern (2-3)   1-3, 1-0
Las Palmas v Slovan Bratislava (3-2)   2-2, 1-0
Ruch Chorzow v Dynamo Dresden (0-4)   0-1, 0-3
Frem Copenhagen v FC Twente (0-9)   0-5, 0-4

**Third Round**
Ararat Erevan v Kaiserslautern† (2-2)   2-0, 0-2
Cologne v Bor Moenchengladbach (0-5)   0-0, 0-5
Tottenham H v Red Star Belgrade (2-1)   2-0, 0-1
FC Twente v Las Palmas (4-2)   3-0, 1-2
OFK Belgrade v Beroe Stara (3-1)   0-0, 3-1

Vitoria Setubal v Inter-Milan (2-1)   2-0, 0-1
Dynamo Berlin v Liverpool (1-3)   0-0, 1-3
Porto v Dynamo Dresden (1-3)   1-2, 0-1

**Quarter-Final**
Kaiserslautern v Bor Moenchengladbach (2-9)   1-2, 1-7
OFK Belgrade v FC Twente (3-4)   3-2, 0-2
Tottenham H* v Vitoria Setubal (2-2)   1-0, 1-2
Liverpool v Dynamo Dresden (3-0)   2-0, 1-0

**Semi-Final**
Liverpool* v Tottenham H (2-2)   1-0, 1-2
Bor Moenchengladbach v FC Twente (5-1)   3-0, 2-1

*Won on away goals rule.*   † *Won on penalty kicks.*

### Final 1972–73: Liverpool 3, Borussia Moenchengladbach 0
(At Liverpool, 10 May, 1973, 41,169)

*Liverpool:* Clemence; Lawler, Lindsay, Smith, Lloyd, Hughes, Keegan, Cormack, Toshack, Heighway (Hall), Callaghan.
*Borussia Moenchengladbach:* Kleff; Danner, Michallik, Vogts, Bonhof, Kulik, Jensen, Wimmer, Rupp (Simonsen), Netzer, Heynckes.
*Scorers:* Liverpool – Keegan 2, Lloyd.

### Borussia Moenchengladbach 2, Liverpool 0
(At Moenchengladbach, 23 May, 1973, 35,000)

*Borussia Moenchengladbach:* Kleff; Vogts, Surau, Netzer, Bonhof, Danner, Wimmer, Kulik, Jensen, Rupp, Heynckes.
*Liverpool:* Clemence; Lawler, Lindsay, Smith, Lloyd, Hughes, Keegan, Cormack, Heighway (Boersma), Toshack, Callaghan.
*Scorer:* Bor Moenchengladbach – Heynckes 2.

## UEFA CUP 1973–74

**First Round**
Fredrikstad v Dynamo Kiev (0-5)   0-1, 0-4
Ruch Chorzow v Wuppertal (8-6)   4-1, 4-5
BK 1903 Copenhagen v AIK (3-2)   2-1, 1-1
Carl Zeiss Jena v Mikkelin (6-0)   3-0, 3-0
Stroemgodset v Leeds U (2-7)   1-1, 1-6
Oesters v Feyenoord (2-5)   1-3, 1-2
Hibernian v Keflavik (3-1)   2-0, 1-1
Nice v Barcelona (3-2)   3-0, 0-2
Fortuna Dusseldorf v Naestved (3-2)   1-0, 2-2
Grasshoppers v Tottenham H (2-9)   1-5, 1-4
Aberdeen v Finn Harps (7-2)   4-1, 3-1
Dundee v FC Twente (3-7)   1-3, 2-4
Espanol v RWD Molenbeek (2-4)   0-3, 2-1
Belenenses v Wolverhampton W (1-4)   0-2, 1-2
US Luxembourg v Marseille (1-12)   0-5, 1-7
Setubal v Beerschot (4-0)   2-0, 2-0
Ipswich T v Real Madrid (1-0)   1-0, 0-0
Lazio v Sion (4-3)   3-0, 1-3
Sliema Wanderers v Lokomotiv Plovdiv (0-3)   0-2, 0-1
Fiorentina v Univ Craiova (0-1)   0-0, 0-1
Ferencvaros v Gwardia Warsaw (1-3)   0-1, 1-2
Stuttgart v Olympiakos Nicosia (13-0)   9-0, 4-0
Tatran Presov v Velez (5-3)   4-2, 1-1
Dynamo Tbilisi v Slavia Sofia (4-3)   4-1, 0-2
Panathinaikos v OFK Belgrade* (2-2)   1-2, 1-0
Admira-Wacker* v Inter-Milan (2-2)   1-0, 1-2
Fenerbahce v Agres Pitesti (6-2)   5-1, 1-1
VSS Kosice v Honved (3-5)   1-0, 2-5
Torino v Lokomotiv Leipzig (2-4)   1-2, 1-2
Eskisehirspor v Cologne (0-2)   0-0, 0-2
Panachaiki v AK Graz (3-1)   2-1, 1-0
Ards v Standard Liège (4-8)   3-2, 1-6

**Second Round**
Admira-Wacker v Fortuna Dusseldorf (2-4)   2-1, 0-3

Aberdeen v Tottenham H (2-5)   1-1, 1-4
Dynamo Tbilisi v OFK Belgrade (8-1)   3-0, 5-1
Nice v Fenerbahce (4-2)   4-0, 0-2
Lokomotiv Leipzig* v Wolverhampton W (4-4)   3-0, 1-4
Panachaiki v FC Twente (1-8)   1-1, 0-7
Setubal* v RWD Molenbeek (2-2)   1-0, 1-2
Marseille v Cologne (2-6)   2-0, 0-6
Ipswich T v Lazio (6-4)   4-0, 2-4
Dynamo Kiev v BK 1903 Copenhagen (3-1)   1-0, 2-1
Lokomotiv Plovdiv v Honved (5-7)   3-4, 2-3
Ruch Chorzow v Carl Zeiss Jena (3-1)   3-0, 0-1
Stuttgart v Tatran Presov (8-4)   3-1, 5-3
Leeds U† v Hibernian (0-0)   0-0, 0-0
Feyenoord v Gwardia Warsaw (3-2)   3-1, 0-1
Standard Liège v Univ Craiova (3-1)   2-0, 1-1

**Third Round**
Dynamo Kiev v Stuttgart (2-3)   2-0, 0-3
Dynamo Tbilisi v Tottenham H (2-6)   1-1, 1-5
Ipswich T v FC Twente (3-1)   1-0, 2-1
Honved v Ruch Chorzow (2-5)   2-0, 0-5
Leeds U v Setubal (2-3)   1-0, 1-3
Fortuna Dusseldorf v Lokomotiv Leipzig (2-4)   2-1, 0-3
Nice v Cologne (1-4)   1-0, 0-4
Standard Liège v Feyenoord* (3-3)   3-1, 0-2

**Quarter-Final**
Ipswich T v Lokomotiv Leipzig† (1-1)   1-0, 0-1
Cologne v Tottenham H (1-5)   1-2, 0-3
Stuttgart v Setubal (3-2)   1-0, 2-2
Ruch Chorzow v Feyenoord (2-4)   1-1, 1-3

**Semi-Final**
Lokomotiv Leipzig v Tottenham H (1-4)   1-2, 0-2
Feyenoord v Stuttgart (4-3)   2-1, 2-2

*Won on away goals.*   † *Won on penalties.*

### Final 1973–74: Tottenham Hotspur 2, Feyenoord 2
(At White Hart Lane, 21 May, 1974, 46,281)

*Tottenham:* Jennings; Evans, Naylor, Pratt, England, Beal, McGrath, Perryman, Chivers, Peters, Coates.
*Feyenoord:* Treytel; Rijsbergen, Van Daele, Israel, Vos, De Jong, Jansen, Van Hanegem, Ressel, Schoenmaker, Kristensen.
*Scorers:* Tottenham – England, Van Daele og; Feyenoord – Van Hanegem, De Jong.

### Feyenoord 2, Tottenham Hotspur 0
(At Rotterdam, 29 May, 1974, 68,000)

*Feyenoord:* Treytel; Rijsbergen, Van Daele, Israel, Vos, Ramljak, Jansen, De Jong, Ressel, Schoenmaker, Kristensen (Boskamp) (Wery).
*Tottenham:* Jennings; Evans, Naylor, Pratt (Holder), England, Beal, McGrath, Perryman, Chivers, Peters, Coates.
*Scorers:* Feyenoord – Rijsbergen, Ressel.

## UEFA CUP 1974-75

**First Round, First Leg**
Lyon 7 (*Lacombe 3, Maillard 3, Maniero*), Red Boys 0
Valur 0, Portadown 0
Derby Co 4 (*Hector 2, Daniel, Lee*), Servette 1 (*Petrovic*)
Ipswich T 2 (*Talbot, Hamilton*), Twente 2 (*Zuidema, Pahlplatz*)
Stoke C 1 (*Smith*), Ajax 1 (*Krol*)
RWD Molenbeek 1 (*Wellens*), Dundee 0
Rosenborg 2 (*Iversen 2*), Hibernian 3 (*Stanton, Gordon, Cropley*)
Porto 4 (*McAlle og, Cubillas, Flavio, Gomes*), Wolverhampton W 1 (*Bailey*)
Etar 0, Inter-Milan 0
Gornik Zabrze 2 (*Kurzeja, Kwasny*), Partizan Belgrade 2 (*Zavitic, Vukotic*)
Start 1 (*Mathiesen M.*), Djurgaarden 2 (*Svensson M., Skotte*)
Boluspor 0, Dynamo Bucharest 1 (*Deleanu*)
Spartak Moscow 3 (*Piscarov, Gladulin, Lovchev*), Velez Mostar 1 (*Bajevic*)
Besiktas 2 (*Sinan, Tezcan*), Steagul Brasov 0
SW Innsbruck 2 (*Flindt 2*), Borussia Moenchengladbach 1 (*Heynckes*)
Sturm Graz 2 (*Stendal, Kulmer*), Antwerp 1 (*Heyligen*)
Randers Freja 1 (*Nielsen*), Dynamo Dresden 1 (*Dorner*)
Hamburg 3 (*Volkert 2, Kaltz*), Bohemians 0
Rapid Vienna 3 (*Pajenk, Ritter, Krankl*), Aris Salonika 1 (*Alexiadis*)
Real Sociedad 0, Banik Ostrava 1 (*Micka*)
Lokomotiv Plovdiv 3 (*Kourbanov, Bonev, Stamboliev*), Raba ETO 1 (*Glazer*)
Oesters 2 (*Mattsson 2, Nordenberg pen*), Dynamo Moscow 2 (*Koslov, Pavlenkov*)
Nantes 2 (*Rampillon, Michel*), Legia Warsaw 2 (*Bialad 2*)
Napoli 2 (*Massa, Pogliana*), Videoton 0
Vorwaerts 2 (*Schutz, Krautzk*), Juventus 1 (*Capello*)
Grasshoppers 2 (*Elsener, Grahn*), Panathinaikos 0
Torino 1 (*Pulici*), Fortuna Dusseldorf 1 (*Zewe*)
Cologne 5 (*Muller 2, Flohe 2, Lohr*), Kokkolan 1 (*Makela*)
FC Amsterdam 5 (*Jansen 2, Otto, Koopman, Husers*), Hibernian Malta 0
KB Copenhagen 3 (*Sorensen, Holstrom, Bernborg*), Atlético Madrid 2 (*Ayala, Salcedo*)
Vitoria Setubal 1 (*Vicente*), Real Zaragoza 1 (*Arrua*)

**First Round, Second Leg**
Red Boys 1 (*Cristophe*), Lyon 4 (*Domenech 2, Mariot, Bernard*)
Portadown 2 (*McFaul, Morrison pen*), Valur 1 (*Albertson*)
Servette 1 (*Martin*), Derby Co 2 (*Lee, Hector*)
Twente 1 (*Bos*), Ipswich T 1 (*Hamilton*)
Ajax 0, Stoke C 0
Dundee 2 (*Duncan, Jocky Scott*), RWD Molenbeek 4 (*Teugels, Boskamp, Wellens 2*)
Hibernian 9 (*Harper 2, Munro 2, Stanton 2, Cropley 2, Gordon*), Rosenborg 1 (*Iversen*)
Wolverhampton W 3 (*Richards, Dougan, Daley*), Porto 1 (*Cubillas*)
Inter-Milan 3 (*Oriali, Boninsegna 2*), Etar 0
Partizan Belgrade 3 (*Dordevic, Vukotic, Todozevic*), Gornik Zabrze 0
Djurgaarden 5 (*Skotte, Stenbach, Karlsson 2, Samuelsson*)
Start 1 (*Mathiesen*)
Dynamo Bucharest 3 (*Dinu, Dumitrache, Lucescu*), Boluspor 0
Velez Mostar 2 (*Colic, Popic*), Spartak Moscow 0
Steagul Brasov 3 (*Serbaniou 3*), Besiktas 0
Borussia Moenchengladbach 3 (*Heynckes, Jensen, Vogts*), SW Innsbruck 0
Antwerp 1 (*Kodat*), Sturm Graz 0
Dynamo Dresden 0, Randers Freja 0
Bohemians 0, Hamburg 1 (*Bertl*)
Aris Salonika 1 (*Alexiadis*), Rapid Vienna 0
Banik Ostrava 4 (*Vojacek, Slany, Albrecht, Kolecko*), Real Sociedad 0
Raba ETO 3 (*Sebo, Penzes, Proczik*), Lokomotiv Plovdiv 1 (*Kichekov*)
Dynamo Moscow 2 (*Evryuzhkhin, Petrushin*), Oesters 1 (*Svensson*)
Legia Warsaw 0, Nantes 1 (*Merigot*)

Videoton 1 (*Wollek*), Napoli 1 (*Braglia*)
Juventus 3 (*Anastasi, Altafini, Hause og*), Vorwaerts 0
Panathinaikos 2 (*Antoniadis 2*), Grasshoppers 1 (*Santrac*)
Fortuna Dusseldorf 3 (*Zimmerman, Seel, Geye pen*), Torino 1 (*Agroppi*)
Kokkolan 1 (*Lamberg*), Cologne 4 (*Neumann, Lohr, Simmet 2*)
Hibernian Malta 0, FC Amsterdam 7 (*Karte 2, Jansen 2, Franz, Husers, Dekkers*)
Atlético Madrid 4 (*Leal, Garate, Irureta 2*), KB Copenhagen 0
Real Zaragoza 4 (*Arrua, Diarte, Castany, Leiros*), Vitoria Setubal 0
Dukla Prague had a walkover when Pezoporikos withdrew

**Second Round, First Leg**
Derby Co 2 (*Nish, Rioch pen*), Atlético Madrid 2 (*Luis pen, Ayala*)
Hibernian 2 (*Stanton, Cropley*), Juventus 4 (*Gentile, Altafini 2, Cuccurredu*)
Partizan Belgrade 5 (*Kosic 2, Zavajic, Nikolic, Vukotic*), Portadown 0
Nantes 1 (*Bossis*), Banik Ostrava 0
Dynamo Bucharest 1 (*Dinu*), Cologne 1 (*Luscher*)
Raba ETO 2 (*Varsanyi, Stolz*), Fortuna Dusseldorf 0
Rapid Vienna 1 (*Ritter*), Velez Mostar 1 (*Halaldiz*)
Dynamo Dresden 1 (*Sasche*), Dynamo Moscow 0
Grasshoppers 2 (*Grahn, Santrac*), Real Zaragoza 1 (*Arrua*)
Borussia Moenchengladbach 1 (*Simonsen*), Lyon 0
Hamburg 8 (*Volkert 2, Bertl, Zaczyk, Memering, Nogly, Ripp, Krobach*), Steagul Brasov 0
Twente 2 (*Thijseen, Van der Vall*), RWD Molenbeek 1 (*Koens*)
Djurgaarden 0, Dukla Prague 2 (*Nehoda, Gajdusek*)
Inter-Milan 1 (*Boninsegna*), FC Amsterdam 2 (*Jansen 2*)
Napoli 1 (*Orlandini*), Porto 0
Ajax 1 (*Gerrie Muhren*), Antwerp 0

**Second Round, Second Leg**
Atlético Madrid 2 (*Luis 2*), Derby Co 2 (*Rioch, Hector*)
*Derby won 7-6 on penalties*
Juventus 4 (*Bettega, Anastasi 2, Altafini*), Hibernian 0
Portadown 1 (*Malcolmson*), Partizan Belgrade 1 (*Tordevic*)
Banik Ostrava 1 (*Klement 2*), Nantes 0
Cologne 3 (*Overath, Muller, Neumann*), Dynamo Bucharest 2 (*Custov, Georgescu*)
Fortuna Dusseldorf 3 (*Herzog, Szernotzky, Brucken*), Raba ETO 0
Velez Mostar 1 (*Halaldiz*), Rapid Vienna 0
Dynamo Moscow 1 (*Korneev*), Dynamo Dresden 0
Real Zaragoza 5 (*Rubial 2, Soto, Oldhauser og, Niggl og*), Grasshoppers 0
Lyon 2 (*Valette, Domenech R.*), Borussia Moenchengladbach 5 (*Bonhof 2, Simonsen 2, Kulik*)
Steagul Brasov 1 (*Curbaniou*), Hamburg 2 (*Kaltz, Bjornmose*)
RWD Molenbeek 0, Twente 1 (*Zuidema*)
Dukla Prague 3 (*Nehoda 2, Macela*), Djurgaarden 1 (*Svensson*)
FC Amsterdam 0, Inter-Milan 0
Porto 0, Napoli 1 (*Juliano*)
Antwerp 2 (*Kodat, Riedl pen*), Ajax 1 (*Geels*)

**Third Round, First Leg**
Napoli 0, Banik Ostrava 2 (*Albrecht, Kolecko*)
Hamburg 4 (*Bjornmose 2, Volkert, Nogly*), Dynamo Dresden 1 (*Schmuck*)
Dukla Prague 3 (*Dvorak, Krumich, Nehoda*), Twente 1 (*Jeuring*)
Partizan Belgrade 1 (*Vukotic*), Cologne 0
Borussia Moenchengladbach 5 (*Heynckes 2, Simonsen 2, Bonhof*), Real Zaragoza 0
FC Amsterdam 3 (*Husers 2, Kriegler og*), Fortuna Dusseldorf 0

Juventus 1 (*Damiani*), Ajax 0
Derby Co 3 (*Bourne 2, Hinton*), Velez Mostar 1 (*Vladic*)

Velez Mostar 1 (*Kvesic*), Twente 0
Banik Ostrava 0, Borussia Moenchengladbach 1 (*Heynckes*)

**Third Round, Second Leg**
Banik Ostrava 1 (*Slany*), Napoli 1 (*Ferrandini*)
Dynamo Dresden 2 (*Dorner, Hafner*), Hamburg 2 (*Bertl 2*)
Twente 5 (*Zuidema 3, Notten 2*), Dukla Prague 0
Cologne 5 (*Overath, Lohr, Muller, Glowacz, Flohe*), Partizan Belgrade 1 (*Povlovic*)
Real Zaragoza 2 (*Vileta, Galdos*), Borussia Moenchengladbach 4 (*Simonsen, Heynckes 2, Stielike*)
Fortuna Dusseldorf 1 (*Seel*), FC Amsterdam 2 (*Husers, Jansen*)
Ajax 2 (*Blankenburg, Gerrie Muhren*), Juventus 1 (*Damiani pen*)
Velez Mostar 4 (*Bajevic pen, Pecelj, Vladic, Primorac pen*), Derby Co 1 (*Hector*)

**Quarter-Finals, Second Leg**
Hamburg 0, Juventus 0
Borussia Moenchengladbach 3 (*Micka og, Heynckes, Vogts*), Banik Ostrava 1 (*Hudecek*)
FC Amsterdam 2 (*Jansen 2*), Cologne 3 (*Strack, Muller, Lohr*)
Twente 2 (*Zuidema, Overweg*), Velez Mostar 0

**Semi-Finals, First Leg**
Twente 3 (*Jeuring, Zuidema 2*), Juventus 1 (*Altafini*)
Cologne 1 (*Lohr*), Borussia Moenchengladbach 3 (*Simonsen 2, Danner*)

**Quarter-Finals, First Leg**
Juventus 2 (*Capello, Viola*), Hamburg 0
Cologne 5 (*Flohe 2 [1 pen], Muller 3*), FC Amsterdam 1 (*Visser*)

**Semi-Finals, Second Leg**
Juventus 0, Twente 1 (*Zuidema*)
Borussia Moenchengladbach 1 (*Danner*), Cologne 0

### Final 1974–75: Borussia Moenchengladbach 0, Twente Enschede 0
(At Dusseldorf, 7 May, 1975, 45,000)

*Borussia Moenchengladbach:* Kleff; Wittkamp, Stielike, Vogts, Surau, Bonhof, Wimmer, Danner (Del Haye), Kulik (Schaffer), Simonsen, Jensen.
*Twente Enschede:* Gross; Drost, Van Ierssel, Overweg, Oranen, Thijssen, Pahlplatz, Van der Vall, Bos, Jeuring (Achterberg), Zuidema.

### Twente Enschede 1, Borussia Moenchengladbach 5
(At Enschede, 21 May, 1975, 24,500)

*Twente Enschede:* Gross; Drost, Van Ierssel, Overweg, Oranen, Bos (Muhren), Thijssen, Pahlplatz (Achterberg), Van der Vall, Jeuring, Zuidema.
*Borussia Moenchengladbach:* Kleff; Wittkamp, Vogts, Surau (Schafer), Klinkhammer, Bonhof, Wimmer (Koppel), Danner, Simonsen, Jensen, Heynckes.
*Scorers:* Borussia Moenchengladbach – Heynckes 3, Simonsen 2 (1 pen); Twente Enschede – Drost.

# UEFA CUP 1975—76

**First Round, First Leg**

Duisburg 7 (*Mertakas og, Lehmann 3, Worm 2, Thies*), Paralimni 1 (*Chatzyannis*)
Glentoran 1 (*Jamieson*), Ajax 6 (*Geels 4, Meyer, Notten*)
Grasshoppers 3 (*Elsener, Santrac, Bosco*), Real Sociedad 3(*Satrustegui 2, Murillo*)
PAOK Salonika 1 (*Koudas*), Barcelona 0
AIK Stockholm 1 (*Leback pen*), Spartak Moscow 1 (*Lovchev*)
Antwerp 4 (*Heylingen, Kodat 3*), Aston Villa 1 (*Graydon*)
Bohemians Prague 1 (*Masnik*), Honved 2 (*Pinter, Toth*)
Carl Zeiss Jena 3 (*Sengewald 2, Kurbjuweit*), Marseille 0
Uni Craiova 1 (*Oblemenco*), Red Star Belgrade 3 (*Filipovic 2, Savic*)
Everton 0, AC Milan 0
Feyenoord 1 (*De Jong*), Ipswich T 2 (*Whymark, Johnson*)
GAIS Gothenburg 2 (*Palsson 2 [l pen]*) Slask Wroclaw 1 (*Kwaitkowski*)
Hertha Berlin 4 (*Kostedde 2, Hoor 2*), HJK Helsinki 1 (*Kangaslorpi*)
Hibernian 1 (*Harper*), Liverpool 0
Holbaek 0, Stal Mielec 1 (*Domarski*)
Cologne 2 (*Glowacz, Lohr*), B 1903 Copenhagen 0
Lyon 1 (*Jodar, Millard 2, Mihajlovic*), Bruges 3 (*Van der Eycken 3 [l pen]*)
Molde 1 (*Wetterdahl*), Oesters Vaxjo 0
Tirgu Mures 2 (*Muresan, Faxekas*), Dynamo Dresden 2 (*Schade, Heidler*)
Chernomonretz Odessa 1 (*Doroschenko*), Lazio 0
Porto 7 (*Julio, Cubillas 2 [l pen], Oliveira, Octavio, Gomes*), Avenir Beggen 0
Rapid Vienna 1 (*Widmann*), Galatasaray 0
Roma 2 (*Pellegrini, Petrini*), Dounav Russe 0
Moscow Torpedo 4 (*Grishken 2, Sakharov pen, Belenkov*), Napoli 1 (*Savoldi*)
VOEST Linz 2 (*Scharmann, Stering*), Vasas Budapest 0
Vojvodina 0, AEK Athens 0
Young Boys 0, Hamburg 0
Athlone T 3 (*Martin, Davis 2*), Valerengen 1 (*Olsen*)
Inter Bratislava 5 (*Levicky, Luprich, Petras, Jurkemik, Sajanek*), Zaragoza 0
Keflavik 1, Dundee U 2 (*Narey 2*)
Levski Spartak 3 (*Spassov 2, Panov*), Eskisehirspor 0
Sliema Wanderers 1 (*Azzopardi*), Sporting Lisbon 2 (*Marinho, Fernandez*)

**First Round, Second Leg**

Paralimni 2 (*Konstantinou A., Mertakas*), Duisburg 3 (*Dietz, Krause, Seliger*)
Dundee U 4 (*Hall 2, Hegarty pen, Sturrock*), Keflavik 0
Liverpool 3 (*Toshack 3*), Hibernian 1 (*Edwards*)
AEK Athens 3 (*Papaioannou, Papadopoulos, Wagner*), Vojvodina 1 (*Buikov*)
Ajax 8 (*Notten, Van Dord, Geels 3, Gerrie Muhren, Brokamp 2*), Glentoran 0
Aston Villa 0, Antwerp 1 (*Kodat*)
Barcelona 6 (*Neeskens 2 pens, Rexach 2, Cruyff*), PAOK Salonika 1 (*Anastasiadis*)
Bruges 3 (*Van der Eycken, Valette og, Chnier og*), Lyon 0
Avenir Beggen 0, Porto 3 (*Julio, Grilli og, Seninho*)
Marseille 0, Carl Zeiss Jena 1 (*Irmscher*)
B 1903 Copenhagen 2 (*Christiansen 2*), Cologne 3 (*Brucken 3*)
Dounav Russe 1 (*Ivanov*), Roma 0
Dynamo Dresden 4 (*Heidler 3, Kreische*), Tirgu Mures 1 (*Muresan*)
Eskisehirspor 1 (*Mehmet*), Levski Spartak 4 (*Spassov 2, Panov, Milanov*)
Galatasaray 3 (*Sevki, Gokmen 2*), Rapid Vienna 1 (*Krankl*)
Hamburg 4 (*Reimann, Bertl 2, Bjornmose*), Young Boys 2 (*Siegenthaler 2*)
HJK Helsinki 1 (*Salo*), Hertha Berlin 2 (*Sidka, Grau*)
Honved 1 (*Kocsis pen*), Bohemians Prague 1 (*Panenka*)
Ipswich T 2 (*Woods, Whymark*), Feyenoord 0
Lazio 3 (*Chinaglia 3 [l pen]*), Chernomoretz Odessa 0
AC Milan 1 (*Calloni pen*), Everton 0
Napoli 1 (*Braglia*), Moscow Torpedo 1 (*Filatov*)
Oesters Vaxjo 6 (*Svensson, Matsson 2, Evesson, Ejderstedt, Isaxsson*), Molde 0

Red Star Belgrade 1 (*Filipovic pen*), Uni Craiova 1 (*Krizan*)
Real Sociedad 1 (*Urreisti*), Grasshoppers 1 (*Santrac*)
Slask Wroclaw 4 (*Sybis 3, Pawlowski*), GAIS Gothenburg 2 (*Hans Johanson 2*)
Moscow Spartak 1 (*Andreyey*), AIK Stockholm 0
Sporting Lisbon 3 (*Baltazar, Da Costa, Manuel Fernandes pen*), Sliema Wanderers 1 (*Loporto*)
Stal Mielec 2 (*Karas, Krawczyk*), Holbaek 1 (*Torben Hansen*)
Valerengen 1 (*Dag Olvavason*), Athlone T 1 (*Martin*)
Vasas Budapest 4 (*Varadi 2, Kovacs, Izso*), VOEST Linz 0
Zaragoza 2 (*Pepe Gonzalez pen, Arrua*), Inter Bratislava 3 (*Jurkemik, Petras, Mraz*)

**Second Round, First Leg**

Duisburg 3 (*Schneider W., Worm, Krause*), Levski Spartak 2 (*Panov 2*)
Athlone 0, AC Milan 0
Carl Zeiss Jena 1 (*Kurbjuweit*), Stal Mielec 0
Dundee U 1 (*Rennie*), Porto 2 (*Oliveira, Seninho*)
Galatasaray 2 (*Sevki, Gokmen*), Moscow Torpedo 4 (*Enver og, Hrobroskin, Sakharov pen, Maksimenkov*)
Hertha Berlin 1 (*Kostedde*), Ajax 0
Honved 2 (*Weimper 2*), Dynamo Dresden 2 (*Heidler 2*)
Inter Bratislava 2 (*Luprich pen, Mraz*), AEK Athens 0
Ipswich T 3 (*Gates, Peddelty, Austin*), Bruges 0
Spartak Moscow 2 (*Lovchev 2*), Cologne 0
Oesters Vaxjo 1 (*Evansson*), Roma 0
Real Sociedad 1 (*Amas*), Liverpool 3 (*Highway, Callaghan, Thompson*)
Red Star Belgrade 1 (*Susic*), Hamburg 1 (*Bjornmose*)
Slask Wroclaw 1 (*Pawlowski*), Antwerp 1 (*Houwaart*)
Vasas Budapest 2 (*Kovacs 2, Varad pen*), Sporting Lisbon 1 (*Chico*)
Lazio 0, Barcelona 3 (*Lazio refused to play because of possible political demonstrations against the Spaniards. FIFA thus awarded the game to Barcelona 3-0*).

**Second Round, Second Leg**

Levski Spartak 2 (*Ivkov, Panov pen*), Duisburg 1 (*Worm*)
Liverpool 6 (*Toshack, Kennedy 2, Fairclough, Highway, Neal*), Real Sociedad 0
Ajax 4 (*Brokamp, Geels 2 [l pen], Meyer*), Hertha Berlin 1 (*Kostedde*)
Antwerp 1 (*De Schrijver*), Slask Wroclaw 2 (*Sybis, Pawlowski*)
AEK Athens 3 (*Tassos 2 [l pen], Wagner*), Inter Bratislava 1 (*Novotny*)
Barcelona 4 (*Sotil, Cruyff, Neeskens, Fortes*), Lazio 0
Bruges 4 (*Lambert 1 pen, De Cubber, Le Fevre, Van der Eycken*), Ipswich T 0
Dynamo Dresden 1 (*Dorner pen*), Honved 0
Hamburg 4 (*Reimann 2, Ettmayer, Memering*), Red Star Belgrade 0
Cologne 0, Moscow Spartak 1 (*Andreyev*)
AC Milan 3 (*Vincenzi, Benetti 2 [l pen]*), Athlone T 0
Moscow Torpedo 3 (*Degtyarev, Sahkarov pen, Budulakin*), Galatasaray 0
Porto 1 (*Seninho*), Dundee U 1 (*Hegarty*)
Roma 2 (*Pellegrini, Boni*), Oesters Vaxjo 0
Sporting Lisbon 2 (*Manuel Fernandes 2*), Vasas Budapest 1 (*Grass*)
Stal Mielec 1 (*Karas*), Carl Zeiss Jena 0

**Third Round, First Leg**

Ajax 2 (*Geels, Steffenhagen*), Levski Spartak 1 (*Voinov*)
Barcelona 3 (*Migueli, Rexach, Neeskens*), Vasas Budapest 1 (*Muller*)
Bruges 1 (*Cools*), Roma 0
Dynamo Dresden 3 (*Riedel 2, Kreische*), Moscow Torpedo 0
Hamburg 2 (*Zaczyk, Volkert pen*), Porto 0
Inter Bratislava 1 (*Saljanek*), Stal Mielec 0
Slask Wroclaw 1 (*Pawlowski*), Liverpool 2 (*Faber og, Toshack*)

AC Milan 4 (*Calloni 2, Bigon, Maldera*), Moscow Spartak 0

Dynamo Dresden 0, Liverpool 0
Hamburg 1 (*Bertl*), Stal Mielec 1 (*Oratowski*)

**Third Round, Second Leg**
Levski Spartak 2 (*Panov 2*), Ajax 1 (*Geels*)
Liverpool 3 (*Case 3*), Slask Wroclaw 0
Moscow Spartak 2 (*Papayev, Ovchev*), AC Milan 0
Moscow Torpedo 3 (*Dedtyaryov 2, Petrenko*), Dynamo Dresden 1 (*Heidler*)
Porto 2 (*Julio, Cubillas*), Hamburg 1 (*Reimann*)
Roma 0, Bruges 1 (*Lambert*)
Stal Mielec 2 (*Sekulski, Karas*), Inter Bratislava 0
Vasas Budapest 0, Barcelona 1 (*Fortes*)

**Quarter-Finals, First Leg**
Barcelona 4 (*Neeskens pen, Marcial, Asensi, Heredia*), Levski Spartak 0
Bruges 2 (*Le Fevre, Krieger*), AC Milan 0

**Quarter-Finals, Second Leg**
Levski Spartak 5 (*Panov 2 [1 pen], Yordanov 2, Spassov*), Barcelona 4 (*Marcial, Asensi, Heredia, Neeskens pen*)
Liverpool 2 (*Case, Keegan*), Dynamo Dresden 1 (*Heidler*)
AC Milan 2 (*Chiarugi 2*), Bruges 1 (*Sanders*)
Stal Mielec 0, Hamburg 1 (*Nogly*)

**Semi-Finals, First Leg**
Barcelona 0, Liverpool 1 (*Toshack*)
Hamburg 1 (*Reimann*), Bruges 1 (*Lambert*)

**Semi-Finals, Second Leg**
Bruges 1 (*Kaltz og*), Hamburg 0
Liverpool 1 (*Thompson*), Barcelona 1 (*Rexach*)

### Final 1975-76: Liverpool 3, Bruges 2

(At Anfield, 28 April, 1976, 56,000)

*Liverpool:* Clemence; Smith, Neal, Thompson, Kennedy, Hughes, Keegan, Fairclough, Heighway, Toshack (Case), Callaghan.
*Bruges:* Jensen; Bastyns, Krieger, Leekens, Volders, Cools, Van der Eycken, De Cubber, Van Gool, Lambert, Le Fevre.
*Scorers:* Liverpool – Kennedy, Case, Keegan (pen); Bruges – Lambert, Cools.

### Bruges 1, Liverpool 1

(At Olympia Stadium, Bruges, 19 May, 1976, 32,000)

*Bruges:* Jensen; Bastyns, Krieger, Leekens, Volders, Cools, Van der Eycken, Van Gool, Lambert (Sanders), De Cubber (Hinderyckx), Le Fevre.
*Liverpool:* Clemence; Smith, Neal, Thompson, Kennedy, Hughes, Keegan, Case, Heighway, Toshack (Fairclough), Callaghan.
*Scorers:* Bruges – Lambert (pen); Liverpool – Keegan.

# UEFA CUP 1976-77

**First Round, First Leg**

Porto 2 (*Rodolfo, Cubillas*), Schalke 04 2 (*Erwin Kremers, Fischer*)
Fram Reykjavik 0, Slovan Bratislava 3 (*Haraslin 2, Mrva*)
Glentoran 3 (*Feeney 2, Dickinson*), Basle 2 (*Maissen, Ramseier*)
Paralimni 1 (*Mertakas*), Kaiserslautern 3 (*Rinderl, Meier, Spiergeri*)
AEK Athens 2 (*Nikoloudis, Papaioannou*), Moscow Dynamo 0
Ajax 1 (*Krol*), Manchester U 0
Austria Salzburg 5 (*Schwarz 3 [1 pen], Haider 2*), Adanaspor 0
Belenenses 2 (*Quaresma, Horta*), Barcelona 2 (*Heredia 2*)
Celtic 2 (*McDonald, Dalglish*), Wisla Krakow 2 (*Kmiecik, Wrobel*)
Derby Co 12 (*Hector 5, Rioch, James 3, George 3*), Finn Harps 0
Dinamo Bucharest 0, AC Milan 0
Eintracht Brunswick 7 (*Hollmann, Stoltenburg 2, Frank 3, Gersdorff*), Holbaek 0
Espanol 3 (*Cuesta, Maranon, Caszely*), Nice 1 (*Toko*)
Feyenoord 3 (*Schneider pen, Kreuz, Vreysen*), Djurgaarden 0
Fenerbahce 2 (*Cemil 2*), Videoton 1 (*Nagy*)
Grasshoppers 7 (*Bosco, Ponte, Seller 2, Bauer, Cornioley 2 [1 pen]*), Hibernian Malta 0
Hibernian 1 (*Brownlie*), Sochaux 0
Internazionale 0, Honved 1 (*Kozma*)
Cologne 2 (*Flohe pen, Van Gool*), GKS Tychy 0
Kuopion Palloseura 3 (*Toernroos, Rissanen 2*), Oester Vaxjo 2 (*Stromberg, Ejderstedt*)
Magdeburg 3 (*Steinbach, Streich 2 [1 pen]*), Cesena 0
Manchester C 1 (*Kidd*), Juventus 0
Naestved 0, RWD Molenbeek 3 (*Boskamp, Wellens 2*)
QPR 4 (*Bowles 3, Masson*), Brann Bergen 0
Red Boys Differdange 0, Lokeren 3 (*Verheyen 2, Dalving*)
Slavia Prague 2 (*Herda, Radolsky*), Akademik Sofia 0
Schachtjor Donetzk 3 (*Rogovsky, Sokolvsky, Starukhin*), Dynamo Berlin 0
Sportul Studentesc 3 (*Grosu, Ionescu 2*), Olympiakos 0
SW Innsbruck 2 (*Sterig, Pezzey*), Start Kristiansand 1 (*Mathiesen pen*)
ASA Tirgu Mures 0, Dynamo Zagreb 1 (*Jurisic*)
Ujpest Dozsa 1 (*Dunai I.*), Atlético Bilbao 0
Lokomotiv Plovdiv 2 (*Fidanov, Bonev*), Red Star Belgrade 1 (*Filipovic*)

**First Round, Second Leg**

Adanaspor 2 (*Isa, Sener*), Austria Salzburg 0
Akademik Sofia 3 (*Dimitrov 2, Yankov*), Slavia Prague 0
Barcelona 3 (*Rexach, Asensi, Clares*), Belenenses 2 (*Vasques, Rocha*)
Basle 3 (*Nielsen, Mundschin, Demarmels*), Glentoran 0
Dynamo Berlin 1 (*Noak*), Schachtjor Donetzk 1 (*Rogowski*)
Atlético Bilbao 5 (*Rojo 2, Dani 3*), Ujpest Dozsa 0
Brann Bergen 0, QPR 7 (*Webb; Givens 2, Bowles 3, Thomas*)
Cesena 3 (*Mariani, Pepe, Macchi*), Magdeburg 1 (*Sparwasser*)
Djurgaarden 2 (*Karlsson K., Stenbaek*), Feyenoord 1 (*Nico Jansen*)
Dynamo Zagreb 3 (*Sensen 2, Bogdan*), ASA Tirgu Mures 0
Finn Harps 1 (*McFarland og*), Derby Co 4 (*Hector 2, George 2*)
Hibernian Malta 0, Grasshoppers 2 (*Sieler, Cornioley pen*)
Holbaek 1 (*Tofte*), Eintracht Brunswick 0
Honved 1 (*Poczik*), Internazionale 1 (*Mariani*)
Juventus 2 (*Scirea, Boninsegna*), Manchester C 0
Lokeren 3 (*Mommens, Hansen, Lubanski*), Red Boys Differdange 1 (*Flenghi pen*)
Manchester U 2 (*Macari, McIlroy*), Ajax 0
Moscow Dynamo 2 (*Bubnov, Yukubik pen*), AEK Athens 1 (*Tassos pen*)
Nice 2 (*Toko, Bjekovic*), Espanol 1 (*Aquino pen*)
Oester Vaxjo 2 (*Stromberg, Svensson*), Kuopion Palloseura 0
Olympiakos 2 (*Galakos, Karavitis pen*), Sportul Studentesc 1 (*Radacanu*)

RWD Molenbeek 4 (*Koons, Boskamp 2 [1 pen], Cordier*), Naestved 0
Schalke 04 3 (*Fichtel, Abramczik, Fischer*), Porto 2 (*Oliveira 2*)
Slovan Bratislava 5 (*Pekarik, Ondrus, Barto, Capkovic, Atlasson og*), Fram Reykjavik 0
Sochaux 0, Hibernian 0
Start Kristiansand 0, SW Innsbruck 5 (*Koncilia 2, Sterling 2 [1 pen], Witzl*)
GKS Tychy 1 (*Ogaza*), Cologne 1 (*Muller*)
Videoton 4 (*Wollek, Kovacs J., Szalmasy 2*), Fenerbahce 0
Wisla Krakow 2 (*Kmiecik 2*), Celtic 0
Kaiserslautern 8 (*Toppmuller 4, Pirrung 2, Meier, Riedl*), Paralimni 0
AC Milan 2 (*Calloni, Silva*), Dinamo Bucharest 1 (*Satmareanu*)
Red Star Belgrade 4 (*Bolicevic, Filipovic 2, Stamenkovic*), Lokomotiv Plovdiv 1 (*Bonev*)

**Second Round, First Leg**

AEK Athens 2 (*Wagner 2*), Derby Co 0
Akademik Sofia 4 (*Paunov 2, Manolov, Dimitrov*), AC Milan 3 (*Capello 2, Colovatti*)
Austria Salzburg 2 (*Schwarz P., Schwarz W. pen*), Red Star Belgrade 1 (*Filipovic*)
Barcelona 2 (*Cruyff, Clares*), Lokeren 0
Basle 1 (*Marti*), Atlético Bilbao 1 (*Madariaga*)
Eintracht Brunswick 2 (*Frank, Stolzenburg*), Espanol 1 (*Maranon*)
Hibernian 2 (*Blackley, Brownlie*), Oester Vaxjo 0
SW Innsbruck 1 (*Sterling*), Videoton 1 (*Czeczeli pen*)
Kaiserslautern 2 (*Briegel 2*), Feyenoord 2 (*De Jong, Nico Jansen*)
Cologne 2 (*Konopka, Muller*), Grasshoppers 0
Magdeburg 2 (*Steinbach, Zapf*), Dynamo Zagreb 0
Manchester U 1 (*Hill*), Juventus 0
Schachtjor Donetzk 3 (*Shevluch, Starukhin, Vasin*), Honved 0
Slovan Bratislava 3 (*Novotny, Haraslin, Ondrus*), QPR 3 (*Bowles 2, Givens*)
Sportul Studentesc 0, Schalke 04 1 (*Fischer*)
Wisla Krakow 1 (*Kapka*), RWD Molenbeek 1 (*Olsen*)

**Second Round, Second Leg**

Atlético Bilbao 3 (*Villar, Carlos, Rojo 1*), Basle 1 (*Marti*)
Derby Co 2 (*George, Rioch*), AEK Athens 3 (*Nikoloudis, Tassos, Wagner*)
Dynamo Zagreb 2 (*Krunjcar 2*), Magdeburg 2 (*Streich, Pommerenke*)
Espanol 2 (*Jeremias, Ortiz Aquino pen*), Eintracht Brunswick 0
Feyenoord 5 (*Wim Jansen, Nico Jansen, De Jong, Van Deinsen, Schneider pen*), Kaiserslautern 0
Grasshoppers 2 (*Bauer pen, Bosco*), FC Cologne 3 (*Muller, Larsen 2*)
Honved 2 (*Kozma 2 [1 pen]*), Schachtjor Donetzk 3 (*Shevluik, Reznik 2*)
Juventus 3 (*Boninsegna 2, Benetti*), Manchester U 0
AC Milan 2 (*Calloni, Morini*), Akademik Sofia 0
Oester Vaxjo 4 (*Linderoth 2, Ejderstedt 2*), Hibernian 1 (*Smith*)
QPR 5 (*Givens 3 [1 pen], Bowles, Clement*), Slovan Bratislava 2 (*Ondrus, Jan Capkovic*)
Red Star Belgrade 1 (*Filipovic*), Austria Salzburg 0
RWD Molenbeek 1 (*Nielsen*), Wisla Krakow 1 (*Maculewicz*)
Schalke 04 4 (*Bongartz 2, Fischer 2*), Sportul Studentesc 0
Videoton 1 (*Nagy*), SW Innsbruck 0
Lokeren 2 (*Verheyen, Dalving*), Barcelona 1 (*Cruyff*)

**Third Round, First Leg**

AEK Athens 2 (*Papaioannou, Marvos*), Red Star Belgrade 0
Atlético Bilbao 4 (*Dani 2 [1 pen], Carlos 2*), AC Milan 1 (*Capello*)

Espanol 0, Feyenoord 1 (*De Felipe og*)
Juventus 3 (*Bettega, Tardelli, Boninsegna*), Schachtjor Donetzk 0
Magdeburg 5 (*Streich, Tyll 2, Mewes, Pommerenke*), Videoton 0
Oester Vaxjo 0, Barcelona 3 (*Clares 2, Neeskens*)
QPR 3 (*Givens, Webb, Bowles*), Cologne 0
RWD Molenbeek 1 (*Lafont*), Schalke 04 0

**Third Round, Second Leg**
Cologne 4 (*Muller 2, Lohr, Weber*), QPR 1 (*Masson*)
Barcelona 5 (*Clares, Cruyff, Asensi 2, Heredia*), Oester Vaxjo 1 (*Everson*)
Feyenoord 2 (*Krauz, Nico Jansen*), Espanol 0
AC Milan 3 (*Calloni 2 [1 pen], Biasiolo*), Atlético Bilbao 1 (*Madariaga pen*)
Red Star Belgrade 3 (*Baralic, Filipovic, Savic*), AEK Athens 1 (*Wagner*)
Schalke 04 1 (*Abramczik*), RWD Molenbeek 1 (*Teugels*)
Schachtjor Donetsk 1 (*Shevluk*), Juventus 0
Videoton 1 (*Nagy J.*), Magdeburg 0

**Quarter-Final, First Leg**
Atlético Bilbao 2 (*Churruca, Dani pen*), Barcelona 1 (*Asensi*)

Feyenoord 0, RWD Molenbeek 0
Magdeburg 1 (*Streich*), Juventus 3 (*Cuccureddu, Benetti, Boninsegna*)
QPR 3 (*Francis 2 pens, Bowles*), AEK Athens 0

**Quarter-Final, Second Leg**
AEK Athens 3 (*Mavros 2, Papaioannou*), QPR 0
Barcelona 2 (*Cruyff 2*), Atlético Bilbao 2 (*Irureta 2*)
Juventus 1 (*Cuccureddu*), Magdeburg 0
RWD Molenbeek 2 (*Wellens, Teugels pen*), Feyenoord 1 (*De Jong*)

**Semi-Final, First Leg**
RWD Molenbeek 1 (*Teugels*), Atlético Bilbao 1 (*Churruca*)
Juventus 4 (*Cuccureddu, Bettega 2, Causio*), AEK Athens 1 (*Papadopoulos*)

**Semi-Final, Second Leg**
AEK Athens 0, Juventus 1 (*Bettega*)
Atlético Bilbao 0, RWD Molenbeek 0

### Final 1976–77: Juventus 1, Atlético Bilbao 0
(In Turin, 4 May, 1977, 75,000)

*Juventus:* Zoff; Cuccureddu, Gentile, Scirea, Morini, Tardelli, Furino, Benetti, Causio, Boninsegna (Gori), Bettega.
*Atlético Bilbao:* Iribar; Villar, Escalza, Guoicoechea, Guisasola, Quaderra, Irureta, Rojo II, Dani, Churruca, Rojo I.
*Scorer:* Juventus – Tardelli.

### Atlético Bilbao 2, Juventus 1
(In Bilbao, 18 May, 1977, 43,000)

*Atlético Bilbao:* Iribar; Lasa (Carlos), Guisasola, Alesanco, Escalza, Villar, Churruca, Irureta, Amarrortu, Dani, Rojo I.
*Juventus:* Zoff; Cuccureddu, Morini, Scirea, Gentile, Causio, Tardelli, Furino, Benetti, Boninsegna (Spinosi), Bettega.
*Scorers:* Atlético Bilbao – Irureta, Carlos; Juventus – Bettega.
*Juventus won on away goals rule.*

## UEFA CUP 1977—78

### First Round, First Leg

Eintracht Frankfurt 5 (*Nickel 2, Wenzel, Kraus, Grabowski*), Sliema Wanderers 0
AZ 67 11 (*Van Hanegem, Arntz, Nygaard 3, Peters 4, Kist 2*), Red Boys 1 (*Christoph pen*)
Aston Villa 4 (*Gray, Deehan 2, Little*), Fenerbahce 0
Barcelona 5 (*Heredia 2, Cruyff pen, Clares, Zuviria*), Steaua 1 (*Nastase*)
Bastia 3 (*Felix 3*), Sporting Lisbon 2 (*Jordao pen, Fraguito*)
Bayern Munich 8 (*Oblak, Rummenigge 3, Hoeness, Müller 3*), Mjondalen 0
Boavista 1 (*Jorge Gomes*), Lazio 0
Bohemians 0, Newcastle U 0
Carl Zeiss Jena 5 (*Trocha 2, Vogel 2 [1 pen], Topfer*), Altay Izmir 1 (*Mustafa pen*)
Dundee U 1 (*Sturrock*), KB Copenhagen 0
Fiorentina 0, Schalke 04 0
Frem Copenhagen 0, Grasshoppers 2 (*Elsener, Becker*)
Glenavon 2 (*Malone pen, McDonald*), PSV Eindhoven 6 (*Van der Kuylen 2, Van Kraay, Deijkers, Deacy, Lubse*)
Gornik Zabrze 5 (*Gizil 3, Radecki, Wasilewski*), Haka Valkeakosken 3 (*Jarzyna og, Vimomen, Pivinen*)
Internazionale 0, Dynamo Tbilisi 1 (*Kipiani*)
Dynamo Kiev 1 (*Vermeeyev*), Eintracht Brunswick 1 (*Frank*)
Landskrona 0, Ipswich T 1 (*Whymark*)
Las Palmas 5 (*Maciel 2 [1 pen], Juani, Morete 2*), Sloboda Tuzla 0
Lens 4 (*Bosudira, Francoise, Djeballi, Elie*), Malmö FF 1 (*Sjoberg*)
Linz ASK 3 (*Koegelberger 2, Vokovic*), Ujpest Dozsa 2 (*Torocsik 2*)
Odra Opole 1 (*Decker*), Magdeburg 2 (*Sparwasser 2*)
Olympiakos Piraeus 3 (*Karavisis, Losanda, Galakos*), Dynamo Zagreb 1 (*Zedec*)
Manchester C 2 (*Barnes, Channon*), Widzew Lodz 2 (*Boniek 2 [1 pen]*)
Marek Stanke Dimitrov 2 (*Pargov, Petrov 2*), Ferencvaros 0
Rapid Vienna 1 (*Walzer*), Inter Bratislava 0
RWD Molenbeek 0, Aberdeen 0
Servette 1 (*Barberis*), Atlético Bilbao 0
Standard Liège 1 (*Nickel*), Slavia Prague 0
Start Kristiansand 6 (*Myhre, Skuse, Haugen 2, Mathisen 2 [1 pen]*), Fram Reykjavik 0
ASA Tirgu Mures 1 (*Fanici*), AEK Athens 0
Torino 3 (*Pulici 2, Claudio Sala*), Apoel 0
Zurich 1 (*Risi*), CSKA Sofia 0

### First Round, Second Leg

Aberdeen 1 (*Jarvie*), RWD Molenbeek 2 (*Gores, Wellens*)
AEK Athens 3 (*Papaioannou, Viera, Moussouris*), ASA Tirgu Mures 0
Altay Izmir 4 (*Mustafa 2, Murat 2*), Carl Zeiss Jena 1 (*Lindemann*)
Apoel 1 (*Marcou*), Torino 1 (*Garritano*)
Atlético Bilbao 2 (*Dani, Amorrortu*), Servette 0
CSKA Sofia 1 (*Markov*), Zurich 1 (*Cuccinotta*)
Eintracht Brunswick 0, Dynamo Kiev 0
Fenebahce 0, Aston Villa 2 (*Deehan, Little*)
Ferencvaros 2 (*Pusztai, Ebedli pen*), Marek Stanke 0
Grasshoppers 6 (*Meyer 2, Becker, Elsener, Ponte 2*), Frem Copenhagen 1 (*Mikkelsen*)
Inter Bratislava 3 (*Novotny 2, Levicky 2*), Rapid Vienna 0
Ipswich T 5 (*Whymark 4 [1 pen], Mariner*), Landskrona 0
Lazio 5 (*Garlaschelli 2, Giordano 3*), Boavista 0
Magdeburg 1 (*Streich*), Odra Opole 1 (*Kiose*)
Malmö FF 2 (*Cervin, Ljungberg*), Lens 0
Mjondalen 0, Bayern Munich 4 (*Rausch, Gruber, Kunkel, Niedermaier*)
Newcastle U 4 (*Gowling 2, Craig T. 2*), Bohemians 0
PSV Eindhoven 5 (*Rene Van der Kerkhof, Lubse 2, Deijkers 2*), Glenavon 0
Schalke 04 2 (*Abramczik, Helmut Kremers*), Fiorentina 1 (*Desolati*)
Slavia Prague 3 (*Vesely, Notovy, Nachtman*), Standard Liège 2 (*Nickel, Sigurvinsson*)
Sliema Wanderers 0, Eintracht Frankfurt 0
Sloboda Tuzla 4 (*Gec, Kovacevic 2, Mulahasonovic*), Las Palmas 3 (*Morete 2, Maciel*)

Sporting Lisbon 1 (*Manuel Fernandes*), Bastia 2 (*Rep, Desvignes*)
Steaua 1 (*Dumitru pen*), Barcelona 3 (*Cruyff, Asensi, Sanchez*)
Dynamo Tbilisi 0, Internazionale 0
Ujpest Dozsa 7 (*Fazekas 2, Toth 2, Torocsik, Sarlos, Fekete*), Linz ASK 0
Valkeakosken 0, Gornik Zabrze 0
Widzew Lodz 0, Manchester C 0
Dynamo Zagreb 5 (*Cerin 2, Senzen, Zajec pen, Bonic*), Olympiakos Piraeus 1 (*Caravitis pen*)
Start Kristiansand 2 (*Skuseth, Ole Olsen*), Fram Reykjavik 0
Red Boys 0, AZ 67 5 (*Kist 3, Van Hanegem, Van Rijnsoer*)
KB Copenhagen 3 (*Andersen 3*), Dundee U 0

### Second Round, First Leg

AEK Athens 2 (*Mavros, Nikoloudis*), Standard Liège 1 (*Sigurvinsson, Poul*)
AZ 67 1 (*Nygaard*), Barcelona 1 (*Neeskens*)
Aston Villa 2 (*McNaught 2*), Gornik Zabrze 0
Bastia 2 (*Papi 2*), Newcastle U 1 (*Cannell*)
Bayern Munich 3 (*Müller, Rummenigge 2*), Marek Stanke 0
Inter Bratislava 1 (*Sajanek*), Grasshoppers 0
Ipswich T 1 (*Gates*), Las Palmas 0
KB Copenhagen 1 (*Laudrup*), Dynamo Tbilisi 4 (*Chivadze, Kipiani, Chelebadze, Shengekiya*)
Lazio 2 (*Wilson, Giordano*), Lens 0
Magdeburg 4 (*Sparwasser 3, Steinbach*), Schalke 04 2 (*Demange, Abramczik*)
RWD Molenbeek 1 (*Wellens*), Carl Zeiss Jena 1 (*Lindemann*)
Start Kristiansand 1 (*Helge Haugen*), Eintracht Brunswick 0
Torino 3 (*Pulici, Patrizio Sala, Pecci*), Dynamo Zagreb 1 (*Cerin*)
Ujpest Dozsa 2 (*Torocsik, Viczko*), Atlético Bilbao 0
Widzew Lodz 3 (*Rozborsky, Kowenicki, Boniek*), PSV Eindhoven 5 (*Deijkers 2, Deacy, Van der Kuylen, Francois*)
Zurich 0, Eintracht Frankfurt 3 (*Holzenbein, Wenzel 2*)

### Second Round, Second Leg

Barcelona 1 (*Rexach pen*), AZ 67 1 (*Kist*)
*Barcelona won on penalties 5-4.*
Atlético Bilbao 3 (*Dani 2, Tirapu*), Ujpest Dozsa 0
Eintracht Brunswick 4 (*Breitner, Handschuh, Hollman 2*), Start Kristiansand 0
Carl Zeiss Jena 1 (*Lindemann pen*), RWD Molenbeek 1 (*Alhino*)
*Carl Zeiss Jena won on penalties 6-5.*
Dynamo Zagreb 1 (*Senzen*), Torino 0
Eintracht Frankfurt 4 (*Kraus, Grabowski, Stepanovic, Krobach*), Zurich 3 (*Risi 2 [1 pen], Torstensson*)
Gornik Zabrze 1 (*Marcinkowski*), Aston Villa 1 (*Gray*)
Grasshoppers 5 (*Elsener 2, Ponte, Sulser, Hey*), Inter Bratislava 1 (*Jurkemik*)
Marek Stanke 2 (*Petrov, Pargov*), Bayern Munich 0
Las Palmas 3 (*Morete 2, Felix*), Ipswich T 3 (*Mariner 2, Tibbott*)
Lens 6 (*Six 3, Bousdira, Djebali 2*), Lazio 0
Newcastle U 1 (*Gowling*), Bastia 3 (*De Zerbi, Rep 2*)
PSV Eindhoven 1 (*Deijkers*), Widzew Lodz 0
Schalke 04 1 (*Kremers*), Magdeburg 3 (*Pommerenke 2, Steinbach*)
Standard Liège 4 (*Labarbe, Riedl, Nickel, Gorez*), AEK Athens 1 (*Ardizoglou*)
Dynamo Tbilisi 2 (*Kipiani, Chelebadze*), KB Copenhagen 1 (*Andersen*)

### Third Round, First Leg

Aston Villa 2 (*Iribar og, Deehan*), Atlético Bilbao 0
Bastia 2 (*Papi, Rep*), Torino 1 (*Pulici*)
Carl Zeiss Jena 2 (*Schnuphase, Lindemann*), Standard Liège 0

Eintracht Frankfurt 4 (*Grabowski, Holzenbein, Kraus, Skala*), Bayern Munich 0
Ipswich T 3 (*Gates, Whymark, Talbot*), Barcelona 0
Magdeburg 4 (*Zapf, Pommerenke pen, Mewes, Steinbach*), Lens 0
PSV Eindhoven 2 (*Lubse, Van der Kuylen*), Eintracht Brunswick 0
Dynamo Tbilisi 1 (*Shengelia*), Grasshoppers 0

**Third Round, Second Leg**
Atlético Bilbao 1 (*Dani*), Aston Villa 1 (*Mortimer*)
Barcelona 3 (*Cruyff 2, Rexach pen*), Ipswich T 0
*Barcelona won on penalties 3-1.*
Bayern Munich 1 (*Rummenigge*), Eintracht Frankfurt 2 (*Wenzel, Holzenbein*)
Eintracht Brunswick 1 (*Bruns*), PSV Eindhoven 2 (*Van Kraay, Deijkers*)
Grasshoppers 4 (*Sulser, Ponte 2 [1 pen], Elsener*), Dynamo Tbilisi 0
Lens 2 (*Bousdira 2*), Magdeburg 0
Standard Liège 1 (*Nickel*), Carl Zeiss Jena 2 (*Szengewald, Weise pen*)
Torino 2 (*Graziani 2*), Bastia 3 (*Larios, Krimau 2*)

**Quarter-Final, First Leg**
Aston Villa 2 (*McNaught, Deehan*), Barcelona 2 (*Cruyff, Zuviria*)

Bastia 7 (*Larios, Papi, Mariot, Felix 2, Cazes, Franceschetti*), Carl Zeiss Jena 2 (*Raab 2*)
Magdeburg 1 (*Streich*), PSV Eindhoven 0
Eintracht Frankfurt 3 (*Kraus, Holzenbein 2 [1 pen]*), Grasshoppers 2 (*Bosco, Ponte pen*)

**Quarter-Final, Second Leg**
Grasshoppers 1 (*Ponte pen*), Eintracht Frankfurt 0
Carl Zeiss Jena 4 (*Raab, Lindemann, Vogel, Topfer pen*), Bastia 2 (*Papi, Krimau*)
PSV Eindhoven 4 (*Brandst 2, Seguin og, Lubse*), Magdeburg 2 (*Hoffman, Pommerenke*)
Barcelona 2 (*Migueli, Asensi*), Aston Villa 1 (*Little*)

**Semi-Final, First Leg**
Grasshoppers 3 (*Hermann, Ponte pen, Montandon*), Bastia 2 (*Krimau, Papi pen*)
PSV Eindhoven 3 (*Olmo og, Lubse, Postuma*), Barcelona 0

**Semi-Final, Second Leg**
Barcelona 3 (*Rexach 2 pens, Fortes*), PSV Eindhoven 1 (*Deacy*)
Bastia 1 (*Papi*), Grasshoppers 0

## Final 1977–78: Bastia 0, PSV Eindhoven 0
(In Corsica, 26 April, 1978, 15,000)

*Bastia:* Hiard; Burkhard, Guesdon, Orlanducci, Cazes, Papi, Lacuseta (Felix), Larios, Rep, Krimau, Mariot.

*PSV Eindhoven:* Van Beveren; Van Kraay, Krijgh, Stevens, Brandts, Poortvliet, Van der Kuylen, Willy Van der Kerkhof, Deijkers, Rene Van der Kerkhof, Lubse.

## PSV Eindhoven 3, Bastia 0
(In Eindhoven, 9 May, 1978, 27,000)

*PSV Eindhoven:* Van Beveren; Krijgh, Stevens, Van Kraay (Deacy), Brandts, Willy Van der Kerkhof, Poortvliet, Van der Kuylen, Lubse, Deijkers, Rene Van der Kerkhof.

*Bastia:* Hiard (Weller); Marchioni, Orlanducci, Guesdon, Cazes, Lacuesta, Larios, Papi, Rep, Krimau, Mariot (De Zerbi).

*Scorers:* PSV Eindhoven – Willy Van der Kerkhof, Deijkers, Van der Kuylen.

# UEFA CUP 1978-79

**First Round, First Leg**
Dukla Prague 1 (*Nehoda*), Lanerossi Vicenza 0
AC Milan 1 (*Novellino*), Lokomotiv Kosice 0
CSKA Sofia 2 (*Djevizov, Christov*), Valencia 1 (*Solsona*)
Borussia Moenchengladbach 5 (*Bruns 2, Gores, Nielsen, Simonsen*), Sturm Graz 1 (*Jurtin*)
Arges Pitesti 3 (*Toma, Moiceanu 2*), Panathinaikos 0
Atlético Bilbao 2 (*Van Dord og, Vidal*), Ajax 0
Everton 5 (*King 2, Thomas, Walsh, Latchford*), Finn Harps 0
Jeunesse Esch 0, Lausanne 0
Nantes 0, Benfica 2 (*Chalana, Nene*)
Gijon 3 (*Ferrero, Moran 2*), Torino 0
Sporting Braga 5 (*Chico Gordo 4, Lito*), Hibernians 0
Galatasaray 1 (*Fatih*), WBA 3 (*Robson, Regis, Cunningham*)
Dynamo Berlin 5 (*Riediger 3, Netz, Brillat*), Red Star Belgrade 2 (*Sestic, Savic*)
Palloseura 2 (*Monkkanen, Eiskanen*), 1903 Copenhagen 1 (*Haarby*)
Basle 2 (*Tanner, Stohler*), Stuttgart 3 (*Ohlicher 2, Dieter Hoeness*)
Torpedo Moscow 4 (*Vassilev, Mironov, Grijsin, Sutsijlin*), Molde 0
Elfsborg 2 (*Svensson, Magnusson*), Strasbourg 0
Duisburg 5 (*Jara, Alhaus, Bussers, Worm 2*), Lech Poznan 0
Standard Liège 1 (*Denier*), Dundee U 0
Start Kristiansand 0, Esbjerg 0
Arsenal 3 (*Stapleton 2, Sunderland*), Lokomotiv Leipzig 0
Carl Zeiss Jena 1 (*Topfer*), Lierse 0
Glentoran 0, IBV Vestmann 0
Twente 1 (*Thorsen*), Manchester C 1 (*Watson*)
Hibernian 3 (*Higgins 2, Temperley*), IFK Norrköping 2 (*Ohlsson, Andersson*)
Timisoara 2 (*Cotec, Paltinisan*), MTK Budapest 0
Pezoporikos 2 (*Teofonu 2*), Slask Wroclaw 2 (*Pawlowski, Sybis*)
Olympiakos 2 (Kritikopoulos, Kaltzas), Levski Spartak 1 (*Panov*)
Dynamo Tbilisi 2 (*Kipiani, Shengelja*), Napoli 0
Hajduk Split 2 (*Kop, Luchetin*), Rapid Vienna 0
Hertha Berlin 0, Trakia Plovdiv 0
Honved 6 (*Lukacs, Weimper 2, Gijmesi, Bodoyni, Nagy*), Adanaspor 0

**First Round, Second Leg**
Lanerossi Vicenza 1 (*Briaschi*), Dukla Prague 1 (*Roselli og*)
Lokomotiv Kosice 1 (*Kozak*), AC Milan 0
Valencia 4 (*Saura 2, Kempes, Felman*), CSKA Sofia 1 (*Christov*)
Sturm Graz 1 (*Schilcher*), Borussia Moenchengladbach 2 (*Simonsen, Bruns*)
Panathinaikos 1 (*Gonios*), Arges Pitesti 2 (*Duru, Radu*)
Ajax 3 (*Clarke 2, Lerby*), Atlético Bilbao 0
Finn Harps 0, Everton 5 (*King, Latchford, Walsh, Ross, Dobson*)
Lausanne 2 (*Dizerens, Sanpedro*), Jeunesse Esch 0
Benfica 0, Nantes 0
Torino 1 (*Graziani*), Gijon 0
Hibernians 3 (*Spiteri Gonzi, Mizzi 2*), Sporting Braga 2 (*Chico Gordo, Reinaldo*)
WBA 3 (*Robson, Cunningham, Trewick*), Galatasaray 1 (*Turgay*)
Red Star Belgrade 4 (*Borovnicka 2, Savic, Sestic*), Dynamo Berlin 1 (*Riediger*)
1903 Copenhagen 4 (*Christensen, Smidt, Larsen, Dam*), Palloseura 4 (*Eiskanen 2, Heinalainen, Rautio*)
Stuttgart 4 (*Kelsch 3, Hansi Muller*), Basle 1 (*Schonberger*)
Molde 3 (*Brakstad, Bjoraa, Fuglseth*), Torpedo Moscow 3 (*Vassilev 2, Zotijlin*)
Strasbourg 4 (*Piasecki, Tanter, Marx, Wagner*), Elfsborg 1 (*Ahlstrom*)
Lech Poznan 2 (*Kasalik, Okonski*), Duisburg 5 (*Bussers, Worm 2, Wenten, Buttgereit*)
Dundee U 0, Standard Liège 0
Esbjerg 1 (*Iversen*), Start Kristiansand 0
Lokomotiv Leipzig 1 (*Stapleton og*), Arsenal 4 (*Price, Sunderland, Stapleton 2*)

Lierse 2 (*Bosche, Van den Bergh*), Carl Zeiss Jena 2 (*Schupase, Topfer*)
IBV Westmann 1 (*Oskarsson*), Glentoran 1 (*McFall*)
Manchester C 3 (*Kidd, Bell, Overweg og*), Twente 2 (*Wildschut, Gritter*)
IFK Norrköping 0, Hibernian 0
MTK Budapest 2 (Koritar, Nadu og), Timisoara 1 (*Petrescu*)
Slask Wroclaw 5 (*Garlowski, Faber, Olesiak, Kwiatkowski, Sybis*), Pezoporikos 1 (*Lambrou*)
Levski Spartak 3 (*Milkov, Panov, Voinov*), Olympiakos 1 (*Kaltzas*)
Napoli 1 (*Savoldi*), Dynamo Tbilisi 1 (*Daraselia*)
Rapid Vienna 2 (*Krejcirik, Francker*), Hajduk Split 1 (*Zungul*)
Trakia Plovdiv 1 (*Argirov*), Hertha Berlin 2 (*Granitza 2*)
Adanaspor 2 (*Irfan, Necip*), Honved 2 (*Sener og, Pinter*)

**Second Round, First Leg**
Ajax 1 (*Lerby*), Lausanne 0
Benfica 0, Borussia Moenchengladbach 0
Everton 2 (*Latchford, King*), Dukla Prague 1 (*Macela*)
Arges Pitesti 2 (*Dobrin, Moiceanu*), Valencia 1 (*Felman*)
Sporting Braga 0, WBA 2 (*Regis 2*)
Torpedo Moscow 2 (*Vassilev, Sakharov*), Stuttgart 1 (*Dieter Hoeness*)
Strasbourg 2 (*Gemmrich, Piasecki*), Hibernian 0
Gijon 0, Red Star Belgrade 1 (*Misa og*)
Carl Zeiss Jena 0, Duisburg 0
Palloseura 0, Esbjerg 2 (*Bach, Nielsen*)
IBV Westmann 0, Slask Wroclaw 2 (*Kwiatkowski, Halgrimsson og*)
Manchester C 4 (*Hartford, Palmer, Kidd 2*), Standard Liège 0
Honved 4 (*Weimper 2, Gijmesi, Pinter*), Timisoara 0
Hertha Berlin 2 (*Nussing, Granitza*), Dynamo Tbilisi 0
Hajduk Split 2 (*Kop, Djordjevic*), Arsenal 1 (*Brady*)
Levski Spartak 1 (*Milkov*), AC Milan 1 (*Chiodi*)

**Second Round, Second Leg**
WBA 1 (*Brown A.*), Sporting Braga 0
Stuttgart 2 (*Hansi Muller, Volkert*), Torpedo Moscow 0
Hibernian 1 (*MacLeod*), Strasbourg 0
Red Star Belgrade 1 (*Petrovic*), Gijon 1 (*Borovnika og*)
Duisburg 3 (*Dietz, Jara, Fruck*), Carl Zeiss Jena 0
Esbjerg 4 (*Berthelsen, Thoresen, Stergaard, Bach*), Palloseura 1 (*Loikkanen*)
Slask Wroclaw 2 (*Nocko, Kwiatkowski*), IBV Westmann 1 (*Halgrimsson*)
Standard Liège 2 (*Sigurvinsson 2*), Manchester C 0
Timisoara 2 (*Rosca, Paltinislan*), Honved 0
Dynamo Tbilisi 1 (*Shengelia*), Hertha Berlin 0
Arsenal 1 (*Young*), Hajduk Split 0
AC Milan 3 (*Maldera, Bigon, Chiodi*), Levski Spartak 0
Dukla Prague 1 (*Gajdusek*), Everton 0
Lausanne 0, Ajax 4 (*Erkens, Clarke 2, Arnesen*)
Valencia 5 (*Kempes 2, Bonhof, Saura, Solsona*), Arges Pitesti 2 (*Moiceanu, Doru Nicolae*)
Borussia Moenchengladbach 2 (*Bruns pen, Klinkhammer*), Benfica 0

**Third Round, First Leg**
Stuttgart 4 (*Volkert 2 [1 pen], Kelsch, Ohlicher*), Dukla Prague 1 (*Gajdusek*)
Honved 4 (*Nagy 2, Lukacs, Weimper pen*), Ajax 1 (*Clarke pen*)
Red Star Belgrade 1 (*Blagojevic*), Arsenal 0
Esbjerg 2 (Hansen pen, Jaspersen), Hertha Berlin 1 (*Milewski*)
Borussia Moenchengladbach 1 (*Kulik pen*), Slask Wroclaw 1 (*Olesiak*)
Valencia 1 (*Felman*), WBA 1 (*Cunningham*)
Strasbourg 0, Duisburg 0
AC Milan 2 (*Bigon 2*), Manchester C 2 (*Kidd, Power*)

**Third Round, Second Leg**
Dukla Prague 4 (*Dieter Hoeness og, Vizek, Pelc pen, Gajdusek*), Stuttgart 0

Ajax 2 (*Clarke pen, Tahamata*), Honved 0
Arsenal 1 (*Sunderland*), Red Star Belgrade 1 (*Savic*)
Hertha Berlin 4 (*Milewski 4*), Esbjerg 0
Slask Wroclaw 2 (*Pawlowski 2 [1 pen]*), Borussia Moenchengladbach 4 (*Simonsen 3, Nielsen*)
WBA 2 (*Brown T. 2*), Valencia 0
Duisburg 4 (*Worm, Weber 2, Fruck*), Strasbourg 0
Manchester C 3 (*Booth, Hartford, Kidd*), AC Milan 0

**Quarter-Finals, First Leg**
Honved 2 (*Varga 11, Weimper pen*), Duisburg 3 (*Worm 2, Seliger*)
Red Star Belgrade 1 (*Savic*), WBA 0
Manchester C 1 (*Channon*), Borussia Moenchengladbach 1 (*Lienen*)
Hertha Berlin 1 (*Nussing*), Dukla Prague 1 (*Pelc*)

**Quarter-Finals, Second Leg**
Duisburg 1 (*Bussers*), Honved 2 (*Karalyos, Pal*)

WBA 1 (*Regis*), Red Star Belgrade 1 (*Sestic*)
Borussia Moenchengladbach 3 (*Kulik, Bruns, Del Haye*), Manchester C 1 (*Deyna*)
Dukla Prague 1 (*Nehoda*), Hertha Berlin 2 (*Agerbeck, Milewski*)

**Semi-Finals, First Leg**
Red Star Belgrade 1 (*Savic*), Hertha Berlin 0
Duisburg 2 (*Worm, Fruck*), Borussia Moenchengladbach 2 (*Simonsen, Lausen*)

**Semi-Finals, Second Leg**
Hertha Berlin 2 (*Beer, Sidka*), Red Star Belgrade 1 (*Milosavljevic*)
Borussia Moenchengladbach 4 (*Simonsen 2, Kulik, Lienen*), Duisburg 1 (*Bussers*)

**Final 1978–79: Red Star Belgrade 1, Borussia Moenchengladbach 1**
(In Belgrade, 9 May, 1979, 87,500)

*Red Star Belgrade:* Stojanovic; Jovanovic, Miletovic, Jurisic, Jovin, Muslin (Krmpotic), Petrovic, Blagojevic, Milosavljevic (Milovanovic), Savic, Sestic.
*Borussia Moenchengladbach:* Kneib; Vogts, Hannes, Schaffer, Ringles, Schafer, Kulik, Nielsen (Danner), Wohlers (Gores), Simonsen, Lienen.
*Scorers:* Red Star Belgrade – Sestic; Borussia Moenchengladbach – Juristic og.

**Borussia Moenchengladbach 1, Red Star Belgrade 0**
(In Dusseldorf, 23 May, 1979, 45,000)

*Borussia Moenchengladbach:* Kneib; Vogts, Hannes, Schaffer, Ringles, Schafer, Kulik (Koppel), Gores, Wohlers, Simonsen, Lienen.
*Red Star Belgrade:* Stojanovic; Jovanovic, Miletovic, Jurisic, Jovin, Muslin, Petrovic, Blagojevic, Milovanovic (Sestic), Savic, Milosavljevic.
*Scorer:* Borussia Moenchengladbach – Simonsen (pen).

## UEFA CUP 1979—80

**First Round, First Leg**
Perugia 1 (*Vujadinovic og*), Dinamo Zagreb 0
Inter-Milan 3 (*Muraro, Baresi, Marini*), Real Sociedad 0
Napoli 2 (*Damiani, Agostinelli*), Olympiakos 0
Stuttgart 1 (*Danova og*), Torino 0
Dundee U 0, Anderlecht 0
Glenavon 0, Standard Liège 1 (*Edstroem*)
Dinamo Kiev 2 (*Bessonov, Demianenko*), CSKA Sofia 1
(*Metodiev*)
Lokomotiv Sofia 3 (*Stankov, Velickov, Szokolov*), Fer-
encvaros 0
Kalmar 2 (*Sunesson, Sandberg*), IBK Keflavik 1 (*Mergeis-
son*)
KPT Kuopio 1 (*Pirinen*), Malmö 2 (*Andersson, Prytz pen*)
Dinamo Bucharest 3 (*Multescu, Georgescu, Vrinceanu*),
Alki Larnaca 0
Bohemians Prague 0, Bayern Munich 2 (*Kraus, Rummen-
igge*)
Zbrojovka Brno 6 (*Mazura, Janecka 2, Kroupa, Jarusek
2*), Esbjerg 0
Valletta 0, Leeds U 4 (*Graham 3, Hart*)
Orduspor 2 (*Cihan, Arif*), Banik Ostrava 0
Wiener SK 0, Uni Craiova 0
Widzew Lodz 2 (*Boniek, Kowienicki*), St Etienne 1 (*Pla-
tini*)
Aris Salonika 3 (*Cuis, Pallas pen, Zindros*), Benfica 1
(*Reinaldo*)
Carl Zeiss Jena 2 (*Schnuphase, Lindemann*), WBA 0
Atlético Madrid 1 (*Ruben Cano*), Dinamo Dresden 2
(*Hafner, Weber*)
Aarhus 1 (*Olesen*), Stal Mielec 1 (*Karas*)
Feyenoord 1 (*Notten*), Everton 0
Skeid Oslo 1 (*Rein*), Ipswich T 3 (*Mills, Turner, Mariner*)
Gijon 0, PSV Eindhoven 0
Galatasaray 0, Red Star Belgrade 0
Aberdeen 1 (*Harper*), Eintracht Frankfurt 1 (*Bum Kun
Cha*)
Rapid Vienna 0, Diosgyor 1 ( *Fuko*)
Borussia Moenchengladbach 3 (*Lienen, Nickel pen,
Kulik*), Viking 0
Sporting Lisbon 2 (*Fernandes 2*), Bohemians 0
Zurich 1 (*Zwicher*), Kaiserslautern 3 (*Neues, Bongartz,
Wolff*)
Shakhtjor 2 (*Sokolovsky 2*), Monaco 1 (*Petit*)
Progres Niedercorn 0, Grasshoppers 2 (*Herbert Hermann,
Egli*)

**First Round, Second Leg**
Dinamo Zagreb 0, Perugia 0
Real Sociedad 2 (*Satrustegui 2*), Inter-Milan 0
Olympiakos 1 (*Karavitis*), Napoli 0
Torino 2 (*Sala, Graziani*), Stuttgart 1 (*Ohlicher*)
Anderlecht 1 (*Nielsen*), Dundee U 1 (*Kopel*)
Standard Liège 1 (*Edstrom*), Glenavon 0
CSKA Sofia 1 (*Metodiev pen*), Dinamo Kiev 1 (*Buryak*)
Ferencvaros 2 (*Pusztai, Fogany*), Lokomotiv Sofia 0
IBK Keflavik 1 (*Andreasson og*), Kalmar 0
Malmö 2 (*Arvidsson 2*), KPT Kuopio 0
Alki Larnaca 0, Dinamo Bucharest 9 (*Georgescu 3, Vrin-
ceanu 2, Augustin, Talanar, Multescu, Moldovan*)
Bayern Munich 2 (*Rummenigge, Breitner pen*), Bohe-
mians Prague 2 (*Ondrus, Prokas pen*)
Esbjerg 1 (*Bach*), Zbrojovka Brno 1 (*Jarusek*)
Leeds U 3 (*Curtis, Hankin, Hart*), Valletta 0
Banik Ostrava 6 (*Knapp, Vojacek, Nemec, Licka 2,
Danek*), Orduspor 0
Uni Craiova 3 (*Camataru 2, Geolganu*), Wiener SK 1
(*Drabits*)
St Etienne 3 (*Rep 3 [1 pen]*), Widzew Lodz 0
Benfica 2 (*Reinaldo, Gomes*), Aris Salonika 1 (*Semertzi-
dis*)
WBA 1 (*Wile*), Carl Zeiss Jena 2 (*Lindemann, Raab pen*)
Dinamo Dresden 3 (*Riedl, Ruiz og, Weber*), Atlético
Madrid 0
Stal Mielec 0, Aarhus 1 (*Jensen*)
Everton 0, Feyenoord 1 (*Budding*)
Ipswich T 7 (*Wark, Muhren 2, McCall 2, Mariner,
Thijssen*), Skeid Oslo 0
PSV Eindhoven 1 (*Van der Kerkhof W.*), Gijon 0
Red Star Belgrade 3 (*Savic 2, Milovanovic*), Galatasaray
1 (*Gungor*)

Eintracht Frankfurt 1 (*Holzenbein*), Aberdeen 0
Diosgyor 3 (*Szalai, Fekete, Tatar*), Rapid Vienna 2 (*Keg-
levits, Sallmayer*)
Viking 1 (*Bjensen*), Borussia Moenchengladbach 1
(*Kulik*)
Bohemians 0, Sporting Lisbon 0
Kaiserslautern 5 (*Melzer 2, Kaminke, Wendt, Geye*), Zur-
ich 1 (*Zappa*)
Monaco 2 (*Onnis, Dalger*), Shakhtjor 0
Grasshoppers 4 (*Ponte, Pfister, Egli, Heinz Hermann*),
Progres Niedercorn 0

**Second Round, First Leg**
Aris Salonika 1 (*Semertzidis*), Perugia 1 (*Rossi*)
Standard Liège 2 (*Riedl, Sigurvinsson pen*), Napoli 1
(*Capone*)
Borussia Moenchengladbach 1 (*Hannes*), Inter-Milan 1
(*Altobelli*)
Dinamo Bucharest 2 (*Multescu pen, Augustin*), Eintracht
Frankfurt 0
Uni Craiova 2 (*Balaci, Irimescu*), Leeds U 0
Zbrojovka Brno 3 (*Kotasek 2, Janecka*), IBK Keflavik 1
(*Georgsson*)
Red Star Belgrade 3 (*Savic pen, Muslin, Sestic*), Carl Zeiss
Jena 2 (*Raab 2 [1 pen]*)
Lokomotiv Sofia 4 (*Mihailov 4 [2 pens]*), Monaco 2
(*Onnis 2 [J pen]*)
Dundee U 0, Diosgyor 1 (*Fekete*)
Aarhus 1 (*Sander*), Bayern Munich 2 (*Rummenigge 2*)
Grasshoppers 0, Ipswich T 0
Feyenoord 4 (*Petursson 3 [J pen], Van Diesen*), Malmö 0
PSV Eindhoven 2 (*Van der Kerkhof R., Moster*), St
Etienne 0
Sporting Lisbon 1 (*Fernandes*), Kaiserslautern 1 (*Bon-
gartz*)
Dinamo Dresden 1 (*Weber pen*), Stuttgart 1 (*Forster*)
Banik Ostrava 1 (*Nemec*), Dinamo Kiev 0

**Second Round, Second Leg**
Perugia 0, Aris Salonika 3 (*Cuis, Semcrtzidis, Zindros*)
Napoli 1 (*Damiani*), Standard Liège 1 (*Riedl*)
Inter-Milan 2 (*Altobelli 2*), Borussia Moenchengladbach
3 (*Nickel 2 [J pen], Ringells*)
Eintracht Frankfurt 3 (*Bum Kun Cha, Holzenbein,
Nickel*), Dinamo Bucharest 0
Leeds U 0, Uni Craiova 2 (*Ciriu, Beldeanu*)
IBK Keflavik 1 (*Olafsson*), Zbrojovka Brno 2 (*Kroupa,
Kotasek*)
Carl Zeiss Jena 2 (*Trocha, Topfer*), Red Star Belgrade 3
(*Kurbjuweit og, Filipovic, Blagojevic*)
Monaco 2 (*Christophe, Onnis*), Lokomotiv Sofia 1
(*Mihailov*)
Diosgyor 3 (*Borostyan, Tatar 2 [J pen]*), Dundee U 1
(*Kopel*)
Bayern Munich 3 (*Hoeness D. 2, Breitner*), Aarhus 1
(*Mickelsen*)
Ipswich T 1 (*Beattie*), Grasshoppers 1 (*Sulser*)
Malmö 1 (*Arvidsson*), Feyenoord 1 (*Petursson*)
St Etienne 6 (*Larios, Santini, Platini 2, Roussey, Rep pen*),
PSV Eindhoven 0
Kaiserslautern 2 (*Bongartz, Neues pen*), Sporting Lisbon
0
Stuttgart 0, Dinamo Dresden 0
Dinamo Kiev 2 (*Demianenko, Kapsalis*), Banik Ostrava
0

**Third Round, First Leg**
Bayern Munich 2 (*Rummenigge, Janzon*), Red Star Bel-
grade 0
Grasshoppers 0, Stuttgart 2 (*Klotz, Hadewicz*)
Borussia Moenchengladbach 2 (*Nickel 2*), Uni Craiova 0
Diosgyor 0, Kaiserslautern 2 (*Wendt, Bongartz*)
Eintracht Frankfurt 4 (*Bum Kun Cha, Nickel, Muller,
Lotterman*), Feyenoord 1 (*Stafieu*)
Standard Liège 1 (*Voordeckers*), Zbrojovka Brno 2 (*Svo-
boda, Dosek*)
St Etienne 4 (*Platini, Larios, Firos og, Roussey*), Aris
Salonika 1 (*Semertzidis*)
Lokomotiv Sofia 1 (*Mihailov*), Dinamo Kiev 0

**Third Round, Second Leg**

Red Star Belgrade 3 (*Savic, Petrovic, Repcic*), Bayern Munich 2 (*Hoeness 2*)

Stuttgart 3 (*Muller, Martin, Kelsh*), Grasshoppers 0

Uni Craiova 1 (*Irimescu*), Borussia Moenchengladbach 0

Kaiserslautern 6 (*Neues, Melzer, Brummer, Kaminke, Bongartz, Stabel pen*), Diosgyor 1 (*Borostyan*)

Feyenoord 1 (*Peters*), Eintracht Frankfurt 0

Zbrojovka Brno 3 (*Jarusel, Kroupa, Janecka*), Standard Liège 2 (*Edstrom, De Matos*)

Aris Salonika 3 (*Larios og, Pallas pen, Venos*), St Etienne 3 (*Larios, Zimako, Rep*)

Dinamo Kiev 2 (*Blochin, Kapsalis*), Lokomotiv Sofia 1 (*Doychev*)

**Quarter-Final, First Leg**

St Etienne 1 (*Platini*), Borussia Moenchengladbach 4 (*Nielsen 2, Nickel, Lienen*)

Kaiserslautern 1 (*Brummer*), Bayern Munich 0

Eintracht Frankfurt 4 (*Nachtweih, Lorant pen, Nickel, Karger*), Zbrojovka Brno 1 (*Horny*)

Stuttgart 3 (*Muller, Volkert 2 [1 pen]*), Lokomotiv Sofia 1 (*Kolev*)

**Quarter-Final, Second Leg**

Borussia Moenchengladbach 2 (*Thychosen, Hannes*), St Etienne 0

Bayern Munich 4 (*Hoeness 2, Janzon, Breitner pen*), Kaiserslautern 1 (*Wendt*)

Zbrojovka Brno 3 (*Horny, Kotasek, Kopenec*), Eintracht Frankfurt 2 (*Karger, Neuberger*)

Lokomotiv Sofia 0, Stuttgart 1 (*Ohlicher*)

**Semi-Final, First Leg**

Stuttgart 2 (*Ohlicher, Volkert pen*), Borussia Moenchengladbach 1 (*Nickel*)

Bayern Munich 2 (*Hoeness, Breitner pen*), Eintracht Frankfurt 0

**Semi-Final, Second Leg**

Borussia Moenchengladbach 2 (*Matthaus, Schaefer*), Stuttgart 0

Eintracht Frankfurt 5 (*Pezzey 2, Karger 2, Lorant pen*), Bayern Munich 1 (*Dremmler*)

### Final 1979–80: Borussia Moenchengladbach 3, Eintracht Frankfurt 2
(In Moenchengladbach, 7 May, 1980, 25,000)

*Borussia Moenchengladbach:* Kneib; Hannes, Schaefer, Schaeffer, Ringels, Matthaus, Kulik, Nielsen (Thychosen), Del'Haye (Boedeker), Harald Nickel, Lienen.

*Eintracht Frankfurt:* Pahl; Pezzey, Neuberger, Koerbel, Ehrmanntraut, Lorant, Holzenbein (Nachtweih), Borchers, Bernd Nickel, Tscha, Karger (Trapp).

*Scorers:* Borussia Moenchengladbach – Kulik 2, Matthaus; Eintracht Frankfurt – Karger, Holzenbein.

### Eintracht Frankfurt 1, Borussia Moenchengladbach 0
(In Frankfurt, 21 May, 1980, 60,000)

*Eintracht Frankfurt:* Pahl; Pezzey, Neuberger, Koerbel, Ehrmanntraut, Lorant, Holzenbein, Borchers, Bernd Nickel, Tscha, Nachtweih (Schaub).

*Borussia Moenchengladbach:* Kneib; Hannes, Fleer, Schaefer, Ringels, Matthaus (Thychosen), Boedeker, Kulik, Nielsen (Del'Haye), Harald Nickel, Lienen.

*Scorer:* Eintracht Frankfurt – Schaub.

*Eintracht Frankfurt won on away goals.*

## UEFA CUP 1980—81

**First Round, First Leg**

AZ 67 Alkmaar 6 (*Hovenkamp, Nygaard, Peters 2, Welzl, Tol*), Red Boys 0

IA Akranes 0, Cologne 4 (*Kroth, Littbarski, Muller, Strack*)

Sliema Wanderers 0, Barcelona 2 (*Canito, Landaburu*)

Ujpest Dozsa 1 (*Kardos*), Real Sociedad 1 (*Alonso*)

Arges Pitesti 0, Utrecht 0

Ballymena U 2 (*McQuiston, Sloan*), Vorwaerts Frankfurt 1 (*Geyer*)

Bohemians Prague 3 (*Bicovsky 2, Levy*), Gijon 1 (*Ferrero*)

Dynamo Dresden 1 (*Weber*), Napredak 0

Elfsborg 1 (*Nilsson*), St Mirren 2 (*Somner, Abercromby*)

Grasshoppers 3 (*Meyer 3 [2 pens]*), KB Copenhagen 1 (*Eigenbrod*)

Hamburg 4 (*Kaltz, Hrubesch 2, Hartwig*), Sarajevo 2 (*Susic 2*)

Ipswich T 5 (*Wark 4 [3 pens], Mariner*), Aris Salonika 1 (*Pallas pen*)

Juventus 4 (*Scirea, Verza, Bettega, Cabrini pen*), Panathinaikos 0

Kaiserslautern 1 (*Funkel*), Anderlecht 0

Dynamo Kiev 1 (*Buryak pen*), Levski Spartak 1 (*Spassov*)

PSV Eindhoven 3 (*Brandts, Van Kraay, Van der Koylen pen*), Wolverhampton W 1 (*Gray*)

Kuopion Palloseura 0, St Etienne 7 (*Paganelli 2, Hyvarinen og, Platini 2, Roussey, Janvion*)

Linz ASK 1 (*Krieger*), Radnicki Nis 2 (*Stojlkovic, Pantelic pen*)

Lokeren 1 (*Verheyen pen*), Moscow Dynamo 1 (*Gassayev*)

Magdeburg 2 (*Hoffman, Pommerenke pen*), Moss 1 (*Henriksen*)

Manchester U 1 (*McIlroy*), Widzew Lodz 1 (*Surlit*)

Porto 1 (*Souza*), Dundalk 0

RWD Molenbeek 1 (*De Wolf*), Torino 2 (*Mariani, Graziani*)

Shakhtor Donetsk 1 (*Starukhin*), Eintracht Frankfurt 0

Slask Wroclaw 0, Dundee U 0

Sochaux 2 (*Jeskowiak, Ivezic pen*), Servette 0

Standard Liège 1 (*Dardenne*), Steaua Bucharest 1 (*Raducanu*)

Stuttgart 6 (*Klotz 3, Allgower 2, Kelsch*), Pezoporikos 0

Twente 5 (*Bos, Carlsson og, Kila 2, Jol*), IFK Gothenburg 1 (*Nilsson*)

Vasas 0, Boavista 2 (*Eliseu, Julio*)

Zbrojovka Brno 3 (*Kroupa, Mikulicka, Mazura*), Voest Linz 1 (*Haider*)

Fenerbahce 0, Beroe Stara Zagora 1 (*Peyev*)


**First Round, Second Leg**

St Etienne 7 (*Rep 4 [1 pen], Lestage, Paganelli, Lopez*), Kuopion Palloseura 0

Servette 2 (*Cuccinotta, Bizzini*), Sochaux 1 (*Genghini*)

Red Boys 0, AZ 67 Alkmaar 4 (*Kist 3 [1 pen], Welzl*)

Steaua Bucharest 1 (*Raducanu*), Standard Liège 2 (*Voordeckers, Edstrom*)

Aris Salonika 3 (*Tsirmokos, Drambis, Zeleidis*), Ipswich T 1 (*Gates*)

Radnicki Nis 4 (*Mitosevic, Stolijovic 2, Panajotovic*), Linz ASK 1 (*Siegl*)

Napredak 0, Dynamo Dresden 1 (*Muller pen*)

Moscow Dynamo 0, Lokeren 1 (*Verheyen*)

Vorwaerts Frankfurt 3 (*Conrad, Jarmuskiewicz, Krautzig*), Ballymena U 0

Boavista 0, Vasas 1 (*Kiss*)

IFK Gothenburg 2 (*Nilsson 2*), Twente 0

Sarajevo 3 (*Lukic, Pasic 2*), Hamburg 3 (*Hrubesch 3*)

Voest Linz 0, Zbrojovka Brno 2 (*Janecka, Kroupa*)

St Mirren 0, Elfsborg 0

Dundee U 7 (*Dodds 2, Hegarty, Pettigrew 2, Stark, Payne pen*), Slask Wroclaw 2 (*Pawlowski 2*)

Widzew Lodz 0, Manchester U 0

KB Copenhagen 2 (*Fossgaard, Hansen pen*), Grasshoppers 5 (*Heinz Hermann 3, Zanetti, Sulser*)

Moss 2 (*Kollshaugen 2*), Magdeburg 3 (*Streich, Mewes, Wildebrand*)

Levski Spartak 0, Kiev Dynamo 0


Beroe Stara Zagora 2 (*Petkov, Dragolov*), Fenerbahce 1 (*Selcuk*)

Anderlecht 3 (*Nielsen 3, [1 pen]*), Kaiserslautern 2 (*Gaye, Wendt*)

Real Sociedad 1 (*Satrustegui*), Ujpest Dozsa 0

Barcelona 1 (*Rexach pen*), Sliema Wanderers 0

Eintracht Frankfurt 3 (*Holzenbein, Cha Kun Bum 2*), Shakhtor Donetsk 0

Utrecht 2 (*Van der Lem, Carbo*), Arges Pitesti 0

Dundalk 0, Porto 0

Cologne 6 (*Engels, Muller 4, Okudera*), IA Akranes 0

Wolverhampton W 1 (*Eves*), PSV Eindhoven 0

Gijon 2 (*Ferrero, Jimenez*), Bohemians 1 (*Nemec*)

Panathinaikos 4 (*Gentile og, Andreucchi, Luvanthinos, Delikaris*), Juventus 2 (*Bettega, Fanna*)

Torino 2 (*D'Amico, Graziani*), RWD Molenbeek 2 (*De Bolle, Van de Korput og*)

Pezoporikos 1 (*Theophanous P.*), Stuttgart 4 (*Tuefekci 2, Klotz, Allgower*)


**Second Round, First Leg**

Sochaux 2 (*Genghini, Ravelli*), Boavista 2 (*Julio, Eliseu*)

St Mirren 0, St Etienne 0

Torino 3 (*Sala P., Pecci, Mewes og*), Magdeburg 1 (*Steinbach*)

Twente 1 (*Rohde*), Dynamo Dresden 1 (*Heidler*)

Widzew Lodz 3 (*Grebosz, Pieta, Smolarek*), Juventus 1 (*Bettega*)

Dundee U 1 (*Pettigrew*), Lokeren 1 (*Mommens*)

Utrecht 2 (*Carbo, Dr Kruyk pen*), Eintracht Frankfurt 1 (*Borchers*)

Ipswich T 3 (*Wark 2, Beattie*), Bohemians Prague 0

Levski Spartak 1 (*Spassov*), AZ 67 Alkmaar 1 (*Kist*)

PSV Eindhoven 1 (*Van der Kuylen*), Hamburg 1 (*Hrubesch*)

Cologne 0, Barcelona 1 (*Quini*)

Stuttgart 5 (*Tuefekci, Martin pen, Scuth og, Allgower, Klotz*), Vorwaerts Frankfurt 1 (*Krautzig*)

Kaiserslautern 1 (*Wendt*), Standard Liège 2 (*Wellens, Plessers*)

Beroe Stara Zagora 0, Radnicki Nis 1 (*Halilovic*)

Zbrojovka Brno 1 (*Murillo og*), Real Sociedad 1 (*Uraide*)

Porto 2 (*Teixeira, Albertino*), Grasshoppers 0


**Second Round, Second Leg**

AZ 67 Alkmaar 5 (*Tol 2, Nygaard pen, Kist, Peters*), Levski Spartak 0

Radnicki Nis 2 (*Stojikovic, Mitosevic*), Beroe Stara Zagora 1 (*Stojanov*)

Dynamo Dresden 0, Twente 0

St Etienne 2 (*Larios 2*), St Mirren 0

Boavista 0, Sochaux 1 (*Durkalic*)

Magdeburg 1 (*Tyll*), Torino 0

Juventus 3 (*Tardelli, Furino, Brady*), Widzew Lodz 1 (*Pieta*)

Eintracht Frankfurt 3 (*Karger, Nachtweih, Pezzey*), Utrecht 1 (*Neuberger og*)

Hamburg 2 (*Groh, Hrubesch*), PSV Eindhoven 1 (*Van der Kuylen*)

Standard Liège 2 (*Edström, Graf*), Kaiserslautern 1 (*Briegel*)

Barcelona 0, Cologne 4 (*Strack, Engels, Littbarski, Muller*)

Vorwaerts Frankfurt 1 (*Lindemann*), Stuttgart 2 (*Allgower, Hansi Muller pen*)

Real Sociedad 2 (*Satrustegui 2*), Zbrojovka Brno 1 (*Kotasek*)

Grasshoppers 3 (*Sulser, Koller, Pfister pen*), Porto 0

Lokeren 0, Dundee U 0

Bohemians 2 (*Micinec, Panenka*), Ipswich T 0


**Third Round, First Leg**

Eintracht Frankfurt 4 (*Neuberger, Borchers, Holzenbein, Nachtweih*), Sochaux 2 (*Genghini, Pezzey og*)

Hamburg 0, St Etienne 5 (*Hartwig og, Platini 2, Larios, Zimako*)

Stuttgart 3 (*Hansi Muller 2 [1 pen], Karl-Heinz Forster*), Cologne 1 (*Konopka*)

Lokeren 1 (*Lato*), Real Sociedad 0
Grasshoppers 2 (*Heinz Hermann, Koller*), Torino 1 (*Sclosa*)
Radnicki Nis 2 (*Pantelic pen, Panajotovic*), AZ 67 Alkmaar 2 (*Tol, Kist*)
Standard Liège 1 (*Plessers*), Dynamo Dresden 1 (*Heidler*)
Ipswich T 5 (*Wark 3, Brazil, Mariner*), Widzew Lodz 0

**Third Round, Second Leg**
Sochaux 2 (*Patrick Revelli 2*), Eintracht Frankfurt 0
St Etienne 1 (Paganelli), Hamburg 0
Cologne 4 (*Dieter Muller, Strack 2, Woodcock*), Stuttgart 1 (*Konopka og*)
Widzew Lodz 1 (*Pieta*), Ipswich T 0
Dynamo Dresden 1 (*Dorner*), Standard Liège 4 (*Sigurvinsson 3, Tahamata*)
Torino 2 (*Graziani, Pulici*), Grasshoppers 1 (*Terraneo og*)
Real Sociedad 2 (*Lopez Ufarte pen, Zamora*), Lokeren 2 (*Larsen 2*)
AZ 67 Alkmaar 5 (*Kist 3, Nygaard, Welzl*), Radnicki Nis 0

**Quarter-Final, First Leg**
Standard Liège 0, Cologne 0
AZ 67 Alkmaar 2 (*Tol, Welzl*), Lokeren 0
St Etienne 1 (*Rep*), Ipswich T 4 (*Mariner 2, Muhren, Wark*)
Grasshoppers 0, Sochaux 0

**Quarter-Final, Second Leg**
Ipswich T 3 (*Butcher, Wark pen, Mariner*), St Etienne 1 (*Zimako*)
Cologne 3 (*Dieter Muller, Bonhof pen, Littbarski*), Standard Liège 2 (*Graf, Vandersmissen*)
Sochaux 2 (*Durkalic, Genghini*), Grasshoppers 1 (*Koller*)
Lokeren 1 (*Verheyen*), AZ 67 Alkmaar 0

**Semi-Final, First Leg**
Ipswich T 1 (*Wark*), Cologne 0
Sochaux 1 (*Genghini*), AZ 67 Alkmaar 1 (*Arntz*)

**Semi-Final, Second Leg**
Cologne 0, Ipswich T 1 (*Butcher*)
AZ 67 Alkmaar 3 (*Metgod, Jonker, Peters*), Sochaux 2 (*Genghini, Meyer*)

### Final 1980–81: Ipswich T (1) 3, AZ 67 Alkmaar (0) 0
(At Ipswich, 6 May, 1981, 27,532)

*Ipswich T:* Cooper; Mills, McCall, Thijssen, Osman, Butcher, Wark, Muhren, Mariner, Brazil, Gates.

*AZ 67 Alkmaar:* Treytel; Van der Meer, Spelbos, Metgod, Hovenkamp, Peters, Jonker, Arntz, Nygaard (Welzl), Kist, Tol.

*Scorers:* Ipswich T – Wark pen, Thijssen, Mariner.

### AZ 67 Alkmaar (3) 4, Ipswich T (2) 2
(In Amsterdam, 20 May, 1981, 28,500)

*AZ 67 Alkmaar:* Treytel; Reynders, Spelbos, Metgod, Hovenkamp, Peters, Welzl (Kist), Arntz, Jonker, Nygaard, Tol.

*Ipswich T:* Cooper; Mills, McCall, Thijssen, Osman, Butcher, Wark, Muhren, Mariner, Brazil, Gates.

*Scorers:* AZ 67 Alkmaar – Welzl, Metgod, Tol, Jonker; Ipswich T – Thijssen, Wark.

# EUROPEAN CUP 1981–82

**Preliminary Round**
St Etienne 1 (*Lopez*), Dynamo Berlin 1 (*Lopez og*)
Dynamo Berlin 2 (*Neta, Riediger*), St Etienne 0

**First Round, First Leg**
Widzew Lodz 1 (*Smolarek*), Anderlecht 4 (*Lozano 2, Hansen, Petursson*)
Dynamo Berlin 2 (*Schulz, Riediger*), Zurich 0
Ferencvaros 3 (*Pogany 2, Szokolai*), Banik Ostrava 2 (*Licka, Knapp*)
Celtic 1 (*MacLeod*), Juventus 0
Hibernians 1 (*Spiteri-Gonzi*), Red Star Belgrade 2 (*Jurisic, Savic*)
OPS Oulu 0, Liverpool 1 (*Dalglish*)
Oster 0, Bayern Munich 1 (*Rummenigge*)
Benfica 3 (*Nenè, Filipovic, Mansel*), Omonia 0
Austria Vienna 3 (*Steinkogler, Gasselich 2*), Partizani 1 (*Tomori*)
Dynamo Kiev 1 (*Blokhin*), Trabzonspor 0
Start 1 (*Haugen*), AZ 67 3 (*Peters 2, Kist*)
Aston Villa 5 (*Morley, Withe 2, Donovan 2*), Valur 0
Niedercorn 1 (*Meunier*), Glentoran 1 (*Cleary*)
KB Copenhagen 1 (*Tune*), Athlone Town 1 (*O'Connor*)
CSKA Sofia 1 (*Yonchev*), Real Sociedad 0
Uni Craiova 3 (*Cirtu, Irmescu, Ticleanu*), Olympiakos 0

**First Round, Second Leg**
Anderlecht 2 (*Brylle, Geurts*), Widzew Lodz (*Smolarek*)
Zurich 3 (*Jerkovic 3*), Dynamo Berlin 1 (*Ullrich*)
Banik Ostrava 3 (*Sreiner, Knapp 2*), Ferencvaros 0
Juventus 2 (*Virdis, Bettega*), Celtic 0
Red Star Belgrade 8 (*Goracinov, Petrovic 2, Sestic, Savic D. 2, Savic R. 2*), Hibernians 1 (*Spiteri-Gonzi*)
Liverpool 7 (*Dalglish, McDermott 2, Kennedy R., Johnson, Rush, Lawrenson*), OPS Oulu 0
Bayern Munich 5 (*Hoeness 2, Rummenigge 2, Niedermayer*), Oster 0
Omonia 0, Benfica 1 (*Chalana*)
Partizani 1 (*Ballgjini*), Austria Vienna 0
Trabzonspor 1 (*Metin*), Dynamo Kiev 1 (*Bessonov*)
AZ 67 1 (*Metgod*), Start 0
Valur 0, Aston Villa 2 (*Shaw 2*)
Glentoran 4 (*Blackledge 2, Jameson, Manley*), Niedercorn 0
Athlone Town 2 (*Davis 2*), KB Copenhagen 2 (*Larsen, Andersen*)
Real Sociedad 0, CSKA Sofia 0
Olympiakos 2 (*Mitropoulos, Anastopoulos*), Uni Craiova 0

**Second Round, First Leg**
Banik 3 (*Licka 2, Knapp*), Red Star Belgrade 1 (*Krmpotic*)
Anderlecht 3 (*Geurts 2, Vercauteren*), Juventus 1 (*Marocchino*)
AZ 67 2 (*Kist, Tol*), Liverpool 2 (*Johnson, Lee*)
CSKA Sofia 2 (*Dimitrov A., Zdravkov pen*), Glentoran 0
KB Copenhagen 1 (*Foosgard*), Uni Craiova 0
Benfica 0, Bayern 0
Austria Vienna 0, Dynamo Kiev 1 (*Bal*)
Dynamo Berlin 1 (*Riediger*), Aston Villa 2 (*Morley 2*)

**Second Round, Second Leg**
Red Star Belgrade 3 (*Djurovski B., Savic D., Petrovic*), Banik 0
Juventus 1 (*Brio*), Anderlecht 1 (*Geurts*)
Liverpool 3 (*McDermott pen, Rush, Hansen*), AZ 67 2 (*Kist, Thompson og*)
Glentoran 2 (*Cleary, Manley*), CSKA Sofia 1 (*Dimitrov A.*)
Uni Craiova 4 (*Crisan, Balaci, Beldeanu, Camataru*), KB Copenhagen 1 (*Andersen*)
Bayern Munich 4 (*Hoeness 3, Breitner*), Benfica 1 (*Nenè pen*)
Dynamo Kiev 1 (*Buryak pen*), Austria Vienna 1 (*Petkov*)
Aston Villa 0, Dynamo Berlin 1 (*Terletzki*)

**Quarter-Finals, First Leg**
Anderlecht 2 (*Geurts, Lozano*), Red Star Belgrade 1 (*Djurovski B.*)
Dynamo Kiev 0, Aston Villa 0
Liverpool 1 (*Whelan*), CSKA Sofia 0
Uni Craiova 0, Bayern Munich 2 (*Breitner, Rummenigge*)

**Quarter-Finals, Second Leg**
Red Star Belgrade 1 (*Savic D. pen*), Anderlecht 2 (*Hofkens, Vercauteren*)
Aston Villa 2 (*Shaw, McNaught*), Dynamo Kiev 0
CSKA Sofia 2 (*Mladenov 2*), Liverpool 0
Bayern Munich 1 (*Hoeness*), Uni Craiova 1 (*Geolgau*)

**Semi-Finals, First Leg**
CSKA Sofia 4 (*Dimitrov G., Yonchev 2, Zdravkov pen*), Bayern Munich 3 (*Durnberger, Hoeness, Breitner*)
Aston Villa 1 (*Morley*), Anderlecht 0

**Semi-Finals, Second Leg**
Bayern Munich 4 (*Breitner 2 [1 pen], Rummenigge 2*), CSKA Sofia 0
Anderlecht 0, Aston Villa 0

**Final 1981–82: Aston Villa (0) 1, Bayern Munich (0) 0**
(In Rotterdam, 26 May, 1982, 46,000)

*Aston Villa:* Rimmer (Spink); Swain, Williams, Evans, McNaught, Mortimer, Bremner, Shaw, Withe, Cowans, Morley.
*Bayern Munich:* Muller; Dremmler, Horsmann, Weiner, Augenthaler, Kraus (Niedermayer), Durnberger, Breitner, Hoeness, Mathy (Guttler), Rummenigge.
*Scorer:* Aston Villa – Withe.

## FIFA GENERAL SECRETARY
On 15 January 1982, the FIFA Executive Committee elected Joseph 'Sepp' Blatter as General Secretary of FIFA. A former Swiss amateur footballer and a general secretary of the Swiss Ice Hockey Federation, Mr Blatter had served as director of the Technical Department of FIFA since 1977.

# EUROPEAN CUP-WINNERS' CUP 1981–82

**Preliminary Round**
Poli Timisoara 2 (*Anghel, Nedelcu*), Lok Leipzig 0
Lok Leipzig 5 (*Baum, Moldt, Zoetzsche, Kuhn 2*), Poli Timisoara 0

**First Round, First Leg**
Ajax 1 (*Lerby*), Tottenham H 3 (*Falco 2, Villa*)
KTP 0, Bastia 0
Eintracht Frankfurt 2 (*Pezzey, Koerbel*), PAOK Salonika 0
Dynamo Tbilisi 2 (*Zhvania, Shengelia*), Grazer AK 0
Barcelona 4 (*Quini, Simonsen 2, Schuster*), Trakia Plovdiv 1 (*Slavkov*)
Swansea C 0, Lok Leipzig 1 (*Kinne*)
Valerengen 2 (*Jacobsen 2*), Legia Warsaw 2 (*Majevsky, Okonski*)
SKA Rostov 3 (*Varov 2, Andreyev*), Ankaragucu 0
Paralimni 1 (*Goumenos*), Vasas 0
Ballymena U 0, AS Roma 2 (*Chierico, Ancelotti*)
Lausanne 2 (*Parietti, Kok*), Kalmar 1 (*Magnusson*)
Jeunesse Esch 1 (*Scheichlev*), Velez 1 (*Mueahasanovic*)
Floriana 1 (*Aquilina*), Standard Liège 3 (*Meeuws, Voordeckers, Vandermissen*)
Fram 2 (*Torfarsson, Sveinjonsson*), Dundalk 1 (*Fairclough*)
Dukla Prague 3 (*Rada, Stambachr, Nehoda*), Glasgow Rangers 0
Vejle 2 (*Andersen, Gert*), Porto 1 (*Romero*)

**First Round, Second Leg**
Tottenham 3 (*Galvin, Falco, Ardiles*), Ajax 0
Bastia 5 (*Cazes, Ihily 2, Ponte, Milla*), KTP 0
PAOK Salonika 2 (*Kostikos 2*), Eintracht Frankfurt 0
Grazer AK 2 (*Riedl, Schicker*), Dynamo Tbilisi 2 (*Shengelia 2*)
Trakia Plovdiv 1 (*Slavkov*), Barcelona 0
Lok Leipzig 2 (*Kinne, Moldt*), Swansea C 1 (*Charles*)
Legia Warsaw 4 (*Baran, Adamczyk, Topoiskim, Milosevic*), Valerengen 1 (*Moen*)
Ankaragucu 0, SKA Rostov 2 (*Andreyev, Vanadiev*)
Vasas 8 (*Varadi 3, Kiss 2, Szebergyinszky, Iszo 2*), Paralimni 0
AS Roma 4 (*Spinosi, Pruzzo 2, Giovanelli*), Ballymena U 0
Kalmar 3 (*Ohllson 2, Persson*), Lausanne 2 (*Parietti, Kok*)
Velez 6 (*Okuka 2, Skocajic, Natijevic 2, Bajevic*), Jeunesse Esch 1 (*Scheitler*)
Standard Liège 9 (*Voordeckers 3, Plessers 2, Vandermissen, Tahamata, Haan, Meeuws*), Floriana 0
Dundalk 4 (*Flanagan pen, Fairclough, Lawlor, Dubb*), Fram 0

Glasgow Rangers 2 (*Bett, MacDonald*), Dukla Prague 1 (*Stambachr*)
Porto 3 (*Jaime 2, Sousa*), Vejle 0

**Second Round, First Leg**
Legia Warsaw 2 (*Adamczyk, Baran*), Lausanne 1 (*Kok*)
SKA Rostov 1 (*Yashin*), Eintracht Frankfurt 0
Dukla Prague 1 (*Kozak*), Barcelona 0
Porto 2 (*Walsh, Costa*), AS Roma 0
Dundalk 1 (*Fairclough*), Tottenham H 1 (*Crooks*)
Vasas 0, Standard Liège 2 (*Tahamata 2*)
Lok Leipzig 1 (*Zoetzsche*), Velez 1 (*Vukoje*)
Bastia 1 (*Milla*), Dynamo Tbilisi 1 (*Gutsayev*)

**Second Round, Second Leg**
Lausanne 1 (*Ley-Ravello*), Legia Warsaw 1 (*Baran*)
Eintracht Frankfurt 2 (*Pezzey, Lorant pen*), SKA Rostov 0
Barcelona 4 (*Moran, Sanchez, Alesanco, Schuster*), Dukla Prague 0
AS Roma 0, Porto 0
Tottenham H 1 (*Crooks*), Dundalk 0
Standard Liège 2 (*Voordeckers 2*), Vasas 0
Velez 1 (*Bajevic*), Lok Leipzig 1 (*Zotzsche pen*)
Dynamo Tbilisi 3 (*Shengelia 2, Sulakvelidze*), Bastia 1 (*Milla*)

**Quarter-Finals, First Leg**
Legia Warsaw 0, Dynamo Tbilisi 1 (*Sulakvelidze*)
Lok Leipzig 0, Barcelona 3 (*Quini, Moran, Simonsen*)
Standard Liège 2 (*Englebert, Gabriel og*), Porto 0
Tottenham H 2 (*Miller, Hazard*), Eintracht Frankfurt 0

**Quarter-Finals, Second Leg**
Barcelona 1 (*Moran*), Lok Leipzig 2 (*Schone, Bernschein*)
Dynamo Tbilisi 1 (*Shengelia*), Legia Warsaw 0
Eintract Frankfurt 2 (*Borchers, Cha Bum Kun*), Tottenham H 1 (*Hoddle*)
Porto 2 (*Jacques, Walsh*), Standard Liège 2 (*Lecloux, Vandermissen*)

**Semi-Finals, First Leg**
Tottenham H 1 (*Roberts*), Barcelona 1 (*Olmo*)
Dynamo Tbilisi 0, Standard Liège 1 (*Daerden*)

**Semi-Finals, Second Leg**
Barcelona 1 (*Simonsen*), Tottenham H 0
Standard Liège 1 (*Daerden*), Dynamo Tbilisi 0

**Final 1981–82: Barcelona (1) 2, Standard Liège (1) 1**
(In Barcelona, 12 May, 1982, 100,000)

*Barcelona:* Urruti; Gerardo, Migueli, Alesanco, Manolo, Sanchez, Moratalla, Esteban, Simonsen, Quini, Carrasco.

*Standard Liège:* Preud'homme; Gerets, Poel, Meeuws, Plessers, Vandermissen, Daerden, Haan, Botteron, Tahamata, Wendt.

*Scorers:* Barcelona – Simonsen, Quini; Standard Liège – Vandermissen.

## INTERNATIONAL FOOTBALL ASSOCIATION BOARD 1981
The annual meeting of the International Football Association Board was held at Ruthin, Wales, on 13 June 1981. No changes of any great import were made to the Laws of the Game.

The apparent policy of 'random editing' was maintained with a transposition of words in Law XII (Fouls and Misconduct) to conform with wording in Law V (Referees). There are further examples of 'tidying up', unnoted in *FIFA News*, sometimes of sections that have been nonsense for years, providing further evidence that the Laws of the Game are badly in need of a complete overhaul.

# UEFA CUP 1981–82

**First Round, First Leg**
Adanaspor 1 (*Ozer*), Inter-Milan 3 (*Serena, Bini, Altobelli*)
Napoli 2 (*Damiani, Musella*), Radnicki 2 (*Stojanovic, Aleksic*)
Bohemians 0, Valencia 1 (*Saura*)
Nantes 1 (*Halilodzic*), Lokeren 1 (*Dobias*)
Limerick 0, Southampton 3 (*Moran 2, Armstrong*)
Sporting Lisbon 4 (*Oliveira, Carlos, Manuel, Jordao*), Red Boys 0
PSV Eindhoven 7 (*Van de Kerkof R., Van de Kerkof W., Thoresen, Geels 3, Young Mo Hooa*), Naestved 0
Boavista 4 (*Vital, Jorge Silva, Coelho, Palhares*), Atlético Madrid 1 (*Pablo*)
Rapid 2 (*Weber, Panenka*), Videoton 2 (*Szabo, Vegh*)
Neuchatel Xamax 4 (*Luthi 2, Pellegrini, Trinchero*), Sparta Prague 0
Dynamo Tirana 1 (*Zeri*), Carl Zeiss Jena 0
Tatabanya 2 (*Weimper, Csapo*), Real Madrid 1 (*Santillana*)
Aris Salonika 4 (*Panos, Kouis 3*), Sliema Wanderers 0
Malmo 2 (*Nillsson, Kinnvall*), Wisla Krakow 0
SV Hamburg 0, Utrecht 1 (*Carbo*)
Grasshoppers 1 (*Fimian*), WBA 0
Vikingur 0, Bordeaux 4 (*Fernandez, Trésor, Gemmrich, Lacombe*)
Feyenoord 2 (*Bouwens, Nielsen*), Szombierki 0
Ipswich T 1 (*Thijssen*), Aberdeen 1 (*Hewitt*)
Bryne 0, Winterslag 2 (*Berger, Weiss*)
Zenit Leningrad 1 (*Zheludkov*), Dynamo Dresden 2 (*Dorner, Heidler*)
Magdeburg 3 (*Hoffmann, Streich, Mathaus og*), Borussia Moenchengladbach 1 (*Mill*)
Haka 2 (*Kujanpas 2*), IFK Gothenburg 3 (*Fredriksson, Corneliusson, Karlsson*)
Beveren 3 (*Shoenberger, Albert, Martens*), Linfield 0
Monaco 2 (*Edstrom, Bellone*), Dundee U 5 (*Kirkwood, Dodds 2, Bannon 2 [1 pen]*)
Panathinaikos 0, Arsenal 2 (*McDermott, Meade*)
Spartak Moscow 3 (*Svetsov 2, Gavrilov*), FC Bruges 1 (*Sorensen*)
Kaiserslautern 1 (*Brehme*), Akademik 0
Apoel 1 (*Andronicou*), Arges Pitesti 1 (*Ignat*)
Hajduk 3 (*Zoran Vujovic, Zlatko Vujovic 2*), Stuttgart 1 (*Rozic og*)
Dynamo Bucarest 3 (*Georgescu 2, Dragonea*), Levski Spartak 0
Sturm Graz 1 (*Schauss*), CSKA Moscow 0

**First Round, Second Leg**
Inter-Milan 4 (*Beccalossi, Bagni, Serena, Altobelli*), Adanaspor 1 (*Ahmet*)
Radnicki 0, Napoli 0
Valencia 1 (*Solsona*), Bohemians 0
Lokeren 4 (*Larsen 2, Snelders, Verheyen*), Nantes 2 (*Baronchelli, Bibard*)
Southampton 1 (*Keegan*), Limerick 1 (*Morris*)
Red Boys 0, Sporting Lisbon 7 (*Oliveira, Inacio, Jordao, Jorge 2, Freire*)
Naestved 2 (*Hansen 2*), PSV Eindhoven 1 (*Thoresen*)
Atlético Madrid 3 (*Dirceu 2, Cano*), Boavista 1 (*Dianmantino*)
Videoton 0, Rapid 2 (*Krankl 2*)
Sparta Prague 3 (*Griga 2, Jarolim*), Neuchatel Xamax 2 (*Trinchero, Pellegrini*)
Carl Zeiss Jena 4 (*Raab, Schnuphase, Bielau, Trocha*), Dynamo Tirana 0
Real Madrid 1 (*Isidro*), Tatabanya 0
Sliema Wanderers 2 (*Tortell, Losco*), Aris Salonika 4 (*Semertzidis, Kouis, Zelidis, Panov*)
Wisla Krakow 1 (*Kapka*), Malmo 3 (*Palmer, Prytz, Nilsson*)
Utrecht 3 (*Carbo, Kruyk, Van Veen*), Hamburg 6 (*Milewski 2, Wehmeyer, Hartwig, Bastrup, Groh*)
WBA 1 (*Robertson*), Grasshoppers 1 (*Fimian, Koller, Jara*)
Bordeaux 4 (*Fernandez, Martinez, Relmy, Trésor*), Vikingur 0
Szombierki 1 (*Ogaza*), Feyenoord 1 (*Bouwens*)
Aberdeen 3 (*Strachan pen, Weir 2*), Ipswich T 1 (*Wark pen*)

Winterslag 1 (*Billen*), Bryne 2 (*Mailand, Hellvich*)
Dynamo Dresden 4 (*Trauttman, Schmuck, Ming, Heidler*), Zenit Leningrad 1 (*Kasashchen*)
Borussia Moenchengladbach 2 (*Pinkall, Matthaus*), Magdeburg 0
IFK Gothenburg 4 (*Schiller, Nilsson, Karlsson, Holmgren*), Haka 0
Linfield 0, Beveren 5 (*Martens 4, Pfaff D.*)
Dundee U 1 (*Milne*), Monaco 2 (*Edstrom, Bellone*)
Arsenal 1 (*Talbot*), Panathinaikos 0
FC Bruges 1 (*Wellens*), Spartak Moscow 3 (*Radionou, Schaavlov, Gavrilov*)
Akademik 1 (*Gorev*), Kaiserslautern 2 (*Metzgerin, Briegel*)
Arges Pitesti 4 (*Turcu, Banta, Cirstea, Callo*), Apoel 0
Stuttgart 2 (*Schaffer, Muller D.*), Hajduk 2 (*Bogdanovic, Jelinik*)
Levski Spartak 2 (*Kurdon 2*), Dynamo Bucarest 1 (*Augustin*)
CSKA Moscow 2 (*Chesnokov, Tarkhanov*), Sturm Graz 1 (*Bakota*)

**Second Round, First Leg**
Southampton 2 (*Keegan pen, Channon*), Sporting Lisbon 4 (*Jordao, Holmes og, Fernandes 2*)
Real Madrid 3 (*Garcia Cortes, Gallego, Isidro*), Carl Zeiss Jena 2 (*Bielau, Kurbjuweit*)
Grasshoppers 2 (*Jara, Sulser*), Radnicki 0
Aris Salonika 1 (*Kollis*), Lokeren 1 (*Larsen*)
Rapid Vienna 1 (*Panenka*), PSV Eindhoven 0
Valencia 2 (*Roberto, Welzl*), Boavista 0
Malmo 0, Neuchatel Xamax 1 (*Pellegrini*)
Bordeaux 2 (*Genimerick, Soler*), SV Hamburg 1 (*Kaltz*)
Spartak Moscow 2 (*Rolgnov, Gavrilov*), Kaiserslautern 1 (*Funkel*)
Winterslag 1 (*Berger*), Arsenal 0
Aberdeen 3 (*Strachan, Weir, Hewitt*), Arges Pitesti 0
Feyenoord 2 (*Kaczor, Vermeulen*), Dynamo Dresden 1 (*Heidler*)
Inter-Milan 1 (*Pasinato*), Dynamo Bucarest 1 (*Custov*)
Sturm Graz 2 (*Breber, Niederbacher*), IFK Gothenburg 2 (*Nilsson 2*)
Borussia Moenchengladbach 2 (*Schaffer, Hannes*), Dundee U 0
Beveren 2 (*Theunis, Van Moer*), Hajduk 3 (*Gudelj, Vujovic, Sliskovic*)

**Second Round, Second Leg**
Sporting Lisbon 0, Southampton 0
Carl Zeiss Jena 0, Real Madrid 0
Radnicki 2 (*Djordjevic, Savic*), Grasshoppers 0
Lokeren 4 (*Gudjohnsen, Lato, Larsen, Mommens*), Aris Salonika 0
PSV Eindhoven 2 (*Poortvliet 2*), Rapid Vienna 1 (*Krankl*)
Boavista 1 (*Diamantino*), Valencia 0
Neuchatel Xamax 1 (*Pellegrini*), Malmo 0
SV Hamburg 2 (*Hrubesch 2*), Bordeaux 0
Kaiserslautern 4 (*Funkel, Briegel 2, Geye*), Spartak Moscow 0
Arsenal 2 (*Hollins, Rix*), Winterslag 1 (*Billen*)
Arges Pitesti 2 (*Radu, Barbulescu*), Aberdeen 2 (*Strachan pen, Hewitt*)
Dynamo Dresden 1 (*Lippman*), Feyenoord 1 (*Van Deinsen*)
Dynamo Bucarest 3 (*Georgescu, Augustin, Orac*), Inter-Milan 2 (*Altobelli, Prohaska*)
IFK Gothenburg 3 (*Olgren, Nilsson, Fredriksson*), Sturm Graz 2 (*Stendarl, Bakota*)
Dundee U 5 (*Milne, Kirkwood, Sturrock, Hegarty, Bannon*) Borussia Moenchengladbach 0
Hajduk 1 (*Pasic*), Beveren 2 (*Krowe, Anters*)

**Third Round, First Leg**
Lokeren 1 (*Lato*), Kaiserslautern 0
Rapid Vienna 0, Real Madrid 1 (*Santillana*)
Aberdeen 3 (*Black, Watson, Hewitt*), SV Hamburg 2 (*Hrubesch 2*)
Sporting Lisbon 0, Neuchatel Xamax 0
IFK Gothenburg 3 (*Holmgren, Nilsson 2*), Dynamo Bucarest 1 (*Muttescu*)
Winterslag 0, Dundee U 0
Radnicki 2 (*Radoslavevec, Savic*), Feyenoord 0

Valencia 5 (*Tendillo, Rodriguez 2, Welzl, Arnesen*), Hajduk 1 (*Todac*)

**Third Round, Second Leg**
Kaiserslautern 4 (*Hofeditz, Briegel, Funkel, Eilenfeldt*), Lokeren 1 (*Gudjohnson*)
Real Madrid 0, Rapid Vienna 0
SV Hamburg 3 (*Hrubesch, Memering pen, Jakobs*), Aberdeen 1 (*McGhee*)
Neuchatel Xamax 1 (*Andrey*), Sporting Lisbon 0
Dynamo Bucarest 0, IFK Gothenburg 1 (*Nilsson*)
Dundee U 5 (*Bannon, Narey, Hegarty, Milne 2*), Winterslag 0
Feyenoord 1 (*Nielsen*), Radnicki 0
Hajduk 4 (*Gudelj 3, Primorac*), Valencia 1 (*Saura*)

**Quarter-Finals, First Leg**
SV Hamburg 3 (*Bastrup, Memering, Von Heesen*), Neuchatel Xamax 2 (*Givens, Luthi*)
Real Madrid 3 (*Cunningham, Garcia Hernandez, Juanito*), Kaiserslautern 1 (*Eilenfeldt pen*)
Dundee U 2 (*Narey, Dodds*), Radnicki 0

Valencia 2 (*Arnesen 2 [1 pen]*), IFK Gothenburg 2 (*Corneliusson, Nilsson T.*)

**Quarter-Finals, Second Leg**
Neuchatel Xamax 0, SV Hamburg 0
Kaiserslautern 5 (*Funkel 2, Eilenfeldt, Bongartz, Geye*), Real Madrid 0
Radnicki 3 (*Panajotovic 2, Djordjevic pen*), Dundee U 0
IFK Gothenburg 2 (*Tommy Holmgren, Fredriksson pen*), Valencia 0

**Semi-Finals, First Leg**
Kaiserslautern 1 (*Hofeditz*), IFK Gothenburg 1 (*Corneliusson*)
Radnicki 2 (*Beganovic, Obradovic*), SV Hamburg 1 (*Von Heesen*)

**Semi-Finals, Second Leg**
IFK Gothenburg 2 (*Tommy Holmgren, Fredriksson pen*), Kaiserslautern 1 (*Geye*) aet
SV Hamburg 5 (*Hartwig 2, Von Heesen 2, Magath*), Radnicki 1 (*Panajotovic*)

**Final 1981–82: IFK Gothenburg (0) 1, SV Hamburg (0) 0**
(In Gothenburg, 5 May, 1982, 42,548)

*IFK Gothenburg:* Wernersson; Svensson, Hysen, Karlsson C., Fredriksson, Tord Holmgren, Karlsson J., Stromberg, Corneliusson, Nilsson (Sanberg), Tommy Holmgren (Schiller).
*SV Hamburg:* Stein; Kaltz, Jakobs, Hieronymus, Groh, Hartwig, Wehmeyer, Magath, Von Heesen (Memering), Bastrup, Hrubesch.
*Scorer:* IFK Gothenburg – Tord Holmgren.

**SV Hamburg (0) 0, IFK Gothenburg (1) 3**
(In Hamburg, 19 May, 1982, 60,000)

*SV Hamburg:* Stein; Kaltz (Hidien), Hieronymus, Groh, Wehmeyer, Hartwig, Memering, Magath, Von Heesen, Hrubesch, Bastrup.
*IFK Gothenburg:* Wernersson; Svensson, Hysen (Schiller), Karlsson C., Fredriksson, Tord Holmgren, Stromberg, Karlsson J., Corneliusson (Sandberg), Nilsson, Tommy Holmgren.
*Scorers:* IFK Gothenburg – Corneliusson, Nilsson, Fredriksson pen.


# FIFA REFEREES' COMMITTEE
At the meeting of the Referees' Committee (5 May 1981) that preceded the International Board meeting, a proposal by the Welsh Football Association to include obstruction as an offence punishable by a direct free-kick was rejected because the Committee 'unanimously agreed that an obstruction in the penalty-area should not be penalised by a penalty-kick'.

It is not surprising, then, that in answer to a question from the Swiss FA regarding a goal-kick in which the ball touched the referee, in the penalty-area, but nevertheless went out of the area, the Committee agreed by a majority of votes that the referee should be considered as 'air' and that the ball was in play.

One cannot help observing that, if the referees came down to earth, they might notice a glaring absurdity in that very same law, namely that if a goal-kick is not kicked beyond the penalty-area it must be retaken. Why a player who touches the ball before it leaves the penalty-area cannot be punished by the award of an indirect free-kick remains a mystery, then, for yet another year. – N.S.B.


# GOLDEN BOOT AWARD
Winner of the Golden Boot Award for Europe's leading League goalscorer in 1981–82 was Wim Kieft, the 19-year-old striker of Ajax and Holland, with 32 goals. The runner-up award was shared between his fellow-countryman Kees Kist of AZ 67 Alkmaar with 29, and Delio Onnis from the French club Tours. Joint fourth with 27 goals were the Portuguese striker Jacques from FC Porto and Horst Hrubesch of SV Hamburg.

# BRITISH CLUBS IN EUROPE 1981–82

## EUROPEAN CUP 1981–82

**FIRST ROUND, FIRST LEG**

**16 SEPT**

**Aston Villa (3) 5** *(Morley, Withe 2, Donovan 2)*

**Valur (0) 0**          20,481

*Aston Villa:* Rimmer; Swain, Gibson, Evans, Ormsby, Mortimer, Bremner, Donovan, Withe, Cowans, Morley.
*Valur:* Haraldsson; Sveinsson, Thrainsson, Thorvaldsson (Valsson), Gudmundsson, Jonsson, Eidsson, Sighvatsson, Sigurdsson (Hallgrimsson), Thorbjonsson, Valsson. .

**Celtic (0) 1** *(MacLeod)*

**Juventus (0) 0**          60,017

*Celtic:* Bonner; McGrain, Reid, Aitken, McAdam, MacLeod, Provan, Sullivan, Nicholas, Burns, McCluskey.
*Juventus:* Zoff; Gentile, Cabrini, Furino, Brio, Scirea, Marocchino (Fanna), Tardelli, Bettega, Brady, Bonini.

**KB Copenhagen (1) 1** *(Tune)*

**Athlone T (1) 1** *(O'Connor M.)*      3200

*KB Copenhagen:* Qvist; Hansen, Eriksen, Tune, Eigenbrod, Winfeld, Laudrup, Fosgaard, Busk, Rossel, Andersen.
*Athlone T:* Smyth; Fenuik, O'Connor P., McCue, Conway, Carroll, Wyse, Clarke, Salmon, Devlin, O'Connor M. (Larkin).

**OPS Oulu (0) 0**

**Liverpool (0) 1** *(Dalglish)*        8400

*OPS Oulu:* Rantanen; Kemppainen, Leinenen, Salo, Armstrong, Ahonen, Juntinen, Rissanen (Jalasvaara), Himanka, Smith, Saarinen.
*Liverpool:* Grobbelaar; Neal, Kennedy A., Thompson, Hansen, Lawrenson, Dalglish, Kennedy R., Johnson, Lee, Souness.

**Progres Niedercorn (1) 1** *(Meunier)*

**Glentoran (1) 1** *(Cleary)*       1500

*Progres Niedercorn:* Defrang; Meunier, Margue, Bossi M., Bossi J., Bossi H. (Thill), Nuremberg, Krecke, Back, May, Neumann.
*Glentoran:* Paterson; McCreery, Harrison, Keeley, Strain, Bowers, Kingon, Cleary, Jameson, Blackledge, Manley.

**FIRST ROUND, SECOND LEG**

**30 SEPT**

**Athlone T (0) 2** *(Davis 2)*

**KB Copenhagen (1) 2** *(Larsen T., Andersen)*   10,000

*Athlone T:* Smith; Larkin, Conway, O'Connor M., McCue, Salmon, Carroll, Davis, Wyse, Clarke, Devlin.
*KB Copenhagen:* Qvist; Hansen, Busk (Larsen K.), Tune, Eriksen, Larsen T., Laudrup, Fosgaard, Petersen (Winfield), Rossel, Andersen.

**Glentoran (1) 4** *(Blackledge 2, Jameson, Manley)*

**Progres Niedercorn (0) 0**      5000

*Glentoran:* Paterson; McCreery R., Strain, Harrison, Keeley (Porter), Cleary, Jameson, Bowers, Blackledge, Manley, Kingon.
*Progres Niedercorn:* Defrong; Meunier, Margue, Bossi M., Bossi J., Bossi H. (Schmitz J.), Nuremberg, Krecke (Thill), Back, May, Neumann.

**Juventus (2) 2** *(Virdis, Bettega)*

**Celtic (0) 0**          70,000

*Juventus:* Zoff; Gentile, Cabrini, Furino, Brio, Scirea, Marocchino, Tardelli, Bettega, Brady (Bonini), Virdis (Fanna).
*Celtic:* Bonner; Moyes, Reid, Aitken, McAdam, McLeod, Provan, Sullivan, McGarvey, Burns, McCluskey.

**Liverpool (2) 7** *(Dalglish, McDermott 2, Kennedy R., Johnson, Rush, Lawrenson)*

**OPS Oulu (0) 0**        20,789

*Liverpool:* Grobbelaar; Neal, Kennedy A., Thompson, Kennedy R. (Lawrenson), Hansen, Dalglish, Lee, Johnson (Rush), McDermott, Souness.
*OPS Oulu:* Rantanen; Kemppainen, Puotiniemi, Salo, Armstrong, Ahonen, Juntenen, Rissanen, Jalasvaara, Himanka, Saarinen.

**Valur (0) 0**

**Aston Villa (2) 2** *(Shaw 2)*      3500

*Valur:* Haraldsson; Sveinsson, Thrainsson, Hallgrimsson, Gudmundsson, Jonsson, Petursson, Bergs, Valsson, Sighvatsson, Eidsson.
*Aston Villa:* Rimmer; Swain, Gibson, Evans, Ormsby, Mortimer, Bremner, Shaw, Withe, Cowans, Blair.

**SECOND ROUND, FIRST LEG**

**21 OCT**

**Dynamo Berlin (0) 1** *(Riediger)*

**Aston Villa (1) 2** *(Morley 2)*     31,000

*Dynamo Berlin:* Rudwaleit; Noack, Trieloff, Troppa, Ulrich, Terletzki, Ernst, Strasser (Jungling), Riediger, Schulz, Netz.
*Aston Villa:* Rimmer; Williams (Linton), Ormsby, Evans, Gibson, Mortimer, Bremner, Shaw, Withe, Cowans, Morley.

**CKSA Sofia (2) 2** *(Dimitrov A., Zdravkov pen)*

**Glentoran (0) 0**        55,000

*CSKA Sofia:* Velinov; Bezinski, Zdravkov, Kalburov, Dimitrov G., Iliev, Mladenov, Kerimov (Velkov), Dzevizov, Markov, Dimitrov A. (Bylkov).
*Glentoran:* Paterson; McCreery R., Keely, Harrison, Strain, Porter, Jameson, Bowers, Cleary, Manley (Ron McCreery), Blackledge.

**AZ 67 (0) 2** *(Kist, Tol)*

**Liverpool (1) 2** *(Johnson, Lee)*    15,000

*AZ 67:* Treytel; Van der Meer, Metgod, Spelbos, Hovenkamp (Anema), Arntz, Peters, Rijnders, Jonker, Kist, Tol.
*Liverpool:* Grobbelaar; Neal, Lawrenson, Thompson, Kennedy R., Hansen, Dalglish (Whelan), Lee, Johnson, McDermott, Souness.

**SECOND ROUND, SECOND LEG**

**4 NOV**

**Aston Villa (0) 0**

**Dynamo Berlin (1) 1** *(Terletzki)*    28,175

*Aston Villa:* Rimmer; Swain, Gibson, Evans, Williams, Mortimer, Bremner, Shaw, Withe, Cowans, Morley.
*Dynamo Berlin:* Rudwaleit; Schiegel, Trieloff, Backs, Ernst, Troppa, Terletzki, Ulrich, Riediger, Schulz (Strasser), Netz.

**Glentoran (0) 2** *aet (Cleary, Manley)*

**CSKA Sofia (0) 1** *(Dimitrov A.)* 4021

*Glentoran:* Paterson; McCreery R., Neill (Stewart), Keely, Porter, Cleary, Jameson, Bowers, Blackledge (McDaid), Manley, Kingon.
*CSKA Sofia:* Velinov; Bezinski, Zdravkov, Kalburov, Dimitrov G., Iliev (Dimitrov A.), Mladenov (Voncev), Kerimov, Dzevizov, Markov, Velkov.

**Liverpool (1) 3** *(McDermott pen, Rush, Hansen)*

**AZ 67 (0) 2** *(Kist, Thompson og)* 29,703

*Liverpool:* Grobbelaar; Neal, Lawrenson, Kennedy R., Hansen, Dalglish, Whelan, Rush, McDermott, Souness.
*AZ 67:* Treytel; Van der Meer, Metgod, Spelbos, Hovenkamp, Peters, Tol, Arntz, Kist, Reijnders, Jonker.

## QUARTER-FINALS, FIRST LEG

### 3 MAR

**Dynamo Kiev (0) 0**

**Aston Villa (0) 0** 36,000

At Simferopol
*Dynamo Kiev:* Chanov; Bessonov (Khapsalis), Baltacha, Zhuraviev, Demyanenko, Lozinsky, Buryak, Bal, Khlus, Veremeyev (Yevtushenko), Blokhin.
*Aston Villa:* Rimmer; Swain, Bremner, Blair, McNaught, Williams, Mortimer, Shaw, Withe, Cowans, Morley.

**Liverpool (0) 1** *(Whelan)*

**CSKA Sofia (0) 0** 27,388

*Liverpool:* Grobbelaar; Neal, Kennedy A., Whelan, Lawrenson, Hansen, Dalglish, Lee, Rush, McDermott, Souness.
*CSKA Sofia:* Velinov; Bezinski, Dimitrov D., Tomanov, Dimitrov G., Iliev, Yonchev (Dimitrov A.), Kerimov, Djevizov, Zdravkov, Mladenov.

## QUARTER-FINALS, SECOND LEG

### 17 MAR

**Aston Villa (2) 2** *(Shaw, McNaught)*

**Dynamo Kiev (0) 0** 38,579

*Aston Villa:* Rimmer; Swain, Williams, Evans, McNaught, Mortimer, Bremner, Shaw, Withe, Cowans, Morley.
*Dynamo Kiev:* Chanov; Boiko, Baltacha, Zhuraviev, Demyanenko, Bal, Lozinsky, Yevtushenko, Khlus, Veremeyev (Khapsalis), Blokhin.

**CSKA Sofia (0) 2** *aet (Mladenov 2)*

**Liverpool (0) 0** 60,000

*CSKA Sofia:* Velinov; Bezinski, Dimitrov D., Tomanov (Kerimov), Dimitrov G., Iliev, Yonchev, Mladenov, Djevisov, Markov, Zdravkov (Velkov).
*Liverpool:* Grobbelaar; Neal, Lawrenson, Kennedy, Whelan, Thompson, Dalglish, Lee, Rush (Johnston), McDermott (Johnson), Souness.

## SEMI-FINAL, FIRST LEG

### 7 APRIL

**Aston Villa (1) 1** *(Morley)*

**Anderlecht (0) 0** 38,539

*Aston Villa:* Rimmer; Swain, Williams, Evans, McNaught, Mortimer, Bremner, Shaw, Withe, Cowans, Morley.
*Anderlecht:* Munaron; Peruzovic, Broos, Lozano, De Groote, Vercauteren, De Greff, Renquin (Jovanic), Coeck, Cluytens, Petursson (Geurts).

## SEMI-FINAL, SECOND LEG

### 21 APRIL

**Anderlecht (0) 0**

**Aston Villa (0) 0** 28,000

*Anderlecht:* Munaron; De Greff, De Groote, Peruzovic, Broos, Coeck, Hofkens (Jovanic), Lozano, Vercauteren, Geurts (Frimann), Brylle.
*Aston Villa:* Rimmer; Swain, Williams, Evans, McNaught, Mortimer, Bremner, Shaw, Withe, Cowans, Morley.

## FINAL

### 26 MAY

**Aston Villa (0) 1** *(Withe)*

**Bayern Munich (0) 0** 46,000

*Aston Villa:* Rimmer (Spink); Swain, Williams, Evans, McNaught, Mortimer, Bremner, Shaw, Withe, Cowans, Morley.
*Bayern Munich:* Muller; Dremmler, Weiner, Augenthaler, Horsmann, Mathy (Guttler), Breitner, Kraus (Niedermayer), Durnberger, Rummenigge, Hoeness.

# EUROPEAN CUP-WINNERS' CUP 1981–82

## FIRST ROUND, FIRST LEG

### 16 SEPT

**Ajax (0) 1** *(Lerby)*

**Tottenham H (2) 3** *(Falco 2, Villa)* 27,500

*Ajax:* Schrijvers; Jansen (Wijnberg), Molenaar, Boeve, Ziegler, Olsen, Hamberg, La Ling, Ophof (Vanenberg), Schoenaker.
*Tottenham H:* Clemence; Hughton, Miller, Roberts, Villa, Perryman, Ardiles, Archibald, Galvin, Hoddle, Falco.

**Ballymena U (0) 0**

**AS Roma (0) 2** *(Chierico, Ancelotti)* 3500

*Ballymena U:* Matthews; Beattie, Fox, O'Doherty, McCullogh, McDowell (Smyth), Neill, Sloan, McCusker, Malone, Moffatt (Houston).
*AS Roma:* Tancredi; Nela, Marangon, Turone, Falcao, Boneti, Chierico, Maggiora, Pruzzo, Ancelotti, Conti.

**Dukla Prague (1) 3** *(Rada, Stambachr, Nehoda)*

**Rangers (0) 0** 22,500

*Dukla Prague:* Netolicka; Macela, Novak, Fiala, Rada, Pelc, Vizek, Kozak, Nehoda, Kriz, Stambachr.
*Rangers:* McCloy; Jardine, Dawson, Forsyth, Jackson (Stevens), McClelland, Bett, McLean, Russell, McAdam, Johnstone (Redford).

**Fram (0) 2** *(Torfasson, Sveinjonsson)*

**Dundalk (1) 1** *(Fairclough)* 5000

*Fram:* Baldursson; Haraldsson, Hauksson, Ormslev, Geilsson, Bjarnasson, Arasson, Thorkelsson, Gudmundsson, Torfasson, Sveinjonsson.
*Dundalk:* Blackmore; Gregg, Lawlor, McConville, Dunning, Flanagan, Byrne, Kehoe, Fairclough, Carlyle, Archbold.

Swansea C (0) 0
Lokomotiv Leipzig (0) 1 *(Kinne)*                    10,295
*Swansea C:* Davies; Robinson, Hadziabdic, Rajkovic,
Stevenson, Attley (Evans W.), Curtis, James R., James L.
(Giles), Mahoney, Latchford.
*Lokomotiv Leipzig:* Muller; Joachim, Baum, Dennstedt,
Zotzsche, Kinne, Moldt, Liebers, Altmann, Schone,
Kuhn.

## FIRST ROUND, SECOND LEG

### 29 SEPT

Tottenham H (0) 3 *(Galvin, Falco, Ardiles)*
Ajax (0) 0                                           34,606
*Tottenham H:* Clemence; Hughton, Miller, Roberts, Villa,
Perryman, Ardiles, Archibald, Galvin, Hoddle, Crooks.
*Ajax:* Galje; Jansen, Molenaar, Boeve, Wijnberg, Lerby,
Olsen, Vanenberg, Hamberg, Kieft, Schoenaker.

### 30 SEPT

Dundalk (2) 4 *(Flanagan pen, Fairclough, Lawlor, Duff)*
Fram (0) 0                                           3500
*Dundalk:* Blackmoor; Gregg, Lawlor M., McConville,
Dunning, Flanagan, Byrne S., Kehoe, Fairclough, Car-
lyle, Duff.
*Fram:* Baldursson; Haraldsson, Hauksson, Ormslev,
Geirsson, Bjarnasson, Arasson, Thorkelsson, Gudmunds-
son, Gorfasson, Sveinjonsson.

Lokomotiv Leipzig (2) 2 *(Kinne, Moldt)*
Swansea C (1) 1 *(Charles)*                          22,500
*Lokomotiv Leipzig:* Muller; Baum, Fritzsche, Dennstedt,
Zotzsche, Altmann, Moldt, Liebers, Kinne, Kuhn (Fross-
mann), Bornschein (Schone).
*Swansea C:* Davies; Rajkovic, Attley, Stevenson (Evans
W.), Hadziabdic, James R., Robinson, James L., Latch-
ford (Giles), Charles, Curtis.

Rangers (2) 2 *(Bett, MacDonald)*
Dukla Prague (1) 1 *(Stambachr)*                     20,000
*Rangers:* Stewart; McClelland (Redford), Dawson, Jar-
dine, Forsyth, Bett, Cooper, Russell, McAdam (John-
stone), MacDonald, Johnston.
*Dukla Prague:* Netolicka; Macela, Kapko, Fiala, Rada,
Kozak (Dolezal), Vizek, Rott, Nehoda, Kriz, Stambachr.

AS Roma (2) 4 *(Spinosi, Pruzzo 2, Giovanelli)*
Ballymena U (0) 0                                    24,000
*AS Roma:* Tancredi; Nela, Marangon (Perrone), Spinosi,
Falcao, Bonetti, Chierico, Giovanelli, Pruzzo, Ancelotti,
Conti (Faccini).
*Ballymena U:* Matthews; Beattie, Huston, O'Doherty,
McCullogh, McDowell, Neill, Sloan, McQuiston
(McCusker), Malone, Fox.

## SECOND ROUND, FIRST LEG

### 21 OCT

Dundalk (0) 1 *(Fairclough)*
Tottenham H (0) 1 *(Crooks)*                         17,000
*Dundalk:* Blackmore; Gregg, McConville, Dunning,
Lawlor, Byrne, Flanagan, Kehoe, Duff (Archbold), Fair-
clough, Carlyle.
*Tottenham H:* Clemence; Hughton, Miller, Roberts, Per-
ryman, Hazard, Ardiles, Galvin (Smith), Hod-
dle, Crooks.

## SECOND ROUND, SECOND LEG

### 4 NOV

Tottenham H (0) 1 *(Crooks)*
Dundalk (0) 0                                        33,455
*Tottenham H:* Clemence; Hughton, Miller, Roberts, Haz-
ard, Perryman, Ardiles, Archibald, Galvin, Hoddle,
Crooks.
*Dundalk:* Blackmore; Gregg, Lawlor, McConville, Dun-
ning (Archbold), Flanagan, Byrne, Fairclough, Carlyle
(Reilly), Duff.

## QUARTER-FINALS, FIRST LEG

### 3 MAR

Tottenham H (0) 2 *(Miller, Hazard)*
Eintracht Frankfurt (0) 0                            38,172
*Tottenham H:* Clemence; Hughton, Miller, Price, Hazard,
Perryman, Ardiles, Archibald, Galvin, Hoddle, Crooks
(Falco).
*Eintracht Frankfurt:* Juriens; Sziedat, Pezzey, Neuberger,
Korbel, Lorant, Nickel (Lottermann), Falkenmayer, Cha,
Kunast (Gulich), Nachtweih.

## QUARTER-FINALS, SECOND LEG

### 17 MAR

Eintracht Frankfurt (2) 2 *(Borchers, Cha)*
Tottenham H (0) 1 *(Hoddle)*                         41,000
*Eintracht Frankfurt:* Pahl; Lorant, Pezzey, Sziedat, Lot-
termann (Kunast), Borchers, Neuberger, Nickel, Falken-
mayer, Cha, Nachtweih.
*Tottenham H:* Clemence; Hughton, Miller, Price, Hazard,
Perryman, Ardiles (Roberts), Falco (Villa), Galvin, Hod-
dle, Archibald.

## SEMI-FINAL, FIRST LEG

### 7 APRIL

Tottenham H (0) 1 *(Roberts)*
Barcelona (0) 1 *(Olmo)*                             41,555
*Tottenham H:* Clemence; Price, Hughton, Miller (Jones),
Perryman, Hazard, Roberts, Villa, Galvin, Hoddle,
Crooks.
*Barcelona:* Urruti; Ramos, Olmo, Alesanco, Manolo,
Sanchez, Gerardo, Estella, Simonsen, Carrasco, Moran
(Moratalla).

## SEMI-FINAL, SECOND LEG

### 21 APRIL

Barcelona (0) 1 *(Simonsen)*
Tottenham H (0) 0                                    80,000
*Barcelona:* Urruti; Ramos, Olmo, Manolo, Sanchez, Ale-
sanco, Simonsen (Zuviria), Gerardo, Quini (Esteban),
Moratalla, Carrasco.
*Tottenham H:* Clemence; Hughton, Price (Falco), Rob-
erts, Hazard, Perryman, Villa, Archibald, Galvin, Hod-
dle, Crooks.

## UEFA CUP 1981–82

### FIRST ROUND, FIRST LEG

#### 16 SEPT

**Beveren (1) 3** *(Schoenberger, Albert, Martens)*
**Linfield (0) 0**                                    7000
*Beveren:* Pfaff J.-M.; Jaspers, Garot, Buyl, Backe, Van Moer, Schoenberger, Albert, Theunis, Martens, Weihrauch (Schooff).
*Linfield:* Dunlop; Parks, McCartney, Hayes, Rafferty, Walsh, Nixon, McKee (Murray), Whitten, Dornan, Anderson.

**Ipswich T (1) 1** *(Thijssen)*
**Aberdeen (0) 1** *(Hewitt)*                         18,535
*Ipswich T:* Cooper; Mills, McCall, Thijssen, Osman, Butcher, Wark, Muhren, O'Callaghan (D'Avray), Brazil, Gates.
*Aberdeen:* Leighton; Kennedy, Rougvie, Watson, McLeish, Miller, Strachan, Cooper, McGhee, Hewitt, Weir (Simpson).

**Limerick (0) 0**
**Southampton (0) 3** *(Moran 2, Armstrong)*         10,000
*Limerick:* Fitzpatrick; Nolan, Finucane, Hand, Storan, Meaney, Duggan (McDonald), Hulmes, Kennedy, Walsh, Ward.
*Southampton:* Wells; Golac, Holmes, Baker, Watson, Agboola, Keegan, Channon, Moran, Armstrong, Ball.

**Monaco (0) 2** *(Edstrom, Bellone)*
**Dundee U (2) 5** *(Bannon 2 [1 pen], Dodds 2, Kirkwood)*                                           7609
*Monaco:* Ettori; Liegeon (Perais), Amoros, Courtois, Vitalis, Barberis, Christophe, Edstrom, Couriol, Pecout, Bellone.
*Dundee U:* McAlpine; Holt, Narey, Hegarty, Kopel, Phillip (Gough), Kirkwood, Milne, Bannon, Sturrock, Dodds.

**Panathinaikos (0) 0**
**Arsenal (1) 2** *(McDermott, Meade)*               27,000
*Panathinaikos:* Konstantinou; Kyrastas, Karoulias, Kovis, Kapsis, Anastasiades, Livanthinos, Katsiakos (Delikaris), Galakos, Rocha-Boublis, Dokken.
*Arsenal:* Jennings; Hollins, Sansom, Talbot, O'Leary, Young, Davis, Vaessen (Meade), McDermott, Nicholas, Rix.

**Grasshoppers (1) 1** *(Fimian)*
**WBA (0) 0**                                         8100
*Grasshoppers:* Berbig; Herbert Hermann, Meyer, In-Albon, Wehrli, Egli, Jara, Heinz Hermann, Sulser, Zanetti, Fimian (Pfister).
*WBA:* Godden; Batson, Statham, Moses, Wile, Robertson, Robson, Mills, Regis, Owen, MacKenzie.

### FIRST ROUND, SECOND LEG

#### 29 SEPT

**Linfield (0) 0**
**Beveren (1) 5** *(Martens 4, Pfaff D.)*            2700
*Linfield:* Dunlop; Hayes, McCartney (Beattie), Garrett, Rafferty, Walsh, Nixon, McGaughey, Whitten, Murray, Anderson (Gordon).
*Beveren:* Pfaff J.-M.; Jaspers, Garot, Buyl, Backe, Pfaff D., Schoenberger, Albert (Grieve), Theunis, Martens, Alcock (Van Eycken).

**Southampton (0) 1** *(Keegan)*
**Limerick (0) 1** *(Morris)*                        12,841
*Southampton:* Katalinic; Golac, Holmes, Baker G., Watson, Agboola, Keegan, Channon, Moran, Armstrong, Ball.
*Limerick:* Fitzpatrick; Nolan, Nodwell, Finucane, Storan, Meaney, Duggan, Hulmes (Morris), Kennedy, Walsh, Ward.

#### 30 SEPT

**Aberdeen (1) 3** *(Strachan pen, Weir 2)*
**Ipswich T (1) 1** *(Wark pen)*                     24,000
*Aberdeen:* Leighton; Kennedy, Rougvie, Watson (Bell), McLeish, Miller, Strachan, Cooper, McGhee, Hewitt, Weir.
*Ipswich T:* Cooper; Mills, McCall, Thijssen (O'Callaghan), Osman, Butcher, Wark, Muhren, Mariner, Brazil, Gates.

**Arsenal (0) 1** *(Talbot)*
**Panathinaikos (0) 0**                              23,514
*Arsenal:* Jennings; Devine, Sansom, Talbot, O'Leary (Whyte), Young, Hollins, Sunderland, McDermott, Nicholas, Rix.
*Panathinaikos:* Konstantinou; Kyrastas, Karoulias, Kouis, Simeforidis, Livanthinos, Haralibidis, Kelikaris (Anastasiades), Galakos, Rocha-Boublis (Katsiakos), Dokken.

**Dundee U (0) 1** *(Milne)*
**Monaco (0) 2** *(Edstrom, Bellone)*                12,000
*Dundee U:* McAlpine; Stark, Holt, Phillip, Hegarty, Narey, Bannon, Payne (Milne), Kirkwood, Sturrock, Dodds.
*Monaco:* Ettori; Leignon, Puel, Perais, Nonot, Christophe, Amoros (Recordier), Bigotat, Edstrom, Couriol (Valadier), Bellone.

**WBA (0) 1** *(Robertson)*
**Grasshoppers (2) 3** *(Fimian, Koller, Jara)*      16,745
*WBA:* Godden; Batson, Statham, Mills (Cross), Wile, Robertson (Webb), Robson, Deehan, Regis, Owen, MacKenzie.
*Grasshoppers:* Berbig; In-Albon, Meyer, Egli, Herbert Hermann, Wehrli, Koller, Heinz Hermann, Sulser, Jara, Fimian (Zanetti).

### SECOND ROUND, FIRST LEG

#### 20 OCT

**Winterslag (0) 1** *(Berger)*
**Arsenal (0) 0**                                     8000
*Winterslag:* De Bruyne; Houben, Billen, Vanlessen, Lambrichts, Albertsen, Thijs, Denier, Berger, Weis, Davids.
*Arsenal:* Jennings; Devine, Sansom, Talbot, O'Leary, Young, Hollins, Sunderland, Meade (McDermott), Nicholas, Rix.

**Borussia Moenchengladbach (0) 2** *(Schaffer, Hannes)*
**Dundee U (0) 0**                                    31,000
*Borussia Moenchengladbach:* Kleff; Ringels, Hannes, Schaffer, Fleer, Matthaus, Bruns, Rahn (Veh), Pinkall, Mill, Wuttke.
*Dundee U:* McAlpine; Kopel, Hegarty, Narey, Murray, Philipp, Bannon, Holt, Milne, Kirkwood, Dodds.

**21 OCT**

**Aberdeen (3) 3** *(Strachan, Weir, Hewitt)*

**Arges Pitesti (0) 0**                    18,000

*Aberdeen:* Leighton; Kennedy, Rougvie, Watson, Cooper, Miller, Strachan, McMaster, McGhee, Hewitt, Weir.
*Arges Pitesti:* Arichu (Cristian); Zamfir, Barbulescu, Tulpan, Stancu, Cristea, Baluta, Kalo, Radu, Ignat, Turcu.


**Southampton (0) 2** *(Keegan pen, Channon)*

**Sporting Lisbon (3) 4** *(Jordao, Holmes og, Fernandes 2)*                    18,573

*Southampton:* Wells; Golac, Holmes, Williams, Nicholl, Whitlock (Lawrence), Keegan, Channon, Moran, Armstrong, Ball.
*Sporting Lisbon:* Meszaros; Zezinho (Barao), Inacio, Xavier, Eurico, Ademar, Freire, Nogueira (Virgilio), Fernandes, Oliveira, Jordao.


## SECOND ROUND, SECOND LEG

**3 NOV**

**Arsenal (1) 2** *(Hollins, Rix)*

**Winterslag (1) 1** *(Billen)*                    22,930

*Arsenal:* Jennings; Hollins, Sansom, Talbot, O'Leary, Whyte, McDermott, Vaessen (Davis), Meade, Nicholas, Rix.
*Winterslag:* De Bruyne; Houben, Billen, Vanlessen, Lambrichts, Albertsen, Thijs, Denier, Berger, Weis, Davids.


**Dundee U (2) 5** *(Milne, Kirkwood, Sturrock, Hegarty, Bannon)*

**Borussia Moenchengladbach (0) 0**                    17,500

*Dundee U:* McAlpine; Holt, Narey, Hegarty, Murray, Gough, Bannon, Kirkwood, Milne, Sturrock, Dodds.
*Borussia Moenchengladbach:* Kleff; Ringels, Hannes, Schaffer, Fleer, Matthaus, Veh (Schafer), Bruns, Wuttke, Mill, Pinkall.


**4 NOV**

**Arges Pitesti (2) 2** *(Radu, Barbulescu)*

**Aberdeen (0) 2** *(Strachan pen, Hewitt)*                    16,000

*Arges Pitesti:* Cristian; Barbulescu, Stancu, Cristea, Eduard, Kalo, Badea, Ignat, Baluta, Radu, Turcu.
*Aberdeen:* Leighton; Kennedy, Miller, McLeish, Rougvie, Strachan, Cooper, McMaster (Hewitt), Watson, McGhee, Weir.


**Sporting Lisbon (0) 0**

**Southampton (0) 0**                    50,000

*Sporting Lisbon:* Meszaros; Virgilio, Barao, Xavier, Eurico, Ademar, Freire, Marinho, Fernandes, Oliveira, Jordao.
*Southampton:* Katalinic; Baker S., Holmes, Williams, Nicholl, Agboola, Keegan, Channon, Moran, Lawrence (Wallace), Ball.


## THIRD ROUND, FIRST LEG

**25 NOV**

**Aberdeen (1) 3** *(Black, Watson, Hewitt)*

**Hamburg (0) 2** *(Hrubesch 2)*                    24,000

*Aberdeen:* Leighton; Kennedy, Rougvie (Cooper), Miller, McMaster, Strachan, Watson, Simpson, Black, McGhee (McCall), Hewitt.


*Hamburg:* Stein; Kaltz, Hartwig (Hidien), Beckenbauer, Groh, Milewski (Hieronymus), Wehmeyer, Magath, Memering, Hrubesch, Bastrup.


**1 DEC**

**Winterslag (0) 0**

**Dundee U (0) 0**                    10,000

*Winterslag:* De Bruyne; Bouben, Vanlessen, Lambrichts, Billen, Albertsen, Weis, Thijs, Denier P. (Denier M.), Berger, Van Woerkun.
*Dundee U:* McAlpine; Holt, Stark, Phillip (Kopel), Hegarty, Narey, Bannon, Milne, Gough, Sturrock, Dodds.


## THIRD ROUND, SECOND LEG

**9 DEC**

**Dundee U (3) 5** *(Bannon, Narey, Hegarty, Milne 2)*

**Winterslag (0) 0**                    16,232

*Dundee U:* McAlpine; Holt, Malpas, Phillip, Hegarty, Narey, Bannon, Milne, Kirkwood, Sturrock, Dodds.
*Winterslag:* De Bruyne; Houben, Billen, Vitalen, Lambrichts, Albertsen, Thijs, Denier P., Berger, Weis, Denier M.


**Hamburg (1) 3** *(Hrubesch, Memering pen, Jakobs)*

**Aberdeen (0) 1** *(McGhee)*                    45,600

*Hamburg:* Stein; Wehmeyer, Jakobs, Beckenbauer, Groh, Von Heesen, Memering, Magath, Milewski, Hrubesch, Bastrup.
*Aberdeen:* Leighton; Kennedy, Watson, Miller, McMaster, McLeish, Strachan (Bell), Cooper, Simpson, Black, Hewitt (McGhee).


## QUARTER-FINAL, FIRST LEG

**3 MAR**

**Dundee U (2) 2** *(Narey, Dodds)*

**Radnicki Nis (0) 0**                    16,000

*Dundee U:* McAlpine; Holt, Malpas, Gough, Hegarty, Narey, Bannon, Milne, Kirkwood, Sturrock, Dodds.
*Radnicki Nis:* Milenkovic; Halilovic, Obradovic, Bojovic, Vojinovic, Drizic, Panayotovic, Djordjevic, Radosavljevic (Aleksic), Nikolic, Beganovic.


## QUARTER-FINAL, SECOND LEG

**17 MAR**

**Radnicki Nis (0) 3** *(Panajotovic 2, Djordjevic pen)*

**Dundee U (0) 0**                    15,000

*Radnicki Nis:* Milenkovic; Gravilovic, Obradovic, Bojovic, Vojinovic, Drizic, Stoiljkovic, Djordjevic, Radosavljevic (Panajotovic), Nikolic, Beganovic.
*Dundee U:* McAlpine; Holt, Malpas, Gough, Hegarty, Narey, Milne, Bannon, Kirkwood, Sturrock, Dodds.

# EUROPEAN FOOTBALLER OF THE YEAR 1981

Karl-Heinz Rummenigge, 26, retained his title of European Footballer of the Year, although he received 16 fewer points than he did in 1980 and his margin of success was halved. Even so he finished 42 points clear of runner-up Paul Breitner, his club and country colleague and the prodigal son of the Bundesliga. The poll was another triumph for the West German League System which has provided the last six winners.

Bernd Schuster, runner-up in 1980, gained more points this time, but was placed third, while France's Michel Platini, third in 1980 with 33, gained 3 more points yet dropped to fourth place. However, the comeback man was certainly Oleg Blokhin, the Dynamo Kiev striker who, since winning the award himself in 1975, had been in some decline as far as this poll was concerned.

To emphasise the return to international recognition of the Soviet Union they had three other players in the first thirteen named.

Another oddity came from the failure of the three immediately previous winners, Kevin Keegan (twice), Allan Simonsen and Franz Beckenbauer, to achieve even 1 point between them.

## POINTS AWARDED

106 Karl-Heinz Rummenigge (Bayern Munich)
 64 Paul Breitner (Bayern Munich)
 39 Bernd Schuster (Barcelona)
 36 Michel Platini (St Etienne)
 14 Oleg Blokhin (Dynamo Kiev)
 13 Dino Zoff (Juventus)
 10 Ramaz Shengelia (Dynamo Tbilisi)
  9 Alexander Chivadze (Dynamo Tbilisi)
  7 Liam Brady (Juventus), John Wark (Ipswich Town)
  6 Zbigniew Boniek (Widzew Lodz), Max Bossis (Nantes), David Kipiani (Dynamo Tbilisi), Bruno Pezzey (Eintracht Frankfurt), Andras Toroczik (Ujpest Dozsa)
  5 Horst Hrubesch (Hamburg), Rudi Krol (Napoli), Vladimir Petrovic (Red Star Belgrade)
  4 Trevor Brooking (West Ham United), Zlatko Vujovic (Hajduk Split)
  3 Giancarlo Antognoni (Fiorentina), Luis Arconada (Real Sociedad), Jan Ceulemans (FC Bruges), Kenny Dalglish (Liverpool), Bryan Robson (Manchester United), Wilfried van Moer (Beveren), Frank Stapleton (Manchester United)
  2 Grzegorz Lato (Lokeren), Tibor Nyilasi (Ferencvaros), Wlodzimierz Smolarek (Widzew Lodz), Frans Thijssen (Ipswich Town)
  1 Oliveira (Sporting Lisbon), Uli Stielike (Real Madrid), Jezus Zamora (Real Sociedad)

## PAST WINNERS

1956 Stanley Matthews (Blackpool); 1957 Alfredo di Stefano (Real Madrid); 1958 Raymond Kopa (Real Madrid); 1959 Alfredo di Stefano (Real Madrid); 1960 Luis Suarez (Barcelona); 1961 Omar Sivori (Juventus); 1962 Josef Masopust (Dukla Prague); 1963 Lev Yashin (Dynamo Moscow); 1964 Denis Law (Manchester U); 1965 Eusebio (Benfica); 1966 Bobby Charlton (Manchester U); 1967 Florian Albert (Ferencvaros); 1968 George Best (Manchester U); 1969 Gianni Rivera (Milan); 1970 Gerd Muller (Bayern Munich); 1971 Johan Cruyff (Ajax); 1972 Franz Beckenbauer (Bayern Munich); 1973 Johan Cruyff (Barcelona); 1974 Johan Cruyff (Barcelona); 1975 Oleg Blokhin (Dynamo Kiev); 1976 Franz Beckenbauer (Bayern Munich); 1977 Allan Simonsen (B Moenchengladbach); 1978 Kevin Keegan (Hamburg); 1979 Kevin Keegan (Hamburg); 1980 Karl-Heinz Rummenigge (Bayern Munich).

# BRITISH AND IRISH CLUBS IN EUROPE

**1955–56**
EUROPEAN CUP　　　Hibernian (Semi-Final)

**1955–58**
EUROPEAN
INTER-CITIES　　　London beat Basle, Frankfurt and Lausanne before losing to Barcelona 2-2, 2-6 in the
FAIRS CUP　　　　Final.
　　　　　　　　　Birmingham C knocked out Inter and Zagreb before losing to Barcelona 4-3, 0-1 and 1-2
　　　　　　　　　at Basle.

**1956–57**
EUROPEAN CUP　　　Manchester U (Semi-Final)　　　　Rangers (First Round Proper)

**1957–58**
EUROPEAN CUP　　　Manchester U (Semi-Final)　　　　Glenavon (Preliminary Round)
　　　　　　　　　Rangers (First Round Proper)　　　Shamrock R (Preliminary Round)

**1958–60**
FAIRS CUP　　　　Birmingham C (Runners-Up)　　　　Chelsea (Second Round)

**1958–59**
EUROPEAN CUP　　　Wolverhampton W (First Round)　　Drumcondra (Preliminary Round)
　　　　　　　　　Ards (Preliminary Round)　　　　Hearts (Preliminary Round)
　　　　　　　　　Manchester U were invited to compete, but were withdrawn by the Football League.

**1959–60**
EUROPEAN CUP　　　Rangers (Semi-Final)　　　　　Linfield (Preliminary Round)
　　　　　　　　　Wolverhampton W (Quarter-Final)　Shamrock R (Preliminary Round)

**1960–61**
EUROPEAN CUP　　　Burnley (Quarter-Final)　　　　Limerick (Preliminary Round)
　　　　　　　　　Hearts (Preliminary Round)　　　Glenavon – Withdrew
EUROPEAN
CUP-WINNERS' CUP　Rangers (Runners-Up)　　　　　Wolverhampton W (Semi-Final)
FAIRS CUP　　　　Birmingham C (Runners-Up)　　　Hibernian (Semi-Final)

**1961–62**
EUROPEAN CUP　　　Tottenham H (Semi-Final)　　　Drumcondra (Preliminary Round)
　　　　　　　　　Rangers (Quarter-Final)　　　　Linfield (Preliminary Round)
EUROPEAN　　　　Dunfermline Ath (Quarter-Final)　Swansea T (First Round)
CUP-WINNERS' CUP　Leicester C (Second Round)　　　Glenavon (First Round)
　　　　　　　　　　　　　　　　　　　　　　　St Patrick's Ath (Preliminary Round)
FAIRS CUP　　　　Sheffield W (Quarter-Final)　　Nottingham F (First Round)
　　　　　　　　　Hearts (Second Round)　　　　　Birmingham C (Second Round)
　　　　　　　　　　　　　　　　　　　　　　　Hibernian (Second Round)

**1962–63**
EUROPEAN CUP　　　Dundee (Semi-Final)　　　　　Shelbourne (Preliminary Round)
　　　　　　　　　Ipswich T (First Round)　　　Linfield (Preliminary Round)
EUROPEAN　　　　Tottenham H(Winners)　　　　　Shamrock R (Second Round)
CUP-WINNERS' CUP　Rangers (Second Round)　　　　Bangor C (First Round)
　　　　　　　　　　　　　　　　　　　　　　　Portadown (First Round)
FAIRS CUP　　　　Hibernian (Quarter-Final)　　Everton (First Round)
　　　　　　　　　Dunfermline Ath (Second Round)　Celtic (First Round)
　　　　　　　　　Glentoran (First Round)　　　Drumcondra (Second Round)

**1963–64**
EUROPEAN CUP　　　Rangers (Preliminary Round)　　Dundalk (Preliminary Round)
　　　　　　　　　Everton (Preliminary Round)　　Distillery (Preliminary Round)
EUROPEAN　　　　Celtic (Semi-Final)　　　　　　Borough U (Second Round)
CUP-WINNERS' CUP　Manchester U (Quarter-Final)　Tottenham H (Second Round)
　　　　　　　　　Linfield (Second Round)　　　Shelbourne (First Round)
FAIRS CUP　　　　Partick T (Second Round)　　　Hearts (First Round)
　　　　　　　　　Arsenal (Second Round)　　　　Glentoran (First Round)
　　　　　　　　　Sheffield W (Second Round)　　Shamrock R (First Round)

**1964–65**

| | | |
|---|---|---|
| **EUROPEAN CUP** | Liverpool (Semi-Final)<br>Rangers (Quarter-Final) | Shamrock R (Preliminary Round)<br>Glentoran (Preliminary Round) |
| **EUROPEAN<br>CUP-WINNERS' CUP** | West Ham U (Winners)<br>Cardiff C (Quarter-Final)<br>Dundee (Second Round) | Cork Celtic (First Round)<br>Derry C (First Round) |
| **FAIRS CUP** | Manchester U (Semi-Final)<br>Dunfermline Ath (Third Round)<br>Everton (Third Round) | Celtic (Second Round)<br>Shelbourne (Second Round)<br>Kilmarnock (Second Round) |

**1965–66**

| | | |
|---|---|---|
| **EUROPEAN CUP** | Manchester U (Semi-Final)<br>Derry C (First Round) | Kilmarnock (First Round)<br>Drumcondra (Preliminary Round) |
| **EUROPEAN<br>CUP-WINNERS' CUP** | Liverpool (Runners-Up)<br>Celtic (Semi-Final)<br>West Ham U (Semi-Final) | Limerick (First Round)<br>Cardiff C (First Round)<br>Coleraine (First Round) |
| **FAIRS CUP** | Leeds U (Semi-Final)<br>Chelsea (Semi-Final)<br>Dunfermline Ath (Quarter-Final)<br>Hearts (Third Round) | Everton (Second Round)<br>Glentoran (First Round)<br>Hibernian (First Round)<br>Shamrock R (Second Round) |

**1966–67**

| | | |
|---|---|---|
| **EUROPEAN CUP** | Celtic (Winners)<br>Linfield (Quarter-Final) | Liverpool (First Round)<br>Waterford (Preliminary Round) |
| **EUROPEAN<br>CUP-WINNERS' CUP** | Rangers (Runners-Up)<br>Everton (Second Round)<br>Shamrock R (Second Round) | Glentoran (First Round)<br>Swansea T (First Round) |
| **FAIRS CUP** | Leeds U (Runners-Up)<br>Kilmarnock (Semi-Final)<br>Burnley (Quarter-Final)<br>Dundee U (Third Round) | WBA (Third Round)<br>Dunfermline Ath (Second Round)<br>Drumcondra (First Round) |

**1967–68**

| | | |
|---|---|---|
| **EUROPEAN CUP** | Manchester U (Winners)<br>Dundalk (First Round) | Celtic (First Round)<br>Glentoran (First Round) |
| **EUROPEAN<br>CUP-WINNERS' CUP** | Cardiff C (Semi-Final)<br>Aberdeen (Second Round)<br>Tottenham H (Second Round) | Crusaders (First Round)<br>Shamrock R (First Round) |
| **FAIRS CUP** | Leeds U (Winners)<br>Dundee (Semi-Final)<br>Rangers (Quarter-Final)<br>Hibernian (Third Round) | Liverpool (Third Round)<br>Nottingham F (Second Round)<br>Linfield (First Round)<br>St Patrick's Ath (First Round) |

**1968–69**

| | | |
|---|---|---|
| **EUROPEAN CUP** | Manchester U (Semi-Final)<br>Celtic (Quarter-Final)<br>Manchester C (First Round) | Glentoran (First Round)<br>Waterford (First Round) |
| **EUROPEAN<br>CUP-WINNERS' CUP** | Dunfermline Ath (Semi-Final)<br>WBA (Quarter-Final)<br>Crusaders (First Round) | Cardiff C (First Round)<br>Shamrock R (First Round) |
| **FAIRS CUP** | Newcastle U (Winners)<br>Rangers (Semi-Final)<br>Leeds U (Quarter-Final)<br>Hibernian (Third Round)<br>Aberdeen (Second Round) | Chelsea (Second Round)<br>Dundalk (Second Round)<br>Liverpool (First Round)<br>Linfield (First Round)<br>Morton (First Round) |

**1969–70**

| | | |
|---|---|---|
| **EUROPEAN CUP** | Celtic (Runners-Up)<br>Leeds U (Semi-Final) | Waterford (First Round)<br>Linfield (First Round) |
| **EUROPEAN<br>CUP-WINNERS' CUP** | Manchester C (Winners)<br>Rangers (Second Round)<br>Cardiff C (Second Round) | Ards (First Round)<br>Shamrock R (First Round) |
| **EUROPEAN<br>FAIRS CUP** | Arsenal (Winners)<br>Newcastle U (Quarter-Final)<br>Dunfermline Ath (Third Round)<br>Southampton (Third Round)<br>Liverpool (Second Round) | Kilmarnock (Third Round)<br>Dundee U (First Round)<br>Coleraine (Second Round)<br>Dundalk (First Round)<br>Glentoran (First Round) |

**1970–71**

| | | |
|---|---|---|
| EUROPEAN CUP | Celtic (Quarter-Final)<br>Everton (Quarter-Final) | Waterford (Second Round)<br>Glentoran (First Round) |
| EUROPEAN<br>CUP-WINNERS' CUP | Chelsea (Winners)<br>Manchester C (Semi-Final)<br>Cardiff C (Quarter-Final) | Linfield (First Round)<br>Aberdeen (First Round)<br>Bohemians (Preliminary Round) |
| EUROPEAN<br>FAIRS CUP | Leeds U (Winners)<br>Arsenal (Quarter-Final)<br>Liverpool (Semi-Final)<br>Newcastle U (Second Round)<br>Coleraine (Second Round) | Dundee U (Second Round)<br>Coventry C (Second Round)<br>Cork Hibs (First Round)<br>Rangers (First Round)<br>Kilmarnock (First Round)<br>Hibernian (Third Round) |

**1971–72**

| | | |
|---|---|---|
| EUROPEAN CUP | Arsenal (Quarter-Final)<br>Celtic (Semi-Final) | Linfield (First Round)<br>Cork Hibs (First Round) |
| EUROPEAN<br>CUP-WINNERS' CUP | Liverpool (Second Round)<br>Chelsea (Second Round)<br>Cardiff C (First Round) | Rangers (Winners)<br>Distillery (First Round)<br>Limerick (First Round) |
| UEFA CUP | Tottenham H (Winners)<br>Wolverhampton W (Runners-Up)<br>Leeds U (First Round)<br>Southampton (First Round)<br>Shelbourne (First Round)<br>Glentoran (First Round) | Dundee (Third Round)<br>Aberdeen (Second Round)<br>St Johnstone (Third Round) |

**1972–73**

| | | |
|---|---|---|
| EUROPEAN CUP | Derby Co (Semi-Final)<br>Celtic (Second Round) | Waterford (First Round) |
| EUROPEAN<br>CUP-WINNERS' CUP | Leeds U (Runners-Up)<br>Hibernian (Quarter-Final) | Wrexham (Second Round)<br>Cork Hibs (Second Round) |
| UEFA CUP | Liverpool (Winners)<br>Tottenham H (Semi-Final)<br>Stoke C (First Round)<br>Manchester C (First Round) | Aberdeen (First Round)<br>Partick T (First Round)<br>Bohemians (First Round) |

**1973–74**

| | | |
|---|---|---|
| EUROPEAN CUP | Liverpool (Second Round)<br>Celtic (Semi-Final) | Waterford (First Round)<br>Crusaders (First Round) |
| EUROPEAN<br>CUP-WINNERS' CUP | Sunderland (Second Round)<br>Rangers (Second Round)<br>Cardiff C (First Round) | Glentoran (Quarter-Final)<br>Cork Hibs (First Round) |
| UEFA CUP | Tottenham H (Runners-Up)<br>Ipswich T (Quarter-Final)<br>Leeds U (Third Round)<br>Wolverhampton W (Second Round) | Aberdeen(Second Round)<br>Hibernian (Second Round)<br>Finn Harps (First Round)<br>Ards (First Round) |

**1974–75**

| | | |
|---|---|---|
| EUROPEAN CUP | Leeds U (Runners-Up)<br>Celtic (First Round) | Coleraine (First Round)<br>Cork Celtic (Second Round) |
| EUROPEAN<br>CUP-WINNERS' CUP | Liverpool (Second Round)<br>Ards (First Round)<br>Cardiff C (First Round) | Finn Harps (First Round)<br>Dundee U (Second Round) |
| UEFA CUP | Derby Co (Third Round)<br>Ipswich T (First Round)<br>Stoke C (First Round)<br>Wolverhampton W (First Round) | Bohemians (First Round)<br>Dundee (First Round)<br>Portadown (Second Round)<br>Hibernian (Second Round) |

**1975–76**

| | | |
|---|---|---|
| EUROPEAN CUP | Derby Co (Second Round)<br>Linfield (First Round) | Rangers (Second Round)<br>Bohemians (First Round) |
| EUROPEAN<br>CUP-WINNERS' CUP | West Ham U (Runners-Up)<br>Celtic (Quarter-Final)<br>Home Farm (First Round) | Wrexham (Quarter-Final)<br>Coleraine (First Round) |
| UEFA CUP | Liverpool (Winners)<br>Aston Villa (First Round)<br>Glentoran (First Round)<br>Athlone T (Second Round) | Ipswich T (Second Round)<br>Everton (First Round)<br>Hibernian (First Round)<br>Dundee U (Second Round) |

**1976–77**

| | | |
|---|---|---|
| **EUROPEAN CUP** | Liverpool (Winners) | Dundalk (First Round) |
| | Crusaders (First Round) | Rangers (First Round) |
| **EUROPEAN CUP-WINNERS' CUP** | Southampton (Quarter-Final) | Bohemians (Second Round) |
| | Cardiff C (First Round) | Carrick R (Second Round) |
| | Hearts (Second Round) | |
| **UEFA CUP** | Manchester C (First Round) | Hibernian (Second Round) |
| | Derby Co (Second Round) | Glentoran (First Round) |
| | Manchester U (Second Round) | Celtic (First Round) |
| | QPR (Quarter-Final) | Finn Harps (First Round) |

**1977–78**

| | | |
|---|---|---|
| **EUROPEAN CUP** | Liverpool (Winners) | Celtic (Second Round) |
| | Sligo Rovers (First Round) | Glentoran (Second Round) |
| **EUROPEAN CUP-WINNERS' CUP** | Rangers (First Round) | Cardiff C (First Round) |
| | Dundalk (First Round) | Manchester U (Second Round) |
| | Coleraine (First Round) | |
| **UEFA CUP** | Aston Villa (Quarter-Final) | Ipswich T (Third Round) |
| | Manchester C (First Round) | Newcastle U (Second Round) |
| | Bohemians (First Round) | Dundee U (First Round) |
| | Glenavon (First Round) | Aberdeen (First Round) |

**1978–79**

| | | |
|---|---|---|
| **EUROPEAN CUP** | Nottingham F (Winners) | Rangers (Quarter-Final) |
| | Liverpool (First Round) | Bohemians (Second Round) |
| | Linfield (First Round) | |
| **EUROPEAN CUP-WINNERS' CUP** | Ipswich T (Quarter-Final) | Aberdeen (Second Round) |
| | Ballymena U (First Round) | Shamrock R (Second Round) |
| | Wrexham (First Round) | |
| **UEFA CUP** | Manchester C (Quarter-Final) | WBA (Quarter-Final) |
| | Arsenal (Third Round) | Everton (Second Round) |
| | Dundee U (First Round) | Hibernian (Second Round) |
| | Finn Harps (First Round) | Glentoran (First Round) |

**1979–80**

| | | |
|---|---|---|
| **EUROPEAN CUP** | Nottingham F (Winners) | Dundalk (Second Round) |
| | Liverpool (First Round) | Linfield (Preliminary Round) |
| | Celtic (Quarter-Final) | |
| **EUROPEAN CUP-WINNERS' CUP** | Arsenal (Runners-Up) | Waterford (First Round) |
| | Rangers (Second Round) | Cliftonville (First Round) |
| | Wrexham (First Round) | |
| **UEFA CUP** | Leeds U (Second Round) | Glenavon (First Round) |
| | Ipswich T (Second Round) | Bohemians (First Round) |
| | Dundee U (Second Round) | WBA (First Round) |
| | Aberdeen (First Round) | Everton (First Round) |

**1980–81**

| | | |
|---|---|---|
| **EUROPEAN CUP** | Liverpool (Winners) | Linfield (First Round) |
| | Nottingham F (First Round) | Limerick (First Round) |
| | Aberdeen (Second Round) | |
| **EUROPEAN CUP-WINNERS' CUP** | West Ham U (Quarter-Final) | Crusaders (First Round) |
| | Celtic (First Round) | Waterford (Second Round) |
| | Newport Co (Quarter-Final) | |
| **UEFA CUP** | Ipswich T (Winners) | St Mirren (Second Round) |
| | Manchester U (First Round) | Ballymena U (First Round) |
| | Wolverhampton W (First Round) | Dundalk (First Round) |
| | Dundee U (Second Round) | |

**1981–82**

| | | |
|---|---|---|
| **EUROPEAN CUP** | Aston Villa (Winners) | Glentoran (Second Round) |
| | Liverpool (Quarter-Final) | Athlone T (First Round) |
| | Celtic (First Round) | |
| **EUROPEAN CUP-WINNERS' CUP** | Tottenham H (Semi-Final) | Dundalk (Second Round) |
| | Rangers (First Round) | Ballymena U (First Round) |
| | Swansea C (First Round) | |
| **UEFA CUP** | Arsenal (Second Round) | Dundee U (Quarter-Final) |
| | Southampton (Second Round) | Aberdeen (Third Round) |
| | Ipswich T (First Round) | Linfield (First Round) |
| | WBA (First Round) | Limerick (First Round) |

# Summary of Appearances

## EUROPEAN CUP (1955–82)

**English clubs**
9  Liverpool
5  Manchester U
2  Derby Co, Wolverhampton W, Everton, Leeds U, Nottingham F
1  Burnley, Tottenham H, Ipswich T, Manchester C, Arsenal, Aston Villa

**Scottish clubs**
12  Celtic
9  Rangers
2  Hearts
1  Dundee, Kilmarnock, Hibernian, Aberdeen

**Clubs from Northern Ireland**
10  Linfield
6  Glentoran
2  Crusaders
1  Glenavon, Ards, Distillery, Derry C, Coleraine

**Clubs from Eire**
6  Waterford
4  Dundalk
3  Drumcondra, Shamrock R
2  Bohemians, Limerick
1  Shelbourne, Cork Hibs, Cork Celtic, Sligo Rovers, Athlone T

**Winners: Celtic 1966–67; Manchester U 1967–68; Liverpool 1976–77, 1977–78, 1980–81; Nottingham F 1978–79, 1979–80; Aston Villa 1981–82**

**Finalists: Celtic 1969–70; Leeds U 1974–75**

## EUROPEAN CUP-WINNERS' CUP (1960–82)

**English clubs**
4  West Ham U, Tottenham H
3  Liverpool
2  Chelsea, Manchester C, Manchester U
1  Wolverhampton W, Leicester C, Everton, WBA, Leeds U, Sunderland, Southampton, Ipswich T, Arsenal

**Scottish clubs**
9  Rangers
4  Celtic
3  Aberdeen
2  Dunfermline Ath
1  Dundee, Dundee U, Hibernian, Hearts

**Welsh clubs**
11  Cardiff C
4  Wrexham
3  Swansea C
1  Bangor C, Borough U, Newport Co

**Clubs from Northern Ireland**
3  Coleraine, Crusaders
2  Glentoran, Ards, Linfield, Ballymena U
1  Glenavon, Derry C, Distillery, Portadown, Carrick Rangers, Cliftonville

**Clubs from Eire**
6  Shamrock R
2  Limerick, Cork Hibs, Bohemians, Waterford, Dundalk
1  Shelbourne, Cork Celtic, St Patrick's Ath, Finn Harps, Home Farm

**Winners: Tottenham H 1962–63; West Ham U 1964–65; Manchester C 1969–70; Chelsea 1970–71; Rangers 1971–72**

**Finalists: Liverpool 1965–66; Rangers 1960–61, 1966–67; Leeds U 1972–73; West Ham U 1975–76; Arsenal 1979–80**

## EUROPEAN FAIRS CUP & UEFA CUP (1955–82)

**English clubs**
8  Leeds U
7  Ipswich T
6  Liverpool, Everton
5  Arsenal
4  Manchester C, Birmingham C, Newcastle U, Wolverhampton W, WBA
3  Chelsea, Tottenham H, Manchester U, Southampton
2  Sheffield W, Nottingham F, Stoke C, Derby Co, Aston Villa
1  Burnley, Coventry C, London Rep XI, QPR

**Scottish clubs**
12  Hibernian
8  Dundee U
6  Aberdeen
5  Dunfermline Ath
4  Kilmarnock
3  Hearts, Rangers, Dundee, Celtic
2  Partick T
1  Morton, St Johnstone, St Mirren

**Clubs from Northern Ireland**
8  Glentoran
3  Linfield
2  Coleraine, Glenavon
1  Ards, Portadown, Ballymena U

**Clubs from Eire**
4  Bohemians
3  Finn Harps, Dundalk
2  Shelbourne, Shamrock R, Drumcondra
1  St Patrick's Ath, Cork Hibs, Athlone T, Limerick

**Winners: Leeds U 1967–68, 1970–71; Newcastle U 1968–69; Arsenal 1969–70; Tottenham H 1971–72; Liverpool 1972–73, 1975–76; Ipswich T 1980–81**

**Finalists: Birmingham C 1958–60, 1960–61; Leeds U 1966–67; Wolverhampton W 1971–72; Tottenham H 1973–74**

# RECORDS

## Major British Records

### HIGHEST SCORES

| | | | | | | |
|---|---|---|---|---|---|---|
| **First-Class Match** | | Arbroath | 36 | Bon Accord | 0 | 5.9.1885 |
| | | (*Scottish Cup 1st Round*) | | | | |
| **International Match** | | England | 13 | Ireland | 0 | 18.2.1882 |
| **FA Cup** | | Preston NE | 26 | Hyde U | 0 | 15.10.1887 |
| | | (*1st Round*) | | | | |

### FOOTBALL LEAGUE

| | | | | | | |
|---|---|---|---|---|---|---|
| **Division 1** | (*Home*) | WBA | 12 | Darwen | 0 | 4.4.1892 |
| | | Nottingham F | 12 | Leicester Fosse | 0 | 21.4.1909 |
| | (*Away*) | Newcastle U | 1 | Sunderland | 9 | 5.12.1908 |
| | | Cardiff C | 1 | Wolverhampton W | 9 | 3.9.1955 |
| **Division 2** | (*Home*) | Newcastle U | 13 | Newport Co | 0 | 5.10.1946 |
| | (*Away*) | Burslem PV | 0 | Sheffield U | 10 | 10.12.1892 |
| **Division 3** | (*Home*) | Tranmere R | 9 | Accrington S | 0 | 18.4.1959 |
| | | Brentford | 9 | Wrexham | 0 | 15.10.1963 |
| | (*Away*) | Halifax T | 0 | Fulham | 8 | 16.9.1969 |
| | | Brighton | 2 | Bristol R | 8 | 1.12.1973 |
| **Division 3(S)** | (*Home*) | Luton T | 12 | Bristol R | 0 | 13.4.1936 |
| | (*Away*) | Northampton T | 0 | Walsall | 8 | 2.2.1947 |
| **Division 3(N)** | (*Home*) | Stockport Co | 13 | Halifax T | 0 | 6.1.1934 |
| | (*Away*) | Accrington S | 0 | Barnsley | 9 | 3.2.1934 |
| **Division 4** | (*Home*) | Oldham Ath | 11 | Southport | 0 | 26.12.1962 |
| | (*Away*) | Crewe Alex | 1 | Rotherham U | 8 | 8.9.1973 |

### SCOTTISH LEAGUE

| | | | | | | |
|---|---|---|---|---|---|---|
| **Premier** | (*Home*) | Aberdeen | 8 | Motherwell | 0 | 26.3.1979 |
| **Division** | (*Away*) | Kilmarnock | 1 | Rangers | 8 | 20.9.1980 |
| **Division 1** | (*Home*) | Celtic | 11 | Dundee | 0 | 26.10.1895 |
| | (*Away*) | Airdrieonians | 1 | Hibernian | 11 | 24.10.1959 |
| **Division 2** | (*Home*) | East Fife | 13 | Edinburgh C | 2 | 11.12.1937 |
| | (*Away*) | Alloa Ath | 0 | Dundee | 10 | 8.3.1947 |

### MOST GOALS FOR IN A SEASON

| **FOOTBALL LEAGUE** | | *Goals* | *Games* | *Season* |
|---|---|---|---|---|
| Division 1 | Aston V | 128 | 42 | 1930–31 |
| Division 2 | Middlesbrough | 122 | 42 | 1926–27 |
| Division 3(S) | Millwall | 127 | 42 | 1927–28 |
| Division 3(N) | Bradford C | 128 | 42 | 1928–29 |
| Division 3 | QPR | 111 | 46 | 1961–62 |
| Division 4 | Peterborough U | 134 | 46 | 1960–61 |

| **SCOTTISH LEAGUE** | | | | |
|---|---|---|---|---|
| Premier Division | Celtic | 79 | 36 | 1976–77 |
| Division 1 | Hearts | 132 | 34 | 1957–58 |
| Division 2 | Raith R | 142 | 34 | 1937–38 |

### FEWEST GOALS FOR IN A SEASON

| **FOOTBALL LEAGUE** | (minimum 42 games) | *Goals* | *Games* | *Season* |
|---|---|---|---|---|
| Division 1 | Leicester C | 26 | 42 | 1977–78 |
| Division 2 | Watford | 24 | 42 | 1971–72 |
| Division 3(S) | Crystal Palace | 33 | 42 | 1950–51 |
| Division 3(N) | Crewe Alex | 32 | 42 | 1923–24 |
| Division 3 | Stockport Co | 27 | 46 | 1969–70 |
| Division 4 | Bradford | 30 | 46 | 1967–68 |
| | Workington | 30 | 46 | 1975–76 |
| | Gillingham | 30 | 46 | 1963–64 |

| **SCOTTISH LEAGUE** | (minimum 30 games) | | | |
|---|---|---|---|---|
| Premier Division | Clydebank | 23 | 36 | 1977–78 |
| | Kilmarnock | 23 | 36 | 1980–81 |
| Division 1 | Stirling Alb | 18 | 39 | 1980–81 |
| Division 2 | Lochgelly U | 20 | 38 | 1923–24 |

## MOST GOALS AGAINST IN A SEASON

| FOOTBALL LEAGUE | | Goals | Games | Season |
|---|---|---|---|---|
| Division 1 | Blackpool | 125 | 42 | 1930–31 |
| Division 2 | Darwen | 141 | 34 | 1898–99 |
| Division 3(S) | Merthyr T | 135 | 42 | 1929–30 |
| Division 3(N) | Nelson | 136 | 42 | 1927–28 |
| Division 3 | Accrington S | 123 | 46 | 1959–60 |
| Division 4 | Hartlepools U | 109 | 46 | 1959–60 |

| SCOTTISH LEAGUE | | | | |
|---|---|---|---|---|
| Premier Division | Motherwell | 86 | 36 | 1978–79 |
| Division 1 | Leith Ath | 137 | 38 | 1931–32 |
| Division 2 | Edinburgh C | 146 | 38 | 1931–32 |

## FEWEST GOALS AGAINST IN A SEASON

| FOOTBALL LEAGUE | (minimum 42 games) | Goals | Games | Season |
|---|---|---|---|---|
| Division 1 | Liverpool | 16 | 42 | 1978–79 |
| Division 2 | Manchester U | 23 | 42 | 1924–25 |
| Division 3(S) | Southampton | 21 | 42 | 1921–22 |
| Division 3(N) | Port Vale | 21 | 46 | 1953–54 |
| Division 3 | Rotherham U | 32 | 46 | 1980–81 |
| Division 4 | Lincoln C | 25 | 46 | 1980–81 |

| SCOTTISH LEAGUE | (minimum 30 games) | | | |
|---|---|---|---|---|
| Premier Division | Rangers | 24 | 36 | 1975–76 |
| Division 1 | Celtic | 14 | 38 | 1913–14 |
| Division 2 | Morton | 20 | 38 | 1966–67 |

## MOST POINTS IN A SEASON

| FOOTBALL LEAGUE | (under old system) | Points | Games | Season |
|---|---|---|---|---|
| Division 1 | Liverpool | 68 | 42 | 1978–79 |
| Division 2 | Tottenham H | 70 | 42 | 1919–20 |
| Division 3 | Aston Villa | 70 | 46 | 1971–72 |
| Division 3(S) | Nottingham F | 70 | 46 | 1950–51 |
| | Bristol C | 70 | 46 | 1954–55 |
| Division 3(N) | Doncaster R | 72 | 42 | 1946–47 |
| Division 4 | Lincoln C | 74 | 46 | 1975–76 |

| SCOTTISH LEAGUE | | | | |
|---|---|---|---|---|
| Premier Division | Celtic | 56 | 36 | 1980–81 |
| Division 1 | Rangers | 76 | 42 | 1920–21 |
| Division 2 | Morton | 69 | 38 | 1966–67 |

| FOOTBALL LEAGUE | (three points for a win) | | | |
|---|---|---|---|---|
| Division 1 | Liverpool | 87 | 42 | 1981–82 |
| Division 2 | Luton T | 88 | 42 | 1981–82 |
| Division 3 | Burnley | 80 | 46 | 1981–82 |
| Division 4 | Sheffield U | 96 | 46 | 1981–82 |

## FEWEST POINTS IN A SEASON

| FOOTBALL LEAGUE | (minimum 34 games) | Points | Games | Season |
|---|---|---|---|---|
| Division 1 | Leeds U | 18 | 42 | 1946–47 |
| | QPR | 18 | 42 | 1968–69 |
| | Glossop | 18 | 34 | 1899–1900 |
| | Notts Co | 18 | 34 | 1904–05 |
| | Woolwich Arsenal | 18 | 38 | 1912–13 |
| Division 2 | Doncaster R | 8 | 34 | 1904–05 |
| | Loughborough T | 8 | 34 | 1899–1900 |
| Division 3 | Rochdale | 21 | 46 | 1973–74 |
| Division 3(S) | Merthyr T | 21 | 42 | 1924–25 & 1929–30 |
| | QPR | 21 | 42 | 1925–26 |
| Division 3(N) | Rochdale | 11 | 40 | 1931–32 |
| Division 4 | Bradford | 20 | 46 | 1968–69 |

| SCOTTISH LEAGUE | (minimum 30 games) | | | |
|---|---|---|---|---|
| Premier Division | St Johnstone | 11 | 36 | 1975–76 |
| Division 1 | Stirling A | 6 | 30 | 1954–55 |

## MOST WINS IN A SEASON

| FOOTBALL LEAGUE | | Wins | Games | Season |
|---|---|---|---|---|
| Division 1 | Tottenham H | 31 | 42 | 1960–61 |
| Division 2 | Tottenham H | 32 | 42 | 1919–20 |
| Division 3(S) | Millwall | 30 | 42 | 1927–28 |
| | Plymouth Arg | 30 | 42 | 1929–30 |
| | Cardiff C | 30 | 42 | 1946–47 |
| | Nottingham F | 30 | 46 | 1950–51 |
| | Bristol C | 30 | 46 | 1954–55 |
| Division 3(N) | Doncaster R | 33 | 42 | 1946–47 |
| Division 3 | Aston Villa | 32 | 46 | 1971–72 |
| Division 4 | Lincoln C | 32 | 46 | 1975–76 |

| SCOTTISH LEAGUE | | | | |
|---|---|---|---|---|
| Premier Division | Celtic | 26 | 36 | 1980–81 |
| Division 1 | Rangers | 35 | 42 | 1920–21 |
| Division 2 | Morton | 33 | 38 | 1966–67 |

## RECORD HOME WINS IN A SEASON

Brentford won all 21 games in Division 3(S), 1929–30

## RECORD AWAY WINS IN A SEASON

Doncaster R won 18 of 21 games in Division 3(N), 1946–47

## FEWEST WINS IN A SEASON

| FOOTBALL LEAGUE | | Wins | Games | Season |
|---|---|---|---|---|
| Division 1 | Stoke | 3 | 22 | 1889–90 |
| | Woolwich Arsenal | 3 | 38 | 1912–13 |
| Division 2 | Loughborough T | 1 | 34 | 1899–1900 |
| Division 3(S) | Merthyr T | 6 | 42 | 1929–30 |
| Division 3(N) | Rochdale | 4 | 40 | 1931–32 |
| Division 3 | Rochdale | 2 | 46 | 1973–74 |
| Division 4 | Bradford | 4 | 46 | 1967–68 |

| SCOTTISH LEAGUE | | | | |
|---|---|---|---|---|
| Premier Division | St Johnstone | 3 | 36 | 1975–76 |
| Division 1 | Vale of Leven | 0 | 22 | 1891–92 |
| Division 2 | East Stirlingshire | 1 | 22 | 1905–06 |
| | Forfar Ath | 1 | 38 | 1974–75 |

## MOST DEFEATS IN A SEASON

| FOOTBALL LEAGUE | | Defeats | Games | Season |
|---|---|---|---|---|
| Division 1 | Leeds U | 30 | 42 | 1946–47 |
| | Blackburn R | 30 | 42 | 1965–66 |
| Division 2 | Tranmere R | 31 | 42 | 1938–39 |
| Division 3 | Newport Co | 31 | 46 | 1961–62 |
| Division 3(S) | Merthyr T | 29 | 42 | 1924–25 |
| Division 3(N) | Rochdale | 33 | 40 | 1931–32 |
| Division 4 | Workington | 32 | 46 | 1975–76 |

| SCOTTISH LEAGUE | | | | |
|---|---|---|---|---|
| Premier Division | St Johnstone | 28 | 36 | 1975–76 |
| Division 1 | St Mirren | 31 | 42 | 1920–21 |
| Division 2 | Lochgelly U | 30 | 38 | 1923–24 |
| | Brechin C | 30 | 36 | 1962–63 |
| | Forfar Ath | 30 | 38 | 1974–75 |

## FEWEST DEFEATS IN A SEASON

| FOOTBALL LEAGUE | | Defeats | Games | Season |
|---|---|---|---|---|
| Division 1 | Preston NE | 0 | 22 | 1888–89 |
| | Leeds U | 2 | 42 | 1968–69 |
| Division 2 | Liverpool | 0 | 28 | 1893–94 |
| | Burnley | 2 | 30 | 1897–98 |
| | Bristol C | 2 | 38 | 1905–06 |
| | Leeds U | 3 | 42 | 1963–64 |
| Division 3 | QPR | 5 | 46 | 1966–67 |
| Division 3(S) | Southampton | 4 | 42 | 1921–22 |
| | Plymouth Arg | 4 | 42 | 1929–30 |
| Division 3(N) | Port Vale | 3 | 46 | 1953–54 |
| | Doncaster R | 3 | 42 | 1946–47 |
| | Wolverhampton W | 3 | 42 | 1923–24 |
| Division 4 | Lincoln C | 4 | 46 | 1975–76 |
| | Sheffield U | 4 | 46 | 1981–82 |

| SCOTTISH LEAGUE | | Defeats | Games | Season |
|---|---|---|---|---|
| **Premier Division** | Celtic | 4 | 36 | 1976–77 |
| **Division 1** | Celtic | 0 | 18 | 1897–98 |
| | Rangers | 0 | 18 | 1898–99 |
| | Rangers | 1 | 42 | 1920–21 |
| | Hearts | 1 | 34 | 1957–58 |
| | Celtic | 1 | 34 | 1967–68 |
| | Rangers | 1 | 34 | 1967–68 |
| **Division 2** | Kilmarnock | 0 | 18 | 1898–99 |
| | Clyde | 1 | 36 | 1956–57 |
| | Morton | 1 | 36 | 1963–64 |

## MOST DRAWN GAMES IN A SEASON

| FOOTBALL LEAGUE | | Draws | Games | Season |
|---|---|---|---|---|
| **Division 1** | Norwich C | 23 | 42 | 1978–79 |
| **SCOTTISH LEAGUE** | | | | |
| **Premier Division** | Hibernian | 18 | 36 | 1976–77 |

## MOST GOALS IN A GAME

| FOOTBALL LEAGUE | | |
|---|---|---|
| **Division 1** | Ted Drake (Arsenal) 7 goals v Aston Villa | 14.12.1935 |
| **Division 2** | Tommy Briggs (Blackburn R) 7 goals v Bristol R | 5.2.1955 |
| | Neville Coleman (Stoke C) 7 goals v Lincoln C | 23.2.1957 |
| **Division 3(S)** | Joe Payne (Luton T) 10 goals v Bristol R | 13.4.1936 |
| **Division 3(N)** | Robert Bell (Tranmere R) 9 goals v Oldham Ath | 26.12.1935 |
| **Division 3** | Steve Earle (Fulham) 5 goals v Halifax T | 16.9.1969 |
| | Barrie Thomas (Scunthorpe U) 5 goals v Luton T | 24.4.1965 |
| | Keith East (Swindon T) 5 goals v Mansfield T | 20.11.1965 |
| | Alf Wood (Shrewsbury T) 5 goals v Blackburn R | 2.10.1971 |
| **Division 4** | Herbert Lister (Oldham Ath) 6 goals v Southport | 26.12.1962 |
| **SCOTTISH LEAGUE** | | |
| **Division 1** | Jimmy McGrory (Celtic) 8 goals v Dunfermline Ath | 14.9.1928 |
| **Division 2** | Owen McNally (Arthurlie) 8 goals v Armadale | 1.10.1927 |
| | Jim Dyet (King's Park) 8 goals v Forfar Ath | 2.1.1930 |
| | John Calder (Morton) 8 goals v Raith R | 18.4.1936 |
| **FA CUP** | Ted MacDougall (Bournemouth) 9 goals v Margate (*1st Round*) | 20.11.1971 |
| **SCOTTISH CUP** | John Petrie (Arbroath) 13 goals v Bon Accord (*1st Round*) | 5.9.1885 |

## MOST LEAGUE GOALS IN A SEASON

| FOOTBALL LEAGUE | | Goals | Games | Season |
|---|---|---|---|---|
| **Division 1** | Dixie Dean (Everton) | 60 | 39 | 1927–28 |
| **Division 2** | George Camsell (Middlesbrough) | 59 | 37 | 1926–27 |
| **Division 3(S)** | Joe Payne (Luton T) | 55 | 39 | 1936–37 |
| **Division 3(N)** | Ted Harston (Mansfield T) | 55 | 41 | 1936–37 |
| **Division 3** | Derek Reeves (Southampton) | 39 | 46 | 1959–60 |
| **Division 4** | Terry Bly (Peterborough U) | 52 | 46 | 1960–61 |
| **SCOTTISH LEAGUE** | | | | |
| **Division 1** | William McFadyen (Motherwell) | 52 | 34 | 1931–32 |
| **Division 2** | Jim Smith (Ayr) | 66 | 38 | 1927–28 |

## MOST LEAGUE GOALS IN A CAREER

| FOOTBALL LEAGUE | | Goals | Games | Season |
|---|---|---|---|---|
| **Arthur Rowley** | WBA | 4 | 24 | 1946–48 |
| | Fulham | 27 | 56 | 1948–50 |
| | Leicester C | 251 | 303 | 1950–58 |
| | Shrewsbury T | 152 | 236 | 1958–65 |
| | | —— | —— | |
| | | 434 | 619 | |
| | | —— | —— | |
| **SCOTTISH LEAGUE** | | | | |
| **Jimmy McGrory** | Celtic | 1 | 3 | 1922–23 |
| | Clydebank | 13 | 30 | 1923–24 |
| | Celtic | 396 | 375 | 1924–38 |
| | | —— | —— | |
| | | 410 | 408 | |
| | | —— | —— | |

## MOST GOALS IN AN INTERNATIONAL

| England | | |
|---|---|---|
| | Malcolm Macdonald (Newcastle U) 5 goals v Cyprus, at Wembley | 16.4.1975 |
| | Willie Hall (Tottenham H) 5 goals v Ireland, at Old Trafford | 16.11.1938 |
| | G. O. Smith (Corinthians) 5 goals v Ireland, at Sunderland | 18.2.1899 |
| | Steve Bloomer (Derby Co) 5 goals* v Wales, at Cardiff | 16.3.1896 |
| Scotland | Charles Heggie (Rangers) 5 goals v Ireland, at Belfast | 20.3.1886 |
| Ireland | Joe Bambrick (Linfield) 6 goals v Wales, at Belfast | 1.2.1930 |
| Wales | James Price (Wrexham) 4 goals v Ireland, at Wrexham | 25.2.1882 |
| | Mel Charles (Cardiff C) 4 goals v Ireland, at Cardiff | 11.4.1962 |
| | Ian Edwards (Chester) 4 goals v Malta, at Wrexham | 25.10.78 |

* There are conflicting reports which make it uncertain whether Bloomer scored four or five goals in this game.

## MOST GOALS IN AN INTERNATIONAL CAREER

| | | Goals | Games |
|---|---|---|---|
| England | Bobby Charlton (Manchester U) | 49 | 106 |
| Scotland | Denis Law (Huddersfield T, Manchester C, Torino, Manchester U) | 30 | 55 |
| Ireland | Billy Gillespie (Sheffield U) | 13 | 25 |
| Wales | Trevor Ford (Swansea T, Aston Villa, Sunderland, Cardiff C) | 23 | 38 |

## MOST CUP WINNERS' MEDALS

**FA CUP** – 5 medals each

James Forrest (Blackburn R) 1884, 1885, 1886, 1890, 1891
Hon. A. F. Kinnaird (Wanderers) 1873, 1877, 1878, (Old Etonians) 1879, 1882.
C. H. R. Wollaston (Wanderers) 1872, 1873, 1876, 1877, 1878.

**SCOTTISH CUP** – 7 medals each

Jimmy McMenemy (Celtic) 1904, 1907, 1908, 1911, 1912, 1914, (Partick T) 1921.
Bob McPhail (Airdieonians) 1924, (Rangers) 1928, 1930, 1932, 1934, 1935, 1936.
Billy McNeill (Celtic) 1965, 1967, 1969, 1971, 1972, 1974, 1975.

## RECORD ATTENDANCES

| Football League | 83,260 | Manchester U v Arsenal, Maine Road | 17.1.1948 |
|---|---|---|---|
| Scottish League | 118,567 | Rangers v Celtic, Ibrox Stadium | 2.1.1939 |
| FA Cup Final | 126,047* | Bolton W v West Ham U, Wembley | 28.4.1923 |
| European Cup | 135,826 | Celtic v Leeds U, semi-final at Hampden Park | 15.4.1970 |

* It has been estimated that as many as 70,000 more broke in without paying.

## OTHER RECORDS

The oldest player to appear in the Football League was Neil McBain who played in goal for New Brighton v Hartlepools U, Division 3(N), 15 March, 1947. He was then aged 52 years 4 months.

The oldest player to appear for any of the home countries in a full international was Billy Meredith, who was nearly 46 years of age when he played for Wales v England, 15 March, 1920.

The record for most appearances in the Football League during one season by a player over 40 years of age was created by Bob McGrory. In his last season as a player with Stoke C (1934–35) he appeared in all 42 First Division games. Bob was then 43 years of age.

The record for most consecutive appearances in the Football League was created by Harold Bell, Tranmere R centre-half. From the opening game of season 1946–47 Bell did not miss a single game until August 1955 – a run of 401 consecutive Division 3(N) matches. Including FA Cup, Liverpool Senior Cup and Cheshire Bowl games, Bell enjoyed a run of 459 consecutive first team appearances.

John Trollope created a club record by making 770 League appearances for Swindon T between 1960 and 1980. In the Scottish League the record for most appearances for a single club was created by Bob Ferrier with 626 for Motherwell between 1918 and 1937.

Billy Wright (Wolverhampton W) set up a world record by playing in 70 consecutive internationals for England, from 1951 to 1959.

Since substitutes were introduced into League football in 1965, Bristol C is the club that has played through the longest spell without calling upon one of these players – a run of 52 League games, 4 FA Cup, and 2 League Cup ties from February 1966 to April 1967.

The shortest player to appear in the Football League is outside-right Fred le May, who was only 5ft tall. He played for Thames 1930–31, Watford 1931–32, and Clapton Orient 1932–33. The tallest was Albert Iremonger, Notts Co and Lincoln C goalkeeper 1904–27. He was 6ft 5in tall.

The longest FA Cup tie was the 4th qualifying round match between Alvechurch and Oxford C in 1971. It needed 11 hours (six games) before Alvechurch won 1-0.

The longest single game on record is that between Stockport Co and Doncaster R, 30 March, 1946. In an effort to reach a decisive result, this Third Division (N) Cup tie continued for 203 minutes before bad light forced an abandonment.

Rochdale suffered 14 consecutive home defeats in Division 3(N) in 1931–32. This is a Football League record. After beating New Brighton 3-2 on 7 November, 1931, they did not get another home point until holding Barrow to a goalless draw in their second home game of season 1932–33. During that same period Rochdale suffered one run of 17 consecutive defeats (home and away) – also a Football League record.

In season 1904–05 Manchester U won 14 consecutive Division 2 games. This Football League record was equalled by Bristol C and Preston NE in Division 2 in 1905–06 and 1950–51 respectively.

The Scottish League record for the longest run of consecutive victories was created by Morton in Division 2 in 1963–64 when they won 23 games in a row.

Nottingham F were undefeated in a run of 42 First Division games, November 1977 to December 1978. This is a Football League record.

The longest run without defeat in a single season of Football League games is one of 30 matches by Burnley in Division 1 in 1920–21.

In the Scottish League, Celtic created a record by remaining undefeated in a run of 62 games – November 1915 to April 1917.

Blackburn Rovers hold the record for the longest run of consecutive FA Cup ties without defeat. From December 1883 to December 1886 they were unbeaten in 24 Cup ties and won the trophy three times during this period.

Only two players have scored two goals for each side in a Football League game. Sam Wynne did so in a Division 2 game, 6 October, 1923, scoring twice for Oldham Ath as well as putting two through his own goal for Manchester U. Chris Nicholl (Aston Villa) scored all the goals in a 2-2 draw with Leicester C, Division 1, 20 March, 1976.

Jimmy Cookson reached a first century of Football League goals in the shortest time. He made his début for Chesterfield in 1925 and reached his century in December 1927 with West Bromwich A his 87th Football League game.

The record number of goals scored by a player making his Football League début is five – by George Hilsdon for Chelsea v Glossop, Division 2, 1 September, 1906.

The record for scoring the fastest goal in a Football League game is claimed by Jim Fryatt. According to referee Mr R. J. Simon this player scored for Bradford v Tranmere R only 4 seconds after the kick-off, 25 April, 1964. Fastest own goal was in 6 seconds by Pat Kruse (Torquay U) for Cambridge U, 3 January, 1977.

The fastest goals scored in the FA Cup Final at Wembley were obtained in the first minute. In 1928 John Roscamp put Blackburn R ahead when he charged both the Huddersfield goalkeeper and the ball into the net, and in 1955 Jackie Milburn headed Newcastle U into a first-minute lead over Manchester C.

John McIntyre scored four goals in 5 minutes for Blackburn R v Everton, Division 1, 16 September, 1922.

W. G. Richardson also scored four goals in 5 minutes for WBA, Division 1, 7 November, 1931, but this was even more remarkable because the feat was achieved in an away game – against West Ham U.

The record number of penalties missed by one side in a Football League Division 1 game is three: by Fletcher (2) and Thornley for Manchester C against Newcastle U, 27 January, 1912.

The most penalties scored by a player in a First Division game is three – Billy Walker for Aston Villa v Bradford C, 12 November, 1921; Charlie Mitten for Manchester U v Aston Villa, 8 March, 1950; and Ken Barnes for Manchester C v Everton, 7 December, 1957.

The record number of players from the same club in an England team is seven: Frank Moss, George Male, Eddie Hapgood, Wilf Copping, Raymond Bowden, Ted Drake and Clifford Bastin, all of Arsenal, played against Italy at Highbury, 14 November, 1934.

The England team twice included all Corinthian players in the 1890s but this cannot be considered a record because the Corinthians were a combined eleven, most of their players also appearing with other clubs.

The England team that won the 1966 World Cup created a record for the country by remaining unchanged in six consecutive games – the quarter-final, semi-final and final of the World Cup and their next three games.

England's longest run without defeat is one of 20 games between 1889 and 1896.

The biggest Championship-winning margin for any division of the Football League is 15 points; by Middlesbrough in Division 2 in 1973–74.

The smallest number of players called upon by a club to complete a season of Football League games is 14. Liverpool did so when winning the Championship in 1965–66, and Aston Villa equalled it in 1980–81 when they too won the Championship.

In the Scottish League, Dundee called upon only 15 players throughout season 1961–62, when they won the Championship.

The goalscoring record for a goalkeeper in a single season of Football League games is five (all from penalties) in 1923–24 by Arnold Birch of Chesterfield in Division 3(N).

Five men have both played in and managed Football League Championship winning teams: Ted Drake, Arsenal, centre-forward, 1933–34, 1934–35, 1937–38, Chelsea, manager, 1954–55. Bill Nicholson, Tottenham H, right half-back, 1950–51, manager, 1960–61. Alf Ramsey, right-back, Tottenham H, 1950–51, Ipswich T, manager, 1961–62. Joe Mercer, left-half, Everton 1938–39, Arsenal, 1947–48, 1952–53, Manchester C, manager, 1967–68. Dave Mackay, left-half, Tottenham H, 1960–61, Derby Co, manager, 1974–75. Bob Paisley, Liverpool, left half-back, 1946–47, manager, 1975–76, 1976–77, 1978–79, 1979–80.

In 1973–74 Leeds U created a Football League record for the longest run without defeat from the start of a season – 29 First Division games before losing 2-3 at Stoke. It could be said that this only equalled Liverpool's run in the Second Division in 1893–94 when they were unbeaten in all 28 games. Their 29th game that season was the extra 'Test Match' to decide promotion and relegation between the First and Second Divisions.

The youngest player to appear in the Football League is Albert Geldard who was aged 15 years 156 days when making his début for Bradford against Millwall, Division 2, 16 September, 1929.

The youngest player in an FA Cup Final is Paul Allen, who was aged 17 years 256 days when West Ham U beat Arsenal 1-0, 10 May, 1980.

The highest number of players ordered off in the Football League in a single day is eight, 5 October, 1974. This figure also represents the record for the FA Cup competition. Eight players were ordered off in 1st round matches, 9 January, 1915.

# International Records

## HIGHEST SCORES

| | | | | | |
|---|---|---|---|---|---|
| **World Cup Match** | New Zealand | 13 | Fiji | 0 | 1981 |
| **Olympic Games** | Denmark | 17 | France | 1 | 1908 |
| | Germany | 16 | USSR | 0 | 1912 |
| **International Match** | Germany | 13 | Finland | 0 | 1940 |
| | Spain | 13 | Bulgaria | 0 | 1933 |
| **European Cup** | Feyenoord | 12 | Reykjavik | 2 | 1969 |
| **European Cup-Winners' Cup** | Sporting Lisbon | 16 | Apoel Nicosia | 1 | 1963 |
| **Fairs & UEFA Cups** | IFC Cologne | 13 | Union Luxembourg | 0 | 1965 |

## GOALSCORING RECORDS

| | | |
|---|---|---|
| **World Cup Final** | Geoff Hurst (England) 3 goals v West Germany | 1966 |
| **World Cup Final tournament** | Just Fontaine (France) 13 goals | 1958 |
| **Major European Cup game** | Lothar Emmerich (Borussia Dortmund) v Floriana in Cup-Winners' Cup – 6 goals | 1965 |
| **Career** | Arthur Friedenreich (Brazil) 1329 goals | 1910–30 |
| | Pelé (Brazil) 1281 goals | *1956–78 |
| | Franz 'Bimbo' Binder (Austria, Germany) 1006 goals | 1930–50 |

*Pelé has since scored two goals in Testimonial matches making his total 1283.*

## MISCELLANEOUS

Brazil set up a record for undefeated matches in the World Cup in the 1958 and 1962 finals, playing 13, winning 11, and drawing two. Their run ended when they lost 3-1 to Hungary in the 1966 World Cup.

Hungary went 13 years undefeated at home. After losing 7-2 to Sweden in 1943 they were unbeaten at home until they lost 4-2 to Czechoslovakia in 1956. The Hungarians also had a run of 29 games before losing: from their 5-3 defeat against Austria in May 1950 until they lost the World Cup final 3-2 to West Germany in July 1954.

Real Madrid were undefeated in League matches at home from February 1957, when they lost 3-2 to Atlético Madrid, until beaten again by Atlético 1-0 in March 1965. Between these defeats they won 114 matches and drew eight.

Ferenc Deak was one of the most prolific goalscorers in League football in the years immediately after the war. In 1945–46 he scored 66 goals for Szentlorinci AC in Hungary, 48 in 1946–47, and 59 in 1948–49 when with Ferencvaros.

Players who have won international caps for three different countries are Ladislav Kubala, capped for Hungary, Czechoslovakia, and Spain, and Alfredo Di Stefano for Argentina, Colombia, and Spain.

The Nordahl brothers, Knut, Bertil, and Gunnar, won Olympic gold medals with Sweden in 1948.

In 1955–56 Fiorentina went 33 Italian League matches without defeat.

In what is thought to be the longest match on record, Santos (Brazil) and Penarol (Uruguay) played 3½ hours from 2 August to 3 August after kicking off at 9.30 p.m. The match ended 3-3 after interruptions during play.

The first international played in Europe, other than between British teams, was Austria 5 Hungary 0 on 12 October, 1902. The first match in South America was a 1-1 draw between Argentina and Uruguay in 1905.

The first transfer fee approaching £1 million was £922,300 for Johan Cruyff from Ajax (Holland) to Barcelona (Spain) in 1973.

Diego Maradona was transferred from Argentinos Juniors to Barcelona for £4,235,000 in June 1982.

# Firsts in Football

**Football League**

The first five Football League games were played on 8 September, 1888. Bolton Wanderers were three goals up in about six minutes against Derby Co, but were eventually beaten 6-3. Cox of Aston Villa scored the first 'own goal', giving Wolverhampton W an early lead, but Villa recovered to draw 1-1.

Huddersfield T became the first team to complete a hat-trick of League Championships – 1924–25–26.

**FA Cup**

Tottenham H were the first Southern club to win the Cup when they beat Sheffield U in 1901. Spurs were then members of the Southern League and so were the first and only non-League club to carry off the trophy.

King George V was the first reigning monarch to attend a Cup Final. He saw Burnley beat Liverpool at the Crystal Palace in 1914.

David Jack (Bolton W) scored the first goal in a Wembley Cup Final. This was in 1923 when the crowd broke in to see the Wanderers beat West Ham U 2-0.

Extra time was first played in the Cup Final in 1877. Wanderers and Oxford University were drawing 1-1 at full-time; Wanderers won 2-1.

**Internationals and representative games**

The first representative game was played at Battersea Park, 31 March, 1866, London beating Sheffield by two goals and four touch-downs to nil.

The first official England v Scotland international was played at the West of Scotland Cricket Ground, Partick, 30 November, 1872, and resulted in a goalless draw.

Wales played their first international in 1876, losing 4-0 to Scotland in Glasgow.

Ireland's first international was against England at Bloomfield, Belfast, in 1882 when the visitors won 13-0.

Caps were first awarded for appearances in internationals in 1886.

The Football League played their first representative game in April 1891. It was against the Football Alliance at Sheffield and resulted in a 1-1 draw.

England's first defeat on foreign soil in a full international was 3-4 by Spain in Madrid in 1929.

England's first home defeat by a continental country was at Wembley in 1953 when Hungary won 6-3.

Scotland's first home defeat by a foreign team was at Hampden Park in 1950 when Austria won 1-0.

Billy Wright became the first international in Britain to gain 100 caps when he captained England against Scotland at Wembley in April 1959.

Terry Venables was the first player to win international honours for England at five levels – Schoolboy, Youth, Amateur, Under-23 and Full International. He gained his first full cap in October 1964.

### Floodlit football

The first-ever game by floodlight was between two Sheffield Association teams at Bramall Lane, 14 October, 1878.

The first FA Cup tie under floodlights was a replay between Kidderminster Harriers and Brierley Hill Alliance, 14 September, 1955.

Floodlights were first switched on during an international match in England in November 1955 at Wembley – England v Spain.

The first Football League game under floodlights was Portsmouth v Newcastle U at Fratton Park, 22 February, 1956.

The first full international played entirely under floodlights in Britain took place at Wembley in 1963 when England beat N Ireland 8-3.

### Hat-tricks

The first hat-trick in an FA Cup Final was scored by William Townley for Blackburn R v Sheffield Wednesday in 1890.

### Equipment, etc.

Shinguards were first introduced and registered by Sam Widdowson of Nottingham F in 1874. The cross-bar first replaced the tape in 1875, and the whistle was used by the referee for the first time in 1878. Goalnets were invented and patented by J. A. Brodie of Liverpool in 1890 and were first used in the FA Cup Final in 1892.

### Substitutes

First substitute in a Football League game was Keith Peacock of Charlton Ath, at Bolton, 21 August, 1965.

The first instance of a substitute in a Home International Championship game was at Wrexham in 1889 when Pugh of Rhostyllen took over from the injured S. G. Gillam in the Welsh goal against Scotland.

England's first substitute in a full international was Jimmy Mullen (Wolverhampton W) who took over from the injured Jackie Milburn after 10 minutes of the game against Belgium in Brussels, 18 May, 1950.

The first substitute to score in a Football League game was Bobby Knox (Barrow) v Wrexham, Division 4, 21 August, 1965.

### Transfers

The first four, five, six and seven-figure transfer fees between British clubs were as follows:

£1000 – Alf Common, Sunderland to Middlesbrough, 1905.
£10,890 – David Jack, Bolton W to Arsenal, 1928.
£110,000 – Alan Ball, Blackpool to Everton, 1966.
£1,000,000 – Trevor Francis, Birmingham C to Nottingham F, 1979.

### Radio and TV

The first match broadcast in England was the First Division game between Arsenal and Sheffield U at Highbury, 22 January, 1927.

The first Football League game to be televised was Blackpool v Bolton W, 10 September, 1960.

The first FA Cup tie to be televised – other than the final – was Charlton Ath v Blackburn R, 5th round, 8 February, 1947.

### Corner kick

Billy Smith was the first player to score direct from a corner kick in a Football League game – Huddersfield T v Arsenal, 11 October, 1924.

### Limited Company

The first football club to form itself into a limited liability company was Birmingham C in 1888. At that time they were known as Small Heath.

### Penalty kick

The first player to score from a penalty kick in a Football League match was Heath of Wolverhampton W v Accrington, Division 1, 14 September, 1891.

### Professional

The identity of the first professional footballer may never be definitely established, but it was probably J. J. Lang, a Scot who joined Sheffield Wednesday in 1876 after playing for Clydesdale and Glasgow Eastern.

### Tour

Oxford University were the first to send a football team on an overseas tour when in 1875 they visited Germany.

### Sunday football

The first Football League game to be played on a Sunday was between Millwall and Fulham on the morning of 20 January, 1974. Eleven other Football League games were played later the same day.

# UNIVERSITIES FOOTBALL 1981–82

## UAU CHAMPIONSHIP

**First XI Championship**
**Quarter-Finals**
Birmingham 4, Brunel 0
Bristol 2, Aberystwyth 1
Warwick 4, Loughborough 1
Liverpool 2, Kent 1 aet

**Semi-Finals**
Birmingham 0:2, Bristol 0:1
Liverpool 4, Warwick 2 aet

**Final**
*(at West Bromwich Albion FC)*
Liverpool 2, Birmingham 0

**Second XI Championship**
**Quarter-Finals**
Swansea 2, Bangor 0
Loughborough 2, Hull 1 aet
Newcastle 4, Bristol 0
Liverpool 1, Keele 0

**Semi-Finals**
Swansea 1, Loughborough 0
Newcastle 2, Liverpool 1

**Final**
*(at Keele University)*
Swansea 1, Newcastle 0

**Third XI Championship**
**Quarter-Finals**
Swansea 2, Sheffield 1
Manchester 2, Loughborough 0
Nottingham 4, Exeter 1
Reading 1, Aston 1
*(Reading won 6-5 on pens)*

**Semi-Finals**
Manchester 3:3, Swansea 3:0
Nottingham 2, Reading 0

**Final**
*(at Keele University)*
Manchester 2, Nottingham 1

## BRITISH UNIVERSITIES TOURNAMENT
*At UCNW (Bangor)*

**Pool A**
Scotland 3, Northern Ireland 1
Scotland 1, Wales 1
Scotland 1, UAU II 1
Wales 1, Northern Ireland 0
UAU II 3, Northern Ireland 0
Wales 3, UAU II 1

**Pool B**
UAU I 2, Cambridge 1
Cambridge 2, Oxford 1
Cambridge 4, London 0
UAU I 3, Oxford 0
UAU I 4, London 0
Oxford 3, London 2

**Final**
UAU I 2, Wales 1 aet

**Third Place Match**
Scotland 1 Cambridge 0

**Fifth Place Match**
Oxford 4, UAU II 2 aet

**Seventh Place Match**
London 2, Northern Ireland 1

## REPRESENTATIVE FIXTURES

English Universities 1, Welsh Universities 0
UAU 3, British Colleges 0
UAU 2, British Polytechnics 3
UAU 0, FA XI 3
UAU 2, Dutch Universities 2

## UNIVERSITY MATCH

*(at Wembley, 9 December, 1981)*
Oxford 2, Cambridge 0

# YOUTH FOOTBALL 1981-82

## FA YOUTH CHALLENGE CUP 1981-82

**Preliminary Round**

| | |
|---|---|
| Stockton v York City | |
| *York City received w.o.* | |
| Guisborough Town v Darlington | 0-3 |
| Formby v Marine | 3-1 |
| Preston North End v Barrow | 1-0 |
| Chadderton v Chorley | 0-6 |
| Wigan Athletic v Crewe Alexandra | 1-0 |
| Irlam Town v Bury | 0-5 |
| Chesterfield v Spalding United | 8-0 |
| Boston w.o.; Louth United withdrew | |
| Hednesford Town v Corby Town | 0-1 |
| Enderby Town v Stamford | 2-1 |
| Desborough Town v Paget Rangers | 0-4 |
| Alvechurch v Tamworth | 2-0 |
| Banbury United v Milton Keynes City | 0-0 |
| Wellingborough Town v Kettering Town | 4-2 |
| Ely Crusaders v Sawston Enterprises | 4-1 |
| Colchester United v Harwich & Parkeston | 5-1 |
| Baldock Town v The '61' | 1-2 |
| Royston Town v Cambridge City | 7-0 |
| Loughton BC v Letchworth Garden City | 3-1 |
| Hendon v Hillingdon Borough | 3-2 |
| Haringey Borough v Ford United | 1-0 |
| Molesey v Southall | 2-1 |
| Croydon v Brentford | 2-1 |
| Harpenden Town v Enfield Rolenmil | |
| *Enfield Rolenmil received w.o.* | |
| Stevenage Youth v Stotfold | 2-1 |
| Welwyn Garden v Chalfont St Peter | |
| *Welwyn Garden received w.o.* | |
| Faversham Town v Greenwich Borough | 0-4 |
| Maidstone United v Ashford Town | 3-2 |
| Camberley Town v Hampton | 3-5 |
| Walton & Hersham v Ringmer | 7-0 |
| Burgess Hill Town v Windsor & Eton | |
| *Windsor & Eton received w.o.* | |
| Horley Town v Fleet Town | 6-2 |
| Waterlooville v Aldershot | 0-1 |
| Bognor Regis Town v Gosport Borough | 2-2 |
| Abingdon United v Wokingham Town | 3-2 |
| Chesham United v Oxford City | 1-2 |
| AFC Bournemouth v Melksham Town | 6-0 |
| Trowbridge Town v Dorchester Town | 3-1 |

**Preliminary Round – Replays**

| | |
|---|---|
| Milton Keynes City v Banbury United | 1-2 |
| Gosport Borough v Bognor Regis Town | 3-2 |

**First Round Qualifying**

| | |
|---|---|
| Consett v Darlington | 1-7 |
| York City v Bradford City | 2-1 |
| Chorley v Preston North End | 2-2 |
| Formby v Halifax Town | 2-0 |
| Southport v Bury | 1-2 |
| Wigan Athletic v Rhyl | 5-0 |
| Scunthorpe United v Boston | 1-1 |
| Chesterfield v Syston Juniors | 2-0 |
| Mansfield Town v Enderby Town | 1-0 |
| Corby Town v Bedworth United | 4-0 |
| Oldbury United v Alvechurch | 1-3 |
| Paget Rangers v Northampton Town | 1-2 |
| Coventry Sporting v Wellingborough Town | 3-0 |
| Banbury United v Cambridge United | 0-1 |
| Gorleston v Colchester United | 3-1 |
| Ely Crusaders v Harlow Town | 2-3 |
| Loughton BC v Royston Town | 3-0 |
| The '61' v Tring Town | 1-1 |
| Enfield v Haringey Borough | 2-3 |
| Hendon v Feltham | 2-0 |
| Maidenhead United v Croydon | 2-0 |
| Molesey v Addlestone & Weybridge Town | 1-1 |
| Welwyn Garden v Stevenage Youth | 1-4 |
| Enfield Rolenmil v Edgware | 5-0 |
| Folkestone v Maidstone United | 2-5 |
| Greenwich Borough v Bromley | 0-1 |

| | |
|---|---|
| Worthing v Walton & Hersham | 2-4 |
| *(Match awarded to Worthing; Walton &* | |
| *Hersham played ineligible players)* | |
| Hampton v Sutton United | 2-2 |
| Fareham Town v Horley Town | |
| *Horley Town received w.o.* | |
| Windsor & Eton v Leatherhead | 2-1 |
| Bournemouth v Gosport Borough | 1-2 |
| Aldershot v Woking | 2-3 |
| Gloucester City v Oxford City | 0-2 |
| Abingdon United v Burnham | 3-1 |
| Exeter City v Trowbridge Town | 6-1 |
| AFC Bournemouth v Swindon Town | 1-0 |

**First Round Qualifying – Replays**

| | |
|---|---|
| Preston North End v Chorley | 7-1 |
| Boston v Scunthorpe United | 0-5 |
| Tring Town v The '61' | 1-0 |
| Addlestone & Weybridge Town v Molesey | 0-1 |
| Sutton United v Hampton | 3-1 |

**Second Round Qualifying**

| | |
|---|---|
| Darlington v York City | 1-3 |
| Preston North End v Formby | 1-3 |
| Bury v Wigan Athletic | 3-2 |
| Scunthorpe United v Chesterfield | 1-5 |
| Mansfield Town v Corby Town | 3-2 |
| Alvechurch v Northampton Town | 5-0 |
| Coventry Sporting v Cambridge United | 1-8 |
| Gorleston v Harlow Town | 1-0 |
| Loughton BC v Tring Town | 3-0 |
| Haringey Borough v Hendon | 1-1 |
| Maidenhead United v Molesey | 4-3 |
| Stevenage Youth v Enfield Rolenmil | 2-3 |
| Maidstone United v Bromley | 3-3 |
| Worthing v Sutton United | 4-4 |
| Horley Town v Windsor & Eton | 3-4 |
| Gosport Borough v Woking | 4-4 |
| Oxford City v Abingdon United | 3-1 |
| Exeter City v AFC Bournemouth | 3-4 |

**Second Round Qualifying – Replays**

| | |
|---|---|
| Hendon v Haringey Borough | 1-2 |
| Bromley v Maidstone United | 1-3 |
| Sutton United v Worthing | 7-2 |
| Woking v Gosport Borough | 4-1 |

**First Round**

| | |
|---|---|
| York City v Barnsley | 0-5 |
| Grimsby Town v Hull City | 1-2 |
| Huddersfield Town v Rotherham United | 1-2 |
| Burnley v Hartlepool United | 1-0 |
| Blackburn Rovers v Doncaster Rovers | 1-2 |
| Formby v Yorkshire Amateur | 1-1 |
| Bury v Notts County | 6-1 |
| Oldswinford v Oldham Athletic | 2-5 |
| Tranmere Rovers v Shrewsbury Town | 2-4 |
| Liverpool v Wrexham | 4-1 |
| Wolverhampton Wanderers v Mansfield Town | 3-0 |
| Alvechurch v Nottingham Forest | 0-3 |
| Coventry City v Sutton Coldfield Town | 8-0 |
| Sheffield United v Port Vale | 0-1 |
| Chesterfield v Birmingham City | 0-6 |
| Walsall v Nuneaton Borough | 1-0 |
| Norwich City v Orient | 1-1 |
| Southend United v Cambridge United | 2-4 |
| Queen's Park Rangers v Barking | 2-0 |
| Loughton BC v Gorleston | 4-1 |
| Haringey Borough v St Albans City | 1-1 |
| Aylesbury United v Enfield Rolenmil | 1-2 |
| Dover v Redhill | 0-2 |
| Wimbledon v Maidenhead United | 2-1 |
| Maidstone United v Woking | 6-3 |
| Windsor & Eton v Reading | 4-0 |

| | |
|---|---|
| Gillingham v Dartford | 3-0 |
| Oxford City v Fulham | 0-3 |
| Brighton & Hove Albion v Sutton United | 2-1 |
| Welling United v Portsmouth | 1-1 |
| Plymouth Argyle v Torquay United | 3-1 |
| Newport County v Oxford United | 2-5 |
| AFC Bournemouth v Cardiff City | 2-3 |
| Swansea City v Bristol Rovers | 1-1 |

**First Round – Replays**

| | |
|---|---|
| Yorkshire Amateur v Formby | aet 1-3 |
| Orient v Norwich City | 4-0 |
| St Albans City v Haringey Borough | 2-3 |
| Portsmouth v Welling United | 3-0 |
| Bristol Rovers v Swansea City | 3-1 |

**Second Round**

| | |
|---|---|
| Bolton Wanderers v Leeds United | 1-1 |
| Blackpool v Burnley | 0-1 |
| Hull City v Sunderland | 0-1 |
| Doncaster Rovers v Newcastle United | 1-1 |
| Formby v Bury | 0-2 |
| Barnsley v Middlesbrough | 2-2 |
| Sheffield Wednesday v West Bromwich Albion | 4-3 |
| Stoke City v Derby County | 2-0 |
| Aston·Villa v Nottingham Forest | 2-2 |
| Oldham Athletic v Coventry City | 0-4 |
| Manchester City v Everton | 0-1 |
| Port Vale v Chester | 0-0 |
| Rotherham United v Liverpool | 2-3 |
| Shrewsbury Town v Leicester City | 0-0 |
| Walsall v Manchester United | 1-3 |
| Hereford United v Birmingham City | 0-4 |
| Lincoln City v Wolverhampton Wanderers | 0-3 |
| Enfield Rolenmil v Millwall | 0-4 |
| Queen's Park Rangers v Windsor & Eton | 4-2 |
| Cambridge United v Brighton & Hove Albion | 2-0 |
| Charlton Athletic v Luton Town | 2-0 |
| Fulham v Ipswich Town | 2-0 |
| Loughton BC v Redhill | 1-0 |
| Arsenal v Gillingham | 3-0 |
| West Ham United v Orient | 4-0 |
| Watford v Oxford United | 2-0 |
| Crystal Palace v Chelsea | 0-1 |
| Wimbledon v Tottenham Hotspur | 1-4 |
| Haringey Borough v Maidstone United | 4-3 |
| Bristol Rovers v Southampton | 1-3 |
| Cardiff City v Plymouth Argyle | 3-1 |
| Portsmouth v Bristol City | 1-0 |

**Second Round – Replays**

| | |
|---|---|
| Leeds United v Bolton Wanderers | aet 2-0 |
| Newcastle United v Doncaster Rovers | 2-0 |
| Middlesbrough v Barnsley | 2-0 |
| Nottingham Forest v Aston Villa | 2-4 |
| Chester v Port Vale | 2-0 |
| Leicester City v Shrewsbury Town | 4-1 |

**Third Round**

| | |
|---|---|
| Sunderland v Chester | 1-1 |
| Leicester City v Middlesbrough | 0-3 |
| Coventry City v Burnley | 0-0 |

| | |
|---|---|
| Stoke City v Wolverhampton Wanderers | 1-1 |
| Bury v Sheffield Wednesday | 2-0 |
| Everton v Aston Villa | 0-2 |
| Newcastle United v Leeds United | 2-2 |
| Manchester United v Liverpool | 0-0 |
| Haringey Borough v Charlton Athletic | 0-3 |
| Queen's Park Rangers v Portsmouth | 10-0 |
| Tottenham Hotspur v Fulham | 1-1 |
| Birmingham City v West Ham United | 2-1 |
| Loughton BC v Watford | 0-4 |
| Cambridge United v Millwall | 3-1 |
| Chelsea v Cardiff City | 1-1 |
| Arsenal v Southampton | 0-1 |

**Third Round – Replays**

| | |
|---|---|
| Chester v Sunderland | 0-1 |
| Burnley v Coventry City | 2-1 |
| Wolverhampton Wanderers v Stoke City | 4-1 |
| Leeds United v Newcastle United | 3-2 |
| Liverpool v Manchester United | 0-1 |
| Fulham v Tottenham Hotspur | 1-2 |
| Cardiff City v Chelsea | 2-0 |

**Fourth Round**

| | |
|---|---|
| Queen's Park Rangers v Burnley | 3-0 |
| Birmingham City v Cambridge United | 3-0 |
| Tottenham Hotspur v Sunderland | 0-0 |
| Wolverhampton Wanderers v Charlton Athletic | 1-0 |
| Bury v Middlesbrough | 4-7 |
| Watford v Southampton | 3-0 |
| Leeds United v Manchester United | 0-0 |
| Aston Villa v Cardiff City | 3-3 |

**Fourth Round Replays**

| | |
|---|---|
| Sunderland v Tottenham Hotspur | 1-0 |
| Manchester United v Leeds United | 1-0 |
| Cardiff City v Aston Villa | 2-5 |

**Fifth Round**

| | |
|---|---|
| Birmingham City v Manchester United | 0-0, 0-2 |
| Aston Villa v Sunderland | 1-2 |
| Queen's Park Rangers v Wolverhampton Wanderers | 3-3, 1-2 |
| Watford v Middlesbrough | 5-0 |

**Semi-Finals – First Leg**

| | |
|---|---|
| Watford v Wolverhampton Wanderers | 2-1 |
| Manchester United v Sunderland | 1-0 |

**Semi-Finals – Second Leg**

| | |
|---|---|
| Wolverhampton Wanderers v Watford | 1-5 |
| Sunderland v Manchester United | 1-2 |

**Final – First Leg**

| | |
|---|---|
| Manchester United v Watford | 2-3 |

**Final – Second Leg**

| | |
|---|---|
| Watford v Manchester United | aet 4-4 |

*Watford won 7-6 on aggregate.*

# FA COUNTY YOUTH CUP 1981–82

**First Round**

| | |
|---|---|
| Northumberland v North Riding | aet 2-4 |
| Westmorland v Manchester | 0-2 |
| Liverpool v Derbyshire | 0-1 |
| Sheffield & Hallam v Leicestershire & Rutland | 4-0 |
| Staffordshire v Northamptonshire | 5-5 |
| Suffolk v Cambridgeshire | 2-1 |
| Huntingdonshire v RAF | 6-2 |
| Bedfordshire v Army | 0-3 |
| Hertfordshire v Oxfordshire | 6-0 |
| Kent v Sussex | 4-2 |
| Hampshire v Devon | 0-2 |
| Berks & Bucks v Herefordshire | 0-2 |

| | |
|---|---|
| Shropshire v Gloucestershire | 0-2 |
| Dorset v Cornwall | 4-0 |

**First Round – Replay**

| | |
|---|---|
| Northamptonshire v Staffordshire | 4-1 |

**Second Round**

| | |
|---|---|
| Cumberland v North Riding | 0-2 |
| Lancashire v Durham | aet 3-4 |
| West Riding v Manchester | 4-3 |
| Lincolnshire v East Riding | 1-2 |

| | |
|---|---|
| Cheshire v Derbyshire | 1-1 |
| Nottinghamshire v Sheffield & Hallam | 1-0 |
| Birmingham v Northamptonshire | 6-3 |
| Norfolk v Suffolk | 5-1 |
| Essex v Huntingdonshire | 2-9 |
| Middlesex v Army | 3-2 |
| London v Hertfordshire | 0-2 |
| Surrey v Kent | 3-3 |
| Royal Navy v Devon | 0-1 |
| Wiltshire v Herefordshire | 1-0 |
| Worcestershire v Gloucestershire | 0-4 |
| Somerset & Avon (South) v Dorset | 4-0 |

**Second Round – Replays**

| | |
|---|---|
| Derbyshire v Cheshire | 3-4 |
| Kent v Surrey | 3-2 |

**Third Round**

| | |
|---|---|
| North Riding v Durham | aet 3-1 |
| West Riding v East Riding | 1-0 |
| Cheshire v Nottinghamshire | 3-0 |
| Birmingham v Huntingdonshire | 4-4 |
| Norfolk v Hertfordshire | 1-4 |

| | |
|---|---|
| Middlesex v Kent | 1-3 |
| Devon v Somerset & Avon (South) | 2-1 |
| Wiltshire v Gloucestershire | aet 3-1 |

**Third Round – Replay**

| | |
|---|---|
| Huntingdonshire v Birmingham | 3-1 |

**Fourth Round**

| | |
|---|---|
| Cheshire v North Riding | 6-1 |
| Huntingdonshire v West Riding | 5-2 |
| Devon v Wiltshire | 3-0 |
| Kent v Hertfordshire | 3-1 |

**Semi-Finals**

| | |
|---|---|
| Devon v Cheshire (at Tiverton) | 3-1 |
| Kent v Huntingdonshire (at Maidstone) | 4-1 |

**Final**

| | |
|---|---|
| Kent v Devon | 0-0, 2-3 |

# ENGLAND YOUTH INTERNATIONAL MATCHES 1947–82

*Professionals. † Abandoned. UYT UEFA Youth Tournament. WYT World Youth Tournament.*

### v SCOTLAND

| | | | E | S |
|---|---|---|---|---|
| 1947 | 25 Oct | Doncaster | 4 | 2 |
| 1948 | 30 Oct | Aberdeen | 1 | 3 |
| UYT1949 | 21 Apr | Utrecht | 0 | 1 |
| 1950 | 4 Feb | Carlisle | 7 | 1 |
| 1951 | 3 Feb | Kilmarnock | 6 | 1 |
| 1952 | 15 Mar | Sunderland | 3 | 1 |
| 1953 | 7 Feb | Glasgow | 4 | 3 |
| 1954 | 6 Feb | Middlesbrough | 2 | 1 |
| 1955 | 5 Mar | Kilmarnock | 3 | 4 |
| 1956 | 3 Mar | Preston | 2 | 2 |
| 1957 | 9 Mar | Aberdeen | 3 | 1 |
| 1958 | 1 Mar | Hull | 2 | 0 |
| 1959 | 28 Feb | Aberdeen | 1 | 1 |
| 1960 | 27 Feb | Newcastle | 1 | 1 |
| 1961 | 25 Feb | Elgin | 3 | 2 |
| 1962 | 24 Feb | Peterborough | 4 | 2 |
| *UYT1963 | 19 Apr | White City | 1 | 0 |
| 1963 | 18 May | Dumfries | 3 | 1 |
| 1964 | 22 Feb | Middlesbrough | 1 | 1 |
| 1965 | 27 Feb | Inverness | 1 | 2 |
| 1966 | 5 Feb | Hereford | 5 | 3 |
| 1967 | 4 Feb | Aberdeen | 0 | 1 |
| *UYT1967 | 1 Mar | Southampton | 1 | 0 |
| *UYT1967 | 15 Mar | Dundee | 0 | 0 |
| 1968 | 3 Feb | Walsall | 0 | 5 |
| 1969 | 1 Feb | Stranraer | 1 | 1 |
| 1970 | 31 Jan | Derby | 1 | 2 |
| 1971 | 30 Jan | Greenock | 1 | 2 |
| 1972 | 30 Jan | Bournemouth | 2 | 0 |
| 1973 | 20 Jan | Kilmarnock | 3 | 2 |
| 1974 | 26 Jan | Brighton | 2 | 2 |
| *UYT1981 | 27 May | Aachen | 0 | 1 |
| *UYT1982 | 23 Feb | Glasgow | 0 | 1 |
| *UYT1982 | 23 Mar | Coventry | 2 | 2 |

### v WALES

| | | | E | W |
|---|---|---|---|---|
| 1948 | 28 Feb | High Wycombe | 4 | 2 |
| UYT1948 | 15 Apr | Shepherds Bush | 4 | 0 |
| 1949 | 26 Feb | Swansea | 0 | 0 |

| | | | | |
|---|---|---|---|---|
| 1950 | 25 Feb | Worcester | 1 | 0 |
| 1951 | 17 Feb | Wrexham | 1 | 1 |
| 1952 | 23 Feb | Plymouth | 6 | 0 |
| 1953 | 21 Feb | Swansea | 4 | 2 |
| 1954 | 20 Feb | Derby | 2 | 1 |
| 1955 | 19 Feb | Milford Haven | 7 | 2 |
| 1956 | 18 Feb | Shrewsbury | 5 | 1 |
| 1957 | 9 Feb | Cardiff | 7 | 1 |
| 1958 | 15 Feb | Reading | 8 | 2 |
| 1959 | 14 Feb | Portmadoc | 3 | 0 |
| 1960 | 19 Mar | Canterbury | 1 | 1 |
| 1961 | 18 Mar | Newtown | 4 | 0 |
| 1962 | 17 Mar | Swindon | 4 | 0 |
| 1963 | 16 Mar | Haverfordwest | 1 | 0 |
| 1964 | 15 Mar | Leeds | 2 | 1 |
| 1965 | 20 Mar | Newport | 2 | 2 |
| 1966 | 19 Mar | Northampton | 4 | 1 |
| 1967 | 18 Mar | Cwmbran | 3 | 3 |
| 1968 | 16 Mar | Watford | 2 | 3 |
| 1969 | 15 Mar | Haverfordwest | 3 | 1 |
| *UYT1970 | 25 Feb | Newport | 0 | 0 |
| *UYT1970 | 18 Mar | Leyton | 1 | 2 |
| 1970 | 20 Apr | Reading | 0 | 0 |
| 1971 | 20 Feb | Aberystwyth | 1 | 2 |
| 1972 | 19 Feb | Swindon | 4 | 0 |
| 1973 | 24 Feb | Portmadoc | 4 | 1 |
| *UYT1974 | 9 Jan | West Bromwich | 1 | 0 |
| 1974 | 2 Mar | Shrewsbury | 2 | 1 |
| *UYT1974 | 13 Mar | Cardiff | 0 | 1 |
| *UYT1976 | 11 Feb | Cardiff | 1 | 0 |
| *UYT1976 | 3 Mar | Maine Rd | 2 | 3 |
| *UYT1977 | 9 Mar | West Bromwich | 1 | 0 |
| *UYT1977 | 23 Mar | Cardiff | 1 | 1 |

### v NORTHERN IRELAND

| | | | E | NI |
|---|---|---|---|---|
| 1948 | 15 May | Belfast | 2 | 2 |
| UYT1949 | 18 Apr | Haarlem | 3 | 3 |
| 1949 | 14 May | Hull | 4 | 2 |
| 1950 | 6 May | Belfast | 0 | 1 |
| 1951 | 5 May | Liverpool | 5 | 2 |
| 1952 | 19 Apr | Belfast | 0 | 2 |

| | | | | |
|---|---|---|---|---|
| 1953 | 11 Apr | Wolverhampton | 0 | 0 |
| UYT1954 | 10 Apr | Bruehl | 5 | 0 |
| 1954 | 8 May | Newtownards | 2 | 2 |
| 1955 | 14 May | Watford | 3 | 0 |
| 1956 | 12 May | Belfast | 0 | 1 |
| 1957 | 11 May | Leyton | 6 | 2 |
| 1958 | 10 May | Bangor | 2 | 4 |
| 1959 | 9 May | Liverpool | 5 | 0 |
| 1960 | 14 May | Portadown | 5 | 2 |
| 1961 | 13 May | Manchester | 2 | 0 |
| 1962 | 12 May | Londonderry | 1 | 2 |
| *UYT1963 | 23 Apr | Wembley | 4 | 0 |
| 1963 | 11 May | Oldham | 1 | 1 |
| 1964 | 25 Jan | Belfast | 3 | 1 |
| 1965 | 22 Jan | Birkenhead | 2 | 3 |
| 1966 | 26 Feb | Belfast | 4 | 0 |
| 1967 | 25 Feb | Stockport | 3 | 0 |
| 1968 | 23 Feb | Belfast | 0 | 2 |
| 1969 | 28 Feb | Birkenhead | 0 | 2 |
| 1970 | 28 Feb | Lurgan | 1 | 3 |
| 1971 | 6 Mar | Blackpool | 1 | 1 |
| 1972 | 11 Mar | Chester | 1 | 1 |
| *UYT1972 | 17 May | Sabadell | 4 | 0 |
| 1973 | 24 Mar | Telford | 3 | 0 |
| 1974 | 19 Apr | Birkenhead | 1 | 2 |
| *UYT1975 | 13 May | Kriens | 3 | 0 |
| *UYT1980 | 16 May | Arnstadt | 1 | 0 |

### v ARGENTINA

| | | | E | A |
|---|---|---|---|---|
| *WYT1981 | 5 Oct | Sydney | 1 | 1 |

### v AUSTRIA

| | | | E | A |
|---|---|---|---|---|
| UYT1949 | 19 Apr | Zeist | 4 | 2 |
| UYT1952 | 17 Apr | Barcelona | 5 | 5 |
| UYT1957 | 16 Apr | Barcelona | 0 | 3 |
| 1958 | 4 Mar | Highbury | 3 | 2 |
| 1958 | 1 June | Graz | 4 | 3 |
| UYT1960 | 20 Apr | Vienna | 0 | 1 |
| *UYT1964 | 1 Apr | Rotterdam | 2 | 1 |
| 1980 | 6 Sept | Pazin | 0 | 1 |
| *UYT1981 | 29 May | Bonn | 7 | 0 |
| 1981 | 3 Sept | Umag | 3 | 0 |

### v AUSTRALIA

| | | | E | A |
|---|---|---|---|---|
| *WYT1981 | 8 Oct | Sydney | 1 | 1 |

### v BELGIUM

| | | | E | B |
|---|---|---|---|---|
| UYT1948 | 16 Apr | West Ham | 3 | 1 |
| UYT1951 | 22 Mar | Cannes | 1 | 1 |
| UYT1953 | 31 Mar | Brussels | 2 | 0 |
| †1956 | 7 Nov | Brussels | 3 | 2 |
| 1957 | 13 Nov | Sheffield | 2 | 0 |
| *UYT1965 | 15 Apr | Ludwigshafen | 3 | 0 |
| *UYT1969 | 11 Mar | West Ham | 1 | 0 |
| *UYT1969 | 26 Mar | Waregem | 2 | 0 |
| UYT1972 | 13 May | Palma | 0 | 0 |
| UYT1973 | 4 June | Viareggio | 0 | 0 |
| *UYT1973 | 19 May | Lokeren | 1 | 0 |
| 1979 | 17 Jan | Brussels | 4 | 0 |
| 1980 | 8 Sept | Labia | 6 | 1 |

### v BULGARIA

| | | | E | B |
|---|---|---|---|---|
| UYT1956 | 28 Mar | Salgotarjan | 1 | 2 |
| UYT1960 | 16 Apr | Graz | 0 | 1 |

| | | | | |
|---|---|---|---|---|
| UYT1962 | 24 Apr | Ploesti | 0 | 0 |
| *UYT1968 | 7 Apr | Nimes | 0 | 0 |
| *UYT1979 | 31 May | Vienna | 0 | 1 |

### v CAMEROON

| | | | E | C |
|---|---|---|---|---|
| *WYT1981 | 3 Oct | Sydney | 2 | 0 |

### v CZECHOSLOVAKIA

| | | | E | C |
|---|---|---|---|---|
| UYT1955 | 7 Apr | Lucca | 0 | 1 |
| *UYT1966 | 21 May | Rijeka | 2 | 3 |
| *UYT1969 | 20 May | Leipzig | 3 | 1 |
| *UYT1979 | 24 May | Bischofshofen | 3 | 0 |
| 1979 | 8 Sept | Pula | 1 | 2 |
| 1982 | 11 Apr | Cannes | 0 | 1 |

### v DENMARK

| | | | E | D |
|---|---|---|---|---|
| *1955 | 1 Oct | Plymouth | 9 | 2 |
| 1956 | 20 May | Esbjerg | 2 | 1 |
| *UYT1979 | 31 Oct | Esbjerg | 3 | 1 |
| *UYT1980 | 26 Mar | Coventry | 4 | 0 |

### v EGYPT

| | | | E | Eg |
|---|---|---|---|---|
| *WYT1981 | 11 Oct | Sydney | 4 | 2 |

### v FINLAND

| | | | E | F |
|---|---|---|---|---|
| *UYT1975 | 19 May | Berne | 1 | 1 |

### v FRANCE

| | | | E | F |
|---|---|---|---|---|
| 1957 | 24 Mar | Fontainebleau | 1 | 0 |
| 1958 | 22 Mar | Eastbourne | 0 | 1 |
| *UYT1966 | 23 May | Rijeka | 1 | 2 |
| *UYT1967 | 11 May | Istanbul | 2 | 0 |
| *1968 | 25 Jan | Paris | 0 | 1 |
| *UYT1978 | 8 Feb | Selhurst Park | 3 | 1 |
| *UYT1978 | 1 Mar | Paris | 0 | 0 |
| *UYT1979 | 2 June | Vienna | 0 | 0 |
| 1982 | 12 Apr | Cannes | 0 | 1 |

### v EAST GERMANY

| | | | E | EG |
|---|---|---|---|---|
| UYT1958 | 7 Apr | Neunkirchen | 1 | 0 |
| 1959 | 8 Mar | Zwickau | 3 | 4 |
| 1960 | 2 Apr | Portsmouth | 1 | 1 |
| *UYT1965 | 25 Apr | Essen | 2 | 3 |
| *UYT1969 | 22 May | Magdeburg | 0 | 4 |
| *UYT1973 | 10 June | Florence | 3 | 2 |

### v WEST GERMANY

| | | | E | WG |
|---|---|---|---|---|
| UYT1953 | 4 Apr | Boom | 3 | 1 |
| UYT1954 | 15 Apr | Gelsenkirchen | 2 | 2 |
| UYT1956 | 1 Apr | Sztalinvaros | 2 | 1 |
| 1957 | 31 Mar | Oberhausen | 4 | 1 |
| 1958 | 12 Mar | Bolton | 1 | 2 |
| 1961 | 12 Mar | Flensberg | 0 | 2 |
| *1962 | 31 Mar | Northampton | 1 | 0 |
| *1967 | 14 Feb | Moenchenglad-bach | 1 | 0 |
| UYT1972 | 22 May | Barcelona | 2 | 0 |
| 1975 | 25 Jan | Las Palmas | 4 | 2 |

| 1976 | 14 Nov | Monte Carlo | 1 | 1 |
| *UYT1979 | 28 May | Salzburg | 2 | 0 |
| 1979 | 1 Sept | Pula | 1 | 1 |

### v GREECE

| | | | E | G |
|---|---|---|---|---|
| UYT1957 | 18 Apr | Barcelona | 2 | 3 |
| UYT1959 | 2 Apr | Dimitrovo | 4 | 0 |
| UYT1977 | 23 May | Beveren | 1 | 1 |

### v HUNGARY

| | | | E | H |
|---|---|---|---|---|
| UYT1954 | 11 Apr | Dusseldorf | 1 | 3 |
| UYT1956 | 31 Mar | Tatabanya | 2 | 4 |
| *1956 | 23 Oct | Tottenham | 2 | 1 |
| *1956 | 25 Oct | Sunderland | 2 | 1 |
| *UYT1965 | 21 Apr | Wuppertal | 5 | 0 |
| *UYT1975 | 16 May | Olten | 3 | 1 |
| *UYT1977 | 10 Oct | Las Palmas | 3 | 0 |
| 1979 | 5 Sept | Pula | 2 | 0 |
| 1980 | 11 Sept | Pula | 1 | 2 |
| 1981 | 7 Sept | Porec | 4 | 0 |

### v ICELAND

| | | | E | I |
|---|---|---|---|---|
| *UYT1973 | 31 May | Viareggio | 2 | 0 |
| *UYT1977 | 21 May | Turnhout | 0 | 0 |

### v REPUBLIC OF IRELAND

| | | | E | RI |
|---|---|---|---|---|
| UYT1953 | 5 Apr | Leuven | 2 | 0 |
| *UYT1964 | 30 Mar | Middleburg | 6 | 0 |
| *UYT1968 | 7 Feb | Dublin | 0 | 0 |
| *UYT1968 | 28 Feb | Portsmouth | 4 | 1 |
| *UYT1970 | 14 Jan | Dublin | 4 | 1 |
| *UYT1970 | 4 Feb | Luton | 10 | 0 |
| *UYT1975 | 9 May | Brunnen | 1 | 0 |
| *UYT1981 | 11 Feb | Walsall | 1 | 0 |
| *UYT1981 | 11 Mar | Belfast | 3 | 0 |

### v ISRAEL

| | | | E | I |
|---|---|---|---|---|
| *1962 | 20 May | Tel Aviv | 3 | 1 |
| *1962 | 22 May | Haifa | 1 | 2 |

### v ITALY

| | | | E | I |
|---|---|---|---|---|
| UYT1958 | 13 Apr | Luxembourg | 0 | 1 |
| UYT1959 | 25 Mar | Sofia | 0 | 3 |
| UYT1961 | 4 Apr | Braga | 2 | 3 |
| *UYT1965 | 23 Apr | Marl-Huels | 3 | 1 |
| *UYT1966 | 25 May | Rijeka | 1 | 1 |
| *UYT1967 | 5 May | Izmir | 1 | 0 |
| 1973 | 14 Feb | Cava dei Tirreni | 0 | 1 |
| 1973 | 14 Mar | Highbury | 1 | 0 |
| *UYT1973 | 6 June | Viareggio | 1 | 0 |
| 1978 | 19 Nov | Monte Carlo | 1 | 2 |
| *UYT1979 | 28 Feb | Rome | 1 | 0 |
| *UYT1979 | 4 Apr | Villa Park | 2 | 0 |

### v LUXEMBOURG

| | | | E | L |
|---|---|---|---|---|
| UYT1950 | 25 May | Vienna | 1 | 2 |
| UYT1954 | 17 Apr | Bad Neuenahr | 0 | 2 |
| 1957 | 2 Feb | West Ham | 7 | 1 |

| 1957 | 17 Nov | Luxembourg | 3 | 0 |
| UYT1958 | 9 Apr | Eschsalzette | 5 | 0 |

### v MALTA

| | | | E | M |
|---|---|---|---|---|
| *UYT1969 | 18 May | Wolfen | 6 | 0 |
| *UYT1979 | 26 May | Salzburg | 3 | 0 |

### v NETHERLANDS

| | | | E | N |
|---|---|---|---|---|
| UYT1948 | 17 Apr | Tottenham | 3 | 2 |
| UYT1951 | 26 Mar | Cannes | 2 | 1 |
| *1954 | 21 Nov | Arnhem | 2 | 3 |
| *1955 | 5 Nov | Norwich | 3 | 1 |
| 1957 | 2 Mar | Brentford | 5 | 5 |
| UYT1957 | 14 Apr | Barcelona | 1 | 2 |
| 1957 | 2 Oct | Amsterdam | 3 | 2 |
| 1961 | 9 Mar | Utrecht | 0 | 1 |
| *1962 | 31 Jan | Brighton | 4 | 0 |
| UYT1962 | 22 Apr | Ploesti | 0 | 3 |
| *UYT1963 | 13 Apr | Wimbledon | 5 | 0 |
| *UYT1968 | 9 Apr | Nimes | 1 | 0 |
| *UYT1974 | 13 Feb | West Bromwich | 1 | 1 |
| *UYT1974 | 27 Feb | The Hague | 1 | 0 |
| *UYT1979 | 23 May | Halle | 1 | 0 |
| 1982 | 9 Apr | Cannes | 1 | 0 |

### v POLAND

| | | | E | P |
|---|---|---|---|---|
| UYT1960 | 18 Apr | Graz | 4 | 2 |
| *UYT1964 | 26 Mar | Breda | 1 | 1 |
| *UYT1971 | 26 May | Presov | 0 | 0 |
| UYT1972 | 20 May | Valencia | 1 | 0 |
| 1975 | 21 Jan | Las Palmas | 1 | 1 |
| *UYT1978 | 9 May | Chorzow | 0 | 2 |
| 1979 | 3 Sept | Porac | 0 | 1 |
| *UYT1980 | 25 May | Leipzig | 2 | 1 |

### v PORTUGAL

| | | | E | P |
|---|---|---|---|---|
| UYT1954 | 18 Apr | Bonn | 0 | 2 |
| UYT1961 | 2 Apr | Lisbon | 0 | 4 |
| *UYT1964 | 3 Apr | The Hague | 4 | 0 |
| *UYT1971 | 30 May | Prague | 3 | 0 |
| 1978 | 13 Nov | Monte Carlo | 2 | 0 |
| *UYT1980 | 18 May | Rosslau | 1 | 1 |
| 1982 | 7Apr | Cannes | 3 | 0 |

### v QATAR

| | | | E | Q |
|---|---|---|---|---|
| *WYT1981 | 14 Oct | Sydney | 1 | 2 |

### v RUMANIA

| | | | E | R |
|---|---|---|---|---|
| 1957 | 15 Oct | Tottenham | 4 | 2 |
| UYT1958 | 11 Apr | Luxembourg | 1 | 0 |
| UYT1959 | 31 Mar | Pazardjic | 1 | 2 |
| *UYT1963 | 15 Apr | Highbury | 3 | 0 |
| *WYT1981 | 17 Oct | Adelaide | 0 | 1 |

### v SAAR

| | | | E | S |
|---|---|---|---|---|
| UYT1954 | 13 Apr | Dortmund | 1 | 1 |
| UYT1955 | 9 Apr | Prato | 3 | 1 |

## v SPAIN

| | | | E | S |
|---|---|---|---|---|
| UYT1952 | 15 Apr | Barcelona | 1 | 4 |
| 1957 | 26 Sept | Birmingham | 4 | 4 |
| UYT1958 | 5 Apr | Saarbrucken | 2 | 2 |
| *1958 | 8 Oct | Madrid | 4 | 2 |
| UYT1961 | 30 Mar | Lisbon | 0 | 0 |
| *1964 | 27 Feb | Murcia | 2 | 1 |
| *UYT1964 | 5 Apr | Amsterdam | 4 | 0 |
| *UYT1965 | 17 Apr | Heilbronn | 0 | 0 |
| *1966 | 30 Mar | Swindon | 3 | 0 |
| *UYT1967 | 7 May | Manisa | 2 | 1 |
| *1971 | 31 Mar | Pamplona | 2 | 3 |
| *1971 | 20 Apr | Luton | 1 | 1 |
| 1972 | 9 Feb | Alicante | 0 | 0 |
| 1972 | 15 Mar | Sheffield | 4 | 1 |
| *UYT1975 | 25 Feb | Bristol | 1 | 1 |
| *UYT1975 | 18 Mar | Madrid | 1 | 0 |
| 1976 | 12 Nov | Monte Carlo | 3 | 0 |
| *UYT1978 | 7 May | Bukowno | 1 | 0 |
| 1978 | 17 Nov | Monte Carlo | 1 | 1 |
| *UYT1981 | 25 May | Siegen | 1 | 2 |

## v SWEDEN

| | | | E | S |
|---|---|---|---|---|
| *UYT1971 | 24 May | Poprad | 1 | 0 |
| 1981 | 5 Sept | Pazin | 3 | 2 |

## v SWITZERLAND

| | | | E | S |
|---|---|---|---|---|
| UYT1950 | 26 May | Stockerau | 2 | 1 |
| UYT1951 | 27 Mar | Nice | 3 | 1 |
| UYT1952 | 13 Apr | Barcelona | 4 | 0 |
| UYT1955 | 11 Apr | Florence | 0 | 0 |
| 1956 | 11 Mar | Schaffhausen | 2 | 0 |
| 1956 | 13 Oct | Brighton | 2 | 2 |
| 1958 | 26 May | Zurich | 3 | 0 |
| *1960 | 8 Oct | Leyton | 4 | 3 |
| *†1962 | 22 Nov | Coventry | 1 | 0 |

| | | | | |
|---|---|---|---|---|
| *1963 | 21 Mar | Bienne | 7 | 1 |
| *UYT1973 | 2 June | Forte dei Marim | 2 | 0 |
| *UYT1975 | 11 May | Buochs | 4 | 0 |
| 1980 | 4 Sept | Rovinj | 3 | 0 |

## v TURKEY

| | | | E | T |
|---|---|---|---|---|
| UYT1959 | 29 Mar | Dimitrovo | 1 | 1 |
| *UYT1978 | 5 May | Wodzislaw | 1 | 1 |

## v URUGUAY

| | | | E | U |
|---|---|---|---|---|
| 1977 | 9 Oct | Las Palmas | 1 | 1 |

## v USSR

| | | | E | USSR |
|---|---|---|---|---|
| *UYT1963 | 17 Apr | Tottenham | 2 | 0 |
| *UYT1967 | 13 May | Istanbul | 0 | 1 |
| *UYT1968 | 11 Apr | Nimes | 1 | 1 |
| *UYT1971 | 28 May | Prague | 1 | 1 |
| 1978 | 10 Oct | Las Palmas | 1 | 0 |

## v YUGOSLAVIA

| | | | E | Y |
|---|---|---|---|---|
| UYT1953 | 2 April | Liège | 1 | 1 |
| 1958 | 4 Feb | Chelsea | 2 | 2 |
| UYT1962 | 20 Apr | Ploesti | 0 | 5 |
| *UYT1967 | 9 May | Izmir | 1 | 1 |
| *UYT1971 | 22 May | Bardejor | 1 | 0 |
| UYT1972 | 18 May | Barcelona | 1 | 0 |
| 1976 | 16 Nov | Monte Carlo | 0 | 3 |
| 1978 | 15 Nov | Monte Carlo | 1 | 1 |
| *UYT1980 | 20 May | Altenburg | 2 | 0 |
| 1981 | 10 Sept | Pula | 5 | 0 |

---

## ENGLAND YOUTH INTERNATIONAL MATCHES 1981–82

## UEFA YOUTH TOURNAMENT 1981–82

### Group A

| | |
|---|---|
| Austria v USSR | 1-4 |
| West Germany v Eire | 1-0 |
| Austria v West Germany | 4-1 |
| USSR v Eire | 2-0 |
| Austria v Eire | 4-2 |
| USSR v West Germany | 1-0 |

### Group B

| | |
|---|---|
| Spain v Bulgaria | 1-2 |
| Poland v Belgium | 1-0 |
| Spain v Poland | 0-1 |
| Bulgaria v Belgium | 0-1 |
| Spain v Belgium | 1-3 |
| Bulgaria v Poland | 0-0 |

### Group C

| | |
|---|---|
| Portugal v Hungary | 2-1 |
| Czechoslovakia v Finland | 2-1 |
| Portugal v Czechoslovakia | 1-1 |
| Hungary v Finland | 2-3 |
| Portugal v Finland | 1-1 |
| Hungary v Czechoslovakia | 0-2 |

### Group D

| | |
|---|---|
| Scotland v Albania | 3-0 |
| Turkey v Netherlands | 1-3 |
| Scotland v Turkey | 2-0 |
| Albania v Netherlands | 1-3 |
| Scotland v Netherlands | 1-1 |
| Albania v Turkey | 1-1 |

### Semi-Finals

| | |
|---|---|
| USSR v Czechoslovakia | 0-1 |
| Poland v Scotland | 0-2 |

### Third Place Match

| | |
|---|---|
| USSR v Poland | 3-1 |

### Final

| | |
|---|---|
| Czechoslovakia v Scotland | 1-3 |

## UEFA YOUTH TOURNAMENT FINALS 1948–82

| Year | Winners | | Runners-up | | Venue |
|------|---------|---|-----------|---|-------|
| 1948 | England | 3 | Netherlands | 2 | London |
| 1949 | France | 4 | Netherlands | 1 | Rotterdam |
| 1950 | Austria | 3 | France | 2 | Vienna |
| 1951 | Yugoslavia | 3 | Austria | 2 | Cannes |
| 1952 | Spain* | 0 | Belgium | 0 | Barcelona |
| 1953 | Hungary | 2 | Yugoslavia | 0 | Brussels |
| 1954 | Spain* | 2 | West Germany | 2 | Cologne |
| 1955–56 | Played in groups only | | | | |
| 1957 | Austria | 3 | Spain | 2 | Madrid |
| 1958 | Italy | 1 | England | 0 | Luxembourg |
| 1959 | Bulgaria | 1 | Italy | 0 | Sofia |
| 1960 | Hungary | 2 | Rumania | 1 | Vienna |
| 1961 | Portugal | 4 | Poland | 0 | Lisbon |
| 1962 | Rumania | 4 | Yugoslavia | 1 | Bucharest |
| 1963 | England | 4 | Northern Ireland | 0 | London |
| 1964 | England | 4 | Spain | 0 | Amsterdam |
| 1965 | East Germany | 3 | England | 2 | Essen |
| 1966 | Italy† | 0 | USSR | 0 | Belgrade |
| 1967 | USSR | 1 | England | 0 | Istanbul |
| 1968 | Czechoslovakia | 2 | France | 1 | Cannes |
| 1969 | Bulgaria* | 1 | East Germany | 1 | Leipzig |
| 1970 | East Germany* | 1 | Netherlands | 1 | Glasgow |
| 1971 | England | 3 | Portugal | 0 | Prague |
| 1972 | England | 2 | West Germany | 0 | Barcelona |
| 1973 | England | 3 | East Germany | 2 | Florence |
| 1974 | Bulgaria | 1 | Yugoslavia | 0 | Malmo |
| 1975 | England | 1 | Finland | 0 | Berne |
| 1976 | USSR | 1 | Hungary | 0 | Budapest |
| 1977 | Belgium | 2 | Bulgaria | 1 | Brussels |
| 1978 | USSR | 3 | Yugoslavia | 0 | Krakow |
| 1979 | Yugoslavia | 1 | Bulgaria | 0 | Vienna |
| 1980 | England | 2 | Poland | 1 | Leipzig |
| 1981 | West Germany | 1 | Poland | 0 | Dusseldorf |
| 1982 | Scotland | 3 | Czechoslovakia | 1 | Helsinki |

* Won on toss of a coin.  † Joint holders.

## FIFA WORLD YOUTH CHAMPIONSHIP 1981

**Group A**

| Poland v Qatar | 0-1 |
|---|---|
| USA v Uruguay | 0-3 |
| USA v Qatar | 1-1 |
| Uruguay v Poland | 1-0 |
| Qatar v Uruguay | 0-1 |
| Poland v USA | 4-0 |

**Group B**

| Italy v South Korea | 1-4 |
|---|---|
| Rumania v Brazil | 1-1 |
| Rumania v South Korea | 1-0 |
| Brazil v Italy | 1-0 |
| South Korea v Brazil | 0-3 |
| Italy v Rumania | 0-1 |

**Group C**

| Spain v Egypt | 2-2 |
|---|---|
| West Germany v Mexico | 1-0 |
| West Germany v Egypt | 1-2 |
| Mexico v Spain | 1-1 |
| Egypt v Mexico | 3-3 |
| Spain v West Germany | 2-4 |

**Group D**

| England v Cameroon | 2-0 |
|---|---|
| Australia v Argentina | 2-1 |
| Australia v Cameroon | 3-3 |
| Argentina v England | 1-1 |
| Cameroon v Argentina | 0-1 |
| England v Australia | 1-1 |

**Quarter-finals**

| Uruguay v Rumania | 1-2 |
|---|---|
| Brazil v Qatar | 2-3 |
| West Germany v Australia | 1-0 |
| England v Egypt | 4-2 |

**Semi-finals**

| Rumania v West Germany | aet 0-1 |
|---|---|
| Qatar v England | 2-1 |

**Third Place Match**

| Rumania v England | 1-0 |
|---|---|

**Final**

| West Germany v Qatar | 4-0 |
|---|---|

## ENGLAND MATCHES

3 October, 1981, Sydney

**England 2** (*Finnigan, Dey*)
**Cameroon 0**                                    20,000

*England:* Kendall; Southey, Crosby, Robson, Banfield, Peake, Allen, Dey, Finnigan (Webb), Wallace, Kinsey (Small).

5 October, 1981, Sydney

**England 1** (*Small*)
**Argentina 1**                                    16,700

*England:* Kendall; Greenall, Crosby, Robson, Banfield, Peake, Allen, Webb, Finnigan, Wallace, Small.

8 October, 1981, Sydney
**England 1** (*Small*)
**Australia 1**                                      29,500
*England:* Kendall; Greenall, Crosby, Robson, Banfield, Peake, Allen, Webb, Finnigan, Wallace, Small.

14 October, 1981, Sydney
**England 1** (*Small*)
**Qatar 2**                                          13,000
*England:* Kendall; Greenall, Kinsey, Robson, Allen, Peake, Dey, Webb, Cooke, Wallace, Small (Finnigan).

11 October, 1981, Sydney
**England 4** (*Webb 3, Cooke*)
**Egypt 2**                                          8500
*England:* Kendall; Greenall, Crosby (Kinsey), Robson, Banfield, Peake, Dey, Webb, Finnigan (Cooke), Wallace, Small.

17 October, 1981, Adelaide
**England 0**
**Rumania 1**                                        10,000
*England:* Gosney; Banfield, Greenall, Robson, Webb, Allen (Dey), Kinsey (Southey), Peake, Gage, Cooke, Muir.

## EUROPEAN YOUTH CHAMPIONSHIP

**QUALIFYING ROUND FIRST LEG**
23 February, 1982, Glasgow Rangers FC
**Scotland 1**
**England 0**                                        7700
*England:* Francis; Yallop, Winterburn, Singleton (Lewis), Elliott, Robson, Snodin I., Dey, Foster, Harle (Stewart), Walters.

**QUALIFYING ROUND SECOND LEG**
23 March, 1982, Coventry City FC
**England 2** (*Pearson, Walters*)
**Scotland 2**
*England:* Francis; Parker, Pickering, Duffield, Elliott, Robson, Singleton, Steven (Bell), Pearson, Walters, Childs.

## YOUTH TOURNAMENT, YUGOSLAVIA

3 September, 1981, Umag
**England 3** (*Robson, Singleton, Schaivi*)
**Austria 0**                                        1500
*England:* Gosney (Benstead); Yallop, Templeton, Elliott, Robson, Gage (Williams), Singleton, Walker, Wallace (Gilligan), Dey, Schiavi.

7 September, 1981, Porec
**England 4** (*Wallace 3, Singleton*)
**Hungary 0**                                        500
*England:* Gosney; Yallop, Templeton, Elliott, Robson, Gage (Childs), Singleton, Walker, Wallace, Dey (Williams), Schiavi (Gilligan).

**FINAL**
10 September, 1981, Pula

5 September, 1981, Pazin
**England 3** (*Gage, Wallace, Schiavi*)
**Sweden 2**                                         500
*England:* Gosney; Yallop (Parker), Templeton, Elliott, Robson, Gage (Childs), Singleton, Walker, Wallace, Dey, Schiavi (Gilligan).

**England 5** (*Wallace, Robson, Dey 2, Schiavi*)
**Yugoslavia 0**                                     5000
*England:* Gosney; Yallop (Parker), Templeton, Elliott, Robson, Gage (Williams), Singleton (Childs), Walker, Wallace, Dey, Schiavi.

## YOUTH TOURNAMENT, CANNES

7 April, 1982, Pierre de Collbertin Stadium
**England 3** (*Bell 2* [1 pen], *Kerslake*)
**Portugal 0**
*England:* Andrews (Greygoose); Brown, Culverhouse, Duce, McClure (Ridley), Comfort, Kerslake, Lewis, Little, Bell (Frain), Lee.

11 April, 1982, Pierre de Collbertin Stadium
**England 0**
**Czechoslovakia 1**
*England:* Greygoose; Culverhouse, McClure, North, Comfort, Kerslake, Little, Williams, Ridley, Lee, Frain.

**FINAL**
12 April, 1982, Pierre de Collbertin Stadium
**England 0**
**France 1**

9 April, 1982, Pierre de Collbertin Stadium
**England 1** (*Little*)
**Netherlands 0**
*England:* Andrews; Brown, Culverhouse, Duce, McClure, Comfort, Kerslake, Lewis, Little, Bell, Lee.

*England:* Andrews; Brown, Culverhouse (Ridley), Duce, McClure, Comfort, Kerslake, Lewis (Frain), Little, Bell, Lee.

# NON-LEAGUE FOOTBALL 1981–82

## FA CHALLENGE TROPHY 1981–82

**Preliminary Round**

| | |
|---|---|
| Rhyl v Caernarfon Town | 1-1 |
| Colwyn Bay v Kirkby Town | 1-0 |
| Emley v Bridlington Trinity | 4-1 |
| Sutton Town v New Mills | 2-0 |
| Sutton Coldfield Town v Mexborough Town Athletic | 2-2 |
| Alfreton Town v Darlaston | 4-2 |
| (at Matlock Town FC) | |
| Bilston v Arnold | 3-1 |
| Belper Town v Lye Town | 3-0 |
| Dudley Town v Eastwood Town | 3-0 |
| Heanor Town v Ilkeston Town | 1-0 |
| Long Eaton United v Highgate United | 1-1 |
| St Albans City v Lowestoft Town | 4-1 |
| Sudbury Town v Aveley | 2-1 |
| Hertford Town v Hornchurch | 2-0 |
| Chatham Town v Wembley | 1-2 |
| Sheppey United v Tilbury | 2-1 |
| Walton & Hersham v Farnborough Town | 0-1 |
| Sittingbourne v Chesham United | 0-2 |
| Ware v Finchley | 1-3 |
| Hampton v Lewes | 0-1 |
| Feltham v Kingstonian | 0-2 |
| Metropolitan Police v Camberley Town | 7-0 |
| Maidenhead United v Oxford City | 2-4 |
| Knighton Town v Haverfordwest County | 0-1 |
| Clandown v Llanelli | 0-2 |
| Cinderford Town v Maesteg Park | 3-4 |
| Clevedon Town v Glastonbury | 2-0 |
| Dawlish v Shepton Mallet Town | 4-5 |
| Bridport v Bideford | 1-3 |
| Keynsham Town v Welton Rovers | 1-2 |

| | |
|---|---|
| Chesham United v Dunstable | 3-2 |
| Clapton v St Albans City | 0-3 |
| Hertford Town v Corby Town | 2-0 |
| Banbury United v King's Lynn | 2-3 |
| Hillingdon Borough v Oxford City | 2-1 |
| Wellingborough Town v Witney Town | 2-1 |
| Chelmsford City v Cambridge City | 1-0 |
| Harrow Borough v Wealdstone | 2-2 |
| Finchley v Boreham Wood | 1-2 |
| Billericay Town v Sudbury Town | 4-0 |
| Harlow Town v Wembley | 1-0 |
| Milton Keynes City v Spalding United | 0-1 |
| Addlestone & Weybridge Town v Crawley Town | 2-1 |
| Gosport Borough v Farnborough Town | 1-1 |
| Kingstonian v Hounslow | 4-1 |
| Lewes v Canterbury City | 2-2 |
| Wokingham Town v Hayes | 3-1 |
| Tonbridge AFC v Andover | 2-1 |
| Bromley v Folkestone | 3-0 |
| Fareham Town v Sheppey United | 2-1 |
| Waterlooville v Staines Town | 2-2 |
| Croydon v Ashford Town | 2-0 |
| Metropolitan Police v Basingstoke Town | 0-3 |
| Epsom & Ewell v Thanet United | 6-0 |
| Welton Rovers v Bideford | 0-1 |
| Gloucester City v Salisbury | 2-1 |
| Trowbridge Town v Shepton Mallet Town | 2-1 |
| Saltash United v Weston-super-Mare | 1-0 |
| Poole Town v Llanelli | 5-1 |
| Mangotsfield United v Taunton Town | 0-1 |
| Maesteg Park v Clevedon Town | 2-1 |
| Barnstaple Town v Haverfordwest County | 3-2 |

**Preliminary Round – Replays**

| | |
|---|---|
| Caernarfon Town v Rhyl | 4-1 |
| Mexborough Town Athletic v Sutton Coldfield Town | 1-1 |
| Highgate United v Long Eaton United | 0-1 |

**Preliminary Round – Second Replay**

| | |
|---|---|
| Sutton Coldfield Town v Mexborough Town Athletic | 3-2 |

**First Round Qualifying**

| | |
|---|---|
| Horden CW v Fleetwood Town | 2-1 |
| Workington v Droylsden | 3-1 |
| Whitley Bay v North Shields | 0-0 |
| Emley v Whitby Town | 0-0 |
| West Auckland Town v Rossendale United | 1-3 |
| Penrith v Tow Law Town | 3-1 |
| Netherfield v Willington | 1-0 |
| Horwich RMI v Ashton United | 3-0 |
| South Bank v Burscough | 1-2 |
| Darwen v Crook Town | 5-0 |
| Shildon v St Helens Town | 4-2 |
| Evenwood Town v Ferryhill Athletic | 0-0 |
| Goole Town v Consett | 3-1 |
| Gateshead v Durham City | 1-0 |
| South Liverpool v Caernarfon Town | 1-4 |
| Colwyn Bay v Brereton Social | 9-2 |
| Nantwich Town v Southport | 2-1 |
| Oswestry Town v Prescot Cables | 1-0, 0-2 |
| (first match abandoned after 45 minutes) | |
| Formby v Hyde United | 0-3 |
| Bilston v Bootle | 1-0 |
| Stourbridge v Sutton Coldfield Town | 1-2 |
| Telford United v Moor Green | 1-1 |
| Hednesford Town v Bedworth United | 1-2 |
| Heanor Town v Macclesfield Town | 1-0 |
| Redditch United v Dudley Town | 1-3 |
| Sutton Town v Boston | 1-2 |
| Belper Town v Buxton | 0-2 |
| Tamworth v Worksop Town | 1-1 |
| Grantham v Bromsgrove Rovers | 0-2 |
| Long Eaton United v Leek Town | 0-1 |
| Enderby Town v AP Leamington | 3-1 |
| Alfreton Town v Curzon Ashton | 1-1 |

**First Round Qualifying – Replays**

| | |
|---|---|
| North Shields v Whitley Bay | 2-0 |
| Whitby Town v Emley | 2-1 |
| Ferryhill Athletic v Evenwood Town | 8-0 |
| Moor Green v Telford United | 0-2 |
| Worksop Town v Tamworth | 3-1 |
| Curzon Ashton v Alfreton Town | 1-2 |
| Wealdstone v Harrow Borough | 4-0 |
| Farnborough Town v Gosport Borough | 3-3 |
| Canterbury City v Lewes | 2-5 |
| Staines Town v Waterlooville | 1-0 |

**First Round Qualifying – Second Replay**

| | |
|---|---|
| Gosport Borough v Farnborough Town | 2-2 |

**First Round Qualifying – Third Replay**

| | |
|---|---|
| Farnborough Town v Gosport Borough | 1-2 |

**Second Round Qualifying**

| | |
|---|---|
| Shildon v Goole Town | 0-0 |
| Darwen v Horwich RMI | 2-2 |
| Horden CW v North Shields | 5-0 |
| Workington v Gateshead | 1-0 |
| Ferryhill Athletic v Rossendale United | 1-1 |
| Penrith v Netherfield | 2-1 |
| Burscough v Whitby Town | 3-1 |
| Worksop Town v Leek Town | 1-1 |
| Buxton v Heanor Town | 4-0 |
| Caernarfon Town v Nantwich Town | 0-1 |
| Colwyn Bay v Alfreton Town | 5-1 |
| Bromsgrove Rovers v Hyde United | 0-0 |
| Bilston v Telford United | 1-2 |
| Dudley Town v Prescot Cables | 0-1 |
| St Albans City v Chelmsford City | 2-1 |
| Billericay Town v Hillingdon Borough | 5-0 |
| Chesham United v Spalding United | 1-1 |
| Boreham Wood v Sutton Coldfield Town | 0-1 |
| Hertford Town v Enderby Town | 1-2 |
| King's Lynn v Boston | 2-2 |
| Bedworth United v Wealdstone | 1-1 |
| Harlow Town v Wellingborough Town | 1-1 |

| | |
|---|---|
| Basingstoke Town v Gosport Borough | 2-2 |
| Kingstonian v Croydon | 2-2 |
| Fareham Town v Staines Town | 1-2 |
| Wokingham Town v Bromley | 4-1 |
| Addlestone & Weybridge Town v Lewes | 2-0 |
| Epsom & Ewell v Tonbridge AFC | 3-1 |
| Gloucester City v Maesteg Park | 4-0 |
| Trowbridge Town v Barnstaple Town | 4-0 |
| Bideford v Poole Town | 0-0 |
| Saltash United v Taunton Town | 1-1 |

**Second Round Qualifying – Replays**

| | |
|---|---|
| Goole Town v Shildon | aet 4-3 |
| Horwich RMI v Darwen | 3-2 |
| Rossendale United v Ferryhill Athletic | 3-0 |
| *(at Droylsden FC)* | |
| Leek Town v Worksop Town | 4-1 |
| Hyde United v Bromsgrove Rovers | 1-0 |
| Spalding United v Chesham United | 0-1 |
| Boston v King's Lynn | 0-2 |
| Wealdstone v Bedworth United | 5-1 |
| Wellingborough Town v Harlow Town | 1-2 |
| Gosport Borough v Basingstoke Town | 2-1 |
| Croydon v Kingstonian | 1-0 |
| Poole Town v Bideford | 1-3 |
| Taunton Town v Saltash United | 2-0 |

**Third Round Qualifying**

| | |
|---|---|
| Morecambe v Bishop Auckland | 0-2 |
| Workington v Frickley Athletic | 0-1 |
| Horwich RMI v Chorley | 0-1 |
| Burscough v Horden CW | 1-3 |
| Goole Town v Lancaster City | 0-1 |
| Rossendale United v Penrith | 3-1 |
| *(at Mossley FC)* | |
| Prescot Cables v Buxton | 0-1 |
| Witton Albion v Matlock Town | 2-0 |
| Stalybridge Celtic v Gainsborough Trinity | 5-1 |
| Kidderminster Harriers v Leek Town | 1-0 |
| Colwyn Bay v Hyde United | 1-1 |
| Burton Albion v Winsford United | 1-0 |
| Telford United v Nantwich Town | 5-0 |
| King's Lynn v Harlow Town | 1-1 |
| Enderby Town v St Albans City | 4-4 |
| Barking v Chesham United | 1-0 |
| Alvechurch v Billericay Town | 3-0 |
| Hitchin Town v Leytonstone & Ilford | 3-0 |
| Sutton Coldfield Town v Wealdstone | 0-0 |
| Hendon v Barnet | 2-1 |
| Tooting & Mitcham United v Dover | 2-0 |
| Leatherhead v Addlestone & Weybridge Town | 2-2 |
| Staines Town v Wokingham Town | 2-2 |
| Carshalton Athletic v Dorchester Town | 0-0 |
| Croydon v Gosport Borough | 3-2 |
| Epsom & Ewell v Gravesend & Northfleet | 1-1 |
| Maidstone United v Bognor Regis Town | 2-1 |
| Bridgend Town v Gloucester City | 0-3 |
| Minehead v Trowbridge Town | 3-1 |
| Frome Town v Taunton Town | 1-1 |
| Bath City v Bridgwater Town | 3-0 |
| Bideford v Merthyr Tydfil | 0-3 |

**Third Round Qualifying – Replays**

| | |
|---|---|
| Hyde United v Colwyn Bay | 4-0 |
| Harlow Town v King's Lynn | 2-1 |
| St Albans City v Enderby Town | 3-1 |
| Wealdstone v Sutton Coldfield Town | 2-1 |
| Addlestone & Weybridge Town v Leatherhead | 0-1 |
| Wokingham Town v Staines Town | 0-2 |
| Dorchester Town v Carshalton Athletic | 2-0 |
| Gravesend & Northfleet v Epsom & Ewell | 3-3 |
| Taunton Town v Frome Town | 4-2 |

**Third Round Qualifying – Second Replay**

| | |
|---|---|
| Gravesend & Northfleet v Epsom & Ewell | 0-1 |

**First Round**

| | |
|---|---|
| Stalybridge Celtic v Chorley | 0-1 |
| Boston United v Hyde United | 0-1 |
| Telford United v Burton Albion | 1-0 |

| | |
|---|---|
| Marine v Scarborough | 0-1 |
| Frickley Athletic v Bishop Auckland | 0-1 |
| Lancaster City v Spennymoor United | 2-0 |
| Ashington v Blyth Spartans | 1-2 |
| Runcorn v Stafford Rangers | 2-0 |
| Kidderminster Harriers v Barrow | 0-0 |
| Northwich Victoria v Bangor City | 3-2 |
| Kettering Town v Mossley | 0-1 |
| Horden CW v Witton Albion | 1-1 |
| Altrincham v Nuneaton Borough | 1-0 |
| Buxton v Rossendale United | 1-2 |
| Alvechurch v Croydon | 1-3 |
| Woking v Barking | 2-1 |
| Hendon v Taunton Town | aet 5-1 |
| *(at Queen's Park Rangers FC)* | |
| Cheltenham Town v Epsom & Ewell | 2-3 |
| Slough Town v Bath City | 4-2 |
| Minehead v Worcester City | 1-1 |
| Aylesbury United v Sutton United | 2-4 |
| Wealdstone v Gloucester City | 3-1 |
| Weymouth v Enfield | 0-1 |
| Dartford v Leatherhead | 2-1 |
| Walthamstow Avenue v Wycombe Wanderers | 1-1 |
| Yeovil Town v Bishop's Stortford | 2-3 |
| Dulwich Hamlet v St Albans City | 1-1 |
| Maidstone United v Hastings United | 1-1 |
| Dagenham v Hitchin Town | 1-0 |
| Merthyr Tydfil v Dorchester Town | 2-1 |
| Bedford Town v Staines Town | 1-1 |
| Tooting & Mitcham United v Harlow Town | 0-0 |

**First Round – Replays**

| | |
|---|---|
| Barrow v Kidderminster Harriers | 2-2 |
| Witton Albion v Horden CW | 2-2 |
| Worcester City v Minehead | 5-2 |
| Wycombe Wanderers v Walthamstow Avenue | 1-1 |
| St Albans City v Dulwich Hamlet | 4-3 |
| Hastings United v Maidstone United | 0-2 |
| Staines Town v Bedford Town | aet 3-2 |
| Harlow Town v Tooting & Mitcham United | 2-1 |

**First Round – Second Replays**

| | |
|---|---|
| Witton Albion v Horden CW | 2-1 |
| Wycombe Wanderers v Walthamstow Avenue | 5-1 |

**Second Round**

| | |
|---|---|
| Woking v Mossley | 0-0 |
| Slough Town v Rossendale United | 1-0 |
| Wealdstone v Dagenham | 1-2 |
| Chorley v Bishop Auckland | 0-1 |
| St Albans City v Scarborough | 0-1 |
| Kidderminster Harriers v Blyth Spartans | 2-1 |
| Harlow Town v Sutton United | 0-1 |
| Hyde United v Wycombe Wanderers | 0-0 |
| Epsom & Ewell v Altrincham | 0-1 |
| Bishop's Stortford v Maidstone United | 3-0 |
| Telford United v Bedford Town | 0-0 |
| Runcorn v Lancaster City | 4-0 |
| Merthyr Tydfil v Enfield | 1-6 |
| Worcester City v Croydon | 4-1 |
| Witton Albion v Hendon | 1-0 |
| Dartford v Northwich Victoria | 0-2 |

**Second Round Replays**

| | |
|---|---|
| Mossley v Woking | 5-0 |
| Wycombe Wanderers v Hyde United | 3-2 |
| Bedford Town v Telford United | 0-3 |

**Third Round**

| | |
|---|---|
| Wycombe Wanderers v Bishop Auckland | 4-1 |
| Altrincham v Mossley | 2-0 |
| Kidderminster Harriers v Dagenham | 4-3 |
| Telford United v Enfield | 0-1 |
| Bishop's Stortford v Witton Albion | 6-1 |
| Scarborough v Slough Town | 1-1 |
| Northwich Victoria v Runcorn | 3-0 |
| Sutton United v Worcester City | 1-1 |

**Third Round Replays**

| | |
|---|---|
| Slough Town v Scarborough | 1-2 |
| Worcester City v Sutton United | aet 5-2 |

**Fourth Round**

| | |
|---|---|
| Altrincham v Bishop's Stortford | 2-2, 3-1 |
| Northwich Victoria v Worcester City | 2-1 |
| Kidderminster Harriers v Wycombe Wanderers | 0-1 |
| Enfield v Scarborough | 4-2 |

**Semi-Finals – First Leg**

| | |
|---|---|
| Northwich Victoria v Enfield | 0-0 |
| Altrincham v Wycombe Wanderers | 1-1 |

**Semi-Finals – Second Leg**

| | |
|---|---|
| Enfield v Northwich Victoria | 1-0 |
| Wycombe Wanderers v Altrincham | 0-3 |

**Final** (*at Wembley*)

**Enfield 1** (*Taylor*)
**Altrincham 0**                                          20,000

*Enfield:* Jacobs; Marrett, Tone, Jennings, Waite, Ironton, Ashford, Taylor, Holmes, Oliver (Flint), King S.

*Altrincham:* Connaughton; Crossley, Davison, Daley, Cuddy, King J. (Whitbread), Allan, Heathcote, Johnson, Rogers, Howard.

**Previous Finals**

| | |
|---|---|
| 1970 | Macclesfield T 2, Telford U 0 (28,000) |
| 1971 | Telford U 3, Hillingdon B 2 (29,500) |
| 1972 | Stafford R 3, Barnet 0 (24,000) |
| 1973 | Scarborough 2, Wigan Ath 1 (23,000) |
| 1974 | Morecambe 2, Dartford 1 (19,000) |
| 1975 | Matlock T 4, Scarborough 0 (21,000) |
| 1976 | Scarborough 3, Stafford R 2 (21,000) |
| 1977 | Scarborough 2, Dagenham 1 (20,000) |
| 1978 | Altrincham 3, Leatherhead 1 (19,999) |
| 1979 | Stafford R 2, Kettering T 0 (32,000) |
| 1980 | Dagenham 2, Mossley 1 (26,000) |
| 1981 | Bishop's Stortford 1, Sutton U 0 (22,578) |

# BOB LORD CHALLENGE TROPHY 1981–82

*Byes:* Altrincham, Barrow, Bath C, Boston U, Frickley Ath, Kettering T, Maidstone U, Northwich Victoria, Scarborough, Weymouth.

**First Round**

| | |
|---|---|
| Automotive Products Leamington v Enfield | 1-4, 0-4 |
| Dagenham v Barnet | 1-0, 1-2 |
| *(Dagenham won on away goals rule)* | |
| Dartford v Trowbridge T | 0-1, 3-1 |
| Stafford Rangers v Runcorn | 2-2, 0-2 |
| Worcester C v Telford U | 2-4, 1-2 |
| Yeovil T v Gravesend & Northfleet | 0-2, 0-0 |

**Second Round**

| | |
|---|---|
| Barrow v Altrincham | 2-1, 2-4 |
| Boston U v Frickley Ath | 0-0, 3-1 |
| Dagenham v Bath C | 5-0, 2-2 |

| | |
|---|---|
| Dartford v Weymouth | 2-3, 1-2 |
| Gravesend and Northfleet v Maidstone U | 1-1, 2-2 |
| *(Gravesend & Northfleet won on away goals rule)* | |
| Northwich Victoria v Kettering T | 3-3, 2-0 |
| Runcorn v Scarborough | 2-1, 2-2 |
| Telford U v Enfield | 1-1, 1-2 |

**Third Round**

| | |
|---|---|
| Altrincham v Northwich Victoria | 1-0, 3-1 |
| Boston U v Runcorn | 2-1, 0-1 |
| *(Runcorn won on away goals rule)* | |
| Dagenham v Enfield | 1-2, 1-2 |
| Gravesend & Northfleet v Weymouth | 0-1, 0-2 |

**Semi-Finals**

| | |
|---|---|
| Runcorn v Enfield | 1-1, 0-2 |
| Weymouth v Altrincham | 1-0, 4-2 |

**Final – First Leg: Enfield 1, Weymouth 2**
(20 April, 1982, attendance 1003)

*Enfield:* Jacobs; Barrett, Tone, Jennings, Waite, Ironton, Ashford, Taylor, Holmes (Flint), Oliver, King.
*Weymouth:* Baker; Arnold, Morrell, Elliott, Merrick, Finnigan, McCafferty (Pearson), Paterson, Iannone, Dove, Borthwick.
*Scorers:* Enfield – Ashford; Weymouth – Paterson, Dove.

**Second Leg: Weymouth 4, Enfield 3**
(3 May, 1982, attendance 1709)

*Weymouth:* Baker; Arnold, Morrell, Elliott, Merrick, Finnigan, McCafferty, Dyer, Pearson, Dove, Borthwick.
*Enfield:* Jacobs; Barrett, Flint, Jennings, Turner, Ironton, Ashford, Taylor, Holmes, Oliver, King.
*Scorers:* Weymouth – Morrell, Finnigan, McCafferty, Pearson; Enfield – Flint, Turner, King.

# ALLIANCE PREMIER LEAGUE CHALLENGE SHIELD 1981

**Altrincham 4, Kettering T 2**
(At Altrincham, 24 August, 1981, attendance 1150)

Played between 1980–81 champions – Altrincham – and the Bob Lord Trophy runners-up – Kettering T – as Altrincham also won the Trophy.

## ALLIANCE PREMIER LEAGUE 1981–82

| | Altrincham | Automotive Products Leamington | Barnet | Barrow | Bath City | Boston United | Dagenham | Dartford | Enfield | Frickley Athletic | Gravesend and Northfleet | Kettering | Maidstone United | Northwich Victoria | Runcorn | Scarborough | Stafford Rangers | Telford United | Trowbridge Town | Weymouth | Worcester | Yeovil |
|---|---|---|---|---|---|---|---|---|---|---|---|---|---|---|---|---|---|---|---|---|---|---|
| Altrincham | — | 2-3 | 2-0 | 1-1 | 1-0 | 1-1 | 1-1 | 2-0 | 1-0 | 1-1 | 3-1 | 2-1 | 1-2 | 0-2 | 2-2 | 2-0 | 0-1 | 3-0 | 1-2 | 0-0 | 6-3 | 7-1 |
| Automotive Products Leamington | 0-1 | — | 0-2 | 1-1 | 2-1 | 7-0 | 0-4 | 0-2 | 2-3 | 1-0 | 3-3 | 3-3 | 1-1 | 0-2 | 1-1 | 1-2 | 1-5 | 0-2 | 0-1 | 2-2 | 0-1 | 2-5 |
| Barnet | 0-0 | 0-0 | — | 1-2 | 2-1 | 2-1 | 1-2 | 2-0 | 4-1 | 0-0 | 2-0 | 2-1 | 1-1 | 0-1 | 1-3 | 1-1 | 0-2 | 1-0 | 0-0 | 0-3 | 1-2 | 0-0 |
| Barrow | 1-0 | 2-1 | 1-2 | — | 0-0 | 0-0 | 0-0 | 2-0 | 0-1 | 2-0 | 2-0 | 2-1 | 2-0 | 6-1 | 1-1 | 3-2 | 1-1 | 2-0 | 2-0 | 2-0 | 0-0 | 3-1 |
| Bath City | 1-1 | 7-0 | 0-1 | 0-1 | — | 1-2 | 2-2 | 1-1 | 0-1 | 1-3 | 1-0 | 3-2 | 1-1 | 1-1 | 0-2 | 2-0 | 2-1 | 1-2 | 1-1 | 2-1 | 2-3 | 2-0 |
| Boston United | 1-1 | 2-0 | 2-1 | 0-0 | 4-0 | — | 3-4 | 3-2 | 1-0 | 3-1 | 2-2 | 4-2 | 6-0 | 2-0 | 0-1 | 2-0 | 2-2 | 4-2 | 1-0 | 0-0 | 3-2 | 0-0 |
| Dagenham | 2-0 | 0-0 | 1-1 | 0-0 | 0-1 | 0-3 | — | 2-1 | 2-4 | 2-0 | 0-1 | 2-1 | 1-1 | 2-1 | 0-1 | 2-2 | 2-0 | 3-2 | 1-2 | 2-1 | 1-2 | 3-0 |
| Dartford | 0-1 | 2-2 | 0-2 | 0-2 | 0-1 | 2-1 | 0-3 | — | 0-2 | 1-0 | 0-1 | 2-2 | 2-1 | 1-2 | 1-2 | 0-1 | 1-1 | 2-0 | 1-0 | 1-0 | 0-2 | 5-0 |
| Enfield | 1-1 | 6-1 | 0-1 | 7-2 | 2-1 | 1-0 | 3-2 | 0-2 | — | 3-0 | 4-0 | 1-1 | 3-2 | 1-0 | 2-0 | 1-4 | 2-0 | 3-4 | 0-0 | 0-0 | 1-2 | 2-0 |
| Frickley Athletic | 1-1 | 4-0 | 0-1 | 2-1 | 5-1 | 2-2 | 3-1 | 3-0 | 1-1 | — | 1-1 | 3-2 | 0-3 | 1-0 | 2-0 | 2-3 | 2-0 | 0-0 | 2-1 | 3-0 | 1-2 | 2-1 |
| Gravesend and Northfleet | 5-4 | 4-1 | 2-3 | 3-1 | 1-3 | 1-0 | 1-2 | 1-0 | 1-2 | 1-1 | — | 1-3 | 1-1 | 0-1 | 2-4 | 3-0 | 1-1 | 0-2 | 2-0 | 0-1 | 0-1 | 1-1 |
| Kettering | 0-0 | 1-2 | 5-2 | 0-2 | 2-0 | 1-0 | 3-1 | 4-4 | 0-1 | 4-1 | 1-1 | — | 2-2 | 2-4 | 0-0 | 1-2 | 3-0 | 1-3 | 1-1 | 2-1 | 0-1 | 1-1 |
| Maidstone United | 2-0 | 4-0 | 1-1 | 1-0 | 1-0 | 1-0 | 2-2 | 5-1 | 1-4 | 0-3 | 1-1 | 2-0 | — | 3-1 | 1-2 | 0-2 | 1-2 | 2-2 | 4-0 | 1-2 | 2-2 | 1-2 |
| Northwich Victoria | 5-4 | 3-0 | 1-1 | 2-0 | 2-1 | 3-0 | 3-0 | 1-2 | 2-1 | 0-0 | 0-1 | 3-2 | 3-1 | — | 1-1 | 2-1 | 1-0 | 2-2 | 3-0 | 0-1 | 3-0 | 0-1 |
| Runcorn | 1-3 | 3-0 | 1-0 | 0-0 | 5-1 | 1-0 | 1-0 | 4-2 | 2-0 | 1-0 | 1-0 | 1-0 | 1-1 | 1-1 | — | 2-0 | 1-1 | 2-3 | 0-0 | 0-2 | 0-1 | 1-3 |
| Scarborough | 2-0 | 6-1 | 2-0 | 2-0 | 1-1 | 1-1 | 2-2 | 2-0 | 1-4 | 0-1 | 5-0 | 1-1 | 0-0 | 0-4 | 2-0 | — | 1-0 | 0-0 | 2-0 | 3-1 | 5-2 | 2-1 |
| Stafford Rangers | 4-3 | 3-1 | 1-1 | 1-1 | 0-0 | 1-1 | 0-0 | 1-4 | 0-1 | 0-0 | 1-1 | 1-0 | 1-1 | 2-2 | 3-0 | 1-1 | — | 1-2 | 3-1 | 2-1 | 1-0 | 3-1 |
| Telford United | 0-2 | 2-0 | 3-0 | 0-0 | 1-0 | 2-1 | 0-2 | 2-0 | 2-0 | 7-1 | 1-0 | 0-1 | 1-2 | 2-1 | 1-1 | 1-1 | 0-3 | — | 2-0 | 2-0 | 2-1 | 1-2 |
| Trowbridge Town | 1-0 | 2-1 | 1-1 | 2-0 | 1-1 | 0-1 | 0-1 | 2-0 | 2-2 | 2-0 | 2-0 | 2-3 | 3-0 | 1-0 | 0-0 | 1-3 | 1-1 | 2-0 | — | 1-1 | 1-1 | 2-4 |
| Weymouth | 4-3 | 1-2 | 2-0 | 3-0 | 2-0 | 2-1 | 1-1 | 2-1 | 2-2 | 5-0 | 2-1 | 1-1 | 1-0 | 1-0 | 0-1 | 3-1 | 1-1 | 0-1 | 1-0 | — | 3-2 | 1-1 |
| Worcester | 4-3 | 4-3 | 3-1 | 4-0 | 2-0 | 2-1 | 2-1 | 2-0 | 1-2 | 3-2 | 1-2 | 1-1 | 4-1 | 0-1 | 0-1 | 2-4 | 1-1 | 2-1 | 3-1 | 0-0 | — | 3-0 |
| Yeovil | 2-1 | 3-2 | 4-1 | 0-0 | 2-0 | 3-2 | 1-4 | 1-1 | 1-2 | 1-2 | 2-1 | 1-1 | 1-0 | 4-1 | 1-3 | 0-0 | 2-1 | 1-2 | 2-0 | 1-4 | 3-0 | — |

## ALLIANCE PREMIER LEAGUE 1981–82

| | P | W | D | L | F | A | Pts |
|---|---|---|---|---|---|---|---|
| Runcorn | 42 | 28 | 9 | 5 | 75 | 37 | 93 |
| Enfield | 42 | 26 | 8 | 8 | 90 | 46 | 86 |
| Telford United | 42 | 23 | 8 | 11 | 70 | 51 | 77 |
| Worcester City | 42 | 21 | 8 | 13 | 70 | 60 | 71 |
| Dagenham | 42 | 19 | 12 | 11 | 69 | 51 | 69 |
| Northwich Victoria | 42 | 20 | 9 | 13 | 56 | 46 | 69 |
| Scarborough | 42 | 19 | 11 | 12 | 65 | 52 | 68 |
| Barrow | 42 | 18 | 11 | 13 | 59 | 50 | 65 |
| Weymouth | 42 | 18 | 9 | 15 | 56 | 47 | 63 |
| Boston United | 42 | 17 | 11 | 14 | 61 | 57 | 62 |
| Altrincham | 42 | 14 | 13 | 15 | 66 | 56 | 55 |
| Bath City | 42 | 15 | 10 | 17 | 50 | 57 | 55 |
| Yeovil Town | 42 | 14 | 11 | 17 | 56 | 68 | 53 |
| Stafford Rangers | 42 | 12 | 16 | 14 | 48 | 47 | 52 |
| Frickley Athletic | 42 | 14 | 10 | 18 | 47 | 60 | 52 |
| Maidstone United | 42 | 11 | 15 | 16 | 55 | 59 | 48 |
| Trowbridge Town | 42 | 12 | 11 | 19 | 38 | 54 | 47 |
| Barnet | 42 | 9 | 14 | 19 | 36 | 52 | 41 |
| Kettering Town | 42 | 9 | 13 | 20 | 64 | 76 | 40 |
| Gravesend & Northfleet | 42 | 10 | 10 | 22 | 51 | 69 | 40 |
| Dartford | 42 | 10 | 9 | 23 | 47 | 69 | 39 |
| AP Leamington | 42 | 4 | 10 | 28 | 40 | 105 | 22 |

## ALLIANCE PREMIER LEAGUE LEADING GOALSCORERS 1981–82

| | |
|---|---|
| 27 | Williams (Scarborough) |
| 24 | Mather (Telford U) |
| 23 | Iannone (Weymouth) |
| 20 | Ironton (Enfield) |
| 19 | Ashford (Enfield) |
| 19 | Atkins (Barnet) |
| 19 | Burton (Dagenham) |
| 19 | Reid (Northwich Victoria) |

## BERGER ISTHMIAN LEAGUE 1981–82

### PREMIER DIVISION

| | P | W | D | L | F | A | Pts |
|---|---|---|---|---|---|---|---|
| Leytonstone & Ilford | 42 | 26 | 5 | 11 | 91 | 52 | 83 |
| Sutton United | 42 | 22 | 9 | 11 | 72 | 49 | 75 |
| Wycombe Wanderers | 42 | 21 | 10 | 11 | 63 | 48 | 73 |
| Staines Town | 42 | 21 | 9 | 12 | 59 | 46 | 72 |
| Walthamstow Avenue | 42 | 21 | 7 | 14 | 81 | 62 | 70 |
| Harrow Borough | 42 | 18 | 13 | 11 | 77 | 55 | 67 |
| Tooting & Mitcham | 42 | 19 | 10 | 13 | 58 | 47 | 67 |
| Slough Town | 42 | 17 | 13 | 12 | 64 | 54 | 64 |
| Leatherhead | 42 | 16 | 12 | 14 | 57 | 52 | 60 |
| Hayes | 42 | 16 | 10 | 16 | 58 | 52 | 58 |
| Croydon | 42 | 16 | 9 | 17 | 59 | 57 | 57 |
| Barking | 42 | 14 | 14 | 14 | 53 | 51 | 56 |
| Hendon | 42 | 13 | 13 | 16 | 56 | 65 | 52 |
| Dulwich Hamlet | 42 | 14 | 10 | 18 | 47 | 59 | 52 |
| Bishop's Stortford | 42 | 15 | 5 | 22 | 50 | 70 | 50 |
| Carshalton Athletic | 42 | 14 | 8 | 20 | 58 | 86 | 50 |
| Billericay Town | 42 | 11 | 16 | 15 | 41 | 50 | 49 |
| Hitchin Town | 42 | 12 | 11 | 19 | 56 | 77 | 47 |
| Bromley | 42 | 13 | 7 | 22 | 63 | 79 | 46 |
| Woking | 42 | 11 | 13 | 18 | 57 | 75 | 46 |
| Harlow Town | 42 | 10 | 11 | 21 | 50 | 73 | 41 |
| Boreham Wood | 42 | 8 | 13 | 21 | 47 | 58 | 37 |

### DIVISION ONE

| | P | W | D | L | F | A | Pts |
|---|---|---|---|---|---|---|---|
| Wokingham Town | 40 | 29 | 5 | 6 | 86 | 30 | 92 |
| Bognor Regis Town | 40 | 23 | 10 | 7 | 65 | 34 | 79 |
| Metropolitan Police | 40 | 22 | 11 | 7 | 75 | 48 | 77 |
| Oxford City | 40 | 21 | 11 | 8 | 82 | 47 | 74 |
| Feltham | 40 | 20 | 8 | 12 | 65 | 49 | 68 |
| Lewes | 40 | 19 | 7 | 14 | 73 | 66 | 64 |
| Hertford Town | 40 | 16 | 10 | 14 | 62 | 54 | 58 |
| Wembley | 40 | 14 | 15 | 11 | 69 | 55 | 57 |
| Farnborough Town | 40 | 15 | 11 | 14 | 71 | 57 | 56 |
| Epsom & Ewell | 40 | 16 | 8 | 16 | 53 | 44 | 56 |
| Kingstonian | 40 | 16 | 7 | 17 | 57 | 56 | 55 |
| Hampton | 40 | 15 | 9 | 16 | 52 | 52 | 54 |
| Hornchurch | 40 | 13 | 15 | 12 | 42 | 50 | 54 |
| Aveley | 40 | 14 | 10 | 16 | 46 | 58 | 52 |
| St Albans City | 40 | 14 | 9 | 17 | 55 | 55 | 51 |
| Maidenhead United | 40 | 11 | 10 | 19 | 49 | 70 | 43 |
| Tilbury | 40 | 9 | 15 | 16 | 49 | 67 | 42 |
| Walton & Hersham | 40 | 10 | 11 | 19 | 43 | 65 | 41 |
| Chesham United | 40 | 9 | 9 | 22 | 39 | 71 | 36 |
| Clapton | 40 | 9 | 7 | 24 | 44 | 73 | 34 |
| Ware | 40 | 5 | 2 | 33 | 29 | 105 | 17 |

### DIVISION TWO

| | P | W | D | L | F | A | Pts |
|---|---|---|---|---|---|---|---|
| Worthing | 40 | 29 | 6 | 5 | 95 | 25 | 93 |
| Cheshunt | 40 | 25 | 7 | 8 | 79 | 33 | 82 |
| Hungerford Town* | 40 | 22 | 10 | 8 | 89 | 42 | 74 |
| Barton Rovers | 40 | 22 | 8 | 10 | 65 | 32 | 74 |
| Windsor & Eton | 40 | 22 | 6 | 12 | 69 | 49 | 72 |
| Corinthian Casuals | 40 | 19 | 12 | 9 | 67 | 50 | 69 |
| Harwich & Parkeston | 40 | 19 | 12 | 9 | 64 | 47 | 69 |
| Letchworth Garden City | 40 | 15 | 11 | 14 | 67 | 55 | 56 |
| Dorking Town | 40 | 13 | 17 | 10 | 52 | 44 | 56 |
| Hemel Hempstead | 40 | 15 | 9 | 16 | 54 | 49 | 54 |
| Basildon United | 40 | 16 | 5 | 19 | 64 | 51 | 53 |
| Finchley | 40 | 14 | 9 | 17 | 57 | 68 | 51 |
| Southall | 40 | 12 | 14 | 14 | 36 | 42 | 50 |
| Epping Town | 40 | 12 | 11 | 17 | 48 | 62 | 47 |
| Molesey | 40 | 13 | 7 | 20 | 61 | 73 | 46 |
| Egham Town | 40 | 11 | 9 | 20 | 56 | 64 | 42 |
| Rainham Town | 40 | 11 | 9 | 20 | 53 | 83 | 42 |
| Tring Town | 40 | 9 | 13 | 18 | 49 | 78 | 40 |
| Eastbourne United | 40 | 9 | 12 | 19 | 51 | 73 | 39 |
| Horsham | 40 | 10 | 9 | 21 | 42 | 79 | 39 |
| Camberley Town | 40 | 3 | 2 | 35 | 21 | 140 | 11 |

* 2 points deducted.

# NORTHERN PREMIER LEAGUE BASS CHALLENGE CUP 1981–82

*Byes:* Burton Albion, Buxton, Gainsborough Trinity, Gateshead, Goole T, Marine, Mossley, South Liverpool, Witton Albion, Workington.

**First Round**

| | |
|---|---|
| Bangor C v Oswestry T | 1-2, 2-2 |
| Grantham v Matlock T | 1-1, 4-1 |
| Morecambe v Lancaster C | 2-0, 0-1 |
| Southport v Netherfield | 4-3, 2-1 |
| Tamworth v Macclesfield T | 0-2, 1-3 |
| Worksop T v King's Lynn | 1-1, 1-3 |

**Second Round**

| | |
|---|---|
| Gainsborough Trinity v Gateshead | 2-0 |
| Grantham v Burton Albion | 0-0 |
| King's Lynn v Witton Albion | 2-0 |
| Marine v South Liverpool | 5-0 |
| Morecambe v Mossley | 0-2 |
| Oswestry T v Buxton | 5-1 |
| Southport v Goole T | 3-1 |
| Workington v Macclesfield T | 2-2 |

**Second Round Replays**

| | |
|---|---|
| Burton Albion v Grantham | 2-1 |
| Macclesfield T v Workington | 0-2 |

**Third Round**

| | |
|---|---|
| Burton Albion v Oswestry T | 2-1 |
| Gainsborough Trinity v Marine | 2-1 |
| Mossley v King's Lynn | 0-0 |
| Workington v Southport | 1-1 |

**Third Round Replays**

| | |
|---|---|
| King's Lynn v Mossley | 1-3 |
| Southport v Workington | 1-2 |

**Semi-Finals**

| | |
|---|---|
| Gainsborough Trinity v Burton Albion | 0-0, aet 2-2 |
| (*Gainsborough Trinity won 7-5 on pens*) | |
| Workington v Mossley | 0-4, 1-2 |

**Final: Gainsborough Trinity 1, Mossley 0**

(At Maine Road, 20 April, 1982, attendance 1658)

*Gainsborough Trinity:* Blackburn; Jones, White, Lodge, Benniworth, Harris, Glaves, Wignall, Owen (Spencer), Seal, Brolly.

*Mossley:* Sherlock; Gorman, Gallagher, Deakin (Hughes), Vaughan, Duff, Szabo, Derbyshire, Page, O'Connor, Garmory.

*Scorer:* Gainsborough Trinity – Wignall.

# NORTHERN PREMIER LEAGUE BASS CHALLENGE SHIELD 1981

**Runcorn 2, Mossley 1**

(*Score after 90 minutes 1-1*)
(At Runcorn, 20 October, 1981)

Played between the 1980–81 League Champions – Runcorn – and the Cup runners-up – Mossley – as Runcorn were also the Cup winners.

## NORTHERN PREMIER LEAGUE 1981–82

| | P | W | D | L | F | A | Pts |
|---|---|---|---|---|---|---|---|
| Bangor City | 42 | 27 | 8 | 7 | 108 | 60 | 62 |
| Mossley | 42 | 27 | 11 | 7 | 76 | 43 | 59 |
| Witton Albion | 42 | 22 | 10 | 10 | 75 | 44 | 54 |
| Gateshead | 42 | 19 | 14 | 9 | 65 | 49 | 52 |
| King's Lynn | 42 | 19 | 12 | 11 | 61 | 36 | 50 |
| Grantham | 42 | 18 | 13 | 11 | 65 | 53 | 49 |
| Burton Albion | 42 | 19 | 9 | 14 | 71 | 62 | 47 |
| Southport | 42 | 16 | 14 | 12 | 63 | 55 | 46 |
| Marine | 42 | 17 | 12 | 13 | 64 | 57 | 46 |
| Macclesfield Town | 42 | 17 | 9 | 16 | 67 | 58 | 43 |
| Workington | 42 | 18 | 7 | 17 | 62 | 60 | 43 |
| Worksop Town | 42 | 15 | 13 | 14 | 52 | 60 | 43 |
| South Liverpool | 42 | 13 | 13 | 16 | 55 | 57 | 39 |
| Goole Town | 42 | 13 | 13 | 16 | 56 | 60 | 39 |
| Oswestry Town | 42 | 14 | 11 | 17 | 55 | 59 | 39 |
| Buxton | 42 | 14 | 11 | 17 | 48 | 56 | 39 |
| Lancaster City | 42 | 13 | 12 | 17 | 47 | 50 | 38 |
| Gainsborough Trinity | 42 | 10 | 13 | 19 | 60 | 69 | 33 |
| Tamworth | 42 | 10 | 9 | 23 | 31 | 56 | 29 |
| Morecambe | 42 | 9 | 11 | 22 | 43 | 86 | 29 |
| Matlock Town | 42 | 7 | 12 | 23 | 38 | 72 | 26 |
| Netherfield | 42 | 5 | 9 | 28 | 31 | 91 | 19 |

## NORTHERN PREMIER LEAGUE LEADING GOALSCORERS 1981–82

| | |
|---|---|
| 41 | Bennett (Bangor C) |
| 30 | Leadbeatter (Grantham) |
| 27 | Cooper (Southport) |
| 27 | Gauden (Burton Albion) |
| 21 | Owen (Gainsborough Trinity) |
| 21 | White (Witton Albion) |
| 19 | Chapman (King's Lynn) |
| 19 | Smith (Workington) |
| 17 | Carter (South Liverpool) |
| 17 | Thornton (South Liverpool) |
| 16 | Fisher (Worksop T) |
| 16 | Lewis (Oswestry T) |
| 16 | McClatchey (Marine) |
| 15 | Derbyshire (Mossley) |
| 15 | Jackson (Witton Albion) |
| 15 | Reach (Workington) |
| 14 | Walker (Macclesfield T) |

## NORTHERN PREMIER LEAGUE 1981-82

| | Bangor City | Burton Albion | Buxton | Gainsborough Trinity | Gateshead | Goole Town | Grantham | King's Lynn | Lancaster City | Macclesfield Town | Marine | Matlock Town | Morecambe | Mossley | Netherfield | Oswestry Town | South Liverpool | Southport | Tamworth | Witton Albion | Workington | Worksop Town |
|---|---|---|---|---|---|---|---|---|---|---|---|---|---|---|---|---|---|---|---|---|---|---|
| Bangor City* | — | 3-2 | 3-1 | 2-1 | 3-1 | 3-0 | 3-1 | 2-0 | 2-1 | 4-4 | 2-1 | 2-1 | 5-2 | 2-1 | 2-0 | 0-0 | 3-1 | 4-2 | 0-0 | 1-1 | 4-1 | 2-1 |
| Burton Albion | 2-2 | — | 1-0 | 2-0 | 1-1 | 3-1 | 1-1 | 1-0 | 0-0 | 4-1 | 1-1 | 2-2 | 3-1 | 0-2 | 5-1 | 3-1 | 4-2 | 0-2 | 0-3 | 2-1 | 2-2 | 2-0 |
| Buxton | 1-0 | 5-1 | — | 2-1 | 0-0 | 1-0 | 2-3 | 1-0 | 2-1 | 0-4 | 1-2 | 2-1 | 1-2 | 1-2 | 1-1 | 1-0 | 1-2 | 3-1 | 1-1 | 3-3 | 2-1 | 6-1 |
| Gainsborough Trinity | 4-5 | 4-3 | 0-0 | — | 1-1 | 2-2 | 4-1 | 2-0 | 1-2 | 0-4 | 3-2 | 2-1 | 1-2 | 0-1 | 3-1 | 4-0 | 2-0 | 0-0 | 2-0 | 0-1 | 4-1 | 3-0 |
| Gateshead | 3-3 | 2-4 | 2-0 | 3-2 | — | 0-0 | 1-1 | 2-0 | 0-0 | 2-1 | 3-2 | 1-0 | 4-0 | 0-1 | 4-0 | 0-0 | 2-1 | 0-0 | 2-0 | 1-1 | 4-1 | 0-0 |
| Goole Town | 0-1 | 4-1 | 2-1 | 2-2 | 3-0 | — | 0-2 | 0-4 | 3-1 | 1-4 | 1-1 | 2-1 | 4-0 | 1-1 | 0-1 | 4-1 | 2-0 | 2-2 | 0-1 | 1-0 | 1-0 | 0-3 |
| Grantham | 2-2 | 1-2 | 2-0 | 3-0 | 2-1 | 1-1 | — | 2-2 | 1-0 | 1-0 | 2-1 | 2-0 | 2-0 | 1-2 | 0-0 | 2-2 | 1-1 | 2-1 | 0-2 | 1-1 | 4-2 | 1-1 |
| King's Lynn | 2-0 | 3-0 | 4-1 | 1-0 | 1-0 | 2-0 | 3-0 | — | 2-1 | 1-0 | 1-2 | 2-2 | 1-1 | 0-0 | 0-1 | 0-0 | 2-2 | 1-0 | 1-0 | 1-0 | 3-1 | 1-1 |
| Lancaster City | 0-3 | 1-0 | 2-1 | 1-1 | 2-3 | 0-0 | 1-2 | 1-2 | — | 1-0 | 3-2 | 2-0 | 2-1 | 1-1 | 2-0 | 1-1 | 1-2 | 1-2 | 1-2 | 2-1 | 0-1 | 1-0 |
| Macclesfield Town | 4-0 | 1-2 | 3-1 | 1-1 | 0-1 | 1-1 | 2-0 | 2-1 | 4-2 | — | 1-1 | 0-1 | 2-1 | 3-0 | 3-0 | 3-2 | 2-1 | 1-1 | 3-1 | 0-2 | 0-3 | 4-2 |
| Marine | 2-1 | 1-1 | 2-1 | 2-2 | 3-1 | 2-0 | 0-4 | 1-0 | 0-0 | 3-0 | — | 1-1 | 2-0 | 2-0 | 2-2 | 0-1 | 3-1 | 1-4 | 2-1 | 2-3 | 1-0 | 1-1 |
| Matlock Town | 2-7 | 0-1 | 0-0 | 0-1 | 1-5 | 2-0 | 0-4 | 1-3 | 3-0 | 0-1 | 3-0 | — | 1-1 | 2-2 | 1-0 | 0-1 | 0-2 | 1-4 | 2-0 | 1-2 | 1-2 | 0-1 |
| Morecambe | 0-9 | 1-2 | 0-0 | 0-2 | 2-3 | 2-2 | 3-1 | 0-0 | 3-0 | 1-0 | 3-0 | 0-3 | — | 1-2 | 2-1 | 2-1 | 0-0 | 0-0 | 1-3 | 1-3 | 0-0 | 0-0 |
| Mossley | 6-1 | 1-0 | 3-0 | 5-2 | 1-1 | 2-1 | 3-1 | 1-3 | 1-4 | 1-0 | 3-1 | 1-1 | 3-2 | — | 4-2 | 2-0 | 4-1 | 4-2 | 4-0 | 2-2 | 1-3 | 1-0 |
| Netherfield | 1-5 | 0-5 | 0-0 | 1-1 | 2-3 | 0-2 | 2-2 | 0-2 | 1-3 | 1-1 | 0-1 | 3-0 | 1-5 | 2-2 | — | 0-1 | 1-0 | 1-3 | 0-1 | 0-2 | 1-2 | 1-3 |
| Oswestry Town | 1-2 | 2-1 | 5-2 | 1-1 | 3-0 | 2-0 | 2-2 | 2-3 | 0-0 | 4-0 | 2-2 | 4-0 | 1-2 | 1-1 | 1-1 | — | 2-3 | 1-4 | 2-1 | 0-2 | 1-2 | 0-2 |
| South Liverpool | 3-3 | 3-1 | 0-1 | 3-0 | 1-1 | 0-3 | 0-4 | 0-0 | 1-0 | 3-0 | 0-3 | 3-0 | 0-0 | 1-0 | 4-0 | 2-0 | — | 0-1 | 0-1 | 1-2 | 3-2 | 0-1 |
| Southport | 2-1 | 2-1 | 0-1 | 1-1 | 2-0 | 2-1 | 2-1 | 1-1 | 2-3 | 1-1 | 1-0 | 1-1 | 2-1 | 1-0 | 0-2 | 2-2 | 1-1 | — | 1-1 | 2-1 | 3-2 | 2-0 |
| Tamworth | 1-4 | 2-3 | 0-0 | 2-1 | 0-1 | 0-0 | 1-2 | 0-2 | 1-0 | 0-2 | 0-1 | 2-1 | 0-1 | 0-2 | 3-0 | 2-0 | 1-3 | 4-2 | — | 1-2 | 0-0 | 4-1 |
| Witton Albion | 1-0 | 1-2 | 0-1 | 2-1 | 0-1 | 2-3 | 1-1 | 1-0 | 1-1 | 0-2 | 5-2 | 2-1 | 5-1 | 0-2 | 6-0 | 2-0 | 2-1 | 0-3 | 0-3 | — | 0-0 | 1-1 |
| Workington | 0-1 | 1-0 | 0-1 | 0-0 | 3-4 | 2-4 | 1-1 | 2-1 | 3-2 | 0-0 | 1-0 | 7-1 | 7-1 | 1-0 | 1-0 | 2-1 | 2-2 | 3-2 | 5-1 | 2-1 | — | 3-0 |
| Worksop Town | 1-6 | 0-0 | 1-2 | 1-0 | 1-1 | 3-3 | 0-1 | 2-1 | 1-0 | 3-2 | 2-2 | 2-1 | 2-1 | 0-2 | 3-0 | 2-1 | 2-2 | 1-1 | 2-0 | 3-0 | 2-1 | — |

* Relegated from Alliance Premier League.

## SOUTHERN LEAGUE CHALLENGE CUP, 1981–82

**First Round**

| | |
|---|---|
| Alvechurch v Stourbridge | 0-0, 3-1 |
| Ashford T v Folkestone | 3-2, 1-1 |
| Aylesbury U v Addlestone & Weybridge T | 2-1, 2-1 |
| Banbury U v Cambridge C | 0-1, 1-4 |
| Basingstoke T v Salisbury | 1-2, 2-2 |
| Canterbury C v Dover | 3-2, 0-1 |
| Cheltenham T v Bridgend T | 0-3, 1-1 |
| Corby T v Bedford T | 2-1, 1-3 |
| Crawley T v Tonbridge AFC | 0-1, 1-2 |
| Dorchester T v Taunton T | 4-0, 3-1 |
| Dunstable v Welling U | 2-2, 0-4 |
| Gloucester C v Merthyr Tydfil | 0-0, 1-1 |
| Gosport Borough v Fareham T | 1-2, 0-0 |
| Hillingdon Borough v Hounslow | 5-2, 1-1 |
| Kidderminster Harriers v Bedworth U | 2-0, 0-1 |
| Milton Keynes C v Wellingborough T | 0-1, 2-0 |
| Minehead v Poole T | 2-0, 1-2 |
| Nuneaton Borough v Bromsgrove Rovers | 2-1, 2-1 |
| Redditch U v Enderby T | 1-2, 3-6 |
| Thanet U v Hastings U | 0-1, 1-8 |
| Waterlooville v Andover | 0-4, 2-3 |
| Wealdstone v Chelmsford C | 5-1, 4-2 |
| Witney T v Barry T | 3-1, 0-1 |

**First Round Replays**

| | |
|---|---|
| Canterbury C v Dover | 0-1 |
| Merthyr Tydfil v Gloucester C | 0-0 |
| *(Gloucester C won 6-5 on pens)* | |

**Second Round**

*Byes:* Aylesbury U, Bridgend T, Dorchester T, Dover, Gloucester C, Hastings U, Hillingdon Borough, Nuneaton Borough, Wealdstone.

| | |
|---|---|
| Andover v Fareham T | 1-2 |
| Ashford T v Tonbridge AFC | 0-2 |
| Bedford T v Welling U | 4-2 |

| | |
|---|---|
| Enderby T v Alvechurch | 2-0 |
| Milton Keynes C v Cambridge C | 2-0 |
| Minehead v Salisbury | 2-3 |
| Witney T v Kidderminster Harriers | 1-1 |

**Second Round Replay**

| | |
|---|---|
| Kidderminster Harriers v Witney T | 0-2 |

**Third Round**

| | |
|---|---|
| Bedford T v Aylesbury U | 1-2 |
| Dorchester T v Bridgend T | 3-0 |
| Enderby T v Nuneaton Borough | 2-2 |
| Gloucester C v Salisbury | 2-0 |
| Hastings U v Fareham T | 1-3 |
| Milton Keynes C v Witney T | 1-3 |
| Tonbridge AFC v Dover | 0-0 |
| Wealdstone v Hillingdon Borough | 2-1 |

**Second Round Replays**

| | |
|---|---|
| Dover v Tonbridge AFC | 3-1 |
| Nuneaton Borough v Enderby T | 4-1 |

**Fourth Round**

| | |
|---|---|
| Dorchester T v Fareham T | 4-1 |
| Dover v Wealdstone | 0-2 |
| Gloucester C v Witney T | 1-1 |
| Nuneaton Borough v Aylesbury U | 2-3 |

**Fourth Round Replay**

| | |
|---|---|
| Witney T v Gloucester C | 0-2 |

**Semi-Finals**

| | |
|---|---|
| Dorchester T v Wealdstone | 1-3, 0-2 |
| Gloucester C v Aylesbury U | 0-0, 1-0 |

### Final – First Leg: Gloucester C 0, Wealdstone 1
(5 April, 1982, attendance 2200)

*Gloucester C:* Cornwell; Brown, Parsons, Bruton, Layton, Griffiths, Paterson, Evans, Doyle, Wheeler, Burford.
*Wealdstone:* Goddard; Perkins, Pearce, Byatt, Bowgett, Barwick, Waites, Wainwright, Cordice A., Knowles, Davies.
*Scorer:* Wealdstone – Pearce.

### Second Leg: Wealdstone 1, Gloucester C 0
(14 April, 1982, attendance 2200)

*Wealdstone:* Goddard; Perkins, Pearce, Byatt, Bowgett, Barwick, Cordice N., Wainwright, Cordice A., Knowles, Davies.
*Gloucester C:* Cornwell; Brown, Mockridge, Burton, Layton, Griffiths, Paterson, Evans, Doyle (Lewis), Wheeler, Burford.
*Scorer:* Wealdstone – Bowgett.

## CHAMPIONSHIP MATCH 1981

### Alvechurch 3, Bedford Town 1
(At Alvechurch, 27 October, 1981)

Played between the 1980–81 League champions – Alvechurch – and the Cup winners – Bedford T.

## CHAMPIONS OF SOUTHERN LEAGUE

In order to determine the champions, the winners of the Midland Division – Nuneaton Borough – played the winners of the Southern Division – Wealdstone – on a home and away basis.

### First Leg: Nuneaton Borough 1, Wealdstone 0
(8 May, 1982)

### Second Leg: Wealdstone 2, Nuneaton Borough 1 aet
(10 May, 1982)

The scores being equal after extra time, a penalty competition was held which Wealdstone won.

## SOUTHERN LEAGUE – MIDLAND DIVISION 1981–82

Column numbers correspond to the same team order as the rows: 1 Alvechurch, 2 Banbury United, 3 Barry Town, 4 Bedford Town, 5 Bedworth United, 6 Bridgend Town, 7 Bromsgrove Rovers, 8 Cambridge City, 9 Cheltenham Town, 10 Corby Town, 11 Enderby Town, 12 Gloucester City, 13 Kidderminster Harriers, 14 Merthyr Tydfil, 15 Milton Keynes City, 16 Minehead, 17 Nuneaton Borough, 18 Redditch United, 19 Stourbridge, 20 Taunton Town, 21 Wellingborough Town, 22 Witney Town.

| | 1 | 2 | 3 | 4 | 5 | 6 | 7 | 8 | 9 | 10 | 11 | 12 | 13 | 14 | 15 | 16 | 17 | 18 | 19 | 20 | 21 | 22 |
|---|---|---|---|---|---|---|---|---|---|---|---|---|---|---|---|---|---|---|---|---|---|---|
| Alvechurch | — | 1-1 | 2-2 | 5-0 | 1-0 | 3-1 | 4-0 | 5-1 | 1-1 | 1-0 | 3-1 | 3-0 | 0-0 | 3-1 | 1-0 | 5-1 | 0-3 | 5-2 | 0-2 | 3-0 | 1-1 | 0-2 |
| Banbury United | 0-3 | — | 1-3 | 2-0 | 2-1 | 1-3 | 1-1 | 2-2 | 2-3 | 2-1 | 1-1 | 0-4 | 1-3 | 1-0 | 2-0 | 3-1 | 2-2 | 8-3 | 0-3 | 0-0 | 3-4 | 0-2 |
| Barry Town | 3-0 | 5-2 | — | 1-0 | 1-0 | 0-0 | 5-1 | 6-1 | 2-0 | 1-0 | 0-2 | 3-0 | 2-1 | 1-0 | 0-0 | 2-1 | 0-2 | 2-0 | 1-1 | 2-2 | 1-3 | 0-2 |
| Bedford Town | 0-2 | 2-0 | 1-0 | — | 1-2 | 2-1 | 1-1 | 4-1 | 1-0 | 0-4 | 1-3 | 0-0 | 0-2 | 3-3 | 1-1 | 0-2 | 0-2 | 2-0 | 3-1 | 1-1 | 2-0 | 0-0 |
| Bedworth United | 1-0 | 2-2 | 1-0 | 1-2 | — | 1-1 | 2-1 | 3-0 | 2-2 | 0-1 | 0-2 | 0-1 | 1-3 | 0-0 | 3-0 | 4-0 | 0-2 | 5-1 | 1-3 | 3-0 | 1-3 | 1-0 |
| Bridgend Town | 2-2 | 3-1 | 0-0 | 2-1 | 1-1 | — | 1-3 | 3-1 | 2-0 | 1-1 | 2-2 | 0-1 | 0-4 | 0-0 | 1-0 | 2-1 | 2-4 | 2-2 | 2-1 | 4-1 | 1-1 | 1-2 |
| Bromsgrove Rovers | 1-2 | 3-2 | 2-0 | 1-1 | 0-1 | 1-0 | — | 4-0 | 1-2 | 1-3 | 3-0 | 1-0 | 0-0 | 2-4 | 0-0 | 2-4 | 3-3 | 2-0 | 0-1 | 3-0 | 1-2 | 2-2 |
| Cambridge City | 1-1 | 1-1 | 2-0 | 6-1 | 3-0 | 2-2 | 4-0 | — | 3-1 | 3-3 | 3-3 | 0-0 | 1-1 | 2-1 | 0-0 | 5-0 | 0-2 | 1-1 | 1-2 | 2-2 | 2-0 | 0-1 |
| Cheltenham Town | 1-1 | 6-0 | 1-0 | 1-0 | 2-2 | 2-0 | 1-2 | 3-1 | — | 1-3 | 2-0 | 1-1 | 1-2 | 0-0 | 2-1 | 0-1 | 1-0 | 1-1 | 0-1 | 2-2 | 0-1 | 0-1 |
| Corby Town | 0-3 | 4-2 | 1-0 | 0-4 | 1-4 | 1-1 | 1-3 | 3-3 | 1-3 | — | 1-1 | 0-1 | 0-4 | 1-0 | 1-1 | 2-0 | 2-2 | 5-0 | 1-4 | 2-0 | 1-2 | 3-2 |
| Enderby Town | 2-3 | 2-1 | 2-0 | 1-1 | 0-1 | 6-0 | 3-0 | 2-1 | 2-0 | 1-1 | — | 5-1 | 1-3 | 2-1 | 1-0 | 2-0 | 0-3 | 5-3 | 1-1 | 2-4 | 2-2 | 0-3 |
| Gloucester City | 0-1 | 3-0 | 2-2 | 1-3 | 0-0 | 3-0 | 1-0 | 4-0 | 1-3 | 1-0 | 5-1 | — | 1-0 | 5-1 | 0-0 | 2-0 | 1-3 | 1-0 | 5-2 | 3-0 | 1-5 | 2-0 |
| Kidderminster Harriers | 0-0 | 3-0 | 1-0 | 2-0 | 2-1 | 3-0 | 4-2 | 4-0 | 0-4 | 3-3 | 1-0 | 1-0 | — | 0-0 | 3-2 | 5-0 | 0-2 | 3-1 | 1-1 | 3-3 | 3-1 | 1-1 |
| Merthyr Tydfil | 0-0 | 3-0 | 4-0 | 3-1 | 0-0 | 0-0 | 2-3 | 3-0 | 2-3 | 0-1 | 2-1 | 2-2 | 2-2 | — | 2-1 | 0-1 | 2-2 | 3-0 | 1-0 | 3-3 | 3-1 | 1-3 |
| Milton Keynes City | 0-3 | 0-3 | 1-1 | 1-3 | 3-0 | 0-1 | 0-2 | 2-1 | 3-0 | 2-1 | 1-2 | 1-3 | 0-0 | 2-2 | — | 1-0 | 0-3 | 2-1 | 0-4 | 2-4 | 2-0 | 3-2 |
| Minehead | 1-0 | 1-5 | 1-1 | 1-0 | 0-1 | 1-0 | 0-2 | 2-2 | 2-2 | 1-0 | 1-1 | 3-0 | 1-1 | 2-1 | 3-2 | — | 1-3 | 2-0 | 1-2 | 3-3 | 2-2 | 2-0 |
| Nuneaton Borough | 0-0 | 2-3 | 1-1 | 1-0 | 2-1 | 5-1 | 2-2 | 2-1 | 3-2 | 1-0 | 3-2 | 0-2 | 0-0 | 0-1 | 0-3 | 1-1 | — | 2-0 | 2-1 | 0-1 | 2-0 | 1-1 |
| Redditch United | 0-1 | 2-1 | 1-7 | 1-3 | 0-2 | 0-1 | 3-2 | 2-0 | 1-1 | 1-5 | 0-3 | 2-0 | 3-0 | 4-1 | 1-0 | 1-0 | 2-0 | — | 1-2 | 2-1 | 2-0 | 1-0 |
| Stourbridge | 1-3 | 1-1 | 1-0 | 3-0 | 0-3 | 0-1 | 0-2 | 2-0 | 3-1 | 0-4 | 4-1 | 1-3 | 1-2 | 0-1 | 3-0 | 1-0 | 2-1 | 4-0 | — | 1-3 | 3-0 | 1-2 |
| Taunton Town | 1-3 | 3-5 | 2-1 | 0-3 | 0-1 | 2-0 | 0-3 | 2-0 | 3-2 | 0-0 | 4-1 | 1-3 | 1-0 | 4-2 | 1-1 | 2-2 | 0-2 | 3-0 | 1-3 | — | 2-0 | 2-0 |
| Wellingborough Town | 0-1 | 2-0 | 0-0 | 1-1 | 0-0 | 0-1 | 2-1 | 2-1 | 1-1 | 0-0 | 0-2 | 2-0 | 3-0 | 0-1 | 2-2 | 3-0 | 0-3 | 3-1 | 3-0 | 3-0 | — | 1-0 |
| Witney Town | 1-2 | 3-0 | 1-1 | 0-1 | 1-2 | 4-1 | 6-2 | 4-1 | 2-2 | 2-4 | 2-4 | 1-2 | 0-1 | 3-4 | 2-1 | 4-1 | 1-1 | 4-0 | 1-2 | 2-0 | 1-0 | — |

# SOUTHERN LEAGUE – SOUTHERN DIVISION 1981–82

| Home \ Away | Addlestone and Weybridge Town | Andover | Ashford Town | Aylesbury United | Basingstoke Town | Canterbury City | Chelmsford City | Crawley Town | Dorchester Town | Dover | Dunstable | Fareham Town | Folkestone | Gosport Borough | Hastings United | Hillingdon Borough | Hounslow | Poole Town | Salisbury | Thanet United | Tonbridge AFC | Waterlooville | Wealdstone | Welling United |
|---|---|---|---|---|---|---|---|---|---|---|---|---|---|---|---|---|---|---|---|---|---|---|---|---|
| Addlestone and Weybridge Town | — | 2-0 | 2-3 | 0-0 | 1-2 | 0-1 | 2-2 | 0-6 | 1-1 | 3-3 | 1-4 | 1-1 | 2-0 | 3-2 | 2-1 | 2-0 | 0-2 | 2-2 | 2-6 | 1-3 | 1-0 | 1-1 | 1-0 | 0-0 |
| Andover | 0-1 | — | 0-1 | 2-2 | 5-1 | 3-1 | 3-0 | 2-1 | 5-0 | 2-2 | 1-0 | 3-1 | 4-3 | 6-0 | 2-1 | 0-1 | 1-1 | 1-0 | 0-2 | 3-4 | 0-2 | 1-1 | 0-1 | 2-4 |
| Ashford Town | 1-1 | 5-1 | — | 3-1 | 0-0 | 1-2 | 3-0 | 1-1 | 2-1 | 1-0 | 3-1 | 2-0 | 1-2 | 1-0 | 5-1 | 1-1 | 1-1 | 1-1 | 2-3 | 2-4 | 0-1 | 0-0 | 0-0 | 0-1 |
| Aylesbury United | 0-0 | 4-1 | 5-1 | — | 2-2 | 2-1 | 1-0 | 2-0 | 1-1 | 4-0 | 0-2 | 2-0 | 1-4 | 0-3 | 1-0 | 0-0 | 1-0 | 4-3 | 4-1 | 0-0 | 3-1 | 0-0 | 3-0 | 2-1 |
| Basingstoke Town | 1-4 | 3-0 | 2-0 | 2-2 | — | 2-1 | 1-1 | 1-0 | 1-1 | 0-0 | 1-3 | 1-1 | 2-0 | 3-1 | 1-0 | 1-2 | 1-3 | 1-3 | 1-3 | 0-1 | 1-1 | 0-0 | 2-3 | 0-0 |
| Canterbury City | 0-1 | 3-1 | 1-2 | 2-2 | 0-1 | — | 0-1 | 2-0 | 4-0 | 2-3 | 2-0 | 0-1 | 3-2 | 2-0 | 4-2 | 2-2 | 1-6 | 1-1 | 1-1 | 0-0 | 3-1 | 2-1 | 0-5 | 2-3 |
| Chelmsford City | 2-2 | 3-0 | 3-0 | 1-1 | 2-1 | 0-0 | — | 2-0 | 3-0 | 0-0 | 0-2 | 2-2 | 2-1 | 2-0 | 0-1 | 2-0 | 3-1 | 0-2 | 1-2 | 4-0 | 0-2 | 3-1 | 0-2 | 0-5 |
| Crawley Town | 0-6 | 2-1 | 1-1 | 1-3 | 3-1 | 2-0 | 3-1 | — | 3-3 | 1-2 | 2-0 | 1-1 | 0-0 | 2-3 | 0-0 | 1-3 | 2-0 | 2-1 | 3-0 | 3-0 | 1-0 | 1-5 | 1-2 | 1-2 |
| Dorchester Town | 1-1 | 5-0 | 2-1 | 4-2 | 4-0 | 2-3 | 3-0 | 1-2 | — | 1-3 | 1-0 | 5-1 | 0-3 | 2-1 | 0-1 | 0-0 | 0-1 | 2-2 | 2-1 | 6-0 | 5-1 | 2-1 | 2-2 | 0-1 |
| Dover | 3-3 | 2-2 | 1-0 | 1-0 | 4-1 | 0-2 | 1-0 | 3-1 | 1-0 | — | 5-2 | 0-0 | 1-4 | 4-0 | 0-1 | 2-0 | 2-0 | 1-1 | 2-3 | 5-0 | 1-0 | 3-1 | 0-0 | 2-2 |
| Dunstable | 1-4 | 1-0 | 3-1 | 0-2 | 1-0 | 2-2 | 0-0 | 2-0 | 1-0 | 1-0 | — | 0-0 | 1-2 | 4-0 | 4-1 | 0-1 | 3-4 | 1-1 | 2-0 | 5-1 | 2-0 | 1-0 | 1-2 | 4-1 |
| Fareham Town | 1-1 | 3-1 | 2-0 | 2-0 | 1-1 | 0-2 | 2-0 | 2-2 | 5-1 | 2-3 | 0-2 | — | 0-0 | 1-2 | 1-2 | 0-0 | 1-0 | 3-2 | 1-1 | 5-1 | 4-2 | 1-2 | 0-1 | 2-2 |
| Folkestone | 2-0 | 4-3 | 1-2 | 2-3 | 1-4 | 0-3 | 2-0 | 2-1 | 0-0 | 1-4 | 4-0 | 0-0 | — | 2-1 | 0-2 | 2-0 | 1-3 | 1-6 | 1-3 | 3-0 | 0-1 | 0-2 | 2-1 | 4-2 |
| Gosport Borough | 3-2 | 6-0 | 1-0 | 0-3 | 3-1 | 2-0 | 2-1 | 2-3 | 1-1 | 0-2 | 4-1 | 1-2 | 0-2 | — | 0-1 | 0-1 | 2-1 | 2-2 | 1-1 | 3-1 | 2-0 | 0-2 | 1-3 | 3-0 |
| Hastings United | 2-1 | 2-1 | 5-1 | 1-0 | 1-1 | 4-2 | 0-1 | 0-1 | 1-0 | 0-0 | 4-1 | 0-0 | 1-4 | 0-2 | — | 0-1 | 3-0 | 2-4 | 3-1 | 2-1 | 3-1 | 0-0 | 0-0 | 1-0 |
| Hillingdon Borough | 2-0 | 0-1 | 1-1 | 0-0 | 0-0 | 2-2 | 2-0 | 1-3 | 0-0 | 2-0 | 0-1 | 0-0 | 0-1 | 0-1 | 0-1 | — | 5-0 | 4-3 | 1-0 | 2-1 | 0-1 | 4-1 | 1-0 | 1-1 |
| Hounslow | 0-2 | 1-1 | 1-1 | 1-0 | 5-0 | 1-6 | 3-1 | 2-0 | 2-0 | 3-4 | 0-1 | 0-0 | 1-3 | 2-1 | 5-0 | 1-0 | — | 1-1 | 2-0 | 4-2 | 3-2 | 3-0 | 1-2 | 2-1 |
| Poole Town | 2-2 | 1-0 | 1-1 | 2-1 | 1-0 | 1-1 | 2-2 | 2-1 | 2-2 | 1-1 | 1-1 | 0-0 | 1-6 | 2-2 | 2-4 | 4-3 | 1-1 | — | 4-3 | 4-1 | 4-1 | 2-1 | 1-2 | 0-1 |
| Salisbury | 2-6 | 0-2 | 2-3 | 2-1 | 4-0 | 3-1 | 1-2 | 3-0 | 1-0 | 2-3 | 3-1 | 3-2 | 1-3 | 1-1 | 3-1 | 1-0 | 2-4 | 4-3 | — | 2-0 | 0-1 | 0-4 | 2-4 | 2-1 |
| Thanet United | 1-3 | 3-4 | 2-4 | 2-1 | 3-0 | 0-0 | 4-0 | 0-1 | 6-0 | 5-0 | 5-1 | 1-1 | 3-0 | 3-1 | 2-1 | 1-0 | 0-2 | 0-3 | 2-0 | — | 2-0 | 0-1 | 0-2 | 1-3 |
| Tonbridge AFC | 4-2 | 3-2 | 2-4 | 2-1 | 3-1 | 1-1 | 3-1 | 0-2 | 5-1 | 1-0 | 1-0 | 0-0 | 2-0 | 4-2 | 0-2 | 0-1 | 4-0 | 0-3 | 5-3 | 2-1 | — | 0-4 | 0-2 | 1-3 |
| Waterlooville | 2-1 | 2-0 | 3-1 | 6-1 | 4-0 | 2-1 | 3-0 | 4-1 | 1-0 | 3-1 | 3-1 | 1-0 | 1-2 | 0-2 | 2-4 | 1-0 | 4-1 | 3-3 | 3-0 | 1-0 | 1-1 | — | 0-1 | 1-0 |
| Wealdstone | 0-0 | 4-0 | 3-0 | 3-0 | 3-0 | 2-3 | 0-2 | 1-2 | 1-2 | 2-2 | 1-2 | 0-1 | 2-1 | 1-3 | 0-0 | 3-0 | 3-0 | 4-1 | 4-1 | 6-1 | 1-2 | 0-1 | — | 0-2 |
| Welling United | 2-0 | 2-0 | 0-2 | 3-0 | 6-0 | 0-0 | 0-1 | 2-3 | 4-1 | 4-2 | 4-2 | 2-0 | 4-2 | 3-0 | 1-1 | 3-0 | 2-0 | 0-1 | 4-1 | 2-0 | 1-1 | 2-3 | 1-1 | — |

# SOUTHERN LEAGUE 1981–82

## MIDLAND DIVISION

| | P | W | D | L | F | A | Pts |
|---|---|---|---|---|---|---|---|
| Nuneaton Borough | 42 | 27 | 11 | 4 | 88 | 32 | 65 |
| Alvechurch | 42 | 26 | 10 | 6 | 79 | 34 | 62 |
| Kidderminster Harriers | 42 | 22 | 12 | 8 | 71 | 40 | 56 |
| Stourbridge | 42 | 21 | 10 | 11 | 69 | 47 | 52 |
| Gloucester City | 42 | 21 | 9 | 12 | 64 | 48 | 51 |
| Bedworth United | 42 | 20 | 10 | 12 | 59 | 40 | 50 |
| Enderby Town | 42 | 20 | 10 | 12 | 79 | 66 | 50 |
| Witney Town | 42 | 19 | 8 | 15 | 71 | 49 | 46 |
| Barry Town | 42 | 16 | 14 | 12 | 59 | 46 | 46 |
| Corby Town | 42 | 19 | 8 | 15 | 70 | 59 | 46 |
| Merthyr Tydfil | 42 | 16 | 12 | 14 | 63 | 54 | 44 |
| Wellingborough Town | 42 | 15 | 12 | 15 | 50 | 45 | 42 |
| Bridgend Town | 42 | 13 | 13 | 16 | 50 | 62 | 39 |
| Bromsgrove Rovers | 42 | 15 | 8 | 19 | 57 | 63 | 38 |
| Bedford Town | 42 | 12 | 13 | 17 | 45 | 54 | 37 |
| Cheltenham Town | 42 | 11 | 14 | 17 | 65 | 68 | 36 |
| Taunton Town | 42 | 12 | 8 | 22 | 46 | 76 | 32 |
| Banbury United | 42 | 11 | 8 | 23 | 63 | 91 | 30 |
| Minehead | 42 | 12 | 6 | 24 | 38 | 69 | 30 |
| Cambridge City | 42 | 10 | 8 | 24 | 38 | 80 | 28 |
| Milton Keynes City | 42 | 6 | 11 | 25 | 34 | 70 | 23 |
| Redditch United | 42 | 8 | 5 | 29 | 37 | 103 | 21 |

### Leading Goalscorers
29 Brooks (Witney T)
26 Smith S. (Enderby T)
22 Robson (Nuneaton Borough)
20 Lewis (Gloucester C)
18 Gough (Cheltenham T)
18 Roberts (Corby T)
18 Stevens (Alvechurch)

## SOUTHERN DIVISION

| | P | W | D | L | F | A | Pts |
|---|---|---|---|---|---|---|---|
| Wealdstone | 46 | 32 | 8 | 6 | 100 | 32 | 72 |
| Hastings United | 46 | 31 | 9 | 6 | 79 | 34 | 71 |
| Dorchester Town | 46 | 21 | 18 | 7 | 76 | 41 | 60 |
| Gosport Borough | 46 | 26 | 8 | 12 | 76 | 45 | 60 |
| Fareham Town | 46 | 20 | 14 | 12 | 58 | 48 | 54 |
| Poole Town | 46 | 19 | 15 | 12 | 92 | 63 | 53 |
| Waterlooville | 46 | 22 | 9 | 15 | 75 | 53 | 53 |
| Welling United | 46 | 19 | 13 | 14 | 70 | 48 | 51 |
| Addlestone & Weybridge Town | 46 | 17 | 17 | 12 | 71 | 53 | 51 |
| Chelmsford City | 46 | 20 | 11 | 15 | 64 | 53 | 51 |
| Aylesbury United | 46 | 19 | 12 | 15 | 79 | 61 | 50 |
| Basingstoke Town | 46 | 18 | 12 | 16 | 75 | 61 | 48 |
| Dover | 46 | 19 | 8 | 19 | 61 | 63 | 46 |
| Ashford Town | 46 | 16 | 14 | 16 | 52 | 56 | 46 |
| Tonbridge AFC | 46 | 19 | 7 | 20 | 62 | 70 | 45 |
| Dunstable | 46 | 18 | 8 | 20 | 63 | 68 | 44 |
| Salisbury | 46 | 16 | 10 | 20 | 64 | 81 | 42 |
| Hounslow | 46 | 15 | 11 | 20 | 59 | 83 | 41 |
| Hillingdon Borough | 46 | 14 | 10 | 22 | 46 | 58 | 38 |
| Canterbury City | 46 | 10 | 16 | 20 | 49 | 78 | 36 |
| Crawley Town | 46 | 9 | 12 | 25 | 46 | 81 | 30 |
| Folkestone | 46 | 10 | 6 | 30 | 49 | 101 | 26 |
| Andover | 46 | 4 | 11 | 31 | 39 | 100 | 19 |
| Thanet United | 46 | 5 | 7 | 34 | 37 | 110 | 17 |

### Leading Goalscorers
31 Courtney (Poole T)
27 Senior (Dorchester T)
25 Cordice A. (Wealdstone)
23 Batten (Hastings U)
22 Finneston (Addlestone & Weybridge T)
20 Bowkett (Wealdstone)
20 Eddie (Basingstoke T)
19 Fuller (Dunstable)
19 Hampshare (Hastings U)
19 Thompson (Salisbury)
18 Jolley (Dover)

# OTHER LEAGUE TABLES 1981–82

## ATHENIAN LEAGUE

| | P | W | D | L | F | A | Pts |
|---|---|---|---|---|---|---|---|
| Leyton-Wingate | 36 | 28 | 8 | 0 | 87 | 19 | 64 |
| Edgware | 36 | 20 | 10 | 6 | 76 | 52 | 50 |
| Uxbridge | 36 | 20 | 9 | 7 | 56 | 27 | 49 |
| Burnham | 36 | 19 | 7 | 10 | 64 | 44 | 45 |
| Redhill | 36 | 14 | 13 | 9 | 43 | 38 | 41 |
| Harefield United | 36 | 14 | 12 | 10 | 52 | 47 | 40 |
| Ruislip Manor | 36 | 15 | 9 | 12 | 58 | 55 | 39 |
| Banstead Athletic | 36 | 13 | 12 | 11 | 51 | 39 | 38 |
| Chertsey Town | 36 | 11 | 14 | 11 | 43 | 44 | 36 |
| Woodford Town | 36 | 13 | 8 | 15 | 48 | 45 | 34 |
| Marlow | 36 | 12 | 8 | 16 | 40 | 46 | 32 |
| Kingsbury Town | 36 | 11 | 10 | 15 | 43 | 52 | 32 |
| Whyteleafe | 36 | 8 | 15 | 13 | 30 | 41 | 31 |
| Horley Town | 36 | 10 | 10 | 16 | 40 | 45 | 30 |
| Hoddesdon Town | 36 | 11 | 7 | 18 | 50 | 57 | 29 |
| Grays Athletic | 36 | 10 | 8 | 18 | 41 | 62 | 28 |
| Chalfont St Peter | 36 | 8 | 10 | 18 | 42 | 50 | 26 |
| Fleet Town | 36 | 7 | 9 | 20 | 38 | 76 | 23 |
| Haringey Borough | 36 | 4 | 9 | 23 | 27 | 90 | 17 |

## THE CENTRAL LEAGUE

| | P | W | D | L | F | A | Pts |
|---|---|---|---|---|---|---|---|
| Liverpool | 42 | 29 | 9 | 4 | 87 | 30 | 67 |
| Everton | 42 | 30 | 3 | 9 | 98 | 32 | 63 |
| Aston Villa | 42 | 25 | 7 | 10 | 94 | 45 | 57 |
| Nottingham F | 42 | 23 | 10 | 9 | 102 | 37 | 56 |
| Newcastle U | 42 | 19 | 10 | 13 | 61 | 57 | 48 |
| Wolverhampton W | 42 | 19 | 10 | 13 | 79 | 69 | 48 |
| WBA | 42 | 17 | 13 | 12 | 57 | 44 | 47 |
| Sheffield U | 42 | 16 | 14 | 12 | 51 | 43 | 46 |
| Manchester U | 42 | 18 | 8 | 16 | 58 | 44 | 44 |
| Derby Co | 42 | 18 | 8 | 16 | 60 | 54 | 44 |
| Leeds U | 42 | 18 | 5 | 19 | 60 | 53 | 41 |
| Sheffield W | 42 | 18 | 5 | 19 | 75 | 76 | 41 |
| Coventry C | 42 | 15 | 11 | 16 | 49 | 59 | 41 |
| Stoke C | 42 | 11 | 15 | 16 | 50 | 61 | 37 |
| Bury | 42 | 13 | 9 | 20 | 48 | 74 | 35 |
| Blackpool | 42 | 14 | 7 | 21 | 56 | 85 | 35 |
| Blackburn R | 42 | 10 | 14 | 18 | 58 | 81 | 34 |
| Manchester C | 42 | 12 | 9 | 21 | 43 | 73 | 33 |
| Preston NE | 42 | 12 | 8 | 22 | 60 | 86 | 32 |
| Huddersfield T | 42 | 12 | 5 | 25 | 45 | 87 | 29 |
| Burnley | 42 | 7 | 11 | 24 | 42 | 88 | 25 |
| Bolton W | 42 | 6 | 9 | 27 | 54 | 109 | 21 |

## CHESHIRE COUNTY LEAGUE

### DIVISION ONE

| | P | W | D | L | F | A | Pts |
|---|---|---|---|---|---|---|---|
| Hyde United | 38 | 27 | 8 | 3 | 91 | 34 | 62 |
| Chorley | 38 | 23 | 9 | 6 | 70 | 34 | 55 |
| Burscough | 38 | 21 | 10 | 7 | 70 | 39 | 52 |
| Winsford United | 38 | 21 | 9 | 8 | 68 | 43 | 51 |
| Rossendale United | 38 | 18 | 10 | 10 | 62 | 44 | 46 |
| Glossop | 38 | 13 | 19 | 6 | 52 | 30 | 45 |
| Darwen* | 38 | 16 | 10 | 12 | 63 | 62 | 40 |
| Curzon Ashton | 38 | 12 | 15 | 11 | 57 | 50 | 39 |
| Prescot Cables* | 38 | 16 | 8 | 14 | 51 | 45 | 38 |
| Stalybridge Celtic | 38 | 14 | 9 | 15 | 71 | 66 | 37 |
| Fleetwood Town | 38 | 12 | 13 | 13 | 42 | 55 | 37 |
| Formby | 38 | 12 | 11 | 15 | 42 | 55 | 35 |
| Accrington Stanley | 38 | 11 | 11 | 16 | 40 | 57 | 33 |
| Nantwich Town* | 38 | 10 | 13 | 15 | 48 | 49 | 31 |
| Leek Town | 38 | 10 | 11 | 17 | 39 | 45 | 31 |
| Horwich RMI | 38 | 12 | 7 | 19 | 58 | 72 | 31 |
| Bootle | 38 | 11 | 12 | 15 | 49 | 47 | 30 |
| St Helens Town | 38 | 7 | 11 | 20 | 34 | 71 | 25 |
| Ashton United | 38 | 8 | 6 | 24 | 38 | 77 | 22 |
| Droylsden | 38 | 3 | 4 | 31 | 26 | 96 | 10 |

*2 points deducted for fielding ineligible players.*

### DIVISION TWO

| | P | W | D | L | F | A | Pts |
|---|---|---|---|---|---|---|---|
| Congleton Town | 38 | 25 | 9 | 4 | 67 | 20 | 59 |
| Rhyl | 38 | 24 | 10 | 4 | 84 | 29 | 58 |
| Irlam Town | 38 | 23 | 10 | 5 | 67 | 27 | 56 |
| Leyland Motors | 38 | 19 | 14 | 5 | 79 | 45 | 52 |
| Maghull | 38 | 20 | 7 | 11 | 64 | 48 | 47 |
| Radcliffe Borough | 38 | 18 | 7 | 13 | 64 | 39 | 43 |
| Kirkby Town | 38 | 17 | 9 | 12 | 53 | 42 | 43 |
| Warrington Town | 38 | 17 | 8 | 13 | 52 | 35 | 42 |
| Eastwood (Hanley)* | 38 | 16 | 9 | 13 | 62 | 41 | 39 |
| Middlewich Athletic* | 38 | 15 | 11 | 12 | 42 | 34 | 39 |
| Atherton LR | 38 | 14 | 11 | 13 | 46 | 46 | 39 |
| Ford Motors | 38 | 13 | 10 | 15 | 48 | 59 | 36 |
| Prescot BI | 38 | 14 | 7 | 17 | 64 | 70 | 35 |
| Ellesmere Port & Neston | 38 | 13 | 6 | 19 | 43 | 55 | 32 |
| Skelmersdale United* | 38 | 13 | 5 | 20 | 32 | 49 | 29 |
| Salford | 38 | 9 | 6 | 23 | 34 | 65 | 24 |
| Atherton Collieries | 38 | 8 | 7 | 23 | 41 | 85 | 23 |
| Ashton Town | 38 | 6 | 9 | 23 | 40 | 76 | 21 |
| New Mills | 38 | 6 | 8 | 24 | 31 | 93 | 20 |
| Prestwich Heys | 38 | 6 | 7 | 26 | 30 | 75 | 15 |

*2 points deducted for fielding ineligible players.*

## ESSEX SENIOR LEAGUE

| | P | W | D | L | F | A | Pts |
|---|---|---|---|---|---|---|---|
| Heybridge Swifts | 32 | 26 | 4 | 2 | 74 | 21 | 56 |
| Wivenhoe Town | 32 | 20 | 4 | 8 | 66 | 35 | 44 |
| Brentwood | 32 | 19 | 5 | 8 | 61 | 32 | 43 |
| Bowers United | 32 | 16 | 8 | 8 | 56 | 33 | 40 |
| Witham Town | 32 | 16 | 6 | 10 | 49 | 27 | 38 |
| Sawbridgeworth | 32 | 16 | 5 | 11 | 55 | 35 | 37 |
| Canvey Island | 32 | 15 | 7 | 10 | 42 | 38 | 37 |
| Brightlingsea United | 32 | 12 | 9 | 11 | 34 | 44 | 33 |
| Stansted | 32 | 11 | 10 | 11 | 42 | 41 | 32 |
| Halstead Town | 32 | 13 | 4 | 15 | 52 | 49 | 30 |
| Chelmsford Res | 32 | 8 | 10 | 14 | 36 | 53 | 26 |
| Coggeshall Town | 32 | 9 | 8 | 15 | 39 | 56 | 26 |
| Ford United | 32 | 11 | 3 | 18 | 36 | 70 | 25 |
| East Thurrock United | 32 | 6 | 10 | 16 | 25 | 47 | 22 |
| Maldon Town | 32 | 6 | 9 | 17 | 36 | 59 | 21 |
| Eton Manor* | 32 | 7 | 7 | 18 | 26 | 60 | 20 |
| East Ham United | 32 | 3 | 7 | 22 | 29 | 56 | 13 |

*1 point deducted*

## THE FOOTBALL COMBINATION

| | P | W | D | L | F | A | Pts |
|---|---|---|---|---|---|---|---|
| QPR | 38 | 27 | 5 | 6 | 90 | 40 | 59 |
| Southampton | 38 | 26 | 6 | 6 | 88 | 36 | 58 |
| Ipswich Town | 38 | 25 | 6 | 7 | 84 | 37 | 56 |
| Watford | 38 | 20 | 9 | 9 | 57 | 46 | 49 |
| Fulham | 38 | 16 | 15 | 7 | 58 | 30 | 47 |
| Norwich City | 38 | 18 | 9 | 11 | 67 | 52 | 45 |
| West Ham United | 38 | 18 | 7 | 13 | 74 | 48 | 43 |
| Tottenham Hotspur | 38 | 16 | 10 | 12 | 56 | 46 | 42 |
| Birmingham City | 38 | 16 | 10 | 12 | 48 | 40 | 42 |
| Luton Town | 38 | 13 | 11 | 14 | 52 | 52 | 37 |
| Arsenal | 38 | 10 | 12 | 16 | 47 | 51 | 32 |
| Orient | 38 | 11 | 9 | 18 | 53 | 59 | 31 |
| Swindon Town | 38 | 11 | 9 | 18 | 52 | 66 | 31 |
| Chelsea | 38 | 11 | 9 | 18 | 42 | 58 | 31 |
| Leicester City | 38 | 10 | 10 | 18 | 47 | 64 | 30 |
| Plymouth Argyle | 38 | 10 | 9 | 19 | 41 | 64 | 29 |
| Crystal Palace | 38 | 12 | 2 | 24 | 46 | 78 | 26 |
| Bristol Rovers | 38 | 10 | 6 | 22 | 35 | 80 | 26 |
| Oxford United | 38 | 8 | 7 | 23 | 38 | 68 | 23 |
| Reading | 38 | 7 | 9 | 22 | 39 | 99 | 23 |

## GLOUCESTERSHIRE COUNTY LEAGUE

| | P | W | D | L | F | A | Pts |
|---|---|---|---|---|---|---|---|
| Shortwood United | 32 | 22 | 6 | 4 | 92 | 49 | 50 |
| Almondsbury Greenway | 32 | 21 | 7 | 4 | 88 | 32 | 49 |
| Lydbrook Athletic | 32 | 17 | 11 | 4 | 69 | 36 | 45 |
| Wilton Rovers | 32 | 18 | 6 | 8 | 66 | 44 | 42 |
| Imm Bristol St George* | 32 | 19 | 5 | 8 | 75 | 42 | 41 |
| Port of Bristol | 32 | 16 | 6 | 10 | 70 | 53 | 38 |
| Old Georgians | 32 | 16 | 6 | 10 | 56 | 39 | 38 |
| Hambrook | 32 | 13 | 8 | 11 | 54 | 57 | 34 |
| Sharpness | 32 | 11 | 10 | 11 | 60 | 49 | 32 |
| Oldland | 32 | 10 | 9 | 13 | 44 | 57 | 29 |
| Hanham Athletic | 32 | 6 | 15 | 11 | 41 | 50 | 27 |
| Yate Town | 32 | 8 | 8 | 16 | 53 | 81 | 24 |
| Newent Town | 32 | 7 | 9 | 16 | 29 | 54 | 23 |
| Matson Athletic | 32 | 8 | 6 | 18 | 43 | 72 | 22 |
| Frampton United | 32 | 6 | 8 | 18 | 41 | 60 | 20 |
| Cadbury Heath | 32 | 4 | 8 | 20 | 27 | 74 | 16 |
| Stonehouse | 32 | 3 | 6 | 23 | 34 | 93 | 12 |

*2 points deducted.*

## HAMPSHIRE LEAGUE

### DIVISION ONE

| | P | W | D | L | F | A | Pts |
|---|---|---|---|---|---|---|---|
| AFC Totton | 38 | 24 | 7 | 7 | 67 | 33 | 55 |
| Sholing Sports | 38 | 23 | 6 | 9 | 65 | 28 | 52 |
| Newport | 38 | 20 | 9 | 9 | 56 | 40 | 49 |
| Eastleigh | 38 | 19 | 8 | 11 | 53 | 29 | 46 |
| Southampton A | 38 | 18 | 7 | 13 | 56 | 49 | 43 |
| Brockenhurst | 38 | 15 | 12 | 11 | 64 | 47 | 42 |
| Horndean | 38 | 15 | 11 | 12 | 51 | 48 | 41 |
| Havant Town | 38 | 15 | 10 | 13 | 56 | 65 | 40 |
| Downton | 38 | 14 | 11 | 13 | 51 | 57 | 39 |
| Portsmouth RN | 38 | 14 | 9 | 15 | 53 | 56 | 37 |
| Pegasus | 38 | 14 | 9 | 15 | 47 | 50 | 37 |
| Brading Town | 38 | 13 | 11 | 14 | 42 | 56 | 37 |
| Gosport Borough | 38 | 11 | 12 | 15 | 45 | 53 | 34 |
| Fareham Town | 38 | 9 | 16 | 13 | 30 | 41 | 34 |
| Netley Central Sports | 38 | 8 | 15 | 15 | 45 | 62 | 31 |
| Romsey Town | 38 | 10 | 10 | 18 | 38 | 55 | 30 |
| Waterlooville | 38 | 11 | 7 | 20 | 45 | 58 | 29 |
| Moneyfield Sports | 38 | 9 | 11 | 18 | 56 | 75 | 29 |
| Pirelli General | 38 | 8 | 12 | 18 | 41 | 50 | 28 |
| East Cowes Vics | 38 | 9 | 9 | 20 | 50 | 60 | 27 |

# HELLENIC LEAGUE

## PREMIER DIVISION

| | P | W | D | L | F | A | Pts |
|---|---|---|---|---|---|---|---|
| Forest Green Rovers | 30 | 23 | 1 | 6 | 71 | 20 | 47 |
| Moreton Town | 30 | 13 | 13 | 4 | 44 | 32 | 39 |
| Wantage Town | 30 | 14 | 10 | 6 | 42 | 28 | 38 |
| Newbury Town | 30 | 14 | 8 | 8 | 62 | 38 | 36 |
| Maidenhead Town | 30 | 14 | 6 | 10 | 46 | 34 | 34 |
| Fairford Town | 30 | 12 | 10 | 8 | 41 | 29 | 34 |
| Abingdon Town | 30 | 13 | 7 | 10 | 34 | 32 | 33 |
| Flackwell Heath | 30 | 11 | 10 | 9 | 27 | 30 | 32 |
| Thame United | 30 | 9 | 10 | 11 | 40 | 39 | 28 |
| Bicester Town | 30 | 9 | 10 | 11 | 40 | 42 | 28 |
| Wallingford Town | 30 | 11 | 5 | 14 | 40 | 54 | 27 |
| Clanfield | 30 | 8 | 8 | 14 | 33 | 53 | 24 |
| Northwood | 30 | 9 | 3 | 18 | 35 | 47 | 21 |
| Hazells | 30 | 7 | 7 | 16 | 26 | 51 | 21 |
| Didcot Town | 30 | 5 | 10 | 15 | 18 | 40 | 20 |
| Kidlington | 30 | 6 | 6 | 18 | 26 | 56 | 18 |

## DIVISION ONE

| | P | W | D | L | F | A | Pts |
|---|---|---|---|---|---|---|---|
| Lambourn Sports | 30 | 21 | 4 | 5 | 65 | 30 | 46 |
| Abingdon United | 30 | 18 | 6 | 6 | 68 | 40 | 42 |
| Viking Sports | 30 | 17 | 6 | 7 | 59 | 40 | 40 |
| Milton Keynes Borough | 30 | 17 | 5 | 8 | 63 | 36 | 39 |
| Badminton | 30 | 16 | 5 | 9 | 65 | 35 | 37 |
| Brackley Town | 30 | 15 | 7 | 8 | 47 | 29 | 37 |
| Cirencester Town | 30 | 12 | 10 | 8 | 54 | 37 | 34 |
| Rayners Lane | 30 | 14 | 6 | 10 | 47 | 35 | 34 |
| Morris Motors | 30 | 13 | 6 | 11 | 57 | 59 | 32 |
| Lydney Town | 30 | 8 | 15 | 7 | 38 | 34 | 31 |
| Thatcham Town | 30 | 11 | 6 | 13 | 54 | 53 | 28 |
| Pressed Steel | 30 | 6 | 9 | 15 | 39 | 50 | 21 |
| Lowty Staverton | 30 | 7 | 6 | 18 | 31 | 57 | 19 |
| Worrall Hill | 30 | 7 | 5 | 18 | 40 | 81 | 19 |
| AFC Aldermaston | 30 | 3 | 8 | 19 | 31 | 75 | 14 |
| Easington Sports | 30 | 2 | 3 | 25 | 21 | 88 | 7 |

# KENT LEAGUE

## DIVISION ONE

| | P | W | D | L | F | A | Pts |
|---|---|---|---|---|---|---|---|
| Erith & Belvedere | 30 | 17 | 10 | 3 | 45 | 22 | 44 |
| Sittingbourne | 30 | 16 | 11 | 3 | 65 | 33 | 43 |
| Chatham | 30 | 18 | 5 | 7 | 61 | 34 | 41 |
| Sheppey United | 30 | 16 | 5 | 9 | 60 | 40 | 37 |
| Crockenhill | 30 | 11 | 13 | 6 | 54 | 41 | 35 |
| Slade Green | 30 | 11 | 13 | 6 | 45 | 32 | 35 |
| Whitstable Town | 30 | 11 | 12 | 7 | 48 | 37 | 34 |
| Cray Wanderers | 30 | 13 | 6 | 11 | 51 | 40 | 32 |
| Deal Town | 30 | 11 | 10 | 9 | 44 | 36 | 32 |
| Ramsgate | 30 | 9 | 9 | 12 | 44 | 47 | 27 |
| Hythe Town | 30 | 10 | 7 | 13 | 48 | 52 | 27 |
| Darenth Heathside | 30 | 10 | 4 | 16 | 37 | 50 | 24 |
| Tunbridge Wells | 30 | 8 | 6 | 16 | 36 | 58 | 22 |
| Herne Bay | 30 | 7 | 6 | 17 | 36 | 65 | 20 |
| Faversham Town | 30 | 4 | 8 | 18 | 26 | 50 | 16 |
| Kent Police | 30 | 2 | 7 | 21 | 35 | 98 | 11 |

# LANCASHIRE COMBINATION

| | P | W | D | L | F | A | Pts |
|---|---|---|---|---|---|---|---|
| Caernarfon Town | 34 | 23 | 8 | 3 | 71 | 27 | 54 |
| Colne Dynamoes | 34 | 24 | 4 | 6 | 72 | 33 | 52 |
| Nelson | 34 | 19 | 7 | 8 | 66 | 44 | 45 |
| Wren Rovers | 34 | 18 | 7 | 9 | 67 | 47 | 43 |
| Clitheroe | 34 | 13 | 16 | 5 | 67 | 40 | 42 |
| Great Harwood Town | 34 | 16 | 8 | 10 | 61 | 47 | 40 |
| Chadderton | 34 | 17 | 5 | 12 | 62 | 43 | 39 |
| Blackpool Mechanics | 34 | 14 | 9 | 11 | 47 | 34 | 37 |
| Vulcan Newton | 34 | 13 | 8 | 13 | 61 | 46 | 34 |
| Padiham | 34 | 14 | 6 | 14 | 47 | 47 | 34 |
| Lytham | 34 | 11 | 11 | 12 | 74 | 66 | 33 |
| Oldham Dew | 34 | 12 | 6 | 16 | 48 | 61 | 30 |
| Wigan Rovers | 34 | 11 | 7 | 16 | 44 | 53 | 29 |
| Bacup Borough | 34 | 9 | 8 | 17 | 47 | 77 | 26 |
| Whitworth Valley | 34 | 5 | 12 | 17 | 42 | 68 | 22 |
| Daisy Hill | 34 | 5 | 9 | 20 | 31 | 64 | 19 |
| Bolton ST | 34 | 7 | 4 | 23 | 40 | 86 | 18 |
| Ashton Athletic | 34 | 4 | 7 | 23 | 22 | 76 | 15 |

# LEICESTERSHIRE SENIOR LEAGUE

## DIVISION ONE

| | P | W | D | L | F | A | Pts |
|---|---|---|---|---|---|---|---|
| Anstey Nomads* | 30 | 22 | 7 | 1 | 81 | 25 | 49 |
| Birstall United | 30 | 19 | 6 | 5 | 64 | 29 | 44 |
| Enderby Reserves | 30 | 19 | 4 | 7 | 53 | 36 | 42 |
| Stapenhill* | 30 | 19 | 2 | 9 | 74 | 43 | 38 |
| Wigston Fields | 30 | 16 | 3 | 11 | 56 | 39 | 35 |
| Oadby Town | 30 | 16 | 2 | 12 | 54 | 36 | 34 |
| Earl Shilton Albion | 30 | 15 | 3 | 12 | 56 | 43 | 33 |
| Friar Lane Old Boys | 30 | 15 | 3 | 12 | 63 | 54 | 33 |
| Melton Town | 30 | 13 | 5 | 12 | 62 | 40 | 31 |
| Harborough Town | 30 | 11 | 4 | 15 | 43 | 59 | 26 |
| Wigston Town | 30 | 8 | 7 | 15 | 41 | 45 | 23 |
| Desford Colliery | 30 | 7 | 9 | 14 | 51 | 69 | 23 |
| Lutterworth Town | 30 | 10 | 3 | 17 | 27 | 46 | 23 |
| Quorn | 30 | 6 | 8 | 16 | 31 | 73 | 20 |
| Hinckley Town* | 30 | 5 | 5 | 20 | 33 | 73 | 13 |
| Thringstone MW | 30 | 2 | 3 | 25 | 20 | 89 | 7 |

* 2 points deducted.

# LONDON SPARTAN LEAGUE

## PREMIER DIVISION

| | P | W | D | L | F | A | Pts |
|---|---|---|---|---|---|---|---|
| Fisher Athletic | 26 | 17 | 7 | 2 | 60 | 18 | 41 |
| Bracknell Town | 26 | 15 | 5 | 6 | 47 | 30 | 35 |
| Merstham | 26 | 14 | 4 | 8 | 41 | 28 | 32 |
| Malden Vale | 26 | 13 | 6 | 7 | 41 | 30 | 32 |
| Beckton United | 26 | 10 | 8 | 8 | 39 | 31 | 28 |
| Waltham Abbey | 26 | 11 | 5 | 10 | 41 | 28 | 27 |
| Alma Swanley | 26 | 10 | 7 | 9 | 47 | 49 | 27 |
| Beckenham Town | 26 | 8 | 8 | 10 | 28 | 24 | 24 |
| Chingford | 26 | 10 | 4 | 12 | 47 | 57 | 24 |
| Swanley Town | 26 | 8 | 6 | 12 | 32 | 45 | 22 |
| Amersham Town | 26 | 6 | 9 | 11 | 33 | 53 | 21 |
| Berkhamsted Town | 26 | 7 | 5 | 14 | 26 | 43 | 19 |
| Greenwich Borough | 26 | 6 | 5 | 15 | 29 | 49 | 17 |
| Ambrose Fleming | 26 | 5 | 5 | 16 | 29 | 55 | 15 |

## MIDLAND COUNTIES LEAGUE

### PREMIER DIVISION

| | P | W | D | L | F | A | Pts |
|---|---|---|---|---|---|---|---|
| Shepshed Charterhouse | 34 | 22 | 7 | 5 | 78 | 26 | 51 |
| Alfreton Town | 34 | 20 | 7 | 7 | 64 | 24 | 47 |
| Eastwood Town | 34 | 19 | 8 | 7 | 62 | 34 | 46 |
| Spalding United | 34 | 14 | 14 | 6 | 49 | 35 | 42 |
| Guisborough Town | 34 | 16 | 9 | 9 | 49 | 37 | 41 |
| Appleby Frodingham | 34 | 16 | 8 | 10 | 53 | 50 | 40 |
| Heanor Town | 34 | 12 | 15 | 7 | 40 | 32 | 39 |
| Mexborough Town Athletic | 34 | 14 | 8 | 12 | 45 | 41 | 36 |
| Boston | 34 | 12 | 11 | 11 | 45 | 35 | 35 |
| Skegness Town | 34 | 12 | 11 | 11 | 32 | 37 | 35 |
| Long Eaton United | 34 | 11 | 12 | 11 | 44 | 50 | 34 |
| Belper Town | 34 | 10 | 13 | 11 | 47 | 49 | 33 |
| Bridlington Trinity | 34 | 10 | 9 | 15 | 48 | 56 | 29 |
| Ilkeston Town | 34 | 8 | 9 | 17 | 35 | 46 | 25 |
| Brigg Town | 34 | 6 | 11 | 17 | 30 | 60 | 23 |
| Arnold | 34 | 9 | 4 | 21 | 46 | 74 | 22 |
| Sutton Town | 34 | 5 | 8 | 21 | 27 | 67 | 18 |
| Ashby | 34 | 4 | 8 | 22 | 24 | 64 | 16 |

## MIDLAND FOOTBALL COMBINATION

### DIVISION ONE

| | P | W | D | L | F | A | Pts |
|---|---|---|---|---|---|---|---|
| Chipping Norton Town | 42 | 27 | 9 | 6 | 106 | 43 | 63 |
| Highgate United | 42 | 27 | 6 | 9 | 85 | 46 | 60 |
| Mile Oak Rovers | 42 | 24 | 10 | 8 | 78 | 49 | 58 |
| Cinderford Town | 42 | 19 | 16 | 7 | 71 | 40 | 54 |
| Oldbury United | 42 | 22 | 8 | 12 | 67 | 44 | 52 |
| Bridgnorth Town | 42 | 20 | 12 | 10 | 65 | 47 | 52 |
| Moor Green | 42 | 22 | 7 | 13 | 84 | 59 | 51 |
| Knowle | 42 | 16 | 16 | 10 | 64 | 50 | 48 |
| Walsall Sportsco | 42 | 18 | 10 | 14 | 68 | 54 | 46 |
| Racing Club Warwick | 42 | 16 | 13 | 13 | 68 | 64 | 45 |
| West Midlands Police | 42 | 14 | 14 | 14 | 70 | 70 | 42 |
| Boldmere St Michaels | 42 | 14 | 14 | 14 | 59 | 60 | 42 |
| Coleshill Town | 42 | 16 | 8 | 18 | 57 | 68 | 40 |
| Stratford Town | 42 | 12 | 12 | 18 | 37 | 49 | 36 |
| Smethwick Highfield | 42 | 13 | 10 | 19 | 49 | 64 | 36 |
| Northfield Town | 42 | 15 | 6 | 21 | 56 | 76 | 36 |
| Solihull Borough | 42 | 11 | 13 | 18 | 46 | 68 | 35 |
| Cradley Town | 42 | 12 | 10 | 20 | 60 | 80 | 34 |
| Paget Rangers | 42 | 10 | 14 | 18 | 43 | 63 | 34 |
| Walsall Wood | 42 | 9 | 8 | 25 | 40 | 82 | 26 |
| Evesham United | 42 | 6 | 9 | 27 | 40 | 83 | 21 |
| Hurley Daw Mill | 42 | 3 | 7 | 32 | 42 | 96 | 13 |

## SOUTH MIDLANDS LEAGUE

### PREMIER DIVISION

| | P | W | D | L | F | A | Pts |
|---|---|---|---|---|---|---|---|
| Pirton | 32 | 21 | 6 | 5 | 59 | 25 | 48 |
| Arlesey Town | 32 | 21 | 6 | 5 | 61 | 28 | 48 |
| Stotfold | 32 | 20 | 7 | 5 | 73 | 33 | 47 |
| 61 FC (Luton) | 32 | 21 | 3 | 8 | 65 | 31 | 45 |
| Winslow United | 32 | 16 | 7 | 9 | 59 | 44 | 39 |
| Baldock Town | 32 | 15 | 6 | 11 | 49 | 37 | 36 |
| Royston Town | 32 | 15 | 4 | 13 | 48 | 42 | 34 |
| Walden Rangers | 32 | 13 | 6 | 13 | 35 | 43 | 32 |
| Shillington | 32 | 11 | 8 | 13 | 44 | 41 | 30 |
| Vauxhall Motors | 32 | 10 | 8 | 14 | 50 | 52 | 28 |
| Sandy Albions | 32 | 12 | 4 | 16 | 43 | 57 | 28 |
| Biggleswade Town | 32 | 9 | 8 | 15 | 45 | 53 | 26 |
| Selby | 32 | 12 | 2 | 18 | 43 | 55 | 26 |
| Waterlows | 32 | 9 | 7 | 16 | 34 | 57 | 25 |
| Hatfield Town | 32 | 6 | 10 | 16 | 34 | 64 | 22 |
| BAC | 32 | 4 | 7 | 21 | 26 | 65 | 15 |
| Harpenden Town | 32 | 4 | 7 | 21 | 30 | 82 | 13 |

## WEST MIDLANDS (REGIONAL) LEAGUE

### PREMIER DIVISION

| | P | W | D | L | F | A | Pts |
|---|---|---|---|---|---|---|---|
| Shifnal Town | 42 | 26 | 11 | 5 | 82 | 36 | 63 |
| Sutton Coldfield Town | 42 | 26 | 9 | 7 | 80 | 43 | 61 |
| Halesowen Town | 42 | 24 | 8 | 10 | 84 | 45 | 56 |
| Bilston | 42 | 23 | 8 | 11 | 70 | 49 | 54 |
| Ledbury Town | 42 | 19 | 14 | 9 | 83 | 58 | 52 |
| Rushall Olympic | 42 | 16 | 18 | 8 | 72 | 54 | 50 |
| Willenhall Town | 42 | 18 | 11 | 13 | 64 | 46 | 47 |
| VS Rugby | 42 | 20 | 7 | 15 | 67 | 51 | 47 |
| Blakenall | 42 | 20 | 7 | 15 | 59 | 53 | 47 |
| Dudley Town | 42 | 17 | 12 | 13 | 61 | 52 | 46 |
| Wednesfield Social | 42 | 15 | 13 | 14 | 43 | 42 | 43 |
| Lye Town | 42 | 15 | 12 | 15 | 59 | 49 | 42 |
| Hednesford Town | 42 | 17 | 8 | 17 | 61 | 57 | 42 |
| Coventry Sporting | 42 | 13 | 11 | 18 | 43 | 54 | 37 |
| Gresley Rovers | 42 | 13 | 9 | 20 | 50 | 59 | 35 |
| Hinckley Athletic | 42 | 12 | 10 | 20 | 43 | 66 | 34 |
| Tividale | 42 | 13 | 6 | 23 | 56 | 82 | 32 |
| Malvern Town | 42 | 11 | 10 | 21 | 49 | 78 | 32 |
| Armitage | 42 | 10 | 11 | 21 | 43 | 69 | 31 |
| Oldswinford | 42 | 9 | 11 | 22 | 48 | 74 | 29 |
| Brereton Social | 42 | 7 | 10 | 25 | 47 | 100 | 24 |
| Darlaston | 42 | 6 | 8 | 28 | 37 | 84 | 20 |

## NORTHERN ALLIANCE

| | P | W | D | L | F | A | Pts |
|---|---|---|---|---|---|---|---|
| Percy Main | 34 | 23 | 5 | 6 | 77 | 38 | 51 |
| Morpeth Town | 34 | 21 | 6 | 7 | 74 | 49 | 48 |
| Bedlington Terriers | 34 | 19 | 6 | 9 | 81 | 37 | 44 |
| Forest Hall | 34 | 18 | 8 | 8 | 68 | 33 | 44 |
| High Pit Social | 34 | 18 | 8 | 8 | 63 | 47 | 44 |
| Esh Winning Pine | 34 | 17 | 7 | 10 | 58 | 41 | 41 |
| Darlington CL BR | 34 | 15 | 8 | 11 | 52 | 42 | 32 |
| Dudley Welfare | 34 | 15 | 8 | 11 | 42 | 42 | 38 |
| Ryhope CA | 34 | 16 | 5 | 13 | 52 | 46 | 37 |
| Carlisle City | 34 | 13 | 6 | 15 | 47 | 58 | 32 |
| Wigton | 34 | 11 | 9 | 14 | 50 | 50 | 31 |
| Shotton Comrades | 34 | 10 | 10 | 14 | 42 | 50 | 30 |
| Cramlington New Town | 34 | 14 | 2 | 18 | 49 | 64 | 30 |
| Stockton Town | 34 | 10 | 7 | 17 | 40 | 55 | 27 |
| Wallsend Town | 34 | 7 | 6 | 21 | 43 | 68 | 20 |
| Stobswood Welfare | 34 | 7 | 6 | 21 | 26 | 82 | 20 |
| Alnwick Town | 34 | 7 | 5 | 22 | 59 | 90 | 19 |
| Wallington | 34 | 6 | 6 | 22 | 34 | 77 | 18 |

## NORTHERN LEAGUE

| | P | W | D | L | F | A | Pts |
|---|---|---|---|---|---|---|---|
| Blyth Spartans | 38 | 25 | 8 | 5 | 77 | 31 | 83 |
| Whitby Town | 38 | 23 | 11 | 4 | 64 | 21 | 80 |
| South Bank | 38 | 20 | 7 | 11 | 72 | 44 | 67 |
| Tow Law Town | 38 | 18 | 8 | 12 | 76 | 58 | 62 |
| Spennymoor United | 38 | 16 | 13 | 9 | 59 | 37 | 61 |
| Billingham Synthonia | 38 | 17 | 9 | 12 | 57 | 46 | 60 |
| Bishop Auckland | 38 | 17 | 8 | 13 | 63 | 51 | 59 |
| Durham City | 38 | 17 | 5 | 16 | 75 | 67 | 56 |
| Shildon | 38 | 16 | 8 | 14 | 57 | 53 | 56 |
| North Shields | 38 | 14 | 13 | 11 | 67 | 61 | 55 |
| Ferryhill Athletic | 38 | 16 | 6 | 16 | 57 | 59 | 54 |
| Horden Colliery Welfare | 38 | 15 | 6 | 17 | 55 | 58 | 51 |
| Crook Town | 38 | 15 | 6 | 17 | 60 | 69 | 51 |
| Evenwood Town | 38 | 13 | 9 | 16 | 57 | 66 | 48 |
| Penrith* | 38 | 13 | 10 | 15 | 63 | 66 | 46 |
| Consett | 38 | 10 | 10 | 18 | 46 | 64 | 40 |
| West Auckland Town | 38 | 9 | 10 | 19 | 42 | 67 | 37 |
| Ashington | 38 | 9 | 8 | 21 | 50 | 87 | 35 |
| Whitley Bay | 38 | 8 | 7 | 23 | 47 | 83 | 31 |
| Willington | 38 | 3 | 10 | 25 | 46 | 102 | 19 |

* 3 points deducted.

## SOUTH-EAST COUNTIES
### SENIOR LEAGUE

|  | P | W | D | L | F | A | Pts |
|---|---|---|---|---|---|---|---|
| Queen's Park Rangers | 30 | 22 | 7 | 1 | 80 | 23 | 51 |
| West Ham United | 30 | 20 | 5 | 5 | 94 | 31 | 45 |
| Tottenham Hotspur | 30 | 16 | 7 | 7 | 63 | 42 | 39 |
| Norwich City | 30 | 13 | 12 | 5 | 47 | 29 | 38 |
| Ipswich Town | 30 | 12 | 11 | 7 | 50 | 35 | 35 |
| Charlton Athletic | 30 | 13 | 9 | 8 | 38 | 28 | 35 |
| Gillingham | 30 | 10 | 10 | 10 | 38 | 43 | 30 |
| Arsenal | 30 | 14 | 2 | 14 | 45 | 44 | 30 |
| Watford | 30 | 11 | 5 | 14 | 56 | 63 | 27 |
| Crystal Palace | 30 | 10 | 6 | 14 | 40 | 54 | 26 |
| Millwall | 30 | 8 | 10 | 12 | 32 | 47 | 26 |
| Chelsea | 30 | 11 | 4 | 15 | 30 | 47 | 26 |
| Portsmouth | 30 | 10 | 5 | 15 | 40 | 51 | 25 |
| Fulham | 30 | 8 | 5 | 17 | 44 | 74 | 21 |
| Southend United | 30 | 5 | 5 | 20 | 26 | 67 | 15 |
| Orient | 30 | 4 | 3 | 23 | 47 | 92 | 11 |

## SOUTH-WESTERN LEAGUE

|  | P | W | D | L | F | A | Pts |
|---|---|---|---|---|---|---|---|
| Newquay | 36 | 24 | 5 | 7 | 89 | 43 | 53 |
| Millbrook | 36 | 23 | 6 | 7 | 75 | 38 | 52 |
| Torpoint | 36 | 22 | 7 | 7 | 106 | 66 | 51 |
| St Blazey | 36 | 23 | 4 | 9 | 81 | 44 | 50 |
| Torrington | 36 | 22 | 6 | 9 | 74 | 38 | 48 |
| Wadebridge Town | 36 | 18 | 10 | 8 | 77 | 39 | 46 |
| Plymouth Civil Service | 36 | 21 | 3 | 12 | 53 | 40 | 45 |
| Penzance | 36 | 19 | 5 | 12 | 63 | 48 | 43 |
| Bugle | 36 | 14 | 10 | 12 | 78 | 70 | 38 |
| Launceston | 36 | 14 | 8 | 14 | 75 | 65 | 36 |
| St Austell | 36 | 10 | 10 | 16 | 47 | 70 | 30 |
| Plymouth Argyle | 36 | 12 | 5 | 19 | 69 | 76 | 29 |
| Tavistock | 36 | 10 | 9 | 17 | 51 | 72 | 29 |
| Newton Abbot | 36 | 10 | 8 | 18 | 38 | 51 | 28 |
| Appledore | 36 | 10 | 8 | 18 | 49 | 72 | 28 |
| Clyst Rovers | 36 | 7 | 10 | 19 | 41 | 78 | 24 |
| Bodmin Town | 36 | 8 | 7 | 21 | 54 | 85 | 23 |
| Truro City | 36 | 5 | 7 | 24 | 40 | 89 | 17 |
| Holsworthy | 36 | 1 | 12 | 23 | 32 | 108 | 14 |

*Plymouth Command withdrew on 6 April, 1982, owing to the Falklands crisis.*

## SUSSEX COUNTY LEAGUE
### DIVISION ONE

|  | P | W | D | L | F | A | Pts |
|---|---|---|---|---|---|---|---|
| Peacehaven & Telscombe* | 30 | 22 | 5 | 2 | 66 | 20 | 48 |
| Littlehampton Town | 30 | 17 | 8 | 5 | 67 | 32 | 42 |
| Burgess Hill Town | 30 | 14 | 10 | 6 | 58 | 48 | 38 |
| Steyning Town | 30 | 16 | 5 | 9 | 65 | 37 | 37 |
| Pagham | 30 | 13 | 9 | 8 | 49 | 36 | 35 |
| Three Bridges | 30 | 13 | 9 | 8 | 40 | 38 | 35 |
| Arundel | 30 | 10 | 11 | 9 | 40 | 36 | 31 |
| Hastings Town | 30 | 11 | 6 | 13 | 39 | 40 | 28 |
| Chichester City | 30 | 8 | 12 | 10 | 40 | 47 | 28 |
| Hailsham Town | 30 | 8 | 11 | 11 | 45 | 58 | 27 |
| Ringmer | 30 | 11 | 5 | 14 | 36 | 52 | 27 |
| Southwick* | 30 | 9 | 10 | 11 | 39 | 37 | 26 |
| Eastbourne Town | 30 | 11 | 3 | 16 | 38 | 43 | 25 |
| Whitehawk | 30 | 7 | 8 | 15 | 38 | 54 | 22 |
| Horsham YMCA | 30 | 3 | 10 | 17 | 19 | 50 | 16 |
| Shoreham | 30 | 2 | 7 | 21 | 37 | 88 | 11 |

* Points adjusted.

## TOWN AND COUNTRY LEAGUE

|  | P | W | D | L | F | A | Pts |
|---|---|---|---|---|---|---|---|
| Tiptree United | 42 | 28 | 9 | 5 | 78 | 32 | 66 |
| Sudbury Town | 42 | 25 | 10 | 7 | 82 | 38 | 60 |
| Gorleston | 42 | 24 | 8 | 10 | 91 | 44 | 56 |
| Great Yarmouth Town | 42 | 22 | 11 | 9 | 84 | 44 | 55 |
| Wisbech Town | 42 | 21 | 9 | 12 | 66 | 40 | 51 |
| Saffron Walden Town | 42 | 21 | 9 | 12 | 75 | 57 | 51 |
| Newmarket Town | 42 | 19 | 11 | 12 | 72 | 56 | 49 |
| Brantham Athletic | 42 | 18 | 13 | 11 | 59 | 50 | 49 |
| Chatteris Town | 42 | 17 | 15 | 10 | 58 | 49 | 49 |
| Colchester United Res | 42 | 15 | 14 | 13 | 67 | 63 | 44 |
| Haverhill Rovers | 42 | 12 | 17 | 13 | 52 | 53 | 41 |
| March Town United | 42 | 13 | 15 | 14 | 58 | 62 | 41 |
| Lowestoft Town | 42 | 15 | 9 | 18 | 68 | 63 | 39 |
| Felixstowe Town | 42 | 14 | 10 | 18 | 60 | 81 | 38 |
| Ely City | 42 | 12 | 13 | 17 | 55 | 78 | 37 |
| Histon | 42 | 12 | 12 | 18 | 48 | 72 | 36 |
| Thetford Town | 42 | 9 | 18 | 15 | 51 | 70 | 36 |
| Bury Town | 42 | 12 | 10 | 20 | 53 | 77 | 34 |
| Braintree | 42 | 10 | 8 | 24 | 53 | 86 | 28 |
| Clacton Town | 42 | 7 | 9 | 26 | 43 | 73 | 23 |
| Soham Town Rangers | 42 | 6 | 9 | 27 | 47 | 74 | 21 |
| Stowmarket | 42 | 5 | 11 | 26 | 42 | 83 | 21 |

## UNITED COUNTIES LEAGUE
### PREMIER DIVISION

|  | P | W | D | L | F | A | Pts |
|---|---|---|---|---|---|---|---|
| Stamford | 36 | 25 | 5 | 6 | 71 | 28 | 55 |
| Irthlingborough Diamonds | 36 | 23 | 8 | 5 | 73 | 34 | 54 |
| Rushden Town | 36 | 19 | 7 | 10 | 61 | 32 | 45 |
| Buckingham Town | 36 | 19 | 7 | 10 | 63 | 43 | 45 |
| Bourne Town | 36 | 18 | 7 | 11 | 64 | 44 | 43 |
| Potton United | 36 | 14 | 11 | 10 | 41 | 30 | 41 |
| Ampthill Town | 36 | 14 | 11 | 11 | 73 | 67 | 39 |
| Long Buckby | 36 | 14 | 10 | 12 | 57 | 60 | 38 |
| Holbeach United | 36 | 14 | 9 | 13 | 53 | 46 | 37 |
| Wootton Blue Cross | 36 | 14 | 9 | 13 | 57 | 58 | 37 |
| Kempston Rovers | 36 | 13 | 10 | 13 | 63 | 62 | 36 |
| Stevenage Borough | 36 | 12 | 9 | 15 | 50 | 49 | 33 |
| Desborough Town | 36 | 10 | 13 | 13 | 49 | 55 | 33 |
| S & L Corby | 36 | 10 | 12 | 14 | 46 | 57 | 32 |
| Rothwell Town | 36 | 12 | 6 | 18 | 48 | 60 | 30 |
| Brit Timken Duston | 36 | 11 | 8 | 17 | 46 | 67 | 30 |
| Eynesbury Rovers | 36 | 8 | 9 | 19 | 35 | 58 | 25 |
| Wolverton Town | 36 | 8 | 4 | 24 | 36 | 68 | 20 |
| St Neots Town | 36 | 2 | 7 | 27 | 25 | 91 | 11 |

## WEARSIDE LEAGUE

|  | P | W | D | L | F | A | Pts |
|---|---|---|---|---|---|---|---|
| Seaham CW Red Star | 38 | 27 | 5 | 6 | 67 | 27 | 59 |
| Peterlee Newtown | 38 | 24 | 8 | 6 | 81 | 31 | 56 |
| Chester-le-Street Town | 38 | 24 | 7 | 7 | 69 | 34 | 55 |
| Reyrolles | 38 | 23 | 7 | 8 | 82 | 50 | 53 |
| Blue Star | 38 | 21 | 9 | 8 | 88 | 40 | 51 |
| Brandon United | 38 | 21 | 8 | 9 | 73 | 48 | 50 |
| Whickham | 38 | 19 | 11 | 8 | 81 | 46 | 49 |
| South Shields | 38 | 22 | 7 | 10 | 66 | 48 | 49 |
| Hartlepool Res | 38 | 18 | 8 | 12 | 69 | 50 | 44 |
| Easington | 38 | 17 | 9 | 12 | 66 | 53 | 43 |
| Roker | 38 | 13 | 13 | 12 | 63 | 68 | 39 |
| Washington | 38 | 12 | 9 | 17 | 50 | 56 | 33 |
| Heaton Stannington | 38 | 13 | 5 | 20 | 53 | 76 | 31 |
| Eppleton CW | 38 | 8 | 9 | 21 | 42 | 58 | 25 |
| Annfield Plain | 38 | 7 | 9 | 22 | 50 | 84 | 23 |
| Wingate | 38 | 9 | 4 | 25 | 59 | 75 | 22 |
| Murton | 38 | 6 | 9 | 23 | 29 | 79 | 21 |
| Stockton | 38 | 8 | 5 | 25 | 46 | 100 | 21 |
| Ryhope CW | 38 | 6 | 7 | 25 | 44 | 89 | 19 |
| Boldon CA | 38 | 4 | 9 | 25 | 38 | 94 | 17 |

## WESTERN LEAGUE

### PREMIER DIVISION

| | P | W | D | L | F | A | Pts |
|---|---|---|---|---|---|---|---|
| Bideford | 38 | 26 | 10 | 2 | 88 | 20 | 62 |
| Barnstaple Town* | 38 | 26 | 8 | 4 | 78 | 31 | 59 |
| Bridgwater Town | 38 | 16 | 16 | 6 | 70 | 46 | 48 |
| Clandown | 38 | 17 | 12 | 9 | 49 | 37 | 46 |
| Melksham Town | 38 | 17 | 11 | 10 | 58 | 50 | 45 |
| Frome Town | 38 | 16 | 9 | 13 | 67 | 58 | 41 |
| Weston-super-Mare | 38 | 15 | 11 | 12 | 47 | 42 | 41 |
| Saltash United | 38 | 15 | 7 | 16 | 47 | 53 | 37 |
| Devizes Town | 38 | 14 | 7 | 17 | 53 | 60 | 35 |
| Dawlish | 38 | 11 | 13 | 14 | 45 | 53 | 35 |
| Liskeard Athletic | 38 | 11 | 12 | 15 | 39 | 48 | 34 |
| Bridport | 38 | 12 | 10 | 16 | 43 | 54 | 34 |
| Clevedon Town* | 38 | 11 | 12 | 15 | 58 | 60 | 33 |
| Chippenham Town | 38 | 12 | 9 | 17 | 33 | 39 | 33 |
| Falmouth Town | 38 | 12 | 9 | 17 | 46 | 55 | 33 |
| Portway-Bristol | 38 | 9 | 13 | 16 | 40 | 47 | 31 |
| Wellington | 38 | 10 | 11 | 17 | 50 | 62 | 31 |
| Keynsham Town | 38 | 9 | 13 | 16 | 39 | 55 | 31 |
| Mangotsfield United | 38 | 11 | 6 | 21 | 30 | 59 | 28 |
| Welton Rovers | 38 | 7 | 7 | 24 | 37 | 88 | 21 |

* 1 point deducted for playing an ineligible player.

### DIVISION ONE

| | P | W | D | L | F | A | Pts |
|---|---|---|---|---|---|---|---|
| Shepton Mallet Town | 36 | 25 | 8 | 3 | 88 | 30 | 58 |
| Exmouth Town | 36 | 24 | 8 | 4 | 74 | 31 | 56 |
| Swanage Town & Herston | 36 | 21 | 5 | 10 | 90 | 47 | 47 |
| Wimborne Town | 36 | 19 | 9 | 8 | 67 | 35 | 47 |
| Bath City | 36 | 19 | 6 | 11 | 72 | 46 | 44 |
| Elmore | 36 | 19 | 6 | 11 | 58 | 45 | 44 |
| Paulton Rovers | 36 | 17 | 6 | 13 | 54 | 48 | 40 |
| Bristol Manor Farm | 36 | 15 | 9 | 12 | 58 | 50 | 39 |
| Torquay United | 36 | 15 | 9 | 12 | 50 | 44 | 39 |
| Tiverton Town | 36 | 13 | 8 | 15 | 62 | 63 | 34 |
| Chard Town | 36 | 12 | 10 | 14 | 43 | 55 | 34 |
| Odd Down | 36 | 14 | 5 | 17 | 51 | 57 | 33 |
| Radstock Town | 36 | 10 | 11 | 15 | 44 | 67 | 31 |
| Glastonbury | 36 | 12 | 6 | 18 | 63 | 69 | 30 |
| Heavitree United | 36 | 11 | 7 | 18 | 39 | 69 | 29 |
| Yeovil Town | 36 | 10 | 8 | 18 | 40 | 53 | 28 |
| Larkhall Athletic | 36 | 10 | 5 | 21 | 42 | 84 | 25 |
| Ottery St Mary | 36 | 6 | 3 | 27 | 28 | 79 | 15 |
| Ilminster Town | 36 | 3 | 5 | 28 | 20 | 70 | 11 |

## YORKSHIRE LEAGUE

### DIVISION ONE

| | P | W | D | L | F | A | Pts |
|---|---|---|---|---|---|---|---|
| Emley | 30 | 16 | 9 | 5 | 57 | 27 | 41 |
| Guiseley | 30 | 17 | 5 | 8 | 52 | 33 | 39 |
| Leeds Ashley Road | 30 | 15 | 9 | 6 | 44 | 30 | 39 |
| Scarborough | 30 | 15 | 7 | 8 | 51 | 38 | 37 |
| Bentley VW | 30 | 13 | 9 | 8 | 46 | 37 | 35 |
| Lincoln United | 30 | 13 | 8 | 9 | 47 | 35 | 34 |
| Winterton Rangers | 30 | 13 | 8 | 9 | 37 | 30 | 34 |
| Thackley | 30 | 13 | 7 | 10 | 51 | 35 | 33 |
| Ossett Albion | 30 | 10 | 11 | 9 | 28 | 26 | 31 |
| North Ferriby United | 30 | 10 | 7 | 13 | 46 | 46 | 27 |
| Sheffield | 30 | 10 | 7 | 13 | 33 | 46 | 27 |
| Hallam | 30 | 10 | 6 | 14 | 46 | 53 | 26 |
| Frecheville CA | 30 | 11 | 3 | 16 | 39 | 48 | 25 |
| Farsley Celtic | 30 | 10 | 2 | 18 | 38 | 54 | 22 |
| Liversedge | 30 | 6 | 5 | 19 | 24 | 52 | 17 |
| York RI | 30 | 5 | 3 | 22 | 28 | 77 | 13 |

### DIVISION TWO

| | P | W | D | L | F | A | Pts |
|---|---|---|---|---|---|---|---|
| Harrogate Town | 30 | 16 | 8 | 6 | 56 | 29 | 40 |
| Ossett Town | 30 | 17 | 6 | 7 | 51 | 29 | 40 |
| Garforth Miners | 30 | 14 | 11 | 5 | 44 | 27 | 39 |
| Bradley Rangers | 30 | 14 | 10 | 6 | 42 | 31 | 38 |
| Maltby MW | 30 | 13 | 8 | 9 | 48 | 39 | 34 |
| BSC (Parkgate) | 30 | 13 | 8 | 9 | 43 | 40 | 34 |
| Norton Woodseats | 30 | 14 | 5 | 11 | 35 | 28 | 33 |
| Hatfield Main | 30 | 10 | 10 | 10 | 42 | 41 | 30 |
| Hall Road Rangers | 30 | 11 | 8 | 11 | 32 | 37 | 30 |
| Harworth Colliery | 30 | 11 | 7 | 12 | 40 | 37 | 29 |
| Bridlington Town | 30 | 9 | 6 | 15 | 35 | 55 | 24 |
| Grimethorpe MWES | 30 | 7 | 9 | 14 | 39 | 42 | 23 |
| Pilkington Recreation | 30 | 5 | 12 | 13 | 29 | 41 | 22 |
| Yorkshire Amateur | 30 | 9 | 4 | 17 | 27 | 53 | 22 |
| Kiveton Park | 30 | 7 | 7 | 16 | 37 | 52 | 21 |
| Fryston CW | 30 | 5 | 11 | 14 | 36 | 56 | 21 |

## FA VASE 1981—82

**Extra Preliminary Round**

| | |
|---|---|
| Dormans Athletic v Bedlington Terriers | 1-4 |
| Wigton v Hebburn Reyrolle | 2-1 |
| Roker v Windscale United | 4-0 |
| Gt Harwood Town v York Railway Inst | 1-0 |
| Milton v Pilkington Recreation | 0-3 |
| Hucknall CW v Grasmere Rovers | aet 1-2 |
| Graham Street Prims v Sutton Trinity | 4-2 |
| Lutterworth Town v Newhall United | 0-1 |
| Yaxley v Atherstone United | 0-2 |
| Barkingside v Bury Town | 2-1 |
| Waterlows v Wivenhoe Town | 0-2 |
| Midland Bank v Highfield | 4-1 |
| Swanage & Herston v Horndean | 2-0 |
| AFC Totton v Warminster Town | 4-0 |
| Hengrove Athletic v Penhill | 0-1 |
| Wilton Rovers v Timsbury Athletic | 4-0 |
| Exmouth Town v Newquay | 2-2 |

**Extra Preliminary Round – Replay**

| | |
|---|---|
| Newquay v Exmouth Town | 4-2 |

**Preliminary Round**

| | |
|---|---|
| Bedlington Terriers v Billingham Social | 4-1 |
| Annfield Plain v High Pit Social | 1-6 |
| Heaton Stannington v Cleator Moor Celtic | 2-1 |
| Percy Main v Boldon CA | 1-0 |

| | |
|---|---|
| Appleby v Wallsend Town | 4-3 |
| Smith's Dock v Brandon United | 1-1 |
| Roker v Darlington RA | 4-0 |
| Chester-le-Street v South Shields | 3-0 |
| Ryhope CA v Norton & Stockton Ancients | 2-1 |
| Ryhope CW v Hartlepool BW | aet 4-2 |
| Gretna v Wingate | aet 2-1 |
| Stockton Buffs v Redcar Albion | 0-3 |
| Seaham CW Red Star v Haig Colliery | 2-1 |
| Eppleton CW v Wigton | 2-1 |
| Stobswood Welfare v Peterlee Newtown | 1-2 |
| Nunthorpe Athletic v Harrogate Town | 1-1 |
| Birkenshawe Rovers v Pickering Town | 1-2 |
| Leyland Motors v Blackpool Rangers | 0-1 |
| Abbey Hey WMC v Salford | 1-2 |
| Padiham v Great Harwood Town | 3-2 |
| Pilkington Recreation v Clitheroe | 3-0 |
| Atherton Collieries v Bradley Rangers | 1-0 |
| Sheffield v Irlam Town | 0-2 |
| Rylands v Dalton United | 1-2 |
| Burnley Belvedere v Brook Sports | aet 1-2 |
| Wren Rovers v Prestwich Heys | 5-0 |
| Maghull v H B & H Newton | 3-2 |
| Chadderton v Ossett Town | 2-0 |
| Wythenshawe Amateurs v Hoylake Athletic | 2-3 |
| Heswall v Lytham | 3-4 |
| Linotype v New Brighton | 2-0 |
| Stork v North Withington | 3-1 |
| Kidsgrove Athletic v Prescot BI | 1-5 |

| | |
|---|---|
| Waterloo Dock v Skelmersdale United | 2-1 |
| Eastwood (Hanley) v BSC (Parkgate) | 2-0 |
| Warrington Town v Stocksbridge Soc | 4-0 |
| Appleby Frodingham v Immingham Town | aet 5-3 |
| Garforth Miners v Yorkshire Amateurs | 0-1 |
| Brigg Town v Harworth Colliery Inst | aet 3-1 |
| Denaby United v North Ferriby United | 0-1 |
| Barton Town v Hatfield Main | 2-3 |
| Hall Road Rangers v Clay Cross Works | 0-0 |
| Bentley Victoria v Grasmere Rovers | 2-1 |
| Fryston Colliery Welfare v Louth United | 2-1 |
| Gresley Rovers v Clipstone Welfare | 1-3 |
| Bourne Town v Anstey Nomads | 2-1 |
| Long Eaton Grange v Graham Street Prims | 2-1 |
| Stapenhill v Mirrlees Blackstone | 2-1 |
| Arnold Kingsell v Paget Rangers | aet 3-2 |
| Armitage v Rainworth Miners Welfare | 1-3 |
| Blakenall v Oakham United | 2-1 |
| Kimberley Town v Mile Oak Rover & Y | aet 5-2 |
| Newhall United v Birstall United | 3-2 |
| Oadby Town v Hinckley Town | aet 1-2 |
| Bridgnorth Town v Wednesfield Social | 1-1 |
| Oldswinford v Knowle | 0-3 |
| Rushall Olympic v Northfield | 0-2 |
| Boldmere St Michaels v VS Rugby | 1-1 |
| Thringstone Miners Welfare v Quorn | 3-1 |
| Oldbury United v Tividale | 2-0 |
| Racing Club Warwick v Rothwell Town | 7-1 |
| Smethwick Highfield v Malvern Town | 0-1 |
| Walsall Wood v Moreton Town | 5-1 |
| Solihull Borough v Wolverton Town | 4-3 |
| West Midlands Police v Bicester Town | 4-3 |
| Holbeach United v Chatteris Town | 1-0 |
| Melton Town v Haverhill Rovers | 1-3 |
| Great Yarmouth Town v Downham Town | 6-1 |
| Diss Town v Wroxham | 2-2 |
| Stowmarket v Ely City | 1-4 |
| Huntingdon United v Hadleigh United | 0-3 |
| Brantham Athletic v Wisbech Town | 1-1 |
| Watton v Histon | 3-0 |
| Soham Town Rangers v Crane Sports | 2-0 |
| Beccles v Tiptree United | aet 3-5 |
| Somersham Town v Felixstowe Town | 0-3 |
| Coggeshall Town v Bungay Town | 1-2 |
| Braintree v St Neots Town | 2-0 |
| March Town United v Clacton Town | 1-0 |
| Brightlingsea United v Heybridge Swifts | 0-2 |
| Harwich & Parkeston v Saffron Walden Town | 5-2 |
| Ampthill Town v Sandy Albions | 5-2 |
| Letchworth Garden City v Atherstone United | 2-0 |
| Potton United v Stansted | aet 0-1 |
| Maldon Town v Wivenhoe Town | 1-3 |
| Selby v Harpenden Town | 4-4 |
| Crown & Manor v Arlesey Town | 0-1 |
| Witham Town v Hoddesdon Town | 3-1 |
| Hemel Hempstead v Wootton Blue Cross | 2-1 |
| Baldock Town v Edgware | 2-3 |
| Barkingside v Epping Town | 5-4 |
| Pirton v Kingsbury Town | 0-1 |
| Amersham Town v Tansley | 2-1 |
| Sawbridgeworth Town v Old Esthameians | 1-5 |
| Greenwich Borough v Woodford Town | aet 2-4 |
| Shillington v Chalfont St Peter | 3-1 |
| Beckton United v Willesden | |
| (Willesden withdrew; Beckton United received w.o.) | |
| Stotfold v East Thurrock United | 2-1 |
| Berkhamsted Town v Hazells (Aylesbury) | 2-1 |
| Welling United v Crockenhill | 2-1 |
| Canvey Island v Midland Bank | 2-0 |
| Deal Town v Redhill | 1-3 |
| Bexhill Town v Tunbridge Wells | 0-0 |
| Herne Bay v Burgess Hill Town | 1-2 |
| Horley Town v Whitstable Town | 3-3 |
| Horsham v Hastings Town | 3-3 |
| Faversham Town v West Wickham | 1-0 |
| Swanley Town v Hythe Town | 3-2 |
| Horsham YMCA v Eastbourne Town | 0-1 |
| Fisher Athletic v East Grinstead | 1-2 |
| Slade Green v Peacehaven & Telscombe | 0-3 |
| Corinthian Casuals v Worthing | 3-1 |
| Three Bridges v Old Salesians | 2-1 |
| Merstham v Chessington United | 2-1 |
| Ulysses v Erith & Belvedere | 0-2 |
| Dorking Town v Steyning Town | 1-0 |
| Arundel v Farnham Town | 2-0 |

| | |
|---|---|
| Frimley Green v Chichester City | 1-2 |
| Malden Town v Shoreham | 1-3 |
| British Aerospace Weybridge v Southwick | aet 2-3 |
| Chobham v Wick | 1-0 |
| Maidenhead Town & Youth v Brockenhurst | 1-3 |
| Eastleigh v Didcot Town | 0-1 |
| Ash United v Littlehampton Town | 5-5 |
| Beckenham Town v Eton Manor | 1-1 |
| Banstead Athletic v Darenth Heathside | 2-1 |
| Egham Town v Thame United | 4-0 |
| Kew Association v Clanfield | 0-1 |
| Chertsey Town v Guildford & Worplesdon | 2-0 |
| Flackwell Heath v Kidlington | 2-1 |
| Marlow v Abingdon Town | 4-2 |
| Southall v Wallingford Town | 2-1 |
| Leighton Town v Chipping Norton Town | 0-5 |
| Bracknell Town v Cirencester Town | 3-1 |
| Portfield v AFC Totton | aet 1-2 |
| Swanage & Herston v Calne Town | 3-0 |
| Pagham v St Martins | 7-0 |
| Pirelli General v Sholing Sports | 1-2 |
| Amesbury v Flight Refuelling | 3-1 |
| Melksham Town v Romsey Town | 2-1 |
| Imm Bristol St George v Evesham United | 1-0 |
| Chippenham Town v Westbury United | 2-0 |
| Shortwood v Fairford Town | 3-2 |
| Portway-Bristol v Matson Athletic | 4-1 |
| Forest Green Rovers v Worrall Hill | 5-1 |
| Wilton Rovers v Park | 2-1 |
| Ledbury Town v Cadbury Heath | 8-2 |
| Bristol Manor Farm v Malmesbury Vic | 6-3 |
| Lydney Town v Imperial Bristol | 1-1 |
| Larkhall Athletic v Glenside St Gab | 2-0 |
| Yate Town v Robinsons DRG | 3-3 |
| Radstock Town v Penhill | 2-4 |
| Sharpness v Backwell United | 0-0 |
| Avon Bradford v Odd Down | 1-4 |
| Appledore v Paulton Rovers | 0-1 |
| Ilminster v Peasedown Athletic | 1-0 |
| Newquay v Torrington | 2-0 |
| Ottery St Mary v Wadebridge Town | 0-6 |

**Preliminary Round – Replays**

| | |
|---|---|
| Brandon United v Smith's Dock | 1-1 |
| Harrogate Town v Nunthorpe Athletic | 2-2 |
| Clay Cross Works v Hall Rd Rangers | aet 3-2 |
| Wednesfield Social v Bridgnorth Town | 1-0 |
| VS Rugby v Boldmere St Michaels | 2-1 |
| Wroxham v Diss Town | 3-0 |
| Wisbech Town v Brantham Athletic | 4-0 |
| Harpenden Town v Selby | 1-1 |
| Tunbridge Wells v Bexhill Town | 2-1 |
| Whitstable Town v Horley Town | 2-1 |
| Hastings Town v Horsham | 2-3 |
| Littlehampton Town v Ash United | 2-4 |
| Eton Manor v Beckenham Town | 1-0 |
| Imperial Bristol v Lydney Town | 4-2 |
| Robinsons DRG v Yate Town | 0-1 |
| Backwell United v Sharpness | 1-0 |

**Preliminary Round – Second Replays**

| | |
|---|---|
| Brandon United v Smith's Dock | aet 3-2 |
| Nunthorpe Athletic v Harrogate Town | 0-1 |
| Harpenden Town v Selby | aet 4-2 |

**First Round**

| | |
|---|---|
| Bedlington Terriers v Appleby | 1-0 |
| Brandon United v Ryhope CW | 4-2 |
| High Pit Social v Chester-le-Street | 0-2 |
| Gretna v Seaham CW Red Star | aet 2-3 |
| Heaton Stannington v Percy Main | 2-0 |
| Redcar Albion v Eppleton CW | 1-2 |
| Roker v Ryhope CA | 1-2 |
| Peterlee Newtown v Nunthorpe Athletic | 2-1 |
| Pickering Town v Salford | 0-0 |
| Padiham v Norton Woodseats | 1-0 |
| Thackley v Tadcaster Albion | 0-0 |
| Blackpool Rangers v Atherton Coll | 1-0 |
| Ossett Albion v Kiveton Park | 4-1 |
| Irlam Town v Dalton United | 2-0 |
| Leeds Ashley Rd v Pilkington Recreation | 5-2 |
| Wren Rovers v Prescot BI | 2-1 |

| | |
|---|---|
| Brook Sports v Maghull | 1-1 |
| Hoylake Athletic v Yorkshire Amateurs | aet 1-0 |
| Appleby Frodingham v Hall Road Rangers | 2-1 |
| Bentley Victoria v Clipstone Welfare | 1-1 |
| Staveley Works v Brigg Town | 8-3 |
| North Ferriby United v Fryston CW | 7-0 |
| Winterton Rangers v Ashby Institute | 0-0 |
| Rainworth MW v Hatfield Main | 3-2 |
| Waterloo Dock v Stork | 3-0 |
| Chadderton v Middlewich Athletic | 0-1 |
| Glossop v Lytham | 1-0 |
| Linotype v Warrington Town | 0-1 |
| Shifnal Town v Eastwood (Hanley) | 4-2 |
| Stapenhill v Wednesfield Social | 3-3 |
| Hinckley Athletic v Bourne Town | 2-0 |
| Long Eaton Grange v Walsall Wood | 2-1 |
| Walsall Sportsco v Arnold Kingswell | 2-0 |
| (at Walsall Wood FC) | |
| Blakenall v Hinckley Town | 4-0 |
| Coventry Sporting v Kimberley Town | 0-2 |
| Knowle v Thringstone Miners Welfare | 6-0 |
| Halesowen Town v Oldbury United | 2-1 |
| Racing Club Warwick v Newhall United | aet 2-4 |
| Desborough Town v Solihull Borough | 4-0 |
| VS Rugby v Northfield | 0-2 |
| Malvern Town v West Midlands Police | 1-2 |
| Buckingham Town v Wilton Rovers | 3-2 |
| Gorleston v Holbeach United | 4-1 |
| Wroxham v March Town United | aet 2-1 |
| Great Yarmouth Town v Hadleigh United | 6-1 |
| Wivenhoe Town v Haverhill Rovers | aet 2-1 |
| Watton v Ely City | 4-0 |
| Tiptree United v Heybridge Swifts | 2-1 |
| Wisbech Town v Soham Town Rangers | 1-0 |
| Bungay Town v Harwich & Parkeston | 3-9 |
| Letchworth GC v Arlesey Town | aet 1-2 |
| Braintree v Felixstowe Town | 3-5 |
| Barton Rovers v Stansted | 3-1 |
| Harpenden Town v Edgware | 2-1 |
| Bowers United v Ampthill Town | 0-4 |
| Hemel Hempstead v Barkingside | 2-0 |
| Royston Town v Rainham Town | 1-2 |
| Witham Town v Kingsbury Town | 0-0 |
| Haringey Borough v Shillington | 3-1 |
| Beckton United v Canvey Island | 3-1 |
| Ford United v Old Esthameians | aet 2-1 |
| Woodford Town v Stotfold | 6-3 |
| Amersham Town v Harefield United | 4-4 |
| Egham Town v Flackwell Heath | 0-2 |
| Ruislip Manor v Corinthian Casuals | 3-1 |
| Erith & Belvedere v Eton Manor | 2-1 |
| Uxbridge v Chipping Norton Town | aet 0-1 |
| Didcot Town v Berkhamsted Town | 0-1 |
| Whyteleafe v Faversham Town | 2-1 |
| Swanley Town v Eastbourne Town | 0-1 |
| Eastbourne United v East Grinstead | 4-2 |
| Peacehaven & Tels v Whitstable Town | 1-3 |
| Ringmer v Merstham | 0-1 |
| Dorking Town v Southwick | 0-2 |
| Chobham v Tunbridge Wells | 2-1 |
| Horsham v Banstead Athletic | 2-1 |
| Redhill v Burgess Hill Town | 1-1 |
| Three Bridges v Welling United | 1-0 |
| Southall v Chertsey Town | 2-0 |
| Shoreham v Pagham | 2-2 |
| Chichester City v Ash United | 1-1 |
| Marlow v Bracknell Town | 2-1 |
| First Tower United v Sholing Sports | 0-1 |
| Brockenhurst v Arundel | 2-1 |
| Newport IOW v AFC Totton | 1-0 |
| Swanage & Herston v Amesbury | 1-0 |
| Melksham Town v Portway-Bristol | 2-0 |
| Forest Green Rovers v Ledbury Town | 2-1 |
| Chippenham Town v Imperial Bristol | 2-0 |
| Port of Bristol v Clanfield | 2-1 |
| Yate Town v Larkhall Athletic | 2-1 |
| Bristol Manor Farm v Imm Bristol St George | 0-0 |
| Odd Down v Backwell United | 4-3 |
| Penhill v Shortwood | 0-1 |
| Paulton Rovers v Ilminster | 2-1 |
| Newquay v Wadebridge Town | 1-0 |

**First Round – Replays**

| | |
|---|---|
| Salford v Pickering Town | aet 2-1 |

| | |
|---|---|
| Tadcaster Albion v Thackley | 0-2 |
| Maghull v Brook Sports | 2-1 |
| Clipstone Welfare v Bentley Victoria | 3-2 |
| Ashby Institute v Winterton Rangers | 1-2 |
| Wednesfield Social v Stapenhill | 2-1 |
| Kingsbury Town v Witham Town | 1-0 |
| Harefield United v Amersham Town | 5-2 |
| Burgess Hill Town v Redhill | 0-1 |
| Pagham v Shoreham | 7-0 |
| Ash United v Chichester City | aet 3-1 |
| Imm Bristol St George v Bristol Manor Farm | 2-1 |

**Second Round**

| | |
|---|---|
| Eppleton CW v Thackley | 1-0 |
| Ryhope CA v Blue Star | 0-2 |
| Peterlee Newtown v Leeds Ashley Road | 4-1 |
| Bedlington Terriers v Whickham | 3-0 |
| Ossett Albion v Heaton Stannington | 2-1 |
| Chester-le-Street v Guisborough Town | 1-3 |
| Padiham v Brandon United | 1-0 |
| Seaham CW Red Star v Guiseley | 3-1 |
| Hoylake Athletic v Maghull | 1-1 |
| (at Maghull FC) | |
| Wren Rovers v Congleton Town | aet 5-4 |
| Irlam Town v Blackpool Rangers | 2-0 |
| (at Marine FC) | |
| Salford v Frecheville Community | 1-2 |
| Glossop v Waterloo Dock | aet 0-1 |
| Warrington Town v Hallam | 0-0 |
| Appleby Frodingham v Clipstone Welfare | 2-0 |
| Staveley Works v Lincoln United | 2-1 |
| Rainworth MW v North Ferriby United | aet 2-1 |
| Winterton Rangers v Skegness Town | 1-2 |
| Walsall Sportsco v Blakenall | 1-1 |
| Middlewich Athletic v Shepshed Charterhouse | 2-1 |
| Newhall United v West Midlands Police | 0-3 |
| (at Burton Albion FC) | |
| Kimberley Town v Willenhall Town | 1-6 |
| (at Eastwood Town FC) | |
| Northfield v Wednesfield Social | 1-2 |
| Shifnal Town v Friar Lane OB | 4-1 |
| Desborough Town v Halesowen Town | 0-6 |
| Long Eaton Grange v Wigston Fields | 3-2 |
| Knowle v Wisbech Town | 2-1 |
| Hinckley Athletic v Rushden Town | 1-1 |
| Wroxham v Wivenhoe Town | 0-2 |
| Gt Yarmouth Town v Irthlingborough Diamonds | aet 1-1 |
| Harwich & Parkeston v Watton | 9-0 |
| Gorleston v Stamford | 2-1 |
| Rainham Town v Haringey Borough | 3-1 |
| Tiptree United v Kempston Rovers | 2-0 |
| Ford United v Felixstowe Town | 3-3 |
| Arlesey Town v Basildon United | 2-0 |
| Woodford Town v Barton Rovers | 0-1 |
| Ampthill Town v East Ham United | 4-2 |
| Buckingham Town v Berkhamsted Town | 4-3 |
| Kingsbury Town v Cheshunt | 0-2 |
| Flackwell Heath v Hemel Hempstead | 0-0 |
| Harpenden Town v Grays Athletic | 2-4 |
| Horsham v Beckton United | 3-0 |
| Erith & Belvedere v Leyton-Wingate | 0-1 |
| Whyteleafe v Eastbourne Town | 4-0 |
| Whitstable Town v Alma Swanley | 4-1 |
| (at Canterbury City FC) | |
| Chobham v Eastbourne United | 1-2 |
| Redhill v Cray Wanderers | aet 2-1 |
| Merstham v Marlow | 2-1 |
| (at Marlow FC) | |
| Southwick v Molesey | 0-2 |
| Three Bridges v Ash United | 4-1 |
| Ruislip Manor v Malden Vale | 3-1 |
| Sholing Sports v Harefield United | 2-0 |
| Southall v Burnham | 0-0 |
| Melksham Town v Newport IOW | 0-0 |
| Pagham v Windsor & Eton | 1-2 |
| Brockenhurst v Yate Town | 1-0 |
| Swanage & Herston v Newbury Town | 0-2 |
| Forest Green Rovers v Chippenham Town | 4-1 |
| Shortwood United v Hungerford Town | 4-2 |
| Chipping Norton Town v Odd Down | 0-1 |
| Imm Bristol St George v Almondsbury Greenway | 1-4 |
| Port of Bristol v Paulton Rovers | 1-3 |
| Newquay v Devizes Town | 1-4 |

**Second Round – Replays**

| | |
|---|---|
| Maghull v Hoylake Athletic | 2-0 |
| Hallam v Warrington Town | 1-0 |
| Blakenall v Walsall Sportsco | 0-2 |
| Rushden Town v Hinckley Athletic | 1-2 |
| Felixstowe Town v Ford United | 2-3 |
| Hemel Hempstead v Flackwell Heath | 2-0 |
| Burnham v Southall | 0-1 |
| Newport IOW v Melksham Town | 0-1 |

**Third Round**

| | |
|---|---|
| Padiham v Ossett Albion | 0-0 |
| Peterlee Newtown v Guisborough Town | 3-4 |
| Blue Star v Eppleton Colliery Welfare | 3-0 |
| Bedlington Terriers v Seaham CW Red Star | 1-3 |
| *(at Seaham CW Red Star FC)* | |
| Hallam v Wren Rovers | 3-1 |
| Frecheville Community v Waterloo Dock | 2-1 |
| Irlam Town v Maghull | aet 2-0 |
| Rainworth MW v Appleby Frodingham | aet 4-1 |
| Staveley Works v Skegness Town | 0-1 |
| *(at Eastwood Town FC)* | |
| Shifnal Town v Hinckley Athletic | aet 5-3 |
| Middlewich Athletic v Walsall Sportsco | 3-2 |
| *(at Winsford United FC)* | |
| Knowle v Halesowen Town | 3-1 |
| Wednesfield Social v Willenhall Town | 0-2 |
| *(at Willenhall Town FC)* | |
| West Midlands Police v Long Eaton Grange | 4-3 |
| *(at Burton Albion FC)* | |
| Ford United v Barton Rovers | 2-2 |
| Grays Athletic v Arlesey Town | 2-1 |
| Harwich & Parkeston v Gorleston | 0-1 |
| Buckingham Town v Wivenhoe Town | 2-1 |
| Hemel Hempstead v Rainham Town | aet 3-2 |
| Cheshunt v Tiptree United | 1-0 |
| Irthlingborough Diamonds v Ampthill Town | 2-1 |
| Marlow v Windsor & Eton | 3-4 |
| Leyton Wingate v Horsham | 8-0 |
| Southall v Ruislip Manor | 4-0 |
| Redhill v Whitstable Town | 1-0 |
| Whyteleafe v Sholing Sports | 0-1 |
| Three Bridges v Eastbourne United | 3-1 |
| *(at Eastbourne United FC)* | |
| Molesey v Melksham Town | 4-1 |
| Paulton Rovers v Odd Down | 1-3 |
| Forest Green Rovers v Almondsbury Greenway | aet 2-1 |
| Newbury Town v Brockenhurst | 0-1 |
| Shortwood United v Devizes Town | 3-1 |

**Third Round – Replays**

| | |
|---|---|
| Ossett Albion v Padiham | 1-1 |
| Barton Rovers v Ford United | 4-1 |

**Third Round – Second Replay**

| | |
|---|---|
| Padiham v Ossett Albion | 1-3 |

**Fourth Round**

| | |
|---|---|
| Blue Star v Ossett Albion | 2-1 |
| Seaham CW Red Star v Guisborough Town | 0-1 |
| Irlam Town v Hallam | 2-1 |
| Rainworth MW v Frecheville Community | 1-0 |

| | |
|---|---|
| West Midlands Police v Skegness Town | 1-3 |
| Knowle v Middlewich Athletic | 4-1 |
| Willenhall Town v Shifnal Town | 0-0 |
| Buckingham Town v Grays Athletic | 3-1 |
| Irthlingborough Diamonds v Gorleston | 2-0 |
| Southall v Three Bridges | 1-2 |
| Hemel Hempstead v Redhill | aet 2-1 |
| Windsor & Eton v Cheshunt | 0-1 |
| Leyton-Wingate v Barton Rovers | 0-2 |
| Shortwood United v Sholing Sports | 2-0 |
| Forest Green Rovers v Odd Down | 3-1 |
| Brockenhurst v Molesey | 1-1 |

**Fourth Round Replays**

| | |
|---|---|
| Shifnal Town v Willenhall Town | 0-1 |
| Molesey v Brockenhurst | 1-0 |

**Fifth Round**

| | |
|---|---|
| Willenhall Town v Irlam Town | 1-0 |
| Rainworth MW v Skegness Town | 1-0 |
| Guisborough Town v Blue Star | 0-1 |
| Molesey v Three Bridges | 2-1 |
| Barton Rovers v Knowle | 2-1 |
| Shortwood United v Forest Green Rovers | 0-1 |
| Irthlingborough Diamonds v Buckingham Town | 2-1 |
| Hemel Hempstead v Cheshunt | 1-3 |

**Sixth Round**

| | |
|---|---|
| Blue Star v Cheshunt | 1-1, 1-0 |
| Molesey v Rainworth MW | 0-1 |
| Willenhall Town v Forest Green | aet 1-2 |
| Irthlingborough Diamonds v Barton Rovers | 1-1, 0-1 |

**Semi-Finals – First Leg**

| | |
|---|---|
| Blue Star v Forest Green Rovers | 1-4 |
| Barton Rovers v Rainworth MW | 0-0 |

**Semi-Finals – Second Leg**

| | |
|---|---|
| Forest Green Rovers v Blue Star | 0-1 |
| Rainworth MW v Barton Rovers | 2-1 |

**Final** *(at Wembley)*

| | |
|---|---|
| **Forest Green Rovers 3** *(Leitch 2, Norman)* | |
| **Rainworth MW 0** | 12,500 |

*Forest Green Rovers:* Moss; Norman, Day, Turner, Higgins (Dangerfield), Jenkins, Burns, Guest, Millward, Leitch, Doughty.

*Rainworth MW:* Watson; Hallam, Hodgson, Slater, Sterland, Oliver, Knowles, Raine, Radzki, Reah, Comerford.

**PREVIOUS FINALS**

| | |
|---|---|
| 1975 | Hoddesdon 2, Epsom 1 (10,000) |
| 1976 | Billericay T 1, Stamford 0 (12,000) |
| 1977 | Billericay T (1) 2, Sheffield (1) 1 (15,150) |
| 1978 | Blue Star 2, Barton R 1 (16,000) |
| 1979 | Billericay T 4, Almondsbury Greenway 1 (16,792) |
| 1980 | Stamford 2, Guisborough T 0 (11,500) |
| 1981 | Whickham 3, Willenhall T 2 (12,000) |

# FA SUNDAY CUP 1981–82

**First Round**

| | |
|---|---|
| Morpeth St Georges v Hartlepool Lion Hotel | 0-1 |
| Newbiggin Sports Centre v Murton Victoria | 5-0 |
| Hartlepool Workmens v Newbiggin Dolphin | 3-1 |
| Boldon SC v Shildon Elm Road WMC | 1-0 |
| Winlaton-West-End v Highgate | 0-3 |
| Warwick Southpool v Bricklayers Sports | |
| *Bricklayers Sports received w.o.* | |
| Inter Volante v Grassendale United | 1-2 |
| Brereton Town v North Liverpool | 3-1 |
| Bobbies Lane Sports v Dingle Rail | 1-6 |
| Old Horns v Eden Vale | 0-3 |

| | |
|---|---|
| Cobblers v Woodpecker | 3-2 |
| Aireville v Raysel & Lister Athletic | 3-1 |
| Eagle v Phoenix | 2-1 |
| AD Bulwell v Hoval-Farrar | 1-0 |
| Olympic Star v Four Ashes United | 4-2 |
| Bordesley Rovers v Swanfield | 0-1 |
| Deborah United v Greyhound Bilston | 1-3 |
| Hallen Sunday v Slade Celtic | 1-0 |
| Robin Hoods Retreat v Ollis Transport Combined | 0-1 |
| Sandwell v Rediffusion Bedminster Down Sunday | aet 4-3 |
| Byron & Counts XI v Undeb United | 2-1 |
| Laverstoke Park Albion v Willmotts Sports | 1-0 |

| | |
|---|---|
| Corby Kingfisher v Arras | 0-2 |
| Evergreen v Quebec Rovers | 2-1 |
| Girton Eagles v Temperance United | 2-4 |
| Ely Crusaders v Carlton United | 3-1 |
| Continental v Dortmund | 3-2 |
| Lion Rangers v Black Horse | 1-0 |
| Rainham WMC v Forresters United | 1-2 |
| Fryerns Community v Elco | 0-3 |
| Artois United v Bowsport | 2-2 |
| Croft City v Sun | |
| *Sun received w.o.* | |
| Walmer v Lakeside | 1-5 |
| Road Sea v Caribb | 3-2 |
| Wrythe Athletic v Durrington | 1-3 |
| North Stoneham v Colden Common | 0-1 |

### First Round – Replay

| | |
|---|---|
| Bowsport v Artois United | 3-2 |

*Byes to Second Round*
Adelaide Park, Bedford Midlanders, Breaks, Cannon Hotel, Club Lafayette, East Levenshulme CC, Finns (Steeplejacks) Knottingley, Gillford Park, Jumbos XI, Lodge Cottrell, Marklynn Motors, Marston Sports, Northampton Abington Athletic, Odhams OB, Oxford Road Social, Quality Carpets, Sheffield House Rangers, Troy Athletic.

*Exempt to Second Round*
Blue Star, Clifda, Croxteth & Gillmoss RBL, Fantail, Lee Chapel North, Mackintosh, Park Rangers (Wednesfield), Tabular-Beaufort, Twin Foxes, Two-Seven-Nine.

### Second Round

| | |
|---|---|
| Gillford Park v Highgate | 2-3 |
| Eden Vale v Croxteth & Gillmoss RBL | 1-5 |
| Marklynn Motors v Hartlepool Workmens | 2-1 |
| Newbiggin Sports Centre v Boldon Social | 2-0 |
| Swanfield v Dingle Rail | 0-1 |
| Eagle v Grassendale United | 2-1 |
| Fantail v Finns (Steeplejacks) Knottingley | 2-1 |
| Byron & Counts XI v Adelaide Park | 4-1 |
| Olympic Star v East Levenshulme CC | 3-0 |
| Park Rangers (Wednesfield) v Marston Sports | 2-2 |
| Bricklayers Sports v Cobblers | 2-2 |
| AD Bulwell v Lodge Cottrell | 3-1 |
| Brereton Town v Aireville | 2-3 |
| Club Lafayette v Northampton Abington Athletic | 1-1 |
| Lion Rangers v Sandwell | 3-2 |
| Tabular-Beaufort v Quality Carpets | 1-2 |
| Greyhound Bilston v Hallen Sunday | 0-3 |
| Jumbos XI v Ollis Transport Combined | 0-3 |
| Clifda v Continental | 2-1 |
| Mackintosh v Arras | 0-1 |
| Bedford Midlanders v Twin Foxes | 3-4 |
| Lee Chapel North v Breaks | 2-1 |
| Evergreen v Forresters United | 2-0 |
| Odhams OB v Sheffield House Rangers | 0-3 |
| Temperance United v Ely Crusaders | aet 3-4 |
| Colden Common v Two-Seven-Nine | 0-2 |
| Road Sea v Elco | 5-1 |
| Lakeside v Durrington | 2-0 |
| Sun v Troy Athletic | 1-0 |
| Laverstoke Park Albion v Bowsport | 3-0 |

### Second Round – Replays

| | |
|---|---|
| Marston Sports v Park Rangers (Wednesfield) | 0-3 |
| Cobblers v Bricklayers Sports | aet 2-1 |
| Northampton Abington Athletic v Club Lafayette | 0-1 |

*Byes to Third Round*
Hartlepool Lion Hotel, Oxford Road Social.

### Third Round

| | |
|---|---|
| AD Bulwell v Croxteth & Gillmoss RBL | 1-2 |
| Fantail v Marklynn Motors | 0-1 |
| Newbiggin Sports Centre v Aireville | 1-1 |
| Dingle Rail v Hartlepool Lion Hotel | 3-1 |
| Highgate v Eagle | 1-3 |
| Hallen Sunday v Park Rangers (Wednesfield) | 2-2 |
| Club Lafayette v Cobblers | 2-7 |
| Lion Rangers v Ollis Transport Combined | 1-0 |
| Olympic Star v Quality Carpets | 2-0 |
| Evergreen v Twin Foxes | 0-2 |
| Road Sea v Byron & Counts XI | 1-1 |
| Sun v Arras | 2-2 |
| Lakeside v Lee Chapel North | 0-3 |
| Sheffield House Rangers v Laverstoke Park Albion | 2-0 |
| Ely Crusaders v Oxford Road Social | 0-2 |
| Clifda v Two-Seven-Nine | 1-1 |

### Third Round – Replays

| | |
|---|---|
| Aireville v Newbiggin Sports Centre | 2-1 |
| Park Rangers (Wednesfield) v Hallen Sunday | 1-3 |
| Byron & Counts XI v Road Sea | 2-2 |
| Arras v Sun | 4-0 |
| Two-Seven-Nine v Clifda | 3-0 |

### Third Round – Second Replay

| | |
|---|---|
| Byron & Counts XI v Road Sea | 4-0 |

### Fourth Round

| | |
|---|---|
| Eagle v Marklynn Motors | 4-3 |
| Dingle Rail v Aireville | 1-0 |
| Cobblers v Croxteth & Gillmoss RBL | 1-3 |
| Hallen Sunday v Lion Rangers | 4-0 |
| Two-Seven-Nine v Lee Chapel North | 1-2 |
| Sheffield House Rangers v Twin Foxes | 0-3 |
| Byron & Counts XI v Olympic Star | 0-1 |
| Oxford Road Social v Arras | 1-4 |

### Fifth Round

| | |
|---|---|
| Olympic Star v Croxteth & Gillmoss RBL | 0-2 |
| Dingle Rail v Eagle | 1-0 |
| Arras v Hallen Sunday | 2-1 |
| Lee Chapel North v Twin Foxes | 0-1 |

### Semi-Finals

| | |
|---|---|
| Croxteth & Gillmoss RBL v Dingle Rail | 1-2 |
| (*at Formby FC*) | |
| Twin Foxes v Arras | 3-1 |
| (*at Letchworth Garden City FC*) | |

### Final (*at Hitchin Town FC*)

| | |
|---|---|
| Twin Foxes v Dingle Rail | 1-2 |

## AMATEUR FOOTBALL ALLIANCE 1981–82

## ARTHURIAN LEAGUE

### PREMIER DIVISION

| | P | W | D | L | F | A | Pts |
|---|---|---|---|---|---|---|---|
| Carthusians | 14 | 11 | 1 | 2 | 51 | 20 | 23 |
| Brentwoods | 14 | 11 | 1 | 2 | 40 | 22 | 23 |
| Lancing OB | 14 | 8 | 5 | 1 | 36 | 12 | 21 |
| Chigwellians | 14 | 7 | 1 | 6 | 25 | 20 | 15 |
| Cholmeleians | 14 | 6 | 0 | 8 | 20 | 30 | 12 |
| Foresters | 14 | 3 | 3 | 8 | 23 | 33 | 9 |
| Malvernians | 14 | 2 | 2 | 10 | 15 | 39 | 6 |
| Wellingburians | 14 | 1 | 1 | 12 | 15 | 49 | 3 |

### DIVISION ONE

| | P | W | D | L | F | A | Pts |
|---|---|---|---|---|---|---|---|
| Aldenhamians | 16 | 14 | 1 | 1 | 58 | 20 | 29 |
| Bradfieldians | 15 | 11 | 0 | 4 | 36 | 24 | 22 |
| Westminsters | 16 | 8 | 2 | 6 | 31 | 30 | 18 |
| Reptonians | 15 | 7 | 3 | 5 | 37 | 33 | 17 |
| Wykehamists | 16 | 6 | 5 | 5 | 27 | 27 | 17 |
| Harrovians | 16 | 7 | 2 | 7 | 23 | 25 | 16 |
| Salopians | 16 | 6 | 1 | 9 | 34 | 41 | 13 |
| Etonians | 16 | 3 | 0 | 13 | 21 | 41 | 6 |
| Ardinians | 16 | 1 | 2 | 13 | 22 | 48 | 4 |

## SOUTHERN AMATEUR LEAGUE

### DIVISION ONE

| | P | W | D | L | F | A | Pts |
|---|---|---|---|---|---|---|---|
| West Wickham | 22 | 14 | 5 | 3 | 46 | 20 | 33 |
| Old Esthameians | 22 | 11 | 6 | 5 | 37 | 19 | 28 |
| Midland Bank | 22 | 12 | 4 | 6 | 37 | 25 | 28 |
| Norsemen | 22 | 10 | 5 | 7 | 33 | 34 | 25 |
| Old Bromleians | 22 | 8 | 6 | 8 | 45 | 37 | 22 |
| Crouch End Vampires | 22 | 9 | 4 | 9 | 34 | 35 | 22 |
| East Barnet OG | 22 | 7 | 7 | 8 | 33 | 29 | 21 |
| Lloyds Bank | 22 | 6 | 7 | 9 | 26 | 43 | 19 |
| Winchmore Hill | 22 | 6 | 6 | 10 | 27 | 34 | 18 |
| Catford Wanderers | 22 | 7 | 4 | 11 | 35 | 43 | 18 |
| Kew Association | 22 | 6 | 6 | 10 | 17 | 32 | 18 |
| South Bank Poly | 22 | 5 | 2 | 15 | 26 | 45 | 12 |

### DIVISION TWO

| | P | W | D | L | F | A | Pts |
|---|---|---|---|---|---|---|---|
| Old Parkonians | 22 | 13 | 4 | 5 | 49 | 31 | 30 |
| Nat West Bank | 22 | 13 | 2 | 7 | 55 | 37 | 28 |
| Polytechnic | 22 | 9 | 5 | 8 | 33 | 30 | 23 |
| Southgate Olympic | 22 | 9 | 4 | 9 | 36 | 32 | 22 |
| Old Westminster Cits | 22 | 9 | 4 | 9 | 33 | 42 | 22 |
| Old Actonians Ass | 22 | 7 | 7 | 8 | 30 | 33 | 21 |
| Brentham | 22 | 6 | 9 | 7 | 32 | 41 | 21 |
| Civil Service | 22 | 8 | 4 | 10 | 44 | 46 | 20 |
| Lensbury | 22 | 7 | 6 | 9 | 33 | 38 | 20 |
| Britannic House | 22 | 7 | 6 | 9 | 28 | 36 | 20 |
| Carshalton | 22 | 6 | 7 | 9 | 32 | 33 | 19 |
| Barclays Bank | 22 | 7 | 4 | 11 | 33 | 39 | 18 |

### DIVISION THREE

| | P | W | D | L | F | A | Pts |
|---|---|---|---|---|---|---|---|
| Old Stationers | 22 | 15 | 4 | 3 | 68 | 17 | 34 |
| Alleyn Old Boys | 22 | 14 | 6 | 2 | 56 | 20 | 34 |
| Bank of England | 22 | 14 | 2 | 6 | 47 | 32 | 30 |
| Old Lyonians | 22 | 9 | 8 | 5 | 28 | 31 | 26 |
| Pearl Assurance | 22 | 10 | 4 | 8 | 47 | 36 | 24 |
| Broomfield | 22 | 7 | 7 | 8 | 31 | 37 | 21 |
| Alexandra Park | 22 | 7 | 5 | 10 | 37 | 47 | 19 |
| Ibis | 22 | 5 | 7 | 10 | 33 | 42 | 17 |
| Cuaco | 22 | 6 | 5 | 11 | 23 | 38 | 17 |
| Merton | 22 | 6 | 4 | 12 | 33 | 54 | 16 |
| Old Latymerians | 22 | 4 | 6 | 12 | 32 | 58 | 14 |
| Reigate Priory | 22 | 4 | 4 | 14 | 21 | 44 | 12 |

## NEMEAN AMATEUR LEAGUE

### DIVISION ONE

| | P | W | D | L | F | A | Pts |
|---|---|---|---|---|---|---|---|
| Tansley | 20 | 15 | 1 | 4 | 54 | 25 | 31 |
| Old Isleworthians | 20 | 10 | 8 | 2 | 42 | 27 | 28 |
| Parkfield | 20 | 10 | 5 | 5 | 41 | 20 | 25 |
| Albanian | 20 | 10 | 4 | 6 | 39 | 32 | 24 |
| Old Greenfordians | 20 | 9 | 5 | 6 | 28 | 21 | 23 |
| Old Hamptonians | 20 | 10 | 2 | 8 | 37 | 27 | 22 |
| Ealing Association | 20 | 10 | 2 | 8 | 44 | 38 | 22 |
| Hale End Athletic | 20 | 7 | 3 | 10 | 31 | 41 | 17 |
| Economicals | 20 | 4 | 2 | 14 | 19 | 34 | 10 |
| Old Tiffinians | 20 | 3 | 4 | 13 | 35 | 56 | 10 |
| Wood Green Old Boys | 20 | 4 | 0 | 16 | 24 | 73 | 8 |

### DIVISION TWO

| | P | W | D | L | F | A | Pts |
|---|---|---|---|---|---|---|---|
| Parkfield Reserves | 20 | 12 | 5 | 3 | 61 | 28 | 29 |
| Hampstead Heathens | 20 | 11 | 6 | 3 | 52 | 30 | 28 |
| Old Hendonians | 20 | 12 | 3 | 5 | 55 | 31 | 27 |
| Tansley Reserves | 20 | 9 | 5 | 6 | 38 | 40 | 23 |
| Old Hamptonians Reserves | 20 | 9 | 4 | 7 | 38 | 31 | 22 |
| Duncombe Sports | 20 | 8 | 2 | 10 | 57 | 54 | 18 |
| London Airways | 20 | 7 | 4 | 9 | 39 | 40 | 18 |
| Albanian Reserves | 20 | 8 | 1 | 11 | 38 | 50 | 17 |
| Ealing Association Res | 20 | 5 | 4 | 11 | 30 | 55 | 14 |
| Old Greenfordians Res | 20 | 5 | 3 | 12 | 32 | 52 | 13 |
| Old Elysians | 20 | 4 | 3 | 13 | 25 | 54 | 11 |

## OLD BOYS' LEAGUE

### PREMIER DIVISION

| | P | W | D | L | F | A | Pts |
|---|---|---|---|---|---|---|---|
| Salesians | 20 | 16 | 1 | 3 | 48 | 17 | 33 |
| Enfield | 20 | 11 | 6 | 3 | 41 | 31 | 28 |
| Ignatians | 20 | 11 | 3 | 6 | 39 | 28 | 25 |
| Aloysians | 20 | 9 | 4 | 7 | 36 | 27 | 22 |
| Strandians | 20 | 7 | 6 | 7 | 42 | 42 | 20 |
| Minchendenians | 20 | 7 | 6 | 7 | 33 | 38 | 20 |
| Wokingians | 20 | 4 | 9 | 7 | 28 | 28 | 17 |
| Suttonians | 20 | 8 | 1 | 11 | 29 | 44 | 17 |
| Meadonians | 20 | 4 | 6 | 10 | 25 | 34 | 14 |
| Camdenians | 20 | 4 | 5 | 11 | 27 | 43 | 13 |
| Clapham | 20 | 3 | 5 | 12 | 35 | 51 | 11 |

### SENIOR DIVISION ONE

| | P | W | D | L | F | A | Pts |
|---|---|---|---|---|---|---|---|
| Fincunians | 22 | 17 | 2 | 3 | 60 | 22 | 36 |
| Sinjuns | 22 | 12 | 5 | 5 | 47 | 31 | 29 |
| O. Hill | 22 | 12 | 5 | 5 | 40 | 26 | 29 |
| Highburians | 22 | 10 | 5 | 7 | 60 | 44 | 25 |
| Latymer | 22 | 9 | 4 | 9 | 33 | 32 | 22 |
| Josephians | 22 | 8 | 6 | 8 | 28 | 27 | 22 |
| Tenisonians | 22 | 5 | 10 | 7 | 17 | 26 | 20 |
| Tollingtonians | 22 | 6 | 7 | 9 | 40 | 39 | 19 |
| Glyn | 22 | 7 | 4 | 11 | 27 | 33 | 18 |
| Salesians Res | 22 | 4 | 10 | 8 | 28 | 43 | 18 |
| Leyton | 22 | 5 | 7 | 10 | 30 | 40 | 17 |
| Westhamians | 22 | 3 | 3 | 16 | 21 | 68 | 9 |

### SENIOR DIVISION TWO

| | P | W | D | L | F | A | Pts |
|---|---|---|---|---|---|---|---|
| Buckwellians | 22 | 16 | 4 | 2 | 74 | 18 | 36 |
| Manorians | 22 | 14 | 5 | 3 | 65 | 36 | 33 |
| Camdenians Res | 22 | 12 | 7 | 3 | 57 | 33 | 31 |
| Salvatorians | 22 | 10 | 7 | 5 | 61 | 38 | 27 |
| Uffingtonians | 22 | 9 | 6 | 7 | 34 | 30 | 24 |
| Wokingians Res | 22 | 7 | 7 | 8 | 30 | 38 | 21 |
| Uxonians | 22 | 6 | 6 | 10 | 34 | 40 | 18 |
| Addeyans | 22 | 6 | 6 | 10 | 35 | 42 | 18 |
| Vaughanians | 22 | 6 | 5 | 11 | 43 | 50 | 17 |
| Pelhamians | 22 | 5 | 7 | 10 | 32 | 65 | 17 |
| Paludians | 22 | 4 | 4 | 14 | 30 | 56 | 12 |
| Suttonians Res | 22 | 3 | 4 | 15 | 29 | 78 | 10 |

## SOUTHERN OLYMPIAN LEAGUE

### SENIOR SECTION

### DIVISION ONE

| | P | W | D | L | F | A | Pts |
|---|---|---|---|---|---|---|---|
| Old Grammarians | 22 | 17 | 2 | 3 | 70 | 37 | 36 |
| Old Parmiterians | 22 | 13 | 1 | 8 | 59 | 40 | 27 |
| Old Bealonians | 22 | 12 | 2 | 8 | 52 | 37 | 26 |
| Witan | 22 | 8 | 9 | 5 | 49 | 42 | 25 |
| Old Monovians | 22 | 10 | 4 | 8 | 49 | 35 | 24 |
| Old Woodhouseians | 22 | 10 | 3 | 9 | 42 | 38 | 23 |
| Old Finchleians | 22 | 10 | 2 | 10 | 55 | 53 | 22 |
| Old Fairlopians | 22 | 9 | 3 | 10 | 47 | 45 | 21 |
| Mill Hill Village | 22 | 8 | 4 | 10 | 53 | 50 | 20 |
| Old Wilsonians | 22 | 8 | 4 | 10 | 35 | 44 | 20 |
| Southgate County | 22 | 6 | 2 | 14 | 39 | 65 | 14 |
| Mayfield Athletic | 22 | 2 | 2 | 18 | 27 | 91 | 6 |

### DIVISION TWO

| | P | W | D | L | F | A | Pts |
|---|---|---|---|---|---|---|---|
| St Mary's College | 24 | 18 | 4 | 2 | 67 | 24 | 40 |
| Colposa | 24 | 16 | 4 | 4 | 69 | 31 | 36 |
| Bourneside | 24 | 12 | 6 | 6 | 41 | 32 | 30 |
| Old Colfeians | 24 | 14 | 2 | 8 | 38 | 36 | 30 |
| Wandsworth Borough | 24 | 11 | 7 | 6 | 64 | 36 | 29 |
| Centymca | 24 | 10 | 6 | 8 | 47 | 41 | 26 |
| London Welsh | 24 | 12 | 2 | 10 | 44 | 43 | 26 |
| Old Owens | 24 | 10 | 2 | 12 | 41 | 46 | 22 |
| GWR | 24 | 7 | 6 | 11 | 32 | 42 | 20 |
| Old Edmontonians | 24 | 6 | 7 | 11 | 41 | 53 | 19 |
| Fulham Compton OB | 24 | 5 | 4 | 15 | 33 | 52 | 14 |
| Inland Revenue | 24 | 5 | 2 | 17 | 33 | 66 | 12 |
| Old Libertians | 24 | 3 | 2 | 19 | 23 | 71 | 8 |

## CUP FINALS

**Senior:** Old Grammarians 2, Old Parmiterians 1 *after 0-0 draw aet*
**Middlesex Senior:** Old Ignatians 3, Enfield Old Grammarians 1
**Surrey Senior:** Southbank Polytechnic 1, Old Westminster Citizens 0 *aet*
**Essex Senior:** Old Bealonians 2, Old Parmiterians 1
**W. E. Greenland Memorial Trophy:** Liverpool Victoria 1, Linkater Paine 0

# FA REPRESENTATIVE MATCHES 1934–82

### FA XI v ROYAL NAVY

| Year | Month | Venue | FA | RN |
|---|---|---|---|---|
| 1934 | Dec | Portsmouth | 0 | 0 |
| 1935 | Dec | Plymouth | 3 | 4 |
| 1936 | Dec | Chatham | 7 | 0 |
| 1937 | Dec | Devonport | 5 | 0 |
| 1938 | Dec | Portsmouth | 6 | 2 |
| 1947 | Feb | Portsmouth | 3 | 0 |
| 1947 | Dec | Portsmouth | 4 | 0 |
| 1948 | Dec | Plymouth | 1 | 1 |
| 1949 | Dec | Plymouth | 4 | 1 |
| 1950 | Dec | Portsmouth | 1 | 2 |
| 1951 | Dec | Portsmouth | 4 | 1 |
| 1952 | Dec | Plymouth | 4 | 0 |
| 1953 | Dec | Portsmouth | 1 | 0 |
| 1954 | Dec | Portsmouth | 2 | 1 |
| 1955 | Dec | Portsmouth | 5 | 5 |
| 1957 | Jan | Portsmouth | 5 | 1 |
| 1957 | Dec | Portsmouth | 5 | 2 |
| 1958 | Dec | Portsmouth | 4 | 1 |
| 1959 | Dec | Portsmouth | 5 | 3 |
| 1960 | Dec | Portsmouth | 6 | 2 |
| 1961 | Dec | Portsmouth | 7 | 3 |
| 1962 | Dec | Portsmouth | 4 | 0 |
| 1963 | Dec | Portsmouth | 2 | 0 |
| 1964 | Dec | Portsmouth | 4 | 1 |
| 1965 | Dec | Portsmouth | 9 | 1 |
| 1966 | Nov | Portsmouth | 1 | 0 |
| 1967 | Nov | Portsmouth | 3 | 0 |
| 1968 | Nov | Portsmouth | 2 | 0 |
| 1969 | Nov | Portsmouth | 1 | 0 |
| 1970 | Dec | Portsmouth | 2 | 2 |
| 1971 | Dec | Portsmouth | 3 | 2 |
| 1972 | Nov | Portsmouth | 2 | 1 |
| 1973 | Nov | Portsmouth | 2 | 0 |

### FA XI v THE ARMY

| Year | Month | Venue | FA | Army |
|---|---|---|---|---|
| 1934 | Nov | Tidworth | 1 | 1 |
| 1935 | Nov | Colchester | 4 | 4 |
| 1936 | Nov | Aldershot | 6 | 3 |
| 1937 | Nov | Aldershot | 4 | 2 |
| 1938 | Nov | Colchester | 1 | 1 |
| 1946 | Nov | Stoke | 3 | 8 |
| 1947 | Nov | Brighton | 4 | 0 |
| 1948 | Nov | Ipswich | 0 | 2 |
| 1949 | Nov | Charlton | 4 | 1 |
| 1950 | Nov | Highbury | 3 | 2 |
| 1951 | Nov | Highbury | 4 | 2 |
| 1952 | Nov | Leeds | 4 | 1 |
| 1953 | Nov | Newcastle | 3 | 1 |
| 1954 | Nov | Sheffield | 1 | 1 |
| 1955 | Nov | Newcastle | 2 | 2 |
| 1956 | Nov | Manchester | 7 | 3 |
| 1957 | Oct | Manchester | 6 | 3 |
| 1958 | Oct | Newcastle | 4 | 1 |
| 1959 | Oct | Newcastle | 3 | 1 |
| 1960 | Oct | Sheffield | 2 | 1 |
| 1961 | Oct | Sunderland | 1 | 2 |
| 1962 | Oct | Aldershot | 6 | 2 |
| 1963 | Oct | Aldershot | 4 | 2 |
| 1964 | Feb | Catterick | 2 | 2 |
| 1964 | Oct | Aldershot | 1 | 4 |
| 1965 | Feb | Catterick | 1 | 2 |
| 1965 | Oct | Aldershot | 1 | 1 |
| 1966 | Oct | Aldershot | 1 | 1 |
| 1967 | Oct | Aldershot | 3 | 1 |
| 1968 | Oct | Aldershot | 1 | 1 |
| 1969 | Oct | Aldershot | 3 | 0 |
| 1970 | Oct | Aldershot | 2 | 0 |
| 1972 | Oct | Aldershot | 3 | 2 |
| 1973 | Oct | Bordon | 0 | 4 |

### FA XI v OXFORD UNIVERSITY

| Year | Month | Venue | FA | OU |
|---|---|---|---|---|
| 1934 | Nov | Oxford | 6 | 1 |
| 1935 | Nov | Oxford | 3 | 2 |
| 1936 | Nov | Oxford | 5 | 1 |
| 1937 | Nov | Oxford | 6 | 2 |
| 1938 | Nov | Oxford | 2 | 0 |
| 1945 | Nov | Oxford | 7 | 0 |
| 1946 | Nov | Oxford | 4 | 3 |
| 1947 | Nov | Oxford | 2 | 0 |
| 1948 | Nov | Oxford | 1 | 1 |
| 1949 | Nov | Oxford | 2 | 1 |
| 1950 | Nov | Oxford | 3 | 3 |
| 1951 | Nov | Oxford | 2 | 1 |
| 1952 | Nov | Oxford | 4 | 2 |
| 1953 | Nov | Oxford | 4 | 2 |
| 1954 | Nov | Oxford | 5 | 0 |
| 1955 | Nov | Oxford | 2 | 1 |
| 1956 | Nov | Oxford | 3 | 0 |
| 1957 | Nov | Oxford | 1 | 1 |
| 1958 | Nov | Oxford | 5 | 0 |
| 1959 | Nov | Malvern | 4 | 1 |
| 1960 | Nov | Eastbourne | 3 | 1 |
| 1961 | Nov | Oxford | 6 | 0 |
| 1962 | Nov | Eastbourne | 3 | 3 |
| 1963 | Nov | Oxford | 4 | 0 |
| 1964 | Oct | Eastbourne | 4 | 1 |
| 1965 | Nov | Oxford | 6 | 0 |
| 1966 | Nov | Eastbourne | 3 | 0 |
| 1967 | Nov | Oxford | 6 | 0 |
| 1968 | Nov | Eastbourne | 5 | 0 |
| 1969 | Nov | Oxford | 0 | 1 |
| 1970 | Nov | Eastbourne | 1 | 0 |
| 1971 | Nov | Oxford | 1 | 0 |
| 1972 | Nov | Eastbourne | 5 | 0 |
| 1973 | Nov | Oxford | 5 | 0 |
| 1976 | Nov | Oxford | 1 | 0 |
| 1977 | Nov | Oxford | 4 | 0 |
| 1978 | Nov | Oxford | 3 | 1 |
| 1979 | Nov | Oxford | 6 | 1 |
| 1980 | Nov | Witney Town | 3 | 1 |
| 1981 | Nov | Oxford City | 0 | 2 |

### FA XI v UNIVERSITIES ATHLETIC UNION

| Year | Month | Venue | FA | UAU |
|---|---|---|---|---|
| 1934 | Feb | Newcastle | 5 | 2 |
| 1935 | Feb | Manchester | 0 | 5 |
| 1936 | Feb | Manchester | 2 | 2 |
| 1937 | Feb | Exeter | 1 | 4 |
| 1938 | Feb | Leeds | 4 | 1 |
| 1939 | Feb | Southampton | 0 | 2 |
| 1946 | Feb | Darlington | 10 | 1 |
| 1947 | Feb | Southampton | 4 | 1 |
| 1948 | Feb | Bristol | 2 | 1 |
| 1949 | Feb | Sheffield | 2 | 0 |
| 1950 | Feb | Exeter | 4 | 0 |
| 1951 | Feb | Hull | 2 | 1 |
| 1952 | Mar | Doncaster | 1 | 4 |
| 1953 | Feb | Nottingham | 4 | 1 |
| 1954 | Feb | Bristol | 3 | 1 |
| 1955 | Feb | Sheffield | 5 | 0 |
| 1956 | Feb | Reading | 0 | 3 |
| 1957 | Mar | Stoke | 4 | 1 |
| 1958 | Mar | Leicester | 1 | 1 |
| 1959 | Mar | Peterborough | 1 | 2 |
| 1960 | Mar | Norwich | 3 | 0 |
| 1961 | Feb | Reading | 1 | 2 |
| 1963 | Apr | Sheffield | 3 | 0 |
| 1964 | Feb | Birmingham | 8 | 0 |
| 1965 | Mar | Coventry | 1 | 3 |
| 1966 | Mar | Rugby | 5 | 0 |
| 1967 | Mar | Sheffield | 2 | 1 |

| 1968 | Feb | Nottingham | 1 | 1 |
|---|---|---|---|---|
| 1969 | Apr | Sheffield | 6 | 0 |
| 1970 | Feb | Morecambe | 3 | 1 |
| 1971 | Apr | Durham | 1 | 1 |
| 1971 | Oct | Aldershot | 0 | 2 |
| 1973 | Feb | Newcastle | 2 | 3 |
| 1974 | Feb | Nuneaton | 2 | 2 |
| 1976 | Feb | York | 2 | 2 |
| 1977 | Mar | York | 2 | 2 |
| 1978 | Mar | Altrincham | 2 | 1 |
| 1979 | Mar | Altrincham | 1 | 1 |
| 1980 | Mar | Altrincham | 4 | 2 |
| 1982 | Mar | Altrincham | 3 | 0 |

## FA XI v ROYAL AIR FORCE

| | | | FA | RAF |
|---|---|---|---|---|
| 1934 | Jan | Cranwell | 2 | 0 |
| 1935 | Jan | Watford | 4 | 0 |
| 1936 | Jan | Uxbridge | 3 | 3 |
| 1937 | Jan | Uxbridge | 9 | 1 |
| 1937 | Nov | Uxbridge | 4 | 4 |
| 1938 | Dec | Cranwell | 3 | 2 |
| 1946 | Oct | Reading | 4 | 1 |
| 1947 | Oct | Highbury | 3 | 0 |
| 1948 | Oct | Highbury | 9 | 2 |
| 1949 | Oct | Fulham | 2 | 1 |
| 1950 | Oct | Fulham | 6 | 1 |
| 1951 | Oct | Stamford Bridge | 4 | 0 |
| 1952 | Oct | Stamford Bridge | 8 | 1 |
| 1953 | Oct | Tottenham | 4 | 0 |
| 1954 | Oct | Highbury | 3 | 1 |
| 1955 | Oct | Bristol | 9 | 0 |
| 1956 | Oct | Sheffield | 2 | 1 |
| 1957 | Oct | Nottingham | 5 | 2 |
| 1958 | Oct | Bristol | 1 | 4 |
| 1959 | Oct | Norwich | 9 | 2 |
| 1960 | Oct | Manchester | 2 | 2 |
| 1961 | Oct | Peterborough | 13 | 0 |
| 1962 | Oct | Uxbridge | 4 | 2 |
| 1963 | Oct | Uxbridge | 4 | 2 |
| 1964 | Sept | Uxbridge | 5 | 1 |
| 1969 | Oct | Halton | 2 | 2 |
| 1970 | Oct | Halton | 5 | 0 |
| 1971 | Oct | Halton | 1 | 0 |
| 1972 | Oct | Uxbridge | 2 | 1 |
| 1973 | Oct | Uxbridge | 4 | 0 |
| 1976 | Jan | Wealdstone | 2 | 1 |

## FA XI v CAMBRIDGE UNIVERSITY

| | | | FA | CU |
|---|---|---|---|---|
| 1934 | Nov | Cambridge | 5 | 0 |
| 1935 | Nov | Cambridge | 6 | 1 |
| 1936 | Nov | Cambridge | 5 | 0 |
| 1937 | Nov | Cambridge | 3 | 1 |
| 1938 | Nov | Cambridge | 6 | 2 |
| 1946 | Feb | Cambridge | 5 | 1 |
| 1946 | Nov | Cambridge | 3 | 2 |
| 1947 | Nov | Cambridge | 6 | 1 |
| 1948 | Nov | Cambridge | 7 | 1 |
| 1949 | Nov | Cambridge | 3 | 1 |
| 1950 | Nov | Cambridge | 4 | 2 |
| 1951 | Nov | Cambridge | 4 | 1 |
| 1952 | Nov | Cambridge | 8 | 0 |
| 1953 | Nov | Cambridge | 2 | 3 |
| 1954 | Nov | Cambridge | 4 | 2 |
| 1955 | Nov | Cambridge | 5 | 1 |
| 1956 | Nov | Cambridge | 6 | 1 |
| 1957 | Nov | Cambridge | 5 | 0 |
| 1958 | Nov | Cambridge | 1 | 1 |
| 1959 | Nov | Eastbourne | 1 | 2 |
| 1960 | Nov | Cambridge | 3 | 4 |
| 1961 | Nov | Eastbourne | 3 | 2 |
| 1962 | Nov | Cambridge | abandoned | |
| 1963 | Oct | Eastbourne | 2 | 0 |
| 1964 | Nov | Cambridge | 3 | 1 |

| 1965 | Nov | Cambridge | 5 | 1 |
|---|---|---|---|---|
| 1967 | Nov | Eastbourne | 1 | 1 |
| 1968 | Nov | Cambridge | 2 | 1 |
| 1969 | Nov | Eastbourne | 3 | 0 |
| 1970 | Nov | Cambridge | 7 | 0 |
| 1971 | Nov | Eastbourne | 4 | 0 |
| 1972 | Nov | Cambridge | 1 | 0 |
| 1973 | Nov | Eastbourne | 3 | 0 |
| 1976 | Nov | Cambridge | 1 | 0 |
| 1977 | Nov | Cambridge | 4 | 0 |
| 1978 | Nov | Cambridge | 6 | 1 |
| 1979 | Nov | Cambridge | 2 | 1 |
| 1980 | Nov | Cambridge | 1 | 1 |
| 1981 | Nov | Cambridge | 1 | 1 |

## FA XI v LONDON UNIVERSITY

| | | | FA | LU |
|---|---|---|---|---|
| 1958 | Mar | Motspur Park | 7 | 1 |
| 1959 | Mar | Motspur Park | 0 | 1 |
| 1960 | Mar | Motspur Park | 5 | 1 |
| 1961 | Mar | Kingston | 2 | 2 |
| 1962 | Mar | Motspur Park | 7 | 0 |
| 1964 | Mar | Kingston | 5 | 1 |
| 1965 | Mar | Motspur Park | 6 | 2 |
| 1966 | Mar | Motspur Park | 2 | 1 |
| 1967 | Mar | Hayes | 3 | 1 |
| 1968 | Mar | Motspur Park | 3 | 0 |
| 1969 | Mar | Motspur Park | 3 | 0 |
| 1970 | Mar | Woking | 9 | 0 |
| 1971 | Mar | Motspur Park | 4 | 0 |
| 1973 | Mar | Motspur Park | 4 | 1 |
| 1974 | Mar | Motspur Park | 8 | 1 |
| 1976 | Mar | Kingston | 4 | 1 |
| 1976 | Dec | Wealdstone | 3 | 0 |
| 1977 | Dec | Metropolitan Police FC | 2 | 0 |
| 1978 | Dec | Harrow Borough FC | 5 | 1 |
| 1979 | Dec | Hayes | 3 | 0 |
| 1980 | Dec | Sutton United | 3 | 1 |

## FA XI v AMATEUR FOOTBALL ALLIANCE

| | | | FA | AFA |
|---|---|---|---|---|
| 1958 | Jan | Maidstone | 4 | 2 |
| 1959 | Jan | Barking | 3 | 1 |
| 1960 | Feb | Maidstone | 5 | 0 |
| 1961 | Feb | Bromley | 2 | 2 |
| 1962 | Feb | Wimbledon | 3 | 1 |
| 1963 | Feb | Kingston | 7 | 1 |
| 1964 | Feb | Tooting | 3 | 0 |
| 1965 | Feb | Wealdstone | 2 | 2 |
| 1966 | Feb | Kingston | 3 | 0 |
| 1967 | Feb | Bromley | 1 | 2 |
| 1968 | Feb | Enfield | 1 | 0 |
| 1969 | Feb | Dulwich | Ground unfit | |
| 1970 | Feb | Clapton | 2 | 2 |
| 1971 | Feb | Tooting | 4 | 0 |
| 1973 | Feb | Bishop's Stortford | 3 | 1 |
| 1974 | Feb | Leytonstone | 2 | 1 |
| 1976 | Apr | Dulwich | 4 | 0 |
| 1977 | Mar | Leytonstone | 2 | 2 |
| 1978 | Feb | Wealdstone | 4 | 1 |
| 1979 | Feb | Metropolitan Police FC | 5 | 2 |
| 1980 | Jan | Metropolitan Police FC | 2 | 1 |
| 1981 | Feb | Metropolitan Police FC | 5 | 1 |
| 1982 | Feb | Harrow Borough | 1 | 1 |

## FA XI v BERGER ISTHMIAN LEAGUE

| | | | FA | BIL |
|---|---|---|---|---|
| 1980 | Mar | | 0 | 3 |

## FA XI v BRITISH COLLEGES SPORTS ASSOCIATION

| | | | FA | BC |
|---|---|---|---|---|
| 1972 | Dec | Chorley | 2 | 1 |
| 1973 | Dec | Spennymoor | 0 | 1 |

| 1976 | Mar | Cheltenham | 0 | 1 |
|------|-----|------------|---|---|
| 1977 | Feb | Cheltenham | 4 | 0 |
| 1978 | Feb | Cheltenham | 0 | 1 |
| 1980 | Feb | Stafford Rangers | 2 | 0 |

### FA XI v BRITISH POLICE

| | | | FA | BP |
|------|-----|---|----|----|
| 1979 | Oct | | 1 | 1 |
| 1980 | Oct | | 1 | 0 |

### FA XI v SUNDERLAND

| | | | FA | Sund |
|------|-----|-----------|----|------|
| 1973 | Dec | Sunderland | 0 | 4 |

### FA XI v COMBINED SERVICES

| | | | FA | CS |
|------|-----|-----------|----|----|
| 1977 | Apr | Aldershot | 2 | 2 |
| 1978 | Apr | Aldershot | 1 | 1 |
| 1979 | Apr | Aldershot | 1 | 1 |
| 1980 | Apr | Aldershot | 1 | 2 |
| 1981 | Apr | Aldershot | 1 | 1 |

### FA XI v NORTHERN LEAGUE

| | | | FA | NL |
|------|-----|----------------|----|----|
| 1977 | Mar | Blyth Spartans | 2 | 3 |
| 1978 | Apr | Consett | 2 | 3 |
| 1979 | Apr | North Shields | 0 | 2 |
| 1980 | Feb | Blyth Spartans | 1 | 3 |
| 1981 | Apr | Consett | 0 | 0 |
| 1982 | Mar | North Shields | 2 | 0 |

### FA XI v SOUTH-WEST COUNTIES

| | | | FA | SWC |
|------|-----|-----------------|----|-----|
| 1977 | Oct | Exeter City FC | 0 | 1 |
| 1978 | Oct | Southampton FC | 1 | 1 |
| 1979 | Oct | Bath City FC | 5 | 1 |
| 1981 | Oct | Swindon Town FC | 2 | 1 |

### FA XI v NORTHERN PREMIER LEAGUE

| | | | FA | NPL |
|------|------|-------------------------|----|-----|
| 1980 | Sept | Runcorn FC | 0 | 0 |
| 1981 | Nov | Gainsborough Trinity FC | 1 | 1 |

### FA XI v WESTERN LEAGUE

| | | | FA | WL |
|------|------|---------------|----|----|
| 1980 | Sept | Frome Town FC | 0 | 0 |

### FA XI v JERSEY FA

| | | | FA | J |
|------|-----|------------|----|---|
| 1980 | Oct | Springfield | 3 | 0 |
| | | St Helier | | |

### FA XI v BRITISH POLYTECHNICS

| | | | FA | BP |
|------|-----|-------------|----|----|
| 1982 | Feb | Nuneaton FC | 4 | 3 |

## International Semi-Professional Tournament 1982

Played in Scotland (Aberdeen)

**1 JUNE**

**England 0**
**Italy 0**

*England:* Clarke; Thompson, Davison, Jennings, Barrett, Johnson, Stephens, Watson, Howard, Williams (Rogers), Smith.

**Scotland 2**
**Netherlands 1**

**3 JUNE**

**England 1** (*Ashford*)
**Netherlands 0**

*England:* Clarke; Thompson, Davison, Jennings, Barrett, Johnson, Stephens, Watson, Howard, Ashford, Smith (Sellers).

**Scotland 2**
**Italy 2**

**5 JUNE**

**England 1** (*Johnson*)
**Scotland 1**

*England:* Clarke; Thompson (Stephens), Davison, Jennings, Barrett, Sellers, Watson, Johnson, Howard, Ashford, Rogers.

**Netherlands 4**
**Italy 2**

**FINAL TABLE**

| | P | W | D | L | F | A | Pts |
|-------------|---|---|---|---|---|---|-----|
| Scotland | 3 | 1 | 2 | 0 | 5 | 4 | 4 |
| England | 3 | 1 | 2 | 0 | 2 | 1 | 4 |
| Netherlands | 3 | 1 | 0 | 2 | 5 | 5 | 2 |
| Italy | 3 | 0 | 2 | 1 | 4 | 6 | 2 |

*Previous winners:* 1979 England; 1980 Scotland; 1981 England.

# SCHOOLS FOOTBALL 1981–82

## ENGLISH SCHOOLS' INTER-ASSOCIATION TROPHY 1981–82

**Fifth Round**

| | |
|---|---|
| Grimsby v Sheffield | 0-7 |
| Newcastle v Wigan | 2-1 |
| High Wycombe v Swindon | 4-1 |
| Basingstoke v Brent | 1-2 |
| Walsall v Liverpool | 1-1, 1-4 |
| Barnsley v Derby | 0-0, 1-2 |
| Newham v Kettering & Corby | 4-0 |
| West London v Slough | 0-2 |
| Warrington v Kingston upon Hull | 0-4 |
| Chester v Coventry | 1-3 |
| Manchester v Rotherham | 3-2 |
| Salford v Leeds | 5-1 |
| Brighton v Southend | 5-1 |
| Enfield v Ipswich | 3-3, 1-0 |
| Reading v Oxford | 2-3 |
| Norwich v Bristol | 2-1 |

**Sixth Round**

| | |
|---|---|
| Sheffield v Newcastle | 2-1 |
| High Wycombe v Brent | 2-2, 0-4 |

| | |
|---|---|
| Liverpool v Derby | 3-2 |
| Newham v Slough | 1-0 |
| Kingston upon Hull v Coventry | 0-1 |
| Manchester v Salford | 2-1 |
| Brighton v Enfield | 1-2 |
| Oxford v Norwich | 1-0 |

**Quarter-Finals**

| | |
|---|---|
| Sheffield v Brent | 3-0 |
| Liverpool v Newham | 4-1 |
| Coventry v Manchester | 2-1 |
| Enfield v Oxford | 1-0 |

**Semi-Finals**

| | |
|---|---|
| Sheffield v Liverpool | 3-1 |
| Coventry v Enfield | 3-0 |

**Final**

| | |
|---|---|
| Sheffield v Coventry | 1-0, 4-1 |

## ENGLISH SCHOOLS' TROPHY FINALISTS 1905–82

| | Winners | Runners up | | Winners | Runners up |
|---|---|---|---|---|---|
| 1905 | London | Sheffield | 1948 | Stockport* | Liverpool* |
| 1906 | Sheffield | Manchester | 1949 | Barnsley | Derby County |
| 1907 | West Ham | Sunderland | 1950 | Swansea | Manchester |
| 1908 | Derby | Oxford | 1951 | Liverpool | Brierley Hill & |
| 1909 | Sheffield | Birmingham N | | | Sedgeley |
| 1910 | Sunderland | Walsall | 1952 | Ilford | Swansea |
| 1911 | Chester-le-Street | Tottenham | 1953 | Swansea | Chesterfield |
| 1912 | West Ham | Birkenhead | 1954 | Liverpool | Southampton |
| 1913 | Watford | Sunderland | 1955 | Swansea | Manchester |
| 1914 | Sheffield | West Ham | 1956 | Liverpool | Brighton |
| 1915 | Cardiff | Manchester | 1957 | Southampton* | Barnsley* |
| 1916 | Bradford | West Ham | 1958 | Bristol | Swansea |
| 1917 | West Ham | Grimsby | 1959 | Brierley Hill, Sedgeley | |
| 1918 | Liverpool | West Ham | | & Tipton* | Doncaster* |
| 1919 | Grimsby | Sunderland | 1960 | Manchester | East London |
| 1920 | Reading | Grimsby | 1961 | Barnsley | Liverpool |
| 1921 | Liverpool | West Ham | 1962 | Stoke | Liverpool |
| 1922 | S London | Grimsby | 1963 | Stoke | Bristol |
| 1923 | Sheffield | Birmingham | 1964 | Erdington | |
| 1924 | N Staffs | Reading | | and Saltley | Chester-le-Street |
| 1925 | Sheffield | Brighton | 1965 | Swansea* | Leicester* |
| 1926 | Grimsby | Liverpool | 1966 | East London | Oxford |
| 1927 | E Northumberland | Rotherham | 1967 | Liverpool | East London |
| 1928 | N Staffordshire | Brighton | 1968 | Manchester* | Waltham Forest* |
| 1929 | S Northumberland | Southampton | 1969 | Liverpool | Swindon |
| 1930 | Newcastle | Chesterfield | 1970 | Liverpool | East London |
| 1931 | Islington | Wolverhampton | 1971 | Huyton | Stoke |
| 1932 | Manchester* | Southampton* | 1972 | Chelmsford | Oxford |
| 1933 | Sunderland | Edmonton | 1973 | Liverpool | Chelmsford |
| 1934 | Manchester | Swansea | 1974 | Manchester | Oxford |
| 1935 | Manchester | Swansea | 1975 | Barking | Havering |
| 1936 | Preston* | West Ham* | 1976 | Liverpool | Slough |
| 1937 | Liverpool | Blyth (Northumberland) | 1977 | South London | Islington |
| 1938 | Manchester | Bootle | 1978 | Newham | Ealing |
| 1939 | Swansea | Chesterfield | 1979 | Bristol | Croydon |
| 1940 | Abandoned | | 1980 | Middlesbrough | Reading |
| 1941–5 | No Competition | | 1981 | High Wycombe | Sunderland |
| 1946 | Leicester | Stockton-on-Tees | 1982 | Sheffield | Coventry |
| 1947 | Salford | Leicester | | | |

*Joint winners.*

# ESFA NATIONAL COMPETITIONS 1981–82

## ASSOCIATED BISCUITS TROPHY

### Second Round

| | |
|---|---|
| Middlesex A v Kent | 2-4 |
| Hampshire A v Middlesex B | 2-5 |
| Cambridgeshire v Suffolk | 1-2 |
| Inner London B v Bedfordshire | 2-1 |
| Somerset v Devon | 0-3 |
| South Glamorgan v Hereford & Worcs | 1-0 |
| Oxfordshire v Berkshire | 4-1 |
| Hampshire B v Surrey B | 1-2 |
| Lancashire A v Greater Manchester A | 2-1 |
| Cheshire A v Clwyd | 4-1 |
| Durham A v Cleveland | 0-3 |
| Durham B v North Yorkshire | 1-1, 0-1 |
| South Yorkshire A v Derbyshire | 1-3 |
| West Midlands A v Merseyside B | 3-2 |
| Lincolnshire A v South Yorkshire B | 2-4 |
| Leicestershire v Northamptonshire | 3-2 |

### Third Round

| | |
|---|---|
| Kent v Middlesex B | 1-2 |
| Suffolk v Inner London B | 1-0 |
| Devon v South Glamorgan | 1-2 |
| Oxfordshire v Surrey B | 1-1, 0-1 |
| Lancashire A v Cheshire A | 1-2 |
| Cleveland v North Yorkshire | 2-0 |
| Derbyshire v West Midlands A | 2-0 |
| South Yorkshire v Leicestershire | 1-0 |

### Fourth Round

| | |
|---|---|
| Middlesex B v Suffolk | 1-2 |
| South Glamorgan v Surrey B | 2-0 |
| Cheshire A v Cleveland | 5-2 |
| Derbyshire v South Yorkshire B | 1-0 |

### Semi-Finals

| | |
|---|---|
| Suffolk (Sir John Leman High School, Beccles) v South Glamorgan (Fitzalan School, Cardiff) | 1-2 |
| Cheshire A (Beamont High, Warrington) v Derbyshire (Mortimer Wilson School, Alfreton) | 2-0 |

### Final

| | |
|---|---|
| South Glamorgan v Cheshire A | 2-1 |

## DENTYNE COMPETITION

Greater Manchester B 7, Surrey A 1

## BUKTA COUNTY CHAMPIONSHIPS

Humberside 1, Merseyside 0

## SMITH'S FOODS SIX-A-SIDE CHAMPIONSHIPS

### Semi-Finals

Dedworth Middle School, Windsor, Berks 2, Holy Name RC Middle School, Leeds 0
St Mary's & St Michael's RC Middle School, London E1 1, Milby Middle School, Nuneaton, Worcs 1
(*Milby Middle School won 3-1 on pens*)

### Third Place Match

St Mary's & St Michael's RC Middle School 1, Holy Name RC Middle School 0

### Final

Dedworth Middle School 1, Milby Middle School 1
(*Dedworth Middle School won on corners*)

## ENGLISH SCHOOLS INTERNATIONALS

### UNDER 15

| | | |
|---|---|---|
| England v Northern Ireland | 6 March, Barnsley | won 4-0 |
| v Wales | 12 March, Reading | won 3-2 |
| v Netherlands | 27 March, Wembley | won 7-0 |
| v Switzerland | 3 April, York | won 1-0 |
| v Scotland | 24 April, Kirkcaldy | lost 0-3 |
| v West Germany | 11 May, Berlin | lost 1-2 |
| v West Germany | 13 May, Frankfurt | lost 0-3 |
| v Scotland | 5 June, Wembley | drawn 0-0 |

*Scorers:* Purdie 4, Beckford 3, Fairbrother 2, Hutchings 2, Keen 2, Priest 1, Seagraves 1, own goal 1.

### VICTORY SHIELD 1981–82

| | P | W | D | L | F | A | Pts |
|---|---|---|---|---|---|---|---|
| Scotland | 3 | 2 | 1 | 0 | 6 | 2 | 5 |
| England | 3 | 2 | 0 | 1 | 7 | 5 | 4 |
| Wales | 3 | 1 | 0 | 2 | 6 | 6 | 2 |
| Northern Ireland | 3 | 0 | 1 | 2 | 0 | 6 | 1 |

### CENTENARY SHIELD (Under-18)

| | P | W | D | L | F | A | Pts |
|---|---|---|---|---|---|---|---|
| England | 2 | 2 | 0 | 0 | 2 | 0 | 4 |
| Scotland | 2 | 1 | 0 | 1 | 2 | 1 | 2 |
| Wales | 2 | 0 | 0 | 2 | 0 | 3 | 0 |

# COACHING AND THE COACHES

Coaching in England is organised by the English Football Association through their Coaching Department. All the official coaching awards emanate from there, and such available awards in descending order are: the Full Coaching Award, the Intermediate Coaching Award (to be introduced in 1984), the Preliminary Coaching Badge, the Local Team Manager's Award, the Youth Team Manager's Certificate, and the School Team Manager's Certificate. In addition, the FA have devised an award for schoolchildren known as the Super Skills Awards.

On the administrative side there are additionally 43 County Coaching Associations plus the three Armed Services, all with County Secretaries who deal with the day-to-day running of coaching at the lower levels and various delegated aspects of the system.

The FA Coaching Headquarters are at the FA's offices at 16 Lancaster Gate, London W2 3LW.

Around the country there are various Regional Coaches supported by Coaching Organisers, and each Regional Coach or Organiser has under his control a number of Coaching Associations formed for the purpose of bringing coaches together to discuss fresh coaching ideas and to take part in refresher courses.

The Regional Coaches and Coaching Organisers are:

## Regional Coaches

**North-East Region:** Mr Jack Detchon, 2nd Floor, 22 High Street, Sheffield S1 2GD.
**North-West Region:** Mr Richard Bate, 31a Wellington Street (St John's), Blackburn, Lancs BB1 8AU.
**Midlands-West Region:** Mr Kevin Verity, 25 Gresham Chambers, 14 Lichfield Street, Wolverhampton WV1 1DG, Staffs.
**Midlands-East Region:** Mr Keith Wright, 29b High Street, Oakham, Rutland.
**Mid-West Region:** Mr David Burnside, 9 Brunswick Square, Bristol B23 4PE.
**London Region (North):** Mr Colin Murphy, c/o The FA Regional Offices, 16 Lancaster Gate, London W2 3LW.
**London Region (South):** Mr Robin Russell, c/o The FA Regional Offices, 16 Lancaster Gate, London W2 3LW.

## COACHING ORGANISERS

**East Anglia Region:** Mr Graham Morgan, Roundwell Cottage, 1 Grove Road, Hethersett, Norwich, Norfolk.
**South-West Region:** Mr Peter Amos, 20 Tuckers Meadow, Crediton, Devon.

The aforementioned are supplemented by the Staff Coaches who are awarded that status for their efforts and hard work in relation to coaching. The Staff Coaches are:
Adams, J. W.; Adamson, J.; Ainsley, G. E.; Allen, D.; Armfield, J.; Bate, R.; Beaglehole, E. W.; Blenkinsop, E. B.; Blunt, K. R. W.; Bond, C. E.; Bramley, J.; Brown, A.; Brown, A. W.; Burnside, D.; Burton, K.; Calvert, J. S.; Cann, S. T.; Cartwright, J.; Casey, T.; Charlton, J.; Churchill, T.; Curtis, G.; Detchon, J.; Dobson, C.; Ford, F.; Furphy, K.; Goodwin, J. W.; Gordon, J.; Gradi, D.; Greaves, I. C. R.; Greenwood, R.; Hardisty, J. R. E.; Hassall, H. W.; Henderson, J. R. E.; Hill, J. W. T.; Houghton, R.; Howe, D.; Hughes, C. F. C.; Jago, G.; Jarman, J. E.; Jones, C.; Kelly, M. J.; Lawrence, T. E.; Lee, B. R.; Lewin, R.; McCluskey, E.; McAnearney, J.; Mansel, J.; Megson, D. H.; Mercer, J.; Minshull, R.; Nicholson, W. E.; Powell, E. W.; Robson, R. W.; Saunders, T. W.; Sayer, C.; Sexton, D. J.; Shannon, L.; Shoulder, J.; Sirrell, J.; Slater, W. J.; Smith, G. C.; Smith, M. J.; Summers, G.; Taylor, G.; Tranter, T. G.; Truman, J. B.; Wade, A.; Waiters, A. K.; Walker, M.; Wardle, G.; Watson, T,; Welton, P.; Wigmore, S. T.; Wilkinson, H.; Williams, B.; Woosnam, P. A.; Worthington, E. S.; Wright, W. A.

Regular coaching periodicals are *Soccer Insight*, the coaching insert to the Football Association Publication *Football Today*, and *Soccer Coach* magazine published by the London Football Coaches Association Editor, Mr Ken Goldman.

## LEAGUE SPONSORSHIP

In August 1981, Pepsi-Cola launched a cash-for-goals scheme worth £70,000. The chief award, a trophy and £5000 for one team in each division, was based on one point for each home goal, two for each away goal, and three bonus points for scoring three goals or more in a League match. There were also prizes of £1000 for the top-scoring team in each division every month and in addition, the top individual goalscorer in each division at the end of the season would win a trophy and £1000. Clubs winning the monthly awards would share them with a charity of their choice.

Later in the season, the National Dairy Council upstaged Pepsi-Cola with a sponsorship deal for the Football League Cup – announced less than two weeks before the final. For a substantial – but undisclosed – amount, the League Cup became the Milk Cup, and the winners, Liverpool, took two trophies back to Anfield.

# LAWS OF THE GAME

*The Laws of the Game and Decisions of the International Board that follow are reproduced with the special permission of FIFA, and the text is the official text as published by FIFA.*

### LAW I
### THE FIELD OF PLAY

The Field of Play and appurtenances shall be as shown in the following plan:

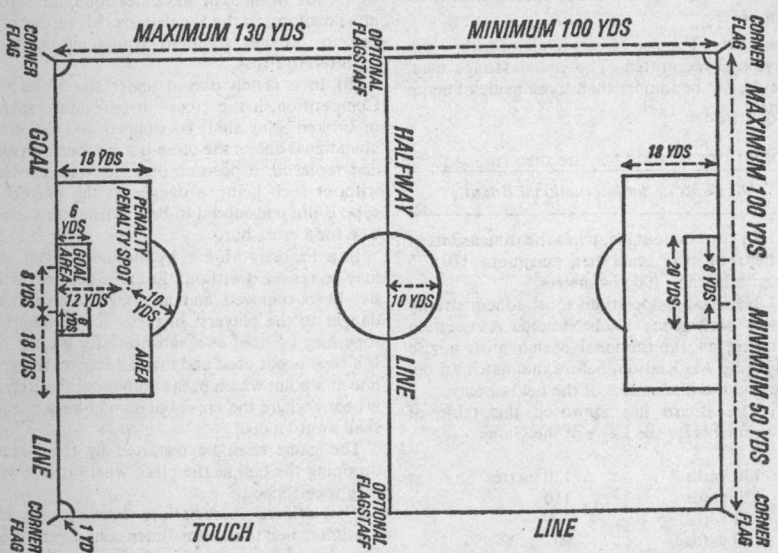

(1) **Dimensions.** The field of play shall be rectangular, its length being not more than 130 yards nor less than 100 yards and its breadth not more than 100 yards nor less than 50 yards. (In International Matches the length shall be not more than 120 yards nor less than 110 yards and the breadth not more than 80 yards nor less than 70 yards.) The length shall in all cases exceed the breadth.

(2) **Marking.** The field of play shall be marked with distinctive lines, not more than 5 inches in width, not by a V-shaped rut, in accordance with the plan, the longer boundary lines being called the touch-lines and the shorter the goal-lines. A flag on a post not less than 5ft high and having a non-pointed top, shall be placed at each corner; a similar flag-post may be placed opposite the halfway line on each side of the field of play, not less than 1 yard outside the touch-line. A halfway-line shall be marked out across the field of play. The centre of the field of play shall be indicated by a suitable mark and a circle with a 10 yards radius shall be marked round it.

(3) **The Goal-Area.** At each end of the field of play two lines shall be drawn at right-angles to the goal-line, 6 yards from each goal-post. These

shall extend into the field of play for a distance of 6 yards and shall be joined by a line drawn parallel with the goal-line. Each of the spaces enclosed by these goal lines and the goal-line shall be called a goal-area.

(4) **The Penalty-Area.** At each end of the field of play two lines shall be drawn at right-angles to the goal-line, 18 yards from each goal-post. These shall extend into the field of play for a distance of 18 yards and shall be joined by a line drawn parallel with the goal-line. Each of the spaces enclosed by these lines and the goal-line shall be called a penalty-area. A suitable mark shall be made within each penalty-area, 12 yards from the mid-point of the goal-line, measured along an undrawn line at right-angles thereto. These shall be the penalty-kick marks. From each penalty-kick mark an arc of a circle, having a radius of 10 yards, shall be drawn outside the penalty-area.

(5) **The Corner-Area.** From each corner-flag post a quarter circle, having a radius of 1 yard, shall be drawn inside the field of play.

(6) **The Goals.** The goals shall be placed on the centre of each goal-line and shall consist of two upright posts, equidistant from the corner-flags and 8 yards apart (inside measurement), joined

by a horizontal cross-bar the lower edge of which shall be 8ft from the ground. The width and depth of the goal-posts and the width and depth of the cross-bars shall not exceed 5 inches (12cm). The goal-posts and the cross-bars shall have the same width.

Nets may be attached to the posts, cross-bars and ground behind the goals. They should be appropriately supported and be so placed as to allow the goal-keeper ample room.

*Footnote*

**Goal nets.** The use of nets made of hemp, jute or nylon is permitted. The nylon strings may, however, not be thinner than those made of hemp or jute.

---

*Decisions of the International Board*

---

(1) In International matches the dimensions of the field of play shall be: maximum 110×75 metres; minimum 100×64 metres.

(2) National Associations must adhere strictly to these dimensions. Each National Association organising an International Match must advise the visiting Association, before the match, of the place and the dimensions of the field of play.

(3) The Board has approved this table of measurements for the Laws of the Game:

| | | |
|---|---|---|
| 130 yards | . . . | 120 metres |
| 120 yards | . . . | 110 |
| 110 yards | . . . | 100 |
| 100 yards | . . . | 90 |
| 80 yards | . . . | 75 |
| 70 yards | . . . | 64 |
| 50 yards | . . . | 45 |
| 18 yards | . . . | 16.50 |
| 12 yards | . . . | 11 |
| 10 yards | . . . | 9.15 |
| 8 yards | . . . | 7.32 |
| 6 yards | . . . | 5.50 |
| 1 yard | . . . | 1 |
| 8 feet | . . . | 2.44 |
| 5 feet | . . . | 1.50 |
| 28 inches | . . . | 0.71 |
| 27 inches | . . . | 0.68 |
| 9 inches | . . . | 0.22 |
| 5 inches | . . . | 0.12 |
| ¾ inch | . . . | 0.019 |
| ½ inch | . . . | 0.0127 |
| ⅜ inch | . . . | 0.010 |
| 14 ounces | . . . | 396 grams |
| 16 ounces | . . . | 453 grams |
| 15 lb/sq in | . . . | 1 kg/cm² |

(4) The goal-line shall be marked the same width as the depth of the goal-posts and the cross-bar, so that the goal-line and goal-post will conform to the same interior and exterior edges.

(5) The 6 yards (for the outline of the goal-area) and the 18 yards (for the outline of the pen-alty-area) which have to be measured along the goal-line, must start from the inner sides of the goal-posts.

(6) The space within the inside areas of the field of play includes the width of the lines marking these areas.

(7) All Associations shall provide standard equipment, particularly in International Matches, when the Laws of the Game must be complied with in every respect and especially with regard to the size of the ball and other equipment which must conform to the regulations. All cases of failure to provide standard equipment must be reported to FIFA.

(8) In a match played under the Rules of a Competition, if the cross-bar becomes displaced or broken, play shall be stopped and the match abandoned unless the cross-bar has been repaired and replaced in position or a new one provided without such being a danger to the players. A rope is not considered to be a satisfactory substitute for a cross-bar.

In a Friendly Match, by mutual consent, play may be resumed without the cross-bar provided it has been removed and no longer constitutes a danger to the players. In these circumstances, a rope may be used as a substitute for a cross-bar. If a rope is not used and the ball crosses the goal-line at a point which in the opinion of the Referee is below where the cross-bar should have been he shall award a goal.

The game shall be restarted by the Referee dropping the ball at the place where it was when play was stopped.

(9) National Associations may specify such maximum and minimum dimensions for the cross-bars and goal-posts, within the limits laid down in Law I, as they consider appropriate.

(10) Goal-posts and cross-bars must be made of wood, metal or other approved material as decided from time to time by the International FA Board. They may be square, rectangular, round, half-round or elliptical in shape. Goal-posts and cross-bars made of other materials and in other shapes are not permitted.

(11) 'Curtain-raisers' to International Matches should only be played following agreement on the day of the match, and taking into account the condition of the field of play, between representatives of the two Associations and the Referee (of the International Match).

(12) National Associations, particularly in International Matches, should

— restrict the number of photographers around the field of play,

— have a line ('photographers' line') marked behind the goal-lines at least two metres from the corner flag going through a point situated at least 3.5 metres behind the intersection of the goal-line with the line marking the goal area to a point situated at least six metres behind the goal-posts,

— prohibit photographers from passing over these lines,

— forbid the use of artificial lighting in the form of 'flashlights'.

## LAW II – THE BALL

The ball shall be spherical; the outer casing shall be of leather or other approved materials. No material shall be used in its construction which might prove dangerous to the players.

The circumference of the ball shall not be more than 28in and not less than 27in. The weight of the ball at the start of the game shall not be more than 16oz nor less than 14oz. The pressure shall be equal to 0.6–0.7 atmosphere, which equals 9.0–10.5lb/sq in (= 600–700gr/cm²) at sea level. The ball shall not be changed during the game unless authorised by the Referee.

---

### Decisions of the International Board

---

(1) The ball used in any match shall be considered the property of the Association or Club on whose ground the match is played, and at the close of play it must be returned to the Referee.

(2) The International Board, from time to time, shall decide what constitutes approved materials. Any approved material shall be certified as such by the International Board.

(3) The Board has approved these equivalents of the weights specified in the Law: 14 to 16 ounces = 396 to 453 grammes.

(4) If the ball bursts or becomes deflated during the course of a match, the game shall be stopped and restarted by dropping the new ball at the place where the first ball became defective.

(5) If this happens during a stoppage of the game (place-kick, goal-kick, corner-kick, free-kick, penalty-kick or throw-in) the game shall be restarted accordingly.

## LAW III – NUMBER OF PLAYERS

(1) A match shall be played by two teams, each consisting of not more than eleven players, one of whom shall be the goalkeeper.

(2) Substitutes may be used in any match played under the rules of a competition, subject to the following conditions:

(a) that the authority of the international association(s) or national association(s) concerned, has been obtained,

(b) that, subject to the restriction contained in the following paragraph (c), the rules of a competition shall state how many, if any, substitutes may be used, and

(c) that a team shall not be permitted to use more than two substitutes in any match.

(3) Substitutes may be used in any other match, provided that the two teams concerned reach agreement on a maximum number, not exceeding five, and that the terms of such agreement are intimated to the Referee, before the match. If the Referee is not informed, or if the

teams fail to reach agreement, no more than two substitutes shall be permitted.

(4) Any of the other players may change places with the goalkeeper, provided that the Referee is informed before the change is made, and provided also, that the change is made during a stoppage in the game.

(5) When a goalkeeper or any other player is to be replaced by a substitute, the following conditions shall be observed:

(a) the Referee shall be informed of the proposed substitution, before it is made,

(b) the substitute shall not enter the field of play until the player he is replacing has left, and then only after having received a signal from the Referee,

(c) he shall enter the field during a stoppage in the game, and at the half-way line.

*Punishment:*

(a) Play shall not be stopped for an infringement of paragraph 4. The players concerned shall be cautioned immediately the ball goes out of play.

(b) For any other infringement of this law, the player concerned shall be cautioned, and if the game is stopped by the Referee, to administer the caution, it shall be restarted by an indirect free-kick, to be taken by a player of the opposing team, from the place where the ball was, when play was stopped. If the free-kick is awarded to a side within its own goal-area, it may be taken from any point within that half of the goal-area in which the ball was when play was stopped.

---

### Decisions of the International Board

---

(1) The minimum number of players in a team is left to the discretion of National Associations.

(2) The Board is of the opinion that a match should not be considered valid if there are fewer than seven players in either of the teams.

(3) A competition may require that the referee shall be informed, before the start of the match, of the names of not more than five players, from whom the substitutes (if any) must be chosen.

(4) A player who has been ordered off before play begins may be replaced only by one of the named substitutes. The kick-off must not be delayed to allow the substitute to join his team.

A player who has been ordered off after play has started may not be replaced.

A named substitute who has been ordered off, either before or after play has started, may not be replaced (this decision relates only to players who are ordered off under Law XII. It does not apply to players who have infringed Law IV).

(5) A player who has been replaced shall not take any further part in the game.

(6) A substitute shall be deemed to be a player and shall be subject to the authority and jurisdiction of the Referee whether called upon to play or not. For any offence committed on the field of play a substitute shall be subject to the same pun-

ishment as any other player whether called upon or not.

## LAW IV – PLAYERS' EQUIPMENT

(1) A player shall not wear anything which is dangerous to another player.

(2) Footwear (boots or shoes) must conform to the following standard:

(a) Bars shall be made of leather or rubber and shall be transverse and flat, not less than half an inch in width and shall extend the total width of the sole and be rounded at the corners.

(b) Studs which are independently mounted on the sole and are replaceable shall be made of leather, rubber, aluminium, plastic or similar material and shall be solid. With the exception of that part of the stud forming the base, which shall not protrude from the sole more than one quarter of an inch, studs shall be round in plan and not less than half an inch in diameter. Where studs are tapered, the minimum diameter of any section of the stud must not be less than half an inch. Where metal seating for the screw type is used, this seating must be embedded in the sole of the footwear and any attachment screw shall be part of the stud. Other than the metal seating for the screw type of stud, no metal plates even though covered with leather or rubber shall be worn, neither studs which are threaded to allow them to be screwed on to a base screw that is fixed by nails or otherwise to the soles of footwear, nor studs which, apart from the base, have any form of protruding edge rim or relief marking or ornament should be allowed.

(c) Studs which are moulded as an integral part of the sole and are not replaceable shall be made of rubber, plastic, polyurethane or similar soft materials. Provided that there are no fewer than ten studs on the sole, they shall have a minimum diameter of three-eighths of an inch (10mm). Additional supporting material to stabilise studs of soft materials, and ridges which shall not protrude more than 5mm from the sole and moulded to strengthen it, shall be permitted provided that they are in no way dangerous to other players. In all other respects they shall conform to the general requirements of this Law.

(d) Combined bars and studs may be worn, provided the whole conforms to the general requirements of this Law. Neither bars nor studs on the soles shall project more than three-quarters of an inch. If nails are used they shall be driven in flush with the surface.

(3) The goalkeeper shall wear colours which distinguish him from the other players and from the Referee.

*Punishment:* For any infringement of this Law, the player at fault shall be sent off the field of play to adjust his equipment and he shall not return without first reporting to the Referee, who shall satisfy himself that the player's equipment is in order; the player shall only re-enter the game at a moment when the ball has ceased to be in play.

---

*Decisions of the International Board*

---

(1) The usual equipment of a player is a jersey or shirt, shorts, stockings and footwear. In a match played under the rules of a competition, players need not wear boots or shoes, but shall wear jersey or shirt, shorts, or track suit or similar trousers, and stockings.

(2) The Law does not insist that boots or shoes must be worn. However, in competition matches Referees should not allow one or a few players to play without footwear when all the other players are so equipped.

(3) In International Matches, International Competitions, International Club Competitions and friendly matches between clubs of different National Associations, the Referee, prior to the start of the game, shall inspect the players' footwear, and prevent any player whose footwear does not conform to the requirements of this Law from playing until such time as it does comply.

The rules of any competition may include a similar provision.

(4) If the Referee finds that a player is wearing articles not permitted by the Laws and which may constitute a danger to other players, he shall order him to take them off. If he fails to carry out the Referee's instruction, the player shall not take part in the match.

(5) A player who has been prevented from taking part in the game or a player who has been sent off the field for infringing Law IV must report to the Referee during a stoppage of the game and may not enter or re-enter the field of play unless and until the Referee has satisfied himself that the player is no longer infringing Law IV.

(6) A player who has been prevented from taking part in a game or who has been sent off because of an infringement of Law IV, and who enters or re-enters the field of play to join or rejoin his team, in breach of the conditions of Law XII, shall be cautioned. If the Referee stops the game to administer the caution, the game shall be restarted by an indirect free-kick, taken by a player of the opposing side, from the place where the ball was when the Referee stopped the game. If the free-kick is awarded to a side within its own goal-area, it may be taken from any point within that half of the goal-area in which the ball was when play was stopped.

## LAW V – REFEREES

A Referee shall be appointed to officiate in each game. His authority and the exercise of the powers granted to him by the Laws of the Game commence as soon as he enters the field of play.

His power of penalising shall extend to offences committed when play has been temporarily suspended, or when the ball is out of play. His decision on points of fact connected with the play shall be final, so far as the result of the game is concerned. He shall:

(a) Enforce the Laws.

(b) Refrain from penalising in cases where he is satisfied that, by doing so, he would be giving an advantage to the offending team.

(c) Keep a record of the game, act as timekeeper and allow the full or agreed time, adding thereto all time lost through accident or other cause.

(d) Have discretionary power to stop the game for any infringement of the Laws and to suspend or terminate the game whenever, by reason of the elements, interference by spectators, or other cause, he deems such stoppage necessary. In such a case he shall submit a detailed report to the competent authority, within the stipulated time, and in accordance with the provisions set up by the National Association under whose jurisdiction the match was played. Reports will be deemed to be made when received in the ordinary course of post.

(e) From the time he enters the field of play, caution any player guilty of misconduct or ungentlemanly behaviour and, if he persists, suspend him from further participation in the game. In such cases the Referee shall send the name of the offender to the competent authority, within the stipulated time, and in accordance with the provisions set up by the National Association under whose jurisdiction the match was played. Reports will be deemed to be made when received in the ordinary course of post.

(f) Allow no person other than the players and linesmen to enter the field of play without his permission.

(g) Stop the game if, in his opinion, a player has been seriously injured; have the player removed as soon as possible from the field of play, and immediately resume the game. If a player is slightly injured, the game shall not be stopped until the ball has ceased to be in play. A player who is able to go to the touch or goal-line for attention of any kind, shall not be treated on the field of play.

(h) Send off the field of play, any player who, in his opinion, is guilty of violent conduct, serious foul play, or the use of foul or abusive language.

(i) Signal for recommencement of the game after all stoppages.

(j) Decide that the ball provided for a match meets with the requirements of Law II.

---

*Decisions of the International Board*

---

(1) Referees in International Matches shall wear a blazer or blouse the colour of which is distinct from the colours worn by the contesting teams.

(2) Referees for International Matches will be selected from a neutral country unless the countries concerned agree to appoint their own officials.

(3) The Referee must be chosen from the official list of International Referees. This need not apply to Amateur and Youth International Matches.

(4) The Referee shall report to the appropriate authority misconduct or any misdemeanour on the part of spectators, officials, players, named substitutes or other persons which take place either on the field of play or in its vicinity at any time prior to, during, or after the match in question so that appropriate action can be taken by the authority concerned.

(5) Linesmen are assistants of the Referee. In no case shall the Referee consider the intervention of a Linesman if he himself has seen the incident and from his position on the field, is better able to judge. With this reserve, and the Linesman neutral, the Referee can consider the intervention and if the information of the Linesman applies to that phase of the game immediately before the scoring of a goal, the Referee may act thereon and cancel the goal.

(6) The Referee, however, can only reverse his first decision so long as the game has not been restarted.

(7) If the Referee has decided to apply the advantage clause and to let the game proceed, he cannot revoke his decision if the presumed advantage has not been realised, even though he has not, by any gesture, indicated his decision. This does not exempt the offending player from being dealt with by the Referee.

(8) The Laws of the Game are intended to provide that games should be played with as little interference as possible, and in this view it is the duty of Referees to penalise only deliberate breaches of the Law. Constant whistling for trifling and doubtful breaches produces bad feeling and loss of temper on the part of the players and spoils the pleasure of spectators.

(9) By para. (d) of Law V the Referee is empowered to terminate a match in the event of grave disorder, but he has no power or right to decide, in such event, that either team is disqualified and thereby the loser of the match. He must send a detailed report to the proper authority who alone has power to deal further with this matter.

(10) If a player commits two infringements of a different nature at the same time, the Referee shall punish the more serious offence.

(11) It is the duty of the Referee to act upon the information of neutral Linesmen with regard to incidents that do not come under the personal notice of the Referee.

(12) The Referee shall not allow any person to enter the field until play has stopped, and only then, if he has given him a signal to do so, nor shall he allow coaching from the boundary lines.

## LAW VI – LINESMEN

Two Linesmen shall be appointed, whose duty (subject to the decision of the Referee) shall be to indicate when the ball is out of play and which side is entitled to the corner-kick, goal-kick or throw-in. They shall also assist the Referee to control the game in accordance with the Laws. In the event of undue interference or improper conduct by a Linesman, the Referee shall dispense with his services and arrange for a substitute to be appointed. (The matter shall be reported by the Referee to the competent authority.) The Linesmen should be equipped with flags by the Club on whose ground the match is played.

*Decisions of the International Board*

(1) Linesmen, where neutral, shall draw the Referee's attention to any breach of the Laws of the Game of which they become aware if they consider that the Referee may not have seen it, but the Referee shall always be the judge of the decision to be taken.

(2) National Associations are advised to appoint official Referees of neutral nationality to act as Linesmen in International Matches.

(3) In International Matches, Linesmen's flags shall be of a vivid colour, bright reds and yellows. Such flags are recommended for use in all other matches.

(4) A Linesman may be subject to disciplinary action only upon a report of the Referee for unjustified interference or insufficient assistance.

## LAW VII – DURATION OF THE GAME

The duration of the game shall be two equal periods of 45 minutes, unless otherwise mutually agreed upon, subject to the following: (a) Allowance shall be made in either period for all time lost through accident or other cause, the amount of which shall be a matter for the discretion of the Referee; (b) Time shall be extended to permit a penalty-kick being taken at or after the expiration of the normal period in either half.

At half-time the interval shall not exceed five minutes except by consent of the Referee.

*Decisions of the International Board*

(1) If a match has been stopped by the Referee, before the completion of the time specified in the rules, for any reason stated in Law V it must be replayed in full unless the rules of the competition concerned provide for the result of the match at the time of such stoppage to stand.

(2) Players have a right to an interval at half-time.

## LAW VIII – THE START OF PLAY

(a) **At the beginning of the game,** choice of ends and the kick-off shall be decided by the toss of a coin. The team winning the toss shall have the option of choice of ends or the kick-off. The Referee having given a signal, the game shall be started by a player taking a place-kick (i.e., a kick at the ball while it is stationary on the ground in the centre of the field of play) into his opponents' half of the field of play. Every player shall be in his own half of the field and every player of the team opposing that of the kicker shall remain not less than 10 yards from the ball until it is kicked-off; it shall not be deemed in play until it has travelled the distance of its own circumference. The kicker shall not play the ball a second time until it has been touched or played by another player.

(b) **After a goal is scored,** the game shall be restarted in like manner by a player of the team losing the goal.

(c) **After half-time:** when restarting after half-time, ends shall be changed and the kick-off shall be taken by a player of the opposite team to that of the player who started the game.

*Punishment:* For any infringement of this Law, the kick-off shall be retaken, except in the case of the kicker playing the ball again before it has been touched or played by another player; for this offence, an indirect free-kick shall be taken by a player of the opposing team from the place where the infringement occurred, unless the offence is committed by a player in his opponent's goal-area, in which case the free-kick shall be taken from a point anywhere within that half of the goal-area in which the offence occurred. A goal shall not be scored direct from a kick-off.

(d) **After any other temporary suspension:** when restarting the game after a temporary suspension of play from any cause not mentioned elsewhere in these Laws, provided that immediately prior to the suspension the ball has not passed over the touch or goal-lines, the Referee shall drop the ball at the place where it was when play was suspended and it shall be deemed in play when it has touched the ground; if, however, it goes over the touch or goal-lines after it has been dropped by the Referee, but before it is touched by a player, the Referee shall again drop it. A player shall not play the ball until it has touched the ground. If this section of the Law is not complied with the Referee shall again drop the ball.

*Decisions of the International Board*

(1) If, when the Referee drops the ball, a player infringes any of the Laws before the ball has touched the ground, the player concerned shall be cautioned or sent off the field according to the seriousness of the offence, but a free-kick cannot be awarded to the opposing team because the ball was not in play at the time of the offence. The ball shall therefore be again dropped by the Referee.

(2) Kicking-off by persons other than the players competing in a match is prohibited.

## LAW IX – BALL IN AND OUT OF PLAY

The ball is out of play:

(a) When it has wholly crossed the goal-line or touch-line, whether on the ground or in the air.

(b) When the game has been stopped by the Referee.

The ball is in play at all other times from the start of the match to the finish including:

(a) If it rebounds from a goal-post, cross-bar or corner-flag post into the field of play.

(b) If it rebounds off either the Referee or Linesmen when they are in the field of play.

(c) In the event of a supposed infringement of the Laws, until a decision is given.

---

*Decisions of the International Board*

---

(1) The lines belong to the areas of which they are the boundaries. In consequence, the touch-lines and the goal-lines belong to the field of play.

## LAW X – METHOD OF SCORING

Except as otherwise provided by these Laws, a goal is scored when the whole of the ball has passed over the goal-line, between the goal-posts and under the cross-bar, provided it has not been thrown, carried or intentionally propelled by hand or arm, by a player of the attacking side, except in the case of a goalkeeper, who is within his own penalty-area.

The team scoring the greater number of goals during a game shall be the winner; if no goals, or an equal number of goals are scored, the game shall be termed a 'draw'.

---

*Decisions of the International Board*

---

(1) Law X defines the only method according to which a match is won or drawn; no variation whatsoever can be authorised.

(2) A goal cannot in any case be allowed if the ball has been prevented by some outside agent from passing over the goal-line. If this happens in the normal course of play, other than at the taking of a penalty-kick: the game must be stopped and restarted by the Referee dropping the ball at the place where the ball came into contact with the interference.

(3) If, when the ball is going into goal, a spectator enters the field before it passes wholly over the goal-line, and tries to prevent a score, a goal shall be allowed if the ball goes into goal unless the spectator has made contact with the ball or has interfered with play, in which case the Referee shall stop the game and restart it by dropping the ball at the place where the contact or interference occurred.

## LAW XI – OFF-SIDE

(1) A player is in an off-side position if he is nearer to his opponents' goal-line than the ball, **unless:**

(a) He is in his own half of the field of play, or

(b) There are at least two of his opponents nearer their own goal-line than he is.

(2) A player shall only be declared off-side and penalised for being in an off-side position, if, at the moment the ball touches, or is played by, one of his team, he is, in the opinion of the referee

(a) interfering with play or with an opponent, or

(b) seeking to gain an advantage by being in that position.

(3) A player shall not be declared off-side by the referee

(a) merely because of his being in an off-side position, or

(b) if he receives the ball, direct, from a goal-kick, a corner-kick, a throw-in, or when it has been dropped by the referee.

(4) If a player is declared off-side, the referee shall award an indirect free-kick, which shall be taken by a player of the opposing team from the place where the infringement occurred, unless the offence is committed by a player in his opponents' goal-area, in which case, the free-kick shall be taken from a point anywhere within that half of the goal-area in which the offence occurred.

---

*Decisions of the International Board*

---

(1) Off-side shall not be judged at the moment the player in question receives the ball, but at the moment when the ball is passed to him by one of his own side. A player who is not in an off-side position when one of his colleagues passes the ball to him or takes a free-kick, does not therefore become off-side if he goes forward during the flight of the ball.

## LAW XII – FOULS AND MISCONDUCT

A player who intentionally commits any of the following nine offences:

(a) Kicks or attempts to kick an opponent;

(b) Trips an opponent, i.e., throwing or attempting to throw him by the use of the legs or by stooping in front of or behind him;

(c) Jumps at an opponent;

(d) Charges an opponent in a violent or dangerous manner;

(e) Charges an opponent from behind unless the latter be obstructing;

(f) Strikes or attempts to strike an opponent;

(g) Holds an opponent;

(h) Pushes an opponent;

(i) Handles the ball, i.e., carries, strikes or propels the ball with his hand or arm. (This does not apply to the goalkeeper within his own penalty-area);

shall be penalised by the award of a direct free-kick to be taken by the opposing side from the place where the offence occurred, unless the offence is committed by a player in his opponents' goal-area in which case, the free-kick shall be taken from a point anywhere within that half of the goal-area in which the offence occurred.

Should a player of the defending side intentionally commit one of the above nine offences within the penalty-area he shall be penalised by a **penalty-kick**.

A penalty-kick can be awarded irrespective of the position of the ball, if in play, at the time an offence within the penalty-area is committed.

A player committing any of the five following offences:

(1) Playing in a manner considered by the Referee to be dangerous, e.g., attempting to kick the ball while held by the goalkeeper;

(2) Charging fairly, i.e., with the shoulder, when the ball is not within playing distance of the players concerned and they are definitely not trying to play it;

(3) When not playing the ball, intentionally obstructing an opponent, i.e. running between the opponent and the ball, or interposing the body so as to form an obstacle to an opponent;

(4) Charging the goalkeeper except when he

(a) is holding the ball;

(b) is obstructing an opponent;

(c) has passed outside his goal-area;

(5) When playing as goalkeeper and within his own penalty area,

(a) from the moment the ball comes under his control he takes more than four steps without releasing the ball into play and – having released it – he touches the ball again before it has been touched or played by another player, or

(b) indulges in tactics which, in the opinion of the Referee, are designed merely to hold up the game and thus waste time and so give an unfair advantage to his own team – shall be penalised by the award of an **indirect free-kick** to be taken by the opposing side from the place where the infringement occurred, unless the offence is committed by a player in his opponents' goal-area, in which case the free-kick shall be taken from a point anywhere within that half of the goal-area in which the offence occurred.

A player shall be **cautioned** if:

(j) he enters or re-enters the field of play to join or rejoin his team after the game has commenced, or leaves the field of play during the progress of the game (except through accident) without, in either case, first having received a signal from the Referee showing him that he may do so. If the Referee stops the game to administer the caution the game shall be restarted by an indirect free-kick taken by a player of the opposing team from the place where the ball was when the Referee stopped the game. If the free-kick is awarded to a side within its own goal-area it may be taken from any point within the half of the goal-area in which the ball was when play was stopped. If, however, the offending player has committed a more serious offence he shall be penalised according to that section of the law he infringed;

(k) he persistently infringes the Laws of the Game;

(l) he shows by word or action, dissent from any decision given by the Referee;

(m) he is guilty of ungentlemanly conduct.

For any of these last three offences, in addition to the caution, an **indirect free-kick** shall also be awarded to the opposing side from the place where the offence occurred unless a more serious infringement of the Laws of the Game was committed. If the offence is committed by a player in his opponents' goal-area, a free-kick shall be taken from a point anywhere within that half of the goal-area in which the offence occurred.

A player shall be **sent off** the field of play, if:

(n) in the opinion of the Referee he is guilty of violent conduct or serious foul play;

(o) he uses foul or abusive language;

(p) he persists in misconduct after having received a caution.

If play be stopped by reason of a player being ordered from the field for an offence without a separate breach of the Law having been committed, the game shall be resumed by an **indirect free-kick** awarded to the opposing side from the place where the infringement occurred, unless the offence is committed by a player in his opponents' goal-area, in which case, the free-kick shall be taken from a point anywhere within that half of the goal-area in which the offence occurred.

---

### Decisions of the International Board

---

(1) If the goalkeeper either intentionally strikes an opponent by throwing the ball vigorously at him or pushes him with the ball while holding it, the Referee shall award a penalty-kick, if the offence took place within the penalty-area.

(2) If a player deliberately turns his back to an opponent when he is about to be tackled, he may be charged but not in a dangerous manner.

(3) In case of body-contact in the goal-area between an attacking player and the opposing goalkeeper not in possession of the ball, the Referee, as sole judge of intention, shall stop the game if, in his opinion, the action of the attacking player was intentional, and award an indirect free-kick.

(4) If a player leans on the shoulders of another player of his own team in order to head the ball, the Referee shall stop the game, caution the player for ungentlemanly conduct and award an indirect free-kick to the opposing side.

(5) A player's obligation when joining or rejoining his team after the start of the match to 'report to the Referee' must be interpreted as meaning 'to draw the attention of the Referee from the touch-line'. The signal from the Referee shall be made by a definite gesture which makes the player understand that he may come into the field of play; it is not necessary for the Referee to wait until the game is stopped (this does not apply in respect of an infringement of Law IV), but the Referee is the sole judge of the moment in which he gives his signal of acknowledgement.

(6) The letter and spirit of Law XII do not oblige the Referee to stop a game to administer a caution. He may, if he chooses, apply the advan-

tage. If he does apply the advantage, he shall caution the player when play stops.

(7) If a player covers up the ball without touching it in an endeavour not to have it played by an opponent, he obstructs but does not infringe Law XII para. 3 because he is already in possession of the ball and covers it for tactical reasons whilst the ball remains within playing distance. In fact, he is actually playing the ball and does not commit an infringement; in this case, the player may be charged because he is in fact playing the ball.

(8) If a player intentionally stretches his arms to obstruct an opponent and steps from one side to the other, moving his arms up and down to delay his opponent, forcing him to change course, but does not make 'bodily contact' the Referee shall caution the player for ungentlemanly conduct and award an indirect free-kick.

(9) If a player intentionally obstructs the opposing goalkeeper, in an attempt to prevent him from putting the ball into play in accordance with Law XII, 5(a), the Referee shall award an indirect free-kick.

(10) If after a Referee has awarded a free-kick a player protests violently by using abusive or foul language and is sent off the field, the free-kick should not be taken until the player has left the field.

(11) Any player, whether he is within or outside the field of play, whose conduct is ungentlemanly or violent, whether or not it is directed towards an opponent, a colleague, the Referee, a Linesman or other person, or who uses foul or abusive language, is guilty of an offence, and shall be dealt with according to the nature of the offence committed.

(12) If, in the opinion of the Referee a goalkeeper intentionally lies on the ball longer than is necessary, he shall be penalised for ungentlemanly conduct and

(a) be cautioned and an indirect free-kick awarded to the opposing team;

(b) in case of repetition of the offence, be sent off the field.

(13) The offence of spitting at opponents, officials or other persons, or similar unseemly behaviour shall be considered as violent conduct within the meaning of section (n) of Law XII.

(14) If, when a Referee is about to caution a player, and before he has done so, the player commits another offence which merits a caution, the player shall be sent off the field of play.

# LAW XIII – FREE-KICK

Free-kicks shall be classified under two headings: 'Direct' (from which a goal can be scored direct against the offending side), and 'Indirect' (from which a goal cannot be scored unless the ball has been played or touched by a player other than the kicker before passing through the goal).

When a player is taking a direct or an indirect free-kick inside his own penalty-area, all of the opposing players shall remain outside the area, and shall be at least ten yards from the ball whilst the kick is being taken. The ball shall be in play immediately it has travelled the distance of its own circumference and is beyond the penalty-area. The goalkeeper shall not receive the ball into his hands, in order that he may thereafter kick it into play. If the ball is not kicked direct into play, beyond the penalty-area, the kick shall be retaken.

When a player is taking a direct or an indirect free-kick outside his own penalty-area, all of the opposing players shall be at least ten yards from the ball, until it is in play, unless they are standing on their own goal-line, between the goal-posts. The ball shall be in play when it has travelled the distance of its own circumference.

If a player of the opposing side encroaches into the penalty-area, or within ten yards of the ball, as the case may be, before a free-kick is taken, the Referee shall delay the taking of the kick, until the Law is complied with.

The ball must be stationary when a free-kick is taken, and the kicker shall not play the ball a second time, until it has been touched or played by another player.

Notwithstanding any other reference in these Laws to the point from which a free-kick is to be taken, any free-kick awarded to the defending side, within its own goal-area, shall be taken from any point within that half of the goal-area in which the free-kick has been awarded.

*Punishment.* If the kicker, after taking the free-kick, plays the ball a second time before it has been touched or played by another player an indirect free-kick shall be taken by a player of the opposing team from the spot where the infringement occurred.

---

### Decisions of the International Board

(1) In order to distinguish between a direct and an indirect free-kick, the Referee, when he awards an indirect free-kick, shall indicate accordingly by raising an arm above his head. He shall keep his arm in that position until the kick has been taken and retain the signal until the ball has been played or touched by another player or goes out of play.

(2) Players who do not retire to the proper distance when a free-kick is taken must be cautioned and on any repetition be ordered off. It is particularly requested of Referees that attempts to delay the taking of a free-kick by encroaching should be treated as serious misconduct.

(3) If, when a free-kick is being taken, any of the players dance about or gesticulate in a way calculated to distract their opponents, it shall be deemed ungentlemanly conduct for which the offender(s) shall be cautioned.

## LAW XIV – PENALTY-KICK

A penalty-kick shall be taken from the penalty-mark and, when it is being taken, all players with the exception of the player taking the kick, and the opposing goal-keeper, shall be within the field of play but outside the penalty-area, and at least 10 yards from the penalty-mark. The opposing goalkeeper must stand (without moving his feet) on his own goal-line, between the goal-posts, until the ball is kicked. The player taking the kick must kick the ball forward; he shall not play the ball a second time until it has been touched or played by another player. The ball shall be deemed in play directly it is kicked, i.e., when it has travelled the distance of its circumference, and a goal may be scored direct from such a penalty-kick. If the ball touches the goalkeeper before passing between the posts, when a penalty-kick is being taken at or after the expiration of half-time or full-time, it does not nullify a goal. If necessary, time of play shall be extended at half-time or full-time to allow a penalty-kick to be taken.

*Punishment*

For any infringement of this Law:

(a) by the defending team, the kick shall be retaken if a goal has not resulted.

(b) by the attacking team other than by the player taking the kick, if a goal is scored it shall be disallowed and the kick retaken.

(c) by the player taking the penalty-kick, committed after the ball is in play, a player of the opposing team shall take an indirect free-kick from the spot where the infringement occurred. If, in the case of paragraph (c), the offence is committed by the player in his opponents' goal-area, the free-kick shall be taken from a point anywhere within that half of the goal-area in which the offence occurred.

---

### Decisions of the International Board

---

(1) When the Referee has awarded a penalty-kick, he shall not signal for it to be taken, until the players have taken up position in accordance with the Law.

(2) (a) If, after the kick has been taken, the ball is stopped in its course towards goal, by an outside agent, the kick shall be retaken.

(b) If, after the kick has been taken, the ball rebounds into play, from the goalkeeper, the cross-bar or a goal-post, and is then stopped in its course by an outside agent, the Referee shall stop play and restart it by dropping the ball at the place where it came into contact with the outside agent.

(3) (a) If, after having given the signal for a penalty-kick to be taken, the Referee sees that the goalkeeper is not in his right place on the goal-line, he shall, nevertheless, allow the kick to proceed. It shall be retaken, if a goal is not scored.

(b) If, after the Referee has given the signal for a penalty-kick to be taken, and before the ball has been kicked, the goal-keeper moves his feet, the Referee shall, nevertheless, allow the kick to proceed. It shall be retaken, if a goal is not scored.

(c) If, after the Referee has given the signal for a penalty-kick to be taken, and before the ball is in play, a player of the defending team encroaches into the penalty-area, or within ten yards of the penalty-mark, the Referee shall, allow the kick to proceed. It shall be retaken, if a goal is not scored.

The player concerned shall be cautioned.

(4) (a) If, when a penalty-kick is being taken, the player taking the kick is guilty of ungentlemanly conduct, the kick, if already taken, shall be retaken, if a goal is scored.

The player concerned shall be cautioned.

(b) If, after the Referee has given the signal for a penalty-kick to be taken, and before the ball is in play, a colleague of the player taking the kick encroaches into the penalty-area or within ten yards of the penalty-mark, the Referee shall, nevertheless, allow the kick to proceed. If a goal is scored, it shall be disallowed, and the kick retaken.

The player concerned shall be cautioned.

(c) If, in the circumstances described in the foregoing paragraph, the ball rebounds into play from the goalkeeper, the crossbar or a goal-post, the Referee shall stop the game, caution the player and award an indirect free-kick to the opposing team from the place where the infringement occurred.

(5) (a) If, after the referee has given the signal for a penalty-kick to be taken, and before the ball is in play, the goalkeeper moves from his position on the goal-line, or moves his feet, and a colleague of the kicker encroaches into the penalty-area or within 10 yards of the penalty-mark, the kick, if taken, shall be retaken.

The colleague of the kicker shall be cautioned.

(b) If, after the Referee has given the signal for a penalty-kick to be taken, and before the ball is in play, a player of each team encroaches into the penalty-area, or within 10 yards of the penalty-mark, the kick, if taken, shall be retaken.

The players concerned shall be cautioned.

(6) When a match is extended, at half-time or full-time, to allow a penalty-kick to be taken or retaken, the extension shall last until the moment that the penalty-kick has been completed, i.e. until the Referee has decided whether or not a goal is scored.

A goal is scored when the ball passes wholly over the goal-line.

(a) direct from the penalty-kick,

(b) having rebounded from either goal-post or the cross-bar, or

(c) having touched or been played by the goal-keeper.

The game shall terminate immediately the Referee has made his decision.

(7) When a penalty-kick is being taken in extended time:

(a) the provisions of all of the foregoing paragraphs, except paragraphs (2)(b) and (4)(c) shall apply in the usual way, and

(b) in the circumstances described in paragraphs (2)(b) and (4)(c) the game shall terminate immediately the ball rebounds from the goalkeeper, the cross-bar or the goal-post.

## LAW XV – THROW-IN

When the whole of the ball passes over a touch-line, either on the ground or in the air, it shall be thrown in from the point where it crossed the line, in any direction, by a player of the team opposite to that of the player who last touched it. The thrower at the moment of delivering the ball must face the field of play and part of each foot shall be either on the touch-line or on the ground outside the touch-line. The thrower shall use both hands and shall deliver the ball from behind and over his head. The ball shall be in play immediately it enters the field of play, but the thrower shall not again play the ball until it has been touched or played by another player. A goal shall not be scored direct from a throw-in.

*Punishment:*

(a) If the ball is improperly thrown in the throw-in shall be taken by a player of the opposing team.

(b) If the thrower plays the ball a second time before it has been touched or played by another player, an indirect free-kick shall be taken by a player of the opposing team from the place where the infringement occurred, unless the offence is committed by a player in his opponents' goal-area, in which case, the free-kick shall be taken from a point anywhere within that half of the goal-area in which the offence occurred.

*Decisions of the International Board*

(1) If a player taking a throw-in, plays the ball a second time by handling it within the field of play before it has been touched or played by another player, the Referee shall award a direct free-kick.

(2) A player taking a throw-in must face the field of play with some part of his body.

(3) If, when a throw-in is being taken, any of the opposing players dance about or gesticulate in a way calculated to distract or impede the thrower, it shall be deemed ungentlemanly conduct, for which the offender(s) shall be cautioned.

## LAW XVI – GOAL-KICK

When the whole of the ball passes over the goal-line excluding that portion between the goal-posts, either in the air or on the ground, having last been played by one of the attacking team, it shall be kicked direct into play beyond the penalty-area from a point within that half of the goal-area nearest to where it crossed the line, by a player of the defending team. A goalkeeper shall not receive the ball into his hands from a goal-kick in order that he may thereafter kick it into play. If the ball is not kicked beyond the penalty-area, i.e., direct into play, the kick shall be retaken. The kicker shall not play the ball a second time until it has touched – or been played by – another player. A goal shall not be scored direct from such a kick. Players of the team opposing that of the player taking the goal-kick shall remain outside the penalty-area whilst the kick is being taken.

*Punishment:*

If a player taking a goal-kick plays the ball a second time after it has passed beyond the penalty-area, but before it has touched or been played by another player, an indirect free-kick shall be awarded to the opposing team, to be taken from the place where the infringement occurred, unless the offence is committed by a player in his opponents' goal-area, in which case, the free-kick shall be taken from a point anywhere within that half of the goal-area in which the offence occurred.

*Decisions of the International Board*

(1) When a goal-kick has been taken and the player who has kicked the ball touches it again before it has left the penalty-area, the kick has not been taken in accordance with the Law and must be retaken.

## LAW XVII – CORNER-KICK

When the whole of the ball passes over the goal-line, excluding that portion between the goal-posts, either in the air or on the ground, having last been played by one of the defending team, a member of the attacking team shall take a corner-kick, i.e., the whole of the ball shall be placed within the quarter circle at the nearest corner-flag post, which must not be moved, and it shall be kicked from that position. A goal may be scored direct from such a kick. Players of the team opposing that of the player taking the corner-kick shall not approach within 10 yards of the ball until it is in play, i.e., it has travelled the distance of its own circumference, nor shall the kicker play the ball a second time until it has been touched or played by another player.

*Punishment:*

(a) If the player who takes the kick plays the ball a second time before it has been touched or played by another player, the Referee shall award an indirect free-kick to the opposing team, to be taken from the place where the infringement occurred, unless the offence is committed by a player in his opponents' goal-area, in which case the free-kick shall be taken from a point anywhere within that half of the goal-area in which the offence occurred.

(b) For any other infringement the kick shall be retaken.

# ADDRESSES

**The Football Association:** 16 Lancaster Gate, London W2 3LW

**Scotland:** Ernie Walker, 6 Park Gardens, Glasgow G3 7YE
**Northern Ireland** (Irish FA): W. J. Drennan, J.P., M.B.E., 20 Windsor Avenue, Belfast BT9 6EG
**Wales:** Trevor Morris, O.B.E., 3 Fairy Road, Wrexham LL13 7PS

**Republic of Ireland** (FA of Ireland): P. J. O'Driscoll, 80 Merrion Square, Dublin 2
**International Federation** (FIFA): S. Blatter, FIFA House, Hitzigweg 11, CH-8032 Zurich, Switzerland
**Union of European Football Associations:** H. Bangerter, PO Box 16, CH-3000 Berne 15, Switzerland

## THE LEAGUES

**The Football League:** R. H. G. Kelly, F.C.I.S., The Football League, Lytham St Annes, Lancs. FY8 1JG. *0253-729421. Telex 67675*
**The Scottish League:** J. Farry, 188 West Regent Street, Glasgow G2 4RY. *041-248 3844/5*
**The Irish League:** J. H. Long, 16 Donegall Square South, Belfast
**Alliance Premier League:** P. D. Hunter, 24 Barnehurst Road, Bexleyheath, Kent DA7 6EZ. *Crayford 22616*
**Athenian League:** G. G. Dell, 'Ardranech', Monument Lane, Chalfont St Peter, Bucks. *Chalfont St Giles 3819*
**Central League:** D. J. Grimshaw, 118 St Stephens Road, Deepdale, Preston, Lancs., PR1 6TD. *Preston 55898*
**North West Counties League:** C. R. Mahood, Burscough Nurseries, Ring O'Bells Lane, Lathom, Ormskirk, Lancs L40 5US. *Rufford 822688*
**Town & Country League:** A. W. G. Rudd, 'Heathercliff', Gunton Cliff, Lowestoft. *Lowestoft 5996*
**Football Combination:** T. P. R. Kirkup, 15 Oulton Rise, Spinney Hill, Northampton NN3 1EW. *0604-47831*
**Hellenic League:** D. A. G. Harrison, 107 Thame Road, Haddenham, Aylesbury, Bucks. *Haddenham 290590*
**Kent League:** D. Baker, 17 Sterling Road, Sittingbourne, Kent. *Sittingbourne 25105*
**Lancashire Amateur League:** H. Heap, 'Maraldo', Carlton Road, Hale, Altrincham, Cheshire, WA15 8RH. *061-980 2344*
**Lancashire Football League:** H. E. Lambert, 3 Cravans Avenue, Ewood, Blackburn BB2 4LB. *Blackburn 58561*
**Leicestershire Senior League:** P. Henwood, 63 Carisbrooke Rd, Leicester LE2 3PF. *Leicester 705475*
**London Spartan:** D. Cordell, 44 Greenleas, Waltham Abbey, Essex. *Lea Valley 712428*
**Manchester League:** T. W. Gilgryst, 7 Bowlee Close, Unsworth, Bury, Lancs. *061-766 3082*
**Midland Combination:** L. W. James, 175 Barnet Lane, Kingswinford, Brierley Hill, West Midlands. *Kingswinford 3459*
**Mid-Week Football League:** Frank P. White, 11 Tulip Way, Clacton-on-Sea, Essex. *Clacton 32750*
**Nemean Amateur League:** W. Chivers, 58 Laurel Avenue, Potters Bar, Herts. EN6 2AB. *Potters Bar 54969*

**Northern Intermediate League:** F. R. Vicary, 12 Holmefield Avenue, Thornes, Wakefield, Yorks WF2 7AF. *Wakefield 75013*
**Northern League:** G. Nicholson, 99 Watling Road, Bishop Auckland, Co. Durham. *Bishop Auckland 2167*
**Northern Premier League:** R. D. Bayley, 22 Woburn Drive, Hale, Altrincham, Cheshire WA15. *061-980-7007*
**North Midlands League:** G. Thompson, 7 Wren Park Close, Ridgway, Sheffield
**Old Boys Football League:** B. Aldous, Clemitis Cottage, Ongar Road, White Roding, Dunmow, Essex. *White Roding 278*
**Peterborough and District League:** A. V. Brown, 27 Gloucester Road, Old Fletton, Peterborough
**Isthmian League:** A. C. F. Turvey, 'Ladymead', 18 Apple Way, Basing, Basingstoke, Hants. *Basingstoke 61789*
**Southern Amateur League:** F. J. Banner, 10 Oakwood Road, Orpington, Kent. *Farnborough 58720*
**South-East Counties League:** R. A. Bailey, 10 Highlands Road, New Barnet, Herts. EN5 5AB. *01-449 5131*
**Southern League:** D. J. Strudwick, 49 Woodlands Way, Southwater, Horsham, West Sussex, RH13 7HT
**South Midlands League:** C. Moyse, 33 Markham Crescent, Dunstable, Beds. LU5 4SS. *Dunstable 64682*
**South Western League:** G. Gazzard, 6 Coastguard Crescent, Penzance, Cornwall. *Penzance 61397*
**United Counties League:** G. Ellitson, 2 St Marks Close, Rushden, Northants. *Rushden 313106*
**Wearside:** J. R. Walsh, 85 Hartington St, Roker, Sunderland, Tyne & Wear. *Sunderland 75513*
**Western League:** J. Veale, 5 Everest Road, Bristol BS16 2BX. *0272-652699*
**The Welsh League:** Anthony W. Griffiths, 13 Llynfi Road, Maesteg, Bridgend, Mid Glamorgan CF34 9DS. *0656 734096*
**West Midlands Regional League:** K. H. Goodfellow, 152 Garrison Lane, Small Heath, Birmingham. *021-772-0375*
**West Yorkshire League:** W. Keyworth, 2 Hill Court Grove, Branley, Yorks. L13 2AP. *Pudsey 74465*
**Northern Counties (East):** B. Wood, 5 Restmore Avenue, Guiseley, Nr Leeds, LS20 9DG. *Guiseley 4558 (home); Bradford 29595 (9 a.m. to 5 p.m.)*

## COUNTY FOOTBALL ASSOCIATIONS

**Bedfordshire:** P. Burns, 13 Wendover Way, Luton, Beds. LU2 7LS. *Luton 30829*
**Berks and Bucks:** C. J. Twelftree, 42 Bourtonville, Buckingham, Bucks. *Buckingham 2137*
**Birmingham County:** W. F. Pennick, County F.A. Offices, Rayhall Lane, Great Barr, Birmingham B43 6JE *021-357-4278*
**Cambridgeshire:** R. E. Rogers, 20 Aingers Road, Histon, Cambridge. *Histon 2803*
**Cheshire:** F. Foden, 549 Crewe Road, Wistaston, Crewe, CW2 6PU. *Crewe 69429*

**Cornwall:** W. Parnell, 12 Higher Tremena, St Austell PL25 5QQ. *St Austell 3236*
**Cumberland:** R. Johnson, 72 Victoria Road, Workington, Cumberland. *Workington 3979*
**Derbyshire:** H. L. P. Holmes, 82 Friar Gate, Derby. *Derby 25835*
**Devon County:** C. H. Norsworthy, 8 Belair Road, Peverell, Plymouth PL2 3QH. *Plymouth 73550*
**Dorset County:** P. Hough, 110 Dorchester Rd, Oakdale, Poole, Dorset BH15 3SD *0202 746244*

**Durham:** G. L. Pearce, 'Codeslaw', Ferens Park, Durham DH1 1JZ. *Durham 3653*

**East Riding County:** C. Branton, 83 Belvedere Road, Hessel, Hull HU13 9JH *Hull 649294*

**Essex County:** M. S. Jeffers, 54A Eastwood Road, Goodmayes, Ilford, Essex. *01-590 7893*

**Gloucestershire:** E. J. Marsh, 46 Douglas Road, Horfield, Bristol BS7 0JD. *Bristol 46430*

**Guernsey:** R. Truslum, Carleeta, Marette Du Haut, St Martins, Guernsey C.I. *0481-36529*

**Hampshire:** R. G. Barnes, 367 Winchester Road, Southampton. *Southampton 766884*

**Herefordshire:** R. A. Doody, Longwynd, Paradise Green, Marden, Hereford. *Sutton St Nicholas 674*

**Hertfordshire:** G. W. Daulby, 158 Hazelwood Drive, St Albans, Herts. AL4 OU2

**Hunts County:** M. M. Armstrong, 1 Chapel End, Great Giddings, Huntingdon, Cambs. *Winwick 262*

**Isle of Man:** Mrs R. Raley, 129 Bucks Road, Douglas, I.O.M.

**Jersey:** Miss S. Mourant, Racqueberg Farm, Samares Lane, St Clement, Jersey, C.I.

**Kent County:** K. T. Masters, 69 Maidstone Road, Chatham, Kent ME4 6DT. *Medway 43824*

**Lancashire:** J. Kenyon, 31A, Wellington St, St John's, Blackburn, Lancs. BB1 8AU *Blackburn 64333*

**Leicestershire and Rutland:** R. E. Barston, 67 Melton Road, Leicester

**Lincolnshire:** F. S. Richardson, 9 The Avenue, Lincoln. *Lincoln 24917*

**Liverpool County:** S. A. Rudd, 23 Greenfield Road, Old Swann, Liverpool 13. *051-526-9515*

**London:** A. F. Monger, 4 Aldworth Grove, London SE13 6HY. *01-690-9626*

**Manchester County:** S. Holliday, 87 Hart Road, Fallowfield, Manchester 14. *061-224-5185*

**Middlesex County:** A. L. Smith, 68 Squires Lane, London N3 2AP *01-346 7565*

**Norfolk County:** R. Kiddell, 39 Beaumont Road, Costessey, Norwich NR5 0HG. *Norwich 742421*

**Northamptonshire:** B. Walden, 37 Harding Terrace, Northampton. *Northampton 39584*

**North Riding County:** J. Sturgeon, 284 Linthorpe Road, Middlesbrough. *Middlesbrough 224585*

**Northumberland:** J. A. Forster, 30 St Mary's Place, Newcastle upon Tyne, NE1 7P2. *Newcastle 610779*

**Nottinghamshire:** W. T. Annable, 7 Clarendon Street, Nottingham. *Nottingham 48954*

**Oxfordshire:** P. J. Ladbrook, 3 Wilkins Road, Cowley, Oxford

**Sheffield and Hallamshire:** G. Thompson, Clegg House, 253 Pittsmoor Road, Sheffield 3. *Sheffield 27817*

**Shropshire:** A. W. Brett, High Street Chambers, 10–11, High Street, Shrewsbury

**Somerset County:** L. G. Webb, 32 North Road, Midsomer Norton, Bath BA3 2QQ. *Midsomer Norton 3176*

**Staffordshire:** T. Myatt, County Offices, Miller Street, Newcastle-under-Lyme ST5 1HB. *Newcastle-under-Lyme 622585*

**Suffolk County:** B. A. H. Collings, 15 Taunton Close, Henley Rise, Ipswich IP1 6NL. *Ipswich 714676*

**Surrey County:** L. F. J. Smith, 2 Fairfield Avenue, Horley, Surrey RH6 7PD *Horley 4945*

**Sussex County:** R. F. Reeve, County Office, Culver Road, Lancing, Sussex BN15 9AX

**Westmorland:** J. R. Plumbe, 24 Crescent Green, Kendal LA9 6DR *Kendal 23227*

**West Riding County:** R. M. Robin, 77 Great George Street, Leeds LS1 3DR

**Wiltshire:** F. J. Peart, 161 Grange Drive, Stratton St Margaret, Swindon. *Stratton St Margaret 2239*

**Worcestershire:** P. Rushton, 84 Windermere Drive, Warndon, Worcester WR4 9JB. *Worcester 51166*

## OTHER USEFUL ADDRESSES

**Amateur Football Alliance:** W. P. Goss, Room 33, 3rd Floor, 6 Langley Street, London WC2 *01-240 3837/8*

**English Schools FA:** A. Rice, 4A Eastgate Street, Stafford ST16 2NN. *0785-51142*

**Oxford University:** Sir Harold Thompson, C.B.E., F.R.S., St John's College, Oxford

**Cambridge University:** J. C. Irons, Trinity Hall, Cambridge

**Army:** Major A. Dobson, M.B.E., Ministry of Defence (A.S.C.B.), Clayton Barracks, Aldershot, Hants.

**Royal Air Force:** Sq/Ldr J. A. Miller, 7 Canberra Drive, RAF Scampton, Lincoln

**Royal Navy:** Lt-Cdr H. A. Sheppard, R.N. Sports Office, H.M.S. Nelson, Portsmouth, Hants. PO1 3HH

**Universities Athletic Union:** Alun Evans, U.A.U., 28 Woburn Square, London WC1 *01-637 4828*

**Central Council of Physical Recreation:** General Secretary, 70 Brompton Road, London, SW3 1HE. *01-584 6651*

**British Olympic Association:** 6 John Prince's Street, W1M 0DH *01-408 2029*

**National Federation of Football Supporters' Clubs:** Head Office: 1 Saville Row, Bath, Avon BA1 2QP *0225-318592*. General Secretary: Malcolm Gamlen, 69 Fourth Avenue, Chelmsford, Essex *0245-63305*

**National Playing Fields Association:** Col R. Satterthwaite, O.B.E., 578 Catherine Place, London, SW1

**The Scottish Football Commercial Managers Association:** J. E. Hillier (Chairman), c/o Keith FC Promotions Office, 60 Union Street, Keith, Banffshire, Scotland

**Professional Footballers' Association:** G. Taylor, 124 Corn Exchange Buildings, Hanging Ditch, Manchester M4 3BN. *061-834 7554*

**Referees' Association:** O. J. Venning, Summerhill, Kingswinford, West Midlands

**The Association of Football League Referees and Linesmen:** R. Hall, Secretary, 59 Woodcock Hill, Kenton, Harrow, Middlesex HA3 0JH

**Women's Football Association:** Miss P. Gregory, 27 Myddleton Avenue, Forty Hill, Enfield, Middx. *01-363 1152*

**The Association of Provincial Football Supporters' Clubs in London:** E. Norfolk, 79 Dellow Close, Ilford, Essex

**The Association of Football League Commercial Managers:** G. H. Dimbleby, Secretary WBA FC, The Hawthorns, Halfords Lane, West Bromwich B71 4LF

**The Association of Football Statisticians:** R. J. Spiller, 5 Hempstalls, Basildon, Essex. *0268 282556*

**The Football Programme Directory:** David Stacey, 'The Beeches', 66 Southend Road, Wickford, Essex SS11 8EN.

**England Football Supporters Association:** Hon. Publicity Officer, David Stacey, 66 Southend Road, Wickford, Essex SS11 8EN

**The Football League Executive Staffs Association:** Westwood House, 80 Warwick Street, Leamington Spa, Warwickshire CV32 4QG. *0926 313651/36418*

**The Ninety-Two Club:** 104 Gilda Crescent, Whitchurch, Bristol BS14 9LD

# FOOTBALL LEAGUE FIXTURES 1982–83

*These fixtures are the copyright of The Football League and may not be reproduced without permission. The Editor wishes to remind readers that these fixtures are subject to alteration and that it is advisable to check that a particular fixture still stands before travelling.*

## DIVISION ONE

| | Arsenal | Aston Villa | Birmingham C | Brighton & HA | Coventry C | Everton | Ipswich T | Liverpool | Luton T | Manchester C | Manchester U | Norwich C | Nottingham F | Notts Co | Southampton | Stoke C | Sunderland | Swansea C | Tottenham H | Watford | WBA | West Ham U |
|---|---|---|---|---|---|---|---|---|---|---|---|---|---|---|---|---|---|---|---|---|---|---|
| Arsenal | — | 7.12 | 30.10 | 5.2 | 9.4 | 13.11 | 19.2 | 4.9 | 19.3 | 23.4 | 2.5 | 31.8 | 18.9 | 5.3 | 2.4 | 15.1 | 18.12 | 1.1 | 27.12 | 27.11 | 16.10 | 2.10 |
| Aston Villa | 14.5 | — | 4.4 | 13.11 | 19.3 | 12.2 | 29.12 | 18.12 | 8.9 | 23.10 | 20.11 | 5.3 | 11.9 | 19.2 | 3.1 | 30.4 | 15.1 | 25.9 | 30.10 | 16.10 | 16.4 | 9.12 |
| Birmingham C | 12.3 | 27.12 | — | 2.5 | 18.9 | 23.4 | 23.10 | 31.8 | 9.10 | 16.10 | 15.1 | 9.4 | 26.2 | 26.3 | 11.12 | 4.9 | 30.4 | 27.11 | 7.5 | 2.10 | 6.11 | 5.2 |
| Brighton & HA | 7.9 | 2.5 | 25.9 | — | 23.4 | 9.4 | 28.8 | 12.3 | 22.1 | 4.9 | 15.1 | 11.12 | 2.10 | 26.3 | 27.12 | 4.12 | 16.4 | 30.10 | 7.5 | 1.1 | 12.2 | 23.10 |
| Coventry C | 11.9 | 19.3 | 18.9 | 23.4 | — | 25.9 | 3.1 | 26.3 | 6.11 | 2.10 | 12.2 | 27.12 | 9.4 | 22.1 | 9.4 | 31.8 | 26.2 | 13.11 | 16.10 | 5.3 | 30.4 | 14.5 |
| Everton | 26.3 | 12.2 | 4.12 | 25.9 | 9.4 | — | 14.5 | 6.11 | 18.12 | 22.1 | 28.8 | 18.9 | 5.4 | 16.10 | 12.3 | 18.12 | 23.4 | 5.3 | 13.11 | 15.1 | 20.11 | 30.4 |
| Ipswich T | 9.10 | 2.4 | 5.3 | 11.12 | 14.5 | 13.11 | — | 2.10 | 18.12 | 4.4 | 18.9 | 28.8 | 16.10 | 26.2 | 20.11 | 22.1 | 25.9 | 2.10 | 31.8 | 7.5 | 30.10 | 3.5 |
| Liverpool | 3.1 | 7.5 | 31.8 | 12.3 | 26.3 | 6.11 | 2.10 | — | 18.9 | 28.12 | 4.9 | 27.11 | 28.8 | 2.4 | 4.12 | 1.1 | 23.4 | 15.1 | 13.11 | 11.12 | 28.8 | 19.2 |
| Luton T | 6.11 | 9.4 | 9.10 | 22.1 | 16.10 | 18.12 | 28.12 | 18.9 | — | 2.10 | 11.12 | 26.2 | 20.11 | 2.4 | 26.3 | 25.9 | 13.11 | 23.4 | 2.5 | 27.12 | 5.3 | 31.8 |
| Manchester C | 4.12 | 18.9 | 16.10 | 18.12 | 2.10 | 22.1 | 28.8 | 28.12 | 2.10 | — | 23.10 | 11.12 | 1.1 | 9.4 | 11.9 | 5.3 | 2.5 | 26.2 | 5.2 | 4.9 | 28.12 | 16.4 |
| Manchester U | 25.9 | 18.9 | 8.9 | 15.1 | 11.9 | 28.8 | 18.12 | 4.9 | 19.3 | 30.4 | — | 7.5 | 4.12 | 2.10 | 26.3 | 13.11 | 19.2 | 27.11 | 1.1 | 23.4 | 3.1 | 12.3 |
| Norwich C | 16.4 | 1.1 | 9.4 | 11.12 | 27.11 | 18.9 | 28.8 | 27.11 | 26.2 | 11.12 | 7.5 | — | 2.10 | 5.2 | 2.10 | 9.10 | 20.11 | 2.4 | 15.1 | 19.2 | 25.9 | 26.3 |
| Nottingham F | 23.10 | 25.9 | 26.2 | 2.10 | 9.4 | 5.4 | 16.10 | 28.8 | 20.11 | 1.1 | 4.12 | 2.10 | — | 23.4 | 11.9 | 20.11 | 1.1 | 11.12 | 16.10 | 18.9 | 19.2 | 15.1 |
| Notts Co | 22.1 | 19.2 | 26.3 | 26.3 | 22.1 | 16.10 | 26.2 | 2.4 | 2.4 | 9.4 | 2.10 | 5.2 | 23.4 | — | 23.4 | 2.10 | 3.1 | 11.9 | 12.3 | 30.10 | 4.4 | 18.12 |
| Southampton | 28.12 | 3.1 | 11.12 | 27.12 | 9.4 | 12.3 | 20.11 | 4.12 | 26.3 | 11.9 | 26.3 | 2.10 | 11.9 | 23.4 | — | 4.12 | 23.4 | 5.3 | 2.10 | 31.8 | 18.12 | 16.10 |
| Stoke C | 28.8 | 30.4 | 4.9 | 4.12 | 31.8 | 18.12 | 22.1 | 1.1 | 25.9 | 5.3 | 13.11 | 9.10 | 20.11 | 2.10 | 4.12 | — | 12.3 | 11.9 | 19.3 | 2.5 | 8.9 | 6.11 |
| Sunderland | 18.12 | 15.1 | 30.4 | 16.4 | 26.2 | 23.4 | 30.10 | 23.4 | 13.11 | 2.5 | 19.2 | 20.11 | 1.1 | 1.9 | 23.4 | 4.12 | — | 19.3 | 11.12 | 26.3 | 14.5 | 4.9 |
| Swansea C | 20.11 | 3.5 | 27.11 | 30.10 | 13.11 | 5.3 | 25.9 | 15.1 | 23.4 | 26.2 | 27.11 | 2.4 | 11.12 | 11.9 | 5.3 | 11.9 | 19.3 | — | 12.2 | 19.3 | 26.3 | 5.4 |
| Tottenham H | 4.4 | 27.11 | 7.5 | 7.5 | 16.10 | 13.11 | 13.11 | 13.11 | 2.5 | 5.2 | 1.1 | 15.1 | 16.10 | 12.3 | 2.10 | 19.3 | 11.12 | 12.2 | — | 2.10 | 4.12 | 20.11 |
| Watford | 30.4 | 12.3 | 2.10 | 27.11 | 5.2 | 5.3 | 23.4 | 30.4 | 9.4 | 2.10 | 23.4 | 9.4 | 2.10 | 5.2 | 2.5 | 16.4 | 11.12 | 19.3 | 16.10 | — | 11.9 | 29.12 |
| WBA | 26.2 | 26.2 | 12.2 | 20.11 | 13.11 | 2.10 | 9.10 | 2.5 | 9.4 | 22.1 | 16.4 | 12.3 | 22.1 | 7.5 | 5.2 | 13.11 | 25.9 | 7.9 | 19.3 | 23.4 | — | 18.9 |
| West Ham U | 12.2 | 23.4 | 11.9 | 5.3 | 11.12 | 27.11 | 7.9 | 9.10 | 4.1 | 25.9 | 30.10 | 13.11 | 7.5 | 26.2 | 19.3 | 2.5 | 13.11 | 27.12 | 1.1 | 2.4 | 22.1 | — |

# DIVISION TWO

| | Wolverhampton W | Shrewsbury T | Sheffield W | Rotherham U | QPR | Oldham Ath | Newcastle U | Middlesbrough | Leicester C | Leeds U | Grimsby T | Fulham | Derby Co | Crystal Palace | Chelsea | Charlton Ath | Carlisle U | Cambridge U | Burnley | Bolton W | Blackburn R | Barnsley |
|---|---|---|---|---|---|---|---|---|---|---|---|---|---|---|---|---|---|---|---|---|---|---|
| Barnsley | 5.2 | 30.10 | 27.12 | 26.2 | 9.10 | 4.9 | 2.5 | 19.3 | 2.4 | 27.11 | 1.1 | 2.10 | 19.10 | 15.1 | 13.11 | 7.5 | 11.12 | 9.4 | 18.9 | 5.3 | 23.4 | — |
| Blackburn R | 15.1 | 14.5 | 2.10 | 18.12 | 26.3 | 29.12 | 1.9 | 30.4 | 18.9 | 23.10 | 5.2 | 19.2 | 2.5 | 16.4 | 16.10 | 12.3 | 6.11 | 4.9 | 4.4 | 20.11 | — | 4.12 |
| Bolton W | 18.9 | 6.11 | 9.4 | 9.10 | 12.3 | 28.9 | 4.9 | 26.2 | 27.11 | 2.4 | 2.5 | 5.2 | 26.3 | 2.10 | 7.5 | 11.12 | 27.12 | 23.4 | 15.1 | — | 1.1 | 23.10 |
| Burnley | 2.4 | 25.9 | 1.1 | 11.9 | 12.2 | 30.10 | 19.3 | 3.1 | 11.12 | 9.4 | 7.5 | 5.3 | 27.11 | 9.10 | 23.4 | 26.2 | 7.9 | 13.11 | — | 28.8 | 27.12 | 21.1 |
| Cambridge U | 23.10 | 4.12 | 16.10 | 22.1 | 30.4 | 14.5 | 30.4 | 17.12 | 6.11 | 12.2 | 12.3 | 5.4 | 19.2 | 25.12 | 28.8 | 11.9 | 25.9 | — | 26.3 | 4.12 | 3.1 | 7.9 |
| Carlisle U | 2.10 | 29.4 | 28.9 | 13.11 | 5.3 | 5.3 | 20.11 | 28.12 | 5.2 | 26.2 | 4.9 | 18.12 | 15.1 | 18.9 | 30.10 | 9.10 | — | 3.5 | 16.4 | 5.4 | 19.3 | 14.5 |
| Charlton Ath | 2.5 | 20.11 | 4.9 | 30.4 | 29.12 | 16.4 | 4.12 | 13.11 | 15.1 | 9.10 | 18.9 | 28.9 | 2.10 | 1.4 | 5.3 | — | 12.3 | 5.2 | 16.10 | 14.5 | 30.10 | 18.12 |
| Chelsea | 31.8 | 7.9 | 2.5 | 4.9 | 22.1 | 18.9 | 16.4 | 14.5 | 4.9 | 13.11 | 2.10 | 28.12 | 6.11 | 5.3 | — | 5.3 | 9.4 | 15.1 | 4.12 | 18.12 | 26.2 | 26.3 |
| Crystal Palace | 27.11 | 29.12 | 11.12 | 3.1 | 4.4 | 16.10 | 5.3 | 25.9 | 1.1 | 22.1 | 23.4 | 30.10 | 18.12 | — | 6.11 | 23.10 | 2.4 | 2.4 | 18.12 | 12.2 | 11.9 | 28.8 |
| Derby Co | 12.3 | 3.1 | 19.3 | 4.12 | 7.5 | 20.11 | 4.4 | 11.9 | 23.10 | 9.10 | 7.5 | 7.5 | — | 6.11 | 12.2 | 27.12 | 16.10 | 9.4 | 12.2 | 13.11 | 25.9 | 16.4 |
| Fulham | 1.1 | 11.9 | 27.11 | 28.8 | 3.1 | 6.11 | 26.2 | 22.1 | 23.4 | 2.10 | 14.5 | — | 7.5 | 18.12 | 19.2 | 6.11 | 11.9 | 27.12 | 19.2 | 25.9 | 28.8 | 12.2 |
| Grimsby T | 19.3 | 18.12 | 5.3 | 4.4 | 7.9 | 30.4 | 28.12 | 16.4 | 12.3 | 23.4 | — | 14.5 | 16.10 | 12.3 | 3.1 | 28.8 | 2.4 | 30.10 | 20.10 | 28.12 | 7.9 | 20.11 |
| Leeds U | 4.9 | 12.2 | 5.2 | 26.2 | 14.5 | 5.4 | 30.10 | 20.11 | 23.4 | — | 26.3 | 13.11 | 18.9 | 4.12 | 11.12 | 26.3 | 19.3 | 2.10 | 14.5 | 30.4 | 26.2 | 30.4 |
| Leicester C | 26.2 | 19.2 | 30.10 | 28.12 | 4.12 | 2.10 | 5.2 | 5.4 | — | 1.1 | 19.2 | 16.4 | 5.3 | 26.3 | 11.9 | 23.4 | 1.1 | 27.11 | 4.9 | 16.10 | 27.11 | 28.12 |
| Middlesbrough | 23.4 | 22.1 | 15.1 | 14.5 | 25.9 | 19.2 | 5.4 | — | 2.5 | 8.9 | 20.11 | 4.12 | 9.4 | 20.11 | 9.4 | 25.9 | 11.9 | 19.3 | 3.1 | 3.1 | 22.1 | 6.11 |
| Newcastle U | 11.12 | 16.10 | 18.9 | 16.4 | 23.10 | 9.10 | — | 8.9 | 27.12 | 1.1 | 28.12 | 16.10 | 27.12 | 2.5 | 27.12 | 22.3 | 23.10 | 7.5 | 16.10 | 22.1 | 3.1 | 25.9 |
| Oldham Ath | 13.11 | 5.3 | 2.4 | 12.3 | 28.8 | — | 9.10 | 12.2 | 26.3 | 12.3 | 30.10 | 9.3 | 1.1 | 23.10 | 25.9 | 27.11 | 27.11 | 11.12 | 12.3 | 12.3 | 9.4 | 19.2 |
| QPR | 7.5 | 26.3 | 23.4 | 7.9 | — | 5.2 | 5.2 | 8.9 | 27.10 | 23.4 | 9.10 | 2.5 | 23.4 | 26.2 | 27.11 | 7.9 | 26.3 | 31.8 | 2.10 | 2.10 | 1.4 | 16.10 |
| Rotherham U | 9.4 | 16.10 | 13.11 | — | 11.9 | 2.5 | 2.10 | 5.3 | 31.8 | 6.11 | 27.12 | 15.1 | 6.11 | 28.9 | 9.4 | 3.1 | 22.1 | 18.9 | 5.2 | 30.10 | 13.11 | 4.4 |
| Sheffield W | 9.10 | 26.3 | — | 19.3 | 6.11 | 18.12 | 18.12 | 28.8 | 12.3 | 2.4 | 23.10 | 30.4 | 2.4 | 4.9 | 25.9 | 27.11 | 23.4 | 26.3 | 20.11 | 2.10 | 7.5 | 12.3 |
| Shrewsbury T | 27.12 | — | 26.3 | 28.12 | 16.4 | 4.12 | 18.9 | 9.10 | 2.10 | 30.10 | 8.4 | 4.9 | 30.10 | 14.5 | 1.1 | 7.9 | 27.11 | 28.9 | 3.5 | 19.3 | 11.12 | 4.4 |
| Wolverhampton W | — | 4.4 | 18.12 | 23.10 | 18.12 | 15.1 | 14.5 | 11.9 | 16.10 | 3.1 | 6.11 | 20.11 | 20.11 | 30.4 | 22.1 | 7.9 | 12.2 | 5.3 | 28.12 | 16.4 | 28.8 | 11.9 |

# DIVISION THREE

| | AFC B'mouth | Bradford C | Brentford | Bristol R | Cardiff C | Chesterfield | Doncaster R | Exeter C | Gillingham | Huddersfield T | Lincoln C | Millwall | Newport Co | Orient | Oxford U | Plymouth Arg | Portsmouth | Preston NE | Reading | Sheffield U | Southend U | Walsall | Wigan Ath | Wrexham |
|---|---|---|---|---|---|---|---|---|---|---|---|---|---|---|---|---|---|---|---|---|---|---|---|---|
| AFC B'mouth | — | 27.11 | 1.1 | 2.11 | 9.10 | 9.4 | 2.5 | 25.9 | 23.10 | 6.11 | 23.4 | 22.1 | 26.3 | 2.4 | 8.1 | 15.2 | 26.2 | 12.3 | 27.12 | 11.9 | 28.9 | 28.8 | 7.5 | 12.2 |
| Bradford C | 30.4 | — | 19.3 | 12.2 | 16.2 | 26.2 | 23.10 | 13.11 | 3.1 | 14.5 | 12.3 | 16.4 | 11.9 | 8.1 | 3.11 | 9.10 | 4.12 | 4.4 | 28.8 | 18.12 | 25.9 | 29.9 | 22.1 | 28.12 |
| Brentford | 14.5 | 6.11 | — | 28.8 | 3.1 | 9.10 | 26.2 | 18.12 | 28.12 | 26.3 | 23.10 | 25.9 | 28.9 | 22.1 | 15.2 | 11.3 | 1.4 | 2.11 | 12.2 | 30.4 | 11.9 | 16.4 | 8.1 | 4.12 |
| Bristol R | 1.3 | 2.10 | 1.1 | — | 14.5 | 29.1 | 4.9 | 29.12 | 7.9 | 30.4 | 18.9 | 19.10 | 19.2 | 5.3 | 5.4 | 5.2 | 13.11 | 16.4 | 30.10 | 4.1 | 19.3 | 4.12 | 16.10 | 18.12 |
| Cardiff C | 19.2 | — | 30.4 | 11.9 | — | 27.11 | 9.4 | 28.9 | 16.10 | 15.3 | 26.3 | 19.10 | 27.12 | 7.5 | 28.9 | 2.4 | 30.10 | 6.11 | 1.3 | 25.9 | 23.4 | 22.1 | 11.9 | 28.8 |
| Chesterfield | 4.12 | 5.3 | — | 11.9 | 30.4 | — | 12.3 | 16.4 | 16.10 | 4.4 | 6.11 | 14.5 | 27.12 | 7.5 | 28.9 | 23.10 | 18.12 | 26.3 | 22.1 | 5.4 | 12.2 | 1.3 | 25.9 | 28.8 |
| Doncaster R | 3.1 | 16.10 | 7.5 | 8.1 | 4.12 | 30.10 | — | 10.9 | 25.3 | 1.3 | 19.2 | 18.12 | 28.8 | 12.2 | 16.4 | 5.11 | 30.4 | 28.12 | 25.9 | 5.4 | 22.1 | 14.5 | 28.9 | 3.1 |
| Exeter C | 5.2 | 5.3 | 7.5 | 2.4 | 29.1 | 2.10 | 7.5 | — | 4.9 | 15.1 | 2.3 | 16.10 | 1.1 | 27.11 | 12.3 | 27.12 | 8.9 | 18.9 | 8.4 | 5.4 | 2.5 | 1.3 | 28.9 | 3.1 |
| Gillingham | 5.3 | 23.4 | 2.9 | 7.5 | 29.1 | 2.10 | 7.5 | 4.9 | — | 30.10 | 1.1 | 11.9 | 1.1 | 27.11 | 28.8 | 27.12 | 19.3 | 18.9 | 28.9 | 22.1 | 2.5 | 6.11 | 3.11 | 19.2 |
| Hudd. T | 19.3 | 3.5 | 1.1 | 27.11 | 23.10 | 15.2 | 2.11 | 28.8 | 12.3 | — | 2.4 | 12.2 | 7.5 | 25.9 | 30.4 | 26.2 | 16.2 | 3.1 | 11.9 | 29.9 | 8.1 | 4.4 | 2.5 | 8.1 |
| Lincoln C | 18.12 | 30.10 | 5.3 | 13.11 | 22.1 | 19.3 | 9.10 | 2.4 | 12.3 | 28.12 | — | 4.12 | 2.5 | 25.9 | 30.4 | 26.2 | 16.2 | 3.1 | 11.9 | 29.9 | 8.1 | 4.4 | 28.8 | 16.4 |
| Millwall | 8.9 | 8.5 | 15.2 | 5.9 | 9.10 | 1.1 | 23.4 | 14.5 | 4.12 | 2.10 | 3.1 | — | 2.5 | 26.12 | 9.10 | 2.11 | 6.2 | 15.1 | 28.11 | 12.3 | 2.4 | 23.10 | 28.8 | 6.11 |
| Newport Co | 13.11 | 19.9 | 6.2 | 9.10 | 4.4 | 1.1 | 28.8 | 14.5 | 1.3 | 16.4 | 3.1 | 3.1 | — | 26.2 | 28.12 | 7.9 | 6.4 | 15.2 | 19.3 | 12.3 | 23.10 | 16.10 | 27.3 | 6.11 |
| Orient | 4.9 | 2.3 | 19.9 | 20.10 | 27.12 | 8.1 | 19.2 | 9.4 | 9.4 | 16.10 | 27.11 | 26.2 | 2.5 | — | 4.12 | 2.11 | 16.2 | 23.4 | 28.9 | 25.9 | 9.4 | 22.1 | 8.1 | 2.4 |
| Oxford U | 4.9 | 20.10 | 15.2 | 8.9 | 17.12 | 7.5 | 26.3 | 12.3 | 28.8 | 4.12 | 13.5 | 9.10 | 4.12 | 9.4 | — | 26.3 | 18.1 | 17.12 | 20.2 | 13.5 | 13.3 | 16.11 | 6.11 | 8.1 |
| Plymouth Arg | 19.2 | 30.10 | 19.9 | 5.2 | 2.4 | 23.10 | 5.11 | 27.12 | 23.4 | 9.4 | 26.2 | 2.11 | 7.9 | 26.3 | 26.3 | — | 8.9 | 18.9 | 20.2 | 12.3 | 2.4 | 2.5 | 2.10 | 25.9 |
| Portsmouth | 16.10 | 1.3 | 28.9 | 13.11 | 30.10 | 18.12 | 30.4 | 8.9 | 19.3 | 16.2 | 6.2 | 16.4 | 18.1 | 18.9 | 4.12 | 1.1 | — | 14.5 | 5.3 | 15.1 | 1.10 | 4.9 | 19.10 | 11.9 |
| Preston NE | 30.10 | 9.4 | 27.12 | 26.3 | 12.3 | 23.4 | 13.11 | 19.2 | 16.10 | 18.12 | 9.10 | 15.1 | 17.12 | 29.1 | 13.11 | 26.3 | 23.10 | — | 2.10 | 4.9 | 3.12 | 7.9 | 14.5 | 28.9 |
| Reading | 4.4 | 15.1 | 1.3 | 12.3 | 3.11 | 13.11 | 2.4 | 22.1 | 16.4 | 18.12 | 29.1 | 30.4 | 6.11 | 9.10 | 3.1 | 4.9 | 28.12 | 2.10 | — | 16.2 | 13.11 | 15.10 | 9.4 | 14.5 |
| Sheffield U | 29.1 | 23.4 | 27.11 | 2.5 | 5.2 | 18.9 | 27.11 | 12.2 | 19.2 | 7.9 | 7.5 | 30.10 | 1.3 | 1.1 | 19.3 | 18.1 | 15.1 | 4.9 | 16.2 | — | 26.3 | 19.2 | 9.4 | 16.10 |
| Southend U | 16.4 | 5.2 | 29.1 | 3.1 | 17.12 | 6.9 | 18.9 | 14.1 | 13.5 | 2.11 | 4.9 | 14.1 | 16.10 | 29.10 | 13.5 | 2.5 | 1.10 | 3.12 | 15.10 | 26.3 | — | 29.4 | 18.2 | 28.2 |
| Walsall | 15.1 | 7.5 | 9.4 | 2.5 | 26.2 | 6.9 | 1.1 | 19.3 | 5.2 | 29.1 | 27.12 | 5.3 | 23.4 | 15.2 | 26.2 | 2.5 | 4.9 | 7.9 | 13.11 | 9.10 | 27.11 | — | 29.12 | 30.10 |
| Wigan Ath | 18.9 | 7.9 | 4.9 | 26.2 | 16.4 | 7.9 | 29.1 | 2.4 | 3.11 | 18.2 | 6.11 | 12.2 | 6.11 | 24.11 | 6.11 | 2.10 | 4.9 | 14.5 | 5.3 | 19.2 | 29.4 | 12.3 | — | 4.4 |
| Wrexham | 2.10 | 2.4 | 8.4 | 22.4 | 15.1 | 2.5 | 15.2 | 7.9 | 18.9 | 4.9 | 12.3 | 19.3 | 27.11 | 13.11 | 23.10 | 7.5 | 29.1 | 5.2 | 1.1 | 26.2 | 2.11 | 12.3 | 27.12 | — |

# DIVISION FOUR

| | Aldershot | Blackpool | Bristol C | Bury | Chester | Colchester U | Crewe Alex | Darlington | Halifax T | Hartlepool U | Hereford U | Hull C | Mansfield T | Northampton T | Peterborough U | Port Vale | Rochdale | Scunthorpe U | Stockport Co | Swindon T | Torquay U | Tranmere R | Wimbledon | York C |
|---|---|---|---|---|---|---|---|---|---|---|---|---|---|---|---|---|---|---|---|---|---|---|---|---|
| Aldershot | — | 27.11 | 30.10 | 9.4 | 13.11 | 2.4 | 19.10 | 1.3 | 7.5 | 5.3 | 2.5 | 25.9 | 1.1 | 12.2 | 11.9 | 28.9 | 23.4 | 8.1 | 16.10 | 27.12 | 22.1 | 28.8 | 19.2 | 19.3 |
| Blackpool | 30.4 | — | 16.4 | 7.9 | 29.1 | 5.2 | 6.11 | 2.10 | 9.10 | 14.5 | 23.10 | 4.12 | 15.1 | 26.3 | 3.1 | 12.3 | 26.2 | 18.12 | 1.4 | 4.9 | 2.11 | 28.12 | 18.9 | 15.2 |
| Bristol C | 12.3 | 11.9 | — | 23.4 | 2.11 | 27.11 | 7.5 | 2.5 | 15.2 | 26.2 | 2.4 | 28.8 | 26.3 | 22.1 | 12.2 | 27.12 | 9.4 | 25.9 | 6.11 | 1.1 | 28.9 | 8.1 | 23.10 | 9.10 |
| Bury | 4.12 | 22.1 | 18.12 | — | 19.3 | 30.10 | 11.9 | 5.3 | 25.9 | 28.12 | 28.8 | 1.3 | 19.2 | 3.1 | 16.4 | 8.1 | 12.2 | 30.4 | 19.10 | 16.10 | 13.11 | 28.9 | 14.5 | 4.4 |
| Chester | 26.3 | 29.9 | 2.3 | 6.11 | — | 5.3 | 28.8 | 19.2 | 12.2 | 4.12 | 25.9 | 30.4 | 16.10 | 16.4 | 20.10 | 11.2 | 8.1 | 14.5 | 28.12 | 30.10 | 11.9 | 4.4 | 3.1 | 18.12 |
| Colchester U | 28.12 | 25.9 | 29.4 | 12.3 | 22.10 | — | 21.1 | 15.10 | 28.8 | 3.1 | 7.1 | 17.12 | 5.11 | 4.4 | 1.4 | 22.10 | 10.9 | 15.4 | 17.12 | 18.2 | 13.5 | 25.3 | 2.11 | 3.12 |
| Crewe Alex | 15.2 | 19.3 | 7.9 | 29.1 | 15.1 | 17.9 | — | 3.9 | 11.3 | 15.4 | 11.9 | 7.1 | 1.10 | 4.4 | 1.4 | 25.9 | 28.8 | 28.9 | 3.1 | 5.2 | 3.12 | 13.5 | 30.4 | 2.11 |
| Darlington | 1.3 | 2.10 | 2.5 | 5.3 | 19.2 | 15.10 | 3.9 | — | 22.1 | 4.4 | 11.9 | 17.12 | 12.3 | 30.4 | 28.12 | 22.10 | 28.8 | 28.9 | 26.3 | 6.11 | 16.4 | 15.2 | 4.12 | 14.5 |
| Halifax T | 18.9 | 18.2 | 19.10 | 5.2 | 1.10 | 14.1 | 29.10 | 7.9 | — | 29.4 | 5.11 | 4.4 | 3.9 | 3.12 | 1.3 | 15.10 | 4.3 | 28.9 | 13.5 | 28.1 | 3.1 | 17.12 | 25.3 | 12.3 |
| Hartlepool U | 23.10 | 1.1 | 16.10 | 2.4 | 12.3 | 13.11 | 29.10 | 27.12 | 29.4 | — | 26.3 | 22.1 | 8.10 | 11.9 | 8.1 | 29.4 | 7.5 | 28.8 | 19.2 | 18.12 | 26.2 | 30.4 | 5.3 | 2.10 |
| Hereford U | 3.1 | 5.3 | 28.12 | 15.1 | 5.2 | 4.9 | 16.10 | 29.1 | 13.11 | — | — | 20.10 | 18.9 | 18.12 | 14.5 | 19.2 | 7.5 | 2.5 | 28.8 | 2.5 | 9.10 | 12.3 | 4.9 | 7.9 |
| Hull C | 5.2 | 9.4 | 15.1 | 2.11 | 27.11 | 9.10 | 7.1 | 2.4 | 27.12 | 8.1 | 14.3 | — | 3.1 | 23.10 | 6.11 | 26.3 | 25.9 | 18.10 | 4.12 | 5.3 | 17.12 | 16.4 | 4.9 | 25.9 |
| Mansfield T | 14.5 | 28.8 | 26.2 | 9.10 | 26.2 | 19.3 | 12.2 | 30.10 | 8.1 | 14.3 | 5.3 | 3.1 | — | 28.12 | 27.9 | 11.9 | 25.9 | 18.10 | 4.12 | 23.10 | 17.12 | 16.4 | 5.4 | 30.4 |
| N'hamp. T | 2.10 | 13.11 | 19.9 | 21.9 | 7.9 | 19.10 | 27.12 | 28.11 | 10.4 | 29.1 | 23.4 | 5.3 | 2.4 | — | 30.10 | 1.1 | 15.2 | 20.3 | 5.2 | 28.9 | 12.3 | 10.10 | 15.1 | 4.9 |
| Peterboro' U | 29.1 | 4.5 | 2.10 | 18.9 | 16.2 | 27.12 | 2.4 | 23.4 | 3.11 | 4.9 | 1.1 | 19.3 | 12.3 | 2.3 | — | 1.1 | 13.11 | 20.3 | 15.1 | 26.2 | 23.10 | 10.10 | 8.9 | 7.9 |
| Port Vale | 16.4 | 30.10 | 4.4 | 4.9 | 18.9 | 6.9 | 5.3 | 5.2 | 29.1 | 18.10 | 1.1 | 9.10 | 31.1 | 14.5 | 30.4 | — | 16.4 | 14.2 | 2.10 | 15.1 | 28.12 | 4.12 | 8.12 | 3.1 |
| Rochdale | 18.12 | 16.10 | 4.4 | 4.9 | 18.9 | 29.1 | 4.9 | 15.1 | 23.10 | 8.10 | 7.9 | 14.5 | 5.2 | 26.3 | 18.2 | 6.11 | — | 4.4 | 16.4 | 18.9 | 30.4 | 3.1 | 1.3 | 28.12 |
| Scunthorpe U | 4.9 | 23.4 | 5.2 | 27.11 | 1.1 | 2.10 | 22.4 | 7.5 | 12.11 | 8.10 | 8.4 | 15.10 | 1.3 | 6.11 | 18.2 | 2.11 | 6.5 | — | 7.9 | 11.2 | 12.3 | 23.10 | 29.1 | 19.9 |
| Stockport Co | 26.2 | 27.12 | 18.3 | 14.2 | 2.4 | 22.4 | 2.5 | 12.11 | 1.1 | 8.10 | 1.11 | 10.9 | 8.4 | 24.9 | 28.8 | 6.5 | 27.9 | 11.2 | — | 2.5 | 7.1 | 21.1 | 11.3 | 22.10 |
| Swindon T | 4.4 | 8.1 | 14.5 | 26.2 | 12.3 | 10.10 | 25.9 | 19.3 | 11.9 | 18.12 | 12.2 | 16.4 | 23.10 | 8.5 | 4.12 | 28.8 | 22.1 | 3.1 | 30.4 | — | 15.2 | 2.11 | 28.12 | 13.11 |
| Torquay U | 8.9 | 2.3 | 29.1 | 26.3 | 7.5 | 1.1 | 9.4 | 18.9 | 2.5 | 2.10 | 27.12 | 19.2 | 23.4 | 16.10 | 5.3 | 2.4 | 27.11 | 30.10 | 4.9 | 20.10 | — | 6.11 | 5.2 | 15.1 |
| Tranmere R | 15.1 | 2.4 | 4.9 | 7.5 | 27.12 | 13.11 | 1.1 | 18.10 | 23.4 | 5.2 | 6.9 | 30.10 | 6.9 | 19.2 | 16.10 | 8.4 | 2.5 | 5.3 | 18.9 | 28.2 | 18.3 | — | 2.10 | 29.1 |
| Wimbledon | 9.10 | 7.5 | 5.3 | 1.1 | 2.5 | 4.9 | 19.2 | 9.4 | 13.11 | 19.3 | 28.9 | 8.1 | 27.12 | 28.8 | 22.1 | 23.4 | 19.10 | 11.9 | 30.10 | 1.4 | 25.9 | 12.2 | — | 26.2 |
| York C | 6.11 | 19.10 | 19.2 | 27.12 | 23.4 | 9.4 | 1.3 | 1.1 | 28.9 | 30.10 | 7.5 | 12.2 | 27.11 | 8.1 | 25.9 | 2.5 | 2.4 | 22.1 | 5.3 | 26.3 | 28.8 | 11.9 | 16.10 | — |

# INTERNATIONAL, REPRESENTATIVE AND CUP DATES 1982–83

*Note:* Provisional dates for British International Championship – 23–31 May.

## 1982

### August

21 FA Charity Shield

### September

1 Football League Cup – 1st round, 1st leg
4 FA Challenge Cup – preliminary round
11 FA Challenge Trophy – preliminary round
FA Challenge Vase – extra preliminary round
FA Youth Challenge Cup – 1st round qualifying
15 European Cups – 1st round, 1st leg
Football League Cup – 1st round, 2nd leg
18 FA Challenge Cup – 1st round qualifying
21 England v West Germany (*UEFA Under-21 Competition, 1980–82 final, first leg*)
22 Denmark v England (*European Championship*)
Wales v Norway (*European Championship*)
29 European Cups – 1st round, 2nd leg
FA XI v Western League

### October

2 FA Challenge Cup – 2nd round qualifying
3 FA Sunday Cup – 1st round
6 Football League Cup – 2nd round, 1st leg
9 FA Challenge Vase – preliminary round
FA Youth Challenge Cup – 2nd round qualifying
12 West Germany v England (*UEFA Under-21 Competition, 1980–82 final, second leg*)
13 England v West Germany
Scotland v East Germany (*European Championship*)
Austria v Northern Ireland (*European Championship*)
16 FA Challenge Cup – 3rd round qualifying
20 European Cups – 2nd round, 1st leg
FA XI v British Police
23 FA Challenge Trophy – 1st round qualifying
26 FA XI v Northern Premier League
27 Football League Cup – 2nd round, 2nd leg
30 FA Challenge Cup – 4th round qualifying
FA County Youth Challenge Cup – 1st round
31 FA Sunday Cup – 2nd round

### November

3 European Cups – 2nd round, 2nd leg
6 FA Challenge Vase – 1st round
FA Youth Challenge Cup – 1st round proper
10 Football League Cup – 3rd round
FA XI v Oxford University
16 Greece v England (*UEFA Under-21 Competition*)
17 Greece v England (*European Championship*)
Switzerland v Scotland (*European Championship*)
Northern Ireland v West Germany (*European Championship*)
20 FA Challenge Cup – 1st round proper
24 UEFA Cup – 3rd round, 1st leg
FA XI v Cambridge University
27 FA Challenge Trophy – 2nd round qualifying
28 FA Sunday Cup – 3rd round

### December

1 Football League Cup – 4th round
4 FA Challenge Vase – 2nd round
FA Youth Challenge Cup – 2nd round proper
FA County Youth Challenge Cup – 2nd round
8 UEFA Cup – 3rd round, 2nd leg
FA XI v London University
11 FA Challenge Cup – 2nd round proper
15 England v Luxembourg (*European Championship*)
Belgium v Scotland (*European Championship*)
Albania v Northern Ireland (*European Championship*)
Yugoslavia v Wales (*European Championship*)
18 FA Challenge Trophy – 3rd round qualifying

## 1983

### January

1 FA Challenge Vase – 3rd round
8 FA Challenge Cup – 3rd round qualifying
FA Youth Challenge Cup – 3rd round proper
9 FA Sunday Cup – 4th round
12 FA XI v Combined Services
15 FA Challenge Trophy – 1st round proper
FA County Youth Challenge Cup – 3rd round
19 Football League Cup – 5th round
22 FA Challenge Vase – 4th round
29 FA Challenge Cup – 4th round proper

### February

2 FA XI v British Colleges Sports Association
5 FA Challenge Trophy – 2nd round proper
FA Youth Challenge Cup – 4th round proper
6 FA Sunday Cup – 5th round
9 Football League Cup – semi-final, 1st leg
12 FA Challenge Vase – 5th round
16 Football League Cup – semi-final, 2nd leg
FA XI v Amateur Football Alliance
19 FA Challenge Cup – 5th round proper
FA County Youth Challenge Cup – 4th round
26 FA Challenge Trophy – 3rd round proper

### March

1 FA XI v Universities Athletic Union
2 European Cups – 3rd round, 1st leg
UEFA Cup – 4th round, 1st leg
5 FA Challenge Vase – 6th round
FA Youth Challenge Cup – 5th round proper
12 FA Challenge Cup – 6th round proper
13 FA Sunday Cup – semi-final
15 FA XI v Northern League
16 European Cups – 3rd round, 2nd leg
UEFA Cup – 4th round, 2nd leg
19 FA Challenge Trophy – 4th round proper
26 Football League Cup Final
FA Challenge Vase – semi-final, 1st leg
29 England v Greece (*UEFA Under-21 Competition*)
30 England v Greece (*European Championship*)
Scotland v Switzerland (*European Championship*)
Northern Ireland v Turkey (*European Championship*)

### April

2 FA Challenge Vase – semi-final, 2nd leg
FA Youth Challenge Cup – semi-final
FA County Youth Challenge Cup – semi-final
6 European Cups – semi-final, 1st leg
9 FA Challenge Trophy – semi-final, 1st leg
16 FA Challenge Cup – semi-final
FA Challenge Trophy – semi-final, 2nd leg
20 European Cups – semi-final, 2nd leg
26 England v Hungary (*UEFA Under-21 Competition*)
27 England v Hungary (*European Championship*)
Northern Ireland v Albania (*European Championship*)
Wales v Bulgaria (*European Championship*)
FA XI v Guernsey FA
30 FA Challenge Vase – Final
FA Youth Challenge Cup – Final

### May

1 FA Sunday Cup – Final
4 UEFA Cup – Final, 1st leg
7 FA County Youth Challenge Cup – Final
11 European Cup Winners' Cup – Final
13 European Youth Championship in England (*ends 22 May*)
14 FA Challenge Trophy – Final
18 UEFA Cup – Final, 2nd leg
21 FA Challenge Cup – Final
25 European Champion Club's Cup – Final

### June

4 World Youth Championship in Mexico (*ends 19 June*)
8 Brazil v England